PAGE
36

ON THE ROAD

YOUR COMPLETE DESTINATION GUIDE
In-depth reviews, detailed listings
and insider tips

D1422341

THIS EDITION WRITTEN AND RESEARCHED BY

Duncan Garwood

Alexis Averbuck, James Bainbridge, Paul Clammer,
Jayne D'Arcy, Peter Dragičević, Mark Elliott, Steve Fallon,
Anthony Ham, Virginia Maxwell, Craig McLachlan,
Anja Mutić, Josephine Quintero, Regis St Louis,
Nicola Williams, Neil Wilson

welcome to
Mediterranean
Europ

Natural Wonders

For many people the Mediterranean's main appeal is the promise of summer sun and long, lazy days on the beach. Each year up to 200 million visitors pour into the region, making it the world's top tourist destination. While not all head straight for the beach, many do – and with good reason. The Mediterranean's beaches are superb, ranging in style from big, sporty sands on Portugal's western seaboard to idyllic Sardinian hideaways, and rocky platforms on Croatia's craggy Dalmatian coast. But there's more to the Med than the beach, and, away from the coast, the region's ancient landscape offers some truly spectacular natural sights – snow-clad Alpine peaks, Saharan sand dunes, bizarre rock formations, even a stunning fjord in Montenegro.

Cultural Calling

Alongside great natural beauty, the Mediterranean boasts an unparalleled cultural legacy. Spanning 14,000 years, this priceless patrimony provides a thrilling window onto the region's long and dramatic past. Prehistoric paintings reveal the preoccupations of France's primeval cave dwellers; Greek and Roman monuments testify to the power and ambition of the ancient superpowers; Islamic art tells of Moorish sophistication; Gothic cathedrals, Renaissance palaces and baroque facades record the great artistic movements of history.

Golden sun-kissed beaches, dreamy seascapes, ancient ruins and awe-inspiring art – Mediterranean Europe is a visual and sensual feast. Visit once and you'll be hooked for life.

(left) People relaxing on Sveti Stefan beach, Montenegro (p618).
(bottom) Roman amphitheatre at night, Pula, Croatia (p135).

The region's celebrated galleries and museums are pretty special too, housing a considerable chunk of the Western world's combined art collection.

Food, Glorious Food

The region's passion for the finer things in life also extends to the kitchen. Eating well is part and parcel of everyday life on the Med, as well as one of its great pleasures, and it doesn't have to cost a bomb. Picnicking on a loaf of freshly baked bread with cheese and olives and a bottle of wine bought from the local market could well turn out to be a holiday highlight. For dedicated foodies, France and Italy are the obvious destinations but each country has its own culinary specialities – think tapas in Spain, tajine in Morocco, kebaps in Turkey. And for wine buffs, the Mediterranean cellar is really quite something, with everything from world famous vintages to thousands of cheerful local labels.

No Problem

Capping everything is the fact that Mediterranean Europe is an easy region in which to travel. Sure, services might not always be what you're used to, and some areas can be expensive, particularly in summer, but English is widely spoken, public transport more or less works, and with so many accommodation and eating options to choose from, you're sure to find somewhere to suit your style.

❭ Mediterranean Europe

Eiffel Tower, Paris, France
From any angle this iconic tower is magic to behold (p211)

Canals, Venice, Italy
Impossibly beautiful yet easily loved (p504)

Alfama, Lisbon, Portugal
Discover the ancient labyrinth of the Alfama (p696)

Djemaa el-Fna, Marrakesh, Morocco
Bask in exotic sights, sounds and smells (p671)

Forum, Rome, Italy
Ancient Rome legends, remarkable ruins and haunting views (p461)

Dubrovnik, Croatia
The Balkan's finest old town is simply spectacular (p162)

La Sagrada Família, Barcelona, Spain
Visit the fanciful, proud La Sagrada Família (p827)

800 km
500 miles

NORWAY
Oslo
SWEDE
Skagerrak
DENMARK
Copenhagen
North Sea
SCOTLAND
Edinburgh
NORTHERN IRELAND
Belfast
Dublin
Irish Sea
BRITAIN
IRELAND
WALES
ENGLAND
NETHERLANDS
Berlin
Cardiff
London
Amsterdam
GERMANY
St George's Channel
Brussels
Rhine
BELGIUM
English Channel
LUXEMBOURG
Seine
Paris
Luxembourg City
Danube
ATLANTIC OCEAN
Elb
LIECHTENSTEIN
FRANCE
Bern
Vaduz
SWITZERLAND
Loire
Mt Blanc (4807m)
ALPS
Venice
Bay of Biscay
Po
ITALY
PYRENEES
Monaco
Ligurian Sea
San Marino
Douro
Andorra la Vella
ANDORRA
Golfe du Lion
Corsica (France)
Rom
PORTUGAL
Madrid
Ebro
Barcelona
Tyrrhenian Sea
SPAIN
Sardinia (Italy)
Lisbon
Balearic Islands (Spain)
Mediterranean Sea
Strait of Gibraltar
Rabat
MOROCCO
Marrakesh
ATLAS MOUNTAINS
TUNISIA
ALGERIA
WESTERN SAHARA

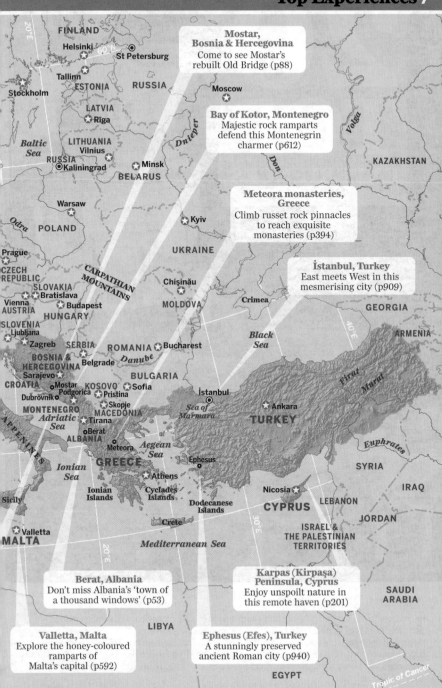

Mostar,
Bosnia & Hercegovina
Come to see Mostar's
rebuilt Old Bridge (p88)

Bay of Kotor, Montenegro
Majestic rock ramparts
defend this Montenegrin
charmer (p612)

Meteora monasteries,
Greece
Climb russet rock pinnacles
to reach exquisite
monasteries (p394)

İstanbul, Turkey
East meets West in this
mesmerising city (p909)

Berat, Albania
Don't miss Albania's 'town of
a thousand windows' (p53)

Karpas (Kirpaşa)
Peninsula, Cyprus
Enjoy unspoilt nature in
this remote haven (p201)

Valletta, Malta
Explore the honey-coloured
ramparts of
Malta's capital (p592)

Ephesus (Efes), Turkey
A stunningly preserved
ancient Roman city (p940)

20 TOP EXPERIENCES

Ancient Rome, Italy

1 Rome's famous seven hills – in fact, there are nine – offer some superb vantage points. A favourite is the Palatino (p464), a gorgeous green expanse of evocative ruins, towering umbrella pines, and unforgettable views over the Roman Forum. This is where it all began, where Romulus supposedly founded the city and where the ancient Roman emperors lived in unimaginable luxury. Nowadays, it's a truly haunting spot, and as you walk the dusty paths you can almost sense the ghosts in the air.

La Sagrada Família, Barcelona, Spain

2 One of Spain's top sights, the Modernista brainchild of Antoni Gaudí remains a work in progress more than 80 years after its creator's death. Fanciful and profound, inspired by nature and barely restrained by a Gothic style, Barcelona's quirky temple (p827) soars skyward with an almost playful majesty. The improbable angles and departures from architectural convention will have you shaking your head in disbelief, but the detail of the decorative flourishes on the Passion and Nativity Facades are worth studying for hours.

Bay of Kotor, Montenegro

3 There's a sense of secrecy and mystery to the Bay of Kotor (p612). Grey mountain walls rise steeply from steely blue waters, getting higher and higher as you progress through their folds to the hidden reaches of the inner bay. Here, ancient stone settlements hug the shoreline, with Kotor's ancient alleyways concealed in its innermost reaches behind hefty stone walls. Talk about drama! But you wouldn't expect anything else of the Balkans, where life is exuberantly Mediterranean and lived full of passion on these ancient streets.

İstanbul, Turkey

4 Straddling Europe and Asia, İstanbul's curriculum vitae includes stints as capital of the Byzantine and Ottoman Empires. It's quite simply one of the world's greatest cities. The historical highlights cluster in Sultanahmet (p909) – the Aya Sofya, Blue Mosque, Topkapı Palace and Grand Bazaar. After marvelling at their ancient domes and glittering interiors, it's time to experience this 13-million-strong metropolis's vibrant contemporary life. Cross the Galata Bridge, passing ferries and fish kebap stands, to Beyoğlu, a nightlife hot spot full of chic rooftop bars and rowdy taverns.

SARAJANE CLELAND / LONELY PLANET IMAGES ©

Djemaa el-Fna, Marrakesh, Morocco

5 Marrakesh's central square, the Djemaa el-Fna (p671), is the 1001 Nights writ large. By day it's an unassuming place, surrounded with carts selling the freshest squeezed orange juice imaginable, but not much else. As the sun dips however, the place comes alive. Noises, smells, colours and action abound: there's the reedy drone of snake charmers, brightly clad water sellers roaming with leather bags and brass cups, crowds gathering around storytellers and acrobats, and the cooking smoke of dozens of open-air food stalls and restaurants everywhere. It's a sensory overload – dive right in.

Eiffel Tower, Paris, France

6 Seven million people visit the Eiffel Tower (p211) annually, but few disagree that each visit is unique. From an evening ascent amid twinkling lights to lunch in the company of a staggering city panorama, there are 101 ways to 'do' it. Pedal beneath it, skip the lift and hike up, buy a crêpe from a stand or a key ring from the street, snap yourself in front of it, visit at night or – our favourite – experience the odd special occasion when all 324m of it glows a different colour.

GLENN BEANLAND / LONELY PLANET IMAGES ©

Venice, Italy

7 There's something magical about Venice (p504) on a sunny winter's day. With far fewer tourists around and the light sharp and clear, it's the perfect time to lap up the city's unique and magical atmosphere. Ditch your map and wander Dorsoduro's shadowy backlines while imagining secret assignations and whispered conspiracies at every turn. Then visit two of Venice's top galleries, the Galleria dell'Accademia (p508) and the Collezione Peggy Guggenheim (p508), which houses works by many of the giants of 20th-century art.

GLENN BEANLAND / LONELY PLANET IMAGES ©

Berat, Albania

8 This wine-producing region's town (p53) reigns supreme in terms of Ottoman-style wonder and magic. From the river below, the multiwindowed white and black Unesco-listed houses look down at you. Wander on up the cobblestone paths to see what they're really about and meander through its living and breathing castle area complete with a museum filled with stunning iconography by Onufri. Stay in Berat's Ottoman-style hostel or one of two traditional-homes-turned-hotels and participate in the evening walk along the promenade for a truly enlivening experience.

PATRICK SYDER / LONELY PLANET IMAGES ©

Alhambra, Granada, Spain

9 The palace complex of the Alhambra (p879) is one of the most refined examples of Islamic art anywhere in the world and an enduring symbol of 800 years of Moorish rule of Al-Andalus. From afar, the Alhambra's red fortress towers dominate the Granada skyline, set against a backdrop of the Sierra Nevada's snow-capped peaks. Up close, the Alhambra's perfectly proportioned Generalife gardens complement the exquisite detail of the Palacio Nazariés. Put simply, this is Spain's most beautiful monument.

JOHN ELK III / LONELY PLANET IMAGES ©

Valletta, Malta

10 Malta's miniature capital city (barely 600m across) was constructed by the Knights of St John in the 16th and 17th centuries, 'a city built by gentlemen, for gentlemen'. Its orderly grid of shaded streets and steep staircases is lined with historic buildings made from Malta's honey-coloured limestone. Walk the perimeter of the city along the top of the massive fortifications – curtain walls, bastions, gun batteries and vast ditches – with views across the Grand Harbour, once home to the knights' galleys, and later the British Mediterranean fleet.

JEAN-PIERRE LESCOURRET / LONELY PLANET IMAGES ©

Ancient Landmarks, Greece

11 From the renowned magnificence of Athens' Acropolis to the monastery-crowned rock spires of Meteora, Greece (p367) offers some of Europe's most impressive historical sights. Top temples include oracular Delphi, perched above the sparkling Gulf of Corinth, and Olympia, home to the first Olympic Games. The acoustically perfect theatre of Epidavros sits alongside the mystical Sanctuary of Asclepius, an ancient healing centre. Olive and orange groves surround the vast ruins of Mystras, the one-time capital of the Byzantine Empire. Start with the Acropolis and follow the path of history over Greece's landscape.

Island hopping in the Adriatic, Croatia

12 From short jaunts between nearby islands to overnight rides along the length of the Croatian coast, travel by sea is a great and inexpensive way to see the Croatian side of the Adriatic (p145). Take in the scenery of this stunning coastline as you whiz past some of Croatia's 1244 islands, and if you have cash to splash, take it up a couple of notches and charter a sailboat to see the islands in style, propelled by winds and sea currents.

Ephesus (Efes), Turkey

13 The eastern Mediterranean's best-preserved classical city is unique among historical sights: the tourists surging down the Curetes Way actually enhance the experience, evoking life in this busy Roman city. The capital of the Roman province of Asia, Ephesus (p939) had 250,000-plus inhabitants, many of them worshippers of the goddess Artemis. After 150 years of excavations, it is the place to get a feel for Greco-Roman times. Near the jaw-dropping Library of Celsus, with its two storeys of pillars, are the Terraced Houses, the luxurious pads of the Roman elite.

Mostar, Bosnia & Hercegovina

14 If the 1993 bombardment of Mostar's iconic 16th-century stone bridge underlined the heartbreaking pointlessness of Yugoslavia's brutal civil war, its painstaking reconstruction has proved symbolic of a peaceful new era. Although parts of Mostar (p88) are still dotted with shockingly bombed-out buildings, the town continues to dust itself off. Its charming Ottoman quarter has been especially convincingly rebuilt and is once again a delightful patchwork of stone mosques, souvenir peddlers and inviting cafes and today it's tourists rather than militias that besiege the place.

JEAN-PIERRE LESCOURRET / LONELY PLANET IMAGES ©

Alfama, Lisbon, Portugal

15 The Alfama (p696), with its labyrinthine alleyways, hidden courtyards and curving, shadow-filled lanes, is a magical place to lose all sense of direction and delve into the soul of the city. On the journey, you'll pass breadbox-sized grocers, brilliantly tiled buildings and cosy taverns filled with easy-going chatter, with the scent of chargrilled sardines and the mournful rhythms of fado drifting in the breeze. Then you round a bend and catch sight of steeply pitched rooftops leading down to the glittering Tejo and you know you're hooked...

Walking the old city walls at dusk, Dubrovnik, Croatia

WAYNE WALTON / LONELY PLANET IMAGES ©

16 Get up close and personal with the city by walking Dubrovnik's spectacular city walls (p162), as history is unfurled from the battlements. No visit is complete without a leisurely walk along these ramparts, the finest in the world and Dubrovnik's main claim to fame. Built between the 13th and 16th centuries, they are still remarkably intact today and the vistas over the terracotta rooftops and the Adriatic Sea are sublime, especially at dusk when the sundown turns the hues dramatic and the panoramas unforgettable.

Provence, France

BETHUNE CARMICHAEL / LONELY PLANET IMAGES ©

17 Captured on canvas by Van Gogh and Cézanne, Provence (p316) is a picture of bold primary colours and bucolic landscapes. Travel the area and you'll pass scented lavender fields, chestnut forests and silvery olive groves as you make for beautiful medieval cities and hilltop villages. But it's not all rural chic and perfect panoramas. On the southern coast, Marseille, the region's tough, compelling capital exudes a gruff, edgy charm. One of the Mediterranean's great ports, this is the ideal place to try bouillabaisse, Provence's legendary fish dish.

Mt Triglav & Vršič Pass, Slovenia

18 They say you're not really Slovene until you've climbed Mt Triglav (p761). There's no rule about which particular route you take – there are about 20 ways up – but if you're a novice, ascend with a guide from the Pokljuka Plateau north of Bohinj. If time is an issue and you're driving head for the Vršič Pass (p763), which stands (literally) head and shoulders above the rest and leads from alpine Gorenjska, past Mt Triglav itself and down to sunny Primorska and the bluer-than-blue Soča River in one hair-raising, spine-tingling hour.

Meteora, Greece

19 Meteora's towering rock spires are a stunning natural sight. But what makes them even more incredible are the elaborate 14th-century monasteries (p394) built on top of them. There were originally 24 monasteries (one for each pinnacle) but nowadays only six remain, accessible by stairs cut into the rock. Make the ascent and you're rewarded with breathtaking views of the surrounding landscape and, on quiet days, a sense of almost otherworldly serenity. For a completely different experience, Meteora's vertical peaks provide superb rock climbing.

Karpas Peninsula, Cyprus

20 Lace up those hiking boots or whip out the mountain bike as the wild Karpas Peninsula (p201) in the northeast of the island is a fabulous place for walking and cycling. Explore this rare region of Cyprus where Turks and Greeks continue to live alongside each other and where the island's first eco village, Büyükkonuk. is located. This is an area of unspoilt natural beauty with picturesque virgin beaches, pine-clad rolling hills and rural villages where there are more goats than folk. Wild donkeys, turtles and more than 350 species of bird also hang out here, so don't forget the binoculars.

need to know

Buses
» Extensive network across the region; bus travel is often preferable in mountainous Eastern Europe.

Trains
» High-speed links across Western Europe; coverage patchy and services slow in Balkan countries.

When to Go

- desert, dry climate
- warm summer, mild winter
- mild year round
- mild summer, cold winter
- cold climate

Paris
GO Apr–Jun

Barcelona
GO May–Jun & Sep

Dubrovnik
GO May–Sep

İstanbul
GO Apr–May

Rome
GO Apr–Jun & Sep

Athens
GO May–Jun

Marrakesh
GO mid-Mar–May

Your Daily Budget

Budget less than
€60

» Dorm beds: €5-30.

» Budget pensions: up to €55 for a double.

» Plentiful markets and supermarkets for self-caterers.

» Check for discount cards, city and transport passes.

Midrange
€60–€150

» Double room in a midrange hotel: €55–150.

» B&Bs are often better value for money than hotels.

» Restaurant meals from about €15 per person.

Top end over
€150

» Double room in a top-end hotel: from €120.

» Top restaurants often have cheaper fixed-price lunch menus.

» Car hire: from €45 per day.

High Season
(Jun–Aug)

» Hot sunny days and packed beaches.

» Peak rates in coastal areas; inland cities may have discounts in August.

» Also coincides with the ski season (December to late March), Christmas, New Year and Easter.

Shoulder
(Apr–May & Sep–Oct)

» Sunny spring days in April and May; September is still hot enough for the beach.

» Crowds and high prices in many cities; more space and lower prices on the coast.

Low Season
(Nov–Mar)

» The coldest and wettest time of the year with snow in mountainous areas.

» Prices are at their lowest.

» Many coastal resorts shut up for the winter.

Driving

» Car hire readily available across the region; tolls apply on many motorways; road conditions not great in Albania and Bosnia and Hercegovina (BiH).

Ferries

» Good safe network in the Mediterranean; book ahead for popular routes in peak season.

Bicycles

» Bike hire is widely available; can take bikes on trains and ferries for a small extra fee.

Planes

» National airlines and up to 42 low-cost carriers fly Europe, ensuring a comprehensive network and competitive fares.

Websites

» **Lonely Planet** (www.lonelyplanet.com/europe) Destination coverage, hotel bookings, traveller forum and much more.

» **Cheap Flights** (www.flycheapo.com) Lists budget airlines and their routes.

» **Ferry** (www.aferry.com) Research and book ferry tickets.

» **Seat 61** (www.seat61.com) About train travel.

» **Visit Europe** (www.visiteurope.com) Has practical advice and useful links.

» **Michelin** (www.viamichelin.com) Good for road directions and online maps.

Money

» The euro is used in Cyprus (Republic), France, Greece, Italy, Malta, Montenegro, Portugal, Slovenia and Spain.

» **Albania** Lekë; euros, ATM card.

» **BiH** Convertible mark; euros, ATM card.

» **Croatia** Kuna; euros, ATM card, credit card.

» **Morocco** Dirham; euros, UK pounds or US dollars, ATM card, credit card.

» **North Cyprus** Turkish lira; euros or UK pounds, ATM card.

» **Turkey** Turkish lira; euros or US dollars, ATM card.

Visas

» No visas are required for most people for stays of up to 90 days in Schengen countries, and Albania, BiH, Croatia, Montenegro and Morocco.

» Citizens of Australia, the US, Canada and New Zealand need a visa for stays of longer than 90 days in the Schengen area.

» Australian, Canadian, UK and US citizens need a visa for Turkey – buy it on arrival.

Arriving in the Med

Services to city:

» **Roissy Charles de Gaulle Airport, Paris** Bus: every 15 minutes 5.30am to midnight, hourly from 12.30am

» **Leonardo da Vinci Airport, Rome** Train: every 30 minutes 6.30am to 11.40pm Bus: 8.30am to 12.30pm, four services 1.15am to 5am

» **Atatürk International Airport, İstanbul** Bus: half-hourly 4am to 1am Metro & Tram: frequent 5.40am to 1.40am

» **Barajas Airport, Madrid** Bus: every 15 to 30 minutes 24 hours Metro: frequent 6.05am to 2am

What to Take

» Travel insurance – make sure it covers any activities you might be doing.

» Your driving licence and, if necessary, International Driving Permit.

» Photocopies of all important documents – so you're covered in case of theft.

» Plug adaptor, power transformer and mobile-phone recharger – so you can stay connected.

» Smart set of clothes – for that 'oh so chic' French restaurant.

» Sandals or thongs – for showers and pebbly beaches.

» Hat, cap and shades – lifesavers when it's 35°C in the shade.

» Rain gear – it does rain in the Med, in some months a lot.

if you like...

Coastal Beauty

When it comes to spectacular scenery and shimmering seascapes, few areas can rival the Mediterranean. Its coastline is a magical mix of silky beaches, dreamy coves and precipitous cliffs, all lapped by lukewarm waters in a thousand shades of blue.

Amalfi Coast Italy's coastal pin-up is pure Mediterranean bliss with cliffs plunging into sparkling azure waters and villages hanging onto vertiginous slopes (p554).

Côte d'Azur Join the European jet set on the French Riviera as it snakes along the lavender-scented coast from one celebrity hot spot to the next (p329).

Turquoise Coast A boat cruise is a popular way of exploring the clear blue waters, hidden coves and ancient ruins of Turkey's western Mediterranean coast (p945).

Dalmatia Hundreds of verdant, unspoilt islands clutter the crystal-clear waters off Croatia's Adriatic coast (p145).

Karpas Peninsula Pad around virgin sand dunes and spy on nesting turtles in Cyprus' remote northeastern tip (p201).

Food & Drink

There's no finer place to indulge your appetites than the Mediterranean. With so many local specialities and traditional tipples to try, lovers of fine food and drink will be in seventh heaven.

Port Get to grips with Portugal's national drink in the riverside city of Porto, gateway to the port-producing Douro valley (p732).

Wine French wines have been setting the gold standard for centuries. Treat yourself to a taste by touring Burgundy's Côte d'Or vineyards (p278).

Pizza Italy's culinary classic is best when prepared in a wood-fired oven and served with an ice-cold beer in a Neapolitan pizzeria (p549).

Kebap This mainstay of Turkish cuisine comes in various forms, from the classic *döner* to the more sophisticated *İskender* (p908).

Tapas Bar-hopping in Madrid becomes a culinary experience when eating tapas, Spain's legendary bar snacks (p800).

Moroccan Spices Dine on exotic street food from stalls at Marrakesh's mind-blowing Djemaa el-Fna (p674).

Outdoor Activities

With its warm seas, snowy mountains and favourable climate, the Med is a sports lover's paradise. Whether you're after perfect snow powder or roaring surf, you'll find plenty of opportunities to feed your adrenalin habit.

Skiing Most of the region's top resorts are in the French and Italian Alps, but there's great value skiing in Slovenia (p778) and near Sarajevo (p86).

Hiking There's excellent hiking across much of the region, particularly in mountainous areas such as Morocco's High Atlas Mountains (p676).

Diving Warm shallow waters and the calcified wreck of a 3rd-century Roman ship make for fabulous diving off Croatia's Mljet Island (p161).

Surfing Surfers head to the western edge of the continent for the thundering waves that crash in on central Portugal's Atlantic beaches (p723).

Rafting Rafting along the Tara River in the Durmitor National Park is one of the most popular outdoor pursuits in Montenegro (p628).

» Carnevale in Venice, Italy (p509)

RUTH EASTHAM & MAX PAOLI / LONELY PLANET IMAGES ©

Partying

Ever since ancient Greek philosophers raised the pursuit of pleasure to a philosophy, the Med has been a party hot spot. Modern-day hedonists are spoilt for choice with everything from cutting edge clubs to seafront bars and bacchanalian beach parties.

Ios & Mykonos Summer revellers flock to the bars and clubs in Ios and gay-friendly Mykonos, two of Greece's premier party destinations (p401).

Ibiza Long a clubbing mecca, the Spanish island boasts some of the world's top clubs and regularly hosts big-name DJs (p866).

Hvar Town The main town on Hvar Island rocks in summer, serving up the best nightlife on the Dalmatian coast (p158).

Paceville Malta's in-your-face party scene centres on the pubs, clubs and bars of this popular district north of Valletta (p597).

Paris Catch a cabaret, dance till dawn or swoon over jazz in a shadowy basement bar – Paris by night offers limitless possibilities (p239).

Festivals & Celebrations

Showcasing the region's fiery passions and spiritual nature, the Mediterranean's great festivals range from solemn religious processions to wild street parties, costumed balls and glitzy film fests.

Carnival The lead-up to Lent is marked by carnival celebrations across the region, including Carnevale in Venice, a week-long fancy dress party dating to the 13th century (p509).

Sanfermines Festival Every July bulls are let loose on Pamplona's historic streets and every July hundreds of hyper-charged nutters run with them (p849).

Cannes Film Festival Every May Hollywood big shots don their glad rags and cruise the Croisette at the world's most prestigious film festival (p335).

Fez Festival of World Sacred Music One of the best world music festivals on the circuit, this hugely popular event features top musicians from across the globe (p662).

T-Mobile INmusic Festival Huge crowds and major European acts make for a superb atmosphere at Zagreb's three-day music bonanza (p124).

Architecture

Mediterranean Europe is a dream destination for architecture buffs. Ancient temples stand alongside hulking Gothic churches, majestic mosques, baroque piazzas and avant-garde museums.

Pantheon Rome's emblematic monument is a staggering achievement and the high point of ancient Roman engineering (p469).

Cathédrale de Notre Dame de Paris Paris' most famous and most visited cathedral is a towering masterpiece of early Gothic architecture (p219).

Blue Mosque Islamic style finds perfect form in the domes and minarets of the Blue Mosque, one of İstanbul's most recognisable buildings (p909).

St Peter's Square The Vatican's magnificent central piazza is a dazzling work of baroque urban design (p469).

La Sagrada Família Still a work in progress, Barcelona's showpiece church was designed by Antonio Gaudí, the most famous exponent of 20th-century Catalan modernism (p832).

Museo Guggenheim Since it was opened in Bilbao in 1997, Frank Gehry's striking Museo Guggenheim has quickly become a modern icon (p848).

If you like...spectacular desert scenery, camel treks depart from Merzouga in Morocco (p683) for the Erg Chebbi, a magnificent chain of drifting Saharan sand dunes.

Museums & Galleries

Home to some of the world's most celebrated art, the region's great museums and galleries boast works by French Impressionists, Spanish surrealists and the maestros of the Italian Renaissance, as well as many other revered artists.

Musée du Louvre One of the world's most famous museums, the Louvre has an enormous collection, yet most eyes are drawn to Leonardo da Vinci's *Mona Lisa* (p223).

Vatican Museums Michelangelo's Sistine Chapel frescoes are the highlight of the Vatican's mammoth museum complex (p469).

Galleria degli Uffizi There's nowhere better to feast on Italian art than Florence, the city where the Renaissance started in the late 15th century (p525).

Museo del Prado Madrid's top art gallery features works by Spanish giants Goya, Velázquez, El Greco and many more (p785).

National Archaeological Museum Finds from archaeological sites across Greece are exhibited at Athens' most prestigious museum (p371).

Ancient Ruins

The cradle of Western civilisation, Mediterranean Europe is littered with reminders of its ancient past. Ruined, and not-so-ruined, temples, amphitheatres, even entire towns, stand testament to the vision and skill of ancient Greece and Rome's pioneering engineers.

Parthenon Dating to the 5th century BC, Athens' staggering Doric temple encapsulates the glory of the once-powerful Greek empire (p370).

Pompeii Almost 2000 years after it was destroyed by Mt Vesuvius, Italy's most perfectly preserved ancient town is a thrilling sight (p551).

Ephesus Centred on a remarkable 25,000-seat theatre, the compelling ruins of Ephesus are Turkey's top ancient site (p939).

Diocletian's Palace Built for a Croatian-born Roman emperor, this monumental palace covers much of Split's historic centre (p150).

Les Arènes Nimes' stirring Roman amphitheatre once staged all sorts of gory gladiatorial games; nowadays it hosts bullfights and historical recreations (p313).

Medieval Towns

Against a backdrop of almost constant conflict, art and architecture flourished in the Middle Ages, giving rise to some truly wonderful medieval towns and cities.

Siena Offering one of Italy's finest medieval cityscapes, Siena radiates out from Piazza del Campo, setting of the city's famous Palio horse race (p535).

Dubrovnik Dubrovnik's majestic medieval walls date to its heyday as an independent republic and rival to the powerful Venetians (p162).

Santiago de Compostela Lording over Santiago's beautiful medieval centre is the city's landmark cathedral, a triumphant mix of architectural styles (p852).

Fez A tangled web of shady, twisting alleyways, Fez's medina is the largest and best preserved medieval city in the Arab-Muslim world (p660).

Kotor Situated at the head of a stunning fjord, walled Kotor is dramatically wedged between the sea and the steeply rising grey mountainside (p614).

month by month

1 **Carnival**, February

2 **Easter**, late March or April

3 **Fez Festival of World Sacred Music**, June

4 **Il Palio**, July

5 **Sanfermines**, July

January

As the New Year celebrations die down, the winter cold digs in. This is a fine time to hit the ski slopes with good fresh snow in the Alps and Pyrenees.

Skiing, Regionwide

Fresh snowfalls mean excellent conditions for skiing and snowboarding. The region's most famous resorts are in the French and Italian Alps but there's also excellent, and cheaper, skiing in the Pyrenees and Balkan countries. Slovenia and Bosnia & Hercegovina both offer exciting pistes.

February

The cold weather continues to provide ideal skiing conditions, while down below, the winter quiet is shattered by high-spirited carnival celebrations. Book accommodation if you're heading to a big carnival destination.

Carnival, Regionwide

In the period before Lent, carnival is a big deal in southern Europe, celebrated with wild processions, costumed parties and much eating and drinking. Events are held all over, but festivities are particularly high-spirited in Cádiz (Spain; p887), Rijeka (Croatia; p140), Nice (France; p333) and Venice (Italy; p509).

March

The onset of spring brings blooming flowers, rising temperatures and unpredictable rainfall. Unless Easter falls in late March, it is still fairly quiet, even in the mountains where the ski season is starting to tail off.

Las Fallas de San José, Spain

Valencia is the place to be in the week leading up to 19 March. The city's annual party marathon (p858) is an explosive event of partying, pageants and fireworks, culminating in the torching of hundreds of giant effigies in the central square.

April

Weather-wise April is glorious – sunshine and pleasant temperatures – but it can be busy, depending on when Easter falls. If travelling over Easter, expect crowds, memorable celebrations and high-season prices.

Easter, Regionwide

Across the region, Easter week is marked by parades, solemn processions and passion plays. In Rome, the Pope leads a Good Friday procession around the Colosseum and, on Easter Sunday, he gives his traditional blessing in St Peter's Square. See p480.

Maggio Musicale Fiorentino, Italy

The curtain goes up on Italy's oldest arts festival, a month-long spectacle of theatre, classical music, jazz and dance held at Florence's Teatro del Maggio Musicale Fiorentino between late-April and June. See p529.

 Music Biennale Zagreb

Held every odd-numbered year, Zagreb's headline event (p124) is one of Europe's top contemporary music festivals. Since it was established in 1961, it has grown in reputation and now attracts world-class performers from a range of musical backgrounds. See www.mbz.hr.

Feria de Abril, Spain

April is a festive time in Seville. The week before Easter, Semana Santa, is marked by sinister processions, while the Feria de Abril is a week-long fiesta of folklore, flamenco, tapas and sherry. (See p871).

May

Beautiful sunny weather makes this a wonderful time to visit the region. Life on the coast is slowly starting up as hotels begin to open for the season and the festival calendar moves into top gear.

May Day, Regionwide

A public holiday across much of the region, May Day traditions differ from country to country. The French give each other *muguets* (lilies of the valley), the Greeks gather wildflowers and the Italians descend on Rome for a vast open-air rock concert (p480).

Queima das Fitas, Portugal

In the week following the first Thursday in May students and townsfolk of Coimbra (p726) raucously celebrate the end of the academic year. Events kick off with a traditional fado serenade and climax with a parade of extravagantly decorated floats.

Cannes Film Festival, France

Mid-month, the world's most influential and glamorous film festival rolls out the red carpet for the Hollywood A-list. Onlookers crowd la Croisette (p337) to catch a glimpse of their celluloid heroes and debate potential Palme d'Or winners.

Fiesta de San Isidro, Spain

From the Friday preceding 15 May until the following Sunday, Madrid celebrates its patron saint with typical abandon (p795). Roll up for costumed processions, concerts, bullfights and plenty of late night revelry.

Druga Godba, Slovenia

Ljubljana's flamboyant festival of alternative and world music (p747) features everything from new jazz to contemporary folk music. Alongside a rich concert program, there are also film screenings, workshops, debates and seminars. See www.drugagodba.si.

June

The summer has arrived and with it hot, sunny weather and a full festival schedule. This is a great time for sunning yourself on the beach before the holiday hordes descend and prices skyrocket.

Fez Festival of World Sacred Music, Morocco

With an international cast of top performers, this is one of the Med's most popular world-music festivals (p662). Sell-out concerts are held in a number of atmospheric locations, including the palatial Batha Museum. See www.fesfestival.com.

Palio delle Quattro Antiche Repubbliche Marinare, Italy

Historic rivalries are rekindled in the form of boat races between Italy's four ancient maritime republics: Pisa, Genoa, Amalfi and Venice (p509). Before the races, representatives from each city don medieval garb and parade through the host city.

International İstanbul Music Festival, Turkey

Catch a classical concert in a sultan's palace or jazz in a 4th-century church during İstanbul's month-long music fest. In 2010 about 20,000 people watched concerts by some 600 artists, including the Vienna Philharmonic Orchestra. See www.iksv.or/muzik.

Estate Romana, Italy

Between June and September, Rome's ruins, piazzas and parks stage events organised as part of this sweeping annual festival (p480). The program is eclectic featuring everything from film screenings to children's concerts, book readings and theatrical performances.

T-Mobile INmusic Festival, Croatia

One of the top music festivals in the Balkans, this two-day event near Lake Jarun in Zagreb (p124) features a strong international line-up – in recent years Massive Attack, Moby, Kraftwerk and Lily Allen have all played. Details from www.t-mobileinmusicfestival.com.

Festa de Santo António, Portugal

On 12 and 13 June, Lisbon commemorates St Anthony with parades, street parties and unfeasible quantities of grilled sardines (p700). The event comes as part of the wide-ranging cultural event, Festas de Lisboa. See www.egeac.pt for details.

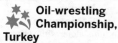

Hellenic Festival, Greece

The ancient theatre at Epidavros and the Theatre of Herodes Atticus are the headline venues of Athens' annual cultural shindig (p375). The festival, which runs from mid-June to August, features music, dance, theatre, and much more besides. See www.greekfestival.gr.

Oil-wrestling Championship, Turkey

Huge crowds gather in Edirne in late June/early July to cheer greased-up wrestlers as they slap each other around during the Kırkpınar wrestling festival (p926). Dating back to the 14th century, this is the world's oldest wrestling event. See www.kirkpinar.com.

July

Temperatures start to peak as schools break up for the long summer vacation. The coastal resorts are pretty busy by now and there are any number of festivals to check out.

Festival d'Avignon, France

Avignon's renowned arts festival is the oldest of its type in France and one of Europe's most famous. A month-long feast of drama, music, dance and poetry (p325), it runs alongside the alternative fringe festival, Festival Off (www.avignonleoff.com). See www.festival-avignon.com.

Baščaršijske Noći, Bosnia & Hercegovina

Dance, music and theatre take to the streets of Sarajevo for the month-long Baščaršija Nights festival (p80). All tastes are catered to with everything from ballet and opera to film screenings, book readings and kids events.

Marrakesh Popular Arts Festival, Morocco

A jubilant celebration of traditional Moroccan music, this is a hugely popular event, drawing musicians from all over the country, as well as belly dancers, snake charmers and fortune-tellers. Concerts are held at venues across town, including the Palais el-Badi (p671).

Zagreb Summer Evenings, Croatia

Zagreb's Upper Town buzzes to the sound of music and drama for much of July. The city's traditional summer festival (p671) showcases a range of musical forms from classical to blues, jazz and world music. Details from www.kdz.hr.

Ljubljana Festival, Slovenia

Thousands flock to Slovenia's capital, Ljubljana, for the country's most important arts festival. Held throughout July and August, it has something for everyone with world-class concerts, dance performances, lectures, children's workshops and exhibitions (p747). Check out the website, www.ljubljanafestival.si.

Il Palio, Italy

Siena's legendary horse race Il Palio (p537) is held twice annually, on 2 July and 16 August. Accompanied by great pomp and medieval festivities, it is a ferocious affair, contested by jockeys riding bareback around the city's central square. For more information see www.ilpalio.org.

Sanfermines, Spain

One of Europe's most famous festivals, Pamplona's annual bull running (p849) is not for the faint-hearted (or sane). Every morning between 6 and 14 July bulls are let loose to charge through the city accompanied by a crowd of crazy runners.

Dubrovnik Summer Festival, Croatia

Dubrovnik's beautiful streets set the scintillating stage for Croatia's biggest summer arts festival (p165). Local and international musicians, actors and artists perform at venues across the city throughout July and August. Get details at www.dubrovnik-festival.hr.

Festa del Redentore, Italy

On the third weekend in July, gondola regattas serve as the build-up to a spectacular fireworks display in Venice (p509). The much beloved festival was inaugurated in the 16th century to give thanks for the end of a plague epidemic.

 Mostar Bridge Diving Competition, Bosnia & Hercegovina

Crowds throng the rocky banks of the Neretva River to watch daredevil divers leap off Mostar's iconic bridge, Stari Most (p88), and plunge into the green waters 21m below.

Nice Jazz Festival, France

International jazz greats lead this week-long party on the French Riviera (p333). Louis Armstrong, Dizzy Gillespie and BB King have all headlined here, and the festival is a key date on the European jazz calendar. See www.nicejazzfestival.fr.

August

The height of the summer. Much of the region is on holiday – most people in France and Italy take their annual vacation this month – making for packed resorts, quiet cities and traffic jams on coast-bound roads.

Feast of the Assumption, Regionwide

Celebrated on 15 August, the Feast of the Assumption is the busiest holiday day of the year. Across the region, beaches are jam packed, cities slow to a standstill, and everyone basks in the summer sun.

Sarajevo Film Festival, Bosnia & Hercegovina

Since it was inaugurated in 1995, the Sarajevo Film Festival (p80) has become one of the largest film festivals in Europe and a major showcase for southeastern European movies. Commercial and art-house flicks are screened, almost all with English subtitles. For details see www.sff.ba.

Mostra del Cinema di Venezia, Italy

At the end of the month, movie big shots alight at Venice for the world's oldest film festival (p509). The focus of attention is the Palazzo del Cinema on the Lido, a small slither of an island in Venice's lagoon.

September

September is a lovely month to be on the Med. The August crowds have gone home but it's still hot enough for sunbathing and swimming and there's great hiking in the region's many national parks.

Braderie de Lille, France

Held on the first weekend in September, Lille's annual flea market is one of the largest in Europe, attracting up to two million visitors. Stalls sell everything from books to stuffed animals while restaurants compete to serve the most mussels.

Bienal de Flamenco, Spain

Give yourself up to the passion of Spain's largest flamenco festival (p871), held in Seville every even-numbered year. The world's top flamenco stars strut their stuff before passionate fans in venues across the city.

Festes de la Mercè, Spain

Barcelona's great annual bash (p830) is a bombastic affair, held over four days around 24 September. Highlights include eight-storey human towers and a procession of dragons which parades the streets accompanied by deafening fireworks and bangers. See www.bcn.cat/merce.

Hiking, Regionwide

Autumn, along with spring, is the ideal period for hiking. At higher altitudes, peaks are usually free of snow between June and September, making for great trekking in the Italian Dolomites (p522), Morocco's High Atlas Mountains (p676) and the Spanish Pyrenees (p841).

October

As coastal resorts wind down for the season, the focus returns inland. Warm weather and autumnal colours make for pleasant sightseeing, particularly in southerly areas, and accommodation rates start to drop.

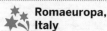

Romaeuropa, Italy

Established international performers join emerging stars at Rome's autumn festival of theatre, opera and dance (p480). Events, staged between late September and October, range from full-on raves and avant-garde dance performances to installations, multimedia shows, recitals and readings. Get details on http://romaeu ropa.net.

Adventure Race Montenegro

Montenegro's gruelling Adventure Race (p613) is not the only way to enjoy the Bay of Kotor's dramatic beauty, but it's certainly the toughest. Held in late September/early October, it involves an entire day of kayaking, mountain biking, trekking and orienteering. Check out www.adventure-racemontenegro.com.

November

The wettest month of the year, November is a quiet time with not a whole lot going on. On the plus side, accommodation is cheap and there are few tourists around.

International Jazz Festival, Bosnia & Hercegovina

One of the few events in November, Sarajevo's week-long jazz fest (p80) has a strong international reputation. Well-known musicians from around the world perform to enthusiastic crowds across the Bosnian capital. Get program details on www.jazzfest.ba.

December

The build-up to Christmas is a jolly time. Crowds brave the cold temperatures to shop at markets and enjoy the festive lights that adorn many towns and cities. Up in the mountains, the ski season kicks off mid-month.

Fête des Lumières, France

A public holiday in many countries, 8 December is an important religious date, the Feast of the Immaculate Conception. In Lyon it coincides with the Festival of Lights (p287), a spectacular sound and light show in the city's historic centre.

Christmas, Regionwide

Christmas is accompanied by the usual gift-giving traditions and family get-togethers. Highlights of the Christmas period include Strasbourg's famous Christmas market, the Marché de Noël (p264) in France, and Naples' elaborate *presepi* (nativity scenes; p544).

itineraries

Whether you've got six days or 60, these itineraries provide a starting point for the trip of a lifetime. Want more inspiration? Head online to lonelyplanet. com/thorntree to chat with other travellers.

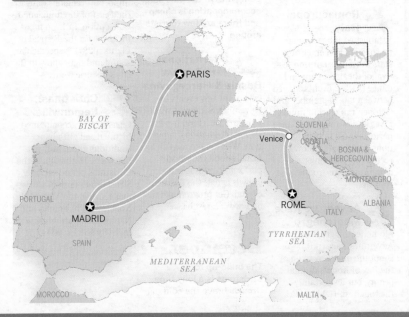

Two Weeks
City Highlights

With only two weeks to travel, the challenge is to see as much as possible whilst doing justice to each place you visit. This whirlwind tour concentrates on four of the region's most seductive cities.

Start with three days in the French capital, **Paris**. Check out the big sights – the Eiffel Tower, Notre Dame, the Louvre – and lap up the lifestyle in buzzing Montmartre and the Marais. Armed with your newly acquired savoire-faire, head southwards to **Madrid**, Spain's passionate capital. Admire the vast art collection at the Museo del Prado and pop into the king's royal palace, before an evening bar-hopping from one tapas joint to the next. After a couple of days, fly over to **Venice**, Italy's haunting and impossibly beautiful canal city. Here you'll have fun losing yourself in atmospheric lanes and postcard perfect piazzas, perhaps taking a gondola down the Grand Canal. From Venice, push on down to Italy's magnificent Eternal City. They say a lifetime's not enough for **Rome**, but three days should give you just enough time for the big sights – the Colosseum, Roman Forum, Vatican and Sistine Chapel.

One Month
A Tale of Two Continents

Marvel at amazing architecture, get lost in medinas and kick back on Atlantic beaches as you make your way round Portugal, Morocco and Spain on this intercontinental tour.

Start off in **Lisbon**, Portugal's laid-back capital and one of Europe's oft-overlooked cities. Explore the tangled lanes of the colourful Alfama district and tune in to the city sound at a fado club before heading down to The Algarve for a taste of Portuguese beach life. There are loads of beaches to choose from, including several around **Lagos**, a small fishing town with a vibrant summer scene. From Lagos, overnight trains run across the border to **Seville** in Spain. A sultry, fiery city famous for its full-blooded lifestyle and explosive festivals, Seville provides the perfect introduction to southern Spanish life. From Seville continue on to **Tarifa**, where you can catch a ferry to the Moroccan port of **Tangier**. After a quick nose around this lively, energetic city push on down the coast to cosmopolitan **Casablanca** and, beyond that, the hip resort of **Essaouira**, a perennial favourite with travellers. Next, venture inland to **Marrakesh**, one of Morocco's highlights. Watch the sun set on the blood-red walls and enjoy the nightly spectacle at Djemaa el-Fna before pressing on to **Fez** and its labyrinthine medina, the world's largest medieval Islamic city. Once you've found your way out of the maze and taken in the colourful (and smelly) tanneries, head up to **Melilla** on the north coast for an overnight ferry to **Málaga** in Spain. Hang around for a day or two to visit the wonderful Museo Picasso Málaga and enjoy the exuberant nightlife and then head up to **Granada** to visit the remarkable Alhambra. A masterpiece of medieval Islamic architecture, this is one of Spain's most celebrated Moorish marvels, along with the Mezquita at **Córdoba**. Yet more architectural wonders await in the beautiful cathedral town of **Toledo**, where historic streets are crammed with monuments and reminders of a turbulent past. The last stop is **Madrid**, Spain's thumping capital, where you can ogle world-class art, eat like a prince and party into the small hours.

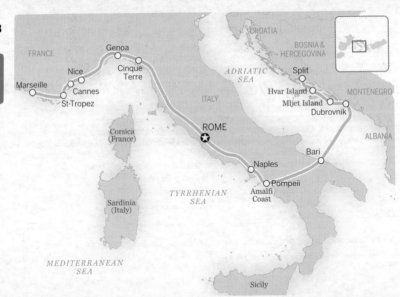

One Month
A Coastal Jaunt

> Passing through the French Riviera, several Unesco-listed national parks and a number of full-blooded Mediterranean ports, this three-country route takes in some of the region's finest coastal scenery.

Start in **Marseille**, France's edgy, multiethnic Mediterranean port. A far cry from the postcard-pretty landscape that characterises much of the surrounding Provence region, it's a gritty, atmospheric city with some great sights and wonderful restaurants where you can sample a bowl of bouillabaisse. From Marseilles, follow the coast eastwards along the fabled French Riviera. Top up your tan at **St-Tropez** and catch a film at **Cannes** as you wend your way along the coast to **Nice**, the Côte d'Azur's busy, cosmopolitan capital. From Nice, take a train to **Genoa** where you can wander the same salty streets that once inspired local boy Christopher Columbus, and eyeball sharks at Europe's second largest aquarium. For more sea thrills take a day or two to explore the **Cinque Terre**, one of Italy's most spectacular stretches of coastline. The road now leads to **Rome**, as all eventually do. Take in the big headline sights before continuing south to manic, in-your-face **Naples**. This sprawling city is not to everyone's taste but amidst the chaos it harbours some truly amazing works of art, many taken from the nearby ruins of **Pompeii**. Continuing on, you'll come to the **Amalfi Coast**, a dreamy stretch of shimmering seascapes and plunging cliffs. From the Mediterranean coast, cross over to the Adriatic port of **Bari** where you can catch a ferry for Croatia. While you wait to set sail, visit the Basilica di San Nicola and see where the bones of St Nicholas, aka Santa Claus, are buried. Over in Croatia, the first stop is **Dubrovnik**, the undisputed star of the Dalmatian coast. Once you've marvelled at the city's marble streets and baroque buildings, jump on a boat for some island hopping. Nearby, peaceful **Mljet Island** is a seductive mix of forests, vineyards and small villages, while further north **Hvar Island** boasts sunshine, beaches and a vibrant nightlife. From Hvar, it's a short ferry ride to **Split**, Croatia's second largest city and home to the Unesco-listed Diocletian's Palace, one of Eastern Europe's greatest Roman monuments.

A Balkan Odyssey

Mountainous and covered in great swathes of forest, Slovenia and the Balkan countries present the tougher, more rugged side of the Mediterranean. This 1045km eastern European odyssey leads through stunning mountain landscapes and beautiful towns as it snakes southwards from Slovenia to Albania.

To get you in the mood start with a few days in **Ljubljana**, Slovenia's cultured capital, enjoying the cafe life and exploring the city's landmark castle. Once done, head northwest to the lakeside town of **Bled**. A gorgeous spot in its own right, Bled makes a great base for hiking in the surrounding Julian Alps. From Bled double back to Ljubljana to pick up a bus to the Croatian capital, **Zagreb**. Hang around for a coffee or two in the Upper Town before pushing on to Bosnia & Hercegovina and **Bihać**, a pretty staging post on the road to Sarajevo. Before reaching the Bosnian capital, take time to stop off at **Jajce**, famous for its catacombs, citadel and waterfall, and **Travnik**, home to some impressive castle ruins. After a few days enjoying **Sarajevo**'s charming Turkish quarter and hip east-west vibe continue south to **Mostar** and its scene-stealing bridge. Known as the Stari Most, this is one of BiH's most iconic sights, along with the divers who hurl themselves from it during the July diving competition. From Mostar, it's a straightforward bus journey to **Herceg Novi**, an attractive walled town on Montenegro's coast at the mouth of the Bay of Kotor. A spectacular road winds its way along the bay to the magnificent medieval town of **Kotor**, wedged between dark mountains at the head of southern Europe's deepest fjord. The route here turns inland, through the thrilling Lovćen National Park, and on to Montenegro's former capital **Cetinje**. Continuing eastwards brings you to **Podgorica**, the nation's low-key modern capital. About 65km from Podgorica on the southeastern tip of Lake Shkodra, ancient **Shkodra** provides a good introduction to Albania as well as a convenient base for exploring the remote mountains around Theth. The last stretch of the tour leads south to the capital **Tirana**, once a model of drab Soviet-style urban blandness, now a crazy, colourful, buzzing city.

Three Weeks
Greek Island Hopping

Two Weeks
Turkish Delights

With their beautiful beaches, ancient ruins and endless pleasures, the Greek Islands have been seducing travellers for millennia. Ferry services are reduced in winter, so this a trip best undertaken in summer.

The obvious starting point is **Athens**, home to some of Europe's most iconic monuments. From nearby **Piraeus**, jump on a ferry for **Mykonos**, one of Greece's top island destinations. A hedonistic hot spot, it boasts action-packed beaches and a pretty whitewashed town. Before leaving, take time for a day trip to **Delos**, the mythical birthplace of the god Apollo. From Mykonos, sail south to **Naxos**, the largest and greenest of the Cyclades islands. It's much more than a beach stop, and its enticing main town and striking interior make it well worth exploring. From Naxos, it's a quick ferry ride to **Paros** and the popular beaches of **Antiparos**. Continuing southwards, **Santorini** is one of the Aegean's most impressive islands, its volcanic cliffs sheering up from the limpid blue sea. Greece's most southerly island, Crete makes a fitting finale. Just southwest of the main city **Iraklio** is **Knossos**, the ancient capital of Minoan Crete where the mythical Minotaur is supposed to have lived.

Bridging the gap between East and West, Turkey is a compelling cauldron of culture and style.

The place to start is **İstanbul**, one of the world's great cities, whose highlights include Topkapı Palace, Aya Sofya and Blue Mosque. Further round the Aegean coast **Çanakkale** is a popular base for visiting nearby **Gallipoli**, scene of vicious fights during WWI, and the legendary town of **Troy**. Following the coast, you arrive at **Bergama**, celebrated for the ruins of ancient Pergamum, once a powerful Middle Eastern kingdom. More classical treasures await at **Ephesus (Efes)**, Turkey's version of Pompeii, near **Selçuk**, home to the scarce remains of the Temple of Artemis, one of the Seven Wonders of the Ancient World. From Selçuk, push on to **Patara**, where you can share a magnificent 20km-long beach with breeding turtles. Spend a day or two hanging out in a tree house in **Olympos** before heading on to **Antalya**, with its historic Ottoman district and ancient Roman harbour. At this point head inland to **Konya**, which gave birth to the 13th-century whirling dervishes and also boasts some fine Seljuk architecture. Further northeast, the eerie, rocky landscape around **Göreme** is one of Turkey's most incredible sights.

Food, Port & Provence
Artistic Glories

Three Weeks
Food, Port and Provence

Taking in Portugal, Spain and France, this Franco-Iberian tour works either as a stand-alone itinerary or as half of a longer pan-Mediterranean tour.

The starting point is **Lisbon**, Portugal's fascinating and charming capital. When you've done exploring its Moorish ramparts and twisting tumbledown alleys, head north to the country's second largest city, **Porto**, the ideal place to taste the national tipple, port. From Porto get an overnight train to **Bilbao** in the Spanish Basque Country, where you'll find one of southern Europe's most recognisable buildings, the stunning Museo Guggenheim. East of Bilbao, **San Sebastián** is an elegant seafront city celebrated as one of Spain's great foodie destinations. Once sated, continue on to **Barcelona** for a blast of metropolitan style and a look at the city's unique Modernisme architecture. Next, jump on a train to **Nîmes**, a vibrant city that houses some of France's finest Roman ruins. To the east, **Avignon** provides an elegant introduction to Provence, France's showcase region renowned for its blistering colours and beautiful landscapes. As you head to the gripping Mediterranean port of **Marseille**, take a day to enjoy the bohemian chic of **Aix-En-Provence**, birthplace of Paul Cézanne and author Émile Zola.

Three Weeks
Artistic Glories

Depending on how much time you have, this whistle-stop tour of Italy and Greece can either be undertaken as a trip in its own right or as a continuation of the previous tour of Portugal, Spain and France.

Kick off in **Florence**, the birthplace of the Renaissance and one of Italy's great art cities. After a few days ogling priceless treasures, drag yourself away for a quick stopover at **Pisa**, home to the world-famous Leaning Tower, en route to **Rome** and more mind-boggling artistic treasures. From Rome, pick up a train to the Adriatic port of **Bari** and a ferry for Patra. Once docked, head straight for **Olympia**, venue of the first Olympic Games in 776 BC. After a night there continue southeast to **Mystras**, famed for the beauty of its Byzantine palaces and monasteries. Next day, head to the charming seafront town of **Nafplio** for a day or two, before pushing on to mythical **Mycenae** and the ruins of **Ancient Corinth**. Across the water, **Athens** is a chaotic mix of the ancient and the modern. Not to be missed, the Parthenon dominates the cityscape from its position over the Acropolis, while the National Archaeological Museum houses the country's most important collection of ancient artefacts.

countries at a glance

Stretching from Portugal in the west to Turkey's eastern reaches, Mediterranean Europe encompasses a huge variety of peoples and places. The vast majority of visitors head to the big holiday hot spots – France, Spain, Italy, Greece and Turkey – for the classic cocktail of sun, sea, culture, great food and timeless scenery. In North Africa, Morocco is another popular destination with its age-old medinas and Saharan landscapes. Far fewer travellers venture off the beaten track to experience the heartfelt hospitality and stunning natural beauty of the eastern Adriatic countries – Slovenia, Croatia, Bosnia & Hercegovina, Montenegro and Albania.

Albania

Beaches ✓✓
Scenery ✓✓✓
Culture ✓✓

Once isolated Albania has some of the last undeveloped coastline on the Mediterranean, its mountains are some of Europe's most spectacular, and the Koman ferry is possibly the region's most beautiful boat ride. **p39**

Bosnia & Hercegovina

Scenery ✓✓
Adventure Holidays ✓✓✓
History ✓✓

One of the best-known European destinations for active holidays, Bosnia is a great place for kayaking, skiing, hiking and mountain biking. With its mixed Muslim and Christian heritage, it's also a fascinating blend of cultures. **p71**

Croatia

Cuisine ✓✓
Architecture ✓✓✓
Scenery ✓✓✓

A dazzling coastline and thousands of islands, Dubrovnik's legendary old town, Diocletian's Palace in Split, the extraordinary Plitvice Lakes National Park and Istria's foodie offerings – you're spoilt for choice in Croatia. **p115**

Cyprus

History ✓✓✓
Beaches ✓✓
Culture ✓✓

Mythical birthplace of the goddess Aphrodite, Cyprus' ancient landscape is thick with Graeco-Roman ruins, Byzantine monasteries and historic mosques. Away from the main resorts, you'll find beautiful, unspoilt beaches and tracts of inspiring countryside. **p180**

France

Food ✓✓✓
Cities ✓✓✓
Wine ✓✓✓

There's Paris and then there's Paris and that's enough reason to visit France. But consider all the other extraordinary towns and regions (such as Lyon and Provence). In all of them you can enjoy fabulous French food and wine. **p209**

Greece

Monuments ✓✓✓
Islands ✓✓✓
Food ✓

The Acropolis is the iconic symbol of an ancient civilisation that is a basis for ours. Civilisation is of little concern at the scores of beguiling islands with their beaches, tavernas and ultra-fresh seafood. **p367**

Italy

History ✓✓✓
Culture ✓✓✓
Food ✓✓✓

History (Roman Empire), tick. Culture (Renaissance et al), tick. Food (Italian cuisine), tick, tick, tick! Really, there's so much to love about the Boot that who knows where to begin – so just take the plunge. **p457**

Malta

Diving & Snorkelling ✓✓✓
Beaches ✓✓
History ✓✓

Warm, crystal clear waters make Malta a top diving and snorkelling spot, while plentiful beaches ensure great sunbathing. History buffs will enjoy the island's strange megalithic temples, the ancient Hypogeum and honey-coloured capital Valletta. **p589**

Montenegro

Scenery ✓✓✓
Historic Sites ✓✓
Outdoor Pursuits ✓✓

Montenegro crams an awful lot into a very small space: jagged mountains, sheer-walled river canyons, extreme sports, long sandy beaches and the spectacular Bay of Kotor, where the mountains dip their toes into the sea. **p609**

Morocco

Culture ✓✓✓
Food ✓✓
Trekking ✓✓✓

Dive into Fez's seething medina or Marrakesh's magical souqs for a blast of North African Muslim culture. Dine on tajine and mint tea as you hike between Berber villages in the High Atlas Mountains. **p635**

Portugal

Towns ✓✓
Culture ✓✓
Beaches ✓

Coimbra has it all: a lively university town where the medieval backstreets yield odd little clubs for fado music. It's an intoxicating mix – if you can escape the pull of Lisbon or the beaches. **p693**

Slovenia

Scenery ✓✓✓
Outdoor Sports ✓✓✓
Wine ✓✓

Even serial visitors to Slovenia regularly stop and stare, mesmerised by the sheer beauty of this tiny country. Don't miss Mt Triglav, Vršič Pass, Lake Bled, the Karst, or the Postojna and Škocjan caves. **p743**

Spain

Cities ✓✓✓
Food ✓✓
Beaches ✓

Ever sunny, Spain works its spell from Basque tapas bars to the never-ending nights of vibrant Barcelona to the impossibly photogenic hill towns and famous beaches of Andalucía. Plus you really can smell the orange blossoms in Seville. **p783**

Turkey

History ✓✓✓
Ruins ✓✓✓
Beaches ✓✓✓

From İstanbul's bustling bazaars and towering minarets to the evocative ruins of Ephesus and sumptuous beaches on the Turquoise Coast, Turkey is a beguiling mix of Mediterranean charm and Eastern promise. **p907**

Look out for these icons:

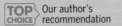 Our author's recommendation

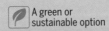 A green or sustainable option

FREE No payment required

See the Index for a full list of destinations covered in this book.

On the Road

Albania

Includes »

Best Places to Stay

» Berat Backpackers (p55)
» B&B Tedeschini (p52)
» Hotel Kalemi (p61)

Best Places to Eat

» Kujtimi (p61)
» Era (p45)
» Tradita G+T (p50)

Why Go?

Alps sprout in the background, plains and lakes surround the central mountain ranges, and coastal areas provide the traveller to Albania (or Shqipëria, as the locals call it) with dramatically different cultural and geographical landscapes. City slickers can down coffee in busy, always surprising Tirana before heading to an exhibition or nightclub.

After years of government-enforced isolation, Albanians welcome travellers with sincere hospitality. Upgraded roads swirl past the new houses and bar/restaurant/hotel developments that demonstrate the country's newfound prosperity.

August sees quiet seaside spots morph into loud disco-laden towns where every day is a thumping weekend. Head north and you might spot locals in traditional dress, sworn virgins and shepherds guiding flocks in the otherwise inhospitable mountains.

Albania is unforgettable: donkeys tethered to concrete bunkers, houses crawling up each other to reach the hilltops in Berat and Gjirokastra, and isolated beaches.

When to Go

Tirana

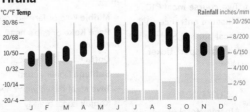

June Enjoy the Mediterranean climate and deserted beaches.

August Beaches are packed and overseas-based Albanians return to holiday with their families.

December See features and shorts at the Tirana Film Festival. Snowshoe to Theth.

Fast Facts

» **Area** 28,748 sq km

» **Capital** Tirana

» **Telephone** country code 355

» **Emergency** police 129, fire 128, ambulance 127

Exchange Rates

Australia	A$1	102.5 lekë
Canada	C$1	101.8 lekë
euro	€1	141.8 lekë
Japan	¥100	116.5 lekë
New Zealand	NZ$1	77.1 lekë
UK	UK£1	159.3 lekë
USA	US$1	97.9 lekë

Set Your Budget

» **Budget hotel** €12-15 per person

» **Two-course meal** €10

» **Museum entrance** €1-3

» **Local beer** €1.50

» **City transport ticket** 30 lekë

Resources

» **Albania-Hotel** (www.albania-hotel.com)

» **Balkanology** (www.balkanology.com/albania)

» **National Tourist Organisation** (www.albaniantourism.com)

Connections

Albania has daily bus connections with Kosovo, Montenegro, Macedonia, Italy (bus and ferry) and Thessaloniki and Athens in Greece. Albania's Saranda is a short ferry trip from Greece's Corfu. Travellers heading south from Croatia can pass through Montenegro to Shkodra (via Ulcinj), and can loop the country before heading into Macedonia via Pogradec or Kosovo via the Lake Koman ferry or new superfast Albania–Kosovo highway.

ITINERARIES

Three Days

Drink frappé at Tirana's trendy Blloku cafes, check oput the museum and art gallery, then spend the night dancing in packed nightclubs. On day two, head up the Djati Express and dine on roast lamb in the clean mountain air of Mt Djati National Park. Return to Tirana in time for the two-hour trip to the Ottoman-era town of Berat. Stay in a character-filled hotel or hostel in the town's old quarters. On day three, Kruja is a good detour on the way to the airport; check out one of the country's best ethnographic museums and buy souvenirs in its authentic little bazaar.

One Week

Spend a day in Tirana, head south to Berat for a few days, then pass through the scenic Llogaraja Pass. Take on beachside Drymades or Jal before making a pit stop at Saranda to prepare for a stroll around Butrint's ruins. Pause at the Blue Eye Spring en route to the Ottoman-era town of Gjirokastra.

Essential Food & Drink

» **Byrek** Pastry with cheese or meat

» **Fergesë** Baked peppers, egg and cheese and occasionally meat

» **Midhje** Wild or farmed mussels, often served fried

» **Paçë Koke** Sheep's head soup usually served for breakfast

» **Qofta** Flat or cylindrical minced-meat rissoles

» **Sufllaqë** Doner kebab

» **Tavë** Meat baked with cheese and egg

» **Konjak** Local brandy

» **Raki** Popular spirit made from grapes

» **Raki mani** Spirit made from mulberries

MONTENEGRO

Peja

Plav

KOSOVO

Valbonë

Theth

Bajram
Curri

Valbonë
National
Park

Theth
National
Park

Drin

Fierzë

E851

E65

Lake
Skadar

Lake
Fierza

Lake
Koman

Kukës

Tetovo

E762

Puka

E851

Koman

Shkodra

Rreshen

Lura
National Park

Mavrovo
National Park

Peshkopia

Milot

E851

Drin River

E65

Qafe Shtama
National
Park

Bulqiza

Kruja

MACEDONIA

Zall Gjocaj
National Park

E65

Mt Dajti
National Park

Tirana

Ohrid

Durrës

E852

E852

Lake
Ohrid

Kavaja

Elbasan

Lake
Prespa

E853

Shkumbini

Divjaka
National Park

Lushnja

Lake Prespa
National Park

E853

Kuçova

Mt Tomorri
National Park

Apollonia

Berat

Fier

Mt Tomorri
(2415m)

Korça

Drenova
National Park

Vjosa River

Sazan

Vlora

Këlcyra

Karaburun
Peninsula

E853

Llogaraja Pass
National Park

Dhërmi

Drymades

Vuno

Himara

Gjirokastra

Jal

Livadhi

Blue Eye
Spring

E90

GREECE

E853

Saranda

Mesopotamia

Ksamil

IONIAN SEA

Butrint
National Park

Ioannina

Corfu

Kerkira

GREECE

N

0   40 km
0   20 miles

Albania Highlights

1 Feast your eyes on the wild colour schemes and experience the hip Blloku cafe culture in **Tirana** (p42)

2 Explore the Unesco World Heritage–listed museum cities of calm **Berat** (p53) and slate-roofed **Gjirokastra** (p61)

3 Catch some sun at **Drymades** (p57), just one of beaches on the south's dramatic Ionian Coast

4 Travel back in time to the ruins of **Butrint** (p60), hidden in the depths of a forest in a serene lakeside setting

5 Catch the Lake Koman ferry to near Valbone and trek the northern Alps (aka Accursed Mountains) to the village of **Theth** (p50)

TIRANA

📞 04 / POP 600,000

Lively, colourful Tirana has changed beyond belief in the last decade from the dull, grey city it once was (see pre-'90s Albanian movies for a glimpse). It's amazing what a lick of paint can do – it covers one ugly tower block with horizontal orange and red stripes, another with concentric pink and purple circles, and plants perspective-fooling cubes on its neighbour.

Trendy Blloku buzzes with well-dressed *nouvelle bourgeoisie* hanging out in bars or zipping between boutiques. Quite where their money comes from is the subject of much speculation in this economically deprived nation, but thankfully you don't need much of it to have a fun night out in the city's many bars and clubs.

The city's grand central boulevards are lined with fascinating relics of its Ottoman, Italian and communist past – from delicate minarets to loud socialist murals. Tirana's traffic does daily battle with both itself and pedestrians in a constant scene of unmitigated chaos. Loud, crazy, colourful, dusty – Tirana is simply fascinating.

Tirana

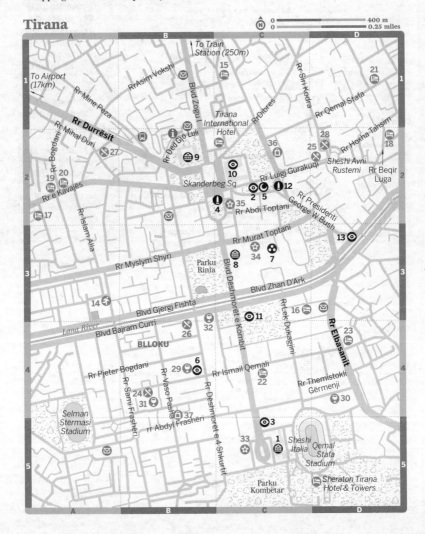

⊙ Sights & Activities

Running through Tirana is Blvd Zogu I, which becomes Dëshmorët e Kombit as it crosses the Lana River. At its northern end is Tirana's train station, head south and you're at the Tirana University. The main sites of interest are on or very close to this large boulevard, including, roughly halfway along, the orientation point of Skanderbeg Sq.

NORTH OF THE RIVER

Sheshi Skënderbej   SQUARE
Skanderbeg Sq is the best place to start witnessing Tirana's daily goings-on. Until it was pulled down by an angry mob in 1991, a 10m-high bronze statue of Enver Hoxha stood here, watching over a mainly car-free square. Now only the **equestrian statue of Skanderberg** remains, deaf to the cacophony of screeching horns as cars four-lanes deep try to shove their way through the battlefield below. The square's recent redevelopment may turn the cacophony into a murmur.

Et'hem Bey Mosque   MOSQUE
(☉8am–noon) If you stop to examine Skanderbeg's emblematic goat's-head helmet, the minaret of the 1789–1823 Et'hem Bey Mosque will catch your eye. The small and elegant mosque is one of the oldest buildings left in the city, spared from destruction during the atheism campaign of the late '60s because of its status as a cultural monument. Take your shoes off to look inside at the beautifully painted dome.

Clock Tower   MONUMENT
(Kulla e Sahatit; Rr Luigi Gurakqi; admission 50 lekë; ☉9am–1pm Mon, 9am–1pm & 4-6pm Thu) Behind the mosque is the tall Clock Tower, which you can climb for views of the square. Further on, the socialist realist **Statue of the Unknown Partisan** attracts day labourers waiting for work, some with their own jackhammers – a fitting image of the precarious position of the postcommunist Albanian worker.

Palace of Culture   NOTABLE BUILDING
(Pallate Kulturës; Sheshi Skënderbej) To the east of Sheshi Skënderbej is the white stone Palace of Culture, which has a theatre, shops and art galleries. Construction of the palace began as a gift from the Soviet people in

Tirana

1960 and was completed in 1966, years after the 1961 Soviet-Albanian split.

National History Museum

MUSEUM

(Muzeu Historik Kombëtar; Sheshi Skënderbej; admission 200 lekë; ⊙10am-5pm Tue-Sat, to 2pm Sun) On the northwestern side of the square is the National History Museum. This, the largest museum in Albania, holds most of the country's archaeological treasures and a replica of Skanderbeg's massive sword (how he held it, rode his horse and fought at the same time is a mystery). The mosaic mural entitled *Albania* adorning the museum's facade shows Albanians victorious and proud from Illyrian times through to WWII. There's a terrific exhibition of icons by Onufri, the renowned 16th-century master of colour. A sombre and controversial gallery devoted to the miseries of the communist regime was being updated at the time of research. Note there's no entry half an hour before closing time.

National Art Gallery

ART GALLERY

(Galeria Kombëtare e Arteve; Blvd Dëshmorët e Kombit; admission 200 lekë; ⊙10am-5pm Tue-Sat, to 2pm Sun) The National Art Gallery is packed with bright Soviet realism paintings featuring smiling 'aren't we happy to be here!' workers in their various places of employ. No entry 20 minutes before closing time.

Fortress of Justinian

RUINS

(Rr Murat Toptani) If you turn up Rr Murat Toptani, behind the National Art Gallery, you'll pass the 6m-high walls of the Fortress of Justinian, the last remnants of a Byzantine-era castle. These days half a cinema/nightclub overflows over the top. East from here, on the corner of Rr Presidenti George W Bush and the Lana River, is **Tanners' Bridge**, a small 19th-century slippery-when-wet stone bridge.

FREE Mosaic of Tirana

RUINS

(Rr Naim Frashëri 1; www.drkkt.com) It's a little tricky to find (it was only discovered itself in 1972) but this 3rd-century AD mosaic and other surviving relics are proof of an early ancient settlement in Tirana.

SOUTH OF THE RIVER

Pyramid

NOTABLE BUILDING

(Blvd Dëshmorët e Kombit) The Pyramid was designed by Enver Hoxha's daughter and son-in-law and completed in 1988. It was formerly the Enver Hoxha Museum, and more recently a convention centre and nightclub; its white-marble sides are slowly falling apart and it appears that the Pyramid's disintegration will be complete before renovation occurs.

Congress Building

NOTABLE BUILDING

(Blvd Dëshmorët e Kombit) Another creation of the former dictator's daughter and son-in-law is the square Congress Building, just a little down the boulevard from the Pyramid. Follow Rr Ismail Qemali two streets north of the Congress Building and enter the once totally forbidden but now totally trendy **Blloku** area. This former Communist Party elite hang-out was opened to the general public for the first time in 1991. Security still guards the **former residence of Enver Hoxha** (cnr Rr Dëshmorët e 4 Shkurtit & Rr Ismail Qemali).

Archaeological Museum

MUSEUM

(Muzeu Arkeologik; Sheshi Nënë Tereza; admission €1; ⊙10.30am-2.30pm Mon-Fri) The staff may bemoan the unrenovated condition of the Archaeological Museum, but it does manage to house an extensive collection of antiquities and provide information about recent archaeological digs.

Martyrs' Cemetery

CEMETERY

At the top of Rr Elbasanit is the Martyrs' Cemetery, where some 900 partisans who died in WWII are buried. The views over the city and surrounding mountains (including Mt Dajti to the east) are excellent, as is the sight of the immense, beautiful and strangely androgynous Mother Albania statue (1972). Hoxha was buried here in 1985 but in 1992 he was exhumed and interred in an ordinary graveyard elsewhere. Catch a municipal bus heading up Rr Elbasanit; the grand driveway is on your left.

☞ Tours

Get off the beaten track or discover Albania's tourist attractions with the following Tirana-based tour companies:

Albanian Experience

TOURS

(⏺2272 055; www.albania-experience.al; Sheraton Tirana Hotel, Sheshi Italia; ⊙8.30am-7pm Mon-Fri, 8.30am-5pm Sat) Organises tours of Albania with knowledgeable guides.

Outdoor Albania

TOURS

(⏺2227 121; www.outdooralbania.com; Metropol Bldg, Rr Sami Frashëri; ⊙9am-5pm Mon-Fri) Excellent trailblazing adventure tour agency offering hiking, rafting, snowshoeing, sea and white-water kayaking and, in summer, hikes through the Alps.

Festivals & Events

Tirana International Film Festival   CINEMA
(www.tiranafilmfest.com) This festival is held each December and features both short and feature films from its international competition winners, as well as new cinematic work from Albanian filmmakers.

🛏 Sleeping

Tirana Backpacker Hostel   HOSTEL €
(☏068 2167 357; www.tiranahostel.com; Rr Elbasanit 85; dm €12;＠) Albania's first hostel opened in 2005 in a 70-year-old villa close to the city centre. Its 25 beds are spread over four rooms and its bathrooms have great showers. It has big balconies, a garden and a cosy outdoor kitchen. Helpful managers can link you in to their summer hostel in Vuno (p58) and Hostel 2, which is also in Tirana.

Milingona   HOSTEL €
(☏069 2260 775, 069 2049 836; www.milingona hostel.com; Rr Qemal Stafa 277; dm €12;＠) Run by uber-enthusiastic and multilingual sisters Zhujeta and Rozana, Milingona (meaning 'ant') is clean and homey, with a 'never going to leave' terrace up top which, thanks to the sisters' local musical connections, occasionally doubles as a music venue. There's no breakfast but there is an excellent kitchen for self-caterers. They offer bike rental and tours of Tirana, and they'll meet you in Tirana when you arrive.

Hostel Albania   HOSTEL €
(☏067 2783 798; www.hostel-albania.com; Rr Beqir Luga 56; dm €11-13;❄＠⚲) This hostel has small four- and six-person dorms, though the basement's 14-bed dorm (€11) is the coolest spot in summer and dividers hide the fact that there are so many bunks down there. There's room for a couple of tents (€7 per person). Zen space is in the outdoor shoes-off oriental lounge, and a filling breakfast with filter coffee is included. Great information about the local art scene can be found here.

Green House   BOUTIQUE HOTEL €€€
(☏2222 632; www.greenhouse.al; Rr Jul Varibova 6; s/d €85/110; ❄⚲) In a cool spot in Tirana sits this modern hotel with downlit, modern rooms that scream celebrity. Its restaurant is a modern and friendly expat hang-out with a varied menu and a long wine list. It looks up at one of Tirana's quirkiest buildings.

Hotel Nirvana   HOTEL €€
(☏2235 270; Rr e Kavajës 96/2; s/d incl breakfast €60/80;❄＠) With its ostentatious marble

staircase and walls dripping with art (apparently this is nothing compared with the owner's house), this hotel may have delusions of grandeur, but thankfully the price remains reasonably humble and the staff are friendly and helpful. Free parking.

Pension Andrea   PENSION €€
(☏069 2094 915; Rr Anton Harapi 103; s/d €25/30) Grandmother Gina runs this quiet pension with limited English but loads of enthusiasm. All rooms have TVs and a couple have air-con. There's a safe storage area for bicycles. From Rr Jeronim de Rada take the first right down the court; you'll find Gina through the gate on your right.

Freddy's Hostel   HOTEL €
(☏068 2035 261, 2266 077; www.freddyshostel. com; Rr Bardhok Biba 75; dm/r €12/32) Freddy's isn't really a hostel (there's no communal area) but the clean, basic bunk-free rooms have lockers and come in different configurations. It's well signposted on a suburban street running parallel to Blvd Zogu I. Can also arrange long-term apartments.

Hotel Serenity   HOTEL €€
(☏2267 152; Rr Bogdani 4; d €50;❄＠) This simple villa-style hotel is in a quiet and central location. Rooms have tiled floors, minibars and TVs and offer excellent value.

Rogner Hotel Europapark Tirana HOTEL €€€
(☏2235 035; www.europapark.com; Blvd Dëshmorët e Kombit; s €150-180, d €170-200, ste €240-270; ❄＠❄⚲) With an unbeatable location in the heart of the city, the Rogner is a peaceful oasis with a huge garden, tennis court and free wi-fi in the lobby as well as onsite banks, travel and car-rental agencies. The rooms are spacious and comfortable and have flat-screen TVs.

🍴 Eating

If you thought that cuisine in Tirana's restaurants might be monotonous or that eating out would be a downmarket experience, you were wrong.

Most of the eating and drinking action is at Blloku, a square of some 10 blocks of shops, restaurants, cafes and hotels situated one block west of Dëshmorët and along the Lana River in south Tirana.

TOP CHOICE **Era**   TRADITIONAL €
(☏2266 662; Rr Ismail Qemali; mains from 200 lekë; ⊙11am-midnight) Serves traditional Albanian and Italian fare in the heart of Blloku. Be warned: it's hard to move on once you've

eaten here. It's also sometimes quite hard to get a seat. Does delivery and takeaway.

Oda
TRADITIONAL €€
(Rr Luigj Gurakuqi; meals 800 lekë) Bright flashing lights will guide you to this endearing little restaurant down a lane near Sheshi Avni Rustemi. It's up there in the traveller popularity stakes, and offers diners (if there's room) an authentic vibe, interesting Albanian dishes, and extra, extra-strong restaurant-distilled raki.

Pasticeri Française
BAKERY €
(Rr Dëshmorët e 4 Shkurtit 1; breakfast from 300 lekë; ☉8am-10pm; 🛜) It's no wonder this French cafe has a slimming advertisement hanging on its wall; its sweet pastries (and macarons) are irresistible.

Shpia Jon
TRADITIONAL €€
(Rr Kont Urani; meals 800 lekë; ☉7am-10pm, closed Sun) This new restaurant is hidden in a fairly suburban part of town but serves light and fluffy *qofte* and *qifqi* (meatballs and rice-balls) and piping-hot *tavë* (blend of cheese, peppers, tomato and eggplant with an egg). The serves are generous and, bar the moving wall of water in the courtyard, the house is decorated with tradition in mind.

Stephen Centre
CAFE €€
(Rr Hoxhim Tahsim 1; mains 500 lekë; ☉8am-8pm, closed Sun; 🛜) If you like your fries thin, your wi-fi free and the spirit Christian, here's the cafe for you. The accommodation upstairs comes in single-bed configurations (single/double €30/40).

🍷 Drinking
Most of Tirana's nightspots will have you partying on to the wee hours.

Radio
BAR
(Rr Ismail Qemali 29/1) Set back from the street is this very, very cool yet understated bar. Check out the owner's collection of antique Albania-made radios while sipping cocktails with groovy locals.

Charl's
BAR
(Rr Pjetër Bogdani 36) Charl's is a consistently popular bar with Tirana's students because of its ever-varying live music on the weekends, and disco/dance crowd-pleasers the rest of the time. The relaxed vibe is enhanced by the bar's open-air garden.

Kaon Beer Garden
BEER HALL
(Rr Assim Zeneli; ☉noon-1am) For those who hate the hassle of ordering beer after beer,

here's Kaon. Its popular 'keg-on-the-table' approach means it can be hard to get a table in the evening (queuing is normal), but once you get in, it's a pleasant outdoor bar and restaurant in the fancy villa-filled part of town. You won't go hungry; Albanian meals start from 200 lekë. Locally brewed beer comes in standard glasses, or tabletop two- and three-litre 'roxys'.

Sky Club Bar
BAR
(Sky Tower, Rr Dëshmorët e 4 Shkurtit) Start your night here for spectacular city views from the revolving bar on top of one of the highest buildings in town.

☆ Entertainment
There is a good choice of entertainment options in Tirana, in the form of bars, clubs, cinema, performances, exhibitions and even ten-pin bowling. For the low-down on events and exhibitions, check posters around town. For alternative events ask at Milingona hostel and Hostel Albania.

Folie
CLUB
(Rr Murat Toptani) This is where the big-name DJs come to play, and though the crowd can be a little more concerned with being seen than actually enjoying themselves, it's a great outdoor venue for a loud night out.

FREE Marubi Film & Multimedia School
CINEMA
(www.afmm.edu.al; Rr Aleksander Moisiu 76; ☉7pm Thu) Shows free art-house movies on Thursdays during the semester. It's near the last Kino Studio bus stop in the city's northeast.

Kinema Millennium 2
CINEMA
(www.ida-millennium.com; Rr Murat Toptani; tickets 300-500 lekë) Current-release movies that are cheaper the earlier in the day you go. At night it's a nightclub.

Theatre of Opera & Ballet
THEATRE
(☎2224 753; Sheshi Skënderbej; tickets from 300 lekë; ☉performances from 7pm, from 6pm winter) Check the listings and posters outside the theatre for performances.

Academy of Arts
THEATRE
(☎2257 237; www.artacademy.al; Sheshi Nënë Tereza) Classical music and other performances take place throughout the year in either the large indoor theatre or the small open-air faux-classical amphitheatre; both are part of the university. Prices vary according to the program.

🛍 Shopping

Souvenir shops on Rr Durrësit and Blvd Zogu I sell red Albanian flags, red T-shirts, red lighters, bunker ashtrays and lively traditional textiles.

Adrion International Bookshop BOOKS
(Palace of Culture; ⊙9am-9pm Mon-Sat) The place to head for maps, guides and English-language books.

Market FOOD & DRINK
(Sheshi Avni Rustemi) Buy fruit, vegetables and deli produce here; nearby Qemal Stafa has second-hand stalls selling everything from bicycles to bedheads.

Natyral & Organik FOOD & DRINK
(Rr Vaso Pasha) This tiny store in Blloku not only supports small village producers by stocking their organic olive oil, honey, herbs, tea, eggs, spices, raki and cognac (these make great gifts, but be aware of customs regulations in the countries you're travelling through); it's also a centre for environmental activism.

ℹ Information

Tirana has plenty of ATMs linked to international networks.

ABC Clinic (☑2234 105; www.abchealth.org; Rr Qemal Stafa 260; ⊙9am-1pm Mon, Wed & Fri, 9am-5pm Tue & Thu) Has English-speaking Christian doctors and a range of services, including brief (600 lekë) and normal (1200 lekë) consultations.

DHL (☑2268 755; Rr Ded Gjo Luli 6; ⊙8am-6pm Mon-Fri, 8am-noon Sat) Parcel-sending service.

Hygeia Hospital Tirana (☑2390 000; www.hygeia.al; Tirana-Durrës Hwy) This new Greek-owned private hospital has a 24-hour emergency department.

Post office (☑2228 262; Rr Çameria; ⊙8am-8pm) A shiny and clean oasis in a street jutting west from Sheshi Skënderbej. Smaller offices operate around the city.

Tirana in Your Pocket (www.inyourpocket.com) Has a local team of writers providing up-to-date coverage of Tirana. It can be downloaded free or bought at bookshops, hotels and some of the larger kiosks for 500 lekë.

Tirana tourist information centre (☑2223 313; Rr Ded Gjo Luli; www.tirana.gov.al; ⊙9am-7pm Mon-Fri, 9am-4pm Sat & Sun) Friendly staff make getting information easy at this new-to-Tirana government-run initiative.

ℹ Getting There & Around

A large number of agencies and airline offices sell air and bus tickets along Rr Mine Peza and Blvd Zogu 1, close to the National History Museum.

Air

Nënë Tereza International Airport (Mother Teresa Airport, Rinas airport, Tirana Airport; www.tirana-airport.com.al) is at Rinas, 17km northwest of Tirana. The new, glossy passenger terminal opened in 2006. The Rinas Express airport bus operates an hourly (6am to 6pm) service from Rr Mine Peza on the western side of the National History Museum for 250 lekë one way. The going taxi rate is €17. The airport is 20 minutes' drive away, but plan for possible traffic delays.

Bicycle

This was the main form of transport for Albanians until the early '90s, and it's having a comeback (cyclists seem to make more headway in Tirana's regular traffic snarls). Bike hire is available from several hostels.

Bus

You have the option of buses or *furgons* (minibuses). There is no official bus station in Tirana, though there's a makeshift bus station beside the train station where some buses drop passengers off and depart from. Confusingly, other buses and *furgons* depart from ever-changing places in and around the city, so check locally for the latest departure points. You can almost guarantee that taxi drivers will be in the know; however, you may have to dissuade them from taking you the whole way.

Furgons are usually slightly more expensive than buses and leave when full. Buses for Pristina in Kosovo (€10, five hours, three daily) leave from beside the museum on Blvd Zogu 1. To Macedonia, there are buses via Struga (€13, five hours) to Tetovo (€15, seven to eight hours) and Skopje (€20, eight hours) from the same spot. Buses to Ulcinj (€20) and Budva (€30) in Montenegro depart from 6am in front of the tourist information centre. If you're heading to Athens (€35, 15 hours), buses leave at around either 8am or 7pm from outside the travel agencies on Blvd Zogu 1.

Most bus services are fairly casual; you turn up and pay the driver. However, you can also buy tickets the day before from **Drita Travel and Tours** (☑2251 277; www.dritatravel.com; Rr Ded Gjo Luli) for services to Athens (8am, €35), Montenegro (6am, €30), Kosovo (6am, €10) and Macedonia (7.30pm, €20).

Car

Lumani Enterprise (☑04-2235 021; www.lumani-enterprise.com) is a local car-hire

DOMESTIC BUSES FROM TIRANA

DESTINATION	COST (LEKË)	DURATION (HR)	DISTANCE (KM)
Berat	400	2½	122
Durrës	100	1	38
Elbasan	300	1½	54
Fier	300	2	113
Gjirokastra	1000	7	232
Korça	800	4	181
Kruja	200	½	32
Pogradec	700	3½	150
Saranda	1200	7	284
Shkodra	400	2	116
Vlora	400	4	147

company. International companies in Tirana include the following (each also has an outlet at the airport):

Avis (☑2235 011, 068 2062 161; Rogner Hotel Europapark, Blvd Dëshmorët e Kombit)

Europcar (☑2227 888, 068 2093 908; Rr Durrësit 61)

Hertz (☑2255 028; Tirana Hotel International, Sheshi Skënderbej)

Sixt (☑2259 020, 068 2068 500; Rr e Kavajës 116)

Train

The run-down train station is at the northern end of Blvd Zogu I. Albania's trains range from sort of OK to very decrepit. Albanians travel by train if they can't afford to travel by bus. Seven trains daily go to Durrës (70 lekë, one hour, 36km). Trains also depart for Elbasan (190 lekë, four hours, 2.10pm), Pogradec (2km out of town; 295 lekë, eight hours, 5.30am), Shkodra (145 lekë, 3½ hours, 1.15pm) and Vlora (250 lekë, 5¾ hours, 4.30pm). Check timetables at the station the day before travelling. Purchase tickets before hopping on the train.

Taxi

Taxi stands dot the city, and taxis charge 300-400 lekë for a ride inside Tirana and 600 lekë at night and to destinations outside the city centre. Reach agreement on price with the driver before setting off. **Radio Taxi** (☑377 777), with 24-hour service, is particularly reliable.

AROUND TIRANA

Just 25km east of Tirana is **Mt Dajti National Park** (1611m). It is the most accessible mountain in the country, and many Tiranans go there to escape the city rush and have a spit-roast lamb lunch. A sky-high, Austrian-made cable car, **Dajti Express** (www.dajtiekspres.com; 700 lekë return; ☑9am-9pm Tue-Sun), takes 15 minutes to rise to (almost) the top. It's a scenic trip over bunkers, forest, farms and hilltops. Once there, you can avoid all the touts and their minibuses and take the opportunity to stroll through lovely, shady beech and pine forests. There are grassy picnic spots along the road to the right, but if you didn't pack a picnic, try the lamb roast and spectacular views from the wide terrace of the **Panorama Restaurant** (meals 800 lekë).

To get to the Dajti Express departure point, take the public bus from outside Tirana's Clock Tower to 'Porcelain' (30 lekë). From here, it's a 1.5km walk uphill, or you can wait for a free bus transfer. Taxis seem to charge what they want to the Dajti Express drop-off point, but the trip from Tirana should only cost 600 lekë. It's also possible to drive or cycle to the top.

NORTHERN ALBANIA

The northern Albanian landscape has rich wildlife, swamps and lagoons around Shkodra and Lezha and high mountains around Theth in the northeast (named the 'accursed mountains', Bjeshkët e Namuna, in Albanian). Blood feuds may occupy some locals' minds, but pose little risk to tourists (see the boxed text, p49).

Shkodra

📱 022 / POP 91,300

Shkodra (Shkodër), the traditional centre of the Gheg cultural region, is one of the oldest cities in Europe. Rozafa Fortress has stunning views, and the Marubi permanent photography exhibition in town is small but fascinating. A section of town has benefited from sensitive renovations of its historic buildings, and Shkodra's locals are more likely to ride a bicycle than drive a car.

Travellers pass through here on the way between Tirana and Ulcinj in Montenegro, but most use the town as a base for forays into the alpine areas of Theth and Valbonë and the isolated wonder of Lake Koman.

As the Ottoman Empire declined in the late 18th century, Shkodra became the centre of a semi-independent *pashalik* (region governed by a pasha, an Ottoman high official), which led to a blossoming of commerce and crafts. In 1913 Montenegro attempted to annex Shkodra (it succeeded in taking Ulcinj), a move not approved of by the international community, and the town changed hands often during WWI. Badly damaged by an earthquake in 1979, Shkodra was subsequently repaired and is Albania's fourth-largest town. The communist-era Hotel Rozafa in the town centre does little to welcome guests, but it makes a good landmark: restaurants, the information centre and most of the town's sights are close by.

⊙ Sights

Rozafa Fortress
CASTLE

(admission 200 lekë; ⊙8am-10pm) Three kilometres southwest of Shkodra, near the southern end of Lake Shkodra, is the Rozafa Fortress, founded by the Illyrians in antiquity and rebuilt much later by the Venetians and Turks. The fortress derives its name from a woman named Rozafa, who was allegedly walled into the ramparts as an offering to the gods so that the construction would stand. The story goes that Rozafa asked that two holes be left in the stonework so that she could continue to breastfeed her baby. There's a spectacular wall sculpture of her near the entrance of the castle's **museum** (admission 150 lekë; ⊙8am-7pm). Some nursing women come to the fortress to smear their breasts with the milky water that seeps from the wall during some months of the year. Municipal buses (30 lekë) stop near the turn-off to the castle, and it's a short walk up from there.

Marubi Permanent Photo Exhibition
ART GALLERY

(Rr Muhamet Gjollesha; admission 100 lekë; ⊙8am-4pm Mon-Fri) Hidden behind a block of shops and flats, the Marubi Permanent Photo Exhibition has fantastic photography by the Marubi 'dynasty', Albania's first and foremost photographers. The first-ever photograph taken in Albania is here, taken by Pjetër Marubi in 1858. The exhibition shows fascinating portraits, places and events. Not only is this a rare insight into what things looked like in old Albania, it is also a small collection of mighty fine photographs. To get here, go northeast of the clock tower to Rr Çlirimi; Rr Muhamet

---

FAMILY FEUD WITH BLOOD AS THE PRIZE

The *Kanun* (Code) was formalised in the 15th century by powerful northern chieftain Lekë Dukagjin. It consists of 1262 articles covering every aspect of daily life: work, marriage, family, property, hospitality, economy and so on. Though the *Kanun* was suppressed by the communists, there has been a revival of its strict precepts in northern Albania.

According to the *Kanun,* the most important things in life are honour and hospitality. If a member of a family (or one of their guests) is murdered, it becomes the duty of the male members of that clan to claim their blood debt by murdering a male member of the murderer's clan. This sparks an endless cycle of killing that doesn't end until either all the male members of one of the families are dead, or reconciliation is brokered through respected village elders.

Hospitality is so important in these parts of Albania that the guest takes on a godlike status. There are 38 articles giving instructions on how to treat a guest – an abundance of food, drink and comfort is at his or her disposal, and it is also the host's duty to avenge the murder of his guest, should this happen during their visit. It's worth reading *Broken April*, by Ismail Kadare, a brilliant exploration of people living under the *Kanun*.

Gjollesha darts off to the right. The exhibition is on the left in an unmarked building, but locals will help you find it if you ask.

🛏 Sleeping & Eating

TOP CHOICE **Tradita G&T**

BOUTIQUE HOTEL, TRADITIONAL RESTAURANT **€€**
(Tradita Gegë dhe Toskë; ✆068 2086 056, 2240 537; www.traditagt.com; Rr Skënderbeu 4; s/d/t €35/50/55; ❋) Hooray, this restaurant has expanded into a hotel and the rooms are a delight. Family rooms have two levels and basic facilities, and there's a homemade, home-grown breakfast waiting for guests in the morning. The restaurant serves excellent fish dishes (meals 1100 lekë) in an ethnographic museum atmosphere. If you're heading Lake Koman way, the owner can arrange for the bus to pick you up from the hotel.

Hotel Kaduku   HOTEL **€**
(HK; ✆42 216; Sheshi 5 Heronjtë; s/d incl breakfast €23/32) This popular hotel is behind Raiffeisen Bank on the roundabout near Hotel Rozafa. Its two wings have been renovated, but the best reason to stay here is for the information provided by staff about getting to and from Theth. If it's full, owners have access to cheap rooms elsewhere.

Piazza Park   PIZZA **€**
(Rr 13 Dhjetori; mains 300-1000 lekë) Where the locals return to, night after night, day after day. Once you get past security, people-watch (or be watched) next to the fountains and kids' playground.

Hotel Europa   BAR
(Sheshi 2 Prilli) Check out the accursed mountains from the bar on level five of this luxury hotel. Its outdoor ground-floor bar is also a relaxing spot next to a park and playground.

ℹ Information

The **information office** (a stand-alone booth) near Piazza Park is open daily, and until 9pm in summer.

ℹ Getting There & Away

BUS There are hourly *furgons* and buses to and from Tirana (350 lekë, two hours, 6am to 4pm). From Shkodra, *furgons* depart from outside Radio Shkodra near Hotel Rozafa. *Furgons* to Ulcinj in Montenegro leave at 9am and 4pm (600 lekë, two hours) from the other side of the park abutting Grand Hotel Europa. They fill quickly. From Ulcinj, buses leave for Shkodra at 6am and 12.30pm. Catch the 7am bus to Lake Koman (800 lekë, two hours) in time for the wonderful ferry trip along the lake to Fierza (400 lekë, two hours) near Kosovo. *Furgons* depart for Theth daily at 7am (700 lekë).

TAXI It costs between €40 and €45 for the trip from Shkodra to Uncinj in Montenegro.

TRAIN Trains depart Tirana daily at 1.15pm (145 lekë), and arrive in Shkodra at 4.50pm, but you'll need to be up early to catch the 5.40am train back. *Furgons* meet arriving trains.

Theth & Valbonë

These small villages deep in the 'accursed mountains' are all but deserted in winter (Theth locals head south to live in Shkodra) but come summer, they're a magnet for those seeking beauty, isolation, mystery and adventure. From Theth, three circular hikes are marked out with red and white markers. It's possible to hike in the region without a guide, but they're helpful and you can expect to pay an informal guide between 3000 and 4000 lekë per day. Formal guides charge €50.

The main hike is from Theth to Valbonë (or vice versa). It takes around three hours to trek from Theth's centre (742m) to Valbonë pass (1812m), then a further two hours to the houses of Rragam and 1½ hours along a riverbed to near Bajram Curri.

◉ Sights

Kulla   HISTORIC BUILDING
(Theth; admission €1) Visit this 'lock-in tower' in central Theth where men waited, protected, during a blood feud (see boxed text p49).

🛏 Sleeping & Eating

Recent investment has resulted in many of Theth's homes becoming B&Bs (complete with Western-style bathrooms with hot showers). Due to the absence of restaurants in town, families include breakfast, lunch and dinner in the deal. Try www.shkoder-albanian-alps.com (linked with Outdoor Albania, p44) for accommodation.

Guesthouse Mëhill Çarku   GUEST HOUSE **€€**
(✆069 3164 211; www.guesthouse-thethi-carku.com; Theth; per person 2500 lekë; ☉Apr-Oct) Book in advance for a bed in this home with thick stone walls, timber floors, a garden and farm.

Guesthouse Tërthorja   GUEST HOUSE **€€**
(✆069 3840 990; www.terthorja-guesthouse-tethi.com; Theth; per person lekë 2500) This renovated guest house has a sports field, sports equipment and a resident cow.

BUNKER LOVE

On the hillsides, beaches and generally most surfaces in Albania, you will notice small concrete domes (often in groups of three) with rectangular slits. Meet the bunkers: Enver Hoxha's concrete legacy, built from 1950 to 1985. Weighing in at five tonnes of concrete and iron, these little mushrooms are almost impossible to destroy. They were built to repel an invasion and can resist full tank assault – a fact proved by their chief engineer, who vouched for his creation's strength by standing inside one while it was bombarded by a tank. The shell-shocked engineer emerged unscathed, and tens of thousands were built. Today, some are creatively painted, one houses a tattoo artist, and maybe one day the more spectacularly located ones will house tourists.

Hotel Rilindja   HOTEL
(☑067 3014 637; www.journeytovalbona.com; Valbonë; r incl breakfast per person €15, per tent €6) Good accommodation and food. The family can organise hikes, picnics and transport.

ⓘ Getting There & Around

BUS Though Theth is only 70km from Shkodra, expect the occasionally hair-raising *furgon* trip to take four hours. The *furgon* leaves from outside Café Rusi in Shkodra at 7am.

TAXI To Theth from Shkodra by taxi expect to pay €100.

FERRY A popular route is to take the 7am *furgon* from Shkodra to the Koman Ferry, travel by ferry (two hours) then jump on a *furgon* from the ferry to Bajram Curri (20 minutes, 150 lekë) in time for the 2.30pm *furgon* to Valbonë (200 lekë). This route can also be driven (the ferry charges €25 for a car and five people). The *furgon* leaves Valbonë at 7am for Bajram Curri, while the return ferry departs Fierzë at 2pm. If you're heading into Kosovo, it takes roughly 50 minutes to the border by car from the ferry terminal.

CENTRAL ALBANIA

Central Albania crams it all in. Travel an hour or two from Tirana and you can be Ottoman house-hopping in brilliant Berat, musing over ancient ruins in deserted Apollonia or haggling for antiques in an Ottoman bazaar in Kruja.

Kruja

☑0511 / POP 20,000
From the road below, Kruja's houses appear to sit in the lap of a mountain. An ancient castle juts out to one side, and the massive Skanderbeg Museum juts out of the castle itself. The local plaster industry is going strong so expect visibility-reducing plumes of smoke to cloud views of the Adriatic Sea.

Kruja is Skanderbeg's town. Yes, Albania's hero was born here, and although it was over 500 years ago, there's still a great deal of pride in the fact that he and his forces defended Kruja from the Ottomans until his death. As soon as you get off the *furgon* you're face to knee with a statue of Skanderbeg wielding his mighty sword with one hand, and it just gets more Skanderdelic after that.

At a young age Kastrioti, the son of an Albanian prince, was handed over as a hostage to the Turks, who converted him to Islam and gave him a military education at Edirne in Turkey. There he became known as Iskander (after Alexander the Great) and Sultan Murat II promoted him to the rank of *bey* (governor), thus the name Skanderbeg.

In 1443 the Turks suffered a defeat at the hands of the Hungarians at Niš in present-day Serbia, and nationally minded Skanderbeg took the opportunity to abandon the Ottoman army and Islam and rally his fellow Albanians against the Turks. Skanderbeg made Kruja his seat of government between 1443 and 1468. Among the 13 Turkish invasions he subsequently repulsed was that led by his former commander, Murat II. Pope Calixtus III named Skanderbeg the 'captain general of the Holy See' and Venice formed an alliance with him. The Turks besieged Kruja four times. Though beaten back in 1450, 1466 and 1467, they finally took control of Kruja in 1478 (after Skanderbeg's death).

Kruja's sights can be covered in a few hours, making this an ideal town to visit en route to Tirana's airport.

⊙ Sights

Castle   CASTLE
(⊙24hr) Inside Kruja's castle grounds are Albania flag sellers, pizza restaurants and an

array of interesting sights, though few actually castle-related.

Skanderbeg Museum
MUSEUM

(admission 200 lekë; ⊙9am-1pm & 4-7pm Tue-Sun) Designed by Enver Hoxha's daughter and son-in-law, this museum opened in 1982, and its spacious seven-level interior displays replicas of armour and paintings depicting Skanderbeg's struggle against the Ottomans. The museum is something of a secular shrine, and takes itself very seriously indeed, with giant statues and dramatic battle murals.

Ethnographic Museum
MUSEUM

(admission 300 lekë; ⊙9am-1pm & 4-7pm, closed Mon) This traditional home in the castle complex below the Skanderbeg Museum is one of the best in the country. Set in an original 19th-century Ottoman house that belonged to the affluent Toptani family, this museum shows the level of luxury and self-sufficiency the household maintained by producing its own food, drink, leather and weapons. They even had their very own mini-*hammam* (Turkish bath) and watermill. The walls are lined with original frescos from 1764. The English-speaking guide's detailed explanations are excellent; offer a tip if you can.

Teqe
CHURCH

A short scramble down the cobblestone lane are the remains of a small *hammam* as well as a functioning *teqe* – a small place of worship for those practising the Bektashi branch of Islam. This beautifully decorated *teqe* has been maintained by successive generations of the Dollma family since 1789. Skanderbeg himself reputedly planted the knotted olive tree at the front.

Bazaar
MARKET

This Ottoman-style bazaar is the country's best place for souvenir shopping and has WWII medical kits, antique gems and quality traditional ware, including beautifully embroidered tablecloths, copper coffee pots and plates. You can watch women using looms to make *kilims* (rugs) and purchase the results.

ⓘ Getting There & Away

Kruja is 32km from Tirana. Make sure your *furgon* from Tirana (200 lekë) is going to Kruja, not just Fush Kruja, below. It is very easy to reach the airport (100 lekë, 15 minutes) by *furgon* or taxi from here, and it's en route to Shkodra, though you'll need to pull over a bus on the busy Tirana–Shkodra highway as they don't stop in the town itself.

Durrës

Durrës was once Albania's capital. Its 10km-long beach is a lesson in unplanned development; hundreds of hotels stand side by side, barely giving breathing space to the beach and contributing to the urban-waste problem that causes frequent outbreaks of skin infections in swimmers. Despite this, it has some good sights in the older part of town and makes a decent place for day-trippers.

◉ Sights

Archaeological Museum
MUSEUM

(Muzeu Arkeologik; Rr Taulantia; admission 300 lekë; ⊙9am-3pm Tue-Sat, 10am-3pm Sun) The Archaeological Museum on Durrës' waterfront has an impressive collection of artefacts from the Greek, Hellenistic and Roman periods, and guides who will explain it all. Durrës was a centre for the worship of Venus, and the museum has a cabinet full of little busts of the love goddess.

Amphitheatre of Durrës
RUINS

(Rr e Kalasë; admission 300 lekë; ⊙9am-7pm) The Amphitheatre of Durrës was built on the hillside inside the city walls in the early 2nd century AD. In its prime it had the capacity to seat 15,000 to 20,000 spectators, but these days a few inhabited houses occupy the stage, a reminder of its recent rediscovery (in 1966) and excavation. The Byzantine chapel in the amphitheatre has several beautiful mosaics.

⌕ Sleeping & Eating

B&B Tedeschini
TOP CHOICE
B&B €€

(☎224 343, 068 2246 303; ipmcrsp@icc.al.eu.org; Rr Dom Nikoll Kaçorri 5; s/d without bathroom incl breakfast €15/30) This gracious 19th-century former Italian consulate is a homey B&B with airy rooms, containing antique furniture. Owner (and doctor) Alma prepares great breakfasts in the country-style kitchen. From the Great Mosque walk past the town hall and take a right, then a quick left. Use the doorbell next to the green gates.

Hotel Pepeto
HOTEL €€

(☎224 190; Rr Mbreti Monun 3; s/d/ste incl breakfast €25/35/50; ❋@🕸) A well-run (and well-signposted) guest house at the end of a court, just off the square fronting the Great Mosque. The rooms are decent and quiet, some have baths and balconies and the suite is an attic-dweller's dream. There's a spacious lounge and bar area downstairs.

Bar Torra BAR €
(Sheshi Mujo Ulqinaku) This Venetian tower was opened by a team of local artists and was one of the first private cafes in Albania. There are art displays (and cozy nooks) downstairs, and in summer you can gaze around Durrës from the top of the tower.

Picante INTERNATIONAL €
(Rr Taulantia; mains 700-7000 lekë) Upping the trendy ante on the redeveloped waterfront is this stark white restaurant with a chilli theme and good, though budget-stretching, meals.

❶ Getting There & Away

BOAT Agencies around the train station sell tickets for the many ferry lines plying the Durrës–Bari route (single deck €40, eight hours). **Venezia Lines** (☎225 338) has the fastest boat to Bari (€60, 3½ hours). Ferries also depart Durrës for Ancona most days in summer (€65, 17 hours) and at least three days a week throughout the year.

BUS & FURGON *Furgons* (150 lekë, one hour) and buses (100 lekë, one hour) to Tirana leave from beside the train station when they're full. Buses leave for Shkodra at 7.30am and 1.30pm (400 lekë, three hours). In summer, long-distance buses and *furgons* going to and from Saranda, Gjirokastra, Fier and Berat (400 lekë, 1½ hours) bypass this station, picking up and dropping off passengers at the end of Plazhi i Durrësi, east of the harbour, which can be reached by the 'Plepa' orange municipal bus (30 lekë, 10 minutes). In July and August many buses connect Durrës with Pristina in Kosovo (€10, five hours).

TRAIN Six trains a day head to Tirana (70 lekë, one hour, 6.15am, 8.45am, 9.20am, 1.05pm, 3.12pm, 4.45pm and 8.05pm). Trains also depart for Shkodra (1.05pm), Pogradec (6.45am), Elbasan (6.45am, 3.25pm) and Vlore (5.35pm). Check at the station for changes in departure times.

Apollonia

The ruined city of ancient **Apollonia** (admission 700 lekë; ⊙9am-5pm) is 12km west of Fier, which is 90km south of Durrës. Apollonia is set on rolling hills among olive groves, and the plains below stretch for kilometres. Apollonia (named after the god Apollo) was founded by Greeks from Corinth and Corfu in 588 BC and quickly grew into an important city-state, which minted its own currency and benefited from a robust slave trade. Under the Romans (from 229 BC) the city became a great cultural centre with a famous school of philosophy.

Julius Caesar rewarded Apollonia with the title 'free city' for supporting him against Gnaeus Pompeius Magnus (Pompey the Great) during the civil war in the 1st century BC, and sent his nephew Octavius, the future Emperor Augustus, to complete his studies here.

After a series of military and natural disasters (including an earthquake in the 3rd century AD that turned the river into a malarial swamp), the population moved southward into present-day Vlora, and by the 5th century AD only a small village with its own bishop remained at Apollonia.

There is far less to see at Apollonia than there is at Butrint, but there are some picturesque ruins within the 4km of city walls, including a small original theatre and the elegant pillars on the restored facade of the city's 2nd-century AD administrative centre. You may be able to see the 3rd-century BC **House of Mosaics** from a distance, though they're often covered up with sand for protection from the elements. Inside the **Museum of Apollonia** complex is the Byzantine monastery and Church of St Mary, which has gargoyles on the outside pillars. Much of the site remains to be excavated, but recent discoveries include a necropolis outside the castle walls with graves from the Bronze and Iron Ages.

❶ Getting There & Away

Apollonia is best visited on a day trip from Tirana, Durrës, Vlora or Berat.

Furgons depart for the site (50 lekë) from Fier's '24th August Bar' (ask locals for directions). From Fier, *furgons* head to Durrës (200 lekë, 1½ hours), Tirana (300 lekë, two hours), Berat (300 lekë, one hour) and Vlora (200 lekë, 45 minutes).

If you'd prefer not to wait for the *furgon*, a taxi will charge 500 lekë one way from Fier.

Berat

☑032 / POP 45,500
A highlight of any trip to Albania is a visit to beautiful Berat. Its most striking feature is the collection of white Ottoman houses climbing up the hill to its castle, earning it the title of 'town of a thousand windows' and helping it join Gjirokastra on the list of Unesco World Heritage sites in 2008. Its rugged mountain setting is particularly evocative when the clouds swirl around the tops of the minarets, or break up to show the icy top of Mt Tomorri.

WHERE'S THE ROOF?

Half-completed houses dot Albania's roadsides, and while many look deserted, the reality is they're being built one level at a time, with immigrants returning each summer armed with more cash to add another level, or to finally put the finishing touch – a roof – on their multilevel home. While the house is a work in progress, look up: you'll most certainly spot a weatherbeaten stuffed teddy bear adorning its highest level. A lost child's toy? No, it's an attempt to ward off the evil eye.

The old quarters are lovely ensembles of whitewashed walls, tiled roofs and cobblestone roads. Surrounding the town, olive and cherry trees decorate the gentler slopes, while pine woods stand on the steeper inclines. In true Albanian style, an elegant mosque with a pencil minaret is partnered on the main square by a large new Orthodox church. Bridges over the Osumi River include a 1780 seven-arched stone footbridge.

In the 3rd century BC an Illyrian fortress called Antipatrea was built here on the site of an earlier settlement. The Byzantines strengthened the hilltop fortifications in the 5th and 6th centuries, as did the Bulgarians 400 years later. The Serbs, who occupied the citadel in 1345, renamed it Beligrad, or 'White City'. In 1450 the Ottoman Turks took the town. After a period of decline, in the 18th and 19th centuries the town began to thrive as a crafts centre specialising in woodcarving.

⊙ Sights

Kalasa   CASTLE
(admission 100 lekë; ⊘24hr) The neighbourhood inside the castle's walls still lives and breathes; you'll see old Mercedes-Benz cars struggling up the cobblestone roads to return locals home. If you walk around this busy, ancient neighbourhood for long enough you'll invariably stumble into someone's courtyard thinking it's a church or ruin (no one seems to mind, though). In spring and summer the fragrance of chamomile is in the air (and underfoot), and wildflowers burst from every gap between the stones. The highest point is occupied by the **Inner Fortress**, where ruined stairs lead to a Tolkienesque water reservoir; take a torch (flashlight) and watch your step.

Onufri Museum   ART GALLERY
(admission 200 lekë; ⊘9am-1pm & 4-7pm May-Sep, 9am-4pm Oct-Apr, closed Mon) Kala was traditionally a Christian neighbourhood, but fewer than a dozen of the 20 churches remain. The quarter's biggest church, **Church of the**

Dormition of St Mary (Kisha Fjetja e Shën Mërisë), is the site of the Onufri Museum. The church itself dates from 1797 and was built on the foundations of a 10th-century church. Onufri's spectacular 16th-century artworks are displayed on the ground level along with a beautifully gilded iconostasis.

Churches & Chapels   CHURCHES
Ask at the Onufri Museum if you can see the other churches and tiny chapels in Kala, including **St Theodore** (Shën Todher), close to the citadel gates; the substantial and picturesque **Church of the Holy Trinity** (Kisha Shën Triades), below the upper fortress; and the little chapels of **St Mary Blachernae** (Shën Mëri Vllaherna) and **St Nicholas** (Shënkolli). Some of the churches date back to the 13th century. Also keep an eye out for the **Red Mosque**, by the southern Kala walls, which was the first in Berat and dates back to the 15th century.

Chapel of St Michael   CHURCH
Perched on a cliff ledge below the citadel is the artfully positioned little chapel of St Michael (Shën Mihell), best viewed from the Gorica quarter.

Ethnographic Museum   MUSEUM
(admission 100 lekë; ⊘9am-1pm & 4-7pm May-Sep, 9am-4pm Oct-30 Apr, closed Mon) Down from the castle, this museum, in an 18th-century Ottoman house that's as interesting as the exhibits. The ground floor has displays of traditional clothes and the tools used by silversmiths and weavers, while the upper storey has kitchens, bedrooms and guest rooms decked out in traditional style. Check out the *mafil*, a kind of mezzanine looking into the lounge where the women of the house could keep an eye on male guests (and see when their cups needed to be filled). There are information sheets in Italian, French and English.

Mosques   NEIGHBOURHOOD
Down in the traditionally Muslim Mangalem quarter, there are three grand mosques. The 16th-century **Sultan's Mosque** (Xhamia

e Mbretit) is one of the oldest in Albania. The **Helveti teqe** behind the mosque has a beautiful carved ceiling and was specially designed with acoustic holes to improve the quality of sound during meetings. The Helveti, like the Bektashi, are a dervish order, or brotherhood, of Muslim mystics. The big mosque on the town square is the 16th-century **Lead Mosque** (Xhamia e Plumbit), so named because of the lead coating its sphere-shaped domes. The 19th-century **Bachelors' Mosque** (Xhamia e Beqarëvet) is down by the Osumi River; look for the enchanting paintings on its external walls. This mosque was built for unmarried shop assistants and junior craftsmen and is perched between some fine Ottoman-era shopfronts along the river.

🏃 Activities

Bogove Waterfall · HIKING
Catch the 8am or 9am *furgon* to Bogove via Skrappar, or a later bus to Polican then transfer to a *furgon* to Bogove. Lunch at Taverna Dafinat above the bus stop, then follow the path along the river (starting on the Berat side) to this icy waterfall.

Cobo Winery · WINE TASTING
The Cobo family winery has one of the only cellar doors in Albania, and it's worth checking it. Try its Sheshi i Bardhe, Trebiano, Shesh i Izi and Kashmer wines, and, of course, its Raki me Arra. Any bus/*furgon* heading to Tirana can drop you off at the winery for 100 lekë.

Albanian Rafting Group · RAFTING
(📞069 2035 634; www.albrafting.org) Organises one- and two-day rafting trips along the Osumi River and canyons.

🛏️ Sleeping & Eating

TOP CHOICE · Berat Backpackers · HOSTEL €
(📞069 3064 429; www.beratbackpackers.com; Gorica; dm incl breakfast €12; ⊘Apr-Nov) Albania's best backpackers is the brainchild of Englishman Scott; he's transformed a traditional house in the Gorica quarter (across the river from Mangalem) into a vine-clad hostel with a basement bar, alfresco drinking area and a cheery, relaxed atmosphere that money can't buy. There's a shaded camping area on the terrace (€5 per person), two airy dorms with original ceilings, and one excellent-value double room (€13 per person).

Hotel Mangalemi · HOTEL €€
(📞32 093, 068 2429 803; www.mangalemihotel.com; Rr e Kalasë; s/d incl breakfast €20/35) Tomi Mio

(the hotel is known locally as Hotel Tomi) and his son run this iconic hotel in two sprawling Ottoman houses (they recently bought and renovated the house next door). Its terrace restaurant has great Albanian food with bonus views of Mt Tomorri. It's on the left side of the cobblestone road leading to the castle.

Hotel Guva · HOTEL €
(📞30 014; Mangalem; s/d incl breakfast €15/30) The four rooms of this 'new kid on the block' have tremendous views of Gorica, as does its upstairs terrace bar. One room has four single beds for €10 per person. It's a hike up stairs near St Michael.

Bujar's · TRADITIONAL €
(meals 200 lekë) In the market area near the Osumi River you'll find this simple restaurant with cheap and traditional lunches. The restaurant doesn't have menus, just a selection of daily offerings. Look for a single-storey, light-blue building down a lane.

Antigoni · TRADITIONAL €€
(Gorica; mains 600 lekë) This bustling restaurant may have an unusual style of service (some call it ignoring), but the Mangalem and Osumi River views from its upper levels are outstanding, and the food and local wine, when you finally get to order it, is good.

ℹ️ Information

The town's **information centre** (www.bashki aberat.com) is located in the council building, parallel to the Osumi River in new Berat.

ℹ️ Getting There & Away

Buses and *furgons* run between Tirana and Berat (400 lekë, 2½ hours) hourly until 3pm. From Tirana, buses leave from the 'Kombinati' station (catch the municipal bus from Sheshi Skënderbej to Kombinati for 30 lekë). In Berat, buses depart from and arrive at the bus station next to the Lead Mosque. There are buses to Vlora (300 lekë, 2½ hours), Durrës (400 lekë, 1½ hours) and Saranda via Gjirokastra (1000 lekë, six hours, two daily at 8am and 2pm).

SOUTHERN COAST

With rough mountains falling headfirst into bright-blue seas, this area is wild and ready for exploration. Some beaches are jam-packed in August, yet there's plenty of space, peace and happy-to-see-you faces in the low season. With careful government planning, the southern coast could shine. In the meantime, if the rubbish lying next to you on the beach gets you down, you only have to bend your neck a bit to see the snowcapped mountain peaks and wide green valleys zigzagged by rivers.

Vlora

☑ 033 / POP 124,000

It's here in sunny Vlora (the ancient Aulon) that the Adriatic Sea meets the Ionian, but the beaches are muddy and grubby, and the port town has really outgrown itself. History-buffs should come here for its museums and historic buildings, while beach lovers should hold their horses for horses for Dhermi, Drymades or Jal, all further south.

◉ Sights

Sheshi i Flamurit SQUARE

At Sheshi i Flamurit (Flag Sq), near the top of Sadik Zotaj, a magnificent socialist-realist **Independence Monument** stands proud against the sky with the flag bearer hoisting the double-headed eagle into the blue. Near the base of the monument lies the grave of local Ismail Qemali, the country's first prime minister.

Ethnographic Museum MUSEUM

(Sheshi i Flamurit; admission 50 lekë; ⊘9am-noon Mon-Sat) This ethnographic museum is jam-packed with relics of Albanian life. It's hidden behind an inconspicuous metal fence.

Muzeu Historik MUSEUM

(Sheshi i Flamurit) This antiquities museum opposite the ethnographic museum was undergoing renovation at the time of research.

Muradi Mosque MOSQUE

The 16th-century Muradi Mosque is a small elegant structure made of red and white stone, with a modest minaret; its exquisite design is attributed to one of the greatest Ottoman architects, Albanian-born Sinan Pasha.

National Museum of Independence MUSEUM

(admission 100 lekë; ⊘9am-1pm & 5-8pm) Down by the harbour, the National Museum of Independence is housed in the villa that became the headquarters of Albania's first government in 1912. The preserved offices, historic photographs and famous balcony make it an interesting place to learn about Albania's short-lived, but long-remembered, 1912 independence.

☐ Sleeping

Hotel Konomi HOTEL €

(☑229 320; Rr e Uji i Ftohtë; r €20) Set on top of a hill with views of the party end of town, this stark former workers' camp is good for the socialist idealism experience. Catch an orange municipal bus to Uji i Ftohtë (30 lekë) and walk along the beach road until the second pedestrian crossing; the stairs start behind the cafe.

ⓘ Information

Colombo Travel & Tours (☑232 377; Hotel Sazani) Books tours and provides information.

ⓘ Getting There & Away

BUS & FURGON Buses (400 lekë, four hours) and *furgons* (500 lekë, three hours) to Tirana and Durrës (500 lekë, 2½ hours) whiz back and forth from 4am until 7pm. Buses to Saranda (800 lekë, six hours) and on to Gjirokastra (900 lekë, seven hours) leave at 7am and 12.30pm. There are nine buses a day to Berat (300 lekë, two hours). Buses leave from Rr Rakip Malilaj; departures to Athens (€25) and cities in Italy (from €70) depart from Muradi Mosque.

FERRY Vlora to Brindisi in Italy takes around six hours. From Monday to Saturday there are departures from Brindisi at 11pm and Vlora at noon (deck €35).

TRAIN The daily train departs Tirana for Vlora at 4.30pm and Vlora for Tirana at 4.30am (250 lekë, five hours).

Llogaraja Pass National Park

Reaching the pinetree-clad Llogaraja Pass National Park (1025m) is a highlight of travels in Albania. If you've been soaking up the sun on the southern coast's beaches, it seems impossible that after a steep hairpin-bend climb you'll be up in the mountains tucking into spit-roasted lamb and homemade wine. There's great scenery up here, including the *pisha flamur* (flag pine) – a tree resembling the eagle design on the Albanian flag. Watch clouds descending onto the mountain, shepherds on the plains guiding their herds, and thick forests where deer, wild boar and wolves roam. Check out the resident deer at the Tourist Village before heading across the road to the cute family-run cabins at **Hotel Andoni** (☑068 240 0929; cabins 4000 lekë). The family do a wonderful lamb roast lunch (800 lekë) here.

Drymades

As you zigzag down the mountain from the Llogaraja Pass National Park, the white crescent-shape beaches and azure waters lure you from below. The first beach before the alluvial fan is Palasa, and it's one of the last bar/restaurant/hotel free beaches around.

The next beach along is **Drymades beach**. Turn right just after the beginning of the walk down to Dhërmi beach and you'll be on the sealed road that twists through olive groves. After a 20-minute walk you'll be on its rocky white beach.

🛏️ Sleeping & Eating

TOP CHOICE | **Sea Turtle**　CAMPING GROUND €
(☑069 4016 057; per person 1000 lekë; ☺Jun-Sep) This great little set-up is run by two brothers. Each summer they turn the family orange orchard into a vibrant tent city, and the price includes the tent (with mattresses, sheets and pillows), breakfast and a family-cooked dinner (served up in true camp style). Hot showers are under the shade of old fig trees.

Drymades Hotel　CAMPING GROUND €
(☑069 2074 000; campsites 700 lekë, cabins incl breakfast 7000 lekë) A constellation of cabins and rooms under the shade of pine trees just a step away from the blue sea. You can stay indoors or camp. There's a bar, restaurant and shaded playground, plus a classic beach bar with a straw roof. Prices halve off peak.

Lollipop　CLUB
(Drymades Beach) This very loud beach club (part of an Albanian chain of clubs) has DJs bopping along with their headphones on during long August days and nights, and a certain hammock and cocktail (500 lekë) appeal.

Dhërmi

Dhërmi beach is well and truly under the tourist trance in summer: expect booked-out accommodation and an almost unbearable rubbish problem. Despite this, there is fun to be had, and, if techno isn't your style, peace and quiet to be had, too. It's made up of lovely rocky outcrops, Mediterranean-blue water and tiny coves. The beach is 1.5km below the Vlora–Saranda road, so ask the driver to stop at the turn-off on the Llogaraja side of the village. From here it's an easy 10-minute walk downhill.

🛏️ Sleeping & Eating

Hotel Riviera　HOTEL €€
(☑068 2633 333; Dhërmi Beach; d €40-80;🕸@) This hotel has had a leopardskin-curtain makeover and is now ultra too-cool-for-school, with orange, lime-green and brown walls. The futon-style beds and flat-screen TVs make it all acceptable. An ubercool bar, the Yacht Club, is perched on the water's edge.

Blu Blu　HOTEL €€
(☑068 6055 371; Dhërmi Beach; r €80;☺May-Oct; 🕸🛜) Hello? Whose stroke of genius is this? Turn left at the bottom of the road to Dhërmi, and follow the road almost to its end. Here you'll find one of the best 'no disco' beachside spots in Albania. Little white cabins with sea views sit among growing banana trees, and the bar/restaurant serves great food. Start your dream day with a freshly squeezed orange juice. Rooms start at €30 in May.

Hotel Luciano　RESTAURANT €€
(mains 500 lekë) Sure, the mosaic on the wall of this waterfront pizza and pasta joint says 'no', but it's a resounding 'yes' to its woodfired pizzas. It's the first place you'll find after walking down the hill from the main road.

Himara

☑0393 / POP 4500
This sleepy town has fine beaches, a couple of pleasant Greek seafood tavernas, some hi-tech, good-looking hotels and an interesting Old Town high on the hill. Most of the ethnic Greek population left in the 1990s, but many have returned – Greek remains the mother tongue of its people. The lower town comprises three easily accessible rocky beaches and the town's hotels and restaurants. The main Vlora–Saranda road passes the entrance to the hilltop castle, which, like Berat's, still houses many people. A taxi to the castle from Himara costs 300 lekë.

🛏️ Sleeping

Rapo's Resort　LUXURY HOTEL €€€
(☑22 856; www.raposresorthotel.com; d €110-140;🏊) This top-end resort has smart interior design and sparkling bathrooms, and it also houses a massive swimming pool. For €5 anyone can relax by the pool for the day.

Kamping Himare　CAMPING GROUND €
(☑068 5298 940; www.himaracamping.com; per person €4; ☺Jun-Sep) Midnight movies in an open-air cinema add to the appeal of this

fairly central camping ground in an olive and orange grove. Tent rate include mattresses, sheets and pillows. Try the restaurant's sublime pancakes (100 lekë) for breakfast.

Manolo
BOUTIQUE HOTEL €€

(☑22 375; d €50) Above a cool, but not too cool, bar are four contemporary rooms that show good attention to detail and have sea views.

Kamping Mediterraneo
CAMPING GROUND €

(☑067 2184 518; per person incl breakfast & dinner €8) This camping ground is at Livadhi beach, a 30-minute walk north from Himara. The beach's northern water is warmer and sandier, but it's the southern side that houses the camping ground. It's got disco in its soul, so don't expect a quiet night. Taxis here from Himara are 400 lekë.

🛈 Getting There & Away

Buses towards Saranda and Vlora pass through Himara in the early morning; check with locals exactly when. The Himara–Saranda bus departs at 1pm from near Manolo.

Vuno & Jal

Less than 10 minutes' drive from Himara is Vuno, a tiny hillside village above a picturesque beach (Jal, pronounced Yal). Outdoor Albania (p44) renovated Vuno's primary school, and each summer its classrooms are filled with blow-up beds and it becomes **Shkolla Hostel** (☑068 3133 451; www.tirana hostel.com; dorm bed €7; ☉Jul & Aug). What it lacks in infrastructure and privacy it makes up for with its goat-bell soundtrack and evening campfire. From Vuno walk over the bridge and follow the rocky path to your right past the cemetery.

It's a challenging 40-minute signed walk through olive groves to picturesque Jal, or a 5km walk along the main beach road. Jal was a victim of the permit police a few years ago, and since then new structures have taken on a temporary tone. Jal has two beaches; one has free camping while the other has a camping ground set back from the sea (including tent 2000 lekë). Fresh seafood is bountiful in Jal and there are plenty of beachside restaurants in summer.

Saranda

☑0852 / POP 32,000

Saranda has grown rapidly in the past few years; skeletal high-rises crowd around its horseshoe shape and hundreds more are being built in the outlying region. Saranda is bustling in summer – buses are crowded with people carrying swimming paraphernalia and the weather means it's almost obligatory to go for a swim. A daily stream of Corfu holidaymakers take the 45-minute ferry trip to Albania, add the Albanian stamp to their passports and hit Butrint or the Blue Eye Spring before heading back.

The town's name comes from Ayii Saranda, an early monastery dedicated to 40 saints; its bombed remains (including some preserved frescos) are still high on the hill above the town. The town was called Porto Edda for a period in the 1940s, after Mussolini's daughter.

Saranda's stony beaches are quite decent and there are plenty of sights in and around town, including the mesmerising ancient archaeological site of Butrint and the hypnotic Blue Eye Spring. Between Saranda and Butrint, the lovely beaches and islands of Ksamil are perfect for a dip after a day of exploring.

◉ Sights

Synagogue
RUINS

(Rr Skënderbeu; ☉24hr) This 5th-century synagogue is centrally located and is evidence of one of the earliest Balkan-Jewish communities.

Museum of Archaeology
MUSEUM

(Rr Flamurit; ☉9am-2pm & 4-9pm) This office-like building houses a well-preserved mosaic floor in its basement. If you are lucky, you will hear the manager's flute.

Castle of Lëkurësit
CASTLE

This former castle is now a restaurant with superb views over Saranda and Butrint lagoon, especially at sunset. A taxi there costs about 1000 lekë return; arrange a time for the driver to pick you up, or it's a 15-minute walk up from the Saranda–Tirana road.

🛌 Sleeping

Hairy Lemon
HOSTEL €

(☑069 3559 317; dm incl breakfast €12; ☎) With a prime 8th-floor location, a clean beach at its base and a friendly, helpful atmosphere, this Irish-run backpacker hostel is a good place to chill out. There's an open-plan kitchen and lounge, and two dorm rooms with fans and sea breezes. Follow the port road for around 10 minutes and continue when it becomes dirt; it's the orange-and-yellow apart-

Over the past years, rampant development combined with land ownership issues have resulted in a fierce crackdown on what are perceived to be 'illegal' buildings throughout the country. Owners of buildings deemed to be constructed illegally (particularly in beachside areas, but including Tirana) are given written notice before the bulldozers and dynamite experts are called in to render the building uninhabitable. The rubble remains long after the bulldozers have gone, making some villages look like an earthquake has hit, though some of the lopsided skeletal remains could be modern art.

ment block on your right, above Dora E Art. Pancakes for breakfast.

Hotel Palma   HOTEL €€
(✆22 929; Rr Mithat Hoxha; s/d incl breakfast €30/50;❄) Right next to the port, this hotel has carpets that don't fit, but some rooms have great views with large balconies and the location is handy. If you're up for it, guests get free entry into the onsite summer disco.

Hotel Gjika   HOTEL €
(✆22 413; Lagjia nr 1; s/d incl breakfast €15/20) Up the hill from the main road is this simple family-run hotel with clean rooms with sea views. It's a quiet spot in a reasonably low-rise neighbourhood and is a good budget option for couples.

Bunker Hostel   HOSTEL €
(✆069 4345 426; dm incl breakfast €12; ❋) Practically kissing the port, this hostel is run by local Rino (it's also known as Rino's bunker), who has all the past and present gossip of the town (where to find hidden bunkers, for a start). The rooms, however, are bland, the common area is windowless and there is only one bathroom for the 18 beds.

✖ Eating

Tani   SEAFOOD €
(mains 250-550 lekë) This portside seafood restaurant is run by chef Tani, who prides himself on serving dishes he's invented himself. The oven-baked filled mussels are a cheesy delight, and it's in a cool vine-draped location.

Dropulli   TRADITIONAL €
(cnr Rruga Skënderbeu & Rr Mitro Dhmertika; veg dishes around 300 lekë) A local restaurant that has Albanian holidaymakers returning to it day after day has to be good, and vegetarians will love the melt-in-your-mouth stuffed peppers with tasty rice; ask for it to be served with potatoes.

Beque   TRADITIONAL €
(Sheshi Qendror I Qytetit; mains 300-500 lekë) Listen to the mosque call over the park while eating some of Saranda's cheapest and best Albanian-style food. Try the traditional soup and local seafood, or *tasqebap* (meat in sauce).

Pupi   SEAFOOD €€
(Rr Saranda-Butrint; seafood dishes around 650 lekë) Pupi has an unusual name but serves good seafood dishes on terraces under pine trees. It's on the road to Butrint, after Hotel Grand. In summer diners can take a swim at its private beach.

❶ Information

Four main streets arc around Saranda's bay, including the waterfront promenade that becomes prime *xhiro* (evening walk) territory in the evening. Banks with ATMs line the sea road (Rr 1 Maji) and the next street inland (Rr Skënderbeu).

ZIT information centre (Rr Skënderbeu; ⏱8am-4pm Mon-Fri, 9am-2pm & 4-9pm Sat & Sun Oct-Jun, 8.30am-2pm & 4-10pm Jul-Sep) Saranda's ZIT information centre is the most established in Albania and provides information about transport and local sights. The newer, bigger tourist information centre on the promenade sells travel guides, souvenirs, Ismail Kadare novels and maps.

❶ Getting There & Away

The ZIT information centre opposite the synagogue ruins has up-to-date bus timetables.

Bus

The main bus station is uphill from the ruins on Rr Vangjel Pando. Municipal buses go to Butrint via Ksamil on the hour from 7am to 5pm (100 lekë, 30 minutes), leaving from the roundabout near the port and opposite ZIT. Buses to Tirana (1200 lekë, seven hours) leave at 5am, 6.30am, 8.30am, 9.30am, 10.30am, 2pm and 10pm. The 5.30am Tirana bus takes the coastal route (1200 lekë, nine hours). There are two buses and *furgons* an hour to Gjirokastra's new town (300 lekë, 1½ hours) – they all pass the turn-off to the

Blue Eye Spring. Buses to Himara (600 lekë, two hours) leave at 6am, 2pm, 2.30pm and 3pm, and the daily service to Korça (1200 lekë, eight hours) leaves at 5.30am. Buses to the Greek border near Konispoli leave Saranda at 8am and 11am (200 lekë), otherwise you can reach the Greek border via Gjirokastra.

Ferry

Finikas (⌨260 57; finikaslines@yahoo.com; Rr Mithat Hoxha) at the port sells tickets for the **Ionian Cruises** (www.ionian-cruises.com) fast boat, the *Flying Dolphin*, which leaves for Corfu at 10.30am daily except Mondays (€19, 45 minutes). A slower boat departs daily at 4.30pm (€19, 90 minutes) and in summer a third ferry departs Saranda at 12.45pm Tuesday to Sunday and 10.30am Monday. From Corfu there are three ferries: the *Flying Dolphin* departs 9am, *Sotiraquis* at 9.30am and *Kaliopi* at 6.30pm. Greek time is one hour ahead of Albanian time.

Taxi

Taxis wait for customers at the bus stop and opposite Central Park on Rr Skënderbeu. A taxi to the Greek border at Kakavija costs 4000 lekë.

Around Saranda

BUTRINT

The ancient ruins of **Butrint** (www.butrint.org; admission 700 lekë; ⊘8am-dusk), 18km south of Saranda, are renowned for their size, beauty and tranquillity. They're in a fantastic natural setting and are part of a 29-sq-km national park. Set aside at least two hours to explore this fascinating place.

Although the site had been inhabited long before, Greeks from Corfu settled on the hill in Butrint (Buthrotum) in the 6th century BC. Within a century Butrint had become a fortified trading city with an acropolis. The lower town began to develop in the 3rd century BC, and many large stone buildings had already been built by the time the Romans took over in 167 BC. Butrint's prosperity continued throughout the Roman period, and the Byzantines made it an ecclesiastical centre. The city went into decline and was abandoned until 1927, when Italian archaeologists arrived. These days Lord Rothschild's UK-based Butrint Foundation helps maintain the site.

As you enter the site the path leads to the right, to Butrint's 3rd-century-BC **Greek theatre**, secluded in the forest below the acropolis. Also in use during the Roman period, the theatre could seat about 2500 people. Close by are the small **public baths**, where geometric mosaics are buried under a layer of mesh and sand to protect them from the elements.

Deeper in the forest is a wall covered with crisp Greek inscriptions, and the 6th-century palaeo-Christian **baptistry** decorated with colourful mosaics of animals and birds, again under the sand. Beyond are the impressive arches of the 6th-century **basilica**, built over many years. A massive **Cyclopean wall** dating back to the 4th century BC is further on. Over one gate is a relief of a lion killing a bull, symbolic of a protective force vanquishing assailants.

The top of the hill is where the **acropolis** once was. There's now a castle here, housing an informative **museum** (⊘8am-4pm). The views from the museum's courtyard give you a good idea of the city's layout, and you can see the Vivari Channel connecting Lake Butrint to the Straits of Corfu. There are community-run stalls inside the gates where you can buy locally produced souvenirs.

ⓘ Getting There & Away

The municipal bus from Saranda to Butrint costs 100 lekë and leaves hourly from 7am to 5pm. It passes through Ksamil.

KSAMIL

Ksamil, 17km south of Saranda, has three small, dreamy islands within swimming distance and dozens of beachside bars and restaurants that open in the summer. The public Saranda–Butrint bus stops twice in the town (100 lekë; leaves hourly 1am to 5pm); either stop will get you to the pristine waters, though if you look closely you'll realise that the sand is trucked in.

Hotel Joni (⌨069 2091 554; s/d €15/20) is a clean hotel near the roundabout. There are plenty of 'rooms to rent' in private homes closer to the water and seafood restaurants perch along the beachfront in summer.

BLUE EYE SPRING

Twenty-two kilometres east of Saranda, the **Blue Eye Spring** (Syri i Kaltër; admission per person 50 lekë, per car 200 lekë) is a hypnotic pool of deep-blue water surrounded by electric-blue edges like the iris of an eye. It feeds the Bistrica River and its depth is unknown. It's a pleasant spot; blue dragonflies dash around the water, and the surrounding shady oak trees make a pleasant picnic spot. There's a restaurant and cabins nearby. If you don't mind a 2km walk, any bus travelling between Saranda and Gjirokastra can drop you off at the spring's turn-off. **Terini Travel Agency** (📞24 985; Rr 4 Mitat Haxha, Saranda) by Saranda's port runs bus tours to the spring leaving the port at 10am on Tuesday and Saturday (€15), otherwise try a taxi.

EASTERN ALBANIA

Close to the Greek border and accessible from the Tirana–Athens bus route or from Saranda is the Unesco town of Gjirokastra. Expect bunker-covered mountains, wintertime snowfields and plenty of roads leading to Greece.

Gjirokastra

📞084 / POP 35,000

Defined by its castle, roads paved with chunky limestone and shale, imposing slate-roofed houses, and views out to the Drina Valley, Gjirokastra is an intriguing town described beautifully by local-born author Ismail Kadare (b 1936) in *Chronicles of Stone*. Archaeological evidence suggests there's been a settlement here for 2500 years, though these days it's the 600 'monumental' houses in town that attract visitors. Some of these magnificent houses, a blend of Ottoman and local architectural influence, have caved in on themselves, and Unesco funding is being spent to maintain them. Repairing each roof costs around $US20,000 – a sum out of reach for many of the homes' owners. Gjirokastra-born former dictator Enver Hoxha made sure his hometown was listed as a museum city, but after the fall of the communist regime the houses fell into disrepair.

⊙ Sights

Gjirokastra Castle　　　　　　　CASTLE
(admission 200 lekë; ⊙8am-8pm) The town's moody castle hosts an eerie collection of armoury and is the setting for Gjirokastra's folk festival (held every four or five years). It was built by Ali Pasha of Tepelena. It's an extra 200 lekë to visit its interior **Museum Kombetar** and see prison cells and more armoury. A new museum on the history of Gjirokastra was being planned at the time of research.

Ethnographic Museum　　　　　　MUSEUM
(admission 200 lekë; ⊙9am-7pm) This museum houses local homewares and was built on the site of Enver Hoxha's former house.

Zekate House　　　　　HISTORIC BUILDING
(admission €1) This incredible three-storey house dates from 1811 and has twin towers and a double-arched facade. The owners live next door and collect the payments. Check with the information centre for opening hours.

Bazaar　　　　　　　　　HISTORIC AREA
The 'Neck of the Bazaar' makes up the centre of the Old Town and contains artesian shops that support masters of the local stone- and wood-carving industries. Walk up to find the steps leading to Gjirokastra castle.

🛏 Sleeping

Stay in the scenic Old Town if possible, though there are accommodation options in the new town.

TOP CHOICE **Hotel Kalemi**　　　　HOTEL €€
(📞263 724; draguak@yahoo.com; Lagjia Palorto Gjirokastra; r €35; @🛜❄) This delightful, large Ottoman-style hotel has spacious rooms adorned with carved ceilings and large communal areas, including a broad veranda with Drina Valley views. Breakfast (juice, tea, a boiled egg, and bread with delicious fig jam) is included.

Guest House Haxhi Kotoni　　　B&B €
(📞263 526, 069 2366 846; www.kotonihouse.com; s/d incl breakfast €20/25;❄) The fact that these rooms are 220 years old makes up for their small size, and attached bathrooms and air-conditioning are bonuses. Hosts Haxhi and Vita love Gjirokastra and are happy to pass information on, as well as pack picnics for guests' day trips. Ask about fishing trips and hikes. Wheelchair friendly.

Hotel Cajupi　　　　　　　　HOTEL €€
(📞269 010; www.cajupi.com; s/d incl breakfast €30/40;❄) A revamp has turned this mammoth communist-era hotel into a decent place to stay, though the bathroom blocks the view in some badly planned rooms.

✕ Eating

TOP CHOICE **Kujtimi**　　　　TRADITIONAL €
(mains 250-400 lekë; ⊙11am-late) On the left-hand side of the path to Fantazia Restaurant is this unassuming outdoor restaurant, run by the Dumi family. Try the *trofte* (fried trout; 400 lekë), the *midhje* (fried mussels; 350 lekë) and the local red wine.

Kurveleshi　　　　　　　TRADITIONAL €
(mains 200 lekë; ⊙9am-dinner) This small cafe-style restaurant in the neck of the bazaar is

a good spot for lunch. Local specialities include minty rice *qifqi* (200 lekë) and there's beer on tap (60 lekë).

ℹ️ Information

The new town (no slate roofs here) is on the main Saranda–Tirana road, and a taxi up to or back from the Old Town is 300 lekë.

Information Centre (⊙8am-4pm Mon-Fri, 9am-2pm & 4-9pm Sat & Sun Oct-Jun, 8.30am-2pm & 4-10pm Jul-Sep) Opposite Cajupi Hotel behind the statue of the partisans.

ℹ️ Getting There & Away

Buses pass through the new town on their way to Tirana and Saranda, and *furgons* also go to Saranda (400 lekë, one hour). It takes about an hour to get to the Blue Eye Spring from Gjirokastra; buses to and from Saranda pass by its entrance, which is 2km from the spring itself. Buses to Tirana leave on the hour from 5am – the last one passes through after 11pm.

UNDERSTAND ALBANIA

History

Albanians call their country Shqipëria, and trace their roots to the ancient Illyrian tribes. Their language is descended from Illyrian, making it a rare survivor of the Roman and Slavic influxes and a European linguistic oddity on a par with Basque. The Illyrians occupied the western Balkans during the 2nd millennium BC. They built substantial fortified cities, mastered silver and copper mining, and became adept at sailing the Mediterranean. The Greeks arrived in the 7th century BC to establish self-governing colonies at Epidamnos (now Durrës), Apollonia and Butrint. They traded peacefully with the Illyrians, who formed tribal states in the 4th century BC.

Roman, Byzantine & Ottoman Rule

Inevitably the expanding Illyrian kingdom of the Ardiaei, based at Shkodra, came into conflict with Rome, which sent a fleet of 200 vessels against Queen Teuta in 229 BC. A long war resulted in the extension of Roman control over the entire Balkan area by 167 BC.

Under the Romans, Illyria enjoyed peace and prosperity, though large agricultural estates were worked by slaves. The Illyrians preserved their own language and traditions despite Roman rule. Over time the populace slowly replaced their old gods with the new Christian faith championed by Emperor Constantine. The main trade route between Rome and Constantinople, the Via Egnatia, ran from the port at Durrës.

When the Roman Empire was divided in AD 395, Illyria fell within the Eastern Empire, later known as the Byzantine Empire. Three early Byzantine emperors (Anastasius I, Justin I and Justinian I) were of Illyrian origin. Invasions by migrating peoples (Visigoths, Huns, Ostrogoths and Slavs) continued through the 5th and 6th centuries.

In 1344 Albania was annexed by Serbia, but after the defeat of Serbia by the Turks in 1389 the whole region was open to Ottoman attack. The Venetians occupied some coastal towns, and from 1443 to 1468 the national hero Skanderbeg (Gjergj Kastrioti) led Albanian resistance to the Turks from his castle at Kruja. Skanderbeg won all 25 battles he fought against the Turks, and even Sultan Mehmet-Fatih, the conqueror of Constantinople, could not take Kruja. After Skanderbeg's death the Ottomans overwhelmed Albanian resistance, taking control of the country in 1479, 26 years after Constantinople fell.

Ottoman rule lasted 400 years. Muslim citizens were favoured and were exempted from the janissary system, whereby Christian households had to give up one of their sons to convert to Islam and serve in the army. Consequently many Albanians embraced the new faith.

Independent Albania

In 1878 the Albanian League at Prizren (in present-day Kosovo) began a struggle for autonomy that the Turkish army put down in 1881. Further uprisings between 1910 and 1912 culminated in a proclamation of independence and the formation of a provisional government led by Ismail Qemali at Vlora in 1912. These achievements were severely compromised when Kosovo, roughly one-third of Albania, was ceded to Serbia in 1913. The Great Powers tried to install a young German prince, Wilhelm of Wied, as ruler, but he wasn't accepted and returned home after six months. With the outbreak of WWI, Albania was occupied in succession by the armies of Greece, Serbia, France, Italy and Austria-Hungary.

In 1920 the capital city was moved from Durrës to less vulnerable Tirana. A republican government under the Orthodox priest

Fan Noli helped to stabilise the country, but in 1924 it was overthrown by the interior minister, Ahmed Bey Zogu. A northern warlord, he declared himself King Zogu I in 1928, but his close collaboration with Italy backfired in April 1939 when Mussolini ordered an invasion of Albania. Zogu fled to Britain with his young wife, Geraldine, and newborn son, Leka, and used gold looted from the Albanian treasury to rent a floor at London's Ritz Hotel.

On 8 November 1941 the Albanian Communist Party was founded with Enver Hoxha as first secretary, a position he held until his death in April 1985. The communists led the resistance against the Italians and, after 1943, against the Germans.

The Rise of Communism

In January 1946 the People's Republic of Albania was proclaimed, with Hoxha as president and 'Supreme Comrade'.

In September 1948 Albania broke off relations with Yugoslavia, which had hoped to incorporate the country into the Yugoslav Federation. Instead, it allied itself with Stalin's USSR and put into effect a series of Soviet-style economic plans – raising the ire of the USA and Britain, which made an ill-fated attempt to overthrow the government.

Albania collaborated closely with the USSR until 1960, when a heavy-handed Khrushchev demanded that a submarine base be set up at Vlora. Breaking off diplomatic relations with the USSR in 1961, the country reoriented itself towards the People's Republic of China.

From 1966 to 1967 Albania experienced a Chinese-style cultural revolution. Administrative workers were suddenly transferred to remote areas and younger cadres were placed in leading positions. The collectivisation of agriculture was completed and organised religion was completely banned.

Following the Soviet invasion of Czechoslovakia in 1968, Albania left the Warsaw Pact and embarked on a self-reliant defence policy. Some 60,000 igloo-shaped concrete bunkers (see boxed text, p51) serve as a reminder of this policy. Under the communists, some malarial swamps were drained, hydroelectric schemes and railway lines were built, and the literacy level was raised. Albania's people, however, lived in fear of the Sigurimi (secret police) and were not permitted to leave the country, and many were tortured, jailed or murdered for misdemeanours such as listening to foreign radio stations.

With the death of Mao Zedong in 1976 and the changes that followed in China after 1978, Albania's unique relationship with China also came to an end, and the country was left isolated and without allies. The economy was devastated and food shortages became more common.

Post-Hoxha

Hoxha died in April 1985 and his associate Ramiz Alia took over the leadership. Restrictions loosened (Albania was opened up to tourists in organised groups) but people no longer bothered to work on the collective farms, leading to food shortages in the cities. Industries began to fail and Tirana's population tripled as people took advantage of being able to freely move to the city.

In June 1990, inspired by the changes that were occurring elsewhere in Eastern Europe, around 4500 Albanians took refuge in Western embassies in Tirana. After a brief confrontation with the police and the Sigurimi, these people were allowed to board ships for Brindisi in Italy, where they were granted political asylum.

Following student demonstrations in December 1990, the government agreed to allow opposition parties, and the Democratic Party, led by heart surgeon Sali Berisha, was formed.

The March 1992 elections ended 47 years of communist rule, with parliament electing Sali Berisha president. Former president Alia was later placed under house arrest for writing articles critical of the Democratic government, and the leader of the Socialist Party, Fatos Nano, was also arrested on corruption charges.

During this time Albania switched from a tightly controlled communist regime to a rambunctious free-market free-for-all. A huge smuggling racket sprang up in which stolen Mercedes-Benz cars were brought into the country, and the port of Vlora became a major crossing point for illegal immigrants from Asia and the Middle East into Italy.

In 1996, 70% of Albanians lost their savings when private pyramid-investment schemes, believed to have been supported by the government, collapsed. Riots ensued, elections were called, and the victorious Socialist Party under Nano – who had been freed from prison by a rampaging mob – was able to restore some degree of security and investor confidence.

In 1999 a different type of crisis struck when 465,000 Kosovars fled to Albania as a result of a Serbian ethnic-cleansing campaign. The influx had a positive effect on Albania's economy, and strengthened the relationship between Albania and Kosovo.

For the past decade Albania has found itself in a kind of mini boom, with much money being poured into construction projects and infrastructure renewal. The general election of 2005 saw a return of Berisha's Democratic Party to government, and in 2009 they narrowly won again, forming a coalition with the Socialist Movement for Intergration (LSI). The LSI's leader, Ilir Meta, formerly of the Socialist Party, is Albania's deputy prime minister. Albania managed to manoeuvre itself around the crippling economic crisis that gripped other European countries in 2008 and economic growth has continued. Despite this, infrastructure deficiencies still plague the country.

Albania joined NATO in 2009, and EU membership beckons.

The Albanians

Albania's population is made up of approximately 95% Albanians, 3% Greeks and 2% 'other' – comprising Vlachs, Roma, Serbs, Macedonians and Bulgarians.

Albanians are generally kind, helpful and generous. If you ask for directions, don't be surprised if you're guided all the way to your destination. The majority of young people speak some English, but speaking a few words of Albanian (or Italian, and, on the south coast, Greek) will be useful.

Albanians shake their heads sideways to say yes *(po)* and usually nod and 'tsk' to say no (jo – pronounced 'yo'). Albanians familiar with foreigners often take on the nod-for-yes way, which increases confusion.

The Ghegs in the north and the Tosks in the south have different dialects, music, dress and the usual jokes about each other's weaknesses.

Albanians are nominally 70% Muslim, 20% Christian Orthodox and 10% Catholic, but more realistic statistics estimate that up to 75% of Albanians are nonreligious. Religion was ruthlessly stamped out by the 1967 cultural revolution, when all mosques and churches were taken over by the state. By 1990 only about 5% of Albania's religious buildings were left intact. The rest had been turned into cinemas or army stores, or were destroyed. Albania remains a very secular society.

The Muslim faith has a branch called Bektashism, similar to Sufism, and its world headquarters were in Albania from 1925 to 1945. Bektashi followers go to *teqe* (temple-like buildings without a minaret), which are found on hilltops in towns where those of the faith fled persecution. Most Bektashis live in the southern half of the country.

The Arts

Literature

One Albanian writer who is widely read outside Albania is Ismail Kadare (b 1936). In 2005 he won the inaugural Man Booker International Prize for his body of work. His books are a great source of information on Albanian traditions, history and social events, and exquisitely capture the atmosphere of the country's towns, as in the lyrical descriptions of Kadare's birthplace, Gjirokastra, in *Chronicle in Stone* (1971). *Broken April* (1990), set in the northern highlands before the 1939 Italian invasion, describes the life of a village boy who is next in line in a desperate cycle of blood vendettas.

There is no substantial body of Albanian literature before the 19th century besides some Catholic religious works. Oral epic poetry was the most popular literary form during the period leading up to Albanian independence in 1912. A group of romantic patriotic writers at Shkodra, including Migjeni (1911–38) and Martin Çamaj (1925–92), wrote epics and historical novels.

Perhaps the most interesting writer of the interwar period was Fan Noli (1880–1965). Educated as a priest in the US, Noli became premier of Albania's Democratic government until it was overthrown in 1924, when he returned to head the Albanian Orthodox Church in the US. Although many of his books have religious themes, the introductions he wrote to his own translations of Cervantes, Ibsen, Omar Khayyám and Shakespeare established him as Albania's foremost literary critic.

Cinema

During Albania's isolationist years the only Western actor approved by Hoxha was UK actor Sir Norman Wisdom (he became quite a cult hero). However, with so few international movies to choose from, the local film industry had a captive audience. While much of its output was propagandist, by the

1980s this little country was turning out an extraordinary 14 films a year. Despite a general lack of funds, two movies have gone on to win awards at international film festivals. Gjergj Xhuvani's comedy *Slogans* (2001) is a warm and touching account of life during communist times. This was followed in 2002 by *Tirana Year Zero*, Fatmir Koci's bleak look at the pressures on the young to emigrate.

Another film worth seeing is *Lamerica* (1995), a brilliant and stark look at Albania around 1991. Woven loosely around a plot about a couple of Italian scam artists and Albanians seeking to escape to Italy, the essence of the film is the unshakeable dignity of the ordinary Albanian in the face of adversity.

Renowned Brazilian director Walter Salles *(The Motorcycle Diaries)* adapted Ismail Kadare's novel *Broken April*. Keeping the novel's main theme, he moved the action to Brazil in *Behind the Sun* (2001). *Lorna's Silence* (2008), a film about Albanians living in Belgium, was awarded in the 2008 Cannes Film Festival.

Music

Blaring from cars, bars, restaurants and mobile phones – music is something you get plenty of in Albania. Most modern Albanian music has clarinet threaded through it and a goatskin drum beat behind it. Polyphony, the blending of several independent vocal or instrumental parts, dates from ancient Illyrian times, and can still be heard, particularly in the south.

Visual Arts

One of the first signs of the Albanian arts scene are the multicoloured buildings of Tirana, a project organised by the capital's mayor, Edi Rama, himself an artist. The building's residents don't get a say in the colour or design, and come home to find their homes daubed in spots, paintings of trees, or even paintings of laundry drying under their windowsills.

Remnants of socialist realism adorn the walls and gardens of some galleries and museums, although most were destroyed in a backlash after the fall of the communist government.

One of the most delicious Albanian art treats is to be found in Berat's Onufri Museum (p54). Onufri was the most outstanding Albanian icon painter of the 16th and 17th centuries, and his work is noted for its unique intensity of colour, derived from natural dyes that are as fresh now as the day he painted with them.

Churches around the country also feature amazing original frescos.

The Landscape

Albania consists of 30% vast interior plains, 362km of coast and a mountainous spine that runs its length. Mt Korab, at 2764m, is Albania's highest peak. Forest covers just under 40% of the country, with Mediterranean shrubs at up to 600m, an oak forest belt between 600m and 1000m, and beech and pine forests between 1000m and 1600m.

The country's large and beautiful lakes include the Balkans' biggest, Lake Shkodra, which borders Montenegro in the north, and the ancient Lake Ohrid in the east (one-third Albanian, two-thirds Macedonian). Albania's longest river is the Drin (280km), which originates in Kosovo and is fed by melting snow from mountains in Albania's north and east. Hydroelectricity has changed Albania's landscape: Lake Koman was once a river, and the blue water from the Blue Eye Spring near Saranda travels to the coast in open concrete channels via a hydroelectricity plant. Agriculture makes up a small percentage of land use, and citrus and olive trees spice up the coastal plains. Most rural householders grow their own food.

National Parks & Wildlife

The number of national parks in Albania has risen from six to 15 since 1966 and include Dajti, Llogara, Tomorri, Butrint, Valbonë and Theth. Most are protected only by their remoteness, and tree-felling and hunting still take place. Hiking maps of the national parks are available, though they can be hard to find (try *Wanderkarte Nordalbanien* for Theth).

Albania's Alps have become a 'must-do' for hikers, and they're home to brown bear, wolf, otter, marten, wild cat, wild boar and deer. Falcons and grouse are also alpine favourites, and birdwatchers can also flock to wetlands at Lake Butrint, Karavasta Lagoon and Lake Shkodra (though the wetlands aren't pristine).

Lake Ohrid's trout is endangered (but still eaten), and endangered loggerhead turtles nest on the Ionian Coast and on the Karaburun

Peninsula, where there have also been sightings of critically endangered Mediterranean monk seals.

Environmental Issues

During communism, there were around 2000 cars in the country. The number of roaring automobiles has since risen to Western European levels and rises by 10% annually. Many of Albania's older cars are diesel Mercedes-Benzes stolen from Western Europe. As a consequence of the explosion, air-pollution levels in Tirana are five to 10 times higher than in Western European countries.

Illegal logging and fishing reached epidemic proportions during the 1990s, and there are signs of it today; fishing for the endangered *koran* trout in Lake Ohrid continues, as does fishing with dynamite along the coast.

Badly maintained oilfields around Fier leak sludge into the surrounding environment, and coastal regions discharge raw sewage into seas and rivers. The rapid development of beach areas has compounded the issue, though projects are in place to improve waste disposal in environmentally sensitive areas like Lake Ohrid.

Albania was practically litter-free until the early '90s, as everything was reused or recycled, but today there's literally rubbish everywhere. Walk around the perimeter of a hotel in a picturesque location and you'll come across its very unpicturesque dumping ground. Some Albanians are doing their bit to improve these conditions, and a 'raising awareness' campaign against litter was started by well-known Albanians in 2010. Several organic food organisations are also trying to make a difference.

Food & Drink

In coastal areas the calamari, mussels and fish will knock your socks off, while high-altitude areas like Llogaraja have roast lamb worth climbing a mountain for.

Offal is popular; *fërgesë Tiranë* is a traditional Tirana dish of offal, eggs and tomatoes cooked in an earthenware pot.

Italian influences mean vegetarians will probably become vegitalians, and many restaurants serve pizza, pasta or grilled and stuffed vegetables.

Most restaurants allow smoking, though some may have designated nonsmoking areas.

Local Drinks

Raki is very popular. The two main types are grape *raki* (the most common) and *mani* (mulberry) *raki*. Ask for homemade if possible *(raki ë bërë në shtëpi)*. If wine is more your cup of tea, seek out the Çobo winery near Berat and its Shesh i bardhe white. Local beers include Tirana, Norga (from Vlora) and Korça. Korça's beer fest takes place each August (www.visit-korca.com). Most days start with an espresso.

SURVIVAL GUIDE

Directory A–Z

Accommodation

With almost every house, bar and petrol station doubling as a hotel you might think you'll never have trouble finding a bed in Albania, and you're right, though seaside towns are often booked out in August.

The number of backpacker hostels has tripled in recent years and you'll find them in Tirana, Vuno, Saranda and Berat. Check for new ones on www.hostelworld.com.

Homestays abound in Theth (www.shkoder-albanian-alps.com). The number of camping grounds is increasing; you'll find them at Himare, Livadhi, Dhërmi and Drymades (from €4 per person). Most have hot showers, onsite restaurants and entertainment.

Prices included are for high season. You can expect the following from Albania's hotels:

€ usually decent and clean; a simple breakfast and wi-fi often included

€€ bigger rooms, onsite restaurant and possibly swimming pool

€€€ include modern decor, fitness centre, satellite TV and swimming pool

Activities

Hiking and adventure sports are gaining popularity in Albania, and Outdoor Alba-

---

SLEEPING PRICE RANGES

» € – under €30 per night for a double room

» €€ – €30 to €100

» €€€ – cheapest double over €100

nia (www.outdooralbania.com) is an excellent organisation at the forefront of the industry. Smaller operatives are starting up: the **Albania Rafting Group** (www.albrafting.org) runs rafting tours of the Osumi River and canyons in Berat. Hiking in the Alps is popular (with and without guides), as is mountain biking around the country.

Beachwise, south of Vlora the sandy Adriatic gives it up for its rockier Ionian counterpart, but the swimming is better and the scenery more picturesque.

Business Hours

If opening hours are not listed in reviews they are as follows:

Banks 9am-3.30pm Mon-Fri

Cafes & Bars 8am-midnight

Offices 8am-5pm Mon-Fri

Restaurants 8am-midnight

Shops 8am-7pm; siesta time can be any time between noon and 4pm

Embassies & Consulates

There is no Australian, New Zealand or Irish embassy in Albania. The following embassies and consulates are in Tirana:

Canada (☑04-2257 275; canadalb@canada.gov.al; Rr Dëshmorët e 4 Shkurti)

France (☑04-2233 750; www.ambafrance-al.org; Rr Skënderbej 14)

Germany (☑04-2274 505; www.tirana.diplo.de; Rr Skënderbej 8)

Netherlands (☑04-2240 828; www.mfa.nl/tir; Rr Asim Zeneli 10)

UK (☑04-2234 973; www.ukinalbania.fco.gov.uk; Rr Skënderbej 12)

US (☑04-2247 285; http://tirana.usembassy.gov; Rr Elbasanit 103)

Food

The average cost of a main course in a restaurant is 100 to 200 lekë for budget (€), 200 to 500 lekë for midrange (€€) and more than 500 lekë for top end (€€€). See also p66.

Gay & Lesbian Travellers

Extensive anti-discrimination legislation became law in 2010, but did not extend to legalising same-sex marriage. Gay and lesbian life in Albania is alive and well but is not yet organised into clubs or organisations. It's no problem to be foreign and affectionate with your same-sex partner in the street, but keep

in mind that no couples are overly demonstrative in public in Albania so any public sexual behaviour beyond holding hands and kissing will be a spectacle. Gaydar will serve gay and lesbian visitors well here: you'll have to ask on the street where the parties are. The alternative music and party scene is queer-friendly.

Holidays

New Year's Day 1 January

Summer Day 16 March

Nevruz 23 March

Catholic Easter March or April

Orthodox Easter March or April

May Day 1 May

Bajram i Madh September

Mother Teresa Day 19 October

Bajram i Vogël November

Independence Day 28 November

Liberation Day 29 November

Christmas Day 25 December

Internet Access

If you've brought your own smartphone or laptop you can access free wi-fi around the country. Internet cafes (often dominated by teens playing shoot-'em-up games) cost around 100 lekë per hour.

Money

The lekë is the official currency, though the euro is widely accepted; you'll get a better rate in general if you use lekë. Accommodation is quoted in euros but can be paid in either currency. ATMs (found in most of Albania's towns, bar Theth and small beaches) usually offer to dispense cash in either currency.

Albanian banknotes come in denominations of 100, 200, 500, 1000, 2000 and 5000 lekë. There are five, 10, 20, 50 and 100 lekë coins.

In 1964 the currency was revalued 10 times; prices are sometimes quoted at the old rate (3000 lekë instead of 300). Happily, if you hand over 3000 lekë you will probably be handed 2700 lekë in change.

Albanian lekë can't be exchanged outside the country, so exchange them or spend them before you leave.

Credit cards are accepted only in the larger hotels, shops and travel agencies, and few of these are outside Tirana.

It's polite to leave your change as a tip.

Post

The postal system is fairly rudimentary – there are no postcodes, for example – and it certainly does not enjoy a reputation for efficiency.

Telephone

Albania's country phone code is ☑355 (dial + or 00 first from a mobile phone).

Three established mobile-phone providers are Vodafone, AMC and Eagle, and a fourth licence has been promised. Don't expect isolated areas to have coverage (though Theth does). Prepaid SIM cards cost around 600 lekë and include credit. Calls within the country cost roughly 30 to 60 lekë a minute. Mobile numbers begin with ☑06. To call an Albanian mobile number from abroad, dial ☑+355 then either 67, 68 or 69 (ie drop the 0).

Tourist Information

Tourist information offices operate in Tirana, Shkodra, Saranda, Gjirokastra (www.gjirokastra.org) and Berat (www.bashkia-berat.net). You can purchase city maps of Tirana in bookshops, and maps of Vlora, Saranda, Gjirokastra, Durrës and Shkodra from the respective town's travel agencies or hotels.

Travellers with Disabilities

High footpaths and unannounced potholes make life difficult for mobility-impaired travellers. Tirana's top hotels do cater to people with disabilities, and some smaller hotels are making an effort to be more accessible. The roads and castle entrances in Gjirokastra, Berat and Kruja are cobblestone, although taxis can get reasonably close to the action.

Visas

Visas are not required for citizens of EU countries or nationals of Australia, Canada, New Zealand, Japan, South Korea, Norway, South Africa or the USA. Travellers from other countries should check www.mfa.gov.al. Passports are stamped for a 90-day stay. A €10 entry and exit fee was abolished some years ago; do not be conned into paying this by taxi drivers at border crossings.

Women Travellers

Albania is a safe country for women travellers, but outside Tirana it is mainly men who go out and sit in bars and cafes in the evenings. You may tire of being asked why you're travelling alone.

Getting There & Away

Air

Nënë Tereza International Airport (Mother Teresa Airport, Rinas airport, Tirana Airport; www.tirana-airport.com.al) is 17km northwest of Tirana. There are no domestic flights within Albania. The following airlines fly to and from Albania:

Adria Airways (JP; ☑04-2272 666; www.adria.si) Flies to Madrid, Barcelona, Paris, Zurich, Munich, Frankfurt, Brussels, London, Manchester, Ljubljana, Amsterdam, Copenhagen, Warsaw, Moscow, Stockholm, Sarajevo and Vienna.

Air One (AP; ☑04-2230 023; www.flyairone.it) Flies to Milan.

Albanian Air (LV; ☑04-2235 162; www.albanianair.com) Flies to Pisa, Bologna, Turin, Pisa, Bergamo, Milan, London, Frankfurt, Istanbul, Antalya, Dubai and Jeddah.

Alitalia (AZ; ☑04-2230 023; www.alitalia.com) Flies to Rome, Verona, Turin, Naples, Florence, Genoa, Milan, Catania, Venice, Brussels, London, Madrid, Paris, Barcelona, Amsterdam and Munich.

Austrian Airlines (OS; ☑04-2235 029; www.austrian.com) Flies to Vienna.

BelleAir (LZ; ☑04-2240 175; www.belleair.it) Flies to Pristina, Ancona, Rimini, Forli, Bari, Pescara, Naples, Trieste, Perugia, Milan, Treviso, Turin, Parma, Bologna, Pisa, Florence, Rome, Geneva, Zurich, Stuttgart and Liege.

British Airways (BA; ☑04-2381 991; www.britishairways.com) Flies to London.

Bulgaria Air (FB; ☑04-2230 410; www.air.bg) Flies to Sofia, June to September only.

Lufthansa (LH; ☑04-2258 010; www.lufthansa.com) Flies to Vienna and Munich.

Malév Hungarian Airlines (MA; ☑04-2234 163; www.malev.hu) Flies to Budapest.

Olympic Air (OA; ☑04-2228 960; www.olympicair.com) Flies to Athens.

Turkish Airlines (TK; ☑04-2258 459; www.turkishairlines.com) Flies to İstanbul.

Land

Border Crossings

There are no passenger trains into Albania, so your border-crossing options are buses, *furgons*, taxis or walking to a border and picking up transport on the other side.

Montenegro The main crossings link Shkodra to Ulcinj (Muriqan) and to Podgorica (Hani i Hotit).

Kosovo The closest border crossing to the Koman Ferry terminal is Morina, and further north is Qafë Prush. Near Kukës use Morinë.

Macedonia Use Blato to get to Debar, quiet Qafë e Thanës to the north of Lake Ohrid, or Sveti Naum, near Pogradec, to its south. There's also a crossing at Stenje.

Greece The main border crossing to and from Greece is Kakavija on the road from Athens to Tirana. It's about half an hour from Gjirokastra and 250km west of Tirana, and can take up to three hours to pass through during summer. Kapshtica (near Korça) also gets long lines in summer. Konispoli is near Butrint in Albania's south.

Bus
From Tirana, regular buses head to Pristina, Kosovo; to Struga, Tetovo and Skopje in Macedonia; to Budva and Ulcinj in Montenegro; and to Athens and Thessaloniki in Greece. *Furgons* and buses leave Shkodra for Montenegro, and buses head to Kosovo from Durrës. Buses travel to Greece from Albanian towns on the southern coast and buses to Italy leave from Vlora.

Car & Motorcycle
To enter, you'll need a Green Card (proof of third-party insurance, issued by your insurer); check that your insurance covers Albania.

Taxi
Heading to Macedonia, taxis from Pogradec will drop you off just before the border at Tushëmisht/Sveti Naum. Alternatively, it's an easy 4km walk to the border from Pogradec. It's possible to organise a taxi (or, more usually, a person with a car) from where the Koman Ferry stops in Fierzë to Gjakove in Kosovo. Taxis commonly charge €40 from Shkodra to Ulcinj in Montenegro.

Sea
Two or three ferries per day ply the route between Saranda and Corfu, in Greece, and there are plenty of ferry companies making the journey to Italy from Vlora and Durrës – see those sections for detailed information.

Bicycle
Cycling in Albania is tough but certainly feasable. Expect lousy road conditions including open drains, some abysmal driving from fellow road users and roads that barely qualify for the title. Organised groups head north for mountain biking, and cyclists are even spotted cycling the long and tough Korça–Gjirokastra road. Shkodra, Durrës and Tirana are towns where you'll see locals embracing the bike, and Tirana even has bike lanes.

Bus
The first bus/*furgon* departure is often at 5am and things slow down around lunchtime. There are many buses catering to the crowds along the coast in July and August. Fares are low (eg Tirana–Durrës costs 150 lekë), and you either pay the conductor on board or when you hop off.

Municipal buses operate in Tirana, Durrës, Shkodra and Vlora, and trips cost 30 lekë. Watch your possessions.

Car & Motorcycle
Albania's drivers are not the best in the world, mostly due to the communist era, when car ownership required a permit from the government, and only two were issued to non-party members. As a result, the government didn't invest in new roads, and most Albanians were inexperienced motorists. Nowadays the road infrastructure is improving; there's a super highway from Tirana to Kosovo, and the coastal route from the Montenegro border to Butrint, near Saranda, is in good condition. That said, drivers are still highly unpredictable.

Tourists are driving cars, motorbikes and mobile homes into the country in greater numbers, and, apart from bad roads and bad drivers, the only hazards some report are being caught speeding.

Off the main routes a 4WD is a good idea. Driving at night is particularly hazardous, and driving on mountain 'roads' at any time is a whole new field of extreme sport. Cars, *furgons*, trucks and buses *do* go off the edge.

The **Automobile Club of Albania** (ACA; ☎04- 2257 828; www.aca.al; Rr Ismail Quemali 32/1, Tirana) offers emergency assistance (☎04-2262 263) around the country for 300 lekë per year and has links with international automobile associations.

Driving Licence

Foreign driving licences are permitted, but it is recommended to have an International Driving Permit as well.

Fuel & Spare Parts

There are petrol stations in the cities and increasing numbers in the country. Unleaded fuel is available along all major roads, but fill up before driving into the mountainous regions. A litre of unleaded petrol costs 150 lekë, eurodiesel is 145 lekë. As the range of cars being driven around Albania increases, so does the availability of spare parts, but it almost goes without saying that if you're driving an old Mercedes-Benz there will be parts galore.

Car Hire

See p47 for car-hire companies operating out of Tirana. Hiring a small car costs from €35 per day, a 4WD costs around €100 per day.

Road Rules

Drinking and driving is forbidden, and there is zero tolerance for blood-alcohol readings.

Both motorcyclists and passengers must wear helmets. Speed limits are as low as 30km per hour in built-up areas and 35km per hour on the edges and there are plenty of speed cameras monitoring the roads. Keep your car's papers with you, as police are active checkers.

Hitchhiking

Though never entirely safe, hitchhiking is quite a common way for travellers to get around – though it's rare to see locals doing it.

Train

Albanians prefer bus and *furgon* travel, and when you see the speed and the state of the (barely) existing trains, you'll know why. However, the trains are dirt cheap and travelling on them is an adventure. Daily passenger trains leave Tirana for Durrës, Shkodra, Fier, Vlora, Elbasan and a few kilometres out of Pogradec. Check timetables at the station in person, and buy your ticket 10 minutes before departure. Albania is not connected to neighbouring countries by train.

Bosnia & Hercegovina

Best Places to Stay

» Muslibegović House (p92)
» Kostelski Buk (p107)
» Hotel Platani (p98)
» Hotel Centar (p100)
» Hotel Blanca (p102)

Best Places to Eat

» Mala Kuhinja (p82)
» Bridge-view restaurants, Mostar (p94)
» Riverside restaurants on the Una (p139)

Why Go?

This craggily beautiful land retains some lingering scars from the heartbreaking civil war in the 1990s. But today visitors will more likely remember Bosnia and Hercegovina (BiH) for its deep, unassuming human warmth and for the intriguing East-meets-West atmosphere born of fascinatingly blended Ottoman and Austro-Hungarian histories.

Major drawcards are the reincarnated antique centres of Sarajevo and Mostar, where rebuilt historical buildings counterpoint fashionable bars and wi-fi–equipped cafes. Elsewhere Socialist architectural monstrosities are surprisingly rare blots on predominantly rural landscapes. Many Bosnian towns are lovably small, wrapped around medieval castles and surrounded by mountain ridges or cascading river canyons. Few places in Europe offer better rafting or such accessible, inexpensive skiing.

When to Go
Sarajevo

Spring Beat the heat in Herzegovina, blooming flowers in Bosnia, peak-flowing rivers.

Summer Accommodation fills up but for beginners the rafting is best in July.

Mid-December to mid-March Olympic-standard skiing. Prices drop in late March.

Fast Facts

» **Area** 51,129 sq km

» **Capital** Sarajevo

» **Telephone country code** 387

» **Emergency** ambulance 124, fire 123, police 122, roadside assistance 1282, 1288

Exchange Rates

Australia	A$1	1.41KM
Canada	C$1	1.40KM
euro	€1	1.95KM
Japan	¥100	1.60KM
New Zealand	NZ$1	1.06KM
UK	UK£1	2.20KM
USA	US$1	1.35KM

Set Your Budget

» **Budget hotel room** 60KM

» **Two-course meal** 17KM

» **Museum entrance** 1.50KM to 5KM

» **Beer** 2KM to 3KM

» **City transport ticket** 1.80KM

Resources

» **BiH Tourism** (www.bhtourism.ba)

» **Bosnian Institute** (www.bosnia.org.uk)

» **Office of the High Representative** (www.ohr.int)

Connections

Regular buses link the Croatian coast to Mostar and Sarajevo plus there's a little-publicised Trebinje–Dubrovnik service. Trains link Sarajevo to Zagreb, Belgrade and Budapest-Keleti, the only direct overland link to Hungary. There are numerous bus connections to Serbia and Montenegro from Sarajevo, Višegrad and Trebinje.

ITINERARIES

Six days

Arriving from Dubrovnik (coastal Croatia), roam Mostar's Old Town and join a day tour visiting Počitelj, Blagaj and the Kravice waterfalls. After two days in Sarajevo head for Jajce then bus down to Split (Croatia). Or visit Višegrad en route to Mokra Gora and Belgrade (Serbia).

Two weeks

As above, but add quaint Trebinje and (if driving) historic Stolac between Dubrovnik and Mostar. Ski or go cycling around Bjelašnica, visit the controversial Visoko pyramid and old-town Travnik en route to Jajce, and consider adding in some high-adrenaline rafting from Banja Luka, Bihać or Foča.

Essential Food & Drink

» **Ćevapčići** Grilled minced meat formed into cylindrical little *ćevapi* or patty-shaped *pljeskavica*.

» **Ćevabdžinica** *Ćevapi* specialist-eateries but almost all restaurants serve them along with *šnicla* (steak/schnitzel), *kotleti* (normally veal), *ražnjići* (shish kebab), *pastrmka* (trout) and *ligne* (squid).

» **Dolme** Cabbage leaves or vegetables stuffed with minced meat.

» **lonac** Cabbage and meat hotpot.

» **Hurmastica** Syrup-soaked sponge fingers.

Bosnia & Hercegovina Highlights

1 Nose about Mostar's atmospheric Old Town seeking ever-new angles from which to photograph young men throwing themselves off the magnificently rebuilt **Stari Most** (Old Bridge; p88)

2 Raft dramatic canyons down one of BiH's fast-flowing rivers – whether from **Foča** (p99), **Bihać** (p106) or **Banja Luka** (p104)

3 Ski the 1984 Olympic pistes at **Jahorina** (p86) or **Bjelašnica** (p87) or explore the wild uplands behind them

4 Potter around the timeless Turkish- and Austrian-era pedestrian lanes of **Sarajevo** (p74), sample its fashionable cafes and eclectic nightlife or gaze down on the mosque-dotted, red-roofed cityscape from Biban restaurant

SARAJEVO

✏ 033 / POP 737,000

In the 1990s Sarajevo was on the edge of annihilation. Today it's a cosy, vibrant capital with humanity, attractive contours and East-meets-West ambience that are increasingly making it a favourite summer traveller destination. And in winter it's brilliantly handy for some of Europe's best-value skiing.

The city is tightly wedged into the steep, narrow valley of the modest Miljacka River. Attractive Austro-Hungarian–era avenues Ferhadija/Maršala Tita and Obala Kulina Bana converge at the very atmospheric Baščaršija, 'Turkish Town'. Surrounding slopes are fuzzed with red-roofed Bosnian houses and prickled with uncountable minarets, climbing towards green-topped mountain ridges. Westward, Sarajevo sprawls for over 10km through Novo Sarajevo and dreary Dobrijna past contrastingly dismal ranks of bullet-scarred apartment blocks. At the westernmost end of the tramway spine, affluent Ilidža gives the city a final parkland flourish.

History

Romans had bathed at Ilidža's sulphur springs a millennium earlier, but Sarajevo was officially 'founded' by 15th-century Turks. It rapidly grew wealthy as a silk-importing entrepôt and developed considerably during the 1530s when Ottoman governor Gazi-Husrevbey lavished the city with mosques and built the covered bazaar that still bears his name (see p75). In 1697 the city was burnt by Eugene of Savoy's Austrian army. When rebuilt, Sarajevo cautiously enclosed its upper flank in a large, fortified citadel, the remnants of which still dominate the Vratnik area.

The Austro-Hungarians were back more permanently in 1878 and erected many sturdy central European-style buildings. However, their rule was put on notice by Gavrilo Princip's fatal 1914 pistol shot that killed Archduke Franz Ferdinand, plunging the world into WWI.

Less than a decade after hosting the 1984 Winter Olympics, Sarajevo endured an infamous siege that horrified the world. Between 1992 and 1995, Sarajevo's heritage of six centuries was pounded into rubble and its only access to the outside world was via a metre-wide, 800m-long tunnel under the airport (p80). Bosnian Serb shelling and sniper fire killed over 10,500 Sarajevans and wounded 50,000 more. Uncountable white-stoned graveyards on Kovači and up near Koševo Stadium are a moving testimony to those terrible years.

The Entities of Bosnia & Hercegovina

Plunge into the pedestrianised 'Turkish' lanes of **Baščaršija** and the street cafes of **Ferhadija**. From the spot where a 1914 assassination kicked off WWI cross the cute **Latin Bridge** for a beer at **Pivnica HS** or dinner overlooking the city rooftops at **Biban**.

Next day ponder the horrors of the 1990s siege era at the moving **History Museum** and unique **Tunnel Museum**. Recover with a drink at eccentrically Gothic **Zlatna Ribica** and a feisty gig at **Bock/FIS**.

⊙ Sights & Activities

BAŠČARŠIJA & AROUND

The bustling old Turkish quarter is a warren of marble-flagged pedestrian lanes with open courtyards full of mosques, copper workshops, jewellery shops and inviting little restaurants. The area's charms are best discovered by untargeted wandering between the many street cafes.

Pigeon Square   NEIGHBOURHOOD
(Map p78) Nicknamed Pigeon Sq for all the birds, Baščaršija's central open space centres on the Sebilj, an ornate 1891 drinking fountain. It leads past the lively (if tourist-centric) coppersmith alley, Kazandžiluk, to the picturesque garden-wrapped 16th-century Baščaršija mosque (Bravadžiluk) and the six-domed Bursa Bezistan (www.muzejsarajeva.ba; Abadžiluk 10; admission 2KM; ◎10am-6pm Mon-Fri, 10am-3pm Sat). Originally a silk-trading bazaar, this 1551 stone building is now a museum with bite-sized overviews of the city's history and a compelling model of Sarajevo as it looked in 1878.

Gazi-Husrevbey Vakuf Buildings
                        ARCHITECTURAL ENSEMBLE
(Map p78) Ottoman governor Gazi-Husrevbey's splendid 16th-century complex includes a madrassa (religious school; Saraći 33-49), a stone-vaulted covered bazaar and the imposing Gazi-Husrevbey Mosque (www.vakuf-gazi.ba; Saraći 18; admission 2KM; ◎9am-noon, 2.30-4pm & 5.30-7pm May-Sep, closed Ramadan). Its cylindrical minaret contrasts photogenically with the elegant stone clock tower across Mudželeti Veliki alley.

Old Orthodox Church   CHURCH
(Map p78; Mula Mustafe Bašeskije 59; ◎8am-6pm Mon-Sat, 8am-4pm Sun) This outwardly austere little 1740 stone church has an impressive gilded iconostasis (wall of icons) and a three-room cloister-museum (admission 2KM; ◎8am-3pm Tue-Sun) displaying historic icons, old manuscripts and church paraphernalia.

BJELAVE & VRATNIK

Svrzo House   HOUSE-MUSEUM
(Svrzina Kuća; Map p78; ☑535264; Glođina 8; admission 2KM; ◎10am-6pm Mon-Fri, 10am-3pm Sat). This brilliantly restored 18th-century house-museum retains its courtyards and *doksat* (overhanging box windows).

Vratnik   NEIGHBOURHOOD
(Map p76) For great views over town continue up towards the once-vast Vratnik Citadel, built in the 1720s and reinforced in 1816. Its Kula Ploče tower (Ploča bb; admission 2KM; ◎10am-6pm Mon-Fri, 10am-3pm Sat) houses a fascinating little museum to BiH's first president Alija Izetbegović and allows access to a short city-wall walk (exit at Kula Širokac tower). But the best panoramas are from the grassy-topped Yellow Bastion (Žuta Tabija; Jekovac bb). Minibus 55 runs to Vratnik.

FERHADIJA & AROUND

In summer, street cafes fill virtually every open space around Ferhadija, a pedestrianised avenue lined with grand Austro-Hungarian buildings. There's also plenty of sternly triumphalist early-20th-century architecture along Maršala Tita beyond an eternal flame that commemorates victims of WWII. The city's socially harmonious pre-1990s past is well illustrated by the close proximity of three places of worship.

Catholic Cathedral   CHURCH
(Katedrala; Map p78; Trg Fra Grge Martića 2; ◎9am-4pm) The 1889 neo-Gothic Catholic Cathedral is where Pope John Paul II served mass during his 1997 visit.

Orthodox Cathedral   CHURCH
(Saborna Crkva; Map p78; Trg Oslobođenja) The large 1872 Orthodox Cathedral, built in Byzantine-Serb style, is artfully lit at night.

Jewish Museum   MEDIEVAL SYNAGOGUE
(Map p78; Mula Mustafe Bašeskije 40; admission 2KM; ◎10am-6pm Mon-Fri, 10am-1pm Sun) More religiously open-minded than most of Western Europe in its day, the 15th-century Ottoman

Greater Sarajevo

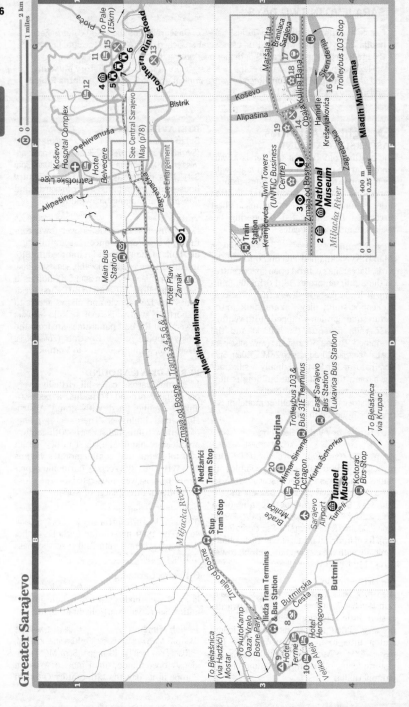

To Pale (15km)

Ploče

Southern Ring Road

Bistrik

Koševo Hospital Complex

Pehlivanuša

Hotel Belvedere

See Central Sarajevo Map (p78)

See Enlargement

Patriotske Lige

Alipašina

Main Bus Station

Hotel Plavi Zamak

Zmaja od Bosne

Mladih Muslimana

Miljacka River

Zmaja od Bosne

Trams 3, 4, 5, 6 & 7

Nedžarići Tram Stop

Dobrinja

Trolleybus 103 & Bus 31E Terminus

East Sarajevo Bus Station (Lukavica Bus Station)

To Bjelašnica via Krupac

Mimar Sinana

Hotel Octagon

Kurta Schorka

Tunnel Museum

Kotorac Bus Stop

Sarajevo Airport

Tunel Station

Braće Mulića

Stup Tram Stop

Bosne

Zmaja od Zmaja

Ilidža Tram Terminus & Bus Station

Butmirska Cesta

Butmir

To AutoKamp Oaza', Vrelo Bosne Park

To Bjelašnica (via Hadžići), Mostar

Hotel Terme

Hotel Hercegovina

Velika Aleja

Enlargement

Maršala Tita

Branilaca Sarajeva

Trolleybus 103 Stop

Koševo

Alipašina

Skenderija

Mladih Muslimana

Hamidije

Kreševljakovića

Obala Kulina Bana

Zagrebačka

Twin Towers (UNITIC Business Centre)

National Museum

Zmaja od Bosne

Miljacka River

Train Station

Kranjčevića

BOSNIA & HERCEGOVINA

Empire offered refuge to the Sephardic Jews who had been evicted en masse from Spain in 1492. While conditions varied, Bosnian Jews mostly prospered, until WWII that is, when most of the 14,000-strong community fled or were murdered by Nazis. The community's story is well told in this 1581 Sephardic synagogue that still sees active worship during Rosh Hashana (Jewish New Year).

THE RIVERBANK
National Library   ARCHITECTURAL MONUMENT
(Map p76) Bosnia's once-glorious National Library started life as the 1892 City Hall (Vijećnica). A century later it was deliberately hit by a Serb incendiary shell and its irreplaceable collection of manuscripts and Bosnian books was destroyed. Today the building is just a skeleton with scaffolding partly hiding its storybook Moorish facades. However, long overdue reconstruction work has finally restarted.

Sarajevo 1878–1918 Museum
                              HISTORICAL MUSEUM
(Map p78; Zelenih Beretki 2; admission 2KM; ⊙10am-6pm Mon-Fri, 10am-3pm Sat) This one-room exhibition examines the city's Austro-Hungarian–era history and the infamous 1914 assassination of Franz Ferdinand that happened right outside, ultimately triggering WWI.

Obala Kulina Bana   HISTORICAL STREET
The riverside drive is patchily flanked with fine Austro-Hungarian–era buildings, including the **main post office** (Map p78; Obala

Kulina Bana 8; ⊙7am-8pm Mon-Sat) with its soaring interior and old-fashioned brass counter-dividers. Next door, the **University Rectorate** (Map p78; Obala Kulina Bana 7) is similarly grand. Across the river the Gothic Revival–style **Academy of Arts** (Map p76; Obala Maka Dizdara) looks like a mini version of Budapest's magnificent national parliament building.

NOVO SARAJEVO
During the 1992–95 siege, the wide road from the airport (Zmaja od Bosne) was dubbed 'sniper alley' because Serb gunmen in surrounding hills could pick off civilians as they tried to cross it. The distinctive, pudding-and-custard coloured **Holiday Inn** (Map p76; www.holidayinn.com/sarajevo; Zmaja Od Bosne 4) famously housed most of the embattled journalists covering that conflict.

National Museum   MUSEUM
(Zemaljski Muzej Bosne-i-Hercegovine; Map p76; www.zemaljskimuzej.ba; Zmaja od Bosne 3; adult/student 5/1KM; ⊙10am-5pm Tue-Fri, 9am-1pm Sat, 10am-2pm Sun) Large and very impressive, the National Museum is a quadrangle of four splendid neoclassical buildings purpose-built in 1913. The ancient history section displays Illyrian and Roman carvings in a room that looks dressed for a toga party. Upstairs, peep through the locked, high-security glass door of room 37 to glimpse the world-famous **Sarajevo Haggadah**, a 14th-century Jewish codex estimated to be worth around a billion US dollars. Geraldine

Central Sarajevo

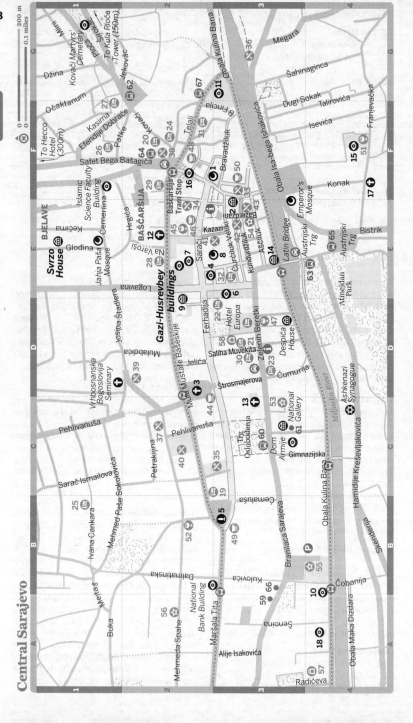

Brooks' 2007 historical novel *People of the Book* is a part-fictionalised account of how the Nazis failed to grab it during WWII.

Across a peaceful botanical garden are sections on natural history and minerals, plus an ethnography building with mannequin scenes of traditional Bosnian life set in gorgeous wooden interiors rescued from real 19th-century houses. At the front are some exceptional medieval *stećci* (carved grave slabs).

History Museum   MUSEUM

(Map p76; Zmaja od Bosne 5; foreigner/local 4/2KM; ☉11am-7pm Mon-Fri, 10am-2pm Sat & Sun) More than half of the small but engrossing History Museum 'non-ideologically' charts the course of the 1990s conflict. Affecting personal exhibits include ID cards of 'lost' medics, examples of food aid, stacks of Monopoly-style 1990s dinars and a makeshift siege-time 'home'. The effect is emphasised by the building's miserable and still partly war-damaged 1970s

Central Sarajevo

architecture. Directly behind, the amusingly tongue-in-cheek **Tito Cafe** (www.caffetito.ba; ⊘7am-midnight) comes replete with Tito photos, stormtrooper-helmet lampshades and garden seating amid WWII artillery pieces.

ILIDŽA & BUTMIR

 Tunnel Museum   WAR MUSEUM
(Map p76; Tuneli 1, Butmir; admission 5KM; ⊘9am-3pm, closed some Sun in winter) For much of the 1990s' war, Sarajevo was virtually surrounded by hostile Serb forces. Butmir was the last Bosniak-held part of the city still linked to the outside world. However, between Butmir and Sarajevo lies the airport runway. Although it was supposedly neutral and under tenuous UN control, crossing it would have been suicidal during the conflict. The solution, in extremis, was a hand-dug 800m tunnel beneath the runway. That alone proved just enough to keep Sarajevo supplied with arms and food during the three-year siege. Most of the tunnel has since collapsed, but this unmissable museum retains a 20m section and gives visitors just a glimpse of its hopes and horrors. Photos are displayed around the shell-pounded house that hides the tunnel entrance and there's a 20-minute video wordlessly showing footage of city bombardment and the wartime tunnel experience.

Joining a Sarajevo city tour (organised by most hostels) is generally cheaper than coming by taxi and your guide can add a lot of useful insight. Alternatively take tram 3 to Ilidža (35 minutes, 11km from Baščaršija), then switch to the Kotorac bus (10 minutes, twice hourly). Get off at the last stop, walk across the bridge, then turn immediately left down Tuneli for 600m.

Termalna Rivijera   SWIMMING
(Map p76; www.terme-ilidza.ba/en; Butmirska Cesta 18; adult/child Mon-Fri 13/10KM, Sat & Sun 15/12KM; ⊘9am-10pm Sun-Fri, 9am-2am Sat) A complex of indoor and outdoor swimming pools 500m east of Ilidža tram terminus.

Vrelo Bosne   PARK
The focus of this extensive park is a pretty patchwork of lush mini-islands where the source of the Bosna River is a hole in a rocky cliff. While it's not worth a special trip from central Sarajevo, if you're staying in Ilidža the park makes a pleasant outing accessible by horse-cart or on foot along Velika Aleja, a tree-lined pedestrian avenue stretching 3km from Ilidža's main hotel area.

☞ Tours

A 90-minute, €7 **Sarajevo Discovery** (☑061190591; www.sarajevo-discovery.com) walking tour departs daily at 5pm from the main tourist office. Book ahead from either tourist office for the daily Tunnel Tour (€12, 2pm) and excellent three-hour 'Times of Misfortune' (€25, 11am), visiting sites related to the 1990s conflict.

Assuming a minimum group size, many hostels also offer tunnel and/or city tours, often fascinatingly accompanied by siege survivors.

For trips further afield, ecotourism specialist **Green Visions** (☑717290; www.sarajevo-travel.ba; opposite Radnička 66; ⊘9am-5pm Mon-Fri) offers a wide range of weekend and tailor-made hiking trips into the Bosnian mountains and villages.

✸ Festivals & Events

Baščaršijske Noći (Baščaršija Nights; www.bascarsijskenoci.ba) Wide-ranging arts fest lasting all July.

Jazz Festival (www.jazzfest.ba) Local and international jazz in early November.

Sarajevo Film Festival (www.sff.ba) Globally acclaimed with commercial and art-house movies, most with English subtitles. Held in late July

🛏 Sleeping

CITY CENTRE

Hotel Michele   BOUTIQUE GUEST HOUSE €€€
(Map p78; ☑560310; www.hotelmichele.ba; Ivana Cankara 27; r €75-105, apt €120-150) Behind the exterior of a contemporary townhouse, this marvellously offbeat eight-room guest house excites with a lobby-bar full of portraits and elegant furniture and follows up with accommodation that's mostly in vast, exotically furnished apartments with antique if sometimes mismatching furniture. Recent celebrity guests have included Morgan Freeman and Kevin Spacey.

Hotel Kovači   NEO-TRADITIONAL HOUSE-HOTEL €€
(Map p78; ☑573700; www.hotelkovaci.com; Kovači 12; s/d/tr/apt €50/70/90/100; ▣🛜) This wonderfully central family hotel blends a chic, understated modernism with the basic design of a traditional *doksat* house, its fresh white rooms softened with photos

of 19th-century Sarajevo on protruding panels.

Hotel Central
SPORTS HOTEL €€€

(Map p78; ☎561800; www.hotelcentral.ba; Cumurija 8; s\d/tr 200/240/300KM; ✳🖥) Behind the grand Austro-Hungarian facade, most of this newly renovated 'hotel' is in fact an amazing three-floor gym complex with professional-standard cardio and weight rooms and a big indoor pool with hot tub and saunas. All this along with qualified sports training staff is included in the rates for the 15 huge, fashionably appointed guest rooms leading off corridors painted lugubriously deep purple.

Hotel Hecco
HOTEL €€

(Map p76; ☎273730; www.hotel-hecco.net; Medresa 1; s/tw/d/tr/apt 80/110/130/150/160KM; @🖥) Twenty-nine bright, airy rooms lead off an artfully designed warren of corridors that are dotted with armchairs and feel a little like a Mondrian painting in three dimensions. Staff are obliging, there's limited car parking but no lift and only the top floor has air-con. Minibus 58 stops outside.

Residence Rooms
HOSTEL €

(Map p78; ☎200157; www.residencerooms.ba; 1st fl, Saliha Muvekita 1; dm/d €15/40; @🖥) High ceilings, ample common areas and widely spaced beds in the dorms all make for a convivial hostel experience and there are plenty of lively bars within stumbling distance.

HCC Sarajevo Hostel
HOSTEL €

(Map p78; ☎503294; www.hcc.ba; 3rd fl, Saliha Muvekita 2; dm 25-29KM, s/d 40/65KM; @🖥) This sociable new hostel has a brilliant kitchen and a smaller communal TV lounge/lobby with DVDs to watch and a guitar to strum. Don't be put off by the speakerphone entrance and four flights of ragged access stairs.

Sobe Divan
BUDGET ROOMS €

(Map p78; ☎061420254; Brandžiluk 38; tw €30) Above an Ali Baba's cave of a restaurant, these 10 twin rooms are painted in sunny Provencal colours and are all equipped with new, private bathrooms. There's no reception or common room, but at such bargain prices one can't complain. Off season, single use is just €15.

Haris Hostel
HOSTEL €

(Map p76; ☎232563; www.hyh.ba; Vratnik Mejdan 29; dm €15; @🖥) If you can handle the sweaty 10-minute climb from town, Haris is a friendly budget choice with three six-bed dorms sharing a decent kitchen, sitting area

ℹ TO BOOK OR NOT TO BOOK?

In midsummer the best places fill fast so reservations can be wise. However, many Sarajevo accommodation rates have fallen so significantly of late that prices quoted on flyers, hotel websites and booking engines can prove 30% higher than for walk-ins, especially at pricier places; so off-season it can really pay to wait. The best hostels should be reserved ahead but there are many others, each offering an unpredictable mixture of good and bad, central and less central. At the numerous cheap places around Baščaršija tram stop, it's generally preferable to look before you book.

and a rough concrete terrace with rooftop views and occasional barbeques. Check availability at the hostel's **Old Town office** (Map p78; Kovači 7; ⊙8am-7pm Mon-Fri, 8am-4pm Sat).

Hotel Art
BUSINESS HOTEL €€

(Map p78; ☎232855; www.hotelart.ba; Ferhadija 30a; s/d 165/186KM; ✳@🖥P) Wrought-iron bedsteads and Persian rugs contrast with the functional plastic-wood veneer furniture in pastel-toned rooms that come with in-room computer, safe and trouser press.

Villa Wien
BUSINESS HOTEL €€

(Ćurčiluk Veliki 3; d 146KM) More original, slightly cheaper and just as central as the co-run Hotel Art, it has six indulgently pseudo–*belle époque* rooms above the Wiener Café. Check in at the main hotel.

City Boutique Hotel
BOUTIQUE HOTEL €€

(Map p78; ☎566850; www.cityhotel.ba; Mula Mustafe Bašekije 2; r €67-71 Fri-Sun, €101-112 Mon-Thu; ✳🖥) Contemporary, designer rooms in rectilinear modernist style feature striking colours and backlit ceiling panels. There's a 6th-floor self-serve lounge-cafe and rooftop terrace with limited views. Busy road outside.

Hotel Safir
FAMILY HOTEL €€

(Map p78; ☎475040; www.hotelsafir.ba; Jagodića 3; s/d €60/82; 🖥) Off stairways featuring vibrantly colour-suffused flower photos, well-tended rooms come with little window mirrors, conical basins and beam-me-up-Scotty shower booths. Six out of eight have a kitchenette.

Hotel Telal
MINI-HOTEL €

(Map p78; ☎525125; www.hotel-telal.ba; Abdesthana 4; s/d/tr/apt €25/35/45/60)

Reception feels a little claustrophobic but the rooms are unexpectedly smart and well tended for the price.

Ljubičica Hostel   BUDGET ACCOMMODATION €
(Map p78; ☑232109, 061131813; www.hostel ljubicica.net; Mula Mustafe Bašeskije 65; dm €10, homestay s/d from €15/20; ⏰5.30am-11pm, 8am-10pm winter) This agency can usually find you a homestay room somewhere within the old city and has several sites with packed-full dorms. The dorms at Mula Mustafe Bašeskije 49 are new but as functional as you'd expect for €10. Numerous other cheap options lie within 100m.

ILIDŽA

Several grand yet well-priced hotels lie in green, pleasant Ilidža. Parking is easier here than downtown but it's a 35-minute tram-ride from Sarajevo's old centre.

TOP CHOICE   Casa Grande   ELEGANT HOTEL €€
(Map p76; ☑639280; www.casagrande -bih.com; Velika Aleja 2; s/d/tr/q 68/113/138/165KM; ❋❄P) Designed like an aristocratic 1920s villa, the Casa Grande sits amid the plane trees right at the start of Ilidža's classic avenue, Velika Aleja. Rooms range from spacious to huge and are remarkably luxurious for the price. Expect satellite TV, 30-nozzle full-body shower pods and framed (if sometimes dreadful) imitations of 'classic' art.

AutoKamp Oaza   CAMPING GROUND €
(☑636140; hoteloaza@live.com; per person 10KM plus per tent/car/campervan 7/8/12KM) Tree-shaded camping and caravan hook-ups (electricity 3KM extra) tucked behind the Hotel Imzit, 1.5km west of Ilidža tram terminus.

✖ Eating

CITY CENTRE
Mala Kuhinja   FUSION €€
(Map p78; ☑061144741; www.malakuhinja.ba; Josipa Štadlera 6; meals 15-20KM; ⏰9am-6pm Mon-Fri, 9am-5pm Sat) There's no menu at this tiny, fusion-food gem where TV celebrity chef Muamer Kurtagic asks you what you fancy, hands you a shot of homemade *loza* (local grappa) and sets about creating culinary magic. Sit at the three-stool 'bar' to watch the show in all its glory. Reservations advisable.

Karuzo   VEGETARIAN, SEAFOOD €€
(Map p78; ☑444647; www.karuzorestaurant.com; Dženetića Čikma 2; veg mains 15-18KM; ⏰noon-3pm Mon-Fri, 6-11pm Mon-Sat) This friendly

little restaurant, styled vaguely like a yacht's interior, is one of the few places in Bosnia to offer a meat-free menu. This includes imaginative vegetarian meals like spicy chickpea pockets with tahini sauce and a range of fish dishes (17KM to 35KM) and sushi (3KM to 5KM per piece). The owner is both waiter and chef so don't be in a hurry.

Dveri   BOSNIAN €€
(Map p78; ☑537020; www.dveri.co.ba; Prote Bakovića 10; meals 10-16KM; ⏰10am-11pm; ❋) A narrow, easily missed streetfront entrance leads through into this tourist-friendly 'country cottage' eatery hung with loops of garlic, corn cobs and gingham-curtained windows. Inky risottos or veggie-stuffed eggplant wash down a treat with 6KM glasses of the house red, an excellent Hercegovinian Blatina. Beware if offered 'homemade bread': it's good but costs 5KM extra.

To Be or Not to Be   ECCLECTIC €€
(Map p78; ☑233265; Čizmedžiluk 5; meals 10-22KM; ⏰11am-11pm) Arched metal shutters creak open to reveal a tiny two-table room lovably decorated in traditional Bosnian style. Try the daring, tongue-tickling steak in chilli chocolate (20KM). The name, with 'Not to Be' crossed out as a message of positivity, was originally a poster slogan for the 1994 Sarajevo Winter Festival, held against all odds during the siege.

Inat Kuća   CLASSIC BOSNIAN €€
(Spite House; Map p78; ☑447867; www.inatkuca.ba; Velika Alifakovac 1; mains 12-20KM, snacks 10KM) In a classic Ottoman-era house, this Sarajevo institution is a veritable museum piece with a great riverside terrace. The menu tells the story of its odd name but much of the typical Bosnian food (stews, *dolme*) is pre-prepared and slightly lacklustre.

GREATER SARAJEVO
Hot Wok Café   ASIAN FUSION €€
(Map p76; ☑203322; Maršala Tita 12; meals 12-17KM; ⏰11am-11pm Mon-Fri, 11am-1am Sat) Pull up an over-tall stool-seat and watch the chef wok up your meal on an antique stove that contrasts with the *Kill Bill* modernism of the decor. The menu is pun-tastic and the South-ast Asian fusion food is full of unexpected flavour combinations that confuse the palate but leave you wanting to lick the plate.

Biban   BOSNIAN €€
(Map p76; ☑232026; Hošin Brijeg 95a; mains 7-16KM; ⏰10am-10pm) Biban offers panoramic city views similar to those from better-

known Park Prinčeva, but it's cheaper and more relaxed without the latter's scurrying army of waistcoated waiters. Perfectly cooked squid (13KM) and various Bosnian dishes come in generously sized portions. Walk 600m uphill from Park Prinčeva, turning left after Nalina 15.

Park Prinčeva
BOSNIAN €€€

(Map p76; ☎222708; www.parkprinceva.ba; Iza Hidra 7; meals 12-23KM; ☺9am-11pm) Like Bono and Bill Clinton before you, gaze down from this picture-perfect ridgetop perch for fabulous views of Sarajevo's rooftops, mosques and twinkling lights. Get there by minibus 56 from Latin Bridge.

Quick Eats

Close to Pigeon Sq you'll find a Konzum Supermarket, a 24-hour bakery and dozens of street-terrace cafes. For inexpensive snack meals look along Bradžiluk or Kundurdžiluk where the best-known *ćevabdžinica* (albeit not the sexiest) is **ŽelJo** (Map p78; Kundurdžiluk 17 & 20; ćevapi 3-7KM; ☺8am-10pm).

Markale
MARKET

(Map p78; Mula Mustafe Bašeskije; ☺7am-5pm Mon-Sat, 7am-2pm Sun) The central market comprises the covered 1894 Gradska Tržnica hall selling meat and dairy goods while across a busy road is Markale's huddle of vegetable stalls. Marketgoers were massacred here on several occasions by Serb mortar attacks in the 1990s, including a 1995 assault that proved a 'last straw', triggering NATO air strikes against the forces besieging Sarajevo.

Butik-Badem
SWEETS, NUTS

(Map p78; Abadžiluk 12; ☺8am-11pm) This super little health-food shop sells luscious *lokum* (Turkish delight; per kg 6KM to 10KM), nuts and a variety of tempting snack foods by weight.

Drinking

As chilly April melts into sunny May, terraces blossom and central Sarajevo becomes one giant street cafe.

Bars

Zlatna Ribica
BAR

(Map p78; Kaptol 5; ☺10am-2am) This marvellously Gothic cafe-bar is loaded with eccentricities, including drinks menus hidden away in old books that dangle from lampshades. The uniquely stocked toilet will have you laughing out loud. Expect soft jazz and free nibbles, perhaps grapes or dried figs.

Pivnica HS
BREWERY BAR-RESTAURANT

(Map p78; Franjevačka 15; ☺10am-1am) If Willy Wonka built a beer hall it might look like this. It's the only place you can be sure of finding excellent Sarajevskaya dark beer (brewed next door) and there's superb food too (pastas 8KM, mains from 13KM).

Pravda
COCKTAILS & COFFEE

(Map p76; www.pravda.ba; Radićeva 4c; ☺8am-midnight) Choose from marigold-patterned chill-out sofas or white-enamel perch-stools, then strike your pose amid Sarajevo's gilded youth. Oh no, don't say they've all gone next door to Cafe Nivea?!

City Pub
PUB

(Map p78; Despićeva bb; ☺8am-2am) Despite a could-be-anywhere pub interior, this friendly place is a very popular meeting point, with occasional live music.

Barhana
RAKIJA, PIZZERIA

(Đugalina 8; ☺10am-midnight) A selection of flavoured local shots (from 3KM) served in a hidden courtyard off a lane with several other bar-restaurants.

Cafes

Kuća Sevdaha
CAFE

(Map p78; www.artkucasevdaha.ba/en/; Halači 5; ☺10am-11pm) Sip Bosnian coffee, juniper sherbet or rose water while nibbling local sweets and listening to the lilting wails of *sevdah*, traditional Bosnian music. The ancient building that surrounds the cafe's glassed-in fountain courtyard is now used as a museum celebrating great 20th-century *sevdah* performers (admission 2KM).

Caffe Divan
CARAVANSERAI

(Map p78; Morića Han, Saraći 77; ☺8am-midnight) Relax in wicker chairs beneath the wooden beams of a gorgeous, historic caravanserai courtyard whose stables now contain an alluring Iranian carpet shop.

Hecco Deluxe
CAFE

(Map p78; www.heccodeluxe.com; 10th fl, Ferhadije 2; coffee 2-3KM, mains 8-25KM; ☺7am-11pm) For memorable 360-degree views of the city centre take the lift to the 9th-floor Hecco Deluxe Hotel, then climb the stairs one floor further. Good coffee, no alcohol.

Alfonso
COFFEE HOUSE

(Map p78; Trg Fra Grge Martica 4; ☺8am-11pm) Great espressos served at open-air pavement seating that sprawls around the Catholic cathedral, or inside where a hip interior includes a catwalk between cushioned sunken seat spaces. Music gets louder after dark.

Dibek
HUBBLE-BUBBLE BAR

(Map p78; Laledžina 3; ☺8am-11pm) Smoking a hookah (nargile water pipe; 10KM) is back in fashion as you'll see in this DJ-led bar on a super-quaint little Old Town square.

☆ Entertainment
Nightclubs & Live Music

Bock/FIS
ALTERNATIVE/URBAN

(Map p76; www.bock.ba; Musala bb; ☺6pm-2am) There's no easy-to-spot sign for this little basement venue, where you might find live punk or alternative bands on weekdays and 'urban' party music at weekends.

The Club
DJS, LIVE MUSIC

(Map p76; ☏550550; www.theclub.ba; Maršala Tita 7; beer 4KM; ☺10am-4am) This subterranean trio of stone cavern rooms includes a restaurant that serves till 3am (with live Serbian folk music), a lounge that would seem better suited to a gentlemen's club, and a bar where DJs or cramped live concerts pull in crowds after midnight (entrance 5KM includes drink). Around the back, Pivnica Sarajevo has a cushioned garden-bar.

Club Jež
TURBOFOLK

(Map p78; www.jez.ba; Zelenih Beretki 14; drinks 2.50KM; ☺6pm-late) This intimate stone-vaulted cavern club heaves with young local revellers overdosing on turbofolk. Cover charges (around 3KM) include one drink.

Sloga
STUDENT DISCO

(Map p78; Seljo, Mehmeda Spahe 20; beer from 4KM; ☺8pm-3am) This cavernous, blood-red club-disco-dance hall caters to an excitable, predominantly student crowd but dancing is oddly impeded by rows of tables (only moved on Mondays for salsa night). Cover charge 5KM at weekends.

Hacienda
DJ-BAR, RESTAURANT

(Map p78; www.placetobe.ba; Bazerdzani 3; ☺10am-very late) The not-quite Mexican food could be spicier. Not so the ambience at 2am, by which time this cane-ceilinged cantina has metamorphosed into one of the Old Town's most happening nightspots. Several other bars in the block are equally buzzing.

Performing Arts

National Theatre
PERFORMING ARTS

(Narodno Pozorište; Map p78; ☏221682; www.nps. ba; Obala Kulina Bana 9; tickets from 10KM; ☺box office 9am-noon & 4-7.30pm) Classically adorned with fiddly gilt mouldings, this proscenium-arched theatre hosts a ballet, opera, play or philharmonic concert virtually every night from mid-September to mid-June.

🛍 Shopping

Baščaršija's pedestrian lanes are full of jewellery stalls and wooden-shuttered souvenir shops flogging slippers, Bosnian flags, carpets, archetypal copperware and wooden spoons, though if you're heading to Mostar, you might find prices better there. The attractive, one-street, stone-domed Gazi-Husrevbey Covered Bazaar (Map p78; www.vakufgazi.ba; ☺8am-8pm Mon-Fri, 9am-2pm Sat) sells relatively inexpensive souvenirs, fake brand-name bags and sunglasses (from 5KM).

Some Sarajevo bookshops still stock the darkly humorous Sarajevo Survival Guide (23.40KM), originally published during the 1992–3 siege, as well as guidebooks, magazines and English-language books on ex-Yugoslavia.

BuyBook (Map p76; ☏716450; www.buybook. ba; Radićeva 4; ☺9am-10pm Mon-Sat)

Šahinpašić (Map p78; ☏667210; www.btcsahinpasic.com; Vladislava Skarića 8; ☺9am-9pm Mon-Sat)

ℹ Information
Internet Access
Albatros (Map p78; Sagradžije 27; per hr 2KM; ☺10am-midnight)

Internet Caffe Baščaršija (Map p78; Aščiluk bb; per hr 2KM; ☺7am-midnight)

Internet Resources
Sonar (www.sonar.ba) Has listings and information.

Medical Services
Klinički Centar Univerziteta Sarajevo (Map p76; ☏297000; 1st fl, DIP Bldg, Stepana Tomića bb; ☺8am-2pm Mon-Fri) VIP (ie English-speaking) Clinic within the vast Koševo Hospital complex. Take bus 14 from Dom Armije to Hotel Belvedere and then walk 300m northwest.

Money
There are ATMs outside the bus station, inside the airport and sprinkled all over the city centre. There's nowhere to exchange money at the stations but several banks on Ferhadija around the Catholic Cathedral can oblige. UniCredit Bank (Map p78; Zelenih Beretki 24; ☺8am-6pm Mon-Fri, 8.30am-1pm Sat) changes travellers cheques.

Tourist Information

Tourist information centre (Map p78; 220724; www.sarajevo-tourism.com) Baščaršija (Sarači 58; 10am-2pm & 3-8pm Mon-Fri, 10am-4pm Sat-Sun); Main office (Zelenih Beretki 22a; 9am-5.30pm Mon-Fri, 9am-3pm Sat) Helpful with maps, brochures and ready answers for many an awkward question. Recommended daily walking and war-era city tours.

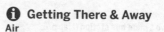

Getting There & Away

Air

Sarajevo's modest international **airport** (Map p76; 234841; www.sarajevo-airport.ba; Kurta Schorka 36) is about 12km southwest of Baščaršija. For flight details see p113.

BUSES FROM SARAJEVO

DESTINATION	STATION	PRICE (KM)	DURATION (HR)	DEPARTURES
Banja Luka	M	31	5	5am, 7.45am, 9.15am, 2.30pm, 3.30pm, 4.30pm, 6.30pm
	L	31	5	9.30am, 11.30am
Bihać	M	42	6½	7.30am, 1.30pm, 10pm
Belgrade	M	47	7½	6am
	L	40-55	8-11	8am, 9.45am, 12.30pm, 3pm, 10pm
Dubrovnik	M	44	7	7.15am, 10am, plus 2.30pm, 10.30pm summer
Foča	L	9	1½	7.45am, 9.30am, 11am, 6.25pm; or use Trebinje & Višegrad services
Herceg Novi	M	49	7½	11am (summer only)
Jajce	ML	23.50	3½	take Banja Luka buses
Ljubljana	M	92	8½	8.40pm Tue, Fri, Sun
Mostar	M	18	2½	15 daily
Munich	M	134	19	8am
Niš	L	46	11	8.40am, 6pm
Novi Pazar	M	32	7-8	9am, 3pm, 6pm, 9pm, 10pm
Pale	L	3.50	40min	12 daily Mon-Fri, 3.15pm only Sat & Sun
	M	5.40	25min	7am, 10am, 2pm
Podgorica	L	35	6	8.15am, 2pm, 10.30pm
Split (via Mostar)	M	51	7½	10am, 9pm, plus 7am in summer
Split (via Livno)	M	51	7¼	6am via Livno
Travnik	M	15.50	2	nine daily
Trebinje	L	26	5	7.45am, 1pm, 4.05pm (via Sutjeska National Park)
Tuzla	M	20	3¼	nine daily
Visoko	M	5.70	50min	at least hourly by Kakanj bus
Vienna (Beć)	M	100	14½	11.15am
Zagreb	M	54	9½	6.30am, 12.30pm, 10pm
	M	54	8½	9.30am via Bosanski Brod

M = main bus station, L = East Sarajevo Bus Station

Bus

Sarajevo's **main bus station** (Map p76; 213100; Put Života 8) primarily serves locations in the Federation, Croatia and Western Europe. Most services to the Republik Srpsk (RS) and Serbia leave from **East Sarajevo Bus Station** (Map p76; 057-317377; Nikole Tesle bb), commonly known as Lukovica bus station. The latter lies way out in the suburb of Dobrinja, 400m beyond the western terminus stop of trolleybus 103 and bus 31E. To some destinations, buses leave from both stations.

Train

From the **train station** (Map p76; 655330; Put Života 2) useful services include:

Belgrade (33KM, nine hours) Departs 11.35am.

Budapest (105.90KM, 12 hours) Departs 6.55am, routed via Doboj, Šamac and Osijek (Croatia). Returns from Budapest-Keleti at 9.45am.

Mostar (9.90KM, three hours) Departs 7.05am and 6.18pm on trains bound for Ploče (23.50KM, four hours) on the Croatian coast.

Zagreb (58.90KM, 9½ hours) Trains depart 10.42am and 9.27pm. There is no longer any couchette service.

❶ Getting Around

To/From the Airport

Bus 36 departs from directly opposite the terminal but only runs to Nedžarići (part way along the Ilidža–Baščaršija tram line) and at best runs only twice an hour. More frequent and convenient trolleybus 103 and bus 31E both run to the centre, picking up around 700m from the terminal. To find the stop turn right out of the airport then take the first left. Shimmy right-left-right past Hotel Octagon, then turn right at the Panda car wash (Brače Mulića 17). Just before the Mercator Hypermarket (Mimar Sinana 1) cross the road and take the bus-trolleybus going back the way you've just come.

Airport taxis charge at least 7KM to Ilidža and 25KM to Baščaršija.

Bicycle

Rent-A-Bike (062547364; www.girbikerental.com.ba; Dženitića Čikma bb; per hr/day/week 3/15/50KM; 9am-2pm & 3.30-9pm Wed-Mon)

Car

One-way systems and parking are awkward and Baščaršija is largely pedestrianised. Many hotels advertising parking have just a few spaces available. However, while central Sarajevo isn't driver-friendly, a car certainly makes it much easier to reach the surrounding mountain areas. Many hotels have their own small car-rental agencies. See also p114.

Public Transport

Many lines (including tram 1, trolley 103 and minibus 56) operate 6am to 11pm daily, but some stop after 7pm, and all have reduced services on Sunday. For timetables, click 'Redove Voznje' on www.gras.co.ba then select mode of transport.

Single-ride tickets, 1.60/1.80KM from kiosks/drivers, must be stamped once aboard. Inspectors have no mercy on 'ignorant foreigners'. Day tickets (5.60KM) are valid on almost all buses, trams and trolleybuses. They're sold at the kiosk facing the Catholic Cathedral.

USEFUL ROUTES

Tram 3 (every four to seven minutes) From Ilidža passes the Holiday Inn then loops one way (anticlockwise) around Baščaršija. Last tram back to Ilidža departs around midnight.

Tram 1 (every 12 to 25 minutes) Does the same loop as the more frequent Tram 3 but starts from the train station (from where you could alternatively walk to the nearest Tram 3 stop in about seven minutes).

Trolleybus 103 (every six to 12 minutes) Runs along the southern side of the city from Austrijski Trg passing near Green Visions en route to Dobrinja (30 minutes). Handy for East Sarajevo (Lukovica) bus station and the airport.

Bus 31E (three per hour, 6.30am to 10pm) Vijećnica to Dobrinja (for Lukovica bus station).

Taxi

All of Sarajevo's taxis have meters; **Žuti Taxis** (Yellow Cab; 663555) actually turn them on. Taxis cost 2KM plus about 1KM per kilometre. Handy central taxi ranks are near Latin Bridge, Hotel Kovači and outside Zelenih Beretki 5.

AROUND SARAJEVO

Mountains rise directly behind the city, offering convenient access to winter skiing or summer rambles but landmine dangers remain, so stick to well-used paths.

Jahorina

057

Jahorina's mixture of open grasslands, forested patches and wide views makes it the most visually attractive of BiH's three main ski resorts. The world-class pistes at this **resort** (www.oc-jahorina.com; ski pass per half/full day 20/30KM, ski-set rentals per day 25-40KM) were designed for the 1984 Winter Olympics. All accommodation is within 300m of one of Jahorina's six main ski lifts.

In summer you can rent mountain bikes from Hotel Termag (per half/full day 7/10KM).

🛏 Sleeping & Eating

Hotels are widely strung out along 2.5km of wiggling lane. This starts with a little seasonal shopping 'village' where you'll find the cheaper *pansions* (all closed out of season). The Termag Hotel is 300m above, then around 1km beyond the road S-bends past the Hotel Dva Javora and the post office. Beyond the still-ruined Hotel Jahorina the lane tunnels beneath Rajska Vrata before dead-ending at the top of the Skočine Lift. Quoted ski-season rates are for mid-January to March with half board; summer rates include breakfast only.

Termag Hotel   SKI HOTEL €€€
(📞270422; www.termaghotel.com; s/d/ste 115/152/200KM, ski season from d/ste 240/300KM; 🛜🍴P) Within an oversized mansion built in Scooby Doo Gothic style, the Termag is a beautifully designed fashion statement where traditional ideas and open fireplaces are given a stylish, modernist twist. Rooms use thick wooden boards to artistic effect and many have glowing bedside tables. Underground parking available.

Rajska Vrata   RESTAURANT, ROOMS €€
(📞272020; www.jahorina-rajskavrata.com; mains 7-14KM) Beside the longest piste in town, this perfect alpine ski-in cafe-restaurant has rustic sheepskin benches around a centrally flued real fire. The cosy pine-walled bedrooms (doubles/triples €50/75) are only available in summer.

Hotel Dva Javora   SKI HOTEL €€
(📞270481; www.hoteldvajavora.com; s/d/tr €24/40/56, ski season from €38/62/86; 🛜) Above a seasonal shopping centre, the modern lobby bar has glowing fireplaces. The rooms, while fairly plain, come with new pine beds and clean checkerboard bathrooms. In season, apartments sleeping up to six people cost just €72 without meals.

Pansion Sport   SKI LODGE €€
(📞270333; www.pansion-sport.com; s 39-92KM, d 54-124KM; ⊙19 Dec-10 Apr) Pleasant Swiss chalet-style guest house at the bottom 'village area' of the resort.

ℹ Getting There & Away

Jahorina is 13km from Pale, or alternatively 27km from Sarajevo via a scenic mountainside lane. Buses run in ski season only, departing from Pale (3KM, 25 minutes) at 7am and 2pm and returning at 8am and 3pm. Some winter weekends buses depart Sarajevo's main bus station at 9am, returning at 3.45pm. A taxi from Pale costs 30KM.

Bjelašnica
📞033

BiH's second Olympic ski field rises above the two-hotel resort of **Bjelašnica** (www.bjelasnica.ba; ski pass per day/night/week 30/18/200KM), around 30km south of Sarajevo. In summer Bjelašnica's numerous apartments mostly lie empty but you can still rent bicycles (per hour/day 4/25KM) from the excellent new **Hotel Han** (📞584150; www.hotelhan.ba; s/d summer 70/100KM, winter 105/170KM; 🛜), a stylish yet reasonably priced 2010 construction facing the main piste. For groups it can also arrange hiking and quad biking.

Fronted by what looks like a giant Plexiglas pencil, the friendly but older **Hotel Maršal** (📞584100; www.hotel-marsal.ba; d/ste €54/80, winter from €80/110; @) rents skis, boots and poles (guests/nonguests per day 15/20KM) in season.

The good-value, brand-new **Hostel Feri** (📞775555; www.feri.ba; Veliko Polje; per person 42.60-67KM, s 64-100KM; 🛜) charges the same per person whether you're in a double or six-bedded room, all unexpectedly luxurious for a 'hostel' with flat-screen TV and wi-fi. It's set in a meadow 5km northwest of Bjelašnica, too far from the lifts for downhill skiing but other assorted sporting activities are available.

Minibus 85 leaves from Sarajevo's Ilidža bus station on Monday, Tuesday and Saturday at 8am plus 4pm Friday. It returns from Bjelašnica around 10.15am Monday and Saturday (not Tuesday) and 6.15pm Friday. On weekends in ski season there's also a 9am bus from Sarajevo's National Museum, returning at 4pm.

HERCEGOVINA

Hercegovina is the part of BiH that no one in the West ever mentions, if only because they can't pronounce it. The arid, Mediterranean landscape has a distinctive beauty punctuated with barren mountain ridges and photogenic river valleys. Famed for its fine wines and sun-packed fruits, Hercegovina is sparsely populated, but it has several

WORTH A TRIP

UMOLJANI

If you're driving, don't miss exploring the web of rural lanes tucked away in the grassy uplands above Bjelašnica. Although most villages here suffered severely in the war, with little traditional architecture left, their mountain settings are truly lovely. Try heading for **Umoljani village** (16km from Bjelašnica), where there's rustic accommodation (single/twin/triple/quad 20/40/60/80KM) available in a new, three-bedroom log house behind the cute little **Restoran Studeno Vrelo** (☑061709540; coffee/snack 1.50/5KM). The approach road to Umoljani is beautiful and there are *stećci* just above the road around 2.5km before the village. The road to **Milišići** has even more dramatic views. **Green Visions** (www.sarajevo-travel.ba) organises summer weekend trips to war-spared **Lukomir**, the nation's highest and most isolated village.

intriguing historic towns and the Adriatic coast is just a skip away.

Mostar

☑036 / POP 94,000

At dusk the lights of numerous millhouse restaurants twinkle across gushing streamlets. The impossibly quaint Kujundžiluk 'gold alley' bustles joyously with trinket sellers. And in between, the Balkans' most celebrated bridge forms a truly majestic stone arc between reincarnated medieval towers. It's a magical scene.

Meanwhile, behind the cobbled lanes of the attractively restored Ottoman quarter, a less palatable but equally unforgettable 'attraction' lies in observing the devastating urban scars that still recall the city's brutal 1990s conflict all too vividly.

Add in a selection of day trips for which Mostar makes an ideal base and it's not surprising that this fascinating little city is starting to attract a growing throng of summer visitors.

History

Mostar means 'bridge-keeper', and the crossing of the Neretva River here has always been its raison d'être. In the mid-16th century, Mostar boomed as a key transport gateway within the powerful, expanding Ottoman Empire. Some 30 *esnafi* (craft guilds) included tanners (for whom the Tabhana was built), and goldsmiths (hence Kujundžiluk, 'gold alley'). In 1557, Suleyman the Magnificent ordered a swooping stone arch to replace the suspension bridge whose wobbling had previously terrified tradesmen as they gingerly crossed the fast-flowing Neretva River. The beautiful Stari Most (Old Bridge) that resulted was finished in 1566 and came to be appreciated

as one of the era's engineering marvels. It survived the Italian occupation of WWII, but after standing for 427 years the bridge was destroyed in November 1993 by Bosnian Croat artillery in one of the most poignant and depressingly pointless moments of the whole Yugoslav civil war.

Ironically Muslims and Croats had initially fought together against Serb and Montenegrin forces that had started bombarding Mostar in April 1992. However, on 9 May 1993, a bitter conflict erupted between the former allies. Bosnian Croat forces expelled many Bosniaks from their homes: some were taken to detention camps, others fled across the Neretva to the very relative safety of the Muslim east bank. For two years the two sides swapped artillery fire and the city was pummelled into rubble.

By 1995 Mostar resembled Dresden after WWII, with all its bridges destroyed and all but one of its 27 Ottoman-era mosques utterly ruined. Vast international assistance efforts rebuilt almost all of the Unesco-listed old city core, including the classic bridge, painstakingly reconstructed using 16th century–style building techniques and stone from the original quarry. However, nearly two decades after the conflict, significant numbers of shattered buildings remain as ghostlike reminders. The psychological scars will take generations to heal and the city remains oddly schizophrenic, with two bus stations, two postal systems and, until very recently, two fire services – one Bosniak and the other Croat.

◉ Sights

Stari Most   MEDIEVAL BRIDGE

The world-famous **Stari Most** (Old Bridge) is the indisputable visual focus that gives Mostar its special magic. The bridge's pale stone magnificently throws back the golden glow of sunset or the tasteful nighttime floodlighting. Numerous well-positioned cafes and restaurants, notably behind the **Tabhana** (an Ottoman-era enclosed courtyard), tempt you to admire the scene from a dozen varying angles. Directly west in a semicircular gunpowder tower is the **Bridge-Divers' Clubhouse** (admission 2KM; ☺10am-dusk, variable). Its members are an elite group of young men who will plunge 21m off the bridge's parapet into the icy Neretva River below once their hustlers have collected enough photo money from onlookers. If you want to jump yourself (from €25), they can organise a wet suit and basic training (highly advisable). When you're ready to go, two divers wait below in case of emergencies. Visiting the clubhouse you can read a few information boards about the bridge's history and descend for a brief glimpse of the unadorned Turkish jail-pit below. The tower's top two floors house a separate exhibition of around 50 black-and-white photos depicting city life during the war – great but hardly justifying the extra 5KM entry fee.

Across the bridge, the **Old Bridge Museum** (adult/student 5/3KM; ☺11am-2pm winter, 10am-6pm summer, closed Mon) has two parts, both offering only sparse exhibits. First you climb up a five-storey stone defence tower for partial views and interesting but limited displays about the bridge's context and construction. Climb back down to walk through the bridge's archaeological bowels, emerging on Kujundžiluk. There's a slow-moving 15-minute video of the bridge's destruction/reconstruction but a better-paced DVD is shown (and for sale, €10) at the free-admission **Galerija Sava Neimarevic** in a former mosque right on the bridge's southwest parapet.

The annual bridge-diving competition is held in July.

Old Town   NEIGHBOURHOOD
Layered down a mini-valley around the quaint little **Crooked Bridge** (Kriva Ćuprija), stairways link quaint old houses and stone mills, now mostly used as restaurants. Above, pretty old shopfronts line **Prječka Čaršija** and **Kujundžiluk**, the picturesque cobbled alleys that join at Stari Most. Entered from a gated courtyard, the originally 1618 **Koski Mehmed Paša Mosque** (Mala Tepa 16; mosque/mosque & minaret 4/8KM; ☺8am-7pm Apr-Oct, 9am-3pm Nov-Mar) has interior decor that lacks finesse, but climbing its claustrophobic minaret offers commanding Old Town panoramas.

Braće Fejića   NEIGHBOURHOOD
Mostar's main shopping street, Braće Fejića, links the modest **Tepa Vegetable Market** (☺6.30am-2pm) to **Trg Musala**, once the grand heart of Austro-Hungarian Mostar, now scarred by the war-ruined shell of Hotel Neretva (under reconstruction). Braće Fejića's architecture is predominantly banal but features the expertly rebuilt 1557 **Karađozbeg Mosque** (mosque/mosque & minaret 4/8KM; ☺9am-7pm Apr-Oct, 9am-5pm Nov-Mar, closed during prayers) with its distinctive lead-roofed wooden veranda and four-domed madrassa annexe (now a clinic). The early-17th-century **Roznamedži Ibrahimefendi Mosque** was the only mosque to survive the 1993–5 shelling relatively unscathed. Its associated **madrassa**, demolished in 1960, has also been rebuilt and hosts shops and a cafe.

Down a side lane, the charmingly ramshackle **Bišćevića Ćošak** (Turkish House; ☎550677; Bišćevića 13; admission 4KM; ☺9am-3pm Nov-Feb, 8am-8pm Mar-Oct) is a 350-year-old Ottoman-Bosnian home with a colourfully furnished interior sporting a selection of traditional metalwork and carved wooden furniture. For interesting comparisons also visit the grander 18th/19th-century **Muslibegović House** (admission 4KM; ☺10am-6pm mid-Apr–mid-Oct), which now doubles as a boutique hotel (see p92).

Former Front Line   WAR DAMAGE
It's thought-provoking and intensely moving to see that over 15 years after the conflict, many buildings are still bullet pocked and some remain skeletal wrecks. Several of these lie along Mostar's former front line across which Croat and Muslim communities bombarded each other during the civil war. Every year more are restored but you'll still see several tragic ruins around Spanski Trg, including the bombed-out nine-storey tower that was once **Ljubljanska Banka** (Kralja Zvonimira bb).

Bajatova   NEIGHBOURHOOD
The little **Museum of Hercegovina** (http://muzejhercegovine.com; Bajatova 4; admission 5KM; ☺8am-2pm Mon-Fri, 10am-noon Sat) is housed in the former home of Džemal Bijedić, an ex-head of the Yugoslav government who died in mysterious circumstances in 1978. There are small archaeological and ethnographic sections plus a well-paced 10-minute film featuring pre- and post-1992 bridge-diving plus war footage that shows the moment Stari Most was blown apart.

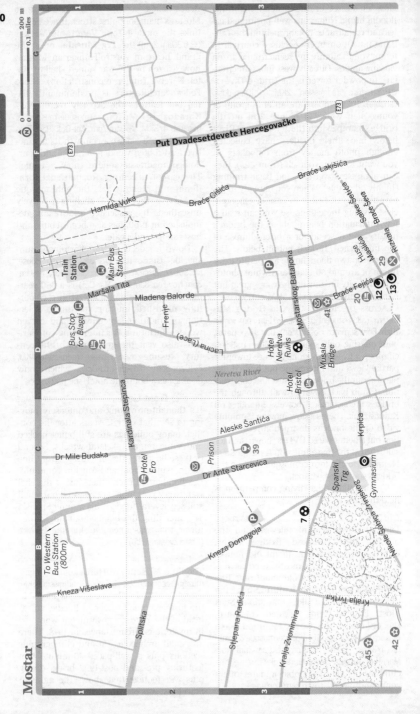

Mostar

0 ――― 200 m
0 ――― 0.1 miles

Put Dvadesetdevete Hercegovačke

E73

E73

Braće Lakišića

Braće Ćišića

Hamida Vuka

Husé Maslića
Salke Šestea
Braće Ševa

29

Rizkala

13

12

Braće Feiića

20

Mostarskog Bataljona

41

Train Station

Main Bus Station

Maršala Tita

Mladena Balorde

Frenje

Lacina (Lace)

Bus Stop for Blagaj

25

Hotel Neretva Ruins

Musala Bridge

Neretva River

Hotel Bristol

Aleske Šantića

Kardinala Stepinca

Dr Mile Budaka

Hotel Ero

Prison

Dr Ante Starcevica

39

Krpića

Spanski Trg

Gymnasium

Nikole Šubića Zrinskog

7

To Western Bus Station (800m)

Kneza Domagoja

Kneza Višeslava

Splitska

Stjepana Radića

Kralja Zvonimira

Kralja Tvrtka

45

42

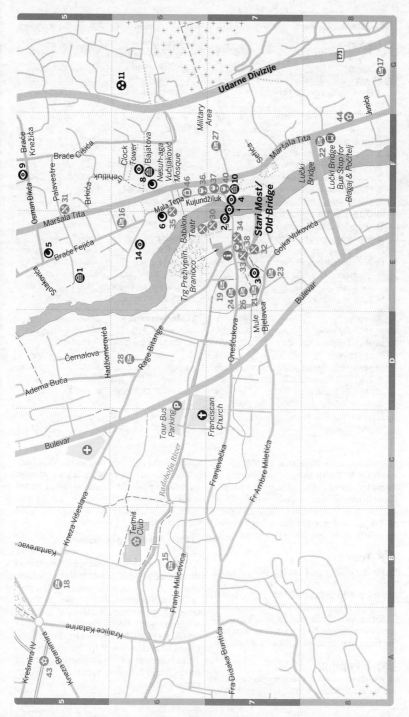

Udarne Divizije

Military Area

Stari Most/ Old Bridge

Clock Tower

Nesuh-aga Vučijaković Mosque

Mala Tepa

Kujundžiluk

Trg Preživjelih, Babilon, Teatr Branioco

Lučki Bridge

Lučki Bridge Bus Stop for Blagaj & Počitelj

Maršala Tita

Maršala Tita

Braće Knežića

Braće Ćišića

Palavestre

Osman Dikća

Brkića

Braće Fejića

Šolakovića

Čemalova

Adema Buća

Hadžiomerovića

Rage Bitange

Tour Bus Parking

Radobolia River

Franciscan Church

Franjevačka

Fr Ambre Miletića

Onešćukova

Mule

Bjelava

Gojka Vukovića

Bulevar

Bulevar

Tennis Club

Franje Milićevica

Franje Milićevica

Kneza Višeslava

Kantarevac

Kraljice Katarine

Kralja Branimira IV

Krešmira IV

Fra Didaka Buntića

Sećira

Jusića

E73

G17

44

22

11

9

9

31

5

1

8

6

35

16

14

46

36

37

40

10

4

2

30

34

38

32

33

3

23

19

24

26

21

28

15

18

43

Stairway lane **Bajatova** climbs on towards the M17 with an underpass leading towards the site of a once imposing **Orthodox church** almost totally destroyed by Croat shelling in 1993. The site is currently fenced off for planned reconstruction but when accessible it offers extensive city views.

☞ Tours

Some homestays and hostels offer walking tours around town and/or great-value €25 day trips visiting Blagaj, Međugorje, Počitelj and the Kravice waterfalls. **Almira Travel** (☏551873; www.almira-travel.ba; Mala Tepa 9) offers alternative options including wine-tasting tours in a range of European languages.

🛏 Sleeping

If you're stumped for accommodation the tourist information centre (p95) and travel agencies can help you find a bed. Most budget options are in people's homes without reception or full-time staff, so calling ahead is wise. In low season some are virtually dormant but you might get a whole room for the dorm price.

TOP CHOICE **Muslibegović House**

HERITAGE HOUSE €€

(☏551379; www.muslibegovichouse.com; Osman Đikća 41; s/d/ste €50/85/100; ✳ 🛜) In summer, tourists pay to visit this restored 18th-century Ottoman courtyard house. But it's simultaneously an extremely convivial boutique homestay-hotel. Room sizes and styles vary significantly, mixing excellent modern bathrooms with elements of traditional Bosnian, Turkish or even Moroccan design, notably in rooms 2 and 3. Double rooms cost €70 during low season.

Hotel Old Town BOUTIQUE HOTEL €€

(☎558877; www.oldtown.ba; Rad Bitange 9a; d/tr from 160/240KM; ✳ P ⑨) This super-central boutique hotel is designed to look like a typical Bosnian house and sports handmade, specially designed wooden furniture. Meanwhile its state-of-the-art ecofriendly energy-saving systems include waste-burning furnaces for water-heating and air circulation to save on air-con wastage. Deluxe rooms (single/double 190/280KM) are marginally larger than standard ones.

Hostel Majdas HOUSE-HOSTEL €

(☎061382940, 062265324; www.hostelmajdas. com; 1st fl, Franje Milicevica 39; dm/d without bathroom €12.90/27; ✳ @ ⑨) By sheer force of personality, and a very human awareness of traveller needs, the host family has transformed this once dreary tower-block apartment into Mostar's cult hostel. Space is tight in the colour-coordinated bunk dorms and little communal areas, but it's a great place to meet fellow travellers; there are lockers, FAQ and cultural-tip sheets, €3 laundry, a book exchange and a taxi sign-up sheet. Sharp-witted Bata runs popular full-day regional tours several times weekly (€25).

Pansion Oscar BUDGET ROOMS €

(☎580237; Oneščukova 33; s/d €30/40, s/d/tr/q without bathroom €20/30/45/60; ✳) This brilliantly located family *pansion* has six rooms in two reconstructed Old Town houses, separated by parasol-shaded summer seating. The cheaper but more appealing rooms are set into sloping eaves. Two of the unsophisticated en suites share a balcony. The lovely contoured garden below becomes a *nargile* (hubble-bubble) cafe in summer, but there's no indoor sitting room or internet.

Motel Emen OLD TOWN ROOMS €€

(☎581120, 061848734; www.motel-emen.com; Oneščukova 32; s/d/tr/q 82/124/154/212KM; ✳ @) The term 'motel' is quite misleading for what are in fact six tastefully appointed new rooms above a restaurant on one of Old Mostar's most popular pedestrian lanes. The decor has an understated chic and prices are reasonable for such a prized address. Room 103 (double 144KM) has a large private terrace.

Kriva Ćuprija MILLHOUSE ROOMS €€

(☎550953; www.motel-mostar.ba; s/d/apt from €30/55/65; ✳) Soothe yourself with the sounds of gushing streams in new, impeccably clean (if not necessarily large) rooms ranged above this stone millhouse restaurant overlooking the Crooked Bridge. The new annexe, **Kriva Ćuprija 2** (Maršala Tita 186) is stylish and features two hot tubs on a rear deck but it lacks the perfect location of the original and is right beside a busy main road.

Shangri-La B&B €€

(☎551819; www.shangrila.com.ba; Kalhanska 10; d without/with breakfast €34/44; ✳ ⑨ P) Charming English-speaking hosts are welcoming but not intrusive, while their four rooms are better appointed than those of many Mostar hotels. Quiet yet very central with limited free (if awkward) parking.

Motel Deny MINI-HOTEL €€

(☎578317; www.mdmostar.com; Kapetanovina 1; s/d/tr 70/100/150KM May-Sep, 60/90/130KM Oct-Apr; ✳ ⑨ P) Four of the six neat, well-furnished rooms overlook the Old Town's mill area, the best balcony views being from the smallest rooms (102 and 202). At night the lobby flickers alluringly with candlelight.

Hotel Pellegrino APARTMENT HOTEL €€

(☎062969000, 061480784; www.hotel-pellegrino. ba; Faladžića 1c; r €50-120; ✳) Above a large, neo-Tuscan restaurant-lounge (guests only), expansive rooms have excellent anti-allergenic bedding and kitchenette. Each room has its own oddity, be it a giant black lacquer vase, a bundle-of-twigs lamp or a whole-cow mat.

Villa Fortuna B&B €€

(☎551888; www.villafortuna.ba; Rade Bitange 34; s/d/tr €30/40/55, incl breakfast €35/50/70; ✳ ⑨ P) Seven fresh, air-con rooms with elements of pseudo-aged 'country' furniture are set above Fortuna Travel in a hidden courtyard with gated parking for small cars. The backyard sitting area is decorated with old Bosnian metalwork.

Hostel Nina FAMILY HOSTEL €

(☎061382743; www.hostelnina.ba; Čelebica 18; dm/ s/d without bathroom €10/15/20; @ ✳) Popular homestay-hostel run by an obliging English-speaking lady whose husband, a war survivor and former bridge jumper, runs regional tours that often end up over bargain beers at his bar in the Tabhana. Note that the overflow annexe is in a dowdy apartment block across town near the Rondo.

Pansion Aldi HOUSE-HOSTEL €

(☎552185, 061273457; www.pansion-aldi.com; Laćina 69a; dm/d without bathroom €10/20; ✳ @ P) Handy for the bus station, this family-run hostel has 17 beds in five large if simple rooms; all but one is double, with air-con. There's a shared kitchenette and three small toilet-shower cubicles. A highlight is the riverside garden terrace where a small splash pool is installed among the roses in summer.

Hostel Miturno
HOSTEL €

(☑552408; www.hostel-miturno.ba, www.miturno.ba; Braće Felića 67; dm/d €10/20; ❄☎) Run by a youthful, music-loving crew, this central mini-hostel has a handful of rooms and small dorms above a main-street shop. The TV room-lobby is cramped but colourful and social.

✗ Eating

Cafes and restaurants with divine views of the river cluster along the riverbank near Stari Most. Although unapologetically tourist-oriented, their meal prices are only a *maraka* or two more than any ordinary dive. Along Mala Tepe and Braće Fejića you'll find a morning vegetable market, supermarkets and several inexpensive places for *ćevapi* and other Bosnian snacks.

Restaurant Bella Vista
BOSNIAN €€

(Tabhana; pizzas 7-10KM; mains 8-18KM) Along with Restaurants Babilon and Teatr next door, the Bella Vista has stupendous terrace views across the river to the Old Town and Stari Most. The food might be less impressive than the views, but some of the set 'tourist menus' are excellent value.

Konoba Stari Mlin
BOSNIAN €

(Jusovina bb; meals 5-12KM; ☺8am-10pm) Down a hidden stairway, this millhouse restaurant includes one table tucked into a rocky alcove and several more on a tree-shaded terrace looking up at the crooked bridge, albeit across a litter-strewn stream. Exceptionally good-value meals include garlic calf's liver with French fries (5KM) and well-cooked trout (10KM) and the house white wine (per litre 15KM) is better than many competitors'.

Hindin Han
FISH, BOSNIAN €€

(Jusovina bb; fish 10-18KM, grills 6-12KM; ☺11am-11pm) Perched pleasantly but not spectacularly high above a side stream, this rebuilt historic building can be beaten for views but rarely for the quality of its fish meals.

Šadrvan
BOSNIAN €€

(Jusovina 11; meals 10-20KM) On a quaint, vine- and tree-shaded corner where the pedestrian lane from Stari Most divides, this tourist favourite has tables set around a trickling fountain made of old Turkish-style metalwork. The menu covers all Bosnian bases and takes a stab at some vegetarian options.

Meat-free *đuveć* (KM7) tastes like ratatouille on rice.

Urban Grill
ČEVABDŽINICA €

(www.urbangrill.ba; Mala Tepa; 5/10 ćevapi 3.50/6KM; ☺8am-11pm) Can *ćevapi* ever be cool? They think so here. And hidden away beneath the hip main servery is a little terrace with an unexpectedly excellent Old Bridge view.

ABC
ITALIAN €

(☑061194656; Braće Fejića 45; pizza & pasta 6-9KM, mains 12-15KM; ☺8am-11pm Mon-Fri, noon-11pm Sat & Sun) Above a popular cakeshop-cafe, this relaxed pastel-toned Italian restaurant is decorated with photos of old Mostar and dotted with aspidistras. Pizzas are bready but the pastas come with an extra bucketful of parmesan. Try plate-lickingly creamy Aurora tortellini.

Eko-Eli
BOSNIAN PIES €

(Maršala Tita 115; mains 2-3KM; ☺7am-11pm) Typical Bosnian snacks including *krompirača*, *sirnica*, *burek* and *zeljanica* are cooked fresh over hot coals and served up for pennies at sit-and-scoff tables. Zero luxury and no tourists.

♥ Drinking

Ali Baba
CAVE BAR

(Kujundžiluk; ☺24hr Jun-Sep, closed winter) Take a cavern in the raw rock, add colourful low lighting, fat beats and sensibly priced drinks and hey presto, you've got this wacky party bar. A dripping tunnel leads out to a second entrance on Maršala Tita.

OKC Abrašević
ALTERNATIVE BAR

(☑561107; www.okcabrasevic.org; Alekse Šantića 25) This understatedly intellectual smoky box of a bar offers Mostar's most vibrantly alternative scene and has an attached venue for offbeat gigs. It's hidden away in an unsigned courtyard on the former front line. Draft beer from 2KM. Hours vary.

Bijeli Bar
BAR-CAFE

(Stari Most 2; ☺7am-11pm) The ubercool main lounge zaps you with wicked white-on-white Clockwork Orange decor. Meanwhile, around the corner the same bar owns an utterly spectacular perch-terrace from which the old bridge and towers appear from altogether new angles. The latter is entered from Maršala Tita, through a wrought-iron gate marked Atelje Novalić: cross the Japanese-style garden and climb the stone roof-steps.

Caffe Marshall BAR-CAFE
(Oneščukova bb; ☺8am-midnight) Minuscule box bar with an electronic jukebox and a ceiling draped with musical instruments.

Wine & More WINE-TASTING CAFE
(Mala Tepa; ☺9am-11pm) Play Bacchus, sampling Trebinje's famous Turdoš Monastery wines (per glass 5KM) at barrel tables on the Old Town's time-polished stone stairways. Inside the icon decor is less interesting.

☆ Entertainment

OKC Abrašević hosts occasional concerts and Ali Baba fills its summer cave with contemporary dance sounds, particularly on weekend party nights. There are several DJ cafes and nightclubs in a mall area near the Rondo.

Club Oxygen NIGHTCLUB
(www.biosphere.ba/biosfere-stranice-oxigen-en.html; Braće Fejića bb; ☺variable) Oxygen has movie nights, DJ-discos and Mostar's top live gigs. In summer its rooftop SkyBar takes over as the place to party.

Dom Herceg Stjepan Kosaća
CULTURAL CENTRE
(✆323501; Rondo; 🖥) Diverse shows and concerts include occasional touring operas, ballets and theatre from Croatia. There's a weekend turbofolk club behind.

Pavarotti Music Centre STUDIO VENUE
(✆550750; Maršala Tita 179) Originally funded by the famous tenor as a post-war rehabilitation program, this music school and recording studio has a cafe and holds occasional concerts in its open courtyard.

🛍 Shopping

The stone-roofed shop-houses of Kujundžiluk throw open metal shutters to sell colourfully inexpensive Turkish and Indian souvenirs including glittery velveteen slippers (€7), pashmina-style wraps (from €5), fezzes (€5), *boncuk* (evil-eye) pendants and Russian-style nested dolls. Look for pens fashioned from old bullets and watch while master coppersmith **Ismet Kurt** (Kujundžiluk 5; ☺9am-8pm) hammers old mortar-shell casings into works of art.

❶ Information

Most businesses accept euros and Croatian kuna as well as marakas. Along Braće Fejića are banks, ATMs, a pharmacy, supermarkets and two internet cafes (both in side lanes). Mostar website include the **Hercegovina Tourist Board** (www.hercegovina.ba) and **Visit Mostar** (www.visitmostar.org).

Bosniak post office (Braće Fejića bb; ☺8am-8pm Mon-Fri, 8am-6pm Sat)

Croat post office (Dr Ante Starčevića bb; ☺7am-7pm Mon-Sat, 8am-noon Sun)

Europa Club (Huse Maslića 10; per hr 1KM; ☺7am-midnight) Internet cafe beneath a stationery shop.

Tourist information centre (✆397350; Trg Preživjelih Branioco; ☺9am-9pm Jun-Sep, 10am-6pm Oct, closed Nov-May)

❶ Getting There & Around
Air

Mostar airport (code OMO; ✆350992; www.mostar-airport.ba), 6km south of town off the Čapljina road, has no scheduled flights.

BUSES FROM MOSTAR'S MAIN BUS STATION

DESTINATION	PRICE (KM)	DURATION (HR)	DEPARTURES
Banja Luka (via Jajce)	25	6	1.30pm
Belgrade	53	11	7.30pm, 9pm
Čapljina	6	40min	twice-hourly Mon-Fri, six daily Sun
Dubrovnik	27	3-4	7am, 10.15am, 12.30pm
Herceg Novi	46	4½	7am
Sarajevo	18	2½	hourly 6am-3pm plus 6.15pm & 8.30pm
Split	31	4½	7am, 10.15am, 12.50pm, 11.25pm
Stolac	6	1	hourly till 6.15pm
Trebinje (via Nevesinje)	21	3	6.15am Mon-Sat, 3.30pm, 5.30pm
Vienna	110	12	8.30am
Zagreb	43	9½	7am, 9am, 8.15pm

Bicycle

Polo Travel (☑061547827; Trg Preživjelih Branioco; ⊗9am-9pm) rents bicycles (per half/full day €10/15).

Bus

Most long-distance buses use the **main bus station** (☑552025; Trg Ivana Krndelja) beside the train station. However, Renner buses to Stolac, a 4.30pm bus to Split (25KM) and seven weekday services to Međugorje (4KM, 45 minutes) start from the inconveniently located, half-built **western bus station** (Autobusni Kolodvor; ☑348680; Vukovarska bb). Yellow **Mostar Bus** (☑552250; www.mostarbus.ba/linije.asp) services to Blagaj start from opposite the train station and pick up passengers more conveniently at the Lučki Most stop.

Car

Hyundai Rent-A-Car (☑552404; www.hyundai.ba; main bus station; per day/week from 75/390KM; ⊗8am-6pm Mon-Fri, 9am-noon Sat) hire charges include full insurance without deductible and free option to drop off in Sarajevo. Add 17% tax in some cases and 30KM extra to collect or drop off the car after hours.

Train

Trains to Sarajevo (9.90KM, 2¾ hours) depart at 7.59am and 6.40pm daily, puffing alongside fish farms in the dammed gorge of the pea-green Neretva River before struggling up a series of switchbacks behind Konjic to reach Sarajevo after 65 tunnels.

Around Mostar

By joining a tour or hiring a car you could visit Blagaj, Počitelj, Međugorje and the Kravice waterfalls all in one day.

BLAGAJ
☑036 / POP 4000

The most iconic sight in pretty Blagaj village is a very picturesque, half-timbered **Tekija** (Dervish House; ☑573221; admission 4KM; ⊗8am-10pm) standing at the foot of a soaring cliff that's topped, way above, by the **Herceg Stjepan Fortress** ruins. The Tekija's ground floor is used as a souvenir shop and cafe but upstairs the wobbly wooden interior entombs two Tajik 15th-century dervishes and attracts pious pilgrims. Outside, the surreally blue-green Buna River gushes out of a cave in the cliff base and flows past a series of riverside restaurants linked by footbridges.

Walking to the Tekija takes 10 minutes from the seasonal **tourist information booth** (☑061687575; blagaj_city@yahoo.com; ⊗10am-7pm

WINE DIVINE

Hercegovina's homegrown wines are a delightful surprise. Local **živalka** grapes yield unexpectedly dry yet fruit-filled whites while suitably aged **blatina** reds can be a sturdy and complex. In restaurants, ordering *domaći* ('house') wine by carafe (ie 'open') costs from just 12KM per litre, far less than by bottle, and ensures that you're drinking a really local drop. It's possible to visit a selection of rural wineries (see www.wine route.ba) but it pays to phone ahead.

in season), which rents bicycles. Easy to miss behind a stone wall en route is the artistically appointed **Oriental House** (Velagomed, Velagic House; ☑572712; Velagicevina bb; admission 2KM), an 18th-century Ottoman homestead ensemble set behind island-meadow gardens. Hours are sporadic. At times they have been known to rent out guest rooms. Otherwise try the friendly unmarked **Kayan Pansion** (☑572299; nevresakajan@yahoo.com; per person €10; ❀), offering two well-kept four-bed rooms above a family home. It's unmarked, set back across a side road opposite the octagonal 1892 **Sultan Sulejman Mosque**.

Camp Bara (☑061627803; www.camp-bara.com) is just a scraggy patch of riverside grass with two simple bathrooms down a steep, narrow lane. It overlooks a fish farm but it's a cheap, central spot for camping.

Mostar Bus (www.mostarbus.ba/linije.asp) routes 10, 11 and 12 from Mostar all run to (or very near) Blagaj (2.10KM, 30 minutes), with 16 services on weekdays but only a handful at weekends. There's no direct public transport from Blagaj to Počitelj.

MEĐUGORJE
☑036 / POP 4300

On 24 June 1981 a vision appeared to six local teenagers in Međugorje (www.medjugorje.hr). What they believe they saw was a manifestation of the Holy Virgin. As a result, this formerly poor wine-making backwater has been utterly transformed into a bustling Catholic pilgrimage centre and continues to grow even though Rome has not officially acknowledged the visions' legitimacy. Today Međugorje has that odd blend of honest faith and cash-in tackiness that is reminiscent of Lourdes (France) or Fatima (Portugal) but there's little of beauty here and for nonpilgrims a one-hour visit often proves ample to get the idea. The town's focus is double-towered 1969 **St James' Church** (Župna Crkva). In a garden 200m behind that, the mesmerising **Resurrected Saviour** (Uskrsli Spasitej) is a masterpiece of contemporary sculpture showing a 5m-tall metallic Christ standing crucified yet cross-less, his manhood wrapped in scripture. At times the statue's right knee 'miraculously' weeps a colourless liquid that pilgrims queue to dab onto specially inscribed pads.

A 3km (5KM) taxi ride away at **Podbrdo** village, streams of the faithful climb **Brdo Ukazanja** (Apparition Hill). Red-earth paths studded with sharp stones access a white statue of the Virgin Mary marking the site of the original 1981 visions. If you're fit you could nip up and back in 20 minutes but pilgrims spend an hour or more contemplating and praying at way stations, a few walking barefoot in deliberately painful acts of penitence.

Download artists'-eye town maps from the **tourist association** (www.tel.net.ba/tzm -medjugorje/1%20karta100.jpg).

POČITELJ
📞 036 / POP 350
This stepped Ottoman-era fortress village is one of the most picture-perfect architectural ensembles in BiH. Cupped in a steep rocky amphitheatre, it was systematically despoiled in the 1990s conflicts but its finest 16th-century buildings are now rebuilt, including the **Šišman Ibrahim Madrassa**, the 1563 **Hadži Alijna Mosque** and the 16m **clock tower** (Sahat Kula). The upper village culminates in the still part-ruined **Utvrda** (Fort) containing the iconic octagonal **Gavrakapetan Tower**.

Two lovely new pine-walled **apartments** (d/tr €40/60; ❄) just beside the city gate-tower include breakfast on a vine-shaded view-terrace. Pre-book through English-speaking **Mediha Oruč** (📞062481844), summer only. Year-round, Razira Kajtaz offers simple **homestay rooms** (📞826468, 062230023; per person €10) in an unlabelled, stone-roofed house with partial air-con.

Muta Restaurant (snacks 5-7KM, mains 12-20KM) serves schnitzels, *dolme* or trout in a stonewalled house opposite the mosque. The vine-shaded terrace is great for a drink.

Počitelj is right beside the main Split–Mostar road, 5km north of Čapljina. Mostar–Split and Mostar–Čapljina buses pass by, but southbound only the latter (roughly hourly on weekdays) will usually accept Počitelj-bound passengers. If day-tripping in

summer, arrive early to avoid the heat and the Croatian tour groups.

KRAVICE WATERFALLS
In spring this stunning mini-Niagara of 25m cascades pounds itself into a dramatic, steamy fury. In summer the falls themselves are less impressive but surrounding pools become shallow enough for swimming. The falls are 15 minutes' walk from a car park that's 4km down a dead-end road turning off the M6 (Čapljina–Ljubuški road) at km42.5. There's no public transport.

Neum

Driving between Split and Dubrovnik, don't forget your passport as you'll pass through BiH's tiny toehold of Adriatic coastline. Buses often make a refreshment break on the Neum bypass (kuna accepted), but Neum itself is crammed with concrete apartment-hotels and the Adriatic is more inviting elsewhere in neighbouring Croatia.

Stolac

📞 036 / POP 12,000
Backed by a steep, bald mountain ridge, the attractive castle town of Stolac was the site of Roman Diluntum (3rd century AD). A prominent citadel from the 15th century, Stolac suffered serious conflict in 1993. The displaced population has returned and several of the town's greatest historical buildings have been painstakingly reconstructed, though war damage is still painfully evident.

In the town centre, the 1735 **Šarić House** faces memorable mural-fronted **Čaršija Mosque**, rebuilt to look just like the 1519 original. A derelict supermarket in front is less photogenic. Upstream are several picturesque but increasingly ruinous 17th-century stone **mill-races**. Downstream, the tree-lined main street, Hrvatske-Brante (aka Ada), passes a diagonal switchback lane that leads up to the hefty **castle ruins**. Around 300m further is another group of historic buildings, some rebuilt. Across the bridges, views of the castle site are most memorable from near the Auro petrol station, 50m south of the graffiti-covered bus station.

Beside the Mostar road 3km west of Stolac, **Radimlja Necropolis** (admission free) looks at first glimpse like a marble quarryman's yard, and the backdrop of dreary cafes and low-rise

20th-century buildings doesn't help. On closer inspection the group of around 110 blocks are actually some of Bosnia's most important *stećci* grave-markers (see p110), though only a few have outstanding carvings.

Stolac's only hotel, **Villa Ragusa** (☑853700; s/d/tr 35/70/105KM), offers unremarkable but spruced up old rooms just across a small bridge from the town centre.

Except on Sunday, buses run from Mostar to Stolac at least hourly. The intriguing Stolac-Trebinje road crosses a war-scarred former no-man's-land passing the still bombed-out hilltop hamlet of Žegulja. There's no bus link but you might persuade the town's one taxi to take you to Ljubinje (20km), from where a 4.30pm bus runs to Trebinje (10KM, 1½ hours).

EASTERN BOSNIA & HERCEGOVINA

To get quickly yet relatively easily off the main tourist trail, try linking Sarajevo or Mostar to Dubrovnik via Trebinje, or head to Belgrade via Višegrad. For much of these journeys you'll be passing through the Republika Srpska, where's it's fascinating to hear about BiH's 1990s traumas from the 'other side'.

Trebinje

☑059 / POP 36.000

A beguiling quick stop between Dubrovnik (28km) and Višegrad (or Mostar), Trebinje has a small, walled **Old Town** (Stari Grad) where inviting, unpretentious cafes offer a fascinating opportunity to meet friendly local residents and hear Serb viewpoints on divisive recent history. Old Town ramparts back onto the riverside near a 19th-century former Austro-Hungarian barracks which now houses the eclectic **Hercegovina Museum** (www.muzejhercegovine.org; Stari Grad 59; admission 2KM; ⊘8am-2pm Mon-Fri, 10am-2pm Sat).

Parts of Trebinje feel a little like southern France, nowhere more so than on the lovely stone-flagged **Trg Svobode**, which is shaded by plane and chestnut trees and lined with street cafes with wrought-iron overhangs.

Trebinje's 1574 **Arslanagić Bridge** (Perovića Most) is a unique double-backed structure sadly let down by the unexotic suburban location (700m northeast of Hotel Leotar) to which it was moved in the 1970s.

For phenomenal views take the 2km winding lane leading east of Hotel In to hilltop **Hercegovacka Gracanica**, where the compact but eye-catching **Presvete Bogorodice Church** was erected in 2000 to rehouse the bones of local hero Jovan Dučić. Its design is based on the 1321 Gračanica monastery in Kosovo, a building that's symbolically sacred to many Serbs.

🛏 Sleeping

TOP CHOICE **Hotel Platani** BOUTIQUE HOTELS €€
(www.hotelplatani.info; Trg Svobode; s/d/tr old building 71/104/126KM, new building 82/134/157KM; ❄🐾) The Platani consists of two outwardly similar buildings with iconic glass and wrought-iron overhangs that help give Trebinje's tree-lined main square its Gallic character. Rooms in the old building are unimpeachably clean but slightly dated. However, in the new building they're contrastingly stylish and contemporary with Klimt-esque art works. Highly recommended.

Hotel Porto Bello GUEST ROOMS €€
(☑223344; www.portobellotrebinje.com; s/d €30/45; ❄@) Five try-hard rooms with decent facilities but without much character above a restaurant within the walls of the Old Town.

Hotel In MOTEL €€
(☑261443; www.etagehotel.com; Dušanova; s/d/tr 60/90/120KM; ❄P) Across the river near the hospital, the 'In' is set back from the main road so it's quieter than its parent, Motel Etage. Brand new at the time of research, it was clean and fresh but without particular interest and some rooms were a squeeze.

🍴 Eating & Drinking

Pizza Castello ITALIAN €
(☑260245; Trg Travunije 3; pizzas 6-12KM; ⊘8am-11pm Mon-Sat, 6-11pm Sun) Castello's terrace is great for people-watching, jovial hosts Snezhan and Dušan speak great English, and the thin-crust pizza is excellent. Castello is on the left as you enter the Old Town square from the Platani.

Galerija Veritas CAFE
(Stari Grad 17; ⊘9am-11pm) This brick-domed vaulted cavern cafe has a beamed upper level and a floating barge-bar terrace on the river at the back, partly beneath the Kameni Bridge.

Azzovo CAFE

(Stari Grad 114; ☉8am-11pm Mon-Sat, 10am-11pm Sun) Old Town blues-oriented bar with ceilings of bamboo and vine stems.

ℹ Information

Balkan Investment Bank (Preobraženska 6; ☉8am-3.30pm Mon-Fri, 8am-11.30am Sat) Changes money, has an ATM.

Online City Map (www.trebinje.info/trebinje/mape/plan-grada.html)

Tourist office (📞273410; Jovan Dučića bb; www.trebinjeturizam.com; ☉8am-8pm Mon-Fri, 8am-3pm Sat) Facing the Hotel Platani near the Old Town's western gate.

ℹ Getting There & Away

The '**bus station**' (Vojvode Stepe Stepanovića) is simply a pair of bus shelters in a parking area. Walk north then immediately east (200m) to find the Old Town's west gate.

Trebinje to Višegrad

Trebinje–Belgrade and Trebinje–Sarajevo buses pass through the glorious **Sutjeska National Park** (www.npsutjeska.srbinje.net, in Bosnian), where the magnificent grey rock sides of the Sutjeska canyon rise like Chinese paintings either side of the road. Further north the canyon opens out near an impressively vast concrete **Partizans' Memorial** commemorating the classic WWII battle of Tjentište. Mountaineers and hikers can explore more of the national park's scenic wonders with extreme-sports outfit **Encijan** (📞211220, 211150; www.pkencijan.com; Kraljapetra-I 1; ☉9am-5pm Mon-Sat), based in **Foča**. It also organise world-class **rafting** on the Tara River that cascades out of Europe's deepest canyon (across the Montenegrin border) then thunders over 21 rapids (class III to class IV in summer, class IV to class V in April).

Višegrad

📞058 / POP 20,000

Višegrad is internationally famous for its 10-arch **Mehmet Paša Sokolović Bridge**, built in 1571 and immortalised in Andrić's classic *Bridge on the Drina*. Celebrated Sarajevo-born film director Emir Kusturica is reportedly planning a movie based on the Andric book with filming to coincide with long-overdue repair work to the great bridge's foundations (probably 2012). Filming may create a stone ethno-village in Višegrad to be used first as a set and later as a tourist resort much as happened with Drvengrad (www.mecavnik.info) in Serbia.

The town is otherwise architecturally unexciting but it's set between some of Bosnia's most impressive river canyons. If you're driving, there's a great **viewpoint** 3.6km down a side road to Ruda that branches off the Višegrad–Goražde highway 9km south of town.

Boat trips (from 30KM per person including lunch) from Višegrad depart around 10am in summer, and will probably become more frequent in coming years but for now pre-booking is usually essential. Check details with the helpful **tourist office** (📞620821, 620950; www.visegradturizam.com; ☉8am-4pm Mon-Fri, 8am-3pm Sat) near the southern end of the old bridge. The website has a town map.

BUSES FROM TREBINJE

There are no longer buses to Stolac or Herceg Novi.

DESTINATION	PRICE (KM)	DURATION (HR)	DEPARTURES
Belgrade (via Višegrad)	48	11	8am, 6pm
Dubrovnik	10	45min	10am Mon-Sat (returns at 1.30pm)
Foča	18	2½	take Belgrade, Pale or Sarajevo bus
Ljubinje	10	1½	2.10pm Mon-Fri, 7pm daily
Mostar (via Nevesinje)	20	3	6.15am, 10am, 2.30pm
Novi Sad	53	12	5.30pm
Pale	28	4½	5am
Podgorica (via Nikšič)	33	3½	8.30am, 3pm, 4.30pm
Sarajevo	26	4	5am, 7.30am, 11am

Reconstructed in 2010, the narrow-gauge railway to Mokra Gora (Serbia) links up with the popular Šargan 8 tourist train. Daily services could start by the time you read this, allowing a stop at the historic **Dobrun Monastery** (km11.5, Višegrad–Belgrade road). From outside that complex looks like a latter-day hacienda hotel but the site is of deeply historical resonance for Serbs as Karađorđe hid here immediately before launching the 1804 Serb uprising. The monastery was almost entirely destroyed in WWII but the original porch of the central 14th-century chapel survives.

🛏 Sleeping & Eating

Hotel Višegrad   HOTEL €€
(☎631051; www.hotel.visegrad24.info; Trg Palih Boraca; s/d/tr 49/83/123KM) Behind a sickly yellow facade, the Višegrad is ideally central and staff are helpful but despite a 2009 renovation it remains less than luxurious. Rooms are clean enough but showers are feeble and power points are wantonly inconvenient. Its restaurant (mains 7KM to 14KM) is a blandly boxlike affair pumping out loud Europop but the terrace has picture-perfect views of the classic bridge and the kitchen produces unexpectedly excellent dinners, with fresh trout at just 30KM per kg. Two other motels are both around 1km from the centre, and there's a third at km8 on the Dobrun road.

ℹ Getting There & Away

A bus station is planned near the 'new bridge' 1.5km northeast of centre. Until it's built, buses to Foča (9.30am), Banja Luka (8am), Užice (11.30am and 6pm via Dobrun and Mokra Gora) and the 5.15am bus to Belgrade start from outside the Hotel Višegrad. Other buses, which are in transit through town, stop briefly near the north side of the old bridge and at Motel Okuka (1km northeast of the centre) where some make a refreshment break. Such routes include Trebinje (via Foča and Sutjeska National Park) at 10am and 11.15pm, Sarajevo at 4am and 12.45pm, Niš around 9.20pm and Belgrade at 9.45am, 1.30pm and 10.45pm.

CENTRAL & WESTERN BOSNIA

West of Sarajevo lies a series of mildly interesting historic towns, green wooded hills, rocky crags and dramatic rafting canyons. The area offers ample opportunities for exploration and adrenaline-rush activities.

Visoko

📞032 / POP 17,000

Once the capital of medieval Bosnia and the spiritual centre of the controversial Bosnian Church, this unremarkable leather-tanning town had been largely forgotten during the 20th century. Then Bosnian archaeologist Semir Osmanagic hatched a bold theory that Visoko's 250m-high Visočica Hill is in fact the **World's Greatest Pyramid** (Sun Pyramid; www.piramidasunca.ba; admission 2KM), built approximately 12,000 years ago by a long-disappeared superculture. Other nearby hills are mooted to be lesser pyramids too, and archaeologists are busily investigating prehistoric subterranean labyrinths, notably the **Tunnel Ravne** (☎062730299; admission 5KM; ⊙call ahead), of which over 200m can already be visited on guided hard-hat tours.

The mainly forested 'Sun Pyramid' does indeed have a seemingly perfect pyramidal shape when viewed from some angles (despite a long ridge at the back) and plates of bafflingly hard ancient 'concrete' found here are cited as having once covered the hill, creating an artificially smoothed surface. Visits to the site's **archaeological excavations** (admission 2KM) start with a stiff 20-minute climb from an info point-ticket booth near Bistro Vidikovac, itself around 15 minutes' walk from Visoko bus station. Start by crossing the river towards the **Motel Piramida-Sunca** (☎731460; www.motelpiramidasunca.co.ba; 6th fl, Musala 1; s/d/tr/q 50/80/120/160KM; ❊) and turn immediately left down Visoko's patchily attractive main street, Alije Izetbegovića, passing the excellent if semidormant **Hotel Centar** (☎061108427; www.hotelcentar.ba; s/d 70/130KM, apt 110-160KM; ⊙call ahead; ❊🖥). Renamed Čaršijska, the street then curves to point directly towards the pyramid summit. After the bazaar veer left into Tvrtka/Mule Hodžić then, opposite Mule Hodžić 25, climb steeply up winding Pertac/Fetahagića, turning left at the top. The info point is just beyond.

ℹ Getting There & Away

Visoko is a stop for buses between Sarajevo (5.70KM, 50 minutes) and Kakanj (4.70KM, 35 minutes) running 18 times daily (seven times Sundays). For Travnik and Jajce, direct buses depart Visoko at 8.10am, 9.50am, 2.10pm and 4.10pm or change in Zenica (14 buses on weekdays).

Dotted among the faceless industrial towns of virtually untourist ed northeastern Bosnia are several very photogenic medieval castle ruins.

» **Doboj** The city is an ugly railway junction but the castle hosts costumed festivals and there's a great little cafe-tower.

» **Gradačac** Gradačac town centre is dominated by a partly reconstructed castle with a restaurant on top.

» **Srebrenik** Truly dramatic crag-top setting 6km east of Srebrenik town.

» **Tešanj** Powerful ruins rise above a loveable Old Town square.

» **Vranduk** Small ruins set in BiH's most idyllic castle village, around 10km north of Zenica.

Travnik

☑030 / POP 27,500

Once the seat of Bosnia's Turkish viziers (Ottoman governors), Travnik is now best known for its sheep cheese – and as the birthplace of Nobel prize–winning author Ivo Andrić, who set his classic *Bosnian Chronicle* here. It's a pleasant place to briefly break the journey between Sarajevo and Jajce, and in winter there's skiing at nearby Vlašić. Funnelled through the narrow, forest-sided Lavša Valley, Travnik straddles the M5 highway, paralleled by the main commercial street, Bosanska. To find Bosanska from the bus station, exit through the platform-side yellow fencing, turn left and walk four minutes east continuing when Prnjavor becomes a footpath alley just beyond the BHT/post office building. You should emerge on Bosanska near the dome-sheltered **Viziers' Turbe**, the best known of several Travnik tomb posts. Turn right here to find the helpful **tourist office** (☑511588; www.tzsbk.com; Bosanska 75; ⊙8am-4pm Mon-Fri) facing the distinctive **Sahat Kula** stone clocktower. Turn left for all other sights.

◉ Sights & Activities

Stari Grad   FORTRESS RUINS
(adult/student 2/1.50KM; ⊙8am-8pm May-Sep, 9am-6pm Oct & Apr)

Towards the town's eastern end, a sizeable castle ruin encloses a reconstructed multi-sided keep that houses a modest museum featuring local costumes and sketching the area's history. Around the castle site lies Travnik's most attractive historical district. At its base, **Plava Voda** (Blue Water) is a picturesque gaggle of summer restaurants beside a merrily gurgling stream criss-crossed by small bridges.

Many Coloured Mosque   HISTORIC MOSQUE
(Šasend Džamija; Bosanska 203) Built in 1757 and reconstructed a century later, its famous facade murals have faded but the mosque is remarkable for the *bezistan* (mini-bazaar) built into the arches beneath the main prayerhouse. Behind the mosque is a pedestrian underpass beneath the M5 from which Varoš leads up to Stari Grad.

Ivo Andrić Museum   MEMORIAL MUSEUM
(☑518140; Zenjak 13; adult/student 2/1.50KM; ⊙9.30am-5pm) Readers who enjoyed *Bosnian Chronicle* might like this old-style house designed to simulate Andrić's birthplace. Labels are in Bosnian but the enthusiastic curator speaks English. The museum is one block off Bosanska (north between 171 and 169).

Vlašić   SKI RESORT
(www.babanovac.net; ski passes per day/night/week 19/12/120KM) This three-lift ski field is above Babanovac village, 27km northwest of Travnik.

🛏 Sleeping

Central hotels suffer from road rumble as do half a dozen other motels strung 10km along the eastbound M5.

CENTRAL TRAVNIK
Motel Aba   HOTEL €
(☑511462; www.aba.ba; Šumeća 166a; s 35-40KM, d/tr/q 50/70/80KM; 🕾) Handily near to Plava Voda, Aba provides highly acceptable, unfussy en suite rooms at unbelievably reasonable prices. There's free wi-fi and limited free parking but breakfast costs 10KM extra.

The stairs and road noise are minor niggles but it's fabulous value.

Hotel Lipa
HOTEL €€

(☎511604; Lažajeva 116; s/d/tr 52/84/111KM) Neat, if blandly remodelled, little rooms lead off the dingy corridors at this Yugo-salvian-era hotel, but at least the location is relatively central, directly behind the Vi-ziers' Turbe.

VLAŠIĆ

Blanca
RESORT & SPA €€€

(☎519900; www.blancaresort.com; s €52-165, d €74-242, tr €132-273) Right at the base of the ski-jump, this 2010 complex uses wooden chalet elements to soften an overall sense of poised designer cool. Guests get free use of four different saunas, the indoor swimming pool has recliner chairs at view windows and unlike virtually every other Vlašić ho-tel it's open year round. 'Classic' rooms have no view whatsoever while 'superior' rooms are huge. 'Premium' rooms strike the best balance.

Hotel Central
SKI HOTEL €€

(☎540165; www.hotel-central-vlasic.net; per person 52-82KM) Homey, seasonal ski hotel that's about the nearest Vlašić gets to 'budget ac-commodation'.

✕ Eating

Along Bosanska you'll find supermarkets, bakeries and several shops (such as num-ber 157) selling Travnik's trademark white cheese (*Travnički Sir*).

Restaurant Divan
TRADITIONAL BOSNIAN €€

(Zenjak 13; meals 5-16KM; ☺9am-11pm) Dine on fish, squid or Bosnian grills around the piano in thick-walled, timber-beamed rooms beneath the Ivo Andrić museum or in the enclosed courtyard behind.

Lutvina Kahva
HISTORIC CAFE €

(Plava Voda; ćevapi 2-7KM, mains 9-11KM; ☺7am-10pm) Decorated with copperware, this Moor-ish cube of cafe featured in Andrić's novel and has perfectly situated streamside seating.

Konoba Plava Voda
TRADITIONAL BOSNIAN €€

(Šumeće bb; meals 5.50-15KM; ☺7am-10pm) Three restaurants, all called Plava Voda, each have lovely summer terraces overlooking the at-tractive springs area. This one offers an Eng-lish menu and generous portions.

❶ Getting There & Away

Travnik's **bus station** (☎792761) is off Sehida (the M5 highway) around 500m west of centre.

Jajce

☎030 / POP 30,000

Above an impressive waterfall, Jajce's forti-fied Old Town climbs a steep rocky knoll to the powerful, ruined castle where Bosnia's medieval kings were once crowned. The sur-rounding array of glorious mountains, lakes and canyons make Jajce a great exploration base, while curious catacombs and a Mithra-ic temple might intrigue fans of mysterious 'lost' religions. But don't expect too much from the town centre; despite the surround-ing fortifications, it's a mainly banal collec-tion of 20th-century architecture.

❍ Sights

Old Town Jajce's attractions can be seen in a two-hour ramble, assuming you can locate the sites' various keyholders.

Catacombs
MEDIEVAL CARVINGS

(Svetog Luke bb; admission 1KM) Built around 1400, this two-level half-lit crypt is small and roughly hewn but notable for the boldly sculpted sun and crescent moon motif, a rare surviving memorial to the independent

BUSES FROM TRAVNIK

DESTINATION	PRICE (KM)	DURATION (HR)	DEPARTURES
Bihać	26-32	6	6, 6.50am, 9.30am, 3.30pm, 4.20pm, 11.50pm
Babanovac	4	45min	7.15am, 11.30am, 6pm, 7.30pm
Jajce	8-12.70	1½	7.25am, 11.10am, 5.15pm, plus all Bihać buses
Sarajevo	15.50	2	about hourly till noon, 3.40pm, 6.20pm, 7.10pm
Split (via Bugojno)	23-31	4½	up to 6 daily
Zenica	4.50-7	1	25 daily

Bosnian Church. Tito is said to have hidden here during 1943. Request the key from the little cafe-hairdresser opposite, which is built onto the side of the sturdy round **Bear Tower** (Medvjed Kula).

Tvrđava
FORTIFIED CITADEL

To explore the remnant Old Town, walk up past the **Tower of St Luke**, a 15th-century campanile attached to a now ruined church. Turn right at the tiny, boxlike Dizdar Džamija (Women's Mosque) and climb stairs to the portal of the sturdy main **fortress** (adult/child 1/0.50KM; ⏱10am-7pm). Inside is mostly bald grass but the ramparts offer sweeping views of the valleys and crags that surround Jajce's urban sprawl.

From the **Velika Tabija** (Gornja Mahala) a further section of citadel wall descends to the **Midway Tower** (Mala Tabija) facing the attractively renovated **Old Kršlak House**.

Waterfalls
VIEWPOINT

Jajce's impressive 21m-high **waterfalls** mark the confluence of the Pliva and Vrbas Rivers. For the classic tourist-brochure photo, cross the big Vrbas bridge and turn left on the Banja Luka road. Walk 500m, then at the third lay-by on the left climb over the low crash barrier and double back 150m down a footpath through the pinewoods to the viewpoint.

Mithraeum
ANCIENT SCULPTURE

(Mitrasova 12) Hidden in a drab 20th-century building are remnants of a 4th-century sculpture featuring Mithras fighting a bull watched by an audience of ladies and centurions. Once worshipped in a now-mysterious, forgotten religion, Mithras was a pre-Zoroastrian Persian sun god 'rediscovered' by mystical Romans. Peep in through the glassless window with a torch or request the key from the tourist booth (1KM per person).

AVNOJ Museum
SOCIALIST HISTORY

(admission 2KM; ⏱9am-5pm) In 1943 the second congress of Antifascist Council of the People's Liberation of Yugoslavia (AVNOJ) formulated Yugoslavia's postwar socialist constitution. This momentous event occurred in a banal Jajce building rather like a school hall on whose stage now stands a large brooding statue of partisan Tito made of gold-painted polystyrene. Sparse photographic info boards have partial translations in barely intelligible English.

Plivsko Jezero
LAKES

Some 5km west of Jajce, wooded mountains reflect idyllically in the picture-perfect Pliva Lakes (Plivsko Jezero). A water-meadow park between the two contains a super-quaint collection of 17 miniature **watermills** that form one of Bosnia's most photographed scenes. Take Jezero-bound buses to Plaža Motel (km91 on the M5), then walk 15 minutes back along the lakeside. Plaža Motel rents **rowing boats** (per hr 6KM). Rent bicycles at AutoKamp (per hr/day 2/10KM; ⏱7am-11pm).

🛏 Sleeping & Eating

Eko-Pliva (📞564100, 065632110; www.plivatourism.ba) and the tourist information booth can both arrange simple **homestays** (per person 20-30KM). One such is **Pašagina Avlija's place** (📞657048; per person €10) right beside the Bear Tower.

CENTRAL JAJCE

Hotel Stari Grad CENTRAL HOTEL €€
(📞654006; www.jajcetours.com; Svetog Luke 3; s/d 57/84KM, apt 82-154KM; ❄@🛜) Although it's not actually old, beams, wood panelling and a heraldic fireplace give this comfortable little hotel a look of suavely modernised antiquity. Beneath the part-glass floor of the appealing lobby-restaurant (mains 10KM to 14KM) are the excavations of an Ottoman-era *hammam* (Turkish bath).

Hotel Tourist 98 URBAN MOTEL €€
(📞658151; www.hotel-turist98.com; Kraljice Katerine bb; s/d/tr/q 58/86/109/138KM; ❄) This bright-red box beside Jajce's big hypermarket offers new, very straightforward rooms with pearl-in-shell lamps. Four apartments (from 122KM) have air-con.

LAKES AREA

Plaža Motel LAKESIDE MOTEL €
(📞647200; www.motel-plaza.com; s/d 40/70KM, pizza 7-11KM, mains 9-14KM) Clean, inexpensive rooms, but the main attraction is dining on trout, pizza or *ćevapi* right at the waterfront beside the hotel's small jetty.

AutoKamp CAMPING GROUND €
(www.jajcetours.com; campsite per person from 10KM; ⏱mid-Apr–Sep) Well-maintained site set 300m back from the lake and watermills.

🍷 Drinking

Travnik Gate CAFE-BAR
(Sadije Softića 1; ⏱7am-11pm) This unpretentiously local bar is hidden in the bare stone tower of the medieval Travnik Gate. Enter through the historic Omerbegović House,

BOSNIA & HERCEGOVINA CENTRAL & WESTERN BOSNIA

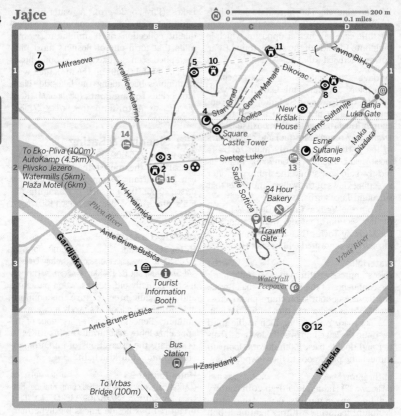

the first unmarked wooden door on Sadije Softića, and climb.

ℹ️ Information

Several central banks change money and have ATMs.

Network (Trg Jajačkih Branitelja; internet per hr 2KM; ⏰8.30am-midnight)

Tourist information booth (☎658268; ⏰9am-6pm Mon-Fri, 10am-6pm Sat May-Sep) Off season the office moves into the AVNOJ Museum building.

ℹ️ Getting There & Away

See the table, opposite.

Banja Luka

☎051 / POP 232,000

Probably Europe's least-known 'capital' (of the Republika Srpska since 1998), Banja Luka is lively more than lovely but it's a fine base for organising rafting, canyoning, cycling or hiking on landmine-free trails in the surrounding countryside. To organise any of the above contact **Guideline** (☎466411; www.guidelinebl.com; Cerska 54; ⏰9am-5pm) or discuss things with the enthusiastic **tourist office** (☎232760; www.banjaluka-tourism.com; Kralja Petra 87; ⏰8am-6pm Mon-Fri, 9am-2pm Sat). The latter is conveniently central on the city's main drag (Kralja Petra) opposite the iconic 1933 Hotel Palace. Mountain bikes can be rented from **Cycling Shop** (Gundulićeva 106; per hr/day 2/15KM), 1.3km northeast. You can download extensive if slightly dated city listings from http://www.inyourpocket.com/bosniaherzegovina/banja-luka.

Historic Banja Luka was ravaged by a 1969 earthquake then, late in the civil war, was flooded by Serb refugees from Croatia who dynamited over a dozen historic mosques. The most famous of these, the **Ferhadija**

Jajce

⊙ Sights

Džamija, is now being painstakingly reconstructed using traditional masonry techniques. On the riverside directly southeast are the chunky walls of a large, squat 16th-century **castle** (kaštel) enclosing parkland. Summer festivities held here include the famous **Demofest** (www.demofest.org), a playoff competition between up-and-coming raw garage bands held in late July.

Otherwise, the only two central blocks with much architectural appeal are around the memorable **Orthodox Church of Christ Saviour** (Crkva Hrista Spasitelja); its brick belltower looks like a Moroccan minaret on Viagra.

🛏 Sleeping & Eating

Running parallel to Kralja Petra, there are cheap snack bars in courtyards off Veselina Maslaše and many street cafes on its northern extension, Bana Milosavlevica.

Vila Vrbas BOUTIQUE HOTEL €€
(☎433840; Brace Potkonjaka 1; s/d/ste 70/110/120KM; ❋🛜) Polished new rooms above an upmarket restaurant peep through the plane trees at the castle ramparts from across the river.

Hotel Atina BUSINESS HOTEL €€
(☎334800; www.atinahotel.com; Slobodana Kokanovica 5; web rate s/d 140/180KM, walk-in rate s/d/apt 102/104/204KM; ❋❋🛜) Smart without undue extravagance; the main features are stylish rectilinear fittings and a helpfully central yet quiet location just east of the castle.

Hostel Banja Luka HOUSE-HOSTEL €
(☎065831131; www.hostelbanjaluka.com; Srpskih Ustanika 26; dm/tw/tr without bathroom €10/20/30; 🛜) Guests pay per person in four simple two- or three-bed rooms above the Pigal Cafe. The kitchen is tiny and the location blandly suburban but owner Vladimir's brimming enthusiasm for Banja Luka is contagious. His place is 1.7km southeast of the castle with bakeries, ATMs, forest hikes, an internet cafe and the Guideline office all within easy walking distance. Take bus 14 from the centre or 14B from the bus station alighting at 'Integral'.

City Smile Hostel HOSTEL €
(☎214187; www.citysmilehostel.com; Skendera Kulenovića 16; dm 22KM; 🛜) Bunk beds can be tight packed at this small hostel but there's a decent kitchen and sitting area and it's only

BUSES FROM JAJCE

DESTINATION	PRICE (KM)	DURATION (HR)	DEPARTURES
Banja Luka	8.50-12	1½	7.30am, 9.15am, 1pm, 4.20pm, 5.20pm, 6.50pm
Bihać	19-25	3½	8.30am, 11.15am, 12.30pm, 5.25pm
Jezero	1.5-2	15min	7.30am, 8.30am, 11.30am, 12.30pm, 4.30pm
Mostar	18.50-25	4	2.20pm, 6.15pm
Sarajevo	23.50	3½	7am, 9.15am, 10.20am, 5.15pm
Split	30.50	4½	6am (from Split departs at 12.30pm)
Travnik	8-12.70	1¼	take Zenica or Sarajevo buses
Zenica	14	2¼	8.15am, 8.50am, 1.40pm, 3.15pm, 3.50pm
Zagreb	36	8½	10am, 11.15am, 12.30pm

BUSES FROM BANJA LUKA

DESTINATION	PRICE (KM)	DURATION (HR)	DEPARTURES
Belgrade	41.5	5¾-7½	many 5am-5pm plus 9pm & 11.30pm
Bihać	20	3	5.30am, 7.30am, 1pm, 2pm
Jajce	11.50	1½	6.40am, 7.45am, 1pm, 2pm, 4pm
Sarajevo	31	5	6.30am, 7.45am, 2.30pm, 4pm, 5pm, 12.30pm
Zagreb	31	7	3.15am, 6.30am, 8.45am, 9.10am, 11.30am, 4pm, 5.30pm

BOSNIA & HERCEGOVINA CENTRAL & WESTERN BOSNIA

800m south of the centre. The entrance is hidden on Duška Koščige.

ⓘ Getting There & Away

The **airport** (✆535210; www.banjaluka-airport.com) is 22km north. That's 50KM by taxi or a 1.2km walk east of the Gradiška bus route (1.50KM). **Adria Airlines** (www.adria.si) connects four times weekly via Ljubljana to much of Europe. BH Airlines flies to Zürich (thrice weekly).

The **main bus and train station** (✆315555; Prote N Kostića 38) are together, 3km north using buses 6, 8 or 10 from near Hotel Palace.

Useful rail connections include Zagreb (27KM, 4¼ hours) at 3.49pm and Sarajevo (24.70KM, five hours) at 1.15pm.

Around Banja Luka
VRBAS CANYONS

Between Jajce and Banja Luka the Vrbas River descends through a series of lakes and gorges that together form one of BiH's foremost adventure-sport playgrounds. **Karanovac Rafting Centre** (✆882085, 065420000; www.guidelinebl.com), 11km from Banja Luka by bus 8A, is a reliable, well-organised outfit offering guided **canyoning** (€25), **kayaking** and especially top-class **rafting** (€33 per person). Rafting requires at least four people but joining a group is usually easy enough in summer and some weekends there's a rare opportunity for some floodlit **night-rafting**.

Set 800m off the road at **Krupa** (25km), where a pretty set of cascades tumbles down between little wooden mill-huts, nearby canyons and grottoes attract mountaineers and cavers. The Jajce road winds steeply on past a high dam overlooked by the rocky knob of what was once **Bočac Citadel**.

Bihać
✆037 / POP 80,000

In central Bihać, a closely clumped **church tower**, **turbe** and 16th-century stone **tower-museum** (✆223214; admission 2KM; ⊙call ahead) look very photogenic viewed through the trees across gushing rapids. But that's about all there is to see here apart from nearby **Fethija Mosque**, converted from a rose-windowed medieval church in 1595. Bihać could make a staging post for reaching Croatia's marvellous Plitvice Lakes (www.np-plitvicka-jezera.hr; p147) just 30km away. Otherwise grab a map and brochure from Bihać's **tourist booth** (www.tzusk.net; Bosanska 1; ⊙8am-4pm) or from the Hotel Park opposite. Then head out into the lovely Una Valley, preferably on a raft!

⊙ Sights & Activities
Una River   VALLEY

In the lush green gorges of the **Una Valley**, the adorable Una River goes through varying moods. Sections are as calm as mirrored opal, others gush over widely fanned rapids or down pounding cascades, most dramatically at **Štrcački Buk**. There are lovely watermill restaurants at **Bosanska Krupa** and near **Otoka Bosanska**. Up 4km of hairpins above the valley, spookily Gothic **Ostrožac Fortress** (✆061236641; www.ostrozac.com; admission 1KM; ⊙8am-6pm) is the most inspiring of several castle ruins. Phone the caretaker for admission.

Various adventure-sports companies offer rafting (€27 to €52, six person minimum) and kayaking. Each has its own campsite and provides transfers from Bihać since none are central. Try **Una Kiro Rafting** (✆361110; www.una-kiro-rafting.com; Golubić), **Una-Aqua** (✆061604313; www.una-aqua.com; Račić) or **Bjeli Una Rafting** (✆380222,

061138853; www.una-rafting.ba; Klokot). The festive **Una Regatta** in late July sees hundreds of kayaks and rafts following a three-day course from Kulen-Vakuf to Bosanska Krupa via Bihać.

For caving, climbing, cycling and canyoning contact extreme-sports club **Limit** (☑061144248; www.limit.co.ba; Džanića Mahala 7, Bihać).

🛏 Sleeping & Eating

CENTRAL BIHAĆ

Villa Una GUEST HOUSE **€€**
(☑311393; villa.una@bih.net.ha; Bihaćkih Branilaca 20; s/d/tr 52/74/96KM; superior s/d 62/84KM; ❄🛜📶🅿) In this very friendly *pansion* homey standard rooms (some with air-con) suffer from road noise but much newer 'superior' rooms are quiet and well appointed with little balconies and great showers. It's halfway between the bus station and the Una Bridge; the frontage is painted to look half-timbered.

Hotel Paviljon RESTAURANT, ROOMS **€€**
(☑220882; www.hotel-paviljon.com; Una Bridge; s/d 69/125KM; ❄🛜) Red carpet and two-colour woods give a strikingly modern feel to 13 new if sometimes cramped rooms above central Bihać's most polished riverside restaurant (grills 3KM to 8KM, mains 7KM to 23KM). It's set in parkland beside the main Una Bridge. Several rooms have semiprivate riverview terraces.

Opal Exclusive RIVERSIDE HOTEL **€€**
(☑228586, 224182; www.hotelopalexclusive.net; Krupska bb; s/d/apt 89/138/192M; ❄🛜🅿) The staff are gruffly uncommunicative and getting here you'll pass briefly through a rather off-putting area of town just north of the centre. However, the spacious rooms are the best in central Bihać, and there are paintings in gilt frames, indulgent settees on the landings and lovely river views.

Motel Avlija MINI-HOTEL **€€**
(☑220882; www.avlija-motel.ba; Trg Maršala Tita 7; s/d/tr/apt 59/111/131/132KM; ❄🛜) Pleasantly crafted new guest rooms set above a busy cafe-bar behind the central, well-marked UniCredit Bank.

Restaurant River Una WATERSIDE RESTAURANT **€€**
(☑310014; Džemala Bijedića 12; mains 12-17KM; ☺7am-11pm) Fish 'fly' inside this pseudo-rustic restaurant situated just across the Una Bridge from central Bihać, but it's the summer seating right at the water's edge

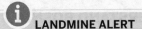
The Bihać area was mined during the war so stick to paths and concreted areas.

that puts it one step ahead of several nearby rivals.

UNA VALLEY

TOP CHOICE | **Kostelski Buk** RIVERSIDE HOTEL **€€**
(☑302340; www.kostelski-buk.com; M14, Kostela; s/d from 63/96KM; ❄🛜📶🅿) The Louis XVI chairs, copper-coloured curtains and leather-padded doors might be a little glitzy for some tastes but the rooms are superbly equipped, amply sized and come with artistic bronze-coloured panelling that's somewhere between Klimt and William Morris. Beds have luxurious mattresses worthy of a five-star hotel. The cosiest of three restaurants (mains 10KM to 18KM) overlooks some waterfall rapids and serves excellent seafood platters (30KM for two people) washed down with a very good Hercegovinian Riesling (per 500ml 9KM). It's 9km from Bihać towards Banja Luka.

Motel Estrada FAMILY HOTEL **€**
(☑531320; Ostrožac; s/d 30/40KM) Homestay-style en suite rooms in the fifth unmarked house on the left up the Prečići road; 300m southwest of Ostrožac castle.

ⓘ Getting There & Away

Disguised as a mini-casino, Bihać's **bus station** (☑311939) is 1km west of the centre, just off Bihaćkih Branilaća. Destinations include:

Banja Luka (20KM, three hours) Departs 5.30am, 7.30am, 1pm and 3pm via Bosanska Krupa and Otoka Bosanska.

Kostela (2.50KM, 10 minutes) Use Cazin-bound buses, 10 times daily on weekdays, 8.50am, 11.30am and 3.30pm Saturday, 3.30pm only Sunday. Use same buses for Ostražac (3.50KM, 25 minutes).

Plitvice Jezero Take the 7am Slunjski bus to Grabovac (10KM, 45 minutes, no service Sunday), cross the road to the AutoKamp then catch the 8.45am shuttle to the lake park's entrance gate.

Sarajevo (42KM, seven hours) Departs 12.45am, 7.30am, 2.30pm and 10pm, via Travnik.

Zagreb (21-24KM, 2½ hours) Departs 4.45am (no service Sunday), 10.20am, 2pm and 4.45pm.

UNDERSTAND BOSNIA & HERCEGOVINA

History

Be aware that much of BiH's history remains highly controversial and is seen very differently according to one's ethno-religious viewpoint.

In AD 9 ancient Illyrian Bosnia was conquered by the Romans. Slavs arrived from the late 6th century and were dominant by 1180, when Bosnia first emerged as an independent entity under former Byzantine governor Ban Kulina. BiH had a patchy golden age between 1180 and 1463, peaking in the late 1370s when Bosnia's King Tvtko gained Hum (future Hercegovina) and controlled much of Dalmatia.

Blurring the borderline between Europe's Catholic west and Orthodox east, sparsely populated medieval Bosnia had its own independent church. This remains the source of many historical myths, but the long-popular idea that it was 'infected' by the Bulgarian Bogomil heresy is now largely discounted.

Turkish Ascendancy

Turkish raids whittled away at the country throughout the 15th century and by the 1460s most of Bosnia was under Ottoman control. Within a few generations, easygoing Sufi-inspired Islam became dominant among townspeople and landowners, many Bosnians converting as much to gain civil privileges as for spiritual enlightenment. However, a sizeable proportion of the serfs *(rayah)* remained Christian. Bosnians also became particularly prized soldiers in the Ottoman army, many rising eventually to high rank within the imperial court. The early Ottoman era also produced great advances in infrastructure, with fine mosques and bridges built by charitable bequests. Later, however, the Ottomans failed to follow the West's industrial revolution. By the 19th century the empire's economy was archaic, and all attempts to modernise the feudal system in BiH were strenuously resisted by the entrenched Bosnian-Muslim elite. In 1873 İstanbul's banking system collapsed under the weight of the high-living sultan's debts. To pay these debts the sultan demanded added taxes. But in 1874 BiH's harvests failed, so paying those taxes would have meant starving. With nothing left to lose the mostly Christian Bosnian peasants revolted, leading eventually to a messy tangle of pan-Balkan wars.

Austro-Hungarian Rule

These wars ended with the farcical 1878 Congress of Berlin, at which the Western powers carved up the western Ottoman lands. Austria-Hungary was 'invited' to occupy BiH, which was treated like a colony even though it theoretically remained Ottoman under sovereignty. An unprecedented period of development followed. Roads, railways and bridges were built. Coal mining and forestry became booming industries. Education encouraged a new generation of Bosnians to look towards Vienna. But new nationalist feelings were simmering: Bosnian Catholics increasingly identified with neighbouring Croatia (itself within Austria-Hungary) while Orthodox Bosnians sympathised with recently independent Serbia's dreams of a greater Serbian homeland. In between lay Bosnia's Muslims (40%), who belatedly started to develop a distinct Bosniak consciousness.

While Turkey was busy with the 1908 Young Turk revolution Austria-Hungary annexed BiH, undermining the aspirations of those who had dreamed of a pan-Slavic or greater Serbian future. The resultant scramble for the last remainders of Ottoman Europe kicked off the Balkan Wars of 1912 and 1913. No sooner had these been (unsatisfactorily) resolved than the heir to the Austrian throne was shot dead while visiting Sarajevo. One month later Austria declared war on Serbia and WWI swiftly followed.

World Wars, Communism & Political Tension

WWI killed an astonishing 15% of the Bosnian population. It also brought down both the Turkish and Austro-Hungarian empires, leaving BiH to be absorbed into proto-Yugoslavia.

During WWII, BiH was occupied partly by Italy and partly by Germany, then absorbed into the newly created fascist state of Croatia. Croatia's Ustaše decimated Bosnia's Jewish population, and they also persecuted Serbs and Muslims. Meanwhile a pro-Nazi group of Bosnian Muslims committed their own atrocities against Bosnian Serbs while Serb Četniks and Tito's Communist Partizans put up some stalwart resistance to the Germans (as well as fighting each other). The BiH mountains proved ideal territory for Tito's flexible guerrilla army, whose greatest victories are still locally commemorated with vast memorials. In 1943, Tito's antifascist council meeting at Jajce (p103) famously formulated a constitution for an inclusive postwar, socialist Yugoslavia. BiH was granted republic status within that Yugoslavia but up until 1971 (when *Muslim* was defined as a Yugoslav 'ethnic group'), Bosniaks were not considered a distinct community and in censuses had to register as Croat, Serb or 'Other/Yugoslav'. Despite considerable mining in the northeast and the boost of the 1984 Sarajevo Winter Olympics, BiH's economy remained relatively undeveloped.

The 1990s Conflict

In the post-Tito era, as Yugoslavia imploded, religio-linguistic (often dubbed 'ethnic') tensions were ratcheted up by the ultranationalist Serb leader Slobodan Milošević and equally radical Croatian leader Franjo Tuđman. Although these two were at war by spring 1991, they reputedly came up with a de facto agreement in which they planned to divide BiH between breakaway Croatia and rump Yugoslavia.

Under president Alija Izetbegović, BiH declared independence from Yugoslavia on 15 October 1991. Bosnian Serb parliamentarians wanted none of this and withdrew to set up their own government at Pale, 20km east of Sarajevo. BiH was recognised internationally as an independent state on 6 April 1992 but Sarajevo was already under siege both by Serb paramilitaries and by parts of the Yugoslav army (JNA).

Over the next three years a brutal and extraordinarily complex civil war raged. Best known is the campaign of ethnic cleansing in northern and eastern BiH creating the 300km 'pure'-Serb Republika Srpska (RS). But locals of each religion will readily admit that 'there were terrible criminals on our side too'. In western Hercegovina the Croat population armed itself with the help of neighbouring Croatia, eventually ejecting Serbs from their villages in a less reported but similarly brutal war.

Perhaps unaware of the secret Tuđman-Milošević understanding, Izetbegović had signed a formal military alliance with Croatia in June 1992. But by early 1993 fighting had broken out between Muslims and Croats, creating another war front. Croats attacked Muslims in Stolac and Mostar, bombarding their historic monuments and blasting Mostar's famous medieval bridge into the river. Muslim troops, including a small foreign mujahedin force, desecrated churches and attacked Croat villages, notably around Travnik.

UN Involvement

With atrocities on all sides, the West's reaction was confused and erratic. In August 1992, pictures of concentration-camp and rape-camp victims (mostly Muslim) found in northern Bosnia spurred the UN to create Unprofor, a protection force of 7500 peacekeeping troops. Unprofor secured the neutrality of Sarajevo airport well enough to allow the delivery of humanitarian aid, but overall proved notoriously impotent.

Ethnic cleansing of Muslims from Foča and Višegrad led the UN to declare safe zones around the Muslim-majority towns of Srebrenica, Župa and Goražde. But rarely has the term 'safe' been so misused. When NATO belatedly authorised air strikes to protect these areas, the Serbs responded by capturing 300 Unprofor peacekeepers and chaining them to potential targets to keep the planes away.

In July 1995 Dutch peacekeepers could only watch as the starving, supposedly 'safe' area of Srebrenica fell to a Bosnian Serb force led by the infamous Ratko Mladić. An estimated 8000 Muslim men were slaughtered in Europe's worst mass killings since WWII. Miraculously, battered Goražde held out thanks to sporadically available UN food supplies. By this stage, Croatia had renewed its own internal offensive, expelling Serbs from the Krajina region of Croatia in August 1995. At least 150,000 of these dispossessed people then moved to the Serb-held areas of northern Bosnia.

Finally, another murderous Serb mortar attack on Sarajevo's main market (Markale) kickstarted a shift in UN and NATO politics. An ultimatum to end the Serbs' siege of Sarajevo was made more persuasive through two weeks of NATO air strikes in September 1995. US president Bill Clinton's proposal for a peace conference in Dayton, Ohio, was accepted soon after.

The Dayton Agreement

While maintaining BiH's pre-war external boundaries, Dayton divided the country into today's pair of roughly equally sized 'entities' (see the boxed text, p110), each with limited autonomy. Finalising the border required considerable political and cartographic creativity and was only completed in 1999 when the last sticking point, Brčko, was belatedly given a self-governing status all of its own. Meanwhile BiH's curious rotating tripartite presidency has been kept in check by the EU's powerful High Representative (www.ohr.int).

ℹ WHAT'S IN A NAME?

Geographically Bosnia and Hercegovina (BiH) comprises Bosnia (in the north) and Hercegovina (pronounced Her-tse-GO-vina, in the south), although the term 'Bosnian' refers to anyone from BiH, not just from Bosnia proper. Politically, BiH is divided into two entirely different entities. Southwest and central BiH falls mostly within the Federation of Bosnia and Hercegovina, usually shortened to 'the Federation'. Meanwhile most areas bordering Serbia, Montenegro and the northern arm of Croatia are within the Serb-dominated Republika Srpska (abbreviated RS). A few minor practicalities (stamps, phonecards) appear in different versions and the Cyrillic alphabet is more prominent in the RS but these days you'll often struggle to notice which one you're in.

For refugees (1.2 million abroad, and a million displaced within BiH), the Dayton Agreement emphasised the right to return to (or to sell) their pre-war homes. International agencies donated very considerable funding to restore BiH's infrastructure, housing stock and historical monuments.

An embarrassing problem post-Dayton was the failure to find Ratko Mladić and the Bosnian Serb leader Radovan Karadžić (president of the RS until July 1996). Both were due to face trial as war criminals. Despite five million dollar rewards offered for their arrest, Karadžić was only apprehended in 2008, while Mladić remains at large, probably protected by supporters who perceive him to be an honest patriot.

Bosnia & Hercegovina Today

Less radically nationalist politicians now run the RS, while under EU and American pressure BiH has centralised considerably in a movement away from the original Dayton 'separate powers' concept. BiH now has a unified army and common passports. Both entities now have indistinguishable car licence plates and use the same currency, albeit with banknotes in two variants. Many (though by no means all) refugees have returned and rebuilt their pre-war homes.

Deep scars remain and the communities remain socially divided but violence has long since stopped. Today economics is the greatest concern for most Bosnians. Those few socialist-era factories that weren't destroyed in the 1990s conflicts have downsized to fit tough 21st-century global realities. New 'business-friendly' government initiatives, including a recent wave of privatisations, are eyed with suspicion; the populace fears growing corruption. People assume that one day BiH will join the EU, though for many, nearby Slovenia's experience suggests that EU membership will just push up prices and make life harder. 'Life's tough' one war widow told us, 'but at least there's peace'.

The People of Bosnia-Hercegovina

Bosniaks (Bosnian Muslims, 40% of the population), Bosnian Serbs (Orthodox Christians, 31%) and Bosnian Croats (Catholics, 15%) differ by religion but are all Southern Slavs. Physically they are indistinguishable (so the term 'ethnic cleansing' applied so often during the war, should more accurately have been called 'religio-linguistic forced expulsions'). The pre-war population was mixed, with intermarriage common in the cities. Stronger divisions have inevitably appeared since the 'ethnic cleansing' of the 1990s. The war resulted in massive population shifts, changing the size and linguistic balance of many cities. Bosniaks now predominate in Sarajevo and central BiH, Bosnian Croats in western and southern Hercegovina, and Bosnian Serbs in the RS, which includes Istochno (East) Sarajevo and Banja Luka. Today social contact between members of the three groups remains limited and somewhat wary. Religion is taken seriously as a badge of 'ethnicity' but spiritually most people are fairly secular.

The Arts

Crafts

BiH crafts from *kilims* (woollen flat-weaves) to copperware and decoratively repurposed bullet casings are widely sold in Mostar's Kujundžiluk and Sarajevo's Baščaršija. *Stećci* (singular *stećak*) are archetypal Bosnian forms of oversized medieval gravestones. The best-known examples are found at Radimlja near Stolac. However, those collected outside Sarajevo's National Museum are finer, while a group near Umoljani has a much more visually satisfying setting.

Literature

Bosnia's best-known writer, Ivo Andrić (1892–1975), won the 1961 Nobel Prize in Literature. With extraordinary psychological agility, his epic novel, the classic *Bridge on the Drina*, retells 350 years of Bosnian history as seen through the eyes of unsophisticated townsfolk in Višegrad. His *Travnik Chronicles* (aka *Bosnian Chronicle*) is also rich with human insight, though its portrayal of Bosnia is through the eyes of jaded 19th-century foreign consuls in Travnik.

Many thought-provoking essays, short stories and poems explore the prickly subject of the 1990s conflict, often contrasting horrors against the victims' enduring humanity. Quality varies greatly but recommended collections include Miljenko Jergović's *Sarajevo Marlboro* and Semezdin Mehmedinović's *Sarajevo Blues*.

Movies

The relationship between two soldiers, one Muslim and one Serb, caught alone in the same trench during the Sarajevo siege was the theme for Danis Tanović's Oscar-winning 2002 film *No Man's Land*. The movie *Go West* takes on the deep taboo of homosexuality as a wartime Serb-Bosniak gay couple become a latter-day Romeo and Juliet. *Gori Vatra* (aka *Fuse*) is an irony-packed dark comedy set in the pretty Bosnian castle town of Tešanj just after the war, parodying efforts to hide corruption and create a facade of ethnic reintegration for the sake of a proposed visit by US president Bill Clinton.

Music

Sevdah (traditional Bosnian music) typically uses heart-wrenching vocals to recount tales of unhappy amours, though singing it was once used as a subtle courting technique. Sarajevo has an annual jazz festival (November). The post-industrial city of Tuzla has vibrant rap and metal scenes.

The Landscape

BiH is predominantly mountainous. The mostly arid south (Hercegovina) dips one tiny toe of land into the Adriatic Sea at Neum then rises swiftly into bare limestone uplands carved with deep grey canyons. The central mountain core has some 30 peaks rising between 1700m and 2386m.

Further north and east the landscape becomes increasingly forested with waterfalls and alpine valleys, most famously in the magnificent Sutjeska National Park. In the far northeast the peaks subside into rolling bucolic hills flattening out altogether in the far north.

SURVIVAL GUIDE

Directory A–Z

Accommodation

Except in hostels, all quoted room prices assume a private bathroom and breakfast unless otherwise indicated.

Our price ranges for a double room are budget (€; less than 80KM), midrange (€€; 80KM to 190KM) and top end (€€€; more than 190KM).

High season means June to September generally but late December to early March in ski resorts. In Mostar and Sarajevo summer prices rise 20% to 50% and touts appear at the bus stations.

Accommodation Types

Homestays Somebody's spare room. Slip-on shoes and plentiful clean socks are a boon since it's normal courtesy to remove footwear on entering a private house. Hosts will provide slippers.

Hostels Usually bunk rooms in a semi-converted private home. Many lack signs but can be booked through international hostel-booking sites. Essentially Mostar and Sarajevo only.

Hotels Often inhabiting the husk of old Tito-era concrete monsters, many are now elegantly remodelled but some remain gloomy and a little forbidding.

BOOKS

Bosnia: A Short History by Noel Malcolm is a very readable introduction to the complexities of Bosnian history. In *Not My Turn To Die* by Savo Heleta the memoirs of a besieged family at Goražde give insights into the strange mixture of terror, boredom and resignation of the 1990s conflict.

BuyBook (www.buybook.ba) produces several regional guidebooks.

GAY & LESBIAN TRAVELLERS

Although homosexuality was decriminalised per se in 1998 (2000 in the RS), attitudes remain very conservative. Sarajevo's only high-profile LGTB event (the Queer Festival of 2008) was violently attacked by anti-gay protesters. **Association Q** (www.queer.ba) nonetheless attempts to empower the self-reliance of the gay community in BiH and the English-language **Gay Romeo** (www.gayromeo.com) chat site reportedly has several hundred Sarajevo members.

Motels Generally new and suburban and ideal for those with cars. However, occasionally the term simply implies a lower midrange hotel so don't automatically assume there's parking.

Pansions Anything from a glorified homestay to a little boutique hotel.

Ski Hotels Between Christmas and 15 January availability is very stretched and prices will be around 50% higher. Some demand minimum stays during ski season, though since the economic downturn this rule is being less rigorously enforced. Most close during low season.

Activities

Skiing Inexpensive yet world-class at Jahorina, Bjelašnica or Vlašić.

Rafting Reaches terrifyingly difficult class V in April/May but is more suitable for beginners in summer. Top spots are around Foča, Bihać and Banja Luka.

Hiking and mountain biking Compromised since the 1990s by the presence of landmines, but many upland areas and national parks now have safe, marked trails. Ecotourism organisation Green Visions (p80) offers seasonal hiking excursions from Sarajevo.

Business Hours

Office hours 8am-4pm Mon-Fri

Banks 8am-6pm Mon-Fri, 8.30am-1.30pm Sat

Shops 8am-6pm daily

Restaurants 11.30am-10.30pm, often later in summer.

Whatever signs might say, actual restaurant closing time depends on customer demand more than fixed schedules. Restaurants opening in the morning usually operate as a cafe only until lunchtime.

Dangers & Annoyances

Landmines and unexploded ordnance, still thought to affect around 3% of BiH's area, caused nine deaths and 19 recorded injuries in 2009. Stick to asphalt/concrete surfaces or well-worn paths in affected areas and don't enter war-damaged buildings. **BHMAC** (www.bhmac.org) has more information.

Food

The average cost of a main courses in a restaurant is under 8KM for budget (€), 8KM to 15KM for midrange (€€) and more than 15KM for top end (€€€).

Holidays

Major Islamic festivals are observed in parts of the Federation where the Feast of Sacrifice is known as Kurban Bajram and the end-of-Ramadan celebration is Ramazanski Bajram. Orthodox Easter (variable) and Christmas (6 January) are observed in the RS. Western Easter (variable) and Christmas (25 December) are celebrated in the Federation. Nationwide holidays:

New Year's Day 1 January

Independence Day 1 March

May Day 1 May

National Statehood Day 25 November

Internet Access

Most hotels and some cafes now offer wi-fi; it's free unless otherwise mentioned.

LANGUAGE

The people of BiH speak essentially the same language but it's referred to as 'Bosnian' (Bosanski) in Muslim parts, 'Croatian' (Hrvatski) in Croat-controlled areas and 'Serbian' (Српски) in the RS. The Federation uses the Latin alphabet. The RS uses predominantly Cyrillic (Ћирилица) but Latin (Latinica) is gaining wider parallel usage there too. Brčko uses both alphabets equally.

Key Bosnian phrases: *zdravo* (hello); *hvala* (thanks); *molim* (please).

Maps

Freytag & Berndt's very useful if flawed 1:250,000 BiH road map costs 12KM in Sarajevo bookshops. City maps are patchily available from bookshops, kiosks or tourist information centres. Many cities post town plans on their websites.

Money

ATMs Machines accepting Visa and MasterCard are ubiquitous.

Cash Bosnia's convertible mark (KM or BAM) is pronounced *kai-em* or *maraka* and divided into 100 fenig. It's tied to the euro at approximately €1=1.96KM. Many businesses unblinkingly accept euros and for minor purchases you'll often get a favourable 1:2 rate. Croatian kuna are accepted in some places too.

Travellers cheques Exchange usually requires the original purchase receipt.

Post

BiH fascinates philatelists by having three parallel postal organisations, each issuing their own stamps: **BH Post** (www.bhp.ba) and **Srpske Poste** (www.filatelija.rs.ba) for the RS, and the Croat **HP Post** (www.post.ba) based in western Mostar.

Telephone

Mobile-phone companies BH Mobile (☏061- and ☏062-), HT/EroNet (☏063-) and M-Tel (☏065-) all have virtually nationwide coverage.

Phonecards (10KM) for payphones are sold at post offices and some street kiosks. Beware that different cards are required for the Federation and for RS.

Country code ☏387

International operator ☏1201

Local directory information ☏1188

Travellers with Disabilities

Bosnia's most charming townscapes are full of stairways and steep, rough streets that are very awkward if you're disabled. A few places have wheelchair ramps in response to all the war wounded, but smaller hotels won't have lifts and disabled toilets remain extremely rare.

Visas

Stays of under 90 days require no visa for citizens of most Europeans countries and Australia, Brunei, Canada, Japan, Malaysia, New Zealand, Singapore, South Korea, Turkey and the USA. Other nationals should see www.mva.ba for visa details and where to apply. For South Africans that's London or Tripoli! Visas usually require a letter of invitation or a tourist-agency voucher of EU, and most other European, countries.

Getting There & Away

Air

As an alternative to flying direct, consider budget flights to Dubrovnik, Split or Zagreb (Croatia) and connecting to BiH by bus or train.

Airlines

Adria (JP; www.adria.si) Via Ljubljana (also serves Banja Luka).

Austrian (OS; www.austrian.com) Via Vienna.

BH Airlines (JA; Map p78; ☏033-550125, 768335; www.bhairlines.ba; Branilaca Sarajeva 15, Sarajevo; ⊙9am-5pm Mon-Fri, 9am-2pm Sat) Pronounced 'Bay-Ha', this is the national carrier. It flies from Sarajevo to Belgrade, Copenhagen, Frankfurt, Gothenburg, İstanbul, Stockholm, Vienna and Zürich. Some Frankfurt and Vienna services go via Banja Luka.

Croatia Airlines (OU; www.croatiaairlines.com) Via Zagreb.

germanwings (4U; www.germanwings.com) Stuttgart and Köln-Bonn.

JAT (JU; Map p78; www.jat.com) Via Belgrade.

Lufthansa (LH; www.lufthansa.com) Via Munich.

Malév (MA; www.malev.com) Via Budapest.

Norwegian (DY; www.norwegian.no) Weekly to Stockholm.

Turkish (TK; www.thy.com) Via İstanbul.

Land

Bus

There are buses to Zagreb and/or Split (Croatia) at least daily from most towns in the Federation and to Serbia and/or Montenegro from many RS towns. Buses to Vienna and Germany run several times weekly from bigger BiH cities.

Car & Motorcycle

Drivers need Green Card insurance and an EU or International Driving Permit. Transiting Neum in a Croatian hire car is usually hassle-free.

Train

The modest international network links Sarajevo to Belgrade, Zagreb (via Banja Luka), Budapest (via Osijek, Croatia) and to Ploče (coastal Croatia via Mostar).

Getting Around

Bicycle

For tough cyclists BiH's calm if hilly secondary routes can prove a delight. Several mountain areas now have suggested off-road trails for mountain bikers but beware of straying off-route: landmines remain a danger.

Bus

Frequency drops drastically at weekends on shorter-hop routes, some stopping altogether on Sundays.

Bus stations pre-sell tickets but it's normally easy enough to wave down any bus en route. Advance reservations are sometimes necessary for overnight routes or at peak holiday times.

Fares are around 7KM per hour travelled. Return tickets can prove significantly cheaper than two singles but you'll be inconveniently limited to one specific company. Expect to pay 2KM extra per stowed bag. Most bus station ticket offices have a 'garderob' for left luggage (from 2KM).

Car & Motorcycle

There's minimal public transport to BiH's most spectacular remote areas so having wheels can really transform your trip. Bosnian winding roads are lightly trafficked and a delight for driving if you aren't in a hurry. **BIHAMK** (☏222 210; bihamk.ba; Skenderija 23, Sarajevo; annual membership 25KM; ◷8am-4.30pm Mon-Fri, 9am-noon Sat) offers road as-

sistance and towing services (call ☏1282 or ☏1288).

Hire

International chains are represented while smaller local outfits are often based at hotels. Most companies add 17% VAT. A good deal is **Hyundai Rent-A-Car** (www.hyundai.ba; from 75/390KM per day/week); its standard rates include full insurance, theft protection and CDW. Pick up/drop off is possible at Mostar, Sarajevo or Sarajevo airport without extra charge for open-jaws.

Road Rules

Drive on the right. First-aid kit, warning triangle and spare bulb-kits are compulsory.

Blood-alcohol limit 0.031%

Headlights Must be kept on day and night

LPG Availability very limited

Parking Awkward in Mostar and Sarajevo, contrastingly easy elsewhere. In town centres expect to pay 1KM per hour to an attendant.

Petrol Typically around 2.05KM per litre (Federation), 1.95KM (RS)

Seatbelts Compulsory

Snow chains Compulsory on some mountain roads (November to April) and wherever snow is over 5cm deep

Speed limits 100kmh (dual carriageways), 80kmh (rural), 60kmh or less (in town). Absurdly slow limits are often posted with no obvious logic but police spot-checks are common.

Winter Tyres Compulsory mid-November to mid-April

Train

Trains are slower and less frequent than buses but generally around 30% cheaper. **RS Railways** (www.zrs-rs.com/red_voznje.php) has full, up-to-date rail timetables.

Croatia

Why Go?

Croatia has been touted as the 'new this' and the 'new that' for years since its re-emergence on the tourism scene, but it's now clear that it's a unique destination that holds its own and then some: this is a country with a glorious 1778km-long coast and a staggering 1244 islands. The Adriatic coast is a knockout: its sapphire waters draw visitors to remote islands, hidden coves and traditional fishing villages, all while touting the glitzy beach and yacht scene. Istria captivates with its gastronomic delights and wines, and the bars, clubs and festivals of Zagreb, Zadar and Split remain little-explored gems. Eight national parks showcase primeval beauty with their forests, mountains, rivers, lakes and waterfalls. Punctuate all this with dazzling Dubrovnik in the south – just the right finale. Best of all, Croatia hasn't given in to mass tourism: there are pockets of authentic culture and plenty to discover off the grid.

Best Places to Stay

» Arcotel Allegra (p125)
» Hotel Peristil (p151)
» Lešić Dimitri Palace (p159)
» Hotel Bellevue (p166)

Best Places to Eat

» Vinodol (p126)
» Konoba Batelina (p138)
» Foša (p148)
» Konoba Trattoria Bajamont (p153)

When to Go
Zagreb

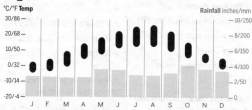

July & August
Lots of sunshine, warm sea and summer festivals. Many tourists and highest prices.

June Best time to visit: beautiful weather, fewer people, lower prices, the festival season kicks off.

May & September Good weather, few tourists, full local events calendar, great for hiking.

Exchange Rates

Australia	A$1	5.32KN
Canada	C$1	5.29KN
euro	€1	7.36KN
Japan	¥100	6.04KN
New Zealand	NZ$1	4.01KN
UK	UK£1	8.27KN
USA	US$1	5.08KN

Set Your Budget

» **Budget room** 450KN

» **Two-course meal** 150KN

» **Museum entry** 10-40KN

» **Beer** 15KN

» **City transport ticket** 10KN

Resources

» **Adriatica.net** (www.adriatica.net)

» **Croatian National Tourist Board** (www.croatia.hr)

Connections

Croatia is a convenient transport hub for southeastern Europe and the Adriatic. Zagreb is connected by train and/or bus to Venice, Budapest, Belgrade, Ljubljana and Sarajevo. Down south there are easy bus connections from Dubrovnik to Mostar and Sarajevo (Bosnia and Hercegovina), and to Kotor (Montenegro). There are a number of ferries linking Croatia with Italy, including routes from Dubrovnik to Bari, and Split to Ancona.

ITINERARIES

One week

After a day in dynamic Zagreb, delving into its simmering nightlife, fine restaurants and choice museums, head down to Split for a day and night at Diocletian's Palace, a living part of this exuberant seafront city. Then hop over to chic Hvar and windsurf in pretty Bol on Brač. Next take it easy down the winding coastal road to magnificent Dubrovnik, for the final two days, taking a day trip to Mljet or the nearby Elafiti Islands.

Two weeks

After two days in Zagreb, head to Istria for a three-day stay, with Rovinj as the base, and day trips to Pula and Poreč. Go southeast next to the World Heritage–listed Plitvice Lakes National Park, a verdant maze of turquoise lakes and cascading waterfalls. After a quick visit, move on to Zadar, a real find of a city: historic, modern, active and packed with attractions. Then go on south to Split for a day or two. From here, take ferries to Hvar, Brač and then Korčula, spending a day or more on each island before ending with three days in Dubrovnik and an outing to Mljet.

Essential Food & Drink

» **Ćevapčići** Small spicy sausages of minced beef, lamb or pork.

» **Pljeskavica** An ex-Yugo version of a hamburger.

» **Ražnjići** Small chunks of pork grilled on a skewer.

» **Burek** Pastry stuffed with ground meat, spinach or cheese.

» **Rakija** Strong Croatian brandy comes in different flavors, from plum to honey.

» **Beer** Two top types of Croatian *pivo* (beer) are Zagreb's Ožujsko and Karlovačko from Karlovac.

ZAGREB

♪ 01 / POP 779,145

Everyone knows about Croatia's coast and islands, but a mention of the country's capital still draws the question: 'Is it worth going to?' Here is the answer: Zagreb is a great destination, with culture, arts, music, architecture, gastronomy and everything else that make a quality capital.

Visually, Zagreb is a mixture of straight-laced Austro-Hungarian architecture and rough-around-the-edges socialist structures; its character is a sometimes uneasy combination of these two elements. This mini metropolis is made for strolling, drinking coffee in the permanently full cafes, popping into museums and galleries, and enjoying the theatres, concerts and cinema. It's a year-round outdoor city: in spring and summer everyone scurries to Jarun Lake in the southwest to swim, boat or dance the night away at lakeside discos, while in autumn and winter Zagrebians go skiing at Mt Medvednica, only a tram ride away, or hiking in nearby Samobor.

History

Zagreb's known history begins in the medieval times with two hills: Kaptol, now the site of Zagreb's cathedral, and Gradec. When the two merged in the mid-16th century, Zagreb was born.

The space now known as Trg Josipa Jelačića became the site of Zagreb's lucrative trade fairs, spurring construction around its edges. In the 19th century the economy expanded and cultural life blossomed with the development of a prosperous clothing trade and a rail link connecting Zagreb with Vienna and Budapest.

Between the two world wars, working-class neighbourhoods emerged in Zagreb between the railway and the Sava River, and new residential quarters were built on the southern slopes of Mt Medvednica. In April 1941, the Germans invaded Yugoslavia and entered Zagreb without resistance. Ante Pavelić and the Ustaše moved quickly to proclaim the establishment of the Independent State of Croatia (Nezavisna Država Hrvatska), with Zagreb as its capital.

In postwar Yugoslavia, Zagreb (to its chagrin) took second place to Belgrade but continued to expand. Zagreb was made the capital of Croatia in 1991, the same year that the country became independent.

⊙ Sights

As the oldest part of Zagreb, the Upper Town (Gornji Grad) offers landmark buildings and churches from the earlier centuries of Zagreb's history. The Lower Town (Donji Grad) has the city's most interesting art museums and fine examples of 19th- and 20th-century architecture.

UPPER TOWN

Cathedral of the Assumption of the Blessed Virgin Mary   CHURCH

(Katedrala Marijina Uznešenja; Kaptol; ⊙10am-5pm Mon-Sat, 1-5pm Sun) Kaptol Sq is dominated by the twin neo-Gothic spires of this 1899 cathedral, formerly known as St Stephen's. Elements of an earlier medieval cathedral, destroyed by an earthquake in 1880, can be seen inside, including 13th-century frescoes, Renaissance pews, marble altars and a baroque pulpit. Note that you might be turned away if you're not dressed appropriately: no bare legs or shoulders.

Dolac Market   MARKET

(⊙6am-3pm Mon-Sat, 6am-1pm Sun) Zagreb's colourful Dolac is just north of Trg Josipa Jelačića. This buzzing centre of Zagreb's daily activity since the 1930s draws in traders

---

ZAGREB IN TWO DAYS

Start your day with a stroll through Strossmayerov Trg, Zagreb's oasis of greenery. While there, take a look at the Strossmayer Gallery of Old Masters and then walk to Trg Josipa Jelačića, the city's centre. Head up to Kaptol for a look at the Cathedral of the Assumption of the Blessed Virgin Mary, the focus of Zagreb's (and Croatia's) spiritual life. While you're in the Upper Town, pick up some fruit at the Dolac market. Then get to know the work of Croatia's best sculptor at Meštrović Atelier and take in a contemporary art exhibition at Galerija Klovićevi Dvori. See the lay of the city from the top of Lotršćak Tower and then enjoy a bar-crawl along Tkalčićeva.

On the second day, tour the Lower Town museums, reserving two hours for the Museum Mimara, then have lunch at Tip Top. Early evening is best at Trg Petra Preradovića before dining at one of the Lower Town restaurants and sampling some of Zagreb's nightlife.

Croatia Highlights

1 Gape at the Old Town wall of **Dubrovnik** (p162), which surrounds luminous marble streets and finely ornamented buildings

2 Admire the Venetian architecture and vibrant nightlife of **Hvar Town** (p157)

3 Indulge in the lively and historic delights of Diocletian's Palace in **Split** (p150)

4 Explore the lakes, coves and island monastery of **Mljet** (p161)

5 Stroll the cobbled streets and unspoiled fishing port of **Rovinj** (p132)

6 Take in the wild landscapes of **Rt Kamenjak** (p137) cape near Pula

7 Marvel at the turquoise lakes and waterfalls in **Plitvice Lakes National Park** (boxed text, p147)

Zagreb

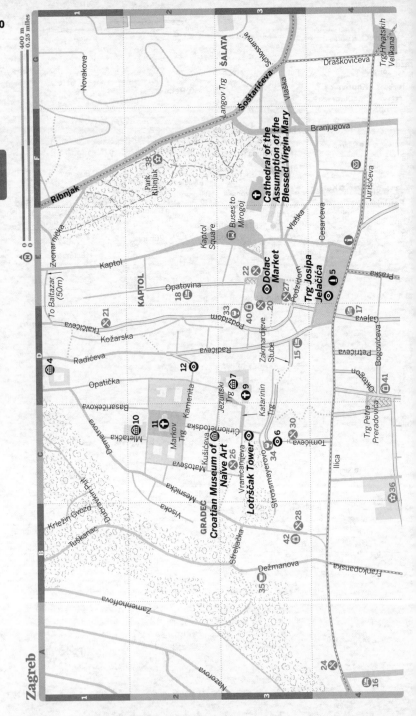

N
400 m
0.25 miles

Ribnjak

ŠALATA

Šoštarićeva

Novakova

Langov Trg

Schlosserove

Draškovićeva

Trg Hrvatskih
Velikana

Park
Ribnjak

38

Zvonarnička

Kaptol

KAPTOL

Opatovina

18

Buses to
Mirogoj

Kaptol
Square

**Cathedral of the
Assumption of the
Blessed Virgin Mary**

Branjugova

Vlaška

Jurišićeva

Vlaška

Cesarčeva

**Dolac
Market**

22

27

**Trg Josipa
Jelačića**

5

To Baltazar
(50m)

Tkalčićeva

21

Kožarska

Radićeva

Tkalčićeva

Podzidom

33

40

20

Podzidom

17

Gajeva

Praška

i

4

Opatička

12

Bašaričekova

Radićeva

Zakmardijeve
Stube

15

Petrićeva

Bogovićeva

Oktogon

41

Dežmanova

Mletačka

10

11

Markov
Trg

Matoševa

Kamenita

Jezuitski
Trg

7

9

Katarinin
Trg

Cirilometodska

**Croatian Museum of
Naïve Art**

26

34

6

30

Tomićeva

Trg Petra
Preradovića

Demetrova

Kušlićeva

Lotrščak Tower

Vranicanijeva

Strossmayerovo

Ilica

36

Mesnička

Visoka

GRADEC

Streljačka

28

42

Krležin Gvozd

Dubravkin put

Tuškanac

35

Frankopanska

Zamenhofova

Nazorova

24

16

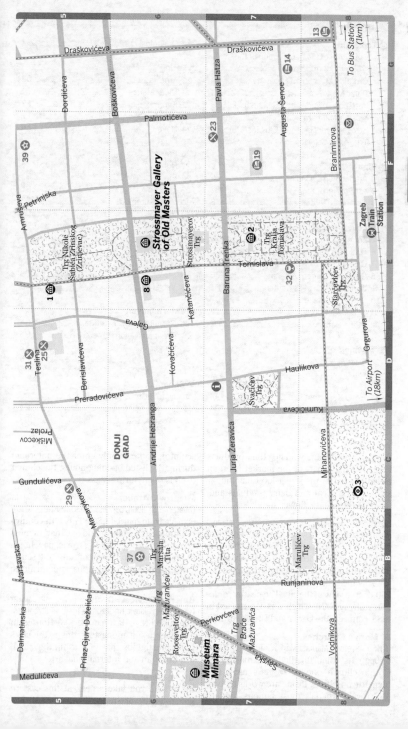

Draškovićeva

Draškovićeva

To Bus Station (1km)

Đorđićeva

Boškovićeva

Pavla Hatza

Augusta Šenoe

Palmotićeva

Branimirova

23

39

14

19

Petrinjska

Amruševa

Strossmayer Gallery of Old Masters

Zagreb Train Station

Strossmayerov Trg

Trg Nikole Šubića Zrinskog (Zrinjevac)

2

Trg Kralja Tomislava

8

Baruna Trenka

Tomislava

32

Katančićeva

Starčevićev Trg

Galeva

1

Bernslavićeva

Kovačićeva

To Airport (18km)

Grgurova

Haulikova

31

25

Teslina

Šnačićev Trg

Preradovićeva

Andrije Hebranga

Jurija Žerovića

Kumičeva

Miškecov Prolaz

DONJI GRAD

Mihanovićeva

Gundulićeva

29

Marulićev Trg

3

Varšavska

Dalmatinska

Prilaz Gjure Deželića

37

Trg Maršala Tita

Runjaninova

Medulićeva

Roosveltov Trg

Mažuranićev Trg

Perkovčeva

Trg Braće Mažuranića

Vodnikova

Museum Mimara

Savska

from all over Croatia who flog their products here. The main part of the market is on an elevated square; the street level has indoor stalls selling meat and dairy products and, towards the square, flower stands.

Lotrščak Tower HISTORIC BUILDING
(Kula Lotrščak; Strossmayerovo Šetalište 9; adult/concession 10/5KN; ☉10am-8pm) From Radićeva 5, off Trg Jelačića, a pedestrian walkway called Stube Ivana Zakmardija leads to this medieval tower, which can be climbed for a sweeping 360-degree view of the city. The nearby **funicular railway** (4KN), which was constructed in 1888, connects the Lower and Upper Towns.

St Mark's Church CHURCH
(Crkva Svetog Marka; Markov Trg; ☉7.30am-6.30pm) Its colourful tiled roof makes this Gothic church one of Zagreb's most emblematic buildings. Inside are works by Ivan Meštrović, Croatia's most famous modern

sculptor. You can only enter the anteroom during the listed opening hours; the church itself is open during Mass.

Meštrović Atelier ART GALLERY
(Mletačka 8; adult/concession 30/15KN; ☉10am-6pm Tue-Fri, to 2pm Sat & Sun) This 17th-century building, the former home of Croatia's most recognised artist, Ivan Meštrović, now houses an excellent collection of some 100 sculptures, drawings, lithographs and furniture created by the artist.

Galerija Klovićevi Dvori ART GALLERY
(www.galerijaklovic.hr; Jezuitski Trg 4; adult/concession 30/20KN; ☉11am-7pm Tue-Sun) Housed in a former Jesuit monastery, this is the city's most prestigious space for exhibiting modern Croatian and international art.

Stone Gate LANDMARK
Make sure you take a peek at this eastern gate to medieval Gradec Town, now a shrine.

According to legend, a great fire in 1731 destroyed every part of the wooden gate except for the painting of the *Virgin and Child* by an unknown 17th-century artist.

City Museum
MUSEUM

(Muzej Grada Zagreba; www.mgz.hr; Opatička 20; adult/concession 20/10KN; ⊙10am-6pm Tue-Fri, 11am-7pm Sat, 10am-2pm Sun) Check out the scale model of old Gradec, atmospheric background music and interactive exhibits that fascinate kids. There are summaries in English in each room of the museum, which is in the former Convent of St Claire (1650).

Croatian Museum of Naïve Art
MUSEUM

(Hrvatski Muzej Naivne Umjetnosti; www.hmnu.org; Ćirilometodska 3; adult/concession 20/10KN; ⊙10am-6pm Tue-Fri, to 1pm Sat & Sun) If you like Croatia's naïve art or want a good intro to it, head to this small museum. It houses over 1000 paintings, drawings and some sculpture by the discipline's most important artists.

LOWER TOWN

Trg Josipa Jelačića
SQUARE

Zagreb's main orientation point and its geographic heart is Trg Josipa Jelačića. It has an **equestrian statue** of Jelačić, the 19th-century *ban* (viceroy or governor) who led Croatian troops into an unsuccessful battle with Hungary in the hope of winning more autonomy for his people. The square is Zagreb's principal meeting point; sit in one of the cafes for quality people-watching.

Museum Mimara
MUSEUM

(Muzej Mimara; Rooseveltov Trg 5; adult/concession 40/30KN; ⊙10am-7pm Tue-Fri, to 5pm Sat, to 2pm Sun) Ante Topić Mimara donated his diverse collection to Croatia. Housed in a neo-Renaissance palace, it includes icons, glassware, sculpture, Oriental art and works by renowned painters such as Rembrandt, Velázquez, Raphael and Degas.

Strossmayer Gallery of Old Masters
MUSEUM

(Strossmayerova Galerija Starih Majstora; www.mdc.hr/strossmayer; Trg Nikole Šubića Zrinskog 11; adult/concession 10/5KN; ⊙10am-7pm Tue, to 4pm Wed-Fri, to 1pm Sat & Sun) Inside the neo-Renaissance Croatian Academy of Arts and Sciences, it showcases the impressive fine-art collection donated to Zagreb by Bishop Strossmayer in 1884. When it's closed, enter the interior courtyard to see the Baška Slab (1102) from Krk Island, one of the oldest inscriptions in the Croatian language.

Archaeological Museum
MUSEUM

(Arheološki Muzej; www.amz.hr; Trg Nikole Šubića Zrinskog 19; adult/concession 20/10KN; ⊙10am-5pm Tue, Wed & Fri, to 8pm Thu, to 1pm Sat & Sun) The fascinating Archaeological Museum has a wide-ranging display of artefacts from prehistoric times through to the medieval period. Behind the museum is a garden of Roman sculpture turned into a pleasant open-air cafe in the summer.

Gallery of Modern Art
ART GALLERY

(Moderna Galerija; www.moderna-galerija.hr; Andrije Hebranga 1; adult/concession 40/20KN; ⊙10am-6pm Tue-Fri, to 1pm Sat & Sun) With a glorious display of Croatian artists of the last 200 years, it offers an excellent overview of Croatia's vibrant arts scene.

Art Pavilion
ART GALLERY

(Umjetnički Paviljon; www.umjetnicki-paviljon.hr; Trg Kralja Tomislava 22; adult/concession 30/15KN; ⊙11am-7pm Tue-Sat, 10am-1pm Sun) The yellow Art Pavilion in a stunning 1897 art nouveau building presents changing exhibitions of contemporary art. It shuts down from mid-July through late August.

FREE THRILLS

Though you'll have to pay to get into most of Zagreb's galleries and museums, there are some gorgeous parks and markets to be enjoyed for nowt – and there's always window shopping!

» Taste bits of food for free at Dolac – but don't be too cheeky!

» Smell the herbs at the Botanical Gardens.

» Enjoy the long walks around Maksimir Park.

» See the magnificent Mirogoj cemetery.

» Pop inside the gorgeous baroque Jesuit Church of St Catherine and the ever-renovated cathedral.

MARKET DAYS

The Sunday **antiques market** (⊙9am-2pm) on Britanski Trg is one of central Zagreb's joys, but to see a flea market that's unmatched in the whole of Croatia, you have to head to **Hrelić** (⊙7am-3pm). This huge open space is packed with anything – from car parts, cars and antique furniture to clothes, records, kitchenware, you name it. Shopping aside, it's also a great place to experience the truly Balkan part and chaotic fun of Zagreb – Roma music, bartering, grilled-meat smoke and general gusto. If you're going in the summer months, take a hat and slap on sunscreen – there's no shade. Take bus 295 to Sajam Jakuševac from behind the train station.

Botanical Garden   GARDEN
(Botanički Vrt; Mihanovićeva bb; admission free; ⊙9am-2.30pm Mon-Tue, 9am-7pm Wed-Sun Apr-Oct) Laid out in 1890, the garden has 10,000 plant species, including 1800 tropical flora specimens. The landscaping has created restful corners and paths that seem a world away from bustling Zagreb.

OUTSIDE THE CENTRE

Museum of Contemporary Art   MUSEUM
(Muzej Suvremene Umjetnosti; www.msu.hr; Avenija Dubrovnik 17; adult/concession 30/15KN, free 1st Wed of month; ⊙11am-7pm Tue-Sun, 11am-10pm Thu) Housed in a dazzling functionalist building by local architect Igor Franić, this swanky new museum in Novi Zagreb, across the Sava River, puts on solo and thematic group shows by Croatian and international artists. The year-round schedule is packed with film, theatre, concerts and performance art.

Mirogoj   CEMETERY
(⊙6am-8pm Apr-Sep, 7.30am-6pm Oct-Mar) A 10-minute ride north of the city centre on bus 106 from the cathedral (or a half-hour walk through leafy streets) takes you to one of Europe's most beautiful cemeteries. This verdant resting place was designed in 1876 by Austrian-born architect Herman Bollé, who created numerous buildings around Zagreb. The sculpted and artfully designed tombs lie beyond a majestic arcade topped by a string of cupolas.

Maksimir Park   PARK
(Maksimirska bb; www.park-maksimir.hr; ⊙9am-dusk) Another green delight is Maksimir Park, a peaceful wooded enclave covering 18 hectares; it is easily accessible by trams 4, 7, 11 and 12. Opened to the public in 1794, it was the first public promenade in southeastern Europe. There's also a modest **zoo** (www.zoo.hr; adult/child 30/20KN; ⊙9am-8pm) here.

⛭ Tours

ZET   BUS TOURS
(www.zet.hr) Zagreb's public transportation network operates open-deck tour buses (70KN) departing from Kaptol on a hop-on hop-off basis from April through September.

Zagreb Inside   WALKING TOURS
(www.zagrebinside.com) Runs weekly thematic tours (adult/student 90KN/70KN) such as Women of Zagreb and Do You Speak Croatian?, which teaches you basic language skills. The meeting point is outside the tourist info centre; no tours in August.

Blue Bike Tours   BIKE TOURS
(www.zagrebbybike.com) Has three-hour tours (170KN) departing twice daily.

⚑ Festivals & Events

For a complete listing of Zagreb events, see www.zagreb-convention.hr.

Music Biennale Zagreb   MUSIC
(www.mbz.hr) Croatia's most important contemporary music event is held during odd-numbered years, in April.

Queer Zagreb Festival   GAY & LESBIAN
(www.queerzagreb.org) Camp out and party in late April/early May, with theatre, film, dance and music.

T-Mobile INmusic Festival   MUSIC
(www.t-mobileinmusicfestival.com) A three-day extravaganza every June, this is Zagreb's highest-profile music festival, with multiple stages by the Jarun Lake.

World Festival of Animated Film   FILM
(www.animafest.hr) This prestigious festival has been held in Zagreb since 1972, now annually in June.

Cest is D'Best   STREET FESTIVAL
(www.cestisdbest.com) In early June, it features five stages around the city centre, around 200 international performers and

acts that include music, dance, theatre, art and sports.

Eurokaz
THEATRE

(www.eurokaz.hr) The International Festival of New Theatre showcases innovative theatre troupes and cutting-edge performances from around the world in the second half of June.

International Folklore Festival
FOLKLORE

(www.msf.hr) Each July, it features folk dancers and singers from Croatia and other European countries, plus free workshops in dance, music and art.

Zagreb Summer Evenings
MUSIC

A cycle of concerts in the Upper Town each July, with the atrium of Galerija Klovićevi Dvori and the Gradec stage used for the performances of classic music, jazz, blues and world tunes.

🛏 Sleeping

Zagreb's accommodation scene has been undergoing a small but noticeable change with the arrival of some of Europe's low-cost airlines: the budget end of the market is consequently starting to get a pulse. Although the new hostels cater mainly to the backpacker crowd, it's a good beginning. For midrangers and those wanting more privacy and a homey feel, there are private rooms and apartments.

Prices stay the same in all seasons but be prepared for a 20% surcharge if you arrive during a festival, especially the autumn business fair in mid- to late September.

If you intend to stay in a private house or apartment, try not to arrive on Sunday, because most of the agencies will be closed. Prices for doubles run from about 300KN and studio apartments start at 400KN per night. There's usually a surcharge for one-night stays. Some agencies:

Evistas (☑48 39 554; www.evistas.hr; Augusta Šenoe 28; s from 210KN, d/apt 295/360KN) Recommended by the tourist office.

InZagreb (☑65 23 201; www.inzagreb.com; Remetinečka 13; apt 471-616KN) Centrally located apartments with a minimum three-night stay. The price includes bike rental, wireless internet and pick-up and drop-off from the train and/or bus station.

Never Stop (Nemoj Stati; ☑091 637 8111; www.nest.hr; Crvenog Križa 31; apt 430-596KN) Has apartments in the centre of town, with a minimum three-night stay.

Arcotel Allegra
BOUTIQUE HOTEL €€€

(☑46 96 000; www.arcotel.at/allegra; Branimirova 29; s/d from 730/840KN; P❄@🖥) Zagreb's first designer hotel has a marble-and-exotic-fish reception and airy rooms where bed throws come with printed faces of Kafka, Kahlo and other iconic personalities. There's a top-floor spa, and a good onsite restaurant. Look out for summer specials.

Hotel Dubrovnik
HOTEL €€€

(☑48 63 555; www.hotel-dubrovnik.hr; Gajeva 1; s/d from 980/1200KN; P❄🖥) Smack on the main square, this glass city landmark has 245 elegant units with old-school classic style and, from some, great views of the square.

Hotel Ilica
HOTEL €€

(☑37 77 522; www.hotel-ilica.hr; Ilica 102; s/d/apt 349/449/749KN; P❄🖥) A great central option, with quiet rooms ranging from super kitsch to lushly decorous. Trams 6, 11 and 12 stop right outside the entrance, or walk down buzzy Ilica for 15 minutes.

Hobo Bear Hostel
HOSTEL €

(☑48 46 636; www.hobobearhostel.com; Medulićeva 4; dm/d from 122/400KN; ❄@🖥) Inside a duplex apartment, this sparkling seven-dorm hostel has exposed-brick walls, hardwood floors, free lockers, kitchen, common room and book exchange. Three doubles are across the street.

Krovovi Grada
PENSION €

(☑48 14 189; Opatovina 33; s/d 200/300KN; @🖥) Basic but charming, this restored old house is set back from the street a minute from bustling Tkalčićeva. Rooms have creaky floors, vintage furniture and grandma blankets. Get the upstairs room for vistas of Old Town rooftops.

Fulir Hostel
HOSTEL €

(☑48 30 882; www.fulir-hostel.com; Radićeva 3a; dm 130-140KN; @🖥) Seconds away from Trg Josipa Jelačića, the Fulir has 28 beds, friendly owners, self-catering (it's right by Dolac market), lockers, a DVD-packed common room and free internet, tea and coffee.

Buzzbackpackers
HOSTEL €

(☑23 20 267; www.buzzbackpackers.com; Babukićeva 1b; dm/d from 130/450KN; ❄@🖥) Out of the centre but clean with bright rooms, free internet, a shiny kitchen and a BBQ area. Take tram 4 or 9 from the train station to the Heinzelova stop, from where it's a short walk. The owners also run an apartment-style hostel in the city centre.

Omladinski Hostel HOSTEL €

(☑48 41 261; www.hfhs.hr; Petrinjska 77; 6-/3-bed dm 113KN, s/d 203/286KN; 🛜) Although spruced up not too long ago, this socialist-era spot still maintains a bit of its old gloomy feel. The rooms are sparse and clean; it's central and the cheapest in town.

✗ Eating

You'll have to love Croatian and (below par) Italian food to enjoy Zagreb's restaurants, but new places are branching out to include Japanese and other world cuisines. The biggest move is towards elegantly presented haute cuisine at haute prices, many with a slow-food twist.

You can pick up excellent fresh produce at Dolac market.

TOP CHOICE **Vinodol** CROATIAN €€

(Teslina 10; mains from 70KN) Well-prepared Central European fare much loved by local and overseas patrons. On warm days, eat on the covered patio entered through an ivy-clad passageway off Teslina. Highlights include the succulent lamb or veal and potatoes *under peka* (baked in a coal oven).

Tip Top SEAFOOD €€

(Gundulićeva 18; mains from 55KN; ⊙Mon-Sat) The excellent Dalmatian food is served by wait staff sporting old socialist uniforms. Every day has its own set menu of mainstays; the Thursday octopus goulash is particularly tasty.

Amfora SEAFOOD €

(Dolac 2; mains from 40KN; ⊙to 3pm Mon-Sat, to 1pm Sun) This locals' lunch fave serves super-fresh seafood straight from the market across the way, paired with off-the-stalls veggies. It's a hole-in-the-wall place with a few tables outside and an upstairs gallery with a market vista.

Kerempuh CROATIAN €€

(Kaptol 3; mains from 75KN; ⊙lunch Mon-Sun) Overlooking Dolac market, this is a fabulous place to taste well-cooked and simple Croatian cuisine. The set menu changes daily, according to what the chef picked out at the market.

Prasac MEDITERRANEAN €€€

(☑48 51 411; Vranicanijeva 6; mains from 87KN; ⊙Mon-Sat) Creative Mediterranean fare is conjured up by the Croatian-Sicilian chef at this intimate spot with wooden beamed ceilings. The market-fresh food is superb but the service slow and the portions small. Reserve ahead.

Stari Fijaker 900 CROATIAN €

(Mesnička 6; mains from 50KN; ⊙closed Sun evening summer) Tradition reigns in the kitchen of this restaurant-beer hall with a decor of banquettes and white linen, so try the homemade sausages, bean stews and *štrukli* (dumplings filled with cottage cheese), or one of cheaper daily dishes.

Ivica i Marica CROATIAN €€

(Tkalčićeva 70; mains from 70KN) Based on the Hansel and Gretel story, this restaurant-cake shop is made to look like the gingerbread house from the tale, with waiters clad in traditional costumes. It has veggie and fish dishes plus meatier fare. The cakes and *štrukli* are great.

Konoba Čiho SEAFOOD €€

(Pavla Hatza 15; mains from 80KN) An old-school Dalmatian *konoba* (simple family-run establishment), where, downstairs, you can get fish (by the kilo) and seafood grilled or stewed. Try the wide range of *rakija* (grape brandy) and house wines.

Vallis Aurea CROATIAN €

(Tomićeva 4; mains from 37KN; ⊙Mon-Sat) This true local eatery has some of the best home cooking you'll find in town, so it's no wonder it gets chock-a-block at lunchtime for its *gableci* (traditional lunches). Right by the lower end of the funicular.

Karijola PIZZA €

(Kranjčevićeva 16a; pizzas from 42KN) Locals swear by the thin-crust crispy pizza churned out of a clay oven at this no-frills spot. Pizzas come with high-quality ingredients such as smoked ham, top olive oil, cherry tomatoes, rocket and oyster mushrooms. It's near the Cibona Tower (take tram 12 from the main square, direction Ljubljanica).

Baltazar CROATIAN €€€

(Nova Ves 4; mains from 120KN; ⊙Mon-Sat) Meats – duck, lamb, pork, beef and turkey – are grilled and prepared the Zagorje and Slavonia way in this upmarket old-timer. The summer terrace is the place to dine under the stars.

Nova VEGETARIAN €€

(Ilica 72; mains from 60KN; ⊙Mon-Sat) This elegant macrobiotic restaurant is the place for those of the vegan persuasion, with great-value set menus.

Pingvin SANDWICH STAND €

(Teslina 7; ⊙9am-4am Mon-Sat, 6pm-2am Sun) This quick-bite institution, around since 1987, offers tasty designer sandwiches and salads which locals savour on a handful of bar stools.

Rubelj
FAST FOOD €

(Dolac 2; mains from 25KN) One of the many Rubeljs across town, this Dolac branch is a great place for a quick portion of *ćevapi* (small spicy sausage of minced beef, lamb or pork).

🍷 Drinking

In the Upper Town, the chic Tkalčićeva throbs with bars and cafes. In the Lower Town, Trg Petra Preradovića (known locally as Cvjetni Trg) is the most popular spot for street performers and occasional bands in mild weather. One of the nicest ways to see Zagreb is to join in on the *špica* – Saturday-morning pre-lunch coffee drinking on the terraces along Bogovićeva, Preradovićeva and Tkalčićeva.

TOP CHOICE Bacchus
BAR

(www.bacchusjazzbar.hr; Trg Kralja Tomislava 16) You'll be lucky if you score a table at Zagreb's funkiest courtyard garden – lush and hidden in a passageway. After 10pm, the action moves indoors, inside the artsy subterranean space that hosts jazz concerts, poetry readings and oldies' nights.

Booksa
COFFEE HOUSE

(www.booksa.hr; Martićeva 14d; ⊘11am-8pm Tue-Sun, closed 3 weeks from late Jul) Bookworms and poets, writers and performers, oddballs and artists and other creative types come to chat over coffee, buy books and hear readings at this lovely bookshop. There are English-language readings too. It's a 10-minute stroll east of the main square.

Stross
BAR

(Strossmayerovo Šetalište) From June to September a makeshift bar is set up at the Strossmayer promenade in the Upper Town, with cheap drinks and live music most nights. Come for the mixed-bag crowd, great city views and leafy ambience.

Cica
BAR

(Tkalčićeva 18) This tiny storefront bar is as underground as it gets on Tkalčićeva. Sample one or – if you dare – all of 15 kinds of *rakija* (homemade brandy) that the place is famous for.

Velvet
CAFE

(Dežmanova 9; ⊘8am-10pm Mon-Fri, to 3pm Sat, to 2pm Sun) Stylish spot for a good cup of java and a quick bite amid the minimalist chic interior decked out by owner Saša Šekoranja, Zagreb's hippest florist.

☆ Entertainment

Zagreb doesn't register highly on a nightlife Richter scale, but it does have an ever-developing art and music scene. Its theatres and concert halls present a variety of programs throughout the year. Many are listed in the monthly brochure *Zagreb Events & Performances,* which is available from the main tourist office

Nightclubs

Nightclub entry ranges from 20KN to 100KN. Clubs open around 10pm but most people show up around midnight. Most clubs open only from Thursday to Saturday.

Aquarius
CLUB

(www.aquarius.hr; Jarun Lake) A truly fab place to party, this enormously popular spots opens onto a huge terrace on the lake. During summer, Aquarius sets up shop at Zrće on Pag.

Močvara
CLUB

(www.mochvara.hr, in Croatian; Trnjanski Nasip bb) In a former factory on the banks of the Sava River, 'Swamp' is one of the best venues in town for the cream of alternative music and attractively dingy charm.

KSET
CLUB

(www.kset.org, in Croatian; Unska 3) Located in the neighbourhood of Trnje, this is Zagreb's best music venue, with anyone who's anyone performing here – from ethno to hip-hop acts.

Jabuka
CLUB

(Jabukovac 28) 'Apple' is an old-time favourite, with 1980s hits played to a 30-something crowd that reminisces about the good old days when they were alternative. It's in the leafy residential neighborhood of Tuškanac.

Medika
CLUB

(www.pierottijeva11.org; Pierrotijeva 11) This artsy venue in an old pharmaceutical factory, just to the west of Savska, is the city's first legalized squat, with concerts, art exhibits and parties fuelled with cheap beer.

Purgeraj
CLUB

(www.purgeraj.hr; Park Ribnjak 1) Live rock, blues and avant-garde jazz is on the music menu at this funky space. The popular Saturday night hosts a fusion of disco, funk, pop and '80s.

Gay & Lesbian Venues

The gay and lesbian scene in Zagreb is finally becoming more open than it has previously been, although 'freewheeling' it isn't. Many gay men discreetly cruise the south beach around Jarun Lake and are welcome in most discos.

David
GAY & LESBIAN

(www.sauna-aquateam.hr; Ulica Ivana Broza 8a; ☺5-11pm) This men-only sauna, bar and video room, to the west of Savska, is a popular spot on Zagreb's gay scene. The day ticket is 80KN.

Rush Club
GAY & LESBIAN

(Amruševa 10) A younger gay and lesbian crowd mixes at this fun club in the city centre, with free entry on Thursday and themed nights such as karaoke.

Sport

Basketball is popular in Zagreb, home to Cibona basketball team. Pay homage to the team's most famous player at the **Dražen Petrović Memorial Museum** (✆48 43 333; www.cibona.com; Savska 30; tickets for games 20-100KN), located south along Savska, on a small square just to the west. Games take place frequently; tickets can be purchased at the door or online at www.cibona.com.

Dinamo is Zagreb's most popular football (soccer) team and it plays matches at **Stadion Maksimir** (Maksimirska 128; tickets from 30KN), on the eastern side of Zagreb. Games are played on Sunday afternoons between August and May. Take trams 4, 7, 11 or 12 to Bukovačka.

Performing Arts

Make the rounds of the theatres in person to check their programs. Tickets are usually available for even the best shows.

Croatian National Theatre
THEATRE

(✆48 88 418; www.hnk.hr; Trg Maršala Tita 15) This neo-baroque theatre, established in 1895, stages opera and ballet performances.

Vatroslav Lisinski Concert Hall
LIVE MUSIC

(✆61 21 166; www.lisinski.hr; Trg Stjepana Radića 4) The city's most prestigious venue for symphony concerts, jazz and world music performances. It's tucked away behind the main train station.

Croatian Music Institute
LIVE MUSIC

(✆48 30 822; Gundulićeva 6a) Another good venue for classical music concerts, it often feature Croatian composers performed by Croatian musicians.

Shopping

Ilica is Zagreb's main shopping street.

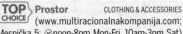 Prostor
CLOTHING & ACCESSORIES

(www.multiracionalnakompanija.com; Mesnička 5; ☺noon-8pm Mon-Fri, 10am-3pm Sat) A fantastic little art gallery and clothes shop, featuring some of the city's best independent artists and young designers. In a courtyard off Mesnička.

Bronić Sisters
CLOTHING

(www.bronic.biz) Don't miss the versatile textured interpretations of multitalented twins Josipa and Marijana, who sell their inspired garments and accessories at their home studio.

Natura Croatica
FOOD & DRINK

(www.naturacroatica.com; Skalinska 2a) All-natural Croatian products and souvenirs – from handcrafted soaps and fragrant bath oils to *rakija*, wines, chocolates, jams and spices.

Sherrif & Cherry
CLOTHING

(www.sheriffandcherry.com; Medvedgradska 3) Snag a par of revamped and super-trendy Yugo-era Startas trainers at this boutique-creative studio headed up by Rovinj-born designer Mauro Massarotto. Continue north along Tkalčićeva for five minutes.

Profil Megastore
BOOKS

(Bogovićeva 7; ☺9am-10pm Mon-Sat) Inside an entryway, this most atmospheric of Zagreb bookstores has a great selection of books (many in English) and a nice cafe.

❶ Information

Discount Cards

Zagreb Card (www.zagrebcard.fivestars.hr; 24/72hr 60/90KN) Provides free travel on all public transport, a 50% discount on museum and gallery entries, plus discounts in some bars and restaurants, and on car rental. The card is sold at the main tourist office and many hostels, hotels, bars and shops.

Emergency

Police (✆45 63 311; Petrinjska 30)

Internet Access

Several cafes around town offer free wi-fi, including Booksa.

Sublink (www.sublink.hr; Teslina 12; per hr 15KN; ☺9am-10pm Mon-Sat, 3-10pm Sun) The city's first cybercafe remains its best.

Left Luggage

Garderoba bus station (1st 4hr 20KN, then per hr 2.50KN; ☺5am-10pm Mon-Sat, 6am-10pm Sun); train station (lockers per 24hr 15KN; ☺24hr)

Medical Services

Dental Emergency (☑48 03 200; Perkovčeva 3; ☺24hr)

KBC Rebro (☑23 88 888; Kišpatićeva 12; ☺24hr) East of the city, it provides emergency aid.

Pharmacy (☑48 16 198; Trg Josipa Jelačića 3; ☺24hr)

Money

There are ATMs at the bus and train stations, the airport, and at numerous locations around town. Some banks in the train and bus stations accept travellers cheques. Exchange offices can be found in many locations around town.

Post

Main post office (☑48 11 090; Jurišićeva 13; ☺7am-8pm Mon-Fri, 7am-1pm Sat) Has a telephone centre.

Tourist Information

Main tourist office (☑48 14 051; www. zagreb-touristinfo.hr; Trg Josipa Jelačića 11; ☺8.30am-9pm Mon-Fri, 9am-6pm Sat & Sun) Distributes free city maps and leaflets, and sells the Zagreb Card.

Plitvice National Park office (☑46 13 586; Trg Kralja Tomislava 19; ☺8am-4pm Mon-Thu, 8am-3.30pm Fri) Has details and brochures mainly on Plitvice but also on Croatia's other national parks.

Seasonal tourist office annex (airport; ☺9am-9pm Mon-Fri, 10am-5pm Sat & Sun Jun-Sep) By International Arrivals.

Tourist office annex (train station; ☺8.30am-8pm Mon-Fri, 12.30-6.30pm Sat & Sun) Same services as the main tourist office.

Travel Agencies

Atlas Travel Agency (☑48 07 300; www. atlas-croatia.com; Zrinjevac 17) Tours around Croatia.

Croatia Express (☑49 22 237; Trg Kralja Tomislava 17) Train reservations, car rental, air and ferry tickets, hotel bookings and a daily trip to the beach from June to September (90KN round trip to Crikvenica).

❶ Getting There & Away

Air

For information about international flights to and from Croatia, see p268.

Zagreb Airport (☑45 62 222; www.zagreb-airport.hr) Located 17km southeast of Zagreb, this is one of the country's major airports, offering a range of international and domestic services.

Bus

Zagreb's **bus station** (☑060 313 333; www. akz.hr; Avenija M Držića 4) is 1km east of the train station. Trams 2, 3 and 6 run from the bus station to the train station. Tram 6 goes to Trg Josipa Jelačića.

Before buying a bus ticket, ask about the arrival time – some of the buses take local roads and stop in every town en route.

International destinations include Belgrade (199KN to 204KN, six hours, six daily), Munich (352KN, 9½ hours, two daily), Sarajevo (188KN to 244KN, seven to eight hours, four to five daily) and Vienna (250KN, five to six hours, two daily).

Train

The **train station** (☑060 333 444; www.hznet. hr) is in the southern part of the city. As you come out of it, you'll see a series of parks and pavilions directly in front of you, which lead into

DOMESTIC BUSES FROM ZAGREB

DESTINATION	FARE (KN)	DURATION (HR)	DAILY SERVICES
Dubrovnik	215-228	9½-11	9-10
Korčula	239	11	1
Krk	163-194	3-4½	8
Mali Lošinj	267-284	5-6	3
Plitvice	72-83	2-2½	11
Poreč	150-221	4-4½	11
Pula	162-185	3½-5½	14-17
Rijeka	104-155	2½-3	20-25
Rovinj	146-185	3-6	9-11
Split	165-181	5-8½	32-34
Zadar	99-138	3½-5	31

INTERNATIONAL TRAINS FROM ZAGREB

DESTINATION	FARE (KN)	DURATION (HR)	DAILY SERVICES
Banja Luka	100	4½	2
Belgrade	159	6½	4
Budapest	223	6-7	3
Ljubljana	100	2½	7
Mostar	282	11½	1
Munich	674	8½-9	3
Plŏe	313	13½	1
Sarajevo	222	9½	2
Venice	303	7½	1
Vienna	446	5½-6½	2

the town centre. It's advisable to book train tickets in advance because of limited seating.

Domestic trains head to Rijeka (97KM, four to five hours, five daily), Split (166KM, 5½ to eight hours, five daily) and Zadar (161KM, eight hours, one daily).

ⓘ Getting Around

Zagreb is a fairly easy city to navigate. Traffic is bearable and the efficient tram system should be a model for other polluted, traffic-clogged European capitals.

To/From the Airport

BUS The Croatia Airlines bus to the airport (30KN) leaves from the bus station every half-hour or hour from about 5am to 8pm, and returns from the airport on the same schedule.

TAXI Costs between 150KN and 300KN.

Car

Zagreb is a fairly easy city to navigate by car (boulevards are wide and parking in the city centre, although scarce, costs 12KN per hour). Watch out for trams buzzing around.

Motorists can call **Hrvatski Autoklub** (HAK; Croatian Auto Club; ☑46 40 800; www.hak. hr; Avenija Dubrovnik 44) on ☑987 for help on the road.

International car-hire companies include **Budget Rent-a-Car** (☑45 54 936; www.budget.hr; 1. Pile 1 and at airport) and **Hertz** (☑48 46 777; www.hertz.hr; Vukotinovićeva 4). Local companies usually have lower rates; try **H&M** (☑37 04 535; www.hm-rentacar.hr; Grahorova 11), which also has a desk at the airport.

Public Transport

Public transport is based on an efficient network of trams, although the city centre is compact enough to make them unnecessary.

Buy tickets at newspaper kiosks for 8KN. Tickets can be used for transfers within 90 minutes, but only in one direction. Note that you can ride the tram for free two stations in each direction from the main square.

A *dnevna karta* (day ticket), valid on all public transport until 4am the next morning, is available for 25KN at most newspaper kiosks.

Make sure you validate your ticket when you get on the tram by inserting it in the yellow box.

Taxi

Zagreb's taxis all have meters, which begin at 19KN and then ring up 7KN per kilometre. On Sunday and at night (10pm to 5am) there's a 20% surcharge. Waiting time is 50KN per hour. The baggage surcharge is 3KN per bag.

You'll have no trouble finding idle taxis, usually at blue-marked taxi stops, or you can call for one at ☑060 800 800.

ISTRIA

☑052

Continental Croatia meets the Adriatic in Istria (Istra to Croats), the heart-shaped 3600-sq-km peninsula just south of Trieste in Italy. While the bucolic interior of rolling hills and fertile plains attracts artsy visitors to its hilltop villages, rural hotels and farmhouse restaurants, the verdant indented coastline is enormously popular with the sun'n'sea set. Vast hotel complexes line much of the coast and its rocky beaches are not Croatia's best, but the facilities are wide-ranging, the sea is clean and secluded spots are still plentiful.

The coast, or 'Blue Istria', as the tourist board calls it, gets flooded with tourists in summer, but you can still feel alone and undisturbed in 'Green Istria' (the interior), even in mid-August. Add acclaimed gastronomy (starring fresh seafood, prime white truffles, wild asparagus, top-rated olive oils and award-winning wines), sprinkle it with historical charm and you have a little slice of heaven.

Poreč

POP 17,460

Poreč (Parenzo in Italian) sits on a low, narrow peninsula halfway down the western coast of Istria. The ancient Roman town is the centrepiece of a vast system of resorts that stretch north and south, entirely devoted to summer tourism. While this is not the place for a quiet getaway (unless you come out of season), there is a World Heritage–listed basilica, a medley of Gothic, Romanesque and baroque buildings, well-developed tourist infrastructure and the pristine Istrian interior within easy reach.

◉ Sights

The compact Old Town, called Parentium by the Romans, is based on a rectangular street plan. The ancient Decumanus with its polished stones is the main street running through the peninsula's middle, lined with shops and restaurants. Hotels, travel agencies and excursion boats are on the quay, Obala Maršala Tita, which runs from the small-boat harbour to the tip of the peninsula.

Euphrasian Basilica   CHURCH
(Eufrazijeva bb; admission free, belfry 10KN; ☉7am-8pm Apr–mid-Oct or by appointment) The main reason to visit Poreč is the 6th-century Euphrasian Basilica, one of Europe's finest intact examples of Byzantine art. What packs in the crowds are the glittering wall mosaics in the apse, veritable masterpieces featuring biblical scenes, archangels and martyrs. The belfry affords an invigorating view of the Old Town.

Also worth a visit is the adjacent **Bishop's Palace** (admission 10KN; ☉10am-7pm Apr–mid-Oct or by appointment), which contains a display of ancient stone sculptures, religious paintings and 4th-century mosaics from the original oratory.

Trg Marafor   SQUARE
Trg Marafor is where the Roman forum used to stand and public gatherings took place. West of this rectangular square, inside a small park, are the ruins of the 2nd-century **Temple of Neptune**, dedicated to the god of sea.

Sveti Nikola   ISLAND
From May to October passenger boats (adult/child 20/10KN) travel to Sveti Nikola, the small island that lies opposite Poreč harbour. They depart every 30 minutes (from 6.45am to 1am) from the wharf on Obala Maršala Tita.

🏃 Activities

Many recreational activities are to be found outside the town in either Plava Laguna or Zelena Laguna. For details, pick up the annual *Poreč Info* booklet from the tourist office.

From May to early October, a tourist train operates regularly from Šetalište Antuna Štifanića by the marina to Plava Laguna (15KN) and Zelena Laguna (15KN). An hourly passenger boat makes the same run from the ferry landing (15KN).

The well-marked paths make **cycling** and **hiking** a prime way to explore the region. The tourist office issues a free map of roads and trails. You can rent a bike at agencies around town for about 70KN per day.

There is good **diving** in and around shoals and sandbanks in the area, as well as at the nearby *Coriolanus*, a British Royal Navy warship that sank in 1945. At **Diving Centre Poreč** (☑433 606; www.divingcenter-porec.com), boat dives start at 110KN (more for caves or wrecks) or 310KN with full equipment rental.

🛏 Sleeping

Accommodation in Poreč is plentiful but gets booked ahead of time, so advance reservations are essential if you come in July or August.

If you want to find private accommodation, consult the travel agencies we've listed (p132). Expect to pay between 200KN and 250KN for a double room in the high season or 280KN to 350KN for a two-person apartment, plus a 30% surcharge for stays of less than four nights. There are a limited number of rooms in the Old Town, where there's no parking. Look for the *Domus Bonus* certificate of quality in private accommodation.

Valamar Riviera Hotel   LUXURY HOTEL €€€
(☑408 000; www.valamar.com; Obala Maršala Tita 15; s 990-1400KN; d 1300-1990KN; P❋@) This new harbourfront property is a swanky four-star choice, with a private beach on Sveti Nikola. Look out for specials and packages.

Hotel Hostin
HOTEL €€

(☎408 800; www.hostin.hr; Rade Končara 4; s/d 683/966KN; P❄@☲) At this charmer, in verdant parkland steps from the bus station, each room has a balcony. There's an indoor swimming pool, and a pebble beach only 70m away.

Hotel Poreč
HOTEL €

(☎451 811; www.hotelporec.com; Rade Končara 1; s/d 475/720KN;❄) While the rooms inside this concrete box have uninspiring views over the bus station and the shopping centre opposite, they're acceptable and an easy walk from the Old Town.

Camp Zelena Laguna
CAMPING GROUND €

(☎410 700; www.plavalaguna.hr; Zelena Laguna; per adult/campsite 55/77KN; ☺Apr-Sep; ☲) Well equipped for sports, this camping ground 5km from the Old Town can house up to 2700 people. It has access to many beaches, including a naturist one.

✖ Eating

A large supermarket and department store are situated next to Hotel Poreč, near the bus station.

Peterokutna Kula
INTERNATIONAL €€

(Decumanus 1; mains from 70KN) Inside the medieval Pentagonal Tower, this upmarket restaurant has two alfresco patios in a stone vault, and a roof terrace. It serves a full spectrum of fish and meat but has erratic service.

Dva Ferala
ISTRIAN €

(Obala Maršala Tita 13a; mains from 60KN) Savour well-prepared Istrian specialities, such as *istarski tris* for two – a copious trio of homemade pastas – on the terrace of this pleasant *konoba*.

Nono
PIZZA €

(Zagrebačka 4; pizzas 40-80KN) Nono serves the best pizza in town, with puffy crusts and toppings such as truffles. Other dishes are tasty too.

Buffet Horizont
SEAFOOD €

(Eufrazijeva 8; mains from 30KN) For cheap and tasty seafood snacks like sardines, shrimp and calamari, look out for this yellow house with wooden benches outside.

♟ Drinking & Entertainment

Lapidarium
BAR

(Svetog Maura 10) This gorgeous bar with a large courtyard has a series of antique-filled inner rooms. Wednesday is jazz night in summer, with alfresco live music.

Byblos
CLUB

(www.byblos.hr; Zelena Laguna bb) On Fridays, celeb guest DJs such as David Morales crank out house tunes at this humongous open-air club, one of Croatia's hottest places to party.

Torre Rotonda
CAFE-BAR

(Narodni Trg 3a) Take the steep stairs to the top of the historic Round Tower and grab a table at the open-air cafe to watch the action on the quays.

❶ Information

You can change money at any of the many travel agencies or banks. There are ATMs all around town.

Atlas Travel Agency (☎434 933; www.atlas -croatia.com; Eufrazijeva 63) Books excursions.

CyberM@c (Mire Grahalića 1; per hr 42KN; ☺10am-10pm) A full-service computer centre.

Di Tours (☎432 100; www.di-tours.hr; Prvomajska 2) Finds private accommodation.

Left luggage (per hour 6KN; ☺7am-8.30pm) At the bus station.

Medical Centre (☎451 611; Maura Gioseffija 2)

Post office (Trg Slobode 14; ☺8am-noon & 6-8pm Mon-Fri, 8am-noon Sat) Has a telephone centre.

Sunny Way (☎452 021; sunnyway@pu.t-com. hr; Alda Negrija 1) Specialises in boat tickets and excursions to Italy and around Croatia.

Tourist office (☎451 293; www.to-porec.com; Zagrebačka 9; ☺8am-9pm Mon-Sat, 9am-1pm & 6-9pm Sun)

❶ Getting There & Away

From the **bus station** (☎432 153; Rade Končara 1) just outside the Old Town, behind Rade Končara, there are buses to Rovinj (42KN, 45 minutes, six daily), Zagreb (218KN, four hours, seven daily), Rijeka (85KN, two hours, seven daily) and Pula (54KN, one to 1½ hours, eight daily).

There are four fast catamarans to Venice daily in high season (two hours) by **Commodore Cruises** (www.commodore-cruises.hr), **Astarea** (☎451 100) and **Venezia Lines** (www.venezia lines.com). Prices range from 225KN to 474KN for a one-way journey, and 300KN to 880KN for return trip. **Ustica Line** (www.usticalines.it) runs catamarans to Trieste every day except Monday (160KN, 1½ hours).

Rovinj
POP 14,234

Rovinj (Rovigno in Italian) is coastal Istria's star attraction. While it can get overrun with tourists in the summer months and residents are developing a sharp eye for maximising their profits (by upgrading the hotels and restaurants to four-star status), it remains one of the last true Mediterranean fishing ports. Fishermen haul their catch into the harbour in the early morning, followed by a horde of squawking gulls, and mend their nets before lunch.

The massive Church of St Euphemia, with its 60m-high tower, punctuates the peninsula. Wooded hills and low-rise hotels surround the Old Town, which is webbed by steep, cobbled streets and piazzas. The 13 green, offshore islands of the Rovinj archipelago make for a pleasant afternoon away, and you can swim from the rocks in the sparkling water below Hotel Rovinj.

◎ Sights

The Old Town of Rovinj is contained within an egg-shaped peninsula, with the bus station just to the southeast. There are two harbours – the northern open harbour and the small, protected harbour to the south.

Church of St Euphemia   CHURCH
(Sveta Eufemija; Petra Stankovića; ⊙10am-6.30pm May-Oct, sporadic hours rest of year) The town's showcase is the imposing Church of St Euphemia that dominates the Old Town from its hilltop location. Built in 1736, it's the largest baroque building in Istria, reflecting the period during the 18th century when Rovinj was its most populous town, an important fishing centre and the bulwark of the Venetian fleet.

Inside the church behind the right-hand altar, don't miss the marble **tomb of St Euphemia**, Rovinj's patron saint martyred in AD 304, whose body mysteriously appeared in Rovinj according to legend. The mighty 60m **bell tower** is topped by a copper statue of St Euphemia, which shows the direction of the wind by turning on a spindle. You can climb it for 10KN.

Batana House   MUSEUM
(Pina Budicina 2; adult/child 10/5KN, with guide 15KN; ⊙10am-3pm & 7-11pm Jun-Aug, 10am-1pm Tue-Sun Sep-May, closed Jan & Feb) On the harbour, Batana House is a multimedia museum dedicated to the *batana,* a flat-bottomed fishing boat that stands as a symbol of Rovinj's seafaring and fishing tradition.

Grisia   HISTORIC AREA
Lined with galleries where local artists sell their work, this cobbled street leads uphill from behind the elaborate 1679 **Balbi Arch** to St Euphemia. The winding narrow back-streets around Grisia are an attraction in themselves. Windows, balconies, portals and squares are a pleasant confusion of styles – Gothic, Renaissance, baroque and neoclassical. On the second Sunday in August each year, Grisia becomes an open-air **art exhibition**, with anyone from children to professional painters displaying their work.

Heritage Museum   MUSEUM
(www.muzej-rovinj.com; Trg Maršala Tita 11; adult/concession 15/10KN; ⊙10am-2pm & 6-10pm Tue-Fri, 10am-2pm Sat & Sun) In a baroque palace, it contains a collection of contemporary art and old masters from Croatia and Rovinj, as well as archaeological finds and a maritime section. Hours are shorter outside summer.

Punta Corrente Forest Park   PARK
Follow the waterfront on foot or by bike past Hotel Park to this verdant area, locally known as Zlatni Rat, about 1.5km south. It's covered in oak and pine groves and boasts 10 species of cypress. You can swim off the rocks or just sit and admire the offshore islands.

⚑ Activities

Most people hop aboard a boat for **swimming**, **snorkelling** and **sunbathing**. In summer, there are hourly boats to Sveta Katarina (return 30KN, 10 minutes) and to Crveni Otok (return 40KN, 15 minutes). They leave from just opposite Hotel Adriatic and also from the Delfin ferry dock near Hotel Park.

Nadi Scuba Diving Centar (☏813 290; www.scuba.hr) and **Petra** (☏812 880; www.diving petra.hr) offer daily boat dives. The main attraction is the **Baron Gautsch wreck**, a 1914 Austrian passenger steamer sunk in 40m of water.

Biking around Rovinj and the Punta Corrente Forest Park is a superb way to spend an afternoon. You can rent bikes at many agencies around town, for about 20KN per hour or 60KN per day.

☞ Tours

Most travel agencies in Rovinj sell day trips to Venice (400KN to 500KN), Plitvice (550KN to 600KN) and Brijuni (380KN to 430KN). There are also fish picnics (250KN), panoramic cruises (100KN) and boat outings to Limska Draga Fjord (150KN). These can be slightly cheaper if booked through one of the independent operators that line the waterfront; **Delfin** (☏848 265) is reliable.

For kayaking, such as an 8km jaunt around the Rovinj archipelago, book a trip through **Istrian Kayak Adventures** (☑095 838 3797; Carera 69).

🛏 Sleeping

Rovinj has become Istria's destination of choice for hordes of summertime tourists, so reserving in advance is strongly recommended. Prices have been rising steadily and probably will continue to do so.

If you want to stay in private accommodation, there is little available in the Old Town, plus there is no parking and the cost is higher. Double rooms start at 220KN in the high season, with a small discount for single occupancy; two-person apartments start at 330KN. Out of season, prices go down considerably.

The surcharge for a stay of less than three nights is up to 50% and guests who stay only one night are sometimes punished with a 100% surcharge during summer months. You can book directly through a travel agency.

Except for a few private options, most hotels and camping grounds in the area are managed by **Maistra** (www.maistra.com), including Rovinj's swankiest hotel, **Monte Mulini** (www.montemulinihotel.com).

TOP CHOICE **Hotel Heritage Angelo D'Oro**
BOUTIQUE HOTEL €€€
(☑840 502; www.rovinj.at; Via Švalba 38-42; s/d 916/1580KN; P❋❋🛜) In a renovated Venetian townhouse, the 23 plush rooms and suites of this boutique hotel have lots of antiques plus mod cons aplenty. There's a tanning room, bikes for rent and a lush interior terrace, a great place for a drink amid ancient stone.

Casa Garzotto GUEST HOUSE €€
(☑814 255; www.casa-garzotto.com; Via Garzotto 8; s/d 758/1010KN;P❋🛜) Each of the four studio apartments inside this historic town house has original details like fireplaces and wooden beams. There are two annexes nearby: one with more basic rooms (650KN) and another with four-person apartments (1440KN).

Vila Lili HOTEL €€
(☑840 940; www.hotel-vilalili.hr; Mohorovičića 16; s/d 380/788KN;❋@) Bright rooms have all the three-star perks, including air-con and minibars, in a small modern house a short walk out of town. There are also a couple of pricier suites.

Hotel Adriatic HOTEL €€
(☑803 510; www.maistra.com; Pina Budicina bb; s/d 676/1007KN;❋@🛜) The location right on the harbour is excellent and the rooms spick-and-span and well equipped, but on the kitschy side. The pricier sea-view rooms have more space.

Porton Biondi CAMPING GROUND €
(☑813 557; www.portonbiondi.hr; per person/tent 41/24KN; ☺Mar-Oct) This camping ground that sleeps 1200 is about 2km from the Old Town.

🍴 Eating

Most of the restaurants that line the harbour offer the standard fish and meat mainstays at similar prices. For a more gourmet experience, you'll need to bypass the water vistas. Note that many restaurants shut their doors between lunch and dinner.

Picnickers can get supplies at the supermarket next to the bus station or at one of the Konzum stores around town.

TOP CHOICE **Ulika** ISTRIAN €€
(Vladimira Švalbe 34; mains from 80KN) For an evening snack of local cheese, cured meats and tasty small bites, head to this tiny tavern a few doors down from Angelo D'Oro.

Kantinon SEAFOOD €
(Alda Rismonda 18; mains from 53KN) A fishing theme runs through this high-ceilinged canteen that specialises in fresh seafood at low prices. The Batana fish plate for two is great value, as are the set menus.

La Puntulina MEDITERRANEAN €€€
(☑813 186; Svetog Križa 38; mains from 100KN) Sample creative Med cuisine on three alfresco terraces. Pasta dishes are more affordable (from 80KN). At night, grab a cushion and sip a cocktail on the rocks below this converted townhouse. Reservations recommended.

Veli Jože SEAFOOD €
(Svetog Križa 3; mains from 50KN) Graze on good Istrian standards, either in the eclectic interior crammed with knick-knacks or at the outdoor tables with water views.

🍷 Drinking & Entertainment

While there are plenty of spots for a quiet drink during the day, come night most action takes place at **Monvi Centar** (www.monvicenter.com; Luja Adamovića bb), a stroll out of the centre. This entertainment complex has lounge bars, restaurants and clubs that regularly host open-air concerts and celebrity DJs.

Havana BAR
(Aldo Negri bb) Tropical cocktails, Cuban cigars, straw parasols and the shade of tall pine trees make this open-air cocktail bar

DESTINATION	FARE (KN)	DURATION	DAILY SERVICES
Dubrovnik	589	15hr	1
Labin	80	2hr	3
Poreč	41	45min	11
Pula	38	50min	23
Rijeka	94	3hr	8
Split	416	11hr	1
Trieste, Italy	88	2hr	3
Zagreb	193	5hr	10

a popular spot to chill and watch the ships go by.

Piassa Granda   WINE BAR
(Veli Trg 1) This stylish little wine bar with red walls and wooden beamed ceilings has 150 wine labels, mainly Istrian. Try the truffle grappa and the delicious snacks and salads.

Valentino   BAR
(Svetog Križa 28) Premium cocktail prices on the terrace of this high-end cocktail and champagne spot include fantastic sunset views, on the water's edge.

❶ Information
There's an ATM next to the bus-station entrance, and banks all around town. Most travel agencies will change money.

Futura Travel (☑817 281; www.futura-travel.hr; Matteo Benussi 2) Private accommodation, money exchange, excursions and transfers.

Globtour (☑814 130; www.globtour-turizam.hr; Alda Rismonda 2) Excursions, private accommodation and bike rental.

Left luggage (per day 6KN; ☺6am-8pm Mon-Fri, 7.45am-7.30pm Sat & Sun) *Garderoba* is at the bus station. Note the half-hour breaks at 9.15am and 4.40pm.

Medical Centre (☑813 004; Istarska bb)

Planet (☑840 494; www.planetrovinj.com; Svetog Križa 1) Doubles has a internet cafe (6KN per 10 minutes) and has a printer. Good bargains on private accommodation, too.

Post office (Matteo Benussi 4; ☺7am-8pm Mon-Fri, to 2pm Sat)

Tourist office (☑811 566; www.tzgrovinj.hr; Pina Budicina 12; ☺8am-10pm Jun-Sep, 8am-3pm Mon-Fri, 8am-1pm Sat Oct-May) Just off Trg Maršala Tita, it has plenty of brochures and maps.

❶ Getting There & Away
The bus station is just to the southeast of the Old Town.

Pula
POP 60,000

The wealth of Roman architecture makes the otherwise workaday Pula (ancient Polensium) a standout among Croatia's larger cities. The star of the Roman show is the remarkably well-preserved Roman amphitheatre, which dominates the streetscape and doubles as a venue for summer concerts and performances. Historical attractions aside, Pula is a busy commercial city on the sea that has managed to retain a friendly small-town appeal. A series of beaches and good nightlife are just a short bus ride away at the resorts that occupy the Verudela Peninsula to the south. Further south along the indented shoreline, the Premantura Peninsula hides a spectacular nature area, the protected cape of Kamenjak.

❍ Sights
The oldest part of the city follows the ancient Roman plan of streets circling the central citadel. Most sights are clustered in and around the Old Town, as well as on Giardini, Carrarina and Istarska as well as the Riva, which runs along the harbour.

Roman Amphitheatre   ANCIENT SITE
(Arena; Flavijevska bb; adult/concession 40/20KN; ☺8am-9pm summer, 9am-8pm spring & autumn, 9am-5pm winter) Pula's most famous and imposing sight is this 1st-century amphitheatre overlooking the harbour northeast of the Old Town. Built entirely from local limestone, the amphitheatre with seating for up

to 20,000 spectators was designed to host gladiatorial contests. In the chambers downstairs is a small **museum** with a display of ancient olive oil equipment. Every summer the **Pula Film Festival** is held here, as are pop and classical concerts.

Temple of Augustus   RUINS

(Forum; adult/concession 10/5KN; ⏰9am-8pm Mon-Fri, 10am-3pm Sat & Sun summer, or by appointment) This is the only visible remnant from the Roman era on Forum, Pula's central meeting place from antiquity through the Middle Ages. This temple, erected from

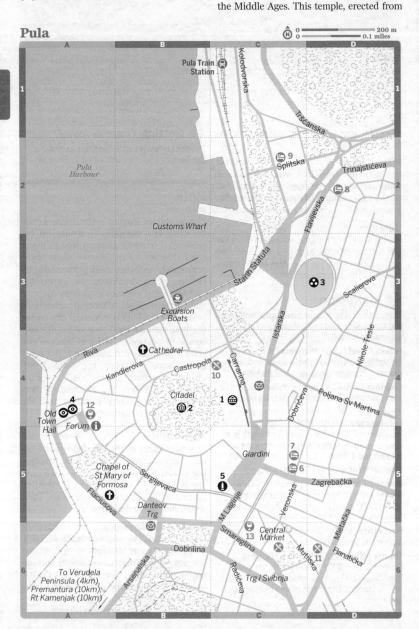

Pula

2 BC to AD 14, now houses a small historical museum with captions in English.

Archaeological Museum   MUSEUM
(Arheološki Muzej; Carrarina 3; adult/concession 20/10KN; ⊙9am-8pm Mon-Sat, 10am-3pm Sun May-Sep, 9am-2pm Mon-Fri Oct-Apr) This museum presents archaeological finds from all over Istria. Even if you don't enter the museum, be sure to visit the large **sculpture garden** around it, and the **Roman theatre** behind. The garden, entered through 2nd-century twin gates, is the site of concerts in summer.

Triumphal Arch of Sergius   RUINS
Along Carrarina are Roman walls, which mark the eastern boundary of old Pula. Follow these walls south and continue down Giardini to this majestic arch erected in 27 BC to commemorate three members of the Sergius family who achieved distinction in Pula.

Museum of History   MUSEUM
(Povijesni Muzej Istre; Gradinski Uspon 6; adult/concession 15/7KN; ⊙8am-9pm Jun-Sep, 9am-5pm Oct-May) In a 17th-century Venetian fortress on a hill above the Old Town's centre, it has meagre exhibits that deal mostly with the maritime history of Pula, but the views from the citadel walls are worth a stop.

Beaches
Pula is surrounded by a half-circle of rocky beaches, each one with its own fan club. The most tourist-packed are undoubtedly

those surrounding the hotel complex on the **Verudela Peninsula**, although some locals will dare to be seen at the small turquoise-coloured **Hawaii Beach** near the Hotel Park.

For seclusion, head out to the wild **Rt Kamenjak** (www.kamenjak.hr, in Croatian; pedestrians & cyclists free, per car/scooter 25/15KN; ⊙7am-10pm) on the Premantura Peninsula, 10km south of town. Istria's southernmost point, this gorgeous, entirely uninhabited cape has wildflowers (including 30 species of orchid), 30km of virgin beaches and coves, and a delightful beach bar, **Safari** (snacks 25-50KN; ⊙May-Sep), half-hidden in the bushes near the beach, about 3.5km from the entrance to the park. Watch out for strong currents if swimming off the southern cape.

Windsurf Bar (www.windsurfing.hr) in Premantura rents bikes and windsurfing equipment (board and sail from 70KN per hour). Take bus 26 from Pula to Premantura (15KN), then rent a bike to get inside the park.

🏃 Activities
At the **Orca Diving Center** (📞224 422; Hotel Histria) on the Verudela Peninsula, you can arrange boat and wreck dives. In addition to windsurfing, **Windsurf Bar** (📞091 512 3646; www.windsurfing.hr; Camping Village Stupice) in Premantura offers biking (250KN) and kayaking (300KN) excursions.

An easy 41km **cycling trail** from Pula to Medulin follows the path of Roman gladiators. Check out **Istria Bike** (www.istria-bike.com), a tourist board–run website outlining trails, packages and agencies that offer biking trips.

🛏 Sleeping
Pula's peak tourist season runs from the second week of July to late August. During this period it's wise to make advance reservations. The tip of the Verudela Peninsula, 4km southwest of the city centre, has been turned into a vast tourist complex replete with hotels and apartments.

Any travel agency can give you information and book you into one of the hotels, or you can contact **Arenaturist** (📞529 400; www.arenaturist.hr; Splitska 1a).

The travel agencies in Pula can find you private accommodation, but there is little available in the town centre. Count on paying from 250KN to 490KN for a double room and from 300KN to 535KN for a two-person apartment. You can also browse the list of private accommodation at www.pulainfo.hr.

Hotel Scaletta
HOTEL €€

(☎541 599; www.hotel-scaletta.com; Flavijevska 26; s/d 505/732KN;❄️🅿️🛜) There's a friendly family vibe here, the recently spruced up rooms have tasteful decor and a bagful of trimmings (such as minibars), and the restaurant serves decent food. Plus it's just a hop and a skip from town.

Hotel Galija
HOTEL €€

(☎383 802; www.hotelgalija.hr; Epulonova 3; s/d 505/732KN;❄️🛜) A stone's throw from the market in the town centre, this small family-run hotel has comfortably outfitted rooms that come in different sizes and colours, some with hydromassage showers.

Hotel Omir
HOTEL €

(☎218 186; www.hotel-omir.com; Dobricheva 6; s/d 450/600KN;🛜) The best budget option smack in the heart of town, Hotel Omir has modest but clean and quiet rooms with TV. The more expensive units have air-con. There's no elevator.

Riviera Guest House
HOTEL €

(☎211 166; www.arenaturist.hr; Splitska 1; s/d 350/555KN) This once grand property in a neo-baroque 19th-century building is in dire need of a thorough overhaul. The saving grace: it's in the centre and the front rooms have water views.

Youth Hostel
HOSTEL €

(☎391 133; www.hfhs.hr; Valsaline 4; dm 117KN, caravan 137KN;@) This hostel overlooks a beach in Valsaline Bay, 3km south of central Pula. There are dorms and caravans split into two tiny four-bed units, each with bathroom. To get here, take bus 2A or 3A to the 'Piramida' stop, walk back towards the city to the first street, then turn left and look for the hostel sign.

Camping Stoja
CAMPING GROUND €

(☎387 144; www.arenacamps.com; Stoja 37; per person/tent 57/34KN; ☺Apr-Oct) The closest camping ground to Pula, 3km southwest of the centre, has lots of space on the shady promontory, with a restaurant and diving centre. Take bus 1 to Stoja.

🍴 Eating

There are a number of decent eating places in the city centre, although most locals head out of town for better value and fewer tourists.

TOP CHOICE ⟩ Milan
MEDITERRANEAN €€

(www.milan1967.hr; Stoja 4; mains from 70KN) An exclusive vibe, seasonal speciali-

ties, four sommeliers and even an olive-oil expert on staff all create one of the city's best dining experiences. The five-course fish menu is well worth it.

Vodnjanka
ISTRIAN €

(Vitezića 4; mains from 40KN; ☺closed Sat dinner & Sun) Locals swear by the real-deal home cooking at this cash-only no-frills spot. Its small menu concentrates on simple Istrian dishes. To get here, walk south on Radićeva to Vitezića.

Konoba Batelina
SEAFOOD €€

(Cimulje 25, Banjole; mains from 70KN; ☺dinner) The superb food that awaits at this family-run tavern is worth a trek to the village of Banjole, 3km east of Pula. The owner, fisherman and chef David Skoko, dishes out seafood that's some of the best, most creative and lovingly prepared you'll find in Istria.

Kantina
INTERNATIONAL €€

(Flanatička 16; mains from 70KN; ☺Mon-Sat) The beamed stone cellar of this Habsburg building has been redone in a modern style. The ravioli Kantina, stuffed with *skuta* (ricotta) and prosciutto, are delicious.

Jupiter
PIZZA €

(Castropola 42; pizzas 25-84KN) The thin crusts here would make any Italian mama proud; the pasta is yummy, too. There's a terrace upstairs and a 20% discount on Wednesday.

🍸 Drinking & Entertainment

You should try to catch a concert in the spectacular amphitheatre; the tourist office has schedules. Although most of the nightlife is out of the town centre, in mild weather the cafes on the Forum and along the pedestrian streets Kandlerova, Flanatička and Sergijevaca are lively people-watching spots.

TOP CHOICE ⟩ Scandal Express
CAFE-BAR

(Ciscuttijeva 15) Mingle with a mixed-bag crowd of locals at this popular gathering spot with a cool train carriage vibe, lots of posters and smoking allowed.

Cabahia
BAR

(Širolina 4) This artsy hideaway in Veruda has a cosy wood-beamed interior, eclectic decor, dim lighting, South American flair and a great garden terrace out the back. It hosts concerts and gets packed on weekends.

Rojc
ART CENTRE

(Gajeva 3) For the most underground experience, check the program at this converted army barracks, just south of the city centre,

DESTINATION	FARE (KN)	DURATION	DAILY SERVICES
Dubrovnik	557	15hr	1
Poreč	50-65	1-1½hr	14
Rovinj	35	45min	20
Split	387-392	10hr	3
Zadar	255	7hr	3
Zagreb	170-216	4-5½hr	15

that houses a multimedia art centre and art studios with occasional concerts, exhibitions and other events.

Cvajner CAFE
(Forum 2) Snag a prime alfresco table at this artsy cafe right on the buzzing Forum and check out rotating exhibits in the funky interior that showcases works by up-and-coming local artists.

❶ Information

Active Travel Istra (☑215 497; www.activa-istra.com; Scalierova 1) Excursions around Istria, adventure trips and concert tickets.

Hospital (☑376 548; Zagrebačka 34)

IstrAction (☑383 369; www.istraction.com; Prilaz Monte Cappelletta 3) Offers half-day tours to Kamenjak and around Pula's fortifications as well as medieval-themed full-day excursions around Istria.

Left luggage (Garderoba; per hr 2.50KN; ⊙4am-10.30pm Mon-Sat, 5am-10.30pm Sun) At the bus station, however, hours are unreliable.

Main post office (Danteov Trg 4; ⊙7.30am-7pm Mon-Fri, to 2.30pm Sat) You can make long-distance calls here. Check out the cool staircase inside!

MMC Luka (Istarska 30; per hr 25KN; ⊙8am-midnight Mon-Fri, 8am-3pm Sat) Internet access.

Tourist Ambulance (Flanatička 27; ⊙8am-9.30pm Mon-Fri Jul & Aug)

Tourist information centre (☑212 987; www.pulainfo.hr; Forum 3; ⊙8am-9pm Mon-Fri, 9am-9pm Sat & Sun) Knowledgeable staff here provide maps, brochures and schedules of events in Pula and around Istria. Pick up *Domus Bonus*, a booklet listing the best-quality private accommodation in Istria.

❶ Getting There & Away

Boat

Pula's harbor is located west of the bus station. **Jadroagent** (☑210 431; www.jadroagent.hr;

Riva 14; ⊙7am-3pm Mon-Fri) has schedules and tickets for boats connecting Istria with the islands and south of Croatia.

Commodore Cruises (☑211 631; www.commodore-travel.hr; Riva 14) sells tickets for a catamaran between Pula and Zadar (100KN, five hours), which runs five times weekly from July through early September and twice weekly in June and late September. There's a Wednesday boat service to Venice (430KN, 3½ hours) between June and September.

Bus

From the Pula **bus station** (☑060 304 091; Trg 1 Istarske Brigade bb), located 500m northeast of the town centre, there are buses heading to Rijeka (77KN to 88KN, two hours) almost hourly. In summer, reserve a seat a day in advance.

Train

The train station is near the sea, less than 1km north of town. There is one direct train daily to Ljubljana (144KN, 4½ hours) and three to Zagreb (140KN, nine hours), but you must board a bus for part of the trip, from Lupoglav to Rijeka.

❶ Getting Around

The city buses of use to visitors are 1, which runs to Camping Stoja, and 2A and 3A to Verudela. The frequency varies from every 15 minutes to every half-hour (from 5am to 11.30pm). Tickets are sold at *tisak* (newsstands) for 6KN, or 11KN from the driver.

KVARNER REGION

☑051

The Kvarner Gulf (Quarnero in Italian) covers 3300 sq km between Rijeka and Pag Island in the south, protected by the Velebit Range in the southeast, the Gorski Kotar in the east and the Učka massif in the northwest. Covered with luxuriant forests, lined with beaches and dotted with islands, the region has a mild gentle climate and a wealth of vegetation.

The metropolitan focus is the busy commercial port of Rijeka, Croatia's third-largest city, only a few kilometres from the aristocratic Opatija Riviera. The islands of Krk, Rab, Cres and Lošinj offer picture-perfect Old Towns just a ferry ride away, as well as plenty of beaches for scenic swimming.

Rijeka

POP 137,860

While Rijeka (Fiume in Italian) doesn't quite fit the bill as a tourist destination, it does offer an insightful glimpse into the workaday life of Croatia's largest port. Most people rush through en route to the islands or Dalmatia but, for those who pause, a few assets await. Blend in with the coffee-sipping locals on the bustling Korzo pedestrian strip, stroll along the tree-lined promenade that fronts the harbour, and visit the imposing hilltop fortress of Trsat. Rijeka also boasts a burgeoning nightlife, and hosts Croatia's biggest and most colourful Carnival celebration every year.

Much of the centre contains the ornate, imposing public buildings you would expect to find in Vienna or Budapest, evidence of the strong Austro-Hungarian influence. The industrial aspect is evident from the boats, cargo and cranes that line the waterfront. As one of Croatia's most important transportation hubs, Rijeka has buses, trains and ferries that connect Istria and Dalmatia with Zagreb.

Korzo runs through the city centre, roughly parallel to Riva (seafront). The intercity bus station is at the western edge of Riva. The train station is a five-minute walk west of the intercity bus station, along Krešimirova.

◎ Sights

Trsat Castle & Church CASTLE
(adult/concession 15/5KN; ⊘9am-8pm May-Oct, to 5pm Nov-Apr) High on a hill above the city is this semi-ruined 13th-century fortress that houses two galleries and great vistas from the open-air cafe. During the summer, the fortress features concerts and theatre performances. The other hill highlight is the **Church of Our Lady of Trsat** (Crkva Gospe Trsatske; Frankopanski Trg; ⊘8am-5pm), a centuries-old magnet for believers that showcases an apparently miraculous icon of Virgin Mary.

City Tower MONUMENT
Rijeka's main orientation point is this distinctive yellow tower on the Korzo, originally a gate from the seafront to the city and one of the few monuments to have survived the devastating earthquake of 1750.

Maritime & History Museum MUSEUM
(Pomorski i Povijesni Muzej Hrvatskog Primorja; www.ppmhp.hr; Muzejski Trg 1; adult/concession 10/5KN; ⊘9am-8pm Mon-Fri, to 1pm Sat) Housed in the Hungarian-style Governor's Palace, this museum gives a vivid picture of life among seafarers, with model ships, sea charts, navigation instruments and portraits of captains.

Astronomical Centre ASTRONOMICAL CENTRE
(Astronomski Centar; www.rijekasport.hr; Sveti Križ 33; ⊘8am-11pm Tue-Sat) High on a hill in the city's east, Croatia's first astronomical centre is a striking modern complex encompassing an observatory, planetarium and study centre. Catch bus 7A from the centre.

Museum of Modern & Contemporary Art MUSEUM
(Muzej Moderne i Suvremene Umjetnosti; www.mmsu.hr; Dolac 1; adult/concession 10/5KN; ⊘10am-1pm & 6-9pm Mon-Fri, 10am-1pm Sat) On the 2nd floor of the University Library, this small L-shaped museum puts on high-quality rotating shows, from street photography to contemporary Croatian artists.

✦ Festivals & Events

The **Rijeka Carnival** (www.ri-karneval.com.hr) is the largest in Croatia, with two weeks of pageants, street dances, concerts, masked balls, exhibitions and parades. It occurs anywhere between late January and early March, depending on when Easter falls.

Hartera (www.hartera.com) is an annual electronic music festival with DJs and artists from across Europe. It's held in a former paper factory on the banks of the Rječina River over three days in mid-June.

🛏 Sleeping

Prices in Rijeka hotels generally stay the same year-round, except at popular Carnival time, when you can expect to pay a surcharge. There are few private rooms in Rijeka itself; the tourist office lists these on its website. Opatija is a much better choice for accommodation.

Best Western Hotel Jadran HOTEL €€
(☏216 600; www.jadran-hoteli.hr; Šetalište XIII Divizije 46; s/d from €97/114; P❀✳@⧉) Located 2km east of the centre, this attractive four-star hotel has seaview rooms where you can revel in the tremendous Adriatic vistas from

your balcony right above the water. There's a tiny beach below.

Youth Hostel
HOSTEL €

(☏406 420; www.hfhs.hr; Šetalište XIII Divizije 23; dm/s/d 165/192/330KN; ⊜@☎) In the leafy residential area of Pečine 2km east of the centre, this renovated 19th-century villa has clean, spacious (if plain) rooms and a communal TV area. Reserve ahead.

Hotel Neboder
HOTEL €€

(☏373 538; www.jadran-hoteli.hr; Strossmayerova 1; s/d from €63/79; P ❋ @) This modernist tower block offers small, neat and modish rooms, most with balconies and amazing views; only the superior rooms have air-conditioning.

Hotel Continental
HOTEL €€

(☏372 008; www.jadran-hoteli.hr; Andrije Kačića Miošića 1; s/d/ste €72/90/110; P ❋ @) At this landmark hotel, the ground-floor reception and bar areas are dated and staff can be uninterested. That said, the recently renovated rooms are comfortable and the location excellent.

Eating

If you want a meal on a Sunday, you'll be relegated to either fast food, pizza or a hotel restaurant, as nearly every other place in Rijeka is closed.

Foodies should consider heading to the nearby village of Volosko, 2km east of Opatija, where there's a clutch of fantastic restaurants.

For self-caterers, there's a large supermarket between the bus and train stations, and a **city market** (btwn Vatroslava Lisinskog & Trninina) open till 2pm daily (noon Sunday). Also check out **Mlinar** (Grdenićeva 27) bakery for delicious filled baguettes, wholemeal bread, croissants and *burek*.

Na Kantunu
SEAFOOD €€

(Demetrova 2; mains from 45KN) If you're lucky enough to grab a table at this tiny lunchtime spot on an industrial stretch of the port, you'll be treated to superlative daily catch.

Kukuriku
FINE DINING €€

(☏691 519; www.kukuriku.hr; Trg Matka Laginje 1a, Kastav; 6-course meals 380-550KN; ⊙closed Mon Nov-Easter) Among the pioneers of the slow-food movement in Croatia, this gastronomic destination in the Old Town of Kastav, Rijeka's hilltop suburb, offers delectable meals amid lots of rooster-themed decoration. It's worth the splurge and the trek on bus 18 from Rijeka or buses 33 and 37 from Opatija.

Zlatna Školjka
SEAFOOD €€

(Kružna 12; mains 65-95KN) Savour the superbly prepared seafood and choice Croatian wines at this classy maritime-themed restaurant. The adjacent **Bracera**, by the same owners, serves crusty pizza, even on Sunday.

Restaurant Spagho
ITALIAN €

(Ivana Zajca 24A; mains from 40KN) A stylish, modern Italian with exposed brickwork, art and hip seating that offers delicious, filling portions of pasta, pizza, salads, and meat and fish dishes.

Drinking

The main drags of Riva and Korzo are the best bet for a drink, with everything from lounge bars to no-nonsense pubs.

Gradina
CAFE

(Trsat; ☎) Set in the grounds of the castle, this happening cafe-bar with chill-out music, great views and friendly service would rate anywhere.

Karolina
BAR

(Gat Karoline Riječke bb) Occupying a striking glass structure on the waterfront, this destination bar is good for daytime coffee and for hanging out with the in-crowd to DJ-spun music on summer nights.

Hemingway
BAR

(Korzo 28) This stylish venue for coffee-sipping, cocktail-drinking and people-watching pays homage to its namesake with large B&W photos of the white-bearded one.

Information

There are ATMs and exchange offices along Korzo and at the train station.

Erste Club (Korzo 22; ⊙7am-11pm Mon-Sat, 8am-10pm Sun) Four terminals where you can surf the net for free for short periods. There's free wireless access along Korzo and in parts of Trsat.

Hospital (☏658 111; Krešimirova 42)

Left luggage intercity bus station (per day 15KN; ⊙5.30am-10.30pm); train station (per day locker 15KN; ⊙4.30am-10.30pm) The bus-station *garderoba* is at the cafe next door to the ticket office.

Post office (Korzo 13; ⊙7am-8pm Mon-Fri, to 2pm Sat) Has a telephone centre and an exchange office.

Tourist Information Centre (☏335 882; www.tz-rijeka.hr; Korzo 33a; ⊙8am-8pm Mon-Sat) Has good colour city maps, lots of brochures and private accommodation lists.

Rijeka

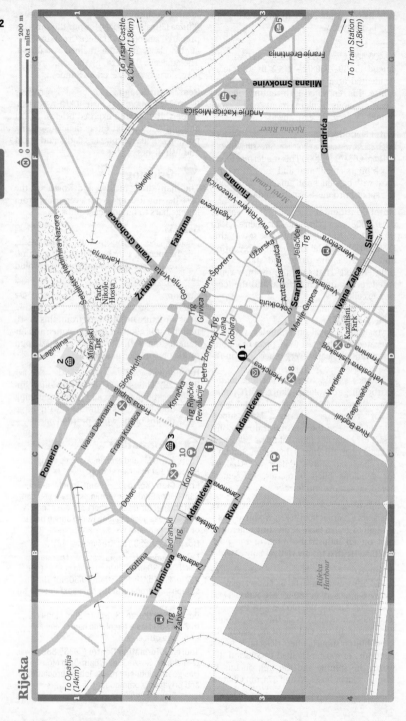

CROATIA KVARNER REGION

To Opatija
(14km)

To Trsat Castle
& Church (1.8km)

To Train Station
(1.8km)

Miliana Smokvine

Andrije Kačića Miošića

Franje Brentinija

Cindrića

Riječina River

Mrtvi Canal

Fašizma

Fiumara

Ivana Grohovca

Žrtava

Agatićeva

Pava Rittera Vitezovica

Užarska

Ante Starčevića

Jelačićev
Trg

Slavka

Scarpina

Ivana Zajca

Venzelova

Vlastistka

Veslarska

Školjić

Kalvarija

Šetalište Vladimira Nazora

Park
Nikole
Hosta

Mljekarski
Trg

Laginjina

Dure Šporera

Gnova Vrata

Trg
Grivica

Sokolkula

Matije Gupca

Kazališni
Park

Trninina

Trg
Ivana
Koblera

Henckea

Vatroslava Lisinskog

Verdieva

Zagrebačka

Riva Boduli

Petra Zoranica

Sloginkula

Frana Supila

Kovačka

Trg Riječke
Revolucije

Adamićeva

Dolac

Korzo

Henckea

Adamićeva

Zanonova

Riva

Splitska

Jadranski
Trg

Trpimirova

Zadarska

Ciottina

Rijeka
Harbour

Trg
Žabica

Ivana Dežmana

Frana Kurelca

Pomerio

Rijeka

⊙ Sights

⊜ Sleeping

⊗ Eating

⊙ Drinking

❶ Getting There & Away

Boat
All ferries depart from the new ferry terminal.

Jadroagent (☑211 626; www.jadroagent.hr; Trg Ivana Koblera 2) Has information on all boats around Croatia.

Jadrolinija (☑211 444; www.jadrolinija.hr; Riječki Lukobran bb; ⊙8am-8pm Mon-Fri, 9am-5pm Sat & Sun) Sells tickets for the large coastal ferries that run all year between Rijeka and Dubrovnik on their way to Bari in Italy, via Split, Hvar, Korčula and Mljet.

Bus
If you fly into Zagreb, there is a Croatia Airlines van that goes directly from Zagreb airport to Rijeka daily (155KN, 3.30pm, two hours). It goes back to Zagreb from Rijeka at 5am. There are three daily buses to Trieste (50KN, 2½ hours) and one daily bus to Ljubljana (170KN, five hours). To get to Plitvice (130KN, four hours), you have to change in Otočac.

The **intercity bus station** (☑060 302 010; Trg Žabica 1) is west of the town centre.

Car
AMC (☑338 800; www.amcrentacar.hr; Lukobran 4) Based in the new ferry terminal building, has cars starting from 243KN per day.

Dollar & Thrifty Rental Car (☑325 900; www.subrosa.hr) Has a booth inside the intercity bus station, also competitively priced.

Train
The **train station** (☑213 333; Krešimirova 5) is a ten-minute walk east of the city centre. Seven daily trains run to Zagreb (100KN, four to five hours). There's one daily connection to Split (170KN, eight hours), though it involves a change at Ogulin. Two direct daily services head to Ljubljana (98KN, three hours) and one daily train goes to Vienna (319KN to 525KN, nine hours).

❶ Getting Around
Taxis are very reasonable in Rijeka (if you use the right firm). **Cammeo** (☑313 313) cabs are modern, inexpensive, have meters and are highly recommended; a ride in the central area costs 20KN.

Opatija
POP 7872

Opatija stretches along the coast, just 15km west of Rijeka, its forested hills sloping down to the sparkling sea. It was this breathtaking location and the agreeable all-year climate that made Opatija the most fashionable seaside resort for the Viennese elite during the days of the Austro-Hungarian empire. The grand residences of the wealthy have since been revamped and turned into upscale hotels, with a particular accent on spa and health holidays. Foodies have been flocking from afar too, for the clutch of terrific restaurants in the nearby fishing village of Volosko.

BUSES FROM RIJEKA

DESTINATION	FARE (KN)	DURATION (HR)	DAILY SERVICES
Dubrovnik	357-496	12-13	3-4
Krk	56	1-2	14
Pula	92	2¼	8
Rovinj	86	1-2	4
Split	253-324	8	6-7
Zadar	161-203	4-5	6-7
Zagreb	137-155	2¼-3	13-15

Opatija sits on a narrow strip of land sandwiched between the sea and the foothills of Mt Učka. Ulica Maršala Tita is the main road that runs through town; it's lined with travel agencies, ATMs, restaurants, shops and hotels.

⊙ Sights & Activities

Lungomare   SEAFRONT
The pretty Lungomare is the region's showcase. Lined with plush villas and ample gardens, this shady promenade winds along the sea for 12km from Volosko to Lovran. Along the way are innumerable rocky outgrowths – a better option than Opatija's concrete beach.

Villa Angiolina   HISTORIC BUILDING
(Park Angiolina 1; ⊙9am-1pm & 4.30-9.30pm Tue-Sun summer, shorter hr rest of yr) The restored Villa Angiolina houses the **Croatian Museum of Tourism**, a grand title for a modest travel-related collection of old photographs, postcards, brochures and posters. Don't miss a stroll around the park, overgrown with gingko trees, sequoias, holm oaks and Japanese camellia, Opatija's symbol.

Učka Nature Park   NATURE RESERVE
Opatija and the surrounding region offer some wonderful opportunities for hiking and biking around the Učka mountain range; the tourist office has maps and information.

🛏 Sleeping & Eating

There are no real budget hotels in Opatija, but there's plenty of value in the midrange and top end. Private rooms are abundant but a little more expensive than in other areas; expect to pay around 170KN to 240KN per person.

Maršala Tita is lined with serviceable restaurants that offer pizza, grilled meat and fish. The better restaurants are away from the main strip. Head to nearby Volosko for fine dining and regional specialities.

Villa Ariston   HOTEL €€
(⌨271 379; www.villa-ariston.com; Ulica Maršala Tita 179; s 350-480KN; d 600-800KN; P❄@☎) With a gorgeous location beside a rocky cove, this historic hotel with period charm has celeb cachet in spades (Coco Chanel and the Kennedys are former guests).

Hotel Opatija   HOTEL €€
(⌨271 388; www.hotel-opatija.hr; Trg Vladimira Gortana 2/1; r €52-66; P❄❄@) The setting in a Habsburg-era mansion is the star at this large hilltop three-star with comfortable rooms, an amazing terrace, a small indoor seawater pool and lovely gardens.

Medveja   CAMPING GROUND €
(⌨291 191; medveja@liburnia.hr; per adult/tent 44/32KN; ⊙Easter–mid-Oct) It lies on a pretty pebble cove 10km south of Opatija and has apartments and mobile homes for rent too.

Istranka   ISTRIAN €
(Bože Milanovića 2; mains from 55KN) Graze on flavourful Istrian mainstays like *maneštra* (vegetable and bean soup) and *fuži* (hand-rolled pasta) at this rustic-themed tavern in a small street just up from Maršala Tita.

Bevanda   MEDITERRANEAN €€€
(Zert 8; mains from 180KN) A marble pathway leads to this gorgeous restaurant, which has a huge ocean-facing terrace with Grecian columns and a short modern menu featuring terrific fresh fish and meat dishes.

♀ Drinking & Entertainment

Opatija is a pretty sedate place, its Viennese-style coffee houses and hotel terraces popular with the mature clientele, though there are a few stylish bars. Check out the slightly bohemian **Tantra** (Lido), which juts out into the Kvarner Gulf, and **Hemingway** (Zert 2), the original venue of what is now a nation-wide chain of sleek cocktail bars.

❶ Information

Da Riva (⌨272 990; www.da-riva.hr; Ulica Maršala Tita 170) A good source for private accommodation and excursions around Croatia.

Linea Verde (⌨701 107; www.lineaverde-croatia.com; Andrije Štangera 42, Volosko) Specialist agency with trips to Učka Nature Park and gourmet tours around Istria.

Tourist office (⌨271 310; www.opatija-tourism.hr; Ulica Maršala Tita 128; ⊙8am-10pm Mon-Sat, 5-9pm Sun Jul & Aug, 8am-7pm Mon-Sat Apr-Jun & Sep, 8am-4pm Mon-Sat Oct-Mar) This office has lots of maps, leaflets and brochures.

❶ Getting There & Away

Bus 32 runs through the centre of Rijeka along Adamićeva to the Opatija Riviera (18KN, 15km) as far as Lovran every 20 minutes daily until late in the evening.

Krk Island

POP 16,400

Croatia's largest island, 409-sq-km Krk (Veglia in Italian) is also one of the busiest in the summer. It may not be the most beautiful or lush island in Croatia – in fact, it's largely overdeveloped and stomped over – but its decades of experience in tourism make it an easy place to visit, with good transport connections and well-organised infrastructure.

❶ Getting There & Around

The Krk toll bridge links the northern part of the island with the mainland, and a regular car ferry links Valbiska with Merag on Cres (passenger/car 18KN/115KN, 30 minutes) in summer.

Krk is also home to **Rijeka airport** (www.rijeka-airport.hr), the main hub for flights to the Kvarner region, which consist mostly of low-cost and charter flights during summer.

Rijeka and Krk Town (56KN, one to two hours) are connected by nine to 13 daily bus services. Services are reduced on weekends.

Six daily buses run from Zagreb to Krk Town (179KN to 194KN, three to four hours). Note that some bus lines are more direct than others, which will stop in every village en route. **Autotrans** (www.autotrans.hr) has two quick daily buses.

Out of the summer season, all services are reduced.

KRK TOWN
POP 3373

The picturesque Krk Town makes a good base for exploring the island. It clusters around a medieval walled centre and, spreading out into the surrounding coves and hills, a modern development that includes a port, beaches, camping grounds and hotels.

◉ Sights

Highlights include the Romanesque **Cathedral of the Assumption** (Trg Svetog Kvirina) and the fortified **Kaštel** (Trg Kamplin) facing the seafront on the northern edge of the Old Town. The narrow cobbled streets that make up the pretty old quarter are worth a wander, although they're typically packed.

🛏 Sleeping & Eating

There is a range of accommodation in and around Krk, but many hotels only open between April and October. Private rooms can be organised through any of the agencies, including **Autotrans** (☑222 661; www.autotrans-turizam.com; Šetalište Svetog Bernardina 3) in the bus station.

Hotel Marina　　　　　BOUTIQUE HOTEL €€€
(☑221 357; www.hotelikrk.hr; Obala Hrvatske Mornarice 6; r 890-1606KN; P❋@🤶) The only hotel in the Old Town, with a prime waterfront location and 10 deluxe contemporary units.

Bor　　　　　　　　　　　　　HOTEL €€
(☑220 200; www.hotelbor.hr; Šetalište Dražica 5; s/d from 290/581KN; ◷Apr-Oct; P🤶) The 22

rooms are modest and without trimmings at this low-key hotel, but the seafront location amid pine forests makes it a worthwhile stay.

Autocamp Ježevac　　　CAMPING GROUND €
(☑221 081; camping@valamar.com; Plavnička bb; per adult/campsite 47/59KN; ◷mid-Apr–mid-Oct) Beachfront camping ground with shady pitches located on old farming terraces, with good swimming and barbecue sites. It's a 10-minute walk southwest of town.

Konoba Nono　　　　　　　　CROATIAN €
(Krčkih Iseljenika 8; mains from 40KN) Savour local specialities like *šurlice* (homemade noodles) topped with goulash or scampi, just a hop and a skip from the Old Town.

Galija　　　　　　　　　　　　PIZZA €
(www.galija-krk.com; Frankopanska 38; mains from 45KN) Munch your margarita or vagabondo pizza, grilled meat or fresh fish under beamed ceilings of this convivial part-*konoba*, part-pizzeria.

❶ Information

The **seasonal tourist office** (☑220 226; www.tz-krk.hr, in Croatian; Obala Hrvatske Mornarice bb; ◷8am-8pm Mon-Sat, 8am-2pm Sun Jun-Oct & Easter-May) distributes brochures and materials, including a map of hiking paths, and advice in many languages. Out of season, go to the **main tourist office** (☑220 226; Vela Placa 1; ◷8am-3pm Mon-Fri) nearby. You can change money at any travel agency and there are numerous ATMs around town.

The bus from Rijeka stops at the station (no left-luggage office) by the harbour, a few minutes' walk from the Old Town.

DALMATIA

Roman ruins, spectacular beaches, old fishing ports, medieval architecture and unspoilt offshore islands make a trip to Dalmatia (Dalmacija) unforgettable. Occupying the central 375km of Croatia's Adriatic coast, Dalmatia offers a matchless combination of hedonism and historical discovery. The jagged coast is speckled with lush offshore islands and dotted with historic cities.

Split is the largest city in the region and a hub for bus and boat connections along the Adriatic, as well as home to the late-Roman Diocletian's Palace. Nearby are the early Roman ruins in Solin (Salona). Zadar has yet more Roman ruins and a wealth of churches. The architecture of Hvar and Korčula recalls the days when these islands

LOŠINJ & CRES ISLANDS

Separated by an 11m-wide canal (with a bridge), these two highly scenic islands in the Kvarner archipelago are often treated as a single entity. On Lošinj, the more populated of the two, the pretty ports of Mali Lošinj and Veli Lošinj, ringed by pine forests and lush vegetation, attract plenty of summertime tourists. Consequently, there are varied sleeping and eating options. The waters around Lošinj are the first protected marine area for dolphins in the entire Mediterranean, watched over by the Mali Lošinj-based **Blue World** (www.blue-world.org) NGO.

Wilder, more barren Cres has a natural allure that's intoxicating and inspiring. Sparsely populated, it's covered in dense primeval forests and lined with a craggy coastline of soaring cliffs, hidden coves and ancient hilltop towns. The northern half of Cres, known as Tramuntana, is prime cruising terrain for the protected griffon vulture; see these giant birds at **Eco-Centre Caput Insulae** (www.supovi.hr), an excellent visitor centre in Beli on the eastern coast. The main seaside settlements lie on the western shore of Cres, while the highlands showcase the astounding medieval town of Lubenice.

The main maritime port of entry for the islands is Mali Lošinj, which is connected to Rijeka, Pula, Zadar and Venice in the summer. A variety of car ferries and catamaran boats are run by **Jadrolinija** (www.jadrolinija.hr), **Split Tours** (www.splittours.hr) and **Venezia Lines** (www.venezialines.com).

were outposts of the Venetian empire. None can rival majestic Dubrovnik, a cultural and aesthetic jewel, while magical Mljet features isolated island beauty.

Zadar

☏023 / POP 73,442

Boasting a historic Old Town of Roman ruins and medieval churches, cosmopolitan cafes and excellent museums, Zadar is really beginning to make its mark. It's not too crowded and has two unique attractions: the sound-and-light spectacle of the Sea Organ and Sun Salutation, which need to be seen and heard to be believed.

It's not a postcard-perfect kind of place. Stroll the Old Town and you'll pass unfortunate Yugo-era office blocks juxtaposed with elegant Hapsburg architecture – this is no Dubrovnik. Zadar is a working town, not a museum piece, and a key transport hub with superb ferry connections to Croatia's Adriatic islands, Kvarner, southern Dalmatia and Italy.

It's also recently been dubbed Croatia's 'city of cool' for its clubs, bars and festivals run by international music stars.

◎ Sights & Activities

Sea Organ & Sun Salutation   LANDMARK
Zadar's incredible **Sea Organ** (Morske Orgulje), designed by local architect Nikola Bašić, has a hypnotic effect. Set within the perforated stone stairs that descend into the sea is a system of pipes and whistles that exudes wistful sighs when the movement of the sea pushes air through it.

Right next to it is the **Sun Salutation** (Pozdrav Suncu), another wacky and wonderful Bašić creation. It's a 22m circle cut into the pavement, filled with 300 multilayered glass plates that collect the sun's energy during the day, and, together with the wave energy that makes the Sea Organ's sound, produce a trippy light show from sunset to sunrise.

Church of St Donat   CHURCH
(Crkva Svetog Donata; Šimuna Kožičića Benje; admission 12KN; ⊙9am-9pm May-Sep, 9am-4pm Oct-Apr) This circular 9th-century Byzantine structure was built over the Roman forum. Slabs from the ancient forum are visible in the church and there is a pillar from the Roman era on the northwestern side. In summer, ask about the musical evenings held here (featuring Renaissance and early baroque music).

Museum of Ancient Glass   MUSEUM
(www.mas-zadar.hr; Poljana Zemaljskog Odbora 1; adult/concession 30/10KN; ⊙9am-9pm May-Sep, 9am-7pm Mon-Sat Oct-Apr) Zadar's newest attraction is this well-designed museum, which explains the history and invention of glass with thousands of pieces on display: tools, blowpipes and early vessels from Egypt and Mesopotamia, goblets, jars, vials, jewellery and amulets.

St Simeon's Church CHURCH
(Crkva Svetog Šime; Trg Šime Budinica; ⊙8am-noon & 6-8pm Jun-Sep) Reconstructed in the 16th and 17th centuries on the site of an earlier structure, this church has a 14th-century sarcophagus, a masterpiece of medieval goldsmith work.

Cathedral of St Anastasia CATHEDRAL
(Katedrala Svete Stošije; Trg Svete Stošije; ⊙8am-noon & 5-6.30pm Mon-Fri) The 13th-century Romanesque Cathedral of St Anastasia has some fine Venetian carvings in the choir stalls and a **belltower** (10KN) that you can climb for stunning Old Town views.

Museum of Church Art MUSEUM
(Trg Opatice Čike bb; adult/concession 20/10KN; ⊙10am-12.45pm & 6-8pm Mon-Sat, 10am-noon Sun) In the Benedictine monastery opposite St Donatus, this impressive museum offers two floors of elaborate gold and silver reliquaries, marble sculptures, religious paintings, icons and embroidery.

Beaches BEACHES
You can swim from the steps off the promenade and listen to the sound of the Sea Organ. There's a swimming area with diving boards, a small park and a cafe on the coastal promenade off Zvonimira. Bordered by pine trees and parks, the promenade takes you to a beach in front of Hotel Kolovare and then winds on for about a kilometre up the coast.

⚲ Tours
Travel agencies offer boat cruises to Telašćica Bay and the beautiful Kornati Islands, which include lunch and a swim in the sea or a salt lake. **Aquarius Travel Agency** (☎212 919; www.juresko.hr; Nova Vrata bb) charges 250KN per person for a full-day trip or ask around on Liburnska Obala (where the excursion boats are moored).

Organised trips to the national parks of Paklenica, Krka and Plitvice Lakes are also popular.

✦ Festivals & Events
Between July and September, the Zadar region showcases some of the globe's most celebrated electronic artists, bands and DJs. The ringmaster for these festivals is the Zadar-based **Garden** bar, but the festivals are held in nearby Petrčane up the coast, 10km north of town. The original event, the **Garden Festival** (www.thegardenzadar.com) has been running since 2006. By 2010, four other festivals (Soundwave, Suncebeat, Electric Elephant and Stop Making Sense) had joined the Petrčane party.

🛏 Sleeping
Most visitors head out to the 'tourist settlement' at Borik, 3km northwest of Zadar, on the Puntamika bus 5 or 8 (8KN, every 20 minutes from the bus station, hourly on Sunday). Here there are hotels (most dating from the Yugo days), a hostel, a camping ground, big swimming pools, sporting opportunities and numerous *sobe* (rooms) signs; you can arrange a private room through a travel agency in town.

Hotel Bastion BOUTIQUE HOTEL €€€
(☎494 950; www.hotel-bastion.hr; Bedemi Zadarskih Pobuna 13; s/d/ste from 905/1140/

WORTH A TRIP

PLITVICE LAKES NATIONAL PARK

Midway between Zagreb and Zadar, **Plitvice Lakes National Park** (☎751 015; www.np-plitvicka-jezera.hr; adult/concession Apr-Oct 110/80KN, Nov-Mar 80/60KN; ⊙7am-8pm) comprises 19.5 hectares of wooded hills and 16 turquoise lakes, all connected by a series of waterfalls and cascades. The mineral-rich waters carve new paths through the rock, depositing tufa (new porous rock) in continually changing formations. Wooden footbridges follow the lakes and streams over, under and across the rumbling water for an exhilaratingly damp 18km. Swimming is not allowed. Your park admission (prices vary by season) is valid for the entire stay and also includes the boats and buses you need to use to see the lakes. There is hotel accommodation only onsite, and private accommodation just outside the park. Check the options with the Plitvice National Park office in Zagreb (p129).

We've received complaints regarding bus transport to Plitvice: note that not all Zagreb–Zadar buses stop here, as the quicker ones use the motorway. Check schedules at www.akz.hr. The journey takes three hours from Zadar (75KN to 89KN) and 2½ hours from Zagreb (62KN to 70KN), and there are 10 daily services. Luggage can be left at the **tourist information centre** (⊙7am-8pm) at the park's main entrance.

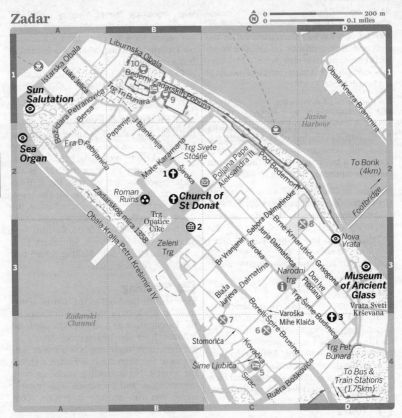

CROATIA DALMATIA

1290KN;⊖❋@🔊) Built over the remains of a fortress at the heart of the Old Town, the Bastion radiates character, with a pleasing art deco design theme, 28 well-finished rooms, and a top-drawer restaurant and basement spa.

Villa Hrešć PENSION €€
(📞337 570; www.villa-hresc.hr; Obala Kneza Trpimira 28; s 550-650KN, d 750-850KN; P❋❄🔊) This condo-style villa is about a 20-minute walk from Zadar's historic sights. There's a coastal garden with an Old Town vista, and good-value rooms and apartments with attractive decor. Some also have massive terraces.

Venera Guest House PENSION €
(📞214 098; www.hotel-venera-zd.hr; Šime Ljubića 4a; d 350-450KN) A modest guest house that has two things going for it: a good location on a quiet street in the Old Town and friendly family owners.

Student Hostel HOSTEL €
(📞224 840; Obala Kneza Branimira bb; dm 147KN; ⊙Jul & Aug) This student dormitory turns into a hostel in July and August. It's centrally located – right across the footbridge – and has no-frills three-bed rooms and shared bathrooms.

Autocamp Borik CAMPING GROUND €
(📞332 074; per adult 38-56KN, per campsite 94-146KN; ⊙May-Oct) A good option for those who want easy access to Zadar, this camping ground is steps away from the shore at Borik. Pitches are shaded by tall pines and facilities are good.

✖ Eating

Zadar's morning **market** (⊙6am-3pm) is one of Croatia's best.

Foša FINE DINING €€€
(www.fosa.hr; Kralja Dmitra Zvonimira 2; mains from 85KN) A classy place with a gorgeous terrace

Zadar

◉ Top Sights

◉ Sights

◉ Sleeping

◉ Eating

◉ Drinking

jutting out into the harbour and a sleek interior. Start by tasting the olive oils, and move on to a grilled Adriatic fish of your choice, and mean meat dishes too.

Zalogajnica Ljepotica CANTEEN €
(Obala Kneza Branimira 4b; mains from 35KN) The cheapest place in town prepares three to four dishes a day (think risotto, pasta and grilled meat) at knockout prices in a no-frills setting.

Trattoria Canzona ITALIAN €
(Stomorića 8; mains from 40KN) Simple, enjoyable trattoria with pavement tables laid with gingham tablecloths. Best for an inexpensive meal; it has very substantial and juicy gnocchi.

Na po ure DALMATIAN €
(Borelli Špire Brusine 8; mains from 40KN) Hungry? This unpretentious family-run *konoba* is the place to sate that appetite with from-the-heart Dalmatian cooking: grilled lamb, calves' liver and fresh fish served with potatoes and vegetables.

🍷 Drinking & Entertainment

Zadar has pavement cafes, lounge bars, boho bars and everything in between. Head to the district of Varoš on the southwest side of the Old Town for interesting little dive bars popular with students and arty types.

Garden BAR
(www.thegardenzadar.com; Bedemi Zadarskih Pobuna; ⊙late May-Oct) One of the reasons many of Croatia's youngsters rate Zadar as 'a really cool place' is this remarkable bar-club-garden-restaurant perched on top of the old city walls. It's owned and run by UB40's producer Nick Colgan and drummer James Brown. Daytime is relaxed; the real fun begins at night.

Arsenal BAR
(www.arsenalzadar.com; Trg Tri Bunara 1) A large renovated shipping warehouse now hosts this brilliant cultural centre, with a large lounge bar-restaurant-concert hall in the centre that has a small stage for live music and shows.

❶ Information

Aquarius Travel Agency (⌂212 919; www.juresko.hr; Nova Vrata bb) Books, accommodation and excursions.

Geris.net (Federica Grisogona 8 1; per hr 25KN) The city's best cybercafe.

Hospital (⌂315 677; Bože Peričića 5)

Left luggage (Garderoba; per day 15KN) bus station (⊙6am-10pm Mon-Fri); Jadrolinija dock (⊙7am-8.30pm Mon-Fri, to 3pm Sat); train station (⊙24hr)

Miatours (⌂/fax 212 788; www.miatours.hr; Vrata Svetog Krševana) Arranges excursions and accommodation.

Post office (Poljana Pape Aleksandra III; ⊙7.30am-9pm Mon-Sat, to 2pm Sun) You can make phone calls and there's an ATM.

Tourist office (⌂316 166; www.tzzadar.hr; Mihe Klaića 5; ⊙8am-10pm Mon-Fri, to 9pm Sat & Sun Jun-Sep, 8am-8pm Oct-May) Publishes a good colour map and the free *Zadar City Guide*.

❶ Getting There & Away

Air

Zadar's airport, 12km east of the city, is served by **Croatia Airlines** (⌂250 101; www.croatiaairlines.hr; Poljana Natka Nodila 7) and **Ryanair** (www.ryanair.com). A Croatia Airlines bus meets all flights and costs 20KN. For a taxi, call the very efficient and cheap **Lulić** (⌂494 494).

Boat

On the harbour, **Jadrolinija** (⌂254 800; Liburnska Obala 7) has tickets for all local ferries. Buy international tickets from **Jadroagent** (⌂211 447; jadroagent-zadar@zd.t-com.hr; Poljana Natka Nodila 4), just inside the city walls.

Bus

The **bus station** (⌂211 035; www.liburnija-zadar.hr, in Croatian) is a 10-minute walk southeast of the harbour and the Old Town and has daily buses to Zagreb (95KN to 143KN, 3½ to seven hours, every 30 minutes). Buses marked 'Po-luotok' run from the bus station to the harbour.

Train

The **train station** (☑212 555; www.hznet.hr; Ante Starčevića 3) is adjacent to the bus station. There are six daily trains to Zagreb, but the journey time is very slow indeed; the fastest take over eight hours.

Split

☑021 / POP 188.694

The second-largest city in Croatia, Split (Spalato in Italian) is a great place to see Dalmatian life as it's really lived. Free of mass tourism, this always buzzing city has just the right balance of tradition and modernity. Step inside Diocletian's Palace – a Unesco World Heritage site and one of the world's most impressive Roman monuments – and you'll see dozens of bars, restaurants and shops thriving amid the atmospheric old walls where Split life has been going on for thousands of years. Split's unique setting and exuberant nature make it one of the most delectable cities in Europe. The dramatic coastal mountains are the perfect backdrop to the turquoise waters of the Adriatic and you'll get a chance to appreciate the gorgeous Split cityscape when making a ferry journey to or from the city.

The Old Town is a vast open-air museum and the new information signs at the important sights explain a great deal of Split's history. The seafront promenade, Obala Hrvatskog Narodnog Preporoda, better known as Riva, is the best central reference point.

History

Split achieved fame when Roman emperor Diocletian (AD 245–313) had his retirement palace built here from 295 to 305. After his death the great stone palace continued to be used as a retreat by Roman rulers. When the neighbouring colony of Salona was abandoned in the 7th century, many of the Romanised inhabitants fled to Split and barricaded themselves behind the high palace walls, where their descendants continue to live to this day.

⊙ Sights

DIOCLETIAN'S PALACE

Diocletian's Palace   HISTORIC AREA

Facing the harbour, Diocletian's Palace is one of the most imposing Roman ruins in existence. Don't expect a palace though, nor a museum – this palace is the living heart of the city, and its labyrinthine streets are packed with people, bars, shops and restaurants.

It was built as a strong rectangular fortress, with walls measuring 215m from east to west, 181m wide at the southernmost point and reinforced by square corner towers. The imperial residence, mausoleum and temples were south of the main street, now called Krešimirova, connecting the east and west palace gates.

Town Museum   MUSEUM

(Muzej Grada Splita; www.mgst.net; Papalićeva 1; adult/concession 10/5KN; ⊙9am-9pm Tue-Fri, 9am-4pm Sat-Mon) Built for one of the many noblemen who lived within the palace in the Middle Ages, the Papalić Palace that houses the museum is considered a fine example of late-Gothic style. Its three floors showcase a tidy collection of artefacts, paintings, furniture and clothes from Split; captions are in Croatian. Shorter hours outside summer.

Ethnographic Museum   MUSEUM

(Etnografski Muzej; www.etnografski-muzej-split.hr, in Croatian; Severova 1; adult/concession 10/5KN; ⊙9am-9pm Mon-Fri, 9am-1pm Sat) This mildly interesting museum has a collection of photos of old Split, traditional costumes and memorabilia of important citizens, housed in two floors and an attic. For great Old Town views, make sure you climb the staircase that leads to the terrace on the southern edge of the vestibule. Shorter hours outside summer.

Cathedral of St Domnius   CHURCH

(Katedrala Svetog Duje; Kraj Svetog Duje 5; admission free; ⊙8am-8pm Mon-Sat, 12.30-6.30pm Sun Jun-Sep, sporadic hrs Oct-May) On the eastern side of the Peristil, Split's cathedral was built as Diocletian's mausoleum. The oldest monuments inside are the remarkable 13th-century scenes from the life of Christ carved on the wooden entrance doors. The choir is furnished with 13th-century Romanesque seats that are the oldest in Dalmatia. The **treasury** (admission 10KN) is rich in reliquaries, icons, church robes and illuminated manuscripts. You can climb the Romanesque **belfry** (admission 10KN).

Peristil   SQUARE

This picturesque colonnaded square, with a neo-Romanesque cathedral tower rising above, is a great place for a break in the sun. The **vestibule**, an open dome above the ground-floor passageway at the southern end of the Peristil, is overpoweringly grand and cavernous.

Temple of Jupiter
RUIN

(admission 5KN; ☺8am-8pm Jun-Sep) The temple once had a porch supported by columns, but the one column you see today dates from the 5th century. Below the temple is a crypt, which was once used as a church.

Basement Halls
MONUMENT

(adult/concession 25/10KN; ☺9am-9pm Jun-Sep, shorter hrs Oct-May) Although mostly empty, the rooms and corridors underneath Diocletian's Palace emit a haunting sense of timelessness that is well worth the price of the ticket.

OUTSIDE THE PALACE WALLS

Gregorius of Nin
LANDMARK

(Grgur Ninski) This 10th-century statue is of the Croatian bishop who fought for the right to use old Croatian in liturgical services. Notice that his left big toe has been polished to a shine – it's said that rubbing the toe brings good luck.

Gallery of Fine Arts
MUSEUM

(Galerija Umjetnina Split; www.galum.hr; Kralja Tomislava 15; adult/concession 20/10KN; ☺11am-7pm Tue-Sat, 10am-1pm Sun) Split's newest museum in a former hospital exhibits nearly 400 works of art spanning almost 700 years. Upstairs is the permanent collection; temporary exhibits downstairs change every few months. The cafe has a terrace overlooking the palace.

OUTSIDE CENTRAL SPLIT

Archaeological Museum
MUSEUM

(Arheološki Muzej; www.armus.hr; Zrinsko-Frankopanska 25; adult/concession 20/10KN; ☺9am-2pm & 4-8pm Mon-Sat) North of town, this is a fascinating supplement to your walk around Diocletian's Palace and around ancient Salona. The history of Split is traced from Illyrian times to the Middle Ages, in chronological order, with explanations in English.

Meštrović Gallery
ART GALLERY

(Galerija Meštrović; Šetalište Ivana Meštrovića 46; adult/concession 30/15KN; ☺9am-7pm Tue-Sun May-Sep, shorter hrs Oct-Apr) At this stellar art museum, below Marjan to the west of the city centre, you'll see a comprehensive, nicely arranged collection of works by Ivan Meštrović, Croatia's premier modern sculptor.

Marjan
NATURE RESERVE

For an afternoon away from the city buzz, Marjan (178m) is the perfect destination. This hilly nature reserve offers trails through fragrant pine forests, scenic lookouts and ancient chapels. There are different ways

of reaching Marjan. One is to hike straight up from the Meštrović Gallery. Otherwise, you can start closer to the centre, from the stairway (Marjanske Skale) in Varoš, right behind the Church of Sveti Frane. Alternatively, walk along the seafront of Marjan to get to some quiet beaches, such as Kašjuni cove.

Bačvice
BEACH

The most popular city beach is on the eponymous inlet. This biggish pebbly beach has good swimming, a lively ambience, a great cafe-bar and plenty of water games. There are showers and changing rooms at both ends of the beach.

★ Festivals & Events

This traditional February **Carnival** event sees locals dressing up and dancing in the streets for two very fun days. Otherwise known as Split Day, the 7 May **Feast of St Duje** involves much singing and dancing all around the city. From mid-July to mid-August, the **Split Summer Festival** (www.splitsko-ljeto.hr) features opera, drama, ballet and concerts on open-air stages.

🛏 Sleeping

Good budget accommodation has become more available in Split in the last couple of years but it's mostly hostels. Private accommodation is again the best option, and in the summer you may be deluged at the bus station by people offering *sobe* (rooms available). Make sure you are clear about the exact location of the room or you may find yourself several bus rides from the town centre.

The best thing to do is to book through one of the travel agencies, but there is little available within the heart of the Old Town. Expect to pay between 200KN and 400KN for a double room; in the cheaper ones you will probably share the bathroom with the proprietor.

Hotel Peristil
HOTEL €€€

(☎329 070; www.hotelperistil.com; Poljana Kraljice Jelene 5; s/d 1000/1200KN; ❄@☎) This lovely hotel overlooks the Peristil, in the midst of Diocletian's Palace, with its 12 gorgeous rooms – all with hardwood floors, antique details, good views and warm service.

Hotel Bellevue
HOTEL €€

(☎345 644; www.hotel-bellevue-split.hr; Bana Josipa Jelačića 2; P@) This atmospheric old classic has seen better days, but it remains one of the more dreamy hotels in town, with its regal patterned wallpaper, dark-brown

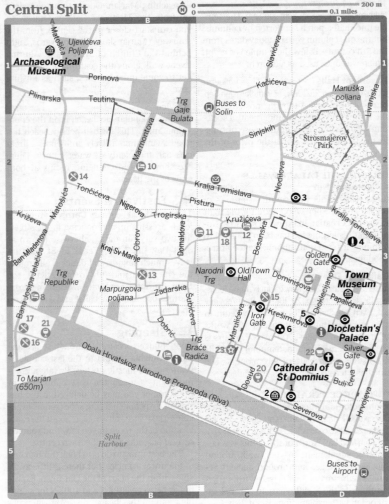

Central Split map showing streets and numbered locations including Archaeological Museum, Diocletian's Palace, Cathedral of St Domnius, Town Museum, Split Harbour, Buses to Airport.

wood, art deco elements, billowing curtains and faded but well-kept rooms.

Villa Varoš PENSION €
(☎483 469; www.villavaros.hr; Miljenka Smoje 1; d/ ste 500/800KN; ❄@🖘) Owned by a New Yorker Croat, Villa Varoš, just to the west of Bana Josipa Jelačića, is central, the rooms are simple, bright and airy, and the apartment is excellent (with a well-equipped kitchen, Jacuzzi and small terrace).

Hotel Adriana HOTEL €€
(☎340 000; www.hotel-adriana.com; Obala Hrvatskog Narodnog Preporoda 8; s/d 700/1000KN;

❄🖘) Good value, excellent location. The rooms are not massively exciting, with navy curtains and beige furniture, but some have sea views – a real bonus in Split's Old Town.

Silver Central Hostel HOSTEL €
(☎490 805; www.silvercentralhostel.com; Kralja Tomislava 1; dm 150-180KN; ❄@🖘) In an up-stairs apartment, this light yellow-coloured boutique hostel has four dorm rooms, free internet and cable TV in the pleasant lounge. There's another hostel, **Silver Gate** (☎322 857; www.silvergatehostel.com; Hrvojeva 6; dm 165KN), near the food market, with the same facilities.

Split Hostel Booze & Snooze HOSTEL €
(342 787; www.splithostel.com; Narodni Trg 8; dm 150-180KN; 🌐@🛜) Run by a pair of Aussie Croat women, this party place at the heart of town has 25 beds in four dorms, a terrace, book swap and free internet. Their brand-new outpost, **Fiesta Siesta** (Kružićeva 5; dm 150-180KN, d 440-500KN; 🌐@🛜) has five sparkling dorms and one double above the popular Charlie's Backpacker Bar.

🍴 Eating

TOP CHOICE Konoba Trattoria Bajamont

DALMATIAN €
(Bajamontijeva 3; mains from 60KN; ⊙closed dinner Sun) At this one-room joint with a handful of tables and no sign above the door, the menu features excellent Dalmatian mainstays, such as small fried fish, squid-ink risotto and *brujet* (seafood stew with wine, onions and herbs, served with polenta).

Kod Fife DALMATIAN €
(Trumbićeva Obala 11; mains from 40KN) Dragan presides over a motley crew of sailors, artists and misfits who drop in for his simple, Dalmatian home cooking (especially the *pašticada*), and his own brand of grumpy slow but loving hospitality. Go west of the Riva, which turns into Trumbićeva Obala.

Perun DALMATIAN €€
(Senjska 9; mains from 70KN) This adorable spot in Varoš has a leafy terrace amid ancient stone, a rustic low-key vibe and seafood (and meat) done *na gradele* (on the grill), depending on what's fresh that day.

Šperun SEAFOOD €€
(Šperun 3; mains from 70KN) A sweet little restaurant decked out with rustic details, this favourite among the foreigners churns out decent Dalmatian classics. **Šperun Deva** across the street is a charming corner bistro with a few tables outside, offering breakfasts and a great daily menu (from 50KN).

Makrovega VEGETARIAN €
(Leština 2; mains from 40KN; ⊙9am-8pm Mon-Fri, to 5pm Sat) A meat-free haven with a clean, spacious (nonsmoking!) interior and delicious buffet and à la carte food that alternates between macrobiotic and vegetarian.

Galija PIZZA €
(Tončićeva 12; pizzas from 20KN) The most popular place on Split's pizza scene for several decades now, it's the sort of joint that locals take you to for a simple but good meal.

Art & Čok SANDWICH BAR €
(Obrov 2; sandwiches from 14KN; ⊙Mon-Sat) Excellent sandwiches on handcrafted bread.

Try the *porchetta* (aromatic pork, roasted red peppers and gherkins).

Drinking & Entertainment

Split is great for nightlife, especially in the spring and summer months. The palace walls are generally throbbing with loud music on Friday and Saturday nights.

Žbirac
CAFE

(Bačvice bb) This beachfront cafe is like the locals' open-air living room, a cult hang-out with great sea views, swimming day and night, and occasional concerts.

Bifora
CAFE-BAR

(Bernardinova 5) A quirky crowd of locals frequents this artsy spot on a lovely little square, much loved for its intimate low-key vibe.

Ghetto Club
BAR

(Dosud 10) Head for Split's most bohemian bar in an intimate courtyard amid flowerbeds, a trickling fountain, great music and a friendly atmosphere.

Galerija
CAFE-BAR

(Vuškovićeva bb) Catch up with friends in the granny-chic interior, with pretty floral sofas and armchairs, paintings and little lamps everywhere.

Luxor
CAFE-BAR

(Kraj Sv Ivana 11) Touristy, yes, but having coffee in the courtyard of the cathedral is great: cushions are laid out on the steps and you can watch the locals go about their business.

Vidilica
CAFE

(Nazorov Prilaz 1) Worth the climb up the stone stairs through the ancient Varoš quarter for a sunset drink at this hilltop cafe with amazing city and harbour views.

Libar
CAFE-BAR

(Trg Franje Tuđmana 3) A relaxed place away from the palace buzz, this little spot has a lovely upper terrace, great breakfasts and tapas all day.

Fluid
BAR-CLUB

(Dosud 1) This chic spot is a jazzy party bar. Right up the stairs, which get jammed with people on weekend nights, the sleek **Puls** draws more of an electronic-music crowd.

 Information

Discount Cards

Split Card (1 day 35KN) Get the Split Card for one day and you can use it for three days without paying anything extra. You get free and reduced admissions to Split attractions and discounts on car rental, restaurants, shops and hotels.

Internet Access

Several cafes around town offer free wi-fi access, including Luxor.

Backpackers Cafe (☎338 548; Obala Kneza Domagoja 3; per hr 30KN; ⊗7am-9pm) Also sells used books and provides information for backpackers. There's happy hour for internet between 3pm and 5pm, when it's 50% off.

Left Luggage

Garderoba bus station (1st hr 5KN, then 1.50KN per hr; ⊗6am-10pm); train station (per day 15KN; ⊗6am-11.30pm)

Medical Services

KBC Firule (☎556 111; Spinčićeva 1) Split's hospital.

Money

You can change money at travel agencies or the post office. There are ATMs around the bus and train stations and throughout the city.

Post

Main post office (Kralja Tomislava 9; ⊗7.30am-7pm Mon-Fri, 7.30am-2.30pm Sat)

Tourist Information

Croatian Youth Hostel Association (☎396 031; www.hfhs.hr; Domilijina 8; ⊗8am-4pm Mon-Fri) Sells HI cards and has information about youth hostels all over Croatia.

Tourist office (☎345 606; www.visitsplit.com; Peristil; ⊗8am-8.30pm Jul-Aug, 8am-8.30pm Mon-Sat, 8am-1.30pm Sun Jun & Sep, 9am-5pm Mon-Fri Oct-May) Has information on Split and sells the Split Card.

Travel Agencies

Atlas Airtours (☎343 055; www.atlasairtours.com; Bosanska 11) Tours, private accommodation and money exchange.

Maestral (☎470 944; www.maestral.hr; Boškovića 13/15) Monastery stays, horseback-riding excursions, lighthouse holidays, hiking, sea kayaking and more.

Turist Biro (☎347 100; www.turistbiro-split.hr; Obala Hrvatskog Narodnog Preporoda 12) Its main area is private accommodation.

 Getting There & Away

Air

Split airport (www.split-airport.hr) is 20km west of town, just 6km before Trogir. **Croatia Airlines** (☎362 997; www.croatiaairlines.hr; Obala Hrvatskog Narodnog Preporoda 9; ⊗8am-8pm Mon-Fri, 9am-noon Sat) operates one-hour flights to Zagreb several times a day and a weekly flight to Dubrovnik.

A couple of low-cost airlines fly to Split, including **Easyjet** (www.easyjet.com) and **germanwings** (www.germanwings.com).

Boat

Jadrolinija (📞338 333; Gat Sv Duje bb), in the large ferry terminal opposite the bus station, handles most of the coastal ferry lines and catamaran boats that operate between Split and the islands. There is also the twice-weekly ferry service between Rijeka and Split, which goes on to Bari (406KN) in Italy. Four times weekly a car ferry goes from Split to Ancona in Italy (361KN, nine to 11 hours).

In addition to Jadrolinija's boats, there is a fast passenger boat, the **Krilo** (www.krilo.hr), that goes to Hvar Town (22KN, one hour) daily and on to Korčula (55KN, 2¾ hours).

SNAV (📞322 252; www.snav.it) has daily ferries to Ancona (Italy) from mid-June through September (five hours) and to Pescara (Italy) from late July through August (6½ hours). Also departing to Ancona from Split are **BlueLine** (www.blueline-ferries.com) car ferries (from 333KN per person, 450KN per car, 10 to 12 hours).

Car ferries and passenger lines depart from separate docks; the passenger lines leave from Obala Lazareta and car ferries from Gat Sv Duje. You can buy tickets from either the main Jadrolinija office in the large ferry terminal opposite the bus station, or at one of the two stalls near the docks. In summer it's necessary to reserve at least a day in advance for a car ferry and you are asked to appear several hours before departure.

Bus

Advance bus tickets with seat reservations are recommended. Most buses leave from the main **bus station** (📞060 327 777; www.ak-split.hr) beside the harbour.

Bus 37 goes to Split airport and Trogir (20KN, every 20 minutes), also stopping at Solin; it leaves from a local bus station on Domovinskog Rata, 1km northeast of the city centre, but it's faster and more convenient to take an intercity bus heading north to Zadar or Rijeka.

Train

There are five daily trains between Split **train station** (📞338 525; www.hznet.hr; Obala Kneza Domagoja 9) and Zagreb (179KN to 189KN, 5½ to eight hours), which is just behind the bus station, two of which are overnight. There are also two trains a day from Split to Zadar (88KN, five hours) via Knin.

❶ Getting Around

Buses by **Pleso Prijevoz** (www.plesoprijevoz. hr) and **Promet Žele** (www.split-airport.com.hr) depart to Split airport (30KN) from Obala Lazareta several times daily. You can also take bus 37 from the local bus station on Domovinskog Rata (20KN, 50 minutes).

Buses run about every 15 minutes from 5.30am to 11.30pm. A one-zone ticket costs 10KN for one trip in central Split; it's 20KN to the surrounding districts. You can buy tickets on the bus and the driver can make change.

Trogir

📞021 / POP 12,995

Gorgeous and tiny Trogir (formerly Trau) is beautifully set within medieval walls, its streets knotted and maze-like. It's fronted by a wide seaside promenade lined with bars and cafes and luxurious yachts docking in the summer. Trogir is unique among Dalmatian towns for its profuse collection of Romanesque and Renaissance architecture (which flourished under Venetian rule), and this,

BUSES FROM SPLIT

DESTINATION	FARE (KN)	DURATION (HR)	DAILY SERVICES
Dubrovnik	105-157	4½	20
Medugorje*	100	3-4	4
Mostar*	114	3½-4½	8
Pula	397	10-11	3
Rijeka	305	8-8½	11
Sarajevo*	190	6½-8	4
Zadar	120	3-4	27
Zagreb	185	5-8	29

*Bosnia & Hercegovina

along with its magnificent cathedral, earned it status as a World Heritage site in 1997.

Trogir is an easy day trip from Split and a relaxing place to spend a few days, taking a trip or two to nearby islands.

◉ Sights

The heart of the Old Town, which occupies a tiny island in the narrow channel between Čiovo Island and the mainland, is a few minutes' walk from the bus station. After crossing the small bridge near the station, go through the north gate. Trogir's finest sights are around Narodni Trg to the southeast. Most sights can be seen on a 15-minute walk around this island.

Cathedral of St Lovro   CHURCH
(Katedrala Svetog Lovre; Trg Ivana Pavla II; admission 20KN; ⊙8am-8pm Mon-Sat, 2-8pm Sun Jun-Sep, shorter hrs Oct-May) The showcase of Trogir is this three-naved Venetian cathedral built from the 13th to 15th centuries. Its glory is the Romanesque portal of *Adam and Eve* (1240) by Master Radovan, the earliest example of the nude in Dalmatian sculpture. Enter the building through an obscure back door to see the richly decorated **Renaissance Chapel of St Ivan** and the choir stalls, pulpit and **treasury**, which contains an ivory triptych. You can climb the 47m cathedral **tower** for a delightful view.

Kamerlengo Fortress   FORTRESS
(Tvrđava Kamerlengo; admission 15KN; ⊙9am-9pm May-Oct) Once connected to the city walls, the fortress was built around the 15th century. Today it hosts concerts during the Trogir Summer festival.

Town Museum   MUSEUM
(Gradski Muzej; Kohl-Genscher 49; admission 15KN; ⊙10am-5pm Jul-Sep, shorter hrs Oct-May) Housed in the former Garagnin-Fanfogna palace, the museum has five rooms which exhibit books, documents, drawings and period costumes from Trogir's long history.

❶ Information

Atlas Trogir (✆881 374; www.atlas-trogir.hr; Obala Kralja Zvonimira 10) This travel agency arranges private accommodation and runs excursions.

Portal Trogir (✆885 016; www.portal-trogir.com; Obala Bana Berislavića 3) Finds private accommodation; rents bikes, scooters and kayaks; books excursions and has an internet corner.

WORTH A TRIP

SOLIN (SALONA)

The ruin of the ancient city of Solin (known as Salona by the Romans), among the vineyards at the foot of mountains just northeast of Split, is the most interesting archaeological site in Croatia. Salona was the capital of the Roman province of Dalmatia from the time Julius Caesar elevated it to the status of colony. It held out against the barbarians and was only evacuated in AD 614 when the inhabitants fled to Split and neighbouring islands in the face of Avar and Slav attacks.

Begin your visit at the main entrance near Caffe Bar Salona, where you'll see an info-map of the complex. **Tusculum Museum** (admission 20KN; ⊙9am-7pm Mon-Sat, 9am-1pm Sun Jun-Sep, 9am-3pm Mon-Fri, 9am-1pm Sat Oct-May) is where you pay admission for the entire archaeological reserve (you'll get a brochure with a map) as well as for the small museum with interesting sculpture embedded in the walls and in the garden. Some of the highlights inside the complex include **Manastirine**, the fenced area behind the car park, a burial place for early Christian martyrs prior to the legalisation of Christianity; the excavated remains of **Kapljuč Basilica** – one of the early Christian cemeteries in Salona – and the 5th-century **Kapjinc Basilica** that sits inside it. Also look out for the **covered aqueduct** from the 1st century AD; the 5th-century **cathedral** with an octagonal **baptistery**; and the huge 2nd-century **amphitheatre**.

The ruins are easily accessible on Split city bus 1 (12KN), which goes directly to Caffe Bar Salona (sit on the right side and look out for the blue and white sign pointing to Salona) every half-hour from Trg Gaje Bulata.

From the amphitheatre at Solin it's easy to continue on to Trogir by catching a westbound bus 37 from the nearby stop on the adjacent highway (buy a four-zone ticket for 20KN in Split if you plan to do this). If, on the other hand, you want to return to Split, use the underpass to cross the highway and catch an eastbound bus 37.

❶ Getting There & Away

City bus 37 from Split (28km) leaves half-hourly from the local bus station, with a stop at Split airport en route to Trogir. You can buy the four-zone ticket (20KN) from the driver. There are boats to Split four times daily (20KN), from Čiovo island (150m to the left of the bridge).

Southbound buses from Zadar (130km) will drop you off in Trogir, as will most northbound buses from Split going to Zadar, Rijeka and Zagreb.

Hvar Island

♪ 021 / POP 11,459

Hvar is the number-one carrier of Croatia's superlatives: it's the most luxurious island, the sunniest place in the country and, along with Dubrovnik, the most popular tourist destination. Hvar is also famed for its verdancy and its lavender fields, as well as other aromatic herbs such as rosemary.

The island's hub and busiest destination is Hvar Town, estimated to draw around 30,000 people a day in the high season. It's odd that they can all fit in the small bay town, but fit they do. Visitors wander along the main square, explore the sights on the winding stone streets, swim on the numerous beaches or pop off to get into their birthday suits on the Pakleni Islands, but most of all they party at night. There are several good restaurants and a number of top hotels, as well as a couple of hostels.

Car ferries from Split deposit you in Stari Grad but local buses meet most ferries in summer for the trip to Hvar Town. The town centre is Trg Sv Stjepana, 100m west of the bus station. Passenger ferries tie up on Riva (seafront promenade), the eastern quay.

◉ Sights & Activities

Franciscan Monastery & Museum
MONASTERY
(admission 20KN; ◷9am-1pm & 5-7pm Mon-Sat) At the southeastern end of Hvar Town you'll find this 15th-century Renaissance monastery, with a wonderful collection of Venetian paintings in the adjoining church and a cloister garden with a cypress tree said to be more than 300 years old.

Arsenal
HISTORIC BUILDING
(Trg Svetog Stjepana; admission arsenal & theatre 20KN; ◷9am-9pm) Smack in the middle of Hvar Town is the imposing Gothic arsenal, and upstairs is Hvar's prize, the **Renaissance theatre** built in 1613 – reported to be

the first theatre in Europe open to plebs and aristocrats alike.

Cathedral of St Stephen
CHURCH
(Katedrala Svetog Stjepana; Trg Svetog Stjepana; ◷30min before twice-daily Mass) Forming a stunning backdrop to Trg Sv Stjepana, the cathedral was built in the 16th and 17th centuries at the height of the Dalmatian Renaissance.

Fortica
FORTRESS
(admission 20KN; ◷8am-9pm Jun-Sep) On the hill high above Hvar Town, this Venetian fortress (1551) is worth the climb up to appreciate the sweeping panoramic views. The fort was built to defend Hvar from the Turks, who sacked the town in 1539 and 1571. There's a lovely cafe at the top.

🛏 Sleeping

Accommodation in Hvar Town is extremely tight in July and August: a reservation is highly recommended. Try the travel agencies for help. Expect to pay anywhere from 150KN to 300KN per person for a room with a private bathroom in the town centre. Outside the high season you can negotiate a better price.

Hotel Riva
LUXURY HOTEL €€€
(♪750 100; www.suncanihvar.com; Riva bb; s/d 1401/1497KN; ❄@) Now the luxury veteran on the Hvar Town lodging scene, this 100-year-old hotel has 54 smallish contemporary rooms and a great location right on the harbour, perfect for watching the yachts glide up and away.

Hotel Croatia
HOTEL €€
(♪742 400; www.hotelcroatia.net; Majerovica bb; s/d 810/1080KN; P❅@❄) Only a few steps from the sea, this medium-size, rambling 1930s building sits among gorgeous, peaceful gardens. The rooms are simple and fresh, many with balconies overlooking the gardens and the sea.

Luka's Lodge
HOSTEL €
(♪742 118; www.lukalodgehvar.hostel.com; Lučica bb; dm 140KN, d per person 120-175KN; @❅❄) Friendly owner Luka takes good care of his guests at this homey hostel a five-minute walk from town. All rooms come with fridges, some with balconies. There's a living room, two terraces and a kitchen.

Green Lizard
HOSTEL €
(♪742 560; www.greenlizard.hr; Ulica Domovinskog Rata 13; dm 140KN, d per person 120-175KN; ◷Apr-Oct; @❅) This private hostel is a friendly and cheerful budget option, a short walk from the ferry. Dorms are simple and clean, there's a

communal kitchen and laundry service and a few doubles with private and shared facilities.

Camping Vira CAMPING GROUND €
(☑741 803; www.campingvira.com; per adult/campsite 50/87KN; ⊙May–mid-Oct; 🐾) This four-star camping ground on a wooded bay 4km from town is one of the best in Dalmatia. There's a gorgeous beach, a lovely cafe and restaurant, and a volleyball pitch. The facilities are well kept.

✗ Eating

The pizzerias along the harbour offer predictable but inexpensive eating. Self-caterers can head to the supermarket next to the bus station, or pick up fresh supplies at the next-door vegetable market.

Konoba Menego DALMATIAN €€
(Put Grode bb; tapas-style dishes 45-70KN) At this rustic old house, everything is decked out in Hvar antiques and the staff wear traditional outfits. Try the marinated cheeses and vegetables, prepared the old-fashioned Dalmatian way.

Konoba Luviji DALMATIAN €€
(mains from 70KN) Food churned out of the wood oven at this wine-focused tavern is simple, unfussy and tasty. Downstairs is the *konoba* where Dalmatian-style tapas is served; the upstairs restaurant has Old Town and harbour views.

Zlatna Školjka FINE DINING €€€
(Petra Hektorovića 8; www.zlatna.skoljka.com; mains from 120KN) This slow-food family-run hideaway stands out for its creative fare conjured up by a local chef-celebrity. Try the unbeatable *gregada*, traditional fish stew with lobster and sea snails; order in advance.

🍷 Drinking

Hvar has some of the best nightlife on the Adriatic coast.

Falko Bar BEACH BAR
(⊙10am-10pm mid-May–mid-Sep) A 20-minute seafront walk from the town centre, past Hula Hula, brings you to this adorable hideaway in a pine forest just above the beach. Think low-key artsy vibe, homemade *rakija*, hammocks and occasional concerts, exhibits and other fun events.

Carpe Diem BAR-CLUB
(www.carpe-diem-hvar.com; Riva) This swanky harbourfront spot is the mother of Croatia's coastal clubs, with house music spun nightly by resident DJs. The new **Carpe Diem Beach**

on the island of Stipanska is the hottest place to party (June to September), with daytime beach fun and occasional full-moon parties.

Hula-Hula BEACH BAR
(www.hulahulahvar.com) THE spot to catch the sunset to the sound of techno and house music, Hula-Hula is known for its apres-beach party (4pm to 9pm) where all of young trendy Hvar descends for sun-downer cocktails. To find it, head west along the seafront.

V-528 CLUB
(www.v-528.com; ⊙from 9.30pm) A former fortress on the slope above the seafront, this open-air venue has a stunning look, great sound system, DJ-fuelled parties and an oxygen room in an ancient chapel.

❶ Information

Atlas Hvar (☑741 911; www.atlas-croatia.com) On the western side of the harbour, it finds private accommodation.

Clinic (☑741 300; Sv Katarine) Medical clinic about 700m from the town centre.

Del Primi (☑095 998 1235; www.delprimi-hvar.com; Burak 23) Travel agency specialising in private accommodation.

Francesco (Burak bb; per hr 30KN; ⊙8am-midnight) Internet cafe and call centre.

Pelegrini Tours (☑742 743; www.pelegrini-hvar.hr; Riva bb) Private accommodation, boat tickets to Italy with SNAV and Blue Line, excursions (daily trip to Pakleni Otoci), and bike, scooter and boat rental.

Secret Hvar (☑717 615; www.secrethvar.com) Great offroad tours of the island's scenic interior, with abandoned villages, dramatic canyons and endless lavender fields.

Tourist office (☑742 977; www.tzhvar.hr; ⊙8am-2pm & 3-9pm Jun & Sep, 8am-2pm & 3-10pm Jul-Aug, 8am-2pm Mon-Sat Sep-May) On Trg Svetog Stjepana.

❶ Getting There & Away

The local Jadrolinija car ferry from Split calls at Stari Grad (47KN, two hours) six times a day in summer months. Jadrolinija also has a catamaran daily to Hvar Town (22KN, one hour). In addition, **Krilo** (www.krilo.hr), the fast passenger boat, travels once a day between Split and Hvar Town (22KN, one hour) in the summer months; it also goes to Korčula (55KN, 2¾ hours). You can buy tickets at Pelegrini Tours.

There are at least 10 car ferries (fewer in the low season) running from Drvenik, on the mainland, to Sućuraj (16KN, 35 minutes) on the tip of Hvar Island. The **Jadrolinija agency** (☑741 132; www.jadrolinija.hr) is beside the landing in Stari Grad.

There are also connections to Italy in the summer season. The Jadrolinija ferries that operate between Rijeka and Dubrovnik call at Hvar twice a week during summer, stopping in Stari Grad before continuing on to Korčula, Dubrovnik and ultimately Bari in Italy. During the summer, two Jadrolinija ferries per week go from Stari Grad to Ancona in Italy. **SNAV** (www.snav.com) and **BlueLine** (www.blueline-ferries.com) also run regular boats to Ancona from Hvar Town. Pelegrini Tours in Hvar sells these tickets.

❶ Getting Around

Buses meet most ferries that dock at Stari Grad and go to Hvar Town (25KN, 50 minutes). A taxi costs from 150KN to 350KN. **Radio Taxi Tihi** (☑ 098 338 824) is cheaper if there are a number of passengers to fill up the minivan.

Korčula Island

☑ 020 / POP 16,200

Rich in vineyards and olive trees, the island of Korčula was named Korkyra Melaina (Black Korčula) by the original Greek settlers because of its dense woods and plant life. As the largest island in an archipelago of 48, it provides plenty of opportunities for scenic drives, particularly along the southern coast.

Swimming opportunities abound in the many quiet coves and secluded beaches, while the interior produces some of Croatia's finest wine, especially dessert wines made from the *grk* grape cultivated around Lumbarda. Local olive oil is another product worth seeking out.

On a hilly peninsula jutting into the Adriatic sits Korčula Town, a striking walled town of round defensive towers and red-roofed houses. Resembling a miniature Dubrovnik, the gated, walled Old Town is crisscrossed by narrow stone streets designed to protect its inhabitants from the winds swirling around the peninsula.

The big Jadrolinija car ferry drops you off either in the west harbour next to the Hotel Korčula or the east harbour next to Marko Polo Tours. The Old Town lies between the two harbours. The large hotels and main beach lie south of the east harbour, and the residential neighbourhood Sveti Nikola (with a smaller beach) is southwest of the west harbour. The town bus station is 100m south of the Old Town centre.

◉ Sights

Other than following the circuit of the city walls or walking along the shore, sightseeing in Korčula centres on Trg Sv Marka (St Mark's Sq).

St Mark's Cathedral   CHURCH
(Katedrala Svetog Marka; Statuta 1214; ⊘9am-9pm Jul & Aug, Mass only Sep-Jun) Dominating Trg Svetog Marka, the 15th-century Gothic-Renaissance cathedral features two paintings by Tintoretto (*Three Saints* on the altar and *Annunciation* to one side).

Town Museum   MUSEUM
(Gradski Muzej; ☑711 420; Statuta 1214; admission 15KN; ⊘9am-9pm daily Jun-Aug, 9am-1pm Mon-Sat Sep-May) The 16th-century Gabriellis Palace opposite the cathedral houses the museum, with exhibits of Greek pottery, Roman ceramics and home furnishings, all with English captions.

Marco Polo Museum   MUSEUM
(Ulica De Polo; admission 15KN; ⊘9am-7pm Jun-Sep, 10am-4pm May & Oct) It's said that Marco Polo was born in Korčula in 1254; you can visit what is believed to have been his house and climb the tower for an eagle's-eye vista over the Korčula peninsula and Adriatic.

Treasury Museum   MUSEUM
(Statuta 1214; admission 15KN; ⊘9am-7.30pm Mon-Sat May-Nov) Located in the 14th-century Abbey Palace, this museum with its hall of Dalmatian art is worth a look.

☞ Tours

Both Atlas Travel Agency and Marko Polo Tours offer a variety of boat tours and island excursions, including day trips to Mljet. In summer, water taxis at the east harbour collect passengers to visit **Badija Island**, which features a historic 15th-century Franciscan Monastery, plus **Orebić** (p160) and the nearby village of **Lumbarda**, both of which have sandy beaches.

🛏 Sleeping & Eating

Korčula's hotel scene is on the bulky and resort side. If you don't fancy staying in any of the big hotels, a more personal option is a guest house. Atlas Travel Agency and Marko Polo Tours arrange private rooms (from 250KN in high season).

Lešić Dimitri Palace   BOUTIQUE HOTEL €€€
(☑715 560; www.lesic-dimitri.com; Don Pavla Poše 1-6; apt 2731-8741KN; ❋☺☞) Exceptional in every way (including its rates). Spread over several town mansions, the six 'residences' have been finished to an impeccable standard, while keeping original detail.

WORTH A TRIP

OREBIĆ

Orebić, on the southern coast of the Pelješac Peninsula between Korčula and Ploče, offers better beaches than those found at Korčula, 2.5km across the water. The easy access by ferry from Korčula makes it the perfect place to go for the day. The best beach in Orebić is Trstenica cove, a 15-minute walk east along the shore from the port.

In Orebić the ferry terminal and the bus station are adjacent to each other. Korčula buses to Dubrovnik, Zagreb and Sarajevo stop at Orebić.

Hotel Bon Repos   HOTEL €€
(☎726 800; www.korcula-hotels.com; d 524KN; P🅿︎⛵@🏋) On the road to Lumbarda, this huge decent-value hotel has manicured grounds, a large pool overlooking a small beach and water-taxi service to Korčula Town.

Villa DePolo   APARTMENTS €
(☎711 621; tereza.depolo@du.t-com.hr; Svetog Nikole bb; d 330KN;❄🈂️) These small, simple but attractive modern rooms (and one apartment) come with comfortable beds; one has a terrace with amazing views. It's a short walk from the Old Town.

Pansion Hajduk   PENSION €
(☎711 267; olga.zec@du.t-com.hr; d from 430KN; ❄🈂️🏋) It's a couple of kilometres from town on the road to Lumbarda, but you get a warm welcome, air-conditioned rooms with TVs and even a swimming pool.

Autocamp Kalac   CAMPING GROUND €
(☎711 182; www.korculahotels.com; per person/campsite 54/48KN; ❂May-Oct) This attractive camping ground with tennis courts is a 30-minute walk away from the Old Town, in a dense pine grove near the beach.

TOP CHOICE **Konoba Komin**   DALMATIAN €€
(☎716 508; Don Iva Matijace; mains from 45KN) This family-run *konoba* looks almost medieval, with its *komin* (roaring fire), roasting meat, ancient stone walls and solid wooden tables. The menu is simple and delicious and the space tight so book ahead.

LD   FINE DINING €€
(☎715 560; www.lesic-dimitri.com; Don Pavla Poše 1-6; mains from 45KN) Korčula's finest restaurant, with tables right above the water, of-fers a modern, metropolitan-style menu and many wonderful Croatian wines.

Konoba Maslina   DALMATIAN €€
(Lumbarajska cesta bb; mains from 50KN) Everything you'd want from a rural *konoba*; this traditional place 3km out of town on the road to Lumbarda offers honest country cooking – fresh fish, lamb and veal, and local ham and cheese.

ℹ Entertainment

Between June and September there's **moreška sword dancing** (tickets 100KN; ❂9pm Mon & Thu) by the Old Town gate; performances are more frequent during July and August. The clash of swords and the graceful movements of the dancers/fighters make an exciting show. The tourist office, Atlas and Marko Polo Tours sell tickets.

ℹ Information

There are several ATMs around town, including one at HVB Splitska Banka. You can also change money at the post office or at any of the travel agencies.

Atlas Travel Agency (☎711 231; atlas-korcula@du.htnet.hr; Trg 19 Travnja bb) Represents American Express, runs excursions and finds private accommodation.

Hospital (☎711 137; Kalac bb) About 1km past the Hotel Marko Polo.

Kantun Tours (☎715 622; www.kantun-tours.com; Plokata 19 Travnja bb) Probably the best-organised and largest agency, it offers private accommodation, excursions, car hire and boat tickets. Also has luggage storage.

PC Centrar Doom (Obvjeknik Vladimir DePolo; per hr 25KN) Internet access and cheapish international phone calls.

Tourist office (☎715 701; www.korcula.net; Obala Franje Tuđmana 4; ❂8am-3pm & 5-8pm Mon-Sat, 9am-1pm Sun Jul-Aug, 8am-2pm Mon-Sat Sep-Jun) On the west harbour; an excellent source of information.

ℹ Getting There & Away

Transport connections to Korčula are good. There are buses to Dubrovnik (85KN, three hours, one to three daily) and one to Zagreb (239KN, 11 hours). Book ahead in summer.

The island has two major entry ports by boat – Korčula Town and Vela Luka. All the Jadrolinija ferries between Split and Dubrovnik stop in Korčula Town. There's a **Jadrolinija office** (☎715 410) about 25m down from the west harbour.

There's a daily fast boat, the **Krilo** (www.krilo.hr), which runs from Split to Korčula (55KN, 2¾ hours) all year round, stopping at Hvar en route. Jadrolinija runs a passenger catamaran daily from June to September from Split to Vela Luka (60KN, two hours), stopping at Hvar. There's also a regular afternoon car ferry between Split and Vela Luka (45KN, three hours) that stops at Hvar most days.

From the Pelješac Peninsula, regular boats link Orebić and Korčula. Passenger launches (15KN, 10 minutes, 13 daily June to September, at least five daily rest of year) sail to Korčula Town. Car ferries (17KN, 15 minutes, at least 14 daily year-round) also run this route, but use the deeper port of Dominče, 3km away from Korčula Town. (As bus connections are poor and taxis fares are extortionate – 80KN for a 3km journey – try to use the catamaran boats if you're on foot.)

Scooters (291KN for 24 hours) and boats (580KN per day) are available from Rent a Đir (☏711 908; www.korcula-rent.com; Biline 5).

Mljet Island

☏020 / POP 1232

Of all the Adriatic islands, Mljet (Meleda in Italian) may be the most seductive. Much of the island is covered by forests and the rest is dotted with fields, vineyards and villages. The northwestern half of the island forms Mljet National Park, where lush vegetation, pine forests and two saltwater lakes offer a scenic hideaway. It's an unspoiled oasis of tranquillity that, according to legend, captivated Odysseus for seven years.

The island is 37km long, and has an average width of about 3km. The main points of entry are Pomena and Polače, two tiny towns about 5km apart.

Most people visit the island on excursions from Korčula or Dubrovnik, but it is possible to take a passenger boat from Dubrovnik or come on the regular ferry from Dubrovnik and stay a few days for hiking, cycling and boating.

◉ Sights & Activities

The highlights of the island are Malo Jezero and Veliko Jezero, the two lakes on the island's western end connected by a channel. In the middle of Veliko Jezero is an islet with a 12th-century Benedictine monastery, which contains a pricey but atmospheric restaurant.

There's a boat from Mali Most (about 1.5km from Pomena) on Malo Jezero that leaves for the island monastery every hour at 10 minutes past the hour. It's not possible to walk right around the larger lake as there's no bridge over the channel connecting the lakes to the sea. If you decide to swim it, keep in mind that the current can be strong.

Renting a bicycle (20/100KN per hour/day) is an excellent way to explore the national park. Several places including Hotel Odisej in Pomena have bikes. Be aware that Pomena and Polače are separated by a steep hill. The bike path along the lake is an easier and very scenic pedal, but it doesn't link the two towns. You can rent a paddleboat and row over to the monastery but you'll need stamina.

The island offers some unusual opportunities for **diving**. There's a Roman wreck dating from the 3rd century in relatively shallow water. The remains of the ship, including amphorae, have calcified over the centuries and this has protected them from pillaging. There's also a German torpedo boat from WWII and several walls to dive. Contact Kronmar Diving (☏744 022; Hotel Odisej).

🛏 Sleeping & Eating

The Polače tourist office arranges private accommodation (from around 260KN per double), but it's essential to make arrangements before peak season. You'll find more *sobe* signs around Pomena than Polače, and practically none at all in Sobra. Restaurants rent out rooms too.

Stermasi   APARTMENTS €
(☏098 939 0362; Saplunara; apt 401-546KN; P❄)
On the 'other' side of Mljet, these apartments are ideal for those wanting to enjoy the simple life and natural beauty of the island. Well presented and bright, the nine modern units have terraces or private balcony. Sandy beaches are on your doorstep and the onsite restaurant is one of Dalmatia's best.

MLJET: INS & OUTS

Sightseeing boats from Korčula and the Dubrovnik catamarans arrive at Polače wharf in high season; Jadrolinija ferries use the port of Sobra close to the centre of the island. The entry point for Mljet National Park (www.np-mljet.hr; adult/concession 90/40KN) is between Pomena and Polače. Your ticket includes a bus and boat transfer to the Benedictine monastery. If you stay overnight on the island you only pay the park admission once.

Soline 6
HOTEL €€

(☎744 024; www.soline6.com; Soline; d 546KN) This very green place is the only accommodation within the national park, with everything built from recycled products, organic waste composted, waterless toilets and no electricity. The four studios are modern and equipped with private bathrooms, balconies and kitchens.

Camping Mungos
CAMPING GROUND €

(☎745 300; www.mungos-mljet.com; Babino Polje; per person 52KN; ⊙May-Sep) Close to the beach and the lovely grotto of Odysseus, this camping ground has a restaurant, currency exchange and a mini-market.

Hotel Odisej
HOTEL €€€

(☎744 022; www.hotelodisej.hr; Pomena; d from 580KN; P⊙❀✴@⊙) The only conventional hotel option in Mljet isn't great. A lingering Yugo flavour endures, service can be stone-faced and decor is little changed from the 1970s. That said, rates are not outrageous and it's rarely booked up.

Melita
DALMATIAN €€

(www.mljet-restoranmelita.com; St Mary's Island, Veliko Jezero; mains from 60KN) A more romantic (and touristy) spot can't be found on the island – this is the restaurant attached to the church on the little island in the middle of the big lake.

❶ Information

The **tourist office** (☎744 186; www.mljet.hr; ⊙8am-1pm & 5-7pm Mon-Sat, 9am-noon Sun Jun-Sep, 8am-1pm Mon-Fri Oct-May) is in Polače and there's an ATM next door (and another at Hotel Odisej in Pomena). There are free brochures and a good walking map for sale.

Babino Polje, 18km east of Polače, is the island capital. It's home to another **tourist office** (☎745 125; www.mljet.hr; ⊙9am-5pm Mon-Fri) and a post office.

❶ Getting There & Away

Jadrolinija ferries stop only at Sobra (32KN, two hours) but the **Melita catamaran** (☎313 119; www.gv-line.hr; Vukovarska 34, Dubrovnik) goes to Sobra (22KN, one hour) and Polače (50KN, 1½ hours) in the summer months, leaving Dubrovnik's Gruž harbour twice daily (9.15am and 6.15pm) and returning daily from Polače at 4pm and twice daily from Sobra (6.15am and 4.40pm). You *cannot* reserve tickets in advance so get to the harbour ticket office well in advance in high season to secure a seat. Tour boats from Korčula also run to Polače harbour in high season. Infrequent buses connect Sobra and Polače.

Dubrovnik
⊡020 / POP 29,995

No matter whether you are visiting Dubrovnik for the first time or if you're returning again and again to this marvellous city, the sense of awe and beauty when you set eyes on the Stradun (the Old Town's main street) never fades. It's hard to imagine anyone, even the city's inhabitants, becoming jaded by its marble streets and baroque buildings, or failing to be inspired by a walk along the ancient city walls that once protected a civilised, sophisticated republic for five centuries and that now look out onto the endless shimmer of the peaceful Adriatic.

History

Founded 1300 years ago by refugees from Epidaurus in Greece, medieval Dubrovnik (Ragusa until 1918) shook off Venetian control in the 14th century, becoming an independent republic and one of Venice's more important maritime rivals, trading with Egypt, Syria, Sicily, Spain, France and later Turkey. The double blow of an earthquake in 1667 and the opening of new trade routes to the east sent Ragusa into a slow decline, ending with Napoleon's conquest of the town in 1808.

The deliberate shelling of Dubrovnik by the Yugoslav army in 1991 sent shockwaves through the international community but, when the smoke cleared in 1992, traumatised residents cleared the rubble and set about repairing the damage. Reconstruction has been extraordinarily skilful.

After a steep postwar decline in tourism, Dubrovnik has bounced back and become a major tourist destination once again.

❂ Sights

All the sights are in the Old Town, which is closed to cars. Looming above the city is Srđ Hill, which is connected by cable car to Dubrovnik. The main street in the Old Town is Placa (better known as Stradun).

OLD TOWN
City Walls & Forts
LANDMARK

(Gradske Zidine; adult/concession 70/30KN; ⊙9am-6.30pm Apr-Oct, 10am-3pm Nov-Mar) No visit to Dubrovnik would be complete without a leisurely walk around the spectacular city walls, the finest in the world and Dubrovnik's main claim to fame. Built between the 13th and 16th centuries, they are still intact today. They enclose the entire city in a protective veil more than 2km long and up to 25m high, with two round and 14 square towers, two corner fortifications and a large fortress. The views over the town and sea are great – this walk could be the high point of your visit. The main entrance and ticket office to the walls is by the **Pile Gate**. You can also enter at the **Ploče Gate** in the east (a wise move at really busy times of day).

War Photo Limited PHOTO GALLERY
(www.warphotoltd.com; Antuninska 6; admission 30KN; ⊘9am-9pm daily Jun-Sep, 9am-3pm Tue-Sat, 9am-1pm Sun May & Oct) An immensely powerful experience, this state-of-the-art photographic gallery has changing exhibitions curated by the gallery owner and former photojournalist Wade Goddard. In addition to temporary shows, there's a permanent exhibition on the upper floor devoted to the war in Yugoslavia. It closes between November and April.

Franciscan Monastery & Museum MONASTERY
(Muzej Franjevačkog Samostana; Placa 2; adult/concession 30/15KN; ⊘9am-6pm) Inside the monastery complex is a mid-14th-century **cloister**, one of the most beautiful late-Romanesque structures in Dalmatia. Further inside is the third-oldest functioning **pharmacy** in Europe, in business since 1391. The small monastery **museum** has a collection of relics, liturgical objects and pharmacy items.

Dominican Monastery & Museum MONASTERY
(Muzej Dominikanskog Samostana; off Ulica Svetog Dominika 4; adult/concession 20/10KN; ⊘9am-6pm May-Oct, to 5pm Nov-Apr) This imposing 14-century structure in the northeastern corner of the city is a real architectural highlight, with a forbidding fortress-like exterior that shelters a rich trove of paintings from Dubrovnik's finest 15th- and 16th-century artists.

Rector's Palace PALACE
(Pred Dvorom 3; adult/concession 35/15KN, audio guide 30KN; ⊘9am-6pm May-Oct, to 4pm Nov-Apr) This Gothic-Renaissance palace built in the late 15th century houses a museum with furnished rooms, baroque paintings and historical exhibits. Today, the atrium is often used for concerts during the Summer Festival.

Cathedral of the Assumption of the Virgin CHURCH
(Stolna Crkva Velike Gospe; Poljana M Držića; ⊘morning & late-afternoon Mass) Completed in 1713 in a baroque style, the cathedral is notable for its fine altars. The cathedral **treasury**

(Riznica; adult/concession 10/5KN; ⊘8am-5.30pm Mon-Sat, 11am-5.30pm Sun May-Oct, 10am-noon & 3-5pm Nov-Apr) contains relics of St Blaise and a number of religious paintings.

Sponza Palace PALACE
The 16th-century Sponza Palace was originally a customs house, then a minting house, a state treasury and a bank. Now it houses the State Archives and the **Memorial Room of the Defenders of Dubrovnik** (⊘10am-10pm Mon-Fri, 8am-1pm Sat), a heartbreaking collection of portraits of young people who perished between 1991 and 1995.

St Blaise's Church CHURCH
(Crkva Svetog Vlahe; Luža Sq; ⊘morning & late-afternoon Mass Mon-Sat) Imposing church built in 1715 in a baroque style; the ornate exterior contrasts strongly with the sober residences surrounding it.

Onofrio Fountain MONUMENT
One of Dubrovnik's most famous landmarks, the Onofrio Fountain was built in 1438 as part of a water-supply system that involved bringing water from a well 12km away.

Serbian Orthodox Church & Museum CHURCH
(Muzej Pravoslavne Crkve; Od Puča 8; adult/concession 10/5KN; ⊘9am-2pm Mon-Sat) This 1877 Orthodox church has a fascinating collection of icons dating from the 15th to 19th centuries.

Synagogue SYNAGOGUE
(Sinagoga; Žudioska 5; admission 10KN; ⊘10am-8pm May-Oct Mon-Fri, to 3pm Nov-Apr) The oldest Sephardic and second-oldest synagogue in the Balkans, dating back to the 15th century, has a small museum inside.

Orlando Column MONUMENT
This popular meeting place used to be the spot where edicts, festivities and public verdicts were announced.

EAST OF THE OLD TOWN

TOP CHOICE **Cable Car** CABLE CAR
(Petra Krešimira IV; www.dubrovnikcablecar.com; adult/concession 40/20KN; ⊘9am-10pm Tue-Sun May-Oct, shorter hrs Nov-Apr) Reopened after 19 years, the cable car whisks you from just north of the city walls up to Mount Srđ in under four minutes, for a stupendous perspective from a lofty 405m, down to the terracotta-tiled rooftops of the Old Town and the island of Lokrum, with the Adriatic Sea and distant Elafiti islands filling the horizon.

CROATIA DALMATIA

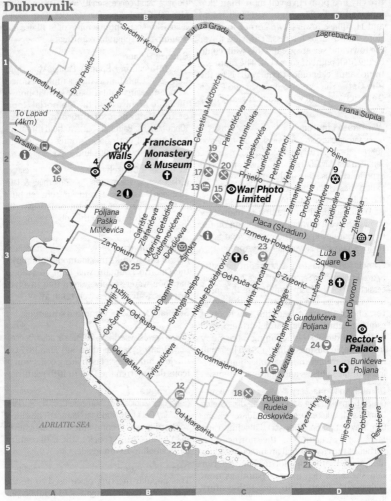

THE COAST

Banje Beach, not far from Ploče Gate, used to be the most popular city beach, though it's less popular now a section has been roped off for the exclusive EastWest Club. Just southeast is **Sveti Jakov**, a good local beach that doesn't get rowdy. Buses 5 and 8 will get you here. The nicest beach that's walkable from the Old Town is below Hotel Bellevue. **Lapad Bay** brims with hotel beaches that you can use without a problem; try the bay by Hotel Kompas. A little further on is the good shallow **Copacabana Beach** on Babin Kuk peninsula. In

the Old Town, you can also swim below the two Buža bars.

An even better option is to take the ferry that shuttles hourly in summer to lush **Lokrum Island** (return 40KN, last boat back 6pm), a national park with a rocky nudist beach (marked FKK), a botanical garden and the ruins of a medieval Benedictine monastery.

🏊 Activities

Navis Underwater Explorers (☎099 35 02 773; www.navisdubrovnik.com; Copacabana Beach) offers recreational dives (including the wreck of the *Taranto*) and courses.

to Mljet, Korčula and the Elafiti Islands (250KN) are also offered.

✷ Festivals & Events

The **Feast of St Blaise** is held on 3 February, and **Carnival** is also held in February.

Dubrovnik Summer Festival (www.dubrovnik-festival.hr) is a major cultural event over five weeks in July and August, with theatre, music and dance performances at different venues in the Old Town.

🛏 Sleeping

Private accommodation is generally the best option in Dubrovnik, which is the most expensive destination in Croatia. Beware the scramble of private owners at the bus station and ferry terminal: some provide what they say they offer while others are scamming. Expect to pay from 300KN for a double room, and from 500KN for an apartment in high season.

OLD TOWN

TOP CHOICE **Karmen Apartments** APARTMENT €€
(☑323 433, 098 619 282; www.karmendu.com; Bandureva 1; apt 437-1165KN;❄🛜) Run by an Englishman who has lived in Dubrovnik for decades, these four inviting apartments with plenty of character enjoy a great location a stone's throw from Ploče harbour. Book well ahead.

Fresh Sheets HOSTEL €
(☑091 79 92 086; www.igotfresh.com; Sv Šimuna 15; dm/d 210/554KN; ❄@🛜) The only hostel in the Old Town is a warm, welcoming place right by the city walls; all rooms and reception areas are painted in zany colours and there's space for socialising downstairs. It's run by a party-hard crew who organise legendary booze-ups.

Hotel Stari Grad BOUTIQUE HOTEL €€€
(☑322 244; www.hotelstarigrad.com; Od Sigurate 4; s/d 1180/1580KN; ❄❄🛜) This Old Town hotel is all about location – it's very close to the Pile Gate and just off the Stradun. Its eight rooms are smallish but neat and attractive. Staff are sweet and views from the rooftop terrace are dramatic.

Apartments Amoret APARTMENTS €€
(☑091 53 04 910; www.dubrovnik-amoret.com; Dinke Ranjine 5; apt 655-874KN;❄❄🛜) Spread over three historic buildings in the heart of the Old Town, Amoret offers 11 high-quality renovated studio apartments with wi-fi, elegant

Contact **Adriatic Kayak Tours** (☑091 72 20 413; www.adriatickayaktours.com; Zrinsko Frankopanska 6) for kayak excursions (from a half-day paddle to a week-long trip).

☞ Tours

Dubrovnik Walks CITY TOURS
(☑095 80 64 526; www.dubrovnikwalks.com) Excellent guided walks in English. One-hour Old Town tours (70KN) run twice daily.

Adriatic Explore TOURS
(☑323 400; www.adriatic-explore.com; Bandureva 4) Day trips to Mostar and Montenegro (both 380KN) are very popular; excursions

Dubrovnik

decor, a dash of art, parquet wood flooring and kitchenette-style cooking facilities.

OUTSIDE THE OLD TOWN

Hotel Bellevue LUXURY HOTEL €€€
(☎330 000; www.hotel-bellevue.hr; Petra Čingrije 7; d from 1835KN; P🐾❄☀@🛜) Ignore the dated tinted-glass frontage; this is a very classy hotel, positioned on a cliff over the Adriatic, boasting all balconied rooms. The restaurant, Vapor, is top-notch and there's a gem of a beach below, accessible by the hotel's lift. It's a 15-minute walk west of the Pile Gate.

Begović Boarding House PENSION €
(☎435 191; www.begovic-boarding-house.com; Primorska 17; dm/r/apt 146/292/364KN; P@) A steep walk uphill from Lapad harbourfront, this welcoming family-run place has smallish but clean pine-trimmed rooms, some opening out onto a communal garden with amazing views. There's free pick-up from the bus or ferry, free internet, a kitchen and excursions.

YHA Hostel HOSTEL €
(☎423 241; dubrovnik@hfhs.hr; Vinka Sagrestana 3; dm 148KN; @) Its location is pretty good, in a quiet area 1km west of the Old Town.

This mid-sized hostel has decent, spacious if plain dorms (and one double) and a rooftop terrace. Rates include breakfast. Book ahead.

Hotel Ivka HOTEL €€
(☎362 600; www.hotel-ivka.com; Put Sv Mihajla 21; s/d 585/760KN; P☀@🛜) Modern three-star hotel with spacious modern rooms that have wooden floors and free wi-fi; most come with balconies, too. Comfort levels are high given the prices. It's closer to Lapad and the ferry terminal than the Old Town, but on a regular bus route.

🍴 Eating

Weed out tourist traps and choose carefully, and you'll find fabulous food in the Old Town.

Lucín Kantun CROATIAN €€
(☎321 003; Od Sigurate bb; meals around 140KN) A modest-looking place with shabby-chic decor, a few pavement tables and some of the most creative food in Dubrovnik. Everything on the short mezze-style menu is freshly cooked from an open kitchen so you may have to wait a while at busy times.

Wanda
ITALIAN €€€

(☑098 94 49 317; www.wandarestaurant.com; Prijeko 8; mains from 70KN) This is a very classy Italian, with good Croatian wines and dishes such as osso buco with saffron risotto and beautifully crafted pastas. Eat from the fixed-priced tasting menus (150KN to 580KN) to see what the chefs are really capable of.

Dubravka 1836
CAFE €€

(www.dubravka1836.hr; Brsalje 1; mains from 49KN) This place has arguably Dubrovnik's best dining terrace, right by the Pile Gate with stunning wall and sea views. Though it draws quite a touristy clientele, locals still rate the fresh fish, risottos and salads, pizza and pasta.

Nishta
VEGETARIAN €

(www.nishtarestaurant.com; Prijeko bb; mains from 59KN; ☺ closed Mon) A casual enjoyable vegetarian restaurant, Nishtu raids the globe for dishes so you'll find miso soup, nachos, Indian food, Thai curries and chow mein.

Buffet Skola
CAFE €

(Antuninska 1; snacks from 17KN) For a quick bite between sightseeing spots, you can't do better. The ham and cheese sandwich is the thing to order.

🍷 Drinking

Buža
BAR

(Ilije Sarake) Finding this isolated bar-on-a-cliff feels like a discovery as you duck and dive around the city walls and finally see the entrance tunnel. It showcases tasteful music and a mellow crowd soaking up the vibes, views and sunshine.

Buža II
BAR

(Crijevićeva 9) Just a notch more upmarket than the original, this one is lower on the rocks and has a shaded terrace where you can snack on crisps, peanuts or sandwiches.

The Gaffe
PUB

(Miha Pracata bb) The busiest place in town, this huge pub has a homey interior, a long covered side terrace and friendly staff.

Troubadur
BAR

(Bunićeva Poljana 2) Come to this corner bar, a legendary Dubrovnik venue, for live jazz concerts in the summer.

EastWest Club
BAR-CLUB

(www.ew-dubrovnik.com; Frana Supila bb) By day this outfit on Banje Beach rents out beach chairs and umbrellas and serves drinks to the bathers. When the rays lengthen, the cocktail bar opens.

☆ Entertainment

TOP CHOICE | Lazareti
CULTURAL CENTRE

(www.lazareti.com; Frana Supila 8) Dubrovnik's best cultural centre, Lazareti hosts cinema nights, club nights, live music, gigs and pretty much all the best things in town.

Open-Air Cinema
CINEMA

(Kumičića, Lapad) In two locations, it's open nightly in July and August with screenings starting after sundown. Also at Za Rokom in the Old Town.

ℹ Information

There are numerous ATMs in town, in Lapad and at the ferry terminal and bus station. Travel agencies and post office will also exchange cash.

Atlas Travel Agency (www.atlas-croatia.com) Gruž Harbour (☑418 001; Obala Papa Ivana Pavla II 1); Pile Gate (☑442 574; Sv Đurđa 1) Organises excursions within Croatia and to Mostar and Montenegro. Also finds private accommodation.

Hospital (☑431 777; Dr Roka Mišetića) A kilometre south of Lapad Bay.

Left luggage (Garderoba; 1st hr 5KN, then each hr 1.50KN; ☺4.30am-10pm) At the bus station.

Main post office (cnr Široka & Od Puča)

Netcafé (www.netcafe.hr; Prijeko 21; per hr 30KN) This cybercafe has fast connections, CD/DVD burning, wi-fi, photo printing and scanning.

OK Travel & Trade (☑418 950; okt-t@du.t-com.hr; Obala Stjepana Radića 32) Near the Jadrolinija ferry terminal.

Tourist office (www.tzdubrovnik.hr; ☺8am-8pm daily Jun-Sep, 8am-3pm Mon-Fri, 9am-2pm Sat Oct-May) bus station (☑417 581; Obala Pape Ivana Pavla II 44a); Gruž Harbour (☑417 983; Obala Stjepana Radića 27); Lapad (☑437 460; Šetalište Kralja Zvonimira 25); Old Town (☑323 587; Široka 1); Old Town 2 (☑ 323 887; Ulica Svetog Dominika 7) Maps, information and the indispensable Dubrovnik Riviera guide. The smart new head office that's under construction just west of the Pile Gate should open by the time you read this.

ℹ Getting There & Away

Air

Daily flights to/from Zagreb are operated by **Croatia Airlines** (☑01-66 76 555; www.croatia airlines.hr). Fares vary between 270KN for promo fares and around 760KN for flexi fares. The trip takes about an hour. Croatia Airlines also operate nonstop flights to Frankfurt and seasonal routes to cities, including Rome, Paris and Amsterdam.

Dubrovnik airport is served by over 20 other airlines from across Europe.

Boat

A twice-weekly **Jadrolinija** (☎418 000; www. jadrolinija.hr; Gruž Harbour) coastal ferry heads north to Korčula, Hvar, Split, Zadar and Rijeka. There's a local ferry that leaves Dubrovnik for Sobra and Polače on Mljet (60KN, 2½ hours) throughout the year; in summer there are two ferries a day. Several daily ferries run year-round to the outlying Elafiti Islands of Koločep, Lopud and Šipan.

Ferries also go from Dubrovnik to Bari, in southern Italy; there are six a week in the summer season (291KN to 401KN, nine hours) and two in the winter months.

Jadroagent (☎419 000; Obala Stjepana Radića 32) books ferry tickets and has information.

Bus

The Jadrolinija ferry terminal and the bus station are next to each other at Gruž, several kilometres northwest of the Old Town.

Buses out of Dubrovnik **bus station** (☎060 305 070; Obala Pape Ivana Pavla II 44a) can be crowded, so book tickets ahead in summer.

Split–Dubrovnik buses pass briefly through Bosnian territory, so keep your passport handy for border-crossing points.

All bus schedules are detailed at www.libertas dubrovnik.hr.

ℹ Getting Around

Čilipi international airport (www.airport -dubrovnik.hr) is 24km southeast of Dubrovnik. Atlas buses (35KN) leave from the main bus station irregularly, supposedly two hours before Croatia Airlines domestic flights, but it's best to check the latest schedule at the Atlas travel agency by the Pile Gate. Buses leave the airport for Dubrovnik bus station (via the Pile Gate in this direction) several times a day and are timed to coincide with arrivals. A taxi costs around 240KN.

Dubrovnik's buses run frequently and generally on time. The fare is 10KN if you buy from the driver but only 8KN if you buy it at a kiosk.

UNDERSTAND CROATIA

History

Croatia has a long and torrid history, which has helped define the Croats and contributed much to the fabric of the country. Since time immemorial, people have come and gone, invading, trading and settling. For long periods, the Croats have been ruled by and have fought off others – Venetians, Ottomans, Hungarians, Habsburgs, the French, the Germans. The creation of Yugoslavia after WWII brought some semblance of unity into the south Slavic nations. Yet it didn't last long. After the death of Yugoslav leader Tito in 1980, Yugoslavia slowly disintegrated, and a brutal civil war ensued.

War & Peace

With political changes sweeping Eastern Europe, many Croats felt the time had come to separate from Yugoslavia and the elections of April 1990 saw the victory of Franjo Tuđman's Croatian Democratic Union (Hrvatska Demokratska Zajednica; HDZ). On 22 December 1990 a new Croatian con-

BUSES FROM DUBROVNIK

DESTINATION	FARE (KN)	DURATION (HR)	DAILY SERVICES
Korčula	95	3	2
Kotor	96	2½	2-3
Mostar	105	3	3
Orebić	84	2½	2
Plitvice	330	10	1
Rijeka	357-496	13	4-5
Sarajevo	210	5	2
Split	122	4½	19
Zadar	174-210	8	8
Zagreb	250	11	7-8

stitution was promulgated, changing the status of Serbs in Croatia from that of a 'constituent nation' to a national minority.

The constitution's failure to guarantee minority rights and mass dismissals of Serbs from the public service stimulated the 600,000-strong ethnic Serb community within Croatia to demand autonomy. In early 1991 Serb extremists within Croatia staged provocations designed to force federal military intervention. A May 1991 referendum (boycotted by the Serbs) produced a 93% vote in favour of independence, but when Croatia declared independence on 25 June 1991, the Serbian enclave of Krajina proclaimed its independence from Croatia.

Under pressure from the EC (now the EU), Croatia declared a three-month moratorium on its independence, but heavy fighting broke out in Krajina, Baranja (the area north of the Drava River opposite Osijek) and Slavonia. The Serb-dominated Yugoslav People's Army intervened in support of Serbian irregulars, under the pretext of halting ethnic violence.

When the Croatian government ordered a blockade of 32 federal military installations in the republic, the Yugoslav navy blockaded the Adriatic coast and laid siege to the strategic town of Vukovar on the Danube. During the summer of 1991, a quarter of Croatia fell to Serbian militias and the Yugoslav People's Army.

In early October 1991 the federal army and Montenegrin militia moved against Dubrovnik to protest the blockade of their garrisons in Croatia, and on 7 October the presidential palace in Zagreb was hit by rockets fired by Yugoslav air-force jets in an unsuccessful assassination attempt on President Tuđman. When the three-month moratorium on independence ended, Croatia declared full independence. On 19 November the city of Vukovar fell after a bloody three-month siege. During six months of fighting in Croatia 10,000 people died, hundreds of thousands fled and tens of thousands of homes were destroyed.

To fulfil a condition for EC recognition, in December the Croatian Sabor (Parliament) belatedly amended its constitution to protect minority groups and human rights. A UN-brokered ceasefire from 3 January 1992 generally held. In January 1992 the EC, succumbing to strong pressure from Germany, recognised Croatia. This was followed three months later by US recognition; in May 1992 Croatia was admitted to the UN.

The fighting continued until the Dayton Accord, signed in Paris in December 1995, recognised Croatia's traditional borders and provided for the return of eastern Slavonia, which was effected in January 1998. The transition proceeded relatively smoothly, but the two populations still regard each other with suspicion.

Although the central government in Zagreb has made the return of Serb refugees a priority in accordance with the demands of the international community, Serbs intending to reclaim their property face an array of legal impediments.

Franjo Tuđman's combination of authoritarianism and media control, and tendency to be influenced by the far right, no longer appealed to the postwar Croatian populace. By 1999 opposition parties united to work against Tuđman and the HDZ. Tuđman was hospitalised and died suddenly in late 1999, and planned elections were postponed until January 2000. Still, voters turned out in favour of a centre-left coalition, ousting the HDZ and voting in the centrist Stipe Mesić, who held the presidential throne for ten years.

Croatia on the Cusp

Sitting between the Balkans and Central Europe, Croatia has been suffering from something of a love-hate-love affair with the EU and its neighbours as well as with its own politicians.

The biggest drama in Croatia's contemporary politics took place in July 2009 when the then prime minister Ivo Sanader announced his resignation and withdrawal from politics out of the blue and, rumours had it, went off sailing on his yacht. The parliament quickly approved his deputy, former journalist Jadranka Kosor, as prime minister; she was the first woman in Croatia's history to hold this post. In a move unpopular with the opposition, Kosor formed the government with pretty much the same cabinet members as Sanader's.

A major change happened in Croatia when Ivo Josipović of the opposition party, the Social Democratic Party of Croatia (SDP), won the presidential election in January 2010, beating the independent candidate Milan Bandić (Zagreb's mayor, who is serving his fourth term) with 60.26% of the vote in the runoffs. He was inaugurated as Croatia's third president in February 2010. Many Croats see Josipović as ineffective, a puppet of a corrupt regime. Others regard him as pro-European, in his (some say weak) attempts to employ a zero-tolerance policy towards corruption and inspire foreign investment.

Membership talks with the EU continue, as Croatia deals with the repercussions of global recession on its home turf as well as widespread governmental corruption and elements of rabid nationalism. It aims to join the EU in 2012, although that largely depends on negotiations and the accession treaty being ratified by the 27 members.

Attitudes towards Croatia joining the EU are divided. Many people are enthusiastic, though the enthusiasm has dropped with what some locals see as 'an endless list of rules' presented to the country. Predictably, it's the younger generations who are more geared towards joining the EU; the older generations lament the loss of industrial and agricultural independence that will inevitably happen when the country joins up.

It remains to be seen whether Croatia will manage to clean up its act. Until then, Croatia is still on the brink of Europe, which is part of its appeal and its curse.

The People of Croatia

According to the most recent census (2001), Croatia had a population of roughly 4.5 million people, a decline from the prewar population of nearly five million. Some 59% live in urban areas. About 280,000 Serbs (50% of the Serbian population) departed in the early 1990s; an estimated 110,000 have returned. In the postindependence economic crunch, 120,000 to 130,000 Croats emigrated, but a roughly equal number of ethnic Croat refugees arrived from Bosnia and Hercegovina and another 30,000 or so came from the Vojvodina region of Serbia. Italians are concentrated in Istria, while Albanians, Bosniaks and Roma can be found in Zagreb, Istria and some Dalmatian towns. The largest cities in Croatia are Zagreb (780,000), Split (188,700), Rijeka (138,000), Osijek (85,200) and Zadar (73,500).

Religion

According to the most recent census, 87.8% of the population identified itself as Catholic, 4.4% Orthodox, 1.3% Muslim, 0.3% Protestant and 6.2% others and unknown. Croats are overwhelmingly Roman Catholic, while all Serbs belong to the Eastern Orthodox Church, a division that has its roots in the fall of the Roman Empire.

It would be difficult to overstate the extent to which Catholicism shapes the Croatian national identity. The Church is the most trusted institution in Croatia, rivalled only by the military. Religious holidays are celebrated with fervour and Sunday Mass is strongly attended.

Food & Drink

Croatian food is a savoury smorgasbord of taste, echoing the varied cultures that have influenced the country over the course of its history. You'll find a sharp divide between the Italian-style cuisine along the coast and the flavours of Hungary, Austria and Turkey in the continental parts.

Staples & Specialities

Zagreb and northwestern Croatia favour the kind of hearty meat dishes you might find in Vienna. Juicy spit-roasted and baked meat features *janjetina* (lamb), *svinjetina* (pork) and *patka* (duck), often accompanied by *mlinci* (baked noodles) or *pečeni krumpir* (roast potatoes).

Coastal cuisine is typically Mediterranean, using a lot of olive oil, garlic, fresh fish and shellfish, and herbs. Along the coast, look for lightly breaded and fried *lignje* (squid) as a main course. For a special appetiser, try *paški sir*, a pungent hard cheese from the island of Pag. Dalmatian *brodet* (stewed mixed fish served with polenta) is another regional treat.

Istrian cuisine has been attracting international foodies for its long gastronomic tradition, fresh foodstuffs and unique specialities. Typical dishes include *maneštra*, a thick vegetable-and-bean soup, *fuži*, hand-rolled pasta often served with truffles or game meat, and *fritaja* (omelette often served with seasonal vegies). Istrian wines and olive oil are highly rated.

It's customary to have a small glass of brandy before a meal and to accompany the food with one of Croatia's many wines. Croatians often mix their wine with water, calling it *bevanda*. *Rakija* (brandy) comes in different flavours. The most commonly drunk are *loza* (grape brandy), *šljivovica* (plum brandy) and *travarica* (herbal brandy).

The two top types of Croatian *pivo* (beer) are Zagreb's Ožujsko and Karlovačko from

Karlovac. You'll probably want to practise saying *živjeli!* (cheers!).

Where to Eat & Drink

Most restaurants cluster in the middle of the price spectrum – few are unbelievably cheap and few are exorbitantly expensive. A restaurant *(restoran)* is at the top of the food chain, generally presenting a more formal dining experience. A *gostionica* or *konoba* is usually a traditional family-run tavern. A *pivnica* is more like a pub, with a wide choice of beer. A *kavana* is a cafe. Self-service cafeterias are quick, easy and inexpensive, though the quality of the food tends to vary.

Restaurants are open long hours, often noon to 11pm (some midnight), with Sunday closings outside of peak season.

Vegetarians & Vegans

Outside of major cities like Zagreb, Rijeka, Split and Dubrovnik, vegetarian restaurants are few but Croatia's vegetables are usually locally grown and quite tasty. *Blitva* (swiss chard) is a nutritious side dish often served with potatoes. The hearty *štrukli* (baked cheese dumplings) are a good alternative too.

The Arts

Literature

Croatia's towering literary figure is 20th-century novelist and playwright Miroslav Krleža (1893–1981). His most popular novels include *The Return of Philip Latinovicz* (1932), which has been translated into English.

Some contemporary writers worth reading include expat writer Dubravka Ugrešić, best known for her novels *The Culture of Lies* and *The Ministry of Pain*. Slavenka Drakulić's *Café Europa – Life After Communism* is an excellent read, while Miljenko Jergović's *Sarajevo Marlboro* and *Mama Leone* powerfully conjure up the atmosphere of life in pre-war Yugoslavia.

Music

Although Croatia has produced many fine classical musicians and composers, its most original musical contribution lies in its rich tradition of folk music. The instrument most often used in Croatian folk music is the *tamburica,* a three- or five-string mandolin that is plucked or strummed. Translated as 'group of people', *klapa* is an outgrowth of church-choir singing. The form is most pop-

In July and August there are summer festivals in Dubrovnik, Split, Pula and Zagreb. Dubrovnik's summer music festival emphasises classical music, with concerts in churches around town, while Pula hosts a variety of pop and classical stars in the Roman amphitheatre and also hosts a film festival. Mardi Gras celebrations have recently been revived in many towns with attendant parades and festivities, but nowhere is it celebrated with more verve than in Rijeka.

ular in rural Dalmatia and can involve up to 10 voices singing in harmony.

There's a wealth of homegrown talent on Croatia's pop and rock music scene. Some of the most prominent pop, fusion and hip-hop bands are Hladno Pivo (Cold Beer), Pips Chips & Videoclips, TBF, Edo Maajka, Vještice (The Witches), Gustafi and the deliciously insane Let 3.

Visual Arts

Vlaho Bukovac (1855–1922) was the most notable Croatian painter in the late 19th century. Important early-20th-century painters include Miroslav Kraljević (1885–1913) and Josip Račić (1885–1908). Post-WWII artists experimented with abstract expressionism but this period is best remembered for the naive art that was typified by Ivan Generalić (1914–92). Recent trends have included minimalism, conceptual art and pop art. Contemporary Croatian artists worth checking out include Lovro Artuković, Sanja Iveković, Dalibor Martinis, Andreja Kulunčić, Sandra Sterle and Renata Poljak.

Environment

Croatia is shaped like a boomerang: from the Pannonian plains of Slavonia between the Sava, Drava and Danube Rivers, across hilly central Croatia to the Istrian peninsula, then south through Dalmatia along the rugged Adriatic coast.

The narrow Croatian coastal belt at the foot of the Dinaric Alps is only about 600km long as the crow flies, but it's so indented that the actual length is 1778km. If the 4012km of coastline around the offshore islands is added to the total, the length becomes 5790km. Most of the 'beaches' along this jagged coast consist of slabs of rock sprinkled with naturists. Don't come expecting to find sand, but the waters are sparkling clean, even around large towns.

Croatia's offshore islands are every bit as beautiful as those off the coast of Greece. There are 1244 islands and islets along the tectonically submerged Adriatic coastline, 50 of them inhabited. The largest are Cres, Krk, Mali Lošinj, Pag and Rab in the north; Dugi Otok in the middle; and Brač, Hvar, Korčula, Mljet and Vis in the south.

Wildlife

Deer are plentiful in the dense forests of Risnjak National Park, as are brown bears, wild cats and *ris* (lynx), from which the park gets its name. Occasionally a wolf or wild boar may appear but only rarely. Plitvice Lakes National Park, however, is an important refuge for wolves. A rare sea otter is also protected in Plitvice, as well as in Krka National Park.

The griffon vulture, with a wingspan of 2.6m, has a permanent colony on Cres, and Paklenica National Park is rich in peregrine falcons, goshawks, sparrow hawks, buzzards and owls. Krka National Park is an important migration route and winter habitat for marsh birds as well as rare golden eagles and short-toed eagles.

National Parks

When the Yugoslav federation collapsed, eight of its finest national parks ended up in Croatia. These have a total area of 96,135 sq km, of which 74,260 sq km is land and 21,875 sq km is water. 7.94% of the entire surface of Croatia is protected land.

The dramatically formed karstic gorges and cliffs make Paklenica National Park along the coast a rock-climbing favourite. More rugged is the mountainous Northern Velebit National Park, a stunning patchwork of forests, peaks, ravines and ridges that backs northern Dalmatia and the Šibenik-Knin region. The abundant plant and animal life, including bears, wolves and deer, in the Plitvice Lakes National Park between Zagreb and Zadar has warranted its inclusion on Unesco's list of World Natural Heritage sites. Both Plitvice Lakes and Krka National Parks (near Šibenik) feature a dramatic series of cascades and incredible turquoise lakes.

The Kornati Islands consist of 140 sparsely inhabited and vegetated islands, islets and reefs scattered over 300 sq km – an Adriatic showpiece easily accessible on an organised tour from Zadar. The northwestern half of the island of Mljet has been named a national park due to its two highly indented saltwater lakes surrounded by lush vegetation. The Brijuni Islands near Pula are the most cultivated national park since they were developed as a tourist resort in the late 19th century and were the getaway paradise for Tito.

Environmental Issues

The lack of heavy industry in Croatia has had the happy effect of leaving its forests, coasts, rivers and air generally fresh and unpolluted, but, as ever, an increase in investment and development brings forth problems and threats to the environment. With the tourist boom, the demand for fresh fish and shellfish has risen exponentially. As it is no longer possible to fish their way out of the problem, the only alternative for Croats is to grow their own seafood. The production of farmed sea bass, sea bream and tuna (for export) is rising substantially, resulting in environmental pressure along the coast. In particular, Croatian tuna farms capture the young fish for fattening before they have a chance to reproduce and replenish the wild fish population.

Coastal and island forests face particular problems. The dry summers and brisk *maestrals* (strong, steady westerly winds) also pose substantial fire hazards along the coast.

SURVIVAL GUIDE

Directory A–Z

Accommodation

In this chapter, budget accommodation (€) includes camping grounds, hostels and some guest houses, and costs up to 450KN for a double. Midrange accommodation (€€) costs 450KN to 800KN a double, while the top end (€€€) starts from 800KN and can go as high as 4000KN per double. Reviews are listed in order of preference. For hotels, we list the starting B&B price in high season.

Note that private accommodation is a lot more affordable in Croatia; it's very often great value. If you don't mind foregoing hotel facilities, it's a great way to go about vacationing in Croatia.

Note that many establishments add a 30% charge for less than three-night stays and include 'residence tax', which is around

7KN per person per day. Prices in this book do not include the residence tax.

Along the coast, accommodation is priced according to four seasons, which vary from place to place:

November to March The cheapest months. There may only be one or two hotels open in a coastal resort but you'll get great rates – often no more than 350KN for a double in a good three-star hotel and 250KN in a lesser establishment.

April, May and October Generally the next-cheapest months.

June and September The shoulder season.

July and August Book in advance (especially along the coast) and count on paying top price, especially in the peak period, which starts in late July and lasts until mid- or late August.

Camping

Nearly 100 camping grounds are scattered along the Croatian coast. Camping grounds are generally open from mid-April to mid-September, give or take a few weeks. The exact times change from year to year, so it's wise to call in advance if you're arriving at either end of the season.

Nudist camping grounds (marked FKK) are among the best, as their secluded locations ensure peace and quiet. Bear in mind that freelance camping is officially prohibited. A good site for camping information is www.camping.hr.

Hostels

The **Croatian YHA** (☎01-48 29 291; www.hfhs. hr; Savska 5/1, Zagreb) operates youth hostels in Rijeka, Dubrovnik, Punat, Zadar, Zagreb and Pula. Nonmembers pay an additional 10KN per person per day for a stamp on a welcome card; six stamps entitle you to membership. The Croatian YHA can also provide information about private youth hostels in Krk, Zadar, Dubrovnik and Zagreb.

Prices given in this book are for the high season in July and August; prices fall the rest of the year.

Hotels

Hotels are ranked from one to five stars with most in the two- and three-star range. Features such as satellite TV, direct-dial phones, high-tech bathrooms, minibars and air-con are standard in four- and five-star hotels, and one-star hotels have at least a bathroom in

the room. Many two- and three-star hotels offer satellite TV but you'll find better decor in the higher categories. In August, some hotels may demand a surcharge for stays of less than three or four nights, but this is usually waived during the rest of the year, when prices drop steeply. In Zagreb prices are the same all year.

Breakfast is included in the prices quoted for hotels in this chapter, unless stated otherwise.

Private Rooms

Private rooms or apartments are the best-value accommodation in Croatia. Service is excellent and the rooms are usually extremely well kept. You may very well be greeted by offers of *sobe* (rooms) or *apartmani* (apartments) as you step off your bus and boat, but rooms are most often arranged by travel agencies or the local tourist office. Booking through an agency will ensure that the place you're staying in is officially registered and has insurance.

It makes little sense to price shop from agency to agency, since prices are fixed by the local tourist association. Whether you deal with the owner directly or book through an agency, you'll pay a 30% surcharge for stays of less than four or three nights and sometimes 50% or even 100% more for a one-night stay, although you may be able to get them to waive the surcharge if you arrive in the low season. Some will even insist on a seven-night minimum stay in the high season.

Whether you rent from an agency or rent from the owners privately, don't hesitate to bargain, especially for longer stays.

Activities

There are numerous outdoorsy activities in Croatia.

Cycling Croatia has become a popular destination for cycle enthusiasts. See www.bicikl.hr and www.pedala.com.hr.

Diving Most of the coastal and island resorts mentioned in this chapter have dive shops. For more info see the **Croatian Association of Diving Tourism** (www.croprodive.info), **Croatian Diving Federation** (www.diving-hrs.hr, in Croatian) and **Pro Diving Croatia** (www.diving.hr).

Hiking For information about hiking in Croatia, see the **Croatian Mountaineering Association** (www.plsavez.hr).

Kayaking and rafting Zagreb-based **Huck Finn** (www.huck-finn.hr) is a good contact for sea and river kayaking packages as well as rafting.

Rock climbing and caving For details, contact the **Croatian Mountaineering Association** (www.plsavez.hr) or check its speleological department website at www.speleologija.hr.

Windsurfing For info about windsurfing in Croatia, see www.hukjd.hr or www.windsurfing.hr.

Yachting A good source of information is the **Association of Nautical Tourism** (Udruženje Nautičkog Turizma; ☎051-209 147; Bulevar Oslobođenja 23, Rijeka), which represents all Croatian marinas.

Business Hours

Banks 9am-7pm Mon-Fri, 8am-1pm or 9am-2pm Sat

Bars 9am-midnight

Offices 8am-4pm or 9am-5pm Mon-Fri, 8am-1pm or 9am-2pm Sat

Restaurants noon-11pm or midnight, closed Sun out of peak season

Shops 8am-8pm Mon-Fri, to 2pm Sat

Embassies & Consulates

The following are all in Zagreb.

Albania (☎01-48 10 679; Jurišićeva 2a)

Australia (☎01-48 91 200; Kaptol Centar, Nova Ves 11)

Bosnia & Hercegovina (☎01-45 01 070; Torbarova 9)

Bulgaria (☎01-46 46 609; Nike Grškovića 31)

Canada (☎01-48 81 200; Prilaz Gjure Deželića 4)

Czech Republic (☎01-61 77 246; Radnička Cesta 47/6)

France (☎01-48 93 600; Andrije Hebranga 2)

Germany (☎01-63 00 100; Ulica Grada Vukovara 64)

Hungary (☎01-48 90 900; Pantovčak 257)

Ireland (☎01-63 10 025; Miramarska 23)

Netherlands (☎01-46 42 200; Medvešćak 56)

New Zealand (☎01-46 12 060; Vlaška 50a/V)

Poland (☎01-48 99 444; Krležin Gvozd 3)

Romania (☎01-46 77 550; Mlinarska ulica 43)

Serbia (☎01-45 79 067; Pantovčak 245)

Slovakia (☎01-48 77 070; Prilaz Gjure Deželića 10)

Slovenia (☎01-63 11 000; Alagovićeva 30/annex)

UK (☎01-60 09 100; I Lučića 4)

USA (☎01-66 12 200; Thomasa Jeffersona 2)

Food

Price ranges are: budget (€; under 50KN), midrange (€€; 50KN to 80KN) and top end (€€€; over 80KN).

Gay & Lesbian Travellers

Homosexuality has been legal in Croatia since 1977 and is tolerated, but not welcomed with open arms. Public displays of affection between same-sex couples may be met with hostility, especially beyond the major cities.

Exclusively gay clubs are a rarity outside Zagreb, but many of the large discos attract a mixed crowd. Raves are also a good way for gay men and women to meet. On the coast, gay men gravitate to Rovinj, Hvar, Split and Dubrovnik, and tend to frequent naturist beaches.

In Zagreb, late April/early May is the **Queer Zagreb Festival** (www.queerzagreb.org) and the last Saturday in June is Gay Pride Zagreb day. Gay-friendly venues are listed throughout this book.

Most Croatian websites devoted to the gay scene are in Croatian only, but a good starting point is http://travel.gay.hr.

Holidays

New Year's Day 1 January

Epiphany 6 January

Easter Monday March/April

Labour Day 1 May

Corpus Christi 10 June

Day of Antifascist Resistance 22 June; marks the outbreak of resistance in 1941

Statehood Day 25 June

Homeland Thanksgiving Day 5 August

Feast of the Assumption 15 August

Independence Day 8 October

All Saints' Day 1 November

Christmas 25 & 26 December

Money

Credit Cards

Amex, MasterCard, Visa and Diners Club cards are widely accepted in large hotels, stores and many restaurants, but don't count on cards to pay for private accommodation or meals in small restaurants. You'll find ATMs accepting MasterCard, Maestro, Cirrus, Plus and Visa in most bus and train stations, airports, all major cities and most small towns.

Lonely Planet's *Croatia* is a comprehensive guide to the country.

Interesting reads about Croatia include Rebecca West's *Black Lamb and Grey Falcon,* a classic travel book which recounts the writer's journeys through Croatia, Serbia, Bosnia, Macedonia and Montenegro in 1941. British writer Tony White retraced West's journey in *Another Fool in the Balkans* (2006), juxtaposing modern life in Serbia and Croatia with the region's political history. *Croatia: Travels in Undiscovered Country* (2003), by Tony Fabijančić, recounts the life of rural folks in a new Croatia. *Plum Brandy: Croatian Journeys* by Josip Novakovich is a sensitive exploration of his family's Croatian background.

Currency

Croatia uses the kuna (KN). Commonly circulated banknotes come in denominations of 500, 200, 100, 50, 20, 10 and five kuna. Each kuna is divided into 100 lipa. You'll find silver-coloured 50- and 20-lipa coins, and bronze-coloured 10-lipa coins.

Tax

Travellers who spend more than 740KN in one shop are entitled to a refund of the value-added tax (VAT), which is equivalent to 22% of the purchase price. In order to claim the refund, the merchant must fill out the Tax Cheque (required form), which you must present to the customs office upon leaving the country. Mail a stamped copy to the shop within six months, which will then credit your credit card with the appropriate sum.

Tipping

If you're served well at a restaurant, you should round up the bill, but a service charge is always included. Bar bills and taxi fares can also be rounded up. Tour guides on day excursions expect to be tipped.

Telephone

Mobile Phones

If you have an unlocked 3G phone, you can buy a SIM card for about 50KN. You can choose from four network providers: VIP (www.vip.hr), T-Mobile (www.t-mobile.hr), Tomato (www.tomato.com.hr) and Tele2 (www.tele2.hr).

Phone Codes

To call Croatia from abroad, dial your international access code, then ☏385 (the country code for Croatia), then the area code (without the initial 0) and the local number.

To call from region to region within Croatia, start with the area code (with the initial zero); drop it when dialling within the same code.

Phone numbers with the prefix ☏060 are either free or charged at a premium rate, so watch the small print. Phone numbers that begin with ☏09 are mobile phone numbers.

Phonecards

To make a phone call from Croatia, go to the town's main post office. You'll need a phone card to use public telephones. Phonecards are sold according to *impulsa* (units), and you can buy cards of 25 (15KN), 50 (30KN), 100 (50KN) and 200 (100KN) units. These can be purchased at any post office and most tobacco shops and newspaper kiosks.

Tourist Information

Croatian National Tourist Board (www.croatia.hr) is a good source of info. There are regional tourist offices that supervise tourist development, and municipal tourist offices that have free brochures and information.

Travellers with Disabilities

Due to the number of wounded war veterans, more attention is being paid to the needs of disabled travellers in Croatia. Public toilets at bus stations, train stations, airports and large public venues are usually wheelchair accessible. Large hotels are wheelchair accessible, but very little private accommodation is. Bus and train stations in Zagreb, Zadar, Rijeka, Split and Dubrovnik are wheelchair accessible, but the local Jadrolinija ferries are not. For further information, get in touch with **Hrvatski Savez Udruga Tjelesnih Invalida** (☏01-48 12 004; www.hsuti.hr; Šoštarićeva 8, Zagreb), the Croatian union of associations for physically disabled persons.

Visas

Citizens of the EU, USA, Canada, Australia, New Zealand, Israel, Ireland, Singapore and the UK do not need a visa for stays of up to 90 days. South Africans must apply for a 90-day visa in Pretoria. Contact any Croatian embassy, consulate or travel agency abroad for information.

Getting There & Away

Getting to Croatia is becoming ever easier, especially if you're arriving in summer. Low-cost carriers are finally establishing routes to Croatia, and a plethora of bus and ferry routes shepherd holidaymakers to the coast.

Air

There are direct flights to Croatia from a number of European cities; however, there are no nonstop flights from North America to Croatia.

There are several major airports in Croatia.

Dubrovnik (www.airport-dubrovnik.hr) Nonstop flights from Brussels, London (Gatwick), Manchester, Hannover, Frankfurt, Cologne, Stuttgart and Munich

Pula (www.airport-pula.com) Nonstop flights from Manchester and London (Gatwick).

Rijeka (www.rijeka-airport.hr) Nonstop flights from Cologne and Stuttgart.

Split (www.split-airport.hr) Nonstop flights from London, Frankfurt, Munich, Cologne, Prague and Rome.

Zadar (www.zadar-airport.hr) Nonstop flights from London, Brussels, Munich, Bari, Dublin and more.

Zagreb (www.zagreb-airport.hr) Direct flights from all European capitals, plus Hamburg, Stuttgart and Cologne.

Land

Croatia has border crossings with Hungary, Slovenia, Bosnia & Hercegovina, Serbia and Montenegro.

Bus

Buses run to destinations throughout Europe.

From Austria, **Eurolines** (www.eurolines.com) operates buses from Vienna to several destinations in Croatia.

Rijeka €43, nine hours, two weekly

Split €51, 11½ hours, two weekly

Zadar €43, 8¼ hours, two weekly

Zagreb €32, five to seven hours, two daily (one direct, the other via Varaždin)

Bus services between Germany and Croatia are good, and fares are cheaper than the train. All buses are handled by **Deutsche Touring GmbH** (www.deutsche-touring.de); there are no Deutsche Touring offices in Croatia, but numerous travel agencies and bus stations sell its tickets.

Scheduled departures to/from Germany:

Istria From Frankfurt weekly; from Munich twice weekly.

Split From Cologne, Dortmund, Frankfurt, Main, Mannheim, Munich, Nuremberg and Stuttgart daily; from Berlin (via Rijeka) twice a week.

Rijeka From Berlin twice weekly.

Zagreb From Cologne, Dortmund, Frankfurt, Main, Mannheim, Munich, Nuremberg and Stuttgart daily; from Berlin four times a week.

Trieste in Italy is well connected with the Istrian coast. Note that there are fewer buses on Sundays. In addition to the following, there's also a bus from Padua that passes Venice, Trieste and Rovinj and ends up in Pula (235KN, six hours). It runs Monday to Saturday.

Dubrovnik 410KN, 15 hours, one daily

Rijeka 65KN, two hours, five daily

Rovinj 88KN, three hours, two daily

Poreč 69KN, two hours, three daily

Pula 105KN, 2½-3¾ hours, six daily

Split 279KN, 10½ hours, two daily

Zadar 188KN, 7½ hours, one daily

For Montenegro, there are three daily buses from Kotor to Dubrovnik (100KN, 2½ hours) that starts at Bar and stops at Herceg Novi.

There are six daily buses from Zagreb to Belgrade, Serbia (199KN to 204KN, six hours). At Bajakovo on the border, a Serbian bus takes you on to Belgrade.

Slovenia is well connected with the Istrian coast. Buses from Ljubljana head to Rijeka (180KN, 2½ hours, two daily), Rovinj (173KN, four hours, three daily) and Split (310KN, 10 hours, one daily). There's also one bus each weekday that connects Rovinj with Koper (87KN, 2¾ hours), stopping at Poreč, Portorož and Piran.

Car & Motorcycle

If you rent a car in Italy, many insurance companies will not insure you for a trip into

Croatia. Border officials know this and may refuse you entry unless permission to drive into Croatia is clearly marked on the insurance documents.

Most car-rental companies in Trieste and Venice are familiar with this requirement and will furnish you with the correct stamp. Otherwise, you must make specific inquiries.

Train

There are two daily and two overnight trains between Vienna and Zagreb, via Slovenia and via Hungary. The price is between €47 and €57 and the journey takes between 5¾ and 6½ hours.

For BiH, trains from Sarajevo service Ploče (via Mostar and Banja Luka; €13, four hours, four daily) and Zagreb (€30, 9½ hours, two daily)

There are three trains daily from Munich, Germany to Zagreb (€39 to €91, 8½-nine hours) via Salzburg and Ljubljana. Reservations are required southbound but not northbound.

There are three daily trains from Zagreb to Budapest, Hungary (€30 return, six to seven hours).

Between Venice, Italy and Zagreb (€25 to €40, 7½ hours), there is one direct train at night and several more that run through Ljubljana.

Four daily trains connect Zagreb with Belgrade, Serbia (159KN, 6½ hours).

From Slovenia, trains run from Ljubljana to Rijeka (100KN, 2½ hours, two daily) and Zagreb (100KN to 160KN, 2½ hours, seven daily).

Sea

Regular boats from the following companies connect Croatia with Italy:

Blue Line (www.blueline-ferries.com)

Commodore Cruises (www.commodore-cruises.hr)

Emilia Romagna Lines (www.emiliaromagnalines.it)

Jadrolinija (www.jadrolinija.hr)

Split Tours (www.splittours.hr)

SNAV (www.snav.com)

Termoli Jet (www.termolijet.it)

Ustica Lines (www.usticalines.it)

Venezia Lines (www.venezialines.com)

Air

Croatia Airlines (☎01-66 76 555; www.croatiaairlines.hr) is the only carrier for flights within Croatia. There are daily flights between Zagreb and Dubrovnik, Pula, Split and Zadar.

Bicycle

Cycling can be a great way to explore the islands. Relatively flat islands such as Pag and Mali Lošinj offer the most relaxed biking, but the winding, hilly roads on other islands offer spectacular views. Bicycles are easy to rent along the coast and on the islands. Some tourist offices, especially in the Kvarner and Istria regions, have maps of routes and can refer you to local bike-rental agencies. Even though it's not fully translated into English yet, www.pedala.hr is a great reference for cycling routes around Croatia.

Boat

Jadrolinija Ferries

Jadrolinija operates an extensive network of car ferries and catamarans along the Adriatic coast. Ferries are a lot more comfortable than buses, though somewhat more expensive.

Services operate year-round, though they are less frequent in winter. Cabins should be booked a week ahead. Deck space is usually available on all sailings.

You must buy tickets in advance at an agency or a Jadrolinija office. Tickets are not sold on board. In summer months, you need to check in two hours in advance if you bring a car.

Somewhat mediocre fixed-price menus in onboard restaurants cost about 100KN; the cafeteria only offers ham-and-cheese sandwiches for 30KN. Do as the Croatians do: bring some food and drink with you.

Local Ferries

Local ferries connect the bigger offshore islands with each other and with the mainland, but you'll find many more ferries going from the mainland to the islands than from island to island.

On most lines, service is less frequent between October and April. Extra passenger boats are added in the summer; these are usually faster, more comfortable and more expensive.

On some shorter routes (eg Jablanac to Mišnjak), ferries run nonstop in summer and advance reservation is unnecessary.

Buy tickets at a Jadrolinija office or at a stall near the ferry (usually open 30 minutes prior to departure). There are no ticket sales on board. In summer, arrive one to two hours prior to departure, even if you've already bought your ticket.

Cars incur a charge; calculated according to the size of car, and often very pricey. Reserve as far in advance as possible. Check in several hours in advance. Bicycles incur a small charge.

There is no meal service; you can buy drinks and snacks on board. Most locals bring their own food.

Bus

Bus services are excellent and relatively inexpensive. There are often a number of different companies handling each route so prices can vary substantially. Luggage stowed in the baggage compartment under the bus costs extra (7KN a piece, including insurance).

Bus Companies

The companies listed here are among the largest.

Autotrans (☑051-660 300; www.autotrans. hr) Based in Rijeka. Connections to Istria, Zagreb, Varaždin and Kvarner.

Brioni Pula (☑052-535 155; www.brioni. hr) Based in Pula. Connections to Istria, Trieste, Padua, Split and Zagreb.

Contus (☑023-315 315; www.contus.hr) Based in Zadar. Connections to Split and Zagreb.

Croatiabus (☑01-61 13 213; www.croatiabus.hr) Connecting Zagreb with towns in Zagorje and Istria.

Samoborček (☑01-48 19 180; www.samo borcek.hr) Connecting Zagreb with towns in Dalmatia.

Tickets & Schedules

At large stations, bus tickets must be purchased at the office, not from drivers. Try to book ahead to be sure of a seat, especially in the summer.

Departure lists above the various windows at bus stations tell you which window sells tickets for your bus. On Croatian bus schedules, *vozi svaki dan* means 'every day' and *ne vozi nedjeljom i blagdanom* means 'no service Sunday and holidays'.

Some buses travel overnight, saving you a night's accommodation. Don't expect to get much sleep, though, as the inside lights will be on and music will be blasting the whole night. Take care not to be left behind at meal or rest stops, which usually occur about every two hours.

Car & Motorcycle

Croatia has recently made a major investment in infrastructure, the highlight of which is a new motorway connecting Zagreb with Split. The 'autoroute' is expected to reach Dubrovnik at some stage. Zagreb and Rijeka are now connected by motorway, and an Istrian motorway has shortened the travel time to Italy considerably.

Although the new roads are in excellent condition, there are stretches where service stations and facilities are few and far between.

Car Hire

In order to rent a car you must be 21 or over, with a valid driving licence and a valid credit card.

Independent local companies are often much cheaper than the international chains, but the big companies offer one-way rentals. Sometimes you can get a lower car-rental rate by booking the car from abroad, or by booking a fly-drive package.

Car Insurance

Third-party public liability insurance is included by law with car rentals, but make sure your quoted price includes full collision insurance, known as a collision damage waiver (CDW). Otherwise, your responsibility for damage done to the vehicle is usually determined as a percentage of the car's value, beginning at around 2000KN.

Driving Licence

Any valid driving licence is sufficient to drive legally and rent a car; an international driving licence is not necessary.

The **Hrvatski Autoklub** (HAK; Croatian Auto Club; ☑01-46 40 800; www.hak.hr; Avenija Dubrovnik 44, Zagreb) offers help and advice. For help on the road, you can contact the nationwide **HAK road assistance** (Vučna Služba; ☑987).

On the Road

Petrol stations are generally open from 7am to 7pm and often until 10pm in summer. Petrol is Eurosuper 95, Super 98, normal or diesel. See www.ina.hr for up-to-date fuel prices.

You have to pay tolls on all motorways, to use the Učka tunnel between Rijeka and Istria, to use the bridge to Krk Island, and on the road from Rijeka to Delnice.

For general news on Croatia's motorways and tolls, see www.hak.hr. The radio station HR2 broadcasts traffic reports in English every hour on the hour from July to early September.

Road Rules

In Croatia you drive on the right, and use of seatbelts is mandatory. Unless otherwise posted, the speed limits for cars and motorcycles are 50km/h in built-up areas, 100km/h on main highways and 130km/h on motorways.

On two-lane highways, it's illegal to pass long military convoys or a line of cars caught behind a slow-moving truck.

It's illegal to drive with blood alcohol content higher than 0.5%.

You are required to drive with your headlights on even during the day.

Local Transport

The main form of local transport is bus (although Zagreb and Osijek also have well-developed tram systems).

Buses in major cities such as Dubrovnik, Rijeka, Split and Zadar run about once every 20 minutes, less on Sunday. A ride is usually around 8KN, with a small discount if you buy tickets at a *tisak* (newsstand).

Small medieval towns along the coast are generally closed to traffic and have infrequent links to outlying suburbs.

Bus transport within the islands is infrequent since most people have their own cars.

Train

Trains are less frequent than buses but more comfortable. For information about schedules, prices and services, contact **Croatian Railways** (Hrvatske Željeznice; ☎060-333 444; www.hznet.hr).

Zagreb is the hub for Croatia's less-than-extensive train system. No trains run along the coast and only a few coastal cities are connected with Zagreb. For travellers, the main lines of interest are the following:

» Zagreb–Rijeka–Pula (via Lupoglava, where passengers switch to a bus)
» Zagreb–Zadar–Šibenik–Split
» Zagreb–Varaždin–Koprivnica
» Zagreb–Osijek

Domestic trains are either 'express' or 'passenger' (local). Express trains have 1st- and 2nd-class cars, plus smoking and nonsmoking areas. A reservation is advisable for express trains.

Express trains are more expensive than passenger trains; prices in this book are for unreserved 2nd-class seating.

There are no couchettes on domestic services. There are sleeping cars on overnight trains between Zagreb and Split.

Baggage is free on trains; most stations have left-luggage services charging around 15KN a piece per day.

EU residents who hold an InterRail pass can use it in Croatia for free travel, but you're unlikely to take enough trains to justify the cost.

Cyprus

Best Places to Eat

» Shiantris (p186)
» Dino Art Café (p193)
» Fetta's (p196)

Best Places to Stay

» Classic Hotel (p185)
» Chrielka (p193)
» Semiramis (p194)

Why Go?

Cyprus (Κύπρος) captures the imagination. This is not your standard Mediterranean island cliché; Cyprus reflects its proximity to Asia and the Middle East in its culture, cuisine and history. Similarly evocative is the contrast between old and new, particularly evident in the capital, Lefkosia (South Nicosia). Here you can see the merging of traditional and modern Cyprus, with dusty dilapidated buildings round the corner from smart boutiques and arty bars. The flip side of this is the tourist-driven areas of Kato Pafos and Agia Napa although, thankfully, development has remained relatively low rise.

Get away from the clamour and head for the green peaks of the Troodos, or the iconic northern Cyprus resort of Kyrenia (Girne), with its picturesque harbour, medieval churches and castles. Most importantly, visit both sides of the island – you'll get a fuller picture of the complex and fractured Cypriot identity. Talks on peace and unification continue: watch this space.

When to Go
Lefkosia (Nicosia)

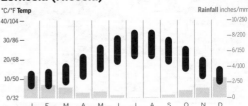

| March–April Glorious weather and the top religious festival for Greek Cypriots: Easter Week. | June–August Art, culture and the superb International Music Festival in Lemesos in July. | September–October Striking autumn colours along the hiking trails in the Troodos mountains. |

Connections

The main place to get to and from Cyprus by boat is Turkey – go between Girne and Taşucu or Alanya in summer, and Gazimağusa to Mersin overnight (for details, see p206). Ferries to the Republic of Cyprus were suspended in the 1990s but are expected to resume in 2011, with a route opening between Lemesos and Laurion in the south east of Attica in Greece. Meanwhile mini three-day cruises to Egypt are one option for those wanting to take to the seas (see p206). Most visitors arrive in Cyprus via air to Pafos or Larnaka airports in the (Greek) Republic, and to Ercan airport in the (Turkish) North. Note that the latter is not recognised by the international airline authorities so you can only fly there via Turkey.

ITINERARIES

One Week

With just a week in Cyprus, head to the capital to explore north and south Lefkosia. Cross the border for an overnight trip to Girne, then head south to Lemesos and Pafos for the island's best Graeco-Roman ruins, with a stop in the scenic Troodos Massif.

Two Weeks

With more time, hire a car and explore Frankish ruins in Gazimağusa (Famagusta) and drive up to Polis and the wild Karpas region. If you're up for some more untamed nature, head to the rugged Akamas Peninsula. Then visit Larnaka to pay your respects at the grave of Lazarus.

Essential Food & Drink

» **Meze** A healthy and sociable way to enjoy a wide variety of different foods and flavours, a meze comprises around 30 small plates of food, including dips, vegetables and a wide range of traditional fish and meat dishes, like *calamare* (squid), *keftedes* (meatballs) and *sheftalia* (pork and lamb rissoles).

» **Halloumi** This quintessential Cypriot cheese made from goat's or sheep's milk, or a combination of both, appears everywhere. Enjoy it grilled as a side dish or stuffed in pita bread with salad, or just as it comes with cucumbers and tomatoes.

» **Kebabs** Tuck into the original doner kebab, especially in the north where the traditional shredded lamb is usually wrapped in flat bread and served with salad. *Urfa* kebab comes with onions and black pepper, while *adana* is slightly hot with spicy red pepper.

AT A GLANCE

» **Currency** Republic: euro (€); North Cyprus: Turkish lira (TL)

» **Official languages** Greek and Turkish

» **Money** ATMs are plentiful

» **Visas** Not needed for EU citizens

Fast Facts

» **Area** 9250 sq km

» **Capital** Republic: Lefkosia; North Cyprus: Lefkoşa

» **Telephone area codes** Republic ☐357, North Cyprus ☐90 392

» **Emergency** ☐112

Exchange Rates

Australia	A$1	TL1.69
Canada	C$1	TL1.64
euro	€1	TL2.25
Japan	¥100	TL1.96
New Zealand	NZ$1	TL1.27
UK	UK£1	TL2.58
USA	US$1	TL1.60

Set Your Budget

» **Budget hotel** Republic: €45; North Cyprus: €35

» **Two-course meal** Republic: €15; North Cyprus: €11

» **Museum entrance** Republic: €2.50; North Cyprus: €2

Resources

» **Tourism in North Cyprus** (www.northcyprus.cc)

» **Official Republic of Cyprus website** (www.visitcyprus.com)

0 50 km
0 30 miles

To Alanya (Turkey)

To Tašucu (Turkey)

Koruçam Burnu (Cape Kormakitis)

Lapta
Akdeniz (Ayia Irini)
St Hilarion ❶
Girne (Kyrenia)
Bellapa

Kyrenia (Pentadactylos) Mountains
Bufaven

UN Buffer Zone (Green Line)
Guzelyurt (Morfou)
Agios Dometios
Lefkoša (North Nicosia)

Kato Pyrgos
Morfou Bay
Astromeritis
Ledra Palace Checkpoint
Lefkosia (South Nicosia)

Chrysochou Bay
Soli

Cape Arnaoutis
Baths of Aphrodite

Lara Beach (Turtle Beach)
Latsi
Polis
Kykkos Monastery
Agios Nikolaos tis Stegis
REPUBLIC OF CYPRUS

Agios Georgios
Kykkos (1318m)
Pedoulas
Kakopetria
Olympus (1952m)
Stavrovouni Monastery (688m)

Akamas Peninsula ❹
Avakas Gorge
Archangelos
Agros
Pano Lefkara

Coral Bay
Tombs of the Kings
Platres
Plateia Troodos
Troodos Massif ❸

Pafos ❷
Ktima
Omodos

Kouklia
Aphrodite's Sanctuary
Sanctuary of Apollon Ylatis
Lemesos (Limassol)
Kalymr Beach
Governor' Beach

Pafos International Airport
Petra Tou Romiou
Pissouri Beach
Kourion
Episkopi Bay
Kolossi ❶

Akrotiri UK Sovereign Base
Salt Lake
Akrotiri Bay

To Rhodes (Greece); Piraeus (Greece)
To Haifa (Israel)

Cyprus Highlights

❶ Be king of the castle at the Crusader fortresses of **Kolossi** (p192), **Kantara** (p201) and **St Hilarion** (p199)

❷ Bring history to life at the fabulous Graeco-Roman ruins of **Pafos** (p195)

❸ Step back to Byzantine times in the **Troodos Massif** (p193)

❹ Trek the wild trails of the **Akamas Peninsula** (p196)

⑤ Walk along beaches in the splendidly isolated **Karpas Peninsula** (p201)

⑥ Visit the craft shops in the beautiful **Büyük Han** (Great Inn; p197)

⑦ Taste a fantastic kebab at one of **Lefkoşa** old city's eateries (p197)

THE REPUBLIC OF CYPRUS

Covering the southern 63% of the island, the Republic of Cyprus has the lion's share of the beaches and historical treasures. While development is evident at the main beach resorts, head inland and you'll find pretty stone villages that have hardly changed for centuries.

Lefkosia (South Nicosia)
ΛΕΥΚΩΣΙΑ

POP 240,000

Lefkosia is an enticing city and ideal for experiencing what modern Cyprus is all about. The ancient walls, traditional eateries and a growing multicultural core effectively showcase the city's basic make-up. Almost everything of interest lies within the city's walls, with its labyrinth of narrow streets hiding churches, mosques and evocative, often crumbling, colonial houses. The country's best museum is also here, housing an extensive archaeological collection. The city has been labelled with the beaten cliché of 'the last divided capital', a reality that, although still present, is slowly changing thanks to 24-hour checkpoint crossings into its northern half, Lefkoşa. It's now possible to see Lefkosia as one city, though it may still be years until it's truly that way.

See p196 for details on Lefkoşa (North Nicosia) in North Cyprus.

◉ Sights & Activities

Pick up the free booklet *Cyprus 10000 Years of History & Civilisation* from the tourist office and consider taking one of its free tours (see p185). Note that a massive redesign project has currently cordoned off much of Lefkosia's Plateia Eleftherias. Completion is scheduled for 2013 when the area will encompass a park and a pedestri-

Lefkosia (South Nicosia)

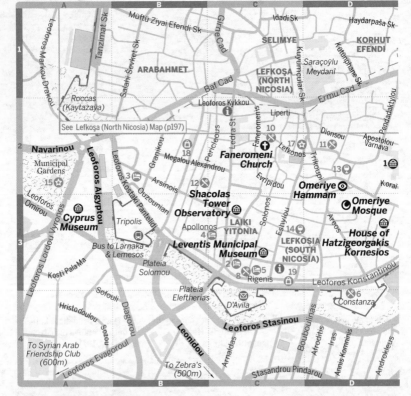

an walkway flanked by palm trees and the ancient Venetian walls.

TOP CHOICE Cyrus Museum
MUSEUM

(Leoforos Mouseiou 1; admission €4; ⊙9am-5pm Mon-Sat, 10am-1pm Sun) Located near the old Pafos Gate, this is the best archaeological museum on the island. Covering the Neolithic to Byzantine periods, exhibits include an incredible collection of pots, statues and tomb offerings, including the famous Aphrodite statue from Soloi.

Shacolas Tower Observatory
OBSERVATORY

(11th fl, Shakolas Tower, cnr Ledra & Arsinois; admission €0.85; ⊙10am-6.30pm) Incongruously, a part of the Debenhams department store building, take the lift to the 11th floor where the observatory offers sweeping city views, including across the Green Line and the distant mountain, its side bearing a vast painted Turkish flag.

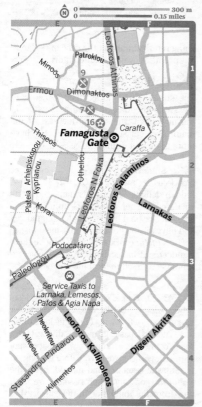

House of Hatzigeorgakis Kornesios
MUSEUM

(Patriarchou Grigoriou 20; admission €1.70; ⊙8am-2pm Mon-Fri, 9am-1pm Sat) This well-preserved 18th-century house belonged to Kornesios, the Great Dragoman (interpreter between the Ottoman and Orthodox authorities). Rooms are extravagantly decked out with original Ottoman furnishings.

Archbishop's Palace
MUSEUMS

There are three museums within the palace's compound on Plateia Archiepiskopou Kyprianou. St John's Cathedral (⊙9am-1pm Mon-Sat, 2-4pm Mon-Fri) has stunning frescoes from 1662; the Ethnographic Museum (Plateia Archiepiskopou Kyprianou; admission €1.70; ⊙9am-5pm Mon-Fri, 10am-1pm Sat) displays traditional Cypriot folk art; and the Byzantine Museum (Plateia Archiepiskopou Kyprianou; admission €1.70; ⊙9am-4.30pm Mon-Fri, to 1pm Sat) has a superb collection of ancient icons and frescoes.

Omeriye Mosque
MOSQUE

(Plateia Tillirias; ⊙outside prayer times) A little deeper into the historic quarter is this well-restored mosque.

FREE Leventis Municipal Museum
MUSEUM

(Ippokratous 17; ⊙10am-4.30pm Tue-Sun) Traces the history of Lefkosia from prehistoric to present times.

Faneromeni Church
CHURCH

(Onasagorou) Superb 17th-century icons.

☞ Tours

Cyprus Tourism Organisation (CTO)
WALKING TOUR

The CTO runs free guided walks on Mondays, Thursdays and Fridays, all starting at 10am, from the CTO Office (p188) in the old city. 'Chrysaliniotissa & Kaimakli: the Past Restored' is a bus-and-walking guided tour that runs on Mondays; on Thursdays, it's a walk through Old Lefkosia; and Friday's 'Nicosia – Outside the Walls' is a bus-and-walking guided tour. All walks last two hours and 45 minutes, and have a 30-minute break in the middle.

🛏 Sleeping

TOP CHOICE Classic Hotel
BOUTIQUE HOTEL €€€

(☎2266 4006; www.classic.com.cy; Rigenis 94; s/d €80/97; P❄🐾) This three-star hotel, close to Pafos Gate, is a member of the 'Small Luxury Hotels of the World' group, and you can see why. Everything, from the reception to the rooms, is decorated in relaxing creamy colours; the design is minimalist and the rooms are smart and comfortable. The 59 Knives restaurant, part of the hotel, specialises in haute cuisine, adding its own contribution to the Classic's luxuries.

Royiatiko   HOTEL €€€
(☑2244 5445; www.royiatikohotel.com.cy; Apollonos 27; s/d €89/100; P❄ 🤚⏹) Opened in early 2010, this hotel deserves more than its two-star rating. The rooms are elegantly decorated in tones of brown and cream with large luxurious cushions on the beds. There are fridges, kettles and stylish bathrooms with steely grey floor tiles, plus a well-equipped gym.

Sky Hotel   HOTEL €
(☑2266 6880; www.skyhotel.ws; Solonos 7c; s/d €49/60; ❄) The best budget place in Lefkosia, Sky is bang in the centre of the old town-surrounded by souvenir shops and cafes frequented by hubble bubble aficionados. Rooms are carpeted and spacious with pine furniture and pale paintwork; most have large balconies overlooking the rooftops.

Centrum Hotel   HOTEL €€
(☑2245 6444; www.centrumhotel.net; Pasikratous 15; s/d €65/70; ❄@🤚) A fairly stylish hotel, with spacious rooms, that's a cross between a boutique and business hotel; it was under-

going refurbishment at the time of research, but promises even greater comfort.

✗ Eating

The streets surrounding historic Ledra St have a good choice of restaurants while, in the new town, the streets due east of the main Archiepiskopou Makariou 111 have more upmarket dining choices.

⟦TOP CHOICE⟧ **Shiantris**   CYPRIOT €€
(Pericleous 38; mains from €8; ⏰12.30-4pm) A hidden delight, Shiantris is named after its vociferous owner who cooks up a fantastic array of seasonal beans with lemon, parsley and olive oil and, for carnivores, meat dishes such as *afelia* (pork stew with wine and coriander) and baked lamb. A great place to immerse yourself in local life and cuisine.

Egeon   MEZE €€
(☑2243 3297; Ektoros 40; meze from €17; ⏰Mon-Sat 8pm-11pm) The discreet yet very popular Egeon draws a following of mainly local devotees. The food, basically meze, is divine. Order some courgettes scrambled with egg or potent, rich garlicky yoghurt, before moving on to fantastic vegetable and meat dishes – the *sheftalia* (pork and lamb rissoles) are fresh and aromatic. You'll dine in the courtyard of

CITY WITH A PLAN

In an effort to bring North Cyprus and the Republic closer together, close to 100 Ottoman, Frankish and Byzantine buildings in Lefkosia have been faithfully restored with funding from the UN and EU. The **Nicosia Masterplan** covers churches and mosques, *hammams* (Turkish baths) and tombs, mansions and monuments, museums and cultural centres – the aim is to promote understanding of the shared history between the two sides. Just by the Ledra Palace Hotel checkpoint, the **Masterplan office** (www.lefkosia.org.cy; ⊗8am-6pm Mon-Fri, 9am-5pm Sat & Sun) can provide information sheets on each project, as well as a free booklet *Walled Nicosia: A Guide to its Historical and Cultural Sites.*

places to eat in Lefkosia, this is an ideal place for vegetarians. The meze is massive, so approach it with respect, and if you come for lunch, you won't be eating dinner that night. Offerings include green beans, chickpeas, tabouleh and plenty of meat, too. Try the delicious *mahalabia* (a light rice custard, which is served cold) for dessert and, once you're so stuffed you can't move, puff on a *nargileh* (water pipe). To find the restaurant head west of the Cyprus Museum along Chilonos. The restaurant is on a cross street, to the left, after around 600m.

Mattheos   CYPRIOT €
(Plateia 28 Oktovriou 6; mains from €6; ⊗lunch Mon-Sat) Another simple local lunch place; decked out with chequered tablecloths, this place is super atmospheric. The food is not as good as Shiantris but Mattheos does have a delightful outside eating space, right behind the little mosque, next to Faneromeni Church.

Municipal Market   MARKET €
(Plateia Dimarchias; ⊗Mon-Sat) In the heart of the old town. Alternatively, drop in on the fantastic **fruit and veg market** (Constanza bastion; ⊗8am-2pm Wed).

Fanous   LEBANESE €€
(Solonos 7; mains from €7) Lebanese specialties, including four different versions of hummus, plus falafel, tabouleh and stuffed vine leaves.

Zebra's   INTERNATIONAL €€
(Klimentos 43; mains €10-15) In the new town, 500m south of the Constanza bastion, famed for its steaks and seafood platters with prawns, mussels, calamari and fish.

the atmospheric old house in summer, and inside the house in winter. Bookings essential.

Inga's Veggie Heaven   VEGETARIAN €€
(Chrisaliniotissa Crafts Centre, Dimonaktos 2; mains €8; ⊗Tue-Sat 9am-5pm) Inga's is an invaluable addition to Lefkosia's eating scene. It's a simple Nordic eatery, with half a dozen tables sitting under the tall eaves of the old roof. Inga is a friendly Icelandic chef who prepares several fresh dishes of the day, such as almond stuffed peppers or a delicious lentil burger, always served with a salad and homemade bread. Desserts are legendary, especially her vegan raspberry and chocolate cake. There's a small terrace outside surrounded by arts and crafts studios.

Syrian Arab Friendship Club   MEZE €€
(Vassilisa Amalia 17; meze from €15; ⊗11am-midnight) In addition to being one of the best

Drinking & Entertainment

Hammam   CAFE, BAR
(Soutsou 9) Located within a heavenly old colonial house behind the main mosque,

---

LEFKOSIA IN...

One Day

Start your day by popping into **Faneromeni Church**. Check out what is visible of the magnificent **Venetian walls** (currently part of a massive architectural project), the city's guardians for centuries, then go to **Famagusta Gate**, where concerts and other events are held. The best part of the day is spent simply wandering around the streets of the old city and checking out the old colonial houses, now falling into decay. Trace the Green Line and have lunch at **Shiantris**, where you can have a real Cypriot meal alongside the city's working men. Then go to the **Cyprus Museum**, where the oldest artefact dates back to 8000 BC. Have a luxurious Turkish bath in the **Omeriye Hammam** and then eat some of the finest meze on the island at **Egeon**. Finish with drinks at **Hammam**.

DON'T MISS

OMERIYA HAMMAM

Have a good sweat and scrub up at **Omeriya Hammam** (www.hamambaths. com; Plateia Tyllirias 8; admission & Turkish bath €20, 20min body scrub €20, massage €40-50; ⊙9am-9pm, men only Tue, Thu & Sat, women only Wed, Fri & Sun, tours only 11am-5pm Mon), luxurious and aesthetically restored Turkish baths next to the Omeriye Mosque. Exquisitely marbled throughout, there are traditional Turkish steam baths and the option of a body scrub and/or aromatherapy or Chinese massage. Candles, mirrors and the hint of exotic perfumes create just the right ambience for a tad of self-pampering. The baths are segregated with same-sex masseurs, and separate days and times for men and women.

with a grand arched door and beautifully tiled floors; the perfect place for sitting under the stars and sipping a cocktail beneath a spreading fig tree.

Oktana   CAFE, BAR
(Aristidou 6) Decorated with edgy art deco posters, there are regular art exhibitions and poetry readings, plus a delightful sunken patio out back. The rambling interior has a bookshop and various rooms, including a basement space favoured by the *nargileh* smokers.

Brew   CAFE, BAR
(Ippocratous 30; ⊙Tue-Sun) Another gorgeous space, Brew stretches through the ground floor of an old mansion. It's an airy, spacious place, with good music and white-painted wooden furniture. Come here for exotic herb teas, like green tea with scented apple, rose and almond; cocktails and light snacks.

Film & Theatre

There are several cinemas that show international films (the *Cyprus Mail* has full listings).

Weaving Mill   CINEMA
(www.ifantourgio.org.cy; Lefkonos 67-71) Located in the old town, art-house movies are shown at this suitably bohemian cinema.

Lefkosia Municipal Theatre   THEATRE
(Leoforos Mouseiou 4) Opposite the Cyprus Museum, the popular Lefkosia Municipal

Theatre is the venue for quality musical and theatrical productions.

Theatro Ena   THEATRE
(Leforos Athinas 4) Try this theatre in the old city, which may have productions in other languages.

Contact the CTO (p188) for more information on theatre performances.

 Shopping

In the historic quarter, pedestrianised Ledra St is the city's main shopping area; while in the newer part of town, Archiepiskopou Makariou 111 is the high street for upmarket fashion and those familiar international chains.

Cyprus Handicrafts Centre   HANDICRAFTS
(Athalassis 186; ⊙7.30am-2.30pm Mon-Fri, 3-6pm Thu) Cypriot lace and embroidery at decent prices, as well as leatherware, mosaics, ceramics and pottery.

Antique shops   ANTIQUES
(Vasileou Voulgaroktonou 5 & 6) For antiques, visit two very dusty, fun shops on opposite sides of the street (you may have to ring the owner to come down for you to browse). You'll find lots of great stuff, from retro bits and pieces, to lovely ceramics, paintings, ornaments and more.

 Information

Cyprus Tourism Organisation (CTO; www. visitcyprus.com; Laïki Yitonia; ⊙8.30am-4pm Mon-Fri, to 2pm Sat)

Nicosia Municipality Office (Ledra St; ⊙7.30am-2.30pm Thu-Tue, 7.30am-2.30pm & 3-6pm Wed) At the Ledra St crossing, this new municipality office has multilingual leaflets about the city.

Getting There & Around

Intercity (www.intercity-buses.com) Runs frequent services to Lemesos (€4, one hour), Larnaka (€3, 45 minutes), Agia Napa (€4, one hour) and Pafos (€5, 1½ hours) from the main stand at Plateia Solomou.

Petsas (☎7777 1515; www.petsas.com.cy; Kostaki Pantelidi 24; per day from €25) Car hire is near Plateia Solomou.

Travel & Express (☎7777 7474; www.travel express.com.cy; Salaminos) Close to Podocataro Bastion, has half-hourly service taxis to Lemesos (€12, one hour), with connections to Pafos (€22, 1½ hours), Larnaka (€9, one hour) and Agia Napa (€18, one hour). Private taxis are at Plateia Eleftherias.

ⓘ NEW BUS SYSTEM

In mid-2010 there was a major shake-up of the former, reputedly unreliable bus system in the Republic of Cyprus. Simply put, each of the five districts now operates its own bus company. Fares are government subsidised and have been pegged at €1 per ride, €2 per day, €10 per week and €30 for a month of unlimited journeys within the respective district, which include rural villages. All five companies have comprehensive websites. These are: Lefkosia district, **Osel Buses** (www.osel.com.cv); Lemesos district, **Limassol Buses** (www.limassolbuses.com); Pafos district, **Pafos Buses** (www.pafosbuses.com); Famagusta district, **Zinonas Buses** (www.zinonasbuses.com); and Larnaca district, **Osea Buses** (www.oseabuses.com). In addition, buses that connect the cities are run by the appropriately named **Intercity Bus Company** (www.intercity-buses.com), which is also government subsidised and, thus, very reasonable, given the distances involved. Each intercity route will also offer discounted fares on multiple journeys over a day/week/month or year. You can buy your tickets on the bus.

Larnaka ΛΑΡΝΑΚΑ

POP 73,200

Calmer and friendlier than the other coastal resorts, Larnaka is famous as the final resting place of Agios Lazaros, who rose from the dead in the Bible. There's a palm-fringed promenade fronting a popular beach, an atmospheric Turkish neighbourhood and an older quarter of town centred round the Zenonos Kitieos shopping street. The Republic's main airport is 5km south of town, near the salt lake.

◉ Sights & Activities

Aside from the sights listed here, Larnaka is famed for its pottery. Quality ceramics are produced in well-signposted small workshops based around Ak Deniz in the old Turkish quarter. Larnaka is also known for its offshore wrecks and there are several outfits which organise dives and boat trips, operating from the jetty by the marina.

Agios Lazaros Church CHURCH
(Agiou Lazarou; ⊙8am-12.30pm & 3.30-6.30pm) The old town is dominated by the stately Byzantine-era church, which contains fabulous icons (and Titanic-sized chandeliers), plus the tomb of the esteemed Lazaros. There's also a small **museum** (admission €1; ⊙8.30am-1pm & 3-5.30pm Mon, Tue, Thu, Fri & Sun, 8.30am-1pm Wed & Sat) housed in the monastery cells with ancient icons and similar.

Larnaka Castle CASTLE
(Leoforos Athinon; admission €1.70; ⊙fort & museum 9am-7pm Mon-Fri) Down on the waterfront, the castle has a medieval museum with exhibits spread over three rooms that include ceramics, photos and swashbuckling swords dating from the 15th century. Used as a prison during British colonial rule, the site of the original gallows makes harrowing viewing; they were last used in 1945.

Pierides Museum MUSEUM
(Zinonos Kitieos 4; admission €2; ⊙9am-4pm Mon-Thu, 9am-1pm Fri & Sat) Opposite the tourist office, this excellent museum has a superb collection of ceramics, maps and folk art amassed by several generations of the Pierides family. Demetrios Pierides started the collection in the early 19th century to prevent important artefacts from being pillaged. There are six chronologically arranged rooms in the museum and the exhibition includes a comprehensive history of Cyprus.

Larnaka Mosques MOSQUES
Islamic monuments include the **Grand Mosque** (Büyük Cami) in old Larnaka and the **Hala Sultan Tekke** dramatically situated among an oasis of palm trees near the salt lake. Considered an important shrine in the Muslim world, it contains the mausoleum of Hala Sultan, the foster-aunt of the prophet Mohammed. Both mosques accept visitors outside prayer times and accept donations.

Stavrovouni MONASTERY
(⊙6am-noon & 3-6pm) About 30km west of Larnaka, the monastery is perched atop a 688m buttress with panoramic views over the island – unfortunately, only men can enter.

Larnaka Archaeological Museum MUSEUM
(Kalogreon; admission €2; ⊙9am-2.30pm Mon-Fri, 3-5pm Thu) Includes a reconstructed Neolithic tomb.

ⓘ DRESS CODE FOR VISITING MOSQUES

If you are planning to visit a mosque or monastery anywhere on the island, be aware that modest dress is obligatory. Neither men nor women should wear shorts or short-sleeved shirts and women, in particular, should cover up as much as possible. The good news is that, increasingly, mosques and monasteries are supplying expansive capes, or similar, for visitors to borrow free of charge: a veritable godsend if it's a hot sightseeing day.

🛏 Sleeping & Eating

Many hotels here offer rooms with small kitchenettes which are especially convenient for families. Most of the restaurants on the promenade serve overpriced international cuisine, although the wide terraces are a good place for a sundowner. Seafood lovers should head for the seafront restaurants east of the salt lake, near the small harbour.

Petrou Bros　　　　　　APARTMENT €
(☑2465 0600; www.petrou.com.cy; Armenikis Eklisias; 2-bed apt €45-60; P⚹@🛜) Good value and central with sizeable, if starkly lit, kitchenettes with a fridge, two hotplates and plenty of pots and pans. The bedrooms are small by comparison, but pleasantly furnished with private terraces.

Augusta Apartments　　　　APARTMENT €
(☑2465 1802; Leoforos Athinon 102; 2-bed apt €55-75; ⚹) Attractive blue-carpeted rooms with small balconies, sea views and tightly packed kitchenettes.

Prasino Amaxoudi　　　　　KEBABS €
(Agias Faneromenis; mains €5-8) This diner-style restaurant is the top place in Larnaka for kebabs. Go with friendly owner Dimitris' recommendations, like succulent grilled halloumi (firm, salty white cheese) in hot pita bread with salad. The tender chicken kebabs are equally scrumptious. It's by the Grand Mosque in the old Turkish quarter.

1900 Art Café　　　　　　CYPRIOT €€
(Stasinou 6; mains from €8; ⊙6-11pm Wed-Mon) Atmospheric rooms with high ceilings, and walls papered with posters, black-and-white prints and paintings. Don't expect art on a plate though; the food is filling homestyle cooking with hearty vegetable soups and a choice of meat, fish and vegetarian dishes.

Militzis　　　　　　　　CYPRIOT €€
(Piale Pasa 42; mains from €9) Across from the waves, Militzis is good for authentic Greek Cypriot fare.

Zephyros Beach Tavern　　　SEAFOOD €€
(Piale Pasa 37; fish meze €18.50) Overlooking the picturesque harbour, to the south, the tavern's fish meze (for two) is legendary in this town.

ⓘ Information

CTO (www.visitcyprus.com; Plateia Vasileos Pavlou; ⊙8.15am-2.30pm & 3-6.15pm Mon-Fri, 8.15am-1pm Sat, closed Wed afternoon) Has the usual maps and brochures. Free walking tours of the city leave the CTO office at 10am on Wednesdays and Larnaka Castle on Fridays.

ⓘ Getting There & Around

Intercity (www.intercity-buses.com) Has regular daily buses to Lemesos (€3, 45 minutes), Lefkosia (€3, 45 minutes) and Agia Napa (€3, one hour). From the airport to central Larnaka, take local buses 431 and 440 (€1, 30 minutes, Monday to Saturday).

Travel & Express (☑7777 7474; www.travel express.com.cy; Papakyriakou) Operates service taxis every half-hour to Lemesos (€11, one hour) and Lefkosia (€9, one hour).

Agia Napa (Ayia Napa)

In just three decades Agia Napa has grown from a tiny fishing village to a florescent resort dedicated solely to seasonal, mainly British, tourism. On the plus side, the buildings are predominantly low rise, rather than Benidorm-style blocks. Most hotels and restaurants close from November until April.

⊙ Sights & Activities

Monastery of Agia Napa　　　MONASTERY
(Plateia Seferi; ⊙9am-6pm) The beautifully cloistered monastery is incongruously sited next to the pub-and-club centre of the adjoining square. Best visited in the early morning, the monastery is an oasis of calm amid the in-your-face commercialism of Agia Napa's entertainment scene.

Thalassa Museum　　　　　MUSEUM
(Leoforos Kryou Nerou 14; adult/child €3/1; ⊙9am-1pm & 6-10pm Wed-Sun & 6-10pm Tue) As well as

the busy beach, you can visit this comprehensive museum dedicated to the maritime history of Cyprus, with its replica of the 4th-century AD Kyrenia wreck.

CTO TOURS
(Kyrou Nerou 12; ⊙8.30am-2.30pm & 3-6pm Mon-Fri, closed Wed afternoon) Has information on tours to North Cyprus and other activities. It also organises walks on Mondays and Fridays from 8.30am to 1.30pm from Cape Greco and including the archaeological site of Makronisos.

🛏 Sleeping & Eating

There are loads of holiday apartments for rent in the area. Restaurants are plentiful, but many are strictly seasonal.

Faros HOTEL €€€
(☑2372 3838; www.faroshotel.com.cy; Leoforos Archiepiskopou Makariou III; d €110, garden ste €180; 🛜🌊) A three-storey modern hotel near the harbour, with 96 sleek, bright rooms in the main building and a further 34 slightly more expensive garden suites surrounding the pool. Note that there is a four-night minimum stay in July and August.

Green Bungalows APARTMENT €
(☑2372 1511; www.greenbungalows.com; Katalymata 19; 2-person apt from €50; ⊙Apr-Oct; ❄🌊)

A superior B-class apartment hotel with a poolside bar offering cosy apartments and breakfast from €5.

TOP CHOICE Xylino CYPRIOT €
(Vrysoulles; mains €7; ⊙closed Sun) Situated outside of Agia Napa, in the small modern town of Vrysoulles. Dine under the orange trees on specialities like mousakka, *tsippoura* (sea bream) or more earthy choices, like liver with onions. It is across from the church.

Limelight CYPRIOT €€
(Lipertis 10; mains €10; ⊙2pm-late) Family run since 1983, this restaurant has a large rustic-style dining room fronted by a terrace. Choices include plenty to keep carnivorous folk chomping, including suckling pig, grilled duck and steak. Moussaka, dolmades (stuffed vine leaves) and *souzoukakia* (meat balls in a tomato and garlic sauce) are also on the menu.

☆ Entertainment

In the '90s, clubbers flocked to Agia Napa and it fast gleaned a questionable reputation for being another Magaluf-style Mediterranean resort famed for binge-drinking Brits. Although Agia Napa is still known for its clubbing, it has a less frenetic scene these days.

WORTH A TRIP

CRAFTS, CULTURE & CUISINE

If you are based in Larnaka and have wheels, an enjoyable day out starts in the lace-making village of **Lefkara**, about 30km southwest of town. You won't want to hang around too long though as, although it's a pretty place, it's very touristy and much of the lace comes from China these days! No worries, there are two worthwhile museums and you can enjoy the surrounding scenery as you head for **Kato Dhrys**, a couple of kilometres due south. Right on the road is the traditional **Platanos** bar and restaurant with its vast terrace under the plane trees. Rev up your adrenalin levels with a Cypriot coffee before continuing along the F112, via pretty Vavla, towards Lemesos. After 3km, stop at the **Ayios Minas** convent. Pick up a bag of macadamia nuts from the stalls fronting the entrance and take a look at this 15th-century convent with its exquisite, highly patterned icons painted by the nuns. Follow the road towards Lemesos for 9km until you see the turn-off for the fascinating Neolithic site of **Chirokitia** (admission €1.70; ⊙8am-5pm), a Unesco World Heritage site dating back 9000 years and one of the earliest permanent human settlements in Cyprus. The Chirokitians lived in round stone huts; the remains of around 60 are on view with comprehensive descriptions of their features. If you're feeling peckish, continue towards Lemesos taking the number 15 exit to **Zygi** where some of this coast's best seafood restaurants are located: **Zygiana** (Afxeniou 71) is a favourite with the locals. Return to Larnaka via the secondary B4 road that hugs beaches which are remarkably undeveloped. Stop at **Cape Kiti** to see the 19th-century lighthouse, before returning to Larnaka and (ideally) the sun setting over the salt plains creating a mesmerising pink hue.

For the highest concentration of clubs, head for Plateai Seferi and the surrounding streets (signposted the 'Cosmopolitan Area') where clubs like **Black and White**, **Soul Swing** (R&B) and **Loveshack Club** are interspersed with the inevitable kebab and Chinese takeaways.

❶ Getting There & Around

Intercity (www.intercity-buses.com) Has regular daily buses to Lefkosia (€4, one hour) and Larnaka (€3, one hour) from where you can take onward buses to Lemesos and Pafos.

Travel & Express (☑7777 7474; www.travel express.com.cy) Operates service taxis between Paralimni and Larnaka with pick-up and drop-off in Agia Napa.

Dozens of places in town rent out mopeds, cars and jeeps for around €30 per day.

Lemesos (Limassol)
ΛΕΜΕΣΟΣ

POP 201,257

Part beach resort, part economic hub, Lemesos is the second-largest town in Cyprus. It is becoming an increasingly sophisticated city, fast gaining a reputation for its fine innovative dining. The long-awaited luxurious new marina is due to open in 2014, after suffering innumerable delays. The historic centre has plenty of atmosphere with pedestrian shopping streets that are only truly busy when the cruise ships disgorge their passengers. The city is at the centre of one of the richest areas for exploration, with archaeological remains, beaches and the verdant mountains of the Troodos nearby.

The town rose to prominence after Richard the Lionheart married Berengaria of Navarre here in 1191.

◉ Sights & Activities

Most of the main sights are within walking distance of the old port. The main shopping street is St Andrew's St, one street back from the waterfront. Beach lovers will have to head west out of town where a string of unexceptional beach resorts are strung along the coast. Windsurfers and kitesurfers should head to unspoilt Kourion Beach. Less choppy is Avdimou Beach, although both stretches of sand lack shade, so pack a parasol.

FREE **Lemesos Castle**   CASTLE
(Eirinis; ◷9am-5pm Mon-Sat, 10am-1pm Sun) The main attraction in Lemesos is the solid-looking castle. Inside there are lovely shady gardens and a **museum** where exhibits include Crusader gravestones, Ottoman pottery, suits of armour and an interesting display of black-and-white photos of Byzantine sites all over Cyprus.

Grand Mosque   MOSQUE
(Genethliou Mitella) Surrounded by palms and used by the remaining Turkish Cypriot population, the mosque is open to visitors, outside of prayer time. Nearby is the tiny mixed-sex **Hammam** (Loutron 3; steam bath & sauna/massage €15; ◷2-10pm).

Archaeological Museum   MUSEUM
(cnr Vyronos & Kaningos; admission €1.70; ◷9am-5pm Mon-Sat, 10am-1pm Sun) The district archaeological museum pales in comparison with Lefkosia's Cyprus Museum but is worth a brief visit. Highlights include terracotta figures thought to be the remains of votive offerings, and curious-looking glass bottles and vials.

Kourion & Castle   HISTORIC AREA
(Kourion; admission €1.70; ◷8am-7.30pm) A few kilometres west, the Graeco-Roman site at Kourion has Roman baths, an *agora* (public forum) and a famous amphitheatre backed by the setting sun. Get here before 10am to beat the crowds, or arrive in the afternoon to appreciate the sunset (though it might be a bit busier). Just northeast of here is the robust keep of **Kolossi Castle** (admission €1.70; ◷9am-7.30pm), built in Crusader times.

Sanctuary of Apollon Ylatis   RUINS
(Episkopi; admission €1.70; ◷9am-7.30pm) Five kilometres due west from Kourion are the partly restored remains of the sacred sanctuary created by a cult of Apollo worshippers in Graeco-Roman times.

Petra tou Romiou   HISTORIC AREA
The old coast road to Pafos is dotted with sites linked to Aphrodite, the Greek goddess of love. About 26km towards Pafos, is the legendary birthplace of the goddess – it's a scenic spot with huge, white-marble boulders on a pebble beach with great skimming stones.

🛏 Sleeping

There are some excellent accommodation choices in the city, including the island's very first couture hotel.

TOP **Chrielka** APARTMENT €€
(☑2535 8366; www.chrielka.com.cy; Olympion 7; studio €60-70, 2-person apt €85-110; ❋✿) Staying at Chrielka is a bit like staying with a well-travelled great uncle; owner Mr Nikitas has collected some wonderful Asian ceramics and various artefacts from his travels, and developed a fine wine cellar (yes, there *is* a bar). The 33 apartments has tastefully decorated and include a balcony, kitchenette and satellite TV; some overlook the Municipal Gardens. The small pool is an unexpected plus.

Luxor Guest House GUEST HOUSE €
(☑2536 2265; www.luxorlimassol.com; Agiou Andreou 101; dm €12, d €35; @) The Luxor is the only place in the city, and possibly in the country, that has a real backpacking atmosphere – in a positive sense. The rooms are airy, with painted wood-board ceilings and small balconies overlooking this bustling pedestrian street. There is one en suite double.

Londa BOUTIQUE HOTEL €€€
(☑2586 5555; www.londahotel.com; George A St 72, Potamos Yermasoyias Yermasoyia; r €170; ❋✿) The island's first couture hotel, the Italian-owned Londa sports custom-made furnishings ranging from hand-carved headboards to Cavallino carpets. Rooms are spacious, with lashings of white linen and cool earth colours. Extensive facilities include a spa, infinity pool and the Caprice Bar, which flips to a smoochy club in the evening when the resident DJ takes centre stage. It's 550m east of the historic centre.

✗ Eating & Drinking

TOP **Dino Art Café** INTERNATIONAL €€
(☑2576 2030; Irinis 62-66; mains from €8; ☺lunch & dinner Tue-Sat, lunch Sun) Dino's has a great reputation and many a follower among Cypriots thanks to its fashionable decor, friendly boss and great food. The massive salads (€12) are fantastic, with the duck and orange salad holding a special place in our hearts (and bellies). There's a good sandwich selection and some delicate sushi, too. Reservations are recommended.

127 INTERNATIONAL €€
(Elenis Paleologinas 5; salad/sandwiches from €7.50) This place has a late-night lounge atmosphere with its edgy artwork, black sofas, high ceilings and elegant terrace out back. There is a choice of 10 innovative salads, as well as hot dishes – and cool cocktails.

il Castello INTERNATIONAL €€
(Irinis 22; salads €8.50-12.50) Great place for a greenery fix, with superb salads like avocado, mango and hazelnuts, plus quiche, filled jacket potatoes and burgers.

Draught Microbrewery MICROBREWERY €€
(Vasilissis) Serves a range of lagers, ales and wheat beers, as well as light munchies like fajitas. There's a resident DJ at weekends.

Adiexodo CAFE €
(Salaminos 8) Grab a table under the ancient ficus tree and challenge one of the elderly regulars to a backgammon game.

ⓘ Information

CTO (cnr Spyros Araouzou & Dimitriou Nikolaidi; ☺8.15am-2.30pm & 3-6.15pm Mon-Fri, to 1.30pm Wed & Sat, closed Wed afternoon) On the waterfront, a few blocks east of the old harbour.
CyberNet (Eleftherias 79; per hr €2.50; ☺1-11pm Mon-Fri, 10am-11pm Sat & Sun) Internet access.

ⓘ Getting There & Around

Intercity (www.intercity-buses.com) Has regular daily buses to Lefkosia (€4, one hour), Larnaka (€3, 45 minutes) and Pafos (€3, one hour) from its bus stop north of the castle. The district bus company **Limassol Buses** (www.limassolbuses.com) operates buses to the Troodos.
Travel & Express (☑7777 7474; www.travelexpress.com.cy; Thessalonikis 21) Has regular service taxis to Lefkosia (€12, 1½ hours), Larnaka (€11, one hour) and Pafos (€10.50, one hour). They will also drop you off at Larnaka airport (€13.50) and Pafos airport (€12.50). Another taxi option is **Acropolis Service Taxis** (☑2536 6766; Spyrou Araouzou 65), which departs regularly for the same destinations.

Troodos Massif (Troodos)
ΤΡΟΟΔΟΣ

The last great wilderness in the Republic, the Troodos Massif mountain range is a haven for walkers and nature buffs. Dotted among the black pines are small wine-making villages and Unesco World Heritage–listed Byzantine monasteries. The highest point is Mt Olympus (1952m), crowned by NATO radar beacons. The former colonial government had its summer headquarters in Plateia Troodos (Troodos Sq) – most visitors these days stay in Platres, about 7km south. The mountains are criss-crossed by walking

WORTH A TRIP

TIMIOS STAVROS MONASTERY

About 30km south of Pedoulas, Omodos is a small, pretty village of stone houses, cobbled streets and stalls selling everything from lacework to honey – all centred around the magnificent Timios Stavros Monastery (☉8am-4pm). The monastery has a lavish altar with colourful icons, plus three small museums off the rear courtyard, including the quaintly named EOKA Straggle Museum (sic) with its harrowing photos and text about the 1955–59 National Organisation of Freedom Fighters (EOKA) independence struggle. There are also fine lace and ecclesiastical museums, and an art gallery for temporary exhibitions by mainly local painters.

trails, and walkers can pick up walking-trail brochures from the Troodos Visitor Centre near Plateia Troodos. One of the most popular walks is the 1km hike from Platres to pretty Kaledonia Falls.

◉ Sights & Activities

Kykkos Monastery MONASTERY
(www.kykkos-museum.cy.net; ☉10am-dusk) About 20km northwest of Pedoulas, this is the most famous monastery in the Troodos. The walls of the cloisters on several floors are faced with beautiful and vividly coloured mosaics and frescoes dating back to the early 19th century. There's also a distillery here that produces *komandaria* (sweet, traditional wine) and *zivania* (strong spirit), which is available for purchase. The **museum** (admission €5; ☉10am-6pm) has displays of relic cases and other intriguing bits of religious paraphernalia. Archbishop Makarios III is buried in a guarded mausoleum, about 2km uphill.

FREE **Byzantine Museum** MUSEUM
(Pedoulas; ☉10am-1pm & 2.30-5pm) This modest icon museum is in the lower part of the village. Ask for the key to the small stone **Church of Archangelos** opposite, which contains hellfire-and-brimstone frescoes that date from 1474.

Agios Nikolaos tis Stegis CHURCH
(admission by donation; ☉9am-4pm Tue-Sat, 11am-4pm Sun) Located near Kakopetria, this church has even older frescoes depicting stern-looking saints, dating from the 12th century.

🛏 Sleeping & Eating

PLATRES

Platres is a small leafy town and the most popular place to stay. Half a dozen tavernas on the lower main street offer inexpensive, if unexceptional, Cypriot grills and stews.

TOP CHOICE **Semiramis** BOUTIQUE HOTEL €€
(☎2542 27277; www.semiramishotelcyprus.com; Spyrou Kyprianou 55; s/d half-board only Jul & Aug €50/90) In a historic building with panoramic treetop views, this latest addition has upped the accommodation stakes in town. The rooms all have plenty of character, with sumptuous antique bedheads and wardrobes, lofty ceilings and soothing pastel walls. Prices drop by half the rest of the year.

Skylight INTERNATIONAL €€
(Archbishop Makarios 524; mains from €8) A restaurant plus swimming pool (admission per day €5), Skylight is family friendly with good grills, Cypriot dishes, pasta, baked potatoes and burgers. Enjoy your meal between swimming and lounging on the sunny terrace.

PLATEIA TROODOS

Plateia Troodos is a one-street town with no real year-round population. Services are aimed at visitors who come for the walking in summer and skiing in winter. It has several simple restaurants on the main road offering anglicised Cypriot meals.

Jubilee Hotel HOTEL €€
(☎2542 0107; www.jubileehotel.com; s/d €74/110; P❄🛜) A stylish and elegant hotel, 350m from the village along the Prodromos road. Outside the hotel there are deck chairs for you to recline in and enjoy the fresh air. Inside is a soothing lounge in dark wood, furnished with inviting armchairs. There is also a games room with a billiards table and summer activity programs for children.

Troodos Camping Ground CAMPING GROUND €
(☎2242 1624; campsites €4; ☉May-Oct) Below town on the Lefkosia road, this camping ground has pines for shade and a small cafe.

PEDOULAS

This is a quieter alternative to Platres, with lots of historic treasures.

Two Flowers   GUEST HOUSE **€**

(☑2295 2372; full board only d €50, August €100) A lovely little B&B with 19 simple, clean and bright rooms, five of which sit in an old house around 300m down the road that overlooks the valley. The rest of the rooms are in the main building (where the restaurant is, too), each with a private bathroom. The owners are friendly and, outside of the more expensive month of August, it's great value.

TOP CHOICE **Platanos**   CYPRIOT **€**

(mains €8) Platanos offers a real slice of rural life – there's often an intense backgammon game going on in the corner and the shade of the *platanos* (plane trees) offers atmospheric seating. You can get good Cypriot dishes such as moussaka and *afelia*, as well as some juicy kebabs. Located in the lower part of the village.

❶ Information

Troodos Visitor Centre (admission €0.85; ☺10am-4pm) Located just south of Plateia Troodos with a nature museum, video show and information leaflets.

For skiing information, contact the **Cyprus Ski Federation** (www.cyprusski.com).

❶ Getting There & Around

Villages in the Troodos are widely spaced so a rental car is the best way to get around. **Limassol Buses** (www.limassolbuses.com) has daily buses from Lemesos to Troodos and Platres (1¾ hours).

Rural taxis in Platres can ferry you around the monasteries. A taxi from Lemesos to Platres will cost around €40.

Pafos ΠΑΦΟΣ

POP 48,300

The former capital of Cyprus, Pafos is packed with historical relics…and tourists. If you find the beach strip at Kato Pafos too developed, head up to Ktima on the hillside which has an atmospheric Cypriot feel and good choice of shops, restaurants and cafes. More beach resorts are strung out north along the coast towards Agios Georgios. To escape the crowds, rent a car and head for the wonderfully untouched Akamas Peninsula.

If you are into clubbing, head for the pedestrian Andono St, near the tourist office, home to the best-loved music bars

and clubs. If you prefer shopping to shimmying, Ktima's central municipal market is packed with craft stores.

◉ Sights

TOP CHOICE **Pafos Archaeological Sites**   RUINS

(admission €3.60; ☺8am-7.30pm) It's worth braving the crowds to see this site with its astounding Roman mosaics, many featuring the rambunctious exploits of Dionysos, the god of wine. Within the same compound are the ruins of a castle and amphitheatre. There's another castle on the harbour and more impressive Roman ruins, **Hrysopolitissa Basilica** (☺dawn-dusk), just up the hill near the Pyramos Hotel.

Tombs of the Kings   ANCIENT SITE

(admission €2; ☺8.30am-7.30pm) This is a Unesco World Heritage site and Pafos' main attraction. The site contains a set of well-preserved underground tombs and chambers used by residents of Nea Pafos from the 3rd century BC to the 3rd century AD, during the Hellenistic and Roman periods. It's about 2km north of Kato Pafos.

Byzantine Museum   MUSEUM

(Andrea Ioannou 5, Ktima; admission €2; ☺9am-4pm Mon-Fri, 9am-1pm Sat) Impressive icons, including the oldest on the island dating from the 9th century.

Ethnographic Museum   MUSEUM

(Exo Vrysis 1, Ktima; admission €2; ☺9am-6pm Mon-Sat, 9am-1pm Sun) A folklorish jumble, including costumes and kitchen utensils.

🛏 Sleeping & Eating

Ktima has the best hotels for walk-ins during high season. For seafood head to the string of restaurants opposite the harbour.

TOP CHOICE **Pyramos Hotel**   HOTEL **€**

(☑2693 0222; www.pyramos-hotel.com; Agias Anastasias 4, Kato Pafos; s/d €35/45; 🌸) For something different, grab a room overlooking the fascinating adjacent archaeological site of Hrysopolitissa Basilica. Soothingly decked out with cream walls, orange throws and classy mosaic-tiled bathrooms, this is one of the best small hotels in Kato Pafos.

Axiothea Hotel   HISTORIC HOTEL **€**

(☑2693 2866; www.axiotheahotel.com; Ivis Malioti 2, Ktima; s/d €40/50; 🌸) This dusky pink hotel, just southeast of the CTO office, has a vast reception area and lounge with

WORTH A TRIP

POLIS & THE AKAMAS

Built over the ruins of ancient Marion in the northwest of the Republic, **Polis** is the Mediterranean everyone remembers – orange groves above a pretty beach and small tavernas clustered around the village square. It also makes a great base for hiking or mountain biking in the Akamas. This stunning natural wilderness is protected as a national park and the hills are criss-crossed by dirt tracks and walking trails – pick up the CTO's *European Long Distance Path* brochure. **Avakas Gorge** on the west side of the cape is a particularly rewarding hike.

There are also some wild, isolated beaches near here – gorgeous **Lara Beach** has a turtle research station operating from June to September, accessible by car from Agios Georgios.

original stone floors and comfy sofas to enjoy the panoramic views of the town and sea. Rooms are carpeted and comfortable, but vary in size; those in the back are smaller.

Kiniras HOTEL €
(☎2694 1604; www.kiniras.cy.net; Archiepiskopou Makariou III 91, Ktima; s/d €60/70; ❋) Bang in the centre of Ktima, Kiniras is passionately run by its house-proud owner. The rooms are decorated with colourful frescoes, and have telephone, radio, TV, fridge and safe box. If you're hungry, the hotel's downstairs restaurant, Kiniras Garden, is an atmospheric place to eat.

[TOP CHOICE] **Fetta's** CYPRIOT €€
(☎2693 7822; Ioanni Agroti 33, Ktima; mains €9-17; ☺12.30-4pm) Often proclaimed as one of Cyprus's best traditional restaurants, Fetta's is a real treat. A *yaya* (grandma) prepares fantastic meze (€17) and grilled meat, dishing them out from a low, smoky window on the side of the house, while efficient waiters dart between the kitchen and the pavement or a small park, where the tables are sprawled.

Muse INTERNATIONAL €€
(www.muse-kitchen-bar.com; Mousallas, Ktima; snacks €8-9; ☺9am-2am) A hip new place with sweeping views for a mid-morning frappé, midday light lunch, or an evening cocktail

when the place morphs into a fashionable lounge bar. Menu choices include sushi, salads, quesadillas and sandwiches.

ⓘ Information

CTO (Gladstonos 3; ☺8.15am-2.30pm & 3-6.15pm Mon-Fri, 8.15am-1.30pm Sat, closed Wed afternoon) Just down from Ktima's main square. There's a second office on Poseidonos in Kato Pafos.

ⓘ Getting There & Around

Intercity (www.intercity-buses.com) Regular daily buses to Lefkosia (€5, 1½ hours) and Lemesos (€3, 45 minutes).

Travel & Express (☎0777 7474; www.travel express.com.cy; Leoforos Evagora Pallikaridi 9, Ktima) Operates service taxis to Lemesos (€10, one hour), Larnaka (change at Lemesos, €20, 1½ hours) and Lefkosia (change at Lemesos, €22, 1½ hours).

NORTH CYPRUS

Growing numbers of tourists are exploring the Turkish Republic of Northern Cyprus (TRNC), but the state is recognised only by mainland Turkey. Historic ruins abound, beaches are breathtaking and locals are friendly, but the legacy of 1974 casts a long shadow in the form of looted churches and neglected national treasures.

Lefkoşa (North Nicosia)

POP 85,579

The northern half of Lefkosia is another world. Approaching from the smart boutiques in Ledra St, the avenue fractures into a medina-style market of stalls and kebab houses. Thanks to the Nicosia Masterplan (see boxed text, p187), many of the historic buildings are being restored and the area around the Selimiye Mosque has a real sense of heritage. Overall, though, life moves slowly and the dusty streets are lined with ancient mosques and Frankish ruins. With the relaxing of border restrictions, many people take a day trip across from the Republic (and vice versa) via the Ledra Palace or Ledra St checkpoints.

See p184 for details on Lefkosia in the Republic of Cyprus.

◉ Sights & Activities

To visit and appreciate the historic renovation that is taking place here, pick up a

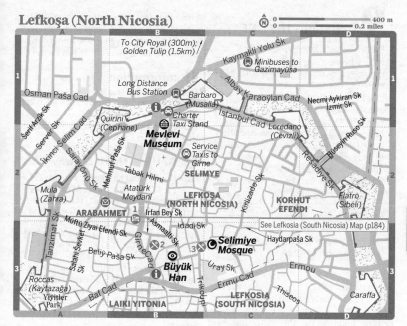

copy of the *Nicosia Trail* brochure from the tourist office or visit the Nicosia Masterplan headquarters at the Ledra Palace Hotel.

Mevlevi Museum MUSEUM
(Mevlevi Tekke Müzesi; Girne Caddesi; adult/child TL5/2; ⊙9am-12.30pm & 1.30-4.45pm) Just inside the walls, the museum is dedicated to the whirling Sufi dervishes (Muslim mystics), who were based here until the 1950s. Traditional *sema* (devotional dances) take place during the Shebu Arus celebrations in December.

Selimiye Mosque MOSQUE
(Selimiye Camii; Selimiye Meydani) The Selimiye quarter is dominated by this imposing mosque that was originally built as a cathedral between 1209 and 1326.

Büyük Han HANDICRAFTS
(www.buyukhan-art.com; Tarihi Büyük Hamam, Great Baths; Irfan Bey Sokak 9) A few blocks west of the mosque is this atmospheric one-time Ottoman inn that now contains a stylish arts and crafts market spread over two floors. Prices are fair and there are some great gift options, including embroidered bags, handmade cards and filigree silver jewellery.

🛏 Sleeping & Eating

Accommodation in Lefkoşa is limited and the few budget options available are not recommended for lone female travellers.

Golden Tulip LUXURY HOTEL €€€
(☑610 5064; www.goldentulipnicosia.com; Dereboyu St; s/d €100/120; P❋@☀) At last – a seriously posh hotel has arrived on the scene. Ultra modern with several restaurants, plus valet service, fitness centre, pool, spa and a suitably glittery casino, the Golden Tulip is Turkish-owned but under Swiss management. The hotel is outside the walls, around 500m northwest of Kyrenia Gate.

ⓘ CROSSING THE LINE

Border restrictions in Cyprus were relaxed in December 2003, allowing overnight trips across the Green Line. In theory, foreign tourists are permitted to cross from south to north (or vice versa) and stay for up to three months, but it's not currently possible to enter Cyprus on one side of the line and leave from the other. Pedestrian crossings are at Ledra St and Ledra Palace Hotel in Lefkosia. There are seven access points in total linking the Greek Cypriot and Turkish Cypriot sides; the latest is the Limnitis –Yesilrmak crossing in the northwest which opened in October 2010. Hire cars can only be taken from south to north; see the boxed text (p201) for car insurance options and advice.

Saray Hotel　　　　　　　HOTEL **€€**
(☑228 3115; saray@northcyprus.net; Atatürk Meydanı; s/d €50/70; ❄) Once a star on the Lefkoşa hotel scene, this hotel has long had a sense of faded glory. However, it was undergoing an extensive renovation at the time of research so, chances are all has improved. It is right in the centre of the old city, on Atatürk Meydanı.

City Royal　　　　　　　HOTEL **€€**
(☑228 7621; www.city-royal.com; Gazeteci Kemal Aşik Caddesi; r from €70; ❄🐾🌐) A popular choice with travellers on business and with casino lovers. Rooms are carpeted and spacious with minibar, phone, satellite TV, and even a phone in the bathroom. There is also a swimming pool and a gym. To reach here, head northeast of the Kyrenia Gate for around 300m.

TOP CHOICE **Sabor**　　　　　MEDITERRANEAN **€€**
(Selimiye Meydanı 29; mains around TL15) Right next to Selimiye Mosque, this is Lefkoşa's best choice for those who can't eat another kebab. The menu specialises in Italian and Spanish food, with some Asian noodle dishes. The portions are generous, the prices are low and the staff (and resident cat population) are friendly.

Bereket　　　　　　　　TURKISH **€**
(Irfan Bey Sokak; pide & lahmacun TL7-10; ⊙4am-1.30pm) A rough and ready kiosk a few metres away from the grand Büyük Han, Bereket is run by Ilker, who makes the best

pide and *lahmacun* (Turkish-style pizza, topped with minced lamb and parsley) in town in his stone oven. There are a couple of chairs outside or you can munch on the go.

ⓘ Information

Tourist office (Kyrenia Gate; ⊙8am-5pm Mon-Fri, to 3pm Sat & Sun) Has free maps and brochures.
Tourist kiosk (Ledra St crossing; ⊙8am-5pm Mon-Fri, to 3pm Sat & Sun)

ⓘ Getting There & Away

Girneliler Seyahat has regular minibuses to Girne (TL4, 30 minutes), while **Akva/Ulusoy** goes frequently to Güzelyurt (TL5.50, 45 minutes). **Virgo Trans** minibuses to Gazimağusa (TL4, one hour) leave half-hourly from Kaymakli Yolu Sokak, just east of Kyrenia Gate. The long-distance bus station is a 15-minute walk north along Gazeteci Kemal Aşik Caddesi.

Kombos service taxis that take up to seven people run to Girne (TL5, 30 minutes) from Mevlevi Tekke Sokak near the Kyrenia Gate in the old city. A private taxi (departing from the charter taxi stand) to Ercan airport will cost TL35 (40 minutes).

A reliable car-hire outfit is **Sun Rent-a-Car** (☑227 2303; www.sunrentacar.com; Abdi Ipekci Caddesi 10; per day from TL45), 500m north of Kyrenia Gate. Note that all car rental agencies in Northern Cyprus have a minimum of three-day rental.

Girne (Kyrenia)
POP 20,000

This is the Mediterranean as it used to be – a picturesque stone harbour, ending abruptly at a looming Byzantine castle. The old part of Girne is delightful but, in the surrounding hills, hundreds of British expats are living the dream of owning a summer villa, so visit now before the whole area vanishes under a sea of holiday homes.

Most things in Girne are sandwiched between the harbour and Ramadan Cemil Meydani, the main roundabout.

⊙ Sights & Activities

Head to the waterfront, near the tourist office if you fancy a boat-and-barbecue trip. A number of operators have kiosks there. Just uphill from the castle is Girne's main mosque, **Aga Cafer Paşa Cami**. Minibuses run from the main roundabout to the pretty hill village of **Lapta**, a popular retirement spot for British expats.

Kyrenia Castle & Shipwreck Museum

CASTLE

(Girne Kalesi; adult/child TL13/4; ⊙9am-12.30pm & 1.30-4.45pm) Dominating the harbour is Girne's main attraction, an impressively preserved castle with archaeological displays, Neanderthal exhibits, gloomy dungeons, and the remains of the world's oldest shipwreck to be brought to the surface – thought to have sunk in a storm around 300 BC.

Castles

CASTLES

Draped along the highest, rockiest ridge above Kyrenia, **St Hilarion Castle** (adult/child TL7/3; ⊙9am-12.30pm & 1.30-4.45pm) is an archetypal Crusader castle. Views are stupendous but it sits in the middle of an army base, so the only way in is by hire car or taxi (TL25 return from Girne). On a 4WD track off the Girne–Gazimağusa road, the remote Crusader castle of **Buffavento** offers more breathtaking views.

Bellapais

RUINS

(adult/child TL9/3; ⊙9am-12.30pm & 1.30-4.45pm) A TL50 return taxi ride from Girne (they will wait for you for an hour) gets you to the late-Byzantine abbey ruins at Bellapais, the setting for Lawrence Durrell's *Bitter Lemons*.

🛏 Sleeping & Eating

There are some good accommodation choices in town but book ahead if you are planning to visit in July and August. The waterfront has dozens of expensive tourist restaurants serving kebabs and Anatolian interpretations of a Greek meze. There's a cluster of cheaper kebab houses just west of Ramadan Cemil Meydani.

TOP **CHOICE** **White Pearl Hotel** HOTEL **€€**

(☑815 4677; www.whitepearlhotel.com; Girne Limanı; s/d €50/68; ﷯) The nine rooms in this small hotel exude cleanliness and understated style, and are very good value. The rooms at the front are smaller, but preferable, as they have balconies with fabulous five-star views of the harbour. The breakfast is more extensive than most.

Nostalgia Hotel

BOUTIQUE HOTEL **€€**

(☑815 3079; www.nostalgiahotel.com; Cafer Paşa Sokak 7; d €60; ﷯) The owner here is a classic car enthusiast, hence the Morris Minor bonnet suspended from the wall! The rooms are decorated in a similarly classic style. Romantics should go for the Heritage Suite

with its sumptuous four-poster bed. The hotel's restaurant uses organic eggs and vegetables grown on the owner's farm.

Sidelya Hotel

HOTEL **€**

(☑815 6051; fax 815 6052; Nasır Güneş Sokak 7; s/d €17/27; ﷯) This is a good budget option which was having a total makeover at the time of research. The rooms are spacious, with views of the sea and the lighthouse on the pier.

Niazi's

MEDITERRANEAN **€€**

(☑815 2160; www.niazis.com; Kordonboyu Sokak; mains TL20) Located across from the Dome Hotel, this elegant restaurant is popular with ladies who lunch. Although it has gained its reputation with its juicy kebabs, the vegetarian meze is similarly delicious and the wholewheat pasta dishes will keep you smiling as well.

Cyprus Dorms

BUDGET HOTEL **€**

(☑887 2007; www.cyprusdorms.com; Bozaklar Sok 6; dm €8, d €25) A sparkling clean hostel near the harbour.

Set Restorante Italiano

ITALIAN **€€**

(Aga Cafér Sokak; mains from TL20; ⊙Apr-Oct) Serves authentic Italian food in a Romanesque stone courtyard.

🛈 Information

Tourist office (⊙9am-5pm) At the west end of the harbour.

Café Net (Efeler Sokak; per hr TL3; ⊙10am-midnight) Internet access

🛈 Getting There & Away

Buses and service taxis stop near the main roundabout. **Girneliler Seyahat** has regular minibuses to Lefkoşa (TL4, 30 minutes). Hourly **Virgo Trans** minibuses to Gazimağusa (TL7, one hour) leave from an office on the south side of Ramadan Cemil Meydani. **Kibhas** has six daily buses to the airport at Ercan (TL10, one hour).

Kombos (Ramadan Cemil Meydani) has service taxis for up to seven people that run to Lefkoşa (TL5, 30 minutes) and Gazimağusa (TL8, one hour).

The ferry terminal is a TL6 taxi ride from town – see p206 for boats to Turkey.

Güzelyurt (Morfou)

A backwater, even by Cyprus standards, Güzelyurt is a faded, citrus-producing town, close to a rugged, rocky coast. Few tourists come here but the **Museum of Archaeology**

& Nature (Ecevit Caddesi; admission TL7; ☺8am-4.30pm) has the only collection of any size in the north. Nearby, lovely **Ayios Mamas Church** (Ecevit Caddesi) has been preserved in its original condition, largely through the efforts of the exiled bishop of Morfou. The restored amphitheatre at **Soli** (Soli Harabeleri; adult/child TL7/3; ☺9am-12.30pm & 1.30-4.45pm) is accessible by chartered taxi.

There's nowhere to stay, but Güzelyurt is an easy day trip from Lefkoşa by bus (TL5, 45 minutes) or service taxi (TL8, one hour).

Gazimağusa (Famagusta) ΑΜΜΟΧΩΣΤΟΣ

POP 36,400

Despite burgeoning villa developments along the coast, within the ancient city walls Gazimağusa still feels medieval. Bound by mighty Venetian walls, the city was one of the last places to fall in the Ottoman invasion and little has changed here in centuries. The old town is dotted with looming Frankish and Venetian ruins. Ferries run to Mersin on mainland Turkey. There are three entrances through the city walls, two by the waterfront and one near the main roundabout. From the inland gate, İstiklal Caddesi runs down to Kemal Meydanı (the main square), lined with shops, banks and foreign-exchange offices.

◉ Sights

Lala Mustafa Paşa   MOSQUE
(Erenler Sokak; admission by donation; ☺outside prayer times) Gazimağusa is awash with Frankish ruins, and several medieval churches have been converted into mosques, including this famous church where the Frankish kings were crowned. The original church was modelled on the Cathedral of Rheims in France; it's probably the finest example of Gothic architecture in Cyprus and dominates the skyline of the old town. Although the interior has been whitewashed in typical Islamic fashion, the soaring Gothic architectural lines may still be appreciated.

Othello's Tower   NOTABLE BUILDING
(Othello Kalesi; adult/child TL7/3; ☺9am-12.30pm & 1.30-4.45pm) Right on the city walls, this tower is where the Venetian governor Cristofo Moro is said to have killed his wife Desdemona in a fit of jealous rage. The incident inspired Shakespeare's *Othello* but the bard mistakenly assumed that Cristofo

was a Moor, thereby adding an unexpected racial twist to the tale. These days, visitors climb the tower to enjoy the views over the town, best sampled in the early morning or evening.

Salamis   ANCIENT SITE
(Salamis Harabeleri; adult/child TL9/5; ☺9am-12.30pm & 1.30-4.45pm) About 9km north of Gazimağusa are the impressive but poorly maintained Graeco-Roman ruins of Salamis. You can see mosaics, columns and a huge amphitheatre, and there's a pleasant sandy beach here with interesting snorkelling. A return taxi from Gazimağusa will cost TL35.

Salamis Necropolis   CEMETERY
(Salamis Mezarlık Alanı; adult/child TL5/3; ☺9am-12.30pm & 1.30-4.45pm) Across the highway is the necropolis, intriguingly famous for its horse-chariot burials.

⌔ Sleeping & Eating

The camping ground near the ruins at Salamis is open to tourists intermittently – check with the tourist office. The hotels in town are very basic, you may want to stay elsewhere. Half a dozen al fresco restaurants on the main square serve pizzas, burgers and other Western meals. For homestyle kebabs and halloumi pitas, there are several *salonus* (diners) on Liman Yolu, just north of the mosque.

Altun Tabya Hotel   GUESTHOUSE €
(☎366 2585; cnr Altun Tabya & Kizilkule Sokak; d €30; ▣) Tucked inside the city walls, this family-owned place is a rare reliable option with its collection of simple, spotless rooms. To get here, turn right after you pass through the inland gate.

Portofino   HOTEL €
(☎366 4392; Feyzi Çakmak Bulvan 9; s/d €24/36; ▣) This hotel has never been great, although it did have a spanking new paint job when we visited.

TOP CHOICE **Ginkgo**   INTERNATIONAL €€
(Liman Yolu Sokak 1; mains TL10-20) Next to the mosque, with a sprawling terrace and atmospheric interior in a former *madrasa* (Islamic religious school), the menu here includes some innovative options like rosemary soup and chicken with white lemon sauce.

Petek   BAKERY €
(Yeşil Deniz Sokak 1; snacks & sweets from TL5) This is an Aladdin's cave of a cake shop,

CAR INSURANCE AT THE BORDER

If you have a rented car from the Republic and you want to drive to North Cyprus, you will not be allowed across the border unless you have Turkish car insurance which can be purchased at the respective crossing. This will cost you from €25 for one day and €35 for a month of multiple entries. However, although relatively costly, this is only third party insurance and will not cover you if you are involved in an accident where you are at fault. In this scenario you could end up spending time and a considerable sum before you are allowed to leave. Plus, the car rental agency in the Republic will not be much help as, although there is no official ruling, they do not approve of their cars being taken across the Green Line. A less worrisome alternative is to rent a car from the Turkish side once you have crossed the border.

selling sweet and savoury pastries, cakes, Turkish delight and strong, sweet Turkish coffee.

❶ Information

Tourist office (⊘7.30am-4pm Mon-Fri, 9am-6pm Sat & Sun) Housed in the Akkule Bastion at the south end of İstiklal Caddesi.

❶ Getting There & Away

İtimat runs minibuses to Lefkoşa (TL6, one hour), leaving every half-hour from the main roundabout. **Virgo Trans/Göçmen** has minibuses to Girne (TL5, one hour) that leave hourly from Gazi Mustafa Kemal Bulvarı.

Kombos runs share taxis to Girne (TL6, one hour), leaving from Eşref Bitlis Caddesi, about 500m northwest of the city walls.

The ferry terminal is about 500m southeast of the centre – see p206 for information on ferries to Turkey. **KT Denizcilik** has an office on Bülent Ecevit Bulvarı.

Karpas (Kirpaşa) Peninsula

For a taste of what Cyprus was like before partition, hire a car and head to the remote Karpas Peninsula. This wild area has barely been touched by tourism but the tiny **tourist office** (⊘9am-5pm) in the post office in Yeni Erenköy can point you towards archaic tombs and basilicas.

At the west end of the Karpas, reached via a winding, bumpy road, the swooningly romantic Crusader-era castle of **Kantara** (Kantara Kalesi; adult/child TL5/3; ⊘9am-12.30pm & 1.30-4.45pm) hovers above the Mesaoria plain.

Over on the south coast, **Altinkum Beach** (aka Golden Beach or Turtle Beach) is a sea of golden dunes with hardly a human footprint on the sand. Turtles nest here from June to August. On the north coast, there's another nice beach and a ruined Roman/Byzantine basilica at **Agios Filon**, and more beaches and ruined basilicas at **Aphendrika**.

The enclaved Greek Cypriot population here was able to protect some of the churches and monasteries after 1974, and you can see ancient icons in the slightly forlorn-looking monastery of **Apostolos Andreas** at the tip of the peninsula.

UNDERSTAND CYPRUS

History

Blessed with natural resources but cursed by a strategic location, Cyprus has been a pawn in the games of empires since ancient times. Greek culture arrived in 1400 BC with the Mycenaeans but the ancient Greek cities at Pafos, Salamis and Kourion were massively expanded by the Romans, who converted the island to Christianity.

As Roman influence declined, Cyprus was incorporated into the Byzantine Empire, and Orthodox Christianity became the dominant religion. King Richard the Lionheart of England annexed Cyprus on his way to the Third Crusade in 1191. The island passed to the castle-building Knights Templar, then to the Catholic Franks, followed by the Venetians who built huge walls around Lefkosia and Gazimağusa to protect themselves from Arab marauders. This failed to stop the Ottomans from invading in 1570 and dominating Cyprus for the next 300 years.

In 1878 Turkey sold Cyprus to Britain but the majority Greek Cypriot population demanded *enosis* (independence from

CYPRUS KARPAS (KIRPAŞA) PENINSULA

BÜYÜKKONUK ECO VILLAGE

Büyükkonuk is a small settlement at the bottom end of the Karpas Peninsula. Cyprus' first eco village, Büyükkonuk was selected to start up a movement for sustainable development, agritourism and an eco-friendly lifestyle. So far the village's 800 residents have used close to €2 million from the USAID (United States Agency for International Development), the UN and Turkey since the beginning of the project to renovate a number of traditional buildings. The most notable is the aesthetically restored **Old Olive Mill** (☺8am-8pm daily, admission free), on the main road through the village. The mill is an example of traditional local architecture that aims to revive and highlight the role of olive farming as the epicentre of Cypriot agricultural life. If you want to experience life in the village, you can stay at **Lois & Ismail Cemal's B&B** (www.ecotourismcyprus.com; r per person €20), where the decor is simple but activities are plentiful: you can learn how to make traditional food, explore one of the local walking trails or go birdwatching in spring. The Canadian-Cypriot couple also runs a traditional craft shop where you can pick up some unusual souvenirs.

foreign rule and union with Greece). In response, the British created a Turkish Cypriot police force to subdue the Greek Cypriots. Such 'divide and rule' politics paved the way for civil war.

Over the next 60 years, ripples of violence spread across the island, spearheaded by the National Organisation of Freedom Fighters (EOKA) and the Turkish Defence Organisation (TMT); the latter aimed to divide Greek and Turkish Cypriot populations as a stepping stone towards *taksim* – the partition of Cyprus. Britain finally granted independence to Cyprus in August 1960 but the violence continued.

Forces from mainland Greece launched a coup against the government of Archbishop Makarios III on 15 July 1974, killing dozens of Turkish Cypriots. In response, Turkish forces occupied the northern third of the island, driving 180,000 Greek Cypriots from their homes and killing 8000 more. Some 65,000 Turkish Cypriots were displaced in the opposite direction before the island was partitioned into Greek and Turkish states.

Over the following decades, all traces of Greek culture were removed from the north and the area was flooded with thousands of illegal settlers from mainland Turkey. Despite a series of international resolutions, Cyprus remains a divided island. The Turkish Republic of Northern Cyprus, created by Turkish Cypriot leader Rauf Denktash in 1983, is recognised only by Turkey. There have been moves, however, towards reunification.

The Green Line (the ceasefire line that divides Cyprus into two, cutting through the capital) was opened in 2003 to allow refugees from both sides to revisit their homes and, in 2004, the two communities held a referendum on UN proposals for reunification. This was accepted by 65% of Turkish Cypriots, but rejected by 75% of Greek Cypriots. As a result, the southern Republic of Cyprus entered the EU alone in May 2004. Since then, border restrictions have eased, allowing easy travel between the two sides, but wounds are still fresh. A four-year stalemate on peace and unification talks was revived when the Republic's left-wing president Demetris Christofias (elected in February 2008) met with the Turkish-Cypriot leader Mehmet Ali Talat in September 2008 for new peace talks. However, the subsequent election in April 2010 of the 72-year-old veteran politician Dervis Eroglu has concerned some analysts who see Eroglu as a hardliner. As before, the most difficult, pressing and perennial issues for the two leaders to resolve remain power-sharing, land ownership – and compensation.

People

Since partition, the vast majority of Greek Cypriots live in the Republic but a few hundred Greek Cypriot farmers cling on in the remote Karpas Peninsula. In the north, the Turkish Cypriot population is now heavily outnumbered by Anatolian settlers from the Turkish mainland.

Cypriots on both sides of the line are friendly, honest and law-abiding, if nationalistic. Family life, marriage and children still play a central role in society, as does religion. The population of the Republic has recently become much more diverse, with the arrival of large numbers of migrant workers from southeast Asia and the Indian subcontinent.

More than 99% of the North Cyprus population is Sunni Muslim, while the Republic is 94% Greek Orthodox, with small but growing communities of Maronites, Roman Catholics, Hindus and Muslims.

Arts

The definitive art of Cyprus is the production of icons – the paintings of saints that grace Greek Orthodox churches. You can see examples dating back to the Byzantine period in many churches and monasteries. Performing arts have been big in Cyprus since ancient times, and several Roman amphitheatres are still used for performances. Relics of Cyprus' architectural heritage can be seen all over the island, from Stone Age settlements to vast Roman cities and Frankish cathedrals.

Environment

Cyprus is divided by two mountain ranges: the Kyrenia (Pentadactylos) Mountains in North Cyprus and the Troodos Massif in the centre of the Republic. The most important nature reserves in the Republic are the Troodos National Forest Park and Akamas Peninsula. The north has just one reserve, in the Karpas.

On both sides of the divide, the construction of tourist villas is putting a huge strain on natural resources – as long as expats continue to buy holiday homes, the concrete jungle will keep on growing. Tourism is the island's main polluter, but urbanisation and hunting are affecting wildlife populations, including the rare mouflon (wild sheep).

Food & Drink

Cypriot food is a combination of Greek, Turkish and Middle Eastern cuisines, based primarily on meat, vegetables and bread. Popular Cypriot dishes include *souvlakia* (pork kebabs), *sheftalia* (pork and lamb rissoles), *kleftiko ofto* (lamb baked in a sealed oven), *afelia* (pork stew with wine and coriander), *stifado* (beef and onion stew) and *koupepia* (stuffed vine leaves). These dishes are often served together in a huge meal known as a meze.

The north relies on Anatolian cuisine, with numerous variations on the kebab theme. Vegetarians can rely on meat-free dishes in meze, as well as beans and other pulses, often stewed alone, with olive oil, lemon and herbs. For a quick picnic anywhere in Cyprus, grab some bread, halloumi, olives, juicy Cypriot tomatoes and some fresh figs.

The wine from the Troodos Massif mountain range is decent – sweet *komandaria* is the traditional wine, while *zivania* (a strong spirit distilled from grape pressings) is the local firewater.

SURVIVAL GUIDE

Directory A-Z

Accommodation

Accommodation in Cyprus ranges from huts on the beach to super luxurious five-star hotels complete with glossy marble spas. Prices vary between the south and the north, the latter mostly offering cheaper accommodation across all budgets.

PRICE RANGES

The accommodation price ranges used in this chapter are based on the cost of a double room with a private bathroom and breakfast included, during the high season (July to August).

Republic of Cyprus

€   Up to €60

€€   €60 to €90

€€€   More than €90

North Cyprus

€   Up to €40

€€   €40 to €70

€€€   More than €70

CAMPING

The Republic has six licensed camping grounds, including good sites at Polis, Plateia Troodos and Governor's Beach (near Lemesos)

The four official camping grounds in the north are often closed, but wild camping is popular in the Karpas.

Activities

» All the seaside resorts offer water sports such as banana-boat rides, scuba dives, boat trips and paragliding.

» The Akamas Peninsula and Troodos Massif in the Republic, and the Karpas Peninsula and Kyrenia Mountains in North Cyprus, offer fantastic hiking and mountain biking.

» The European Long Distance path from Pafos to Larnaka connects with similar trails across Europe – pick up the *European Long Distance Path* brochure from a CTO office or the visitor centre in Plateia Troodos.

Business Hours

Note that the hours for the sights listed in this chapter are for high season and there may be some deviation at other times of the year.

Banks 8.30am-12.30pm Mon to Fri, plus 3.15-4.45pm Mon afternoons in the Republic

Bars 11am-midnight

Businesses and shops Shops close early on Wed and Sat and many places close at lunchtime in summer

Clubs 9pm-late Thu-Sat

Post offices 7.30am-1.30pm & 4-7pm Mon, Tue, Thu, Fri; 7.30am-1.30pm Wed, 8.30-10.30am Sat

Restaurants 11am to 2pm and from 7.30pm to 11pm daily (smaller restaurants close on Sun)

Children

Most attractions in Cyprus offer discounts for children and hotels can arrange extra beds in rooms for a small additional charge. The coastal resorts have the most to offer children – Agia Napa and Pafos are packed with family-friendly attractions and activities.

Customs Regulations

The Republic joined the EU in 2004; see the Regional Directory, p1004, for standard EU allowances. In North Cyprus you can bring in 500g of tobacco or 400 cigarettes, plus 1L of spirits or wine and 100mL of perfume duty free.

Embassies & Consulates

The Republic of Cyprus is represented worldwide, while North Cyprus has just a few overseas offices. See p205 for visa information.

Countries with diplomatic representation in Lefkosia in the Republic of Cyprus include the following:

Australia (☎2275 3001/3; Leoforos Stasinou & Annis Komninis 4, 2nd fl)

France (☎2258 5300; Saktouri 14-16, Agiou Omologites)

Germany (☎2245 1145; Nikitara 10)

Greece (☎2244 5111; Leoforos Lordou Vyronos 8-10)

Italy (☎2235 7635; 25th Martiou 11, Egkomi)

Spain (☎2245 0410; Strovolou 32, Strovolos)

UK (☎2286 1100; Alexandrou Palli)

USA (☎2239 3939; Gonia Metochiou & Ploutarchou, Egkomi)

Countries with diplomatic representation in Lefkoşa in North Cyprus include:

Australia (☎227 7332; Güner Türkmen Sokak 20)

Germany (☎227 5161; 28 Kasım Sokak 15)

Turkey (☎227 2314; Bedreddin Demirel Caddesi)

UK (☎227 4938; Mehmet Akif Caddesi 23)

USA (☎227 8295; Saran Sokak 6, K Kaymakli)

Food

For more information on food and drink, see p203. The price ranges used in this book are based on the cost of a main course and listings are ordered by preference.

Republic of Cyprus

€   Up to €7

€€   €7 to €12

€€€   More than €12

North Cyprus

€   Up to TL10

€€   TL10 to TL20

€€€   More than TL120

Money

CURRENCY

The Republic's currency is the euro (€).

The unit of currency in North Cyprus is the revalued Turkish lira (TL), but euros and UK pounds are widely accepted.

EXCHANGE

Most currencies and travellers cheques are accepted, and almost all banks have exchange facilities and ATMs that take international cards.

Public Holidays

Holidays in the Republic are the same as those in Greece, with the addition of **Greek Cypriot Day** (1 April) and **Cyprus Independence Day** (1 October).

North Cyprus has a three-day holiday to celebrate the end of Ramadan, starting on 20 July 2012 and 9 July 2013. There is also a four-day holiday for the Muslim festival of Eid al Adha, starting on 6 November 2011, 26 October 2012 and 15 October 2013. Annual holidays:

National Sovereignty/Children's Day 23 April (Republic)

Labour Day 1 May (Republic and North Cyprus)

Youth & Sport Day 19 May (Republic and North Cyprus)

Peace & Freedom Day 20 July (Republic and North Cyprus)

TMT Day 1 August (North Cyprus)

Victory Day 30 August (North Cyprus)

Turkish Republic Day 29 October (North Cyprus)

Proclamation of the Turkish Republic of Northern Cyprus Day 15 November (North Cyprus)

Telephone
PAY PHONES

» In the Republic (country code ☎357), phone booths use CYTA phonecards, which are available from shops. Calling abroad with these cards costs €0.0621 per minute to a landline and €0.15 per minute to mobile phones. For more info, see www.cyta.com.cy.

» In North Cyprus, pay phones take KKTC Telekomünikasyon phonecards, which are available from shops – calls cost TL0.80 per minute to Europe and TL1.50 to the USA. To call North Cyprus from abroad, first dial ☎90 (the country code for Turkey), then the regional code ☎392, and then the number.

» To call North Cyprus from the Republic, dial its country code followed by the local number. To call the Republic from North Cyprus, call its country code followed by the local number. Regional area codes form part of the phone number throughout Cyprus.

MOBILE PHONES

» Roaming GSM phones can be used all over Cyprus. Prepaid phone SIM packs are available from shops and phone offices.

Tourist Information

The **Cyprus Tourism Organisation** (CTO; www.visitcyprus.org.cy) has offices at Larnaka and Pafos airport, and in all major towns in the Republic, with excellent maps and information leaflets.

North Cyprus Tourism (www.holidayin-northcyprus.com) has offices in Lefkoşa, Gazimağusa, Girne, Ercan airport and Yeni Erenköy, with limited brochures and information.

Visas

» Nationals of Australia, New Zealand, the US, Canada, Japan and all European Economic Area countries can enter and stay in either the Republic or North Cyprus for up to three months without a visa.

» Citizens of Greece, the Republic of Cyprus and Armenia need a visa for North Cyprus, and Turkish citizens need a visa for the Republic.

» With the thawing of political relations, tourists are now allowed to cross the Green Line and stay on the opposite side. No special visa is required and immigration stamps are made on a separate piece of paper to avoid future problems entering the Republic – see the boxed text, p198, for more information.

Getting There & Away

Cyprus is a convenient gateway between Europe and the Middle East. There are air connections to major cities in Europe and the Middle East, and ferries between North Cyprus and Turkey. It has recently become much easier to travel between the Republic of Cyprus and North Cyprus, but you must enter and leave Cyprus from the same side of the Green Line. See the boxed text, p198, for more information.

Ferry services to the Republic are currently suspended, so almost all travellers arrive by air. Departure tax varies with the destination and is always included in the ticket price.

Air

The Republic's international airports are at Larnaka and Pafos. From Larnaka airport, buses 431, 436 and 440 run roughly half-hourly to the port, Prodomos area and Makenzy Beach respectively. A taxi costs approximately €15. From Pafos airport, bus

612 is scheduled to meet flights and runs to Pafos harbour, the Tomb of the Kings, the coastal road and, ultimately, to Coral Bay. A taxi to the centre of Pafos costs around €20.

The main airport in North Cyprus is Ercan, but flights sometimes land at Geçitkale.

TO/FROM REPUBLIC OF CYPRUS

There are budget, scheduled and charter flights from major cities throughout Europe and the Middle East with Cyprus Airways as well as other carriers. Fares from London to Cyprus cost between UK£80 and £200, depending on the season. As well as the following scheduled airlines, budget carriers **easyJet** (U2; ☑+44 871 244 2366; www.easyjet. com), **Aegean Airlines** (A3; ☑2265 4000; www. aegeanair.com) and **Monarch** (ZB; ☑800 95242; http://flights.monarch.co.uk) all have discount flights to Larnaka from the UK, Greece and central Europe.

Airlines flying to the Republic:

British Airways (BA; www.britishairways.com)

Cyprus Airways (CY; www.cyprusairways.com)

Egypt Air (MS; www.egyptair.com.eg)

El Al Israel Airlines (LY; www.elal.co.il)

Emirates (EK; www.emirates.com)

Gulf Air (GF; www.gulfairco.com)

KLM (KL; www.klm.com)

Lufthansa (LH; www.lufthansa.com)

Olympic Airlines (OA; www.olympicairlines.com)

TO/FROM NORTH CYPRUS

Flights to Ercan airport in North Cyprus start in Turkey so you must fly there first. Fares from London to Ercan (via İstanbul) start at UK£250. A return ticket to Ercan from İstanbul costs around US$150.

Airlines flying to North Cyprus:

Atlasjet (KK; www.atlasjet.com)

Cyprus Turkish Airlines (YK; www.kthy.net)

Pegasus Airlines (PG; www.flypgs.com)

Turkish Airlines (TK; www.thy.com)

Sea

Services to the Republic's main port at Lemesos are currently suspended. However, they may restart as soon as 2011. Check with **Salamis Shipping** (www.salamisinternational. com) and **Louis Cruise Lines** (www.louiscruises. com). Short cruises to Egypt are available from Lemesos. **Lefkothea** (lefkothea.travel@ cytanet.com.cy) is a reliable agent.

FERRIES FROM NORTH CYPRUS

Fergün Denizcilikik (www.fergun.net) operates a daily express boat and a slower car ferry between Girne and Taşucu (TL69 to TL150, 2½ to 7½ hours). In summer there are additional ferries between Girne and Alanya, Antalya and Anamur. There are also sailings from Gazimağusa to Mersin (TL80, 10 hours) three times a week operated by **Cyprus Turkish Shipping** (cypship@super online.com).

Tickets & Taxes

Tickets can be bought from the passenger lounge at the port or from the main ferry agents **Mavi-Tur** (☑815 2344; Ziya Rizki Caddesi 6/2c; Kyrenia). Note that there is an additional tax of TL32 per passenger for all ferry routes originating in Northern Cyprus.

Getting Around

Bicycle

The **Cyprus Cycling Federation** (www.cyprus cycling.com; Kimonos 1, Egkomi, Lefkosia) can provide information regarding cycle routes.

The **CTO** (www.visitcyprus.com) produces a *Cycling Routes* brochure with 39 itineraries, plus information on accredited guides and cycling organisations.

Bus

The bus service in the Republic has had a major overhaul, see the boxed text, p189. North Cyprus has a baffling number of bus companies, listings are under the respective towns.

Car & Motorcycle

COSTS

» You can hire cars and motorbikes in most towns.

» Rates start at around €25 per day for cars and €10 per day for mopeds and motorcycles.

LICENCES & INSURANCE

» Most car and motorcycle licences are valid in the Republic but only British and international licences are accepted in North Cyprus.

» The minimum age for hiring a car is 21; drivers under 25 pay extra insurance fees. You must be 17 or over to ride a motorcycle (18 or over for engines bigger than 50cc); these restrictions apply in both the Republic and North Cyprus.

» Cars hired in the Republic can be temporarily insured for travel within North Cyprus at the border but this can be problematic. See the boxed text, p201 for more information.

» Hire cars cannot be taken in the opposite direction.

» If you travel with your car to Cyprus on the ferry from Turkey, you are eligible to obtain a three-month duty waiver and local insurance upon your arrival.

» For assistance, contact **Cyprus Automobile Association** (☎22 31 32 33; www.cyprusaa.org)

Taxi

» Service taxis take up to eight people and run between major towns.

» In the Republic, all service taxis are run by **Travel & Express** (www.travelexpress .com.cy)

» In North Cyprus, **Kombos** (☎227 2929) connects Lefkoşa, Girne and Gazimağusa.

» There are urban taxis in all large towns and rural taxis connect rural villages.

France

Best Places to Eat

» Chez Janou (p233)

» Pink Flamingo (boxed text, p237)

» La Table de Ventabren (boxed text, p324)

» Auberge de la Truffe (boxed text, p302)

» Les Vieilles Luges (p292)

Best Places to Stay

» Hôtel Amour (p232)

» L'Apostrophe (p230)

» Hôtel de l'Illwald (boxed text, p267)

» L'Épicerie (p323)

» Hôtel 7e Art (p337)

Why Go?

Few countries provoke such passion as La Belle France. Love it or loathe it, everyone has their own opinion about this Gallic goliath. Snooty, sexy, superior, chic, infuriating, arrogant, officious and inspired in equal measures, the French have long lived according to their own idiosyncratic rules, and if the rest of the world doesn't always see eye-to-eye with them, well, *tant pis* (too bad) – that's the price you pay for being a culinary trendsetter, artistic pioneer and cultural icon.

If ever there was a country of contradictions, this is it. France is a deeply traditional place: castles, chateaux and ancient churches litter the landscape, while centuries-old principles of rich food, fine wine and joie de vivre underpin everyday life. Yet it is also a country that has one of Western Europe's most multicultural make-ups, not to mention a well-deserved reputation for artistic experimentation and architectural invention. Enjoy!

When to Go

Paris

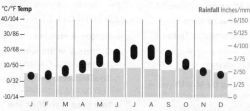

Dec–Mar Hit the French Alps, Jura or Pyrenees for some serious ski action. Or eat truffles.

Apr–Jun France at springtime best, *sans* crowds; June's Fête de la Musique gets you jigging.

Sep Cooling temperatures, abundant produce and the grape harvest; perfect for cycling through Provence.

AT A GLANCE

» **Currency** euro (€)

» **Language** French

» **Money** ATMs can be found everywhere.

» **Visas** Schengen rules apply

Fast Facts

» **Area** 551,000 sq km

» **Population** 64.4 million

» **Capital** Paris

» **Telephone** country code🖉33; international access code 🖉00

» **Emergency** 🖉112

Exchange Rates

Australia	A$1	€0.74
Canada	C$1	€0.74
Japan	¥100	€0.87
New Zealand	NZ$1	€0.56
UK	UK£1	€1.16
USA	US$1	€0.67

Set Your Budget

» **Budget hotel room** from €70

» **Two-course dinner** €15–50

» **Museum entrance** €4–8

» **Glass of wine** €2–5

» **Paris metro ticket** €1.70

Resources

» **Paris by Mouth** (www.parisbymouth.com) Capital dining and drinking

» **France 24** (www.france24.com/en/france) French news in English

» **France.fr** (www.france.fr) Official country website

Connections

High-speed trains link Paris' Gare du Nord with London St Pancras (via the Channel Tunnel/Eurostar rail service) in just over two hours; Gare du Nord is also the point of departure for speedy trains to Brussels, Amsterdam and Cologne. Many more trains make travelling between the French capital and pretty much any city in every neighbouring country a real pleasure. Ferry links from Cherbourg, St-Malo, Calais and other north-coast ports travel to England and Ireland; and ferries from Marseille and Nice provide regular links with seaside towns in Corsica, Italy and North Africa.

Regular bus and rail links cross the French–Spanish border via the Pyrenees, and the French–Italian border via the Alps and the southern Mediterranean coast. For more see p359.

ITINERARIES

One Week

Start with a few days exploring Paris, taking in the Louvre, Eiffel Tower, Musée d'Orsay, Notre Dame, Montmartre and a boat trip along the Seine. Then head out to Normandy, Monet's garden at Giverny, and Versailles; or throw yourself into the Renaissance high life at chateaux in the Loire Valley.

Two Weeks

With Paris and surrounds having taken up much of the first week, concentrate on exploring one or two regions rather than trying to do too much in a whistlestop dash. High-speed TGV (train à grande vitesse) trains zip from Paris to practically every province: for prehistoric interest, head to the Dordogne; for architectural splendour, you can't top the Loire Valley; for typical French atmosphere, try the hilltop villages of Provence; and for sunshine and seafood, the French Riviera on the sparkling Med is the only place to be.

Essential Food & Drink

» **Fondue & raclette** Warm cheese dishes in the French Alps.

» **Oysters & white wine** Everywhere on the Atlantic coast, but especially in Cancale and Bordeaux.

» **Bouillabaisse** Marseille's signature hearty fish stew, eaten with croutons and rouille (garlic-and-chilli mayonnaise).

» **Foie gras & truffles** The Dordogne features goose and 'black diamonds' from December to March. Provence is also good for indulging in the aphrodisiacal fungi.

» **Piggy-part cuisine** Lyon is famous for its juicy andouillette (pig-intestine sausage) and Côtes du Rhône red.

» **Champagne** Tasting in century-old cellars is an essential part of Champagne's bubbly experience.

PARIS

POP 2.21 MILLION

What can be said about the sexy, sophisticated City of Lights that hasn't already been said a thousand times before? Quite simply, this is one of the world's great metropolises – a trendsetter, market leader and cultural capital for over a thousand years and still going strong. This is the place that gave the world the cancan and the cinematograph, a city that reinvented itself during the Renaissance, bopped to the beat of the jazz age and positively glittered during the belle époque (literally, 'beautiful era').

As you might expect, Paris is strewn with historic architecture, glorious galleries and cultural treasures galore. But the modern-day city is much more than just a museum piece: it's a heady hotchpotch of cultures and ideas – a place to stroll the boulevards, shop till you drop, flop riverside, or simply do as Parisians do and watch the world buzz by from a streetside cafe. Savour every moment.

History

The Parisii, a tribe of Celtic Gauls, settled the Île de la Cité in the 3rd century BC. Paris prospered during the Middle Ages and flourished during the Renaissance, when many of the city's most famous buildings were erected.

The excesses of Louis XVI and his queen, Marie-Antoinette, led to an uprising of Parisians on 14 July 1789, and the storming of the Bastille prison – kick-starting the French Revolution.

In 1851 Emperor Napoleon III oversaw the construction of a more modern Paris, complete with wide boulevards, sculptured parks and a sewer system. Following the disastrous Franco-Prussian War and the establishment of the Third Republic, Paris entered its most resplendent period, the belle époque, famed for its art nouveau architecture and artistic and scientific advances. By the beginning of the 1930s, Paris had become a centre for the artistic avant-garde, and it remained so until the Nazi occupation of 1940–44.

After WWII, Paris regained its position as a creative centre and nurtured a revitalised liberalism that climaxed in student-led uprisings in 1968.

During the 1980s President François Mitterrand initiated several *grands projets,* building projects that garnered widespread approval even when the results were popular failures. In 2001 Bertrand Delanoë, a socialist with support from the Green Party, became Paris' – and a European capital's – first openly gay mayor. He returned to power for another term in the 2008 elections.

⊙ Sights

LEFT BANK

Eiffel Tower   LANDMARK
(Map p214; www.tour-eiffel.fr; lifts to 2nd fl adult/child €8.10/4, to 3rd fl €13.10/9, stairs to 2nd

---

PARIS IN...

Two Days

Join a **morning tour** then focus on those Parisian icons: **Notre Dame**, the **Eiffel Tower** and the **Arc de Triomphe**. Late afternoon have a coffee or pastis on **av des Champs-Élysées**, then mooch to **Montmartre** for dinner. Next day enjoy the **Musée d'Orsay**, **Ste-Chapelle** and the **Musée Rodin**. Brunch on **place des Vosges** and enjoy a night of mirth and gaiety in the nightlife-buzzy **Marais**.

Four Days

With another two days, consider a **cruise** along the Seine or **Canal St-Martin** and meander further afield to **Cimetière du Père Lachaise** or **Parc de la Villette**. By night take in a concert or opera at the **Palais Garnier** or **Opéra Bastille**, and go on a bar-and-club crawl along Ménilmontant's **rue Oberkampf**. The **Bastille** area also translates as another great night out.

A Week

Seven days allows you to see a good many of the major sights listed in this chapter and also visit places around Paris, such as **Chartres** with its beautiful cathedral, and the queen of French chateaux, **Versailles**.

France Highlights

1 Gorge on the iconic sights and sophistication of Europe's most hopelessly romantic city, **Paris** (p211)

2 Relive the French Renaissance with extraordinary chateaux built by kings and queens in the **Loire Valley** (p271)

3 Do a Bond swooshing down slopes in the shadow of Mont Blanc in **Chamonix** (p290)

4 Dodge tides, stroll moonlit sand and immerse yourself in legend at island abbey **Mont St-Michel** (p255)

5 Savour ancient ruins, modern art, markets, lavender and hilltop villages in slow-paced **Provence** (p316)

6 Taste bubbly in ancient *caves* (cellars) in **Reims** (p260) and **Épernay** (p262), the heart of Champagne

7 Tuck into France's halest, piggy-driven cuisine in traditional **Lyonnais bouchons** (p288)

8 Soak up the mystery of the world's best megaliths from the back of a Breton bicycle around **Carnac** (boxed text, p257)

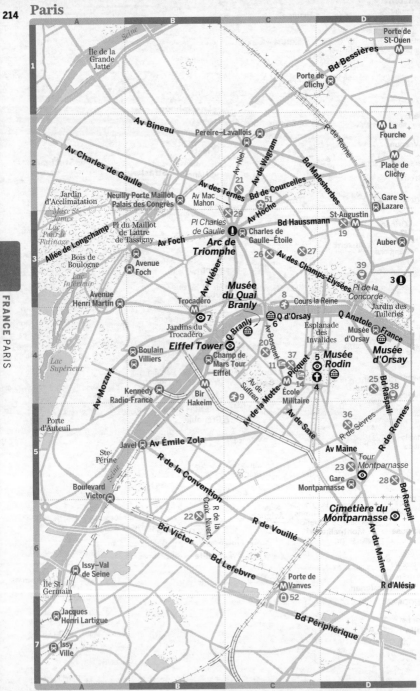

FRANCE PARIS

Seine

Porte de
St-Ouen

Île de la
Grande
Jatte

Bd Bessières

Porte de
Clichy

R de Rennes

M La
Fourche

Av Bineau

Pereire–Lavallois

Av Niel

Av de Wagram

M Place de
Clichy

Av Charles de Gaulle

21

Av des Ternes

Bd de Courcelles

Bd Malesherbes

Gare St-
Lazare

Jardin
d'Acclimatation

Neuilly Porte Maillot
Palais des Congrès

Av Mac
Mahon

51

Av Hoche

Bd Haussmann

St-Augustin

M

Parc St-
James

Pl du Maillot
de Lattre
de Tassigny

29

Pl Charles
de Gaulle

Charles de
Gaulle–Étoile

19

Auber

Lac
Pour le
Patinage

Av Foch

Arc de
Triomphe

26

27

39

Allée de Longchamp

Avenue
Foch

Av des Champs-Élysées

Pl de la
Concorde

3

Bois de
Boulogne

Av Kléber

Musée
du Quai
Branly

8

Cours la Reine

Jardin des
Tuileries

Lac
Inférieur

Avenue
Henri Martin

Trocadéro

M

7

Q d'Orsay

Q Anatole
France

Musée
d'Orsay

Jardins du
Trocadéro

Q Branly

6

Av Bosquet

Esplanade
des
Invalides

Musée
d'Orsay

Lac
Supérieur

Boulain
Villiers

Eiffel Tower

20

37

Musée
Rodin

Champ de
Mars Tour
Eiffel

11

Av Picquet

14

5

25

38

Bd Raspail

Av Mozart

Kennedy
Radio-France

Bir
Hakeim

9

Av de Suffren

École
Militaire

4

36

Bd Raspail

Porte
d'Auteuil

Javel

Av Émile Zola

Av de la Motte-

Av de Saxe

R de Sèvres

R de Rennes

Ste-
Périne

R de la Convention

Av Maine

Tour
Montparnasse

23

28

Boulevard
Victor

R de la
Croix Nivert

Gare
Montparnasse

Av du Maine

Issy-Val
de Seine

22

R de Vouillé

Cimetière du
Montparnasse

Île St-
Germain

Bd Victor

Bd Lefebvre

Jacques
Henri Lartigue

Porte de
Vanves

M

R d'Alésia

Issy
Ville

52

Bd Périphérique

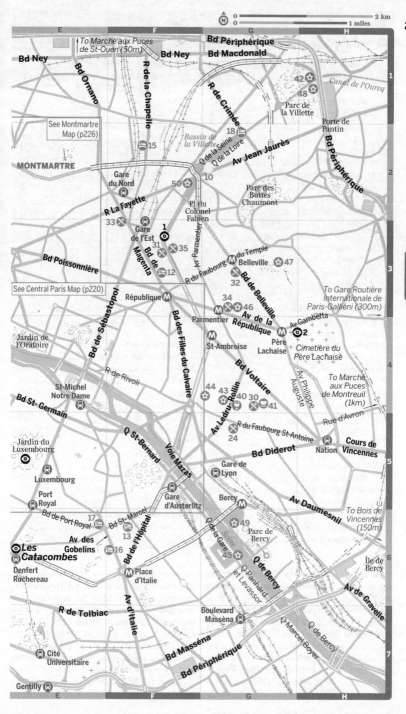

△ N 0 — 2 km
0 — 1 miles

See Montmartre Map (p226)

See Central Paris Map (p220)

Bd Ney
To Marché aux Puces de St-Ouen (50m)
Bd Ney
Bd Périphérique
Bd Macdonald

Bd Ornano
R de la Chapelle
R de Crimée
Canal de l'Ourcq

42
48
Parc de la Villette
Porte de Pantin

Bassin de la Villette
18
Q de la Seine
Q de la Loire
Av Jean Jaurès
Bd Périphérique

MONTMARTRE

Gare du Nord
50
10

Parc des Buttes Chaumont

R La Fayette
33
Pl du Colonel Fabien

Gare de l'Est
1
31
35
Av Parmentier
du Temple
Belleville
47

Bd Poissonnière
Bd de Magenta
12
R du Faubourg
32
Bd de Belleville

République
34
46
Parmentier
Av de la République
Père Lachaise
2
Cimetière du Père Lachaise

Jardin de l'Oratoire
St-Ambroise
Av Gambetta

Bd de Sébastopol
Bd des Filles du Calvaire
To Gare Routière Internationale de Paris-Galliéni (300m)

St-Michel Notre Dame
R de Rivoli
Bd Voltaire
To Marché aux Puces de Montreuil (1km)

Bd St- Germain
44
43
40 30
41
Av Ledru-Rollin
Rue d'Avron

Jardin du Luxembourg
Q St-Bernard
Voie Mazas
R du Faubourg St-Antoine
24
Bd Diderot
Nation
Cours de Vincennes

Luxembourg
Av Philippe Auguste

Port Royal
Gare de Lyon
Av Daumesnil

Bd de Port Royal
17
Gare d'Austerlitz
Bercy
To Bois de Vincennes (150m)

Les Catacombes
13
Bd St-Marcel
Bd de l'Hôpital
49
Parc de Bercy
Île de Bercy

Denfert Rochereau
16
Av des Gobelins
Place d'Italie
45
Q de Bercy

R de Tolbiac
Av d'Italie
Boulevard Massèna
Q de Bercy
Av de Gravelle

Cité Universitaire
Bd Masséna
Q Marcel Boyer
Bd Périphérique

Gentilly

PARIS PARIS

fl €4.50/3; ⊙lifts & stairs 9am-midnight mid-Jun–Aug, lifts 9.30am-11pm, stairs 9.30am-6pm Sep–mid-Jun; Ⓜ Champ de Mars–Tour Eiffel or Bir Hakeim) It's impossible now to imagine Paris (or France, for that matter) without La Tour Eiffel, the Eiffel Tower, but the 'metal asparagus', as some Parisians snidely called it, faced fierce opposition from Paris' artistic elite when it was built for the 1889 Exposition Universelle (World Fair). The tower was almost torn down in 1909, and was only

saved by the new science of radiotelegraphy (it provided an ideal spot for transmitting antennas). Named after its designer, Gustave Eiffel, the tower is 324m high, including the TV antenna at the tip. This figure can vary by as much as 15cm, however, as the tower's 7300 tonnes of iron, held together by 2.5 million rivets, expand in warm weather and contract when it's cold.

The three levels are open to the public (entrance to the 1st level is included in all admission tickets), though the top level closes in heavy wind. You can either take the lifts (east, west and north pillars), or, if you're feeling fit – don't blame us if you run out of steam halfway up – the stairs in the south pillar up to the 2nd platform. Buy tickets in advance online to avoid monumental queues at the ticket office.

Spreading out around the Eiffel Tower are the **Jardins du Trocadéro** (MTrocadéro), whose fountains and statue garden are grandly illuminated at night.

Musée du Quai Branly   MUSEUM
(Map p214; www.quaibranly.fr; 37 quai Branly, 7e; adult/child €8.50/free; ⊙11am-7pm Tue, Wed & Sun, to 9pm Thu-Sat; MPont de l'Alma or Alma-Marceau) The architecturally impressive but unimaginatively named Quai Branly Museum introduces the art and cultures of Africa, Oceania, Asia and the Americas through innovative displays, film and musical recordings. With '*Là où dialoguent les cultures*' ('Where cultures communicate') as its motto, the museum is one of the most dynamic and forward-thinking in the world. The anthropological explanations are kept to a minimum; what is displayed here is meant to be viewed as art. Don't miss the views from the 5th-floor restaurant, **Les Ombres**.

Musée d'Orsay   ART MUSEUM
(Map p214; www.musee-orsay.fr; 62 rue de Lille, 7e; adult/child €8/free; ⊙9.30am-6pm Tue, Wed & Fri-Sun, 9.30am-9.45pm Thu; MMusée d'Orsay or Solférino) The Musée d'Orsay, housed in a turn-of-the-century train station overlooking the Seine, displays France's national collection of paintings, sculptures and other art produced between the 1840s and 1914. The museum is especially renowned for its Impressionist and art nouveau collections: the upper level contains a celebrated collection of Impressionist paintings by Monet, Pissarro, Renoir, Sisley, Degas and Manet, plus post-Impressionist works by Cézanne, Van Gogh, Seurat and Matisse. Art nouveau aficionados will want to linger on the middle level, while on the ground floor, look out for early works by Manet, Monet, Renoir and Pissarro.

Tickets are valid all day, so you can come and go as you please. A reduced entrance fee of €5.50 applies to everyone after 4.15pm (6pm on Thursday). A combined ticket including the Musée Rodin costs €12.

[TOP CHOICE] Jardin du Luxembourg   PARK
(Map p220; ⊙7.30 or 8.15am–5 or 10pm according to the season; MLuxembourg) When the

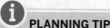
weather is fine, Parisians of all ages come flocking to the formal terraces and chestnut groves of this 23-hectare city park to read, relax, stroll through urban **orchards** and visit the honey-producing **Rucher du Luxembourg** (Luxembourg Apiary).

The **Palais du Luxembourg** (Map p220; rue de Vaugirard, 6e), at the northern end of the garden, was built for Marie de Médicis, Henri IV's consort; it has housed the **Sénat** (Senate), the upper house of the French parliament, since 1958.

Top spot for sun-soaking – always loads of chairs here – is the southern side of the palace's 19th-century, 57m-long **Orangery** (1834), where lemon and orange trees, palms, grenadiers and oleanders shelter from the cold.

[TOP CHOICE] Musée Rodin   GARDEN, ART MUSEUM
(Map p214; www.musee-rodin.fr; 79 rue de Varenne, 7e; adult/child incl garden €7-10/free, garden only €1; ⊙10am-5.45pm Tue-Sun; MVarenne) One of our favourite cultural attractions, the Rodin Museum is both a sublime museum and one of the most relaxing spots in the city, with a lovely sculpture garden in which to lounge. The 18th-century house displays some of Rodin's most famous works, including *The Burghers of Calais (Les Bourgeois de Calais), Cathedral, The Thinker (Le Penseur)* and *The Kiss (Le Baiser)*.

Les Catacombes   OSSUARY
(Map p214; www.catacombes.paris.fr, in French; 1 av Colonel Henri Roi-Tanguy, 14e; adult/child €8/4; ⊙10am-5pm Tue-Sun; MDenfert Rochereau)

WANT MORE?

For in-depth information, reviews and recommendations at your fingertips, head to the Apple App Store to purchase Lonely Planet's *Paris City Guide* iPhone app.

Alternatively, head to **Lonely Planet** (www.lonelyplanet.com/france/paris) for planning advice, author recommendations, traveller reviews and insider tips.

There are few spookier sights in Paris than the Catacombes, one of three underground cemeteries created in the late 18th century to solve the problems posed by Paris' overflowing cemeteries. Twenty metres below street level, the catacombs consist of 1.7km of winding tunnels stacked from floor to ceiling with the bones and skulls of millions of Parisians – guaranteed to send a shiver down your spine.

If your ghoulish appetite yearns for more, check out lots more famous graves at **Cimetière du Montparnasse** (Map p214; cnr blvd Edgar Quinet & rue Froidevaux, 14e; ⌚8am-5.30 or 6pm Mon-Fri, 8.30am-6pm Sat, 9am-6pm Sun; Ⓜ Edgar Quinet or Raspail), including French crooner Serge Gainsbourg, poet Charles Baudelaire, writer Guy de Maupassant, playwright Samuel Beckett, photographer Man Ray and philosopher Jean-Paul Sartre.

Musée des Égouts de Paris MUSEUM

(Map p214; place de la Résistance, 7e; adult/child €4.20/3.40; ⌚11am-5pm Sat-Wed May-Sep, 11am-4pm Sat-Wed Oct-Dec & Feb-Apr; Ⓜ Pont de l'Alma) A working museum whose entrance – a rectangular maintenance hole topped with a kiosk – is across the street from 93 quai d'Orsay, 7e. Raw sewage flows beneath your feet as you walk through 480m of odoriferous tunnels, passing artefacts illustrating the development of Paris' waste-water disposal system. A visit here quite takes your breath away.

Panthéon MONUMENT

(Map p220; place du Panthéon, 5e; adult/child €8/free; ⌚10am-6.30pm Apr-Sep, to 6pm Oct-Mar; Ⓜ Luxembourg) This domed landmark was commissioned around 1750 as an abbey church, but because of financial and structural problems it wasn't completed until 1789 (not a good year for opening churches in France). The crypt houses the tombs of Voltaire, Jean-Jacques Rousseau, Victor Hugo, Émile Zola, Jean Moulin and Nobel Prize–winner Marie Curie, among many others. Inside the gloomy Panthéon itself, a working model of Foucault's Pendulum demonstrates the rotation of the earth; it wowed the scientific establishment when it was presented here in 1851.

Hôtel des Invalides MONUMENT, MUSEUM

(Map p214; Ⓜ Varenne or La Tour Maubourg) Hôtel des Invalides was built in the 1670s as housing for 4000 *invalides* (disabled war veterans). On 14 July 1789, a mob forced its way into the building and seized 28,000 rifles before heading to the prison at Bastille, starting the French Revolution.

North of the main courtyard is the **Musée de l'Armée** (Map p214; Army Museum; www.invalides.org; 129 rue de Grenelle, 7e; adult/child €9/free; ⌚10am-6pm Mon & Wed-Sat, to 9pm Tue), home to the nation's largest collection on the history of the French military.

South are **Église St-Louis des Invalides**, once used by soldiers, and **Église du Dôme**, which contains the extraordinarily extravagant **Tombeau de Napoléon 1er** (Napoleon I's Tomb; ⌚10am-6pm Apr-Sep, 10am-5pm Oct-Mar): six coffins fit into one another rather like a Russian stacking doll.

Palais de Chaillot PALACE, MUSEUM

(Map p214; 17 place du Trocadéro et du 11 Novembre, 16e; Ⓜ Trocadéro) The two curved, colonnaded wings of this palace and the terrace in between them afford an exceptional panorama of the **Jardins du Trocadéro**, the Seine and the Eiffel Tower. The palace's eastern wing houses the standout **Cité de l'Architecture et du Patrimoine** (Map p214; www.citechaillot.fr, in French; 1 place du Trocadéro et du 11 Novembre, 16e; adult/child €8/free; ⌚11am-7pm Mon, Wed & Fri-Sun, to 9pm Thu), devoted to French architecture and heritage.

Jardin des Plantes GARDEN

(Map p220; 57 rue Cuvier & 3 quai St-Bernard, 5e; ⌚7.30am-7pm; Ⓜ Gare d'Austerlitz, Censier Daubenton or Jussieu) Paris' 24-hectare Jardin des Plantes was founded in 1626 as a medicinal herb garden for Louis XIII. On its southern fringe is the city's main natural-history museum, the **Musée National d'Histoire Naturelle** (Map p220; www.mnhn.fr, in French; ⌚10am-5pm Wed-Mon; Ⓜ Censier Daubenton or Gare d'Austerlitz), with several galleries covering evolution, geology, palaeontology and the history of human evolution.

Église St-Germain des Prés CHURCH
(Map p220; 3 place St-Germain des Prés, 6e; ⊙8am-7pm Mon-Sat, 9am-8pm Sun; Ⓜ St-Germain des Prés) Paris' oldest church, the Romanesque Église St-Germain des Prés, was built in the 11th century on the site of a 6th-century abbey and was the dominant church in Paris until the arrival of Notre Dame.

Église St-Sulpice CHURCH
(Map p220; place St-Sulpice, 6e; ⊙7.30am-7.30pm; Ⓜ St-Sulpice) Lined with 21 side chapels, this beautiful Italianate church was built between 1646 and 1780. The facade, designed by a Florentine architect, has two rows of superimposed columns and is topped by two towers. The neoclassical decor of the vast interior is influenced by the Counter-Reformation.

THE ISLANDS
Paris' twin set of islands could not be more different. Île de la Cité is bigger, full of sights and very touristed (few people live here).

Smaller Île St-Louis is residential and quieter, with just enough boutiques and restaurants – and a legendary ice-cream maker – to attract visitors. The area around Pont St-Louis, the bridge across to the Île de la Cité, and Pont Louis Philippe, the bridge to the Marais, is one of the most romantic spots in Paris.

ÎLE DE LA CITÉ
The site of the first settlement in Paris, around the 3rd century BC, and later the Roman town of Lutèce (Lutetia), Île de la Cité remained the centre of royal and ecclesiastical power throughout the Middle Ages. The seven decorated arches of Paris' oldest bridge, Pont Neuf (Map p220; Ⓜ Pont Neuf), have linked Île de la Cité with both banks of the River Seine since 1607.

Cathédrale de Notre Dame de Paris
CHURCH
(Map p220; www.cathedraledeparis.com; 6 place du Parvis Notre Dame, 4e; audioguide €5; ⊙8am-6.45pm Mon-Fri, 8am-7.15pm Sat & Sun; Ⓜ Cité) Notre Dame is the true heart of Paris: distances from Paris to all parts of metropolitan France are measured from place du Parvis Notre Dame, the square in front of this masterpiece of French Gothic architecture.

Notre Dame – the most visited site in Paris, with 10 million people crossing its threshold each year – is famed for its stunning stained-glass rose windows, leering gargoyles and elegant flying buttresses, as

well as a monumental 7800-pipe organ. Constructed on a site occupied by earlier churches (and, a millennium before that, a Gallo-Roman temple), it was begun in 1163 but not completed until the mid-14th century. Architect Viollet-le-Duc carried out extensive renovations in the mid-19th century. Free 1½-hour tours in English run at noon on Wednesday, 2pm Thursday and 2.30pm Saturday.

The entrance to its famous towers, the **Tours de Notre Dame** (Map p220; rue du Cloître Notre Dame; adult/child €7.50/free; ⊙10am-6.30pm daily Apr-Jun & Sep, 9am-7.30pm Mon-Fri, 9am-11pm Sat & Sun Jul & Aug, 10am-5.30pm daily Oct-Mar) is from the North Tower, to the right and around the corner as you walk out of the cathedral's main doorway. A narrow spiral staircase – 422 steps – takes you to the top of the west facade for face-to-face views of countless gargoyles, the massive 13-tonne 'Emmanuel' bell in the South Tower and an unforgettable bird's-eye view of Paris. No hunchbacks, though, despite what you may have heard from Victor Hugo.

 Ste-Chapelle CHURCH
(Map p220; 4 blvd du Palais, 1er; adult/child €8/free; ⊙9.30am-6pm Mar-Oct, 9am-5pm Nov-Feb; Ⓜ Cité) Paris' most exquisite Gothic monument is tucked within the Palais de Justice (Law Courts). The 'walls' of the **upper chapel** are sheer curtains of richly coloured and finely detailed **stained glass**, which bathe the chapel in extraordinary coloured light on a sunny day. Conceived by Louis IX to house his sacred relics, the chapel was consecrated in 1248.

ⓘ IT'S FREE

Paris' national museums are something of a bargain: admission is reduced for those aged over 60 years and 18 to 25; and completely free for **EU residents under 26** years of age, anyone **under 18** years, and **everyone on the first Sunday of each month**. These include: the Louvre, Musée National d'Art Moderne in the Pompidou, Musée du Quai Branly, Musée d'Orsay, Musée Rodin and Cité de l'Architecture et du Patrimoine.

Ditto for the following except they are only free the first Sunday of the month from November to March: Arc de Triomphe, Conciergerie, Panthéon, Ste-Chapelle and the Tours de Notre Dame.

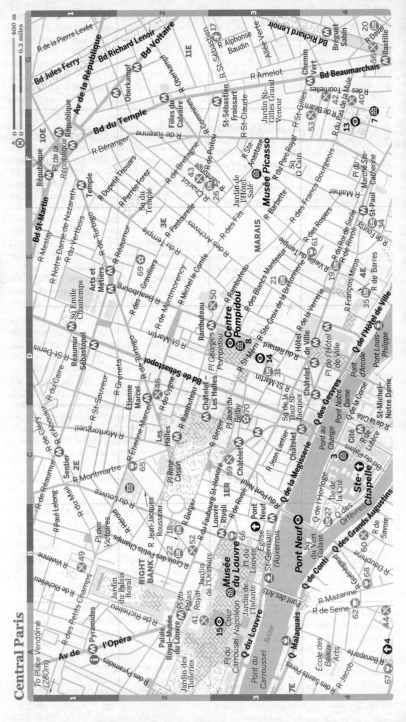

Central Paris

FRANCE PARIS

400 m
0.2 miles

To Place Vendôme
(280m)

Av de l'Opéra

R des Pyramides

R de Richelieu
R Vivienne

R de Richelieu

R des Petits Champs
Pl des Victoires

RIGHT BANK

Jardin du Palais Royal

Palais Royal-Musée du Louvre

Pl du Palais Royal

Jardin des Tuileries

Cour Napoléon

Pl du Carrousel

Pont du Carrousel

Seine

Jardin de l'Infante

Pont des Arts

Q du Louvre

Q Malaquais

École des Beaux-Arts

R des Saints-Pères

R Bonaparte

R Jacob

R de Seine

R Mazarine

R Dauphine

R Guénégaud

Q de Conti

Q des Grands Augustins

Q de la Mégisserie

Q des Gesvres

Q de l'Hôtel de Ville

Pont Neuf

Pont au Change

Pont Notre Dame

Pont d'Arcole

Pl du Pont Neuf

Sq du Vert Galant

Île de la Cité

Q de l'Horloge

Q des Orfèvres

Ste-Chapelle

Cité

Châtelet

Pl du Châtelet

Sq de la Tour St-Jacques

Centre Pompidou

Pl Georges Pompidou

St-Merri

Rambuteau

Hôtel de Ville

Pl de l'Hôtel de Ville

Q de la Corse

Pont de la Tournelle

Bd du Palais

Bd de Sébastopol

Les Halles

Châtelet Les Halles

Étienne Marcel

Réaumur Sébastopol

Arts et Métiers

St-Martin

Bd St-Martin

Bd St-Denis

République

Pl de la République

Bd du Temple

Temple

Oberkampf

Bd Jules Ferry

Av de la République

Bd Richard Lenoir

Bd Voltaire

St-Sébastien Froissart

Bd Beaumarchais

Bd Richard Lenoir

Bastille

MARAIS

Musée Picasso

St-Paul

4E

3E

2E

1ER

7E

10E

11E

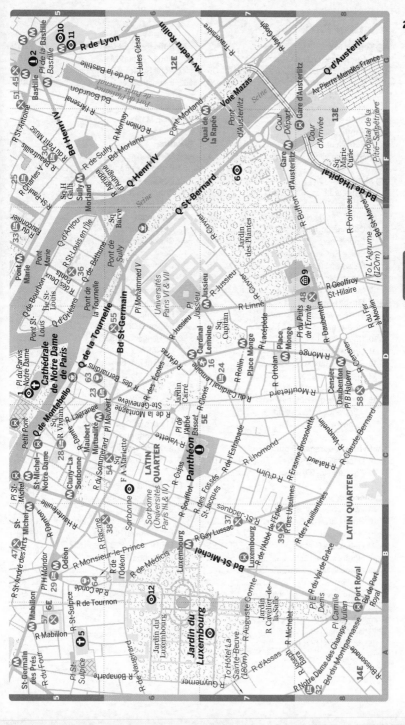

Central Paris

Conciergerie
MONUMENT

(Map p220; 2 blvd du Palais, 1er; adult/child €7/ free; ⊙9.30am-5 or 6pm; MCité) Built as a royal palace in the 14th century for the concierge of the Palais de la Cité, this was the main prison during the Reign of Terror (1793–94), used to incarcerate alleged enemies of the Revolution before they were brought before the Revolutionary Tribunal in the Palais de Justice next door. Among the 2700 prisoners held here before being sent to the guillotine was Queen Marie-Antoinette – see a reproduction of her cell.

The Rayonnant Gothic, 14th-century **Salle des Gens d'Armes** (Cavalrymen's Hall) is the largest surviving medieval hall in Europe.

A joint ticket with Ste-Chapelle costs €11.

RIGHT BANK

Musée du Louvre
ART MUSEUM

(Map p220; www.louvre.fr; permanent collections/permanent collections & temporary exhibits €9.50/14, after 6pm Wed & Fri €6/12; ⊙9am-6pm Mon, Thu, Sat & Sun, 9am-10pm Wed & Fri; MPalais Royal-Musée du Louvre) The vast Palais du Louvre, overlooking the fashionable **Jardin des Tuileries** gardens, was constructed as a fortress by Philippe-Auguste in the 13th century and rebuilt in the mid-16th century for use as a royal residence. In 1793 the Revolutionary Convention transformed it into the nation's first national museum.

The Louvre's staggering 35,000 exhibits are spread across three wings: Sully, Denon and Richelieu. It's reckoned you'd need about nine months to see everything, so trying to pack it all into a single afternoon isn't a particularly clever idea: you'll get much more out of it if you concentrate on a single section or period that interests you.

The collection is mind-bogglingly diverse, ranging from Islamic art works and Egyptian artefacts through to a fabulous collection of Greek and Roman antiquities (including the *Venus de Milo* and the *Winged Victory of Samothrace*). But it's the celebrated paintings that draw most visitors; highlights include signature works by Raphael, Botticelli, Delacroix, Titian, Géricault and of course Leonardo da Vinci's slyly smiling *Mona Lisa* (Denon Wing, 1st floor, room 6). If you have time, peek at the section devoted to objets d'art, which houses a series of fabulously extravagant salons, including the apartments of Napoleon III's Minister of State, a collection of priceless Sèvres porcelain and Louis XV's dazzling crown jewels.

The gallery's main entrance and ticket windows in the Cour Napoléon are covered by the iconic 21m-high **Pyramide du Louvre**, a glass pyramid designed by the Chinese-American architect IM Pei. Skip the pyramid-entrance queue by entering via the Porte des Lions entrance or the Carrousel du Louvre shopping centre.

Arc de Triomphe
LANDMARK

(Map p214; viewing platform adult/child €9/free; ⊙10am-10.30 or 11pm; MCharles de Gaulle-Étoile) The Arc de Triomphe stands in the middle of the world's largest traffic roundabout, **place de l'Étoile**, officially known as place Charles de Gaulle. The 'triumphal arch' was commissioned in 1806 by Napoleon to commemorate his victories, but remained unfinished when he started losing battles, and wasn't completed until 1836. Since 1920, the body of an **unknown soldier** from WWI has lain beneath the arch; a memorial flame is rekindled each evening around 6.30pm.

The **viewing platform** (50m up via 284 steps and well worth the climb) affords wonderful views of the dozen avenues that radiate out from the arch, many of which are named after Napoleonic generals. **Av Foch** is Paris' widest boulevard, while **av des Champs Élysées** leads south to **place**

ℹ THE LOUVRE: TICKETS & TOURS

Buy tickets in advance from ticket machines in the Carrousel du Louvre shopping centre (99 rue de Rivoli) or, for an extra €1 to €1.60, from Fnac or Virgin Megastores *billetteries* (ticket offices), and walk straight in without queuing. Tickets are valid for the whole day, meaning you can come and go as you please. By 2012 you should be able to buy tickets direct on www.louvre.fr.

Before hitting the collections, pick up a free English-language *plan* (map) of the labyrinthine Louvre from the information desk in the centre of the Hall Napoléon. At the entrance to each wing rent a self-paced audioguide (€6).

English-language **guided tours** (☑01 40 20 52 63) depart at 11am, 2pm and (sometimes) 3.45pm Monday and Wednesday to Saturday. Tickets cost €5 in addition to the cost of admission. Sign up at least 30 minutes before departure time.

BOHEMIAN SOULS IN MONTMARTRE

No address better captures the quartier's rebellious, bohemian and artsy past than **Musée de Montmartre** (Map p226; www.museedemontmartre.fr; 12 rue Cortot, 18e; adult/child €7/free; ⊘11am-6pm Tue-Sun; ⓜLamarck Caulaincourt), one-time home to painters Renoir, Utrillo and Raoul Dufy. The 17th-century manor house–museum displays paintings, lithographs and documents; hosts art exhibitions by contemporary artists currently living in Montmartre; and in its excellent bookshop sells bottles of the wine produced from grapes grown in the quartier's very own vineyard, **Clos Montmartre**.

Later, pay your respects to bohemian souls – writers Émile Zola, Alexandre Dumas and Stendhal, composer Jacques Offenbach, artist Edgar Degas, film director François Truffaut and dancer Vaslav Nijinsky among others – laid to rest in the **Cimetière de Montmartre** (Map p226; ⊘8am-5.30 or 6pm Mon-Fri, from 8.30am Sat, from 9am Sun; ⓜPlace de Clichy). Around since 1798, the cemetery is Paris' most famous cemetery after Père Lachaise (p225).

de la Concorde and its famous 3300-year-old pink granite obelisk, which once stood in the Temple of Ramses at Thebes (present-day Luxor).

Centre Pompidou
ART MUSEUM
(Map p220; www.centrepompidou.fr; place Georges Pompidou, 4e; ⓜRambuteau) Opened in 1977, this is one of central Paris' most iconic modern buildings; it was one of the first structures to have its 'insides' turned out. Its main attraction, the **Musée National d'Art Moderne** (Map p220; adult/child €10-12/free; ⊘11am-9pm Wed-Mon), showcases France's national collection of post-1905 art, with surrealists, cubists, fauvists and pop artists all brilliantly represented.

Outside, street performers congregate around lively **place Georges Pompidou**. Nearby **place Igor Stravinsky** delights with its fanciful mechanical fountains of skeletons, a treble clef and a pair of ruby-red lips.

Basilique du Sacré Cœur
LANDMARK
(Map p226; www.sacre-coeur-montmartre.com; place du Parvis du Sacré Cœur, 18e; ⊘6am-10.30pm; ⓜAnvers) The gleaming white **dome** (admission €5; ⊘9am-7pm daily Apr-Sep, 9am-6pm Oct-Mar) of this iconic basilica has one of Paris' most spectacular city panoramas. It sits plump in the heart of hillside Montmartre, a neighbourhood that lured bohemian writers and artists in the late 19th and early 20th centuries. Between 1908 and 1912 Picasso lived at the studio called **Bateau Lavoir** (Map p226; 11bis place Émile Goudeau; ⓜAbbesses).

After WWI the artsy activity shifted to Montparnasse, but Montmartre nonetheless retains an upbeat ambience that all the tourists in the world couldn't spoil. Cafes, restaurants, endless tourists and a concentrated cluster of caricaturists and painters fill its main square, **place du Tertre** (Map p226; ⓜAbbesses) – if you're seeking your portrait painted in Paris, this is the spot.

Just a few blocks southwest of the tranquil residential streets of Montmartre is lively, neon-lit **Pigalle** (9e and 18e), one of Paris' two main sex districts. A funicular connects it to the top of Butte de Montmartre (Montmartre Hill).

Opéra & Grands Boulevards
HISTORIC BUILDING, NOTABLE STREETS
Place de l'Opéra is the site of Paris' world-famous (and original) opera house, **Palais Garnier** (Map p226; ⌖guided tours 08 25 05 44 05; www.operadeparis.fr; place de l'Opéra, 9e; ⓜOpéra). Around it fan out eight contiguous 'Great Boulevards' – Madeleine, Capucines, Italiens, Montmartre, Poissonnière, Bonne Nouvelle, St-Denis and St-Martin – laid out in the 17th century, and later the cultural hub of the city during the belle époque. Blvd Haussmann is the heart of the city's commercial district and boasts many famous department stores.

Place Vendôme
SQUARE
(ⓜTuileries or Opéra) The octagonal place Vendôme has long been one of the city's smartest addresses, famous for its 18th-century architecture, exclusive boutiques and the superposh Hôtel Ritz-Paris. The 43.5m-tall **Colonne Vendôme** (Map p214) was fashioned from cannons captured by Napoleon at the Battle of Austerlitz in 1805; the general stands on top of the column dressed in suitably imperial garb.

Musée Picasso
ART MUSEUM

(Map p220; www.musee-picasso.fr, in French; 5 rue de Thorigny, 3e; ⊗9.30am-6pm Wed-Mon; ⓂSt-Paul or Chemin Vert) One of Paris' best-loved art museums, the Picasso Museum contains more than 3500 of the *grand maître*'s engravings, paintings, ceramics and sculptures, as well as works from his own art collection by Braque, Cézanne, Matisse, Modigliani, Degas and Rousseau. At the time of printing, it was scheduled to reopen after extensive renovations in 2012.

Place des Vosges
SQUARE

(Map p220; ⓂSt-Paul or Bastille) The Marais, the area of the Right Bank north of Île St-Louis in the 3e and 4e, was originally a marsh before it was transformed into one of the city's most fashionable districts by Henri IV, who constructed elegant *hôtels particuliers* (private mansions) around place Royale – today known as place des Vosges.

Novelist Victor Hugo lived here from 1832 to 1848, and his home is now the **Maison de Victor Hugo** (Map p220; www.musee-hugo.paris.fr, in French; adult/child €7/free; ⊗10am-6pm Tue-Sun), with drawings, paintings and memorabilia relating to the author.

Place de la Bastille
SQUARE

(Map p220; ⓂBastille) The Bastille is the most famous monument in Paris that no longer exists; the notorious prison was demolished by a Revolutionary mob on 14 July 1789, and the place de la Bastille where the prison once stood is now a busy traffic roundabout. The 52m-high **Colonne de Juillet** (July Column) was erected in memory of Parisians killed during the July Revolution of 1830.

Opéra Bastille
OPERA HOUSE

(Map p220; www.opera-de-paris.fr, in French; 2-6 place de la Bastille, 12e; ⓂBastille) Paris' giant 'second' opera house, the Opéra Bastille, designed by the Canadian architect Carlos Ott, was inaugurated on 14 July 1989, the 200th anniversary of the storming of the Bastille. Check online for departure times of 1¼-hour **guided tours** (☑01 40 01 19 70; adult/child €11/6). Tickets go on sale 10 minutes before departure at the **box office** (Map p220; 130 rue de Lyon, 12e; ⊗10.30am-6.30pm Mon-Sat).

TOP CHOICE Cimetière du Père Lachaise
CEMETERY

(Map p214; www.pere-lachaise.com; ⊗8am-6pm Mon-Fri, from 8.30am Sat, from 9am Sun; ⓂPhilippe Auguste, Gambetta or Père Lachaise) The world's most-visited graveyard, Cimetière du Père Lachaise opened its one-way doors in 1804. Among the 800,000 people buried here are Chopin, Molière, Balzac, Proust, Gertrude Stein, Colette, Pissarro, Seurat, Modigliani, Sarah Bernhardt, Yves Montand, Delacroix, Édith Piaf and even the 12th-century lovers Abélard and Héloïse, whose remains were disinterred and reburied here together in 1817 beneath a neo-Gothic tombstone. The graves of **Oscar Wilde** (Division 89) and **Jim Morrison** (Division 6) are perennially popular.

🏃 Activities

Cycling

Paris now counts some 370km of cycling lanes in the city, plus many sections of road are shut to motorised traffic on Sundays and holidays. Pick up wheels with **Vélib'** (p243), join an organised bike tour (see p226) or rent your own wheels and DIY with:

DON'T MISS

CANAL ST-MARTIN

The shaded towpaths of the tranquil, 4.5km-long **Canal St-Martin** (Map p214; ⓂRépublique, Jaurès or Jacques Bonsergent) are a wonderful place for a romantic stroll or a bike ride past nine locks, metal bridges and ordinary Parisian neighbourhoods. The canal's banks have undergone a real urban renaissance, and the southern stretch in particular is an ideal spot for cafe lounging, quayside summer picnics and late-night drinks. Hip new bistros have moved into the area (most are closed Sunday and often Monday) and if you're in Paris to tempt your taste buds, you'll wind up in these eastern suburbs sooner rather than later.

Linking the 10e arrondissement with **Parc de la Villette** in the 19e via the **Bassin de la Villette** and **Canal de l'Ourcq**, the canal makes its famous dogleg turn in the 10e arrondissement. Parts of the waterway – which was built between 1806 and 1825 in order to link the Seine with the 108km-long Canal de l'Ourcq – are actually higher than the surrounding land. If you want to savour the real flavour of the canal, take a tour on a **canal boat** (see p227).

Montmartre

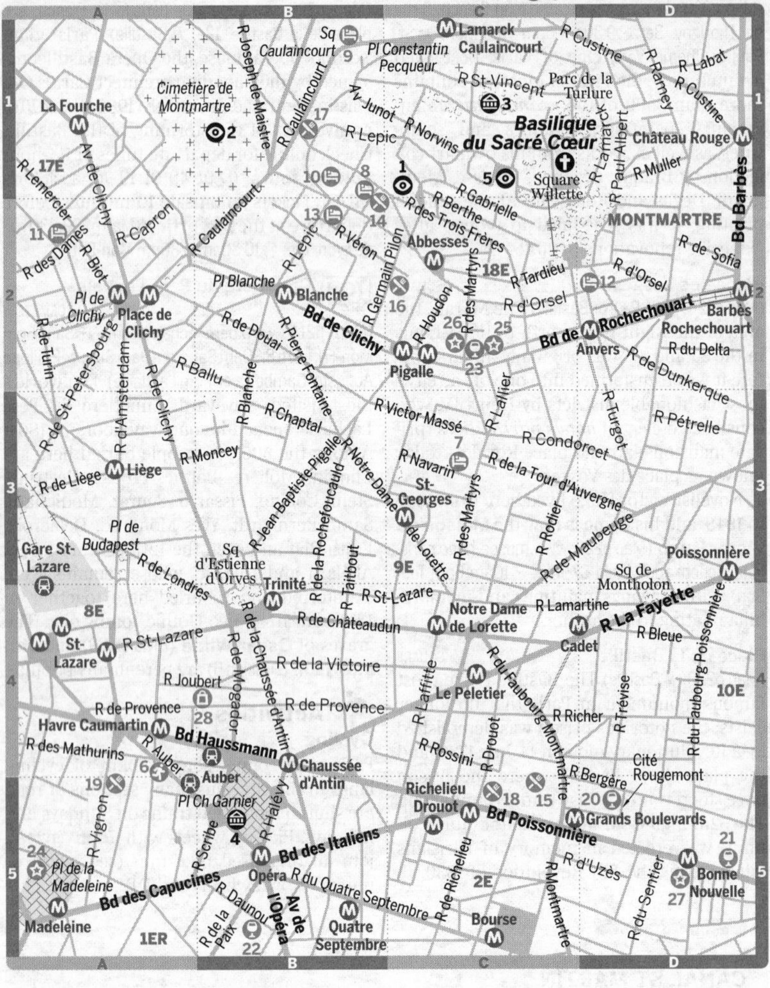
0 400 m
0 0.2 miles
A
B
C
D
1
2
3
4
5
La Fourche
Cimetière de Montmartre
Sq Caulaincourt
Pl Constantin Pecqueur
Lamarck Caulaincourt
R Custine
R Labat
R Ramey
Parc de la Turlure
R St-Vincent
Basilique du Sacré Cœur
Square Willette
Château Rouge
MONTMARTRE
Bd Barbès
R Joseph de Maistre
R Caulaincourt
Av Junot
R Lepic
R Norvins
R Lamarck
R Paul Albert
R Muller
R Gabrielle
R Berthe
R des Trois Frères
R Véron
Abbesses
17E
R Lemercier
R des Dames
R Capron
Av de Clichy
R Biot
Pl Blanche
Blanche
R Germain Pilon
R des Martyrs
18E
R Tardieu
R d'Orsel
R de Sofia
Barbès Rochechouart
Pl de Clichy
Place de Clichy
R de Turin
R de St-Pétersbourg
R de Douai
Bd de Clichy
R Houdon
Bd de Rochechouart
Anvers
R du Delta
R de Dunkerque
R Pierre Fontaine
Pigalle
R Ballu
R Blanche
R d'Amsterdam
R de Clichy
R Chaptal
R Victor Massé
R Lallier
R Turgot
R Pétrelle
R Condorcet
R Moncey
Liège
R de Liège
R Navarin
St-Georges
R de la Tour d'Auvergne
R Jean Baptiste Pigalle
R Notre Dame de Lorette
R de la Rochefoucauld
R Rodier
R de Maubeuge
Poissonnière
Pl de Budapest
Gare St-Lazare
R de Londres
Sq d'Estienne d'Orves
Trinité
R Taitbout
9E
R St-Lazare
Notre Dame de Lorette
R Lamartine
Sq de Montholon
R La Fayette
Cadet
R Bleue
8E
St-Lazare
R de Châteaudun
R de la Chaussée d'Antin
R de Mogador
R de la Victoire
R Laffitte
R du Faubourg Montmartre
R du Faubourg Poissonnière
R Trévise
10E
R Joubert
R de Provence
Le Peletier
R Richer
Havre Caumartin
Bd Haussmann
R des Mathurins
R Auber
Auber
Chaussée d'Antin
R Rossini
R Drouot
R Bergère
Cité Rougemont
Pl Ch Garnier
R Halévy
Richelieu Drouot
Bd Poissonnière
Grands Boulevards
R Vignon
R Scribe
Bd des Italiens
R d'Uzès
Pl de la Madeleine
Opéra
R du Quatre Septembre
R de Richelieu
2E
R Montmartre
R du Sentier
Bonne Nouvelle
Bd des Capucines
R Daunou
Av de l'Opéra
R de la Paix
Quatre Septembre
Bourse
Madeleine
1ER

Gepetto et Vélos CYCLING
(Map p220; www.gepetto-et-velos.com, in French; 59 rue du Cardinal Lemoine, 5e; per day/weekend €15/25; ⏲9am-1pm & 2-7.30pm Tue-Sat; Ⓜ Cardinal Lemoine)

Paris à Vélo, C'est Sympa! CYCLING
(Map p220; www.parisvelosympa.com; 22 rue Alphonse Baudin, 11e; per day/weekend €15/25; ⏲9.30am-1pm & 2-6pm Mon-Fri, 9am-1pm & 2-7pm Sat & Sun, shorter hours in winter; Ⓜ St-Sébastien Froissart)

☞ Tours

Fat Tire Bike Tours BICYCLE
(Map p214; ☎01 56 58 10 54; www.fattirebiketours.com; 24 rue Edgar Faure, 15e; Ⓜ La Motte-Picquet Grenelle) Bike tours by day (€28; four hours) and night; to Versailles, Monet's garden (Giverny) and the Normandy beaches. Participants generally meet opposite the Eiffel Tower at the start of the Champ de Mars. Costs include the bicycle and rain gear. Reserve in advance.

Bateaux Mouches BOAT
(Map p214; ☎01 42 25 9610; www.bateauxmouches.com; Port de la Conférence, 8e; adult/child €10/5; ⏲Mar-Nov; Ⓜ Alma Marceau) Based on the Right Bank, Paris' most famous riverboat company runs 1000-seat tour boats. Cruises (70 minutes) run regularly from 10.15am to 11pm April to September and

13 times a day between 11am and 9pm the rest of the year.

Paris Canal Croisières   BOAT
(Map p214; ☏01 42 40 96 97; www.pariscanal. com; Bassin de la Villette, 19-21 quai de la Loire, 19e; adult/child €17/10; ⊗Mar-Nov; Ⓜ Jaurès or Musée d'Orsay) This company runs daily 2½-hour cruises departing from near the Musée d'Orsay (quai Anatole France, 7e) for Bassin de la Villette, 19e, via the charming Canal St-Martin and Canal de l'Ourcq.

L'Open Tour   BUS
(Map p226; ☏01 42 66 56 56; www.pariscity rama.com; 13 rue Auber, 9e; 1 day adult/child €29/15; Ⓜ Havre Caumartin or Opéra) This company runs open-deck buses along four circuits and you can jump on/off at more than 50 stops. Buy tickets from the driver.

Eye Prefer Paris   WALKING
(www.eyepreferparistours.com; €195 for 3 people) New Yorker turned Parisian leads offbeat tours of the city; cooking classes too.

Paris Walks   WALKING
(www.paris-walks.com; adult/child €12/8) Thematic tours (fashion, chocolate, the French Revolution) in English.

🎊 Festivals & Events

Grande Parade de Paris   NEW YEAR
(www.parisparade.com) The Great Paris Parade, with marching and carnival bands, dance acts and so on, takes place on the afternoon of New Year's Day.

Fashion Week   FASHION
(www.pretparis.com) Prêt-à-Porter, the ready-to-wear fashion salon that is held twice a year in late January and again in September, is a must for fashion buffs. It's held at the Parc des Expositions at Porte de Versailles, 15e (Ⓜ Porte de Versailles).

Paris Jazz Festival   JAZZ
(www.parcfloraldeparis.com; www.paris.fr) Free jazz concerts every Saturday and Sunday afternoon in June and July in Parc Floral de Paris.

Paris Plages   BEACH
(www.paris.fr) 'Paris Beaches' sees three waterfront areas transformed into sand-and-pebble 'beaches', complete with sunbeds, beach umbrellas, atomisers, lounge chairs and palm trees. Four weeks from mid-July to mid-August.

Nuit Blanche   EVENT
(www.paris.fr) 'White Night' is when Paris becomes 'the city that doesn't sleep', with museums across town joining bars and

BOIS DE BOULOGNE & VINCENNES

Flee the smoke for a gad around Paris' twinset of green woods – **Bois de Vincennes** and the **Bois de Boulogne** – where Parisians picnic, sunbathe and escape the city hustle.

On Paris' western fringe, 845-hectare **Bois de Boulogne** (Map p214; blvd Maillot, 16e; **M**Porte Maillot) was inspired by Hyde Park in London. Attractions include formal gardens, a lake with rowing boats, **kids' amusement park** (www.jardindacclimatation.fr) and 18th-century chateau, **Château de Bagatelle** (route de Sèvres à Neuilly, 16e; adult/child €6/free; ⊘tours 3pm Sat & Sun Apr-Sep, 9am-5pm Oct-Mar), with spectacular flower gardens. The **Fondation Louis Vuitton pour la Création** (www.fondationlouisvuitton.fr), a fine-arts centre designed by Frank Gehry, will open here by the end of 2012. Steer clear after dark, when Bois de Boulogne morphs into a playground for female and transvestite prostitutes.

To the southeast of the centre is the 995-hectare **Bois de Vincennes** (off Map p214; blvd Poniatowski, 12e; **M**Porte de Charenton or Porte Dorée), which encompasses its own fortified castle, **Château de Vincennes** (www.chateau-vincennes.fr; av de Paris, 12e; ⊙10am-5 or 6pm May-Aug, 10am-5pm Sep-Apr; **M**Château de Vincennes); it's free to explore the grounds, but the keep and royal chapel can only be visited by guided **tour** (adult/child €8/free). Nearby there's also a huge **floral park** (www.parcfloraldeparis.com, in French) with a butterfly garden, a **zoo** (www.mnhn.fr) and an **aquarium** (www.acquarium-portedoree.fr).

clubs and staying open till the very wee hours on the first Saturday and Sunday of October.

Fete des Vendanges de Montmartre
HARVEST

(www.fetedesvendangesdemontmartre.com, in French) This five-day festival during the second weekend in October celebrates Montmartre's grape harvest with costumes, speeches and a parade.

🛏 Sleeping

The Paris Convention & Visitors Bureau (p242) can find you a place to stay (no booking fee, but you need a credit card), though queues can be long in high season.

For B&B accommodation try **Alcôve & Agapes** (www.bed-and-breakfast-in-paris.com), **Good Morning Paris** (www.goodmorningparis.fr) or **B&B Paris** (www.2binparis.com).

LOUVRE & LES HALLES

This area is central but don't expect tranquillity or many bargains. Although it's most disposed to welcoming top-end travellers, there are some decent midrange places too.

TOP CHOICE Hôtel St-Merry HISTORIC HOTEL **€€**
(Map p220; ☑01 42 78 14 15; www.hotel marais.com; 78 rue de la Verrerie, 4e; r €135-230, tr €205-275; ❄⏀; **M**Châtelet) The interior of

this 12-room hostelry, with beamed ceilings, church pews and wrought-iron candelabra, is a neo-goth's wet dream; you have to see the architectural elements of room 9 (flying buttress over the bed) and the furnishings of 12 (choir-stall bed board) to believe them. Only some of the rooms come with air-conditioning.

BVJ Paris-Louvre HOSTEL **€**
(Map p220; ☑01 53 00 90 90; www.bvjhotel.com; 20 rue Jean-Jacques Rousseau, 1er; dm/d €29/70; @⏀; **M**Louvre-Rivoli) This modern, 200-bed hostel has doubles and bunks in a single-sex room for four to 10 people, with showers down the corridor. Guests must be aged 18 to 35 years. Rooms are accessible from 2.30pm on the day you arrive and all day after that. No kitchen.

Hôtel de Lille BUDGET HOTEL **€**
(Map p220; ☑01 42 33 33 42; 8 rue du Pélican, 1er; s €39-43, d €50-55, tr €85; **M**Palais Royal-Musée du Louvre;) This old-fashioned but spotlessly clean 13-room hotel is down a quiet side street from the Louvre in a 17th-century building.

MARAIS & BASTILLE

Budget accommodation is a forte of the Marais. East of Bastille, the untouristed 11e provides a glimpse up close of working-class Paris.

TOP CHOICE Hôtel du Petit Moulin

BOUTIQUE HOTEL €€€

(Map p220; ☎01 42 74 10 10; www.hoteldupetit
moulin.com; 29-31 rue de Poitou, 3e; r €190-290;
✳@🛜; MFilles du Calvaire) This scrumptious
boutique hotel (OK, we're impressed that
it was a bakery at the time of Henri IV)
was designed by Christian Lacroix. Choose
from medieval and rococo Marais sporting
exposed beams and dressed in toile de Jouy
wallpaper, to more-modern surrounds with
contemporary murals and heart-shaped
mirrors just this side of kitsch.

Hôtel Daval HOTEL €€

(Map p220; ☎01 47 00 51 23; www.hoteldaval.com; 21
rue Daval, 11e; s €81, d €89-98, tr/q €109/127; ✳🛜;
MBastille) Always a favourite, this 23-room
property is a very central option if you're
looking for almost-budget accommodation
just off place de la Bastille. What's more, a
refit has brought it well into the 21st century.
Rooms and bathrooms are on the small side
and if you're looking for some peace and quiet, choose a back room (eg room 13).

Hôtel de la Bretonnerie HOTEL €€

(Map p220; ☎01 48 87 77 63; www.bretonnerie.
com; 22 rue Ste-Croix de la Bretonnerie, 4e; r €135-
165, tr & q €190; 🛜; MHôtel de Ville) This very
charming midrange hotel in the heart of
the Marais nightlife area dates from the
17th century. The decor of its 29 rooms and
suites is unique; some have four-poster and
canopy beds.

Hôtel Caron de Beaumarchais

BOUTIQUE HOTEL €€

(Map p220; ☎01 42 72 34 12; www.carondebeau
marchais.com; 12 rue Vieille du Temple, 4e; r €125-
162; ✳🛜; MSt-Paul) Decorated like an 18th-
century private house, this themed hotel
must be seen to be believed. In the palatial
lobby an 18th-century pianoforte, gaming
tables, gilded mirrors and candelabras set
the tone for a stay that will be unique.

**Maison Internationale de la Jeunesse et
des Étudiants** HOSTEL €

(MIJE; ☎01 42 74 23 45; www.mije.com; dm/s/d/tr
per person €30/49/36/32; @) The MIJE runs
three hostels in attractively renovated 17th-
and 18th-century *hôtels particuliers* in the
heart of the Marais, and it's difficult to think
of a better budget deal in Paris. **MIJE Mau-
buisson** (Map p220; 12 rue des Barres, 4e; MHôtel
de Ville or Pont Marie) – the pick of the three – is
half a block south of the *mairie* (town hall)
of the 4e and has 99 beds. With 200 beds,

MIJE Le Fourcy (Map p220; 6 rue de Fourcy, 4e;
MSt-Paul) is the largest of the three and has
a cheap eatery serving a three-course fixed-
price *menu* including a drink for €10.50.
MIJE Le Fauconnier (Map p220; 11 rue du Fauconnier, 4e; MSt-Paul or Pont Marie), two blocks
south, sleeps 125.

Rooms are closed from noon to 3pm, and
the curfew is 1am to 7am. Annual membership costs €2.50.

Hôtel du 7e Art THEMED HOTEL €€

(Map p220; ☎01 44 54 85 00; www.paris-hotel
-7art.com; 20 rue St-Paul, 4e; s €75-150, d €95-
155; 🛜; MSt-Paul) Film buffs, this fun place
with a black-and-white-movie theme running throughout its 23 rooms is for you.

Hôtel St-Louis Marais HISTORIC HOTEL €€

(Map p220; ☎01 48 87 87 04; www.saintlouis
marais.com; 1 rue Charles V, 4e; s €99, d & tw
€115-140, tr €150; 🛜; MSully Morland) This
especially charming hotel in a converted
17th-century convent sports lots of wooden
beams, terracotta tiles and heavy brocade
drapes. Four floors but no lift; wi-fi €5.

THE ISLANDS
Île St-Louis is the more romantic of the
Seine's two islands and is strung with excel-
lent top-end hotels. Or try:

> ℹ️ **RENTING AN
> APARTMENT**
>
> Be it a night, a week or longer, this is
> increasingly the modish way to stay in
> Paris. Consult agencies listed on www.
> parisinfo.com or try:
>
> » **Haven in Paris** (www.haveninparis.
> com) Luxury apartments from €575
> per week
>
> » **Paris Accommodation Service**
> (www.paris-accommodation-service.com)
> Over 500 properties; studios from
> €520 per week
>
> » **Paris Apartments Services**
> (www.paris-apts.com) Studios from
> €100 per day
>
> » **Paris Attitude** (www.parisattitude.
> com) 3000 properties; studios from
> €325 per week
>
> » **Paris Stay** (www.paristay.com) Over
> 200 vacation flats (ie convenient
> location), with studios from €300 per
> week

Hôtel Henri IV

BUDGET HOTEL €

(Map p220; ☎01 43 54 44 53; www.henri4hotel.
fr; 25 place Dauphine, 1er; r €42-69, tr €77-81; ☎;
ⓂPont Neuf or Cité) This place, known for its
15 worn and very cheap rooms, has always
been popular for its romantic location on
the tip of Île de la Cité. What we long expected has happened: under new management
the hotel is cleaning up its act and refitting
its rooms. Views over the square are wonderful. Book well in advance.

LATIN QUARTER

Midrange hotels in this good-value Left
Bank neighbourhood are particularly popular with visiting academics, making rooms
hardest to find during conferences (March
to June and October).

Port Royal Hôtel

BUDGET HOTEL €

(Map p214; ☎01 43 31 70 06; www.hotelportroyal.
fr; 8 blvd de Port Royal, 5e; s €41-89, d €52.50-89;
ⓂLes Gobelins) This 46-room hotel has been
run by the same family since 1931. Its six
floors are served by a lift, but the cheapest
(washbasin-clad) rooms share a toilet and
shower (buy a €2.50 token at reception).
Rooms are spotless and quiet, especially
those peeping down on a glassed-in courtyard. Predictably, this value-for-money place
is no secret, so book ahead. No credit cards.

Hôtel La Demeure

BOUTIQUE HOTEL €€

(Map p214; ☎01 43 37 81 25; www.hotel
-paris-lademeure.com; 51 blvd St-Marcel, 13e; s/d
€165/202; ❋@☎; ⓂGobelins) This elegant
little number is the domain of a charming
father/son team who speak perfect English
and are always at hand. Warm red and orange tones lend a 'clubby' feel to public areas; wraparound balconies add extra appeal
to corner rooms; and then there's those extra touches – an iPod dock in every room,
wineglasses for guests who like to BYO
('bring your own'), art to buy on the walls...

Oops

DESIGN HOSTEL €

(Map p214; ☎01 47 07 47 00; www.oops-paris.com;
50 av des Gobelins, 13e; dm €28-35; @☎; ⓂGobe-
lins) It might be discreetly wedged between
cafe terraces and shop fronts but inside
there is nothing discreet about this address.
A lurid candyfloss-pink lift scales its six
floors. Doubles (which can be booked in advance) are well sized and stylish dorms max
out at four to six beds. Breakfast is a generous affair and in keeping with that true hostel spirit guests must evacuate their room
between 11am and 5pm. Reserve online.

Hôtel de Notre Dame Maître Albert

HOTEL €€

(Map p220; ☎01 43 26 79 00; www.hotel-paris
-notredame.com; 19 rue Maître Albert, 5e; d €170-
280; ❋@☎; ⓂMaubert Mutualité) A lovely little
number hidden down a quiet street paces
from the Seine, this quaint hotel is something of a labyrinth with its long corridors
bedecked in striking cobblestone-patterned
carpet and rooms with low beamed ceilings;
occasionally sloping.

Hôtel Henri IV Rive Gauche

HOTEL €€€

(Map p220; ☎01 46 33 20 20; www.henri-paris
-hotel.com; 9-11 rue St-Jacques, 5e; s/d/tr €159/
185/210; ❋@☎; ⓂSt-Michel Notre Dame or Cluny
La Sorbonne) This 'country chic' hotel with 23
rooms awash with antiques, old prints and
fresh flowers is steps from Notre Dame and
the Seine – think manor house in Normandy. Front rooms have stunning views of Église St-Séverin and its buttresses. Rates are
cheapest online.

Hôtel des Grandes Écoles

GARDEN HOTEL €€

(Map p220; ☎01 43 26 79 23; www.hotel-grandes
-ecoles.com; 75 rue du Cardinal Lemoine, 5e; d €115-
140; @☎; ⓂCardinal Lemoine or Place Monge)
This wonderful 51-room hotel with its own
garden is tucked into a courtyard of a medieval street. Choose a room in one of three
buildings: our favourites are rooms 29 to 33
with direct garden access.

ST-GERMAIN, ODÉON & LUXEMBOURG

Staying in chic St-Germain des Prés (6e) is
a delight. But beware – budget places just
don't exist in this part of the Left Bank.

TOP CHOICE L'Apostrophe

DESIGN HOTEL €€

(Map p220; ☎01 56 54 31 31; www.
apostrophe-hotel.com; 3 rue de Chevreuse, 6e; d
€150-350; ❋@☎; ⓂVavin) This art hotel has
style. Its 16 rooms pay homage to the written word: graffiti tags one wall of room U
(for 'urbain'), which has a ceiling shaped
like a skateboard ramp; and room P (for
'Paris parody') sits in the clouds overlooking Paris' rooftops. Clever design features
such as double sets of imprinted curtains
(one for day, one for night) or the 'bar table'
on wheels that slots over the bed, top off
this design-driven ensemble.

TOP CHOICE Hôtel Relais St-Germain

HOTEL €€€

(Map p220; ☎01 43 29 12 05; www.hotel
-paris-relais-saint-germain.com; 9 Carrefour de
l'Odéon, 7e; s/d €220/285; ❋@☎; ⓂOdéon)
What rave reports this 17th-century town

house with flower boxes and baby-pink awning gets. Ceilings are beamed, furniture is antique and fabrics are floral. Mix this with a chic contemporary air, ample art works to admire and one of Paris' most talked-about bistros, **Le Comptoir du Relais** (p235), as next-door neighbour. Delicious, darling!

Hôtel La Sainte-Beuve
HOTEL €€

(off Map p220; ☎01 45 48 20 07; www.parishotel charme.com; 9 rue Ste-Beuve, 6e; d €159-365; ✳@☎; Ⓜ Rue Notre Dame des Champs) 'Home away from home' is the motto of this 22-room *hôtel-maison* southwest of Jardin du Luxembourg. Rooms are a riot of colour: pick from fuchsia-pink stylishly mixed with lime-green and taupe, or racing green wed with oyster-grey and burgundy.

FAUBOURG ST-GERMAIN & INVALIDES

The 7e is a lovely arrondissement to call home, although it's slightly removed from the action.

Cadran Hôtel
BOUTIQUE HOTEL €€

(Map p214; ☎01 40 62 67 00; www.paris-hotel -cadran.com; 10 rue du Champ de Mars, 7e; d €144-225; ✳☎; Ⓜ École Militaire) An address for gourmets, this concept hotel seduces guests with a clock theme and an open-plan reception spilling into a *bar à chocolat* (chocolate bar) that sells – yes – chocolate and seasonally flavoured *macarons*. Rooms are futuristic, with all the mod cons.

Hôtel Muguet
FAMILY HOTEL €€

(Map p214; ☎01 47 05 05 93; www.hotelmuguet. com; 11 rue Chevert, 7e; s/d/tr €110/145/195; ✳☎; Ⓜ La Tour Maubourg) Functional decor and generous-sized triples, with armchair-bed converting a separate lounge area into kid's bedroom, make this a great family choice. From the 4th floor, the Eiffel Tower starts to sneak into view. Back down on ground level, a trio of rooms opens onto a delightful courtyard garden.

Hôtel du Champ-de-Mars
BUDGET HOTEL €

(Map p214; ☎01 45 51 52 30; www.hotelduchamp demars.com; 7 rue du Champ de Mars, 7e; s/d/ tr €91/98/128; @☎; Ⓜ École Militaire) This charming 25-room hotel, which lies in the shadow of the Eiffel Tower, is on everyone's wish list – you'll need to book a month or two ahead.

CLICHY & GARE ST-LAZARE

These areas have some excellent midrange choices. The best deals are away from Gare St-Lazare, but there are several places beside the station along rue d'Amsterdam worth checking out.

TOP CHOICE Hôtel Eldorado
QUIRKY HOTEL €

(Map p226; ☎01 45 22 35 21; www.el doradohotel.fr; 18 rue des Dames, 17e; s €35-60, d €70-80, tr €80-90; ☎; Ⓜ Place de Clichy) This bohemian place is one of Paris' greatest finds: a welcoming, well-run place with 23 colourfully decorated and (often) ethnically themed rooms. We love rooms 1 and 2 in the garden annexe. Cheaper-category singles have washbasin only. The hotel's excellent **Bistro des Dames** is a bonus.

GARE DU NORD, GARE DE L'EST & RÉPUBLIQUE

The areas around the Gare du Nord and Gare de l'Est are far from the prettiest parts of Paris, but decent-value hotels are a dime a dozen.

TOP CHOICE St Christopher's Inn
HOSTEL €

(Map p214; ☎01 40 34 34 40; www.st-christ ophers.co.uk; 68-74 quai de la Seine, 19e; dm incl breakfast €15-38, d from €35; @☎; Ⓜ Riquet or Jaurès) This is certainly one of Paris' best, biggest (300 beds) and most up-to-date hostels. It features a modern design, three types of dorms (10-bed, eight-bed, six-bed) as well as doubles with or without bathroom. Other perks include a canalside cafe, free (temperamental) wi-fi, breakfast, internet cafe, a female-only floor and bar. Seasonal prices vary wildly; check the website for an accurate quote. No kitchen.

Kube Hôtel
BOUTIQUE HOTEL €€€

(Map p214; ☎01 42 05 20 00; www.muranoresort. com; 1-5 passage Ruelle, 18e; s €250, d €300-400; ✳@☎; Ⓜ La Chapelle) The easternmost edge of the 18e, virtually on the lap of Gare du Nord, is the last place you'd expect to find an ubertrendy boutique hotel. The theme is, of course, three-dimensional square – from the glassed-in reception box in the entrance courtyard to the cube-shaped furnishings in the 41 guestrooms and the ice in the cocktails at its celebrated **Ice Kube** bar.

Hôtel du Nord
HOTEL €

(Map p214; ☎01 42 01 66 00; www.hoteldunord -leparivelo.com; 47 rue Albert Thomas, 10e; r/q €69/105; ☎; Ⓜ République) A cosy place with 23 personalised rooms all decorated with flea-market antiques, Hôtel du Nord's other winning attribute is its prized location near place République. Borrow a bike from reception.

République Hôtel THEMED HOTEL €€
(Map p214; 01 42 39 19 03; www.republique
hotel.com; 31 rue Albert Thomas, 10e; s/d/tr/q
€75/88/108/159; M République) This hip
spot is heavy on the pop art and UK paraphernalia – the Union Jack and the Beatles
turn up an awful lot – but you cannot fault
the inexpensive rates and fantastic location
off place République.

MONTMARTRE & PIGALLE
What a charmer Montmartre is with its
varied accommodation scene embracing everything from boutique to bohemian, hostel
to *hôtel particulier*. The area east of Sacré
Cœur can be rough – avoid Château Rouge
metro station at night.

Hôtel Amour BOUTIQUE HOTEL €€
(Map p226; 01 48 78 31 80; www.hotel
amourparis.fr; 8 rue Navarin, 9e; s/d €100/150-280;
M St-Georges or Pigalle) Planning a romantic escapade to Paris? Say no more. One of
the 'in' hotels of the moment, the inimitable
black-clad Amour is very much worthy of
the hype – you won't find a more original
place to lay your head in Paris at these pric-

---

es. Of course, you'll have to forgo TV (none),
but who needs a box when you're in love?

Hôtel des Arts HOTEL €€
(Map p226; 01 46 06 30 52; www.arts-hotel-paris.
com; 5 rue Tholozé, 18e; s/d €95/140; @ M Abbesses or Blanche) Hôtel des Arts has comfortable midrange rooms done up in a traditional style (lots of floral motifs). Just up the
street is the old-style windmill Moulin de la
Galette – how's that for location?

Hôtel Bonséjour Montmartre BUDGET HOTEL €
(Map p226; 01 42 54 22 53; www.hotel-bonsejour
-montmartre.fr; 11 rue Burq, 18e; s €33-69, d €56-
69; @ M Abbesses) At the top of a quiet street,
the 'Good Stay' is a perennial favourite. It's
simple but welcoming, comfortable and very
clean. Some rooms have balconies and No 55
glimpses Sacré Cœur. Hall showers €2.

Le Village Hostel HOSTEL €
(Map p226; 01 42 64 22 02; www.villagehostel.fr;
20 rue d'Orsel, 18e; per person dm €28-38, d €70-
90, tr €96-115, q €112-140; @ M Anvers) A fine,
25-room address with beamed ceilings, lovely terrace and Sacré Cœur views. Kitchen
facilities are available, and there's a popular
bar too. Rooms are closed between 11am and
4pm; no curfew.

Plug-inn Hostel HOSTEL €
(Map p226; 01 42 58 42 58; www.plug-inn.fr; 7
rue Aristide Bruant, 18e; dm €20-30, d €60-80, tr
€90; @ M Abbesses or Blanche) This 2010
hostel has several things going for it,
central Montmartre location for starters.
Lockout by day; no curfew by night.

Hotel Caulaincourt Square BUDGET HOTEL €
(Map p226; 01 46 06 46 06; www.caulaincourt.
com; 2 square Caulaincourt, 18e; dm €25, s
€50-60, d & tw €63-76, tr €89; @ M Lamarck
Caulaincourt) This hotel with dorm rooms
is perched on the backside of Montmartre,
beyond the tourist hoopla in a real Parisian neighbourhood.

Eating
As the culinary centre of the most aggres-
sively gastronomic country in the world,
the city has more 'generic French', regional,
and ethnic restaurants than any other place
in France. In pricier restaurants, ordering
a *menu* (set two- or three-course meal at a
fixed price) at lunchtime is invariably extraordinary good value.

LOUVRE & LES HALLES
This area is filled with trendy restaurants,
though few are outstanding – most cater to

PARISIAN EAT STREETS

» **Av de Choisy, av d'Ivry** & **rue Baudricourt** Chinatown: cheap Chinese and Southeast Asian (especially
Vietnamese) eateries

» **Blvd de Belleville** Middle Eastern
(Algerian, Tunisian) food, especially
couscous

» **Rue de Belleville** Asian, especially
Thai and Vietnamese

» **Rue du Faubourg St-Denis**
Indian, Pakistani and Bangladeshi

» **Passage Brady** Magnet for Indian,
Pakistani and Bangladeshi dishes

» **Rue Cadet, rue Richer** & **rue
Geoffroy Marie** Triangle of streets;
Jewish (mostly Sephardic) and kosher
food

» **Rue Montorgueil** Pedestrian market street packed with tip-top quality,
quick eats

» **Rue Ste-Anne** The heart of Paris'
Japantown

» **Rue Rosiers** Hunting ground for
Ashkenazic Jewish kosher food, especially falafel

TOP FIVE PÂTISSERIES

» **Ladurée** (Map p214; www.laduree.fr, in French; 75 av des Champs-Élysées, 8e; MGeorge V) The most famous and decadent of Parisian patisseries; inventor of the *macaron* to boot.

» **Le Nôtre** (Map p220; www.lenotre.fr, in French; 10 rue St- Antoine, 4e; MBastille) Delectable pastries and chocolate; 10 more outlets around town.

» **La Pâtisserie des Rêves** (Map p214; www.lapatisseriedesreves.com; 93 rue du Bac, 7e; MRue du Bac) Extraordinary cakes and tarts showcased beneath glass at the chic 'art' gallery of big-name *pâtissier* Philippe Conticini.

» **Bruno Solques** (Map p220; 248 rue St-Jacques, 5e; MLuxembourg) Paris' most inventive *pâtissier*, Bruno Solques excels at oddly shaped flat tarts and fruit-filled brioches.

» **Dalloyau** (Map p220; www.dalloyau.fr; 5 blvd Beaumarchais, 4e; MBastille) Specialities include *pain aux raisins* (raisin bread), *millefeuille* (pastry layered with cream), *tarte au citron* (lemon tart) and *opéra* (coffee-flavoured almond cake and chocolate).

tourists. Streets lined with places to eat include rue des Lombards, the narrow streets north and east of Forum des Halles, and foodie streets rue Montorgueil and rue Ste-Anne. Find supermarkets around Forum des Halles.

Le Grand Colbert　　　　FRENCH €€€
(Map p220; ☎01 42 86 87 88; www.legrandcolbert. fr; 2-4 rue Vivienne, 2e; lunch menus €22.50 & €29.50; ⊗noon-1am; MPyramides) This former workers' *cafétéria* transformed into a fin-de-siècle showcase is a convenient spot for lunch if visiting the *passages couverts* (covered passages) or cruising the streets late at night (last orders: 1am).

Café Marly　　　　FRENCH, CAFÉ €€€
(Map p220; ☎01 46 26 06 60; cour Napoléon du Louvre, 93 rue de Rivoli, 1er; mains €20-30; ⊗8am-2am; MPalais Royal-Musée du Louvre) This classic venue facing the Louvre's inner courtyard serves contemporary French fare throughout the day under the palace colonnades. Views of the glass pyramid (and French starlets) are priceless.

Saveurs Végét' Halles　　　　VEGETARIAN €
(Map p220; ☎01 40 41 93 95; www.saveursveget halles.fr; 41 rue des Bourdonnais, 1er; menus €9.90-18.90; ⊗Mon-Sat; MChâtelet; ☑) This strictly vegan eatery is egg-free and serves a fair few mock-meat dishes like *poulet végétal aux champignons* ('chicken' with mushrooms) and *escalope de seitan* (wheat gluten 'escalope'). No alcohol.

Le Petit Mâchon　　　　LYONNAIS €€
(Map p220; ☎01 42 60 08 06; 158 rue St-Honoré, 1er; mains €14-22; ⊗Tue-Sun; MPalais Royal-Musée du Louvre) Close to the Louvre, this

upbeat bistro serves some of the best Lyonnais specialities in town.

Joe Allen　　　　AMERICAN €€
(Map p220; ☎01 42 36 70 13; 30 rue Pierre Lescot, 1er; lunch menus €14, dinner menus €18.10 & €22.50; ⊗noon-1am; MÉtienne Marcel) An institution since 1972, Joe Allen is a little bit of New York in Paris. The ribs are particularly recommended.

MARAIS & BASTILLE

The Marais is one of Paris' premier dining neighbourhoods; book ahead for weekend dining. Towards République is decent ethnic cuisine: Chinese noodle shops and restaurants on rue Au Maire, 3e (MArts et Métiers); and Jewish restaurants cooking up specialities from Central Europe, North Africa and Israel along rue des Rosiers, 4e (MSt-Paul). Takeaway falafel and shawarma are available at several places along the same street.

Bastille is equally chock-a-block with restaurants; then there is its fabulous open-air market (see boxed text, p234).

TOP CHOICE **Chez Janou**　　　　PROVENÇAL €€
(Map p220; ☎01 42 72 28 41; www.chezja-nou.com; 2 rue Roger Verlomme, 3e; mains €14.50-19; MChemin Vert) This lovely little spot just east of place des Vosges attracts celebs (last seen: John Malkovich) with its inspired cooking from the south of France, 80 types of pastis and excellent service.

TOP CHOICE **Le Hangar**　　　　FRENCH, BISTRO €€
(Map p220; ☎01 42 74 55 44; 12 impasse Berthaud, 3e; mains €16-20; ⊗Tue-Sat; MLes Halles) Unusual for big mouths like us, we almost baulk at revealing details of this

TOP FIVE FOOD MARKETS

» **Marché Bastille** (Map p220; blvd Richard Lenoir, 11e; ⊙7am-2.30pm Thu & Sun; ⓂBastille or Richard Lenoir) Paris' best outdoor food market.

» **Marché Belleville** (Map p214; blvd de Belleville btwn rue Jean-Pierre Timbaud & rue du Faubourg du Temple, 11e & 20e; ⊙7am-2.30pm Tue & Fri; ⓂBelleville or Couronnes) Fascinating entry into the large, vibrant communities of the eastern neighbourhoods, home to artists, students and immigrants from Africa, Asia and the Middle East.

» **Marché Couvert St-Quentin** (Map p214; 85 blvd de Magenta, 10e; ⊙8am-1pm & 3.30-7.30pm Tue-Sat, 8.30am-1pm Sun; ⓂGare de l'Est) Iron-and-glass covered market built in 1866, lined with gourmet food stalls.

» **Rue Cler** (Map p214; rue Cler, 7e; ⊙8am-7pm Tue-Sat, 8am-noon Sun; ⓂÉcole Militaire) Commercial street market with an almost party-like atmosphere at weekends.

» **Rue Mouffetard** (Map p220; rue Mouffetard; ⊙8am-7.30pm Tue-Sat, 8am-noon Sun; ⓂCensier Daubenton) The city's most photogenic market street.

---

perfect little restaurant. It serves all the bistro favourites – rillettes, foie gras, steak tartare – in relaxing surrounds. The terrace is a delight in fine weather.

La Gazzetta FRENCH €€€
(Map p214; ✆01 43 47 47 05; www.lagazzetta.fr; 29 rue de Cotte, 12e; lunch menus €16, dinner menus €38 & €50; ⊙lunch Tue-Sat, dinner Mon-Sat; ⓂLedru Rollin) This neo-brasserie has gained a substantial following under the tutelage of Swedish chef Peter Nilsson, who is as comfortable producing dishes such as scallops with cress and milk-fed lamb confit and iced Bleu d'Auvergne cheese as he is mini anchovy pizzas. Excellent-value, lunchtime *menu*.

Le Petit Marché FRENCH, BISTRO €€
(Map p220; ✆01 42 72 06 67; 9 rue de Béarn, 3e; mains €16-24, lunch menus €12.50; ⓂChemin Vert) This great little bistro just up from place des Vosges fills up at lunch and dinner with a mixed crowd who come to enjoy its hearty cooking and friendly service.

TOP CHOICE Café Hugo FRENCH, CAFE €
(Map p220; ✆01 42 72 64 04; 22 place des Vosges, 4e; mains €10.70-13.30; ⊙8am-2am; ⓂChemin Vert) Go for brunch (€16.20) or the *plat du jour* (dish of the day) with a glass of wine (€12.50) at our favourite affordable eatery on Paris' most beautiful square – and you'll love Paris forever.

Chez Nénesse FRENCH, BISTRO €
(Map p220; ✆01 42 78 46 49; 17 rue Saintonge, 3e; mains €18; ⊙Mon-Fri; ⓂFilles du Calvaire) The atmosphere here is charmingly 'old Parisian' and unpretentious. Dishes are prepared with fresh, high-quality ingredients and pose good value for money.

Marche ou Crêpe FRENCH, BRETON €
(Map p214; ✆01 43 57 04 78; www.marcheoucrepe.com; 88 rue Oberkampf, 11e; crêpes & galettes €2.20-7.80; ⊙6pm-midnight Tue-Thu, 6pm-2am Fri & Sat, 5pm-midnight Sun; ⓂParmentier) This little outlet near nightlife-busy rue Jean-Pierre Timbaud serves delicious savoury galettes, sweet crêpes, homemade soups, and salads – until late, very late.

LATIN QUARTER & JARDIN DES PLANTES

From cheap-eat student haunts to chandelier-lit palaces loaded with history, the 5e has something to suit every budget and culinary taste. Rue Mouffetard is famed for its food market and food shops; while its side streets, especially pedestrianised rue du Pot au Fer, cook up fine budget dining.

TOP CHOICE Bistroy Les Papilles FRENCH, BISTRO €€
(Map p220; ✆01 43 25 20 79; www.lespapillesparis.fr, in French; 30 rue Gay Lussac, 5e; menus €22-31; ⊙Tue-Sat; ⓂLuxembourg) This hybrid bistro, wine cellar and *épicerie* (specialist grocer) is one of those fabulous dining experiences that packs out the place (reserve a few days in advance to guarantee a table). Dining is at simply dressed tables wedged beneath bottle-lined walls, and fare is market-driven. But what really sets it apart is its exceptional wine list.

TOP CHOICE L'Agrume FRENCH, BISTRO €€
(off Map p220; ✆01 43 31 86 48; 15 rue des Fossés St-Marcel, 5e; mains €30, lunch menus €14 & €16, dinner menu €35; ⊙Tue-Sat; ⓂCensier Daubenton) Lunching at this pocket-sized contemporary bistro is magnificent value and a real gourmet experience. Watch chefs work

with seasonal products in the open kitchen while you dine; reserve several days ahead.

Le Pré Verre   FRENCH, BISTRO €€
(Map p220; ☑01 43 54 59 47; 25 rue Thénard, 5e; 2-/3-course menus €13.50/28; ⊗Tue-Sat; ⓂMaubert Mutualité) Noisy, busy and buzzing, this jovial bistro plunges diners into the heart of a Parisian's Paris. At lunchtime join the flock and go for the fabulous-value *formule déjeuner* (€13). The wine list features France's small independent vignerons.

La Mosquée de Paris   NORTH AFRICAN €€
(Map p220; ☑01 43 31 38 20; 39 rue Geoffroy St-Hilaire, 5e; mains €15-20; ⓂCensier Daubenton or Place Monge) Dig into a couscous, *tajine* or meaty grill within the walls of the city's **central mosque**. Or spoil yourself with a peppermint tea and oriental pastry in its **tearoom** (⊗9am-11.30pm), or lunch, body scrub and massage in its *hammam* (Turkish bath).

ST-GERMAIN, ODÉON & LUXEMBOURG

There's far more to this fabled pocket of Paris than the literary cafes of Sartre or the picnicking turf of Jardin de Luxembourg. Rue St-André des Arts (ⓂSt-Michel or Odéon) is lined with places to dine lightly or lavishly, as is the stretch between Église St-Sulpice and Église St-Germain des Prés (especially rue des Canettes, rue Princesse and rue Guisarde).

TOP CHOICE **Le Comptoir du Relais**
                              FRENCH, BISTRO €€€
(Map p220; ☑01 44 27 07 97; 9 Carrefour de l'Odéon, 6e; dinner menus €50; ⓂOdéon) The

HIPPY GROOVE CUISINE

Tiny but almost perfect, **Le Mouton Noir** (Map p214; ☑01 48 07 05 45; www.lemoutonnoir.fr; 65 rue de Charonne, 11e; menus €29; ⊗dinner Tue-Sat, lunch Sat & Sun; ⓂCharonne) is no *mouton noir* (black sheep). Fabulously unique, this dining address with a mere two dozen seats west of Bastille is a neighbourhood secret that we've just gone and blown. The idea is to use unusual products in traditional French cooking – 'cuisine hippy groove', the chef calls it. Try crab bisque with red curry and lentils, sea bass with cheese, or eggplant with thyme. Brunch (€19) is a fine weekend tradition.

235

THE GOURMET GLACIER

Berthillon (Map p220; 31 rue St-Louis en l'Île, 4e; ice creams €2.10-5.40; ⊗10am-8pm Wed-Sun; ⓂPont Marie) on Île St-Louis is the place to head to for Paris' finest ice cream. There are 70 flavours to choose from, ranging from fruity cassis to chocolate, coffee, *marrons glacés* (candied chestnuts), *Agenaise* (Armagnac and prunes), *noisette* (hazelnut) and *nougat au miel* (honey nougat). One just won't be enough…

culinary handiwork of top chef Yves Camdeborde, this gourmet bistro serves seasonal dishes with a creative twist. Bagging a table without an advance reservation at lunchtime is doable providing you arrive sharp at 12.30pm, but forget more gastronomic evening dining without a reservation (weeks in advance for weekends).

TOP CHOICE **Quatrehommes**   CHEESE SHOP €
(Map p214; 62 rue de Sèvres, 6e; ⓂVanneau) Buy the best of every French cheese, many with an original take (eg Mont d'Or flavoured with black truffles), at this king of *fromageries* (cheese shops). The smell alone upon entering is heavenly.

KGB   FUSION €€
(Map p220; ☑01 46 33 00 85; http://zekitchen-galerie.fr, in French; 25 rue des Grands Augustins, 6e; lunch menus €27 & €34; ⊗Tue-Sat; ⓂSt-Michel) KGB (as in 'Kitchen Galerie Bis') is the latest creation of William Ledeuil of **Ze Kitchen Galerie** (Map p220; 4 rue des Grands Augustins, 6e; lunch/dinner menus €26.50/65; ⊗Mon-Fri, dinner Sat; ⓂSt-Michel) fame. Overtly art-gallery in feel, this small dining space plays to a hip crowd with its casual platters of Asian-influenced *zors d'œuvres,* creative pastas and meats cooked in a *marmite* (earthenware pot).

Bouillon Racine   CLASSICAL FRENCH €€
(Map p220; ☑01 44 32 15 60; 3 rue Racine, 6e; lunch/dinner menus €14.90/29.50; ⓂCluny-La Sorbonne) This 'soup kitchen' built in 1906 to feed city workers is an art nouveau palace. Age-old recipes such as roast snails, *caille confite* (preserved quail) and lamb shank with liquorice inspire the menu. End your foray into gastronomic history with an old-fashioned sherbet.

Cosi SANDWICH BAR €

(Map p220; 54 rue de Seine, 6e; sandwich menus €10-15; ⊘noon-11pm; MOdéon) With sandwich names such as Stonker, Tom Dooley and Naked Willi, Cosi could easily run for Paris' most imaginative sandwich maker.

Marché St-Germain MARKET €

(Map p220; 4-8 rue Lobineau, 6e; ⊘8.30am-1pm & 4-7.30pm Tue-Sat, 8.30am-1pm Sun; MMabillon) Covered food market.

EIFFEL TOWER AREA & 16E

The museum- and monument-rich 16e arrondissement has some fine dines too. Around Mademoiselle Eiffel grab picnic supplies on foodie street rue Cler or pick from several restaurants on rue de Montessuy.

TOP CHOICE **Café Constant** FRENCH, CONTEMPORARY €€

(Map p214; www.cafeconstant.com, in French; 139 rue Ste-Dominique, 7e; mains €16; ⊘Tue-Sun; MÉcole Militaire or Port de l'Alma) Take a former Michelin-starred chef, a dead-simple corner cafe and what do you get? A Christian Constant hit with original mosaic floor, worn wooden tables and a massive queue out the door every mealtime. The cafe doesn't take reservations, but you can enjoy a drink at the bar while you wait. Cuisine is creative bistro.

Les Cocottes FRENCH, CONCEPT €€

(Map p214; www.leviolondingres.com; 135 rue Ste-Dominique, 7e; starters/cocottes & mains/desserts €11/16/7; ⊘Mon-Sat; MÉcole Militaire or Port de l'Alma) *Cocottes* are casseroles, and that is what this chic space – jam-packed day and night – is all about. Get here sharp at noon or 7.15pm (or before) to get a table; no reservations.

MONTPARNASSE

Since the 1920s, Montparnasse has been one of Paris' premier avenues for enjoying cafe life, though younger Parisians deem the quarter démodé (out of fashion) these days.

TOP CHOICE **Jadis** FRENCH, BISTRO €€€

(Map p214; ☑01 45 57 73 20; www.bistrot-jadis.com, in French; 202 rue de la Croix Nivert, 15e; lunch menus €25 & €32, dinner menus €45 & €65; ⊘Mon-Fri; MBoucicaut) This neo-bistro is one of Paris' most raved about. Traditional French dishes pack a modern punch thanks to rising-star chef Guillaume Delage, who dares to do things like braise pork cheeks in beer and use black rice instead of white. The lunch *menu* is extraordinary good value and the chocolate soufflé sheer heaven.

TOP CHOICE **La Cabane à Huîtres** FRENCH, OYSTERS €

(Map p214; ☑01 45 49 47 27; 4 rue Antoine Bourdelle, 14e; menus €18; ⊘Wed-Sat; MMontparnasse-Bienvenüe) One of Paris' best oyster addresses, this earthy wooden-styled *cabane* (cabin) with just nine tables is the pride and joy of fifth-generation oyster farmer Françis Dubourg, who splits his week between the capital and his oyster farm in Arcachon on the Atlantic coast.

Le Dôme HISTORIC BRASSERIE €€€

(Map p214; ☑01 43 35 25 81; 108 blvd du Montparnasse, 14e; starters/mains €20/40; MVavin) A 1930s art deco extravaganza, the Dome is a monumental place for a meal of the formal white-tablecloth and bow-tied waiter variety. Stick with the basics at this historical venue and end on a high with *millefeuille* – a decadent extravaganza not to be missed.

ÉTOILE & CHAMPS-ÉLYSÉES

The 8e arrondissement around the Champs-Élysées is known for its big-name chefs (Alain Ducasse, Pierre Gagnaire, Guy Savoy) and culinary icons (Taillevent), but there are all sorts of under-the-radar restaurants scattered in the backstreets where Parisians who live and work in the area dine.

Bistrot du Sommelier FRENCH €€€

(Map p214; ☑01 42 65 24 85; www.bistrotdu-sommelier.com; 97 blvd Haussmann, 8e; lunch menus €33, incl wine €43, dinner menus €65-110; ⊘Mon-Fri; MSt-Augustin) The whole point of this attractive eatery is to match wine with food, aided by one of the world's foremost sommeliers, Philippe Faure-Brac. Sample his wine/food pairings on Friday, when a three-course tasting lunch with wine is €50 and a five-course dinner with wine is €75.

Le Boudoir FRENCH €€€

(Map p214; ☑01 43 59 25 29; 25 rue du Colisée, 8e; lunch/dinner menus €19/50; ⊘lunch Mon-Fri, dinner Tue-Sat; MSt-Philippe du Roule or Franklin D Roosevelt) Spread across two floors, the quirky salons here – Marie Antoinette, Palme d'Or and the Red Room – are individual works of art with a style befitting the name. In a move towards yesteryear decadence, a private smoking room is hidden on the premises. The *prix fixe* (fixed-price) lunch is an excellent deal.

Le Hide FRENCH €€

(Map p214; ☑01 45 74 15 81; www.lehide.fr; 10 Rue du Général Lanrezac, 17e; menus €22 & €29; ⊘lunch Mon-Fri, dinner Mon-Sat; MCharles de Gaulle-Étoile) A reader favourite, Le Hide

CANAL ST-MARTIN: A PARISIAN-PERFECT PICNIC

Pink Flamingo (Map p214; ☑01 42 02 31 70; www.pinkflamingopizza.com; 67 rue Bichat, 10e; pizzas €10.50-16; ☺until 11pm Tue-Sat, 1pm-11pm Sun; ⓂJacques Bonsergent) is not just another pizza place. *Mais non, chérie!* Once the weather warms up, the Flamingo un-veils its secret weapon – pink helium balloons that the delivery guy uses to locate you and your perfect canalside picnic spot. Nip into the canalside pizzeria to order Paris' most inventive pizza (duck, apple and chèvre perhaps, or what about gorgonzola, figs and cured ham?), grab a balloon, and stroll off along the canal to your perfect picnic spot.

To make your picnic Parisian perfect, buy a bottle of wine from nearby **Le Verre Volé** (Map p214; ☑01 48 03 17 34; 67 rue de Lancry, 10e; mains €12; ⓂJacques Bonsergent), a wine shop with a few tables, excellent wines (€5 to €60 per bottle, €4.50 per glass) and ex-pert advice.

is a tiny neighbourhood bistro serving scrumptious traditional French fare: snails, baked shoulder of lamb, monkfish in lemon butter.

Fromagerie Alléosse   CHEESE SHOP €
(Map p214; 13 rue Poncelet, 17e; ⓂTernes) This is the best cheese shop in Paris; well worth a trip across town.

OPÉRA & GRANDS BOULEVARDS
The neon-lit area around blvd Montmartre forms one of the Right Bank's most animat-ed cafe and dining districts.

TOP CHOICE **Les Pâtes Vivantes**   CHINESE €
(46 du Faubourg Montmartre, 9e; noodles €9.50-12; ☺Mon-Sat; ⓂLe Peletier) This is one of the few spots in Paris for sampling hand-pulled noodles (*là miàn*) made to order in the age-old northern Chinese tradition. There's also a **Latin Quarter branch** (Map p220; ☑01 40 46 84 33; 22 blvd St-Germain, 5e; ⓂCardinal Lemoine).

Le Roi du Pot au Feu   FRENCH, BISTRO €€
(Map p226; 34 rue Vignon, 9e; menus €24-29; ☺noon-10.30pm Mon-Sat; ⓂHavre Caumartin) The typical Parisian bistro atmosphere adds to the charm of the 'King of Hotpots', but what you really come here for is its *pot-au-feu* (beef, root vegetable and herb stew), the stock as starter and the meat and veg as main. No bookings.

Chartier   FRENCH, BISTRO €
(Map p226; ☑01 47 70 86 29; www.restaurant -chartier.com; 7 rue du Faubourg Montmartre, 9e; menus with wine €19.40; ⓂGrands Boulevards) Chartier started life as a *bouillon* (soup kitchen) in 1896 and is a real belle époque gem. For a taste of old-fashioned Paris, it's unbeatable. No reservations.

Le J'Go   SOUTHWEST FRENCH €€
(Map p226; ☑01 40 22 09 09; www.lejgo.com; 4 rue Drouot, 9e; menus €15-20; ☺lunch Mon-Fri, dinner Mon-Sat; ⓂRichelieu Droit) This con-temporary, Toulouse-style bistro magics diners away to southwestern France. Fla-vourful regional cooking revolves around a *rôtissoire* (meat on a spit) – minimum 20 minutes' roasting.

MONTMARTRE & PIGALLE
You'll still find some decent eateries in Montmartre, but beware the tourist traps. Towards place Pigalle there are plenty of grocery stores, many open until late; try side streets off blvd de Clichy such as rue Lepic.

Chez Toinette   FRENCH €€
(Map p226; ☑01 42 54 44 36; 20 rue Germain Pilon, 18e; mains €17-22; ☺dinner Mon-Sat; ⓂAb-besses) Chez Toinette keeps alive the tradi-tion of old Montmartre with its simplicity and culinary expertise. Partridge, doe and duck are house specialities.

Café Burq   FRENCH, BISTRO €€
(Map p226; ☑01 42 52 81 27; 6 rue Burq, 18e; menus €26 & €30; ☺7pm-2am Tue-Sat; ⓂAb-besses) This convivial, retro bistro is always buzzing; book ahead. But don't come for the decor or space – both are nonexistent.

Le Café qui Parle   FRENCH €€
(Map p226; ☑01 46 06 06 88; 24 rue Caulain-court, 18e; menus €12.50 & €17; ☺Mon-Sat, lunch Sun; ☏; ⓂLamarck Caulaincourt or Blanche) We love the Talking Cafe's wall art and ancient safes below (the building was once a bank), but not as much as we love its weekend brunch (€17).

🍷 Drinking

The line between bars, cafes and bistros is blurred at best. Sitting at a table costs more than standing at the counter, more on a fancy square than a backstreet, more in the 8e than in the 18e. After 10pm many cafes charge a pricier *tarif de nuit* (night rate).

LOUVRE & LES HALLES

Le Fumoir
COCKTAIL BAR

(Map p220; 6 rue de l'Amiral Coligny, 1er; ⊙11am-2am; MLouvre-Rivoli) The 'Smoking Room' is a huge, stylish colonial-style bar-cafe opposite the Louvre – a fine place to sip top-notch gin while nibbling on olives.

Le Cochon à l'Oreille
BAR, CAFE

(Map p220; 15 rue Montmartre, 1er; ⊙10am-11pm Tue-Sat; MLes Halles or Étienne Marcel) A Parisian jewel, this heritage-listed hole-in-the wall retains its belle époque tiles with market scenes of Les Halles, and just eight tiny tables.

MARAIS & BASTILLE

Le Pure Café
CAFE

(Map p214; 14 rue Jean Macé, 11e; ⊙7am-2am; MCharonne) This old cafe moonlights as a restaurant, but we like it as it was intended to be, especially over a *grand crème* (large

white coffee) and the papers on Sunday morning.

Le Bistrot du Peintre
WINE BAR

(Map p214; 116 av Ledru-Rollin, 11e; ⊙8am-2am; MBastille) Lovely belle époque bistro and wine bar, with 1902 art nouveau bar, elegant terrace and spot-on service.

Au Petit Fer à Cheval
BAR

(Map p220; 30 rue Vieille du Temple, 4e; ⊙8am-2am; MHôtel de Ville or St-Paul) The original horseshoe-shaped zinc counter (1903) leaves little room for much else at this genial bar, but nobody seems to mind.

La Chaise Au Plafond
BAR

(Map p220; 10 Rue du Trésor, 4e; ⊙10am-2am; ⊙Hôtel de Ville or St-Paul) The Chair on the Ceiling is a peaceful, warm place with terrace – a real oasis from the frenzy of the Marais and worth knowing about in summer.

LATIN QUARTER & JARDIN DES PLANTES

Curio Parlor Cocktail Club
COCKTAIL BAR

(Map p220; 16 rue des Bernardins, 5e; ⊙7pm-2am Tue-Thu, 7pm-4am Fri & Sat; MMaubert Mutualité) This hybrid bar-club looks to the interwar *années folles* (crazy years) of 1920s Paris, London and New York for inspiration. Go to its Facebook page to track the next party.

ST-GERMAIN, ODÉON & LUXEMBOURG

🔺 TOP CHOICE Au Sauvignon
WINE BAR

(Map p214; 80 rue des Sts-Pères, 7e; ⊙8am-midnight; MSèvres-Babylone) To savour the full flavour of this 1950s wine bar, order a plate of *casse-croûtes au pain Poilâne* – sandwiches made with the city's most famous bread.

Prescription Cocktail Club
COCKTAIL CLUB

(Map p220; 23 rue Mazarine, 6e; ⊙7pm-2am Mon-Thu, 7pm-4am Fri & Sat; MOdéon) With bowler and flat-top hats as lampshades and a 1930s speakeasy New York air to the place, this cocktail club is Parisian-cool. Watch Facebook for events.

Le 10
CELLAR PUB

(Map p220; 10 rue de l'Odéon, 6e; ⊙5.30pm-2am; MOdéon) Plot the next revolution or conquer a lonely heart at this local institution that groans with students, smoky ambience and cheap sangria.

Café La Palette
HISTORIC CAFE

(Map p220; 43 rue de Seine, 6e; ⊙8am-2am Mon-Sat; MMabillon) In the heart of gal-

---

ⓘ BAR-HOPPING STREETS

Prime Parisian drinking spots, perfect for evening meandering to soak up the scene:

» **Rue Vieille du Temple & surrounding streets, 4e** Marais cocktail of gay bars and chic cafes.

» **Rue Oberkampf & rue Jean-Pierre Timbaud, 11e** Hip bars, bohemian hang-outs and atmospheric cafes.

» **Rue de la Roquette, rue Keller & rue de Lappe, 11e** Whatever you fancy, Bastille has the lot.

» **Rue Montmartre, 2e** Modern, slick bars and pubs.

» **Canal St-Martin, 10e** Heady summer nights in casual canalside cafes.

» **Rue Princesse & rue des Canettes, 6e** Pedestrian duo of student, sports 'n' tapas bars and pubs on the Left Bank.

lery land, this cafe where Cézanne and Braque drank attracts fashionable people and art dealers. Its summer terrace is as beautiful.

Les Deux Magots
HISTORIC CAFE

(Map p220; www.lesdeuxmagots.fr; 170 blvd St-Germain, 6e; ⊗7am-1am; ⓂSt-Germain des Prés) St-Germain's most famous cafe, where Sartre, Hemingway and Picasso hung out.

ÉTOILE & CHAMPS-ELYSÉES

Buddha Bar
COCKTAIL BAR

(Map p214; 8-12 rue Boissy d'Anglas, 8e; ⊗noon-2am Sun-Thu, 4pm-3am Fri & Sat; ⓂConcorde) The decor is spectacular, with a two-storey golden Buddha and millions of candles, at this A-list cocktail bar known for its Zen lounge music.

OPÉRA & GRANDS BOULEVARDS

DeLaVille Café
BAR, CAFE

(Map p226; 34 blvd de Bonne Nouvelle, 10e; ⊗11am-2.30am; ☎; ⓂBonne Nouvelle) This erstwhile brothel fuses history (original mosaic tiles, distressed walls) with industrial chic. Its terrace is among the best along the grands boulevards and DJs play Thursday to Saturday, making it a hot 'before' venue for the nearby Rex Club (p241).

TOP CHOICE Harry's New York Bar
AMERICAN BAR

(Map p226; 5 rue Daunou, 2e; ⊗10.30am-4am; ⓂOpéra) Lean upon the bar where F Scott Fitzgerald and Ernest Hemingway drank and gossiped, while white-smocked waiters mix killer martinis and Bloody Marys.

TOP CHOICE Au Limonaire
WINE BAR

(Map p226; ☎01 45 23 33 33; http://limonaire.free.fr; 18 cité Bergère, 9e; ⊗7pm-midnight Mon, 6pm-midnight Tue-Sun; ⓂGrands Boulevards) This little wine bar is one of the best places to listen to traditional French *chansons* (songs) and local singer/songwriters. Reservations recommended.

MONTMARTRE & PIGALLE

La Fourmi
BAR

(Map p226; 74 rue des Martyrs, 18e; ⊗8am-2am Mon-Thu, to 4am Fri & Sat, 10am-2am Sun; ⓂPigalle) A Pigalle stayer, 'The Ant' always hits the mark: hip but not snobby, with a laid-back crowd and a rock-oriented playlist.

☆ Entertainment

From jazz cellars to comic theatre, garage beats to go-go dancers, world-class art gal-

If you go on the day of a performance, you can snag a half-price ticket (plus €3 commission) for ballet, theatre, opera and other performances at the discount-ticket outlet **Kiosque Théâtre Madeleine** (Map p226; www.kiosquetheatre.com; opp 15 place de la Madeleine, 8e; ⊗12.30-8pm Tue-Sat, to 4pm Sun; ⓂMadeleine).

French-language websites www.billetreduc.com, www.ticketac.com and www.webguichet.com all sell discounted tickets.

leries to avant-garde artist squats, Paris is *the* capital of savoir-vivre, with spectacular entertainment to suit every budget, every taste. To find out what's on, surf **Figaroscope** (www.figaroscope.fr) or buy *Pariscope* (€0.40) or *Officiel des Spectacles* (€0.35; www.offi.fr, in French) at Parisian news kiosks. *Billeteries* (ticket offices) in **Fnac** (www.fnacspectacles.com, in French) and **Virgin Megastores** (www.virginmega.fr, in French) sell tickets.

Live Music

Palais Omnisports de Paris-Bercy (Map p214; www.bercy.fr, in French); **Le Zénith** (Map p214; www.le-zenith.com, in French) and **Stade de France** (www.stadefrance.com) are Paris' big-name venues. But it's the smaller concert halls loaded with history and charm that most fans favour.

Le Vieux Belleville
FRENCH CHANSONS

(Map p214; ☎01 44 62 92 66; www.le-vieux-belleville.com; 12 rue des Envierges, 20e; admission free; ⊗performances 8pm Thu-Sat; ⓂPyrénées) This old-fashioned bistro at the top of Parc de Belleville is an atmospheric venue for performances of *chansons,* featuring accordions and an organ grinder, three times a week. It's a lively favourite with locals; book ahead.

Cabaret Sauvage
WORLD, LATINO

(Map p214; ☎01 42 09 03 09; www.cabaretsauvage.com; Parc de la Villette, 221 av Jean Jaurès, 19e; tickets €8-34; ⊗7pm-2am Tue-Sun; ⊗Porte de la Villette) This super-cool space (it looks like a gigantic yurt) hosts African, reggae and raï concerts as well as DJ nights that last till dawn; occasional hip-hop and indie acts pass through.

FREE SHOWS

Paris' eclectic gaggle of clowns, mime artists, living statues, acrobats, rollerbladers, buskers and other street entertainers can be bags of fun and costs substantially less than a theatre ticket (a few coins in the hat is a sweet gesture). Some excellent musicians perform in the long echo-filled corridors of the metro, a privilege that artists have to audition for. Outside, you can be sure of a good show at:

» **Place Georges Pompidou, 4e** In front of the Centre Pompidou.

» **Pont St-Louis, 4e** Bridge linking Paris' two islands (best enjoyed with Berthillon ice cream in hand).

» **Pont au Double, 4e** Pedestrian bridge linking Notre Dame with the Left Bank (ditto; see boxed text, p235).

» **Place Jean du Bellay, 1er** Musicians and fire-eaters near the Fontaine des Innocents.

» **Parc de la Villette, 19e** African drummers at the weekend.

» **Place du Tertre, Montmartre, 18e** Montmartre's original main square wins hands down as Paris' busiest street-artist stage.

L'Attirail WORLD, LATINO
(Map p220; ☎01 42 72 44 42; www.lattirail.com; 9 rue au Maire, 3e; admission free; ☺10.30am-1.30am Mon-Sat, 3pm-1.30am Sun; Ⓜ Arts et Métiers) There are free concerts of *chansons françaises* and world music almost every evening at this cosmopolitan enclave. Manic but friendly customers crowd the Formica bar with its cheap *pots* (460mL bottle) of wine.

Le Baiser Salé JAZZ
(Map p220; www.lebaisersale.com, in French; 58 rue des Lombards, 1er; admission free-€20; ☺5pm-6am; ☺ Châtelet) One of several jazz clubs located on this street, the Salty Kiss hosts concerts of jazz, Afro and Latin jazz and jazz fusion, and is known for discovering new talents. Sets start at 7.30pm and 10pm. Monday's jam session is free.

Salle Pleyel CLASSICAL
(Map p214; ☎01 42 56 13 13; www.sallepleyel.fr; 252 rue du Faubourg St-Honoré, 8e; concert tickets €10-85; ☺ box office noon-7pm Mon-Sat, to 8pm on day of performance; Ⓜ Ternes) Dating from the 1920s, this highly regarded hall hosts many of Paris' finest classical-music events, including concerts by the Orchestre de Paris (www.orchestredeparis.com, in French).

Point Éphémère ROCK, INDIE
(Map p214; ☎01 40 34 02 48; www.pointephe mere.org; 200 quai de Valmy, 10e; admission free-€21; ☺ bar noon-2am Mon-Sat, 1-9pm Sun; Ⓜ Louis Blanc) This 'centre for dynamic artists' has a great location by Canal St-

Martin, with indie concerts and the odd electro dance night. Bar, restaurant and exhibit area too.

La Cigale ROCK, JAZZ
(Map p226; ☎01 49 25 81 75; www.lacigale.fr; 120 blvd de Rochechouart, 18e; admission €25-60; Ⓜ Anvers or Pigalle) Now classed as a historical monument, this music hall dates from 1887 but was redecorated 100 years later by Philippe Starck.

Nightclubs

Unfortunately, Paris is *not* up to the likes of London, Berlin or New York when it comes to clubbing. Lacking a mainstream scene, the scene tends to be underground and mobile, making the web the smartest way of keeping on top of it.

TOP CHOICE La Scène Bastille CLUB
(Map p214; www.scenebastille.com; 2bis rue des Taillandiers, 11e; admission €12-15; ☺ Mon-Sat; Ⓜ Bastille or Ledru Rollin) The unpretentious Bastille Scene is the kind of place where local DJs go to relax and listen to music.

TOP CHOICE Le Batofar TUGBOAT
(Map p214; www.batofar.org, in French; opp 11 quai François Mauriac, 13e; admission free-€15; ☺9pm-midnight Mon & Tue, to 4am or later Wed-Sun; Ⓜ Quai de la Gare or Bibliothèque) This much-loved tugboat has a rooftop bar that's great in summer, while the club underneath provides memorable underwater acoustics between its metal walls and portholes.

Le Divan du Monde
CULTURAL CENTRE

(Map p226; www.divandumonde.com; 75 rue des Martyrs, 18e; admission €10-15; ⊗11pm-5am Fri & Sat; ⓂPigalle) Cinematographic events, Romani music gatherings, *nouvelles chansons françaises* (new French songs), air-guitar face-offs, rock parties... Inventive and open-minded is what this excellent cross-cultural venue in Pigalle is.

Le Balajo
DANCE CLUB

(Map p214; www.balajo.fr; 9 rue de Lappe, 11e; admission from €12; ⊗10pm-2am Tue & Thu, 11pm-5am Fri & Sat, 3-7.30pm Sun; ⓂBastille) This historic ballroom is devoted to salsa classes and Latino music on weekdays and DJ-spun rock, disco, funk, R&B and house at weekends.

Le Nouveau Casino
CLUB

(Map p214; www.nouveaucasino.net, in French; 109 rue Oberkampf, 11e; admission €5-10; ⊗7.30pm or midnight to 2 or 5am Tue-Sun; ⓂParmentier) This club is known for its live-music concerts and lively weekend club nights. The program is eclectic, underground and up-to-the-minute.

Le Rex Club
CLUB

(Map p226; www.rexclub.com; 5 blvd Poissonnière, 2e; admission free-€12; ⊗11.30pm-6am Wed-Sat; ⓂBonne Nouvelle) The Rex reigns majestic in the house and techno scene – always has and always will.

🛍 Shopping

As in most capital cities, shops are spread across different neighbourhoods, inspiring very different styles of shopping. Annual, month-long *soldes* (sales) see prices slashed by as much as 50%; they start up in mid-January and again in mid-June.

Key areas to mooch with no particular purchase in mind are the maze of backstreet lanes in the Marais (3e and 4e), around St-Germain des Prés (6e), and parts of Montmartre and Pigalle (9e and 18e). Or perhaps you have something specific to buy?

Designer haute couture The world's most famous designers stylishly jostle for window space on Av Montaigne, av Georges V and rue du Faubourg St-Honoré, 8e.

Chain-store fashion Find Gap, H&M, Zara and other major, super-sized chain stores on Rue de Rivoli in the 1er, Les Halles in the 2e, and av des Champs-Élysées, 8e.

Department stores On and around Blvd Haussmann, 9e, including Paris' famous

Track tomorrow's hot 'n' happening soirée with these Parisian nightlife links:

» www.gogoparis.com (in English)
» www.lemonsound.com
» www.novaplanet.com
» www.parisbouge.com
» www.parissi.com
» www.tribudenuit.com

Galeries Lafayette (Map p226) at No 40 and **Printemps** (Map p226) at No 64.

Factory outlets Price-cut fashion for men, women and kids the length of Rue d'Alésia, 14e.

Hip fashion & art Young designers crowd Rue Charlot, 3e, and beyond in the northern Marais.

Fine art & antiques Right Bank place des Vosges, 4e, and Left Bank Carré Rive Gauche, 6e.

Design Eames, eat your heart out! Boutique galleries specialising in modern furniture, art and design (1950s to present) stud rue Mazarine and rue de Seine, 6e.

ⓘ Information

Dangers & Annoyances

Paris is generally safe. Metro stations best avoided late at night include: Châtelet-Les Halles and its corridors; Château Rouge in Montmartre; Gare du Nord; Strasbourg St-Denis; Réaumur Sébastopol; and Montparnasse Bienvenüe.

Pickpocketing and thefts from handbags and packs is a problem wherever there are crowds (especially of tourists). Be careful around Montmartre's Sacré Cœur; Pigalle; the areas around Forum des Halles and Centre Pompidou; the Latin Quarter; below the Eiffel Tower; and on the metro during rush hour.

Internet Resources

Mairie de Paris (www.paris.fr)

Paris by Mouth (www.parisbymouth.com)

Paris Convention & Visitors Bureau (www.parisinfo.com)

My Little Paris (www.mylittleparis.com)

Medical Services

American Hospital of Paris (☑01 46 41 25 25; www.american-hospital.org; 63 blvd Victor Hugo, 92200 Neuilly-sur-Seine; ⓂPont de Levallois Bécon)

DON'T MISS

FLEA MARKETS

» **Marché aux Puces de Montreuil** (off Map p214; av du Professeur André Lemière, 20e; ☺8am-7.30pm Sat-Mon; Ⓜ Porte de Montreuil) Particularly known for its second-hand clothing, designer seconds, engravings, jewellery, linen, crockery and old furniture.

» **Marché aux Puces de St-Ouen** (off Map p214; rue des Rosiers, av Michelet, rue Voltaire, rue Paul Bert & rue Jean-Henri Fabre, 18e; ☺9am-6pm Sat, 10am-6pm Sun, 11am-5pm Mon; Ⓜ Porte de Clignancourt) Around since the late 19th century, and said to be Europe's largest.

» **Marché aux Puces de la Porte de Vanves** (Map p214; av Georges Lafenestre & av Marc Sangnier, 14e; ☺7am-6pm or later Sat & Sun; Ⓜ Porte de Vanves) The smallest and, some say, friendliest of the trio.

Hôpital Hôtel Dieu (☎01 42 34 82 34; www.aphp.fr; 1 place du Parvis Notre Dame, 4e; Ⓜ Cité) One of the city's main government-run public hospitals; after 8pm use the emergency entrance on rue de la Cité, 4e.

Pharmacie Les Champs (☎01 45 62 02 41; Galerie des Champs, 84 av des Champs-Élysées, 8e; ☺24hr; Ⓜ George V)

Tourist Information

Paris Convention & Visitors Bureau (Map p220; www.parisinfo.com; 25-27 rue des Pyramides, 1er; Ⓜ Pyramides; ☺9am-7pm Jun-Oct, 10am-7pm Mon-Sat & 11am-7pm Sun Nov-May) Main tourist office, with a clutch of smaller centres elsewhere in the city.

ⓘ Getting There & Away

Air

Aéroport d'Orly (ORY; ☎01 70 36 39 50; www.aeroportsdeparis.fr) Older and smaller of Paris' two major airports, 18km south of the city.

Aéroport Roissy Charles de Gaulle (CDG; ☎01 70 36 39 50; www.aeroportsdeparis.fr) Three terminal complexes – Aérogare 1, 2 and 3 – are located 30km northeast of Paris in the suburb of Roissy.

Aéroport Beauvais (BVA; ☎08 92 68 20 66; www.aeroportbeauvais.com) Located 80km north of Paris; used by charter companies and budget airlines

Bus

Eurolines (☎01 43 54 11 99; www.eurolines.fr; 55 rue St-Jacques, 5e; Ⓜ Cluny-La Sorbonne) Reservations and tickets for international buses to Western and Central Europe, Scandinavia and Morocco.

Gare Routière Internationale de Paris-Galliéni (off Map p214; ☎08 92 89 90 91; 28 av du Général de Gaulle; Ⓜ Galliéni) Paris' international bus terminal in the eastern suburb of Bagnolet.

Train

Paris has six major train stations. For mainline train information around the clock, contact **SNCF** (☎08 91 36 20 20, timetables ☎08 91 67 68 69; www.sncf.fr).

Gare d'Austerlitz (Map p220; blvd de l'Hôpital, 13e; Ⓜ Gare d'Austerlitz) Trains to/from Spain and Portugal; Loire Valley and non-TGV trains to southwestern France (eg Bordeaux and Basque Country).

Gare de l'Est (Map p214; blvd de Strasbourg, 10e; Ⓜ Gare de l'Est) Trains to/from Luxembourg, parts of Switzerland (Basel, Lucerne, Zurich), southern Germany (Frankfurt, Munich) and points further east; regular and TGV Est trains to areas of France east of Paris (Champagne, Alsace and Lorraine).

Gare de Lyon (Map p214; blvd Diderot, 12e; Ⓜ Gare de Lyon) Trains to/from parts of Switzerland (eg Bern, Geneva, Lausanne), Italy and points beyond; regular and TGV Sud-Est and TGV Midi-Méditerranée trains to areas southeast of Paris, including Dijon, Lyon, Provence, the Côte d'Azur and the Alps.

Gare Montparnasse (Map p214; av du Maine & blvd de Vaugirard, 15e; Ⓜ Montparnasse Bienvenüe) Trains to/from Brittany and places en route from Paris (eg Chartres, Angers, Nantes); TGV Atlantique Ouest and TGV Atlantique Sud-Ouest trains to Tours, Nantes, Bordeaux and other destinations in southwestern France.

Gare du Nord (Map p214; rue de Dunkerque, 10e; Ⓜ Gare du Nord) Trains to/from the UK, Belgium, northern Germany, Scandinavia, Moscow etc (terminus of the high-speed Thalys trains to/from Amsterdam, Brussels, Cologne and Geneva and Eurostar to London); trains to the northern suburbs of Paris and northern France, including TGV Nord trains to Lille and Calais.

Gare St-Lazare (Map p214; rue St-Lazare & rue d'Amsterdam, 8e; Ⓜ St-Lazare) Normandy (eg Dieppe, Le Havre, Cherbourg).

❶ Getting Around
To/From the Airports

Getting into town is straightforward and inexpensive thanks to a fleet of public-transport options. Bus drivers sell tickets. Children aged four to nine years pay half-price on most services.

AÉROPORT D'ORLY

Air France bus 1 (☎08 92 35 08 20; http://videocdn.airfrance.com/cars-airfrance; single/return €11.50/18.50; ☺6.15am-11.15pm from Orly, 6am-11.30pm from Invalides) This *navette* (shuttle bus) runs every 30 minutes to/from Gare Montparnasse (rue du Commandant René Mouchotte, 15e; Ⓜ Montparnasse Bienvenüe) and Aérogare des Invalides (Ⓜ Invalides) in the 7e.

Noctilien bus 31 (☎32 46; www.noctilien.fr; adult €6.80 or 4 metro tickets; ☺12.30am-5.30pm) Part of the RATP night service, Noctilien hourly bus 31 links Orly-Sud with Gare de Lyon, Place d'Italie and Gare d'Austerlitz (45 mins).

Orlybus (☎32 46; www.ratp.fr; adult €6.60; ☺6am-11.20pm from Orly, 5.35am-11.05pm from Paris) RATP bus every 15 to 20 minutes to/from metro Denfert Rochereau (20 to 30 minutes) in the 14e.

Orlyval (☎32 46; www.ratp.fr; adult €10.25; ☺6am-11pm) This RATP service links Orly with the city centre via a shuttle train and the RER (p244). Automatic rail (€7.90) to the RER B station Antony, then RER B4 north (€2.35; 35 to 40 minutes to Châtelet, every four to 12 minutes). Orlyval tickets are valid for the subsequent RER and metro journey.

RATP bus 183 (☎32 46; www.ratp.fr; adult €1.70 or 1 metro/bus ticket; ☺5.35am-8.35pm) Cheapest way of getting to/from Orly Sud: very slow public bus linking only Orly-Sud (one hour) with metro Porte de Choisy every 30 minutes.

RATP bus 285 (☎32 46; www.ratp.fr; adult €6.80 or 4 metro tickets; ☺5.05am-midnight from Orly, 5am-12.40am from Paris) Every 10 to 30 minutes to/from metro Villejuif Louis Aragon (55 minutes).

RER C & shuttle (☎32 46; www.ratp.fr; adult €6.20; ☺5.30am-11.30pm) Shuttle bus every 15 to 30 minutes to RER line C station, Pont de Rungis-Aéroport d'Orly RER station, then RER C2 train to Paris' Gare d'Austerlitz (50 minutes).

AÉROPORT ROISSY CHARLES DE GAULLE

Air France bus 2 (☎08 92 35 08 20; http://videocdn.airfrance.com/cars-airfrance; single/return €15/24; ☺5.45am-11pm) Links airport every 30 minutes with the Arc de Triomphe outside 1 av Carnot, 17e (45 minutes), and Porte Maillot metro station, 17e (35 to 50 minutes).

Air France bus 4 (☎08 92 35 08 20; http://videocdn.airfrance.com/cars-airfrance; adult single/return €16.50/27; ☺7am-9pm from Roissy Charles de Gaulle, 6.30am-9.30pm from Paris) Links airport every 30 minutes with **Gare de Lyon** (20bis blvd Diderot, 12e; Ⓜ Gare de Lyon) and **Gare Montparnasse** (rue du Commandant René Mouchotte, 15e; Ⓜ Montparnasse Bienvenüe); journey times 50 to 55 minutes.

Noctilien buses 140 & 143 (☎32 46; www.noctilien.fr; adult €5.10 or 3 metro tickets; ☺12.30am-5.30pm) Hourly night buses to/from Gare de l'Est (140 & 143) and Gare du Nord (143).

RATP bus 350 (☎32 46; www.ratp.fr; adult €5.10 or 3 metro tickets ☺5.30am-11pm) Every 30 minutes to/from Gare de l'Est and Gare du Nord (both one hour).

RER B (☎32 46; www.ratp.fr; adult €8.70; ☺5.20am-midnight) Under extensive renovation at the time of research, with replacement buses on duty; RER line B3 usually links CDG1 and CDG2 with the city every 10 to 15 minutes (30 minutes).

Roissybus (☎32 46; www.ratp.fr; adult €9.40; ☺5.30am-11pm) Direct bus every 30 minutes to/from **Opéra** (cnr rue Scribe & rue Auber, 9e; Ⓜ Opéra).

BETWEEN ORLY & CHARLES DE GAULLE

Air France shuttle bus 3 (www.cars-airfrance.com, in French; adult €19; ☺6am-10.30pm) Every 30 minutes; free for connecting Air France passengers; journey time one hour.

Orlyval (☎32 46; www.ratp.fr; adult €17.60; ☺6am-11pm) RER line B3 from Charles de Gaulle to the Antony station, then Orlyval automatic metro to Orly.

AÉROPORT PARIS-BEAUVAIS

Navette Officielle (Official Shuttle Bus; ☎08 92 68 20 64, airport 08 92 68 20 66; adult €14) Leaves Parking Pershing, west of the Palais des Congrès de Paris, 3¼ hours before flight departures (board 15 minutes before) and leaves the airport 20 minutes after arrivals, dropping passengers south of the Palais des Congrès on place de la Porte Maillot. Journey time 1¼ hours; buy tickets at sales point just outside the terminal and from a kiosk in the car park.

Bicycle

Vélib' (www.velib.paris.fr; day/week subscription €1/5, bike hire per 1st/2nd/additional 30min free/€2/4) With this self-service bike scheme you can pick up a pearly-grey bike for peanuts from one roadside Vélib' station and drop it off at another. Its almost 1500 bike *stations* are accessible around the clock. iPhone users can download the Vélib' application. To get a bike, open a Vélib' account: one- and seven-day subscriptions can be done at any station with any credit card that has a micro-chip. If the station you want to return your bike to is full, swipe your card across the multilin-gual terminal to get 15 minutes for free to find another station. Bikes are geared to cyclists aged 14 and over, and are fitted with gears, antitheft lock with key, reflective strips and front/rear lights. Helmets are not compulsory; bring your own if you want to wear one.

Boat

Batobus (☏ 08 25 05 01 01; www.batobus.com; adult 1-/2-/3-day pass €13/17/20; ☉10am-9.30pm May-Aug, shorter hr rest of year) A fleet of glassed-in trimarans dock at eight small piers along the Seine every 15 to 30 minutes; buy tickets at each stop or tourist offices, and jump on and off as you like.

Car & Motorcycle

If driving a car in Paris doesn't destroy your holiday sense of spontaneity, parking will. If you must drive, the fastest way to get across the city is usually via the blvd Périphérique, the ring road encircling the city.

Major car-rental companies have offices at airports and train stations. Another option is the self-service, pay-as-you-go scheme provided by **Connect by Hertz** (☏ 08 00 45 04 00; www.connectbyhertz.com): for a €120 annual mem-bership fee you can use their website to book a car in your neighbourhood; rates start at €4/32 per hour/day plus €0.35 per kilometre and include insurance and petrol. The Mairie de Paris also hopes to have a fleet of 3000-odd electric rental cars parked around the city by 2012, to be called Autolib' (ie the car equivalent of Vélib').

Street parking in central Paris is limited to two hours (€1.50 to €3 per hour); to pay, buy a Paris Carte worth €10 or €30 at *tabacs* (tobac-conists). Municipal car parks cost €2 to €3.50 per hour or around €25 per 24 hours.

Got the urge to look like you've just stepped into (or out of) a 1950s French film? Grab a pastel-coloured Vespa XLV 50cc scooter from **Left Bank Scooters** (www.leftbankscooters.com); they'll deliver/pick up from your hotel and arrange tours (from €130) as far as Versailles.

Public Transport

Paris' public transit system is operated by the **RATP** (www.ratp.fr). The same RATP tickets are valid on the metro, RER, buses, trams and Montmartre funicular. A single ticket/*carnet* of 10 costs €1.70/12.

One ticket covers travel between any two metro stations (no return journeys) for 1½ hours; you can transfer between buses and between buses and trams, but not from metro to bus or vice versa.

ON YOUR WAY

The official **Paris Île de France** (www.nouveau-paris-ile-de-france.fr) website is a treasure trove of information on the area.

Keep your ticket until you exit the station; ticket inspectors can fine you if you can't pro-duce a valid ticket.

BUS Paris' bus system runs from 5.30am to 8.30pm Monday to Saturday, after which certain *service en soirée* (evening service) lines continue until midnight or 12.30am, when **Noctilien** (www.noctilien.fr) night buses, departing every hour between 12.30am and 5.30am, kick in. Two circular lines (the NO1 and NO2) link the four main train stations – St-Lazare, Gare de l'Est, Gare de Lyon and Montparnasse – plus popular nightspots such as Bastille, the Champs-Élysées, Pigalle and St-Germain. Look for blue *N* or 'Noctilien' signs.

Short bus rides (ie rides in one or two bus zones) cost one metro/bus ticket (€1.70 or €1.80 direct from the driver); longer rides re-quire two. Remember to cancel *(oblitérer)* single-journey tickets in the *composteur* (cancelling machine) next to the driver.

METRO & RER Paris' underground network consists of the 14-line metro and the RER, a network of suburban train lines. Each metro train is known by the name of its terminus. The last metro train on each line begins sometime between 12.35am and 1.04am, before starting up again around 5.30am.

TOURIST PASSES The Mobilis card allows unlimited travel for one day in two to six zones (€6.10 to €17.30) on the metro, the RER, buses, trams and the Montmartre funicular; while the Paris Visite pass allows unlimited travel (including to/from airports) plus discounted entry to museums and activities and costs €8.80/14.40/19.60/28.30 for one to three zones for one/two/three/five days.

TRAVEL PASSES Navigo (www.navigo.fr, in French), like London's Oyster or Hong Kong's Octopus cards, consists of a weekly, monthly or yearly unlimited pass that can be recharged at Navigo machines in most metro stations; swipe the card across the electronic panel to go through turnstiles. Standard Navigo passes, available to anyone with an address in Île de France, are free but take up to three weeks to be issued. Otherwise pay €5 for a Nagivo Dé-couverte (Navigo Discovery) card, issued on the spot. Both require a passport photo and can be recharged for periods of one week or more.

Otherwise, weekly tickets (*coupon hebdomadaire*) cost €17.20 for zones 1 and 2, valid Monday to Sunday; monthly tickets (*coupon mensuel;* €56.60 for zones 1 and 2) run from the first day of the month.

Taxi

The flag fall is €2.10, plus €0.89 per kilometre within the city limits from 10am and 5pm Monday to Saturday (Tarif A; white light on meter), and €1.14 per kilometre from 5pm to 10am, all day Sunday, and public holidays (Tarif B; orange light on meter).

Central taxi switchboard (📞01 45 30 30 30)

Alpha Taxis (📞01 45 85 85 85; www.alpha taxis.com)

Taxis Bleus (📞01 49 36 29 48, 08 91 70 10 10; www.taxis-bleus.com)

Taxis G7 (📞01 47 39 47 39; www.taxisg7.fr, in French).

AROUND PARIS

Bordered by five rivers – the Epte, Aisne, Eure, Yonne and Marne – the area around Paris looks rather like a giant island, and indeed is known as Île de France. Centuries ago this was where French kings retreated to extravagant chateaux in Versailles and Fontainebleau. These days such royal castles have been joined by a kingdom of an altogether different kind.

Disneyland Paris

In 1992, Mickey Mouse, Snow White and chums set up shop on reclaimed sugar-beet fields 32km east of Paris at a cost of €4.6 billion. Though not quite as over-the-top as its American cousin, France's Disneyland packs in the crowds nonetheless.

The main **Disneyland Park** (🕙9am-11pm summer, 10am-8pm Mon-Fri, 9am-8pm Sat & Sun winter) comprises five *pays* (lands), including an idealised version of an American **Main St**, a recreation of the American Wild West in **Frontierland** with the legendary Big Thunder Mountain ride, futuristic **Discoveryland**, and the exotic-themed **Adventureland**, where you'll find the Pirates of the Caribbean and the spiralling 360-degrees roller coaster, Indiana Jones and the Temple of Peril. Pinocchio, Snow White and other fairy-tale characters come to life in candy-coated heart of the park, **Fantasyland**.

Adjacent **Walt Disney Studios Park** (🕙9am-6pm summer, 10am-6pm Mon-Fri, 9am-6pm Sat & Sun winter) has a sound stage, backlot and animation studios illustrating how films, TV programs and cartoons are produced.

Standard admission fees at **Disneyland Resort Paris** (www.disneylandparis.com; adult/child €52/44) only cover one park – to visit both buy a one-day pass costing €65/57 per adult/child. Multiday equivalents are also available, as are a multitude of special offers and accommodation/transport packages.

Marne-la-Vallée/Chessy, Disneyland's RER station, is served by line A4; trains run every 15 minutes or so from central Paris (€6.55, 35 to 40 minutes) with the last train back to Paris just after midnight. By car follow route A4 from Porte de Bercy (direction Metz-Nancy) and take exit 14.

Versailles

POP 88,930

The prosperous and leafy suburb of Versailles, 28km southwest of Paris, is the site of France's grandest and most famous chateau. It served as the kingdom's political capital and the seat of the royal court for more than a century – from 1682 until 1789 when Revolutionary mobs massacred the palace guard and dragged Louis XVI and Marie Antoinette back to Paris, where they eventually had their heads separated from their shoulders.

Dodge the worst of the crowds by visiting early morning or late afternoon, and buy your ticket in advance online (www.chateauversailles.fr) or from Fnac. Queues are longest on Tuesday (when many of Paris' museums are closed) and on Sunday.

SUMMER MAGIC

The palace gardens' largest fountains are the 17th-century **Bassin de Neptune** (Neptune's Fountain), a dazzling mirage of 99 spouting gushers 300m north of the palace. Watch them 'dance' in all their glory during summer's **Grandes Eaux Musicales** (adult/child €8/6; 🕙11am-noon & 3.30-5pm Tue, Sat & Sun Apr-Sep) or after-dark **Grandes Eaux Nocturnes** (adult/child €21/17; 🕙9-11.30pm Sat & Sun mid-Jun–Aug). Both 'dancing water' displays set to baroque and other classical music of the era are nothing sort of magical.

◉ Sights

Château de Versailles PALACE

(www.chateauversailles.fr; adult/child & EU resident under 26yr €15/free; ⊙9am-6.30pm Tue-Sun summer, 9am-5.30pm Tue-Sun winter) Built in the mid-17th century by Louis XIV to project the absolute power of the French monarchy, Versailles palace was jointly designed by the architect Louis Le Vau, the painter and interior designer Charles Le Brun, and the landscape artist André Le Nôtre. It's a fabulous monument to the wealth and ambition of the French aristocracy.

The 580m-long palace is split into several wings, each with an astonishing array of grand halls, wood-panelled corridors and sumptuous bedchambers, including the **Grand Appartement du Roi** (King's Suite) and **Galerie des Glaces** (Hall of Mirrors), a 75m-long ballroom with 17 huge mirrors on one side. Outside are vast **landscaped gardens**, filled with canals, pools and neatly trimmed box hedges, and two outbuildings, the **Grand Trianon** and the **Petit Trianon**.

Standard admission includes an English-language audioguide and entry to the state apartments, the chapel, **Appartements du Dauphin et de la Dauphine** and various galleries. A **Passeport** (adult/child & EU resident under 26yr €18-25/free) includes the same, plus the two Trianons and, in high season, the Hameau de la Reine and the Grandes Eaux Musicales fountain displays.

The current €400-million restoration project is Versailles' most ambitious yet and until 2020 at least a part of the palace is likely to be clad in scaffolding.

❶ Getting There & Away

RER line C5 (€2.95, every 15 minutes) goes from Paris' Left Bank RER stations to Versailles-Rive Gauche, 700m southeast of the chateau.

SNCF operates up to 70 trains daily from Paris' Gare St-Lazare (€3.70) to Versailles-Rive Droite, 1.2km from the chateau. Versailles-Chantiers is served by half-hourly SNCF trains daily from Gare Montparnasse (€2.95); trains continue to Chartres (€11.50, 30 to 60 minutes).

Chartres

POP 45,600

The magnificent 13th-century cathedral of Chartres, crowned by two very different spires – one Gothic, the other Romanesque – rises from rich farmland 88km southwest of Paris and dominates the medieval town. With its astonishing blue stained glass and other

ZOOM IN

To study the extraordinary detail of Chartres' cathedral close up, rent binoculars (€2) from Chartres **tourist office** (☑02 37 18 26 26; www.chartres-tourisme.com; place de la Cathédrale; ⊙9am-7pm Mon-Sat, 9.30am-5.30pm Sun summer, 10am-6pm Mon-Sat, 10am-1pm & 2.30-4.30pm Sun winter), across the square from the cathedral's main entrance.

treasures, France's best-preserved medieval basilica is a must-see.

◉ Sights

Cathédrale Notre Dame de Chartres

CHURCH

(www.diocese-chartres.com, in French; place de la Cathédrale; ⊙8.30am-7.30pm daily, to 10pm Tue, Fri & Sun summer) The 130m-long Chartres cathedral takes your breath away. The original Romanesque cathedral was devastated in a fire in 1194, but remnants of it remain in the **Portail Royal** (Royal Portal) and the 103m-high **Clocher Vieux** (Old Bell Tower, also known as the South Tower). The rest of the cathedral predominantly dates from the 13th century, including many of the 172 glorious **stained-glass windows**, which are renowned for the depth and intensity of their 'Chartres blue' tones.

A visit up the lacy Flamboyant Gothic, 112m-tall **Clocher Neuf** (New Bell Tower; adult/child €7/free, free to all 1st Sun of certain months; ⊙9.30am-12.30pm & 2-6pm Mon-Sat, 2-6pm Sun summer, to 5pm winter) rewards with superb views of the three-tiered flying buttresses and the 19th-century copper roof, turned green by verdigris.

❶ Getting There & Away

Some three dozen SNCF trains a day link Paris' Gare Montparnasse (€13.60, 55 to 70 minutes) with Chartres via Versailles-Chantiers (€11.50, 45 minutes to one hour).

LILLE, FLANDERS & THE SOMME

When it comes to culture, cuisine, beer, shopping and dramatic views of land and sea, the friendly Ch'tis (residents of France's northern tip) and their region compete with the best France has to offer: Flemish-style Lille, the cross-Channel shopping centre of Calais, and the moving battlefields and cemeteries of WWI.

Lille

POP 232,000

Lille (Rijsel in Flemish) may be the country's most underrated major city. In recent decades this once-grimy industrial metropolis has transformed itself – with generous government help – into a glittering and self-confident cultural and commercial hub. Highlights of the city include an attractive Old Town with a strong Flemish accent, three renowned art museums, stylish shopping and a cutting-edge, student-driven nightlife.

◎ Sights

Vieux Lille
OLD TOWN

Lille's Old Town, which begins just north of place du Général de Gaulle, is justly proud of its restored 17th- and 18th-century houses. Those along **rue de la Monnaie** house the city's chicest boutiques and the **Hospice Comtesse Museum** (32 rue de la Monnaie; adult €3.50; ⊙10am-12.30pm & 2-6pm, closed Mon morning & Tue), featuring mainly religious art.

Nearby, the 1652 **Vieille Bourse** (Old Stock Exchange; place du Général de Gaulle; Ⓜ Rihour) consists of 24 houses decorated with caryatids and cornucopia.

Palais des Beaux Arts
ART MUSEUM

(Fine Arts Museum; www.pba-lille.fr; place de la République; adult/child €5.50/free; ⊙2-6pm Mon, 10am-6pm Wed-Sun; Ⓜ République Beaux Arts) Lille's world-renowned fine-arts museum has a first-rate collection of 15th- to 20th-century paintings, including works by Rubens, Van Dyck and Manet.

La Piscine Musée d'Art et d'Industrie
ART MUSEUM

(www.roubaix-lapiscine.com; 23 rue de l'Espérance, Roubaix; adult/child €4.50/free; ⊙11am-6pm Tue-Thu, 11am-8pm Fri, 1-6pm Sat & Sun; Ⓜ Gare Jean Lebas) Housed in an art deco swimming pool (built 1927–32), this gallery 12km northeast of Gare Lille-Europe, showcases fine arts, applied arts and sculpture in a delightfully watery environment.

🛌 Sleeping

⎯TOP⎯ L'Hermitage Gantois
CHOICE

DESIGN HOTEL €€€

(☑03 20 85 30 30; www.hotelhermitagegantois. com; 224 rue de Paris; d €215-325; @ 🛜; Ⓜ Mairie

de Lille) We love the highly civilised atrium and 67 huge, luxurious rooms at this mix of Flemish-Gothic facade and refined ultra-modernist interiors. Starck accessories mingle with Louis XV–style chairs, and bathrooms sparkle with Carrara marble. The still-consecrated chapel was built in 1637.

Hôtel Brueghel
HOTEL €€

(☑03 20 06 06 69; www.hotel-brueghel.com; 5 parvis St-Maurice; d €89; 🛜; Ⓜ Gare Lille-Flandres) The 65 rooms here mix vaguely antique furnishings with modern styling, though they don't have as much Flemish charm as the lobby. Some south-facing rooms have sunny views of the adjacent church.

Hôtel du Moulin d'Or
HOTEL €€

(☑03 20 06 12 67; www.hotelmoulindor.com, in French; 15 rue du Molinel; d/tr €87/98; ❄🛜; Ⓜ Gare Lille-Flandres) Rich yellow and blue tones welcome you warmly to this family-run establishment with 14 rooms, some flowery, others striped. The cute little breakfast room feels like a B&B. No lift.

Auberge de Jeunesse
HOSTEL €

(☑03 20 57 08 94; www.hihostels.com; 12 rue Malpart; dm incl breakfast €18, d €37; ⊙Feb–mid-Dec; @🛜; Ⓜ Mairie de Lille) This central former maternity hospital has 163 beds in rooms for two to eight, kitchen facilities and free parking. A few doubles have en-suite showers. Lockout 11am to 3pm (4pm Friday to Sunday).

🍴 Eating

Keep an eye out for *estaminets* (traditional eateries) serving Flemish specialities such as *carbonnade* (beef braised with Flemish beer, spice bread and brown sugar).

ⓘ OLD TOWN EAT STREETS

» **Rue de Gand** Small, moderately priced French and Flemish restaurants.

» **Rue de la Monnaie** Quirky restaurants here and on neighbouring side streets.

» **Rue Royale** Ethnic cuisine (couscous, Japanese etc).

» **Rue Solférino** & **rue Masséna** Lively, student-dominated cheap eats near the Palais des Beaux-Arts.

Chez la Vieille　　　　　TRADITIONAL €

(☎03 28 36 40 06; 60 rue de Gand; mains €9.50-12; ⓢTue-Sat) One of the best places in Lille to tuck into Flemish specialities. Old-time prints, antiques and fresh hops hanging from the rafters create the ambience of a Flemish village c 1900. The vibe is informal but it's a good idea to call ahead.

À l'Huîtrière　　　　　SEAFOOD €€€

(☎03 20 55 43 41; www.huitriere.fr, in French; 3 rue des Chats Bossus; lunch menus €45; ⓢMon-Sat, lunch Sun Sep-Jul) On the 'Street of the Hunchback Cats', this sophisticated restaurant is as well known for its stunning art deco trappings – think sea-themed mosaics and stained glass – as for its fabulous seafood and wine cellar.

Meert　　　　　TEAROOM €

(www.meert.fr; 27 rue Esquermoise; ⓢ9.30am-7.30pm Tue-Fri, 9am-7.30pm Sat, 9am-1pm & 3-7pm Sun; ⓜRihr) Vanilla-flavoured *gaufres* (waffles; €2.30 each) are the speciality of this luxury tearoom-cum-pastry-and-sweets-shop, in the biz since 1761. Its adjacent **chocolate shop** (per kg €89) transports you to 1839.

ⓉⓄⓅ CHOICE **Marché de Wazemmes**

　　　　　FOOD MARKET €

(place de la Nouvelle Aventure; ⓢ8am-2pm Tue-Thu, 8am-8pm Fri & Sat, 8am-3pm Sun & holidays; ⓜGambetta) Beloved foodie space, 1.7km southwest of the tourist office in Lille's working-class quarter of Wazemmes.

🍷 Drinking

Think two key nightlife zones: Vieux Lille's small, chic bars, and the student-oriented bars around rue Masséna and rue Solférino. In summer, pavement cafe terraces render

---

DON'T MISS

NORTHERN BREWS

French Flanders brews some truly excellent *bière blonde* (lager) and *bière ambrée* (amber beer) with an alcohol content of up to 8.5%. Brands that give the Belgian brewers a run for their money include 3 Monts, Amadeus, Ambre des Flandres, Brasserie des 2 Caps, Ch'ti, Enfants de Gayant, Grain d'Orge, Hellemus, Jenlain, L'Angellus, La Wambrechies, Moulins d'Ascq, Raoul, Septante 5, St-Landelin, Triple Secret des Moines and Vieux Lille.

---

place de la Théâtre in front of the opera prime beer-sipping terrain.

L'Illustration Café　　　　　BAR, CAFE

(www.bar-lillustration.com, in French; 18 rue Royale; ⓢ12.30pm-3am Mon-Sat, 2pm-3am Sun) Adorned with art nouveau woodwork and changing exhibits by local painters, this laid-back bar attracts artists, musicians, budding intellectuals and teachers in the mood to read, exchange weighty ideas – or just shoot the breeze. The mellow soundtrack mixes Western classical with jazz, French *chansons* and African beats.

ℹ Information

Tourist office (☎from abroad 03 59 57 94 00, in France 08 91 56 20 04; www.lilletourism. com; place Rihour; ⓢ9.30am-6.30pm Mon-Sat, 10am-noon & 2-5pm Sun; ⓜRihr) Sells the Lille City Pass (one-/two-/three-day €20/30/45) covering Lille's museums and public transport.

ℹ Getting There & Away

Eurolines (☎08 92 89 90 91; www.eurolines. com; 23 parvis St-Maurice; ⓜGare Lille-Flandres) Serves cities such as Brussels (€17, 1½ hours), Amsterdam (€42, five hours) and London (€35, 5½ hours; by day via the Channel Tunnel, at night by ferry). Buses depart from blvd de Leeds near Gare Lille-Europe.

Lille has two train stations: Gare Lille-Flandres for regional services and Paris' Gare du Nord (€40 to €55, one hour, 14 to 18 daily), and ultramodern Gare Lille-Europe for all other trains, including Eurostars to London and TGVs/Eurostars to Brussels-Nord (€18 to €26, 35 minutes, 12 daily).

ℹ Getting Around

Lille's two metro lines, tramways and bus lines are run by **Transpole** (www.transpole.fr). Tickets (€1.30) are sold on buses but must be purchased (and validated in the orange posts) *before* boarding a metro or tram. A Pass Journée (all-day pass) costs €3.60.

Calais

POP 76,200

As Churchill might have put it, 'Never in the field of human tourism have so many travellers passed through a place and so few stopped to visit'. Over 15 million people pass through Calais en route to the cross-Channel ferries, but few explore the town itself – it's worth it, if only to see Rodin's famous sculpture, *The Burghers of Calais*.

Sights

Burghers of Calais
SCULPTURE

By the time you read this, it should be possible to ride a lift up to the top of the Unesco World Heritage–listed **belfry** crowning Calais' Flemish Renaissance-style **town hall** (1911–25). Inside is the town's main sight: Rodin's *Les Bourgeois de Calais* (The Burghers of Calais; 1895), honouring six local citizens who, in 1347, held off the besieging English forces for more than eight months. Edward III was so impressed he ultimately spared the Calaisiens and their six leaders.

TOP CHOICE Musée de la Dentelle et de la Mode
LACE MUSEUM

(www.cite-dentelle.fr; 135 quai du Commerce; €5; ☺10am-5 or 6pm Wed-Mon) Watch a century-old mechanical loom with 3500 vertical threads and 11,000 horizontal ones bang, clatter and clunk according to instructions given by perforated Jacquard cards at Calais' cutting-edge Lace and Fashion Museum.

Sleeping

TOP CHOICE Hôtel Meurice
HOTEL €€

(☎03 21 34 57 03; www.hotel-meurice. fr; 5-7 rue Edmond Roche; d €85-150; @☎) Meurice is a veteran hotel with 39 rooms and plenty of atmosphere thanks to its grand lobby staircase, antique furnishings, Hemingwayesque bar and breakfast room with garden views.

Auberge de Jeunesse
HOSTEL €

(☎03 21 34 70 20; www.auberge-jeunesse-calais. com; av Maréchal de Lattre de Tassigny; s/d incl breakfast €26/38; ☎) Modern, well equipped and just 200m from the beach. Take bus 3, 5 or 9.

Eating

Restaurants ring place d'Armes and are plentiful just south of there along rue Royale.

Histoire Ancienne
BISTRO €

(☎03 21 34 11 20; www.histoire-ancienne.com; 20 rue Royale; lunch/dinner menus from €13/19; ☺Tue-Sat, lunch Mon) Specialising in French and regional dishes, some grilled over an open wood fire, this 1930s Paris-style bistro has treats such as *escargots à l'ail* (garlic snails).

Information

Tourist office (☎03 21 96 62 40; www.calais -cotedopale.com; 12 blvd Georges Clemenceau; ☺9 or 10am-6 or 7pm, closed Sun mid-Sep–Mar)

Getting There & Around

Boat

Daily some 40-odd car ferries from Dover dock at Calais' bustling car-ferry terminal, 1.5km northeast of place d'Armes.

P&O Ferries Calais town centre (www.poferries .com; 41 place d'Armes); car-ferry terminal (☺6am-10pm); car-ferry car park (☺24hr) The only ferry company that still takes foot passengers across the Strait of Dover.

SeaFrance Calais town centre (www.seafrance. com; 2 place d'Armes); car-ferry car park (☺24hr)

Shuttle buses (€2, hourly 11am to 6 or 7pm) link Gare Calais-Ville (train station) and place d'Armes (stopping in front of Café de la Tour) with the car-ferry terminal. Departure times are posted at stops.

Bus

Ligne BCD (☎08 00 62 00 59; www.ligne-bcd. com, in French) links Calais' train station (hours posted) with Dunkirk (€8, 50 minutes, 11 daily Monday to Friday, three on Saturday).

Car & Motorcycle

To reach the Channel Tunnel's vehicle-loading area at Coquelles, 6km southwest of the town centre, follow the road signs on the A16 to 'Tunnel Sous La Manche' (exit 42).

Train

Calais has two train stations: **Gare Calais-Ville**, 650m south of main square place d'Armes; and TGV station **Gare Calais-Fréthun**, 10km southwest near the Channel Tunnel entrance. Trains and shuttle buses (€2, free with train ticket) link the two.

Gare Calais-Ville serves Amiens (€24, 2½ to 3½ hours, six to eight daily), Boulogne (€7.50, 30 minutes, up to 19 daily), Dunkirk (€8, 50 minutes, two to five Monday to Saturday) and Lille-Flandres (€16, 1¼ hours, eight to 19 daily).

Gare Calais-Fréthun is served by TGVs to Paris' Gare du Nord (€41 to €62, 1½ hours, three to six daily) and Eurostars to London St-Pancras (€149, one hour, three daily).

Dunkirk
POP 69,500

Made famous and flattened almost simultaneously in 1940, Dunkirk (Dunkerque) was unfortunately rebuilt during one of the most uninspired periods in Western architecture. Admire a spectacular view of it from the 15th-century, 58m-high **belfry** (adult €2.90) housing the **tourist office** (☎03 28 66 79 21; www.lesdunesdeflandre.fr; rue de l'Amiral Ronarc'h);

FRANCE DUNKIRK

CÔTE D'OPALE

For a dramatic and beautiful intro to France, head to the 40km of majestic cliffs, sand dunes and beaches between Calais and Boulogne. Known as the Côte d'Opale (Opal Coast) because of the ever-changing interplay of greys and blues in the sky and sea, it is a kaleidoscope of wind-buffeted coastal peaks, wide beaches and rolling farmland. The remains of Nazi Germany's Atlantic Wall, a chain of fortifications and gun emplacements built to prevent the Allied invasion that in the end took place in Normandy, stud the shore, much loved by British beach-goers since Victorian times.

Protected by the **Parc Naturel Régional des Caps et Marais d'Opale** (www.parc-opale.fr), the area is criss-crossed by hiking paths, including the **GR120 Littoral trail** (red-and-white trail markings) that snakes along the coast – except where the cliffs are in danger of collapse. Some trails are open to mountain bikers and those on horseback. Each village along the Côte d'Opale has at least one camping ground, and most have places to eat.

By car, the D940 offers some truly spectacular vistas – or hop aboard Inglard's bus 44, which links the string of villages between Calais and Boulogne.

its melodious, 50-bell carillon inside sounds every quarter-hour.

Ship-model lovers will enjoy this port city's **Musée Portuaire** (Harbour Museum; www.museeportuaire.com; 9 quai de la Citadelle; adult/family €5/13; ⊙10am-12.45pm & 1.30-6pm Wed-Mon), housed in a one-time tobacco warehouse. **Guided tours** (adult/family incl museum €10/15) take visitors aboard a lighthouse ship, a *peniche* (barge) and a three-masted training ship built for the German merchant marine in 1901.

Malo-les-Bains, 2km northeast of Dunkirk city centre, is a turn-of-the-20th-century seaside resort whose broad, sandy beach, **Plage des Alliés**, honours Allied troops evacuated to England during Operation Dynamo. Stretching east to the Belgian border, the **Dunes Flamandes** (Flemish Dunes) represent a unique ecosystem harbouring hundreds of plant species, including rare orchids. Tides permitting, walk or cycle along the wet sand or path from Malo-les-Bains to Leffrinckoucke, Zuydcoote and Bray-Dunes.

Most trains from Dunkirk's train station, 1km southwest of the tourist office, stop at Gare Lille-Flandres (€13, 30 to 80 minutes, up to 20 daily).

NORMANDY

Famous for cows, cider and Camembert, this largely rural region (www.normandie-tourisme.fr) is one of France's most traditional – and most visited thanks to world-renowned

sights such as the Bayeux Tapestry, historic D-Day beaches, Monet's garden at Giverny and spectacular Mont St Michel.

Rouen

POP 120,000

With its elegant spires, beautifully restored medieval quarter and soaring Gothic cathedral, the ancient city of Rouen is a Normandy highlight. Devastated several times during the Middle Ages by fire and plague, the city was later badly damaged by WWII bombing raids, but has been meticulously rebuilt over the last six decades. The city makes an ideal base for exploring the northern Normandy coast.

◉ Sights

Église Jeanne d'Arc　　　　CHURCH
(place du Vieux Marché) The old city's main thoroughfare, rue du Gros Horloge, runs from the cathedral west to **place du Vieux Marché**. Dedicated in 1979, the thrillingly bizarre Église Jeanne d'Arc, with its fish-scale exterior, marks the spot where 19-year-old Joan of Arc was burned at the stake in 1431.

Cathédrale Notre Dame　　　CATHEDRAL
(place de la Cathédrale; ⊙2-7pm Mon, 7.30am-7pm Tue-Sat, 8am-6pm Sun) Rouen's stunning Gothic cathedral, with its polished, brilliant-white facade, is the famous subject of a series of paintings by Monet. Its 75m-tall **Tour de Beurre** (Butter Tower) was financed by locals who donated to the cathedral in re-

turn for being allowed to eat butter during Lent – or so the story goes.

Musée des Beaux-Arts ART MUSEUM
(esplanade Marcel Duchamp; adult/child €5/free; ⏱10am-6pm Wed-Mon) Housed in a grand structure erected in 1870, Rouen's fine-arts museum features canvases by Caravaggio, Rubens, Modigliani, Pissarro, Renoir, Sisley (lots) and (of course) several works by Monet.

Musée Le Secq des Tournelles MUSEUM
(☑02 35 88 42 92; 2 rue Jacques Villon; adult/child €3/free; ⏱10am-1pm & 2-6pm Wed-Mon) Inside a desanctified 16th-century church, this riveting museum examines the blacksmith's craft.

🛏 Sleeping

Hôtel des Carmes HOTEL €
(☑02 35 71 92 31; www.hoteldescarmes.com, in French; 33 place des Carmes; d €49-65, tr €67-77; @🛜) This sweet little number has a dozen rooms with bright, quirky decor; some have cerulean-blue cloudscapes painted on the ceilings. Burn off some Camembert calories by taking one of the cheaper, 4th-floor rooms.

TOP CHOICE **Hôtel de Bourgtheroulde**
 HOTEL €€€
(☑02 35 14 50 50; www.hotelsparouen.com; 15 place de la Pucelle; r €215-380; ❄🛜🏊) This stunning conversion of an old private mansion brings a dash of glamour and luxury to Rouen's hotel scene. Rooms are

DON'T MISS

251

THE CIDER ROAD

Normandy's signposted 40km **Route du Cidre**, about 20km east of Caen, wends its way through the Pays d'Auge, a rural area of orchards, pastures, hedgerows, half-timbered farmhouses and stud farms, through picturesque villages such as Cambremer and Beuvron-en-Auge. Along the way, signs reading 'Cru de Cambremer' indicate the way to about 20 small-scale, traditional producers who are happy to show you their facilities and sell you their home-grown cider (€3 a bottle) and Calvados.

large, gorgeously designed and feature beautiful bathrooms.

Hôtel de la Cathédrale HOTEL €
(☑02 35 71 57 95; www.hotel-de-la-cathedrale.fr; 12 rue St-Romain; s €56-79, d €66-96, q €119; 🛜) Hiding behind a 17th-century half-timbered facade, this atmospheric hotel has 27 stylishly refitted rooms, mostly overlooking a quiet plant-filled courtyard.

Hôtel Dandy HOTEL €€
(☑02 35 07 32 00; www.hotels-rouen.net; 93 rue Cauchoise; d €80-105; 🛜) Decorated in a grand Louis XV style, this charming place has individually designed rooms brimming

WORTH A TRIP

KILLING FIELDS

The **Battle of the Somme**, a WWI Allied offensive waged northeast of Amiens, was planned with the goal of relieving the pressure on the beleaguered French troops at Verdun. On 1 July 1916, two-dozen divisions of British, Commonwealth and French troops went 'over the top' in a massive assault along a 34km front. But German positions proved virtually unbreachable, and on the first day alone 21,392 Allied troops were killed and another 35,492 were wounded.

By the time the offensive was called off in mid-November, some 1.2 million lives had been lost: the British had advanced just 12km, the French 8km. The Battle of the Somme has since become a symbol of the meaningless slaughter of war and its killing fields and cemeteries have since become a site of pilgrimage (see www.somme-battlefields.co.uk). The tourist offices in **Amiens** (☑03 22 71 60 50; www.amiens.com/tourisme) and **Arras** (☑03 21 51 26 95; www.ot-arras.fr) supply maps, guides and minibus tours.

Cheap, spartan but oozing soul are the dorm facilities in Arras at **Maison St-Vaast** (☑03 21 21 40 38; http://arras.catholique.fr/page-15065.html, in French; 103 rue d'Amiens; dm per person €21; 🛜). A convent in the 1600s and rebuilt after WWI, the atmospheric building has a lovely cloister and a 1920s chapel with stained glass and a frequently played pipe organ.

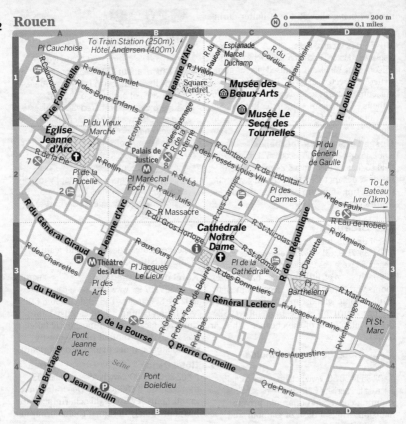

with character and is passionately run by a friendly family.

Hôtel Andersen　　HOTEL €
(☎02 35 71 88 51; www.hotelandersen.com; 4 rue Pouchet; s €45-56, d €56-63; ☎) Ensconced in an early-19th-century mansion, this quietly stylish hotel with old-world atmosphere, classical music and 15 spare but imaginative rooms is one of a half-dozen hotels around the train station.

✗ Eating

Little eateries crowd the north side of rue Martainville. For ethnic cuisine head two blocks south to rue des Augustins. More restaurants can be found along rue de Fontenelle (a block west of Église Jeanne d'Arc), and a few blocks east along rue Ecuyère.

TOP CHOICE **Les Nymphéas**　　NORMAN €€
(☎02 35 89 26 69; www.lesnympheas -rouen.com, in French; 7-9 rue de la Pie; menus €30-70; ☺Tue-Sat) Its formal table settings arrayed under 16th-century beams, this fine restaurant serves cuisine based on fresh local ingredients, giving a rich Norman twist to dishes such as farm-raised wild duck, scallops and lobster.

Gill　　GASTRONOMIC €€
(☎02 35 71 16 14; www.gill.fr; 8-9 quai de la Bourse; menus €35-92; ☺Tue-Sat) *The* place to go in Rouen for French cuisine of the highest order, served in an ultrachic, modern space. Specialities include Breton lobster, scallops with truffles, Rouen-style pigeon and, for dessert, *millefeuille à la vanille*.

Le P'tit Bec　　BISTRO €
(☎02 35 07 63 33; www.leptitbec.com, in French; 182 rue Eau de Robec; menus €13-15.50; ☺lunch Mon-Sat, dinner Fri & Sat, also open dinner Tue-Thu Jun-Aug; ☑) The down-to-earth menu here is stuffed with pasta, salads, *œufs cocottes* (eggs with grated cheese baked in cream),

Rouen

⊙ Top Sights

Cathédrale Notre Dame	C3
Église Jeanne d'Arc	A2
Musée des Beaux-Arts	C1
Musée Le Secq des Tournelles	C1

🛏 Sleeping

1	Hôtel Dandy	A1
2	Hôtel de Bourgtheroulde	A2
3	Hôtel de la Cathédrale	C3
4	Hôtel des Carmes	C2

🍴 Eating

5	Gill	B4
6	Le P'tit Bec	D2
7	Les Nymphéas	A2
8	Pascaline	B2

several vegetarian options and homemade desserts. Its summer terrace sits on one of Rouen's most picturesque side streets.

Pascaline　　　　　　　　BISTRO €
(☎02 35 89 67 44; 5 rue de la Poterne; mains €10-20) A top spot for a great-value lunch, this bustling bistro serves up traditional French cuisine in typically Parisian surroundings. Live piano nightly and jazz on Thursdays.

ℹ Information

Tourist office (☎02 32 08 32 40; www.rouen tourisme.com; 25 place de la Cathédrale; ⊙9am-7pm Mon-Sat, 9.30am-12.30pm & 2-6pm Sun) Hotel reservations cost €3; audioguides (€5).

ℹ Getting There & Away

TRAIN Some direct train services from **Gare Rouen-Rive Droite** (rue Jeanne d'Arc):

Amiens €18.20, 1¼ hours, four or five daily.
Caen €23.30, 1½ hours, eight to 10 daily.
Dieppe €10.40, 45 minutes, up to 16 daily.
Le Havre €13.60, 50 minutes, 10 to 18 daily.
Paris St-Lazare €20.50, 1¼ hours, up to 25 daily.

Bayeux

POP 14,350

Bayeux has become famous throughout the English-speaking world thanks to a 68m-long piece of painstakingly embroidered cloth: the 11th-century Bayeux Tapestry, whose 58 scenes vividly tell the story of the Norman invasion of England in 1066. The town is also one of the few in Normandy to have survived WWII practically unscathed, with a centre crammed with 13th- to 18th-century buildings, wooden-framed Norman-style houses, and a spectacular Norman Gothic cathedral.

⊙ Sights

TOP CHOICE **Bayeux Tapestry**　　　TAPESTRY
(www.tapisserie-bayeux.fr; rue de Nesmond; admission incl audioguide €7.80; ⊙9am-6.30pm mid-Mar–mid-Nov, to 7pm May-Aug, 9.30am-12.30pm & 2-6pm mid-Nov–mid-Mar) The world's most celebrated embroidery recounts the conquest of England from an unashamedly Norman perspective. Fifty-eight scenes fill the central canvas, and religious allegories and illustrations of everyday 11th-century life fill the borders. The final showdown at the Battle of Hastings is depicted in graphic fashion, complete with severed limbs and decapitated heads (along the bottom of scene 52); Halley's Comet, which blazed across the sky in 1066, appears in

FRANCE BAYEUX

DON'T MISS

MAISON DE CLAUDE MONET

Monet's home for the last 43 years of his life is now the delightful **Maison et Jardins de Claude Monet** (☎02 32 51 28 21; www.fondation-monet.com; adult/child €6/3.50; ⊙9.30am-6pm Apr-Oct), where you can view the Impressionist's pastel-pink house and famous gardens with lily pond, Japanese bridge draped in purple wisteria, and so on. Early to late spring, daffodils, tulips, rhododendrons, wisteria and irises bloom in the flowery gardens, followed by poppies and lilies. By June, nasturtiums, roses and sweet peas are in flower, while September is the month to see dahlias, sunflowers and hollyhocks.

The gardens are in Giverny, 66km southeast of Rouen. Several trains (€10.10, 40 minutes) leave Rouen before noon; with hourly return trains between 5pm and 10pm (9pm Sat). From Paris' Gare St-Lazare two early-morning trains run to Vernon (€12.50, 50 minutes), 7km to the west of Giverny, from where **shuttle buses** (☎08 25 07 60 27; www.mobiregion.net; €4 return) shunt passengers to Giverny.

scene 32. Scholars believe the 68.3m-long tapestry was commissioned by Bishop Odo of Bayeux, William the Conquerer's half-brother, for the opening of Bayeux' cathedral in 1077. For an animated version of the Bayeux Tapestry, check out David Newton's creative short film on YouTube.

Musée Mémorial de la Bataille de Normandie
WAR MUSEUM

(Battle of Normandy Memorial Museum; blvd Fabien Ware; adult/student €6.50/3.80; ⊗9.30am-6.30pm May-Sep, 10am-12.30pm & 2-6pm Oct-Apr) Using well-chosen photos, personal accounts, dioramas and wartime objects, this first-rate museum offers an excellent introduction to WWII in Normandy. Don't miss the 25-minute film on the Battle of Normandy, screened in English up to five times daily. Nearby, the Bayeux War Cemetery (blvd Fabien Ware) contains the graves of 4848 soldiers from the UK and 10 other countries (including Germany).

🛌 Sleeping

Family Home
HOSTEL €

(☑02 31 92 15 22; 39 rue Général de Dais; dm/s €19/30) One of France's most charming hostels, this place sports a 17th-century dining room, a delightful 16th-century courtyard, and 80 beds in rooms for one to four people. Check in any time of day – if reception isn't staffed, phone and someone will pop by.

Château de Bellefontaine
CHATEAU HOTEL €€

(☑02 31 22 00 10; www.hotel-bellefontaine.com; 49 rue de Bellefontaine; d €125-150; 🛰) Swans and a bubbling brook welcome you to this majestic 18th-century chateau, surrounded by a 2-hectare private park 1.5km southeast of town. Decor mixes tradition with modernity, and the rural location couldn't be more pastoral.

Hôtel Reine Mathilde
HOTEL €

(☑02 31 92 08 13; www.hotel-bayeux-reinemathilde. fr; 23 rue Larcher; d €60-63, tr/q €73/85; 🛰) Located above a bustling cafe, this charming little hotel is an excellent bet, right in the centre of town. Rooms, smallish but comfortable, are named after Norman folk of yore.

🍴 Eating

Rue St-Jean and rue St-Martin are home to cheap eateries and food shops. Appropriately, rue des Cuisiniers (north of the cathedral) is another handy, restaurant-busy street. Be

DON'T MISS

CAEN MÉMORIAL

Caen's hi-tech, hugely impressive Mémorial – Un Musée pour la Paix (Memorial – A Museum for Peace; www.memorial-caen.fr; Esplanade Général Eisenhower; adult/child €17.50/free; ⊗9am-7pm Mar-Oct, 9.30am-6pm Tue-Sun Nov-Feb) uses sound, lighting, film, animation and lots of exhibits to graphically explore and evoke the events of WWII, D-Day landings and the ensuing Cold War. Tickets remain valid for 24 hours. The museum also runs D-Day beach tours.

sure to sample local speciality *cochon de Bayeux* (Bayeux-style pork).

La Reine Mathilde
CAKE SHOP €

(47 rue St-Martin; cakes from €2.50; ⊗8.30am-7.30pm Tue-Sun) A sumptuous, c 1900-style patisserie and *salon de thé* (tearoom) that's ideal if you've got a hankering for something sweet. There's seating here, making it prime breakfast and afternoon-tea terrain.

La Rapière
NORMAN €€

(☑02 31 21 05 45; 53 rue St-Jean; menus €15-33.50; ⊗Fri-Tue) Housed in a late-1400s mansion held together by its original oak beams, this restaurant specialises in hearty home cooking – the *timbale de pêcheur* (fisherman's stew) is served up piping hot in a cast-iron pan. For dessert, an excellent option is *trou normand* (apple sorbet with a dash of Calvados).

ℹ️ Information

Tourist office (☑02 31 51 28 28; www.bayeux -bessin-tourism.com; pont St-Jean; ⊗9.30am-12.30pm & 2-6pm)

ℹ️ Getting There & Away

Trains link Bayeux with Caen (€5.80, 20 minutes, up to 13 daily), from where there are connections to Paris' Gare St-Lazare (€31.20, two hours) and Rouen (€22.70, 1½ hours).

D-Day Beaches

The D-Day landings, code-named 'Operation Overlord', were the largest military operation in history. Early on 6 June 1944, Allied troops stormed ashore along 80km of beaches north of Bayeux, code-named (from west to east) Utah, Omaha, Gold, Juno and Sword. The landings on D-Day – called Jour J in French – were followed by the Battle of Normandy, which ultimately led to the liberation of Europe from Nazi occupation. Memorial museums in Caen (see the boxed text, p254) and Bayeux (p254) provide a comprehensive overview, and there are many small D-Day museums dotted along the coast. For context, see www.normandiememoire.com and www.6juin1944.com.

The most brutal fighting on D-Day took place 15km northwest of Bayeux along the stretch of coastline now known as **Omaha Beach**, today a glorious stretch of fine golden sand partly lined with sand dunes and summer homes. **Circuit de la Plage d'Omaha**, trail-marked with a yellow stripe, is a self-guided tour along the beach, surveyed from a bluff above by the huge **Normandy American Cemetery & Memorial** (www.abmc.gov; Colleville-sur-Mer; ⊙9am-5pm). Featured in the opening scenes of Steven Spielberg's *Saving Private Ryan,* this is the largest American cemetery in Europe.

Tours

Mémorial   MINIBUS
(www.memorial-caen.fr; tours €69) Excellent year-round minibus tours (four to five hours). Rates include entry to Mémorial. Book online.

Normandy Sightseeing Tours
                                     WALKING, MINIBUS
(☑02 31 51 70 52; www.normandywebguide.com) Half-/full-day tours (€40/75) of various beaches and cemeteries.

ⓘ Getting There & Away

Bus Verts (www.busverts.fr, in French) bus 70 (two or three daily Monday to Saturday, more in summer) goes northwest from Bayeux to Colleville-sur-Mer and Omaha Beach (€2.15, 35 minutes).

Mont St-Michel

On a rocky island opposite the coastal town of Pontorson, connected to the mainland by a narrow causeway, the sky-scraping turrets of the abbey of **Mont St-Michel** (☑02 33 89 80 00; www.monuments-nationaux.fr; adult/child incl guided tour €8.50/free; ⊙9am-7pm May-Aug, 9.30am-6pm Sep-Apr, last entry 1hr before closing) provide one of France's iconic sights. The surrounding bay is notorious for its fast-rising tides: at low tide the Mont is surrounded by

bare sand for miles around; at high tide, just six hours later, the bay, causeway and nearby car parks can be submerged.

From the **tourist office** (☑02 33 60 14 30; www.ot-montsaintmichel.com; ⊙9am-7pm Jul & Aug, 9am-12.30pm & 2-6.30pm Mon-Sat, 9am-noon & 2-6pm Sun Apr-Jun & Sep, shorter hours winter), at the base of the mount, a cobbled street winds up to the **Église Abbatiale** (Abbey Church), incorporating elements of both Norman and Gothic architecture. Other notable sights include the arched **cloître** (cloister), the barrel-roofed **réfectoire** (dining hall), and the Gothic **Salle des Hôtes** (Guest Hall), dating from 1213. A one-hour tour is included with admission; English tours run hourly in summer, twice daily (11am and 3pm) in winter. In July and August, Monday to Saturday, there are illuminated *nocturnes* (night-time visits) with music from 7pm to 10pm.

Bus 6 (☑08 00 15 00 50; www.mobi50.com, in French) links Mont St-Michel with Pontorson (€2, 13 minutes), from where there are two to three daily trains to/from Bayeux (€20.80, 1¾hr) and Cherbourg (€25.90, three hours).

BRITTANY

Brittany is for explorers. Its wild, dramatic coastline, medieval towns, thick forests and eeriest stone circles this side of Stonehenge make a trip here well worth the detour from the beaten track. This is a land of prehistoric mysticism, proud tradition and culinary wealth, where locals still remain fiercely independent, where Breton culture (and cider) is celebrated and where Paris feels a very long way away indeed.

KNOW THE TIDE

Check the *horaire des marées* (tide table) at the tourist office. When the tide is out, you can walk all the way around Mont St-Michel, a distance of about 1km. Stray too far from the Mont and you risk getting stuck in wet sand – from which Norman soldiers are depicted being rescued in one scene of the Bayeux Tapestry – or being overtaken by the incoming tide, providing your next of kin with a great cocktail-party story.

Quimper

POP 67,250

Small enough to feel like a village – with its slanted half-timbered houses and narrow cobbled streets – and large enough to buzz as the troubadour of Breton culture, Quimper (pronounced *kam-pair*) is the thriving capital of Finistère (meaning 'land's end'; in Breton *Penn ar Bed*, meaning 'head of the world').

◎ Sights

Most of Quimper's historic architecture is concentrated in a tight triangle formed by place Médard, rue Kéréon, rue des Gentilhommes and its continuation, rue du Sallé, to place au Beurre.

Cathédrale St-Corentin   CHURCH
(☺9.30am–noon & 1.30–6.30pm) At the centre of the city is the cathedral with its distinctive

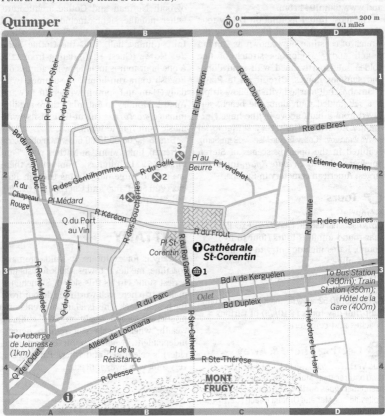

Quimper

FRANCE BRITTANY

kink, said to symbolise Christ's inclined head as he was dying on the cross. Construction began in 1239 but the cathedral's dramatic twin spires weren't added until the 19th century. High on the west facade, look out for an equestrian statue of King Gradlon, the city's mythical 5th-century founder.

Musée Départemental Breton   MUSEUM
(1 rue du Roi Gradlon; adult/child €4/free; ☺9am–6pm daily) Beside the cathedral, recessed

THE MORBIHAN MEGALITHS

Pre-dating Stonehenge by about a hundred years, **Carnac** comprises the world's greatest concentration of megalithic sites. There are more than 3000 of these upright stones scattered across the countryside between **Carnac-Ville** and **Locmariaquer** village, most of which were erected between 5000 BC and 3500 BC. No one's quite sure what purpose these sites served, although theories abound. A sacred site? Phallic fertility cult? Or maybe a celestial calendar? Even more mysterious is the question of their construction – no one really has the foggiest idea how the builders hacked and hauled these vast granite blocks several millennia before the wheel arrived in Brittany, let alone mechanical diggers.

Because of severe erosion, the sites are usually fenced off to allow vegetation to regrow. **Guided tours** (€4) run in French year-round and in English at 3pm Wednesday, Thursday and Friday early July to late August. Sign up at the **Maison des Mégalithes** (☑02 97 52 89 99; rte des Alignements; ⊙9am-8pm Jul & Aug, to 5.15pm Sep-Apr, to 7pm May & Jun). Opposite, the largest menhir field – with no fewer than 1099 stones – is the **Alignements du Ménec**, 1km north of Carnac-Ville. From here, the D196 heads northeast for about 1.5km to the **Alignements de Kermario**. Climb the stone observation tower midway along the site to see the alignment from above. Another 500m further on are the **Alignements de Kerlescan**, while the **Tumulus St-Michel**, 400m northeast of the Carnac-Ville tourist office, dates back to at least 5000 BC.

For background, Carnac's **Musée de Préhistoire** (10 place de la Chapelle, Carnac-Ville; adult/child €5/2.50; ⊙10am-6pm) chronicles life in and around Carnac from the Palaeolithic and neolithic eras to the Middle Ages.

behind a magnificent stone courtyard, this museum showcases Breton history, furniture, costumes, crafts and archaeology in a former bishop's palace.

🛏 Sleeping

Hôtel Manoir des Indes MANOR HOUSE €€

(☑02 98 55 48 40; www.manoir-hoteldesindes. com; 1 allée de Prad ar C'hras; s €105-150, d €150-170; ⊛❄❅) This stunning hotel conversion, located in an old manor house just a short drive from the centre of Quimper, has been restored with the original world-traveller owner in mind. Decor is minimalist and modern with Asian objets d'art and lots of exposed wood.

Hôtel de la Gare HOTEL €

(☑02 98 90 00 81; www.hoteldelagarequimper. com; 17 av de la Gare; s/d €49/54; ❄) This cheap, friendly place opposite the train station is the best deal in town. There's a pleasant cafe feel to the lobby, free parking and a small courtyard garden.

Auberge de Jeunesse HOSTEL €

(☑02 98 64 97 97; www.fuaj.org/quimper; 6 av des Oiseaux; camping €6, dm incl breakfast from €12.70, sheets €3; ⊙Apr-Sep) Seasonal hostel with self-catering facilities.

🍴 Eating

Le Cosy Restaurant REGIONAL CUISINE €

(☑02 98 95 23 65; 2 rue du Sallé; mains €10-14.50; ⊙lunch Tue-Sat, dinner Wed, Fri & Sat) Make your way through the *épicerie* crammed with locally canned sardines, ciders and other Breton specialities to this eclectic dining room where you can tuck into top-quality gratins and *tartines*.

Crêperie La Krampouzerie CRÊPERIE €

(9 rue du Sallé; galettes €2-7; ⊙Tue-Sat, dinner Sun) Crêpes and galettes made from organic flours and regional ingredients like *algues d'Ouessant* (seaweed), Roscoff onions and homemade ginger caramel are king here. Tables on the square out front create a real street-party atmosphere.

Le Petit Gaveau BISTRO €

(☑02 98 64 29 86; 16 rue des Boucheries; mains €8-15 ⊙lunch Mon-Sat, dinner Wed-Sat) This sleek conversion of an old stone house plays host to simple yet excellent food. Live jazz Thursday to Saturday (€3 supplement).

ℹ Information

Tourist office (☑02 98 53 04 05; www. quimper-tourisme.com, in French; place de la Résistance; ⊙9.30am-12.30pm & 1.30-6.30pm)

ℹ Getting There & Away

CAT/Viaoo (www.viaoo29.fr) bus destinations include Brest (€6.50, 1¼ hours); **Le Coeur** (☏02 98 54 40 15) runs to Concarneau (€2, 45 minutes, seven to 10 daily).

Frequent trains serve Brest (€15.40, 1¼ hours), Rennes (€38, 2½ hours) and Paris' Gare Montparnasse (€74.80, 4¾ hours).

St-Malo

POP 50,200

The mast-filled port of fortified St-Malo is inextricably tied up with the deep briny blue: the town became a key harbour during the 17th and 18th centuries, functioning as a base for merchant ships and government-sanctioned privateers, and these days it's a busy cross-Channel ferry port and summertime getaway.

◉ Sights

Walking on top of the city's sturdy 17th-century ramparts (1.8km) affords fine views of the old walled city known as Intra-Muros ('within the walls') or Ville Close – access the ramparts from any of the city gates.

Cathédrale St-Vincent   CATHEDRAL
(place Jean de Châtillon; ☺9.30am-6pm) The city's centrepiece was constructed between the 12th and 18th centuries. The battle to liberate St-Malo destroyed around 80% of the old city during August 1944, and damage to the cathedral was particularly severe. A mosaic plaque on the floor of the nave marks the spot where Jacques Cartier received the blessing of the bishop of St-Malo before his 'voyage of discovery' to Canada in 1535.

Fort National   RUINS
(www.fortnational.com; adult/child €5/3; ☺Easter & Jun-Sep) From the city ramparts, spot the remains of St-Malo's former prison and the rocky islet of **Île du Grand Bé**, where the great St-Malo-born 18th-century writer Chateaubriand is buried. (You can walk across at low tide, but check the tide times with the tourist office.)

Musée du Château   HISTORY MUSEUM
(adult/child €5/2.80; ☺10am-noon & 2-6pm Apr-Sep, Tue-Sun Oct-Mar) Within **Château de St-Malo**, built by the dukes of Brittany in the 15th and 16th centuries, this museum looks at local cod fishing and photos of St-Malo after WWII.

Aquarium   AQUARIUM
(www.aquarium-st-malo.com; av Général Patton; adult/child €15.50/9.50; ☺10am-6pm Feb-Oct & Dec, to 8pm Jul & Aug) Allow around two hours to spend at St-Malo's excellent aquarium, 4km south of the city centre. It's a great wet-weather alternative for kids, with a minisubmarine descent and a *bassin tactile* (touch pool), where you can actually fondle sea creatures such as rays and turbot – and even a baby shark. Bus C1 from the train station passes by every half-hour.

⌖ Sleeping

Hôtel San Pedro   HOTEL €
(☏02 99 40 88 57; www.sanpedro-hotel.com; 1 rue Ste-Anne; s €52-54, d €63-73; ☏) Tucked at the back of the old city, the San Pedro has cool, crisp, neutral-toned decor with subtle splashes of colour, friendly service and superb sea views.

Camping Aleth   CAMPING GROUND €
(☏06 78 96 10 62; www.camping-aleth.com; allée Gaston Buy, St-Servan; €13.40 per 2-person tent; ☺May-Sep) Perched on a peninsula, Camping Aleth has panoramic 360-degree views and is close to beaches and some lively bars.

Auberge de Jeunesse Éthic Étapes   HOSTEL €
(☏02 99 40 29 80; www.centrevarangot.com; 37 av du Père Umbricht; dm incl breakfast €17.50-19.80; @) This efficient place has a self-catering kitchen and free sports facilities. Take bus C1 from the train station.

✗ Eating

Restaurants abound between Porte St-Vincent, the cathedral and the Grande Porte.

FRANCE BRITTANY

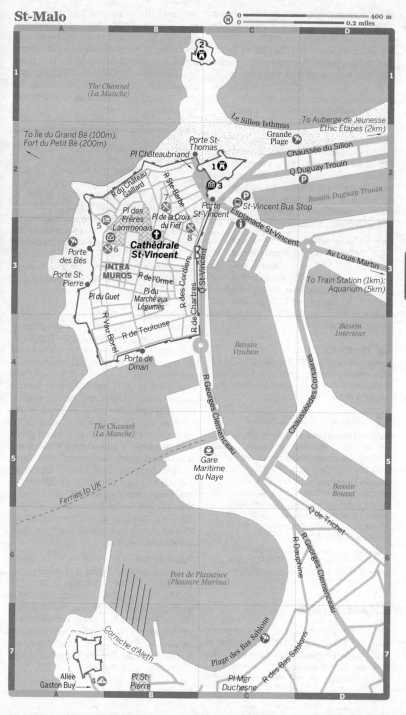

0   400 m
0   0.2 miles

A **B** **C** **D**

1

The Channel
(La Manche)

To Île du Grand Bé (100m);
Fort du Petit Bé (200m)

Le Sillon Isthmus

To Auberge de Jeunesse
Éthic Étapes (2km)

Grande
Plage

Chaussée du Sillon

Porte St-
Thomas

Pl Châteaubriand

2

Q Duguay Trouin

R du Château
Gaillard

R Ste-Barbe

7

Porte
St-Vincent

1

3

St-Vincent Bus Stop

Bassin Duguay Trouin

Pl des
Frères
Lammenais

Pl de la Croix
du Fief

8

Esplanade St-Vincent

5

6

**Cathédrale
St-Vincent**

Porte
des Bés

**INTRA
MUROS**

R de l'Orme

Q St-Vincent

R des Cordiers

Av Louis Martin

To Train Station (1km);
Aquarium (5km)

Porte St-
Pierre

Pl du Guet

Pl du
Marché aux
Légumes

R de Chartres

Bassin
Intérieur

R Vau Borel

R de Toulouse

3

Porte de
Dinan

R Georges Clemenceau

Bassin
Vauban

Bassin
Bouvet

4

The Channel
(La Manche)

Gare
Maritime
du Naye

Chaussée des Corsaires

5

Ferries to UK

Q de Trichet

R Georges Clemenceau

R Dauphine

6

Port de Plaisance
(Pleasure Marina)

7

Corniche d'Aleth

Plage des Bas Sablons

R des Bas Sablons

Allée
Gaston Buy

4

Pl St-
Pierre

Pl Mgr
Duchesne

TOP CHOICE **Restaurant Delaunay** GASTRONOMIC €€
(☎02 99 40 92 46; www.restaurant-delaunay.com; 6 rue Ste-Barbe; menus €28-65; ☑dinner Mon-Sat, closed Mon winter) Chef Didier Delaunay creates standout gastronomic cuisine within aubergine-painted walls at this superb yet unassuming-looking restaurant. The menu features succulent dishes both from the surf (Breton lobster's a speciality) and turf (tender lamb).

Le Chalut SEAFOOD €€
(☎02 99 56 71 58; 8 rue de la Corne-du-Cerf; menus €25-68; ☺Wed-Sun) This unremarkable-looking establishment is, in fact, St-Malo's most celebrated restaurant. Its kitchen overflows with the best the Breton coastline has to offer – buttered turbot, line-caught sea bass and scallops in champagne sauce.

La Bouche en Folie FRENCH, MODERN €
(☎06 72 49 08 89; 14 rue du Boyer; menus €12.90-29; ☺Wed-Sun) Well off the tourist trail, this sleek joint oozes Gallic gorgeousness and casts a modern spin on French staples – lamb is fricasséed with garlic and artichokes; monkfish is partnered by peas, black olives and asparagus.

ℹ Information

Tourist office (☎08 25 13 52 00, 02 99 56 64 43; www.saint-malo-tourisme.com; Esplanade St-Vincent; ☺9am-7.30pm Mon-Sat, 10am-6pm Sun Jul & Aug)

ℹ Getting There & Away

Brittany Ferries (www.brittany-ferries.com) sails between St-Malo and Portsmouth; **Condor Ferries** (www.condorferries.co.uk) runs to/from Poole and Weymouth via Jersey or Guernsey.

Keolis Emeraude (www.keolis-emeraude.com) has buses to/from Mont St-Michel (€3.30, 1½ hours, three to four daily). **Illenno** (www.illenoo-services.fr) has buses to Dinard (€1.70, 30 minutes, hourly) and Rennes (€3, one to 1½ hours, up to six daily).

TGV train services include to/from Rennes (€11.60, one hour) and Paris' Gare Montparnasse (€62.40, three hours, up to 10 daily).

CHAMPAGNE

Known in Roman times as Campania, meaning 'plain', the agricultural region of Champagne is synonymous these days with its world-famous bubbly. This multimillion-dollar industry is strictly protected under French law, ensuring that only grapes grown in designated Champagne vineyards can truly lay a claim to the hallowed title. The town of Épernay, 30km south of the regional capital of Reims, is the best place to head for *dégustation* (tasting), and a special 'Champagne Route' wends its way through the region's most celebrated vineyards.

Reims

POP 187,650

Over the course of a millennium (816 to 1825), some 34 sovereigns – among them two dozen kings – began their reigns in Reims' famed cathedral. Meticulously reconstructed after WWI and again following WWII, the city – whose name is pronounced something like 'rance' and is often anglicised as Rheims – is endowed with handsome pedestrian zones, well-tended parks, lively nightlife and a state-of-the-art tramway.

⊙ Sights

Cathédrale Notre Dame CHURCH
(www.cathedrale-reims.com, in French; place du Cardinal Luçon; ☺7.30am-7.30pm) Begun in 1211, this cathedral served for centuries as the venue for all French royal coronations – including that of Charles VII, who was crowned here on 17 July 1429, with Joan of Arc at his side. Heavily restored since WWI, the 139m-long cathedral is a Unesco World Heritage site. Its most famous features include the western facade's 12-petalled **great rose window**, a 15th-century wooden **astronomical clock** and several decorative windows by painter Marc Chagall. Climb the 250 steps (guided tour only) of the **cathedral tower** (adult/child €7/free; ☺at least hourly 10am-5pm Tue-Sat & Sun morning mid-Mar–Oct) for a stunning 360-degree view across France's flattest region; book tours next door at Palais du Tau.

Palais du Tau MUSEUM
(www.palais-du-tau.fr; 2 place du Cardinal Luçon; adult/child €7/free; ☺9.30am-12.30pm & 2-5.30pm Tue-Sun) This former archbishop's residence dating to 1690 was where French princes stayed before their coronations – and where they hosted sumptuous banquets afterwards. It is now a museum of truly exceptional statuary, liturgical objects and tapestries from the cathedral.

CENT SAVER

The **Reims City Card** (€15), sold at the tourist office, gets you a tour of a Champagne house, a DIY audioguide tour of the cathedral and admission into Reims' municipal museums.

TOP CHOICE Basilique St-Rémi   CHURCH

(place du Chanoine Ladame) This Benedictine abbey church, a Unesco World Heritage site, mixes Romanesque elements with early Gothic. It honours Bishop Remigius, who baptised Clovis and 3000 Frankish warriors in 498. The 12th-century-style chandelier has 96 candles, one for each year of the life of St Rémi, whose tomb lies in the choir. It's situated about 1.5km south-southeast of the tourist office; take the Citadine 1 or 2 or bus A or F to the St-Rémi stop.

🏃 Activities

The bottle-filled cellars (10°C to 12°C – bring a sweater!) of eight Reims-area Champagne houses can be visited by guided tour which ends, *naturellement,* with a tasting session.

Mumm   CHAMPAGNE HOUSE

(www.mumm.com; 34 rue du Champ de Mars; tours €10; ⊘9am-11am & 2-5pm Mar-Oct, Sat Nov-Feb) Mumm (pronounced 'moom', founded in 1827, is the world's third-largest Champagne producer. Engaging and edifying one-hour tours take you through cellars filled with 25 million bottles of bubbly. Tours with tutored tastings of special vintages cost €15 to €20.

Taittinger   CHAMPAGNE HOUSE

(www.taittinger.com; 9 place St-Nicaise; tours €10; ⊘9.30-11.50am & 2pm-4.20pm, closed Sat & Sun mid-Nov–mid-Mar) Parts of these cellars, 1.5km southeast of the cathedral, occupy 4th-century Roman stone quarries; other bits were excavated by 13th-century Benedictine monks.

🛏 Sleeping

Hôtel de la Paix   HOTEL €€

(✆03 26 40 04 08; www.bestwestern-lapaix-reims.com; 9 rue Buirette; d €155-205; ❄@🛜🏊) An island of serenity just steps from hopping place Drouet d'Erlon, this modern, Best Western–affiliated hostelry has 169 classy, comfortable rooms. Mellow out in the pool, Jacuzzi, *hammam* or Japanese courtyard garden.

Hôtel de la Cathédrale   HOTEL €

(✆03 26 47 28 46; www.hotel-cathedrale-reims.fr; 20 rue Libergier; s/d/q from €56/59/79; 🛜) Graciousness and a resident Yorkshire terrier greet guests at this hostelry, run by a music-loving couple. Rooms, spread over four floors (no lift) are smallish but pleasingly chintz; room 43 peeps at Basilique St-Rémi and the hills.

Latino Hôtel   HOTEL €

(✆03 26 47 48 89; www.latinocafe.fr, in French; 33 place Drouet d'Erlon; d €58-79, ste €130; ❄@🛜) Above a buzzy cafe filled with a Latin beat, this almost-boutique hotel features some fun furnishings, a warm welcome from the staff and pithy quotes from the great and the good (Gandhi, Oscar Wilde) sgraffitoed on the hall walls.

WORTH A TRIP

CULINARY CANCALE

No day trip from St-Malo is tastier than one to **Cancale** (www.cancale-tourisme.fr), an idyllic Breton fishing port 14km to the east that's famed for its offshore *parcs à huîtres* (oyster beds).

Learn all about oyster farming at the **Ferme Marine** (www.ferme-marine.com; corniche de l'Aurore; adult/child €6.80/3.60; ⊘mid-Feb–Oct, English guided tours 2pm Jul–mid-Sep) and shop for oysters fresh from their beds at the **Marché aux Huîtres** (12 oysters from €3.50, lunch platters €20; ⊘9am-6pm), the local oyster market atmospherically clustered around the Pointe des Crolles lighthouse.

Le Coquillage (✆02 99 89 64 76; www.maisons-de-bricourt.com; 1 rue Duguesclin; menus €26-90; ⊘Mar-Dec), the fabulous, Michelin three-star kitchen of superchef Olivier Roellinger, is housed in the equally fabulous Château Richeux, 4km south of Cancale. Crown the culinary experience with lunch or dinner here.

Keolis (www.keolis-emeraude.com) runs buses from St-Malo (€2, 30 minutes) that stop in Cancale at Port de la Houle, next to the pungent fish market.

FRANCE REIMS

✖ Eating

Place Drouet d'Erlon is lined with inexpensive restaurants and pub-cafes. More-discerning diners head to rue de Mars, adjacent to rue du Temple and place du Forum.

TOP CHOICE Le Foch   FISH €€
(📞03 26 47 48 22; www.lefoch.com; 37 blvd Foch; menus €31-80; ⏰Tue-Fri, dinner Sat, lunch Sun) Considered by many to be one of France's best fish restaurants, elegant Le Foch – holder of one Michelin star – serves up classic cuisine that's as beautiful as it is delicious.

Brasserie Le Boulingrin   BRASSERIE €€
(📞03 26 40 96 22; www.boulingrin.fr; 48 rue de Mars; menus €18-28; ⏰Mon-Sat) An old-time brasserie – the decor and zinc bar date to 1925 – whose ambience and cuisine make it an enduring favourite. September to June, the culinary focus is *fruits de mer* (seafood).

Côté Cuisine   TRADITIONAL, FRENCH €
(📞03 26 83 93 68; 43 blvd Foch; mains €11.80-22.50; ⏰Mon-Sat) A spacious, modern place with well-regarded traditional French cuisine – especially good value for lunch. Try to snag a table overlooking Sq Colbert.

❶ Information

Tourist office (www.reims-tourisme.com; 2 rue Guillaume de Machault; ⏰9am-7pm Mon-Sat, 10am-6pm Sun)

❶ Getting There & Away

Direct trains link Reims with Épernay (€6, 20 to 36 minutes, at least 14 daily), Laon (€9, 35 to 55 minutes, up to eight daily) and Paris' Gare de l'Est (€24, 1¾ hours, 10 to 15 daily), half of which are speedy TGVs (€32 to €41, 45 minutes).

Épernay

POP 25,225

Prosperous Épernay, 25km south of Reims, is the self-proclaimed *capitale du champagne* and home to many of the world's most celebrated Champagne houses. Beneath the town's streets, some 200 million of bottles of Champagne are slowly being aged, just waiting around to be popped open for some fizz-fuelled celebration.

◉ Sights & Activities

Many of Épernay's *maisons de champagne* (Champagne houses) are based along the handsome and eminently strollable av de

Champagne. Cellar tours end with tasting and a visit to the factory-outlet bubbly shop.

Moët & Chandon   CHAMPAGNE HOUSE
(📞03 26 51 20 20; www.moet.com; adult/child €14.50/9; 20 av de Champagne; ⏰9.30-noon & 2-4.30pm, closed Sat & Sun mid-Nov–mid-Mar, closed Jan) This prestigious *maison* offers some of the region's best cellar tours. Feeling flush? Buy a jeroboam (3L bottle) of 1998 superpremium Dom Pérignon, *millésime* (vintage Champagne) for €2100.

Mercier   CHAMPAGNE HOUSE
(📞03 26 51 22 22; www.champagnemercier. com; 68-70 av de Champagne; adult/child €9/5; ⏰9.30-11.30am & 2-4.30pm, closed mid-Dec–mid-Feb) Everything here is flashy, including the 160,000L barrel that took two decades to build, the lift that transports visitors 30m underground, and the laser-guided touring train.

De Castellane   CHAMPAGNE HOUSE
(📞03 26 51 19 11; www.castellane.com, in French; 64 av de Champagne; adult/child €8.50/ free; ⏰10-11am & 2-5pm mid-Mar–Dec, closed Jan–mid-Mar) Tours take in an informative bubbly museum, and the reward for climbing the 237 steps up the 66m-high tower (1905) is a fine panorama.

🛏 Sleeping

Le Clos Raymi   HISTORIC HOTEL €€
(📞03 26 51 00 58; www.closraymi-hotel.com; 3 rue Joseph de Venoge; d from €100; @) Staying at this delightful three-star place is like being a personal guest of Monsieur Chandon himself, who occupied this luxurious home over a century ago. Seven romantic rooms have giant beds, 3.7m-high ceilings, ornate mouldings and parquet floors.

La Villa St-Pierre   HOTEL €
(📞03 26 54 40 80; www.villasaintpierre.fr; 14 av Paul Chandon; d €45-50; 🛜) In an early-20th-century mansion, this homely hotel with 11 simple rooms retains much of the charm of yesteryear.

✖ Eating

Épernay's main dining area is Rue Gambetta and adjacent place de la République.

TOP CHOICE La Cave à Champagne
                              FRENCH, REGIONAL €€
(📞03 26 55 50 70; www.la-cave-a-champagne.com, in French; 16 rue Gambetta; menus €17-32; ⏰Thu-Mon, lunch Tue) 'The Champagne Cellar' is well regarded by locals for its *champenoise* cuisine, served in a warm, traditional, bour-

TROYES

What a fine and dandy spot to get a sense of what Europe looked like back when Molière was penning his finest plays and the Three Musketeers were swashbuckling! One of Champagne's historic capitals, lively little **Troyes** (www.tourisme-troyes.com) is graced with some of France's finest medieval and Renaissance half-timbered buildings. Explore lanes such as **rue Paillot de Montabert**, **rue Champeaux**, **rue de Vauluisant**, **rue de la Pierre** and **rue Général Saussier** to throw yourself in the heart of it.

Tiny **ruelle des Chats** (Alley of the Cats) feels like stepping back into the Middle Ages, while pharmacy **Apothicaire de l'Hôtel-Dieu-le-Comte** (quai des Comtes de Champagne; adult/child €2/free; ⏱10 or 11am-1pm & 2-7pm Thu-Sun & Wed afternoon May-Sep, 10am-noon & 2-5pm Fri-Sun Oct-Apr) is a fabulous blast from the past with its original wood panelling dating to 1721, and old-fashioned remedies. Traditional crafts made obsolete by the Industrial Revolution fill the **Maison de l'Outil et de la Pensée Ouvrière** (Museum of Tools & Crafts; www.maison-de-l-outil.com; 7 rue de la Trinité; adult/child €6.50/free; ⏱10am-6pm), housed in the magnificent Renaissance-style Hôtel de Mauroy, built in 1556. Then there is the **Cathédrale St-Pierre et St-Paul** (place St-Pierre) with its hotchpotch of Champenois Gothic architecture, medieval **stained glass**, fantastical baroque **organ** and tiny **treasury**.

The people of Troyes are enormously proud of their local speciality, *andouillette de Troyes* (pork or veal tripe sausage), something of an acquired taste best sampled over lunch at **Au Jardin Gourmand** (☎03 25 73 36 13; 31 rue Paillot de Montabert; mains €19-23; ⏱Tue-Sat, dinner Mon). It's elegant and intimate with a lovely summer terrace, and there are no fewer than 11 varieties of *andouillette* on the menu.

geois atmosphere. You can sample three different Champagnes for €21. To avoid disappointment, book your table a couple of weeks in advance.

Bistrot Le 7   FRENCH €€
(☎03 26 55 28 84; 13 rue des Berceaux; menus €17-23; ⏱daily) One of the restaurants at Hôtel Les Berceaux has earned a Michelin star, the other (this one) serves excellent French cuisine amid semiformal, Mediterranean-chic decor. The escargots in a basil, butter and cream sauce are superior, and the chocolate desserts are to die for.

Restaurant Le Théâtre
                         TRADITIONAL, FRENCH €€
(☎03 26 58 88 19; www.epernay-rest-letheatre. com, in French; menus €17-46; ⏱dinner Mon & Thu-Sat, lunch Tue & Sun) Traditional cuisine is served in a corner dining room built a century ago with 4.2m ceilings and floor-to-ceiling windows. The market-driven menu changes every three weeks.

ⓘ Information
Tourist office (☎03 26 53 33 00; www. ot-epernay.fr; 7 av de Champagne; ⏱9.30am-12.30pm & 1.30-7pm Mon-Sat, 11am-4pm Sun, closed Sun mid-Oct–mid-Apr) Details on cellar visits, car touring and walking/cycling options.

Rents GPS units (€7 per day) with DIY vineyard-driving tours in English.

ⓘ Getting There & Away
Direct trains link Reims (€6.20, 20 to 36 minutes, 11 to 18 daily) and Paris' Gare de l'Est (€21, 1¼ hours, five to 10 daily).

ALSACE & LORRAINE

Alsace is a one-off cultural hybrid. With its Germanic dialect and French sense of fashion, love of foie gras and *choucroute* (sauerkraut), fine wine *and* beer, this distinctive region often leaves you wondering quite where you are. Where are you? In the land of living fairy tales, where vineyards fade into watercolour distance, and hilltop castles mingle with the region's emblematic storks and half-timbered villages.

Lorraine has high culture and effortless grace thanks to its historic roll-call of dukes and art nouveau pioneers, who had an eye for grand designs and good living. Its blessedly underrated cities, cathedrals and art collections leave first-timers spellbound, while its WWI battlefields render visitors speechless.

FOODIE TRAILS

No matter whether you're planning to get behind the wheel for a morning or pedal leisurely through the vineyards for a week, the picture-book **Route des Vins d'Alsace** (Alsace Wine Route) is a must. Swinging 170km from Marlenheim to Thann, the road is like a 'greatest hits' of Alsace, with its pastoral views, welcoming *caves* (cellars) and half-timbered villages. Go to www.alsace-route-des-vins.com to start planning.

Fancy cheese with your wine? Hit **Munster** to taste the pungent, creamy fromage first made by Benedictine monks. The tourist office (www.la-vallee-de-munster.com) arranges farmstays and dairy tours.

Having polished off the cheese and wine, it would be rude not to pass the chocolates, or gingerbread, or macaroons, on the **Route du Chocolat et des Douceurs d'Alsace**, 200km of sweet-toothed travels. Pick up a map at Strasbourg tourist office (p267), from where the trail wends 80km north to Bad Bergzabern and 125km south to Heimsbrunn near Mulhouse. Before departure, stock up on *pain d'épices* (gingerbread) from heavenly shop **Mireille Oster** (www.mireille-oster.com; 14 rue des Dentelles), *beerawecka* (Alsatian fruit cake) from **Coco LM** (www.coco-lm.com; 16 rue du Dôme) and sumptuous truffles, pralines, macaroons and edible Strasbourg landmarks from renowned chocolatier **Christian** (www.christian.fr; 12 rue de l'Outre).

Strasbourg

POP 276,000

Prosperous, cosmopolitan Strasbourg ('City of the Roads') is the intellectual and cultural capital of Alsace, as well as the unofficial seat of European power – the European Parliament, the Council of Europe and the European Court of Human Rights are all based here. The city's most famous landmark is its pink sandstone cathedral, towering above the restaurants, *winstubs* (traditional Alsatian eateries) and pubs of the lively old city.

Mulled wine, spicy *bredele* (biscuits) and a Santa-loaded children's village make a trip to Strasbourg's sparkly Marché de Noël a must.

◉ Sights

TOP CHOICE **Grande Île**   OLD TOWN

With its bustling squares and up-market shopping streets, the Grande Île – Unesco-listed since 1988 – is a paradise for the aimless ambler. Its narrow streets are especially enchanting at night, while the half-timbered buildings and flowery canals around **Petite France** on the Grande Île's southwestern corner are fairy-tale pretty. Drink in views of the River Ill and the mighty 17th-century **Barrage Vauban** (Vauban Dam), undergoing renovation at the time of writing, from the much-photographed **Ponts Couverts** (Covered Bridges) and their trio of 13th-century towers.

Cathédrale Notre-Dame   CHURCH

(place de la Cathédrale; ⊙7am-7pm) Strasbourg's lacy, candy-coloured Gothic cathedral is one of the marvels of European architecture. Its west facade was completed in 1284, but the 142m spire wasn't finished till 1439. Inside the south entrance, the 30m-high, 16th-century **astronomical clock** (adult/child €2/free; ⊙tickets sold from 11.50am) strikes solar noon at 12.30pm, with a parade of carved wooden figures portraying the different stages of life and Jesus with his apostles.

A spiral staircase twists up to the 66m-high **platform** (adult/child €4.70/2.30; ⊙9am-7.15pm), which provides a stork's-eye view of Strasbourg.

Musée d'Art Moderne et Contemporain

ART MUSEUM

(place Hans Jean Arp; adult/child €6/free; ⊙noon-7pm Tue, Wed & Fri, noon-9pm Thu, 10am-6pm Sat & Sun) This striking glass-and-steel cube showcases an outstanding collection of fine art, graphic art and photography. Kandinsky, Picasso, Magritte and Monet canvases hang out alongside curvaceous works by Strasbourg-born abstract artist Hans Jean Arp.

Palais Rohan   HISTORIC RESIDENCE

(2 place du Château; adult/child €5/free; ⊙noon-6pm Mon & Wed-Fri, 10am-6pm Sat & Sun) Hailed as a mini Versailles, this opulent 18th-century residence was built for the city's princely bishops. Its basement archaeology museum spans the Palaeolithic period to AD 800; and rooms adorned with Hannong

ceramics and silverware evoke the lavish lifestyle of 18th-century nobility in the ground-floor decorative arts museum.

☞ Tours

Cave des Hospices de Strasbourg WINE
(www.vins-des-hospices-de-strasbourg.fr, in French; 1 place de l'Hôpital; ⊙8.30am-noon & 1.30-5.30pm Mon-Fri, 9am-12.30pm Sat) A hospice back in the days when wine was considered a cure for all ills, this brick-vaulted wine cellar produces first-rate Alsatian wines deep in the bowels of Strasbourg's hospital.

Batorama BOAT
(www.batorama.fr, in French; adult/child €8.50/4.50; ⊙half-hourly 9.30am-9pm) Scenic boat trips along the storybook canals of Petite France, taking in the Vauban Dam and the glinting EU institutions. Tours depart from in front of Palais Rohan.

Brasseries Heineken BEER
(☑03 88 19 57 55; 4 rue St-Charles; ⊙hourly 9am-4pm Mon-Fri) Free two-hour tours of the Heineken brewery (some in English; reserve ahead), 2.5km north of Grande Île; take bus 4 to the Schiltigheim Mairie stop.

✺ Festivals & Events

Vin chaud (mulled wine), spicy *bredele* and a Santa-loaded children's village feature in Strasbourg's sparkly **Marché de Noël** (Christmas Market; www.noel.strasbourg.eu), from the last Saturday in November to 24 December.

Raise a glass to Alsatian beer at October's **Mondial de la Bière** (www.mondialbierestras bourg.com) or to wine at March's **Riesling du Monde** (www.riesling-du-monde.com).

🛏 Sleeping

Camping de la Montagne Verte
CAMPING GROUND €
(☑03 88 30 25 46; www.camping-montagne-verte -strasbourg.com; 2 rue Robert Forrer; campsites €14-18.50) Pitch up at this quiet camping ground, a 10-minute stroll from Montagne Verte tram stop, 3km west of Petite France. It's right next to the cycling lane leading into town.

Hôtel du Dragon SMALL HOTEL €€
(☑03 88 35 79 80; www.dragon.fr; 12 rue du Dragon; s €79-112, d €89-124; @☎) Step through a tree-shaded courtyard into the blissful calm of this bijou hotel. Crisp interiors, attentive service and prime location near Petite France.

Hôtel Gutenberg HISTORIC HOTEL €€
(☑03 88 32 17 15; www.hotel-gutenberg.com; 31 rue des Serruriers; r €75-135; ✳@☎) Right in the flower-filled heart of Petite France, this hotel blends 250 years of history with contemporary design – think clean lines, zesty colours and the occasional antique.

Romantik Hôtel Beaucour HISTORIC HOTEL €€
(☑03 88 76 72 00; www.hotel-beaucour.com; 5 rue des Bouchers; s €75-110, d €135-165; ✳@☎) With its antique flourishes and a cosy salon centred on a fireplace, this place oozes half-timbered romance. Jacuzzi bathtubs!

✗ Eating

Appetising restaurants abound on Grande Île: try canalside Petite France for Alsatian fare and half-timbered romance; Grand' Rue for curbside kebabs and *tarte flambée;* and rue des Veaux or rue des Pucelles for hole-in-the-wall eateries serving the world on a plate.

TOP CHOICE **La Choucrouterie** ALSATIAN €€
(☑03 88 36 52 87; www.choucrouterie. com, in French; 20 rue St Louis; choucroute €12-16; ⊙lunch Mon-Fri, dinner daily) Naked ladies straddling giant sausages (on the menu, we hasten to add) and eccentric chefs juggling plates of steaming *choucroute garnie* are

---

DON'T MISS

WHEN HELL WAS HELL

Hollywood gore seems tame compared with the tortures back when Hell really was hell. Sure to scare you into a life of chastity is *Les Amants Trépassés* (The Deceased Lovers), painted in 1470, showing a grotesque couple being punished for their illicit lust: both of their entrails are being devoured by dragon-headed snakes.

Track it down in room 23 of Strasbourg's fabulous **Musée de l'Œuvre Notre Dame** (3 place du Château; adult/child €4/free; ⊙noon-6pm Tue-Fri, 10am-6pm Sat & Sun). Occupying a cluster of sublime 14th- and 16th-century buildings, the world-renowned ecclesiastical museum boasts one of Europe's premier collections of Romanesque, Gothic and Renaissance sculptures, 15th-century paintings and stained glass.

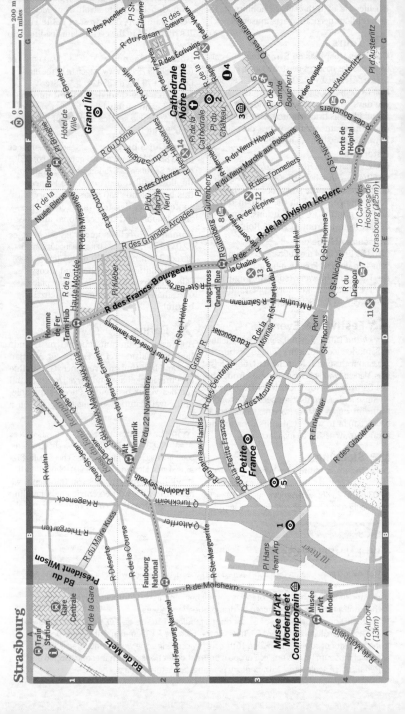

Strasbourg

200 m
0.1 miles

FRANCE ALSACE & LORRAINE

Grand Île

Cathédrale Notre Dame

Hôtel de Ville

Pl Broglie

R de la Nuée Bleue

R des Francs-Bourgeois

R de la Division Leclerc

Petite France

Musée d'Art Moderne et Contemporain

Musée d'Art Moderne

Train Station

Gare Centrale

Pl de la Gare

Bd de Metz

Bd du Président Wilson

R de Molsheim

Ill River

Pl Hans Jean Arp

To Airport (13km)

To Cave des Hospices de Strasbourg (425m)

Porte de l'Hôpital

Pl d'Austerlitz

Strasbourg

just the tip of the theatrical iceberg at this inimitable bistro and playhouse double act.

La Cloche á Fromage   CHEESE SHOP €€
(☏03 88 23 13 19; www.cheese-gourmet.com; 27 rue des Tonneliers; fondues €21-25; ☺Tue-Sun) *Au revoir* diet... Loosen your belt for Strasbourg's gooiest fondues and raclette at this temple to cheese, saving an inch for the 200-variety cheeseboard of Guinness Book of World Records fame.

Maison Kammerzell   ALSATIAN €€
(☏03 88 32 42 14; www.maison-kammerzell.com; 16 place de la Cathédrale; menus €27-46) Medi-

eval icon Maison Kammerzell serves well-executed Alsatian cuisine such as *baeckeoffe* and *choucroute*. A staircase spirals up to frescoed alcoves and the 1st floor where the views – oh the views! – of the floodlit cathedral are sensational.

L'Assiette du Vin   BISTRO €€
(☏03 88 32 00 92; www.assietteduvin.fr, in French; 5 rue de la Chaîne; lunch menus €19, dinner menus €32-55; ☺Tue-Fri, dinner Sat-Mon) Market-fresh cuisine with a twist, discreet service and an award-winning wine list lure discerning foodies to this rustic-chic bistro in the Old Town. The plat du jour is a snip at €8.50.

Bistrot et Chocolat   CAFE €
(www.bistrotetchocolat.net, in French; 8 rue de la Râpe; snacks €4-8, brunches €10-19; ☺10.30am-7pm Tue-Sun) Chocolate fondue, organic hot chocolate with ginger, chocolate soup sprinkled with gingerbread croutons... This boho-chic bistro is an ode to the cocoa bean. Weekend brunches are a treat.

ⓘ Information
Tourist office (☏03 88 52 28 28; www. otstrasbourg.fr; 17 place de la Cathédrale; ☺9am-7pm) Runs an annexe in the southern wing of Strasbourg train station, 400m west of Grande Île.

ⓘ Getting There & Away
Air
Strasbourg's international **airport** (www.strasbourg.aeroport.fr) is 17km southwest of the city centre (towards Molsheim), near the village of Entzheim.

Ryanair links London Stansted with **Karlsruhe/Baden Baden airport** (www.badenairpark.de), 58km northeast of Strasbourg, across the Rhine in Germany.

Train
DOMESTIC Destinations include Paris' Gare de l'Est (€67, 2¼ hours, 17 daily), Lille (€94, four hours, 13 daily), Lyon (€52, six hours, five

---

WORTH A TRIP

FOREST FANTASY

Get back to nature at the **Hôtel de l'Illwald** (☏03 90 56 11 40; www.illwald.fr; Schnellenbuhl; d €72-85; ☜), a dreamy hotel bordering the lushly forested Ill'Wald nature reserve, which has France's largest population of wild deer. This half-timbered, red-sandstone hotel keeps the mood intimate in gorgeous rooms: some sleek with hardwood floors and four-poster beds, others rustic with warm pine, antique furnishings and downy bedding. After a day walking or cycling, have drinks by an open fire and dinner in the frescoed restaurant. The hotel is 60km south of Strasbourg, off the D424 in Schnellenbuhl.

KATZENTHAL

Tiptoe off the tourist trail to Alsatian village **Katzenthal** (population 550), 9km west of Colmar and 80km south of Strasbourg. *Grand cru* vines ensnare the hillside, topped by the medieval ruins of Château du Wineck, from where walking trails into forest and vineyard begin.

Then there is the fabulous, family-run **Vignoble Klur** (☎03 89 80 94 29; www.klur. net; 105 rue des Trois Epis; d €80-110), an organic winery and guest house that hosts wine tastings, Alsatian cookery classes, herb walks in the vineyards, creative workshops and tandems to pedal through the vines *á deux*. Make yourself at home in a sunny apartment with kitchenette, read a book by an open fire in the salon, or unwind in the organic sauna. Oh, and don't miss Jean-Louis Frick's hilarious mural of hedonistic wine lovers above the entrance – it has raised a few local eyebrows, apparently.

daily), Marseille (€87, eight hours, five daily), Metz (€23, two hours, 20 daily) and Nancy (€22, 1½ hours, 25 daily).

INTERNATIONAL Cities with direct services include Basel SNCF (Bâle; €21, 1¼ hours, 25 daily), Brussels-Nord (€70, 5¼ hours, three daily), Karlsruhe (€22, 40 minutes, 16 daily) and Stuttgart (€43, 1¼ hours, four TGVs daily). If you take the Eurostar via Paris or Lille, London is just five hours and 15 minutes away, city centre to city centre.

ROUTE DES VINS From Strasbourg, there are trains to Route des Vins destinations including Colmar (€10.50, 30 minutes, 30 daily), Dambach-la-Ville (€8, one hour, 12 daily), Obernai (€5.50, 30 minutes, 20 daily) and Sélestat (€7.50, 30 minutes, 46 daily).

Nancy

POP 107,250

Delightful Nancy has a refined air found nowhere else in Lorraine. With its resplendent central square, fine museums, medieval Old Town, formal gardens and shop windows sparkling with crystal, the former capital of the dukes of Lorraine catapults visitors back to the opulence of the 18th century (when much of the city centre was built).

⊙ Sights

Place Stanislas SQUARE
This neoclassical square, laid out in the 1750s, is one of Europe's most dazzling public spaces. The rococo fountains, gilded gateways and opulent buildings form one of France's finest ensembles of 18th-century architecture.

Musée de l'École de Nancy MUSEUM
(School of Nancy Museum; www.ecole-de-nancy. com; 36-38 rue du Sergent Blandan; adult/child

€6/4; ⊙10am-6pm Wed-Sun) A highlight of a visit to Nancy, the School of Nancy Museum brings together an exquisite collection of art nouveau interiors, curvaceous glass and landscaped gardens. Find it in a 19th-century villa, 2km southwest of the centre.

Musée des Beaux-Arts ART MUSEUM
(3 place Stanislas; adult/child €6/free; ⊙10am-6pm Wed-Mon) Star attractions at this fine-arts museum include a superb collection of art nouveau glass and paintings from the 14th to 18th centuries.

🛏 Sleeping

TOP CHOICE **Hôtel des Prélats** HISTORIC HOTEL €€
(☎03 83 30 20 20; www.hoteldesprelats. com; 56 place Monseigneur Ruch; s/d €69/109; ❄@🛜) Sleep in a 17th-century bishop's palace next to the cathedral. Prélats plays up the romance with stained-glass windows, four-poster beds and shimmery drapes.

Hôtel de Guise BOUTIQUE HOTEL €€
(☎03 83 32 24 68; www.hoteldeguise.com; 18 rue de Guise; s €63, d €75-100; 🛜) Boutique chic meets 17th-century elegance at this hotel on an old-town backstreet. There's a walled garden for quiet moments.

La Résidence TRADITIONAL HOTEL €€
(☎03 83 35 42 34; www.hotel-laresidence-nancy. fr, in French; 30 blvd Jean-Jaurès; r €70-85; 🛜) This convivial hotel is one of Nancy's best deals, with an inviting salon and a leafy courtyard for an alfresco breakfast.

🍽 Eating

Eats street rue des Maréchaux dishes up everything from French to Italian, tapas, seafood, Indian and Japanese. Then there's Grande Rue, peppered with sweet bistros.

Chez Tony DELI €
(place Henri Mengin; mains €6-11; ⊘Tue-Sat) Generously heaped plates of antipasti, freshly made pasta, colourful garden chairs, big smiles all round – it's a Tuscan garden party every lunchtime at Chez Tony in Nancy's covered market. Toast your find with a glass of olive liqueur or Chianti.

Brasserie Excelsior BRASSERIE €€
(⊘03 83 35 24 57; 50 rue Henri Poincaré; menus €23-38; ⊘8am-12.30am Mon-Sat, 8am-11pm Sun) As opulent as a Fabergé egg with its stucco and stained glass, Excelsior whisks you back to the decadent era of art nouveau. Brusquely efficient waiters serve brasserie classics: oysters, steaks and seafood platters.

Aux Délices du Palais BISTRO €
(⊘03 83 30 44 19; 69 Grande Rue; mains €9; ⊘Mon-Fri, dinner Sat) Purple walls and glitter balls, this shabby-chic bistro serves whatever the jovial chef fancies cooking – from flavoursome tagines to fajitas. Great value, hence the enthusiastic local following.

ⓘ Information

Tourist office (⊘03 83 35 22 41; www.ot -nancy.fr; place Stanislas; ⊘9am-7pm Mon-Sat, 10am-5pm Sun) Free brochures detailing walking tours of Nancy's art nouveau architecture.

ⓘ Getting There & Away

The **train station** (place Thiers), 800m southwest of place Stanislas, is on the line linking Paris' Gare de l'Est (€54, 1½ hours, 11 daily) with Strasbourg (€22, 1½ hours, 12 daily). Other destinations include Baccarat (€9.50, 45 minutes, 15 daily) and Metz (€9.50, 40 minutes, 48 daily).

Metz

POP 125,720

Straddling the confluence of the Moselle and Seille Rivers, Metz is Lorraine's graceful capital. Its Gothic marvel of a cathedral,

DON'T MISS

CENTRE POMPIDOU-METZ

This architecturally innovative **museum** (www.centrepompidou-metz.fr; 1 parvis des Droits de l'Homme; adult/child €7/ free; ⊘11am-6pm Mon, Wed & Sun, 11am-8pm Thu, Fri & Sat), dazzling white and sinuous, is the satellite branch of Paris' Centre Pompidou. Its gallery draws on Europe's largest collection of modern art to stage ambitious temporary exhibitions. The dynamic space also hosts top-drawer cultural events.

Michelin star-studded dining scene, beautiful yellow-stone Old Town and regal Quartier Impérial (up for Unesco World Heritage status) have long managed to sidestep the world spotlight. But all that has changed with the show-stopping arrival of Centre Pompidou-Metz.

⊙ Sights

Cathédrale St-Étienne CHURCH
(place St-Étienne; ⊘8am-6pm) As delicate as Chantilly lace, the golden spires of this Gothic cathedral crown the town's skyline. Exquisitely lit by kaleidoscopic curtains of 13th- to 20th-century stained glass, the cathedral is nicknamed 'God's lantern'. Flamboyant **Chagall** windows in reds, yellows and blues in the ambulatory harbour the **treasury** (adult/child €2/1; ⊘10am-12.30pm & 2-5pm), and a sculpture of a dragon said to have terrified pre-Christian Metz lurks in the 15th-century **crypt** (adult/child €2/1; ⊘10am-12.30pm & 2-5pm).

Quartier Impérial HISTORIC QUARTER
The stately boulevards and bourgeois villas of the German Imperial Quarter, including rue Gambetta and av Foch, are the brainchild

FRANCE METZ

MASSIF DES VOSGES

The sublime **Parc Naturel Régional des Ballons des Vosges** covers 3000 sq km in the southern Vosges range. In the warm months, the gentle, rounded mountains, deep forests, glacial lakes and rolling pastureland are a walker's paradise, with an astounding 10,000km of marked trails and cycle routes, and in winter you'll discover three dozen inexpensive skiing areas.

For information on the park, contact the **Maison du Parc Naturel Régional des Ballons des Vosges** (www.parc-ballons-vosges.fr, in French; 1 cour de l'Abbaye; ⊘10am-noon & 2-6pm Tue-Sun) in Munster, a small streamside town famous for its notoriously smelly and eponymous cheese, Munster (meaning 'monastery').

of Kaiser Wilhelm II. Built to trumpet the triumph of Metz' post-1871 status as part of the Second Reich, the architecture is a whimsical mix of art deco, neo-Romanesque and neo-Renaissance influences. The area's unique ensemble of Wilhelmian architecture has made it a candidate for Unesco World Heritage status. Philippe Starck lamp posts juxtapose Teutonic sculptures, whose common theme is German imperial might, at the monumental Rhenish neo-Romanesque train station (1908).

Sleeping

TOP CHOICE **Péniche Alclair** HOUSEBOAT €
(06 37 67 16 18; www.chambrespenichemetz.com; allée St Symphorien; r incl breakfast €65;) Cécile and Xavier Bonfils have transformed an old barge into this stylish blue houseboat with snazzy bathrooms and watery views. Find it moored a pleasant 15-minute riverside stroll south of the centre.

Hôtel de la Cathédrale HISTORIC HOTEL €€
(03 87 75 00 02; www.hotelcathedrale-metz.fr; 25 place de Chambre; d €75-110;) This classy little hotel occupies a 17th-century town house opposite the cathedral. Climb the wrought-iron staircase to your classically elegant room, with high ceilings, hardwood floors and antique trappings.

La Citadelle DESIGN HOTEL €€€
(03 87 17 17 17; www.citadelle-metz.com; 5 av Ney; d €205-265;) A 16th-century citadel given a boutique makeover, luxurious La Citadelle blends history with Zen-style sleekness. The hotel's pride and joy is its Michelin-starred restaurant, **Le Magasin aux Vivres**.

Eating

Metz has scores of appetising restaurants, many along and near the river. Place St-Jacques becomes one giant open-air cafe when the sun's out. Cobbled rue Taison and the arcades of place St-Louis shelter moderately priced bistros, pizzerias and cafes.

Restaurant Thierry FUSION €€
(03 87 74 01 23; www.restaurant-thierry.fr; 5 rue des Piques; menus €24-34; Mon, Tue & Thu-Sat) Walking into this spice-scented, lantern-lit restaurant is like stepping into the glammest of Marrakchi riads. An open fire crackles in the salon, where an aperitif works up an appetite for Asian- and Moroccan-inflected dishes, such as delicate prawn *nems* (spring rolls), seafood tagines and beautifully cooked sole with tempura.

La Voile Blanche MODERN FRENCH €€
(03 87 20 66 66; 1 parvis des Droits de l'Homme; menus €25-35; Wed-Mon, lunch Sun) Art on a plate is the aim at Centre Pompidou-Metz' kaleidoscope-inspired restaurant, designed by architects Patrick Jouin and Sanjit Manku.

Maire TRADITIONAL FRENCH €€
(03 87 32 43 12; www.restaurant-maire.com, in French; 1 rue des Ponts des Morts; menus €37-45; Wed-Mon, dinner Wed) This smart riverside restaurant serves up cathedral views, market-fresh dishes and 500 bottles in its wine cellar.

Information

Tourist office (03 87 55 53 76; http://tourisme.mairie-metz.fr; 2 place d'Armes; 9am-7pm Mon-Sat, 10am-5pm Sun)

Getting There & Away

Train it from Metz' ornate early-20th-century **train station** (pl du Général de Gaulle) to Paris' Gare de l'Est (€53, 80 minutes, 13 daily), Nancy (€9.50, 40 minutes, 48 daily) and Strasbourg (€23, 1¾ hours, 14 daily).

DON'T MISS

GO TO MARKET

If only every market were like Metz' grand **Marché Couvert** (Covered Market; place de la Cathédrale; 8am-6.30pm Tue-Sat). Once a bishop's palace, now a temple to fresh local produce, this is the kind of place where you pop in for a baguette and struggle out an hour later with bags overflowing with charcuterie, ripe fruit and five different sorts of fromage.

Make a morning of it, stopping for an early, inexpensive lunch and a chat with the market's larger-than-life characters. At **Chez Mauricette** (sandwiches €2-4.50, antipasti plate €5-7), Mauricette tempts with Lorraine goodies from herby saucisson to local charcuterie and mirabelle pâté. Her neighbour is **Soupes á Soups** (soups €2.80-5.50), where Patrick ladles out homemade soups, from mussel to creamy mushroom varieties.

CHATEAUX TOURS

Many of the big-name Loire Valley chateaux are covered by the **Pass'-Châteaux**, which offers savings of between €1.20 and €5.30 depending on which chateaux you visit; contact the tourist offices in Blois, Cheverny and Chambord.

Hard-core indie travellers might baulk at the idea, but if you don't have your own wheels a minibus tour can be the most time-efficient way of taking in the Loire Valley biggies.

Blois tourist office and TLC (☎02 54 58 55 44; www.tlcinfo.net, in French; ☻3 morning departures Apr-Aug) run a shuttle (€6) from Blois to Chambord and Cheverny.

Several companies offer a choice of itineraries, packaging Azay-le-Rideau, Villandry, Cheverny, Chambord and Chenonceau (plus wine-tasting tours) in various combinations. Half-day trips cost €18 to €33; full-day trips €43 to €50. Admission to the chateaux isn't included, but you get discount on tickets. Reserve at Tours tourist office, from where most tours depart:

- » **Acco-Dispo** (www.accodispo-tours.com)
- » **Alienor** (www.alienor.com)
- » **Quart de Tours** (www.quartdetours.com)
- » **St-Eloi Excursions** (www.saint-eloi.com)
- » **Touraine Evasion** (www.tourevasion.com)
- » **Loire Valley Tours** (www.loire-valley-tours.com)

THE LOIRE VALLEY

One step removed from the French capital, the Loire was historically the place where princes, dukes and notable nobles established their country getaways, and the countryside is littered with some of the most extravagant architecture outside Versailles. From sky-topping turrets and glittering banquet halls to slate-crowned cupolas and crenellated towers, the hundreds of chateaux dotted along this valley, a Unesco World Heritage site, comprise 1000 years of astonishingly rich architectural and artistic treasures.

Blois

POP 40,057

Blois' historic chateau was the feudal seat of the powerful counts of Blois, and its grand halls, spiral staircases and sweeping courtyards provide a whistlestop tour through the key periods of French architecture. Sadly for chocoholics, the town's historic chocolate factory, Poulain, is off-limits to visitors.

◉ Sights

Blois' old city, heavily damaged by German attacks in 1940, retains its steep, twisting medieval streets.

Château Royal de Blois   CASTLE
(www.chateaudeblois.fr; place du Château; adult/child €8/4; ☻9am-7pm Jul & Aug, 9am-6.30pm Apr-Jun & Sep, 9am-12.30pm & 1.30-5.30pm Oct-Mar) Blois' Royal Chateau makes an excellent introduction to the chateaux of the Loire Valley, with elements of Gothic (13th century); Flamboyant Gothic (1498–1503), early Renaissance (1515–24) and classical (1630s) architecture in its four grand wings.

Maison de la Magie   MUSEUM
(www.maisondelamagie.fr, in French; 1 place du Château; adult/child €9/5; ☻10am-12.30pm & 2-6.30pm, closed mornings Mon-Fri Sep) Opposite the chateau is the former home of watchmaker, inventor and conjurer Jean Eugène Robert-Houdin (1805–71), after whom the great Houdini named himself. It now offers daily magic shows and optical trickery.

Musée de l'Objet   ART MUSEUM
(www.museedelobjet.org, in French; 6 rue Franciade; adult/child €4/2; ☻1.30-6.30pm Wed-Sun late Jun-Aug, Fri-Sun Mar-late Jun & Sep-Oct, closed Dec-Feb) This eye-catching museum has modern art made from everyday materials, with works by Dalí and Man Ray.

🛏 Sleeping

Côté Loire   HOTEL €
(☎02 54 78 07 86; www.coteloire.com; 2 place de la Grève; d €55-76; ☎) If it's charm and

THE LOIRE BY BIKE

The Loire Valley is mostly flat – it's excellent cycling country. **Loire à Vélo** (www.loireavelo.fr) maintains 800km of signposted routes. Pick up a guide from tourist offices, or download route maps, audioguides and bike-hire details online.

Détours de Loire (☎02 47 61 22 23; www.locationdevelos.com) has bike-rental shops in Tours and Blois (☎02 54 56 07 73; train station); can deliver bikes; and allows you to collect/return bikes along the route for a small surcharge. Classic bikes cost €14/59 per day/week; tandems €45 per day.

Les Châteaux à Vélo (☎02 54 78 62 52; www.chateauxavelo.com) has a bike-rental circuit between Blois, Chambord and Cheverny, 300km of marked trails and can shuttle you by minibus. Free route maps online (also 40 downloadable MP3 guides) and at tourist offices.

colours you want, head for the Loire Coast. Its rooms come in cheery checks, bright pastels and the odd bit of exposed brick; and breakfast is served on a wooden-decking patio.

Hôtel Anne de Bretagne　HOTEL €
(☎02 54 78 05 38; http://annedebretagne.free.fr; 31 av du Dr Jean Laigret; s €45-51, d €54-56, tr €60-72; ☎) This creeper-covered hotel has friendly staff and a bar full of polished wood and vintage pictures. Modern rooms are finished in flowery wallpaper and stripy bedspreads.

Le Monarque　HOTEL €
(☎02 54 78 02 35; 61 rue Porte Chartraine; s €38, d €58-59; ❉☎) Modern, bright and no-nonsense, this hotel sits at the edge of the old city, and offers comfort, cleanliness and a restaurant.

✗ Eating & Drinking

L'Orangerie　GASTRONOMIC €€€
(☎02 54 78 05 36; www.orangerie-du-chateau.fr; 1 av du Dr Jean Laigret; menus €33-77) The Orangery is cloud nine for connoisseurs of haute cuisine. Plates are artfully stacked (duck liver, langoustine, foie gras) and the sparkling *salon* would make Louis XIV envious. On summer nights, dine in the courtyard.

Les Banquettes Rouges　TRADITIONAL, FRENCH €€
(☎02 54 78 74 92; 16 rue des Trois Marchands; menus €14.50-32; ☺Tue-Sat) Handwritten slate menus and wholesome food distinguish the Red Benches: rabbit with marmalade, duck with lentils and salmon with apple vinaigrette, all done with a spicy twist.

Le Castelet　TRADITIONAL, FRENCH €€
(☎02 54 74 66 09; 40 rue St-Lubin; menus €15-32; ☺Tue-Sat & Mon; ☑) Rusticana and rural frescos cover the walls of this country restaurant that emphasises seasonal ingredients, organics and vegetarian options.

ℹ Information

Tourist office (☎02 54 90 41 41; www.bloispaysdechambord.com; 23 place du Château; ☺9am-7pm)

ℹ Getting There & Away

Bus

TLC (☎02 54 58 55 44; www.tlcinfo.net) runs a chateau shuttle (see boxed text, p271) and buses from Blois' train station (tickets €2 on board). Some destinations:

BEAUGENCY Line 16, 55 minutes, four Monday to Saturday, one Sunday

CHAMBORD Line 3, 40 minutes, four Monday to Saturday, one Sunday

CHEVERNY Line 4, 45 minutes, six to eight Monday to Friday, two Saturday, one Sunday

Train

AMBOISE €11, 20 minutes, 10 daily

ORLÉANS €13 to €20, 45 minutes, hourly

TOURS €13 to €19, 40 minutes, 13 daily

PARIS' GARES D'AUSTERLITZ & MONT-PARNASSE €34 to €57, two hours, 26 daily

Around Blois

CHÂTEAU DE CHAMBORD

For full-blown chateau splendour, you can't top **Chambord** (☎02 54 50 50 20; www.chambord.org; adult/child €9.50/free; ☺9am-7.30pm mid-Jul–mid-Aug, 9am-6.15pm mid-Mar–mid-Jul & mid-Aug–Sep, 9am-5.15pm Jan–mid-Mar & Oct-Dec), constructed from 1519 by François I as a lavish base for hunting game in the Sologne forests, but eventually used for just 42 days during the king's 32-year reign (1515–47). Pick up the multilingual audioguide (adult/child €4/2), if only to avoid getting lost in Chambord's endless rooms and corridors.

The chateau's most famous feature is its **double-helix staircase**, attributed by some

WORTH A TRIP

LUNCH BREAK

Need a moment to yourself between chateaux? Head to Bracieux, 7km south of Chambord, for lunch at **Au Fil de Temps** (☎02 54 46 03 84; 11 place de la Halle; €18-22; ☺Fri-Wed). Its simple specialities such as tender white asparagus with beurre blanc or savoury salmon filets beat the tourist traps into the dust.

to Leonardo da Vinci, who lived in Amboise (34km southwest) from 1516 until his death three years later. The Italianate **rooftop terrace**, surrounded by cupolas, domes, chimneys and slate roofs, was where the royal court assembled to watch military exercises and hunting parties returning at the end of the day.

Several times daily there are 1½-hour **guided tours** (€4) in English, and during school holidays **costumed tours** entertain kids. The *son et lumière* show **Chambord, Rêve de Lumières** (adult/child €12/10, ☺Jul–mid-Sep), projected on the chateau's facade nightly, is a real summer highlight, as is the daily **equestrian show** (☎02 54 20 31 01; www.ecuries-chambord.com, in French; adult/child €9.50/7; ☺May-Sep).

Chambord is 16km east of Blois, 45km southwest of Orléans and 17km northeast of Cheverny. For public transport options see p272 and the boxed text, p271.

CHÂTEAU DE CHEVERNY
Thought by many to be the most perfectly proportioned chateau of all, **Cheverny**

(☎02 54 79 96 29; www.chateau-cheverny.fr; adult/child €7.50/3.60; ☺9.15am-6.45pm Jul & Aug, 9.15am-6.15pm Apr-Jun & Sep, 9.45am-5.30pm Oct, 9.45am-5pm Nov-Mar) represents the zenith of French classical architecture, the perfect blend of symmetry, geometry and aesthetic order. It has hardly been altered since its construction between 1625 and 1634. Inside is a formal dining room, bridal chamber and children's playroom (complete with Napoleon III–era toys), as well as a guards' room full of pikestaffs, claymores and suits of armour.

Near the chateau's gateway, the kennels house pedigreed French pointer/English foxhound hunting dogs still used by the owners of Cheverny; feeding time is the **Soupe des Chiens** (☺5pm Apr-Sep, 3pm Oct-Mar).

Behind the chateau is the 18th-century **Orangerie**, where many priceless art works (including the *Mona Lisa*) were stashed during WWII. Hergé used the castle as a model for Moulinsart (Marlinspike) Hall, the ancestral home of Tintin's sidekick, Captain Haddock. **Les Secrets de Moulinsart** (combined ticket with chateau adult/child €12/7) explores the Tintin connections.

Cheverny is 16km southeast of Blois and 17km southwest of Chambord. For buses to/from Blois see its Getting There & Away section.

CHÂTEAU DE CHAUMONT
It's a brisk climb up to resolutely medieval **Château de Chaumont-sur-Loire** (www.domaine-chaumont.fr, in French; adult/child €9/3.50; ☺10am-6.30pm Apr-Sep, to 5 or 6pm Oct-Mar), set on a bluff overlooking the Loire. The entrance, across a wooden drawbridge between two wide towers, opens onto an inner courtyard from where there are stunning

DON'T MISS

A CHAMBORD GAD-ABOUT

Chambord is not just about its chateau: **Domaine National de Chambord**, the vast hunting reserve ensnaring it, is a must-explore. While most of its 54 sq km is reserved strictly for high-ranking French government officials (hard to imagine Sarkozy astride a galloping stallion), 10 sq km of its **walking**, **cycling** and **equestrian trails** are open to anyone.

A real highlight is **wildlife-spotting**, especially in September and October during the rutting season, when you can watch stags, boars and red deer woo and mate. Observation towers dot the park; set out at dawn or dusk to spot.

Or pedal around: hire bikes at the **rental kiosk** (☎02 54 33 37 54; per hr/half-/full day €6/10/13; ☺Apr-Oct) near the jetty on the Cosson River (where you can also rent boats). **Guided bike tours** (adult/child €10/6 plus bike hire) depart mid-August to September. Alternatively, join a **Land Rover Safari** (☎02 54 50 50 06; adult/child €18/10; ☺Apr-Sep).

STAYING OVER

Tucked at the foot of Cheverny's driveway amid grassland, renovated 19th-century farmhouse **La Levraudière** (☎02 54 79 81 99; http://lalevraudiere. free.fr; 1 chemin de la Levraudière; incl breakfast s €59, d €62-65, tr €80-85) is a perfect blend of tradition and modernity. Breakfast is around a slab-like wooden table laden with fabulous homemade jams, while rooms are all about crisp linens and meticulous presentation.

views. Opposite the main entrance are the luxurious stables, built in 1877.

Chaumont-sur-Loire is 17km southwest of Blois and 20km northeast of Amboise. Onzain, a 2.5km walk from Chaumont across the Loire, has trains to Blois (€11, 10 minutes, 13 daily) and Tours (€11 to €15, 35 minutes, 10 daily).

Tours

POP 140,000

Hovering somewhere between the style of Paris and the conservative sturdiness of central France, Tours is a key staging post for exploring chateaux country. It's a smart, vivacious kind of town, filled with wide 18th-century boulevards, parks and imposing public buildings, as well as a busy university of some 25,000 students.

⊙ Sights

Musée des Beaux-Arts   ART MUSEUM

(18 place François Sicard; adult/child €4/2; ⊙9am-12.45pm & 2-6pm Wed-Mon) Arranged around the courtyard of the archbishop's gorgeous palace, this fine-arts museum flouts grand rooms decorated to reflect the period of the art works on display. Look for works by Delacroix, Degas and Monet, as well as a rare Rembrandt miniature and a Rubens Madonna and Child.

Cathédrale St-Gatien   CHURCH

(place de la Cathédrale; ⊙9am-7pm) With its twin towers, flying buttresses and gargoyles, this cathedral's a show-stopper. It's known for its stained glass; the interior dates from the 13th to 16th centuries, and the domed tops of the two 70m-high towers are Renaissance.

Musée du Compagnonnage   MUSEUM

(8 rue Nationale, in Cloître St-Julien; adult/child €5/3.30; ⊙9am-noon & 2-6pm, closed Tue mid-Sep–mid-Jun) France's skilled labourers, including pastry chefs, coopers and locksmiths, are celebrated here. Displays range from handmade clogs to booby-trapped locks, vintage barrels and cakes.

🛏 Sleeping

L'Adresse   BOUTIQUE HOTEL €€

(☎02 47 20 85 76; www.hotel-ladresse.com; 12 rue de la Rôtisserie; s €50, d €70-100; ❄@🕏) Looking for Parisian style in provincial Tours? Then you're in luck – 'The Address' is a boutique bonanza, with rooms finished in sleek slates and ochres, topped off with wi-fi, flat-screen TVs and designer sinks.

Hôtel de l'Univers   HOTEL €€€

(☎02 47 05 37 12; www.hotel-univers.fr; 5 blvd Heurteloup; d €198-270; ❄@🕏) Everyone from Ernest Hemingway to Édith Piaf has bunked at the Universe over its 150-year history. Previous guests gaze down from the frescoed balcony above the lobby, and rooms are appropriately glitzy: huge beds, gleaming bathrooms.

Hôtel Mondial   HOTEL €€

(☎02 47 05 62 68; www.hotelmondialtours.com; 3 place de la Résistance; s €52-72, d €64-87; 🕏) Overlooking place de la Résistance, this hotel boasts a fantastic city-centre position. The modernised, metropolitan attic rooms in funky greys, browns and scarlets are the nicest, but even the older-style ones are decent. Reception is on the 2nd floor and there's no lift.

Hôtel Ronsard   BOUTIQUE HOTEL €

(☎02 47 05 25 36; www.hotel-ronsard.com; 2 rue Pimbert; s €53-67, d €59-72; ❄@🕏) This hotel translates as centrally located and comfortable value. Think sleek modern rooms dressed in slate-grey and sparkling white linen.

🍴 Eating

In the old city, place Plumereau, rue du Grand Marché and rue de la Rôtisserie are crammed with cheap eats (quality variable).

Cap Sud   GASTRO BISTRO €€

(☎02 47 05 24 81; 88 rue Colbert; menus €14.50-36; ⊙Tue-Sat) A hot-mod red interior combines nicely with genial service here, and the food! The food! Sensitive, refined creations are made from the freshest ingredients presented in style. Reserve in advance.

Tartines & Co GOURMET SANDWICHES €

(6 rue des Fusillés; mains €9-12; ⊙lunch Tue-Sat, dinner Wed-Fri) This snazzy little bistro re-invents the traditional *croque* (toasted sandwich) amidst jazz and friendly chatter. Choose your topping and it's served up quick-as-a-flash on toasted artisanal bread.

L'Atelier Gourmand GASTRO BISTRO €€

(☑02 47 38 59 87; 37 rue Étienne Marcel; menus €23; ⊙lunch Tue-Fri, dinner Mon-Sat) Another foodie address, but bring dark glasses: the puce-and-silver colour scheme is straight out of a Brett Easton Ellis novel. There's no quibbling with the food: hunks of roast lamb, green-pepper duck and authentic bouillabaisse, delivered with a modern spin.

Le Zinc TRADITIONAL FRENCH €€

(☑02 47 20 29 00; 27 place du Grand Marché; menus €19-25.50; ⊙Mon, Tue & Thu-Sat, dinner Sun) More concerned with market-fresh classic staples than Michelin stars and haute cuisine cachet, this bistro is attractive, authentic and tasty.

Drinking

Place Plumereau and the surrounding streets are plastered with grungy bars and drinking dens, all of which get stuffed to bursting on hot summer nights.

Bistro 64 JAZZ BAR

(64 rue du Grand Marché; ⊙11am-2am Mon-Sat) One step removed from the place Plum hustle. Scuffed-up decor, jazz combos and plenty of house beers entertain a local crowd.

La Canteen WINE BAR

(10 rue de la Grosse Tour; ⊙noon-2.30pm & 7.30-11pm Mon-Sat) For something smoother and sexier, swing by this designer wine bar with rough stone walls, leather sofas, razor-sharp tables and neon-lit bar.

Information

Tourist office (☑02 47 70 37 37; www.ligeris. com; 78-82 rue Bernard Palissy; ⊙8.30am-7pm Mon-Sat, 10am-12.30pm & 2.30-5pm Sun)

ⓘ Getting There & Away

Air

Tours-Val de Loire Airport (www.tours.aero port.fr), 5km northeast, is linked to London's Stansted, Dublin, Marseille and Porto by Ryanair.

Bus

The **information desk** (⊙8am-6.30pm Mon-Fri, 8.30am-12.30pm & 1.30-6.30pm Sat) for **Touraine Fil Vert** (☑02 47 31 14 00; www. touraine-filvert.com, in French) is at the bus

---

WORTH A TRIP

TOP CHATEAUX TRIPS

From Tours a clutch of fabulous castles beg to be discovered:

» **Chenonceau** (www.chenonceau.com; adult/child €10.50/8; ⊙9am-8pm Jul & Aug, 9am-7.30pm Jun & Sep, 9am-7pm Apr & May, 9.30am-5 or 6pm Oct-Mar) This 16th-century castle is one of the Loire's most architecturally attractive – and busiest. Framed by a glassy moat and sweeping gardens, and topped by turrets and towers, it's straight out of a fairy tale. Don't miss the yew-tree labyrinth and the 60m-long Grande Gallerie spanning the Cher River.

» **Azay-le-Rideau** (☑02 47 45 42 04; adult/child €7.50/free; ⊙9.30am-6pm, to 7pm Jul & Aug, 10am-12.30pm & 2-5.30pm Oct-Mar) Built in the 1500s on an island in the Indre River, this romantic, moat-ringed wonder flouts geometric windows, ordered turrets and decorative stonework. Don't miss: its famous loggia staircase and summertime *son et lumière*.

» **Langeais** (☑02 47 96 72 60; adult/child €8.50/5; ⊙9.30am-6.30pm, to 5.30pm Feb & Mar, 9am-7pm Jul & Aug) For medieval atmosphere, head for this 15th-century fortress complete with working drawbridge, crenellated battlements and ruined 10th-century donjon. Don't miss the ruined keep (France's oldest) built by 10th-century warlord, Count Foulques Nerra.

» **Villandry** (www.chateauvillandry.com; adult/child €9/5, gardens only €6/3.50; ⊙chateau 9am-6pm, to 5.30pm Mar, to 5pm Feb & early Nov, gardens 9am-5pm to 7.30pm year-round) One of the last major Renaissance chateaux to be built in the Loire, this one is more famous for what's outside than in. Its gardens are nothing short of glorious. Don't miss the Ornamental Garden or the *potager* (kitchen garden).

FRANCE THE LOIRE VALLEY

Tours

200 m
0.1 miles

To Rochecorbon (3km);
Amboise (23km)

R François Clouet

Bd Heurteloup

Bd Heurteloup

R du Rempart

To St-Pierre-des-Corps;
Train Station (5km)

R Albert Thomas

Cathédrale St-Gatien

Musée des Beaux-Arts

Flower Garden

R des Ursulines

R Jules Simon

R Édouard Vaillant

Pl du Général Leclerc

R Lavoisier

Pl de la Cathédrale

R Bernard Palissy

Av Charles Gilles

R de la Barre

R du Cygne

R Colbert

Pl François Sicard

Jardin de la Préfecture

R de Bordeaux

R Corneille

Pl de la Préfecture

R de Buffon

R Victor Laloux

R Berthelot

R Pimbert

R de la Scellerie

R Émile Zola

Pl Jean Jaurès

Av de Grammont

R Voltaire

Musée du Compagnonnage

R Nationale

R de la Préfecture

R des Minimes

To Tours-Val de
Loire Airport
(12km)

R du Commerce

Pl de la Résistance

R des Déportés

R Marceau

R de Cloche

Bd Béranger

Bd Béranger

To Azay-le-Rideau (25km);
Loches (42km); Chinon (46km)

R de Constantine

R de Jérusalem

R Néricault Destouches

R de la Grandière

R des Orfèvres

R de la Monnaie

R de la Rôtisserie

R Descartes

R Rapin

R Rabelais

R Léonard de Vinci

R de la Paix

Pl Plumereau

R du Châteauneuf

R del Arbalète

Pl Gaston Paillhou

R Briçonnet

R du Mûrier

Pl du Grand Marché

R des Halles

R Chanoineau

R des Tanneurs

Q du Pont Neuf

R Bretonneau

R Étienne Marcel

Pl du Grand Marché

R des Balais

R de la Grosse Tour

R Eugène Sue

Pl de la Victoire

R de la Victoire

Tours

station, next to the train station. Line C links Tours with Amboise (€1.60, 35 minutes, 12 daily Monday to Saturday) and Chenonceaux (€1.60, 1¼ hours, two daily).

Train

Tours is the Loire's main rail hub. The train station is linked to St-Pierre-des-Corps, Tours' TGV train station, by frequent shuttle trains.

AMBOISE €11, 20 minutes, 12 daily

ANGERS €23 to €34, one hour, 26 daily

BLOIS €9.10, 40 minutes, 12 daily

BORDEAUX €40 to €62, 2¾ hours

CHENONCEAUX €11, 30 minutes, eight daily

LOCHES €11, 50 minutes, one or two daily

NANTES €28 to €55, 1½ hours

ORLÉANS €24 to €35, one to 1½ hours, hourly

PARIS' GARE D'AUSTERLITZ €41 to €62, two to 2¾ hours, five daily, slow trains

PARIS' GARE MONTPARNASSE €44 to €83, 1¼ hours, 30 daily, high-speed TGVs

SAUMUR €14 to €21, 35 minutes, hourly

Amboise

POP 12,900

The childhood home of Charles VIII and final resting place of Leonardo da Vinci, elegant Amboise, 23km northeast of Tours, is pleasantly perched along the southern bank of the Loire and overlooked by its fortified chateau. With some seriously posh hotels and a wonderful weekend market, Amboise is a very popular base for exploring nearby chateaux; coach tours arrive en masse to visit da Vinci's Clos Lucé.

◉ Sights

Château Royal d'Amboise   CASTLE
(place Michel Debré; adult/child €9.70/6.30; ⊙9am-6pm Apr–mid-Nov, 9am-5.30pm Mar, 9am-12.30pm & 2-4.45pm Jan-Feb & mid-Nov–Dec) Sprawling across a rocky escarpment above town, this easily defendable castle presented a formidable prospect to would-be attackers – but saw little military action. It was more often used as a weekend getaway from the official royal seat at nearby Blois. Charles VIII (r 1483–98), born and bred here, was responsible for the chateau's Italianate remodelling in 1492. Today, just a few of the original 15th- and 16th-century structures survive, notably the **Flamboyant Gothic wing** and **Chapelle St-Hubert**, believed to be the final resting place of da Vinci. Exit the chateau through the circular **Tour Hurtault** with its ingenious sloping spiral ramp for easy carriage access.

Le Clos Lucé   HISTORIC MANOR
TOP CHOICE (www.vinci-closluce.com; 2 rue du Clos Lucé; adult/child €12.50/7.50; ⊙9am-7pm Feb-Oct, to 6pm Nov-Dec, 10am-6pm Jan) Leonardo da Vinci took up residence in the grand manor house at Le Clos Lucé in 1516 on the invitation of François I, and its interior and gardens are chock-a-block with scale models of the artist's many wacky inventions.

Pagode de Chanteloup   PAGODA
(www.pagode-chanteloup.com, in French; adult/child €8.50/6.50; ⊙10am-7pm) Two kilometres south of Amboise, this curiosity was built between 1775 and 1778 when the odd blend of classical French architecture and Chinese motifs were all the rage. Clamber to the top for glorious views. In summer, picnic hampers (€12 to €26) are sold, you can rent rowing boats, and play free outdoor games.

🛏 Sleeping

La Pavillon des Lys   BOUTIQUE HOTEL €€
(☎02 47 30 01 01; www.pavillondeslys.com; 9 rue d'Orange; d €98-160; ❄) Consider this: take

EASE THE PAIN

Buy tickets in advance at the tourist office and visit early in the day to avoid crowds.

a cappuccino-coloured, 18th-century town house and fill it with designer lamps, roll-top baths, hi-fi stereos and deep sofas – chuck in a locally renowned restaurant and an elegant patio garden and wow, you've got yourself one beautiful hotel!

Le Clos d'Amboise
HISTORIC HOTEL €€

(02 47 30 10 20; www.leclosamboise.com; 27 rue Rabelais; r €97-149;) Another posh pad finished with oodles of style and lashings of luxurious fabrics. Features range from wood-panelling to antique beds; some rooms have separate sitting areas, others original fireplaces. Sauna and gym in the old stables.

Villa Mary
B&B €€

(02 47 23 03 31; www.villa-mary.fr; 14 rue de la Concorde; d incl breakfast €90-120) Four tip-top rooms in an impeccably furnished 18th-century town house, crammed with beeswaxed antiques, glittering chandeliers and antique rugs.

Centre Charles Péguy-Auberge de Jeunesse
HOSTEL €

(02 47 30 60 90; www.mjcamboise.fr; Île d'Or; dm €12; reception 2-8pm Mon-Fri, 5-8pm Sat & Sun;) Efficient boarding-school-style hostel on Île d'Or, with 72 beds mostly in three- or four-bed dorms. Table tennis and bike hire available.

Hôtel Le Blason
HOTEL €

(02 47 23 22 41; www.leblason.fr; 11 place Richelieu; s/d/tr €45/55/70;) Quirky, creaky budget hotel on a quiet square with 25 higgledy-piggledy rooms, wedged in around corridors: most are titchy, flowery and timber-beamed.

Eating

Chez Bruno
REGIONAL CUISINE €

(02 47 57 73 49; place Michel Debré; menus from €12; lunch Tue-Sun, dinner Tue-Sat) Uncork a host of local vintages in a coolly contemporary setting, accompanied by honest regional cooking.

L'Épicerie
TRADITIONAL FRENCH €€

(02 47 57 08 94; 46 place Michel Debré; menus €22-34; Wed-Sun) A more time-honoured atmosphere with rich wood, neo-Renaissance decor and filling fare such as *cuisse de lapin* (rabbit leg) and *tournedos de canard* (duck fillet).

Bigot
TEAROOM €

(2 rue Nationale; 9am-7.30pm Tue-Fri, 8.30am-7.30pm Sat & Sun) Since 1913 this award-winning chocolatier and patisserie has been whipping up some of the Loire's creamiest cakes and gooiest treats: multicoloured *macarons,* buttery biscuits, handmade chocolates and petits fours.

ℹ️ Information

Tourist office (02 47 57 09 28; www.amboise-valdeloire.com; 9am-7pm Mon-Sat, 10am-1pm & 2-6pm Sun) In a riverside building opposite 7 quai du Général de Gaulle.

ℹ️ Getting There & Around

Bicycle

Cycles Richard (02 47 57 01 79; 2 rue de Nazelles; €15/day; 9am-noon & 2.30-7pm Tue-Sat)

Bus

Touraine Fil Vert's Line C (see Tours' Getting There & Away section) links Amboise's post

---

WORTH A TRIP

A TRIP BETWEEN VINES

Burgundy's most renowned vintages come from the **Côte d'Or** (Golden Hillside), a range of hills made of limestone, flint and clay that runs south from Dijon for about 60km. The northern section, the **Côte de Nuits**, stretches from Marsannay-la-Côte south to Corgoloin and produces reds known for their robust, full-bodied character. The southern section, the **Côte de Beaune**, lies between Ladoix-Serrigny and Santenay and produces great reds and whites.

Tourist offices can provide local brochures: *The Burgundy Wine Road,* an excellent free booklet published by the Burgundy Tourist Board (www.bourgogne-tourisme.com); and a useful map, *Roadmap to the Wines of Burgundy* (€0.50). There's also the **Route des Grands Crus** (www.road-of-the-fine-burgundy-wines.com), a signposted road route of some of the most celebrated Côte de Nuits vineyards.

Wine & Voyages (www.wineandvoyages.com; €48-58) and **Alter & Go** (www.alterandgo.fr; €60-80), with an emphasis on history and winemaking methods, run minibus tours in English; reserve online or at the Dijon tourist office.

office with Tours' bus terminal (€1.60, 45 minutes, 12 daily Monday to Saturday). Two go to Chenonceaux (15 minutes, Monday to Saturday).

Train

BLOIS €11, 20 minutes, 14 daily

TOURS €11, 20 minutes, 10 daily

PARIS' GARE D'AUSTERLITZ €38 to €56, 2¼ hours, 14 daily

PARIS' GARE MONTPARNASSE €107, 1¼ hours, 10 daily, TGV

BURGUNDY & THE RHÔNE VALLEY

If there's one place in France where you're really going to find out what makes the nation tick, it's Burgundy. Two of the country's enduring passions – food and wine – come together in this gorgeously rural region, and if you're a sucker for hearty food and the fruits of the vine, you'll be in seventh heaven.

Dijon

POP 250,000

Dijon is one of France's most appealing cities. Filled with elegant medieval and Renaissance buildings, dashing Dijon is Burgundy's capital, and spiritual home of French mustard. Its lively Old Town is wonderful for strolling, especially if you like to leaven your cultural enrichment with excellent food, fine wine and shopping.

Dijon has plenty of green spaces including **Jardin de l'Arquebuse**, whose stream, pond and formal gardens are across the tracks from the train station.

⊙ Sights & Activities

Palais des Ducs et des États de Bourgogne
PALACE

(Palace of the Dukes & States of Burgundy) Once home to Burgundy's powerful dukes, this monumental palace with neoclassical facade overlooks **place de la Libération**, Old Dijon's magnificent central square dating from 1686. The palace's eastern wing houses the outstanding **Musée des Beaux-Arts**, whose entrance is next to the **Tour de Bar**, a squat 14th-century tower that once served as a prison.

Just off the **Cour d'Honneur**, the 46m-high, mid-15th-century **Tour Philippe le Bon** (adult/child €2.30/free; ⊗guided tours every

THE LUCKY OWL

Dijon's **Rue de la Chouette** is named after the small stone *chouette* (owl) carved into the exterior corner of the chapel, diagonally across from No 24. It's said to grant happiness and wisdom to those who stroke it, so generations of fortune-seekers have worked it quite smooth! All sorts of superstitions surround the owl: some insist that walking by the dragon in the lower left corner of the grille of the adjacent window annuls your wish; others insist that approaching the dragon helps your wish come true.

45min 9am-noon & 1.45-5.30pm, closed Mon-Tue & morning Wed, also Thu-Fri late Nov–Easter) affords fantastic views over the city. Spot Mont Blanc on a clear day.

Église Notre Dame
CHURCH

A block north of the Palais des Ducs, this church was built between 1220 and 1240. Its extraordinary facade's three tiers are lined with leering gargoyles separated by two rows of pencil-thin columns. Atop the church, the 14th-century **Horloge à Jacquemart**, transported from Flanders in 1383 by Philip the Bold who claimed it as a trophy of war, chimes every quarter-hour.

Cathédrale St-Bénigne
CHURCH

(place St-Philibert) Built over the tomb of St Benignus (believed to have brought Christianity to Burgundy in the 2nd century), Dijon's Burgundian Gothic-style cathedral was built around 1300 as an abbey church. Some of Burgundy's great figures are buried in its crypt.

Musée de la Vie Bourguignonne
MUSEUM

(17 rue Ste-Anne; ⊗9am-noon & 2-6pm Wed-Mon) Housed in a 17th-century Cistercian convent, this museum explores village and town life in Burgundy in centuries past with evocative tableaux illustrating dress and traditional crafts.

⌒ Sleeping

Hôtel Le Jacquemart
HOTEL €

(☎03 80 60 09 60; www.hotel-lejacquemart.fr; 32 rue Verrerie; d €49-65; @) In the heart of old Dijon, this two-star hotel has tidy, comfortable rooms; the pricier ones come with marble fireplaces.

Dijon

0 200 m
0 0.1 miles

G

R Vannerie

R Chaudronnerie

R Auguste Comte

R Verrerie ⊞ 3

R Jeannin

Pl St-
Michel

R Vaillant

R Buffon

F

Pl de la
Banque

R de la
Chouette

R de la
Préfecture

Église Notre Dame ✚

Palais des Ducs et des
États de Bourgogne ⊞ 1

R Rameau

Pl du
Théâtre

R des
Bons Enfants

R du Palais

R Chabot Chamy

To Airport (6km)

R Pasteur

E

R Bannelier

Impasse Quentin ✕ 9

Pl de la
Libération

R Musette

R des Forges

R Jules Mercier

R du Bourg

R Vauban

R Amiral Roussin

Pl des
Cordeliers

R Turgot

R Ste-Anne

Musée de la Vie
Bourguignonne ⊞

✕ 9

R Victor Dumay

D

Bd de Brosses

R Devosge

Pl
Grangier ⊞
L'Espace
Bus

R Mably

R du
Chapeau Rouge

R de la Liberté

R Bossuet

R Piron

R Brulard

⊞ 10

✕ 7

Pl
Bossuet

Pl Émile
Zola

R Berbisey

R Crébillon ✕ 8

C

Av de la
1ère Armée

Pl
Darcy

Jardin
Darcy

R Dr Chaussier

R du Docteur Maret

Porte Guillaume
(Triumphal Arch)

R Michelet

R Danton

Pl St-
Philibert

Cathédrale
St-Bénigne ✚

R Monge ⊞ 5

R Condorcet

R de la
Manutention

B

R des Perrières

Transco
Bus Stops

Av Maréchal Foch

⊞ 4

R du Dr-Remy

Bd de Sévigné

R Mariotte

Rempart Miséricorde

To Beaune
(45km)

A

To Puits de Moïse (1.3km);
Avallon (105km)

Av Albert 1er

R de l'Arquebuse

Musée
d'Histoire
Naturelle ⊞

Jardin
de l'Arquebuse

R Jehan-de-Marville

Av de l'Ouche

1

2

3

4

Dijon

Hôtel Chambellan   HOTEL €
(☎03 80 67 12 67; www.hotel-chambellan.com; 92 rue Vannerie; s/d from €45/50) Built in 1730, this Old Town address has a vaguely medieval feel. Rooms come in cheerful tones of red, orange, pink and white; some have courtyard views.

Hôtel Le Sauvage   HOTEL €
(☎03 80 41 31 21; www.hotellesauvage.com, in French; 64 rue Monge; s €46-55, d €51-61, tr €80; ☎) Set in a 15th-century *relais de poste* (post-relay house) that ranges around a cobbled, vine-shaded courtyard, this little hotel just off the lively rue Monge is definitely good value.

Hôtel Le Jura   HOTEL €€
(☎03 80 41 61 12; www.oceaniahotels.com; 14 av Maréchal Foch; d €70-92, q €179; 🌡🔒) Near the train station, this no-nonsense hotel has friendly staff and some rooms overlooking a central courtyard. 'Superior' rooms are really that. Room prices fluctuate; check online.

🍴 Eating

Eat streets loaded with restaurants include buzzy rue Berbisey, place Émile Zola, rue Amiral Roussin and around the perimeter of the covered market. Outdoor cafes fill place de la Libération.

Café Chez Nous   CAFE €
(impasse Quentin; lunch menus €8; ☺lunch noon-2pm, bar 10am-2am, 11am-2pm Sun, closed Mon) This quintessentially French *bar du coin* (neighbourhood bar), often crowded, hides down an alleyway near the covered market. Lunches are generally organic and wine by the glass is a bargain (€1.20 to €2.40). Check the chalkboard for dinners and live music.

Le Petit Roi de la Lune   BISTRO €€
(☎03 80 49 89 93; 28 rue Amiral Roussin; lunch menus €10, mains €15-18; ☺lunch Tue-Sat, dinner Mon-Sat) A hip, younger crowd comes for French cuisine that, explains the chef, has been *revisitée, rearrangée et decalée* (revisited, rearranged and shifted). The hugely popular breaded-and-fried Camembert served with blackberry jelly tops the list.

La Mère Folle   BURGUNDIAN €€
(☎03 80 50 19 76; 102 rue Berbisey; menus €10-23; ☺Tue-Sat) Look past the OTT medieval decor to find Burgundian specialities such as *magret de canard au miel, thym et mirabelles* (fillet of duck with honey, thyme and cherry plums). Weekday lunches are a steal and include terrine straight from the crock.

La Dame d'Aquitaine   REGIONAL CUISINE €€
(☎03 80 30 45 65; 23 place Bossuet; menus €21-43; ☺lunch Tue-Sat, dinner Mon-Sat, closed lunch mid-Jul–mid-Aug) Excellent local cuisine is served under the sumptuously lit bays of a 13th-century *cave*. Classical music filters through and the wine list is extensive.

ℹ Information

Tourist office (☎08 92 70 05 58; www.visit dijon.com; ☺9am-6.30pm Mon-Sat, 10am-6pm Sun) Main office (11 rue des Forges); Annexe (train station)

FRANCE DIJON

DON'T MISS

DIJON MUSTARD

If there is one pilgrimage to be made on Dijon's main shopping area, rue de la Liberté, it is to **Moutarde Maille** (32 rue de la Liberté; ☺10am-7pm Mon-Sat), the factory boutique of the company that makes Dijon's most famous mustard. The tangy odours of the sharp sauce assault your nostrils instantly upon entering and there are 36 different kinds to buy, including cassis-, truffle- or celery-flavoured. Three on tap (from €2.40 per 200ml) can be sampled.

ⓘ Getting There & Away

Bus

Transco (☏08 00 10 20 04; www.mobigo
-bourgogne.com) Buses stop in front of the
train station. Bus 60 (€1.50) links Dijon with
the northern Côte de Nuits wine villages of
Marsannay-la-Côte, Couchey, Fixin and Gevrey-
Chambertin (30 minutes).

Eurolines (☏03 80 68 20 44; 53 rue Guillaume
Tell) International travel.

Train

LYON-PART DIEU €36 to 90, two hours, 25
daily

PARIS' GARE DE LYON €52 to €136, 1¾
hours by TGV, three hours regular train, 20
daily

NICE €106 to €213, 6¼ hours by TGV, two
direct daily

STRASBOURG €55 to €126, 3½ hours, nine
daily

ⓘ Getting Around

Bicycle

Main tourist office (€18/day) Rentals with free
helmets.

Velodi (www.velodi.net, in French) 400 bikes at
33 stations around town.

Beaune

POP 22,720

Beaune (pronounced 'bone'), 44km south
of Dijon, is the unofficial capital of the Côte
d'Or. This thriving town's raison d'être and
the source of its joie de vivre is wine: making
it, tasting it, selling it, but most of all, drinking it. Consequently Beaune is one of the
best places in all of France for wine tasting.

The jewel of Beaune's old city is the magnificent Hôtel-Dieu, France's most splendif-
erous medieval charity hospital.

◉ Sights & Activities

Beaune's amoeba-shaped old city is enclosed
by **stone ramparts** sheltering wine cellars.
Lined with overgrown gardens and ringed
by a pathway, they make for a lovely stroll.

TOP CHOICE | **Hôtel-Dieu des Hospices de
Beaune**   GOTHIC HOSPITAL
(rue de l'Hôtel-Dieu; adult/child €6.50/2.80;
⊙9am-6.30pm) Built in 1443, this magnificent Gothic hospital (until 1971) is famously
topped by stunning turrets and pitched
rooftops covered in multicoloured tiles. Interior highlights include the barrel-vaulted
Grande Salle (look for the dragons and

peasant heads up on the roof beams); the
mural-covered **St-Hughes Room**; an 18th-
century **pharmacy** lined with flasks once
filled with elixirs and powders such as
beurre d'antimoine (antimony butter) and
poudre de cloportes (woodlouse powder);
and the multipanelled masterpiece **Polyp-
tych of the Last Judgement** by 15th-centu-
ry Flemish painter Rogier van der Weyden,
depicting Judgment Day in glorious technicolour.

Cellar Visits   WINE TASTING

Millions of bottles of wine age to perfection in cool dark cellars beneath Beaune's
buildings, streets and ramparts. Tasting
opportunities abound and dozens of cellars can be visited by guided tour. Our favourites include the candlelit cellars of the
former Église des Cordeliers, **Marché aux
Vins** (www.marcheauxvins.com, in French; 2 rue
Nicolas Rolin; admission €10; ⊙9.30-11.45am &
2-5.45pm, no midday closure mid-Jun–Aug), where
15 wines can be sampled; and **Cellier de la
Vieille Grange** (www.bourgogne-cellier.com, in
French; 27 blvd Georges Clemenceau; ⊙9am-noon
& 2-7pm Wed-Sat, by appointment Sun-Tue), where
locals flock to buy Burgundy wines *en vrac*
(in bulk) for as little as €1.25 per litre (from
€3.40 per litre for AOC). Tasting is done
direct from barrels using a pipette. Bring
your own jerrycan or buy a vinibag. **Patri-
arche Père et Fils** (www.patriarche.com; 5 rue
du Collège; audioguide tour €10; ⊙9.30-11.30am &
2-5.30pm), lined with about five million bottles of wine, has Burgundy's largest cellars.

🛏 Sleeping

Hôtel des Remparts   HISTORIC HOTEL €€
(☏03 80 24 94 94; www.hotel-remparts-beaune.
com; 48 rue Thiers; d €75-112; ✳@ 🛜) Set
around two delightful courtyards, rooms
in this 17th-century town house have red-
tiled floors, simple antique furniture and
luxurious bathrooms. Friendly staff can
also hire out bikes.

Hôtel Rousseau   HOTEL €
(☏03 80 22 13 59; 11 place Madeleine; d incl
breakfast €58, s/d with washbasin only from €40,
hall shower €3) An endearingly old-fashioned, 12-room hotel where the lady who
has run the place since 1959 occasionally
shuts reception without warning so she
can go shopping.

Abbaye de Maizières   HISTORIC HOTEL €€
(☏03 80 24 74 64; www.beaune-abbaye
-maizieres.com; 19 rue Maizières; d €112; @)

It is not in town, but in beautiful stone-laced vintner villages around Dijon and Beaune that some of Burgundy's most sought-after sleeping addresses are hidden:

» **Villa Louise Hôtel** (☑ 03 80 26 46 70; www.hotel-villa-louise.fr, in French; Aloxe-Corton; d €100-195; @ 🖃 🗷) Who needs city life when you can stow away in vineyard-side luxury? This tranquil mansion on the Côte de Beaune houses dreamy rooms, expansive garden, sauna, pool and wine cellar.

» **Domaine Corgette** (☑ 03 80 21 68 08; www.domainecorgette.com; rue de la Perrière, St-Romain; d incl breakfast €80-90; 🖃) The sun-drenched terrace at this village winery faces dramatic cliffs. Rooms are light and airy with crisp linens, fireplaces and wooden floors.

» **Maison des Abeilles** (☑ 03 80 62 95 42; http://perso.wanadoo.fr/maison-des-abeilles, in French; Magny-les-Villars; d incl breakfast €58-64, q €90; @) Sweet and jolly Jocelyne maintains this impeccably clean *chambre d'hôte* (B&B) in a small village in the Haute Côte. Rooms are colourful and breakfast is a homemade feast.

Think an idiosyncratic hotel inside a 12th-century abbey with 13 rooms featuring brickwork and wooden beams.

✖ Eating

Beaune harbours a host of excellent restaurants; you'll find many around place Carnot, place Félix Ziem and place Madeleine.

Caves Madeleine BURGUNDIAN €€
(☑ 03 80 22 93 30; 8 rue du Faubourg Madeleine; menus €14-24; ⊙ Mon-Wed & Sat, dinner Fri) This is a convivial Burgundian restaurant where locals tuck into regional classics like *boeuf bourguignon* and *cassolette d'escargots* at long shared tables surrounded by wine racks.

Le Bistrot Bourguignon BURGUNDIAN €€
(☑ 03 80 22 23 24; 8 rue Monge; mains €16-19; ⊙ Tue-Sat) This lively bistro and wine bar serves hearty regional cuisine and 17 Burgundy wines by the glass (€3 to €9). Hosts live jazz at least once a month.

Le P'tit Paradis MODERN BURGUNDIAN €€
(☑ 03 80 24 91 00; 25 rue Paradis; menus €19-36; ⊙ Tue-Sat) Find this intimate restaurant, known for *cuisine elaborée* (creative cuisine) made with local products, on a medieval street. Summer terrace.

❶ Information

Tourist office (☑ 03 80 26 21 30; www.beaune-burgundy.com; 6 blvd Perpreuil; ⊙ 9am-7pm Mon-Sat, 9am-6pm Sun)

❶ Getting There & Away
Bus
Bus 44 links Beaune with Dijon (€1.50, 1½ hours, up to seven daily), stopping at Côte d'Or

villages like Vougeot, Nuits-St-Georges and Aloxe-Corton.

Train
DIJON €11, 25 minutes, 40 daily
LYON-PART DIEU €31 to €46, 1¾ hours, 16 daily
MÂCON €12.90, 50 minutes, 16 daily
NUITS-ST-GEORGES €11, 10 minutes, 40 daily
PARIS' GARE DE LYON €64 to €118, 2¼ hours by TGV, 20 daily, two direct TGVs daily

Lyon
POP 480,660

Gourmets, eat your heart out: Lyon is *the* gastronomic capital of France, with a lavish table of piggy-driven dishes and delicacies to savour. The city has been a commercial, industrial and banking powerhouse for the past 500 years, and is still France's second-largest conurbation, with outstanding art museums, a dynamic nightlife, green parks and a Unesco-listed Old Town.

◉ Sights
VIEUX LYON
Old Lyon, with its cobblestone streets and medieval and Renaissance houses below Fourvière hill, is divided into three quarters: St-Paul at the northern end, St-Jean in the middle and St-Georges in the south. Lovely old buildings languish on **rue du Bœuf**, **rue St-Jean** and **rue des Trois Maries**.

The partly Romanesque **Cathédrale St-Jean** (place St-Jean, 5e; ⊙ 8am-noon & 2-7.30pm Mon-Fri, 8am-noon & 2-7pm Sat & Sun; Ⓜ Vieux Lyon), seat of Lyon's 133rd bishop, was built from the late 11th to the early 16th centuries.

FRANCE BURGUNDY & THE RHÔNE VALLEY

Lyon

0
0

400 m
0.2 miles

To La Dombes
& Lyon-St-Exupéry
Airport (25km);
Pérouges (27km)

Pont
Morand

Pl Louis
Pradel

Croix
Paquet

Montée St-Sébastien

R du Griffon

R du Romarin

R Terrailles

Le Village
des Créateurs

R des Tables Claudiennes

R René Leynaud

R Burdeau

R des Capucins

R Ste-Catherine

To Croix
Rousse (1km)

Montée de la
Grande Côte

R Terme

Jardin des
Plantes

R de l'Annonciade

R du Jardin des Plantes

Pl
Sathonay

R Sergent Blandan

R Pareille

Pl de la
Comédie

21

R Verdi

8

R de la Bourse

To Rive
Gauche (50m);
Les Halles de
Lyon (1.5km)

Pont
Lafayette

Pl de la
Bourse

Cordeliers

Hôtel de Ville

R de l'Arbre Sec

PRESQU'ÎLE

R du Bât d'Argent

R Neuve

R Gentil

Pl
Francisque
Régaud

12

Musée des
Beaux-Arts

Fountain

3

R Paul Chenavard

17

9

R de la
Fromagerie

R Dubois

R Paul Chenavard

10

7

R d'Algérie

R Constantine

R Lanterne

R de la Plâtière

R Mercière

15

20

R de la Pêcherie

Q de la Pêcherie

16

Pont
Alphonse
Juin

11

Suône

Q Romain Rolland

Q de Bondy

Pl St-
Paul

R Octavio Mey

R Juiverie

Montée
St-Barthélemy

R de
Gadagne

R du
Gouvernement

Gare St-Paul

ST-PAUL

Pl du
Petit Collège

Q Pierre Scize

Q de Bondy

R Roger Radisson

5E

Fourvière
Hill

5

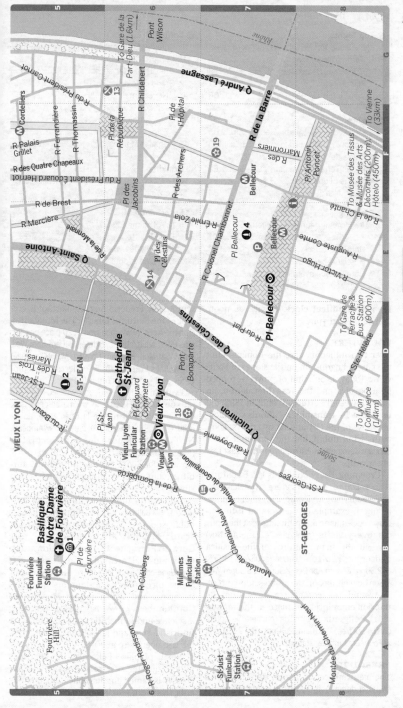

285

FRANCE LYON

Lyon

Its **astronomical clock** chimes at noon, 2pm, 3pm and 4pm.

FOURVIÈRE

Over two millennia ago, the Romans built the city of Lugdunum on the slopes of Fourvière. Today, Lyon's 'hill of prayer' – topped by a basilica and the **Tour Métallique**, an Eiffel Tower–like structure built in 1893 and used as a TV transmitter – affords spectacular views of the city and its two rivers. Footpaths wind uphill, but the **funicular** (place Édouard Commette; €2.40 return) is the least taxing way up.

Crowning Fourvière hill is the **Basilique Notre Dame de Fourvière** (www.fourviere. org; ⊘8am-7pm), an iconic, 27m-high basilica, a superb example of exaggerated 19th-century ecclesiastical architecture. One-hour **discovery visits** (adult/child €2/1; ⊘Apr-Nov) take in the main features of the basilica and crypt; **rooftop tours** (adult/child €5/3; ⊘2.30pm & 4pm Apr-Oct, 2.30pm & 3.30pm Wed & Sun Nov) climax on the stone-sculpted roof.

Around the corner, treasures from its interior enjoy pride of place in the **Musée d'Art Religieux** (8 place de Fourvière, 5e; adult/child €5/free; ⊘10am-12.30pm & 2-5.30pm; ⓂFourvière funicular station).

PRESQU'ÎLE

The centrepiece of **place des Terreaux** (ⓂHôtel de Ville) is a 19th-century fountain sculpted by Frédéric-Auguste Bartholdi, creator of the Statue of Liberty. The **Musée des Beaux-Arts** (www.mba-lyon.fr; 20 place des Terreaux, 1er; adult/child €76/free; ⊘10am-6pm Wed, Thu & Sat-Mon, 10.30am-6pm Fri; ⓂHôtel de Ville) showcases France's finest collection of sculptures and paintings outside Paris.

Lyonnais silks are showcased at the **Musée des Tissus** (www.musee-des-tissus. com, in French; 34 rue de la Charité, 2e; adult/child €7/4; ⊘10am-5.30pm Tue-Sun; ⓂAmpère). Next door, the **Musée des Arts Décoratifs** (free with Musée des Tissus ticket; ⊘10am-noon & 2-5.30pm Tue-Sun) displays 18th-century furniture, tapestries, wallpaper, ceramics and silver.

Laid out in the 17th century, **place Bellecour** (ⓂBellecour) – one of Europe's largest public squares – is pierced by an equestrian **statue of Louis XIV**. South of here, past **Gare de Perrache**, lies the once-downtrodden industrial area of **Lyon Confluence** (www.lyon-confluence.fr), where the Rhône and Saône meet. Trendy restaurants now line its quays, and the ambitious **Musée des Confluences** (www.museedesconfluences.fr), a science-and-humanities museum inside a futuristic steel-and-glass transparent crystal, will open here in 2014.

North of place Bellecour, the charmful hilltop quarter of **Croix Rousse** (ⓂCroix Rousse) is famed for its bohemian inhabitants, lush outdoor food market and silk-weaving tradition, illustrated by the **Maison des Canuts** (www.maisondescanuts.com; 10-12 rue d'Ivry, 4e; adult/child €6/3; ☉10am-6pm Tue-Sat, guided tours 11am & 3.30pm; Ⓜ Croix Rousse).

RIVE GAUCHE

Parc de la Tête d'Or PARK
(blvd des Belges, 6e; Ⓜ Masséna) Spanning 117 hectares, France's largest urban park was landscaped in the 1860s. It's graced by a lake (rent a rowing boat), botanic garden with greenhouses, rose garden, zoo and **puppet theatre** (☎04 78 93 71 75; www.theatre-guignol. com). Its northern realms are ensnared by the post-1960 art of the **Musée d'Art Contemporain** (www.moca-lyon.org; 81 quai Charles de Gaulle, 6e; adult/child €8/free; ☉noon-7pm Wed-Fri, 10am-7pm Sat & Sun).

Buses 41 and 47 link the park with metro Part-Dieu.

Musée Lumière FILM MUSEUM
(www.institut-lumiere.org; 25 rue du Premier Film, 8e; adult/child €6/5; ☉11am-6.30pm Tue-Sun; Ⓜ Monplaisir-Lumière) Cinema's glorious beginnings are showcased at the art nouveau home of Antoine Lumière, who moved to Lyon with sons Auguste and Louis in 1870. The brothers shot the first reels of the world's first motion picture, *La Sortie des Usines Lumières* (Exit of the Lumières Factories) here in one of their father's photographic factories in the grounds on 19 March 1895. The former factory is the Hangar du Premier Film cinema today.

Centre d'Histoire de la Résistance et de la Déportation MILITARY MUSEUM
(www.chrd.lyon.fr; 14 av Berthelot, 7e; adult/child €4/free; ☉9am-5.30pm Wed-Sun; Ⓜ Perrache or Jean Macé) The WWII headquarters of Gestapo commander Klaus Barbie evokes Lyon's role as the 'Capital of the Resistance' through moving multimedia exhibits.

WANT MORE?

For in-depth information, reviews and recommendations at your fingertips, head to the Apple App Store to purchase Lonely Planet's *Lyon City Guide* iPhone app.

Alternatively, head to **Lonely Planet** (www.lonelyplanet.com/france/burgundy-and-the-rhone/lyon) for planning advice, author recommendations, traveller reviews and insider tips.

The **Lyon City Card** (www.lyon-france. com; 1/2/3 days adult €20/30/40, child €11/15/20) covers admission to every Lyon museum and the roof of Basilique Notre Dame de Fourvière, as well as a guided city tour, a river excursion (April to October) and discounts on other selected attractions, exhibitions and shops.

The card also includes unlimited travel on city buses, trams, the funicular and metro (cheaper cards not incorporating transport are available). Pre-book online or buy from the tourist office.

⚜ Festivals & Events

Les Nuits de Fourvière MUSIC
(Fourvière Nights; www.nuitsdefourviere. fr, in French) Open-air concerts atmospherically set in Fourvière's Roman amphitheatre; early June to late July.

Fête des Lumières LIGHT
(Festival of Lights; www.lumieres.lyon.fr) Over several days around the Feast of the Immaculate Conception (8 December), sound-and-light shows are projected onto key buildings.

🛏 Sleeping

Péniche Barnum B&B €€
(☎06 63 64 37 39; www.peniche-barnum.com; 3 quai du Général Sarrail, 6e; d €120-150; ❄@🛜; Ⓜ Foch) Moored on the Rhône between Pont Morand and the Passerelle du Collège footbridge, Lyon's most unique B&B is a navy-and-timber barge with two smart en suite guestrooms, a book-filled lounge, and shaded terrace on deck. Organic breakfast €10.

Hôtel Le Boulevardier HOTEL €
(☎04 78 28 48 22; www.leboulevardier.fr; 5 rue de la Fromagerie, 1er; s €45-51, d €47-53; 🛜; Ⓜ Hôtel de Ville) Sporting quirky touches such as old skis and tennis racquets adorning the hallways, Le Boulevardier is a bargain 11-room hotel with snug, spotless rooms. It's up a steep spiral staircase above a cool little bistro and jazz club of the same name, which doubles as reception.

Hotelo HOTEL €€
(☎04 78 37 39 03; www.hotelo-lyon.com; 37 cours de Verdun, 2e; d from €70; Ⓜ Perrache) Our hot

choice around Gare de Perrache, this one stands out for its crisp contemporary design. Studios have a kitchenette and one room is perfectly fitted out for travellers with disabilities.

Hôtel de Paris
HOTEL €€

(04 78 28 00 95; www.hoteldeparis-lyon.com; 16 rue de la Platière, 1er; s €49-59, d €65-90; ❄@🛜; MHôtel de Ville) At this fantastic-value hotel in a 19th-century bourgeois building, the funkiest rooms' retro '70s decor incorporates a palette of chocolate-and-turquoise or candyfloss-pink.

Auberge de Jeunesse du Vieux Lyon
HOSTEL €

(04 78 15 05 50; lyon@fuaj.org; 41-45 montée du Chemin Neuf, 5e; dm incl breakfast €18; ⏱reception 7am-1pm, 2-8pm & 9pm-1am; @🛜; MVieux Lyon) Stunning city views unfold from the terrace of Lyon's only hostel, and from many of the (mostly six-share) dorms.

Hôtel Iris
HOTEL €

(04 78 39 93 80; www.hoteliris.fr; 36 rue de l'Arbre Sec, 1er; s €43-55, d €56-80; MHôtel de Ville) This basic but colourful dame in a centuries-old convent couldn't be better placed: its street brims with hip places to eat and drink.

Eating

A flurry of big-name chefs presides over a sparkling restaurant line-up that embraces all genres: French, fusion, fast and international, as well as traditional Lyonnais *bouchons* (literally meaning 'bottle stopper' or 'traffic jam', but in Lyon a small, friendly bistro serving the city's local cuisine). See www.lyonresto.com (in French) for reviews, videos and ratings.

EAT STREETS

» **Rue St-Jean** A surfeit of restaurants jam Vieux Lyon's pedestrian main street.

» **Cobbled rue Mercière, rue des Marronniers** & **place Antonin Poncet, 2e** Ride the metro to Bellecour and these buzzing streets, chock-a-block with eating options (of widely varying quality) and pavement terraces overflowing in summer.

» **Rue du Garet** & **Rue Verdi, 1er** This twinset of parallel streets sits snug by Lyon's opera house on the Presqu'île.

TOP CHOICE **Le Bec**
FRENCH, FUSION €€€

(04 78 42 15 00; www.nicolaslebec.com, 2e; 14 rue Grolée; lunch menus €40, dinner menus €90-135; ⏱Tue-Sat) With two Michelin stars, this is the flagship restaurant of Lyon's hottest chef Nicolas Le Bec, famed for his seasonal, world-influenced cuisine. Sunday brunch (€45) at his other address, innovative concept space **Rue Le Bec** (04 78 92 87 87; 43 quai Rambaud, 2e; mains €9-30; ⏱Tue-Sun; 🚋1, Montrochet stop), on the Confluence, is equally hot.

TOP CHOICE **Magali et Martin**
LYONNAIS €€

(04 72 00 88 01; 11 rue Augustins, 1er; lunch/dinner menus €19.60/35; ⏱Mon-Fri; MHôtel de Ville) Watch chefs turn out traditional but lighter, more varied *bouchon*-influenced cuisine, at this sharp dining address.

Café des Fédérations
BOUCHON €€

(04 78 28 26 00; www.lesfedeslyon.com, in French; 8 rue Major Martin, 1er; menus €19-42; ⏱Mon-Sat; MHôtel de Ville) Black-and-white

---

A MARKET LUNCH

Shopping and munching some lunch at the market is an unmissable part of the Lyon experience.

Pick up a round of impossibly runny St Marcellin from legendary cheesemonger Mère Richard, or a knobbly Jésus de Lyon from pork butcher Collette Sibilia at Lyon's famed indoor market **Les Halles de Lyon** (http://halledelyon.free.fr, in French; 102 cours Lafayette, 3e; ⏱8am-7pm Tue-Sat, 8am-noon Sun; MPart-Dieu). Or simply sit down and enjoy a lunch of local produce, lip-smacking *coquillages* (shellfish) included, at one of its stalls.

Alternatively, meander up to the hilltop quarter of Croix Rousse and, December to April, indulge in oysters and a glass of white Cotes de Rhône on a cafe pavement terrace – before or after shopping at its fabulous **outdoor food market** (blvd de la Croix Rousse, 4e; ⏱Tue-Sun morning; MCroix Rousse).

photos of old Lyon hang on wood-panelled walls at this Lyonnais bistro, unchanged for decades.

Le Comptoir des Filles
LYONNAIS €€

(☑04 78 38 03 30; 8 quai des Celestins, 2e; mains €15-23; ☺Tue-Sat; Ⓜ Bellecour) *Quenelles* (Lyonnais dumplings) are the speciality of this elegant, Saône-side spot. Six varieties are available each day along with other market-prepared dishes.

Comptoir-Restaurant des Deux Places
BOUCHON €€

(☑04 78 28 95 10; 5 place Fernand Rey, 1er; lunch/dinner menus €13/28; ☺Tue-Sat; Ⓜ Hôtel de Ville) Checked curtains, antique-crammed interior and ink-scribed menu contribute to the overwhelmingly traditional feel of this neighbourhood bistro with an idyllic terrace beneath trees.

Grand Café des Négociants
BRASSERIE €€

(www.cafe-des-negociants.com, in French; 2 place Francisque Regaud, 2e; mains €17.50-34; ☺7am-3am; Ⓜ Cordeliers) This cafe-style brasserie with mirror-lined walls and tree-shaded terrace has been a favourite meeting point with Lyonnais since 1864. Don't miss its thick hot chocolate (cheaper before noon).

🍷 Drinking & Entertainment

Cafe terraces on place des Terreaux buzz with all-hours drinkers, as do the British, Irish and other-styled pubs on nearby rue Ste-Catherine, 1er, and rue Lainerie and rue St-Jean, 5e, in Vieux Lyon.

Weekly what's on guides include **Lyon Poche** (www.lyonpoche.com, in French; at newsagents €1) and **Le Petit Bulletin** (www.petit-bulletin.fr, in French; free on street corners). Track nightclub offerings at www.lyonclubbing.com, www.lyon2night.com and www.night4lyon.com (all in French).

You can buy theatre and concert tickets at **Fnac Billetterie** (www.fnac.com/spectacles; 85 rue de la République, 2e; ☺10am-7pm Mon-Sat; Ⓜ Bellecour).

Ninkasi Gerland
LIVE MUSIC

(www.ninkasi.fr, in French; 267 rue Marcel Mérieux, 7e; Ⓜ Stade de Gerland) Spilling over with a fun, frenetic crowd, this microbrewery near Lyon's football stadium is one of several Ninkasi addresses around town. Entertainment ranges from DJs and bands to film projections amid a backdrop of fish-and-chips, build-your-own burgers and other un-French food.

DRINKS AFLOAT
289

Floating bars with DJs and live bands rock until around 3am aboard the string of *péniches* (river barges) moored along the Rhône's left bank. Scout out the section of quai Victor Augagneur between Pont Lafayette (metro Cordeliers or Guichard) and Pont de la Guillotière (metro Guillotière).

Our favourites: laid-back **Passagère** (21 quai Victor Augagneur, 7e; ☺daily); classy **La Pie** (http://lapieresto.com, in French; 2 quai Victor Augagneur, 3e; ☺Wed-Sat); party-hard **Le Sirius** (www.lesirius.com, in French; 4 quai Victor Augagneur, 3e; ☺daily; 🐾); and electro-oriented **La Marquise** (www.marquise.net, in French; 20 quai Victor Augagneur, 3e; ☺Tue-Sun).

Le Wine Bar d'à Côté
WINE BAR

(www.cave-vin-lyon.com, in French; 7 rue Pleney, 1er; ☺Tue-Sat; Ⓜ Cordeliers) Hidden in a tiny alleyway, this cultured wine bar feels like a rustic English gentlemen's club with leather sofa seating and library.

Le Voxx
BAR

(1 rue d'Algérie, 1er; Ⓜ Hôtel de Ville) Minimalist riverside bar packed with a real mix of people, from students to city slickers.

Opéra de Lyon
OPERA HOUSE

(www.opera-lyon.com, in French; place de la Comédie, 1er; Ⓜ Hôtel de Ville) Premier venue for opera, ballet and classical music.

(L'A)Kroche
LIVE MUSIC

(8 rue Monseigneur Lavarenne, 5e; ☺Tue-Sun; Ⓜ Vieux Lyon) Hip concert cafe-bar with DJs spinning electro, soul, funk and disco; bands too.

Hot Club de Lyon
LIVE MUSIC

(www.hotclubjazz.com, in French; 26 rue Lanterne, 1er; admission €5-18; ☺Tue-Sat; Ⓜ Hôtel de Ville) Lyon's leading jazz club, around since 1948.

Le Transbordeur
LIVE MUSIC

(www.transbordeur.fr, in French; 3 blvd de Stalingrad, Villeurbanne) In an old industrial building, Lyon's prime concert venue draws international acts on the European concert-tour circuit.

ℹ Information
Tourist office (☑04 72 77 69 69; www.lyon-france.com; place Bellecour, 2e; ☺9am-6pm; Ⓜ Bellecour)

ⓘ Getting There & Away

Air

Lyon-St-Exupéry Airport (www.lyon.aeroport.fr), 25km east of the city, serves 120 direct destinations across Europe and beyond, including many budget carriers.

Bus

Eurolines (☑04 72 56 95 30; www.eurolines.fr; Gare de Perrache)

Linebús (☑04 72 41 72 27; www.linebus.com, in Spanish; Gare de Perrache)

Train

Lyon has two main-line train stations: **Gare de la Part-Dieu** (Ⓜ Part-Dieu) and **Gare de Perrache** (Ⓜ Perrache). Some destinations by direct TGV:

BEAUNE €23.10, 2¼ hours, up to nine daily

DIJON €30.20, two hours, at least 12 daily

LILLE-EUROPE €92, 3¼ hours, nine daily

MARSEILLE €58.60, 1¾ hours, every 30 to 60 minutes

PARIS GARE DE LYON €64.30, two hours, every 30 to 60 minutes

STRASBOURG €55.90, 4¾ hours, five daily

ⓘ Getting Around

Tramway **Rhonexpress** (www.rhonexpress.net, in French) links the airport with Part-Dieu train station in under 30 minutes. Trams depart approximately every 15 minutes between 6am and 9pm, and every 30 minutes from 5am to 6am and 9pm to midnight. A single/return ticket costs €13/23.

Buses, trams, a four-line metro and two funiculars linking Vieux Lyon to Fourvière are run by **TCL** (www.tcl.fr). Public transport runs from around 5am to midnight. Tickets cost €1.60/13.70 for one/*carnet* of 10; bring coins as machines don't accept notes (or some international credit cards). Time-stamp tickets on all forms of public transport or risk a fine.

Bikes are available from 200-odd bike stations thanks to **vélo'v** (www.velov.grandlyon.com; first 30min free, first/subsequent hr €1/2).

THE FRENCH ALPS & JURA

Whether it's paragliding among the peaks, hiking the trails or hurtling down a mountainside strapped to a pair of glorified toothpicks, the French Alps is the undisputed centre of adventure sports in France. Under Mont Blanc's 4810m of raw wilderness lies the country's most spectacular outdoor playground, and if the seasonal crowds get too much, you can always take refuge in the little-visited Jura, a region of dark wooded hills and granite plateaux stretching for 360km along the French–Swiss border.

Chamonix

POP 9400 / ELEV 1037M

With the pearly white peaks of the Mont Blanc massif as sensational backdrop, being an icon comes naturally to Chamonix. First 'discovered' by Brits William Windham and Richard Pococke in 1741, this is the mecca of mountaineering. Its knife-edge peaks, plunging slopes and massive glaciers have enthralled generations of adventurers and thrill-seekers ever since. Its après-ski scene is equally pumping.

◉ Sights

Aiguille du Midi MOUNTAIN PEAK, CABLE CAR

A jagged pinnacle of rock 8km from the domed summit of Mont Blanc, the **Aiguille du Midi** (3842m) is one of Chamonix' iconic landmarks. If you can handle the height, the 360-degree panorama from the top of the French, Swiss and Italian Alps is unforgettable.

The vertiginous **Téléphérique du l'Aiguille du Midi** (☑04 50 53 30 80, advance reservations 24hr 04 50 53 22 75; 100 place de l'Aiguille du Midi; adult/child return Aiguille du Midi €41/33, Plan de l'Aiguille €24/19.20; ☺8.30am-4.30pm) links Chamonix with the Aiguille du Midi. Mid-station Plan de l'Aiguille (2317m) is a terrific place to start hikes or paraglide. In summer you will need to obtain a boarding card (marked with the number of your departing *and* returning cable car) in addition to a ticket. Advance phone reservations incur a €2 booking fee. Bring warm clothes, as even in summer the temperature rarely rises above -10°C at the top.

Mid-May to mid-September the unrepentant can continue for a further 30 minutes of mind-blowing scenery – think suspended glaciers and spurs, seracs and shimmering ice fields – in the smaller bubbles of the

TICKET TO RIDE

Public transport is free in the Chamonix valley if you have a **carte d'hôte** – free from your hotel or camping ground when you check in! The card includes reductions on some activities too.

ERIC FAVRET: MOUNTAIN GUIDE

Ever since Mont Blanc, the highest peak in the Alps, was first climbed in 1786, Chamonix has attracted travellers worldwide. And there is something really special about it: not only does it sit amid extremely condensed mountaineering opportunities, it's also a perfectly balanced combination of pure landscape alignment and dramatic mountain views.

Aiguille du Midi

The Aiguille du Midi, with one of the highest cable cars in the world, cannot be missed. Beyond the summit ridge is a world of snow and ice offering some of the greatest intermediate off-piste terrain in the Alps.

Off-Piste Thrills

The Vallée Blanche has to be seen. But the Aiguille du Midi also has amazing off-piste runs, such as Envers du Plan, a slightly steeper and more advanced version of Vallée Blanche, offering dramatic views in the heart of the Mont Blanc range. There is also the less frequented run of the 'Virgin' or 'Black Needle'; a striking glacial run, offering different views and a close-up look at the Giant's seracs.

Best-Ever Mont Blanc View

No hesitation: the Traverse from Col des Montets to Lac Blanc. It's as popular as the Eiffel Tower for hikers in summer. I love swimming in mountain lakes, so I like to stop at Lac des Chéserys, just below, where it is quieter: what's better than a swim in pure mountain water, looking at Mont Blanc, the Grandes Jorasses and Aiguille Verte? This is what I call mountain landscape perfection!

Télécabine Panoramic Mont Blanc (adult/child return from Chamonix €65/52; ⊙8.30am-3.45pm) to **Pointe Helbronner** (3466m) on the French–Italian border. From here another cable car descends to the Italian ski resort of Courmayeur.

Le Brévent   MOUNTAIN PEAK
The highest peak on the western side of the valley, **Le Brévent** (2525m) offers fabulous views of the Mont Blanc massif. It can be reached via the **Télécabine du Brévent** (29 rte Henriette d'Angeville; adult/child €24/19.50; ⊙8.50am-4.45pm Jun-Aug, 8.45am-4.45pm mid-Dec–Apr), which is found at the end of rue de la Mollard.

Mer de Glace   GLACIER
The glistening **Mer de Glace** (Sea of Ice) is the second-largest glacier in the Alps, 14km long, 1800m wide and up to 400m deep. A quaint red mountain train links **Gare du Montenvers** (35 place de la Mer de Glace; adult/child €24/19; ⊙10am-4.30pm) in Chamonix with Montenvers (1913m), from where a cable car transports tourists in summer down to the glacier and the **Grotte de la Mer de Glace** (⊙Dec-May & mid-Jun–Sep), an ice cave where frozen tunnels and ice sculptures – carved anew every year since 1946 –

change colour like mood rings. A quaint red mountain train trundles up from **Gare du Montenvers** (35 place de la Mer de Glace; adult/child €24/19; ⊙10am-4.30pm) in Chamonix to Montenvers (1913m), from where a cable car takes you down to the glacier and cave. Tickets cover the 20-minute journey, entry to the caves and the cable car.

The Mer de Glace can be reached on foot via the Grand Balcon Nord trail from Plan de l'Aiguille. The two-hour uphill trail from Chamonix starts near the summer luge track. Traversing the crevassed glacier requires proper equipment and an experienced guide.

🏃 Activities

The **Maison de la Montagne** (190 place de l'Église; ⊙8.30am-noon & 3-7pm), across the square from the tourist office, supplies comprehensive details on hiking, skiing and every other imaginable pastime in the Mont Blanc area.

🛏 Sleeping

TOP CHOICE **Auberge du Manoir**   CHALET €€
(☑04 50 53 10 77; www.aubergedumanoir .com, in French; 8 rte du Bouchet; s €94-108, d €104-150, q €165; ☎) This beautifully converted

farmhouse, ablaze with geraniums in summer, ticks all the perfect-Alpine-chalet boxes: pristine mountain views, pine-panelled rooms and an inviting bar where an open fire keeps things cosy.

Hotel Slalom
BOUTIQUE HOTEL €€

(04 50 54 40 60; www.hotelslalom.net; 44 rue de Bellevue, Les Houches; r €158;) The rooms are the epitome of boutique chic – sleek, snowy white and draped with Egyptian cotton linens – at this gorgeous chalet-style hotel, situated nicely at the foot of the slopes in Les Houches.

Le Vert Hôtel
PARTY HOTEL €€

(04 50 53 13 58; www.verthotel.com; 964 rte des Gaillands; s/d/tr/q €75/96/120/140, minimum 3-night stay) Self-proclaimed 'Chamonix' house of sports and creativity', this party house 1km south of town has no-frills rooms, some with microscopic bathrooms. But what people really come for is the hotel's all-happening, ultrahip bar, a regular venue for top DJs and live music.

Hôtel El Paso
PARTY HOTEL €

(04 50 53 64 20; www.cantina.fr; 37 impasse des Rhododendrons; s/d/tr/q €49/64/75/90) What you'll get is a threadbare mattress and four scuffed walls reminiscent of good times – small sacrifices given that El Paso is cheap, central and *the* place to party, dude. Tex-Mex feasts and DJs downstairs keep the place rocking, so invest in earplugs if sleeping is a priority.

Hotel L'Oustalet
FAMILY HOTEL €€

(04 50 55 54 99; www.hotel-oustalet.com; 330 rue du Lyret; d/q €140/180;) You'll pray for snow at this Alpine chalet near Aiguille du Midi cable car, just so you can curl up by the fire with a *chocolat chaud* (hot chocolate) and unwind in the sauna and whirlpool. Rooms are snugly decorated in solid pine and open onto balconies with Mont Blanc views. There's a pool in the garden for summertime chilling.

SAVVY SLEEPS

Book ahead in winter, when hotel beds are at a premium. Many places close from mid-April to May and from November to mid-December. Room rates nosedive in the low season and summer; expect discounts of up to 50% on high-season prices.

Hôtel Faucigny
SMALL HOTEL €€

(04 50 53 01 17; www.hotelfaucigny-chamonix. com; 118 place de l'Église; s/d/tr/q €55/86/98/124;) This bijou hotel is one of the sweetest deals in town. Relax by an open fire in winter and out on the flower-clad terrace with Mont Blanc views in summer.

Les Deux Glaciers
CAMPING GROUND €

(04 50 53 15 84; www.les2glaciers.com; 80 rte des Tissières; campsites €14.50; mid-Dec–mid-Nov;) Oh, what a beautiful morning! Draw back your tent flap and be dazzled by Mont Blanc and glaciated peaks at this almost year-round camping ground in Les Bossons, 3km south of Chamonix. Take the train to Les Bossons, or the Chamonix bus to Tremplin-le-Mont.

Eating

Les Vieilles Luges
TOP CHOICE
TRADITIONAL FRENCH €€

(www.lesvieillesluges.com; Les Houches; menus €20-35) Like a scene from a snow globe, this childhood dream of a 250-year-old farmhouse can only be reached by slipping on skis or taking a scenic 20-minute hike from Maison Neuve chairlift.

Le Bistrot
GASTRONOMIC €€€

(04 50 53 57 64; www.lebistrotchamonix.com, in French; 151 av de l'Aiguille du Midi; menus €17-65) Sleek and monochromatic, this is a real foodie's place. Michelin-starred chef Mickey experiments with textures and seasonal flavours to create taste sensations like pan-seared Arctic char with chestnuts, and divine warm chocolate macaroon with raspberry and red pepper coulis.

Le GouThé
TEAROOM €

(95 rue des Moulins; menus €9; 9am-6.30pm Fri-Mon) Philippe's hot chocolates with pistachio and gingerbread infusions, bright macaroons and crumbly homemade tarts are just the sugar fix for the slopes. He's a dab hand with *galettes* (buckwheat crêpes), too.

Le Chaudron
REGIONAL CUISINE €€

(04 50 53 57 64; 79 rue des Moulins; menus €20-23; dinner) Funky cowskin-clad benches are the backdrop for a feast of Savoyard fondues and lamb slow-cooked in red wine to melting perfection at this chic chalet.

Munchie
FUSION €€

(04 50 53 45 41; www.munchie.eu; 87 rue des Moulins; mains €18-24; dinner) Think pan-Asian fusion at this trendy Swedish-run hang-out where sittings go faster than

A LOFTY LUNCH

Feast on fine cuisine and even finer mountain views at these high-altitude favourites:

» **La Crémerie du Glacier** (www.lacremerieduglacier.fr, in French; 766 chemin de la Glacière; mains €10-19; ⊘Tue-Mon) World-famous *croûtes au fromage* (toast topped with melted cheese). Ski here with the red Pierre à Ric piste in Les Grands Montets.

» **Le 3842** (☑04 50 55 82 23; Aiguille du Midi; mains €12-21; ⊘restaurant mid-Jun–mid-Sep, snack bar all year) Dining and drinking with knockout views at what claims to be Europe's highest cafe atop the Aiguille du Midi.

» **Le Panoramic** (☑04 50 53 44 11; Le Brévent; menus from €15; ⊘mid-Dec–Apr & late Jun–Sep) Cheeses, cured meats, BBQ fare and knockout MB views.

musical chairs (making it worth a try even without a reservation).

Drinking & Entertainment

Nightlife rocks. In the centre, riverside rue des Moulins boasts a line-up of drinking holes. Get the low-down on the slopeside scene on www.lepetitcanardchx.com.

Most après-ski joints serve food as well as booze.

Chambre Neuf   BAR
(272 av Michel Croz; 🕾) Cover bands, raucous après-ski drinking and Swedish blondes dancing on the tables make Room Nine one of Chamonix's liveliest party haunts. Conversations about epic off-pistes and monster jumps that are, like, totally mental, man, dominate at every table.

Monkey Bar   MUSIC BAR
(81 place Edmond Desailloud; ⊘1pm-2am; 🕾) Slightly grungy, very cool, this party hot spot has live gigs and DJs several times a week. There's a mad rush to the bar at 4.45pm, when pints are €1.50 for 15 minutes!

MBC   MICROBREWERY
(www.mbchx.com; 350 rte du Bouchet; ⊘4pm-2am) Be it with burgers, cheesecake, live music or amazing locally brewed beers, this trendy microbrewery delivers.

Information

Tourist office (☑04 50 53 00 24; www.chamonix.com; 85 place du Triangle de l'Amitié; ⊘8.30am-7pm)

Getting There & Away

Bus

From **Chamonix bus station** (www.sat-montblanc.com; place de la Gare), next to the train station, two to three buses run daily to/from Geneva airport (one way/return €33/55, 1½ to two hours) and Courmayeur (one way/return €13/20, 45 minutes). Advanced booking only.

Train

From Chamonix-Mont Blanc **train station** (place de la Gare) the Mont Blanc Express narrow-gauge train trundles to/from St-Gervais-Le Fayet (€9.50, 40 minutes, nine to 12 daily), from where there are trains to most major French cities.

Annecy

POP 53,000 / ELEV 447M

Lac d'Annecy is one of the world's purest lakes, receiving only rainwater, spring water and mountain streams. Swimming in its sapphire depths, surrounded by snowy mountains, is a real Alpine highlight. Strolling the geranium-strewn streets of the historic Vieille Ville (Old Town) is not half bad either.

Sights & Activities

Vieille Ville & Lakefront   OLD TOWN, LAKE
Wandering around the Vieille Ville and the lakefront is the essence of Annecy. Behind the town hall are the **Jardins de l'Europe**, linked to the park of **Champ de Mars** by the **Pont des Amours** (Lovers' Bridge).

With labyrinthine narrow streets and colonnaded passageways, the Old Town retains much of its 17th-century appearance. On the central island, imposing **Palais de l'Isle** (3 passage de l'Île; adult/child €4.90/2.30; ⊘10.30am-6pm) was a prison, but now hosts local-history displays.

In the 13th- to 16th-century castle above town, the museum inside **Château d'Annecy** (adult/child €4.90/2.30; ⊘10.30am-6pm) explores traditional Savoyard art, crafts and Alpine natural history.

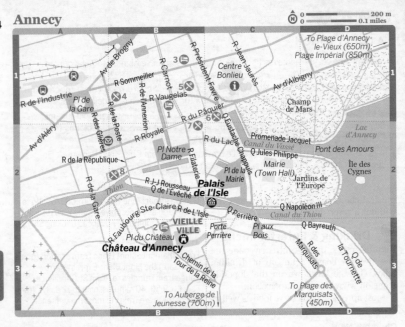

0 ——— 200 m
0 ——— 0.1 miles

Annecy

⊙ Top Sights

🛏 Sleeping

🍴 Eating

Parks line the lakefront. Public beach **Plage d'Annecy-le-Vieux** is 1km east of Champ de Mars. Closer to town, the private **Plage Impérial** (€3.50; ☺Jul & Aug) sits beneath the pre-WWI **Impérial Palace**. **Plage des Marquisats** (☺Jul & Aug) is 1km south of the Vieille Ville along rue des Marquisats.

🛏 Sleeping

Hôtel Alexandra   FAMILY HOTEL €
(☏04 50 52 84 33; www.hotelannecy-alexandra.fr; 19 rue Vaugelas; s/d/tr/q €48/59/70/89; 🛜) Nice

surprise: Annecy's most charming hotel is also among its most affordable. The welcome is five-star and rooms are spotless – a few extra euros gets you a balcony and canal view.

Le Pré Carré   BOUTIQUE HOTEL €€€
(☏04 50 52 14 14; www.hotel-annecy.net; 27 rue Sommeiller; s/d €172/202; ✷@🛜) Chic Le Pré Carré keeps things contemporary with Zen colours in rooms, a jacuzzi and business corner. The staff know Annecy inside out, so you're in very good hands.

Hôtel du Château   HOTEL €
(☏04 50 45 27 66; www.annecy-hotel.com; 16 rampe du Château; s/d/tr/q €49/68/75/85; 🛜) Nestled at the foot of the castle, this hotel's trump card is its sun-drenched, panoramic breakfast terrace. Pine-furnished rooms are small but sweet.

Camping Les Rives du Lac
          CAMPING GROUND €
(☏04 50 52 40 14; www.lesrivesdulac-annecy. com; 331 chemin des Communaux; campsites €21; ☺mid-Apr–mid-Oct) Pitch your tent near the lakefront at this shady camping ground, 5km south of town in Sévrier. A cycling track runs into central Annecy from here.

Auberge de Jeunesse   HOSTEL €
(☏04 50 45 33 19; www.fuaj.org, in French; 4 rte du Semnoz; dm incl breakfast & sheets €19.50;

⊘mid-Jan–Nov; 🛜) Annecy's smart wood-clad hostel has great facilities and chipper staff. Dorms have en suite showers. It's a 10-minute walk south of the centre.

✖ Eating

The quays along Canal du Thiou in the Vieille Ville are jam-packed with touristy cafes and pizzerias. Crêpes, kebabs, classic French cuisine – you'll find it all along pedestrianised rue Carnot, rue de L'Isle and rue Faubourg Ste-Claire.

La Cuisine des Amis   BISTRO €€

(📞04 50 10 10 80; 9 rue du Pâquier; mains €16.50-25) Walking into this bistro is somewhat like gatecrashing a private party – everyone is treated like one big jolly *famille*. Pull up a chair, *prendre un verre* (have a drink), scoff regional fare, pat the dog and see if your snapshot ends up on the wall of merry *amis*.

Nature & Saveur   ORGANIC €€

(📞04 50 45 82 29; place des Cordeliers; lunch menus with/without wine €42/32; ⊘lunch Tue-Sat) Laurence Salomon's 100% organic restaurant attracts a real boho-chic clientele. Inspired by the seasons, the menu uses wholesome ingredients from local farms, ranging from obscure legumes to locally reared meat.

La Ciboulette   MODERN FRENCH €€

(📞04 50 45 74 57; www.laciboulette-annecy.com; cour du Pré Carré, 10 rue Vaugelas; menus €31-46; ⊘Tue-Sat) Such class! Crisp white linen and gold-kissed walls set the scene at this surprisingly affordable Michelin-starred place, where chef Georges Paccard cooks fresh seasonal specialities, such as slow-roasted Anjou pigeon with Midi asparagus. Reservations are essential.

Contresens   FUSION €€

(📞04 50 51 22 10; 10 rue de la Poste; mains €15; ⊘Tue-Sat) The menu reads like a mathematic formula but it soon becomes clear: starters are A, mains B, sides C and desserts D. The food is as experimental as the menu – think sun-dried tomato, Beaufort cheese and rocket salad burger, mussel ravioli, 'deconstructed' Snickers – and totally divine. Kid nirvana.

L'Étage   TRADITIONAL FRENCH €€

(📞04 50 51 03 28; 13 rue du Pâquier; mains €14-22, 3-course menus €18) Cheese, glorious cheese... *Fromage* is given pride of place in the spot-on fondues and raclette at L'Étage, where a backdrop of mellow music and cheerful staff keep the ambience relaxed.

FREE WHEELER

295

Pick up a set of wheels to gad along the silky-smooth cycling path ensnaring Lake Annecy from **Vélonecy** (place de la Gare; €15 per day) at the train station; train ticket holders pay €5 per day. Or, in summer, simply head for the water and hire a bike lakeside from one of the many open-air stalls.

❶ Information

Tourist office (📞04 50 45 00 33; www.lac-annecy.com; Centre Bonlieu, 1 rue Jean Jaurès; ⊘9am-6.30pm Mon-Sat, 10am-1pm Sun)

❶ Getting There & Away

Bus

From the **bus station** (rue de l'Industrie), adjoining the train station, **Billetterie Crolard** (www.voyages-crolard.com) sells tickets for roughly hourly buses to villages around the lake, local ski resorts and Lyon St-Exupéry airport (one-way/return €33/50, 2¼ hours). **Autocars Frossard** (www.frossard.eu) sells tickets for Geneva (€10.50, 1¾ hours, 16 daily).

Train

From Annecy's **train station** (place de la Gare), there are frequent trains to many destinations, including Lyon (€23, 2¼ hours) and Paris' Gare de Lyon (€75, four hours).

Grenoble

POP 159,400

Wherever you turn in big-city Grenoble, you'll be treated to intoxicating Alpine views. But Grenoble isn't just a mountain base: since the 1960s the city has been a leading technology hub and cultural centre, with outstanding museums, a lively arts scene and some 60,000 students to lap it all up.

◉ Sights

Fort de la Bastille   FORTRESS

(www.bastille-grenoble.com) Looming above the old city on the northern side of the Isère River, this grand 16th-century fort is Grenoble's best-known landmark. Views are spectacular, with vast mountains on every side and the grey waters of the Isère River below. On China-blue ski days you can ogle Mont Blanc's snowy hump. To get to the fort, ride the riverside **Téléphérique Grenoble Bastille** (quai Stéphane Jay; adult/child single €4.50/2.90, return €6.50/4.05; ⊘Feb-Dec).

FRANCE THE FRENCH ALPS & JURA

Grenoble

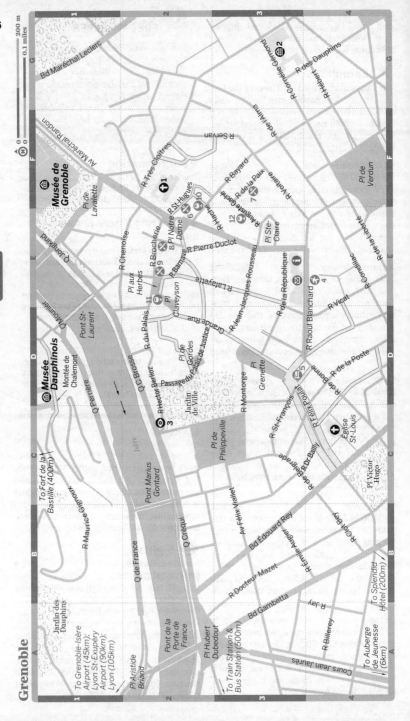

0.1 miles
200 m

To Grenoble-Isère
Airport (45km);
Lyon St-Exupéry
Airport (90km);
Lyon (105km)

Jardin des
Dauphins

To Fort de la
Bastille (400m)

R Maurice Gignoux

Musée
Dauphinois

Montée de
Chalemont

Q Perrière

Pont St-
Laurent

Q Brosse

Q Mounier

Q Jongkind

Pl de
Lavalette

Musée
de Grenoble

Av Maréchal Randon

Bd Maréchal Leclerc

R Très Cloîtres

R Chenoise

R Brocherie

R du Palais

R Hector Berlioz

Passage du Palais de Justice

Pl de
Gordes

Pl
Claveyson

Pl aux
Herbes

R Barnave

Grande Rue

R Pierre Duclot

Pl Notre
Dame

R St-Hugues

R Haxo

R Hache

R Auguste Genin

R Lafayette

R Jean Jacques Rousseau

R de la République

R Raoul Blanchard

R Vicat

Pl Ste
Claire

R Voltaire

R de la Paix

R Bayard

R Servan

R de l'Alma

R Fontaine Gagnon

R des Dauphins

R Hébert

Pl de
Verdun

R de la Liberté

Q Créqui

Q de France

Pont Marius
Gontard

Pont de la
Porte de France

Pl Aristide
Briand

Pl Hubert
Dubedout

To Train Station &
Bus Station (500m)

Cours Jean Jaurès

R Billerey

R Jay

Bd Gambetta

R Docteur Mazet

Av Félix Viallet

Bd Édouard Rey

Pl Victor
Hugo

To Auberge
de Jeunesse
(6km)

To Splendid
Hôtel (200m)

R Émile Augier

Pl de
Philippeville

R Montorge

Pl
Grenette

R St-François

R de Belgrade

R du Dr Bailly

R Félix Poulat

R de Bonne

R de la Poste

Église
St-Louis

R Oiot Bey

Q Conditilc

Jardin
de Ville

Grenoble

Musée de Grenoble — MUSEUM
(www.museedegrenoble.fr, in French; 5 place de Lavalette; adult/child €5/free; ◎10am-6.30pm Wed-Mon) The sleek glass-and-steel exterior of Grenoble's boldest museum is renowned for its distinguished modern collection, including star pieces by Chagall, Matisse, Canaletto, Monet and Picasso.

Magasin Centre National d'Art Contemporain — ART MUSEUM
(www.magasin-cnac.org; 155 cours Berriat; adult/child €3.50/2; ◎2-7pm Tue-Sun) Ensconced in a cavernous glass-and-steel warehouse built by Gustave Eiffel, this is among Europe's leading centres of contemporary art. Many of its cutting-edge exhibitions are designed specifically for the space. Ride tram A to the Berriat-Le Magasin stop.

Musée de l'Ancien Évêché — MUSEUM
(www.ancien-eveche-isere.com, in French; 2 rue Très Cloîtres; ◎9am-6pm Wed-Sat & Mon, 10am-7pm Sun, 1.30-6pm Tue) On place Notre Dame, Grenoble's Italianate **Cathédrale Notre Dame** and adjoining 13th-century **Bishops' Palace** – originally home to Grenoble's bishops – form this history museum. Its rich collection takes visitors beneath the cathedral square to a crypt safeguarding old Roman walls and a 4th- to 10th-century baptistery.

Musée Dauphinois — MUSEUM
(www.musee-dauphinois.fr, in French; 30 rue Maurice Gignoux; ◎10am-7pm Wed-Mon) Set in a 17th-century convent, this museum documents the cultures, crafts and traditions of Alpine life, including a fantastic exhibition devoted to the region's skiing history.

Musée de la Résistance et de la Déportation de l'Isère — MUSEUM
(www.resistance-en-isere.com, in French; 14 rue Hébert; ◎9am-6pm Mon & Wed-Fri, 1.30-6pm Tue, 10am-6pm Sat & Sun) This emotive museum examines the deportation of Jews and other 'undesirables' from Grenoble to Nazi camps during WWII in a cool-headed way.

🛏 Sleeping

Auberge de Jeunesse — HOSTEL €
(☑04 76 09 33 52; www.fuaj.org, in French; 10 av du Grésivaudan; dm incl breakfast €19; @) Clean and ultramodern, Grenoble's ecoconscious hostel sits in parkland, 5km from town. Top-notch facilities include bar, kitchen and sun deck. Take bus 1 to La Quinzaine stop or tram A to La Rampe stop and walk for 15 minutes.

Splendid Hôtel — HOTEL €€
(☑04 76 46 33 12; www.splendid-hotel.com; 22 rue Thiers; s/d €59/75-95; ※ 🛜) Colourful, fresh and jazzed up with funky paintings, this is a welcome break from Grenoble's otherwise dreary two-star scene. Take a seat in the leafy courtyard for a copious breakfast with fresh pastries and fruit.

Hôtel de l'Europe — HISTORIC HOTEL €
(☑04 76 46 16 94; www.hoteleurope.fr; 22 place Grenette; s €31-45, d €41-70) Set on Grenoble's

ACTION!

Get the scoop on mountain activities around Grenoble – skiing, snowboarding, ice climbing, walking, mountain biking, rock climbing and more – from knowledgeable staff at Grenoble's **Maison de la Montagne** (www.grenoble-montagne.com; 3 rue Raoul Blanchard).

If you're heading out for the day to one of the town's nearby ski resorts, jump lift-pass queues by buying your pass in advance from Grenoble's tourist office.

liveliest square, this 17th-century haunt retains some charm. The snazzy hot-pink breakfast room and grand spiral staircase promise good things, making the rooms something of an anticlimax with their '70s-style wallpaper and postage-stamp bathrooms.

✗ Eating

Grenoble's most atmospheric bistros huddle on backstreets in the *quartier des Antiquaires* (Antiques Quarter). Don't miss local dish *gratin dauphinois* (finely sliced potatoes oven-baked in cream and a pinch of nutmeg).

TOP CHOICE Chez Mémé Paulette
CAFE €

(2 rue St-Hugues; mains €8; ⊘noon-midnight Tue-Sat) This is an old curiosity shop of a cafe, crammed with antique books, milk jugs, cuckoo clocks and other eye-catching collectables. It draws a young, arty crowd with its boho vibe and wallet-friendly soul food, from chunky soups to *tartines* and home-made tarts.

L'Épicurien
MODERN FRENCH €€

(📞04 76 51 96 06; 1 place aux Herbes; menus €25-41) Chandeliers cast flattering light on the leather banquettes, exposed stone and twisting wrought-iron staircase of this chic split-level restaurant. An aperitif at the bar whets your appetite for flavours such as creamy *gratin dauphinois* and herb-crusted lamb.

Ciao a Te
ITALIAN €€

(📞04 76 42 54 41; 2 rue de la Paix; mains €15; ⊘Tue-Sat Jul-Jun) Stylish and relaxed, this Grenoblois favourite dishes up handmade pasta, crispy *panzerotti* (filled pastries), tender veal and the freshest seafood in town.

La Fondue
FRENCH €€

(📞04 76 15 20 72; 5 rue Brocherie; fondues €17-20; ⊘Tue-Sat, dinner Mon) Gorge on so-smooth fondues laced with kirsch, Génépi and chartreuse or chocolate.

🍷 Drinking

Like every good student city, Grenoble does a mean party. See www.grenews.com and www.petit-bulletin.fr for what's happening.

Le 365
WINE BAR

(3 rue Bayard; ⊘Tue-Sat) If Dionysus (god of wine) had a house, this is surely what it would look like: an irresistible clutter of bottles, oil paintings and candles that create an ultrarelaxed setting for quaffing wine.

Le Couche Tard
BAR

(1 rue du Palais) If you're too cool for school, check out Go to Bed Late, a grungy pub that actively encourages you to graffiti its walls. The merrier you become during happy hour (until 10pm daily), the more imaginative those doodles are...

Le Tord Boyaux
WINE BAR

(4 rue Auguste Gaché; ⊘6pm-2am) More than 30 flavoured wines, some quite extrava-

---

WORTH A TRIP

GREAT ESCAPES

Southwest of Grenoble, the gently rolling pastures and chiselled limestone peaks of the 1750-sq-km **Parc Natural Régional du Vercors** are the stuff of soft adventure. Quieter and cheaper than neighbouring Alpine resorts, the wildlife-rich park is a magnet for enthusiasts of fresh air, cross-country skiing, snowshoeing, caving and hiking. Its accommodation, moreover, is the stuff of Alpine dreams:

» **Les Allières** (www.aubergedesallieres.com, in French; Lans-en-Vercors; half-board per person €45) This 1476m-high forest chalet offers no-frills digs (bunk beds, shared toilets) and wondrous mountain food (mains €16 to €25). The wood-fire raclette and *tarte aux myrtilles* (blueberry tart) are divine.

» **À la Crécia** (www.gite-en-vercors.com, in French; 436 chemin des Cléments, Lans-en-Vercors; s/d/tr/q €52/57/72/87) Goats, pigs and poultry rule the roost at this 16th-century, solar-powered farm. Rooms are stylishly rustic with beams, earthy hues and mosaic bathrooms. Dinner (€17) is a farm-fresh feast.

» **Gîte La Verne** (http://gite.laverne.free.fr, in French; La Verne, Méaudre; apt for 4/8 people per week €500/750) Fitted with fully equipped kitchens, this *gîte*'s beautiful apartments blend Alpine cosiness with mod cons. Whether you opt for self-catering or half-board, you'll luurv the *hammam* and outdoor Norwegian bath.

gant (violet, chestnut, Génépi, fig), and a blind test every Tuesday night to see how many your taste buds can recognise.

ℹ Information
Tourist office (☎04 76 42 41 41; www.grenoble-tourisme.com; 14 rue de la République; ⊗9am-6.30pm Mon-Sat, 10am-1pm & 2-5pm Sun)

ℹ Getting There & Away
Air
Several budget airlines, including Ryanair and easyJet, fly to/from **Grenoble Isère airport** (www.grenoble-airport.com), 45km northwest and linked by **shuttle bus** (www.grenoble-altitude.com; single/return €12.50/22, 45 minutes, twice daily Tue-Sat).

Bus
From the **bus station** (rue Émile Gueymard), next to the train station, **VFD** (www.vfd.fr, in French) and **Transisère** (www.transisere.fr, in French) run buses to/from various destinations including Geneva (€43, 2½ hours) and Lyon St-Exupéry (€22, one hour) airports.

Train
From the **train station** (rue Émile Gueymard), frequent trains run to/from Paris' Gare de Lyon (from €76, 3½ hours) and Lyon (€19, 1½ hours, five daily).

Besançon
POP 121,850

Despite a swoon-worthy Old Town, first-rate restaurants and happening bars pepped up by students, this cultured capital of the Franche-Comté region – astraddle several hills and the banks of the Doubs River – is refreshingly modest and untouristy. In Gallo-Roman times, it was a key stop on trade routes between Italy, the Alps and the Rhine. Time-travel to 2012, when Besançon TGV train station opens 10km north in the village of Auxon.

◉ Sights
Citadelle de Besançon   CITADEL
(www.citadelle.com; rue des Fusillés de la Résistance; adult/child €8/4.60; ⊗9am-6pm) Besançon's crowning glory, dramatically lit by night, is its Unesco-listed **citadel**, a formidable feat of 17th-century engineering by the prolific Vauban. Inside are three museums covering local traditions, natural history and the rather more harrowing rise of Nazism, fascism and the French Resistance movement.

Musée des Beaux-Arts   MUSEUM
(www.musee-arts-besancon.org, in French; 1 place de la Révolution; adult/child €5/free; ⊗9.30am-noon & 2-6pm Wed-Mon) This is France's oldest museum, founded in 1694 when the Louvre was but a twinkle in Paris' eye. The collection spans archaeology with its Egyptian mummies, Neolithic tools and Gallo-Roman mosaics; a cavernous drawing cabinet whose 5500 works include Dürer, Delacroix and Rodin masterpieces; and 14th- to 20th-century painting with standouts by Titian, Rubens, Goya and Matisse.

🛏 Sleeping
Hôtel de Paris   DESIGN HOTEL €€
(☎03 81 81 36 56; www.besanconhoteldeparis.com; 33 rue des Granges; s €60, d €75-105; @🖥🛜) Hidden in the Old Town, this former 18th-century coaching inn reveals a razor-sharp eye for design. Corridors lit by leaded windows lead to slinky, silver-kissed rooms, a small fitness room and shady inner courtyard.

Charles Quint Hôtel   HISTORIC HOTEL €€
(☎03 81 82 05 49; www.hotel-charlesquint.com; 3 rue du Chapitre; d €89-145; @🏊) This 18th-century town house turned nine-room boutique hotel is sublime. Find it slumbering in the shade of the citadel, behind the cathedral.

Maison de Verre   B&B €€
(☎03 81 81 82 27; www.lamaisondeverre.com, in French; 26 rue Bersot; s/d 75/85; 🛜) Katherine Bermond has cleverly converted a car factory into this nouveau-chic *chambre d'hôte* with industrial twist.

🍴 Eating
TOP CHOICE **Le Saint-Pierre**   MODERN FRENCH €€
(☎03 81 81 20 99; www.restaurant-saint pierre.com, in French; 104 rue Battant; menus €35-60; ⊗lunch Mon-Fri, dinner Mon-Sat) This arty restaurant is among Besançon's most coveted. Crisp white linen, exposed stone and subtle lighting are the backdrop for intense flavours, expertly paired with regional wines. The three-course *menu marché* is a steal at €35.

A WINE LOVER'S TRIP

No road trip is tastier than the **Route des Vins de Jura** (Jura Wine Rd; www.laroutedesvin sdujura.com), a driving itinerary that corkscrews through 80km of well-tended vines and pretty stone villages. Route planners and winery guide are online.

Linger in **Arbois**, Jura wine capital, over a glass of *vin jaune*. The history of this nutty 'yellow wine' is told in the **Musée de la Vigne et du Vin** (adult/child €3.50/2.70; ⏰10am-12pm & 2-6pm Wed-Mon), in the whimsical, turreted Château Pécauld. Don't miss the 2.5km-long **Chemin des Vignes** walking trail and 8km-long **Circuit des Vignes** mountain-bike routes through vines.

La Balance Mets et Vins (☎03 84 37 45 00; 47 rue de Courcelles; menus €23-55; ⏰Thu-Mon, lunch Tue) at Arbois offers the perfect coda to this wine lover's trip; lunch here, on local, organic produce. Its signature *coq au vin jaune et aux morilles*, casserole and crème brûlée doused in *vin jaune* are musts, as is the wine menu with five glasses of either Jurassienne wine (€15) or *vin jaune* (€25, including a vintage one). Kids can sniff, swirl and sip, too, with three kinds of organic grape juice (€7.50).

High above Arbois is tiny **Pupillin**, a cuter-than-cute, yellow-stone village famous for its wine production. Several *caves* (wine cellars) can be visited.

Arbois **tourist office** (☎03 84 66 55 50; www.arbois.com; 17 rue de l'Hôtel de Ville; ⏰9am-noon & 2-6pm Mon-Sat) has walking and cycling information and a list of *caves* for tastings.

Trains link Arbois and Besançon (€8.50, 45 minutes, 10 daily).

La Table des Halles MODERN FRENCH €€
(☎03 81 50 62 74; 22 rue Gustave Courbet; menus €15-29; ⏰Tue-Sat) The urban loft decor at this fashionable restaurant wouldn't look out of place in New York's meat-packing district. But what lands on your plate is resolutely French and regional.

Mirabelle CAFE €
(5 rue Mégevand; mains €11-14; ⏰lunch Mon-Fri, dinner Mon-Sat) Bird boxes dangle from the ceiling and the cheese menu is chalked on a mouse-shaped blackboard at this kinda kitsch, kinda cool cafe. A boho crowd flock here for gratins, *croûtes* and scrummy tarts made with seasonal, mostly organic ingredients.

ℹ Information

Tourist office (☎03 81 80 92 55; www .besancon-tourisme.com; place du 8 Septembre; ⏰10am-6pm Mon-Sat, 10am-1pm Sun)

ℹ Getting There & Away

From the **train station** (av du Général de Gaulle), trains serve Paris (€41, 2¾ hours, 26 daily), Dijon (€14, 70 minutes, 20 daily) and Lyon (€28, 3½ hours, 25 daily).

Around Besançon

SALINE ROYALE

Envisaged by its designer, Claude-Nicolas Ledoux, as the 'ideal city', the 18th-century **Saline Royale** (Royal Saltworks; www.saline royale.com, in French; adult/child €7.50/3.50; ⏰9am-noon & 2-6pm) in Arc-et-Senans, 35km southwest of Besançon, is a showpiece of early Industrial Age town planning. The semicircular saltworks is a Unesco World Heritage site.

Trains link Besançon and Arc-et-Senans (€6.50, 30 minutes, 10 daily).

MÉTABIEF

Métabief (population 890, elevation 1000m), 75km south of Besançon, is the Jura's leading cross-country ski resort. From atop Mont d'Or (1463m), a fantastic panorama stretches over the foggy Swiss plain to Lake Geneva, the Matterhorn and Mont Blanc.

Then there is *vacherin Mont d'Or,* the only French cheese to be wrapped in spruce bark and eaten with a spoon – hot from a box. Arrive with the milk lorry around 9am at the **Fromagerie du Mont d'Or** (www .fromageriedumontdor.com, in French; 2 rue Moulin; ⏰9am-12.15pm & 3-7pm Mon-Sat, 9am-noon Sun) to watch it being made.

Online see www.tourisme-metabief.com.

Parc Naturel Régional du Haut-Jura

Experience the Jura at its rawest in the Haut-Jura Regional Park, an area of 757 sq km stretching from Chapelle-des-Bois almost to the western tip of Lake Geneva. Each year in February its lakes, mountains and low-lying valleys host the Transjurassienne, the world's second-longest cross-country skiing race.

Highlights include **Les Rousses** (population 2850, elevation 1100m), the park's main sports hub in winter (skiing) and summer (walking and mountain biking); and the incredible views from the **Telesiège Val Mijoux** (chairlift return €6; ☺10.30am-1pm & 2.15-5.30pm Sat & Sun mid-Jul–mid-Aug) linking Mijoux with Mont Rond (1533m). Even more stunning is the far-reaching vista over Lake Geneva from the **Col de la Faucille**, 20km south of Les Rousses.

Château de Voltaire (allée du Château; adult/child €5/free; ☺tours in French hourly 10.30am-4.30pm Tue-Sun mid-May–mid-Sep), where the great writer lived from 1759 until his return to Paris and death in 1778, is also worth visiting. Guided tours take in the chateau, chapel and 7-hectare park.

Public transport in the park is almost nonexistent, so you'll need wheels. A great place to start is in Lajoux at the **Maison du Parc** (www.parc-haut-jura.fr; adult/child €5/3; ☺10am-12.30pm & 2-6.30pm Tue-Fri, 2-6.30pm Sat & Sun), an interactive sensorial museum that explores the region through sound, touch and smell.

THE DORDOGNE & THE LOT

If it's French heart and soul you're after, look no further. Tucked in the country's southwestern corner, the neighbouring regions of the Dordogne and Lot combine history, culture and culinary sophistication in one unforgettably scenic package. The Dordogne is best known for its sturdy *bastides* (fortified towns), clifftop chateaux and spectacular prehistoric cave paintings, while the Mediterranean-tinged region of the Lot is home to endless vintage vineyards and the historic city of Cahors.

Sarlat-La-Canéda

POP 9950

A gorgeous tangle of honey-coloured buildings, alleyways and secret squares make up this unmissable Dordogne village – a natural if touristy launch pad into the Vézère Valley.

Part of the fun of Sarlat is getting lost in its twisting alleyways and backstreets. **Rue Jean-Jacques Rousseau** or the area around **Le Présidial** are good starting points, but for the grandest buildings and *hôtels particuliers* you'll want to explore **rue des Consuls**. Whichever street you take, sooner or later you'll hit the **Cathédrale St-Sacerdos** (place du Peyrou), a real mix

---

DON'T MISS

CROSS-BORDER

Hôtel Franco-Suisse (☏03 84 60 02 20; www.arbezie-hotel.com; La Cure; s/d/tr/q incl half-board €88/127/166/254), a unique bistro inn right on the French-Swiss border, lets you sleep sweet with your head in Switzerland and your feet in France. At home here since 1920, the Arbez family take huge pride in their cosy rooms and regional cuisine. Find them wedged between France's Col de la Faucille and Switzerland's Col de la Givrine in the hamlet of La Cure, 2.5km from Les Rousses.

DON'T MISS

GOOSE FEST

Three gold-hued, bronze-sculpted geese on **place du Marché aux Oies** ('geese market' square) attest to the enduring economic and gastronomic role of these birds in the Dordogne. Both the covered market and Sarlat's chaotic **Saturday-morning market** (place de la Liberté & rue de la République) – a full-blown French market experience 'must' – sell a smorgasbord of goose-based goodies.

In local restaurants, feast on foie gras and other goose-based specialities such as *grillons* (coarse-textured goose pâté), *magret* (goose breast), *aiguillettes* (fine slivers of *magret*) and *civet* (stew).

Gaggles of live geese fill Sarlat during its **Fest'Oie** (goose festival) on the third Sunday in February, accompanied by stalls, music and goose-fuelled banquet.

TRUFFLE CAPITAL

For culinary connoisseurs there is just one reason to visit the Dordogne: black truffles (*truffes*). A subterranean fungi that thrives on the roots of oak trees, this mysterious little mushroom is notoriously capricious. The art of truffle-hunting is a closely guarded secret and vintage crops fetch as much as €1000 per kg. Truffles are sought after by top chefs for an infinite array of gourmet dishes, but black truffles are often best eaten quite simply in a plain egg omelette, shaved over buttered pasta or sliced on fresh crusty bread.

Truffles are hunted by dogs (and occasionally pigs) from December to March and sold at special truffle markets in the Dordogne, including in Périgueux, Sarlat and most notably, the 'world's truffle capital', **Sorges** (population 1234). This tiny village, 23km northeast of Périgueux on the N21, is the place to get up on truffle culture, at the **Ecomusée de la Truffe** (www.ecomusee-truffe-sorges.com; Le Bourg, Sorges; adult/child €4/2; ☺10am-noon & 2-5pm, closed Mon Oct-Jan) and hook yourself up with a truffle hunt. **La Truffe Noire de Sorges** (☎06 08 45 09 48; www.truffe-sorges.com; 1½hr tours €10; ☺by reservation Dec-Feb & Jun-Sep) runs tours of *truffiéres* (the areas where truffles are cultivated), followed by tasting.

Then there is **Auberge de la Truffe** (☎05 53 05 02 05; www.auberge-de-la-truffe.com, in French; Sorges; s €52-105, d €56-120; ✳☻) in the village centre, with its stylish and renowned **restaurant** (menus €23-57) serving sensational seasonal cuisine. For culinary connoisseurs there is just one fixed menu to order, the *menu truffe* (€100).

of architectural styles and periods: the belfry and western facade are the oldest parts.

Nearby, the former **Église Ste-Marie** (place de la Liberté) houses Sarlat's mouthwatering **Marché Couvert** (covered market) and a state-of-the-art **panoramic lift** (elevator) in its bell tower. It was designed by top French architect Jean Nouvel (whose parents live in Sarlat).

The **tourist office** (☎05 53 31 45 45; www.sarlat-tourisme.com; rue Tourny; ☺9am-6pm Mon-Sat, 10am-1pm & 2-5pm Sun) neighbours the cathedral.

🛏 Sleeping

Hôtel La Couleuvrine　　　　HOTEL €€
(☎05 53 59 27 80; www.la-couleuvrine.com; 1 place de la Bouquerie; d €56-88; @) Gables, chimneys and red-tile rooftops adorn this rambling hotel, originally part of Sarlat's city wall. It's old, odd and endearingly musty; a couple of rooms are in the hotel's turret.

Hôtel Les Récollets　　　　　HOTEL €
(☎05 53 31 36 00; www.hotel-recollets-sarlat.com; 4 rue Jean-Jacques Rousseau; d €45-69; ✳🛜) Lost in the Old Town medieval maze, the Récollets is a budget beauty. Nineteen topsy-turvy rooms and a charming vaulted breakfast room are rammed in around the medieval *maison*.

Clos La Boëtie　　　　　BOUTIQUE HOTEL €€€
(☎05 53 29 44 18; www.closlaboetie-sarlat.com; 95-97 av de la Selves; d €210-280; ✳@🛜☻) Each

of the 11 rooms at this 19th-century mansion, a five-minute walk north of the Cité Médiévale, is a jewel. Some have terraces and all come with soothing, hydromassage showers and balneotherapy ('water healing') baths.

🍴 Eating

Bistro de l'Octroi　　　REGIONAL CUISINE €€
(☎05 53 30 83 40; www.lebistrodeloctroi.fr, in French; 111 av de Selves; menus €18-26) This local's tip is a little way out of town, but don't let that dissuade you. Sarladais pack into this cosy town house for the artistically presented, accomplished cooking that doesn't sacrifice substance for style.

Le Grand Bleu　　　　　　GASTRONOMIC €€€
(☎05 53 29 82 14; www.legrandbleu.eu, in French; 43 av de la Gare; menus €33-90; ☺lunch Thu-Sun, dinner Tue-Sat) Every menu at this Michelin-starred temple includes a choice of meat (such as veal sweetbreads with truffles) or seafood (such as lobster risotto with roast eggplant and truffle mousse). Cooking courses, too.

Le Présidial　　　　　REGIONAL CUISINE €€
(☎05 53 28 92 47; 6 rue Landry; menus from €29; ☺lunch Tue-Sat, dinner Mon-Sat Apr-Nov) What was a 17th-century courthouse now flaunts the city's most romantic dining terrace. Goose, duck and foie gras dominate the menu, and the wine list is packed with Sarlat and Cahors vintages.

Le Bistrot

REGIONAL CUISINE €€

(☑05 53 28 28 40; place du Peyrou; menus €18.50-24.50; ⊘Mon-Sat) Red-checked tablecloths and twinkling fairy lights create an intimate atmosphere at this diminutive bistro. Don't miss the *pommes sarlardaises* (potatoes cooked in duck fat).

ℹ Getting There & Away

The **train station** (ave de la Gare), 1.3km south of the old city, serves Périgueux (change at Le Buisson; €13.90, 1¾ hours, three daily) and Les Eyzies (change at Le Buisson; €8.60, 50 minutes to 2½ hours, three daily).

Les Eyzies-de-Tayac-Sireuil

POP 860

A hot base for touring the Vézère Valley's extraordinary cave collection, this village is essentially a clutch of touristy shops strung along a central street. Its **Musée National de Préhistoire** (www.musee-prehistoire-eyzies.fr, in French; 1 rue du Musée adult/child €5/free, 1st Sun of month free; ⊘9.30am-6pm Wed-Mon), rife with amazing prehistoric finds, makes a great introduction to the area.

About 250m north of the museum is the Cro-Magnon shelter of **Abri Pataud** (www.mnhn.fr, in French; 20 rue du Moyen Âge; adult/child €5/3; ⊘10am-noon & 2-6pm Sun-Thu), with an ibex carving dating from about 19,000 BC. Admission includes a guided tour (some in English).

Train services link Les Eyzies with Sarlat-la-Canéda.

Cahors

POP 21,128

Sheltered in a U-shape curve in the Lot River, bustling Cahors has the feel of a sun-baked Mediterranean town. Pastel-coloured buildings line shaded squares in the old medieval quarter, criss-crossed by a labyrinth of alleyways, dead ends and riverside quays. The town's most famous landmark is the **Pont Valentré**, one of France's finest medieval bridges, built from six arches and three towers.

🛏 Sleeping

[TOP CHOICE] **Hôtel Jean XXII**   HOTEL €

(☑05 65 35 07 66; www.hotel-jeanxxii.com, in French; 2 rue Edmond-Albé; s €48, d €58-65; 🕾) This excellent little hotel mixes original stone, greenery and well-worn wood with a dash of metropolitan minimalism. Smart rooms have muted colours, and there's a

WORTH A TRIP

PREHISTORIC PAINTINGS

Fantastic prehistoric **caves** with some of the world's finest **cave art** is what makes the Vézère Valley so very special. Most of the caves are closed in winter, and get very busy in summer. Visitor numbers are strictly limited, so you'll need to reserve well ahead.

Of the valley's 175 known sites, the most famous include **Grotte de Font de Gaume** (www.eyzies.monuments-nationaux.fr; adult/child €7/free; ⊘9.30am-12.30pm & 2-5.30pm Sun-Fri), 1km northeast of Les Eyzies. About 14,000 years ago, prehistoric artists created the gallery of over 230 figures, including bison, reindeer, horses, mammoths, bears and wolves, of which 25 are on permanent display.

About 7km east of Les Eyzies, **Abri du Cap Blanc** (www.eyzies.monuments-nationaux.fr; adult/child €7/free; ⊘9.30am-12.30 & 2-5.30pm Sun-Fri) showcases an unusual sculpture gallery of horses, bison and deer.

Then there is **Grotte de Rouffignac** (www.grottederouffignac.fr; adult/child €6.30/4; tours in French ⊘10-11.30am & 2-5pm), sometimes known as the 'Cave of 100 Mammoths' because of its painted mammoths. Access to the caves, hidden in woodland 15km north of Les Eyzies, is aboard a trundling electric train.

Star of the show goes hands down to **Grotte de Lascaux** (Lascaux II; ☑05 53 51 95 03; www.semitour.com; adult/child €8.80/6; ⊘9.30am-6pm), 2km southeast of Montignac, featuring an astonishing menagerie including oxen, deer, horses, reindeer and mammoth, as well as an amazing 5.5m bull, the largest cave drawing ever found. The original cave was closed to the public in 1963 to prevent damage to the paintings, but the most famous sections have been meticulously recreated in a second cave nearby – a massive undertaking that required some 20 artists and took 11 years.

reading area on the 1st floor where you can unwind in leather armchairs.

Auberge de Jeunesse HOSTEL €
(☏05 65 35 64 71; fjt46@wanadoo.fr; 222 rue Joachim Murat; dm €13.20; ☺9am-12.30pm & 2-7pm; ☎) In an old convent, Cahors' hostel is basic but friendly and functional. Dorms sleep four to ten, and there's a rambling garden.

✕ Eating

L'O à la Bouche FRENCH €€
(☏05 65 35 65 69; 134 rue St-Urcisse; menus €19.50-26.50; ☺Tue-Sat) 'Cuisine creative' are the watchwords at this refined address where classic ingredients get a fresh spin: cod in a peanut crust and 'tout coco' chocolate pudding anyone?

Le Marché FUSION €€
(☏05 65 35 27 27; www.restaurantlemarche.com; 27 place Jean-Jacques Chapon; menus €19-50; ☺Tue-Sat) Puce-and-cream armchairs, razor-edge wood and slate walls set the designer tone at the Market, where the menu's just as swish.

Marie Colline VEGETARIAN €
(☏05 65 35 59 96; 173 rue Georges Clemenceau; mains €8.50; ☺lunch Tue-Fri Sep-Jul; ☑) This little bistro has such a traditional feel it's a surprise to discover that its menu is meat- and fish-free. Solo diners are seated at a sociable shared table.

ℹ Information

Tourist office (☏05 65 53 20 65; www.tourisme-cahors.com; in French; place François Mitterrand; ☺9.30am-6.30pm Mon-Sat)

ℹ Getting There & Away

Cahors' **train station** (place Jouinot Gambetta) is on the main line (eight to 10 daily) to Paris' Gare d'Austerlitz (€67.70, five hours) via Brive-la-Gaillarde (€18.20, one hour), Limoges (€30.50, two hours) and Souillac (€13.10, 40 minutes), from where SNCF coaches continue to Sarlat (€2, 40 minutes, two daily).

THE ATLANTIC COAST

Though the French Riviera is France's most popular beach spot, the many seaside resorts along the Atlantic coast are fast catching up. If you're a surf nut or a beach bum, then the sandy bays around Biarritz will be right up your alley, while oenophiles can sample the fruits of the vine in the high temple of French winemaking, Bordeaux. Towards the Pyrenees you'll find the Basque Country, which in many ways is closer to the culture of northern Spain than to the rest of France.

Nantes

POP 291,000

You can take Nantes out of Brittany (as happened when regional boundaries were redrawn during WWII), but you can't take Brittany out of its long-time capital, Nantes ('Naoned' in Breton). Spirited and innovative, this city has a long history of reinventing itself. Founded by Celts, the city later became France's foremost port, industrial centre and shipbuilding hub, and has recently reinvented itself again as a cultural centre and youthful metropolis – one in two Nantais is under 40!

◉ Sights

TOP CHOICE **Les Machines de l'Île de Nantes** GALLERY
(www.lesmachines-nantes.fr; adult/child €7/5.50, elephant ride adult/child €7/5.50; ☺10am-8pm Jul-Aug, hours vary rest of year) Nantes' quirkiest sight! Prance around like a Maharajah on a 45-tonne elephant with a secret lounge in its belly or sail a boat through dangerous oceans rife with oversized squid at this surreal gallery that would have Jules Verne smiling in his grave! Admission covers the workshop where the larger-than-life, fantastical contraptions are built.

Musée Jules Verne MUSEUM
(www.julesverne.nantes.fr, in French; 3 rue de l'Hermitage; adult/child €3/1.50; ☺10am-noon & 2-6pm Mon & Wed-Sat, 2-6pm Sun) Overlooking the river 2km southwest of the tourist office, this magical museum displays 1st-edition books, hand-edited manuscripts and cardboard cut-outs inspired by the work of Jules Verne of *Around the World in 80 Days* fame, born in Nantes in 1828.

Château des Ducs de Bretagne CASTLE, MUSEUM
(www.chateau-nantes.fr; adult/child €5/3; ☺9.30am-8pm Jul-Aug, shorter hr rest of year) Forget fusty furnishings – the stripped, light-filled interior of the restored Château des Ducs de Bretagne houses multimedia-rich new exhibits detailing the city's history.

NANTES CITY PASS

Sold at the tourist office for €18/28/36 per 24/48/72 hours, this pass gets you unlimited travel on buses and trams, entry into museums and monuments, a guided tour, shopping discounts and various other handy extras.

Musée des Beaux-Arts MUSEUM
(10 rue Georges Clemenceau; adult €3.50; ◷10am-6pm Wed & Fri-Mon, to 8pm Thu) One of the finest collections of French paintings outside Paris hangs here, with works by Chagall, Monet, Picasso and Kandinsky among others.

🛏 Sleeping

TOP CHOICE **Hôtel Pommeraye** BOUTIQUE HOTEL €€
(☑02 40 48 78 79; www.hotel-pommeraye. com; 2 rue Boileau; s €54-99, d €59-129; 🕿) Sleek and chic, this is more art gallery than hotel. The rooms have shimmering short-pile carpets and textured walls, while eye-catching art seriously distracts in reception and other common areas.

Hôtel Graslin BOUTIQUE HOTEL €€
(☑02 40 69 72 91; www.hotel-graslin.com; 1 rue Piron; r €75-105; 🕿) An unlikely (but very Nantes) marriage of art deco and 1970s is what this refurbished hotel is all about. Love the edgy colour combos and shag carpets in the attic rooms.

La Manu HOSTEL €
(☑02 40 29 29 20; nanteslamanu@fuaj.org; 2 place de la Manu; dm incl breakfast €18.20; ◷reception closed noon-4pm; @) Housed in a converted factory, this well-equipped, 123-bed hostel is a 15-minute walk from the centre. Alas, there's a lock-out from noon to 4pm. Take tram 1 to the Manufacture stop.

Hôtel des Colonies BOUTIQUE HOTEL €
(☑02 40 48 79 76; www.hoteldescolonies.fr; 5 rue du Chapeau Rouge; s €58-78, d €65-78; 🕿) Local art exhibitions, cherry-red public areas and rooms in purple, green and orange make this an attractive option.

Hôtel La Pérouse DESIGN HOTEL €€
(☑02 40 89 75 00; www.hotel-laperouse.fr; 3 allée Duquesne; r €118; ❄🕿) Styled to reflect the city's shipbuilding traditions, this hotel has a wooden gangway entrance, stone-and-wood lobby and 46 rooms with zigzag chairs and canvas sail curtains.

🍴 Eating

Nantes' most cosmopolitan dining is in the medieval Bouffay quarter around rue de la Juiverie, rue des Petites Écuries and rue de la Bâclerie. Rue Jean Jacques Rousseau and rue Santeuil are other busy eat streets.

In March and November, buy sardines at street stalls all over town.

TOP CHOICE **Le Bistrot de l'Écrivain**
MODERN FRENCH €€
(☑02 51 84 15 15; 15 rue Jean Jacques Rousseau; menus €14.50-18.50; ◷Mon-Sat) Splashed in shades of red, the Writer's Bistro is an easygoing place with bottle-lined walls and creative Nantaise cuisine.

Un Coin en Ville MODERN FRENCH €€
(☑02 40 20 05 97; 2 place de la Bourse; menus from €12.90; ◷lunch Tue-Fri, dinner Tue-Sat) Flickering candles, soulful jazz and blues, and cooking that fuses local produce with exotic styles is what gives this place sex appeal.

Le 1 GASTRONOMIC €€
(☑02 40 08 28 00; 1 rue Olympe de Gouges; menus €14.90-23) The wine cellar – a see-through affair with 2000-odd bottles stacked on stainless-steel racks – is a big drawcard of this contemporary dining space overlooking the Loire.

🍷 Drinking

Let the party begin! Nantes has no shortage of edgy spots and there is no better place to start than the **Hangar à Bananes** (www. hangarabananes.com, in French; 21 quai des Antilles; ◷daily till late), a rejuvenated banana-ripening warehouse on Île de Nantes with more than a dozen restaurants, bars and clubs (and combinations thereof), each hipper than the next. The front terraces of most face Daniel Buren's art installation **Anneaux de Buren** (quai des Antilles), illuminated at night.

Or try industrial-chic **Le Lieu Unique** (www.lelieuunique.com, in French; 2 rue de la Biscuiterie), the one-time LU biscuit factory-turned-performance arts space where you can catch dance, theatre and contemporary art. Its restaurant and polished concrete bar buzzes.

If you get French, **leBoost** (www.leboost. com, in French) has local listings.

ℹ Information

Tourist office (www.nantes-tourisme.com; 2 place St-Pierre & cours Olivier de Clisson; ◷10am-6pm Mon-Sat, from 10.30am Thu)

FRANCE NANTES

ℹ️ Getting There & Away

Air

Aéroport International Nantes-Atlantique
(www.nantes.aeroport.fr) is 12km southeast of town. Shuttle buses (€7, 20 minutes) link it with the Gare Centrale bus-tram hub and the train station's southern entrance from about 6.45am to 11pm.

Train

The **train station** (27 blvd de Stalingrad) is well connected to most of the country. Destinations include Paris' Gare Montparnasse (€57.90, two hours, 15 to 20 daily), Bordeaux (€44.60, four hours, three or four daily) and La Rochelle (€24.10, 1¾ hours, three or four daily).

Poitiers

POP 91,900

Inland from the coast, history-steeped Poitiers rose to prominence as the former capital of Poitou, the region governed by the Counts of Poitiers in the Middle Ages. Poitiers has one of the oldest universities in the country, first established in 1432 and today a lynchpin of this lively city.

◉ Sights

Église Notre Dame la Grande　　　CHURCH
(place Charles de Gaulle) Every evening from 21 June until the third weekend in September, spectacular colours are cinematically projected onto the western facade of this beautiful Romanesque church next to Poitier's covered market. The oldest parts date from the 11th century and the only original frescos are the faint 12th- or 13th-century works that adorn the U-shaped dome above the choir.

Baptistère St-Jean　　　CHURCH
(rue Jean Jaurès; adult/child €2/1; ☺10.30am-12.30pm & 3-6pm Wed-Mon Apr-Oct) Constructed in the 4th and 6th centuries on Roman foundations, this baptistery, 100m south of Poitier's Gothic-style cathedral **Cathédrale St-Pierre** (rue de la Cathédrale), was redecorated in the 10th century and used as a parish church. The octagonal hole beneath the frescos was used for total-immersion baptisms until the 7th century.

Futuroscope　　　THEME PARK
(www.futuroscope.com; adult/child €35/26; ☺10am-11.15pm Jul-Aug, shorter hr Sep-Dec & Feb-Jun) This cinematic theme park, 10km north of Poitiers in Jaunay-Clan, takes you whizzing through space, diving into the deep blue ocean depths and on a close encounter with futuristic creatures. To keep things cutting edge, one-third of the attractions change annually. Many are motion-seat setups requiring a minimum height of 120cm. From Poitiers' train station take bus 9 or E (€1.30, 30 minutes).

🛏️ Sleeping & Eating

Hôtel de l'Europe　　　HISTORIC HOTEL €
(☎05 49 88 12 00; www.hotel-europe-poitiers.com; 39 rue Carnot; s/d €55/61; 🛜) The main building of this elegant hotel, with sweeping staircase, oversized rooms and refined furnishings, dates from 1710.

WORTH A TRIP

GREEN VENICE

Floating along emerald waterways – tinted green in spring and summer by duckweed – in a kayak or rowing boat is a real Zen highlight. Dubbed *Venise Verte* (Green Venice), the **Parc Naturel Interrégional du Marais Poitevin** is a tranquil, bird-filled wetland covering some 800 sq km of wet and drained marshland, threaded with canals, cycling paths and the odd waterside village.

Boating and **cycling** are the only ways to explore and there is no shortage of bikes (€6/13 per hour/half-day) and flat-bottomed boats (from €15/38) or kayaks (from €12/30) to rent from the Marais Poitevin's two main bases: tiny, honey-coloured **Coulon** and (our favourite, being a sucker for romance), the pretty village of **Arçais**. Try **Arçais Venise Verte** (www.veniseverteloisirs.fr, in French), **Au Martin Pecheur** (www.aumartin pecheur.com, in French) or **Bardet-Huttiers** (www.marais-arcais.com, in French).

To ensure complete and utter head-over-the-heels love, stay overnight at the environmentally friendly **Maison Flore** (☎05 49 76 27 11; www.maisonflore.com; rue du Grand Port, Arçais; s/d €57/72; 🛜). Romantically set on Arçais' waterfront, the 10-room boutique hotel is painted the colours of local marsh plants such as pale-green Angelica and bright-purple Iris. Books and board games in the lounge add a cosy touch and you can rent boats.

Getting to Green Venice is painful in anything other than your own car.

Thirsty? The 1000-sq-km wine-growing area around the city of Bordeaux is, along with Burgundy, France's most important producer of top-quality wines. Whet your palate with Bordeaux tourist office's introduction wine-and-cheese courses (€24).

Serious students of the grape can enrol in a two-hour (€25) or two- to three-day course (€335 to €600) at the *école du vin* (wine school) inside the **Maison du Vin de Bordeaux** (3 cours du 30 Juillet). Courses include chateaux visits.

Bordeaux has over 5000 estates where grapes are grown, picked and turned into wine. Smaller chateaux often accept walk-in visitors, but at many places, especially better-known ones, you have to reserve in advance. If you have your own wheels, one of the easiest to visit is **Château Lanessan** (☑05 56 58 94 80; www.lanessan.com; Cussac-Fort-Medoc; adult/child €8/2; ⊘advance reservation).

Favourite vine-framed villages brimming with charm and tasting/buying opportunities include medieval **St-Émilion** (www.saint-emilion-tourisme.com), port town **Pauillac** (www.pauillac-medoc.com) and **Listrac-Médoc**. In **Arsac-en-Médoc**, Philippe Raoux's vast glass-and-steel wine centre, **La Winery** (☑05 56 39 04 90; www.lawinery.fr, in French; Rond-point des Vendangeurs, D1), stuns with concerts and contemporary art exhibitions alongside tastings to determine your *signe œnologique* ('wine sign'; booking required).

Many chateaux close during October's *vendange* (grape harvest).

Hôtel Central HOTEL €
(☑05 49 01 79 79; www.centralhotel86.com, in French; 35 place du Maréchal Leclerc; d €38-65) At the southern edge of Poitier's charming pedestrian district of half-timbered houses, this two-star place is a terrific little bargain. Rooms are snug but sunlit.

La Serrurerie TRADITIONAL €
(☑05 49 41 05 14; 28 rue des Grandes Écoles; mains €10-17.50; ⊘8am-2am) Showcasing local art, sculpture and retro toys, this mosaic-and-steel bistro-bar is Poitiers' communal lounge-dining room. A chalked blackboard menu lists specialities such as *tournedos* (thick slices) of salmon, sensational pastas and a divine crème brûlée.

ⓘ Information

Tourist office (☑05 49 41 21 24; www.ot-poitiers.fr; 45 place Charles de Gaulle; ⊘10am-11pm Mon-Sat, 10am-6pm & 7-11pm Sun 21 Jun-Aug, shorter hr rest of year)

ⓘ Getting There & Away

The **train station** (blvd du Grand Cerf) has direct links to Bordeaux (€35, 1¾ hours), Nantes (€27.50, 3¼ hours) and Paris' Gare Montparnasse (€50, 1½ hours, 12 daily).

Bordeaux

POP 238,900

The new millennium was a turning point for the city long nicknamed La Belle au Bois Dormant (Sleeping Beauty), when the mayor, ex-

Prime Minister Alain Juppé, roused Bordeaux, pedestrianising its boulevards, restoring its neoclassical architecture, and implementing a hi-tech public-transport system. Today the city is a Unesco World Heritage site and, with its merry student population and 2.5 million-odd annual tourists, scarcely sleeps at all.

⊙ Sights

Cathédrale St-André CHURCH
This Unesco-listed cathedral is almost over-shadowed by the gargoyled, 50m-high Gothic belfry, **Tour Pey-Berland** (adult/child €5/free; ⊘10am-1.15pm & 2-6pm Jun-Sep, shorter hr rest of year). Erected between 1440 and 1466, its spire was later topped off with the statue of Notre Dame de l'Aquitaine. Scaling the tower's 232 narrow steps rewards you with a spectacular panorama of the city.

Museums MUSEUMS
Bordeaux's museums have free entry for permanent collections. Gallo-Roman statues and relics dating back 25,000 years are among the highlights at the impressive **Musée d'Aquitaine** (20 cours Pasteur; temporary exhibitions €3; ⊘11am-6pm Tue-Sun), while more than 700 post-1960s works by 140 European and American artists are on display at the **CAPC Musée d'Art Contemporain** (Entrepôt 7, rue Ferrére; ⊘11am-6pm Tue, Thu-Sun, to 8pm Wed, closed Mon).

The evolution of Occidental art from the Renaissance to the mid-20th century is on view at Bordeaux's **Musée des Beaux-Arts**

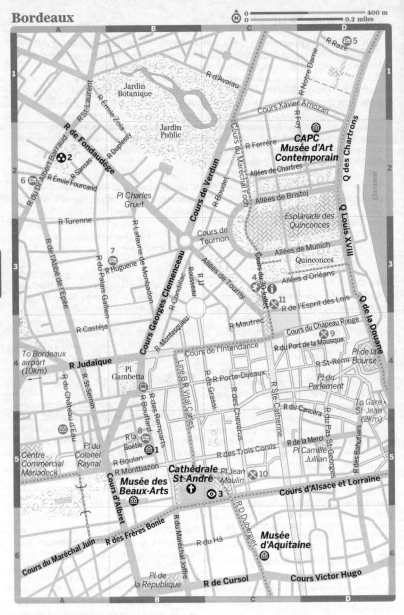

(20 cours d'Albret; ⏰11am-6pm Wed-Mon), while *faïence* pottery, porcelain, gold, iron, glasswork and furniture are displayed at the **Musée des Arts Décoratifs** (39 rue Bouffard; ⏰museum 2-6pm Wed-Mon, temporary exhibits from 11am Mon-Fri).

Palais Gallien RUINS
(rue du Docteur Albert Barraud; adult/child €3/2.50; ⏰2-7pm Jun-Sep) The only remains of the Roman city of Burdigala are these crumbling ruins of what was once its 3rd-century amphitheatre.

Bordeaux

Jardin Public   GARDEN

(cours de Verdun) Home to a lovely botanical garden since 1855, the Jardin Public was laid out in 1755 and reworked in the English style a century later.

🛏 Sleeping

Ecolodge des Chartrons `TOP CHOICE`   B&B €€

(☑05 56 81 49 13; www.ecolodgedeschartrons.com; 23 rue Raze; s/d incl breakfast €98/110) Hidden on a side street off the quays in Bordeaux's Chartrons wine merchants district, this *chambre d'hôte* spearheads ecofriendly sleeping in the city: think solar-heated water, hemp-based soundproofing and recycled antique furniture.

La Maison Bord'eaux   BOUTIQUE HOTEL €€

(☑05 56 44 00 45; www.lamaisonbord-eaux.com; 113 rue du Docteur Albert Barraud; s/d from €130/150; ☜) You'd expect to find a sumptuous 18th-century chateau with conifer-flanked courtyard and stable house in the countryside, but this one is smack-bang in the city. Dine after dusk on request (from €30).

La Maison du Lierre   BOUTIQUE HOTEL €€

(☑05 56 51 92 71; www.maisondulierre.com; 57 rue Huguerie; d €68-128; ☜) A beautiful Bordelaise stone staircase (no lift) leads to sunlit rooms with polished floorboards, rose-printed fabrics and sparkling bathrooms at the delight-

ful House of Ivy. The vine-draped garden is dreamy.

Auberge de Jeunesse   HOSTEL €

(☑05 56 33 00 70; www.auberge-jeunesse-bordeaux.com; 22 cours Barbey; dm incl sheets & breakfast €22; ⊙reception 7.30am-1.30pm & 3.30-9.30pm; ☜) Bordeaux's hostel is in an ultramodern building. From the train station, follow cours de la Marne for 300m and turn left opposite the park; the hostel is about 250m further.

Une Chambre en Ville   BOUTIQUE HOTEL €€

(☑05 56 81 34 53; www.bandb-bx.com; 35 rue Bouffard; s/d €103/115) A Room in Town blends in well with the antique and art shops on the same street. Each of the five rooms is a work of art.

🍴 Eating

Place du Parlement, rue du Pas St-Georges, rue des Faussets and place de la Victoire are loaded with dining addresses, as is the old waterfront warehouse district around quai des Marques – great for a sunset meal or drink.

Le Cheverus Café `TOP CHOICE`   BISTRO €

(☑05 56 48 29 73; 81-83 rue du Loup; menus from €10.50; ⊙Mon-Sat) Friendly, cosy and chaotically busy (be prepared to wait for a table at lunchtime) best describes this neighbourhood bistro, smack in the city centre. Lunch in particular is an all-out bargain.

La Tupina `TOP CHOICE`   REGIONAL CUISINE €€

(☑05 56 91 56 37; 6 rue Porte de la Monnaie; mains €18-40) Filled with the smell of soup simmering in an old *tupina* ('kettle' in Basque) over an open fire, this white-tableclothed place is feted far and wide for its seasonal regional specialities: minicasserole of foie gras and eggs, milk-fed lamb or goose wings with potatoes and parsley. Lunch here weekdays for €16.

L'Entrecôte   BRASSERIE €€

(☑05 56 81 76 10; 4 cours du 30 Juillet; menus €16.50) Opened in 1966, this unpretentious place doesn't take reservations, and it has just one menu option: succulent thin-sliced meat, heated by tealights, cooked in a special shallot sauce and accompanied by homemade *frites* (French fries).

La Boîte à Huîtres   OYSTERS €

(☑05 56 81 64 97; 36 cours du Chapeau Rouge; mains €8) This rickety wood-panelled little place is the best spot in Bordeaux to slurp fresh Arcachon oysters, traditionally served with sausage.

DON'T MISS

OYSTERS ON SATURDAY

A classic Saturday-morning Bordeaux experience is slurping oysters and white wine from one of the seafood stands at the market, **Marché des Capucins** (six oysters & glass of wine €6; ⊙7am-noon).

L'Estaquade   GASTRONOMIC €€€
(☑05 57 54 02 50; quai de Queyries; mains €22-26) Set on stilts jutting out from the riverbank, this restaurant is known for its seafood and magical views of Bordeaux's lovely neoclassical architecture.

❶ Information

Tourist office (☑05 56 00 66 00; www. bordeaux-tourisme.com; 12 cours du 30 Juillet; ⊙9am-7.30pm Mon-Sat, 9.30am-6.30pm Sun Jul & Aug, shorter hr rest of yr) Runs a smaller but helpful branch by the train station.

❶ Getting There & Away

Air

Bordeaux airport (www.bordeaux.aeroport. fr) is in Mérignac, 10km west of the city centre, with domestic and some international services. **Jet'Bus** (☑05 56 34 50 50) shuttle buses (€7, 45 minutes, every 45 minutes) links it with the train station, place Gambetta and main tourist office in town.

Bus

Citram Aquitaine (www.citram.fr, in French) Regional buses.
Eurolines (☑05 56 92 50 42; 32 rue Charles Domercq) International lines.

Train

From Bordeaux's Gare St-Jean, 3km from the centre:

PARIS' GARE MONTPARNASSE €69.80, three hours, at least 16 daily

NANTES €44.60, four hours

POITIERS €35.20, 1¾ hours

TOULOUSE €33, 2¼ hours

Biarritz

POP 27,500

Edge your way south along the coast towards Spain and you arrive in stylish Biarritz, just as ritzy as its name suggests. The resort took off in the mid-19th century (Napoleon III had a rather soft spot for the place) and it still shimmers with architectural treasures from the belle époque and art deco eras. Big waves – some of Europe's best – and a beachy lifestyle are a magnet for Europe's hip surfing set.

◉ Sights & Activities

Beaches   BEACHES
Biarritz' fashionable beaches, particularly **Grande Plage** and **Plage Miramar**, are end-to-end bodies on hot summer days. Rent a stripey 1920s style beach tent for €9.50 a day. North of Pointe St-Martin, the adrenaline-pumping surfing beaches of **Anglet** continue northwards for over 4km. Ride eastbound bus 9 from av Verdun (just near av Édouard VII).

Beyond long, exposed **Plage de la Côte des Basques**, some 500m south of Port Vieux, are **Plage de Marbella** and **Plage de la Milady**. Take westbound bus 9 from rue Gambetta where it crosses rue Broquedis.

Musée de la Mer   MUSEUM
(www.museedelamer.com; Esplanade du Rocher de la Vierge; adult/child €8/5.50; ⊙9.30am-midnight Jul-Aug, shorter hr rest of year) Biarritz' history as a fishing and whaling port is explored at the Musée de la Mer, alongside underwater life collected from the Bay of Biscay (Golfe de Gascogne).

🛏 Sleeping

Hôtel Mirano   BOUTIQUE HOTEL €€
(☑05 59 23 11 63; www.hotelmirano.fr, in French; 11 av Pasteur; d €100-110) Squiggly purple, orange and black wallpaper and oversize orange-perspex light fittings are just a few of the groovy rad '70s touches at this boutique retro hotel, found a 10-minute stroll from the town centre.

Villa Le Goëland   HISTORIC HOTEL €€€
(☑05 59 24 25 76; www.villagoeland.com; 12 plateau de l'Atalaye; r from €170; ☏) This stunning family home with chateau-like spires is perched high on a plateau above Pointe Atalaye. Rooms have panoramic views of town, the sea and across to Spain.

Hôtel Edouard VII   HISTORIC HOTEL €€
(☑05 59 22 39 80; www.hotel-edouardvii.com; 21 av Carnot; d from €118; ☏) From the ornate dining room full of tick-tocking clocks to the pots of lavender designed to match the wallpaper, this beautiful and intimate hotel screams 1920s Biarritz chic.

Hôtel Les Alizès
BOUTIQUE HOTEL €

(☑05 59 24 11 74; www.alizes-biarritz.com; 13 rue du Port Vieux; s/d €62/90; 🕾) With its brash and blushing shades clashing brilliantly with old-fashioned desks and wardrobes, this funky family-run hotel is one of the town's most memorable cheapies. Its beach-facing location is spot on.

Auberge de Jeunesse de Biarritz
HOSTEL €

(☑05 59 41 76 00; www.hibiarritz.org; 8 rue Chiquito de Cambo; dm incl sheets & breakfast €19.50; ⊗reception 8.30-11.30am & 6-9pm, to noon & 10pm May-Sep, closed mid-Dec–early Jan; @🕾) This popular place offers outdoor activities including surfing. Rooms for two to four hostellers have an en suite bathroom. To get here from the train station, follow the railway westwards for 800m.

 Eating

See-and-be-seen cafes and restaurants line Biarritz' beachfront. Anglet is also becoming increasingly trendy, with cafes strung along the waterfront.

Casa Juan Pedro
TOP CHOICE | SEAFOOD €

(☑05 59 24 00 86; Port des Pêcheurs; mains €5-15) Situated down by the old port – something of a hidden village of wooden fishing cottages – this cute shack restaurant cooks up tuna, sardines and squid with bags of friendly banter. There are several similar neighbouring places.

Le Crabe-Tambour
SEAFOOD €€

(☑05 59 23 24 53; 49 rue d'Espagne; menus €13-18) Named after the famous 1977 film (the owner was the cook for the film set), this local address serves great seafood at a price that is hard to fault.

Bistrot des Halles
BASQUE €€

(☑05 59 24 21 22; 1 rue du Centre; mains €14.50-17) One of several decent restaurants set along the rue du Centre that get their fruit and veg fresh from the nearby covered produce market, this bustling place serves up excellent fish as well as other fresh fare, in an interior adorned with old metallic advertising posters.

WORTH A TRIP

LOURDES

In the heart of the Pyrenees, **Lourdes** (www.lourdes-infotourisme.com), population 15,700, has been one of the world's most important pilgrimage sites since 1858, when 14-year-old Bernadette Soubirous (1844–79) saw the Virgin Mary in a series of 18 visions that came to her in a grotto. The town now feels dangerously close to a religious theme park, with a roll-call of over six million miracle-seeking visitors and endless souvenir shops selling statues and Virgin Mary–shaped plastic bottles (just add holy water at the shrine). But the commercialism doesn't extend to the *sanctuaires* (sanctuaries) themselves, mercifully souvenir-free.

Grotte de Massabielle (Massabielle Cave) is the most revered site in the area. The Esplanade des Processions, which is lined with enormous flickering candles left by previous pilgrims, leads along a river to the grotto's entrance, where people queue up to enter the cave or to dip in one of the 19 holy **baths** (⊗generally 9-11am & 2.30-4pm Mon-Sat, 2-4pm Sun & holy days). It's not for wallflowers: once you're behind the curtain, you're expected to strip off before being swaddled in a sheet and plunged backwards into the icy water.

The main 19th-century section of the sanctuaries is divided between the neo-Byzantine **Basilique du Rosaire**, the **crypt** and spire-topped **Basilique Supérieure** (Upper Basilica). From Palm Sunday to mid-October, nightly torchlight processions start from the Massabielle Grotto at 9pm, while at 5pm there's the **Procession Eucharistique** (Blessed Sacrament Procession) along Esplanade des Processions.

When the crowds of pilgrims get too much for you, seek refuge on the rocky 94m-high pinnacle of **Pic du Jer** – the panorama of Lourdes and the Pyrenees is inspiring. Walk three hours along a marked trail or ride six minutes in the century-old **funicular** (www.picdujer.info; blvd d'Espagne; adult/child €9.50/8; ⊗9.30am-6 or 7pm Mar-Nov). The summit is a superb picnic spot.

Lourdes is well connected by train; destinations include Bayonne (€21, 1¾ hours, up to four daily), Toulouse (€25.10, 1¾ hours, six daily) and Paris' Gare Montparnasse (€89.30, 6½ hours, four daily).

EAT STREETS

The area around covered market **Les Halles** (rue des Halles, rue du Centre, rue du Vieux Port) is the Biarritz hot spot for character-infused tapas joints, bar loaded with tasty treats.

Le Clos Basque
BASQUE €€

(05 59 24 24 96; 12 rue Louis Barthou; menus €24; ⊙lunch Tue-Sun, dinner Tue-Sat) With its exposed stonework strung with abstract art, this tiny place could have strayed from Spain. Cuisine is traditional Basque with a contemporary twist. Reserve to snag a table on the terrace.

Drinking
Great bars stud rue du Port Vieux, place Clemenceau and the central food-market area.

Ventilo Caffé
BAR €

(rue du Port Vieux; ⊙closed Tue out of season) Dressed up like a tart's boudoir, this fun and funky place continues its domination of the Biarritz bar scene.

Arena Café Bar
BAR €

(Plage du Port Vieux; ⊙9am-2am Apr-Sep, 10am-2am Wed-Sun Oct-Mar) Tucked in a tiny cove, this beachfront hangout combines style-conscious restaurant (mains €15 to €22) with fuchsia- and violet-tinged bar and DJs.

Milk Bar
BAR €

(17 blvd du Géneral de Gaulle; ⊙Tue-Sun) If you're on the hunt for a surfer, or are a surfer at heart, then this place just back from the beach is the place to get your wax out.

ⓘ Information
Tourist office (05 59 22 37 00; www.biarritz.fr; Square d'Ixelles; ⊙9am-7pm Jul & Aug, 9am-6pm Mon-Sat, 10am-5pm Sun Sep-Jun)

ⓘ Getting There & Away
Air

Biarritz-Anglet-Bayonne Airport (www.biarritz.aeroport.fr), 3km southeast of Biarritz, is served by easyJet, Ryanair and other low-cost carriers. STAB bus No 6 (line C on Sunday) links it once or twice hourly with Biarritz.

Bus

ATCRB buses (www.transdev-atcrb.com) runs services down the coast to the Spanish border.

Train

Biarritz-La Négresse train station, 3km south of town, is linked to the centre by buses 2 and 9 (B and C on Sundays).

LANGUEDOC-ROUSSILLON

Languedoc-Roussillon comes in three distinct flavours: Bas-Languedoc (Lower Languedoc), land of bullfighting, rugby and robust red wines, where the region's major sights are found; sunbaked Nîmes with its fine Roman amphitheatre; and fairy-tale Carcassonne, crowned with a ring of witch-hat turrets.

Inland, Haut Languedoc (Upper Languedoc) is a mountainous, sparsely populated terrain made for lovers of the great outdoors; while south sits Roussillon, snug against the rugged Pyrenees and frontier to Spanish Catalonia. Meanwhile Languedoc's traditional centre, Toulouse, was shaved off when regional boundaries were redrawn almost half a century ago, but we've chosen to include it in this section.

Carcassonne
POP 49,100

With its witch's-hat turrets and walled city, from afar Carcassonne looks like a fairy-tale fortress – but the medieval magic's more than a little tarnished by an annual influx of over four million visitors. It can be a tourist hell in high summer, so arrive out of season to see the town at its best (and quietest).

Pick up an audioguide (€3 for two hours) to **La Cité** (Old City) at the **tourist office** (04 68 10 24 30; www.carcassonne-tourisme.com; 28 rue de Verdun; ⊙9am-6 or 7pm Mon-Sat, 9am-noon or 1pm Sun) or its **annexe** (La Cité Porte Narbonnaise).

The old city is dramatically illuminated at night and enclosed by two **rampart walls** punctuated by 52 stone towers, Europe's largest city fortifications. Successive generations of Gauls, Romans, Visigoths, Moors, Franks and Cathars reinforced the walls, but only the lower sections are original; the rest, including the turrets, were stuck on by the 19th-century architect Viollet-le-Duc.

A drawbridge leads to the old gate of **Porte Narbonnaise** and rue Cros Mayrevieille en route to place Château and the 12th-century **Château Comtal** (adult/child €8.50/free; ⊙10am-6.30pm Apr-Sep). Admission includes a castle meander, a short film and an optional 30- to 40-minute guided tour of the ramparts (tours in English July and August). South is **Basilique St-Nazaire** (☉9-11.45am & 1.45-5 or 5.30pm), illuminated by delicate medieval rose windows.

Carcassonne is on the main rail line to/ from Toulouse (€14, 50 minutes).

Nîmes

POP 146,500

This buzzy city boasts some of France's best-preserved classical buildings, including a famous Roman amphitheatre, although the city is most famous for its sartorial export, *serge de Nîmes* – better known to cowboys, clubbers and couturiers as denim.

◎ Sights

Les Arènes ROMAN AMPHITHEATRE
(adult/child €7.80/4.50; ☉9am-6.30pm) Nîmes' magnificent Roman amphitheatre, the best preserved in the Roman Empire, was built around AD 100 to seat 24,000 spectators. It hosted animal fights to the death, stag hunts, man against lion or bear confrontations and, of course, gladiatorial combats. In the contemporary arena, it's only the bulls that get killed. There's a mock-up of the gladiators' quarters and, if you time it right, you'll see a couple of actors in full combat gear slugging it out in the arena.

Maison Carrée ROMAN TEMPLE
(place de la Maison Carrée; adult/child €4.50/3.70; ☉10am-6.30pm) The Square House is a remarkably preserved rectangular Roman temple, constructed around AD 5 to honour Emperor Augustus' two adopted sons. Inside, a 22-minute 3D film staring heroes from the city's history is screened every half-hour.

Carré d'Art MUSEUM
(www.carreeartmusee.com, in French; place de la Maison Carrée; permanent collection free, temporary exhibitions adult/child €5/3.70; ☉10am-6pm Tue-Sun) The striking glass-and-steel build-

ℹ **BILLET NÎMES ROMAINE** 313

Buy a **combination ticket** (adult/child €9.90/7.60), valid for three days, covering all three of Nîmes major sights. Buy one at the first sight you visit.

ing facing the Maison Carrée was designed by British architect Sir Norman Foster. Inside is the **municipal library** and **Musée d'Art Contemporain**, with both permanent and temporary modern and contemporary art exhibitions from the 1960s on. End your visit with lunch (€16 to €28) on the Art Square's wonderful rooftop restaurant terrace, **Le Ciel de Nîmes**.

🛏 Sleeping

Royal Hôtel HOTEL €€
(☎04 66 58 28 27; www.royalhotel-nimes.com, in French; 3 blvd Alphonse Daudet; r €60-80; ❄🐾) You can't squeeze this 21-room hotel, popular with visiting artists and raffishly bohemian, into a standard mould. Rooms are furnished with flair and mainly overlook place d'Assas, a work of art in its own right.

Hôtel Amphithéâtre HOTEL €
(☎04 66 67 28 51; http://perso.wanadoo.fr/hotel-amphitheatre; 4 rue des Arènes; s €41-45, d €53-70) A pair of 18th-century mansions, the Amphitheatre Hotel just down the road from its namesake has 15 rooms, each named after a writer or painter. Montesquieu and Arrabal each have a balcony.

Auberge de Jeunesse HOSTEL €
(☎04 66 68 03 20; www.hinimes.com; 257 chemin de l'Auberge de Jeunesse, La Cigale; dm/d €13.50/34; ☉Feb-Dec) This sterling, well-equipped hostel with self-catering facilities has houses for two to six in its extensive grounds, as well as regular dorms. Find it 3.5km northwest of the train station; take bus I, direction Alès or Villeverte, to the Stade stop.

FRANCE NÎMES

FESTIVE NÎMES

Nîmes becomes more Spanish than French during its two *férias* (bullfighting festivals): the five-day **Féria de Pentecôte** (Whitsuntide Festival) in June, and the three-day **Féria des Vendanges** celebrating the grape harvest on the third weekend in September. Each is marked by daily *corridas* (bullfights). Buy tickets in situ or online at the **Billeterie des Arènes** (www.arenesdenimes.com; 2 rue de la Violette).

PONT DU GARD

A Unesco World Heritage site, this three-tiered Roman aqueduct is exceptionally well preserved. It's part of a 50km-long system of canals built about 19 BC by the Romans to bring water from near Uzès to Nîmes. The scale is huge: the 35 arches of the 275m-long upper tier, running 50m above the Gard River, contain a watercourse designed to carry 20,000 cubic metres of water per day and the largest construction blocks weigh over five tonnes.

Pick up an audioguide (€6) from the **visitors centre** (www.pontdugard.fr; ◎9.30am-7pm May-Sep, to 5 or 6pm Oct-Apr) on the left, northern bank and allow around 1½hr to take in the vast, hugely informative and innovative museum **Musée de la Romanité** inside. Afterwards, walk the **Mémoires de Garrigue**, a 1.4km trail with explanatory panels through typical Mediterranean bush and scrubland.

A day ticket covering the above plus parking in one of the car parks on either side of the Gard River is €15 for up to five passengers (€10 November to March). In July and August pay an extra €2 to teeter along the aqueduct's top tier with a guide (every half-hour from 10am to 11.30am and 2pm to 5.30pm). Admission to the site is free once the museum has closed.

The best view of the Pont du Gard is from upstream, beside the river, where you can swim on hot days.

✗ Eating

Nîmes' gastronomy owes as much to Provence as to Languedoc. Look out for *cassoulet* (pork, sausage and white bean stew, sometimes served with duck), aïoli and *rouille* (a spicy chilli mayonnaise).

Le Marché sur la Table   FRENCH €€
(☑04 66 67 22 50; 10 rue Littré; mains €17-19; ◎Wed-Sun) You *could* just pop in for a glass of wine at this first-class bistro, but you'd be missing out on Éric Vidal's market-fuelled food. Dining in the quiet rear courtyard is delightful.

Le 9   FRENCH €€
(☑04 66 21 80 77; 9 rue de l'Étoile; mains €15-18; ◎Mon-Sat & lunch Sun May-Sep) Have a meal or drop in for a drink at this mildly eccentric place, tucked behind high green doors. Eat in vast, arched former stables or in the leafy, vine-clad courtyard.

Carré d'Art   CLASSIC FRENCH €€
(☑04 66 67 52 40; www.restaurant-lecarredart. com, in French; 2 rue Gaston Boissier; menus €19-29; ◎Mon-Sat) Enjoy exceptional cuisine in sublimely tasteful surroundings – gilded mirrors, moulded ceilings, fresh flowers, feather-light chandeliers and contemporary art work.

Au Plaisir des Halles   FRENCH €€
(☑04 66 36 01 02; 4 rue Littré; mains €24-30; ◎Tue-Sat) Near the covered market, ingredients here are locally sourced and the lunchtime three-course *menu* (€20) is excellent value. Local winegrowers feature both on the walls and in the wine racks.

ℹ Information

Tourist office (☑04 66 58 38 00; www. ot-nimes.fr; 6 rue Auguste; ◎8.30am-6.30pm Mon-Fri, 9am-6.30pm Sat, 10am-5pm Sun)

ℹ Getting There & Away

Air

Ryanair is the only airline to use Nîmes' **airport** (☑04 66 70 49 49), 10km southeast of the city on the A54.

Bus

Bus station (☑04 66 38 59 43; rue Ste-Félicité)
PONT DU GARD €1.50, 30 minutes, two to seven daily
UZÈS €1.50, 45 minutes, four to 10 daily

Train

ALÈS €8.50, 40 minutes
ARLES €7.50, 30 minutes
AVIGNON €8.50, 30 minutes
MARSEILLE €19, 1¼ hours
PARIS' GARE DE LYON €52 to €99.70, three hours

Toulouse

POP 446,200

Elegantly set at the confluence of the Canal du Midi and the River Garonne, this vibrant southern city – nicknamed *la ville rose* (the pink city) after the distinctive hot-pink stone used in many buildings – is one of France's liveliest metropolises. Busy, buzzy and bustling with students, this riverside dame has a history stretching back over 2000 years and has been a hub for the aerospace industry since the 1930s. With a thriving cafe and cultural scene, a wealth of impressive *hotels particuliers* and an enormously atmospheric old quarter, France's fourth-largest city is one place you'll definitely want to linger.

⊙ Sights

Place du Capitole
SQUARE

(place du Capitole) On the ceiling of the arcades on this bustling square's western side are 29 vivid **illustrations** of Toulouse history by contemporary artist Raymond Moretti. On the square's eastern side is the 128m-long facade of the **Capitole**, Toulouse's city hall built in the 1750s.

Basilique St-Sernin
CHURCH

(place St-Sernin; ⊙8.30am-noon & 2-6pm Mon-Sat, 8.30am-12.30pm & 2-7.30pm Sun) The magnificent octagonal tower and spire of Toulouse's famous red-brick basilica pop up above the rooftops all over the city. This is France's largest and best-preserved example of Romanesque architecture: inside, the soaring nave and delicate pillars lead towards the ornate tomb of St-Sernin himself, sheltered beneath a sumptuous canopy.

Cité de l'Espace
MUSEUM

(www.cite-espace.com/en; av Jean Gonord; adult/ child €22/15.50; ⊙9.30am-7pm mid-Jul–Aug, 9.30am-5 or 6pm Sep-Dec & Feb-Jun, closed Jan) On the city's eastern outskirts, this museum explores the city's interstellar credentials with a wealth of hands-on exhibits, from space shuttle simulators and 3D-theatres to a full-scale replica of the Mir Space Station and a 53m-high Ariane 5 space rocket.

Musée des Augustins
ART MUSEUM

(www.augustins.org; 21 rue de Metz; adult/child €3/ free, temporary exhibitions €6/free; ⊙10am-6pm Thu-Tue, 10am-9pm Wed) Toulouse's fabulous fine-arts museum in an old Augustinian monastery with cloister gardens spans the centuries from the Romans to the early 20th century. View works by Delacroix, Ingres and Courbet, Toulouse-Lautrec and Monet.

Les Abattoirs
ART MUSEUM

(www.lesabattoirs.org; 76 allées Charles de Fitte; admission €3-10; ⊙11am-7pm weekends, 10-6pm Wed-Fri) This red-brick structure was the city's main abattoir, since reinvented as cutting-edge art gallery and venue for concerts and exhibitions.

🛏 Sleeping

Hôtel St-Sernin
BOUTIQUE HOTEL €€

`TOP CHOICE` (☑05 61 21 73 08; www.hotelstsernin.com; 2 rue St-Bernard; d €111-131; ☜) A swish little number in the shade of Basilique St-Sernin, this hotel is beautifully finished with slate-grey walls, crisp white sheets and splashes of zesty colour. Book well ahead to snag a basilica view.

Le Clos des Potiers
HOTEL €€

(☑05 61 47 15 15; www.le-clos-des-potiers.com; 12 rue des Potiers; d €100-125; ☜) This little-known hideaway in a *hôtel particulier* near the cathedral is one of Toulouse's best-kept secrets. Rooms blend the bespoke feel of an upmarket B&B (antique rugs, characterful furniture, original mantelpieces) with the comfort and efficiency of a smart hotel (private garden, lovely lounge, treat tray).

Hôtel La Chartreuse
HOTEL €

(☑05 61 62 93 39; www.chartreusehotel.com; 4bis blvd de Bonrepos; s/d/tr €41/47/57) This super, family-run establishment by the station is a really welcome surprise: clean, friendly and surprisingly quiet, with a lovely little breakfast room and back garden patio. Sure, rooms are a tad fusty, but for this price, what do you expect?

✕ Eating

Blvd de Strasbourg, place St-Georges and place du Capitole are perfect spots for summer dining alfresco. Rue Pargaminières

---

DON'T MISS

ALL AFLOAT

Toulouse is a river city, and you couldn't possibly leave without venturing out onto the water. March to November, several operators run scenic hour-long boat trips (adult/child €8/5) along the Garonne from quai de la Daurade; in summer trips also pass through the St-Pierre lock onto the Canal du Midi and Canal de Brienne.

Buy tickets on the boat, up to 10 minutes before departure, from **Les Bateaux Toulousains** (www.bateaux-toulousains.com), **Toulouses Croisières** (www.toulouse-croisieres.com) or **L'Occitania** (www.loccitania.fr).

is the street for kebabs, burgers and other late-night student grub.

TOP CHOICE Chez Navarre
REGIONAL CUISINE €€

(☑05 62 26 43 06; 49 Grande Rue Nazareth; menus €13-20; ⊘Mon-Fri) Wanna dine with locals? Then come to this wonderful *table d'hôtes* where honest Gascon cuisine is dished up beneath a hefty beamed ceiling. Dining is around communal, candlelit tables and there's usually just one main meal choice plus soup and terrine.

Au Jardins des Thés
CAFE €€

(16 pl St-Georges; menus €12.50-15.50) A perennially packed terrace on one of the city's smartest squares testifies to just how good the salads, *tartes salées* (savoury tarts) and other little lunchy treats are at these Tea Gardens.

Les Halles Victor Hugo
BISTRO €

(place Victor Hugo; menus €10-20; ⊘lunch Tue-Sun) For a quintessentially French experience, join the punters at the string of tiny restaurants on the 1st floor of the Victor Hugo food market. Food is simple, unfussy and full of character.

Faim des Haricots
VEGETARIAN €

(www.lafaimdesharicots.fr; 3 rue du Puits Vert; ⊘Mon-Sat; ☑) Everything's served *á volonte* (all you can eat) at this 100% veggie/wholefood restaurant, where €15.50 buys you a savoury tart, salad, hot dishes, dessert and a *pichet* (pitcher) of wine.

🍷 Drinking & Entertainment

Almost every square in the Vieux Quartier has at least one cafe, busy day and night. Other hot after-dark streets include rue Castellane, rue Gabriel Péri and near the river around place St-Pierre.

Toulouse has a cracking live music and clubbing scene. Check what's on at www.toulouse.sortir.eu.

Au Père Louis
HISTORIC BAR

(45 rue des Tourneurs; ⊘8.30am-3pm & 5-10.30pm Mon-Sat) Top of our list for irresistible old-fashioned charm, 'Father Louis' is Toulouse's oldest bar (franked 1889).

Bodega Bodega
TAPAS BAR

(1 rue Gabriel Péri; tapas €4.50-10; ⊘7pm-2am Mon-Fri, 7pm-6am Sat, 8pm-2am Sun) Revel in all the fun of the *féria* in a historic building where the tax authority once was. Weekends means live music and the tapas is tip-top.

La Maison
BAR

(9 rue Gabriel Péri; ⊘5pm-2am Sun-Fri, 5pm-5am Sat) The House is a hip, shabby-chic hangout for students and trendies, with plenty of vintage fireplace, scruffy sofas and secondhand chairs dotted around the living room.

Opus Café
CLUB

(24 rue Bachelier; admission free; ⊘midnight-5am Mon-Wed, 11pm-6am Thu-Sat) Dance until dawn at this much-loved venue for seasoned clubbers.

Le Bikini
MUSIC CLUB

(www.lebikini.com; rue Hermès, Ramonville St-Agne) The stuff of Toulousien legend for 25 years or so; at the end of metro line B (Ramonville metro stop).

Le Cri de la Mouette
CLUB, BAR

(www.lecridelamouette.com; 78 allée de Barcelone) The Cry of the Seagull is a cool club-bar and gig venue aboard a canalboat.

ℹ Information

Tourist office (☑05 61 11 02 22; www.toulouse-tourisme.com; square Charles de Gaulle; ⊘9am-7pm Mon-Sat, 10.30am-5.15pm Sun Jun-Sep, shorter hr rest of year)

ℹ Getting There & Away

Air

Toulouse-Blagnac Airport (www.toulouse.aeroport.fr/en), 8km northwest of the centre, has frequent flights to Paris and other large French and European cities. easyJet, bmibaby, Ryanair, KLM, Flybe and germanwings fly here. A **shuttle bus** (www.tisseo.fr) (€5, 20 minutes, every 20 minutes) links it with town.

Train

Gare Matabiau (blvd Pierre Sémard), 1km northeast of the centre, is served by frequent fast TGVs west to Bordeaux (€36.90, two hours), with connections to Bayonne, Paris and the southwest), and east to Carcassonne (€12, one hour) and beyond.

PROVENCE

Provence conjures up images of rolling lavender fields, blue skies, gorgeous villages, wonderful food and superb wine. It certainly delivers on all those fronts, but it's not just worth visiting for the good looks – dig a little deeper and you'll also discover the multicultural metropolis of Marseille, the artistic haven of Aix-en-Provence and the old Roman city of Arles.

Marseille

POP 860,350

There was a time when Marseille was the butt of French jokes. No more. The *cité phocéenne* has made an unprecedented comeback, undergoing a vast makeover. Marseillais will tell you that the city's rough-and-tumble edginess is part of its charm and that, for all its flaws, it is a very endearing place. They're right: Marseille grows on you with its unique history, souklike markets, millennia-old port and spectacular *corniches* (coastal roads) – all good reasons indeed why Marseille was chosen as European Capital of Culture in 2013.

⊙ Sights

Vieux Port   OLD PORT

Ships have docked for more than 26 centuries at Marseille's colourful Vieux Port. Although the main commercial docks were transferred to the Joliette area on the coast north of here in the 1840s, it still overflows with fishing craft, yachts and local ferries.

Guarding the harbour are **Fort St-Nicolas** on the southern side and, across the water, **Fort St-Jean**, founded in the 13th century by the Knights Hospitaller of St John of Jerusalem. Wedged between restaurants on the cafe-lined quays is **La Maison du Pastis** (108 quai du Port), a distillery where you can sample 90 varieties of the local aniseed-flavoured firewater, pastis.

Standing guard between the old and the 'new' port, is the striking Byzantine-style **Cathédrale de la Major**, at the heart of the current dynamic dockland redevelopment around **La Joliette**. The cathedral's distinct striped facade is built from local white Cassis stone and green marble from Florence in Italy.

Basilique Notre Dame de la Garde   CHURCH
(montée de la Bonne Mère; ⊙7am-7pm, longer hr summer) Be blown away by the celestial views and knockout 19th-century architecture at the hilltop Basilique Notre Dame de la Garde, the resplendent Romano-Byzantine basilica 1km south of the Vieux Port that dominates Marseille's skyline. The domed basilica was built between 1853 and 1864 and is ornamented with coloured marble, murals and mosaics restored in 2006. Take bus 60 from the Vieux Port or walk up (30 minutes).

Château d'If   ISLAND CASTLE
(www.if.monuments-nationaux.fr; adult/child €5/free; ⊙9.30am-6.30pm, shorter hr & closed Mon winter) Immortalised in Alexandre Dumas' 1840s novel *Le Comte de Monte Cristo* (The Count of Monte Cristo), the 16th-century island prison of Château d'If sits 3.5km west of the Vieux Port. Political prisoners of all persuasions were incarcerated here, along with Protestants, the Revolutionary hero Mirabeau and the Communards of 1871.

Frioul If Express (www.frioul-if-express.com; 1 quai des Belges, 1er) boats (€10, 20 minutes) sail from the corner of quai de la Fraternité and quai de Rive Neuve at the Vieux Port.

⌐TOP⌐ Le Panier   HISTORIC QUARTER
CHOICE North of the Vieux Port, Marseille's old Le Panier quarter translates as 'the basket', and was the site of the Greek *agora* (marketplace). Today, its winding, narrow streets are a jumble of old stone houses, candy-coloured wooden shutters and artisans' shops: **72% Pétanque** (10 rue du Petit Puits), known for its brilliantly scented soaps, chocolate or tomato-leaf included, is a real favourite. Be prepared to get lost and don't miss the stunning **Centre de la Vieille Charité** (2 rue de la Charité, 2e; ⓜJoliette), built as a charity shelter for the town's poor and now home to a twinset of museums covering Mediterranean archaeology and African, Oceanic and American Indian Art. Later, hang out at a cafe on people-watching square **place de Lenche**.

⌐ Sleeping

⌐TOP⌐ Casa Honoré   BOUTIQUE B&B €€€
CHOICE (☎04 96 11 01 62; www.casahonore.com; 123 rue Sainte, 7e; d incl breakfast €150-200; ✳⌐⌐⌐; ⓜVieux Port) Los Angeles meets Marseille at this four-room *maison d'hôte*, built around a central courtyard with lap pool shaded by banana trees. The style reflects the owner's love for contemporary interior design.

CENT SAVER

The **Marseille City Pass** (1-/2-day pass €22/29) gets you admission to Marseille's museums, a guided tour of town, unlimited public transport travel, a boat trip, entrance to Château d'If and a load of discounts. Buy it at the tourist office.

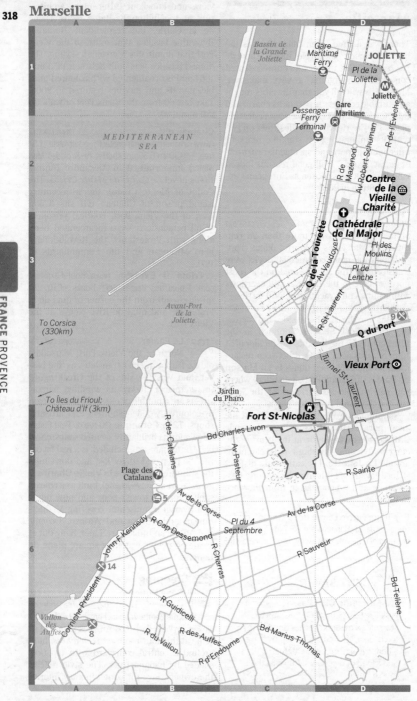

FRANCE PROVENCE

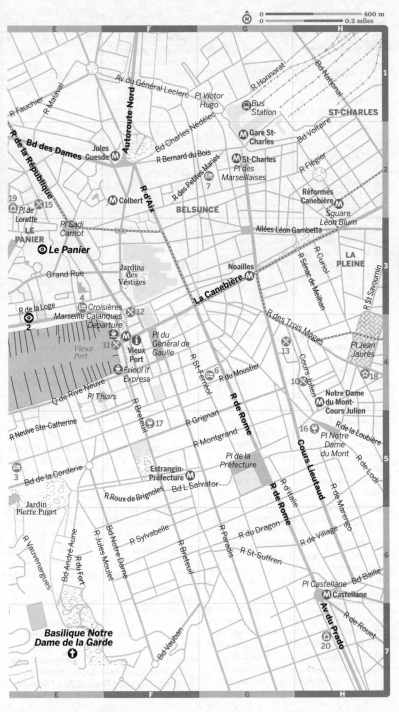

0 — 400 m
0 — 0.2 miles

FRANCE MARSEILLE

R Fauchier
R Malaval
R de la République
Bd des Dames
Av du Général Leclerc
Pl Victor Hugo
R Honnorat
Bd National
ST-CHARLES

Autoroute Nord
Jules Guesde
Bd Charles Nédélec
R Bernard du Bois
Gare St-Charles
Bd Voltaire

Colbert
R d'Aix
R des Petites Maries
St-Charles
Pl des Marseillaises
R Fléger
Réformés Canebière
Square Léon Blum

19 Pl de Lorette
15
BELSUNCE

Pl Sadi Carnot
LE PANIER
Le Panier

Grand Rue
Jardins des Vestiges
Noailles
La Canebière
Allées Léon Gambetta
R Curiol
R Sénac de Meilhan
LA PLEINE
R St Savournin

R de la Loge
4
Croisières Marseille Calanques Departure
12
Pl du Général de Gaulle
R des Trois Mages
Pl Jean Jaurès

2
Vieux Port
11
Vieux Port
Frioul If Express
R St-Ferréol
6 R du Moustier
13
Cours Julien
18

Q de Rive Neuve
Pl Thiars
R Breteuil
17
R Grignan
R de Rome
10
Notre Dame du Mont-Cours Julien

R Neuve Ste-Catherine
R Montgrand
16 Pl Notre Dame du Mont
R de la Loubière
R de Lodi

3
Bd de la Corderie
Estrangin-Préfecture
Pl de la Préfecture
R de Rome
R d'Aille

Jardin Pierre Puget
R Roux de Brignoles
Bd L Salvator
R de Marengo

R Vauvenargues
Bd André Aune
R du Fort
Bd Notre Dame
R Jules Moulet
R Sylvabelle
R Breteuil
R Paradis
R du Dragon
R St-Suffren
R de Village
Cours Lieutaud

Pl Castellane
Bd Baille
Castellane

Basilique Notre Dame de la Garde

Bd Vauban
Av du Prado
20
R de Rouet

Vertigo BOUTIQUE HOSTEL €

(☑04 91 91 07 11; www.hotelvertigo.fr; 42 rue des Petites Maries, 1er; dm €25-27, d €60-70; @; Ⓜ Gare St-Charles SNCF) This snappy boutique hostel kisses goodbye to dodgy bunks and hospital-like decor, and says 'hello' to vintage posters, designer chrome kitchen, groovy communal spaces and polite multilingual staff.

Hôtel Saint-Ferréol HOTEL €€

(☑04 91 33 12 21; www.hotelsaintferreol.com; 19 rue Pisançon, 1er; d €99-120; ❋@☏; Ⓜ Vieux Port) On the corner of the city's prettiest pedestrianised street, this plush hotel has individually decorated rooms inspired by artists. Service is exceptional.

Hôtel Belle-Vue HOTEL €€

(☑04 96 17 05 40; www.hotel-bellevue-marseille. fr; 34 quai du Port, 2e; d €84-135; ❋@☏; Ⓜ Vieux Port) Rooms at this old-fashioned hotel are decorated with mid-budget simplicity, but have million-dollar portside views. La Caravelle, one of Marseille's coolest bars, is downstairs.

Hôtel Le Richelieu BEACH HOTEL €€

(☑04 91 31 01 92; www.lerichelieu-marseille. com; 52 corniche Président John F Kennedy, 7e; d €53-88, tr €91-110; ❋@☏) The best rooms at this economical seaside hotel face the sea, lending the place a beach-house feel. Breakfast on the water-view terrace is idyllic.

✗ Eating

The Vieux Port overflows with restaurants, but choose carefully. Head to Cours Julien and its surrounding streets for world cuisine; and to the near Marché des Capucins area for cheap-eat pizza and couscous (under €10).

When in Marseille eat bouillabaisse (fish stew) and *supions* (squid pan-fried with garlic, parsley and lemon).

Jardin des Vestiges ARMENIAN-MEDITERRANEAN €

(15 rue Reine Elizabeth, 1er; mains €7-13; ☉9am-6pm Mon-Sat; Ⓜ Vieux Port) Our favourite budget choice draws on Armenian, Greek and Lebanese kitchens to create dishes such as kebabs, stuffed eggplant, moussaka and tabouleh. Buy to-go sandwiches here (€4 to €6) before boarding ferries to the islands.

Chez Jeannot MARSEILLAIS, FRENCH €€

(☑04 91 52 11 28; 129 rue du Vallon des Auffes; mains €12-25; ☉Tue-Sat, lunch Sun) An institution among Marseillais, the jovial rooftop terrace overlooking the port of Vallon des Auffes books out days ahead (but you can usually score an inside table). Stick to thin-crust pizzas and *supions* ('chippirons' on the menu).

Péron CONTEMPORARY €€€

(☑04 91 52 15 22; www.restaurant-peron.com, in French; 56 corniche Président John F Kennedy, 7e; mains €35; ☉lunch Tue-Sun, dinner Tue-Sat)

Perched on the sea's edge with magnificent views of Château d'If, Péron is one of Marseille's top seafood tables. Arrive before dark to watch the sunset.

La Cantinetta ITALIAN €€
(04 91 48 10 48; 24 cours Julien; mains €9-19; Tue-Sat; Notre Dame du Mont-Cours Julien) Our top choice on cours Julien serves perfectly al dente housemade pasta and other Italian goodies. Tables inside are cheek-by-jowl; we prefer the sun-dappled, tiled patio garden.

Chez Madie Les Galinettes PROVENÇAL €€
(04 91 90 40 87; 138 quai du Port, 2e; menus €25-35; Mon-Sat, closed Sat lunch summer; Vieux Port) This portside terrace is always packed, as is its arty interior when the weather isn't cooperating. Bouillabaisse needs to be ordered 48 hours ahead.

Pizzaria Chez Étienne MARSEILLAIS, ITALIAN €€
(43 rue de Lorette, 2e; mains €12-15; Mon-Sat; Colbert) This family-style neighbourhood haunt serves Marseille's best wood-fired pizza, beef steak and *supions* (pan-fried squid). Pop in beforehand to reserve in person (no phone). No credit cards.

Drinking & Entertainment

Options for a coffee or something stronger abound on both quays at the Vieux Port.

Cafes crowd cours Honoré d'Estienne d'Orves (1e), a large open square two blocks south of quai de Rive Neuve. Another cluster overlooks place de la Préfecture, at the southern end of rue St-Ferréol (1er).

DON'T MISS

MARSEILLE MARKETS

The small but enthralling **fish market** (quai des Belges; 8am-1pm; Vieux Port) is a daily fixture at the Vieux Port. **Cours Julien** hosts a Wednesday-morning organic fruit and vegetable market and **Prado Market** (av du Prado; 8am-1pm; Castellane or Périer) is the place to go for anything and everything other than food.

La Caravelle BAR
(34 quai du Port, 2e; 7am-2am; Vieux Port) Look up or miss this upstairs hideaway with miniature portside terrace. Live jazz Friday from 9pm.

TOP CHOICE La Part des Anges WINE BAR
(33 rue Sainte; mains €15, lunch Mon-Sat, dinner daily) The wine list at this happening wine bar and restaurant is an oenologist's dream.

Dame Noir BAR
(30 place Notre Dame de Mont, 6e; 5pm-2am Tue-Sat; Notre Dame du Mont-Cours Julien) Hip cats spill onto the sidewalk from this neighbourhood bar. DJs spin Thursday to Saturday. No sign; look for the red lights by the door.

L'Intermédiaire DIVE CLUB
(63 place Jean Jaurès, 6e; 7pm-2am; Notre Dame du Mont-Cours Julien) Grungy venue

WORTH A TRIP

LES CALANQUES

Marseille abuts the wild and spectacular Les Calanques, a protected 20km stretch of high, rocky promontories rising from the bright turquoise sea. Sheer cliffs are occasionally interrupted by idyllic beach-fringed coves, many only possible to reach with kayak. They've been protected since 1975 and are slated to become a national park by 2011.

Calanque de Sormiou is the largest rocky inlet, with two seasonal restaurants cooking up fabulous views: **Le Château** (04 91 25 08 69; mains €18-24; Apr–mid-Oct) – the better food – and **Le Lunch** (04 91 25 05 39, 04 91 25 05 37; http://wp.resto.fr/lelunch; mains €16-28; Apr–mid-Oct) – nearer the water; both require advance reservation. By bus, take No 23 from the Rond Point du Prado metro stop to La Cayolle, from where it's a 3km walk (note diners with a table reservation can drive through; otherwise, the road is open to cars weekdays only September to June).

Marseille's tourist office leads guided hikes in Les Calanques and has information on walking trails (shut July and August due to forest-fire risk). For great views from out at sea hop aboard a boat trip to the wine-producing port of **Cassis** (www.ot-cassis.com), 30km east along the coast, with **Croisières Marseille Calanques** (www.croisieres-marseille-calanques.com, in French; 74 quai du Port, 2e).

WANT MORE?

Head to **Lonely Planet** (www.lonely planet.com/france/provence/marseille) for planning advice, author recommendations, traveller reviews and insider tips.

with graffitied walls is one of the best for live bands or DJs (usually techno or alterna).

ℹ Information

Dangers & Annoyances

Marseille isn't a hotbed of violent crime, but petty crimes and muggings are common. Avoid the Belsunce area (southwest of the train station, bounded by La Canebière, cours Belsunce and rue d'Aix, rue Bernard du Bois and blvd d'Athènes) at night. Walking La Canebiére is annoying, but generally not dangerous; expect to encounter kids peddling hash.

Tourist information

Tourist office (📞 04 91 13 89 00; www. marseille-tourisme.com; 4 La Canebière, 1er; ⊙9am-7pm Mon-Sat, 10am-5pm Sun; Ⓜ Vieux Port)

ℹ Getting There & Away

Air

Aéroport Marseille-Provence (www.marseille. aeroport.fr), 25km northwest in Marignane, has numerous budget flights to various European destinations. **Shuttle buses** (Marseille 📞04 91 50 59 34; airport 📞04 42 14 31 27; www. lepilote.com) link it with Marseille train station (€8.50; 25 minutes, every 20 minutes from 5am to 11.30pm).

Boat

Gare Maritime (passenger ferry terminal; www.marseille-port.fr; Ⓜ Joliette)

SNCM (www.sncm.fr; 61 blvd des Dames, 2e; Ⓜ Joliette) Ferries to/from Corsica, Sardinia, Algeria and Tunisia.

Algérie Ferries (📞04 91 90 89 28; 58 blvd des Dames, 2e; Ⓜ Colbert) Ferries to/from Algeria.

Bus

The **bus station** (3 rue Honnorat, 3e; Ⓜ Gare St-Charles) is behind the train station.

AIX-EN-PROVENCE €4.90, 35 to 60 minutes, every five to 10 minutes

AVIGNON €18.50, two hours, one daily

CANNES €25, two hours, up to three daily

NICE €26.50, three hours, up to three daily

Train

From Marseille's **Gare St-Charles**, trains including TGVs go all over France and Europe.

AVIGNON €22.80, 35 minutes, 27 daily

LYON €47.30, 1¾ hours, 16 daily

NICE €29.70, 2½ hours, 21 daily

PARIS' GARE DE LYON €84.20, three hours, 21 daily

ℹ Getting Around

Pick up a bike from 100-plus stations across the city with **Le Vélo** (www.levelo-mpm.fr). A one-week 'subscription' costs €1; the first 30 minutes of each ride are free, then pay €1 per hour.

Marseille has two metro lines, two tram lines and an extensive bus network, all run by **RTM** (6 rue des Fabres, 1er; ⊙8.30am-6pm Mon-Fri, 9am-12.30pm & 2-5.30pm Sat; Ⓜ Vieux Port), where you can obtain information and transport tickets (€1.50). The metro runs from 5am to 10.30pm Monday to Thursday, and until 12.30am Friday to Sunday; the tram runs between 5am and 1am daily.

Aix-en-Provence

POP 146,700

Aix-en-Provence is to Provence what the Left Bank is to Paris: a pocket of bohemian chic crawling with students. It's hard to believe that 'Aix' (pronounced ex) is just 25km from chaotic, exotic Marseille. The city has been a cultural centre since the Middle Ages (two of the town's most famous sons are painter Paul Cézanne and novelist Émile Zola) but for all its polish, it's still a laid-back Provençal town at heart.

◉ Sights

Circuit de Cézanne   ARTIST TRAIL

Art, culture and architecture abound in Aix, especially thanks to local lad Paul Cézanne (1839–1906). To see where he ate, drank, studied and painted, you can follow the Circuit de Cézanne, marked by footpath-embedded bronze plaques inscribed with the letter C. A free English-language guide to the plaques, *Cézanne's Footsteps*, is available from the tourist office.

The trail takes in Cézanne's last studio, **Atelier Paul Cézanne** (www.atelier-cezanne.com; 9 av Paul Cézanne; adult/child €5.50/2; ⊙10am-noon & 2-6pm, closed Sun winter), 1.5km north of the tourist office. It's painstakingly preserved as it was at the time of his death, strewn with tools and still-life models; his admirers claim this is where Cézanne is most present.

The other two main Cézanne sights in Aix are the **Bastide du Jas de Bouffan**, the family home where Cézanne started painting, and the **Bibémus quarries**, where he did most of his Montagne Ste-Victoire paintings. Head to the tourist office for bookings (required) and information.

Cathédrale St-Sauveur   CHURCH
(rue Laroque; ⊙8am-noon & 2-6pm) A potpourri of styles, Aix cathedral was begun in the 12th century and successively enlarged over the next few hundred years: it's worth a visit for the memorable Gregorian chants, usually sung at 4.30pm Sunday.

Musée Granet   MUSEUM
(www.museegranet-aixenprovence.fr, in French; place St-Jean de Malte; adult/child €4/free; ⊙11am-7pm Tue-Sun) Housed in a 17th-century priory, this museum's pride and joy are its nine Cézanne paintings and works by Picasso, Léger, Matisse, Tal Coat and Giacometti.

✯✰ Festivals & Events
Life seems to be one long festival in festive Aix; the tourist office has a festival list.

Festival International d'Art Lyrique d'Aix-en- Provence   PERFORMING ARTS
(International Festival of Lyrical Art; www.festival -aix.com) The highlight of Aix's sumptuous cultural calendar. In July, this month-long festival brings classical music, opera and buskers.

Festival de le Roque d'Anthéron
PIANO MUSIC
(www.festival-piano.com) Mid-July to mid-August, from Aix to the Luberon.

🛏 Sleeping
Book accommodation through the **Centrale de Réservation** (☑04 42 16 11 84; www.aixen provencetourism.com).

TOP **L'Épicerie**   B&B €€
CHOICE (☑06 08 85 38 68; www.unechambreen ville.eu; 12 rue du Cancel; s incl breakfast €80-120, d €100-130; 🛜) This retro B&B is the fabulous creation of born-and-bred Aixois lad, Luc. His breakfast room recreates a 1950s grocery store, and the flowery garden out back is a dream for evening dining (book ahead). Breakfast is a veritable feast gargantuan enough to last all day.

Hôtel Cézanne   BOUTIQUE HOTEL €€€
(☑04 42 91 11 11; http://cezanne.hotelaix.com; 40 av Victor Hugo; d €179-249; ❋@🛜) Aix's hippest hotel is a study in clean lines, with sharp-edged built-in desks and loveseats that feel a touch Ikea. Best is breakfast (€19), which includes smoked salmon and Champagne.

Auberge de Jeunesse du Jas de Bouffan
HOSTEL €
(☑04 42 20 15 99; www.auberge-jeunesse-aix.fr; 3 av Marcel Pagnol; dm incl breakfast & sheets €19-22; ⊙reception 7am-2.30pm & 4.30pm-midnight, closed mid-Dec–Jan) Shiny-new with a bar, tennis courts, bike shed and massive summer BBQs, this HI hostel is 2km west of the centre; shame about the motorway. Take bus 4 from La Rotonde to the Vasarely stop.

Hôtel les Quatre Dauphins   SMALL HOTEL €€
(☑04 42 38 16 39; www.lesquatredauphins.fr; 54 rue Roux Alphéran; s €55-60, d €70-85; ❋🛜) Close to cours Mirabeau, this sweet 13-room hotel, a former private mansion, was redone in 2010 and looks fresh and clean, with new bathrooms and rainfall showerheads. The tall terracotta-tiled staircase (no elevator) leads to four attic rooms, with sloped beamed ceilings.

Hôtel Cardinal   HOTEL €
(☑04 42 38 32 30; www.hotel-cardinal-aix. com; 24 rue Cardinale; s/d €60/70) Beneath stratospheric ceilings, Hôtel Cardinal's 29 romantic rooms are beautifully furnished with antiques, tasselled curtains, and newly tiled bathrooms.

✗ Eating
Aix' sweetest treat is the marzipan-like local speciality, *calisson d'Aix,* a small, diamond-shaped, chewy delicacy made with ground almonds and fruit syrup. The daily **produce market** (place Richelme) sells olives, goat's cheese, garlic, lavender, honey, peaches, melons and other sun-kissed products.

Le Petit Verdot   FRENCH €€
(☑04 42 27 30 12; www.lepetitverdot.fr; 7 rue En-trecasteaux; mains €15-25; ⊙dinner Mon-Sat, lunch Sat) Wine is the primary focus at this earthy restaurant, where tabletops are made of cast-off wine crates. The meat-heavy menu is designed to marry with the wines, not the other way round.

La Chimère Café   SUPPER CLUB €€
(☑04 42 38 30 00; www.lachimerecafe.com; 15 rue Brueys; menus €28-32) Aix's party crowd laps up the cabaret feel of this former nightclub: starry-night vaulted ceiling in the underground room and grand chandeliers with crimson velvet on the main floor. Food is classic French.

WORTH A TRIP

A CULINARY DETOUR

Hilltop village **Ventabren** (population 5000), 16km west of Aix, provides the perfect lazy-day detour. Meander sun-dappled cobbled lanes; peep inside a 17th-century church; and get drunk on dizzying views of Provence from old chateau ruins before a superb lunch or dinner at **La Table de Ventabren** (☑04 42 28 79 33; www.latabledeventabren. com; 1 rue Cézanne; menus €41-50; ☺lunch Wed-Sun, dinner Tue-Sun). Chef Dan Bessoudo, honoured with a coveted Michelin star, creates inventive wholly modern French dishes and knockout desserts – served in summer on a romantic terrace facing distant mountains and starry skies. Get here before the prices double; reservations essential.

Le Poivre d'Ane   CONTEMPORARY **€€**
(☑04 42 21 32 66; www.restaurantlepoivredane. com; 40 place des Cardeurs; menus €28-45; ☺dinner Thu-Tue) Fancy a haddock milkshake, duck sushi or thyme-and-cinnamon apple tart with Baileys whipped cream? Summer tables are smack dab on one of Aix's loveliest pedestrian squares; reservations essential.

Amphitryon   PROVENÇAL **€€**
(☑04 42 26 54 10; www.restaurant-amphitryon.fr; 2-4 rue Paul Doumer; menus €25-40; ☺Tue-Sat) Amphitryon enjoys a solid reputation, particularly in summer for its market-driven cooking and alfresco dining in the cloistergarden. Attached **Comptoir de l'Amphi** (mains €12-17) is less expensive.

❶ Information

Tourist office (www.aixenprovencetourism. com; 2 place du Général de Gaulle; ☺8.30am-7pm Mon-Sat, 10am-1pm & 2-6pm Sun, longer hr summer)

❶ Getting There & Away

Bus

From Aix' **bus station** (av de l'Europe), a 10-minute walk southwest from La Rotonde, routes include Marseille (€4.90, 35 minutes via the autoroute or one hour via the D8), Arles (€9, 1½ hours) and Avignon (€14.70, 1¼ hours).

Half-hourly shuttle buses go to/from Aix TGV station and Aéroport Marseille-Provence.

Train

The only useful train from Aix' **city centre train station** (av Victor Hugo) is to/from Marseille (€7, 50 minutes). Other services use **Aix TGV station**, 15km away.

AVIGNON €6.60, 20 minutes

MARSEILLE €13, 55 minutes

NÎMES €7.50, 30 minutes

Avignon

POP 93,560

Hooped by 4.3km of superbly preserved stone ramparts, this graceful city is the belle of Provence's ball. Famed for its annual performing arts festival and fabled bridge, Avignon is an ideal spot from which to step out into the surrounding region. Wrapping around the city, Avignon's defensive ramparts were built between 1359 and 1370, and are punctuated by a series of sturdy *portes* (gates).

◉ Sights

Palais des Papes   PAPAL PALACE
(www.palais-des-papes.com; place du Palais; adult/child €6/3; ☺9am-8pm Jul & early–mid-Sep, to 9pm Aug, to 7pm mid-Mar–Jun & mid-Sep–Oct, to 6.30pm early–mid-Mar, to 5.45pm Nov-Feb) This Unesco World Heritage site, the world's largest Gothic palace, was built when Pope Clement V abandoned Rome in 1309 and settled in Avignon. The immense scale of the palace, with its cavernous stone halls and vast courtyards, testifies to the wealth of the popes; the 3m-thick walls, portcullises and watchtowers emphasise their need for defence.

Pont St-Bénezet   BRIDGE
(adult/child €4.50/3.50; ☺9am-8pm, 9.30am-5.45pm Nov-Mar) This fabled bridge, immortalised in the French nursery rhyme *Sur le Pont d'Avignon,* was completed in 1185. The 900m-long wooden bridge was repaired and rebuilt several times before all but four of its 22 spans were washed away in the mid-1600s. If you don't feel like paying, you can see it for free from the Rocher des Doms park, Pont Édouard Daladier or from across the river on the Île de la Barthelasse's chemin des Berges.

Musée du Petit Palais MUSEUM

(www.petit-palais.org; place du Palais; adult/child €6/free; ☉10am-1pm & 2-6pm Wed-Mon) The bishops' and archbishops' palace during the 14th and 15th centuries now houses an outstanding collection of lavish 13th- to 16th-century Italian religious paintings by artists including Botticelli, Carpaccio and Giovanni di Paolo.

Musée Angladon ART MUSEUM

(www.angladon.com; 5 rue Laboureur; adult/child €6/4; ☉1-6pm Tue-Sun Apr-Nov, 1-6pm Wed-Sun Jan-Mar, closed Dec) This charming museum harbours Impressionist treasures, including the only Van Gogh painting in Provence *(Railway Wagons),* and works by Cézanne, Manet, Degas and Picasso.

📷 Festivals & Events

Hundreds of artists take to the stage and streets during the world-famous **Festival d'Avignon** (www.festival-avignon.com), held every year from early July to early August. Don't miss the more experimental (cheaper) fringe **Festival Off** (www.avignonleoff.com, in French) that runs alongside the main fest.

🛌 Sleeping

TOP CHOICE **Le Limas** B&B €€

(☎04 90 14 67 19; www.le-limas-avignon.com; 51 rue du Limas; d/tr incl breakfast from €120/200; ❄@) Behind its discreet lavender door, this chic address in an 18th-century town house is like something out of *Vogue Living.* It's everything interior designers strive for when mixing old and new. Breakfast by the fireplace or on a sun-drenched terrace!

Hôtel de l'Horloge HOTEL €€

(☎04 90 16 42 00; www.hotels-ocre-azur.com; place de l'Horloge; r €95-180; ❄☎) Most rooms at this supercentral hotel are straightforward (comfortable, all mod cons), but the five terrace rooms have the edge with sophisticated furnishings and views: ask for 505 with its incredible view of the Palais des Papes.

YMCA-UCJG HOSTEL €€

(☎04 90 25 46 20; www.ymca-avignon.com; 7bis chemin de la Justice; dm €36, without bathroom €25; ☉reception 8.30am-6pm, closed Dec–early Jan; ☎☀) This spotless hostel across the river, just outside Villeneuve-lès-Avignon, has some private rooms and a swimming pool and terrace with panoramic views of the city. Take bus 10 to the Monteau stop.

Hôtel Boquier HOTEL €

(☎04 90 82 34 43; www.hotel-boquier.com, in French; 6 rue du Portail Boquier; d €50-70; ❄☎) The infectious enthusiasm of owners Sylvie and Pascal Sendra sweeps through this central little place, bright, airy and spacious.

Lumani B&B €€

(☎04 90 82 94 11; www.avignon-lumani.com; 37 rue du Rempart St-Lazare; d incl breakfast €100-170; ❄☎) This fabulous *maison d'hôte* run by Elisabeth, whose art is hung throughout the stunning house, is a fount of inspiration for artists. Love the fountained garden.

🍴 Eating

Place de l'Horloge's touristy cafes have so-so food. Restaurants open seven days during summer-festival season, when reservations

---

WORTH A TRIP

VAN GOGH'S ARLES

If the winding streets and colourful houses of Arles seem familiar, it's hardly surprising – Vincent van Gogh lived here for much of his life in a yellow house on place Lamartine, and the town regularly featured in his canvases. His original house was destroyed during WWII, but you can still follow in Vincent's footsteps on the **Van Gogh Trail**, marked out by footpath plaques and a brochure handed out by the **tourist office** (main office ☎04 90 18 41 20; www.tourisme.ville-arles.fr; esplanade Charles de Gaulle; ☉9am-6.45pm Apr-Sep, 9am-4.45pm Mon-Sat, 10am-12.45pm Sun Oct-Mar; train station ☎04 90 43 33 57; ☉9am-1.30pm & 2.30-4.45pm Mon-Fri Apr-Sep).

Two millennia ago, Arles was a major Roman settlement. The town's 20,000-seat amphitheatre and 12,000-seat theatre, known as the **Arénes** and the **Théâtre Antique**, are nowadays used for cultural events and bullfights.

Telleschi (☎04 42 28 40 22) buses go to/from Aix-en-Provence (€9, 1½ hours) and there are regular trains to/from Nîmes (€7.50, 30 minutes), Marseille (€13.55, 55 minutes) and Avignon (€6.60, 20 minutes).

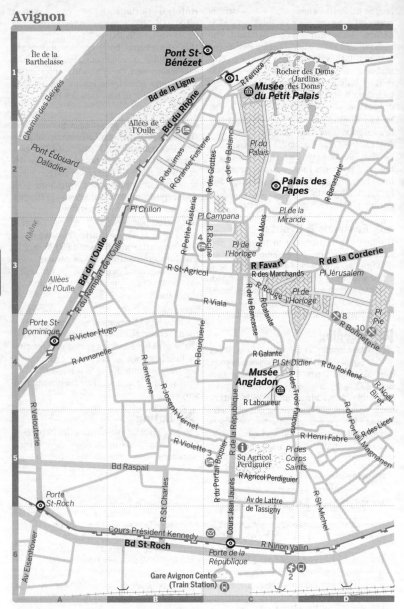

FRANCE PROVENCE

become essential. *Papaline d'Avignon* is a pink, chocolate ball filled with potent Mont Ventoux herbal liqueur.

Cuisine du Dimanche   PROVENÇAL €€
(✆04 90 82 99 10; www.lacuisinedudimanche.com, in French; 31 rue Bonneterie; mains €15-25; ✆closed

Sun & Mon Oct-May) Spitfire chef Marie shops every morning at Les Halles to find the freshest ingredients for her earthy flavour-packed cooking. The market-driven menu changes daily, but specialities include scallops and a simple roast chicken with pan gravy.

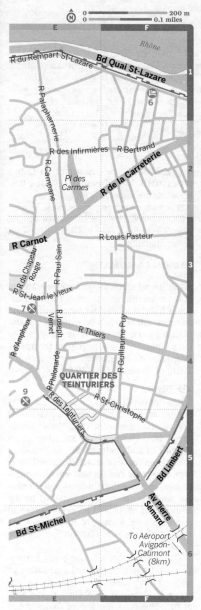

FRANCE AVIGNON

L'Epice and Love FRENCH €

(☑ 04 90 82 45 96, 30 rue des Lices; mains €11-12; ☺ dinner Mon-Sat) Stews, roasts and other homestyle French dishes is what makes this tiny bohemian restaurant, decorated with antique kitchen ware and mismatched chairs, so appealing. No credit cards.

❶ Information

Tourist office (www.avignon-tourisme.com; 41 cours Jean Jaurès; ☺ 9am-5pm Mon-Sat, 9.45am-5pm Sun)

❶ Getting There & Away

Air

Aéroport Avignon-Caumont (www.avignon. aeroport.fr), 8km southeast, has seasonal flights to/from Britain and Ireland.

Bus

From the **bus station** (blvd St-Roch), down the ramp to the right as you exit the train station:

AIX-EN-PROVENCE €14, 1¼ hour

ARLES €7.70, 1½ hours

MARSEILLE €20, two hours

NÎMES €8.10, 1¼ hours

Train

Avignon has two stations: **Gare Avignon TGV**, 4km southwest in Courtine; and central **Gare**

Au Tout Petit CONTEMPORARY FRENCH €€

(☑ 04 90 82 38 86; 4 rue d'Amphoux; menus €11-24; ☺ Tue-Sat) This teensy place with just eight tables packs big flavours into every imaginative dish: simple, smart cooking, maximising the use of spice.

LES HALLES

There is no better spot to shop for that perfect Provence picnic to scoff atop bluff-top park **Rocher des Doms** (tasty views of the Rhône, Avignon and Mont Ventoux) than at the market. Bursting with local life and a fabulous vegetal wall by green designer Patrick Blanc (of Musée du Quai Branly fame), **Les Halles** (place Pie; www.avignon -leshalles.com; ⊘7am-1pm Tue-Sun) is a gourmand paradise of fruit, veg, meat, cheese, herbs, olive oil and other local seasonal produce. Each Saturday at 11am, moreover, during **La Petite Cuisine des Halles**, a local chef gives a cooking demo and lesson; details online.

Avignon Centre (42 blvd St-Roch) with trains to/from:

ARLES €6.70, 20 minutes

NÎMES €8.70, 30 minutes

Some TGVs to/from Paris stop at Gare Avignon Centre, but TGVs for Marseille (€22.80, 35 minutes) and Nice (€54.40, three hours) only use Gare Avignon TGV.

In July and August there's a direct **Eurostar** (www.eurostar.com) service on Saturdays from London (from €135 return, six hours) to Gare Avignon Centre. See p360 for more details.

Around Avignon

LES BAUX DE PROVENCE

At the heart of the Alpilles, spectacularly perched above picture-perfect rolling hills of vineyards, olive groves and orchards, is the hilltop village of Les Baux de Provence. Van Gogh painted it and if you stroll around the deep dungeons, up crumbling towers and around the maze-like ruins of **Château des Baux** (www.chateau-baux-provence.com; adult/child €7.60/5.70; ⊘9am-6pm, to 8pm Jul & Aug) you'll see why.

For a real splurge lunch at legendary **L'Ousta de Baumanière** (☎04 90 54 33 07; www.oustaudebaumaniere.com; menus €95-150)

CARPENTRAS MARKET

Don't miss **Carpentras**, 25km northeast of Avignon, on a Friday morning when its streets and squares spill over with hundreds of market stalls laden with breads, honeys, cheeses, olives, fruit and a rainbow of *berlingots* (the local striped, pillow-shaped hard-boiled sweet). Late November to March, pungent black-truffle stalls murmur with hushed-tones transactions.

or the Michelin-star restaurant **La Cabro d'Or** (☎04 90 54 33 21), also in Les Baux. Reservations are imperative for both.

The **tourist office** (☎04 90 54 34 39; www. lesbauxdeprovence.com; ⊘9.30am-5pm Mon-Fri, 10am-5.30pm Sat & Sun) has information on accommodation.

VAISON-LA-ROMAINE
POP 6392

A traditional market town for aeons, Vaison la Romaine still has a thriving Tuesday market, delightful cobbled medieval quarter and an extraordinarily rich Roman legacy. It also makes a great base for hiking and cycling jaunts into the limestone ridge of the nearby **Dentelles de Montmirail** and also up the 'Giant of Provence', **Mont Ventoux** (1912m).

◎ Sights

Gallo-Roman Ruins ARCHAEOLOGICAL SITE
(adult/child €8/3.50; ⊘closed Jan–early Feb) The ruined remains of Vasio Vocontiorum, the Roman city that flourished here from the 6th to 2nd centuries BC, fill two sites. At **Puymin** (av du Général de Gaulle; ⊘9.30am-6pm, closed noon-2pm Oct-Mar) see noblemen's houses, mosaics, the still-functioning **Théâtre Antique** (built around AD 20 for an audience of 6000) and an **archaeological museum** with a swag of fine statues, including likenesses of Hadrian and his wife Sabina.

Colonnaded shops, public baths' foundations and a limestone-paved street with an underground sewer are visible at **La Villasse** (⊘10am-noon & 2.30-6pm), to the west of the same road. **Maison au Dauphin** has splendid marble-lined fish ponds.

Your ticket also includes entry to the peaceful 12th-century Romanesque cloister at **Cathédrale Notre-Dame de Nazareth** (cloister €1.50; ⊘10am-12.30pm & 2-6pm, closed Jan & Feb), found a five-minute walk west of La Villasse.

CHÂTEAUNEUF-DU-PAPE

Carpets of vineyards unfurl around this tiny medieval village, the summer residence of Avignon's popes who had a summer residence – all but one ruined wall today – built atop the hill here.

Most Châteauneuf-du-Pape wine is red, and strict regulations govern production. Reds come from 13 different grape varieties – grenache is the biggie – and are aged at least five years. Sample them over a free tasting *(dégustation gratuite)* at more than two dozen shops and cellars in the village, or at the **Musée du Vin** (www.brotte.com; rte d'Avignon; admission free; ⊙9am-1pm & 2-7pm). The **tourist office** (www.paysprovence.fr, in French; place du Portail; ⊙9.30am-6pm Mon-Sat Jun-Sep, closed Wed & Sun Oct-May) has a list of wine-producing estates that do cellar visits, tastings, tours and so on.

Perched beneath the ruined chateau, **Le Verger des Papes** (✆04 90 83 50 40; 4 rue du Château; menus €20-30; ⊙hours vary) has a leafy terrace with knockout vistas and the best traditional French cooking in town, with bread made in a wood-fired oven.

Cité Médiévale   MEDIEVAL CITY
Across the pretty **Pont Romain** (Roman Bridge), cobblestone alleyways known as *calades* carve through the stone walls up to an imposing 12th-century **chateau** (guided tours in French, €2; ⊙check with tourist office) built by the counts of Toulouse, from where there are eagle-eye views.

🛏 Sleeping & Eating

Hôtel Le Burrhus   DESIGN HOTEL €
(✆04 90 36 00 11; www.burrhus.com; 1 place de Montfort; d €55-87; 🛜) Smack bang on Vaison's vibrant central square, this looks like a quaint old place from the outside, but is cutting-edge designer inside.

La Lyriste   PROVENÇAL €€
(✆04 90 36 04 67; 45 cours Taulignan; menus €18-36; ⊙Wed-Sun) In summer book a table on the terrace at this tasty contemporary bistro, known for its seasonal dishes and local classics such as *bourride* (fish stew).

❶ Getting There & Away
From the **bus station**, 400m east of the town centre on ave des Choralies, **Autocars Lieutaud/Trans Vaucluse** (www.cars-lieutaud.fr) runs buses to/from Avignon (€6, 1½ hours).

THE FRENCH RIVIERA & MONACO

With its glistening seas, idyllic beaches and lush hills, the French Riviera (Côte d'Azur in French) screams exclusivity, extravagance and excess. It has been a favourite getaway for the European jet set since Victorian times and there is nowhere more chichi or glam in France than St-Tropez, Cannes and super-rich, sovereign Monaco.

But it's not just a high-roller's playground. Every year millions of visitors descend on the southern French coast to bronze their bodies, smell the lavender and soak up that hip Mediterranean vibe.

Nice
POP 352,400
Riviera queen Nice is what good living is all about – shimmering shores, the very best of Mediterranean food, a unique historical heritage, free museums, a charming Old Town, exceptional art and Alpine wilderness within an hour's drive. No wonder so many young French people aspire to live here while the tourists just keep flooding in.

To get stuck-in straight away, make a beeline upon arrival for Promenade des Anglais, Nice's curvaceous palm-lined seafront that follows its busy pebble beach for 6km from the city centre to the airport.

⊙ Sights
Vieux Nice   OLD TOWN
Ditch the map and lose yourself in the Old Town's tangle of 18th-century pedestrian passages and alleyways, historic churches and hole-in-the-wall joints selling Niçois tapas. Cours Saleya, running parallel to the seafront, hosts one of France's most vibrant, vividly hued **food markets** (⊙6am-1.30pm Tue-Sun), trestle tables groaning with shiny fruit and veg, pastries, *fruits confits* (glazed or candied fruits such as figs, ginger, pears etc). Baroque **Cathédrale Ste-Réparate** (place Rossetti) with its glazed terracotta

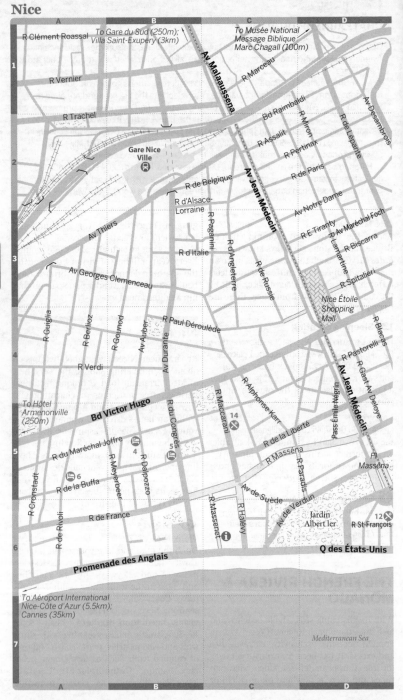

To Gare du Sud (250m);
Villa Saint-Exupery (3km)

To Musée National
Message Biblique
Marc Chagall (100m)

R Clément Roassal

R Vernier

R Trachel

Av Malaaussena

R Marceau

Bd Raimbaldi

R Miron

R de Lépante

Av Desambrois

R Assalit

R Pertinax

Gare Nice
Ville

R de Belgique

Av Jean Médecin

R de Paris

R d'Alsace-
Lorraine

Av Notre Dame

R E Tiranty

Av Marechal Foch

Av Thiers

R Paganini

R d'Italie

R d'Angleterre

R de Russie

Lamartine

R Biscarra

Av Georges Clemenceau

R Spitalieri

Nice Étoile
Shopping
Mall

R Guiglia

R Berlioz

R Gounod

Av Auber

R Paul Déroulède

R Blacas

R Pastorelli

Av Gast Av Deloye

R Verdi

Av Durante

Av Jean Médecin

To Hôtel
Armenonville
(250m)

Bd Victor Hugo

R Alphonse Karr

R Maccarani

14

Pass Émile Négrin

R du Maréchal Joffre

R Meyerbeer

R du Congrès

R Dalpozzo

4

5

R de la Liberté

R Mass250

Pl
Masséna

R Cronstadt

R de la Buffa

6

Av de Suède

Av de Verdun

R Paradis

R de Rivoli

R de France

R Massenet

R Halévy

Jardin
Albert Ier

12

R St-François

To Aéroport International
Nice-Côte d'Azur (5.5km);
Cannes (35km)

Promenade des Anglais

Q des États-Unis

Mediterranean Sea

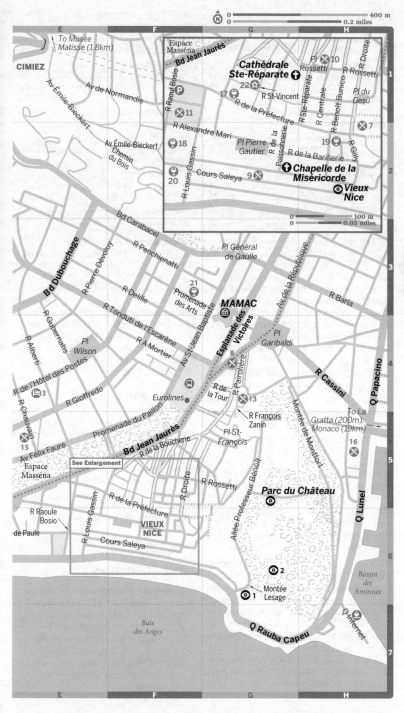

FRANCE NICE

dome (1650) and **Chapelle de la Miséricorde** (cours Saleya) are equally exuberant.

At the eastern end of quai des États-Unis, steep steps and a cliffside **ascenseur** (lift; €1.10; ⊙9am-7pm Apr-Sep, shorter hr rest of year) climb up to **Parc du Château**, a hilltop park with great views over Old Nice and the beachfront. The chateau itself was razed by Louis XIV in 1706 and never rebuilt.

Musée Matisse   MUSEUM
(www.musee-matisse-nice.org; 164 av des Arènes de Cimiez; ⊙10am-6pm Wed-Mon) Housed in a 17th-century Genoese mansion, this small museum reveals Henri Matisse's evolution as an artist rather than wowing the crowds with masterpieces. You can view well-known works such as his blue paper cutouts *Blue Nude IV* and *Woman with Amphora* alongside less-well-known sculptures and experimental pieces. Take bus 17 from the bus station or bus 22 from Place Masséna to the Arènes stop.

MAMAC   ART MUSEUM
(Musée d'Art Moderne et d'Art Contemporain; www.mamac-nice.org; promenade des Arts; ⊙10am-6pm Tue-Sun) This one is worth a visit for its stunning architecture alone, but it also houses some fantastic avant-garde art from the 1960s to the present, including iconic pop art from Roy Lichtenstein and Andy Warhol's 1965 *Campbell's Soup Can*. An awesome panorama of Vieux Nice unfolds from the rooftop garden-gallery.

Musée National Message Biblique Marc Chagall   ART MUSEUM
(www.musee-chagall.fr, in French; 4 av Dr Ménard; adult/child €7.50/5.50; ⊙10am-5pm Wed-Mon Oct-Jun, to 6pm Jul-Sep) This small museum houses the largest public collection of the Russian-born artist's seminal paintings of *Old Testament* scenes.

🏃 Activities

Beaches   BEACHES
You'll need at least a beach mat to cushion your tush from Nice's beaches, which are made up of round pebbles. Free sections of beach alternate with 15 sunlounge-lined **private beaches** (www.plagesdenice.com, in French; ⊙May-Sep), where you pay to rent a sunlounger (around €15 a day).

On the beach, operators hire out catamarans, paddleboats and jet skis; you can also

---

DON'T MISS

THE CORNICHES

Some of the Riviera's most spectacular scenery stretches east between Nice and Monaco. A trio of *corniches* (coastal roads) hugs the cliffs between the two seaside cities, each higher up the hill than the last. The middle *corniche* ends in Monaco; the upper and lower continue to Menton near the French-Italian border.

parascend, waterski or paraglide. There are showers and toilets on every beach.

✯ Festivals & Events

Carnaval de Nice   CARNIVAL
(www.nicecarnaval.com) This two-week carnival, held in February, is particularly famous for its 'battles of the flowers', where thousands of blooms are tossed into the crowds from passing floats, as well as its fantastic fireworks display.

Nice Jazz Festival   MUSIC
(www.nicejazzfestival.fr) In July, Nice swings to the week-long jazz festival at the Arènes de Cimiez, amid the Roman ruins.

🛏 Sleeping

Nice has a suite of places to sleep, from stellar independent backpacker hostels to international art-filled icons. Prices rocket upwards in the summer season.

TOP CHOICE Villa Rivoli   BOUTIQUE HOTEL €€
(☎04 93 88 80 25; www.villa-rivoli.com; 10 rue de Rivoli; s/d/q from 85/99/210; ❄@🐾) Built in 1890, this stately villa feels like your own pied-à-terre in the heart of Nice. Rooms are character-rich, some with fabric walls, gilt-edged mirrors, and marble fireplaces. Breakfast in the garden or belle-époque salon.

Hôtel Windsor   BOUTIQUE HOTEL €€
(☎04 93 88 59 35; www.hotelwindsornice.com; 11 rue Dalpozzo; d €120-175; ❄@🐾🏊) Graffiti casts aggressive splashes of colour on the edgy, oversize rooms of the Windsor – a real nod to contemporary art. Rooms overlooking the backyard tropical garden have a particularly lush view.

Nice Garden Hôtel   BOUTIQUE HOTEL €€
(☎04 93 87 35 63; www.nicegardenhotel.com; 11 rue du Congrès; s/d €75/100; ❄🐾) Nine beautifully appointed rooms blend old and new and overlook a delightful garden with a glorious orange tree – pure, unadulterated charm and peacefulness just two blocks from the promenade.

Villa Saint-Exupéry   HOSTEL €
(☎04 93 84 42 83; www.villahostels.com; 22 av Gravier; dm €25-30, s/d €45/90; @🐾) Why can't all hostels be like this? Set in a lovely converted monastery in the north of the city, this backpacker palace features a 24-hour common room in a converted chapel, state-of-the-art-kitchens, barbecue terraces

WORTH A TRIP

THE PINE CONE TRAIN

Chugging between mountains and the sea, narrow-gauge railway **Train des Pignes** (Pine Cone Train; www.trainprovence.com) is one of France's most picturesque train rides. Rising to 1000m, with breathtaking views, the 151km-long track between Nice and Digne-les-Bains passes through the scarcely populated back country of little-known Haute Provence.

Day-trip suggestion: a picnic and meander around the historical centre and citadel of the beautiful medieval village of **Entrevaux** (€18 return, 1½ hours).

and lovely dorms; they'll even pick you up from the nearby Comte de Falicon tram stop or St Maurice stop for bus 23 (from the airport).

Hôtel Wilson   BOUTIQUE HOTEL €
(☎04 93 85 47 79; www.hotel-wilson-nice.com; 39 rue de l'Hôtel des Postes; s/d €50/55; 🐾) Many years of travelling, an experimental nature and exquisite taste have turned Jean-Marie's rambling flat into a compelling place to stay. Mind the two resident tortoises as you sit down for a breakfast.

Hôtel Armenonville   HOTEL €€
(☎04 93 96 86 00; www.hotel-armenonville.com; 20 av des Fleurs; d €86-105; @🐾) Shielded by its large garden, this grand early-20th-century mansion has sober rooms, three (12, 13 and 14) with a huge terrace overlooking *le jardin*.

🍴 Eating

Niçois nibbles include *socca* (a thin layer of chickpea flour and olive oil batter), *salade niçoise* and *farcis* (stuffed vegetables). Restaurants in Vieux Nice are a mixed bag, so choose carefully.

La Merenda   NIÇOIS €€
(4 rue Raoul Bosio; mains €12-15; ⏰Mon-Fri) This pocket-sized bistro serves some of the most unusual fare in town: stockfish (dried cod soaked in running water for a few days and then simmered with onions, tomatoes, garlic, olives and potatoes) and tripe. It also serves Bellet wines, a rare local vintage. No credit cards.

DON'T MISS

NICE FAST FOOD

When locals crave a quick bite, they grab a *pan bagnat* (loosely translated as sopped bread), the local version of a tuna sandwich made with crusty round bread, chunks of cold tuna, lettuce, tomatoes, onions, radish and egg, all drizzled with loads of olive oil. The best come from portside snack-bar **La Gratta** (2 blvd Franck Pilatte; sandwiches €4.50; ⊘lunch). Find a spot by the water to dangle your feet over the quay and watch masts bob in the harbour while you drip olive oil down your chin.

Chez René Socca　　　　NIÇOIS €
(2 rue Miralhéti; dishes from €2; ⊘9am-9pm Tue-Sun, to 10.30pm Jul & Aug, closed Nov) This address is about taste, not presentation or manners. Grab some *socca* or *petits farçis* and head across the street to the bar for a *grand pointu* (glass) of red, white or rosé.

Zucca Magica　　　　VEGETARIAN €€
(☑04 93 56 25 27; www.lazuccamagica.com; 4bis quai Papacino; menus €30; ⊘Tue-Sat; ⍊) The 'Magic Pumpkin' is a rarity in France – a vegetarian restaurant that non-vegetarians like! Bring an appetite: fixed-price meals comprise four set dishes (five for dinner) plus dessert, all sourced at the market.

La Table Alziari　　　　NIÇOIS €
(☑04 93 80 34 03, 4 rue François Zanin; mains €9-15, ⊘Tue-Sat) Run by the grandson of the famous Alziari olive-oil family, this citrus-coloured restaurant chalks up local specialities such as *morue à la niçoise* (cod served with potatoes, olives and a tomato sauce) and *daube* (stew) on its blackboard.

Acchiardo　　　　BISTRO €
(38 rue Droite; mains €14-20; ⊘Mon-Fri) Going strong since 1927; locals flock here to Acchiardo for the plat du jour (daily special), a glass of wine and a load of gossip served straight up on the counter.

TOP CHOICE **Fenocchio**　　　　ICE CREAM €
(2 place Rossetti; from €2; ⊘9am-midnight Feb-Oct) Beat the summer heat with Nice's most fabulous *glacier* (ice-cream maker). Eschew predictable favourites and indulge in new tastes: black olive, tomato-basil, rhubarb, avocado, rosemary, *calisson* (almond biscuit frosted with icing sugar),

lavender, ginger or liquorice. There are 50 flavours in all to choose from.

TOP CHOICE **Luc Salsedo**　　　MODERN FRENCH €€€
(☑04 93 82 24 12; www.restaurant-salsedo.com, in French; 14 rue Maccarani; mains €26; ⊘lunch Fri & Sun-Tue, dinner Thu-Tue Jun-Sep, dinner only Jul-Aug) The cuisine of young chef Salsedo is local and seasonal, served without pomp on plates, rustic boards or cast-iron pots. The wine list is another French hit.

Luna Rossa　　　　ITALIAN €€
(☑04 93 85 55 66; www.lelunarossa.com; 3 rue Chauvain; mains €15-25; ⊘Tue-Fri, dinner Sat) The Red Moon translates as fresh pasta, perfectly cooked seafood, sun-kissed veg (artichoke hearts, sun-dried tomatoes, asparagus tips etc) and succulent meats.

La Petite Maison　　　FRENCH, NIÇOIS €€€
(☑04 93 92 59 59; www.lapetitemaison-nice.com; 11 rue St-François de Paule; mains €20-40; ⊘Mon-Sat) Nice's hottest tables draw celebs and politicians for its happening scene and elegantly executed Niçois specialities – tops for a splashy night out.

🍷 Drinking & Entertainment

Vieux Nice's streets are stuffed with bars and cafes, serving anything from morning espresso to lunchtime pastis (the aperitif tipple in these parts).

Smarties　　　　LOUNGE BAR
(http://nicesmarties.free.fr; 10 rue Defly; ⊘6pm-2am Tue-Sat) We love Smarties' sexy-'70s swirly orange style, which draws a hot-looking straight/gay crowd. On weekends, the tiny dance floor fills when DJs spin deep house, electro, techno and occasionally disco; weekdays are mellower. Free buffet with happy hour (6pm to 9pm).

Les Distilleries Idéales　　　　CAFE
(24 rue de la Préfecture; ⊘9am-12.30am) Whether you're after a coffee on your way to cours Saleya or a sundowner, the atmosphere in this brilliant bistro is infectious: you're bound to leave with a skip in your step.

Le Bar des Oiseaux　　　　CABARET
(www.bardesoiseaux.com, in French; 5 rue St-Vincent; ⊘lunch Mon-Sat, dinner Tue-Sat) Artists dig this bohemian bar (and adjoining theatre) for live jazz, *chansons françaises* (French songs) and cabaret nights. Cover costs around €5 when there's entertainment; you can also dine here (*menus* around €20).

Ma Nolan's
PUB

(www.ma-nolans.com; 2 rue St François de Paule; ⊘noon-2am Mon-Fri, 11pm-2am Sat & Sun) This Irish pub is a backpacker favourite, with a Monday-night pub quiz, televised sport, nightly live music and full English brekkie.

Le Six
GAY BAR

(www.le6.fr; 6 rue Raoul Bosio; ⊘Tue-Sun 10pm-4:30am) Primped and pretty A-gays crowd shoulder to shoulder at Nice's compact, perennially popular 'mo bar. Climb the ladder to the mezzanine.

Chez Wayne's
BAR

(www.waynes.fr; 15 rue de la Préfecture; ⊘2.30pm-12.30am) This raucous watering hole has live bands every night.

ⓘ Information

Main tourist office (www.nicetourisme.com; 5 promenade des Anglais; ⊘8am-8pm Mon-Sat, 9am-7pm Sun Jun-Sep, 9am-6pm Mon-Sat Oct-May) By the beach.

Train station tourist office (av Thiers; ⊘8am-8pm Mon-Sat, 9am-7pm Sun Jun-Sep, 8am-7pm Mon-Sat, 10am-5pm Sun Oct-May)

ⓘ Getting There & Away

Air

Aéroport International Nice-Côte d'Azur (www.nice.aeroport.fr), 6km west of the centre, is served by numerous carriers, including several low-cost ones.

Ligne d'Azur runs two airport buses (€4). Route 99 shuttles approximately every half-hour direct between Gare Nice Ville and both airport terminals daily from around 8am to 9pm. Route 98 takes the slow route and departs from the bus station every 20 minutes (30 minutes Sunday) from around 6am to around 9pm.

A second tram line is planned to connect Nice's centre with the airport.

Boat

The fastest, cheapest ferries to Corsica (p344) depart from Nice.

SNCM (www.sncm.fr; ferry terminal, quai du Commerce)

Corsica Ferries (www.corsicaferries.com; quai Lunel)

WANT MORE?

For in-depth information, reviews and recommendations at your fingertips, head to the Apple App Store to purchase Lonely Planet's *Nice City Guide* iPhone app.

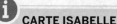

CARTE ISABELLE
335

Between July and September, the SNCF's **Carte Isabelle** (€14) covers unlimited train trips in a single day (except TGV trains) from Fréjus to Ventimiglia in Italy, and from Nice inland to Tende.

Bus

From the **bus station** (5 blvd Jean Jaurès) a single €1 fare takes you anywhere in the Alpes-Maritimes *département* (with a few exceptions, such as the airport) and includes one connection, within 74 minutes. Buses run daily to Antibes (one hour), Cannes (1½ hours), Monaco (45 minutes), Vence (one hour) and St-Paul de Vence (55 minutes).

Eurolines (www.eurolines.com) Operates from the bus station.

Train

From **Gare Nice Ville** (av Thiers), 1.2km north of the beach, there are frequent services to Antibes (€4, 30 minutes), Cannes (€6.10, 40 minutes), Menton (€4.60, 35 minutes) and Monaco (€3.40, 20 minutes). Direct TGV trains link Nice with Paris' Gare de Lyon (€115, 5½ hours).

Cannes

POP 71,800

Everyone's heard of Cannes and its celebrity film festival. The latter only lasts for two weeks in May, but the buzz and glitz linger all year thanks to regular visits from celebrities who come here to indulge in designer shopping, beaches and the palace hotels of the Riviera's glammest seafront, blvd de la Croisette.

Offshore lie the idyllic islands, Îles de Lérins, the unexpected key to 2000-plus years of history – from Ligurian fishing communities (200 BC) to one of Europe's oldest religious communities (5th century AD) and the enigmatic Man in the Iron Mask.

⊙ Sights & Activities

Beaches
BEACHES

The central, sandy beaches along blvd de la Croisette are sectioned off for hotel patrons. Many accept day guests, who pay from €20 per day for a mattress and yellow-and-white parasol on **Plage du Gray d'Albion** (⊘10am-5pm Mar-Oct), to €50-odd for a pearl-white lounge on the pier of super-stylish **Z Plage** (⊘9.30am-6pm May-Sep), the beach of Hôtel Martinez.

Cannes

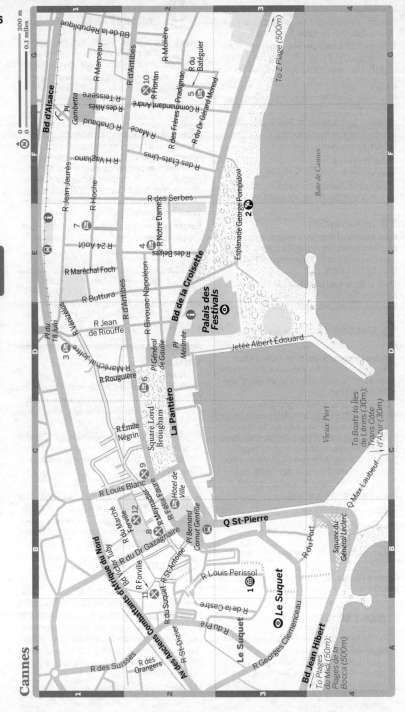

R des Suisses
R des Orangers
R St-Dizier
R du Pré
Av des Anciens Combattants d'Afrique du Nord
Bd d'Victor Ruby
R Forville
R du Suquet
R St-Antoine
R Georges Clemenceau
Bd Jean Hibert

To Plages du Midi (50m);
Plages de la Bocca (500m)

Le Suquet

◎ Le Suquet
R de la Castre
R Louis Perissol
1

R du Marché Forville
R du Dr Gazagnaire
R Meynadier
R Félix Faure
Pl Bernard Cornut Gentille
12
8
Q St-Pierre
R du Port
Square du Général Leclerc
Q Max Laubeuf

To Boats to Îles de Lérins (30m); Trans Côte d'Azur (30m)

Vieux Port

9
R Louis Blanc
Hôtel de Ville
R Émile Négrin
Square Lord Brougham
La Pantiéro
6
R Rouguière
R Maréchal Joffre
3
Pl du 18 Juin
R Venizélos
R Jean de Riouffe
R Buttura
R Maréchal Foch
R d'Antibes
R Bivouac Napoléon
Pl Général de Gaulle
Pl Mérimée

Jetée Albert Édouard

Palais des Festivals
i

Bd de la Croisette

R des Belges
R Notre Dame
4
R 24 Août
7
R des Serbes
R Hoche
R Jean Jaurès
R H Vagliano
R des États-Unis
R Maréchal Foch

Esplanade George Pompidou
2

Baie de Cannes

Bd d'Alsace

Pl Gambetta
R Chabaud
R Mace
R Teisseire
R des Alliés
10
R Marceau
R d'Antibes
R Molière
R du Batéguier
R Florian
R Commandant André
R des Frères Pradignac
R du Dr Gérard Monod
5

Bd de la République

To Z Plage (500m)

N
0   200 m
0   0.1 miles

Cannes

A microscopic strip of sand near the Palais des Festivals is free, but you'll find better free sand on **Plages du Midi** and **Plages de la Bocca**, west from the Vieux Port along blvd Jean Hibert and blvd du Midi.

Palais des Festivals   LANDMARK
(Festival Palace; blvd de la Croisette) At the western end of La Croisette, this concrete bunker is the unlikely host of the world's most glamorous film festival. The tourist office runs **guided tours** (adult/child €3/free; 1½ hrs; ⊙2.30pm Jun-Apr) several times a month; book ahead.

Le Suquet   OLD TOWN
Cannes' historic quarter, pre-dating the glitz and glam of the town's festival days, retains a quaint village feel with its steep, meandering alleyways. There are wonderful views of the Baie de Cannes from the top of the hill, and the fascinating **Musée de la Castre** (place de la Castre; adult/child €3.20/free; ⊙10am-7pm Jul & Aug, 10am-1pm & 2-5pm Tue-Sun Sep-Jun), an ethnographic museum.

Îles de Lérins   ISLANDS
Although just 20 minutes away by boat, these tranquil islands feel far from the madding crowd. **Île Ste-Marguerite**, where the mysterious Man in the Iron Mask was incarcerated during the late 17th century, is known for its bone-white beaches, eucalyp-

tus groves and small marine museum. Tiny **Île St-Honorat** has been a monastery since the 5th century: visit small chapels, stroll through vineyard and forest and lunch or take afternoon tea at monk-run restaurant **La Tonnelle** (☏04 92 99 18 07; mains €25; ⊙lunch).

Boats leave Cannes from quai des Îles on the western side of the harbour. **Riviera Lines** (ww.riviera-lines.com; adult/child €11.50/6 return) runs ferries to Île Ste-Marguerite and **Compagnie Planaria** (www.cannes-iles delerins.com; adult/child €12/6) covers Île St-Honorat.

🛏 Sleeping

Hotel prices in Cannes fluctuate wildly according to the season, and soar during the film festival, when you'll need to book months in advance.

TOP CHOICE | **Hôtel 7e Art**   BOUTIQUE HOTEL €
(☏04 93 68 66 66; www.7arthotel.com; 23 rue Maréchal Joffre; s €68, d €60-98; ❄️🛜) Cannes' newest star puts boutique style within reach of budgeteers. The owners schooled in Switzerland and their snappy design of putty-coloured walls, padded headboards and pop art far exceeds what you'd expect at this price.

Hôtel Le Mistral   BOUTIQUE HOTEL €€
(☏04 93 39 91 46; www.mistral-hotel.com; 13 rue des Belges; d from €89; ❄️🛜) This small hotel, a mere 50m from La Croisette, wins the *palme d'or* for best value in town: rooms are in red and plum tones and bathrooms feature designer fittings.

Hotel Le Romanesque   BOUTIQUE HOTEL €€
(☏04 93 68 04 20; www.hotelleromanesque.com; 10 rue Batéguier; r €90-150; ❄️🛜) Every room is individually decorated at this eight-room boutique charmer in the heart of Cannes' nightlife district. Favourites include Charlotte, with its sun-drenched bath; and Elizabeth, the former maid's quarters, with low, sloping, beamed ceilings.

Villa Tosca   HOTEL €€
(☏04 93 38 34 40; www.villa-tosca.com; 11 rue Hoche; s/d €80/100; ❄️🛜) This elegant, bourgeois town house sits on a semi-pedestrianised street in Cannes' shopping area. Rooms with balcony are perfect for people-watching.

Hôtel Splendid   BOUTIQUE HOTEL €€€
(☏04 97 06 22 22; www.splendid-hotel-cannes. com; 4-6 rue Félix Faure; s/d from €160/190; ❄️) The hotel in this elaborate 1871 building has

THE SCENT OF THE CÔTE D'AZUR

Mosey some 20km northwest of Cannes to inhale the sweet smell of lavender, jasmine, mimosa and orange-blossom fields. In **Grasse**, one of France's leading perfume producers, dozens of perfumeries create essences to sell to factories (for aromatically enhanced foodstuffs and soaps) as well as to prestigious couture houses – the highly trained noses of local perfume-makers can identify 3000 scents in a single whiff.

Fragonard (www.fragonard.com; 20 blvd Fragonard; ☉9am-6pm Feb-Oct, 9am-12.30pm & 2-6pm Nov-Jan) is the easiest perfumery to reach by foot. The tourist office has information on other perfumeries and field trips to local flower farms, including the flower-strewn **Domaine de Manon** (☏04 93 60 12 76; www.domaine-manon.com; admission €6). Roses are picked mid-May to mid-June, jasmine July to late October.

everything it takes to rival Cannes' posher palaces: beautifully decorated rooms, fabulous location, stunning views and more, in the form of self-catering kitchenettes.

✖ Eating

You'll find the least-expensive restaurants around rue du Marché Forville. Hipper, pricier establishments are in Le Suquet and the 'Carré d'Or' (the 'golden square' streets between La Croisette and rue d'Antibes). Square Lord Brougham, next to the Vieux Port, is the place to picnic.

Mantel TOP CHOICE MODERN EUROPEAN €€
(☏04 93 39 13 10; www.restaurantmantel. com; 22 rue St-Antoine; menus €25-38; ☉Fri-Mon, dinner Tue & Thu) The Italian maître d' here will make you feel like a million dollars and you'll melt for Noël Mantel's divine cuisine and great-value prices. Best of all, you get not one but two desserts with your menu (oh, the pannacotta...).

Le Riad MOROCCAN €€
(☏04 93 38 60 95; www.restaurant-le-riad.fr; 6 impasse Florian; mains €13-26; ☉noon-midnight Tue-Sat) Le Riad imports Moroccan hospitality and authentic cooking, with *tagine* classics and a real *pastilla* (pigeon pie) – rare even in Morocco. On weekend nights a bellydancer sets a party mood. Excellent service.

Coquillages Brun SEAFOOD €€
(☏04 93 39 21 87; www.astouxbrun.com; 27 rue Félix Faure; menus from €28; ☉12pm-1am) Cannes' most famous brasserie is *the* place to indulge in oysters, mussels, prawns, crayfish and other delightfully fresh shells with a glass of crisp white wine.

Aux Bons Enfants TRADITIONAL FRENCH €€
(80 rue Meynadier; menus €23; ☉Tue-Sat) This familial little place buzzes. The lucky ones

who get a table (arrive early or late) can feast on top-notch regional dishes.

ℹ Information

Tourist office (☏04 92 99 84 22; www.cannes. travel; blvd de la Croisette; ☉9am-8pm Jul & Aug, 9am-7pm Mon-Sat Sep-Jun) On the ground floor of Palais des Festivals; runs an annexe next to the train station.

ℹ Getting There & Away

Bus

From the **bus station** (place Bernard Cornut Gentille) buses serve Nice (bus 200, €1, 1½ hours) and Nice airport (bus 210, €15, 50 minutes, half-hourly)

Train

GRASSE €3.80, 30 minutes

MARSEILLE €22, two hours

NICE €6.10, 40 minutes

St-Tropez

POP 5700

In the soft autumn or winter light, it's hard to believe the pretty terracotta fishing village of St-Tropez is a stop on the Riviera celebrity circuit. It seems far removed from its glitzy siblings further up the coast, but come spring or summer, it's a different world: the population increases tenfold, prices triple and fun-seekers pile in to party till dawn, strut around the luxury-yacht-packed Vieux Port and enjoy the creature comforts of exclusive A-listers' beaches in the Baie de Pampelonne.

If you can at all avoid visiting in July and August, do. But if not, take heart: it's always fun to play 'I spy...' (a celebrity).

☉ Sights & Activities

Musée de l'Annonciade   ART MUSEUM
(place Grammont, Vieux Port; adult/child €6/4;
⊙10am-noon & 2-6pm Wed-Mon Oct & Dec-May,
10am-noon & 3-7pm Wed-Mon Jun-Sep) Displayed
in a disused chapel at the Vieux Port (Old
Port), this small water-facing museum displays works by Matisse, Bonnard, Dufy and
pointillist Signac, who set up his home and
studio in St-Tropez.

Plage de Pampelonne   BEACH
The golden sands of **Plage de Tahiti**, 4km
southeast of town, morph into the 5km-long,
celebrity-studded **Plage de Pampelonne**,
which sports a line-up of exclusive beach
restaurants and clubs in summer. The bus
to Ramatuelle stops at various points along
a road, 1km inland from the beach. Beach
mats can be rented for around €15 per day.

Citadelle   CITADEL
(admission €2.50; ⊙10am-6.30pm Apr-Sep,
10am-12.30pm & 1.30-5.30pm Oct-Mar) The
panoramas of St-Tropez's iconic church
tower and glistening bay from this lofty
17th-century fortress are definitely worth
the climb.

🛏 Sleeping

St-Tropez is no shoestring destination, but
multistar camping grounds abound on the
road to Plage de Pampelonne.

Hôtel Le Colombier   HOTEL €€
(☏04 94 97 05 31; impasse des Conquettes; r €84-
158, without bath €76; ▣) An immaculate converted house five minutes' walk from place
des Lices, the Colombier's fresh summery decor is feminine and uncluttered. Not all rooms

have air-con. Rooms without baths share a
toilet, but have bidet, sink and shower.

Hôtel Ermitage   BOUTIQUE HOTEL €€€
(☏04 94 27 52 33; www.ermitagehotel.fr; av Paul
Signac; r €180-300; ▣🛜@) Kate Moss and
Lenny Kravitz favour this rocker crash pad
inspired by St-Tropez in the 1950s to 1970s
– disco meets mid-century modern. Its out-
of-town, hillside location only ups the exclusivity factor and proffers knockout views
over town.

Lou Cagnard   HOTEL €€
TOP CHOICE (☏04 94 97 04 24; www.hotel-lou-cag
nard.com; 18 av Paul-Roussel; d/tr €69-140/160;
▣🛜) Book well ahead for this great-value
courtyard charmer, shaded by lemon and
fig trees. Rooms are spotlessly kept and
five have garden terraces.

Pastis   ART HOTEL €€€
(☏04 98 12 56 50; www.pastis-st-tropez.com; 61
av du Général Leclerc; d from €200-350; ▣▣)
This stunning hotel with pop-art-inspired
interior is the brainchild of an English
couple passionate about modern art. Swim
in the emerald-green pool and snooze
under centenary palm trees.

Les Palmiers   BOUTIQUE HOTEL €€
(☏04 94 97 01 61; www.hotel-les-palmiers.com;
26 blvd Vasserot; d €89-189; ▣) In an old villa
with courtyard garden overlooking place
des Lices, Les Palmiers has friendly service
and simple rooms. Skip the annexe for the
main building.

🍴 Eating

Quai Jean Jaurès at the Vieux Port is littered
with restaurants and cafes.

DON'T MISS

TOP FIVE BEACH EATS

Book lunch (well ahead) at the following, open May to September and around €15 to €40
for a main.

» **Club 55** (www.leclub55.fr; 43 blvd Path) St-Tropez's oldest-running beach club, this
1950s address was the crew canteen for the filming of *And God Created Woman* with
Brigitte Bardot. The rich and famous flock here to be seen, although the food – rather
remarkably – is nothing special.

» **Nikki Beach** (www.nikkibeach.com/sttropez; rte de l'Epi) Favoured by dance-on-the-
bar celebs such as Paris Hilton and Pamela Anderson, the deafening scene ends at
midnight.

» **Moorea Plage** (www.moorea-plage-st-tropez.com; rte des Plages) Ideal for conversation
and backgammon (supplied); tops for steak.

» **Liberty Plage** (www.plageleliberty.com; chemin des Tamaris; ⊙year-round) Clothing
optional – eat naked.

MASSIF DE L'ESTÉREL

Punctuated by pine, oak and eucalyptus trees, the rugged red mountain range Massif de l'Estérel contrasts dramatically with the brilliant blue sea.

Extending east from St-Raphaël to Mandelieu-La Napoule (near Cannes), a curling coastal road, the famous corniche de l'Estérel (also known as the corniche d'Or and N98), passes through summer villages and dreamy inlets perfect for a quick dip. Try **Le Dramont**, where the 36th US Division landed on 15 August 1944, or **Agay**, a sheltered bay with excellent beach. More than 100 hiking trails criss-cross the Massif de l'Estérel's interior and views from the top of **Pic de l'Ours** (496m) and **Pic du Cap Roux** (452m), both accessible via marked trails, are breathtaking.

End your foray in style with dinner or a drink in neighbouring **St-Raphaël** (population 35,000) at **Les Charavins** (☑04 94 95 03 76; 36 rue Charabois; mains €18-26; ☺dinner Thu-Tue, lunch Thu, Fri, Mon & Tue). Run by Philippe Furnémont, a former Michelin-starred chef and wine connoisseur, this jolly wine bar is fabulously French. The cuisine is resolutely traditional, and don't even *think* about turning down whatever wine suggestion Philippe offers you.

Brasserie des Arts MODERN FRENCH €€
(☑04 94 40 27 37; www.brasseriedesarts.com; 5 place des Lices; mains €20) Wedged in a line-up of eating/drinking terraces jockeying for attention on St-Tropez's people-watching square, BA, as it is known, is where the locals go. Its fixed three-course menu is gourmet and excellent value.

Auberge des Maures PROVENÇAL €€
(☑04 94 97 01 50; 4 rue du Docteur Boutin; mains €31-39; ☺dinner) St-Trop's oldest restaurant remains the locals' choice for consistently good, copious portions of earthy Provençal cooking. Book a table (essential) in the leafy courtyard.

Le Sporting BRASSERIE €€
(☑04 94 97 00 65; place des Lices; mains €14-24; ☺8am-1am) There's a bit of everything on the menu at always-packed Le Sporting,

but the speciality is hamburger topped with foie gras and creamy morel sauce. Reservations essential.

ℹ Information

Tourist office (☑04 94 97 45 21; www.ot-saint-tropez.com; quai Jean Jaurès; ☺9.30am-8pm Jul & Aug, 9.30am-12.30pm & 2-7pm Apr-Jun & Sep–mid-Oct, 9.30am-12.30pm & 2-6pm mid-Oct–Mar)

ℹ Getting There & Away

Boat
Trans Côte d'Azur (www.trans-cote-azur.com) Day trips from Nice and Cannes, Easter to September.

Bus
From the **bus station** (av Général de Gaulle), buses run by **VarLib** (www.varlib.fr, in French) serve Ramatuelle (€2, 35 minutes) and St-Raphaël train station (€2, 1¼ hours) via Grimaud, Port Grimaud and Fréjus. There are four daily buses to Toulon-Hyères airport (€15; 1½ hours).

THE MARKET

One of southern France's busiest and best, St-Tropez's **place des Lices market** (☺mornings Tue & Sat) is a highlight of local life, with colourful stalls groaning under the weight of plump fruit and veg, mounds of olives, local cheeses, chestnut purée and fragrant herbs. Afterwards meander to the port and duck beneath the stone arch to the bijou **fish market** (☺mornings Tue-Sun, daily summer), hidden between stone walls on place aux Herbes.

Monaco

☑377 / POP 32,000

Your first glimpse of this pocket-sized principality will probably make your heart sink: after all the gorgeous medieval hilltop villages, glittering beaches and secluded peninsulas of the surrounding area, Monaco's concrete high-rises and astronomic prices come as a shock.

But Monaco is beguiling. The world's second-smallest state (a smidgen bigger

That's what Brazilian triple-world champion Nelson Piquet famously likened driving Monaco's **Formula One Grand Prix** to! Monaco's cachet nonetheless means it's the most coveted trophy, and the narrow lanes, tortuous road layout and hairpin bends along Monaco's streets means spectators can get closer to the action than at most circuits. Buy trackside tickets (from €70/270 standing/seated) for the event, held each year in May, from the **Automobile Club de Monaco** (www.formula1monaco.com), but get in early as demand is steeper than the near-vertical streets. If you're dead keen, you can walk the 3.2km circuit; the tourist office has maps.

than the Vatican), it is as famous for its tax-haven status as for its glittering casino, sports scene (Formula One, world-famous circus festival and tennis open) and a royal family on a par with British royals for best gossip fodder. For visitors, it just means an exciting trip: from an evening at the stunning casino to a visit of the excellent Musée Océanographique to a spot of celebrity/royalty spotting, Monaco is a fun day out on the Riviera.

In terms of practicalities, Monaco is a sovereign state but has no border control. It has its own flag (red and white), national holiday (19 November) and telephone country code (377), but the official language is French and the country uses the euro even though it is not part of the European Union.

Sights & Activities

Casino de Monte Carlo CASINO
(www.casinomontecarlo.com; place du Casino; ☺European Rooms from noon Sat & Sun, from 2pm Mon-Fri) Living out your James Bond fantasies just doesn't get any better than at Monte Carlo's monumental, richly decorated showpiece, the 1910-built casino. Admission is €10 for the European Rooms, with poker/slot machines, French roulette and *trente et quarante* (a card game), and €20 for the Private Rooms, which offer baccarat, blackjack, craps and American roulette. Jacket-and-tie dress code kicks in after 10pm. Minimum entry age for both types of rooms is 18; bring photo ID.

TOP CHOICE Musée Océanographique de Monaco AQUARIUM
(www.oceano.org; av St-Martin; adult/child €13/6.50; ☺9.30am-7pm) Propped on a sheer cliff-face, this classic-looking museum was built in 1910 and houses a fantastic aquarium. The spectacular views from the rooftop terrace are especially not to be missed. Ex-

hibit signs are translated into English, Italian and German.

Palais du Prince ROYAL PALACE
(www.palais.mc; adult/child €8/3.50; ☺10am-6pm Apr-Sep) For a glimpse into royal life, tour the state apartments with an audioguide. The palace is what you would expect of any aristocratic abode: lavish furnishings and expensive 18th- and 19th-century art. Guards are changed outside the palace at 11.55am every day.

Cathédrale de Monaco CHURCH
(4 rue Colonel) An adoring crowd continually shuffles past Prince Rainier's and Princess Grace's graves inside the choir of Monaco's Romanesque-Byzantine cathedral. Its famous boys' choir sings Sunday Mass at 10am from September to June.

Sleeping

If your shoestring budget's fraying, stay in Nice and train it the 20 minutes to Monaco.

Ni Hôtel BOUTIQUE HOTEL €€
(☎97 97 51 51; www.nihotel.com; 1bis rue Grimaldi; s/d from €120/150; ❄⊛) This uberhip design hotel makes bold use of flashy primary colours (shower walls, chairs and stairs are made of transparent coloured plastic) mixed with sobering black and white. The roof terrace is in a prime spot for evening drinks.

TRAFFIC-JAM DODGER

To skip the worst of July and August's high-season traffic, motorists get off the A8 at Le Muy (exit 35), take the D558 road through the Massif des Maures and via La Garde Freinet to Port Grimaud, park and hop aboard a **Bateaux Verts** (www.bateauxverts.com) shuttle boat (adult/child €6.50/3.50, 15 minutes) to St-Tropez.

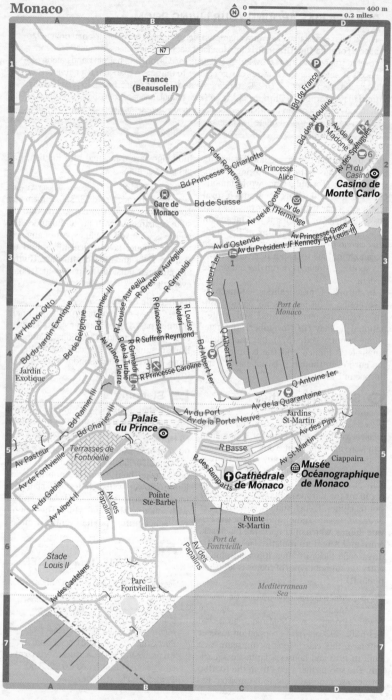

0   400 m
0   0.2 miles

France
(Beauseil)

N7

Bd de France

Bd des Moulins

Av de la Madone
Av des Spélugues

Pl du Casino

Casino de Monte Carlo

R de Roqueville

Av Princesse Alice

Bd Princesse Charlotte

Av de la Costa

Av de

Av de l'Hermitage

Bd de Suisse

Gare de Monaco

Av Princesse Grace

Av d'Ostende

Av du Président JF Kennedy Bd Louis-II

Av du

Port de Monaco

Q Albert 1er

R Grimaldi

R Bretelle Auréglia

R Louise Auréglia

Bd Rainier III

Bd de Belgique

Av du Jardin Exotique

Av Hector Otto

R Princesse

R Louise Notari

R Suffren Reymond

Q Albert 1er

Bd Albert 1er

Q Antoine 1er

Av de la Quarantaine

Jardin Exotique

Av Prince Pierre

R Grimaldi

R de la Turbie

R Princesse Caroline

Av du Port

Av de la Porte Neuve

Jardins St-Martin

Av des Pins

Bd Rainier III

Palais du Prince

R Basse

Av St-Martin

Bd Charles III

Av Pasteur

Terrasses de Fontvieille

R des Remparts

Cathédrale de Monaco

Musée Océanographique de Monaco

Ciappaira

Av de Fontvieille

R du Gabian

Av Albert II

Pointe Ste-Barbe

Av des Papalins

Pointe St-Martin

Stade Louis II

Av des Castelans

Parc Fontvieille

Av des Papalins

Port de Fontvieille

Mediterranean Sea

Monaco

Hôtel Miramar
HOTEL €€

(☎93 30 86 48; www.miramar.monaco-hotel.com; 1 av du Président JF Kennedy; d €145; ✳☎📶) This 1950s-vintage seaside hotel, replete with rooftop terrace bar for lazy breakfasts, lunches and evening drinks, is a fabulous option located right by the port. Seven of the 11 rooms have fabulous balconies overlooking the yachts.

✖ Eating & Drinking

TOP CHOICE Le Nautique
CAFE €

(3 av Président Kennedy; mains €9-13; ☺Mon-Sat lunch) The clubhouse of Monaco's rowing club has million-dollar views and €10 lunches, served in a sunny linoleum-floored dining room. Look for the gym equipment at street level and the inconspicuous sign marked 'Société Nautique Fédération Monégasque Sport Avion Snack Bar'.

Tip Top
PIZZERIA €

(11 rue Spélugues; mains 12-24; ☺24hr) Tip Top is where local Monégasques gather all night long for pizza, pasta and gossip.

Huit & Demi
ITALIAN €€

(☎93 50 97 02; www.huit-et-demi.com; rue Princesse Caroline; mains €13-27; ☺noon-3pm & 7-11pm Mon-Fri, 7-11pm Sat) Chic and popular, this is the hot spot to savour Italian fare amid crimson-coloured walls lined with celebrity B&W portraits. We prefer the street terrace.

Brasserie de Monaco
MICROBREWERY

(www.brasseriedemonaco.com; 36 rte de la Piscine; ☺11am-1pm Sun-Thu, 11am-3am Fri & Sat) Tourists and locals rub shoulders at Monaco's only microbrewery, which crafts rich organic ales and lager alongside tasty (pricy) antipasti plates.

Stars 'n' Bars
AMERICAN

(www.starsnbars.com; 6 quai Antoine 1er; ☺noon-2.30am, closed Mon Oct-May) Any star worth his/her reputation has partied at this American western saloon. Monstrous burgers and other food too.

Café de Paris
CAFE

(www.montecarloresort.com; place du Casino; mains €17-53; ☺7am-2am) Sip grossly over-priced coffee and limo-spot on this sprawling 300-seat terrace next to the casino.

❶ Information

Telephone

Calls between Monaco and France are international calls. Dial 00 followed by Monaco's country code (377) when calling Monaco from France or elsewhere abroad. To phone France from Monaco, dial 00 and France's country code (33).

Tourist information

Tourist office (www.visitmonaco.com; 2a blvd des Moulins; ☺9am-7pm Mon-Sat, 11am-1pm

THE MONACO MONARCHY

Originally from Genoa in neighbouring Italy, the Grimaldi family has ruled Monaco since 1297, except for its occupation during the French Revolution. Its independence was again recognised by France in 1860, and it's been an independent state ever since.

Since the marriage of Prince Rainier III of Monaco (r 1949–2005) to Hollywood actress Grace Kelly in 1956, Monaco's ruling family has been a non-stop feature in gossip magazines. Even Albert II, who has been prince since his father's death in 2005, hasn't escaped media scrutiny: he has two illegitimate children and no legitimate heirs, but his achievements as an athlete (he played for Monaco football team and is a judo black belt), his charity work and promotion of the arts have earned him favourable press. In mid-2010 he announced his engagement and impending marriage in 2011 to South African Olympic swimmer and former model Charlene Wittstock.

DON'T MISS

BACKPACKER PARADISE

If you're not up for the Nice–Monaco train trip, check into **Relais International de la Jeunesse Thalassa** (✆04 93 81 27 63; www.clajsud.fr; 2 av Gramaglia, Cap d'Ail; dm incl sheets & breakfast €18; ⊙Apr-Oct), Monaco's closest hostel, smack on the seashore in a beautiful spot on Cap d'Ail.

Sun) From mid-June to late September additional tourist-info kiosks mushroom around the harbour and train station.

ⓘ Getting There & Away

Monaco's **train station** (av Prince Pierre) has frequent trains to Nice (€3.40, 20 minutes), and east to Menton (€1.90, 10 minutes) and beyond into Italy.

CORSICA

The rugged island of Corsica (Corse in French) is officially a part of France, but remains fiercely proud of its own culture, history and language. It's one of the Mediterranean's most dramatic islands, with a bevy of beautiful beaches, glitzy ports and a mountainous, maquis-covered interior to explore, as well as a wild, independent spirit all of its own.

The island has long had a love-hate relationship with the mother mainland – you'll see plenty of anti-French slogans and 'Corsicanised' road signs – but that doesn't seem to deter the millions of French tourists who descend on the island every summer. Prices skyrocket and accommodation is at a premium during the peak season between July and August, so you're much better off saving your visit for spring and autumn.

Bastia

POP 44,000

Filled with heart, soul and character, the ramshackle old port of Bastia is a good surprise. Sure, it might not measure up to Ajaccio's sexy style or the architectural appeal of Bonifacio, but this lived-in, well-loved city is what modern-day Corsica is all about. Allow yourself at least a day to climb narrow alleyways from the seething old harbour to the dramatic 16th-century citadel, currently undergoing one of the largest (and costliest) renovation projects in the island's history.

◉ Sights & Activities

Even by Corsican standards, Bastia is a pocket-sized city. The 19th-century central square of **place St-Nicholas** sprawls along the seafront between the ferry port and harbour. Named after the patron saint of sailors – a nod to Corsica's seagoing heritage – the square is lined with plane trees, busy cafes and a **statue of Napoleon Bonaparte**, Corsica's famous son.

A network of narrow lanes leads south towards the old port and the neighbourhood of **Terra Vecchia**, a muddle of crumbling apartments and balconied blocks. Further south is the Vieux Port (Old Port), ringed by pastel-coloured tenements and buzzy brasseries, as well as the twin-towered **Église St-Jean Baptiste**. The best views of the harbour are from the **Jetée du Dragon** (Dragon Jetty) or from the hillside park of **Jardin Romieu** (Romieu Garden), reached via a twisting staircase from the waterfront. Behind the garden looms Bastia's sunbaked **citadel**, built from the 15th to 17th centuries as a stronghold for the city's Genoese masters. One of the citadel's landmarks, the **Palais des Gouverneurs** (Governors' Palace; place du Donjon) now houses Bastia's top-notch local history museum, **Musée d'Histoire de Bastia** (€5; ⊙10am-6pm Tue-Sun).

⌂ Sleeping

Hôtel Central   HOTEL €€
(✆04 95 31 71 12; www.centralhotel.fr; 3 rue Miot; d €85-100; 🕸) This family-run number in a stately 19th-century building has 21 rooms wrapped with a retro feel.

Hôtel Les Voyageurs   HOTEL €€
(✆04 95 34 90 80; www.hotel-lesvoyageurs.com; 9 av Maréchal Sébastiani; s €75-95, d €90-115; ✳🕸) What sets The Travellers apart is the buttermilk walls, modern-art prints and blindingly white bathrooms that contrast sharply with the more austere facade.

✕ Eating

You'll find endless restaurants around the Vieux Port and quai des Martyrs.

Chez Vincent   TRADITIONAL CORSICAN €€
(✆04 95 31 62 50; 12 rue St-Michel; mains €9-22; ⊙Mon-Fri, dinner Sat) Corsican staples and wood-fired pizzas are what beckon here. The

assiette du bandit Corse (€18.50) features a smorgasbord of local nosh, including stewed veal chestnuts, cured meats, ewe's-milk cheese, wild boar pâté and roast *figatellu* (liver sausage).

A Casarella MODERN CORSICAN €€
(☑04 95 32 02 32; 6 rue Ste-Croix; mains €15-28; ⊘Tue-Sun) Tuck into innovative dishes built from organic produce on Bastia's loveliest terrace, poised above the port in the citadel, twinkling harbour lights below.

❶ Information

Tourist office (www.bastia-tourisme.com; place St-Nicolas; ⊘8.30am-8pm Apr-Sep, shorter hr rest of year)

❶ Getting There & Away

Air

Aéroport Bastia-Poretta (www.bastia.aeroport.fr) is 24km south of the city. Buses (€8.50, 30 minutes, 10 daily) depart from outside the Préfecture building; timetables are posted at the stop.

Boat

Bastia's two **ferry terminals** are connected by a free **shuttle bus**. All the ferry companies have information offices in the southern terminal, which usually open for same-day ticket sales a couple of hours before each sailing.

Ferries sail to/from Marseille, Toulon and Nice on mainland France, and several ports in Italy.

Corsica Ferries (www.corsicaferries.com; 15bis rue Chanoine Leschi)

La Méridionale (www.lameridionale.fr)

Moby Lines (www.moby.it; 4 rue du Commandant Luce de Casabianca)

SNCM (www.sncm.fr; inside Southern Terminal)

Bus

Beaux Voyages (☑04 95 65 11 35) Buses to Île Rousse (€13, 90 minutes) and Calvi (€16, 2½ hours) daily except Sunday. Buses leave from the train station.

Eurocorse (☑04 95 31 73 76) Buses to Ajaccio (€21, three hours) via Corte (€11.50, two hours) twice daily except on Sundays from Bastia's 'bus station', a car park north of place St-Nicholas.

Autocars Cortenais (☑04 95 46 02 12) Travels to Corte (€11, two hours) once daily on Monday, Wednesday and Friday. Buses leave from the train station.

Les Rapides Bleus (☑04 95 31 03 79; 1 av Maréchal Sébastiani) Buses leave from in front of the post office to Porto-Vecchio (€22, three hours) twice daily except Sundays and holidays.

Train

From the **train station** (av Maréchal Sébastiani) main destinations include Ajaccio (€25, 3¾ hours, four daily) via Corte (1¾ hours), and Calvi (three hours, three or four daily) via Île Rousse.

Calvi

POP 5600

Basking between the fiery orange bastions of its 15th-century citadel and the glittering waters of a moon-shaped bay, Calvi feels closer to the chichi sophistication of a Côte d'Azur resort than a historic Corsican port – and has sky-high prices to match. Palatial yachts dock along its harbourside, while above the quay the watchtowers of the town's Genoese stronghold stand guard, proffering sweeping views inland to Monte Cinto (2706m). Visit in the shoulder seasons, when you can stroll the citadel's cobbled alleys in relative peace and quiet.

The **tourist office** (☑04 95 65 16 67; www. balagne-corsica.com; Port de Plaisance; ⊘9amnoon & 3-6.30pm Jul & Aug, 9am-noon & 2-6pm Mon-Sat May, Jun, Sep & Oct, 9am-noon & 2-6pm Mon-Fri Nov-Apr) is opposite the marina.

Calvi's 15th-century **citadel** – also known as the Haute Ville (Upper City) – sits on a rocky promontory above the Basse Ville (Lower Town). The **Palais des Gouverneurs** (place d'Armes), once the seat of power for the Genoese administration, now serves as a base for the French Foreign Legion. Uphill from Caserne Sampiero is the 13th-century **Église St-Jean Baptiste**, rebuilt in 1570.

Calvi's stellar 4km **beach** begins at the marina and runs east around the Golfe de Calvi. Rent out kayaks and windsurfing gear from **Calvi Nautique Club** (www.calvinc.org; Base Nautique, Port de Plaisance; ⊘May-Oct).

🛏 Sleeping

Most hotels shut in winter.

MONEY MATTERS

Many restaurants and hotels in Corsica don't accept credit cards, and *chambres d'hôtes* (B&Bs) hardly ever: those that do quite frequently refuse card payments for amounts typically less than €15.

TRAMWAY DE LA BALAGNE

The best way to dip into the glittering beaches and rocky coves lacing the Balagne coast between Calvi and Île Rousse is aboard the clattering **Tramway de la Balagne** – an unforgettable train journey (€5.50, 45 minutes, up to eight daily Easter to September). Nicknamed the *trinighellu* (the trembler), the dinky little train stops at 15 stations (all by request only) en route between the two towns; for sand, leave the train at Algajola or Plage de Bodri, the last stop before Île Rousse.

Hôtel Belvedere
HOTEL €€

(04 95 65 01 25; www.resa-hotels-calvi.com; place Christophe Colomb; d €70-120; ❄️ 📶) With a top-town position striking distance from the citadel and 24 comfortable yet small-ish rooms, the Viewpoint won't disappoint. Rooms on the 3rd floor gloat at top-notch views of the Golfe de Calvi.

Hôtel du Centre
HOTEL €

(04 95 65 02 01; 14 rue d'Alsace Lorraine; d without bathroom €32-47; ☺Jun-Sep) Not the most charming choice – furnishings are seriously dated – but at this price and in such a brilliant location it would be churlish to quibble.

Camping La Pinède
CAMPING GROUND €

(04 95 65 17 80; www.camping-calvi.com; rte de la Pinède; campsites €9; ☺Apr-Oct; 🏊) Handy for Calvi town and the beach.

✗ Eating

Calvi's quayside is chock-a-block with restaurants, quality variable.

TOP CHOICE Emile's
GASTRONOMIC €€€

(04 95 65 09 60; quai Landry; mains €38-46; ☺Apr-Oct) This top-end darling of central Calvi overlooks the quayside. If you've never tried grilled lobster, this is *the* place to do it, washed down with an ice-cold bottle of white.

Le Tire-Bouchon
BISTRO €€

(04 95 65 24 41; rue Clémenceau; mains €12-20; ☺Jun-Sep, closed Wed Apr, May & Oct) This buzzy option is a gourmand's playpen. Perch yourself on the balcony overlooking the crowds milling below and order from the chalkboard: veal stew perhaps, or tagliatelle with broccius, a cheese platter and a luscious local tipple.

ⓘ Getting There & Away

Air

Aéroport Calvi Ste-Catherine (www.calvi.aeroport.fr), 7km southeast, has no airport bus: allow €20-odd for a **taxi** (04 95 65 03 10).

Boat

SNCM and Corsica Ferries run boats to/from Nice from Calvi's **ferry terminal** (quai Landry).

Bus

Les Beaux Voyages (04 95 65 15 02; place de la Porteuse d'Eau) runs daily buses to Bastia (€16, 2½ hours) via Île Rousse (€4, 15 minutes).

Train

Calvi's **train station** connects with Ajaccio (five hours, two daily) via Corte (€15.10, four hours two daily) and Bastia (three hours), both with change of train in Ponte Leccia.

Ajaccio
POP 52,880

With its sweeping bay and buzzing centre replete with mellow-toned buildings, cafes and yacht-packed marina, Ajaccio, Corsica's main metropolis, is all class and seduction. Looming over this elegant port city is the spectre of Corsica's great general: Napoleon Bonaparte was born here in 1769 and the city is dotted with statues and museums relating to the diminutive dictator (starting with the main street in Ajaccio, cours Napoléon).

⊙ Sights & Activities

Musée National de la Maison Bonaparte
MUSEUM

(rue St-Charles; adult/child €5/3.50; ☺2-5.50pm Mon, 9-11.30am & 2-5.30pm Tue-Sun Apr-Sep, 2-4.15pm Mon, 10-11.30am & 2-4.15pm Tue-Sun Oct-Mar) The Napoleonic saga begins here, the grand house where Napoléon spent the first nine years of his life. View memorabilia of the emperor and his siblings, including a glass medallion containing a lock of his hair.

Palais Fesch – Musée des Beaux-Arts
ART MUSEUM

(www.musee-fesch.com; adult/child €8/5; 50-52 rue du Cardinal Fesch; ☺10.30-5pm Mon, Wed & Sat, noon-5pm Thu, Fri & Sun) Established by

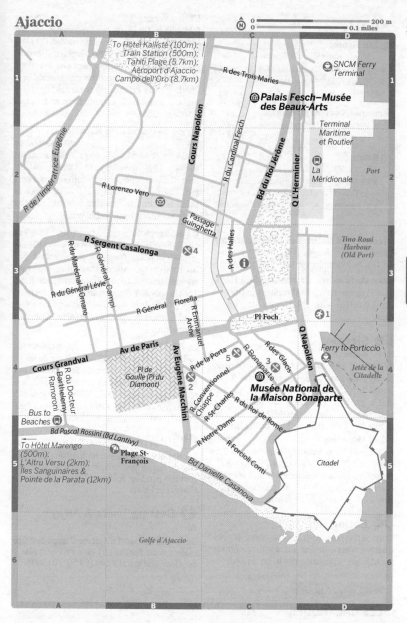

N
0 — 200 m
0 — 0.1 miles

To Hôtel Kallisté (100m);
Train Station (500m);
Tahiti Plage (5.7km);
Aéroport d'Ajaccio-
Campo dell'Oro (8.7km)

R des Trois Maries

SNCM Ferry
Terminal

🏛 **Palais Fesch–Musée
des Beaux-Arts**

Terminal
Maritime
et Routier

R du Cardinal Fesch

Cours Napoléon

La
Méridionale

Port

Bd du Roi Jérôme

Q L'Herminier

R Lorenzo Vero

Passage
Guinghetta

Tino Rossi
Harbour
(Old Port)

R Sergent Casalonga

✕4

R des Halles

ℹ

R du Général Campi

R du Maréchal Ornano

R du Général Lévie

R Général Fiorella

R Emmanuel Arène

Pl Foch

Q Napoléon

✪1

Ferry to Porticcio

Av de Paris

Av Eugène Macchini

R de la Porta

5

R des Glacis

R Bonaparte

3

Jetée de la
Citadelle

Cours Grandval

R du Docteur Barthélemy Ramoroni

Pl de
Gaulle (Pl du
Diamant)

✕2

R Conventionnel
Chiappe

R St-Charles

🏛 **Musée National de
la Maison Bonaparte**

R du Roi de Rome

Bus to
Beaches 🚍

Bd Pascal Rossini (Bd Lantivy)

R Notre Dame

R Forcioli Conti

To Hôtel Marengo
(500m);
L'Altru Versu (2km);
Îles Sanguinaires &
Pointe de la Parata (12km)

ℹ **Plage St-
François**

Bd Danielle Casanova

Citadel

Golfe d'Ajaccio

R de l'Impératrice Eugénie

FRANCE AJACCIO

Napoléon's uncle, this Corsica must-see has France's largest collection of Italian paintings outside the Louvre. Don't miss Botticelli's *La Vierge à l'Enfant Soutenu par un Ange* (Mother & Child Supported by an Angel).

Boat Trips   TOURS
Boat trips around the Golfe d'Ajaccio and Îles Sanguinaires (€27), and excursions to the Scandola Nature Reserve (adult/child €50/35), depart daily from the quay opposite place Foch.

Ajaccio

◎ Top Sights

Musée National de la Maison
Bonaparte C4
Palais Fesch–Musée des
Beaux-Arts C1

Activities, Courses & Tours

1 Découvertes Naturelles D3
 Nave Va ....(see 1)

◎ Eating

2 Le 20123..B4
3 Le Bilboq – Chez Jean Jean...............C4
4 Le Grand Café Napoléon.....................B3
5 U Pampasgiolu..................................C4

Découvertes Naturelles (www.decouvertes-naturelles.net; ◎May-Sep) Highlight: a sunset Îles Sanguinaires cruise (€27).

Nave Va (www.naveva.com; ◎May-Sep) Highlight: voyage down to Bonifacio (adult/child €58/40) with a four-hour stop on shore.

🛏 Sleeping

Hôtel Kallisté   HOTEL €€
(☑04 95 51 34 45; www.hotel-kalliste-ajaccio.com; 51 cours Napoléon; s €67-77, d €85-105; ❀🖥) Exposed brick, neutral tones, terracotta tiles and a glass lift conjure a neo-boutique feel at the Kallisté, and the facilities are fab – wifi, satellite TV and a stonking buffet brekkie.

Hôtel Marengo   HOTEL €
(☑04 95 21 43 66; www.hotel-marengo.com; 2 rue Marengo; d €61-83; ◎Apr-Oct; ❀) Expect pastel rooms (all with balconies) and a quiet courtyard, all a stroll from the beach, at this jolly, hospitably run little bolthole.

🍴 Eating

Tiny streetside restaurants cram the old quarter where dining on a sultry summer night is an experience not to be missed.

L'Altru Versu   GASTRONOMIC €€
(☑04 95 50 05 22; rte des Sanguinaires, Les Sep Chapelles; mains €22-30; ◎closed Mon Oct-May) Creative cuisine and the Mezzacqui brothers – passionate gastronomes and excellent singers (they hitch on their guitars and serenade guests Friday and Saturday nights) – make a formidable combination at this top Corsican table.

TOP CHOICE | **Le Grand Café Napoléon**
     MEDITERRANEAN €€
(☑04 95 21 42 54; 10-12 cours Napoléon; mains €23-30) This one-of-a-kind Ajaccio institution in a belle époque ballroom scores a perfect 10 on our 'charm meter'. The decor is mind-blowing, the cuisine refined, and the weekday lunch unbeatable value.

U Pampasgiolu   TRADITIONAL CORSICAN €€
(☑06 09 39 26 92; 15 rue de la Porta; mains €14-28; ◎dinner Mon-Sat) The rustic arch-vaulted dining room of this Ajaccio institution is always packed thanks to first-rate Corsican food. Try the *planche spuntinu* (snack selection) or *planche de la mer* (fish and seafood selection) – wooden platters of assorted Corsican specialities.

Le 20123   TRADITIONAL CORSICAN €€
(☑04 95 21 50 05; www.20123.fr; 2 rue du Roi de Rome; menus €32; ◎dinner Tue-Sun) Decked out like a traditional village (complete with water pump, washing line and central square), this is a good bet for authentic Corsican fare. There's just a single menu, presented orally.

❶ Information

Tourist office (www.ajaccio-tourisme.com; 3 blvd du Roi Jérôme; ◎9am-6pm Mon-Sat, 9am-1pm Sun Jun-Sep, 8.30am-12.30pm & 2-5pm Mon-Fri Oct-May)

❶ Getting There & Away

Air

Bus 8 links **Aéroport d'Ajaccio-Campo dell'Oro** (www.ajaccio.aeroport.fr), 8km east, with Ajaccio's train and bus stations (€4.50, 20 minutes).

WORTH A TRIP

LES CALANQUES

One of Corsica's most iconic natural sights, **Les Calanques de Piana**, 85km south of Calvi, are a spectacular landscape of flaming-red granite cliffs and spiky outcrops, carved into bizarre shapes by the sea and wind. Vivid green pine and chestnut forests on less-rocky areas contrast dramatically with the technicoloured granite.

Several walking trails wend through these dramatic rock formations, many starting near the Pont de Mezzanu road bridge, 3km from **Piana** (www.otpiana.com) along the D81.

RÉSERVE NATURELLE DE SCANDOLA

There's no vehicle access or footpath into the magnificent **Réserve Naturelle de Scandola** – Corsica's only Unesco-protected marine reserve, midway between Ajaccio and the coastal town of **Porto** – so the only way to get up close is by sea. From April to October several companies based on the quayside at Porto's marina sail through its shimmering sapphire waters to the base of its cliffs. Expect to pay around €40 for the privilege.

Predictably, this is paradise for **diving** and **snorkelling**, and several companies organise introductory dives for beginners (from €45) and snorkelling trips (€15) to the fringe of Scandola. At Porto's quay, try diving outfits **Centre de Plongée du Golfe de Porto** (www.plongeeporto.com), **Génération Bleue** (www.generation-bleue.com) or **Méditerranée Porto Sub** (www.plongeecose.fr).

Boat

Boats to/from Toulon, Nice and Marseille depart from/arrive at **Terminal Maritime et Routier** (quai l'Herminier):

Corsica Ferries (www.corsicaferries.com)

La Méridionale (www.lameridionale.fr)

SNCM (www.sncm.fr)

Bus

Local bus companies have kiosks inside the ferry terminal building.

Autocars Ceccaldi (✆04 95 22 41 99) Travels to Porto (2½ hours, two daily, no Sunday buses Sep-Jun) via Piana (1½ hours).

Eurocorse (✆04 95 21 06 30) Travels to Bastia (three hours, two daily) via Corte (two hours), and Bonifacio (four hours, one or two daily).

Train

From the **train station** (place de la Gare):

BASTIA (four hours, three to four daily)

CALVI (five hours, two daily; change at Ponte Leccia)

CORTE (two hours, three to four daily)

Bonifacio

POP 2700

With its glittering harbour, creamy-white cliffs and stout citadel, this dazzling port is an essential stop. Just a short hop from Sardinia, Bonifacio has a distinctly Italianate feel: sun-bleached town houses, washing lines and murky chapels cram the old citadel, while down below on the harbourside, brasseries and boat-kiosks tout their wares to the droves of day trippers.

A steep staircase links the harbour with the citadel's old gateway, the **Porte de Gênes**, complete with its original 16th-century drawbridge. Inside the gateway is

the 13th-century **Bastion l'Étendard**, which houses a small historical museum exploring Bonifacio's past. Along the ramparts, fabulous panoramic views unfold from **place du Marché** and **place Manichella**. From the citadel, the **Escalier du Roi d'Aragon** (King of Aragon's stairway; admission €2.50; ⊗9am-7pm Apr-Oct) staggers down the cliff.

Boat trips to the remote beaches and gin-clear waters of the offshore **Îles Lavezzi** (Lavezzi Islands) run from the quayside. Bonifacio is surrounded by beaches, including **Piantarella** (popular with windsurfers) and shingly **Calalonga**. The horseshoe bay of **Rondinara** is about 18km northeast, and tree-fringed **Palombaggia** is about 30km northeast near Porto-Vecchio.

🛏 Sleeping

Hôtel des Étrangers　　　　　HOTEL **€**
(✆04 95 73 01 09; www.hoteldesetrangers.fr; av Sylvère Bohn; d €46-65; ⊗Apr–mid-Oct; ❋🐾) Bonifacio's only budget option is the 'Foreigners' Hotel'. Spick-and-span rooms, all with tiled floors, clean bathrooms and simple colour schemes almost make up for the road racket.

Hôtel Le Colomba　　　　　HOTEL **€€**
(✆04 95 73 73 44; www.hotel-bonifacio-corse.fr; rue Simon Varsi; d €100-160; ⊗Mar-Nov; ❋🐾) A not-quite-boutique hotel in a picturesque side street, in the heart of the citadel. Wrought-iron bedsteads and country fabrics in some rooms, carved bedheads and chequerboard tiles in others.

🍴 Eating

Swish terrace restaurants pack the quayside, but the food isn't always as fancy as the ambience suggests.

DON'T MISS

THE PERFECT SNAPSHOT

If you're after that perfect picture, don't miss the fantastic, three-hour return walk along cliffs from Bonifacio to **Phare de Pertusato** (Pertusato Lighthouse), from where the seamless views of the cliffs, Îles Lavezzi, Bonifacio and Sardinia will sweep you off your feet. The starting point (signposted) is just to the left of the sharp bend on the hill up to Bonifacio's citadel. Complete the experience with lunch at Domaine de Licetto.

Cantina Doria   CORSICAN €
(☑04 95 73 50 49; 27 rue Doria; mains €10-14; ⊙Apr-Oct) This is *the* place in Bonifacio for Corsican country food, which is served at wooden benches amid copper pots, rustic tools and dented signs. Try typical *lasagnes au fromage Corse* (lasagne with Corsican cheese) or *aubergines à la Bonifacienne* (aubergines stuffed with breadcrumbs and cheese), and you'll leave patting your tummy contentedly.

Domaine de Licetto   TRADITIONAL CORSICAN €€
(☑04 95 73 03 59; rte du Phare; menus €36; ⊙dinner Mon-Sat Apr-Jul & Sep–mid-Oct, daily Aug) For the authentic Corsican experience this restaurant is hard to beat. The five-course menu is a culinary feast of local ingredients (suckling lamb, cheese-stuffed eggplant...) produced by small-scale farmers. Find it in the maquis on the way to Phare de Pertusato.

Kissing Pigs   MODERN CORSICAN €€
(☑04 95 73 56 09; quai Banda del Ferro; mains €8-15) Diners pack into this cosy wine bar by the harbour, famed for its platters of Corsican meats and cheeses. The wine list and swinging sausages are also hits.

❶ Information

Tourist office (www.bonifacio.fr; 2 rue Fred Scamaroni; ⊙9am-8pm May–mid-Oct, 9am-noon & 2-6pm Mon-Fri mid-Oct–Apr)

❶ Getting There & Away
Air

A taxi into town from **Aéroport de Figari** (www.figari.aeroport.fr), 21km north, costs about €40 (no public transport).

Boat

Saremar (www.saremar.it, in Italian) and **Moby Lines** (www.moby.it) sail between Bonifacio and Santa Teresa di Gallura (on the neighbouring island of Sardinia) in summer.

Bus

Eurocorse (☑04 95 70 13 83) runs buses to Porto-Vecchio (30 minutes), with onward connections to Ajaccio (four hours).

UNDERSTAND FRANCE

France Today

Presidential elections in 2007 ushered in big change for France in the shape of Nicolas Sarkozy (b 1955) of Chirac's centre-right party UMP (*Union pour un Mouvement Populaire*). Dynamic, ambitious and far from media-shy, Sarko (as he was quickly dubbed by the popular press) wooed punters with big talk of job creation, lower taxes, crime crackdown and help for France's substantial immigrant population. Yet controversy dogged Sarko's first period in office, infamously marked by him splitting with his second wife and swiftly wedding sexy Italian chanteuse and multimillionaire supermodel Carla Bruni.

Beyond Sarkozy's high-profile private life, there have been major political developments too, including the banning of smoking in public places (2007) and the ratification of a new EU treaty (2008). More controversially, the wearing of crucifixes, the Islamic headscarf and other overtly religious symbols has been banned in state schools since 2004 and the wearing of face-covering veils in public since 2010 – much to the consternation of France's notable Muslim community (around 10% of the population).

For a few fleeting months in 2009 France joined much of the rest of Europe in recession and by mid-2010 the unemployment rate was hovering at a disconcerting 10%. Hard-line attempts were made the same year to raise the retirement age from 60 to 62 and full state pension age from 65 to 67, thereby reforming a pension system unchanged since 1982, which simply sparked widespread horror and a series of national strikes and protests.

Sarko's honeymoon was clearly over.

Prehistory

Neanderthals were the first to live in France (about 90,000 to 40,000 BC). Cro-Magnons followed 35,000 years ago and left behind cave paintings and engravings, especially around the Vézère Valley in the Dordogne. Neolithic people (about 7500 to 4000 years ago) created France's incredible menhirs (standing stones) and dolmens (megalithic tombs), especially in Brittany.

The Celtic Gauls arrived between 1500 and 500 BC, and were superseded by the Romans for around five centuries after Julius Caesar took control around 52 BC, until the Franks and Alemanii overran the country.

The Frankish Merovingian and Carolingian dynasties ruled from the 5th to the 10th century AD. In 732 Charles Martel defeated the Moors, preventing France from falling under Muslim rule. Martel's grandson, Charlemagne (742–814), extended the power and boundaries of the kingdom and was crowned Holy Roman Emperor in 800.

The Early French Kings

The tale of William the Conqueror's invasion of England in 1066 is recorded in the Bayeux Tapestry, sowing the seeds for a fierce rivalry between France and England that peaked with the Hundred Years War (1337–1453).

Following the occupation of Paris by the English-allied dukes of Burgundy, John Plantagenet was made regent of France on behalf of England's King Henry VI in 1422. Less than a decade later he was crowned king at Paris' Notre Dame cathedral. Luckily for the French, a 17-year-old warrior called Jeanne d'Arc (Joan of Arc) came along in 1429. She persuaded Charles VII that she had a divine mission from God to expel the English from France. Following her capture by the Burgundians and subsequent sale to the English in 1430, Joan was convicted of witchcraft and heresy and burned at the stake in Rouen, on the site now marked by the city's cathedral.

The arrival of Italian Renaissance culture during the reign of François I (r 1515–47) ushered in some of France's finest chateaux, especially in the Loire Valley.

The period from 1562 to 1598 was one of the bloodiest periods in French history. Ideological disagreement between the Huguenots (French Protestants) and the Catholic

The Sun King

Louis XIV, Le Roi Soleil (the Sun King), ascended the throne in 1643, and spent the next 60 years in a series of bloody wars. He also constructed the fabulous palace at Versailles.

Louis XV ascended to the throne in 1715 and shifted the royal court back to Paris. As the 18th century progressed, the ancien régime became increasingly out of step with the needs of the country. Antiestablishment and anticlerical ideas expressed by Voltaire, Rousseau and Montesquieu further threatened the royal regime.

Revolution to Republic

Social and economic crisis marked the 18th century. Discontent among the French populace turned violent when a Parisian mob stormed the prison at Bastille. France was declared a constitutional monarchy and Louis XVI was publicly guillotined in January 1793 on Paris' place de la Concorde.

The Reign of Terror between September 1793 and July 1794 saw religious freedoms revoked, churches closed, cathedrals turned into 'Temples of Reason' and thousands beheaded. In the chaos a dashing young Corsican general named Napoleon Bonaparte (1769–1821) stepped from the shadows.

In 1799 Napoleon assumed power and in 1804 he was crowned emperor of France at Notre Dame. Napoleon waged several wars in which France gained control over most of Europe. Two years later, Allied armies entered Paris, exiled Napoleon to Elba and restored the French throne at the Congress of Vienna (1814–15).

In 1815 Napoleon escaped, entering Paris on 20 May. His glorious 'Hundred Days' back in power ended with the Battle of Waterloo and his exile to the island of St Helena, where he died in 1821.

Second Republic to Second Empire

The subsequent years were marked by civil strife and political unrest, with monarchists and revolutionaries vying for power. Louis-Philippe (r 1830–48), a constitutional monarch, was chosen by parliament but ousted by the 1848 Revolution. The Second Republic was established and Napoleon's nephew, Louis Napoleon Bonaparte, was elected president. But in 1851 Louis Napoleon led a coup d'état and proclaimed himself Emperor Napoleon III of the Second Empire (1852–70).

France enjoyed significant economic growth. Paris was transformed under urban planner Baron Haussmann (1809–91), who created the 12 huge boulevards radiating from the Arc de Triomphe. But Napoleon III embroiled France in various catastrophic conflicts, including the Crimean War (1853–56) and the Franco-Prussian War (1870–71), which ended with Prussia taking the emperor prisoner. Upon hearing the news, defiant Parisian masses took to the streets demanding a republic be declared – enter the Third Republic.

The World Wars

The 20th century was marked by two of the bloodiest conflicts in the nation's history, beginning with the Great War (WWI). The northeastern part of France bore the brunt of the devastating trench warfare between Allied and German forces: 1.3 million French soldiers were killed and almost one million injured, and the battlefields of the Somme have become powerful symbols of the unimaginable costs and ultimate futility of modern warfare.

After the war, the Treaty of Versailles imposed heavy reparations on the defeated nations, including the return of Alsace-Lorraine, which the French had lost to Germany in 1871. These punitive terms sowed the seeds for future unrest, when the fanatic leader Adolf Hitler rose to power and promised to restore the German nation's pride, power and territory. Despite constructing a lavish series of defences (the so-called Maginot Line) along its German border, France was rapidly overrun and surrendered in June 1940. The occupying Germans divided France into an Occupied Zone (in the north and west) and a puppet state in the south, centring on the spa town of Vichy.

The British Army was driven from France during the Battle of Dunkirk in 1940. Four years later, on 6 June 1944, Allied forces stormed the coastline of Normandy in the D-Day landings. The bloody Battle of Normandy followed and Paris was liberated on 25 August.

The Fourth Republic

In the first postwar election in 1945, the wartime leader of the Free French, Général Charles de Gaulle, was appointed head of the government, but quickly sensed that the tide was turning against him and in 1946 he resigned.

Progress rebuilding France's shattered economy and infrastructure was slow. By 1947 France was forced to turn to the USA for loans as part of the Marshall Plan to rebuild Europe. The economy gathered steam in the 1950s but the decade marked the end of French colonialism in Vietnam and in Algeria. The Algerian war of independence (1954–62) was particularly brutal, characterised by torture and massacre meted out to nationalist Algerians.

The Modern Era

De Gaulle assumed the presidency again in 1958, followed by his prime minister Georges Pompidou (in power 1969–74), Valéry Giscard d'Estaing (in power 1974–81), François Mitterrand (in power 1981–95), and the centre-right president Jacques Chirac, who (among other things) oversaw the country's adoption of the euro in 1999.

Arts

Literature

France has made huge contributions to European literature. The philosophical work of Voltaire (1694–1778) and Jean-Jacques Rousseau dominated the 18th century. A century later the poems and novels of Victor Hugo – Les Misérables and Notre Dame de Paris (The Hunchback of Notre Dame) among them – became landmarks of French Romanticism.

In 1857 two literary landmarks were published: Madame Bovary by Gustave Flaubert (1821–80) and Charles Baudelaire's collection of poems, Les Fleurs du Mal (The Flowers of Evil). Émile Zola (1840–1902) meanwhile strove to convert novel-writing from an art to a science in his series Les Rougon-Macquart.

Symbolists Paul Verlaine (1844–96) and Stéphane Mallarmé (1842–98) aimed to express mental states through their poetry. Verlaine's poems, with those of Arthur Rimbaud (1854–91), are seen as French literature's first modern poems.

After WWII, the existentialist movement developed around the lively debates of Jean-Paul Sartre (1905–80), Simone de Beauvoir (1908–86) and Albert Camus (1913–60) over coffee and cigarettes in Paris' Left Bank cafes.

Contemporary authors include Françoise Sagan, Pascal Quignard, Anna Gavalda, Emmanuel Carrère, Stéphane Bourguignon and Martin Page, whose novel *Comment Je Suis Devenu Stupide* (How I Became Stupid) explores a 25-year-old Sorbonne student's methodical attempt to become stupid. No French writer better delves into the mind, mood and politics of the country's ethnic population than Faïza Guène (b 1985; www.faiza-guene-lesgensdubalto.fr), the latest literary sensation born and bred on a ghetto housing estate outside Paris.

Cinema

Cinematographic pioneers the Lumière brothers shot the world's first-ever motion picture in March 1895 and French film flourished in the following decades. The post-WWII *nouvelle vague* (new wave) filmmakers, such as Claude Chabrol, Jean-Luc Godard and François Truffaut, pioneered the advent of modern cinema, using fractured narratives, documentary camerawork and highly personal subjects.

Big-name stars, slick production values and nostalgia were the dominant motifs in the 1980s, as filmmakers switched to costume dramas, comedies and 'heritage movies'. Claude Berri's depiction of prewar Provence in *Jean de Florette* (1986), Jean-Paul Rappeneau's *Cyrano de Bergerac* (1990) and *Bon Voyage* (2003), set in 1940s Paris – all starring France's best-known (and biggest-nosed) actor, Gérard Depardieu – found huge audiences in France and abroad.

La Haine (1995), directed by Mathieu Kassovitz, documents the bleak reality of life in the Parisian suburbs. At the other end of the spectrum, massive international hit *Le Fabuleux Destin de Amélie Poulain* (*Amélie;* 2001) is a feel-good story about a Parisian do-gooder. Or watch *Bienvenue chez les Ch'tis* (2008), another big box-office hit of recent years, which debunks grim stereotypes about the industrialised regions of the north of France with high jinks and hilarity.

Music

French musical luminaries Charles Gounod (1818–93), César Franck (1822–90) and *Carmen* creator Georges Bizet (1838–75) among them were a dime a dozen in the 19th century. Claude Debussy (1862–1918) revolutionised classical music with *Prélude à l'Après-Midi d'un Faune* (Prelude to the Afternoon of a Faun); while Maurice Ravel (1875–1937) peppered his work, including *Boléro,* with sensuousness and tonal colour.

Jazz was the hot sound of 1920s Paris with the likes of Sidney Bechet, Kenny Clarke, Bud Powell and Dexter Gordon filling clubs in the capital.

The *chanson française,* a folkish tradition dating from medieval troubadours, was revived in the 1930s by Edith Piaf and Charles Trenet. In the 1950s Paris' Left Bank cabarets nurtured *chansonniers* (cabaret singers) like Léo Ferré, Georges Brassens, Claude Nougaro, Jacques Brel and the much-loved crooner Serge Gainsbourg.

Electronic music (think Daft Punk and Air) has a global following, while French rap never stops breaking new ground, pioneered in the 1990s by MC Solaar and continued by young French rappers such as Disiz La Peste, Monsieur R, Rohff (www.roh2f.com), the trio Malekal Morte, Marseille's home-grown IAM (www.iam.tm.fr) and five-piece band KDD from Toulouse. Cyprus-born Diam's (short for *'diamant'* meaning 'diamond'; www.diams-lesite.com), who arrived in Paris aged seven, is one of France's few female rappers, while Brittany's Manau (www.manau.com) trio engagingly fuses hip hop with traditional Celtic sounds.

French pop music has evolved massively since the 1960s *yéyé* (imitative rock) days of Johnny Hallyday. Particularly strong is world music, from Algerian raï and other North African music (artists include Natacha Atlas) to Senegalese *mbalax* (Youssou N'Dour) and West Indian zouk (Kassav, Zouk Machine). Musicians who combine many of these elements include Paris-born Manu Chao (www.manuchao.net) and Franco-Algerian Rachid Taha (www.rachidtaha.fr).

No artist has cemented France's reputation in world music more than Paris-born, Franco-Congolese rapper, slam poet and three-time Victoire de la Musique-award winner, Abd al Malik (www.abdalmalik.fr). Hot on the heels of his first two albums, *Gibraltar* (2006) and *Dante* (2008) – both classics – is his fabulous *Château Rouge* (2010).

Architecture

Southern France is the place to find France's Gallo-Roman legacy, especially at the Pont du Gard, and the amphitheatres in Nîmes and Arles.

THE MENU

In France a menu is not the card given to you in restaurants listing what's cooking (that's called *la carte* in French). Rather, *un menu* is a pre-set, three-course meal at a fixed price – by far the best-value dining around and something that is available in 99% of restaurants.

Lunch *menus* often include a glass of wine and/or coffee, and are a great way of dining at otherwise unaffordable gastronomic addresses.

All but top-end places often have *une formule* on offer too, a cheaper lunchtime option usually comprising the plat du jour (dish of the day) plus starter or dessert.

Several centuries later, architects adopted Gallo-Roman motifs in masterpieces such as Poitier's Église Notre Dame la Grande.

Impressive 12th-century Gothic structures include Avignon's pontifical palace, Chartres' cathedral, and of course, Notre Dame in Paris.

Art nouveau (1850–1910) combined iron, brick, glass and ceramics in new ways. See it for yourself at Paris' metro entrances and in the Musée d'Orsay.

Contemporary buildings to look out for include the once-reviled (now much-revered) Centre Pompidou and IM Pei's glass pyramid at the Louvre. In the provinces, notable buildings include Strasbourg's European Parliament, a 1920s art deco swimming pool-turned-art museum in Lille, and the stunning new Centre Pompidou in Metz.

Painting

An extraordinary flowering of artistic talent occurred in 19th- and 20th-century France. The Impressionists, who endeavoured to capture the ever-changing aspects of reflected light, included Edouard Manet, Claude Monet, Edgar Degas, Camille Pisarro, and Pierre-Auguste Renoir. They were followed by the likes of Paul Cézanne (who lived in Aix-en-Provence) and Paul Gauguin, as well as the fauvist Henry Matisse (a resident of Nice on the French Riviera) and cubists including Spanish-born Pablo Picasso and Georges Braque (1882–1963).

Environment

The Land

Hexagon-shaped France is the largest country in Europe after Russia and Ukraine. The country's 3200km-long coastline ranges from chalk cliffs (Normandy) to fine sand (Atlantic coast) and pebbly beaches (Mediterranean coast).

Europe's highest peak, Mont Blanc (4810m), crowns the French Alps along France's eastern border, while the rugged Pyrenees define France's 450km-long border with Spain, peaking at 3404m. The country's major river systems include the Garonne, Rhône, Seine, and France's longest river, the Loire.

Wildlife

France has more mammals (around 110) than any other country in Europe. Couple this with 363 bird species, 30 types of amphibian, 36 varieties of reptile and 72 kinds of fish, and wildlife-watchers are in paradise. Several distinctive animals can still be found in the Alps and Pyrenees, including the marmot, *chamois* (mountain antelope), *bouquetin* (Alpine ibex) and *mouflon* (wild mountain sheep), introduced in the 1950s. The *loup* (wolf) disappeared from France in the 1930s, but was reintroduced to the Parc National du Mercantour in 1992. The *aigle royal* (golden eagle) is a rare but hugely rewarding sight in the French mountain parks.

National Parks

The proportion of protected land is low relative to the country's size: six national parks (www.parcsnationaux-fr.com) fully protect just 0.8% of the country. Another 13% is protected by 45 regional parks (www.parcs-naturels-regionaux.tm.fr) and a further few per cent by 320 smaller nature reserves (www.reserves-naturelles.org).

Environmental Issues

Summer forest fires are an annual hazard. Wetlands, essential for the survival of a great number of species, are shrinking. More than two million hectares – 3% of French territory – are considered important wetlands, but only 4% of this land is protected.

France generates around 80% of its electricity from nuclear power stations – the highest ratio in the world – with the rest coming from carbon-fuelled power stations and renewable resources (mainly wind farms and hydroelectric dams). Latest projects include Europe's largest solar-powered electricity-generating station in a village in Provence (2011), and new nuclear reactor on Normandy's west coast (2012) under the world's most ambitious nuclear-power program.

Food & Drink

France means food. Every region has its distinctive cuisine, from the rich classic dishes of Burgundy, the Dordogne, Lyon and Normandy, to the sun-filled Mediterranean flavours of Provence, Languedoc and Corsica. Broadly speaking, the south tends to favour olive oil, garlic and tomatoes, while the cooler pastoral north favours cream and butter. Coastal areas brim with mussels, oysters and saltwater fish.

The number-one essential is *pain* (bread), typically eaten with every meal. Order in a restaurant and within minutes a basket should be on your table. Except in a handful of top-end gastronomic restaurants, butter (unsalted) is never an accompaniment. The long, thin baguette (and fatter *flûte*) is the classic 'loaf', but there are countless others.

France *is* cheese land and the local *fromagerie* (cheese shop) is always the pongiest place in town. There are nearly 500 varieties of *fromage* (cheese), ranging from world-known classics such as Brie, Camembert and Époisses de Bourgogne (France's smelliest cheese?) to local unknowns available only in the regions where they're made. At mealtimes cheese is always served after the main course and before dessert.

Charcuterie – hams, *saucissons* (salamis), sausages, black pudding and the fabulous *andouillette* (pig intestine sausage) – is the backbone of any self-respecting French picnic. Traditionally it is made only from pork, though other meats (beef, veal, chicken or goose) go into sausages, salamis, blood puddings and other cured and salted meats. Vegetarians and vegans note: specialist vegetarian restaurants are few and far between in France; most menus are meat-heavy.

There are dozens of wine-producing regions throughout France, but the principal regions are Alsace, Bordeaux, Burgundy, Champagne, Languedoc-Roussillon, the Loire region and the Rhône. Areas such as Burgundy comprise many well-known districts, including Chablis, Beaujolais and Mâcon, while Bordeaux encompasses Médoc,

 WHERE TO EAT & DRINK

» **Auberge** Country inn serving traditional country fare, often attached to a rural B&B or small hotel.

» **Ferme auberge** Working farm that cooks up meals built squarely from local farm products; usually served *table d'hôte* (literally 'host's table'), meaning in set courses with little or no choice.

» **Bistro** (also spelled *bistrot*) Anything from a pub or bar with snacks and light meals to a small, fully fledged restaurant.

» **Brasserie** Very much like a cafe except it serves full meals, drinks and coffee from morning till 11pm or even later. Classic fare includes *choucroute* (sauerkraut) and *moules-frites* (mussels and fries).

» **Cafe** Serves basic food as well as drinks, most commonly a chunk of baguette filled with Camembert or pâté and *cornichons* (mini gherkins), a *croque-monsieur* (grilled ham and toasted-cheese sandwich) or *croque-madame* (a toasted-cheese sandwich topped with a fried egg).

» **Crêperie** (also *galetteries*) Casual address specialising in sweet crêpes and savoury galettes.

» **Restaurant** Born in Paris in 1765 when Monsieur Boulanger opened a small business on rue Bailleul, 1er, selling soups, broths and other *restaurants* ('restoratives'). Restaurants today serve lunch and dinner five or six days; for standard opening hours see p357.

» **Salon de Thé** Trendy tearoom often serving light lunches (quiche, salads, cakes, tarts, pies and pastries) as well as black and herbal teas.

St-Émilion and Sauternes among many others. Northern France and Alsace meanwhile produce some excellent local beers; *bière à la pression* (draught beer) is served by the *demi* (about 33cL).

Coffee and mineral water are drunk by the gallon in France. In restaurants save cents by asking for a jug of tap water *(une carafe d'eau)* rather than pricier bottled water. The most common coffee, simply called *un café* in French, is espresso – ordering anything other than this at the end of a meal is a real faux pas.

SURVIVAL GUIDE

Directory A–Z

Accommodation

France has accommodation to suit every taste and pocket. In this guide we've listed reviews by author preference.

As a rule of thumb, budget covers everything from bare-bones hostels to simple family-run places; midrange means a few extra creature comforts such as satellite TV, air-conditioning and free wi-fi; while top-end places stretch from luxury five-star chains with the mod cons and swimming pools to boutique-chic chalets in the Alps.

Accommodation costs vary wildly between regions: what will buy you a night in a romantic *chambre d'hôte* (B&B) in the countryside may only get you a dorm bed in major cities and ski resorts; see individual sections to gauge costs.

Many tourist offices make room reservations, often for a fee of €5, but many only do so if you stop by in person. In the French Alps, ski resort tourist offices operate a central reservation service.

PRICE RANGES

Our reviews refer to the cost of a double room with a private bathroom, except in hostels or where otherwise specified. Quoted rates are for high season, which is July and August in southern France (Provence and the French Riviera, Languedoc-Roussillon, Corsica) and December to March in the French Alps. Prices exclude breakfast unless otherwise noted.

€€€	more than €175 (€180 in Paris)
€€	€70 to €175 (€80 to €180 in Paris)
€	below €70 (€80 in Paris)

B&BS

For charm, a heartfelt *bienvenue* (welcome) and home cooking, it's hard to beat a *chambre d'hôtes* (B&B). Pick up lists at local tourist offices or online:

Bienvenue à la Ferme (www.bienvenue-a-la -ferme.com) Sleep on a farm.

Chambres d'Hôtes France (www.chambres dhotesfrance.com)

Fleurs de Soleil (www.fleursdesoleil.fr, in French)

Gîtes de France (www.gites-de-france. fr) Umbrella organisation for B&Bs and self-catering properties *(gîtes);* check their catalogue *Gîtes de Charme* (www.gites-de -france-charme.com).

Samedi Midi Éditions (www.samedimidi. com)

CAMPING

Camping has never been more *en vogue*. Gîtes de France and Bienvenue à la Ferme coordinate camping on farms.

» Most camping grounds open March or April to October.

» Euro-economisers should look for good-value but no-frills *campings municipaux* (municipal camping grounds).

» Camping in nondesignated spots *(camping sauvage)* is illegal in France. Easy-to-navigate websites with campsites searchable by location and facilities:

Camping en France (www.camping.fr)

Camping France (www.campingfrance.com)

Guide du Camping (www.guideducamping. com)

HPA Guide (http://camping.hpaguide.com)

Les Cabanes de France (www.cabanes-de -france.com, in French) Tree houses.

HOSTELS

Hostels range from funky to threadbare.

» A dorm bed in an *auberge de jeunesse* (youth hostel) costs about €25 in Paris, and anything from €10 to €28 in the provinces; sheets are always included and often breakfast too.

» To prevent outbreaks of bed bugs, sleeping bags are no longer permitted.

» All hostels are nonsmoking.

HOTELS

French hotels vary greatly in quality, ranging from low-budget no-star places to full-blown pleasure palaces.

» French hotels almost never include breakfast in their advertised nightly rates.
» Hotels in France are rated with one to five stars; ratings are based on objective criteria (eg size of entry hall), not service, decor or cleanliness.
» A double room has one double bed (or two singles pushed together); a room with twin beds is more expensive, as is a room with bathtub instead of shower.

Activities

From glaciers, rivers and canyons in the Alps to porcelain-smooth cycling trails in the Dordogne and Loire Valley – not to mention 3200km of coastline stretching from Italy to Spain and from the Basque country to the Straits of Dover – France's landscapes beg exhilarating outdoor escapes.

» The French countryside is criss-crossed by a staggering 120,000km of *sentiers balisés* (marked walking paths), which pass through every imaginable terrain in every region of the country. No permit is needed to hike.

» Probably the best-known trails are the *sentiers de grande randonnée* (GR), long-distance paths marked by red-and-white-striped track indicators.

» For details on regional activities, courses, equipment rental, clubs and companies, see this book's destination listings and contact local tourist offices.

ORGANISATIONS

Whether you are a peak bagger, surfer dude or thrill-seeking mountain biker, the following organisations can help you plan your petit adventure:

Club Alpin Français (French Alpine Club; www.ffcam.fr, in French) Groups 280 mountain-sports clubs and arranges professional guides for escapades in *alpinisme* (mountaineering), *escalade* (rock climbing), *escalade de glace* (ice climbing) and other highland activities. Runs *refuges* (mountain huts) in the French Alps too.

École du Ski Français (ESF; www.esf.net) French ski school.

Fédération Française de Cyclisme (www.ffc.fr, in French) Founded in 1881, the French Cycling Federation is *the* authority on competitive cycling in France and mountain biking (VTT; *vélo tout terrain*).

Fédération Française de Vol Libre (www.federation.ffvl.fr, in French) Groups regional clubs specialising in *deltaplane* (hang-gliding), *parapente* (paragliding) and *le kite-surf* (kitesurfing).

Véloroutes et Voies Vertes (www.af3v.org) A database of 250 signposted *véloroutes* (bike paths) and *voies vertes* (greenways) for cycling and in-line skating.

Business Hours

French business hours are regulated by a maze of government regulations, including the 35-hour working week.

» The midday break is uncommon in Paris but, in general, gets longer the further south you go.

» French law requires most businesses to close Sunday; exceptions include grocery stores, *boulangeries*, florists and businesses catering to the tourist trade.

» In many places shops close on Monday.

» Many service stations open 24 hours a day and stock basic groceries.

» Restaurants generally close one or two days of the week.

» Most (but not all) national museums are closed on Tuesday, while most local museums are closed on Monday, though in summer some open daily. Some museums close for lunch.

» In this book we've only listed business hours where they differ from the following standards:

Banks 9 or 9.30am-1pm & 2-5pm Mon-Fri or Tue-Sat

Bars 7pm to 1am Mon-Sat

Cafes 7 or 8am-10 or 11pm Mon-Sat

Nightclubs 10pm-3, 4 or 5am Thu-Sat

Post offices 8.30 or 9am to 5 or 6pm Mon-Fri, 8am-noon Sat

Restaurants lunch noon-2.30 or 3pm, dinner 7-10 or 11pm

Shops 9 or 10am-noon & 2-6 or 7pm Mon-Sat

Supermarkets 9am to 7 or 8pm Mon-Sat

Embassies & Consulates

All foreign embassies are in Paris. Many countries have consulates in other major cities such as Bordeaux, Lyon, Nice, Marseille and Strasbourg. To find a consulate or embassy visit look up *'ambassade'* in France's **Pages Jaunes** (Yellow Pages; www.pagesjaunes.fr, in French).

Australia (☑01 40 59 33 00; www.france.embassy.gov.au; 4 rue Jean Rey; ⓂBir Hakeim)

Canada (☎01 44 43 29 00; www.amb-canada.fr; 35 av Montaigne; Ⓜ Franklin D Roosevelt)

Japan (☎01 48 88 62 00; www.amb-japon.fr in French & Japanese; 7 av Hoche; Ⓜ Courcelles)

New Zealand (☎01 45 01 43 43; www.nzemb assy.com; 7ter rue Léonard de Vinci; Ⓜ Victor Hugo)

UK (☎01 44 51 31 00; www.ukinfrance.fco.gov.uk; 35 rue du Faubourg St- Honoré; Ⓜ Concorde)

USA (☎01 43 12 22 22; http://france.usembassy. gov; 4 av Gabriel; Ⓜ Concorde)

Food

Eating reviews throughout this chapter are ordered by preference. Price ranges for a two-course evening meal are:

€€€   more than €50

€€   €15 to €50

€   below €15

Gay & Lesbian Travellers

Gay mayors (including Paris' very own Bertrand Delanoë), artists and film directors, camper-than-camp fashion designers...the rainbow flag flies high in France, one of Europe's most liberal countries when it comes to homosexuality.

» Most major gay and lesbian organisations are based in Paris.

» Bordeaux, Lille, Lyon, Toulouse and many other towns have active communities.

» Attitudes towards homosexuality tend to be more conservative in the countryside and villages.

» Gay Pride marches are held in major French cities from mid-May to early July.

» Online try:

French Government Tourist Office (www. us.franceguide.com/special-interests/gay-friendly) Information about 'the gay-friendly destination par excellence'.

France Queer Resources Directory (www.france.qrd.org, in French) Gay and lesbian directory.

Gay Travel France (www.gaytravelfrance.com) Gay and lesbian accommodation.

Paris Gay (www.paris-gay.com) Everything about gay Paree.

Language Courses

The government site www.diplomatie.gouv. fr (under 'Francophony') and www.europa -pages.com/france list language schools in France.

All manner of French language courses are available in Paris and provincial towns and cities; many arrange accommodation. Some schools you might consider:

Alliance Française (www.alliancefr.org; 101 blvd Raspail, 6e, Paris; Ⓜ St-Placide) Venerable institution for the worldwide promotion of French language and civilisation, with intensive and extensive classes, including literature and business French.

Centre Méditerranéen d'Études Françaises (www.monte-carlo.mc/centremed; chemin des Oliviers, Cap d'Ail) French Riviera school dating to 1952, with an open-air amphitheatre designed by Jean Cocteau overlooking the sparkling blue Med.

Eurocentre d'Amboise (www.eurocentres. com; 9 mail St-Thomas, Amboise) Small, well-organised school in the charming Loire Valley; branches in La Rochelle and Paris.

Université de Provence (http://sites.univ -provence.fr/wscefee; 29 av Robert Schumann, Aix-en-Provence) A hot choice in lovely Aix.

Legal Matters

French police have wide powers of stop-and-search and can demand proof of identity at any time. Foreigners must be able to prove their legal status in France (eg passport, visa, residency permit).

Money

» Credit and debit cards, accepted almost everywhere in France, are convenient, relatively secure and usually offer a better exchange rate than travellers cheques or cash exchanges.

» Some places (eg 24hr petrol stations, some autoroute toll machines) only take French-style credit cards with chips and PINs.

» Commercial banks charge €3 to €5 fee per foreign-currency transaction – if they even bother to offer exchange services any more.

» In Paris and major cities, *bureaux de change* (exchange bureaux) are faster and easier, open longer hours and give better rates.

For lost cards, call:

Amex (☎01 47 77 72 00)

Diners Club (☎08 10 31 41 59)

MasterCard (☎08 00 90 13 87)

Visa (Carte Bleue; ☎08 00 90 11 79)

Public Holidays

New Year's Day (Jour de l'An) 1 January

Easter Sunday & Monday (Pâques & lundi de Pâques)

May Day (Fête du Travail) 1 May – traditional parades.

Victoire 1945 8 May – commemorates the Allied victory in Europe that ended WWII.

Ascension Thursday (Ascension) May – celebrated on the 40th day after Easter.

Pentecost/Whit Sunday & Whit Monday (Pentecôte & lundi de Pentecôte) Mid-May to mid-June – celebrated on the seventh Sunday after Easter.

Bastille Day/National Day (Fête Nationale) 14 July – *the* national holiday.

Assumption Day (Assomption) 15 August

All Saints' Day (Toussaint) 1 November

Remembrance Day (L'onze novembre) 11 November – marks the WWI armistice.

Christmas (Noël) 25 December

Telephone
MOBILE PHONES

» French mobile phones numbers begin with ☎06 or ☎07.

» France uses GSM 900/1800, compatible with the rest of Europe and Australia but not with the North American GSM 1900 or the totally different system in Japan (though some North Americans have tri-band phones that work here).

» It may be cheaper to buy your own French SIM card (€20 to €30) sold at ubiquitous outlets run by France's three mobile phone companies, **Bouygues** (www.bouyguestelecom.fr), France Telecom's **Orange** (www.orange.com) and **SFR** (www.sfr.com, in French).

» Recharge cards are sold at most *tabacs* and newsagents; domestic prepaid calls cost about €0.50 per minute.

PHONE CODES

Calling France from abroad Dial your country's international access code, ☎33 (France's country code), and the 10-digit local number *without* the initial 0.

Calling internationally from France Dial ☎00 (the international access code), the country code, area code (without the initial zero if there is one) and local number.

Directory inquiries For France Telecom's *service des renseignements* (directory inquiries) dial ☎11 87 12. For help in English with all France Telecom's services, see www.francetelecom.com or call ☎09 69 36 39 00.

International directory inquiries For numbers outside France, dial ☎11 87 00.

Emergency number ☎112, can be dialled from public phones without a phonecard.

Toilets

» Public toilets, signposted WC or *toilettes,* are not always plentiful in France.

» Love them (sci-fi geek) or loathe them (claustrophobe), France has its fair share of 24hr self-cleaning toilets, €0.50 in Paris and free elsewhere.

» Some older cafes and restaurants still have the hole-in-the-floor squat toilets.

» The French are blasé about unisex toilets, so save your blushes when tiptoeing past the urinals to reach the ladies' loo.

Visas

For up-to-date details on visa requirements, visit the **French Foreign Affairs Ministry** (www.diplomatie.gouv.fr).

» EU nationals and citizens of Iceland, Norway and Switzerland need only a passport or national identity card to enter France and stay in the country, even for stays of over 90 days. Citizens of new EU member states may be subject to various limitations on living and working in France.

» Citizens of Australia, the USA, Canada Israel, Hong Kong, Japan, Malaysia, New Zealand, Singapore, South, Korea and many Latin American countries do not need visas to visit France as tourists for up to 90 days. For long stays of over 90 days, contact your nearest French embassy or consulate.

» Other people wishing to come to France as tourists have to apply for a **Schengen Visa** (p1015).

» Tourist visas cannot be changed into student visas after arrival. However, short-term visas are available for students sitting university-entrance exams in France.

Getting There & Away
Entering the Country

Entering France from other parts of the EU is a breeze – no border checkpoints or customs thanks to Schengen Agreements signed by all of France's neighbours except the UK, the Channel Islands and Andorra. For these three entities, old-fashioned document and customs checks remain the norm, at least when exiting France (when entering France in the case of Andorra).

Air

For a list of airports in France, see the boxed text below.

Land

BUS

Eurolines (✆08 92 89 90 91; www.eurolines. eu), a group of 32 long-haul coach operators (including the UK's National Express), links France with cities across Europe and in Morocco and Russia. Discounts are available to people under 26 and over 60. Make advance reservations, especially in July and August.

The standard Paris–London fare is €46 (€57 including high-season supplements) but the trip – including a Channel crossing either by ferry or the Chunnel – can cost as little €15 if you book 45 days ahead.

CAR & MOTORCYCLE

A right-hand-drive vehicle brought to France from the UK or Ireland must have deflectors affixed to the headlights to avoid dazzling oncoming traffic.

Departing from the UK, **Eurotunnel shuttle trains** (✆in UK 08443-35 35 35, in France 08 10 63 03 04; www.eurotunnel.com) whisk bicycles, motorcycles, cars and coaches from Folkestone through the Channel Tunnel to Coquelles, 5km southwest of Calais, in just 35 minutes. The shuttle services run 24 hours a day. The earlier you book, the cheaper the fare. Standard fares for a car, including up to nine passengers, start at UK£53.

TRAIN

Rail services link France with virtually every country in Europe. Tickets and information are handled by **Rail Europe** (www.raileurope. com) or in France, by **SNCF** (✆in France 36 35, from abroad +33 8 92 35 35 35; www.sncf.com).

Certain services between France and its continental neighbours are marketed under separate brand names:

» **Alleo** Rail travel to Germany.
» **Artésia** (www.artesia.eu) Italian cities such as Milan and, overnight, Venice, Florence and Rome.
» **Elipsos** (www.elipsos.com) Luxurious 'train-hotel' services to Spain.
» **TGV Lyria** (www.tgv-lyria.fr) Switzerland
» **Thalys** (www.thalys.com) Links Paris' Gare du Nord with Brussels (82 minutes), Amsterdam CS (3⅓hr), Cologne Hauptbahnhof (3¼ hours) and other destinations.
» **Eurostar** (✆in UK 08432 186 186, in France 08 92 35 35 39; www.eurostar.com) Runs from London St-Pancras station to Paris Gare du Nord in 2¼ hours, with easy onward connections available to destinations all over France. Ski trains connecting England with the French Alps run weekends mid-December to mid-April.

SEA

Regular ferries travel to France from Italy, the UK, Channel Islands and Ireland. Several ferry companies ply the waters between Corsica and Italy. For details, see the boxed text, p362.

INTERNATIONAL AIRPORTS

AIRPORT	PHONE	WEBSITE
Paris	France 39 50; abroad +33 1 70 36 39 50	www.aeroportsdeparis.fr
Bordeaux	05 56 34 50 50	www.bordeaux.aeroport.fr
Lille	08 91 67 32 10	www.lille.aeroport.fr
Lyon	08 26 80 08 26	www.lyon.aeroport.fr
Marseille	04 42 14 14 14	www.mrsairport.com
Nantes	02 40 84 80 00	www.nantes.aeroport.fr
Nice	08 20 42 33 33	www.nice.aeroport.fr
Strasbourg	03 88 64 67 67	www.strasbourg.aeroport.fr
Toulouse	08 25 38 00 00	www.toulouse.aeroport.fr

SAMPLE TRAIN FARES

ROUTE	FULL FARE (€)	DURATION (HR)
Amsterdam–Paris	79	3¼
Barcelona–Montpellier	57	4½
Berlin–Paris	238	8
Brussels–Paris	44–64	1½
Frankfurt–Paris	106	4
Geneva–Lyon	25	2
Geneva–Marseille	65	3½
Vienna–Strasbourg	149	9

Getting Around

Air

France's vaunted high-speed train network has made rail travel between some cities (eg from Paris to Lyon and Marseille) faster and easier than flying.

Air France (☏36 54; www.airfrance.com) and its subsidiaries **Brit Air** (☏36 54; www.britair.fr) and **Régional** (☏36 54; www.regional.com) control the lion's share of France's long-protected domestic airline industry. Good deals can be had if you buy your ticket well in advance (at least 42 days ahead for the very best deals), stay over a Saturday night and don't mind tickets that can't be changed or reimbursed.

Budget carriers offering flights within France include **easyJet** (www.easyjet.com), **Airlinair** (www.airlinair.com), **Twin Jet** (www.twinjet.net) and **CCM** (www.aircorsica.com).

Bus

You're nearly always better off travelling by train in France if possible, as the SNCF domestic railway system is heavily subsidised by the government and is much more reliable than local bus companies. Nevertheless, buses are widely used for short-distance travel within *départements,* especially in rural areas with relatively few train lines (eg Brittany and Normandy).

Bicycle

France is a great place to cycle. Not only is much of the countryside drop-dead gorgeous, but the country has a growing number of urban and rural *pistes cyclables* (bike paths and lanes; www.voiesvertes.com, in French) and an extensive network of second-ary and tertiary roads with relatively light traffic. French train company SNCF does its best to make travelling with a bicycle easy and has a special website for cyclists (www.velo.sncf.com, in French).

Most French cities and towns have at least one bike shop that rents out mountain bikes (VTT; €10 to €20 a day), road bikes (VTCs) and cheaper city bikes. You have to leave ID and/or a deposit (often a credit-card slip) that you forfeit if the bike is damaged or stolen. A growing number of cities have automatic bike rental systems.

Car & Motorcycle

A car gives you exceptional freedom and allows you to visit more-remote parts of France. But it can be expensive and, in cities, parking and traffic are frequently a major headache. Motorcyclists will find France great for touring, with winding roads of good quality and lots of stunning scenery.

BRINGING YOUR OWN VEHICLE

All foreign motor vehicles entering France must display a sticker or licence plate identifying its country of registration. If you're bringing a right-hand-drive vehicle remember to fix deflectors on your headlights to avoid dazzling oncoming traffic.

Driving Licence & Documents

All drivers must carry a national ID card or passport; a valid driving licence (*permis de conduire;* most foreign licences can be used in France for up to a year); car-ownership papers, known as a *carte grise* (grey card); and proof of third party (liability) insurance.

FUEL & TOLLS

Essence (petrol), also known as *carburant* (fuel), costs around €1.40/L for 95 unleaded

INTERNATIONAL FERRY COMPANIES

CONNECTION	FERRY COMPANY	PHONE NUMBER(S)
England–Normandy, England–Brittany, Ireland–Brittany	Brittany Ferries	in UK 0871-244 0744; in Ireland 021 4277 801; in France 08 25 82 88 28
Ireland–Normandy	Celtic Link Ferries	in Ireland 053-916 2688
Morocco–France	Comanav & Comarit	in Sète (SNCM) 04 67 46 68 00
England–Normandy, England–Brittany, Channel Islands–Brittany	Condor Ferries	in UK 0845-609 1024; in France 08 25 13 51 35
Tunisia–France	CTN	Marseille 04 91 91 55 71
Ireland–Normandy, Ireland–Brittany	Irish Ferries	in Ireland 0818 300 400; in France 08 10 00 13 57; in Cherbourg 02 33 23 44 44; in Roscoff 02 98 61 17 17
England–Channel Ports, England–Normandy	LD Lines	in UK 0844-576 8836; in France 08 25 30 43 04
Channel Islands–Normandy	Manche Îles Express	on Jersey 01534-880 756; on Guernsey 01481-832 059; in France 08 25 13 10 50
England–Channel Ports	Norfolk Line	in UK 0844-847 5042; outside UK +44-208-127 8303 in France 03 28 59 01 01
England–Channel Ports	P&O Ferries	in UK 08716 645 645; in France 08 25 12 01 56
England–Channel Ports	SeaFrance	in UK 0871-423 7119; in France 08 25 82 50 00
Algeria–France, Sardinia–France, Tunisia–France	SNCM	in France 32 60; outside France +33 825 88 80 88;
England–Normandy	Transmanche Ferries	in UK 0844-576 8836; in France 08 25 30 43 04

(Sans Plomb 95 or SP95, usually available from a green pump), and €1.30 for diesel (*diesel, gazole* or *gasoil,* usually available from a yellow pump). Filling up *(faire le plein)* is most expensive along autoroutes and cheapest at supermarkets on town outskirts.

Many French motorways (autoroutes) are fitted with toll *(péage)* stations that charge a fee based on the distance you've travelled; factor in these costs when driving.

HIRE

To hire a car you'll usually need to be over 21 and in possession of a valid driving licence and a credit card. Auto transmissions are *very* rare in France; you'll need to order one well in advance.

See p1024 for a list of major car rental companies with offices across France and Europe.

INSURANCE

Unlimited third-party liability insurance is mandatory in France. Third-party liability insurance is provided by car-rental companies, but collision-damage waivers (CDW) vary between companies. When comparing rates check the *franchise* (excess). Your credit card may cover CDW if you use it to pay for the car rental.

ROAD RULES

Cars drive on the right in France. Speed limits on French roads are as follows:
» 50km/h in built-up areas

WEBSITE	PORTS OUTSIDE FRANCE	PORTS IN FRANCE
www.brittany-ferries.co.uk; www.brittanyferries.ie	Cork, Plymouth, Poole, Portsmouth	Caen (Ouistreham), Cherbourg, Roscoff, St-Malo
www.celticlinkferries.com	Rosslare	Cherbourg
www.aferry.to/comanav.htm; www.aferry.to/comarit.htm	Nador, Tanger	Sète
www.condorferries.com	Poole, Portsmouth, Weymouth, Guernsey, Jersey	Cherbourg, St-Malo
www.ctn.com.tn	Tunis	Marseille
www.irishferries.ie; www.shamrock-irlande.com, in French	Rosslare	Cherbourg, Roscoff
www.ldlines.co.uk	Dover, Portsmouth	Boulogne-sur-Mer, Le Havre
www.manche-iles-express.com	Alderney, Guernsey, Jersey	Barneville-Carteret, Diélette, Granville
www.norfolkline.com	Dover	Dunkirk (Loon Plage)
www.poferries.com	Dover	Calais
www.seafrance.com	Dover	Calais
www.sncm.fr	Alger, Annaba, Bejaia, Oran, Porto Torres, Skikda, Tunis	Marseille
www.transmancheferries.com	Newhaven	Dieppe

» 90km/h (80km/h if it's raining) on N and D highways

» 110km/h (100km/h if it's raining) on dual carriageways

» 130km/h (110km/h if it's raining) on autoroutes.

Other key rules of the road:

» All passengers must wear seatbelts.

» Children who weigh less than 18kg must travel in backward-facing child seats.

» It is illegal to drive with a blood-alcohol concentration over 0.05% – the equivalent of two glasses of wine for a 75kg adult.

» Mobile phones may only be used when accompanied by a hands-free kit or speakerphone.

» All vehicles must carry a reflective safety jacket (stored inside the car, not boot) and a reflective triangle.

» Riders of any type of two-wheeled vehicle with a motor (except motor-assisted bicycles) must wear a helmet.

» North American drivers, remember: turning right on a red light is illegal.

Train

France's superb rail network is operated by the state-owned **SNCF** (www.sncf.com); many rural towns not on the SNCF train network are served by SNCF buses.

The flagship trains on French railways are the superfast TGVs, which reach speeds in excess of 200mph and can whisk you from Paris to the Côte d'Azur in as little as three hours.

SNCF TRAIN FARES & DISCOUNTS

The Basics

» Full-fare return travel costs twice as much as a one-way fare.

» 1st-class travel, where still available, costs 20% to 30% extra.

» Ticket prices for many trains are pricier during peak periods.

» The further in advance you reserve, the lower the fare.

» Children aged 4 to 11 pay half price, under 4s travel for free.

Discount Tickets

» **Prem's** The SNCF's most heavily discounted, use-or-lose tickets, sold online, by phone and at ticket windows/machines a maximum of 90 days and minimum 14 days before you travel.

» **Bons Plans** A grab-bag of cheap options for different routes/dates, advertised online under the tab 'Dernière Minute' (Last Minute).

» **iDTGV** Cheap tickets aimed at the iPod generation on advance-purchase TGV travel between about 30 cities; only sold at www.idtgv.com.

Discount Cards

Reductions of 25% to 60% are available with several discount cards (valid for one year):

» **Carte 12-25** (www.12-25-sncf.com in, French; €49) For travellers aged 12 to 25 years.

» **Carte Enfant Plus** (www.enfantplus-sncf.com, in French; €70) For one to four adults travelling with a child aged four to 11 years.

» **Carte Escapades** (www.escapades-sncf.com, in French; €85) Discounts on return journeys of at least 200km that include a Saturday night away or only involve travel on a Saturday or Sunday; for 26- to 59-year-olds.

» **Carte Sénior** (www.senior-sncf.com, in French; €56) Over 60 years.

Many non-high-speed lines are also served by TGV trains; otherwise you'll find yourself aboard a non-TGV train, referred to as a *corail* or TER *(train express régional)*. TGV lines and key stations:

TGV Nord, Thalys & Eurostar These link Paris' Gare du Nord with Arras, Lille, Calais, Brussels (Bruxelles-Midi), Amsterdam, Cologne and, via the Channel Tunnel, Ashford, Ebbsfleet and London St Pancras.

TGV Est Européen Connects Paris' Gare de l'Est with Reims, Nancy, Metz, Strasbourg, Zurich and Germany, including Frankfurt and Stuttgart. At present super-high-speed track stretches only as far east as Lorraine, but it's supposed to reach Strasbourg in 2016.

TGV Sud-Est & TGV Midi-Méditerranée These lines link Paris' Gare de Lyon with the southeast, including Dijon, Lyon, Geneva, the Alps, Avignon, Marseille, Nice and Montpellier.

TGV Atlantique Sud-Ouest & TGV Atlantique Ouest These link Paris' Gare Montparnasse with western and southwestern France, including Brittany (Rennes, Brest, Quimper), Tours, Nantes, Poitiers, La Rochelle, Bordeaux, Biarritz and Toulouse.

TICKETS

Buying online at the various SNCF websites can reward with you some great reductions

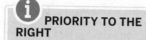

PRIORITY TO THE RIGHT

Under the *priorité à droite* (priority to the right) rule, any car entering an intersection from a road on your right has the right of way, unless the intersection is marked '*vous n'avez pas la priorité*' (you do not have right of way) or '*cédez le passage*' (give way).

VALIDATE YOURSELF

Before boarding any train, you must validate *(composter)* your ticket by time-stamping it in a *composteur*, one of those yellow posts located on the way to the platform. If you forget (or don't have a ticket for some other reason), find a conductor on the train before they find you – or risk an unwelcome fine.

on fares, but be warned – these are generally intended for domestic travellers, and if you're buying abroad be aware of the pit-

falls. Many tickets can't be posted outside France, and if you buy with a non-French credit card, you might not be able to use it in the automated ticket collection machines at many French stations. Buying from a ticket office may not secure you the cheapest fare, but at least you'll be sure of being able to pick up your ticket…

RAIL PASSES

The **InterRail One Country Pass** (www.inter railnet.com; 3/4/6/8 days €194/209/269/299, 12–25 yr €126/136/175/194), valid in France, entitles residents of Europe who do not live in France to unlimited travel on SNCF trains for three to eight days over a month.

Greece Ελλάδα

Best Places to Eat

» Marco Polo Café (p423)
» Tassia (p440)
» Tzitzikas & Mermingas (p378)
» Spondi (p380)
» Taverna Lava (p412)

Best Places to Stay

» 1700 (p399)
» Amfitriti Pension (p388)
» Hotel Grande Bretagne (p377)
» Pension Sofi (p407)
» Hotel Afendoulis (p428)

Why Go?

Don't let headline-grabbing financial woes put you off going to Greece. The elements that have made Greece one of the most popular destinations on the planet are still all there, and now is as good a time as ever to turn up for some fun in the sun. That alluring combination of history and hedonism continues to beckon. Within easy reach of magnificent archaeological sites are breathtaking beaches and relaxed tavernas serving everything from ouzo to octopus. Wanderers can island-hop to their heart's content, while party types can enjoy pulsating nightlife in Greece's vibrant modern cities and on islands such as Mykonos, Ios and Santorini. Throw in welcoming locals with an enticing culture and it's easy to see why most visitors head home vowing to come back. Travellers to Greece inevitably end up with a favourite site they long to return to – get out there and find yours.

When to Go
Athens

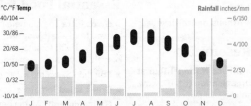

| May & Jun Greece opens the shutters in time for Orthodox Easter; the best months to visit. | Jul & Aug Be prepared to battle summer crowds, high prices and soaring temperatures. | Sep & Oct The season winds down; a relaxing and pleasant time to head to Greece. |

Fast Facts

» **Area** 131,944 sq km

» **Population** 11.2 million

» **Capital** Athens

» **Telephone** country code ☑30; international access code ☑00

» **Emergency** ☑112

Exchange Rates

Australia	A$1	€0.74
Canada	C$1	€0.74
Japan	¥100	€0.87
New Zealand	NZ$1	€0.56
UK	UK£1	€1.16
USA	US$1	€0.67

Set Your Budget

» **Budget hotel room** €50

» **Two-course dinner** €20

» **Museum entrance** €5

» **Beer** €2.50

» **Athens metro ticket** €2

Resources

» **Greece National Tourist Organisation** (GNTO; www.gnto.gr)

» **Ministry of Culture** (www.culture.gr)

» **Ancient Greece** (www.ancientgreece.com)

» **Greek Ferries** (www.greekferries.gr)

Connections

For those visiting Greece as part of a trip around Europe, there are various exciting options for reaching onward destinations overland or by sea.

There are regular ferry connections between Greece and the Italian ports of Ancona, Bari, Brindisi and Venice. Similarly, there are ferries operating between the Greek islands of Rhodes, Symi, Kos, Samos, Chios and Lesvos and the Aegean coast of Turkey. Island-hopping doesn't have to take you back to Athens.

Overland, it's possible to reach Albania, Bulgaria, Macedonia and Turkey from Greece. If you've got your own wheels, you can drive through border crossings with these four countries. There are bus connections with Albania, Bulgaria and Turkey, and train connections with Bulgaria, Macedonia and Turkey. In summer there are direct train services to Moscow.

ITINERARIES

One Week

Explore Athens' museums and ancient sites on day one before spending a couple of days in the Peloponnese visiting Nafplio, Mycenae and Olympia; ferry to the Cyclades and enjoy Mykonos and spectacular Santorini.

One Month

Give yourself some more time in Athens and the Peloponnese, then visit the Ionian Islands for a few days. Explore the Zagoria Villages before travelling back to Athens via Meteora and Delphi. Take a ferry from Piraeus south to Mykonos, then island-hop via Santorini to Crete. After exploring Crete, take the ferry east to Rhodes, then north to Symi, Kos and Samos. Carry on north to Chios, then head on to Lesvos. Take the ferry back to Piraeus when you're out of time or money.

Essential Food & Drink

» **Gyros Pitta** The ultimate in cheap eats. Pork or chicken shaved from a revolving stack of sizzling meat is wrapped in pitta bread with tomato, onion, fried potatoes and lashings of tzatziki (yoghurt, cucumber and garlic). Costs €2 to €3.

» **Souvlaki** Skewered meat, usually pork.

» **Greek salad** Tomatoes, cucumber, onion, feta and olives.

» **Grilled octopus** All the better with a glass of ouzo.

» **Ouzo** Sipped slowly, this legendary Greek aniseed-flavoured tipple turns a cloudy white when ice and water is added.

» **Raki** Cretan firewater produced from grape skins.

» **Greek coffee** A legacy of Ottoman rule, Greek coffee should be tried at least once by all visitors.

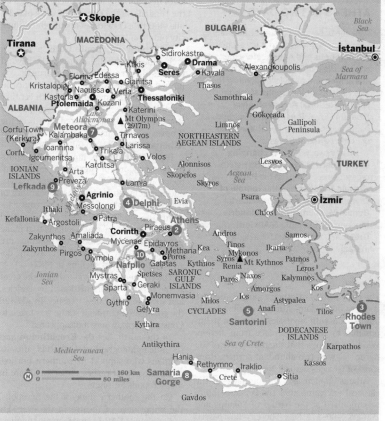

Greece Highlights

❶ **Island-hop** (p454) at your own pace under the Aegean sun

❷ In **Athens** (p369), trace the ancient to the modern from the Acropolis to booming nightclubs

❸ Lose yourself within the medieval walls of **Rhodes Old Town** (p423)

❹ Search for the oracle amidst **Delphi's** (p393) dazzling ruins

❺ Stare dumbfounded at the dramatic volcanic caldera of incomparable **Santorini** (p410)

❻ Sup on **ouzo** (p446) while munching on grilled octopus

❼ Climb russet rock pinnacles to the exquisite monasteries of **Meteora** (p394)

❽ Hike through Crete's stupendous **Samaria Gorge** (p419)

❾ Let your cares float away from the pristine west-coast beaches of **Lefkada** (p438)

❿ Use quaint **Nafplio** (p388) as a base for exploring the back roads and ruins of the Pelopponese

ATHENS AΘHNA

POP 3.8 MILLION

Stroll around Athens and you'll quickly stumble across breathtaking archaeological treasures, reminders of the city's enormous historical influence on Western civilisation. With the makeover that accompanied the 2004 Olympics, Athens presented its cosmopolitan-modern side to the world, and with Greece's financial difficulties in 2010 it has revealed its more restive aspect. Though the city still suffers from traffic congestion, pollution and urban sprawl, take the time to look beneath her skin and you will discover a complex metropolis full of vibrant subcultures.

ATHENS IN TWO DAYS

Walk the deserted morning streets of the charming Plaka district to reach the **Acropolis** and **Agora** before the crowds. Dig in to *mezedhes* at **Tzitzikas & Mermingas** before spending the afternoon at the **Acropolis Museum** and the **National Archaeological Museum**. Enjoy **Parthenon** views and haute cuisine over dinner at **Varoulko** or sup on gyros at **Savas**.

On day two, watch the **changing of the guard** at Syntagma Sq before crossing the gardens to the **Panathenaic Stadium** and the **Temple of Olympian Zeus**. Visit the wonderful **Benaki Museum** or the **Goulandris Museum of Cycladic & Ancient Greek Art**, then rest up for a night out in **Gazi**.

History

The early history of Athens, named after the goddess of wisdom, Athena, is inextricably interwoven with mythology, making it impossible to disentangle fact from fiction. What is known is that the hilltop site of the Acropolis, with two abundant springs, drew some of Greece's earliest Neolithic settlers.

Athens' golden age, the pinnacle of the classical era, came after the Persian empire was repulsed at the battles of Salamis and Plataea (480–479 BC). The city has passed through many hands and cast off myriad invaders from Sparta to Philip II of Macedon, the Roman and Byzantine Empires, and, most recently, the Ottoman Empire. In 1834 Athens superseded Nafplio as the capital of independent Greece.

○ Sights

Acropolis   ANCIENT SITE
(Map p376; ☏210 321 0219; adult/child €12/free; ⊙8.30am-8pm Apr-Oct, 8am-5pm Nov-Mar; Ⓜ Akropoli) Arguably the most important ancient monument in the Western world, the Acropolis attracts multitudes of tourists, so visit in the early morning or late afternoon.

The site was inhabited in Neolithic times and the first temples were built during the Mycenaean era in homage to the goddess Athena. People lived on the Acropolis until the late 6th century BC, but in 510 BC the Delphic oracle declared that the Acropolis should be the province of the gods. When all of the buildings were reduced to ashes by the Persians on the eve of the Battle of Salamis (480 BC), Pericles set about rebuilding a city purely of temples.

Enter near the **Beule Gate**, a Roman arch added in the 3rd century AD. Beyond this lies the **Propylaea**, the enormous columned gate that was the city's entrance in ancient times. Damaged in the 17th century when lightning set off a Turkish gunpowder store, it's since been restored. South of the Propylaea, the small, graceful **Temple of Athena Nike** was been fully restored.

It's the **Parthenon**, however, that epitomises the glory of ancient Greece. Completed in 438 BC, it's unsurpassed in grace and harmony. To achieve the appearance of perfect form, columns become narrower towards the top and the bases curve upward slightly towards the ends – effects that make them look straight. Above the columns are the remains of a Doric frieze, partly destroyed by Venetian shelling in 1687.

The Parthenon was built to house the great statue of Athena commissioned by Pericles, and to serve as the new treasury. In AD 426 the gold-plated 12m-high statue was taken to Constantinople, where it disappeared.

To the north, lies the **Erechtheion** and its much-photographed Caryatids, the six maidens who support its southern portico. These are plaster casts – the originals are in the Acropolis Museum.

On the southern slope of the Acropolis, the importance of theatre in the everyday lives of ancient Athenians is made manifest in the enormous **Theatre of Dionysos** (Map p376). Built between 340 and 330 BC on the site of an earlier theatre dating to the 6th century BC, it held 17,000 people. The **Stoa**

ℹ CHEAPER BY THE HALF-DOZEN

The €12 ticket at the Acropolis (valid for four days) includes entry to the other significant ancient sites: Ancient Agora, Roman Agora, Keramikos, Temple of Olympian Zeus and the Theatre of Dionysos.

Anyone aged under 19 years or with an EU student card gets in free. Also free: Sundays from November to March, the first Sunday of April, May, June and October, and national holidays.

of Eumenes (Map p372), built as a shelter and promenade for theatre audiences, runs west to the **Theatre of Herodes Atticus** (Map p376), built in Roman times (open only for performances).

TOP CHOICE **Acropolis Museum**   MUSEUM
(Map p372; ☎210 900 0901; www.the acropolismuseum.gr; Dionysiou Areopagitou 15; admission €5; ☺8am-8pm Tue-Sun; ☏; Ⓜ Akropoli) Don't miss this superb museum on the southern base of the hill, and magnificently reflecting the Parthenon on its glass facade; it houses the surviving treasures of the Acropolis.

Bathed in natural light, the 1st-floor **Archaic Gallery** is a forest of statues, including stunning examples of 6th-century *kore* (maidens). Finds from temples pre-dating the Parthenon include sculptures such as Heracles slaying the Lernaian Hydra, and a lioness devouring a bull.

The museum's crowning glory is the top-floor **Parthenon Gallery**, a glass hall built in alignment with the Parthenon, visible through the windows. It showcases the temple's metopes and 160m frieze shown in sequence for the first time in over 200 years. Interspersed between the golden-hued originals, white plaster replicates the controversial Parthenon Marbles removed by Lord Elgin in 1801 and later sold to the British Museum.

Other highlights include five **Caryatids**, the maiden columns that held up the Erechtheion (the sixth is in the British Museum), a giant floral acroterion and a **movie** illustrating the history of the Acropolis.

The surprisingly good-value **restaurant** has superb views; there's a fine museum **shop**.

Ancient Agora   ANCIENT SITE
(Map p376; ☎210 321 0185; Adrianou 24; adult/child €4/free; ☺8.30am-8pm Apr-Oct, 8am-5.30pm Nov-Mar; Ⓜ Monastiraki) The Ancient Agora was the marketplace of early Athens and the focal point of civic and social life; Socrates spent time here expounding his philosophy. The main monuments of the Agora are the well-preserved **Temple of Hephaestus**, the 11th-century **Church of the Holy Apostles** and the reconstructed **Stoa of Attalos**, which houses the site's excellent museum.

Roman Agora   ANCIENT SITE
(Map p376; ☎210 324 5220; cnr Pelopida & Eolou; adult/child €2/free; ☺8.30am-8pm Apr-Oct, 8am-5.30pm Nov-Mar; Ⓜ Monastiraki) The Romans

---

FREE THRILLS   **371**

A simple wander through the streets brings eye candy galore, or take in:

» National Gardens
» Changing of the Guard
» Monastiraki Flea Market
» Sunday Market
» Lykavittos Hill

built their agora just east of the ancient Athenian Agora. The wonderful **Tower of the Winds** was built in the 1st century BC by Syrian astronomer Andronicus. Each side represents a point of the compass and has a relief carving depicting the associated wind.

Temple of Olympian Zeus & Panathenaic Stadium   ANCIENT SITES
(Map p372; ☎210 922 6330; adult/child €2/free; ☺8.30am-8pm Apr-Oct, 8am-5.30pm Nov-Mar; Ⓜ Akropoli) Begun in the 6th century BC, Greece's largest temple is impressive for the sheer size of its Corinthian columns: 17m high with a base diameter of 1.7m. It took more than 700 years to build, with Emperor Hadrian overseeing its completion in AD 131, and sits behind **Hadrian's Arch**. East of the temple, the Panathenaic Stadium, built in the 4th century BC as a venue for the Panathenaic athletic contests, hosted the first modern Olympic Games in 1896.

National Archaeological Museum   MUSEUM
(☎210 821 7717; www.namuseum.gr; 28 Oktovriou-Patision 44; adult/child €7/free; ☺1.30-8pm Mon, 8am-8pm Tue-Sun Apr-Oct, 8.30am-3pm Nov-Mar; Ⓜ Viktoria) One of the world's great museums, the National Archaeological Museum contains significant finds from major archaeological sites throughout Greece. The vast collections include exquisite gold artefacts from Mycenae, spectacular Minoan frescos from Santorini and aquiline Cycladic figurines.

Benaki Museum   MUSEUM
(Map p372; ☎210 367 1000; www.benaki.gr; cnr Leoforos Vasilissis Sofias & Koumbari 1; adult/child €6/free, free Thu; ☺9am-5pm Mon, Wed, Fri & Sat, 9am-midnight Thu, to 3pm Sun; Ⓜ Syntagma) This superb museum houses the extravagant collection of Antoine Benaki, the son of an Alexandrian cotton magnate. Splendid displays include ancient sculpture, Persian, Byzantine and Coptic objects, Chinese ce-

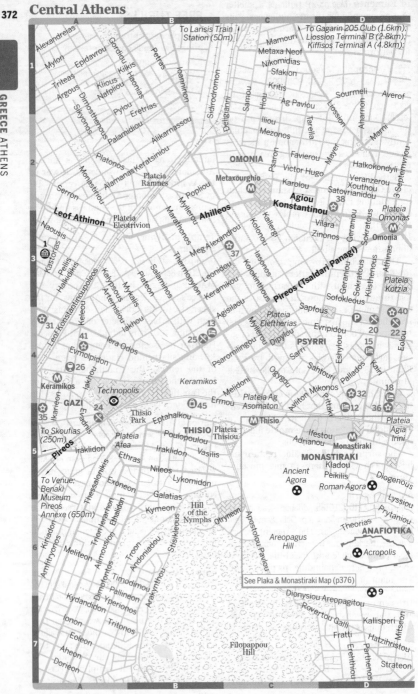

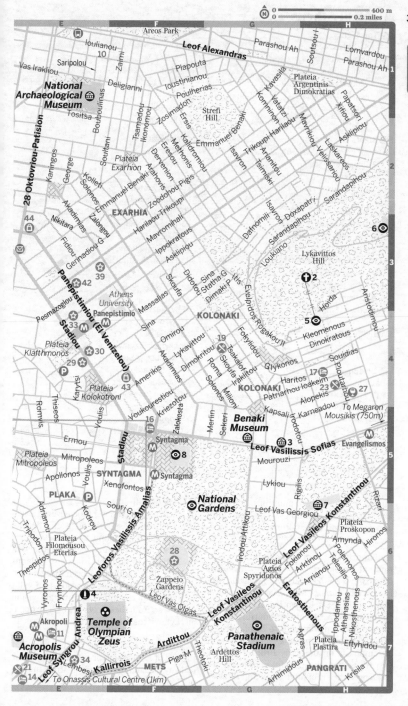

Areos Park

Leof Alexandras

Parashou Ah
Soutsou
Lomvardou
Parashou Ah

Vas Irakliou
Saripolou

Ioulianou
10
Zaimi
Plapouta
Ioustinianou
Poulherias

Plateia
Argentinis
Dimokratias
Papatsori
Xifou
Asklipiou

**National
Archaeological
Museum**

Tositsa
Bouboulinas
Deligianni
Zosimadon

Kavasila
Vatatzi
Komninon
Mavrikiou Velissariou
Liskareos

Strefi
Hill
Emmanuel Benaki

Trikoupi Harilaou
Arianitou
Tsimiski

28 Oktovriou-Patision

Souftani

Plateia
Exarhion
Emmanuel Benaki
Zoodohou Pigis

Isavron

Kaningos
George
Kolleti
Solonos
Akadimias
Zalongou

Ersis
Methonis
Eressou
Dervenion
Arahovis
Harilaou Trikoupi

Kallidromiou

Isavron
Dafnomili
Doxapatri
Sarandapihou

44
Nikitara
Fidiou
Gennadiou G

EXARHIA

Mavromihali
Ippokratous
Asklipiou

Sarandapihou

Loukianou

6

Panepistimiou
42
39

Athens
University
Skoufa

Didotou
Sina
Statha G
Itis
Dimaki P

Evelpidon Rogakou II

Lykavittos
Hill

2

Pesmazoglou
33
Panepistimio
Panepistimiou (El Venizelou)

Massalias

KOLONAKI

Hoida
Aristodimou

Stadiou

Sina
Omirou

Akadimias
Lykavittou
Dimokritou

Fokylidou

5
Kleomenous
Dinokratous

Plateia
Klafthmonos

30

19

Tsakalof
Skoufa
Iraklitou
Glykonos

Souidias

Roma
Miltou

Haritos
Patriarhou Ioakeim
17

Ploutarhou
23
27

29
Karytsi
Plateia
Kolokotroni
43
Amerikis
Solonos

KOLONAKI

Kapsali
Alopekis
Karneadou

To Megaron
Mousikis (750m)

Thiseos
Romvis
Voulis

Voukourestiou
Kriezotou
Zalokosta

Merlin
Sekeri
Irodotou

Ermou
16
Syntagma

**Benaki
Museum**
3
Leof Vasilissis Sofias
Evangelismos

Plateia
Mitropoleos
Mitropoleos
Apollonos
Stadiou
Syntagma
8

Mourouzi
Rizari

PLAKA
SYNTAGMA
Xenofontos
Syntagma

Lykiou

7

Voulis
Souri G

**National
Gardens**

Leof Vas Georgiou

Plateia
Proskopon
Amynda
Hironos

Adrianou
Tripodon
Kodrou

Plateia
Filomousou
Eterias

Leoforos Vasilissis Amalias

Irodou Attikou

Plateia
Agios
Spyridonos

Fokianou
Arktinou

Leof Vasileos Konstantinou

Polemonos
Telesilis

Thespidos
Vyronos
Frynihou

28

Zappeio
Gardens
Leof Vas Olgas

Arrianou

Ippodamou
Athanasias
Nikosthenous

4

**Temple of
Olympian
Zeus**

Leof Vasileos
Konstantinou

Agras
Plateia
Plastira
Eftyhidou

Akropoli
11

Leof Syngrou Andrea

**Panathenaic
Stadium**

Eratosthenous

**Acropolis
Museum**

34
Kallirrois

Ardittou
Piga M
Theotoki

Ardettos
Hill

PANGRATI

21
14

Lembesi
METS
To Onassis Cultural Centre (1km)

Arhimidous
Krisila

◎ **Top Sights**

Acropolis Museum	E7
Benaki Museum	G5
National Archaeological Museum	E1
National Gardens	F6
Panathenaic Stadium	G7
Temple of Olympian Zeus	E7

◎ **Sights**

1	Athinais	A3
2	Chapel of Agios Georgios	H3
3	Goulandris Museum of Cycladic & Ancient Greek Art	G5
4	Hadrian's Arch	E6
5	Lykavittos Funicular Railway	H4
6	Lykavittos Theatre	H3
7	National Museum of Contemporary Art	H6
8	Parliament	F5
9	Stoa of Eumenes	D6

Activities, Courses & Tours

10	Trekking Hellas	E1

🛏 **Sleeping**

11	Athens Backpackers	E7
12	Athens Style	D5
13	Eridanus	B4
14	Hera Hotel	E7
15	Hotel Cecil	D4
16	Hotel Grande Bretagne	F5
17	Periscope	H4
18	Tempi Hotel	D4

✪ **Eating**

19	Entryfish	G4
20	Fruit & Vegetable Market	D4
21	Mani Mani	E7
22	Meat Market	D4
23	Oikeio	H4
24	Sardelles	A5
25	Varoulko	B4

🍸 **Drinking**

26	Hoxton	A4
27	Mai Tai	H4

✪ **Entertainment**

28	Aigli Cinema	F6
29	Apollon Cinema	E4
30	Astor Cinema	E4
31	BIG	A4
32	Envy	D4
33	Hellenic Festival Box Office	E4
34	Lamda Club	E7
35	Letom	A5
36	Magaze	D5
37	Mirovolos	C3
38	National Theatre	D2
39	Olympia Theatre	E3
40	Rembetika Stoa Athanaton	D4
41	Sodade	A4
42	Ticket House	E3

🛍 **Shopping**

43	Eleftheroudakis Books	F4
44	Metropolis Music	E3
45	Sunday Market	B5

ramics, icons, El Greco paintings, and fabulous traditional costumes. The museum's annexes around the city contain Islamic art, archives and rotating exhibitions.

Goulandris Museum of Cycladic & Ancient Greek Art   MUSEUM
(Map p372; ☎210 722 8321; www.cycladic.gr; Neofytou Douka 4; adult/child €7/free; ⊙10am-5pm Mon, Wed, Fri & Sat, to 8pm Thu, 11am-5pm Sun; ☎; MEvangelismos) This wonderful private museum was custom-built to display its extraordinary collection of Cycladic art, with an emphasis on the early Bronze Age. It's easy to see how the graceful marble statues influenced the art of Modigliani and Picasso.

Lykavittos Hill   PARK
(Map p372; MEvangelismos) Pine-covered Lykavittos is the highest of the eight hills dotting Athens. Make the climb up to the summit for absolutely stunning views of the city, the Attic basin and the islands of Salamis and Aegina (pollution permitting). The little **Chapel of Agios Giorgios** is floodlit at night and resembles a fairy-tale vision when seen from the streets below. The open-air **Lykavittos Theatre** hosts concerts in summer.

The main path to the summit starts at the top of Loukianou, or take the **funicular railway** (return €6; ⊙9am-3am) from the top of Ploutarhou.

Parliament & Changing of the Guard

CULTURAL RITUAL

(Map p372) In front of the parliament building on Plateia Syntagmatos (Syntagma Sq), the traditionally costumed *evzones* (guards) of the **Tomb of the Unknown Soldier** change every hour on the hour. On Sunday at 11am, a whole platoon marches down Vasilissis Sofias to the tomb, accompanied by a band.

National Gardens

PARK

(Map p372; entrances on Leoforos Vasilissis Sofias & Leoforos Vasilissis Amalias; ⏰7am-dusk; ⓂSyntagma) A delightful, shady refuge during summer, these gardens contain a large playground, a duck pond and a tranquil cafe.

Tours

Athens Sightseeing Public Bus Line

BUS

(Bus Route 400; tickets €5) Stops at 20 key sites. Buy tickets (valid for 24 hours on all public transport, excluding airport services) on board.

CitySightseeing Athens

BUS

(☎210 922 0604; www.city-sightseeing.com; adult/concession €18/8; ⏰every 30min 9am-6pm) Open-top double-decker buses on a 90-minute circuit.

Athens Happy Train

TROLLEY

(☎210 725 5400; adult/concession €6/4; ⏰9am-midnight) Hour-long minitrain tours leaving from the top of Ermou.

Trekking Hellas

OUTDOOR ACTIVITIES

(☎210 331 0323; www.outdoorsgreece.com; Saripolou 10, Plaka; ⓂSyntagma) Activities from Athens walking tours (€22) to bungee jumping in the Corinth Canal (€60).

Festivals & Events

Hellenic Festival

PERFORMING ARTS

(Map p372; ☎210 327 2000; www.greekfestival.gr; box office Panepistimiou 39, Syntagma; ⏰8.30am-4pm Mon-Fri, 9am-2pm Sat; ⓂPanepistimio) The city's most important cultural event runs from mid-June to August. International music, dance and theatre fill venues across Athens and Epidavros' ancient theatre.

Sleeping

Discounts apply in low season, for longer stays and on the internet. Book well ahead for July and August.

CONTEMPORARY ART

Athens is not all ancient art. For a taste of the contemporary, visit:

» **Taf** (The Art Foundation; Map p376; ☎210 323 8757; www.theartfoundation.gr; Normanou 5, Monastiraki) Eclectic art and music gallery.

» **Onassis Cultural Centre** (off Map p372; ☎210 924 9090; www.sgt.gr; Leoforos Syngrou 109, Tavros) This multimillion-euro visual and performing arts centre features theatre, music and dance performances, as well as art exhibits and talks.

» **National Museum of Contemporary Art** (Map p372; ☎210 924 2111; www.emst. gr; Leoforos Vas Georgiou B 17-19, enter from Rigilis; admission €3; ⏰11am-7pm) In 2011, the museum will be moving to the old Fix brewery on Leoforos Syngrou.

Or hit the Gazi neighbourhood for:

» **Technopolis** (☎210 346 7322; Gazi) Former gasworks turned cultural centre.

» **Benaki Museum Pireos Annexe** (☎210 345 3111; www.benaki.gr; Pireos 138, cnr Andronikou, Rouf; ⏰10am-6pm Wed-Sun) Arts and cultural exhibitions.

» **Athinais** (☎210 348 0000; www.athinais.com.gr; Kastorias 36, Gazi; ⏰9am-9pm) Local and international artists. Call ahead for schedule.

Festivals include:

» **Art-Athina** (www.art-athina.gr) International contemporary art fair in May.

» **Athens Biennial** (www.athensbiennial.org) Every two years from June to October.

» **ReMap** (www.remap.org) Parallel event to the Biennial, exhibiting in abandoned buildings.

Plaka & Monastiraki

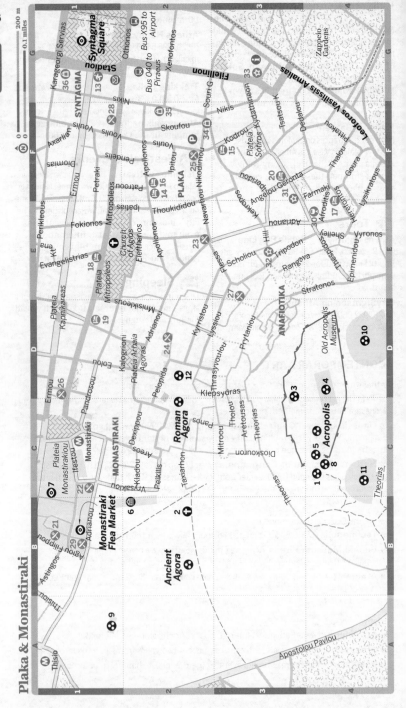

200 m
0.1 miles

Syntagma Square
Stadiou
SYNTAGMA
Karageorgi Servias
Othonos
Bus X95 to Airport
Xenofontos
Filellinon
Bus 040 to Piraeus
Souri G
Nikis
Vassilissis Amalias
Leoforos
Zappeio Gardens
Nikis
Skoufou
Plateia Kydathineon
Sotiros
Tsatsou
Kodrou
Voulis
Voulis
Plateia
Dedalou
Axarlion
Voulis
Apollonos
Ipitou
PLAKA
Pittakou
Sotiros
Farmaki
Thalou
Goura
Patroou
Navarhou Nikodimou
Angelou Geronta
Afroditis
Lysikratous
Pendelis
Petraki
Ipatias
Thoukididou
Kekropos
Adrianou
Iperidou
Diomias
Ermou
Mitropoleos
Apollonos
Shelley
Iosipidsetti
Heretidou
Epimenidou
Fokionos
Church of Agios Eleftherios
Tessa
Scholiou
Tripodon
Vyronos
Perikleous
Kiti
Evangelistrias
Plateia Mitropoleos
Mnisikleous
Adrianou
Kyrristou
Lysiou
Rangova
Stratonos
ANAFIOTIKA
Plateia Kapnikareas
Plateia Mitropoleos
Plateia Athaia Agoras
Pelopida
Klepsydras
Prytaniou
Thrasyvoulou
Old Acropolis Museum
Eolou
Kalogrioni
Panos
Tholou
Aretousas
Theorias
Ermou
Pandrosou
Areos
Dexippou
Kladiou
Pelikilis
Taxiarhon
Vrysakiou
Mitroou
Dioskouron
Theorias
Acropolis
Pireos
Plateia Monastirakiou
Ifestou
Monastiraki
Monastiraki Flea Market
Aiou Filippou
Adrianou
Astingos
Thisio
Trisiou
Roman Agora
Ancient Agora
Aposolou Pavlou
Theorias
Theorias

Plaka & Monastiraki

SYNTAGMA & MONASTIRAKI

⌖ Hotel Grande Bretagne

LUXURY HOTEL €€€

(Map p372; ☎210 333 0000; www.grandebreta gne.gr; Vasileos Georgiou 1, Syntagma; r/ste from €275/420; P❋@🛜❄; MSyntagma) Dripping with elegance and old-world charm, *the* place to stay in Athens has always has been these deluxe digs. Built in 1862 to accommodate visiting heads of state, it ranks among the great hotels of the world. From the decadent, chandeliered lobby, to the exquisite guestrooms, divine spa and rooftop restaurant, this place is built for pampering.

Magna Grecia

BOUTIQUE HOTEL €€

(Map p376; ☎210 324 0314; www.magnagrecia hotel.com; Mitropoleos 54, Monastiraki; s/d incl breakfast from €110/130; ❋@🛜; MSyntagma) Enjoy Acropolis views from the front rooms and rooftop terrace in a historic building opposite the cathedral. Rooms sport comfortable mattresses and minibars.

Plaka Hotel

HOTEL €€

(Map p376; ☎210 322 2096; www.plakahotel.gr; Kapnikareas 7 & Mitropoleos, Monastiraki; s/d/tr incl breakfast €109/135/145; ❋@; MMonastiraki) Folks come here not for the tidy, bland rooms but for the excellent Acropolis views from the rooftop garden and top-floor digs.

Hotel Cecil

HOTEL €€

(Map p372; ☎210 321 7079; www.cecil.gr; Athinas 39, Monastiraki; s/d €75/105; ❋; MMonastiraki) Aromatic spices waft into the lobby from nearby Asian markets, but double-pane windows keep the high-ceilinged rooms in this old classical building quiet. Close to Psyrri nightlife.

Tempi Hotel

HOTEL €€

(Map p372; ☎210 321 3175; www.tempihotel.gr; Eolou 29, Monastiraki; d/tr €64/78, s/d without bathroom €43/57; 🛜; MMonastiraki) No-frills rooms may be tiny, but some have balconies overlooking Plateia Agia Irini. A communal kitchen and nearby markets make it ideal for self-caterers.

PLAKA, MAKRYGIANNI & KOUKAKI

⌖ Central Hotel

BOUTIQUE HOTEL €€

(Map p376; ☎210 323 4357; www.cen tralhotel.gr; Apollonos 21, Plaka; r incl breakfast

€93-155; ⊜✳@; MSyntagma) Pass through the sleek lobby and by the attentive staff to spacious white rooms hung with original art and decked out with all the mod cons. Some balconies have Acropolis views, as does the rooftop, where you can sunbake and relax in the Jacuzzi.

TOP CHOICE Hera Hotel
BOUTIQUE HOTEL €€

(Map p372; ☏210 923 6682; www.hera hotel.gr; Falirou 9, Makrygianni; r from €115; ✳@; MAkropoli) The interior of this exquisite boutique hotel matches its lovely neoclassical facade. The rooftop garden, restaurant and bar boast spectacular views and it is a short walk to the Acropolis and Plaka.

Athens Backpackers
HOSTEL €

(Map p376; ☏210 922 4044; www.backpack ers.gr; Makri 12, Makrygianni; dm €24-29, studio from €90; ✳@☎; MAkropoli) This excellent, popular hostel boasts a rooftop party bar with Acropolis views, kitchen, daily movies, and the friendly Aussie management hosts (free!) barbecues. Breakfast and nonalcoholic drinks are included; long-term storage, laundry and airport pick-up available.

Hotel Acropolis House
HOTEL €€

(Map p376; ☏210 322 2344; www.acropolishouse .gr; Kodrou 6-8, Plaka; s incl breakfast €53-73, d €68-91, tr €119; ✳✳; MSyntagma) This well-situated hotel in a 19th-century house feels more pension than hotel, with a comfy sitting room and hospitable management. Guests chat amicably over breakfast.

Marble House Pension
HOTEL €

(off Map p372; ☏210 922 8294; www.marble house.gr; Zini 35, Koukaki; s/d/tr €39/49/59, d/ tr without bathroom €45/55; ✳@☎; MSyngrou-Fix) This long-standing Athens favourite is on a quiet cul-de-sac 10 minutes' walk from Plaka. Step through the garden to quiet, spotless rooms. For air-con add €9.

Hotel Hermes
BOUTIQUE HOTEL €€

(Map p376; ☏210 323 5514; www.hermeshotel. gr; Apollonos 19, Plaka; s/d/tr incl breakfast €109/135/145; ⊜✳@; MSyntagma) Next to the Central, with similar amenities, but not quite as swish.

Hotel Phaedra
HOTEL €€

(Map p376; ☏210 323 8461; www.hotelphaedra. com; Herefontos 16, Plaka; r €65-80; ✳@; MAkropoli) Many of the tasteful, small rooms at this family-run hotel have balconies with Acropolis or church views. Great rooftop terrace.

Student & Travellers' Inn
HOSTEL €

(Map p376; ☏210 324 4808; www.studenttravell ersinn.com; Kydathineon 16, Plaka; dm €20-25, d €63, without bathroom €58; ✳@☎; MAkropoli) The mixed-sex dorms may be spartan and housekeeping a bit lean, but extras (laundry, left luggage) make up for it.

PSYRRI & GAZI

Athens Style
HOSTEL €

(Map p372; ☏210 322 5010; www.athenstyle.com; Agias Theklas 10, Psyrri; dm incl breakfast €21-25, s/d €51/84, studios €90-124; ✳@☎; MMonastiraki) This bright, arty hostel, the newest in town, has dorm beds and well-equipped studios. The cool basement lounge holds art exhibitions, a pool table and home cinema; the rooftop bar has Acropolis views.

Eridanus
BOUTIQUE HOTEL €€€

(Map p372; ☏210 520 5360; www.eridanus.gr; Pireos 78, Gazi; d incl breakfast from €195; P✳@☎; MKeramikos) After a late night partying in Gazi or nearby Psyrri, soak in your marble bathtub and lounge around in a fluffy white robe. Helpful staff cater to your every whim; the rooftop garden has Acropolis views.

KOLONAKI

Periscope
BOUTIQUE HOTEL €€€

(Map p372; ☏210 729 7200; www.periscope. gr; Haritos 22, Kolonaki; r from €135; ⊜✳@☎; MEvangelismos) A hip hotel with a cool, edgy look (Mini Cooper seats for chairs in the cafe-bar), this place has comfortable minimalist rooms with all the mod cons and a quiet location.

🍴 Eating

In addition to mainstay tavernas, Athens has bistros and swank eateries. Wear your most stylish togs at night: Athenians dress up to eat out. Eat streets include Mitropoleos, Adrianou and Navarchou Apostoli in Monastiraki, the area around Plateia Psyrri and Gazi, near Keramikos metro.

Listings without opening hours specified are open for lunch and dinner daily during high season. For standard business hours, see p448.

The **fruit and vegetable market** (Map p372) on Athinas is opposite the **meat market** (Map p372).

SYNTAGMA & MONASTIRAKI

TOP CHOICE Tzitzikas & Mermingas
MEZEDHES €€

(Map p376; Mitropoleos 12-14, Syntagma; mezedhes €6-8; MSyntagma) Greek merchandise lines the walls of this cheery, modern *mezedhopoleio*. The great range of delicious and creative *mezedhes* draws a bustling local crowd. Don't miss the decadent honey-coated fried cheese with ham...it's the kind of special dish that will haunt your future dreams.

Café Avyssinia
MEZEDHES €€

(Map p376; ☎210 321 7407; Kynetou 7, Monastiraki; mains €8.50-14.50; ⓜMonastiraki) Hidden away on the edge of grungy Plateia Avyssinias in the middle of the flea market, this *mezedhopoleio* gets top marks for atmosphere, and the food is not far behind. Often has live music on weekends.

Savas
SOUVLAKI €

(Map p376; Mitropoleos 86-88, Monastiraki; gyros €2; ⓜMonastiraki) This joint serves enormous grilled-meat plates (€8.50) and the tastiest gyros (pork, beef or chicken) in Athens. Take away or sit down in what becomes one of the city's busiest eat streets late at night.

Also recommended:

Viasos
MODERN GREEK €

(Map p376; Adrianou 19) Young local crowds chat over juicy gyros (€2) and generous *mezedhes* (€7 to €12) on one of Athens' most atmospheric pedestrian streets.

Dioskouri
MODERN GREEK €

(Map p376; Adrianou 37) Another Adrianou option.

PLAKA & MAKRYGIANNI

Taverna tou Psarra
TAVERNA €€

(Map p376; ☎210 321 8734; Eretheos 16, Plaka; mains €8-23; ⓜMonastiraki) On a path leading up towards the Acropolis, this gem of a taverna is one of Plaka's best, serving scrumptious *mezedhes* and excellent fish and meat classics on a tree-lined terrace.

Paradosiako
TAVERNA €

(Map p376; ☎210 321 4121; Voulis 44a, Plaka; mains €7-14; ⓜSyntagma) For great traditional fare, you can't beat this inconspicuous, no-frills taverna on the periphery of Plaka. Choose from daily specials such as delicious shrimp *saganaki*.

Mani Mani
REGIONAL CUISINE €

(Map p372; ☎210 921 8180; Falirou 10, Makrygianni; mains €9.50-17; ⓧclosed Jul & Aug; ⓜAkropoli) Sample cuisine from Mani in the Peloponnese, such as tangy sausage with orange. Most dishes can be ordered as half-serves (at half-price), allowing you to try a wide range.

O Platanos
TAVERNA €

(Map p376; ☎210 322 0666; Diogenous 4, Monastiraki, Plaka; mains €7-9; ⓜMonastiraki) Laid-back O Platanos (Plane Tree) serves tasty, home-cooked-style Greek cuisine. The lamb dishes are delicious and we love the leafy courtyard.

Eat
MODERN GREEK €€

(Map p376; ☎210 324 9129; Adrianou 91, Plaka; mains €8-17; ⓜSyntagma) A sleek alternative to the endless traditional tavernas, Eat serves interesting salads and pastas and modern interpretations of Greek classics such as shrimp dolmas with sun-dried tomatoes (€9).

PSYRRI, THISSIO & GAZI

Skoufias
REGIONAL CUISINE €

(☎210 341 2252; Vasiliou tou Megalou 50, Rouf; mains €5-9; ⓧ9pm-late; ⓜKeramikos) This gem of a taverna near the railway line is a little off the beaten track but worth seeking out. The Cretan-influenced menu features eclectic dishes rarely found in the tourist joints: from superb rooster with ouzo to lamb *tsigariasto* (braised) with *horta* (wild greens).

Varoulko
SEAFOOD €€€

(Map p372; ☎210 522 8400; www.varoulko.gr; Pireos 80, Gazi; mains €22-30; ⓧclosed Sun; ⓜKeramikos) For a magical Greek dining experience, you can't beat the winning combination of Acropolis views and delicious seafood by celebrated chef Lefteris Lazarou. This Michelin-starred seafood restaurant remains popular with Athenian celebrities and foodies, who sup on sublime crayfish dolmas wrapped in sorrel leaves in an airy, glass-fronted dining room.

Sardelles
SEAFOOD €

(☎210 347 8050; Persefonis 15, Gazi; mains €9.50-15; ⓜKeramikos) As the name (sardines) suggests and the novel fishmonger paper tablecloths confirm, this modern fish taverna specialises in seafood *mezedhes*. Outside tables face the illuminated gasworks.

KOLONAKI & PANGRATI

TOP CHOICE Oikeio
BISTRO €

(Map p372; ☎210 725 9216; Ploutarhou 15, Kolonaki; mains €8-11; ⓜEvangelismos) With excellent home-style cooking, this modern taverna lives up to its name ('Homey'). The intimate bistro atmosphere spills out to tables on the pavement for glitterati-watching without the normal high Kolonaki bill. Reservations recommended.

Spondi
GOURMET GREEK €€€

(210 756 4021; www.spondi.gr; Pyrronos 5, Pangrati; mains €36-50; 8pm-midnight) Dining in this superb restaurant's gorgeous vaulted cellar or in its bougainvillea-draped courtyard in summer is quite an understatedly elegant affair. Chef Arnaud Bignon has won two Michelin stars, creating extravagant seasonal menus using local ingredients and adhering to French technique but embodying vibrant Greek flavours.

Entryfish
GOURMET MEZEDHES €€

(Map p372; 210 361 7666; Skoufa 52, Kolonaki; mezedhes €11-20; Syntagma) Brush shoulders with CEOs at this packed, swank seafood salon. Funky newsprint and art glass line the walls, and the *mezedhes* all have exquisitely delicate flavours. Reservations recommended.

🍷 Drinking

Athenians know how to party. Everyone has their favourite *steki* (hang-out), but expect people to show up after midnight. Head to Psyrri (around Agatharchou), Gazi (around Voutadon and the Keramikos metro station) and Kolonaki (around Ploutarhou and Haritos or Skoufa and Omirou) and explore!

Omonia is best avoided late at night, and although Exarhia has a bohemian bar scene, the neighbourhood has been affected recently by street demonstrations.

Kolonaki has a mind-boggling array of cafes off Plateia Kolonakiou on Skoufa and Tsakalof. Another cafe-thick area is Adrianou, along the Ancient Agora.

TOP CHOICE Hoxton
BAR

(off Map p372; Voutadon 42, Gazi; Keramikos) Kick back on overstuffed leather couches under modern art in this industrial space that fills up late with bohemians, ruggers and the occasional pop star.

Brettos
BAR

(Map p376; 210 323 2110; Kydathineon 41, Plaka; Syntagma) This distillery and bar is back-lit by an eye-catching collection of coloured bottles.

Mai-Tai
BAR

(Map p372; Ploutarhou 18, Kolonaki; Evangelismos) Jam-packed with well-heeled young Athenians, this is just one in a group of happening spots in Kolonaki.

☆ Entertainment

The *Kathimerini* supplement inside the *International Herald Tribune* contains event listings and a cinema guide, or check www.breathtakingathens.gr, www.ticketservices.gr and www.tickethour.com. **Ticket House** (Map p372; 210 360 8366; Panepistimiou 42) sells concert tickets.

Nightclubs

Athenians go clubbing after midnight and dress up. In summer try beachfront venues.

Venue
DANCE CLUB

(off Map p372; 210 341 1410; www.venue-club.com; Pireos 130, Rouf; Fri & Sat) Arguably the city's biggest dance club: three-stage dance floor and an energetic crowd.

Envy
DANCE CLUB

(Map p372; 210 331 7801; Agias Eleousis 3 & Kakourgodikiou, Psyrri; Wed-Sat) The name changes at this popular club, which plays the latest dance music in Psyrri during winter and takes place at ever-changing beachside spots in summer.

Letom
DANCE CLUB

(6992240000; Dekeleon 26, Gazi) Late-night clubbers flock to the dance parties with top international and local DJs, and a gay-friendly, hip young crowd.

Akrotiri
DANCE CLUB

(210 985 9147; Vasileos Georgiou B 5, Agios Kosmas; 10pm-5am) Beach-side with a capacity for 3000, bars and lounges cover multiple levels.

Lava Bore
DANCE CLUB

(Map p376; 210 324 5335; Filellinon 25, Plaka) A popular place for tourists; open year-round.

Gay & Lesbian Venues

Gay bars cluster in Makrygianni, Psyrri, Gazi, Metaxourghio and Exarhia. Check out www.athensinfoguide.com, www.gay.gr or a copy of the *Greek Gay Guide* booklet at *periptera* (newspaper kiosks).

Lamda Club
DANCE CLUB

(Map p372; 210 942 4202; Lembesi 15, cnr Leoforos Syngrou, Makrygianni) Athens' best gay dance club gets crowded late.

Sodade
DANCE CLUB

(www.sodade.gr; Triptolemou 10, Gazi) Attracts a younger crowd.

BIG
BAR

(www.bigbar.gr; Iera Odos 67, Gazi) Hub of Athens' lively bear scene.

Mirovolos
RESTAURANT, BAR

(Map p372; 210 522 8806; Giatrakou 12, Metaxourghio) Popular lesbian cafe-bar-restaurant.

Magaze CAFE, BAR
(Map p372; Eolou 33, Monastiraki) All-day hang-out with Acropolis views from pavement tables; becomes a lively bar after sunset.

Live Music
In summer, concerts rock plazas and parks; some clubs shut down.

JAZZ, ROCK & WORLD MUSIC

TOP CHOICE **Half Note Jazz Club** JAZZ CLUB
(☎210 921 3310; www.halfnote.gr; Trivonianou 17, Mets) Dark, smoky venue for serious jazz.

Gagarin 205 Club MUSIC CLUB
(☎210 854 7601; www.gagarin205.gr; Liossion 205) The city's coolest space attracts interesting international and local acts.

Alavastro Café MUSIC CLUB
(☎210 756 0102; Damareos 78, Pangrati) Eclectic mix of modern jazz, ethnic and Greek music in a casual, intimate venue.

REMBETIKA
Most authentic *rembetika* venues close during summer, but you can see a popularised version at some tavernas in Psyrri.

Rembetika Stoa Athanaton TRADITIONAL MUSIC
(Map p372; ☎210 321 4362; Sofokleous 19; ⊗3.30-6pm & midnight-late Mon-Sat Oct-May) Located above the meat market, this is still *the* place to listen to *rembetika*.

Classical Music, Theatre & Dance
In summer, the excellent Hellenic Festival (p375) swings into action.

Megaron Mousikis CONCERT HALL
(off Map p372; ☎210 728 2333; www.megaron.gr; cnr Leoforos Vasilissis Sofias & Kokkali) Superb concert venue hosting winter performances by local and international artists.

National Theatre DRAMA
(Map p372; ☎210 522 3243; www.n-t.gr; Agiou Konstantinou 22-24, Omonia) Contemporary plays and ancient theatre on the main stage and other venues.

Olympia Theatre OPERA, BALLET
(Map p372; ☎210 361 2461; www.nationalopera.gr; Akadimias 59, Exarhia) November to June: ballet, symphony and the Greek National Opera (www.nationalopera.gr).

Dora Stratou Dance Company DANCE
(Map p376; ☎210 921 4650; www.grdance.org; Filopappou Hill, ticket office Scholiou 8; tickets €15; ⊗9.30pm Tue-Sat, 8.15pm Sun May-Sep)

Traditional folk-dancing shows feature more than 75 musicians and dancers in an open-air amphitheatre.

Cinemas
Most cinemas show recent releases in English; tickets cost around €8. In summer, take your movie-going outdoors at Aigli and Cine Paris.

Apollon CINEMA
(Map p372; ☎210 323 6811; Stadiou 19)

Astor CINEMA
(Map p372; ☎210 323 1297; Stadiou 28)

Aigli CINEMA
(Map p372; ☎210 336 9369) Historic open-air cinema in the verdant Zappeio Gardens.

Cine Paris CINEMA
(Map p376; ☎210 322 0721; Kydathineon 22, Plaka) Nab a seat with Acropolis views.

🔒 Shopping
Athens is the place to shop for cool jewellery, clothes and shoes, and souvenirs such as backgammon sets, hand-woven textiles, olive oil beauty products, worry beads and ceramics. Find boutiques around Syntagma, from the Attica department store past Voukourestiou and on Ermou; designer brands and cool shops in Kolonaki; and souvenirs, folk art and leather in Plaka and Monastiraki.

Monastiraki Flea Market MARKET
(Map p376) Enthralling; spreads daily from Plateia Monastirakiou (Monastiraki Sq).

Sunday Market MARKET
(Map p372; ⊗7am-2pm Sun) At the end of Ermou, towards Gazi.

Metropolis Music MUSIC
(Map p372; ☎210 383 0804; Panepistimiou 64, Omonia) Well stocked with Greek and international CDs.

Compendium Books BOOKS
(Map p376; ☎210 322 1248; Nikis 28, Plaka; MSyntagma) English-language books; excellent selection of Greek history and literature.

Public ELECTRONICS, BOOKS
(Map p376; ☎210 324 6210; Plateia Syntagma; MSyntagma) English-language books on 3rd floor.

Eleftheroudakis Books BOOKS
Plaka (Map p376; ☎210 322 9388; Nikis 20; MSyntagma); Syntagma (Map p372; ☎210 325 8440; Panepistimiou 17; MSyntagma)

ⓘ Information

Dangers & Annoyances

Like any big city, Athens has its hot spots. Plateia Omonias (Omonia Sq) is home to pickpockets, prostitutes and drug dealers; women should avoid walking alone here at night. Also watch for pickpockets on the metro and at the markets. When there are strikes, picketers tend to march in Plateia Syntagmatos.

When taking taxis, ask the driver to use the meter or negotiate a price in advance. Ignore stories that the hotel you've chosen is closed or full: they're angling for a commission from another hotel.

Bar scams are commonplace, particularly in Plaka and Syntagma. They go something like this: friendly Greek approaches solo male traveller, discovers traveller is new to Athens, and reveals that he, too, is from out of town. However, friendly Greek knows a great bar where they order drinks and equally friendly owner offers another drink. Women appear and more drinks are served; at the end of the night the traveller is hit with an exorbitant bill.

With the recent financial reforms in Greece have come frequent strikes in Athens. If there is a strike while you are here, confirm that the sights you wish to see will be open and the transport you are planning to use will be running.

Emergency

Athens Police Station Central (☎210 770 5711/17; Leoforos Alexandras 173, Ambelokipi; Ⓜ Ambelokipi); Plateia Syntagmatos (☎210 725 7000)

Police Emergency (☎100)

Tourist Police (☎24hr 171, 210 920 0724; Veïkou 43-45, Koukaki; ⊙8am-10pm)

Visitor Emergency Assistance (☎112) Toll-free, 24 hours; in English.

Internet Access

There are free wireless hot spots at Plateia Syntagmatos, Thisio, Gazi, the port of Piraeus, Starbucks cafes and on the 3rd floor of Public (p381).

Internet Resources

Official visitor site www.breathtaking athens.gr

Media

Kathimerini (www.ekathimerini.com) and *Athens News* (www.athensnews.gr) have English-language coverage.

Medical Services

Ambulance/First-Aid Advice (☎166)

Duty Pharmacies & Hospitals (☎1434, in Greek) Published in *Kathimerini*. Check pharmacy windows for nearest duty pharmacy.

SOS Doctors (☎1016, 210 821 1888; ⊙24hr) Pay service with English-speaking doctors.

Money

Most banks have branches around Plateia Syntagmatos.

Eurochange Syntagma (☎210 331 2462; Karageorgi Servias 2; ⊙8am-9pm; Ⓜ Syntagma); Monastiraki (☎210 322 2657; Areos 1)

Telephone

Public phones take phonecards, available from kiosks, as are prepaid SIM cards for mobiles.

Tourist Information

EOT (Greek National Tourist Organisation; ☎210 870 7000; www.gnto.gr) Syntagma (Map p376; ☎210 331 0392; Leoforos Vasilissis Amalias 26; ⊙9am-7pm Mon-Fri, 10am-4pm Sat & Sun; Ⓜ Syntagma); airport (☎210 353 0445; Arrivals Hall; ⊙9am-7pm Mon-Fri, 10am-4pm Sat & Sun); head office (Tsoha 24; ⊙9am-2pm Mon-Fri; Ⓜ Ambelokipi)

ⓘ Getting There & Away

Air

Modern **Eleftherios Venizelos International Airport** (ATH; ☎210 353 0000; www.aia.gr), 27km east of Athens, has a 24-hour information desk. For domestic flights:

Aegean Airlines (☎210 626 1000; www.aegeanair.com; Othonos 10, Syntagma)

Athens Airways (☎210 669 6600; www.athensairways.com)

Olympic Air (☎210 926 4444; www.olympicair.com; Filellinon 15, Syntagma)

Boat

Most ferries, hydrofoils and high-speed catamarans leave from the massive port at Piraeus. Some services depart from smaller ports at Rafina and Lavrio.

Bus

Athens has two main intercity **KTEL** (www.ktel.org) bus stations, one 5km and one 7km to the north of Omonia. Get timetables at tourist offices.

Kifissos Terminal A (☎210 512 4910; Kifissou 100) Buses to the Peloponnese, Igoumenitsa, Ionian Islands, Florina, Ioannina, Kastoria, Edessa and Thessaloniki, among other destinations. Bus 051 goes to central Athens (junction of Zinonos and Menandrou, near Omonia) every 15 minutes from 5am to midnight. Taxis to Syntagma cost about €8.

Liossion Terminal B (☎210 831 7153; Liossion 260) Buses to Trikala (for Meteora), Delphi, Larissa, Thiva, Volos and other destinations. To get here, take bus 024 from outside the main gate of the National Gardens on Amalias and ask to get off at Praktoria KTEL. Get off the bus at Liossion 260, turn right onto Gousiou and you'll see the terminal.

Buses for destinations in southern Attica leave from the **Mavromateon Terminal** (☎210 880 8000; Alexandras & 28 Oktovriou-Patision, Pedion Areos), about 250m north of the National Archaeological Museum.

Car & Motorcycle

Syngrou Rd, just south of the Temple of Olympian Zeus, is lined with car-hire firms.

Avis (☎210 322 4951; Leoforos Vasilissis Amalias 48, Makrygianni)

Budget (☎210 921 4771; Leoforos Syngrou 8, Makrygianni)

Europcar (☎210 924 8810; Leoforos Syngrou 43, Makrygianni)

Train

Intercity trains to central and northern Greece depart from the central **Larisis train station**, about 1km northwest of Plateia Omonias.

For the Peloponnese, take the suburban rail to Kiato and change for other OSE services, or check for available lines at the Larisis station.

OSE Offices (☎1110; www.ose.gr) Syntagma (☎210 362 4402; Sina 6; ⊗8am-3pm Mon-Sat); Omonia (☎210 524 0647; Karolou 1; ⊗8am-3pm Mon-Fri)

Getting Around

To/From the Airport

The 24-hour airport information desks are loaded with transport information.

BUS Tickets cost €3.20. Services:

Plateia Syntagmatos Bus X95, 60 to 90 minutes, every 30 minutes, 24 hours (The Syntagma stop is on Othonos St; see Map p376)

Terminal A (Kifissos) Bus Station Bus X93, 35 minutes, every 30 minutes

Metro Line 3 at Ethniki Amyna Bus X94, 25 minutes, every 10 minutes, 7.30am to 11.30pm

Piraeus (Plateia Karaïskaki) Bus X96, 90 minutes, every 20 minutes, 24 hours

METRO Line 3 links the airport to the city centre in around 40 minutes; it operates from Monasti-

raki from 5.50am to midnight, and from the airport from 5.30am to 11.30pm. Tickets (€6) are valid for all public transport for 90 minutes. Fare for two or more passengers is €5 each.

TAXI Fares vary according to the time of day and level of traffic; expect at least €30 from the airport to the centre, and €40 to Piraeus. Both trips can take up to an hour.

Public Transport

The metro, tram and bus system makes getting around central Athens and to Piraeus easy. Athens' road traffic can be horrendous. Tickets (€1), good for 90 minutes, and a 24-hour travel pass (€3) work on all forms of public transport except for airport services; or get a travel pass. Children aged under six years travel free. People under 18 and over 65 pay half-fare.

Get maps and timetables at EOT tourist offices, **Athens Urban Transport Organisation** (OASA; ☎185; www.oasa.gr; Metsovou 15, Exarhia/Mouseio) or from their website.

BUS & TROLLEYBUS Buses and electric trolleybuses operate every 15 minutes from 5am to midnight. Purchase tickets before boarding (from the metro, a bus-ticket booth or a kiosk). Validate as you board.

Piraeus Buses operate 24 hours: every 20 minutes from 6am to midnight, and then hourly. From Syntagma and Filellinon (see Map p376) to Akti Xaveriou catch Bus 040; from Omonia end of Athinas to Plateia Themistokleous, catch Bus 049.

METRO Trains operate from 5am to midnight: every three minutes during peak periods and every 10 minutes off-peak. Get timetables at www.ametro.gr. Validate tickets as you enter the platforms.

Taxi

Athenian taxis are yellow and hard to hail. The flag fall is €1.05 with an additional surcharge of €1 from ports and train and bus stations, and €3.40 from the airport; then the day rate (tariff 1 on the meter) is €0.60 per kilometre. The night rate (tariff 2 on the meter) is €1.05 per kilometre between midnight and 5am. Baggage costs €0.35 per item over 10kg. The minimum fare is €2.80. Booking a radio taxi costs €1.70 extra.

Athina 1 (☎210 921 2800)

Enotita (☎801 115 1000)

Ikaros (☎210 515 2800)

Train

Fast **suburban rail** (☎1110; www.trainose.com) links Athens with the airport, Piraeus, the outer regions and the northern Peloponnese. It connects to the metro at Larisis, Doukissis Plakentias and Nerantziotissa stations, and goes from the airport to Kiato.

TRAVEL PASS

For short-stay visits, consider the €15 tourist ticket, valid for three days of unlimited travel on all of Athens' public transport, including the metro airport service, and the Athens Sightseeing bus.

AROUND ATHENS

Piraeus Πειραιάς

POP 175,700

The highlights of Greece's main port and ferry hub are the otherworldly rows of ferries, ships and hydrofoils filling its seemingly endless quays. It takes around 30 minutes to get here (10km) from Athens' centre by metro, so there's no reason to stay in shabby Piraeus. The Mikrolimano (Small Harbour), with its cafes and fish restaurants, reveals the city's gentler side.

🛏 Sleeping

Pireaus Theoxenia   LUXURY HOTEL **€€€**
(☏210 411 2550; www.theoxeniapalace.com; Karaoli Dimitriou 23; d €110-265; ❈@🛜) Pireaus' swank, central hotel with plump bathrobes and satellite TV; get the best deals online.

Hotel Triton   HOTEL **€€**
(☏210 417 3457; www.htriton.gr; Tsamadou 8; d €60-68; ❈@) This refurbished hotel with sleek executive-style rooms is a treat compared with Pireaus' usual run-down joints.

🍴 Eating

If you're killing time, take trolleybus 20 to Mikrolimano for harbourfront seafood.

Rakadiko   TAVERNA **€**
(☏210 417 8470; Stoa Kouvelou, Karaoli Dimitriou 5; mains €12-20; ⊙Tue-Sat) Dine, quietly, under grapevines, on *mezedhes* from all over Greece. Live *rembetika* on weekends.

Mandragoras   MARKET **€**
(Gounari 14; ⊙7.30am-4pm Mon, Wed, Sat, to 8pm Tue, Thu & Fri) Fantastic array of fresh Greek products.

General Market   MARKET **€**
(⊙6am-4pm Mon-Fri) On Dimosthenous.

Piraeus

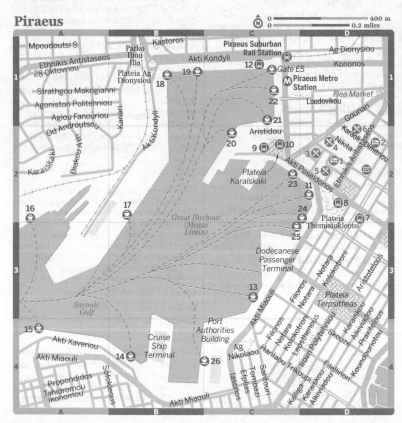

Piraikon   SUPERMARKET €
(Ippokratous 1; ⊘8am-8pm Mon-Fri, 8am-4pm
Sat)

Information

INTERNET ACCESS Free wi-fi around the port.
LEFT LUGGAGE At the metro station (€3 for
24 hours).

ℹ Getting There & Away
Boat

All ferry companies have online timetables and
booths on the quays. The main branch of EOT
in Athens has a weekly schedule. Schedules are
reduced in April, May and October, and are radically cut in winter, especially to smaller islands.
When buying tickets, confirm the departure
point. See the Getting There & Away sections
for each island for more details or contact the
Piraeus Port Authority (☏1441; www.olp.gr).

Hellenic Seaways (☏210 419 9000; www.
hellenicseaways.gr; cnr Akti Kondyli & Elotikou)
operates high-speed hydrofoils and catamarans
to the Cyclades from early April to the end of
October, and year-round services to the Saronic
Gulf Islands. Other high-speed services include
Aegean Speedlines (☏210 969 0950; www.
aegeanspeedlines.gr).

Bus

See p454 for Athens buses. The X96 Piraeus–
Athens Airport Express (€3.20) leaves from the
southwestern corner of Plateia Karaïskaki.

Metro

The fastest and most convenient link to Athens
is the metro (€1, 30 minutes, every 10 minutes,
5am to midnight), near the ferries.

Train

Piraeus has a station for Athens' suburban rail.

ℹ Getting Around

Local bus 904 runs between the metro station
and Zea Marina.

THE PELOPONNESE
ΠΕΛΟΠΟΝΝΗΣΟΣ

The Peloponnese encompasses a breathtaking array of landscapes, villages and ruins,
where much of Greek history has played
out. It's home to Olympia, birthplace of the
Olympic Games; the ancient archaeological
sites of magical Epidavros, Mycenae and
Corinth; the fairy-tale Byzantine city of Mystras; and ancient Sparta.

Two of Greece's most gorgeous towns
grace its shores: Venetian-style Nafplio and
romantic Monemvasia. The isolated Mani
Peninsula, best known for its wild landscape
and people, bristles with fortified tower
settlements and is blanketed with a colourful collection of spectacular wildflowers in
spring.

Patra ΠΑΤΡΑ

POP 185,700

Greece's third-largest city, Patra is the principal ferry port for the Ionian Islands and Italy. Despite its 3000-year history, ancient sites and vibrant social life, few travellers linger here longer than necessary to transfer to their ferries.

⊙ Sights

Kastro CASTLE
(admission free; ⊗8.30am-3pm Tue-Sun) The Byzantine castle, built by the Emperor Justinian, has excellent views to the Ionian Islands.

Archaeological Museum of Patras MUSEUM
(cnr Amerikis & Patras-Athens National Rd; admission free; ⊗8.30am-3pm Tue-Sun) The contemporary buildings here make up the country's second-largest museum and feature objects from prehistoric to Roman times.

Roman Odeon RUINS
(cnr Germanou & Sotiriadou; ⊗8am-3pm Tue-Sun) This impressive place is a magical spot to see a performance.

✱✰ Festivals

Patras Carnival MARDI GRAS
(www.carnivalpatras.gr) Wild weekend of costume parades and floats in spring.

🛏 Sleeping

Primarolia Art Hotel BOUTIQUE HOTEL €€
(☑2610 624 900; www.arthotel.gr; Othonos Amalias 33; s/d incl breakfast €99/140; ✻@) This stylish place oozes individuality, with sleeping spaces ranging from the bold, contemporary and minimalist to the florid, romantic and baroque.

Pension Nikos HOTEL €
(☑2610 623 757; cnr Patreos 3 & Agiou Andreou 121; s/d/tr €28/38/45, s/d without bathroom €23/33) Marble stairs lead to spotlessly clean rooms smack in the city centre.

🍴 Eating & Drinking

There are scores of stylish cafes and fast-food eateries lying between Kolokotroni and Ermou; drinking hot spots cluster on Agios Nikolaos and Radinou (off Riga Fereou). Pedestrianised Trion Navarhon is lined with tavernas.

Kitchen of Kornelia BISTRO €
(☑2610 272 987; Plateia Kapodistrio 4; mains €8-14; ⊗1.30pm-midnight Tue-Sat, to 5pm Sun) Dig in to Turkish braised beef with aubergine puree (€14) and other delicate specialities in this cool bistro tucked in the corner of a quiet square.

Mythos TAVERNA €
(☑2610 329 984; cnr Trion Navarhon 181 & Riga Fereou; mains €8-14; ⊗7pm-late) Friendly waiters serve excellent home-cooked Greek classics in a chandelier-strewn town house.

Dia Discount Supermarket SUPERMARKET €
(Agiou Andreou 29; ⊗Mon-Sat) Handy for grabbing some food before your ferry departs.

ℹ Information

Tourist office (☑2610 461 741; www.infocenter patras.gr; Othonos Amalias 6; ⊗8am-10pm) Friendly multilingual staff run Greece's best tourist office, with information on transport, free bicycles and internet access. A kiosk in central Plateia Trion Symahon is open 9am to 4pm.

Tourist Police (☑2610 455 833; Gounari 52; ⊗7am-9pm)

ℹ Getting There & Away

Boat

Schedules vary; the tourist office provides timetables. Ticket agencies line the waterfront.

Strintzis (☑2610 240 000; www.strintzis ferries.gr) routes:

Kefallonia €17.80, 2¾ hours, two daily
Ithaki €17.80, four hours, one daily

Minoan Lines (☑2610 426 000; www.minoan. gr) and **ANEK Lines** (☑2610 226 053; www. anek.gr) sail to Corfu (€30.50, seven hours, one daily).

For details of services to Italy, see p452.

Bus

Services from **KTEL Achaia bus station** (☑2610 623 886; cnr Zaimi 2 & Othonos Amalias):

Athens €17, three hours, half-hourly, via Corinth
Ioannina €20.90, 4½ hours, two daily
Kalamata €20, four hours, two daily
Kalavryta €7.50, two hours, two daily
Pyrgos (for Olympia) €8.80, two hours, 10 daily
Thessaloniki €40, seven hours, four daily

Buses to the Ionian Islands, via the port of Kyllini, leave from the **KTEL Lefkada & Zakynthos bus station** (☎2610 220 993; Othonos Amalias 48) or nearby **KTEL Kefallonia bus station** (☎2610 274 938; Othonos Amalias 58).

Train

Services from **Patra train station** (☎2610 639 108; Othonos Amalias 27):

Athens' Kiato station (connects to suburban rail) regular/intercity express (IC) €3.70/6.90, 2½ hours

Diakofto regular/IC €2.30/4.90, 45 minutes/one hour

Kalamata normal/IC €6.60/11.30, five hours

Pyrgos (for Olympia) normal/IC €3.70/6.30, three/1½ hours

Diakofto–Kalavryta Railway ΔΙΑΚΟΦΤΟ ΚΑΛΑΒΡΥΤΑ

This spectacular rack-and-pinion **train** (☎26910 43228), built in the 1890s, crawls up the deep gorge of the Vouraïkos River from the small coastal town of Diakofto to the mountain resort of Kalavryta, 22km away. It's a thrilling one-hour journey, with dramatic scenery best viewed from any forward-facing seat. There are five trains a day (€9.50) in each direction. They book up, so buy tickets in advance at any train station in Greece. Diakofto is one hour east of Patra on the main train line to Athens (€7). See www.odontotos.com for more information.

Corinth ΚΟΡΙΝΘΟΣ

POP 29,800

Drab, modern Corinth (*ko*-rin-thoss), 6km west of the Corinth Canal, is an uninspiring town; it's better to stay in the village near Ancient Corinth if visiting the ruins.

🛌 Sleeping

Hotel Apollon　　　　　　　HOTEL **€**
(☎27410 22587; www.hotelapollongr.com; Damaskinou 2; s/d €35/45; ❄) Basic, handily situated near the bus station and offering good discounts; the best option in town.

Blue Dolphin Camping　CAMPING GROUND **€**
(☎27410 25766; www.camping-blue-dolphin.gr; campsites per tent/adult €5/6.50; ☺Apr-Sep; ▧) Has a beach and decent facilities and offers tours. It's at Lecheon, about 4km west of Corinth, just after the ancient Corinth turn-off. Staff will pick you up from train or bus stations.

ℹ Getting There & Away

BUSES Buses to Athens (€7.50, 1½ hours, half-hourly) and Ancient Corinth (€1.40, 20 minutes, hourly) leave from the **KTEL Korinthos bus station** (☎27410 75425; Dimocratias 4). Buses to the rest of the Peloponnese leave from the **Corinth Isthmus (Peloponnese) KTEL bus station** (☎27410 83000) on the Peloponnese side of the Corinth Canal. To get there from Corinth, catch one of the frequent local buses to Loutraki.

TRAIN Trains go to Patra (regular/IC €5.70/8.90) and Athens (14 daily, four of which are IC services). The handy *proastiako* suburban train runs goes to Athens airport (€10, one hour, eight daily). At the time of research the inland line to Tripoli was under repair.

Ancient Corinth & Acrocorinth ΑΡΧΑΙΑ ΚΟΡΙΝΘΟΣ & ΑΚΡΟΚΟΡΙΝΘΟΣ

Seven kilometres southwest of Corinth's modern city, the ruins of **Ancient Corinth** (☎27410 31207; site & museum €6; ☺8am-8pm Apr-Oct, to 3pm Nov-Mar) and its lovely museum

---

WORTH A TRIP

THE WINE ROAD

The Nemea region, in the rolling hills southwest of Corinth, is one of Greece's premier wine-producing areas, famous for its full-bodied reds from the local *agiorgitiko* grape and a white from *roditis* grapes. Some wineries offer tastings:

» **Skouras** (☎27510 23688; www.skouraswines.com) Northwest of Argos.

» **Ktima Palivou** (☎27460 24190; www.palivos.gr; Ancient Nemea)

» **Lafkioti** (☎27460 31244; www.lafkiotis.gr; Ancient Kleonai) Located 3km east of Ancient Nemea.

» **Gaia Wines** (☎27460 22057; www.gaia-wines.gr; Koutsi) North of Nemea.

lie at the edge of a small village in the midst of fields sweeping to the sea. It was one of ancient Greece's wealthiest cities, but earthquakes and invasions have left only one Greek monument remaining: the imposing **Temple of Apollo**; the rest of the ruins are Roman. **Acrocorinth** (admission free; ⊘8am-3pm), the remains of a citadel built on a massive outcrop of limestone, looms majestically over the site.

The great-value digs at **Tasos Taverna & Rooms** (✆27410 31225; s/d/tr €30/45/55; ❄), 200m from the museum, are spotlessly clean and above an excellent eatery serving Greek classics.

Nafplio ΝΑΥΠΛΙΟ

POP 14,500

Elegant Venetian houses and neoclassical mansions dripping with crimson bougainvillea cascade down Nafplio's hillside to the azure sea. Vibrant cafes, shops and restaurants fill winding pedestrian streets. Crenulated Palamidi Fortress perches above it all. What's not to love?

◉ Sights

Palamidi Fortress   FORTRESS
(✆27520 28036; admission €4; ⊘8am-6.45pm Jun-Aug, to 2.45pm Sep-May) Enjoy spectacular views of the town and surrounding coast from the magnificent hilltop fortress built by the Venetians between 1711 and 1714.

Archaeological Museum   MUSEUM
(Plateia Syntagmatos; ⊘8.30am-3pm Tue-Sun; adult/concession €2/1) Fine exhibits include fire middens from 32,000 BC and bronze armour from near Mycenae (12th to 13th centuries BC).

Peloponnese Folklore Foundation Museum   MUSEUM
(✆27520 28379; 1 Vas Alexandrou St; admission €4; ⊘9am-2.30pm & 5.30-10.30pm) One of Greece's best small museums, with displays of vibrant regional costumes and rotating exhibitions.

⊨ Sleeping

Exquisite hotels abound in Nafplio. The Old Town is *the* place to stay, but it has a limited number of budget options. Friday to Sunday town fills up and prices rise; book ahead. Cheaper spots dot the road to Argos and Tolo.

TOP CHOICE **Amfitriti Pension**   PENSION €€
(✆27520 96250; www.amfitriti-pension.gr; Kapodistriou 24; d incl breakfast €85-110) Quaint antiques fill these intimate rooms in a house in the Old Town. You can also enjoy stellar views at its nearby sister hotel, **Amfitriti Belvedere**, which is chock full of brightly coloured tapestries and emits a feeling of cheery serenity.

Pension Marianna   PENSION €€
(✆27520 24256; www.pensionmarianna.gr; Potamianou 9; s/d/tr incl breakfast €70/85/100; P❄🖛) Welcoming owners epitomise Greek *filoxenia* (hospitality) and serve delicious organic breakfasts. Up a steep set of stairs, and tucked under the fortress walls, a dizzying array of rooms intermix with sea-view terraces.

Pension Dimitris Bekas   PENSION €
(✆27520 24594; Efthimiopoulou 26; s/d/tr €23/29/40) The only good, central budget option. Clean, homey rooms have a top-value location on the slopes of the Akronafplia, and the owner has a killer baseball-cap collection.

Hotel Grande Bretagne   LUXURY HOTEL €€€
(✆27520 96200; www.grandebretagne.com.gr; Filellinon Sq; s/d incl breakfast €130/180) In the heart of Nafplio's cafe action and overlooking the sea, this splendidly restored hotel with high ceilings, antiques and chandeliers radiates plush opulence.

Kapodistrias   PENSION €€
(✆27520 29366; www.hotelkapodistrias.gr; Kokinou 20; s/d incl breakfast €50/75; ❄🖛) Beautiful rooms, many with elegant canopy beds, come with sea or old-town views.

Adiandi   BOUTIQUE HOTEL €€
(✆27520 22073; www.hotel-adiandi.com; Othonos 31; r incl breakfast €110-120; ❄🖛) Rooms in this fun and upmarket place are quirkily decorated with artistic door bedheads and contemporary decor. Fantastic farm-fresh breakfasts.

Hotel Byron   PENSION €€
(✆27520 22351; www.byronhotel.gr; Platonos 2; d €60-80; ❄) Tucked into two fine Venetian buildings, iron bedsteads, rich carpets and period furniture fill immaculate rooms.

✕ Eating

Nafplio's Old Town streets are loaded with standard tavernas; those on Staïkopoulou and those overlooking the port on Bouboulinas get jam-packed on weekends.

Taverna Aeolos TRADITIONAL GREEK €
(27520 26828; V Olgas 30; mains €5-13) This
boisterous taverna lined with copper pans
gets packed with locals sharing generous
mixed-grill plates (€8.50). Live music during summer.

Omorfi Poli GREEK, ITALIAN €
(27520 29452; Bouboulinas 75; mains €6-16;
dinner) Greek favourites and *mezedhes*
(€5) with a slight Italian twist (there's
mushroom risotto), plus friendly service
and good wine list.

Antica Gelateria di Roma ICE CREAM €
(27520 23520; cnr Farmakopoulou 6 &
Komninou) The best (yes, best) traditional
gelati outside Italy.

To Kenitrikon CAFE €
(27520 29933; Plateia Syntagmatos; mains
€4-10) Relax under the shady trees on this
pretty square during extensive breakfasts.

Shopping
Nafplio shopping is a delight, with jewellery workshops, boutiques and wonderful
regional products, such as honey, wine and
handicrafts.

Metallagi JEWELLERY
(27520 21267; Sofroni 3) Young jeweller
Maria Koitsoidaki handcrafts elegant
nature-inspired jewellery from silver, fine
metals, gems and stones.

Art Shop CREATIVE ART
(27520 29546; Ypsilantou 14) This airy boutique carries a range of carefully selected
original art, ceramics, clothes, and kids'
painting supplies and games.

Odyssey BOOKS
(27520 23430; Plateia Syntagmatos) International papers, magazines and novels.

Information
EMERGENCY Tourist Police (27520 28131;
Kountouridou 16)

**TOURIST INFORMATION Kasteli Travel
& Tourist Agency** (27520 29395; 38 Vas
Konstantinou; 9am-2pm year-round & 6-8pm
Jun-Sep) At Syngrou; friendly English-speaking.

Municipal Tourist Office (27520 24444; 25
Martiou; 9am-1pm & 4-8pm) Generally unhelpful. A kiosk in Fillenon Sq offers free headsets for
walking tours (10am to 1pm and 6pm to 8pm).

Getting There & Away
Services from **KTEL Argolis Bus Station**
(27520 27323; Syngrou 8):

Argos (for Peloponnese connections) €1.40, 30
minutes, half-hourly

Athens €12, 2½ hours, hourly (via Corinth)

Epidavros €2.60, 45 minutes, four daily

Mycenae €2.60, one hour, two daily

Epidavros ΕΠΙΔΑΥΡΟΣ
Spectacular World Heritage–listed **Epidavros** (27530 22006; admission €6; 8am-7pm
Apr-Sep, to 5pm Oct-Mar) was the sanctuary of
Asclepius, god of medicine. Amid pine-covered hills, the magnificent **theatre** is still a
venue during the Hellenic Festival, but don't
miss the peaceful **Sanctuary of Asclepius**,
an ancient spa and healing centre.

For an early-morning visit to the site,
stay at the **Hotel Avaton** (27530 22178; s/d
€45/69; P), just 1km away, at the junction
of the road to Kranidi, or go as a day trip
from Nafplio (€2.60, 45 minutes, four buses
daily).

Mycenae ΜΥΚΗΝΕΣ
Although settled as early as the 6th millennium BC, **Ancient Mycenae** (27510 76585;
admission €8; 8am-8pm Jun-Sep, to 6pm Oct, to
3pm Nov-May) was at its most powerful from
1600 to 1200 BC. Mycenae's entrance, the
Lion Gate, is Europe's oldest monumental
sculpture. Homer accurately described Mycenae as being 'rich in gold': excavations of
Grave Circle A by Heinrich Schliemann in
the 1870s uncovered magnificent gold treasures, such as the Mask of Agamemnon, now
on display at Athens' National Archaeological Museum.

Most people visit on day trips from
Nafplio, but the bare **Belle Helene Hotel**
(27510 76225; Christou Tsounta; d incl breakfast
€40) is where Schliemann lived during the
excavations.

Two buses go daily to Mycenae from Argos (€1.60, 30 minutes) and Nafplio (€2.60,
one hour).

Sparta ΣΠΑΡΤΗ
POP 14,356
Cheerful, unpretentious modern Sparta
(*spar*-tee) is at odds with its ancient Spartan image of discipline and deprivation. Although there's little to see, the town makes a
convenient base from which to visit Mystras.

GORGE YOURSELF

The picturesque prefecture of **Arkadia** occupies much of the central Peloponnese and is synonymous with grassy meadows, forested mountains and gurgling streams. West of Tripoli, a tangle of medieval villages and narrow winding roads weave into valleys of dense vegetation beneath the Menalon Mountains. These areas are best accessed by car.

Wonderful walks along the **Lousios Gorge** leave from **Dimitsana** (population 230), a delightful medieval village built amphitheatrically on two hills at the beginning of the gorge. It sits 11km north of **Stemnitsa** (population 412), another gorge gateway and a striking village of stone houses and Byzantine churches.

Trekking Hellas of Arcadia (27910 25978, 6974459753; www.trekkinghellas.gr) offers rafting (€50 to €80) on the nearby Lousios and Alfios Rivers, and gorge hikes (€20 to €50).

Leonidio (population 3224), 90km east of Sparta, is dramatically set at the mouth of the **Badron Gorge**. Some older residents still speak Tsakonika, a distinctive dialect from the time of ancient Sparta.

Modern **Hotel Lakonia** (27310 28951; www.lakoniahotel.gr; Palaeologou 89; s/d incl breakfast €45/70; ❄️📶) maintains comfy, welcoming rooms with spotless bathrooms.

In a cheery yellow building, **Hotel Cecil** (27310 24980; Palaeologou 125; s/d €40/55; ❄️) has austere rooms with balconies overlooking the quiet end of the strip.

The sweet smell of spices inundates **Restaurant Elysse** (Palaeologou 113; mains €5.50-12), which is run by a friendly Greek-Canadian family. Locals chill out next door at **Café Ouzeri** (mains €2-6).

The **Tourist Police** (27310 20492; Theodoritou 20) can provide information.

Sparta's **KTEL Lakonias bus station** (27310 26441; cnr Lykourgou & Thivronos), on the east edge of town, services Athens via Corinth (€17.60, 3½ hours, eight daily), Gythio (€4, one hour, five daily), Monemvasia (€9, two hours, three daily) and Mystras (€1.40, 30 minutes, 10 daily).

Mystras ΜΥΣΤΡΑΣ

Magical **Mystras** (27310 83377; adult/child €6/3; ⏰8am-7.30pm Apr-Oct, 8.30am-3pm Nov-Mar) was once the effective capital of the Byzantine Empire. Ruins of palaces, monasteries and churches, most of them dating from between 1271 and 1460, nestle at the base of the Taÿgetos Mountains, and are surrounded by verdant olive and orange groves.

Allow half a day to explore the site. While only 7km from Sparta, staying in the village nearby allows you to get there early before it heats up. Enjoy exquisite views and a beautiful swimming pool at **Hotel Byzan-**

tion (27310 83309; www.byzantionhotel.gr; s/d €45/65; ❄️@📶), near the main square. Have a decadent escape at **Hotel Pyrgos Mystra** (27310 20870; www.pyrgosmystra.com; Manousaki 3; s/d incl breakfast €170/220; ❄️), with its lovingly appointed rooms in a restored mansion.

Camp at **Castle View** (27310 83303; www.castleview.gr; campsites per adult/tent/car €6/4/4, 2-person bungalow €30; ⏰Apr-Oct; ❄️) about 1km before Mystras village and set in olive trees, or **Camping Paleologio Mystras** (27310 22724; campsites per adult/tent/car €7/4/4; ❄️), 2km west of Sparta and approximately 4km from Mystras. Buses will stop outside either if you ask.

Several tavernas serve traditional Greek meals.

Gefyra & Monemvasia
ΓΕΦΥΡΑ & ΜΟΝΕΜΒΑΣΙΑ
POP 1320

Slip out along a narrow causeway, up around the edge of a towering rock rising dramatically from the sea and arrive at the exquisite walled village of Monemvasia. Enter the *kastro* (castle), which was separated from mainland Gefyra by an earthquake in AD 375, through a narrow tunnel on foot, and emerge into a stunning (carless) warren of cobblestone streets and stone houses. Beat the throngs of day trippers by staying over.

Signposted steps lead up to the ruins of a **fortress** built by the Venetians in the 16th century, and the Byzantine **Church of Agia Sophia**, perched precariously on the edge of the cliff. Views are spectacular, and wildflowers shoulder-high in spring.

Sleeping & Eating

Staying in a hotel in the *kastro* could be one of the most romantic things you ever do (ask for discounts in low season), but if you're on a tight budget stay in Gefyra.

TOP CHOICE **Hotel Malvasia** HISTORIC HOTEL €€
(☑27320 61113; d/apt from €80/160; ❄️🏠) A variety of cosy, traditionally decorated rooms and apartments (most with sea views) are scattered around the Old Town.

Hotel Aktaion HOTEL €
(☑27320 61234; s/d €30/40) This clean, sunny hotel, on the Gefyra end of the causeway, has balconies and views of the sea and 'the rock'.

Three traditional Greek tavernas sit cheek to cheek in Monemvasia's old town: **Matoula** (☑27320 61660), **Marianthi** (☑2732 61371) and **To Kanoni** (☑27320 61387). You can't really go wrong (mains €8 to €13).

Taverna O Botsalo TAVERNA
(☑27320 61491; mains €4-9) Just down the wharf on the mainland; serves savoury meals.

Getting There & Away

Buses stop in Gefyra at the friendly **Malvasia Travel** (☑27320 61752), where you can buy tickets. Four daily buses travel to Athens (€27, six hours) via Corinth and Sparta (€9, 2½ hours).

Gythio ΓΥΘΕΙΟ

POP 4490

Gythio (*yee*-thih-o) was once the port of ancient Sparta. Now it's an earthy fishing town on the Lakonian Gulf and gateway to the rugged, much more beautiful Mani Peninsula.

Peaceful **Marathonisi islet**, linked to the mainland by a causeway, is said to be ancient Cranae, where Paris (prince of Troy) and Helen (the wife of Menelaus of Sparta) consummated the love affair that sparked the Trojan War. You'll find the tiny **Museum of Mani History** (☑27330 24484; admission €2; ◷8am-2.30pm) here in an 18th-century tower.

Sleeping

Camping Meltemi CAMPING GROUND €
(☑27330 23260; www.campingmeltemi.gr; campsites per tent/adult €5/6; ◷Apr-Oct; 🛜🏊) Birds chirp in these idyllic silver olive groves, 3km south of Gythio; private beach, swimming pool and summer beauty contests! The Areopoli bus stops here.

Hotel La Boheme BOUTIQUE HOTEL €
(☑27330 21992; www.labohemehotel.gr; Tzani Tzanitaki; s/d €50/60; 🅿️❄️@) Sea views, upmarket rooms and a zippy downstairs bar-restaurant draw the crowds.

Xenia Karlaftis Rooms to Rent PENSION €
(☑27330 22719; opposite Marathonisi islet; s/d €25/40) Friendly owner Voula keeps clean rooms and offers kitchen access. Several nearby places are of similar quality if you can't get in here.

Eating

The waterfront is packed with fish tavernas and cafes.

I Gonia TAVERNA €
(Vassilis Pavlou; mains €6-15) Watch all the action while supping on delectable Greek standards. On the corner, opposite the port.

Nissus TAVERNA €
(☑6973384176; mains €10-15; ◷dinner) Take in fantastic views from this tiny bar-restaurant on Marthonisi islet.

Getting There & Away

BOAT ANEN Lines (www.anen.gr) has a weekly summertime ferry to Kissamos, Crete (€22, seven hours) via Kythira (€10, 2½ hours) and Antikythira. Schedules change; check with **Rozakis Travel** (☑27330 22207; rosakigy@otenet.gr; Pavlou 5).

BUS KTEL Lakonia bus station (☑27330 22228; cnr Vasileos Georgios & Evrikleos) is on the square near Hotel Aktion. Services:

Areopoli €2.40, 30 minutes, four daily

Athens €21.50, 4½ hours, six daily

Diros Caves €3.30, one hour, one daily

Sparta €3.90, one hour, four daily

The Mani Η ΜΑΝΗ

The exquisite Mani completely lives up to its reputation for rugged beauty, abundant wildflowers in spring and dramatic juxtapositions of sea and the Taÿgetos Mountains (threaded with wonderful walking trails). The Mani occupies the central peninsula of the southern Peloponnese and is divided into two regions: the arid Lakonian (inner) Mani in the south and the verdant Messinian (outer) Mani in the northwest near Kalamata. Explore the winding roads by car.

LAKONIAN MANI

For centuries the Maniots were a law unto themselves, renowned for their fierce independence and their spectacularly murderous internal feuds. To this day, bizarre tower settlements built as refuges during clan wars dot the rocky slopes of Lakonian Mani.

Areopoli (population 774), 30km southwest of Gythio and named after Ares, the god of war, is a warren of cobblestone and ancient towers. Enter a dreamlike courtyard to reach the excellent **Pyrgos Kapetanakas** (☑27330 51233; access off Kapetan Matepan; s/d/tr €50/60/80; ✳), in a splendid tower house built by the powerful Kapetanakas family in 1865. **Tsimova Rooms** (☑27330 51301; Kapetan Matepan; s/d €55/60) is in a renovated tower tucked behind the Church of Taxiarhes.

Step behind the counter to choose from the scrumptious specials at **Nicola's Corner Taverna** (☑27330 51366; Plateia Athanaton; mains €8-10), on the central square.

The **bus station** (☑27330 51229; Plateia Athanaton) services Gythio (€2.80, 30 minutes, four daily), Itilo (for the Messinian Mani, €2, 20 minutes, three daily Monday to Saturday), Gerolimenas (€3.30, 45 minutes, three daily) and the Diros Caves (€1.40, 15 minutes, one daily).

Eleven kilometres south, the extensive, though touristy **Diros Caves** (☑27330 52222; adult/child €12/7; ☺8.30am-5.30pm Jun-Sep, to 3pm Oct-May) contain a subterranean river. In neighbouring **Pyrgos Dirou**, stay over at chic **Vlyhada** (☑27330 52469; www.vlyhada.gr; d incl breakfast €70; P✳).

Gerolimenas, a tranquil fishing village on a sheltered bay 20km further south, is home to the exceedingly popular boutique **Kyrimai Hotel** (☑27330 54288; www.kyrimai. gr; d from €100; P✳✳). Groovy music and mood lighting fill this exquisitely renovated castle with a seaside swimming pool and top-notch restaurant.

MESSINIAN MANI

Stone hamlets dot aquamarine swimming coves. Silver olive groves climb the foothills to the snow-capped Taÿgetos Mountains. Explore the splendid meandering roads and hiking trails from Itilo to Kalamata.

The people of the enchanting seaside village of **Kardamyli**, 37km south of Kalamata, know how good they've got it. Sir Patrick Leigh Fermor famously wrote about his rambles here in *Mani: Travels in the Southern Peloponnese*. Trekkers come for the magnificent **Vyros Gorge**. Walks are well organised and colour-coded.

Kardamyli has a good choice of small hotels and private rooms for all budgets; book ahead for summer.

Notos Hotel (☑27210 73730; www.notos hotel.gr; studios €95-110; ✳) is really a boutique hamlet of individual stone houses, perched on a hill overlooking the village, the mountains, and the sea! Each elegantly decorated wee house has a fully equipped kitchen, a verandah and a view.

Run by the former housekeeper to Patrick Leigh Fermor, **Lela's Rooms** (☑27210 73541; r €55; ✳) has basic charming rooms on the sea, while the adjoining Lela's Taverna serves up tasty home-style Greek cuisine (mains €10) under pergolas on the water's edge.

Olympia Koumounakou Rooms (☑27210 73623; s/d €30/35) is basic but clean and popular with backpackers, who like the communal kitchen and courtyard.

Beautiful **Elies** (☑27210 73140; mains €6.50-10; ☺lunch), right by the beach 1km north of town, is worth a lunchtime stop.

Kardamyli is on the main bus route from Itilo to Kalamata (€3.10, one hour) and two to three buses stop daily at the central square.

Olympia ΟΛΥΜΠΙΑ

POP 1000

Tucked alongside the Kladeos River, in fertile delta country, the modern town of Olympia supports the extensive ruins of the same name. The first Olympics were staged here in 776 BC, and every four years thereafter until AD 394 when Emperor Theodosius I banned them. During the competition the city states were bound by a sacred truce to stop fighting and take part in athletic events and cultural exhibitions.

Ancient Olympia (☑26240 22517; adult/child €6/3, site & museum €9/5; ☺8am-8pm Apr-Oct, 8.30am-3pm Nov-Mar) is dominated by the immense ruined **Temple of Zeus**, to whom the games were dedicated. Don't miss the statue of **Hermes of Praxiteles**, a classical sculpture masterpiece, at the exceptional **Archaeological Museum** (adult/child €6/3; ☺1.30-8pm Mon, 8am-8pm Tue-Sun Apr-Oct, to 3pm Nov-Mar).

Sparkling-clean **Pension Posidon** (☑26240 22567; www.pensionposidon.gr; Stefanopoulou 9; s/d/tr €35/45/60; ✳) and quiet, spacious **Hotel Pelops** (☑/fax 26240 22543;

www.hotelpelops.gr; Varela 2; s/d/tr incl breakfast €48/60/84; ⊝❄@🖥) offer the best value in the centre. Family-run **Best Western Europa** (📞26240 22650; www.hoteleuropa.gr; Drouva 1; s/d €90/130; P❄@🖥🏊) perches on a hill above town and has gorgeous sweeping vistas from room balconies and the wonderful swimming pool.

Pitch your tent in the leafy grove at **Camping Diana** (📞26240 22314; campsites per tent/adult €6/8; 🏊), 250m west of town.

Tucked beneath the trees, **Taverna Gefsis Melathron** (📞26240 22916; George Douma 3; mains €5-8; 🍴) is the best of the ho-hum tavernas for traditional cuisine, including scrumptious vegetarian options and organic wines.

Olympia Municipal Tourist Office (📞26240 23100; Praxitelous Kondyli; ⊙9am-3pm Mon-Fri May-Sep) has transport schedules.

Catch buses at the stop on the north end of town. Northbound buses go via Pyrgos (€1.90, 30 minutes), where you connect to buses for Athens, Corinth and Patra. Two buses go east from Olympia to Tripoli (€11.10, 2½ hours). Trains run daily to Pyrgos (€1, 30 minutes), where you can switch for Athens, Corinth and Patra.

CENTRAL GREECE
ΚΕΝΤΡΙΚΗ ΕΛΛΑΔΑ

This dramatic landscape of deep gorges, rugged mountains and fertile valleys is home to the magical stone pinnacle-topping monasteries of Meteora and the iconic ruins of ancient Delphi, where Alexander the Great sought advice from the Delphic oracle. Established in 1938, **Parnassos National Park** (www.routes.gr), to the north of Delphi, attracts naturalists, hikers and skiers.

Delphi ΔΕΛΦΟΙ
POP 2800
Modern Delphi and its adjoining ruins hang stunningly on the slopes of Mt Parnassos overlooking the shimmering Gulf of Corinth.

The ancient Greeks regarded Delphi as the centre of the world. According to mythology, Zeus released two eagles at opposite ends of the world and they met here. By the 6th century BC, **Ancient Delphi** (📞22650 82312; site or museum €6, combined adult/child €9/5, free Sun Nov-Mar; ⊙1.30-7.45pm Mon, 8am-7.45pm Tue-Sun Apr-Oct, 8.30am-2.45pm Nov-Mar) had become the Sanctuary of Apollo. Thousands of pilgrims flocked here to consult the middle-aged female oracle who sat at the mouth of a fume-emitting chasm. After sacrificing a sheep or goat, pilgrims would ask a question, and a priest would translate the oracle's response into verse. Wars, voyages and business transactions were undertaken on the strength of these prophecies. From the entrance, take the **Sacred Way** up to the **Temple of Apollo**, where the oracle sat. From here the path continues to the **theatre** and **stadium**.

Opposite the main site and down the hill some 100m, don't miss the **Sanctuary of Athena** and the much-photographed **Tholos**, a 4th-century-BC columned rotunda of Pentelic marble.

In the town centre, the welcoming **Hotel Hermes** (📞22650 82318; Vasileon Pavlou-Friderikis 27; s/d incl breakfast €45/60; ❄) has spacious rooms sporting balconies with stunning valley views.

Apollon Camping (📞22650 82762; www.apolloncamping.gr; campsites per person/tent €7.50/4; P@🖥🏊), 2km west of town, has great facilities, including a restaurant and minimarket.

Specialities at **Taverna Vakhos** (📞22650 83186; Apollonos 31; mains €4.50-11) include stuffed zucchini flowers and rabbit stew. Locals pack **Taverna Gargadouas** (📞22650 82488; Vasileon Pavlou & Friderikis; mains €4-9) for grilled meats and slow-roasted lamb (€7.50).

The **bus station** (📞22660 82317), post office, banks and **tourist office** (📞22650 82900; ⊙7.30am-2.30pm Mon-Fri, 8am-2pm Sat) are all on modern Delphi's main street, Vasileon Pavlou. Six buses a day go to Athens (€13.60, three hours). Take a bus to Lamia (€8.20, two hours, two daily) or Trikala (€13.80, 4½ hours, two daily) to transfer for Meteora.

> **WORTH A TRIP**
>
> ## PELION PENINSULA
>
> The **Pelion Peninsula**, a dramatic mountain range whose highest peak is Pourianos Stavros (1624m), was inhabited, according to mythology, by half-man and half-horse *kentavri* (centaurs). Today it is a verdant mecca for trekkers. The largely inaccessible eastern flank consists of high cliffs that plunge into the sea. The gentler western flank coils round the Pagasitikos Gulf.

Meteora ΜΕΤΕΩΡΑ

Meteora (meh-*teh*-o-rah) should be a certified Wonder of the World with its magnificent late-14th-century monasteries perched dramatically atop enormous rocky pinnacles. Try not to miss it. The tranquil village of **Kastraki**, 2km from Kalambaka, is the best base for visiting.

While there were once monasteries on all 24 pinnacles, only six are still occupied: **Megalou Meteorou** (Grand Meteoron; ☺9am-5pm Wed-Mon Apr-Oct, to 4pm Thu-Mon Nov-Mar), **Varlaam** (☺9am-4pm Wed-Mon Apr-Oct, Thu-Mon Nov-Mar), **Agiou Stefanou** (☺9am-1.30pm & 3.30-5.30pm Tue-Sun Apr-Oct, 9.30am-1pm & 3-5pm Nov-Mar), **Agias Triados** (Holy Trinity; ☺9am-5pm Fri-Wed Apr-Oct, 10am-3pm Nov-Mar), **Agiou Nikolaou Anapafsa** (☺9am-3.30pm Sat-Thu) and **Agias Varvaras Rousanou** (☺9am-6pm Thu-Tue Apr-Oct, to 4pm Nov-Mar). Admission is €2 for each monastery and strict dress codes apply (no bare shoulders or knees and women must wear skirts; borrow a long skirt at the door if you don't have one). Walk the footpaths between monasteries or drive the back road.

Meteora's stunning rocks are also a climbing mecca. Licensed mountain guide **Lazaros Botelis** (☎24320 79165, 6948043655; meteora@nolimits.com.gr; Kastraki) and mountaineering instructor **Kostas Liolos** (☎6972567582; kliolios@kalampaka.com; Kalambaka) show the way.

🛏 Sleeping & Eating

TOP CHOICE ⟩ **Doupiani House**   HOTEL €
(☎24320 75326; www.doupianihouse. com; s/d/tr incl breakfast €40/50/60; P ✳ @ ⛱) Gregarious hosts Thanassis and Toula Nakis offer this comfy home from which to explore or simply enjoy the panoramic views. Request a balcony room.

Vrachos Camping   CAMPING GROUND €
(☎24320 22293; www.campingmeteora.gr; campsites per tent/adult €7/free; ✺) Great views, excellent facilities and a good taverna; a short stroll from Kastraki.

Taverna Paradisos   TRADITIONAL GREEK €
(☎24320 22723; mains €4-7.50) Look for outstanding traditional meals with spectacular views.

Taverna Gardenia   TRADITIONAL GREEK €
(☎24320 22504; Kastrakiou St; mains €4-8) Freshest Greek food served with aplomb and more splendid views. The owners also

have good-value, spacious rooms (single/double/triple €35/45/55).

ℹ Getting There & Around

Local buses shuttle between Kalambaka and Kastraki (€1.90); a bus goes up to the monasteries in the morning. Hourly buses from Kalambaka go to the transport hub of Trikala (€2, 30 minutes), from where buses go to Ioannina (€13.10, three hours, two daily) and Athens (€27, 4½ hours, seven daily). From Kalambaka, express trains run to Athens (regular/IC €14.60/24.30, 5½hr/4½, two/two daily) and Thessaloniki (€12.10, four hours, three daily).

NORTHERN GREECE
ΒΟΡΕΙΑ ΕΛΛΑΔΑ

Northern Greece is stunning, graced as it is with magnificent mountains, thick forests, tranquil lakes and archaeological sites. Most of all, it's easy to get off the beaten track and experience aspects of Greece noticeably different to other mainland areas and the islands.

Thessaloniki
ΘΕΣΣΑΛΟΝΙΚΗ
POP 800,800

Dodge cherry sellers in the street, smell spices in the air and enjoy waterfront breezes in Thessaloniki (thess-ah-lo-*nee*-kih), also known as Salonica. The second city of Byzantium and of modern Greece boasts countless Byzantine churches, a smattering of Roman ruins, engaging museums, shopping to rival Athens, fine restaurants and a lively cafe scene and nightlife.

◉ Sights

Historical Sights   MONUMENT, CHURCH
Check out the seafront **White Tower** (Lefkos Pyrgos; www.lpth.org; admission free; ☺8am-3pm Tue-Sun) and wander *hanmams* (Turkish baths) and churches such as the enormous, 5th-century **Church of Agios Dimitrios** (Agiou Dimitriou 97; admission free; ☺8am-10pm).

Art & Culture
MUSEUMS, GALLERY
The award-winning **Museum of Byzantine Culture** (☎2313 306 400; www.mbp.gr; Leoforos Stratou 2; admission €4; ☺8am-8pm Tue-Sun, 1.30-8pm Mon) beautifully displays splendid sculptures, mosaics, icons and other intriguing artefacts. The **Archaeological Museum**

(☎2310 830 538; Manoli Andronikou 6; admission €6; ⊙8.30am-8pm) showcases prehistoric, ancient Macedonian and Hellenistic finds.

The compelling **Thessaloniki Centre of Contemporary Art** (www.cact.gr; admission free; ⊙11am-7pm Tue-Sun) and hip **Museum of Photography** (www.thmphoto.gr; admission free; ⊙11am-7pm Tue-Sun), beside the port, are worth an hour.

🛏 Sleeping

Steep discounts abound during summer; prices rise during conventions.

Electra Palace Hotel   LUXURY HOTEL €€
(☎2310 294 000; www.electrahotels.gr; Plateia Aristotelous 9; d €130-210; 🅿@🛜🏊) Dive into five-star seafront pampering: impeccable service, plush rooms, a rooftop bar, indoor and outdoor swimming pools and a *hammam*.

Hotel Pella   HOTEL €
(☎2310 524 221; www.pella-hotel.gr; Ionos Dragoumi 63; s/d €40/50; 🅿) Quiet and family-run, with spotless rooms.

Hotel Tourist   BUSINESS HOTEL €€
(☎2310 270 501; www.touristhotel.gr; Mitropoleos 21; s/d incl breakfast €55/70; 🅿@) Spacious rooms in a charming, central, neoclassical building are maintained by friendly staff.

City Hotel   BUSINESS HOTEL €€
(☎2310 269 421; www.cityhotel.gr; Komninon 11; s/d incl breakfast €120/135; 🅿@🛜) Ask for a light-filled front room in this excellently located sleek, stylish hotel.

Backpacker's Refuge   HOSTEL €
(☎6983433591; backpackers _refuge@hotmail. com; Botsari 84; dm per person €15; 🛜) Snug, hostel-like flat with a two-bed and a four-bed dorm. Call, email or SMS ahead, as it's frequently booked.

Hotel Orestias Kastorias   HOTEL €
(☎2310 276 517; www.okhotel.gr; Agnostou Stratiotou 14; s/d/tr €38/49/59; 🅿@) A friendly favourite with cosy, clean rooms.

🍴 Eating

Tavernas dot Plateia Athonos and cafes pack Leoforos Nikis. Head to **Modiano Market** for fresh fruit and vegetables.

Zythos   TRADITIONAL GREEK €
(Katouni 5; mains €6-12) Popular with locals, this excellent taverna with friendly staff serves up delicious standards, interesting regional specialities, good wines by the glass and beers on tap. Its second outlet is **Dore**

Zythos (☎2310 279 010; Tsirogianni 7), near the White Tower.

Kitchen Bar   ECLECTIC INTERNATIONAL €
(☎2310 502 241; Warehouse B, Thessaloniki Port; mains €7-13) This perennial favourite offers both drinks and artfully prepared food, in a sumptuously decorated, renovated warehouse with waterfront tables. Chefs, like style-conscious clientele, are always on display.

O Arhontis   FOOD STAND €
(Ermou 26; mains €5; ⊙11am-5pm) Eat delicious grilled sausages and potatoes off butcher's paper at this popular working-class eatery in Modiano Market.

Myrsini   CRETAN €
(☎2310 228 300; Tsopela 2; mains €7-10; ⊙Sep-Jun) Hearty portions of delicious Cretan dishes such as roast rabbit and *myzithropitakia* (flaky filo triangles with sweet sheep's milk cheese).

Paparouna   CREATIVE GREEK €
(☎2310 510 852; www.paparouna.com; Syngrou 7; mains €8-16; ⊙1pm-1am; 🛜) Built a century ago as a bank, this lively restaurant whips up inventive cuisine like chicken with peppermint and honey.

Turkenlis   BAKERY €
(Aristotelous 4) Renowned for *tzoureki* (sweet bread) and a mind-boggling array of sweet-scented confections.

🍷 Drinking & Entertainment

Funky bars line Plateia Aristotelous and Leoforos Nikis, while Syngrou and Valaoritou Sts have newer drinking holes.

Spiti Mou   BAR
(cnr Egnatia & Leontos Sofou 26; ⊙1pm-late; 🛜) Unmarked entrance and relaxed vibe, with big couches and eclectic tunes.

Lido   DISCO
(Frixou 5, Sfageia; ⊙9pm-late) Pumps out R&B, house and more. Like most nightclubs, in summer it operates out on the airport road.

ℹ Information

EMERGENCY First-Aid Centre (☎2310 530 530; Navarhou Koundourioti 10)

Tourist Police (☎2310 554 871; 5th fl, Dodekanisou 4; ⊙7.30am-11pm)

TOURIST INFORMATION Office of Tourism Directorate (☎2310 221 100; tour-the@otenet. gr; Tsimiski 136; ⊙8am-8pm Mon-Fri, to 2pm Sat)

Getting There & Away

Air

Makedonia Airport (SKG; ☑2310 473 212) is 16km southeast of the centre and served by local bus 78 (€0.60, one hour, from 5am to 10pm). Taxis cost €15 (20 minutes).

Olympic Air (☑2310 368 666; Navarhou Koundourioti 1-3) and **Aegean Airlines** (☑2310 280 050; El Venizelou 2) fly throughout Greece. **Astra Airlines** (☑2310 489 392; www.astra-airlines.gr) flies to Chios.

Boat

Weekly ferries go to, among others, Limnos (€25, eight hours), Lesvos (€36, 14 hours) and Chios (€37, 19 hours). **Karaharisis Travel & Shipping Agency** (☑2310 524 544; Navarhou Koundourioti 8) handles tickets.

Bus

The **main bus station** (☑23105 95408; Monastiriou 319) services Athens (€35, 6¼ hours, 10 daily), Ioannina (€28.50, 4¾ hours, six daily) and other destinations. Buses to the Halkidiki Peninsula leave from the **Halkidiki bus terminal** (☑23103 16555; Karakasi 68).

OSE (☑2310 599 100; Aristotelous 26) runs buses to Sofia (€22, seven hours, two to four times daily) and Tirana (€31, twice daily). You can buy tickets from the office on the eastern side of the train station. Buses from the small **KTEL-Asprovalta station** (☑2310 536 260, Irinis 17) serve İstanbul (€45, 9½ hours, two daily).

Train

The **train station** (☑2310 599 421; Monastiriou) serves Athens (regular/IC €28/36, 6¾/5½ hours, seven/10 daily), Alexandroupolis (€13.60, six hours, three daily) and destinations beyond. International trains from Athens (heading to Belgrade, Sofia, İstanbul etc) stop at Thessaloniki. You can get schedules from the **train ticket office** (OSE; ☑2310 598 120; Aristotelous 18) or the station.

Thessaloniki

Halkidiki ΧΑΛΚΙΔΙΚΗ

Beautiful pine-covered Halkidiki is a three-pronged peninsula that extends into the Aegean Sea, southeast of Thessaloniki. Splendid, if built-up, sandy beaches rim its 500km of coastline. The middle **Sithonian Peninsula** is most spectacular. With camping and rooms to rent, it is more suited to independent travellers than overdeveloped **Kassandra Peninsula**, although Kassandra has the summertime **Sani Jazz Festival** (www.sanifestival.gr). You'll need your own wheels to explore Halkidiki properly.

Halkidiki's third prong is occupied by the all-male Monastic Republic of **Mt Athos** (known in Greek as the Holy Mountain), where 20 monasteries full of priceless treasures stand amid an impressive landscape of gorges, mountains and sea. Only men may visit, a permit is required and the summer waiting list is long. Start months in advance by contacting the Thessaloniki-based **Mt Athos Pilgrims' Bureau** (☑2310 252 578; fax 2310 222 424; pilgrimsbureau@c-lab.gr; Egnatia 109; ◷9am-2pm Mon-Fri, 10am-noon Sat).

Alexandroupolis
ΑΛΕΞΑΝΔΡΟΥΠΟΛΗ

POP 49,200

Alexandroupolis (ah-lex-an-*dhroo*-po-lih) and nearby Komotini (ko-mo-tih-*nee*) enjoy lively student atmospheres that make for a satisfying stopover on the way to Turkey or Samothraki.

Lavish, waterfront **Hotel Bao Bab** (☑25510 34823; Alexandroupoli-Komotini Hwy; s/d/tr €40/60/70; P✳@), 1km west of town, has large, comfortable rooms and an excellent restaurant. Downtown, **Hotel Marianna** (☑25510 81456; Malgaron 11; s/d €45/60) has small, clean rooms.

Tuck into today's fresh catch at **Psarotaverna tis Kyra Dimitras** (cnr Kountourioti & Dikastirion; fish €6-11).

Alexandroupoli's cool nightspots change with the whims of its students. Leoforos Dimokratias has trendy bars; cafes line the waterfront.

The **Municipal tourist office** (☑25510 64184; Leoforos Dimokratias 306; ◷7.30am-3pm) is helpful.

⊙ Getting There & Away

AIR & BOAT Dimokritos Airport is 7km east of town and served by Olympic Air and Aegean Airlines. **Sever Travel** (☑25510 22555; sever1@otenet.gr; Megalou Alexandrou 24) handles ferry (to Samothraki and Limnos) and airline tickets.

BUS Bus station (☑25510 26479; Eleftheriou Venizelou 36). Services:

Athens €61, 10 hours, one daily

Thessaloniki €26.50, 3¾ hours, nine daily

İstanbul (Turkey) OSE bus €15, six hours, one daily Tuesday to Sunday

TRAIN Train station (☑25510 26395). Services:

Athens €49, 14 hours, one daily

Thessaloniki €9, seven hours, six daily

İstanbul €38, seven hours, three daily

Svilengrad (Bulgaria) €7, four hours, one daily

Mt Olympus ΟΛΥΜΠΟΣ
ΟΡΟΣ

Just as it did for the ancients, Greece's highest mountain, the cloud-covered lair of the Greek pantheon, fires the visitor's imagination today. The highest of Olympus' eight peaks is **Mytikas** (2917m), popular with trekkers, who use **Litohoro** (elevation 305m), 5km inland from the Athens–Thessaloniki highway, as their base. The main route up takes two days, with a stay overnight at one of the **refuges** (⊙May-Oct). Good protective clothing is essential, even in summer. **EOS** (Greek Alpine Club; ☑23520 84544; Plateia Kentriki; ⊙9.30am-12.30pm & 6-8pm Mon-Sat Jun-Sep) has information on treks.

The romantic guest house **Xenonas Papanikolaou** (☑23520 81236; xenpap@otenet.gr; Nikolaou Episkopou Kitrous 1; s/d €45/50; ✱⊛) sits in a flowery garden up in the backstreets, a world away from the tourist crowds.

Olympos Beach Camping (☑23520 22111; www.olympos-beach.gr; Plaka Litohorou; campsites per adult/tent €7/6, bungalows €45; ⊙Apr-Oct) has a funky waterfront lounge and a pleasant beach.

TOP CHOICE **Gastrodromio En Olympio** (☑23520 21300; Plateia Eleftherias; mains €7-13), one of Greece's best country restaurants, serves up specialities such as *soutzoukakia* (minced meat with cumin and mint) and delicious wild mushrooms with an impressive regional wine list and gorgeous Olympus views.

From the **bus station** (☑23520 81271) 13 buses daily go to Thessaloniki (€8, 1¼ hours) and three to Athens (€28, 5½ hours). Litohoro's **train station**, 9km away, gets 10 daily trains on the Athens–Volos–Thessaloniki line.

Ioannina ΙΩΑΝΝΙΝΑ

POP 61,700

Charming Ioannina (ih-o-*ah*-nih-nah) on the western shore of Lake Pamvotis at the foot of the Pindos Mountains, was a major intellectual centre during Ottoman rule. Today it's a thriving university town with a lively waterfront cafe scene.

☉ Sights

Kastro OLD QUARTER

The narrow stone streets of the evocative old quarter sit on a small peninsula jutting into the lake. Within its impressive fortifications, **Its Kale**, an inner citadel with lovely grounds and lake views, is home to the splendid **Fetiye Cami** (Victory Mosque), built in 1611, and the gemlike **Byzantine Museum** (☑26510 25989; admission €3; ⊙8am-5pm Tue-Sun).

Lake Pamvotida LAKE

The lake's serene *nisi* (island) shelters four **monasteries** among its trees. Frequent ferries (€2) leave from near Plateia Mavili.

🛏 Sleeping

TOP CHOICE **Filyra** BOUTIQUE HOTEL €€

(☑26510 83560; http://hotelfilyra.gr; alley off Andronikou Paleologou 18; r €65; ✱) Five Old Town self-catering suites that fill up fast. The affiliated **Traditional Hotel Dafni** (Ioustinianou 12; s/d/q €45/65/90; ✱) is built into the Kastro's outer walls.

Hotel Kastro PENSION €€

(☑26510 22866; Andronikou Paleologou 57; s/d €75/90; P✱) Ask for a high-ceilinged upstairs room at this quaint hotel, across from Its Kale.

Limnopoula Camping CAMPING GROUND €

(☑26510 25265; Kanari 10; campsites per tent/adult €4/8; ⊙Apr-Oct) Tree-lined and splendidly set on the edge of the lake 2km northwest of town.

✗ Eating & Drinking

Scores of cafes and restaurants line the waterfront. Enjoy a cold beer on a sunny day in Its Kale, at its exquisitely situated cafe (mains €4 to €8).

Taberna To Manteio TRADITIONAL GREEK €

(Plateia Georgiou 15; mains €7-8) Join local families along the flower-filled Its Kale wall for deliciously simple *mezedhes,* salads and grills.

Es Aei GREEK €

(☑26510 34571; Koundouriotou 50; mains €8-12) This favourite haunt of local and foreign gastronomes combines an Ottoman flair with a unique, glass-roofed dining room.

Ananta BAR

(cnr Anexartisias & Stoa Labei; ⊙9pm-3am) Rock out in the shadows of the long bar.

ℹ Information

EOT (tourist office; ☑26510 41142; Dodonis 39; ⊙7.30am-2.30pm Mon-Fri)

EOS (Greek Alpine Club; ☑26510 22138; Despotatou Ipirou 2; ⊙7-9pm Mon-Fri)

ℹ Getting There & Away

AIR Aegean Airlines (☑26510 64444) and **Olympic Air** (☑26510 26518) fly to Athens. Slow buses ply the 2km road into town.

BUS The **station** (☑26510 26286; Georgiou Papandreou) is 300m north of Plateia Dimokratias. Services:

Athens €35.20, 6½ hours, nine daily

Igoumenitsa €8.80, 1¼ hours, eight daily

Thessaloniki €28.50, 4¾ hours, six daily

Trikala €13.10, 2¼ hours, two daily

Zagorohoria & Vikos Gorge ΤΑ ΖΑΓΟΡΟΧΩΡΙΑ & ΧΑΡΑΔΡΑ ΤΟΥ ΒΙΚΟΥ

Do not miss the spectacular Zagori region, with its deep gorges, abundant wildlife, dense forests and snowcapped mountains. Some 46 charming villages, famous for their grey-slate architecture, and known collectively as the Zagorohoria, are sprinkled across a large expanse of the Pindos Mountains north of Ioannina. These beautifully restored gems were once only connected by stone paths and arching footbridges, but paved roads now wind between them. Get information on walks from Ioannina's EOT and EOS offices. Book ahead during high season (Christmas, Greek Easter and August); prices plummet in low season.

Tiny, carless **Dilofo** makes for a peaceful sojourn, especially if you lodge at excellent **Gaia** (✆26530 22570; www.gaia-dilofo.gr; s/d from €60/100) or **Arhontiko Dilofo** (✆26530 22455; www.dilofo.com; d incl breakfast from €65) and tuck into a delicious meal at **Taverna Lidthos** (mains €6-8), overlooking the village.

Delightful **Monodendri**, known for its special pitta bread, is a popular departure point for treks through dramatic 12km-long, 900m-deep **Vikos Gorge**, with its sheer limestone walls. Get cosy at quaint **Archontiko Zarkada** (✆26530 71305; www.monodendri.com; s/d incl breakfast €40/60), one of Greece's best-value small hotels.

Exquisite inns with attached tavernas abound in remote (but popular) twin villages **Megalo Papingo** and **Mikro Papingo**. Visit the **WWF Information Centre** (Mikro Papingo; ⊙10.30am-6pm Fri-Wed) to learn about the area.

In Megalo Papingo, simple **Lakis** (✆26530 41087; d incl breakfast €65) is a *domatia* (B&B), taverna and store. Stylish **Tsoumani** (✆26530 41893; www.tsoumanisnikos.gr; d from €85) also serves some of the best food around. Two friendly brothers run charming **Xenonas tou Kouli** (✆26530 41115; d €90).

Hide away in Mikro Papingo's sweetly rustic **Xenonas Dias** (✆26530 41257; s/d €60/80) or fabulous, sumptuously minimalist **1700** (✆26530 41179; www.mikropapigo.gr; d from €100) and elegantly appointed **Antalki** (✆26530 41441; www.antalki.gr; d €80-120).

Infrequent buses run to Ioannina from Dilofo (€3.50, three weekly), Monodendri (€3.10, one hour, twice weekly) and the Papingos (€5, two hours, three weekly).

Igoumenitsa ΗΓΟΥΜΕΝΙΤΣΑ

POP 9110

Though tucked beneath verdant hills and lying on the sea, this characterless west-coast port is little more than a ferry hub: keep moving.

If you must stay over, look for *domatia* signs or have a '70s flashback at **Hotel Oscar** (✆26650 23338; Ag Apostolon 149; s/d €30/40; ✺), across from the Corfu ticket booths.

Taverna Emily Akti (Podou 13; mains €6-8) ekes out some character under a pergola near the Corfu ferry quay.

The **bus station** (✆26650 22309; Kyprou 29) services Ioannina (€8.20, 2½ hours, nine daily) and Athens (€33, eight hours, five daily).

Several companies operate **ferries to Corfu** (✆26650 99460) between 5am and 10pm (person/car €7/33, 1½hr, hourly), and hydrofoils in summer. International ferries go to the Italian ports of Ancona, Bari, Brindisi and Venice. Ticket agencies line the port.

SARONIC GULF ISLANDS
ΝΗΣΙΑ ΤΟΥ ΣΑΡΩΝΙΚΟΥ

Scattered about the Saronic Gulf, these islands are within easy reach of Athens. The Saronics are named after the mythical King Saron of Argos, a keen hunter who drowned while chasing a deer that had swum into the gulf to escape.

You can either island-hop through the group then return to Piraeus, or carry on to the Peloponnese from any of the islands mentioned.

Aegina ΑΙΓΙΝΑ

POP 13,500

Once a major player in the Hellenic world, thanks to its strategic position at the mouth of the gulf, Aegina (*eh-yee-nah*) now enjoys its position as Greece's premier producer of pistachios. Pick up a bag before you leave!

Bustling **Aegina Town**, on the west coast, is the island's capital and main port. There is no official tourist office, but information can be gleaned at www.aeginagreece.com.

The impressive **Temple of Aphaia** (adult/under 18yr €4/free; ⊙8am-6.30pm) is a well-preserved Doric temple 12km east of Aegina Town. It's said to have served as a model for the construction of the Parthenon. Standing on a pine-clad hill with imposing views out over the gulf, it is well worth a visit. Buses from Aegina Town to the small resort of Agia Marina can drop you at the site.

In Aegina Town, **Hotel Rastoni** (☑22970 27039; www.rastoni.gr; d/tr €90/120; P✴@☎), a boutique hotel with excellent service, gets a big thumbs up for its quiet location, spacious rooms and lovely garden. **Electra Pension** (☑22970 26715; s/d €45/50; ✴) is in a quiet corner of town with rooms that are impeccable and comfy.

A flotilla of ferries (€9.50, 70 minutes) and hydrofoils (€14, 40 minutes) ply the waters between Aegina and Piraeus with great regularity. You can head back to Piraeus, carry on through the Saronic Gulf Islands or take a boat to Methana (€5.70, 40 minutes) on the Peloponnese. There is a good public bus service on the island.

Poros ΠΟΡΟΣ

POP 4500

Only a few hundred metres from the village of Galatas on the shores of the mountainous Peloponnese, Poros is an attractive island with a friendly feel that is worth the effort. **Poros Town**, on the island's southern coast, is a haven for yachties, and with boats from all over tied up along the waterfront, there is a happy mood in the air.

HELLENIC WILDLIFE HOSPITAL

While some Greeks may not appear too environmentally minded, others are making a sterling effort to face the country's ecological problems head on. The **Hellenic Wildlife Hospital** (☑22970 28367; www.ekpaz.gr; ☉10am-7pm) on the Saronic Gulf island of Aegina is one such place. The centre tackles the damage caused to wild birds and animals due to hunting and pollution, and runs projects such as the release of raptors into the wilds of Crete and Northern Greece. You can visit the centre for free, though donations are appreciated. Better yet, the centre welcomes volunteers and accommodation is supplied.

Seven Brothers Hotel (☑22980 23412; www.7brothers.gr; s/d/tr €55/65/75; ✴@) is conveniently close to the hydrofoil dock. This modern hotel has bright, comfy rooms with balconies and tea- and coffee-making facilities.

There is no tourist office, but also no shortage of businesses hoping to sell you your onward ticket. Hit www.poros.com.gr for extensive information.

There are four ferry (€13.30, 2½ hours) and four hydrofoil (€25.20, one hour) services daily between Poros and Piraeus. The ferries go via Aegina (€8.60, 1¼ hours), while the hydrofoils go direct. Many of the outbound boats head on to Hydra and Spetses. Small boats shuttle back and forth between Poros and Galatas (€1, five minutes) on the Peloponnese.

Hydra ΥΔΡΑ

POP 2900

The catwalk queen of the Saronics, Hydra (*ee*-drah) is a delight. **Hydra Town** has a picturesque horseshoe-shaped harbour with gracious white and pastel stone mansions stacked up the rocky hillsides that surround it. The island is known as a retreat for artists, writers and celebrities, and wears its celebrity with panache.

A major attraction is Hydra's tranquillity. Forget noisy motorbikes keeping you awake half the night! There are no motorised vehicles – apart from two sanitation trucks – and the main forms of transport are foot and donkey.

TOP CHOICE **Pension Erofili** (☑22980 54049; www.pensionerofili.gr; Tombazi; s/d/tr €45/55/65; ✴), tucked away in the inner town, has clean, comfortable rooms and an attractive courtyard. The young friendly owners add a friendly sparkle. **Hotel Miranda** (☑22980 52230; www.mirandahotel.gr; Miaouli; s/d incl breakfast €120/140; ✴) is worth a splurge. Originally built in 1810 as the mansion of a wealthy Hydriot sea captain, this stylish place retains much of its historical character and is a National Heritage building.

Hydra Town is on the island's north coast. There is no tourist office, but check out www.hydradirect.com for detailed information.

High-speed boat services (€28.40, 1½ hours) connect Hydra with Piraeus seven times daily. There are also services to Ermioni and Porto Heli on the Peloponnese mainland and outbound boats to Spetses.

Spetses ΣΠΕΤΣΕΣ

POP 4000

Spetses is an appealing island that is packed with visitors in summer. Its attractiveness is largely thanks to Spetses-born philanthropist Sotirios Anargyrios, who made a fortune in the US after emigrating in 1848. Anargyrios returned in 1914, bought two-thirds of the then-barren island, planted Aleppo pines, financed the island's road system, and commissioned many of the town's grandest buildings.

Spetses Town, the main port, sprawls along half the northeast coast of the island.

Opposite the small town beach to the east of the ferry quay, **Villa Marina** (☎22980 72646; www.villamarinaspetses.com; s/d €60/75; ✺) is a welcoming place with tidy rooms containing a fridge. Ask for a sea view.

There is no tourist office. See the website www.spetsesdirect.com for more information.

At least six high-speed boats head daily to Piraeus (€39, 2¼ hours). Another option is to carry on to the Peloponnese mainland on boats to Ermioni (€10, one hour) or Porto Heli (€7, 10 minutes).

CYCLADES ΚΥΚΛΑΔΕΣ

The Cyclades (kih-*klah*-dez) are Greek islands to dream about. Named after the rough *kyklos* (circle) they form around the island of Delos, they are rugged outcrops of rock in the azure Aegean, speckled with white cubist buildings and blue-domed Byzantine churches. Throw in sun-blasted golden beaches, more than a dash of hedonism and a fascinating culture, and it's easy to see why many find the Cyclades irresistible.

Some of the islands, such as Mykonos, Ios and Santorini, have seized tourism with great enthusiasm. Prepare to battle the crowds if you turn up at the height of summer. Others are little more than clumps of rock, with a village, secluded coves and a few curious tourists. Ferry services rarely run in winter, while from July to September the Cyclades are vulnerable to the *meltemi*, a fierce northeasterly wind that can cull ferry schedules.

History

Said to have been inhabited since at least 7000 BC, the Cyclades enjoyed a flourishing Bronze Age civilisation (3000–1100 BC),

---

ⓘ CYCLADIC CONNECTIONS

For planning purposes, it's worth noting that once the season kicks in, **Hellenic Seaways** (www.hsw.gr) runs daily catamarans up and down the Cyclades, starting from both Piraeus (for Athens) and Iraklio on Crete.

One boat heads south daily from Piraeus to Paros, Naxos, Ios and Santorini, returning along the same route. There's also a daily run from Piraeus to Syros, Tinos and Mykonos.

Heading north from Iraklio, another catamaran runs to Santorini, Ios, Paros, Mykonos and return.

Island-hopping through the Cyclades from Piraeus to Crete (or vice-versa) is getting easier and easier – though ease of travel means there are more people out there doing it!

---

more or less concurrent with the Minoan civilisation. From the 4th century AD, the islands, like the rest of Greece, suffered a series of invasions and occupations. The Turks turned up in 1537 but neglected the Cyclades to the extent that they became backwaters prone to raids by pirates – hence the labyrinthine character of their towns, which was meant to confuse attackers. On some islands the whole population moved into the mountainous interior to escape the pirates, while on others they braved it out on the coast. Consequently, the *hora* (main town) is on the coast on some islands, while on others it is inland.

The Cyclades became part of independent Greece in 1827. During WWII they were occupied by the Italians. Before the revival of the islands' fortunes by the tourist boom that began in the 1970s, many islanders lived in poverty and many more headed for the mainland or emigrated to America or Australia in search of work.

Mykonos ΜΥΚΟΝΟΣ

POP 9700

Sophisticated Mykonos glitters happily under the Aegean sun, shamelessly surviving on tourism. The island has something for everyone, with marvellous beaches, romantic sunsets, chic boutiques, excellent restaurants and bars, and its long-held reputation as a mecca for gay travellers. The maze of white-walled streets in Mykonos Town was designed to confuse pirates, and it certainly manages to captivate and confuse the crowds that consume the island's capital in summer.

⊙ Sights & Activities

Mykonos Town   NEIGHBOURHOOD
A stroll around Mykonos Town, shuffling through snaking streets with blinding white walls and balconies of flowers is a must for any visitor. **Little Venice**, where the sea laps up to the edge of the restaurants and bars, and Mykonos' famous hilltop row of **windmills** should be included in the spots-to-see list. You're bound to run into one of Mykonos' famous resident pelicans on your walk.

Beaches
The island's most popular beaches are on the southern coast. **Platys Gialos** has wall-to-wall sun lounges, while nudity is not uncommon at **Paradise Beach**, **Super Paradise**, **Agrari** and gay-friendly **Elia**.

🛌 Sleeping

Mykonos has two camping areas, both on the south coast. Minibuses from both meet the ferries and buses go regularly into town. Rooms in town fill up quickly in high season.

Hotel Philippi   HOTEL €€
(📞22890 22294; chriko@otenet.gr; 25 Kalogera, Mykonos Town; s €60-90, d €75-120; ✳🛜) In the heart of the *hora*, Philippi has spacious, bright, clean rooms that open onto a railed verandah overlooking a lush garden. Free wi-fi. An extremely pleasant place to stay.

Paradise Beach Camping   CAMPING €
(📞22890 22852; www.paradisemykonos.com; campsites per tent/person €5/10; @🛇) There are lots of options here, including camping, beach cabins and apartments, as well as bars, a swimming pool, games etc. It is skin-to-skin mayhem in summer with a real party atmosphere. The website has it all.

Hotel Lefteris   HOTEL €€
(📞22890 27117; www.lefterishotel.gr; 9 Apollonas, Mykonos Town; s/d €95/120, studios €220-260; ✳) Tucked away just up from Taxi Sq, Lefteris has bright, comfy rooms, and a relaxing sun terrace with superb views over town. A good international meeting place.

Poseidon Hotel   HOTEL €€
(📞22890 22437; www.poseidonhotelmykonos. gr; Agiou Ioannou, Mykonos Town; s/d/ste €110/130/300; P✳@🛇) In a great location a few hundred metres up from the southern bus station, Poseidon presents more-than-adequate rooms, plush suites and a superb pool area.

🍴 Eating

There is no shortage of places to eat and drink in Mykonos Town. Cheap eateries are found around Taxi Sq and the southern bus station. Restaurants offering abundant (but pricey) seafood abound in Little Venice and towards the Delos excursion boats. Mykonos' top touts are its two resident pelicans, who wander the restaurants looking for handouts, often with visitors following them.

[TOP CHOICE] Fato a Mano   MEDITERRANEAN €
(📞22890 26256; Meletopoulou Sq; mains €8-15) In the middle of the maze, this place is worth taking the effort to find. It serves up tasty Mediterranean and traditional Greek dishes with pride.

🍷 Drinking & Entertainment

The waterfront is perfect for sitting with a drink and watching an interesting array of passers-by, while Little Venice has bars with dreamy views and water lapping below your feet.

Cavo Paradiso   CLUB
(📞22890 27205; www.cavoparadiso.gr) For those who want to go the whole hog, this place 300m above Paradise Beach picks up around 2am and boasts a pool the shape of Mykonos. A bus transports clubbers from town in about 15 minutes in summer.

Long feted as a gay travel destination, there are many gay-centric clubs and hang-outs:

Kastro   BAR
(Agion Anargyron) In Little Venice, this the spot to start the night with cocktails as the sun sets.

Pierro's   CLUB
(Agias Kiriakis) Near Taxi Sq; a popular dance club for rounding off the night.

ℹ Information

Tourist information office (📞22890 25250; www.mykonos.gr; ☉9am-9pm Jul & Aug, 10am-5pm Easter-Jun, Sep & Oct) At the western end of the waterfront, just up from the Delos boat ticket office.

Island Mykonos Travel (📞22890 22232; www. discovergreece.org) On Taxi Sq, where the port

Mykonos

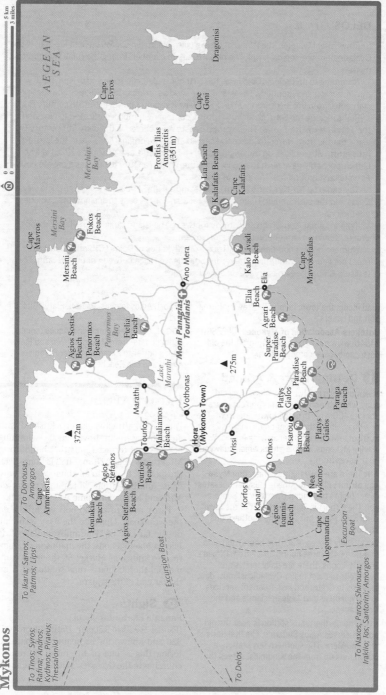

To Tinos; Syros;
Rafina; Andros;
Kythnos; Piraeus;
Thessaloniki

To Ikaria; Samos;
Patmos; Lipsi

To Donousa;
Amorgos

To Naxos; Paros; Shinousa;
Iraklio; Ios; Santorini; Amorgos

To Delos

AEGEAN
SEA

5 km
3 miles

Dragonisi

Cape
Evros

Cape
Goni

Profitis Ilias
Anomeritis
(351m)

Lia Beach

Cape
Kalafatis

Kalafatis Beach

Merchtias
Bay

Cape
Mavros

Mersini
Bay

Fokos
Beach

Mersini
Beach

Kalo Livadi
Beach

Cape
Mavrokefalas

Ano Mera

Moni Panagias
Tourlianis

Elia
Elia Beach

Agios Sostis
Beach

Panormos
Beach

Ftelia
Beach

Panormos
Bay

Lake
Marathi

Agrari
Beach

Super
Paradise
Beach

275m

Paradise
Beach

Vothonas

Platys
Gialos

Paraga
Beach

Marathi

372m

Tourlos

Malaliamos
Beach

Hora
(Mykonos Town)

Vrissi

Ornos

Platys
Gialos

Psarou
Psarou
Beach

Agios
Stefanos

Tourlos
Beach

Agios Stefanos
Beach

Cape
Armenistis

Houlakia
Beach

Korfos

Kapari

Agios
Ioannis
Beach

Nea
Mykonos

Cape
Alogomandra

Excursion
Boat

Excursion Boat

Excursion
Boat

WORTH A TRIP

DELOS ΔΗΛΟΣ

Southwest of Mykonos, the island of **Delos** (sites & museum €5; ⊙9am-3pm Tue-Sun) is the Cyclades' archaeological jewel. The opportunity to clamber among the ruins shouldn't be missed.

According to mythology, Delos was the birthplace of Apollo – the god of light, poetry, music, healing and prophecy. The island flourished as an important religious and commercial centre from the 3rd millennium BC, reaching its apex of power in the 5th century BC.

Ruins include the **Sanctuary of Apollo**, containing temples dedicated to him, and the **Terrace of the Lions**. These proud beasts were carved in the early 6th century BC using marble from Naxos to guard the sacred area. The original lions are in the island's **museum**, with replicas on the original site. The **Sacred Lake** (dry since 1926) is where Leto supposedly gave birth to Apollo, while the **Theatre Quarter** is where private houses were built around the **Theatre of Delos**.

The climb up **Mt Kynthos** (113m), the island's highest point, is a highlight. The view of Delos and the surrounding islands is spectacular, and it's easy to see how the Cyclades got their name.

Take a sunhat, sunscreen and sturdy footwear. The island's cafeteria sells food and drinks. Staying overnight on Delos is forbidden.

Numerous boat companies offer trips from Mykonos to Delos (€15 return, 30 minutes) between 9am and 1pm. The return boats leave Delos between noon and 3pm. There is also a €5 per person entry fee on arrival at Delos.

road meets the town; helpful for travel information and tickets.

Hoteliers Association of Mykonos (☑22890 24540; www.mha.gr; ⊙8am-4pm) At the old port; can book accommodation.

ⓘ Getting There & Around

Mykonos Town has two ferry quays. The old quay, where the smaller ferries and catamarans dock, is 400m north of the town waterfront. The new quay, where the bigger boats dock, is 2.5km north of town. Buses meet arriving ferries. When leaving Mykonos, double-check which quay your boat leaves from.

AIR There are daily flights connecting **Mykonos airport** (JMK) to Athens. easyJet operates direct flights to London from May to September. The airport is 3km southeast of the town centre; €1.50 by bus from the southern bus station.

BOAT Daily ferries (€30, five hours) and catamarans (€45, three hours) arrive from Piraeus. From Mykonos, there are daily ferries and hydrofoils to most major Cycladic islands, daily services to Crete, and less-frequent services to the northeastern Aegean Islands and the Dodecanese.

BUS The northern bus station is near the old port. It serves Agios Stefanos, Elia, Kalafatis and Ano Mera. The southern bus station, a 300m walk up from the windmills, serves the

airport, Agios Ioannis, Psarou, Platys Gialos and Paradise Beach.

LOCAL BOATS In summer, caiques (small fishing boats) from Mykonos Town and Platys Gialos putter to Paradise, Super Paradise, Agrari and Elia Beaches.

Paros ΠΑΡΟΣ

POP 13,000

Paros is an attractive, laid-back island with an enticing main town, good swimming beaches and terraced hills that build up to Mt Profitis Ilias (770m). It has long been prosperous, thanks to an abundance of pure white marble (from which the *Venus de Milo* and Napoleon's tomb were sculpted).

Paros' main town and port is **Parikia**, on the west coast. Opposite the ferry terminal, on the far side of Windmill roundabout, is Plateia Mavrogenous, the main square. Agora, also known as Market St, the main commercial thoroughfare, runs southwest from the far end of the square.

⊙ Sights

Panagia Ekatontapyliani   CHURCH
(Parikia; ⊙7.30am-9.30pm) Dating from AD 326 and known for its beautiful ornate interior, this is one of the most impressive churches in the Cyclades. Within the church

Paros & Antiparos

5 km
3 miles

To Naxos

To Iraklia

Santa Maria
Cape Agias Marias

Moni Agiou Ioannou
Monastiri
Plastira Bay

Cape Korakas

Lageri
Ampelas

Cape Antikefalos
Molos
Moni Agiou Antonios

Kolimvythres
Naoussa

Marmara
Logaras
Punda

Kamares

Kostos

Marpissa
Piso Livadi
Golden Beach
Nea Hrysi Akti

Marathi

Lefkes
Prodromos

Marble Quarries

Dryos

Livadia

Paros

Moni Agiou Ioannou

Mt Profitis Ilias (770m)

Krios
Parikia

To Naxos; Dounousa;
Little Cyclades; Sikinos;
Amorgos; Ikaria;
Samos; Dodecanese

Cape Agios Fokas

Agios Fokas

Excursion Boat

Petaloudes (Valley of the Butterflies)

Cape Mavros

Parasporos

Kamari

Akrotiri

To Mykonos; Tinos;
Andros; Rafina

Pounta

Angeria

Aliki
Aliki Beach

Cape Skilos

Antiparos
Glyfa

Apandima

Sunset
Antiparos

AEGEAN SEA

Cave of Antiparos

Agios Georgios
Agios Georgios

Soros

To Syros; Piraeus;
Thessaloniki

To Sifnos; Iraklio; Ios;
Kimolos; Folegandros;
Serifos; Milos;
Santorini; Anafi

compound, the **Byzantine Museum** (admission €1.50; ⊙9.30am-2pm & 6-9pm) has an interesting collection of icons and artefacts.

🏃 Activities

A great option on **Paros** is to rent a scooter or car at one of the many outlets in Parikia and cruise around the island. There are sealed roads the whole way, and the opportunity to explore villages such as **Naoussa, Marpissa** and **Aliki**, and swim at beaches such as **Logaras, Punda** and **Golden Beach**. Naoussa is a cute little fishing village on the northeastern coast that is all geared up to welcome tourists.

Less than 2km from Paros, the small island of **Antiparos** has fantastic beaches, which have made it wildly popular. Another attraction is its **Cave of Antiparos** (admission €3.50; ⊙10.45am-3.45pm Jun-Sep), considered to be one of Europe's best.

🛏 Sleeping

Rooms Mike   ROOMS €
(☑22840 22856; Parikia; www.roomsmike.com; s/d/tr €35/45/60) A popular and friendly place, Mike's offers good location and local advice. There are options of rooms with shared facilities through to fully self-contained units with kitchens. Mike's sign is easy to spot from the quay, away to the left.

Pension Sofia   PENSION €€
(☑22840 22085; Parikia; www.sofiapension-paros. com; s/d €100/120; P❋@) If you've got a few extra euros and don't mind a stroll to town, this place, with a beautifully tended garden and immaculate rooms, is a great option that won't be regretted.

Rooms Rena   ROOMS €
(☑22840 22220; www.cycladesnet.gr; Epitropakis; s/d/tr €35/45/60; ❋🛜) The quiet, well-kept rooms here are excellent value. Turn left from the pier then right at the ancient cemetery and follow the signs.

Koula Camping   CAMPING GROUND €
(☑22840 22801; www.campingkoula.gr; campsites per tent/person €4/8; ⊙Apr-Oct; P🛜) A pleasant shaded spot behind the beach at the north end of the waterfront.

🍴 Eating & Drinking

Budget eating spots are easy to find near the Windmill roundabout in Parikia. Head along the waterfront to the west of the ferry quay to find a line-up of restaurants and drinking establishments that gaze out at the setting sun. It's hard to beat **Pebbles Jazz Bar** for ambience. There are also a number of good eating and drinking options along Market St, which more or less parallels the waterfront.

TOP CHOICE **Ephessus**   GREEK €
(mains €6-12) On the road back behind Rooms Mike; serves tasty Greek cuisine and has a top reputation with locals.

ℹ Information

There is no tourist office. See the website www. parosweb.com for information.

Santorineos Travel (☑22840 24245; bookings @santorineos-travel.gr) On the waterfront near the Windmill roundabout; good for ticketing and information.

ℹ Getting There & Around

AIR Paros' airport (PAS) has daily flight connections with Athens. The airport is 8km south of Parikia; €1.50 by bus.

BOAT Parikia is a major ferry hub with daily connections to Piraeus (€30, five hours) and frequent ferries and catamarans to Naxos, Ios, Santorini, Mykonos and Crete. The fast boats generally take half the time but are more expensive, eg a fast boat to Piraeus costs €40. The Dodecanese and the northeastern Aegean Islands are also well serviced from here.

BUS From Parikia there are frequent bus services to the entire island.

LOCAL BOATS In summer there are excursion boats to Antiparos from Parikia port, or you can catch a bus to Pounta and ferry across.

Naxos ΝΑΞΟΣ

POP 18,200

The largest of the Cyclades islands, Naxos could probably survive without tourism – unlike many of its neighbouring islands. Green and fertile, Naxos produces olives, grapes, figs, citrus, corn and potatoes. The island is well worth taking the time to explore with its fascinating main town, excellent beaches and striking interior.

Naxos Town, on the west coast, is the island's capital and port. The ferry quay is at the northern end of the waterfront, with the bus terminal out front.

👁 Sights & Activities

Kastro   CASTLE
Behind the waterfront in Naxos Town, narrow alleyways scramble up to the spectacu-

lar hilltop 13th-century *kastro*, where the Venetian Catholics lived. The *kastro* looks out over the town, and has a well-stocked **archaeological museum** (admission €3; ☺8.30am-3pm Tue-Sun).

Beaches

The beach of **Agios Georgios** is a 10-minute walk south from the main waterfront. Beyond it, wonderful sandy beaches stretch as far south as **Pyrgaki Beach**. **Agia Anna Beach**, 6km from town, and **Plaka Beach** are lined with accommodation and packed in summer.

Villages

A hire car or scooter will help reveal Naxos' dramatic landscape. The **Tragaea** region has tranquil villages, churches atop rocky crags and huge olive groves. **Filoti**, the largest inland settlement, perches on the slopes of **Mt Zeus** (1004m), the highest peak in the Cyclades. The historic village of **Halki**,

one-time centre of Naxian commerce, is well worth a visit.

Apollonas is a lovely spot near Naxos' northern tip. There's a **beach**, excellent **taverna**, and the mysterious 10.5m **kouros** (naked male statue), constructed in the 7th century BC, lying abandoned and unfinished in an ancient marble quarry.

🛏 Sleeping

TOP CHOICE **Pension Sofi** PENSION €€
(☎22850 23077; www.pensionsofi.gr; r €30-75; ❄) Run by members of the friendly Koufopoulos family, Pension Sofi is in Naxos Town, while their **Studios Panos** (☎22850 26078; www.studiospanos.com; Agios Georgios Beach; r €30-60; ❄) is a 10-minute walk away near Agios Georgios Beach. Prepare yourself to be showered with affection. Guests are met with a glass of family-made wine, and rooms are immaculate with bathroom and kitchen. Highly recommended; rates

KETI VALLINDROS: KITRON-MAKER

Keti lives and works in Halki, 16km east of Naxos Town, and is a 5th-generation maker of Kitron, a liqueur unique to Naxos that is usually consumed cold after meals. The fruit of the citron (Citrus Medica) may be barely edible in its raw state, but when the leaves are boiled with pure alcohol, the result is a tasty concoction that has been keeping Naxians happy since Keti's great-great grandfather came up with it in the 1870s. While the exact recipe is top secret, Keti is keen to see visitors enjoy her family's Kitron as much as Naxians do. She and her extended family run tours and tasting at **Vallindras Distillery** (☎22850 31220; ⊙10am-11pm Jul-Aug 10am-6pm May-Jun & Sep-Oct) in Halki's main square. They have a **Kitron Museum** (entry free) that has ancient jars and copper stills, complimentary **tastings**, and a **shop** selling the distillery's products. If you can't get enough of the stuff, there's good news, because the family also runs the **Kitron Bar and Café** on the Naxos Town waterfront.

at both places halve out of the high season. Call ahead for a pick-up at the port. Sofi is open year-round; Panos opens from April to October.

Hotel Grotta HOTEL €€
(☎22850 22215; www.hotelgrotta.gr; s/d incl breakfast €70/85; P❋@🛜🏊) Overlooking Grotta Beach at the northern end of town, this modern hotel has comfortable and immaculate rooms, a Jacuzzi and minipool, and offers great sea views. Service is friendly and internet use, including wi-fi, is free.

Camping Maragas CAMPING GROUND €
(☎22850 42552; www.maragascamping.gr; campsites €9, d €45, studio €70) On Agia Anna Beach to the south of town, this place has all sorts of options, including camping, rooms and studios, and there is a restaurant and mini-market on site.

🍴 Eating & Drinking

Naxos Town's waterfront is lined with eating and drinking establishments. Head into Market St in the Old Town, just down from the ferry quay, to find quality tavernas. South of the waterfront, but only a few minutes' walk away, Main Sq is home to plenty of excellent eateries.

Metaximas TAVERNA €
(Market St) Serving seafood at its best.

Picasso Mexican Bistro TEX-MEX €
(Agiou Arseniou) Dine on superlative Tex-Mex; near Main Sq.

East West Asian Restaurant ASIAN €
(Odos Komiakis) All your Thai, Chinese and Indian favourites; near Main Sq.

Venetico TAVERNA €
(Apollonas) If you're exploring, every village on the island has a taverna. This one,

on the waterfront at Apollonas, near the northern tip of Naxos, is a great option.

ℹ️ Information

There's no official tourist information office. Try the website www.naxos-greece.net for more information.

Naxos Tourist Information Centre (NTIC; ☎22850 25201; ⊙8am-midnight) This privately owned organisation just opposite the port offers help with accommodation, tours, luggage storage and laundry.

Zas Travel (☎22850 23330; www.zas-travel-naxos.gr; ⊙8am-midnight) Sells ferry tickets.

ℹ️ Getting There & Around

AIR Naxos airport (JNX) has daily flight connections with Athens. The airport is 3km south of town; no buses – a taxi costs €15.

BOAT There are daily ferries (€30, five hours) and catamarans (€45, 3¾ hours) from Naxos to Piraeus, and good ferry and hydrofoil connections to most Cycladic islands and Crete. There are also ferries to Rhodes (€32, 14 hours, twice weekly).

BUS Buses travel to most villages regularly from the bus terminal in front of the port.

CAR & MOTORCYCLE Car and motorcycle rentals are readily available.

Ios ΙΟΣ

POP 1900

Ios has long held a reputation as 'Party Island'. There are wall-to-wall bars and nightclubs in 'the village' (Hora) that thump all night, and fantastic fun facilities at Milopotas Beach that entertain all day. You won't leave disappointed if you're there to party.

But there's more to Ios than just hedonistic activities. British poet and novelist Lawrence Durrell thought highly of Ios as a place of poetry and beauty, and there is an enduring claim that Homer was buried here, with his alleged tomb in the north of the island.

Ios' three population centres are close together on the west coast. Ormos is the port, where ferries arrive. Two kilometres inland and up overlooking the port is 'the village', Hora, while 2km down from Hora to the southeast is Milopotas Beach.

Sights & Activities

The village has an intrinsic charm with its labyrinth of white-walled streets, and it's very easy to get lost, even if you haven't had one too many. Milopotas has everything a resort beach could ask for and parties hard. More and more roads are being upgraded on the island, and a rental car or scooter is becoming a good option for exploring Ios.

Skarkos
ARCHAEOLOGICAL SITE

('The Snail'; admission free; ⊙8.30am-3pm Tue-Sun) This new attraction is also an award-winning archaeological triumph for Ios. This Bronze Age settlement crowns a low hill in the plain just to the north of Hora, and its excavations have been opened to the public.

Manganari Beach
BEACH

This isolated beach on the south coast is reached by rental vehicle, or by excursion boat or bus in summer. It's a beautiful spot and the drive on Ios' newest sealed road is an experience in itself.

Homer's Tomb
TOMB

You'll need your own wheels to get here, 12km north of Hora.

Meltemi Water Sports
WATER SPORTS

(☎22860 91680; www.meltemiwatersports. com) This outfit at Milopotas Beach's far end has rental windsurfers, sailboats and canoes.

Ios

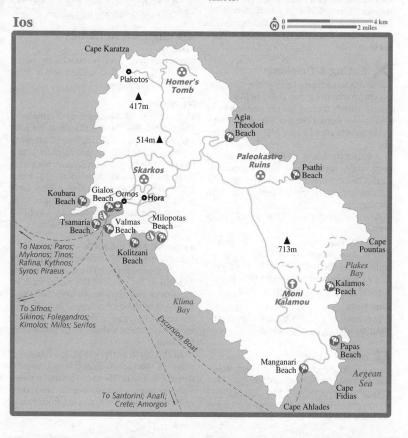

🛏 Sleeping

TOP **Francesco's** ROOMS €
CHOICE
(☎22860 91223; www.francescos.net;
Hora; dm/s/d €15/40/50; ❄@) A lively meeting
place in the village with superlative views
from its terrace bar, legendary Francesco's is
convenient for party-going, and rates halve
out of high season. The party spirit rules
here, especially in the new 'giant Jacuzzi'.

Far Out Camping & Beach Club
CAMPING GROUND €
(☎22860 91468; www.faroutclub.com; Milopotas;
campsites per person €12, bungalows €10-20, studios €90; @❄) Right on Milopotas Beach,
this place has tons of options. Facilities include camping, bungalows and hotel rooms,
and its pools are open to the public. Details
are on the website. It also has rental cars,
quad bikes and scooters.

Hotel Nissos Ios HOTEL €€
(☎22860 91610; www.nissosios-hotel.com;
Milopotas; s/d/tr €50/70/85; ❄@) This cheerful place is on Milopotas Beach. Rooms
feature huge colourful wall murals, and
the excellent **Bamboo Restaurant & Pizzeria** on site.

🍴 Eating & Drinking

There are numerous places in the village to
get cheap eats like gyros. Down at Milopotas
Beach, there's a great bakery and stacks of
options for during the day. The restaurants
in the village are of a very high standard for
later.

Another option is to head down to the
port, where the tavernas serve superb seafood. The port may be filled with visitors in
the day, but it's the locals who head there in
the evening.

At night, the compact little village erupts
with bars.

TOP **Pithari** GREEK €
CHOICE
(Hora; mains from €8) Behind the
cathedral at the entrance to the Hora, offers an excellent array of tasty dishes; the
seafood spaghetti is especially good.

Blue Note BAR
A perennial village favourite, where Happy
Hour continues all night long!

ℹ Information

There's no tourist office. See the website www.
iosgreece.com for more information.

Acteon Travel (☎22860 91343; www.acteon.
gr) has offices in Ormos, the village and Milopotas and is helpful.

ℹ Getting There & Around

BOAT Ios has daily ferry connections with Piraeus (€31.50, seven hours), and being strategically placed between Mykonos and Santorini,
there are frequent catamarans and ferries to
the major Cycladic islands and Crete.

BUS There are buses every 15 minutes between the port, the village and Milopotas Beach
until early morning. Buses head to Manganari
Beach in summer (€3 each way).

Santorini (Thira)
ΣΑΝΤΟΡΙΝΗ (ΘΗΡΑ)

POP 13,500

Stunning Santorini is unique and should
not be missed. The startling sight of the submerged caldera almost encircled by sheer
lava-layered cliffs – topped off by clifftop
towns that look like a dusting of icing sugar –
will grab your attention and not let it go. If
you turn up in high season, though, be prepared for relentless crowds and commercialism – Santorini survives on tourism.

⊙ Sights & Activities

FIRA

Santorini's main town perches on top of the
caldera; the stunning caldera views from
Fira are unparalleled.

Museums

The exceptional **Museum of Prehistoric
Thira** (admission €3; ⊙8.30am-8pm Tue-Sun),
which has wonderful displays of artefacts
predominantly from ancient Akrotiri, is two
blocks south of the main square. **Megaron
Gyzi Museum** (admission €3.50; ⊙10.30am-
1pm & 5-8pm Mon-Sat, 10.30am-4.30pm Sun),
behind the Catholic cathedral, houses local
memorabilia, including photographs of Fira
before and after the 1956 earthquake.

AROUND THE ISLAND

Excavations in 1967 uncovered the remarkably well-preserved Minoan settlement of
Akrotiri at the south of the island, with its
remains of two- and three-storey buildings.
A section of the roof collapsed in 2005, killing one visitor, and at the time of research,
the site's future as a visitor attraction was up
in the air.

At the north of the island, the intriguing
village of **Oia** (ee-ah), famed for its postcard
sunsets, is less hectic than Fira and a must-
visit. Its caldera-facing tavernas are superb
spots for brunch. There's a path from Fira to

Oia along the top of the caldera that takes three to four hours to walk.

Santorini's black-sand **beaches** of **Perissa** and **Kamari** sizzle – beach mats are essential.

Of the surrounding islets, only **Thirasia** is inhabited. Visitors can clamber around on volcanic lava on **Nea Kameni** then swim into warm springs in the sea at **Palia Kameni**; there are various excursions available to get you there.

TOP CHOICE Santo Wines (☎22860 22596; www.santowines.gr; Pyrgos) is a great spot to try the delectable Assyrtico crisp dry white wine while savouring unbelievable views. Santorini is home to an increasing number of excellent wineries.

🛏 Sleeping

Hotel Keti　　　　TRADITIONAL HOTEL €€
(☎22860 22324; www.hotelketi.gr; Agiou Mina, Fira; d/tr €95/120; ❉@) Overlooking the caldera, with views to die for, Hotel Keti has traditional rooms carved into the cliffs. Some rooms have Jacuzzis. Head down just before Hotel Atlantis and follow the signs.

Hotel Atlantis　　　　HOTEL €€€
(☎22860 22232; www.atlantishotel.gr; Fira; s/d incl breakfast €200/300; ᴘ❉@☎) Perfectly

Santorini (Thira)

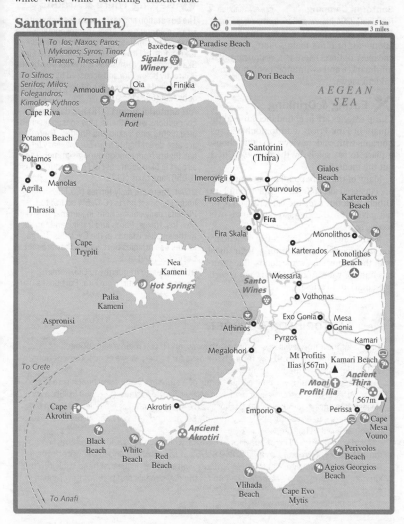

positioned and epitomising Santorini style, Atlantis is the oldest and most impressive place in Fira. With bright, airy rooms, swimming pool, relaxing terraces and lounges, it is a superb place to stay.

Pension Petros
PENSION €

(☎22860 22573; www.hotelpetros-santorini.gr; Fira; s/d/tr €60/70/85; ❋) Three hundred metres east of the square, Petros offers decent rooms at good rates, free airport and port transfers, but no caldera views. It's a good budget option, with rates halving outside high season. The friendly family also has other hotels.

Santorini Camping
CAMPING GROUND €

(☎22860 22944; www.santorinicamping.gr; Fira; campsites per person €9; P @ ❋) This place, 500m east of Fira's main square, is the cheapest option. There is a restaurant, bar, minimarket and swimming pool, but no caldera views.

Eating & Drinking

Cheap eateries are in abundance around the square in Fira. Prices tend to double at restaurants with caldera views, so don't choose a place to eat solely by the outlook. Check out the menu first.

Many of the more popular bars and clubs are clustered along Erythrou Stavrou in Fira. Others look out over the caldera; you're often paying for the view, so don't glaze over too early.

Many diners head out to Oia, legendary for its superb sunsets, timing their meal with the setting sun, while good-value tavernas line the waterfronts at the beach resorts of Kamari and Perissa.

Fanari
GREEK €

(☎22860 25107; www.fanari-restaurant.gr) On the street leading down to the old port, serves up both tasty traditional dishes and superlative views.

❶ Information

There is no tourist office. Try the website www.santorini.net for more information.

Dakoutros Travel (☎22860 22958; www.dakoutrostravel.gr; ⏱8.30am-10pm) Opposite the taxi station in Fira; extremely helpful and good for ticketing.

❶ Getting There & Around

The bus station and taxi station are just south of Fira's main square, Plateia Theotokopoulou. The new port of Athinios, where most ferries dock, is 10km south of Fira by road. The old port of Fira Skala, used by cruise ships and excursion boats, is directly below Fira and accessed by cable car (adult/child €4/2 one way), donkey (€5, up only) or by foot (588 steps)

AIR **Santorini airport** (JTR) has daily flight connections with Athens, plus seasonal scheduled flights with Iraklio and Rhodes. There are also direct flights from Europe; easyJet has flights from London during summer. The airport is 5km southeast of Fira; frequent buses (€1.50) and taxis (€12).

BOAT There are daily ferries (€33.50, nine hours) and fast boats (€47, 5¼ hours) to Piraeus; daily connections in summer to Mykonos, Ios, Naxos, Paros and Iraklio; and ferries to the smaller islands in the Cyclades. Large ferries use Athinios port, where they are met by buses (€2) and taxis.

BUS Buses go frequently to Oia, Kamari, Perissa and Akrotiri from Fira. Port buses usu-

---

❶ **SANTORINI ON A BUDGET**

Spectacular Santorini will take your breath away, and if you're on a tight budget, its prices might too. Expect to pay through the nose for caldera views at accommodation and eating establishments in and around Fira.

A budget alternative with the added bonus of a stunning black-sand beach is to head out to Perissa, on the southeast coast, and stay at **Stelios Place** (☎22860 81860; www.steliosplace.com; r €30-80; P ❋ ❋). Stelios is an excellent option one block back from the beach. There's a refreshing pool, very friendly service and free port and airport transfers. Rates halve out of high season.

All of your needs will be catered for in Perissa, which has bars and restaurants lining the waterfront. **Taverna Lava** (☎22860 81776), at the southern end of the waterfront, is an island-wide favourite that features a mouth-watering menu. Or just head back into the kitchen, see what Yiannis has conjured up for the day's meals and pick whatever looks good.

Public buses run regularly into Fira.

ally leave Fira, Kamari and Perissa one to 1½ hours before ferry departures.

CAR & MOTORCYCLE A rental car or scooter is a great option on Santorini.

CRETE ΚΡΗΤΗ

POP 540,000

Crete is Greece's largest and most southerly island and its size and distance from the rest of Greece give it the feel of a different country. With its dramatic landscape and unique cultural identity, Crete is a delight to explore.

The island is split by a spectacular chain of mountains running east to west. Major towns are on the more hospitable northern coast, while most of the southern coast is too precipitous to support large settlements. The rugged mountainous interior, dotted with caves and sliced by dramatic gorges, offers rigorous hiking and climbing.

While Crete's proud, friendly and hospitable people have enthusiastically embraced tourism, they continue to fiercely protect their traditions and culture – and it is the people that remain a major part of the island's appeal.

For more detailed information, snap up a copy of Lonely Planet's *Crete*. Good websites on Crete include www.interkriti.org, www.infocrete.com and www.explorecrete.com.

History

Crete was the birthplace of Minoan culture, Europe's first advanced civilisation, which flourished between 2800 and 1450 BC. Very little is known of Minoan civilisation, which came to an abrupt end, possibly destroyed by Santorini's volcanic eruption in around 1650 BC. Later, Crete passed from the warlike Dorians to the Romans, and then to the Genoese, who in turn sold it to the Venetians. Under the Venetians, Crete became a refuge for artists, writers and philosophers, who fled after it fell to the Turks. Their influence inspired the young Cretan painter Domenikos Theotokopoulos, who moved to Spain and there won immortality as the great El Greco.

The Turks conquered Crete in 1670. In 1898 Crete became a British protectorate after a series of insurrections and was united with independent Greece in 1913. There was fierce fighting during WWII when a German airborne invasion defeated Allied forces in the 10-day Battle of Crete. A fierce resistance movement drew heavy German reprisals, including the slaughter of whole villages.

Iraklio ΗΡΑΚΛΕΙΟ

POP 131,000

Iraklio (ee-*rah*-klee-oh; often spelt Heraklion), Crete's capital, is a bustling modern city and the fifth-largest in Greece. It has a lively city centre, an excellent archaeological museum and is close to Knossos, Crete's major visitor attraction.

Iraklio's harbours face north into the Sea of Crete. The old harbour is instantly recognisable as it is protected by the old Venetian fortress. The new harbour is 400m east. Plateia Venizelou, known for its Lion Fountain, is the heart of the city, 400m south of the old harbour up 25 Avgoustou.

◉ Sights

Archaeological Museum   MUSEUM
(Map p416; Xanthoudidou 2; adult/student €6/3; ◷8am-1pm Mon, 8am-8pm Tue-Sun) The outstanding Minoan collection here is second only to that of the national museum in Athens. The museum was under long-term reconstruction at the time of research.

Koules Venetian Fortress   FORTRESS
(Map p416; admission €2; ◷9am-6pm Tue-Sun) Protecting the old harbour, this impressive fortress is also known as Rocca al Mare, which, like the city walls, was built by the Venetians in the 16th century.

Battle of Crete Museum   MUSEUM
(Map p416; cnr Doukos Beaufort & Hatzidaki; admission free; ◷8am-3pm) Chronicles the historic WWII battle with photographs, letters, uniforms and weapons.

⌂ Sleeping

TOP CHOICE **Lato Boutique Hotel**
BOUTIQUE HOTEL €€
(Map p416; ☎28102 28103; www.lato.gr; Epimenidou 15; s/d €100/127; ❋@) This stylish boutique hotel overlooking the waterfront is a top place to stay. Ask for a room with harbour views. The contemporary interior design extends to the bar, breakfast restaurant and **Brilliant** (☎28103 34959), the superb fine-dining restaurant on the ground floor.

Hotel Mirabello   HOTEL €
(Map p416; ☎28102 85052; www.mirabello-hotel.gr; Theotokopoulou 20; s/d €35/45; ❋@) A pleasant, relaxed budget hotel on a quiet street in the centre of town, this place is run by an

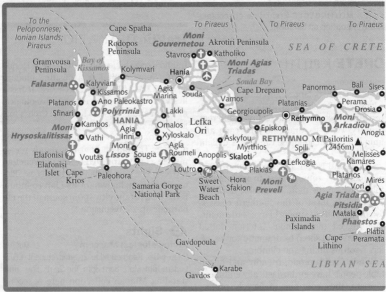

ex-sea captain who has travelled the world. A good-value option. Check out the excellent website.

Rent Rooms Hellas ROOMS €
(Map p416; ☎28102 88851; Handakos 24; dm/d/ tr without bathroom €12/30/42) A popular budget choice, this place has a lively atmosphere, packed dorms, a rooftop bar and a bargain breakfast (from €3).

Eating & Drinking

There's a congregation of cheap eateries, bars and cafes in the Plateia Venizelou (Morosini Fountain) and El Greco Park area. The places around the park are packed at night. A bustling, colourful market runs all the way along 1866, with a number of reasonably priced tavernas. Head down towards the old harbour for plenty of seafood options.

Giakoumis Taverna TAVERNA €
(Map p416) One of the best, offering up Cretan specialities hot off the grill.

Ippokambos Ouzerie SEAFOOD €
(Map p416) A local favourite that attracts crowds of seafood lovers.

Café Plus BAR
(Map p416) At the nexus of the pedestrianised zones, this place overflows with locals, especially in the early evening.

ℹ️ Information

TOURIST INFORMATION Tourist office
(Map p416; ☎28102 46299; Xanthoudidou 1; ⊙8.30am-8.30pm Apr-Oct, to 3pm Nov-Mar) Opposite the Archaeological Museum.

TRAVEL AGENCIES Skoutelis Travel
(☎28102 80808; www.skoutelis.gr; 25 Avgoustou 20) Between Plateia Venizelou and the old harbour; handles airline and ferry bookings, and rents cars.

WEBSITES www.heraklion-city.gr

ℹ️ Getting There & Around

AIR There are many flights departing daily from Iraklio's **Nikos Kazantzakis airport** (HER) for Athens and, in summer, regular flights to Thessaloniki and Rhodes. easyJet has scheduled flights to seven destinations across Europe. Summer sees even more charter flights arrive from all over. The airport is 5km east of town. Bus 1 travels between the airport and city centre (Map p416; €1.20) every 15 minutes from 6am to 1am. It stops at Plateia Eleftherias, across the road from the Archaeological Museum.

BOAT Daily ferries service Piraeus (€37, seven hours), and catamarans head daily to Santorini and continue on to other Cycladic islands. Twice weekly, ferries sail east to Rhodes (€28, 12 hours) via Agios Nikolaos, Sitia, Kassos, Karpathos and Halki.

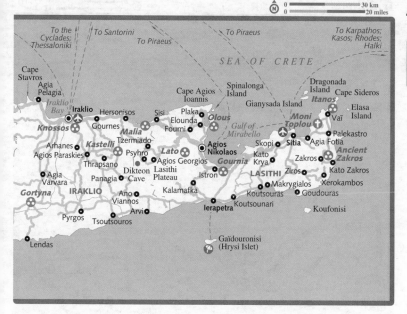

BUS **KTEL** (www.ktel.org) Runs the buses on Crete; has useful tourist information inside Bus Station A.

Iraklio has two bus stations. The main **Bus Station A** (Map p416) is just inland from the new harbour and serves eastern Crete (Agios Nikolaos, Ierapetra, Sitia, Malia and the Lasithi Plateau), as well as Hania and Rethymno.

Bus Station B (off Map p416), 50m beyond the Hania Gate, serves the southern route (Phaestos, Matala and Anogia).

Check out www.ktel.org for long-distance bus information.

Knossos ΚΝΩΣΣΟΣ

Five kilometres south of Iraklio, **Knossos** (☏28102 31940; admission €6; ☉8am-7pm Jun-Oct, to 3pm Nov-May) was the capital of Minoan Crete, and is now the island's major tourist attraction.

Knossos (k-nos-os) is the most famous of Crete's Minoan sites and is the inspiration for the myth of the Minotaur. According to legend, King Minos of Knossos was given a magnificent white bull to sacrifice to the god Poseidon, but decided to keep it. This enraged Poseidon, who punished the king by causing his wife Pasiphae to fall in love with the animal. The result of this odd union was

the Minotaur – half-man and half-bull – who lived in a labyrinth beneath the king's palace, munching on youths and maidens.

In 1900 Arthur Evans uncovered the ruins of Knossos. Although archaeologists tend to disparage Evans' reconstruction, the buildings – incorporating an immense palace, courtyards, private apartments, baths, lively frescos and more – give a fine idea of what a Minoan palace might have looked like.

Buses to Knossos (€1.30, three per hour; 20min) leave from Bus Station A.

Phaestos & Other Minoan Sites ΦΑΙΣΤΟΣ

Phaestos (☏29820 42315; admission €6; ☉8am-7pm May-Oct, to 5pm Nov-Apr), 63km southwest of Iraklio, is Crete's second-most important Minoan site. While not as impressive as Knossos, Phaestos (fes-tos) is still worth a visit for its stunning views of the surrounding Mesara plain and Mt Psiloritis (2456m; also known as Mt Ida). The layout is similar to Knossos, with rooms arranged around a central courtyard. Eight buses a day head to Phaestos from Iraklio's Bus Station B (€5.90, 1½ hours).

Other important Minoan sites can be found at **Malia**, 34km east of Iraklio, where

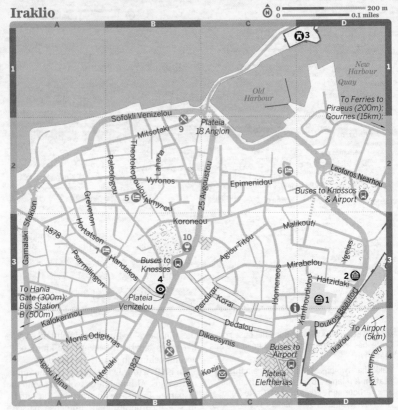

there's a palace complex and adjoining town, and **Zakros**, 40km southeast of Sitia, the last Minoan palace to have been discovered, in 1962.

Rethymno ΡΕΘΥΜΝΟ

POP 28,000

Rethymno (*reth*-im-no) is Crete's third-largest town. It's also one of the island's architectural treasures, due to its stunning fortress and mix of Venetian and Turkish houses in the old quarter. A compact town, most spots of interest are within a small area around the old Venetian harbour.

The old quarter is on a peninsula that juts out into the Sea of Crete; the fortress sits at its head, while the Venetian harbour, ferry quay and beach are on its eastern side. El Venizelou is the main strip along the waterfront and beach. Running parallel behind it is Arkadiou, the main commercial street.

Rethymno's 16th-century **Venetian fortezza** (fortress; Paleokastro Hill; admission €3; ⊙8am-8pm May-Oct) is the site of the city's ancient acropolis and affords great views across the town and mountains. The main gate is on the eastern side of the fortress, opposite the interesting **archaeological museum** (☎28310 54668; admission €3; ⊙8.30am-3pm Tue-Sun), which was once a prison.

Happy Walker (☎28310 52920; www.happy walker.com; Tombazi 56) runs an excellent program of daily walks in the countryside and also longer walking tours.

Sea Front (☎28310 51981; www.rethym noatcrete.com; Arkadiou 159; d €35-50; ❉) has all sorts of sleeping options and is ideally positioned with beach views and spacious rooms. **Hotel Fortezza** (☎28310 55551; www.fortezza.gr; Melissinou 16; s/d incl breakfast €70/85; P❉☰) is more upmarket; with a refreshing pool, it's in a refurbished old building in the heart of the Old Town. **Rethymno**

Iraklio

⊙ Sights
1 Archaeological Museum D3
2 Battle of Crete Museum......................D3
3 Koules Venetian Fortress D1
4 Lion Fountain B3

🛌 Sleeping
5 Hotel Mirabello.....................................B2
6 Lato Boutique Hotel C2
7 Rent Rooms Hellas A3

✖ Eating
Brilliant .... (see 6)
8 Giakoumis Taverna B4
9 Ippokambos Ouzeri............................B2

🍷 Drinking
10 Café Plus B3

Youth Hostel (☎28310 22848; www.yhrethym no.com; Tombazi 41; dm €10) is a well-run place with crowded dorms, free hot showers and no curfew.

The **municipal tourist office** (☎28310 29148; www.rethymno.gr; Eleftheriou Venizelou; ⊘9am-8.30pm), on the beach side of El Venizelou, is convenient and helpful. **Ellotia Tours** (☎28310 24533; www.rethymnoatcrete. com; Arkadiou 155) will answer all transport, accommodation and tour inquiries.

There are regular ferries between Piraeus and Rethymno (€30, nine hours), and a high-speed service in summer. Buses depart regularly to Iraklio (€6.5, 1½ hours) and Hania (€6, one hour).

Hania XANIA

POP 53,500

Crete's most romantic, evocative and alluring town, Hania (hahn-*yah*; often spelt Chania) is the former capital and the island's second-largest city. There is a rich mosaic of Venetian and Ottoman architecture, particularly in the area of the old harbour, which lures tourists in droves. Modern Hania retains the exoticism of a city caught between East and West, and is an excellent base for exploring nearby idyllic beaches and a spectacular mountainous interior.

⊙ Sights & Activities

Old Harbour   HISTORIC DISTRICT
From Plateia 1866, the old harbour is a short walk down Halidon. A stroll around here is a must for any visitor to Hania. It is worth the 1.5km walk around the sea wall to get to the Venetian **lighthouse** (Map p418) at the entrance to the harbour.

Archaeological Museum   MUSEUM
(Map p418; Halidon 30; admission €2; ⊘8.30am-3pm Tue-Sun) The museum is housed in a 16th-century Venetian church that the Turks made into a mosque. The building became a movie theatre in 1913 and then was a munitions depot for the Germans during WWII.

Food Market   MARKET
(Map p418) Hania's covered food market, in a massive cross-shaped building, is definitely worth an inspection.

🛌 Sleeping

TOP CHOICE **Pension Lena**   PENSION €
(Map p418; ☎28210 86860; www.lena chania.gr; Ritsou 5; s/d €35/55; ❄) For some real character in where you stay, Lena's pension in an old Turkish building near the mouth of the old harbour is the place to go. Help yourself to one of the appealing rooms if proprietor Lena isn't there – pick from the available ones on the list on the blackboard.

Amphora Hotel   HOTEL €€
(Map p418; ☎28210 93224; www.amphora.gr; Parodos Theotokopoulou 20; s/d €95/110; ❄) Most easily found from the waterfront, this is Hania's most historically evocative hotel. Amphora is in an impressively restored Venetian mansion with elegantly decorated rooms around a courtyard. The hotel also runs the **waterfront restaurant**, which ranks as the best along that golden mile.

Camping Hania   CAMPING GROUND €
(off Map p418; ☎28210 31138; campsites per tent/ person €4/5; P❄) Take the Kalamaki Beach bus from the east corner of Plateia 1866 (every 15 minutes) to get to this camping ground, which is 3km west of town on the beach. There is a restaurant, bar and mini-market.

✖ Eating & Drinking

The entire waterfront of the old harbour is lined with restaurants and tavernas, many of which qualify as tourist traps. Watch out for touts trying to reel you in. There are a number of good options one street back.

Taverna Tamam   TAVERNA €€
(Map p418; ☎28210 58639; Zambeliou 49; ✎) A taverna in an old converted Turkish bathhouse, with tables that spill out onto the

GREECE CRETE

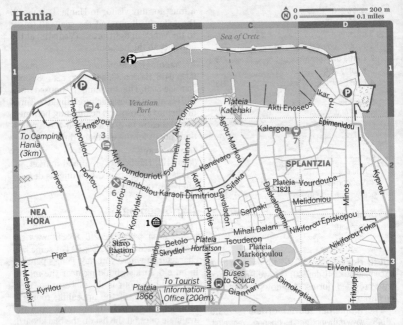

Hania

⊙ Sights
1 Archaeological Museum	B3
Food Market	(see 5)
2 Lighthouse	B1

⊜ Sleeping
3 Amphora Hotel	A2
4 Pension Lena	A1

⊗ Eating
Amphora	(see 3)
5 Food Market	C3
Michelas	(see 5)
6 Taverna Tamam	B2

⊙ Drinking
7 Café Kriti	C2

street. This place has tasty soups and a superb selection of vegetarian specialities.

TOP CHOICE Michelas CRETAN €
(Map p418; ☑28210 90026; ⊙10am-4pm Mon-Sat) Has authentic Cretan specialities at reasonable prices. This family-run place uses only Cretan ingredients and cooks up a great selection each day that you can peruse, then choose from.

Café Kriti BAR
(Map p418; Kalergon 22; ⊙8pm-late) Near the eastern end of the Venetian harbour, this place is known for its down-to-earth atmosphere and live traditional Cretan music.

ⓘ Information

TOURIST INFORMATION Tourist information office (off Map p418; ☑28210 36155; Kydonias 29; ⊙8am-2.30pm) Under the Town Hall; is helpful and provides practical information and maps.

TRAVEL AGENCIES Tellus Travel (☑28210 91500; www.tellustravel.gr; Halidon 108; ⊙8am-11pm) Schedules and ticketing; rents out cars.

WEBSITES www.chania.gr

ⓘ Getting There & Away

AIR There are several flights a day between **Hania airport** (CHQ) and Athens and five flights a week to Thessaloniki. An increasing number of budget airlines are flying directly into Hania; easyJet has flights from London. The airport is 14km east of town on the Akrotiri Peninsula. Taxis to town cost €15; there are few buses.

BOAT Daily ferries sail between Piraeus (€30, nine hours) and the port of Souda, 9km southeast of Hania. There are also increasing numbers of faster boats. Frequent buses (Map p418; €1.30) and taxis (€10) connect town and Souda.

BUS Frequent buses run along Crete's northern coast to Iraklio (€11, 2¾ hours, half-hourly), Rethymno (€6, one hour, half hourly) and Kastelli-Kissamos (€4, one hour, 14 daily); buses run less frequently to Paleohora (€6.50, one hour 50 minutes, four daily), Omalos (€5.90, one hour, three daily) and Hora Sfakion (€6.50, 1½ hours, three daily) from the main bus station on Kydonias.

Hania's bus station is on Kydonias, two blocks southwest of Plateia 1866, one of the city's main squares. Buses for the beaches west of Hania leave from the eastern side of Plateia 1866.

Samaria Gorge ΦΑΡΑΓΓΙ ΤΗΣ ΣΑΜΑΡΙΑΣ

The **Samaria Gorge** (☏28250 67179; admission €5; ☉6am-3pm May–mid-Oct) is one of Europe's most spectacular gorges and a superb hike. Walkers should take rugged footwear, food, drinks and sun protection for this strenuous five- to six-hour trek.

You can do the walk as part of an excursion tour, or independently by taking the Omalos bus from the main bus station in Hania (€5.90, one hour) to the head of the gorge at Xyloskalo (1230m) at 7.30am, 8.30am and 2pm. It's a 16.7km walk out (all downhill) to Agia Roumeli on the coast, from where you take a boat to Hora Sfakion (€8, 1¼ hours, three daily) and then a bus back to Hania (€6.50, 1½ hours, three daily). You are not allowed to spend the night in

the gorge, so you need to complete the walk in a day.

Paleohora & the Southwest Coast ΠΑΛΑΙΟΧΩΡΑ

POP 2200

Paleohora (pal-ee-o-*hor*-a) has a sleepy end-of-the-line feel about it. Isolated and a bit hard to get to, the village is on a peninsula with a sandy beach to the west and a pebbly beach to the east. On summer evenings the main street is closed to traffic and the tavernas move onto the road. If you're after a relaxing few days, Paleohora is a great spot to chill out.

Heading south from the bus stop, you'll find the main street, which is called Eleftheriou Venizelou.

The ruins of the 13th-century **Venetian castle** are worth clambering over, although there's not much left after the fortress was destroyed by the Turks, the pirate Barbarossa in the 16th-century and then the Germans during WWII.

Homestay Anonymous (☏28230 41509; www.cityofpaleochora.gr/cp; s/d/tr €23/28/32; ☀) is a great option with its warm service and communal kitchen. Across the road from the sandy beach, the refurbished **Poseidon Hotel** (☏28230 41374; www.interkriti.net/hotel/paleohora/poseidon; s/d/apt €35/40/50; ☀@) has a mix of tidy double rooms, studios and apartments. **Camping Paleohora** (☏28230 41120; campsites per tent/person €3/5) is 1.5km

BEAT THE CROWDS AT SAMARIA

The Samaria Gorge walk is extremely popular and can get quite crowded, especially in summer. Most walkers have given the gorge a day and are on a rushed trip from Hania and other northern-coast cities.

If you've got a bit of time on your hands, and decide to do things on your own, there are a couple of excellent options.

One is to take the 2pm bus from Hania and spend the night in the Cretan mountains at 1200m above sea level in **Omalos** (population 30) at the very pleasant **Neos Omalos Hotel** (☏28210 67269; www.neos-omalos.gr; s/d €20/30). The hotel's restaurant serves excellent Cretan cuisine and local wine by the litre (€6); there's a shuttle to the start of the gorge track the next morning. Keen hikers may want to stay here a couple of nights and tackle Mt Gingilos (2080m; five hours return from Xyloskalo) before hiking the gorge.

Another option is to leave from Hania in the morning, but let the sprinters go and take your time hiking through this stupendous gorge. When you hit the coast at **Agia Roumeli** (population 125), down a cool beer, take a dip in the refreshing Libyan Sea, savour the tasty Cretan specials at **Faragi Restaurant & Rooms** (☏28250 91225; s/d/tr €20/30/35; ☀) and stay the night in the tidy rooms above the restaurant. The next day you can take a ferry either west to Sougia or Paleohora, or east to Loutro or Hora Sfakion.

northeast of town, near the pebble beach. There's a taverna but no minimarket here.

There are plenty of eating options on the main street. Vegetarians rave about **Third Eye** (mains from €5; 🖉), just inland from the sandy beach. Specialities include a tempting range of Greek-Asian fusion dishes.

There's a welcoming **tourist office** (🖉28230 41507; ⊙10am-1pm & 6-9pm Wed-Mon May-Oct) on the pebble beach road near the harbour and ferry quay. The opening hours listed here are indicative only! Back on the main street, **Notos Rentals/Tsiskakis Travel** (🖉28230 42110; www.notoscar.com; ⊙8am-10pm) handles almost everything, including tickets, rental cars/scooters and internet access.

There are six buses daily between Hania and Paleohora (€6.50, two hours). A bus for Samaria Gorge hikers leaves for Omalos (€5.50, two hours) each morning at 6.15am.

Further east along Crete's southwest coast are **Sougia**, **Agia Roumeli** (at the mouth of the Samaria Gorge), **Loutro** and **Hora Sfakion**. No road links the coastal resorts, but a daily boat from Paleohora to Sougia (€7.50, one hour), Agia Roumeli (€11, 1½ hours), Loutro (€13, 2½ hours) and Hora Sfakion (€14, three hours) connects the villages in summer. The ferry leaves Paleohora at 9.45am and returns from Hora Sfakion at 1pm. It's also possible to walk right along this southern coast.

WORTH A TRIP

LOUTRO

The tiny village of **Loutro** (population 90) is a particularly picturesque spot, curled around the only natural harbour on the southern coast of Crete. It's a great place for a break. With no vehicle access, the only way in is by boat or on foot. Ferries drop in daily from Hora Sfakion to the east, and from Paleohora, Sougia and Agia Roumeli to the west.

Hotel Porto Loutro (🖉28250 91433; www.hotelportoloutro.com; s/d/tr incl breakfast €45/55/65; ❄) has tasteful rooms with balconies overlooking the harbour. The village beach, excellent walks, rental kayaks, and boat transfers to Sweetwater Beach will help to fill in a peaceful few days. Take a book and chill out.

Lasithi Plateau ΟΡΟΠΕΔΙΟ ΛΑΣΙΘΙΟΥ

The impressive mountain-fringed Lasithi Plateau in eastern Crete is laid out like an immense patchwork quilt. At 900m above sea level, it is a vast flat expanse of orchards and fields, once dotted with thousands of stone windmills with white canvas sails. There are still plenty of windmills, but most are now of the rusted metal variety and don't work.

There are 20 villages around the periphery of the plain, the largest being **Tzermiado** (population 750), **Agios Georgios** (population 550) and **Psyhro** (population 210).

The **Dikteon Cave** (🖉28440 31316; admission €4; ⊙8am-6pm) is where, according to mythology, Rhea hid the newborn Zeus from Cronos, his offspring-gobbling father. The cave, which covers 2200 sq metres and features numerous stalactites and stalagmites, is 1km from the village of Psyhro.

There are daily buses to the area from Iraklio (€5, two hours), though having your own wheels would make life a lot easier.

Agios Nikolaos ΑΓΙΟΣ ΝΙΚΟΛΑΟΣ

POP 11,000

Agios Nikolaos (ah-yee-os nih-ko-laos) is an attractive former fishing village on Crete's northeast coast. The de facto town centre is around the picturesque **Voulismeni Lake**, which is ringed with cafes and tavernas, and is linked to the sea by a short canal. The ferry port is 150m past the canal.

The two nice little beaches in town, **Kytroplatia** and **Ammos**, get a bit crowded in summer. **Almyros Beach**, about 1km south, gets less so. Agios Nikolaos acts as a base for excursion tours to **Spinalonga Island**. The island's massive fortress was built by the Venetians in 1579 but taken by the Turks in 1715. It later became a leper colony. Nowadays it's a fascinating place to explore. Tours cost around €25.

Pergola Hotel (🖉28410 28152; Sarolidi 20; s/d €35-40; ❄) is a friendly family-run place out near the ferry port, with clean rooms, balconies and sea views. **Du Lac Hotel** (🖉28410 22711; www.dulachotel.gr; Oktovriou 17; s/d €40/60) is a refurbished hotel in a great location with views out over the lake.

Finding a place to eat will not be a problem. **Taverna Itanos** (🖉28410 25340; Kyprou 1;

mains €4-10), tucked away on a backstreet off the main square, is superb, has reasonable prices and offers the opportunity to wander into the kitchen and see what looks good.

The very helpful **municipal tourist office** (☎28410 22357; www.agiosnikolaos.gr; ⊙8am-9pm Apr-Nov) is on the north side of the bridge over the canal and does a good job of finding sleeping options.

Ferries depart for Rhodes (€30, 11 hours) via Sitia, Kasos, Karpathos and Halki twice a week. There are also two weekly ferries to Piraeus (€34, 12 hours). Buses to Iraklio run every 30 minutes (€6.50, 1½ hours).

Sitia ΣΗΤΕΙΑ

POP 8750

Sitia (si-*tee*-a) is a laid-back little town in the northeastern corner of Crete that has escaped much of the tourism frenzy along the north coast. It is on an attractive bay flanked by mountains, and is an easy place to unwind.

The main square, Plateia Iroon Plytehniou, is in the corner of the bay, and recognisable by its palm trees and statue of a dying soldier. The ferry port is about 500m to the northeast.

Porto Belis Travel (☎28430 22370; www. portobelis-crete.gr; Karamanli Aven 34), on the waterfront just before the start of the town beach, is a one-stop shop, handling ticketing, rental cars and scooters, and accommodation bookings in town. It also runs **Porto Belis House** (☎28430 22370; d/q €34/57; ✴) above the travel agency. These rooms are immaculate, have kitchens and look straight out onto the beach.

Hotel Arhontiko (☎28430 28172; Kondylaki 16; d/studio €30/35), two blocks uphill from the port, has spotless rooms with shared bathrooms in a beautifully maintained neoclassical building. **Itanos Hotel** (☎28430 22900; www.itanoshotel.com; Karamanli 4; s/d incl breakfast €42/56; ✴@) is an upmarket establishment next to the square with its own excellent **Itanos Taverna** on the waterfront outside the front door.

The waterfront is lined with tavernas. **Balcony** (☎28430 25084; Foundalidou 19; mains €10-18), a couple of streets back from the waterfront, is the finest dining in Sitia. It's in a charmingly decorated neoclassical building.

The helpful **tourist office** (☎28430 28300; Karamanli; ⊙9.30am-2.30pm & 5-8.30pm Mon-Fri, 9.30am-2pm Sat), on the waterfront, has town maps.

Sitia airport (JSH) has flights to Athens. There are two ferries per week via Kasos, Karpathos and Halki to Rhodes (€27, 14 hours), and two to Piraeus (€32, 14½ hours). There are five buses daily to Iraklio (€13.10, 3½ hours) via Agios Nikolaos (€6.90, 1½ hours).

DODECANESE
ΔΩΔΕΚΑΝΗΣΑ

Strung out along the coast of western Turkey, the 12 main islands of the Dodecanese (*dodeca* means 12) have suffered a turbulent past of invasions and occupations that has endowed them with a fascinating diversity.

Conquered successively by the Romans, the Arabs, the Knights of St John, the Turks, the Italians, then liberated from the Germans by British and Greek commandos in 1944, the Dodecanese became part of Greece in 1947. These days, tourists rule.

The islands themselves range from the verdant and mountainous to the rocky and dry. While Rhodes and Kos host highly developed tourism, the more remote islands await those in search of traditional island life.

Rhodes ΡΟΔΟΣ

POP 98,000

Rhodes (Rodos in Greek) is the largest island in the Dodecanese. According to mythology, the sun god Helios chose Rhodes as his bride

TALKING TURKEY

Turkey is so close that it looks like you could swim there from many of the Dodecanese and Northeastern Aegean islands. Here are the boat options:

» Rhodes to Marmaris (see p422)

» Symi to Datça (see p426)

» Kos to Bodrum (see p428)

» Samos to Kuşadasi (near Ephesus; see p429)

» Chios to Çeşme (near İzmir; see p432)

» Lesvos to Dikili (near Ayvalık; see p432)

and bestowed light, warmth and vegetation upon her. The blessing seems to have paid off, for Rhodes produces more flowers and sunny days than most Greek islands. Throw in an east coast of virtually uninterrupted sandy beaches and it's easy to understand why sun-starved northern Europeans flock here.

❶ Getting There & Away

AIR There are plenty of flights daily between Rhodes' **Diagoras airport** (RHO) and Athens, plus less regular flights to Karpathos, Kasos, Kastellorizo, Thessaloniki, Iraklio and Samos. Options are growing. International charter flights swarm in summer, plus budget airlines such as easyJet arrive with scheduled flights.

The airport is on the west coast, 16km south-west of Rhodes Town; 25 minutes and €2.20 by bus.

BOAT Rhodes is the main port of the Do-decanese and there is a complex array of departures. There are daily ferries from Rhodes to Piraeus (€53, 13 hours). Most sail via the Dodecanese north of Rhodes, but at least twice a week there is a service via Karpathos, Crete and the Cyclades.

In summer, catamaran services run up and down the Dodecanese daily from Rhodes to Symi, Kos, Kalymnos, Nisyros, Tilos, Patmos and Leros.

TO TURKEY There are boats between Rhodes and Marmaris in Turkey (one-way/return includ-

Rhodes

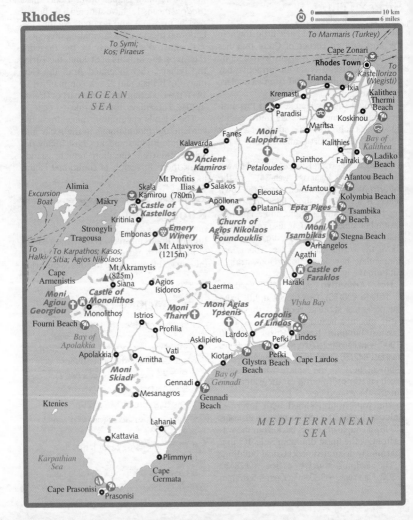

DON'T MISS

OLD TOWN

A wander around Rhodes' World Heritage–listed Old Town is a 'must'. It is reputedly the world's finest surviving example of medieval fortification, with 12m-thick walls. Throngs of visitors pack its busier streets and eating, sleeping and shopping options abound.

The Knights of St John (see p427) lived in the Knights' Quarter in the northern end of the Old Town.

The cobbled **Odos Ippoton** (Ave of the Knights; Map p424) is lined with magnificent medieval buildings, the most imposing of which is the **Palace of the Grand Masters** (Map p424; ☏22410 23359; admission €6; ⏱8.30am-3pm Tue-Sun), which was restored, but never used, as a holiday home for Mussolini.

The 15th-century Knight's Hospital now houses the **Archaeological Museum** (Map p424; ☏22410 27657; Plateia Mousiou; admission €3; ⏱8am-4pm Tue-Sun). The splendid building was restored by the Italians and has an impressive collection that includes the ethereal marble statue *Aphrodite of Rhodes*.

The pink-domed **Mosque of Süleyman** (Map p424), at the top of Sokratous, was built in 1522 to commemorate the Ottoman victory against the knights, then rebuilt in 1808.

You can take a pleasant walk around the imposing walls of the Old Town via the wide and pedestrianised moat walk.

---

ing port taxes €51/75, 50 minutes). Check www.marmarisinfo.com for up-to-date details.

RHODES TOWN
POP 56,000

Rhodes' capital is Rhodes Town, on the northern tip of the island. Its **Old Town**, the largest inhabited medieval town in Europe, is enclosed within massive walls and is a joy to explore. To the north is **New Town**, the commercial centre. The **town beach**, which looks out at Turkey and can get very crowded in summer, runs around the peninsula at the northern end of New Town.

The main port, **Commercial Harbour**, is east of the Old Town, and is where the big interisland ferries dock. Northwest of here is **Mandraki Harbour**, lined with excursion boats and smaller ferries, hydrofoils and catamarans. It was the supposed site of the Colossus of Rhodes, a 32m-high bronze statue of Apollo built over 12 years (294–282 BC). The statue stood for a mere 65 years before being toppled by an earthquake.

🛏 Sleeping

TOP CHOICE **Marco Polo Mansion**
BOUTIQUE HOTEL €€

(Map p424; ☏22410 25562; www.marcopolomansion.gr; Agiou Fanouriou 40, Old Town; d €90-150) In a 15th-century building in the Turkish quarter of the Old Town, this place is rich in Ottoman-era colours and features in glossy European magazines. Take a look at the rooms online. Attached is the highly recommended Marco Polo Café, (see boxed text, p425).

Mango Rooms
ROOMS €

(Map p424; ☏22410 24877; www.mango.gr; Plateia Dorieos 3, Old Town; s/d/tr €40/50/60; ❄@) A good-value, friendly one-stop shop near the back of the Old Town, Mango has a restaurant, bar and internet cafe down below, six well-kept rooms above, and a sun terrace on top.

Hotel Andreas
PENSION €€

(Map p424; ☏22410 34156; www.hotelandreas.com; Omirou 28d, Old Town; s/d €55/70; ❄❄🛜) Tasteful Hotel Andreas has individually decorated rooms and terrific views from its terrace. Rates differ by room; check it all out online, and choose your room before you go. There's a minimum two-night stay, but most stay longer.

Hotel International
HOTEL €

(Map p424; ☏22410 24595; diethnes@otenet.gr; 12 Kazouli St, New Town; s/d/tr €45/60/75) In New Town, the International is a friendly family-run operation with immaculately clean and good-value rooms only a few minutes from Rhodes' main town beach. It's a 10-minute stroll to Old Town, and prices drop by a third out of high season.

🍴 Eating & Drinking

There's food and drink everywhere you look in Rhodes. Outside the city walls are many cheap places in the New Market, at the southern end of Mandraki Harbour. Head further north into New Town for countless restaurants and bars.

GREECE DODECANESE

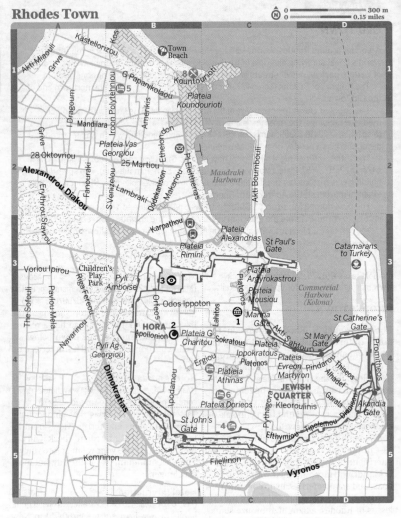

Inside the walls, Old Town has it all in terms of touts and over-priced tavernas trying to separate less savvy tourists from their euro. The back alleys tend to throw up better quality eateries and prices. Delve into the maze and see what you can come up with.

TOP CHOICE To Meltemi   TAVERNA, SEAFOOD **€**
(Map p422; Kountourioti 8; mains €5-12) At the northern end of Mandraki Harbour is one place worth heading to. Gaze out on Turkey from this beachside taverna where the seafood is superb. Try the grilled calamari stuffed with tomato and feta, and inspect the old photos of Rhodes.

ℹ Information

TOURIST INFORMATION Tourist information office (EOT; Map p424; ☎22410 35226; cnr Makariou & Papagou; ⊗8am-2.45pm Mon-Fri) Has brochures, maps and *Rodos News*, a free English-language newspaper.

TRAVEL AGENCIES Triton Holidays (☎22410 21690; www.tritondmc.gr; Plastira 9, Mandraki) In the New Town, this place is exceptionally helpful, handling accommodation bookings, ticketing and rental cars. The island-hopping experts, Triton can provide up-to-date advice in these times of constantly changing flight and boat schedules. E-mail ahead for advice.

WEBSITES www.rodos.gr

Rhodes Town

❶ Getting Around

BUS Rhodes Town has two bus stations a block apart next to the New Market. The **west-side bus station** serves the airport, Kamiros (€4.60, 55 minutes) and the west coast. The **east-side bus station** serves the east coast, Lindos (€4.70, 1½ hours) and the inland southern villages.

AROUND THE ISLAND

The **Acropolis of Lindos** (admission €6; ⊙8.30am-6pm Tue-Sun), 47km south from Rhodes Town, is an ancient city spectacularly perched atop a 116m-high rocky outcrop. Below is the town of **Lindos**, a tangle of streets with elaborately decorated 17th-century houses.

The extensive ruins of **Kamiros** (admission €4; ⊙8am-5pm Tue-Sun), an ancient Doric city on the west coast, are well preserved, with the remains of houses, baths, a cemetery and a temple, but the site should be visited as much for its lovely setting on a gentle hillside overlooking the sea.

Between Rhodes Town and Lindos, the **beaches** are packed. Venture further south to find good stretches of deserted sandy beach.

Karpathos ΚΑΡΠΑΘΟΣ

POP 6000

The elongated, mountainous island of Karpathos (*kar*-pah-thos), midway between Crete and Rhodes, is a scenic, hype-free place with a cosy port, numerous beaches and unspoilt villages. It is a wealthy island, reputedly receiving more money from emigrants living abroad (mostly in the USA) than any other Greek island.

The main port and capital is **Pigadia**, on the southeast coast. Karpathos has spectacular beaches with some of the clearest turquoise waters to be seen anywhere, particularly **Apella** and **Ahata**, both north of Pigadia, and **Ammoöpi**, 8km south of the capital. The northern village of **Olymbos** is like a living museum. Locals wear traditional outfits and the facades of houses are decorated with bright plaster reliefs. A great option on Karpathos is to hire a car and tour the island in a day on its excellent roads. The 19km stretch from Spoa to Olymbos is expected to finally be sealed by summer 2011.

TOP CHOICE **Elias Rooms** (☑22450 22446; www. eliasrooms.com; s/d €30/35 s/d apt €35/40) is an excellent accommodation option. Owner Elias is a mine of information and his rooms have great views while being in a quiet part of town. There's a choice of smaller rooms or bigger apartments that are clean and simple. Elias' website can tell you all you need to know about Karpathos and he is happy to provide information by email.

In Pigadia, a booth on the harbour serves as **municipal tourist office** (☑22450 23835; ⊙Jul & Aug). For more information on the island, check out www.inkarpathos.com. **Possi Travel** (☑22450 22148; possitvl@hotmail.com) on pedestrianised Apodimon Karpathion can suggest local tours and handles air and ferry tickets.

In summer, **Karpathos airport** (AOK), 13km southwest of Pigadia, has daily flights to Rhodes and Athens. With a huge new terminal, international charter flights also wing their way in. There are two ferries a week to Rhodes (€22, four hours) and two to Piraeus (€58, 19 hours) via Crete and the Cyclades. In summer there are daily excursion boats from Pigadia to Ahata and Apella beaches.

DON'T MISS

MARCO POLO CAFÉ

A top spot to eat in Rhodes, and one of our top restaurants for Greece, **Marco Polo Café** (Map p424; ☑22410 25562; www.marcopolomansion.gr; Agiou Fanouriou 40, Old Town) is worth finding in the backstreets of the Old Town. Owner Efi is as tastefully colourful as her mansion and garden restaurant. This place serves its guests with a rare passion – and the desserts are exquisite!

TAVERNA UNDER THE TREES *CRAIG MCLACHLAN*

Driving back down the west coast of Karpathos after a swim at Apella, the beach my wife describes as her favourite in Greece, we dropped into Taverna Under the Trees, a stand-alone place on the remote coastal road which had been highly recommended. I'd been looking for a place under some big trees (as the name suggests!), but as Kosta Ikonomidas explained later, this was his second version of Taverna Under the Trees and as this one had only been open a little over a year, the trees at his new place hadn't grown yet.

My wife and I chose a table with a marvellous view west out over the sea. The only other customers were seated looking east at Karpathos' rugged central mountains. I pointed this out to Kosta.

'Yes, they are Germans and they come every day. One day they look out at the sea, the next they have their backs to it. They have come every day for two weeks!' There's no better recommendation than this, I thought to myself.

Kosta is a Karpathanian character. Along with his family, he immigrated to the US at the age of 17, spent 27 years as a butcher in New York city, then came back to his home village of Piles 14 years ago.

'Karpathos is the second richest Greek island after Chios,' he explained. 'Chios made its money from shipping, but Karpathos became rich by the hard work of its emigrants. People immigrated to the US, Canada and Australia, worked hard, built up businesses, bought property, and Karpathos reaped the benefits. Many sent money to their relatives and family here, while others came back to Karpathos but still earn huge incomes from businesses and properties abroad.'

Taverna Under the Trees is a top spot. Kosta grows his own vegetables and is proud of the quality of the food he serves.

'People come from all over the island for my lamb dishes,' he said proudly. 'I only use the best quality here. Come look in my kitchen!' We had been chatting for a while, and Kosta knew I am a Kiwi. 'Yes, only the best quality,' he said, winking while pulling a vacuum-pack of New Zealand lamb out of the refrigerator!

Look for Kosta and **Taverna Under the Trees** (☎69779 84791) on the coastal road south of Lefkos, but north of the junction to Piles. His calamari is superb, and his smile infectious.

There are also excursions from Pigadia to Diafani, at the north of the island, that include a bus trip to Olymbos.

Local buses can drop you at Ammoöpi beach, but a rental vehicle is a good option.

Symi ΣΥΜΗ

POP 2600

Simply superb, Symi is an inviting island to the north of Rhodes that should be on all island-hopper itineraries. The port town of Gialos is a Greek treasure, with pastel-coloured mansions heaped up the hills surrounding the protective little harbour. Symi is swamped by day trippers from Rhodes, and it's worth staying over to enjoy the island in cruise control. The town is divided into Gialos, the port, and the tranquil *horio* (village) above it, accessible by taxi, bus or 360 steps from the harbour.

There is no tourist office. The best source of information is the free, widely available monthly English-language *Symi Visitor* (www.symivisitor.com), which includes maps of the town.

The **Monastery of Panormitis** (admission free; ☉dawn–sunset) is a hugely popular complex at the southern end of the island. Its **museum** (admission €1.50) is impressive, but try to avoid the hordes of day trippers who arrive at around 10.30am on excursion boats from Rhodes.

Budget accommodation is scarce. **Rooms Katerina** (☎22460 71813, 69451 30112; d €30; ❄) is excellent, but get in quick as there are only three rooms. There is a communal kitchen with breathtaking views down over the port, and helpful Katerina is happy to answer all your questions.

Pension Catherinettes (☎22460 71671; Julie-symi@otenet.gr; s/d €40/58; ❄@) has airy rooms on the north side of the harbour. It's where the treaty surrendering the Dodecanese to the Allies was signed in 1945. On the waterfront next to the clock tower, **Hotel Nireus** (22460 72400; www.nireus-hotel.gr; s/d incl breakfast €80/115; ✳@) is bright, friendly, has free wi-fi and the bonus of being able to swim right out front.

The narrow streets back up the valley from the harbour provide some excellent eating and drinking options. Try to avoid the waterfront spots that cater to flag-following day trippers.

Kalodoukas Holidays (22460 71077; www.kalodoukas.gr) handles accommodation bookings, ticketing and has a book of walking trails on the island.

There are frequent boats between Rhodes and Kos that stop at Symi, as well as daily excursion boats from Rhodes. **Symi Tours** (www.symitours.com) runs excursions on Saturdays to Datça in Turkey for €40.

Small taxi boats visit inaccessible east-coast beaches daily in summer, including spectacular Agios Georgious, backed by a 150m sheer cliff.

Kos ΚΩΣ

POP 17,900

Captivating Kos, only 5km from the Turkish peninsula of Bodrum, is popular with history buffs as the birthplace of Hippocrates (460–377 BC), the father of medicine. The island also attracts an entirely different crowd – sun-worshipping beach lovers from northern Europe who flock in on charter flights during summer. Tourism rules the roost, and whether you are there to explore the Castle of the Knights or to party till you drop, Kos should keep you happy for at least a few days.

Kos Town is based around a circular harbour, protected by the imposing Castle of the Knights, at the eastern end of the island. The ferry quay is north of the castle. Akti Koundourioti is the main drag around the harbourfront.

⊙ Sights & Activities

Castle of the Knights   CASTLE
(22420 27927; admission €4; ⊙8am-2.30pm Tue-Sun) Built in the 14th century, this castle protected the knights from the encroaching Ottomans, and was originally separated from town by a moat. That moat is now Finikon, a major street. Entrance to the castle is over the stone bridge behind the Hippocrates Tree.

Asklipieion   RUINS
(22420 28763; adult/student €4/3; ⊙8am-7:30pm Tue-Sun) On a pine-clad hill 4km southwest of Kos Town stand the extensive ruins of the renowned healing centre where Hippocrates practised medicine. Groups of doctors come from all over the world to visit.

Ancient Agora   RUINS
The ancient agora, with the ruins of the **Shrine of Aphrodite** and **Temple of Hercules**, is just off Plateia Eleftherias. North of the agora is the **Hippocrates Plane Tree**, under which the man himself is said to have taught his pupils.

Archaeological Museum   MUSEUM
(22420 28326; Plateia Eleftherias; admission €3; ⊙8am-2.30pm Tue-Sun) The focus of the collection here is sculpture from excavations around the island.

If the history is all too much, wander around and relax with the Scandinavians at the town **beach** past the northern end of the harbour.

Kos Town has recently developed a number of **bicycle paths** and renting a bike from one of the many places along the waterfront is a great option for getting around town and seeing the sights.

THE KNIGHTS OF ST JOHN

Do some island-hopping in the Dodecanese and you'll quickly realise that the Knights of St John left behind a whole lot of castles.

Originally formed as the Knights Hospitaller in Jerusalem in 1080 to provide care for poor and sick pilgrims, the knights relocated to Rhodes (via Cyprus) after the loss of Jerusalem in the First Crusade. In Rhodes, they ousted the ruling Genoese in 1309, built a stack of castles to protect their new home, then set about irking the neighbours by committing acts of piracy against Ottoman shipping. Sultan Süleyman the Magnificent, not a man you'd want to irk, took offence and set about dislodging the knights from their strongholds. Rhodes capitulated in 1523 and the remaining knights relocated to Malta. They set up there as the Sovereign Military Hospitaller of Jerusalem, of Rhodes, and of Malta.

Sleeping

TOP CHOICE **Hotel Afendoulis** HOTEL €
(22420 25321; www.afendoulishotel.com; Evripilou 1; s/d €35/50; ✳@) In a pleasant, quiet area about 500m south of the ferry quay, this well-kept hotel won't disappoint. Run by the charismatic English-speaking Alexis, this is a great place to relax and enjoy Kos. Port and bus station transfers are complimentary, and you can get your laundry done here.

Pension Alexis PENSION €
(22420 28798; www.pensionalexis.com; Irodotou 9; s/d €25/35; ✳) This highly recommended place has long been a budget favourite with travellers. It has large rooms, some with shared facilities, and a relaxing veranda and garden. They'll pick you up at the port or bus station for free and there are laundry facilities on site. It's back behind the Dolphin roundabout.

Eating & Drinking

Restaurants line the central waterfront of the old harbour, but you might want to hit the backstreets for value. There are plenty of cheap places to eat on the beach to the north of the harbour, and a dozen discos and clubs around the streets of Diakon and Nafklirou, just north of the agora.

TOP CHOICE **Stadium Restaurant** SEAFOOD €
(22420 27880; mains €9-16) On the long waterfront 500m southeast of the castle, Stadium serves succulent seafood at good prices, along with excellent views of Turkey.

ℹ Information

TOURIST INFORMATION Municipal tourist office (22420 24460; www.kosinfo.gr; Vasileos Georgiou 1; ⊗8am-2.30pm & 3-10pm Mon-Fri, 9am-2pm Sat) On the waterfront directly south of the port; provides maps and accommodation information.

TRAVEL AGENCIES Exas Travel (22420 28545; www.exas.gr) Near the Archaeological Museum, in the heart of town, to the southwest of the harbour; handles schedules, ticketing and excursions.

WEBSITES www.kosinfo.gr

ℹ Getting There & Around

AIR There are daily flights to Athens from Kos' **Ippokratis airport** (KGS), which is 28km southwest of Kos Town. International charters wing in throughout the summer and easyJet operates scheduled flights from London. Get to/from the airport by bus (€4) or taxi (€25).

BOAT There are frequent ferries from Rhodes to Kos that continue on to Piraeus (€46, 10 hours), as well as ferries heading the opposite way. Daily fast-boat connections head north to Patmos and Samos, and south to Symi and Rhodes.

TO TURKEY In summer boats depart daily for Bodrum in Turkey (€34 return, one hour).

BUS There is a good public bus system on Kos, with the bus station on Kleopatras, near the ruins at the back of town.

MINI-TRAIN Next to the tourist office is a blue mini-train for Asklipion (€5 return, hourly) and a green mini-train that does city tours (€4, 20 minutes).

Patmos ΠΑΤΜΟΣ
POP 3050

Patmos has a sense of 'spirit of place', and with its great beaches and relaxed atmosphere, is a superb place to unwind. For the religiously motivated it is not to be missed. Orthodox and Western Christians have long made pilgrimages to Patmos, for it was here that John the Divine ensconced himself in a cave and wrote the Book of Revelation.

The main town and port of Skala is about halfway down the east coast of Patmos, with a protected harbour. Towering above Skala to the south is the *hora,* crowned by the immense Monastery of St John the Theologian.

◉ Sights & Activities

St John Sites RELIGIOUS SITES
The **Cave of the Apocalypse** (admission free, treasury €6; ⊗8am-1.30pm daily & 4-6pm Tue, Thu & Sun), where St John wrote his divinely inspired Book of Revelation, is halfway between the port and *hora*. Take a bus from the port or hike up the **Byzantine path**, which starts from a signposted spot on the Skala–*hora* road.

The **Monastery of St John the Theologian** (admission free; ⊗8am-1.30pm daily & 4-6pm Tue, Thu & Sun) looks more like a castle than a monastery and tops Patmos like a crown. It exhibits all kinds of monastic treasures.

Beaches BEACHES
Patmos' coastline provides secluded coves, mostly with pebble beaches. The best is **Psili Ammos**, in the south, reached by excursion boat from Skala port. **Lambi Beach**, on the north coast, is a pebble-beach lover's dream come true.

Sleeping

Yvonni Studios ROOMS €
(📞22470 33066; www.12net.gr/yvonni; s/d
€35/50) On the western side of Skala, these
exceptionally clean and pleasant studios are
fully self-contained and big on privacy. Call
ahead for a booking or drop into Yvonni's
gift shop in Skala and ask for Theo.

Katina's Rooms ROOMS €
(📞22470 31327, 69734 17241; s/d €35/50) The
smiling Katina meets most boats and is
happy to provide a ride to her four immaculately clean rooms at the northern end of
the harbour. Enthusiastic and helpful, she
has contacts with other tidy rooms in her
neighbourhood if hers are full.

Blue Bay Hotel BOUTIQUE HOTEL €€
(📞22470 31165; www.bluebaypatmos.gr; s/d/tr
€78/116/144; ❅⊛@) At the quieter southern
end of Skala, this waterfront hotel has
superb rooms, internet access, and breakfast included in its rates (which tumble
outside of high season).

ℹ Information

TOURIST INFORMATION Tourist office
(📞22470 31666; ⊗8am-6pm Mon-Fri Jun-Sep)
In the white building opposite the port in Skala,
along with the post office and police station.

TRAVEL AGENCIES Apollon Travel (📞22470
31324; apollontravel@stratas.gr) On the waterfront; handles schedules and ticketing.

WEBSITES www.patmosweb.gr; www.patmos
-island.com

ℹ Getting There & Away

BOAT Patmos is well connected, with ferries
to Piraeus (€35, eight hours, two weekly) and
south to Rhodes (€32, 7½ hours, two weekly).
In summer daily catamarans head south to Kos
and Rhodes, and north to Samos.

NORTHEASTERN AEGEAN ISLANDS
ΤΑ ΝΗΣΙΑ ΤΟΥ ΒΟΡΕΙΟ ΑΝΑΤΟΛΙΚΟ ΑΙΓΑΙΟΥ

One of Greece's best-kept secrets, these far-
flung islands are strewn across the northeastern corner of the Aegean, closer to Turkey than mainland Greece. They harbour unspoilt scenery, welcoming locals, fascinating
independent cultures, and remain relatively
calm even when other Greek islands are sag-
ging with tourists at the height of summer.

Samos ΣΑΜΟΣ
POP 32,800

A lush mountainous island only 3km from
Turkey, Samos has a glorious history as the
legendary birthplace of Hera, wife and sister
of god-of-all-gods Zeus. Samos was an important centre of Hellenic culture, and the
mathematician Pythagoras and storyteller
Aesop are among its sons. The island has
beaches that bake in summer, and a hinterland that is superb for hiking. Spring brings
with it pink flamingos, wildflowers, and orchids that the island grows for export, while
summer brings throngs of package tourists.

ℹ Getting There & Around

AIR There are daily flights to Athens from
Samos airport (SMI), 4km west of Pythagorio,
plus less regular flights to Iraklio and Thessaloniki. Charter flights wing in from Europe in
summer.

BOAT Samos has two main ports: Vathy
(Samos Town) in the northeast and Pythagorio
on the southeast coast. Those coming from the
south by boat generally arrive in Pythagorio.
Big ferries use Vathy. Once you're on Samos
and have onward tickets, double-check where
your boat is leaving from. Buses between the
two take 25 minutes.

A maritime hub, Samos offers daily ferries to
Piraeus (€35, 13 hours), plus ferries heading
north to Chios, west to the Cyclades and south
to the Dodecanese. Catamarans head south to
Patmos (€20, one hour), carrying on to Leros,
Kalymnos and Kos (€34, 3½ hours).

BUS You can get to most of the island's villages
and beaches by bus.

CAR & MOTORCYCLE Rental cars and scooters are readily available around the island.

TO TURKEY There are daily ferries to Kuşadasi
(for Ephesus) in Turkey (€35/45 one-way/
return plus €10 port taxes). Day excursions are
also available from April to October. Check with
ITSA Travel (📞22730 23605; www.itsatravel-
samos.gr) in Vathy for up-to-date details.

VATHY (SAMOS TOWN) ΒΑΘΥ ΣΑΜΟΣ
POP 2030

Busy Vathy is an attractive working port
town. Most of the action is along Themistokleous Sofouli, the main street that runs
along the waterfront. The main square, Plateia Pythagorou, in the middle of the waterfront, is recognisable by its four palm trees
and statue of a lion.

The rarely open and hard-to-find **tourist
office** (📞22730 28582; ⊗Jun-Sep) is in a side
street one block north of the main square.

ITSA Travel (22730 23605; www.itsatravel. com), opposite the quay, is helpful with travel inquiries, excursions, accommodation and luggage storage. To get to Vathy's bus station, follow the waterfront south and turn left onto Lekati, 250m south of Plateia Pythagorou (just before the police station).

The **Archaeological Museum** (adult/student €3/2; ⊙8.30am-3pm Tue-Sun), by the municipal gardens, is first rate. The highlight is a 5.5m *kouros* statue.

TOP CHOICE **Pythagoras Hotel** (22730 28601; www.pythagoras-hotel.com; Kallistratou 12; s/d/tr €20/35/45; ❷@⑤) is a friendly, great-value place with a convivial atmosphere, run by English-speaking Stelio. There is a restaurant serving tasty home-cooked meals; a bar; satellite TV; and internet access on site. Facing inland, the hotel is 400m to the left of the quay. Call ahead for free pick-up on arrival.

Ino Village Hotel (22730 23241; www. inovillagehotel.com; Kalami; s/d/tr incl breakfast €65/80/100; ❷❀@❀) is an impressive, elegant place in the hills north of the ferry quay. Its **Elea Restaurant** on the terrace serves up both invigorated Greek cuisine and views over town and the harbour.

Garden Taverna (22730 24033; Manolis Kalomiris; mains €4-9) serves good Greek food in a lovely garden setting; it's up to the left behind the main square.

PYTHAGORIO ΠΥΘΑΓΟΡΕΙΟ
POP 1300

Pretty Pythagorio, 25 minutes south of Vathy by bus, is where you'll disembark if you've come by boat from Patmos. It is a small, enticing town with a yacht-lined harbour and a holiday atmosphere.

The excellent **statue of Pythagoras** and his triangle, on the waterfront opposite the ferry quay, should have you recalling his theorem from your high school maths days. If not, buy a T-shirt emblazoned with it to remind you.

The 1034m-long **Evpalinos Tunnel** (adult/student €4/2; ⊙8.45am-2.45pm Tue-Sun), built in the 6th century BC, was dug by political prisoners and used as an aqueduct to bring water from Mt Ampelos (1140m). In the Middle Ages, locals hid out in it during pirate raids. Part of it can still be explored. It's a 20-minute walk north of town.

Hotel Alexandra (22730 61429; Metamorfosis Sotiros 22; d €35), not far from the castle, is a friendly place with cosy rooms and an attractive garden. **Pension Despina** (22730 61677; A Nikolaou; s/d €35/50), a block back from the waterfront, offers simple studios and rooms, some with balconies and kitchenettes.

Tavernas and bars line the waterfront. **Poseidon Restaurant** (22730 62530; mains from €5), on the small town beach, past the jetty with the Pythagoras statue on it, offers superb seafood. **Iliad Bar** (22730 62207; cocktails from €5), on the waterfront, serves wicked cocktails till the wee hours and is run by an expat Kiwi.

The cordial **municipal tourist office** (22730 61389; deap5@otenet.gr; ⊙8am-9.30pm) is two blocks from the waterfront on the main street, Lykourgou Logotheti. The bus stop is two blocks further inland on the same street, next to the post office.

AROUND SAMOS

Ireon (adult/student €4/3; ⊗8.30am-3pm Tue-Sun), the legendary birthplace of the goddess Hera, is 8km west of Pythagorio. The temple at this World Heritage site was enormous – four times the Parthenon – though only one column remains.

The captivating villages of **Vourliotes** and **Manolates**, on the slopes of imposing Mt Ampelos, northwest of Vathy, are excellent walking territory and have many marked pathways.

Choice beaches include **Tsamadou** on the north coast, **Votsalakia** in the southwest and **Psili Ammos** to the east of Pythagorio. The latter is sandy and stares straight out at Turkey, barely a couple of kilometres away.

Chios ΧΙΟΣ

POP 54,000

Due to its thriving shipping and mastic industries (mastic produces the resin used in chewing gum), Chios (*hee*-os) has never really bothered much with tourism. If you are an off-the-beaten-track type of Greek Islands traveller, you'll find Chios all the more appealing.

Chios Town, on the island's eastern coast, is a working port and home to half the island's inhabitants. A main street runs in a semicircle around the port, with most ferries docking at its northern end. The *kastro* (old Turkish quarter) is to the north of the ferry quay, and Plateia Vounakiou, the main square, is just south and inland from the quay.

⊙ Sights & Activities

In Chios Town, **Philip Argenti Museum** (Korais; admission €1.50; ⊗8am-2pm Mon-Thu, 8am-2pm & 5-7.30pm Fri, 8am-12.30pm Sat) contains the treasures of the wealthy Argenti family.

World Heritage–listed **Nea Moni** (New Monastery; admission free; ⊗8am-1pm & 4-8pm) is 14km west of Chios Town and reveals some of the finest Byzantine art in the country, with mosaics dating from the 11th century. The mosaics survived, but the resident monks were massacred by the Turks in 1822. You can see their dented skulls in the chapel at the monastery's entrance.

Those in the ghost village of **Anavatos**, 10km from Nea Moni and built on a precipitous cliff, preferred a different fate, hurling themselves off the cliff rather than being taken captive by the Turks.

Pyrgi, 24km southwest of Chios Town, is one of Greece's most unusual villages. The facades of the town's dwellings are decorated with intricate grey-and-white geometric patterns and motifs. The tiny medieval town of **Mesta**, 10km from Pyrgi and nestled within fortified walls, features cobbled streets, overhead arches and a labyrinth of streets designed to confuse pirates.

🛏 Sleeping

Chios Rooms ROOMS €
TOP CHOICE (☎22710 20198; www.chiosrooms.gr; Leoforos Egeou 110; s/d/tr €25/35/45) A top location to stay, this place is upstairs in a restored neoclassical house on the waterfront at the southern end of the harbour. It has bright, airy rooms, some with en suite bathrooms, and is being restored lovingly by its Kiwi owner, Don, who is a mine of information on Chios.

Hotel Kyma HOTEL €€
(☎22710 44500; kyma@chi.forthnet.gr; Evgenias Handris 1; s/d/tr incl breakfast €71/90/111; ❄) Around the corner from Chios Rooms, this place occupies a charismatic century-old mansion and is run by the enthusiastic multilingual Theodoris. Ask for a room overlooking the sea.

GUM-CHEWERS FROM WAY BACK

Chios is home to the world's only gum-producing mastic trees and the southern *mastihohoria* (mastic villages) were wealthy for centuries. Not only were they wealthy, but the mastic trees are also said to have saved them when the Turks came and slaughtered the rest of the island's residents. The sultan's reputed fondness for mastic chewing gum – and the rumour that his harem girls used it for keeping their teeth clean and their breath fresh – meant that the *mastihohoria* were spared.

These days, **Masticulture Ecotourism Activities** (☎22710 76084; www.masticulture.com) in the southern village of Mesta, introduces visitors to the local history and culture, including mastic cultivation tours. In Chios Town, on the waterfront, **Mastihashop** sells products such as mastic chewing gum, toothpaste and soaps, and **Mastic Spa** sells mastic-based cosmetics.

✖ Eating

The waterfront has ample options in the way of way of eateries and bars, though for cheap eats, head one street back onto El Venizelou, which is lined with shops. The Plateia Vounakiou area, inland from where the ferries dock, also throws up some good options.

Hotzas Taverna TAVERNA €
(☎22710 42787; Kondyli 3; mains from €5) Up the back of town, Hotzas is known by locals to provide the best Greek fare on the island. Get a local to mark it on a map, and enjoy the walk. It's worth the effort of finding.

ℹ Information

TOURIST INFORMATION Municipal tourist office (☎22710 44389; infochio@otenet.gr; Kanari 18; ⊙7am-10pm Apr-Oct, to 4pm Nov-Mar) On the street that runs inland to the main square; provides information on accommodation, schedules and rentals.

TRAVEL AGENCIES Agean Travel (☎22710 41277; aegeantr@otenet.gr; Leoforos Egeou 114) At the southern end of the harbour; handles ticketing.

WEBSITES www.chios.gr

ℹ Getting There & Around

AIR There are daily flights from **Chios airport** (JKH) to Athens and five per week to Thessaloniki. The airport is 4km south of Chios Town; there's no bus; a taxi costs €6.

BOAT Ferries sail daily to Piraeus (€32.50, six hours) and Lesvos (€19.50, two hours 15 minutes), and weekly to Thessaloniki (€40, 18 hours). There are one or two ferries a week south to Samos (€15, three hours).

BUS Chios Town has two bus stations. Blue buses go regularly to local villages and Karfas Beach, and leave from the local bus station at the main square. Buses to Pyrgi (€2.50) and Mesta (€3.50) and other distant points leave from the long-distance bus station on the waterfront near the ferry quay.

TO TURKEY Boats to Turkey run all year from Chios, with daily sailings from July to September to Çeşme (one-way/return €20/30), near İzmir. For details, check out **Miniotis Lines** (☎22710 24670; www.miniotis.gr; Neorion 24).

Lesvos (Mytilini) ΛΕΣΒΟΣ (ΜΥΤΙΛΗΝΗ)

POP 93,500

Lesvos, or Mytilini as it is often called, tends to do things in a big way. The third-largest of the Greek Islands after Crete and Evia, Lesvos produces half the world's ouzo and is home to over 11 million olive trees. Mountainous yet fertile, the island presents excellent hiking and birdwatching opportunities, but remains relatively untouched in terms of tourism development.

Lesvos has always been a centre of philosophy and artistic achievement, and to this day is a spawning ground for innovative ideas in the arts and politics. An excellent source of information on the island is www. greeknet.com.

The two main towns on the island are the capital, Mytilini, on the southeast coast, and attractive Mithymna on the north coast.

ℹ Getting There & Away

AIR Written up on flight schedules as Mytilene, Lesvos' **Odysseas airport** (MJT) has daily connections with Athens, plus flights to Thessaloniki and Iraklio. The airport is 8km south of Mytilini town; a taxi costs €8.

BOAT In summer there are daily boats to Piraeus (€30, 12 hours) via Chios, and three boats a week to Thessaloniki (€35, 13 hours).

TO TURKEY There are four ferries a week to Dikeli port, which serves Ayvalik in Turkey (one-way/return €30/45), plus other options. Stop by Zoumboulis Tours (p433) for ticketing and schedules.

MYTILINI ΜΥΤΙΛΗΝΗ
POP 27,300

The capital and main port, Mytilini, is built between two harbours (north and south) with an imposing fortress on the promontory to the east. All ferries dock at the southern harbour, and most of the town's action is around this waterfront. With a large university campus, Mytilini is a lively place year-round.

⊙ Sights & Activities

Museums MUSEUMS
Mytilini's excellent neoclassical **Archaeological Museum** (8 Noemvriou; adult/child €3/2; ⊙8.30am-3pm) has a fascinating collection from Neolithic to Roman times.

Theophilos Museum (admission €2; ⊙9am-1pm & 4.30-8pm Tue-Sun), 4km south of Mytilini in Varia village, is a shrine to the prolific folk painter Theophilos. Next door is the **Teriade Museum** (☎22510 23372; admission €2; ⊙8.30am-2pm &5-8pm Tue-Sun), with an astonishing collection of paintings by world-renowned artists.

Fortress FORTRESS
(adult/student €2/1; ⊙8am-2.30pm Tue-Sun) Mytilini's impressive fortress was built in early Byzantine times and enlarged by the

Sappho, one of Greece's great ancient poets, was born on Lesvos during the 7th century BC. Most of her work was devoted to love and desire, and the objects of her affection were often female. Because of this, Sappho's name and birthplace have come to be associated with female homosexuality.

These days, Lesvos is visited by many lesbians paying homage to Sappho. The whole island is very gay-friendly, in particular the southwestern beach resort of Skala Eresou, which is built over ancient Eresos, where Sappho was born. The village is well set up to cater to lesbian needs and has a 'Women Together' festival held annually in September. Check out www.sapphotravel.com for details.

There is an excellent statue of Sappho in the main square on the waterfront in Mytilini.

Turks. The pine forest surrounding it is a superb place for a stroll or to have a picnic.

🛏 Sleeping

Pension Thalia ROOMS €
(☎22510 24640; Kinikiou 1; s/d €25/30) This pension has clean, bright rooms in a large house. It is about a five-minute walk north of the main square, up Ermou, the road that links the south and north harbours. Follow the signs from the corner of Ermou and Adramytiou.

Hotel Sappho HOTEL €€
(☎22510 22888; Kountourioti 31; s/d/tr €45/60/70) On the waterfront, rooms here are simple but clean. It's easy to find, and has the attraction of a 24-hour reception as ferries into Mytilini tend to arrive at nasty hours.

Porto Lesvos 1 Hotel HOTEL €€
(☎22510 41771; www.portolesvos.gr; Komninaki 21; s/d €60/90; ❄@) This hotel has good rooms and service – right down to robes and slippers – in a restored building one block back from the waterfront.

✕ Eating & Drinking

Mytilini's top spots are a road or two back at the northern end of the harbour.

O Diavlos GREEK €
(☎22510 22020; Ladadika 30) Come here for the best in both local cuisine and art; paintings by local artists line the walls and can be purchased should you get the urge.

Ocean Eleven Bar BAR
(☎22510 27030; Kountourioti 17) Enjoy a cocktail here while watching the mayhem on the waterfront.

❶ Information

TOURIST INFORMATION Tourist office
(☎22510 42512; 6 Aristarhou; ⏱9am-1pm Mon-Fri) Located 50m up Aristarhou inland from the quay; offers brochures and maps, but its opening hours are limited.

TRAVEL AGENCIES Tourist Police (☎22510 22776) At the entrance to the quay; helpful if you're outside tourist-office hours.

Zoumboulis Tours (☎22510 37755; Kountourioti 69) On the waterfront, handles flights, boat schedules, ticketing and excursions to Turkey.

WEBSITES www.lesvos.net

❶ Getting Around

BUS Mytilini has two bus stations. For local buses, head along the waterfront to the main square. For long-distance buses, walk 600m from the ferry along the waterfront to El Venizelou and turn right until you reach Agia Irinis park, which is next to the station. There are regular services in summer to Mithymna, Petra, Agiasos, Skala Eresou, Mantamados and Agia Paraskevi.

MITHYMNA ΜΗΘΥΜΝΑ
POP 1500

The gracious, preserved town of Mithymna (known by locals as Molyvos) is 62km north of Mytilini. Cobbled streets canopied by flowering vines wind up the hill below the impressive castle. The town is full of cosy tavernas and genteel stone cottages.

The noble **Genoese castle** (admission €2; ⏱8.30am-7pm Tue-Sun) perches above the town like a crown and affords tremendous views out to Turkey. Pebbly **Mithymna Beach** sits below the town and is good for swimming. Don't forget to stroll down to the harbour.

Eftalou hot springs (public/private bath per person €3.50/5; ⏱public bath 6-8am & 6-10pm, private bath 9am-6pm), 4km from town on the beach, is a superb bathhouse complex with a whitewashed dome and steaming, pebbled pool. There are also private baths where you don't need a bathing suit.

TOP CHOICE **Nassos Guest House** (📞22530 71432; www.nassosguesthouse.com; Arionis; d & tr €20-35; 🛜) is an airy, friendly place with shared facilities and a communal kitchen, in an old Turkish house oozing with character. With rapturous views, it's highly recommended. It's easy to spot as it's the only blue house below the castle.

Betty's Restaurant (📞22530 71421; Agora) has superb home-style Greek food, views and atmosphere in a building that was once a notorious bordello. Betty also has a couple of **cottages** (📞22530 71022; www.bettys cottages.molivos.net) with kitchens in her garden that sleep up to four for €50.

From the bus stop, walk straight ahead towards the town for 100m to the helpful **municipal tourist office** (www.mithymna.gr; ⏰8am-9pm Mon-Fri, 9am-7pm Sat & Sun), which has good maps. Some 50m further on, the cobbled main thoroughfare of 17 Noemvriou heads up to the right. Go straight to get to the colourful fishing port.

Buses to Mithymna (€5) take 1¾ hours from Mytilini, though a rental car is a good option.

AROUND THE ISLAND

Southern Lesvos is dominated by **Mt Olympus** (968m) and the very pretty village of **Agiasos**, which has good artisan workshops making everything from handcrafted furniture to pottery.

Western Lesvos is known for its petrified forest, with petrified wood at least 500,000 years old, and for the gay-friendly town of Skala Eresou, the birthplace of Sappho.

SPORADES ΣΠΟΡΑΔΕΣ

Scattered to the southeast of the Pelion Peninsula, to which they were joined in prehistoric times, the 11 islands that make up the Sporades group have mountainous terrain, dense vegetation and are surrounded by scintillatingly clear seas.

The main ports for the Sporades are Volos and Agios Konstantinos on the mainland.

Skiathos ΣΚΙΑΘΟΣ

POP 6150

Lush and green, Skiathos has a beach-resort feel about it. Charter flights bring loads of package tourists, but the island still oozes enjoyment. Skiathos Town and some excellent beaches are on the hospitable south coast, while the north coast is precipitous and less accessible. Skiathos Town was used as a shooting location in the filming of *Mamma Mia*.

Skiathos Town's main thoroughfare is Papadiamanti, named after the 19th-century novelist and short-story writer Alexandros Papadiamanti, who was born here. It runs inland opposite the quay.

⊙ Sights & Activities

Beaches

Skiathos has superb beaches, particularly on the south coast. **Koukounaries** is popular with families. A stroll over the headland, **Big Banana Beach** is stunning, but if you want an all-over tan, head a tad further to **Little Banana Beach**, where bathing suits are a rarity.

Boat Trips

At the Old Port in Skiathos Town, there are all sorts of offerings in terms of **boat excursions** – trips to nearby beaches (€10), trips around Skiathos Island (€25) and full-day trips that take in Skopelos, Alonnisos and the Marine Park (€35).

🛏 Sleeping

Pension Pandora ROOMS €
(📞24270 24357, 6944137377; www.skiathosinfo. com/accomm/pension-pandora; r €30-70; P❄) Run by the effervescent Georgina, this family-run place is 10 minutes' walk north of the quay. The spotless rooms have TV, kitchens and balconies. Georgina also has two exceptional apartments just off Papadiamanti.

Camping Koukounaries CAMPING €
(📞24270 49250; campsites per tent/person €4/10) This place, 30 minutes from town by bus at the southwestern end of the island, is at beautiful Koukounaries Beach. There are good facilities, a minimarket and a taverna.

Villa Orsa BOUTIQUE ROOMS €€
(📞24270 22430; s/d incl breakfast €70/80; ❄) Perched above the old harbour, this mansion features traditionally styled rooms and a garden terrace overlooking the sea.

🍴 Eating & Drinking

Skiathos Town is brimming with eateries. There are seafood options around the old harbour, and some excellent places up the stairs from there behind the small church.

Skiathos is popular with English visitors who don't want to miss their football; there

MOVIES UNDER THE STARS

Greece has such great weather in summer that not only does it have a history of open-air theatre, there is also an open-air cinema culture. **Cinema Attikon** (☑24720 22352; €7), on Skiathos Town's main street of Papadiamanti, is a great example. You can catch current English-language movies under the stars, sip a beer and practise speed-reading Greek subtitles at the same time! Films are usually shown in their original language in Greece, not dubbed.

A number of other islands have similar outdoor cinemas.

are ample opportunities to consume fish and chips and watch the premier league along Papadiamanti!

Piccolo   PIZZA €
(☑24270 22780; mains from €7) Does exquisite pizzas and pastas in a lovely setting.

1901   GREEK €
(☑69485 26701; mains from €7) A superb fine-dining restaurant with a glowing reputation.

Kentavros   BAR
(☑24270 22980) A popular drinking spot just off Plateia Papadiamanti. Expect a mellow ambience and mixture of rock, jazz and blues.

ℹ Information

TOURIST INFORMATION **Tourist information booth** (☑24270 23172) At the port, but it opens irregularly.

TRAVEL AGENCIES **Heliotropio Travel** (☑24270 22430; www.heliotropio.gr) Opposite the ferry quay; handles ticketing and rents cars and scooters.

WEBSITES skiathosinfo.com

ℹ Getting There & Around

AIR Along with numerous charter flights from northern Europe, in summer there is a daily flight from Athens to Skiathos. **Skiathos airport** (JSI) is 2km northeast of Skiathos Town.

BOAT There are frequent daily hydrofoils to/from the mainland ports of Volos (€30, 1¼ hours) and Agios Konstantinos (€33, two hours), as well as cheaper ferries. The hydrofoils head to and from Skopelos (€16, 35 minutes) and Alonnisos (€18, one hour). In summer

there is a daily hydrofoil to Thessaloniki (€55, 3½ hours).

BUS Crowded buses ply the south-coast road between Skiathos Town and Koukounaries every 30 minutes between 7.30am and 11pm year-round, stopping at all the beaches along the way. The bus stop is at the eastern end of the harbour.

Skopelos ΣΚΟΠΕΛΟΣ

POP 4700

A mountainous island, Skopelos is covered in pine forests, vineyards, olive groves and fruit orchards. While the northwest coast is exposed with high cliffs, the southeast is sheltered and harbours pleasant pebbled beaches. The island's main port and capital of Skopelos Town, on the east coast, skirts a semicircular bay and clambers in tiers up a hillside, culminating in a ruined fortress.

Recent claims to fame for Skopelos are the legendary Skopelos pie, which can be bought all over Greece, and its use as a location for the filming of *Mamma Mia*. The crew took over Skopelos Town's accommodation for a month and filmed at Agnontas and Kastani beaches on the western coast.

TOP CHOICE **Pension Sotos** (☑24240 22549; www.skopelos.net/sotos; s & d €35-55; ❄@☎), in the middle of the waterfront, has big rooms in an enchanting old Skopelete building. There's also a communal kitchen, terrace and courtyard. Check out individual rooms and its different prices online before you go. **Hotel Regina** (☑24240 22138; www.skopelosweb.gr/regina; s/d incl breakfast €40/55; ❄) has bright and cheery rooms with balconies. The hotel's rooftop signage is easily spotted from the waterfront.

Head to Souvlaki Sq, 100m up from the dock, for cheap eats such as gyros and souvlaki. The top spot in town to chill out is under the huge plane tree at **Platanos Jazz Bar** (☑24240 23661) on the waterfront. It's open all day, plays wicked jazz and blues until the late hours, and is the ideal place to recover from, or prepare for, a hangover. Next door is **Taverna Ta Kimata O Angelos** (☑24240 22381), a traditional taverna that is the oldest one on the island.

In Skopelos Town, there is no tourist office, but **Thalpos Holidays** (☑24240 29036; www.holidayislands.com), on the waterfront between the ferry quay and the excursion-boat quay, is handy for accommodation and tours. The bus station is next to the port.

ECOTOURISM ON THE RISE

In a country not noted for its ecological long-sightedness, locals (especially the fishermen) initially struggled with the idea of the **National Marine Park of Alonnisos** when it was established in 1992 to protect the highly endangered Mediterranean monk seal and to promote the recovery of fish stocks.

These days, though, the people of the Sporades have caught on to the advantages of having such a park on their doorstep. Ecotourism is on the rise, with daily excursions on licensed boats into the park from Skiathos, Skopelos and Alonnisos. Though your odds of seeing the shy monk seal aren't great – it's on the list of the 20 most endangered species worldwide – the chances of cruising among pods of dolphins (striped, bottlenose and common) are high.

Excursion boats along the waterfront offer trips into the Marine Park.

Flying Dolphin hydrofoils dash several times a day to Skiathos (€15.50, 45 minutes), Alonnisos (€8.50, 20 minutes), Volos (€26.30, 2¼ hours) and Agios Konstantinos (€44, 2½ hours). Most hydrofoils also call in at Loutraki, the port below Glossa on the northwest coast of the island. There is also a daily ferry along the same route that costs less but takes longer. There are frequent buses from Skopelos Town to Glossa (€4.30, one hour) stopping at all beaches along the way.

Alonnisos ΑΛΟΝΝΗΣΟΣ

POP 2700

Green, serene, attractive Alonnisos is at the end of the line and is thereby the least visited of the Sporades' main islands. The west coast is mostly precipitous cliffs, but the east coast is speckled with pebble-and-sand beaches. The island is well known as a walking destination.

The port village of Patitiri was slapped together in 1965 after an earthquake destroyed the hilltop capital of Alonnisos Town. There are two main thoroughfares; facing inland from the ferry quay, Pelasgon is to the left and Ikion Dolopon is to the far right.

The tiny *hora*, **Old Alonnisos**, is a few kilometres inland. Its streets sprout a profusion of plant life, alluring villas of eclectic design and dramatic vistas.

Pension Pleiades (☏24240 65235; www.pleiadeshotel.gr; s/d €45/50; ❄@) looks out over the harbour and is visible from the quay. The rooms are immaculate, balconied, bright and cheerful. There's also a good restaurant. **Liadromia Hotel** (☏24240 65521; www.liadromia.gr; d/tr/ste €50/70/95; P❄@) is an excellent-value place with tons of char-

acter, overlooking Patitiri's harbour. Follow the stairway opposite the National Bank. **Camping Rocks** (☏24240 65410; campsites per person €6) is a shady, basic camping ground. It is a steep hike about 1.5km from the port; go up Pelasgon and take the first road on your left.

There is no tourist office, but on the waterfront, **Alonnisos Travel** (☏24240 66000; www.alonnisostravel.gr) handles boat scheduling and ticketing. **Ikos Travel** (☏24240 65320; www.ikostravel.com) runs a popular round-the-island excursion. The bus stop is on the corner of Ikion Dolopon and the waterfront.

There are ferries with varying regularity connecting Alonnisos to Volos and Agios Konstantinos via Skopelos and Skiathos. Flying Dolphin hydrofoils provide the most regular schedules between the islands. They travel several times a day to Skopelos Town (€9, 20 minutes), Skiathos (€16, 1½ hours), Volos (€38.50, three hours) and Agios Konstantinos (€44, three hours).

The local bus (€1.20) runs to the *hora* every hour.

IONIAN ISLANDS
ΤΑ ΕΠΤΑΝΗΣΑ

The idyllic cypress- and fir-covered Ionian Islands stretch down the western coast of Greece from Corfu in the north to Kythira, off the southern tip of the Peloponnese. Mountainous, with dramatic cliff-backed beaches, soft light and turquoise water, they're more Italian in feel, offering a contrasting experience to other Greek islands. Invest in a hire car to get to small villages tucked along quiet back roads. Prices drop in low season.

Corfu ΚΕΡΚΥΡΑ

POP 122,670

Many consider Corfu, or Kerkyra (*ker*-kih-rah) in Greek, to be Greece's most beautiful island – the unfortunate consequence of which is that it's often overrun with crowds.

ℹ️ **Getting There & Away**

AIR Ioannis Kapodistrias Airport (CFU; ☎26610 30180) is 3km from Corfu Town. **Olympic Air** (☎26610 22962) and **Aegean Airlines** (☎26610 27100) fly daily to Athens and a few times a week to Thessaloniki.

BOAT Ferries go to Igoumenitsa (€7, 1½ hours, hourly). In summer daily ferries and hydrofoils

go to Paxi, and international ferries (see p451) stop in Patra (€38, six hours).

BUS Daily buses to Athens (€49, 8½ hours) and Thessaloniki (€45, eight hours) leave from **Avrami long-distance bus station** (☎26610 28927; I Theotoki).

CORFU TOWN

POP 28,692

Built on a promontory and wedged between two fortresses, Corfu's Old Town is a tangle of narrow walking streets through gorgeous Venetian buildings. Explore the winding alleys and surprising plazas in the early morning or late afternoon to avoid the hordes of day trippers seeking souvenirs.

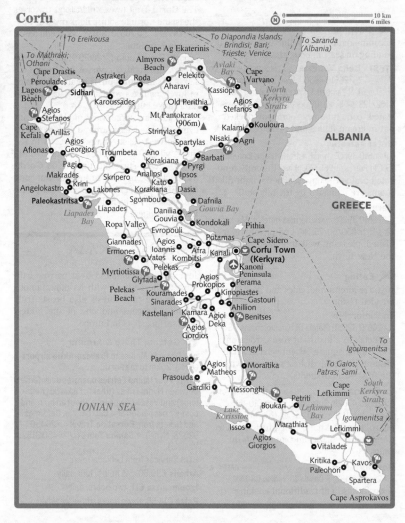

Corfu

◉ Sights

Palaio Frourio   FORTRESS
(Old Fortress; adult/concession €4/2; ⊙8.30am-7pm May-Oct, to 3pm Nov-Mar) The Palaio Frourio stands on an eastern promontory; the **Neo Frourio** (New Fortress) lies to the northwest.

Archaeological Museum   MUSEUM
(Vraïla 5; admission €4; ⊙8.30am-3pm Tue-Sun) Houses a collection of finds from Mycenaean to classical times.

Church of Agios Spiridon   CHURCH
(Agios Spiridonos) This richly decorated church displays the remains of St Spiridon, paraded through town four times a year.

🛏 Sleeping

Accommodation prices fluctuate wildly depending on season; book ahead.

TOP CHOICE ▸ Bella Venezia   BOUTIQUE HOTEL €€
(☑26610 46500; www.bellavenezia hotel.com; N Zambeli 4; s/d incl breakfast from €102/123; ❄✳🅰) Impeccable and understated; contemporary rooms are decked out in cream linens and marbles.

Hotel Astron   HOTEL €€
(☑26610 39505; hotel_astron@hol.gr; Donzelot 15, Old Port; s/d €65/70; ✳🅰) Recently renovated and with some sea views, light-filled rooms are managed by friendly staff.

Hermes Hotel   HOTEL €
(☑26610 39268; www.hermes-hotel.gr; Markora 12; s/d/tr €50/60/75; ✳) Completely refurbished, pleasant, well-appointed rooms in the New Town.

🍴 Eating

If you're after a bite, cafes and bars line the arcaded Liston.

To Dimarchio   ITALIAN, GREEK €€
(☑26610 39031; Plateia Dimarchio; mains €8-25) Relax in a luxurious rose garden on a charming square. Attentive staff serve elegant, inventive dishes, prepared with the freshest ingredients.

La Cucina   ITALIAN, CORFIOT €
(☑26610 45029; Guilford 17; mains €10-15) Every detail is cared for at this intimate bistro, from the hand-rolled tortellonis to the inventive pizzas and murals on the walls.

Rouvás   GREEK €
(☑26610 31182; S Desilla 13; mains €8-14; ⊙lunch) Resilient traditional cooking

makes this a favourite lunch stop for locals. It even caught the eye of UK celebrity chef Rick Stein for a TV cooking program.

ℹ Information

Tourist Police (☑26610 30265; 3rd fl, Samartzi 4)

ℹ Getting Around

Blue buses (€0.90 to €1.30) for villages near Corfu Town leave from Plateia San Rocco. Services to other destinations leave from Avrami terminal. A taxi from the airport to the centre costs around €15.

AROUND THE ISLAND

The **Corfu Trail** (www.corfutrail.org) traverses the island north to south. Book dives at **Corfu Divers** (☑26630 81038; www.corfu-divers.com) in **Kassiopi**.

Casa Lucia (☑26610 91419; www.casa-lucia-corfu.com; studios & cottages €60-120; 🅿✳), in **Sgombou**, is a garden complex of lovely cottages with a strong artistic and alternative ethos.

To gain an aerial view of the gorgeous cypress-backed bays around **Paleokastritsa**, the west coast's main resort, go to the quiet village of **Lakones**. Further south, good beaches surround tiny **Agios Gordios**. Backpackers head to low-key **Sunrock** (☑26610 94637; Pelekas Beach; dm/r per person €18/24; @✳) for its full-board hostel and genial atmosphere.

Lefkada ΛΕΥΚΑΔΑ

POP 22,500

Joined to the mainland by a narrow isthmus, fertile Lefkada with its mountainous interior and pine forests also boasts truly splendid beaches and one of the hottest windsurfing spots in Europe.

ℹ Getting There & Around

AIR Olympic Air flies to **Preveza-Aktio airport** (PVK), 20km to the north.

BOAT Four Island Ferries operates daily ferries between Nydri, Frikes (Ithaki), Fiskardo (Keffalonia) and Vasiliki. Trips take about an hour and cost €7 per person and €30 per car. Get times and tickets from **Borsalino Travel** (☑26450 92528; Nydri) or **Samba Tours** (☑26450 31520; Vasiliki).

BUS Services from Lefkada Town:

Athens €30.50, 5½ hours, four daily

Igoumenitsa €11, two hours, daily

Patra €14.50, three hours, three weekly

Preveza €2.70, 30 minutes, six daily

Thessaloniki €39.10, eight hours, two weekly

CAR Rent cars in Lefkada Town, Nydri or Vasiliki.

LEFKADA TOWN

Most travellers' first port of call, Lefkada Town remains laid-back except for August high season. The town's unique earthquake-resistant corrugated-steel architecture somehow blends with its attractive marina, waterfront cafes and vibrant pedestrian thoroughfares.

🛏 Sleeping & Eating

Restaurants and cafes line the main street, Dorpfeld, central Lefkas Sq and the waterfront.

Hotel Santa Maura HOTEL €€
(☑26450 21308; Dorpfeld; s/d/tr incl breakfast €55/75/85; ☀) Think tropical Bahamas with sky-blue and shell-pink interiors and breezy balconies; best rooms on the top floor.

Pension Pirofani HOTEL €€
(☑26450 25844; Dorpfeld; d €95; ☀) Renovated, sleek rooms have balconies for prime people-watching.

Faei Kairos TRADITIONAL GREEK €
(☑26450 24045; Golemi; mains €4.50-11) Unashamed nostalgia for the good old days of cinema defines this excellent eatery on Lefkada Town's waterfront.

AROUND THE ISLAND

With its lovely bay, **Nydri** is somewhat blighted by tacky souvenir shops and touristy tavernas. Escape instead to exquisite **Nhion** (☑26450 41624; Kiafa village; www.neion.gr; d/tr incl breakfast €95/125; ☀), a pristine mountain retreat with stellar views and restored stone buildings.

Lefkada's true gifts are its west-coast beaches. Cliffs drop to broad sweeps of white sand and turquoise waters. Explore! Tiny, bohemian **Agios Nikitas** village draws travellers, but gets very crowded in summer.

Southernmost eucalyptus-scented **Vasiliki** is popular with windsurfers. Organise lessons through **Club Vass** (☑26450 31588; www.clubvass.com), or guided treks, kayaking and other activities through **Trekking Hellas** (☑26450 31130; www.trekking.gr). Overlooking the port, **Pension Holidays** (☑26450 31426; s/d €60/65; ☀) has great-value rooms with kitchens.

POP 3700

Odysseus' long-lost home in Homer's *Odyssey*, Ithaki (ancient Ithaca) remains a verdant, pristine island blessed with cypress-covered hills and beautiful turquoise coves.

ℹ Getting There & Away

Ferries run between Frikes, Fiskardo (Keffalonia), Nydri and Vasiliki (Lefkada). Buy tickets at the Frikes dock just before departure. Trips take about 90 minutes and cost €7 per person and €33 per car. Other ferries run to Sami (Keffalonia) and Patras. Check ever-changing routes and schedules at **Delas Tours** (☑26740 32104; www.ithaca.com.gr; Vathy).

KIONI

Tucked in a tiny, tranquil bay, Kioni is a wonderful place to chill for a few days.

Individuals rent **rooms** (☑26740 31014; r €40, without bathroom €30), some with kitchens and sea views. **Captain's Apartments** (☑26740 31481; www.captains-apartments.gr; studio/apt €65/90; ☀) is owned by an affable former merchant navy captain. His shipshape, spacious apartments come with kitchens, satellite TV and balconies overlooking the valley and village.

Several tavernas dot the harbour. Try **Mythos** (mains €6-8) for excellent *pastitsio* and Greek staples. Comfy **Cafe Spavento** also has internet (per hour €4).

AROUND THE ISLAND

The dusty, relaxed port of **Frikes**, where the ferries dock, is a funkier alternative to Kioni and has rooms to rent.

Vathy, Ithaki's small, bustling capital, is the spot for hiring cars and getting cash (no banks in Kioni). Elegant mansions rise from around its bay and **Hotel Perantzada** (☑26740 33496; www.arthotel.gr/perantzada; Odyssea Androutsou; s/d incl breakfast from €130/150; ☀@☀) occupies two with sensational individually decorated rooms. Charming **Hotel Familia** (☑26740 33366; www.hotel-familia.com; Odysseos 60; d incl breakfast €140-160; ☺☀☎), in a renovated olive press, offers bikes and a bodacious breakfast.

Kefallonia ΚΕΦΑΛΛΟΝΙΑ

POP 39,500

Tranquil cypress- and fir-covered Kefallonia has not succumbed to package tourism to the extent that some of the other Ionian

KEFALLONIA HIGH-SEASON FERRIES

FROM	TO	FARE (€)	DURATION (HR)
Argostoli	Kyllini (Peloponnese)	14	3
Pesada	Agios Nikolaos (Zakynthos)	7	1½
Poros	Kyllini	10	1½
Sami	Bari (Italy)	45	12
Sami	Patra (Peloponnese)	17	2¾
Sami	Piso Aetos & Vathy (Ithaki)	6	45min

Islands have. This largest Ionian island is breathtakingly beautiful with rugged mountain ranges, rich vineyards, soaring coastal cliffs and golden beaches; it remains low-key outside resort areas. Due to the widespread destruction of an earthquake in 1953, much of the island's historic architecture was levelled; Fiskardo is the exception.

ⓘ Getting There & Around

AIR **Olympic Air** (☎26710 41511) flights go to Athens from **Keffalonia Airport** (EFL; ☎26710 41511), 9km south of Argostoli.

BOAT **Four Island Ferries** operates seasonal routes between Fiskardo, Frikes (Ithaki), Nydri and Vasiliki (Lefkada). In Fiskardo, get tickets from **Nautilus Travel** (☎26740 41440) or the dock before departure. Trips average 90 minutes and cost €7 per person and €30 per car.

BUS Four daily buses connect Argostoli with Athens (€37.10, seven hours), via Patra (€21, four hours)

CAR A car is best for exploring Kefallonia. **Pama Travel** (☎26740 41033; www.pamatravel.com; Fiskardo) rents cars and boats, books accommodation and has internet access.

FISKARDO

Pretty Fiskardo, with its pastel-coloured Venetian buildings set around a picturesque bay, was the only Kefallonian village not to be destroyed by the 1953 earthquake. Despite its popularity with European yachties and upmarket package tourists, it's still peaceful enough to appeal to independent travellers, and is a sublime spot to hang for a few days. Take lovely walks to sheltered coves for swimming.

🛏 Sleeping

Archontiko HISTORIC PENSION €€
(☎26740 41342; r from €80; ❄) Overlooking the harbour, people-watch from the balconies of these luxurious rooms in a restored stone mansion.

Faros Suites BOUTIQUE HOTEL €€
(☎26740 41355; www.myrtoscorp.com; ste incl breakfast from €115; ❄@❄) Apartments with fully equipped kitchens, some with sea views, in the next bay over from the village.

Regina's Rooms PENSION €€
(☎26740 41125; d €50-70) On the car park overlooking the village, this budget bargain is ideal for self-caterers. Some of its colourful, breezy rooms have gorgeous bay views or kitchenettes.

🍴 Eating

Fiskardo has no shortage of excellent waterside restaurants.

TOP CHOICE **Tassia** SEAFOOD, GREEK €€
(☎26740 41205; mains €10-25) This unassuming but famous Fiskardo institution run by Tassia Dendrinou, celebrated chef and writer, serves up excellent seafood and Greek dishes.

Café Tselenti ITALIAN €€
(☎26740 41344; mains €8-23) Enjoy outstanding Italian classics served by friendly waiters at this place tucked back a bit in a romantic plaza.

Vasso's SEAFOOD €€
(☎26740 41276; mains €10-40) Whether it's fresh grilled fish or pasta with crayfish, Vasso's is *the* place to head for exceptional seafood.

AROUND THE ISLAND

In **Argostoli**, the capital, stay over at **Vivian Villa** (☎26710 23396; www.kefalonia-vivianvilla.gr; Deladetsima 9; s/d/tr €55/70/85, apt €120; ❄) with its big, bright rooms and friendly owners. Sample top Kefallonian cuisine at **Arhontiko** (☎26710 27213; 5 Risospaston; mains €6.50-8.80).

Straddling a slender isthmus on the northwest coast, the petite pastel-coloured village of **Assos** watches over the ruins of a Venetian fortress perched upon a pine-covered peninsula. Splendid **Myrtos Beach**, 13km south of Assos, is spellbinding from above, with postcard views from the precarious roadway.

Zakynthos ΖΑΚΥΝΘΟΣ

POP 38,600

The beautiful island of Zakynthos, or Zante, has stunning coves, dramatic cliffs and extensive beaches, but unfortunately is swamped by package-tour groups, so only a few special spots warrant your time.

❶ Getting There & Around

AIR The **airport** (ZTH; ☑26950 28322) is 6km from Zakynthos Town. **Olympic Air** (☑26950 28322) has daily flights to Athens. easyJet offers occasional flights to Gatwick.

BOAT Get tickets at **Zakynthos Shipping Co-operative** (☑26950 22083/49500; Lombardou 40) in Zakynthos Town. Occasional ferries go to Brindisi, Italy (€69, 15½ hours).

BUS **KTEL bus station** (☑26950 22255) is west of Zakynthos town. Services:

Athens €23.20, six hours, three daily.

Kefallonia In high season two daily buses go from Pesada to Argostoli, and just two per week go from Agios Nikolaos. Alternatively, cross to Kyllini and catch another ferry to Kefallonia.

Patra €6.80, 3½ hours, four daily.

CAR As bus services are poor, explore the island by car.

Europcar (☑26950 41541; Plateia Agiou Louka, Zakynthos Town).

ZAKYNTHOS TOWN

The island's attractive Venetian capital and port was painstakingly reconstructed after the 1953 earthquake. Its elegant arcades and lively cafe scene make it the best base from which to explore the island.

The peaceful, pine-tree-filled **Kastro** (☑26950 48099; admission €3; ☺8.30am-2.30pm Tue-Sun), a ruined Venetian fortress high above town, makes for a pleasant outing. The **Byzantine Museum** (☑26950 42714; Pla-

teia Solomou; admission €3; ☺8.30am-3pm Tue-Sun) houses fabulous ecclesiastical art rescued from churches razed in the earthquake.

⛏ Sleeping & Eating

Avoid eating on the touristy Plateia Agiou Markou and do what the locals do: hit Alexandrou Roma for cheap eats. Sweet stores sell *mandolato*, the local soft nougat.

Hotel Strada Marina   HOTEL **€€**
(☑26950 42761; www.stradamarina.gr; Lombardou 14; s/d €60/90; ✳☒) Well-situated, portside rooms have balconies with sea views.

Camping Zante   CAMPING GROUND **€**
(☑26950 61710; www.zantecamping.gr; Ampula Beach; campsites per person/tent €6/5; @☒) Decent beachside camping 5km north of Zakynthos Town.

Green Boat Taverna   SEAFOOD, GREEK **€**
(☑26950 22957; Krionerou 50; mains €4-15) Fish and excellent Greek dishes, about 1km north along the waterfront.

Arekia   GREEK **€**
(☑26950 26346; Krioneriou 92; mains €3-10) Munch Greek specialities to the melodies of live *kantades* (serenades), north on the waterfront.

2D   SOUVLAKI **€**
(Alexandrou Roma 32; gyros from €2.50) Delicious gyros and juicy roast chickens.

AROUND THE ISLAND

The **Vasilikos Peninsula** is the pretty green region southeast of Zakynthos Town and fringing **Laganas Bay** with its long, lovely **Gerakas Beach**. The area has been declared a national marine park in order to protect the endangered loggerhead turtles that come ashore to lay their eggs in August, the peak of the tourist invasion. Inform yourself before exploring so as not to accidentally disrupt buried eggs.

TOP CHOICE **Logothetis Organic Farm** (☑26950 35106; http://logothetisfarm.gr; Vasilikos; 1-/2-bedroom cottage €70/150;

ZAKYNTHOS HIGH-SEASON FERRIES

FROM	TO	FARE (€)	DURATION (HR)
Zakynthos Town	Kyllini (Peloponnese)	8.50	1½
Agios Nikolaos	Pesada (Kefallonia)	7	1½
Poros	Kyllini	10	1½

🛜📶) offers tasteful cottages and bicycles, sells organic produce, and arranges horse-riding and sailing.

Cape Keri, near the island's southernmost point, has spectacular views of sheer cliffs and splendid beaches. Keri Beach is overrated. **Tartaruga Camping** (📞26950 51967; www.tartaruga-camping.com; campsites per adult/car/tent €5/3/3.60, r per person €20-50; P❄@), well signed on the road from Laganas to Keri, sprawls through terraced olive groves, pines and plane trees next to the sea.

Continue north and try to arrive early at gorgeous **Limnionas** for swimming in crystal-clear turquoise coves, as there's barely any space to sunbathe on the rocks. The only eatery at the cove, **Taverna Porto Limnionas** (mains €3-15) serves up delicious Greek classics in a sublime setting overlooking the sea.

Many people head to overhyped **Shipwreck Beach** in the northwest. For a sea-level look take a boat from Cape Skinari near Agios Nikolaos, Porto Vromi or Alykes.

UNDERSTAND GREECE

History

With its strategic position at the crossroads of Europe and Asia, Greece has endured a long and turbulent history. During the Bronze Age (3000–1200 BC in Greece), the advanced Cycladic, Minoan and Mycenaean civilisations flourished. The Mycenaeans were swept aside in the 12th century BC by the warrior-like Dorians, who introduced Greece to the Iron Age. The next 400 years are often referred to as the dark ages, a period about which little is known.

By 800 BC, when Homer's *Odyssey* and *Iliad* were first written down, Greece was undergoing a cultural and military revival with the evolution of the city states, the most powerful of which were Athens and Sparta. Greater Greece, Magna Graecia, was created, with southern Italy as an important component. The unified Greeks repelled the Persians twice, at Marathon (490 BC) and Salamis (480 BC). Victory over Persia was followed by unparalleled growth and prosperity known as the classical (or golden) age.

The Golden Age

During this period, Pericles commissioned the Parthenon, Sophocles wrote *Oedipus the King* and Socrates taught young Athenians to think. The golden age ended with the Peloponnesian War (431–404 BC), when the militaristic Spartans defeated the Athenians. They failed to notice the expansion of Macedonia under King Philip II, who easily conquered the war-weary city states.

Philip's ambitions were surpassed by those of his son, Alexander the Great, who marched triumphantly into Asia Minor, Egypt, Persia and what are now parts of Afghanistan and India. In 323 BC he met an untimely death at the age of 33, and his generals divided his empire between themselves.

Roman Rule & the Byzantine Empire

Roman incursions into Greece began in 205 BC. By 146 BC Greece and Macedonia had become Roman provinces. After the subdivision of the Roman Empire into eastern and western empires in AD 395, Greece became part of the Eastern (Byzantine) Empire, based at Constantinople.

In the centuries that followed, Venetians, Franks, Normans, Slavs, Persians, Arabs and, finally, Turks, took turns chipping away at the Byzantine Empire.

ORIGINAL OLYMPICS

The Olympic tradition emerged around the 11th century BC as a paean to the Greek gods, in the form of contests of athletic feats that were attended initially by notable men – and women – who assembled before the sanctuary priests and swore to uphold solemn oaths. By the 8th century BC, the attendance had grown to include a wide confederacy of city states, and the festival morphed into a male-only major event lasting five days at the site of Olympia. A ceremonial truce was enforced for the duration of the games. Crowds of spectators lined the tracks, where competitors vied for victory in athletics, chariot races, wrestling and boxing. Three millennia later, while the scale and scope of the games may have expanded considerably, the basic format has remained essentially unchanged.

The Ottoman Empire & Independence

After the end of the Byzantine Empire in 1453, when Constantinople fell to the Turks, most of Greece became part of the Ottoman Empire. Crete was not captured until 1670, leaving Corfu as the only island not occupied by the Turks. By the 19th century the Ottoman Empire was in decline. The Greeks, seeing nationalism sweep through Europe, fought the War of Independence (1821–22). Greek independence was proclaimed on 13 January 1822, only for arguments among the leaders who had been united against the Turks to escalate into civil war. The Turks, with the help of the Egyptians, tried to re-take Greece, but the great powers – Britain, France and Russia – intervened in 1827, and Ioannis Kapodistrias was elected the first Greek president.

Kapodistrias was assassinated in 1831 and the European powers stepped in once again, declaring that Greece should become a monarchy. In January 1833 Otho of Bavaria was installed as king. His ambition, called the Great Idea, was to unite all the lands of the Greek people to the Greek motherland. In 1862 he was peacefully ousted and the Greeks chose George I, a Danish prince, as king.

During WWI Prime Minister Venizelos allied Greece with France and Britain. King Constantine (George's son), who was married to the kaiser's sister Sophia, disputed this and left the country.

Smyrna & WWII

After the war Venizelos resurrected the Great Idea. Underestimating the new-found power of Turkey under the leadership of Atatürk (Mustafa Kemal), he sent forces to occupy Smyrna (the present-day Turkish port of İzmir), with its large Greek population. The army was heavily defeated and this led to a brutal population exchange between the two countries in 1923.

In 1930 George II, Constantine's son, was reinstated as king; he appointed the dictator General Metaxas as prime minister. Metaxas' grandiose ambition was to combine aspects of Greece's ancient and Byzantine past to create a Third Greek Civilisation. However, his chief claim to fame is his celebrated *ohi* (no) to Mussolini's request to allow Italian troops into Greece in 1940.

Greece fell to Germany in 1941 and resistance movements, polarised into royalist and communist factions, staged a bloody civil war lasting until 1949. The civil war was the trigger for a mass exodus that saw almost one million Greeks head off to countries such as Australia, Canada and the USA. Entire villages were abandoned as people gambled on a new start in cities such as Melbourne, Toronto, Chicago and New York.

The Colonels' Coup

Continuing political instability led to the colonels' coup d'état in 1967. The colonels' junta distinguished itself with its appalling brutality, repression and political incompetence. In 1974 it attempted to assassinate Cyprus' leader, Archbishop Makarios, and when he escaped the junta replaced him with the extremist Nikos Samson, prompting Turkey to occupy North Cyprus. The continued Turkish occupation of Cyprus remains one of the most contentious issues in Greek politics. The junta had little choice but to hand back power to the people. In November 1974 a plebiscite voted against restoration of the monarchy. Greece became a republic with the right-wing New Democracy (ND) party taking power.

The 1980s & 1990s

In 1981 Greece entered the European Community (now the EU) as its 10th, smallest and poorest member. Andreas Papandreou's Panhellenic Socialist Movement (Pasok) won the next election, giving Greece its first socialist government. Pasok, which ruled for most of the next two decades, promised the removal of US air bases and withdrawal from NATO, but delivered only rising unemployment and spiralling debt.

Elections in 1990 brought the ND party back to power, but tough economic reforms made the government unpopular and in 1993, Greeks again turned to Pasok and the ailing Papandreou. He had little option but to continue with the austerity program and became equally unpopular until he stood down in 1996 due to ill health. Pasok then abandoned its leftist policies, elected economist and lawyer Costas Simitis as leader, and romped to victory later that year.

The New Millennium

Simitis' government focused strongly on further integration with Europe and in January 2001 admission to the euro club was approved; Greece duly adopted the currency in 2002 and prices have been on the rise ever since.

Greece tilted to the right and in March 2004 elected the ND party led by Costas Karamanlis. This new broom was fortuitous, as the Olympic preparations were running late and suffering budget problems. While the Olympics were successful, Greece is still counting the cost.

During the long hot summer of 2007, forest fires threatened Athens and caused untold damage in the western Peloponnese, Epiros and Evia. Later that year, Karamanlis' government was returned to power for a second term, but amid growing discontent that included massive general strikes and riots, was turfed out in elections in October 2009 in favour of Pasok and George Papandreou, son and grandson of former prime ministers.

Textbooks are being written on Greece's 2010 financial crisis. Simply put, Greece almost fell over from years of over-borrowing, overspending and breaking eurozone rules on deficit management. Financially crippled and looking likely to drag other failing eurozone economies down with it, in May 2010 Greece was on the receiving end of a €110-billion bail-out package to help right the ship. Time will tell if it stays afloat. Needless to say, austerity measures to help balance the budget were not popular, with citizens angry about cuts in spending, pensions and salaries, along with higher taxes.

Greece's foreign policy is dominated by a perceptibly warming, yet still sensitive relationship with Turkey – with Greece continuing to support Turkey's bid to join the EU, despite concerns over Turkish plans to explore for oil and gas in the eastern Aegean.

People

Greece's population has exceeded 11.1 million, with around one-third of the people living in the Greater Athens area and more than two-thirds living in cities – confirming that Greece is now a primarily urban society. Less than 15% live on the islands, the most populous being Crete, Evia and Corfu. Greece has an ageing population and declining birth rate, with big families a thing of the past. Population growth over the last couple of decades is due to a flood of migrants, both legal and illegal.

About 95% of the Greek population belongs to the Greek Orthodox Church. The remainder is split between the Roman Catholic, Protestant, Evangelist, Jewish and Muslim faiths. While older Greeks and those in rural areas tend to be deeply religious, most young people are decidedly more secular.

The Greek year is centred on the saints' days and festivals of the church calendar. Name days (celebrating your namesake saint) are celebrated more than birthdays. Most people are named after a saint, as are boats, suburbs and train stations.

Orthodox Easter is usually at a different time than Easter celebrated by Western churches, though generally in April/May.

RECOGNISE THAT TWANG?

Don't be surprised if your hotel receptionist or waiter speaks perfect English with an Australian twang. A growing stream of young second- and third-generation Greeks are repatriating from the USA, Australia, Canada and other reaches of the Greek diaspora. A huge number of Greeks emigrated during their country's tumultuous history and it is said that over five million people of Greek descent live in 140 countries around the world. Strong sentimental attractions endure and many expat Greeks are involved in the political and cultural life of their ancestral islands, and many retire in Greece.

Arts

The arts have been integral to Greek life since ancient times, with architecture having had the most profound influence. Greek temples, seen throughout history as symbolic of democracy, were the inspiration for architectural movements such as the Italian Renaissance. Today masses of cheap concrete apartment blocks built in the 20th century in Greece's major cities belie this architectural legacy.

Thankfully, the great works of Greek literature are not as easily besmirched. The first and greatest Ancient Greek writer was Homer, author of *Iliad* and *Odyssey,* telling the story of the Trojan War and the subsequent wanderings of Odysseus.

Pindar (c 518–438 BC) is regarded as the pre-eminent lyric poet of ancient Greece and was commissioned to recite his odes at the Olympic Games. The great writers of love poetry were Sappho (6th century BC) and

Alcaeus (5th century BC), both of whom lived on Lesvos. Sappho's poetic descriptions of her affections for women gave rise to the term 'lesbian'.

The Alexandrian Constantine Cavafy (1863–1933) revolutionised Greek poetry by introducing a personal, conversational style. Later, poet George Seferis (1900–71) won the Nobel Prize for literature in 1963, as did Odysseus Elytis (1911–96) in 1979. Nikos Kazantzakis, author of *Zorba the Greek* and numerous novels, plays and poems, is the most famous of 20th-century Greek novelists.

Greece's most famous painter was a young Cretan called Domenikos Theotokopoulos, who moved to Spain in 1577 and became known as the great El Greco. Famous painters of the 20th century include Konstantinos, Partenis and, later, George Bouzianis, whose work can be viewed at the National Art Gallery in Athens.

Music has been a facet of Greek life since ancient times. When visiting Greece today, your trip will inevitably be accompanied by the plucked-string sound of the ubiquitous bouzouki. The bouzouki is one of the main instruments of *rembetika* music – which is in many ways the Greek equivalent of the American blues and has its roots in the sufferings of refugees from Asia Minor in the 1920s.

Dance is also an integral part of Greek life. Whether at a wedding, nightclub or village celebration, traditional dance is widely practised.

Drama continues to feature in domestic arts, particularly in Athens and Thessaloniki. In summer Greek dramas are staged in the ancient theatres where they were originally performed.

Greek film has for many years been associated with the work of film-maker Theo Angelopoulos, who won Cannes' Palme d'Or in 1998 with *An Eternity and One Day*.

Greek TV is dominated by chat shows, sport and foreign movies, only to be interrupted by localised versions of the latest American 'reality TV' hit.

Environment

The Land

Greece sits at the southern tip of the Balkan Peninsula. Of its 1400 islands, only 169 are inhabited. The land mass is 131,944 sq km

and Greek territorial waters cover a further 400,000 sq km. Nowhere in Greece is much more than 100km from the sea.

Around 80% of the land is mountainous, with less than a quarter of the country suitable for agriculture.

Greece sits in one of the most seismically active regions in the world – the eastern Mediterranean lies at the meeting point of three continental plates: the Eurasian, African and Arabian. Consequently, Greece has had more than 20,000 earthquakes in the last 40 years, most of them very minor.

Wildlife

The variety of flora in Greece is unrivalled in Europe, with a dazzling array of spectacular wildflowers best seen in the mountains of Crete and the southern Peloponnese.

You won't encounter many animals in the wild, mainly due to hunting. Wild boar, still found in the north, is a favourite target. Squirrels, rabbits, hares, foxes and weasels are all fairly common on the mainland. Reptiles are well represented by snakes, including several poisonous viper species.

Lake Mikri Prespa in Macedonia has the richest colony of fish-eating birds in Europe, while the Dadia Forest Reserve in Thrace counts such majestic birds as the golden eagle and the giant black vulture among its residents.

The brown bear, Europe's largest land mammal, still survives in very small numbers in the mountains of northern Greece, as does the grey wolf.

Europe's rarest mammal, the monk seal, once very common in the Mediterranean Sea, is now on the brink of extinction in Europe. There are about 400 left in Europe, half of which live in Greece. About 40 frequent the Ionian Sea and the rest are found in the Aegean.

The waters around Zakynthos are home to Europe's last large sea turtle colony, that of the loggerhead turtle *(Careta careta)*. The **Sea Turtle Protection Society of Greece** (✏/fax 21052 31342; www.archelon.gr) runs monitoring programs and is always on the look-out for volunteers.

National Parks

While facilities in Greek national parks aren't on par with many other countries, all have refuges and some have marked hiking trails. The most visited parks are Mt Parnitha, north of Athens, and the Samaria

Gorge on Crete. The others are Vikos-Aoös and Prespa National Parks in Epiros; Mt Olympus on the border of Thessaly and Macedonia; and Parnassos and Iti National Parks in central Greece. There is also a national marine park off the coast of Alonnisos, and another around the Bay of Laganas area off Zakynthos.

Environmental Issues

Greece is belatedly becoming environmentally conscious but, regrettably, it's too late for some regions. Deforestation and soil erosion are problems that go back thousands of years, with olive cultivation and goats being the main culprits. Forest fires are also a major problem, with an estimated 250 sq km destroyed every year.

General environmental awareness remains at a depressingly low level, especially where litter is concerned. The problem is particularly bad in rural areas, where roadsides are strewn with aluminium cans and plastic packaging hurled from passing cars. It is somewhat surprising that the waters of the Aegean are as clear as they are considering how many cigarette butts are tossed off ferries.

Food & Drink

Snacks

Greece has a great range of fast-food options. Foremost among them are gyros and souvlaki. The gyros is a giant skewer laden with seasoned meat that grills slowly as it rotates, the meat being steadily trimmed from the outside. Souvlaki are small cubes of meat cooked on a skewer. Both are served wrapped in pitta bread with salad and lashings of tzatziki (a yogurt, cucumber and garlic dip). Other snacks are pretzel rings, spanakopita (spinach and cheese pie) and *tyropitta* (cheese pie).

Starters

Greece is famous for its appetisers, known as *mezedhes* (literally, 'tastes'; meze for short). Standards include tzatziki, *melitzanosalata* (aubergine dip), taramasalata (fish-roe dip), dolmadhes (stuffed vine leaves; dolmas for short), *fasolia* (beans) and *oktapodi* (octopus). A selection of three or four starters represents a good meal and makes an excellent vegetarian option.

Main Dishes

You'll find moussaka (layers of aubergine and mince, topped with béchamel sauce and baked) on every menu, alongside a number of other taverna staples. They include *moschari* (oven-baked veal and potatoes), *keftedes* (meatballs), *stifado* (meat stew), *pastitsio* (baked dish of macaroni with minced meat and béchamel sauce) and *yemista* (either tomatoes or green peppers stuffed with minced meat and rice).

Kalamaria (fried squid) is the most popular (and cheapest) seafood, while *barbouni* (red mullet) and *sifias* (swordfish) tend to be more expensive than meat dishes.

Fortunately for vegetarians, salad is a mainstay of the Greek diet. The most popular is *horiatiki salata,* normally listed on English-language menus as Greek salad. It's a delicious mixed salad comprising cucumbers, peppers, onions, olives, tomatoes and feta cheese. For the full scoop on Greece's legendary feta cheese, check out www.feta.gr.

Desserts

Most Greek desserts are Turkish in origin and variations on pastry soaked in honey, such as baklava (thin layers of pastry filled with honey and nuts). Delicious Greek yogurt also makes a great dessert, especially with honey.

THE ART OF OUZO

Ouzo is Greece's most famous but misunderstood tipple. While it can be drunk as an aperitif, for most Greeks ouzo has come to embody a way of socialising – best enjoyed during a lazy, extended summer afternoon of seafood *mezedhes* (appetisers) by the beach. Ouzo is sipped slowly and ritually to clean the palate between tastes. It is served in small bottles or *karafakia* (carafes) with water and a bowl of ice cubes – and is commonly drunk on the rocks, diluted with water (it turns a cloudy white). Mixing it with cola is a foreign abomination!

Made from distilled grapes, ouzo is also distilled with residuals from fruit, grains and potatoes, and flavoured with spices, primarily aniseed, giving it that liquorice flavour. The best ouzo is produced on Lesvos and there are more than 360 brands!

NO MORE SMOKE

Legislation that brought in anti-smoking laws similar to those throughout Europe in 2009 was not exactly popular with Greeks, the EU's biggest smokers. Smoking is now officially banned inside public places with the penalty fines placed on the business owners.

Drinks

Bottled mineral water is cheap and available everywhere, as are soft drinks and packaged juices.

Mythos, in its distinctive green bottle, and Alfa, are popular Greek beers.

Greece is traditionally a wine-drinking society. An increasingly good range of wines made from traditional grape varieties is available. Wine enthusiasts should take a look at www.allaboutgreekwine.com. Retsina, wine flavoured with pine-tree resin, is a tasty alternative – though an acquired taste for some. Most tavernas will offer locally made house wines by the carafe.

Metaxa, Greece's dominant brandy, is sweet, while if you are offered some raki, make sure to take a small sip first!

'Greek' coffee should be tried at least once. Don't drink the mudlike grounds at the bottom!

Where to Eat & Drink

The most common variety of restaurant in Greece is the taverna, traditionally an extension of the Greek home table. *Estiatorio* is Greek for restaurant and often has the same dishes as a taverna but with higher prices. A *psistaria* specialises in charcoal-grilled dishes, while a *psarotaverna* specialises in fish. *Ouzeria* (ouzo bars) often have such a range of *mezedhes* that they can be regarded as eateries. For opening hours of restaurants and cafes, see p448. Restaurant listings in this chapter without specified business hours are open for lunch and dinner daily during high season.

Kafeneia are the smoke-filled cafes where men gather to drink 'Greek' coffee, play backgammon and cards, and engage in heated political discussion. Every Greek town you'll visit now has at least one cafe-bar where Greece's youth while away hours over a frappé (frothy ice coffee).

Buying and preparing your own food is easy in Greece – every town of consequence has a supermarket, as well as fruit and vegetable shops.

To have a go at producing your own Greek culinary masterpieces, check out www.gourmed.gr. You'll also find information on the healthy Greek diet at www.mediterranean-diet.gr, while www.oliveoil.gr can tell you all about one of Greece's best-known products.

SURVIVAL GUIDE

Directory A–Z

Accommodation

Hotels Classified as deluxe, or A, B, C, D or E class; ratings seldom seem to have much bearing on the price, which is determined more by season and location.

Domatia Greek equivalent of a B&B, minus the breakfast; don't worry about finding them – owners will find you as they greet ferries and buses shouting 'room!'.

Youth hostels In most major towns and on some islands; Greek Youth Hostel Organisation (☏21075 19530;www.athens-yhostel.com).

Camping grounds Generally open from April to October; standard facilities include hot showers, kitchens, restaurants and minimarkets – and often a swimming pool; Panhellenic Camping Association (www.panhellenic-camping-union.gr).

Mountain refuges Listed in *Greece Mountain Refuges & Ski Centres,* available free of charge at EOT and EOS (Ellinikos Orivatikos Syndesmos, the Greek Alpine Club) offices.

HAPHAZARD OPENING HOURS

It's worth noting that with businesses associated with tourists, opening hours can be rather haphazard. In high season when there are plenty of visitors around, restaurants, cafes, nightclubs and souvenir shops are pretty much open whenever they think they can do good business. If there are few people around, some businesses will simply close early or won't bother opening at all. And in low season, some places, including some sleeping options, may close up for months at a time.

PRICE RANGES

In this chapter we have used the following price ranges for sleeping options. Prices quoted in listings are for high season (usually July and August) and include a private bathroom.

€€€ more than €150

€€ €60 to €150

€ less than €60

Business Hours

Banks 8am-2.30pm Mon-Thu, 8am-2pm Fri (in cities, also: 3.30-6.30pm Mon-Fri, 8am-1.30pm Sat)

Cafes 10am-midnight

Post offices 7.30am-2pm Mon-Fri (in cities 7.30am-8pm Mon-Fri, 7.30am-2pm Sat)

Restaurants 11am-3pm & 7pm-1am (varies greatly)

Supermarkets 8am-8pm Mon-Fri, 8am-3pm Sat

Street kiosks (*periptera*) early-late Mon-Sun

Children

» It's safe and easy to travel with children in Greece.
» Greeks are very family-orientated.
» Be very careful crossing roads with kids!
» Travel on ferries, buses and trains is free to age four years; half-fare to age 10 (ferries) or 12 (buses and trains).
» You'll find plenty of kids' menus.
» See www.greece4kids.com.

Customs

You may bring the following into Greece duty-free:

» 200 cigarettes or 50 cigars
» 1L of spirits or 2L of wine
» 50ml of perfume
» 250ml of eau de cologne.

It is strictly forbidden to export antiquities (anything over 100 years old) without an export permit.

Embassies & Consulates

Australia (☑210 870 4000; www.greece. embassy.gov.au; 6th fl, Thon Building, cnr Leoforos Alexandras & Leoforos Kifisias, Ambelokipi, Athens)

Canada (☑210 727 3400; www.greece.gc.ca; Genadiou 4, Athens)

Japan (☑210 670 9900; www.gr.emb-japan. go.jp; Ethnikís Antistáseos 46, Halandri, Athens)

New Zealand (☑210 692 4136; www.nz embassy.com; costacot@yahoo.com; Kifisias 76, Ambelokipi, Athens)

UK (☑210 727 2600; http://ukingreece.fco.gov. uk; Ploutarhou 1, Athens)

USA (☑210 721 2951; http://athens.usembassy. gov; Leoforos Vasilissis Sofias 91, Athens)

Food

In this chapter we have used the following price ranges for Eating options:

€€€ more than €40

€€ €15 to €40

€ less than €15

Gay & Lesbian Travellers

» The church plays a significant role in shaping society's views on issues such as sexuality, and homosexuality is generally frowned upon.
» It is wise to be discreet and to avoid open displays of togetherness. That said, Greece is a popular destination for gay travellers.
» Athens has a busy gay scene that packs up and heads to the islands for summer.
» Mykonos has long been famous for its bars, beaches and hedonism.
» A visit to Eresos on Lesvos has become something of a pilgrimage for lesbians.

SEASONAL PRICES

The prices quoted in this chapter for sleeping options are for 'high season' (usually July and August). If you turn up in the 'middle' or 'shoulder seasons' (May and June; September and October) expect to pay significantly less. During 'low season' (late October to late April) prices can be up to 50% cheaper, but a lot of places, especially on the islands, virtually close their shutters for winter. Websites will usually display these differences in price.

Greek accommodation is subject to strict price controls, and by law a notice must be displayed in every room stating the category of the room and the seasonal price. If you think there's something amiss, contact the Tourist Police.

KALIMERA!

Greece is one of those countries where a big smile and some local language can go a long way. If you make an effort, so will the locals. For some more phrases, see the Language chapter (p1030) but also try these basics on for size – they're likely to be all you'll need, and are best if they come with a smile:

» ka·li·me·ra	Good morning
» yia su	Hello
» ef·kha·ri·sto	Thank you
» pa·ra·ka·lo	Please/You're welcome
» stin i·yia mas	Cheers!

Greece is also one of those countries where it pays not to get upset if things don't go your way. There's no point in getting angry with anyone if the ferry is late (or if it doesn't come at all!). You'll likely be met with a stone face and unhelpful service. Relax! You're in Greece!

Internet Access

» Greece has embraced the internet big-time.

» Charges differ wildly (as does the speed of access).

» Some midrange and most top-end hotels will offer their guests some form of internet connection.

» Laptop-wielding visitors will often be able to connect to wi-fi at hotels and most internet cafes.

Language Courses

For intensive language courses check out the Athens Centre (www.athenscentre.gr).

Money

ATMs Everywhere except the smallest villages.

Bargaining While souvenir shops will generally bargain, prices in other shops are normally clearly marked and non-negotiable; accommodation is nearly always negotiable outside peak season, especially for longer stays.

Cash Currency is king at street kiosks and small shops, and especially in the countryside.

Changing currency Banks, post offices and currency exchange offices are all over the places; exchange all major currencies.

Credit cards Generally accepted, but may not be on smaller islands or in small villages.

Tipping The service charge is included on the bill in restaurants, but it is the custom to 'round up the bill'; same for taxis.

Post

» *Tahydromia* (post offices) are easily identified by the yellow sign outside.

» Regular postboxes are yellow; red postboxes are for express mail.

» The postal rate for postcards and airmail letters within the EU is €0.60, to other destinations it's €0.80.

Public Holidays

New Year's Day 1 January

Epiphany 6 January

First Sunday in Lent February

Greek Independence Day 25 March

Good Friday/Easter Sunday March/April

May Day (Protomagia) 1 May

Feast of the Assumption 15 August

Ohi Day 28 October

Christmas Day 25 December

St Stephen's Day 26 December

Safe Travel

» Crime is traditionally low in Greece, but on the rise.

» Watch out for bar scams and *bombes* (spiked drinks).

» Be careful of pickpockets on the Athens metro, around Omonia and at the flea market.

» Thefts from tourists are often committed by other tourists.

Telephone

» Maintained by Organismos Tilepikoinonion Ellados, known as OTE (o-*teh*).

» Public phones are easy to use; pressing the 'i' button brings up the operating instructions in English.

» Public phones are everywhere and all use phonecards.

» For directory inquiries within Greece, call ☏131 or ☏132; for international directory inquiries, it's ☏161 or ☏162.

MOBILE PHONES

» Mobile phones have become the must-have accessory in Greece.

» If you have a compatible GSM phone from a country with a global roaming agreement with Greece, you will be able to use your phone there.

» Make sure you have global roaming activated before you leave your country of residence.

» There are several mobile service providers in Greece; CosmOTE (www.cosmote.gr) has the best coverage.

» You can purchase a Greek SIM card for around €20.

PHONE CODES

» Telephone codes are part of the 10-digit number within Greece.

» The landline prefix is 2 and for mobiles it's 6.

PHONECARDS

» All public phones use OTE phonecards; sold at OTE offices and street kiosks.

» Phonecards come in €3, €5 and €10 versions; local calls cost €0.30 for three minutes.

» Discount-card schemes are available, offering much better value for money.

Time

» One time zone throughout Greece.

» Two hours ahead of GMT/UTC.

» Three hours ahead on daylight-savings time: from the last Sunday in March to the last Sunday in October.

MOVING ON?

For tips, recommendations and reviews beyond Greece, head to shop.lonelyplanet.com, where you can purchase downloadable PDFs of the Albania and Turkey chapters from Lonely Planet's *Mediterranean Europe* guide, or the Macedonia and Bulgaria chapters from *Eastern Europe*.

Toilets

» Public toilets are rare, except at airports and bus and train stations.

» Most places have Western-style toilets.

» Some public toilets may be Asian-style squat toilets.

» Greek plumbing can't handle toilet paper! Anything larger than a postage stamp will cause a blockage. Put your used toilet paper, sanitary napkins and tampons in the small bin provided next to every toilet.

Tourist Information

Greek National Tourist Organisation (GNTO; www.gnto.gr) Known as EOT within Greece.

EOT office or **local tourist office** In almost every town of consequence and on many of the islands.

Tourist Police In popular destinations, and can also provide information; head here if you think you've been ripped off.

Travellers with Disabilities

» Most hotels, museums and ancient sites are not wheelchair accessible; the uneven terrain is an issue even for able-bodied people.

» Few facilities for the visually or hearing impaired.

» Check out www.greecetravel.com/handicapped.

Visas

» Visitors from most countries don't need a visa for Greece.

» Countries whose nationals can stay in Greece for up to three months include Australia, Canada, all EU countries, Iceland, Israel, Japan, New Zealand and the USA.

Getting There & Away

Air

» Most visitors arrive by air, mostly into Athens.

» Seventeen international airports in Greece; most handle only summer charter flights to the islands.

» Growing number of scheduled services by budget airlines, eg easyJet flies into Athens, Corfu, Hania, Iraklio, Kos, Mykonos, Rhodes, Santorini, Thessaloniki and Zakynthos

CITY	AIRPORT	DESIGNATION
Aktion (for Lefkada)	Aktion National Airport	PVK
Athens	Eleftherios Venizelos Airport	ATH
Corfu	Corfu Intl Airport	CFU
Hania (Crete)	Hania Intl Airport	CHQ
Iraklio	Nikos Kazantzakis Airport	HER
Kalamata	Kalamata Intl Airport	KLX
Karpathos	Karpathos National Airport	AOK
Kavala	Alexander the Great Airport	KVA
Kefallonia	Kefallonia Intl Airport	EFL
Kos	Hippocrates Intl Airport	KGS
Mykonos	Mykonos National Airport	JMK
Rhodes	Diagoras Airport	RHO
Samos	Samos Intl Airport	SMI
Santorini (Thira)	Santorini National Airport	JTR
Skiathos	Skiathos National Airport	JSI
Thessaloniki	Macedonia Airport	SKG
Zakynthos	Zakynthos Intl Airport	ZTH

Greek Airlines flying international routes:

Olympic Air (OA; www.olympicair.com) Privatised version of former Olympic Airlines.

Aegean Airlines (A3; www.aegeanair.com)

Land
BORDER CROSSINGS
You can drive or ride through the following border crossings (the main one is Kakavia):

From Albania:
» Kakavia (60km northwest of Ioannina)
» Sagiada (28km north of Igoumenitsa)
» Mertziani (17km west of Konitsa)
» Krystallopigi (14km west of Kotas)

From Bulgaria:
» Promahonas (109km northeast of Thessaloniki)
» Ormenio (in northeastern Thrace)
» Exohi (50km north of Drama)

From Macedonia:
» Evzoni (68km north of Thessaloniki)
» Niki (16km north of Florina)
» Doïrani (31km north of Kilkis)

From Turkey:
» Kipi (43km east of Alexandroupolis)
» Kastanies (139km northeast of Alexandroupolis)

BUS
The **Hellenic Railways Organisation** (OSE; www.ose.gr) operates:

To Albania Overnight bus between Athens and Tirana (16 hours, daily) via Ioannina and Gjirokastra.

To Bulgaria Athens–Sofia bus (15 hours, six weekly); Thessaloniki-Sofia (7½ hours, four daily).

To Turkey Athens to İstanbul (22 hours, six weekly); stops at Thessaloniki (seven hours) and Alexandroupolis (13 hours).

TRAIN
To Bulgaria Daily train between Sofia and Athens (18 hours) via Thessaloniki.

To Macedonia Two trains daily from Thessaloniki to Skopje (five hours).

To Turkey Daily trains operate between İstanbul and Thessaloniki (12 hours).

To Russia Summer-only direct weekly service from Thessaloniki to Moscow (70 hours).

Sea
Check out ferry routes, schedules and services online at www.greekferries.gr.

ALBANIA

Saranda Petrakis Lines (☎26610 38690; www.ionian-cruises.com) has daily hydrofoils to Corfu (25 minutes).

ITALY

Ancona In summer, there are three daily sailings to Patra (20 hours).

Bari Daily sailings to Patra (14½ hours) via Corfu (eight hours) and Keffalonia (14 hours); also daily to Igoumenitsa (11½ hours).

Brindisi Operates only between April and early October; services to Patra (15 hours), calling in at Igoumenitsa.

Venice In summer, up to 12 weekly sailings to Patra (30 hours) via Corfu (25 hours).

TURKEY

Boat services operate between Turkey's Aegean coast and the Greek Islands:

Rhodes to Marmaris Daily in summer, twice weekly in winter; 50 minutes.

Symi to Datça Saturdays in summer; one hour.

Kos to Bodrum Daily in summer; one hour.

Samos to Kuşadası Daily in summer, weekly in winter; one hour.

Chios to Çeşme Daily in summer; one hour.

Lesvos to Ayvalik Four times weekly in summer; one hour.

Getting Around

Greece has a comprehensive transport system and is easy to get around.

LONDON TO ATHENS OVERLAND

For overland enthusiasts, a trip from London to Athens can be accomplished in two days, taking in some gorgeous scenery along the way. A sample itinerary from London would see you catching the Eurostar to Paris and then an overnight sleeper train to Bologna in Italy. From there, a coastal train takes you to Bari, where there's an overnight boat to Patra on the Peloponnese. From Patra, it's a 4½-hour train journey to Athens.

Air

Domestic air travel has been very price competitive of late, and it's sometimes cheaper to fly than take the ferry, especially if you book ahead online. A plan to merge Olympic Air and Aegean Airlines was prohibited by the European Commission in January 2011 due to its potential effect on competition and prices.

Domestic Air Carriers

Aegean Airlines (A3; www.aegeanair.com) The big competition offers newer aircraft and similar prices on popular routes.

Astra Airlines (A2; www.astra-airlines.gr) Based in Thessaloniki; a newcomer flying limited routes.

Athens Airways (ZF; www.athensairways. com) New kid on the block.

Olympic Air (OA; www.olympicair.com) Recently privatised; has the most extensive network.

Sky Express (SHE; www.skyexpress.gr) Based in Iraklio, Crete; mainly flies routes that the big two don't.

Bicycle

» Greece has very hilly terrain.
» Summer heat can be stifling.
» Many drivers totally disregard the road rules.

Bicycle tours See www.cyclegreece.gr; bicycles are carried for free on ferries.

Rental bicycles Available at most tourist centres, but these are generally for pedalling around town rather than for serious riding. Prices generally range from €10 to €20 per day.

Boat

FERRY

» Ferries come in all shapes and sizes, from state-of-the-art 'superferries' that run on the major routes, to ageing open ferries that operate local services to outlying islands.
» Newer high-speed ferries are slashing travel times, but cost much more.
» 'Classes' on ferries are largely a thing of the past; you have the option of 'deck class', which is the cheapest ticket, or 'cabin class' with air-con cabins and a decent lounge and restaurant.
» When buying tickets you will automatically be given deck class.

» Tickets can be bought at the last minute at the dock, but in high season, some boats may be full – plan ahead.

CATAMARAN

» High-speed catamarans have become an important part of the island travel scene.
» Much less prone to cancellation in rough weather.
» Catamaran fares are generally more expensive than ferries and about the same as hydrofoils.

HYDROFOIL

» A faster alternative to ferries on some routes; take half the time, but cost twice as much.
» Most routes will operate only during the high season.
» Tickets for hydrofoils must be bought in advance and they are often sold with seat allocation.

Bus

» Long-distance buses are operated by **KTEL** (Koino Tamio Eispraxeon Leoforion; www. ktel.org).
» Fares are fixed by the government; service routes can be found on the company's website.
» Comfortable, generally run on time, and frequent services on all major routes.
» Reasonably priced – eg Athens–Volos (€25, five hours) and Athens–Patra (€17, three hours).
» Tickets should be bought at least an hour in advance to ensure a seat.
» Buses don't have toilets and refreshments, but stop for a break every couple of hours.

Car & Motorcycle

» A great way to explore areas in Greece that are off the beaten track.

ISLAND-HOPPING

For many, the idea of meandering from island to island by boat in the Greek Islands is the ultimate dream. It's still a lot of fun, but to some extent not what it used to be. Many of those slow, romantic old ferries you may have seen in the movies have disappeared, replaced by big modern people-movers. If you turn up in high season you might find it just as stressful as rush hour back home.

It's still possible to get away from it all, but it will require some thought – head to smaller islands off the beaten path before high season kicks in. Every island has a boat service of some sort!

Boat operations are highly seasonal and based on the tourist trade, so there's not a lot happening in winter. Services pick up from April, and during July and August Greece's seas are a mass of wake and wash.

Summer also brings the *meltemi,* a strong dry northerly wind that can blow for days and cause havoc to ferry schedules.

In any season, changes to schedules can take place at the last minute. Be prepared to be flexible. Boats seldom arrive early, but often arrive late! And some don't come at all. Think of it as part of the fun.

Check out www.greekferries.gr for schedules, costs and links to individual boat company websites.

» Be careful – Greece has the highest road-fatality rate in Europe.

» The road network has improved dramatically in recent years.

» Freeway tolls are fairly hefty.

» Almost all islands are served by car ferries, but they are expensive; costs vary by the size of the vehicle.

» The Greek automobile club, **ELPA** (www.elpa.gr), generally offers reciprocal services to members of other national motoring associations. If your vehicle breaks down, dial ☑104.

» EU-registered vehicles are allowed free entry into Greece for six months without road taxes being due; a green card (international third party insurance) is all that's required.

HIRE
Rental cars

» Available just about anywhere in Greece.

» Better rates with local companies than with the big multinational outfits.

» Check the insurance waivers closely; check how they can assist in case of a breakdown.

» High-season weekly rates start at about €280 for the smallest models, dropping to €200 in winter – add tax and extras.

» Major companies will request a credit-card deposit.

» Minimum driving age in Greece is 18, but most car-hire firms require a driver of 21 or over.

Mopeds & Motorcycles

» Available for hire everywhere.

» Regulations stipulate that you need a valid motorcycle licence stating proficiency for the size of motorcycle you wish to rent – from 50cc upwards.

» Mopeds and 50cc motorcycles range from €10 to €25 per day or from €25 per day for a 250cc motorcycle.

» Outside high season, rates drop considerably.

» Ensure that the bike is in good working order and the brakes work well.

» Check that your travel insurance covers you for injury resulting from motorcycle accidents.

ROAD RULES

» Drive on the right.

» Overtake on the left (not all Greeks do this!).

» Compulsory to wear seatbelts in the front seats, and in the back if they are fitted.

» Drink-driving laws are strict; a blood alcohol content of 0.05% incurs a fine of around €150 and over 0.08% is a criminal offence.

Public Transport

Bus All major towns have local bus systems.

Metro Athens is the only city with a metro system.

Taxi

» Widely available and reasonably priced.
» Yellow city cabs are metered; rates double between midnight and 5am. Grey rural taxis do not have meters; settle on a price before you get in.
» Athens taxi drivers are gifted in their ability to somehow make a little bit extra with every fare. If you have a complaint, note the cab number and contact the Tourist Police.
» Rural taxi drivers are generally honest, friendly and helpful.

Train

» Greece has only two main lines: Athens north to Thessaloniki and Alexandroupolis, and Athens to the Peloponnese
» There are a number of branch lines, eg Pyrgos–Olympia line and the spectacular Diakofto–Kalavryta mountain railway.
» **Greek Railways Organisation** (OSE; www.ose.gr)
» Inter-Rail and Eurail passes are valid; you still need to make a reservation.
» In summer make reservations at least two days in advance.

Italy

Best Places to Eat

» Pizzeria da Baffetto (p483)

» Osteria de' Poeti (p520)

» L'Osteria di Giovanni (p531)

» Civico 25 (p542)

» Piccolo Napoli (p562)

Best Places to Stay

» Hotel in Pietra (p556)

» Daphne Inn (p481)

» Ca' Angeli (p510)

» Hostel of the Sun (p548)

» Albergo Miramare (p554)

Why Go?

The land that has turned its lifestyle into a designer accessory, Italy is one of Europe's great seducers. Ever since the days of the 18th-century Grand Tour, travellers have been falling under its spell and still today it stirs strong emotions. The rush of seeing the Colosseum for the first time or cruising down Venice's surreal canals are feelings you'll remember for life.

Of course, Italy is not all about Michelangelo masterpieces and frescoed churches. There's also the food, imitated the world over, and a landscape that boasts beautiful Alpine peaks, stunning coastlines and remote, silent valleys. So if the cities don't do it for you, if their noise, heat and chaos start getting to you – as they get to many locals – change gear and head out to the country for a taste of the sun-kissed slow life.

When to Go
Rome

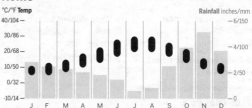

| Apr & May Per-fect spring temps and a week of free museums and cultural events. | Jul Summer means beach weather and a packed festival calendar. | Oct Enjoy the coast without crowds and some fabulous autumn food. |

Fast Facts

» **Area** 301,230 sq km

» **Population** 60.34 million

» **Capital** Rome

» **Telephone** country code ☑39; international access code ☑00

» **Emergency** ☑112

Exchange Rates

Australia	A$1	€0.74
Canada	C$1	€0.74
Japan	¥100	€0.87
New Zealand	NZ$1	€0.56
UK	UK£1	€1.16
USA	US$1	€0.67

Set Your Budget

» **Budget hotel room** €55–110 (double)

» **Two-course dinner** from €20 (pizza €10–15)

» **Museum entrance** €6.50–15

» **Beer** €2.50–5

» **Daily transport ticket (Rome)** €4

Resources

» **Delicious Italy** (www.deliciousitaly.com) For foodies

» **Italia** (www.italia.it) Official tourism site

» **Lonely Planet** (www.lonelyplanet.com/italy)

Connections

Milan and Venice are northern Italy's two main transport hubs. From Milan, trains run to cities across Western Europe, including Barcelona, Paris, Zürich and Vienna. Venice is better placed for Eastern Europe, with rail connections to Ljubljana, Zagreb, Belgrade and Budapest. You can also pick up ferries in Venice for Corfu, Igoumenitsa and Patra. Down the east coast, there are ferries from Bari to various Greek ports, as well as to Bar and Dubrovnik. At the other end of the country, Genoa has ferries to Barcelona and Tunis.

ITINERARIES

One week

A one-week whistle-stop tour of Italy is enough to take in some of the country's main cities. After a couple of days exploring Venice's unique canal-scape, head south to Florence, Italy's great Renaissance city. Two days is not long there but it'll whet your appetite for the artistic and architectural treasures that await in Rome.

Two weeks

After the first week, continue south for some sea and southern passion. Spend a day dodging traffic in Naples, a day investigating the ruins at Pompeii and a day or two admiring the Amalfi Coast. Then backtrack to Naples for a ferry to Palermo and the gastronomic delights of Sicily – or perhaps Cagliari and Sardinia's magical beaches, depending on your preference.

Essential Food & Drink

» **Pizza** Two varieties: Roman, with a thin crispy base; and Neapolitan, with a higher, more doughy base. The best are always prepared in a *forno a legna* (wood-fired oven).

» **Gelato** Popular ice-cream flavours include *fragola* (strawberry), *nocciola* (hazelnut) and *stracciatella* (milk with chocolate shavings).

» **Wine** Ranges from big-name reds such as Piedmont's Barolo to light whites from Sardinia and sparkling *prosecco* from the Veneto.

» **Caffè** Join the locals for a morning cappuccino or post-lunch espresso, both taken standing at a bar.

Italy Highlights

1 Lap up the dolce vita in mesmerising **Rome** (460)

2 Take a vaporetto ride past grand but crumbling canalside palaces in **Venice** (p504)

3 Marvel at the Medicis' art collection in the **Uffizi Gallery** (p525) in Florence

4 Dive dreamy waters off **Cala Gonone** (p573) on Sardinia's east coast

5 Hike up an active volcano in the **Aeolian Islands** (p564)

6 Work up an appetite for pizza exploring the baroque backstreets of **Naples** (p544)

7 Blow your mind on baroque architecture in elegant **Lecce** (p558)

8 Explore imperious **Turin** (p495), so much more than Fiat and factories!

9 Delve into frescoed Etruscan tombs in **Tarquinia** (p491)

10 Enjoy a bike ride and picnic atop the medieval city walls in **Lucca** (p538)

ROME

POP 2.72 MILLION

An epic, monumental metropolis, Rome has been in the spotlight for close to 3000 years. As the showcase seat of the Roman Empire, it was the all-powerful *Caput Mundi* (Capital of the World). Later, as the Renaissance capital of the Catholic world, its name sent shivers of holy terror through believers and infidels alike. Some 500 years on, its name still exerts a powerful hold. Fortunately, its reality is every bit as enticing as its reputation. With its architectural and artistic treasures, its romantic corners and noisy, colourful markets, Rome is a city that knows how to impress.

They say a lifetime's not enough for Rome (*Roma, non basta una vita*). And while it's true that few cities can match its cultural legacy, you don't need to be an expert to enjoy it. In fact, all you have to do is walk its animated streets. Even without trying you'll be swept up in the emotion of a city that has been inspiring artists and lovers since time immemorial.

History

According to legend Rome was founded by Romulus and Remus in 753 BC. Historians debate this, but they do acknowledge that Romulus was the first king of Rome and that the city was an amalgamation of Etruscan, Latin and Sabine settlements on the Palatino, Esquilino and Quirinale Hills. Archaeological discoveries have confirmed the existence of a settlement on the Palatino in that period.

In 509 BC the Roman Republic was founded. Civil war put an end to the republic following the murder of Julius Caesar in 44 BC and a bitter civil war between Octavian and Mark Antony. Octavian emerged victorious and was made the first Roman emperor with the title Augustus.

By AD 100 Rome had a population of 1.5 million and was the *Caput Mundi* (Capital of the World). But by the 5th century decline had set in and in 476 Romulus Augustulus, the last emperor of the Western Roman Empire, was deposed.

By this time Rome's Christian roots had taken firm hold. Christianity had been spreading since the 1st century AD, and under Constantine it received official recognition. Pope Gregory I (590–604) did much to strengthen the Church's grip over the city, laying the foundations for its later role as capital of the Catholic Church.

Under the Renaissance popes of the 15th and 16th centuries, Rome was given an extensive facelift. But trouble was never far away and in 1527 the city was sacked by Spanish forces under Charles V.

Once again Rome needed rebuilding and it was to the 17th-century baroque masters Bernini and Borromini that the city turned. With their exuberant churches, fountains and *palazzi,* these two bitter rivals changed the face of the city. The building boom following the unification of Italy and the declaration of Rome as its capital also profoundly influenced the look of the city, as did Mussolini and hasty post-WWII expansion.

Sights

With more world-class sights than many small nations, Rome can be a daunting prospect. The trick is to relax and not worry about seeing everything – half the fun of the city is just hanging out, enjoying the at-

COLOSSEUM TIPS

Follow these tips to beat the Colosseum queues:

» Buy your ticket from the Palatino entrance (about 250m away at Via di San Gregorio 30) or the Roman Forum entrance (Largo della Salara Vecchia).

» Get the Roma Pass, which is valid for three days and a whole host of sites.

» Book your ticket online at www.pierreci.it (plus booking fee of €1.50).

» Join an official English-language tour – €4 on top of the regular Colosseum ticket price.

Outside the Colosseum, you'll almost certainly be hailed by centurions offering to pose for a photo. They are not doing this for love and will expect payment. There's no set rate but €5 is a perfectly acceptable sum – and that's €5 period, not €5 per person. To avoid ugly scenes always agree on a price beforehand.

Two Days

Get to grips with ancient Rome at the **Colosseum**, the **Roman Forum** and **Palatino (Palatine Hill)**. Spend the afternoon exploring the **Musei Capitolini** before an evening in **Trastevere**. On day two, hit the Vatican. Marvel at **St Peter's Basilica** and the **Sistine Chapel** in the vast **Vatican Museums**. Afterwards, ditch your guidebook and get happily lost in the animated streets around **Piazza Navona** and the **Pantheon**.

Four Days

With another couple of days you should definitely book a visit to the **Museo e Galleria Borghese** and venture out to **Via Appia Antica** and the catacombs. If you can handle more art, the **Galleria Doria Pamphilj** and the **Museo Nazionale Romano: Palazzo Massimo alle Terme** both merit a visit. In the evenings, join the student drinkers and fashionable diners in San Lorenzo, or let your hair down with a concert at the **Auditorium Parco della Musica**.

mosphere. Most sights are concentrated in the area between Stazione Termini and the Vatican. Halfway between the two, the Pantheon and Piazza Navona lie at the heart of the *centro storico* (historic centre). To the southeast, the Colosseum is an obvious landmark.

ANCIENT ROME

Colosseum   RUINS

(Map p466; ☏06 3996 7700; Piazza del Colosseo; adult/EU child incl Roman Forum & Palatino €12/free, audioguide €4; ⊙8.30am-1hr before sunset; ⒨Colosseo) Rome's iconic monument is a thrilling sight. The 50,000-seat Colosseum was ancient Rome's most feared arena and is today one of Italy's top draws, attracting between 16,000 and 19,000 people on an average day.

Originally known as the Flavian Amphitheatre, the Colosseum was started by Emperor Vespasian in AD 72 and finished by his son Titus in AD 80. It was clad in travertine and covered by a huge canvas awning that was held aloft by 240 masts. Inside, tiered seating encircled the sand-covered arena, itself built over underground chambers where animals were caged. Games involved gladiators fighting wild animals or each other. But contrary to Hollywood folklore, bouts between gladiators rarely ended in death, as the games' sponsor was required to pay the owner of a killed gladiator 100 times the gladiator's value.

The top tier and underground corridors, known as the hypogeum, have recently been opened to the public. Visits, which cost €8 on top of the normal Colosseum ticket and are by guided tour only, require advance booking.

To the west of the Colosseum, the **Arco di Costantino** was built to celebrate Constantine's victory over rival Maxentius at the battle of Milvian Bridge in 312.

Roman Forum   RUINS

(Map p466; Largo della Salara Vecchia; adult/EU child incl Colosseum & Palatino €12/free, audioguide €4; ⊙8.30am-1hr before sunset; ⒨Colosseo) Now a collection of fascinating, if rather confusing, ruins, the Roman Forum (Foro Romano) was once the showpiece centre of the Roman Republic. Originally an Etruscan burial ground, it was first developed in the 7th century BC, expanding to become the social, political and commercial core of the Roman world. Its importance declined after the fall of the Roman Empire, until eventually the site was used as pastureland and plundered for marble. The area was system-

ROMA PASS

The **Roma Pass** (www.romapass.it; 3 days €25) provides free admission to two museums or sites (choose from a list of 38), as well as reduced entry to extra sites, unlimited city transport and discounted entry to other exhibitions and events. If you use this for the more expensive sights such as the Colosseum or Musei Capitolini you will save money.

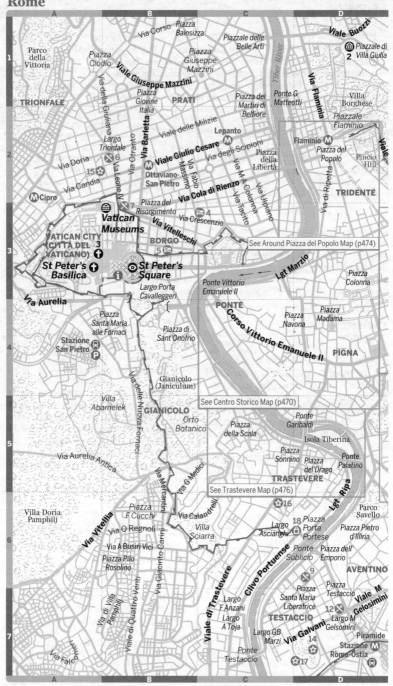

ITALY ROME

A | B | C | D

Parco della Vittoria

Via Corso

Piazza Bainsizza

Piazzale delle Belle Arti

Piazza Clodio

Viale Giuseppe Mazzini

Piazza Giuseppe Mazzini

Viale Buozzi

Piazzale di Villa Giulia 2

TRIONFALE

Via della Giuliana

Piazza Giovine Italia

PRATI

Piazza dei Martiri di Belfiore

Ponte G Matteotti

Via Flaminia

Villa Borghese

Viale delle Milizie

Via Barletta

Largo Trionfale 6

Via Otranto

Lepanto

Viale Giulio Cesare

Piazza del Popolo

Flaminio M

Piazza del Popolo

Pincio Hill

Viale

Via Doria

Via Candia

15

Ottaviano-San Pietro

Via Fabio Massimo

Via degli Scipioni

Via M A Colonna

Piazza della Libertà

Via di Ripetta

TRIDENTE

Cipro M

Via Leone IV

7

Piazza del Risorgimento

Via Cola di Rienzo

Via Ulpiano

Via Tacito

Vatican Museums

Via Vitelleschi

Via Crescenzio 4

VATICAN CITY (CITTÀ DEL VATICANO) 3

BORGO 5

See Around Piazza del Popolo Map (p474)

St Peter's Basilica

St Peter's Square

Lgt Marzio

Piazza Colonna

Via Aurelia

Largo Porta Cavalleggeri

Ponte Vittorio Emanuele II

PONTE

Stazione San Pietro

Piazza Santa Maria alle Fornaci

Piazza di Sant'Onofrio

Corso Vittorio Emanuele II

Piazza Navona

Piazza Madama

PIGNA

Villa Abamelek

Via delle Nuova Fornaci

Gianicolo (Janiculum)

GIANICOLO

See Centro Storico Map (p470)

Orto Botanico

Piazza della Scala

Ponte Garibaldi

Isola Tiberina

Piazza Sonnino

Piazza del Drago

Ponte Palatino

Via Aurelia Antica

Via Mercantini

Via G Medici

See Trastevere Map (p476)

TRASTEVERE

Lgt Ripa

Parco Savello

Villa Doria Pamphilj

Piazza F Cucchi

Via O Regnoli

Via A Busiri Vici

Piazza Pilo Rosolino

Via Giacinto Carini

Via Calandrelli

Villa Sciarra

16

Largo Ascianghi

18 Piazza Porta Portese

Ponte Sublicio

Piazza dell' Emporio

Piazza Pietro d'Illiria

AVENTINO

Via Vitellia

Via di Villa Pamphilj

Viale di Quattro Venti

Viale di Trastevere

Clivo Portuense

9

Piazza Santa Maria Liberatrice

Piazza Testaccio

Piazza Testaccio

12

Largo M Gelsomini

Viale M Gelosimini

Via Falco

Largo F Anzani

Largo A Toja

Largo GB Marzi

TESTACCIO

Via Galvani

14

Stazione Roma-Ostia M

Piramide M

Ponte Testaccio

17

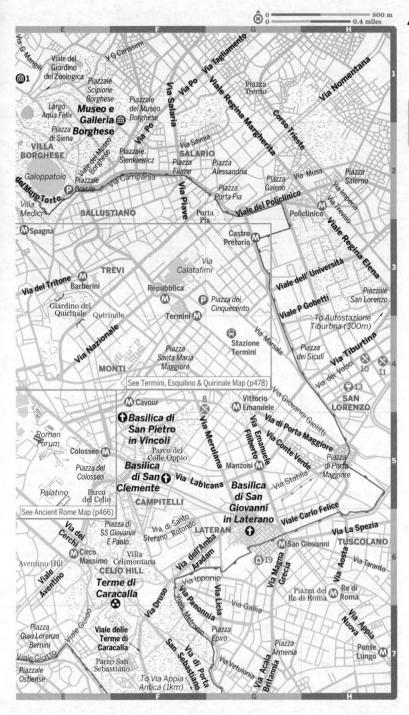

ITALY ROME

atically excavated in the 18th and 19th centuries and excavations continue.

As you enter from Largo della Salaria Vecchia, ahead to your left is the **Tempio di Antonino e Faustina**, built by the senate in 141 and transformed into a church in the 8th century. To your right, the **Basilica Aemilia**, built in 179 BC, was 100m long with a two-storey porticoed facade lined with shops. At the end of the short path, **Via Sacra** traverses the Forum from northwest to southeast. Opposite the Basilica Aemilia stands the **Tempio di Giulio Cesare**, erected by Augustus in 29 BC on the site where Caesar's body had been burned.

Head right up Via Sacra and you reach the **Curia**, once the meeting place of the Roman senate and later converted into a church. In front is the **Lapis Niger**, a large piece of black marble that purportedly covered Romulus' grave.

At the end of Via Sacra, the **Arco di Settimio Severo** was erected in 203 to honour Emperor Septimus Severus and his two sons and celebrate victory over the Parthians. Nearby, the **Millarium Aureum** marked the centre of ancient Rome, from which distances to the city were measured.

Southwest of the arch, eight granite columns are all that remain of the **Tempio di Saturno**, one of ancient Rome's most important temples. Inaugurated in 497 BC, it was later used as the state treasury.

To the southeast, you'll see the **Piazza del Foro**, the Forum's main market and meeting place, marked by the 7th-century **Colonna di Foca** (Column of Phocus). To your right are the foundations of the **Basilica Giulia**, a law court built by Julius Caesar in 55 BC. At the end of the basilica is the **Tempio di Castore e Polluce**, built in 489 BC in honour of the Heavenly Twins, Castor and Pollux. It is easily recognisable by its three remaining columns.

Back towards Via Sacra, the **Casa delle Vestali** was home of the virgins whose job it was to keep the sacred flame alight in the adjoining **Tempio di Vesta**. The vestal virgins were selected at the age of 10 for their beauty and virtue and were required to stay chaste and committed to keeping the flame for 30 years.

Continuing up Via Sacra, you come to the vast **Basilica di Costantino**, also known as the Basilica di Massenzio, whose impressive design inspired Renaissance architects. The **Arco di Tito**, at the Colosseum end of the Forum, was built in AD 81 in honour of the victories of the emperors Titus and Vespasian against Jerusalem.

TOP CHOICE **Palatino (Palatine Hill)** RUINS
(Map p466; Via di San Gregorio 30; adult/EU child incl Colosseum & Roman Forum €12/free, audioguide €4; ⊗8.30am-1hr before sunset; MColosseo) Rising above the Roman Forum, this beautiful area is where Romulus is said to have

founded the city in 753 BC. Archaeological evidence shows that the earliest settlements in the area were in fact on the Palatino and date back to the 8th century BC. This was ancient Rome's poshest neighbourhood and the emperor Augustus lived here all his life. After Rome's fall, it fell into disrepair and in the Middle Ages churches and castles were built over the ruins. During the Renaissance, members of wealthy families established gardens on the hill. Most of the Palatino is covered by the ruins of Emperor Domitian's vast complex, which served as the main imperial palace for 300 years. Divided into the **Domus Flavia** (imperial palace), **Domus Augustana** (the emperor's private residence) and a **stadio** (stadium), it was built by the architect Rabirius in the 1st century AD.

Among the best-preserved buildings on the Palatino is the **Casa di Livia**, home of Augustus' wife Livia, and, in front, Augustus' separate residence, the **Casa di Augusto** (⊙11am-3.30pm Mon, Wed, Sat & Sun), which boasts exceptional frescos.

Museo dei Fori Imperiali   MUSEUM
(Map p478; www.mercatiditraiano.it; Via IV Novembre 94; adult/child €9/free; ⊙9am-7pm Tue-Sun; 🚇Via IV Novembre) This striking museum brings to life the **Mercati di Traiano**, emperor Trajan's great 2nd-century market complex. From the main hallway, a lift whisks you up to the **Torre delle Milizie** (Militia Tower), a 13th-century red-brick tower, and the upper levels of the vast three-storey semicircular construction that once housed hundreds of traders. From the top there are sweeping views over the Imperial Forums.

Piazza del Campidoglio   SQUARE
(Map p466; 🚇Piazza Venezia) This striking piazza sits atop the Capitoline Hill (Campidoglio), the lowest of Rome's seven hills. In ancient times, it was home to the city's two most important temples: one dedicated to Juno Moneta and another to Jupiter Capitolinus, where Brutus is said to have hidden after assassinating Caesar. The Michelangelo-designed piazza, accessible by the graceful **Cordonata** staircase, is bordered by **Palazzo Nuovo** on the left, **Palazzo dei Conservatori** on the right, and **Palazzo Senatorio**, the seat of city government since 1143. In the centre, the bronze **statue of Marcus Aurelius** is a copy; the original is in Palazzo Nuovo.

Musei Capitolini   MUSEUM
(Capitoline Museums; Map p466; www.museicapitolini.org; Piazza del Campidoglio; adult/child €7.50/free, audioguide €5; ⊙9am-8pm Tue-Sun, last entry 7pm; 🚇Piazza Venezia) Housed in Palazzo Nuovo and Palazzo dei Conservatori, the Capitoline Museums are the oldest public museums in the world, dating from 1471. Their collection of classical art is one of Italy's finest, including masterpieces such as the *Lupa capitolina* (She-wolf), a sculpture of Romulus and Remus under a wolf, and the *Galata morente* (Dying Gaul), a moving depiction of a dying Gaul. The **pinacoteca** (art gallery) on the 2nd floor contains paintings by Titian, Tintoretto, Van Dyck, Rubens and Caravaggio.

Chiesa di Santa Maria d'Aracoeli   CHURCH
(Map p466; Piazza del Campidoglio 4; ⊙9am-12.30pm & 3-6.30pm; 🚇Piazza Venezia) Marking the high point of the Campidoglio, this 6th-century church sits on the site of the Roman temple to Juno Moneta. According to legend it was here that the Tiburtine Sybil told Augustus of the coming birth of Christ, and still today the church has a strong association with the nativity.

Carcere Mamertino   CHURCH
(Mamertine Prison; Map p466; ⊙closed for restoration; 🚇Piazza Venezia) From Piazza del Campidoglio, stairs to the left of Palazzo Senatorio lead down to this ancient prison, now church, where St Peter is said to have miraculously baptised his jailers whilst imprisoned here.

Piazza Venezia   SQUARE
Piazza Venezia is dominated by the mountain of white marble that is **Il Vittoriano** (Map p466; 🚇Piazza Venezia), aka the Altare della Patria. Begun in 1885 to commemorate Italian unification and honour Victor Emmanuel II, it incorporates the **tomb of the Unknown Soldier**, as well as the **Museo Centrale del Risorgimento** (admission free; ⊙9.30am-6.30pm), documenting Italian unification. For Rome's best 360-degree views, take the **panoramic lift** (adult/concession €7/3.50; ⊙9.30am-6.30pm Mon-Thu, to 7.30pm Fri-Sun) to the top.

Over the square, the 15th-century **Palazzo Venezia** (Via del Plebiscito 118; adult/concession €4/2; ⊙8.30am-7.30pm Tue-Sun) was the first of Rome's great Renaissance *palazzi*. Mussolini had his office here and there's now a museum of medieval and Renaissance art.

Bocca della Verità   OFFBEAT SIGHT
(Map p466; Piazza Bocca della Verità 18; ⊙10am-5pm; 🚇Via dei Cerchi) A round piece of marble once used as an ancient manhole cover, the Bocca della Verità (Mouth of Truth) is one of Rome's great curiosities. According to

ITALY ROME

Ancient Rome

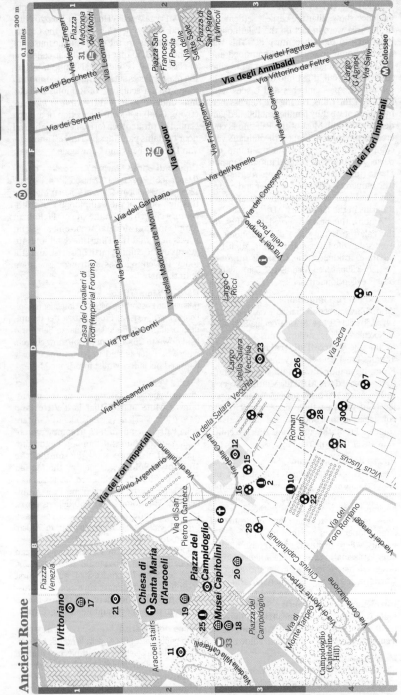

200 m
0.1 miles

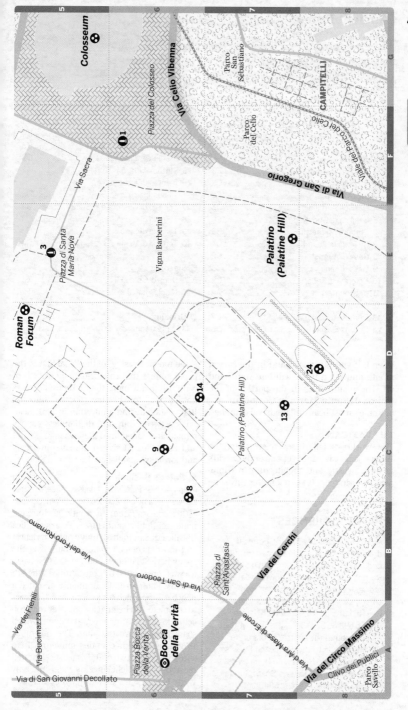

Ancient Rome

legend, if you put your hand in the carved mouth and tell a lie, it will bite your hand off. The mouth lives in the portico of the **Chiesa di Santa Maria in Cosmedin**, one of Rome's most beautiful medieval churches.

THE VATICAN

The world's smallest sovereign state, the Vatican jealously guards of one of the world's greatest artistic and architectural patrimonies. Covering just 0.44 sq km, this tiny state is the modern vestige of the Papal States, the papal empire that ruled Rome and much of central Italy for more than a thousand years until it was forcibly incorporated into the Italian state during unification in 1861. Relations between Italy and the landless papacy remained strained until 1929 when Mussolini and Pope Pius XI signed the Lateran Treaty and formally established the Vatican State.

St Peter's Basilica   CHURCH
(Map p462; St Peter's Sq; admission free, audioguide €5; ⊙7am-7pm Apr-Sep, to 6.30pm Oct-Mar; MOttaviano-San Pietro) In a city of churches, none can hold a candle to St Peter's Basilica (Basilica di San Pietro), Italy's biggest, richest and most spectacular church. Built over the spot where St Peter was buried, the first basilica was consecrated by Constantine in the 4th century. Later, in 1503, Bramante designed a new basilica, which took more than 150 years to complete. Michelangelo took over the project in 1547, designing the grand dome, which soars 120m above the altar. The cavernous 187m-long interior contains numerous treasures, including two of Italy's most celebrated masterpieces: Michelangelo's *Pietà*, the only work to carry his signature; and Bernini's 29m-high baldachin over the high altar.

PAPAL AUDIENCES

At 11am on Wednesday, the Pope addresses his flock at the Vatican (in July and August in Castel Gandolfo near Rome). For free tickets, download the request form from the Vatican website (www.vatican.va) and fax it to the **Prefettura della Casa Pontificia** (fax 06 698 85 863). Pick them up at the office through the bronze doors under the colonnade to the right of St Peter's.

When he is in Rome, the Pope blesses the crowd in St Peter's Sq on Sunday at noon. No tickets are required.

Entrance to the **dome** (🕐8am-6pm Apr-Sep, 8am-5pm Oct-Mar) is to the right as you climb the stairs to the basilica's atrium. Make the climb on foot (€5) or by lift (€7).

Note that the basilica is one of Rome's busiest attractions, so expect queues in peak periods. Dress rules and security are stringently enforced, so no shorts, miniskirts or sleeveless tops, and be prepared to have your bags searched.

St Peter's Square   SQUARE
(Map p462; ⓂOttaviano-San Pietro) The Vatican's central piazza, St Peter's Sq (Piazza San Pietro) was designed by baroque artist Gian Lorenzo Bernini and laid out between 1656 and 1667. Seen from above it resembles a giant keyhole: two semicircular colonnades, each consisting of four rows of Doric columns, bound by a giant ellipse that straightens out to funnel believers into the basilica. The effect was deliberate – Bernini described the colonnade as representing 'the motherly arms of the church'.

In the centre, the 25m obelisk was brought to Rome by Caligula from Heliopolis in Egypt and later used by Nero as a turning post for the chariot races in his circus.

Vatican Museums   ART MUSEUM
(Map p462; ☎06 6988 4676; Viale Vaticano; adult/child €15/free, admission free last Sun of month, audioguide €7; 🕐9am-6pm, last entry 4pm Mon-Sat, to 2pm, last entry 12.30pm last Sun of month; ⓂOttaviano-San Pietro) Boasting one of the world's great art collections, the Vatican Museums are housed in the Palazzo Apostolico Vaticano, a vast 5.5-hectare complex comprising two palaces and three internal courtyards. You'll never manage to explore it all in one day – you'd need several hours just for the highlights – so it pays to be selective. There are several suggested itineraries from the Quattro Cancelli area near the entrance.

Home to some spectacular classical statuary, the **Museo Pio-Clementino** is a must-see. Highlights include the *Apollo belvedere* and the 1st-century *Laocoön,* both in the Cortile Ottagono. Further on, the 175m-long **Galleria delle Carte Geografiche** (Map Gallery) is hung with 40 huge topographical maps. Beyond that are the magnificent **Stanze di Raffaello** (Raphael Rooms), which were once Pope Julius II's private apartments and are decorated with frescos by Raphael. Of the paintings, *La scuola d'Atene* (The School of Athens) in the **Stanza della Segnatura** is considered one of Raphael's great masterpieces.

> ℹ **QUEUE JUMPING AT THE VATICAN MUSEUMS**
>
> Here's how to jump the ticket queue – although we can't help with lines for the security checks.
>
> » Book tickets at http://biglietteri amusei.vatican.va/musei/tickets (plus booking fee of €4). You can also book authorised guided tours (adult/concession €31/25).
>
> » Time your visit: Wednesday mornings are a good bet, as everyone is at the Pope's weekly audience at St Peter's; lunchtime is better than the morning; avoid Mondays, when many other museums are shut.

Sistine Chapel
This is the one place in the Vatican Museums that not one of the 4.5 million annual visitors wants to miss. Home to two of the world's most famous works of art, the 15th-century **Sistine Chapel** (Cappella Sistina) is where the papal conclave is locked to elect the Pope. It was originally built in 1484 for Pope Sixtus IV, after whom it is named, but it was Pope Julius II who commissioned Michelangelo to decorate it in 1508. Over the next four years, the artist painted the remarkable *Genesis* (Creation; 1508–12) on the barrel-vaulted ceiling. Twenty-two years later he returned at the behest of Pope Clement VII to paint the *Giudizio universale* (Last Judgment; 1534–41) on the end wall.

The other walls of the chapel were painted by artists including Botticelli, Ghirlandaio, Pinturicchio and Signorelli.

Castel Sant'Angelo   CASTLE
(Map p470; Lungotevere Castello 50; adult/EU child €8.50/free; 🕐9am-8pm Tue-Sun; 🚌Piazza Pia) An instantly recognisable landmark, the chunky, round-keeped Castel Sant'Angelo was commissioned by Emperor Hadrian in 123 BC as a mausoleum for himself and his family. In the 6th century, it was converted into a papal fortress, and it's now a museum with an assorted collection of sculptures, paintings, weapons and furniture. The terrace offers fine views.

HISTORIC CENTRE

FREE **Pantheon**   MONUMENT
(Map p470; Piazza della Rotonda; audioguide €5; 🕐8.30am-7.30pm Mon-Sat, 9am-6pm Sun, 9am-1pm holidays; 🚌Largo di Torre Argentina) A

ITALY ROME

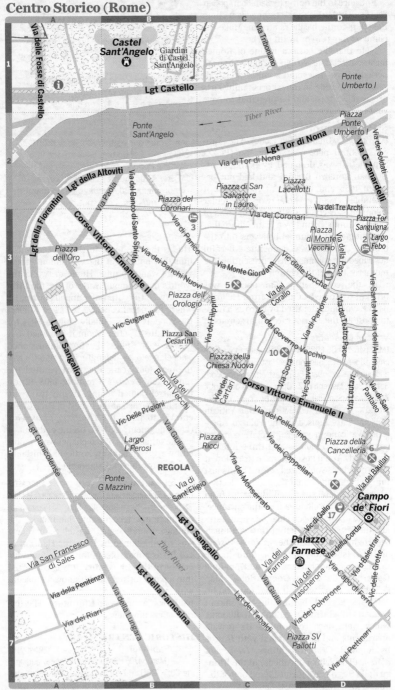

Via delle Fosse di Castello

Castel Sant'Angelo 🏛

Giardini di Castel Sant'Angelo

Via Triboniano

Lgt Castello

Ponte Umberto I

Tiber River

Ponte Sant'Angelo

Piazza Ponte Umberto I

Lgt Tor di Nona

Via G. Zanardelli

Via dei Soldati

Lgt della Altoviti

Via di Tor di Nona

Via Paola

Via del Banco di Santo Spirito

Piazza di San Salvatore in Lauro

Piazza Lacellotti

Lgt della Fiorentini

Piazza del Coronari

3

Via dei Coronari

Via dei Tre Archi

Piazza Tor Sanguigna

Corso Vittorio Emanuele II

Via di Panico

Via dei Banchi Nuovi

Via Monte Giordana

Piazza di Monte Vecchio

Via della Pace

2 Largo Febo

Piazza dell'Oro

Via Santa Maria dell'Anima

Vic delle Vacche

13

Lgt D Sangallo

Via dei Filippini

5 ✗

Via del Corallo

Piazza dell' Orologio

Via del Governo Vecchio

Via del Teatro Pace

Vic Sugarelli

Piazza San Cesarini

Via di Parione

10 ✗

Via del Pantaleo

Piazza della Chiesa Nuova

Via Sora

Vic Savelli

Corso Vittorio Emanuele II

Via dei Cartari

Via dei Banchi Vecchi

Via del Pellegrino

Vic Delle Prigioni

Via Giulia

Largo L Perosi

Piazza Ricci

REGOLA

Via del Monserrato

Via dei Cappellari

Piazza della Cancelleria

6 ✗

Via dei Baullari

7 ✗

Ponte G Mazzini

Via di Sant'Eligio

Lgt Gianicolense

Campo de' Fiori ◉

Vic di Gallo

17

Via della Corda

Lgt D Sangallo

Palazzo Farnese 🏛

Via dei Farnesi

Via Capo di Ferro

Via d Balestrari

Vic delle Grotte

Via del Mascherone

Tiber River

Via San Francesco di Sales

Via della Penitenza

Lgt della Farnesina

Via Giulia

Via dei Polverone

Via dei Tebaldi

Via dei Pettinari

Via dei Riari

Via della Lungara

Piazza SV Pallotti

A | B | C | D

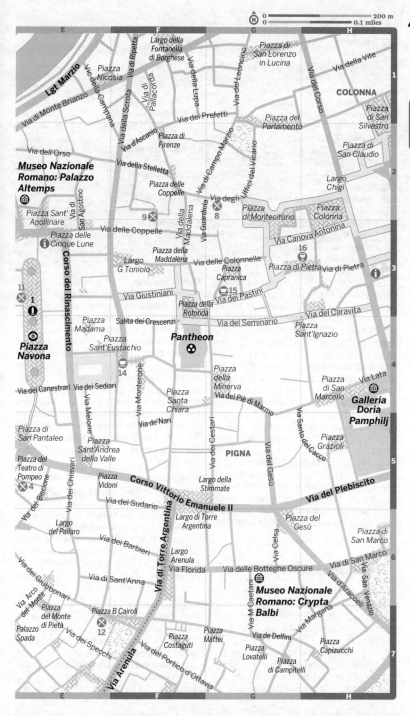

ITALY ROME

0 200 m
0 0.1 miles

E

Lgt Marzio

Via di Monte Brianzo

Via di Ripetta

Piazza
Nicosia

Vicolo della Campana

Largo della
Fontanella
di Borghese

Via di Pallacorda

Via della Scrofa

Via della Lupa

Piazza di
San Lorenzo
in Lucina

Via dei Leoncino

Via del Corso

Via della Vite

COLONNA

Via di
Pallacorda

Via dei Prefetti

Piazza del
Parlamento

Piazza
di San
Silvestro

Via dell'Orso

Via d'Ascanio

Piazza di
Firenze

Via di Campo Marzio

Ufficio del Vicario

Piazza di
San Claudio

Via della Stelletta

**Museo Nazionale
Romano: Palazzo
Altemps**

Via di Sant'Agostino

Piazza delle
Coppelle

Largo
Chigi

Piazza Sant'
Apollinare

Via degli

Piazza
di Montecitorio

Piazza
Colonna

Piazza delle
Cinque Lune

Via delle Coppelle

9

8

Via della Maddalena

Via Guardiola

Via Canova Antonina

16

Piazza della
Maddalena

Via delle Colonnelle

Piazza di Pietra

Via di Pietra

Largo
G Toniolo

Piazza
Capranica

Via Giustiniani

15

Via dei Pastini

Corso del Rinascimento

11

1

Piazza della
Rotonda

Via del Caravita

Salita dei Crescenzi

Via del Seminario

Piazza
Madama

Piazza
Sant'Eustachio

Pantheon

Piazza
Sant'Ignazio

Piazza
Navona

14

Via Monterone

Piazza
della
Minerva

Piazza
di San
Marcello

Via Lata

**Galleria
Doria
Pamphilj**

Via dei Canestrari

Via dei Sediari

Piazza
Santa
Chiara

Via del Piè di Marmo

Piazza di
San Pantaleo

Via de' Nari

Via Melone

Via de' Cestari

Piazza
Sant'Andrea
della Valle

PIGNA

Piazza
Grazioli

Via Santo del Cacco

Piazza del
Teatro di
Pompeo

4

Via dei Chiavari

Piazza
Vidoni

Corso Vittorio Emanuele II

Largo della
Stimmate

Via del Gesù

Via del Plebiscito

Via dei Bisciome

Via del Sudario

Largo di Torre
Argentina

Piazza del
Gesù

Piazza di
San Marco

Largo
del Pallaro

Via dei Barbieri

Largo
Arenula

Via Florida

Via Celsa

Via di San Marco

Via dei Giubbonari

Via di Sant'Anna

Via delle Botteghe Oscure

Via di San Marco

Via d'Aracoeli

Via Arco
del Monte

Piazza
del Monte
di Pietà

Piazza B Cairoli

12

**Museo Nazionale
Romano: Crypta
Balbi**

Palazzo
Spada

Via dei Specchi

Via di Torre Argentina

Piazza
Costaguti

Piazza
Mattei

Via de Delfini

Piazza
Capizucchi

Via M Caetani

Via Margana

Piazza
Lovatelli

Via del Portico d'Ottavia

Via Arenula

Piazza
di Campitelli

Via San Venanzio

F

G

H

Centro Storico (Rome)

striking 2000-year-old temple, now church, the Pantheon is the best preserved of ancient Rome's great monuments. In its current form it dates to around AD 120 when the Emperor Hadrian built over Marcus Agrippa's original 27 BC temple (Agrippa's name remains inscribed on the pediment). The dome, considered the Romans' most important architectural achievement, was the largest in the world until the 15th century and is still the largest unreinforced concrete dome ever built. It's a beautiful, perfectly symmetrical structure whose diameter is exactly equal to the Pantheon's interior height of 43.3m. Light (and rain, which drains away through 22 specially built holes) enters through an oculus, which also acts as a compression ring, absorbing and redistributing the dome's vast structural forces. Inside, you'll find the tomb of Raphael, alongside those of kings Vittorio Emanuele II and Umberto I.

WANT MORE?

For in-depth information, reviews and recommendations at your fingertips, head to the Apple App Store to purchase Lonely Planet's *Rome City Guide* iPhone app.

Alternatively, head to **Lonely Planet** (www.lonelyplanet.com/italy/rome) for planning advice, author recommendations, traveller reviews and insider tips.

Piazza Navona   SQUARE

(Map p470; 🚌Corso del Rinascimento) With its ornate fountains, baroque *palazzi,* pavement cafes and colourful cast of street artists, hawkers, tourists and pigeons, Piazza Navona is central Rome's most celebrated square. Built over the ruins of the 1st-century Stadio di Domiziano (Domitian's Stadium), it was paved over in the 15th century and for almost 300 years was the city's main market. Of the piazza's three fountains, the grand centrepiece is Bernini's 1651 **Fontana dei Quattro Fiumi** (Fountain of the Four Rivers), a monumental affair depicting the rivers Nile, Ganges, Danube and Plate.

Campo de' Fiori   SQUARE

(Map p470; 🚌Corso Vittorio Emanuele II) 'Il Campo', as it's known locally, is a major focus of Roman life: by day it hosts a noisy market, by night it becomes a vast, open-air pub. For centuries, this was the site of public executions, and it was here that the philosophising monk Giordano Bruno (the hooded figure in Ettore Ferrari's sinister statue) was burned at the stake in 1600.

Palazzo Farnese   HISTORIC BUILDING

(Map p470; 📞06 6889 2818; visitefarnese@ france-italia.it; guided tours free, booking obligatory; 🚌Corso Vittorio Emanuele II) Towering over Piazza Farnese, this is one of Rome's most impressive Renaissance buildings. Named after Cardinal Alessandro Farnese, it was started in 1514 by Antonio da Sangallo, carried on by Michelangelo and completed by Giacomo della Porta. Inside, frescos by Annibale Carracci are considered to be on a par with Michelangelo's in the Sistine Chapel. Visits are by guided tour only as the *palazzo* is home to the French Embassy. The twin fountains in the piazza are enormous granite baths taken from the Terme di Caracalla.

Galleria Doria Pamphilj   ART MUSEUM

(Map p470; www.doriapamphilj.it; Via del Corso 305; adult/concession €9.50/7; ⊙10am-5pm; ▣Piazza Venezia) Behind the grey walls of Palazzo Doria Pamphilj is one of Rome's finest private art collections, with works by Raphael, Tintoretto, Brueghel and Titian. The undisputed masterpiece is the Velázquez portrait of Pope Innocent X, who grumbled that the depiction was 'too real'.

Trevi Fountain   FOUNTAIN

(Map p478; ⓜBarberini) Immortalised by Anita Ekberg's sensual dip in Fellini's *La dolce vita,* the Fontana di Trevi is Rome's largest and most famous fountain. The flamboyant baroque ensemble was designed by Nicola Salvi in 1732 and depicts Neptune's chariot being led by Tritons, with sea horses representing the moods of the sea. The water comes from the *aqua virgo,* a 1st-century-BC underground aqueduct, and the name 'Trevi' refers to the *tre vie* (three roads) that converge at the fountain. The custom is to throw a coin into the fountain, thus ensuring your return to Rome. On average about €3000 is chucked away every day.

Galleria Nazionale d'Arte Antica   ART MUSEUM

(Map p478; www.galleriaborghese.it; Via delle Quattro Fontane 13; adult/EU child €5/free; ⊙9am-7.30pm Tue-Sun; ⓜBarberini) A must for anyone into Renaissance and baroque art, this sumptuous gallery is housed in Palazzo Barberini, one of Rome's most spectacular *palazzi.* Inside, you'll find works by Raphael, Caravaggio, Guido Reni, Bernini, Filippo Lippi and Holbein, as well as Pietro da Cortona's breathtaking *Trionfo della Divina Provvidenza* (Triumph of Divine Providence) in the main salon.

Spanish Steps   MONUMENT

(Map p478; Piazza di Spagna; ⓜSpagna) Rising above **Piazza di Spagna**, the Spanish Steps, aka the Scalinata della Trinità dei Monti, have been a magnet for foreigners since the 18th century. The piazza was named after the Spanish embassy to the

Holy See, although the staircase, which was built with French money in 1725, leads to the French church, **Chiesa della Trinità dei Monti**. At the foot of the steps, the fountain of a sinking boat, the *Barcaccia* (1627), is believed to be by Pietro Bernini, father of the more famous Gian Lorenzo. Opposite, **Via dei Condotti** is Rome's top shopping strip.

Piazza del Popolo   SQUARE

(Map p474; ⓜFlaminio) This elegant landmark square was laid out in 1538 at the point of convergence of three roads – Via di Ripetta, Via del Corso and Via del Babuino – at what was then Rome's northern entrance. Guarding its southern approach are the twin 17th-century churches of **Santa Maria dei Miracoli** and **Santa Maria in Montesanto**, while on the northern flank is the **Porta del Popolo**, created by Bernini in 1655. In the centre, the 36m-high **obelisk** was brought by Augustus from Heliopolis in ancient Egypt. Rising above the piazza, **Pincio Hill** affords great views.

On the piazza's northern flank, the **Chiesa di Santa Maria del Popolo** (Map p474; ⊙7am-noon & 4-7pm Mon-Sat, 8am-1.30pm & 4.30-7.30pm Sun) is one of Rome's earliest and richest Renaissance churches. The first chapel was built in 1099 to exorcise the ghost of Nero, who was buried on this spot and whose ghost was said to haunt the area, but in its current form it dates to 1472. Inside, the star attractions are the two magnificent Caravaggio paintings: the *Conversione di San Paolo* (Conversion of St Paul) and the *Crocifissione di San Pietro* (Crucifixion of St Peter).

Museo dell'Ara Pacis Augustae   MUSEUM

(Map p474; www.arapacis.it; Lungotevere in Augusta; adult/child €6.50/free; ⊙9am-7pm Tue-Sun;

FREE THRILLS

Surprisingly, some of Rome's most famous sights are free:

» Trevi Fountain

» Spanish Steps

» Pantheon

» Bocca della Verità

» All churches, including St Peter's Basilica

» Vatican Museums on the last Sunday of the month.

ITALY ROME

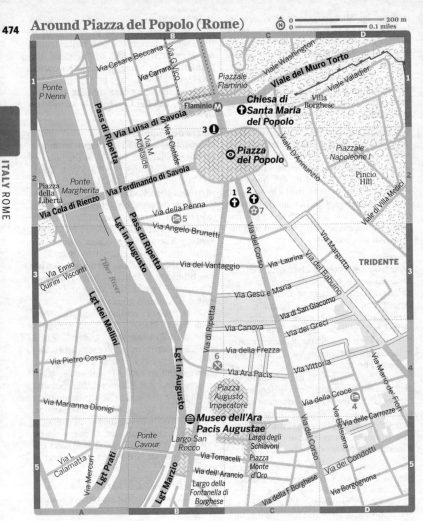

Ⓜ Flaminio) The first modern construction in Rome's historic centre, Richard Meier's controversial white pavilion houses the **Ara Pacis Augustae (Altar of Peace)**, one of the most important works of ancient Roman sculpture. The vast marble altar (it measures 11.6m by 10.6m by 3.6m) was completed in 13 BC as a monument to the peace that Augustus established both at home and abroad.

VILLA BORGHESE

Just north of the historic centre, Villa Borghese is Rome's best-known park, a good spot for a picnic and a breath of fresh air. The grounds, which were created in the 17th century by Cardinal Scipione Borghese, are accessible from Piazzale Flaminio, Pincio Hill, and the top of Via Vittorio Veneto. Bike hire is available at various points, typically costing about €5 per hour.

🔝 **Museo e Galleria Borghese**

MUSEUM, ART MUSEUM

(Map p462; ☎ 06 3 28 10; www.galleriaborghese. it; Piazzale del Museo Borghese; adult/EU child €8.50/2; ⏰ 8.30am-7.30pm Tue-Sun; 🚍 Via Pinciana) If you only have time, or inclination, for one art gallery in Rome, make it this one.

Housing the 'queen of all private art collections', it boasts paintings by Caravaggio, Botticelli and Raphael, as well as some spectacular sculptures by Gian Lorenzo Bernini. There are too many highlights to list here, but try not to miss Bernini's *Ratto di Proserpina* (Rape of Persephone) and *Apollo e Dafne*, Antonio Canova's *Venere Vincitrice* (Victorious Venus) and the six Caravaggios in room VII. Note that you must book your ticket in advance.

Museo Nazionale Etrusco di Villa Giulia
MUSEUM
(Map p462; Piazzale di Villa Giulia; adult/EU child €4/free; ⊘8.30am-7.30pm Tue-Sun; 🚋Viale delle Belle Arti) Italy's finest collection of Etruscan treasures is beautifully housed in the 16th-century Villa Giulia. Many of the exhibits come from Etruscan burial tombs in northern Lazio, with standouts including a polychrome terracotta statue of *Apollo* and the 6th-century-BC *Sarcofago degli Sposi* (Sarcophagus of the Betrothed).

Galleria Nazionale d'Arte Moderna
ART MUSEUM
(Map p462; www.gnam.beniculturali.it; Viale delle Belle Arti 131; adult/EU child €8/free; ⊘8.30am-7.30pm Tue-Sun; 🚋Viale delle Belle Arti) In this vast belle époque palace, you'll find works by some of the most important exponents of modern art, including Canova, Modigliani, De Chirico, Klimt, Pollock and Henry Moore.

TRASTEVERE
Trastevere is one of central Rome's most vivacious neighbourhoods, a tightly packed warren of ochre *palazzi*, ivy-clad facades and photogenic lanes, ideal for aimless wandering. Taking its name from the Latin *trans Tiberium*, meaning over the Tiber, it was originally a working-class district but it has since been gentrified and it is today a trendy hang-out full of bars, trattorias and restaurants.

Basilica di Santa Maria in Trastevere
CHURCH
(Map p476; Piazza Santa Maria in Trastevere; ⊘7.30am-8pm; 🚋Viale di Trastevere) Nestled in a quiet corner of Piazza Santa Maria in Trastevere, Trastevere's picturesque focal square, this exquisite basilica is believed to be the oldest Roman church dedicated to the Virgin Mary. The original church dates to the 4th century, but a 12th-century makeover saw the addition of a Romanesque bell tower and frescoed facade. Inside it's the glittering 12th-century mosaics that are the main drawcard.

Basilica di Santa Cecilia in Trastevere
CHURCH
(Map p476; Piazza di Santa Cecilia; basilica/fresco free/€2.50; ⊘basilica 9.30am-1pm & 4-7.15pm, fresco visits 10.15am & 12.30pm Mon-Fri; 🚋Viale di Trastevere) The last resting place of St Cecilia, the patron saint of music, this church merits a visit for its spectacular 13th-century fresco – Pietro Cavallini's *The Last Judgement.* Under the main basilica, you can visit excavations of several Roman houses.

TERMINI & ESQUILINO
The largest of Rome's seven hills, Esquilino (Esquiline) extends from the Colosseum up to Stazione Termini, Rome's main transport hub.

Basilica di San Pietro in Vincoli CHURCH
(Map p462; Piazza di San Pietro in Vincoli; ⊘8am-12.30pm & 3-7pm; Ⓜ Cavour) Pilgrims and art lovers flock to this church, just off Via Cavour, for two reasons: to see the chains worn by St Peter before his crucifixion (hence the church's name – St Peter in Chains) and to marvel at Michelangelo's magnificent *Moses,* the centrepiece of his unfinished tomb of Pope Julius II.

Trastevere (Rome)

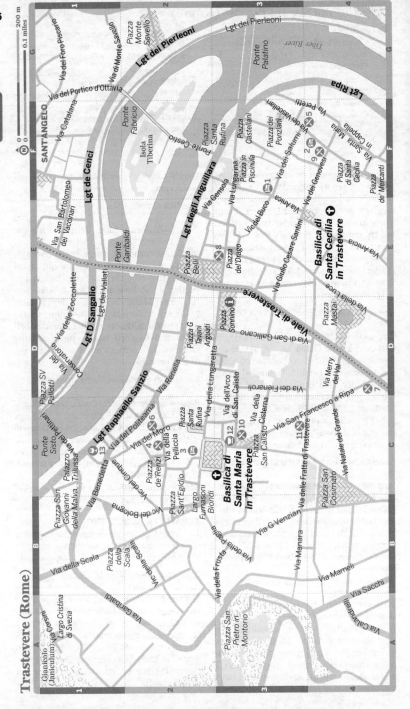

Via Garibaldi

Gianicolo
(Janiculum)

Largo Cristina
di Svezia

Via Corsini

Piazza San
Giovanni
della Malva

Palazzo
Corsini

Piazza SV
Pallotti

Via del
Conservatorio

Lgt D Sangallio

Via delle Zoccolette

Lgt dei Vallati

Lgt de Cenci

Lgt degli Anguillara

Lgt dei Pierleoni

Via San
Bartolomeo
dei Vaccinari

Via Catalana

Via del Portico d'Ottavia

Piazza
Monte
Savello

Via del Foro Piscario

Via di Monte Savello

SANT'ANGELO

Lgt dei Pierleoni

Lgt dei Pierleoni

Tiber River

Ponte
Palatino

Lgt Ripa

Ponte
Fabricio

Isola
Tiberina

Ponte Cestio

Piazza
Santa
Rufina

Piazza in
Piscinula

Via Lungarina

Piazza
Castellani

Piazza dei
Ponziani

Via dei Vascellari

Via Santa Maria in Cappella

Via Peretti

Piazza
di Santa
Cecilia

Piazza
de' Mercanti

Via Anicia

Via dei Salumi

Via dei Genovesi

Via Giulio Cesare Santini

Basilica di
Santa Cecilia
in Trastevere

Via Anicia

Ponte
Garibaldi

Via Gensola

Piazza
Belli

Piazza
del Drago

Vic del Buco

Viale di Trastevere

Piazza
Sonnino

Via di San Gallicano

Piazza
Mastai

Via della Luce

Ponte
Sisto

Via dei Pettinari

Lgt Raphaello Sanzio

Via Renella

Via del Politeama

Via del Moro

Via della
Pelliccia

Piazza
de' Renzi

Vic del Cinque

Piazza
Santa
Rufina

Via del Arco
di San Calisto

Via della Lungaretta

Piazza G
Tavani
Arquati

Via dei Fienaroli

Piazza
San Calisto

Via della
Cisterna

Via Merry
del Val

Via San Francesco a Ripa

Via della Scala

Piazza
San
Pietro in
Montorio

Piazza
della
Scala

Vic delle Scala

Via Benedetta

Largo
Fumasoni
Biondi

Piazza
Sant'Egidio

Basilica di
Santa Maria
in Trastevere

Via della Paglia

Via della Frusta

Via G Venzian

Via San Cosimato

Piazza San
Cosimato

Via Natale del Grande

Via delle Fratte di Trastevere

Via Manara

Via Mameli

Via Sacchi

Via Calandrelli

Trastevere (Rome)

Basilica di Santa Maria Maggiore CHURCH
(Map p478; Piazza Santa Maria Maggiore; ☉7am-7pm; ◻Piazza Santa Maria Maggiore) One of Rome's four patriarchal basilicas, this hulking church was built in 352 on the site of a miraculous snowfall. An architectural hybrid, it has a 14th-century Romanesque belfry, an 18th-century baroque facade, a largely baroque interior and some stunning 5th-century mosaics on the triumphal arch and nave.

Chiesa di Santa Maria degli Angeli CHURCH
(Map p478; Piazza della Repubblica; ☉7am-6.30pm Mon-Sat, to 7.30pm Sun; ◻Repubblica) Facing onto Piazza della Repubblica, this cavernous church occupies what was once the central hall of Diocletian's enormous baths complex. Its most interesting feature is the double meridian in the transept.

SAN GIOVANNI & CELIO
Basilica di San Giovanni in Laterano
CHURCH
(Map p462; Piazza di San Giovanni in Laterano 4; ☉7am-6.30pm; ◻San Giovanni) For a thousand years, this huge white basilica was the most important church in Christendom. Consecrated in 324, it was the first Christian basilica to be built in Rome and until the late 14th century was the Pope's principal residence. Nowadays it's Rome's official cathedral and the Pope's seat as Bishop of Rome. It has been rebuilt various times over the centuries, most notably in the late 18th century, when the monumental facade was added.

Basilica di San Clemente CHURCH
(Map p462; Via di San Giovanni in Laterano; admission basilica/excavations free/€5; ☉9am-12.30pm & 3-6pm Mon-Sat, noon-6pm Sun; ◻Colosseo) Nowhere better illustrates the various stages of Rome's ancient history than this fascinating, multi-layered church. Near the Colosseum (head up the hill towards San Giovanni), the 12th-century church at street level was built

---

MUSEO NAZIONALE ROMANO

Spread over four sites, the **Museo Nazionale Romano** (National Roman Museum) houses one of the world's most important collections of classical art and statuary. A combined ticket including each of the sites costs adult/EU child €7/free and is valid for three days.

» **Palazzo Massimo alle Terme** ART MUSEUM
(Map p478; Largo di Villa Peretti 1; ☉9am-7.45pm Tue-Sun; ◻Termini) A fabulous museum with amazing frescos and wall paintings.

» **Terme di Diocleziano** MUSEUM
(Map p478; Via Enrico de Nicola 79; ☉9am-7.45pm Tue-Sun; ◻Termini) Housed in the Terme di Diocleziano (Diocletian's Baths), ancient Rome's largest baths complex.

» **Palazzo Altemps** MUSEUM
(Map p470; Piazza Sant'Apollinare 44; ☉9am-7.45pm Tue-Sun; ◻Corso del Rinascimento) Boasts the best of the museum's classical sculpture, including the famous Ludovisi collection.

» **Crypta Balbi** MUSEUM
(Map p470; Via delle Botteghe Oscure 31; ☉9am-7.45pm Tue-Sun; Largo di Torre Argentina) Set atop an ancient Roman theatre, the Teatro di Balbus (13 BC).

Termini, Esquilino & Quirinale (Rome)

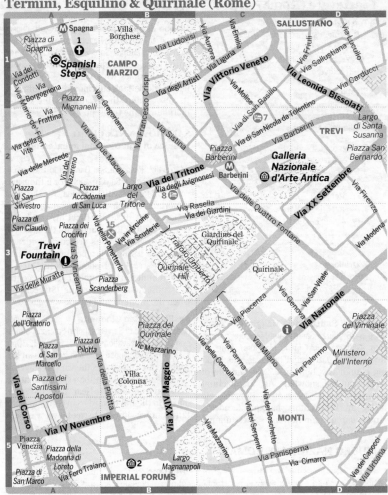

over a 4th-century church that was, in turn, built over a 1st-century Roman house with a temple dedicated to the pagan god Mithras.

Terme di Caracalla
RUINS

(Map p462; Via delle Terme di Caracalla 52; adult/ EU child €6/free; ⊙9am-1hr before sunset Tue-Sun, to 2pm Mon; MCirco Massimo) The vast ruins of the Terme di Caracalla are an awe-inspiring sight. Begun by Caracalla and inaugurated in 217, the 10-hectare leisure complex could hold up to 1600 people and included richly decorated pools, gymnasiums, libraries, shops and gardens. The ruins are now used to stage summer opera.

VIA APPIA ANTICA

The *regina viarum* (queen of roads), Via Appia Antica (Appian Way) is one of the world's oldest roads. Named after Appius Claudius Caecus, who laid the first 90km section in 312 BC, it was extended in 190 BC to reach Brindisi some 540km away on the Adriatic coast. The road, flanked by exclusive residential villas, is rich in ruins and history – this is where Spartacus and 6000 of his slave rebels were crucified in 71 BC, and it's here that you'll find Rome's most celebrated catacombs. These were built as communal burial grounds by the

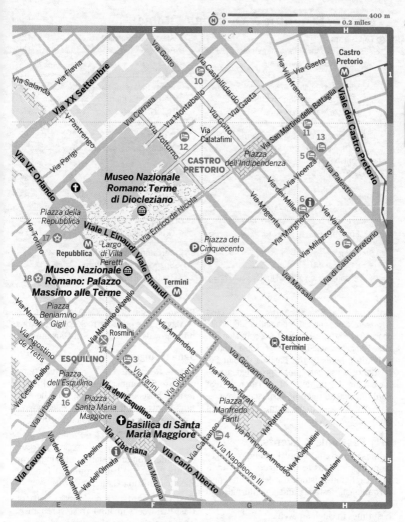

early Christians. Their belief in the Resurrection meant that they couldn't cremate their dead, as was the custom at the time, while persecution meant that they needed somewhere hidden to bury their dead. Roman law also forbade burial within the city walls.

To get to Via Appia Antica, take Metro Line A to Colli Albani, then bus 660, or bus 118 from the Piramide metro station. It's traffic-free on Sunday if you want to walk or cycle it. For information, bike hire or to join a guided tour, head to the **Appia Antica Regional Park Information Point** (☏06 513 53 16; www.parcoappiaantica.org; Via Appia Antica 58-60; ☉9.30am-1.30pm & 2-5.30pm; ☐Via Appia Antica).

Catacombs of San Callisto CATACOMBS
(www.catacombe.roma.it; Via Appia Antica 110; adult/child €8/free; ☉9am-noon & 2-5pm Thu-Tue, closed Feb; ☐Via Appia Antica) These are Rome's largest, most famous and busiest catacombs. Dating to the end of the 2nd century, they once formed part of a tunnel complex extending for some 20km. Excavations have so far unearthed the tombs of 16 popes and thousands of early Christians.

Catacombs of San Sebastiano   CATACOMBS
(www.catacombe.org; Via Appia Antica 136; adult/
concession €8/5; ⊙9am-noon & 2-5pm Mon-Sat,
closed mid-Nov–mid-Dec; 🚌Via Appia Antica)
Extending beneath the Basilica di San Sebastiano, these catacombs provided a safe
haven for the remains of St Peter and St
Paul during the reign of Vespasian. Frescos,
stucco work and mausoleums can be seen
on the second level.

✦ Festivals & Events

Rome's year-round festival calendar ranges
from the religious to the ribald, with traditional religious/historical celebrations, per-
forming-arts festivals and an international
film festival. Summer and autumn are the
best times to catch an event.

March to May

Easter   RELIGIOUS CELEBRATION
On Good Friday the Pope leads a candlelit
procession around the Colosseum. At noon
on Easter Sunday he blesses the crowds in
St Peter's Sq.

Settimana della Cultura   CULTURE WEEK
(April & May) Public museums and galleries
open free of charge during culture week.

Natale di Roma   HISTORIC FESTIVITIES
(21 April) Rome celebrates its birthday
with music, historical recreations, fireworks and free entry to many museums.

Primo Maggio   ROCK CONCERT
(1 May) A free open-air rock concert attracts
huge crowds to Piazza di San Giovanni.

June to August

Estate Romana   CULTURAL FESTIVAL
(June to September) Rome's big cultural
festival hosts events ranging from book
fairs to raves and gay parties – see www.
estateromana.comune.roma.it for details.

Festa dei Santi Pietro e Paolo
   RELIGIOUS CELEBRATION
(29 June) Romans celebrate their patron
saints Peter and Paul around St Peter's
Basilica and Via Ostiense.

Festa di Noantri   NEIGHBOURHOOD PARTY
(last two weeks in July) Trastevere's annual party involves plenty of food, wine,
prayer and dancing.

Festa della Madonna della Neve
   RELIGIOUS CELEBRATION
(5 August) A miraculous 4th-century
snowfall is celebrated at the Basilica di
Santa Maria Maggiore.

September to November

Romaeuropa   MUSIC & DANCE FESTIVAL
(late September to November) International performers take to the stage for
Rome's premier music and dance festival –
listings on http://romaeuropa.net.

Festival Internazionale del Film di Roma

FILM FESTIVAL

(late October) Held at the Auditorium Parco della Musica, Rome's film festival rolls out the red carpet for big-screen big shots – see www.romacinemafest.it.

🛏 Sleeping

While there's plenty of choice, accommodation in Rome tends to be expensive. If you can afford it, the best place to stay is in the *centro storico*, but if you're on a tight budget you'll probably end up in the Termini area, where most of the hostels and cheap *pensioni* (guest houses) are located. You'll find a full list of accommodation options (with prices) at www.060608.it.

Always try to book ahead, even if it's just for the first night. But if you arrive without a booking, there's a hotel reservation service (📞06 699 10 00; booking fee €3; ⊙7am-10pm) next to the tourist office at Stazione Termini.

ANCIENT ROME

Nicolas Inn
B&B €€

(Map p466; 📞06 976 18 483; www.nicolasinn.com; Via Cavour 295; d €100-180; ❄🛜) Visitors love this bright B&B at the bottom of Via Cavour, a stone's throw from the Imperial Forums. Run by a welcoming couple, it has four big guestrooms, each with homely furnishings, colourful pictures and en suite bathrooms.

Duca d'Alba
HOTEL €€€

(Map p466; 📞06 48 44 71; www.hotelducadalba.it; Via Leonina 14; s €70-210, d €80-260; ❄🛜) A refined four-star hotel on an atmospheric cobbled street near Cavour metro station. It's a tight squeeze but the individually decorated guestrooms are sleek and stylish and facilities include a basement fitness room.

THE VATICAN

Hotel Bramante
HOTEL €€€

(Map p462; 📞06 688 06 426; www.hotelbramante. com; Via delle Palline 24; s €100-160, d €140-230; ❄🛜) Housed in a Renaissance *palazzo* in the shadow of the Vatican walls, this charming hotel is a model of classical elegance. Antique furniture, wood-beamed ceilings, marble bathrooms and fresh flowers combine to create an inviting small-inn feel.

Colors Hotel & Hostel
HOSTEL, HOTEL €

(Map p462; 📞06 687 40 30; www.colorshotel.com; Via Boezio 31; dm €25-27, s €50-100, d €55-135; ❄@🛜) Fresh from a recent makeover, this laid-back hostel-cum-hotel near the Vatican has cheery, multicoloured dorms (for 18- to

DON'T MISS

THROUGH THE KEYHOLE

Up in the **Aventino** district you'll find one of Rome's best views. At the southern end of Via Santa Sabina stands the **Priorato dei Cavalieri di Malta**, the headquarters of the Cavalieri di Malta (Knights of Malta). The building is closed to the public but look through its keyhole and you'll see the dome of St Peter's perfectly aligned at the end of a hedge-lined avenue.

35-year-olds only), attractive private rooms and welcoming staff. Rooms with shared bathrooms are available at cheaper rates. Cash only.

HISTORIC CENTRE

TOP CHOICE Daphne Inn
BOUTIQUE HOTEL €€

(Map p478; 📞06 874 50 086; www.daphne -rome.com; Via di San Basilio 55 & Via degli Avignonesi 20; s €110-160, d €90-200, ste €320-550; ❄@🛜) Daphne is a gem. Spread over two sites near Piazza Barberini, it offers value for money, exceptional service and chic rooms. These come in various shapes and sizes but the overall look is minimalist modern with cooling earth tones and linear, unfussy furniture. Extras include irons and boards, bathrobes and tea- and coffee-making sets.

Hotel Panda
HOTEL €

(Map p474; 📞06 678 01 79; www.hotelpanda.it; Via della Croce 35; s €65-80, d €85-110, tr €120-140, ❄🛜) A superb position near the Spanish Steps, attractive high-ceilinged rooms and honest rates ensure a year-round stream of travellers to this budget classic. Air-con costs €6 and you can get breakfast at a nearby bar for €5. Cheaper rooms with shared bathrooms are available.

Okapi Rooms
HOTEL €€

(Map p474; 📞06 3260 9815; www.okapirooms. it; Via della Penna 57; s €65-80, d €85-120; ❄🛜) Occupying a 19th-century town house near Piazza del Popolo, the Okapi is an excellent low-midrange choice. Rooms, which are small and simple, come with cream walls, terracotta-tiled floors and double-glazed windows. Some also have ancient-style carvings and several have tiny terraces.

Relais Palazzo Taverna
BOUTIQUE HOTEL €€

(Map p470; 📞06 203 98 064; www.relaispalaz zotaverna.com; Via dei Gabrielli 92; s €70-140, d €100-180; ❀🛜) This cracking boutique hotel is superbly located in the heart of the historic centre. Its 11 individually decorated rooms sport a contemporary look with grey parquet floors, hand-printed wallpaper and funky, floral motifs.

Hotel Raphaël
LUXURY HOTEL €€€

(Map p470; 📞06 68 28 31; www.raphaelhotel.com; Largo Febo 2; s €160-300, d €220-350; ❀@) An ivy-clad landmark just off Piazza Navona, the Raphaël is a Roman institution. With its gallery lobby – look out for the Picasso ceramics and Miro lithographs – sleek Richard Meier–designed rooms and panoramic rooftop restaurant, it knows how to lay out the red carpet. Breakfast costs extra.

TRASTEVERE

TOP CHOICE Maria-Rosa Guesthouse
B&B €

(Map p476; 📞338 770 00 67; www.maria-rosa.it; Via dei Vascellari; s €60-70, d €75-85, q €120-130; ❀@🛜) A home away from home, this is a delightful little B&B on the 3rd floor of a Trastevere town house. It's a simple affair with two guestrooms sharing a single bathroom and a small common area, but the sunlight, pot plants and books create a lovely, warm atmosphere. The owner, Sylvie, is a fount of local knowledge and goes out of her way to help.

Arco del Lauro
B&B €€

(Map p476; 📞06 978 40 350; www.arcodellauro.it; Via Arco de' Tolomei 27-29; d €85-145, q €130-180; ❀@🛜) This friendly B&B is in a medieval palazzo in Trastevere's quieter eastern half. The five decent-sized double rooms, all on the ground floor, sport an understated modern look with white walls, parquet and modern furnishings, while the one quad retains a high, wood-beamed ceiling. Reception is open until 3pm, after which you'll need to phone.

Villa della Fonte
HOTEL €€

(Map p476; 📞06 580 37 97; www.villafonte.com; Via della Fonte dell'Olio 8; s €90-130, d €130-190; ❀🛜) Near Piazza Santa Maria in Trastevere, this charming little hotel is housed in an ivy-clad 17th-century palazzo. Its five rooms are small but tastefully decorated with white walls, earth-coloured floors and modern en suite bathrooms.

TERMINI & ESQUILINO

Beehive
HOSTEL €

(Map p478; 📞06 447 04 553; www.the-beehive.com; Via Marghera 8; dm €20-25, d €70-80; @🛜) A brilliant boutique hostel run by an environmentally conscious American couple, the Beehive boasts stylish decor, a vegetarian cafe (open only for breakfast and Sunday brunch) and a small yoga studio. Beds are in a spotless, eight-person mixed dorm or in one of six double rooms.

58 Le Real B&B
B&B €€

(Map p478; 📞06 482 35 66; www.lerealdeluxe.com; Via Cavour 58; r €70-155; ❀🛜) This swish nine-room B&B is on the 4th floor of a town house on busy Via Cavour. Rooms are small but stylish with leather armchairs, plasma TVs, Murano chandeliers, polished-wood bedsteads and parquet floors. The same people also run the nearby Relais Conte di Cavour (Map p478; 📞06 482 16 38; www.relaiscontedicavour.com; Via Farini 16; r €100-250).

Welrome
PENSION €

(Map p478; 📞06 478 24 343; www.welrome.it; Via Calatafimi 15-19; s €50-100, d €60-110; 🛜) This is a lovely, low-key hotel not far from Termini. Owner Mary takes great pride in looking after her guests, and her seven rooms provide welcome respite from Rome's relentless streets. Breakfast costs extra, but there are kettles and fridges for guest use.

Hotel Dolomiti
HOTEL €€

(Map p478; 📞06 495 72 56; www.hotel-dolomiti.it; Via San Martino della Battaglia 11; s €60-100, d €80-150; ❀@🛜) A warm, family-run hotel, the Dolomiti is a reliable choice. Rooms, which are colour coordinated in shades of cream, red and cherry-wood, are spread over three floors of a big palazzo not far from Termini.

Funny Palace
HOSTEL €

(Map p478; 📞06 447 03 523; www.funnyhostel.com; Via Varese 33; dm €15-25, s €30-70, d €55-100; @) To find this great little backpacker hostel head for the Splashnet laundry, which doubles as the reception and internet point. Upstairs, the mixed dorms are big and well maintained, while the private rooms reveal a simple, homey look. No credit cards.

Alessandro Palace Hostel
HOSTEL €

(Map p478; 📞06 44 61 958; www.hostelsalessandro.com; Via Vicenza 42; dm €18-25, d €66-120, tr €58-120; ❀@🛜) A long-standing favourite in the Termini area, this slick hostel offers spick-and-span hotel-style rooms, as well as dorms sleeping from four to eight. It's run by a friendly international crew, has 24-hour reception and there's a bar with satellite TV. On the other side of Termini, **Alessandro**

Downtown Hostel (Map p478; ☑06 443 40 147; Via Cattaneo 23) offers more of the same.

Yellow HOSTEL €
(Map p478; ☑06 493 82 682; www.the-yellow. com; Via Palestro 44; dm €18-35; ❈@🛜) In the Termini district, this popular hostel caters to a young, party-loving crowd (there's an age limit – 18 to 40). Dorms, which sleep from four to 12 people in bunk beds, are mixed, and while clean and reasonably sized, they can be noisy. There's no common room but most people hang out in the bar next door.

Hotel Castelfidardo PENSION €
(Map p478; ☑06 446 46 38; www.hotelcastel fidardo.com; Via Castelfidardo 31; s €40-70, d €60-100; ❈🛜) A simple, old-school outfit not far from Stazione Termini.

🍴 Eating

Eating out is one of the great joys of visiting Rome and everywhere you go you'll find trattorias, pizzerias and restaurants. The focus is very much on traditional Italian cooking, and the vast majority of places, particularly the smaller family-run trattorias, keep to tried-and-tested Roman dishes.

The best places to eat are in the historic centre and Trastevere, but there are also excellent choices in San Lorenzo (the area east of Stazione Termini) and Testaccio. You'll need to choose carefully in the Termini neighbourhood and around the Vatican, as both areas are full of overpriced tourist traps.

Roman specialities include *trippa alla romana* (tripe with potatoes, tomato and pecorino cheese), *fiori di zucca* (fried courgette flowers) and *carciofi alla romana* (artichokes with garlic, mint and parsley). Of the pastas, *cacio e pepe* (with pecorino cheese, black pepper and olive oil) and *all'amatriciana* (with tomato, pancetta and chilli) are Roman favourites.

THE VATICAN

Dino e Tony TRATTORIA €€
(Map p462; ☑06 3973 3284; Via Leone IV 60; mains €12; ⊗Mon-Sat) Something of a rarity, Dino e Tony is an authentic trattoria in the Vatican area. Kick off with the monumental antipasto, a minor meal in its own right, before plunging into its signature dish, *rigatoni all'amatriciana*. Finish up with a *granita di caffè*, a crushed iced coffee served with a full inch of whipped cream.

GELATO GALORE

To get the best out of Rome's *gelaterie* (ice-cream shops) look for the words *'produzione proprio'*, meaning 'own production'. As a rough guide, expect to pay between €1.50 and €3.50 for a *cono* (cone) or *coppa* (tub). Here is a choice of the city's finest:

» **San Crispino** (Map p478; Via della Panetteria 42) Near the Trevi Fountain, it serves natural, seasonal flavours – think crema with honey – in tubs only.

» **Old Bridge** (Map p462; Via Bastioni di Michelangelo 5) Just right for a pick-me-up after the Vatican Museums.

» **Tre Scalini** (Map p470; Piazza Navona 30) A Piazza Navona spot famous for *tartufo nero*, a €10 ball of chocolate ice cream filled with chunks of choc and served with cream.

» **Gelateria Giolitti** (Map p470; Via degli Uffici del Vicario 40) Rome's most famous gelateria, near the Pantheon.

HISTORIC CENTRE

TOP CHOICE Pizzeria da Baffetto PIZZA €
(Map p470; Via del Governo Vecchio 114; pizzas €6-9; ⊗6.30pm-midnight) For the full-on Roman pizza experience get down to this local institution. Meals here are raucous, chaotic and fast, but the thin-crust pizzas are good and the vibe is fun. To partake, join the queue and wait to be squeezed in wherever there's room. There's also a **Baffetto 2** (Map p470; Piazza del Teatro di Pompeo 18; ⊗6.30pm-12.30am, 12.30-3.30pm & 6.30pm-12.30am Sat & Sun) near Campo de' Fiori.

Maccheroni TRATTORIA €€
(Map p470; ☑06 6830 7895; Piazza delle Coppelle 44; mains €13; ⊗Mon-Sat) With its classic vintage interior, attractive setting near the Pantheon, and traditional menu, this is the archetypal *centro storico* trattoria. Locals and tourists alike flock here to dine on Roman stalwarts such as *tonnarelli al cacio e pepe* (pasta with cheese and pepper) and *carciofo alla romana* (Roman style artichoke).

Forno di Campo de' Fiori BAKERY €
(Map p470; Campo de' Fiori 22; pizza slices from €2) This is one of Rome's best bakeries, serving bread, panini and delicious straight-from-the-oven pizza *al taglio* (by the slice).

Aficionados claim you should order pizza *bianca* (white pizza), although the panini and pizza *rossa* (with tomato) are just as good.

Ditirambo
TRATTORIA €€

(Map p470; ☑06 687 16 26; Piazza della Cancelleria 72; mains €16; ⊘closed Mon lunch; ☑) This hugely popular new-wave trattoria near Campo de' Fiori offers a laid-back, unpretentious atmosphere and innovative, organic cooking. Vegetarians are well catered for, as are seafood fans, with dishes such as turbot roulade with aubergine and mint. Book ahead.

Vineria Roscioli
DELICATESSEN, RESTAURANT €€€

(Map p470; ☑06 687 52 87; Via dei Giubbonari 21; mains €20; ⊘Mon-Sat) This deli/restaurant is a foodie paradise. Under the brick arches, you'll find a mouth-watering array of olive oils, conserves, cheeses and hams, while out back the chic restaurant serves sophisticated Italian dishes. Wine buffs can peruse the 1100-strong wine list. Reservations recommended.

Gusto
PIZZA, RESTAURANT €€

(Map p474; ☑06 322 62 73; Piazza Augusto Imperatore 9; pizzas/buffet menus €9/10) All exposed brickwork and industrial chic, this big, '90s-style warehouse operation is a lunchtime favourite with office workers, serving everything from thick-crust pizza to cheese platters, salads and overpriced fusion food. At lunch the set menus are a bargain.

Da Tonino
TRATTORIA €

(Map p470; Via del Governo Vecchio 18; mains €7; ⊘Mon-Sat) Defiantly old-school, this traditional neighbourhood trattoria sits among the bohemian boutiques and trendy bars on Via del Governo Vecchio. Don't expect frills (or even menus), just tasty Roman cooking served fast and served cheap.

TRASTEVERE

Hostaria dar Buttero
TRATTORIA €€

(Map p476; ☑06 580 05 17; Via della Lungaretta; mains €11; ⊘Mon-Sat) On Trastevere's touristy main strip – on the quieter eastern side, though – this is a friendly old-school trattoria. The menu lists all the usual pastas, grilled meats and pizzas (evenings only), but the food is well cooked, the atmosphere is convivial and the prices are inviting. In summer, go for a table in the small back garden.

Osteria da Lucia
TRATTORIA €€

(☑06 580 36 01; Vicolo del Mattinato 2; mains €12.50; ⊘Tue-Sun) Hidden away on an atmospheric cobbled backstreet, da Lucia is a terrific neighbourhood trattoria. It's a wonderful place to get your teeth into some authentic Roman soul food, such as *spaghetti alla gricia* (with pancetta and cheese) and tiramisu.

Paris
RESTAURANT €€€

(Map p476; ☑06 581 53 78; Piazza San Calisto 7; mains €18; ⊘lunch & dinner Tue-Sat, lunch Sun) Outside of the Jewish Ghetto, this elegant, old-fashioned restaurant is the best place for traditional Roman-Jewish cooking. Specialities include *carciofi alle giudia* (deep-fried artichoke) and *fritto misto con baccalà* (fried vegetables with salted cod).

Da Enzo
TRATTORIA €

(Map p476; ☑06 581 83 55; Via dei Vascellari 29; mains €9; ⊘Mon-Sat) Lunching locals queue for a bowl of hearty pasta at this cheery trattoria in Trastevere's eastern streets. It's not the place for a long, lingering meal but for a no-nonsense *rigatoni alla carbonara* (pasta carbonara) it'll do just fine.

Da Augusto
TRATTORIA €

(Map p476; Piazza de' Renzi 15; mains €8; ⊘lunch & dinner Mon-Fri, lunch Sat) With a few rickety tables outside and a crowded interior, this earthy Trastevere trattoria is the real McCoy. The menu is rigorously Roman, so expect stalwarts such as *rigatoni all'amatriciana* and *ossobuco con piselli* (ossobuco with peas). Cash only.

Le Mani in Pasta
RESTAURANT €€€

(Map p476; ☑06 581 60 17; Via dei Genovesi 37; mains €18; ⊘Tue-Sun) This rustic Trastevere restaurant has an open kitchen that serves up delicious fresh pasta dishes, grilled meats and fresh seafood. It's a well-known spot, so try to book ahead for dinner.

Pizzeria Ivo
PIZZERIA €

(Map p476; Via di San Francesco a Ripa 158; pizzas €6; ⊘5.30pm-midnight Wed-Mon) A perennially popular pizzeria, Ivo fits the stereotype. With the TV on in the corner and waiters skilfully manoeuvring plates over the noisy hordes, diners chow down on classic thin-crust pizzas.

Also recommended:

Frontoni
DELICATESSEN €

(Map p476; Viale di Trastevere 52-56; pastas €6) Grab a panino at the downstairs deli or head upstairs for a bowl of pasta.

Forno la Renella
BAKERY €

(Map p476; Via del Moro 15-16; pizza slices from €2) Choose from the daily batch of wood-fired pizza, bread, and biscuits.

TESTACCIO

Pizzeria Remo
PIZZA €

(Map p462; Piazza Santa Maria Liberatice 44; pizzas €6; ⏱7.30pm-1am Mon-Sat) This rowdy Testaccio spot is one of the city's most popular pizzerias. Queues are the norm but the large, thin-crust pizzas and delicious bruschetta (toasted bread drizzled with olive oil and selected toppings) make the wait bearable.

Volpetti Più
TAVOLA CALDA €

(Map p462; Via Volta 8; mains €6; ⏱Mon-Sat) Next to the ravishing deli of the same name, this upmarket canteen is one of the few places in town where you can sit down and eat well for less than €15. Grab a tray and choose from the sumptuous spread of pizza, pasta, soup, meat, vegetables and fried nibbles.

TERMINI & ESQUILINO

Pommidoro
TRATTORIA €€

(Map p462; ☏06 445 26 92; Piazza dei Sanniti 44; mains €12; ⏱Mon-Sat) A long-standing favourite in the San Lorenzo area east of Termini, Pommidoro continues to win diners over with its no-fuss traditional food. Celebs sometimes drop by – Nicole Kidman and Fabio Capello have both dined here – but it remains an unpretentious spot with a laid-back vibe and excellent food.

Tram Tram
TRATTORIA €€

(Map p462; ☏06 49 04 16; Via dei Reti 44; mains €16; ⏱Tue-Sun) Dressed up to look like an old-fashioned trattoria, and named after the trams that rattle past outside, this is a trendy San Lorenzo eatery. It offers traditional dishes with a focus on seafood and rustic southern Italian cuisine. There's also an excellent wine list highlighting Italian producers.

TOP CHOICE Panella L'Arte del Pane
BAKERY €

(Map p462; Via Merulana 54; pizza slices from €2.50; ⏱8am-midnight Mon-Wed, Fri & Sat, to 2pm Thu, 8.30am-2pm Sun) Not far from the Basilica di Santa Maria Maggiore, this fabulous bakery is a great place for a quick lunch. Once you've chosen from the opulent array of sliced pizza, focaccia, crêpes, and *arancini* (fried rice balls), adjourn to an outdoor table or perch on a stool inside.

La Gallina Bianca
RESTAURANT €€

(Map p478; ☏06 474 37 77; Via Rosmini 9; pizzas from €8, mains €15) On a small street off Via Cavour, this choice restaurant offers a welcome respite from the tourist rip-off joints near Termini. It specialises in grilled vegetables and meats, although its supersized salads (€9.50) make for a lovely lunch. Pizza is also available.

485

 Drinking

Drinking in Rome is all about looking the part and enjoying the atmosphere. There are hundreds of bars and cafes across the city, ranging from neighbourhood hang-outs to elegant streetside cafes, dressy lounge bars and Irish-theme pubs. During the day, bars are generally for a quick coffee, often taken standing, while early evening sees the city's hip young drinkers descend on the fashionable watering holes for an *aperitivo* (aperitif).

Much of the action is in the *centro storico*. Campo de' Fiori is popular with young drinkers and can get very rowdy. For a more upmarket scene check out the bars in the lanes around Piazza Navona. Over the river, Trastevere is another popular spot with dozens of bars and pubs. To the east of Termini, San Lorenzo is a favourite of students and bohemian uptowners.

Salotto 42
BAR

(Map p470; www.salotto42.it; Piazza di Pietra; ⏱10am-2am Tue-Sat, to midnight Sun) Run by a Swedish model and her Italian partner, this hip, glamorous lounge bar sports soft sofas, coffee-table books and an excellent *aperitivo* spread. Brunch is also served at weekends.

Caffè Sant'Eustachio
CAFE

(Map p470; Piazza Sant'Eustachio 82; ⏱8.30am-1am) This small unassuming place, generally three-deep at the bar, boasts Rome's best coffee. Served sugared and with a layer of froth, the espresso is a smooth, creamy blend with a reassuringly strong caffeine kick.

Freni e Frizioni
BAR

(Map p476; Via del Politeama 4-6; www.freniefrizioni.com; ⏱10am-2am) A favourite Trastevere hang-out, housed in a former garage (hence the name – 'brakes and clutches') and spilling out onto a small piazza. The crowd is young and fashionable, the mojitos are great and the *aperitivo* spread well worth investigating.

La Tazza d'Oro
CAFE

(Map p470; Via degli Orfani 84-86; ⏱Mon-Sat) A busy, stand-up bar that serves a superb espresso and a range of delicious coffee concoctions, such as *granita di caffè*, a crushed-ice coffee with a big dollop of cream, and *parfait di caffè*, a €3 coffee mousse.

Vineria Reggio WINE BAR

(Map p470; Campo de' Fiori 15; ☺8.30am-2am Mon-Sat) The coolest of the Campo de' Fiori bars, this place is a good spot to watch the nightly *campo* circus. It has a small, bottle-lined interior and several outside tables.

Caffè Capitolino CAFE

(Map p466; Piazzale Caffarelli) Hidden behind the Capitoline Museums, this stylish rooftop cafe commands memorable views. It's a good place for a museum time out, although you don't need a ticket to drink here – it's accessible via an entrance behind Piazza dei Conservatori.

Bar San Calisto BAR

(Map p476; Piazza San Calisto; ☺6am-2.30am Mon-Sat) Intellectuals, bohemians, local alcoholics, foreign students – they all flock to this down-at-heel Trastevere landmark for the cheap prices and laid-back atmosphere. It's famous for its chocolate, drunk hot or eaten as ice cream.

Bar della Pace CAFE

(Map p470; Via della Pace 3-7; ☺8.30am-3am Tue-Sun, 5pm-3am Mon) The archetypal dolce vita bar. With its art nouveau interior, ivy-clad facade and well-dressed customers, it's the very epitome of Italian style.

Bar Arco degli Aurunci BAR

(Map p462; Via degli Aurunci 42; ☺8am-2am) On a car-free piazza in San Lorenzo, this attractive modern bar is a cool spot for a drink or light meal. Aperitifs are served between 7pm and 9pm.

☆ Entertainment

Rome has a thriving cultural scene, with a year-round calendar of concerts, performances and festivals. In summer, the Estate Romana festival sponsors hundreds of cultural events, many of which are staged in atmospheric parks, piazzas and churches. Autumn is another good time, with festivals dedicated to dance, drama and jazz.

Listings guides include *Roma C'è* (www.romace.it, in Italian; €1) and *Trova Roma,* a free insert with *La Repubblica* newspaper every Thursday. Both are available at newsstands. Up-coming events are also listed on www.turismoroma.it and wwwinromenow.com.

Two good ticket agencies are **Orbis** (Map p478; ☎06 482 74 03; Piazza dell'Esquilino 37; ☺9.30am-1pm & 4-7.30pm Mon-Fri, 9.30am-1pm Sat), which accepts cash payment only, and the online agency **Hello** (☎800 90 70 80; www.helloticket.it, in Italian).

Classical Music & Opera

Rome's cultural hub and premier concert complex is the **Auditorium Parco della Musica** (☎06 8024 1281; www.auditorium.com; Viale Pietro de Coubertin 34). With its three concert halls and 3000-seat open-air arena, it stages everything from classical-music concerts to tango exhibitions, book readings and film screenings. The auditorium is also home to Rome's top orchestra, the world-class **Orchestra dell'Accademia Nazionale di Santa Cecilia** (☎box office 06 808 20 58; www.santacecilia.it).

The **Accademia Filarmonica Romana** (☎06 320 17 52; www.filarmonicaromana.org) organises classical- and chamber-music concerts, as well as opera, ballet and multimedia events at the **Teatro Olimpico** (☎06 326 59 91; www.teatroolimpico.it; Piazza Gentile da Fabriano 17).

Rome's opera season runs from December to June. The main venue is the **Teatro dell'Opera** (Map p478; ☎box office 06 481 60 255; www.operaroma.it; Piazza Beniamino Gigli 7), which also houses the city's ballet company. Ticket prices tend to be steep. In summer, opera is performed outdoors at the spectacular Terme di Caracalla.

Nightclubs & Live Music

Rome is not one of Europe's great clubbing capitals, but there is action out there. The scene is centred on Testaccio and the Ostiense area, although you'll also find places in Trastevere and the *centro storico*. You'll need to dress the part for the big clubs, which can be tricky to get into, especially for groups of men. Gigs are often listed for 10pm but don't kick off until 11pm, while clubs rarely hot up much before midnight or 1am. Admission is often free but drinks are expensive, typically €10 to €15. Note also that many clubs shut between mid-June and mid-September.

Circolo degli Artisti CLUB, LIVE MUSIC

(www.circolodegliartisti.it; Via Casilina Vecchia 42; ☺Tue-Sun) Out in the up-coming Pigneto district – to the southeast of Stazione Termini – this fantastic club is a centre of the city's underground music scene, staging big names and emerging talents. It also hosts multimedia performances, film projections and cultural events.

Alexanderplatz
JAZZ CLUB

(Map p462; ☎06 397 42 171; www.alexanderplatz.it; Via Ostia 9) Rome's top jazz joint attracts top international performers and a passionate, knowledgeable crowd. In July and August the club ups sticks and transfers to the grounds of Villa Celimontana.

Goa
CLUB

(Via Libetta 13; ☺Tue-Sun) Top international DJs whip the crowd into a frenzy at Rome's top megaclub. Big nights include the Thursday Ultrabeat session, Saturday funky house and the 'Venus Rising' lesbian night every last Sunday of the month.

Villaggio Globale
SOCIAL CENTRE

(Map p462; www.vglobale.biz; Lungotevere Testaccio) For a warehouse-party vibe, head to Rome's best-known *centro sociale* (social centre), housed in an ex-slaughterhouse. Live music and DJ sets focus on dancehall, reggae, dubstep and drum'n'bass.

Big Mama
BLUES CLUB

(Map p462; ☎06 581 24 51; www.bigmama.it; Vicolo di San Francesco a Ripa 18; ☺Tue-Sun) This Trastevere basement is Rome's self-styled home of blues. It plays host to the world's top blues musicians and stages soul, jazz and funk.

AKAB
CLUB

(Map p462; www.akabcave.com; Via Monte Testaccio 68-69; ☺Tue-Sat) This is one of the most popular clubs on the Testaccio clubbing strip, with an underground cellar, a chilled garden and a steady supply of house, R&B and techno.

Cinema

Several cinemas show films in English, including the **Space Cinema Moderno** (Map p478; ☎892 11 11; Piazza della Repubblica 45/46), which screens Hollywood blockbusters and big Italian films, and the **Metropolitan** (Map p474; ☎06 320 09 33; Via del Corso 7), a four-screen multiplex near Piazza del Popolo. Expect to pay €7 to €7.50, with discounts on Wednesday.

🔒 Shopping

With everything from designer flagship stores to antique emporiums, flea markets and bohemian boutiques, shopping is fun in Rome. For the big-gun designer names head to Via dei Condotti and the area between Piazza di Spagna and Via del Corso. Moving down a euro or two, Via Nazionale, Via del Corso, Via dei Giubbonari and Via Cola di Rienzo are good for midrange clothing stores. For something more left field, try the small fashion boutiques and vintage clothes shops on Via del Governo Vecchio and around Campo de' Fiori. If you're looking for high-quality (read expensive) antiques or gifts, head to Via dei Coronari and Via Margutta. Rome's markets are a great place for bargain hunting. The most famous, **Porta Portese** (Map p462; Piazza Porta Portese; ☺6am-2pm Sun) is held every Sunday morning near Trastevere, and sells everything from antiques to clothes, bikes, bags and furniture. Near Porta San Giovanni, the **Via Sannio market** (Map p462; Via Sannio; ☺9am-1.30pm Mon-Sat) sells new and secondhand clothes.

For the best bargains, time your visit to coincide with the *saldi* (sales). Winter sales run from early January to mid-February and summer sales from July to early September.

ℹ Information

Emergency

Police station (Questura; ☎06 4 68 61; Via San Vitale 15)

Internet Access

Free wi-fi is now widely available in hostels, B&Bs and hotels across the city. Some also provide laptops/computers for guests' use. You'll find internet cafes across town, although with the recent spread of wi-fi many have shut.

Medical Services

For emergency treatment, go straight to the *pronto soccorso* (casualty) section of an *ospedale* (hospital). Pharmacists will serve prescriptions and can provide basic medical advice.

Ospedale Santo Spirito (☎06 6 83 51; Lungotevere in Sassia 1) Near the Vatican; multilingual staff.

Pharmacy Piazza dei Cinquecento (Piazza dei Cinquecento 49-51; ☺24hr); Stazione Termini (next to platform 1; ☺7.30-10.30pm)

Policlinico Umberto I (☎06 499 71; Viale del Policlinico 155) Rome's largest hospital.

Money

ATMs are liberally scattered around the city.

American Express (☎06 6 76 41; Piazza di Spagna 38; ☺9am-5.30pm Mon-Fri, 9am-12.30pm Sat) Has an ATM and offers exchange facilities and travel services.

Tourist Information

Centro Servizi Pellegrini e Turisti (Map p462; ☎06 698 81 662; St Peter's Sq; ☺8.30am-6.15pm Mon-Sat) The Vatican's official tourist office.

Enjoy Rome (Map p478; ☑06 445 18 43; www.enjoyrome.com; Via Marghera 8a; ◷8.30am-7pm Mon-Fri, to 2pm Sat) A private tourist office that arranges tours, airport transfers and hotel reservations.

I Fori di Roma Centro Espositivo Informativo (Map p466; Via dei Fori Imperiali; ◷9.30am-6.30pm) An information centre dedicated to the Forums.

The Comune di Roma runs a multilingual **tourist information line** (☑06 06 08; ◷9am-9pm) and information points across the city:

Ciampino airport (International Arrivals; ◷9am-6.30pm)

Castel Sant'Angelo (Map p470; Piazza Pia; ◷9.30am-7pm)

Fiumicino airport (International Arrivals; ◷9am-6.30pm)

Piazza Cinque Lune (Map p470; ◷9.30am-7pm) Near Piazza Navona.

Piazza Sonnino (Map p476; ◷9.30am-7pm) In Trastevere.

Santa Maria Maggiore (Map p478; Via dell'Olmata; ◷9.30am-7pm) Near the Basilica di Santa Maria Maggiore.

Stazione Termini (◷8am-8.30pm) In the hall parallel to platform 24.

Via Marco Minghetti (Map p470; ◷9.30am-7pm) Near the Trevi Fountain.

Via Nazionale (◷9.30am-7pm) In front of the Palazzo delle Esposizioni.

Websites

060608 (www.060608.it) A comprehensive and up-to-date site listing accommodation, attractions, events, and much more.

Pierreci (www.pierreci.it) Has the latest on museums, monuments and exhibitions. Book tickets online here.

Turismo Roma (www.turismoroma.it) Rome Tourist Board's extensive website has plenty of practical information, links and suggestions.

Vatican (www.vatican.va) The Holy See's official website, with practical information on Vatican sites.

Getting There & Away
Air

Rome's main international airport **Leonardo da Vinci** (FCO; ☑06 6 59 51; www.adr.it), better known as Fiumicino, is on the coast 30km west of the city. The much smaller **Ciampino airport** (CIA; ☑06 6 59 51; www.adr.it), 15km southeast of the city centre, is the hub for low-cost carriers including **Ryanair** (www.ryanair.com) and **easyJet** (www.easyjet.com).

Left-luggage (International Arrivals, Terminal 3; per 24hr €6; ◷6.30am-11.30pm) is available at Fiumicino.

Boat

Rome's port is at Civitavecchia, about 80km north of Rome. The main ferry companies:

Grimaldi Lines (☑081 464 444; www.grimaldi-lines.com) To/from Catania (Sicily), Trapani (Sicily), Porto Torres (Sardinia), Barcelona (Spain), Malta, and Tunis (Tunisia).

Sardinia Ferries (☑199 400 500; www.corsica-ferries.it) To/from Golfo Aranci (Sardinia).

SNAV (☑076 636 63 66; www.snav.it) To/from Palermo (Sicily) and Olbia (Sardinia).

Tirrenia (☑89 21 23; www.tirrenia.it) To/from Arbatax, Cagliari and Olbia (all Sardinia).

Bookings can be made at the Termini-based **Agenzia 365** (◷7am-9pm), at travel agents or online at www.traghettionline.net. You can also buy directly at the port.

Half-hourly trains depart from Roma Termini to Civitavecchia (€4.50 to €12.50, one hour). On arrival, it's about 700 to the port (to your right) as you exit the station.

Bus

Long-distance national and international buses use the **Autostazione Tiburtina** (Piazzale Tiburtina) in front of Stazione Tiburtina. Take metro line B from Termini to Tiburtina.

You can get tickets from the offices next to the bus terminus or at travel agencies. Bus operators:

Interbus (☑091 34 25 25; www.interbus.it, in Italian) To/from Sicily.

Marozzi (☑080 579 01 11; www.marozzivt.it, in Italian) To/from Sorrento, Bari, Matera and Lecce.

SENA (☑0861 199 19 00; www.senabus.it) To/from Siena and Tuscany.

Sulga (☑800 099 661; www.sulga.it, in Italian) To/from Perugia, Assisi and Ravenna.

Car & Motorcycle

Driving into central Rome is a challenge, involving traffic restrictions, one-way systems, a shortage of street parking, and aggressive drivers.

Rome is circled by the Grande Raccordo Anulare (GRA), to which all autostradas (motorways) connect, including the main A1 north–south artery (the Autostrada del Sole), and the A12, which connects Rome to Civitavecchia and Fiumicino airport.

CAR HIRE Rental cars are available at the airport and Stazione Termini:

Avis (☏06 481 43 73; www.avis.com)

Europcar (☏06 488 28 54; www.europcar.com)

Hertz (☏06 474 03 89; www.hertz.com)

Maggiore National (☏06 488 00 49; www.maggiore.com).

Near Termini, **Bici & Baci** (☏06 482 84 43; www.bicibaci.com; Via del Viminale 5; ☺8am-7pm) is one of many agencies renting out scooters. Bank on from €19 per day.

Train

Almost all trains arrive at and depart from **Stazione Termini** (Map p478). There are regular connections to other European countries, all major Italian cities, and many smaller towns. Train information is available from the **Sala Viaggiatori** (☺6am-midnight) next to platform 1, online at www.ferroviedellostato.it, or, if you speak Italian, by calling ☏89 20 21. **Left luggage** (1st 5hr €4, 6-12hr per hr €0.60, 13hr & over per hr €0.20; ☺6am-11.50pm) is on the lower-ground floor under platform 24.

Rome's second train station is **Stazione Tiburtina**, a short ride away on metro line B.

ℹ Getting Around

To/From the Airport

FIUMICINO The easiest way to get to/from the airport is by train but there are also bus services.

Cotral bus (www.cotralspa.it; one-way €4.50 or €7 if bought on bus) Runs to/from Stazione Tiburtina via Stazione Termini. Eight daily departures including night services from Tiburtina at 12.30am, 1.15am, 2.30am and 3.45am and from the airport at 1.15am, 2.15am, 3.30am and 5am. Journey time is 45 minutes to an hour.

FR1 train (one-way €8) Connects the airport to Trastevere, Ostiense and Tiburtina stations. Departures from the airport every 15 minutes (hourly on Sunday and public holidays) between 5.57am and 11.27pm, from Tiburtina between 5.05am and 10.33pm.

Leonardo Express train (adult/child €14/free) Runs to/from platforms 27 and 28 at Stazione Termini. Departures from Termini every 30 minutes between 5.52am and 10.52pm, from the airport between 6.36am and 11.36pm. Journey time is 30 minutes.

SIT bus (☏06 591 68 26; www.sitbusshuttle.it; one-way €8) Regular departures from Via Marsala outside Stazione Termini between 5am and 8.30pm, from the airport between 8.30am and 12.30pm. Tickets available on the bus. Journey time is one hour.

Taxi The set fare to/from the city centre is €40, which is valid for up to four passengers with luggage.

CIAMPINO The best option is to take one of the regular bus services into the city centre. You can also take a bus to Ciampino train station and then pick up a train to Stazione Termini.

Cotral bus (www.cotralspa.it; one-way/return €3.90/6.90) Runs frequent services to/from Ciampino train station (€1.20), where you can connect with trains to Stazione Termini (€1.30) or Anagnina metro station (€1.20).

SIT bus (www.sitbusshuttle.com; one-way/return €6/8) Regular departures from Via Marsala outside Stazione Termini between 4.30am and 9.30pm, from the airport between 7.45am and 11.15pm. Tickets available on the bus. Journey time is 45 minutes.

Taxi The set rate to/from the airport is €30.

Terravision bus (www.terravision.eu; one-way/return €4/8) Twice-hourly departures to/from Via Marsala outside Stazione Termini. From the airport, services are between 8.15am and 12.15pm, from Via Marsala between 4.30am and 9.20pm. Buy tickets at Terracafè in front of the Via Marsala bus stop. Journey time is 40 minutes.

Car & Motorcycle

Most of the historic centre is closed to normal traffic from 6.30am to 6pm Monday to Friday, from 2pm to 6pm Saturday, and from 11pm to 3am Friday to Sunday – see http://atacmobile.it for further details.

PARKING Blue lines denote pay-and-display parking spaces with tickets available from meters (coins only) and *tabacchi* (tobacconists). Expect to pay up to €1.20 per hour between 8am and 8pm (11pm in some places). After 8pm (or 11pm) parking is free until 8am the next morning. If your car gets towed away, check with the **traffic police** (☏06 6 76 91).

Car parks:

Piazzale Partigiani (per hr/day €0.77/5; ☺6am-11pm)

Stazione Termini (Via Marsala 30; per hr/day €3/26; ☺6am-1am)

Stazione Tiburtina (Via Pietro l'Eremita; per hr €2; ☺6am-10pm)

Villa Borghese (Viale del Galoppatoio; per hr/day €1.70/20; ☺24hr).

Public Transport

Rome's public transport system includes buses, trams, metro and a suburban train network.

TICKETS Valid for all forms of transport and come in various forms:

Single (BIT; €1) Valid for 75 minutes, during which time you can use as many buses or trams as you like but only go once on the metro.

Daily (BIG; €4) Unlimited travel until midnight of the day of purchase.

Three-day (BTI; €11) Unlimited travel for three days.

Weekly (CIS; €16) Unlimited travel for seven days.

Buy tickets at *tabacchi*, newsstands and from vending machines at main bus stops and metro stations. They must be purchased before you start your journey and validated in the yellow machines on buses, at the entrance gates to the metro or at train stations. Ticketless riders risk an on-the-spot €50 fine.

BUSES Buses and trams are run by **ATAC** (📞06 57 003; www.atac.roma.it). The **main bus station** (Map p478; Piazza dei Cinquecento) is in front of Stazione Termini, where there's an **information booth** (⏰7.30am-8pm). Largo di Torre Argentina, Piazza Venezia and Piazza San Silvestro are also important hubs. Buses generally run from about 5.30am until midnight, with limited services throughout the night.

METRO There are two metro lines, A and B, which both pass through Termini. Take line A for the Trevi Fountain (Barberini), Spanish Steps (Spagna), and Vatican (Ottaviano-San Pietro); and line B for the Colosseum (Colosseo) and Circus Maximus (Circo Massimo). Trains run between 5.30am and 11.30pm (to 1.30am on Friday and Saturday).

Taxi

Official licensed taxis are white with the symbol of Rome on the doors. Always go with the metered fare, never an arranged price (the set fares to and from the airports are exceptions). Official rates are posted in taxis.

You can hail a taxi, but it's often easier to wait at a rank or phone for one. There are major taxi ranks at the airports, Stazione Termini and Largo di Torre Argentina. You can book a taxi by phoning the Comune di Roma's automated **taxi line** (📞06 06 09) or calling a taxi company direct:

La Capitale (📞06 49 94)

Pronto Taxi (📞06 66 45)

Radio Taxi (📞06 35 70)

Samarcanda (📞06 55 51)

Tevere (📞06 41 57)

AROUND ROME

Ostia Antica

An easy day trip from Rome, Ostia Antica is well worth a visit. Ostia was ancient Rome's port, and the clearly discernible ruins of restaurants, laundries, shops, houses and public meeting places give a good impression of what life must once have been like in the 100,000-strong town. Founded in the 4th century BC, the port thrived until the 5th century AD, when barbarian invasions and an outbreak of malaria led to its abandonment and slow burial in river silt, thanks to which it has survived so well.

The **ruins** (adult/concession €6.50/3.25; ⏰8.30am-7pm Tue-Sun Apr-Oct, to 6pm Mar, to 5pm Nov, Dec, Jan & Feb) are spread out and you'll need a few hours to do them justice. Highlights include the **Terme di Nettuno** (Baths of Neptune) and adjacent **amphitheatre**, built by Agrippa and later enlarged to hold 3000 people. Behind it, the **Piazzale delle Corporazioni** (Forum of the Corporations) housed Ostia's merchant guilds and is decorated with well-preserved mosaics.

To get to Ostia Antica from Rome take the Ostia Lido train (25 minutes, half-hourly) from Stazione Porta San Paolo next to the Piramide metro station. The journey is covered by standard public-transport tickets. By car, take Via del Mare or Via Ostiense.

Tivoli

POP 55,700

An ancient resort town and playground for the Renaissance rich, hilltop Tivoli is home to two Unesco-listed sites: Villa Adriana, Emperor Hadrian's sprawling summer residence, and Villa d'Este, a Renaissance villa famous for its garden fountains. You can cover both in a day trip from Rome, but it'll be a long day.

👁 Sights

Villa Adriana   RUINS

(Hadrian's Villa; adult/EU child €6.50/free, plus possible €3.50 for exhibition; ⏰9am-1hr before sunset) Five kilometres from Tivoli proper, Hadrian's vast 2nd-century complex was one of the largest and most sumptuous villas in the Roman Empire. It was subsequently plundered for building materials, but enough remains to convey its magnificence. Allow several hours to explore it.

Villa d'Este   HISTORIC BUILDING, GARDEN

(www.villadestetivoli.info; Piazza Trento; adult/EU child €6.50/free, plus possible €3.50 for exhibition; ⏰8.30am-1hr before sunset Tue-Sun) Up in Tivoli's historic centre, the Renaissance Villa d'Este was built in the 16th century for Cardinal Ippolito d'Este. More than the villa itself, it's the elaborate gardens and their spectacular fountains, including one that plays an organ, that are the main attraction.

Parco Villa Gregoriana   PARK
(adult/child €4/2.50; ☉10am-6.30pm Tue-Sun Apr–mid-Oct, to 2.30pm mid-Oct–Nov & Mar, by appointment rest of year) A short walk from Villa d'Este, this historic park descends down a steep gorge, over which water crashes to the bottom 100m below.

❶ Information

Information is available at the **tourist information kiosk** (☑0774 31 35 36; www.tibursuperbum.it; Piazzale delle Nazioni Unite; ☉9.30am-5.30pm Tue-Sun) near the bus stop in the historic centre.

❶ Getting There & Away

Tivoli is 30km east of Rome and accessible by Cotral bus (€2, one hour, every 20 minutes) from outside Ponte Mammolo metro station. The fastest route by car is on the Rome–L'Aquila autostrada (A24).

To get to Villa Adriana from Tivoli town centre, take CAT bus 4X (€1, 10 minutes, half-hourly) from Largo Garibaldi.

Tarquinia

POP 16,500

Some 90km northwest of Rome, Tarquinia is an absolute gem, the pick of Lazio's Etruscan towns. The highlight is the magnificent Unesco-listed necropolis, but there's also a fascinating Etruscan museum (the best outside of Rome) and an atmospheric medieval town centre.

Founded in the 12th century BC, Tarquinia grew to rival Athens, and its kings were among the first rulers of the nascent city of Rome. It reached its prime in the 4th century BC, before a century of struggle ended with surrender to Rome in 204 BC.

◉ Sights

TOP CHOICE **Necropolis**   ETRUSCAN TOMBS
(Via Ripagretta; admission €6, incl Museo Nazionale Tarquiniense €8; ☉8.30am-30min before sunset Tue-Sun) This remarkable 7th-century-BC necropolis is one of Italy's most important Etruscan sites. There are reckoned only to be 200 painted Etruscan tombs in the entire country and some 140 of those are in Tarquinia. Of the 6000 tombs that have been excavated since 1489, 19 are currently open to the public, including the **Tomba della Caccia e della Pesca**, the richly decorated

Tomba dei Leopardi and the **Tomba della Fustigazione** with its erotic depiction of a little friendly S&M.

To get to the necropolis, about 1.5km outside of the town centre, you can either take bus D (€0.60, nine daily) from outside the tourist office or walk – head up Corso Vittorio Emanuele, turn right into Via Porta Tarquinia and follow straight into Via Ripagretta; it'll take about 15 minutes.

Museo Nazionale Tarquiniense   MUSEUM
(Piazza Cavour; admission €6, incl necropolis €8; ☉8.30am-30min before sunset Tue-Sun) Beautifully housed in the 15th-century Palazzo Vitelleschi, this lovely museum is a treasure trove of Etruscan artefacts. Highlights include a stunning terracotta frieze of winged horses (the Cavalli Alati); a room full of painted friezes; displays of sarcophagi, jewellery and amphorae; and some plates embellished with illustrations of acrobatic sex.

⏮ Sleeping & Eating

Tarquinia is a long day trip from Rome. If you want to stay overnight, the tourist office can provide accommodation lists. For a bite to eat, **Ristorante Arcadia** (☑0766 85 55 01; Via Mazzini 6; mains €12, tourist menus €14; ☉Tue-Sun), just behind the museum, is a friendly place serving excellent pasta, seafood and juicy grilled meats.

❶ Information

The helpful **tourist information office** (☑0766 84 92 82; www.tarquiniaturismo.it; Barriera San Giusto; ☉9am-1pm & 5-10pm Jul & Aug, shorter afternoon hr rest of year) is inside the town's medieval gate.

❶ Getting There & Away

The easiest way to get to Tarquinia from Rome is to take the Pisa train from Termini (€6.20, 1¼ hours, eight daily). At Tarquinia station take bus BC (€0.80, every 30 to 50 minutes) to the town centre.

By car, take the autostrada for Civitavecchia and then Via Aurelia (SS1).

Cerveteri

POP 35,400

With its hilltop *centro storico* and haunting Etruscan tombs, Cerveteri makes a rewarding day trip from Rome. Cerveteri was one of the most important commercial centres in the Mediterranean from the 7th to the 5th century BC. But as Roman power grew, so

Cerveteri's fortunes faded, and in 358 BC the city was annexed by Rome.

Cerveteri's Etruscan tombs are concentrated in the Unesco-listed **Necropoli di Banditaccia** (Piazzale Moretti; admission €6, incl museum €8; ☉9am-1hr before sunset Tue-Sun), just outside the town centre. The tombs are built into *tumoli* (mounds of earth with carved stone bases), laid out in the form of a town. The best preserved is the 6th-century-BC **Tomba dei Rilievi**, adorned with painted reliefs depicting household items and cooking implements. To get to the necropolis take the white shuttle bus G (€0.77) from next to the tourist information point.

In town, you can dine on tasty regional food at the **Antica Locanda Le Ginestre** (✆06 994 06 72; Piazza Santa Maria 5; mains €20; ☉Tue-Sun), one of the Lazio region's top restaurants. For a cheaper alternative try **Cavallino Bianco** (✆06 994 06 72; Piazza Risorgimento; mains €8; ☉closed Tue).

The superhelpful **tourist information point** (✆06 9955 2637; www.etruriaguide.it; Piazza Aldo Moro; ☉9.30am-12.30pm daily & 5.30-7.30pm Fri & Sat Jun-Sep, 9.30am-12.30pm Mon-Sat Oct-May), by the entrance to the historic centre, has information on local sites, accommodation and transport.

Cerveteri is accessible from Rome by Cotral bus (€3.10, 1¼ hours, every 45 minutes) from outside Cornelia station on metro line A.

NORTHERN ITALY

Italy's well-heeled north is a fascinating area of historical wealth and natural diversity. Bordered by the northern Alps and boasting some of the country's most spectacular coastline, it also encompasses Italy's largest lowland area, the decidedly nonpicturesque Po valley plain. Of the cities it's Venice that hogs the limelight, but in their own way Turin, Genoa and Bologna offer plenty to the open-minded traveller. Verona is justifiably considered one of Italy's most beautiful cities, while the medieval centres of Padua, Ferrara and Ravenna all reward the visitor.

Genoa

POP 611,200

One of the Mediterranean's great ports, Genoa (Genova) is an absorbing city of aristocratic *palazzi,* dark, malodorous alleyways, Gothic architecture and industrial sprawl. Birthplace of Christopher Columbus (1451–1506) and home to Europe's second-largest aquarium (the largest is in Valencia), it was once a powerful maritime republic known as La Superba; nowadays it's a fascinating port that's well worth a stopover, particularly as it's the gateway to the magnificent Cinque Terre National Park.

◉ Sights

Central Genoa is concentrated between the city's two main train stations: Stazione Brignole and Stazione Principe, with most sights in the *centro storico* and Porto Antico (Old Port).

Piazza de Ferrari   SQUARE
Genoa's central square is a good place to start exploring the city. Grandiose and impressive, it's centred on an exuberant fountain and flanked by imposing *palazzi* – **Palazzo della Borsa**, Italy's former stock exchange, **Teatro Carlo Felice**, the city's historic opera house, and the huge **Palazzo Ducale** (www.palazzoducale.genova.it; entrance Piazza Giacomo Matteotti), once the seat of the city's rulers but now used to host major art exhibitions. Admission prices and hours depend on the exhibition.

Cattedrale di San Lorenzo   CHURCH
(Piazza San Lorenzo; ☉9am-noon & 3-6pm) A short walk west of Piazza de Ferrari, Genoa's dramatic cathedral is most notable for its black-and-white-triped Italian Gothic facade. It was consecrated in 1118 but the two bell towers and cupola were added in the 16th century.

Acquario di Genova   AQUARIUM
(✆010 234 56 78; www.acquariodigenova.it; Ponte Spinola; adult/child €18/12; ☉8.30am-10pm daily Jul & Aug, 9am-7.30pm Mon-Fri, 8.45am-8.30pm Sat & Sun Mar-Jun, Sep & Oct, 9.30am-7.30pm Mon-Fri, 9.30am-8.30pm Sat & Sun Jan, Feb, Nov & Dec) The main attraction in Genoa's Porto Antico is Europe's second-largest aquarium. Designed by Italian architect Renzo Piano, it houses 5000 animals in six million litres of water.

Renzo Piano was also responsible for two of the port's other landmarks: the **Biosfere** (adult/child €5/3.50; ☉10am-7pm Apr-Oct, to 5pm Nov-Mar), a giant glass ball housing a tropical ecosystem; and the **Bigo** (adult/child €4/3; ☉10am-11pm Tue-Sun, 4-11pm Mon Jun-Aug, 10am-6pm Tue-Sun, 2-6pm Mon rest of year), an eye-catching panoramic lift.

Musei di Strada Nuovo
MUSEUMS

(Via Garibaldi; adult/concession €8/6; ⊙9am-7pm Tue-Fri, from 10am Sat & Sun) Genoa's main museums are in a series of *palazzi* on Via Garibaldi. The three most important, known collectively as the **Musei di Strada Nuova**, are housed in **Palazzo Bianco** (www.museo palazzobianco.it; Via Garibaldi 11), **Palazzo Rosso** (www.museopalazzorosso.it; Via Garibaldi 18) and **Palazzo Doria-Tursi** (www.museopalaz zotursi.it; Via Garibaldi 9). The first two feature works by Flemish, Dutch, Spanish and Italian old masters, while the third displays the personal effects of Niccolò Paganini, Genoa's legendary violinist. Tickets, valid for all three museums, are available from the bookshop in Palazzo Doria-Tursi.

🛏 Sleeping

TOP CHOICE **Locanda di Palazzo Cicala**
BOUTIQUE HOTEL €€€

(⊡010 251 88 24; www.palazzocicala.it; Piazza San Lorenzo 16; s €114-391, d €144-391; ❋@🛜) Located in a 16th-century *palazzo* opposite the cathedral, this welcoming boutique hotel has huge high-ceilinged rooms replete with parquet and slick designer furniture. There are also eight apartments available in nearby buildings.

Hotel Bel Soggiorno
HOTEL €€

(⊡010 54 28 80; www.belsoggiornohotel.com; 2nd fl, Via XX Settembre 19; s €65-110, d €75-135; P❋@🛜) Located on Genoa's main shopping strip, this old favourite is an endearing mix of the modern and the antique, with airy, comfortable rooms and modern amenities such as satellite TV and wi-fi.

Albergo Carola
PENSION €

(⊡010 839 13 40; www.pensionecarola.com; 3rd fl, Via Gropallo 4; s without bathroom €28-35, d €56-70; 🛜) Conveniently close to Stazione Brignole, this is a classic old-school *pensione* with simple, well-kept rooms on the 3rd floor of a towering old building. Rates don't include breakfast.

Ostello di Genova
HOSTEL €

(⊡010 242 24 57; www.ostellogenova.it; Via Costanzi 120; per person dm/s/d €17/27/25) Genoa's HI hostel is a functional, modern affair, some 2km up from the city centre – take bus 40 from Stazione Principe to the end of the line. Check-in is from 2.30pm to midnight and there's a lockout between 11.30am and 2.30pm.

🍴 Eating

Ligurian specialities include pesto (a sauce of basil, garlic, pine nuts and Parmesan) served with *trofie* (pasta curls), and focaccia (flat bread made with olive oil). There are numerous restaurants and trattorias in the *centro storico*, while the Porto Antico area is good for cheap takeaways.

Regina Margherita
RESTAURANT, PIZZA €€

(⊡010 595 57 53; Piazza della Vittoria 89-103; mains €14, pizzas from €5.50) A bright, modern set-up with a two-floor interior and a small outdoor terrace. It's not in a particularly enticing location – on Piazza della Vittoria – but the food is excellent and the service is friendly and efficient. Speciality of the house is the wood-fired Neapolitan pizza.

Osteria San Matteo
RESTAURANT €€

(⊡010 247 32 82; Piazza San Matteo 4r; mains €12) With its wood beams and exposed-brick walls, this is an inviting *osteria* in the heart of the historic centre. It serves a full menu but it's the reasonably priced seafood that stands out. Particularly tasty are the *acciughe* (anchovies) with potatoes, pine nuts and basil, and the *crema catalana* (crème brûlée).

Antica Cantina i Tre Merli
RESTAURANT €€€

(⊡010 247 40 95; Vico dietro il Coro Maddalena 26r; mains €19; ⊙closed Sat lunch & Sun) An atmospheric option just off Via Garibaldi, 'The Three Crows' serves Ligurian cuisine with an emphasis on fish. There are a number of regional specialities on offer, including the classic *trofie con pesto* (pasta curls with pesto).

Ristorante Da Rina
SEAFOOD €€€

(⊡010 246 64 75; www.ristorantedarina.it; Mura delle Grazie 3r; mains €18; ⊙closed Mon & Aug) If you're keen to sample local seafood, this famous place overlooking the port fits the bill. It opened in 1946 and has been a favourite with locals ever since. Reservations recommended.

🍷 Drinking & Entertainment

Action centres on the *centro storico*, with a number of good bars clustered around Piazza delle Erbe.

Mcafé
CAFE

(Piazza Giacomo Matteotti 9; ⊙8am-10pm Mon-Thu, to 1am Fri, 10am-1am Sat & Sun) This swish cafe by the entrance to the Palazzo Ducale is a good place to sip on something cool as you eye up fellow drinkers. Upstairs is a restaurant serving set lunch menus (€12) on weekdays and brunch (€16) at the weekend.

Storico Lounge Café   CAFE
(Piazza de Ferrari 34/36r; ⊙6am-3am) The *aperitivo* buffet here (5pm to 10pm) is a favourite with the city's fashionable young things, who love congregating at the pavement tables overlooking the Teatro Carlo Felice. There's also a DJ set on Friday and Saturday nights.

Teatro Carlo Felice   THEATRE
(☑010 538 12 24; www.carlofelice.it; Passo Eugenio Montale 4) Genoa's historic theatre stages a year-round program of opera, ballet and classical music. Tickets start at about €25.

❶ Information
Tourist offices Airport (☑010 601 52 47; ⊙9am-1pm & 1.30-5.30pm); City centre (☑010 860 61 22; www.turismo.comune.genova. it; Largo Pertini 13; ⊙9.30am-1pm & 2.30-6.30pm); Via Garibaldi (☑010 557 29 03; Via Garibaldi 12r; ⊙9.30am-1pm & 2.30-6.30pm); Antico Porto (⊙10am-7pm)

❶ Getting There & Around
Air
Genoa's **Cristoforo Colombo airport** (GOA; ☑010 6 01 51; www.airport.genova.it; Sestri Ponente) is 6km west of the city. To get there take the **Volabus** (€6, 30min, hourly 5.20am-11.20pm) from Stazione Brignole or Stazione Principe. Buy tickets on board or at tourist offices. A taxi costs €7 per person from Stazione Principe and €8 from Brignole.

Boat
Ferries sail to/from Spain, Sicily, Sardinia, Corsica and Tunisia from the **terminal traghetti** (ferry terminal; www.porto.genova. it; Calata Chiappella), west of the city centre. Ferry companies:

Grandi Navi Veloci (☑010 209 45 91; www. gnv.it) To/from Sardinia (Porto Torres from €25, 11 hours; Olbia from €22, nine to 10 hours), Sicily (Palermo from €83, 20 hours), Barcelona (from €81, 18 hours) and Tunis (from €127, 24 hours).

Moby Lines (☑199 30 30 40; www.mobylines. it) To/from Sardinia (Porto Torres from €24, 10 hours).

Tirrenia (☑800 82 40 79; www.tirrenia.it) To/from Sardinia (Porto Torres from €30, 10 hour; Olbia from €30, 9¾ hours; Arbatax from €27, 14½ hours).

Bus
The main bus terminal is on Piazza della Vittoria, south of Stazione Brignole. Book tickets at **Geotravels** (Piazza della Vittoria 57).

Local buses are run by **AMT** (☑800 08 53 11; www.amt.genova.it). Tickets cost €1.20 and are valid for 90 minutes. Bus 33 runs between Stazione Principe and Stazione Brignole, stopping at Piazza de Ferrari en route.

Train
There are direct trains to Milan (€16.50, 1½ hours, up to 25 daily), Pisa (€16, two hours, up to 15 daily), Rome (€38.50, 5½ hours, nine daily) and Turin (€16, two hours, up to 15 daily). Regional trains to La Spezia service Cinque Terre (€5.30, two hours, up to 21 daily).

It generally makes little difference whether you leave from Brignole or Principe.

Cinque Terre

Liguria's eastern Riviera boasts some of Italy's most dramatic coastline, the highlight of which is the Unesco-listed **Parco Nazionale delle Cinque Terre** (Cinque Terre National Park) just north of La Spezia. Stretching for 18km, this awesome stretch of plunging cliffs and vine-covered hills is named after its five tiny villages: Riomaggiore, Manarola, Corniglia, Vernazza and Monterosso.

It gets very crowded in summer, so try to visit in spring or autumn. You can either visit on a day trip from Genoa or La Spezia, or stay overnight in one of the five villages.

⊙ Sights & Activities
The Cinque Terre villages are linked by the 9km **Blue Trail** (Sentiero Azzurro; admission with Cinque Terre Card), a magnificent, mildly challenging five-hour trail. The walk is in four stages, the easiest of which is the first stage from Riomaggiore to Manarola (Via d'Amore, 20 minutes) and the second from Manarola to Corniglia (one hour). For the final two stages, you'll need to be fit and wearing proper walking shoes. The stretch from Corniglia to Vernazza takes approximately 1½ hours and from Vernazza to Monterosso it's two hours. Make sure you bring a hat, sunscreen and plenty of water if walking in hot weather.

The Blue Trail is just one of a network of footpaths and cycle trails that criss-cross the park; details are available from the park offices. If water sports are more your thing, you can hire snorkelling gear (€10 per day) and kayaks (single/double €5/10 per hour) at the **Diving Center 5 Terre** (www.5terrediving.

com; Via San Giacomo) in Riomaggiore. It also offers a snorkelling boat tour for €18.

🛏 Sleeping & Eating

L'Eremo Sul Mare   B&B €

(☑346 019 58 80; www.eremosulmare.com; Sentiero Azzurro, Vernazza; r €80-110; 🌣) This romantic cliffside B&B (its name means Hermitage by the Sea) is beautifully situated on the Blue Trail about 500m uphill from Vernazza train station. It has three rooms, a panoramic sun terrace and a kitchen for guests' use. Cash only.

Ostello 5 Terre   HOSTEL €

(☑0187 92 02 15; www.cinqueterre.net/ostello; Via B Riccobaldi 21, Manarola; dm €20-23, d €55-65; ⊘closed Nov-Feb; @) A popular private hostel in Manarola. Beds are in bright six-person single-sex dorms or private rooms with en suite bathrooms. Extras include breakfast (€6) and dinner (€18), laundry facilities and sports kit rental. Book at least a week ahead.

Hotel Ca' d'Andrean   HOTEL €

(☑0187 92 00 40; www.cadandrean.it; Via Doscovolo 101, Manarola; s €55-72, d €70-100; 🌣) An excellent family-run hotel in the upper part of Manarola. Rooms are big and cool with tiled floors and unobtrusive furniture; some have private terraces. Breakfast (€6) is served in the garden. No credit cards.

Marina Piccola   SEAFOOD €€

(☑0187 92 01 03; www.hotelmarinapiccola.com; Via Birolli 120, Manarola; mains €12) Dine on fresh-off-the-boat seafood overlooking the small bay at Manarola. The harbourside setting is ideal for *zuppa di pesce* (fish soup) or seafood risotto. The adjoining hotel has small but comfortable air-conditioned rooms (single/double €87/115).

Trattoria La Lanterna   SEAFOOD €€

(☑0187 92 05 89; Via San Giacomo 46, Riomaggiore; mains €16) This busy restaurant is perched above the snug harbour in Riomaggiore. Tables are on a small terrace or in a bright, breezy dining room and the menu features seafood pastas and simple fish dishes.

ℹ Information

The park's main **information office** (☑0187 92 06 33; ⊘8am-9.30pm) is to the right as you exit the train station at Riomaggiore. There are other offices in the train stations at Manarola, Corniglia, Vernazza, Monterosso and La Spezia (most open from 8am to 8pm).

Online information is available at www.parco nazionale5terre.it and www.cinqueterre.com.

> ### CINQUE TERRE CARD
>
> To walk the Blue Trail (Sentiero Azzurro) coastal path you'll need a Cinque Terre Card. This comes in three forms:
>
> » **Cinque Terre Card** (adult/child 1 day €5/2.50, 2 days €8/4) Available at all park offices.
>
> » **Cinque Terre Treno Card** (adult/child 1 day €8.50/4.30, 2 days €14.70/7.40) Covers the Blue Trail plus unlimited train travel between Levanto and La Spezia, including all five villages.
>
> » **Cinque Terre Card Batello** (adult/child 1 day €19.50/9.80) The Blue Trail and unlimited boat travel within the Area Marina Protetta 5 Terre.

ℹ Getting There & Away

Boat

Between July and September, **Golfo Paradiso** (☑0185 77 20 91; www.golfoparadiso.it) operates boat excursions from Genoa's Porto Antico to Vernazza, Monterosso and Riomaggiore. These cost €18 one-way, €33 return.

From late March to October, **Consorzio Marittimo Turistico 5 Terre** (☑0187 73 29 87; www.navigazionegolfodeipoeti.it) runs daily ferries between La Spezia and four of the villages (not Corniglia), costing €16 one-way including all the stops. Return trips are covered by a daily ticket (€23/25 weekdays/weekends).

Train

Regional trains run from Genoa Brignole to Riomaggiore (€4.80, 1½ to two hours, 20 daily), stopping at each of the Cinque Terre villages. The last train back from Riomaggiore to Genoa is at 11.19pm.

Between 4.30am and 11.10pm, one to three trains an hour crawl up the coast from La Spezia to Levanto (€3.30, 30 minutes), stopping at all of the villages en route. If you're doing this journey and you want to walk the Blue Trail, you'll save money buying the Cinque Terre Treno Card.

Turin

POP 908,900

First-time visitors are often surprised by Turin (Torino). Expecting a bleak, industrial sprawl dominated by Fiat factories, they are instead confronted with a dynamic and attractive city full of royal *palazzi*, historic cafes, baroque piazzas and world-class museums. Surprise almost inevitably turns to fascination when they learn of the city's occult aspect. Situated on the 45th parallel, it is said to be one of the three apexes of the white-magic triangle with Lyon and Prague, and also the black-magic counterpart of London and San Francisco.

⊙ Sights

Serious sightseers should consider the **Torino & Piedmont Card** (48hr card adult/child €20/10), available at tourist offices, which gives free public transport (not the metro) and discounts or entry to 170 museums, monuments and castles.

Piazza Castello   SQUARE

Turin's grandest square is bordered by porticoed promenades and regal palaces. Dominating the piazza, **Palazzo Madama** (www. palazzomadamatorino.it) was the original seat of the Italian parliament. It is now home to the **Museo Civico d'Arte Antica** (Piazza Castello; adult/child €7.50/free; ⊙10am-6pm Tue-Sat, to 8pm Sun), whose impressive collection includes Gothic and early Renaissance paintings and some interesting majolica work. To the north, statues of Castor and Pollux guard the entrance to the enormous and lavishly decorated **Palazzo Reale** (Royal Palace; Piazza Castello; adult/child €6.50/free; ⊙8.30am-7.30pm Tue-Sun), built for Carlo Emanuele II in the

---

DON'T MISS

HISTORIC CAFES

Turin is home to an impressive array of historic cafes. Don't leave town without propping up the bar and downing an excellent espresso in the following:

Baratti & Milano (Piazza Castello 29; ⊙closed Wed) Serving coffee and confectionary since 1873.

Caffè San Carlo (Piazza San Carlo 156) Dates from 1828.

Caffè Torino (Piazza San Carlo 204) A relative newcomer, this art nouveau gem opened in 1903.

Neuv Caval'd Brônz (Piazza San Carlo 155)

San Tommaso 10 (Via San Tommaso 10; ⊙Mon-Sat) This is where Lavazza started. It now serves an unorthodox array of flavoured coffees as well as all the classics.

---

mid-17th century. The palace's **Giardino Reale** (Royal Garden; admission free; ⊙9am-1hr before sunset) was designed in 1697 by Louis le Nôtre, noted for his work at Versailles.

A short walk away, **Piazza San Carlo**, known as Turin's drawing room, is famous for its cafes and twin baroque churches **San Carlo** and **Santa Cristina**.

Cattedrale di San Giovanni Battista CHURCH
(Piazza San Giovanni; ⊙8am-noon & 3-7pm Mon-Sat, from 7am Sun) Turin's 15th-century cathedral houses the famous Shroud of Turin (*Sindone*), supposedly the cloth used to wrap the crucified Christ. A copy is on permanent display in front of the altar, while the real thing is kept in a vacuum-sealed box and rarely revealed.

Mole Antonelliana   MUSEUM
(Via Montebello 20) Turin's famous landmark towers 167m over the city skyline. Originally intended as a synagogue, the Mole now houses the enormously enjoyable **Museo Nazionale del Cinema** (www.museocinema. it; adult/child €7/2; ⊙9am-8pm Tue-Fri & Sun, to 11pm Sat) and its comprehensive collection of cinematic memorabilia. Don't miss the glass **panoramic lift** (adult/child €5/3.50; ⊙10am-8pm Tue-Fri & Sun, to 11pm Sat), which whisks you up 85m in 59 seconds. Joint tickets for the museum and lift cost €9/4.50.

Museo Egizio   ART MUSEUM
(www.museoegizio.it; Via Accademia delle Scienze 6; adult/child €7.50/free; ⊙8.30am-7.30pm Tue-Sun) This fabulous museum houses an engrossing collection of ancient Egyptian art that is considered the world's most important outside of Cairo and London.

Also recommended:

Pinacoteca Giovanni e Marella Agnelli
                                        ART MUSEUM
(www.pinacoteca-agnelli.it; Via Nizza 262; permanent exhibitions adult/child €4/2.50; ⊙10am-7pm Tue-Sun) A Renzo Piano–designed art gallery in the Lingotto, Fiat's former car factory.

Castello di Rivoli Museo d'Arte Contemporanea ART MUSEUM
(www.castellodirivoli.org; Piazza Mafalda di Savoia; adult/child €6.50/free; ⊙10am-5pm Tue-Thu, to 9pm Fri-Sun) A modern art gallery in a castle a few kilometres outside of Turin.

🛏 Sleeping

TOP CHOICE **Art Hotel Boston** BOUTIQUE HOTEL €€€
(☎011 50 03 59; www.hotelbostontorino. it; Via Massena 70; s €80-150, d €110-190, ste €250-

500; ✳@🛜) The Boston's austere facade gives no clues as to its chic modern interior. The public spaces are littered with impressive works of contemporary art, while many of the 86 individually decorated rooms are themed on subjects such as Lavazza coffee, Ayrton Senna and Pablo Picasso.

Hotel Montevecchio　　HOTEL €€
(☑011 562 00 23; www.hotelmontevecchio.com; Via Montevecchio 13; s €45-90, d €60-120; @🛜) Conveniently located about 300m from Porta Nuova train station, this is a friendly, well-run two-star place. Rooms come in sunny shades of yellow, the breakfast buffet is ample and there's a long list of extras, including a laundry service and wi-fi (€10 per day).

L'Orso Poeta　　B&B €€
(☑011 517 89 96; www.orsopoeta-bed-and-breakfast.it; Corso Vittorio Emanuele II 10; s/d from €70/110; ✳) A welcoming B&B in a historic apartment building by the Po River. Its two small, pastel-shaded rooms have bathrooms and lots of character. Note that it's closed in August, December and January.

Alpi Resort Hotel　　BUSINESS HOTEL €
(☑011 812 96 77; www.hotelalpiresort.it; Via A Bonafous 5; s €54-65, d €69-85; P✳) A business-like three-star place in an excellent location just off Piazza Vittorio Veneto. Its impeccably clean carpeted rooms are quiet and comfortable, if rather characterless.

✗ Eating & Drinking
Turin has a reputation for magnificent gelato, which you can sample at outlets of **Grom** (☺11am-midnight Sun-Thu, to 1am Fri & Sat) at Piazza Paleocapa 1d, Via Accademia delle Scienze 4, and Via Garibaldi 11.

Early evening is the time to make for one of the city's cafes and enjoy an *aperitivo* accompanied by a sumptuous buffet (included in the price). The most happening *aperitivo* precinct is Piazza Emanuele Filiberto and environs: try **Pastis** (Piazza Emanuele Filiberto 9) or **I Tre Galli** (Via Sant'Agostino 25; ☺Mon-Sat). The *aperitivo* drinks cost around €8.

Da Ciro　　PIZZA €
(☑011 53 19 25; Corso Vinzaglio 17; pizzas from €5.50; ☺closed Sat lunch & Sun) A favourite of Juventus footballers – ex-Juve legend Ciro Ferrara is a part-owner – this is a little bit of Naples in the north. Diners pile into the cheery, unpretentious interior to tear into delicious wood-fired pizzas. Booking recommended.

Otto Etre Quarti　　PIZZA, RESTAURANT €€
(☑011 517 63 67; Piazza Solferino 8c; pizzas from €5, mains €12) Claim a table in one of 8¾'s high-ceilinged dining rooms or on the square-side terrace and feast on fab pizzas or tasty pastas such as *paccheri con tonno* (big pasta tubes with tuna).

❶ Information
The city's efficient **tourist office** (☑010 53 51 81; www.turismotorino.org; ☺9am-7pm daily) has branches at Porta Nuova station, Piazza Castello and Via Giuseppe Verdi near the Mole Antonelliana.

❶ Getting There & Around
In Caselle, 16km northwest of the city centre, **Turin airport** (TRN; ☑011 567 63 61; www.turin-airport.com) serves flights to/from European and national destinations. **Sadem** (☑800 801 600; www.sadem.it, in Italian) runs an airport shuttle (€5.50 or €6 on board, 40 minutes, half-hourly) between the airport and Porta Nuova train station. It operates between 5.15am and 11pm. A taxi costs approximately €35 to €40.

Direct trains connect Turin with Milan (€14.50, two hours, up to 30 daily), Florence (€67, three hours, five daily), Genoa (€15, two hours, up to 20 daily), and Rome (€93, 4¼hr, seven daily).

Milan
POP 1.29 MILLION

Few Italian cities polarise opinion like Milan, Italy's financial and fashion capital. Some people love the cosmopolitan, can-do atmosphere, the vibrant cultural scene and sophisticated shopping; others grumble that it's dirty, ugly and expensive. Certainly, it lacks the picture-postcard beauty of many Italian towns, but in among the urban hustle are some truly great sights – Leonardo da Vinci's *Last Supper,* the immense Duomo, the world-famous La Scala opera house.

Originally founded by Celtic tribes in the 7th century BC, Milan was conquered by the Romans in 222 BC and developed into a major trading and transport centre. From the 13th century it flourished under the rule of two powerful families, the Visconti and the Sforza.

◉ Sights
Milan's main attractions are concentrated in the area between Piazza del Duomo and Castello Sforzesco. To get to the piazza from Stazione Centrale, take the yellow MM3 underground line.

Duomo
CHURCH

(Piazza del Duomo; admission free; ⊙7am-7pm)
With a capacity of 40,000 people, this is
the world's largest Gothic cathedral and
the third-largest church in Europe. Commissioned in 1386 to a florid French-Gothic
design and finished nearly 600 years later,
it's a fairy-tale ensemble of 3400 statues, 135
spires and 155 gargoyles. Climb up to the
roof (stairs/elevator €5/8; ⊙stairs 9am-5.20pm,
lift 9am-9.15pm) for memorable city views.

Galleria Vittorio Emanuele II
SHOPPING ARCADE

(Piazza del Duomo) This elegant iron-and-glass
shopping arcade opens off the northern
flank of Piazza del Duomo. Local tradition
claims you can ward off bad luck by grind-
ing your heel into the balls of the mosaic
bull on the floor near the central cross.

Teatro alla Scala
OPERA HOUSE

(www.teatroallascala.org; Piazza della Scala; admission €5; ⊙9am-12.30pm & 1.30-5.30pm) Milan's

legendary opera house hides its sumptuous
six-tiered interior behind a surprisingly severe
facade. You can peek inside as part of a visit to
the theatre's museum providing there are no
performances or rehearsals in progress.

The Last Supper (Cenacolo Vinciano)
PAINTING

(✆02 9280 0360; www.vivaticket.it; Piazza Santa
Maria delle Grazie 2; adult/EU child €6.50/free plus
booking fee of €1.50; ⊙8.15am-6.45pm Tue-Sun)
Milan's most famous tourist attraction –
Leonardo da Vinci's mural of *The Last Supper* – is in the Cenacolo Vinciano, the refec-
tory of the Chiesa di Santa Maria delle Grazie, west of the city centre. To see it you need
to book ahead or take a city tour.

FREE Castello Sforzesco
CASTLE

(www.milanocastello.it; Piazza Castello
3; ⊙7am-7pm) This dramatic 15th-century
castle was the Renaissance residence of the
Sforza dynasty. It now houses the **Musei del**

Central Milan

Castello (adult/child €3/free; ◎9am-5.30pm
Tue-Sun), a group of museums dedicated to
art, sculpture, furniture, archaeology and
music. Entry is free on Friday between 2pm
and 5.30pm and from Tuesday to Sunday between 4.30pm and 5.30pm.

Pinacoteca di Brera   ART MUSEUM
(www.brera.beniculturali.it; Via Brera 28; adult/
EU child €11/free; ◎8.30am-7.15pm Tue-Sun) Art
amassed by Napoleon forms the basis of
the Pinacoteca's heavyweight collection,
which includes Andrea Mantegna's masterpiece, the *Dead Christ* and Raphael's
Betrothal of the Virgin.

👣 Tours

Autostradale (www.autostradale.it) runs three-
hour multilingual bus tours that take in the
major sights and include entry to *The Last
Supper*. Departures are at 9.30am from Piazza del Duomo every day except Monday.
There are also two daily walking tours (€20)
between Monday and Saturday, departing
from the tourist office on Piazza del Duomo
at 10am and 11.30am. Tickets for both tours
are available from the tourist office at Piazza
del Duomo.

🛏 Sleeping

Milan is a business city, which means hotels are expensive and it can be hard to find
a room, particularly when trade fairs are on

(which is often). Booking is essential at all
times.

Antica Locanda Leonardo   HOTEL €€
(☑02 4801 4197; anticalocandaleonardo.com;
Corso Magenta 78; s €69-105, d €99-230; ✲🛜)
A charming little hotel with characterful
rooms and a gregarious, hospitable owner.
Housed in a 19th-century *palazzo* near the
Cenacolo Vinciano, it's decorated in classic
style with polished wood furniture, parquet
floors, rugs, and pot plants.

Hotel De Albertis   HOTEL €€
(☑02 738 34 09; www.hoteldealbertis.it; Via De Albertis 7; s €50-100, d €50-160; @🛜) A little way
out from the centre in a leafy residential
street, this small hotel is a welcoming, family-run affair. There are few frills but rooms
are clean, comfortable and quiet. Take bus
92 from Stazione Centrale or tram 27 from
the Duomo.

Hotel Nuovo   HOTEL €€
(☑02 8646 4444; www.hotelnuovomilano.com;
Piazza Beccaria 6; r €50-150; ✲🛜) In a city
where 'cheap' is an ugly word, the Nuovo is
a bastion of budget accommodation. Rooms
are basic but clean, and the location, just off
Corso Vittorio Emanuele II, is a winner. Air-
con is only in rooms on the 2nd floor and
rates don't include breakfast.

Ariston Hotel   HOTEL €€€
(☑02 7200 0556; www.aristonhotel.com; Largo
Carrobbio 2; s €65-380, d €80-380; 🅿✲@🛜)
Claiming to be Milan's first 'ecological hotel', the centrally located Ariston offers
smart modern rooms and environmentally
friendly touches such as organic breakfasts,
all-natural soaps, and free bike hire. Check
the website for excellent low-season deals.

🍴 Eating & Drinking

Local specialities include *risotto alla milanese* (saffron-infused risotto cooked in bone-
marrow stock) and *cotoletta alla milanese*
(breaded veal cutlet). There are hundreds of
bars and restaurants in Milan but as a general rule, the area around the Duomo is full
of smart business-oriented restaurants, Brera is a fashionable bar haunt and the lively
Navigli canal district caters to all tastes.
Corso Como and environs is another good
area for a stylish drink.

Pizzeria Piccola Ischia   PIZZA €
(☑02 204 76 13; Via Morgani 7; pizzas €6.50;
◎closed Wed & lunch Sat & Sun) You might
be in the heart of Milan, but this bustling,

boisterous pizzeria is pure Naples. Everything from the wonderful wood-fired pizza to the fried antipasti and exuberant decor screams of the sunny south. It's hugely popular, so expect queues. Also does takeaway.

El Brellin RESTAURANT €€€
(☎02 5810 1351; Via Alzaia Naviglio Grande 14; mains €20, set menus €35-40; ⊙lunch daily, Mon-Sat dinner) Atmosphere-laden El Brellin is set in an 18th-century Navigli laundry. Its candlelit garden is a great place to linger over classic Milanese food whilst watching the evening canalside parade. *Aperitivi* (€8) are served in the bar between 7pm and 9pm.

Rinomata GELATERIA €
(Ripa di Porta Ticinese; ice creams €2.50) If dining in Navigli, skip dessert and grab an ice cream from this historic hole-in-the-wall gelateria. Its fabulous interior features old-fashioned fridges and glass-fronted cabinets filled with cones – and the gelato is good, too.

Peck Italian Bar DESIGNER BAR €€€
(Via Cesare Cantù 3; mains €18; ⊙Mon-Sat) Just around the corner from the legendary **Peck Delicatessen** (www.peck.it; Via Spadari 9; ⊙closed Sun & Mon morning), this bar oozes Milanese style. Black-jacketed bar staff serve coffees, wine and a daily menu of pastas and main courses to a moneyed, well-dressed clientele.

Zucca in Galleria CAFE €
(Galleria Vittorio Emanuele II 21) Grab a coffee (but skip the overpriced food) at the cafe where Giuseppe Verdi used to drink after performances at the Teatro all Scala.

☆ Entertainment

Milan offers a rich and vibrant cultural scene, ranging from opera at La Scala to world-class football and cutting-edge club nights. September is a good time for classical-music fans, as the city co-hosts the **Torino Milano Festival Internazionale della Musica** (www.mitosettembremusica.it).

The opera season at **Teatro alla Scala** (☎02 7200 3744; www.teatroallascala.org; Piazza della Scala) runs from November to July, but you can see theatre, ballet and concerts here year-round, with the exception of August. Tickets are available online or from the **box office** (Galleria del Sagrato, Piazza del Duomo; ⊙noon-6pm) beneath Piazza del Duomo. Bank on €26 to €224 for opera and €19 to €138 for ballet performances.

For jazz, **Blue Note** (☎02 6901 6888; www.bluenotemilano.com; Via Borsieri 37; tickets €20-40) stages top international and Italian performers.

🛍 Shopping

For designer clobber head to the so-called Golden Quad, the area around Via della Spiga, Via Sant'Andrea, Via Monte Napoleone and Via Alessandro Manzoni. Street markets are held around the canals, notably on Viale Papiniano on Tuesday mornings and Saturdays.

ℹ Information

Pharmacy (☎02 669 07 35; Stazione Centrale; ⊙24hr)

Police station (Questura; ☎02 6 22 61; Via Fatebenefratelli 11)

Tourist offices Piazza del Duomo (☎02 7740 4343; www.visitamilano.it; Piazza Duomo 19a; ⊙8.45am-1pm & 2-6pm Mon-Sat, 9am-1pm & 2-5pm Sun); Stazione Centrale (☎02 7740 4318; opposite platform 13; ⊙9am-6pm Mon-Sat, to 1pm & 2-5pm Sun) Pick up the free guides *Hello Milano* and *Milanomese*.

ℹ Getting There & Away
Air

Most international flights fly into **Malpensa airport** (MXP; ☎02 23 23 23; www.sea-aeroportimilano.it), about 50km northwest of Milan. Domestic and some European flights use **Linate airport** (LIN; ☎02 23 23 23; www.sea-aeroportimilano.it), about 7km east of the city. Low-cost airlines often use **Orio al Serio airport** (BGY; ☎035 32 63 23; www.sacbo.it), near Bergamo.

FOOTBALL IN MILAN

Milan is home to Italy's two most successful *calcio* (football) teams: the Berlusconi-owned AC Milan and Internazionale, aka Inter. In recent years, Inter has dominated, winning the Italian championship five times between 2006 and 2010 and romping to victory in the 2010 European Champions League. During the season (September to May), the two clubs play on alternate Sundays at the **Stadio Giuseppe Meazza** (Via Piccolomini 5; Ⓜ Lotto), better known as the San Siro. Match tickets (from €23) are available from branches of Banca Intesa (AC Milan) and Banca Popolare di Milano (Inter). To get to the stadium on match days, take the free shuttle bus from the Lotto (MM1) metro station.

Train

Regular daily trains depart **Stazione Centrale** for Venice (€30.15, 2½ hours), Bologna (€41, one hour), Florence (€52, 1¾ hours), Rome (€89, 3½ hours) and other Italian and European cities. Most regional trains stop at Stazione Nord in Piazzale Cadorna. Note that these prices are for the fast Eurostar Alta Velocità services.

ⓘ Getting Around

To/From the Airport

MALPENSA **Malpensa Shuttle** (www.malpensashuttle.it; adult/concession €7.50/3.75) Buses run to/from Piazza Luigi di Savoia next to Stazione Centrale every 20 minutes between 4.15am and 12.30pm. Buy tickets at Stazione Centrale or the airport. Journey time is 50 minutes.

Malpensa Bus Express (www.autostradale.it; adult/concession €7.50/3.75) To/from Piazza Luigi di Savoia half-hourly between 4.30am and 11pm.The trip takes 50 minutes.

Malpensa Express (www.malpensaexpress.it; adult/concession €11/5.50) Trains from Cadorna underground station half-hourly between 5.57am and 11pm, and then a bus at 11.27pm. Journey time is approximately 35 minutes.

LINATE **Starfly** (www.starfly.net; tickets €4) Buses to/from Piazza Luigi di Savoia half-hourly between 5.40am and 9.30pm. Journey time is 30 minutes. Buy tickets at newsstands or on board.

ATM (www.atm-mi.it; tickets €1) Local bus 73 runs every 10 minutes between 5.35am and 12.35pm from Piazza San Babila.

ORIO AL SERIO **Autostradale** (www.autostradale.it; adult/concession €8.90/4.45) Half-hourly buses to/from Piazza Luigi di Savoia between 4am and 11.30pm. Journey time is one hour.

Bus & Metro

Milan's excellent public transport system is run by **ATM** (www.atm-mi.it). Tickets (€1) are valid for one underground ride or up to 75 minutes' travel on city buses and trams. You can buy them at metro stations, *tabacchi* and newsstands.

Verona

POP 265,400

Wander Verona's atmospheric streets and you'll understand why Shakespeare set *Romeo and Juliet* here – this is one of Italy's most beautiful and romantic cities. Known as *piccola Roma* (little Rome) for its importance in imperial days, its heyday came in the 13th and 14th centuries under the rule

of the Della Scala (aka Scaligeri) family, who built *palazzi* and bridges, were patrons to Giotto, Dante and Petrarch, oppressed their subjects and feuded with everyone else. They were eventually deposed in 1387.

◉ Sights

The **Verona Card** (www.veronacard.it; 1/3 days €10/15) covers city transport and the main monuments. It's available from tourist offices and most sights.

Arena di Verona   ROMAN AMPHITHEATRE
(www.arena.it; Piazza Brà; adult/concession €6/4.50; ⊙1.30pm-7.30pm Mon & 8.30am-7.30pm Tue-Sun Oct-May, 8.30am-3.30pm Jun-Aug) In the corner of Piazza Brà, the 1st-century pink marble Arena di Verona is the third-largest Roman amphitheatre in existence, with a capacity of 20,000. These days it's most famous as Verona's summer opera house (see p502).

Casa di Giulietta   LANDMARK
(Via Cappello 23; courtyard free, museum adult/concession €6/4.50; ⊙1.30-7.30pm Mon & 8.30am-7.30pm Tue-Sun) From the Arena, walk along Via Mazzini, the town's premier shopping strip, to Via Cappello and the Casa di Giulietta. This clever tourist attraction was created by local authorities a few decades ago and marketed as Juliet's house. Romantic superstition suggests that rubbing the right breast of Juliet's statue (in the courtyard below the balcony) will bring you a new lover. Further along the street is **Porta Leoni**, one of the city's Roman gates; the other, **Porta Borsari**, is north of the Arena.

Piazzas   SQUARES
Set over the city's Roman forum, **Piazza delle Erbe** is lined with sumptuous *palazzi* and filled with touristy market stalls. Through the **Arco della Costa**, the quieter **Piazza dei Signori** is flanked by the **Loggia del Consiglio**, the medieval town hall regarded as Verona's finest Renaissance structure, and **Palazzo degli Scaligeri**, the former residence of the Della Scala family.

Basilica di San Zeno Maggiore   CHURCH
(Piazza San Zeno; adult/family €2.50/5; ⊙8.30am-6pm Tue-Sat, 12.30pm-6pm Sun Mar-Oct, 10am-1pm & 1.30-5pm Tue-Sat, 12.30-5pm Sun Nov-Feb) This Romanesque church honours the city's patron saint. Look out for the rose window and Mantegna's triptych of the *Maestà della Vergine* (Majesty of the Virgin), above the high altar.

🛏 Sleeping

High-season prices apply during the opera season and it is absolutely essential to book ahead during this period.

Hotel Aurora   HOTEL €€

(☑045 59 47 17; www.hotelaurora.biz; Piazza delle Erbe; s €90-135, d €100-160; ❄🛜) This top-of-the-range two-star place has friendly staff and clean and comfortable rooms with an understated decor. The lavish breakfast can be enjoyed on a lovely terrace overlooking Piazza delle Erbe.

Appartamenti L'Ospite   APARTMENT €€

(☑045 803 69 94; www.lospite.com; Via XX Settembre 3; apt for 1 or 2 persons €55-200, apt for 3 or 4 persons €65-200; ❄🛜) Over the river from the *centro storico*, L'Ospite has six self-contained apartments for up to four people. Simple and bright with fully equipped kitchens, they come with wi-fi and are ideal for families.

Ostello Villa Francescatti   HOSTEL €

(☑045 59 03 60, fax 045 80 09 127; Salita Fontana del Ferro 15; dm incl breakfast €18.50-20, d €37-40; 🅿) This HI hostel is housed in a 16th-century villa set in extensive grounds. To save yourself a steep uphill walk, take bus 73 from the train station (90 on Sunday). There's a strict 11.30pm curfew.

🍴 Eating

Boiled meats are a Veronese speciality, as is crisp Soave white wine.

Antica Bottega del Vino   WINE BAR €€€

(☑045 800 45 35; www.bottegavini.it; Via Scudo di Francia 3; mains €15-35; ⊘closed Tue) Established in 1890, this wine bar–restaurant is one of the essential stops while you're in town. You can enjoy a glass of wine from a mind-boggling array of choices while standing at the bar, or book a table for a meal. The food is rustic and delicious – freshly made *bigoli all'anatra* (pasta with a duck *ragù*), soupy *risotto all'Amarone* (rice cooked with Amarone wine) and a variety of perfectly cooked meat dishes.

Salumeria G Albertini   DELICATESSEN €

(☑045 803 10 74; www.salumeriaalbertini.it; Corso Sant'Anastasia 41; ⊘closed Sun) Albertinis has been the place to source picnic provisions ever since 1939. Its range of local artisan meats, cheese and wine will make an alfresco meal by the river or inside the amphitheatre the stuff of which lasting memories are made.

Al Pompiere   TRATTORIA €€

(☑045 803 05 37; www.alpompiere.com; Vicolo Regina d'Ungheria 5; mains €12-24; ⊘Tue-Sat, dinner Mon) There's no secret to the success of this much-loved trattoria – top-notch seasonally inspired food and welcoming surroundings. It's particularly noted for its platters of cheese and *salumi* (home-cured meats).

☆ Entertainment

The opera season at the Roman **Arena** (☑045 800 51 51; www.arena.it; tickets €23-198)

WORTH A TRIP

MANTUA

The beautiful Unesco-listed town of Mantua (Mantova) is an easy day trip from Verona. Best known as the place where Shakespeare exiled Romeo, it was for centuries (1328 to 1707) the stronghold of the Gonzaga family, one of Italy's most powerful Renaissance dynasties.

The **tourist office** (☑0376 43 24 32; www.turismo.mantova.it; Piazza Andrea Mantegna 6; ⊘9am-6pm) is close to the city's major attraction, the enormous **Palazzo Ducale** (www.ducalemantova.org; Piazza Sordello; adult/EU child €6.50/free; ⊘8.30am-7pm Tue-Sun). The highlight of this former seat of the Gonzaga family is the **Camera degli Sposi** (Bridal Chamber), home to extraordinary 15th-century frescos by Andrea Mantegna. To visit the *Camera* you need to book ahead (☑041 241 18 97).

For lunch, sit beneath 15th-century frescos in the vaulted dining room of **Ristorante Masseria** (Piazza Broletto 7; pizza €5-7.50; mains €13; ⊘closed Thu) to enjoy local specialities such as *penne in giallo con zafferano, salsiccia e rosmarino* (pasta tubes with saffron, sausage and rosemary).

The best way to get to Mantua is by regional train from Verona (€2.55, 45 minutes, 16 daily).

runs from late June to the end of August. If you attend a performance make sure you take your own food and drinks (stuff sold in the Arena is outrageously overpriced) and perhaps something to sit on, as the stone seating can be very uncomfortable.

ℹ Information

Information is available at the three **tourist offices** (www.tourism.verona.it; airport ☑045 861 91 63; ⊙10am-4pm Mon & Tue, to 5pm Wed-Sat; city centre ☑045 806 86 80; Piazza Brà; ⊙9am-7pm Mon-Sat, 10am-4pm Sun; train station ☑045 800 08 61; ⊙9am-7pm Mon-Sat, to 3pm Sun).

ℹ Getting There & Around

Aeroporto di Verona (Valerio Catullo airport; ☑045 809 56 66; www.aeroportodelgarda.it) is 12km outside the city and accessible by bus from the train station (€4.50, 20 minutes, every 20 minutes between 5.40am and 11.10pm). Ryanair flies to **Brescia airport** (VBS; ☑030 965 65 99), from where **CGA** (www.cgabrescia.it) shuttle buses (€11, 45 minutes, one daily) connect to Verona's main train station.

From the main bus terminal in front of the train station, AMT bus 72 leaves Stand F going to Piazza Erbe. Buses 11, 12 and 13 leave Stand A going to the Arena. Tickets cost €1.10 when purchased from the station's *tabacchi* and validated on board and €1.20 if purchased on the bus. A taxi from the train station to the centre costs around €10.

Verona is directly linked by rail to Milan (€17.50, two hours, every 45 minutes), Venice (€18.50, 1¼ hours, half-hourly), Bologna (€13.50, two hours, six daily) and Rome (€64-80.50, 4¼ hours, hourly).

Padua

POP 213,000

The lively university city of Padua (Padova) is a fun place to hang out, but what really makes it special are the stunning frescos in the Cappella degli Scrovegni. From the train station, follow Corso del Popolo and its continuation Corso Garibaldi until you see a park on your left – walk alongside the park, turn left into Via Erimitani and you'll soon come to the *cappella,* which is next to the Chiesa degli Eremitani.

◉ Sights

The **PadovaCard** (www.padovacard.it; 2/3 days for 1 adult & 1 child €15/20), available from tourist offices and participating sights, provides free parking, public transport and entry to many sights, including the Cappella degli Scrovegni (plus €1 booking fee).

Cappella degli Scrovegni CHURCH
(☑049 201 00 20; www.cappelladegliscrovegni.it; Piazza Eremitani 8; tickets incl entry into the adjoining multimedia room & Musei Civici agli Eremitani adult/concession €13/6; ⊙9am-7pm) Don't miss Giotto's extraordinary frescos here; the 38 colourful panels (c 1304–1306) depicting Christ's life cover the chapel from floor to ceiling. It's best to book tickets at least 24 hours in advance, though it's sometimes possible to buy tickets on the spot. Visits are limited to 25 people at one time and last only 15 minutes (20 minutes at night).

From March to November (and also over the Christmas week), the Cappella (but not the Musei Civici agli Eremitani) is open until 10pm every day except Monday. Tickets for these evening openings cost adult/student and child €8/6 – it's also possible to buy a 'double turn' ticket (€12) at these times, which gives you 40 minutes rather than 20.

The picture galleries in the Musei Civici agli Eremitani are home to an impressive collection of paintings and sculptures, including two Giottos.

Basilica di Sant'Antonio CHURCH
(Piazza del Santo; admission free; ⊙6.20am-7.45pm Apr-Oct, to 6.45pm Nov-Feb) On the other side of the *centro storico* to the Capella, this church is home to the surprisingly gaudy **tomb** of St Anthony, Padua's patron saint. It's one of Italy's major pilgrimage sights. To get here, it's a 1km walk from the Cappella degli Scrovegni or a short tram ride on tram No 3, 12 or 18 from the train station (tickets €1.10, available from *tabacchi* or kiosk outside the station).

🛏 Sleeping

Belludi 37 BOUTIQUE HOTEL €€
(☑049 66 56 33; www.belludi37.it; Via Luca Belludi 37; s without bathroom €57-80, d €120-150; P❄@) Overlooking the Basilica di Sant'Antonio, this sleek boutique hotel offers good-sized rooms and is known for its personal service. It offers tours of the city's markets and *enoteche* (wine bars), as well as bike hire.

Ostello Città di Padova HOSTEL €
(☑049 875 22 19; www.ostellopadova.it; Via Aleardo Aleardi 30; dm incl breakfast from €19; 🛜) Padua's HI hostel has an off-putting institutional feel and rigid opening hours (7.15am to 9.30am and 4.30pm to 11.30pm). Two-, four-, six- and eight-bed rooms are on offer; some have

their own bathroom. Take the tram from the train station to Via Cavaletto, turn right into Via Marin, left at the Torresino church and then right into Via Aleardo.

Albergo Verdi HOTEL €€
(☎049 836 41 63; www.albergoverdipadova.it; Via Dondi dall'Orologio 7; s €40-100, d €40-150; ✱) This modern and centrally located option offers quiet and clean rooms with bright colour schemes and mod cons such as wi-fi (€5 per three hours) and satellite TV.

✖ Eating & Drinking

L'Anfora OSTERIA €€
(☎049 65 66 29; www.osterianfora.it, in Italian; Via dei Sconcin 13; mains €10-15; ⊗closed Sun) The menu at this laid-back *osteria* (tavern) with bare wooden tables and racked wine bottles changes daily and is full of products and dishes typical of Venice. There's sometimes live jazz to accompany your meal – check the website for details.

Antica Osteria dal Capo OSTERIA €€
(☎049 66 31 05; Via degli Obizzi, 2; mains €10-16; ⊗closed Sun all day & lunch Mon) Not far from L'Anfora, this *osteria* offers an atmospheric setting and regional menu.

There are a number of stylish contemporary *enoteche* in Padua that are as popular for *aperitivo* as they are for dinner. Recommended:

Godenda WINE BAR
(☎049 877 41 92; www.godenda.it; Via Squarcione, 4; mains €15; ⊗closed Sun year-round & Mon Apr-Sep) Near Piazza dei Signori.

Enoteca Cortes WINE BAR
(☎049 871 97 97; Riviera Paleocapa 7; mains €16-22; ⊗from 6pm Tue-Sun) Located on a pretty canal to the southwest of the centre.

❶ Information

For tourist information and a copy of the useful, free *Padova Today* magazine, go to one of Padua's three **tourist offices** (www.turismo padova.it; Galleria Pedrocchi ☎049 876 79 27; ⊗9am-1.30pm & 3-7pm Mon-Sat; Piazza del Santo ☎049 875 30 87; ⊗9am-1.30pm & 3-6pm Mon-Sat, 10am-1pm & 3-6pm Sun Apr-Oct only; train station ☎049 875 20 77; ⊗9am-7pm Mon-Sat, to 12.30pm Sun).

❶ Getting There & Away

SITA (☎049 820 68 44; www.sitabus.it, in Italian) buses leave from the new bus station immediately east of the train station going to Venice (€3.55, 45 minutes, hourly) and Marco Polo airport (€3.55, 30 minutes, hourly).

There are regional trains to/from Venice (€2.90, 45 minutes, every 20 minutes), Verona (€4.95, 1½ hours, hourly) and Bologna (€7.45, 1½ hours, hourly). Note that the train information office can be hard to find – it's near Platform 1.

Venice

POP 270,100

Venice (Venezia) is a hauntingly beautiful city. At every turn you're assailed by unforgettable images – tiny bridges crossing limpid canals, delivery barges jostling chintzy gondolas, excited tourists posing for photographs under flocks of pigeons. But to reduce Venice to a set of pictures is as impossible as describing it in sound bites. To gain an understanding of its rich and melancholic culture you really need to walk its hidden back lanes. Parts of the Cannaregio, Dorsoduro and Castello *sestieri* (districts) rarely see many tourists, and you can lose yourself for hours in the streets between the Accademia and the train station. Stroll late at night to feel an eerie atmosphere, redolent of dark passions and dangerous secrets.

Despite its romantic reputation, the reality of modern Venice is a city besieged by rising tides and up to 20 million visitors a year. This and the sky-high property prices mean that most locals live over the lagoon in Mestre.

History

Venice's origins date to the 5th and 6th centuries when barbarian invasions forced the Veneto's inhabitants to seek refuge on the lagoon's islands. First ruled by the Byzantines from Ravenna, it wasn't until 726 that the Venetians elected their first *doge* (duke).

Over successive centuries, the Venetian Republic grew into a great merchant power, dominating half the Mediterranean, the Adriatic and the trade routes to the Levant – it was from Venice that Marco Polo set out for China in 1271. Decline began in the 16th century and in 1797 the city authorities opened the gates to Napoleon, who, in turn, handed the city over to the Austrians. In 1866, Venice was incorporated into the Kingdom of Italy.

Orientation

Everybody gets lost in Venice. With 117 islands, 150-odd canals and 400 bridges (only four of which – the Rialto, the Accademia and, at the train station, the Scalzi and the Calatrava – cross the Grand Canal) it's impossible not to.

It gets worse: Venetian addresses are almost meaningless to all but local posties. Instead of a street and civic number, local addresses often consist of no more than the *sestiere* (Venice is divided into six districts: Cannaregio, Castello, San Marco, Dorsoduro, San Polo and Santa Croce) followed by a long number. Some, however, do have street names and where possible we've provided them. You'll still need to know that a street can be a *calle, ruga* or *salizada;* beside a canal it's a *fondamenta.* A canal is a *rio,* a filled canal-turned-street a *rio terrà,* and a square a *campo* (Piazza San Marco is Venice's only piazza).

The most helpful points of reference are Santa Lucia train station and Piazzale Roma in the northwest and Piazza San Marco (St Mark's Square) in the south. The signposted path from the train station *(ferrovia)* to Piazza San Marco (the nearest Venice has to a main drag) is a good 40- to 50-minute walk.

◉ Sights

A good way to whet your sightseeing appetite is to take vaporetto (small passenger ferry) No 1 along the **Grand Canal**, which is lined with rococo, Gothic, Moorish and Renaissance palaces. Alight at Piazza San Marco, Venice's most famous sight.

Piazza San Marco SQUARE
(Map p512) Piazza San Marco beautifully encapsulates the splendour of Venice's past and its tourist-fuelled present. Flanked by the arcaded **Procuratie Vecchie** and **Procuratie Nuove**, it's filled for much of the day with tourists, pigeons and policemen. While you're taking it all in, you might see the bronze *mori* (Moors) strike the bell of the 15th-century **Torre dell'Orologio** (clock tower).

But it's to the remarkable **Basilica di San Marco** (Map p512; www.basilicasanmarco.it; Piazza San Marco; admission free; ⊙9.45am-5pm Mon-Sat & 2-5pm Sun Easter-Oct, 9.45am-5pm Mon-Sat & 2-4pm Sun Nov-Easter) that all eyes are drawn. Sporting spangled spires, Byzantine domes, luminous mosaics and lavish marble work, it was originally built to house the remains of St Mark. The original chapel was destroyed by fire in 932 and a new basilica was consecrated in its place in 1094. For the next 500 years it was a work in progress as successive *doges* added mosaics and embellishments looted from the East. Behind the main altar is the **Pala d'Oro** (admission €2.50; ⊙9.45am-5pm Mon-Sat & 2-5pm Sun Easter-Oct, 9.45am-4pm Mon-Sat & 2-4pm Sun Nov-Easter), a stunning gold altarpiece decorated with priceless jewels.

ADMISSION DISCOUNTS

The **Rolling Venice Card** (www.hellovenezia.com; €4) is for visitors aged 14 to 29 years; it offers discounts on food, accommodation, shopping, transport and museums. You can get it at tourist offices, and at HelloVenezia booths throughout the city. You'll need ID.

The **Venice Card Orange** (www.hellovenezia.com; under 30yr 3/7 days €66/87, 30yr & over €73/96) entitles holders to free entry to 12 city museums (including Palazzo Ducale), free entry to the 16 Chorus churches, unlimited use of ACTV public transport, limited use of public toilets, and reduced admissions to various museums and events. It doesn't always represent a saving, so check before buying. It's sold at tourist and HelloVenezia offices.

To visit the museums on Piazza San Marco you'll need to buy either a **Museum Pass** (www.museicivicveneziani.it; adult/EU senior & EU student under 25yr/child under 6yr €18/12/ free), which gives entry to the museums on Piazza San Marco and eight other civic museums; or a **San Marco Museum Plus Ticket** (adult/EU senior & EU student under 25yr/ child under 6yr €13/7.50/free), which gives entry to the San Marco museums and your choice of one other civic museum. Both are available at participating museums. Discount passes – including an afternoon pass to the museums on Piazza San Marco (adult/EU senior & EU student under 25 years/child under six years €10/4.50/free) – can be purchased in advance at www.veniceconnected.com.

The **Chorus Pass** (www.chorusvenezia.org; adult/student under 29yr/child under 11yr/ family €10/7/20/free) covers admission to 16 of Venice's major churches and is available online or at the churches. Otherwise entry to each church costs €3.

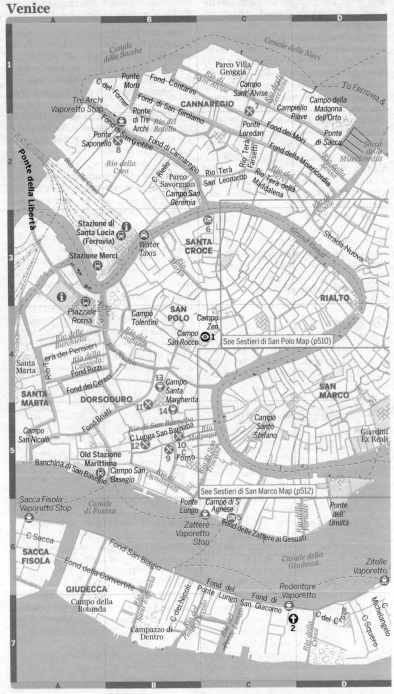

Canale delle Sacche

Canale delle Navi

Parco Villa Groggia

Ponte Moro

Fond Contarini

Rio di Sant'Alvise

Campo Sant'Alvise

Rio degli Vecchini

To Ferrovia &

Tre Archi Vaporetto Stop

C del Forner

Fond di San Girolamo

CANNAREGIO

Campo della Madonna dell'Orto

Ponte di Tre Archi

Rio del Batello

Campiello Piave

Ponte Saponello

Fond di San Giobbe

Ponte Loredan

Fond dei Mori

Ponte di Sacca

8

Fond di Cannaregio

Rio Terà Farsetti

Fond della Misericordia

Sacca della Misericordia

Rio delle Crea

C. Riello

Parco Savorgnan

Rio Terà San Leonardo

Rio Terà della Maddalena

Rio Noale

Campo San Geremia

Stazione di Santa Lucia (Ferrovia)

Water Taxis

SANTA CROCE

Rio Marin

Grand Canal

Strada Nuova

RIALTO

Stazione Merci

Piazzale Roma

Rio delle Burchielle

Rio del Gaffaro

SAN POLO

Campo Tolentini

Campo Zen

Campo San Rocco

1

See Sestieri di San Polo Map (p510)

Santa Marta

erà dei Pensieri

Rio della Cazziola

Fond Rizzi

13

Campo Santa Margherita

SAN MARCO

SANTA MARTA

Fond dei Cereci

DORSODURO

11

14

Campo Santo Stefano

Giardini Ex Reali

Fond Briati

Rio di San Barnaba

Rio Malpaga

Campo San Nicolò

C Lunga San Barnaba

12

10

C Forno

Rio di San Trovaso

9

Old Stazione Marittima

Banchina di San Basegio

Campo San Basegio

Rio di Ognissanti

See Sestieri di San Marco Map (p512)

Sacca Fisola Vaporetto Stop

Canale di Fusina

Ponte Lungo

Campo di S Agnese

Zattere Vaporetto Stop

Fond delle Zattere ai Gesuati

5

Rio della Fornace

Ponte dell' Umiltà

C Sacca

SACCA FISOLA

Fond San Biago

Fond della Convertite

Canale della Giudecca

Zitelle Vaporetto

GIUDECCA

Campo della Rotonda

Fond del Ponte Lunga San Giacomo

Fond di Redentore Vaporetto

C del Croce

C Michelangelo

C Squero

Campazzo di Dentro

2

Rio della Croce

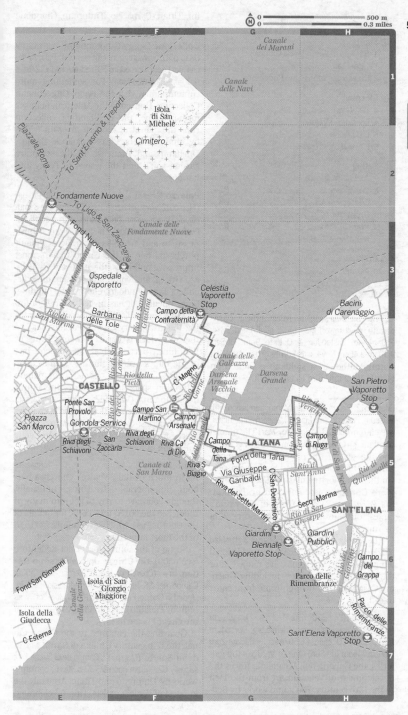

0   500 m
0   0.3 miles

Canale
dei Marani

Canale
delle Navi

Isola
di San
Michele

Cimitero

To Sant'Erasmo & Treporti

Piazzale Roma

Fondamente Nuove

Fond Nuove

To Lido & San Zaccheria

Canale delle
Fondamente Nuove

Ospedale
Vaporetto

Celestia
Vaporetto
Stop

Campo della
Confraternità

Bacini
di Carenaggio

Rio di Santa Giustina

Rio di
San Marina

Barbaria
delle Tole

4

Canale delle
Galeazze

Rio della
Pietà

C Magno

Darsena
Arsenale
Vecchio

Darsena
Grande

San Pietro
Vaporetto
Stop

CASTELLO

Rio di San Lorenzo

Rio dei Greci

3

Campo San
Martino

Campo
Arsenale

Rio delle
Vergini

Campo
di Ruga

Canale di San Pietro

Ponte San
Provolo

Piazza
San Marco

Gondola Service

Riva degli
Schiavoni

San
Zaccaria

Riva degli
Schiavoni

Riva Ca'
di Dio

Campo
della
Tana

LA TANA

Rio di Sant'Anna

Rio di
Quintavalle

Riva S
Biagio

Fond della Tana

Canale di
San Marco

Via Giuseppe
Garibaldi

Riva dei Sette Martiri

C San Domenico

Seco Marina

Rio di San Giuseppe

SANT'ELENA

Fond San Giovanni

Isola di San
Giorgio
Maggiore

Canale della Grazia

Giardini
Biennale
Vaporetto Stop

Giardini
Pubblici

Campo
del
Grappa

Parco delle
Rimembranze

Rio dei Giardini

Isola della
Giudecca

C Esterna

Parco delle
Rimembranze

Sant'Elena Vaporetto
Stop

Venice

The basilica's 99m freestanding **campanile** (bell tower; Map p512; adult/child €8/4; ☺9am-7pm Easter-Jun & Oct, to 9pm Jul-Sep, 9.30am-3.45pm Nov-Easter) dates from the 10th century, although it suddenly collapsed on 14 July 1902 and had to be rebuilt.

Palazzo Ducale   PALACE
(Map p512; Piazzetta di San Marco; admission with Museum Pass or San Marco Museum Plus Ticket; ☺9am-7pm Apr-Oct, to 6pm Nov-Mar) The official residence of the *doges* from the 9th century and the seat of the republic's government, Palazzo Ducale also housed Venice's prisons. On the 2nd floor, the massive **Sala del Maggiore Consiglio** is dominated by Tintoretto's *Paradiso* (Paradise), one of the world's largest oil paintings, which measures 22m by 7m.

The **Ponte dei Sospiri** (Bridge of Sighs; Map p512) connects the palace to an additional wing of the city dungeons. It's named after the sighs that prisoners – including Giacomo Casanova – emitted en route from court to cell.

Gallerie dell'Accademia   ART MUSEUM
(Map p512; www.gallerieaccademia.org; Dorsoduro 1050; adult/EU child €6.50/free; ☺8.15am-2pm Mon, to 7.15pm Tue-Sun) One of Venice's top galleries, the Galleria dell'Accademia traces the development of Venetian art from the 14th to the 18th century. You'll find works by Bell-

ini, Titian, Carpaccio, Tintoretto, Giorgione and Veronese.

Collezione Peggy Guggenheim   ART MUSEUM
(Map p512; www.guggenheim-venice.it; Palazzo Venier dei Leoni, Dorsoduro 701; adult/child €12/free; ☺10am-6pm Wed-Mon) For something more contemporary, visit the Peggy Guggenheim Collection. Housed in the American heiress's former home, the spellbinding collection runs the gamut of modern art with works by, among others, Picasso, Pollock, Braque, Duchamp and Brancusi. In the sculpture garden you'll find the graves of Peggy and her dogs.

Palazzo Grassi   ART MUSEUM
(Map p512; www.palazzograssi.it; Campo San Samuele 3231; admission price varies with exhibitions; ☺10am-7pm Wed-Mon) In 2005, French businessman and art collector François Pinault purchased one of the Grand Canal's most impressive buildings, the 18th-century Palazzo Grassi, and commissioned Japanese architect Tadeo Ando to renovate the building. Since opening, it has hosted a series of impressive temporary exhibitions. After admiring the art, gallery-goers inevitably head to the cafe, which is a great spot for a coffee or light lunch, particularly if you can score one of the tables overlooking the Grand Canal. In 2009 the museum opened a companion exhibition space in Dorsoduro, the **Punta della Dogana** (Map p512; www.palazzograssi.it; Campo San Samuele 3231; admission price varies with exhibitions; ☺10am-7pm Wed-Mon), where pieces from Pinault's extensive and eclectic collection of modern art are on show.

Churches   CHURCHES
As in much of Italy, Venice's churches harbour innumerable treasures; unusually, though, you have to pay to get into many of them. See the boxed text, p505, for details of the Chorus Pass, which gives admission to 16 of the most important.

Scene of the annual Festa del Redentore (see p509), the **Chiesa del Santissimo Redentore** (Church of the Redeemer; Map p506; Campo del SS Redentore 194; admission €3, included in Chorus Pass; ☺10am-5pm Mon-Sat) was built by Palladio to commemorate the end of the Great Plague in 1577.

Guarding the entrance to the Grand Canal, the 17th-century **Chiesa di Santa Maria della Salute** (Map p512; Campo della Salute 1/b; sacristy €2; ☺9am-noon & 3.30-5.30pm) contains works by Tintoretto and Titian. Arguably the greatest of Venice's artists, Titian's celebrated masterpiece the *Assunta* (Assumption; 1518) hangs above the high altar in the **Basilica di Santa Maria Gloriosa dei Frari** (Map p506; Campo dei Frari, San Polo 3004; admission €3, included in Chorus Pass; ⊙10am-6pm Mon-Sat, 1-6pm Sun), the same church in which he's buried.

The Lido
BEACH

Unless you're on the Lido for the Venice Film Festival, the main reason to visit is for the beach. Be warned, though, that it's almost impossible to find space on the sand in summer. It's accessible by vaporetti 1, 2, 8, LN, 51, 52, 61 and 62.

Islands
ISLANDS

Murano is the home of Venetian glass. Tour a factory for a behind-the-scenes look at production or visit the **Glass Museum** (Fondamenta Giustinian 8; adult/EU concession €6.50/3; ⊙10am-5pm Thu-Tue Nov-Mar, to 6pm Apr-Oct); you'll find it near the Museo vaporetto stop. **Burano**, with its cheery pastel-coloured houses, is renowned for its lace. **Torcello**, the republic's original island settlement, was largely abandoned due to malaria and now counts no more than 80 residents. Its not-to-be-missed Byzantine cathedral, **Santa Maria Assunta** (Piazza Torcello; adult/child €5/free; ⊙10.30am-6pm Mar-Oct, 10am-5pm Nov-Feb), is Venice's oldest.

Vaporetti 41 and 42 service Murano from the San Zaccaria vaporetto stop. Vaporetto LN services Murano and Burano from the vaporetto stop at Fondamente Nove in the northeast of the city. Vaporetto T connects Burano and Torcello.

🏃 Activities

Be prepared to pay through the nose for that most quintessential of Venetian experiences, a **gondola ride**. Official rates per gondola (maximum six people) start at €80 (€100 at night) for a short trip including the Rialto but not the Grand Canal, and €120 (€150 at night) for a 50-minute trip including the Grand Canal. Haggling is unlikely to get you a reduction.

If you're a solo traveller in Venice, the cheapest way for you to enjoy a gondola ride is to book in for the two-hour 'Ice-cream & Gondola' tour (€40) offered by **Turismo Ricettivo Veneziano** (www.turive.it). This includes a guided walking tour (conducted in English), a gelato and a 40-minute gondola ride. It leaves from the San Marco tourist office every day at 3pm. The same company offers a 2½hr 'Walking Venice' tour (€35), leaving from the tourist office every day at

9.10am. Both tours run between 1 April and 31 October only.

🎊 Festivals & Events

Carnevale
RELIGIOUS CELEBRATION

The major event of the year, when some Venetians and loads of tourists don Venetian-made masks and costumes for a week-long party in the lead-up to Ash Wednesday. It's been going since 1268.

Palio delle Quattro Repubbliche Marinare
BOAT RACE

Usually held in early June. Venice, Amalfi, Genoa and Pisa take turns to host this historic regatta. It's in Venice in 2015.

Festa del Redentore
RELIGIOUS CELEBRATION

Held on the third weekend in July; celebrations climax with a spectacular fireworks display.

Regata Storica
GONDALA RACES

Costumed parades precede gondola races on the Grand Canal; held on the first Sunday in September.

Venice Architecture Biennale
ARCHITECTURE EXHIBITION

This major architecture shindig is held every even-numbered year from late August to November.

Venice Biennale
ART EXHIBITION

This major exhibition of international visual arts is held every odd-numbered year from June to November.

Venice International Film Festival
FILM FESTIVAL

(Mostra del Cinema di Venezia) Italy's top film fest is held in late August and September at the Lido's Palazzo del Cinema.

🛏 Sleeping

Venice is Italy's most expensive city. It's always advisable to book ahead, especially at weekends, in May and September, and during Carnevale and other holidays.

SAN MARCO

TOP CHOICE **Palazzina Grassi** BOUTIQUE HOTEL €€€ (Map p512; ☑041 528 46 44; www.palazzinagrassi.com; San Marco 3247; rooms from €260; ✳️🌐) Phillipe Stark has endowed this formidably fashionable hotel with his signature style, and we're pleased to report that his design lives up to the magnificent Grand Canal location. Common areas are lavishly decorated with designer furniture and artworks (as befits a hotel owned by the Pinault

operation) and the light-drenched rooms cleverly use mirrors and white furnishings to maximise space. The hotel's Krug champagne bar is the ultimate in exclusiveness.

Novecento   BOUTIQUE HOTEL **€€€**
(Map p512; ☎041 241 37 65; www.novecento.biz; Celle del Dose, Campo San Maurizio 2683; r €150-300; ❋@✆) The decor here is redolent of the exotic East, and the garden is a gorgeous spot for a leisurely breakfast. The hotel sometimes hosts art exhibitions, meaning that you may well bump into artists and local connoisseurs in the enticing communal lounge.

DORSODURO

La Calcina   HOTEL **€€**
(Map p506; ☎041 520 64 66; www.lacalcina.com; Fondamenta Zattere ai Gesuati 780; s €90-140, d €110-310; ❋) Charming La Calcina offers 29 immaculate and elegant rooms with parquet floors and timber furnishings, and a small garden. In summer, breakfast is served on a terrace overlooking the Guidecca Canal.

SAN POLO & SANTA CROCE

TOP CHOICE **Ca' Angeli**   BOUTIQUE HOTEL **€€**
(Map p510; ☎041 523 24 80; www.caangeli. it; Calle del Tragheto della Madoneta, San Polo 1434;

ITALY VENICE

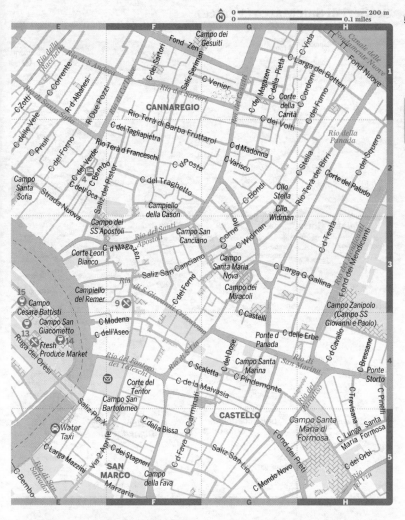

Sestieri di San Polo (Venice)

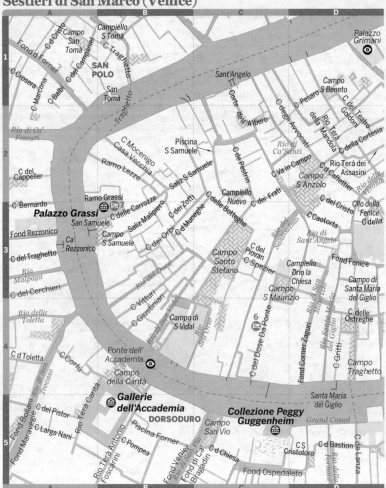

s €85-150, d €105-215, ste €195-315; ❄) A fabulous choice overlooking the Grand Canal, Ca' Angeli is notable for its extremely comfortable rooms, helpful staff and truly magnificent breakfast spread. If you can afford it, opt for a suite overlooking the Grand Canal.

Oltre il Giardino   BOUTIQUE HOTEL €€€
(Map p510; ☏041 275 00 15; www.oltreilgiardino
-venezia.com; Fondamenta Contarini, San Polo 2542;
d €150-250, ste €200-500; ❄@) Once home to
Alma Mahler, the composer's widow, this
gorgeous property boasts a garden with
pomegranate, olive and magnolia trees –
an idyllic spot for a summer breakfast. The
six rooms are charmingly decorated and extremely comfortable.

Hotel Alex   PENSION €
(Map p510; ☏041 523 13 41; www.hotelalexinvenice.
com; Rio Terá, San Polo 2606; s without bathroom
€35-56, d without bathroom €40-90, d €60-120)
The welcoming Alex is in a quiet spot near
Campo dei Frari. Spread over three floors
(no lift), most of the rooms are a decent size
and all are decorated with simple efficiency.

L'Imbarcadero   HOSTEL €
(Map p510; ☏392 584 06 00; www.hostelvenice.
net; cnr Imbarcadero Riva de Biasio & Calle Zen,
Santa Croce; dm/s from €25/65) An easy

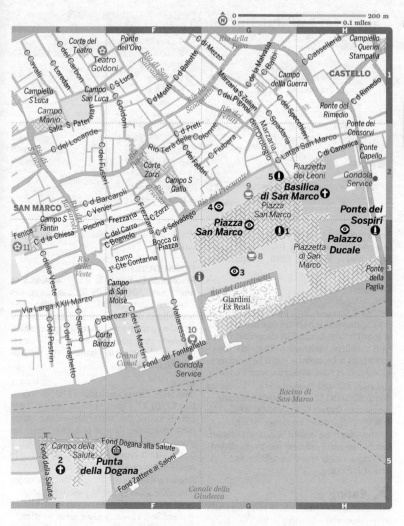

walk from the train station, this friendly hostel in Santa Croce offers clean mixed and female-only dorm rooms and private rooms with shared bathroom.

CANNAREGIO

Hotel Bernardi
HOTEL €

(Map p510; ☎041 522 72 57; www.hotelbernardi.com; SS Apostoli Calle dell'Oca 4366; s without bathroom €25-32, d without bathroom €45-62, s €48-72, d €52-85; ❄@) Comfortable rooms (opt for No 25 or 26), hospitable owners and keen prices mean that this top choice is always heavily booked. A recently opened an-

nexe just around the corner (doubles €57 to €90, family rooms €75 to €130) offers large rooms with modern bathrooms, free wi-fi and disabled access.

CASTELLO

Foresteria Valdese
HOSTEL €

(Map p506; ☎041 528 67 97; www.foresteriavenezia.it; Centro Culturale P Cavagnis 5170; dm/d from €30/92; @) Run by the Waldensian and Methodist Church and housed in a rambling old mansion close to Piazza San Marco, this hostel is one of the cheapest sleeping options in Venice and so is extremely popular.

Sestieri di San Marco (Venice)

Be warned that rooms can get extremely hot in high summer, though. Follow Calle Lunga Santa Maria Formosa from Campo Santa Maria Formosa.

Ca' Valeri B&B €€

(Map p506; ☎041 241 15 30; www.locandacavaleri.com; Ramo Corazzieri 3845; r €69-169, ste €79-179; ❋) The drawcards here are an extremely quiet location and beautifully decorated rooms with excellent bathrooms. The only disappointment is breakfast – you'll be heading to a local cafe as soon as you see what's on offer.

Locanda Ca' del Console B&B €€

(Map p510; ☎041 523 31 64; www.locandacadelconsole.com; Castello 6217; s €90-110, d €120-180; ❋@🛜) This former residence of a 19th-century Austrian consul is now an elegant, family-run hotel offering rooms decorated with rugs, richly coloured fabrics and period furniture.

 Eating

Venetian specialities include *risi e bisi* (pea soup thickened with rice) and *sarde di saor* (fried sardines marinated in vinegar and onions).

DORSODURO

Ristorante La Bitta RESTAURANT €€

(Map p506; ☎041 523 05 31; Calle Lunga San Barnaba 2753a; mains €18-24; ⏾closed Sun) The bottle-lined dining room and attractive internal courtyard are a lovely setting in which to enjoy your choice from a small, meat-dominated menu that changes with the season. No credit cards.

Grom GELATERIA €

(Map p506; Campo San Barnaba 2761; ice creams from €2.20) Ah, Grom. How do we love thee? Let us count the ways: Colombian extra-dark chocolate, Bronte pistachio, marrons glacé, ricotta & fig... There's another outlet on the Strada Nuova in Cannaregio that only opens between April and September.

Enoteca Ai Artisti WINE BAR €€

(Map p506; ☎041 523 89 44; www.enotecaartisti.com; Fondamenta della Toletta 1169a; mains €15; ⏾closed Sun) This tiny place takes its wine seriously (there's a great choice by the glass) and serves delicious cheeses, bruschetta (toast with toppings) and bowls of pasta.

Pizza al Volo PIZZERIA €

(Map p506; Campo Santa Margherita 2944; pizza slices €2-4) In need of a pizza pit stop? Here's your opportunity. You'll be in the company of a steady stream of interns from the Guggenheim.

SAN POLO & SANTA CROCE

Vecio Fritolin RESTAURANT €€€

(Map p510; ☎041 522 28 81; www.veciofritolin.it; Calle della Regina, Santa Croce 2262; mains €25; ⏾dinner Tue, lunch & dinner Wed-Mon) Tradition-

---

WANT MORE?

For in-depth information, reviews and recommendations at your fingertips, head to the Apple App Store to purchase Lonely Planet's *Venice & the Veneto City Guide* iPhone app.

Alternatively, head to **Lonely Planet** (www.lonelyplanet.com/italy/venice) for planning advice, author recommendations, traveller reviews and insider tips.

ally, a *fritolin* was an eatery where diners sat at a common table and tucked into fried seafood and polenta. This is the modern equivalent, only the food is sophisticated, the menu is varied and the decor is stylish rather than rustic. The owners also run a cafe in the Palazzo Grassi.

Osteria La Zucca
WINE BAR, RESTAURANT €€

(Map p510; www.lazucca.it; Calle del Tentor, Santa Croce 1762; mains €10; ⊙closed Sun; 🖋) An unpretentious little restaurant in an out-of-the-way spot, 'The Pumpkin' serves a range of innovative Mediterranean dishes prepared with fresh, seasonal ingredients. Most are small and perfect to share; many are vegetarian.

All'Arco
WINE BAR €

(Map p510; Calle dell'Arco, San Polo 436; chiceti €1.50-4; ⊙7.30am-8pm Mon-Sat) Popular with locals, this tiny *osteria* serves delicious bruschetta and a range of good-quality wine by the glass.

Ae Oche
PIZZA €

(Map p510; www.aeoche.com; Calle del Tentor, Santa Croce 1552a/b; pizzas €4-9.50) Students adore the Tex-Mex decor and huge pizza list at this bustling place. It's on the main path between the *ferrovia* and San Marco.

CANNAREGIO

Da Marisa
TRATTORIA €€

(Map p506; ☎041 72 02 11; Fondamenta di San Giobbe 652b; lunch incl wine & coffee €15, dinner incl wine & coffee €35-40; ⊙lunch daily, dinner Tue & Thu-Sat) You can watch the sun setting over the lagoon from the canalside tables here. Local devotees overlook the fact that service can be brusque, meal times are set (noon and 8pm), credit cards aren't accepted and there's no opportunity to vary the excellent daily menu, which is mostly meat but sometimes seafood.

Fiaschetteria Toscana
RESTAURANT €€€

(Map p510; ☎041 528 52 81; www.fiaschetteriatoscana.it; Salizada S Giovanni Grisostomo 5719; mains €14-32; ⊙closed all day Tue & lunch Wed) Don't worry about the name – this old-fashioned favourite near the Rialto specialises in Venetian dishes but varies the formula with a few Tuscan triumphs such as chianina beef fillet in red-wine sauce. Seafood dominates the menu – the house speciality is fried fish 'Serenissima' style – and the desserts are delectable.

Antica Adelaide
BAR/TRATTORIA €€

(Map p510; Calle Priuli 3728; mains €10-15) Adelaide has been in the food business since as far back as the 18th century. You can pop in

for a drink and *cicheti* (bar snacks) or tuck into a hearty bowl of pasta or full meal.

Anice Stellato
TRATTORIA €€€

(Map p506; ☎041 72 07 44; Fondamenta della Sensa 3272; mains €17.50-23; ⊙closed Mon & Tue) In the little-visited historic Jewish Ghetto, this friendly place serves up huge plates of seafood antipasti, delicious pasta dishes and a super-sized house speciality of fried mixed fish with polenta.

La Cantina
WINE BAR €

(Map p510; Campo San Felice 3689; chicheti €4-10; ⊙closed Mon, 2 weeks Jul & Aug, 2 weeks Jan) Sit at one of the outdoor tables at this *enoteca* (wine bar) and watch the passing traffic promenade up and down the Strada Nuova. A good choice of wines by the glass and classy *chicheti* make it deservedly popular.

🍷 Drinking

Al Mercà
BAR

(Map p510; Campo Cesare Battisti, San Polo 212-213; ⊙closed Sun) One of the city's best bars, this tiny place serves excellent and keenly priced wines by the glass accompanied by a lavish array of *chiceti* – arrive around 6.30pm for the best choice. No seating, just loads of atmosphere.

Muro Venezia
BAR

(Map p510; www.murovinoecucina.it; Campo Cesare Battisti, San Polo 222; ⊙closed Sun) The centre of a happening nightlife scene in the market squares of the Rialto, Muro is the watering hole of choice for young locals, who spill out into the square with their drinks.

Caffè Florian
CAFE

(Map p512; www.caffeflorian.com; Piazza San Marco 56/59) If you think it's worth paying up to four times the usual price for a coffee, emulate Byron, Goethe and Rousseau and pull up a seat at Piazza San Marco's most famous cafe.

Il Caffè
BAR

(Map p506; Campo Santa Margherita, Dorsoduro 2963; ⊙closed Sun) Popular with foreign and Italian students, this is one of Venice's historic drinking spots. Known to locals as Caffè Rosso because of its red frontage, it's got outdoor seating and serves a great *spritz* (Venetian cocktail made with *prosecco* – Venetian sparkling white, soda water and aperol or campari).

Harry's Bar
BAR

(Map p512; www.harrysbarvenezia.com; Calle Vallaresso, San Marco 1323) To drink a Bellini (white-peach pulp and *prosecco*) at the bar that invented them is an expensive experience to tick off the list rather than a holiday highlight. Nevertheless, this bar to the stars is always full.

Ancorà
BAR

(Map p510; Fabbriche Vecchie, San Polo; ⊘closed Sun) Enjoy your *aperitivo* with a Grand Canal view while sitting at one of the three outdoor tables on the waterside terrace here.

Gran Caffè Quadri
CAFE

(Map p512; www.quadrivenice.com; Piazza San Marco 121) Opposite Florian, Caffè Quadri offers more of the same.

Imagina Café
CAFE, BAR

(Map p506; www.imaginacafe.it; Campo San Margherita, Dorsoduro 3126; ⊘closed Sun) A constantly changing exhibition program means that patrons can enjoy art with their *aperitivo* at this hip modern bar.

☆ Entertainment

Tickets for the majority of events in Venice are available from **HelloVenezia ticket outlets** (www.hellovenezia.it; ⊘7am-10.45pm), run by the ACTV transport network. You'll find them in front of the train station and at Piazzale Roma.

Gran Teatro La Fenice
OPERA HOUSE

(Map p512; ☑for guided tours 041 24 24; www.teatrolafenice.it; Campo San Fantin, San Marco 1977; opera tickets from €20) One of Italy's most important opera houses, the fully restored Fenice is back to its sumptuous best after being destroyed by fire in 1996. The opera season runs from May to November.

❶ Information

Emergency
Police station (Questura; ☑041 271 55 11; Fondamenta di San Lorenzo, Castello 5053) There's also a small branch at Piazza San Marco 67.

Medical Services
Twenty-four-hour pharmacies are listed in *Un Ospite a Venezia* (A Guest in Venice), a free guide available in many hotels.
Ospedale Civile (Hospital; ☑041 529 41 04; Campo SS Giovanni e Paolo 6777)

Tourist Information
Pick up the free *Shows & Events* guide at tourist offices. It contains comprehensive city listings and a useful public transport map on the inside back cover. The tourist offices also sell a handy map of the city (€2.50).

Azienda di Promozione Turistica (Venice Tourist Board; ☑central information line 041 529 87 11; www.turismovenezia.it) Lido (Gran Viale Santa Maria Elisabetta 6a; ⊘9am-noon & 3-6pm Jun-Sep); Marco Polo airport (Arrivals Hall; ⊘9am-9pm); Piazza San Marco (Map p512; Piazza San Marco 71f; ⊘9am-3.30pm); Piazzale Roma (Map p506; ⊘9.30am-4.30pm Jun-Sep); train station (Map p506; ⊘8am-6.30pm).

❶ Getting There & Away
Air
Most European and domestic flights land at **Marco Polo airport** (VCE; ☑041 260 92 60; www.veniceairport.it), 12km outside Venice. Ryanair flies to **Treviso airport** (TSF; ☑0422 31 51 11; www.trevisoairport.it), about 30km from Venice.

Boat
Minoan Lines (☑210 414 57 00; www.minoan.gr) runs ferries to Corfu (23½ hours), Igoumenitsa (22 hours) and Patra (36 hours) daily in summer and four times per week in winter. Tickets are priced between €54 and €289.

Bus
ACTV (☑041 24 24; www.actv.it) buses service surrounding areas, including Mestre, Padua and Treviso. Tickets and information are available at the bus station in Piazzale Roma.

Train
Venice's Stazione di Santa Lucia is directly linked by regional trains to Padua (€2.90, 45 minutes, every 20 minutes), Verona (€18.50, 1¼ hours, half-hourly) and Ferrara (€6.15, 1½ hours, every two hours). It is easily accessible from Bologna, Milan, Rome and Florence. You can also reach points in France, Germany, Austria, Switzerland, Slovenia and Croatia from here.

❶ Getting Around
To/From the Airport
To travel between Venice and Marco Polo airport there are various options. **Alilaguna** (www.alilaguna.com) operates four fast-ferry lines between the airport ferry dock and different parts of the city (€13, 70 minutes, approximately every hour); the Rossa (Red) line goes to Piazza San Marco and the Oro (Gold) line goes to both Rialto and San Marco. Follow the signs from the arrivals hall to the ferry dock, where there is a dedicated ticket office. **ATVO** (☑041 520 55 30; www.atvo.it, in Italian) runs 'Venezia Express' buses (€3/5.50 one-way/return, 20 minutes, every half-hour) between the airport and Piazzale Roma, and **ACTV** operates bus 5d (€2.50, 25 minutes, every half-hour). Water taxis from the airport cost €100 for up to five passengers; it's an extra €50 to travel via the Grand Canal.

For Treviso airport, take the ATVO Ryanair bus (€5, 70 minutes, 16 daily) from Piazzale Roma two hours and 10 minutes before your flight departure. The last service is at 7.40pm.

Boat

The city's main mode of public transport is the vaporetto. The most useful routes:

1 From Piazzale Roma to the train station and down the Grand Canal to San Marco and the Lido.

2 From S Zaccaria (near San Marco) to the Lido via Giudecca, Piazzale Roma, the train station and the Rialto.

DM From Piazzale Roma to Murano.

LN From Fondamenta Nuove to S Zaccaria via Murano and Burano.

T Runs between Burano and Torcello.

Tickets, available from ACTV booths at the major vaporetti stops, are expensive: €6.50 for a single trip; €16 for 12 hours; €18 for 24 hours; €23 for 36 hours; €28 for two days; €33 for three days; and €50 for seven days. There are significant discounts for holders of the Rolling Venice Card (eg €18 instead of €33 for the three-day ticket) and all tickets are 15% cheaper if you purchase them online (www.veniceconnected.com) in advance of your trip.

The poor man's gondola, *traghetti* (€0.50 per crossing) are used by Venetians to cross the Grand Canal where there's no nearby bridge.

Car & Motorcycle

Vehicles must be parked on Tronchetto or at Piazzale Roma (cars are allowed on the Lido – take car ferry 17 from Tronchetto). The car parks are not cheap – €27 to €30 every 24 hours – so you're better off leaving your car in Mestre and getting a train over to Venice.

Ferrara

POP 134,500

Ferrara retains much of the austere splendour of its Renaissance heyday, when it was the seat of the powerful Este family (1260–1598). Overshadowed by the menacing Castello Estense, the compact medieval centre is atmospheric and lively.

◉ Sights

If you're planning to visit the major monuments, buy a **Museum Card** (adult/concession €17/10), which gives free entry to all municipal museums. It's available from both the Cathedral Museum and Palazzo Schifanoia.

Castello Estense CASTLE
(www.castelloestense.it; Viale Cavour; adult/child €8/free, Lion's Tower extra €2; ⊙9.30am-5.30pm Tue-Sun) Guarding the northern edge of Ferrara's attractive *centro storico*, the stirring Castello Estense is quite a sight with its square towers, moat and drawbridge. It was begun by Nicolò II d'Este in 1385 and became the Este family's residence. Highlights include the **Sala dei Giganti** (Giant's Room) and **Salone dei Giochi** (Games Salon) with frescos by Camillo and Sebastiano Filippi.

Duomo CHURCH
(Piazza Cattedrale; ⊙7.30am-noon & 3-6.30pm Mon-Sat, 7.30am-12.30pm & 3.30-7.30pm Sun) The pink-and-white 12th-century cathedral is most notable for its superb three-tiered marble facade, which combines Romanesque and Gothic architectural styles. The upper tier features a graphic Gothic depiction of the Last Judgement and heaven and hell.

Palazzo Schifanoia HISTORIC BUILDING
(Via Scandiana 23; adult/child €6/free; ⊙9am-6pm Tue-Sun) Famous for its frescos, this is one of Ferrara's earliest Renaissance buildings and another Este palace. In the **Sala dei Mesi** (Room of the Months), the 15th-century frescos are considered among the best examples of their type in Italy.

🛏 Sleeping & Eating

You won't need to stay overnight to see Ferrara's sights, but it's a cheap alternative to Bologna, and a viable base for Venice.

Hotel de Prati HOTEL **€€**
(☑0532 24 19 05; www.hoteldeprati.com; Via Padiglioni 5; s/d €80/120; ❄🛜) A charming three-star place on the edge of the *centro storico*. Guestrooms are quietly elegant with wrought-iron bedsteads, high ceilings and classic furniture, while downstairs, the yellow and orange walls stage contemporary art exhibitions.

Pensione Artisti PENSION **€**
(☑0532 76 10 38; Via Vittoria 66; s/d without bathroom €28/50, d €60) Ferrara's best budget option features scrubbed old-fashioned rooms, kitchen facilities, free bikes and an excellent location in the *centro storico*. The superfriendly owners also ensure a warm welcome. No breakfast.

Ristorante Osteria Balebùste
BAR, RESTAURANT **€€**
(☑0532 76 35 57; Via Vittoria 44; mains €13; ⊙closed Thu) The exposed-brick walls and

high medieval wood ceiling set the atmospheric backdrop for a relaxed meal of well-presented regional food. Particularly good are the meaty main courses. The adjacent bar also serves evening *aperitvi*.

Al Brindisi Wine Bar   OSTERIA **€€**
(Via Adelardi 11; meals €25-30, set lunch menus from €13; ⊙11am-1am) Apparently the oldest *osteria* in the world, this atmospheric wine bar dates to 1435 – Titian and Copernicus both drank here. Alongside the substantial wine list there's an extensive menu of traditional pastas, mains and snacks.

ℹ Information

The **tourist office** (☎0532 29 93 03; www.ferr arainfo.com; ⊙9am-1pm & 2-6pm Mon-Sat, 9.30am-1pm & 2-5.30pm Sun) is inside Castello Estense.

ℹ Getting There & Around

Ferrara is easy to reach by train. There are regional trains to Bologna (€4, 45 minutes, every 30 to 60 minutes), Venice (€6.15, 1½ hours, every two hours) and nearby Ravenna (€5.70, 1¼ hours, 14 daily).

From the station take bus 1 or 9 for the historic centre.

Bologna

POP 375,000

Boasting a boisterous bonhomie rare in Italy's reserved north, Bologna is worth a few days of anyone's itinerary, not so much for its specific attractions, but for the sheer fun of strolling its animated, arcaded streets. A university town since 1088 (Europe's oldest), it is also one of Italy's foremost foodie destinations. Besides the eponymous *ragù* (bolognese sauce), classic pasta dishes such as tortellini and lasagne were invented here, as was mortadella (aka baloney or Bologna sausage). Treats such as these are enjoyed in welcoming trattorias throughout the city, washed down with fizzy Lambrusco red wine. After dinner, locals love to wander through the city's arcades to their favourite bar or nightclub and party the night away – this is not a town that goes to sleep early.

◉ Sights

Piazza Maggiore   SQUARE
Pedestrianised Piazza Maggiore is Bologna's focal showpiece square. On the southern flank, the Gothic **Basilica di San Petronio** (Piazza Maggiore; ⊙7.45am-12.30pm & 3-6pm), cur-

rently covered in scaffolding, is dedicated to the city's patron saint, Petronius. Its partially complete facade doesn't diminish its status as the world's fifth-largest basilica. Inside, don't miss Giovanni da Modena's bizarre *l'Inferno* fresco in the fourth chapel on the left.

To the west is the **Palazzo Comunale** (Town Hall), home to the city's art collection, the **Collezioni Comunali d'Arte** (admission free; ⊙9am-3pm Tue-Fri, 10am-6.30pm Sat & Sun) and the **Museo Morandi** (admission free; ⊙9am-3pm Tue-Fri, 10am-6.30pm Sat & Sun) dedicated to the work of Giorgio Morandi.

Adjacent to the square, **Piazza del Nettuno** is named after the **Fontana del Nettuno** (Neptune's Fountain), sculpted by Giambologna in 1566 and featuring an impressively muscled Neptune.

Le Due Torri   MEDIEVAL TOWERS
Rising above **Piazza di Porta Ravegnana** are Bologna's two leaning towers, Le Due Torri. The taller of the two, the 97m-high

Torre degli Asinelli (admission €3; ⊙9am-6pm, to 5pm Nov-Mar), was built between 1109 and 1119 and is now open to the public. Climb the 498 steps for some superb city views. The neighbouring **Torre Garisenda** stands at 48m.

Basilica di San Domenico   CHURCH
(Piazza San Domenico 13; ⊙9.30am-12.30pm & 3.30-6.30pm Mon-Sat, 3.30-5.30pm Sun) This 13th-century church is noteworthy for the elaborate sarcophagus of San Domenico, founder of the Dominican order. The tomb stands in the **Capella di San Domenico**,

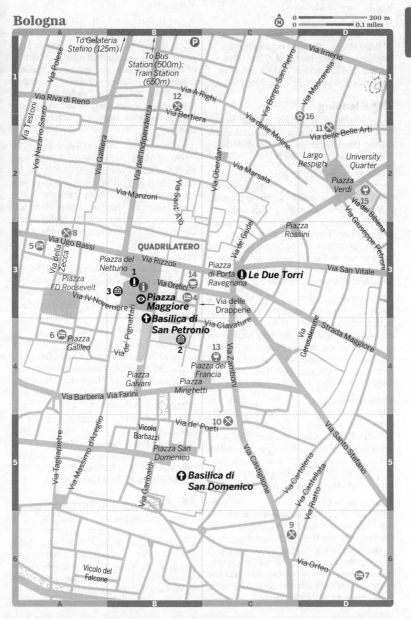

Bologna

which was designed by Nicolò Pisano and later added to by, among others, Michelangelo.

Also recommended:

FREE **Museo Civico Archeologico** MUSEUM
(Via dell'Archiginnasio 2; ⊙9am-3pm Tue-Fri, 10am-6.30pm Sat & Sun) Exhibits Egyptian and Roman artefacts and one of Italy's best Etruscan collections.

FREE **Museo d'Arte Moderna do Bologna** ART MUSEUM
(MAMBO, Museum of Modern Art; www.mambo -bologna-org; Via Don Minzoni 14; ⊙10am-6pm Tue, Wed & Fri-Sun, to 10pm Thu) An excellent modern-art museum in a converted bakery.

🛏 Sleeping

Accommodation is largely geared to the business market. It's expensive (particularly during trade fairs) and can be difficult to find unless you book ahead.

Il Convento dei Fiori di Seta
BOUTIQUE HOTEL €€€
(☑051 27 20 39; www.silkflowersnunnery.com; Via Orfeo 34; d €130-300; ❄@🤶) This seductive boutique hotel is a model of sophisticated design. Housed in a 15th-century convent, it features contemporary furniture juxtaposed against exposed-brick walls and religious frescos, a wine bar in a former sacristy, and Mapplethorpe-inspired flower motifs.

Albergo Panorama
PENSION €
(☑051 22 18 02; www.hotelpanoramabologna.it; 4th flr, Via Livraghi 1; s without bathroom €40-50, d without bathroom €60-70; ❄) An easy walk from Piazza Maggiore, this is a friendly old-school *pensione* with simple, spacious rooms, lovely rooftop views, and fresh flowers in the hallway. Only cash and Visa credit cards.

Hotel Novecento
HOTEL €€€
(☑051 745 73 11; www.bolognarthotels.it; Piazza Galileo 4; s €113-340, d €149-370; ❄❄@🤶) Decorated in the Viennese Succession style, this refined boutique offering is one of four hotels run by Bologna Arts Hotels. All have comfortable and well-equipped rooms, excellent locations and lashings of style.

Albergo delle Drapperie
HOTEL €€
(☑051 22 39 55; www.albergodrapperie.com; Via delle Drapperie 5; d €75-140; ❄) This welcoming three-star hotel enjoys a superb location in the heart of the happening Quadrilatero district. Rooms, which all differ slightly, are attractive with wood-beamed ceilings, wrought-iron beds and the occasional brick arch. Breakfast costs €5 extra.

🍴 Eating

The university district northeast of Via Rizzoli harbours hundreds of restaurants, trattorias, takeaways and cafes catering to hard-up students and gourmet diners alike. For foodie gifts head to the sumptuous delis in the Quadrilatero district east of Piazza Maggiore.

TOP CHOICE Osteria de' Poeti
RESTAURANT €€
(☑051 23 61 66; Via de' Poeti 1b; mains €10; ⊙Tue-Sun) In the cellar of a 14th-century *palazzo,* this atmospheric place is a bastion of old-style service and top-notch regional cuisine. Pasta dishes are driven by what's fresh in the markets, and mains include delicious meat dishes such as succulent roast beef served with rocket and Grana Padano cheese.

Il Saraceno
RESTAURANT, PIZZA €€
(☑051 23 66 28; Via Calcavinazzi 2; pizzas from €5, mains €13,) Popular with lunching locals, this is a good all-purpose eatery just off central Via Ugo Basso. Tables are on a small outdoor terrace or in the yellow air-conditioned interior, and the menu covers all bases, from pizza to pasta, seafood and meats.

Pizzeria Belle Arti
PIZZA €
(☑051 22 55 81; Via delle Belle Arti 14; pizzas €5-9, mains €8) This sprawling place near the university serves delicious wood-fired thin-crust pizzas and a full menu of pastas and main courses. You'll find it near the Odeon cinema.

Trattoria Mariposa
TRATTORIA €
(☑051 22 56 56; Via Bertiera 12; mains €8; ⊙Mon-Sat) A genial, laid-back trattoria, the Mariposa is good for simple homemade favourites such as tortellini with *ragù* or *burro e salvia* (butter and sage).

Bologna also boasts two superb gelaterie:

Gelateria Stefino
GELATERIA
(Via Galleria 49b; ⊙noon-midnight daily)

La Sorbetteria Castiglione
GELATERIA
(Via Castiglione 44; ⊙8am-midnight Tue-Sat, to 11.30pm Mon, to 10.30pm Sun).

🍷 Drinking & Entertainment

Bologna's drinking and nightlife scene is one of the most vibrant in the country, with a huge number of bars, cafe's and clubs. Thirsty students congregate on and around Piazza Verdi, while the fashionable Quadrilatero district hosts a dressier, more up-market scene. Popular spots:

Café de Paris   BAR
(Piazza del Francia 1c; ⊘8am-1am Mon-Thu, to
late Fri & Sat) Modish bar with daily aperitif
between 6pm and 10pm.

La Scuderia   BAR
(Piazza Verdi 2; ⊘8am-3am Mon-Fri, 5pm-3am
Sat) A popular student bar housed in
medieval stables.

Caffè degli Orefici   CAFE
(Via Orefici 6; ⊘Mon-Sat) A modern cafe next
to a historic coffee shop.

Cantina Bentivoglio   JAZZ CLUB
(☑051 26 54 16; www.cantinabentivoglio.it; Via
Mascarella 4b; ⊘8pm-2am) Music lovers
won't want to miss Bologna's top jazz
club; it's also a wine bar and restaurant.

Cassero   CLUB
(www.cassero.it; Via Don Minzoni 18) Legendary
gay and lesbian (but not exclusively) club.
Home of Italy's Arcigay movement.

❶ Information

Ospedale Maggiore (Hospital; ☑051 647 81 11;
Largo Nigrisoli 2)

Police station (Questura; ☑051 640 11 11;
Piazza Galileo 7)

Tourist information (☑051 23 96 60; www.
bolognaturismo.info) Airport (⊘9am-7pm);
Piazza Maggiore 1 (⊘9am-7pm)

❶ Getting There & Around
Air

European and domestic flights arrive at **Guglielmo Marconi airport** (BLQ; ☑051 647 96 15;
www.bologna-airport.it), 6km northwest of the
city. An Aerobus shuttle (€5, 30 minutes, every
10 minutes) departs from the main train station;
buy your ticket at the ATC office behind the taxi
rank or on board.

Bus

National and international coaches depart from
the **bus station** (Piazza XX Settembre), southeast of the train station. However, for most Italy
destinations the train is a better bet.

To get to the centre from the train station take
bus A, 25 or 30 (€1).

Train

Bologna is a major rail hub. From the **central
train station** (Piazza delle Medaglie d'Oro),
fast Eurostar Alta Velocità (ES AV) trains run
to: Venice (€28, 1½ hours, hourly), Florence
(€24, 40 minutes, half-hourly), Rome (€58, 2¾
hours, half-hourly) and Milan (€41, one hour,
hourly).

POP 156,000

Most people visit Ravenna to see its remarkable Unesco-protected mosaics. Relics of the
city's golden age as capital of the Western
Roman and Byzantine Empires, they are
described by Dante in his *Divine Comedy*,
much of which was written here. Easily accessible from Bologna, this refined and polished town is worth a day trip at the very
least. Its national profile is raised each year
during June and July when music concerts
are staged as part of the **Ravenna Festival**
(www.ravennafestival.org). The involvement of
Italy's top conductor, Riccardo Muti, means
the classical component is always strong.

⊙ Sights
Dante's Tomb   TOMB
(Via Dante Alighieri 9; admission free; ⊘9.30am-
6.30pm) Dante spent the last 19 years of his
life in Ravenna after Florence expelled him
in 1302. As a perpetual act of penance, Florence supplies the oil for the lamp that burns
in his tomb.

Early Christian Mosaics   MOSAICS
Ravenna's mosaics are spread over five sites
in the centre: the Basilica di San Vitale, the
Mausoleo di Galla Placida, the Basilica di
Sant'Appollinare Nuovo, the Museo Arcivescovile and the Battistero Neoniano. These
are covered by a single **ticket** (adult/child
€8.50/free), which is available at any of the
five sites. Outside of town you'll find further
mosaics at the Basilica di Sant'Apollinare in
Classe. Note that the hours reported here
are for April to September; outside of these
months they are slightly shorter, typically
9.30am or 10am until 5pm or 5.30pm. Information on Ravenna's main sites is available
online at www.ravennamosaici.it.

On the northern edge of the *centro
storico*, the sombre exterior of 6th-century
Basilica di San Vitalel (Via Fiandrini; ⊘9am-
7pm) hides a dazzling interior with mosaics
depicting Old Testament scenes. In the same
complex, the small **Mausoleo di Galla Pla-
cidia** (Via Fiandrini; ⊘9am-7pm) contains the
city's oldest mosaics. Between March and
mid-September there's an extra €2 booking
fee for the Mausoleo.

Adjoining Ravenna's unremarkable cathedral, **Museo Arcivescovile** (Piazza Arcivesco-
vado; ⊘9am-7pm) boasts an exquisite 6th-
century ivory throne, while next door in the

Battistero Neoniano (Via Battistero; ⊗9am-7pm), the baptism of Christ and the apostles is represented in the domed roof mosaics. To the east, the **Basilica di Sant'Apollinare Nuovo** (Via di Roma; ⊗9am-7pm) boasts, among other things, a superb mosaic depicting a procession of martyrs headed towards Christ and his apostles.

Five kilometres southeast of the city, the apse mosaic of **Basilica di Sant'Apollinare in Classe** (Via Romea Sud, Classe; adult/EU child €3/free; ⊗8.30am-7.30pm Mon-Sat, 1-7.30pm Sun) is a must-see. Take bus 4 (€1) from Piazza Caduti per la Libertà.

🍴 Sleeping & Eating

Cá de Vén
WINE BAR, RESTAURANT €€

(www.cadeven.it; Via Corrado Ricci 24; mains €15; ⊗Tue-Sun) OK, we'll admit it's touristy, but Ravenna's most famous eatery is still an atmospheric spot for a meal and glass of wine. Housed in a cavernous 15th-century *palazzo,* it serves a full menu of regional dishes, including snacks such as *piadine* (flat-bread sandwiches).

Also recommended:

Hotel Sant'Andrea
HOTEL €€

(☎0544 21 55 64; wwwsantandreahotel.com; Via Cattaneo 33; s €80-100, d €110-140; ❄@) A real find, this charming three-star hotel offers elegant accommodation in a converted convent. A grand wooden staircase leads up to smart, carpeted rooms overlooking a lawned garden.

Ostello Galletti Abbiosi
HOSTEL €

(☎0544 313 13; www.galletti.ra.it; Via Roma 140; s €46, d €70-92; ❄🛜) In an 18th-century town house, this is more hotel than hostel. With high-ceilinged, spacious rooms, polite service and an enviable location, it's an excellent deal.

Ostello Dante
HOSTEL €

(☎0544 42 11 64; www.hostelravenna.com; Via Nicolodi 12; dm/s/d €16/22/44; @🛜) Ravenna's modern HI youth hostel. Take bus 80 or the red 'Metrobus' A from the train station.

Locanda del Melarancio
RESTAURANT €€€

(www.locandadelmelarancio.it; Via Mentana 33; mains18; ⊗closed Wed) Sophisticated food at popular eatery.

ℹ️ Information

Tourist offices Main office (☎0544 354 04; www.turismo.ravenna.it; Via Salara 8/12; ⊗8.30am-7pm Mon-Sat, 10am-6pm Sun);

Teodorico (☎0544 45 15 39; Via delle Industrie 14; ⊗9.30am-12.30pm & 3.30-6.30pm); Classe (☎0544 47 36 61; Via Romea Sud 266, Classe; ⊗9.30am-12.30pm & 3.30-6.30pm) Between October and May hours are slightly shorter, typically closing time is an hour or so earlier.

ℹ️ Getting There & Around

Regional trains connect the city with Bologna (€6.20, 1½ hours, 14 daily) and Ferrara (€5.70, 1¼ hours, 14 daily).

In town, cycling is popular. The tourist office runs a free bike-hire service to visitors aged 18 years or over (take ID).

THE DOLOMITES

A Unesco natural heritage site since 2009, the Dolomites stretch across the northern regions of Trentino-Alto Adige and the Veneto. Their stabbing sawtooth peaks provide some of Italy's most thrilling scenery, as well as superb skiing and hiking.

Ski resorts abound, offering downhill and cross-country skiing as well as snowboarding and other winter sports. Facilities are generally excellent and accommodation is widely available. Ski passes cover either single resorts or a combination of slopes; the most comprehensive is the **Superski Dolomiti pass** (www.dolomitisuperski.com; high season 3/6 days €132/233), which accesses 1220km of runs in 12 valleys.

Hiking opportunities run the gamut from kid-friendly strolls to hard-core mountain treks. Trails are well marked with numbers on red-and-white bands on trees and rocks, or by numbers inside coloured triangles for the four *Alte Vie* (High Routes). Recommended areas include the Alpe di Siusi, a vast plateau above the Val Gardena; the area around Cortina; and Pale di San Martino, accessible from San Martino di Castrozza.

ℹ️ Information

Area-wide information can be obtained from tourist offices in **Trento** (☎0461 21 60 00; www.apt.trento.it; Via Manci 2; ⊗9am-7pm) and **Bolzano** (☎0471 30 70 00; www.bolzano-bozen.it; Piazza Walther 8; ⊗9am-1pm & 2-7pm Mon-Fri, 9am-2pm Sat). The best online resource is www.dolomiti.org.

ℹ️ Getting There & Around

Bolzano airport (BZO; ☎0471 25 52 55; www.abd-airport.it) is only served by a couple of European flights. Otherwise the nearest airports are Verona, Bergamo or Innsbruck in Austria, from where trains run south to Bolzano.

The area's excellent bus network is run by **Trentino Trasporti** (☑0461 82 10 00; www.tte sercizio.it) in Trento; **SAD** (☑800 000 471; www. sii.bz.it) in Alto Adige; and **Dolomiti Bus** (www. dolomitibus.it, in Italian) in the Veneto. During winter, most resorts offer 'ski bus' services.

The main towns and the many ski resorts can be reached directly from cities such as Rome, Florence, Venice, Bologna, Milan and Genoa. Information is available from tourist offices and regional bus stations.

Cortina d'Ampezzo

POP 6110 / ELEV 1224M

Surrounded by some of the Dolomites' most dramatic scenery, Cortina is one of Italy's most famous, fashionable and expensive ski resorts. Predictably it boasts first-class facilities (skiing, skating, sledding, climbing) and superb hiking; less obviously, it has some reasonably priced accommodation. Ask at the **tourist office** (☑0436 32 31; www.infodolo miti.it; Piazzetta San Francesco 8; ⊙9am-12.30pm & 3.30-6.30pm) for listings.

SAD (☑800 000 471; www.sii.bz.it) buses connect Cortina with Dobbiaco, where you can change for Bolzano. **Cortina Express** (☑0436 86 73 50; www.cortinaexpress.it) runs seasonal buses to/from Bologna and Venice, and **ATVO** (www.atvo.it) operates buses to/from Venice, daily between June and August and at weekends the rest of the year. Journey time is about two and a quarter hours for Venice and three hours for Bologna.

Canazei

POP 1870 / ELEV 1460M

One of the best-known resorts in the **Val di Fassa**, Canazei is a great spot for serious skiers. It has 120km of downhill and cross-country runs and is linked to the challenging Sella Ronda ski network. There's even summer skiing on the Marmolada glacier, whose stunning 3342m summit marks the highest point in the Dolomites. Further information is available at the **tourist office** (☑0462 60 96 00; www.fassa.com; Piazza Marconi 5; ⊙8.30am-12.30pm & 3-7pm).

For somewhere to stay overnight, try the **Garni Stella Alpina** (☑0462 60 11 27; www. stella-alpina.net; Via Antermont 6; d €68-128; P @), a traditional guest house with seven warm rooms decked out in local Ladin style.

Canazei is served by year-round **Trentino Trasporti** (☑0461 82 10 00; www.ttesercizio.it) buses from Trento (€5.55, 2½ hours) and

WEATHER FORECAST

Even in summer the weather is extremely changeable in the Alps. Even if it's sweltering when you set off, be prepared for cold, wet weather on even the shortest walks. Essentials include good-quality, worn-in walking boots, a waterproof jacket, warm hat and gloves, light food, plenty of water and a decent map. The best maps are the Tabacco 1:25,000 series, widely available throughout the area.

seasonal services from Bolzano and the Val Gardena.

Val Gardena

Branching northeast off the Val di Fassa, the Val Gardena is a popular skiing area with great facilities and accessible prices. In summer hikers head to the Sella Group and the Alpe di Siusi for rugged, high-altitude walks and to the Vallunga for more accessible family strolls.

The valley's main towns are Ortisei, Santa Cristina and Selva Gardena, all offering plenty of accommodation and easy access to runs. Further information is available online at www.valgardena.it, or from the towns' tourist offices:

Ortisei (☑0471 77 76 00; Via Rezia 1; ⊙8.30am-12.30pm & 2.30-6.30pm Mon-Sat, 10am-noon & 5-6.30pm Sun)

Santa Cristina (☑0471 77 78 00; Via Chemun 9; ⊙8am-noon & 2.30-6.30pm Mon-Sat, 9.30am-noon Sun)

Selva Gardena (☑0471 77 79 00; Via Mëisules 213; ⊙8am-noon & 3-6.30pm Mon-Sat, 9am-noon & 4.30-6.30pm Sun)

The Val Gardena is accessible from Bolzano by year-round **SAD** (☑800 000 471; www.sii. bz.it) buses and from the neighbouring valleys in summer.

San Martino di Castrozza

ELEV 1450M

At the foot of the imposing **Pale di San Martino**, the popular town of San Martino di Castrozza acts as a gateway to the **Parco Naturale Paneveggio – Pale di San Martino** (www.parcopan.org). Its **tourist office**

(☎0439 76 88 67; www.sanmartino.com; Via Passo Rolle 165; ☺9am-noon & 3-7pm Mon-Sat, 9.30am-12.30pm Sun) is a mine of useful information.

Trentino Trasporti (☎0461 82 10 00; www.ttesercizio.it) buses run to/from Trento.

TUSCANY

Tuscany is one of those places that well and truly lives up to its press. Its fabled rolling landscape has long been considered the embodiment of rural chic, while its cities are home to a significant portfolio of the world's medieval and Renaissance art. Some people never venture beyond Florence, but with some of Italy's most charming towns an easy trip away, to do so would be a waste, particularly as there are so many chances to sample the region's famous food and wine along the way.

Florence

POP 365,700

Poets of the 18th and 19th centuries swooned at the beauty of Florence (Firenze), and once here you'll appreciate why. An essential stop on everyone's Italian itinerary, this Renaissance treasure trove is busy year-round. Fortunately, the huge crowds fail to diminish the city's lustre. A list of its famous sons reads like a Renaissance who's who – under 'M' alone you'll find Medici, Machiavelli and Michelangelo – and its celebrated cityscape lingers in the memory long after you've said your farewells.

History

Many hold that Florentia was founded by Julius Caesar around 59 BC, but archaeological evidence suggests an earlier village, possibly founded by the Etruscans around 200 BC. A rich merchant city by the 12th century, its golden age arrived in the 15th century. Under the Medici prince Lorenzo il Magnifico (1469–92), the city's cultural, artistic and political fecundity culminated in the Renaissance.

The Medici were succeeded in the 18th century by the French House of Lorraine, which ruled until 1860, when the city was incorporated into the kingdom of Italy. From 1865 to 1870, Florence was, in fact, capital of the fledgling kingdom.

During WWII, parts of the city were destroyed by bombing, including all of its bridges except for Ponte Vecchio. In 1966 a devastating flood destroyed or severely damaged many important works of art. More recently, in 1993, the Mafia exploded a massive car bomb, killing five people and destroying part of the Uffizi Gallery. The gallery is currently undergoing a long-overdue €60 million renovation that will result in its exhibition space being doubled. It remains open while these works are occurring, and the estimated date for their completion is 2013.

☉ Sights & Activities

From the main train station, Santa Maria Novella, it's a 550m walk along Via de' Panzani and Via de' Cerretani to the Duomo. From Piazza di San Giovanni, next to the Duomo, Via Roma leads down to Piazza della Repubblica and continues as Via Calimala and Via Por Santa Maria to the Ponte Vecchio.

There are seven major neighbourhoods in the historic centre: Duomo and Piazza della Signoria, Santa Maria Novella, San Lorenzo, San Marco, Santa Croce, Oltrarno and Boboli/San Miniato al Monte. Most of these owe their names to the significant basilicas located within their borders, which make excellent navigational landmarks.

Piazza del Duomo & Around   CHURCHES
Pictures don't do justice to the exterior of Florence's Gothic **Duomo** (cathedral; www.duomofirenze.it; ☺10am-5pm Mon-Wed & Fri, to 3.30pm Thu, to 4.45pm Sat, to 3.30pm 1st Sat of every month, 1.30-4.45pm Sun). While they reproduce the startling colours of the tiered red, green and white marble facade and the beautiful symmetry of the dome, they fail to give any sense of its monumental size. Officially known as the Cattedrale di Santa Maria del Fiore, its construction begun in 1294 by Sienese architect Arnolfo di Cambio, but it wasn't consecrated until 1436. Its most famous feature, the enormous octagonal **Cupola** (dome; admission €8; ☺8.30am-6.20pm Mon-Fri, to 5pm Sat) was built by Brunelleschi after his design won a public competition in 1420. The interior is decorated with frescos by Vasari and Zuccari, and the stained-glass windows are by Donatello, Paolo Uccello and Lorenzo Ghiberti. The facade is a 19th-century replacement of the unfinished original, pulled down in the 16th century.

Beside the cathedral, the 82m **Campanile** (admission €6; ☺8.30am-6.50pm) was begun by Giotto in 1334 and completed after his death by Andrea Pisano and Francesco Talenti. The views from the top make the 414-step climb worthwhile.

To the west, the Romanesque **Battistero** (Baptistry; Piazza di San Giovanni; admission €4; ⏰12.15-6.30pm Mon-Sat, 8.30am-1.30pm 1st Sat of every month, 8.30am-1.30pm Sun) is one of the oldest buildings in Florence. Built on the site of a Roman temple between the 5th and 11th centuries, it's famous for its gilded-bronze doors, particularly Lorenzo Ghiberti's *Gate of Paradise*.

Surprisingly overlooked by the crowds, the **Museo dell'Opera del Duomo** (Cathedral Museum; www.operaduomo.firenze.it; admission €6; ⏰9am-6.50pm Mon-Sat & 9am-1pm Sun) on the northern (street) side of the cathedral safeguards treasures that once adorned the Duomo, baptistry and campanile and is one of the city's most impressive museums. Ghiberti's *Gate of Paradise* panels (those on the Baptistry doors are copies) and a Pietà by Michelangelo are in the collection here.

Galleria degli Uffizi (Uffizi Gallery)
ART MUSEUM

(www.uffizi.firenze.it; Piazza degli Uffizi 6; adult/EU concession €10/5; ⏰8.15am-6.05pm Tue-Sun) Home to the world's greatest collection of Italian Renaissance art, the Galleria degli Uffizi attracts some 1.5 million visitors annually. They won't all be there when you visit, but unless you've booked a ticket, expect to queue.

The gallery houses the Medici family collection, bequeathed to the city in 1743 on the condition that it never leave the city. Highlights include *La nascita di Venere*

CUTTING THE QUEUES

Sightseeing in Florence inevitably means time spent in queues. You'll never avoid them altogether, but by pre-booking museum tickets you'll save time. For €4 extra per museum you can book tickets for the Uffizi and Galleria dell'Accademia (the two most popular museums) through **Firenze Musei** (☎055 29 48 83; www.firenzemusei.it; ⏰booking line 8.30am-6.30pm Mon-Fri, to 12.30pm Sat, ticket offices 8.15am-6pm daily). Buy ahead of your visit by booking by telephone or online, or purchase in person from the Firenze Musei desks at the Uffizi, Accademia, Palazzo Pitti or Museo di San Marco. There's also a ticket window at the rear of the Chiesa di Orsanmichele.

As this book was going to press, the APT (Azienda di Promozione Turistica) network across Tuscany had just been disbanded, with individual provinces left to run their own tourist information offices. By the time you read this it's possible that some of the tourist offices in this section might have closed or changed location. We recommend enquiring ahead to avoid disappointment.

(Birth of Venus) and *Allegoria della primavera* (Allegory of Spring) in the Botticelli Rooms (10 to 14); Leonardo da Vinci's *Annunciazione* (Annunciation; room 15); Michelangelo's *Tondo doni* (Holy Family; Room 25); and Titian's *Venere d'Urbino* (Venus of Urbino; Room 28). Elsewhere you'll find works by Giotto, Cimabue, Filippo Lippi, Fra' Angelico, Uccello, Raphael, Andrea del Sarto, Tintoretto and Caravaggio. Tickets are cheaper if there are no temporary exhibitions.

Piazza della Signoria
SQUARE

Traditional hub of Florence's political life, Piazza della Signoria is dominated by the **Palazzo Vecchio** (Old Palace; www.palazzovecchio-museoragazzi.it; adult/child €6/2; ⏰9am-7pm Fri-Wed, to 2pm Thu), the historical seat of the Florentine government. Characterised by the 94m **Torre d'Arnolfo**, it was designed by Arnolfo di Cambio and built between 1298 and 1340. The **guided tours** (☎055 276 82 24; info.museoragazzi@comune.fi.it) here are great – particularly those for children. Make sure you book in advance.

The statue of *David* outside the *palazzo* is a copy of Michelangelo's original, which stood here until 1873 but is now in the Galleria dell'Accademia. The nearby **Loggia dei Lanzi** is an open-air showcase of sculpture from the 14th and 16th centuries – look out for Giambologna's *Rape of the Sabine Women* (c1583) and Agnolo Gaddi's *Seven Virtues* (1384–89). The loggia is named after the *Lanzichenecchi* (Swiss Guards) who were stationed here in Cosimo I's time.

Ponte Vecchio
BRIDGE

The 14th-century Ponte Vecchio was originally flanked by butchers' shops, but when the Medici built a corridor through the bridge to link Palazzo Pitti with Palazzo Vecchio, they

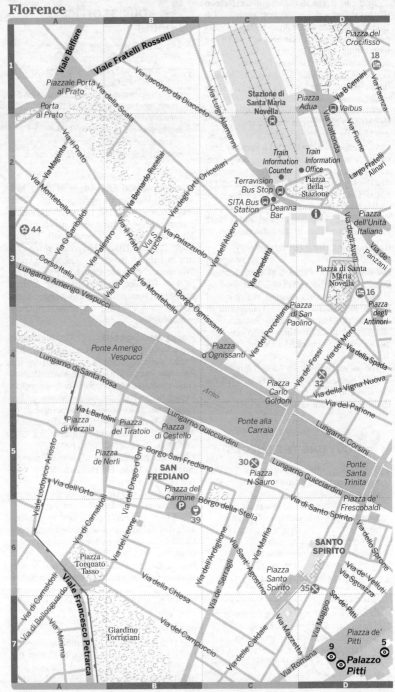

ITALY TUSCANY

Viale Belfiore

Viale Fratelli Rosselli

Via Jacoppo da Diacceto

Piazzale Porta al Prato

Porta al Prato

Via della Scala

Via di Prato

Via Magenta

Via Montebello

Via Luigi Alamanni

Stazione di Santa Maria Novella

Piazza Adua

Vaibus 18

Piazza del Crocifisso

Via B Cennini

Via Faenza

Via Fiume

Via Valfonda

Train Information Counter

Train Information Office

Piazza della Stazione

Largo Fratelli Alinari

Terravision Bus Stop

SITA Bus Station

Deanna Bar

Piazza dell'Unità Italiana

Via degli Avelli

Via de' Panzani

☆ 44

Via G Garibaldi

Via Palestro

Via il Prato

Via S Lucia

Via Bernardo Rucellai

Via degli Orti Oricellari

Via Palazzuolo

Via dell'Albero

Via Benedetta

Piazza di Santa Maria Novella

16

Piazza degli Antinori

Corso Italia

Via Curtatone

Via Montebello

Borgo Ognissanti

Via del Porcellana

Piazza di San Paolino

Lungarno Amerigo Vespucci

Piazza Ognissanti

Piazza d'Ognissanti

Via de' Fossi

Via del Moro

Via della Spada

Ponte Amerigo Vespucci

Arno

Piazza Carlo Goldoni

32

Via della Vigna Nuova

Via del Parione

Lungarno di Santa Rosa

Lungarno Corsini

Via L Bartolini

Piazza di Verzaia

Piazza del Tiratoio

Piazza di Cestello

Lungarno Guicciardini

Ponte alla Carraia

Viale Lodovico Ariosto

Piazza de Nerli

Via del Drago d'Oro

Borgo San Frediano

SAN FREDIANO

30

Piazza N Sauro

Lungarno Guicciardini

Ponte Santa Trinita

Piazza de' Frescobaldi

Via dell'Orto

Via di Camaldoli

Piazza del Carmine

P
39

Borgo della Stella

Via di Santo Spirito

Piazza de' Frescobaldi

Via dello Sprone

Via di Camaldoli

Via di Bellosguardo

Via Minima

Piazza Torquato Tasso

Via del Leone

Via della Chiesa

Via dell'Ardiglione

Via Sant'Agostino

Via de' Serragli

Via Maffia

SANTO SPIRITO

Piazza Santo Spirito

35

Via de' Velluti

Via Sguazza

Sdr de' Pitti

Viale Francesco Petrarca

Giardino Torrigiani

Via del Campuccio

Via delle Caldaie

Via Mazzetta

Via Maggio

Via Romana

Piazza de' Pitti

9

Palazzo Pitti

5

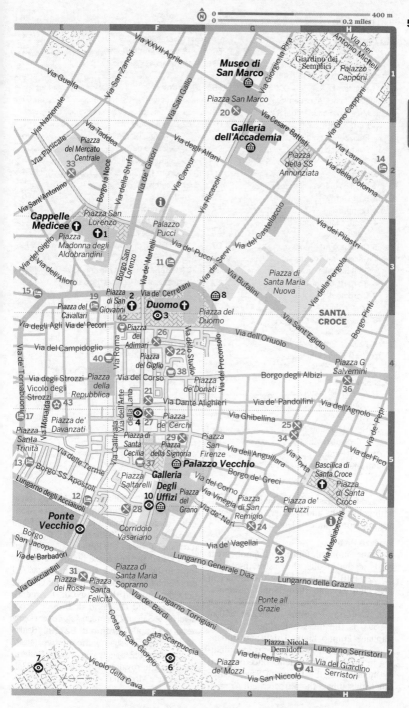

0 — 400 m
0 — 0.2 miles

Via Pier Antonio Micheli

Via XXVII Aprile

Via Giorgio la Pira

Giardino dei Semplici

Palazzo Capponi

Museo di San Marco

Via Guelfa

Via San Zanobi

Via Nazionale

Via San Gallo

Piazza San Marco

20

Via Cesare Battisti

Via Gino Capponi

Via Taddea

Piazza del Mercato Centrale

33

Via Panicale

Via della Stufa

Via de' Ginori

Via degli Alfani

Galleria dell'Accademia

Piazza della SS Annunziata

Via Laura

14

Via della Colonna

Via Sant'Antonino

Borgo la Noce

Via Cavour

Via Ricasoli

Piazza San Lorenzo

Cappelle Medicee

1

Piazza Madonna degli Aldobrandini

Via del Giglio

Via dell'Alloro

Borgo San Lorenzo

Palazzo Pucci

Via de' Martelli

Via de' Pucci

Via dei Servi

Via del Castellaccio

Via dei Pilastri

Via della Pergola

11

Piazza di Santa Maria Nuova

15

19

Piazza di San Giovanni

2

Via de' Cerretani

Via de' Bufalini

8

SANTA CROCE

Piazza del Cavallari

42

Duomo

3

Piazza del Duomo

Via degli Agli

Via de' Pecori

Piazza del Adimari

26

Via dell'Oriuolo

Via Sant'Egidio

Borgo Pinti

Via del Campidoglio

Via Roma

22

Via dello Studio

Via del Proconsolo

40

Piazza del Giglio

38

Piazza de' Donati

Borgo degli Albizi

Piazza G Salvemini

36

Via degli Strozzi

Piazza della Repubblica

Via del Corso

21

Via Dante Alighieri

Via de' Pandolfini

Via dell'Agnolo

Vicolo degli Strozzi

Via de' Tornabuoni

43

Via della Lana

Via dell'Arte della Lana

27

Piazza de' Cerchi

4

Piazza di Santa Cecilia

Via Ghibellina

25

34

Via de' Pepi

17

Piazza de' Davanzati

Via Calimala

29

Piazza della Signoria

Piazza San Firenze

Via dell'Anguillara

Via Torta

Via del Fico

Piazza Santa Trinità

13

Borgo SS Apostoli

Via delle Terme

37

Palazzo Vecchio

Borgo de' Greci

Basilica di Santa Croce

Lungarno degli Acciaiuoli

Piazza Saltarelli

Galleria Degli Uffizi

10

Via del Corno

Piazza de' Peruzzi

Piazza di Santa Croce

12

28

Piazza del Grano

Via Vinegia

Piazza di San Remigio

Via de' Neri

24

Via Magliabechi

Ponte Vecchio

Corridoio Vasariano

Via de' Vagellai

Borgo San Jacopo

Via de' Barbadori

Piazza di Santa Maria Soprarno

23

Lungarno Generale Diaz

31

Piazza dei Rossi

Piazza Santa Felicità

Via de' Bardi

Lungarno delle Grazie

Via Guicciardini

Lungarno Torrigiani

Ponte all Grazie

Costa di San Giorgio

Costa Scarpuccia

7

Vicolo della Cava

6

Piazza Nicola Demidoff

Via dei Renai

Piazza de' Mozzi

Via San Niccolò

Lungarno Serristori

Via del Giardino Serristori

41

◉ **Top Sights**

◉ **Sights**

🛏 **Sleeping**

🍴 **Eating**

🍷 **Drinking**

🎭 **Entertainment**

ordered that the smelly butchers be replaced with goldsmiths and jewellery shops, which are still found along its length.

Palazzo Pitti　　　　　　　　　　PALACE
(Piazza de' Pitti) Built for the Pitti family, great rivals of the Medici, the vast 15th-century Palazzo Pitti was bought by the Medici in 1549 and became their family residence. Today it houses four museums, of which the **Galleria Palatina** (◷8.15am-6.50pm Tue-Sun) is the most important. Works by Raphael, Filippo Lippi, Titian and Rubens adorn lavishly decorated rooms, culminating in the royal apartments once occupied by members of the House of Savoy. Three other museums – the **Museo degli Argenti** (Silver Museum; ◷8.15am-7.30pm Jun-Aug, earlier closing rest of year), the **Galleria d'Arte Moderna** (Gallery of Modern Art; ◷8.15am-6.50pm Tue-Sun) and the **Galleria del Costume** (Costume Gallery; ◷8.15am-6.50pm Tue-Sun) are located in the palace buildings. Ticketing can be confusing: **ticket one** (adult/EU concession €10/5) gets you in to the Galleria del Costume and the Museo degli Argenti, as well as the **Giardino di Boboli** (Boboli Gardens; ◷8.15am-7.30pm Jun-Aug, earlier closing rest of year) and **Giardino di Bardini** (Bardini Gardens; ◷8.15am-sunset); **ticket two** (adult/EU concession €12/6) gets you into the Galleria Palatina, the royal apartments and the Galleria d'Arte Moderna.

Galleria dell'Accademia
ART MUSEUM

(Via Ricasoli 60; adult/concession €10/5; ☺8.15am-6.20pm Tue-Sun) The people queuing outside Galleria dell'Accademia are waiting to see *David,* arguably the Western world's most famous sculpture. Michelangelo carved the giant figure from a single block of marble, finishing it in 1504 when he was just 29. The gallery also displays paintings by Florentine artists spanning the 13th to 16th centuries and regularly hosts temporary exhibitions. Tickets are cheaper if there are no temporary exhibitions.

Basilica di San Lorenzo
CHURCH

(www.basilicasanlorenzofirenze.com, in Italian; Piazza San Lorenzo; admission €3.50; ☺10am-5pm Mon-Sat year-round, 1.30-5pm Sun Mar-Oct) One of the city's finest examples of Renaissance architecture, this basilica was built by Brunelleschi in the 15th century and includes his **Sagrestia Vecchia** (Old Sacristy), with sculptural decoration by Donatello.

Around the corner, at the rear of the basilica, is the sumptuous **Cappelle Medicee** (Medici Chapels; Piazza Madonna degli Aldobrandini; adult/concession €6/3; ☺8.15am-4pm Tue-Sat, 2nd & 4th Mon & 1st, 3rd & 5th Sun of month), the principal burial place of the Medici grand dukes. Its jewel is the incomplete **Sagrestia Nuova**, Michelangelo's first architectural effort, which contains some exquisite sculptures.

Museo di San Marco
ART MUSEUM

(Piazza San Marco 1; adult/concession €4/2; ☺8.15am-1.50pm Tue-Fri, to 4.50pm Sat & 2nd & 4th Sun & 1st, 3rd & 5th Mon of month) Housed in a Dominican monastery, this spiritually uplifting museum is a showcase of the work of Fra' Angelico, who decorated the cells between 1440 and 1441 with deeply devotional frescos to guide the meditation of his fellow friars. Major paintings, including the *Deposition of Christ* (1432) and Fra' Angelico's most famous work, *Annunciation* (c 1440).

☞ Tours

Cycling

The following offer tours of Chianti from Florence, sometimes leaving by minibus and getting on bikes in Chianti and at other times doing the full tour by bike. One-day rides cost between €60 and €90 and are usually available only from March until October.

Florence by Bike
BICYCLE

(☏055 48 89 92; www.florencebybike.it) Guided rides through Chianti plus bike hire (city bike/mountain bike €14.50/21 per day).

I Bike Italy
BICYCLE

(☏055 012 39 94; www.ibikeitaly.com) One- and two-day guided tours in Chianti and a two-hour guided ride around Florence.

I Bike Tuscany
BICYCLE

(☏335 812 07 69; www.ibiketuscany.com) Guided tours around Florence, Chianti and Siena.

Walking Tours

Freya's Florence
WALKING

(☏349 074 89 07; freyasflorence@yahoo.com; €60 per hr for private tours) English-language walking tours with an enthusiastic and expert guide.

Walking Tours of Florence
WALKING

(☏055 264 50 33; www.italy.artviva.com; Via de' Sassetti 1; tours per person from €25) The Artviva outfit offers a range of city tours, all led by English-speaking guides.

☆☆ Festivals & Events

Scoppio del Carro
RELIGIOUS CELEBRATION

(Explosion of the Cart) A cart full of fireworks is exploded in front of the Duomo on Easter Sunday.

Maggio Musicale Fiorentino
MUSIC FESTIVAL

(www.maggiofiorentino.com, in Italian) Italy's longest-running music festival, held from April to June.

Festa di San Giovanni
RELIGIOUS CELEBRATION

(Feast of St John) Florence's patron saint is celebrated on 24 June with costumed soccer matches on Piazza di Santa Croce and fireworks over Piazzale Michelangelo.

⫟ Sleeping

Although there are hundreds of hotels in Florence, it's still prudent to book ahead. Look out for low-season website deals – prices often drop by up to 50%.

WANT MORE?

For in-depth information, reviews and recommendations at your fingertips, head to the Apple App Store to purchase Lonely Planet's *Florence City Guide* iPhone app.

Alternatively, head to **Lonely Planet** (www.lonelyplanet.com/italy/florence) for planning advice, author recommendations, traveller reviews and insider tips.

DUOMO & PIAZZA DELLA SIGNORIA

Relais del Duomo   B&B €€

(☎055 21 01 47; www.relaisdelduomo.it, in Italian; Piazza dell'Olio 2; s €48-85, d €70-130; ❀@☎) Florentine B&Bs don't come much better than this one. Located in the shadow of the Duomo, it has four light and airy rooms with attractive furnishings and lovely little bathrooms. Privacy levels are high and management is extremely helpful.

Hotel Cestelli   B&B €

(☎055 21 42 13; www.hotelcestelli.com; Borgo SS Apostoli 25; s without bathroom €40-60, d without bathroom €50-80, d €70-100; ⊙closed 2 weeks Jan, 3 weeks Aug) Run by Florentine photographer Alessio and his Japanese partner Asumi, this eight-room hotel on the first floor of a 12th-century *palazzo* is wonderfully located. Though dark, the rooms are attractively furnished, quiet and cool.

SANTA MARIA NOVELLA

TOP CHOICE **Hotel Santa Maria Novella** HOTEL €€

(☎055 27 18 40; www.hotelsantamaria novella.it; Piazza di Santa Maria Novella 1; d €135-195, ste €178-235; ❀@☎) The bland exterior of this excellent four-star choice gives no hint of the spacious and elegant rooms within. All are beautifully appointed, featuring marble bathrooms and comfortable beds. The breakfast spread is lavish.

Ostello Archi Rossi   HOSTEL €

(☎055 29 08 04; www.hostelarchirossi.com; Via Faenza 94r; dm €21-27, s €40-60, d €60-90; ⊙closed 2 weeks Dec; @☎) This ever-busy hostel near Stazione di Santa Maria Novella offers bright dorms with three to nine beds; some are single-sex and all have private bathrooms and keyed lockers. Air-conditioning s in private rooms only. The hostel also offers free walking tours.

Hotel Scoti   PENSION €€

(☎055 29 21 28; www.hotelscoti.com; Via de' Tornabuoni 7; s €35-75, d €65-125) On Florence's smartest shopping street, the Scoti is a splendid mix of old-fashioned charm and great value for money. Run with smiling aplomb by Australian Doreen and Italian Carmello, it offers 11 clean and comfortable rooms and an amazing frescoed living room for communal use. Breakfast costs an extra €5.

Continentale   BOUTIQUE HOTEL €€€

(☎055 2 72 62; www.lungarnohotels.com; Viccolo dell'Oro 6r; s €240-300, d €290-530; ❀@) Owned by the Ferragamo fashion house and designed by fashionable Florentine architect Michele Bönan, this glamorous hotel references 1950s Italy in its vibrant decor, and is about as hip as Florence gets.

Hotel Paris   HOTEL €€

(☎055 28 02 81; www.parishotel.it; Via dei Banchi 2; s €80-125, d €90-180; ❀@☎) This pair of 15th-century palaces is linked on the second floor by a glass walkway. Its comfortable three-star rooms sport high ceilings and Renaissance-style furbelows.

SAN LORENZO

Academy Hostel   HOSTEL €

(☎055 23 98 665; www.academyhostel.eu; Via Ricasoli 9; dm €25-38, tw €70-84, s without bathroom €35-45; ❀@☎) The philosophy of this small hostel close to the Duomo is that cheap accommodation shouldn't compromise on comfort. Its dorms (sleeping between three and six) are bright and well set up, with lockers and single beds (no bunks).

Johlea & Johanna   B&B €€

(☎055 463 32 92; www.johanna.it; Via San Gallo 80; s €70-120, d €80-170; ❀) This highly regarded B&B has more than a dozen tasteful, individually decorated rooms housed in five historic residences. There are also two charming suite apartments (€92 to €280).

SAN MARCO

Hotel Morandi alla Crocetta

    BOUTIQUE HOTEL €€

(☎055 234 47 47; www.hotelmorandi.it; Via Laura 50; s €70-109, d €100-169; P❀@☎) This medieval convent-turned-hotel is a stunner. Rooms are charmingly decorated (try for the frescoed No 29) and extremely well equipped. The location is wonderfully quiet.

SAN MINIATO AL MONTE

Campeggio Michelangelo   CAMPING GROUND €

(☎055 681 19 77; Viale Michelangelo 80; www.ec vacanze.it; sites per person with tent €10.80, in onsite elevated tent €15.50; P@) Just off Piazzale Michelangelo, this large and well-equipped camping ground is the nearest to the city centre. Take bus 12 from the train station to Piazzale Michelangelo.

✕ Eating

Classic Tuscan dishes include *ribollita,* a heavy vegetable soup, and *bistecca alla fiorentina* (Florentine steak served rare). Chianti is the local tipple.

DUOMO & PIAZZA DELLA SIGNORIA

TOP CHOICE **'Ino**   SANDWICHES €
(Via dei Georgofili 3r-7r; panini €5-8; ⊙11am-5pm) Short for 'panino', this stylish *paninoteca* (sandwich bar) shop near the Uffizi sources its artisan gourmet ingredients locally and uses them in inventive and delicious ways. A glass of wine is included in the price of every sandwich.

La Canova do Gustavino   WINE BAR €€
(Via della Condotta 29r; mains €8-12) The rear dining room of this atmospheric *enoteca* is lined with shelves full of Tuscan wine – the perfect accompaniment to a simple bowl of soup, a bruschetta, a pasta dish or a hearty main.

Cantinetta dei Verrazzano   WINE BAR €€
(Via dei Tavolini 18-20; platters €4.50-12, focaccias €3-3.50, panini €1.70-3.90; ⊙noon-9pm Mon-Sat) Come here for focaccia fresh from the oven, perhaps topped with caramelised radicchio or porcini mushrooms. And be sure to wash it down with a glass of wine from the Verrazzano estate in Chianti.

I Fratellini   SANDWICHES €
(www.iduefratellini.com; Via dei Cimatori 38r; panini €2.50; ⊙9am-8pm Mon-Sat, closed Fri & Sun 2nd half of Jun & all Aug) I Fratellini is a city institution. Locals flock to its tiny counter for fresh-filled panini ready in the twinkle of an eye, eaten standing in the street.

SANTA MARIA NOVELLA

TOP CHOICE **L'Osteria di Giovanni**   TRATTORIA €€€
(☑055 28 48 97; www.osteriadigiovanni. com, in Italian; Via del Moro 22; mains €18-26; ⊙lunch & dinner Fri-Mon, dinner only Tue-Thu) The house antipasto is a great way to sample Tuscan specialities such as *crostini* and *lardo,* and the *bistecca alla fiorentina* is sensational. Everything a perfect neighbourhood eatery should be, and then some.

Coquinarius   WINE BAR €€
(☑055 230 21 53; Via della Oche 15r; mains €15; ☑) Close to Piazza Signoria, this modern *enoteca* is a perfect spot for lunch or a light dinner. The pasta dishes are uniformly good, and there's almost always a few unusual and delicious salads on the menu. Vegetarians will be very happy after a visit here.

SAN LORENZO

Nerbone   TAVOLA CALDA €
(☑055 21 99 49; inside Mercato Centrale, Piazza del Mercato Centrale; panini €3-4, mains €5-6.50; ⊙7am-2pm Mon-Sat) This unpretentious market stall has been serving its rustic dishes to queues of shoppers and stallholders since 1872. It's a great place to try local staples such as *trippa alla fiorentina* (€6.50) and *panini con bollito* (a boiled beef bun, €3).

SAN MARCO

Accademia Ristorante   TRATTORIA €€
(www.ristoranteaccademia.it, in italian; Piazza San Marco 7r; mains €12-18) There aren't too many decent eateries in this area, which is one of the reasons why this family-run restaurant is perennially packed. Factors such as friendly staff, cheerful decor and consistently good food help, too.

TOP FIVE GELATERIE

There are plenty of places offering *gelato artiginale* (traditional, usually homemade, ice cream and sorbet). Flavours change according to what fruit is in season, and a small cone can cost anywhere from €1.50 to €2.20.

» **La Carraia** (Piazza Nazario Sauro 25; ⊙11am-11pm) Look for the ever-present queue next to the Ponte Carraia, and you will find this fantastic gelateria.

» **Gelateria dei Neri** (22r Via de' Neri; ⊙9am-midnight) Semifreddo-style gelato that is cheaper than its competitors; known for its Giotto (almond, hazelnut and coconut) flavour.

» **Gelateria Vivoli** (Via Isola delle Stinche 7; ⊙7.30am-midnight Tue-Sat, 9am-midnight Sun, closed mid-Aug) Choose a flavour from the huge choice on offer (the chocolate with orange is a perennial favourite) and scoff it in the pretty piazza opposite; tubs only.

» **Grom** (www.grom.it; Via del Campanile at Via delle Oche; ⊙10.30am-11pm, to midnight Apr-Sep) This relative newcomer has taken the city by storm; the flavours are all delectable and many ingredients are organic.

» **Vestri** (www.vestri.it; Borgo degli Albizi 11r; ⊙10.30am-8pm Mon-Sat) Specialises in chocolate; go for the decadent white chocolate with wild strawberries or the chocolate with pepper.

SANTA CROCE

Trattoria Cibrèo (Cibréino) TRATTORIA €€

(www.edizioniteatrodelsalecibreofirenze.it, in Italian; Viadei Macci 122r; mains €13-16; ⊙Tue-Sat, closed Aug) The small dining room here is run with charm and efficiency by a maître d' who will happily explain the menu and suggest a matching wine. *Secondi* comprise a small main dish matched with a side of seasonal vegetables; everything is delicious and exceptionally well priced considering its quality. No reservations and no credit cards.

Del Fagioli TRATTORIA €

(☎055 24 42 85; Corso Tintori 47r; mains €9-10; ⊙Mon-Fri, closed Aug) This Slow Food favourite near the Basilica di Santa Croce is the archetypical Tuscan trattoria. It opened in 1966 and has been serving well-priced bean dishes, soups and roasted meats to throngs of appreciative local workers and residents ever since. No credit cards.

Osteria del Caffè Italiano TRATTORIA €€

(☎055 28 90 20; www.caffeitaliano.it; Via del'Isola delle Stinche 11-13r; mains €16-25; ⊙Tue-Sun) This old-fashioned *osteria* occupies the ground floor of the 14th-century Palazzo Salviati. It's an excellent spot to try the city's famous *bistecca fiorentina*. The adjoining **Pizzeria del Osteria del Caffè Italiano** (pizzas €8; ⊙dinner only) has a simple dining space and offers a limited menu of three types of pizzas: margherita, napoli and marinara.

OLTRANO

TOP CHOICE Le Volpi e L'uva WINE BAR €

(www.levolpieluva.com; Piazza dei Rossi 1; ⊙11am-9pm Mon-Sat) Near the Ponte Vecchio, this intimate *enoteca* has an impressive list of wines by the glass and serves a delectable array of accompanying antipasti, including juicy *prosciutto di Parma*, *lardo*-topped *crostini* and boutique Tuscan cheeses. There's a tiny outdoor terrace and a small number of bar stools.

Trattoria La Casalinga TRATTORIA €

(Via de' Michelozzi 9r; mains €6-9; ⊙closed Sun) Family run and much loved by locals, this unpretentious and always busy place is one of the city's cheapest trattorias. You'll be relegated behind locals in the queue – it's a fact of life and not worth protesting about – with the eventual reward being hearty and dirt-cheap peasant dishes.

🍷 Drinking

Gilli CAFE, BAR

(www.gilli.it; Piazza della Repubblica 39r; ⊙Wed-Mon) The city's grandest cafe, Gilli has been serving excellent coffee and delicious cakes since 1733. Claiming a table on the piazza is *molto* expensive – we prefer standing at the spacious Liberty-style bar.

Old Stove Duomo PUB

(Piazza di San Giovanni 4r) This Irish pub is a magnet for foreign students on holiday, who come here to swill beer and admire the views of the Duomo. Try to snaffle the upstairs balcony table.

James Joyce PUB

(Lungarno Benvenuto Cellini 1r; ⊙6pm-2am, until 3pm Fri & Sat) Guinness on tap and a great beer garden make this somewhat out-of-the-way student favourite worth the walk along the Arno. If you make the trek, consider having dinner at the stylish **Gattabuia Pizzeria** (Lungarno Cellini 13-18r; pizzas €4-12; ⊙dinner daily) next door.

Caffè Rivoire CAFE, BAR

(www.rivoire.it, in Italian; Piazza della Signoria; ⊙closed Mon & 2nd half Jan) Rivoire's terrace has the best view in the city. Settle in for a long *aperitivo* or coffee break – it's worth the high prices.

Chiaroscuro CAFE, BAR

(Via del Corso 36r; ⊙Mon-Sat) Known for its home-roasted coffee, this casual cafe is strategically located between the Duomo and Piazza Signoria. Its *aperitivo* buffet, served between 6pm and 8pm, is excellent.

Dolce Vita BAR

(www.dolcevitaflorence.com; Piazza del Carmine 6r; ⊙5pm-2am Tue-Sun, closed 2 wks Aug) A long-standing Oltrano favourite, 'Sweet Life' serves an *aperitivo* buffet between 7.30pm and 9.30pm, sometimes accompanied by live music.

Negroni BAR

(www.negronibar.com, in Italian; Via dei Renai 17r; ⊙8am-2am Mon-Sat, from 7pm Sun) The famous Florentine cocktail gives its name to this popular bar in the San Nicolò district. Come here after admiring the sun set over the city from Piazzale Michelangelo.

☆ Entertainment

Florence's definitive monthly listings guide, *Firenze Spettacolo* (€1.80), is sold at newsstands.

Concerts, opera and dance are performed year-round at the **Teatro Comunale** (☎800 11 22 11; Corso Italia 16), also the venue for events organised by the Maggio Musicale Fiorentino (see Festivals & Events, p529).

English-language films are screened at the **Odeon Cinehall** (www.cinehall.it, in Italian; Piazza Strozzi 2).

❶ Information

Emergency

Police station (Questura; ☎055 497 71; Via Zara 2)

Medical Services

Dr Stephen Kerr (☎055 28 80 55; www.dr-kerr.com; Piazza Mercato Nuovo 1; ⊙3-5pm Mon-Fri)

Emergency Doctor (Guardia Medica; ☎north of the Arno 055 233 94 56, south of the Arno 055 21 56 16) For a doctor at night, weekends or on public holidays.

Tourist Information

Tourist offices (www.firenzeturismo.it) main office (☎055 29 08 32; Via Cavour 1r; ⊙8.30am-6.30pm Mon-Sat, to 1.30pm Sun); airport (☎055 31 58 74; ⊙8.30am-8.30pm); Santa Croce (☎055 234 04 44; Borgo Santa Croce 29r; ⊙9am-7pm Mon-Sat, to 2pm Sun Mar-Oct, to 5pm Mon-Sat, to 2pm Sun Nov-Feb); Piazza della Stazione (☎055 21 22 45; www.commune.fi.it; Piazza della Stazione 4; ⊙8.30am-7pm Mon-Sat, to 2pm Sun)

❶ Getting There & Away

Air

The main airports serving Florence are **Pisa international airport** (Aeroporto Galileo Galilei; PSA; ☎050 84 93 00; www.pisa-airport.com) and **Bologna airport** (Aeroporto G. Marconi; BLQ; ☎051 647 96 15; www.bologna-airport.it). There's also a small city airport 5km north of Florence, **Florence airport** (Aeroporto Vespucci; FLR; ☎055 306 13 00; www.aeroporto.firenze.it).

Bus

The **SITA bus station** (☎800 37 37 60; www.sitabus.it, in Italian; Via Santa Caterina da Siena 17) is just south of the train station. Buses leave for Siena (€7.10, 1½ hours, every 30 to 60 minutes) and San Gimignano via Poggibonsi (€6.25, 1¼ hours, 14 daily).

Car & Motorcycle

Florence is connected by the A1 *autostrada* to Bologna and Milan in the north and Rome and Naples to the south. The A11 links Florence with Pisa and the coast, and a *superstrada* (expressway) joins the city to Siena.

Train

Florence is well connected by train. There are regular services to/from Pisa (Regional €5.80, 1¼ hours, every 30 minutes), Rome (Eurostar AV, €44, 90 minutes, hourly), Venice (Eurostar AV €52, 1¾ hours, 12 daily) and Milan (Eurostar AV, €16.20, one hour, hourly).

❶ Getting Around

To/From the Airport

Terravision (☎06 321 20 011; www.terravision.it) runs a bus service between the paved bus park in front of the train station and Pisa (Galileo Galilei) airport (adult/child aged five to 12 years €10/4, 70 minutes, 12 daily). Buy your tickets at the Terravision desk inside Deanna Café, opposite. Otherwise there are regular trains (€5.10, 1½ hours, hourly between 6.37am and 8.37pm).

ATAF (☎800 42 45 00; www.ataf.net) runs a shuttle bus (€5, 25 minutes, half-hourly from 5.30am to 11pm) connecting Florence airport with the SITA bus station.

Eurostar's Frecciarossa service travels between Florence and Bologna Centrale train station (€24, 40 minutes, every 30 minutes). Aerobus services travel between Bologna airport and Bologna Centrale (see p521).

Bus

ATAF (☎800 42 45 00; www.ataf.net) buses service the city centre and Fiesole, a small town in the hills 8km northeast of Florence. The most useful terminal is just outside the train station's eastern exit. Take bus 7 for Fiesole, and 12 or 13 for Piazzale Michelangelo. Tickets (90 minutes €1.20) are sold at *tabacchi* and newsstands – you can also buy a 90-minute ticket on board the bus (€2).

Car & Motorcycle

Much of the city centre is restricted to traffic, so the best advice is to leave your car in a car park and use public transport. Details of car parks are available from **Firenze Parcheggi** (☎055 500 19 94; www.firenzeparcheggi.it, in Italian). Note that there is a strict Limited Traffic Zone (ZTL) in the historic centre from 7.30am to 7.30pm Monday to Wednesday and from 7.30am to 6pm and 11.30pm to 4am on Thursday, Friday and Saturday. Fines are hefty if you enter the centre during these times without a special permit having been organised by your hotel in advance. For a map of the ZTL go to www.comune.fi.it/opencms/export/sites/retecivica/materiali/turismo/ztlnov.JPG.

Pisa

POP 87,400

Most people know Pisa as the home of an architectural project gone terribly wrong, but the Leaning Tower is just one of a number of noteworthy sights in this compact and compelling university city.

Pisa's golden age came in the 12th and 13th centuries when it was a maritime power rivalling Genoa and Venice. It was eventually defeated by the Genoese in 1284 and in 1406 it fell to Florence. Under the Medici, the arts and sciences flourished and Galileo Galilei (1564–1642) taught at the university.

Sights & Activities

From Piazza Sant' Antonio, just west of the train station where the bus stands are, the Leaning Tower is a straightforward 1.5km walk – follow Viale F Crispi north, cross the Ponte Solferino over the Arno and continue straight up Via Roma to Campo dei Miracoli.

Pisatour (☎328 144 68 55; www.pisatour. it; adult/child under 15yr €12/free; ☉tours Mon & Thu 3pm, Sat 10.30am) offers excellent two-to-three hour English-language guided walking tours around the historic centre and can also organise guides for the Campo dei Miracoli.

Campo dei Miracoli   CATHEDRALS
(Field of Miracles) Pisans claim that Campo dei Miracoli is among the most beautiful urban spaces in the world. Certainly, the immaculate walled lawns provide a gorgeous setting for the Cathedral, Baptistry and Tower; on the other hand, few places boast so many tat-waving hawkers.

Forming the centrepiece of the Campo's Romanesque trio, the candy-striped **Cathedral** (Duomo; ☉10am-12.45pm & 2-5pm Nov-Feb,

to 6pm Mar, 1to 8pm Apr-Sep, to 7pm Oct), begun in 1063, has a graceful tiered facade and cavernous interior. The transept's bronze doors are by Bonanno Pisano, and the 16th-century entrance doors are by Giambologna.

To the west, the cupcake-like **Baptistry** (Battistero; ☉10am-5pm Nov-Feb, 9am-6pm Mar, 8am-8pm Apr-Sep, 9am-7pm Oct) was started in 1153 and completed by Nicola and Giovanni Pisano in 1260. Inside, note Nicola Pisano's beautiful pulpit.

But it's to the campanile, better known as the **Leaning Tower** (Torre Pendente; ☉10am-4.30pm Dec & Jan, 9.30am-5.30pm Feb, 9am-5.30pm Mar, 8.30am-8pm Apr-Sep, 9am-7pm Oct, 9.30am-5.30pm Nov), that all eyes are drawn. Bonanno Pisano began building in 1173, but almost immediately his plans came a cropper in a layer of shifting soil. Only three of the tower's seven tiers were completed before it started tilting – continuing at a rate of about 1mm per year. By 1990 the lean had reached 5.5 degrees – a tenth of a degree beyond the critical point established by computer models. Stability was finally ensured in 1998 when a combination of biased weighting and soil drilling forced the tower into a safer position. Today it's almost 4.1m off the perpendicular.

Visits are limited to groups of 40 and children under eight years are not allowed entrance; entry times are staggered and queuing is predictably inevitable. It is wise to book ahead.

Flanking the Campo, beautiful **Camposanto cemetery** (☉10am-5pm Nov-Feb, 9am-6pm Mar, 8am-8pm Apr-Sep, 9am-7pm Oct) is said to contain soil shipped from Calvary during the Crusades. Look out for the 14th-century fresco *The Triumph of Death* on the southern cloister wall.

CAMPO DEI MIRACOLI TICKETING

Ticket pricing for Campo dei Miracoli sights is complicated. Tickets to the **Tower** (€15 at ticket office, €17 when booked online) and **Cathedral** (€2 Mar-Oct, free Nov-Feb) are sold individually, but for the remaining sights combined tickets are available. These cost €5/6/10 for one/two/five sights and cover the Cathedral, Baptistry, Camposanto, Museo dell'Opera del Duomo and Museo delle Sinópie. Entry for children aged under 10 years is free for all sights except the tower. Any ticket will also give access to the multimedia and information areas located in the Museo Dell'Opera del Duomo and Museo delle Sinópie.

Tickets are sold at two **ticket offices** (www.opapisa.it) on the piazza: the central ticket office is located behind the tower and a second office is located in the entrance foyer of the Museo delle Sinópie. To ensure your visit to the tower, book tickets via the website at least 15 days in advance.

🛏 Sleeping

Many people visit Pisa on a day trip from Florence, but if you're keen to sample the student bar scene at night there are a few decent overnight options.

Hotel Francesco
HOTEL €€

(☑050 55 54 53; www.hotelfrancesco.com; Via Santa Maria 129; r €60-150; ❄@) The best of the hotels lining busy Via Santa Maria (just off Campo dei Miracoli), the small family-run Francesco offers a warm welcome and bright rooms with mod cons. Breakfast isn't included in the price of the room.

Relais Sotto la Torre
B&B/HOSTEL €

(☑050 55 35 59; www.relaisunderthetower.it; cnr Via Santa Maria & Piazza del Duomo; dm €24-25, d without bathroom €52, d €56; ❄🏠) Literally in the shadow of the Leaning Tower, this cross between a B&B and hostel is spread over two buildings and gets mixed reviews from readers. Rooms are all clean, but a few have no windows and reception hours are irregular. You're unlikely to find anything better at this price, though.

🍴 Eating & Drinking

The best restaurants are bars are located in the streets around Piazza Dante Alighieri, Piazza Vettovaglie and along the riverbank.

Bar Pasticceria Salza
CAFE €

(☑050 58 02 44; Borgo Stretto 44; ⊙8am-8.30pm Apr-Oct, hr vary Tue-Sun Nov-Mar) Salza has been tempting patrons off Borgo Stretto and into sugar-induced wickedness ever since the 1920s. Claim one of the tables in the arcade, or save some money by standing at the bar – the excellent coffee and dangerously delicious cakes and chocolates will satisfy regardless of where they are sampled.

Il Montino
PIZZA €

(Vicolo del Monte 1; cecina €2.40, spuma €1, focaccias €2.50; ⊙10.30am-3pm & 5-10pm Mon-Sat) Students and sophisticates alike adore the *cecina* (chickpea pizza) and *spuma* (sweet, non-alcoholic drink) that are the specialities of this famous pizzeria. Order to go or claim one of the outdoor tables. You'll find it in the laneway behind Caffetiera Ginostra.

Ristoro al Vecchio Teatro
TRATTORIA €€

(☑050 20 21 0; Piazza Dante; set menus €25 & €35, mains €8-12; ⊙lunch Mon-Sat, dinner Tue-Sat) The Vecchio Teatro's genial host is proud of his set menu, and for good reason. The four courses are dominated by local seafood specialities and the dessert finale includes a *castagnaccio* (sweet chestnut cake) that has been known to prompt diners to spontaneous applause.

🍴 Osteria 050
TRATTORIA €€

(☑050 54 31 06; www.zerocinquanta.com, in Italian; Via San Francesco 36; ⊙closed Sun lunch & Tue) Named after Pisa's phone code, this stylish eatery serves regional specialities made with organic products sourced from the local area and used in season.

ℹ Information

For city information, check www.pisaturismo.it or ask at one of the three **tourist offices** (airport ☑050 50 25 18; ⊙9.30am-11.30pm; city centre ☑050 4 22 91; Piazza Vittorio Emanuele II 16; ⊙9am-7pm Mon-Sat, to 4pm Sun; Piazza dei Miracoli ☑334 641 94 08; ⊙9.30am-7.30pm).

ℹ Getting There & Away

The city's **Pisa international airport** (Galileo Galilei airport; PSA; ☑050 84 93 00; www.pisa-airport.com) is linked to the centre by train (€1.10, five minutes, 15 daily), or by the CPT Linea Rossa bus (www.cpt.pisa.it, in Italian; €1, 10 minutes, every 10 minutes). Buy bus tickets at the newsstand at the train station.

Terravision buses depart from the airport to Florence (adult/child five to 12 years €10/4, 70 minutes, 12 daily). **Train Spa** (www.trainspa.it) shuttle buses go to Siena via Empoli (€14, two daily).

Regular trains run to Lucca (Regional €2.40, 30 minutes, every 30 to 60 minutes), Florence (Regional €5.80, 1¼ hours, every 30 minutes), Rome (Eurostar €39.50, three hours, nine daily) and Genoa (InterCity €16, 2½ hours, eight daily).

Siena

POP 54,200

Siena is one of Italy's most enchanting medieval towns. Its walled centre, a beautifully preserved warren of dark lanes punctuated with Gothic *palazzi*, pretty piazzas and eye-catching churches, has at its centre Piazza del Campo (known as Il Campo), the sloping square that is the venue for the city's famous annual horse race, Il Palio.

According to legend, Siena was founded by the sons of Remus. In the Middle Ages its dramatic rise caused political and cultural friction with nearby Florence and the two cities strove to outdo each other with their artistic and architectural achievements. Painters of the Sienese School (most notably in the 13th to 15th centuries) produced significant works of art, many of which are on

ITALY TUSCANY

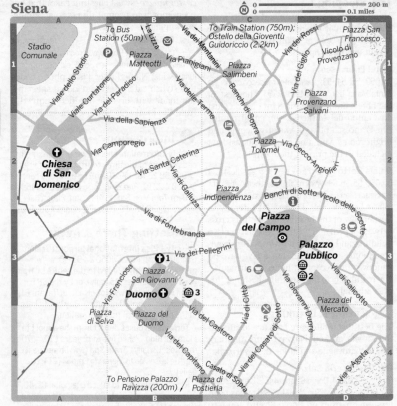

show in the city's impressive museums and churches.

◉ Sights

From the train station take bus 10 (€1) to Piazza Gramsci, from where Piazza del Campo is a short, signposted walk away. From the bus station it's a 10-minute walk up Via La Lizza and Via delle Terme. The centre's main streets – the Banchi di Sopra, Via di Città and Banchi di Sotto – curve around Il Campo. Note that visitors' cars aren't permitted in the centre.

A joint ticket for the Duomo, Battistero, Museo dell'Opera, Diocesan Museum, Crypt and Santa Maria della Scala – all clustered around the Duomo – costs adult/child under 6 years/student/over 65 years €12/free/5/8. See www.operaduomo.siena.it for details.

Piazza del Campo SQUARE
Ever since the 14th century, the slanting, shell-shaped Piazza del Campo has been the city's

civic centre. Forming the base of the piazza, the **Palazzo Pubblico** (Palazzo Comunale) is a good example of Sienese Gothic architecture. Inside, the **Museo Civico** (adult/concession €8/4.50; ⊘10am-6.15pm mid-Mar–Oct, to 4.45pm Nov–mid-Mar) houses some extraordinary frescos, including Simone Martini's famous *Maestà* (Virgin Mary in Majesty) and Ambroglio Lorenzetti's *Allegories of Good and Bad Government*. Soaring above the *palazzo* is the 102m (400-step) **Torre del Mangia** (admission €8; ⊘10am-6.15pm mid-Mar–end Oct, to 3.15pm Nov–mid-Mar), which dates from 1297. A combined ticket to the two costs adult/child under 6 years €13/free and is only available at the Torre del Mangia ticket office.

Duomo CHURCH
(Cathedral; Piazza del Duomo; admission €3; ⊘10.30am-7.30pm Mon-Sat & 1.30-5.30pm Sun Mar-May & Sep-Oct, 10.30am-8pm Mon-Sat & 1.30-6pm Sun Jun-Aug, 10.30am-6.30pm Mon-Sat & 1.30-5.30pm Sun Nov-Feb) The spectacular

Siena

Duomo is one of Italy's Gothic masterpieces. Begun in 1196, it was completed in 1215, although work continued well into the 13th century. Subsequent expansion plans were stymied by the plague of 1348. The striking facade of green, red and white marble was designed by Giovanni Pisano, who also helped his dad, Nicola, craft the cathedral's intricate pulpit. Other noteworthy features include Donatello's bronze of St John the Baptist and statues of St Jerome and Mary Magdalene by Bernini.

Behind the cathedral and down a flight of stairs, the **Battistero** (Baptistry; admission €3; Piazza San Giovanni; ⊕9.30am-7pm Mar-May & Sep-Oct, to 8pm Jun-Aug, 10am-5pm Nov-Feb) has a Gothic facade and a rich interior of 15th-century frescos.

Museo dell'Opera   MUSEUM
(Piazza del Duomo; admission €6; ⊕9.30am-7pm Mar-May & Sep-Oct, to 8pm Jun-Aug, to 5pm Nov-Feb) This museum is home to a large collection of Sienese painting and sculpture, including an entire room dedicated to the work of Duccio di Buoninsegna, the most significant painter of the Sienese School.

Chiesa di San Domenico   CHURCH
(Piazza San Domenico 1; admission free; ⊕7.30am-1pm & 3-6.30pm) On the western edge of the walled city, this is the last resting place of the head and thumb of St Catherine, Siena's patron saint.

🎉 Festivals & Events

Siena's great annual event is the **Palio** (2 Jul & 16 Aug), a pageant culminating in a bareback horse race round Il Campo. The city is divided into 17 *contrade* (districts), of which 10 are chosen annually to compete for the *palio* (silk banner). The only rule in the three-lap race is that jockeys can't tug the reins of other horses.

🛏 Sleeping

It's always advisable to book in advance, but for August and the Palio, it's essential.

Pensione Palazzo Ravizza BOUTIQUE HOTEL €€
(☑0577 28 04 62; www.palazzoravizza.com; Pian dei Mantellini 34; s €95-150, d €115-200; P❄🛜) *Pensione* is a far too modest title for this intimate, sumptuous place. Occupying a delightful Renaissance *palazzo*, frescoed ceilings and antique furniture co-exist with flat-screen TVs and comprehensive wi-fi coverage. Service is courteous and efficient, and there's a small, leafy garden.

Antica Residenza Cicogna   B&B €
(☑347 007 28 88; www.anticaresidenzacicogna.it; Via dei Termini 67; s €75-90, d €85-100; P❄🛜) Springless beds, soundproof windows, ornate frescos, antique furniture and a lavish buffet breakfast make this central option justifiably popular. Reception has limited core hours (8am to 1pm), so arrange your arrival in advance.

Ostello della Gioventù Guidoriccio
                                          HOSTEL €
(☑0577 522 12; siena@ostellionline.org; Via Fiorentina 89; per person €20; P@) An inconvenient 20-minute bus ride from the town centre, Siena's HI hostel has 46 neat but dark two-bed rooms. Take bus 10 or 15 from Piazza Gramsci, or 77 from the train station and tell the driver you're after the *ostello*.

🍴 Eating & Drinking

Among many traditional Sienese dishes are *panzanella* (summer salad of soaked bread, basil, onion and tomatoes), *pappardelle con la lepre* (ribbon pasta with hare) and panforte (a rich cake of almonds, honey and candied fruit).

Osteria Le Logge   RESTAURANT €€€
(☑0577 4 80 13; www.osterialelogge.it; Via dei Porrione 33; mains €19-24; ⊕Mon-Sat) This place changes its menu of creative and delicious Tuscan cuisine almost daily. The downstairs dining room, once a pharmacy, is an

atmospheric space in which to dine and there are also streetside tables.

Hosteria Il Carroccio
TRATTORIA €€

(☎0577 4 11 65; Via del Casato di Sotto 32; mains €13-25; ☺Thu-Tue) Recommended by the prestigious Slow Food movement, Il Carroccio specialises in traditional Sienese cooking. Staples include *pici* (thick spaghetti) and succulent *bistecca di chianina alla brace* (grilled steak).

Caffè Fiorella
CAFE €

(Via di Città 13; ☺Mon-Sat 7am-8pm) Squeeze into this tiny space behind Il Campo to enjoy Siena's best coffee. In summer, the coffee granita with a dollop of cream is a wonderful indulgence.

Pasticceria Nannini
CAFE €

(24 Via Banchi di Sopra; ☺7.30am-11pm) Come here for the finest *cenci* (fried sweet pastry), panforte and *ricciarelli* (almond biscuits) in town, enjoyed with a cup of excellent coffee.

ℹ Information
Tourist office (☎0577 28 05 51; www.terresiena.it; Piazza del Campo 56; ☺9am-7pm).

ℹ Getting There & Away
Siena is not on a main train line, so it's easier to arrive by bus. From the bus station on Piazza Gramsci, **Train SPA** (www.trainspa.it) and SITA buses run to/from Florence (€7.10, 1½ hours, every 30 to 60 minutes), Pisa airport (€14, two daily) and San Gimignano (€5.50, 1¼ hours, hourly), either direct or via Poggibonsi.

Sena (☎0577 28 32 03; www.sena.it) operates services to/from Rome (€21, three hours, 10 daily).

Both Train SPA and Sena have ticket offices underneath the piazza.

Lucca
POP 84,200

Lucca is a love-at-first-sight type of place. Hidden behind monumental Renaissance walls, its historic centre is chock-full of handsome churches, excellent restaurants and tempting *pasticcerie*. Founded by the Etruscans, it became a city state in the 12th century and stayed that way for 600 years. Most of its streets and monuments date from this period.

◉ Sights & Activities
From the train station walk across Piazza Ricasoli, cross Viale Regina Margherita and then follow the path across the grass and through the wall to reach the historic centre.

Opera buffs should visit in July and August, when the **Puccini Festival** (☎0584 35 93 22; www.puccinifestival.it; Lucca ticket office Piazza Anfiteatro, tickets €33-160) is held in a purpose-built outdoor theatre in the nearby settlement of Torre del Lago.

City walls
CITY WALLS

Lucca's 12m-high city walls were built around the old city in the 16th and 17th centuries and were once defended by 126 cannons. In the 19th century they were crowned with a wide, tree-lined footpath that is now the centre of local Lucchese life. To join the locals in walking, jogging, rollerblading or cycling the 4km-long footpath, access it via Piazzale Verdi or Piazza Santa Maria; bike hire is available at the tourist office at Piazzale Verdi (per hour €2.50) or at one of two bike-rental shops (bikes per hour €2.50, tandems €5.50) at Piazza Santa Maria.

Cattedrale di San Martino
CHURCH

(www.museocattedralelucca.it, in Italian; Piazza San Martino; ☺9.30am-5.45pm Mon-Fri, to 6.45pm Sat, 9am-10.45am & noon-6pm Sun Mar-Oct, 9.30am-4.45pm Mon-Fri, to 6.45pm Sat, 11.20am-11.50am & 1-4.45pm Sun Nov-Feb) The predominantly Romanesque cathedral dates to the 11th century. Its exquisite facade was designed to accommodate the pre-existing campanile, and the reliefs over the left doorway of the portico are believed to be by Nicola Pisano. Inside, there's a magnificent *Last Supper* by Tintoretto.

Chiesa e Battistero dei SS Giovanni e Reparata
CHURCH

The 12th-century interior of this deconsecrated church is a hauntingly atmospheric setting for early-evening opera recitals staged by **Puccini e la sua Lucca** (☎340 810 60 42; www.puccinielasualucca.com; adult/concession €17/12), which are held at 7pm every evening from mid-March to October, and on every evening except Thursday from November to mid-March. Professional singers present a one-hour program of arias and duets dominated by the music of Puccini. Tickets are available from the church between 10am and 6pm.

🛏 Sleeping
B&B Ai Cipressi
B&B €

(☎0583 49 65 71; www.aicipressi.it; Via di Tiglio 126; s €55-79, d €69-99; P☀@☎) Outside Porta Elisa opposite the Sanctuary of Santa Gem-

SAN GIMIGNANO

Dubbed the medieval Manhattan, San Gimignano is a tiny hilltop town deep in the Tuscan countryside. A mecca for day trippers from Florence and Siena, it owes its nickname to the 11th-century towers that soar above its pristine *centro storico* (historic centre). Originally 72 were built as monuments to the town's wealth but only 14 remain. To avoid the worst of the crowds try to visit midweek, preferably in deep winter.

The **tourist office** (☎0577 94 00 08; www.sangimignano.com; Piazza del Duomo 1; ⊙9am-1pm & 3-7pm Mar-Oct, to 1pm & 2-6pm Nov-Feb) is a short walk from Piazza dei Martiri di Montemaggio, the nearest San Gimignano has to a bus terminal. On the southern edge of Piazza del Duomo, the **Palazzo Comunale** (Piazza del Duomo; adult/concession €5/4; ⊙9.30am-7pm Mar-Oct, 10am-5.30pm Nov-Feb) houses San Gimignano's art gallery (the **Pinacoteca**) and tallest tower, the **Torre Grossa**. Climb to the top for some unforgettable views.

Nearby, the Romanesque **basilica** (Piazza del Duomo; adult/child €3.50/1.50; ⊙10am-7pm Mon-Fri, to 5.30pm Sat & 12.30-5.30pm Sun Apr-Oct, 10am-5pm Mon-Sat & 12.30-5pm Sun Nov-Mar), known also as the Collegiata, boasts frescos by Ghirlandaio.

While here, be sure to sample the local wine, vernaccia, while marvelling at the spectacular view from the terrace of the **Museo del Vino** (glasses €3-5; ⊙11.30am-6.30pm), located next to the Rocca (fortress).

Regular buses link San Gimignano with Florence (€6.50, 1¼ hours, 14 daily), travelling via Poggibonsi, and Siena (€5.50, 1¼ hours, hourly).

ma Galgani, this motel-style B&B is perfect for travellers with their own car, as it offers free on-site parking. The modern rooms are clean, comfortable and well set up, with good beds and satellite TV.

Affittacamere Stella   PENSION **€**
(☎0583 31 10 22; www.affittacamerestella.com; Via Pisana Traversa 2; s €45-55, d €60-70; P❄☎) Just outside the Porta Sant'Anna, this well-regarded guest house in an early-20th-century apartment building offers comfortable and attractive rooms with wooden ceilings, a kitchen for guests' use and private parking. No breakfast.

Ostello San Frediano   HOSTEL **€**
(☎0583 46 99 57; www.ostellolucca.it; Via della Cavallerizza 12; dm €19-21, d €58; P@) Comfort and service levels are high at this HI-affiliated hostel. There are 141 rooms, a bar and a restaurant. Breakfast costs €3.

 Eating

La Pecora Nera   TRATTORIA **€€**
(☎0583 46 97 38; Piazza San Francesco 4; mains €9-12; ⊙closed Mon, Tue dinner, Sun lunch) The only Lucchese restaurant recommended by the Slow Food movement, La Pecora Nera also scores brownie points for social responsibility, as its profits go to fund workshops for young people with Down syndrome.

Taddeucci   CAFE **€**
(www.taddeucci.com; Piazza San Michele 34; ⊙8.30am-7.45pm, closed Thu Nov-Mar) This *pasticceria* is where the traditional Lucchesi treat of *buccellato* was created in 1881. A ring-shaped loaf made with flour, sultanas, aniseed seeds and sugar, it's the perfect accompaniment to a mid-morning or -afternoon espresso.

Forno Giusti   BAKERY **€**
(Via San Lucia 20; pizzas & filled focaccias per kg €7-16; ⊙7am-1pm & 4-7.30pm, closed Wed afternoon & all day Sun) The best way to enjoy a Lucchese lunch is to picnic on the walls, particularly if you buy delectable provisions from this excellent bakery.

ⓘ Information

For tourist information, go to one of Lucca's three **tourist offices** (☎0583 355 51 00; www.luccatourist.it; Piazza Napoleone (⊙10am-1pm & 2-6pm Mon-Sat); Piazza Santa Maria (⊙9am-7.30pm Apr-Oct, 9am-12.30pm & 3-6.30pm Nov-Mar); Piazza Verdi (⊙9am-7pm).

ⓘ Getting There & Away

The bus station is near Piazzale Giuseppe Verdi, near Porta Vittorio Emanuele Santa Anna. From the bus station VaiBus buses run to/from Pisa airport (€3, one hour, hourly Monday to Saturday and every two hours Sunday).

Lucca is on the Florence–Pisa–Viareggio train line. Regional trains run to/from Florence (Regional €5.20, 1½ hours, every 30 to 90 minutes) and Pisa (€2.40, 30 minutes, every 30 to 60 minutes).

UMBRIA & LE MARCHE

Dubbed the 'green heart of Italy', the predominantly rural region of Umbria harbours some of Italy's best-preserved historic *borghi* (villages) and many important artistic, religious and architectural treasures. The regional capital, Perugia, provides a convenient base, with Assisi an easy day trip away.

To the east, mountainous Le Marche offers more of the same, its appeal encapsulated in the medieval, fairy-tale centre of Urbino.

Perugia

POP 165,300

With its hilltop medieval centre and international student population, Perugia is Umbria's largest and most cosmopolitan city. There's not a lot to see here, but the presence of the University for Foreigners ensures a buzz that's not always apparent in the region's sleepy hinterland. In July, music fans inundate the city for the prestigious **Umbria Jazz festival** (www.umbriajazz.com).

Perugia has a bloody and lively past. In the Middle Ages, the Baglioni and Oddi families fought for control of the city, while later, as a papal satellite, the city fought with its neighbours. All the while art and culture thrived: painter Perugino and Raphael, his student, both worked here.

The historic centre is on top of the hill, the train station is at the bottom and the regional bus station, Piazza dei Partigiani, is halfway between the two. From Piazza Partigiani there are *scale mobili* (elevators) going up to Piazza Italia, where local buses terminate. From Piazza Italia, pedestrianised Corso Vannucci runs up to Piazza IV Novembre, the city's focal point.

◉ Sights

The **Perugia Città Museo Card** (adult/EU concession €10/6) gives one adult and one child aged under 18 years access to five city museums and is valid for 48 hours.

Piazza IV Novembre   SQUARE
Flanking Piazza IV Novembre, the austere 14th-century **Duomo** (Cathedral; Piazza IV Novembre; ⊘7.30am-12.30pm & 4-7pm) has an unfinished two-tone facade and, inside, an altarpiece by Signorelli and sculptures by Duccio.

In the centre of the piazza, the stolid **Fontana Maggiore** was designed by Fra Bevignate and carved by Nicola and Giovanni Pisano between 1275 and 1278.

Palazzo dei Priori   PALACE
The Palazzo dei Priori houses Perugia's best museums, including the **Galleria Nazionale dell'Umbria** (www.gallerianazionaleumbria.it, in Italian; Corso Vannucci 19; adult/EU concession €6.50/3.25; ⊘9.30am-7.30pm Mon, 8.30am-7.30pm Tue-Sun), whose collection contains works by local heroes Perugino and Pinturicchio among many others. Close to the *palazzo*, the impressive **Nobile Collegio del Cambio** (Exchange Hall; Corso Vannucci 25; adult/concession €4.50/2.60; ⊘9am-12.30pm & 2.30-5.30pm Mon-Sat, 9am-1pm Sun, closed Mon pm Nov–mid-Mar) is home to impressive frescos by Perugino.

⚖ Courses

The **Università per Stranieri** (University for Foreigners; ☎075 574 61; www.unistrapg.it; Piazza Fortebraccio 4) runs hundreds of courses in language, art, history, music and architecture.

🛏 Sleeping

Primavera Mini Hotel PENSION €

(📞 075 572 16 57; www.primeveraminihotel.com; Via
Vincioli 8; s €42-65, d €65-75; ✳@🛜) On the top
floor of a 16th-century *palazzo*, this well-run
two-star *pensione* has eight modern rooms

that are as clean as they are comfortable
(ask for the top-floor room with terrace).
Not all rooms have air-con, and breakfast
costs an extra €3 to €6. It's deservedly popular, so book well ahead.

Perugia

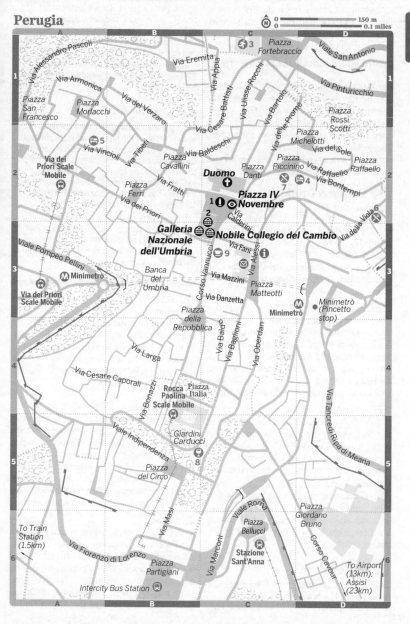

Torre Colombaia
AGRITURISMO €

(☑075 878 73 41; www.torrecolombaia.it; San Biagio delle Valle; per person incl breakfast/half-board €40/60, self-catering apt €90-125) A 15-minute drive southwest from downtown Perugia, this working farm dates back to the 16th century, and guests stay in restored stone hunting lodges. It was the first organic farm in Umbria, and the owners proudly serve meals prepared using their home-grown produce.

Centro Internazionale per la Gioventù
HOSTEL €

(☑075 572 28 80; www.ostello.perugia.it; Via Bontempi 13; dm €15; ☺closed mid-Dec–mid-Jan; @) This is a private hostel with decent four- to six-bed dorms, a frescoed TV room, a kitchen for guests' use and great views from the terrace. The lockout (11am to 3.30pm) and 3.30am curfew are strictly enforced. The price doesn't include breakfast and sheets cost €2.

✗ Eating & Drinking

TOP CHOICE ⟩ Civico 25
WINE BAR €€

(☑075 571 63 76; Via della Viola 25; mains €13.50-14; ☺closed Sun) There's lots to like about this *enoteca* – great jazz on the sound system, friendly staff, delicious food and an excellent range of wine by the glass. The chef creates rustic regional dishes that are full of flavour and extremely well priced. Go.

Pizzeria Mediterranea
PIZZA €

(Piazza Piccinino 11/12; pizzas €4-14; ☺closed Tue) The wood-fired oven in the middle of the dining room is put to excellent use at this busy pizzeria. You can opt for a simple topping or lash out and order delectable *mozzarella di bufala* (fresh buffalo-milk mozzarella) to go on top for a small surcharge.

TOP CHOICE ⟩ Sandri
CAFE €

(Corso Vannucci 32; ☺closed Mon) Sandri has been serving exquisite cakes and the best coffee in town since 1860. Sit at tables on the *corso* or stand at the bar and eye off the decadent cakes, pastries and chocolates on offer.

Punto di Vista
BAR €

(Viale di Indipendenza 2; ☺closed Mon) The term 'stunning view' is bandied around with gay abandon in Tuscany and Umbria, but here it really does apply. Go for a sunset drink.

ℹ Information

City maps are available at the **tourist office** (☑075 573 64 58; www.perugia.umbria2000. it; Piazza Matteotti 18; ☺8.30am-6.30pm). For information about what's on in town, buy a copy of *Viva Perugia* (€0.80) from a local newsstand.

ℹ Getting There & Away

From the intercity bus station on Piazza dei Partigiani, **Sulga** (☑800 09 96 61; www.sulga.it, in Italian) buses depart for Florence (€10.10, two hours, twice weekly), Rome's Tiburtina bus station (€16, 2½ hours, two daily), Fiumicino airport (€23, 3¾ hours, three daily Monday to Saturday, two Sunday), Naples (€25, 4½ hours, two daily) and Assisi (€3.20, 50 minutes, eight daily).

Regional trains connect with Rome (€10.60, 3½ hours, 16 daily) and Florence (€10.55, 2¾ hours, 10 daily).

ℹ Getting Around

From the train station, take the minimetrò (€1) to the Pincetto stop just below Piazza Matteotti, or bus R, TS or TD (€1, €1.50 if purchased on bus) to Piazza Italia. Bus C leaves from outside the UPIM building opposite the station and goes to Piazza Cavallini, near the Duomo. From the intercity bus station on Piazza dei Partigiani, take the free *scala mobila*.

The centre is mostly closed to traffic, so you are best off to park in the free car park at Pian di Massiano and take the minimetrò into the centre. Otherwise, the supervised car park at Piazza Partigiani charges €15 per day.

Assisi

POP 27,600

Seen from afar, the only clue to Assisi's importance is the imposing form of the Basilica di San Francesco jutting over the hillside. Thanks to St Francis, born here in 1182, this quaint medieval town is a major destination for millions of pilgrims.

◉ Sights

Dress rules are applied rigidly at the main religious sights, so no shorts, miniskirts, low-cut dresses or tops. To book guided tours (in English) of the Basilica di San Francesco, telephone its **information office** (☑075 819 00 84; www.sanfrancescoassisi.org; Piazza San Francesco; ☺9am-noon & 2-5pm Mon-Sat) or use the booking form on its website.

Churches
CHURCHES

The **Basilica di San Francesco** (Piazza di San Francesco) comprises two churches. The **upper church** (☺8.30am-6.45pm Easter-Nov, to 5.45pm daily Nov-Easter) was damaged during a severe earthquake in 1997, but has since been restored to its former state. Built between 1230 and 1253 in the Italian Gothic style, it features superb frescos by Giotto and works by Cimabue and Pietro Cavallini.

Downstairs in the dimly lit **lower church** (☺6am-6.45pm Easter-Nov, to 5.45pm Nov-Easter), constructed between 1228 and 1230, you'll find a series of colourful frescos by Simone Martini, Cimabue and Pietro Lorenzetti. The crypt where St Francis is buried is below the church.

The 13th-century **Basilica di Santa Chiara** (☑075 81 22 82; Piazza Santa Chiara; ☺6.30am-noon & 2-7pm Apr-Oct, to 6pm Nov-Mar) contains the remains of St Clare, friend of St Francis and founder of the Order of Poor Clares.

🛏 Sleeping & Eating

You'll need to book ahead during peak times: Easter, August and September, and the Feast of St Francis (3 and 4 October).

Hotel Alexander   HOTEL €€
(☑075 81 61 90; www.hotelalexanderassisi.it; Piazza Chiesa Nuova 6; s €60-80, d €90-120; ❋⊛) Smack-bang in the centre of town, this recently renovated place is a safe choice. There are only nine rooms, but all are clean and well equipped. The roof terrace has great views.

Ostello della Pace   HOSTEL €
(☑075 81 67 67; www.assisihostel.com; Via Valecchie 177; dm €17-19, private room per person €20; ⊛) In a pretty and quiet location between the train station and the Old Town, this family-run HI hostel offers a bar, restaurant, laundry room and bikes for hire.

Trattoria da Erminio   TRATTORIA €
(☑075 81 25 06; www.trattoriadaerminio.it; Via Montecavallo 19; mains €7-11, set menus €16; ☺closed Thu, Feb & first half of Jul) Da Ermino is known for its grilled meats, prepared on a huge fireplace in the main dining area. In summer, tables on the pretty cobbled street are hot property, and no wonder – this is old-fashioned Umbrian dining at its rustic best. You'll find it in the upper town near Piazza Matteotti.

Trattoria Pallotta   TRATTORIA €€
(☑075 81 26 49; Vicolo della Volta Pinta 2; mains €8-16, set menus €16-25; ☺closed Tue) Duck under the frescoed Volta Pinta (Painted Vault) off Piazza del Comune to this brick-vaulted, wood-beamed trattoria. The menu is unapologetically local, featuring homemade *strangozzi* (like tagliatelle), roast pigeon and rabbit stew. There's also an excellent wine list.

ℹ Information

Tourist office (☑075 81 25 34; www.assisi. regioneumbria.eu; Piazza del Comune 22; ☺8am-2pm & 3-6pm Mon-Sat, 10am-1pm Sun) Supplies maps, brochures and practical information.

ℹ Getting There & Away

It is better to travel to Assisi by bus rather than train, as the train station is 4km from Assisi proper, in Santa Maria degli Angeli. Buses arrive at and depart from Piazza Matteotti in the *centro storico*, stopping at Piazza Unita d'Italia below the basilica en route.

Sulga buses connect Assisi with Perugia (€3.20, 50 minutes, eight daily), Rome (€18, three hours, one daily) and Florence (€12.50, 2½ hours, twice weekly).

If you arrive by train, a bus (Linea C, €1, half-hourly) runs between Piazza Matteotti and the station. Regional trains run to Perugia (€2.40, 20 minutes, hourly).

Urbino

POP 15,600

If you visit only one town in Le Marche, make it Urbino. It's difficult to get to, but as you wander its steep, Unesco-protected streets you'll appreciate the effort. Birthplace of Raphael and Bramante and a university town since 1564, it continues to be a bustling centre of culture and learning. In July, it hosts the internationally famous ancient music festival, **Urbino Musica Antica** (www.fima-online.org).

◉ Sights

Interest is centred on Urbino's immaculate hilltop *centro storico*. To get there from the bus terminal on Borgo Mercatale, head up Via Mazzini or take the *ascensore* (lift) up to Via Garibaldi (€0.50).

Palazzo Ducale   PALACE
(Piazza Duca Federico; adult/child €4/free; ☺8.30am-7.15pm Tue-Sun, to 2pm Mon) The town's grand centrepiece is the Renaissance Palazzo Ducale, completed in 1482. Inside, the **Galleria Nazionale delle Marche** features works by Raphael, Paolo Uccello, della Francesca and Verrocchio.

A short walk away is the **Casa Natale di Raffaello** (Via Raffaello 57; admission €3; ☺9am-1pm & 3-7pm Mon-Sat, 10am-1pm Sun), the house where Raphael spent his first 16 years.

🛏 Sleeping & Eating

Albergo Italia
HOTEL €€
(📞0722 27 01; www.albergo-italia-urbino.it; Corso Garibaldi 32; s €48-70, d €75-120; 🏵@) Right in the heart of the walled town, this place has a bland modern interior offset by helpful staff, a pleasant garden terrace and comfortable rooms.

La Trattoria del Leone
TRATTORIA €
(Via Cesare Battisti; mains €10; ☺dinner daily, lunch Sat & Sun) To dine on classic regional food, head to this unassuming trattoria just off the main square. Expect plenty of salamis and cheese, earthy roast meats and full-blooded red wines.

ℹ Information

Tourist offices (📞0722 26 13; www.urbinocul turaturismo.it) Centre (Via Puccinoti 35; ☺9am-7pm); Bus Terminus (☺9am-6pm Mon-Sat) Also useful is www.turismo.pesarourbino.it.

ℹ Getting There & Around

The only way to get to Urbino by public transport is by bus. **Adriabus** (📞800 66 43 32; www. adriabus.eu) runs up to 20 daily buses to Pesaro (€2.75 to €3), from where you can catch a train to Bologna, and two daily services to Rome (€27, 4¼ hours).

Autolinee Ruocco (📞800 90 15 91; www. viaggiruocco.eu) runs a daily bus to Perugia (€15, 1¾ hours), for which it is essential to book in advance.

SOUTHERN ITALY

A sun-bleached land of spectacular coastlines, windswept hills and proud towns, southern Italy is a robust contrast to the genteel north. Its stunning scenery, graphic ruins and fabulous beaches often go hand in hand with urban sprawl and scruffy coastal development, sometimes in the space of a few kilometres.

Yet for all its troubles, *il mezzogiorno* (the midday sun, as southern Italy is known) has much to offer, specifically the fruitful fusion of architectural, artistic and culinary styles that is the legacy of centuries of foreign dominion.

Naples

POP 963,700

A raucous hell-broth of a city, Naples (Napoli) is loud, anarchic, dirty and edgy. Its manic streets and in-your-face energy leave you disoriented, bewildered and hungry for more. Founded by Greek colonists, it became a thriving Roman city and was later the Bourbon capital of the Kingdom of the Two Sicilies. In the 18th century it was one of Europe's great cities, something you'll readily believe as you marvel at its imperious palaces. Many of Naples' finest *palazzi* now house museums and art galleries, the best of which is the Museo Archeologico Nazionale, one of Italy's premier museums and reason enough for a city stopover.

Naples lazes along the waterfront and is divided into *quartieri* (districts). A convenient point of reference is Stazione Centrale, which forms the eastern flank of Piazza Garibaldi, Naples' ugly transport hub. From Piazza Garibaldi, Corso Umberto I skirts the *centro storico,* which is centred on two parallel roads: Via San Biagio dei Librai and its continuation Via Benedetto Croce (together known as Spaccanapoli); and Via dei Tribunali. West of the *centro storico,* Via Toledo, Naples' main shopping strip, leads down to Piazza del Plebiscito. South of here lies the seafront Santa Lucia district; to the west is Chiaia, an upmarket and extremely fashionable area. Above it all, Vomero is a natural balcony with grand views.

◉ Sights

Centro Storico & Around
NEIGHBOURHOOD
If you visit only one museum in southern Italy, make it the **Museo Archeologico Nazionale** (http://museoarcheologiconazionale.cam paniabeniculturali.it, in Italian; Piazza Museo Nazionale 19; adult/EU concession €10/5; ☺9am-7.30pm Wed-Mon), home to one of the world's most important collections of Graeco-Roman antiquities. Many of the exhibits once belonged to the Farnese family, including the colossal *Toro Farnese* (Farnese Bull) and gigantic *Ercole* (Hercules). On the mezzanine floor, *La battaglia di Alessandro contro Dario* (The Battle of Alexander against Darius) is one of many awe-inspiring mosaics from Pompeii.

A short walk south of the museum, Piazza del Gesù Nuovo is flanked by the 16th-century ashlar facade of the **Chiesa del Gesù Nuovo** (☺7am-1pm & 4-7.30pm) and the **Basilica di Santa Chiara** (www.monasterodis antachiara.eu; Via Santa Chiara 49; ☺7.30am-1pm & 4-8pm Mon-Sat). This hulking Gothic complex was restored to its original 14th-century look after being severely damaged by WWII bombing. The main attraction in the basilica complex is the tiled **Chiostro delle Clarisse**

(Nuns' Cloisters; admission €5/3.50; ⏱9.30am-5.30pm Mon-Sat, 10am-2.30pm Sun), adjacent to the main basilica.

Just off Via Benedetto Croce, the **Museo Cappella Sansevero** (www.museosansevero.it; Via de Sanctis 19; adult/concession €7/5; ⏱10am-5.40pm Mon & Wed-Sat, to 1.10pm Sun) reveals a sumptuous baroque interior and the *Cristo velato* (Veiled Christ), Giuseppe Sanmartino's incredibly lifelike depiction of Jesus covered by a veil.

Naples' spiritual heart is the **Duomo** (www.duomodinapoli.com; Via Duomo; ⏱8am-12.30pm & 4.30-7pm Mon-Sat, 8.30am-1pm & 5-7.30pm Sun). Built by the Angevins at the end of the 13th century, it has a 19th-century neo-Gothic facade and a largely baroque interior. Inside, the holy of holies is the 17th-century **Cappella di San Gennaro**, containing the head of St Januarius (the city's patron saint) and two vials of his congealed blood. The saint is said to have saved the city from disasters on various occasions.

At the western end of Via dei Tribunali, **Port' Alba** was one of the city's 17th-century gates.

Chiaia & Santa Lucia NEIGHBOURHOOD
At the bottom of Via Toledo, beyond the glass atrium of the **Galleria Umberto I** shopping arcade, Piazza Trieste e Trento leads onto **Piazza del Plebiscito**, Naples' most ostentatious piazza. Forming one side of the square, the rusty-red **Palazzo Reale** (www.palazzorealenapoli.it; Piazza del Plebiscito I; adult/EU concession €4/2; ⏱9am-7pm Thu-Tue) was the official residence of the Bourbon and Savoy kings and now houses a rich collection of baroque and neoclassical furnishings, statues and paintings.

Overlooking the seafront, **Castel Nuovo** is one of Naples' landmark sites, a hulking 13th-century castle known to locals as the Maschio Angioino (Angevin Keep). Inside, the **Museo Civico** (adult/concession €5/4; ⏱9am-7pm Mon-Sat) displays some interesting 14th- and 15th-century frescos and sculptures.

A second castle, the improbably named **Castel dell'Ovo** (Castle of the Egg; Borgo Marinaro; admission free; ⏱8am-6pm Mon-Sat, to 1pm Sun), originally a Norman castle and then an Angevin fortress, marks the eastern end of the *lungomare* (seaside promenade). The strip of seafront here is known as Borgo Marinaro and is now given over to restaurants and bars.

Vomero NEIGHBOURHOOD
The high point (quite literally) of Neapolitan baroque, the stunning **Certosa di San Martino** is one of Naples' must-see sights. Originally a 14th-century Carthusian monastery, it was given a 17th-century facelift by baroque maestro Cosimo Fanzago, and now houses the **Museo Nazionale di San Martino** (Largo San Martino 5; adult/EU concession €8/4; ⏱8.30am-7.30pm Thu-Tue). Highlights include the main church, the Chiostro Grande (Great Cloister), the 'Images and Memories of Naples' exhibit in the Quarto del Priore (Priors' Quarters), and the Sezione Presepiale, dedicated to rare 18th- and 19th-century *presepi* (nativity scenes).

It's not worth paying the entrance fee to enter the next-door **Castel Sant' Elmo** – its views are the same as those from the Certosa.

The easiest way up to Vomero is to take the Funicolare Centrale (€1.10) from Stazione Cumana di Montesanto, near Via Toledo.

Capodimonte ART MUSEUM
A 30-minute bus ride from the city centre, Capodimonte is worth a day of anyone's time. The colossal 18th-century Palazzo Reale di Capodimonte houses one of southern Italy's top fine-art museums, and the 130-hectare park is a top picnic spot.

The **Museo di Capodimonte** (Parco di Capodimonte; adult/child €10/5; ⏱8.30am-7.30pm Thu-Tue) is spread over three floors and 160 rooms. You'll never see everything, but a morning should be enough for an abridged tour. With works by Bellini, Botticelli, Titian and Andy Warhol, there's no shortage of talking points, but the piece that many come to see is Caravaggio's striking *Flagellazione* (Flagellation).

Take bus 110, M4 or M5 from Stazione Centrale to get here.

✦ Festivals & Events
The **Festa di San Gennaro** honours the city's patron saint and is held three times a year (first Sunday in May, 19 September and 16 December). Thousands pack into the Duomo to witness the saint's blood liquefy, a miracle said to save the city from potential disasters.

🛏 Sleeping
You'll have no problem finding somewhere to stay, though be warned that many places suffer from street noise, and double-glazing isn't common. Most of the budget

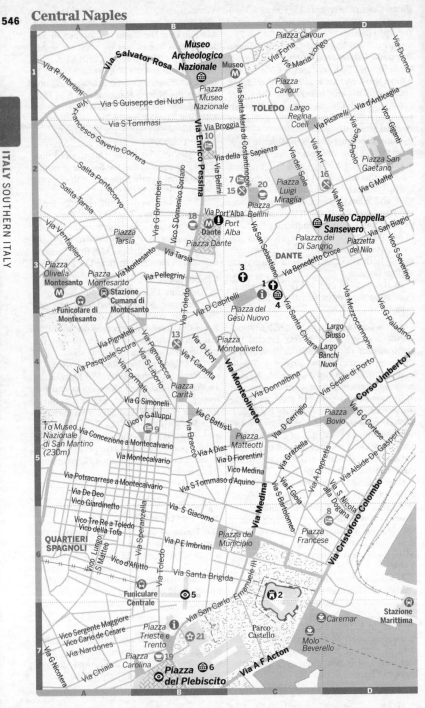

ITALY SOUTHERN ITALY

Museo Archeologico Nazionale

Via Salvator Rosa

Via R Imbriani

Via S Guiseppe dei Nudi

Via S Tommasi

Via Francesco Saverio Correra

Salita Pontecorvo

Salita Tarsia

Via Ventaglieri

Piazza Olivella Montesanto

Piazza Montesanto

Funicolare di Montesanto

Stazione Cumana di Montesanto

Piazza Tarsia

Via G Brombeis

Vico S Domenico Soriano

Via Enrico Pessina

Piazza Museo Nazionale

Museo

Via Santa Maria di Costantinopoli

Via Broggia

Via Bellini

Via della Sapienza

Piazza Cavour

Via Foria

Via S Maria Longo

TOLEDO

Largo Regina Coeli

Via Pisanelli

Via d'Anticaglia

Vico Giganti

Via Duomo

Piazza Cavour

10

7
15

20

Piazza Luigi Miraglia

16

Via del Sole

Via Atri

Via San Paolo

Piazza San Gaetano

Via G Maffei

Via Nilo

Via Port'Alba

Piazza Bellini

Port'Alba

18
Dante

Piazza Dante

Via Tarsia

Via Pellegrini

Via Montesanto

Piazza Montesanto

Via Toledo

13

Via Pignatelli

Via Pasquale Scura

Via Pignasecca

Via S Liborio

Via D Lloy

Via T Caravita

Via D Capitelli

San Sebastiano

Via Benedetto Croce

DANTE

Museo Cappella Sansevero

Palazzo dei Di Sangrio

Piazzetta del Nilo

Via San Biagio

Vico S Severino

3

1
4

Piazza del Gesù Nuovo

Piazza Monteoliveto

Via Santa Chiara

Largo Giusso

Largo Banchi Nuovi

Via Mezzocannone

Via G Paladino

Via Monteoliveto

Via Donnalbina

Via Sedile di Porto

Corso Umberto I

Piazza Carità

Via G Simonelli

Vico P Galluppi

9

To Museo Nazionale di San Martino (230m)

Via Concezione a Montecalvario

Via Montecalvario

Via C Battisti

Via Bracco

Via A Diaz

Piazza Matteotti

Via D Fiorentini

Piazza Bovio

Via G C Cortese

Via D Cerriglio

Piazza Graziella

Via D Depretis

Via Alside De Gasperi

8

Via Potracarrese a Montecalvario

Via De Deo
Vico Giardinetto

Vico Tre Re a Toledo
Vico della Tofa

Via S Tommaso d'Aquino

Vico Medina

Via S Giacomo

Via P E Imbriani

QUARTIERI SPAGNOLI

Vico d'Aflitto

Via Toledo

Via Santa Brigida

Via Speranzella

Via F Gioia

Via S Bartolomeo

Via Medina

Piazza del Municipio

Via S Nicola alla Dogana

Piazza Francese

Via Cristoforo Colombo

Funiculare Centrale

Vico Sergente Maggiore
Vico Cario de Cesare

Via Nardones

Via G Nicotera

Via Chiaia

5

Piazza Trieste e Trento

21

Piazza Carolina

19

Piazza del Plebiscito

6

2

Parco Castello

Caremar

Molo Beverello

Stazione Marittima

Via A F Acton

Via San Carlo Emanuele III

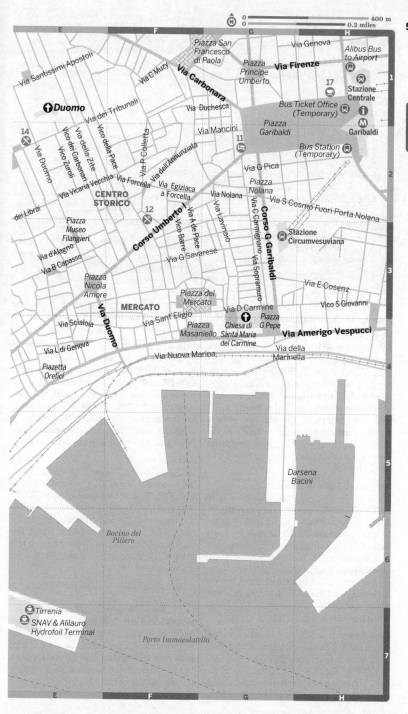

Central Naples

accommodation is in the ugly area around Stazione Centrale and down near the port.

TOP CHOICE Hostel of the Sun
HOSTEL €

(☑081 420 63 93; www.hostelnapoli.com; 7th fl, Via Melisurgo 15; dm €16-20,d without bathroom €50-60, d €60-70; ❋@☎) This award-winning hostel has the lot – great facilities, helpful staff, free tea and coffee, a shared kitchen for guests' use and a breezy, inclusive vibe. Adding to the atmosphere is a vibrant colour scheme that extends to the dorms and hotel-quality private rooms on the 5th floor. Just make sure you have €0.05 for the lift.

Art Resort Galleria Umberto
BOUTIQUE HOTEL €€

(☑081 497 62 81; www.artresortgalleriaumberto. it; 4th fl, Galleria Umberto I 83, Via Toledo, Quartieri Spagnoli; s €110-156, d €140-193; ❋@☎) For a taste of Neapolitan glitz and grandeur, book into this gorgeous boutique hotel secreted on an upper floor of the magnificent Galleria Umberto I. The quiet rooms are lavishly appointed, and the price includes a delicious buffet breakfast and evening *aperitivo*. You'll need €0.10 for the lift.

Constantinopoli 104
BOUTIQUE HOTEL €€€

(☑081 557 10 35; www.constantinopoli104.com; Via Santa Maria di Costantinopoli 104; s/d €170/220; P❋@☎⊛) Set in a neoclassical villa in the city's bohemian heartland, this quiet and elegant place is an excellent choice. The front

terrace, lush garden and small swimming pool are wonderful places to relax after a day spent pounding the pavements.

UNA Napoli
BUSINESS HOTEL €€

(☑081 563 69 01; www.unahotels.it/en/una_hotel_napoli/napoli_hotels.htm; Piazza Garibaldi 10; r €105-148; ❋@☎) A convenient location opposite the train station and excellent online specials mean that it's well worth considering this recently renovated hotel. Rooms are blessedly quiet due to double-glazed windows and have every amenity you will need.

I Fiori di Napoli
B&B €

(☑081 1957 70 83; www.ifioridinapoli.it; 3rd fl, Via Francesco Girardi 92; s with/without bathroom €40/35, d with/without bathroom €80/60; ❋@☎) This sprawling apartment is run by a friendly multilingual crew who go to a lot of trouble to make guests feel at home. The rooms with bathroom also have air-con and satellite TV, and there's a shared kitchen for guests' use. No lift.

La Locanda dell'Arte & Victoria House
B&B €

(☑081 564 46 40; www.bbnapoli.org; Via E Pessina 66; s €45-55, d €60-70; ❋@☎) Spread over two floors in a grand but crumbling *palazzo* near Piazza Dante, the large rooms here have high ceilings, satellite TV and a simple but attractive decor. Excellent value, but remember €0.10 for the lift.

Eating

Neapolitans are justifiably proud of their food. The pizza was created here – there are any number of toppings but locals favour margherita (tomato, mozzarella and basil) or marinara (tomato, garlic, oregano and olive oil), cooked in a wood-fired oven. Pizzerias serving the 'real thing' have a sign on their door – *la vera pizza napoletana* (the real Neapolitan pizza).

For something sweet try a *sfogliatella* (a flaky pastry filled with sweet orange-flavoured ricotta, and ideally served warm).

Pizza

Pizzeria Sorbillo   PIZZA €
(Via dei Tribunali 32; pizzas from €4; ⊙Mon-Sat) The smartest of the Via dei Tribunali pizzerias, the Sorbillo is hugely popular. So much so that eating here is much like sitting down to a meal in rush hour. The hardworking *pizzaioli* (pizza makers) really know their craft – the pizzas are delicious.

Da Michele   PIZZA €
(www.damichele.net; Via Cesare Sersale 1/3; pizzas €4-5; ⊙10am-11pm Mon-Sat) The godfather of Neapolitan pizzerias (it opened in 1870), this place near Piazza Garibaldi takes the no-frills ethos to its extremes. It's dingy, old-fashioned and serves only two types of pizza – margherita and marinara.

Il Pizzaiolo del Presidente   PIZZA €
(Via dei Tribunali 120/121; pizzas from €4; ⊙closed Sun) This is where British uberchef Heston Blumenthal came when he was researching pizza for his TV series *In Search of Perfection,* and for good reason. Be prepared for crowds and service with attitude.

Not Pizza

La Stanza del Gusto   WINE BAR €€
(☑081 40 15 78; www.lastanzadelgusto.com, in Italian; Via Santa Maria di Costantinopoli 100; set menus €35-65, pastas/antipasto platters €14/22; ⊙10.30am-midnight, closed Sun & Mon dinner) Gourmet set menus are served in the upstairs dining room, but the downstairs *enoteca* is more relaxed. We highly recommend the antipasto platters and a thorough investigation of the impressive wine list.

Da Dora   SEAFOOD €€€
(☑081 68 05 19; Via Ferdinando Palasciano 30, Chiaia; mains €12-22; ⊙dinner Mon-Sat, lunch Tue-Sat) This Neapolitan institution is known throughout the city for its fresh seafood. The old-fashioned interior is charming, as are the somewhat elderly waiters and the sing-ing chef. Don't miss the seafood antipasto or Dora's famous linguine, made with lobster, squid, clams and prawns.

Fantasia Gelati   GELATERIA €
(Via Toledo 381; cones from €2; ⊙7.30am-midnight) It claims to be the '*maesti gelatieri in Napoli*' ('master gelato makers in Naples'), and we thoroughly concur. Make your way to this location or the second store in **Vomero** (Piazza Vanvitelli 22; ⊙7.30am-midnight).

Drinking

TOP CHOICE / Caffè Mexico   CAFE
(Piazza Dante 86; ⊙7am-8.30pm Mon-Sat) This retro gem makes the best coffee in the city. The espresso is served *zuccherato* (sweetened), so request it *amaro* if you drink it unadorned. In summer, the *caffè freddo con panna* (iced coffee with cream) is a treat. There's another branch just near Stazione Centrale at Piazza Garibaldi 70.

Gran Caffè Gambrinus   CAFE
(www.caffegambrinus.com; Via Chiaia 1-2; ⊙7am-2am) Naples' most venerable cafe features a showy art nouveau interior and a cast of self-conscious drinkers served by smart, waistcoated waiters. It's great value when you stand at the bar.

Enoteca Belledonne   BAR
(www.enotecabelledonne.com; Vico Belledonne a Chiaia 18; ⊙10am-2pm & 7pm-2am Mon, to 2pm & 4.30pm-2am Tue-Sat, 7pm-2am Sun; ☎) Exposed-brick walls, ambient lighting and bottle-lined shelves set the scene at this much-loved Chiaia wine bar. There's also a tempting grazing menu.

Intra Moenia   CAFE
(www.intramoenia.it, in Italian; Piazza Bellini 70; ⊙10am-2am) Attracting a bohemian crowd, this arty cafe-cum-bookshop is beautifully located on Piazza Bellini. It's a great place to while away a long summer evening with friends and something cool.

Entertainment

You can buy tickets for most sporting and cultural events at **Box Office** (☑081 551 91 88; www.boxofficenapoli.it; Galleria Umberto I 17).

Opera fans will enjoy an evening at **Teatro San Carlo** (☑box office 081 797 23 31; www.teatrosancarlo.it; Via San Carlo 98; box office ⊙10am-7pm Mon-Sat, to 3.30pm Sun; tickets from €25), the oldest opera house in Italy. The opera season runs from December to May and performances of music and ballet are held at other times of the year.

DISCOUNT CARDS

Campania ArteCard (☎800 600 601; www.campaniaartecard.it; €12-30) gives free or discounted admission to museums in Naples and the whole region. Choose the version that suits you best; some include free public transport. The Napoli e Campi Flegrei card is valid for three days, includes free public transport and will give you free entrance to three museums and 50% disount on the entrance charge for 11 others. Available at participating museums, online or through the call centre.

ℹ Information

Dangers & Annoyances

Despite Naples' notoriety as a Mafia hot spot, the city is pretty safe. That said, travellers should be careful about walking alone late at night near Stazione Centrale and Piazza Dante. Petty crime is also widespread – be vigilant for pickpockets and moped bandits, and never leave anything visible in a parked car.

Emergency

Police station (Questura; ☎081 794 11 11; Via Medina 75)

Medical Services

Ospedale Loreto-Mare (Hospital; ☎081 254 27 93; Via Amerigo Vespucci 26) On the waterfront, near the train station.

Tourist Information

There are several **tourist information points** (www.inaples.it) around town: Piazza del Gesù Nuovo (☎081 551 27 01; ⊙9.30am-1.30pm & 2.30-6pm Mon-Sat, 9am-1.30pm Sun); Via Santa Lucia (☎081 240 09 14; ⊙9am-7pm daily); Via San Carlo (☎081 40 23 94; ⊙9.30am-1.30pm & 2.30-6pm Mon-Sat, 9am-1.30pm Sun). All stock *Qui Napoli*, a useful bilingual monthly publication with details of sights, transport, accommodation, and major events.

ℹ Getting There & Away

Air

Capodichino airport (NAP; ☎848 88 87 77; www.gesac.it), 7km northeast of the city centre, is southern Italy's main airport. Flights operate to most Italian cities and up to 30 European destinations, as well as New York. Some 27 airlines serve the airport, including Alitalia, Air One, easyJet, Meridiana, Lufthansa, BMI and Air France.

Boat

A fleet of *traghetti* (ferries), *aliscafi* (hydrofoils) and *navi veloci* (fast ships) connect Naples with Sorrento, the bay islands, the Amalfi Coast, Salerno, Sicily and Sardinia. Hydrofoils leave from Molo Beverello and Mergellina; ferries depart from the Porta di Massa ferry terminal.

Tickets for shorter journeys can be bought at Molo Beverello or Mergellina. For longer journeys try ferry company offices at Porto di Massa or a travel agent. You can also buy online.

Qui Napoli lists timetables for Bay of Naples services. Note, however, that ferry services are pared back in winter and adverse sea conditions may affect sailing schedules.

The major companies servicing Naples:

Ali Lauro (☎081 497 22 38; www.alilauro.it) To/from Sorrento (€10, 35 minutes)

Caremar (☎081 551 38 82; www.caremar.it, in Italian) To/from Capri (€14.50, 1¼ hours)

Metro del Mare (☎199 600 700; www.metro delmare.com) To/from Amalfi (€15, 1½ hours), Positano (€14, 55 minutes), Sorrento (€6.50, 45 minutes) and Salerno (€16, minutes)

NLG (☎081 552 07 63; www.navlib.it, in Italian) To/from Capri (€16, 30 minutes)

Siremar (☎89 21 23; www.siremar.it, in Italian) To/from Lipari (€50, 10½ hours)

SNAV (☎081 428 55 55; www.snav.it, in Italian) To/from Capri (€16, 45 minutes), Palermo (€50, 10 hours)

Tirrenia (☎081 89 21 23; www.tirrenia.com) To/from Palermo (€50, 10 hours) Cagliari (€55, 16¼ hours)

TTT Lines (☎081 580 27 44; www.tttlines.it) To/from Catania (€60, 10½ hours)

Bus

Most buses leave from Piazza Garibaldi. **SITA** (☎199 73 07 49; www.sitabus.it, in Italian) runs buses to Pompeii (€2.40, 40 minutes, hourly), Sorrento (€3.40, one hour 20 minutes, three daily), Positano (€3.40, two hours, three daily), Amalfi (€3.40, two hours, eight daily) and Bari (€20, three hours, one daily). Buy tickets and catch buses from the terminus near Porto di Massa or from the front of Stazione Centrale.

Miccolis (☎081 200 380; www.miccolis-spa. it, in Italian) serves Lecce (€29, 5½ hours) and Brindisi (€26.60, five hours).

Car & Motorcycle

If you value your sanity, skip driving in Naples. If you want to tempt fate, the city is easily accessible from Rome on the A1 *autostrada*. The Naples–Pompeii–Salerno motorway (A3) connects with the coastal road to Sorrento and the Amalfi Coast.

Train

Naples is southern Italy's main rail hub. Most trains stop at Stazione Centrale, which incorporates Stazione Garibaldi. There are up to 30 trains daily to Rome (InterCity €20.50, 2¼ hours) and some 15 to Salerno (InterCity €7, 35 minutes).

The **Circumvesuviana** (☑800 05 39 39; www.vesuviana.it), accessible through Stazione Centrale, operates trains to Sorrento (€3.40, 65 minutes) via Pompeii (€2.40, 35 minutes) and other towns along the coast. There are about 40 trains daily running between 5am and 10.40pm, with reduced services on Sunday.

ⓘ Getting Around

To/From the Airport

By public transport you can either take the regular **ANM** (☑800 639 525; www.anm.it) bus 3S (€1.10, 30 minutes, half-hourly) from Piazza Garibaldi, or the Alibus airport shuttle (€3, 20 minutes, every 20 minutes) from Piazza del Municipio or Stazione Centrale.

Taxi fares are set at €19 to/from the historic centre.

Car & Motorcycle

The public car park outside Castel Nuovo charges €1.50 per hour (€2 for successive hours).

Public Transport

You can travel around Naples by bus, metro and funicular. Journeys are covered by the **Unico Napoli ticket** (www.unicocampania.it), which comes in various forms: the standard ticket, valid for 90 minutes, costs €1.10; a daily pass is €3.10; and a weekend daily ticket is €2.60. Note that these tickets are not valid on the Circumvesuviana line.

Taxi

Taxi fares are set at €10.50 between the historic centre and Piazza Garibaldi and €10 from the centre to the port. There's a €3 surcharge after 10pm (€5.50 on Sunday).

Pompeii

An ancient town frozen in its 2000-year-old death throes, Pompeii was a thriving commercial settlement until Mt Vesuvius erupted on 24 August AD 79, burying it under a layer of *lapilli* (burning fragments of pumice stone) and killing some 2000 people. The Unesco-listed **ruins** (☑081 857 53 47; www.pompeiisites.org; adult/EU concession €11/5.50, audioguide €6.50; ⊙8.30am-7.30pm Apr-Oct, to 5pm Nov-Mar, last entry 1½ hr before closing) provide a remarkable model of a working

Roman city, complete with temples, a forum, an amphitheatre, apartments, a shopping district and a brothel. Dotted around the 44-hectare site are a number of creepy body casts, made in the late 19th century by pouring plaster into the hollows left by disintegrated bodies. They are so lifelike you can still see clothing folds, hair – even the expressions of terror on their faces.

There is a **tourist office** (☑081 536 32 93; www.pompeiiturismo.it; Piazza Porta Marina Inferiore 12; ⊙8am-6pm Mon-Sat, 8.30am-2pm Sun Aug & Sep, 8.30am-3.30pm Mon-Fri, 8.30am-2pm Sat Oct-Jul) just outside the excavations at Porta Marina.

The easiest way to get to Pompeii is by the Ferrovia Circumvesuviana from Naples (€2.40, 35 minutes, half-hourly) or Sorrento (€1.90, 30 minutes, half-hourly). Get off at Pompeii Scavi-Villa dei Misteri; the Porta Marina entrance is nearby.

Capri

POP 7330

The most visited of Naples' Bay islands, Capri is far more interesting than a quick day trip would suggest. Get beyond the glamorous veneer of chichi piazzas and designer boutiques and you'll discover an island of rugged seascapes, desolate Roman ruins and a surprisingly unspoiled rural inland.

Capri's fame dates to Roman times, when Emperor Augustus made it his private playground and Tiberius retired there in AD 27. Its modern incarnation as a tourist destination dates to the early 20th century when it was invaded by an army of European artists, writers and Russian revolutionaries, drawn as much by the beauty of the local boys as the thrilling landscape.

The island is easily reached from Naples and Sorrento. Hydrofoils and ferries dock at Marina Grande, from where it's a short funicular ride up to Capri, the main town. A further bus ride takes you up to Anacapri.

For the best views on the island, take the **seggiovia** (chairlift; one-way/return €7/9; ⊙9.30am-5pm Mar-Oct, 10.30am-3pm Nov-Feb) up from Piazza Vittoria to the summit of **Mt Solaro** (589m), Capri's highest point.

◉ Sights & Activities

Grotta Azzurra   CAVE
(Blue Grotto; admission €4; ⊙9am-3pm) Capri's single most famous attraction is the Blue Grotto, a stunning sea cave illuminated by

an other-worldly blue light. The best time to visit is in the morning. Boats leave from Marina Grande and the return trip costs €19.50 (€12 for the trip and €7.50 for the row boat into the grotto) plus the entrance fee to the grotto; allow a good hour. You can also take a bus from Viale Tommaso de Tommaso in Anacapri (15 minutes) or walk along Viale Tommaso de Tommaso, Via Pagliaro and Via Grotta Azzurra (50 minutes). Note that the grotto isn't visitable when seas are rough or tides are high.

Giardini di Augusto   GARDEN
(Gardens of Augustus; admission free; ☺9am-1hr before sunset) Once you've explored Capri Town's dinky whitewashed streets, head over to the Giardini di Augusto for some breathtaking views. From here the magnificent **Via Krupp** zigzags vertiginously down to Marina Piccola.

Villa Jovis   ANCIENT SITE
(admission €2; ☺9am-1hr before sunset) East of Capri Town, an hour-long walk along Via Tiberio, are the ruins of the largest and most sumptuous of the island's 12 Roman villas, once Tiberius' main Capri residence. A short walk away, down Via Tiberio and Via Matermània, is **Arco Naturale**, a huge rock arch formed by the pounding sea.

Villa San Michele   GARDEN
(☏081 837 14 01; Via Axel Munthe; admission €6; ☺9am-6pm May-Sep, to 5pm Oct & Apr, to 3.30pm Nov-Feb, to 4.30pm Mar) Up in Anacapri, Villa San Michele boasts some Roman antiquities and beautiful, panoramic gardens.

🛏 Sleeping

Capri has plenty of top-end hotels but few genuinely budget options. Always book ahead, as hotel space is at a premium during summer and many places close in winter.

Hotel La Tosca   PENSION €€
(☏081 837 09 89; www.latoscahotel.com; Via Dalmazio Birago 5; s €48-95, d €75-150; ☺Apr-Oct; ❄☂) La Tosca is one of the island's top budget hotels. With 10 sparkling white rooms, a central location and a roof terrace with panoramic views, it presses all the right buttons.

Capri Palace   HOTEL €€€
(☏081 978 01 11; www.capripalace.com; Via Capodimonte 2b; s €270-360, d €350-1450; ☺Apr-Nov; ❄@☂☀) This fashionable retreat has a stylish Mediterranean-style decor and is full of contemporary art. Guests rarely leave the hotel grounds, taking full advantage of the huge pool, on-site health spa and top-notch **L'Olivo** restaurant.

Hotel Bussola di Hermes   HOTEL €€
(☏081 838 20 10; www.bussolahermes.com; Trav La Vigna 14; s €50-110, d €60-150; ❄@) A hospitable outpost on a quiet Anacapri lane, the year-round Bussola offers recently revamped rooms, some with private terraces and sea views.

🍴 Eating & Drinking

Be warned that restaurants on Capri are overpriced and underwhelming. The major exception to this rule (second part only) is L'Olivo restaurant at the Capri Palace Hotel, which is the proud possessor of two Michelin stars.

Da Tonino   RESTAURANT €€€
(☏081 837 67 18; Via Dentecale 12; mains €22-26; ☺closed Wed & Jan-Mar) A tranquil setting and traditional Campanian dishes await at this popular place near Piazzetta della Noci. The menu is dominated by seafood – try the grilled calamari or the salt-and-pepper prawns – and there are delicious lemon profiteroles on offer for dessert.

Le Grottelle   TRATTORIA €€
(☏081 837 57 19; Via Arco Naturale 13; mains €15-22; ☺closed mid-Nov–Mar & Wed Sep-Jul) The simple food plays second fiddle to the atmospheric dining areas at Le Grottelle – one in a cave and the other on a terrace with amazing panoramic views. Chat with the waiter about what's fresh from the sea and don't miss the *torta caprese* for dessert.

Pulalli Wine Bar   WINE BAR €€
(Piazza Umberto I, 4; ☺closed Tue & Nov-Mar) A ritzy spot for a glass of local *limoncello* (lemon liqueur), Pulalli is perched in the clock tower overlooking 'la Piazzetta', Capri Town's main square. For a grandstand view of the action, snaffle a table on the small terrace. For a good cup of coffee, head to next-door **Piccolo Bar** (Piazza Umberto I, 5; ☺5am-1.30am).

R Buonocore   GELATERIA €
(35 Via Vittorio Emanuele; medium cone €3) Come here for the best gelato in town. You'll find it near the corner of Via Carlo Serena.

ℹ Information

Information is available online at www.capri.it, www.capritourism.com or from one of the three **tourist offices** (Anacapri ☏081 837 15 24; Via

G Orlandi 59; ☻9am-3pm Mon-Sat; Capri Town ☑081 837 06 86; Piazza Umberto I; ☻8.30am-8.30pm Mon-Sat, 9am-3pm Sun Apr-Sep, 9am-1pm & 3.30-6.45pm Mon-Sat Nov-Mar; Marina Grande ☑081 837 06 34; ☻9am-1pm & 3.30-6.45pm Mon-Sat). The offices open occasionally on Sundays in summer between 9am and 3pm.

❶ Getting There & Around

There are year-round hydrofoils and ferries to Capri from Naples and Sorrento. Timetables and fare details are available online at www.capritourism.com; look under 'Shipping timetable'. In Naples, sailing times are published in *Qui Napoli;* in Sorrento you can get timetables from the tourist office (see p554).

From Naples, ferries depart from Porto di Massa and hydrofoils from Molo Beverello and Mergellina. Tickets cost €16 (hydrofoil), €14.50 (fast ferry) and €9.60 (ferry) – see p550 for further details.

From Sorrento, there are more than 25 sailings a day (less in winter). You'll pay €14 for the 20-minute hydrofoil crossing, €9.80 for the 25-minute fast ferry trip.

In summer, hydrofoils and ferries connect Capri with Positano (€15.50 to €16.50) and Amalfi (€15 to €17).

On the island, buses run from Capri Town to/from Marina Grande, Anacapri and Marina Piccola. There are also buses from Marina Grande to Anacapri. Single tickets cost €1.40 on all routes, as does the funicular that links Marina Grande with Capri Town in a four-minute trip.

Taxis between Marina Grande and Capri Town cost €16 and can carry up to six people.

A tour around the island by motorboat (stopping for a swim and at the Grotta Azzurra on the way) costs €160 per group. A reputable operator is **Capri Relax** (www.caprirelaxboats.com), which has a small office near the chemist shop at Marina Grande.

Sorrento

POP 16,600

Overlooking the Bay of Naples and Mt Vesuvius, Sorrento is southern Italy's main package holiday resort. Despite this, and despite the lack of a decent beach, it's an appealing place whose laid-back charm defies all attempts to swamp it in souvenir tat. There are few must-see sights but the *centro storico* is lively and the town makes a good jumping-off point for the Amalfi Coast, Pompeii and Capri.

The centre of town is Piazza Tasso, 300m northwest of the Circumvesuviana train and bus station along Corso Italia. From Marina Piccola, where ferries and hydrofoils dock, walk south along Via Marina Piccola then climb the steps to reach the piazza.

◉ Sights & Activities

You'll probably spend most of your time in the *centro storico,* a tight-knit area of narrow streets lined with loud souvenir stores, cafes, churches and restaurants. To the north, the **Villa Comunale park** (admission free; ☻8am-midnight Apr-Sep, to 8pm Nov-Mar) commands grand views over the sea to Mt Vesuvius.

The two main swimming spots are **Marina Piccola** and **Marina Grande**, although neither is especially appealing. Nicer by far is **Bagni Regina Giovanna**, a rocky beach set among the ruins of a Roman villa, 2km west of town. To get there take the SITA bus for Massalubrense.

🛏 Sleeping

Ulisse Deluxe Hostel   HOSTEL €
(☑081 877 47 53; www.ulissedeluxe.com; Via del Mare 22; dm €18-28, d €28-48; ⓟ❄@☎) Masquerading as a three-star hotel, this impeccably run hostel offers smart modern rooms and dorms (all with bathroom), access for travellers with disabilities, an internet point (€5 per hour) and a wellness centre. Breakfast costs an extra €6.

Casa Astarita   B&B €
(☑081 877 49 06; www.casastarita.com; Corso Italia 67; d €70-110; ❄@) The six rooms in this handsome 18th-century building near Piazza Tasso are individually decorated and have all the mod cons you will need.

🍴 Eating & Drinking

Il Buco   RESTAURANT €€€
(☑081 878 23 54; www.ilbucoristorante.it; Il Rampa Marina Piccola 5; mains €35-40; ☻Thu-Tue) Traditional regional specialities are given a modern makeover at Sorrento's best restaurant. Housed in a monks' former wine cellar – hence the name, which means 'the hole' – it well deserves its Michelin star. In summer, seating is outside near one of the city's ancient gates.

L'Antica Trattoria   TRATTORIA €€€
(☑081 807 10 82; www.anticatrattoria.it; Via P Reginaldo 33; set 4-course menu €40-46) Another excellent fine-dining option, this place has been pleasing local palettes since 1930. Choose between the tempting four-course set menus on offer (one from the sea and

another from the land), or opt for a gluten-free or vegetarian version.

Il Fauno CAFE €
(Piazza Tasso 13; ⏱7.30am-9pm) Head to Sorrento's main piazza for the best coffee in town.

❶ Information

Tourist information office (☎081 807 40 33; www.sorrentotourism.com; Via Luigi de Maio 35; ⏱8.45am-6.15pm Mon-Sat, to 12.45 Sun Aug only) In the Circolo dei Forestieri (Foreigners' Club) in front of Marina Piccola.

❶ Getting There & Away

Circumvesuviana trains run half-hourly between Sorrento and Naples (€3.40, 65 minutes) via Pompeii (€1.90). Regular SITA buses leave from the train station for the Amalfi Coast, stopping in Positano (50 minutes) and then Amalfi (1½ hours). Both trips are covered by a 90-minute or greater Unico Costiera travel card.

Sorrento is the main jumping-off point for Capri and ferries/hydrofoils run year-round from Marina Piccola. Get timetables from the tourist office. Tickets cost €14 (hydrofoil) or €9.80 (fast ferry).

Jolly Service and Rent (☎081 877 34 50; www.sorrentorent.com; Via degli Aranci) rents out cars/scooters from €53/32 per day.

Amalfi Coast

Stretching 50km along the southern side of the Sorrentine Peninsula, the Amalfi Coast (Costiera Amalfitana) is a postcard vision of Mediterranean beauty. Against a shimmering blue backdrop, whitewashed villages and terraced lemon groves cling to vertiginous cliffs backed by the craggy Lattari mountains. This Unesco-protected area is one of Italy's top tourist destinations, attracting hundreds of thousands of visitors each year, 70% of them between June and September.

❶ Getting There & Away

There are two main entry points to the Amalfi Coast: Sorrento and Salerno. Regular SITA buses run from Sorrento to Positano (50 minutes) and Amalfi (1½ hours) and from Salerno to Amalfi (1¼ hours). All trips are covered by a 90-minute or greater Unico Costiera travel card.

Between April and September, **Metrò del Mare** runs boats from Naples to Sorrento (€6.50, 45 minutes), Positano (€14, 55 minutes) and Amalfi (€15, 1½ hours). A trip from Amalfi to Positano costs €9; to Sorrento it's €11. **TravelMar** (☎089

81 19 86; www.travelmar.it) runs ferries from Amalfi to Salerno (€6) and Positano (€6) and from Salerno to Positano (€10).

By car, take the SS163 coastal road at Vietri sul Mare.

POSITANO
POP 3970

Approaching Positano by boat, you will be greeted by an unforgettable view of colourful, steeply stacked houses packed onto near-vertical green slopes. In town, the main activities are hanging out on the small beach and browsing the expensive boutiques that are scattered around town.

The **tourist office** (☎089 87 50 67; Via del Saracino 4; ⏱8am-2pm & 3.30-8pm Mon-Sat Apr-Oct, 9am-3pm Mon-Fri Nov-Mar) can provide information on walking in the surrounding hills.

🛏 Sleeping & Eating

TOP CHOICE **Albergo Miramare** HOTEL €€€
(☎089 87 50 02; www.starnet.it/miramare; Via Trara Genoino 29; s €135-150, d €185-250; ⏱Mar-Oct; ❄@�) Every room at this gorgeous hotel has a terrace with sea view, just one of the features that make it a dream holiday destination. Rooms are extremely comfortable, sporting all mod cons, and the common areas include a comfortable lounge and breakfast room with spectacular views.

Villa Flavio Gioia APARTMENT €€
(☎089 87 52 22; www.villaflaviogioia.it; Piazza Flavio Gioia 2; studio apt €139-199, 1-bedroom apt €169-199, 2-bedroom apt €229-310) Eating out is expensive in Positano, so it makes good financial sense to self-cater for some of your stay. Studio-, one- and two-bedroom apartments are available here year-round and come with equipped kitchenette and sea-facing terrace or balcony.

Hostel Brikette HOSTEL €
(☎089 87 58 57; www.brikette.com; Via Marconi 358; dm €22-27, d without bathroom €65-70, d €90-110; ⏱Easter-Nov; @) Near the bus stop on the coastal road, this is one of the very few hostels on the Amalfi Coast. It's decidedly no-frills, with beds in six- to 20-person dorms and modest private rooms, but there's a terrace for drinks and the views are stunning.

Il San Pietro RESTAURANT €€€
(☎089 87 54 55; www.ilsanpietro.it; Via Laurito 2; mains €45-55; ⏱Apr-Oct) Positano's only claim to haute cuisine has fans throughout Europe. Located in the luxe hotel of the same name, it is a perfect spot for a romantic can-

dlelit dinner. The Michelin-starred chef is Belgian, but has well and truly mastered the Italian culinary repertoire.

Da Vincenzo TRATTORIA €€€
(☎089 87 51 28; www.davincenzo.it; Via Pasitea 172-178; mains €18-30; ☺dinner daily, lunch Wed-Mon Apr-Nov) The best of the town's trattorias, Da Vincenzo has been serving *cucina di territorio* (cuisine of the territory) since 1958. It does simple dishes well: the fish is always good and the starter of grilled octopus skewers with fried artichokes is a triumph.

AMALFI
POP 5400

An attractive tangle of souvenir shops, dark alleyways and busy piazzas, Amalfi is the coast's main hub. Large-scale tourism has enriched the town, but it maintains a laid-back, small-town vibe, especially outside of the busy summer months.

Looming over the central piazza is the town's landmark **Duomo** (Piazza del Duomo; admission 10am-5pm €2.50, 7.30am-10am & 5pm-7.30pm free; ☺7.30am-7.30pm), one of the few relics of Amalfi's past as an 11th-century maritime superpower. Between 10am and 5pm, entry is through the adjacent **Chiostro del Paradiso** (Cloisters of Paradise; ☺9am-7.45pm; adult/child €3/1).

Four kilometres west of town, the **Grotta dello Smeraldo** (Emerald Grotto; admission €5; ☺9am-4pm) is the local version of Capri's famous sea cave. One-hour boat trips from Amalfi cost €10 return and operate between 9.20am and 3pm daily.

Get details of these and other activities from the **tourist office** (☎089 87 11 07; www.amalfitouristoffice.it; Corso delle Repubbliche Marinare; ☺9am-1pm & 4-7pm Mon-Fri, to noon Sat).

🛏 Sleeping & Eating

A'Scalinatella Hostel HOSTEL €
(☎089 87 14 92; www.hostelscalinatella.com; Piazza Umberto I 5, Atrani; dm without bathroom €25-30, d €70-90; @) A 10-minute walk from Amalfi, this popular budget operation has four-bed dorms, private rooms and apartments scattered across the village. Extras don't run to frills (this place is really basic) but there's a shared kitchen for guest use.

Hotel Lidomare HOTEL €€
(☎089 87 13 32; www.lidomare.it; Largo Duchi Piccolomini 9; s €55-65, d €103-145; ❇🛜) Housed in a 14th-century building on a petite piazza, the Lidomare is a lovely, family-run hotel. The spacious rooms are full of character,

If you are travelling in Sorrento and along the Amalfi Coast on a SITA bus, it will save money and time to invest in a Unico Costiera travel card, available for durations of 45 minutes (€2.40) 90 minutes (€3.60), 24 hours (€7.20) and 72 hours (€18). The 24-hour and 72-hour tickets also cover one trip on the city sightseeing bus that travels between Amalfi and Ravello and Amalfi and Maiori. Buy the cards from bars, *tabacchi* and SITA or Circumvesuviana ticket offices.

with majolica tiles and fine old antiques. Some also have Jacuzzis and sea views.

La Caravella RESTAURANT €€€
(☎089 87 10 29; www.ristorantelacaravella.it; Via Matteo Camera 12; mains €45-55; ☺Fri-Wed) The location leaves a lot to be desired, but if you're serious about food this is where you should eat when in Amalfi. Michelin starred, it specialises in seafood and has an amazing wine list.

À Sciulia GELATERIA €
(Via Fra Gerardo Sasso 2; ☺10am-2am Mar–mid-Nov; granitas €3.50) For the best lemon granita on the Amalfi Coast (and that's really saying something), head to this hole in the wall. It's on a set of stairs off Via Lorenzo d'Amalfi – look for benches with lemon-coloured cushions.

Pizzeria Donna Stella PIZZA €
(Salita Rascica 2; pizzas from €6, mains €10; ☺Tue-Sun) It's well worth searching out this back-alley pizzeria as it boasts one of Amalfi's loveliest settings – a delightful summer garden enclosed by jasmine-clad walls. The food is adequate, but nothing to get excited about – pizzas are your best bet.

Matera
POP 60,400

Set atop two rocky gorges, Matera is one of Italy's most remarkable towns. Dotting the ravines are the famous *sassi* (cave dwellings), where up to half the town's population lived until the late 1950s. Ironically, the *sassi* are now Matera's fortune, attracting visitors from all over the world and inspiring Mel Gibson to film *The Passion of the Christ* here.

WORTH A TRIP

RAVELLO

The refined, polished town of Ravello commands some of the finest views on the Amalfi Coast. A hair-raising 7km road trip from Amalfi, it has been home to an impressive array of bohemians including Wagner, DH Lawrence, Virginia Woolf and Gore Vidal. The main attractions are the beautiful gardens at **Villa Cimbrone** and **Villa Ruffolo**. The **tourist office** (☎089 85 70 96; www.ravellotime.it; Via Roma 18bis; ⊙9am-8pm) can provide details on these and Ravello's famous summer festival.

Regular SITA buses run from Amalfi to Ravello (€3.60; 70 minutes).

Sights & Activities

Sassi CAVE DWELLINGS

Within Matera there are two *sassi* areas, **Barisano** and **Caveoso**. With a map you can explore them on your own, although you might find an audioguide (€8) from Viaggi Lionetti (Via XX Settembre 9) helpful. There are also plenty of agencies offering tours.

Inhabited since the Paleolithic age, the *sassi* were brought to public attention with the publication of Carlo Levi's book *Cristo si é fermato a Eboli* (Christ Stopped at Eboli, 1954). His description of children begging for quinine to stave off endemic malaria shamed the authorities into action and about 15,000 people were forcibly relocated in the late 1950s. In 1993 the *sassi* were declared a Unesco World Heritage site.

Accessible from Via Ridola, **Sasso Caveoso** is the older and more evocative of the two *sassi*. Highlights include the **chiese rupestre** (rock churches) of **Santa Maria de Idris** and **Santa Lucia alle Malve** (both admission free; ⊙9.30am-1.30pm & 4-10pm) with their well-preserved 13th-century Byzantine frescos.

To see how people lived in the *sassi*, the **Casa-Grotta di Vico Solitario** (off Via Bruno Buozzi; admission €1.50; ⊙9am-9pm Apr-Sep, 9.30am-5.30pm Nov-Mar) has been set up to show a typical cave house of 40 years ago.

The countryside outside of Matera, the **Murgia Plateau**, is littered with dozens of Palaeolithic caves and monastic developments. It's best explored with a guide.

Tours

Viaggi Lionetti (☎0835 33 40 33; www.viaggilionetti.com; Via XX Settembre 9) and **Ferula Viaggi** (☎0835 33 65 72; www.ferulaviaggi.it; Via Cappelluti 34) offer guided tours of the *sassi* – about €13 per person for a three-hour tour – as well as excursions into Basilicata.

Sleeping

TOP CHOICE **Hotel in Pietra** BOUTIQUE HOTEL €€

(☎0835 34 40 40; www.hotelinpietra.it; Via San Giovanni Vecchio 22; s €70, d €110-150; ❄) Housed in a 13th-century church in the Sasso Barisano, this is a fabulously seductive boutique hotel. Everything about the place charms, from the glowing butter-yellow stone walls and soaring arches to the chic minimalist decor and rocky bathrooms. Unforgettable.

Sassi Hotel HOTEL €

(☎0835 33 10 09; www.hotelsassi.it; Via San Giovanni Vecchio 89; s/d €70/90, ste €105-125; ❄) In the Barisano, this friendly *sasso* hotel has a range of rooms in a rambling 18th-century *palazzo*. No two are identical, but the best are bright and spacious with tasteful, modern furniture, terraces and panoramic views.

Le Monacelle HOSTEL, HOTEL €

(☎0835 34 40 97; www.lemonacelle.it; Via Riscatto 9/10; dm/s/d/tr/q €17.60/65/86/105/135; @📶) A former monastery near the Duomo, Le Monacelle is a value-for-money hostel-cum-hotel. Rooms are housed in the former cells and retain an air of elegant austerity, while the terrace offers unforgettable *sassi* views.

Eating & Drinking

Il Cantuccio TRATTORIA €€

(☎0835 33 20 90; Via delle Beccherie 33; mains €13; ⊙Tue-Sun) Family-run Il Cantuccio is a Slow Food–recommended trattoria serving creative regional fare. Speciality of the house is a lavish, seven-dish antipasto, which includes a deliciously creamy ricotta with fig syrup and a tasty *caponata* (a sweet-and-sour aubergine ratatouille).

19a Buca Winery? WINE BAR, RESTAURANT €€

(Via Lombardi 3; mains €15; ⊙6pm-midnight Tue-Sat, 11am-3pm & 6pm-midnight Sun) A modish lounge bar–restaurant in an ancient water cistern 13m below Piazza Vittorio Veneto. It's a showy place with contemporary glass and metal decor and a creative, modern menu.

Il Terrazzino
TRATTORIA €

(Vico San Giuseppe 7; tourist menus €18, evening pizza menus €6; ⊘closed Tue) Just off Piazza Vittorio Veneto, this teeming trattoria does a roaring trade in filling, no-nonsense pastas and simple meat dishes. Get into the swing of things with a rustic antipasto of olives, salami and cheese.

Idris Dolceria
GELATERIA

(Via Bruno Buozzi 62; cones €1.80) For ice cream, this tiny place in the Sasso Caveoso serves superb homemade gelato.

❶ Information

Get *sassi* maps from the **tourist information kiosk** (Via Ridola; ⊘9am-12.30pm & 3-6pm) near the entrance to Sasso Caveoso. Online information is available at www.aptbasilicata.it and www.sassiweb.it.

❶ Getting There & Away

The best way to reach Matera is by bus. From Rome's Stazione Tiburtina, **Marozzi** (www.marozzivt.it, in Italian) runs three daily buses (€34.50, 4½ to 6½ hours). Matera's bus terminus is north of Piazza Matteotti near the train station.

By train, the **Ferrovie Appulo Lucano** (☑080 572 52 29; www.fal-srl.it) runs hourly services to/from Bari (€4, 1¼ hours).

Bari

POP 320,700

Most people visit Bari, Puglia's capital and southern Italy's second city, to pick up a ferry for Greece. And while no one is pretending that this chaotic port is a major must-see destination, it does have a certain, rough-round-the edges charm. There's a buzzing social scene – thanks to the large student population – and a number of architectural gems in the labyrinthine historic centre.

◉ Sights

Bari Vecchia, the Old Town about 1km north of the train station, is where all the major sights are located.

Basilica di San Nicola
CHURCH

(Piazza San Nicola; ⊘7am-8.30pm Mon-Sat, to 10pm Sun) Bari's single most important sight, the Basilica di San Nicola is the the first great Norman church in the south and a wonderful example of Puglia's distinct Romanesque style. It was originally built to house the bones of St Nicholas (aka Father Christmas) that were stolen from Myra (in modern-day Turkey) by Baresi fishermen in 1087. His remains still lie in the crypt, ensuring a regular flow of Catholic and Greek Orthodox pilgrims.

Cattedrale San Sabino
CHURCH

(Piazza dell'Odegitria; ⊘8am-12.30pm & 4-7.30pm Mon-Sat, 8am-12.30pm & 5-8.30pm Sun) From the basilica it's a short walk to the other impressive Romanesque church. Built in the 11th century, but destroyed and rebuilt a century later, this, not the Basilica di San Nicola, is Bari's main seat of worship.

Castello Svevo
CASTLE

(Swabian Castle; Piazza Frederico II di Svevia; admission €2; ⊘8.30am-7.30pm Thu-Tue) On the edge of Bari Vecchia, the brooding, boxlike Castello Svevo dates to Norman times, although much of the present structure was built by Federico II in the 13th century. It now hosts regular art exhibitions.

🛏 Sleeping & Eating

Hotel Pensione Giulia
PENSION €

(☑080 521 66 30; www.hotelpensionegiulia.it; Via Crisanzio 12; s/d €60/75, without bathroom €50/65; ❄) Situated near the train station, this old-fashioned, family-run *pensione* has basic, plainly furnished rooms and a homey feel. Air con is available in the rooms with bathroom for €10 extra.

Hotel Costa
HOTEL €

(☑080 521 00 06; www.hotelcostabari.com; Via Crisanzio 12; s/d €63/90; ❄) A modest three-star place with dated decor, decent-sized rooms and a friendly owner. Optional breakfast is €7.50 extra.

TOP CHOICE Osteria Al Gambero
SEAFOOD €€

(☑080 521 60 18; Corso Antonio de Tullio; mains €13; ⊘Mon-Sat) The seafood in Bari is superb and this characteristic portside restaurant is a cracking place to try it. Join the tourists, devoted locals and occasional celeb for *cavatelli di frutti di mare* (pasta with seafood) followed by oven-baked *spigola* (sea bass).

❶ Information

There's a useful **tourist information point** (☑080 990 93 41; www.infopointbari.com; Piazza Aldo Moro; ⊘9am-7pm Mon-Sat, 9am-1pm Sun) in front of the train station, and another at the port which opens at 9am and closes according to ferry arrival times.

BRINDISI, GATEWAY TO GREECE

About 115km south of Bari, **Brindisi** has been a gateway to Greece since Roman times. These days various companies operate out of the port, sailing to Corfu, Igoumenitsa, Patra, Kefallonia and Paxos. You can check routes and book tickets at www.traghettigrecia. com.

Brindisi is easily accessible by bus and train from Bari, Lecce, Naples and Rome.

ℹ️ Getting There & Away

Air
Bari is served by **Karol Wojtyla airport** (BRI; ☑080 580 03 58; www.seap-puglia.it), 8km northwest of town in Palese. **Tempesta** (www. autoservizitempesta.it) runs an hourly shuttle bus (€4.15, 30 minutes) between the airport and the train station. Alternatively, take local bus 16 (€0.80, 40 minutes).

Boat
Ferries run from Bari to Greece (Corfu, Igoumenitsa, Patra, Keffallonia), Croatia (Split, Dubrovnik) and Montenegro (Bar). Ferry companies have offices at the port, accessible by bus 20 (€0.80) from the train station. You can also get tickets at **Morfimare Travel Agency** (☑080 578 98 11; Corso Antonio de Tullio 36-40) opposite the port.

Train
Bari is on the main east-coast rail line and there are trains to/from Rome (from €33.50, four to 6½ hours), Brindisi (from €6.80, one hour 20 minutes) and Lecce (from €8.60, 1½ to two hours), as well as many smaller towns in Puglia.

Lecce

POP 94, 800

Lecce's bombastic displays of jaw-dropping baroque architecture are one of southern Italy's highlights. Opulent to the point of excess, the local *barocco leccese* (Lecce baroque) style has earned this urbane city a reputation as the 'Florence of the South'. A lively university town with a vibrant bar scene and a graceful historic centre, Lecce is well worth a stopover.

⊙ Sights

Basilica di Santa Croce   CHURCH
(☑0832 24 19 57; Via Umberto I; ⊙8am-1pm & 4-9pm) The most celebrated example of Lecce's baroque architecture is the eye-popping Basilica di Santa Croce. It took a team of 16th- and 17th-century craftsmen more than 100 years to create the swirling facade that you see today. If you look carefully you can actually see a profile of Giuseppe Zimbalo, the chief architect, carved into the facade to the left of the rose window.

Piazza del Duomo   SQUARE
A short walk from the Basilica, Lecce's showpiece square is yet another orgy of architectural extravagance, much of it down to Giuseppe Zimbalo. He restored the 12th-century **cathedral** (⊙8am-12.30pm & 4-8pm), considered by many to be his masterpiece, and fashioned the 68m-high **bell tower**. Facing the cathedral is the 15th-century **Palazzo Vescovile** (Bishop's Palace) and the 17th-century **Seminario**.

Piazza Sant'Oronzo   SQUARE
Lecce's social and commercial hub, Piazza Sant'Oronzo is built round the remains of a 2nd-century **Roman amphitheatre**. Originally this was the largest in Puglia, with a capacity for 15,000 people, but only the lower half of the grandstand survives.

🛏️ Sleeping

Suite 68   BOUTIQUE B&B **€€**
(☑0832 30 35 06; www.kalekora.it; Via Prato 7-9; s €60-80, d €80-120; ❄️) Decorated with works by local artists, the seven stylish rooms at this city-centre B&B have been designed with immaculate taste. Thoughtful, inventive furniture has been set against sandstone walls and white vaulted ceilings to produce a cool North African feel.

B&B Centro Storico Prestige   B&B **€**
(☑0832 24 33 53; www.bbprestige-lecce.it; Via S Maria del Paradiso 4; s €50-60, d €70-90, apt €65-90; @🛜) A cheerful home away from home, this is a cracking little B&B. The irrepressible Renata ushers guests into her lovingly tended 2nd-floor flat, where sunlight floods into understated white guestrooms. There's also a ground-floor apartment for four people and a pretty rooftop terrace.

Centro Storico   B&B **€**
(☑0832 24 27 27; www.bedandbreakfast.lecce.it; Via Vignes 2/b; d €70-80, ste €90-100; 🅿️❄️🛜) A characterful hideaway on the 2nd floor of a 16th-century *palazzo*. The high-ceilinged rooms are bright and colourful, decked out with parquet, wrought-iron beds and thoughtful extras such as kettles and ironing

boards. Upstairs, there's a sun terrace where evening wine tastings are held.

Also recommended:

Azzurretta B&B   B&B
(☑0832 24 22 11; www.bblecce.it; Via Vignes 2/b; s €31-38, d €56-70; ❄) A smart budget B&B run by the same family as the Centro Storico.

✗ Eating & Drinking

Alle due Corti   RESTAURANT €
(☑0832 24 22 23; www.alleduecorti.com; Corte dei Giugni 1; mains €9; ☺Mon-Sat) This traditional restaurant is a fine place to get to grips with Salento's gastronomic heritage. The menu, written in dialect, features classics such as *la taieddha* (rice, potatoes and mussels) and *pupette alla sucu* (meatballs in tomato sauce).

Vico Patarnello   PIZZA, RESTAURANT €
(Vico Mondo Nuovo 2; pizzas €8; ☺8pm-1.30am Tue-Sun) Follow signs to the Chiesa Greca to find this popular pizzeria-cum-restaurant in the backstreets of the historic centre. With outside seating and a modern interior, it's a lovely spot to munch on pizza or pasta dishes such as *linguine all'astice* (thin pasta ribbons with lobster).

Trattoria Le Zie   TRATTORIA €€
(☑0832 24 51 78; Via Colonello Costadura 19; mains €10; ☺closed Mon & dinner Sun) Also known as 'Cucina Casareccia', this family-run trattoria serves exactly what you hope it will – classic, *nonna*-style cooking. Booking essential.

Of the city's many bars, the **Caffè Letterario** (Via Paladini 48) is a happening spot, and **Caffè Alvino** (Piazza Sant'Oronzo 30; ☺closed Tue) is the best place for the traditional Leccese pastry, *pasticciotto*.

❶ Information

Tourist office (☑0832 24 80 92; Corso Vittorio Emanuele 24; ☺9am-1pm & 4-8pm Mon-Sat Apr-Sep, to 7pm Nov-Mar)
Ufficio Informazioni Duomo (☑0832 52 18 77; www.infolecce.it; Piazza del Duomo 2; ☺9.30am-8pm Mon-Fri, 10am-8pm Sat & Sun) Rents out bikes (per hour/day €3/15) and runs guided tours (per person €7).

❶ Getting There & Away

Lecce is the end of the main southeastern rail line and there are frequent direct trains to/from Brindisi (€2.30, 30 minutes, hourly), Bari (€8.60, 1½ to two hours) and Rome (€62, six hours, seven daily), as well as to points throughout Puglia.

By car, take the SS16 to Bari via Monopoli and Brindisi. For Taranto take the SS7.

SICILY

Everything about the Mediterranean's largest island is extreme – the beauty of the rugged landscape, the robust flavours of the regional cuisine, the relentless summer sun and the all-powerful influence of its criminal underbelly.

Over the centuries, Sicily has seen off a catalogue of foreign invaders, ranging from the Phoenicians and ancient Greeks to the Spanish Bourbons and WWII Allies. All have contributed to the island's cultural landscape, leaving in turn Greek temples, Arab domes, Byzantine mosaics, Norman castles, Angevin churches and baroque facades.

This cultural complexity is complemented by Sicily's volcanic geography. Dominating the east coast, Mt Etna (3329m) is Sicily's most famous volcano, although not its most active; Stromboli usually claims that accolade. All round the island aquamarine seas lap at the craggy coastline, while inland, hilltop towns pepper the timeless countryside.

❶ Getting There & Away

AIR Flights from Italy's mainland cities and a number of European destinations land at Sicily's two main air hubs: Palermo's **Falcone-Borsellino airport** (PMO; www.gesap.it; ☑091 702 01 11) and Catania's **Fontanarossa airport** (CTA; ☑095 723 91 11; www.aeroporo.catania.it). Some carriers to Sicily:

Alitalia (☑06 22 22; www.alitalia.it)
Air One (AP; ☑199 207 080; www.flyairone.it)
easyJet (U2; ☑899 234 589; www.easyjet.com)
Meridiana (IG; ☑89 29 28; www.meridiana.it)
Ryanair (FR; ☑899 678 910; www.ryanair.com)

BOAT Regular car and passenger ferries cross to Sicily (Messina) from Villa San Giovanni in Calabria. The island is also accessible by ferry from Genoa, Livorno, Naples and Cagliari, as well as Malta and Tunisia. The main companies:

Grandi Navi Veloci (☑010 209 45 91; www.gnv.it) To Palermo from Genoa, Civitavecchia, Livorno, Tunis and Malta.

Grimaldi Lines (☑081 49 64 44; www.grimaldi-ferries.com) To Palermo from Tunis and Salerno; to Catania from Genoa, Civitavecchia and Malta; to Trapani from Civitavecchia and Tunis.

SNAV (☑091 601 42 11; www.snav.it) To Palermo from Civitavecchia and Naples.

Tirrenia (☑892 123; www.tirrenia.it) To Palermo from Naples and Cagliari; to Trapani from Cagliari.

Timetables are seasonal, so check with a travel agent or online at www.traghettionline.net. Book well in advance during summer, particularly if you have a car.

For information on ferries going directly to the Aeolian Islands, see p565.

BUS Bus services between Rome and Sicily are operated by **SAIS** (☑800 21 10 20; www.saisau tolinee.it, in Italian), **Interbus** (☑0935 224 60; www.interbus.it, in Italian) & **Segesta** (☑091 616 79 19; www.segesta.it in Italian), departing from Rome's Piazza Tiburtina. There are daily buses to Messina (€41, nine hours), Catania (€46, 11 hours), Palermo (€33, 12 hours) and Syracuse (€47, 12 hours).

TRAIN Direct trains run from Milan, Florence, Rome, Naples and Reggio di Calabria to Palermo and Catania. For further information contact **Trenitalia** (☑89 20 21; www.trenitalia.com).

⊙ Getting Around

Generally the best way to get around Sicily is by bus. Services are pretty good and most towns are covered. Trains tend to be cheaper on the major routes, but once you're off the coast, they can be painfully slow.

Roads are generally good and autostradas connect major cities.

Palermo

POP 659,500

Exploring this chaotic yet compelling city can be exhausting, but once you've acclimatised to the congested and noisy streets you'll be rewarded with some of southern Italy's most imposing architecture, impressive art galleries, vibrant street markets and an array of tempting restaurants and cafes.

Palermo's centre is large but it's quite manageable to get around on foot. The main street is Via Maqueda, which runs parallel to Via Roma, the busy road running north from the train station. Corso Vittorio Emanuele crosses Via Maqueda at a junction known as the Quattro Canti (Four Corners). You'll find

Central Palermo

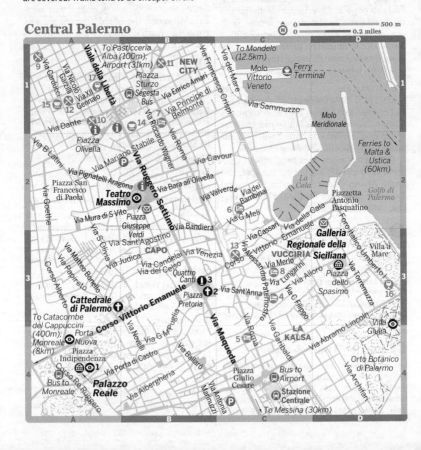

that most sights and hotels are within easy walking distance of this intersection.

◉ Sights

Quattro Canti
LANDMARK

The road junction where Palermo's four central districts converge is a good starting point. Locals call the intersection *Il teatro del sole* (Theatre of the Sun), as each of the baroque facades that surround it is lit up during the course of the day. Nearby, Piazza Pretoria is dominated by the ostentatious **Fontana Pretoria**, whose nude nymphs caused outrage when it was bought from Florence in 1573.

Churches
CHURCHES

Around the corner from Piazza Pretoria, Piazza Bellini is home to three churches: the **Chiesa di Santa Caterina** (admission €2; ⊘9.30am-1pm & 3-7pm Mon-Sat, to 1.30pm Sun Apr-Nov, to 1.30pm daily Dec-Mar), one of the city's most impressive baroque churches; **La Martorana** (Chiesa di Santa Maria dell'Ammiraglio; ☑091 616 1692; donation requested; ⊘8.30am-1pm & 3.30-5.30pm Mon-Sat Nov-Feb, to 1pm & 3.30-7pm Mon-Sat Mar-Oct, to 1pm Sun year-round), Palermo's most famous medieval church; and the red-domed **Chiesa Capitolare di San Cataldo** (admission €1.50; ⊘9am-3.30pm Mon-Fri, to 12.30pm Sat & to 1pm Sun), of interest more for its Arab-Norman exterior than its surprisingly bare interior.

A short walk north up Corso Vittorio Emanuele II brings you to the **Cattedrale di Palermo** (www.cattedrale.palermo.it in Italian; Corso Vittorio Emanuele; admission free; ⊘9.30am-

1.30pm & 2.30-5.30pm Mon-Sat Nov-Feb, to 5.30pm Mon-Sat Mar-Oct, 8am-1.30pm & 4.30-6pm Sun year-round), a visual riot of arches, cupolas, and crenellations. Modified many times over the centuries, it's a stunning example of Sicily's unique Arab-Norman architectural style.

Palazzo Reale
PALACE

(Palazzo dei Normanni; Piazza Indipendenza 1; admission incl Cappella Palatina adult/concession €8.50/6.50; ⊘8.30am-noon & 2-5pm Thu-Sat, Mon & Tue, to 12.30pm Sun) Barely less dramatic than the cathedral is the theatrical seat of the Sicilian parliament. Guided tours lead you to the **Sala di Ruggero II**, the mosaic-decorated bedroom of King Roger II. Downstairs is Palermo's premier tourist attraction, the 12th-century **Cappella Palatina** (Palatine Chapel; ⊘8.15am-5pm Mon-Sat, to 9.45am & 11.15am-12.15pm Sun), a jaw-dropping jewel of Arab-Norman architecture lavishly decorated with exquisite mosaics. Note that if you visit the chapel on a day when the rest of the *palazzo* is closed, the entry price is reduced to adult/concession €7/5.

Galleria Regionale della Siciliana
ART MUSEUM

(Sicilian Regional Gallery; www.regione.sicilia.it/beniculturali/palazzoabatellis; Palazzo Abatellis, Via Alloro 4; adult/concession/child & over 65yr €8/4/free; ⊘9am-12.30pm Tue-Sat) The accolade of 'Palermo's best art gallery' has long been bestowed on the Sicilian Regional Gallery, and it is well deserved. Housed in a gorgeous Catalan-Gothic *palazzo*, it is full of treasures and paintings dating from the Middle Ages to the 18th century.

Central Palermo

Teatro Massimo
THEATRE

(☎091 609 08 31; Piazza Giuseppe Verdi; www.teatromassimo.it, in Italian; tickets €25-125, 25min guided tours adult/concession €5/3; ☻tours 10am-2.30pm Tue-Sun) Supposedly the third-largest 19th-century opera house in Europe after Paris and Vienna, the neoclassical Teatro Massimo took over 20 years to build and, in 1897, opened to celebrate the unification of Italy. The theatre has since become a symbol of the triumph and tragedy of Palermo itself. Appropriately enough, the closing scene of *The Godfather III* was filmed here.

Catacombe dei Cappuccini
CATACOMBS

(Capuchin Catacombs; Piazza Cappuccini 1; admission €3; ☻9am-noon & 3-5.30pm, closed Sun pm Nov-Mar) Southwest of the city centre, these macabre catacombs hold the mummified bodies of some 8000 Palermitans who died between the 17th and 19th centuries. To get here, walk west up Corso Vittorio Emmanuele and Via Cappuccini from Piazza Indipendenza and then north into Via Ippolito Pindemonte.

🛏 Sleeping

If you're on a budget, B&Bs are a better option than the city's motley array of hostels.

Grand Hotel et Des Palmes
HOTEL €€

(☎091 602 81 11; www.grandhoteletdespalmes.it; Via Roma 398; r €115-185; ❂❁) This hotel has been the scene of Palermitan intrigues, double-dealings and liaisons ever since it was built in the late 19th century. The grand Liberty-style salons still impress and the recently renovated rooms offer a high level of comfort and amenity. Check the website for specials.

Al Giardino dell'Allaro
B&B €

(☎091 617 69 04; www.giardinodellalloro.it; Vicolo San Carlo 8, ang Via Alloro 78; s €35-50, d €75-85; ❂❁) Overlooking a tranquil garden in the heart of the Kalsa district, this arty B&B is clean and well maintained. There's a comfortable family suite sleeping four, and five simple doubles, most of which overlook the courtyard.

B&B Panormus
B&B €

(☎091 617 58 26; www.bbpanormus.com; Via Roma 72; s €25-65, d €40-100; ❂) Keen prices, a charming host and attractive rooms decorated in the Liberty style make this one of the city's most popular B&Bs. Each of the five impeccably clean rooms has its own private bathroom down the passageway.

San Francesco
B&B €

(☎091 888 83 91; www.sanfrancescopalermo.it; Via Merlo 30; s €60 d €80-90; ❂) Run by a friendly young couple, the San Francesco has only three rooms but each is atmospheric. The quiet but central location is hard to beat and the breakfast gets rave reviews from guests.

BB22
BOUTIQUE HOTEL €€

(☎335 790 87 33; www.bb22.it; Largo Cavalieri di Malta 22; s €80-100, d €110-160; ❂❁❁) Owner Patty hails from Milan, and has endowed this wonderfully located B&B with a generous allocation of that city's sleek designer style.

🍴 Eating

Like its architecture, Palermo's food is a unique mix of influences. Traditional yet spicy, it marries the island's superb produce – praised by Homer in *The Odyssey* – with recipes imported by the Arab Saracens in the 9th century. The street food is also superb. Two specialities to try are *arancini* (deep-fried rice balls) and cannoli (pastry tubes filled with sweetened ricotta and candied fruit).

TOP CHOICE Piccolo Napoli
SEAFOOD €€€

(☎091 32 04 31; Piazzetta Mulino al Vento 4; mains €20; ☻lunch Mon-Sat, dinner Fri & Sat) Known throughout the city for its spectacularly fresh seafood, delectable olives and excellent house wine, Piccolo Napoli is one destination that serious foodies shouldn't miss. The atmosphere is bustling and the genial owner greets most customers by name – a clear sign that once sampled, the food here exerts a true siren's call. Booking is advised.

Cucina
TRATTORIA €€

(☎091 626 84 16; Via Principe di Villafranca 54; mains €10; ☻closed Sun & 2 weeks Aug) This chic eatery offers a welcome alternative to the battalions of Palermitan restaurants offering identical menus (*involtino,* anyone?). Well-executed modern Italian cuisine is on offer and dishes are light, fresh and flavoursome. The loyal clientele queues for lunch but books for dinner.

Pizzeria Biondo
PIZZA €

(☎091 58 36 62; Via Nicolò Garzilli 27; pizzas €5-12; ☻dinner Thu-Tue, closed Aug–mid-Sep) This long-standing favourite has managed to hold its own against the considerable competition posed by the nearby branch of the excellent Fratelli la Bufala chain. Sit in the simple dining room or claim a table on the street to enjoy your choice of pizza from a huge menu.

Trattoria Il Maestro del Brodo
TRATTORIA €€

(Via Pannieri 7; mains €14; ⏱lunch Tue-Sun, dinner Fri & Sat) A Slow Food–recommended eatery, this no-frills place in the Vucciria offers a sensational antipasto buffet (€5), delicious soups and an array of ultra-fresh seafood.

For an adrenalin-charged food experience, dive into one of Palermo's legendary markets: **Capo** on Via Sant'Agostino, or **Il Ballaró** in the Albergheria quarter, off Via Maqueda. Both are open from 7am to 8pm Monday to Saturday (to 1pm on Wednesday).

 Drinking

Pizzo & Pizzo
WINE BAR €€

(Via XII Gennaio 1-5; ⏱Mon-Sat) Patrons are enticed by an extensive and excellent list of wines by the glass, a buzzing atmosphere and a top-notch array of cheeses, cured meats, foie gras and smoked fish.

Cappello Pasticceria
CAFE

(Via Niccolò Garzilli 10; ⏱7am-9.30pm Thu-Tue) The chocolates and cakes here are true works of art, as beautiful to look at as they are delicious to eat. There's a boudoir-style salon at the back of the shop.

Antico Caffé Spinnato
CAFE

(Via Principe di Belmonte 107-15; ⏱7am-1am) Join Palermo's snappily dressed shoppers for an early-evening drink at this historic cafe. You can sit outside with the pianist or retire to the polished interior to enjoy every imaginable Sicilian drink, ice cream and cake.

Kursaal Kalhesa
CAFE, BAR

(www.kursaalkalhesa.it in Italian; Foro Italico Umberto I 21; ⏱noon-3pm & 6pm-1.30am Tue-Fri, noon-1.30am Sat & Sun) The meeting place of choice for the city's avant-garde, Kursaal Kalhesa occupies a remnant of a handsome early-19th-century palace built into the city walls next to the monumental 16th-century Porta dei Greci e dei Bastioni (Door of the Greeks and Bastions).

 Information
Emergency
Police station (Questura; ☎091 21 01 11; Piazza della Vittoria)

Medical Services
Ospedale Civico (Hospital; ☎091 666 11 11; Via Carmelo Lazzaro)

Tourist information
The **central tourist office** (☎091 605 83 51; www.palermotourism.com; Piazza Castelnuovo 34; ⏱8.30am-2pm & 2.30-6.30pm Mon-Fri) offers a few brochures on Palermo as well as the *Agenda Turismo*, published annually and containing listings for museums, cultural centres, tour guides and transport companies. There are also tourist information points at **Falcone-Borsellino airport** (☎091 59 16 98; in downstairs hall; ⏱8.30am-7.30pm Mon-Sat) and at **Piazza Bellini**, **Piazza Castelnuovo**, **Piazza della Vittoria** and **Via Cavour** (⏱all 9am-1pm & 3-7pm).

 Getting There & Away

National and international flights arrive at **Falcone-Borsellino airport**, 35km west of Palermo. See p584 for details.

The ferry terminal is northeast of the historic centre, off Via Francesco Crispi. Ferries for Cagliari (€51, 14½ hours) and Naples (€50, 10 hours) leave from Molo Vittorio Veneto; for Genoa (€120, 20 hours) from Molo S Lucia. See p584 for further information.

The main intercity bus station is near Via Paolo Balsamo, east of the train station. Sicily's buses are privatised and different routes are serviced by various companies, all of whom have their own ticket offices. Main companies:

Cuffaro (☎091 616 15 10; www.cuffaro.info) To/from Agrigento (€8.10, two hours, nine daily).

Interbus (☎0935 56 51 11; www.interbus.it, in Italian) To/from Syracuse (€13, 3¼ hours, five daily).

SAIS Autolinee (☎091 616 60 28; www.saisautolinee.it, in Italian) To/from Catania (€14.20, 2½ hours, 13 daily).

Regular trains leave from the Stazione Centrale for Messina (€11.55, 3 to 3¾ hours, hourly) via Milazzo (€10.10, 2½ to 3¼ hours), the jumping-off point for the Aeolian Islands. There are also slow services to Catania, Syracuse and Agrigento, as well as to nearby towns such as Cefalù. Long-distance trains go to Reggio di Calabria (€22.40, 5¾ hours, two daily), Naples (€50, 9¼ hours, four daily) and Rome (€61, 11½ hours, seven daily).

 Getting Around
To/From the Airport

A half-hourly bus service run by **Prestia e Comandé** (☎091 58 63 51; www.prestiaecomande.it in Italian) connects the airport with the train station via Piazza Politeama. Tickets for the 50-minute journey cost €5.80 and are available on the bus. There's also the hourly Trinacria Express train service (€5.50, 45 minutes) from Stazione Centrale. A taxi to the airport costs €45 (set fare).

CATTEDRALE DI MONREALE

Just 8km southwest of Palermo, the 12th-century **Cattedrale di Monreale** (Piazza Duomo; admission to cathedral free, north transept & terraces €1.50; ☺cathedral 8am-6pm, north transept 9am-12.30pm & 3.30-5.30pm) is the finest example of Norman architecture in Sicily. The entire 6400-sq-metre ceiling is covered in mosaics depicting 42 Old Testament stories, including the Creation, Adam and Eve, and Noah and his Ark. It's also worth checking out the tranquil **cloisters** (adult/EU concession 18-25yr/EU child & over 65yr €6/3/free; ☺9am-6.30pm Tue-Sun).

To get there, take bus 389 from Piazza Indipendenza in Palermo.

Bus

Walking is the best way to get around Palermo's centre but if you want to take a bus, most stop outside or near the train station. Tickets cost €1.20 (€1.60 on bus) and are valid for 90 minutes. There are two small lines – Gialla and Rossa – that operate in the historic centre.

Aeolian Islands

Rising out of the cobalt-blue seas off Sicily's northeastern coast, the Unesco-protected Aeolian Islands (Isole Eolie) have been seducing visitors since Odysseus' time. With their wild, windswept mountains, hissing volcanoes and rich waters, they form a beautiful outdoor playground, ideal for divers, sun seekers and adrenalin junkies.

Part of a huge volcanic ridge, the seven islands (Lipari, Salina, Vulcano, Stromboli, Alicudi, Filicudi and Panarea) represent the very pinnacle of a 3000m-high outcrop that was formed one million years ago. Lipari is the biggest and busiest of the seven, and the main transport hub. From there you can pick up connections to all the other islands, including Vulcano, famous for its therapeutic mud, and Stromboli, whose permanently active volcano supplies spectacular fire shows.

☉ Sights & Activities

Lipari ISLAND

On Lipari you can explore the volcanic history of the islands at the **Museo Archeologico Eoliano** (adult/child €6/free; ☺9am-1pm & 3-7pm Mon-Sat, 9am-1.30pm Sun) in the Spanish Aragon-built **citadel**. For sunbathing, head to Canneto and the Spiaggia Bianca or to Porticello for Spiaggia Papesca. Snorkelling and diving are popular – contact **Diving Center La Gorgonia** (☎090 981 26 16; www.lagorgoniadiving.it; Salita San Giuseppe; dives from €32) for equipment and guided dives. For tours of the islands, **Da Massimo Dolce Vita Group** (☺090 981 30 86, 333 2986624; www.damassimo.it; Via Maurolico 2) offers various packages, ranging from a €15 tour of Lipari and Vulcano to a €80 summit climb of Stromboli.

Vulcano ISLAND

From Lipari, it's a short boat ride to Vulcano, a malodorous and largely unspoilt island. Most people come here to make the hour-long trek up the **Fossa di Vulcano**, the island's active volcano (€3 for crater entrance), or to wallow in the **Laghetto di Fanghi** mud baths (€2.50 plus €1 for shower).

Stromboli ISLAND

Famous for its spectacular fireworks, Stromboli's **volcano** is the most active in the region, last exploding in February 2007. To make the tough six- to seven-hour ascent to the 920m summit you are legally required to hire a guide. At the top you're rewarded with incredible views of the Sciara del Fuoco (Trail of Fire) and constantly exploding crater. **Magmatrek** (☎090 986 57 68; www.magmatrek.it) organises afternoon climbs for €28 per person (minimum 10 people).

🍴 Sleeping & Eating

Most accommodation is on Lipari. Always try to book ahead, as summer is busy and many places close over winter. Prices fall considerably outside of high season.

LIPARI

Don't immediately dismiss offers by touts at the port – they're often genuine.

Hotel Giardino sul Mare HOTEL €€€
(☎090 981 10 04; www.giardinosulmare.it; Via Maddalena 65; d €80-230; ☺Mar-Nov; ❄❋) This friendly family-run hotel sports chichi decor and a superb clifftop location. The pool terrace, situated on the cliff edge, is fabulous, although if you prefer to swim in the sea there's direct access to a rocky platform below.

Diana Brown PENSION €
(☎090 981 25 84; www.dianabrown.it; Vico Himera 3; s €30-90, d €40-100; ☺year-round; ❋) Down a tiny back lane, Diana has comfortable rooms

decorated in cheerful summery style. Kettles and fridges are provided and the darker downstairs rooms have a small kitchenette. Breakfast (€5) is served on the solarium.

Osteria Mediterranea
TRATTORIA €€

(Corso Vittorio Emanuele; mains €15) Offering excellent value for money, prompt, friendly service and delicious food, this is an excellent choice. Large, juicy olives arrive with the wine, whetting your appetite for the wonderful seafood dishes to follow.

Pescecane
PIZZA €

(Via Vittorio Emanuele 223; pizzas from €4.50) One of a number of pizzerias and trattorias on the main strip, this laid-back place serves excellent wood-fired pizzas and typical island food. There's also a great antipasto buffet.

STROMBOLI

La Locanda del Barbablù

RESTAURANT, B&B €€€

(☑090 98 61 18; www.barbablu.it; Via Vittorio Emanuele 17-19; set menus €38 & €50; ⊘mid-Apr–mid-Oct) One of Stromboli's top restaurants, this place also has six delightfully eccentric rooms (doubles €140 to €240) decorated with period furniture, silk coverlets and antique tiles.

VULCANO

Hotel Les Sables Noirs
HOTEL €€€

(☑090 98 50; www.framonhotels.com; Porto di Ponente; s €95-170, d €150-250; ⊘Apr-Oct; ❉❄) Vulcano's premier hotel sits beachside on the Spiaggia Sabbia Nera. Its large pool is surrounded by gardens and palms, while rooms, many of which have flower-bedecked balconies, are decorated in typical Mediterranean style. The restaurant's panoramic terrace offers sublime sunset views.

Pensione Giara
PENSION €€

(☑090 985 22 29; www.pensionelagiara.it; Via Provinciale 18; d €46-144; ⊘Apr-Oct; ❉) Fronted by lemon trees, this is a cheerful, old-school *pensione* on the road from the port to the volcano. It's a modest affair, with sunny white rooms and a rooftop terrace offering impressive volcano views.

Ritrovo Remigio
BAR €

(Porto di Levante; cannolo €2) Forget the volcanoes, the beaches, the spectacular views. The single most compelling reason to visit Vulcano is to eat a delectable *cannolo* from this otherwise undistinguished bar-gelateria near the port.

SALINA

Hotel Signum
HOTEL €€€ **565**

(☑090 984 42 22; www.hotelsignum.it; Via Scalo 15; d €130-280; ⊘end Mar–Oct; ❉❄) Hidden in the tiny hillside lanes of Malfa, this is Salina's best hotel. Everything about the place is perfect, from the antique-clad rooms to the terrace restaurant, from the fabulous wellness centre – complete with natural spa baths – to the stunning infinity pool looking straight out to smoking Stromboli. Check the website for offers.

❶ Information

The islands' only **tourist office** (☑090 988 00 95; www.aasteolie.191.it, in Italian; Corso Vittorio Emanuele 202; ⊘8.30am-1.30pm & 4.30-7.30pm Mon-Fri, 8.30am-1.30pm Sat & Sun Jul & Aug) is on Lipari.

❶ Getting There & Away

The main departure point for the islands is Milazzo. If arriving in Milazzo by train, you'll need to catch a bus (€0.90) or taxi (€13) to the port, 4km from the station. At the port you'll find ticket offices lined up on Corso dei Mille.

Ustica Lines (☑0923 87 38 13; www.usticalines.it) and **Siremar** (☑892 123; www.siremar.it) run hydrofoils to Vulcano (€14.90, 45 minutes, 17 daily) and on to Lipari (€15.80, one hour). Between June and September departures are almost hourly from 7am to 8pm. There are also direct hydrofoils to Stromboli (€21.45, three hours, eight daily). Siremar also runs ferries to the same destinations. These take up to twice the time and cost about €4 less.

Siremar runs twice-weekly ferries from Naples to Lipari (€50, 10½ hours) and the other islands.

❶ Getting Around

Lipari is the main transport hub, with regular services to Vulcano (ferry/hydrofoil €4.40/5.80, 10/25 minutes), Stromboli (ferry/hydrofoil €12.40/17.80, 1¾/four hours) and the other islands. You can get full timetable information and buy tickets at Lipari's port.

Taormina
POP 11,100

Spectacularly perched on a clifftop terrace, this sophisticated town has a pristine medieval core and grandstand coastal views. Now known as a glitzy resort, it was made famous by Goethe and DH Lawrence, both of whom were former residents. In the 9th century it was Sicily's Byzantine capital.

◉ Sights & Activities

The principal pastime in Taormina is wandering the pretty hilltop streets, browsing the shops and eyeing up fellow holidaymakers.

For a swim you'll need to take the **funivia** (cable car; one-way/return €2/3; ◷9am-8.15pm, to 1am Apr-Sep) down to Taormina's beach, **Lido Mazzarò**, and the tiny **Isola Bella** set in its own picturesque cove.

SAT (☎0942 2 46 53; www.satgroup.it; Corso Umberto I 73) is one of a number of agencies that organises day trips to Mt Etna, as well as tow Syracuse (€45), Palermo and Cefalù (55), and Agrigento (€50).

Teatro Greco   THEATRE
(Via Teatro Greco; adult/concession €6/3; ◷9am-7pm Mar-Aug, to 6.30pm Apr & Sep, to 5pm Oct & Mar, to 4pm Nov-Feb) Take time to visit the stunning Greek theatre. Built in the 3rd century BC and remodelled 400 years later by the Romans, this perfect horseshoe theatre now hosts summer concerts.

Duomo   CHURCH
(◷9am-noon & 4.30-8pm) On Corso Umberto I, the pedestrianised main drag, people congregate around the ornate baroque fountain and Piazza del Duomo. The Norman-Gothic Duomo is on the eastern side of the piazza.

Villa Comunale   GARDEN
(Via Bagnoli Croce; ◷9am-midnight Apr-Sep, to 10pm Nov-Mar) For some great views, head to this immaculate, colourful garden bursting with Mediterranean flora.

🛏 Sleeping & Eating

Hotel Villa Belvedere   HOTEL €€
(☎0942 2 37 91; www.villabelvedere.it; Via Bagnoli Croci 79; s €98-130, d €98-200; ◷end Mar–Nov; ⓟ❋☀) The quiet rooms at this historic hotel are simple yet refined, with cream linens and terracotta floors. Guests adore the luxuriant garden, which has a swimming pool and commands majestic sea views.

Le 4 Fontane   B&B €
(☎347 075 06 24; www.le4fontane.it; Corso Umberto 231; s €40-50, d €60-90; ❋) Run by a friendly couple, this excellent B&B has three spacious, colourful rooms on the top floor of an old *palazzo* (no lift, though). There's a convenient kitchen and it's perfectly located on Taormina's main drag.

Taormina's Odyssey   HOSTEL €
(☎0942 2 45 33; www.taorminaodyssey.com; Via Paternò di Biscari 13; dm/tw from €20/45) Taormina's sole hostel is in a newly con-

structed building just off Corso Umberto I and features two dorms, four private rooms, a communal kitchen and a large terrace. It's open year-round.

La Piazzetta   TRATTORIA €€
(☎094 262 63 17; Via Paladini 5; mains €15-20; ◷closed Mon Nov-Mar) Ask locals for a recommendation and many will reply '*si mangia bene a Piazzetta*' – 'you eat well at La Piazzetta'. A welcoming family-run outfit with tables on a picturesque square, it serves authentic Sicilian food at honest prices.

Tiramisù   PIZZA, TRATTORIA €€
(Via Cappuccini 1, mains €18-24, pizzas from €7; ◷Wed-Mon) Head to this stylish but unpretentious place near Porta Messina for a simple pizza and beer or for something more elaborate. Just make sure you round things off with one of its trademark tiramisus.

Al Duomo   RESTAURANT €€€
(☎094 262 56 56; Vico Ebrei 11; tasting menu €60; ◷Tue-Sun) Right in the heart of the action, Taormina's best restaurant specialises in traditional regional cuisine. Its terrace is a perfect spot for a romantic dinner.

ℹ Information

Tourist office (☎0942 2 32 43; www.gate2 taormina.com; Palazzo Corvaja, Corso Umberto I; ◷8.30am-2pm Mon-Fri & 4-7pm Mon-Thu) Has helpful multilingual staff and plenty of practical information.

ℹ Getting There & Away

Taormina is best reached by bus. From the bus terminus on Via Pirandello, Interbus serves Messina (€3.90, 1½ hours, hourly Monday to Saturday, two on Sunday) and **Etna Trasporti** (☎095 53 27 16; www.etna trasporti.it) connects with Catania airport (€5.60, 1½ hours, six daily Monday to Saturday, four on Sunday).

Taormina's train station is some 2km downhill from the main town, making the train a last resort. If you do arrive this way, catch the Interbus service (€1.50) up to town. They run roughly every 30 to 90 minutes, less often on Sunday.

Mt Etna

The dark silhouette of Mt Etna (3329m) broods ominously over the east coast, more or less halfway between Taormina and Catania. One of Europe's highest and most volatile volcanoes, it erupts frequently, most recently in May 2008, spewing out lava and ash from four summit craters and fissures on the mountain's slopes.

By public transport the best way to get to the mountain is to take the daily AST bus from Catania. This departs from in front of the main train station at 8.30am (returning at 4.30pm; €5.15 return) and drops you at the Rifugio Sapienza (1923m), where you can pick up the **Funivia dell'Etna** (cable car €28.50, cable car, bus & guide €53; ☺9am-4.30pm) to 2500m. From here buses courier you up to the official crater zone (2920m). If you want to walk, allow up to four hours for the round trip.

Gruppo Guide Alpine Etna Sud (☑095 791 47 55; www.etnaguide.com) is one of hundreds of outfits offering guided tours, typically involving 4WD transport and a guided trek. These cost from €45 per person for a half-day tour (usually morning or sunset) and about €60 for a full-day tour.

Armchair excursionists can enjoy Etna views by hopping on a **Ferrovia Circumetnea** train. From Catania it takes two hours to reach Randazzo (www.circumetnea.it; single/ return €4.85/7.80) in the mountain's northern reaches. Further Etna information is available from the **municipal tourist office** (☑095 742 55 73; www.comune.catania.it; Via Vittorio Emanuele II 172; ☺8.15am-7.15pm Mon-Fri, to 12.15pm Sat) in Catania.

If you want to overnight in Catania, **City Lounge B&B** (☑0925 286 17 03; www.city -lounge-bed-and-breakfast.com; Via Gagliani 13; s €35, d €45-65; [P][@]) is an excellent choice. Just five minutes' walk from Piazza del Duomo, it has four thoughtfully decorated guestrooms, a bright communal area and private parking (€5 per night).

Syracuse

POP 124,100

With its gorgeous *centro storico* and gritty ruins, Syracuse (Siracusa) is a baroque beauty with an ancient past. One of Sicily's most visited cities, it was founded in 734 BC by Corinthian settlers and became the dominant Greek city state on the Mediterranean, battling the Carthaginians and Etruscans before falling to the Romans in 212 BC.

If coming by bus, you'll be dropped off at the bus terminal in front of the train station. From here it's about a kilometre walk to Ortygia, the historic centre, where you'll find the best restaurants and hotels – head straight down Corso Umberto. Alternatively, a free shuttle bus connects the station with Piazza Archimede in Ortygia.

◎ Sights

Ortygia   HISTORIC AREA
Connected to the town by bridge, the island of Ortygia is an atmospheric warren of elaborate baroque *palazzi*, lively piazzas and busy trattorias. Just off Via Roma, the 7th-century **cathedral** (Piazza del Duomo; ☺8am-6pm) was built over a pre-existing 5th-century-BC Greek temple, incorporating most of the original columns in its three-aisled structure. Its sumptuous baroque facade was added in the 18th century.

Parco Archeologico della Neapolis
                                              ANCIENT SITE
(Viale Paradiso; adult/concession €8/4, incl Museo Archeologico Paolo Orsi €9; ☺9am-6pm Apr-Sep, to 3pm Mon-Sat, to 1pm Sun Nov-Mar) Syracuse's main attraction is the extensive Parco Archeologico della Neapolis, home to the city's ancient ruins. Hewn out of solid rock, the 5th-century-BC **Greek theatre** is where Aeschylus premiered many of his tragedies. Nearby, the **Orecchio di Dionisio** is an ear-shaped grotto whose perfect acoustics allowed Syracuse's tyrant Dionysius to eavesdrop on his prisoners. On the other side of Via Paradiso, the impressive 2nd-century **Roman amphitheatre** was used for gladiatorial games. The park is a 20-minute walk from the train station.

About 500m east of the archaeological zone, the impressive **Museo Archeologico Paolo Orsi** (Viale Teocrito 66/a; adult/concession €8/4, incl Parco Archeologico della Neapolis €9; ☺9am-6pm daily Apr-Sep, to 3pm Mon-Sat, to 1pm Sun Nov-Mar) houses Sicily's most extensive archaeological collection.

⊨ Sleeping

Alla Giudecca   HOTEL €
(☑0931 2 22 55; www.allagiudecca.it; Via Alagona 52; s €60-75, d €80-120; ✳) Located in Ortygia's old Jewish quarter, this gorgeous hotel boasts 23 suites of various sizes. They all differ slightly but the overall look is rustic chic with brick-tiled floors, exposed wood beams and period antiques, and they all have cooking facilities.

Viaggiatori, Viandanti e Sognatori   B&B €
(☑0931 2 47 81; www.bedandbreakfastsicily.it; Via Roma 156; s €35-50, d €55-65; ✳) Decorated with verve and boasting a prime location in Ortygia, this is Syracuse's best B&B. There's

a lovely bohemian feel, with books and old pieces of antique furniture juxtaposed against silver and purple walls. The same family also runs the more modest **B&B L'Acanto** ([☎]0931 46 11 29; www.bebsicilia.it; Via Roma 15; s €35-50, d €55-65).

Lol Hostel HOSTEL €
([☎]0931 46 50 88; www.lolhostel.com; Via Francesco Crispi 92-96; dm €20-26, d €60-75; [❄][@][☂]) A terrific modern hostel near the train station, with mixed and female-only dorms and sunny, cheerfully furnished private rooms. All have private bathrooms. There's a charge for internet use, but wi-fi is free.

✖ Eating

Solaria Vini & Liquori WINE BAR €
(www.enotecasolaria.com; Via Roma 86; snacks from €5) This wonderful old-school *enoteca* has rows of dark bottles lined up on floor-to-ceiling shelves. Stop by for a glass of wine and a bite to eat – it serves platters of cheese, olives, prosciutto, anchovies and sardines.

La Gazza Ladra TRATTORIA €
([☎]340 060 24 28; Via Cavour 8; mains €12; [☉]Tue-Sun) Hearty, honest fare served in welcoming surroundings at honest prizes. The recipe for success sounds simple but few manage it as well as this friendly, pocket-sized place. Run by a husband-and-wife team, it's recommended by the Slow Food crew.

Jonico-a Rutta 'e Ciauli SEAFOOD €€
([☎]0931 6 55 40; Riviera Dioisio il Grande 194; mains €20, pizzas from €5; [☉]closed Tue) It's a long and not particularly enticing hike to this seafront restaurant, but once you're there you'll appreciate the effort, as the sunny terrace offers cooling sea breezes and dreamy views. Fish features heavily on the menu.

❶ Information

There are two tourist offices: the municipal tourist office ([☎]800 555 000; Via Roma 31; [☉]9am-1pm & 2-5.30pm Mon-Fri, to noon Sat) and the Ortygia tourist office ([☎]0931 46 42 55; Via Maestranza 33; [☉]8am-2pm & 2.30-5.30pm Mon-Fri, to 2pm Sat).

❶ Getting There & Away

In general, buses are quicker and more convenient than trains. Buses use the terminus in front of the train station. Both Interbus and AST ([☎]0931 46 48 20; www.aziendasicilianatrasporti.it) run to/from Catania (€5.70, 1¼ hours, hourly Monday to Saturday, six Sunday) and Palermo (€13, 3¼ hours, two daily Monday to Saturday, three Sunday).

Trains service Taormina (€7.95, two hours, 10 daily), Catania (€6.10, 1¼ hours, 10 daily) and Messina (€9.45, 2¾ hours, eight daily).

Agrigento

POP 59,200

Agrigento enjoys fame and notoriety in equal measure. Fame for its awe-inspiring Greek temples; notoriety for the rampant *abusivismo* (illegal building) that has overrun the medieval hilltop town with highrise tower blocks. Agrigento was founded around 581 BC by Greek settlers and became an important trading centre under the Romans and Byzantines.

Intercity buses arrive on Piazzale Rosselli, where you can catch local bus 1, 2 or 3 to the Valley of the Temples. Up in the main town, the **tourist office** ([☎]800 23 68 37; www.comune.agrigento.it; Piazzale Aldo Moro 1; [☉]8am-2pm Mon-Fri, to 1pm Sat) can provide limited information about the archaeological park.

◉ Sights

Valley of the Temples ARCHAEOLOGICAL SITE
One of the most compelling archaeological sites in southern Europe, this Unesco-listed complex of temples and walls from the ancient city of Akragas was founded here in 581 BC. You'll need a full day to do justice to the **archaeological park** (adult/EU concession €10/free; [☉]8.30am-7pm), divided into eastern and western zones. The most spectacular temples are in the eastern zone. First up is the oldest, the **Tempio di Ercole**, built at the end of the 6th century BC and equivalent in size to the Parthenon. Continuing east, the intact **Tempio della Concordia** was transformed into a Christian church in the 6th century and the **Tempio di Giunone** boasts an impressive sacrificial altar.

Over the road in the western zone, the remains of the 5th-century-BC **Tempio di Giove** suggest just how big the original must have been. In fact, it covered an area of 112m by 56m with 20m-high columns interspersed with *telamoni* (giant male statues), one of which now stands in the Museo Archeologico. Further on, the **Tempio di Castore e Polluce** was partly reconstructed in the 19th century.

North of the temples, on the road up to Agrigento, the **Museo Archeologico** (adult/EU concession €8/free; [☉]9.30am-7pm Tue-Sat, to 1pm Sun & Mon) has a huge collection of well-labelled artefacts.

🛏 Sleeping & Eating

Campeggio Internazionale San Leone
CAMPING GROUND €

(📞0922 41 11 15; www.campingvalledeitempli.com; Viale Emporium 192, San Leone; sites per person/tent/car €7.50/6/3.50; P@🏊) This well-equipped camping ground is on the sea in the small town of San Leone. With a swimming pool, pizzeria and bus shuttle to the temples and nearby beaches, it's got pretty much all you need. Take bus 2 from Agrigento train station.

B&B Atenea 191
B&B €

(📞0922 59 55 94; www.atenea191.com; Via Atenea 191; s €455-60, d €65-85; ❄) A labour of love for the artist owner, the seven rooms at this welcoming B&B are decorated with original paintings and exuberant floral stencils. Two rooms are topped by 18th-century frescos and five have views down to the sea. Breakfast is served on the rooftop patio.

Foresteria Baglio della Luna
HOTEL €€€

(📞0922 51 10 61; www.bagliodellaluna.com; Contrada Maddalusa; s €140-210, d €170-250; P❄) The 13th-century watchtower that guards over this romantic four-star hotel houses its showpiece rooms – all cosy wood-panelling, parquet and antique furniture. Over in the main structure, rooms are less showy and diners flock to the excellent hotel restaurant, Il Déhors.

Trattoria Pizzeria Manhattan
TRATTORIA, PIZZA €

(Salita M Angeli 9; set menus €15-18; ⊙Mon-Sat) Good for straightforward Sicilian cooking, this modest trattoria is halfway up a staircase off Via Ateneo, Agrigento's main street. Help yourself at the antipasto buffet and fill up on spaghetti *alla siciliana* (with tomato, aubergine, basil and salty ricotta). There are two set menus – one with meat, the other with fish.

Café Girasole
CAFE €

(Via Atenea 68-70; ⊙Mon-Sat) You can prop up the bar or sit on the small terrace at this great little wine bar, which is popular with lunching locals and the local *aperitivi* set.

❶ Getting There & Away

For most destinations, the bus is the easiest way to get to and from Agrigento. Cuffaro runs buses to Palermo (€8.10, two hours, nine daily Monday to Saturday, three Sunday) and SAIS services go to Catania and Catania airport (€12.20, three hours, at least 10 daily).

SARDINIA

The Mediterranean's second-largest island, Sardinia is a rugged, beautiful place. Tourist interest is largely focused on the coast, which is one of Italy's most impressive, with stunning sandy beaches, crystalline waters and idyllic coves, but venture inland and you'll discover an altogether different island, an island of untamed nature and proud tradition, of dark granite peaks, dizzying valleys and silent cork forests. Adding a sense of mystery are the 7000 *nuraghi* (circular stone towers), that pepper the landscape, all that's left of Sardinia's mysterious prehistoric past.

Sardinia's top coastal resorts, including the celeb-studded Costa Smeralda (Emerald Coast), are among the most expensive holiday destinations on the Med and get extremely busy in peak season. Visit out of high summer, though, and you'll find that space is not a problem and prices compare very favourably with mainland Italy.

You can get round Sardinia on public transport but you'll discover much more with your own wheels.

❶ Getting There & Away

AIR Flights from Italian and European cities serve Sardinia's three main airports: **Elmas** (CAG; 📞070 211 211; www.sogaer.it) in Cagliari; Alghero's **Fertilia** (AHO; 📞079 93 52 82; www.aeroportodialghero.it); and **Olbia Costa Smeralda** (OLB; 📞0789 56 34 44; www.geasar.it).

BOAT Car and passenger ferries sail year-round from various Italian ports, including Civitavecchia, Genoa, Livorno, Naples and Palermo. Several companies ply these routes and services are at their most frequent between June and September. There are also several summer-only routes from Fiumicino. The major routes and the companies that operate them:

Civitavecchia To/from Olbia (Moby Lines, SNAV, Tirrenia); Cagliari (Tirrenia); Golfo Aranci (Sardinia Ferries).

Genoa To/from Porto Torres (Grandi Navi Veloci, Tirrenia); Olbia (Grandi Navi Veloci, Moby Lines, Tirrenia); Arbatax (Tirrenia).

Livorno To/from Olbia (Moby Lines); Golfo Aranci (Sardinia Ferries).

Naples To/from Cagliari (Tirrenia).

Palermo To/from Cagliari (Tirrenia).

For further details, see listings in individual town entries. Online, you can get up-to-date information and book tickets at www.traghetti online.net.

❶ Getting Around

Getting round Sardinia by public transport is time-consuming, but not impossible. In most cases buses are preferable to trains. The main transport provider, **ARST** (☑800 865 042; www.arst.sardegna.it), operates bus and train services across the island, including the **Trenino Verde** (☑800 460 220; www.treninoverde. com), a tiny tourist train that trundles through Sardinia's most inaccessible countryside.

Cagliari

POP 157,300

Sardinia's capital and most cosmopolitan city, Cagliari rises from the sea in a helter-skelter of golden-hued *palazzi,* domes and facades. Yet for all its splendour, it remains what it always has been – a busy working port with a gritty, down-to-earth atmosphere and a vibrant buzz. With its landmark citadel, great restaurants and popular, sandy beach, Cagliari is very much its own city.

◉ Sights & Activities

Cagliari's sights are concentrated in four central districts: Castello, the medieval citadel that towers over the city; Marina, the bustling seafront area; Stampace, which extends westwards of Largo Carlo Felice, modern Cagliari's showpiece street; and Villanova, east of Castello.

Castello   HISTORIC NEIGHBOURHOOD

Housed in what was once Cagliari's arsenal, the **Citadella dei Musei** is the city's main museum complex. Of its four museums, the most impressive is the **Museo Archeologico Nazionale** (Piazza dell'Arsenale; adult/child €4/2; ◷9am-8pm Tue-Sun), whose fabulous *nuraghi* bronzes provide one of the few clues into the island's mysterious native culture.

Guarding the entrance to the Citadella is the 36m-high **Torre di San Pancrazio** (Piazza Indipendenza; adult/concession €4/2.50; ◷9am-1pm & 3.30-7pm Tue-Sun Apr-Oct, to 4.30pm Tue-Sun Nov-Mar), one of only two existing 14th-century towers.

In the heart of the district stands Cagliari's striking 13th-century cathedral, the **Cattedrale di Santa Maria** (Piazza Palazzo 4; ◷6.30am-noon & 4-8pm Mon-Sat, 8am-1pm & 4.30-8.30pm Sun). Apart from the bell tower, little remains of the original Gothic structure but it's still an impressive sight with its imitation Pisan-Romanesque facade and baroque interior. Inside, note the imposing Romanesque pulpits.

For the best views in the neighbourhood head to the **Bastione San Remy** (Piazza Costituzione), a monumental terrace, formerly a strong point in the defensive walls, which affords huge panoramas over the city and distant lagoons.

Anfiteatro Romano   ROMAN AMPHITHEATRE

(Viale Sant'Ignazio; adult/child €4.30/free; ◷9.30am-1.30pm Tue-Sat, to 1.30pm & 3.30-5.30pm Sun) To the west of the centre, this 2nd-century amphitheatre is the most important Roman monument in Sardinia. During summer, concerts are staged here.

Spiaggia di Poetto   BEACH

A short bus ride from the centre, Cagliari's vibrant beach boasts inviting blue waters and a happening summer bar scene.

✦ Festivals & Events

Cagliari's annual bonanza, the **Festa di Sant'Efisio**, involves four days of costumed processions from 1 May.

🛏 Sleeping

Hotel Miramare   BOUTIQUE HOTEL €€€

(☑070 66 40 21; www.hotelmiramarecagliari.it; Via Roma 59; r €112-280; ❊◉) This boutique four-star place brings a touch of contemporary design to the Sardinian capital. Hidden away in a typical seafront *palazzo*, rooms re-

Cagliari

veal an offbeat look that sets crimson walls and dripping chandeliers against fake zebra-skin chairs and walnut furniture.

Hostel Marina   HOSTEL €
(☎070 450 97 09; www.aighostels.com; Piazza San Sepolcro 3; dm/s/d €22/30/60; 🌐) This crack-

ing HI hostel is in the thick of the Marina district, not a stone's throw from the sea-front. It's housed in a converted 15th-century convent and has spacious, sun-filled single-sex dorms, private rooms, and an internal courtyard.

Cagliari

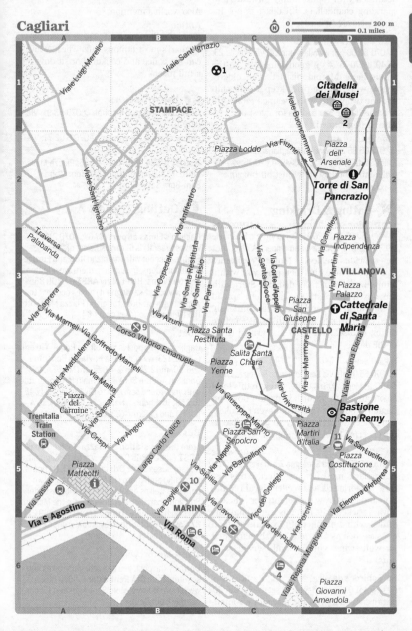

Hotel A&R Bundes Jack PENSION €
([✆] 070 66 79 70; www.hotelbjvittoria.it; Via Roma 75; s €56-58, d €84-88; [❄]) The best budget hotel on the seafront, this is an old-fashioned family-run *pensione*. Run by a garrulous old boy, it has spacious, high-ceilinged rooms decorated with robust family furniture and sparkling chandeliers. Breakfast is not included. No credit cards.

B&B La Marina B&B €
([✆] 070 67 00 65; www.la-marina.it; Via Porcile 23; s €40, d €70-75; [❄]) A good-value B&B in the atmospheric Marina district. The elderly couple who run the place keep a tight ship and the two white, wood-beamed rooms are pristine. There are fridges for guest use.
Also recommended:

Albergo Aurora HOTEL
([✆] 070 65 86 25; www.hotelcagliariaurora.it; Salita Santa Chiara 19; s €43-49, d €70-75; [❄]) A welcoming budget hotel just off buzzing Piazza Yenne.

✕ Eating & Drinking

TOP CHOICE **Monica e Ahmed** SEAFOOD €€
([✆] 070 640 20 45; Corso Vittorio Emanuele 119; mains €14; ⊙closed Sun dinner) A top spot for delicious seafood. Monica welcomes you with a smile and then plies you with a tempting array of fishy delights. Start with the mixed antipasto – a decadent spread of swordfish carpaccio, mussels, cuttlefish, fried calamari and tuna with beans – before diving into seafood pasta and grilled catch of the day.

Il Fantasma PIZZA €
([✆] 070 65 67 49; Via San Domenico 94; pizzas from €6.50; ⊙Mon-Sat) It's quite a trek to this local favourite, but well worth it to chow down on Cagliari's best pizza. If you haven't booked, you'll need to arrive early to get a table in the cheerful, brick-lined interior.

Da Lillicu TRATTORIA €€
([✆] 070 65 29 70; Via Sardegna 78; mains €11) One of Cagliari's most famous eateries, this historic trattoria has an excellent local reputation and its narrow tunnel interior is nearly always packed. The menu is traditional Sardinian with a number of meat and seafood classics such as *burrida* (catfish marinated in white-wine vinegar and served with nuts).

Sa Schironada TRATTORIA €
([✆] 070 451 07 71; Via Baylle 39; set menus €16-30, pizza menus €5-12) Not the place for a romantic dinner, this big, barn-like trattoria is good for a cheap fill-up. There are various menu options but bear in mind that the antipasto spread is a minor meal in itself, with seafood salads, olives, cheese, salamis and stewed snails.

Also worth a mention:

Antico Caffè CAFE €
(Piazza Costituzione; meals €30; ⊙closed Tue) Cagliari's most famous cafe, where you can sip coffee and cocktails or sit down to a full meal.

ⓘ Information

Ospedale Brotzu (Hospital; [✆] 070 53 91; Via Peretti)

Police station (Questura; [✆] 070 6 02 71; Via Amat Luigi 9)

Tourist office ([✆] 070 66 92 55; Piazza Matteotti; ⊙8.30am-1.30pm & 2-8pm Mon-Fri, 8am-8pm Sat & Sun)

ⓘ Getting There & Away

Air

Cagliari's **Elmas airport** (CAG; [✆] 070 211 211; www.sogaer.it) is 6km northwest of the city. Flights connect with mainland Italy and European destinations. In summer, there are additional charter flights. Half-hourly **ARST** ([✆] 800 865 042; www.arst.sardegna.it) buses connect the airport with the bus station on Piazza Matteotti; the 10-minute journey costs €4.

Boat

Cagliari's ferry port is just off Via Roma. **Tirrenia** ([✆] 892 123; www.tirrenia.it; Via dei Ponente 1; ⊙8.30am-12.20pm & 4-6.50pm Mon-Fri, to 6pm Sat, 4-6pm Sun) is the main ferry operator, with year-round services to Civitavecchia (€48 to €58, 16½ hours), Naples (€38 to €44, 16¼ hours) and Palermo (€37 to €44, 14½ hours).

Bus

From the **bus station** on Piazza Matteotti, daily **ARST** ([✆] 800 865 042; www.arst.sardegna.it, in Italian) buses serve Oristano (€6.50, 1½ hours, two daily) and Nuoro (€14.50, 3½ hours, two daily), as well as destinations on the Costa del Sud and Costa Rei. Get tickets from the McDonald's on the square. **Turmo Travel** ([✆] 0789 214 87; www.gruppoturmotravel.com) runs two daily buses to Olbia (€19, 4¼ hours).

Car & Motorcycle

Down by the port, you can rent cars, bikes and scooters from **CIA Rent a Car** ([✆] 070 65 65 03; www.ciarent.it; Via Molo Sant'Agostino 13; car per day from €29).

Train

Trenitalia trains run from the station on Piazza Matteotti to Oristano (€5.95, up to two hours, hourly) and Sassari (€15.75, 4¼ hours, three daily).

Cala Gonone

A popular resort with a small beach and decent accommodation, Cala Gonone makes an excellent base for exploring the spectacular Gulf of Orosei. The coastline, one of Italy's most imperious, is peppered with beaches and sea caves, many of which are only accessible by boat or on foot. Inland, the rugged, difficult terrain is ideal for hikers and climbers.

◉ Sights & Activities

The main activity in Cala Gonone is exploring the coast's coves and caves. You can reach some of these on foot, or by wheeled transport, but the best are only accessible by boat. To hire a boat or join a coastal tour head to the port.

Southern Coast Beaches   BEACHES, CAVES
In town, the small beach **Spiaggia Centrale** is good for a quick dip but the best swimming spots are round the coast. **Cala Fuili**, about 3.5km to the south, is a small, rocky inlet backed by a deep green valley. From here you can hike over the clifftops to the stunning **Cala Luna**, about two hours (4km) away on foot. In between the two is the dazzling **Grotta del Bue Marino** (adult/concession €8/4), a complex of stalactite- and stalagmite-filled caves where monk seals used to pup.

Outdoor Activities   ACTIVITIES
Outdoor activities are big here and there's excellent diving, snorkelling, rock climbing, mountain biking and hiking. There are various agencies that organise activities, including **Prima Sardegna** (☑0784 93 367; www.primasardegna.com; Lungomare Palmasera 32), which also rents out cars (from €78 per day), scooters (€48 per day), mountain bikes (€24 per day) and kayaks (€30 per day). To hire your own boat reckon on €80 to €120 per day for two people plus €25 or so for petrol extra.

☞ Tours

Operating out of the port, the **Nuovo Consorzio Trasporti Marittimi Calagonone** (☑0784 9 33 05; www.calagononecrociere.it) sails to Cala Luna (€12 to €20) and the Grotta del Bue Marino (€16.50 to €19, including Cala Luna €23 to €32) and runs mini-cruises (€26 to €37) along the coast.

Coop Ghivine (☑349 442 55 52; www.ghivine.com; Via Montebello 5) in nearby Dorgali is one of several cooperatives that organise excursions and guided treks, starting at €35 per person.

🛏 Sleeping & Eating

TOP CHOICE **Agriturismo Nuraghe Mannu**
                                    AGRITURISMO €
(☑0784 9 32 64; www.agriturismonuraghemannu.com; off the SP 26 Dorgali-Cala Gonone Rd; per person B&B €26-32, half-board €42-46) Immersed in greenery and with blissful sea views, this is the real McCoy, an authentic working farm with four simple double rooms and five tent pitches (€10 to €12 per person). The superb farmhouse restaurant (meals €25 to €35) features plenty of home-produced cheese, salami, pork and wine. Bookings are essential.

Hotel Su Gologone   HOTEL €€€
(☑0784 28 75 12; www.sugologone.it; s €115-180, r €120-280; P ❋ ☲) About 20km inland from Cala Gonone, this is a fabulous hacienda-style retreat with rustic rooms in a series of whitewashed cottages. Facilities are top notch and the highly rated restaurant specialises in traditional Sardinian cooking, including a delicious *porceddu* (spit-roasted suckling pig).

Hotel Costa Dorada   HOTEL €€
(☑0784 9 33 32; www.hotelcostadorada.it; Lungomare Palmasera 45; per person €54-95; ⊘end Mar–Oct; ❋) The best-looking hotel in town, the flower-clad Costa Dorada offers luxurious sea views and tasteful rooms decorated with local handicrafts. It also has a seafront terrace restaurant (menus €15 to €35) serving fresh seafood and local meat dishes. It's at the southern end of the *lungomare*, just over the road from the beach.

Pop Hotel   HOTEL €€
(☑0784 9 31 85; www.hotelpop.it; d €54-128; ❋) This cheerful year-round hotel is yards from the port. Rooms are spacious and sunny and its roadside restaurant, the **Spaghetteria al Porto**, has a huge menu that includes a number of interesting fusion dishes. There are several set menus, otherwise you're looking at around €25 to €35 for a meal.

Camping Cala Gonone CAMPING GROUND €
(☎0784 9 31 65; www.campingcalagonone.it; sites per person incl car & tent €13-19.50, 2-bed bungalow €48-105; ☻Apr-Oct;⊠) In a pine grove by the entrance to town, this shady camping ground has excellent facilities including a tennis court, bar, barbecue area, pizzeria and swimming pool. Book ahead for August.

Information

Head to the helpful **tourist office** (☎0784 936 96; www.dorgagli.it; Viale Bue Marino 1/a; ☻9am-9pm Jul & Aug, to 1pm & 3-7pm Easter-Jun & Sep-Oct, to noon rest of year) for maps, accommodation lists and contact details for local guides.

Getting There & Away

There are up to six ARST buses a day from Nuoro to Cala Gonone (€3.50, 70 minutes). If travelling by car, you'll need a good road map, such as *Sardegna* published by the Touring Club Italiano.

Alghero

POP 40,900

A picturesque medieval town, Alghero is the main resort on Sardinia's northwest coast. Surprisingly, though, it's not entirely given over to tourism and it is still an important fishing port. Interest is centred on the *centro storico* with its robust stone ramparts and tight-knit lanes.

Alghero was founded in the 11th century by the Genovese and later became an important outpost of the Aragonese Catalans. Still today the local dialect is a form of Catalan, and the town retains something of a Spanish atmosphere.

◉ Sights & Activities

Centro Storico HISTORIC CENTRE
Alghero's medieval core is a charming mesh of narrow cobbled alleys hemmed in by Spanish Gothic *palazzi*. Of the various churches, the most interesting is the **Chiesa di San Francesco** (Via Carlo Alberto; ☻7.30am-noon & 5-8.30pm), with its mix of Romanesque and Gothic styles. A short walk away, the **campanile** (bell tower; admission €2; ☻7pm-9.30pm Tue, Thu & Sat Jul & Aug, 5-8pm Sep, by appointment rest of year) of the Cattedrale di Santa Maria is a fine example of Gothic-Catalan architecture.

Grotte di Nettuno SEA CAVES
(adult/child €12/6; ☻9am-7pm Apr-Sep, to 6pm Oct, to 1pm Nov-Mar, Nov & Dec) From the port

you can take a boat trip along the impressive northern coast to **Capo Caccia** and the grandiose **Grotte di Nettuno** cave complex. The cheapest boat is the **Navisarda ferry** (adult/child return €14/7), which departs hourly between 9am and 5pm from June to September, and three times daily between March and May and in October. Allow 2½ hours for the round trip. Cheaper still, you can get a bus to the caves from Via Catalogna (€3.50 return, 50 minutes, three times daily summer, once winter).

Nuraghe di Palmavera PREHISTORIC RUINS
(admission €3; ☻9am-7pm May-Sep, to 6pm Apr-Oct, 10am-2pm Nov-Mar) Ten kilometres west of Alghero on the road to Porto Conte, this 3500-year-old *nuraghe* village is well worth a visit.

🛏 Sleeping

There's plenty of accommodation in Alghero but you'll need to book between June and September.

Angedras Hotel HOTEL €€
(☎079 973 50 34; www.angedras.it; Via Frank 2; s €53-60, d €75-150; ❋@❅) A model of whitewashed Mediterranean style, the Angedras has cool, airy rooms with big French doors opening on to sunny patios. It's in a quiet residential street within easy walking distance of the historic centre.

Camping La Mariposa CAMPING GROUND €
(☎079 95 03 60; www.lamariposa.it; Via Lido 22; sites per person/tent/car €13/14/6, 4-person bungalows €50-80; ☻Apr-Oct; @) About 2km north of the centre, this popular camping ground is on the beach amid pine and eucalyptus trees. Alongside the usual facilities (shop,

> **WORTH A TRIP**
>
> ## BOSA
>
> As much for the getting there as the town itself, a trip to **Bosa** is well worth your time. The 46km road from Alghero is one of Sardinia's great coastal rides, with unforgettable vistas at every turn. Bosa doesn't disappoint either, with its picturesque Old Town rising up from the Temo River.
>
> For the journey, you can rent cars/motorcycles/bikes from **Cicloexpress** (☎079 98 69 50; www.cicloexpress.com; Via Garibaldi, Alghero) for about €75/35/15 per day.

laundry, internet bar, bike hire), there's also an on-site windsurfing centre (www.ocean tribe.it).

Hotel San Francesco HOTEL €
(☑079 98 03 30; www.sanfrancescohotel.com; Via Ambrogio Machin 2; s €52-63, d €82-101; 🅿@) This year-round hotel is the only one in Alghero's *centro storico*. Housed in an ex-convent, it has plain, modestly decorated rooms set around a 14th-century cloister. Book ahead.

✗ Eating & Drinking

Angedras RESTAURANT €€
(☑079 973 50 78; Bastioni Marco Polo 41; mains €14) Dine in style on Alghero's honey-coloured ramparts. This elegant restaurant, run by the same people as the hotel of the same name, provides a romantic setting for sophisticated and beautifully presented seafood and crisp local wines.

Trattoria Maristella TRATTORIA €€
(☑079 97 81 72; Via Fratelli Kennedy 9; mains €11; ⊙closed Sun dinner) Hospitable and unpretentious, this bustling little trattoria has made a name for itself serving fresh seafood and classic Sardinian staples such as *culurgiones* (ravioli stuffed with potato, pecorino cheese and mint). It gets very busy in peak periods but service is quick and efficient.

Gelateria I Bastioni GELATERIA €
(Bastioni Marco Polo 5; cones €1-3, milkshakes €3.50; ⊙Apr-Oct) It's only a hole in the wall but this gem of a gelateria dishes up superb ice cream. Particularly fab are the fresh fruit flavours, ideally topped by a generous squirt of whipped cream.

Cafe Latino CAFE €
(Bastioni Magelllllano 10) On the ramparts overlooking the marina, this cool bar is the ideal place to kick back with a cool drink and while away the long summer evening.

Also recommended:

Il Ghiotto TAVOLA CALDA €
(Piazza Civica 23; mains €5; ⊙Tue-Sun) A fantastic canteen, serving a daily spread of panini, pastas, salads and mains.

Caffè Costantino CAFE €
(Piazza Civica 30; ⊙Thu-Tue) Alghero's ritziest cafe. Come here for coffee and cakes, not main meals.

❶ Information

On the eastern fringe of the *centro storico,* the superhelpful **tourist office** (☑079 97 90 54; www.comune.alghero.ss.it, in Italian; Piazza Porta Terra 9; ⊙8am-8pm Mon-Sat, 10am-1pm Sun) can answer every imaginable question.

❶ Getting There & Away

Alghero's **Fertilia airport** (AHO; ☑079 93 52 82; www.algheroairport.it) is served by a number of low-cost carriers, with connections to mainland Italy and destinations across Europe.

ARST (☑800 865 042; www.arst.sardegna. it, in Italian) Operates hourly buses (€0.70, 20 minutes) between the airport and the bus terminus on Via Cagliari.

Logudoro Tours (☑079 28 17 28; www. logudorotours.it) Runs two daily buses from the airport to Cagliari (€20, 3½ hours) and vice versa.

UNDERSTAND ITALY

History

Despite a history that dates to classical mythology, Italy is actually a very young country. It only came into being with Italian unification in 1861; until then the Italian peninsula had been a complex patchwork of often warring empires, city states and maritime republics.

The Etruscans & Greeks

Of the many Italic tribes that emerged from the Stone Age, the Etruscans left the most enduring mark. By the 7th century BC their city states – places such as Caere (modern-day Cerveteri) and Tarquinii (Tarquinia) – were the dominant forces in central Italy, important Mediterranean powers rivalled only by the Greeks on the south coast. Greek traders had been settling in Italy since the 8th century BC and over the centuries had founded a number of independent city states, collectively known as Magna Graecia. Despite Etruscan attempts to conquer the Greeks, both groups thrived until the 3rd century BC, when legionnaires from the emerging city of Rome came crashing in.

Rise & Fall of Rome

Rome's origins are mired in myth. Romantics hold that the city was founded by Romulus in 753 BC on the site where he and his twin brother Remus had been suckled by a she-wolf. Few historians accept this as fact, although they acknowledge the existence of a settlement on Palatino Hill dating to the 8th century BC and it's generally accepted that Romulus was the first of Rome's seven kings. The last, the Etruscan Tarquinius Superbus, was ousted in 509 BC, paving the way for the creation of the Roman Republic.

The fledgling republic got off to a shaky start but it soon found its feet and by the 2nd century BC it had seen off all its main rivals – the Etruscans, Greeks and Carthaginians – to become the undisputed master of the Western world. The republic's most famous leader was Julius Caesar, a gifted general and ambitious politician whose lust for power eventually proved his, and the republic's, undoing. His assassination on the Ides of March (15 March) in 44 BC sparked off a power struggle between his chosen successor and great-nephew Octavian and Mark Antony, lover of the Egyptian queen Cleopatra. Octavian prevailed and in 27 BC became Augustus, Rome's first emperor.

Augustus, unlike his crazy successors Caligula and Nero, ruled well and Rome flourished, reaching its zenith in the 2nd century AD. But by the 3rd century economic decline and the spread of Christianity were fuelling discontent. Diocletian tried to stop the rot by splitting the empire into eastern and western halves, but when his successor, Constantine (the first Christian emperor), moved his court to Constantinople, Rome's days were numbered. Sacked by the Goths in 410 and plundered by the Vandals in 455, the Western Empire finally fell in 476.

From the Renaissance to the Risorgimento

Medieval Italy was a period of almost constant warfare. While the Papal States fought the Holy Roman Empire for control over Europe's Catholics, the French and Spanish battled over southern Italy, and Italy's prosperous northern city states struggled for territorial gain. Eventually Milan, Venice and Florence, under the powerful Medici family, emerged as regional powers. Against this fractious background, art and culture thrived, and, in the latter half of the 15th century, the Renaissance broke out in Florence. A sweeping intellectual and artistic movement, the Rinascimento soon spread south to Rome before snowballing into a Europe-wide phenomenon.

By the end of the 16th century most of Italy was in foreign hands – the Spanish in the south and the Austrians in the north. Three centuries later, Napoleon's brief Italian interlude gave rise to the Risorgimento (unification movement). With Count Cavour providing the political vision and Garibaldi the military muscle, the movement culminated in the 1861 unification of Italy under King Vittorio Emanuele. In 1870 Rome was wrested from the papacy and became Italy's capital.

Fascism, WWII & the Italian Republic

Following a meteoric rise to power, Benito Mussolini became Italy's leader in 1925, six years after he'd founded his Fascist Party. Invoking Rome's imperial past, he embarked on a disastrous invasion of Abyssinia (modern-day Ethiopia) and, in 1940, entered WWII on Germany's side. Three years later the Allies invaded Sicily and his nation rebelled: King Vittorio Emanuele III had Mussolini arrested and Italy surrendered soon after. Mussolini was killed by Italian partisans in April 1945.

In the aftermath of the war Italy voted to abolish the monarchy, and in 1946 declared itself a constitutional republic.

A founding member of the European Economic Community, Italy enjoyed a largely successful postwar period. Consistent economic growth survived a period of domestic terrorism in the 1970s and continued well into the 1980s.

The Berlusconi Era

The 1990s heralded a period of crisis. In 1992 a minor bribery investigation ballooned into a nationwide corruption scandal known as Tangentopoli ('kickback city'). Top business figures were imprisoned and the main political parties were reduced to tatters, creating a power vacuum into which billionaire media mogul Silvio Berlusconi deftly stepped. A controversial and deeply divisive figure, Berlusconi has dominated Italian public life since his first foray into government in 1994. After a short period as prime minister in 1994, he won the elections in 2001 and went on to become Italy's longest-serving postwar PM. But his tenure was rarely free of controversy as opponents railed against his hold over Italian TV and support for American intervention in the Iraq conflict. The party came to an end in 2006, when, after an acrimonious election campaign, Romano Prodi's centre-left coalition claimed the narrowest of electoral victories.

The Prodi interlude was short-lived, though, and in April 2008, Il Cavaliere (The Knight, as Berlusconi is known) once again returned to the top job, this time beating Walter Veltroni, the former mayor of Rome. In his third period as PM, Berlusconi is currently playing to type, with controversy and scandal never far from the surface. So far, he has survived newspaper stories alleging relationships that he hosted 'bunga-bunga' orgies at his palatial villa near Milan, he has seen a lifelong ally (Marcello Dell'Utri) sentenced to seven years in prison for Mafia links, and he has watched as Italy struggles to cope with the realities of the post-credit-crunch economy. How long he can hang on for will largely depend on the outcome of four trials that he is currently facing on charges ranging from tax fraud and corruption to paying for sex with an underage prostitute and abuse of power.

People

With a population of 60.34 million, Italy is Europe's fourth most populous country after Germany, France and the UK. Almost half of all Italians live in the industrialised north and almost one in five are aged over 65 years. At the other end of the age scale, Italy is dragging its heels. The country has one of the world's lowest birth rates and the average Italian mamma has only 1.3 children, well short of the two per woman that is considered necessary for a population to maintain itself. In fact, were it not for immigration the Italian population would be in decline. Foreign residents now constitute 6.5% of Italy's population.

Traditionally, Italians are very conscious of their regional identity and very family oriented. Times are changing but it's still common for Italian children to remain at home until they marry.

Religion

Up to 80% of Italians consider themselves Catholic, although only about one in three regularly attends church. Similarly, the Vatican remains a powerful voice in national debate, but can't find enough priests for its parish churches. Still, first Communions, church weddings and regular feast days remain an integral part of Italian life.

There are no official figures but it's estimated that there are about 1.3 million Muslims in Italy, making Islam Italy's second religion. Italy also has small but well-established Orthodox, Protestant and Jewish communities.

Arts

Literature

Italian literature runs the gamut from Virgil's *Aeneid,* to the chilling war stories of Primo Levi and the fantastical tales of Italo Calvino.

Dante, whose *Divina commedia* (Divine Comedy) dates to the early 1300s, was one of three 14th-century greats alongside Petrarch and Giovanni Boccaccio, considered the first Italian novelist.

In ensuing centuries, Machiavelli taught how to manipulate power in *Il principe* (The Prince) and Alessandro Manzoni wrote of star-crossed lovers in *I promessi sposi* (The Betrothed).

Italy's southern regions provide rich literary pickings. Giuseppe Tomasi di Lampedusa depicts Sicily's melancholic resignation in *Il gattopardo* (The Leopard), a theme that Leonardo Sciascia later returns to in *Il giorno della civetta* (The Day of the Owl). Carlo Levi denounces southern poverty in *Cristo si é fermato a Eboli* (Christ Stopped at Eboli), an account of his internal exile under the Fascists. More recently, Andrea Camilleri's Sicilian-based Montalbano detective stories have enjoyed great success.

Cinema

The influence of Italian cinema goes well beyond its success at the box office. In creating the spaghetti western Sergio Leone inspired generations of film-makers, as did horror master Dario Argento and art-house genius Michelangelo Antonioni.

The heyday of Italian cinema was the post-WWII period, when the neo-realists Roberto Rossellini, Vittorio de Sica and Luchino Visconti turned their cameras onto the war-weary Italians. Classics of the genre include *Ladri di biciclette* (Bicycle Thieves; 1948) and *Roma città aperta* (Rome Open City; 1945).

Taking a decidedly different turn, Federico Fellini created his own highly visual style and won an international audience with films such as *La dolce vita* (The Sweet Life; 1959).

GET IN THE MOOD

Whet your appetite for an Italian vacation with these films and books:

» *The Terracotta Dog* (Andrea Camilleri) – food-loving Sicilian detective Salvo Montalbano cracks another murder in this enjoyable read.

» *Gomorrah* (Roberto Saviano) – a disturbing exposé of the Neapolitan Camorra.

» *The Leopard* (Giuseppe Tomasi di Lampedusa) – 50 years after it was first published, this is still the best book about Sicily.

» *The Italians* (Luigi Barzini) – no other book better captures the Italian character.

» *The Dark Heart of Italy* (Tobias Jones) – a no-holds barred study of contemporary Italy.

» *Il Postino* (1994) – spectacular Mediterranean scenery sets the stage for this heart-breaking tale of thwarted dreams.

» *Room with a View* (1985) – all repressed emotions and dreamy shots of early-20th-century Florence.

» *The Talented Mr Ripley* (1999) – intrigue and dark doings set against a series of lush Italian backgrounds.

» *Roman Holiday* (1953) – Gregory Peck and Audrey Hepburn scoot around Rome and never get a hair out of place.

» *Pane e Tulipani* (2000) – an eccentric, feel-good romance set in Venice.

Of Italy's contemporary directors, Roberto Benigni won an Oscar for *La vita è bella* (Life is Beautiful; 1997) and Nanni Moretti won Cannes' Palme D'Or for *La stanza del figlio* (The Son's Room; 2001). In 2008 Paolo Sorrentino's *Il divo* (2008) won the Cannes Jury Prize, and *Gomorrah* (Gomorrah; 2008), Matteo Garrone's film of Roberto Saviano's best-selling book, took the Festival Grand Prix. More recently, Sabina Guzzanti's *Draquila – L'Italia che trema* (Draquila – Italy Trembles; 2010) provoked heated reaction for its satirical take on Berlusconi's response to the L'Aquila earthquake.

Music

Emotional and highly theatrical, opera has always appealed to Italians. Performances of Verdi and Puccini are regularly staged at legendary theatres such as Milan's Teatro alla La Scala and Naples' Teatro San Carlo.

On the classical front, Antonio Vivaldi (1675–1741) created the concerto in its present form and wrote *Le quattro stagione* (The Four Seasons). In more recent times, the Roman singer Eros Ramazzotti has enjoyed considerable international success with his distinct voice and light pop style.

Architecture & Visual Arts

Everywhere you go in Italy you're faced with reminders of the country's convoluted history. Etruscan tombs at Tarquinia and Greek temples at Agrigento tell of glories long past, while Pompeii's skeletal ruins offer insights into the day-to-day life of ancient Romans. Byzantine mosaics in Ravenna, Venice and Palermo reveal influences sweeping in from the East.

Snowballing through 15th- and 16th-century Europe, the Renaissance left an indelible mark, particularly in Florence and Rome. Filippo Brunelleschi defied the architectural laws of the day to create the dome on Florence's Duomo, and Michelangelo Buonarroti swept aside all convention to decorate the Sistine Chapel. Contemporaries Leonardo da Vinci and Raphael further brightened the scene.

Controversial and highly influential, Michelangelo Merisi da Caravaggio dominated the late 16th century with his revolutionary use of light and penchant for warts-and-all portraits. There was little warts and all about the 17th-century baroque style, visible in many of Italy's great churches. Witness the Roman works of Gian Lorenzo Bernini and Francesco Borromini, and Lecce's flamboyant *centro storico*.

Signalling a return to sober classical lines, neoclassicism majored in the late 18th and early 19th centuries. Its most famous Italian exponent was Canova, who carved a name for himself with his smooth sensual style.

Rome's Spanish Steps and Trevi Fountain both date to this period.

In sharp contrast to backward-looking neoclassicism, Italian futurism provided a rallying cry for Modernisme, with Giacomo Balla proving hugely influential. Caught up in the Modernista spirit, the 1920s *razionalisti* (rationalists) provided the architectural vision behind the EUR district in Rome.

Continuing in this modernist tradition are Italy's two superstar architects: Renzo Piano, the visionary behind Rome's Auditorium, and Rome-born Massimiliano Fuksas.

Environment

Bound on three sides by four seas (the Adriatic, Ligurian, Tyrrhenian and Ionian), Italy has more than 8000km of coastline. Inland, about 75% of the peninsula is mountainous – the Alps curve around the northern border and the Apennines extend down the boot.

The peninsula and its surrounding seas harbour a rich fauna. You're unlikely to spot them but there are bears, wolves and wildcats in the national parks of central Italy, as well as over 150 types of bird. Swordfish, tuna and dolphins are common along the coastline and although white sharks are known to exist, attacks are rare.

Italy has 24 national parks, covering about 5% of the country, and more than 400 nature reserves, natural parks and wetlands. It also boasts 45 Unesco World Heritage sites, more than any other country in the world.

Environmental Issues

The three most insidious environmental issues affecting Italy are air pollution, waste disposal and coastal development. Heavy in-dustry and high levels of car ownership have combined to produce dense smog and poor air quality. This affects many Italian cities but is especially widespread in the industrialised north.

Inadequate waste disposal is another major cause of pollution, particularly in Naples, where the sight of rubbish rotting on the streets has become sadly familiar. At the heart of the problem lies a chronic lack of facilities – there are insufficient incinerators to burn the refuse and the landfill sights that do exist are generally full, often with waste dumped illegally by organised crime outfits.

Italy's coast has been subject to almost continuous development since the boom in beach tourism in the 1960s and while this has undoubtedly brought short-term advantages, it has also put a great strain on natural resources.

Food & Drink

Despite the ubiquity of pasta and pizza, Italian cuisine is highly regional. Local specialities abound and regional traditions are proudly maintained, so expect pesto in Genoa, pizza in Naples and *ragù* (bolognese sauce) in Bologna. It's the same with wine – Piedmont produces Italy's great reds, Barolo, Barbaresco and Dolcetto, while Tuscany's famous for its Chianti, Brunello and white Vernaccia.

Vegetarians will find delicious fruit and veg in the hundreds of daily markets, and although few restaurants cater specifically to vegetarians, most serve vegetable-based antipasti (starters), pastas, *contorni* (side dishes) and salads.

EARTHQUAKES & VOLCANOES

Italy is one of the world's most earthquake-prone countries. A fault line runs through the entire peninsula – from eastern Sicily, up the Apennines and into the northeastern Alps. The country is usually hit by minor quakes several times a year and devastating earthquakes are not uncommon in central and southern Italy. The most recent, measuring 6.3 on the Richter scale, struck the central region of Abruzzo on 6 April 2009, killing 295 people and leaving up to 55,000 homeless.

Italy's worst 20th-century earthquake hit southern Italy in 1908, when Messina and Reggio di Calabria were destroyed by a seaquake registering seven on the Richter scale. Some 86,000 people were killed by the quake and subsequent tidal wave.

Italy also has six active volcanoes: Stromboli and Vulcano on the Aeolian Islands; Vesuvius, the Campi Flegrei and the island of Ischia near Naples; and Etna on Sicily. Stromboli and Etna are among the world's most active volcanoes, while Vesuvius has not erupted since 1944.

Where to Eat & Drink

The most basic sit-down eatery is a *tavola calda* (literally 'hot table'), which offers canteen-style food. Pizzerias, the best of which have a *forno a legna* (wood-fired oven), serve the obvious but often a full menu as well. For takeaway, a *rosticceria* sells cooked meats and *pizza al taglio* pizza by the slice.

For wine, make for an *enoteca* (wine bar), many of which also serve light snacks and a few hot dishes. Alternatively, most bars and cafes serve *tramezzini* (sandwiches) and panini (bread rolls). A cheaper option is to go to an *alimentari* (delicatessen) and ask them to make a panino with the filling of your choice. At a *pasticceria* you can buy pastries, cakes and biscuits. *Forni* (bakeries) are another good choice for a cheap snack.

For a full meal you'll want a trattoria or a *ristorante*. Traditionally, trattorias were family-run places that served a basic menu of local dishes at affordable prices and thankfully, a few still are. *Ristoranti* offer more choice and smarter service.

Restaurants, all of which are nonsmoking, usually open for lunch from noon to 3pm and for dinner from 7.30pm, earlier in tourist areas.

On the bill expect to be charged for *pane e coperto* (bread and a cover charge). This is standard and is added even if you don't ask for or eat the bread. Typically it ranges from €1 to €4. *Servizio* (service charge) of 10% to 15% might or might not be included; if it's not, tourists are expected to round up the bill or leave 10%.

Habits & Customs

A full Italian meal consists of an antipasto, a *primo* (first course; pasta or rice dish), *secondo* (second/main course; usually meat or fish) with an *insalata* (salad) or *contorno* (vegetable side dish), *dolci* (dessert) and coffee. When eating out it's perfectly acceptable to mix and match any combination and order, say, a *primo* followed by an *insalata* or *contorno*.

Italians don't tend to eat a sit-down *colazione* (breakfast), preferring instead a cappuccino and *cornetto* (pastry filled with custard, chocolate or jam) at a bar. *Pranzo* (lunch) was traditionally the main meal of the day, although many people now have a light lunch and bigger *cena* (dinner). Italians are late diners, often not eating until after 9pm.

SURVIVAL GUIDE

Directory A–Z

Accommodation

The bulk of Italy's accommodation is made up of *alberghi* (hotels) and *pensioni* – often housed in converted apartments. Other options are youth hostels, camping grounds, B&Bs, *agriturismi* (farm-stays), mountain *rifugi* (Alpine refuges), monasteries and villa/apartment rentals.

Prices fluctuate enormously between high and low season. High-season rates apply at Easter, in summer (mid-June to August), and over the Christmas to New Year period. Peak season in the ski resorts runs from December to March.

The north of Italy is generally more expensive than the south.

Many city-centre hotels offer discounts in August to lure clients from the crowded coast. Check hotel websites for last-minute offers.

Many hotels in coastal resorts shut for winter, typically from November to March.

As a rough guide, reckon on at least €55 for a double room in a budget hotel.

PRICE RANGES

In this chapter prices quoted are the minimum-maximum for rooms with a private bathroom, and unless otherwise stated include breakfast. The following price indicators apply (for a high-season double room):

€€€   more than €200

€€   €110 to €200

€   less than €110

B&BS

» There's a huge number of bed and breakfasts (B&Bs) across the country. Quality varies, but the best offer comfort greater than you'd get in a similarly priced hotel room.

» Prices are typically €70 to €180 for a double room.

» Online booking services include **Bed & Breakfast Italia** (☑06 687 86 18; www.bbitalia. it), which has properties all over the country, and **Cross-pollinate** (www.cross-pollinate. com), which has apartments, B&Bs and guest houses in Rome, Florence and Venice.

CAMPING

» Campers are well catered for in Italy.

» Lists of camping grounds are available from local tourist offices or online at www.

campeggi.com, www.camping.it and www. italcamping.it.

» In high season expect to pay up to €20 per person and a further €25 for a tent pitch.

» Independent camping is not permitted in many places.

CONVENTS & MONASTERIES

» Basic accommodation is often available in convents and monasteries.

» The Rome-based Chiesa di Santa Susanna (www.santasusanna.org) has a list of convents and monasteries throughout the country.

» You can also try www.monasterystays.com, a specialist online booking service.

FARM-STAYS

» An *agriturismo* (farm-stay) is a good option for a country stay, although you will usually need your own transport.

» Accommodation varies from spartan billets on working farms to palatial suites at luxurious rural retreats.

» For information and lists check out www. agriturist.it or www.agriturismo.com.

HOSTELS

» Official HI-affiliated *ostelli per la gioventù* (youth hostels) are run by the Italian Youth Hostel Association (Associazione Italiana Alberghi per la Gioventù; 06 487 11 52; www.aighostels.com; Via Cavour 44, Rome). A valid HI card is required for these; you can get one in your home country or directly at hostels.

» There are many privately run hostels offering dorms and private rooms.

» Dorm rates are typically between €15 and €30, with breakfast usually included. Many places also offer dinner for around €10.

REFUGES

» Italy boasts an extensive network of mountain *rifugi*.

» Open from July to September, refuges offer basic dorm-style accommodation, although some larger ones have double rooms.

» Reckon on €20 to €30 per person per night with breakfast included.

» Further information is available from the Club Alpino Italiano (CAI; www.cai.it), which owns and runs many of the refuges.

RENTAL ACCOMMODATION

The easiest way to rent an apartment or a holiday villa is through one of the hundreds of specialist agencies. Some options:

Cottages & Castles (www.cottagesandcastles .com.au) Oz-based specialist in villa-style accommodation.

Cottages to Castles (www.cottagestocastles. com) UK operator with properties across the country.

Cuendet (www.cuendet.com) Specialises in villa rentals in Tuscany.

Guest in Italy (www.guestinitaly.com) Has apartments and B&Bs in Rome, Florence and Venice.

Long Travel (www.long-travel.co.uk) Has properties in the south of Italy, Sardinia and Sicily.

Activities

Cycling Tourist offices can provide details on trails and guided rides. The best time is spring. Lonely Planet's *Cycling in Italy* offers practical tips and several detailed itineraries.

Diving There are hundreds of schools offering courses and guided dives for all levels.

Hiking & Walking Thousands of kilometres of *sentieri* (marked trails) criss-cross the country. The hiking season is from June to September. Useful websites include www.cai.it and www.parks.it. Lonely Planet's *Walking in Italy* has descriptions of more than 50 walks.

Skiing Italy's ski season runs from December through to March. Prices are generally high, particularly in the top Alpine resorts – the Apennines are cheaper. The best way to save money is to buy a *settimana bianca* (literally 'white week') package deal, covering seven days' accommodation, food and ski passes.

Business Hours

In this chapter, opening hours have only been provided in Information, Eating, Drinking, Entertainment and Shopping sections when they differ from the following standard hours:

Banks 8.30am-1.30pm & 3-4.30pm Mon-Fri

Bars & Cafes 7.30am-8pm; many open earlier and some stay open until the small hours; pubs often open noon-2am

Discos & Clubs 10pm-4am

Pharmacies 9am-1pm & 4-7.30pm Mon-Fri, to 1pm Sat; outside of these hours, pharmacies open on a rotation basis – all are required to post a list of places open in the vicinity

Post offices major offices 8am-7pm Mon-Fri, to 1.15pm Sat; branch offices 8.30am-2pm Mon-Fri, to 1pm Sat

Restaurants noon-3pm & 7.30-11pm or midnight; most restaurants close one day a week

Shops 9am-1pm & 3.30-7.30pm, or 4-8pm Mon-Sat; in larger cities many chain stores and supermarkets open from 9am to 7.30pm Mon-Sat; some also open Sun morning, typically 9am -1pm; food shops are generally closed Thu afternoon; some other shops are closed Mon morning

Many museums, galleries and archaeological sites operate summer and winter opening hours. Typically, winter hours will apply between November and late March or early April.

Embassies

The following embassies are based in Rome.

Australia (☎06 85 27 21, emergencies ☎800 87 77 90; www.italy.embassy.gov.au; Via Antonio Bosio 5; ⊙9am-5pm Mon-Fri)

New Zealand (☎06 853 75 01; www.nzembassy.com/Italy; Via Clitunno 44; ⊙8.30am-12.30pm & 1.30-5pm Mon-Fri)

UK (☎06 422 00 001; http://ukinitaly.fco.gov.uk; Via XX Settembre 80a; ⊙9.15am-1.30pm Mon-Fri)

USA (☎06 467 41; http://italy.usembassy.gov; Via Vittorio Veneto 119a; ⊙8.30am-noon Mon-Fri)

Food

Throughout this chapter, the following price indicators have been used (prices refer to the cost of a main course):

€€€   more than €18

€€   €10 to €18

€   less than €10

Gay & Lesbian Travellers

» Homosexuality is legal in Italy.

» Homosexuality is well tolerated in major cities but overt displays of affection could attract a negative response, particularly in small towns and in the more conservative south.

» Italy's main gay and lesbian organisation is **Arcigay** (www.arcigay.it, in Italian), based in Bologna.

Internet Access

» Wi-fi is increasingly available and many hotels, hostels, B&Bs and *pensioni* now offer it, either free or for a small charge.

» The 🛜 icon in accommodation reviews means wi-fi is available. An @ icon denotes availability of a computer for guest use.

» Access is also available in internet cafes throughout the country, although many have closed in recent years. Charges are typically around €5 per hour.

» To use internet points in Italy you must present photo ID.

Money

» Italy's currency is the euro.

» ATMs, known in Italy as *bancomat,* are widespread and will accept cards displaying the appropriate sign. Visa and MasterCard are widely recognised, as are Cirrus and Maestro; American Express is less common. If you don't have a PIN, some, but not all, banks will advance cash over the counter.

» Credit cards are widely accepted, although they are not as prevalent as in the USA or UK. Many small trattorias, pizzerias and *pensioni* only take cash. Don't assume museums, galleries and the like accept credit cards.

» If your credit/debit card is lost, stolen or swallowed by an ATM, telephone toll-free to block it: **Amex** (☎06 7290 0347); **MasterCard** (☎800 870 866); **Visa** (☎800 81 90 14).

» You're not expected to tip on top of restaurant service charges, but if you think the service warrants it feel free to round up the bill or leave a little extra – 10% is fine. In bars, Italians often leave small change (€0.10 or €0.20).

Post

» Italy's postal system, **Poste Italiane** (☎803 160; www.poste.it), is reasonably reliable.

» The standard service is *posta prioritaria.* Registered mail is known as *posta raccomandata,* insured mail as *posta assicurato.*

» *Francobolli* (stamps) are available at post offices and *tabacchi* (tobacconists) – look for a big white 'T' against a blue/black background. Tobacconists keep regular shop hours.

Public Holidays

Most Italians take their annual holiday in August. This means that many businesses and shops close down for at least a part of the month, usually around Ferragosto (15 August). Easter is another busy holiday.

Public holidays:

New Year's Day (Capodanno) 1 January

Epiphany (Epifania) 6 January

Easter Monday (Pasquetta) March/April

Liberation Day (Giorno delle Liberazione) 25 April

Labour Day (Festa del Lavoro) 1 May

Republic Day (Festa della Repubblica) 2 June

Feast of the Assumption (Ferragosto) 15 August

All Saints' Day (Ognisanti) 1 November

Feast of the Immaculate Conception (Immacolata Concezione) 8 December

Christmas Day (Natale) 25 December

Boxing Day (Festa di Santo Stefano) 26 December

Individual towns also have holidays to celebrate their patron saints:

St Mark (Venice) 25 April

St John the Baptist (Florence, Genoa and Turin) 24 June

Saints Peter and Paul (Rome) 29 June

St Rosalia (Palermo) 15 July

St Janarius (Naples) First Sunday in May, 19 September and 16 December

St Ambrose (Milan) 7 December

Safe Travel

» Petty theft is prevalent in Italy. Be on your guard against pickpockets and moped thieves in popular tourist centres such as Rome, Florence and Venice.

» Watch out for short-changing.

» Road rules are obeyed with discretion, so don't take it for granted that cars will stop at red lights. To cross the road, step confidently into the traffic and walk calmly across.

Telephone

» Area codes are an integral part of all Italian phone numbers and must be dialled even when calling locally. The area codes have been listed in telephone numbers throughout this chapter.

» To call Italy from abroad, dial ☑0039 and then the area code, including the first zero.

EU citizens aged between 18 and 25 years, and students from countries with reciprocal arrangements, generally qualify for a discount (usually half-price) at galleries and museums. Under-18s and over-65s often get in free. In all cases you'll need proof of your age, ideally a passport or ID card.

» To call abroad from Italy, dial ☑00, then the relevant country code followed by the telephone number.

» To make a reverse-charge (collect) international call, dial ☑170. All operators speak English.

» You'll find cut-price call centres in all of the main cities. For international calls, their rates are often cheaper than payphones'.

» Skype is available in many internet cafes.

MOBILE PHONES

» Italy uses the GSM 900/1800 network, which is compatible with the rest of Europe and Australia, but not with the North American GSM 1900 or the Japanese system (although some GSM 1900/900 phones do work here).

» If you have a GSM dual- or tri-band cellular phone that you can unlock (check with your service provider), you can buy a *prepagato* (prepaid) SIM card in Italy.

» Companies offering SIM cards include TIM (Telecom Italia Mobile; www.tim.it), Wind (www.wind.it) and Vodafone (www.vodafone.it). You'll need ID to open an account.

PHONE CODES

» Italy's country code is ☑39.

» Mobile phone numbers begin with a three-digit prefix starting with a 3.

» Toll-free (free-phone) numbers are known as *numeri verdi* and start with 800. These are not always available if calling from a mobile phone.

PHONECARDS

To phone from a public payphone you'll need a *scheda telefonica* (telephone card; (€2.50, €5). Buy these at post offices, *tabacchi* and newsstands.

Tourist Information

For pre-trip information, check out the website of the Ministro del Turismo (www.italia.

it). The ministry also runs a multilingual telephone information service, **Easy Italy** (☏039 039 039; ⊙9am-10pm).

Tourist offices in Italy are listed throughout this chapter.

Travellers with Disabilities

Italy is not an easy country for travellers with disabilities. Cobbled streets, blocked pavements and tiny lifts all make life difficult. Rome-based **Consorzio Cooperative Integrate** (COIN; ☏06 2326 9231; www.coinsociale.it) is the best point of reference for travellers with disabilities.

Other useful websites:

Handyturismo (www.handyturismo.it) Information on Rome.

Milanopertutti (www.milanopertutti.it) Focuses on Milan.

Terre di Mare (www.terredimare.it) Covers Liguria, including Genoa and the Cinque Terre.

If you're travelling by train, **Trenitalia** (www.ferroviedellostato.it) runs a telephone info line (☏199 30 30 60) with details of assistance available at stations.

Visas

» Schengen visa rules apply for entry to Italy.

» Unless staying in a hotel/B&B/hostel etc, all foreign visitors are supposed to register with the local police within eight days of arrival.

» Non-EU citizens who want to study in Italy must obtain a study visa from their nearest Italian embassy or consulate.

» A *permesso di soggiorno* (permit to stay) is required by all non-EU nationals who stay in Italy longer than three months. You must apply within eight days of arriving in Italy. Check the exact documentary requirements on www.poliziadistato.it.

» EU citizens do not require a *permesso di soggiorno*.

Getting There & Away

Getting to Italy is pretty straightforward. It is well served by Europe's low-cost carriers and there are plenty of bus, train and ferry routes into the country. Flights, tours and rail tickets can be booked online at lonelyplanet.com/bookings.

Air

There are direct intercontinental flights to/from Rome and Milan. European flights also serve regional airports.

Italy's main international airports:

Leonardo da Vinci (www.adr.it) Rome; Italy's main airport, also known as Fiumicino.

Malpensa (www.sea-aeroportimilano.it) Milan's principal airport.

Ciampino (www.adr.it) Rome's second airport. For low-cost European carriers.

Pisa International Galileo Galilei (www.pisa-airport.com) Main gateway for Florence and Tuscany.

Venice Marco Polo (www.veniceairport.it)

Bologna Guglielmo Marconi (www.bologna-airport.it)

Cagliari Elmas (www.sogaer.it)

Naples Capodichino (www.gesac.it)

Palermo Falcone-Borsellino (www.gesap.it)

Italy's national carrier is **Alitalia** (www.alitalia.com).

Land
BORDER CROSSINGS

Italy borders France, Switzerland, Austria and Slovenia. The main points of entry:

From France The coast road from Nice; the Mont Blanc tunnel from Chamonix.

From Switzerland The Grand St Bernard tunnel; the Simplon tunnel; Lötschberg Base tunnel.

From Austria The Brenner Pass.

BUS

Eurolines (www.eurolines.com) operates buses from European destinations to Bologna, Florence, Milan, Naples, Rome, Siena, Turin, Verona, Venice and other Italian cities.

CAR & MOTORCYCLE

If traversing the Alps, note that all the border crossings listed above are open year-round. Other mountain passes are often closed in

---

MOVING ON?

For further information, head to shop.lonelyplanet.com to purchase a downloadable PDF of the Tunis chapter from Lonely Planet's *Tunisia* guide.

MAIN INTERNATIONAL FERRY ROUTES

FROM	TO	COMPANY	MIN-MAX FARE (€)	DURATION (HR)
Ancona	Igoumenitsa	Minoan, Superfast	73-108	16
Ancona	Patra	Minoan, Superfast	73-108	15½-22
Ancona	Split	Jadrolinija, SNAV	46-90	4½-11
Bari	Igoumenitsa	Agoudimos, Superfast	64-89	8-12
Bari	Patra	Agoudimos, Superfast	64-89	16
Bari	Corfu	Agoudimos	64-85	11
Bari	Kefallonia	Agoudimos	64-85	15½
Bari	Split	Jadrolinija	51-70.50	22
Bari	Dubrovnik	Jadrolinija	46-63.50	10-12
Bari	Bar	Montenegro	50-55	9
Brindisi	Igoumenitsa	Endeavor	36-67	8
Brindisi	Patra	Endeavor	36-75	14
Brindisi	Corfu	Endeavor, Agoudimos	53-73	6½-11½
Brindisi	Kefallonia	Endeavor	61-83	12½
Genoa	Barcelona	GNV	81	18
Genoa	Tunis	GNV	127	24
Venice	Igoumenitsa	Minoan	77-107	23½
Venice	Patra	Minoan	77-107	29½
Venice	Corfu	Minoan	77-107	22

winter and sometimes even in spring and autumn. Make sure you have snow chains in your car.

When driving into Italy always carry proof of ownership of a private vehicle. You'll also need third-party motor insurance. For road rules and other driving information see p586.

TRAIN
International trains connect with various cities:

Milan To/from Barcelona, Paris, Basel, Geneva, Zürich and Vienna.

Rome To/from Paris, Munich and Vienna.

Venice To/from Paris, Basel, Geneva, Lucerne, Vienna, Ljubljana, Zagreb, Belgrade and Budapest.

There are also international trains from Genoa, Turin, Verona, Bologna, Florence and Naples. Details are available online at www.ferroviedellostato.it.

In the UK, the **Rail Europe Travel Centre** (www.raileurope.co.uk) can provide fare information on journeys to/from Italy, most of which require a change at Paris. Another excellent online resource is **The Man in Seat Sixty-One** (www.seat61.com), with an Italy page that details how to travel from London to Italy.

Eurail and Inter-Rail passes are both valid in Italy.

Sea

Dozens of ferry companies connect Italy with other Mediterranean countries. Timetables are seasonal, so always check ahead – you'll find details of routes, companies and online booking on **Traghettiweb** (www.traghettiweb.it).

Prices quoted here are for a one-way *poltrona* (reclinable seat). Holders of Eurail and Inter-Rail passes should check with the ferry company if they are entitled to a discount or free passage.

Major ferry companies:

Agoudimos (www.agoudimos-lines.com)

Endeavor Lines (www.endeavor-lines.com)

Grandi Navi Veloci (www.gnv.it)

Jadrolinija (www.jadrolinija.hr)

Minoan Lines (www.minoanlines.it)

Montenegro (www.montenegrolines.com)

SNAV (www.snav.it)

Superfast Ferries (www.superfast.com)

Tirrenia (www.tirrenia.it)

Getting Around

Air

Domestic flights serve most major Italian cities and the main islands (Sardinia and Sicily), but are relatively expensive. Airlines serving national routes:

Alitalia (✆06 22 22; www.alitalia.it)

Meridiana (✆89 29 28; www.meridiana.it)

easyJet (✆899 23 45 89; www.easyjet.com)

Ryanair (✆899 01 88 80; www.ryanair.com)

Windjet (✆89 20 20; www.volawindjet.it)

The main airports are in Rome, Pisa, Milan, Bologna, Genoa, Turin, Naples, Venice, Catania, Palermo and Cagliari.

Bicycle

» Cycling is a popular pastime in Italy but as a means of everyday transport it's limited to a few cities in the north.

» Tourist offices can generally provide details of designated bike trails and bike hire (bank on at least €10 per day).

» There are no particular road rules for cyclists, although you'd do well to bring a helmet, lights and a small tool kit.

» Bikes can be taken on regional and international trains carrying the bike logo, but you'll need to pay a bike supplement (€3.50 on regional trains, €12 on international trains). Bikes can be carried free if dismantled and stored in a bike bag.

» Bikes generally incur a small supplement on ferries, typically €5 to €10.

Boat

Navi (large ferries) service Sicily and Sardinia; *traghetti* (smaller ferries) and *aliscafi* (hydrofoils) cover the smaller islands.

The main embarkation points for Sardinia are Genoa, Livorno, Civitavecchia and Naples; for Sicily, it's Naples and Villa San Giovanni in Calabria.

Most long-distance ferries travel overnight.

The major domestic ferry companies:

Grandi Navi Veloci (✆010 209 45 91; www.gnv.it) To/from Sardinia and Sicily.

Moby (✆199 30 30 40; www.mobylines.it) To/from Sardinia and Sicily.

Sardinia Ferries (✆199 400 500; www.corsica-ferries.it) To/from Sardinia.

SNAV (✆081 428 55 55; www.snav.it) To/from Sardinia, Sicily, Aeolian Islands, Capri.

Tirrenia (✆892 123; www.tirrenia.it) To/from Sardinia and Sicily.

For details of routes, refer to individual town entries.

Bus

» Italy boasts an extensive and largely reliable bus network.

» Buses are not necessarily cheaper than trains, but in mountainous areas such as Umbria, Sicily and Sardinia they are often the only choice.

» In larger cities, companies have ticket offices or operate through agencies but in most villages and small towns tickets are sold in bars or on the bus.

» Reservations are usually only necessary for high-season long-haul trips.

Car & Motorcycle

» Roads are generally good throughout the country and there's an excellent system of autostradas (motorways).

» There's a toll to use most autostradas, payable in cash or by credit card at exit barriers.

» Autostradas are indicated by an A with a number (eg A1) on a green background; *strade statali* (main roads) are shown by an S or SS and number (eg SS7) against a blue background.

» Italy's motoring organisation **Automobile Club d'Italia** (ACI; www.aci. it) provides 24-hour roadside assistance (☎803 116).

» Cars use unleaded petrol *(benzina senza piombo)* and diesel *(gasolio)*; both are expensive but diesel is slightly cheaper.

DRIVING LICENCES
All EU driving licences are recognised in Italy. Holders of non-EU licences must get an International Driving Permit (IDP) to accompany their national licence.

HIRE
To hire a car:
» You must have a valid driving licence (plus IDP if required).
» You must have had your licence for at least a year.
» You must be aged 21 years or over. Under-25s will often have to pay a young-driver's supplement on top of the usual rates.
» You must have a credit card.

Make sure you understand what is included in the price (unlimited kilometres, tax, insurance, collision damage waiver etc) and what your liabilities are. For the best rental rates, book your car before leaving home. Note also that most cars have manual gear transmission.

The most competitive multinational car-rental agencies:

Avis (☎06 452 10 83 91; www.avisautono leggio.it)

Budget (☎199 30 73 73; www.budgetautono leggio.it)

Europcar (☎199 30 70 30; www.europcar.it)

Hertz (☎199 11 22 11; www.hertz.it)

Italy by Car (☎091 380 96 76; www.italyby car.it)

Maggiore (☎199 151 120; www.maggiore.it)

You'll have no trouble hiring a scooter or motorcycle (provided you're over 18); there are rental agencies in all Italian cities. Rates start at about €30 a day for a 50cc scooter.

INSURANCE
If you're driving your own car, you'll need an international insurance certificate, known as a Carta Verde (Green Card), available from your insurance company.

ROAD RULES
» Drive on the right, overtake on the left and give way to cars coming from the right.
» It's obligatory to wear seatbelts, to drive with your headlights on outside built-up areas, and to carry a warning triangle and fluorescent waistcoat in case of breakdown.
» Wearing a helmet is compulsory on all two-wheeled vehicles.
» The blood alcohol limit is 0.05%.
» Unless otherwise indicated, speed limits are as follows:

  • *130km/h (in rain 110km/h) on autostradas*

  • *110km/h (in rain 90km/h) on all main, non-urban roads*

  • *90km/h on secondary, non-urban roads*

  • *50km/h in built-up areas*

» Most major Italian cities, including Rome, Bologna, Florence, Milan and Turin, operate restricted traffic zones. You can enter these zones on a *motorino* (moped/scooter) or in a car with foreign registration but not in private or rental cars.

Train
Italy has an extensive rail network. Trains are relatively cheap, and many are fast and comfortable. Most services are run by **Trenitalia** (☎89 20 21; www.ferroviedellostato.it). There are several types of train:

Regionale or interregionale (R) Slow local services.

InterCity (IC) Fast trains between major cities.

Eurostar (ES) Similar to InterCity but faster.

Eurostar Alta Velocità (ES AV) High-speed trains operating on the Turin–Milan–Bologna–Florence–Rome–Naples–Salerno line.

TICKETS
Ticket prices depend on the type of train and class (1st class costs almost double 2nd class). Train prices quoted in this chapter are for the most common trains on any

given route – on some routes that might be a slow Regionale train, on others it could be the fast Eurostar Alta Velocità.

» Regional trains are the cheapest.

» InterCity trains require a supplement, which is incorporated in the ticket price. If you have a standard ticket and board an InterCity you will have to pay the difference on board.

» Eurostar and Alta Velocità trains require prior reservation.

» Generally, it's cheaper to buy all local train tickets in Italy – check for yourself on the Trenitalia website.

» Tickets must be validated – in the yellow machines at the entrance to platforms – before boarding trains.

» Children under four years of age travel free, while kids between four and 12 years are entitled to discounts of between 30% and 50%.

Malta

Best Places to Stay

» Asti Guesthouse (p594)

» Hotel Valentina (p597)

» Point de Vue Guesthouse (p599)

» Maria Giovanna Guesthouse (p602)

Best Places to Eat

» Trabuxu Bistro (p594)

» Kitchen (p598)

» Mahżen XII (p599)

Why Go?

Despite being made up of three tiny islands on the southern edge of Europe, Malta groans under the weight of its rich history and fascinating cultural influences. As a melting pot of Mediterranean culture, Malta merits far deeper exploration than is often given to it by the package crowds whose first priority is hitting the beach.

From ancient stone temples and historic Arabic connections (listen carefully to the local language) to Sicilian-inspired cuisine and an oddly 1950s British atmosphere, Malta will almost certainly surprise you. Valletta and the Three Cities are famed for their grand churches, elegant palaces and honey-coloured limestone fortifications, while nearby Sliema and St Julian are packed with restaurants and bars. And don't forget little Gozo – a pretty, rural island where the pace of life is that much slower – the perfect chill-out spot.

When to Go
Valletta

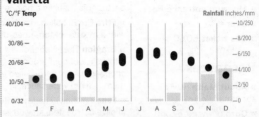

February–March Pleasant temperatures, spring flowers and the festivities of Carnival Week.

September– October Fewer crowds, perfect for sunbathing, sea warm and clear for diving.

December Low accommodation prices, village churches resplendent with fairy lights.

Fast Facts

- » **Area** 316 sq km
- » **Capital** Valletta
- » **Country code** ☎356
- » **Emergency** ☎112

Exchange Rates

Australia	A$1	€0.74
Canada	C$1	€0.74
euro	€1	€1
Japan	¥100	€0.87
New Zealand	NZ$1	€0.56
UK	UK£1	€1.16
USA	US$1	€0.67

Set Your Budget

- » **Budget hotel room** €25 per person
- » **Two-course evening meal** €20
- » **Museum entrance** €5
- » **Beer** €2
- » **Bus ticket** €0.60

Resources

- » **About Malta** (www.aboutmalta.com)
- » **Gozo** (www.gozo.com)
- » **Malta Tourism Authority** (www.visitmalta.com)
- » **StarWeb Malta** (www.starwebmalta.com)

Connections

Malta is well connected to both Sicily and mainland Italy by sea. Catamarans to Pozzallo and Catania in Sicily are the fastest and most frequent connection, while other services link Malta to Palermo, Genoa and Civitavecchia. Ferries operate year-round.

There are frequent flights between Malta and various European destinations, including Sardinia, Larnaca (Cyprus), Istanbul, Athens, Dubrovnik and many cities in Italy, France and Spain.

ITINERARIES

Three Days

Start things off in Valletta to get an overview of the country – wander the streets and soak up some of the history. On your second day, head to the Hypogeum (you'll need to have booked in advance) before enjoying a meal of seafood in Marsaxlokk and the nightlife in Paceville. On the third day visit Mdina and Rabat, then escape to a beach in the northwest.

One Week

As above, then on day four, head for gorgeous Gozo. From here you can take a day trip to Comino, discover your own beaches and enjoy glorious food in Malta's least discovered corner.

Essential Food & Drink

- » **Ġbejniet** You'll either love or hate this small, hard, white cheese traditionally made from unpasteurised sheep's or goat's milk. It is dried in baskets and often steeped in olive oil seasoned with salt and crushed black peppercorns.

- » **Pastizza** (plural *pastizzi*) This traditional Maltese snack is a small parcel of flaky pastry filled with either ricotta cheese or mushy peas. They're available in most bars or from a pastizzerija (usually a hole-in-the-wall takeaway or kiosk).

- » **Ftira** Bread baked in a flat disc and traditionally stuffed with a mixture of tomatoes, olives, capers and anchovies.

- » **Braġioli** These 'beef olives' are prepared by wrapping a thin slice of beef around a stuffing of breadcrumbs, chopped bacon, hard-boiled egg and parsley, then braising them in a red wine sauce.

- » **Fenek** (rabbit) The favourite Maltese dish, whether fried in olive oil, roasted, stewed, served with spaghetti or baked in a pie (*fenek bit-tewm u l-inbid* is rabbit cooked in garlic and wine, *fenek moqli* is fried rabbit, *stuffat tal-fenek* is stewed rabbit).

- » **Kinnie** You'll see its advertising signs are all over the place in Malta – the brand name of a local soft drink, flavoured with bitter oranges and aromatic herbs.

Malta Highlights

1 Absorb centuries of history, enjoy great food and walk the mighty fortifications of delightful **Valletta** (p592)

2 Soak up some sun at the beach – choose between **Golden Bay** (p600) and **Gozo's Ramla Bay** (p602), or snorkelling at **Comino's Blue Lagoon** (p602)

3 Step back in time in the silent streets of the graceful old capital, **Mdina** (p599)

4 Bask in the charms of peaceful, green **Gozo** (p601), and perhaps even dive in its crystalline waters

5 Revel in the picture-postcard coastal scenery of **Dwejra** (p603)

6 Explore the mysterious subterranean necropolis that is the **Hal Saflieni Hypogeum** (p596)

7 Discover Malta's new generation of restaurants specialising in fresh local produce, such as **Trabuxu Bistro** (p594) and **Mahżen XII** (p599)

Valletta

POP 6300

The Maltese capital is an absolute stunner. Whereas careless modern development has blighted much of the rest of Malta's coast, Valletta has retained its architectural unity and ancient charm. Built on a hilly peninsula in the middle of a superb natural harbour, and thick with massive fortifications, Italianate churches and the city's trademark golden limestone buildings, Valletta makes a great base from which to explore the rest of the country and merits a couple of days' exploration in its own right. Commercial activity bustles around Triq ir-Repubblika and Triq il-Merkanti, but the quiet, narrow backstreets are where you'll get a feel for everyday life. The city overlooks the impressive Grand Harbour to the southeast and Marsamxett Harbour to the northwest.

⊙ Sights & Activities

Valletta is a compact town barely 1km long and 600m wide, with a grid of narrow streets. It's an easy city to walk, and the views are spectacular.

St John's Co-Cathedral   CHURCH
(Triq ir-Repubblika; admission incl Cathedral Museum adult/child €6/free; ⊙9.30am-4.30pm Mon-Fri, to 12.30pm Sat, closed Sun, public holidays & during services) Built in the 1570s, Malta's principal church dominates the centre of town. The sombre facade belies a breathtaking baroque interior, the floor covered with colourful marble tombstones marking the resting place of knights and dignitaries. Side chapels built by different orders of the Knights of St John are all fascinating and well explained by the free audioguide. This is a so-called 'co-cathedral', as St Paul's Cathedral in Mdina has historically been the seat of Malta's archbishop, but St John's was raised to an equal level by an 1816 papal

Valletta

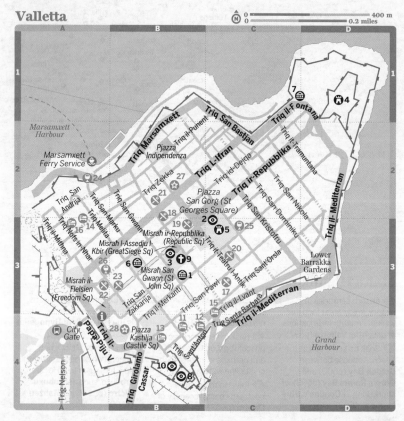

decree. The south aisle leads to the **Cathedral Museum**, dominated by the *Beheading of St John the Baptist* (c 1608) by Caravaggio, one of the artist's most famous and accomplished paintings.

Grand Master's Palace PALACE
(Pjazza San Ġorġ; adult/child €10/5; ☉9am-5pm)
The 16th-century palace built for the leaders of the Knights of St John is now the seat of the Maltese parliament. You can visit the armoury, filled with 16th- to 18th-century weapons and suits of armour, and the grand State Apartments, decorated with paintings of the Grand Masters, and hung with priceless 17th-century Gobelins tapestries.

FREE Upper Barrakka Gardens GARDEN
(Pjazza Kastilja; ☉dawn-dusk) Any walk around Valletta should take in the Upper Barrakka Gardens to soak up the view that puts the 'grand' in Grand Harbour. Stairs lead down to the **Saluting Battery** (www.wirtartna.org; adult/child €5/3; ☉10am-1pm, guided tours at 11am & 12.15pm daily), where cannons once fired salutes to visiting naval vessels. A cannon is now fired every day at noon; guided tours show how the gun is loaded and fired, and there are displays on the history of timekeeping and signalling.

National Museum of Archaeology MUSEUM
(Triq ir-Repubblika; adult/child €5/2.50; ☉9am-7pm) Here you can admire the beautiful objects that have been found at Malta's prehistoric sites – check out the female figurines, known as the 'fat ladies', found at Ħaġar Qim. Best of all is the *Sleeping Lady,* found at the Hypogeum and dating from around 3000 BC.

National War Museum MUSEUM
(Triq il-Fontana; adult/child €6/3; ☉9am-5pm) Next to Fort St Elmo, this museum commemorates Malta's heroic involvement in WWII. The collection includes the jeep Husky used by General Eisenhower, the wreckage of a Spitfire and a Messerschmitt Me-109 fighter aircraft recovered from the seabed, and the George Cross medal that was awarded to the entire population of Malta in 1942.

Fort St Elmo FORTRESS
At the furthest point from City Gate is the fort, built in 1552 by the Knights of the Order of St John; its strategic location was vital to the island's defence. Today it is only open to the public for historical re-enactments, such as **In Guardia** (adult/child €5/3; ☉late Sep-early Jul), a colourful military pageant in 16th-century costume, which is held two to three times a month.

Valletta

VALLETTA IN...

MALTA MALTA

Two Days

Start the day with coffee and *pastizzi* at **Caffé Cordina**, then spend a few hours in Valletta's historic streets, stopping to take in the views over Grand Harbour from the **Upper Barrakka Gardens** where a cannon is fired daily at noon. After lunch, explore **St John's Co-Cathedral** and the **Grand Master's Palace** before dinner at **Trabuxu Bistro**. That evening, take in a show at **Manoel Theatre** or **St James' Cavalier Centre for Creativity**. On day two, spend the morning wandering the historic waterfront and back streets of **Vittoriosa**, before taking a tour of the **Hypogeum**. Round off your visit with dinner at **Rubino**.

Manoel Theatre   THEATRE
(🕿2124 6389; www.teatrumanoel.com.mt; 115 Triq it-Teatru l-Antik; theatre tours €4; ⊙Mon-Sat) This beautiful theatre, built in 1731, is one of the oldest in Europe and functions as Malta's national theatre. There's a varied program of events from October to May (drama, concerts, opera and ballet) or you can take a guided tour (eight daily weekdays, four Saturday) to see the baroque auditorium.

🛏 Sleeping

There's relatively little choice of places to stay in Valletta itself. One alternative is to rent an apartment, which can be done through **Valletta Studio Flats** (🕿2123 6476; www.valletta-studioflats.org).

TOP CHOICE **Asti Guesthouse**   B&B €
(🕿2123 9506; http://mol.net.mt/asti; 18 Triq Sant'Orsla; B&B per person without bathroom €17) You'll get a taste of old-school Valletta charm here in a 350-year-old building converted into a guest house that offers the best-value accommodation in town. Asti has a charming host (though don't cross her!), simple, spacious rooms (each with handbasin), and spotless shared bathrooms. The bargain prices give little indication of the guest house's simple elegance – breakfast is served in a vaulted dining room under a chandelier.

Coronation Guesthouse   B&B €
(🕿2123 7652; 10E Triq M A Vasalli; B&B per person without bathroom from €16) This friendly, family-run place comes complete with wonderfully old royal family paraphernalia. Of the 12 simple rooms, four have balconies with great Valletta views. All bathrooms are shared.

Osborne Hotel   HOTEL €€
(🕿2123 2127/8; www.osbornehotel.com; 50 Triq Nofs in-Nhar; s/d €70/100; ❋🛁🖥🌊) The Osborne, once a hostel to the Knights of St John, adds a dash of style to the Valletta hotel scene. The lobby is a gorgeous and classy affair stuffed full of antiques, and the rooms are thoroughly modern and comfortable. There's a splash pool (with great views) on the roof.

Castille Hotel   HOTEL €€
(🕿2124 3677/8; www.hotelcastillemalta.com; Pjazza Kastilja; s/d from €56/85; ❋🖥) Enjoying a superb position in an old palazzo and with a lobby that feels far more grand than you'd expect for a three-star hotel, the Castille is a great choice. Rooms have more character here than in most local hotels, and the three with traditional wooden balconies are sought-after!

Midland Guesthouse   B&B €
(🕿2123 6024; midlandguesthouse@gmail.com; 255 Triq Sant'Orsla; B&B per person without bathroom from €18) Well-located place spread over several floors of a large town house; rooms are neat and pleasant.

British Hotel   HOTEL €€
(🕿2122 4730; www.britishhotel.com; 40 Triq il-Batterija; s/d from €36/50; ❋@🖥) Rooms may be underwhelming and characterless, but the views, whether from rooms at the front of the building or from the bar, are breathtaking. Air-con costs extra.

🍴 Eating

Cheap and tasty fare can be found at the kiosks beside City Gate bus terminus. Millennium (the first kiosk on your right after you exit City Gate) sells hot *pastizzi* for €0.30 each; next door, the Dates Kiosk sells traditional *mqaret* – delicious pastries stuffed with spiced dates and deep-fried – for €0.20.

TOP CHOICE **Trabuxu Bistro**   MALTESE €€
(🕿2122 0357; www.trabuxu.com.mt; 8-9 Triq Nofs in-Nhar; mains €9-16; ⊙lunch Mon-Fri, dinner Fri & Sat) This cool little bistro, just around the corner from its sister wine bar, serves homecooked, traditional Maltese dishes using fresh seasonal produce – the menu includes octopus salad, pan-fried *lampuka* (a local

fish), rabbit in white wine and garlic, and beef stewed in red wine and port.

Rubino
MALTESE €€

(☏2122 4656; 53 Triq L-Ifran; mains €15; ⊙lunch Tue-Fri, dinner Tue-Sat) Charming, rustic Rubino is a great spot for lunch or dinner, with modern takes on traditional Maltese cooking. There's no menu, just a selection of the day's dishes depending on seasonal produce; Tuesday night is *fenkata* (a communal meal of rabbit) night, for which bookings are advised.

Café Jubilee
CAFE €

(125 Triq Santa Luċija; mains €4-8; ⊙8am-1am Mon-Thu, 8am-3am Fri & Sat; 🔊) A feel-good place you can drop into any time for a breakfast of coffee and *pastizzi*, a lunchtime baguette, or a simple dinner of salad, pasta or risotto. Jubilee is a continental-style bistro with low lighting, cosy nooks and poster-plastered walls; it's also one of the few places where you can eat and drink late in Valletta.

Fumia
CAFE €€

(Manoel Theatre, Triq it-Teatru l-Antik; mains €10-40; ⊙lunch & dinner Tue-Sun) There are two eateries here: the charming Fumia Café in the Manoel Theatre's luminous courtyard where light meals are served up all day; and the stylish Fumia Restaurant in the basement, a refined, dark space housed in a vault and specialising in fish and seafood.

THE KNIGHTS OF WHO?

You'll encounter references to the Knights of the Order of St John all over Malta, so some background information is worth having. The Order of St John was founded during the Christian Crusades of the 11th and 12th centuries to protect Christian pilgrims travelling to and from the Holy Land, and to care for the sick. The knights were drawn from the younger male members of Europe's aristocratic families (those who were not the principal heirs). It was a religious order, with the knights taking vows of celibacy, poverty and obedience, and handing over their patrimonies. The order became extremely prestigious, wealthy and powerful as a military and maritime force, and as a charitable organisation that founded and operated several hospitals.

Caffè Cordina
CAFE €

(244 Triq ir-Repubblika; mains €5-11; ⊙7.30am-7pm Mon-Sat, 7.30am-1pm Sun) The prime location of this local institution makes it a great place for a coffee and cake while you watch the world go by, but make sure you go inside to admire the exquisitely painted vaulted ceiling. The food is passable but nothing special.

Agius Pastizzerija
BAKERY €

(273 Triq San Pawl; pastries €0.25; ⊙7.30am-5.30pm Mon-Sat) Hole-in-the-wall place serving traditional snacks, including *pastizzi* and other carb-loaded treats.

For those staying in apartments and self-catering:

Wembley Stores
SUPERMARKET

(305 Triq ir-Repubblika; ⊙7.45am-7pm Mon-Sat) Stocks a selection of groceries.

Fresh produce market
MARKET

(Triq il-Merkanti; ⊙7am-1pm Mon-Sat) Behind the Grand Master's Palace, where you can buy fruit and vegetables etc.

🍷 Drinking

Valletta is no party town – for real nightlife head to Paceville. But for a pleasant and sophisticated evening look no further.

Trabuxu
WINE BAR

(1 Triq id-Dejqa; ⊙7.30pm-late) Things don't come much simpler or much better than this cellar wine bar (the name means 'corkscrew'). Friendly staff are keen to introduce you to Malta's more accomplished wines, which are complemented by a menu of tasty local tapas, cheese and dips. Perfect.

Kantina
CAFE, BAR

(Triq San Ġwann; ⊙8am-midnight Mon-Sat May-Dec, 8am-8pm Jan-Apr) This cheerful cafe has a great location, with outdoor tables scattered under the trees outside St John's Co-Cathedral. The coffee is up there with the best in town (€2 for a large cappuccino).

2 22
WINE BAR

(222 Triq l-Assedju il-Kbir) This deeply trendy bar is one of Valletta's talking points, combining striking modern design with a setting that is half-in, half-out of a vaulted cavern in St Andrew's Bastion – the outdoor terrace with designer waterfall has a view across the harbour to Sliema.

The Pub
PUB

(136 Triq l-Arċisqof; ⊙11.30am-11pm) Film buffs can raise a glass in memory of the late Oliver

Reed who in 1999 slumped over and died, mid-drink, at this Valletta bar.

☆ Entertainment

St James' Cavalier Centre for Creativity

ARTS CENTRE

(www.sjcav.org; Triq Nofs in-Nhar) Modern arts centre housing exhibition spaces, a theatre for live performances and an art-house cinema. Pick up a program inside for the low-down on what's showing. See also the Manoel Theatre.

❶ Information

Police station (☎2122 5495; Triq Nofs in-Nhar)

Royal Pharmacy (☎2125 2396; 271 Triq ir-Repubblika) Central pharmacy open during shopping hours.

Tourist office City Centre (☎2291 5440; 229 Triq il-Merkanti; ☺9am-5.15pm Mon-Sat, 9am-12.45pm Sun & public holidays); Valletta Waterfront (☎2122 0633; Pinto Wharf; ☺8am-5pm daily)

Ziffa (194 Triq id-Dejqa; per 10min €1; ☺9am-11pm Mon-Sat, 9am-10.30pm Sun) Internet access, wi-fi and good rates for international phone calls.

❶ Getting There & Away

BOAT The **Marsamxetto ferry** crosses between Valletta and Sliema (€0.93, five minutes); boats operate hourly from 8am to 6pm, every 30 minutes from 10am to 4pm. Ferries from Italy (p607) dock at the Sea Passenger Terminal, near Pinto Wharf; the set taxi fare from here to Valletta is €10.

BUS The City Gate bus terminus has services to all parts of the island (see p608). Bus 8 runs between Malta's **airport** (stop outside the

departures hall) to the City Gate bus terminal (€0.47, 40 minutes, every 20 to 30 minutes).

TAXI The set fare for a taxi from the airport to Valletta or Floriana is €15.75. **CT Cabs** (☎2133 3321 or 7933 3321) operates a fleet of eco-friendly electric-powered taxis that ply the streets of Valletta from 7am to 11pm (flat fare €1 per person, maximum three passengers).

Around Valletta

THE THREE CITIES

You'll be awed by views of the Three Cities from Valletta's southern side, but make the effort to visit as well, as these ancient settlements are fast becoming Valletta's most interesting and vibrant neighbours, a world away from the commercialism of Sliema. The Three Cities are **Vittoriosa**, **Senglea** and **Cospicua**, and all three are crowded around Valletta's dockyards. Of the three, Vittoriosa has by far the most to offer visitors, so make this your priority.

Start with the excellent **Maritime Museum** (Vittoriosa Waterfront; adult/child €5/2.50; ☺9am-5pm) where Malta's naval history is celebrated in great detail, from the Romans to the British. From here wander along the renovated waterfront to **Fort St Angelo**, which occupies the end of the peninsula. It housed the Grand Master of the Knights of St John until 1571, and later served as headquarters of la Valette during the Great Siege. Sadly the fortress is not open to the public.

Wandering back through Vittoriosa's backstreets, don't miss the fascinating **Inquisitor's Palace** (Triq il-Mina l-Kbira; adult/child €6/3; ☺9am-5pm), where the inquisition went about its brutal tortures (largely glossed over by the exhibits!) and home now to the National Museum of Ethnography. Nearby is a small maze of charming alleys, collectively known as Il Collachio, with some of the oldest surviving buildings in the city.

From Vittoriosa's waterfront (beneath the prominent church) there are water taxis that will take you across to Valletta for €5, or cruise around the harbour for €10 per person. Buses 1, 2, 4 and 6 from Valletta will take you to the bus stop on Triq 79 beneath the Poste d'Aragon (bus 2 continues to Misrah ir-Rebha). One of these routes leaves Valletta every 15 to 20 minutes; the fare is €0.47.

HAL SAFLIENI HYPOGEUM

The town of Paola, about 4km south of Valletta, is home to the magnificent **Hal Saflieni Hypogeum** (www.heritagemalta.com;

DIY CAPITAL BUS TOUR

Fancy a cheap, quick, DIY bus tour of the capital? Bus 198 is a circular route departing City Gate every half hour from 9.30am to 6pm. It does a clockwise loop around the bastions of Valletta and through Floriana, so you can take in harbour views, Fort St Elmo and the Valletta Waterfront. You'll see the periphery of the capital from the bus, but you'll need to 'fill in the gaps' on foot. A complete circuit takes around 20 minutes; the fare is all of €0.93 (or you can buy a one-day ticket for €3.49 and use the bus as a hop-on hop-off service).

Triq iċ-Ċimiterju; adult/child €25/15; ☉tours hourly 9am-4pm), usually referred to simply as the Hypogeum. It's a fascinating complex of underground burial chambers thought to date from 3600 BC to 3000 BC. Excellent 50-minute tours of the complex are available, but the number of visitors has been restricted in order to preserve this fragile Unesco World Heritage site. Prebooking is therefore *essential* (usually a couple of weeks before you wish to visit); tickets are available in person from the Hypogeum and the National Museum of Archaeology in Valletta, or online at www.heritagemalta.org (€21).

Half a dozen buses leaving from Valletta's City Gate terminus pass through Paola, including bus 1, 2, 3, 4 and 6. Get off at the main square (Pjazza Paola); the Hypogeum is a five-minute signposted walk south.

Sliema, St Julian's & Paceville

Valletta, while nominally Malta's capital, is something of a museum piece. The nearby towns of Sliema, St Julian's and Paceville are where all the action is, and where Malta's younger population flocks to promenade, eat, drink, shop and play. It's also where many tourists base themselves among the growing number of high-rise hotels, apartment blocks, shops, restaurants, bars and nightclubs.

◉ Sights & Activities

There's not a lot to see in Sliema itself, but there are good views of Valletta from Triq ix-Xatt (the Strand), especially at dusk as the floodlights are switched on. Triq ix-Xatt and Triq it-Torri (Tower Rd) make for a pleasant waterfront stroll, with plenty of bars and cafes in which to quench a thirst. Beaches in the area are mostly shelves of bare rock, and clambering in and out of the sea can be a bit awkward. There are better facilities at the many private lidos along the coast, offering swimming pools, sun lounges, bars and water sports; admission costs around €5 to €10 per day.

Captain Morgan Cruises (☏2346 3333; www.captainmorgan.com.mt) operates from the waterfront area of Sliema known as The Ferries. The Captain has a boat trip for every traveller's taste and pocket – there's a popular tour of Grand Harbour (€16), or an all-day cruise around Malta and Comino (€40). Other options include day trips to the Blue Lagoon, a sunset cruise, a sailing cruise on a catamaran or an 'underwater safari' in a glass-bottom boat. There are also popular 4WD jeep safaris (€55/62 to explore Malta/Gozo). Tickets can be purchased at any of the travel agencies on the waterfront.

🛏 Sleeping

TOP CHOICE / **Hotel Valentina**   HOTEL **€€**
(☏2138 2232; www.hotelvalentina.com; Triq Schreiber; s/d from €82/92; ❋🛜) Prices at Valentina are shockingly reasonable and the location is fab. There's a boutique feel, but older rooms have a rustic atmosphere while newer ones have clean, contemporary lines and splashes of vivid colour (an extension will more than double capacity by 2012). Rooms aren't huge, but then neither are the prices. A bargain, especially in low season.

NSTS Hibernia Residence & Hostel
HOSTEL **€**
(☏2133 3859, 2133 5450; www.nsts.org; Triq Mons G Depiro, Sliema; dm €12, s/tw €57/74; @) Malta's only hostel is perfect for those who are after quality budget accommodation. As well as a laundry, kitchens, breakfast room/cafeteria, TV lounge, internet cafe and rooftop sun terrace, there are single-sex dorms or twin studios with private bathroom and kitchenette. From Valletta, take bus 62, 64 or 67 to Balluta Bay and walk 300m up Triq Manwel Dimech; Triq Mons G Depiro is on the left. Low-season prices can be as low as €28/36 per single/twin.

Hotel Juliani   BOUTIQUE HOTEL **€€€**
(☏2138 8000; www.hoteljuliani.com; 12 Triq San Ġorġ, Spinola Bay; s/d from €140/150; ❋@🛜🏊) Hotel Juliani scores points for introducing Malta to the boutique hotel concept. That it's superbly located in Spinola Bay, houses top-notch eateries and is heavily design driven means its overall satisfaction scoresheet is high. There's no beating the views from the gorgeous rooftop pool and terrace.

Ir-Rokna Hotel   HOTEL **€€**
(☏2138 4060; www.roknahotel.com; Triq il-Knisja; s/d from €50/60; ❋🛜) Stay within strolling distance of the treats of St Julian's, but a long way from the Hilton price tag. You're also close to the nightlife, but far enough away to not suffer with noise. Ir-Rokna is decent value, and while the rooms are timeworn and bland, the service is friendly, and the hotel is home to Malta's oldest (and, many claim, its finest) pizzeria (mains €7 to €9).

✕ Eating

St Julian's and the Sliema waterfront are the heart of Malta's fine-dining scene, while Paceville is crammed with cheap and cheerful cafes and fast-food outlets.

TOP CHOICE Kitchen MEDITERRANEAN €€€
(☎2131 1112; 210 Triq it-Torri; mains €16-23; ⏲lunch Thu-Mon, dinner nightly, closed Aug) On a none-too-interesting stretch of the promenade, the Kitchen's owner-chef whips up an exemplary Med-fusion menu in a smart, simple setting. Mouth-watering dishes include white bean soup with truffle oil, and pan-fried prawns with pea puree; there are also some imaginative vegetarian dishes.

Parapett ITALIAN €€
(125 Triq San Ġorġ; mains €7-16; ⏲dinner daily, lunch Sun) This bright and cheerful eatery caters to all tastes with a wide-ranging menu of freshly prepared pasta, pizza, risotto, salad, seafood and grilled meats. There's a separate kids' menu, as well as vegetarian, vegan, dairy-free and gluten-free menus.

Avenue ITALIAN €€
(Triq Gort, Paceville; mains €7-10; ⏲lunch Mon-Sat, dinner daily) Multicoloured and multiroomed, the Avenue is a quiet escape from Paceville's traffic, with a huge pizza and pasta menu, Murano glass and Venetian masks as decor and tons of outdoor tables. With prices this decent it's no surprise that it's enormously popular.

Zest INTERNATIONAL €€€
(☎2138 7600; www.zestflavours.com; 12 Triq San Ġorġ; mains €19-25; ⏲dinner daily; ☎) Zest features one of Malta's most interesting menus, where the theme is 'East meets West'. You can choose from the Western (seared salmon, lamb cutlets) or the Eastern section – perhaps a dim sum platter followed by Indonesian beef rendang. There's also a decent selection of sushi, and great desserts. Bookings are advised; leave small kids at home.

Paparazzi INTERNATIONAL €€
(159 Triq San Ġorġ, Spinola Bay; mains €8-15; ⏲10am-midnight) The sunny terrace here is a prime people-watching spot, with a fine view of Spinola Bay. Fight your way through huge portions from the crowd-pleasing menu of pizzas, pasta and burgers.

Hugo's Lounge ASIAN €€
(Triq San Ġorġ, Paceville; mains €8-16) This very cool, dark cocktail lounge and restaurant serves up well-executed Asian food ranging from Thai curries and satay platters to noodles and stir-fries. It's also a great spot for preclubbing cocktails in the alfresco area on Triq San Ġorġ, Paceville's party street.

For self-caterers:

Arkadia Foodstore GROCERY
(Triq il-Knisja, Paceville; ⏲8am-8pm Mon-Sat) Convenient foodstore.

Tower Foods Supermarket SUPERMARKET
(46 Triq il-Kbira, Sliema; ⏲8am-7.30pm Mon-Sat) Handy supermarket.

🍷 Drinking & Entertainment

The St Julian's and Sliema waterfronts have everything from chichi wine bars to traditional British pubs, while Paceville is the place for partying, with wall-to-wall bars and clubs. Paceville is jam-packed at the weekends year-round (nightly in summer), and all bars and clubs stay open until late – it's an in-your-face scene that won't appeal to everyone. However, change is afoot in Paceville – the long-standing Axis nightclub has been converted to retail and office space, and there are more commercial property developments under way.

Muddy Waters BAR
(56 Triq il-Kbira, St Julian's) On Balluta Bay, Muddies has a great jukebox, rock DJs on Friday and Saturday, and live rock bands on Sunday nights – when things can get pretty rowdy and the tables may act as dance floors. It's a favourite of the student crowd.

Havana CLUB
(www.havanamalta.com;TriqSanĠorġ, Paceville; admission free) Six bars and a soundtrack of R&B, soul and commercial favourites keep the crowds happy here. There are plenty of students and tourists chatting each other up, but plenty of locals too.

Fuego BAR
(www.fuego.com.mt; Triq Santu Wistin, Paceville) Get hot and sweaty dancing up a storm at this popular salsa bar – head first to its free salsa-dancing classes (Mondays to Wednesdays from 8.30pm).

O'Casey's Irish Pub PUB
(Triq Santu Wistin, Paceville) Beneath Hotel Bernard, this pub is crowded, lively and well stocked with cold Guinness. It also screens live football games.

Adam's Bar BAR
(www.adamshotelmalta.com; Ross St, St Julian's) Friendly, laid-back and much-loved gay bar.

Klozet
CLUB

(www.klozetclub.com; Ball St, St Julian's) The island's only gay club.

❶ Information

MelitaNet (Triq Ball, Paceville; per hr €2; ☉24hr) Large internet cafe inside Tropicana Hotel. Also offers good-value rates for international calls.

White House (cnr Paceville Ave & Triq Schreiber, Paceville; per 3hr €5; ☉7am-11pm) Fast internet access with lots of terminals.

❶ Getting There & Away

BOAT From 8am to 6pm the **Marsamxetto ferry** crosses frequently between the Strand in Sliema and the end of Triq San Marku in Valletta (€0.93, five minutes).

BUS Buses 62, 64, 66 and 67 run regularly between Valletta and Sliema, St Julian's and Paceville (€0.47).

Mdina & Rabat

Elegant, aristocratic Mdina, once the capital of Malta, is perched on a rocky outcrop in the southwest of the island. It has been a fortified city for more than 3000 years and was the island's political centre before the knights arrived and chose to settle around Grand Harbour. You can spend hours wandering around the quiet, narrow streets and admiring the exquisite architectural detail. Despite the small honeypots of tourist bustle that have inevitably developed, the city has retained its historical charm. It's at its best of an evening, when the tour buses have gone and you can see just how the town got the nickname 'Silent City'.

The name Mdina comes from the Arabic for 'walled city'. Rabat (population 11,400) is the sprawling town outside the walls to Mdina's south. While it's not a particularly picturesque town, it is full of religious sights including St Paul's Church and two sets of catacombs.

◎ Sights

Palazzo Falson
MUSEUM

(www.palazzofalson.com; Triq Villegaignon; adult/student €10/5; ☉10am-5pm Tue-Sun) If you see only one museum in Mdina, make it this beautifully preserved medieval mansion, which offers a rare glimpse into the private world behind Mdina's anonymous aristocratic walls.

St Paul's Cathedral
CHURCH

(Pjazza San Pawl; adult/student €2.50/1.75, includes museum entry; ☉9.30-4.45pm Mon-Sat, 3-4.45pm Sun) It's not as impressive as St John's in Valletta, but St Paul's is still worth visiting to see the marble tombstones covering the floor and the huge fresco of St Paul's Shipwreck. The **Cathedral Museum** (☑2145 4697; Pjazza San Pawl; ☉9.30am-4.30pm Mon-Fri, to 3.30pm Sat), across the square, is housed in a baroque 18th-century palace, which was originally used as a seminary. It contains collections of coins, silver, vestments, manuscripts and religious paintings.

Domus Romana
MUSEUM

(Wesgħa tal-Mużew; adult/child €6/3; ☉9am-5pm Mon-Sat) Outside Mdina's Greek's Gate is this museum incorporating the excavated remains of a large Roman town house dating from the 1st century BC and featuring impressive mosaic floors.

St Paul's Catacombs
CATACOMBS

(Triq Sant'Agata; adult/child €5/2.50; ☉9am-5pm) From the Domus Romana, walk south along Triq San Pawl for around 600m past St Paul's Church to find the entrance to this series of rock-cut tombs thought to date back to the 3rd century. Entry includes an audioguide.

St Agatha's Crypt & Catacombs
CATACOMBS

(Triq Sant'Agata; adult/child €3.50/1; ☉9am-5pm Mon-Fri, to 1pm Sat) More interesting are the nearby St Agatha's Catacombs, an underground complex of burial chambers boasting some amazing Byzantine frescoes dating from the 12th to the 15th centuries.

🛏 Sleeping & Eating

TOP
CHOICE **Point de Vue Guesthouse**
B&B €€

(☑2145 4117; www.pointdevuemalta.com; 5 Saqqajja, Rabat; B&B per person from €30; @) This century-old 12-room guest house is rightly popular thanks to a combination of affordable rates and its position just metres from Mdina's town walls. Downstairs from the large, spotless rooms (Room 4 is our favourite; it has great island views) are a cafe and restaurant with some unexpected African accents (management is South African-Maltese).

TOP
CHOICE **Mahżen XII**
MALTESE €€

(Triq L-Imhażen; mains €12-15; ☉lunch Fri-Wed, 7-9pm Wed, Fri & Sat) Tucked into a barrel-vaulted powder magazine in Mdina's western walls (the name means 'Magazine

No 12'), this atmospheric little place is a shrine to local produce – much of the food comes from the owner's family farm near Mġarr. Tuck into platters of tomato, bean and basil salad, wild mushrooms, Gozitan cheese, olives and freshly baked bread. You can also buy Maltese wine, honey, organic olive oil, capers, and bajtra (prickly pear) liqueur to take home.

Il Gattopardo   GREEK, ARMENIAN €€
(20 Triq Villegaignon, Mdina; mains €7-10; ☺lunch & dinner Thu-Sat, lunch Mon-Wed Jun-Aug, lunch Mon-Sat Sep-May) The name (meaning 'The Leopard') may be Italian, but this arty bistro set in a lovely old house with a shady courtyard serves up a Greek- and Armenian-inspired menu.

Fontanella Tea Gardens   CAFE €
(Triq is-Sur, Mdina; mains €4-9; ☺10am-6pm winter, to 11pm summer) This place does a roaring lunchtime trade, due largely to its great views (if you can get a terrace table). With a dazzling array of cakes (€2.60 each) to accompany the sandwiches and pizza on the menu, it's a shame about the ordinary service.

ⓘ Getting There & Away

From Valletta, take bus 80 (€0.47) or 81 (€1.16) to reach Rabat; from Sliema and St Julian's bus 65 (€1.16); from Buġibba bus 86 (€1.16). The bus terminus in Rabat is 150m south of Mdina's Main Gate.

Southwest Coast

The views are fantastic from the top of Dingli Cliffs, south of Rabat. While you're here, stop by **Bobbyland Restaurant** (Dingli Cliffs; mains €9-19; ☺10am-3pm & 6.30-11pm, Tue-Sat, 10am-4pm Sun), a local institution with its origins in a wartime Nissen hut-turned-bar. It's regularly crowded with diners munching contentedly on specialities such as traditional Maltese rabbit with garlic.

To the southeast, you'll find the village of Qrendi and the nearby prehistoric temples of **Ħaġar Qim & Mnajdra** (www.heritagemalta. com; adult/child €9/4.50; ☺9am-5pm). Built between 3600 BC and 3000 BC, these are perhaps the best preserved and most evocative of Malta's prehistoric sites. A new visitor centre explains some fascinating theories about the temples and their possible solar and astronomical alignments.

Buses 38 and 138 run from Valletta to the temples (€1.16).

Southeast Coast

Marsaxlokk is a fishing village that sprawls along the side of a photogenic harbour littered with colourful fishing boats. It's renowned for its seafood restaurants and is a magnet for long-lunching locals and tourist busloads, especially on Sundays (fish market day). When the crowds are absent though, it's a charming place.

Duncan Guesthouse (☎2165 7212; www. duncanmalta.com; 33 Xatt is-Sajjieda; d from €45; @☎) is a family-run place offering decent-value rooms, each with bathroom and kitchenette. The minimum stay is four days, which will put some people off.

Of the numerous waterfront eateries here, locals trust **Ir-Rizzu** (☎2165 1569; Xatt is-Sajjieda; mains €10-21) for its fresh fish feasts, as well as nearby **Ix-Xlukkajr** (☎2165 2109; Xatt is-Sajjieda; mains €10-23) where rabbit, as well as fresh fish, is a speciality. For something different, try swanky **Southport** (☎2701 2600; Xatt is-Sajjieda; mains €7-20; ☺lunch & dinner Wed-Mon), which contains no fewer than four restaurants, all catering to the smart set. The views from the upstairs terrace are gorgeous.

Bus 27 runs frequently from Valletta to Marsaxlokk (€0.47); bus 627 runs from Buġibba via Sliema to Marsaxlokk (€1.16, Wednesday and Sunday only).

North Coast

The overdeveloped sprawl of Buġibba and Qawra in the northeast is the heartland of Malta's cheap-and-cheerful package-holiday trade, and it's absolutely mobbed in summer. It's crammed full of hotels, bars and restaurants – fine if you want a week or so of hedonism, but rather lacking in local charm. Buses 49 and 58 run frequently between Valletta and Buġibba (€0.47).

The north is also home to a handful of decent beaches. Beach bums should make a beeline for **Mellieħa Bay** (also known as Għadira Bay), or **Golden Bay** if you like your facilities and water sports laid on thick. If you're after something more low-key, try **Għajn Tuffieħa Bay** and **Ġnejna Bay**.

For Mellieħa Bay, take bus 44 or 45 from Valletta (€0.58), bus 645 from Sliema/St Julian's (€1.16) or bus 48 from Buġibba (€1.16);

TOP SWIMMING SPOTS

There are some great swimming spots scattered around Malta and Gozo, but don't expect to have them all to yourself in high season. The first five in this list are sandy beaches; the others offer rocky ledges for sunbathing. Take a snorkel along.

» **Għajn Tuffieħa Bay** (p600), North Coast

» **Golden Bay** (p600), North Coast

» **Ramla Bay** (p602), Gozo

» **Mellieħa Bay** (p600), North Coast

» **Ġnejna Bay** (p600), North Coast

» **Xlendi Bay** (p603), Gozo

» **Dwejra** (p603), Gozo

» **Blue Lagoon** (p602), Comino

for Golden Bay you'll need bus 47 from Valletta (€0.54), and bus 652 from Sliema/St Julian's and Buġibba (€1.16).

GOZO

Malta's little-sister island has a charm all of its own. More relaxed, more rural and home to some stunning scenery, this tiny place should not be missed on any trip to Malta. Do yourself a favour and spend a few days here, as visiting on a day trip can't really do it justice.

Gozo is a favourite place for scuba diving (p605) and there are several dive operators around the island. You can also take a cruise from resorts such as Marsalforn and Xlendi; this is the best way to enjoy the breathtaking coastline, including the Azure Window and Inland Sea at Dwejra on the west coast.

Victoria (Rabat)

POP 16,600

Victoria, also known as Rabat, is the chief town on Gozo and sits in the centre of the island, 6km from the ferry terminal at Mġarr. Victoria's main attraction is the compact and photogenic citadel, with its cathedral and museums. The town around it is where you'll find most shops and services on the island, and though pleasant enough, it's not usually a place visitors spend much time in.

⊙ Sights

Victoria is built on a hill, crowned by the Citadel (also known as Il-Kastell, or Citadella), a miniature version of Malta's Mdina. At its centre is the **Cathedral of the Assumption** (Misrah il-Katidral; adult/child €3/free; ⊙9am-5pm Mon-Sat) – built between 1697 and 1711, its elegant design is marred only by the fact that funds ran out before completion and the dome was never completed. Inside, the impression of a dome is created by an elaborate trompe l'œil painting on the ceiling. Entry includes an audioguide (deposit required), and admission to the nearby cathedral museum, which displays church gold and religious art.

The handful of small museums inside the Citadel display reasonable collections, but if you're pushed for time, don't feel as though you've missed out – the museums in Valletta are better.

A stroll around the Citadel's walls offers panoramic views of the island. Outside the walls, the main square of Victoria, Pjazza Indipendenza, is a hive of activity, with open-air cafes, treasure-trove craft shops and traders peddling fresh produce.

✗ Eating

Ta'Rikardu MALTESE €
(4 Triq il-Fossos; mains €5-10, platter for 2 €10; ⊙10am-6pm) An institution in Victoria, Ta'Rikardu's sells souvenirs and paintings as well as local produce such as honey, cheese and wine. Take a seat and order a cheap, delicious platter, which includes cheese, bread, locally grown fresh tomatoes, sun-dried tomatoes, capers and olives. Vegie soup or homemade ravioli is also available; wash it all down with a glass or two of Gozitan wine.

ⓘ Information

Aurora Opera House (Triq ir-Reppublika; per 75min €3) Has computers for internet access in its foyer; purchase vouchers from the bar.

Police station (☑2156 2040; Triq ir-Repubblika)

Tourist office (☑2156 1419; Tigrija Palazz, cnr Triq ir-Repubblika & Triq Putirjal; ⊙9am-5.30pm Mon-Sat, to 1pm Sun & public holidays) Inside a shopping arcade, near the bus station.

ⓘ Getting There & Away

See p607 for details of ferry services between Malta and Gozo. Bus 25 runs between Victoria and the ferry, timed with the ferry arrival and departure times.

Gozo's bus terminus is on Triq Putirjal, south off Triq ir-Repubblika and about 10 minutes' walk from the Citadel. All the island's bus routes are circular, starting and finishing at Victoria; the flat fare is €0.47.

Marsalforn

Marsalforn is Gozo's main holiday resort, but it is not an especially lovely town – the bay of this former fishing village is lined with an ugly sprawl of hotels and apartment buildings. Still, it's a low-key resort compared with the fleshpots of Sliema and Buġibba on Malta, and offers some good out-of-season deals on accommodation; it's very popular with divers.

At the head of the bay is a tiny scrap of sand; better swimming and sunbathing can be found on the rocks out to the west, or hike eastward over the hill to Ramla Bay in about 45 minutes.

Maria Giovanna Guesthouse (☎2155 3630; www.gozoguesthouses.com; 41 Triq ir-Rabat; s/d €30/60; @☎) is the pick of budget accommodation on Gozo. This small, extremely welcoming guest house just back from the waterfront retains a loyal clientele who come back again and again. There are 15 rooms, each charmingly decorated in rustic Gozitan style, with private bathrooms; all have balconies, with one exception, and guests are free to use the kitchen.

The best eating option in town is **Il-Kartell** (☎2155 1965; Triq il-Port; mains €10-20), an upmarket waterfront fish restaurant with lots of interesting dishes including braised rabbit in red wine and a superb *aljotta* (fish soup).

Marsalforn is a 4km walk from Victoria, or you can catch bus 21 (€0.47).

Xagħra

The early-19th-century **Church of Our Lady of Victory** looks down on the village square of Xagħra, where old men sit and chat in the shade of the oleanders. Close by are the megalithic temples of **Ġgantija** (www.heritage malta.com; access from Triq L-Imqades; adult/student €8/4; ☉9am-5pm), which has a splendid view over most of southern Gozo and beyond. As the name implies (*ġgantija* means 'giantess'), locals once believed that they had been constructed by giants. These are the largest of the megalithic temples found in the Maltese islands – the walls stand more than 6m high, and together the two temples are 40m wide – and they are believed to be the oldest free-standing structures in the world, built in three stages between 3600 and 3000 BC.

Not far from here is one of Gozo's best beaches, **Ramla Bay**, which has a beautiful red-sand stretch perfect for sunbathing. Follow the signposts from town (bus 42 runs from Victoria to Ramla, July to September).

WORTH A TRIP

COMINO

The tiny island of Comino, smack bang between Malta and Gozo, was once the hideout of pirates and smugglers, but now hosts boatloads of sun-seeking, day-tripping invaders instead. The island is just 2.5km by 1.5km and has a permanent population of four, but the presence of a large hotel and an endless stream of summer visitors will soon dampen your desert-island fantasies. The trick is to stay the night here.

The island's biggest attraction is the photogenic **Blue Lagoon**, a sheltered cove between the west end of the island and the uninhabited islet of Cominotto, with a white-sand seabed and clear turquoise waters. The bay is usually inundated with people enjoying the superb swimming and snorkelling. Most sunbathing is done on the rocky ledges surrounding the cove; take care in the shadeless summer heat. There are public toilets, deckchairs for hire, and kiosks selling drinks and snacks.

Comino Hotel (☎2152 9821; www.cominohotel.com; s/d half-board €89/140; ☉Apr-Oct; ❋@☎) is the only accommodation on the island. It offers bright, simply furnished rooms, a restaurant, cafe and bar, private beach, swimming pools and tennis courts. It also has bike rentals, dive instruction and assorted water sports.

The hotel runs its own ferry service, with crossings from Ċirkewwa in Malta and Mġarr in Gozo; nonguests can use the service, too (€5 each way). Independent water taxis also operate regularly to the island from these two ports – from Mġarr is usually €8 return; from Ċirkewwa is €10 return. Day trips operate to the Blue Lagoon from tourist areas such as Sliema and Buġibba in Malta, and Xlendi and Marsalforn in Gozo.

Xagħra Lodge (☎2156 2362; www.gozo.com/xaghra-lodge;TriqDunĠorġ Preċa; s/d €47/65; ✴✖) is a friendly guest house with decent facilities, including air-con, bathroom, balcony and cable TV in all rooms, plus a swimming pool and an adjacent bar, and a vegetarian-friendly Chinese restaurant. It's a five-minute walk east of the town square.

Oleander (☎2155 7230; Pjazza Vittorija; mains €8-18; ☺lunch & dinner Tue-Sun) is a good place to try authentic Maltese cuisine – regulars rave about the rabbit dishes at this fixture on the pretty village square. The menu has an array of local favourites, including pastas, *braġioli*, fresh fish and fried rabbit in red-wine sauce.

Buses 64 and 65 run between Victoria and Xagħra (€0.47).

Xlendi

Development has turned the fishing village of Xlendi into a popular resort town. Sure, it's busier now, but there's no denying that the bay still enjoys an attractive setting. It's a favourite place for Maltese people taking a weekend break, with good swimming, snorkelling and diving, and plenty of rocks for sunbathing.

San Antonio Guesthouse (☎2156 3555; www.clubgozo.com.mt; Triq it-Torri; s/d €42/66; ✴✖) is perfectly located, a fair climb up the hill on the south side of the bay. Surprisingly (given the price) air-con, cable TV, big private bathrooms and balconies/terraces are standard, and there's a very decent pool.

The pick of the bunch though is **St Patrick's Hotel** (☎2156 2951; www.vjborg.com/stpatricks; Xlendi Waterfront; d from €74; ✴@✖), which is right in the centre of the town and has a rooftop terrace with spa and pool. Sea views come at a premium, but are worth the price.

For eating, try **Stone Crab** (Triq ix-Xatt; mains €5-25; ☺lunch Mar-Oct, dinner Jun-Oct), a cheerful place right on the waterfront that serves up lots of seafood, local dishes and popular pizzas.

Bus 87 runs between Victoria and Xlendi (€0.47).

San Lawrenz

This charming village is famous as the home of writer Nicholas Monsarrat (1910–79), whose novel *The Kappillan of Malta* is considered a classic of Maltese modern literature. The village today is home to the

Ta'Dbieġi Crafts Village (☺10am-4pm), where artisans sell handicrafts, lace, glass and pottery.

You can enjoy a fantastic meal at charming **Tatitas Restaurant** (☎2156 6482; San Lawrenz Sq; mains €14-20; ☺lunch & dinner Apr-Oct), where you can dine alfresco in the square or enjoy the cosy interior. It has a great menu of modern takes on classic Maltese and Mediterranean cookery.

Dwejra

From San Lawrenz it's a 1.5km walk or a short drive (buses are infrequent) to Dwejra, home of Gozo's most famous natural wonder, the **Azure Window**. Here geology and the sea have conspired to produce some of Gozo's most spectacular coastal scenery.

At this dramatic site two vast underground caverns in the limestone have collapsed to create two circular depressions now occupied by Dwejra Bay and the Inland Sea. The **Inland Sea** is a cliff-bound lagoon connected to the open sea by a tunnel that runs for 100m through the headland of Dwejra Point. The tunnel is big enough for small boats to sail through in calm weather and the Inland Sea has been used by fishermen as a haven for centuries. Today the fishermen supplement their income by taking tourists on **boat trips** (per person €3.50) through the cave.

A few minute's walk from the Inland Sea is a huge natural arch in the sea cliffs, known as the Azure Window. In the rocks in front of it is another geological freak called the **Blue Hole** – a vertical chimney in the limestone about 10m in diameter and 25m deep that connects with the open sea through an underwater arch about 8m down. Understandably, it's a very popular dive site, though the snorkelling is also excellent. Between the Inland Sea and the Azure Window is the little **Chapel of St Anne**, built in 1963 on the site of a much older church.

UNDERSTAND MALTA

History

Malta has a fascinating history and is crowded with physical and cultural reminders of its past. The mysterious megalithic temples built between 3600 BC and 2500 BC are the oldest surviving freestanding structures in the world, predating Egypt's Pyramids of Giza by more than 500 years. The best places to view them are on the south coast (p600) and at Xaghra on Gozo.

From around 800 BC to 218 BC, Malta was colonised by the Phoenicians and Carthaginians, and then became part of the Roman Empire. In AD 60, St Paul was shipwrecked on the island, where (according to folklore) he converted the islanders to Christianity.

Arabs from North Africa arrived in AD 870 and tolerated the local Christians. The Arabs were expelled in 1090 by the Norman king, Roger of Sicily. For the next 400 years, Malta's history was linked to Sicily, and its rulers were a succession of Normans, Angevins (French), Aragónese and Castilians (Spanish).

In 1530 the islands were given to the Knights of the Order of St John of Jerusalem by Charles V, Emperor of Spain; the local inhabitants were given no say in the matter. As soon as they arrived in Malta, the knights began to fortify the harbour and to skirmish with Ottoman forces. In May 1565, a huge Ottoman fleet carrying more than 30,000 men laid siege to the island, but 700 knights and 8000 Maltese managed to hold them off. The Great Siege lasted for more than three months, with continuous and unbelievably ferocious fighting. After enormous bloodshed on both sides, help finally arrived from Sicily and the Turks withdrew.

The knights were hailed as the saviours of Europe. Money and honours were heaped upon them by grateful monarchs, and the construction of the new city of Valletta and its enormous fortifications began. With fame and power came corruption, and the knights sank into ostentatious ways, largely supported by piracy. In 1798 Napoleon arrived, seeking to counter the British influence in the Mediterranean, and the knights, who were mostly French, surrendered to him without a fight.

The Maltese defeated the French in 1800 with British assistance, and in 1814 Malta officially became part of the British Empire. The British developed Malta into a major naval base, making it an important target for Axis forces during WWII. Considered a linchpin in the battle for the Mediterranean, Malta was subjected to a German and Italian naval and aerial blockade between 1940 and 1943. In 1942 it suffered five months of day-and-night bombing raids which left 40,000 homes destroyed and the population on the brink of starvation.

In 1947 the devastated island was given a measure of self-government. The country gained independence in 1964, and became a republic in 1974. In recent decades, the Maltese have achieved considerable prosperity, thanks largely to tourism. Every summer the Maltese population triples due to an influx of tourists, and development continues unabated, much to the detriment of the environment.

Malta became a member of the EU in May 2004, and adopted the euro as its national currency in 2008.

People

Malta's population is around 413,000, with most people living in the satellite towns around Valletta, Sliema and the Grand Harbour. Approximately 30,000 live on Gozo, while Comino has a mere handful of farmers. Around 97% of the total population is Maltese-born.

Malta has long been an entry point for illegal immigration into Europe from Africa, but numbers of illegal immigrants have skyrocketed in recent years. This remains a divisive local issue and attitudes are very mixed within the country about how best to deal with the situation.

Despite an easy blend of Mediterranean and British culture throughout the islands, there's still a strong feeling of tradition. The Maltese are fairly conservative in outlook, with strong family values. Around 98% of the population is Roman Catholic, and the Church wields considerable influence – most noticeable on Sundays when many shops and businesses are closed. Abortion and divorce are illegal.

Arts

Lacemaking is thought to have been introduced to Malta during the 16th century when the knights arrived. There are plenty of stalls and shops selling traditional tablecloths and such things in more touristy areas. You should also keep an eye out for beautiful, intricate silver filigree – the art is thought to have come to Malta from Sicily in the 17th century. The Maltese glass-blowing industry has enjoyed increasing success and many pieces are now exported.

Environment

Environmental Issues

Malta's small surface area has been subjected to pressures of population, land use and development, a lack of protection for natural areas and, more recently, a significant increase in pollution. There is also a severe shortage of fresh water. Hunting and trapping of birds remains a (controversial) part of the Maltese way of life.

The Land

The Maltese archipelago consists of three inhabited islands: Malta (246 sq km), Gozo (67 sq km) and Comino (2.7 sq km). It lies in the middle of the Mediterranean, 93km south of Sicily, 290km east of Tunisia and 340km north of Libya.

The densely populated islands are formed of soft, golden limestone, widely used as a building material. There are some low ridges and outcrops, but no major hills. There are few trees and little greenery to soften the sun-bleached landscape; in turn, the sparse vegetation supports little in the way of wildlife. There is almost no surface water and barely any permanent creeks or rivers. The water table is the main source of fresh water, supplemented by several desalination plants.

Food & Drink

Like the Maltese language, local cuisine has been influenced by the many foreign cultures that have ruled the country. The food is rustic and meals are based on seasonal produce and the fisherman's catch.

Malta is not known as a gourmet destination, but the food is generally good and cheap, and at the top end can be excellent. Most restaurants offer inexpensive pizzas and pastas, and there are usually vegetarian options.

Be sure to try the locally caught fish and seafood, and the national dish of *fenek* (rabbit). Also look out for *pastizzi* (small, filled parcels of flaky pastry), a favourite with the locals; you'll pay around €0.30 for one, so they're great for quick, budget snacks.

Local beers are good, particularly Cisk (pronounced 'chisk'), and the range of locally produced wine is surprisingly accomplished.

Most eateries are open from noon to 3pm and 7pm to 11pm Monday to Saturday; most are closed on Sundays. Outside of Valletta and its suburbs, however, be sure to get to a restaurant by 9.30pm at the latest as kitchens can close early.

Smoking is banned in all enclosed spaces, but is still allowed in closed-off, separately ventilated areas.

SURVIVAL GUIDE

Directory A-Z

Accommodation

Malta has a handful of hostels and an array of family-run guest houses that usually represent great value for money. Hotels range from crumbling, characterful old town houses to modern palaces of five-star luxury. The high season is generally June to September, as well as the Christmas to New Year period. Rates are significantly reduced during off-peak periods.

There are loads of internet sites offering information on hotels and other accommodation options in Malta, including:

Holiday Malta (www.holiday-malta.com)

Malta Hotel (www.maltahotel.net)

Malta Hotels (www.malta-hotels.com)

Visit Malta (www.visitmalta.com/booking-page)

PRICE RANGES

Prices are quoted at high-season rates and include private bathroom unless otherwise stated.

€	Less than €50
€€	€50 to €130
€€€	More than €130

Activities

The most popular activities are walking, water sports and scuba diving. Check out www.visitmalta.com and follow the 'What to see & do' link.

Diving conditions here are excellent: visibility often exceeds 30m, there's a wide variety of marine life and warm temperatures mean that diving is possible year-round. Favourite dive spots include Ċirkewwa on Malta, Dwejra on Gozo and various spots around Comino.

There are more than 40 diving schools to choose from. The majority are members of the **Professional Diving Schools Association** (PDSA; www.pdsa.org.mt). See also www.visitmalta.com/diving-malta for comprehensive details of dive sites, regulations and operators.

THE MALTESE FESTA

Each village has a *festa* (feast day) honouring its patron saint, and you can't avoid getting caught up in the celebrations. Religious enthusiasm starts in the days leading up to and during the *festa* as families flock to the churches to give thanks. The streets are illuminated and the festivities culminate in a huge procession, complete with fireworks, marching brass bands and a life-sized statue of the patron saint. *Festa* season runs from May to September. But a *festa* isn't the only excuse to throw a party in Malta, and the website www.maltafestivals.com lists what's on, where and when (including links to *festa* dates and locations).

Most schools offer a half-day 'taster course' or beginner's dive, costing around €40. A course that will give you an entry-level diving qualification (eg PADI Open Water Diver) should take three to five days and cost around €350. Experienced divers can hire equipment and arrange accompanied or unaccompanied dives with most operators.

Potential divers will need to complete a medical questionnaire and may be required to undergo a medical examination (dive centres will help arrange this). If you plan to dive, make sure your travel insurance covers this activity.

Business Hours

Banks 8.30am to 12.30pm Mon to Fri and 8.30am to 11.30am Sat. Slightly longer hours from Jun to Sep.

Museums 9am to 5pm daily; closed major public holidays.

Restaurants noon to 3pm and 7pm to 11pm.

Shops 9am to 1pm and 4pm to 7pm Mon to Sat; closed Sun and public holidays. Some stay open all day in summer, especially in tourist areas.

Food

Malta offers a range of eateries, though most places specialise in Maltese and/or Italian cuisine. Many restaurants open only six days a week, but days of closure vary (Sunday and Monday are popular). Note that some restaurants close for three or four weeks in August.

The prices ranges used in this book are based on the cost of a main course.

€   Less than €8

€€   €8 to €16

€€€ More than €16

Internet Access

Malta has plenty of internet cafes and most hotels and guest houses have a computer available for guests' use. More and more access is via wi-fi, usually free in well-run hotels, but sometimes still charged (around €4 to €6 per hour).

Money

Malta adopted the euro in January 2008. To avoid stealth price hikes, the rate of exchange was fixed at Lm1 (the old Maltese lira) to €2.33, hence the often bizarre prices for museum tickets, public transport and other state-run services.

Banks usually offer better rates of exchange than hotels. There are ATMs and a 24-hour exchange bureau at the airport, and a bank and ATMs at Pinto Wharf. ATMs can be found in almost all towns; credit cards are widely accepted.

It's a good idea to round up a taxi fare or restaurant bill in order to leave a small tip. Shops have fixed prices; hotels and car-hire agencies offer reduced rates in the low and shoulder seasons (October to May).

Public Holidays

New Year's Day 1 January

St Paul's Shipwreck 10 February

St Joseph's Day 19 March

Freedom Day 31 March

Good Friday March/April

Labour Day 1 May

Commemoration of 1919 Independence Riots 7 June

Feast of Sts Peter and Paul (L-Imnarja Festival) 29 June

Feast of the Assumption 15 August

Victory Day 8 September

Independence Day 21 September

Feast of the Immaculate Conception 8 December

Republic Day 13 December
Christmas Day 25 December

Telephone

Public telephones (mostly card-operated) are widely available; buy phonecards at kiosks, post offices and souvenir shops. International calls are discounted after 6pm weekdays and all day Saturday and Sunday. For local telephone inquiries, call ☎1182; for overseas inquiries, call ☎1152.

The international direct dialling code is ☎00. To call Malta from abroad, dial the international access code, ☎356 (the country code for Malta) and the eight-digit number (there are no area codes in Malta).

Most of the population have mobile phones; these numbers begin with either 79 or 99. Malta uses the GSM900 mobile phone network which is compatible with the rest of Europe, Australia and New Zealand, but not with the USA and Canada's GSM1900.

Tourist Information

The Malta Tourism Authority (www.visitmalta.com) has tourist offices at Valletta, Malta international airport and Victoria on Gozo.

Visas

Citizens of EU and EEA (Europe Economic Area) countries do not need a visa for any type of visit. Citizens of Australia, Canada, Israel, Japan, New Zealand and the USA can stay for up to three months without a visa; other nationalities can check their visa requirements on www.foreign.gov.mt (click on the Services/Travelling to Malta link). Malta is part of the Schengen Zone.

Getting There & Away

Air

Malta is well connected to Europe and North Africa. All flights arrive at and depart from Malta international airport (MLA; ☎2124 9600; www.maltairport.com) at Luqa, 8km south of Valletta.

Sea

Malta has regular sea links with Sicily (Pozzallo and Catania), central Italy (Civitavecchia) and northern Italy (Genoa). Ferries dock at the Sea Passenger Terminal beside the Valletta Waterfront in Floriana, underneath the southeast bastions of Valletta.

Virtu Ferries (www.virtuferries.com) Malta (☎2206 9022); Catania (☎095-535 711); Pozzallo (☎0932-954 062) offers the fastest Malta–Sicily crossing with its catamaran service from Pozzallo and Catania. The Pozzallo–Malta crossing takes 90 minutes and operates year-round. The return passenger fare on both routes is €147/88 in high/low season.

Grimaldi Ferries (☎2299 5110; www.grimaldi-ferries.com) operates a weekly service year-round from Genoa and Civitavecchia.

Grandi Navi Veloci (GNV; ☎2569 4550; www.gnv.it) operates a weekly Livorna–Palermo–Malta service.

Ferry schedules tend to change from year to year, and it is best to confirm the information given here, either with the ferry company or with a travel agent.

Getting Around

Air

Harbour Air (☎2122 8302; www.harbourairmalta.com; one way/return €44/80, three daily, 20min) Seaplane service from Valletta Waterfront to Mġarr harbour in Gozo; runs early March to late November.

Heli-Tours Malta (☎2369 6442; www.heli-link-malta.com; one way/return €85/125, 10min) Helicopter service between Malta International Airport and Gozo Helipad; no fixed timetable.

Boat

Malta to Gozo: Gozo Channel (☎2158 0435; www.gozochannel.com) Car ferry services between Ċirkewwa (Malta) and Mġarr (Gozo), with crossings every 45 to 75 minutes from 6am to around 8pm (and every two hours throughout the night). The journey takes 25 minutes, and the return fare for an adult/child is €4.65/1.15; car (including driver) €15.70. Bus 45 runs regularly from Valletta to Ċirkewwa to connect with the ferry to Gozo. Bus 25 runs between Victoria and Mġarr on Gozo. Malta & Gozo to Comino: see p602.

Valletta to Sliema: Marsamxetto ferry service (☎2346 3862) Five-minute crossing with departures every hour (every half-hour from 10am to 4pm) from 8am to 6pm. Ferries depart from Sliema on the hour and half-hour, and leave from Valletta at quarter past and quarter to the hour. The fare one way is €0.93.

BUS FARES

When using the local buses, make sure you have some small denomination coins – handing over a €10 note for a €0.58 fare and expecting change often results in a major strop!

Bus

Malta Public Transport Association (ATP; ☑2125 0007/8; www.atp.com.mt) runs the island bus services. Most routes originate from the chaotic City Gate terminus, just outside Valletta's city gates. Fares are inexpensive and tickets are purchased from the driver. Fares from Valletta cost €0.47 to €0.58; direct routes between tourist areas that bypass Valletta (eg Sliema–Rabat/Mdina, Buġibba–Golden Bay) cost €1.16.

Services are regular and the more popular routes run until 11pm (with night buses operating to/from Paceville until 3am on weekends). Ask at the tourist office or bus terminus for a free timetable.

On Gozo, the bus terminus is in Victoria, just south of Triq ir-Repubblika. All services depart from here and cost €0.47.

Many buses are relics of the 1950s and '60s, supremely stylish kings of the road that are a perennial favourite with visiting photographers. More modern (and less environmentally damaging) vehicles are slowly being introduced, much to many people's consternation, though some of the best vintage models will be retained as tourist attractions.

Car & Motorcycle

Considering the low rental rates it may make economic sense to hire a car, but beware that the Maltese drive in a way that can be politely described as 'after the Italian style'. Road rules are often ignored, roads are confusingly signposted and parking can be difficult. Distance isn't a problem, however, since Malta is so small and Gozo's half the size again. Outside urban areas, driving is a breeze, and your biggest problem will be potholed roads and getting lost due to lack of signposts.

All the major international car-hire companies are at the airport; there are also dozens of local agencies. Shop around – rates depend on season, length of rental period and the size and make of car. Daily rates for the smallest vehicles start from around €22 (for rental of seven days or longer). The age limit for rental drivers is generally 21 to 70, but drivers between 21 and 25 may be asked to pay a supplement.

The Maltese drive on the left. Speed limits are 80km/h on highways and 50km/h in urban areas, but they are rarely observed. The wearing of seatbelts is compulsory for the driver and front-seat passenger. The maximum blood-alcohol concentration (BAC) level allowed in drivers is 0.08%.

There are no right-of-way rules at roundabouts and at intersections priority is given to whoever gets there first. Any accidents must be reported to the nearest police station (and to the rental company) – don't move your vehicle until the police have arrived.

Taxi

Official Maltese taxis are white (with a taxi sign on top) and fitted with meters. Fares are generally expensive. If you arrive at the airport or port, there are kiosks where you pay the set tariffs upfront. Black taxis (no sign) are privately owned and usually offer cheaper rates than official taxis. To order a taxi by phone, ask at your hotel's reception or try **Wembley Motors** (☑2137 4141) for 24-hour service.

Tours

There are loads of companies offering tours around the islands, by boat/bus/4WD or a combination of the three. Half-day tours cost from €25 but prices vary, so shop around. If you're pushed for time, tours can be a good way to see the highlights, but itineraries can often be rushed, with little free time. Day trips to Gozo and Comino are also common.

Captain Morgan Cruises (☑2346 3333; www.captainmorgan.com.mt) runs a range of sailing trips, cruises and jeep safaris, primarily out of Sliema. See p597 for information on harbour tours.

Montenegro Црна Гора

Includes »

Best Places to Eat

» Restoran Stari Mlini (p616)

» Knez Konoba (p618)

» Konoba Feral (p613)

» Stari Most (p623)

» Restoran Kod Marka (p621)

Best Places to Stay

» Palazzo Radomiri (p616)

» Vila Drago (p618)

» Aman Sveti Stefan (p619)

» Eko-Oaza Suza Evrope (p629)

Why Go?

Imagine a place with sapphire beaches as spectacular as Croatia's, rugged peaks as dramatic as Switzerland's, canyons nearly as deep as Colorado's, *palazzi* as elegant as Venice's and towns as old as Greece's. Then wrap it up in a Mediterranean climate and squish it into an area two-thirds the size of Wales, and you start to get a picture of Montenegro.

More adventurous travellers can easily sidestep the peak-season hordes on the coast by heading to the rugged mountains of the north. This is, after all, a country where wolves and bears still lurk in forgotten corners.

Montenegro, Crna Gora, Black Mountain: the name itself conjures up romance and drama. There are plenty of both on offer as you explore this perfumed land, bathed in the scent of wild herbs, conifers and Mediterranean blossoms. Yes, it really is as magical as it sounds.

When to Go

Podgorica

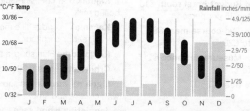

| June Beat the peak-season rush but enjoy the balmy weather; Boka Navy Day in Kotor. | September Warm water, still, but fewer bods to share it with; the Adventure Race takes off. | October The leaves turn golden, making a rich backdrop to walks in the national parks. |

Fast Facts

» **Area** 13,812 sq km

» **Capital** Podgorica

» **Telephone area code** 382

» **Emergency** police 122, fire 123, ambulance 124

Exchange Rates

Australia	A$1	€0.75
Canada	C$1	€0.74
Japan	¥100	€0.89
New Zealand	NZ$1	€0.89
UK	UK£1	€1.18
USA	US$1	€0.74

Set Your Budget

» **Budget hotel room** €10 to €15 per person

» **Two-course meal** €8 to €20

» **Museum entrance** €1 to €5

» **Beer** €1.50

Resources

» **Black Mountain** (www.montenegroholiday.com)

» **Visit Montenegro** (www.visit-montenegro.com)

Connections

Many travellers make the most of the proximity of Dubrovnik's Čilipi airport to Herceg Novi to tie in a visit to Croatia with a Montenegrin sojourn. At the other end of the coast, Ulcinj is the perfect primer for exploring Albania and is connected by bus to Shkodra. Likewise, Rožaje captures elements of Kosovar culture and is well connected to Peć. A train line and frequent bus connections make a trip to Montenegro's closest cousins in Serbia a breeze. Montenegro shares a longer border with Bosnia and Hercegovina (BiH) than any of its neighbours. There are plenty of crossings for drivers, as well as regular bus services from towns. Towns with onward international transport include Herceg Novi, Kotor, Tivat, Bar, Ulcinj and Podgorica.

ITINERARIES

One week

Base yourself in the Bay of Kotor for two nights. Drive through Lovc'en to Cetinje, then the next day continue to Šćepan Polje via Ostrog Monastery. Go rafting the following morning and spend the night in Podgorica. Head to Virpazar for a boat tour of Lake Skadar and then take the scenic lakeside road to Ulcinj. Finish in Sveti Stefan.

Two weeks

Follow the itinerary above, but allow extra time in Kotor, Lake Skadar and Sveti Stefan. From Šćepan Polje head instead to Žabljak and then to Biogradska Gora National Park before continuing to Podgorica.

Essential Food & Drink

» **Njeguški pršut i sir** Smoke-dried ham and cheese from the heartland village of Njeguši.

» **Ajvar** Spicy spread of fried red peppers and eggplant, seasoned with garlic, salt, vinegar and oil.

» **Kajmak** Soft cheese made from the salted cream from boiled milk.

» **Kačamak** Porridge-like mix of cream, cheese, potato and buckwheat or cornflour.

» **Riblja čorba** Fish soup, a staple of the coast.

» **Crni rižoto** Black risotto, coloured with squid ink.

» **Ligne na žaru** Grilled squid, sometimes stuffed (*punjene*) with cheese and smoke-dried ham.

» **Jagnjetina ispod sača** Lamb cooked (often with potatoes) under a metal lid covered with hot coals.

» **Rakija** Domestic brandy, made from nearly anything. The local favourite is grape-based *loza*.

» **Vranac** Local red wine varietal.

» **Krstač** Local white wine varietal.

Montenegro Highlights

1 Marvelling at the majesty and exploring the historic towns hemmed in by the limestone cliffs of the **Bay of Kotor** (p612)

2 Driving the vertiginous route from Kotor to the Njegoš Mausoleum at the top of **Lovćen National Park** (p621)

3 Enjoying the iconic island views while lazing on the sands of **Sveti Stefan** (p618)

4 Seeking the spiritual at peaceful **Ostrog Monastery** (p626)

5 Floating through paradise, rafting between the kilometre-plus walls of the **Tara Canyon** (p628)

6 Wandering through primeval forest mirrored in a tranquil alpine lake at **Biogradska Gora National Park** (p627)

7 Splashing through the floating meadows of water lilies garlanding vast **Lake Skadar** (p623)

BAY OF KOTOR

Coming from Croatia, the Bay of Kotor (Boka Kotorska) starts simply enough, but as you progress through fold upon fold of the bay and the surrounding mountains it gets steeper and steeper and the beauty meter gets close to bursting. It's often described as Southern Europe's most spectacular fjord, and even though the label's not technically correct, the sentiment certainly is.

Herceg Novi Херцег Нови

📞 031 / POP 12.700

It's easy to drive straight through Herceg Novi without noticing anything worth stopping for, especially if you've just come from Croatia with visions of Dubrovnik still dazzling your brain. However, just below the uninspiring roadside frontage hides an appealing Old Town with ancient walls, sunny squares and a lively atmosphere. The water's cleaner here near the mouth of the bay, so the pebbly beaches and concrete swimming terraces are popular.

👁 Sights

Stari Grad   HISTORIC AREA

Herceg Novi's Old Town is at it's most impressive when approached from the pedestrian-only section of ul Njegoševa, paved in the same shiny marble as Dubrovnik and lined in elegant, mainly 19th-century buildings. The street terminates in cafe-ringed **Trg Nikole Đurkovića**, where steps lead up to an elegant crenulated **clocktower** (1667) that was once the main city gate. Just inside the walls is **Trg Herceg Stjepana** (commonly called Belavista Sq), a gleaming white piazza that's perfect for relaxing, drinking and chatting in the shade. At its centre is the Orthodox **Archangel Michael's Church** (built 1883–1905), its lovely proportions capped by a dome and flanked by palm trees. Its Catholic counterpart, **St Jerome's** (1856), is further down the hill, dominating **Trg Mića Pavlovića**.

Kanli-Kula   FORTRESS

(Bloody Tower; admission €1; ⏰8am-midnight) The big fort visible from the main road was a notorious prison during Turkish rule (roughly 1482–1687). You can walk around its sturdy walls and enjoy views over the town. The bastion at the town's seaward edge, **Fortemare**, was rebuilt by the Venetians during their 110-year stint as overlords.

Savina   MONASTERY

(Manastirska 21; ⏰6am-8pm) From its hillside location in the town's eastern fringes, this peaceful Orthodox monastery enjoys wonderful coastal views. It's dominated by the elegant 18th-century **Church of the Dormition**, carved from pinkish stone. Inside there's a gilded iconostasis but you'll need to be demurely dressed to enter (no shorts, sleeveless tops or bikinis). The smaller church beside it has the same name but is considerably older (possibly from the 14th century) and has the remains of frescoes. The monastery is well signposted from the highway.

Regional Museum   MUSEUM

(www.rastko.rs/rastko-bo/muzej/index_e.html; Mirka Komnenovića 9; admission €1.50; ⏰9am-6pm Mon-Sat) Apart from the building itself (a fab bougainvillea-shrouded baroque palace with absolute sea views), this little museum's highlight is its impressive icon gallery.

FREE **Španjola**   FORTRESS

The fortress high above the town, on the other side of the main road, was started and finished by the Turks but named after the Spanish (yep, in 1538 they had a brief stint here as well). If the graffiti and empty bottles are anything to go by, it's now regularly invaded by local teenagers.

🏃 Activities

Herceg Novi is shaping up as the best base for arranging active pursuits, largely due to a network of expats running professional, customer-focused, environmentally aware businesses.

Black Mountain   OUTDOOR PURSUITS

(📞067-640 869; www.montenegroholiday.com; bus station) An agency that can arrange pretty much anything active, including diving, rafting, hiking, paragliding, boat trips and excursions. It offers mountain-bike tours (about €20 per person) and hires out bikes (€10 per day).

Kayak Montenegro   KAYAKING

(📞067-887 436; www.kayakmontenegro.com; Šetalište Pet Danica bb; hire 1/4/8hr €5/15/25) Another excellent outfit run by expats, Kayak Montenegro rents kayaks and offers paddling tours across the bay (half/full day €35/45, including equipment), as well as day trips to explore Lake Skadar from Rijeka Crnojevića.

ADVENTURE RACE MONTENEGRO

Started by a bunch of British expats operating outdoor-adventure businesses out of Herceg Novi, the **Adventure Race** (www.adventureracemontengro.com) should be high on the agenda for anyone who fancies themselves an action man or wonder woman. Held in late September/early October, there are now two separate events. The Coastal Challenge is one day of kayaking, mountain biking, hiking and orienteering amid the exceptional scenery of the Bay of Kotor. For the truly hardcore, the Expedition Challenge is a gruelling two-day, almost nonstop, team-based race that also includes rafting and traversing the northern mountains in the night. It started in 2010, and organisers hope it will join the international circuit as one of the toughest races of its kind in Europe.

Yachting Club 32   EQUIPMENT HIRE
(www.yachtingclub32.com; Šetalište Pet Danica 32) Yachting Club 32 hires jet skis (per 20 minutes €50), paddleboats (per hour €8) and mountain bikes (hour/three hours/day €3/6/15). Windsurfing and parasurfing is also offered.

🛏 Sleeping

In summer there are often people around the bus station touting private accommodation. Black Mountain (p612) can fix you up with rooms starting from around €12 per person, although most of its apartments are more expensive.

Hotel Perla   HOTEL €€
(☏031-345 700; www.perla.me; Šetalište Pet Danica 98; low season s €56-80, d €70-100, high season s €104-163, d €130-204; ❋ P ☏) It's a 15-minute stroll from the centre but if it's beach you're after, Perla's possie is perfect. The helpful staff speak excellent English and the front rooms of this medium-sized modern block have private terraces and sea views.

🍃 Camp Full Monte   CAMPING GROUND €
(☏067 899 208; www.full-monte.com; campsites per person €10; ☉May-Sep) Hidden in the mountains near the Croatian border, this small British-run camping ground offers solar-generated hot water, odourless composting toilets and a whole lot of seclusion. If you hadn't guessed already, clothing is optional. Tents (with full bedding) can be hired for an additional €5 to €15 per person and meals can be arranged (€6.50).

Izvor   HOSTEL €
(☏069-397 957; www.izvor.me; dm €12; P ☏) Four simple shared rooms open out to a terrace overlooking the bay on the slopes above Igalo. The charming young owner speaks excellent English and there's a traditional restaurant (mains €4 to €9) downstairs. There's even a waterfall.

🍴 Eating

If you want to take on the local women in a tussle for the best fresh fruit and vegetables, get to the **market** (Trg Nikole Đurkovića; ☉6am-3pm Mon-Sat, 6am-noon Sun) before 8am.

Konoba Feral   TRADITIONAL €€
(Šetalište Pet Danica 47; mains €8-15) Feral is a local word for a ship's lantern, so it's seafood (not wild cat) that takes pride of place on the menu. The grilled squid is amazing and comes with a massive serving of seasonal vegetables and salads.

Portofino   ITALIAN €€
(Trg Herceg Stjepana; breakfast €2.50-5, mains €6-16) Its blissful location in Herceg Novi's prettiest square makes it tempting to linger here all day, which is exactly what the local expat community seems to do. The menu features creamy pastas and the town's best steaks.

ⓘ Information

You'll find banks with ATMs around Trg Nikola Đurkovića, while ul Njegoševa has the post office and an internet cafe.

Tourist Office (www.hercegnovi.travel; Šetalište Pet Danica bb; ☉9am-11pm May-Sep)

ⓘ Getting There & Around

Bus

Buses stop at the station on the highway, just above the Old Town. There are frequent servies to Kotor (€3.50, one hour), Budva (€5, 1¾ hours) and Podgorica (€8, three hours). International services include Dubrovnik (€10, two hours, two daily), Sarajevo (€24, seven hours, four daily) and Belgrade (€30, 13 hours, nine daily).

Car

A tortuous, often gridlocked, one-way system runs through the town, so you're best to park on the highway. If you're driving to Tivat or Budva, it's usually quicker to take the **ferry** (car/motorcycle/passenger €4/1.50/free; ☉24hr) from Kamenari

(15km northeast of Herceg Novi) to Lepetane (north of Tivat). Queues can be long in summer.

Boat

Taxi boats ply the coast during summer, charging about €7 to the beaches on the Luštica Peninsula.

Perast Пераст

Looking like a chunk of Venice that has floated down the Adriatic and anchored itself onto the bay, Perast hums with melancholy memories of the days when it was rich and powerful. This tiny town boasts 16 churches and 17 formerly grand *palazzi*, one of which has been converted into **Perast Museum** (adult/child €2.50/1.50; ⊙9am-6pm Mon-Sat, to 2pm Sun) and showcases the town's proud seafaring history.

The 55m belltower belongs to **St Nicholas' Church**, which also has a **museum** (admission €1; ⊙10am-6pm) containing relics and beautifully embroidered vestments.

Just offshore are two peculiarly picturesque islands. The smaller St George's Island (Sveti Đorđe) rises from a natural reef and houses a Benedictine monastery shaded by cypresses. Boats (€5) regularly head to its big sister, Our Lady of the Rock Island (Gospa od Škrpjela), which was artificially created in the 15th century. Every year on 22 July the locals row over with stones to continue the task. Its magnificent church was erected in 1630.

Perast makes an atmospheric and peaceful base from which to explore the bay. Several houses rent rooms or you can try the **Hotel Conte Nautilus** (☑032-373687; www.hotel-conte.com; apt €70-250; ❉ ☎), where options range from deluxe studios to two-bedroom seaview apartments in historic buildings around St Nicholas' Church. Its wonderful restaurant (mains €6 to €16) serves fresh fish with lashings of romance on a waterside terrace.

Not far from Perast, **Risan** is the oldest town on the bay, dating to at least the 3rd century BC. Signposts point to some superb **Roman mosaics** (admission €2; ⊙8am-8pm 15 May-15 Oct), discovered in 1930.

Kotor Котор

☑032 / POP 13,500

Those prone to operatic outbursts may find themselves launching into Wagner at their first glimpse of this dramatically beautiful town. Its sturdy walls – started in the 9th century and tweaked until the 18th – arch steeply up the slopes behind it. From a distance they're barely discernable from the mountain's grey hide but at night they're spectacularly lit, reflecting in the water to give the town a golden halo. Within those walls lie labyrinthine marbled lanes, where churches, shops, bars and restaurants surprise you on hidden piazzas.

Kotor's funnel-shaped Stari Grad (Old Town) sits between the bay and the lower slopes of Mt Lovćen. Newer suburbs surround the town, linking up to the old settlements of Dobrota to the north and Muo to the west.

⊙ Sights

The best thing to do in Kotor is to get lost and found again in the maze of streets. You'll soon know every corner, as the town is quite small, but there are plenty of churches to pop into and many coffees to be drunk in the shady squares.

Trg od Oružja   SQUARE

Stepping through the main entrance, **Vrata od Mora** (Sea Gate, 1555), onto Trg od Oružja (Square of Arms) you'll see a strange stone pyramid in front of the **clock tower** (1602) that was once used as a pillory to shame wayward citizens.

St Tryphon Cathedral   CHURCH

(Trg Sv Tripuna; admission €1.50; ⊙8.30am-7pm) The town's most impressive building is the Catholic cathedral, originally built in the 12th century but reconstructed after several earthquakes. The cathedral's gently hued interior is a masterpiece of Romanesque architecture, with slender Corinthian columns alternating with pillars of pink stone, thrusting upwards to support a series of vaulted roofs. Its gilded silver-relief altar screen is considered Kotor's most valuable treasure.

Town Walls   FORTRESS

(admission €2) The energetic can make the 280m ascent via 1350 steps up the fortifications for unforgettable views and a huge sense of achievement. There are entry points near the North Gate and Trg od Salata.

Maritime Museum   MUSEUM

(Trg Bokeljske Mornarice; adult/child incl audioguide €4/1; ⊙8am-7pm Mon-Sat, 9am-1pm Sun) Kotor has a proud history as a naval power and the Maritime Museum celebrates it with three storeys of displays housed in a wonderful early-18th-century palace.

🛏 Sleeping

Although the Stari Grad is a charming place to stay, you'd better pack earplugs. In summer the bars blast music onto the streets

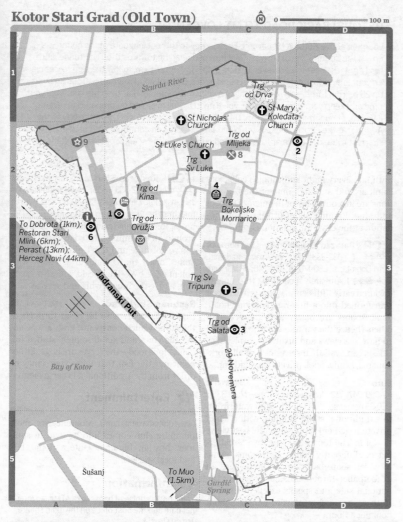

MONTENEGRO KOTOR

Kotor Stari Grad (Old Town)

DETOUR: BACK ROAD TO MT LOVĆEN

Looming above Kotor is Mt Lovćen. The journey to this ancient core of the country is one of the country's great drives. Take the road heading towards the Tivat tunnel and turn right just past the graveyard (there's no sign). After 5km, follow the sign to Cetinje on your left opposite the fort. From here there's 17km of good but narrow road snaking up 25 hairpin turns, each one revealing a vista more spectacular than the last. Take your time and keep your wits about you; you'll need to pull over and be prepared to reverse if you meet oncoming traffic. From the top the views stretch over the entire bay to the Adriatic. At the entrance to Lovćen National Park you can continue straight ahead for the shortest route to Cetinje or turn right and continue on the scenic route through the park.

until 1am every night and rubbish collectors clank around at 6am. Some of the best options are just out of Kotor in quieter Dobrota and Muo. Enquire about private accommodation at the city's information booth.

TOP CHOICE **Palazzo Radomiri** HOTEL €€
(☏032-333 172; www.palazzoradomiri.com; Dobrota; s €60-170, d €80-240; ☺Mar-Sep; ❋P❄🐾) Exquisitely beautiful, this honey-coloured early 18th-century *palazzo* has been transformed into a first-rate boutique hotel. Some rooms are bigger and grander than others (hence the variation in prices), but all 10 have sea views and luxurious furnishings. Guests can avail themselves of a small workout area, sauna, pool, private jetty and bar.

Euro PENSION €
(☏069-047 712; lemaja1@t-com.me; Muo 33; r €20-25 per person; ❋) On the Muo waterfront, this traditional stone building with a small private beach enjoys possibly the best views of Kotor. The top two floors have a scattering of differently configured rooms, some of which share bathrooms. The owner's an ex-footballer turned assistant coach for the national side and speaks excellent English. If there are a few of you, enquire about booking a floor.

Meridian Travel Agency PRIVATE ROOMS €
(☏032-323 448; www.meridiandmc.me) In the lane behind the clock tower, this agency has rooms on its books at around €15 to €30 per person and can also book hotels.

🍴 Eating & Drinking

The Old Town is full of small bakeries, takeaway joints and cafe-bars that spill into the squares and are abuzz with conversation during the day. All chitchat stops abruptly in the evening, when speakers are dragged out onto the ancient lanes and the techno is cranked up to near ear-bleeding volumes.

TOP CHOICE **Restoran Stari Mlini** TRADITIONAL €€€
(☏032-333 555; www.starimlini.com; Jadranska Put, Ljuta; meals €11-21) It's well worth making the 7km trip to Ljuta, just past Dobrota, for this magical restaurant set in and around an old mill by the edge of the bay. If you've got time and don't mind picking out bones, order the Dalmatian fish stew with polenta for two. The steaks are also excellent, as are the bread, wine and service.

Restoran Stari Grad TRADITIONAL €€
(Trg od Mlijeka; mains €8-18) Head through to the stone-walled courtyard, grab a seat under the vines and get absolutely stuffed full of fabulous food – the serves are huge. Either point out the fish that takes your fancy or order from the traditional à la carte menu.

☆ Entertainment

Maximus NIGHTCLUB
(www.discomaximus.com) Montenegro's most pumping club comes into its own in summer, hosting big-name international DJs and local starlets.

ℹ Information

You'll find a choice of banks with ATMs, an internet cafe and the post office on the main square, Trg od Oružja.

Tourist information booth (www.kotor.travel; ☺8am-8pm) Outside Vrata od Mora.

ℹ Getting There & Away

Bus

The bus station is to the south of town, just off the road leading to the Tivat tunnel. Buses to Herceg Novi (€3.50, one hour), Tivat (€2, 20 minutes), Budva (€3, 40 minutes) and Podgorica (€7, two hours) are at least hourly.

Boat

Azzurra Lines (www.azzurraline.com) ferries connect Kotor with Bari, Italy (€65, nine hours, weekly July to August).

Tivat Тиват

📞032 / POP 9,450

In the process of a major makeover, courtesy of the multimillion-dollar redevelopment of its old shipyard into the **Porto Montenegro** (www.portomontenegro.com) superyacht marina, Tivat is becoming more schmick each year. Already the waterfront has been cleaned up, with a new crop of trendy bars and restaurants filling in the gaps between the old stone buildings on the promenade. It's still got a long way to go before it rivals Kotor for charm, but it's a pleasant place to stop.

There are a lot of sweet villages and beaches to explore on the coast between here and Kotor and on the Luštica Peninsula. The helpful **tourist office** (www.tivat.travel; Palih Boraca 8; ⊘8am-9pm Mon-Sat, 8am-noon Sun) can advise you on some terrific walks.

🛏 Sleeping & Eating

Hotel Villa Royal　　　　　HOTEL €€
(📞032-675　310;　villaroyal@t-com.me;　Kalimanj bb; s €42-65, d €68-102, apt €102-141; ❉@🛜) A bright modern block with clean rooms and friendly staff.

Prova　　　　RESTAURANT, BAR €€
(Šetalište Iva Vizina 1; mains €7-14) Shaped like a boat with chandeliers that look like mutant alien jellyfish, this upmarket eatery is the very epitome of the new, increasingly chic Tivat. Excellent pasta.

❶ Getting There & Away

Air

Tivat airport (www.montenegroairports.com) is 3km south of town and 8km through the tunnel from Kotor. Major local and international rental-car companies have counters here. The nearest bus stop is about 1km towards Tivat from the terminal. Taxis cost less than €10 to Tivat, around €15 to Kotor and around €20 to Budva.

Bus

Buses to Kotor (€2, 20 minutes) stop outside a silver kiosk on Palih Boraca. The main stop for longer trips is inconveniently located halfway between Tivat and the airport.

ADRIATIC COAST

Much of Montenegro's determination to re-invent itself as a tourist mecca has focused firmly on its gorgeous Adriatic coastline. In July and August it seems that the entire Serbian world and a fair chunk of its northern Orthodox brethren can be found crammed onto this scant 100km stretch. Avoid these months and you'll find a charismatic set of fortified towns and fishing villages to explore, set against clear Adriatic waters and Montenegro's mountainous backdrop.

Budva Будва

📞033 / POP 10,100

The poster child of Montenegrin tourism, Budva – with its atmospheric Old Town and numerous beaches – certainly has a lot to offer. Yet the child has quickly moved into a difficult adolescence, fuelled by rampant development that has leeched much of the charm from the place. In the height of the season the sands are blanketed with package holidaymakers from Russia and the Ukraine, while by night you'll run the gauntlet of glorified strippers attempting to cajole you into the beachside bars. It's the buzziest place on the coast if you're in the mood to party.

Apart from the Old Town, hardly any streets have names and even fewer have signs. The main beachside promenade is pedestrianised Slovenska Obala, which in summer is lined with fast-food outlets, beach bars, travel agencies hawking tours, internet cafes and a fun park.

⊙ Sights & Activities

Stari Grad　　　　　HISTORIC AREA
Budva's best feature and star attraction is the Stari Grad (Old Town) – a mini-Dubrovnik with marbled streets and Venetian walls rising from the clear waters below. Much of it was ruined by two earthquakes in 1979 but it has since been completely rebuilt and now houses more shops, bars and restaurants than residences. At its seaward end, the **Citadel** (admission €2; ⊘9am-midnight May-Nov) offers striking views, a small museum and a library full of rare tomes and maps. In the square in front of the citadel is a cluster of interesting churches. Nearby is the entry to the **town walls** (admission €1; ⊘9am-5pm).

Archaeological Museum　　　MUSEUM
(Petra I Petrovića 11; adult/child €2/1; ⊘9am-10pm) This museum shows off the town's ancient and complicated history – dating back to at least 500 BC – over three floors of exhibits.

FREE **Museum of Modern Art**　GALLERY
(Cara Dušana 19; ⊘8am-2pm & 5-9pm Mon-Fri, 5-9pm Sat) Also in Stari Grad, this attractive gallery stages temporary exhibitions.

Montenegro Adventure Centre PARAGLIDING
(☑067-580 664; www.montenegrofly.com; Lapčići)
The Montenegro Adventure Centre offers plenty of action from its perch high above Budva. Rafting, hiking, mountain biking and accommodation can all be arranged, as well as paragliding from launch sites around the country. An unforgettable tandem flight landing 750m below at Bečići beach costs €65.

🛏 Sleeping & Eating

Hotel Astoria HOTEL €€€
(☑033-451 110; www.astoriamontenegro.com; Njegoševa 4; s €99-190, d €105-230; ❄@) Water shimmers down the corridor wall as you enter this chic boutique hotel hidden in Stari Grad's fortifications. The rooms are on the small side but they're beautifully furnished. The seaview suite is spectacular and the wonderful guest-only roof terrace is Budva's most magnificent dining area.

Hotel Kangaroo HOTEL €€
(☑033-458 653; www.kangaroo.co.me; Velji Vinogradi bb; s €32-40, d €48-64; ❄P🛜) Bounce into a large clean room with a desk, excellent bathroom and either a terrace or mountain views at this midsized hotel that's a hop, skip and jump from the beach. The owners once lived in Australia, hence the name and the large 3D mural of Captain Cook's *Endeavour* in the popular restaurant below. Attached is a hip new bar for tapas and cocktails, with DJs until midnight on Friday and Saturday – so pack earplugs if you're an early-to-bed type.

Knez Konoba RESTAURANT €€
(Mitrov Ljubiše bb; mains €9-15) Hidden within Stari Grad's tiny lanes, this atmospheric eatery has only three outdoor tables and a handful inside. The traditional dishes are a little more expensive than most but they're beautifully presented and sometimes accompanied with free shots of *rakija* (local brandy).

Saki Apartmani HOSTEL €
(☑067-368 065; www.saki-apartmani.com; IV Proleterska bb; dm/d €10/30; ❄P🛜) Good, clean, cheap apartments and dorm rooms in a quiet location.

Hippo Hostel HOSTEL €
(☑033-458 348; www.hippohostel.com; IV Proleterska 37; dm €10; P@🛜) Social hostel with overgrown garden and buzzy atmosphere.

❶ Information

The post office and a cluster of banks are on and around ulica Mediteranska.

Tourist office (www.budva.travel; Njegoševa bb; ☉9am-9pm Mon-Sat May-Oct) Has brochures on sights and accommodation.

❶ Getting There & Away

The **bus station** (☑033-456 000; Ivana Milutinovića bb) has regular services to Herceg Novi (€5, 1¾ hours), Kotor (€3, 40 minutes), Petrovac (€2.50, 30 minutes) and Cetinje (€3, 40 minutes). **Meridian Rentacar** (☑033-454 105; www.meridian-rentacar.com; Mediteranski Sportski Centar) is opposite the bus station.

You can flag down the Olimpia Express (€1.50) from the bus stops on Jadranska Put to head to Bečići (five minutes) or Sveti Stefan (20 minutes). They depart every 30 minutes in summer and hourly in winter.

Sveti Stefan Свети Стефан

Gazing down on impossibly picturesque Sveti Stefan, 5km south of Budva, provides the biggest 'wow' moment on the entire coast. And gazing on it is all most people will get to do as this tiny island – connected to the shore by a narrow isthmus and crammed full of terracotta-roofed dwellings dating from the 15th century – was nationalised in the 1950s and the whole thing is now a luxurious resort.

Sveti Stefan is also the name of the settlement that's sprung up onshore. From its steep slopes you get to look down at that iconic view all day – which some might suggest is even better than staying in the surreally glamorous enclave below. On the downside, parking is difficult, there are lots of steps and there's little in the way of shops.

The general public can access the main Sveti Stefan beach, which faces the island. From the beach there's a very pleasant walk north to the cute village of **Pržno** where there are some excellent restaurants and another attractive, often crowded beach.

🛏 Sleeping & Eating

TOP CHOICE Vila Drago HOTEL €€
(☑033-468 477; www.viladrago.com; Slobode 32; r low season €35-65, high season €60-100; ❄@🛜) The only problem with this place is that you may never want to leave your terrace, as the views are so sublime. The supercomfy pillows and fully stocked bathrooms are a nice touch, especially at this price. Watch the sunset over the island from the grapevine-covered terrace restaurant (mains €5 to €15) and enjoy specialities from the lo-

cal Paštrovići clan, like roast suckling pig (€15 per kilogram).

Aman Sveti Stefan
RESORT €€€

(☑033-420 000; www.amanresorts.com; ste €700-2500; ❋ P ☀ ⛱ ☎) Truly unique, this iconic island resort offers 50 luxurious suites that showcase the stone walls and wooden beams of the ancient houses. Amazingly there's still a village feel, with cobbled lanes, three churches, lots of indigenous foliage and an open-air cafe on the main piazza. But it's a village where you can order a cocktail by a cliff's-edge swimming pool or slink away for an indulgent massage – and it's not open to the general public. Back on the shore, **Villa Miločer** has a further eight suites in a former royal palace facing lovely Miločer Beach through a curtain of wisteria. This and nearby Queen's Beach are reserved for use by the resort's guests. The public can access the main Sveti Stefan beach and avail themselves of three eateries: the **Olive Tree** at the beach's north end, the **Beach Cafe** at Miločer and **Queen's Chair**, perched on a wooded hill facing Budva.

Vila Levantin
APARTMENTS €€

(☑033-468 206; levantin@t-com.me; Vukice Mitrović 3; r €30-90; ❋ P ☀ ☎) Modern and nicely finished, with red stone walls, blue-tiled bathrooms and an attractive plunge pool on the terrace, Levantin has a range of rooms and apartments at extremely reasonable prices. There's a travel agency attached which can sort you out with tours or rooms in private houses.

❶ Getting There & Away

Olimpia Express buses head to and from Budva (€1.50, 20 minutes) every 30 minutes in summer and hourly in winter, stopping on Ulica Slobode near the Vila Drago.

Petrovac Петровац

The Romans had the right idea, building their summer villas on this lovely bay. The pretty beachside promenade is perfumed with the scent of lush Mediterranean plants, and a picturesque 16th-century **Venetian fortress** guards a tiny stone harbour. This is one of the best places on the coast for families: the accommodation is reasonably priced, the water's clear and kids roam the esplanade at night with impunity.

In July and August you'll be lucky to find an inch of space on the town beach but wander south and there's cypress- and oleander-lined **Lučice Beach** and beyond it the 2.5km-long sweep of **Buljarica Beach**.

🍴 Sleeping & Eating

Hotel W Grand
HOTEL €€

(☑033-461 703; www.wgrandpetrovac.com; s/d low season €48/64, high season €78/104; P ❋ @ ☎) Spacious rooms painted in warm colours and comfortable beds are the hallmark of this modern midsized hotel. Eat up the views from the terrace while tucking into the brilliant breakfast buffet.

Konoba Bonaca
RESTAURANT €€

(mains €8-15) On the main beach drag, this traditional restaurant focuses mainly on seafood but the local cheeses and olives are also excellent. Grab a table under the grapevines on the terrace and gaze out to sea.

Mornar Travel Agency
PRIVATE ROOMS €

(☑033-461 410; www.mornartravel.com; Nerin bb) An excellent local agency offering private accommodation from €23 per person.

❶ Getting There & Away

Petrovac's bus station is near the top of town. Regular services head to Budva and Bar (both €2, 30 minutes).

Bar Бар

☑030 / POP 13,800

Dominated by Montenegro's main port and a large industrial area, Bar is unlikely to be anyone's highlight, but it is a handy transport hub welcoming trains from Belgrade and ferries from Italy. More interesting are the ruins of Stari Bar (Old Bar) in the mountains behind.

◎ Sights

Stari Bar
RUINS

(adult/child €1/0.50; ⊙8am-8pm) Impressive Stari Bar, Bar's original settlement, stands on a bluff 4km northeast, off the Ulcinj road. A steep cobbled hill takes you past a cluster of old houses and shops to the fortified entrance where a short dark passage pops you out into a large expanse of vine-clad ruins and abandoned streets overgrown with grass and wild flowers. A small **museum** just inside the entrance explains the site and its history. The Illyrians founded the city in around 800 BC. It passed in and out of Slavic and Byzantine rule until the Venetians took it in 1443 and held it until it was taken by the Ottomans in 1571. Nearly all the 240 buildings now lie in ruins, a result of Montenegrin shelling, when the town was captured in 1878.

Buses marked Stari Bar depart from the centre of new Bar every hour (€1).

King Nikola's Palace   MUSEUM
(Šetalište Kralje Nikole; admission €1; ⊙8am-2pm & 5-11pm) Presenting an elegant facade to the water, King Nikola's Palace has been converted into a museum housing a collection of antiques, folk costumes and royal furniture. Its shady gardens contain plants cultivated from seeds and cuttings collected from around the world by Montenegro's sailors.

Sleeping & Eating

Hotel Princess   HOTEL €€€
(☑030-300 100; www.hotelprincess-montenegro.com; Jovana Tomaševića 59; s/d low season €70/100, high season €80/120; ❄@🛜P🏊) The standards aren't quite what you'd expect for the price, but this resort-style hotel is the best option in town. Make the most of it at the private beach, swimming pool and spa centre.

Konoba Spilja   RESTAURANT €
(Stari Bar bb; mains €3-15) So rustic you wouldn't be surprised if a goat wandered through, this is a terrific spot for a traditional meal after exploring Stari Bar.

ⓘ Information

There are banks with ATMs around ul Maršala Tita and ul Vladimira Rolovića.

Accident & Emergency Clinic (☑124; Jovana Tomeševića 42)

Post office (Jovana Tomeševića bb)

Tourist information centre (Obala 13 Jula bb; ⊙8am-8pm Jul & Aug, 8am-4pm Mon-Sat Sep-Jun) Helpful staff with good English; stocks useful brochures listing sights and private accommodation.

ⓘ Getting There & Away

The bus station and adjacent train station are 1km southeast of the centre. Bus destinations include Podgorica (€4, seven daily) and Ulcinj (€2.50, three daily). Trains head to Virpazar (€2, 20 minutes, 10 daily), Podgorica (€3.60, one hour, 10 daily) and Kolašin (€8.20, 2½ hours, five daily).

Montenegro Line (☑030-311 164; www.montenegrolines.net) ferries to Bari (€55, nine hours, three weekly) and Ancona (€66, 11 hours, twice weekly in summer) in Italy, and **Azzurra Lines** (www.azzurraline.com) ferries to Bari (€65, nine hours, weekly in summer), leave from the **ferry terminal** (Obala 13 Jula bb) near the centre. You can book your Montenegro Lines ferry tickets here and there's a post office. Az-zurra Lines can be booked at **Mercur** (☑030-313 617; Vladimira Rolovića bb).

Ulcinj Улцињ

☑030 / 10,900

If you want a feel for Albania without actually crossing the border, buzzy Ulcinj's the place to go. The population is 72% Albanian and in summer it swells with Kosovar holidaymakers for the simple reason that it's nicer than most of the Albanian seaside towns. The elegant minarets of numerous mosques give Ulcinj a distinctly Eastern feel, as does the music echoing out of the kebab stands.

For centuries Ulcinj had a reputation as a pirate's lair. By the end of the 16th century as many as 400 pirates, mainly from Malta, Tunisia and Algeria, made Ulcinj their main port of call – wreaking havoc on passing vessels and then returning to party up large on Mala Plaža. Ulcinj became the centre of a thriving slave trade, with people – mainly from North Africa – paraded for sale on the town's main square.

You'll find banks, internet cafes, supermarkets, pharmacies and the post office on Rr Hazif Ali Ulqinaku.

ⓞ Sights & Activities

Stari Grad   HISTORIC AREA
The ancient Stari Grad overlooking Mala Plaža is still largely residential and somewhat dilapidated – a legacy of the 1979 earthquake. A steep slope leads to the Upper Gate, where there's a small **museum** (admission €1; ⊙6am-1pm & 4-9pm Tue-Sun) just inside the walls, containing Roman and Ottoman artefacts.

Beaches   BEACHES
Mala Plaža may be a fine grin of a cove but it's hard to see the beach under all that suntanned flesh in July and August. You're better off strolling south, where a succession of rocky bays offer a little more room to breathe. **Ladies' Beach** (admission €1.50) has a strict women-only policy, while a section of the beach in front of the Hotel Albatross is clothing optional.

The appropriately named **Velika Plaža** (Big Beach) starts 4km southeast of the town and stretches for 12 sandy kilometres. Sections of it sprout deckchairs but there's still plenty of relatively empty space. To be frank, this large flat expanse isn't as picturesque as it sounds and the water is painfully shallow – great for kids but you'll need to walk a fair way for a decent swim.

On your way to Velika Plaža you'll pass the murky **Milena canal**, where local fishermen use nets suspended from long willow rods attached to wooden stilt houses. The effect is remarkably redolent of Southeast Asia. There are more of these contraptions on the banks of the **Bojana River** at the other end of Veliki Plaža.

D'olcinium Diving Club   DIVING
(☎067-319 100; www.uldiving.com; 2 dives incl equipment €40) Divers wanting to explore various wrecks and the remains of a submerged town should contact the D'olcinium Diving Club. It also hires snorkelling (€3) and diving (€15) gear.

🛏 Sleeping

Dvori Balšića & Palata Venezia   HOTEL €€€
(☎030-421 457; www.hotel-dvoribalsica-montene gro.com; Stari Grad; s/d €65/100; ❄🐾) These grand stone *palazzi* are reached by the cobbled lanes and stairs of the Old Town – not great if you're lugging luggage but very atmospheric nonetheless. The sizeable rooms all have kitchenettes, romantic sea views , and stucco and dark wooden interiors.

Hotel Dolcino   HOTEL €€
(☎030-422 288; www.hoteldolcino.com; Hazif Ali Ulqinaku bb; s/d €40/50; ❄🐾) You can't quibble over the exceptionally reasonable prices of this modern business-orientated mini hotel in the centre of town. The quieter rooms at the back have spacious terraces, although the small front balconies are great for watching the passing parade. Signs instruct guests not to flush toilet paper; a rarity in 21st-century Montenegro.

Real Estate Travel Agency   PRIVATE ROOMS €
(☎030-421 609; www.realestate-travel.com; Hazif Ali Ulqinaku bb) Obliging English-speaking staff can help you find private rooms, apartments or hotel rooms. They also rent cars, run tours, organise diving trips and sell maps of Ulcinj.

🍴 Eating

TOP CHOICE **Restoran Kod Marka**   SEAFOOD €€
(☎030-401 720; Bojana River; mains €7-10) Not actually in Ulcinj but well worth the 14km drive, this memorable fish restaurant is one of several that jut out over the Bojana River just before the bridge to Ada Bojana. The specialty, *riblja čorba* (fish soup, €2.50), is sublime: served in a metal pot that will fill your bowl twice over.

Restaurant Pizzeria Bazar TRADITIONAL, PIZZA €
(Hazif Ali Ulqinaku bb; mains €4-10) An upstairs restaurant that's a great idling place when the streets below are heaving with tourists. People-watch in comfort as you enjoy a plate of *lignje na žaru* (grilled squid), the restaurant's speciality.

❶ Getting There & Away

The bus station is on the northeastern edge of town just off Bul Vëllazërit Frashëri. Services head to Bar (€2.50, 30 minutes, three daily), Podgorica (€6, one hour, four daily), Shkodra (Albania; €6, 90 minutes, two daily) and Pristina (Kosovo; €22.50, eight hours, three daily).

CENTRAL MONTENEGRO

The heart of Montenegro – physically, spiritually and politically – is easily accessed as a day trip from the coast but it's well deserving of a longer exploration. Two wonderful national parks separate it from the Adriatic and behind them lie the two capitals, the ancient current one and the newer former one.

Lovćen National Park
Ловћен

Directly behind Kotor is Mt Lovćen (1749m), the black mountain that gave Crna Gora (Montenegro) its name (*crna/negro* means 'black' and *gora/monte* means 'mountain' in Montenegrin and Italian respectively). This locale occupies a special place in the hearts of all Montenegrins. For most of its history it represented the entire nation – a rocky island of Slavic resistance in an Ottoman sea. The old capital of Cetinje nestles in its foothills.

The national park's 6220 hectares are home to 85 species of butterfly, and 200 species of birds and mammals, including endangered brown bears and wolves. It's criss-crossed with well-marked hiking paths.

The **National Park Office** (www.nparkovi. co.me; Ivanova Korita bb; ☺9am-5pm Apr-Oct, shorter hrs winter) is near its centre and offers accommodation in four-bedded bungalows (€40). If you're planning some serious walking, buy a copy of the *Lovćen Mountain Touristic Map* (scale 1:25,000), available from the office and park entries.

Lovćen's star attraction is the magnificent **Njegoš Mausoleum** (admission €3) at the top of its second-highest peak, Jezerski Vrh (1657m). Take the 461 steps up to the entry, where two granite giantesses guard the tomb. Inside, under a golden mosaic canopy, a 28-tonne Vladika Petar II Petrović Njegoš rests in the wings of an eagle, carved from a single block of black granite. The actual tomb lies below and a path at the rear leads to a dramatic circular viewing platform.

If you're driving, the park can be approached from either Kotor or Cetinje (entry fee €2). The back route between the two shouldn't be missed (see the boxed text on p616).

Cetinje Цетиње

☑ 041 / POP 15,200

Rising from a green vale surrounded by rough, grey mountains, Cetinje is an odd mix of former capital and overgrown village, where single-storey cottages and stately mansions share the same street. Pretty Njegoševa is a partly traffic-free thoroughfare lined with interesting buildings, including the **Presidential Palace** and various former embassies marked with plaques. Everything of significance is in the immediate vicinity. There's a **tourist information centre** (☉8am-7pm) on Novice Cerovića.

⊙ Sights

National Museum of Montenegro MUSEUMS
(Narodni muzej Crne Gore; combined ticket adult/child €10/5; ☉9am-5pm, last admission 4.30pm) This is actually a collection of five museums housed in a clump of important buildings. A joint ticket will get you into all of them or you can buy individual tickets.

Two are housed in the former parliament (1910), Cetinje's most imposing building. The fascinating **History Museum** (Istorijski Muzej; Novice Cerovića 7; adult/child €4/2) is very well laid out, following a timeline from the Stone Age to 1955. There are few English signs but the enthusiastic staff will walk you around and give you an overview before leaving you to your own devices.

Upstairs is the equally excellent **Art Museum** (Umjetnički Muzej; adult/child €4/2). There's a small collection of icons, the most important being the precious 9th-century *Our Lady of Philermos*, which was traditionally believed to have been painted by St Luke himself. Elsewhere in the gallery all of Montenegro's great artists are represented, with the most famous having their own separate spaces. Expect a museum staff member to be hovering as you wander around.

While the hovering at the Art Museum is annoying, the **King Nikola Museum** (Muzej kralja Nikole; Trg Kralja Nikole; adult/child €5/2.50) can be downright infuriating. Entry is only by guided tour, which the staff will only give to a group, even if you've pre-paid a ticket and they've got nothing else to do. Still, this 1871 palace of Nikola I, last sovereign of Montenegro, is worth the hassle.

The castle-like **Njegoš Museum** (Njegošev Muzej; Trg Kralja Nikole; adult/child €3/1.50) was the residence of Montenegro's favourite son, prince-bishop-poet Petar II Petrović Njegoš. The hall was built and financed by the Russians in 1838 and housed the nation's first billiard table, hence the museum's alternative name, Biljarda. The bottom floor is devoted to military costumes, photos of soldiers with outlandish moustaches and exquisitely decorated weapons. Njegoš's personal effects are displayed upstairs.

When you leave Biljarda, turn right and follow the walls to the glass pavilion housing a fascinating large scale **relief map** (adult/child €1/0.50) of Montenegro created by the Austrians in 1917.

Occupying the former Serbian embassy, the **Ethnographic Museum** (Etnografski Muzej; Trg Kralja Nikole; adult/child €2/1) is the least interesting of the five, but if you've bought a joint ticket you may as well check it out. The collection of costumes and tools is well presented and has English notations.

Cetinje Monastery MONASTERY
(☉8am-6pm) It's a case of three times lucky for Cetinje Monastery, having been repeatedly destroyed during Ottoman attacks and rebuilt. This sturdy incarnation dates from 1785, with its only exterior ornamentation being the capitals of columns recycled from the original building, founded in 1484.

The chapel to the right of the courtyard holds the monastery's proudest possessions: a shard of the True Cross and the mummified right hand of St John the Baptist. The hand's had a fascinating history, having escaped wars and revolutions and passing through the hands of Byzantine emperors, Ottoman sultans, the Knights Hospitalier, Russian tsars and Serbian kings. It's now housed in a bejewelled golden casket by the chapel's window, draped in heavy fabric. The casket's only occasionally opened for veneration, so if you miss out you can console yourself that it's not a very pleasant sight.

The monastery **treasury** (admission €2; ☉8am-4pm) is only open to groups, but if you are persuasive enough and prepared to wait around, you may be able to get in. It holds a wealth of fascinating objects that form a blur as you're shunted around the rooms by one of the monks. These include jewel-encrusted vestments, ancient handwritten texts, icons, royal crowns and a copy of the 1494 *Oktoih* (Book of the Eight Voices), the first book printed in Serbian.

If your legs, shoulders or cleavage are on display, you'll either be denied entry or given an unflattering smock to wear.

🛏 Sleeping & Eating

Accommodation in Cetinje is limited and there are only a few proper restaurants.

Hotel Grand   HOTEL €€
(☑041-231 651; www.hotelgrand.me; Njegoševa 1; s €46-60, d €66-80) 'Fading grandeur' would be a more accurate moniker but aside from a few pigeons roosting in the walls, Cetinje's only hotel is an OK place to stay. The polished parquet floors, comfy beds and new linen certainly help.

Vinoteka   ITALIAN €
(Njegoševa 103; mains €3-12) The wood-beamed porch looking onto the garden is such a nice spot that the excellent and reasonably priced pizza and pasta feels like a bonus – the decent wine list even more so.

❶ Getting There & Away

Cetinje is on the main highway between Budva and Podgorica and can also be reached by a glorious back road from Kotor via Lovćen National Park. Buses stop at Trg Golootočkih Žrtava, two blocks from the main street. Buses leave every 30 minutes for Podgorica (€3) and hourly for Budva (€3).

Lake Skadar National Park
Скадарско Језеро

The Balkans' largest lake, dolphin-shaped Lake Skadar (Shkodra) has its tail and two-thirds of its body in Montenegro and its nose in Albania. Covering between 370 and 550 sq km (depending on the time of year), it's one of the most important reserves for wetland birds in the whole of Europe. The endangered Dalmatian pelican nests here, along with 256 other species, while 48 known species of fish lurk beneath its smooth surface. On the Montenegrin side, an area of 400 sq km has been protected by a national park since 1983. It's a blissfully pretty area, encompassing steep mountains, hidden villages, historic churches, clear waters and floating meadows of waterlilies.

The **National Park Visitors Centre** (www.nparkovi.co.me; Vranjina bb; admission €2; ☉8am-4pm) is on the opposite side of the causeway heading to Podgorica from Virpazar. This modern facility has excellent displays about all the national parks, not just Lake Skadar, and sells park entry tickets (per day €4) and fishing permits (per day €5). In the busy months, various tour operators set up kiosks in the vicinity, hiring rowboats and speed-boats with drivers.

Just along the causeway are the remains of the 19th-century fortress **Lesendro**. The busy highway and railway tracks prevent land access to the site.

RIJEKA CRNOJEVIĆA ПИЈЕКА ЦРНОЈЕВИЋА

The northwestern end of the lake thins into the serpentine loops of the Crnojević River and terminates near the pretty village of the same name. It's a charming, tucked-away kind of place, accessed by side roads that lead off the Cetinje–Podgorica highway. There's a history display in the **National Park Visitors Centre** (admission €1; ☉10am-6pm), which occupies four wooden huts that jut out over the river on stilts.

You wouldn't expect it but this sleepy place is home to one of Montenegro's best restaurants. **Stari Most** (☑033-239 505; fish per kg €30-50) is well located on the marble river-side promenade, looking towards the photogenic arched stone bridge (1854) from which it derives its name. Fish, particularly eel, is the speciality here and the fish soup alone is enough to justify a drive from Podgorica.

VIRPAZAR ВИРПАЗАР

This little town, gathered around a square and a river blanketed with waterlilies, serves as the main gateway to the national park. Most of the boat tours of the lake depart from here, so the tranquillity is shattered at around 10.30am, when the tour buses from the coast pull in. There's a **National Park kiosk** by the marina that sells entry tickets and fishing permits but doesn't offer much information.

The **Pelikan Hotel** (☑020-711 107; www.pelikan-zec.com; d/tr €58/81; ❄) is a one-stop shop offering accommodation, an excellent traditional restaurant (main €5 to €12) and 2½-hour boat tours that explore the lake's northern reaches (usually around €10 per person, depending on numbers). The rooms are clean and have nice views over the square, although some of them are tiny.

Virpazar doesn't have a bus station but buses on the Bar–Podgorica route stop here. The decrepit train station is off the main road, 800m south of town. There are 10 services daily to Bar (€2, 20 minutes) and Podgorica (€2.20, 40 minutes).

MURIĆI МУРИЋИ

The southern edge of the lake is the most dramatic, with the Rumija Mountains rising precipitously from the water. From Virpazar there's a wonderful drive following the contours of the lake through the mountains towards the border before crossing the range and turning back towards Ulcinj. About halfway, a steep road descends to the village of Murići. This is one of the lake's best swimming spots. Local boatmen offer trips to the monasteries on the nearby islands for around €10 per hour.

The **Murići Vacation Resort** (☑069-688 288; www.nacionalnipark-izletistemurici.com; per person €37) has simple log cabins nestled within in an olive grove. A decent ablutions block is shared and the price includes three meals in the shady outdoor restaurant (mains €5 to €9). It also organises lake tours (€16) that visit the islands and Virpazar.

Podgorica Подгорица

☑020 / POP 136,500

Podgorica's never going to be Europe's most happening capital but if you can get past the sweltering summer temperatures and concrete apartment blocks you'll find a pleasant little city with lots of green space and some excellent galleries and bars.

The city sits at the confluence of two rivers. West of the broad Morača is what passes for the business district. The smaller Ribnica River divides the eastern side in two. To the south is Stara Varoš, the heart of the former Ottoman town. North of the Ribnica is Nova Varoš, an attractive, mainly low-rise precinct of late 19th-century and early 20th-century buildings housing a lively mixture of shops and bars. At its centre is the main square, Trg Republika.

☉ Sights

FREE **Podgorica Museum & Gallery**

MUSEUM

(Marka Miljanova 4; ⊙9am-8pm) Despite Cetinje nabbing most of the national endowment,

the new capital is well served by the Podgorica Museum and Gallery. There's an interesting section on the city's history, including antiquities surviving from its Roman incarnation, Doclea. The gallery features changing exhibitions; look out for Petar Lubarda's large canvas *Titograd* (1956) in the foyer.

FREE **Centre for Contemporary Art**

GALLERIES

The Centre for Contemporary Art operates two galleries in Podgorica. The bottom two floors of the former royal palace **Dvorac Petrovića** (Llubljanska bb; ⊙9am-2pm & 4-9pm Mon-Fri, 10am-2pm Sat) are given over to high-profile exhibitions, while the top floor has an oddball collection of miscellanea. Temporary exhibitions are also staged in the small **Galerija Centar** (Njegoševa 2; ⊙9am-2pm & 5-9pm Mon-Fri, 10am-2pm Sat).

Hram Hristovog Vaskrsenja   CHURCH

(Temple of Christ's Resurrection; Bul Džordža Vašingtona) This immense church is an indicator of the healthy state of Orthodoxy in Montenegro. It's still incomplete after 17 years' construction, but its large dome, white stone towers and gold crosses are a striking addition to Podgorica's skyline.

🛏 Sleeping

Most visitors to Podgorica are here for business, either commerce or government-related. Hotels set their prices accordingly and private accommodation isn't really an option.

Hotel Evropa   HOTEL €€

(☑020-623 444; www.hotelevropa.co.me; Orahovačka 16; s/d €55/90; ❄@☎P) It's hardly a salubrious location, but Evropa is handy to the train and bus stations and offers good clean rooms with comfortable beds, writing desks and decent showers. Despite its diminutive size there's a sauna and fitness room.

Hotel Eminent   HOTEL €€€

(☑020-664 646; www.eminent.co.me; Njegoševa 25; s/d €80/130, apt €90-140; ❄☎) Given its location and excellent facilities, the Eminent seems to be set up for business people keen on an after-work tipple. The front rooms can be noisy but the comfortable mezzanine apartments open onto a covered veranda at the back.

🍴 Eating & Drinking

Head to the little market (Moskovska bb) or the big market (Bratstva Jedinstva bb) for fresh fruit and vegetables.

Podgorica

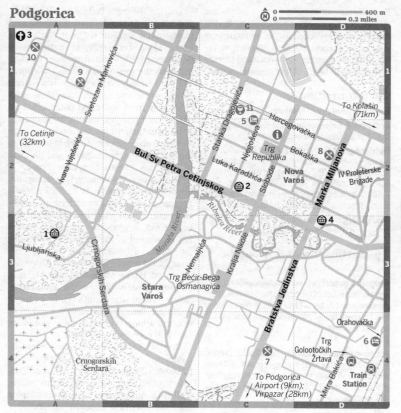

Podgorica

⊙ Sights
1 Dvorac Petrovića A3
2 Galerija Centar C2
3 Hram Hristovog Vaskrsenja A1
4 Podgorica Museum & Gallery D3

🛏 Sleeping
5 Hotel Eminent C2
6 Hotel Evropa D4

🍴 Eating
7 Big Market C4
8 Laterna D2
9 Leonardo A1
10 Little Market A1

🍷 Drinking
11 Buda Bar C1

Leonardo   ITALIAN €€

(Svetozara Markovića bb; mains €5-16) Leonardo's unlikely position at the centre of a residential block makes it a little tricky to find but the effort's well rewarded with accomplished Italian cuisine. The pasta dishes are delicious and reasonably priced, given the upmarket ambience, while the €5 pizzas should leave even those on a budget with a Mona Lisa smile.

Laterna   PIZZA €

(Marka Miljanova 41; mains €4-13; ⊙9am-midnight Mon-Sat) Farm implements hang from the rough stone walls, creating a surprisingly rustic ambience in the centre of the city. A selection of meat and fish grills is offered but it's hard to go past the crispy-based pizza – it's quite possibly Montenegro's best.

MONTENEGRO PODGORICA

Buda Bar
BAR

(Stanka Dragojevića 26; ☺8am-2am) A golden Buddha smiles serenely as you meditate over your coffee or cocktail. This is one slick watering hole; the tentlike semi-enclosed terrace is the place to be on balmy summer nights.

ℹ Information

You'll find plenty of ATMs around the inner city.

Accident & Emergency clinic (Hitna Pomoć; ☑124; Vaka Djurovića bb)

Montenegro Adventures (☑020-208 000; www.montenegro-adventures.com; Jovana Tomaševića 35) The commercial wing of the nonprofit Centre for Sustainable Tourism Initiatives (www.cstimontenegro.org) organises tours, accommodation and the like.

Tourist Organisation Podgorica (TOP; www.podgorica.travel; Slobode 47)

ℹ Getting There & Around

Air

Podgorica airport (www.montenegroairports.com) is 9km south of the city. A shuttle bus (€3) runs between the airport and Trg Republika roughly every 30 minutes. Airport taxis have a standard €15 fare to the centre.

Bus

Podgorica's **bus station** (Trg Goloootočkih Žrtava; ☺5am-10pm) has a left-luggage service, ATM and services to all major towns, including Herceg Novi (€9, three hours), Kotor (€7, two hours) and Ulcinj (€6, one hour).

Car

The major rental-car agencies all have counters at Podgorica airport. Excellent local agency **Meridian Rentacar** (☑020-234 944; www.meridian-rentacar.com; Bul Džordža Vašingtona 85) also has a city office.

Train

Don't expect English or much help from the information desk at the **train station** (Trg Goloootočkih Žrtava 13; ☺5am-11pm), but timetables are posted. Destinations include Bar (€2.60, one hour, 10 daily), Virpazar (€2.20, 40 minutes, 10 daily), Kolašin (€4.80, 1½ hours, five daily) and Belgrade (1st/2nd class €29/20, 7½ hours, three daily).

Ostrog Monastery
Манастир Острог

Resting in a cliff-face 900m above the Zeta valley, the gleaming white **Ostrog Monastery** is the most important site in Montenegro for Orthodox Christians. Even with its masses of pilgrims, tourists and trashy souvenir stands, it's a strangely affecting place.

Leaving the main Podgorica–Nikšić highway 19km past Danilovgrad, a narrow road twists uphill for 7km before it reaches the **Lower Monastery** (1824). In summer you'll be greeted with sweet fragrances emanating from the mountain foliage. The church has vivid frescos and behind it is a natural spring, where you can fill your bottles with deliciously fresh water and potentially benefit from an internal blessing as you sup it. From here the faithful, many of them barefoot, plod up another two steep kilometres to the main shrine. Nonpilgrims and the pure of heart may drive to the upper car park.

The **Upper Monastery** (the really impressive one) is dubbed 'Sv Vasilije's miracle', because noone seems to understand how it was built. Constructed in 1665 within two large caves, it gives the impression that it has grown out of the very rock. Sv Vasilije (St Basil), a bishop from Hercegovina, brought his monks here after the Ottomans destroyed Tvrdos Monastery near Trebinje. Pilgrims queue to go into the atmospheric shrine where the saint's fabric-wrapped bones are kept. To enter you'll need to be wearing a long skirt or trousers (jeans are fine) and cover your shoulders.

One of the only nonsmoking establishments in the country, the **guest house** (☑067-405 258; dm €4) near the Lower Monastery offers tidy single-sex dorm rooms, while in summer many pilgrims lay sleeping mats in front of the Upper Monastery.

There's no public transport but numerous tour buses head here from all of the tourist hot spots. Expect to pay €20 for a day trip from the coast.

NORTHERN MOUNTAINS

This really is the full Monte: soaring peaks, hidden monasteries, secluded villages, steep river canyons and a whole heap of 'wild beauty', to quote the tourist slogan. It's well worth hiring a car for a couple of days to get off the beaten track – some of the roads are truly spectacular.

Kolašin Колашин
☑020 / POP 3000

Kolašin is Montenegro's main mountain resort. Although the skiing's not as reliable as Durmitor, Kolašin's much easier to get to (it's just off the main highway, 71km north of Podgorica) and has far ritzier accommodation. Like most ski towns it looks a lot prettier under a blanket of snow but even in summer it's a handy base for exploring Biogradska Gora National Park or other parts of the Bjelasica Mountains.

Most things of interest, including the banks and post office, are set around the two central squares (Trg Borca and Trg Vukmana Kruščića) and the short street that connects them (ul IV Proleterske).

🏃 Activities

Kolašin 1450 Ski Resort
SKIING

(☑020-717 848; www.kolasin1450.com; skiing half-day/day/week pass €12/20/104) Located 10km east of Kolašin, at an elevation of 1450m, this ski centre offers 30km of runs (graded green, blue, red and black) reached by various ski lifts, as well as a cafe and restaurant in attractive wooden chalets. You can hire a full ski or snowboard kit for €13 per day and there are shuttle buses from the Hotels Lipka and Bianca in the township; they're free if you're a hotel guest or if you purchase your ski pass from the resort. The ski season lasts roughly from December to mid-April but the centre stays open in summer for hikers and offers guided quad-bike trips up the mountain (per half-hour €30).

Hiking
HIKING

Three marked hiking paths start from Trg Borca and head into the Bjelasica mountains. From the ski centre there's a 16km, five-hour loop route through the forest to Mt Ključ (1973m) and back.

Explorer Tourist Agency
OUTDOOR PURSUITS

(☑020-864 200; www.montenegroexplorer.co.me; Mojkovačka bb) Located near the bus station, this agency specialises in action-packed holidays. It can arrange hiking, skiing, rafting, mountain biking, canyoning, caving, mountain climbing, jeep safaris, horse riding, paragliding and fishing expeditions. Mountain bikes can also be hired (per day/week €30/100).

🛏 Sleeping

Hotel Lipka
HOTEL €€

(☑020-863 200; www.hotellipka.com; Mojkovačka 20; s €65-120, d €86-168; 🖭) Going for the designer-rustic look, this modern 72-room hotel is fitted out in wood and stone and liberally scattered with peasant artefacts – there's a spinning wheel in reception, should you get the urge. It's all finished to a very high and comfortable standard.

ℹ Information

Tourist office (Trg Borca 2; ☺8am-4pm) When it's open (it's often not) this impressive wooden information centre, very prominently located on the main street, can help arrange private accommodation, hotels, hiking, rafting, mountain biking and guided jeep tours.

ℹ Getting There & Away

Bus

The **bus station** (Mojkovačka bb) is a shed on the road leading into town about 200m from the centre. There are regular services to Podgorica (€5).

Train

You'll see the town laid out below Kolašin's train station; it's a 1.5km walk to the centre. Five trains head to and from Podgorica (€4.80, 1½ hours) each day. Buy your tickets on the train.

Biogradska Gora National Park Биоградска Гора

Nestled in the heart of the Bjelasica Mountain Range, this pretty national park has as its heart 1600 hectares of virgin woodland – one of Europe's last three remaining primeval forests. The main entrance to the park is between Kolašin and Mojkovac on the Podgorica–Belgrade route. After paying a €2 entry fee you can drive the further 4km to the lake.

You can hire rowboats (per hour €5) and buy fishing permits (per day €20) from the **park office** (www.nparkovi.co.me) by the carpark. Nearby there's a **camping ground** (small/large tent €3/5) with basic squat toilets and a cluster of 11 new windowless log cabins, each with two beds (€20). The ablutions block for the cabins is much nicer. **Restoran Biogradsko Jezero** (mains €5.50-9.20) has a wonderful terrace where you can steal glimpses of the lake through the trees as you tuck into a traditional lamb or veal dish.

The nearest bus stop is an hour's walk away at Kraljevo Kolo and the nearest train station is a 90-minute walk away at Štitarička Rijeka.

Durmitor National Park Дурмитор

☑052 / POP 4900

Magnificent scenery ratchets up to the stupendous in this national park (€2 entry fee per day), where ice and water have carved a dramatic landscape from the limestone. Some 18 glacial lakes known as *gorske oči* (mountain eyes) dot the Durmitor range, with the largest, **Black Lake** (Crno Jezero), a pleasant 3km walk from Žabljak. The rounded mass of **Međed** (The Bear; 2287m) rears up behind the lake flanked by others of the park's 48 peaks over 2000m, including the highest, **Bobotov Kuk** (2523m). In winter (December to March) Durmitor is Montenegro's main ski resort; in summer it's a popular place for hiking, rafting and other active pursuits.

The park is home to enough critters to cast a Disney movie, including 163 species of bird, about 50 types of mammals and purportedly the greatest variety of butterflies in Europe.

Žabljak, at the eastern edge of the range, is the park's principal gateway and the only town within its boundaries. It's not very big and nor is it attractive, but it has a supermarket, post office, bank, hotels and restaurants, all gathered around the parking lot that masquerades as the main square.

✦ Activities

Rafting
RAFTING

Slicing through the mountains at the northern edge of the national park like they were made from the local soft cheese, the **Tara River** forms a canyon that at its peak is 1300m deep. By way of comparison, Colorado's Grand Canyon is only 200m deeper.

Rafting along the river is one of the country's most popular tourist activities, with various operators running trips daily between May and October. The river has a few rapids but don't expect an adrenaline-fuelled white-water experience. You'll get the most excitement in May, when the last of the melting snow still revs up the flow.

The 82km section that is raftable starts from Splavište, south of the impressive 150m-high Tara Bridge, and ends at Šćepan Polje on the Bosnian border. The classic two-day trip heads through the deepest part of the canyon on the first day, stopping overnight at Radovan Luka. Most of the day tours from the coast traverse only the last 18km from Brstanovica – this is outside the national park and hence avoids hefty fees. You'll miss out on the canyon's depths but it's still a beautiful stretch, including most of the rapids. The buses follow a spectacular road along the Piva River, giving you a double dose of canyon action.

If you've got your own wheels you can save a few bucks and avoid a lengthy coach tour by heading directly to Šćepan Polje. It's important to use a reputable operator; in 2010, two people died in one day on a trip with inexperienced guides. At a minimum make sure you're given a helmet and life-jacket – and make sure you wear them.

One good operator is **Kamp Grab** (☑040-200 598; www.tara-grab.com; half-day tour incl lunch €45), with lodgings blissfully located 8km upstream from Šćepan Polje. To get there, you'll need to cross the Montenegrin side of the border crossing and hang a right (tell the guards you're heading to Grab); the last 3.5km is unsealed.

Tara Tour (☑069-086 106; www.tara-tour.com) offers an excellent half-day trip (with/without breakfast and lunch €40/30) and has a cute set of wooden chalets in Šćepan Polje with squat toilets and showers in a separate block; accommodation, three meals and a half-day's rafting costs €55.

Hiking
HIKING

Durmitor is one of the best-marked mountain ranges in Europe. Some suggest it's a little too well labelled, encouraging novices to wander around seriously high-altitude paths that are prone to fog and summer thunderstorms. Check the weather forecast before you set out, stick to the tracks and prepare for sudden drops in temperature. Paths can be as easy as a 4km stroll around the Black Lake.

Skiing
SKIING

On the slopes of **Savin Kuk** (2313m), 5km from Žabljak, you'll find the main ski centre. Its 3.5km run starts from a height of 2010m and is best suited to advanced skiers. On the outskirts of town near the bus station, **Javorovača** is a gentle 300m slope that's good for kids and beginners. The third centre at **Mali Štuoc** (1953m) has terrific views over the Black Lake, Međed and Savin Kuk, and slopes to suit all levels of experience.

One of the big attractions for skiing here is the cost: day passes are around €15, weekly passes are €90, and ski lessons cost between €10 and €20. You can rent ski and snowboard gear from **Sport Trade** (Vuka Karadžića 7, Žabljak) for around €10 per day.

Tara Bungy
BUNGEE JUMPING

(☑067-9010 020; www.bungy.me; jump €79; ☉Jun-Sep) Hurl yourself off the elegant 172m Tara Bridge under the supervision of experienced operators from the UK Bungee Club.

🛏 Sleeping

Eko-Oaza Suza Evrope CABINS €
(☎069-444 590; ekooazatara@gmail.com; Dobrilovina; cabin low/high season €25/50; P) Situated 25km west of Mojkovac at the beginning of the arm of the park that stretches along the Tara River, this family-run 'eco oasis' consists of four comfortable wooden cabins, each sleeping six people. From here you can hike up the mountain and stay overnight in a hut near the glacial Lake Zaboj (1477m). Home-cooked meals are provided on request.

MB Hotel HOTEL €€
(☎052-361 601; mb-turist@yahoo.com; Tripka Đakovića bb, Žabljak; s/d €30/57; P🐾) In a quiet backstreet halfway between the town centre and the bus station, this little hotel offers decent midrange rooms and an attractive restaurant and bar. The restaurant even has a nonsmoking section – something even less likely to be seen in these parts than wolves.

Autokamp Mlinski Potok Mina
CAMPING GROUND €
(☎069-497 625; camp sites per person €3, dm €10) With a fabulously hospitable host (there's no escaping the *rakija* shots), this is a basic camping ground above the National Park Visitors Centre. The owner's house can sleep 12 guests in wood-panelled rooms and he has another house sleeping 11 by the Black Lake.

ℹ Information

Durmitor National Park Visitor Centre (www.nparkovi.co.me; Jovana Cvijića bb; ⊙9am-5pm Mon-Fri) On the road to the Black Lake, this centre includes a wonderful micromuseum focusing on the park's flora and fauna. The knowledgeable English-speaking staff sell local craft, maps and hiking guidebooks.

ℹ Getting There & Away

The most reliable road to Žabljak follows the Tara River west from Mojkovac. In summer this 70km route takes about 90 minutes. If you're coming from Podgorica the quickest route is through Nikšić and Šavnik, but the road can be treacherous in winter. The main highway north from Nikšić follows the dramatic Piva Canyon to Šćepan Polje. There's a wonderful back road through the mountains from the highway near Plužine to Žabljak, but it's impassable as soon as the snows fall.

There's a petrol station near the bus station at the southern end of Žabljak on the Nikšić road. Buses head to Belgrade (€18, nine hours, two daily) and Podgorica (€8, 3½ hours, three daily).

History

Like all the modern states of the Balkan peninsula, Montenegro has a long, convoluted and eventful history. History is worn on the sleeve here and people discuss 600-year-old events (or their not-always-accurate versions of them) as if they happened yesterday. Events such as the split of the Roman Empire, the subsequent split in Christianity between Catholic and Orthodox, and the battles with the Ottoman Turks still have a direct bearing on the politics of today.

Before the Slavs

The Illyrians were the first known people to inhabit the region. By 1000 BC they had established a loose federation of tribes across much of the Balkans. By around 400 BC the Greeks had established some coastal colonies and by AD 10 the Romans had absorbed the entire region into their empire. In 395 the Roman Empire was split into two halves, the western half retaining Rome as capital, the eastern half, which eventually became the Byzantine Empire, centred on Constantinople. Modern Montenegro lay on the fault line between the two entities.

In the early 7th century, the Slavs arrived from north of the Danube. Two main Slavic groups settled in the Balkans: the Croats along the Adriatic coast and the Serbs in the interior. With time most Serbs accepted the Orthodox faith, while the Croats accepted Catholicism.

First Slavic Kingdoms

In the 9th century the first Serb kingdom, Raška, arose near Novi Pazar (in modern Serbia) followed shortly by another Serb state, Duklja, which sprang up on the site of the Roman town of Doclea (present-day Podgorica). Initially allied with Byzantium, Duklja eventually shook off Byzantine influence and began to expand. Over time Duklja came to be known as Zeta, but from 1160 Raška again became the dominant Serb entity. At its greatest extent it reached from the Adriatic to the Aegean and north to the Danube.

Expansion was halted in 1389 at the battle of Kosovo Polje, where the Serbs were defeated by the Ottoman Turks. Thereafter the Turks swallowed up the Balkans and the Serb nobility fled to Zeta, on Lake Skadar. When they were forced out of Zeta by the Ottomans in 1480 they established a stronghold in the mountains at Cetinje on Mt Lovćen.

Montenegro & the Ottomans

This mountainous area became the last redoubt of Serbian Orthodox culture when all else fell to the Ottomans. It was during this time that the Venetians, who ruled Kotor, Budva and much of the Adriatic Coast, began calling Mt Lovćen the Monte Negro (Black Mountain), which lends its name to the modern state. Over time the Montenegrins established a reputation as fearsome warriors. The Ottomans opted for pragmatism, and largely left them to their own devices.

With the struggle against the Ottomans, the previously highly independent tribes began to work collaboratively by the 1600s. This further developed a sense of shared Montenegrin identity and the *vladika,* previously a metropolitan position within the Orthodox Church, began mediating between tribal chiefs. As such, the *vladika* assumed a political role, and *vladika* became a hereditary title: the prince-bishop.

While Serbia remained under Ottoman control, in the late 18th century the Montenegrins under *vladika* Petar I Petrović began to expand their territory, doubling it within the space of a little over 50 years.

A rebellion against Ottoman control broke out in Bosnia and Hercegovina (BiH) in 1875. Montenegrins joined the insurgency and made significant territorial gains as a result. At the Congress of Berlin in 1878 Montenegro and Bosnia officially achieved independence.

In the early years of the 20th century there were increasing calls for union with Serbia and rising political opposition to the ruling Petrović dynasty. The Serbian king Petar Karadjordjević attempted to overthrow King Nikola Petrović and Montenegrin-Serbian relations reached their historic low point.

The Balkans Wars of 1912–13 saw the Montenegrins joining the Serbs, Greeks and Bulgarians and succeeding in throwing the Ottomans out of southeastern Europe. Now that Serbia and Montenegro were both independent and finally shared a border, the idea of a Serbian-Montenegrin union gained more currency. King Nikola pragmatically supported the idea on the stipulation that both the Serbian and Montenegrin royal houses be retained.

The Two Yugoslavias

Before the union could be realised WWI intervened. Serbia quickly entered the war and Montenegro followed in its footsteps. Austria-Hungary invaded Serbia shortly afterwards and swiftly captured Cetinje, sending King Nikola into exile in France. In 1918 the Serbian army reclaimed Montenegro, and the French, keen to implement the Serbian-Montenegrin union, refused to allow Nikola to leave France. The following year Montenegro was incorporated in the Kingdom of the Serbs, Croats and Slovenes, the first Yugoslavia.

Throughout the 1920s some Montenegrins put up spirited resistance to the union with Serbia. This resentment was increased by the abolition of the Montenegrin church, which was absorbed by the Serbian Orthodox Patriarchate.

During WWII the Italians occupied the Balkans. Tito's Partisans and the Serbian Chetniks engaged the Italians, sometimes lapsing into fighting each other. Ultimately, the Partisans put up the best fight and with the diplomatic and military support of the Allies, the Partisans entered Belgrade in October 1944 and Tito was made prime minister. Once the communist federation of Yugoslavia was established, Tito decreed that Montenegro have full republic status and the border of the modern Montenegrin state was set. Of all the Yugoslav states, Montenegro had the highest per-capita membership of the Communist Party and it was highly represented in the armed forces.

The Union & Independence

In the decades following Tito's death in 1980, Slobodan Milošević used the issue of Kosovo to whip up a nationalist storm in Serbia and ride to power on a wave of nationalism. The Montenegrins largely supported their Orthodox co-religionists. In 1991 Montenegrin paramilitary groups were responsible for the shelling of Dubrovnik and parts of the Dalmatian littoral. In 1992, by which point Slovenia, Croatia and BiH had opted for independence, the Montenegrins voted overwhelmingly in support of a plebiscite to remain in Yugoslavia with Serbia.

In 1997 Montenegrin leader Milo Djukanović broke with an increasingly isolated Milošević and immediately became the darling of the West. As the Serbian regime became an international pariah, the Montenegrins increasingly wanted to re-establish their distinct identity.

In 2000 Milošević lost the election in Serbia. Meanwhile Vojislav Koštunica came to power in Montenegro. With Milošević now toppled, Koštunica was pressured to vote for a Union of Serbia and Montenegro. In theory this union was based on equality between the two republics; however, in practice Serbia was such a dominant partner that the union proved unfeasible from the outset. In May 2006 the Montenegrins voted for independence. Since then the divorce of Serbia and Montenegro has proceeded relatively smoothly. Montenegro has rapidly opened up to the West and has instituted economic, legal and environmental reforms with a view to becoming a member of the EU.

The People of Montenegro

In the last census (2003) 43% of the population identified as Montenegrin, 32% as Serb, 8% as Bosniak (with a further 4% identifying as Muslim), 5% as Albanian, 1% as Croat and 0.4% as Roma. Montenegrins are the majority along most of the coast and the centre of the country, while Albanians dominate in the southeast (around Ulcinj), Bosniaks in the far east (Rožaje and Plav), and Serbs in the north and Herceg Novi.

Religion and ethnicity broadly go together in these parts. Over 74% of the population is Orthodox (mainly Montenegrins and Serbs), 18% Muslim (mainly Bosniaks and Albanians) and 4% Roman Catholic (mainly Albanians and Croats).

In 1993 the Montenegrin Orthodox Church (MOC) was formed, claiming to revive the autocephalous church of Montenegro's bishop-princes that was dissolved in 1920 following the formation of the Kingdom of Serbs, Croats and Slovenes. The Serbian Orthodox Church doesn't recognise the MOC and still control most of the country's churches and monasteries.

Visual Arts

Montenegro's visual arts can be divided into two broad strands: religious iconography and Yugoslav-era painting and sculpture. The nation's churches are full of wonderful frescoes and painted iconostases (the screen that separates the congregation from the sanctuary in Orthodox churches). Of the modern painters, an early great was Petar Lubarda (1907–74), whose stylised oil paintings included themes from Montenegrin history.

Environment

The Land

Montenegro is comprised of a thin strip of Adriatic coast, a fertile plain around Podgorica and a whole lot of mountains. The highest peak is Kolac (2534m) in the Prokletije range near Albania. Most of the mountains are limestone and karstic in nature and they shelter large swathes of forest and glacial lakes. Rivers such as the Tara, Piva and Morača have cut deep canyons through them. The oddly shaped Bay of Kotor is technically a drowned river canyon, although it's popularly described as a fjord. Lake Skadar, the largest in the Balkans, spans Montenegro and Albania in the southeast.

Wildlife

Among the mammals that live in Montenegro are otters, badgers, roe deer, chamois, foxes, weasels, moles, groundhogs and hares. Bears, wolves, lynxes and jackals are much rarer sights. Tortoises, lizards and snakes are easier to find and you might spot golden and imperial eagles, white-headed vultures and peregrine falcons above the peaks. The rare Dalmatian pelican nests around Lake Skadar, along with pygmy cormorants, yellow heron and whiskered tern.

National Parks

Montenegro has five national parks covering a total area of 1075 sq km: Lovćen, Durmitor, Biogradska Gora, Lake Skadar and the recently declared Prokletije.

Environmental Issues

For a new country, especially one recovering from a recent war, Montenegro has made some key moves to safeguard the environment, not the least declaring itself an 'ecological state' in its constitution. Yet in the rush to get bums on beaches, the preservation of the nation's greatest selling point sometimes plays second fiddle to development.

The country currently imports 40% of its electricity and ideas mooted for increasing supply have included flooding part of the Morača canyon to build new hydroelectric power stations.

There's little awareness of litter as a problem. It's not just the ubiquitous practice of throwing rubbish out of car windows; we've seen waitresses clear tables by throwing refuse straight into a river and we've heard reports of train employees doing the same. Along the coast, fly-tipping of rubble from building sites is a problem. On an encouraging note, recycling is now established in Herceg Novi and the hunting of the nation's endangered bear population has recently been banned.

Food & Drink

Loosen your belt; you're in for a treat. Eating in Montenegro is generally an extremely pleasurable experience. By default, most of the food is local, fresh and organic, and hence very seasonal. The only downside is a lack of variety. By the time you've been here a week, menu déjà vu is likely to have set in.

The food on the coast is virtually indistinguishable from Dalmatian cuisine: lots of grilled seafood, garlic, olive oil and Italian dishes. Inland it's much more meaty and Serbian influenced.

The village of Njeguši in the Montenegrin heartland is famous for its *pršut* (dried ham) and cheese. Anything with Njeguški in its name is going to be a true Montenegrin dish and stuffed with these goodies.

In the mountains, meat roasted *ispod sača* (under a metal lid covered with hot coals) comes out deliciously tender. You might eat it with *kačamak,* a cheesy, creamy cornmeal or buckwheat dish – heavy going but comforting on those long winter nights.

On the coast, be sure to try the fish soup, grilled squid (served plain or stuffed with *pršut* and cheese) and black risotto (made from squid ink). Whole fish are often presented to the table for you to choose from and are sold by the kilogram.

Fast-food outlets and bakeries *(pekara),* serving *burek* (meat- or spinach-filled pastries), pizza slices and *palačinke* (pancakes) are easy to find. Anywhere that attracts tourists will have a selection of restaurants and *konoba* (small family-run affairs). There is generally no distinction between a cafe and bar. Restaurants open at around 8am and close around midnight, while cafe-bars may stay open until 2am or 3am.

Eating in Montenegro can be a trial for vegetarians and almost impossible for vegans. Pasta, pizza and salad are the best fallback options. Nonsmoking sections are a rumour from distant lands that have yet to trouble the citizens of Montenegro.

Local Drinks

Montenegro's domestic wine is eminently drinkable and usually the cheapest thing on the menu. Vranac and Krstač are the indigenous red and white grapes, respectively. Nikšićko Pivo (try saying that after a few) is the local beer and a good thirst-quencher. Many people distil their own *rakija* (brandy), made out of just about anything (grapes, pears, apples etc). They all come out tasting like rocket fuel.

The coffee is universally excellent. In private houses it's generally served Turkish-style, 'black as hell, strong as death and sweet as love'.

SURVIVAL GUIDE

Directory A–Z

Accommodation

Prices are very seasonal, peaking in July and August on the coast. In this chapter we've listed indicative ranges. Our price ranges for a double room are budget (€; less than €30 per night for the cheapest double room), midrange (€€; €30 to €90) and top end (€€€; more than €90).

The cheapest options are rooms in private houses and apartment rentals. These can be arranged through travel agencies or, in season, you may be approached at the bus stop or see signs hanging outside of houses. Facilities at camping grounds tend to be basic, often with squat toilets and limited water. The national parks have cabin-style accommodation.

An additional tourist tax (less than €2 per night) is added to the rate for all accommodation types. For private accommodation it's sometimes left up to the guest to pay it, but it can be nigh on impossible finding the right authority to pay it to (the procedure varies from area to area). Theoretically you could be asked to provide white accommodation receipt cards (or copies of invoices from hotels) when you leave the country, but in practice this is rarely required.

Activities

Hooking up with activity operators can be difficult due to language difficulties, lack of permanent offices and out-of-date websites. Luckily there are some excellent travel agencies who will do the legwork for you, including Black Mountain in Herceg Novi (p612) and Montenegro Adventure Centre in Budva.

Business Hours

Business hours in Montenegro are a relative concept. Even if hours are posted on the doors of museums or shops, they may not be heeded. Reviews don't list opening hours unless they differ from the following:

Banks Usually 8am-5pm Mon-Fri, until noon Sat

Cafe-bars 8am-midnight (later in high season in busy areas)

Restaurants 8am-midnight

Shops 8am or 9am to 8pm or 9pm; often closed in late afternoon

Embassies & Consulates

The following are all in Podgorica, unless otherwise stated.

Albania (☏020-652 796; Zmaj Jovina 30)

BiH (☏020-618 105; Atinska 58)

Croatia Kotor (☏032-323 127; Trg od Oružja bb); Podgorica (☏020-269 760; Vladimira Ćetkovića 2)

France (☏020-655 348; Atinska 35)

Germany (☏020-667 285; Hercegovačka 10)

Italy (☏020-234 661; Bul Džordža Vašingtona 83)

Serbia (☏020-667 305; Hercegovačka bb)

UK (☏020-618 010; Ulcinjska 8)

USA (☏020-410 500; Ljubljanska bb)

Food

Price ranges: budget (€; under €5), midrange (€€; €5 to €10) and top end (€€€; over €10).

Gay & Lesbian Travellers

Although homosexuality was decriminalised in 1977 and discrimination outlawed in 2010, attitudes to homosexuality remain hostile and life for gay people is extremely difficult. Many gay men resort to online connections (try www.gayromeo.com) or take their chances at a handful of cruisy beaches. Lesbians will find it even harder to access the local community.

Money

Montenegro uses the euro (€). You'll find banks with ATMs in all the main towns, most of which accept Visa, MasterCard, Maestro and Cirrus. Don't rely on restaurants, shops or smaller hotels accepting credit cards.

Tipping isn't expected, although it's common to round up to the nearest euro.

Public Holidays

New Year's Day 1 and 2 January

Orthodox Christmas 6, 7 and 8 January

Orthodox Good Friday & Easter Monday April/May

Labour Day 1 May

Independence Day 21 and 22 May

Statehood Day 13 July

Telephone

The international access prefix is ☏00 or + from a mobile. Mobile numbers start with 06. Local SIM cards are good if you're planning a longer stay. The main providers are T-Mobile, Telenor and M:tel.

Women Travellers

Other than a cursory interest shown by men towards solo women travellers, travelling is hassle free and easy. In Muslim areas some women wear a headscarf but most don't.

Getting There & Away

Air

Montenegro has two international **airports** (www.montenegroairports.com) – **Tivat** (TIV; ☏032-617 337) and **Podgorica** (TGD; ☏020-872 016) – although most tourists arrive via Croatia's Dubrovnik airport, which is very near the border. While various airlines run summer charter flights, the following airlines have regular scheduled flights to/from Montenegro.

Adria Airlines (JP; ☏020-201 201; www.adria. si; Ivana Vujoševića 46, Podgorica) Ljubljana to Podgorica.

Austrian Airlines (OS; ☏020-606 170; www. austrian.com) Vienna to Podgorica (operated by Tyrolean).

Croatia Airlines (OU; ☏020-201 201; www. croatiaairlines.com; Ivana Vujoševića 46, Podgorica) Zagreb to Podgorica.

JAT Airways (JU; ☏020-664 750; www.jat. com; Njegoševa 25, Podgorica) Belgrade to Tivat and Podgorica.

Malév Hungarian Airlines (MA; ☎020-667 480; www.malev.com) Budapest to Podgorica.

Montenegro Airlines (YM; ☎020-664 411; www.montenegroairlines.com; Slobode 23, Podgorica) Belgrade and Moscow to Tivat; Bari, Belgrade, Brussels, Frankfurt, Ljubljana, London, Milan, Moscow, Naples, Niš, Paris, Pristina, Skopje, Vienna and Zürich to Podgorica.

Moskovia Airlines (3R; ☎033-455 967; www.moskovia.aero; Mediteranska 23, Budva) Moscow to Tivat and Podgorica.

S7 Airlines (S7; ☎7-495-777-99-99; www.s7.ru) Moscow to Tivat and Podgorica.

Turkish Airlines (TK; ☎020-653 108; www.turkishairlines.com) Istanbul to Podgorica.

Land
Border Crossings

Albania The main crossings link Shkodra to Ulcinj (Sukobin) and to Podgorica (Hani i Hotit).

BiH The main checkpoints are at Sitnica, Dolovi and Šćepan Polje.

Croatia There's a busy checkpoint on the Adriatic highway between Herceg Novi and Dubrovnik; expect delays in summer. A longer-distance but often quicker checkpoint is Kobila, on the tip of the Prevlaka peninsula.

Kosovo The main crossing is on the road between Rožaje and Peć.

Serbia The busiest crossing is north of Bijelo Polje near Dobrakovo, followed by the checkpoint northeast of Rožaje and another east of Pljevlja.

Bus

There's a well-developed bus network linking Montenegro with the major cities of the region. Podgorica is the main hub but buses stop at most other big towns as well. For some indicative prices, see p613.

Car & Motorcycle

Drivers are recommended to carry an International Driving Permit (IDP) as well as their home country's driving licence. Vehicles need Green Card insurance or insurance must be bought at the border. A €10 eco-tax (valid for one year) is charged on foreign cars entering the country.

Train

Montenegro's only working passenger train line starts at Bar and heads into Serbia. For details on the train to Belgrade, see p626.

Sea

For details on ferries to Italy from Kotor and Bar, see p616 and p620.

Getting Around
Bicycle

Cyclists are a rare species, even in the cities. Don't expect drivers to be considerate. Wherever possible, try to get off the main roads.

Bus

The local bus network is extensive and reliable. Buses are usually comfortable and air conditioned, and are rarely full. It's slightly cheaper to buy your ticket on the bus rather than the station, but a station-bought ticket theoretically guarantees you a seat. Luggage carried below the bus is charged at €1 per piece.

Car & Motorcycle

Independent travel by car or motorcycle is an ideal way to gad about and discover the country; some of the drives are breathtakingly beautiful. Traffic police are everywhere, so stick to speed limits and carry an IDP. Allow more time than you'd expect for the distances involved, as the terrain will slow you down.

The major international car-hire companies have a presence in various centres. **Meridian Rentacar** (☎020-234 944; www.meridian-rentacar.com), which has offices in Budva, Bar, Podgorica and the airports, is a reliable local option; one-day hire starts from €45.

Train

Željeznica Crne Gore (www.zcg-prevoz.me) runs the only passenger train line, heading north from Bar. The trains are old and can be hot in summer but they're priced accordingly and the route through the mountains is spectacular. Useful stops include Virpazar, Podgorica and Kolašin.

Morocco

Why Go?

For many travellers, Morocco might just be a short hop away by ferry or by one of the countless budget airlines from Spain, but it's a much further distance to travel culturally. The regular certainties of Europe are suddenly swept away by the arrival in full technicolour of Africa and Islam. It's a complete sensory overload.

Atlantic winds blow through cosmopolitan Tangier and Casablanca and the whitewashed coastal gems of Asileh and Essaouira. The great imperial cities of Marrakesh and Fez have enough surprises hidden in their winding streets to fill a dozen visits.

The High Atlas Mountains seem custom-made for hiking boots, with trails between Berber villages, and North Africa's highest peak to conquer. Or if you prefer someone else to do the walking, saddle up your camel and ride into the Sahara, to watch the sun setting over an ocean of sand.

Best Places to Eat

» Auberge Dardara Restaurant (p646)

» Outdoor fish grills (p659)

» Café Clock (p666)

» Earth Café (p674)

Best Places to Stay

» Dar Nour (p640)

» Jnane Mogador (p673)

» Dar Raha (p680)

When to Go
Marrakesh

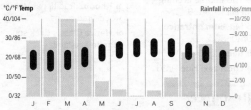

March–June	July–August	November–January
Spring blooms; it's hot but fresh with a chance of rain. Morocco's at its greenest.	It's Ramadan; many restaurants closed in the day and reduced business hours.	Warm days of winter sun that are perfect for Marrakesh and the south.

Fast Facts

» **Area** 446,550 sq km

» **Capital** Rabat

» **Country code** ☎212

» **Emergency** ☎190 Police

Exchange Rates

Australia	A$1	Dh8.45
Canada	C$1	Dh8.22
euro	€1	Dh11.28
Japan	¥100	Dh9.81
New Zealand	NZ$1	Dh6.35
UK	UK£1	Dh12.95
USA	US$1	Dh8.04

Set Your Budget

» **Budget hotel room** from Dh250

» **Two-course evening meal** Dh70–150

» **Museum entrance** Dh10–50

» **Beer** Dh20

» **Local taxi ride** Dh10

Resources

» **The View from Fez** (http://riadzany.blogspot.com)

» **Visit Morocco** (www.visitmorocco.com)

Connections

The cheap flight revolution has well and truly arrived in Morocco, and budget airlines link Casablanca, Marrakesh, Fez and Tangier to the major European air hubs. If you have time, a more enjoyable way of connecting to mainland Europe is by ferry, either zipping across the Straits of Gibraltar from Tangier to Algeciras or Tarifa in Spain, or from Spain's enclaves of Ceuta and Melilla to connect with the Spanish rail network.

ITINERARIES

One week

From Tangier, make a beeline for Fez and Marrakesh, imperial cities in the Moroccan interior that deserve as much time as you can spare. After that, a detour to artsy Essaouira is a wonderful way to step down a gear after the onslaught of Morocco's most clamorous cities.

Two weeks

Follow the itinerary above, but en route south head via chilled-out Chefchaouen. Meknès is a great detour from Fez, but once into the south past Marrakesh, make time either to head into the High Atlas for hiking, or the Saharan sand at Merzouga or M'Hamid.

Essential Food & Drink

» **Tajine** Slow-cooked stew in conical-topped earthenware dish. Classic varieties include chicken with olives and lemon, *kefta* (meatballs), lamb with vegetables and beef with prunes and almonds.

» **Couscous** Slow steamed hand-rolled semolina, served with a light broth and either meat or vegetables. Usually the centrepiece of a meal.

» **B'stilla** Parcel of layered filo pastry, stuffed with pigeon or chicken, nuts and cinnamon.

» **Khoobz** Traditional Moroccan bread, baked in communal wood-fired ovens.

» **Harira** Classic thick soup with onion, lentil, chickpeas, tomato and lamb.

MEDITERRANEAN COAST & THE RIF

Bounded by the red crags of the Rif Mountains and the crashing waves of the Mediterranean, northern Morocco conceals the cosmopolitan hustle of Tangier, the Spanish enclaves of Ceuta and Melilla, the old colonial capital of Tetouan, and the superbly relaxing town of Chefchaouen.

Tangier

POP 650,000

Like the dynamic strait upon which it sits, Tangier is the product of 1001 currents, including Islam, Berber tribes, colonial masters, a highly strategic location, a vibrant port, the Western counterculture and the international jet set. It regularly passed between Moroccan and Western control – for half of the 20th century it was under the dubious control of an international council, making it a byword for licentious behaviour and dodgy dealings.

Many travellers simply pass through, but if you take it head-on and learn to handle the hustlers looking out for tourists fresh off the ferry from Spain, you'll find it a lively, cosmopolitan place with an energetic nightlife.

Tangier's small medina climbs up the hill to the northeast of the city, while the ville nouvelle (new town) surrounds it to the west, south and southeast. The large, central square known as the Grand Socco (officially renamed Place du 9 Avril 1947) provides the link between the two.

◉ Sights

Kasbah   HISTORIC AREA
The kasbah sits on the highest point of Tangier, behind stout walls. Coming from the medina, you enter through Bab el-Aassa, the southeastern gate, to find the **Kasbah Museum** (☑039 932097; admission incl Sultan's Gardens Dh10; ⊙9am-12.30pm Wed-Mon, 3-5.30pm Wed, Thu & Sat-Mon), housed in the 17th-century palace of Dar el-Makhzen. It's now a worthwhile museum devoted to Moroccan arts. Before leaving, take a stroll around the Andalucian-style **Sultan's Gardens**.

**Tangier American Legation
Museum**   MUSEUM
(☑0539 935317; www.legation.org; 8 Rue d'Amerique; admission by donation; ⊙10am-1pm & 3-5pm Mon-Fri) In the southwest corner of the medina, the museum is an intriguing relic of the international zone with a fascinating collection of memorabilia from the international writers and artists who passed through Tangier.

Musée de la Fondation Lorin   MUSEUM
(☑0539 930306; fondationlorin@gmail.com; 44 Rue Touahine; admission by donation; ⊙11am-1pm

---

FRESH OFF THE BOAT?

For many people Tangier is a first: first time in Africa, first time in a Muslim country, first time in a developing country, or some combination of the above. If you've taken the ferry, drawn by the exotic scent from across the strait, here are some tips to ease your arrival (and departure) stress.

The hordes of touts that would descend in packs on unwary travellers have largely disappeared from Tangier's port, but you're still likely to be greeted by a few multilingual 'guides'. The best way to deal with this is to look blasé, claim that you already know the city and politely decline any offers of assistance. Smile and keep moving. It helps to know exactly where you're going, so you can jump quickly into a cab if necessary. A petit taxi (local taxi) into the centre will cost around Dh10 and a grand taxi (shared taxi) around Dh30 between all passengers. Remember to change money on the boat to pay the fare. Tackling anywhere unfamiliar after dark is always more traumatic, so try to arrive early in the day and, above all, with a good sense of humour.

If you're catching the ferry from Tangier and arrive at the port on foot, you'll be approached by touts intent on getting you into one or other of the numerous ticket offices and travel agencies along Ave d'Espagne. To minimise the hassle, you might buy your ticket in advance or take a taxi to the terminal building. In any case, be sure to pick up an exit form with your ticket. The scribes who distribute them at the port will expect a tip for their 'assistance' filling out the form. Allow a good 90 minutes before your boat sails for buying tickets and getting through passport control.

ATLANTIC OCEAN

Azemmour
El- Jadida
Oued Oum

Oualidia

Safi

Ben Guér

Marrakesh

4 Essaouira

Legzira
Plage

Jebel Toubkal
(4167m) 8

Immouzzer
des Ida
Outmane

Tizi n'Test

Taroudannt

Talio

Agadir
Inezgane
Tioute

Jebel
Lekst
(2359m)

Tiznit

Mirleft
Tafraoute

Sidi Ifni

Bouzakarne

Goulmime

CANARY
ISLANDS
(SPAIN)

Cap
Drâa

Tadalt

Tiglite
Assa

Tan Tan
Oued Drâa

ATLANTIC
OCEAN

Tarfaya

Disputed Border

Tinc

Al-Mahbas
Erg Ig

Morocco Highlights

❶ Get lost in the alleys of the **Fez medina** (p661), Islam's greatest living medieval city

❷ Taste 1001 Nights in the open-air spectacle of the **Djemaa el-Fna square** (p671) in Marrakesh

❸ Chill in the Rif Mountains in the dazzling blue town of **Chefchaouen** (p646)

❹ Catch the sea breeze in the port town of **Essaouira** (p657), Morocco's hippest resort

❺ Admire the mosaics, columns and sweeping landscapes of **Volubilis** (p670), Morocco's foremost ancient ruins

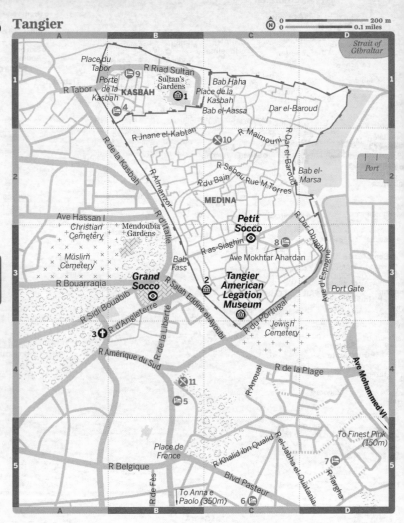

& 3.30-7.30pm Sun-Fri) Housed in a former synagogue, the museum has an engaging collection of photographs, posters and prints of Tangier from 1890 to 1960.

Bab Fass   LANDMARK
Heading uphill, you eventually emerge at the keyhole-shaped gate that opens to the renovated plaza of **Grand Socco**. A short walk up Rue d'Angleterre brings you to one of the more charming oddities of Tangier, the Victorian-era **St Andrews Church** (services Sun 8.30am, 11am), which has the Lord's Prayer in Arabic above the nave.

🛏 Sleeping

TOP CHOICE Dar Nour   GUEST HOUSE $$
(☏0662 112724; www.darnour.com; 20 Rue Gourna, Kasbah; d/ste incl breakfast from Dh720/1300; ☞) With no central courtyard, rooms here branch off two winding staircases, creating a maze of rooms and salons, each more romantic than the last. Rooms are stylishly decorated with a relaxed and homely atmosphere, and the roof has an impressive view over the medina.

Hotel el-Muniria   HOTEL $$
(☏0539 935337; 1 Rue Magellan; s/d Dh200/250, s/d on terrace Dh250/300; ☞) This is your best

Tangier

bit institutional, but well run and strong value for the money. The rooms overlooking the green-tiled roof of the Grande Mosquée are the most picturesque, if you don't mind the muezzin's call.

✖ Eating

In the medina there's a host of cheap eating possibilities around the Petit Socco and the adjacent Ave Mokhtar Ahardan, with rotisserie chicken, sandwiches and brochettes all on offer. In the ville nouvelle, try the streets immediately south of Place de France, which are flush with fast-food outlets, sandwich bars and fish counters.

Populaire Saveur de Poisson

SEAFOOD **$$**

(☎0539 336326; 2 Escalier Waller; set menu Dh150; ⊗lunch & dinner, closed Fri; 🌿) This charming seafood restaurant offers excellent set menus in rustic surroundings. The owner serves a four-course meal of fish soup followed by inventive plates of fresh catch and fresh vegetables, washed down with a homemade juice cocktail. Not just a meal, a whole experience.

Le Nabab

MOROCCAN **$$**

(☎0661 442220; 2 Rue al Kadiria; mains Dh80, menu Dh170; ⊗lunch & dinner) A beautifully restored old *fondouq* (rooming house), all grey *tadelakt* (lime plaster) comfortable seating and swathes of airy pink fabric. Dine around the huge fireplace or in a private alcove. The menu is Moroccan, the welcome friendly and it's licensed.

Anna e Paolo

ITALIAN **$$**

(☎0539 944617; 77 Rue de Prince Heretier; mains from Dh80; ⊗lunch & dinner, closed Sun) This is the top Italian bistro in the city, a family-run restaurant with Venetian owners that feels like you have been invited for Sunday dinner. Expect an international crowd and wholesome food including excellent pizzas and charcuterie.

Restaurant el-Korsan

MOROCCAN **$$$**

(☎0539 935885; El-Minzah Hotel, 85 Rue de la Liberté; mains around Dh160; ⊗dinner) One of Tangier's top restaurants, this chic and classy place inside the El-Minzah offers a smaller, more intimate version of the palace restaurant theme but without the bus tours. Well-presented Moroccan classics are served to soft live music, and often traditional dancing. Reservations are necessary, including one day prior notice for lunch. Dress well.

low-end option in the ville nouvelle, and chock-full of Beat-generation history. French windows and bright, flowery fabrics set it apart, revealing the careful touch of a hands-on family operation.

Hotel de Paris

HOTEL **$**

(☎0539 931877; 42 Blvd Pasteur; s/d incl breakfast low season Dh280/380, high season Dh350/450) This reliable choice in the heart of the ville nouvelle has a classy, old-world aura in its lobby. Rooms are clean and modern, but those overlooking Blvd Pasteur can get noisy.

La Tangerina

GUEST HOUSE **$$**

(☎0539 947731; www.latangerina.com; Rue Sultan, Kasbah; d incl breakfast Dh600-1620; 🛜) This is a perfectly renovated riad at the very top of the kasbah, with 10 rooms of different personality, easily accessible by car (a rarity), with highly attentive hosts. Bathed in light and lined with rope banisters, it feels like an elegant, Berber-carpeted steamship cresting the medina.

Hotel Mamora

HOTEL **$**

(☎0539 934105; 19 Mokhtar Ahardan; s/d with shower Dh60/120, d with toilet Dh200-260) Readers enjoy this hotel near the Petit Socco with its variety of rooms at different rates. It's a

🍷 Drinking

Caid's Bar
BAR

(El-Minzah, 85 Rue de la Liberté; wine from Dh20; ⊙10am-midnight) Welcome to Rick's Café – the real-life model for the bar in *Casablanca*. In the El-Minzah Hotel, it's a classy relic of the grand days of international Tangier, and photos of the famous and infamous adorn the walls. Women are welcome, and the adjacent wine bar is equally good.

Café Hafa
CAFE

(Ave Hadi Mohammed Tazi; ⊙8.30am-11pm Mon-Fri, 8.30am-2am Sat & Sun) Overlooking the strait, you could easily lose an afternoon lazing in this open-air cafe. Locals hang out here to play backgammon. There's no menu, but scrambled eggs, soup and olives are on offer.

☆ Entertainment

Tangier's nightlife picks up in summer. Nightclubs cluster near Place de France and line the beach. Cover charges vary and may be rolled into drink prices.

Loft
NIGHTCLUB

(📞0673 280927; www.loftclub-tanger.com; Rte de Boubana; ⊙10pm-4am, Thu & Sat) This is the premier nightspot, and feels like an enormous silver cruise ship, with upper storey balconies, sparkling metal railings, billowing sail-like curtains, spot lights cutting through artificial fog – and no cover.

Finest Pink
NIGHTCLUB

(Ave Mohammed VI; ⊙11pm till late) Tangier's gay scene has long since departed for Marrakesh, but Finest Pink is gay friendly with a lounge, restaurant, tapas bar and disco opposite the Hotel Shahrazad.

❶ Information

Blvds Pasteur and Mohammed V are lined with numerous banks with ATMs and *bureau de change* counters. Blvd Pasteur also has plenty of internet places.

Clinique du Croissant Rouge (📞0539 942517; 6 Rue al-Mansour Dahabi)

Espace Net (16 Ave Mexique; per hr Dh5; ⊙9.30am-1am)

Main post office (Cnr Rue Quevada & Ave Mohammed V)

ONMT (Délégation Régionale du Tourisme; 📞0539 948050; 29 Blvd Pasteur; ⊙closed Sat & Sun)

❶ Getting There & Away

For ferry options, see p690.

Bus

The **CTM station** is conveniently located beside the port gate. Destinations include Casablanca (Dh130, six hours), Rabat (Dh100, 4½ hours), Marrakesh (Dh230, 10 hours), Fez (Dh110, six hours) and Chefchaouen (Dh40, three hours). Cheaper bus companies operate from the **main bus station** (gare routière; Place Jamia el-Arabia), about 2km south of the city centre.

Taxi

You can hail *grands taxis* (shared taxis) to places outside Tangier from next to the main bus station. The most common destinations are Tetouan (Dh30, one hour), Asilah (Dh20, 30 minutes) and, for Ceuta, Fnideq (Dh40, one hour).

Train

Four trains depart daily from Tanger Ville train station, 3km southeast of the centre (Dh10 in a local *petit taxi*). One morning and one afternoon service go to Casa-Voyageurs in Casablanca (Dh125, 5½ hours); four trains go via Meknès (Dh80, four hours) to Fez (Dh105, five hours), although three involve changing at Sidi Kacem. A night service goes all the way to Marrakesh (seat /couchette Dh205/350, 12 hours).

❶ Getting Around

Petits taxis (blue with yellow stripe) do standard journeys around town for Dh7 to Dh10. From **Ibn Batouta airport** (📞039 393720), 15km southeast of the city, take a cream-coloured *grand taxi* (Dh150).

Around Tangier

Just 14km west of Tangier lies the dramatic **Cap Spartel**, the northwestern extremity of Africa's Atlantic Coast. The lovely beach **Plage Robinson** stretches to the south. Five kilometres along here you reach the **Grottes d'Hercule** (admission Dh5), next to Le Mirage hotel. These caves are said to have been the dwelling place of the mythical Hercules when he mightily separated Europe from Africa.

Ceuta

POP 78,600

Jutting out east into the Mediterranean, this 20 sq km peninsula has been a Spanish enclave since 1640, and its city centre with bars, cafes and Andalucian atmosphere provides a sharp contrast to the other side of the border. Nonetheless, Ceuta is still recognisably African – between a quarter and a third of the population are of Berber origin.

The Plaza de Africa, unmistakable for its giant cathedral, dominates the city centre. The port and ferry terminal are a short walk to the northwest. The border is 2km to the south along the Avenida Martinez Catena.

◎ Sights

FREE **Royal City Walls** LANDMARK
(Ave González Tablas; ⊙10am-2pm & 5-8pm) The impressively restored walls are worth a visit, and contain the striking **Museo de los Murales Reales** art gallery tucked inside.

Museo de la Basilica Tardorromana MUSEUM
(Calle Queipo de Llano; ⊙10am-1.30pm & 5-7.30pm Mon-Sat, 10am-1.30pm Sun) This intriguing underground museum is integrated into the architectural remains of an ancient basilica, discovered during street work in the 1980s, and includes a bridge over open tombs (with skeletons).

⌷ Sleeping

TOP CHOICE **Hostal Central** HOTEL $$
(☎956 51 67 16; www.hostalesceuta.com; Paseo del Revellín; s/d/tr €45/66/76; ❉🖧) This good-value, two-star hotel in an excellent location has ultramodern decor and is very welcoming. Bright rooms are small but spotless.

Parador Hotel La Muralla HOTEL $$$
(☎956 51 49 40; ceuta@parador.es; 15 Plaza de Africa; s/d from €80/100; ❉🖧⛱) Ceuta's top address is this spacious four-star hotel perfectly situated on the Plaza de Africa. Rooms are comfortable, but not luxurious. Balconies overlook a pleasant garden, but the best asset is the value-for-money price.

Hostal Plaza Ruiz HOTEL $$
(☎956 51 67 33; www.hostalesceuta.com; 3 Plaza Ruiz; s/d/tr €45/66/76; ❉🖧) Sister hotel to the Central, this place has a similar, welcoming style and a charming location. Rooms are airy; the best have wrought-iron balconies overlooking the cafes of the plaza.

✕ Eating

The Pablado Marinero (Seamen's Village) beside the yacht harbour is home to a variety of decent restaurants, while tapas bars abound in the streets around Millán Astray to the north of Calle Camoens.

Mucha Kaña TAPAS $
(7 Sargento Mena; tapas from €0.85, mains from €6; ⊙lunch & dinner) Styled as a *cervecería* (bar) but also serving Spanish wines, this is a great place for all ages. There are barstools around barrels as well as tables, and good music. In addition to tapas and raciones, there are pastas and meat dishes.

El Angulo MOROCCAN $$
(1 Muralles Reales; mains from €15; ⊙lunch & dinner, closed Sun) Here's your chance to eat inside the Royal City Walls. The local meats and seafood are as good as the unique atmosphere. White tablecloths and stone fortifications work well, or you can sit outside by the moat.

La Marina SEAFOOD $$
(☎956 51 40 07; 1 Alférez Bayton; ⊙lunch & dinner, closed Sun, closed Feb) This old favourite was closed for renovations at the time of research. No doubt it will continue to specialise in fish dishes, and do a great-value three-course set menu of the chicken/fish and chips variety.

ⓘ Information

To phone Ceuta from outside Spain, dial ☎0034 before the nine-digit phone number. Also remember that Ceuta is on Spanish time and uses the euro.

Banks with ATMs are plentiful around the pedestrianised Paseo de Revellín and Plaza Ruiz.

Cyber Ceuta (Paseo de Colón; per hr €2.50; ⊙11am-2pm & 5-10pm Mon-Sat, 5-10pm Sun)

Main tourist office (☎856 20 05 60; www.ceuta.es, in Spanish; Baluarte de los Mallorquines; ⊙8.30am-8.30pm) Friendly and efficient, with good maps and brochures.

Post office (59 Calle Real; ⊙8.30am-8.30pm Mon-Fri, 9.30am-2pm Sat)

ⓘ Getting There & Away

Bus 7 runs up to the Moroccan *frontera* (border) every 10 minutes from Plaza de la Constitución (€0.70). The large *grand taxi* lot next to Moroccan border control has departures to Tetouan (Dh30, 40 minutes). For Tangier, take a *grand taxi* to Fnideq (Dh5, 10 minutes), just south of the border, and change there.

The **estación marítima** (ferry terminal; Calle Muelle Cañonero Dato) is west of the town centre and from here there are several daily high-speed ferries to Algeciras (p690).

Tetouan

POP 330,000

Tetouan occupies a striking location at the foot of the Rif Mountains. From 1912 until 1956 it was the capital of the Spanish Protectorate in Morocco. This and the town's long relationship with Andalucía have left it with a Hispano-Moorish character that is unique in Morocco. This is physically reflected in the Spanish part of the city (whose white buildings and broad boulevards have recently been restored to their original condition) and the Unesco World Heritage–listed medina.

If you want to see the sea, the port of Martil is a 15-minute cab ride from Tetouan, as is the classy resort village of M'diq.

◉ Sights

Medina   HISTORIC AREA
The whitewashed medina (home to some 40 mosques, of which the **Grande Mosquée** and **Saidi Mosque** are the most impressive) opens through its main gate, Bab er-Rouah, onto Place Hassan II, Tetouan's grand main square. At the opposite end of the medina, the **Musée Marocaine** (Musée Ethnographique; admission Dh10; ◷9am-4pm Mon-Sat) is housed inside the bastion in the town wall.

Artisanal School   NOTABLE BUILDING
(admission Dh10; ◷8.30am-2.30pm Sat-Thu, 8.30-11.30am Fri) Just outside Bab el-Okla is the school offering a fascinating opportunity to see masters teaching apprentices traditional arts, including ornamental woodwork, carved plaster and intricate mosaics.

🛏 Sleeping

TOP CHOICE Blanco Riad   GUEST HOUSE $$$
(☏0539 704202; www.blancoriad.com; 25 Rue Zawiya Kadiria; d incl breakfast Dh880; ✴🛜) This beautiful medina house with its typical Tetouan architecture has been carefully restored and furnished with a blend of modern and antique pieces. The welcome is friendly and help is available to discover the medina.

El Reducto   GUEST HOUSE $$$
(☏0539 968120; www.riadtetouan.com; 38 Zanqat Zawiya; s incl breakfast Dh400-600, d Dh550-850) This superb house is worth a visit just to see

Tetouan

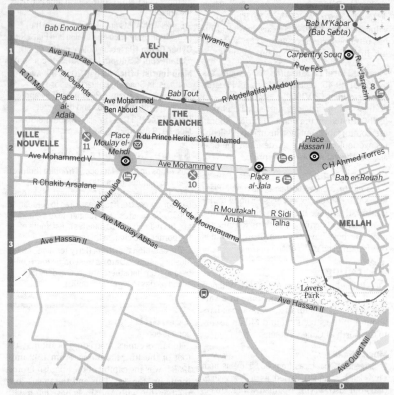

the traditional mosaic tiles with their coppery sheen. The spotless, palatial rooms are truly fantastic (one has a jacuzzi for two). There's also a licensed restaurant with a Spanish touch to the menu.

Pension Iberia HOTEL **$**
(☑0539 963679; 5 Place Moulay el-Mehdi; s/d/tr Dh60/100/150) This is the best budget option, with classic high-ceilinged rooms and shuttered balconies that open out to the Place Moulay el-Mehdi. Bathrooms are shared, and hot showers an extra Dh10.

Eating

Snack Taouss FAST FOOD **$**
(3 Rue 10 Mai; ☺lunch & dinner; mains from Dh25) This snack bar has a Syrian influence and does good felafel and delicious schwarma as well as inexpensive pizzas, salads, *harira*, tajines and more. There's a small seating area upstairs or you can eat on the move.

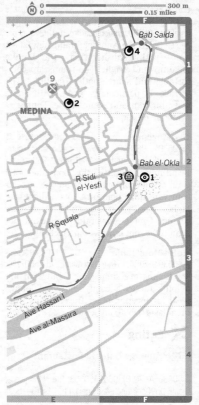

Restaurant Restinga MOROCCAN **$**
(21 Ave Mohammed V; mains from Dh50, beer Dh15; ☺lunch & dinner) The open-air courtyard, shaded by a huge tree, is this charming restaurant's primary attraction – along with the rare alcohol licence. It's a great place to duck out of the crowded boulevard for local seafood.

Palace Bouhlal MOROCCAN **$$**
(☑0670 85 95 63; 48 Jamaa Kebir; set menu Dh100; ☺lunch) A palace restaurant with plush couches, wall rugs, intimate dining spaces gurgling fountains and a grand Moorish arch complementing the usual four-course meal. Follow the lane north around the Grande Mosquée and look for signs directing you down a tiny alley.

ℹ Information

There are plenty of banks with ATMs along Ave Mohammed V.

BMCE foreign exchange office (Place Moulay el-Mehdi; ☺10am-2pm & 4-8pm) Changes cash and travellers cheques outside regular banking hours.

Main hospital (☑0539 972430; Martil Rd) About 2km out of town.

Post office (Place Moulay el-Mehdi; ☺8am-4.30pm Mon-Fri)

Remote Studios (13 Ave Mohammed V; per hr Dh9; ☺9am-midnight) Internet access.

ℹ Getting There & Away

Several bus companies operate from the **bus station** (cnr Rue Sidi Mandri & Rue Moulay Abbas). **CTM** (☑039 961688) has buses running to the usual array of places, including Casablanca (Dh125, six to seven hours, twice daily) via Rabat (Dh100, 4½ hours), Fez (Dh90, four hours), Marrakech (Dh235, 11 hours) and many more.

Grands taxis to Fnideq (for Ceuta; Dh15, 30 minutes) and Martil (Dh5, 15 minutes) leave from Ave Hassan II, which is southeast of the bus station.

Chefchaouen

POP 45,000

Beautifully sited beneath the raw peaks of the Rif, Chefchaouen (known by its diminutive 'Chaouen') is one of the prettiest towns in Morocco. It's an artsy mountain village that feels like its own world. The old medina is a delight of Moroccan and Andalucian influence with red-tiled roofs, bright blue buildings and narrow lanes converging on a delightful square. This is a great place to relax, explore and take day trips in the cool green hills.

Chefchaouen is split into the medina, and the *ciudad nueva*, or new city – a hangover from its occupation by the Spanish. The heart of the medina is Plaza Uta el-Hammam, with its unmistakeable kasbah. The principal route of the *ciudad nueva* is Ave Hassan II. The bus station is a 1km hike southwest of the town centre.

◉ Sights

Plaza Uta el-Hammam   SQUARE
The heart of the medina is the shady, cobbled plaza. This is a peaceful place to relax and watch the world go by, particularly after a long day of exploration. The plaza is dominated by the red-hued walls of the **kasbah** (admission incl museum & gallery Dh10; ◷9am-1pm & 3-6.30pm Wed-Mon, 9am-noon & 3-6.30pm Fri) and the adjacent **Grande Mosqué**, noteworthy for its unusual octagonal minaret. The kasbah is a heavily restored walled fortress that now contains a lovely garden, a small **ethnographic museum** and **art gallery**.

Ras El-Maa   WATERFALLS
Just beyond the far eastern gate of the medina lie the falls of Ras El-Maa. In season there is a popular cafe on the right, just before the bridge. The sound of the water and the verdant hills just beyond the medina wall provide a sudden, strong dose of nature. Continuing over the bridge, you can walk to the ruined 'Spanish' mosque to take in the views.

🛏 Sleeping

TOP CHOICE **Hostal Guernika**   GUEST HOUSE $
(☏0539 987434; hostalgernika@hotmail.com; 49 Onssar; d/tr Dh200/300; 🛜) This is a warm and charming place, with a very caring and attentive owner, not far from the square. There are several great rooms – large and bright, facing the mountains – but others can be dark. All have showers. The terrace has spectacular views. Reserve in summer, Easter and December.

Dar Terrae   GUEST HOUSE $$
(☏0539 98 75 98; www.darterrae.com; Ave Hassan I; s/d/tr incl breakfast Dh290/390/600; 🛜) These funky, cheerfully painted rooms are individually decorated with their own bathroom and fireplace, and hidden up and down a tumble of stairs and odd corners. The Italian owners prepare a fantastic breakfast spread and other meals on request. It's poorly signed – if in doubt ask for the 'Hotel Italiano'.

Dar Baraka   GUEST HOUSE $
(☏0614 682480; www.riad-baraka.com; d incl breakfast Dh280, without bathroom Dh240, q per person Dh120; 🛜) Another brand new guest house with English owners, Dar Baraka is sunny and bright. The rooms are comfortable and share spotless facilities. The terrace is particularly good, with some warming sun and some shade. Dinner is available on request.

Dar Meziana   GUEST HOUSE $$
(☏0539 987806; www.darmezianahotel.com; Rue Zagdud; s/d/tr from Dh475/650/950; ❄🛜) Beautifully decorated, this boutique hotel is an artful creation, with a unique angular courtyard, lush plantings, lots of light, the highest quality furniture and extraordinary ceilings. On the edge of the medina and not signposted, but otherwise perfect.

Hotel Mouritania   GUEST HOUSE $
(☏0539 986184; 15 Rue Qadi Alami; s/d Dh60/120; 🛜) Rooms are simple here, but staff are helpful, there's a comfy courtyard lounge ideal for meeting other travellers, and breakfasts (Dh20) are great.

🍴 Eating

TOP CHOICE **Auberge Dardara Restaurant**
                                    MOROCCAN $$
(☏0539 70 70 07, 0661 150503; Rte Nationale 2; meals Dh90; ◷lunch & dinner) This is the best

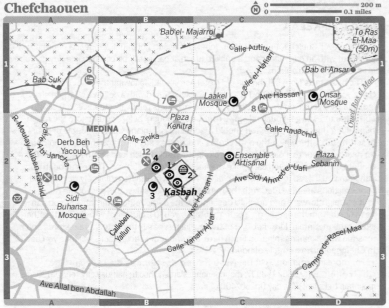

kitchen in the area, and worth the 10-minute drive from town (to Bab Taza, Dh5). The owner uses only the freshest ingredients from the garden, bakes his own bread and makes his own goat's cheese. Try the superb venison cooked with dried figs or the succulent rabbit with quince.

Plaza Cafe-Restaurants AREA $
(Plaza Uta el-Hamman; breakfast from Dh20, mains from Dh30) A popular eating option in Chefchaouen is to choose one of about a dozen on the main square. Menus are virtually identical – continental breakfasts, soups and salads, tajines and seafood – but the food is generally pretty good and the ambience lively.

La Lampe Magique MOROCCAN $
(Rue Targhi; mains from Dh45, set menu Dh75; ☉lunch & dinner) This magical place, which overlooks Plaza Uta el-Hammam, serves delicious Moroccan staples in a grand setting. Three bright-blue floors include a laid-back lounge, a more formal dining area and a roof-top terrace. The menu – featuring favourites like lamb tajine with prunes and some great cooked salads – is much better than average, and the ambience is relaxed.

Chefchaouen

◉ Top Sights
Kasbah...B2

◉ Sights
1 Art Gallery......................................B2
2 Ethnographic Museum..................B2
3 Grande Mosquée...........................B2
4 Plaza Uta el-Hammam..................B2

⊟ Sleeping
5 Dar Baraka......................................A2
6 Dar Meziana....................................A1
7 Dar Terrae.......................................B1
8 Hostal Guernika.............................C1
9 Hotel Mouritania...........................B2

⊗ Eating
10 Assaada..A2
11 La Lampe Magique......................B2
12 Plaza Café-Restaurants..............B2

Assaada MOROCCAN $
(Bab el-Ain; set menu Dh40; ☉lunch & dinner) This reliable cheapie tries hard to please. Located on both sides of the alley just prior to Bab el-Ain, it offers the usual menu *complet,* and recommends its no-cholesterol goat *kefta.* There's a funky graffiti rooftop terrace that

WORTH A TRIP

JEBEL EL-KELAÂ

Looming over Chefchaouen at 1616m, Jebel el-Kelaâ might initially appear a daunting peak, but with an early start and a packed lunch, it can easily be climbed in a day if you're in reasonably good shape.

The hike starts from behind the old Hôtel Asma road, following the 4WD track that takes you to the hamlet of Aïn Tissimlane. Rocks painted with a yellow and white stripe indicate that you're on the right path. The initial hour is relatively steep, as you climb above the trees to get your first views over Chefchaouen, before cutting into the mountains along the steady *piste*. You should reach Aïn Tissemlane within a couple of hours of setting out, after which the path climbs and zigzags steeply through great boulders for nearly an hour to a pass. Turn west along the track, which leads to the saddle of the mountain, from where you can make the final push to the summit. There's a rough path, although you'll need to scramble in places. The peak is attained relatively quickly, and your exertions are rewarded with the most sublime views over this part of the Rif.

It's straightforward and quick to descend by the same route. Alternatively, you can head north from the saddle on a path that takes you to a cluster of villages on the other side of the mountain. El-Kelaâ, one of these villages, has 16th-century grain stores and a mosque with a leaning minaret. From here, a number of simple tracks will take you back to Chefchaouen in a couple of hours.

For more information, visit the **Association des Guides du Tourisme de Chefchaouen** (☑0662 11 39 17; mouddenabdeslam@yahoo.fr; half-day city tour Dh120, mountain treks half-/full day Dh250/400).

exudes urban charm but the staircase isn't for the faint-hearted.

🛍 Shopping

Chefchaouen is a centre for rugs and blankets woven in bright primary colours. Many shops have looms in situ, and although most weaving is now woollen, silk was once the material of choice: the mulberry trees in Plaza Uta el-Hammam are a legacy of these times.

The largest concentration of shops is around the Uta el-Hammam and Place el-Majzen.

ℹ Information

Banque Populaire medina (Plaza Uta el-Hammam) ATM; new city (Ave Hassan II)
Hospital Mohammed V (☑0539 986228; Ave al- Massira al-Khadra)
Post office (Ave Hassan II)
Cyber-Net (Zanqat Sbâa; per hr Dh5; ☺10am-midnight)

ℹ Getting There & Away

Many bus services from Chefchaouen originate elsewhere and are often full on arrival, so buy your ticket a day in advance if possible. **CTM** (☑039 987669) serves Casablanca (Dh115, eight hours), Rabat (Dh85, six hours), Fez (Dh70,

four hours) Tangier (Dh40, three hours) and further destinations.

Grands taxis heading to Tetouan (Dh30, one hour) leave from just below Plaza Mohammed V – change for Tangier or Ceuta.

THE ATLANTIC COAST

Morocco's Atlantic littoral is surprisingly varied, with sweeping beaches and lagoons, and the pretty fishing ports and tourist drawcards of Essaouira and Assilah. It's also the country's economic motor, centred on the political and business capitals of Rabat and Casablanca.

Assilah

POP 30,000

A strategic port since the days of Carthage and Rome, the gorgeous whitewashed resort town of Assilah feels as much like somewhere on a Greek Island than North Africa. It's an intimate, sophisticated introduction to Morocco, with galleries lining the narrow streets. It swarms in summer with holidaying Moroccans and with foreigners trying to find property bargains. Consider visiting out of season to appreciate the charm of this lovely town at its best.

⊙ Sights

Medina   HISTORIC AREA

Assilah's medina is surrounded by the sturdy stone fortifications built by the Portuguese in the 15th century and it is these walls, flanked by palms, that have become the town's landmark. The medina and ramparts have been largely restored in recent years and the tranquil narrow streets lined by whitewashed houses are well worth a wander. Craftspeople and artists have opened workshops along the main streets. The southwestern bastion of the ramparts is the place for views over the ocean.

Paradise Beach   BEACH

Assilah's best beach is 3km south of town and is a gorgeous, pristine spot that really does live up to its name.

🛏 Sleeping

During high season (Easter week and July to September), the town is flooded with visitors so book in advance, but touts meeting the buses or trains offer basic accommodation in the medina for about Dh75.

Hôtel Patio de la Luna   HOTEL $$

(📞0539 416074; 12 Place Zellaka; s/d Dh350/450; 📶) The only accommodation option in Assilah with any local character is this intimate, Spanish-run place secluded behind an unassuming door on the main drag. The somewhat spartan, rustic rooms have wooden furniture, woven blankets and tiled bathrooms and are set around a lovely leafy patio.

Hôtel Azayla   HOTEL $$

(📞0539 416717; www.hotel-azayla.com; 20 Rue ibn Rochd; s/d Dh326/386, Jul & Aug Dh350/486) Big, bright, comfy and well equipped, the rooms here are a good deal. The bathrooms are modern, the decor is tasteful with great photographs of Morocco and Moroccans by the owner, and the giant windows bathe the rooms in light.

Hôtel Sahara   HOTEL $

(📞0539 417185; 9 Rue de Tarfaya; s/d/tr Dh98/150/240, hot showers Dh5) By far the best budget option, this small, immaculately kept hotel offers simple rooms set around an open courtyard, with a very Moroccan atmosphere. Patterned tiles and potted plants adorn the entrance, and the compact rooms, though fairly spartan, are comfortable and well maintained.

🍴 Eating

Assilah has a string of restaurants clustered around Bab Kasaba and along the medina walls on Ave Hassan II. There are a few other cheap options on Rue Ahmed M'dem near the banks on Place Mohammed V.

Restaurant la Place   MOROCCAN, SEAFOOD $$

(📞0539 41726; 7 Ave Moulay Hassan ben el-Mehdi; mains around Dh75; ☀lunch & dinner) Friendly, less formal and more varied than its neighbours, this restaurant offers traditional Moroccan dishes and seafood. The delicious fish tajine provides the best of both worlds.

Casa García   SEAFOOD $$

(📞0539 417465; 51 Rue Moulay Hassan ben el-Mehdi; mains from Dh80; ☀lunch & dinner) Spanish-style fish dishes and fishy tapas are the speciality at this small restaurant opposite the beach, best served with a glass of crisp Moroccan gris wine on the large and breezy terrace. The paella is delicious.

Restaurant Yali   MOROCCAN $

(Ave Hassan II; mains Dh50; ☀lunch & dinner) Although there's little to choose between them, this is one of the most popular of the string of restaurants along the medina walls. It serves up a good selection of fish, seafood, pizza and traditional Moroccan staples.

ℹ Getting There & Away

Assilah is 46km south of Tangier and has good bus connections to most towns. The tiny bus station is on the corner of Ave Moulay Ismail and the Tangier–Rabat Rd. CTM doesn't serve Assilah, but several private bus companies offer services to Casablanca (Dh80, 4½ hours), Marrakech (Dh120, nine hours), Tangier (Dh15, one hour) and Fez (Dh60, 4½ hours).

Three trains run daily to Rabat (Dh83, 3½ hours) and Casablanca (Dh109, 4½ hours), five to Fez (Dh87, four hours) and 10 to Tangier (Dh15, 45 minutes). One overnight train goes direct to Marrakesh (Dh186, nine hours); it originates (and fills up) in Tangier so buy tickets in advance.

Grands taxis to Tangier (Dh20) depart when full from Ave Moulay Ismail, across from the mosque.

Rabat

POP 2.5 MILLION

Rabat has a long and rich history, and plenty of monuments to show for it from the Phoenician, Roman, Almohad and Merenid times. Morocco's political and administrative capital since independence in 1956, Rabat hasn't

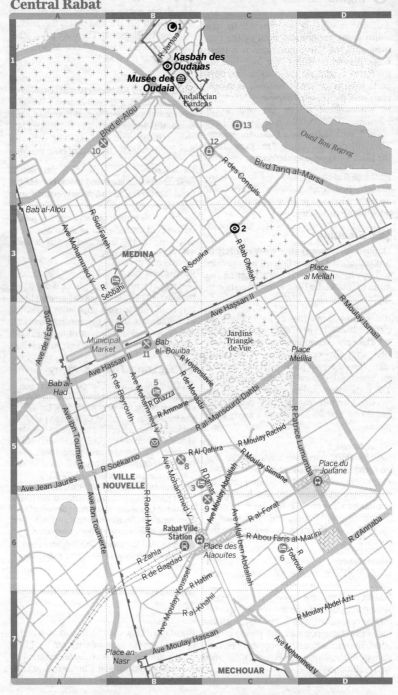

MOROCCO THE ATLANTIC COAST

R. Jamaa

Kasbah des Oudaias

Musée des Oudaia

Andalucían Gardens

Oued Bou Regreg

Blvd el-Alou

10

12

13

R des Consuls

Blvd Tariq al-Marsa

Bab al-Alou

R Sidi Fateh

Ave Mohammed V

MEDINA

R Souika

2

R Bab Chellah

Place al Mellah

R Sebbahi

Ave de l'Égypte

R Moulay Ismaïl

Ave Hassan II

4

Municipal Market

Bab el-Bouiba

11

R Yougoslavie

Jardins Triangle de Vue

Place Melilia

Bab al-Had

Ave Hassan II

R de Beyrouth

Ave Mohammed V

5

R Ghazza

R de Monastir

R al-Mansourd-Dahbi

R Ammane

Place Melilia

Ave Ibn Toumerte

R Soékarno

8

R Al-Qahira

R Moulay Rachid

R Moulay Slimane

R Patrice Lumumba

Place du Joulane

Ave Jean Jaurès

VILLE NOUVELLE

Ave Mohammed V

3

R Damas

9

Ave Moulay Abdallah

Ave Allal ben Abdallah

R al-Forat

R d'Annaba

R Raoul Marc

Rabat Ville Station

Place des Alaouites

R Abou Faris al-Marini

6

R Tobrouk

R Zahla

R de Bagdad

R Hatim

R al-Khahil

R Moulay Abdel Aziz

Ave Moulay Youssef

Ave Moulay Hassan

Ave Mohammed V

Place an-Nasr

MECHOUAR

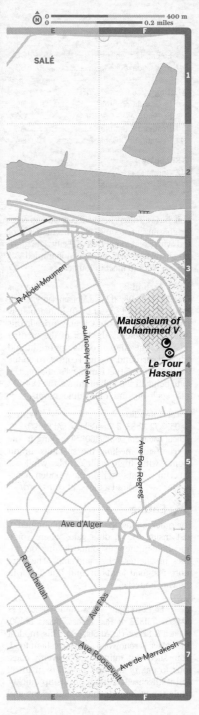

established itself as a tourist destination, but it's a gem of a city. The colonial architecture is stunning (particularly palm-lined Ave Mohammed V) and the atmosphere is cosmopolitan. You'll be blissfully ignored on the streets and souqs, so it's easy to discover the city's monuments and hidden corners at your own pace. The kasbah is also a place to explore with its narrow alleys, art galleries and magnificent ocean views.

Ave Hassan II divides the medina from the ville nouvelle and follows the line of the medina walls to the Oued Bou Regreg, the river that separates the twin cities of Rabat and Salé. Most embassies cluster around Place Abraham Lincoln and Ave Fès east of the centre.

◉ Sights

Medina　　　　　　　　　　　　　　　HISTORIC AREA
Barely 400 years old, Rabat's **medina** is tiny compared to Fez or Marrakesh, although it still piques the senses with its rich mixture of spices, carpets, crafts, cheap shoes and bootlegged DVDs.

The **kasbah** sits high up on the bluff overlooking the Oued Bou Regreg and contains within its walls the oldest **mosque** in Rabat, built in the 12th century and restored in the 18th. The kasbah's southern corner is home to the **Andalusian Gardens** (⊙sunrise-sunset), laid out by the French during the colonial period. The centrepiece is the grand 17th-century palace containing the **Musée des Oudaia** (admission Dh10; ⊙9am-noon & 3-5pm Oct-Apr, to 6pm May-Sep).

Le Tour Hassan　　　　　　　　　　　　LANDMARK
Towering above the Oued Bou Regreg is Rabat's most famous landmark, Le Tour Hassan (Hassan Tower). In 1195 the Almohad sultan Yacoub al-Mansour began constructing an enormous minaret, intending to make it the highest in the Muslim world, but he died before the project was completed. Abandoned at 44m, the beautifully designed and intricately carved tower still lords over the remains of the adjacent mosque.

Mausoleum of Mohammed V　　　　MAUSOLEUM
(⊙sunrise-sunset) The cool marble mausoleum built in traditional Moroccan style, lies opposite the tower. The present king's father (the late Hassan II) and grandfather are laid to rest here, surrounded by intensely patterned *zellij* (tile) mosaics from floor to ceiling.

Central Rabat

Sala Colonia   RUINS
Abandoned, crumbling and overgrown, the combined ancient Roman city of Sala Colonia and **Merenid necropolis of Chellah** (cnr Ave Yacoub al-Mansour & Blvd Moussa ibn Nassair; admission Dh10; ⊘9am-5.30pm) is one of Rabat's most evocative sights. Overgrown with fruit trees and wildflowers, it's an atmospheric place to roam around, although making out some of the structures takes a bit of imagination. An incredible colony of storks has taken over the ruins, lording over the site from their treetop nests.

🛏 Sleeping

TOP CHOICE **Riad Oudaya**   GUEST HOUSE **$$$**
(☏0537 70 23 92; www.riadrabat.com; 46 Rue Sidi Fateh; d/ste Dh1300/1650) Tucked away in the medina, this guest house is a real hidden gem. The rooms around a spectacular courtyard are tastefully decorated with a blend of Moroccan style and Western comfort. Subtle lighting, open fireplaces, balconies and the fountain in the tiled courtyard complete the romantic appeal. Meals here are sublime but need to be ordered in advance.

Le Piétri Urban Hotel   BOUTIQUE HOTEL **$$**
(☏0537 70 78 20; www.lepietri.com; 4 Rue Tobrouk; s/d Dh720/790; ✳🛜) This good-value hotel in a quiet street in a central part of town is modern and chic. The 36 spacious, bright rooms with wooden floors are comfortable, well equipped and decorated in warm colours in a contemporary style. The hotel has an excellent **restaurant**.

Hôtel Balima   HOTEL **$$**
(☏0537 70 77 55; www.hotel-balima.net; Ave Mohammed V; s/d incl breakfast Dh543/716; ✳) The grand dame of Rabat hotels is showing its age

a bit, but still offers newly decorated and comfortable en suite rooms, all immaculately kept and with great views over the city. The glorious shady terrace facing Ave Mohammed V is still the place to meet in Rabat.

Hôtel Dorhmi   HOTEL **$**
(☏0537 72 38 98; 313 Ave Mohammed V; s/d/tr Dh80/130/195, hot shower Dh10) Immaculately kept, very friendly and keenly priced, this family-run hotel is the best of the medina cheapies. The simple rooms are bright and tidy and surround a central courtyard on the 1st floor above the Banque Populaire. Despite being in the hub of things, the Dormhi (also spelt Doghmi) offers quiet rooms.

Hôtel Splendid   HOTEL **$**
(☏0537 72 32 83; 8 Rue Ghazza; s/d Dh190/230, without bathroom Dh125/160) Slap-bang in the heart of the medina, the spacious, bright rooms with high ceilings, big windows, cheerful colours and simple wooden furniture are set around a pleasant courtyard.

✖ Eating

For quick eating, go to Ave Mohammed V just inside the medina gate, where you'll find hole-in-the-wall joints dishing out tajines, brochettes, salads and chips. There are more fast-food joints around Rue Tanta in the ville nouvelle.

TOP CHOICE **Le Petit Beur – Dar Tajine** MOROCCAN **$$**
(☏0537 731322; 8 Rue Damas; mains Dh100; ⊘lunch & dinner, closed Sun; ✐) This modest little place is renowned for its excellent food, from succulent tajines and heavenly couscous to one of the best *pastillas* in town, and it's licensed. At night it fills up quickly, while the waiters double as musicians and

play oud (lute) music to accompany your meal.

Le Grand Comptoir
FRENCH $$$

(☑0537 201514; www.legrandcomptoir.ma; 279 Ave Mohammed V; mains Dh100-160; ☺lunch & dinner; ☏) Sleek, stylish and oozing the charms of an old-world Parisienne brasserie, this suave restaurant and lounge bar woos customers with its chic surroundings and classic French menu. Also good for breakfast or an apéritif.

Restaurant el-Bahia
MOROCCAN $

(Ave Hassan II; mains Dh60; ☺lunch & dinner) Built into the outside of the medina walls and a good spot for people-watching, this laid-back restaurant has the locals lapping up hearty Moroccan fare. Sit on the pavement terrace, in the shaded courtyard or upstairs in the traditional salon.

Restaurant Dinarjat
MOROCCAN $$$

(☑0537 72 42 39; 6 Rue Belgnaoui; meals Dh300-400; ☺lunch & dinner) Stylish and elegant, Dinarjat is a favourite with well-heeled locals and visitors alike. It's set in a superb 17th-century house, and the restaurant is an ode to the Arab-Andalusian art of living with its sumptuous architecture, refined traditional food and peaceful oud music. The tajines, couscous and salads are prepared with the freshest ingredients

🛍 Shopping

Rabat's merchants are a lot more laid-back than in Marrakesh, so you can stroll around the stalls in relative peace, but there's also less space to bargain. The souqs still have a good selection of handicrafts, particularly in and around the Rue des Consuls in the medina, and Blvd Tariq al-Marsa towards the kasbah. Weaving was one of the most important traditional crafts in Rabat, and on Tuesday and Thursday mornings women descend from the villages to auction their carpets to local salesmen at the carpet souq off Rue des Consuls. For fixed prices head for the **Ensemble Artisanal** (Blvd Tariq al-Marsa; ☺9am-noon & 2.30-6.30pm).

ℹ Information

Numerous banks (with ATMs) are concentrated along Ave Mohammed V.

Hôpital Ibn Sina/Avicenna (☑037 672871/037 674450 for emergencies; Place Ibn Sina, Agdal)

Internet (Rue Tanta; per hr Dh8; ☺9am-7.30pm) Next to La Mamma.

Main post office (cnr Rue Soékarno & Ave Mohammed V)

Office National Marocain du Tourisme (ONMT; ☑0537 674013; visitmorocco@onmt.org.ma; cnr Rue Oued el-Makhazine & Rue Zalaka, Agdal; ☺8.30am-noon & 3-6.30pm Mon-Fri) Smiles and vacant faces await at this bureaucratic office.

ℹ Getting There & Away

Rabat Ville train station is in the centre of town (not to be confused with Rabat Agdal station west of the city). Trains run every 30 minutes until 10.30pm to Casa-Port train station in Casablanca (Dh35, one hour), with hourly services to Fez (Dh80, 3½ hours, eight daily) via Meknès (Dh65, 2½ hours), Tangier (Dh95, 4½ hours, eight daily) and Marrakesh (Dh120, 4½ hours, nine daily).

Rabat has two bus stations: the main **gare routière**, where most buses depart and arrive, and the **CTM bus station**. Both are about 5km southwest of the centre on the road to Casablanca. CTM has eight daily services to Casablanca (Dh35, 1½ hours), seven to Fez (Dh70, 3½ hours), three to Marrakesh (Dh130, five hours), five to Tangier (Dh100, 4½ hours) and one to Tetouan (Dh100, five hours). Arriving by bus from the north, you may pass through central Rabat, so it's worth asking if you can be dropped off in town.

Grands taxis leave for Casablanca (Dh40) from just outside the intercity bus station. Other *grands taxis* leave for Fez (Dh60), Meknès (Dh50) and Salé (Dh5) from a space off Ave Hassan II behind the Hôtel Bouregreg.

ℹ Getting Around

Rabat's blue *petits taxis* are plentiful, cheap and quick. A ride around the centre of town will cost about Dh10.

Casablanca

POP 4 MILLION

Many travellers stay in Casablanca just long enough to change planes or catch a train, but Morocco's economic heart offers a unique insight into the country. This sprawling city is home to racing traffic, simmering social problems, wide boulevards, parks and imposing Hispano-Moorish and art deco buildings. Their facades stand in sharp contrast to Casablanca's modernist landmark: the enormous and incredibly ornate Hassan II mosque.

The medina – the oldest part of town – is relatively small and sits close to the port. Nearby is Place des Nations Unies, a large traffic junction that marks the heart of the city. The CTM bus station and Casa-Port train station are in the centre of the city. Casa-Voyageurs station is 2km east of the centre and the airport is 30km southeast of town.

◉ Sights

Hassan II Mosque
MOSQUE

Rising above the Atlantic northwest of the medina, the Hassan II Mosque is the world's third-largest mosque, which was built to commemorate the former king's 60th birthday. The mosque rises above the ocean on a rocky outcrop reclaimed from the sea, a

Central Casablanca

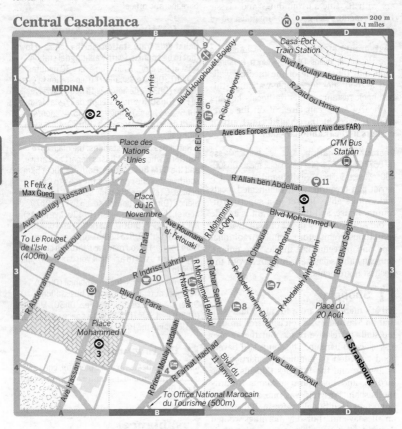

Central Casablanca

◉ Sights
1 Marché Central (Central Market).........D2
2 Medina...A1
3 Place Mohammed V............................A4

🛏 Sleeping
4 Hôtel Astrid...B4
5 Hôtel Guynemer..................................B3
6 Hôtel les Saisons................................C1
7 Hôtel Maamoura..................................C3

8 Hôtel Transatlantique...........................C3

🍽 Eating
Marché Central (Central Market)..(see 1)
9 Taverne du Dauphin..............................C1

🍷 Drinking
10 Café Alba..B3
11 La Bodéga...D2

vast building that holds 25,000 worshippers and can accommodate a further 80,000 in the courtyards and squares around it. If you want to see the interior of the mosque you must take a **guided tour** (adult/child Dh120/30; ⊙9am, 10am, 11am & 2pm Sat-Thu; 9am, 10am & 2pm Fri).

Central Casablanca
AREA

This area is full of great art deco and Hispano-Moorish buildings. The best way to take them all in is by strolling in the area around the **Central Market** (Marché Central) and **Place Mohammed V**. The grand square is surrounded by public buildings that were later copied throughout Morocco, including the law courts, the splendid Wilaya, the Bank al-Maghrib and the main post office. After that, explore the slightly dilapidated 19th-century **medina** near the port.

🛏 Sleeping

TOP
CHOICE Hôtel Guynemer
HOTEL $

(☑0522 275764; www.guynemerhotel.com; 2 Rue Mohammed Belloul; s/d/tr Dh372/538/626; ❋🛜) Readers recommend the friendly and super-efficient family-run Guynemer, in a gorgeous Mauresque building. The 29 well-appointed and regularly updated rooms are tastefully decked out in cheerful colours. Flat-screen TVs, wi-fi access and firm, comfortable beds make them a steal at these rates and the service is way above average.

Hôtel Astrid
HOTEL $

(☑0522 277803; hotelastrid@hotmail.com; 12 Rue 6 Novembre; s/d/tr Dh324/386/486; 🛜) Tucked away on a quiet street south of the centre, the Astrid offers the most elusive element of Casa's budget hotels – a good night's sleep. There's little traffic noise here and the spacious, well-kept rooms are all en suite, with TV, telephone and frilly decor. There's a friendly cafe downstairs and wi-fi in the lobby.

Hôtel Transatlantique
HOTEL $$

(☑0522 294551; www.transatcasa.com; 79 Rue Chaouia; s/d/tr Dh770/925/1025; ❋🛜) Set in one of Casa's architectural gems, the decor at this 1922 hotel is all a bit over the top. It has a snack bar, a shady outdoor seating area and comfortable, but fairly plain, bedrooms. Avoid the 1st floor, as it gets the brunt of noise from the popular **piano bar** and **nightclub**.

Hôtel les Saisons
HOTEL $$$

(☑0522 490901; www.hotellessaisonsmaroc.ma; 19 Rue el Oraïbi Jilali; s/d Dh1100/1400; ❋🛜) This small hotel offers extremely comfortable, well-appointed and quiet rooms with all the usual facilities: a safe, minibar, satellite TV and direct dial phone. It's a more personal place than the larger international hotels and offers good value for money and an excellent location.

Hôtel Maamoura
HOTEL $

(☑0522 45 29 67; www.hotelmaamoura.com; 59 Rue Ibn Batouta; s/d/ste Dh430/570/800; ❋🛜❄) This modern hotel offers excellent value for money. The spotless and spacious rooms may lack period detail, but they are very quiet for this central location, tastefully decorated in muted colours and have neat bathrooms. The staff is friendly and helpful.

🍴 Eating

Rue Chaouia, opposite the central market, is the best place for a quick eat, with its line of rotisseries, stalls and restaurants serving roast chicken, brochettes and sandwiches.

TOP
CHOICE Restaurant du Port de Pêche
SEAFOOD $$

(☑0522 318561; Le Port de Pêche; mains Dh140; ⊙lunch & dinner) This authentic and rustic seafood restaurant in the middle of the fishing harbour is packed to the gills at lunch and dinner as happy diners tuck into fish freshly whipped from the sea and cooked to perfection. The fish and tangy paella are some of the best in town.

Rick's Cafe
MEDITERRANEAN $$

(☑0522 274207; www.rickscafe.ma; 248 Blvd Sour Jdid; mains Dh160; ⊙lunch & dinner; 🛜) Continue northeast from Casa Port train station along Blvd Moulay Abderrahmane to find this beautiful bar, lounge and restaurant run by a former American diplomat, with furniture and fittings inspired by Bogart and Bergman. The menu features excellent French and Moroccan specialities. The pianist will play *As Time Goes By,* and there's a Sunday jam session. You can watch the film again and again on the 1st floor.

Sqala Restaurant
MOROCCAN $$

(☑0522 260960; Blvd des Almohades; mains Dh90-160; ⊙lunch & dinner Tue-Sun, daily in summer) Nestled in the walls of the *sqala,* an 18th-century fortified bastion, this lovely restaurant is a tranquil escape from the city. The cafe has a rustic interior and a delightful garden surrounded by flower-draped trellises. It's a lovely spot for a Moroccan breakfast or a selection of salads for lunch. Tajines are a speciality and the menu features plenty of fish and brochettes.

Taverne du Dauphin SEAFOOD **$$**
(☎0522 22 12 00; 115 Blvd Houphouet Boigny; mains Dh140; ☺lunch & dinner, closed Sun) A Casablanca institution, this traditional Provençal restaurant and bar has been serving up local *fruits de mer* (seafood) since it opened in 1958. This is an old-fashioned family-run place, and one taste of the succulent grilled fish, fried calamari and *crevettes royales* (king prawns) will leave you smitten.

Le Rouget de l'Isle FRENCH **$$$**
(☎0522 29 47 40; 16 Rue Rouget de l'Isle, off Blvd Moulay Hassan I; mains Dh160; ☺lunch Mon-Fri, dinner Mon-Sat) One of Casa's top eateries, Le Rouget is set in a glorious 1930s villa and has a wonderful garden redolent with night-blooming jasmine. Sleek, stylish and charming, it's renowned for its simple but delicious and light French food. Book in advance.

🍸 Drinking & Entertainment

Café Alba CAFE
(59-61 Rue Indriss Lahrizi) High ceilings, swish, modern furniture, subtle lighting and a hint of elegant colonial times mark this cafe out from the more traditional smoky joints around town. It's hassle-free downtime for women and a great place for watching Casa's up-and-coming.

La Bodéga TAPAS BAR
(129 Rue Allah ben Abdellah) Hip, happening and loved by a mixed-aged group of Casablanca's finest, La Bodega is essentially a tapas bar where the music (everything from Salsa to Arabic pop) is loud and the Rioja (Spanish wine) flows freely. It's a fun place with a lively atmosphere and a packed dance floor after 10pm.

Le Trica BAR
(5 Rue el- Moutanabi, Quartier Gauthier; ☺closed Sat lunch & Sun) This bar-lounge, set over two levels with brick walls and 1960s furniture, is the place to feel the beat of the new Morocco. The atmosphere is hot and trendy at night, stirred by the techno beat and a flow of beer and mojitos.

The beachfront suburb of Aïn Diab is the place to go for late-night drinking and dancing in Casablanca. You can expect to pay at least Dh150 to get in and as much again for drinks. Heavy-set bouncers guard the doors and practise tough crowd control – if you don't look the part, you won't get in. Try **Balcon 33** (33 Blvd de la Corniche), **Le Carré Rouge** (Hotel Villa Blanca, Blvd de la Corniche; ☺11.30pm-4am) and **VIP club** (Rue des Dunes).

❶ Information

There are banks – most with ATMS and foreign exchange offices – on almost every street corner in the centre of Casablanca.
Central Market post office (cnr Blvd Mohammed V & Rue Chaouia)
Crédit du Maroc (☎022 477255; 48 Blvd Mohammed V) Separate *bureau de change*.
Gig@net (140 Blvd Mohammed Zerktouni; per hr Dh10; ☺24hr)
LGnet (81 Blvd Mohammed V; per hr Dh8; ☺9am-midnight)
Main post office (cnr Blvd de Paris & Ave Hassan II)

BUS CONNECTIONS FROM CASABLANCA

DESTINATION	COST (DH)	DURATION (HRS)	NO OF DAILY SERVICES
Chefchaouen	125	7	1
Essaouira	145	6	2 with CTM; hourly with private companies
Fez	100	4	8
Marrakesh	90	3½	8
Meknès	90	3½	6
Tangier	145	5½	5 with CTM; regularly with private companies
Tetouan	145	6	5

Office National Marocain du Tourisme
(ONMT; ☏022 271177; 55 Rue Omar Slaoui;
☉8.30am-4.30pm Mon-Fri)
Polyclinique Atlas (☏0522 27 40 39; 27 Rue
Mohammed ben Ali, Quartier Gauthier; ☉24hr)
Medical centre off Rue Jean Jaures.
Wafa Cash (15 Rue Indriss Lahrizi; ☉8am-8pm
Mon-Sat) Open longer hours; has an ATM and
cashes travellers cheques.

❶ Getting There & Away

All long-distance trains, as well as trains to
Mohammed V International Airport, depart from
Casa-Voyageurs train station (☏022 243818).
Destinations include Marrakesh (Dh90, three
hours, nine daily), Fez (Dh110, 4½ hours, 18
daily) via Meknès (Dh90, 3½ hours) and Tangier
(Dh125, five hours, eight daily).

The **Casa-Port train station** is a few hundred
metres northeast of Place des Nations Unies.
Trains from here run to Rabat (Dh35, one hour).

The modern **CTM bus station** (☏022
541010; 23 Rue Léon L'Africain) has daily CTM
departures.

The modern **Gare Routière Ouled Ziane**
(☏022 444470), 4km southeast of the centre, is
the bus station for non-CTM services.

❶ Getting Around

The easiest way to get from Mohammed V International Airport to Casablanca is by train (2nd
class Dh30, 35 minutes); they leave every hour
from 6am to midnight from below the ground
floor of the airport terminal building. A *grand taxi*
between the airport and the city centre costs
Dh300.

Expect to pay Dh10 in or near the city centre
for a trip in one of the red *petits taxis*.

Essaouira

POP 70,000

Perennially popular Essaouira has long
been a favourite on the travellers' trail. It's
laid-back and artsy with sea breezes and
picture-postcard ramparts, all of which conspire to make a short visit from Marrakesh
turn into a stay of several nights. Although
it can appear swamped with visitors in the
height of summer, when the day trippers get
back on the buses there's more than enough
space to sigh deeply and just soak up the
atmosphere.

⊙ Sights & Activities

Medina   HISTORIC AREA
Essaouira's Unesco's World Heritage–listed
18th-century medina is a prime example

of European military architecture in North
Africa. The mellow atmosphere, narrow,
winding streets lined with colourful shops,
whitewashed houses and heavy old wooden
doors make it a wonderful place to stroll.
The easiest place to access the ramparts is
Skala de la Ville, the impressive sea bastion built along the cliffs. Down by the harbour, the **Skala du Port** (adult/child Dh10/3;
☉8.30am-noon & 2.30-6pm) offers picturesque
views over the fishing port and the **Île de
Mogador**.

A number of outlets rent water-sports
equipment and offer instruction along Essaouira's wide, sandy beach. **Océan Vagabond** (☏0524 783934; www.oceanvagabond.com;
☉9am-6pm) rents surfboards (three days
Dh750) and windsurfers (two hours Dh440)
and offers lessons in both as well as kitesurfing. Be aware of strong Atlantic currents.

The **Gnaoua & World Music Festival**
(www.festival-gnaoua.net; 3rd weekend Jun) is a
four-day musical extravaganza that draws
huge crowds.

🛏 Sleeping

Hôtel Beau Rivage   HOTEL $
(☏0524 475925; www.essaouiranet.com/beau
rivage; 14 Place Moulay Hassan; s/d/tr incl breakfast
Dh270/390/510; ☎) Readers recommend this
friendly hotel in a perfect spot, overlooking the main square. The Beau Rivage has
bright, cheerful rooms with modern fittings
and spotless bathrooms. Breakfast is served
on the charming and quiet roof terrace with
views over the port and town.

Lalla Mira   GUEST HOUSE $$
(☏0524 475046; 14 Rue d'Algerie; www.lalla
mira.net; s/d/tr incl breakfast & hammam
Dh436/692/860; ☎) This gorgeous little place,
the town's first eco-hotel, has simple rooms
with ochre *tadelakt* walls, wrought-iron furniture, natural fabrics and solar-powered
underfloor heating. The hotel also has a
hammam and a restaurant serving organic
dishes such as rabbit with peaches and nuts,
or goat with argan oil, and a good selection
of vegetarian food.

Riad Nakhla   GUEST HOUSE $
(☏0524 474940; www.essaouiranet.com/
riad-nakhla; 2 Rue Agadir; s/d/ste incl breakfast
Dh230/360/500; ☎) Riad Nakhla looks like
any other budget place from the outside,
but inside the weary traveller is met with a
beautiful courtyard, with stone columns and
a fountain, more what you'd expect from a

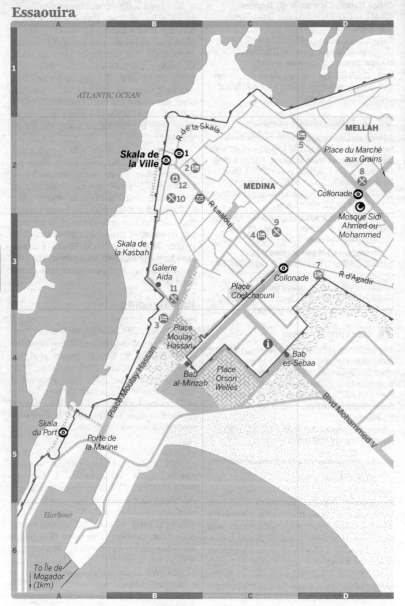

hotel in a higher price bracket. Bedrooms are simple but comfortable and immaculately kept, with bags of local flavour. Enjoy breakfast on the roof terrace with views over the ocean and the town. It's an incredible bargain at this price.

Dar Afram B&B **$$**

(☎0524 785657; www.dar-afram.com; 10 Rue Sidi Magdoul; s Dh200, d Dh300-400, Jun-Sep s Dh250, d Dh400-600) This extremely friendly guest house has simple, spotless rooms, shared bathrooms and a funky vibe. The Aussie-

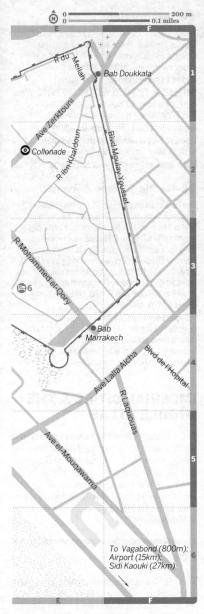

Hidden down a dead-end street, this charming hotel has bright, traditionally styled rooms surrounding a central courtyard painted in cheerful colours. The rooms all have plain white walls, lovely local fabrics and spotless bathrooms. Breakfast is served on the sheltered terrace from where you'll get good views over the medina.

La Casa del Mar   GUEST HOUSE **$$**
(✆0524 475091; www.lacasa-delmar.com; 35 Rue D'Oujda; d incl breakfast Dh825) Delightful guest house that seamlessly blends contemporary design with traditional style and creates a stunning yet simple atmosphere where you can sit back and relax. Retire to your room, join the other guests for a communal Moroccan meal or Spanish paella (by reservation), arrange a home visit from a masseur or henna artist, or just watch the sunset from the seafront terrace.

✗ Eating

Place Moulay Hassan offers plenty of sandwich stands and cafes for lazy breakfasts and lunches.

TOP **Outdoor fish grills**   SEAFOOD **$**
CHOICE
(Place Moulay Hassan; meals Dh40-100) These unpretentious stands at the port end of Place Moulay offer one of the definitive Essaouira experiences. Choose what you want

Moroccan owners are musicians and impromptu sessions often follow evening meals.

Hôtel Les Matins Bleus   GUEST HOUSE **$$**
(✆0524 785363; www.les-matins-bleus.com; 22 Rue de Drâa; s/d/tr incl breakfast Dh310/470/940)

to eat from the colourful displays of freshly caught fish and shellfish at each grill, see it weighed up to arrive at a price, and wait for it to be cooked on the spot and served with a pile of bread and salad.

After 5   MEDITERRANEAN **$$$**
(☑0524 78 47 26; 5 Rue Youssef el-Fassi; mains around Dh200; ⊙7-11pm Wed-Mon, noon-3pm Sat & Sun) Deep-purple seating, warm stone arches and giant lampshades dominate this trendy restaurant which serves well-cooked and original Mediterranean and Moroccan dishes. One of the favourite places to head for dinner.

Taros   MEDITERRANEAN **$$**
(☑0524 47 64 07; 2 Rue du Skala; mains Dh120; ⊙lunch & dinner) One of the most atmospheric terraces in town, you can dine by candlelight inside or out. With great views over the square and port, and an interesting menu specialising in fish, it's a great place to be. There's often live music, too. It's also a good place for afternoon tea, or a drink at the bar.

Restaurant Ferdaous   MOROCCAN **$$**
(☑0524 47 36 55; 27 Rue Abdesslam Lebadi; mains Dh60-80, set menu Dh105; ⊙lunch & dinner, closed Mon) A delightful Moroccan restaurant, and one of the few places in town that serves real, home-cooked, traditional Moroccan food. The seasonal menu offers an innovative take on traditional recipes, the service is very friendly and the low tables and padded seating make it feel like the real McCoy.

Restaurante Les Alizés   MOROCCAN **$$**
(☑0524 47 68 19; 26bis Rue de la Skala; mains Dh120; ⊙lunch & dinner) This popular place, run by a charming Moroccan couple in a 19th-century house, has delicious Moroccan dishes, particularly the couscous with fish and the tajine of *boulettes de sardines* (sardine balls). You'll get a very friendly welcome, and it's a good idea to book ahead. It's above Hotel Smara.

🛍 Shopping

Essaouira is well known for its woodwork and you can visit the string of **woodcarving workshops** near the Skala de la Ville. The exquisite marquetry work on sale is carved from local fragrant thuya wood, unfortunately now endangered. Essaouira also has a reputation as an artists' hub and plenty of galleries around town sell works by local painters.

ⓘ Information

There are several banks with ATMs around Place Moulay Hassan. There are plentiful internet cafes, most opening from 9am to 11pm and charging Dh8 to Dh10 per hour.

Cyber Les Remparts (12 Rue du Rif)
Délégation du Tourisme (☑024 783532; www.essaouira.com; 10 Rue du Caire; ⊙9am-noon & 3-6.30pm Mon-Fri) Very helpful staff.
Espace Internet (8bis, Rue du Caire)
Hôpital Sidi Mohammed ben Abdallah (☑024 475716; Blvd de l'Hôpital) Emergencies.
Main post office (Ave el-Mouqawama)

ⓘ Getting There & Away

The **bus station** is about 400m northeast of the medina, an easy walk during the day but better in a *petit taxi* (Dh10) if you're arriving/ leaving late at night. **CTM** has several buses daily for Casablanca (Dh135, six hours), and to Marrakesh (Dh75, 2½ hours) and Agadir (Dh70, three hours). Other companies run cheaper and more frequent buses to the same destinations as well as Taroudannt (Dh70, six hours) and Rabat (Dh90, six hours).

Supratours (☑024 475317) operates from outside the medina and runs coaches to Marrakesh train station (Dh70, 2½ hours, four daily) to connect with trains to Casablanca. Book in advance, particularly in summer.

IMPERIAL CITIES & THE MIDDLE ATLAS

The rolling plains that sweep across the north along the base of the Middle Atlas are Morocco's most fertile agricultural region, dotted with olive groves and wheat fields. Several of Morocco's most interesting cities are here, including Fez with its teeming medina, imperial Meknès and the Roman ruins of Volubilis.

Fez

POP 1 MILLION

Marrakesh might be modern Morocco's tourist capital, but 1400-year old Fez is Morocco's spiritual beating heart. Its medina (Fès el-Bali) is the largest living medieval Islamic city in the world, and the world's largest car-free urban environment. A first visit can be overwhelming, an assault on the eyes, ears and nose through covered bazaars, winding alleys, mosques and workshops, amid people and pack animals, all of which seem to take you out of the 21st century and back to an imagined era of *1001 Arabian Nights*.

Fez can be neatly divided into three distinct parts: Fès el-Bali (the core of the medina; the main entrance is Bab Bou Jeloud) in the east; Fès el-Jdid (containing the *mellah* and Royal Palace) in the centre; and the ville nouvelle, the modern administrative area constructed by the French, to the southwest.

◉ Sights

THE MEDINA (FÈS EL-BALI)

Within the old walls of Fès el-Bali lies an incredible maze of twisting alleys, blind turns

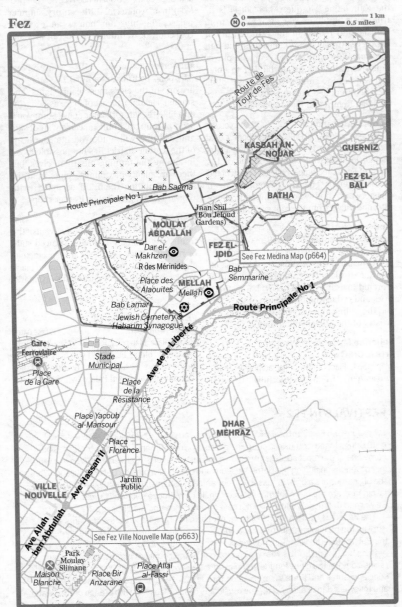

Fez

See Fez Medina Map (p664)

See Fez Ville Nouvelle Map (p663)

MOROCCO FEZ

and hidden souqs. Navigation can be confusing and getting lost at some stage a certainty, but this is part of the medina's charm: you never know what discovery lies around the next corner.

Kairaouine Mosque
MOSQUE

If Fez is the spiritual capital of Morocco, the Kairaouine Mosque (Map p664) is its true heart. Built in 859 by refugees from Tunisia, and rebuilt in the 12th century, it is one of Africa's largest mosques and can accommodate up to 20,000 people at prayer time. Non-Muslims are forbidden to enter and will have to suffice with glimpses of its seemingly endless columns from the gates on Talaa Kebira and Place as-Seffarine.

Medersa Bou Inania
ISLAMIC COLLEGE

(Map p664; admission Dh10; ⏰9am-6pm, closed during prayers) The 14th-century Medersa Bou Inania, 150m east of Bab Bou Jeloud, is the finest of Fez's theological colleges constructed by the Merenids. The *zellij* (tiling), *muqarna* (plasterwork) and woodcarving are elaborate, and views from the roof are impressive.

Medersa el-Attarine
ISLAMIC COLLEGE

(Map p664; admission Dh10; ⏰9am-6pm, closed during prayers) Founded by Abu Said in 1325 in the heart of the medina, the Medersa el-Attarine displays the traditional patterns of Merenid artisanship. The *zellij* base, stucco work and cedar wood at the top of the walls and the ceiling are every bit as elegant as the artistry of the Medersa Bou Inania.

Nejjarine Museum of Wooden Arts & Crafts
MUSEUM

(Map p664; Place an-Nejjarine; admission Dh20; ⏰10am-7pm) In a wonderfully restored *funduq* (a caravanserai for travelling merchants), with a host of fascinating exhibits. The rooftop cafe has great views over the medina. Photography forbidden.

Batha Museum
MUSEUM

(Map p664; ☎035 634116; Rue de la Musée, Batha; admission Dh10; ⏰8.30am-noon & 2.30-6pm Wed-Mon) In a wonderful 19th-century summer palace, the museum houses an excellent collection of traditional Moroccan arts and crafts.

Tanneries
HANDICRAFTS

(Map p664; Derb Chouwara, Blida) The tanneries are one of the city's most iconic sights (and smells). Head northeast of Place as-Seffarine and take the left fork after about 50m; you'll soon pick up the unmistakeable waft of skin and dye that will guide you into the heart of the leather district. It's not possible to get in among the tanning pits themselves, but there are plenty of vantage points from the streets that line them, all occupied (with typical Fassi ingenuity) by leather shops.

Merenid tombs
RUINS

(Map p664) Outside the medina walls, the tombs are dramatic in their advanced state of ruin. The views over Fez are spectacular and well worth the climb. Look for the black smoke in the southern part of the city, marking the potteries.

FEZ EL-JDID (NEW FEZ)

Dar el-Makhzen
PALACE GATES

(Royal Palace; Map p661; Place des Alaouites) Only in a city as old as Fez could you find a district dubbed 'New' because it's only 700 years old. It's home to the Royal Palace, whose entrance

---

FESTIVALS IN FEZ

Every June the **Fez Festival of World Sacred Music** (☎0535 740691; www.fesfestival. com) brings together music groups and artists from all corners of the globe, and has become one of the most successful world-music festivals going. Concerts are held in a variety of venues, including the Batha Museum and the square outside Bab Bou Jeloud. While the big names are a draw (Youssou N'Dour and Ravi Shankar have both played), equally fascinating are the more-intimate concerts held by Morocco's various *tariqas* (Sufi orders). Be warned that tickets can go like hot cakes and accommodation books out early.

The **Festival of Sufi Culture** (www.par-chemins.org) hosts a series of events every April including films and lectures and some spectacular concerts held in the garden of the Batha Museum with Sufi musicians from across the world.

Fez's biggest **religious festival** is also one of the country's largest. The *moussem* (saint's day) of the city's founder, Moulay Idriss, draws huge crowds. Local artisans create special tributes and there's a procession through the medina. Traditional music is played and followers dance and shower the musicians (and onlookers) with orange or rose water.

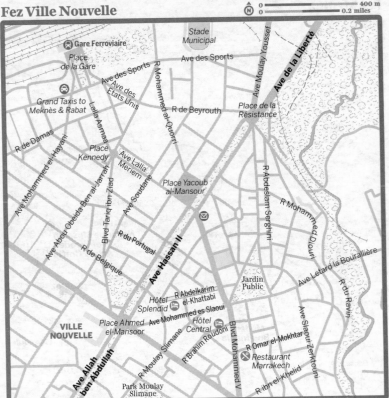

Map showing Fez Ville Nouvelle with streets including Ave des Sports, Ave Moulay Youssef, Ave de la Liberté, Place de la Résistance, R Mohammed al-Quorri, R de Beyrouth, Place de la Gare, Gare Ferroviaire, Stade Municipal, Grand Taxis to Meknès & Rabat, R de Damas, Ave Mohammed el-Hayani, Place Kennedy, Ave Lalla Meriem, Ave Soudane, Place Yacoub al-Mansour, R Abdeslam Serghini, R Mohammed Djouri, Blvd Tariq ibn Ziad, R du Portugal, Ave Hassan II, R de Belgique, Jardin Public, Ave Letard la Bouralière, R du Ravin, Hôtel Splendid, R Abdelkarim el-Khattabi, Ave Mohammed es Slaoui, Ave Slaoui Zerktouni, VILLE NOUVELLE, Place Ahmed el-Mansoor, Hôtel Central, Blvd Mohammed V, R Omar el-Mokhtar, Restaurant Marrakech, Ave Allah ben Abdullah, R Moulay Slimane, R Brahim Roudani, R ibn el-Khelid, Park Moulay Slimane.

MOROCCO FEZ

at Dar el-Makhzen is a stunning example of modern restoration, but the 80 hectares of palace grounds are not open to the public.

Mellah   HISTORIC AREA

In the 14th century, Fès el-Jdid was a refuge for Jews, thus creating a *mellah*. The *mellah's* southwest corner is home to the fascinating **Jewish Cemetery & Habarim Synagogue** (Map p661; donations welcome; ⊙7am-7pm).

🛏 Sleeping

MEDINA

Pension Kawtar   GUEST HOUSE $

(Map p664; ☑0535 740172; pen sion_kaw@yahoo.fr; Derb Taryana, Talaa Seghira; s/d Dh150/250, d with bathroom Dh300; 🛜) Well signed in an alley off Talaa Seghira, the Kawtar is a friendly Moroccan family-run concern. There are 10 rooms tucked into the place – those on the ground floor are a bit gloomy, but they get

better the closer you get to the roof terrace. Great value for the price.

Riad Verus   GUEST HOUSE $

(Map p664; ☑0535 574941 www.riadverus.com; 1 Derb Arset Bennis, Batha; dm Dh280, d Dh890, q Dh1100; 🌡🛜) A relatively new player on the budget scene, rooms here seem to be configured to give the maximum flexibility for the best budget. Everything is open and airy inside, and the young owners play well to the backpacker crowd with regular live music and iPod docks in the rooms.

Dar Bensouda   GUEST HOUSE $$

(Map p664; ☑0535 638939; www.riaddarbensouda.com; 14 Zqaq Labghal, Qettanine; r Dh850-1700; 🛜) A converted palace, Dar Bensouda is the most impressive medina restoration project we've seen in a while. Enter into a large column-flanked courtyard and admire the attention to detail here and in the immaculate rooms. Grand without being overwhelming.

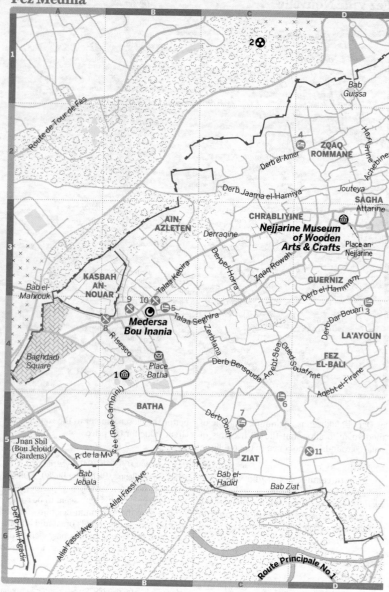

Dar Roumana   GUEST HOUSE $$
(Map p664; ☎0535 741637; www.darroumana.com; 30 Derb el-Amer, Zkak Roumane; r Dh950-1620; ☏) One of those bigger-on-the-inside town-houses, Dar Roumana will always win fans by virtue of its beautiful restoration job and gorgeous roof terrace, commanding one of the finest views across the Fez medina (perfect for taking breakfast or sampling the well-thought-out dinner menus). That's if you even leave the rooms, which are perfect romantic hideaways.

MOROCCO IMPERIAL CITIES & THE MIDDLE ATLAS

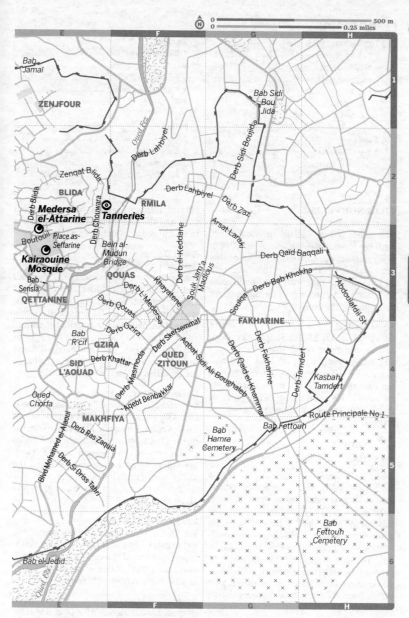

Riad Les Oudayas   GUEST HOUSE **$$$**
(Map p664; ☎0535 636303; www.lesoudayas.com;
4 Derb el Hamiya, Ziat; r from Dh1400; ❀🐾❄)
The Moroccan owner of this riad is a Paris-
based designer, and it certainly shows in
its careful blend of traditional styles and
modern design aesthetic in everything from
the downstairs salons to the chic but com-
fortable bedrooms. Steps lead down from
street level into the courtyard garden, with
a plunge pool and the riad's own hammam
leading off it.

VILLE NOUVELLE

Hôtel Splendid HOTEL $
(Map p663; ✆0535 622148; splendid@iam.net.
ma; 9 Rue Abdelkarim el-Khattabi; s/d Dh350/450;
❋❄) Although in the budget category, this
hotel makes a good claim for three stars. It's
all modern and tidy, with good bathrooms
and comfy beds, plus a pool for the hot days
and a bar for the evenings.

Hôtel Central HOTEL $
(Map p663; ✆0535 622333; 50 Rue Brahim Roudani; s/d with shower Dh140/180) A bright and
airy budget option just off busy Blvd Mohammed V. All rooms have external toilets,
but even those without a shower have their
own sinks. It's good value and popular so
there's sometimes not enough rooms to go
around.

✕ Eating

MEDINA

TOP CHOICE Café Clock CAFE $
(Map p664; ✆035 637855; www.cafeclock.com;
Derb el-Mergana, Talaa Kebira; mains Dh55-80;
⊙9am-10pm; ⊛) In a restored townhouse,
this funky place has a refreshing menu
with offerings such as falafel, grilled sandwiches, some interesting vegetarian options,
a monstrously large camel burger, and delicious cakes and tarts. Cookery, calligraphy
and conversation classes are available, plus
sunset concerts every Sunday (cover charge
around Dh20).

Bou Jeloud restaurants AREA $
(Map p664; Rue Serrajine; mains Dh30-70; ⊙8am-
11pm) Walking in from Bab Bou Jeloud to
the top of Talaa Seghira, you run the gauntlet of a host of restaurants touting for business. They're all pretty much of a muchness,
offering plenty of tajines, couscous, grilled
meat and the like. They're also great places
to sit and people watch over a mint tea.

Fès et Gestes CAFE $$
(Map p664; ✆0535 638532; 39 Arsat el Hamoumi,
Ziat; meals around Dh90; ⊙noon-9.30pm, closed
Wed) In a bustling medina, this converted
French colonial house is a positive oasis:
step through the gates into its pretty, richly
planted garden, with a trickling fountain,
and the cares of the day melt away. Ideal
for light lunches, full tajine-style dinners
or just a refreshing tea or juice to recharge
the batteries in the cool green shade.

Chameau Bleu MOROCCAN $$
(Map p664; ✆0535 638991; 1 Derb Tariana; mains
Dh55-130; ⊙lunch, dinner) Well signed just off
Talaa Kebira, Chameau Bleu is a converted
medina house on several levels, with tables
all the way up to the roof terrace. There
are tajines aplenty, although we found the
grilled meat and fish dishes to be particular
winners; we've also had several good reports
about the pasta.

VILLE NOUVELLE

For quick, filling meals, there are a few
cheap eats on or just off Blvd Mohammed V,
especially around the central market. You'll
also find a good choice of sandwich places
around Place Yacoub al-Mansour.

Restaurant Marrakech MOROCCAN $$
(Map p663; ✆035 930876; 11 Rue Omar el-Mokhtar;
mains from Dh55; ❋) Behind heavy wooden
doors this charming restaurant goes from
strength to strength. Red *tadelakt* walls,
dark furniture and a cushion-strewn salon
at the back add ambience, while the menu's
variety refreshes the palette, with dishes like

chicken tajine with apple and olive, or lamb with aubergine and peppers.

Maison Blanche
FRENCH $$$

(Map p661; ☑0535 944073; 12 Rue Ahmed Chaouki; mains Dh140-220) Making a strong bid for Fez's classiest restaurant, Maison Blanche is all about cool, stylish minimalism, with modern furniture and rough-hewn stone tiles. Food has a strong French classical influence and service is excellent (as is the wine list). Retire to the **upstairs bar** at the end of the evening or swing by between 12.30pm and 2.30pm for the Dh200 lunch menu.

Shopping

Fez is and always has been the artisanal capital of Morocco. The choice of crafts is wide, quality is high and prices are competitive. As usual, it's best to seek out the little shops off the main tourist routes.

Les Potteries de Fès
HANDICRAFTS

(www.artnaji.net; Ain Nokbi; ⊙8am-6pm) On the southwest outskirts of the medina – you'll need to take a *petit taxi* – this is the home of the famous Fassi pottery. You can see the entire production process, from pot throwing to the painstaking hand painting and laying out of *zellij*. It's a joy to behold.

ℹ Information

Internet Access
Cyber Batha (Derb Douh; per hr Dh10; ⊙9am-10pm) Has English as well as French keyboards.
Cyber Club (Blvd Mohammed V; per hr Dh6; ⊙9am-10pm)

Medical Services
Hôpital Ghassani (☑0535 622777) One of the city's biggest hospitals; located east of the ville nouvelle in the Dhar Mehraz district.
Night Pharmacy (☑0535 623493; Blvd Moulay Youssef; ⊙9pm-6am) Located in the north of the ville nouvelle; staffed by a doctor and a pharmacist.

Money
There are plenty of banks (with ATMs) in the ville nouvelle along Blvd Mohammed V. In the medina:
Banque Populaire (Talaa Seghira) ATM and foreign exchange.
Société Générale (Bab Bou Jeloud) ATM and foreign exchange.

Post
Main post office (cnr Ave Hassan II & Blvd Mohammed V)
Post office (Place Batha) In the medina.

Tourist Information
There is no tourist information in the medina.
Tourist Information Office (Syndicat d'Initiative; ☑0535 623460; Place Mohammed V) Not always open, or helpful.

ℹ Getting There & Away

The swanky new **train station** is in the ville nouvelle, a 10-minute walk northwest of Place Florence. Trains depart almost hourly between 7am and 5pm for Casablanca (Dh110, 4½ hours), via Rabat (Dh80, 3½ hours) and Meknès (Dh20, one hour), plus there are two overnight trains. Eight trains travel to Marrakesh (Dh195, eight hours) and one goes to Tangier (Dh105, five hours or four hours if changing at Sidi Kacem).

The main station for **CTM buses** is near Place Atlas in the southern ville nouvelle. CTM runs many daily services to and from Fez.

Non-CTM buses depart from the **gare routiere** outside Bab el-Mahrouk.

Grands taxis for Meknès (Dh18) and Rabat (Dh60) leave from in front of the main bus station (outside Bab el-Mahrouk) and from near the train station.

ℹ Getting Around

Grands taxis from all stands to the airport charge a set fare of Dh120.

Drivers of the red *petits taxis* generally use their meters without any fuss. Expect to pay about Dh9 from the train or CTM station to Bab Bou Jeloud.

BUSES TO/FROM FEZ

DESTINATION	COST (DH)	DURATION (HR)	FREQUENCY
Casablanca	105	5	7 daily
Chefchaouen	45	4	3 daily
Marrakesh	150	9	2 daily
Rabat	70	3½	7 daily
Tangier	115	6	3 daily
Tetouan	100	5	2 daily

Meknès

POP 700,000

Of the four imperial cities, Meknès is the most modest by far. Its proximity to Fez rather overshadows Meknès, which receives fewer visitors than it really should. Quieter and smaller than its grand neighbour, it's also more laid-back, presents less hassle yet still has all the winding narrow medina streets and grand buildings that it warrants as a one-time home of the Moroccan sultanate. Meknès is also the ideal base from which to explore the Roman ruins at Volubilis and the hilltop holy town of Moulay Idriss, two of the country's most significant historic sites.

The valley of the Oued Bou Fekrane divides the old medina in the west and the French-built ville nouvelle in the east. It's a 25-minute walk from the medina to the ville nouvelle, but blue *petits taxis* shuttle between the two. Moulay Ismail's tomb and imperial city are south of the medina.

⊙ Sights

The main sights are tied to Meknès' 17th-century heyday as imperial capital under the Alawite sultan Moulay Ismail.

Place el-Hedim   SQUARE
The heart of the Meknès medina is Place el-Hedim, the large square facing Bab el-Mansour. Built by Moulay Ismail and originally used for royal announcements and public executions, it's a good place to sit and watch the world go by. A small *mellah* is to the west.

Imperial City   HISTORIC AREA
To the south, Moulay Ismail's imperial city opens up through one of the most impressive monumental gateways in all of Morocco, **Bab el-Mansour**.

Mausoleum of Moulay Ismail   MAUSOLEUM
(donations welcome; ⊙8.30am-noon & 2-6pm Sat-Thu) Following the road around to the right, you'll come across the grand Mausoleum of Moulay Ismail with its austere courtyards leading to a lavish tomb.

Heri es-Souani   RUINS
(admission Dh10; ⊙9am-noon & 3-6.30pm) Nearly 2km southeast of the mausoleum, Moulay Ismail's immense granaries and stables, Heri es-Souani are an impressive sight next to the **Agdal Basin**, a stone-lined reservoir and evening promenade spot.

Dar Jamaï Museum   MUSEUM
(Place el-Hedim; admission Dh10; ⊙9am-noon & 3-6.30pm Wed-Mon) Overlooking Place el-Hedim is the 1882 palace that houses the museum. Exhibits include traditional ceramics, jewellery, rugs and some fantastic textiles and embroidery.

Medersa Bou Inania   ISLAMIC COLLEGE
(Rue Najjarine; admission Dh10; ⊙9am-noon & 3-6pm) Deeper in the medina, opposite the Grand Mosque, and typical of the exquisite interior design that distinguishes Merenid monuments.

🛏 Sleeping

TOP CHOICE Hôtel Majestic   HOTEL $
(☏0535 522035; 19 Ave Mohammed V; s/d Dh159/210, with shower Dh231/322) Open for business since 1937, the Majestic is one of the best art deco buildings in Meknès. There's a good mix of rooms (all have sinks), and there's plenty of character to go around from the dark-wood dado to the original art deco light fittings. A hard budget option to beat.

TOP CHOICE Ryad Bahia   GUEST HOUSE $$
(☏0535 554541; www.ryad-bahia.com; Derb Sekkaya, Tiberbarine; r incl breakfast Dh670, ste Dh950-1200; ❀❁⚛) This charming little riad is just a stone's throw from Place el-Hedim. The main entrance opens onto a courtyard (also hosting a great restaurant), and the whole place has an open and airy layout compared to many riads. Rooms are pretty and carefully restored, and the owners (keen travellers themselves) are eager to swap travel stories as well as guide guests in the medina.

Maroc Hôtel   HOTEL $
(☏0535 530075; 7 Rue Rouamzine; s/d/tr Dh100/200/270) A perennially popular shoestring option, the Maroc has kept its standards up over the many years we've been visiting. Friendly and quiet, rooms (with sinks) are simple, and the shared bathrooms are clean. The terrace and courtyard filled with orange trees add to the ambience.

Riad Safir   GUEST HOUSE $$
(☏0535 534785; www.riadsafir.com; 1 Derb Lalla Alamia; r Dh550-750, ste 770-1430; ❀⚛) This delightful and intimate guest house comes in two halves: the original Safir is a homely confection that swaps the traditional *zellij* and plaster of some places for swathes of soft fabrics and carpets in creams and warm

Meknès

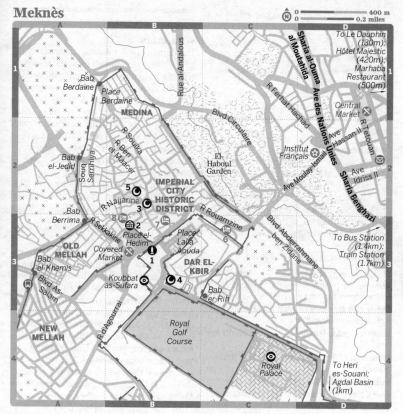

oranges, and plenty of wood. Recently expanded next door, the newer section is all ultramodern chic, with stylishly restrained colours and artful decoration. An unexpected, but winning, contrast.

✗ Eating

Marhaba Restaurant MOROCCAN **$**
(23 Ave Mohammed V; tajines Dh25; ⊗noon-10pm)
We adore this canteen-style place and so does everyone else, judging by how busy it is of an evening. While you can get tajines and the like, do as everyone else does and fill up on a bowl of *harira,* a plate of *makoda* (potato fritters) with bread and hard-boiled eggs – and walk out with change from Dh15. We defy you to eat better for cheaper.

Dar Sultana RESTAURANT **$$**
(☎0535 535720; Derb Sekkaya, Tiberbarine; mains from Dh70, 3-course set menu Dh150) Also going under the name Sweet Sultana, this is a

Meknès

◉ Sights

1	Bab el-Mansour	B3
2	Dar Jamaï Museum	B3
3	Grande Mosquée	B2
4	Mausoleum of Moulay Ismail	B3
5	Medersa Bou Inania	B2

⬠ Sleeping

6	Maroc Hôtel	C3
7	Riad Safir	B3
8	Ryad Bahia	B3

Eating

| | Dar Sultana | (see 8) |

small but charming restaurant in a converted medina house. The tent canopy over the courtyard gives an intimate, romantic atmosphere, set off by walls painted with henna designs and bright fabrics.

The spread of cooked Moroccan salads is a highlight.

Place el-Hedim
AREA $

(sandwiches around Dh30; ⊙7am-10pm) Take your pick of any one of the sandwich stands lining Place el-Hedim, and sit at the canopied tables to watch the scene as you eat. While larger meals such as tajines are available, the sandwiches are usually quick and excellent.

Le Dauphin
FRENCH $$

(☏0535 523423; 5 Ave Mohammed V; mains Dh75-120, set menu Dh150) It might have an uninspiring exterior, but the French dining room and lovely garden give this restaurant one of the nicest dining settings in town. The menu is Continental, with some good meat and fish dishes. Alcohol is served.

❶ Information

There are plenty of banks with ATMs both in the ville nouvelle (mainly on Ave Hassan II and Ave Mohammed V) and the medina (Rue Sekkakine).

Cyber Bab Mansour (Zankat Accra; per hr Dh6; ⊙9am-midnight)

Hôpital Moulay Ismail (☏035 522805; off Ave des FAR)

Main post office (Place de l'Istiqlal) In the ville nouvelle.

Post office (Rue Dar Smen) In the medina.

Quick Net (28 Rue Emir Abdelkader; per hr Dh6; ⊙9am-10pm)

❶ Getting There & Away

Although Meknès has two train stations, head for the more convenient **El-Amir Abdelkader**. There are plentiful trains to Fez (Dh20, 45 minutes) and Casablanca (Dh90, 3½ hours) via Rabat (Dh59, 2¼ hours), with seven for Marrakesh (Dh174, seven hours) and two for Tangier (Dh80, four hours) – or take a westbound train and change at Sidi Kacem.

The **CTM bus station** (Ave des FAR) is about 300m east of the junction with Ave Mohammed V. The main bus station lies just outside Bab el-Khemis, west of the medina. CTM departures include: Casablanca (Dh90, four hours, six daily) via Rabat (Dh55, 2½ hours), Marrakesh (Dh160, eight hours, daily) and Tangier (Dh100, five hours, three daily).

The principal grand taxi rank is next to the bus station at Bab el-Khemis. There are regular departures to Fez (Dh18, one hour) and Rabat (Dh44, 90 minutes). Grands taxis for Moulay Idriss (Dh12, 20 minutes) leave from opposite the Institut Français – the place to organise round-trips to Volubilis.

Around Meknès

VOLUBILIS

The Roman ruins of **Volubilis** (admission Dh20, guide Dh140; ⊙8am-sunset) sit in the middle of a fertile plain about 33km north of Meknès. The city is the best-preserved archaeological site in Morocco and was declared a Unesco World Heritage site in 1997. Its most amazing features are its many beautiful mosaics preserved in situ – look out for the Labours of Hercules and the erotically charged Abduction of Hylas by the Nymphs, as well as the columns of the basilica, which are often topped with storks' nests. Parking costs Dh5.

A half-day outing by grand taxi from Meknès will cost around Dh350, including a stop at Moulay Idriss.

MOULAY IDRISS

This whitewashed holy town is named for a great-grandson of the Prophet Mohammed, the founder of Morocco's first real dynasty in the 8th century, and its most revered saint. His tomb is at the heart of the town, and is the focus of the country's largest moussem every August. Non-Muslims may not enter, but you can climb the twin hills the town straddles for good views. Moulay Idriss's pious reputation deters some travellers, but it's a pretty and relaxed town with a centre free of carpet shops and traffic, giving you a chance to see Morocco as Moroccans experience it.

To the right and uphill from the main shrine, **Dar Zerhoune** (☏0535 544371; www. buttonsinn.com; 42 Derb Zouak Tazgha; dm/s/d incl breakfast Dh200/300/500; 🛜) is a gem of a guest house with a welcoming family flavour. There are a variety of rooms, a terrace with a view to Volubilis, a delicious home-cooked dinner, and tours, bike hire and cookery lessons.

The cheap **food stands** around the main square are all good for a quick snack. The grilled chicken with salad is something of a local speciality.

It's a 5km walk between Moulay Idriss and Volubilis, and there are regular grands taxis to Meknès (Dh12, 20 minutes).

CENTRAL MOROCCO & THE HIGH ATLAS

Marrakesh is the queen bee of Moroccan tourism, but look beyond it and you'll find great hiking in the dramatic High Atlas, and spectacular valleys and gorges that lead to the vast and empty sands of the Saharan dunes.

Marrakesh

POP 2 MILLION

Marrakesh grew rich on the camel caravans threading their way across the desert, but these days it's cheap flights from Europe bringing tourists to spend their money in the souqs that fatten the city's coffers. As many locals have taken the opportunity to move out of the medina into modern housing, so foreigners have arrived to transform those houses into stylish magazine-friendly guest houses.

But Marrakesh's old heart still beats strongly enough, from the time-worn ramparts that ring the city to the nightly spectacle of the Djemaa el-Fna that leaps from the pages of the *1001 Arabian Nights* on the edge of the labyrinthine medina.

Like most Moroccan cities, Marrakesh is divided into new and old sections; it's a short taxi ride or a 30-minute walk from the centre of the ville nouvelle to Djemaa el-Fna.

⊙ Sights

Djemaa el-Fna   SQUARE

The focal point of Marrakesh is Djemaa el-Fna, a huge square in the medina, and the backdrop for one of the world's greatest spectacles. Although it can be lively at any hour of the day, Djemaa el-Fna comes into its own at dusk when the curtain goes up on rows of open-air food stalls smoking the immediate area with mouth-watering aromas. Jugglers, storytellers, snake charmers, musicians, the occasional acrobat and benign lunatics consume the remaining space, each surrounded by jostling spectators.

Koutoubia Mosque   MOSQUE

Dominating the landscape, southwest of Djemaa el-Fna, is the 70m-tall minaret of Marrakesh's most famous and most venerated monument, the Koutoubia Mosque. Visible for miles in all directions, it's a classic example of 12th-century Moroccan-Andalucian architecture.

Ali ben Youssef Mosque   MOSQUE

The largest and oldest-surviving of the mosques inside the medina is the 12th-century Ali ben Youssef Mosque (closed to non-Muslims), which marks the intellectual and religious heart of the medina.

Ali ben Youssef Medersa   ISLAMIC COLLEGE

(Place ben Youssef; admission Dh40; ⊙9am-6pm winter, 9am-7pm summer) Next to the mosque is the 14th-century Ali ben Youssef Medersa, a peaceful and meditative place with some stunning examples of stucco decoration.

Musée de Marrakech   MUSEUM

(www.museedemarrakech.ma; Place ben Youssef; admission Dh40; ⊙9am-6.30pm) Inaugurated in 1997, the Musée de Marrakech is housed in a beautifully restored 19th-century palace, Dar Mnebhi. A combined ticket that also covers Ali ben Youssef Medersa costs Dh60.

Kasbah   HISTORIC AREA

South of the main medina area is the kasbah, which is home to the most famous of the city's palaces, the now-ruined Palais el-Badi (Place des Ferblantiers; admission Dh10; ⊙9am-4.30pm), 'the Incomparable', once reputed to be one of the most beautiful palaces in the world. All that's left are the towering pisé walls taken over by stork nests, and the staggering scale to give an impression of the former splendour. The Palais de la Bahia (Rue Riad Zitoun el-Jedid; admission Dh10; ⊙9am-4.30pm), the 'Brilliant', is the perfect antidote to the simplicity of the nearby el-Badi.

Saadian Tombs   HISTORIC AREA

(Rue de la Kasbah; admission Dh10; ⊙9am-4.45pm) Long hidden from intrusive eyes, the area of the Saadian Tombs alongside the Kasbah Mosque, is home to ornate tombs that are the resting places of Saadian princes.

MARRAKESH IN...

Two Days

Start the day with an orange juice on the **Djemaa el-Fna** and make your way to the **Ali ben Youssef Medersa** and the **Musée de Marrakech**, before plunging into the labyrinthine souqs for an afternoon of shopping. Back at the Djemaa el-Fna, take in the full spectacle before splurging on dinner at **Narwama**. The next day, concentrate on the **Palais de la Bahia**, the **Saadian Tombs** and views of the **Koutoubia Mosque minaret**. Later in the afternoon, head for the ville nouvelle and relax in the tranquillity of the **Jardin Majorelle**. Return to the medina for sunset drinks over the square, before finishing back at Djemaa el-Fna for an utterly memorable meal at its food stands.

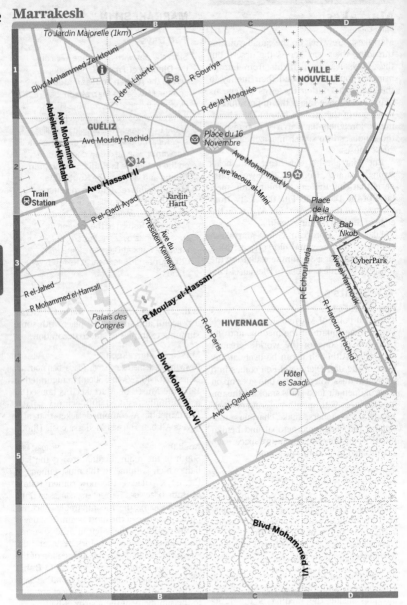

Jardin Majorelle　GARDEN
(☏0524 301852; www.jardinmajorelle.com; cnr Ave Yacoub el-Mansour & Ave Moulay Abdullah; garden Dh30, museum Dh15; ☺8am-6pm summer, to 5.30pm winter) Marrakesh has more gardens than any other Moroccan city, offering the perfect escape from the hubbub of the souqs and the traffic. The rose gardens of Koutoubia Mosque, in particular, offer cool respite near Djemaa el-Fna, while in the ville nouvelle, the Jardin Majorelle is a sublime mix of art deco buildings and psychedelic desert mirage.

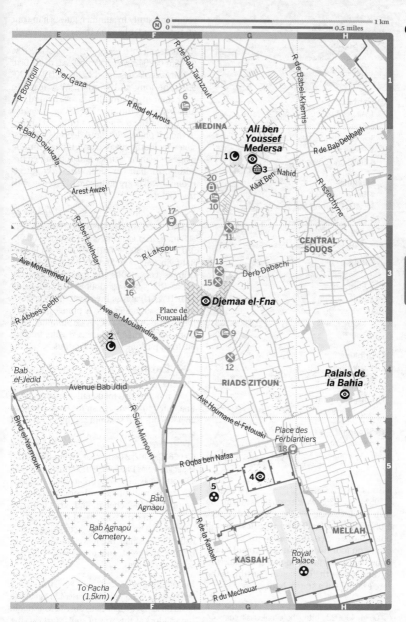

MOROCCO MARRAKESH

Sleeping

TOP CHOICE **Jnane Mogador**   GUEST HOUSE **$**
(☎0524 426324; www.jnanemogador.com; 116 Derb Sidi Bouloukat, off Rue Riad Zitoun el-Kedim; s/d/tr/q Dh360/480/580/660; @) A 19th-century riad with all the 21st-century guest-house fixings: prime location, in-house hammam, tea salon, double-decker roof terraces and owner Mohammed's laid-back hospitality. Book well ahead.

Hôtel Central Palace HOTEL **$$**
(☎0524 440235; www.lecentralpalace.com; 59 Derb Sidi Bouloukat; d without bathroom Dh155, d Dh255-305, ste Dh405; ❄) Sure it's central, but palatial? Actually, yes. With 40 clean rooms on four floors arranged around a burbling courtyard fountain and a roof terrace lording it over the Djemaa el-Fna, this is the rare example of a stately budget hotel.

Hôtel Toulousain BUDGET HOTEL **$**
(☎0524 430033; http://hoteltoulousain.com; 44 Rue Tariq ibn Ziad; s/d with shower & shared toilet Dh150/200, s/d with bathroom Dh180/230-280; ⊚) An easygoing budget hotel run by a kindly Moroccan-American family in a prime Guéliz location, with tasty restaurants, boutiques, laundry, local travel agency and a literary cafe right at your door. When upstairs

rooms get stuffy in summer, guests hang out on patios under banana trees.

Riad Magellan GUEST HOUSE **$$**
(☎0661 082042; www.riadmagellan.com; 62 Derb el Hammam, Mouassine; d incl breakfast Dh770-990) The long and winding alley leads to your door at this hip hideaway behind the Mouassine Fountain. There's a *tadelakt* hot tub on the terrace, multilingual library in the fireplace salon, and deep-tissue massages to soothe away travel kinks. Antique globes, steamer trunks and rocking chairs add retro flair to sleek *tadelakt* guestrooms, which are generously strewn with rose petals.

Dar Soukaina GUEST HOUSE **$$**
(☎0661 245238; www.darsoukaina.com; 19 Derb el-Ferrane, Riad Laârouss; s incl breakfast Dh770-970, d Dh970-1300, tr Dh1115-1400; ❄❄) Fraternal twin riads: the first (Dar I) is all soaring ceilings, cosy nooks and graceful archways, while the spacious double-riad extension (Dar II & III) across the street offers sprawling beds, grand patios, a plunge pool and handsome woodwork. A 20-minute walk from the Djemaa and nearest gate, but not far from parking on Riad Laarous.

✖ Eating

The cheapest and most exotic place to eat in town remains the food stalls on Djemaa el-Fna, piled high with fresh meats and salads, goats' heads and steaming snails.

TOP CHOICE **Earth Café** VEGETARIAN **$**
(☎0661 289402; 2 Derb Zouak, off Rue Riad Zitoun el-Kedim; mains Dh60-80; ⊙11am-11pm) Now for something completely different: a vegetarian spring roll stuffed with organic spinach, pumpkin, blue cheese and grated carrot with a sesame dressing, right in the heart of the souqs. The Earth Café's sunshine-yellow courtyard is small, but its vegie culinary ambitions are great and may make believers out of carnivores.

Mechoui Alley MOROCCAN **$**
(east side of Souq Ablueh; quarter-kilo lamb with bread Dh30-50; ⊙11am-2pm) Just before noon, the vendors at this row of stalls start carving up steaming sides of *mechoui* (slow-roasted lamb), as though expecting King Henry VIII for lunch. Point to the best-looking cut of meat, and ask for a *'nuss'* (half) or *'rubb'* (quarter) kilo. The cook will hack off some falling-off-the-bone lamb and hand it to you

with fresh-baked bread, cumin, salt and olives in a takeaway bag, or serve it to you on paper in a nearby stall.

Tobsil
MOROCCAN $$$
(☑0524 444052; 22 Derb Abdellah ben Hessaien, near Bab Ksour; 5-course menu incl wine Dh600; ☺7.30-11pm Wed-Mon) In this intimate riad, 50 guests max indulge in button-popping, five-course Moroccan menus with aperitifs and wine pairings, as Gnawa musicians strum quietly in the courtyard. No excess glitz or belly dancers distract from noble attempts to finish 11 salads, *bastilla,* tajines and couscous, capped with mint tea, fresh fruit and Moroccan pastries. Booking required.

Haj Mustapha
AREA $
(east side Souq Ablueh; meals Dh35-50; ☺6-10pm) As dusk approaches, several stalls set out paper-sealed crockpots of *tangia* (lamb slow-cooked all day in the ashes of a hammam). This 'bachelor's stew' makes for messy eating, but Haj Mustapha offers the cleanest seating inside a well-scuffed stall. Use bread as your utensil to scoop up *tangia,* sprinkle with cumin and salt, and chase with olives.

Le Chat Qui Rit
ITALIAN $$
(☑0524 434311; 92 Rue Yougoslavie; pizzas Dh50-80, set menu Dh150; ☺7.30-11pm Tue-Sun; ✸) Come here for proper pasta: al dente, tossed with fresh produce and herbs, and drizzled with fruity olive oil. Corsican chef/owner Bernard comes out to ask about everyone's pasta with the delight of a chef who already knows the answer. Seasonal seafood options are a good bet, with fixings just in from the coast daily.

Café des Épices
CAFE $
(☑0254 391770; Place Rahba Kedima; breakfast Dh25, sandwich or salad Dh25-50; ☺8am-9pm) Watch the magic happen as you sip freshly squeezed OJ overlooking Rahba Kedima potion-dealers. Salads and sandwiches are fresh and made to order – try the tangy chicken spiked with herbs, nutmeg and olives – and service is surprisingly efficient, given the steep stairs.

Drinking

The number one spot for a cheap and delicious drink is right on Djemaa el-Fna, where orange juice is freshly squeezed around the clock for just Dh4. Rooftop cafes overlook the square.

Dar Cherifa
CAFE
(☑0524 426463; 8 Derb Chorfa Lakbir, nr Rue Mouassine; tea/coffee Dh20-25; ☺noon-7pm) Revive souq-sore eyes at this serene late-15th-century Saadian riad, where tea and saffron coffee are served with contemporary art and literature either downstairs or with terrace views upstairs.

Kosybar
BAR
(☑0524 380324; http://kozibar.tripod.com; 47 Place des Ferblantiers, medina; ☺noon-1am; ✸) The Marrakesh-meets-Kyoto interiors are full of plush, private nooks, but keep heading upstairs to low-slung canvas sofas and Dh40 to Dh60 wine by the glass on the rooftop terrace. Enjoy drinks with a side of samba, but skip the cardboard-tasting sushi and stick with bar snacks.

☆ Entertainment

Sleeping is overrated in a city where the nightlife begins around midnight. Most of the hottest clubs are in the Hivernage district of the ville nouvelle. Admission ranges from Dh150 to Dh350 including the first drink. Each drink thereafter costs at least Dh50. Dress to impress.

Pacha
NIGHTCLUB
(☑0524 388400; www.pachamarrakech.com; Complexe Pacha Marrakech, Blvd Mohammed VI, Zone Aguedal, Hivernage; admission Mon-Wed before/after 10pm free/Dh150, Thu men/women Dh150/free, Sat & Sun Dh200-300; ☺8pm-1am Mon-Thu, 8pm-2am Fri & Sat; ✸) Pacha Ibiza was the prototype for this clubbing complex that's now Africa's biggest, with DJs mashing up international and Magrebi hits for weekend influxes of Casa hipsters and raging Rabatis. Pacha doesn't come close to hitting its 3000-people occupancy during the week, so bring your own entourage and you might get in free. Ladies arrive en masse Thursdays to drink gratis at Rose Bar; come early to lounge by the pool until the party starts.

Diamant Noir
NIGHTCLUB
(☑0524 446391; Hôtel Marrakech, cnr Ave Mohammed V & Rue Oum Errabia, Guéliz; admission from Dh150, incl first drink; ☺10pm-4am) For its rare gay-friendly clientele on weeknights and seedy charm complete with go-go dancers on weekends, the gravitational pull of 'Le Dia' remains undeniable. The dark dance-floor thumps with hip hop and gleams with mirrors and bronzer-enhanced skin, while professionals lurk at the upstairs bar. Cash only.

🛍 Shopping

Marrakesh is a shopper's paradise; its souqs are full of skilled artisans producing quality products in wood, leather, wool, metal, bone, brass and silver. The trick is to dive into the souqs and treat shopping as a game.

Cooperative Artisanale des Femmes de Marrakesh HANDICRAFTS
(67 Souq Kchachbia; ⊙10am-1pm & 3.30-7pm Sat-Thu) An eye-opening showcase for Marrakesh's women maalems (master artisans), Original, handcrafted designs are a bargain and include handbags made from water-bottle caps wrapped in wool, hand-knit *kissa* (hammam gloves), and black-and-white kaftans edged with red silk embroidery.

ℹ Information

Emergency
Ambulance (☎0524 443724)

Brigade Touristique (tourist police; ☎0524 384601; Rue Sidi Mimoun; ⊙24hr)

Internet Access
Internet cafes ringing the Djemaa el-Fna charge Dh8 to Dh12 per hour; just follow signs reading 'c@fe'.

Cyber Café in CyberPark (Ave Mohammed V; per hr Dh10; ⊙9.30am-8pm)

Hassan Internet (☎0524 441989; Immeuble Tazi, 12 Rue Riad el-Moukha; per hr Dh8; ⊙7am-midnight) A bustling place near the Tazi Hotel with 12 terminals.

Medical Services
Pharmacie de l'Unité (☎024 435982; Ave des Nations Unies, Guéliz; ⊙8.30am-11pm)

Polyclinique du Sud (☎0524 447999; cnr Rue de Yougoslavie & Rue Ibn Aicha, Guéliz; ⊙24hr)

Money
There are plenty of ATMs along Rue de Bab Agnaou off the Djemaa el-Fna.

Crédit du Maroc Medina (Rue de Bab Agnaou; ⊙8.45am-1pm & 3-6.45pm Mon-Sat); Ville Nouvelle (215 Ave Mohammed V)

Post
Main post office (☎024 431963; Place du 16 Novembre; ⊙8.30am-2pm Mon-Sat) In the ville nouvelle.

Post office (Rue Bab Agnaou; ⊙8am-noon & 3-6pm Mon-Fri) A convenient branch office in the medina.

Tourist Information
Office National Marocain du Tourisme (ONMT; ☎024 436179; Place Abdel Moumen ben Ali, Guéliz)

🛈 Getting There & Away

Bus
CTM (Rue Abu Bakr Seddik) operates daily buses to Fez (Dh150, 8½ hours). There are also daily services to Agadir (Dh90, four hours, nine daily), Casablanca (Dh85, four hours, three daily) and Essaouira (Dh70, 2½ hours). Other buses arrive and depart from the main **bus station** (Bab Doukkala) just outside the city walls. A number of companies run buses to Fez (from Dh130, 8½ hours, at least six daily) and Meknès (from Dh120, six hours, at least three daily).

Supratours (☎024 435525; Ave Hassan II), next to the train station, operates six daily coaches to Essaouira (Dh70, 2½ hours).

Train
The glitzy **train station** (cnr Ave Hassan II & Blvd Mohammed VI, Guéliz), has trains to Casablanca (Dh90, three hours, nine daily), Rabat (Dh120, four hours), Fez (Dh195, eight hours, eight daily) via Meknès (Dh160, seven hours) and nightly trains to Tangier (Dh205).

🛈 Getting Around

A *petit taxi* to Marrakesh from the airport (6km) should cost no more than Dh70 (Dh100 at night). Alternatively, airport bus 19 runs every 20 minutes from outside the airport car park to near the Djemaa el-Fna (Dh20). The creamy-beige *petits taxis* around town cost anywhere between Dh8 and Dh20 per journey.

High Atlas Mountains

The highest mountain range in North Africa, the High Atlas runs diagonally across Morocco, from the Atlantic Coast northeast of Agadir all the way to northern Algeria, a distance of almost 1000km. In Berber it's called Idraren Draren (Mountain of Mountains) and it's not hard to see why. Flat-roofed, earthen Berber villages cling tenaciously to the valley sides, while irrigated terraced gardens and walnut groves flourish below.

Hiking

The Moroccan tourist office, Office National Marocain du Tourisme (ONMT), publishes the extremely useful booklet *Morocco: Mountain and Desert Tourism* (2005), which has lists of *bureaux des guides* (guide offices), *gîtes d'étape* (hikers' hostels) and other useful information. Hikes of longer than a couple of days will almost certainly require a guide (Dh300 per day) and mule (Dh100) to carry kit and supplies. There are *bureaux des guides* in Imlil, Setti Fatma,

Azilal, Tabant (Aït Bou Goumez Valley) and El-Kelaâ M'Gouna, where you should be able to pick up a trained, official guide. Official guides carry ID cards. **Club Alpin Français** (CAF; www.caf-maroc.com, in French; Casablanca) operates *refuges* in the Toubkal area. Its website is a good source of information.

JEBEL TOUBKAL

One of the most popular hiking routes in the High Atlas is the ascent of Jebel Toubkal (4167m), North Africa's highest peak. The Toubkal area is just two hours' drive south of Marrakesh and easily accessed by local transport.

You don't need mountaineering skills or a guide to reach the summit, provided you follow the standard two-day route and don't do it in winter. You will, however, need good boots, warm clothing, a sleeping bag, food and water, and you should be in good physical condition before you set out. It's not particularly steep, but it's a remorseless uphill hike all the way (an ascent of 1467m) and it can be very tiring if you haven't done any warm-up walks or spent time acclimatising.

The usual starting point is the picturesque village of **Imlil**, 17km from Asni off the Tizi n'Test road between Marrakesh and Agadir. Most hikers stay overnight in Imlil.

The first day's walk (10km; about five hours) winds steeply through the villages of Aroumd and Sidi Chamharouch to the **Toubkal Refuge** (☏0524 485612; www.caf-maroc.com; campsite incl shower per person/tent Dh30/20, dm CAF & HI members/nonmembers Dh45/60). The refuge sits at an altitude of 2307m and sleeps more than 80 people.

The ascent from the hut to the summit on the second day should take about four hours and the descent about two hours. It can be bitterly cold at the summit, even in summer.

There is plenty of accommodation in Imlil. Try **Hôtel el-Aïne** (☏0524 485625; per person with/without bathroom half-board Dh250/200, d incl breakfast with/without bathroom Dh350/300; ☎) or **Café-Hotel Soleil** (☏0524 485622; www.hotelsoleil.com; per person with/without bathroom half-board Dh250/200, d incl breakfast with/without bathroom Dh350/300; ☎), at the top of the village. Imlil is also well stocked with shops with hiking supplies.

Frequent local buses (Dh15, 1½ hours) and *grands taxis* (Dh30, one hour) leave south of Bab er-Rob in Marrakesh to Asni,

where you change for the final 17km to Imlil (Dh15 to Dh20, one hour).

Other Hikes

In summer it's possible to do an easy one- or two-day hike from the ski resort of **Oukaïmeden**, which also has a Club Alpin Français (CAF) refuge, southwest to Imlil or vice versa. You can get here by *grand taxi* from Marrakesh.

From **Tacheddirt** (where the CAF refuge charges Dh60 for nonmembers) there are numerous hiking options. One of these is a pleasant two-day walk northeast to the village of **Setti Fatma** (also accessible from Marrakesh) via the village of **Timichi**, where there is a welcoming *gîte*. A longer circuit could take you south to **Amsouzerte** and back towards Imlil via **Lac d'Ifni**, Toubkal, **Tazaghart** (also with a refuge and rock climbing) and **Tizi Oussem**.

Tafraoute

Nestled in the enchanting **Ameln Valley** is the village of Tafraoute. Surrounded on all sides by red granite mountains, it's a pleasant and relaxed base for exploring the region. In late February and early March the villages around Tafraoute celebrate the almond harvest with all-night singing and dancing.

☉ Sights & Activities

The best way to get around the beautiful villages of the Ameln Valley is by walking or cycling. Bikes can be rented from **Artisanat du Coin** (per day Dh60). You can also rent mountain bikes or book a mountain-biking trip from **Tafraoute Aventure** (☏0661 387173) and **Au Coin des Nomades** (☏0661 627921), who offer mountain-biking and hiking trips either up Jebel Lekst (2359m) or along the palm-filled gorges of Aït Mansour, leading towards the bald expanses of the southern Anti-Atlas.

🛏 Sleeping & Eating

TOP CHOICE **Hôtel Salama**   HOTEL $
(☏0528 80 00 26; www.hotelsalama.com; s/d/tr Dh178/256/314; ❄☎) An exemplary hotel mixing local materials and modern standards, with an open fire in the lobby and Berber artefacts decorating the corridors. The staff are one of Tafraoute's more impartial sources of information. The roof terrace has mountain views and the **cafe-restaurant**

serves breakfast and full meals overlooking the market square.

Hôtel Les Amandiers
HOTEL **$$**

(☏0528 800088; www.hotel-lesamandiers.com; s/d incl breakfast from Dh400/546; ✳☏❄) This kasbah-like hilltop pile has 60 reasonably attractive rooms with small balconies, offering great views. The hotel needs a renovation, but you may have the place to yourself.

Café Atlas
CAFE **$**

(☏0667 12 02 93; meal Dh60; ⊘breakfast, lunch & dinner) Atlas' covered terrace is more of a local hang-out than the nearby L'Étoile d'Agadir and Marrakech restaurants. Cheese omelette, steak, sandwiches and tajines all feature on the broad menu.

Restaurant L'Étoile du Sud
MOROCCAN **$**

(☏0528 80 00 38; set menu Dh90) L'Étoile du Sud serves a good set menu in a rather kitsch Bedouin-style tent, although you may have to share the place with tour groups, particularly at lunchtime. Still, the lamb tajine is commendable, the service professional and on warm nights it's one of the best places to eat.

❶ Getting There & Away

Buses depart from outside the various company offices on Sharia al-Jeish al-Malaki, including to Agadir (Dh40, six hours, daily), Casablanca (Dh140, 14 hours, five daily) and Marrakesh (Dh100, seven hours, four daily).

Taroudannt

Hidden by magnificent red-mud walls and with the snowcapped peaks of the High Atlas beckoning beyond, Taroudannt appears a touch mysterious at first. It is, however, every inch a market town, with busy souqs where the produce of the rich and fertile Souss Valley is traded.

❂ Sights & Activities

Ramparts
HISTORIC AREA

The 5km of ramparts surrounding Taroudannt are the best preserved in Morocco, their colour changing from golden brown to the deepest red depending on the time of day. They can easily be explored on foot (1½ hours), preferably in the late afternoon.

Tichka Plateau
HIKING

Taroudannt is a great base for hiking in the western High Atlas region and the secluded Tichka Plateau, a delightful meadow of springtime flowers and hidden gorges. There are several agencies in town offering hikes, but beware as there are many stories of rip-offs and unqualified guides.

🛏 Sleeping

Budget hotels on and around the two central squares offer basic accommodation and roof terraces, good for sunbathing and people-watching.

Hôtel Palais Salam
HISTORIC HOTEL **$$**

(☏0528 85 25 01; www.palaisalam.com; kasbah; s/d/apt from Dh562/674/2412; ❄☏) This former pasha's residence, entered through the east wall of the kasbah, lives up to its palatial name, with gardens, pools and fountains (one inhabited by turtles) on various levels. Readers recommend the older, ground-floor rooms for their authenticity, but the newer rooms, behind pink walls and blue shutters, are spacious and pleasant. There's a bar and Moroccan and international restaurants.

Naturally Morocco Guest House: Centre Culturel & Environmental
GUEST HOUSE **$**

(☏0528 55 16 28, 0661 23 66 27 bookings; www.naturallymorocco.co.uk; 422 Derb Afferdou; s/d incl breakfast Dh350/550; ☏) If only there were more places like this medina house, which gives a rare glimpse into Moroccan life and won a responsible tourism award. It offers delicious Moroccan meals and skilled guides. **Activities** include hiking, wildlife trips, coastal excursions and craft workshops, all with an emphasis on cultural contact. The eight-room house has a kitchen for self-catering, a roof terrace with views of the High and Anti Atlas, informative displays in the tiled corridors, and a small library. Packages and bike hire are available.

Hôtel Taroudannt
HOTEL **$**

(☏0528 85 24 16; Ave Mohammed V & Place al-Alaouyine; s/d Dh160/200) This central option has the makings of the best budget hotel in town, with tiled corridors leading past a pleasant restaurant and lush courtyard to rooms with simple bathrooms. The drawbacks are the insalubrious characters in the bar and hustlers hanging around outside.

🍴 Eating

The best place to look for cheap eateries is around Place an-Nasr and north along Ave Bir Zaran, where you find the usual tajine,

AÏT BOU GOUMEZ VALLEY

Aït Bou Goumez Valley is often called 'the Happy Valley' and when you get there you will understand why: there is a touch of Shangri-la about this lush and unusually beautiful valley. East of Marrakesh, beyond Azilal, the Aït Bou Goumez Valley feels remote because it is. A year-round road link was opened in 2001, before which the valley was snowbound for four months a year. Even now the road is rarely busy.

The only real sight in the valley is the marabout of Sidi Moussa, though hiking in the M'Goun Massif is also possible. But the real attraction of the valley is the joy of being in so peaceful a place and seeing this landscape – the rich fertility of the valley floor and terraced hillsides – and the Berber villages, which seem to have grown out of the mud and rock on which they sit. The views over the valley from the shrine, and from the *agadir* (fortified granary) on the adjacent hill, are spectacular.

harira and salads. Several places around Place al-Alaouyine serve sandwiches and simple grills.

Chez Nada MOROCCAN $$
(☎0528 85 17 26; Ave Moulay Rachid; set menu Dh80; ✱) West of Bab el-Kasbah, this 55-year-old restaurant is famous for its tajines, including one with pigeon and a rich one with chicken, egg and prunes. Above the ground-floor cafe and elegant 1st-floor dining room, the roof terrace has views over public gardens. Food is home cooking and excellent. *Pastilla* and royal couscous (Dh60 to Dh95) should be ordered a couple of hours ahead.

Jnane Soussia MOROCCAN $$
(☎0528 85 49 80; mains Dh80; ✱✱) A delightful restaurant, a short walk from the *grand taxi* station, with tented seating areas set around a large pool in a garden adjacent to the ramparts. The house specialities are *mechoui* (whole roast lamb) and pigeon *pastilla*, which have to be ordered in advance, but everything here is good.

❶ Information

There are three banks with ATMs on Place al-Alaouyine, and all have exchange facilities and accept travellers cheques. BMCE also does cash advances. The main **post office** (Rue du 20 Août) is off Ave Hassan II, to the east of the kasbah. Internet access is available at **Roudana Cyber Cafe** (1st fl, Ave Bir Zaran; per hr Dh3; ☺8.30am-midnight).

❶ Getting There & Away

All buses leave from the main bus station outside Bab Zorgane. **CTM** (Hotel Les Arcades, Place al-Alaouyine) has the most reliable buses,

with one departure per day for Casablanca (Dh160, 10 hours) via Marrakesh (Dh80, six hours).

Other companies run services throughout the day to both these cities as well as to Agadir (Dh28, 2½ hours) and Ouarzazate (Dh70, five hours).

Aït Benhaddou

Aït Benhaddou, 32km from Ouarzazate, is one of the most exotic and best-preserved kasbahs in the Atlas region. This is hardly surprising, given the money poured into it as a result of being used for scenes in many films, notably *Lawrence of Arabia*, *Jesus of Nazareth* (for which much of the village was rebuilt) and, more recently, *Gladiator*. The kasbah is now under Unesco protection. It's a very special place.

An all-natural pisé guest house, **Fibule d'Or** (☎0524 887682; www.lafibule-dor.com; d incl breakfast Dh360, per person half-board Dh250) threatens to steal scenes from the glammed-up movie star kasbah directly across the valley. In this nine-room guest house, rooms numbered 6, 5 and 7 are high-ceilinged and bright, but number 8 has the best view of the historic kasbah. Prices are remarkably reasonable for rooms with en suite baths, and thick mudbrick walls keep rooms naturally cool without air-con.

To get here from Ouarzazate, take the main road towards Marrakesh as far as the signposted turn-off (22km); Aït Benhaddou is another 9km down a bitumen road. *Grands taxis* run from outside Ouarzazate bus station when full (Dh20 per person) or cost Dh250 to Dh350 in total for a half-day with return.

Drâa Valley

A ribbon of technicoloured *palmeraies* (palm groves), earth-red kasbahs and stunning Berber villages – the Drâa Valley is a special place. The valley eventually seeps out into the sands of the desert, and it once played a key role in controlling the ancient trans-Saharan trade routes that Marrakesh's wealth was built on.

ZAGORA

The iconic 'Tombouktou, 52 jours' ('Timbuktu, 52 days') signpost was recently taken down in an inexplicable government beautification scheme, but Zagora's fame as a desert outpost is indelible. The Saadians launched their expedition to conquer Timbuktu from Zagora in 1591, and the many desert caravans that passed through this oasis have added to its character.

Jebel Zagora and a *palmeraie* make a dramatic backdrop for the rather drab French colonial outpost buildings and splashy new town hall complex. But for all its recent modernisation, Zagora is still a trading post at heart, with a large **market** on Wednesdays and Sundays selling produce, hardware and livestock.

About 23km south of Zagora, you get your first glimpse of Saharan sand dunes, the **Tinfou Dunes**. If you've never seen a sandy desert, Tinfou is a pleasant spot to take a breather and enjoy a small taste, although the dunes at Merzouga or around M'Hamid are grander.

🏃 Activities

Camel rides are not only possible in Zagora, but practically obligatory. Count on around Dh350 per day if you're camping, and ask about water, bedding, toilets, and how many other people will be sharing your campsite. Decent agencies:

Caravane Desert et Montagne (☎0524 846898; www.caravanedesertetmontagne.com; 112 Blvd Mohammed V) Partners with local nomads to create adventures off the beaten camel track for individuals and small groups.

Caravane Hamada Drâa (☎0524 846930; www.hamadadraa.com, in French; Blvd Mohammed V) English-speaking guides; treks to nomadic camps by licensed guide and native nomad Youssef M'hidi.

Discovering South Morocco (☎0524 846115; www.discoveringsouthmorocco.com) Run by English- and French-speaking, Zagora-born Mohamad Sirirou.

🍽 Sleeping & Eating

All hotels have their own restaurants and will provide set meals (Dh100 to Dh150) to nonguests by prior reservation. Moroccan fare with less flair can be had at cheap, popular restaurants along Blvd Mohammed V.

Dar Raha   GUEST HOUSE **$$**
(☎0524 846993; www.darraha.com; Amezrou; per person incl breakfast/half-board Dh235/310) 'How thoughtful!' is the operative phrase here, from welcoming gifts of dates to oasis-appropriate details like local palm mats, baskets made of recycled plastic bags and thick, straw-reinforced pisé walls eliminating the need for air-con. Comfortable, exposed-mudbrick guestrooms come with *ghandouras* (robes) for lounging around the courtyard, but no en suite baths. Enjoy home-cooked meals and chats in the kitchen, and admire spirited local folk art in the courtyard gallery. Your host gladly arranges visits to the ancient synagogue, 18th-century *ksar* and village self-help organisations.

Villa Zagora   GUEST HOUSE **$$**
(☎0524 846093; www.mavillaausahara.com; Amezrou; d half-board with/without bathroom Dh1030/860, ste Dh1322; ❄☀) This charming, converted country home makes desert living look easy. French doors reveal plush Moroccan carpets underfoot, soaring ceilings overhead, and an eclectic art collection, including Zagora-inspired abstracts. Staff fuss over you like relations you never knew you had, and meals are marathons of dishes made with oasis-fresh ingredients.

Auberge Restaurant Chez Ali   HOTEL **$**
(☎0524 846258; www.chez-ali.com; Ave de l'Atlas Zaouiate El Baraka; garden tents per person Dh40 & showers Dh10, d half-board Dh360-400) While the peacocks stalking the garden can't be bothered, the welcome here is otherwise enthusiastic. Skylit standard rooms upstairs have simple pine furnishings, bathrooms and air-con; tents with pisé walls in the garden sleep four to five and share bathrooms; and 'traditional' rooms have wood-beamed ceilings, mattresses on carpets and shared bathrooms (number 14 has a private terrace).

❶ Information

Banks including **Banque Populaire** and **BMCE** are on Blvd Mohammed V, with ATMs and normal banking hours.

Placenet Cyber Center (95 Blvd Mohammed V; per hr Dh10) Internet access.

Getting There & Away

The **CTM bus station** is at the southwestern end of Blvd Mohammed V, and the main bus and *grand taxi* lot is at the northern end. CTM has a daily service to Marrakesh (Dh120) and Casablanca (Dh195) via Ouazazarte. Other companies also operate buses to Boumalne du Dadès (Dh75). A bus passes through headed to M'Hamid (Dh20, two hours) in the morning; there are also minibuses (Dh25) and *grands taxis* (Dh30).

M'HAMID

Once it was a lonesome oasis, but these days M'Hamid is a wallflower no more. Today the road is flanked with hotels to accommodate travellers lured here by the golden dunes of the Sahara. This one dot on a map actually covers two towns: the M'hamid Jdid is a typical one-street administrative centre with a mosque, a few restaurants, small hotels, craft shops and a Monday market. M'Hamid Bali, the old town, is 3km away across the Oued Drâa. It has an impressive and well-preserved kasbah.

M'hamid's star attraction is **Erg Chigaga**, a mind-boggling 40km stretch of golden Saharan dunes that's the equal of Erg Chebbi near Merzouga. It's 56km away – a couple of hours by 4WD or several days by camel. A closer alternative is Erg Lehoudi, but it's in bad need of rubbish collection. **Sahara Services** (0661 776766; www.saharaservices.info; Kasbah Sahara Services, M'Hamid), 300m on right after M'Hamid entry, and **Zbar Travel** (0668 517280; www.zbartravel.com) are both reliable agencies offering tours – an overnight camel trek should start at about Dh300.

If you're not sleeping with your camel in the desert, **Dar Azawad** (0524 848730; www.darazawad.com; Douar Ouled Driss, M'Hamid; half-board d Dh1600-1800, ste Dh2200-2500;) is a deluxe hotel ideal for Armani-clad nomads, while **Kasbah Sahara Services** (0524 848033; www.hotelmhamid.com; d per person half-board tent/d Dh200/300) offers simpler but still decent fare. It's 300m to the right after M'Hamid entry.

There's a daily CTM bus at 4.30pm to Zagora (Dh20, two hours), Ouarzazate (Dh60, seven hours), Marrakesh (Dh155, 11 to 13 hours) and Casablanca (Dh220, 15 hours), plus an assortment of private buses, minibuses and *grands taxis*.

Dadès Gorge

Those art deco tourism posters you'll see all over southern Morocco showing a striking pink and white kasbah in a rocky oasis aren't exaggerating: the Dadès Gorge really is that impressive.

The main access to the gorge is from **Boumalne du Dadès**, a pleasant, laid-back place with a good Wednesday market. From there, a good sealed road wriggles past 63km of *palmeraies,* fabulous rock formations, Berber villages and some beautiful ruined kasbahs to Msemrir, before continuing as a dirt track to Imilchil in the heart of the High Atlas.

If you have plenty of time, you could easily spend several days pottering about in the gorge – watching nomads bring vast herds of goats down the cliffs to the river, fossicking for fossils and generally enjoying the natural splendour.

There are a number of places to stay; the kilometre markings of the following places refer to the distance into the gorge from Boumalne du Dadès. Nearly all hotels will let you sleep in the salon or on the terrace (even in summer you may need a sleeping bag) for around Dh25, or camp by the river for around Dh10. Most also offer half-board rates and dinner.

River views, good value and a terrace restaurant amid the chirping songbirds make **Hôtel le Vieux Chateau du Dadès** (0524 831261; km25; per person half-board d Dh200-300, ste Dh350) worth going the extra mile to find. The tiled rooms upstairs have better views, but the snug pisé-walled downstairs guest rooms are equally charming.

A bubbly personality overlooking the river, **Auberge des Gorges du Dadès** (0524 830221; www.aubergeaitoudinar.com; km24; campsite per person Dh15, r per person incl breakfast/half-board Dh120/200) has 12 rooms with splashy Amazigh (Moroccan tribe) motifs and big bathrooms plus a pleasantly shaded camping area. The trek leader speaks English, French and Spanish and has more than 23 years' experience.

Romance is in the air at **Les 5 Lunes** (0524 830723; km23, Aït Oudinar; per person half-board Dh200) a snug tree-house-style berth teetering above valley treetops, with four plain but pretty doubles and one triple and a hewn-stone bathroom. Book ahead for dinner.

Chez Pierre (0524 830267; http://chezpierre.ifrance.com; km27, Aït Ouffi; incl breakfast s/d/tr or q Dh470/615/895; closed Nov-Mar;) is a rock-climbing hotel with eight airy rooms and one apartment shimmying right up the gorge. Decor is kept simple to focus attention on what really matters: the view over the valley from flower-filled terraces and poolside sun decks. Picnics and hikes with official guides can be arranged.

Grands taxis and minibuses run up the gorge from Boumalne du Dadès and charge Dh15 per person to the cluster of hotels in the middle of the gorge and Dh30 to Msemrir – ask to be dropped at your chosen hotel. To return, simply wait by the road and flag down a passing vehicle. Boulmane du Dadès itself has good onward connections to major destinations including Zagora (Dh65), Tinerhir (Dh25), Fez (Dh135), Casablanca (Dh150 to Dh190), Erfoud (Dh60) and Marrakesh (Dh70 to Dh90).

Todra Gorge

Being stuck between a rock and a hard place is a fantastic experience to have in the Todra Gorge, where the massive fault dividing the High Atlas from the Jebel Sarhro is at some points just wide enough for a crystal-clear river and some hikers to squeeze through. The road from Tinerhir passes green *palmeraies* and yellowish Berber villages until, 15km along, high walls of pink and grey rock close in around the road. The approach is thrilling and urgent, as though the doors of heaven were about to close before you.

Arrivals at the Todra are best timed for the morning, when the sun briefly alights on the bottom of the gorge, providing your shining golden moment of welcome. In the afternoon it gets very dark and, in winter, bitterly cold.

There's little reason to stay in Tinerhir itself, but you'll find banks, internet cafes and onward transport there. An enormous souq is held about 2.5km west of the centre on Mondays.

◎ Sights & Activities

This is prime hiking and climbing country. About a 30-minute walk beyond the main gorge is the Petite Gorge. This is the starting point of many pleasant day hikes, including one starting by the Auberge Le Festival, 2km after the Petite Gorge. For a more strenuous hike, you could do a three-hour loop from north of the gorge to Tizgui, south of the gorge. Regular donkey and mule traffic keep this path well defined for most of the route.

If you wanted to push on, you could walk to Tinerhir through the *palmeraies* in three or four hours.

Assittif Adventure (☑0668 357792; km14; www.assettif.org), located 700m before the gorge, arranges hikes and horse riding (per hour/day Dh150/500) as well as hiring out bikes (per day Dh100) and mountaineering equipment.

🛏 Sleeping & Eating

🖋 **Auberge Le Festival**   GUEST HOUSE **$$**
(☑0661 267251; www.auberge-lefestival.com; main house s/d Dh300/460, tower room s/d Dh400/700, cave room d/tr Dh700/900, all half-board) Get back to nature in cave guestrooms with fossil-fixture bathrooms dug right into the hillside, or rock-walled, solar-powered lodge rooms surveying the Petit Gorge. After treks and climbs arranged by the multilingual owner, you can relax in the hillside hot tub or dig in the organic garden, helping harvest vegetables for dinner.

Dar Ayour   GUEST HOUSE **$$**
(☑0524 895271; www.darayour.com; km13 Gorges du Todra; per person half-board with/without bathroom Dh250/150, r incl breakfast/half-board Dh200/350) Riads have arrived in Todra with this warm, artsy five-storey guest house that's all Middle Atlas rugs, winking mirror-work pillows and colourful Berber-inspired abstract paintings. Most guestrooms have en suites, and breakfasts with valley views are served on the roof terrace.

Auberge Les Amis   INN, CAMPING **$**
(☑0670 234374; www.amistamtt.wg.vu; km34, Tamtattouchte; campsite per person/car Dh30/30, per person s/d or tr half-board Dh130/200, ste per person half-board Dh230) Your reward for venturing beyond tour-trammelled lower Todra Gorge is this kasbah-style guest house that goes the extra mile for guests, with generous home-cooking, vast, well-polished baths (most en suite), and custom, hand-made guestroom furnishings. Rooms show Berber pride with *tataoui* (woven reed) ceilings, local rugs and crockery jugs repurposed as sink basins. There's camping out back with electrical hookups (Dh10) and laundry (Dh15/load).

❶ Getting There & Away

Buses from Tinerhir leave from the Place Principale to Marrakesh (Dh120, five daily) via Ouarzazate (Dh50), and to Casablanca (Dh175),

TODRA LOOP HIKE

For a vigorous morning hike, try a three-hour loop from north of the gorge to Tizgui, south of the gorge. A 30-minute walk beyond the main gorge is the Petite Gorge, where you'll find a trailhead near Auberge-Camping le Festival. Take the track leading up the hill to the left (south-west); regular donkey and mule traffic keep this path well-defined for most of the route. Head to the pass, and from there, ascend southeast to the next pass. This would be a good place to stray from the main route to look over the rim of the gorge – but be careful, as the winds get mighty powerful up here. From the second pass, descend to the Berber village of Tizgui, where you can stroll through the *palmeraies* back to the gorge.

Erfoud (Dh30, three daily), and Zagora (Dh70). Anything westbound will drop you in Boumalne du Dadès (Dh15). *Grands taxis* run throughout the day to Todra Gorge (Dh7).

Merzouga & the Dunes

Morocco's only genuine Saharan erg is **Erg Chebbi**, an impressive, drifting chain of sand dunes that can reach 160m and seems to have escaped from the much larger dune field across the nearby border in Algeria. The erg is a magical landscape that deserves much more than the sunrise or sunset glimpse many visitors give it. The dunes are a scene of constant change and fascination as sunlight transforms them from pink to gold to red. The largest dunes are near the villages of Merzouga and Hassi Labied. At night, you only have to walk a little way into the sand, away from the light, to appreciate the immense clarity of the desert sky and the brilliance of its stars.

Merzouga, some 50km south of Erfoud is a tiny village, but does have *téléboutiques,* general stores, a mechanic and, of course, a couple of carpet shops. It also has an internet place, **Cyber Shop Le Amis** (per hr Dh5; ☺9am-10pm), and is the focus of fast-expanding tourism in the area. As a result, it is acquiring a reputation for some of the worst hassle in Morocco.

Most hotels offer excursions into the dunes, ranging from Dh80 to Dh250 for two-hour sunrise or sunset camel treks. Overnight trips usually include a bed in a Berber tent, dinner and breakfast, and range from Dh300 to Dh650 per person. Outings in a 4WD are more expensive: up to Dh1200 per day for a car taking up to five passengers.

🛏 Sleeping & Eating

Purists lament the encroachment, but a string of hotels now flanks the western side of Erg Chebbi from the village of Merzouga, north past the oasis village of Hassi Labied. On the upside, many of these places have spectacular dune views from rooms and terraces. Most offer half-board options, and often you can sleep on a terrace mattress or in a Berber tent for Dh30 to Dh50 per person.

Auberge Camping Sahara GUEST HOUSE $
(☎0535 577039; www.aubergesahara.com; d per person half-board Dh200-300, terrace camping per person Dh25; P❋❋) Basic but spotless rooms and Turkish toilets in a friendly Tuareg-run place backing right onto the dunes at the southernmost end of the village. Auberge staff organise excursions and will even help you buy your complete Tuareg outfit in the market.

Kasbah Sable d'Or GUEST HOUSE $
(Chez Isabelle & Rachid; ☎0535 577859; http://kasbah-sable-dor.com; half-board per person with/without bathroom Dh180/150) When the goat bleats welcome, you know you've come to the right place. There are just four rooms here, with hand-painted murals on the doors, fans instead of air-con, and tasty home-cooked dinners in the family salon. You can also camp in a Bedouin tent (Dh25), have a private overnight camel, or get up early to watch the sunrise atop a camel.

Dar el Janoub RESORT $$$
(☎/fax 0535 577852; www.dareljanoub.com; d standard/large/ste per person Dh580/725/800; ❋❋) Neighbouring hotels take the *1001 Arabian Nights* approach to hospitality, but Dar el Janoub is an Amazigh haiku. That splashy graphic pattern on the lobby wall is the Berber alphabet, but otherwise, the place is all clean lines and cool colours, because when you're facing the dunes, why compete? Rates are on the high end, and you'll pay extra for dune-facing rooms – but for the price you're getting half-board, a pool and pure poetry.

MERZOUGA
Most accommodation is south of the village centre, close to the dunes.

Chez Julia GUEST HOUSE **$**

(☏0535 573182; Merzouga centre; s/d/tr/q Dh160/400/600/800) Pure charm in the heart of Merzouga: nine simply furnished rooms in sun-washed colours with soft straw-textured pisé walls, lovingly worn antique mantelpieces, and shiny white-tiled shared bathrooms, plus a furnished family apartment (Dh400 to Dh800) across the street. Ask about birdwatching tours, Saharan music concerts and geology expeditions to seek fossils and *roses des sables,* desert-sand crystals.

Riad Totmaroc GUEST HOUSE **$$**

(☏0670 624136; www.totmaroc.com; Merzouga; per person half-board Dh330; [P]❉) A mod kasbah that provides instant relief from the white-hot desert with five guestrooms in bold, eye-soothing shades of blue and green, shady patios looking right onto the dunes, an open kitchen turning out solid meals, and dromedary overnights with an experienced official local tour leader.

❶ Getting There & Away

Thankfully, the sealed road now continues all the way to Merzouga. Most hotels are at least a kilometre off the road at the base of the dunes, but all are accessible by car. The *pistes* (sandy tracks) can be rough and there is a possibility, albeit remote, of getting stuck in sand, so make sure you have plenty of water for emergencies and a mobile phone. Without your own transport, you'll have to rely on *grands taxis* or on the minivans that run from Merzouga to the transport junction towns of Rissani and Erfoud and back.

UNDERSTAND MOROCCO

History

The Berbers & Romans

Morocco's first-known inhabitants were Near Eastern nomads who may have been distant cousins of the ancient Egyptians. Phoenicians appear to have arrived around 800 BC. When the Romans arrived in the 4th century BC, they called the expanse of Morocco and western Algeria 'Mauretania' and the indigenous people 'Berbers', meaning 'barbarians'.

In the 1st century AD, the Romans built up Volubilis into a city of 20,000 mostly Berber people, but, fed up with the persistently unruly locals, the Roman emperor Caligula declared the end of Berber autonomy in North Africa in 40 AD. But Berbers in the Rif and the Atlas ultimately succeeded through a campaign of near-constant rebellion. As Rome slipped into decline, the Berbers harried and hassled any army that dared to invade to the point where the Berbers were free to do as they pleased.

The Islamic Dynasties

In the second half of the 7th century, the soldiers of the Prophet Mohammed set forth from the Arabian Peninsula and overwhelmed the peoples of North Africa. Within a century, nearly all Berber tribes had embraced Islam, although, true to form, local tribes developed their own brand of Islamic Shi'ism, which sparked rebellion against the eastern Arabs.

By 829, local elites had established an Idrissid state with its capital at Fez, dominating all of Morocco. Thus commenced a cycle of rising and falling Islamic dynasties, which included the Almoravids (1062–1147), who built their capital at Marrakesh; the Almohads (1147-1269), famous for building the Koutoubia Mosque; the Merenids (1269–1465), known for their exquisite mosques and *medersas* (Islamic schools), especially in Fez; the Saadians (1524–1659), responsible for the Palais el-Badi in Marrakesh; and the Alawites (1659–present), who left their greatest monuments in Meknès.

France took control in 1912, making its capital at Rabat and handing Spain a token zone in the north. Opposition from Berber mountain tribes was officially crushed, but continued to simmer away and moved into political channels with the development of the Istiqlal (independence) party.

Morocco since Independence

Under increasing pressure from Moroccans and the Allies, France allowed Mohammed V to return from exile in 1955, and Morocco successfully negotiated its independence from France and Spain in 1956.

When Mohammed V died suddenly of heart failure in 1961, King Hassan II became the leader of the new nation. Hassan II consolidated power by crackdowns on dissent and suspending parliament for a decade. In 1973 the phosphate industry started to boom. Morocco staked its claim to neighbouring Spanish Sahara and its lucrative phosphate reserves with the 350,000-strong

Green March into the territory in 1975, settling the area with Moroccans while greatly unsettling indigenous Sahrawi people agitating for self-determination.

Such grand and patriotic flourishes notwithstanding, the growing gap between the rich and the poor ensured that dissent remained widespread across a broad cross-section of Moroccan society.

Morocco Today

Hassan II died in 1999 and Morocco held its breath. In his first public statement as king, Mohammed VI vowed to right the wrongs of the era known to Moroccans as 'the Black Years'. Today, Morocco's human rights record is arguably the cleanest in Africa and the Middle East, though still not exactly spotless – repressive measures were revived after 9/11 and the 2003 Casablanca bombings. But the commission has nonetheless helped cement human rights advances by awarding reparations to more than 9000 victims of the Black Years.

Mohammed VI has overseen small but real reformist steps, including elections, the introduction of Berber languages in some state schools, and the much-anticipated Mudawanna, a legal code protecting women's rights to divorce and custody. The king has also forged closer ties with Europe and overseen the current tourism boom. The still-disputed territory of Western Sahara continues to be a block on regional political ties.

People

People of Arab-Berber descent make up almost the entire Moroccan population, which is increasingly urbanised, and young to boot – 55% are under 25 years.

Moroccans are inherently sociable and hospitable people. Away from the tourist scrum, a Moroccan proverb tells the story – 'A guest is a gift from Allah'. The public domain may belong to men, but they're just as likely to invite you home to meet the family. If this happens, consider yourself truly privileged but remember: remove your shoes before stepping on the carpet; keep your (ritually unclean) left hand firmly out of the communal dish but feel free to slurp your tea and belch your appreciation loudly.

Morocco is a Muslim country. Fundamentalism is mostly discouraged but remains a presence, especially among the urban poor who have enjoyed none of the benefits of

economic growth. That said, the majority of Muslims do not favour such developments and the popularity of fundamentalism is not as great as Westerners imagine.

Emigration to France, Israel and the US has reduced Morocco's once robust Jewish community to about 7000 from a high of around 300,000 in 1948.

Arts

Architecture

Moroccan religious buildings are adorned with hand-carved detailing, gilded accents, chiselled mosaics and an array of other decorative flourishes. A mosque consists of a courtyard, an arcaded portico and a main prayer hall facing Mecca. Great examples include the 9th-century Kairaouine Mosque in Fez and the colossal Hassan II Mosque in Casablanca. While all but the latter are closed to non-Muslims, the *medersas* (Islamic colleges) that bejewel major Moroccan cities are open for visits.

Although religious architecture dominates, Casablanca in particular boasts local architectural features grafted onto white-washed European art deco edifices in a distinctive crossroads style called mauresque.

The street facade of the Moroccan *riads* (traditional courtyard houses; also called *dars*) usually conceals an inner courtyard that allows light to penetrate during the day and cool air to settle at night. Many guest houses occupy beautifully renovated traditional *riads*.

Music

The most renowned Berber folk group is the Master Musicians of Jajouka, who famously inspired the Rolling Stones and collaborated with them on some truly experimental fusion. Lately the big names are women's, namely the all-female group B'net Marrakech and the bold Najat Aatabou, who sings protest songs in Berber against restrictive traditional roles.

Joyously bluesy with a rhythm you can't refuse, Gnaoua music, which began among freed slaves in Marrakesh and Essaouira, may send you into a trance – and that's just what it's meant to do. To sample the best in Gnaoua, head to Essaouira on the third weekend in June for the Gnaoua & World Music Festival.

Rai, originally from Algeria, is one of the strongest influences on Moroccan contemporary music, incorporating elements of jazz, hip hop and rap.

Environment

Morocco's three ecological zones – coast, mountain and desert – host more than 40 different ecosystems and provide habitat for many endemic species, including the iconic and sociable Barbary macaque (also known as the Barbary ape). Unfortunately, pressure from sprawling urban areas and the encroachment of industrialisation in Morocco's wilderness means that 18 mammal and a dozen bird species are considered endangered.

Pollution, desertification, overgrazing and deforestation are the major environmental issues facing the Moroccan government. The draining of coastal wetlands – which provide important habitats for endangered species – also continues apace to address the rising demand and falling supply of water for irrigation, a problem that becomes increasingly acute with water-hungry tourist developments.

Food & Drink

Influenced by Berber, Arabic and Mediterranean traditions, Moroccan cuisine features a sublime combination of spices and fresh produce.

Al fresco cafes and kiosks put a local twist on a continental breakfast with Moroccan pancakes and doughnuts, French pastries, coffee and mint tea. Follow your nose into the souqs, where you'll find tangy olives and local *jiben* (fresh goat's or cow's milk cheeses) to be devoured with fresh *khoobz* (Moroccan-style flat bread baked in a wood-fired oven).

Lunch is traditionally the biggest meal of the day in Morocco. The most typical Moroccan dish is tajine, a meat and vegetable stew cooked slowly in an earthenware dish. Couscous, fluffy steamed semolina served with tender meat and vegetables, is another staple, while *harira* is a thick soup made from lamb stock, lentils, chickpeas, onions, tomatoes, fresh herbs and spices. *B'stilla,* a speciality of Fez, includes poultry (chicken or pigeon), almonds, cinnamon, saffron and sugar, encased in layers of fine pastry.

Vegetarians shouldn't have too many problems – fresh fruit and vegetables are widely available, as are lentils and chickpeas. Salads are ubiquitous in Morocco, particularly the traditional *salade marocaine* made from diced green peppers, tomatoes and red onion. Ask for your couscous or your tajine *sans viande* (without meat).

Cafe culture thrives. Everyone drinks strong coffee or mint tea, the legendary 'Moroccan whisky', made with Chinese gunpowder tea, fresh mint and copious sugar. It's not advisable to drink tap water in Morocco but fruit juices, especially freshly squeezed orange juice, are the country's greatest bargain. Beer is easy to find in the villes nouvelles; Flag is the most common brand.

Smoking is something of a national pastime for Moroccan men, although most restaurants tend to be reasonably smoke-free.

SURVIVAL GUIDE

Directory A-Z

Accommodation

Auberges de jeunesses (youth hostels) operate in Casablanca, Chefchaouen, Fez, Meknès, Rabat and Tangier. Hotels vary dramatically, ranging from dingy dives to gorgeous guest houses and fancy five-stars (the latter mostly in larger cities). Cities that see many tourists also offer wonderful accommodation in the style of a *riad*.

Advance reservations are highly recommended for all places listed in this chapter, especially in summer.

PRICE RANGES

Places to stay are listed by preference and include a private bathroom unless otherwise stated. Prices given are for high season (June to September) and include tax; always check the price you are quoted is TTC (all taxes included).

$	Up to Dh400
$$	Dh400 to Dh800
$$$	More than Dh800

Pricier towns and cities including Casablanca, Essaouira, Fez, Marrakesh, Rabat and Tangier are exceptions. For these places, price ranges are:

$	Up to Dh600
$$	Dh600 to Dh1200
$$$	More than Dh1200

Activities

CAMEL TREKS & DESERT SAFARIS

Exploring the Moroccan Sahara by camel is one of the country's signature activities and one of the most rewarding wilderness experiences, whether done on an overnight excursion or a two-week trek. The most evocative stretches of Saharan sand include the Drâa Valley, especially the Tinfou Dunes and Erg Chigaga, and the dunes of Erg Chebbi near Merzouga.

Autumn (September to October) and winter (November to early March) are the only seasons worth considering. Prices hover around Dh350 to Dh450 per person per day but vary depending on the number of people, the length of the trek and your negotiating skills.

HAMMAMS

Visiting a *hammam* is a ritual at the centre of Moroccan society and a practical solution for those who don't have hot water at home (or in their hotel). Every town has at least one public *hammam*, and the big cities have fancy spas – both are deep-cleaning and totally relaxing. A visit to a standard *hammam* usually costs Dh20, extra for a massage.

HIKING

Morocco's mountains offer a variety of year-round hiking possibilities. It's relatively straightforward to arrange guides, porters and mules for a more independent adventure. North Africa's highest peak, Jebel Toubkal (4167m), in the High Atlas, attracts the lion's share of visitors, but great possibilities exist throughout the country, including in the Rif Mountains around Chefchaouen. The Dadès and Todra Gorges also offer good hiking opportunities. Spring and autumn are the best seasons for hiking.

SURFING & WINDSURFING

Morocco has some great surfing spots. Essaouira is a centre for windsurfers; see p657 for more information.

Business Hours

Banks 8.30am-6.30pm Mon-Fri

Post offices 8.30am-4.30pm Mon-Fri

Government offices 8.30am-6.30pm Mon-Fri

Restaurants noon-3pm & 7-10pm

Bars 4pm-late

Shops 9am-12.30pm & 2.30-8pm Mon-Sat (often closed longer at midday for prayer)

Children

Moroccans entertain and travel as families, making Morocco a very child-friendly country. Hotels can arrange extra beds in rooms for a small additional charge, and children are welcomed in restaurants.

Embassies & Consulates

Most embassies and diplomatic representation are in Rabat, and open from about 9am until noon, Monday to Friday. The **Moroccan Ministry of Foreign Affairs and Cooperation** (www.maec.gov.ma) has a list of embassies and consulates in Morocco.

EMBASSIES IN RABAT

Algeria (☑0537 76 54 74; www.mae.dz/ma_fr, in French; 46-48 Ave Tariq ibn Zayid) Also has a consulate-general in Casablanca and consulate in Oujda.

Canada (☑0537 68 74 00; www.rabat.gc.ca; 13 Rue Jaafar as-Sadiq, Agdal)

France (☑0537 68 97 00; www.ambafrance-ma.org; 3 Rue Sahnoun, Agdal) Also has consulates in Agadir, Casablanca, Fez, Marrakesh, Rabat and Tangier.

Germany (☑0537 21 86 00; www.rabat.diplo.de, in German & French; 7 Rue Madnine) Also has a consulate in Rabat and honorary consulates in Agadir and Casablanca.

Mauritania (☎0537 65 66 78; www.mauri tania.mr/fr, in French; 6 Rue Thami Lamdaouar, Soussi)

Netherlands (☎0537 21 96 00; www.ambas sadepaysbasrabat.org, in Dutch & French; 40 Rue de Tunis) Also has a consulate-general in Casablanca.

Spain (☎0537 63 39 00; www.maec.es/en; Rue Ain Khalouiya, Route des Zaers, km5300 Soussi) Also has consulates-general in Agadir, Casablanca, Larache, Nador, Rabat, Tangier and Tetouan.

UK (☎0537 63 33 33; http://ukinmorocco.fco. gov.uk/en; 28 Ave SAR Sidi Mohammed, Soussi) Also has honorary consulates in Agadir, Marrakesh and Tangier.

USA (☎0537 76 22 65; http://rabat.us embassy. gov; 2 Ave de Mohammed El Fassi) Also has a consulate-general in Casablanca.

Food

Eating reviews in this book are ordered by preference. Price ranges are based on the cost of an evening main course, excluding drinks and tips:

$ Up to Dh70

$$ Dh70 to Dh150

$$$ More than Dh150

In a midrange restaurant, a set meal including wine would typically cost Dh250–400; in a top-end restaurant, more than Dh400.

Gay & Lesbian Travellers

Homosexual acts (including kissing) are officially illegal – in theory you can go to jail and/or be fined. In most places, discretion is the key and public displays of affection should be avoided (aggression towards gay male travellers is not unheard of) – this advice applies equally to homosexual and heterosexual couples as a means of showing sensitivity to local feelings.

Some towns are certainly more gay-friendly than others, especially Marrakesh and Tangier. That said, gay travellers generally follow the same itineraries as everyone else and although 'gay' bars can be found here and there, Moroccan nightlife tends to include something for everybody.

Lesbians shouldn't encounter any problems, though it's commonly believed by Moroccans that there are no lesbians in their country. Announcing that you're gay probably won't make would-be Romeos magically

disappear. For Moroccan men it may simply confirm their belief that Western men don't measure up in the sexual department.

It is also worth bearing in mind that the pressures of poverty mean than many young men will consider having sex for money or gifts. Needless to say, exploitative relationships form an unpleasant but real dimension of the Moroccan gay scene.

Useful websites include:

Behind the Mask (www.mask.org.za) Detailed information and related news stories for every African country.

Gay & Lesbian Arab Society (www.glas. org) Resources on homosexuality in the Arab world.

Communauté de Femmes Lesbiennes, Bi et Trans du Maroc (www.mennawfena.net, in French) For lesbian, bisexual and transsexual women in Morocco.

Internet Access

Internet access is widely available, efficient and cheap (Dh4 to Dh10 per hour) in internet cafes, usually with pretty impressive connection speeds. One irritant for travellers is the widespread use of French or Arabic (non-qwerty) keyboards.

Most top-end and many midrange hotels offer wi-fi (📶), and it's more or less standard in most *riads* and *maisons d'hôtes*.

Language Courses

There are courses in Arabic – both modern standard and Moroccan – in most major towns in Morocco, with a high concentration in Fez, Rabat and Casablanca – where long- and short-term programs are offered.

Money

The Moroccan currency is the dirham (Dh), which is divided into 100 centimes. It's forbidden to take dirhams out of the country. The Spanish enclaves of Ceuta and Melilla use the euro.

ATMs *(guichets automatiques)* are widespread. Major credit cards are widely accepted in the main tourist centres. Travellers cheques aren't recommended, nor are Australian, Canadian and New Zealand dollars cash.

Tipping and bargaining are integral parts of Moroccan life. Practically any service can warrant a tip, and a few dirham for a service willingly rendered can make your life a lot easier. Tipping between 5% and 10% of a restaurant bill is appropriate.

Post

Post offices are distinguished by the 'PTT' sign or the 'La Poste' logo. You can sometimes buy stamps at *tabacs,* small tobacco and newspaper kiosks.

The postal system is fairly reliable, but not terribly fast. It takes about a week for letters to get to their European destinations, and two weeks or so to get to Australia and North America.

The parcel office, indicated by the sign '*colis postaux*', is generally in a separate part of the post office building. Take your parcel unwrapped for customs inspection.

Public Holidays

All banks, post offices and most shops are shut on the main public holidays:

New Year's Day 1 January

Independence Manifesto 11 January

Labour Day 1 May

Feast of the Throne 30 July

Allegiance of Oued-Eddahab 14 August

Anniversary of the King's and People's Revolution 20 August

Young People's Day 21 August

Anniversary of the Green March 6 November

Independence Day 18 November

In addition to secular holidays there are many national and local Islamic holidays and festivals, all tied to the lunar calendar:

Eid al-Adha Marks the end of the Islamic year. Most things shut down for four or five days.

Eid al-Fitr Held at the end of the month-long dawn to dusk Ramadan fast, which is observed by most Muslims. The festivities last four or five days, during which Morocco grinds to a halt.

Moulid an-Nabi (Mouloud) Celebrates the birthday of the Prophet Mohammed.

Safe Travel

Morocco's era as a hippy paradise is long past. Plenty of *kif* (marijuana) is grown in the Rif Mountains, but drug busts are common and Morocco isn't a good place to investigate prison conditions.

The *brigade touristique* was set up in the principal tourist centres to clamp down on Morocco's notorious *faux guides* and hustlers. Anyone convicted of operating as an unofficial guide faces jail time and/or a huge fine. This has reduced but not eliminated the problem of *faux guides*. You'll still find plenty of these touts hanging around the entrances to medinas and train stations (and even on trains approaching Fez and Marrakesh), and at Tangier port. Remember that their main interest is the commission gained from certain hotels or on articles sold to you in the souqs.

If possible, avoid walking alone at night in the medinas of the big cities. Knife-point muggings aren't unknown.

There is a small risk of terrorism in Morocco. In April 2011, a bomb exploded at Djemaa el-Fna square in Marrakesh, killing several tourists. Reforms initiated by the king have meant that Morocco had (at the time of going to press) avoided the regional upheavals of the 'Arab Spring'.

Toilets

Outside midrange and top-end hotels and restaurants, toilets are mostly of the squat variety, feature a tap, hose or container of water for sluicing – the idea being to wash yourself (with your left hand) after going to the toilet.

There's often no toilet paper (papier hygiénique) so keep a supply with you. Throw the paper in the bin provided.

HOLIDAYS IN MOROCCO

HOLIDAY	2011	2012	2013	2014
Moulid an-Nabi	16 Feb	5 Feb	25 Jan	4 Jan
Ramadan begins	1 Aug	21 Jul	10 Jul	29 Jun
Eid al-Fitr	30 Aug	19 Aug	8 Aug	28 Jul
Eid al-Adha	6 Nov	26 Oct	15 Oct	4 Oct
New Year begins (year)	27 Nov (1433)	16 Nov (1434)	5 Nov (1435)	25 Oct (1436)

Public toilets are rare outside the major cities. Tip the attendant.

Tourist Information

Cities and larger towns have tourist offices, which are normally repositories of brochures manned by uninformed staff. Often the receptionist in your hotel or another local will be more helpful than such bureaus. The best tourist offices are found in smaller destinations that are trying to promote themselves. **L'Office National Marocain du Tourisme** (ONMT; www.visitmorocco.com, www.ruraltourism.ma) runs most tourist offices.

Time

Standard Moroccan time is on GMT/UTC.

Clocks used to move forward one hour for daylight saving. Because the period ends at the beginning of Ramadan, which currently falls during the summer, it's not planned to take place in the coming years.

Time is something that most Moroccans seem to have plenty of; they're not in nearly as much of a hurry to get things done as most Westerners. Learn to go with the flow a little.

Visas

Most visitors to Morocco do not require a visa and are allowed to remain in the country for 90 days on entry. Your passport must be valid for at least six months beyond your date of entry.

Nationals of Israel and many sub-Saharan African countries (including South Africa) must apply in advance for a three-month visa (single/double entry about US$30/50).

Visa extensions are technically possible by applying at the nearest police headquarters (Préfecture de Police) for an extension. In reality, the simplest thing to do is to leave (eg travel to the Spanish enclaves of Ceuta and Melilla) and come back a few days later, ideally re-entering by a different route. The Spanish enclaves have the same visa requirements as mainland Spain.

Women Travellers

Prior to marriage, Moroccan men have little opportunity to meet and get to know women, which is a major reason why Western women receive so much attention. Foreign women are seen as independent and available.

The constant attention is impossible to shake off, no matter what tactic is employed. Be wary but not paranoid – the low-level harassment rarely goes any further.

One benefit of travelling as a woman in Morocco is that, unlike male travellers, you'll have opportunities to meet local women.

Getting There & Away

Air

Morocco's two main international entry points are Mohammed V International Airport, 30km southeast of Casablanca, and Marrakesh's Ménara airport. Other international airports are in Fez, Tangier and Agadir. For information about Moroccan airports and their facilities, visit the website of **Office National des Aéroports** (www.onda.ma).

Royal Air Maroc (RAM; www.royalairmaroc.com) is Morocco's national carrier, with increasing competition from the budget airlines.

Air Arabia (www.airarabia.com)

Air Berlin (www.airberlin.com)

Air Europa (www.air-europa.com)

Air France (www.airfrance.com)

Alitalia (www.alitalia.com)

British Airways (www.ba.com)

easyJet (www.easyjet.com)

Emirates (www.emirates.com)

Iberia (www.iberia.com)

Jet4You (www.jet4you.com)

KLM-Royal Dutch Airlines (www.klm.com)

Lufthansa (www.lufthansa.com)

Ryanair (www.ryanair.com)

Thomson Aiways (http://flights.thomson.co.uk)

Bus

The Moroccan bus company CTM operates buses from Casablanca and most main cities to European destinations as part of the Europe-wide coach consortium **Eurolines** (www.eurolines.com). Another Moroccan bus service with particularly good links to Spanish networks is **Tramesa** (http://perso.menara.ma/tramesa07, in French).

Sea

Regular ferries run to Europe from several ports along Morocco's Mediterranean coast, of which Tangier is the most popular. Algeciras–Tangier ferries (90 minutes) are hourly in summer. Children usually travel half-price. **Direct Ferries** (www.directferries.com) sells tickets for most of the following:

Acciona Transmediterranea, Euroferrys and Ferrimaroc (www.trasmediterranea.es) Almería–Melilla, Almería–Nador, Algeciras–Ceuta, Algeciras–Tangier, Barcelona–Tangier, Málaga–Melilla

Baleària (www.balearia.com) Algeciras–Ceuta, Algeciras–Tangier

Comanav Algeciras–Tangier, Genoa–Tangier, Sète–Nador, Sète–Tangier

Comarit (www.comarit.es, in Spanish) Algeciras–Tangier, Sète–Tangier, Tarifa–Tanger

Getting Around

Air

National carrier **Royal Air Maroc** (RAM; ☏0890 00 08 00; www.royalairmaroc.com) is the main domestic airline, flying from Casablanca to Tangier, Fez, Er-Rachidia, Marrakesh, Essaouira, Agadir and others destinations. For most routes, flying is an expensive and inconvenient option compared to road or rail.

Bus

A dense network of buses operates throughout Morocco, with many private companies competing for business alongside the comfortable and modern coaches of the main national carrier **CTM** (☏0522 45 80 80, in Casablanca).

The **ONCF** (www.oncf.ma, in French) train company runs buses through Supratours to widen its train network, for example running connections from Marrakesh to Essaouira. Morocco's other bus companies are all privately owned and only operate regionally. It's best to book ahead for CTM and Supratours buses, which are slightly more expensive than those of other companies.

Car & Motorcycle

Taking your own vehicle to Morocco is straightforward. In addition to a vehicle registration document and an International Driving Permit (although many foreign licences, including US and EU ones, are also acceptable), a Green Card is required from the car's insurer. Not all insurers cover Morocco.

Renting a car in Morocco isn't cheap, with prices starting at Dh3000 per day for a basic car. International hire companies are well represented; booking in advance online can secure the best deals.

In Morocco you drive on the right-hand side of the road. On a roundabout, give way to traffic entering from the right.

Taxi

Cities and bigger towns have local *petits taxis*, which are a different colour in every city. They are licensed to carry up to three passengers and are usually metered. Fares increase by 50% after 8pm.

The old Mercedes vehicles you'll see belting along roads and gathered in great flocks near bus stations are *grands taxis*. They link towns to their nearest neighbours. *Grands taxis*, take six passengers and leave when full.

Train

Morocco's excellent train network is run by ONCF (www.oncf.ma, in French). There are two lines that carry passengers: from Tangier in the north down to Marrakesh; and from Oujda in the northeast, also to Marrakesh, joining with the Tangier line at Sidi Kacem.

Trains are comfortable, fast and generally preferable to buses. Seats in 2nd-class are more than adequate on any journey. Couchettes are available on the overnight trains between Marrakesh and Tangier. Children aged under four travel free. Those aged between four and 12 years get a reduction of 10% to 50%, depending on the service.

Rail Pass This is available for seven/15/30 days (Dh600/1170/2100 second class, Dh900/1600/3150 first class). Pass prices drop for travellers aged under 26, and again for those under 12.

Carte Fidelité (Dh149) This is for those aged over 26 and gives you 50% reductions on eight return or 16 one-way journeys in a 12-month period.

Portugal

Best Places to Eat

» 100 Maneiras (p706)
» Fortaleza do Guincho (p714)
» Café Ingles (p718)
» A Grade (p731)
» Taberna do Valentim (p734)

Best Places to Stay

» Solar dos Mouros (p701)
» Pensão Residencial Sintra (p713)
» Palace Hotel do Buçaco (p727)
» Guest House Douro (p730)
» Hotel de Peneda (p735)

Why Go?

Medieval castles, frozen-in-time villages, captivating cities and golden-sand beaches: the Portugal experience can mean many things. History, great food and wine, idyllic scenery and blazing nightlife are just the beginning...

Portugal's capital, Lisbon, and its northern rival, Porto, are gems among the urban streetscapes of Europe. Both are magical places for the wanderer, with picturesque views over the river, rattling trams and atmospheric lanes that hide boutiques and old-school record shops, stylish lounges and a vibrant mix of restaurants, fado clubs and open-air cafes.

Outside the cities, Portugal's landscape unfolds in all its variegated beauty. Here you can stay overnight in converted hilltop fortresses fronting age-old vineyards, hike amid granite peaks or explore historic villages of the little-visited hinterland. More than 800km of coast offers more outdoor enticements. You can gaze out over dramatic end-of-the-world cliffs, surf stellar breaks off dune-covered beaches or laze peacefully on sandy islands fronting calm blue seas.

When to Go

Lisbon

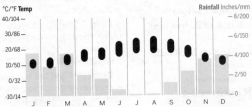

Apr & May
Sunny days and wildflowers set the stage for hiking and outdoor activities.

Jun–Aug
Lovely and lively, with a packed festival calendar and steamy beach days.

Late Sep & Oct
Crisp mornings and sunny days; prices dip, crowds disperse.

Fast Facts

» **Area** 91,470 sq km

» **Population** 10.8 million

» **Capital** Lisbon

» **Telephone** country code ☑351; international access code ☑00

» **Emergency** ☑112

Exchange Rates

Australia	A$1	€0.74
Canada	C$1	€0.74
Japan	¥100	€0.87
New Zealand	NZ$1	€0.56
UK	UK£1	€1.16
USA	US$1	€0.67

Set Your Budget

» **Budget hotel room** €40

» **Two-course dinner** €10–16

» **Museum entrance** €4–6

» **Bottle of Sagres beer** €2–3

» **Lisbon metro ticket** €0.80

Resources

» **Lonely Planet** (www.lonelyplanet.com/portugal/lisbon)

» **Portugal Tourism** (www.visitportugal.com) Official tourism site

Connections

Travelling overland from Portugal entails a trip through Spain. Good places to cross the (invisible) border include ferry crossing from Vila Real de Santo António in The Algarve, with onward connections to Seville. There are also links from Elvas (going across to Badajoz) and rail links from Valença do Minho in the north (heading up to Santiago de Compostela in Galicia). See p739 for more details.

ITINERARIES

One Week

Devote three days to Lisbon, including a night of fado in the Alfama, bar-hopping in Bairro Alto and Unesco-gazing and pastry-eating in Belém. Spend a day taking in the wooded wonderland of Sintra, before continuing to Porto, gateway to the magical wine-growing region of the Douro valley. Wind up your week in the picturesque lanes of Coimbra, Portugal's own Cambridge.

Two Weeks

On week two, stroll the historic lanes of Évora and visit the nearby megaliths. Take in magical hilltop castle towns like Monsaraz and scenic Castelo de Vide before hitting The Algarve. Travel along the coast, visiting the pretty beach-surrounded towns of Tavira, Faro, Lagos and Sagres. End the grand tour with a bang in Lisbon.

Essential Food & Drink

» **Seafood** Char-grilled *lulas* (squid), *polvo* (octopus) or *sardinhas* (sardines). Other treats: *cataplana* (seafood and sausage cooked in a copper pot), *caldeirada* (hearty fish stew) and *açorda de mariscos* (bread stew with shrimp).

» **Cod for all seasons** Portuguese have dozens of ways to prepare *bacalhau* (salted cod). Try *bacalhau a brás* (grated cod fried with potatoes and eggs), *bacalhau espiritual* (cod soufflé) or *bacalhau com natas* (baked cod with cream and grated cheese).

» **Field & fowl** *Porco preto* (sweet 'black' pork), *leitão* (roast suckling pig), *alheira* (bread and meat sausage – formerly Kosher), *cabrito assado* (roast kid) and *arroz de pato* (duck risotto).

» **Drink** Port and red wines from the Douro valley, *alvarinho* and *vinho verde* (crisp, semi-sparkling wine) from the Minho and great, little-known reds from the Alentejo and the Beiras (particularly the Dão region).

» **Pastries** The *pastel de nata* (custard tart) is legendary, especially in Belém. Other delicacies: *travesseiros* (almond and egg pastries) and *queijadas* (mini-cheese pastries).

Portugal Highlights

① Follow the sound of fado spilling from the lamplit lanes of the **Alfama** (p696), an enchanting old-world neighbourhood in the heart of Lisbon

② Take in the laid-back charms of **Tavira** (p716), before hitting some of The Algarve's prettiest beaches

③ Catch live music in a backstreet bar in **Coimbra** (p725), a festive university town with a stunning medieval centre

④ Explore the wooded hills of **Sintra** (p712), studded with fairy-tale-like palaces, villas and gardens

⑤ Conquer the trails of the ruggedly scenic **Parque Nacional da Peneda-Gerês** (p735)

⑥ Enjoy heady beach days in **Lagos** (p717), a surf-loving town with a vibrant drinking and dining scene

⑦ Explore the Unesco World Heritage–listed centre of **Porto** (p727), sampling velvety ports at riverside wine lodges

LISBON

POP 580,000

Spread across steep hillsides that overlook the Rio Tejo, Lisbon has captivated visitors for centuries. Windswept vistas at breathtaking heights reveal the city in all its beauty: Roman and Moorish ruins, white-domed cathedrals and grand plazas lined with sun-drenched cafes. The real delight of discovery, though, is delving into the narrow cobblestone lanes.

As bright-yellow trams clatter through curvy tree-lined streets, Lisboetas (residents of Lisbon) stroll through lamplit old quarters, much as they've done for centuries. Village-life gossip is exchanged over fresh bread and wine at tiny patio restaurants as fado singers perform in the background. In other parts of town, Lisbon reveals her youthful alter ego at stylish dining rooms and lounges, late-night street parties, riverside nightspots and boutiques selling all things classic and cutting-edge.

Just outside Lisbon, there's more to explore: enchanting woodlands, gorgeous beaches and seaside villages – all ripe for discovery.

⊙ Sights

At the riverfront is the grand Praça do Comércio. Behind it march the pedestrian-filled streets of Baixa (lower) district, up to Praça da Figueira and Praça Dom Pedro IV (aka Rossio). From Baixa it's a steep climb west, through swanky shopping district Chiado, into the narrow streets of nightlife haven Bairro Alto. Eastward from Baixa it's another climb to Castelo de São Jorge and the labyrinthine Alfama district around it. The World Heritage sites of Belém lie further west along the river – an easy tram-ride from Praça do Comércio.

BAIXA & ALFAMA

Alfama is Lisbon's Moorish time capsule: a medina-like district of tangled alleys, hidden

LISBOA CARD

If you're planning on doing a lot of sightseeing, this **discount card** represents excellent value. It offers free entry to key museums and attractions, plus unlimited use of public transport. The 24-/48-/72hr versions cost €17/27/34; it's available at tourist offices.

CYCLING THE TEJO

A new **cycling/jogging path** courses along the Tejo for nearly 7km, between Cais do Sodré and Belém. Complete with artful touches – including the poetry of Pessoa printed along parts of it – the path traverses a rapidly changing landscape, taking in ageing warehouses that are being converted into open-air cafes, restaurants and nightspots.

A handy place to rent bikes is a short stroll from Cais do Sodré: **Bike Iberia** (Map p702; www.bikeiberia.com; Largo Corpo Santo 5).

---

palm-shaded squares and narrow terracotta-roofed houses that tumble down to the glittering Tejo. The terrace at **Largo das Portas do Sol** (Map p698) provides a splendid view over the neighbourhood.

Elevador de Santa Justa   ELEVATOR
(Map p702; cnr Rua de Santa Justa & Largo do Carmo; admission €2.80; ⊗7am-11pm) Lisbon's only vertical street lift, this lanky neo-Gothic marvel provides sweeping views over the city's skyline. From the top, it's a short stroll to the fascinating ruins of **Convento do Carmo**, mostly destroyed in an earthquake in 1755.

Castelo de São Jorge   CASTLE RUINS
(Map p702; admission €7; ⊗9am-9pm) Dating from Visigothic times, St George's Castle sits high above the city with stunning views of the city and river. Inside the Ulysses Tower, a **camera obscura** offers a unique 360-degree angle on Lisbon, with demos every half-hour. If you'd rather not walk, take scenic tram 28 from Largo Martim Moniz.

Museu do Fado   MUSEUM
(Largo do Chafariz de Dentro; admission €3; ⊗10am-6pm Tue-Sun) This engaging museum provides vibrant audiovisual coverage of the history of fado from its working-class roots to international stardom.

BELÉM

This quarter, 6km west of Rossio, reflects Portugal's golden age and is home to several iconic sights. In addition to heritage architecture, Belém spreads some of the country's best *pastéis de nata* (custard tarts; see p707).

To reach Belém, hop aboard tram 15 from Praça da Figueira or Praça do Comércio.

Mosteiro dos Jerónimos MONASTERY

(Map p698; Praça do Império; admission €6; ⏲10am-6pm Tue-Sun) Dating from 1496, this Unesco World Heritage site is one of Lisbon's icons, and is a soaring extravaganza of Manueline architecture with stunning carvings and ceramic tiles.

Museu Colecção Berardo ART MUSEUM

(Map p698; www.museuberardo.pt; Praça do Império; admission free; ⏲10am-7pm Sat-Thu, to 10pm Fri) Houses an impressive collection of abstract, surrealist and pop art, along with some of the city's best temporary exhibits. There's also a great indoor-outdoor cafe.

Torre de Belém TOWER

(off Map p698; admission €4; ⏲10am-5pm Tue-Sun) Another of Belém's Unesco World Heritage–listed wonders, the Tower of Belém symbolises the voyages that made Portugal powerful. Brave the cramped winding staircase to the turret for fantastic river views.

SALDANHA

Museu Calouste Gulbenkian MUSEUM

(Map p698; Avenida de Berna 45; admission €4; ⏲10am-6pm Tue-Sun) This celebrated museum showcases an epic collection of Eastern and Western art: Egyptian mummy masks, Mesopotamian urns, Qing porcelain and paintings by Rembrandt, Renoir and Monet.

Centro de Arte Moderna ART MUSEUM

(Modern Art Centre; Map p698; Rua Dr Nicaulau de Bettencourt; admission €4; ⏲10am-6pm Tue-Sun) In a sculpture-dotted garden alongside Museu Calouste Gulbenkian, the modern art museum contains a stellar collection of 20th-century Portuguese art.

SANTA APOLÓNIA & LAPA

The museums listed here are west and east of the city centre, but well worth visiting.

Museu Nacional do Azulejo MUSEUM

(Map p698; Rua Madre de Deus 4; admission €5; ⏲10am-6pm Wed-Sun, 2-6pm Tue) Languishing in a sumptuous 17th-century convent, this museum showcases Portugal's artful *azulejos* (ceramic tiles), with a fascinating 36m-long panel depicting pre-earthquake Lisbon.

Museu Nacional de Arte Antiga

ART MUSEUM

(Ancient Art Museum; Map p698; Rua das Janelas Verdes; admission €5; ⏲10am-6pm Wed-Sun, 2-6pm Tue) Set in a lemon-fronted, 17th-century palace, this museum presents a star-studded collection of European and Asian paintings and decorative arts.

PARQUE DAS NAÇÕES

The former Expo '98 site, a revitalised 2km-long waterfront area in the northeast,

---

LISBON IN...

Two Days

Take a roller-coaster ride on tram 28, hopping off to scale the ramparts of **Castelo de São Jorge**. Sample Portugal's finest at **Wine Bar do Castelo**, then stroll the picturesque lanes of **Alfama**, pausing for a pick-me-up in arty **Pois Café**. Glimpse the fortress-like **Sé** cathedral en route to shopping in pedestrianised **Baixa**. By night, return to lantern-lit Alfama for first-rate fado at Mesa de Frades.

On day two, breakfast on cinnamon-dusted pastries in **Belém**, then explore the fantastical Manueline cloisters of **Mosteiro dos Jerónimos**. River-gaze from the **Torre de Belém** and see cutting-edge art at the **Museu Colecção Berardo**. Head back for sundowners and magical views at **Noobai Café**, dinner at **100 Maneiras** and bar crawling in **Bairro Alto**.

Four Days

Go window-shopping and cafe-hopping in well-heeled **Chiado**, then head to futuristic **Parque das Nações** for riverfront gardens and the head-spinning **Oceanário**. That night, dine at **Bocca** or **Olivier**, then go dancing in clubbing temple **Lux**.

On day four, catch the train to **Sintra**, for walks through boulder-speckled woodlands to fairy-tale palaces. Back in **Rossio**, toast your trip with cherry liqueur at **A Ginjinha** and alfresco dining at **Chapitô**.

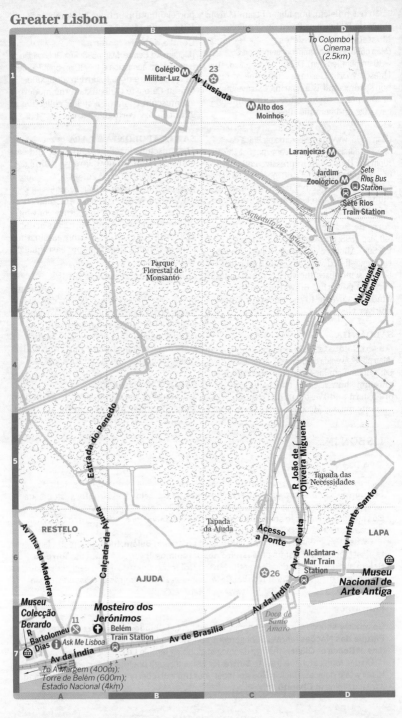

To Colombo
Cinema
(2.5km)

Colégio
Militar-Luz Ⓜ Av Lusiada ⭐ 23

Ⓜ Alto dos
Moinhos

Laranjeiras Ⓜ

Sete
Rios Bus
Station

Jardim
Zoológico Ⓜ

Sete Rios
Train Station

Parque
Florestal de
Monsanto

Aqueduto das Águas Livres

Av Calouste Gulbenkian

Estrada do Penedo

Tapada das
Necessidades

R João de Oliveira Miguens

Av Infante Santo

Calçada da Ajuda

Tapada
da Ajuda

RESTELO

Acesso
a Ponte

LAPA

Alcântara-
Mar Train
Station

Av de Ceuta

Av Ilha da Madeira

AJUDA

⭐ 26

Museu
Nacional de
Arte Antiga

Museu
Colecção
Berardo

Mosteiro dos
Jerónimos ✚

Av da Índia

Av de Brasília

Doca de
Santo
Amaro

R Bartolomeu
Dias 11

Belém
Train Station

Ask Me Lisboa

Av da Índia
To A Margem (400m);
Torre de Belém (600m);
Estadio Nacional (4km)

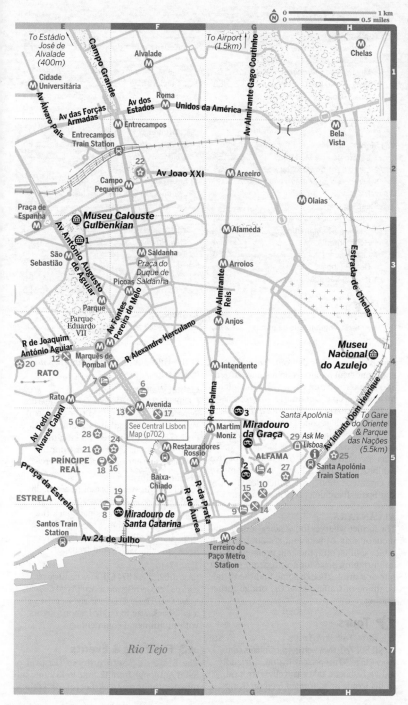

Greater Lisbon

equals a family fun day out. There's weird and wonderful public art on display, gardens and casual riverfront cafes. Other highlights include the epic **Oceanário** (www.oceanario.pt; Doca dos Olivais; adult/child €12/6; ⊙10am-7pm), Europe's second-largest oceanarium, and **Pavilhão do Conhecimento** (Living Science Centre; adult/child €7/4; ⊙10am-6pm Tue-Fri, 11am-7pm Sat & Sun) with over 300 interactive exhibits for kids of all ages. Take the metro to Oriente station – a stunner designed by star Spanish architect Santiago Calatrava.

ALCÂNTARA

The former wharves today house a sleek and modern strip of bars and restaurants with tables spilling onto the long promenade. It's an intriguing place for a waterfront stroll, a bite or a drink, though some find the metallic drone of traffic across the bridge rather grating.

☞ Tours

We Hate Tourism Tours JEEP
(☎911 501 720; www.wehatetourismtours.com; tours €15 to 30 per person) Bruno, a friendly native Lisboeta, takes travellers around in his iconic open-topped jeep on 'King

of the Hills' tours, nightlife outings and beach trips.

Lisbon Walker WALKING
(☎218 861 840; www.lisbonwalker.com; Rua dos Remédios 84; 3hr walk €15; ⊙10am & 2.30pm) Well-informed, English-speaking guides lead fascinating themed walking tours through Lisbon. They depart from the northeast corner of Praça do Comércio.

Lisbon Explorer WALKING
(☎961 198 781; www.lisbonexplorer.com; 2-3hr walk adult/child from €34/free) Top-notch English-speaking guides peel back the many layers of Lisbon's history during three-hour walking tours. Price includes museum admissions and transport.

Transtejo RIVER CRUISE
(Map p702; ☎218 824 671; www.transtejo.pt; Terreiro do Paço ferry terminal; adult/child €20/10; ⊙Apr-Oct) These 2½-hour river cruises are a laid-back way to enjoy Lisbon's sights with multilingual commentary.

Festivals & Events

The **Festa de Santo António** (Festival of Saint Anthony), from 12 June to 13 June, culminates the three-week **Festas de Lisboa**, with processions and dozens of street parties; it's liveliest in the Alfama.

🛏 Sleeping

Lisbon has seriously raised the slumber stakes recently with a new crop of design-conscious boutique hotels and upmarket backpacker digs. Book ahead during high season (July to mid-September).

BAIXA & ROSSIO

Lavra Guest House   GUEST HOUSE €€
(Map p702; ☎218 820 000; www.lavra.pt; Calçada de Santana 182, Rossio; s/d from €40/50; 🛜) Set in a former convent, the Lavra Guest house has a range of rooms, from basic quarters facing onto an inner courtyard, to brighter rooms with wood floors and tiny balconies.

Lisbon Story Guesthouse   GUEST HOUSE €€
(Map p702; ☎211 529 313; www.lisbonstory guesthouse.com; Largo de São Domingos 18, Rossio; d without bathroom incl breakfast €45-80; @🛜) Overlooking the Praça São Domingos is a small, welcoming guest house with small, well-maintained rooms and a shoe-free lounge, with throw pillows and low tables.

Goodnight Hostel   HOSTEL €
(Map p702; ☎213 430 139; www.goodnighthostel. com; Rua dos Correieros 113, Baixa; dm/d €20/50; @🛜) Set in a converted 18th-century town house, this glam hostel rocks with its fab location and retro design. The high-ceilinged dorms offer vertigo-inducing views over Baixa.

Lounge Hostel   HOSTEL €
(Map p702; ☎213 462 061; www.lisbonlounge hostel.com; Rua de São Nicolau 41, Baixa; dm/d incl breakfast €20/60; @) These ultrahip Baixa digs have a party vibe. Bed down in immaculate dorms and meet like-minded travellers in the funky lounge watched over by a wacky moose head.

Travellers House   HOSTEL €
(Map p702; ☎210 115 922; www.travellershouse. com; Rua Augusta 89, Baixa; dm from €22; @) This superfriendly hostel is set in a converted 250-year-old house and offers cosy dorms, a retro lounge with beanbags, an internet corner and a communal kitchen.

Residencial Florescente   GUEST HOUSE €€
(Map p702; ☎213 426 609; www.residencial florescente.com; Rua das Portas de Santo Antão 99, Rossio; s/d from €45/65; ✳@🛜) On a vibrant street lined with alfresco restaurants, lemon-fronted Florescente has comfy rooms in muted tones with shiny new bathrooms. It's a two-minute walk from Rossio.

Pensão Imperial   GUEST HOUSE €
(Map p702; ☎213 420 166; Praça dos Restauradores 78, Rossio; s/d €25/40) Cheery Imperial has a terrific location over the main square. The high-ceilinged rooms with simple wooden furniture are nothing flash, but some have flower-draped balconies overlooking the *praça*.

ALFAMA

Alfama Patio Hostel   HOSTEL €
(Map p698; ☎218 883 127; www.flashhostel.com; Escola Gerais 3; dm/d from €17/60; @🛜) Located in the heart of the Alfama, this place attracts a cool, laid-back crowd. There are loads of activities (pub crawls, day trips to the beach), plus barbecues on the garden-like patio.

Solar dos Mouros   BOUTIQUE HOTEL €€€
(Map p702; ☎218 854 940; www.solardosmouros. pt; Rua do Milagre de Santo António 4; d from €120-240; ✳) Affording river or castle views, the 12 rooms at this boutique charmer bear the imprint of artist Luís Lemos and offer high-end trappings, plus a tiny water garden.

FREE LISBOA

Aside from the Castelo de São Jorge, all the sights in the Lisbon section have free entrance on Sundays from 10am to 2pm. For a free cultural fix on other days, make for Belém's **Museu Colecção Berardo** for great art exhibits, **Museu do Teatro Romano** (Roman Theatre Museum; Map p702; Pátio do Aljube 5; ⊙10am-1pm & 2-6pm Tue-Sun) for Roman theatre ruins, and the fortresslike **Sé** (cathedral; Map p702), built in 1150 on the site of a mosque. For more Roman ruins, take a free tour of the **Núcleo Arqueológico** (Map p702; Rua dos Correeiros 9; ⊙10am-5pm Mon-Sat), which contains a web of tunnels hidden under the Baixa. The new **Museu de Design e da Moda** (Map p702; Rua Augusta 24; ⊙10am-8pm Tue-Sun) exhibits eye-catching furniture, industrial design and couture dating to the 1930s.

Central Lisbon

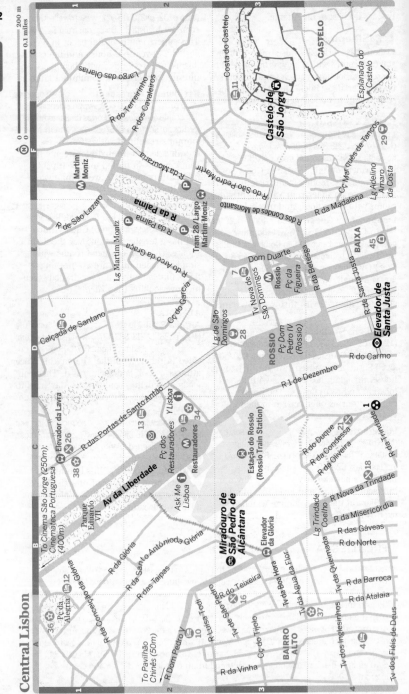

200 m
0.1 miles

G1 Largo das Olarias

R do Terreirinho
R dos Cavaleiros
Martim Moniz M

Costa do Castelo
11 ⊞

Castelo de São Jorge ◎

CASTELO

Esplanada do Castelo

R da Mouraria
R de São Lázaro
R Martim Moniz
Lg Martim Moniz

R da Palma
R da Palma
R do Arco da Graça

Tram 28/Largo Martim Moniz

R do São Pedro Mártir
R dos Condes de Monsanto

R da Madalena

C Marquês de Tancos
Lg Adelino Amaro da Costa
29 ⊗

BAIXA

Dom Duarte
R dos Condes de Monsanto

Calçada de Santano
6 ⊞

Cç do Garcia
Cç do Garcia

7 ⊞
Tv Nova de São Domingos
Pç da Figueira
M São Domingos
R da Betesga

45 ⊞

Lg de São Domingos
28 ⊗

ROSSIO

Pç Dom Pedro IV (Rossio)

R de Santa Justa

Elevador de Santa Justa ◎

R do Carmo
R 1 de Dezembro

Elevador da Lavra ⊞
26 ✦
38 ✦
R das Portas de Santo Antão
13 ⊗
Y Lisboa f
9 ⊗
34 ✦

Pç dos Restauradores
M Restauradores

Estação do Rossio (Rossio Train Station)

1 ◎

R do Duque
21 ⊗
R da Condessa
R da Oliveira
18 ⊗
R da Trindade

Av da Liberdade

Ask Me Lisboa f

R Nova da Trindade
R da Misericórdia
Lg Trindade

Parque Eduardo VII

To Cinema São Jorge (250m);
Cinemateca Portuguesa (400m)

R das Gáveas
R do Norte

Miradouro de São Pedro de Alcântara ◎
Elevador da Glória ⊞

R da Glória
R de Santo António da Glória
R das Taipas

R da Barroca
R da Atalaia

Tv da Boa Hora
Tv da Queimada
R da Condessa Coelho

36 ✦
Pç da Alegria
R da Conceição da Glória

12 ⊞

Tv da Água da Flor

Tv São Pedro
R do Teixeira
16 ⊗

Tv dos Inglesinhos

37 ⊗

BAIRRO ALTO

R Dom Pedro V
10 ⊞
R Luísa Todi
Cç do Tijolo

4 ⊞

Tv dos Fiéis de Deus

To Pavilhão Chinês (50m)

R da Vinha
R da Flor

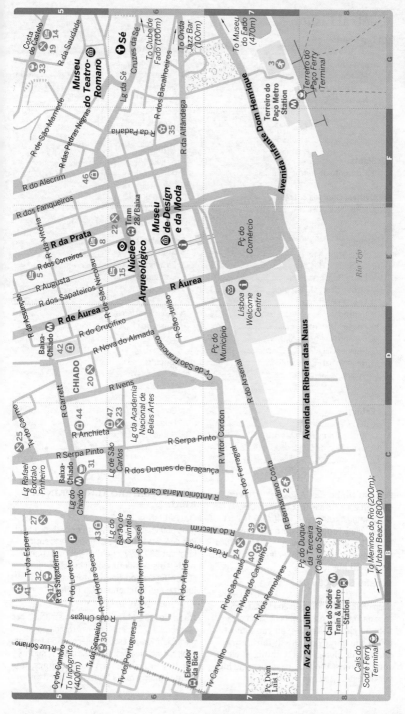

Costa do Castelo
19 14
R da Saudade
33
Museu do Teatro-Romano
Sé
Cruzes da Sé
To Clube de Fado (100m)
To Onda Jazz Bar (100m)
Lg da Sé
R dos Bacalhoeiros
To Museu do Fado (470m)
3
Terreiro do Paço Ferry Terminal
Terreiro do Paço Metro Station
Avenida Infante Dom Henrique
R de São Mamede
R das Pedras Negras
R da Padaria
35
R da Alfândega
R do Alecrim
46
Pç do Comércio
R dos Fanqueiros
R da Vitória
R da Prata
22
8
Tram 28/Baixa
Museu de Design e da Moda
R dos Correiros
Núcleo Arqueológico
5
R Augusta
15
R Áurea
Rio Tejo
R dos Sapateiros
R de São Nicolau
R de Áurea
R da Assunção
R do Crucifixo
R São Julião
Baixa-Chiado
42
R Nova do Almada
Lisboa Welcome Centre
CHIADO
20
Cc de São Francisco
Pç do Município
R Garrett
R Ivens
44
47
23
Pç do Comércio
Lg da Academia Nacional de Belas Artes
R Anchieta
R Serpa Pinto
R Serpa Pinto
R Vítor Cordon
25
Tv do Carmo
R do Arsenal
Avenida da Ribeira das Naus
Baixa-Chiado
31
Lg de São Carlos
R dos Duques de Bragança
R António Maria Cardoso
R do Ferragial
Lg Rafael Bordalo Pinheiro
Lg do Chiado
R do Loreto
R Bernardino Costa
2
27
P
Lg do Barão de Quintela
43
R do Alecrim
39
Tv da Espera
32
R da Horta Seca
R das Flores
24
40
Pç do Duque da Terceira
(Cais do Sodré)
17
R da Salgadeiras
Lg do Barão de Quintela
Tv de Guilherme Coussel
R de São Paulo
R Nova do Carvalho
R Soriano
41
Tv da Bica
30
R das Chagas
R do Ataíde
R dos Remolares
Cais do Sodré Train & Metro Station
Cc do Combro
To Incógnito (400m)
R do Sequeiro
Tv da Portuguesa
To Meninos do Rio (200m);
Urban Beach (800m)
Elevador da Bica
Tv Carvalho
Av 24 de Julho
Cais do Sodré Ferry Terminal
Pç Dom Luís I

Central Lisbon

Top Sights

	Castelo de São Jorge	G3
	Elevador de Santa Justa	D4
	Miradouro de São Pedro de Alcântara	B3
	Museu de Design e da Moda	E6
	Museu do Teatro Romano	G5
	Núcleo Arqueológico	E6
	Sé	G6

Sights

1	Convento do Carmo	C4

Activities, Courses & Tours

2	Bike Iberia	C7
3	Transtejo	G7

Sleeping

4	Anjo Azul	A4
5	Goodnight Hostel	E5
6	Lavra Guest House	D1
7	Lisbon Story Guesthouse	E3
8	Lounge Hostel	E5
9	Pensão Imperial	C2
10	Pensão Londres	A2
11	Pensão Ninho das Águias	G3
12	Residencial Alegria	B1
13	Residencial Florescente	C2
14	Solar dos Mouros	G5
15	Travellers House	E6

Eating

16	100 Maneiras	A3
17	Antigo Primeiro de Maio	B5
18	Cervejaria da Trindade	C4
19	Chapitô	G5
20	Fábulas	D5
21	Faca & Garfo	C4
22	Fragoleto	E6
23	Kaffee Haus	C6
24	Olivier	B7
25	Royale Café	C5
26	Solar dos Presuntos	C1
27	Tavares Rico	B5

Drinking

28	A Ginjinha	D3
29	Bar das Imagens	F4
30	Bicaense	A5
31	Café a Brasileira	C5
32	Maria Caxuxa	B5
33	Wine Bar do Castelo	G5

Entertainment

34	ABEP Ticket Kiosk	C2
35	Bacalhoeiro	F6
36	Cabaret Maxime	A1
37	Catacumbas	A4
38	Crew Hassan	C1
39	Discoteca Jamaica	B7
40	Music Box	B7
41	Zé dos Bois	B5

Shopping

42	Armazéns do Chiado	D5
43	Fábrica Sant'Anna	B5
44	Livraria Bertrand	C5
45	Outra Face da Lua	E4
46	Santos Ofícios	F5
47	Vida Portuguesa	C6

Pensão Ninho das Águias GUEST HOUSE €
(Map p702; ☎218 854 070; Costa do Castelo 74; s/d/tr without bathroom €30/40/60) It isn't called 'eagle's nest' for nothing: this guest house has a Rapunzel-esque turret affording magical 360-degree views over Lisbon. Book well ahead.

Pensão São João da Praça GUEST HOUSE €
(Map p698; ☎218 862 591; 2nd fl, Rua de São João da Praça 97; d €50, without bathroom €35) So close to the *Sé* you can almost touch the gargoyles, this 19th-century guest house has a pick-and-mix of clean, sunny rooms; the best have river-facing verandas.

CHIADO, BAIRRO ALTO & PRÍNCIPE REAL

Oasis Lisboa HOSTEL €
(Map p698; ☎213 478 044; www.oasislisboa.com; Rua de Santa Catarina 24, Principe Real; dm incl breakfast €20; @ 📶) Behind yellow wonder walls, this self-defined backpacker mansion offers wood-floored dorms, a sleek lounge and kitchen, and a rooftop terrace with impressive river views.

Casa de São Mamede GUEST HOUSE €€€
(Map p698; ☎213 963 166; www.casadesaomamede.com; Rua da Escola Politécnica 159, Principe Real; s/d incl breakfast €100/120; ❄) A soothing stay in 18th-century surroundings; this former magistrate's house has handsome

original tiles and elegant antique-clad rooms.

Pensão Londres GUEST HOUSE €€
(Map p702; ☑213 462 203; www.pensaolondres. com.pt; Rua Dom Pedro V 53, Bairro Alto; s/d €50/75) This friendly and popular place has old-fashioned appeal with large, high-ceilinged, carpeted rooms. Those on the 4th floor have fine views.

Anjo Azul GUEST HOUSE €€
(Map p702; ☑213 478 069; www.anjoazul.com; Rua Luz Soriano 75, Bairro Alto; d €50-80; @) This gay-friendly hotel has rooms from scarlet-and-black love nests with heart pillows to chocolate-caramel numbers.

AVENIDA DE LIBERDADE, RATO & MARQUÊS DE POMBAL

Lisbon Dreams GUEST HOUSE €€
(Map p698; ☑213 872 393; www.lisbondreams guesthouse.com; Rua Rodrigo da Fonseca 29, Rato; s/d/tr without bathroom incl breakfast €40/60/75; @☎) On a quiet street lined with jacaranda trees, Lisbon Dreams offers excellent value for its bright modern rooms with high ceilings and high-end mattresses. Bathrooms are shared, but spotlessly clean.

Hotel Britania HOTEL €€€
(Map p698; ☑213 155 016; www.heritage.pt; Rua Rodrigues Sampaio 17; d from €160; ✱@☎) Art deco rules the waves at the affable, top-rated Britania, a boutique gem near Avenida da Liberdade. Cassiano Branco put his modernist stamp on the rooms with chrome lamps, plaid fabrics and shiny marble bathrooms.

Residencial Alegria GUEST HOUSE €€
(Map p702; ☑213 220 670; www.alegrianet.com; Praça da Alegria 12; d €58-78; ✱) Overlooking a palm-dotted plaza, this lemon-fronted belle époque gem has airy and peaceful rooms, with antique-filled corridors.

Eating
New-generation chefs, first-rate ingredients and a generous pinch of old-world spice have put the Portuguese capital on the gastronomic map. You'll find everything from ubercool sushi lounges to designer Michelin-starred restaurants.

BAIXA & ROSSIO

Solar dos Presuntos PORTUGUESE €€€
(Map p702; ☑213 424 253; Rua das Portas de Santo Antão 150, Rossio; mains €15-24; ⊙lunch & dinner Mon-Sat) Renowned for its excellent seafood as well as its smoked and grilled meats, this buzzing restaurant serves up memorable prawn and lobster curry, salt-baked sea bass and delectable seafood paella, among other great picks.

WORTH A TRIP

COSTA DA CAPARICA

Located 10km southwest of Lisbon, Costa da Caparica's seemingly never-ending beach attracts sun-worshipping Lisboetas craving all-over tans, surfer dudes keen to ride Atlantic waves, and day-tripping families seeking clean sea and soft sand. It hasn't escaped development, but head south and the high-rises soon give way to pine forests and mellow beach-shack cafes.

During the summer a **narrow-gauge railway** runs the length of the beach for 20 stops. The nearer beaches, including **Praia do Norte** and **Praia do São Sebastião**, are great for families, while the further ones are younger and trendier, including **Praia da Sereia** (stop 15), with its cool beachfront bar, Bar Waikiki. **Praia do Castelo** (stop 11) and **Praia da Bela Vista** (stop 17) are more-secluded gay and nudist havens.

The **main beach** (called Praia do CDS, or Centro Desportivo de Surf) is lined with cafes, bars and surfing clubs along its promenade.

If you decide to stay overnight, there are a handful of decent lodgings in town, including simple but comfy **Residencial Mar e Sol** (☑212 900 017; www.residencialmaresol.com; Rua dos Pescadores 42; s/d €45/65; ✱@☎).

The best way to get here is by **ferry to Cacilhas** from Lisbon's Cais do Sodré, where bus 135 runs to Costa da Caparica town (€3, 30 to 45 minutes, every 30 to 60 minutes). Sport-minded folk can also get there by bike and ferry, by riding along the **Tejo bike path** 7km from Cais do Sodré to Belém, taking the ferry from there to Trafaria, then continuing on another **new bike path** (also separate from traffic) that runs for another 6km down to Costa da Caparica.

HEAVENLY VIEWS

Lisbon's *miradouros* (view points) provide memorable settings to take in the panorama. Some have outdoor cafes attached.

» **Largo das Portas do Sol** (Map p698) With a stylish bar and cafe.

» **Miradouro da Graça** (Map p698) A pine-fringed square that's perfect for sundowners.

» **Miradouro da Senhora do Monte** (Map p698) The highest lookout, with memorable castle views.

» **Miradouro de São Pedro de Alcântara** (Map p702) Drinks and sweeping views on the edge of Bairro Alto.

» **Miradouro de Santa Catarina** (Map p698) Youthful spot with guitar-playing rebels, artful graffiti and first-rate eating/drinking spot (Noobai Café) attached.

Fragoleto   ICE CREAM €
(Map p702; Rua da Prata 74, Baixa; scoop €1.90; ⊙9am-8pm Mon-Sat) For tasty gelato, head for pint-sized Fragoleto. Manuela makes authentic ice cream using fresh, seasonal fruit.

ALFAMA

Santo António de Alfama   PORTUGUESE €€
(Map p698; ☎218 881 328; Beco de São Miguel 7; mains €13-16; ⊙lunch & dinner) With a lovely front courtyard and atmospheric interior, this bistro is one of the Alfama's stars, with tasty appetisers (gorgonzola-stuffed mushrooms, roasted aubergines with yoghurt), as well as more filling traditional Portuguese dishes.

Chapitô   CONTEMPORARY €€
(Map p702; ☎218 867 334; Costa do Castelo 7; tapas €4-5, mains €10-17; ⊙7.30pm-2am Mon-Fri, noon-2am Sat & Sun) Chapitô's tree-filled courtyard hums with arty types tucking into tapas or barbecued steaks. Zebra and giraffe prints glam up the top-floor restaurant, affording mesmerising views over Lisbon.

Pois Café   CAFE €
(Map p698; Rua de São João da Praça 93; mains €5-12; ⊙11am-8pm Tue-Sun) Boasting a laid-back boho vibe, Pois Café has creative salads, sandwiches and tangy juices. Its sofas invite lazy afternoons spent reading novels and sipping coffee.

Senhora Mãe   CONTEMPORARY €€
(Map p698; Largo de São Martinho 6-7; mains €10-18; ⊙lunch & dinner) A pleasant front patio and a stylish interior set the scene for seasonally inspired dishes, such as ravioli in cuttlefish ink or duck breast with lemongrass.

AVENIDA DE LIBERDADE, RATO & MARQUÊS DE POMBAL

Zé Varunca   PORTUGUESE €€
(Map p698; Rua de São José 54; mains €10-13; ⊙lunch & dinner Mon-Sat) This charming, rustically decorated restaurant specialises in Alentejo cooking, with a changing menu of regional favourites such as roast pork with clam sauce and *migas de bacalhau* (a bread-based dish cooked with cod).

Bocca   FUSION €€€
(Map p698; ☎213 808 383; Rua Rodrigo da Fonseca 87, Marques de Pombal; mains €15-30; ⊙lunch & dinner Tue-Sat) This elegant, award-winning restaurant serves beautifully turned-out meat and seafood dishes. The gastrobar serves inventive plates meant for sharing, as well as tasty cocktails. Superb wine list.

Cervejaria Ribadouro   SEAFOOD €€
(Map p698; ☎213 549 411; Rua do Salitre 2; mains €8-20; ⊙lunch & dinner) This bustling beer hall is popular with local seafood fans. The shellfish are plucked fresh from the tank, weighed and cooked to lip-smacking perfection.

CHIADO, BAIRRO ALTO & PRÍNCIPE REAL

TOP CHOICE **100 Maneiras**   FUSION €€€
(Map p702; ☎210 990 475; Rua do Teixeira 35, Bairro Alta; tasting menus €35; ⊙dinner Mon-Sat) One of Lisbon's best-rated restaurants, 100 Maneiras has no menu, just a 10-course tasting menu that changes daily and features creative, delicately prepared dishes. There's a lively buzz to the elegant and small space. Reservations essential.

Olivier   FRENCH €€€
(Map p702; ☎213 422 916; Rua do Alecrim 23, Chiado; mains €19-27, tasting menus €38; ⊙dinner Mon-Sat) Lisbon masterchef Olivier da Costa continues to wow diners at this intimate Chiado restaurant, with its beautifully prepared French-inspired dishes served

amid gilded banquettes, low-hanging chandeliers and vintage wallpaper. Reservations recommended.

Fábulas
CAFE €

(Map p702; Calçada Nova de São Francisco 14, Chiado; mains €6-10; ⊙10am-midnight Mon-Sat, 10am-8pm Sun; @🕾) Exposed stone walls, low lighting and twisting corridors that open onto cosy nooks and crannies do indeed conjure a storybook fable (*fábula*). Sink into a comfy couch with coffee or wine, or have a meal – salads, pasta, burritos, crêpes and daily specials.

Faca & Garfo
PORTUGUESE €

(Map p702; Rua da Condessa 2, Chiado; mains €6-8; ⊙lunch & dinner Mon-Sat) The sweet *azulejo*-filled Faca & Garfo (which means 'knife and fork') serves carefully prepared Portuguese recipes at reasonable prices. Try the authentic *alheira de Mirandela* (chicken sausage) or the *bife à casa* (steak with cream and port wine sauce).

Terra
VEGETARIAN €€

(Map p698; Rua da Palmeira 15, Principe Real; buffets €15; ⊙lunch Sat & Sun, dinner Tue-Sun; 🖋) Terra is famed for its superb vegetarian buffet (including vegan options) of salads, kebabs and curries, plus organic wines and juices. A fountain gurgles in the tree-shaded courtyard, lit by twinkling lights after dark.

Antigo Primeiro de Maio
PORTUGUESE €€

(Map p702; Rua da Atalaia 8, Bairro Alta; mains €10-12; ⊙dinner Mon-Sat, lunch Mon-Fri) Always packed with regulars, this small festive *tasca* (tavern) serves excellent traditional Portuguese dishes, amid tiled walls, a garrulous crowd and harried-but-friendly waiters.

Tavares Rico
PORTUGUESE €€€

(Map p702; 🖋213 421 112; Rua da Misericórdia 37, Chiado; mains €32-38, tasting menus €90; ⊙lunch & dinner Tue-Sat) Tavares is the fairest of them all, with its all-gold 18th-century interior lit by chandeliers. Signature dishes such as scallops with Alentejo bacon marry well with Portuguese wines.

Kaffee Haus
CAFE €

(Map p702; Rua Anchieta 3, Chiado; mains €6-10; ⊙11am-midnight Tue-Thu, 11am-2am Fri & Sat, 11am-8pm Sun) Overlooking a peaceful corner of Chiado, this cool but unpretentious cafe has daily chalkboard specials – big salads, tasty schnitzels, strudels, cakes and more.

Royale Café
CAFE €

(Map p702; 🖋213 469 125; Largo Rafael Bordalo Pinheiro 29, Chiado; snacks €4-6; ⊙10am-midnight Mon-Sat, to 8pm Sun) This chichi cafe has a pleasant vine-clad courtyard that's ideal for drinks and create-your-own sandwiches.

Cervejaria da Trindade
PORTUGUESE €€

(Map p702; 🖋213 423 506; Rua Nova da Trindade 20c, Chiado; mains €8-20) This 13th-century monastery turned clattering beer hall oozes atmosphere with its vaults and *azulejos*. Feast on humungous steaks or lobster stew, washed down with foaming beer.

BELÉM

A Margem
FUSION €€

(off Map p698; 🖋918 225 584; Doca do Bom Sucesso; salads €10-12; ⊙10am-1am) Well sited near the river's edge, this small, sun-drenched cube of glass and white stone boasts an open patio and large windows facing the Tejo. Locals come for fresh salads, cheese plates, bruschetta and other light bites, as well as wine and cocktails.

Antiga Confeitaria de Belém
PATISSERIE €

(Map p698; 🖋213 637 423; Rua de Belém 86-88) A classically tiled and elegant cafe with probably the best *pastéis de nata* on earth. Delicious! Since 1837, this patisserie has been transporting locals to sugar-coated nirvana with heavenly *pastéis de belém*: crisp pastry nests filled with custard cream, baked at 400 degrees for that perfect golden crust, then lightly dusted with cinnamon. Admire *azulejos* in the vaulted rooms or devour a still-warm tart at the counter to try to guess the secret ingredient.

🍷 Drinking

All-night street parties in Bairro Alto, sunset drinks from high Alfama terraces, and sumptuous art deco cafes scattered about Chiado – Lisbon has many enticing options for imbibers.

WANT MORE?

For in-depth information, reviews and recommendations at your fingertips, head to the Apple App Store to purchase Lonely Planet's *Lisbon City Guide* iPhone app.

Pavilhão Chinês · LOUNGE BAR
(off Map p702; Rua Dom Pedro V 89-91, Principe Real) An old curiosity shop of a bar with oil paintings and model spitfires dangling from the ceiling, and cabinets brimming with glittering Venetian masks and Action Men. Play pool or bag a comfy armchair with port or beer in hand.

Bicaense · BAR
(Map p702; Rua da Bica de Duarte Belo 42a, Bica) Indie kids have a soft spot for this chilled Santa Catarina haunt, kitted out with retro radios, projectors and squishy beanbags. DJs spin house to the preclubbing crowd and the back room stages occasional gigs.

Wine Bar do Castelo · WINE BAR
(Map p702; Rua Bartolomeu de Gusmão 13, Castelo; ☺noon-11pm) Near the entrance to the Castelo de São Jorge, this welcoming place serves more than 150 Portuguese wines by the glass, along with gourmet smoked meats, cheeses, olives and other tasty accompaniments.

Cinco Lounge · LOUNGE BAR
(Map p698; Rua Ruben António Leitão 17, Principe Real; ☺9pm-2am Tue-Sat) Take an award-winning London-born mixologist, add a candlelit, gold-kissed setting and give it a funky twist and you have Cinco Lounge. Come for the laid-back scene and legendary cocktails.

Meninos do Rio · OUTDOOR BAR
(off Map p702; Rua da Cintura do Porto de Lisboa, Armação 255, Santos; ☺12.30pm-1am Sun-Thu, to 4am Fri & Sat) Perched on the river's edge, Meninos do Rio has palm trees, wooden decks, reggae-playing DJs and tropical cocktails, giving it a vibe that's more Caribbean than Iberian.

Maria Caxuxa · BAR
(Map p702; Rua Barroca 6, Bairro Alto; ☺8am-2am) Maria Caxuxa has effortless style, its several rooms decked with giant mixers, *azulejo*-lined walls and 1950s armchairs and sofas, as funk-laden jazz plays overhead.

Café a Brasileira · CAFE, BAR
(Map p702; ☎213 469 547; Rua Garrett 120, Chiado; ☺8am-2am) An historic watering hole for Lisbon's 19th-century greats, with warm wooden innards and a busy counter serving daytime coffees and pints at night.

Bar das Imagens · BAR
(Map p702; Calçada Marquês de Tancos 1, Castelo; ☺11am-2am Tue-Sat, 3-11pm Sun) With a terrace affording vertigo-inducing views over the city, this cheery bar serves potent Cuba libres and other well-prepared cocktails.

Noobai Café · CAFE, BAR
(Map p698; Miradouro de Santa Catarina, Santa Catarina; ☺noon-midnight) Lisbon's best-kept secret is next to Miradouro de Santa Catarina, with a laid-back vibe, jazzy beats and magnificent views from the terrace.

A Ginjinha · BAR
(Map p702; Largo de Saõ Domingos 8, Rossio; ☺9am-10pm) Join a wide swath of society for a refreshingly potent quaff of *ginjinha* (cherry brandy) at this tiny bar-stand-up counter near Rossio.

☆ Entertainment
For the latest goings-on, pick up the weekly *Time Out Lisboa* (www.timeout.pt) from bookstores, or the free monthly *Follow me Lisboa* or the *Agenda Cultural Lisboa* from the tourist office.

Live Music

Zé dos Bois · ALTERNATIVE
(Map p702; ☎213 430 205; www.zedosbois.org; Rua da Barroca 59, Bairro Alto) Focusing on tomorrow's performing arts and music trends, Zé dos Bois is an experimental venue with a laid-back courtyard. This boho haunt has hosted bands such as Black Dice and Animal Collective.

Onda Jazz Bar · JAZZ
(off Map p702; www.ondajazz.com; Arco de Jesus 7, Alfama) This vaulted cellar features a menu of mainstream jazz, plus more-eclectic beats of bands hailing from Brazil and Africa.

Catacumbas · JAZZ
(Map p702; Travessa da Água da Flor 43, Bairro Alta) Moodily lit and festooned with portraits of legends such as Miles Davis, this den is jam-packed when it hosts live jazz on Thursday night.

Nightclubs
Cover charges for nightclubs vary from €5 to €20.

Lux · NIGHTCLUB
(Map p698; www.luxfragil.com; Avenida Infante Dom Henrique, Santo Apolónia) Lisbon's ice-cool, must-see club, Lux is run by ex-Frágil maestro Marcel Reis and is part-owned by John Malkovich. Lux hosts big-name DJs and a fine roof terrace overlooking the Tejo.

Infused by Moorish song and the ditties of homesick sailors, bluesy, bittersweet **fado** encapsulates the Lisbon psyche like nothing else. The uniquely Portuguese style was born in the Alfama, still the best place in Lisbon to hear it live. Minimum consumption charges range from €15 to €25 per person.

» **A Baîuca** (Map p698; Rua de São Miguel 20; ⊘dinner Thu-Mon) On a good night, walking into A Baîuca is like gatecrashing a family party. It's a special place with *fado vadio*, where locals take a turn and spectators hiss if anyone dares to chat during the singing.

» **Clube de Fado** (off Map p702; ☑218 852 704; www.clube-de-fado.com; Rua de São João da Praça; ⊘9pm-2.30am Mon-Sat) Hosts the cream of the fado crop in vaulted, dimly lit surrounds. Big-name *fadistas* perform here alongside celebrated guitarists.

» **Mesa de Frades** (Map p698; ☑917 029 436; www.mesadefrades.com; Rua dos Remédios 139a; admission from €15; ⊘dinner Wed-Mon) A magical place to hear fado, tiny Mesa de Frades used to be a chapel. It's tiled with exquisite *azulejos* and has just a handful of tables. Reserve ahead.

Music Box
NIGHTCLUB

(Map p702; Rua Nova do Carvalho 24, Cais do Sodré; www.musicboxlisboa.com) Under the brick arches on Rua Nova do Carvalho lies one of Lisbon's hottest clubs. Music Box hosts loud and bouncy club nights with music shifting from electro to rock, plus ear-splitting gigs by rising bands.

Incógnito
NIGHTCLUB

(off Map p702; Rua Poiais de São Bento 37, Santa Catarina) No-sign, pint-sized Incógnito offers an alternative vibe and DJs thrashing out indie rock and electro-pop. Sweat it out with a fun crowd on the tiny basement dance floor, or breathe more easily in the loft bar upstairs.

Discoteca Jamaica
NIGHTCLUB

(Map p702; Rua Nova do Carvalho, Cais do Sodré; ⊘11pm-4am) Gay and straight, black and white, young and old – everyone has a soft spot for this offbeat club. It gets going around 2am at weekends with DJs pumping out reggae, hip hop and retro.

Cabaret Maxime
NIGHTCLUB

(Map p702; www.cabaret-maxime.com; Praça da Alegria 58) Young Lisboetas flock to this former strip club for DJ nights of old-school tunes, or loud, sweaty gigs of established and upcoming local bands.

K Urban Beach
NIGHTCLUB

(off Map p702; www.grupo-k.pt; Cais da Viscondessa, Santos) Jutting out over the Tejo, this stylish and airy club has a lively dance floor, a restaurant and outdoor seating that makes fine use of its scenic riverside setting.

Alternative Culture

Lisbon may flirt with high culture and embrace fado, but she also has an ongoing relationship with the underdog. Individuality trumps conformity and alternative culture rules in these offbeat cultural centres.

LX Factory
ART SPACE

(Map p698; www.lxfactory.com; Rua Rodrigues de Faria 103, Alcântara) Lisbon's new hub of creativity hosts a dynamic menu of events from live concerts and film screenings to fashion shows and art exhibitions. There's a rustically cool cafe as well as a restaurant, bookshop and design-minded shops. Weekend nights see parties with a dance- and art-loving crowd.

Crew Hassan
ECLECTIC

(Map p702; Rua das Portas de Santo Antão 159, Rossio; @) Alternative types dig Crew Hassan's graffiti, threadbare sofas, cheap veggie fare and free internet. Its line-up spans films, gigs, exhibitions and DJs playing music from reggae to minimalist techno.

Bacalhoeiro
BAR

(Map p702; ☑218 864 891; Rua dos Bacalhoeiros 125, Baixa; ☎) Nonconformist, laid-back Bacalhoeiro shelters a cosy bar and hosts everything from alternative gigs to film screenings, salsa nights and themed parties. Free wi-fi.

Gay & Lesbian Venues

Lisbon has a relaxed yet flourishing gay scene with an annual Gay Pride Festival in

June. Visit www.gaylisbon4u.com for more listings.

Bar 106 BAR
(Map p698; www.bar106.com; Rua de São Marçal 106) Young and fun with an upbeat, pre-clubbing vibe and crazy events such as Sunday's message party.

Finalmente NIGHTCLUB
(Map p698; Rua da Palmeira 38) This popular club has a tiny dance floor, nightly drag shows and wall-to-wall crowds.

Trumps NIGHTCLUB
(Map p698; www.trumps.pt; Rua da Imprensa Nacional 104b) Lisbon's hottest gay club, with cruisy corners, a sizeable dance floor and events from live music to drag.

Cinemas
Lisbon's cinematic standouts are the grand **São Jorge** (off Map p702; Avenida da Liberdade 175) and, just around the corner, **Cinemateca Portuguesa** (off Map p702; www.cinemateca. pt; Rua Barata Salgueiro 39); both screen off-beat, art-house, world and old films. For Hollywood fare, visit multiscreen **Amoreiras Cinema** (Map p698; Amoreiras Shopping Centre, Avenida Eng Duarte Pacheco) or **Colombo Cinema** (off Map p698; Centro Colombo, Avenida Lusíada).

Sport
Lisbon's football teams are Benfica, Belenenses and Sporting. Euro 2004 led to the upgrading of the 65,000-seat **Estádio da Luz** (Map p698) and the construction of the 54,000-seat **Estádio Nacional** (Map p698). Bullfights are staged on Thursday from May to October at **Campo Pequeno** (Map p698; Avenida da República; tickets €10-75). Tickets are available at **ABEP ticket kiosk** (Map p702; Praça dos Restauradores). State-of-the-art stadium **Estádio José de Alvalade** (off Map p702; Rua Prof Fernando da Fonseca) seats 54,000 and is just north of the university. Take the metro to Campo Grande.

Shopping
Shops in Lisbon are a mix of the classic and the wild, with antiques, stuck-in-time button and tinned-fish shops, and edgy boutiques all sprinkled across the hilly landscape. Rua Garrett and nearby Largo do Chiado, across Rua da Misericórdia, are home to some of Lisbon's oldest and most upmarket boutiques. Meanwhile, Bairro Alto attracts vinyl lovers and vintage fans to its cluster of late-opening boutiques.

Feira da Ladra MARKET
(Map p698; Campo de Santa Clara, Alfama; ☉7am-5pm Sat) You'll find old records, coins, jewellery, vintage postcards, dog-eared poetry books and other attic treasure/trash at this lively Saturday market.

Vida Portuguesa PORTUGUESE PRODUCTS
(Map p702; Rua Anchieta 11, Chiado) With high ceilings and polished cabinets, this store lures nostalgics with all-Portuguese products, from retro-wrapped Tricona sardines to lime-oil soap and Bordallo Pinheiro porcelain swallows.

Santos Oficios HANDICRAFTS
(Map p702; Rua da Madalena 87, Baixa) Touristy but fine selection of Portuguese folk art.

Armazéns do Chiado MALL
(Map p702; Rua do Carmo 2, Chiado) A convenient, well-concealed shopping complex. The Fnac here is good for books, music and booking concert tickets.

Outra Face da Lua VINTAGE
(Map p702; Rua da Assunção 22, Baixa) A fun-to-explore vintage shop in Baixa, with a cafe inside.

Fábrica Sant'Ana HANDICRAFTS
(Map p702; Rua do Alecrim 95, Chiado) Great spot for purchasing fabulous new and old *azulejos*.

Livraria Bertrand BOOKS
(Map p702; ☎213 421 941; Rua Garrett 73, Chiado) Bertrand has Portuguese and foreign-language books amid 18th-century charm.

Information
Emergency
Police, Fire & Ambulance ☎119

Police station (☎217 654 242; Rua Capelo 13)

Tourist police (☎213 421 634; Palácio Foz, Praça dos Restauradores; ☉24hr)

Internet Access
If you're packing a laptop, these cafes offer free wireless surfing:

Mar Adentro (Rua do Alecrim 35)

Brown's Coffee Shop (Rua da Vitória 86)

Fábulas (Calçada Nova de São Francisco 14)

Sans laptop, head to the following places, which charge around €2 to €3 per hour:

Cyber Bica (Rua dos Duques de Bragança; ☉11am-midnight Mon-Fri)

Portugal Telecom (Praça Rossio 68; ☉8am-11pm)

Web Café (Rua do Diário de Notícias 126; ☉7pm-2am)

PARQUE NATURAL DA ARRÁBIDA

Thickly green, hilly and edged by gleamingly clean, golden beaches and chiselled cliffs, the Arrábida Natural Park stretches along the southeastern coast of the Setúbal Peninsula, some 40km south of Lisbon. Highlights here are the long, golden beaches of windsurfer hot-spot **Figueirinha** and the sheltered bay of **Galapo**. Most stunning of all is **Portinho da Arrábida** with fine sand, azure waters and a small 17th-century fort built to protect the monks from Barbary pirates.

Further west lies the former fishing village turned resort town of **Sesimbra**, with a fine beach, a hilltop castle and good seafood restaurants. Keep heading west to reach the haunting **Cabo Espichel**, home to a desolate church and striking ocean views over the cliffs.

Your best option for getting here and exploring the area is to rent a car. Be warned: parking is tricky near the beaches.

Internet Resources
www.timeout.pt Details on upcoming gigs, cultural events and interesting commentary, in Portuguese.

www.askmelisboa.com Multilingual site with info on discount cards.

www.golisbon.com Up-to-date info on sightseeing, eating, nightlife and events.

www.visitlisboa.com Lisbon's comprehensive tourism website, with the low-down on sightseeing, transport and accommodation.

Medical Services
Farmácia Estácio (Rossio 62) A central pharmacy.

British Hospital (📞217 213 400; Rua Tomás da Fonseca) English-speaking staff and doctors.

Money
Cota Câmbios (Rossio 41) One of the best exchange rates in town.

Post
Main post office (Map p702; Praça do Comércio)

Post office (Map p702; Praça dos Restauradores)

Telephone
Portugal Telecom (Rossio 68; ⊙8am-11pm)

Tourist Information
Ask Me Lisboa (Map p702; www.askmelisboa.com; Praça dos Restauradores; ⊙9am-8pm) The largest and most helpful tourist office. Can book accommodation or reserve rental cars.

Y Lisboa (Map p702; www.askmelisboa.com; Praça dos Restauradores; ⊙9am-8pm)

Lisboa Welcome Centre (Map p702; www.visitlisboa.com; Praça do Comércio; ⊙9am-6pm)

Information kiosks (Map p702; near Rua Conceição; ⊙10am-1pm & 2-6pm); Santa Apolónia (door 47, inside train station; ⊙8am-1pm Tue-Sat); Belém (Map p702; Largo dos Jernónimos; ⊙10am-1pm & 2-6pm Tue-Sat); Airport (⊙7am-midnight)

❶ Getting There & Away

Air
Around 6km north of the centre, **Aeroporto de Lisboa** (Lisbon Airport; Map p698; www.ana.pt) operates direct flights to many European cities.

Bus
Lisbon's long-distance bus terminal is **Sete Rios** (Map p698; Rua das Laranjeiras), conveniently linked to both Jardim Zoológico metro station and Sete Rios train station. The big carriers, **Rede Expressos** (📞213 581 460; www.rede-expressos.pt) and **Eva** (📞213 581 466; www.eva-bus.com), run frequent services to almost every major town.

The other major terminal is **Gare do Oriente** (at Oriente metro and train station), concentrating on services to the north and to Spain. The biggest companies operating from here are **Renex** (📞218 956 836; www.renex.pt) and the Spanish operator **Avanza** (📞218 940 250; www.avanzabus.com).

Train
Santa Apolónia station (Map p698) is the terminus for northern and central Portugal. You can catch trains from Santa Apolónia to Gare do Oriente train station, which has departures to The Algarve and international destinations. **Cais do Sodré station** (Map p702) is for Belém, Cascais and Estoril. **Rossio station** (Map p702) is the terminal for trains to Sintra via Queluz.

For fares and schedules visit www.cp.pt.

❶ Getting Around

To/From the Airport

The **AeroBus** (91) runs every 20 minutes from 7.45am to 8.15pm, taking 30 to 45 minutes between the airport and Cais do Sodré; buy your ticket (€3.50) on the bus. A **taxi** into town is about €10 to €14.

Car & Motorcycle

On the outskirts of the city there are cheap (or free) **car parks** near Parque das Nações and Belém. The most central underground car park is at Praça dos Restauradores, costing around €10 to €12 per day. On Saturday afternoons and Sunday, parking is normally free in the pay-and-display areas in the centre.

Public Transport

A 24-hour **Bilhete Carris/Metro** (€3.75) gives unlimited travel on all buses, trams, metros and funiculars. Pick it up from Carris kiosks and metro stations.

BUS, TRAM & FUNICULAR Buses and trams run from 6am to 1am, with a few all-night services. Pick up a transport map from tourist offices or Carris kiosks. A single ticket costs €1.40 on board or €0.81 if you buy a refillable *Viva Viagem* card (€0.50), available at Carris offices and in metro stations.

There are three funiculars:

Elevador da Bica (Map p702)
Elevador da Glória (Map p702)
Elevador do Lavra (Map p702)

Don't leave the city without riding **tram 28** from Largo Martim Moniz through the narrow streets of the Alfama; tram 12 goes from Praça da Figueira out to Belém.

FERRY Car, bicycle and passenger ferries leave frequently from the **Cais do Sodré ferry terminal** (Map p702) to Cacilhas (€0.81, 10 minutes), a transfer point for some buses to Setúbal. From **Terreiro do Paço terminal** catamarans zip across to Montijo (€2.10, every 30 minutes) and Seixal (€1.75, every 30 minutes).

METRO The **metro** (www.metrolisboa.pt; 1-/2-zone single €0.85/1.15; ☺6.30am-1am) is useful for hops across town and to the Parque das Nações. Buy tickets from metro ticket machines, which have English-language menus.

Taxi

Lisbon's taxis are metered and best hired from taxi ranks. Beware of rip-offs from the airport. From Rossio to Belém is around €8 and to the castle about €6. To call one, try **Rádio Táxis** (☎218 119 000) or **Autocoope** (☎217 932 756).

AROUND LISBON

Sintra

POP 26,400

Lord Byron called this hilltop town a 'glorious Eden' and, although best appreciated at dusk when the coach tours have left, it *is* a magnificent place. Less than an hour west of Lisbon, Sintra was the traditional summer retreat of Portugal's kings. Today it's a fairytale setting of stunning palaces and manors surrounded by rolling green countryside.

◉ Sights & Activities

Although the whole town resembles a historical theme park, there are several compulsory eye-catching sights. Most are free or discounted with the Lisboa Card (see p696).

TOP CHOICE **Quinta da Regaleira** VILLA, GARDENS
(www.regaleira.pt; Rua Barbosa du Bocage; adult/child €6/3; ☺10am-8pm) Exploring this neo-Manueline manor and gardens is like delving into another world. The villa has ferociously carved fireplaces, frescos and Venetian glass mosaics with wild mythological and Knights Templar symbols. The playful gardens hide fountains, grottoes, lakes and underground caverns. All routes seem to lead to the 30m-deep initiation well, **Poço Iniciáto**, with mysterious hollowed-out underground galleries lit by fairy lights.

Palácio Nacional de Sintra PALACE
(Largo Rainha Dona Amélia; admission €7; ☺10am-5.30pm Thu-Tue) The whimsical interior of Sintra's iconic twin-chimney palace is a mix of Moorish and Manueline styles, with arabesque courtyards, barley-twist columns and stunning 15th- and 16th-century geometric *azulejos*.

Castelo dos Mouros CASTLE
(adult/child €6/5; ☺10am-8pm) An energetic, 3km greenery-flanked hike from the

---

SINTRA BY BIKE

One new way to see the sights is via electric bicycle, offered by **MVP** (www.mvp.pt; ☺10am-6pm) in the Torre do Relógio near the tourist office in Sintra. Half-day rental costs €19, which is great value considering it includes free admission to four sites, including Castelo dos Mouros, Palácio Nacional da Pena and Monserrate Park.

centre, the 8th-century ruined ramparts of this castle provide fine views.

Palácio Nacional da Pena PALACE
(adult/child €8/6; ⊙10am-7pm) This exuberantly kitsch palace is a further 800m from the Castelo dos Mouros, and is a an architectural extravaganza crammed with curious treasures.

Museu de Arte Moderna MUSEUM
(www.berardocollection.com; Avenida Heliodoro Salgado; admission free; ⊙10am-6pm Tue-Sun) This first-rate museum hosts rotating exhibitions covering the entire modern-art spectrum, from kinetic and pop art to surrealism and expressionism.

Monserrate Park GARDENS, PALACE
(www.parquesdesintra.pt; adult/child €6/5; ⊙9.30am-8pm) This wild, rambling 30-hectare wooded garden 3.5km west of Sintra bristles with exotic foliage. A manicured lawn sweeps up to the whimsical, 19th-century Moorish-inspired *palácio* (⊙10am-1pm & 2-6.30pm).

🛏 Sleeping

Pensão Residencial Sintra GUEST HOUSE €€
(☎219 230 738; www.residencialsintra.blogspot.com; Travessa dos Avaleres 12; d incl breakfast from €80; @🛜🏊) This stately 1850s manor overlooks rambling gardens and an inviting pool, and offers captivating views to the castle. The bright, high-ceilinged rooms are decorated in crisp hues with shiny wood floors.

Lawrence's Hotel GUEST HOUSE €€
(☎219 105 500; www.lawrenceshotel.com; Rua Consiglieri Pedroso 38-40; d/ste from €90/180; ❄@) Lord Byron once stayed at this 18th-century mansion turned boutique hotel. It oozes charm in its lantern-lit, vaulted corridors, snug bar and individually designed rooms, decorated with *azulejos* and antique trunks. Lawrence's has an excellent restaurant.

Casa de Hóspedes Dona Maria da Parreirinha GUEST HOUSE €
(☎219 232 490; Rua João de Deus 12-14; d €45-55) A short walk from the train station, this small, homely guest house has old-fashioned but spotless rooms, with big windows, dark-wood furnishings and floral fabrics.

🍴 Eating & Drinking

Sintra is famous for its luscious pastries, including *queijadas* (crisp pastry shells filled with marzipan-like cheese, sugar, flour and cinnamon) and *travesseiros* (light rolled and folded puff pastries filled with almond-and-egg yolk cream). Sample the goods at **Fábrica das Verdadeiras Queijadas da Sapa** (Alameda Volta do Duche 12; ⊙closed Mon) and **Casa Piriquita** (Rua das Padarias 1-5; ⊙closed Wed).

Tulhas PORTUGUESE €€
(Rua Gil Vicente 4; mains €9-14; ⊙closed Wed) This converted grain warehouse is dark, tiled and quaint, with twisted chandeliers and a relaxed, cosy atmosphere. It's renowned for its *bacalhau com natas* (shredded cod with cream and potato).

Tasca do Xico TAPAS €€
(Rua Arco do Teixeira 6; tapas €4-6; ⊙noon-10pm Tue-Sun) On a quiet lane in the old quarter, the petite Tasca do Xico prepares tasty tapas plates (prawns with garlic, mussels in vinaigrette) as well as a few heartier changing specials such as grilled fresh fish of the day.

Saudade CAFE €
(Avenida Dr Miguel Bombardo 8; snacks €2-4; ⊙8am-10pm Tue-Sun) This former bakery has cherub-covered ceilings and a rambling interior, making it a fine spot for pastries or lighter fare (with a different soup, salad, fish and meat dish of the day). A gallery features changing art exhibitions.

ℹ Information
Tourist office (www.cm-sintra.pt; Praça da República 23; ⊙9am-7pm) Has useful maps and can help with accommodation.

ℹ Getting There & Away
The **Lisbon–Sintra railway** terminates in Sintra, a 1km scenic walk northeast of the town's historic centre. Sintra's **bus station**, and another train station, are a further 1km east in the new town Portela de Sintra. Frequent **shuttle buses** link the historic centre with the bus station.

Train services (€2, 40 minutes, every 15 minutes) run between Sintra and Lisbon's Rossio station. Buses run regularly from Sintra to Cascais (€3.50, 60 minutes), Estoril (€3.50, 40 minutes) and Mafra (45 minutes).

On Fridays to Sundays in summer, Sintra's restored electric tram, the **Elétrico de Sintra** (one-way €2) offers convenient access to the coast, departing about hourly from Rua Alves Roçadas near Portela de Sintra train station, arriving at Praia das Maçãs 45 minutes later.

ℹ Getting Around
A handy bus for accessing the castle is the hop-on, hop-off **Scotturb bus** 434 (€4.60), which runs from the train station via Sintra-Vila

to Castelo dos Mouros (10 minutes), Palácio da Pena (15 minutes) and back.

A **taxi** to Pena or Monserrate costs around €16 return.

Cascais

POP 33,400

Cascais is a handsome seaside resort with elegant buildings, an atmospheric Old Town and a happy abundance of restaurants and bars.

◎ Sights & Activities

Coast & Beaches   COAST, BEACHES

Cascais' three sandy bays – **Praia da Conceição**, **Praia da Rainha** and **Praia da Ribeira** – are great for a sunbake or a tingly Atlantic dip, but attract crowds in summer.

Estoril is a somewhat faded resort 2km east of Cascais with a popular sandy beach and Europe's largest **casino** (www.casino-estoril.pt).

The sea roars into the coast at **Boca do Inferno** (Hell's Mouth), 2km west of Cascais. Spectacular **Cabo da Roca**, Europe's westernmost point, is 16km from Cascais and Sintra and is served by buses from both towns.

Casa das Histórias Paula Rego   GALLERY

(www.casadashistoriaspaularego.com; Avenida da República 300; admission free; ◎10am-8pm) Sintra's stellar new attraction showcases the evocative, twisted fairy-tale-like paintings of Paula Rego, one of Portugal's finest living artists.

Museu Condes de Castro Guimarães

MUSEUM

(admission €2; ◎10am-5pm Tue-Sun) The picturesque gardens of **Parque Marechal Carmona** (Avenida Rei Humberto II) house this museum in a whimsical early-19th-century mansion, complete with castle turrets and Arabic cloister.

🛏 Sleeping & Eating

Fortaleza do Guincho   LUXURY HOTEL €€€

(☎214 870 491; www.guinchotel.pt; Estrada do Guincho; d incl breakfast from €205; 🅿@🛜) Set in a 17th-century fortress perched over the sea, this dramatic five-star guest house has small but beautifully set rooms with solid antique furnishings. The superb **restaurant** (mains around €32) has a Michelin star.

Residencial Solar Dom Carlos

GUEST HOUSE €€

(☎214 828 115; www.solardomcarlos.pt; Rua Latino Coelho 104; s/d €55/70; 🅿❄) Hidden down a sleepy alley, this 16th-century former royal residence turned guest house retains lots of original features, from chandeliers to wood beams, *azulejos* and a frescoed breakfast room.

Cascais Beach Hostel   HOSTEL €

(☎309 906 421; www.cascaisbeachostel.com; Rua da Vista Alegre 10; dm/d €20/50; @🛜🚇) Central for Cascais' beaches and nightlife, this hostel has wood-floored rooms, a lounge, communal kitchen and pool.

Confraria Sushi   JAPANESE €€

(Rua Luís Xavier Palmeirim 16; mains €8-13; ◎noon-midnight Tue-Sun) This art-slung cafe, jazzed up with technicolour glass chandeliers, is a fun spot for sushi and tasty salads. Patio seating.

Apeadeiro   SEAFOOD €€

(Avenida Vasco da Gama 252; mains €7-12) With walls hung with fishing nets, this sunny restaurant is known for its superb char-grilled fish – shrimp piri-piri is delicious.

ℹ Information

Tourist office (www.visiteestoril.com; Rua Visconde de Luz 14) Can provide accommodation lists and bus timetables.

ℹ Getting There & Around

Trains run frequently to Cascais via Estoril (€1.70, 40 minutes) from Cais do Sodré station in Lisbon.

THE ALGARVE

Love it or loathe it, it's easy to see the allure of The Algarve: breathtaking cliffs, golden sands, scalloped bays and long sandy islands. Although overdevelopment has blighted parts of the coast, head inland and you'll land solidly in lovely Portuguese countryside once again. Algarve highlights include the forested slopes of Monchique, pretty riverside town of Tavira and windswept, historic Sagres. Underrated Faro is the regional capital.

BIKE TO THE BEACH

Free bikes are available from 8am to 7pm from a kiosk on Largo da Estação near the train station (bring ID). There's a bicycle path that runs the entire 9km stretch from Cascais to wild **Guincho** beach, a popular surf spot.

The Algarve

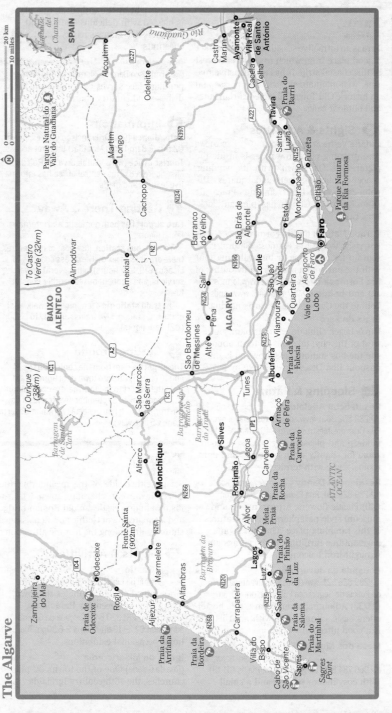

Faro

POP 58,000

Faro is an attractive seaside town and makes a good place from which to explore the rest of this coastal strip. It has an attractive marina, well-maintained parks and plazas and an historic Old Town full of pedestrian lanes and outdoor cafes.

◉ Sights & Activities

Cidade Velha & Waterfront   OLD TOWN
An intriguing place to wander is inside the picturesque Old Town, with its winding, peaceful cobbled streets and squares. The palm-clad **waterfront** around Praça de Dom Francisco Gomes has pleasant kickback cafes.

Parque Natural da Ria Formosa   PARK
For visits to the Ria Formosa Natural Park, sign up for a boating or birdwatching tour with the environmentally friendly outfits of **Ria Formosa** (289 817 466; www.formosamar.pt) and **Lands** (967 073 846; www.lands.pt), both in the Clube Naval in Faro's marina.

Praia de Faro   BEACH
Faro's beach (Ilha de Faro), is 6km southwest of the city; take bus 16 from opposite the bus station. Less crowded is the unspoilt Ilha Deserta, reachable by ferry.

🛏 Sleeping & Eating

Residencial Adelaide   GUEST HOUSE €€
(289 802 383; www.adelaideresidencial.net; Rua Cruz dos Mestres 9; s/d €40/50;❀🛜) This modern and pleasant guest house is good value for slightly worn but clean and light rooms, some with terraces.

Residencial Dandy   GUEST HOUSE €€
(289 824 791; Rua Filipe Alistão 62; d from €40) Plastic flowers, African masks and museum-style paraphernalia are features of this rambling place. The best rooms have antique furniture, high ceilings and wrought-iron balconies.

Pousada da Juventude   HOSTEL €
(289 826 521; www.pousadasjuventude.pt; Rua da Polícia de Segurança Pública 1; dm/d from €14/32) Adjoining a small park, this hostel offers basic, clean rooms with no frills but is a good ultrabudget option.

Mesa dos Mouros

PORTUGUESE, INTERNATIONAL €€€
(966 784 536; Largo da Sé 10; mains €11-18) With cosy indoor seating and a small terrace right by the cathedral, this place is blessed with delicious seafood and gourmet-style mains such as rabbit with chestnuts.

Adega Nova   PORTUGUESE €€
(Rua Francisco Barreto 24; mains €6-14) This popular place serves tasty meat and fish dishes amid country charm.

ℹ Information

Café Aliança (Rua Dr Francisco Gomes; per hr €2.50; ⊙8am-10pm Mon-Sat) Internet access.
Tourist office (www.visitalgarve.pt; Rua da Misericórdia 8) This central office has informative leaflets and maps.

ℹ Getting There & Away

Faro airport has both domestic and international flights.

From the **bus station**, just west of the centre, there are at least six daily express coaches to Lisbon (€19, four hours), plus several slower services, and frequent buses to other coastal towns.

The **train station** is a few minutes' walk west of the bus station. Five trains run daily to Lisbon (€21, four hours).

ℹ Getting Around

The **airport** is 6km from the centre. **Buses** 14 and 16 (€1.65) run into town until 9pm. A **taxi** from the airport to the town centre costs about €12. From May to September, five **ferries** a day run from to/from Ilha Deserta (www.ilha-deserta.com; €5 one-way).

Tavira

POP 12,600

Set on either side of the meandering Rio Gilão, Tavira is a charming town. The ruins of a hilltop castle, an old Roman bridge and a smattering of Gothic and Renaissance churches are among the historic attractions.

◉ Sights & Activities

FREE **Castle**   CASTLE
(Rua da Liberdade; ⊙10am-5pm) Tavira's ruined castle dominates the town. Nearby, the 16th-century **Palácio da Galeria** (281 320 540; Calçada da Galeria; admission €2; ⊙10am-noon & 3-6.30pm Tue-Sat) holds occasional exhibitions.

Igreja da Misericórdia   CHURCH
(Rua da Galeria) One of the town's 30-plus churches, the 16th-century Igreja da

Misericórdia is among the most striking in The Algarve.

Ilha da Tavira ISLAND, BEACH
An island beach connected to the mainland by a ferry at Quatro Águas. Walk the 2km or take the (summer-only) bus from the bus station.

Casa Abilio BIKE HIRE
(Rua João Vaz Corte Real 23; per day around €7) Enjoy pedal power with a rented bike.

Sport Nautica KAYAKING
(Rua Jacques Pessoa 26; per half-/full day €15/25) Rent kayaks for a paddle along the river.

🛏 Sleeping & Eating

Pensão Residencial Lagôas GUEST HOUSE €
(✆281 322 252; Rua Almirante Cândido dos Reis 24; s/d from €20/30) A long-standing favourite, friendly Lagôas has small (some cramped), spotless rooms. There's a plant-filled courtyard and good terrace views.

Residencial Princesa do Gilão
GUEST HOUSE €€
(✆281 325 171; Rua Borda d'Água de Aguiar 10; s/d €50/60; 🅿) This '80s-style place on the river has tight but neat rooms with identical decor. Go for a room with a river view.

Pensão Residencial Castelo
GUEST HOUSE €€
(✆281 320 790; Rua da Liberdade 22; s/d €40/60; 🅿) Castelo offers nicely furnished rooms with spotless tile floors. Some also have balconies and castle views.

Restaurante Bica SEAFOOD €€
(Rua Almirante Cândido dos Reis 24; mains €7-16) Deservedly popular, Bica serves splendid food, such as fresh grilled fish, which diners enjoy with inexpensive but decent Borba wine.

Bistro 'oPorto' INTERNATIONAL €€
(Rua Dr José Pires Padinha 180; mains €10-14; ⊙lunch & dinner Tue-Sat) An intimate bar and a relaxed riverside setting make for a pleasant time at this French-owned spot. Dishes combine Portuguese and French flavours and vegetarians are usually catered for.

ℹ Information

Câmara municipal (town hall; Praça da Republica; ⊙9am-8pm Mon-Fri, 10am-1pm Sat) Free internet access.

Tourist office (Rua da Galeria 9) Can help with accommodation

ℹ Getting There & Away

Some 15 **trains** and six express **buses** run daily between Faro and Tavira (€3.20, one hour).

Lagos
POP 17,500

In summer the pretty fishing port of Lagos has a party vibe; its picturesque cobbled streets and pretty nearby beaches pack with revellers and sun-seekers.

◉ Sights & Activities

Museu Municipal MUSEUM
(Rua General Alberto da Silveira; admission €3; ⊙9.30am-12.30pm & 2-5pm Tue-Sun) The municipal museum houses an eclectic mix of archaeological and ecclesiastical treasures (and oddities). Admission includes the adjacent **Igreja de Santo António**, one of the best baroque churches in Portugal.

Beaches BEACHES
The beach scene includes **Meia Praia**, a vast strip to the east; **Praia da Luz** to the west; and the smaller **Praia do Pinhão**.

Blue Ocean OUTDOOR ACTIVITIES
(✆964 665 667; www.blue-ocean-divers.de) Organises diving, kayaking and snorkelling safaris. Along the promenade, fishermen can offer motorboat jaunts to nearby grottoes.

Kayak Adventures KAYAKING
(www.kayakadventures-lagos.com) Offers kayaking trips from Batata Beach.

🛏 Sleeping

Pensão Marazul GUEST HOUSE €€
(✆282 770 230; www.pensaomarazul.com; Rua 25 de Abril 13; s/d from €40/50; @🤝) Draws a good mix of foreign travellers to its small but cheerfully painted rooms – the best of which offer sea views.

Sol a Sol HOTEL €€
(✆282 761 290; www.residencialsolasol.com; Rua Lançarote de Freitas 22; s/d/tr from €60/65/80) This central, small hotel has neat rooms with tiny balconies and views over the town.

Pousada da Juventude HOSTEL €
(✆282 761 970; www.pousadasjuventude.pt; Rua Lançarote de Freitas 50; dm €16, d €43, without bathroom €35; @) One of Portugal's best, this well-run hostel is a great place to meet other travellers.

✗ Eating

TOP CHOICE **A Forja** PORTUGUESE €€
(Rua dos Ferreiros 17; mains €7-15;
☺lunch & dinner Sun-Fri) This buzzing place
pulls in the crowds for its hearty, top-
quality traditional food. Plates of the day
are always reliable, as are the fish dishes.

Casinha do Petisco PORTUGUESE, SEAFOOD €€
(Rua da Oliveira 51; mains €7-12; ☺Mon-Sat) This
tiny traditional gem comes highly recommended by locals for its seafood grills and
shellfish dishes.

ⓘ Information

Café Gélibar (Rua Lançarote de Freitas 43; per
hr €3; ☺9am-10pm) Sip coffee while emailing.

Tourist office (www.visitalgarve.pt; Praça Gil
Eanes) In the centre of town.

ⓘ Getting There & Away

Bus and **train** services depart frequently for
other Algarve towns, and around eight times
daily to Lisbon (€20, 4¼ hours).

ⓘ Getting Around

A **bus service** (tickets €1-2; ☺7am-8pm Mon-
Sat) provides useful connections to the beaches
of Meia Praia and Luz. Rent bicycles and motorbikes from **Motorent** (☏289 769 716; www.
motorent.pt; Rua Victor Costa e Silva; bike/
motorcycle per day from €10/50).

Monchique

POP 2800

High above the coast, in cooler mountainous woodlands, the picturesque hamlet of
Monchique makes a lovely base for exploring, with some excellent options for walking,
cycling and canoeing.

⊙ Sights & Activities

Caldas de Monchique, 6km south, is a
peaceful hamlet with a **spa resort** (www.
monchiquetermas.com). Some 8km west is The
Algarve's 'rooftop', the 902m **Fóia** peak atop
the Serra de Monchique, with heady views
through a forest of radio masts.

Igreja Matriz CHURCH
(Rua da Igreja) This church features a stunning Manueline portal, with its stone seemingly tied in knots. Keep climbing to reach
the ruins of the 17th-century Franciscan
monastery, **Nossa Senhora do Desterro**,
which overlooks the town from its wooded
hilltop.

Outdoor Tours OUTDOOR ACTIVITIES
(☏282 969 520, 916 736 226; www.outdoor-tours.
com; Mexilhoeira Grande; trips from €20) Offers
cycling, kayaking and walking trips.

🛏 Sleeping & Eating

Residencial Miradouro GUEST HOUSE €
(☏282 912 163; Rua dos Combatentes do Ultra-
mar; s/d/tr €35/40/50) This 1970s hilltop
place offers sweeping, breezy views and
neat rooms, some with balcony.

A Charrete PORTUGUESE €€
(Rua Dr Samora Gil 30-34; mains €9-16; ☺lunch
& dinner Thu-Tue) Touted as the town's best
eatery for its regional specialities, this
place serves reliably good cuisine amid
country rustic charm.

ⓘ Information

Tourist office (Largo de São Sebastião;
☺9.30am-1pm & 2-5.30pm Mon-Fri) Uphill
from the bus stop.

ⓘ Getting There & Away

There are five to nine **buses** daily from Portimão
(€2.80, 45 minutes) to Monchique.

Silves

POP 10,800

The one-time capital of Moorish Algarve,
Silves is a pretty town of jumbling orange
rooftops scattered above the banks of the
Rio Arade. Clamber around the ramparts of
its fairy-tale **castle** for superb views.

🛏 Sleeping & Eating

Residencial Ponte Romana GUEST HOUSE €
(☏282 443 275; Horta da Cruz; s/d €20/35)
Floral-themed rooms beside the Roman
bridge, with castle views and a cavernous bar-restaurant full of old-timers and
Portuguese families.

Quinta da Figueirinha RURAL INN €€
(☏282 440 700; www.qdf.pt; 2-/4-/6-person
apt €64/92/125; ☰) Four kilometres outside
of Silves, this 36-hectare organic farm offers simple apartments in idyllic, farmlike
surroundings.

Café Ingles CAFE, BAR €€
(mains €7-14; ☎) Situated at the castle entrance, this funky English-owned place has
vegetarian dishes, homemade soups, pasta
and wood-fired pizza. In summer there's
live music at weekends.

ℹ Information

No Name Internet (Rua Pintor Bernardo Marques; per hr €2) Internet access.

ℹ Getting There & Away

Silves **train station** is 2km from town; trains from Lagos (€2.15, 35 minutes) stop eight times daily (from Faro, change at Tunes), to be met by local buses. Four to seven **buses** run daily connecting Silves and Albufeira (€3.75, 40 minutes).

Sagres

POP 1940

The small, elongated village of Sagres has an end-of-the-world feel with its sea-carved cliffs and empty, wind-whipped fortress high above the ocean.

⊙ Sights & Activities

Coast & Beaches   COAST, BEACHES

Visit Europe's southwestern-most point, the **Cabo de São Vicente** (Cape St Vincent), 6km to the west. A solitary lighthouse stands on this barren cape.

This coast is ideal for surfing; hire windsurfing gear at sand-dune fringed **Praia do Martinhal**. You can sign up for surfing lessons, hire bikes and arrange canoe trips with **Sagres Natura** (www.sagresnatura.com; Rua São Vicente). **DiversCape** (🖉965 559 073; www.diverscape.com; Porto da Balereira) organises diving trips.

Fortaleza de Sagres   FORT

(adult/child €3/1.50; ⊙10am-8.30pm) Sagres' fort offers breathtaking views over the seaside cliffs. According to legend, this is where Henry the Navigator established his navigation school and primed the early Portuguese explorers.

🛏 Sleeping & Eating

Casa do Cabo de Santa Maria
                    GUEST HOUSE €€

(🖉282 624 722; casacabosantamaria@sapo.pt; Rua Patrão António Faústino; r/apt from €50/80) These squeaky-clean rooms and apartments might not have sweeping views, but they are handsome and nicely furnished.

TOP
CHOICE **A Tasca**   SEAFOOD €€€

(Porto da Baleeira; mains €12-25; ⊙lunch & dinner Thu-Tue) Overlooking the marina, this cosy place whips up tasty *cataplana* (seafood and sausage cooked in a copper pot) and other seafood dishes, best enjoyed on the sunny terrace.

ℹ Information

Tourist office (Rua Comandante Matoso; ⊙Tue-Sat) Central to town.

ℹ Getting There & Away

Frequent **buses** run daily to Sagres from Lagos (€3.50, one hour), with fewer on Sunday. Two continue out to Cabo de São Vicente on weekdays.

CENTRAL PORTUGAL

The vast centre of Portugal is a rugged swath of rolling hillsides, whitewashed villages and olive groves and cork trees. Richly historic, it is scattered with prehistoric remains and medieval castles. It's also home to one of Portugal's most architecturally rich towns, Évora, as well as several spectacular walled villages. There are fine local wines and, for the more energetic, plenty of outdoor exploring in the dramatic Beiras region.

Évora

POP 56,500

Évora is an enchanting place to delve into the past. Inside the 14th-century walls, Évora's narrow, winding lanes lead to a striking medieval cathedral, a Roman temple and a picturesque town square. These old-fashioned good-looks are the backdrop to a lively student town surrounded by wineries and dramatic countryside.

⊙ Sights & Activities

Sé   CHURCH

(Largo do Marquês de Marialva; admission €2-5; ⊙9am-noon & 2-5pm) Évora's cathedral has fabulous cloisters and a museum jam-packed with ecclesiastical treasures.

Templo Romano   RUINS

(Temple of Diana; Largo do Conde de Vila Flor) Once part of the Roman Forum; it's a heady slice of drama right in town.

Capela dos Ossos   OSSUARY

(Praça 1 de Maio; admission €2; ⊙9am-1pm & 2.30-6pm) Built from the skeletons of several thousand people, the ghoulish Chapel of Bones in the Igreja de São Francisco provides a real *Addams Family* day out.

🛏 Sleeping

TOP
CHOICE **Albergaria Calvario**
                    BOUTIQUE HOTEL €€€

(🖉266 745 930; Travessa dos Lagares 3; d/studio incl breakfast €108/125) Elegant, friendly and

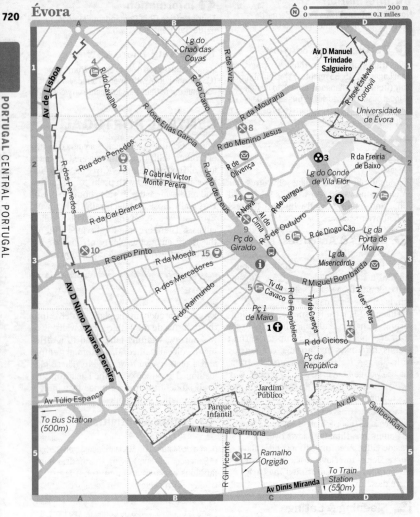

0　　200 m
0　　0.1 miles

comfortable, this place has an ambience that travellers adore. Pleasant lounge areas, books and classical music, plus comfortable beds and flat-screen TVs, ensure a homely stay. Breakfasts are excellent.

Residencial Policarpo　GUEST HOUSE **€€**
(☎266 702 424; www.pensaopolicarpo.com; Rua da Freiria de Baixo 16; d €57, without bathroom €35; P@) This former 16th-century home is charming and atmospheric, if somewhat faded. The guest rooms are decorated with a mix of carved wooden – as well as traditionally hand-painted – Alentejan furniture.

Casa dos Teles　GUEST HOUSE **€**
(☎266 702 453; Rua Romão Ramalho 27; d €30-40; ❄) These nine rooms – mostly light and airy – are good value; quieter rooms at the back overlook a pretty courtyard.

Residencial Diana　GUEST HOUSE **€€**
(☎266 702 008; Rua de Diogo Cão 2; d €55, without bathroom €47; ❄🖥) The Diana is slightly long in the tooth now, with saggy mattresses and grannylike decor. Nevertheless, it's still somewhat charming in a high-ceilinged-and-wood-floored kind of way.

⊙ Sights

◉ Eating

◉ Sleeping

◉◉ Drinking

✕ Eating

Botequim da Mouraria   PORTUGUESE €€
(📞266 746 775; Rua da Mouraria 16a; mains €12.50-
14; ⊙lunch & dinner Mon-Fri, lunch Sat) Poke
around the old Moorish quarter to find this
cosy spot serving some of Évora's finest food
and wine. There are no reservations, just 12
stools at a counter. Rumour is that it's moving to larger premises.

Dom Joaquim   PORTUGUESE €€
(📞266 731 105; Rua dos Penedos 6; mains
€11-13; ⊙lunch & dinner Thu-Tue) Amid stone
walls and modern artwork, Dom Joaquim serves excellent traditional cuisine
including meats (game and succulent,
fall-off-the bone oven lamb) and seafood
dishes.

Vinho e Noz   PORTUGUESE €€
(Ramalho Orgigão 12; mains €9-11; ⊙lunch &
dinner Mon-Sat) This delightful family-run
place has professional service, a large wine
list and good-quality cuisine.

Café Arcada   CAFE, RESTAURANT €
(Praça do Giraldo 10; meals €7-10; ⊙breakfast,
lunch & dinner) An Évora institution, serving
up coffee, crêpes and cakes, with outdoor
tables on the plaza.

Pastelaria Conventual Pão de Rala

        PASTISSERIE €
(Rua do Cicioso 47; ⊙7.30am-8pm) Specialises
in heavenly pastries, all made on the
premises.

◉ Drinking

Cup of Joe   CAFE, BAR €
(Praça de Sertório 3; ⊙noon-2am) Part of a
coffee chain, this attractive cafe has peaceful outdoor seating overlooking a plaza.
Electronic music and a friendly cocktail-
sipping crowd arrive by night.

Bar do Teatro   BAR
(Praça Joaquim António de Aguiar; ⊙8pm-2am)
This small, inviting bar has high ceilings
and old-world decor that sees a friendly
mixed crowd.

Ofcin@Bar   BAR
(Rua da Moeda 27; ⊙8pm-2am Mon-Sat) Attracting all ages, this is a small, relaxed
bar with jazz and blues playing in the
background.

ⓘ Information

Câmara municipal (town hall; ⊙9am-12.30pm
& 2-5pm Mon-Fri) Free internet.

Tourist office (www.cm-evora.pt; Praça do
Giraldo 73) Has an excellent city map.

ⓘ Getting There & Away

Évora has six to 12 **buses** daily to Lisbon (€12,
two hours) and three to Faro (€16, five hours),
departing from the station off Avenida São Sebastião (700m southwest of the centre). At the
time of research the **train station** (600m south
of the Jardim Público) was closed. When operating, trains head to Lisbon, Beja, Lagos and Faro.

Monsaraz

POP 20

In a dizzy setting high above the plain, this
walled village has a moody medieval feel
and magnificent views.

The **Museu de Arte Sacra** (Plaça Dom
Nuno Álvares; admission €1.80; ⊙10am-6pm) has
a good display of religious artefacts; the
15th-century fresco here is quite superb.
Situated 3km north of town is **Menhir of
Outeiro**, one of the tallest megalithic monuments ever discovered.

There are several places to stay in town,
including the friendly **Casa Paroquial**
(📞266 557 181; Rua Direita 4; s/d/tr €35/40/70),

WORTH A TRIP

MEGALITHS

Ancient Greek for 'big stones', **megaliths** are found all over the ancient landscape that surrounds Évora. Such prehistoric structures, built around 5000 to 6000 years ago, dot the European Atlantic coast, but here in Alentejo there is an astounding number of Neolithic remains. Dolmens (Neolithic stone tombs, or *antas* in Portuguese) were probably temples and/or tombs, covered with a large flat stone and usually built on hilltops or near water. Menhirs (individual standing stones) point to fertility rites, while *cromeleques* (cromlechs, stone circles) were also places of worship.

Évora's tourist office sells a *Historical Itineraries* leaflet (€1.05) that details many sites. Dolmen devotees can buy the book *Paisagens Arqueologicas A Oeste de Évora*, which has English summaries.

The star attraction is the **Cromeleque dos Almendres**, the Iberian peninsula's most important megalithic group. The site consists of a huge oval of some 95 rounded granite monoliths – some of which are engraved with symbolic markings – spread down a rough slope. They were erected over different periods, it seems with geometric and astral consideration, probably for social gatherings or sacred rituals. Some 15km west of Évora, it's an extraordinary site to visit.

Two and a half kilometres before Cromeleque dos Almendres stands **Menhir dos Almendres**, a single stone about 4m high, with some very faint carvings near the top. Look for the sign; to reach the menhir you must walk for a few hundred metres from the road.

To get to this area, your only option is to rent a car or bike (note that about 5km of the route is rough and remote). Stop by the tourist office for exact driving directions.

with wooden trimmings, whitewashed walls and heavy wooden furniture.

Eat before 8pm as the town tucks up early to bed. **Cafe-Restaurante Lumumba** (Rua Direita 12; mains €7-9; ☺lunch & dinner) is a small local favourite for its pleasant atmosphere, decent mains and terrace with views.

The **tourist office** (☎266 557 136; Praça Dom Nuno Álvares) can offer advice on accommodation.

Up to four daily **buses** connect Monsaraz with Reguengos de Monsaraz (€3, 35 minutes, Monday to Friday), with connections to Évora.

Estremoz

POP 9000

One of three marble towns in these parts, Estremoz has an attractive centre set with peaceful plazas, orange-tree-lined lanes and a hilltop castle and convent. In its prime, the town was one of the most strongly fortified in Portugal, with its very own palace (now a luxurious *pousada;* upmarket inn).

⊙ Sights

Museu Municipal　　　　　　　　MUSEUM
(Largo D Dinis; adult/child €1.50/free; ☺9am-12.30pm & 2-5.30pm Tue-Sun) In a beautiful 17th-century almshouse, the municipal

museum specialises in fascinating pottery figurines, including an entire Easter parade.

Palácio Ducal　　　　　　　　　　PALACE
(Terreiro do Paça, Vila Viçosa; admission €6; ☺2.30-5.30pm Tue, 10am-1pm & 2.30-5.30pm Wed-Sun) Located in another marble town 17km from Estremoz, this magnificent ancestral home of the dukes of Bragança is rich with *azulejos,* frescoed ceilings and elaborate tapestries.

🛏 Sleeping & Eating

Residencial O Gadanha　　GUEST HOUSE　€
(☎268 339 110; www.residencialogadanha.com; Largo General Graça 56; s/d/tr €20/32.50/42.50; ❄) This whitewashed house offers excellent value for its bright, fresh and clean rooms overlooking the square.

Adega do Isaías　　　　　　PORTUGUESE　€€
(Rua do Almeida 21; mains €8-12; ☺lunch & dinner Mon-Sat) This award-winning, rustic *tasca* serves tender fish, meat and Alentejan specialities inside a wine cellar crammed with tables and huge wine jars.

ⓘ Information

Tourist office (www.cm-estremoz.pt; Rossio Marquês de Pombal) Just south of Rossio.

ℹ️ Getting There & Away

Estremoz is linked to Évora by three local **buses** (€4, 1¼ hours), Monday to Friday.

Peniche

POP 16,000

Popular for its nearby surfing beaches and also as a jumping-off point for the beautiful Ilhas Berlengas nature reserve, the coastal city of Peniche remains a working port, giving it a slightly grittier and more 'lived-in' feel than its beach-resort neighbours. It has a walled historic centre and lovely beaches east of town.

From the bus station, it's a 10-minute walk west to the historic centre.

👁 Sights

Fortress   FORTRESS

(admission free) Peniche's imposing 16th-century fortress served as one of dictator Salazar's infamous jails for political prisoners and was later a temporary home for African refugees. The on-site **museum** (admission €1.50) houses the chilling interrogation chambers and cells on the top floor.

Islands   ISLANDS

About 5km to the northeast of Peniche is the scenic island-village of **Baleal**, connected to the mainland village of Casais do Baleal by a causeway. The fantastic sweep of sandy beach here offers some fine surfing. Surf schools dot the sands, as do several bar-restaurants.

Sitting about 10km offshore from Peniche, **Berlenga Grande** is a spectacular, rocky and remote island, with twisting, shocked-rock formations and gaping caverns. It's the only island of the Berlenga archipelago you can visit; the group consists of three tiny islands surrounded by clear, calm, dark-blue waters full of shipwrecks – great for snorkelling and diving. Several outfits make the 40-minute trip to the island, including **Viamar** (✆262 785 646; www.viamar-berlenga.com; return adult/child €18/10).

🏃 Activities

Surfing

Surf camps offer week-long instruction (from €250 to 450 per week including lodging) as well as individual two-hour classes (€50), plus board and wetsuit hire. Well-established names include **Baleal Surfcamp** (www.baleal surfcamp.com), **Maximum Surfcamp** (www.maximumsurfcamp.com) and **Peniche Surfcamp** (www.penichesurfcamp.com).

Diving

There are good diving opportunities around Peniche, and especially around Berlenga. Expect to pay about €60 to €70 for two dives (less around Peniche) with **Acuasuboeste** (www.acuasuboeste.com; Porto de Pesca) or **Haliotis** (www.haliotis.pt; Avenida Monsenhor Bastos).

Kitesurfing

Kitesurfing is big in Peniche. **Peniche Kite & Surf Center** (www.penichekitecenter.com) offers lessons with equipment for €70.

🛏 Sleeping

TOP CHOICE **Casa das Marés**   B&B €€

(✆262 769 255/200/371; www.casadas mares2.com, www.casadasmares1.com; Praia do Baleal; d €80; 🛜) At the picturesque, windswept tip of Baleal, this imposing house features three unique adjoining B&Bs run by three sisters. The breezy, inviting rooms all have great sea views, and the entire place is loaded with character. Worth reserving ahead.

WORTH A TRIP

CASTELO DE VIDE

A worthy detour north of Estremoz is the hilltop, story-book town **Castelo de Vide**, noted for its picturesque houses with Gothic doorways. Highlights are the **Judiaria** (Old Jewish Quarter), the **medieval backstreets** and (yet another) castle-top **view**. Try to spend a night here heading skywards to **Marvão** (population 190), a fabulous mountain-top walled village 12km from Castelo de Vide. There are charming guest houses in the area, including the good-value **Casa de Hóspedes Melanie** (✆245 901 632; Largo do Paça Novo 3; s/d/tr €25/35/45; ❄) in Castelo de Vide, and the very elegant **Quinta do Barrieiro** (✆245 964 308; www.quintadobarrieiro.com; d from €85; ❄🛜🏊) in Marvão.

On weekdays, three **buses** run from Portalegre to Castelo de Vide (€2.50 to €5, 20 minutes) and two to Marvão (€2.50, 45 minutes). There are three buses connecting Estremoz and Portalegre (€5 to €9, 50 to 80 minutes).

Peniche Hostel
HOSTEL €

(☎969 008 689; www.penichehostel.com; Rua Arquitecto Paulino Montês 6; dm/d €20/45; @🛜) This cosy welcoming hostel, only five minutes' walk from the bus station, has colourfully decorated rooms overlooking the town wall. Surfboards and bikes are available for hire, and there's an attached surf school.

Mar e Sol
HOTEL €€

(☎919 543 105; www.restaurantemaresol.com; d/q €80/130; ⊙mid-Apr–Oct) One of two places to stay on the island of Berlenga Grande, with simple rooms just a few steps above Berlenga's boat dock. Book well ahead.

✖ Eating

Restaurante A Sardinha
SEAFOOD €€

(Rua Vasco da Gama 81; mains €6.50-12.50; ⊙lunch & dinner) This simple place on a narrow street parallel to Largo da Ribeira does a roaring trade with locals and tourists alike.

Hó Amaral
PORTUGUESE €€

(Rua Dr Francisco Seia 7; mains €8-14; ⊙lunch & dinner Fri-Wed) Still going strong after 35 years, this snug wood-panelled eatery reliably does some of the best seafood in Peniche.

❶ Getting There & Away

Peniche's **bus station** (☎968 903 861) is located 400m northeast of the tourist office (cross the Ponte Velha connecting the town to the isthmus). Buses go to Lisbon (€8.20, 1½ hours, every one to two hours), Coimbra (€13, 2¾ hours, three daily) and Óbidos (€2.75, 40 minutes, five to 13 daily).

Óbidos

POP 3100

This exquisite walled village was a wedding gift from Dom Dinis to his wife Dona Isabel (beats a fondue set), and its historic centre is a delightful place to wander. Highlights include the **Igreja de Santa Maria** (Rua Direita), with fine *azulejos*, and views from the town walls.

⌂ Sleeping & Eating

Bar Lagar da Mouraria
BAR, RESTAURANT €

(Rua da Mouraria; mains €8-10; ⊙11am-2am) Housed in a former winery, with beamed ceiling, a flagstone floor and seats around a massive old winepress, this charmer has a menu of tapas, cheese, sausage, sandwiches, fish soup or daily specials.

Casa de São Thiago
B&B €€

(☎262 959 587; www.casas-sthiago.com; Largo de São Thiago; s/d €65/80) This charming labyrinth of trim 18th-century rooms and flower-filled courtyards sits in the shadow of the castle.

Óbido Sol
GUEST HOUSE €

(☎262 959 188; Rua Direita 40; d €40-50) This neatly kept Old Town guest house has cosy and comfortable rooms surrounding a snug living room.

❶ Information

Espaço Internet (Rua Direita 107) Free internet access.

Tourist office (Rua Direita) This helpful tourist office is just outside Porta da Vila, the town's main entrance gate.

❶ Getting There & Away

There are direct **buses** Monday to Friday from Lisbon (€7, 70 minutes).

Nazaré

POP 16,000

With a warren of narrow cobbled lanes running down to a wide, cliff-backed beach, Nazaré is Estremadura's most picturesque coastal resort. The town centre is jammed with seafood restaurants, bars and local women in traditional dress hawking rooms for rent.

◉ Sights & Activities

The **beaches** here are superb, although swimmers should be aware of dangerous currents. Climb or take the funicular to the clifftop **Sítio**, with its cluster of fishermen's cottages and great view.

Historic Monasteries
ARCHITECTURE

Two of Portugal's big-time architectural masterpieces are close by. Follow the signs to Alcobaça where, right in the centre of town, is the immense **Mosteiro de Santa Maria de Alcobaça** (admission €6; ⊙9am-7pm) dating from 1178; don't miss the colossal former kitchen.

Batalha's massive **Mosteiro de Santa Maria de Vitória** (admission €6; ⊙9am-6pm), dating from 1388, is among the supreme achievements of Manueline architecture.

⌂ Sleeping & Eating

Many townspeople rent out rooms; doubles start at €35.

Vila Conde Fidalgo
GUEST HOUSE €
(☑262 552 361; http://condefidalgo.planetaclix.pt; Avenida da Independência Nacional 21a; d/apt from €45/50) This pretty little complex uphill a few blocks from the beach is built around a series of flower-filled courtyards. Rooms all have kitchenettes.

Adega Oceano
HOTEL €€
(☑262 561 161; www.adegaoceano.com, in Portuguese; Avenida da República 51; d €50-60; ❄☎) This little oceanfront place offers pleasantly set rooms – renovated modern rooms in back, beach-view quarters in front.

TOP CHOICE | A Tasquinha
SEAFOOD €€
(Rua Adrião Batalha 54; mains €6.50-11; ☺lunch & dinner Tue-Sun) This enormously popular family-run tavern serves high-quality seafood at reasonable prices. Expect queues on summer nights.

❶ Information
Tourist office (www.cm-nazare.pt) At the end of Avenida da República.

❶ Getting There & Away
Nazaré has numerous **bus** connections to Lisbon (€9.50, two hours).

Tomar
POP 16,000

A charming town straddling a river, Tomar has the notoriety of being home to the Knights Templar; check out their headquarters, the outstanding monastery **Convento de Cristo** (admission €6; ☺9am-6pm). Other rarities include a magnificent 17th-century **Aqueduto de Pegões** (aqueduct) and a medieval **synagogue** (Rua Dr Joaquim Jacinto 73; admission free; ☺10am-7pm Tue-Sun). The town is backed by the dense greenery of the **Mata Nacional dos Sete Montes** (Seven Hills National Forest).

🛏 Sleeping & Eating

Residencial União
GUEST HOUSE €
(☑249 323 161; www.hotel-ami.com/hotel/uniao; Rua Serpa Pinto 94; s/d/q €25/38/45; ☎) Tomar's most atmospheric budget choice, this once-grand town house features large and sprucely maintained rooms with antique furniture and fixtures.

Estalagem de Santa Iria
INN €€
(☑249 313 326; www.estalagemsantairia.com; Mouchão Parque; s/d/ste €65/85/125; ☎)

Centrally located on an island in Tomar's lovely riverside park, this '40s-style inn has large comfortable rooms, most with balconies overlooking the leafy grounds or the river.

Calça Perra
INTERNATIONAL €€
(Rua Pedro Dias 59; mains €8-13; ☺lunch & dinner Tue-Sun) A charming backstreet eatery with a diverse and innovative menu and occasional fado nights.

Restaurante Bela Vista
PORTUGUESE €€
(Rua Marquês de Pombal 68; mains €6-11; ☺lunch & dinner Wed-Sun, lunch Mon) With a lovely riverside terrace and standard Portuguese fare.

❶ Information
Tourist office (Avenida Dr Cândido Madureira) Can provide town and forest maps.

❶ Getting There & Away
Frequent **trains** run to Lisbon (€8.35, two hours).

Coimbra
POP 101,000

Coimbra is a dynamic, fashionable, yet comfortably lived-in city, with a student life centred on the magnificent 13th-century university. Aesthetically eclectic, there are elegant shopping streets, ancient stone walls and backstreet alleys with hidden *tascas* and fado bars. Coimbra was the birth and burial place of Portugal's first king, and was the country's most important city when the Moors captured Lisbon.

◉ Sights & Activities

Igreja de Santa Cruz
MONASTERY
(Praça 8 de Maio; admission €2.50; ☺9am-noon & 2-5pm Mon-Sat) Located at the bottom of the hill in the Old Town, the monastery has a fabulous ornate pulpit and medieval royal tombs. It can be reached via the **elevator** (one-way €1.60) by the market.

Velha Universidade
UNIVERSITY
(Old University; admission €7; ☺10am-noon & 2-5pm) The old university is unmissable in its grandeur. You can visit the library with its gorgeous book-lined hallways and the Manueline chapel dating back to 1517.

O Pioneiro do Mondego
KAYAKING
(www.opioneirodomondego.com) Rents out kayaks for paddling the Rio Mondego between Penacova and Torres de Mondego, an 18km trip costing €20 per person.

ROMAN RUINS

Conimbriga, 16km south of Coimbra, is the site of the well-preserved ruins of a **Roman town** (⊙9am-8pm), including mosaic floors, elaborate baths and trickling fountains. It's a fascinating place to explore, with a good **museum** (admission €4; ⊙10am-6pm Tue-Sun) that describes the once-flourishing and later abandoned town. There's a sunny cafe on site. Frequent buses run to Condeixa, 2km from the site; there are also two direct buses (€2.15) from Coimbra.

✲ Festivals & Events

Coimbra's annual highlight is **Queima das Fitas**, a boozy week of fado and revelry that begins on the first Thursday in May when students celebrate the end of the academic year.

🛌 Sleeping

TOP CHOICE **Casa Pombal Guest House**

BOUTIQUE GUEST HOUSE €€

(☎239 835 175; www.casapombal.com; Rua das Flores 18; d €68, without bathroom €52; @🛜) This winning, Dutch-run guest house squeezes tons of charm into a small space. Ample morning buffet.

Pensão-Restaurante Flôr de Coimbra

GUEST HOUSE €

(☎239 823 865; flordecoimbrahr.com.sapo. pt; Rua do Poço 5; s/d/tr €50/60/70, without bathroom €20/35/45; 🛜) This once-grand 19th-century home with its own restaurant offers loads of character in a great location.

Grande Hostel de Coimbra HOSTEL €

(☎239 108 212; www.grandehostelcoimbra.com; Rua Antero Quental 196; dm/d €18/40; @🛜) You won't find a hostel more laid-back than this and it's hard to beat the location in a grand, century-old town house near the nightlife of Coimbra's university campus.

🍴 Eating & Drinking

Self-caterers should stop by the modern **Mercado Municipal Dom Pedro V** (Rua Olímpio Nicolau Rui Fernandes; ⊙Mon-Sat) for fruit, vegetables and more.

Restaurante Zé Manel PORTUGUESE €€

(Beco do Forno 12; mains €7-9; ⊙lunch & dinner Mon-Fri, lunch Sat) Great food, huge serv-ings and a zany atmosphere, with walls papered with diners' comments, cartoons and poems.

Restaurante Zé Neto PORTUGUESE €€

(Rua das Azeiteiras 8; mains €6-10; ⊙lunch & dinner Mon-Sat) This marvellous family-run place specialises in homemade Portuguese standards, including *cabrito* (kid).

Italia ITALIAN €€

(Parque Dr Manuel de Braga; mains €8-15; ⊙noon-midnight) Expand your midriff at this excellent Italian restaurant on the riverfront with laden dishes of excellent pizza and pasta.

Café Santa Cruz CAFE €€

(Praça 8 de Maio; ⊙Mon-Sat) Former chapel that has been resurrected into one of Portugal's most atmospheric cafes.

☆ Entertainment

Coimbra-style fado is more cerebral than the Lisbon variety, and its adherents are staunchly protective.

TOP CHOICE **Á Capella** FADO HOUSE

(www.acapella.com.pt; Rua Corpo de Deus; admission incl 1 drink €10; ⊙10pm-2am) Housed in a fabulous 14th-century former chapel, Á Capella regularly hosts the city's most renowned fado musicians.

Via Latina DANCE CLUB

(Rua Almeida Garrett 1; ⊙Tue-Sat) Fires up to a steamy dance pit late at night.

ℹ Information

Espaço Internet (Praça 8 de Maio 37; ⊙10am-2pm & 3-8pm) Free internet access.

Tourist office (Praça da Porta Férrea)

ℹ Getting There & Away

At least a dozen **buses** and as many **trains** run daily from Lisbon (€12, 2½ hours) and Porto (€11, 1½ hours), plus frequent buses from Faro and Évora, via Lisbon. The main train stations are **Coimbra B**, 2km northwest of the centre, and central **Coimbra A**. Most long-distance trains call at Coimbra B. The **bus station** (Avenida Fernão Magalhães) is about 400m northeast of the centre.

Luso & the Buçaco Forest

POP 2000

This sylvan region harbours a lush forest of century-old trees surrounded by countryside that's dappled with heather, wildflowers and leafy ferns. There's even a fairy-tale palace here, a 1907 neo-Manueline extravagance, where visitors can dine or stay overnight. Buçaco was chosen as a retreat by 16th-century monks, and it surrounds the lovely spa town of Luso.

The **Maloclinic Spa** (www.maloclinic spa.com; Rua Álvaro Castelões) offers a range of treatments.

🛏 Sleeping & Eating

Palace Hotel do Buçaco HOTEL €€€
(📞231 937 970; www.palacehoteldobussaco.com; Mata Nacional do Buçaco; standard/superior d midweek €150/170, weekend €175/200; P❄) Live a real-life fairy tale and stay at this ostentatious palace complete with gargoyles, ornamental garden and turrets. The elegant restaurant offers seven-course menus for around €40.

Hotelaria Alegre BOUTIQUE HOTEL €€
(📞231 930 256; www.alegrehotels.com; Rua Emídio Navarro 2; s €40-45, d €55-65; P🛜❄) This grand, peach-coloured 19th-century town house has polished period furniture and other appealing touches. There's a formal parlour and vine-draped garden with pool.

ℹ Information

Tourist office (Avenida Emídio Navarro 136; ⊙Mon-Sat) Has maps and leaflets about the forest and trails.

ℹ Getting There & Away

Buses to/from Coimbra (€3.20, 45 minutes) run four times daily each weekday and twice daily on Saturdays.

Serra da Estrela

The forested Serra da Estrela has a raw natural beauty and offers some of the country's best hiking. This is Portugal's highest mainland mountain range (1993m), and the source of its two great rivers: Rio Mondego and Rio Zêzere. The town of Manteigas makes a great base for hiking and exploring the area (plus skiing in winter). The **main park office** (📞275 980 060; pnse@icn.pt; Rua 1 de Maio 2; Manteigas; ⊙Mon-Fri) provides details of popular walks in the Parque Natural da Serra da Estrela; additional offices are at Seia, Gouveia and Guarda.

🛏 Sleeping

Casa das Obras B&B €€
(📞275 981 155; www.casadasobras.pt; Rua Teles de Vasconcelos, Manteigas; r summer/winter

€64/80; P🛜❄) This lovely 18th-century town house has antique-filled rooms, and a pool in a grassy courtyard across the street.

Albergaria Berne HOTEL €€
(📞275 981 351; www.albergariaberne.com; Quinta de Santo António, Manteigas; s/d from €35/55; P❄@🛜❄) Going for a Swiss feel, this lovely hotel has wood-accented rooms, some with balconies and views of Manteigas and the mountains above.

ℹ Getting There & Around

Two regular weekday **buses** connect Manteigas with Guarda, from where there are onward services to Coimbra and Lisbon.No buses cross the park, although you can go around it. At least two buses link Seia, Gouveia and Guarda daily.

THE NORTH

Beneath the edge of Spanish Galicia, northern Portugal is a land of lush river valleys, sparkling coastline, granite peaks and virgin forests. This region is also gluttony for wine lovers: it's the home of the sprightly *vinho verde* wine and ancient vineyards along the dramatic Rio Douro. Gateway to the north is Porto, a beguiling riverside city blending both medieval and modern attractions. Smaller towns and villages also offer cultural allure, from majestic Braga, the country's religious heart, to the seaside beauty Viana do Castelo.

Porto

POP 263,000

At the mouth of the Rio Douro, the hilly city of Porto presents a jumble of styles, eras and attitudes: narrow medieval alleyways, extravagant baroque churches, prim little squares, and wide boulevards lined with beaux-arts edifices. A lively walkable city with chatter in the air and a tangible sense of history, Porto's old-world riverfront district is a Unesco World Heritage site. Across the water twinkle the neon signs of Vila Nova de Gaia, the headquarters of the major port manufacturers.

◉ Sights

Head for the riverfront Ribeira district for an atmospheric stroll around, checking out the gritty local bars, sunny restaurants and river cruises.

Porto

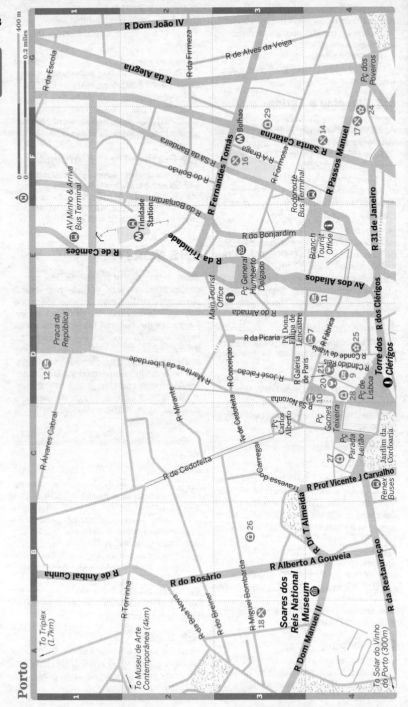

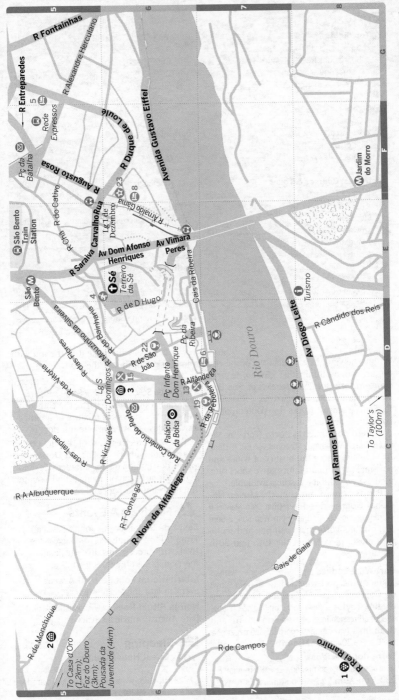

R Fontainhas

R Entreparedes

R Alexandre Herculano

R do Cativo

R Duque de Loule

R Augusto Rosa

R Saraiva Carvalho Rua

Rede Expressos

Pç da Batalha

São Bento Train Station

Avenida Gustavo Eiffel

R Armando Gama

Lg 1 de Dezembro

Av Dom Afonso Henriques

Av Vimara Peres

São Bento

Sé

Terreiro da Sé

R de D Hugo

R de la Bainha

R de Mouzinho da Silveira

R da Vitória

R das Flores

Lg S Domingos

R de São João

Pç da Ribeira

Cais da Ribeira

Turismo

Av Cândido dos Reis

Rio Douro

Av Diogo Leite

Pç Infante Dom Henrique

R Alfândega

R da Reboleira

R do Comércio do Porto

R Virtudes

Palácio da Bolsa

R das Taipas

R A Albuquerque

R-T Gonzaga

R Nova da Alfândega

Cais de Gaia

Av Ramos Pinto

To Taylor's (100m)

Jardim do Morro

R de Monchique

To Casa d'Oro (1.2km); Foz do Douro (3km); Pousada da Juventude (4km)

Cais de Gaia

R de Campos

R Rei Ramiro

Museums   MUSEUMS

Within the verdant gardens west of the city, the arrestingly minimalist **Museu de Arte Contemporânea** (www.serralves.pt; Rua Dom João de Castro 210; admission €5; ⊙10am-7pm Tue-Sun) features works by contemporary Portuguese artists.

Museu do Vinho do Porto (Port Wine Museum; Rua de Monchique 45; admission €2; ⊙11am-7pm Tue-Sun) traces the history of wine- and port-making with an informative short film, models and exhibits. Tastings available.

Porto's best art museum, the **Museu Nacional Soares dos Reis** (Rua Dom Manuel II 44; admission €6; ⊙10am-6pm Wed-Sun, 2-6pm Tue) exhibits Portuguese painting and sculpture masterpieces from the 19th and 20th centuries.

Port-Wine Lodges   TASTINGS

Many of the port-wine lodges in Vila Nova de Gaia offer daily tours and tastings, including **Taylor's** (www.taylor.pt; Rua do Choupelo 250; admission free; ⊙10am-6pm Mon-Fri) and **Graham's** (www.grahamsportlodge.com; per person €3; ⊙9.30am-6pm Mon-Fri).

Torre dos Clérigos   TOWER

(Rua dos Clérigos; admission €2; ⊙10am-noon & 2.30-7pm) Atop 225 steep steps, this tower rewards those who make it to the top with the best panorama of the city.

Sé   CHURCH

(Terreiro da Sé; cloisters €3; ⊙9am-12.30pm & 2.30-7pm) Dominating Porto, the cathedral is worth a visit for its mixture of architectural styles and vast ornate interior.

A few kilometres west of the city centre, the seaside suburb of **Foz do Douro** is a prime destination on hot summer weekends. It has a long beach promenade and a scattering of oceanfront bars and restaurants.

🎆 **Festivals & Events**

Festa de São João (St John's Festival) From 20 to 24 June; Porto's biggest festival, with processions, live music and merry-making all across town.

International Folk Festival A week-long event in late July/early August.

Noites Ritual Rock (www.noitesritual.com) Late August; music festival.

🛏 **Sleeping**

TOP CHOICE **Guest House Douro**
        BOUTIQUE HOTEL €€€

(☏222 015 135; www.guesthousedouro.com; Rua Fonte Taurina 99-101; r €130-170; ❋@☎) In a restored relic overlooking the Douro, these eight rooms have been blessed with gorgeous wood floors, plush queen beds and marble baths; the best have river views. There's a 1am curfew.

TOP CHOICE **6 Only** GUEST HOUSE €€
(☎222 013 971; www.6only.pt; Rua Duque de Loulé 97; d €70-80; @☎) This beautifully restored guest house has just six rooms, all with simple but stylish details that effortlessly blend old (such as wrought-iron decorative balconies) with new (free in-room wi-fi). There's a lounge, a Zen-like courtyard and friendly staff.

Pensão Cristal GUEST HOUSE €
(☎222 002 100; www.pensaocristal.com; Rua Galeria de Paris 48; r €35-60; P❋☎) Pensão Cristal has narrow, artwork-lined corridors and cosy rooms with wood furnishings. It sits on a romantic street that can get rowdy on weekends when the nearby galleries and bars get rolling.

Residencial Rex GUEST HOUSE €
(☎222 074 590; www.residencialrex.com; Praça da República 117; r €48-60; P❋) Residencial Rex is set in a 150 year-old belle-époque manor with a wide range of rooms. Floors two and three are best, with handsome old details, high ceilings and plenty of space.

Pousada da Juventude HOSTEL €
(☎226 177 257; www.microsites.juventude.gov. pt; Rua Paulo da Gama 551; ☺24hr; dm/r €14/30; P@☎) In a bright, modern building on bluffs above the Rio Douro, the crown jewel of Portugal's hostels offers basic but handsome doubles with sweeping views of the river, as well as clean, well-maintained dorms. It's 4km from central Porto.

Hotel Infante de Sagres BOUTIQUE HOTEL €€€
(☎223 398 500; www.hotelinfantesagres.pt; Praça Dona Filipa de Lencastre 62; s/d from €175/195; ❋☎) An exquisite time warp, with well-coiffed doormen, crystal chandeliers and ornately decorated common areas, this place feels like a royal getaway in the heart of the city.

Pensão Astória GUEST HOUSE €
(☎222 008 175; Rua Arnaldo Gama 56; r €25-35) In an austere but elegant town house above the Rio Douro, this spotless place has old-world charm; several rooms have superb views. Reservations recommended.

Residencial dos Aliados GUEST HOUSE €
(☎222 004 853; www.residencialaliados.com; Rua Elísio de Melo 27; r €40-70; ❋☎) Set in one of Porto's marvellous beaux-arts buildings, offering spiffy rooms with polished wooden floors, decent beds and dark wood furnishings.

Porto Downtown Hostel HOSTEL €
(☎222 018 094; www.portodowntownhostel.com; Praça Guilherme Gomes Fernandes 66; r €16-19; P❋☎) This popular hostel has large sunlit dorms with new beds, and common areas with shag rugs and beanbag chairs strewn about.

✕ Eating

TOP CHOICE **A Grade** PORTUGUESE €€
(☎223 321 130; Rua da Saoicolau 9; mains €10-20; ☺lunch & dinner Mon-Sat) Both a humble mum-and-dad operation and a masterwork of traditional fare, with standouts such as baked octopus in butter and wine, roast veal and grilled seafood casseroles. Reservations recommended.

DOP PORTUGUESE €€
(☎222 014 313; www.ruipaula.com; Largo S Domingos 18; mains €25-50; ☺lunch & dinner) Sit at the 'long table' and watch the chef prepare tapas tableside, or find a romantic corner and linger over duck risotto and a bottle of Douro red. Porto's upper crust digs it.

Casa d'Oro ITALIAN €€
(Alameda Bastio Teles 797; pizzas €8-12; ☺lunch & dinner) A concrete and glass clay-oven pizzeria leaning over the Rio Douro just upriver from the mouth. It does terrific pizzas including *diavola* (spicy salami and oregano), *Vesuvio* (sausage and broccoli) and *fichi e prosciutto* (prosciutto and fig).

O Escondidinho PORTUGUESE €€
(www.escondidinho.com.pt; Rua Passos Manuel 144; mains €13-20; ☺lunch & dinner) Amid *azulejos,* dark wood furnishings and starched white place settings, O Escondidinho serves excellent traditional cuisine.

Mercado do Bolhão MARKET €
(Rua Formosa; ☺8am-5pm Mon-Fri, to 1pm Sat) Fruit, vegies, cheese and deli goodies in a 19th-century wrought-iron building.

Café Majestic CAFE €
(Rua Santa Catarina 112; ☺9.30am-midnight Mon-Sat) An art-nouveau extravagance where old souls linger over afternoon tea.

Rota do Chá CAFE €
(Rua Miguel Bombarda 457; ☺noon-8pm Mon-Thu, noon-midnight Fri & Sat, 1-8pm Sun; ☞) This proudly bohemian cafe has a verdant

PORT WINE PRIMER

With its intense flavours, silky textures and appealing sweetness, port wine is easy to love, especially when taken with its proper accompaniments: cheese, nuts and dried fruit.

It was probably Roman soldiers who first planted grapes in the Douro valley some 2000 years ago, but tradition credits the discovery of port itself to 17th-century British merchants. With their country at war with France, they turned to their old ally Portugal to meet their wine habit. According to legend, the British threw in some brandy with grape juice, both to take off the wine's bite and preserve it for shipment back to England – and port wine was the result.

but rustic back garden and a magnificent tea selection.

Drinking

There are dozens of bars on Praça da Ribeira and along the adjacent quay. On warm nights the outdoor tables get packed.

Casa do Livro   LOUNGE BAR
(Rua Galeria de Paris 85; ⊙11.30am-2am Mon-Sat) Vintage wallpaper, gilded mirrors and walls of books give a discreet charm to this perfectly lit bar. On weekends DJs spin funk, soul and retro sounds in the back room for pretty people.

Vinologia   WINE BAR
(Rua de São João 46) This oaky, subterranean wine bar is an excellent place to sample Porto's fine quaffs.

Café Bar O Cais   BAR
(Rua Fonte Taurina 2a) A loyal following crowds the funky, classic-rock-drenched basement bar with old stone walls and vinyl booths.

Solar do Vinho do Porto
                          WINE BAR, RESTAURANT
(Rua Entre Quintas 220) In a 19th-century house near the Palácio de Cristal, this upmarket spot has a manicured garden with picturesque views of the Douro and hundreds of ports by the glass.

Galeria de Paris   BAR, CAFE
(Rua Galeria de Paris 56) A whimsically decorated bar (and daytime lunch buffet), with toys, old phones and other memorabilia lining the walls, which shake to a hip-hop soundtrack.

☆ Entertainment

Plano B   GALLERY, CAFE, BAR
(Rua Cândido dos Reis 30; ⊙closed Aug) This creative space has an art gallery and cafe, with a cosy downstairs space where DJs and live bands hold court.

Maus Hábitos   NIGHTCLUB
(www.maushabitos.com; 4th fl, Rua Passos Manuel 178) This bohemian, multiroom space hosts art exhibits, while live bands and DJs work the back stage.

Triplex   NIGHTCLUB
(www.triplex.com.pt; Avenida Boavista 911) In a pink, three-storey mansion, Triplex has a regular line-up of '80s, electronica and '60s sounds (plus karaoke on Thursday).

Hot Five Jazz & Blues Club   JAZZ
(www.hotfive.eu; Largo Actor Dias 51; ⊙10pm-3am Wed-Sun) Hosts live jazz and blues as well as acoustic, folk and all-out jam sessions.

🔒 Shopping

Major shopping areas are eastward around the Bolhão market and Rua Santa Catarina.

Via Catarina Shopping Centre   MALL
(Rua Santa Catarina) The best central shopping mall, in a tasteful building.

CC Bombarda   GALLERIA
(Rua Miguel Bombarda) For something a little edgier, visit this gallery of stores selling urban wear, stylish home knick-knacks, Portuguese indie rock and other hipster-pleasing delights.

Garrafeira do Carmo   PORT
(Rua do Carmo 17) Port is, naturally, a popular purchase in this town. This knowledgeable shop has a good selection.

Livraria Lello   BOOKS
(Rua das Carmelitas 144) Even if you're not after books, don't miss this 1906 neo-Gothic confection

ⓘ Information

Santo António Hospital (☎222 077 500; Largo Prof Abel Salazar) Has English-speaking staff.

On Web (Praça General Humberto Delgado 291; per hr €1.80; ⊙10am-2am Mon-Sat, 3pm-2am Sun) Internet access.

Main post office (Praça General Humberto Delgado) Across from the main tourist office.

Branch tourist office (Rua Infante Dom Henrique 63) Small but helpful office.

Main tourist office (www.portoturismo.pt; Rua Clube dos Fenianos 25) Opposite the *câmara municipal*.

❶ Getting There & Away

Air

Porto is connected by daily flights from Lisbon and London, and direct links from other European cities, particularly with easyJet and Ryanair.

Bus

Porto has many private bus companies leaving from different terminals; the main tourist office can help. In general, for Lisbon (€18) and The Algarve the choice is **Renex** (www.renex.pt; Campo Mártires de Pátria 37) or **Rede Expressos** (www.rede-expressos.pt; Rua Alexandre Herculano 370).

Three companies operate from or near Praceto Régulo Magauanha, off Rua Dr Alfredo Magalhães: **Transdev-Norte** goes to Braga (€5); **AV Minho** to Viana do Castelo (€7).

Train

Porto is a northern Portugal rail hub with three stations. Most international trains, and all intercity links, start at **Campanhã**, 2km east of the centre. Inter-regional and regional services depart from Campanhã or the central **São Bento station** (Praça Almeida Garrett). Frequent local trains connect these two.

At **São Bento station** you can book tickets to any other destination.

❶ Getting Around

To/From the Airport

The **metro's 'violet' line** provides handy service to the airport. A one-way ride to the centre costs €1.50 and takes about 45 minutes. A daytime **taxi** costs €20 to €25 to/from the centre.

Public Transport

Save money on transport by purchasing a refillable **Andante Card** (€0.50), valid for transport on buses, metro, funicular and tram.

BUS Central hubs of Porto's extensive bus system include Jardim da Cordoaria, Praça da Liberdade and São Bento station. Tickets are cheapest from STCP kiosks or newsagents (€1.80 return within Porto). Tickets bought on the bus are one-way €1.50. There's also a €5 day pass available.

FUNICULAR A panoramic funicular shuttles up and down a steep incline from Avenida Gustavo Eiffel to Rua Augusto Rosa (€0.90, from 8am to 8pm).

METRO Porto's **metro** (www.metrodoporto.pt) currently comprises four metropolitan lines that all converge at the Trinidade stop. Tickets cost €1.50 for a single ride, and €1 with an Andante Card.

TRAM Porto has three antique trams that trundle around town. The most useful line, 1E, travels along the Douro towards the Foz district.

Taxi

To cross town, expect to pay between €5 and €7. There's a 20% surcharge at night, and an additional charge to leave city limits, which includes Vila Nova de Gaia. There are taxi ranks throughout the centre or you can call a **radio taxi** (☎225 076 400).

Along the Douro

Portugal's best-known river flows through the country's rural heartland. In the upper reaches, port-wine grapes are grown on steep terraced hills, punctuated by remote stone villages and, in spring, splashes of dazzling white almond blossom.

The Rio Douro is navigable right across Portugal. Highly recommended is the train journey from Porto to Pinhão (€9, 2½ hours, five trains daily), the last 70km clinging to the river's edge; trains continue to Pocinho (from Porto €10.65, 3½ hours). **Porto Tours** (☎222 000 073; www.portotours.com; Torre Medieval, Calçada Pedro Pitões 15), situated next to Porto's cathedral, can arrange tours, including idyllic Douro cruises. Cyclists and drivers can choose river-hugging roads along either bank, and visit wineries along the way (check out www.rvp.pt for an extensive list of wineries open to visitors). You can also stay overnight in scenic wine lodges among the vineyards.

Viana do Castelo

POP 37,500

The jewel of the Costa Verde (Green Coast), Viana do Castelo has both an appealing medieval centre and lovely beaches just outside the city. In addition to its natural beauty, Viana do Castelo whips up some excellent seafood and hosts some magnificent traditional festivals, including the spectacular **Festa de Nossa Senhora da Agonia** in August.

◉ Sights

The stately heart of town is **Praça da República**, with its delicate fountain and grandiose buildings, including the 16th-century **Misericórdia**, a former almshouse.

Templo do Sagrado Coração de Jesus
CHURCH
(Temple of the Sacred Heart of Jesus; admission free; ☉8am-7pm Apr-Sep) Atop Santa Luzia Hill, the Temple of the Sacred Heart of Jesus offers a grand panorama across the river. It's a steep 2km climb; you can also catch a ride on the newly restored funicular railway (one-way/return €2/3).

Praia do Cabedelo
BEACH
Viana's enormous arcing beach is one of the Minho's best, with little development to spoil its charm. It's across the river from town, best reached by **ferry** (adult/child €1.20/0.60; ☉hourly 9am to 6pm) from the pier south of Largo 5 de Outubro.

🛏 Sleeping

Margarida da Praça
BOUTIQUE HOTEL €€
(📞258 809 630; www.margaridadapraca.com; Largo 5 Outubre; r €65-75; ❄🛜) Fantastically whimsical, this friendly boutique inn offers colourful rooms accented by candelabra lanterns and lush duvets.

Residencial Jardim
GUEST HOUSE €€
(📞258 828 915; www.residencialjardim.com.sapo. pt; Largo 5 de Outubro 68; d €65; ❄🛜) This stately 19th-century town house has spacious rooms with wood floors and French windows overlooking the historic centre or the river.

Pousada da Juventude Gil Eannes
HOSTEL €
(📞258 821 582; www.pousadasjuventude.pt; Gil Eannes; dm/s/d €10/16/24; 🛜) Sleep in the bowels of a huge, creaky hospital ship where men were stitched up and underwent emergency dentistry. This floating hostel scores well for novelty, but has few amenities.

🍴 Eating

TOP CHOICE **Taberna do Valentim**
SEAFOOD €€
(Rua Monsignor Daniel Machado 180; mains €12-15; ☉lunch & dinner Mon-Sat) In the old fishermen's neighbourhood, this fantastic seafood restaurant serves grilled fish by the kilogram, and rich seafood stews – *arroz de tamboril* (monkfish rice) and *caldeirada* (fish stew).

Restaurante Zefa Carqueja
GRILL €
(Campo do Castelo; mains €8-25; ☉lunch & dinner) Barbecue aficionados should seek this casual grill house for some of the best barbecue chicken and ribs in northern Portugal.

ℹ Information

Tourist office (Rua Hospital Velho) Handily located in the old centre.

ℹ Getting There & Away

Five to 10 **trains** go daily to Porto (€5 to €8, two hours), as well as express **buses** (€7, 2¼ hours).

Braga
POP 133,000
Portugal's third-largest city boasts a fine array of churches, their splendid baroque facades looming above the old plazas and narrow lanes of the historic centre. Lively cafes, trim little boutiques, and some good restaurants add to the appeal.

👁 Sights

It's an easy day trip to **Guimarães** with its medieval town centre and a palace of the dukes of Bragança. It's also a short jaunt to **Barcelos**, a town famed for its sprawling Thursday market.

Sé
CHURCH
(Rua Dom Paio Mendes; admission free; ☉8.30am-6.30pm) In the centre of Braga, this is one of Portugal's most extraordinary cathedrals, with roots dating back a thousand years. Within the cathedral you can also visit the **treasury** (€2) and **choir** (€2).

Escadaria do Bom Jesus
RELIGIOUS SITE
At Bom Jesus do Monte, a hilltop pilgrimage site 5km from Braga, is an extraordinary stairway, with allegorical fountains, chapels and a superb view. City bus 2 (€1.50) runs frequently from Braga to the site, where you can climb the steps (pilgrims sometimes do this on their knees) or ascend by funicular railway (€1.20).

🛏 Sleeping

TOP CHOICE **Casa Santa Zita**
GUEST HOUSE €
(📞253 618 331; Rua São João 20; s/d €30/40) This impeccably kept pilgrims' lodge (look for the small tile reading 'Sta Zita') has bright, spotless rooms and an air of palpable serenity. Midnight curfew.

Albergaria da Sé
GUEST HOUSE €€
(📞253 214 502; www.albergaria-da-se.com.pt; Rua Gonçalo Pereira 39; s/d from €45/55; 🅿❄) Around the corner from the cathedral, this friendly three-storey guest house has dark-wood floors and airy rooms.

✗ Eating & Drinking

Livraria Café CAFE €
(Avenida Central 118; mains €4-6; ☺9am-7.30pm Mon-Sat) Tucked inside the bookshop Centésima Página, this charming cafe serves tasty quiches, salads and desserts. Outdoor tables are in the pleasantly rustic garden.

Cozinha da Sé PORTUGUESE €€
(Rua Dom Frei Caetano Brandão 95; mains €7-10; ☺Tue-Sun) Sé serves traditional, high-quality dishes (including one vegetarian selection).

Taperia Palatu SPANISH, PORTUGUESE €€
(Rua Dom Afonso Henrique 35; mains €8-12; ☺Mon-Sat) A Spanish/Portuguese couple serves up delectable Spanish tapas and classic Portuguese dishes in an airy courtyard.

ℹ Information

Tourist office (www.cm-braga.pt; Praça da República 1) Can help with accommodation and maps.

ℹ Getting There & Away

Trains arrive regularly from Lisbon (€31, 3¼ hours), Coimbra (€19, 2¼ hours) and Porto (€2.20, 1¼ hours), and there are daily connections north to Viana do Castelo. Daily **bus** services link Braga to Porto (€4.50, 1¼ hours) and Lisbon (€19, five hours). **Car hire** is available at **AVIC** (☑253 203 910; Rua Gabriel Pereira de Castro 28; ☺Mon-Fri), with prices starting at €35 per day.

Parque Nacional da Peneda-Gerês

Spread across four impressive granite massifs, this vast park encompasses boulder-strewn peaks, precipitous valleys, gorse-clad moorlands and forests of oak and pine. It also shelters more than 100 granite villages that, in many ways, have changed little since Portugal's founding in the 12th century. For nature lovers the stunning scenery here is unmatched in Portugal for camping, hiking and other outdoor adventures. The park's main centre is at Vila do Gerês, a sleepy, hot-spring village.

✗ Activities

Hiking

There are trails and footpaths through the park, some between villages with accommo-

dation. Leaflets detailing these are available from the park offices.

Day hikes around Vila do Gerês are popular. An adventurous option is the **old Roman road** from Mata do Albergaria (10km up-valley from Vila do Gerês), past the **Vilarinho das Furnas** reservoir to Campo do Gerês. More distant destinations include **Ermida** and **Cabril**, both with simple accommodation.

Cycling & Horse Riding

Mountain bikes can be hired in Campo do Gerês (15km northeast of Vila do Gerês) from **Equi Campo** (☑253 357 022, www.equicampo.com; per hr/day €5/18; ☺10am-7pm). Guides here also lead horse-riding trips, hikes and combination hiking/climbing/abseiling excursions.

Water Sports

Rio Caldo, 8km south of Vila do Gerês, is the base for water sports on the Caniçada reservoir. English-run **AML** (Água Montanha e Lazer; ☑965 000 917; www.aguamontanha.com; Lugar de Paredes) rents kayaks, pedal boats, rowing boats and small motorboats. It also organises kayaking trips along the Albufeira de Salamonde.

⌂ Sleeping & Eating

Vila do Gerês has plenty of *pensões* (guest houses), but you may find vacancies are limited; many are block-booked by spa patients in summer.

TOP CHOICE **Hotel de Peneda** BOUTIQUE HOTEL €€
(☑251 460 040; www.hotelpeneda.com; Lugar da Peneda; r €40-75; P �) Set in the Serra da Peneda in the northern reaches of the park, this mountain lodge has a waterfall backdrop, a gushing creek beneath and ultra-cosy rooms with blonde-wood floors and views of quaint Peneda village across the ravine. The restaurant is decent.

Pousada da Juventude de Vilarinho das Furnas HOSTEL €
(☑253 351 339; www.pousadasjuventude.pt; dm/bungalow €13/50; P @) Campo's woodland hostel began life as a temporary dam-workers' camp and now offers a spotless selection of spartan dormitories, simply furnished doubles (with bathrooms) and roomier bungalows with kitchen units.

Quinta Souto-Linho RURAL INN €€
(☑253 392 000; www.oocities.com/souto_linho; d €50-60; P ✱ ✱) This delightful Victorian manor house in Vila do Gerês has four

simply but tastefully remodelled rooms with hardwood floors; some have views. There's also a swimming pool with fine vistas.

Parque Campismo de Cerdeira

CAMPING GROUND €

(📞253 351 005; www.parquecerdeira.com; camping per person/tent/car €5/4/4.50, bungalows €50-65; ☺year-round; P⛄) In Campo de Gerês, this place has oak-shaded sites, laundry, pool, minimarket and a particularly good restaurant. The ecofriendly bungalows have French doors opening onto unrivalled mountain views.

ℹ Information

The head park office is **Adere-PG** (www.adere-pg .pt; ☺Mon-Fri) in Ponte de Barca. Obtain park information and reserve cottages and other park accommodation through here. Other Adere-PG stations are at Mezio and Lamas de Mouro.

ℹ Getting There & Away

Because of the lack of transport within the park, it's good to have your own wheels. You can rent cars in Braga.

UNDERSTAND PORTUGAL

History

Portugal has an early history of occupation, stretching back to 700 BC when the Celts arrived on the Iberian peninsula, followed by the Phoenicians, Greeks, Romans, Visigoths, Moors and Christians.

Life Under the Moors

The Moors ruled southern Portugal for more than 400 years, and some scholars describe that time as a golden age. The Arabs introduced irrigation, previously unknown in Europe. Two Egyptian agronomists came to Iberia in the 10th century and wrote manuals on land management, animal husbandry, plant and crop cultivation and irrigation designs. They also introduced bananas, rice, coconuts, maize and sugar cane. They also encouraged small-scale, cooperatively run communities, specialising in olive oil and wine production and food markets – still embraced in many parts of Portugal.

The Moors opened schools and set about campaigns to achieve mass literacy (in Arabic of course), as well as the teaching of maths, geography and history. Medicine reached new levels of sophistication. There was also a degree of religious tolerance that evaporated when the Christian crusaders came to power. Much to the chagrin of Christian slave owners, slavery was not permitted in the Islamic kingdom – making it a refuge for runaway slaves. Muslims, Christians and Jews all peacefully coexisted, at times even collaborating together, creating the most scientifically and artistically advanced society the world had ever known up until that time.

Age of Discovery

The 15th century marked a golden era in Portuguese history, when Portuguese explorers helped transform the small kingdom into a great imperial power.

The third son of King João I, Henrique 'O Navegador' (Henry the Navigator, 1394–1460) played a pivotal role in establishing Portugal's maritime dominance. As governor of The Algarve he assembled the very best sailors, map-makers, shipbuilders, instrument-makers and astronomers.

By 1431, Portuguese explorers discovered the islands of Madeira and the Azores, followed by Gil Eanes' 1534 voyage beyond Cape Bojador in West Africa, breaking a maritime superstition that this was the end of the world. More achievements followed over the next century. In 1488, Portuguese sailors, under navigator Bartolomeu Dias, were the first Europeans to sail around Africa's southern tip and into the Indian Ocean. This was followed by the epic voyage in 1497–98 when Vasco da Gama reached southern India, and in 1500 when Cabral discovered Brazil. With gold and slaves from Africa and spices from the East, Portugal was soon rolling in riches. As its explorers reached Timor, China and eventually Japan, Portugal cemented its power with garrison ports and trading posts. The monarchy, taking its 'royal fifth' of profits, became the wealthiest in Europe, and the lavish Manueline architectural style symbolised the exuberance of the age.

The Salazar Years

In 1908 King Carlos and his eldest son were assassinated in Lisbon. Two years later Portugal became a republic, which set the stage for an enormous power struggle. Over the next 16 years, chaos ruled, with an astounding 45 different governments coming to power, often the result of military intervention. Another coup in 1926 brought forth new names and faces, most significantly António de Oliveira Salazar, a finance minister who would rise up through the ranks to become prime minister – a post he would hold for 36 years.

Salazar hastily enforced his 'New State' – a republic that was nationalistic, Catholic, authoritarian and essentially repressive. All political parties were banned except for the loyalist National Union, which ran the show, and the National Assembly. Strikes were banned and propaganda, censorship and brute force kept society in order. The new secret police, Polícia Internacional e de Defesa do Estado (PIDE), inspired terror and suppressed opposition by imprisonment and torture. Various attempted coups during Salazar's rule came to nothing. The only good news was a dramatic economic turnaround, with surging industrial growth through the 1950s and 1960s.

Decolonisation finally brought the Salazarist era to a close. Independence movements in Portugal's African colonies led to costly and unpopular military interventions. In 1974, military officers reluctant to continue fighting bloody colonial wars staged a nearly bloodless coup – later nicknamed the Revolution of the Carnations (after victorious soldiers stuck carnations in their rifle barrels). Carnations are still a national symbol of freedom.

Arts

Music

The best-known form of Portuguese music is the melancholy, nostalgic songs called fado (literally 'fate') said to have originated from troubadour and African slave songs. The late Amália Rodrigues was the Edith Piaf of Portuguese fado. Today it is Mariza who has captured the public's imagination with her extraordinary voice and fresh contemporary image. Lisbon's Alfama district has plenty of fado houses (see the boxed text, p709), ranging from the grandiose and tourist-conscious to small family affairs.

Architecture

Unique to Portugal is Manueline architecture, named after its patron King Manuel I (1495–1521). It symbolises the zest for discovery of that era and is hugely flamboyant, characterised by fantastic spiralling columns and elaborate carving and ornamentation.

Visual Arts

Portugal's stunning painted *azulejo* tiles coat contemporary life, covering everything from houses to churches. The art form dates from Moorish times and reached a peak in the late 19th century when the art nouveau and art deco movements provided fantastic facades and interiors. Lisbon has its very own *azulejo* museum (p697).

Environment

Portugal has made astounding gains in transforming itself from a nation powered largely by fossil fuels to one powered by solar, wind and hydropower. In 2005, only 17% of electricity in Portugal's grid came from green energy. By 2010, the figure had risen to 45% – a gain unprecedented elsewhere in Europe. In 2008 the world's largest solar farm opened in the Alentejo, powering 30,000 homes. Portugal also has numerous wind farms and has even launched the world's first 'wave farm' to harness the ocean's power, just north of Porto. By the time you read this, Portugal may have realised its goal of becoming the first country with a nationwide grid of charging stations for electric cars.

SURVIVAL GUIDE

Directory A–Z

Accommodation

There's an excellent range of good-value, inviting accommodation in Portugal. Budget places provide some of Western Europe's cheapest rooms, while you'll find atmospheric, accommodation in farms, palaces, castles, mansions and rustic town houses – usually giving good mileage for your euro.

PRICE RANGES

We list high-season rates for a double room; breakfast is generally not included.

€€€	more than €100
€€	€50 to €100
€	less than €50

ECOTOURISM & FARMSTAYS

Turismo de Habitação (www.turihab.pt) is a private network of historic, heritage or rustic properties, ranging from 17th-century manors to quaint farmhouses or self-catering cottages. Doubles run from about €60 to €120.

SEASONS

Rates in this chapter are for high season.

» **High season:** mid-June to mid-September.

» **Mid-season:** May to mid-June and mid-September to October.

» **Low season:** November to April.

POUSADAS

These are government-run former castles, monasteries or palaces, often in spectacular locations. For details contact tourist offices or **Pousadas de Portugal** (www.pousadas.pt).

GUEST HOUSES

The most common types are the *residencial* and the *pensão:* usually simple, family-owned operations. Some have cheaper rooms with shared bathrooms.

HOSTELS

Portugal has a growing number of hostels, particularly in Lisbon. Nationwide, Portugal has over 30 *pousadas da juventude* (youth hostels; www.pousadasjuventude.pt) within the Hostelling International (HI) system.

CAMPING

For detailed listings of campsites nationwide, pick up the **Roteiro Campista** (www.roteiro-campista.pt; €7), updated annually and sold at bookshops. The swishest places are run by **Orbitur** (www.orbitur.pt) and **Inatel** (www.inatel.pt).

Activities

Cycling and **mountain-biking** trips are becoming popular in Portugal; good starting points are Tavira in The Algarve, Sintra and Setúbal in central Portugal and Parque Nacional da Peneda-Gerês in the north.

Fine country **walks** are found in Parque Nacional da Peneda-Gerês, Serra da Estrela. The ambitious can follow the 240km walking trail **Via Algarviana** (www.viaalgarviana.org) across southern Portugal.

Popular **water sports** include surfing, windsurfing, canoeing, rafting and water skiing. For local specialists, see Lagos, Sagres, Tavira, Coimbra and Parque Nacional da Peneda-Gerês.

Modest alpine **skiing** is possible at Torre in the Serra da Estrela, usually from January through to March.

Business Hours

Reviews in this chapter don't list hours unless they differ from these standard hours:

Banks 8.30am to 3pm Monday to Friday

Bars 7pm to 2am

Cafes 9am to 7pm

Malls 10am to 10pm

Nightclubs 11pm to 4am Thursday to Saturday

Post offices 8.30am to 4pm Monday to Friday

Restaurants noon to 3pm & 7pm to 10pm

Shops 9.30am to noon & 2pm to 7pm Monday to Friday, 10am to 1pm Saturday

Sights 10am to 12.30pm & 2-5pm Tuesday to Sunday

Discount Cards

If you plan to do a lot of sightseeing in Portugal's main cities, the **Lisboa Card** (p696) and **Porto Card** are sensible investments. Sold at tourist offices, these cards offer discounts or free admission to many attractions, and free travel on public transport.

Embassies & Consulates

Australia (☎213 101 500; www.portugal.embassy.gov.au; 2nd fl, Av da Liberdade 200, Lisbon)

Canada Lisbon (☎213 164 600; www.canadainternational.gc.ca; 3rd fl, Av da Liberdade 198, Lisbon); Faro (☎289 803 757; Rua Frei Lourenço de Santa Maria 1, Faro)

Ireland (☎213 929 440; www.embassyofireland.pt; Rua da Imprensa a Estrela 1, Lisbon)

New Zealand Madrid (☎34 915 230 226; www.nzembassy.com) The nearest New Zealand embassy is in Madrid.

UK (☎213 924 000; www.ukinportugal.fco.gov.uk; Rua de Saõ Bernardo 33, Lisbon) Also in Portimaõ.

USA (☎217 273 300; http://portugal.usembassy.gov; Av das Forças Armadas, 1600-081 Lisbon)

Food

There is a great range of offerings for diners of all budgets in Portugal. For a small cost, you'll be able to eat daily specials (pork, chicken, fried fish) at casual, family-style restaurants. Midrange offerings can be found at popular Portuguese eateries serving traditional fare such as *bacalhau* dishes, as well as vegetarian and international fare.

With a budget of €15 per main and up, diners can sample some of the country's best restaurants.

The following price indicators (per main course) are used in this chapter:

€€€   more than €14

€€   €9 to €14

€   less than €9

Money

There are numerous banks with ATMs located throughout Portugal. Credit cards are accepted in midrange and top-end hotels, restaurants and shops.

Public Holidays

New Year's Day 1 January

Carnaval Tuesday February/March – the day before Ash Wednesday

Good Friday March/April

Liberty Day 25 April – celebrating the 1974 revolution

Labour Day 1 May

Corpus Christi May/June – 9th Thursday after Easter

Portugal Day 10 June – also known as Camões and Communities Day

Feast of the Assumption 15 August

Republic Day 5 October – commemorating the 1910 declaration of the Portuguese Republic

All Saints' Day 1 November

Independence Day 1 December – commemorating the 1640 restoration of independence from Spain

Feast of the Immaculate Conception 8 December

Christmas Day 25 December

Telephone

Portugal's country code is ☎351. There are no regional area codes. Mobile phone numbers within Portugal have nine digits and begin with ☎9.

All Portuguese phone numbers consist of nine digits. These include area codes, which always need to be dialled. For general information dial ☎118, and for reverse-charge (collect) calls dial ☎120.

Phonecards are the most reliable and cheapest way of making a phone call from a telephone booth. They are sold at post offices, newsagents and tobacconists in denominations of €5 and €10.

Visas

EU nationals need only a valid passport or identity card for entry to Portugal, and can stay indefinitely. Citizens of Australia, Canada, New Zealand and the US can stay for up to 90 days in any half-year without a visa. Others, including nationals of South Africa, need a visa unless they're the spouse or child of an EU citizen.

Getting There & Away

Air

TAP (www.tap.pt) is Portugal's international flag carrier as well as its main domestic airline. Portugal's main airports:

Lisbon (LIS; ☎218 413 500; www.ana-aeroportos.pt)

Porto (OPO; ☎229 432 400; www.ana-aeroportos.pt)

Faro (FAO; ☎289 800 800; www.ana-aeroportos.pt)

Land

BUS

UK–Portugal and France–Portugal Eurolines services cross to Portugal via northwest Spain; see the boxed text in this section for routes and fares. Some operators:

Alsa (www.alsa.es)

Avanza (www.avanzabus.com)

Damas (www.damas-sa.es)

Eurolines (www.eurolines.com)

Eva (www.eva-bus.com)

CAR & MOTORCYCLE

There is no border control in Portugal. For more information about driving in Portugal, see p740.

TRAIN

The most popular train link from Spain is on the Sud Express, operated by **Renfe** (www.renfe.com; one-way tickets from €59), which has a nightly sleeper service between Madrid and Lisbon. Badajoz (Spain)–Elvas–Lisbon is slow and there is only one regional service daily, but the scenery is stunning. Coming from Galicia, in the northwest of Spain, travellers can go from Vigo to Valença do Minho (Portugal) and continue on to Porto.

SPAIN TO PORTUGAL BUS SERVICES

FROM	TO	VIA	COST (€)	DURATION (HRS)	COMPANY
Madrid	Porto	Guarda	50	8½	Eurolines
Madrid	Lisbon	Évora	50	8	Eurolines, Avanza, Alsa
Barcelona	Lisbon	Évora	100	18	Eurolines
Madrid	Lisbon	Évora	45	8	Eurolines
Sevilla	Lisbon	Évora	48	7	Eurolines, Alsa, Eva, Damas
Sevilla	Faro	Huelva	20	4½	Eva, Damas

From France, there's Lisbon service via Irún (Spain) that takes around 20 hours (one-way tickets from €136). For trains from Paris, contact **SNCF** (www.sncf.com).

Getting Around

Air

TAP Portugal (TAP; www.flytap.com) has daily Lisbon–Faro flights (under an hour) year-round. Overall, however, flights within Portugal are poor value; it is a lot cheaper and not terribly time-consuming to travel by bus or train.

Bicycle

Mountain biking is a fine way to explore the country, although given the Portuguese penchant for overtaking on blind corners, it can be dangerous on lesser roads. Bicycle lanes are rare: veteran cyclists recommend the Parque Nacional da Peneda-Gerês (p735). A handful of towns have bike-hire outfits (from €10 to €20 a day). If you're bringing your own, pack plenty of spare inner tubes. Bicycles can be taken free on all regional and inter-regional trains as accompanied baggage. They can also go on a few suburban services on weekends. Most domestic bus lines won't accept bikes.

Boat

Portugal is not big on water-borne transport as a rule; however, there are river cruises along the Rio Douro from Porto (p733), Lisbon's river trips (p700) and commuter ferries.

Bus

A host of small private bus operators, most amalgamated into regional companies, run a dense network of services across the country. Among the largest companies are **Rede Expressos** (www.rede-expressos.pt), **Rodonorte** (www.rodonorte.pt) and The Algarve line **Eva** (www.eva-bus.com).

Most bus-station ticket desks will give you a computer printout of fares, and services and schedules are usually posted at major stations.

CLASSES

Expressos Comfortable, fast buses between major cities

Rápidas Quick regional buses

Carreiras Marked CR, slow, stopping at every crossroad

COSTS

Travelling by bus in Portugal is fairly inexpensive. A Lisbon–Faro express bus costs around €20; Lisbon–Porto costs about €18. Both take four hours. An under-26 card should get you a small discount on long-distance services.

Car & Motorcycle
AUTOMOBILE ASSOCIATIONS

Automóvel Clube de Portugal (ACP; ☎213 180 100; www.acp.pt) has a reciprocal arrangement with better-known foreign automobile clubs, including AA and RAC. It provides medical, legal and breakdown assistance. The 24-hour emergency help number is ☎707 509 510.

HIRE

To hire a car in Portugal you must be at least 25 years old and have held your home licence for over a year (some companies allow younger drivers at higher rates). To hire a scooter of up to 50cc you must be over 18 years old and have a valid driving licence. For more powerful scooters and motorbikes you must have a valid driving licence covering these vehicles from your home country.

INSURANCE

Although most car-insurance companies within the EU will cover taking your car to Portugal, it is prudent to consider extra cover for assistance in case your car breaks down. The minimum insurance required is third party.

ROAD RULES

The various speed limits for cars and motorcycles are 50km/h within cities and public centres, 90km/h on normal roads and 120km/h on motorways (but 50km/h, 70km/h and 100km/h for motorcycles with sidecars).

Driving is on the right side of the road. Drivers and front passengers in cars must wear seatbelts. Motorcyclists and passengers must wear helmets, and motorcycles must have headlights on day and night. Using a mobile phone while driving could result in a fine.

Drink-driving laws are strict in Portugal, with a maximum legal blood-alcohol level of 0.05%.

Train

Caminhos de Ferro Portugueses (www.cp.pt) is the statewide train network and is generally efficient.

There are four main types of long-distance service. Note that international services are marked IN on timetables.

Regional (marked R on timetables) Slow trains that stop everywhere

Interregional (IR) Reasonably fast trains

Intercidade (IC) or **rápido** Express trains

Alfa Pendular Deluxe, marginally faster and much pricier service.

Slovenia

Best Places to Stay

» Antiq Hotel (p747)
» Hotel Mitra (p775)
» Hotel Triglav Bled (p759)
» Max Piran (p771)
» Celica Hostel (p751)

Best Places to Eat

» Špajza (p752)
» Pri Mari (p771)
» Restavracija Topli Val (p765)
» Restavracija Pungaršek (p760)

Why Go?

It's a pint-sized place, with a surface area of just more than 20,000 sq km and 2 million people. But 'good things come in small packages', and never was that old chestnut more appropriate than in describing Slovenia.

Slovenia has been dubbed a lot of different things by its PR machine – 'Europe in Miniature', 'The Sunny Side of the Alps', 'The Green Piece of Europe' – and they're all true. Slovenia has everything, from beaches, snowcapped mountains, hills awash in grape vines and wide plains blanketed in sunflowers to Gothic churches, baroque palaces and art nouveau public buildings. Its incredible mixture of climates brings warm Mediterranean breezes up to the foothills of the Alps, where it can snow in summer. And with more than half of its total area covered in forest, Slovenia really is one of the 'greenest' countries in the world. In recent years, it has taken on the role as Europe's activities playground.

Come for all these things but come too for the Slovenes themselves – generous, broad-minded and welcoming.

When To Go

Ljubljana

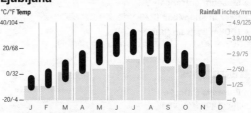

April–June Spring is a great time to be in the lowlands and the flower-carpeted valleys of Gorenjska.

September This is the month made for everything – still warm enough to swim and tailor-made for hiking.

December–March Everyone (and their grandma) dons their skis in this winter-sport mad country.

Fast Facts

» **Area** 20,273 sq km

» **Capital** Ljubljana

» **Telephone country code** 386

» **Emergency** 112

Exchange Rates

Australia	A$1	€0.72
Canada	C$1	€0.71
Japan	¥100	€0.82
New Zealand	NZ$1	€0.54
UK	UK£1	€1.12
USA	US$1	€0.69

Set Your Budget

» **Budget hotel room** €40

» **Two-course meal** €20

» **Museum entrance** €3

» **Beer in shop/bar** €1/3

» **100km by train/bus** €6.03/9.20

Resources

» **E-uprava** (http://e-uprava.gov.si/e-uprava/en/portal.euprava) Official portal with info on everything

» **Slovenian Tourist Board** (www.slovenia.info) Ambitious tourist site

Connections

Border formalities with Slovenia's three European Union neighbours – Italy, Austria and Hungary – are nonexistent and all are accessible by train and (less frequently) bus. Venice can also be reached by boat from Izola and Piran. Expect a somewhat closer inspection of your documents when travelling to/from non-EU Croatia.

ITINERARIES

One Week

Spend a couple of days in Ljubljana, then head north to unwind in Bohinj or romantic Bled beside idyllic mountain lakes. Depending on the season, take a bus or drive over the hair-raising Vršič Pass into the valley of the vivid blue Soča River and take part in some adventure sports in Bovec or Kobarid before returning to Ljubljana.

Two Weeks

Another week will allow you to see just about everything in this chapter: all of the above as well as the Karst caves at Škocjan and Postojna and the Venetian ports of Koper, Izola and Piran on the Adriatic.

Essential Food & Drink

» **Pršut** Air-dried, thinly sliced ham from the Karst region not unlike Italian prosciutto

» **Žlikrofi** Ravioli-like parcels filled with cheese, bacon and chives

» **Žganci** The Slovenian stodge of choice – groats made from barley or corn but usually *ajda* (buckwheat)

» **Potica** A kind of nut roll eaten at teatime or as a dessert

» **Wine** Distinctively Slovenian tipples include peppery red Teran from the Karst region and Malvazija, a straw-colour white wine from the coast

LJUBLJANA

♪ 01 / POP 257,675

Ljubljana (lyoob-*lya*-na) is by far Slovenia's largest and most populous city. It is also the nation's political, economic and cultural capital. As such, virtually everything of national importance begins, ends or is taking place in Ljubljana.

But it can be difficult to get a grip on the place. In many ways the city whose name *al-*

most means 'beloved' (*ljubljena*) in Slovene does not feel like an industrious municipality of national importance but a pleasant, self-contented small town. You might think that way too, especially in spring and summer when cafe tables fill the narrow streets of the Old Town and along the Ljubljanica River and street musicians entertain passers-by on pedestrian Čopova ul and Prešernov trg. Then Ljubljana becomes a little Prague or Kraków

Slovenia Highlights

① Experience the architecture, hilltop castle, green spaces and cafe life of **Ljubljana** (p745), Slovenia's beloved capital

② Wax romantic in picture-postcard **Bled** (p757), with a lake, an island and a castle as backdrop

③ Get into the outdoors or in the bluer-than-blue Soča in the majestic mountain scenery at **Bovec** (p763), one of the country's major outdoor-activities centres

④ Explore the Karst caves at **Škocjan** (p766), with scenes straight out of Jules Verne's *A Journey to the Centre of the Earth*

⑤ Swoon at the wonderful Venetian architecture of the romantic port of **Piran** (p770)

without the crowds. And you won't be disappointed with the museums and galleries, atmospheric bars and varied nightlife either.

History

Legacies of the Roman city of Emona – remnants of walls, dwellings, early churches, even a gilded statuette – can be seen everywhere. Ljubljana took its present form in the mid-12th century as Laibach under the Habsburgs, but it gained regional prominence in 1809, when it became the capital of Napoleon's short-lived 'Illyrian Provinces'. Some fine art nouveau buildings filled up the holes left by a devastating earthquake in 1895, and architect Jože Plečnik continued the remake of the city up until WWII. In recent years the city's dynamic mayor, Zoran Janković, has doubled the number of pedestrian streets, extended a great swathe of the river embankment and spanned the Ljubljanica River with two new footbridges.

◉ Sights

The oldest part of town, with the most important historical buildings and sights (including Ljubljana Castle) lies on the right (east) bank of the Ljubljanica. Center, which has the lion's share of the city's museums and galleries, is on the left (west) side of the river.

CASTLE AREA

Ljubljana Castle   CASTLE
(☏306 4293; www.ljubljanafestival.si; admission free; ◷9am-11pm summer, 10am-9pm winter) Ljubljana Castle crowns a wooded hill that is the city's focal point. It's an architectural mishmash, including fortified walls dating from the early 16th century, a late-15th-century chapel and a 1970s concrete cafe. The best views are from the 19th-century **watchtower** (adult/child €5/2; ◷9am-9pm summer, 10am-6pm winter); admission includes a visit to the **Virtual Museum**, a 23-minute, 3D video tour of Ljubljana though the centuries. More interesting is the new **Slovenia History Exhibition** (with tower & Virtual Museum adult/child €8/4.80) next door, which guides you through the past via iconic objects and multimedia exhibits. The fastest way to reach the castle is via the **funicular** (vzpenjača; return adult/child €3/2; ◷9am-11pm summer, 10am-9pm winter), which ascends from Krekov trg every 10 minutes, though you can also take the hourly **tourist train** (adult/child €3/2; ◷up 9am-9pm, down 9.20am-9.20pm) from south of the tourist informa-

tion centre (TIC) on Stritarjeva ul. It takes about 15 minutes to walk to the castle via Reber ul from the Old Town.

PREŠERNOV TRG & OLD TOWN

Prešernov Trg   SQUARE
This central square is dominated by the **Prešeren monument** (1905), honouring national poet France Prešeren, and the salmon pink, 17th-century **Franciscan Church of the Annunciation** (◷6.40am-noon & 3-8pm). Wander north of the square along Miklošičeva c to admire the fine **art nouveau buildings**, including the landmark Grand Hotel Union at No 1, built in 1905; the former People's Loan Bank (1908) at No 4; and the colourful erstwhile Cooperative Bank from 1922 at No 8.

Triple Bridge   BRIDGE
Leading southward from Prešernov trg is the small but perfectly formed Triple Bridge; prolific architect Jože Plečnik added two side bridges to the 19th-century span in 1931 to create something truly unique.

Old Town   HISTORIC AREA
Ljubljana's oldest and most important district is made up of three elongated 'squares': **Mestni trg**, 'City Square' containing a copy of the baroque **Robba Fountain** (the original is now in the National Gallery) in front of the Gothic **town hall** (1718); **Stari trg** (Old Sq); and **Gornji trg** (Upper Sq).

CENTRAL MARKET AREA

Central Market   MARKET
East of Prešernov trg is a lively open-air market (p753). Walk eastward along the magnificent riverside **Plečnik Colonnade** past the new **Butchers' Bridge**, with wonderful sculptures by Jakov Brdar and miniature padlocks left behind by lovers, to **Dragon Bridge** (Zmajski Most; 1901), a span guarded by four of the mythical creatures that are now the city's mascots.

Cathedral of St Nicholas   CHURCH
(Dolničarjeva ul 1; ◷10am-noon & 3-6pm) Bordering the market, the 18th-century city's main church is filled with pink marble, white stucco, gilt and a panoply of baroque frescos. Check out the magnificent bronze doors (1996) on the west and south sides.

TRG FRANCOSKE REVOLUCIJE AREA

City Museum of Ljubljana   MUSEUM
(☏241 25 00; www.mestnimuzej.si; Gosposka ul 15; adult/child €4/2.50; ◷10am-6pm Tue & Wed, Fri-Sun, 10am-9pm Thu) This excellent museum focuses on Ljubljana's history, culture and

politics via imaginative multimedia and interactive displays. The reconstructed Roman street dating back to the 1st century AD is worth a visit alone.

National & University Library HISTORIC BUILDING
(⚐200 11 09; Turjaška ul 1; ⊙9am-6pm Mon-Fri, 9am-2pm Sat) Diagonally opposite is the National & University Library, Plečnik's masterpiece completed in 1941, with its distinctive horse-head doorknobs and staircase of black marble that leads to a stunning reading room.

MUSEUM AREA

National Museum of Slovenia MUSEUM
(⚐241 44 00; www.nms.si; Prešernova c 20; adult/child €3/2.50, free 1st Sun of month; ⊙10am-6pm Fri-Wed, 10am-8pm Thu) Housed in an elegant 1888 building, the country's most important depository of historical items has rich archaeological and coin collections, including a Roman lapidarium and a Stone Age bone flute discovered near Cerkno in western Slovenia in 1995.

Slovenian Museum of Natural History
MUSEUM
(⚐241 09 40; www2.pms-lj.si; adult/student €3/2.50, inc national museum €5/4) Housed in the same building and keeping the same hours, this museum contains the usual reassembled mammoth and whale skeletons, stuffed birds, reptiles and mammals as well as an excellent mineral collections from the 19th century.

National Gallery MUSEUM
(⚐241 54 18; www.ng-slo.si; Prešernova c 24 & Cankarjeva c 20; adult/child €7/5, free 1st Sun of month; ⊙10am-6pm Tue-Sun) Slovenia's foremost assembly of fine art is housed over two floors both in an old building dating to 1896 and an impressive modern wing.

Ljubljana Museum of Modern Art MUSEUM
(⚐241 68 00; www.mg-lj.si; Tomšičeva ul 14; adult/student €5/2.50; ⊙10am-6pm Tue-Sun) Founded

in 1948, this fine space has been given a massive facelift and is now largely given over to temporary exhibits of modern and contemporary art.

☞ Tours

Two-hour **walking tours** (adult/child €10/5; ⊙10am, 2pm & 5pm Apr-Oct), combined with a ride on the funicular or the tourist train up to the castle or a cruise on the Ljubljanica, are organised by the TIC (p756). They depart daily from the town hall on Mestni trg.

✸ Festivals & Events

There is plenty going on in and around the capital, including **Druga Godba** (www.druga godba.si), a week-long festival of alternative and world music at the Križanke in May; the **Ljubljana Festival** (www.ljubljanafestival. si), the nation's premier cultural event (music, theatre and dance) held from early July to late August; and the **International Ljubljana Marathon** (www.ljubljanskimaraton. si) in late October.

🛏 Sleeping

The TIC (p756) has comprehensive details of private rooms (from s/d €30/50) and apartments (from d/q €55/80) though only a handful are central.

TOP CHOICE **Antiq Hotel** BOUTIQUE HOTEL €€€
(⚐421 35 60; www.antiqhotel.si; Gornji trg 3; s €61-133, d €77-168; ❄@) Ljubljana's original boutique hotel, cobbled together from a series of townhouses in the heart of the Old Town, has 16 rooms and apartments, most of which are very spacious, and a multilevel back garden. The decor is kitsch with a smirk and there are fabulous little nooks and touches everywhere. A short distance west across the Ljubljanica is its sister, the new **Antiq Palace** (⚐08-389 67 00; www.antiqpalace.com; Gosposka ul 10 & Vegova ul 5a; s/d €180/210; ❄@🛜), with 13

LJUBLJANA IN TWO DAYS

From central **Prešernov trg** (p746), walk to Krekov trg and take the funicular up to **Ljubljana Castle** (p746) to get an idea of the lay of the land. After a seafood lunch at **Ribca** (p753), explore the Old Town then cross the Ljubljanica River via St James Bridge and walk north along bust-lined Vegova ul to Kongresni trg. Over a cup of something hot and a slice of something sweet at **Zvezda** (p754), plan your evening: low key at **Jazz Club Gajo** (p755), chichi at **Top: Eat & Party** (p755) or alternative at **Metelkova Mesto** (p754).

On your second day check out some of the city's excellent **museums** (p747), and then stroll or cycle through Park Tivoli, stopping for an oh-so-local horse burger at **Hot Horse** (p753) along the way.

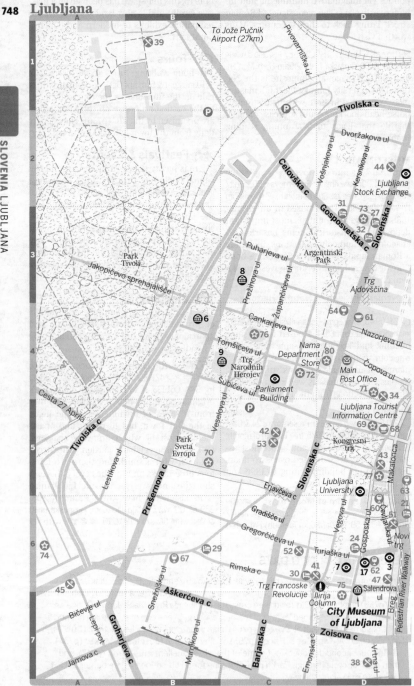

To Jože Pučnik
Airport (27km)

Pivovarniška ul

Tivolska c

Dvoržakova ul

Vošnjakova ul

Kersnikova ul

Gosposvetska c

Slovenska c

44

Ljubljana
Stock Exchange

31

73 **27**

32

Puharjeva ul

Argentinski
Park

Trg
Ajdovščina

8

Preširnova ul

Župančičeva ul

Cankarjeva c

6

54 **61**

76

Nazorjeva ul

Tomšičeva ul

Nama
Department
Store

80

Čopova ul

9
Trg
Narodnih
Herojev

Subičeva ul

Parliament
Building

72

Main
Post Office

71 **34**

Veselova ul

Ljubljana Tourist
Information Centre

69 **68**

42

Kongresni
trg

Cesta 27 Aprila

Tivolska c

53

Park
Sveta
Evropa

70

43

Makalonca

77

Erjavčeva c

Slovenska c

63

Lestikova ul

Ljubljana
University

Vegova ul

Gradišče ul

60

21

Prešernova c

51

Čevljarska c

Gregorčičeva ul

52

Turjaška ul

24

Novi
trg

74

67

Rimska c

30 **41**

7 **17** **62** **3**

Snežniška ul

45

29

Trg Francoske
Revolucije

75

47

Salendrova
ul

Aškerčeva c

Barjanska c

Bičevje ul

Ilirija
Column

**City Museum
of Ljubljana**

Pedestrian River Walkway

Breg

Lepi pot

Grohanjeva c

Murnikova ul

Emonska c

Zoisova c

Jamova c

38

Vrtna ul

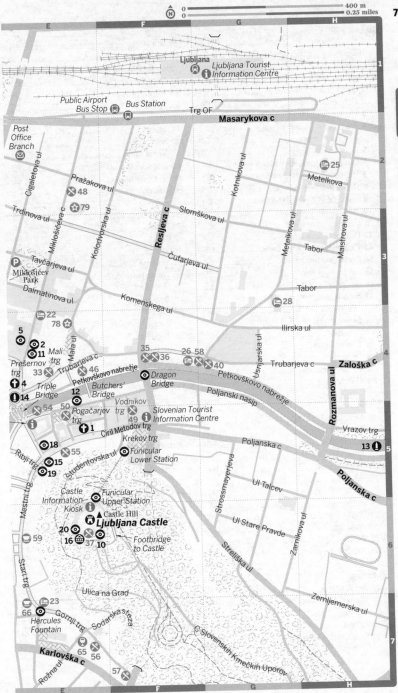

N

0   400 m
0   0.25 miles

Ljubljana

Ljubljana Tourist
Information Centre

Public Airport
Bus Stop   Bus Station

Trg OF

Masarykova c

Post
Office
Branch

Cigaletova ul

Pražakova ul

Trdinova ul

Miklošičeva c

Kolodvorska ul

Resljeva c

Slomškova ul

Kotnikova ul

25

Metelkova

Čufarjeva ul

Metelkova ul

Tabor

Maistrova ul

Tavčarjeva ul

Miklošičev
Park

Dalmatinova ul

Komenskega ul

Tabor

28

Ilirska ul

Usnjarska ul

22
78

5

2
11

Mali
trg

Mala ul

Trubarjeva c

35

36

26 58

40

Trubarjeva c

Zaloška c

Prešernov
trg   33

46

Petkovškovo nabrežje

Dragon
Bridge

Petkovškovo nabrežje

Poljanski nasip

Rozmanova ul

4

Triple
Bridge

14

Butchers'
Bridge

12

Vodnikov
trg

Vrazov trg

13

5

54   50

Pogačarjev
trg

1

49

Slovenian Tourist
Information Centre

Poljanska c

Ciril Metodov trg

Krekov trg

18

55

Studentovska ul

Funicular
Lower Station

Poljanska c

Poljanska c

15

19

Ribji trg

Mestni trg

Castle
Information
Kiosk

Funicular
Upper Station

Castle Hill

Ljubljana Castle

Strossmayerjeva

Ul Talcev

Ul Stare Pravde

Zarnikova ul

20

16   37   10

Footbridge
to Castle

Strelliška ul

59

Stari trg

Ulica na Grad

Zemljemerska ul

6

23

66

Hercules
Fountain

Gornji trg

Sodarska steza

C Slovenskih Kmečkih Uporov

65   56

Karlovška c

Rožna ul

57

SLOVENIA LJUBLJANA

residential suites surrounding two courtyards of a former palace, parts of which date back to the 16th century. The suites are enormous, many retain their original features and are equipped with a full kitchen. The in-house spa facilities over two floors are the flashiest in Ljubljana.

Slamič B&B
PENSION €€

(✆433 82 33; www.slamic.si; Kersnikova ul 1; s €65-75, d €95-100; [P][✳][@]) It's a titch away from the action but Slamič, a B&B above a famous cafe and teahouse, offers 11 bright rooms with antique(ish) furnishings and parquet floors. Choice rooms include the ones looking onto a back garden and Nos 9 and 11 just off an enormous terrace.

Penzion Pod Lipo
PENSION €€

(✆031-809 893; www.penzion-podlipo.com; Borštnikov trg 3; d/tr/q €64/75/100; [@]) Sitting atop one of Ljubljana's oldest *gostilne* along Rimska c, this 10-room inn offers excellent value in a part of the city that is filling up with bars and restaurants. We love the communal kitchen, the original hardwood floors, the computer in each room and the east-facing terrace that catches the morning sun.

🏆 TOP CHOICE Celica Hostel
HOSTEL €€

(✆230 97 00; www.hostelcelica.com; Metelkova ul 8; dm €17-21, s/d/tr cell €53/56/66, 3- to 5-bed r per person €21-26, 7-bed r per person €19-23; [P][@][☎]) This stylishly revamped former prison (built in 1882) in Metelkova has 20 'cells', designed by as many different architects and complete with their original bars; it also has nine rooms and apartments with three to seven beds; and a packed, popular 12-bed dorm. The ground floor is home to cafes (set lunch €4.10 to €6.40; open 7am to midnight), and the hostel boasts its own gallery where everyone can show their own work. Laundry costs €7.

Ljubljana Resort
CAMPING GROUND €

(✆568 39 13; www.ljubljanaresort.si/eng; Dunajska c 270; camping adult €7-13, child €5.25-9.75; [P][✳][@][⚲]) This attractive 6-hectare camping ground-cum-resort 5km north of the centre also offers a 62-room hotel (singles €60 to €75, doubles €75 to €90) and a dozen stationery mobile homes (€84 to €158) accommodating up to five people. Next door is Laguna (www.laguna.si; adult/child from €14/10, ☺May-to Sep), a water park with the works. Take bus 6 or 11 to the Ježica stop.

Zeppelin Hostel
HOSTEL €

(✆051-637 436; www.zeppelinhostel.com; 2 fl, Slovenska c 47; dm €18-24, d €49-60; [@][☎]) Located in the historic Evropa building on the corner of Gosposvetska c, this hostel with three large and bright dorm rooms (four to eight beds) and three doubles (one en suite) is run by an affable Slovenian-Spanish couple.

Pri Mraku
HOTEL €€

(✆421 96 00; www.daj-dam.si; Rimska c 4; s €70-86, d €106-116; [P][✳][@][☎]) Although it calls itself a *gostilna*, 'At Twilight' is really just a smallish hotel with 35 rooms in an old building with a garden. Rooms on the 1st and 4th floors have air-con. It's near the Križanke on Trg Francoske Revolucije – ideal for culture vultures.

Hotel Park
HOTEL €€

(✆300 25 00; www.hotelpark.si; Tabor 9; s €55-90, d €70-130; [P][✳][@]) A recladding outside and a facelift within has turned this 243-room tower-block hotel an even better-value central midrange choice. The 200 pleasant 'standard' and 'comfort' (air-conditioned) rooms are bright and unpretentiously well equipped. Cheaper 'hostel' rooms on the 7th and 12th floors, some of which have shared facilities (but always a toilet), cost €20 to €23 per person in a double and €17 to €19 in a quad. Students with ISIC cards get a 10% discount.

Alibi Hostel
HOSTEL €

(✆251 12 44; www.alibi.si; Cankarjevo nabrežje 27; dm €15-18, d €40-50; [@][☎]) This well-situated 106-bed hostel on the Ljubljanica has brightly painted, airy dorms with four to eight wooden bunks and a dozen doubles. There's a private apartment at the top for six people. Just south of Miklošičev Park, its sister property, the smaller Alibi M14 Hostel (✆232 27 70; www.alibi.si; 2 fl, Miklošičeva c 14; dm €18-20, d €50-60; [✳][@][☎]), has six rooms, including a 10-bed dorm.

H2O
HOSTEL €€

(✆041-662 266; info@simbol.si; Petkovškovo nabrežje 47; dm/d/q €17/50/68; [@][☎]) Also along the Ljubljanica, this six-room hostel wraps around a tiny courtyard, and one room has views of the castle. Rooms, with two to six beds, have their own kitchens.

Hotel Center
PENSION €€

(✆520 06 40, 041 263 347; www.hotelcenter.si; Slovenska c 51; s €45-55, d €60-66; [@]) The decor is simple and functionally modern at this new eight-room pension, but everything is spotless and you can't beat the central location.

The owners run the popular Cafe Compañeros (p754) below.

✕ Eating

TOP CHOICE **Špajza** SLOVENIAN €€
(📞425 30 94; Gornji trg 28; mains €14.60-22; ⏱noon-11pm) A favourite in the Old Town, the 'Pantry' is a nicely decorated rabbit warren of a restaurant with rough-hewn tables and chairs, wooden floors, frescoed ceilings and nostalgic bits and pieces. Try the stupendous *žlikrofi* (pasta stuffed with cheese, bacon and chives; €9 to €12), mushroom dishes in season or the *kozliček iz pečiče* (oven-roasted kid; €14.60). Wines from a dozen different producers from Goriška Brda in Primorska are served.

Pri Škofu SLOVENIAN €€
(📞426 45 08; Rečna ul 8; mains €8-22; ⏱10am-midnight Mon-Fri, noon-midnight Sat & Sun) This wonderful little place in tranquil Krakovo, south of the city centre, serves some of the best prepared local dishes and salads in Ljubljana from an ever-changing menu. Weekday set lunches are €8.

TOP CHOICE **Most** INTERNATIONAL €€
(📞232 81 83; www.restavracija-most.si; Petkovškovo nabrežje 21; mains €13-23) This tastefully decorated, very welcoming restaurant at the foot of Butchers' Bridge serves international dishes that lean toward the Mediterranean. Try the saffron risotto with shrimps and porcini.

Taverna Tatjana SEAFOOD €€
(📞421 00 87; Gornji trg 38; mains €8.50-25; ⏱5pm-midnight Mon-Sat) A wooden-beamed cottage pub with a nautical theme, this is actually a rather exclusive fish restaurant with a lovely back courtyard for the warmer months.

Čompa SLOVENIAN €
(📞040-542 552; Trubarjeva c 40; mains €10-18; ⏱noon-3pm & 7pm-1am Mon-Sat) This new favourite Slovenian restaurant with outside seating along pedestrian Trubarjeva c serves massive platters of meats, cheese and vegetables *na žaru* (on the grill) to happy, very hungry punters.

Gostilna na Gradu SLOVENIAN €
(📞08-205 19 30; www.nagradu.si; Grajska planota 1; dishes €4.50-10) After a wait of what seemed to be forever, the comfortable Inn at the Castle has opened in Ljubljana Castle and – joy of joys – it's serving affordable local dishes such as *jelenov golaž* (venison goulash),

skutni njoki (gnocchi with curd cheese) and *bobiči* (Istrian-style vegetarian soup).

Le Petit Restaurant FRENCH €€
(📞426 14 88; Trg Francoske Revolucije 4; mains €12-20; ⏱7.30am-1am) Opposite the Križanke, what has always been a popular French-style cafe on French Revolution Sq has now opened a wonderful restaurant on the 1st floor with a provincial decor and menu. The pleasant, boho cafe still offers great coffee and a wide range of breakfast goodies (€2.20 to €6.50) and lunches (sandwiches €2.90 to €4.50).

Harambaša BALKAN €
(📞041-843 106; Vrtna ul 8; dishes €4.50-6; ⏱10am-10pm Mon-Fri, noon-10pm Sat, to 6pm Sun) You'll find authentic Bosnian – Sarajevan to be precise – dishes here such as *čevapčiči* (spicy meatballs) and *pljeskavica* (meat patties) served at low tables in a charming modern cottage.

Zhong Hua CHINESE €
(📞230 16 65; Trubarjeva c 50; mains €5.80-12.10; ⏱11am-10.30pm) This place just up from the Ljublanica is just about the most authentic Chinese restaurant in town. Name a dish and they'll make it – and pretty authentically too. The less adventurous will stick with rice and noodle dishes (€4.90 to €6.50).

Sokol SLOVENIAN €
(📞439 68 55; Ciril Metodov trg 18; mains €7-20; ⏱7am-11pm Mon-Sat, 10am-11pm Sun) In an old vaulted house, traditional Slovenian food is served on heavy tables by costumed waiters. Along with traditional dishes such as *obara* (veal stew, €7) and Krvavica sausage with cabbage and turnips (€8.50), there's more exotic fare such as grilled stallion steak (€16).

Namasté INDIAN €€
(📞425 01 59; www.restavracija-namaste.si; Breg 8; mains €6.30-17.90; ⏱11am-midnight Mon-Sat, to 10pm Sun) Should you fancy a bit of Indian, head for this place on the left bank of the Ljubljanica. You won't get high street quality curry but the thalis (from €8) and tandoori dishes (from €9) are good.

Cantina Mexicana MEXICAN €€
(📞426 93 25; www.cantina.si; Knafljev prehod 3; mains €7.90-18.80; ⏱11am-midnight Sun-Thu, to 1am Fri & Sat) The capital's most stylish Mexican restaurant has an eye-catching red-and-blue exterior and hacienda-like decor inside. The fajitas (€8.70 to €14.30) are great.

Quick Eats

Ribca
SEAFOOD €

(☑425 15 44; Adamič-Lundrovo nabrežje 1; dishes €3.30-7.60; ☉8am-4pm Mon-Fri, to 2pm Sat) This basement seafood bar, below the Plečnik Colonnade in Pogačarjev trg, serves tasty fried squid, sardines and herrings to hungry market-goers. Set lunch is €7.50.

Restavracija 2000
SELF-SERVICE €

(☑476 69 25; Trg Republike 1; dishes €2.15-3.70; ☉9am-7pm Mon-Fri, to 3pm Sat) In the basement of the Maximarket department store, this self-service eatery is surprisingly upbeat, and just the ticket if you want something quick while visiting the museums.

Paninoteka
SANDWICH BAR €

(☑059-018 455; Jurčičev trg 3; soups & toasted sandwiches €3-6; ☉8am-1am Mon-Sat, 9am-11pm Sun) Healthy sandwich creations on a lovely little square by the river with outside seating.

Ajdovo Zrno
VEGETARIAN €

(☑040-482 446; www.satwa.si; Trubarjeva c 7; soups & sandwiches €2-4, set lunch €6; ☉10am-7pm Mon-Fri) 'Buckwheat Grain' serves soups, sandwiches, fried vegetables and lots of different salads (self-service, €3 to €10) and casseroles (€3.50). And it has terrific, freshly squeezed juices. Enter from little Mali trg.

Hot Horse
BURGERS €

(☑031-709 716; www.hot-horse.si; Park Tivoli, Celovška c 25; snacks & burgers €2.80-6; ☉9am-6am Tue-Sun, 10am-6am Mon) This kiosk in the city's largest park supplies *Ljubljančani* with one of their favourite treats: horse burgers (€4).

Falafel
STREET FOOD €

(☑041-640 166; Trubarjeva c 40; dishes €3.50-4.50, daily menu €4.50; 11am-midnight Mon-Fri, noon-midnight Sat, 1-10pm Sun) Sandwiches, salads and the eponymous falafel – ideal for veggies on the hoof (though there are meat dishes).

Nobel Burek
STREET FOOD €

(Miklošičeva c 30; burek €2, pizza slices €1.40; ☉24hr) This hole-in-the-wall serves Slovenian-style fast food round-the-clock.

As in all European capitals, Ljubljana is awash in pizzerias (€5 to €8.50).

Pizzeria Foculus (☑421 92 95; www.foculus. com; Gregorčičeva ul 3; ☉11am-midnight) Pick of the crop, which boasts a vaulted ceiling painted with spring and autumn leaves.

Kavalino (☑232 09 90; www.kavalino.si; Trubarjeva c 52; ☉8am-10pm Mon-Thu, to 11pm Fri & Sat)

Trta (☑426 50 66; www.trta.si; Grudnovo nabrežje 21; ☉11am-10pm Mon-Fri, noon-10.30pm Sat) On the right bank of the Ljubljanica.

Mirje (☑426 60 15; Tržaška c 5; ☉10am-10pm Mon-Fri, noon-10pm Sat) Southwest of the city centre.

Self-Catering

Handy supermarkets include a large **Mercator** (Slovenska c 55; ☉7am-9pm) southwest of the train and bus stations and a smaller, more central **Mercator branch** (Kongresni trg 9; ☉7am-8pm Mon-Fri, 8am-3pm Sat & Sun) just up from the river.

The **Maximarket supermarket** (Trg Republike 1; ☉9am-9pm Mon-Fri, 8am-5pm Sat) in the basement of the department store of the same name has the largest selection of food and wine in the city centre.

The **open-air market** (Pogačarjev trg & Vodnikov trg; ☉6am-6pm Mon-Fri, to 4pm Sat summer, 6am-4pm Mon-Sat winter), held across two squares north and east of the cathedral, sells mostly fruit and vegetables and dry goods.

🍷 Drinking

Few cities of this size have central Ljubljana's concentration of inviting cafes and bars, the vast majority with outdoor seating in the warmer months.

Bars & Pubs

Nebotičnik
CAFE-BAR

(☑059-070 395; 12th fl, Štefanova ul 1; ☉8am-3am) After a decade-long hibernation this cafe-bar with its breathtaking terrace atop Ljubljana's famed art deco Skyscraper (1933) has awakened, and the 360-degree views are still spectacular.

Pri Zelenem Zajcu
BAR

(☑031-632 992; Rožna ul 3; ☉9am-midnight Mon-Wed & Sun, to 1am Thu & Sat, to 2am Fri) Ljubljana's only absinthe bar, 'At the Green Rabbit' to you, has its own label and relaxed vibe. It's a bit of a warren of a place (as it would be) but we're sure you'll feel comfortably frisky here.

Open Cafe
GAY & LESBIAN

(☑041-391 371; www.open.si; Hrenova ul 19; ☉4pm-midnight) This very stylish gay cafe south of the Old Town has become the meeting point by Ljubljana's burgeoning gay culture.

Makalonca
CAFE-BAR

(☑030-362 450; Hribarjevo nabrežje 19; ☉8am-1am Mon-Sat, 10am-10pm Sun) This cafe-bar with a 100m-long terrace within the columns of the Ljubljanica embankment is the perfect place to nurse a drink and watch the river roll by.

Žmavc
CAFE-BAR

(☎251 03 24; Rimska c 21; ⏰7.30am-1am Mon-Fri, from 10am Sat, from 6pm Sun) This super popular student hang-out west of Slovenska c, with *manga* comic-strip scenes and graffiti decorating the walls, is always voted tops in cafe-bar polls here.

Dvorni Bar
WINE BAR

(☎251 12 57; www.dvornibar.net; Dvorni trg 2; ⏰8am-1am Mon-Sat, 9am-midnight Sun) This wine bar is an excellent place to taste Slovenian vintages; it stocks more than 100 varieties and has wine tastings every second or third Wednesday of the month (check the website).

Maček
CAFE-BAR

(☎425 37 91; Krojaška ul 5; ⏰9am-12.30am Mon-Sat, to 11pm Sun) *The* place to be seen in Ljubljana on a summer afternoon, the 'Cat' is the most popular venue on the right bank of the Ljubljanica.

LP Bar
CAFE-BAR

(☎041-846 457; Novi trg 2; ⏰8am-midnight Mon-Wed & Sat, to 1am Thu & Fri, 9am-3pm Sun) Within the Academy of Arts and Sciences, LP (no relation to us!) is a civilised place for a libation, with cafe-bar, bookshop and heated seats outside. Great views of the castle.

Cafes & Teahouses

Zvezda
CAFE

(☎421 90 90; Kongresni trg 4 & Wolfova ul 14; ⏰7am-11pm Mon-Sat, 10am-8pm Sun) The 'Star' has all the usual varieties of coffee and tea but is celebrated for its shop-made cakes, especially *skutina pečena* (€2.90), an eggy cheesecake.

Čajna Hiša
TEAHOUSE

(☎421 24 44; Stari trg 3; ⏰9am-10.30pm Mon-Fri, 9am-3pm & 6-10pm Sat; 🕸) If you take your cuppa seriously, come here; the appropriately named 'Tea House' offers a wide range of green and black teas and fruit tisanes (pot €2 to €3.60)

Juice Box
JUICE BAR

(☎051-614 545; Slovenska c 38; juices & smoothies €3.60-4.90; ⏰7am-8pm Mon-Fri, 8am-3pm Sat; 🕸) Of the new crop of juice bars, this is the best, with some excellent fruit and vegetable combinations.

Slaščičarna Pri Vodnjaku
ICE-CREAM PARLOUR

(☎425 07 12; Stari trg 30; ⏰8am-midnight) For ice cream, the 'Confectionery by the Fountain' will surely satisfy – there are almost three dozen flavours (per scoop €1.20), as well as teas (€2) and fresh juices (from €1.40).

⭐ Entertainment

The free bimonthly **Ljubljana in Your Pocket** (www.inyourpocket.com) is your best source of information though the **Ljubljana.info** (www.ljubljana.info) has practical information and listings as well.

Nightclubs

Metelkova Mesto
CLUB

(www.metelkova.org; Masarykova c 24) 'Metelkova Town', an ex-army garrison taken over by squatters after independence, is now a free-living commune. In this two-courtyard block, idiosyncratic clubs, bars and art spaces hide behind brightly tagged doorways, coming to life generally after midnight, daily in summer and at weekends the rest of the year. Venues come in and go out; try to wade though the website or just stroll over and have a look yourself. It's just behind the Celica Hostel (p751).

Cafe Compañeros
CLUB

(☎520 06 40; Slovenska c 51; ⏰11am-5am) Raucous studenty hang-out with a lounge and terrace bar on the ground floor and a wild and crazy club with live music below.

Klub K4
CLUB

(☎438 02 61; www.klubk4.org; Kersnikova ul 4; ⏰10pm-2am Tue, 11pm-4am Wed & Thu, 11pm-6am Fri & Sat, 10pm-4am Sun) This evergreen venue in the basement of the Student Organisation of Ljubljana University (ŠOU) headquarters features rave-electronic music on Fridays and Saturdays, with other styles of music on weeknights, and a popular gay and lesbian night, K4 Roza, on Sundays. It closes in summer.

KMŠ
CLUB

(☎425 74 80; www.klubkms.si; Tržaška ul 2; ⏰8am-5am Mon-Fri, 9pm-5am Sat) Located in the deep recesses of a former tobacco factory complex, the 'Maribor Student Club' is comatose till Saturday when it turns into a lively dance place.

Bachus Center Club
CLUB

(☎241 82 40; www.bachus-center.com; Kongresni trg 3; ⏰8pm-5am Tue-Sat) This place has something for everyone, including a restaurant and bar-lounge, and attracts a mainstream crowd.

Club As
CLUB

(☎425 88 22; www.gostilnaas.si; Čopova 5a, enter from Knafljev prehod; ⏰9am-3am Wed-Sat) DJs transform this candlelit basement bar into a pumping, crowd-pulling nightclub four nights a week.

Top: Eat & Party
CLUB

(☎040-667 722; www.klubtop.si; Tomšičeva ul 2; ⊙11pm-5am) This retro restaurant and cocktail bar on the 6th floor of the Nama department store becomes a popular dance venue nightly and attracts a very chi-chi crowd. Take the glass-bubble lift from along Slovenska c or the lift in the passageway linking Cankarjeva ulica and Tomšičeva ulica.

Live Music

Orto Bar
LIVE MUSIC

(☎232 16 74; www.orto-bar.com; Graboličeva ul 1; ⊙9pm-4am Tue & Wed, to 5am Thu-Sat) A popular bar-club for late-night drinking and dancing with occasional live music, Orto is just five minutes from Metelkova Mesto.

Hugo Barrera Club
LIVE MUSIC

(☎040-177 477; Adamič Lundrovo nabrežje 5; ⊙7am-2am Mon-Wed, to 3am Thu-Sat, 10am-2am Sun) Below the Plečnik Colonnade at the foot of Butchers' Bridge this new venue offers live music from the '60s, '70s and '80s four nights a week.

Sax Pub
LIVE MUSIC

(☎283 9009; Eipprova ul 7; ⊙noon-1am Mon, 10am-1am Tue-Sat, 4-10pm Sun) Over two decades in Trnovo, the colourful Sax has live jazz at around 9pm on Thursday or Sunday from late August to December and February to June. Canned stuff rules at other times.

Jazz Club Gajo
LIVE MUSIC

(☎425 32 06; www.jazzclubgajo.com; Beethovnova ul 8; ⊙7pm-2am Mon-Sat) Established in 1994, Gajo is the city's premier venue for live jazz and attracts both local and international talent. Jam sessions are at 9pm on Monday.

Roxly Cafe Bar
LIVE MUSIC

(☎430 10 21, 041-399 599; www.roxly.si; Mala ul 5; ⊙8am-2am Mon-Wed, to 3am Thu & Fri, 10am-3am Sat) This cafe, bar and restaurant north of the Ljubljanica features live rock music (mostly blues and rock) from 10pm two or three nights a week.

Performing Arts

Cankarjev Dom
LIVE MUSIC

(☎241 71 00, box office 241 72 99; www.cd-cc.si; Prešernova c 10) is Ljubljana's premier cultural centre and has two large auditoriums (the Gallus Hall has perfect acoustics) and a dozen smaller performance spaces.

Križanke
LIVE MUSIC

(☎241 60 00, box office 241 60 26; www.festival-lj. si; Trg Francoske Revolucije 1-2) Hosts concerts of the Ljubljana Festival (p747) and other events at a former 18th-century monastic complex.

Opera House
OPERA, LIVE MUSIC

(☎241 17 40, box office 241 17 66; www.opera.si; Župančičeva ul 1) Opera and ballet are performed at the renovated and extended neo-Renaissance Opera House (1882).

Philharmonic Hall
LIVE MUSIC

(Slovenska Filharmonija; ☎241 08 00; www.filharmonija.si; Kongresni trg 10) This concert hall dating from 1891 is home to the Slovenian Philharmonic Orchestra.

Cinema

Slovenska Kinoteka
CINEMA

(☎434 25 20; www.kinoteka.si; Miklošičeva c 28) The 'Slovenian Cinematheque' screens archival art and classic films in their original languages.

ℹ Information

Discount Cards

The new **Urbana-Ljubljana Tourist Card** (www.visitljubljana.si/en/ljubljana-and-more/ljubljana-tourist-card), available from the tourist offices for 24/48/72 hours (€23/30/35), offers free admission to most museums and galleries, walking and boat tours and unlimited city bus travel.

Internet Access

Web connection is available at virtually every hostel and hotel, the Slovenia Tourist Information Centre (p756; per 30min €1), the STA Travel Cafe (p756; per 20min €1) and the Student Organisation of the University of Ljubljana (p756; free). In addition:

Cyber Cafe Xplorer (☎430 19 91; Petkovškovo nabrežje 23; per 30min/hr €2.50/4; ⊙10am-10pm Mon-Fri, 2-10pm Sat & Sun) Some 10 computers, wi-fi and cheap international phone calls.

DrogArt (☎439 72 70; Kolodvorska ul 20; 1st 15min free, then per 30min/hr €1/1.80; ⊙10am-4pm Mon-Fri) Opposite the train station; three computers.

Portal.si Internet (☎234 46 00; Trg OF 4; per hr €4.20; ⊙5.30am-10.30pm Sun-Fri, 5am-10pm Sat) In the bus station (get code from window 4); three computers.

Internet Resources

City of Ljubljana (www.ljubljana.si) Comprehensive information portal on every aspect of life and tourism.

Left Luggage

Bus station (Trg OF 4; per day €2; ⊙5.30am-10.30pm Sun-Fri, 5am-10pm Sat) Window 3.

Train station (Trg OF 6; per day €2-3; ⊙24hr) Coin lockers on platform 1.

Maps

Excellent free maps are available from the tourist offices. The more detailed 1:20,000-scale *Mestni Načrt Ljubljana* (Ljubljana City Map; €7.70) from **Kod & Kam** (☑600 50 80; www. kod-kam.si; Miklošičeva c 34) is available from newsstands and bookshops.

Medical Services

Central Pharmacy (Centralna Lekarna; ☑244 23 60; Prešernov trg 5; ⊙7.30am-7.30pm Mon-Fri, 8am-3pm Sat)

Health Centre Ljubljana (Zdravstveni Dom Ljubljana; www.zd-lj.si; ☑472 37 00; Metelkova ul 9; ⊙7.30am-7pm) For nonemergencies.

University Medical Centre Ljubljana (Univerzitetni Klinični Center Ljubljana; ☑522 50 50; www3.kclj.si; Zaloška c 2; ⊙24hr) A&E service.

Money

There are ATMs at every turn, including a row of them outside the main TIC office. At the train station you'll find a **bureau de change** (⊙7am-8pm) changing cash (but not travellers cheques) for no commission.

Abanka (Slovenska c 50; ⊙9am-5pm Mon-Fri)

Nova Ljubljanska Banka (Trg Republike 2; ⊙8am-6pm Mon-Fri)

Post

Main post office (Slovenska c 32; ⊙8am-7pm Mon-Fri, to 1pm Sat) Holds poste restante for 30 days and changes money.

Post office branch (Pražakova ul 3; ⊙8am-7pm Mon-Fri, to noon Sat) Just southwest of the bus and train stations.

Tourist Information

Tourist Information Centre Ljubljana Old Town (TIC; ☑306 12 15; www.visitljubljana. si; Kresija Bldg, Stritarjeva ul; ⊙8am-9pm Jun-Sep, 8am-7pm Oct-May); train station (☑433 94 75; Trg OF 6; ⊙8am-10pm Jun-Sep, 10am-7pm Mon-Fri, 8am-3pm Sat Oct-May) Knowledgeable and enthusiastic staff dispense information, maps and useful literature and help with accommodation.

Slovenia Tourist Information Centre (STIC; ☑306 45 76; www.slovenia.info; Krekov trg 10; ⊙8am-9pm Jun-Sep, 8am-7pm Oct-May) Good source of information for the rest of Slovenia, with internet and bicycle rental also available.

Student Organisation of the University of Ljubljana

(Študentska Organizacija Univerze Ljubljani; ŠOU; ☑433 03 20, 051-373 999; www. sou-lj.si; Trubarjeva c 7; ⊙9am-6pm Mon-Thu, 9am-3pm Fri) Information and free internet.

Travel Agency

STA Ljubljana (☑439 16 90, 041-612 711; www.staljubljana.com; 1st fl, Trg Ajdovščina 1; ⊙10am-5pm Mon-Fri) Discount airfares for students; go online at the **STA Travel Cafe** (⊙8am-midnight Mon-Sat).

❶ Getting There & Away

The bus and train stations are 800m north-east of Prešernov trg up Miklošičeva c. Ljubljana's Jože Pučnik Airport is 27km north of the city at Brnik near Kranj.

Bus

The **bus station** (☑234 46 00, information 090-934 230; www.ap-ljubljana.si; Trg OF 4; ⊙5.30am-10.30pm Sun-Fri, 5am-10pm Sat) opposite the train station has bilingual info-phones. Buses serve Bohinj (€8.70, 2¼ hours, 91km, hourly) via Bled (€6.30, 1¼ hours, 57km, hourly). Those to Piran (€12, 2½ to three hours, 140km, up to five daily) go via Koper (€11.10, 1¾ to 2½ hours, 122km) and Postojna (€6, one hour, 54km, half-hourly). There's also service to Maribor (€12.40, three hours, 141km, between two and four daily).

International bus services from Ljubljana include Belgrade (€35, 7¾ hours, 537km, three times daily); Florence (€38, eight hours, 480km, 5.10am daily); Frankfurt (€86, 14 hours, 777km, 6.30pm daily) via Munich (€44, 6¾ hours, 344km); Pula (€22, 4½ hours, 249km, once daily) via Poreč (€21, three hours, 202km) and Rovinj (€21, 2½ hours, 182km); Sarajevo (€38, 10 hours, 566km, twice daily); Skopje (€50, 16 hours, 978km, twice daily); Split (€44, 10½ hours, 528km, daily in summer) via Rijeka (€17, 2½ hours, 136km); Trieste (€11.60, 2¼ hours, 106km, twice daily); and Venice–Mestre (€25, five hours, 230km, three daily).

Train

Ljubljana's **train station** (☑291 33 32; www. slo-zeleznice.si; Trg OF 6; ⊙5am-10pm) has services to Koper (€10, 2½ hours, 153km, up to five daily). Alternatively you can take one of the more frequent Sežana-bound trains and change at Divača (€6.85, 1½ hours, 104km).

Ljubljana–Vienna trains (€63.20, 6¼ hours, 385km, one direct, four via Maribor daily) via Graz (€34.20, 200km, 3½ hours) are expensive, although Spar Schiene fares go as low as €29 on certain trains at certain times.

Three trains depart daily for Munich (€72, six hours, 405km). The 11.50pm departure has sleeping carriages available.

A Venice train (one way/return €25/40, four hours, 244km) via Sežana departs at 2.28am. But it's cheaper to go first to Nova Gorica (€8.50, 3½ hours, 153km, five daily), cross over on foot to the train station in Gorizia and then take an Italian train to Venice (about €9, 2½ hours).

For Zagreb (€13.40, 2½ hours, 154km) there are seven trains daily via Zidani Most. Two trains from the capital at 6.20am and 2.53pm serve Rijeka (€13.80, 2½ hours, 136km) via Postojna.

Trains to Budapest (€53.40, 8¾ hours, 451km, twice daily) go via Ptuj and Hodoš; there are 'Budapest Spezial' fares available for as low as €29 on certain trains at certain times. Belgrade (€25 to €44, 10 hours, 535km) is served by four trains a day.

❶ Getting Around

The cheapest way to/from Ljubljana's **Jože Pučnik Airport** (LJU; ☎04-206 19 81; www. lju-airport.si) at Brnik is by city bus (€4.10, 45 minutes, 27km) from stop 28 at the bus station. These run at 5.20am and hourly from 6.10am to 8.10pm Monday to Friday; on weekends there's a bus at 6.10am and then one every two hours from 9.10am to 7.10pm. A **private airport van** (☎040-771 771, 051- 321 414; www.airport -shuttle.si) also links Trg OF near the bus station (€5) or your hotel (€9) with the airport (30 minutes) up to 11 times daily between 5.10am and 10.30pm. A **taxi** (☎031-216 111; 059-060 777) from Center in Ljubljana will cost €40.

Ljubljana's city buses operate every five to 15 minutes from 5am (6am on Sunday) to 10.30pm, though some start as early as 3.15am and go until midnight and a couple run overnight. The flat fare (€0.80) is paid with a stored-value magnetic Urbana Card (www.jh-lj.si/urbana) which can be purchased at newsstands, tourist offices and the **LPP Information Centre** (☎430 51 75; Slovenska c 56; ☉7am-7pm Mon-Fri) for €2; credit can then be added for from €1 to €50. The central area is perfectly walkable, though, so buses are really only necessary if you're staying way out of town.

Ljubljana Bike (per 2hr/day €1/5; ☉8am-7pm or 9pm Apr-Oct) has two-wheelers available from locations around the city, including outside the STIC and opposite the Antiq Hotel.

JULIAN ALPS

The Julian Alps form Slovenia's dramatic northwest frontier with Italy. Triglav National Park, established in 1924, includes almost all of the Alps lying within Slovenia. The centrepiece of the park is, of course, Mt Triglav (2864m), Slovenia's highest and most sacred mountain, but there are many other peaks here reaching above 2000m. Along with an abundance of fauna and flora, the area offers a wide range of outdoor activities.

Kranj
☑04 / POP 34,620

At the foot of the Kamnik-Savinja Alps, with the snowcapped peak of Storžič (2132m) and others in full view to the north, Kranj is Slovenia's fourth-largest city. The attractive Old Town, perched on an escarpment above the confluence of the Sava and Kokra Rivers, barely measures 250m wide by 1km long.

The frequent buses between Kranj and Ljubljana's airport at nearby Brnik (€1.80, 10 minutes, 10km) make it possible to head straight to the Julian Alps without first going to the capital. While waiting for your on-ward bus to Bled (€3.60, 40 minutes, 29km), have a look at the **Old Town**, a 600m walk south from the bus station. On your way you'll pass the 87-room **Hotel Creina** (☎281 75 00; www.hotel-creina.si; Koroška c 5; s €60-80, d €80-100; P❄@☎), expensive but the only game in town with bikes for rent (per hour/day €1/12). The **tourist office** (☎238 04 50; www.tourism-kranj.si; Glavni trg 2; ☉8am-7pm Mon-Sat, 9am-6pm Sun) can find you a private room from €20 or, in summer, a bed in a student dormitory (from €15).

Pedestrianised streets lead to the **Church of St Cantianus**, with impressive frescos and stained glass. Another 300m further south, the Old Town dead-ends at the Serbian Orthodox **Plague Church**, built during a time of pestilence in 1470, and the 16th-century **defence tower** behind it. Ask the TIC about guided tours of the **tunnels** (adult/child €3/2.50; ☉5pm Tue & Fri, 10am Sat & Sun) under the Old Town built as air-raid shelters during WWII. **Mitnica** (☎040-678 778; Tavčarjeva ul 35; ☉7am-11pm Mon-Wed, 7am-1am Thu, 7am-2am Fri & Sat, 10am-11pm Sun) is a relaxing cafe-bar in a 16th-century toll house with a huge terrace overlooking the river.

Bled
☑04 / POP 5460

With an emerald-green lake, a picture-postcard church on a tiny island, a medieval castle clinging to a rocky cliff, and some of Slovenia's highest peaks as backdrops, Bled seems to have been designed by some god of tourism. Bled can get crowded in season, but it's always an excellent base from which to explore the mountains.

SLOVENIA JULIAN ALPS

Bled

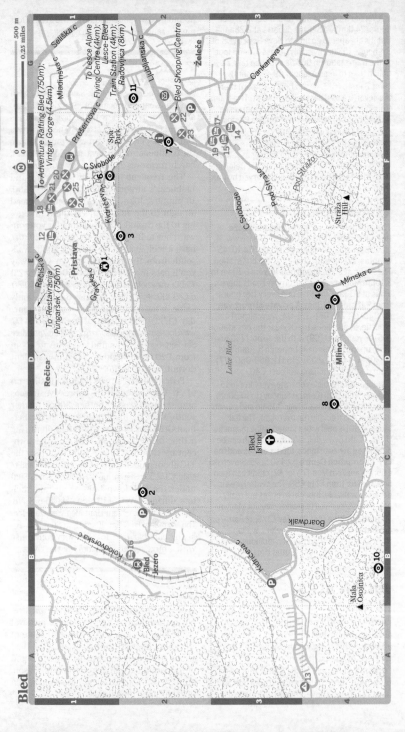

500 m
0.25 miles

To Lesce Alpine
Flying Centre (4km);
Lesce-Bled
Train Station (4km);
Radovljica (8km)

To Adventure Rafting Bled (750m);
Vintgar Gorge (4.5km)

Bled Shopping Centre

Želeče

Ljubljanska c

Cankarjeva c

Seliška c

Mladinska c

Prešernova c

Spa Park

C Svobode

Pod Stražo

Straža Hill

C Svobode

Mlinska c

Mlino

Pod Skalo

Lake Bled

Bled Island

Boardwalk

Pristava

Rečiška c

Grajska c

To Restavracija
Pungaršek (750m)

Rečica

Kidričeva c

Kolodvorska c

Bled Jezero

Kidričeva c

Mala Osojnica

11

22 23

19 15 17

14

7

6 3

18 21 20 25 24

12

1

2

4 9

8

5

10

13

16

Bled

⊙ Sights

Lake Bled
LAKE

A relaxed stroll around the 2km-by-1.4km lake shouldn't take more than a couple of hours, including the short climb to the **Osojnica viewing point** in the southwest. If you prefer, jump aboard the **tourist train** (adult/child €3/2; ⊙9am-9pm May-Oct) just south of the TIC for the 40-minute twirl around the lake.

Bled Island
ISLAND, CHURCH

This tiny, tear-shaped islet is where you'll find Bled's icon, the baroque **Church of the Assumption** (⊙9am-dusk). The trip by piloted **gondola** (pletna; ☑041-427 155; per person €12) allows enough time on the island to look around and ring the 'lucky' bell; all in all, it's about 1½ hours. Do-it-yourself rowing boats for four/six people cost €10/15 per hour.

Bled Castle
CASTLE, MUSEUM

(☑572 9782; www.blejski-grad.si; Grajska c 25; adult/child €7/3.50; ⊙8am-8pm summer, to 6pm

winter) Perched atop a 100m-high cliff, this castle, first mentioned a millennium ago, offers the perfect backdrop to a lake view. One of the easiest ways up on foot leads from behind Bledec Hostel. Admission includes entry to several attractions including the **museum collection** and 16th-century **chapel**.

Vintgar Gorge
GORGE

(adult/child €4/2; ⊙8am-7pm mid-May–Oct) The highlight of visiting the gorge, an easy walk 4km to the northwest of the centre, is the 1600m-long wooden walkway (1893) that criss-crosses the swirling Radovna River for the first 700m or so. Thereafter the scenery becomes tamer and ends at the 16m-high **Šum Waterfall**. From June to September, a daily bus (one way/return €3.50/6.30) leaves Bled bus station for Vintgar at 10am daily, arriving at 10.30am and returning at 12.30pm. Otherwise reach it on foot via the Gostilna Vintgar, an inn just 3km away on quiet roads from the Bledec Hostel.

🏃 Activities

Agencies organise a wide range of outdoor activities in and around Bled, offering everything from mountain biking (from €28) and canyoning (€50) to paragliding (€85). One of the best trips is the Emerald River Adventure (€55), an 11-hour hiking and swimming foray into Triglav National Park and along the Soča River available from **3glav adventures** (☑041-683 184; www.3glav-adventures.com; Ljubljanska c 1; ⊙9am-noon & 4-7pm Apr-Oct). **Adventure Rafting Bled** (☑574 40 41, 051-676 008; www.adventure-rafting.si; Grajska c 21; Hrastova ul 2; ☑Apr-Oct) also organises rafting and canyoning. Both the TIC and Kompas (p761) rent bikes for €3.5/11 per hour/day.

🛏 Sleeping

Kompas (p761) has a list of private rooms and farmhouses, with singles/doubles starting at €24/38.

TOP CHOICE **Hotel Triglav Bled** BOUTIQUE HOTEL €€€
(☑575 26 10; www.hoteltriglavbled.si; Kolodvorska c 33; s €89-159, d €99-179, ste €139-209; P❄@❅☎)This bijou of a boutique hotel is in a painstakingly restored caravanserai that opened in 1906 opposite Bled Jezero train station. Many of the 22 rooms are furnished with antiques, there's an enormous sloped garden that grows the vegetables served in the 1906 terrace restaurant and the views of the lake from everywhere (including the indoor pool) are breathtaking.

RADOVLJICA

A short distance southeast of Bled and well served by bus (€1.80, 15 minutes, 8km), the sleepy town of Radovljica (pop 6025) has a particularly delightful square called **Linhartov trg** in its Old Town, where there are restored and painted houses, an interesting gallery, the fascinating **Beekeeping Museum** (☑532 05 20; Linhartov trg 1; adult/child €3/2; ◷10am-6pm Tue-Sun summer, 8am-3pm Tue, Thu & Fri, 10am-noon & 3-5pm Wed, Sat & Sun winter) and a **tourist office** (☑531 53 00; www.radovljica.si; Gorenjska c 1; 9am-1pm & 2-6pm Mon-Sat summer, 9am-4pm Mon-Fri, to 1pm Sat winter). Have a meal or a drink at **Gostilna Augustin** (☑531 41 63; Linhartov trg 15; mains €9-17), a delightful restaurant and bar with a back terrace affording views of Mt Triglav itself. The square lies 400m southeast of the bus station via Gorenjska c or just 100m up narrow Kolodvorska ul from the train station to the south.

Penzion Mayer
PENSION €€

(☑576 10 58; www.mayer-sp.si; Želeška c 7; s €55, d €75-80, apt €120-150; P@) This flower bedecked 12-room inn in a renovated 19th-century house has a lovely stand-alone cottage with apartments for two to four people. The Mayer's inhouse restaurant is excellent.

Garni Hotel Berc
PENSION €€

(☑576 56 58; www.berc-sp.si; Pod Stražo 13; s €45-50, d €70-80; P@?) This purpose-built place, reminiscent of a Swiss chalet, has 15 rooms on two floors in a quiet location above the lake. Just opposite is a smaller branch, **Garni Penzion Berc** (☑574 18 38; Želeška c 15; s €35-40, d €60-65), with 11 rooms.

Camping Bled
CAMPING GROUND €

(☑575 20 00; www.camping-bled.com; Kidričeva c 10c; adult €8.50-12.50, child €5.95-8.75, huts d €30-40; P@?) This popular 6.5-hectare site fills a small valley at the western end of the lake. The new all-natural A-frame huts on a terrace above the site have become one of Bled's most sought-after addresses.

Traveller's Haven
HOSTEL €

(☑041-396 545; www.travellers-haven.si; Riklijeva c 1; dm/d €19/48; @) This uber-popular hostel in a converted old villa has six rooms with between two and six beds, a great kitchen, laundry, free bikes and a chilled vibe.

Vila Gorenka
PENSION €

(☑574 47 22, 040-958 624; http://freeweb.siol.net/mz2; Želeška c 9; per person €17-25; P@) This budget establishment has 10 double rooms with washbasins – toilets and showers are shared – in a charming old two-story villa dating back to 1909. Some rooms on the 2nd floor have wooden balconies gazing on the lake.

Bledec Hostel
HOSTEL €

(☑574 52 50; www.youth-hostel-bledec.si; Grajska c 17; HI members/nonmembers dm €18/20, d €48/52; P@?) This well-organised HI-affiliated hostel in the shadow of the castle has dorms with four to eight beds with bathrooms, a bar and an inexpensive restaurant. A laundry service (€8.50) is available and bicycle rental is free.

✕ Eating

You'll find a **Mercator** (Ljubljanska c 4; ◷7am-8pm Mon-Sat, 8am-noon Sun) at the eastern end of Bled Shopping Centre. There's a smaller **Mercator branch** (Prešernova c 48; ◷7am-8pm Mon-Sat, 8am-4pm Sun) close to the hostels.

TOP CHOICE ## Restavracija Pungaršek
SLOVENIAN, MEDITERRANEAN €€

(☑059-059 136; www.pungarsek.si; Kolodvorska c 2; mains €13.50-22.50; ◷11am-10.30pm Mon-Sat, to 6pm Sun) North of the lake and equidistant from the Hotel Triglav Bled and hostels, this upmarket restaurant is arguably Bled's finest. Mushrooms dishes are exquisite and desserts to die for. Outside seating under the pines in the warmer months.

Gostilna Pri Planincu
SLOVENIAN, BALKAN €

(☑574 16 13; Grajska c 8; mains €7-22; ◷10am-10pm) 'At the Mountaineers' is a homey pub-restaurant just down the hill from the hostels, with Slovenian mains and grilled Balkan specialities such as čevapčiči (€8.30) and pljeskavica z kajmakom (Serbian-style meat patties with mascarpone-like cream cheese; €9). There's pizza upstairs.

Ostarija Peglez'n
SEAFOOD €€

(☑574 42 18; C Svobode 19a; mains €8.50-27; ◷noon-midnight) The most colourful restaurant in Bled, the 'Iron Inn' is just opposite the landmark Grand Hotel Toplice, with at-

The Julian Alps offer some of Europe's finest hiking. In summer 174 mountain huts (*planinska koča* or *planinski dom*) cater to hikers and none is more than five hours' walk from the next. These huts get very crowded, especially on weekends, so booking ahead is wise.

At €27 per person in a room with up to four beds or €18 in a dormitory in a Category I hut (Category II huts charge €20 and €12 respectively), the huts aren't cheap, but as they serve meals (a simple meal should cost between €4.70 and €6.20 in a Category I hut, and €3.50 and €5 in a Category II hut) you can travel light. Sturdy boots and warm clothes are indispensable, even in midsummer. Trails are generally well marked with a white-centred red circle, but you can still get lost and it's very unwise to trek alone.

For information and maps contact the area's tourist offices or the Alpine Association of Slovenia (p778) in Ljubljana.

tractively retro decor and some of the best fish dishes in town.

Pizzeria Rustika
PIZZA €

(☑576 89 00; Riklijeva c 13; pizza €5.70-9.50; ☺noon-11pm) A marble-roll down the hill from the hostels, this place has its own wood-burning oven and seating on two levels plus an outside terrace.

Slaščičarna Šmon
CAFE €

(☑574 16 16; Grajska c 3; ☺7.30am-10pm) This is the place for Bled's sweet of choice: *kremna rezina* (€2.40), a layer of vanilla custard topped with whipped cream and sandwiched neatly between two layers of flaky pastry.

❶ Information

A Propos Bar (☑574 40 44; Bled Shopping Centre, Ljubljanska c 4; per 15/30/60min €1.25/2.10/4.20; ☺8am-midnight Sun-Thu, to 1am Fri & Sat) Internet access.

Gorenjska Banka (C Svobode 15) Just north of the Park Hotel.

Kompas (☑572 75 00; www.kompas-bled.si; Bled Shopping Centre, Ljubljanska c 4; ☺8am-7pm Mon-Sat, 8am-noon & 4-7pm Sun) Private rooms and bicycles.

Post office (Ljubljanska c 10)

Tourist Information Centre Bled (☑574 11 22; www.bled.si; C Svobode 10; ☺8am-9pm Mon-Sat, 10am-6pm Sun Jul & Aug, 8am-7pm Mon-Sat, 11am-5pm Sun Mar-Jun & Sep-Oct, 8am-6pm Mon-Sat, noon-4pm Sun Nov, 8am-6pm Mon-Fri, 8am-1pm Sun Dec-Feb) Free internet access for 15 minutes or €2.50/4 per 30/60 minutes.

❶ Getting There & Around

Frequent buses to Bohinj (€3.60, 40 minutes, 29km, hourly), Ljubljana (€6.30, 1¼ hours, 57km, hourly) and Kranj (€3.60, 40 minutes,

29km, half-hourly) via Radovljica (€1.80, 15 minutes, 7km) leave from the central bus station.

Trains to Bohinjska Bistrica (€1.70, 20 minutes, 18km, eight daily) and Nova Gorica (€5.90, 1¾ hours, 79km, eight daily) use little Bled Jezero train station, which is 2km west of central Bled – handy for the Hotel Triglav Bled and the camping ground. Trains for Ljubljana (€4.50 to €6.10, 45 minutes to one hour, 51km, up to 19 daily) use Lesce-Bled train station, 4km to the east of town.

Book a taxi on ☑031-705 343.

Bohinj

☑04 / POP 5275

Lake Bohinj, a larger and less-developed glacial lake 26km to the southwest, is a world apart from Bled. Mt Triglav is visible from here and there are activities galore – from kayaking and mountain biking to hiking up Triglav via one of the southern approaches.

Bohinjska Bistrica, the area's largest village, is 6km east of the lake and only interesting for its train station. The main tourist hub on the lake is **Ribčev Laz** at the eastern end, with a supermarket, post office with an ATM and **tourist office** (☑574 60 10; www.bohinj-info.com; Ribčev Laz 48; ☺8am-8pm Mon-Sat, to 6pm Sun summer, 8am-6pm Mon-Sat, 9am-3pm Sun winter), which can help with accommodation and sells fishing licences (€25 per day for the lake, €42 catch and release in the Sava Bohinjka). Central **Alpinsport** (☑572 34 86, 041-596 079; www.alpinsport.si; Ribčev Laz 53; ☺9am or 10am-6pm or 8pm) organises a range of activities, and hires out kayaks, canoes, bikes (per hour/day €4/13.50) and other equipment from a kiosk near the stone bridge. Next door is the delightful **Church of St John the Baptist** (☺10am-noon & 4-7pm summer, by appointment other times), which contains splendid 15th- and 16th-century frescoes.

The nearby village of **Stara Fužina** has an appealing little **Alpine Dairy Museum** (577 01 56; Stara Fužine 181; adult/child €2.50/2; 11am-7pm Tue-Sun Jul & Aug, 10am-noon & 4-6pm Tue-Sun Jan-Jun, Sep & Oct). Just opposite is a cheesemonger called **Planšar** (572 30 95; Stara Fužina 179; noon-8pm summer, by appointment other times), which specialises in homemade dairy products such as hard Bohinj cheese, cottage cheese and curd pie. Just 2km east is **Studor**, a village famed for its *toplarji*, the double-linked hayrack with barns or storage areas at the top, some of which date from the 18th and 19th centuries.

One of the reasons people come to Bohinj is to hike to **Savica Waterfall** (adult/child €2.50/1.25, parking €3; 8am-8pm Jul & Aug; 9am-6pm Apr-Jun, Sep & Oct), which cuts deep into a gorge 60m below and is the source of Slovenia's longest river. It's a 4km hike from Camp Zlatorog in Ukanc at the lake's western end.

From early April to October, the inventively named **Tourist Boat** (041-434 986; adult/child 1 way €8.50/6, return €10/7; 10am-6pm) departs from the pier just opposite the Alpinsport kiosk every 40 minutes (between four and six times a day at other times), terminating a half-hour later at the Ukanc jetty.

The **Cows' Ball** in September is a zany weekend of folk dance, music, eating and drinking to mark the return of the cows from their high pastures down to the valleys. The **International Wildflower Festival** over two weeks in late May/early June includes guided walks and tours, traditional craft markets and concerts. For details on both, go to www.bohinj.si.

🛏 Sleeping & Eating

The tourist office can help arrange accommodation in **private rooms** (per person €13-15) and **apartments** (d €42.50-48.50, q €75-86).

Penzion Gasperin PENSION €€
(059-920 382, 041-540 805; www.bohinj.si/gasperin; Ribčev Laz 36a; per person €25-35; P@🛜) This spotless chalet-style guesthouse with 23 rooms is just 350m east of the tourist office and run by a friendly British-Slovenian couple. Most rooms have balconies.

Hotel Jezero HOTEL €€€
(572 91 00; www.bohinj.si/alpinum/jezero; Ribčev Laz 51; s €60-80, d €100-140; P@🛜🏊) Further renovations have raised the standards even higher at this 76-room place just across from the lake. It has a lovely indoor swimming pool, two saunas and a fitness centre.

Hostel Pod Voglom HOSTEL €
(572 34 61; www.hostel-podvoglom.com; Ribčev Laz 60; dm €17-19, r per person with bathroom € 23-26, without bathroom € 20-22; P@) This budget accommodation 3km west of the centre has 122 beds in 46 somewhat frayed rooms in two buildings. The so-called Hostel Building has doubles, triples and dormitory accommodation with up to four beds and shared facilities; rooms in the Rodica Annexe, with between one and four beds, are en suite.

Camp Zlatorog CAMPING GROUND €
(572 30 64; www.hoteli-bohinj.si/en; Ukanc 2; per person €7-19, tent/campervan €11/23; May-Sep) This pine-shaded 2.5-hectare camping ground accommodating 500 guests is at the lake's western end, 4.5km from Ribčev Laz.

Restavracija Triglav SLOVENIAN €€
(572 35 38; Stara Fužina 23; mains €10.50-17) This country-style place in nearby Stara Fužina serves up hearty Slovenian favourites like lamb and whole pig cooked on the spit and mushrooms on the grill. There's live music from 6pm daily in summer.

Center Bohinj Pizzerija PIZZA €
(572 3170; www.bohinj.si/center; Ribčev Laz 50; pizza €6-10, mains €8.50-14; 9am-10pm) This cheap and kinda cheerful jack-of-all-trades just down from the tourist office is the only eatery in the very centre of Ribčev Laz.

ℹ Getting There & Around

Buses run regularly from Ukanc ('Bohinj Zlatorog' on most schedules) to Ljubljana (€8.70, 2¼ hours, 91km, hourly) via Ribčev Laz, Bohinjska Bistrica and Bled (€4.10, 50 minutes, 34km), with six extra buses daily between Ukanc and Bohinjska Bistrica (€2.30 20 minutes, 12km). From Bohinjska Bistrica, passenger trains to Nova Gorica (€5.20, 1¼ hours, 61km, up to nine daily) make use of a century-old tunnel under the mountains that provides the only direct option for reaching the Soča Valley. In addition there are daily auto trains *(avtovlaki)* from Bohinjska Bistrica to Podbrdo (€8.20, 10 minutes, 7km, five daily) and Most na Soči (€12.50, 40 minutes, 28km, three daily).

Kranjska Gora

04 / POP 1510

Nestling in the Sava Dolinka Valley about some 40km northwest of Bled, Kranjska Gora is Slovenia's largest and best-equipped ski resort. It's at its most perfect under a blanket of snow, but at other times there are endless possibilities for hiking and mountaineering in Triglav National Park, which is right on the town's doorstep to the south. Few travellers will be unimpressed by a trip over the hair-raising Vršič Pass (1611m), the gateway to the Soča Valley.

Sights & Activities

Borovška c, 400m south of where the buses stop, is the heart of the village, with the endearing **Liznjek House** (☑588 19 99; Borovška 63; adult/child €2.50/1.70; ⊙10am-6pm Tue-Sat, to 5pm Sun summer, 9.30am-4pm Tue-Fri, 10am-5pm Sat & Sun winter), an 18th-century museum house with a good collection of household objects and furnishings peculiar to Gorenjska. At its western end is the **Tourist Information Centre Kranjska Gora** (☑580 94 40; www.kranjska-gora.si; Tičarjeva c 2; ⊙8am-7pm Mon-Sat, 9am-6pm Sun Jun-Sep & mid-Dec–Mar, 8am-3pm Mon-Sat Apr, May & Oct–mid-Dec). If you have time (and your own wheels), visit the new **Slovenian Mountaineering Museum** (☑583 35 01; www.planinskimuzej.si; Savska c 1; adult/child €5/3.50; ⊙9am-7pm summer, to 5pm winter) in a startlingly modern structure in Mojstrana, a village 14km to the east.

Kranjska Gora has lots of places offering ski tuition and hiring out equipment, including **ASK Kranjska Gora Ski School** (☑588 53 02; www.ask-kg.com; Borovška c 99a) in the same building as SKB Banka. Rent bikes from one of several **Sport Point** (☑588 48 83; www.sport-point.si; Borovška c 74; per hr/day €3.50/10) outlets. The men's and giant slalom **Vitranc Cup** (www.pokal-vitranc.com) are held here in early March, and the **Ski-Jumping World Cup Championships** (www.planica.info) at nearby Planica later that month.

Sleeping & Eating

Accommodation costs peak from December to March and in midsummer. **Private rooms** (per person €14-24) and **apartments** (d €34-50, q €68-108) can be arranged through the tourist office.

Hotel Kotnik   HOTEL €€
(☑588 15 64; www.hotel-kotnik.si; Borovška c 75; €54-64, d €68-88; @) If you're not into sprawling hotels with hundreds of rooms, choose this charming, bright yellow low-rise property. It has 15 cosy rooms, a great restaurant and pizzeria, and it couldn't be more central.

Brezov Gaj   PENSION €€
(☑588 57 90; www.brezov-gaj.si; Koroška c 7; per person €25-34; P @) The 'Birch Grove' offers some of the best value in Kranjska Gora. Some of the half-dozen rooms have balco-

nies, there's a fitness room and a place to store bikes and skis.

 Natura Eco Camp Kranjska Gora
CAMPING GROUND €
(☑064-121 966; www.naturacamp-kranjskagora.si; adult €8-10, child €5-7, cabin & tree tent €25-30) This wonderful new site some 300m from the main road on an isolated horse ranch in a forest clearing is as close to paradise as we've been for a while. Pitch a tent or stay in one of the little wooden cabins or the unique tree tents, great pouches with air mattresses suspended from the branches.

Hostel Nika   HOSTEL €
(☑588 10 00, 031-644 209; www.porentov-dom.si; Bezje 16; dm €10-11 d €26; P @) This atmospheric, very cheap place on the Sava Dolinka with 23 rooms and 68 beds in Čičare is about 800m northeast of the centre and just across the main road from the TGC Shopping Centre. It's a great starting point for walks into the mountains.

Gostilna Pri Martinu   SLOVENIAN €€
(☑582 03 00; Borovška c 61; mains €6.50-12.50) This atmospheric tavern-restaurant in an old house just beyond Liznjek House is one of the best places to try local specialities such as *telečja obara* (veal stew; €4) and *ričet* (barley stew with smoked pork ribs; €6). Lunch is a snip at just under €7.

Getting There & Away

Buses run hourly to Ljubljana (€8.70, two hours, 91km) via Jesenice (€3.10, 25 minutes, 22m), where you can change for Bled (€3.10, 30 minutes, 21km) as there's just one direct departure to Bled (€4.70, one hour, 40km) on weekdays at 9.15am. A service to Bovec (€6.70, 2¼ hours, 46km) via the Vršič Pass departs five times daily (six at the weekend) from late June to early September.

Soča Valley

The Soča Valley region is defined by the 96km-long Soča River coloured a deep, almost artificial turquoise. The valley has more than its share of historical sights, most of them related to one of the costliest battles of WWI, but the majority of visitors are here for the rafting, hiking, skiing and other active sports.

BOVEC
☑05 / POP 1810
Effectively the capital of the Soča Valley, Bovec has a great deal to offer adventure-sports

enthusiasts. With the Julian Alps above, the Soča River below and Triglav National Park all around, you could spend a week here hiking, kayaking, mountain biking and, in winter, skiing at Mt Kanin (2587m), Slovenia's highest ski station, without ever doing the same thing twice.

The compact village square, Trg Golobarskih Žrtev, has everything you'll need. There are cafes, a hotel, the **Tourist Information Centre Bovec** (☑389 64 44; www.bovec.si; Trg Golobarskih Žrtev 8; ☺8.30am-8.30pm summer, 9am-6pm winter) and a half-dozen adrenaline-raising adventure-sports companies.

🏃 Activities

Organised adventure sports (all prices per person) on offer include **canyoning** (from €45 for two hours) or **caving** (from €40 with guide). Or you could try your hand at **hydrospeed** (like riding down a river on a boogie board); you'll pay €45 to €52 for a 6km to 8km ride. A guided 10km **kayaking** tour costs from €42, or a one-day training course at €70.

From April to October, you can go **rafting** (€37/49 for a 10/20km trip). And in winter you can take a **tandem paraglider flight** (ie as a passenger accompanied by a qualified pilot; €110) from atop the Kanin cable car, 2000m above the valley floor.

The choice of operators is dizzying but the three most experienced are: **Bovec Rafting Team** (☑388 61 28, 041-338 308; www.bovec-rafting-team.com; Mala Vas 106); **Soča Rafting** (☑389 62 00, 041-724 472; www.socarafting.si; Trg Golobarskih Žrtev 14); and **Top Extreme** (☑041-620 636; www.top.si; Trg Golobarskih Žrtev 19).

🛏 Sleeping & Eating

Private rooms (per person €15-30) are easy to come by in Bovec through the TIC.

Martinov Hram   PENSION €€
(☑388 62 14; www.martinov-hram.si; Trg Golobarskih Žrtev 27; s €33-48, d €54-70; P🐾) This lovely guesthouse just 100m east of the centre has a dozen nicely furnished rooms and an excellent restaurant with an emphasis on game, trout and mushroom dishes.

Alp Hotel   HOTEL €€
(☑388 40 00; www.alp-hotel.si; Trg Golobarskih Žrtev 48; s €48-66, d €78-98; P@🐾) This 103-room hotel is fairly good value and as central as you are going to find in Bovec. Guests get to use the swimming pool at the nearby Hotel Kanin.

Kamp Palovnik   CAMPING GROUND €
(☑388 60 07; www.kamp-polovnik.com; Ledina 8; adult €6.50-7.50, child €5-5.75; ☺Apr-mid-Oct; P) Camping facilities are generally better in Kobarid, but this site about 500m southeast of the town centre is much more convenient.

Gostišče Vančar   SLOVENIAN €
(☑389 60 76, 031-312 742; www.penzionvancar.com; Čezsoča 43; mains €ri6-8) This inn 3km south of Bovec is where local people go to taste such local specialities as *kalja* (a sweet-corn pudding) and *bovški krafni* ('raviolis' stuffed with dried pears, raisins and walnuts).

ℹ Getting There & Away

Buses to Nova Gorica (€7.50, two hours, 77km, up to five a day) go via Tolmin (€3.10, 30 minutes, 22km). A service to Kranjska Gora (€6.70, 2¼ hours, 46km) via Vršič Pass departs five times daily (six at the weekend) from late June to early September.

KOBARID
☑05 / POP 1230

Some 21km south of Bovec, quaint Kobarid (Caporetto in Italian) lies in a broad valley on the west bank of the Soča River. Although it's surrounded by mountain peaks higher than 2200m, Kobarid somehow feels more Mediterranean than alpine. The Italian border is a mere 9km to the west.

⊙ Sights

Kobarid Museum   MUSEUM
(☑389 00 00; www.kobariski-muzej.si; Gregorčičeva ul 10; adult/child €5/2.50; ☺9am-6pm Mon-Fri, to 7pm Sat & Sun summer, 10am-5pm Mon-Fri, 9am-6pm Sat & Sun winter) A couple of hundred metres to the southeast is this award-winning museum, devoted almost entirely to the Isonzo (Soča) Front of WWI, which formed the backdrop to Ernest Hemingway's *A Farewell to Arms*.

🏃 Activities

A free pamphlet and map titled *The Kobarid Historical Trail* outlines a 5km-long route that will take you past remnants of WWI troop emplacements to the impressive **Kozjak Stream Waterfalls** and **Napoleon Bridge** built in 1750. More ambitious is the hike outlined in the free *Pot Miru/Walk of Peace* brochure.

There are several outfits on or just off the town's main square that can organise **rafting** (€29 to €37), **canyoning, canoeing** and **paragliding** from April to October. They include:

A2 Rafting (☑041-641 899; www.a2rafting.eu) in a kiosk outside Apartma-Ra.

XPoint (☑388 53 08, 041-692 290; www.xpoint. si; Trg Svobode 6)

Positive Sport (☑040-654 475; www.positive -sport.com; Markova ul 2)

🛏 Sleeping

TOP CHOICE **Hotel Hvala**　　　　　　　HOTEL
(☑389 93 00; wwww.hotel-hvala.si; Trg Svobode 1; s €72-76, d €104-112; P❊@) The best place to stay in town. It has 31 splendid rooms and a unique lift that takes you on a vertical tour of Kobarid.

Kamp Koren　　　　　　CAMPGROUND
(☑389 13 11; www.kamp-koren.si; Drežniške Ravne 33; per person pitch €9.50-11; P@🛜) The oldest (and, some would say, friendliest) camping ground in the valley. It's a 4-hectare site about 500m northeast of Kobarid on the left bank of the Soča River and just beyond the Napoleon Bridge with 100 pitches and six **chalets** (d/tr from €55/60).

Apartma-Ra　　　　　　APARTMENTS
(☑041-641899; apartma-ra@siol.net; Gregorčičeva ul 6c; per person €15-25; P❊@) This welcoming little place lies between the museum and Trg Svobode and has five rooms and apartments.

✖ Eating

In the centre of Kobarid you'll find one of Slovenia's best restaurants, which specialises in fish and seafood.

Restavracija Topli Val (☑389 93 00; www. hotel-hvala.si; Trg Svobode 1; mains €9.50-25; ⊙noon-10pm) Incomparable.

Hiša Franko (☑389 41 20; www.hisafranko. com; Staro Selo 1; mains €20-24; ⊙noon-3pm & 6-11pm Tue-Sun) Another slow-food phenomenon in these parts in the village of Staro Selo some 3km west of town.

❶ Information

Tourist Information Centre Kobarid (☑380 04 90; www.dolina-soce.com; Trg Svobode 16; ⊙9am-8pm Jul & Aug, 9am-1pm & 2-6pm Mon-Fri, 10am-1pm & 3-6pm Sat & Sun Sep-Jun) In the centre of town.

❶ Getting There & Around

Buses, which arrive at and depart from in front of the Cinca Marinca bar on Trg Svobode, link Kobarid with Nova Gorica (€6, 1¼ hours, 55km, up to five daily) and Ljubljana (€11.60, three hours, 131km, up to four daily) passing Most na Soči train station, which is good for Bled and Bohinj.

Buses crossing over the spectacular Vršič Pass to Kranjska Gora (€6.90, three hours, 68km) depart a couple of times a day in July and August.

NOVA GORICA
☑05 / POP 12,240

When the town of Gorica, capital of the former Slovenian province of Goriška, was awarded to the Italians after WWII, the new socialist government in Yugoslavia set out to build a model town on the eastern side of the border. They called it New Gorica and erected a chain-link barrier between the two towns. This rather flimsy 'Berlin Wall' was pulled down to great fanfare in 2004, leaving Piazza della Transalpina (or Trg z Mozaikom on the Slovenian side) straddling the border right behind Nova Gorica's train station. The latter now contains the esoteric **Museum of the Border in Gorica 1945-2004** (☑333 44 00; admission free; ⊙1-5pm Mon-Fri, 9am-5pm Sat, 10am-5pm Sun).

The helpful **Tourist Information Centre Nova Gorica** (☑330 46 00; www.novagorica -turizem.com; Bevkov trg 4; ⊙8am-8pm Mon-Fri, 9am-1pm Sat & Sun summer, 8am-6pm Mon-Fri, 9am-1pm winter) is in the Kulturni Dom (Cultural House).

One of the few inexpensive central options for overnighting, **Prenočišče Pertout** (☑330 75 50, 041-624 452; www.prenocisceper tout.com; Ul 25 Maja 23; s/d €24/34; P@) is a five-room B&B in Rožna Dolina, south of the town centre and scarcely 100m northeast of the Italian border. Some 2km east of the centre along the road to Ajdovščina, the **Siesta** (☑333 12 30; www.hotel-siesta.si; Industrijska c 5; s/d €39/49; P@) is a modern-ish 20-room hotel with bargain-basement rates.

Marco Polo (☑302 97 29; Kidričeva ul 13; mains €6-17; ⊙11am-midnight), an Italian eatery with a delightful back terrace about 250m east of the tourist office, is one of the town's best places to eat, serving pizza (€5.50 to €7.60), pasta (€6 to €12) and more-ambitious dishes.

Buses travel hourly between Nova Gorica and Ljubljana (€10.70 2½ hours, 116km) via Postojna (€6.70, 1½ hours, 63km), and up to five times daily to Bovec (€7.50, two hours, 77km) via Tolmin (€4.70, one hour, 39km).

Trains link Nova Gorica with Bohinjska Bistrica (€5.20, 1½ hours, 61km, up to seven daily), a springboard for Bled, with Postojna (€6.25, two hours, 61km, six daily) via Sežana and Divača, and with Ljubljana (€8.50, 3½ hours, 153km, five daily) via Jesenice.

KARST & COAST

Slovenia's short coast (47km) is an area for both history and recreation. The southernmost resort town of Portorož has some decent beaches, but three important towns famed for their Venetian Gothic architecture – Koper, Izola and Piran – are the main drawcards here. En route from Ljubljana or the Soča Valley, you'll cross the Karst, a huge limestone plateau and a land of olives, ruby-red Teran wine, *pršut* (air-dried ham), old stone churches and deep subterranean caves, including Postojna and Škocjan.

Postojna

☎ 05 / POP 8910

Slovenia's single most-popular tourist attraction, **Postojna Cave** (☎700 01 00; www.post ojnska-jama.si; Jamska c 30; adult/child €20/12; ☉tours hourly 9am-6pm summer, 3 or 4 times from 10am daily winter) is about 1.5km northwest of the town of that name. The 5.7km-long cavern is visited on a 1½-hour tour – 4km of it by electric train and the rest on foot. Inside, impressive stalagmites and stalactites in familiar shapes stretch almost endlessly in all directions.

Just steps south of the cave's entrance is **Proteus Vivarium** (www.turizem-kras.si; adult/child €7/4.20 with cave €25/15; ☉9.30am-5.30pm May-Sep, 10.30am-3.30pm Oct-Apr), a speliobiological research station with a video introduction to underground zoology. A 45-minute tour then leads you into a small, darkened cave to peep at some of the endemic *Proteus anguinus*, a shy (and miniscule) salamander unique to Slovenia.

🛏 Sleeping & Eating

Kompas Postojna   PRIVATE ROOMS €

(☎721 14 80; www.kompas-postojna.si; Titov trg 2a; r per person €17-24; ☉8am-7pm Mon-Fri, 9am-1pm Sat summer, 8am-5pm Mon-Fri, 9am-1pm Sat winter) Private rooms in town and down on the farm.

Hotel Sport   HOTEL, HOSTEL €€

(☎720 22 44; www.sport-hotel.si; Kolodvorska c 1; dm €25, s/d from €55/70; ᴾ@﴾) A hotel of some sort or another since 1880, the Sport offers reasonable value for money, with 37 spic-and-span and very comfortable rooms, including five with nine dorm beds each. There's a kitchen with small eating area. It's 300m north of the centre.

Špajza   SLOVENIAN €€

(☎726 45 06; Ul 1 Maja 1; mains €11-16) A welcome new addition to Postojna's limited eating scene, this attractively decorated *gostilna* 100m southeast of Kompas serves excellent local specialities.

❶ Getting There & Away

Buses from Ljubljana to Koper, Piran and Nova Gorica all stop in Postojna (€6, one hour, 54km, half-hourly). The train is less useful, as the station is 1km east of town (ie almost 3km from the caves).

Buses bound for Postojna Cave and Predjama Castle leave Postojna's train station five times a day between 9.20am and 4.10pm. The bus is free but those with train tickets take precedence. The last bus from the castle is 4.40pm and from the cave at 5.05pm. A taxi to/from the castle, including an hour's wait, will cost €30.

Škocjan Caves

☎ 05

The immense system of **Škocjan Caves** (☎708 21 10; www.park-skocjanske-jame.si; Škocjan 2; adult/child €14/6), a Unesco World Heritage site since 1986, is far more captivating than the larger one at Postojna, and for many travellers a visit here will be a highlight of their trip to Slovenia. With relatively few stalactites, the attraction is the sheer depth of the awesome underground chasm, which you cross by a dizzying little footbridge. To see this you must join a guided walking tour, lasting 1½ to two hours and involving hundreds of steps and a funicular ride at the end. Tours depart hourly from 10am to 5pm from June to September, at 10am, 1pm and 3.30pm in April, May and October, and at 10am and 1pm (with an additional one at 3pm on Sunday) from November to March.

The nearest town with accommodation is **Divača** (population 1325), 5km to the northwest. **Gostilna Malovec** (☎763 12 25; Kraška 30a; s/d €32/48) has a half-dozen basic but renovated rooms in a building beside its traditional **restaurant** (mains €8-15; ☉8am to 10pm) and flashy new 20-room **hotel** (☎763 33 33; www.hotel-malovec.si; s/d €54/80; ᴾ@﴾). The nearby **Orient Express** (☎763 30 10; Kraška c 67; pizza €4.60-14; ☉11am-11pm Sun-Fri, to 2am Sat) is a popular pizzeria and pub.

Bus services running from Ljubljana to Koper and the coast stop at Divača (€7.90, 1½ hours, 82km, hourly) as do trains (€6.85, 1½ hours, 104km, hourly). A van meets incoming trains at 10am, 11.04am, 2pm and

PREDJAMA

The tiny village of Predjama (population 85), some 10km northwest of Postojna, is home to remarkable **Predjama Castle** (☎700 01 00; www.turizem-kras.si; Predjama 1; adult/ child €8/5; ☺9am-7pm summer, 10am-4pm winter), which appears to grow out of a gawping cave. The partly furnished interior spread over four floors boasts costumed wax manne-quins, one of which dangles from the dripping rock-roofed torture chamber. Beneath are stalactite-adorned **caves** (adult/child €7/4.20, with castle €13/8; ☺1-hour tours 11am-5pm May-Sep), which lack Postojna's crowds but also much of its grandeur.

3.10pm and will transport those with bus or train tickets to the caves for free. Otherwise there is a large map indicating the walking route posted outside the station.

Lipica

☑05 / POP 100

Lipica is where Austrian Archduke Charles, son of Ferdinand I, established a stud farm in 1580 to breed horses for the Spanish Rid-ing School in Vienna. The snow-white beau-ties are still raised at the **Lipica Stud Farm** (☎739 15 80; www.lipica.org; Lipica 5; adult/child €10/5), which offers equestrian fans a large variety of tours and riding presentations as well as lessons and carriage rides. Tour times are complicated; see the website for details.

The 85-room **Hotel Klub** (☎739 15 80; s/d €32/49; P@🕾) near the stud farm has a sauna and fitness centre. The nearby **Hotel Maestoso** (☎739 15 80; s/d €80/120; P🕾🕸) has 68 more modern rooms.

Most people visit Lipica as a day trip from Sežana, 5km to the north, or Divača, 10km to the northeast, which are on the Ljubljana–Koper rail line. There is no public transport from either station to Lipica; a taxi will cost between €7 and €15.

Koper

☑05 / POP 24,830

Coastal Slovenia's largest town, Koper (Ca-podistria in Italian) at first glance appears to be a workaday city that scarcely gives tour-ism a second thought. Yet its central core is delightfully medieval and far less over-run than its ritzy cousin Piran, 18km down the coast. Known as Aegida to the ancient Greeks, Koper grew rich as a key port trad-ing salt and was the capital of Istria under the Venetian Republic during the 15th and 16th centuries. It remains Slovenia's most important port.

☉ Sights

Turn back the clock as you pass through **Muda Gate** (1516) leading into Prešernov trg and the bridge-shaped **Da Ponte Fountain** (1666). Carry on north up Župančičeva ul and then Čevljarska ul, the narrow commercial artery, to reach **Titov trg**. This fine square is dominated by the 15th-century **City Tower** (adult/child €2/1.50; ☺9am-2pm & 4-9pm), which can be reached via 204 steps. It is attached to the part-Gothic, part-Renaissance **Cathedral of the Assumption**. The Venetian Gothic and Renaissance **Praetorian Palace** (Titov trg 3; admission free; ☺9am-8pm) contains the town hall, with an old pharmacy and the tourist of-fice on the ground floor and a ornate ceremo-nial hall on the 1st floor. Opposite, the splen-did 1463 **Loggia**, with attached gallery. Next to it is the circular Romanesque **Rotunda of St John the Baptist**, a baptistery with ceil-ing fresco dating from the 12th century.

The **Koper Regional Museum** (☎663 35 70; www.pmk-kp.si; Kidričeva ul 19; adult/child €2/1.50; ☺9am-7pm Tue-Fri, to 1pm Sat & Sun), in-side the Belgramoni-Tacco Palace, contains an Italianate sculpture garden. Kidričeva ul, with its multicoloured **medieval houses**, leads west into Carpacciov trg, the former fish market with a 15th-century **salt warehouse**.

🛏 Sleeping

Museum Hostel   HOSTEL, APARTMENTS €
(☎626 18 70, 041-504 466; bozic.doris@siol.net; Muzejski trg 6; per person €20-25; 🕾) This ex-cellent-value place is more a series of bright apartments with modern kitchens and bath-rooms than a hostel. Reception is at the little Museum Bife, a cafe-bar on Muzejski trg; the rooms are actually at Mladinska ul 7 and Kidričeva ul 34.

Hotel Koper   HOTEL €€€
(☎610 05 00; www.terme-catez.si; Pristaniška ul 3; s €76-92, d €120-150; 🕸@🕸) This 65-room property on the very edge of the historic Old Town is the only central hotel in Koper.

Koper

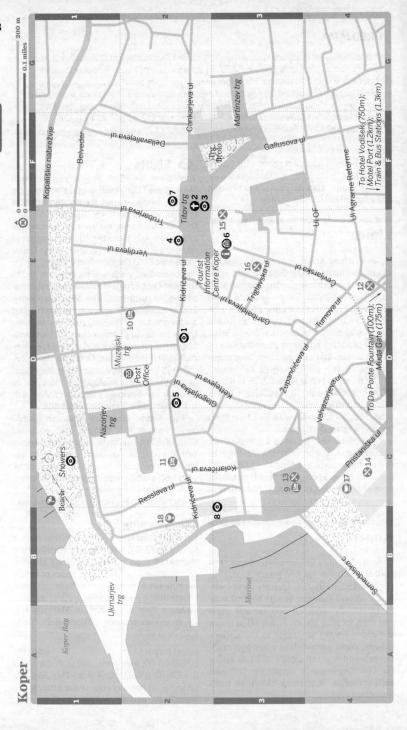

200 m
0.1 miles

Kopališko nabrežje

Belveder

Delavalleleva ul

Cankarjeva ul

Martinzev trg

Gallusova ul

Ul Agrarne Reforme

Ul OF

Trubarjeva ul

Titov trg

Verdijeva ul

Tourist
Information
Centre Koper

Garibaldijeva ul

Čevljarska ul

Triglavska ul

Turnova ul

Kidričeva ul

Muzejski
trg

Post
Office

Gregorčičeva ul

Kettejeva ul

Župančičeva ul

Vaľvazorjeva ul

Nazorjev
trg

Beach

Showers

Resslava ul

Kolarićeva ul

Kidričeva ul

Pristaniška ul

Semedelska c

Ukmarjev
trg

Koper Bay

Marina

To Hotel Vodišek (750m);
Motel Port (1.2km);
Train & Bus Stations (1.3km)

To Da Ponte Fountain (100m);
Muda Gate (175m)

Koper

Sleeping

Hotel Vodišek HOTEL €€

(☎639 24 68; www.hotel-vodisek.com; Kolodvorska c 2; s €48-60, d €72-90; P✳@☎) With 35 small but reasonably priced rooms, this place is in a shopping centre halfway between the Old Town and the train and bus stations. Bicycle use is free for guests.

Motel Port HOTEL, HOSTEL €

(☎611 75 44; www.motel-port.si; Ankaranska c 7; dm €22, s €36/49.50; ◷Jul-Aug; P✳@☎) On the 2nd floor of a shopping centre southeast of the Old Town, this student house, open to visitors in summer, only has 30 rooms, some of them en suite and air-conditioned and others dorm rooms with four to six beds.

✗ Eating

You'll find a small branch of the **Mercator** (Titov trg 2; ◷7am-8pm Mon-Fri, 7am-1pm Sat, 8am-noon Sun) supermarket giant in the Old Town.

Istrska Klet Slavček ISTRIAN, SLOVENIAN €

(☎627 67 29; Župančičeva ul 39; dishes €3-12; ◷7am-10pm Mon-Fri) The 'Istrian Cellar' below an 18th-century palace is one of the most colourful places for a meal in Koper's Old Town. Filling set lunches go for less than €8,

and there's local Malvazija and Teran wine from the barrel.

La Storia ITALIAN €€€

(☎626 20 18; www.lastoria.si; Pristaniška ul 3; mains €8.50-25) This Italian-style *trattoria* with sky-view ceiling frescos inside and a delightful covered terrace outside focuses on salads, pasta and fish dishes.

Pizzeria Atrij PIZZA €€

(☎627 22 55; Čevljarska ul 8, enter from Triglavska ul 2; pizza €3-6.50; ◷9am-9pm Mon-Fri, 10am-10pm Sat) A popular pizzeria down an alleyway no wider than your average quarterback's shoulder spread, the Atrij has a small covered garden out back.

⬤ Drinking

Kavarna Kapitanija CAFE

(☎040-799 000; Ukmarjev trg 8; ◷7am-midnight Mon-Fri, 8am-midnight Sat & Sun) This attractive space, with its wide-open terrace and wicker lounges, would be even more inviting if the tacky souvenir kiosks and parked cars across the grassy strip didn't block the harbour view.

Forum CAFE-BAR

(Pristaniška ul 2; ◷7am-11pm; ☎) Cafe-bar at the northern side of the market and facing a little park and the sea; a popular local hang-out.

❶ Information

Banka Koper (Kidričeva ul 14)

Pina Internet Cafe (☎627 80 72; Kidričeva ul 43; per hr adult/student €4.20/1.20; ◷noon-10pm Mon-Fri, from 4pm Sat & Sun) Central internet cafe with 10 terminals.

Post office (Muzejski trg 3)

Tourist Information Centre Koper (☎664 64 03; www.koper.si; Praetorian Palace, Titov trg 3; ◷9am-8pm Jul & Aug, 9am-5pm Sep-Jun)

❶ Getting There & Away

The joint bus and train station is about 1.5km southeast of central Titov trg. To walk into town, just head north along Kolodvorska c in the direction of the cathedral's distinctive campanile (bell tower).

Buses run to Piran (€2.70, 30 minutes, 18km) every 20 minutes on weekdays and 40 minutes at weekends. Up to five daily buses daily head for Ljubljana (€11.10, 1¾ to 2½ hours, 122km), though the train is more comfortable, with four local services and two faster IC ones (€10, 2¼ hours) at 5.23am and 2.45pm.

Buses to Trieste (€3, 45 minutes, 23km, up to eight per day) run along the coast via Ankaran and Muggia between 6am and 7.30pm from Monday to Saturday. Destinations in Croatia include Rovinj (€11, three hours, 129km, 6.30pm Monday and Friday, 11am Saturday and Sunday, 3.50pm daily June to September) via Poreč (€10, two hours, 88km).

You can order a taxi on ☑040-671 086.

Izola

☑05 / POP 11,545

Overshadowed by more genteel Piran, Izola (Isola in Italian) has a certain Venetian charm, narrow old streets, and excellent (and uncrowded) waterfront restaurants. Ask the helpful **Tourist Information Centre Izola** (☑640 10 50; www.izola.eu; Sončno nabrežje 4; ⊗9am-9pm Jun-Sep, 9am-5pm Mon-Fri, 10am-5pm Sat Oct-May) about **private rooms** (s €19-26, d €30-36) or, in July and August, check out the 174-bed **Riviera** (☑662 1740; branko.miklobusec@guest.arnes.si; Prekomorskih Brigad ul 7; dm €25), a student dormitory overlooking the marina. At the other end of the price range is the 52-room **Hotel Marina** (☑660 41 00; www.hotelmarina.si; Veliki trg 11; s €59-126, d €79-156; **P ❋ @ ⧈**) on the main square and fronting the harbour. **Ribič** (☑641 83 13; www.ribic.biz; Veliki trg 3; mains €9-25; ⊗8am-midnight Mon-Sat, to 10pm Sun) is a landmark seafood restaurant on the waterfront much loved by locals. Out in Izola's industrial suburbs, **Ambasada Gavioli** (☑641 8212, 041-353 722; www.myspace.com/ambasadagavioli; Industrijska c 10; ⊗11pm-6am Fri & Sat) remains coastal Slovenia's top club, showcasing a procession of international and local DJs.

Frequent buses between Koper (€1.80, 15 minutes, 8km) and Piran (€2.30, 20 minutes, 10km) go via Izola.

The **Prince of Venice** (☑05-617 80 00; www.kompas-online.net) catamaran serves Venice (€50 to €70, 2½ hours) from Izola at 7.30am or 8am between one and three times a week (days vary) from April to October.

Piran

☑05 / POP 4515

Picturesque Piran (Pirano in Italian), sitting at the tip of a narrow peninsula, is everyone's favourite coastal town in Slovenia. The Old Town is a gem of Venetian Gothic architecture, but it can be a mob scene at the height of summer. Still, it's hard not to fall in love with the winding Venetian Gothic alleyways and tempting seafood restaurants. It is believed that the town's name comes from the *pyr*, Greek for fire, as fires were once lit at

Punta, the tip of the peninsula, to guide ships to the port at Aegida (now Koper).

◉ Sights

Cathedral of St George   CHURCH
(Adamičeva ul 2) Piran is watched over by the hilltop cathedral mostly dating from the 17th century. If time allows, visit the attached **Parish Museum of St George** (☑673 34 40; admission €1; ⊗10am-1pm & 5-7pm Mon-Fri, 11am-7pm Sat & Sun), which contains church plate, paintings and a lapidary in the crypt. The cathedral's free-standing **bell tower** (admission €2; ⊗10am-2pm & 5-8pm) dates back to 1609 and can be climbed. The octagonal **baptistery** (1650) has imaginatively recycled a 2nd-century Roman sarcophagus as a baptismal font. To the east is a 200m-long stretch of the 15th-century **town wall** complete with loopholes.

Minorite Monastery   MONASTERY
(☑673 44 17; Bolniška ul 20) Parts of this monastery to the east of Tartinijev trg date back to the 14th century; go up the steps and check out the wonderful cloister enlivened with Gregorian chant. Opposite, the **Church of Our Lady of the Snows** has a superb 15th-century arch painting of the Crucifixion.

Sergej Mašera Maritime Museum   MUSEUM
(☑671 00 40; www.pommuz-pi.si; Cankarjevo nabrežje 3; adult/student & senior/child €3.50/2.50/2.10; ⊗9am-noon & 5-9pm Tue-Sun summer, 9am-5pm Tue-Sun winter) The exhibits here focus on the sea, sailing and salt-making – all crucial to Piran's development over the centuries. Check out the 2000-year-old Roman amphorae under glass on the ground floor and the impressive antique ships' models and figureheads upstairs.

Aquarium Piran   AQUARIUM
(☑673 25 72; www.aquariumpiran.com; Kidričevo nabrežje 4; adult/child €7/5; ⊗9am-7pm summer, to 5pm winter) About 100m south of Tartinijev trg and facing the marina, the town's recently renovated aquarium may be on the small side, but there's a tremendous variety of sea life packed into its two-dozen tanks.

Tartinijev trg   SQUARE
At No 4 of this historic central square is the attractive 15th-century **Venetian House**, with its tracery windows and stone lion relief. When built this would have overlooked Piran's inner port, which was filled in 1894 to form the square. Tartinijev trg is named in honour of the 18th-century violinist and composer Giuseppe Tartini (1692–1770), whose statue stands in the centre.

Trg 1 Maja
SQUARE

The name of this square (1st May Sq) may sound like a socialist parade ground, but in fact it's one of Piran's most attractive squares, with a **cistern** dating from the late 18th century. Rainwater from the surrounding roofs flows into it through the fish borne by the stone putti in the corners.

Punta
HISTORIC AREA

Punta, the historical 'snout' of Piran, still has a **lighthouse**, but today's version is small and modern. Attached to it, the round, serrated tower of 18th-century **Church of St Clement** evokes the ancient beacon from which Piran got its name.

🏃 Activities

Most water-related activities take place in Portorož, but if you want to try **diving Noriksub** (🖉673 22 18, 041-590 746; www.sku pinanoriksub.si; Prešernovo nabrežje 24; shore/boat dive €30/40; ⊙10am-noon & 2-6pm Tue-Sun summer, 10am-4pm Sat & Sun winter) organises shore and boat-guided dives and hires out equipment. A 'taster' course is €50.

Bicycles are available for rent from a shop in the Old Town called **Gaastra** (🖉040-255 400; Vidalijeva ul 3; per day €7; ⊙9am-1pm & 5-8pm summer, to 5pm Mon-Sat winter).

🛏 Sleeping

Private rooms (s €18-31.50, d €26-48) and **apartments** (d €40-50, q €65-75) are available through the Maona Tourist Agency (p773) and the **Turist Biro** (🖉673 25 09; www.turistbiro -ag.si; Tomažičeva ul 3; ⊙9am-1pm & 4-7pm Mon-Sat, 10am-1pm Sun), opposite the Hotel Piran.

TOP CHOICE **Max Piran**
B&B €€

(🖉673 34 36, 041-692 928; www.max piran.com; Ul IX Korpusa 26; d €60-70; ❊@🛜) Piran's most romantic accommodation option has just six rooms – each bearing a woman's name rather than a number – in a delightful coral-coloured 18th-century townhouse. It's a short walk from the cathedral.

Miracolo di Mare
B&B €€

(🖉921 76 60, 051-445 511; www.miracolodimare.si; Tomšičeva ul 23; s €50-55, d €60-70; @🛜) A favourite B&B, the 'Wonder of the Sea' has a dozen charming (though smallish) rooms, some of which give on to the most charming raised back garden in Piran.

Hotel Tartini
HOTEL €€€

(🖉671 10 00; www.hotel-tartini-piran.com; Tartinijev trg 15; s €62-86, d €84-124; ❐❊@) This attractive, 45-room property faces Tartinijev trg and manages to catch a few sea views from the upper floors. The staff are especially friendly and helpful. If you've got the dosh, splash out on the eyrie-like suite 40a.

Alibi B11
HOSTEL €

(🖉031-363 666; www.alibi.si; Bonifacijeva ul 11; per person €20-22; ⊙Apr-Dec; @🛜) The flagship of the Alibi stable is not its nicest property but has mostly doubles in eight rooms over four floors and a roof terrace in an ancient townhouse on a narrow street. Reception for all three hostels is here and there's a washing machine. Diagonally opposite is **Alibi B14** (Bonifacijeva ul 14; per person €20-22), an upbeat and colourful four-floor party place with seven rooms, each with two to four beds. More subdued is **Alibi T60** (Trubarjeva ul 60; per person €25; ❊) to the east with a fully equipped double on each of five floors. The view from the terrace of the top room is priceless. The new **Vista Apartment** (Trg 1 Maja 4; per person €25) is a two-room duplex apartment with sea views that sleeps up to eight people.

Val Hostel
HOSTEL €

(🖉673 25 55; www.hostel-val.com; Gregorčičeva ul 38a; per person €22-27; @🛜) This central, partially renovated hostel has 20 rooms, with two to four beds, shared shower, kitchen and washing machine. It's a great favourite with backpackers.

Kamp Fiesa
CAMPING GROUND €

(🖉674 62 30; autocamp.fiesa@siol.net; adult/child €12/4; ⊙May-Sep; ℗) The closest camping ground to Piran is at Fiesa, 4km by road but less than 1km by coastal trail east from the Cathedral of St George. It's tiny and crowded but right on the beach.

🍴 Eating & Drinking

There's an outdoor **fruit and vegetable market** (Zelenjavni trg; ⊙7am-2pm Mon-Sat) in the small square behind the town hall. **Mercator** (Levstikova ul 5; ⊙7am-8pm Mon-Sat, 8am-noon Sun) has a branch in the Old Town. **Ham Ham** (Cankarjevo nabrežje 19; ⊙7am-midnight) is a convenience store opposite the bus station.

TOP CHOICE **Pri Mari**
MEDITERRANEAN, SLOVENIAN €€

(🖉673 47 35, 041-616 488; Dantejeva ul 17; mains €8.50-16; ⊙noon-11pm Tue-Sun summer, noon-10pm Tue-Sat, noon-6pm Sun winter) This stylish and welcoming restaurant run by an Italian-Slovenian couple serves the most inventive Mediterranean and Slovenian dishes in town. Be sure to book ahead.

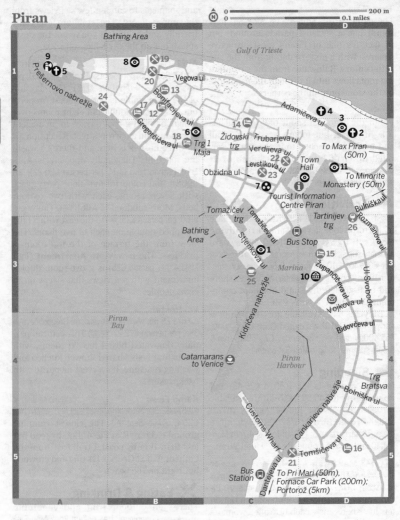

Piran

Riva Piran SEAFOOD €€
(☑673 22 25; Gregorčičeva ul 46; mains €8-28; ☺11.30am-midnight) The best waterfront seafood restaurant and worth patronising is this classy place with the strip's best decor and sea views.

Galeb SEAFOOD €
(☑673 32 25; Pusterla ul 5; mains €8-11; ☺11am-4pm & 6-11pm or midnight Wed-Mon) This excellent family-run restaurant, which has some seafront seating, is located east of the Punta lighthouse. The food is good but takes no risks.

Flora PIZZA €
(☑673 12 58; Prešernovo nabrežje 26; pizza €4-8; ☺10am-1am summer, 10am-10pm winter) The terrace of this simple pizzeria east of the lighthouse has great views of the Adriatic.

Cafe Teater CAFE-BAR
(☑051-694 100; Stjenkova ul 1; ☺8am-3am) Anyone who's anyone in Piran can be found at this cafe with a waterfront terrace and faux antique furnishings.

Žižola Kantina BAR
(Tartinijev trg 10; ☺9am-2am) This simple, nautically themed bar named after the jujube

Piran

(Chinese date) that grows prolifically along the Adriatic has tables right on the main square and serves 15 different flavours of *žganje* (fruit brandy).

❶ Information

Banka Koper (Tartinijev trg 12)

Caffe Neptun (☑041-724 237; www.caffe neptun.com; Dantejeva ul 4; per 20min €1; ⏰7am-1am) Modern cafe near bus station with internet access; free with drink.

Maona Tourist Agency (☑673 45 20; www. maona.si; Cankarjevo nabrežje 7; ⏰9am-8pm Mon-Sat, 10am-1pm & 5-7pm Sun) Rents private rooms, organises activities and cruises.

Post office (Leninova ul 1)

Tourist Information Centre Piran (☑673 02 20, 673 44 40; www.portoroz.si; Tartinijev

---

trg 2; ⏰9am-8pm summer, 9am-5pm winter) Housed in the impressive town hall.

❶ Getting There & Away

Buses from everywhere except Portorož arrive at the bus station, a 300m stroll south along the portside Cankarjevo nabrežje from Tartinijev trg. Trying to drive a car into Piran is insane; vehicles are stopped at a toll gate 200m south of the bus station, where the sensible choice is to use the huge Fornače car park (per hour/day €1.20/12) and ride the frequent shuttle bus into town.

Buses run every 20 to 40 minutes to Koper (€2.70, 30 minutes, 18km) via Izola, while five head for Trieste in Italy (€10, 1¾ hours, 36km) between 6.45am and 6.55pm Monday to Saturday. Between three and five daily buses go to Ljubljana (€12, 2½ to three hours, 140km) via Divača and Postojna.

From the southern end of Tartinijev trg, a shuttle bus (€1) goes every 15 minutes to Portorož.

Venezia Lines (☑05-674 71 60; www.venezia lines.com) catamarans sail to Venice (one way €45-55, return €64-69, 2¼ hours) at 8.30am on Wednesday from May to September. A service run by **Trieste Lines** (www.triestelines.it; one way/return €8.50/15.70) links Piran and Trieste most days during the same period.

Book a taxi on ☑031-730 700.

Portorož
☑05 / POP 2900

Portorož (Portorose in Italian), the biggest coastal resort in Slovenia, is actually quite classy for a seaside town, even along Obala, the main drag. Portorož's sandy beaches are relatively clean, and there are pleasant spas and wellness centres where you can take the waters or cover yourself in curative mud.

At the same time, the vast array of accommodation options makes Portorož a useful fallback if everything's full in Piran; the **Tourist Information Centre Portorož** (☑674 22 20; www.portoroz.si; Obala 16; ⏰9am-8pm summer, 9am-5pm winter) has listings. On the way into Portorož, the summer-only hostel **Prenočišča Korotan** (☑674 54 00; www.sd.upr. si/sdp/prenocisca; Obala 11; s/d €36/49.50; ⏰Jul & Aug; 🅿@) has good-sized en-suite rooms but there's a supplement for stays of one or two nights. At the other end of the scale, the 181-room **Kempinski Palace Portorož** (☑692 70 00; www.kempinski.com/portoroz; Obala 45; s/d from €135/185; 🅿✳@🛜🏊), the art nouveau hotel that put Portorož on the map, has arisen phoenix-like after a protracted renovation and is now the classiest hotel in Slovenia.

There are dozens of pizzerias along Obala, but the venue of choice is **Pizzeria Figarola** (031-313 415; Obala 18; pizza €5.50-8.90), with a huge terrace just up from the main pier. For seafood you won't do better than at **Staro Sidro** (674 50 74; Obala 55; mains €8-19; noon-11pm Tue-Sun) next to the lovely (and landmark) Vila San Marco.

Kavarna Cacao (674 10 35; Obala 14; 8am-1am Sun-Thu, to 3am Fri & Sat) wins the award as the most stylish cafe-bar on the coast and boasts a fabulous waterfront terrace. For live music on Tuesday and Friday from 10pm head for the **Kanela Bar** (674 61 81; Obala 14; 11am-3am), a workhorse of a rock 'n' roll bar secreted between the beach and the Kavarna Cacao.

Portorož is served every 15 minutes by shuttle bus (€1) to/from Piran. Catch it along Obala.

EASTERN SLOVENIA

The rolling vine-covered hills of eastern Slovenia are attractive but much less dramatic than the Julian Alps or, indeed, the coast. If you're heading by train to Vienna via Graz in Austria it saves money to stop in lively Maribor, Slovenia's second-largest city; international tickets are very expensive per kilometre, so doing as much travelling as possible on domestic trains saves cash. While there, consider visiting postcard-perfect Ptuj less than 30km down the road.

Maribor

02 / POP 87,275

Slovenia's second city, chosen as the European Capital of Culture in 2012, really has no unmissable sights but oozes with charm thanks to its delightful (but tiny) Old Town. Pedestrianised central streets buzz with cafes and student life, and in late June/early July the old, riverside Lent district hosts the **Festival Lent** (http://lent.slovenija.net), a two-week extravaganza of folklore and culture.

Maribor Castle (Grajski trg 2), on the main square's northeast corner, contains a magnificent 18th-century **rococo staircase** visible from the street and the **Maribor Regional Museum** (228 35 51; www.pmuzej-mb.si; adult/child €3/2; 9am-4pm Tue-Sat, 9am-2pm Sun), one of Slovenia's richest archaeological and ethnographical collections. To the

southwest, the **cathedral** (Slomškov trg) sits in an oasis of fountain-cooled calm. Follow little Poštna ul southward into **Glavni trg** with its 16th-century **town hall** (Glavni trg 14) and extravagant **plague pillar** erected by townspeople in gratitude for having survived the plague. A block further south down Mesarski prehod and along the Drava River's northern bank is the **Stara Trta** (Vojašniška 8), the world's oldest living grapevine. It's been a source of a dark red wine called Žametna Črnina (Black Velvet) for more than four centuries.

The **Tourist Information Centre Maribor** (234 66 11; www.maribor-pohorje.si; Partinzanska c 6a; 9am-7pm Mon-Fri, to 6pm Sat & Sun) is in a kiosk opposite the Franciscan church. For budget accommodation, try the **Lollipop Hostel** (040-243 160; lollipophostel@yahoo.com; Maistrova ul 17; dm €20; @), with 13 beds in two rooms a short distance from the train station and run by an affable Englishwoman. A short distance to the southeast is the **Grand Hotel Ocean** (234 36 73; www.hotelocean.si; Partizanska c 39; s/d €118/152; P@), a stunning 22-room boutique hotel named after the first train to pass through the city in 1846.

Gril Ranca (252 55 50; Dravska ul 10; dishes €4.80-7.50; 8am-11pm Mon-Sat, noon-9pm Sun) along the Drava in Lent serves simple but scrumptious Balkan grills. For something spicier try nearby **Takos** (252 71 50; Mesarski prehod 3; mains €6.50-12; 11am-11pm Mon-Thu, to 2.30am Fri & Sat), an atmospheric Mexican restaurant that turns into a snappy little night spot at the weekend.

Buses run to Ljubljana (€12.40, three hours, 141km) two to four times a day. Also served are Celje (€6.70, 1½ hours, 65km, four a day) and Ptuj (€3.60, 45 minutes, 27km, hourly). There are daily buses to Munich (€46, 7½ hours, 453km) at 6.30pm and 9.50pm, and one to Vienna (€29, 4½ hours, 258km) at 7.45pm. Of the two-dozen daily trains to/from Ljubljana (€8.50, 2½ hours, 156km), some seven are IC express trains costing €14.40 and taking just under two hours.

Ptuj

02 / POP 19,010

Rising above a wide, fairly flat valley, compact Ptuj – Poetovio to the Romans – forms a symphony of red-tile roofs best viewed from the other side of the Drava River.

⊙ Sights

Ptuj Castle   CASTLE
(Na Gradu 1) Ptuj's pinnacle is well-preserved, containing the fine **Ptuj Regional Museum** (☑787 92 30; www.pok-muzej-ptuj.si; adult/child €4/2.50; ☺9am-6pm Mon-Fri, 9am-8pm Sat & Sun summer, 9am-5pm daily winter).

✤ Festivals

Kurentovanje   CARNIVAL
(www.kurentovanje.net) In February the crowds come to spot the shaggy straw men at Slovenia's foremost traditional carnival. A 'rite of spring', it is celebrated for 10 days up to Mardi Gras, or Shrove Tuesday (February or early March); the museum has some excellent Kurentovanje-related exhibits.

⌂ Sleeping

Hostel Eva   HOSTEL €
(☑771 24 41, 040-226 522; www.bikeek.si; Jadranska ul 22; per person €12-17) If you're looking for budget accommodation, head for this a welcoming place that's connected to a bike shop (rental per hour/day €3.80/11) with six rooms containing two to four beds and a large, light-filled kitchen.

TOP CHOICE **Hotel Mitra**   HOTEL €€
(☑787 74 55, 051-603 069; www.hotel-mitra.si; Prešernova ul 6; s €56-68, d €96-103; [P][✱][@][☎]) If you'd like more comfort, continue walking west on Prešernova ul past a parade of cafes and bars to one of provincial Slovenia's more interesting hotels, with 26 generous-sized guestrooms and three humongous suites, lovely Oriental carpets on the original wooden floors and a wellness centre in an old courtyard cellar.

✗ Eating

Next to the town's open-air **market** (Novi trg; ☺7am-3pm) you'll find a large **Mercator** (Novi trg 3; ☺7.30am-7.30pm Mon-Fri, to 1pm Sat) supermarket.

Amadeus   GOSTILNA €€
(☑771 70 51; Prešernova ul 36; mains €6.50-20; ☺noon-10pm Mon-Thu, noon-11pm Fri & Sat, noon-4pm Sun) A very pleasant *gostilna* above a cafe-bar, it serves *štruklji* (dumplings with herbs and cheese, €4.50), steak and pork dishes.

Gostilna Ribič   GOSTILNA €€
(☑749 06 35; Dravska ul 9; mains €9.50-20; ☺10am-11pm Sun-Thu, to midnight Fri & Sat) The best restaurant in Ptuj has a great riverside terrace and is the ideal spot to have fish.

ⓘ Information

Tourist Information Centre Ptuj (☑779 60 11; www.ptuj.info; Slovenski trg 5; ☺8am-8pm summer, 9am-6pm winter) Facing a medieval tower in the Old Town, it has reams of information and lists of places to stay.

ⓘ Getting There & Away

Buses to Maribor (€3.60, 45 minutes, 27km) run at hourly on weekdays but are less frequent on weekends. You can reach Ptuj up to nine times a day by train from Ljubljana (€8 to €10.50, 2½ hours, 155km) direct or via Zidani Most and Pragersko.

UNDERSTAND SLOVENIA

History

Slovenes can make a credible claim to having invented democracy. By the early 7th century, their Slavic ancestors had founded the Duchy of Carantania (Karantanija), based at Krn Castle (now Karnburg in Austria). Ruling dukes were elected by ennobled commoners and invested before ordinary citizens. This unique model was noted by the 16th-century French political philosopher Jean Bodin, whose work was a key reference for Thomas Jefferson when he wrote the American Declaration of Independence in 1776. Carantania (later Carinthia) was fought over by the Franks and Magyars from the 8th to 10th centuries, and later divided up among Austro-Germanic nobles and bishops. Between the late 13th and early 16th centuries, almost all the lands inhabited by Slovenes, with the exception of the Venetian-controlled coastal towns, came under the control of the Habsburgs.

Indeed, Austria ruled what is now Slovenia until 1918, apart from a brief interlude between 1809 and 1813 when Napoleon created six so-called Illyrian Provinces from Slovenian and Croatian regions and made Ljubljana the capital. Napoleon proved a popular conqueror as his relatively liberal regime de-Germanised the education system. Slovene was taught in schools for the first time, leading to an awakening of national consciousness. In tribute, Ljubljana still has a French Revolution Sq (Trg Francoske Revolucije) with a column bearing a likeness of the French emperor.

Fighting during WWI was particularly savage along the Soča Valley – the so-called Isonzo Front – which was occupied by Italy then dramatically retaken by German-led Austro-Hungarian forces. The war ended with the collapse of Austria-Hungary, which handed western Slovenia to Italy as part of postwar reparations. Northern Carinthia, including the towns of Beljak and Celovec (now Villach and Klagenfurt), voted to stay with Austria in a 1920 plebiscite. What remained of Slovenia joined fellow south *(jug)* Slavs in forming the Kingdom of Serbs, Croats and Slovenes, later Yugoslavia.

Nazi occupation in WWII was for the most part resisted by Slovenian partisans, though after Italy capitulated in 1943 the anti-partisan Slovenian Domobranci (Home Guards) were active in the west. To prevent their nemeses the communists from taking political control in liberated areas, the Domobranci threw their support behind the Germans. The war ended with Slovenia regaining Italian-held areas from Piran to Bovec, but losing Trst (Trieste) and part of Gorica (Gorizia).

In Tito's Yugoslavia, Slovenia, with only 8% of the national population, was the economic powerhouse, creating up to 20% of the national GDP. But by the 1980s the federation had become increasingly Serb-dominated, and Slovenes feared they would lose their political autonomy. In free elections, Slovenes voted overwhelmingly to break away from Yugoslavia and did so on 25 June 1991. A 10-day war that left 66 people dead followed; Yugoslavia swiftly signed a truce in order to concentrate on regaining control of coastal Croatia.

Slovenia was admitted to the UN in May 1992 and became a member of the EU in May 2004. It replaced the tolar with the euro as the national currency in January 2007.

In the national elections of October 2008, Janez Janša's coalition government was narrowly defeated by the Social Democrats under Borut Pahor, who was able to form a coalition with three minority parties. Since 2004, Slovenia has been moving towards a two-party system, with the Social Democrats and Janša's Slovenian Democratic Party as the major political forces.

The Slovenes

The population of Slovenia is largely homogeneous. Just over 83% are ethnic Slovenes, with the remainder Serbs, Croats, Bosnians, Albanians and Roma; there are also small enclaves of Italians and Hungarians, who have special deputies looking after their interests in parliament. Slovenes are ethnically Slavic, typically hardworking, multilingual and extrovert. Just under 58% of Slovenes identify themselves as Catholics.

The Arts

Slovenia's most cherished writer is the Romantic poet France Prešeren (1800–49). His patriotic yet humanistic verse was a driving force in raising Slovene national consciousness. Fittingly, a stanza of his poem 'Zdravljica' (A Toast) forms the lyrics of the national anthem.

Many of Ljubljana's most characteristic architectural features, including its recurring pyramid motif, were added by celebrated Slovenian architect Jože Plečnik (1872–1957), whose work fused classical building principles and folk-art traditions.

Postmodernist painting and sculpture were more or less dominated from the 1980s by the multimedia group Neue Slowenische Kunst (NSK) and the artists' cooperative Irwin. It also spawned the internationally known industrial-music group Laibach, whose leader, Tomaž Hostnik, died tragically in 1983 when he hanged himself from a *kozolec*, the traditional (and iconic) hayrack found only in Slovenia. Slovenia's vibrant music scene embraces rave, techno, jazz, punk, thrash-metal and *chanson* (torch songs from the likes of Vita Mavrič); the most popular local rock group is Siddharta, still going strong after 15 years. There's also been a folk-music revival: keep an ear out for the groups Katice and Katalena, who play traditional Slovenian music with a modern twist, and the vocalist Brina.

Well-received Slovenian films in recent years include *Kruh in Mleko* (Bread & Milk, 2001), the tragic story by Jan Cvitkovič of a dysfunctional small-town family, and Damjan Kozole's *Rezerni Deli* (Spare Parts, 2003) about the trafficking of illegal immigrants through Slovenia from Croatia to Italy by a couple of embittered misfits living in the southern town of Krško, site of the nation's only nuclear power plant. Much lighter fare is *Petelinji Zajtrk* (Rooster's Breakfast, 2007), a romance by Marko Naberšnik set in Gornja Radgona on the Austrian border in northeast Slovenia, and the bizarre US-made documentary *Big River Man* (John Maringouin, 2009) about an overweight dyspeptic marathon swimmer who takes on – wait for it – the Amazon and succeeds.

Environment

Slovenia is amazingly green; indeed, 58% of its total surface area is covered in forest and it's growing. Slovenia is home to almost 3200 plant species – some 70 of which are indigenous. Triglav National Park is particularly rich in native flowering plants. Among the more peculiar endemic fauna in Slovenia is a blind salamander called *Proteus anguinus* that lives deep in Karst caves, can survive for years without eating and has been called a 'living fossil'.

Slovenian Cuisine

Slovenia boasts an incredibly diverse cuisine, but except for a few national favourites such as *žlikrofi* (pasta stuffed with cheese, bacon and chives) and *jota* (hearty bean soup) and incredibly rich desserts like *gibanica*, you're not likely to encounter many of these regional specialities on menus. Dishes like *brodet* (fish soup) from the coast, *ajdovi žganci z ocvirki* (buckwheat 'porridge' with savoury pork crackling) and salad greens doused in *bučno olje* (pumpkinseed oil) are generally eaten at home.

A *gostilna* or *gostišče* (inn) or *restavracija* (restaurant) more frequently serves *rižota* (risotto), *klobasa* (sausage), *zrezek* (cutlet/ steak), *golaž* (goulash) and *paprikaš* (piquant chicken or beef 'stew'). *Riba* (fish) is usually priced by the *dag* (100g). *Postrv* (freshwater trout) generally costs half the price of sea fish, though grilled squid *(lignji na žaru)* doused in garlic butter is usually a bargain.

Common in Slovenia are such Balkan favourites as *cevapčiči* (spicy meatballs of beef or pork) and *pljeskavica* (spicy meat patties), often served with *kajmak* (a type of clotted cream).

You can snack cheaply on takeaway pizza slices or pieces of *burek* (€2), flaky pastry stuffed with meat, cheese or apple. Alternatives include *štruklji* (cottage-cheese dumplings) and *palačinke* (thin sweet pancakes).

Some restaurants have *dnevno kosilo* (set lunches), including *juha* (soup), *solata* (salad) and a main course, for as low as €7.

Wine, Beer & Brandy

Distinctively Slovenian wines include peppery red Teran made from Refošk grapes in the Karst region, Cviček, a dry light red – almost rosé – wine from eastern Slovenia, and Malvazija, a straw-colour white from the coast that is light and dry. Slovenes are justly proud of their top vintages, but cheaper bar-standard 'open wine' (*odprto vino*) sold by the decilitre (100mL) is just so-so.

Pivo (beer), whether *svetlo* (lager) or *temno* (porter), is best on *točeno* (draught) but always available in cans and bottles too.

There are dozens of kinds of *žganje* (fruit brandy) available, including *češnjevec* (made with cherries), *sadjevec* (mixed fruit), *brinjevec* (juniper), *hruška* (pears, also called *viljamovka*) and *slivovka* (plums).

Like many other countries in Europe, Slovenia bans smoking across the board in all public places, including restaurants, bars and hotels.

SURVIVAL GUIDE

Directory A–Z

Accommodation

Very roughly, budget accommodation in Slovenia means a double room under €50. Midrange is €50 to €100 and top end is anything over €100. Accommodation can be a bit more expensive in Ljubljana. Unless otherwise indicated, rooms include toilet and bath or shower and breakfast. Smoking is banned in all hotels and hostels.

Camping grounds generally charge per person, whether you're in a tent or caravan. Almost all sites close from mid-October to mid-April. Camping 'rough' is illegal in Slovenia, and this law is enforced, especially around Bled and on the coast. Seek out the Slovenian Tourist Board's *Camping in Slovenia*.

Slovenia's ever-growing stable of hostels includes Ljubljana's trendy Celica and the Alibi chain found both in the capital and in Piran. Throughout the country there are student dormitories (residence halls) moonlighting as hostels for visitors in July and August. Unless stated otherwise hostel rooms share bathrooms. Hostels usually cost from €17 to €22; prices are at their highest in July and August.

Tourist information offices can usually help you find private rooms, apartments and tourist farms, or they can recommend private agencies that will. Such accommodation can appear misleadingly cheap if you overlook the 30% to 50% surcharge levied on stays of less than three nights. Also be aware that many such properties are in outlying villages with minimal (or no) public transport, and that the cheapest one-star category rooms with shared bathroom are actually very rare, so you'll usually pay well above the quoted minimum. Depending on the season you might save a little money by going directly to any house with a sign reading *sobe* or *Zimmer frei* (indicating 'rooms available' in Slovene and German). For more information check out the STB's *Friendly Countryside* pamphlet listing some 200 farms with accommodation.

Guesthouses, known as a *penzion*, *gostišče*, or *prenočišča*, are often cosy and better value than full-blown hotels. Beware that locally listed rates are usually quoted per person assuming double occupancy. A tourist tax – routinely from €1 per person per day – is usually not included.

Activities

EXTREME SPORTS

Several areas specialise in adrenalin-rush activities – rafting, hydro-speed, kayaking and canyoning – including Bovec (p764) and Bled (p759). Bovec is also a great place for paragliding. Gliding costs are very reasonable from Lesce near Bled. Scuba diving from Piran (p771) is also good value.

HIKING

Hiking is extremely popular, with the **Alpine Association of Slovenia** (www.pzs.si) counting more than 58,000 members and *Ljubljančani* flocking in droves to Triglav National Park (p761) on weekends. There are some 10,000km of marked trails and paths – 8250km of which are mountain trails – and more than 170 mountain huts offer comfortable trailside refuge. Ask for the STB's exhaustive *Hiking in Slovenia*.

SKIING

Skiing is a Slovenian passion, with slopes particularly crowded over the Christmas holidays and in early February. See the STB's *Slovenia Skiing* for more details.

Kranjska Gora (up to 1291m; p762) has some challenging runs, and the world record for ski-jumping was set at nearby Planica, 4km to the west. Above Lake Bohinj, Vogel (up to 1800m) is particularly scenic, as is Kanin (up to 2300m) above Bovec, which can have snow into late spring. Being relatively close to Ljubljana, Krvavec (up to 1971m), northeast of Kranj, can have particularly long lift queues.

Just west of Maribor in eastern Slovenia is a popular choice and the biggest downhill skiing area in the country. Although relatively low (336m to 1347m), the Mariborsko Pohorje is easily accessible, with very varied downhill pistes and relatively short lift queues.

OTHER ACTIVITIES

Mountain bikes are available for hire from travel agencies and some hotels at Bled, Bohinj, Bovec, Kranjska Gora and Postojna.

The Soča River near Kobarid and the Sava Bohinjka near Bohinj are great for fly-fishing April to October. Catch-and-release licences for the latter cost €42 and are sold at the tourist office.

Spas and wellness centres are very popular in Slovenia; the STB publishes a useful brochure called *Health Resorts*. Many towns (eg Portorož) have some spa complexes, and hotels often offer free or low-rate entry to their guests.

Business Hours

Most businesses post their opening times *(delovni čas)* on the door. Many shops close Saturday afternoons. A handful of grocery stores open on Sundays, including some branches of the ubiquitous Mercator supermarket chain. Most museums close on Mondays. Banks often take lunch breaks from noon or 12.30pm to 2pm or 3pm and some open on Saturday mornings. Post offices are generally open from 8am to 6pm weekdays and till noon on Saturday.

Restaurants typically open from 10pm or 11am to 10pm or 11pm. Bars stay open to midnight, though they usually have longer hours on weekends and shorter ones on Sundays.

Embassies & Consulates

Following are among the embassies and consulates in Slovenia. They are all in Ljubljana unless otherwise stated:

Australia (☎01-234 86 75; Železna c 14; ◷9am-1pm Mon-Fri)

Austria (☎01-479 07 00; Prešernova c 23; ◷8am-noon Mon-Thu, 8-10am Fri) Enter from Veselova ul.

Canada (☎01-252 44 44; 12th fl, Trg Republike 3; ◷9am-noon Mon-Fri)

Croatia Ljubljana (☎01-425 62 20; Gruberjevo nabrežje 6; ◷9am-1pm Mon-Fri); Maribor (☎02-234 66 80; Trg Svobode 3; ◷10am-1pm Mon-Fri)

France (☎01-479 04 00; Barjanska c 1; ◷8.30am-12.30pm Mon-Fri) Enter from Zoisova c 2.

Hungary (☎01-512 18 82; ul Konrada Babnika 5; ⊗8am-5pm Mon-Fri)

Ireland (☎01-300 89 70; Palača Kapitelj, Poljanski nasip 6; ⊗9.30am-12.30pm & 2.30-4pm Mon-Fri)

Italy Ljubljana (☎01-426 21 94; Snežniška ul 8; ⊗9-11am Mon-Fri); Koper (☎05-627 37 49; Belvedere 2; ⊗9-11am Mon-Fri)

Netherlands (☎01-420 14 61; Palača Kapitelj, Poljanski nasip 6; ⊗9am-noon Mon-Fri)

New Zealand (☎01-580 30 55; Verovškova ul 57; ⊗8am-3pm Mon-Fri)

South Africa (☎01-200 63 00; Pražakova ul 4; ⊗3-4pm Tue) In the Kompas building.

UK (☎01-200 39 10; 4th fl, Trg Republike 3; ⊗9am-noon Mon-Fri)

USA (☎01-200 55 00; Prešernova c 31; ⊗9-11.30am & 1-3pm Mon-Fri)

Festivals & Events

Major cultural and sporting events are listed under 'Upcoming Events' on the home page of the of the **Slovenian Tourist Board** (www.slovenia.info) website and in the STB's comprehensive *Calendar of Major Events in Slovenia*, issued annually.

Food

Price ranges are: budget (€; under €15), midrange (€€; €15 to €30) and top end (€€€; over €30).

Gay & Lesbian Travellers

Roza Klub (☎01-430 47 40; Kersnikova ul 4) in Ljubljana is made up of the gay and lesbian branches of **ŠKUC** (www.skuc.org), which stands for Študentski Kulturni Center (Student Cultural Centre) but is no longer student-oriented as such.

A more or less monthly publication called **Narobe** (Upside Down; www.narobe.si) is in Slovene only, though you might be able to at least glean from the listings.

Holidays

Slovenia celebrates 14 holidays *(prazniki)* a year. If a holiday falls on a Sunday, then the following Monday becomes the holiday.

New Year 1 & 2 January

Prešeren Day (Slovenian Culture Day) 8 February

Easter & Easter Monday March/April

Insurrection Day 27 April

Labour Day holidays 1 & 2 May

National Day 25 June

Assumption Day 15 August

Reformation Day 31 October

All Saints Day 1 November

Christmas Day 25 December

Independence Day 26 December

Internet Access

Virtually every hostel and hotel now has internet access – a computer for guests' use (free or for a nominal fee), wi-fi, or both. Most cities and towns have at least one internet cafe but they usually only have a handful of terminals. The useful **e-točka** (e-points; www.e-tocke.gov.si) website lists free access terminals, wi-fi hotspots and commercial internet cafes across Slovenia.

Internet Resources

The website of the **Slovenian Tourist Board** (www.slovenia.info) is tremendously useful, as is that of **Mat'Kurja** (www.matkurja.com), a directory of Slovenian web resources. Most Slovenian towns and cities have a website accessed by typing www.town.si (or sometimes www.town-tourism.si). Especially good are **Ljubljana** (www.ljubljana.si), **Maribor** (www.maribor.si) and **Piran/Portorož** (www.portoroz.si).

Money

The official currency is the euro. Exchanging cash is simple at banks, major post offices, travel agencies and *menjalnice* (bureaux de change), although many don't accept travellers cheques. Major credit and debit cards are accepted almost everywhere, and ATMs are ubiquitous.

Post

Local mail costs €0.33 for up to 20g, while an international airmail stamp costs €0.49. Poste restante is free; address it to and pick it up from the main post office at Slovenska c 32, 1101 Ljubljana.

Telephone

Slovenia's country code is ☎386. Public telephones require a phonecard *(telefonska kartica* or *telekartica)*, available at post offices and some newsstands. The cheapest card (€3, 25 units) gives about 20 minutes' calling time to other European countries; the highest value is €14.60 with 300 units. Local SIM cards with €5 credit are available for €12 from **SiMobil** (www.simobil.si), for €15 from **Mobitel** (www.mobitel.si) and for just €3.99 from

EMERGENCY NUMBERS

» **Ambulance** ☎112
» **Fire Brigade** ☎112
» **Police** ☎113
» **Roadside Assistance** ☎1987

new-kid-on-the-block **Tušmobil** (www.tusmo bil.si). Mobile numbers in Slovenia are identified by the prefix ☎030 and ☎040 (SiMobil), ☎031, ☎041, ☎051 and ☎071 (Mobitel) and ☎070 (Tušmobil).

Tourist Information

The Ljubljana-based **Slovenian Tourist Board** (☎01-589 85 50; www.slovenia.info; Dimičeva ul 13) has dozens of tourist information centres (TICs) in Slovenia, and seven branches abroad. See 'STB Representative Offices Abroad' on its website for details.

Visas

Citizens of virtually all European countries, as well as Australia, Canada, Israel, Japan, New Zealand and the USA, do not require visas to visit Slovenia for stays of up to 90 days. Holders of EU and Swiss passports can enter using a national identity card.

Those who do require visas (including South Africans) can get them for up to 90 days at any Slovenian embassy or consulate – see the website of the **Ministry of Foreign Affairs** (www.mzz.gov.si) for a full listing. They cost €35 regardless of the type of visa or length of validity. You'll need confirmation of a hotel booking plus one photo, and you may have to show a return or onward ticket.

Women Travellers

In the event of an emergency call the **police** (☎113) any time or the **SOS Helpline** (☎080 11 55; www.drustvo-sos.si; ☉noon-10pm Mon-Fri, 6-10pm Sat & Sun).

Getting There & Away

Air

Slovenia's only international airport receiving regular scheduled flights at present – Aerodrom Maribor does limited charters only – is Ljubljana's **Jože Pučnik Airport** (LJU; ☎04-206 1981; www.lju-airport.si) at Brnik, 27km north of Ljubljana. From there, the Slovenian flag-carrier, **Adria Airways** (JP; ☎080 13 00, 01-369 10 10; www.adria-airways.

com), serves some 30 European destinations on regularly scheduled flights, with just as many holiday spots served by charter flights in summer. Adria can be remarkably good value and includes useful connections to places like İstanbul, Pristina (Kosovo) and Tirana (Albania).

Other airlines with regularly scheduled flights to and from Ljubljana:

Air France (AF; ☎01-244 34 47; www.airfrance. com) Daily flights to Paris (CDG).

Austrian Airlines (OS; ☎04-202 01 00; www. aua.com) Multiple daily flights with Adria to Vienna.

Brussels Airlines (SN; ☎04-206 16 56; www. brusselsairlines.com) Daily flights with Adria to Brussels.

ČSA Czech Airlines (OK; ☎04-206 17 50; www.czechairlines.com) Flights to Prague.

easyJet (EZY; ☎04-206 16 77; www.easyjet. com) Low-cost daily flights to London Stansted.

Finnair (AY; ☎080 13 00; www.finnair.com) Flights to Helsinki.

JAT Airways (JU; ☎01-231 43 40; www.jat. com) Daily flights to Belgrade.

Turkish Airlines (TK; ☎04-206 16 80; www. turkishairlines.com) Flights to İstanbul.

Land

BUS

International bus destinations from Ljubljana include Serbia, Germany, Croatia, Bosnia & Hercegovina, Macedonia, Italy and Scandinavia; see p781. You can also catch buses to Italy and Croatia from coastal towns, including Piran (p773) and Koper (p769).

TRAIN

It is possible to travel to Italy, Austria, Germany, Croatia and Hungary by train; Ljubljana (p781) is the main hub, although you can, for example, hop on international trains in certain cities like Maribor and Ptuj. International train travel can be expensive. It is sometimes cheaper to travel as far as you can on domestic routes before crossing any borders.

Sea

Piran despatches ferries to Trieste daily and catamarans to Venice at least once a week in season; see p773 for details. There's also a catamaran between nearby Izola and Venice in summer months; see p770.

Getting Around

Bus

Book long-distance buses ahead of time, especially when travelling on Friday afternoons. If your bag has to go in the luggage compartment below the bus, it will cost about €1.50 extra. Check the online bus timetable on the **Avtobusna Postaja Ljubljana** (www.ap-ljubljana.si) website.

Bicycle

Bicycle rental places are generally concentrated in the more popular tourist areas such as Ljubljana, Bled, Bovec and Piran though a fair few cycle shops and repair places hire them out as well.

Car

Daily rates usually start at around €40/210 per day/week, including unlimited mileage, collision-damage waiver and theft protection. Unleaded petrol *(bencin)* costs €1.19 (95 octane) and €1.22 (98 octane), with diesel at €1.13. You must keep your headlights illuminated throughout the day. If you'll be doing a lot of driving consider buying Kod & Kam's 1:100,000 *Avtoatlas Slovenija* (€29).

Tolls are no longer paid separately on the motorways. Instead all cars must display a *vinjeta* (road-toll sticker) on the windscreen. They cost €15/30 for a week/month for cars and €7.50/25 for motorcycles and are available at petrol stations, post offices, some newsstands and tourist information centres. These stickers will already be in place on a rental car, but if you are driving your own vehicle, failure to display such a sticker risks a fine of up to €800.

Further information is available from the **Automobile Association of Slovenia** (☏ 01-530 52 00; www.amzs.si).

Hitching

Hitchhiking is fairly common and legal everywhere in Slovenia except on motorways and a few major highways. But it's never totally safe and Lonely Planet doesn't recommend it.

Train

Slovenian Railways (Slovenske Železnice; ☏ 01-291 33 32; www.slo-zeleznice.si) has a useful online timetable that's easy to use. Buy tickets before boarding or you'll incur a €2.50 supplement. Be aware that EuroCity (EC) and InterCity (IC) trains carry a surcharge of €1.60 on top of standard quoted fares, while InterCity Slovenia ones cost €9.50/6.30 extra in 1st/2nd class.

Spain

Best Places to Eat

» Arzak (p845)

» La Cuchara de San Telmo (p845)

» Mercado de San Miguel (p798)

» Le Pepica (p857)

Best Places to Stay

» Casa Morisca Hotel (p879)

» Pensión Bellas Artes (p844)

» Hospedería La Gran Casa Mudéjar (p813)

» Hotel Constanza (p832)

Why Go?

Passionate, sophisticated and devoted to living the good life, Spain is at once a stereotype come to life and a country more diverse than you ever imagined.

Spanish landscapes stir the soul, from the jagged Pyrenees and wildly beautiful cliffs of the Atlantic northwest to charming Mediterranean coves, while astonishing architecture spans the ages at seemingly every turn. Spain's cities march to a beguiling beat, rushing headlong into the 21st century even as timeless villages serve as beautiful signposts to Old Spain. And then there's one of Europe's most celebrated (and varied) gastronomic scenes.

But above all, Spain lives very much in the present. Perhaps you'll sense it along a crowded after-midnight street when all the world has come out to play. Or maybe that moment will come when a flamenco performer touches something deep in your soul. Whenever it happens, you'll find yourself nodding in recognition: *this* is Spain.

When to Go
Madrid

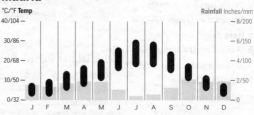

°C/°F **Temp**

40/104 —
30/86 —
20/68 —
10/50 —
0/32 —

J F M A M J J A S O N D

Rainfall Inches/mm
— 8/200
— 6/150
— 4/100
— 2/50
— 0

Mar–Apr Spring wildflowers, Semana Santa processions and mild southern temps

May & Sep Mild and often balmy weather but without the crowds of high summer

Jun–Sep Spaniards hit the coast in warm weather, but quiet corners still abound

Fast Facts

» **Area** 504,782 sq km

» **Population** 46 million

» **Capital** Madrid

» **Telephone** country code ☑34; international access code ☑00

» **Emergency** ☑112

Exchange Rates

Australia	A$1	€0.74
Canada	C$1	€0.74
Japan	¥100	€0.87
New Zealand	NZ$1	€0.56
UK	UK£1	€1.16
USA	US$1	€0.67

Set Your Budget

» **Budget hotel room** €60

» **Two-course dinner** €30

» **Museum entrance** €6–10

» **Beer** €2–3

» **Madrid metro ticket** €9

Resources

» **Tour Spain** (www.tour spain.org) Culture, food, hotels and transport links

» **Turespaña** (www.spain. info) Official tourism site

» **Lonely Planet** (www. lonelyplanet.com/spain)

Connections

Spanish airports are among Europe's best connected, while the typical overland route leads many travellers from France over the Pyrenees into Spain. Rather than taking the main road/rail route along the Mediterranean coast (or between Biarritz and San Sebastián), you could follow lesser known, pretty routes over the mountains. There's nothing to stop you carrying on to Portugal: numerous roads and the Madrid–Lisbon rail line connect the two countries.

The most obvious sea journeys lead across the Strait of Gibraltar to Morocco. The most common routes connect Algeciras or Tarifa with Tangier, from where there's plenty of transport deeper into Morocco. Car ferries also connect Barcelona with Italian (and occasionally Moroccan) ports. For transport details, turn to p903.

There are two main rail lines to Spain from Paris, one to Madrid (to be upgraded to a high-speed service by 2012) via the Basque Country, and another to Barcelona. The latter connects with services to the French Riviera and Switzerland. New rail links are also cutting travel time between southern France and Barcelona.

ITINERARIES

One Week

Marvel at Barcelona's art nouveau–influenced Modernista architecture and seaside style before taking the train to San Sebastián, with a stop in Zaragoza on the way. Head on to Bilbao for the Guggenheim Museum and end the trip living it up in Madrid's legendary night scene.

One Month

Fly into Seville and embark on a route exploring the town and picture-perfect Ronda, Granada and Córdoba. Take the train to Madrid, from where you can check out Toledo, Salamanca and Segovia. Make east for the coast and Valencia, detour northwest into the postcard-perfect villages of Aragón and the Pyrenees, then travel east into Catalonia, spending time in Tarragona before reaching Barcelona. Take a plane or boat for the Balearic Islands, from where you can get a flight home.

Essential Food & Drink

» **Paella** This signature rice dish comes in infinite varieties, although Valencia is its true home.

» **Cured meats** Wafer-thin slices of *chorizo, lomo, salchichón* and *jamón serrano* appear on most Spanish tables.

» **Tapas** These bite-sized morsels range from uncomplicated Spanish staples to pure gastronomic innovation.

» **Olive oil** Spain is the world's largest producer of olive oil.

» **Wine** Spain has the largest area of wine cultivation in the world. La Rioja and Ribera del Duero are the best-known wine-growing regions.

MADRID

POP 3.6 MILLION

No city on earth is more alive than Madrid, a beguiling place whose sheer energy carries a simple message: this city knows how to live. Explore the old streets of the centre, relax in the plazas, soak up the culture in its excellent art museums, and spend at least one night in the city's legendary nightlife scene.

History

Established as a Moorish garrison in 854, Madrid was little more than a muddy, mediocre village when King Felipe II declared it Spain's capital in 1561. That began to change when it became the permanent home of the previously roaming Spanish court.

Despite being home to generations of nobles, the city was a squalid grid of unpaved alleys and dirty buildings until the 18th century, when King Carlos III turned his attention to public works. With 175,000 inhabitants under Carlos' rule, Madrid had become Europe's fifth largest capital.

The postcivil war 1940s and '50s were trying times for the capital, with rampant poverty. When Spain's dictator, General Franco, died in 1975, the city exploded with creativity and life, giving Madrileños the party-hard reputation they still cherish.

Terrorist bombs rocked Madrid in March 2004, just before national elections, and killed 191 commuters on four trains. In 2007 two people died in a Basque terrorist bomb attack at the city's airport. With remarkable aplomb, the city quickly returned to business as usual on both occasions.

Orientation

In Spain, all roads lead to Madrid's Plaza de la Puerta del Sol, kilometre zero. South of the plaza is the oldest part of the city, with Plaza Mayor and Los Austrias to the southwest and the busy streets of the Huertas *barrio* (district or quarter of a town or city) to the southeast. Also to the south lie La Latina and Lavapiés.

North of the plaza is the east–west thoroughfare Gran Vía, the gay *barrio* (neighbourhood) Chueca and gritty Malasaña. East are the city's big three art museums on Paseo del Prado, El Retiro park and upmarket Salamanca.

◉ Sights & Activities

Get under the city's skin by walking its streets, sipping coffee and beer in its plazas and relaxing in its parks. Madrid de los Aus-

trias, the maze of mostly 15th- and 16th-century streets that surround Plaza Mayor, is the city's oldest district. Tapas-crazy La Latina, alternative Chueca, bar-riddled Huertas and Malasaña, and chic Salamanca are other districts that reward pedestrian exploration.

Build in time for three of Europe's top art collections at the Prado, Reina Sofía and Thyssen-Bornemisza museums, as well as a visit to the Palacio Real.

Museo del Prado   ART MUSEUM
(Map p792; www.museodelprado.es; Paseo del Prado; adult/student/child under 18yr & EU senior over 65yr €8/4/free, free to all 6-8pm Tue-Sat & 5-8pm Sun; ⊙9am-8pm Tue-Sun; Ⓜ Banco de España) Spain's premier art museum, the Prado is a seemingly endless parade of priceless works from Spain and beyond. The 1785 neoclassical Palacio de Villanueva opened as a museum in 1819.

The collection is roughly divided into eight major collections: Spanish paintings (1100–1850), Flemish paintings (1430–1700), Italian paintings (1300–1800), French paintings (1600–1800), German paintings (1450–1800), sculptures, decorative arts, and drawings and prints. There is generous coverage of Spanish greats including Goya, Velázquez and El Greco. Prized works include Velázquez' masterpiece *Las Meninas* (depicting maids of honour attending the daughter of King Felipe IV, and Velázquez himself painting portraits of the queen and king) and *El Jardín de las Delicias* (The Garden of Earthly Delights), a three-panelled painting by Hieronymus Bosch of the creation of man, the pleasures of the world, and hell.

Goya's *El Dos de Mayo* and *El Tres de Mayo* rank among Madrid's most emblematic paintings; they bring to life the 1808 anti-French revolt and subsequent execution of insurgents in Madrid. Also worth tracking down is his dark and disturbing *Las Pinturas Negras* (Black Paintings), so-called because of the dark browns and black that dominate and for the distorted animalesque appearance of their characters.

Other masters on show include Peter Paul Rubens, Pieter Bruegel, Rembrandt, Anton van Dyck, Dürer, Rafael, Titian, Tintoretto, Sorolla, Gainsborough, Fra Angelico and Tiepolo.

From the 1st floor of the Palacio de Villanueva, passageways lead to the Edificio Jerónimos, the Prado's modern extension. The main hall contains information counters, a bookshop and a cafe. Rooms A and B

Spain Highlights

1 Explore the **Alhambra** (p879), an exquisite Islamic palace complex in Granada

2 Visit Gaudí's singular work in progress, Barcelona's **La Sagrada Família** (p827), a cathedral that truly defies imagination

3 Wander amid the horseshoe arches of Córdoba's **Mezquita** (p876), close to perfection wrought in stone

4 Eat your way through **San Sebastián** (p844), a gourmand's paradise with an idyllic setting

5 Join the pilgrims making their way to magnificent **Santiago de Compostela** (p852)

6 Soak up the scent of orange blossom, admire the architecture and surrender to the party atmosphere in sunny **Seville** (p870)

7 Discover the impossibly beautiful Mediterranean beaches and coves of **Menorca** (p868)

8 Spend your days in some of Europe's best art galleries and nights amid its best nightlife in **Madrid** (p785)

9 Be carried away by the soulful strains of live **flamenco** (p897)

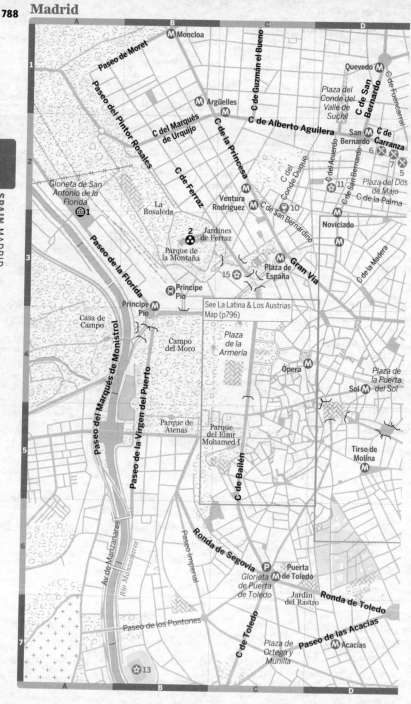

SPAIN MADRID

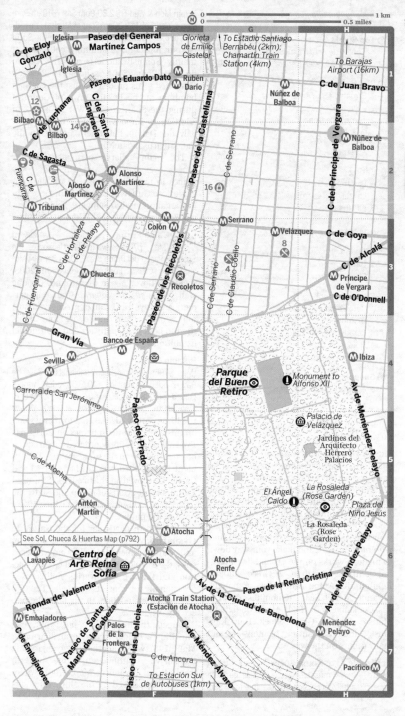

(and Room C on the 1st floor) host temporary exhibitions.

Museo Thyssen-Bornemisza   ART MUSEUM
(Map p792; www.museothyssen.org; Paseo del
Prado 8; adult/student & senior/child under 12yr
€8/5.50/free; ☺10am-7pm Tue-Sun; Ⓜ Banco
de España) Opposite the Prado, the Museo
Thyssen-Bornemisza is an outstanding collection of international masterpieces. Begin
your visit on the 2nd floor, where you'll start
with medieval art, and make your way down
to modern works on the ground level, passing paintings by Titian, El Greco, Rubens,
Rembrandt, Anton van Dyck, Canaletto,
Cézanne, Monet, Sisley, Renoir, Pissarro, Degas, Constable, Van Gogh, Miró, Modigliani,
Matisse, Picasso, Gris, Pollock, Dalí, Kandinsky, Toulouse-Lautrec, Lichtenstein and
many others on the way.

Centro de Arte Reina Sofía   ART MUSEUM
(Map p788; www.museoreinasofia.es; Calle de Santa
Isabel 52; adult/concession €6/free, free to all Sun,

7-9pm Mon & Wed-Fri, 2.30-9pm Sat; ☺10am-9pm
Mon & Wed-Sat, to 2.30pm Sun; Ⓜ Atocha) If modern art is your cup of tea, the Reina Sofía
is your museum. A stunning collection of
mainly Spanish modern art, the Centro
de Arte Reina Sofía is home to Picasso's
Guernica – his protest against the German
bombing of the Basque town of Guernica
during the Spanish Civil War in 1937 – in
addition to important works by surrealist
Salvador Dalí and abstract paintings by the
Catalan artist Joan Miró.

The main gallery's permanent display
ranges over the 2nd and 4th floors. Key
names in modern Spanish art on show include José Gutiérrez Solana, Juan Gris, Pablo Gargallo, Eusebio Sempere, Pablo Palazu-
elo, Eduardo Arroyo and Eduardo Chillida.

FREE **Caixa Forum**   ART MUSEUM
(Map p792; www.fundacio.lacaixa.es, in
Spanish; Paseo del Prado 36; ☺10am-8pm; Ⓜ Atocha) The Caixa Forum, opened in 2008,
seems to hover above the ground. On one
wall is the *jardín colgante* (hanging garden), a lush vertical wall of greenery almost
four storeys high. Inside are four floors
used to hold top-quality art and multimedia
exhibitions.

Palacio Real   PALACE
(Map p796; www.patrimonionacional.es; Calle de
Bailén; adult/concession €10/3.50, adult without
guided tour €8, EU citizens free Wed; ☺9am-6pm
Mon-Sat, to 3pm Sun & holidays; Ⓜ Ópera) When
the 16th-century Alcázar that formerly stood
on this spot went up in flames on Christmas
Eve 1734, King Felipe V ordered construction
of a new palace on the same ground. The opulent Palacio Real was finished in 1755 and
Carlos III moved in during 1764. Still used
for important events of pomp and state, the
palace has 2800-plus rooms, of which 50 are
open to the public.

Look out in particular for the **Salón de
Gasparini**, with its exquisite stucco ceiling
and walls resplendent with embroidered
silks, the 215 clocks of the royal clock collection and the five Stradivarius violins, used
occasionally for concerts and balls. The tapestries and chandeliers throughout the palace are original.

Outside the main palace, poke your head
into the **Farmacia Real** (Royal Pharmacy;
Map p796), where apothecary-style jars line
the shelves. Continue on to the **Armería
Real** (Royal Armoury; Map p796), where
you'll be impressed by the shiny (and sur-

prisingly tiny!) royal suits of armour, most of them from the 16th and 17th centuries.

Plaza Mayor SQUARE

Ringed with cafes and restaurants, and packed with people day and night, the 17th-century arcaded Plaza Mayor (Map p792) is an elegant and bustling square.

Designed in 1619 by Juan Gómez de Mora, the plaza's first public ceremony was the beatification of San Isidro Labrador, Madrid's patron saint. Thereafter, bullfights watched by 50,000 spectators were a recurring spectacle until 1878, while the autos-da-fé (the ritual condemnation of heretics) of the Spanish Inquisition also took place here. Fire largely destroyed the square in 1790, but it was rebuilt and became an important market and hub of city life. Today, the uniformly ochre-tinted apartments with wrought-iron balconies are offset by the exquisite frescos of the 17th-century **Real Casa de la Panadería** (Royal Bakery); the frescos were added in 1992.

Churches CHURCHES

The **Catedral de Nuestra Señora de la Almudena** (Map p796; Calle de Bailén; admission free; ⊙9am-8.30pm; Ópera) is just across the plaza from the Palacio Real. Finished in 1992 after a century, the cathedral is cavernous and laden with more adornment than charm. It's possible to climb to the cathedral's summit with fine views. En route you climb up through the cathedral's museum; follow the signs to the **Museo de la Catedral y Cúpula** (Map p796; adult/child €6/4; ⊙10am-2.30pm Mon-Sat) on the northern facade that faces the Palacio Real.

The cathedral is less captivating than the imposing 18th-century **Basílica de San Francisco El Grande** (Map p796; Plaza de San Francisco 1; adult/concession €3/2; ⊙mass 8am-12.30pm & 4-6pm Mon-Sat; La Latina or Puerta de Toledo).

Convento de las Descalzas Reales CONVENT

(Convent of the Barefoot Royals; Map p792; www.patrimonionacional.es; Plaza de las Descalzas 3; adult/child €5/2.50; ⊙10.30am-12.45pm & 4-5.45pm Tue-Thu & Sat, 10.30am-12.45pm Fri, 11am-1.45pm Sun; Ópera or Sol) Opulent inside though with a rather plain plateresque exterior, the Convento de las Descalzas Reales was founded in 1559 by Juana of Austria. Daughter of Spain's King Carlos I and Isabel of Portugal, Juana transformed one of her mother's palaces into the noblewomen's convent of choice. On the

obligatory guided tour you'll see a gaudily frescoed Renaissance stairway, a number of extraordinary tapestries based on works by Rubens, and a wonderful painting entitled *The Voyage of the 11,000 Virgins*. Some 33 nuns still live here and there are 33 chapels dotted around the convent.

Parque del Buen Retiro GARDENS

(Map p788; ⊙6am-midnight May-Sep, to 11pm Oct-Apr; Retiro, Príncipe de Vergara, Ibiza or Atocha) The splendid gardens of El Retiro are littered with marble monuments, landscaped lawns, the occasional elegant building and abundant greenery. It's quiet and contemplative during the week, but comes to life on weekends.

The focal point for so much of El Retiro's life is the artificial lake (*estanque*), which is watched over by the massive ornamental structure of the **Monument to Alfonso XII** on the east side of the lake, complete with marble lions.

Hidden among the trees south of the lake, the late-19th-century **Palacio de Cristal**, a magnificent metal and glass structure that is arguably El Retiro's most beautiful architectural monument, is now used for temporary exhibitions. Just north of here, the 1883 **Palacio de Velázquez** is also used for temporary exhibitions.

At the southern end of the park, near **La Rosaleda** (Rose Garden) with its more than 4000 roses, is a statue of **El Ángel Caído** (the Fallen Angel, aka Lucifer), one of the few statues to the devil anywhere in the world. It sits 666m above sea level...

In the northeastern corner of the park is the **Ermita de San Isidro**, a small country chapel noteworthy as one of the few, albeit modest, examples of Romanesque architecture in Madrid.

Just outside the park is the **Real Jardín Botánico** (Royal Botanical Garden; Map p792; Plaza de Bravo Murillo 2; adult/concession/child €2.50/1.25/free; ⊙10am-9pm May-Aug; Atocha).

Other Sights

The frescoed ceilings of the **Ermita de San Antonio de la Florida** (Map p788; Glorieta de San Antonio de la Florida 5; admission free; ⊙9.30am-8pm Tue-Fri, 10am-2pm Sat & Sun, hr vary Jul & Aug; Príncipe Pío) are one of Madrid's most surprising secrets. In the southern of the two small chapels you can see Goya's work in its original setting, rendered in 1798. The painter is buried in front of the altar.

SPAIN MADRID

Sol, Chueca & Huertas (Madrid)

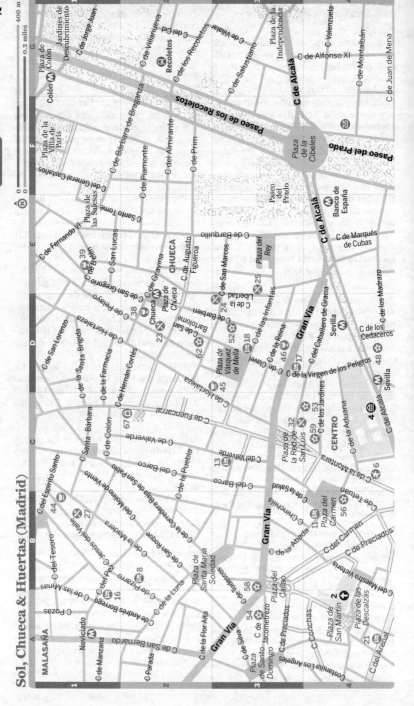

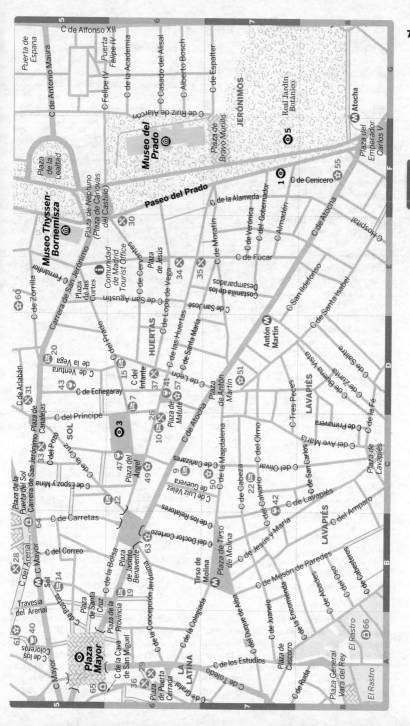

Sol, Chueca & Huertas (Madrid)

The authentically ancient **Templo de Debod** (Map p788; www.munimadrid.es/templodebod; Paseo del Pintor Rosales; admission free; ⊙10am-2pm & 6-8pm Tue-Fri, 10am-2pm Sat & Sun; ⓜVentura Rodríguez) was transferred here stone by stone from Egypt in 1972 as a gesture of thanks to Spanish archaeologists who helped save Egyptian monuments from the rising waters of the Aswan Dam.

The somewhat fusty **Real Academia de Bellas Artes de San Fernando** (Map p792; http://rabasf.insde.es, in Spanish; Calle de Alcalá 13; adult/student/child €3/1.50/free; ⊙9am-5pm Tue-Sat, to 2.30pm Sun & Mon Sep-Jun, hr vary Jul & Aug; ⓜSevilla) offers a broad collection of

WANT MORE?

For in-depth information, reviews and recommendations at your fingertips, head to the Apple App Store to purchase Lonely Planet's *Madrid City Guide* iPhone app.

Alternatively, head to **Lonely Planet** (www.lonelyplanet.com/spain/madrid) for planning advice, author recommendations, traveller reviews and insider tips.

old and modern masters, including works by Zurbarán, El Greco, Rubens, Tintoretto, Goya, Sorolla and Juan Gris.

Madrid also some lovely public squares, among them **Plaza de Oriente** (Map p796; MÓpera), **Plaza de la Villa** (Map p796; MÓpera or Sol), **Plaza de la Paja** (Map p796; MLa Latina) and **Plaza de Santa Ana** (Map p792; MSol, Sevilla or Antón Martín).

⮞ Courses

There's no shortage of places to learn Spanish in Madrid.

Academia Inhispania   LANGUAGE SCHOOL
(Map p792; www.inhispania.com; Calle de la Montera 10-12; MSol)

Academia Madrid Plus   LANGUAGE SCHOOL
(Map p796; www.madridplus.es; 6th fl, Calle del Arenal 21; MÓpera)

⮞ Tours

The Centro de Turismo de Madrid offers **Descubre Madrid** (Discover Madrid; ☑91 588 29 06; www.esmadrid.com/descubremadrid; walking tours adult/concession €3.90/3.12, bus tours €6.45/5.05, bicycle tours €3.90/3.12 plus €6 bike rental), with dozens of guided walking, cycling and bus itineraries.

⭒ Festivals & Events

Madrid's social calendar is packed with festivals and special events. Major holidays and festivals:

Fiesta de San Isidro   CITY FESTIVAL
Street parties, parades, bullfights and other fun events honour Madrid's patron saint on and around 15 May.

Veranos de la Villa   SUMMER FESTIVAL
Madrid's town hall stages a series of cultural events, shows and exhibitions known as Summers in the City, in July and August.

Suma Flamenca   FLAMENCO
A soul-filled flamenco festival that draws some of the biggest names in the genre to the Teatros del Canal in May or June.

🛏 Sleeping

Madrid has high-quality accommodation across all price ranges. Where you decide to stay will play an important role in your experience of Madrid. Los Austrias, Sol and Centro put you in the heart of the busy downtown area, while La Latina (the best *barrio* for tapas), Lavapiés and Huertas (good for nightlife) are ideal for those who love Madrid nights and don't want to stagger too far to get back to their hotel. You don't have to be gay to stay in Chueca, but you'll love it if you are, while Malasaña is another inner-city *barrio* with great restaurants and bars.

LOS AUSTRIAS, SOL & CENTRO

TOP CHOICE **Hotel Meninas**   BOUTIQUE HOTEL €€
(Map p796; ☑91 541 28 05; www.hotelmeninas.com; Calle de Campomanes 7; s/d from €109/129; MÓpera; ✿🛜) Inside a refurbished 19th-century mansion, the Meninas combines old-world comfort with modern, minimalist style. The colour scheme is blacks, whites and greys, with dark-wood floors and splashes of fuchsia and lime-green.

TOP CHOICE **Cat's Hostel**   HOSTEL €
(Map p792; ☑91 369 28 07; www.catshostel.com; Calle de Cañizares 6; dm/d from €15/42; MAntón Martín; ✿@) Forming part of a 17th-century palace, the internal courtyard here is Madrid's finest – lavish Andalucian tilework, a fountain, a spectacular glass ceiling and stunning Islamic decoration, surrounded on four sides by an open balcony. There's a super-cool basement bar with free internet connections and fiestas, often with live music.

Hostal Madrid   BUDGET HOTEL, APARTMENTS €
(Map p792; ☑91 522 00 60; www.hostal-madrid.info; 2nd fl, Calle de Esparteros 6; s €40-60, d €50-78, apt €60-150; MSol) Nineteen excellent apartments here range in size from 33 sq metres to 200 sq metres, each with a fully equipped kitchen, sitting area, bathroom and, in some, an expansive terrace with good rooftop views. The double *hostal* (budget hotel) rooms are comfortable and well-sized, and the service is extremely friendly.

Mad Hostel   HOSTEL €
(Map p792; ☑91 506 48 40; www.madhostel.com; Calle de Cabeza 24; dm from €15; MAntón Martín;

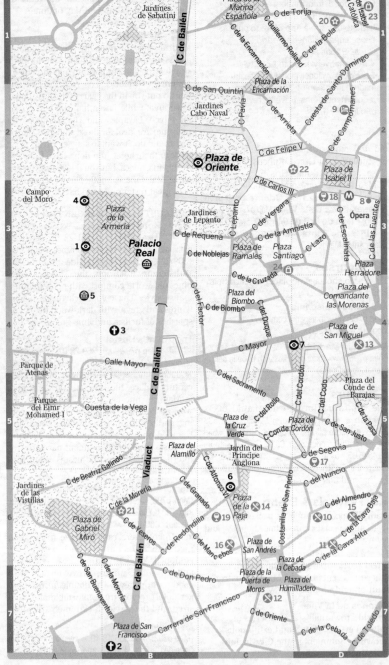

❀@) From the same people who brought you Cat's Hostel, Mad Hostel is less distinguished architecturally but a similar deal. The 1st-floor courtyard – with retractable roof – is a wonderful place to chill, while the four- to eight-bed rooms are smallish but new and clean. There's a small rooftop gym equipped with state-of-the-art equipment.

Hotel Plaza Mayor   HOTEL €€
(Map p792; ☑91 360 06 06; www.h-plazamayor.com; Calle de Atocha 2; s/d from €50/60; Ⓜ Sol or Tirso de Molina; ❀) Stylish decor, charming original elements of a 150-year-old building and helpful staff are selling points here. The rooms are attractive, some with a light colour scheme and wrought-iron furniture. The attic rooms have great views.

Los Amigos Sol Backpackers' Hostel
    HOSTEL €
(Map p792; ☑91 559 24 72; www.losamigoshostel.com; 4th fl, Calle de Arenal 26; dm €17-20; Ⓜ Ópera or Sol; @) If you arrive in Madrid keen for company, this could be the place for you – lots of students stay here, the staff are savvy (and speak English) and there are bright dorm-style rooms (with free lockers). Prices include breakfast and there's a kitchen for use by guests.

Hostal Acapulco   BUDGET HOTEL €
(Map p792; ☑91 531 19 45; www.hostalacapulco.com; Calle de la Salud 13; s/d/tr €52/62/79; Ⓜ Gran Vía; ❀♠) This immaculate little *hostal* has marble floors, renovated bathrooms, double-glazed windows and comfortable beds. Street-facing rooms have balconies overlooking sunny Plaza del Carmen.

Hotel de Las Letras   HOTEL €€
(Map p792; ☑91 523 79 80; www.hoteldelasletras.com; Gran Vía 11; d from €100; Ⓜ Gran Vía) Hotel de las Letras started the rooftop hotel-bar trend in Madrid. The bar's wonderful, but the whole hotel is excellent with individually styled rooms, each with literary quotes scribbled on the walls.

HUERTAS & ATOCHA

TOP CHOICE **Alicia Room Mate**   BOUTIQUE HOTEL €€
(Map p792; ☑91 389 60 95; www.room-matehoteles.com; Calle del Prado 2; d €105-165; Ⓜ Sol, Sevilla or Antón Martín; ❀♠) With beautiful, spacious rooms, Alicia overlooks Plaza de Santa Ana. It has an ultra-modern look and the downstairs bar is oh-so-cool.

Hotel Urban   LUXURY HOTEL €€€
(Map p792; ☑91 787 77 70; www.derbyhotels.com; Carrera de San Jerónimo 34; d from €190; Ⓜ Sevilla; ❀♠♨) The towering glass edifice of Hotel Urban is the epitome of art-inspired designer

cool. Dark-wood floors and dark walls are offset by plenty of light, while the bathrooms have wonderful designer fittings. The rooftop swimming pool is Madrid's best.

Hostal Sardinero BUDGET HOTEL €
(Map p792; ☏91 429 57 56; www.hostalsardinero .com; Calle del Prado 16; s/d from €42/50; Ⓜ Sol or Antón Martín; ❋) A change of owners here has brought more than just a fresh lick of paint, new mattresses and new TVs. The cheerful rooms, which have high ceilings, airconditioning, a safe, hairdryer and renovated bathroom, are complemented nicely by the equally cheerful Nieves and Jimmy who are attentive without being in your face.

Chic & Basic Colors BUDGET HOTEL €€
(Map p792; ☏91 429 69 35; www.chicandbasic .com; 2nd fl, Calle de las Huertas 14; s/d/apt from €62/78/96; Ⓜ Antón Martín; ❋ ⓢ ⌕) It's all about colours here at this fine little *hostal*. The rooms are white in a minimalist style with free internet, flat-screen TVs, dark hardwood floors with a bright colour scheme superimposed on top, with every room a different shade. It's all very comfortable, contemporary and casual.

Hostal Adriano BUDGET HOTEL €
(Map p792; ☏91 521 13 39; www.hostaladriano .com; 4th fl, Calle de la Cruz 26; s/d/tr €53/65/85; Ⓜ Sol) They don't come any better than this bright and cheerful *hostal* wedged in the streets that mark the boundary between Sol and Huertas. Most rooms are well sized and each has its own colour scheme.

MALASAÑA & CHUECA

TOP CHOICE Hotel Óscar BOUTIQUE HOTEL €€
(Map p792; ☏91 701 11 73; www.room -matehoteles.com; Plaza de Vázquez de Mella 12; d €90-200; Ⓜ Gran Vía; ❋ ⓢ ⌕) Simply outstanding, Hotel Óscar's designer rooms ooze style and sophistication. Some have floor-to-ceiling murals, the lighting is always funky and the colour scheme is awash with pinks, limegreens, oranges or a more minimalist blackand-white. The facade – with thousands of hanging Coca-Cola bottles – is a striking local landmark; there's a fine street-level tapas bar and a rooftop terrace.

TOP CHOICE Antigua Posada del Pez HOSTEL €€
(Map p792; ☏91 531 42 96; www.antigua posadadelpez.com; Calle de Pizarro 16; s €40-120, d €50-150; Ⓜ Noviciado) This place inhabits the shell of a historic Malasaña building, but the rooms are slick and contemporary with designer bathrooms. You're also just a few steps up the hill from Calle del Pez, one of Malasaña's most happening streets. It's an exceptionally good deal, even when prices head upwards.

Hotel Abalú BOUTIQUE HOTEL €€
(Map p792; ☏91 531 47 44; www.hotelabalu.com; Calle del Pez 19; s/d/ste from €74/90/140; Ⓜ Noviciado; ❋ ⓢ) Hotel Abalú is an oasis of style amid Malasaña's time-worn feel. Each room has its own design drawn from the imagination of Luis Delgado, from retro chintz to Zen, baroque to pure white, and most aesthetics in between. Some of the suites have jacuzzis and large-screen home cinemas.

Hostal La Zona HOSTEL €
(Map p792; ☏91 521 99 04; www.hostallazona .com; 1st fl, Calle de Valverde 7; s/d/tr €50/60/85; Ⓜ Gran Vía; ❋ ⓢ) Catering primarily to a gay clientele, the stylish Hostal La Zona has exposed brickwork, wooden pillars and a subtle colour scheme. Other highlights include free internet, helpful staff and air-conditioning/ heating in every room.

Albergue Juvenil HOSTEL €
(Map p788; ☏91 593 96 88; www.ajmadrid.es; Calle de Mejía Lequerica 21; dm €19-25; Ⓜ Bilbao or Alonso Martínez; ❋ ⓢ) The Albergue's dorms are spotless, no dorm houses more than six beds (and each has its own bathroom), and facilities include a pool table, a gym, wheelchair access, free internet, laundry and a TV/ DVD room.

✗ Eating

It's possible to find just about any kind of cuisine and eatery in Madrid, from ageless traditional to trendy fusion. Madrid is a focal point of cooking from around the country and is particularly attached to seafood; despite not having a sea, Madrid has the world's second-largest fish market (after Tokyo).

From the chaotic tapas bars of La Latina to countless neighbourhood favourites, you'll have no trouble tracking down specialities like *cochinillo asado* (roast suckling pig) or *cocido madrileño* (a hearty stew made of beans and various animals' innards).

LOS AUSTRIAS, SOL & CENTRO

TOP CHOICE Mercado de San Miguel
FOOD MARKET €€
(Map p796; www.casinodemadrid.es; Plaza de San Miguel; meals €15-35; ⏰10am-midnight Sun-Wed, to 2am Thu-Sat; Ⓜ Sol) One of Madrid's oldest and most beautiful markets, the Mercado de

San Miguel has undergone a stunning major renovation and bills itself as a 'culinary cultural centre'. Within the early-20th-century glass walls, the market has become an inviting space strewn with tables (difficult to nab) where you can enjoy the freshest food or a drink. Apart from the fresh fish corner, you can order tapas at most of the counter bars.

Restaurante Sobrino de Botín

TRADITIONAL SPANISH €€

(Map p792; ☏91 366 42 17; www.botin.es; Calle de los Cuchilleros 17; meals €40-45; Ⓜ La Latina or Sol) It's not every day that you can eat in the oldest restaurant in the world (1725), which also appears in many novels about Madrid, most notably Hemingway's *The Sun Also Rises*. The secret of its staying power is fine *cochinillo* (suckling pig; €22.90) and *cordero asado* (roast lamb; €22.90) cooked in wood-fired ovens. Eating in the vaulted cellar is a treat.

La Gloria de Montera

SPANISH €€

(Map p792; Calle del Caballero de Gracia 10; meals €25-30; Ⓜ Gran Vía) Minimalist style, tasty Mediterranean dishes and great prices mean that you'll probably have to wait in line (no reservations taken) to eat here.

LA LATINA & LAVAPIÉS

This area is best known for its tapas bars; see the boxed text, p800.

TOP CHOICE Naïa Restaurante

FUSION €€

(Map p796; ☏91 366 27 83; www.naia restaurante.com, in Spanish; Plaza de la Paja 3; meals €30-35; ⊙lunch & dinner Tue-Sun; Ⓜ La Latina) On the lovely Plaza de la Paja, Naïa has a real buzz about it, with a cooking laboratory overseen by Carlos López Reyes, delightful modern Spanish food and a chill-out lounge downstairs. The emphasis throughout is on natural ingredients, healthy cooking and exciting tastes.

TOP CHOICE Viva La Vida

VEGETARIAN €

(Map p796; www.vivalavida.vg; Costanilla de San Andrés 16; veg buffet €2.10 per 100g; ⊙noon-midnight; Ⓜ La Latina; ☒) This organic food shop has as its centrepiece an enticing vegetarian buffet with hot and cold food that's always filled with flavour. On the cusp of Plaza de la Paja, it's a great place at any time of the day, especially outside normal Spanish eating hours.

Casa Lucio

TRADITIONAL SPANISH €€

(Map p796; ☏91 365 32 52; www.casalucio.es, in Spanish; Calle de la Cava Baja 35; meals €45-50; ⊙lunch & dinner Sun-Fri, dinner Sat, closed Aug; Ⓜ La Latina) Lucio has been wowing *madrileños* with his light touch, quality ingredients and home-style local cooking for ages – think seafood, roasted meats and eggs (a Lucio speciality) in abundance.

HUERTAS & ATOCHA

TOP CHOICE Vinos González

TAPAS, DELICATESSEN €€

(Map p792; Calle de León 12; meals €20-25; ⊙9am-midnight Tue-Thu, to 1am Fri & Sat; Ⓜ Antón Martín) Ever dreamed of a deli where you could choose a tasty morsel and sit down and eat it right there? Well, here you can. On offer are a tempting array of cheeses, cured meats and other typically Spanish delicacies.

TOP CHOICE Casa Alberto

TRADITIONAL SPANISH €€

(Map p792; ☏91 429 93 56; www.casaal berto.es, in Spanish; Calle de las Huertas 18; meals €25-30; ⊙noon-1.30am Tue-Sat, to 4pm Sun; Ⓜ Antón Martín) One of the most atmospheric old *tabernas* of Madrid, Casa Alberto has been around since 1827. The secret to its staying power is vermouth on tap, excellent tapas and fine sit-down meals; *rabo de toro* (bull's tail) is a good order.

Maceiras

GALICIAN €€

(Map p792; Calle de las Huertas 66; meals €20-30; Ⓜ Antón Martín) Galician tapas (think octopus, green peppers etc) never tasted so good as in this agreeably rustic bar down the bottom of the Huertas hill, especially when washed down with a crisp white Ribeiro.

Lhardy

TRADITIONAL SPANISH €€€

(Map p792; ☏91 521 33 85; www.lhardy.com; Carrera de San Jerónimo 8; meals €60-70; ⊙lunch & dinner Mon-Sat, lunch Sun, closed Aug; Ⓜ Sol or Sevilla) This Madrid landmark (since 1839) is an elegant treasure trove of takeaway gourmet tapas. Upstairs is the upscale preserve of house specialities such as pheasant in grape juice and lemon soufflé. It's expensive, but the quality and service are unimpeachable.

La Finca de Susana

MEDITERRANEAN €€

(Map p792; www.lafinca-restaurant.com; Calle de Arlabán 4; meals €20-25; Ⓜ Sevilla) It's difficult to find a better combination of price, quality cooking and classy atmosphere anywhere in Huertas. The softly lit dining area is bathed in greenery and the sometimes innovative, sometimes traditional food draws a hip young crowd. It doesn't take reservations.

MALASAÑA & CHUECA

TOP CHOICE La Musa

SPANISH FUSION €€

(Map p788; www.lamusa.com.es; Calle de Manuela Malasaña 18; meals €25-30; ⊙9am-1.30am

A TAPAS TOUR OF MADRID

Madrid's home of tapas is La Latina, especially along Calle de la Cava Baja and the surrounding streets. **Almendro 13** (Map p796; Calle del Almendro 13; meals €15-20; MLa Latina) is famous for quality rather than frilly elaborations, with cured meats, cheeses, tortillas and *huevos rotos* (literally, 'broken eggs') the house specialities. Down on Calle de la Cava Baja, **Txacolina** (Map p796; Calle de la Cava Baja 26; meals €15-20; ⊙lunch & dinner Sat, dinner Mon & Wed-Fri; MLa Latina) does some of the biggest *pintxos* (Basque tapas) you'll find. Not far away, **Juanalaloca** (Map p796; Plaza de la Puerta de Moros 4; meals €25-35; ⊙lunch & dinner Tue-Sun, dinner Mon; MLa Latina) does a magnificent *tortilla de patatas* (potato and onion omelette).

In the centre, for *bacalao* (cod) the historic **Casa Labra** (Map p792; Calle de Tetuán 11; meals €15-20; ⊙11am-3.30pm & 6-11pm; MSol) and **Casa Revuelta** (Map p792; Calle de Latoneros 3; meals €15-20; ⊙10.30am-4pm & 7-11pm Mon & Wed-Sat, 10.30am-4pm Sun, closed Aug; MLa Latina or Sol) have no peers.

Down the bottom of the Huertas hill, **Los Gatos** (Map p792; Calle de Jesús 2; meals €25-30; ⊙noon-1am Sun-Thu, to 2am Fri & Sat; MAntón Martín) has eclectic decor and terrific canapés. Nearby, along the Paseo del Prado, there's super-cool **Estado Puro** (Map p792; www.tapasenestadopuro.com, in Spanish; Plaza de Cánovas del Castillo 4; tapas €1.95-9.50; ⊙11am-1am Tue-Sat, to 4pm Sun; MBanco de España or Atocha) with gourmet tapas inspired by Catalonia's world-famous El Bulli restaurant. In Salamanca, **Biotza** (Map p788; Calle de Claudio Coello 27; ⊙9am-midnight Mon-Thu, to 1am Fri & Sat; MSerrano) offers creative Basque *pintxos* in stylish surrounds.

Chueca is another stellar tapas *barrio*. Don't miss **Bocaito** (Map p792; Calle de la Libertad 4-6; meals €20-25; ⊙lunch & dinner Mon-Fri, dinner Sat; MChueca), another purveyor of Andalucian *jamón* (ham) and seafood. **Casa Julio** (Map p792; Calle de la Madera 37; meals €10-15; ⊙lunch & dinner Mon-Sat; MTribunal) is widely touted as the home of Madrid's best *croquetas* (croquettes). Another brilliant choice is **Baco y Beto** (Map p792; www.bacoybeto.com, in Spanish; Calle de Pelayo 24; meals €20-25; ⊙lunch & dinner Fri & Sat, dinner Mon-Thu; MChueca).

Sun-Thu, to 2.30am Fri & Sat; MSan Bernardo) Snug yet loud, a favourite of Madrid's hip young crowd yet utterly unpretentious, La Musa is all about designer decor, lounge music on the sound system and food (breakfast, lunch or dinner) that is always fun and filled with flavour. The menu is divided into three types of tapas – hot, cold and BBQ.

TOP CHOICE **Bazaar**　　　MODERN SPANISH €€
(Map p792; www.restaurantbazaar.com; Calle de la Libertad 21; meals €20-25; MChueca) Bazaar's popularity among the well-heeled and often-famous shows no sign of abating. Its pristine white interior design with theatre lighting may draw a crowd that looks like it stepped out of the pages of *Hola!* magazine, but the food is extremely well priced and innovative. No reservations.

Nina　　　MODERN SPANISH €€
(Map p788; ☎91 591 00 46; Calle de Manuela Malasaña 10; meals €30-40; MBilbao) Sophisticated, intimate and wildly popular, Nina has an extensive menu (available in English) of nouvelle Mediterranean cuisine that doesn't

miss a trick. We like the decor, all exposed brick and subtle lighting, we love just about everything on the menu, but we adore the honey-and-*sobrasada*-sausage-glazed grilled ostrich steak with a salmon and raspberry crust.

La Isla del Tesoro　　　VEGETARIAN €€
(Map p788; ☎91 593 14 40; www.isladeltesoro .net; Calle de Manuela Malasaña 3; meals €30-40; MBilbao;) La Isla del Tesoro is loaded with quirky charm – the dining area is like someone's fantasy of a secret garden come to life. The cooking here is assured and wide-ranging in its influences; the jungle burger is typical in a menu that's full of surprises.

SALAMANCA
Sula Madrid　　　SPANISH FUSION €€€
(Map p788; ☎91 781 61 97; www.sula.es; Calle de Jorge Juan 33; meals €60-70; ⊙lunch & dinner Mon-Sat; MVelázquez) A gastronomic temple that combines stellar cooking with clean-lined sophistication, Sula Madrid – a gourmet food store, super-stylish tapas bar and top-notch restaurant all rolled into one – is

one of our favourite top-end restaurants in Madrid. It serves a range of Mediterranean dishes – some traditional, some with the most creative of twists – that you won't find anywhere else.

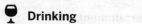 Drinking

Madrid lives life on its streets and plazas, and bar-hopping is a pastime enjoyed by young and old alike. If you're after the more traditional, with tiled walls and flamenco tunes, head to Huertas. For gay-friendly drinking holes, Chueca is the place. Malasaña caters to a grungy, funky crowd, while La Latina has friendly bars that guarantee atmosphere most nights of the week. In summer, the terrace bars that pop up all over the city are unbeatable.

The bulk of Madrid bars open to 2am Sunday to Thursday, and to 3am or 3.30am Friday and Saturday.

LOS AUSTRIAS & CENTRO

TOP CHOICE **Museo Chicote** COCKTAIL BAR
(Map p792; www.museo-chicote.com; Gran Vía 12; ⊙6pm-3am Mon-Thu, to 3.30am Fri & Sat; Ⓜ Gran Vía) The founder of this Madrid landmark is said to have invented more than a hundred cocktails, which the likes of Hemingway, Ava Gardner, Grace Kelly, Sophia Loren and Frank Sinatra all enjoyed at one time or another. It's at its best after midnight when a lounge atmosphere takes over, couples cuddle on the curved benches and some of the city's best DJs do their stuff.

Café del Real BAR-CAFE
(Map p796; Plaza de Isabel II 2; ⊙9am-1am Mon-Thu, to 3am Fri & Sat; Ⓜ Ópera) One of the nicest bar-cafes in central Madrid, this place serves a rich variety of creative coffees and a few cocktails to a soundtrack of chill-out music. The best seats are upstairs, where the low ceilings, wooden beams and leather chairs make a great place to pass an afternoon.

MADRID'S FAVOURITE POSTCLUBBING MUNCHIES

Chocolatería de San Ginés (Map p792; Pasadizo de San Ginés 5; ⊙9.30am-7am Mon-Fri, 9am-7am Fri & Sat; Ⓜ Sol) Join the sugar-searching throngs who end the night at this legendary bar, famous for its freshly fried *churros* (fried sticks of dough) and syrupy hot chocolate.

Delic BAR-CAFE
(Map p796; Costanilla de San Andrés 14; ⊙11am-2am Sun & Tue-Thu, 7pm-2am Mon, 11am-2.30am Fri & Sat; Ⓜ La Latina) We could go on for hours about this long-standing cafe-bar, but we'll reduce it to its most basic elements: nursing an exceptionally good mojito (€8) or three on a warm summer's evening at Delic's outdoor tables on one of Madrid's prettiest plazas is one of life's great pleasures.

La Escalera de Jacob COCKTAIL BAR
(Map p792; Calle de Lavapiés 11; ⊙6pm-2am; Ⓜ Antón Martín or Tirso de Molina) With magicians, storytellers, children's theatre (on Saturdays and Sundays at noon) and live jazz and other musical genres, 'Jacob's Ladder' is one of Madrid's most original bars. And regardless of what's on, it's worth stopping by here for creative cocktails that you won't find anywhere else.

Café del Nuncio BAR-CAFE
(Map p788; Calle de Segovia 9; ⊙noon-2am Sun-Thu, to 3am Fri & Sat; Ⓜ La Latina) Café del Nuncio straggles down a stairway passage to Calle de Segovia. You can drink on one of several cosy levels inside or, better still in summer, enjoy the outdoor seating that one local reviewer likened to a slice of Rome.

HUERTAS & ATOCHA

TOP CHOICE **Penthouse** COCKTAIL BAR
(Map p792; 7th fl, Plaza de Santa Ana 14; ⊙9pm-1.30am Mon-Wed, to 2am Thu, to 2.30am Fri & Sat, 5pm-1.30am Sun; Ⓜ Antón Martín or Sol) High above the Plaza de Santa Ana, this sybaritic rooftop cocktail bar has terrific views over Madrid's rooftops. It's a place for sophisticates, with chill-out areas strewn with cushions, funky DJs and a dress policy designed to sort out the classy from the wannabes.

TOP CHOICE **La Venencia** WINE BAR
(Map p792; Calle de Echegaray 7; ⊙1-3.30pm & 7.30pm-1.30am; Ⓜ Sol) This is how sherry bars should be – old-world, drinks poured straight from the dusty wooden barrels and none of the frenetic activity for which Huertas is famous. La Venencia is a *barrio* classic, with fine sherry from Sanlúcar and *manzanilla* from Jeréz.

El Imperfecto BAR
(Map p792; Plaza de Matute 2; ⊙3pm-2am Sun-Thu, to 3am Fri & Sat; Ⓜ Antón Martín) Its name notwithstanding, the 'Imperfect One' is our ideal Huertas bar, with live jazz most

Tuesdays at 9pm and a drinks menu as long as a saxophone, ranging from cocktails (€6.50) and spirits to milkshakes, teas and creative coffees.

MALASAÑA & CHUECA

TOP CHOICE **Café Comercial**   CAFE
(Map p788; Glorieta de Bilbao 7; ⊙7.30am-midnight Mon, to 1am Tue-Thu, to 2am Fri, 8.30am-2am Sat, 9am-midnight Sun; MBilbao) This glorious old Madrid cafe proudly fights a rearguard action against progress with heavy leather seats, abundant marble and old-style waiters. As close as Madrid came to the intellectual cafes of Paris' Left Bank, Café Comercial now has a clientele that has broadened to include just about anyone.

Splash Óscar   BAR
(Map p792; Plaza de Vázquez de Mella 12; ⊙4.30pm-12.30am; MGran Vía) Another of Madrid's stunning rooftop terraces (although this one with a small swimming pool), atop Hotel Óscar, this chilled space with gorgeous skyline views has become a cause célèbre among A-list celebrities.

Kabokla   BAR
(www.kabokla.es, in Spanish; Calle de San Vicente Ferrer 55; ⊙10pm-1am Tue-Thu, 6pm-3am Fri, 2.30-6.30pm & 10.30pm-3.30am Sat, 2.30pm-10pm Sun; MNoviciado) Run by Brazilians and dedicated to all things Brazilian, Kabokla is terrific. When there's no live music, the DJ gets the crowd dancing. It also serves Madrid's smoothest caipirinhas.

El Jardín Secreto   BAR
(Map p788; Calle del Conde Duque 2; ⊙5.30pm-12.30am Sun-Thu & Sun, 6.30pm-2.30am Fri & Sat; MPlaza de España) 'The Secret Garden' is all about intimacy and romance in a *barrio* that's one of Madrid's best-kept secrets. Lit by Spanish designer candles, draped in organza from India and serving up chocolates from the Caribbean, it never misses a beat.

Café Belén   BAR
(Map p792; Calle de Belén 5; ⊙3.30pm-3am; MChueca) Café Belén is cool in all the right places – lounge and chill-out music, dim lighting, a great range of drinks (the mojitos are especially good) and a low-key crowd that's the height of casual sophistication.

Lolina Vintage Café   CAFE
(Map p792; Calle del Espíritu Santo 9; ⊙10am-1am Sun-Tue, to 2am Wed, to 2.30am Thu-Sat; MTribunal) Lolina Vintage Café seems to have captured the essence of Malasaña in one small space. With a studied retro look (comfy old-style chairs and sofas, gilded mirrors and 1970s-era wallpaper), it confirms that the new Malasaña is not unlike the old but a whole lot more sophisticated.

☆ Entertainment

The **Guía del Ocio** (www.guiadelocio.com, in Spanish; €1) is the city's classic weekly listings magazine. Also good are **Metropoli** (www.abc.es/metropolis, in Spanish) and **On Madrid** (www.elpais.com, in Spanish), respectively *ABC's* and *El País'* Friday listings supplements.

Nightclubs

No *barrio* is without a decent club or disco, but the most popular dance spots are in the centre. Don't expect dance clubs or *discotecas* (nightclubs) to get going until after 1am at the earliest. Standard entry fee is €10, which usually includes the first drink, although megaclubs and swankier places charge a few euros more.

Teatro Joy Eslava   CLUB
(Map p792; www.joy-eslava.com; Calle del Arenal 11; admission €12-15; ⊙11.30pm-6am; MSol) The only things guaranteed at this grand old Madrid dance club (housed in a 19th-century theatre) are a crowd and the fact that it will be open. (The club claims to have opened every single day for the past 29 years.) The music and the crowd are a mixed bag, but queues are long and invariably include locals and tourists, and even the occasional *famoso*.

Charada   CLUB
(Map p796; www.charadaclubdebaile.com, in Spanish; Calle de la Bola 13; admission €10-15; ⊙midnight-6am Thu-Sat; MSanto Domingo) Charada took the Madrid nightlife scene by storm in 2009 and has never looked back. Its decor is New York chic (with no hint of its former existence as a brothel), the cocktails are highly original, the clientele is well-heeled and often famous, and it's the home turntable for some of the best house DJs in town.

Adraba   CLUB
(Map p792; www.fsmgroup.es, in Spanish; Calle de Alcalá 20; admission €15-18; ⊙midnight-6am Wed-Sun; MSevilla) This historic nightclub finally reopened to much fanfare in 2010 and rapidly re-established itself as one of the city's best. The designer decor is stunning and there are five nights of dancing with a sophisticated crowd. Whatever the night, the resident DJs are among the best in Madrid.

Kapital
CLUB

(Map p792; www.grupo-kapital.com, in Spanish; Calle de Atocha 125; admission €20; ⊙6-10pm & midnight-6am Thu-Sun; ⓜAtocha) One of the most famous megaclubs in Madrid, this massive seven-storey nightclub has something for everyone: from cocktail bars and dance music to karaoke, salsa, hip hop and more chilled spaces for R&B and soul, as well as a section devoted to 'Made in Spain' music.

Cinemas

Cine Doré
CINEMA

(Map p792; Calle de Santa Isabel 3; ⊙Tue-Sun; ⓜAntón Martín) The National Film Library offers fantastic classic and vanguard films for just €2.50.

Yelmo Cineplex Ideal
SPANISH CINEMA

(Map p792; www.yelmocines.es, in Spanish; Calle del Doctor Cortezo 6; ⓜSol or Tirso de Molina) Close to Plaza Mayor; offers a wide selection of films.

Theatre

Madrid has a lively cultural scene, with concerts and shows taking place throughout the city.

Teatro de la Zarzuela
THEATRE

(Map p792; ☑91 524 54 00; teatrodelazarzuela. mcu.es; Calle de Jovellanos 4; ⓜBanco de España) This theatre, built in 1856, is the premier place to see *zarzuela,* a very Spanish mixture of dance, music and theatre. It also hosts a smattering of classical music and opera, as well as the cutting-edge Compañía Nacional de Danza.

Teatro Real
OPERA

(Map p796; ☑902 244 848; www.teatro-real.com, in Spanish; Plaza de Oriente; ⓜÓpera) The Teatro Real is the city's grandest stage for elaborate operas and ballets. You'll pay as little as €15 for a spot so far away you will need a telescope, although the sound quality is consistent throughout.

Live Music
FLAMENCO

Many of flamenco's top names perform in Madrid, making it an excellent place to see interpretations of the art.

Corral de la Morería
FLAMENCO

(Map p796; ☑91 365 84 46; www.corraldelamoreria.com; Calle de la Morería 17; admission €27-37; ⊙8.30pm-2.30am, shows 10pm & midnight Sun-Fri, 7pm, 10pm & midnight Sat; ⓜÓpera) One of the most prestigious flamenco stages in Madrid, with 50 years as a leading flamenco venue and top performers most nights. The stage area has a rustic feel, and tables are pushed up close. We'd steer clear of the overpriced restaurant, but the performances have a far higher price to quality ratio.

Las Tablas
FLAMENCO

(Map p788; ☑91 542 05 20; www.lastablasmadrid .com; Plaza de España 9; admission €24; ⊙shows 10.30pm Sun-Thu, 8pm & 10pm Fri & Sat; ⓜPlaza de España) Las Tablas has quickly earned a reputation for quality flamenco. Most nights you'll see a classic flamenco show, with plenty of throaty singing and soul-baring dancing. Antonia Moya and Marisol Navarro, leading lights in the flamenco world, are regular performers.

Casa Patas
FLAMENCO

(Map p792; ☑91 369 04 96; www.casapatas.com, in Spanish; Calle de Cañizares 10; admission €30-35; ⊙shows 10.30pm Mon-Thu, 9pm & midnight Fri & Sat; ⓜAntón Martín or Tirso de Molina) One of the

---

GAY & LESBIAN MADRID

The heartbeat of gay Madrid is the inner-city *barrio* of Chueca, where Madrid didn't just come out of the closet, but ripped the doors off in the process.

A good place to get the low-down is the laid-back **Mamá Inés** (Map p792; www.mama ines.com, in Spanish; Calle de Hortaleza 22; ⊙10am-2pm Sun-Thu, to 3am Fri & Sat; ⓜGran Vía or Chueca). **Café Acuarela** (Map p792; Calle de Gravina 10; ⊙11am-2am Sun-Thu, to 3am Fri & Sat; ⓜChueca) is another dimly lit centrepiece of gay Madrid.

Two of the most popular Chueca nightspots are **Club 54 Studio** (Map p792; www .studio54madrid.com, in Spanish; Calle de Barbieri 7; ⊙11.30pm-3.30am Thu-Sat; ⓜChueca), modelled on the famous New York club Studio 54, and **Liquid Madrid** (Map p792; www .liquid.es; Calle de Barbieri 7; ⊙9am-3am Mon-Thu, to 3.30am Fri & Sat; ⓜChueca). **Why Not?** (Map p792; Calle de San Bartolomé 7; admission €10; ⊙10.30pm-6am; ⓜChueca) is the sort of place where nothing's left to the imagination. Another club popular with a predominantly gay crowd is **Sala Bash/Ohm** (Map p792; Plaza del Callao 4; ⊙midnight-6am Fri & Sat; ⓜCallao).

top flamenco stages in Madrid, this *tablao* always offers unimpeachable quality.

JAZZ

Café Central
JAZZ CLUB

(Map p792; [phone]91 369 41 43; www.cafecentral madrid.com, in Spanish; Plaza del Angel 10; admission €10-15; ⊙1pm-2.30am Sun-Thu, 1.30pm-3.30am Fri & Sat; MAntón Martín or Sol) This art deco bar has consistently been voted one of the best jazz venues in the world by leading jazz magazines, and with almost 9000 gigs under its belt, it rarely misses a beat. Shows start at 10pm and tickets go on sale an hour before the set starts.

FREE Populart
JAZZ CLUB

(Map p792; www.populart.es, in Spanish; Calle de las Huertas 22; ⊙6pm-2.30am Sun-Fri, to 3.30am Fri & Sat; MAntón Martín or Sol) One of Madrid's classic jazz clubs, this place offers a low-key atmosphere and top-quality music – mostly jazz, but with occasional blues, swing and even flamenco thrown into the mix. Shows start at 10.15pm, but if you want a seat get here early.

El Berlín Jazz Club
JAZZ CLUB

(Map p792; [phone]91 521 57 52; www.cafeberlin.es, in Spanish; Calle de Jacometrezo 4; admission €6-10; ⊙7pm-2.30am Tue-Sun; MCallao or Santo Domingo) El Berlín has been something of a Madrid jazz stalwart since the 1950s and it's all about classic jazz with none of the fusion performances that you find elsewhere. The headline acts take to the stage at 11.30pm on Fridays and Saturdays, with other performances sprinkled throughout the week.

OTHER LIVE MUSIC

Costello Café & Niteclub
LIVE MUSIC

(Map p792; www.costelloclub.com; Calle del Caballero de Gracia 10; admission €5-10; ⊙6pm-1am Sun-Wed, to 2.30am Thu-Sat; MGran Vía) Very cool. Costello Café & Niteclub is smooth-as-silk ambience wedded with an innovative mix of pop, rock and fusion in Warholesque surrounds. There's live music every night of the week (except Sundays) at 9.30pm, with resident and visiting DJs until closing time from Thursday to Saturday.

Sala El Sol
LIVE MUSIC

(Map p792; www.elsolmad.com, in Spanish; Calle de los Jardines 3; admission €8-25; ⊙11pm-5.30am Tue-Sat Jul-Sep; MGran Vía) Madrid institutions don't come any more beloved than Sala El Sol. It opened in 1979, and quickly established itself as a leading stage for all the icons of the era. The music rocks and

rolls and usually resurrects the '70s and '80s while soul and funk also get a run.

Café La Palma
LIVE MUSIC

(Map p788; www.cafelapalma.com, in Spanish; Calle de la Palma 62; admission under €12; ⊙4.30pm-3am Sun-Thu, to 3.30am Fri & Sat; MNoviciado) It's amazing how much variety Café La Palma has packed into its labyrinth of rooms. Live shows featuring hot local bands are held at the back, while DJs mix up the front. You might find live music other nights, but there are always two shows at 10pm and midnight from Thursday to Saturday.

Clamores
LIVE MUSIC

(Map p788; www.clamores.es, in Spanish; Calle de Alburquerque 14; admission €5-15; ⊙6pm-3am; MBilbao) This one-time classic jazz cafe has morphed into one of the most diverse live music stages in Madrid. Jazz is still a staple, but world music, flamenco, soul fusion, singer-songwriter, pop and rock all make regular appearances. Live shows can begin as early as 9pm.

FREE Honky Tonk
LIVE MUSIC

(Map p788; www.clubhonky.com, in Spanish; Calle de Covarrubias 24; ⊙9pm-5am; MAlonso Martínez) Despite the name, this is a great place to see local rock 'n' roll, though many acts have a little country or blues thrown into the mix too. It's a fun vibe in a smallish club that's been around since the heady 1980s. Arrive early as it fills up fast.

Sport

Get tickets to football matches and bullfights from box offices or through agents such as **Localidades Galicia** (Map p792; [phone]91 531 91 31; www.bullfightticketsmadrid.com; Plaza del Carmen 1; ⊙9.30am-1pm & 4.30-7pm Mon-Sat, 9.30am-1pm Sun; MSol).

FOOTBALL

Estadio Santiago Bernabéu
FOOTBALL STADIUM

(off Map p788; www.realmadrid.com; Avenida de Concha Espina 1; tour adult/under 14yr €15/10; ⊙10am-7pm Mon-Sat, 10.30am-6.30pm Sun; MSantiago Bernabéu) The legendary Real Madrid plays at this stadium. Fans can visit the stadium and take an interesting tour through the presidential box, dressing room and field. The all-important telephone number for booking game tickets (which you later pick up at Gate 42) is [phone]902 32 43 24, which only works if you're calling from within Spain.

Estadio Vicente Calderón
FOOTBALL STADIUM

(Map p788; www.clubatleticodemadrid.com; Paseo de la Virgin del Puerto; MPirámides) This is home to Atlético de Madrid, whose fans are famed as being some of the country's most devoted.

BULLFIGHTING

Plaza de Toros Las Ventas   BULLFIGHTING
(☎91 356 22 00; www.las-ventas.com, in Spanish; Calle de Alcalá 237; tours €7; ☀tours 10am-2pm; MVentas) Some of Spain's top *toreros* swing their capes in Plaza de Toros Las Ventas, east of Parque del Buen Retiro. Fights are held every Sunday afternoon from mid-May through October. Get tickets (from €5 unshaded standing-room only) at the plaza box office, Localidades Galicia, or from official ticket agents on Calle Victoria close to the Plaza de la Puerta del Sol. For excellent tours of the bullring in English and Spanish, contact Tauro Tour (☎91 556 92 37; gregorio@trazopublicidad.es; 4th fl, Paseo de la Castellana 115).

🔒 Shopping

The key to shopping Madrid-style is knowing where to look. Salamanca is the home of upmarket fashions, with chic boutiques lining up to showcase the best that Spanish and international designers have to offer. Some of it spills over into Chueca, but Malasaña is Salamanca's true alter ego, home to fashion that's as funky as it is offbeat and ideal for that studied underground look that will fit right in with Madrid's hedonistic after-dark crowd. Central Madrid – Sol, Huertas or La Latina – offers plenty of individual surprises.

During *las rebajas*, the annual winter and summer sales, prices are slashed on just about everything. The winter sales begin around 7 January and last well into February. Summer sales begin in early July and last into August.

Shops may (and many do) open on the first Sunday of every month and throughout December.

Antigua Casa Talavera   TRADITIONAL CERAMICS
(Map p796; Calle de Isabel la Católica 2; ☀10am-1.30pm & 5-8pm Mon-Fri, to 1.30pm Sat; MSanto Domingo) The extraordinary tiled facade of this wonderful old shop conceals an Aladdin's Cave of ceramics from all over Spain. This is not the mass-produced stuff aimed at the tourist market, but comes from the small family potters of Andalucía and Toledo.

El Arco Artesanía   SOUVENIRS
(Map p792; Plaza Mayor 9; ☀11am-9pm; MSol or La Latina) This original shop in the southwestern corner of Plaza Mayor sells an outstanding array of homemade designer souvenirs, from stone and glasswork to jewellery and home fittings.

El Flamenco Vive   FLAMENCO
(Map p796; www.elflamencovive.es; Calle Conde de Lemos 7; ☀10am-2pm & 5-9pm Mon-Sat; MÓpera) This temple to flamenco has it all: guitars, songbooks, well-priced CDs, polka-dotted dancing costumes, shoes, colourful plastic jewellery and even literature about flamenco.

Casa de Diego   HANDICRAFTS, ACCESSORIES
(Map p792; www.casadediego.com; Plaza de la Puerta del Sol 12; ☀9.30am-8pm Mon-Sat; MSol) This classic shop has been around since 1858, selling and repairing Spanish fans, shawls, umbrellas and canes. Service is old-style and the staff occasionally grumpy, but the fans are works of antique art.

El Rastro   MARKET
(Map p792; Calle de la Ribera de Curtidores; ☀8am-3pm Sun; MLa Latina, Puerta de Toledo or Tirso de Molina) A Sunday morning at El Rastro, Europe's largest flea market, is a Madrid institution. You could easily spend an entire morning inching your way down the Calle de la Ribera de Curtidores and through the maze of streets that hosts El Rastro flea market every Sunday morning. For every 10 pieces of junk, there's a real gem (we spotted a lost masterpiece: an Underwood typewriter) waiting to be found. A word of warning: pickpockets love El Rastro as much as everyone else.

Agatha Ruiz de la Prada   CLOTHING
(Map p788; www.agatharuizdelaprada.com; Calle de Serrano 27; ☀10am-8.30pm Mon-Sat; MSerrano) This boutique has to be seen to be believed, with pinks, yellows and oranges at every turn. It's fun and exuberant, but it's not just for kids: it's also serious and highly original fashion. Agatha Ruiz de la Prada is one of the enduring icons of 1980s Madrid.

Mercado de Fuencarral   CLOTHING
(Map p792; www.mdf.es, in Spanish; Calle de Fuencarral 45; ☀11am-9pm Mon-Sat; MTribunal) Madrid's home of alternative club cool is still going strong, revelling in its reverse snobbery. With shops like Fuck, Ugly Shop and Black Kiss, it's funky, grungy and filled to the rafters with torn T-shirts and more black leather and silver studs than you'll ever need.

ℹ Information
Dangers & Annoyances
Madrid is a generally safe city although, as in most European cities, you should be wary of

pickpockets in the city centre, on the Metro and around major tourist sights.

Prostitution along Calle de la Montera and in the Casa del Campo park means that you need to exercise extra caution in these areas.

For details about common scams, see the Spain Directory A–Z (p902).

Discount Cards

The **Madrid Card** (☑91 360 47 72; www.madrid card.com; 1/2/3 days €47/60/74) includes free entry to more than 40 museums in and around Madrid and discounts on public transport. The cheaper version (1/2/3 days for €31/35/39) covers just cultural sights.

Emergency
Emergency (☑112)

Policía Nacional (☑091)

Servicio de Atención al Turista Extranjero (Foreign Tourist Assistance Service; ☑91 548 85 37, 91 548 80 08; www.esmadrid.com/satemadrid; Calle de Leganitos 19; ⊙9am-10pm; ▥Plaza de España or Santo Domingo)

Internet Access

Café Comercial (Glorieta de Bilbao 7; per 50min €1; ⊙7.30am-midnight Mon, to 1am Tue-Thu, to 2am Fri, 8.30am-2am Sat, 9am-midnight Sun; ▥Bilbao) One of Madrid's grandest old cafes with internet upstairs.

Centro de Turismo de Madrid (www.esmadrid .com) Free internet for up to 15 minutes at the branch on Plaza Mayor, or free and unlimited access at the Plaza de Colón branch.

Left Luggage

At Madrid's Barajas airport, there are three **consignas** (left-luggage offices; ⊙24hr). In either, you pay €3.85 for the first 24-hour period (or fraction thereof). Thereafter, it costs €3.83/4.93 per day per small/large bag. Similar services operate for similar prices at Atocha and Chamartín train stations (open 7am to 11pm).

Medical Services

Anglo-American Medical Unit (Unidad Medica; ☑91 435 18 23; www.unidadmedica.com; Calle del Conde de Aranda 1; ⊙9am-8pm Mon-Fri, 10am-1pm Sat for emergencies; ▥Retiro) Private clinic with Spanish- and English-speaking staff. Consultations cost around €125.

Farmacia Mayor (☑91 366; Calle Mayor 13; ⊙24hr; ▥Sol)

Money

Like all Spanish cities, Madrid is fairly crawling with bank branches equipped with ATMs. As a rule, exchange bureaux have longer hours but worse rates and steeper commissions.

Post

Main post office (www.correos.es; Plaza de la Cibeles; ⊙8.30am-9.30pm Mon-Fri, to 2pm Sat; ▥Banco de España)

Tourist Information

Centro de Turismo de Madrid (www.esmadrid .com; Plaza Mayor 27; ⊙9.30am-8.30pm; ▥Sol) Excellent city tourist office with a smaller office underneath Plaza de Colón and information points at Plaza de la Cibeles, Plaza de Callao, outside the Centro de Arte Reina Sofía and at the T4 terminal at Barajas airport.

Regional tourist office (www.turismomadrid .es; Calle del Duque de Medinaceli 2; ⊙8am-8pm Mon-Sat, 9am-2pm Sun; ▥Banco de España) Further offices at Barajas airport (T1 and T4), and Chamartín and Atocha train stations.

🛈 Getting There & Away
Air

Madrid's international Barajas airport (MAD), 15km northeast of the city, is a busy place, with flights coming in from all over Europe and beyond.

Bus

Estación Sur de Autobuses (☑91 468 42 00; www.estaciondeautobuses.com, in Spanish; Calle de Méndez Álvaro 83; ▥Méndez Álvaro), just south of the M-30 ring road, is the city's principal bus station. It serves most destinations to the south and many in other parts of the country. Major bus companies:

ALSA (☑902 422 242; www.alsa.es)

Avanzabus (☑902 020 052; www.avanza bus.com)

Car & Motorcycle

The city is surrounded by two main ring roads, the outermost M-40 and the inner M-30; there are also two additional partial ring roads, the M-45 and the more-distant M-50.

Train

Madrid is served by two main train stations. The bigger of the two is **Puerta de Atocha** (▥Atocha Renfe), at the southern end of the city centre. **Chamartín train station** (▥Chamartín) lies in the north of the city. The bulk of trains for Spanish destinations depart from Atocha, especially those going south. International services arrive at and leave from Chamartín. For bookings, contact **Renfe** (☑902 24 02 02; www.renfe.es) at either station.

High-speed Tren de Alta Velocidad Española (AVE) services connect Madrid with Seville (via Córdoba), Valladolid (via Segovia), Toledo, Valencia, Málaga and Barcelona (via Zaragoza and Tarragona).

ⓘ Getting Around

To/From the Airport

METRO Line 8 of the metro (entrances in T2 and T4) runs to the Nuevos Ministerios transport interchange, which connects with lines 10 and 6. It operates from 6.05am to 2am. A single ticket costs €1 (10-ride Metrobús ticket €9); there's an additional €1 supplement if you're travelling to/from the airport. The journey to Nuevos Ministerios takes around 15 minutes, around 25 minutes from T4.

BUS At time of publication, a new 24-hour bus service between Plaza de la Cibeles and the airport was due to start.

AeroCITY (☑91 747 75 70; www.aerocity.com; €5-19 per person) is a private minibus service that takes you door-to-door between central Madrid and the airport.

TAXI A taxi to the city centre will cost you around €25 in total (up to €35 from T4), depending on traffic and where you're going; in addition to what the meter reads, you pay a €5.50 airport supplement.

Public Transport

Madrid's **metro** (www.metromadrid.es) is extensive and well maintained. A single ride costs €1 and a 10-ride ticket is €9. The metro is quick, clean, relatively safe and runs from 6am until 2am.

The bus system is also good; contact **EMT** (www.emtmadrid.es) for more information. Twenty-six night-bus *búhos* (owls) routes operate from midnight to 6am, with all routes originating in Plaza de la Cibeles.

Taxi

You can pick up a taxi at ranks throughout town or simply flag one down. Flag fall is €2.05 from 6am to 10pm daily, €2.20 from 10pm to 6am Sunday to Friday and €3.10 from 10pm Saturday to 6am Sunday. Several supplementary charges, usually posted inside the taxi, apply; these include €5.50 to/from the airport and €2.95 from taxi ranks at train and bus stations.

Radio-Teléfono Taxi (☑91 547 82 00, 91 547 82 00; www.radiotelefono-taxi.com)

Tele-Taxi (☑91 371 21 31, 902 501 130)

AROUND MADRID

The Comunidad de Madrid, the province surrounding the capital, has some of Spain's finest royal palaces and gardens that make for easy day trips from the capital.

Places worth exploring include the royal palace complex at **San Lorenzo de El Escorial** (www.patrimonionacional.es; admission €8, EU citizens free Wed; ◷10am-6pm Apr-Sep, 10am-5pm

Oct-Mar, closed Mon). Check also at www.sanlorenzoturismo.org.

Other worthwhile excursions include **Aranjuez** (www.aranjuez.es, in Spanish), with its **royal palace** (www.patrimonionacional.es; adult/child €5/2.50, EU citizens free Wed, gardens free; ◷palace 10am-6.15pm Tue-Sun, gardens 8am-8.30pm); the traditional village of **Chinchón** (www.ciudad-chinchon.com); and the university town (and birthplace of Miguel de Cervantes), **Alcalá de Henares** (www.turismoalcala.com, in Spanish).

CASTILLA Y LEÓN

Spain's Castilian heartland, Castilla y León is littered with hilltop towns sporting magnificent Gothic cathedrals, monumental city walls and mouth-watering restaurants.

Ávila

POP 56,9000

Ávila's old city, surrounded by imposing city walls comprising eight monumental gates, 88 watchtowers and more than 2500 turrets, is one of the best-preserved medieval bastions in all of Spain. It's a perfect place to spend a day strolling narrow laneways and soaking up history. The city is known as the birthplace of Santa Teresa, a mystical writer and reformer of the Carmelite order.

◉ Sights

Murallas   CITY WALLS

(adult/child €4/2.50; ◷10am-8pm Tue-Sun) Don't even *think* of leaving town without enjoying the walk along the top of Ávila's 12th-century *murallas*. The two access points are at **Puerta del Alcázar** and **Puerta de los Leales**, which allow walks of 300m and 1200m respectively. The same ticket allows you to climb both sections; the last ones are sold at 7.30pm.

Cathedral   CHURCH

(Plaza de la Catedral; admission €4; ◷10am-7pm Mon-Fri, to 8pm Sat, noon-6pm Sun) Embedded into the eastern city walls, the splendid 12th-century cathedral was the first Gothic-style church built in Spain. It boasts rich walnut choir stalls and a long, narrow central nave that makes the soaring ceilings seem all the more majestic.

FREE **Convento de Santa Teresa**   MUSEUM
(◷8.45am-1.30pm & 3.30-9pm Tue-Sun) The convent was built in 1636 at the birth-

place of 16th-century mystic and ascetic, Santa Teresa. It's home to relics, including a piece of the saint's ring finger, as well as a small museum about her life.

🛏 Sleeping

TOP CHOICE Hotel Las Leyendas HISTORIC HOTEL €€

(☎920 35 20 42; www.lasleyendas.es; Calle de Francisco Gallego 3; s/d €69/89; ❋🅿🛜) Occupying the house of 16th-century Ávila nobility, this intimate hotel overflows with period touches (original wooden beams, exposed brick and stonework) wedded to modern amenities.

Hotel El Rastro HISTORIC HOTEL €€

(☎920 35 22 25; www.elrastroavila.com; Calle Cepedas; s/d from €55/65; ❋🛜) Not to be confused with the *hostal* (budget hotel) of the same name, this superb choice is located in a former 16th-century palace. Natural stone, exposed brickwork and a warm colour scheme of earth colours exude a calming understated elegance. The rooms are spacious and stylish.

Hostal Arco San Vicente BUDGET HOTEL €€

(☎920 22 24 98; www.arcosanvicente.com; Calle de López Núñez 6; s/d €55/65; 🅿🛜) This gleaming *hostal* has small blue carpeted rooms with pale paintwork and wrought-iron bed heads. The location, just inside Puerta de San Vicente, and the parking (€10), are additional perks.

🍴 Eating & Drinking

Ávila is famous for its *chuleton de Ávila* (T-bone steak) and *judías del barco de Ávila* (white beans, often with chorizo, in a thick sauce).

Hostería Las Cancelas REGIONAL €€

(☎920 21 22 49; www.lascancelas.com; Calle de la Cruz Vieja 6; meals €30-40; ⊙lunch & dinner Feb-Dec) Part of the hotel of the same name, this courtyard restaurant occupies a delightful interior patio dating back to the 15th century. It's renowned for being a mainstay of Ávila cuisine, and traditional meals are prepared with a salutary attention to detail. Reservations recommended.

Restaurante Reyes Católicos REGIONAL €€

(www.restaurante-reyescatolicos.com, in Spanish; Calle de los Reyes Católicos 6; menú del día €15, meals €25-35) Fronted by a popular tapas bar, this place has bright decor and an accomplished kitchen that churns out traditional dishes that benefit from a creative tweak.

TOP CHOICE La Bodeguita de San Segundo WINE BAR

(www.vinoavila.com, in Spanish; Calle de San Segundo 19; ⊙11am-midnight Thu-Tue) Situated in the 16th-century Casa de la Misericordia, this superb wine bar is standing-room only most nights and more tranquil in the quieter afternoon hours.

ℹ Information

Centro de Recepción de Visitantes (tourist office; www.avilaturismo.com; Avenida de Madrid 39; ⊙8am-8pm)

Regional tourist office (www.turismocastillayleon.com; Calle San Segundo 17; ⊙9am-8pm Sun-Thu, 9am-9pm Fri & Sat).

ℹ Getting There & Away

BUS From Ávila's bus station, there are frequent services to Segovia (€5.45, 55 minutes) and Salamanca (€6.76, 1½ hours).

TRAIN More than 30 trains run daily to Madrid (from €8.25, 1¼ to two hours) and to Salamanca (€9.65, one to 1½ hours, nine daily).

Salamanca

POP 155,600

Whether floodlit by night or bathed in midday sun, Salamanca is a dream destination. This is a city of rare architectural splendour, awash with golden sandstone overlaid with Latin inscriptions in ochre, and with an extraordinary virtuosity of plateresque and Renaissance styles. The monumental highlights are many, with the exceptional Plaza Mayor (illuminated to stunning effect at night) an unforgettable highlight. But this is also Castilla's liveliest city, home to a massive Spanish and international student population who throng the streets at night and provide the city with so much youth and vitality.

⊙ Sights & Activities

TOP CHOICE Plaza Mayor SQUARE

The harmonious Plaza Mayor was completed in 1755 to a design by Alberto Churriguera, one of the clan behind an at times overblown variant of the baroque style that bears their name.

FREE Catedral Nueva & Catedral Vieja CHURCHES

Curiously, Salamanca is home to two cathedrals: the newer and larger cathedral was built beside the old Romanesque one instead of on top of it, as was the norm. The

Catedral Nueva (New Cathedral; Plaza de Anaya; admission free; ☺9am-8pm), completed in 1733, is a late-Gothic masterpiece that took 220 years to build. Its magnificent Renaissance doorways stand out. For fine views over Salamanca, head to the southwestern corner of the cathedral facade and the **Puerta de la Torre** (Ieronimus; Plaza de Juan XXIII; admission €3.25; ☺10am-7.15pm), from where stairs lead up through the tower.

The largely Romanesque **Catedral Vieja** (Old Cathedral; admission €4.75; ☺10am-7.30pm) is a 12th-century temple with a stunning 15th-century altarpiece whose 53 panels depict scenes from the life of Christ and Mary, topped by a representation of the Final Judgement. The entrance is inside the Catedral Nueva.

Universidad Civil
UNIVERSITY

(Calle de los Libreros; adult/student €4/2, Mon morning free; ☺9.30am-1pm & 4-7pm Mon-Fri, 9.30am-1pm & 4-6.30pm Sat, 10am-1pm Sun) The Universidad Civil is a tapestry in sandstone, bursting with images of mythical heroes, religious scenes and coats of arms. It's dominated in the centre by busts of Fernando and Isabel. You can visit the old classrooms and one of the oldest university libraries in Europe.

Other Sights
OTHER SIGHTS

Salamanca's other stand-out buildings include the glorious **Casa de las Conchas** (Calle de la Compañia 2; admission free; ☺9am-9pm Mon-Fri, 9am-2pm & 4-7pm Sat, 10am-2pm & 4-7pm Sun), a city symbol since it was built in the 15th century. The church at the **Convento de San Esteban** (adult/child €3/2; ☺10am-1.15pm & 4-7.15pm) has an extraordinary altar-like facade with the stoning of San Esteban (St Stephen) as its central motif.

Quiet streets lead away to the northeast to the **Convento de Santa Clara** (admission €3; ☺9.30am-2pm & 4.15-7pm Mon-Fri, 9.30am-3pm Sat & Sun). This much-modified convent started life as a Romanesque structure and you can climb up some stairs to inspect at close quarters the 14th- and 15th-century *artesonado* (Mudéjar ceiling).

🛏 Sleeping

TOP CHOICE **Microtel Placentinos**
BOUTIQUE HOTEL €€

(☎923 28 15 31; www.microtelplacentinos.com; Calle de Placentinos 9; s/d incl breakfast €80/95; ❉🖧) One of Salamanca's most charming boutique hotels, Microtel Placentinos is tucked away on a quiet street and has rooms with exposed stone walls and wooden beams. The service is faultless, and the overall atmosphere one of intimacy and discretion.

Aparthotel El Toboso
APARTMENT HOTEL €

(☎923 27 14 62; www.hoteltoboso.com; Calle del Clavel 7; s/d/tr from €30/52/82, 3-/4-/5-person self-contained apt €76/84/93; ❉🖧) These rooms have a homey spare-room feel and are super value, especially the enormous apartments which come with kitchens (including washing machines) and renovated bathrooms.

Hostal Concejo
HOTEL €€

(☎923 21 47 37; www.hconcejo.com, in Spanish; Plaza de la Libertad 1; s/d/tr €45/62/80; Ⓟ❉@🖧) A cut above the average *hostal*, the stylish Concejo has polished-wood floors, tasteful furnishings and a superb central location. Try and snag one of the corner rooms (like number 104) with its traditional glassed-in balcony, complete with table, chairs and people-watching views.

Hostal Catedral
BUDGET HOTEL €

(☎923 27 06 14; Rúa Mayor 46; s/d €30/48; ❉) Just across from the cathedrals, this pleasing *hostal* has just six extremely pretty, clean-as-a-whistle, bright rooms with showers. All look out onto the street or cathedral, which is a real bonus, as is the motherly owner, who treats her visitors as honoured guests.

🍴 Eating & Drinking

Mesón Las Conchas
GRILLED MEATS €€

(Rúa Mayor 16; meals €25-30) Enjoy a choice of outdoor tables (in summer), an atmospheric bar or the upstairs, wood-beamed dining area. The bar caters mainly to locals who know their *embutidos* (cured meats). For sit-down meals, there's a good mix of roasts and *raciones* (large tapas servings).

FIND THE FROG

The university's facade is an ornate mass of sculptures and carvings, and hidden among this 16th-century plateresque creation is a tiny stone frog. Legend says that those who find the frog will have good luck in studies, life and love. If you don't want any help, look away now... It's sitting on a skull on the pillar that runs up the right-hand side of the facade.

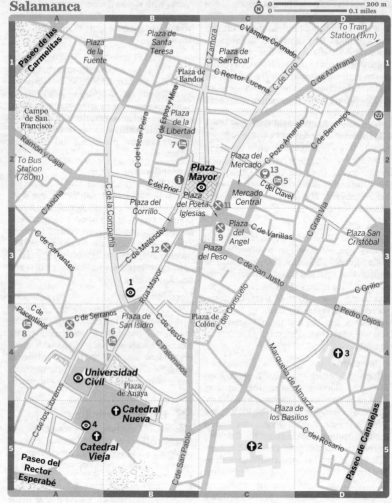

Mesón Cervantes   CASTILIAN €€
(Plaza Mayor 15; meals €15-20; ⊙10am-midnight)
Another great place where you can eat at
the outdoor tables on the plaza, but the dark
wooden beams and atmospheric buzz of the
Spanish crowd on the 1st floor should be experienced at least once. The food's a mix of
salads and *raciones*.

El Pecado   MODERN CREATIVE €€
(☑923 26 65 58; Plaza del Poeta Iglesias 12; meals
€40, menú de degustación €45; ☺) A trendy place
that regularly attracts Spanish celebrities (eg
Pedro Almodóvar and Ferran Adrià), El Pecado ('The Sin') has an intimate dining room

and quirky, creative menu. The hallmarks
are fresh tastes, intriguing combinations and
dishes that regularly change according to
what is fresh in the market that day. Reservations recommended.

Mandala Café   MODERN MEDITERRANEAN €
(Calle de Serranos 9-11; menú €10; ☑☺) Cool
and casual Mandala specialises in a superb
daily menu with choices like black rice with
prawns and *calamares* (squid), and vegetarian moussaka. There are also more salads
than you can shake a carrot stick at, as well
as cakes and fancy ice creams.

◉ **Top Sights**

Catedral Nueva	B5
Catedral Vieja	A5
Plaza Mayor	C2
Universidad Civil	A4

◉ **Sights**

1 Casa de las Conchas	B3
2 Convento de San Esteban	C5
3 Convento de Santa Clara	D4
4 Puerta de la Torre	A5

🛏 **Sleeping**

5 Aparthotel El Toboso	C2
6 Hostal Catedral	B4
7 Hostal Concejo	B2
8 Microtel Placentinos	A4

🍴 **Eating**

9 El Pecado	C3
10 Mandala Café	A4
11 Mesón Cervantes	C2
12 Mesón Las Conchas	B3

🍷 **Drinking**

13 Tío Vivo	C2

TOP CHOICE **Tío Vivo**   MUSIC BAR
(Calle del Clavel 3; ⊘4pm-late) Sip drinks by flickering candlelight to a background of '80s music, enjoying the whimsical decor of carousel horses and oddball antiquities. There's live music Tuesdays to Thursdays from midnight.

ℹ️ Information
Municipal tourist office (www.salamanca.es; Plaza Mayor 14; ⊘9am-2pm & 4.30-8pm Mon-Fri, 10am-8pm Sat, 10am-2pm Sun)
Regional tourist office (www.turismocastillayleon.com; Casa de las Conchas, Rúa Mayor; ⊘9am-8pm Sun-Thu, 9am-9pm Fri & Sat)

ℹ️ Getting There & Away
BUS Buses run from the **bus station** (Avenida de Filiberto Villalobos 71-85) to Madrid (regular/express €14.80/21.90, three/2½ hours, hourly), Ávila (€6.76, 1½ hours, one to four daily) and Segovia (€10.96, 2¾ hours, two daily).
TRAIN Up to eight trains depart daily for Madrid's Chamartín station (€19.10, 2½ hours) via Ávila (€9.65, one hour). The train station is about 1km beyond Plaza de España.

Segovia
POP 56,100

Unesco World Heritage–listed Segovia has a stunning monument to Roman grandeur and a castle said to have inspired Walt Disney, and is otherwise a city of warm terracotta and sandstone hues set amid the rolling hills of Castilla.

◉ Sights
TOP CHOICE **Acueducto**   ROMAN AQUEDUCT
El Acueducto, an 894m-long engineering wonder that looks like an enormous comb of stone blocks plunged into the lower end of old Segovia, is the obvious starting point of a tour of town. This Roman aqueduct is 28m high and was built without a drop of mortar – just good old Roman know-how.

TOP CHOICE **Alcázar**   CASTLE
(www.alcazardesegovia.com; Plaza de la Reina Victoria Eugenia; adult/child €4/3, tower €2, EU citizens free 3rd Tue of month; ⊘10am-7pm Apr-Sep) The fortified and fairytale Alcázar is perched dramatically on the edge of Segovia. Roman foundations are buried somewhere underneath the splendour, but what we see today is a 13th-century structure that burned down in 1862 and was subsequently rebuilt. Inside is a collection of armour and military gear, but even better are the ornate interiors of the reception rooms and the 360-degree views from the **Torre de Juan II**.

Catedral   CHURCH
(Plaza Mayor; adult/child €3/2, free 9.30am-1.15pm Sun; ⊘9.30am-6.30pm) In the heart of town, the resplendent late-Gothic Catedral was started in 1525 and completed a mere 200 years later. The Cristo del Consuelo **chapel** houses a magnificent Romanesque doorway preserved from the original church that burned down.

Iglesia de Vera Cruz   CHURCH
(Carretera de Zamarramala; admission €1.75; ⊘10.30am-1.30pm & 4-7pm Tue-Sun, closed Nov) The most interesting of Segovia's numerous churches, and one of the best preserved of its kind in Europe, is the 12-sided Iglesia de la Vera Cruz. Built in the 13th century by the Knights Templar and based on the Church of the Holy Sepulchre in Jerusalem, it long

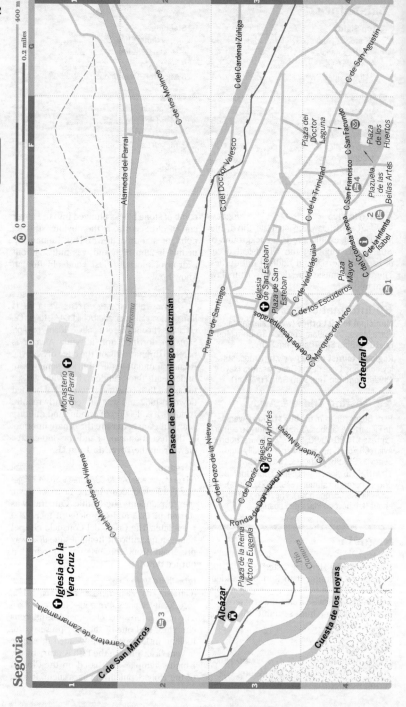

Segovia

N

0   200 m
0   0.2 miles

Iglesia de la Vera Cruz

Monasterio del Parral

Carretera de Zamarramala

C de San Marcos

C del Marqués de Villena

Río Eresma

Alameda del Parral

C de los Molinos

C del Cardenal Zúñiga

C del Doctor Valesco

Paseo de Santo Domingo de Guzmán

Puerta de Santiago

C del Pozo de la Nieve

C de Daoiz

Iglesia de San Andrés

Ciudad Nueva

Ronda de Don Juan II

Plaza de la Reina Victoria Eugenia

Alcázar

Río Clamores

Cuesta de los Hoyas

Iglesia de San Esteban

Plaza de San Esteban

C de los Desamparados

C de los Escuderos

C de Valdeláguila

C del Marqués del Arco

Catedral

Plaza Mayor

C del Cronista Lecea

C de la Infanta Isabel

Plaza del Doctor Laguna

C de la Trinidad

C San Francisco

C San Facundo

Plazuela de las Bellas Artes

Plaza de los Huertos

C de San Agustín

housed what was said to be a piece of the Vera Cruz (True Cross).

🛏 Sleeping

TOP CHOICE **Hospedería La Gran Casa Mudéjar**

HISTORIC HOTEL €€

(☎921 46 62 50; www.lacasamudejar.com; Calle de Isabel la Católica 8; r €90; ❄@🛜) Spread over two buildings, this place has been magnificently renovated, blending genuine 15th-century Mudéjar carved wooden ceilings in some rooms with modern amenities. In the newer wing, where the building dates from the 19th century, the rooms on the top floors have fine mountain views.

Hotel Alcázar BOUTIQUE HOTEL €€€

(☎921 43 85 68; www.alcazar-hotel.com; Calle de San Marcos 5; s/d incl breakfast €135/163; ❄🛜) Sitting by the riverbank in the valley beneath the Alcázar, this charming, tranquil little hotel has lavish rooms beautifully styled to suit those who love old-world luxury. Breakfast on the back terrace is a lovely way to pass the morning, and there's an intimacy and graciousness about the whole experience.

Hostal Fornos BUDGET HOTEL €

(☎921 46 01 98; www.hostalfornos.com, in Spanish; Calle de la Infanta Isabel 13; s/d €41/55; ❄) This tidy little *hostal* is a cut above most places in this price category. It has a cheerful air and rooms with a fresh white-linen-and-wicker-chair look. Some are larger than others, but the value is unbeatable.

Natura – La Hostería BUDGET HOTEL €

(☎921 46 67 10; www.naturadesegovia.com, in Spanish; Calle de Colón 5-7; r €60; ❄🛜) An eclectic choice a few streets back from Plaza Mayor. The owner obviously has a penchant for Dalí prints and the rooms have plenty of character, with chunky wooden furnishings and bright paintwork.

Eating

Segovianos love their pigs to the point of obsession. Just about every restaurant proudly boasts its *horno de asar* (roasts). The main speciality is *cochinillo asado* (roast suckling pig), but *judiones de la granja* (butter beans with pork chunks) also looms large on menus. Reservations are always recommended.

Restaurante El Fogón Sefardí
TOP CHOICE
SEPHARDIC €€

(☑921 46 62 50; www.lacasamudejar.com; Calle de Isabel la Católica 8; meals €30-40; 🖵) This is one of the most original places in town, serving Sephardic cuisine in a restaurant with an intimate patio or in a splendid dining hall with original 15th-century Mudéjar flourishes. The theme in the bar is equally diverse, with dishes from all the continents.

Casa Duque
TOP CHOICE
GRILLED MEATS €€

(☑921 46 24 87; www.restauranteduque. es; Calle de Cervantes 12; menús del día €21-40, meals €25-35) They've been serving *cochinillo asado* here since the 1890s. For the uninitiated, try the *menú segoviano* (€31), which includes *cochinillo*, or the *menú gastronómico* (€40). Downstairs is the informal *cueva* (cave), where you can get tapas and full-bodied *cazuelas* (stews).

Mesón de Cándido
GRILLED MEATS €€

(☑921 42 81 03; www.mesondecandido.es; Plaza del Azoguejo 5; meals €30-40; 🖵) Set in a delightful 18th-century building in the shadow of the aqueduct, Mesón de Cándido is famous throughout Spain for its suckling pig and the more unusual roast boar with apple.

ℹ Information

Centro de Recepción de Visitantes (tourist office; www.turismodesegovia.com; Plaza del Azoguejo 1; ⊗10am-7pm Sun-Fri, 10am-8pm Sat). Guided city tours (two hours 15 minutes, €12 per person) depart daily at 11.15am (minimum of four persons).

Regional tourist office (www.segoviaturismo .es; Plaza Mayor 10; ⊗9am-8pm Sun-Thu, 9am-9pm Fri & Sat)

ℹ Getting There & Away

BUS Buses run half-hourly to Segovia from Madrid's Paseo de la Florida bus stop (€6.70, 1½ hours). Buses also run to/from Ávila (€5.45,

1¼ hours, five daily) and Salamanca (€10.96, 2¾ hours, two daily).

TRAIN Up to nine normal trains run daily from Madrid to Segovia (€6.50 one way, two hours), leaving you at the main train station, 2.5km from the aqueduct. The faster option is the high-speed AVE (€9.90, 35 minutes), which deposits you at the newer Segovia-Guiomar station, 5km from the aqueduct.

León
POP 135,100

León's stand-out attraction is the cathedral, one of the most beautiful in Spain. By day, this pretty city rewards long exploratory strolls. By night, the city's large student population floods into the narrow streets and plazas of the city's picturesque old quarter, the Barrio Húmedo.

◎ Sights

Catedral
TOP CHOICE
CHURCH

(www.catedraldeleon.org, in Spanish; ⊗8.30am-1.30pm & 4-8pm Mon-Sat, 8.30am-2.30pm & 5-8pm Sun) León's 13th-century cathedral, with its soaring towers, flying buttresses and truly breathtaking interior, is the city's spiritual heart. The extraordinary facade has a radiant rose window, three richly sculpted doorways and two muscular towers. After going through the main entrance, lorded over by the scene of the Last Supper, an extraordinary gallery of *vidrieras* (stained-glass windows) awaits. French in inspiration and mostly executed from the 13th to the 16th centuries, the windows evoke an atmosphere unlike that of any other cathedral in Spain; the kaleidoscope of coloured light is offset by the otherwise gloomy interior. There are 128 windows with a surface of 1800 sq metres in all, but mere numbers cannot convey the ethereal quality of light permeating this cathedral.

Real Basílica de San Isidoro
ROMANESQUE CHURCH

Even older than the cathedral, the Real Basílica de San Isidoro provides a stunning Romanesque counterpoint to the former's Gothic strains. The church remains open night and day by historical royal edict.

The attached **Panteón Real** (admission €4, free Thu afternoon; ⊗10am-1.30pm & 4-6.30pm Mon-Sat, 10am-1.30pm Sun) houses the remaining sarcophagi, which rest with quiet dignity beneath a canopy of some of the finest Romanesque frescos in Spain.

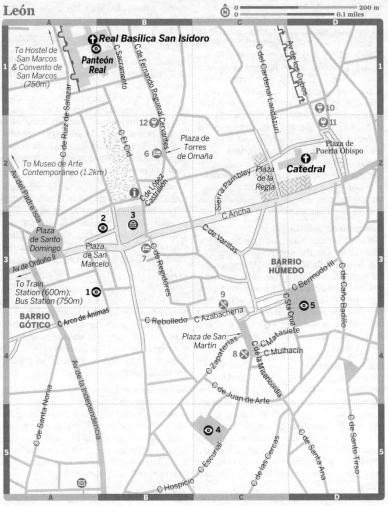

León

⊙ Top Sights
Catedral	D2
Panteón Real	A1
Real Basílica San Isidoro	A1

⊙ Sights
1	Ayuntamiento	A3
2	Casa de Botines	B3
3	Palacio de los Guzmanes	B3
4	Plaza de Santa María del Camino	C5
5	Plaza Mayor	D3

🛏 Sleeping
6	Hostal San Martín	B2
7	La Posada Regia	B3

✕ Eating
8	El Llar	C4
9	La Parrilla del Humedo	C3

🍷 Drinking
10	Big John's	D1
11	Ébanno	D2
12	Ékole Café	B2

FREE **Museo de Arte Contemporáneo**

ART MUSEUM

(Musac; www.musac.org.es; Avenida de los Reyes Leóneses 24; ⏰11am-8pm Tue-Thu, 11am-9pm Fri, 10am-9pm Sat & Sun) León's showpiece Museo de Arte Contemporáneo belongs to the new wave of innovative Spanish architecture. A pleasing square-and-rhombus edifice of colourful glass and steel, it has been acclaimed for the 37 shades of coloured glass that adorn the facade; they were gleaned from the pixelisation of a fragment of one of the cathedral's stained-glass windows.

Although the museum has a growing permanent collection, it mostly houses temporary displays of cutting-edge Spanish and international photography, video installations and other similar art forms.

Convento de San Marcos

CONVENT

More than 100m long and blessed with a glorious facade, the plateresque exterior of this former pilgrims' hospital is sectioned off by slender columns and decorated with delicate medallions and friezes; most of it dates to 1513, by which time the edifice had become a monastery of the Knights of Santiago. Much of the former convent is now a supremely elegant *parador* (luxurious state-owned hotel).

Barrio Gótico

HISTORIC QUARTER

On the fringes of León's Barrio Gótico (old town), Plaza de San Marcelo is home to the **Ayuntamiento** (city hall), which occupies a charmingly compact Renaissance-era palace. The Renaissance theme continues in the form of the splendid **Palacio de los Guzmanes** (1560). Next door is Antoni Gaudí's sober contribution to León's skyline, the castlelike, neo-Gothic **Casa de Botines** (1893).

Down the hill, the delightful **Plaza de Santa María del Camino** (also known as Plaza del Grano) feels like a cobblestone Castilian village square. At the northeastern end of the old town in Barrio Húmedo is the beautiful and time-worn 17th-century **Plaza Mayor**.

🛏️ Sleeping & Eating

TOP CHOICE **Hostal San Martín**

HOTEL €

(☏987 87 51 87; www.sanmartinhostales. com; 2nd fl, Plaza de Torres de Omaña 1; s/d/tr €31/43/55, s without bathroom €20) In a splendid central position, this recently overhauled 18th-century building has light, airy rooms painted in candy colours with small terraces.

TOP CHOICE **La Posada Regia**

HISTORIC HOTEL €€

(☏987 21 31 73; www.regialeon.com, in Spanish; Calle de Regidores 9-11; s/d €65/120; ❄️🛜) You won't find many places better than this hotel in northern Spain. The secret is a 14th-century building, which has been magnificently restored (wooden beams, exposed brick and understated antique furniture), and features individually styled rooms, character that overflows even into the public areas, and supremely comfortable beds and bathrooms.

Hostal de San Marcos

HISTORIC HOTEL €€€

(☏987 23 73 00; www.parador.es; Plaza de San Marcos 7; d from €198; ❄️@🛜) León's sumptuous *parador* is one of the finest hotels in Spain. With palatial rooms fit for royalty and filled with old-world charm, this is one of the Paradores group's flagship properties.

TOP CHOICE **El Llar**

TAPAS €€

(Plaza de San Martín 9; meals €25-30; 🍴) This old León *taberna* is a great place to *tapear* (eat tapas) with an innovative selection of *raciones*. The upstairs restaurant has a fine classic look and the menu includes vegetarian options like fresh leeks prepared in puff pastry and a seven salad choice. There's an excellent wine list.

La Parrilla del Humedo

TAPAS €

(Calle Azabacheria 6; raciones €7-13) This place is always packed with euro-economising *leonéses*, here for the remarkably good house wine and accompanying free and good-size tapa; both for the bargain basement price of €1.50. Head for the dining room out back for heartier portions of local dishes.

🍷 Drinking

The Barrio Húmedo's night-time epicentre is Plaza de San Martín – prise open the door of any bar here or in the surrounding streets (especially Calle de Juan de Arfe and Calle de la Misericordia), inch your way to the bar and you're unlikely to want to leave until closing time.

Tucked away behind the cathedral to the east, **Big John's** (Avenida de los Cubos 4; ⏰7pm-2am) is a jazz hang-out with a vigorous sound mix including bebop, Latin and Dixieland, while adjacent **Ébanno** (Avenida de los Cubos 2; ⏰4pm-late) is classy and as good for laptop-toting wi-fi hunters as for late-night sophisticates. Elsewhere, **Ékole Café** (Plaza de Torres de Omaña; ⌚4.30pm-1.30am Sun-Thu, 4.30pm-3.30am Fri & Sat) is another favourite León drinking hole with an old Parisian feel.

Information

Tourist office (www.turismocastillayleon.com; Calle el Cid 2; ⌚9am-8pm)

Getting There & Away

BUS From the **bus station** (Paseo del Ingeniero Sáez de Miera), there are numerous daily buses to Madrid (€22, 3½ hours) and Burgos (€14.10, 3¾ hours).

TRAIN Regular daily trains travel to Burgos (from €20.10, two hours), Oviedo (from €18.80, two hours), Madrid (from €28.30, 4¼ hours) and Barcelona (from €68.40, nine hours).

Burgos

POP 174,100

The legendary warrior El Cid was born just outside Burgos and is buried in its magnificent cathedral. The grey-stone architecture, fortifying cuisine and extreme climate can make Burgos edgy, but below the surface lies vibrant nightlife, good restaurants and, when the sun's shining, pretty streetscapes.

Sights

TOP CHOICE **Catedral** CHURCH

(Plaza del Rey Fernando; adult/child €5/2.50; ⌚9.30am-6.30pm) The Unesco World Heritage–listed cathedral is a masterpiece. It had humble origins as a modest Romanesque church, but work began on a grander scale in 1221. Remarkably, within 40 years most of the French Gothic structure that you see today had been completed. Probably the most impressive of the portals is the **Puerta del Sarmental**, the main entrance for visitors, although the honour could also go to the **Puerta de la Coronería**, on the northwestern side.

Inside the main sanctuary a host of other chapels showcase the diversity of the interior, from the light and airy **Capilla de la Presentación** to the **Capilla de la Concepción** with its impossibly gilded 15th-century altar. The main altar is a typically overwhelming piece of gold-encrusted extravagance, while directly beneath the star-vaulted central dome lies the **tomb of El Cid**. The **Capilla del Condestable**, behind the main altar, is a remarkable late-15th-century production.

Monasterio de las Huelgas MONASTERY

(guided tours adult/child €5/2.50, free Wed; ⌚10am-1pm & 3.45-5.30pm Tue-Sat, 10.30am-2pm Sun) A 30-minute walk west of the city centre on the southern bank of Río Arlanzón, this monastery was once among the most prominent monasteries in Spain. Founded in 1187 by Eleanor of Aquitaine, daughter of Henry II of England and wife of Alfonso VIII of Castilla, it's still home to 35 Cistercian nuns. This veritable royal pantheon contains the tombs of numerous kings and queens, as well as a spectacular gilded Renaissance altar.

Sleeping & Eating

TOP CHOICE **Hotel Norte y Londres** HISTORIC HOTEL €€

(☎947 26 41 25; www.hotelnorteylondres.com; Plaza de Alonso Martínez 10; s/d €66/100; P @ 📶) Set in a former 16th-century palace and with understated period charm, this fine hotel promises spacious rooms with antique furnishings, polished wooden floors and pretty balconies; those on the 4th floor are more modern.

Hotel Jacobeo HOTEL €

(☎947 26 01 02; www.hoteljacobeo.com; Calle de San Juan 24; s/d incl breakfast €47/58; 🚭 ❄ 📶) This stylish small hotel has gleaming rooms of burgundy-and-white washed walls, terracotta tiles and parquet floors. Bathrooms are well equipped, if on the small side.

Hotel Meson del Cid HISTORIC HOTEL €€

(☎947 20 87 15; www.mesondelcid.es; Plaza de Santa María 8; s/d €70/100; P 🚭 ❄ 📶) Housed in the oldest nonmunicipal building in the city (dating from 1483), the rooms have burgundy-and-cream fabrics, aptly combined with dark wood furnishings and terracotta tiles. Most have stunning front-row views of the cathedral. The dated bathrooms are due for a slick makeover in 2011.

TOP CHOICE **Cervecería Morito** TAPAS €

(Calle de la Sombrerería 27; tapas €3, raciones €5-7) Cervecería Morito is the undisputed king of Burgos tapas bars and it's always crowded. A typical order is *alpargata* (lashings of cured ham with bread, tomato and olive oil) or *calamares fritos* (fried calamari).

La Fabula MODERN CASTILIAN €€

(☎947 26 30 92; Calle de la Puebla 18; menú del día €15, meals €25-30) With local celebrity chef Isabel Alvarez at the helm, fabulous La Fabula offers innovative slimmed-down dishes in a bright, modern dining room filled with classical music.

ℹ️ Information

Municipal tourist office (www.aytoburgos.es, in Spanish; Plaza del Rey Fernando 2; ☺10am-2pm & 4.30-7.30pm Mon-Fri, 10am-1.30pm & 4-7.30pm Sat & Sun)

Regional tourist office (www.turismocastillay leon.com; Plaza de Alonso Martínez 7; ☺9am-8pm Sun-Thu, 9am-9pm Fri & Sat)

ℹ️ Getting There & Away

BUS From Burgos' **bus station** (Calle de Miranda 4) regular buses run to Madrid (€16.25, 2¾ hours), Bilbao (€11.86, two hours) and León (€14.10, 3¾ hours).

TRAIN Burgos is connected to Madrid (from €25.60, four hours, up to seven daily), Bilbao (from €18.70, three hours, five daily), León (from €20.10, two hours, four daily) and Salamanca (from €20.90, 2½ hours, three daily).

CASTILLA-LA MANCHA

Known as the stomping ground of Don Quijote and Sancho Panza, Castilla-La Mancha conjures up images of lonely windmills, medieval castles and bleak, treeless plains. The characters of Miguel de Cevantes provide the literary context, but the richly historic cities of Toledo and Cuenca are the most compelling reasons to visit.

Toledo

POP 82,300

Toledo is Spain's equivalent of a downsized Rome. Commanding a hill rising above the Tajo River, it's crammed with monuments that attest to the waves of conquerors and communities – Roman, Visigoth, Jewish, Muslim and Christian – who have called the city home during its turbulent history. It's one of the country's major tourist attractions.

◉ Sights

TOP CHOICE **Catedral de Toledo** CHURCH
(Plaza del Ayuntamiento; adult/child €7/free; ☺10.30am-6.30pm Mon-Sat, 2-6.30pm Sun) Toledo's cathedral dominates the skyline, reflecting the city's historical significance as the heart of Catholic Spain. Within its hefty stone walls there are stained-glass windows, tombs of kings, and art in the sacristy by the likes of El Greco, Zurbarán, Crespi, Titian, Rubens and Velázquez. Behind the main altar lies a mesmerising piece of 18th-century Churrigueresque baroque, the **Transparente**. Look out for the **Custodia de Arfe**, by the celebrated 16th-century goldsmith Enrique de Arfe. With 18kg of pure gold and 183kg of silver, this 16th-century conceit bristles with some 260 statuettes.

Sinagoga del Tránsito SYNAGOGUE
(www.museosefardi.net, in Spanish; Calle Samuel Leví; adult/child €2.40/1.20, audioguide €3; ☺10am-9pm Tue-Sat, 10am-2pm Sun) Toledo's former *judería* (Jewish quarter) was once home to 11 synagogues. Tragically, the bulk of Toledo's Jews were expelled in 1492. This magnificent synagogue was built in 1355 by special permission of Pedro I (construction of synagogues was prohibited in Christian Spain). The synagogue now houses the **Museo Sefardi** (☺10am-9pm Tue-Sat, 10am-2pm Sun).

San Juan de los Reyes MONASTERY
(Calle San Juan de los Reyes 2; admission €2.30; ☺10am-6pm) North of the synagogues lies the early-17th-century Franciscan monastery and church of San Juan de los Reyes, notable for its delightful cloisters. Provocatively built in the heart of the Jewish quarter, the monastery was founded by Isabel and Fernando to demonstrate the supremacy of the Catholic faith. The rulers had planned to be buried here but, when they took the greater prize of Granada in 1492 they opted for the purpose-built Capilla Real. Throughout the church and cloister the coat of arms of Isabel and Fernando dominates, and the chains of Christian prisoners liberated in Granada dangle from the outside walls. The prevalent late-Flemish Gothic style is enhanced with lavish Isabelline ornament, counterbalanced by Mudéjar decoration.

Sinagoga de Santa María La Blanca
SYNAGOGUE
(Calle de los Reyes Católicos 4; admission €2.30; ☺10am-6pm) This more modest synagogue is characterised by the horseshoe arches that delineate the five naves – classic Almohad architecture.

FREE **Museo de Santa Cruz** MUSEUM
(Calle de Cervantes 3; ☺10am-6.30pm Mon-Sat, 10am-2pm Sun) Just off the Plaza de Zocodover, the 16th-century Museo de Santa Cruz is a beguiling combination of Gothic and Spanish Renaissance styles. The cloisters and carved wooden ceilings are superb, as are the upstairs displays of Spanish ceramics. The ground-level gallery contains a number of El Grecos, a painting attributed to Goya (*Cristo Crucificado*) and

the wonderful 15th-century *Tapestry of the Astrolabes*.

Iglesia de Santo Tomé CHURCH
(www.santotome.org; Plaza del Conde; admission €2.30; ☺10am-6pm) This otherwise modest church contains El Greco's masterpiece, *El Entierro del Conde de Orgaz* (The Burial of the Count of Orgaz). When the count was buried in 1322, Saints Augustine and Stephen supposedly descended from heaven to attend the funeral. El Greco's work depicts the event, complete with miracle guests including himself, his son and Cervantes.

Mezquita del Cristo de la Luz MOSQUE
(Cuesta de Carmelitas Descalzos 10; admission €1.90; ☺2-8pm Fri, 10am-2pm & 3-8pm Sat & Sun) On the northern slopes of town you'll find a modest, yet beautiful, mosque. Built in the 10th century, it suffered the usual fate of being converted to a church (hence the religious frescos), but the original vaulting and arches survived.

🛏 Sleeping

Accommodation is often full, especially from Easter to September.

TOP CHOICE Casa de Cisneros BOUTIQUE HOTEL €€
(☏925 22 88 28; www.hostal-casa-de-cisneros.com; Calle del Cardenal Cisneros; s/d €50/80; ☻✳🛜) Across from the cathedral, this seductive hotel is built on the site of an 11th-century Islamic palace, parts of which can be spied via a glass porthole in the lobby floor. In comparison, this building is a 16th-century youngster with pretty stone-and-wood-beamed rooms and voguish en suite bathrooms.

Hostal Santo Tomé BUDGET HOTEL €
(☏925 22 17 12; www.hostalsantotome.com; Calle de Santo Tomé 13; s/d €42/55; P✳) This good-value *hostal,* above a souvenir shop, has larger-than-most rooms with pale-wood floors and furniture, plus bathrooms with five-star attitude offering extras like shoe polish and hairdryers.

Hostal del Cardenal HISTORIC HOTEL €€
(☏925 22 49 00; www.hostaldelcardenal.com; Paseo de Recaredo 24; s/d €77/113; P✳🛜) A wonderful 18th-century mansion with soft ochre-coloured walls, arches and columns. The rooms are grand, yet welcoming, with dark furniture, plush fabrics and parquet floors. Several overlook the glorious terraced gardens.

La Posada de Manolo BOUTIQUE HOTEL €€
(☏925 28 22 50; www.laposadademanolo.com; Calle de Sixto Ramón Parro 8; s/d incl breakfast €42/66; ✳🛜) This memorable hotel has themed each floor with furnishings and decor reflecting one of the three cultures of Toledo: Christian, Islamic and Jewish. There are stunning views of the old town and cathedral from the terrace.

Parador Nacional Conde de Orgaz
HISTORIC HOTEL €€€
(☏925 22 18 50; www.parador.es; Cerro del Emperador; s/d €171/159; P✳🛜✳) High above the southern bank of Río Tajo, Toledo's low-rise *parador* boasts a classy interior and breathtaking city views. To get here, cross the Puente de Alcántara bridge and follow the signs.

🍴 Eating

TOP CHOICE Aurelio TRADITIONAL SPANISH €€€
(☏925 22 13 92; Plaza del Ayuntamiento 4; meals €35-45; ☺lunch & dinner Tue-Sat, lunch Mon) The three restaurants under this name are among the best of Toledo's top-end eateries (the other locations are Calle de la Sinagoga 1 and 6). Game, fresh produce and traditional dishes are prepared with panache. Reservations recommended.

Alfileritos 24 MODERN INTERNATIONAL €€
(www.alfileritos24.com; Calle de los Alfileritos 24; meals €25-35; ☻) The 14th-century surroundings of columns, beams and barrel-vault ceilings are snazzily coupled with modern artwork and bright dining rooms spread over four floors. The menu demonstrates an innovative flourish in the kitchen.

La Abadía LIGHT DISHES €€
(www.abadiatoledo.com; Plaza de San Nicolás 3; meals €25-30; ☏) In a former 16th-century palace, this atmospheric bar and restaurant has arches, niches and subtle lighting spread over a warren of brick-and-stone-clad rooms. The menu includes various lightweight dishes like *verduras a la parrilla* (grilled fresh vegetables) – perfect for small appetites.

Palacios TRADITIONAL SPANISH €
(Calle Alfonso X el Sabio 3; menú €13.90, meals €14-18) An unpretentious place where stained glass, beams and efficient old-fashioned service combine with traditional no-nonsense cuisine. Hungry? Try a gut-busting bowl of homestyle *judías con perdiz* (white beans with partridge) for starters.

Toledo

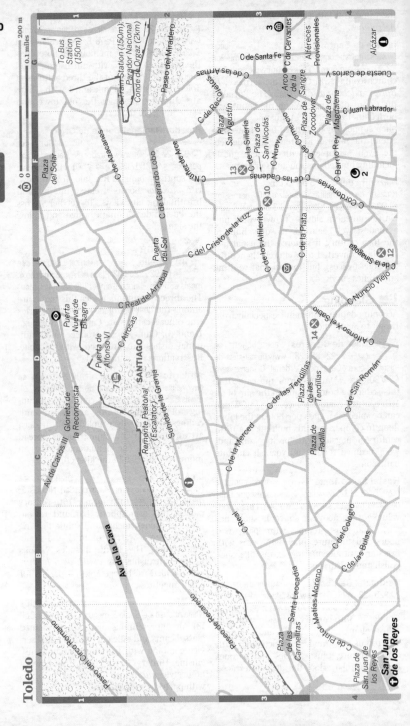

To Bus Station (150m)

To Tram Station (150m);
Parador Nacional
Conde de Orgaz (2km)

Paseo del Miradero

C de Santa Fe   C de Cervantes
Alféreces
Provisionales

Alcázar

Arco ● C de la
Sangre

Cuesta de Carlos V

C de las Armas
C de Recoletos

Plaza
San Agustín

C de la Sillería
Plaza de
San Nicolás

C Nueva

Plaza de
Zocodover

Plaza de
Comercio

C de
Barrio Rey Magdalena

C Juan Labrador

C Núñez de Arce

C de las Cadenas

C de Cordonerías

Plaza del Solar

C de Azacanes

C de Gerardo Lobo

Puerta
del Sol

C del Cristo de la Luz

C de los Alfileritos

C de la Plata

C de la Sinagoga

C de Nuncio Viejo

C Real del Arrabal

Puerta
Nueva de Bisagra

Puerta de
Alfonso VI

C Airosas

SANTIAGO

C Alfonso x el Sabio

Remonte Peatonal
(Escalator)

Subida de la Granja

C de las Tendillas
Plaza de
las Tendillas

C de San Román

Av de Carlos III

Glorieta de
la Reconquista

Paseo del Circo Romano

Av de la Cava

Paseo de Recaredo

C de la Merced

Plaza de
Padilla

C del Colegio

C Real

C de las Bulas

Plaza de las
Carmelitas

Santa Leocadia

C de Pintor Matías Moreno

Plaza de
San Juan de
los Reyes

San Juan
de los Reyes

200 m
0.1 miles

ⓘ Information

Main tourist office (www.toledoturismo.com; Plaza del Ayuntamiento; ☉10.30am-2.30pm Mon, 10.30am-2.30pm & 4.30-7pm Tue-Sun)

Provincial tourist office (www.diputoledo.es; Subida de la Granja; ☉10am-5pm Mon-Sat, 10am-3pm Sun)

ⓘ Getting There & Away

For most major destinations, you'll need to backtrack to Madrid.

BUS From Toledo's **bus station** (Avenida de Castilla La Mancha), buses depart for Madrid (from €5.25, one to 1½ hours) every half-hour from 6am to 10pm daily (less often on Sunday). There are also services on weekdays and Sunday to Cuenca (€11.40, 2¼ hours).

TRAIN The high-speed AVE service runs every hour or so to Madrid (€9.90, 30 minutes).

Cuenca

POP 53,000

A World Heritage site, Cuenca is one of Spain's most memorable small cities, its old centre a stage set of evocative medieval buildings. Most emblematic are the *casas colgadas,* the hanging houses.

◉ Sights & Activities

Casas Colgadas   HISTORIC BUILDINGS

TOP CHOICE Cuenca's *casas colgadas* jut out precariously over the steep defile of Río Huécar. Dating from the 16th century, the houses with their layers of wooden balconies seem to emerge from the rock as if an extension of the cliffs. One of the finest restored examples now houses the **Museo de Arte Abstracto Español** (Museum of Abstract Art; www.march. es; adult/child €3/free; ☉11am-2pm & 4-6pm Tue-Fri, 11am-2pm & 4-8pm Sat, 11am-2.30pm Sun), an impressive contemporary art museum, whose constantly evolving displays include works by Chillida, Tàpies, Millares and the extraordinary landscapes by Eusebio Sempere (1924–85), which really capture the colourful patterned plains of La Mancha. For the best views of the *casas colgadas,* cross the **Puente de San Pablo** footbridge, or walk to the **mirador** at the northernmost tip of the old town.

Museo de la Semana Santa   MUSEUM
(Calle Andrés de Cabrera; adult/child €3/free; ☉11am-2pm & 4.30-7.30pm Wed-Sat; ⊕) The next best thing to experiencing Semana Santa (Easter) first-hand, spread over two floors are audiovisual displays showing the

Toledo

processions by local brotherhoods, against a background of sombre music.

🛏 Sleeping

TOP CHOICE Posada de San José

HISTORIC HOTEL **€**

(☑969 21 13 00; www.posadasanjose.com; Ronda de Julián Romero 4; s/d without bathroom €30/43, d from €82) Owned by Antonio and his Canadian wife, Jennifer, this 17th-century former choir school retains an extraordinary monastic charm with its labyrinth of rooms, crumbling portal, uneven floors and original tiles. The cheaper rooms are in the former priests' cells, while the more costly doubles combine homey comfort with sumptuous old-word charm. Several have balconies with dramatic views of the gorge.

Hostal San Pedro BUDGET HOTEL **€**

(☑969 23 45 43, 628 407601; www.hostalsanpedro. es; Calle San Pedro 34; s/d €35/60) At this well-priced and well-positioned *hostal,* rooms have butter-coloured paintwork, wrought-iron bed heads and rustic wood furniture; the bathrooms are shiny and modern. The owners live elsewhere, so be sure to call before you show up.

Parador HISTORIC HOTEL **€€**

(☑969 23 23 20; www.parador.es; Calle de Hoz de Huécar; d €143; **P**✻) This majestic former convent commands stunning views of the *casas colgadas.* The aesthetically revamped rooms have a luxury corporate feel, while the public areas are headily historic with giant tapestries and antiques.

🍴 Eating

TOP CHOICE La Bodeguilla de Basilio TAPAS **€**

(Calle Fray Luis de León 3; raciones €10-13; ☺lunch & dinner Mon-Sat, lunch Sun) Arrive here with an appetite, as you're presented with a complimentary plate of tapas when you order a drink, and not just a slice of dried-up cheese – typical freebies are a combo of quail eggs, ham, fried potatoes, lettuce hearts and courgettes.

TOP CHOICE Manolo de la Osa

TRADITIONAL SPANISH **€€€**

(☑969 21 95 12; Calle Río Gritos 5, Cerro Molina; meals €40-50) Run by celebrated chef Manuel de la Osa, who creates unique dishes using traditional local ingredients like red partridge salad with butter beans and oyster mushrooms. The decor is suitably elegant. Reservations essential.

Mesón Casas Colgadas

TRADITIONAL SPANISH **€€**

(☑969 22 35 52; Calle de los Canónigos 3; meals €25-35, menú €27) Housed in one of the *casas colgadas,* Cuenca's gourmet pride and joy fuses an amazing location with delicious traditional food on the menu, such as venison stew and the quaintly translated *boned little pork hands stew* (pigs trotters stew!). Reservations recommended.

ℹ️ Information

Main tourist office (www.aytocuenca.org, in Spanish; Plaza Mayor; ☺9am-9pm Mon-Sat, 9am-2.30pm Sun)

Tourist office (Plaza Hispanidad; ☺10am-2pm & 5-8pm Mon-Thu, 10am-8pm Fri-Sun)

ℹ️ Getting There & Away

BUS Services include up to seven buses daily to Madrid (€13.48, two hours).

TRAIN Trains run to Madrid (€11.75, 2½ hours, four to six daily) and Valencia (€12.95, 3¼ hours, four daily).

CATALONIA

Home to stylish Barcelona, ancient Tarragona, romantic Girona, and countless alluring destinations along the coast, in the Pyrenees and in the rural interior, Catalonia (Catalunya in Catalan, Cataluña in Castilian) is a treasure box waiting to be opened.

Barcelona

POP 1.62 MILLION

Barcelona is one of Europe's coolest cities. Despite two millennia of history it's a forward-thinking place, always on the cutting edge of art, design and cuisine. Whether you explore its medieval palaces and plazas, gawk at the Modernista masterpieces, shop for designer duds along its bustling boulevards, sample its exciting nightlife or just soak up the sun on the beaches, you'll find it hard not to fall in love with this vibrant city.

As much as Barcelona is a visual feast, it will also lead you into culinary temptation. Anything from traditional Catalan cooking through the latest in avant-garde new Spanish cuisine will have your appetite in overdrive.

Central Plaça de Catalunya marks the divide between historic and modern Barcelona. From here, the pedestrian boulevard La Rambla shoots southeast to the sea, with the busy Barri Gòtic (Gothic Quarter) and El Raval districts hugging it on either side. To the northwest spreads L'Eixample, laced with Modernista marvels and endless shopping and dining options.

◉ Sights & Activities

La Rambla   HISTORIC AREA

Spain's most famous boulevard, the part-pedestrianised La Rambla, explodes with life. Stretching from **Plaça de Catalunya** (Map p828) to the waterfront, it's lined with street artists, newsstands and vendors selling everything from mice to magnolias.

The colourful **Mercat de la Boqueria** (Map p828; La Rambla; ⊙8am-8pm Mon-Sat; Ⓜ Liceu), a fresh food market with a Modernista entrance, is one of La Rambla's highlights. Nearby, stop for a tour of the **Gran Teatre del Liceu** (Map p828; 🖉93 485 99 14; www.liceu barcelona.com; La Rambla dels Caputxins 51-59; admission with/without guide €8.70/4; ⊙guided tour 10am, unguided visits 11.30am, noon, 12.30pm & 1pm; Ⓜ Liceu), the city's fabulous opera house.

Also stop at the **Plaça Reial** (Map p828; Ⓜ Liceu), a grand 19th-century square surrounded by arcades lined with restaurants and bars. At the waterfront end of La Rambla stands the **Mirador de Colom** (Map p828; Ⓜ Drassanes), a statue of Columbus atop a tall pedestal.

Barri Gòtic   HISTORIC AREA

Barcelona's Gothic **Catedral** (Map p828; Plaça de la Seu; admission free, special visit €5; ⊙8am-12.45pm & 5.15-8pm, special visit 1-5pm Mon-Sat, 2-5pm Sun & holidays; Ⓜ Jaume I) was built atop the ruins of an 11th-century Romanesque church. Highlights include the cool cloister, the crypt tomb of martyr Santa Eulàlia (one of Barcelona's two patron saints), the choir stalls (€2.20), the lift to the rooftop (€2.20) and the modest art collection in the **Sala Capitular** (chapterhouse; admission €2). You only pay the individual prices if you visit outside the special visiting hours.

Not far from the cathedral is pretty **Plaça del Rei** and the fascinating **Museu d'Història de Barcelona** (Map p828; www.museuhistoria.bcn.cat; Carrer del Veguer; adult/senior & student/child under 7yr €7/5/free, free for all from 4pm 1st Sat of month & from 3pm Sun; ⊙10am-8pm Tue-Sun, to 3pm holidays; Ⓜ Jaume I), where you can visit a 4000-sq-metre excavated site of Roman Barcelona under the plaza. The museum encompasses historic buildings including the **Palau Reial Major** (Main Royal Palace), once a residence of the kings of Catalonia and Aragón, and its **Saló del Tinell** (Great Hall).

The area between Carrer dels Banys Nous, to the east of the church, and Plaça de Sant Jaume is known as the Call, and was Barcelona's **Jewish quarter** from at least the 11th century until anti-Semitism saw the Jews expelled from it in 1424. Here the sparse remains of what is purported to be the medieval **Sinagoga Major** (Main Synagogue; Map p828; www.calldebarcelona.org; Carrer de Marlet 5; admission by €2 donation; ⊙10.30am-6pm Mon-Fri, to 3pm Sat & Sun; Ⓜ Liceu) have been revealed.

El Raval   NEIGHBOURHOOD

To the west of La Rambla is El Raval district, a once-seedy, now-funky area overflowing with cool bars and shops. Visit the **Museu d'Art Contemporani de Barcelona** (Macba; Map p828; 🖉93 412 08 10 www.macba.cat; Plaça dels Àngels 1; adult/concession €7.50/6; ⊙11am-8pm Mon & Wed, to midnight Thu-Fri, 10am-8pm Sat, 10am-3pm Sun & holidays; Ⓜ Universitat), which has an impressive collection of international contemporary art.

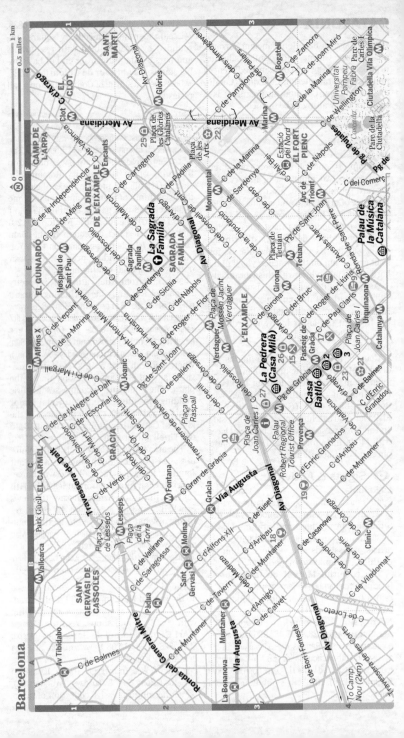

SPAIN CATALONIA

Barcelona

0   1 km
0   0.5 miles

SANT MARTÍ

EL CLOT

CAMP DE L'ARPA

Av d'Aragó

C d'Aragó

Clot (M)

Av Meridiana

Glòries (M)

Av Diagonal

Plaça de les Glòries Catalanes

C de València

25

LA DRETA DE L'EIXAMPLE

EL GUINARDÓ

C de la Independència

Encants

C de Cartagena

C de Dos de Maig

C de Padilla

Plaça de les Arts

C de la Marina

C de Zamora

C de Joan Miró

Parc de Carles I

Bogatell (M)

C de la Marina

Ciutadella Vila Olímpica

C de Pamplona

Av Meridiana

Marina (M)

C de la Marina

C de Wellington

Pompeu Fabra

Parc de Carles I

Hospital de Sant Pau

Sagrada Família

La Sagrada Família

SAGRADA FAMÍLIA

C de Mallorca

C del Rosselló

C de Sardenya

C de Sicília

C de Nàpols

C del Consell de Cent

Av Diagonal

Monumental (M)

C de Sardenya

C de Sardenya

C de Nàpols

Arc de Triomf (M)

C del Comerç

Estació del Nord

EL FORT PIENC

Alfons X (M)

C de Lepant

C de la Marina

C de Sant Antoni Maria Claret

Joanic (M)

C de Pi i Margall

C de Còrsega

Pg de Sant Joan

C de Bailèn

Plaça de Mossèn Jacint Verdaguer

Verdaguer (M)

C de Roger de Flor

Plaça de Tetuan

Pg de Sant Joan

Tetuan (M)

Arc de Triomf

Pg de Pujades

Palau de la Música Catalana

L'EIXAMPLE

C de Girona

C de Girona

Girona (M)

C del Bruc

C de Roger de Llúria

C de Pau Claris

Urquinaona (M)

11

Catalunya (M)

GRÀCIA

EL CARMEL

Travessera de Dalt

Parc Güell

C de Ca l'Alegre de Dalt

C de l'Escorial

C de Sant Lluís

C de Verdi

C del Torrent de l'Olla

C del Perill

Plaça de Raspall

C de Còrsega

Pg de Gràcia

27

La Pedrera (Casa Milà)

26

15

Diputació

17

Casa Batlló

2

3

23

21

Gràcia (M)

Passeig de Gràcia (M)

Plaça de Joan Carles I

C de Balmes

C d'Enric Granados

C de València

Travessera de Gràcia

10

Plaça de Joan Carles I

Palau Robert Regional Tourist Office

Provença (M)

C d'Enric Granados

Fontana (M)

Gran de Gràcia

C de Verdi

Gràcia (K)

Via Augusta

Av Diagonal

Provença

19

C de Muntaner

C d'Aribau

Clínic (M)

SANT GERVASI DE CASSOLES

Vallcarca (M)

Plaça de Lesseps

Lesseps (M)

Plaça de la Torre

C de Saragossa

C de Vallirana

Molina (K)

Sant Gervasi (K)

C d'Alfons XII

C de Muntaner

18

C dels Madrazo

C d'Aribau

C de Casanova

C de Londres

C de París

C de Còrsega

C de París

C de Viladomat

Av Tibidabo (K)

Ronda del General Mitre

C de Balmes

La Bonanova (K)

Pàdua (K)

C de Muntaner

Muntaner (K)

C de Tavern

Via Augusta

C d'Amigó

C de Calvet

C de Bori i Fontestà

Av Diagonal

C de Loreto

C de les Corts

Travessera de les Corts

To Camp Nou (2km)

4. To Camp Nou (2km)

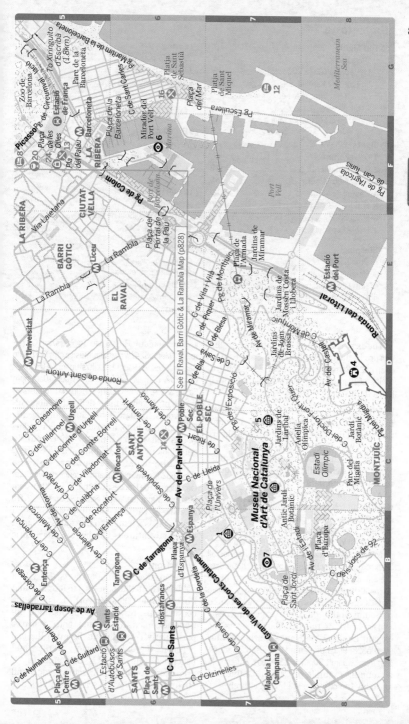

5 6 7 8

G

F

E

D

C

B

A

5 6 7 8

Zoo de Barcelona

To Xiringuito d'Escribà (1.8km)

Pg de Circumval·lació

Pg Martitim de la Barceloneta

Parc de la Barceloneta

Estació de França

Picasso

Plaça de les Olles

Pla del Palau

LA RIBERA

C de Sant Carles

Plaça de la Barceloneta

LA BARCELONETA

Platja de Sant Sebastià

Plaça del Mar

Platja de Sant Miquel

Mediterranean Sea

Pg Escullera

CIUTAT VELLA

Via Laietana

Pg de Colom

Port de Barcelona

Mirador del Port Vell

Mirama

Port Vell

Pg de l'Agricola de Can Tunis

LA RIBERA

BARRI GÒTIC

Liceu

La Rambla

Plaça del Portal de la Pau

Plaça de l'Armada

Jardins de Miramar

Jardins de Mossèn Costa i Llobera

Estació del Port

Ronda del Litoral

Estació del Litoral

La Rambla

EL RAVAL

La Rambla

See El Raval, Barri Gòtic & La Rambla Map (p828)

C de Vilar i Vila

Pg de Montjuïc

C de Piquer

Av de Miramar

Jardins de Joan Brossa

Universitat

C de Blesa

C de Blai

C de Salvà

Ronda de Sant Antoni

EL POBLE SEC

Pg de l'Exposició

Av del Castell

MONTJUÏC

C de Casanova

C de Villarroel

C del Comte d'Urgell

Urgell

Rocafort

SANT ANTONI

C de Tamarit

C de Manso

Poble Sec

C de Ricart

Jardins de Laribal

Aриella Olímpica

Estadi Olímpic

Jardi Botànic

Av del Paral·lel

C de Calàbria

C de Viladomat

C del Comte Borrell

C de Vallença

C de Rocafort

C d'Entença

C de Lleida

Museu Nacional d'Art de Catalunya

Antic Jardí Botànic

Parc del Migdia

Jardí Botànic

C del Doctor Font i Quer

C de Numància

C de Bailèn

C de Guitard

Estació d'Autobusos de Sants

Sants Estació

Plaça de Sants

SANTS

C de Sants

C de Coll del Rec

C de Còrsega

Entença

C de Provença

C de Mallorca

C de València

C de Sepúlveda

Plaça d'Espanya

Espanya

Plaça de l'Univers

Plaça d'Europa

Plaça de Sant Jordi

Av de l'Estadi

Estadi Olímpic

C dels Jocs de 92

Av de Josep Tarradellas

Estació

Hostafrancs

Tarragona

Plaça del Centre

Plaça de Sants

C de Tarragona

Gran Via de les Corts Catalanes

C de la Bordeta

C de Gavà

Magòria La Campana

C d'Olzinelles

Barcelona

The best example of Romanesque architecture in the city, **Església de Sant Pau** (Map p828; Carrer de Sant Pau 101; admission free; ☉cloister 10am-1pm & 4-7pm Mon-Sat; Ⓜ Paral.lel) has a dainty little cloister.

La Ribera NEIGHBOURHOOD
In medieval days, La Ribera was a stone's throw from the Mediterranean and the heart of Barcelona's foreign trade, with homes belonging to numerous wealthy merchants. Now it's a trendy district full of boutiques, restaurants and bars.

A series of palaces where some of those wealthy merchants lived now house the **Museu Picasso** (Map p828; www.museupicasso.bcn.es; Carrer de Montcada 15-23; adult/student/senior & child under 16yr €9/6/free, temporary exhibitions adult/student €5.80/2.90, free for all 3-8pm Sun & all day 1st Sun of month; ☉10am-8pm Tue-Sun & holidays; Ⓜ Jaume I), home to more than 3000 Picassos, most from early in the artist's career. This is one of the most visited museums in the country, so expect queues.

The heart of the neighbourhood is the elegant **Església de Santa Maria del Mar** (Map p828; Plaça de Santa Maria del Mar; admission free; ☉9am-1.30pm & 4.30-8pm; Ⓜ Jaume I), a stunning example of Catalan Gothic and arguably the city's most elegant church.

The opulent **Palau de la Música Catalana** (Map p824; www.palaumusica.org; Carrer de Sant Francesc de Paula 2; adult/student & EU senior/child €12/10/free; ☉hourly 50min tours 10am-6pm Easter & Aug, 10am-3.30pm Sep-Jul; Ⓜ Urquinaona) is one of the city's most delightful Modernista works. Designed by Lluís Domènech i Montaner in 1905, it hosts concerts regularly. It is well worth joining the guided tours to get a look inside if you don't make a concert.

Nearby, the **Mercat de Santa Caterina** (Map p828; www.mercatsantacaterina.net, in Catalan; Avinguda de Francesc Cambó 16; ☉7.30am-2pm Mon, to 3.30pm Tue, Wed & Sat, to 8.30pm Thu & Fri; Ⓜ Jaume I), with its loopily pastel-coloured wavy roof, is a temple to fine foods designed by the adventurous Catalan architect Enric Miralles.

Waterfront SEAFRONT
Barcelona has two major ports: **Port Vell** (Old Port), at the base of La Rambla, and **Port Olímpic** (Olympic Port), 1.5km up the coast. Shops, restaurants and nightlife options are plentiful around both marinas, particularly Port Olímpic. Between the two ports sits the onetime factory workers and fishermen's quarter, **La Barceloneta**. It preserves a delightfully scruffy edge and abounds with crowded seafood eateries.

At the end of Moll d'Espanya in Port Vell is **L'Aquàrium** (Map p824; www.aquarium bcn.com; Moll d'Espanya; adult/senior over 60yr/child 4-12yr/under 4yr €17.50/14.50/12.50/free; ⊙9.30am-11pm Jul & Aug; MDrassanes), with its 80m-long shark tunnel. Short of diving among them (which can be arranged), this is as close as you can get to a set of shark teeth without being bitten.

Barcelona boasts 4km of city *platjas* (beaches), beginning with the gritty **Platja de la Barceloneta** and continuing northeast, beyond Port Olímpic, with a series of cleaner, more attractive strands. All get packed in summer.

L'Eixample
NEIGHBOURHOOD

Modernisme, the Catalan version of art nouveau, transformed Barcelona's cityscape in the early 20th century. Most Modernista works were built in L'Eixample, the gridplan district that was developed from the 1870s on.

Modernisme's star architect was the eccentric Antoni Gaudí (1852–1926), a devout Catholic whose work is full of references to nature and Christianity. His masterpiece, **La Sagrada Família** (Expiatory Temple of the Holy Family; Map p824; ☑93 207 30 31; www.sagrada familia.org; Carrer de Mallorca 401; adult/senior & student/child to 10yr €12/10/free, combined with Casa-Museu Gaudí in Park Güell €14/12/free; ⊙9am-8pm Apr-Sep, to 6pm Oct-Mar; MSagrada Família), is a work in progress and Barcelona's most famous building. Construction began in 1882 and could be completed in 2020. Gaudí spent 40 years working on the church, though he only saw the crypt, the apse and the nativity facade completed. Eventually there'll be 18 towers, all more than 100m high, representing the 12 apostles, four evangelists and Mary, Mother of God, plus the tallest tower (170m) standing for Jesus Christ. Climb high inside some of

the towers (or take the elevator, €2) for a new perspective.

Gaudí's **La Pedrera** (Casa Milà; Map p824; www.fundaciocaixacatalunya.es; Carrer de Provença 261-265; adult/student & EU senior/child under 13yr €10/6/free; ⊙9am-8pm; MDiagonal) is his best-known secular creation, named (it translates as The Quarry) because of its uneven greystone facade, which ripples around the corner of Carrer de Provença. The wave effect is emphasised by elaborate wrought-iron balconies. Inside, you can visit a museum about Gaudí and his work, a Modernista apartment and the surreal rooftop with its bizarre chimneys.

Just down the street is the unique facade of the **Casa Batlló** (Map p824; www.casabatllo. es; Passeig de Gràcia 43; adult/student, child 7-18yr & senior/child under 7yr €17.80/14.25/free; ⊙9am-8pm; MPasseig de Gràcia), an allegory for the legend of St George (Sant Jordi in Catalan) the dragon-slayer. On the same block are two other Modernista gems, **Casa Amatller** (Passeig de Gràcia 41) by Josep Puig i Cadafalch and the **Casa Lleó Morera** (Passeig de Gràcia 35) by Lluís Domènech i Montaner.

High up in the Gràcia district sits Gaudí's enchanting **Park Güell** (Carrer d'Olot 7; admission free; ⊙10am-9pm; MLesseps or Vallcarca, ☐24), originally designed to be a self-contained community with houses, schools and shops. The project flopped, but we're left with a Dr Seuss–style playground filled with colourful mosaics and Gaudí-designed paths and plazas.

The website www.rutadelmodernisme. com is a great resource on Modernisme in Barcelona.

Montjuïc
NEIGHBOURHOOD

Southwest of the city centre and with views out to sea and over the city, Montjuïc serves as a Central Park of sorts and is a great place for a jog or stroll. It's dominated by the **Castell de Montjuïc** (Map p824), a one-time fortress with great views. Buses 50, 55 and 61 all head up here. A local bus, the PM (Parc de Montjuïc) line, does a circle trip from Plaça d'Espanya to the *castell*. Cable cars and a funicular line also access the area.

Museu Nacional d'Art de Catalunya (Map p824; www.mnac.cat; Mirador del Palau Nacional; adult/student/senior & child under 15yr €8.50/6/free, 1st Sun of month free; ⊙10am-7pm Tue-Sat, to 2.30pm Sun & holidays; MEspanya) is a broad panoply of Catalan and European art. The Romanesque frescos are truly stunning.

WANT MORE?

For in-depth information, reviews and recommendations at your fingertips, head to the Apple App Store to purchase Lonely Planet's *Barcelona City Guide* iPhone app.

Alternatively, head to **Lonely Planet** (www.lonelyplanet.com/spain/barcelona) for planning advice, author recommendations, traveller reviews and insider tips.

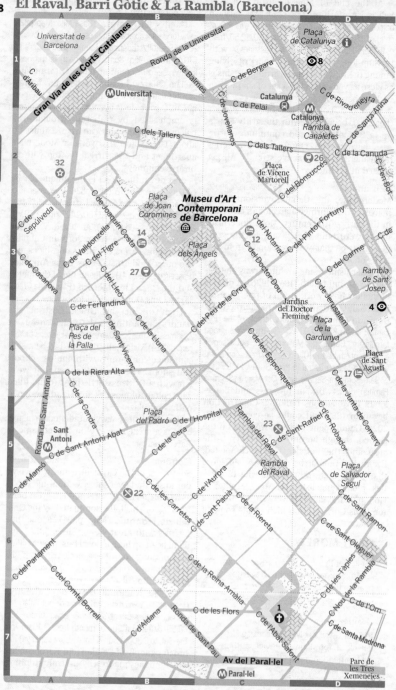

SPAIN CATALONIA

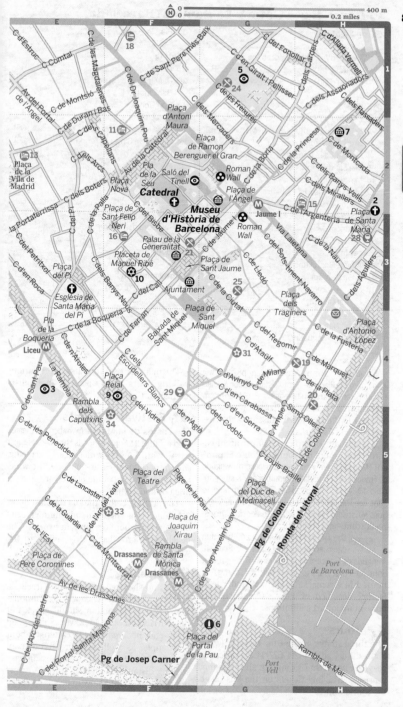

Fundació Joan Miró (Map p824; www.bcn.fjmiro.es; Plaça de Neptu; adult/senior & child €8.50/6, temporary exhibitions €4/3; ◎10am-8pm Tue-Wed, Fri & Sat, to 9.30pm Thu, to 2.30pm Sun & holidays) is the definitive museum showcasing Joan Miró's works.

A showcase of typical Spanish architecture from around the country, **Poble Espanyol** (Map p824; www.poble-espanyol.com; Avinguda de Francesc Ferrer i Guàrdia; adult/senior & student/child 4-12yr €8.50/6.50/5.50; ◎9am-8pm Mon, to 2am Tue-Thu, to 4am Fri, to 5am Sat, to midnight Sun; Ⓜ Espanya, ☒50, 61 or 193) has craft shops, restaurants and nightlife.

FREE **CaixaForum** (Map p824; www.fundacio.lacaixa.es, in Catalan & Spanish; Avinguda de Francesc Ferrer i Guàrdia 6-8; ◎10am-8pm Tue-Fri & Sun, to 10pm Sat; Ⓜ Espanya) is housed in a remarkable former Modernista factory designed by Puig i Cadafalch and puts on major art exhibitions.

☞ Tours

The three routes of the **Bus Turístic** (www.tmb.net; 1 day adult/4-12yr €22/14, 2 consecutive days €29/18; ◎9am-7.30pm) link all the major tourist sights. Buy tickets on the bus or at the tourist office.

The main tourist office also offers various **walking tours** (tours €12.50-19) in English, Spanish or Catalan.

✸ Festivals & Events

The **Festes de la Mercè** (www.bcn.cat/merce), held around 24 September, is the city's biggest party, with four days of concerts, dancing, *castellers* (human castle-builders), fireworks and *correfocs* – a parade of firework-spitting dragons and devils.

The evening before the **Dia de Sant Joan** (24 June) is a colourful midsummer celebration with bonfires and fireworks. The beaches are crowded with revellers to the wee hours.

🛏 Sleeping

There's no shortage of hotels in Barcelona. Those looking for cheaper accommodation close to the action should check out the Barri Gòtic and El Raval. Some good lower-end *pensiones* are scattered about L'Eixample, as well as a broad range of midrange and top-end places, most in easy striking distance of the Old Town. A growing range of options now makes it easier to stay in La Ribera and near the beaches at La Barceloneta.

Numerous private apartment-rental companies operate in Barcelona. These can often be a better deal than staying in a hotel. Start your search at **Aparteasy** (☎93 451 67 66; www.aparteasy.com), **Barcelona On Line** (☎902 887 017, 93 343 79 93; www.barcelona-on-line.es) and **Rent a Flat in Barcelona** (☎93 342 73 00; www.rentaflatinbarcelona.com).

LA RAMBLA & BARRI GÒTIC

Hotel Neri   HOTEL €€€
(Map p828; ☎93 304 06 55; www.hotelneri.com; Carrer de Sant Sever 5; d from €235; MLiceu; ❄@🛜) Occupying a beautifully adapted, centuries-old building, this stunningly renovated medieval mansion combines historic stone walls with sexy plasma TVs. Downstairs is a fine restaurant, and you can take a drink and catch some rays on the roof deck.

Alberg Hostel Itaca   HOSTEL €
(Map p828; ☎93 301 97 51; www.itacahostel.com; Carrer de Ripoll 21; dm €14-20, d €55; MJaume I; @🛜) A bright, quiet hostel near La Catedral, Itaca has spacious dorms (sleeping six, eight or 12 people), with parquet floors, spring colours and a couple of doubles with private bathroom.

Hostal Campi   BUDGET HOTEL €
(Map p828; ☎93 301 35 45; www.hostalcampi.com; Carrer de la Canuda 4; d €67, s/d without bathroom €34/57; MCatalunya) An excellent bottom-end deal. The best rooms are the doubles with their own loo and shower. Although basic, they are extremely roomy and bright.

EL RAVAL

Hotel San Agustín   HOTEL €€
(Map p828; ☎93 318 16 58; www.hotelsa.com; Plaça de Sant Agustí 3; s €123-144, d €171; MLiceu; ❄@🛜) Once an 18th-century monastery, this hotel opened in 1840, making it the city's oldest. The location is perfect: a quick stroll off La Rambla on a curious square. Rooms sparkle, are mostly spacious and light, and have parquet floors.

Hostal Gat Raval   BUDGET HOTEL €€
(Map p828; ☎93 481 66 70; www.gataccommod ation.com; Carrer de Joaquín Costa 44; d €82, s/d without bathroom €58/74; MUniversitat; ❄@🛜) There's a pea-green and lemon-lime colour scheme in this hip, young, 2nd-floor hostel-style lodgings deep in El Raval. Rooms are pleasant, secure and each is behind a green door, but only some have private bathroom.

Casa Camper   HOTEL €€€
(Map p828; ☎93 342 62 80; www.casacamper. com; Carrer d'Elisabets 11; s/d €228/255; MLiceu; ❄❄@) Run by the Mallorcan shoe people in the better end of El Raval, these designer digs offer rooms with a few surprises, like the Vinçon furniture. Across the corridor from each room is a separate, private sitting room, with balcony, TV and hammock.

LA RIBERA & LA BARCELONETA

[TOP CHOICE] Hotel Banys Orientals
                                       BOUTIQUE HOTEL €€
(Map p828; ☎93 268 84 60; www.hotelbanysori entals.com; Carrer de l'Argenteria 37; s/d €93/107; MJaume I; ❄@) Cool blues and aquamarines combine with dark-hued parquet floors to lend this boutique beauty an understated charm. All rooms – admittedly on the small side but impeccably presented – look onto the street or back lanes.

Chic & Basic   HOTEL €€
(Map p824; ☎93 295 46 52; www.chicandbasic .com; Carrer de la Princesa 50; s €96, d €132-171; MJaume I; ❄@) In a completely renovated building are 31 spotlessly white rooms. They have high ceilings, enormous beds (room types are classed as M, L and XL!) and lots of detailed touches (LED lighting, TFT TV screens and the retention of many beautiful old features of the original building, such as the marble staircase).

Pensió 2000   BUDGET HOTEL €
(Map p828; ☎93 310 74 66; www.pensio2000.com; Carrer de Sant Pere més Alt 6; s/d €52/65, without bathroom €35/45; MUrquinaona; @) Sitting in front of the Modernista chocolate box that is the Palau de la Música Catalana, this cheerful *pensión*, with its seven canary-yellow rooms, is a conveniently placed option. Two rooms (the pick) have their own bathroom. You can also take time out on the little terrace.

W Barcelona   HOTEL €€€
(Map p824; ☎93 295 28 00; www.w-barcelona .com; Plaça de la Rosa del Vents 1; r 283-385; MBar celoneta, 🚌17, 39, 57 or 64; P❄@🏊) In an admirable location at the end of a beach, this spinnaker-shaped glass tower offers all sorts of rooms. Guests flit between the gym, infinity pool (with bar) and Bliss@spa. There's avant-garde dining on the 2nd floor in the Bravo restaurant and hip cocktail sipping with stunning views in the Eclipse bar.

L'EIXAMPLE

TOP CHOICE **Hotel Constanza** BOUTIQUE HOTEL €€
(Map p824; 93 270 19 10; www.hotel constanza.com; Carrer del Bruc 33; s/d €110/130; MGirona or Urquinaona; ❄@) Constanza is a boutique belle that has stolen the heart of many a visitor to Barcelona. Even smaller singles are made to feel special with broad mirrors and strong colours (reds and yellows, with black furniture). Suites and studios are further options. The terrace is a nice spot to relax for a while, looking over the rooftops of L'Eixample.

Hostal Goya BUDGET HOTEL €€
(Map p824; 93 302 25 65; www.hostalgoya.com; Carrer de Pau Claris 74; s €70, d €96-113; MPasseig de Gràcia; ❄) The Goya is a gem of a spot on the chichi side of l'Eixample and a short stroll from Plaça de Catalunya. Rooms have parquet floors and a light colour scheme that varies from room to room. In the bathrooms, the original mosaic floors have largely been retained, combined with contemporary design features.

Hotel Casa Fuster HOTEL €€€
(Map p824; 93 255 30 00, 902 202345; www.ho telcasafuster.com; Passeig de Gràcia 132; s/d from €294/321; MDiagonal; P❄❄@❄❄) It is hard to believe the wrecking ball once threatened this Modernista mansion turned luxury hotel. Standard rooms are plush if smallish. Period features have been lovingly restored and complemented with hydromassage tubs and king-sized beds.

✗ Eating

Barcelona is foodie heaven. The city has firmly established itself as one of Europe's gourmet capitals, and innovative, cutting-edge restaurants abound. Some of the most creative chefs are one-time students of world-renowned chef Ferran Adrià, whose influence on the city's cuisine is strong.

Although Barcelona has a reputation as a hot spot of 'new Spanish cuisine', you'll still find local eateries serving up time-honoured local grub, from squid-ink *fideuà* (a satisfying paella-like noodle dish) through pigs' trotters, rabbit with snails, and *butifarra* (a tasty local sausage).

LA RAMBLA & BARRI GÒTIC

Skip the overpriced traps along La Rambla and get into the winding lanes of the Barri Gòtic.

Bar Celta TAPAS €€
(Map p828; 93 315 00 06; Carrer de la Mercè 16; meals €20-25; ❄noon-midnight Tue-Sun; MDrassanes) Specialists in *pulpo* (octopus) and other seaside delights from Galicia in the country's northwest; the waiters waste no time in serving up bottles of crisp white Ribeiro wine to wash down the *raciones*.

Agut CATALAN €€
(Map p828; 93 315 17 09; Carrer d'En Gignàs 16; meals €35; ❄lunch & dinner Tue-Sat, lunch Sun; ❄) Contemporary paintings set a contrast with the fine traditional Catalan dishes offered in this timeless restaurant. You might start with something like the *bouillabaisse con cigalitas de playa* (little seawater crayfish) for €11 and follow with an oak-grilled meat dish.

Pla MODERN SPANISH €€
(Map p828; 93 412 65 52; www.pla-repla.com; Carrer de Bellafila 5; meals €45-50; ❄dinner; ❄) In this modern den of inventive cooking with music worthy of a club, the chefs present deliciously strange combinations such as *bacallà amb salsa de pomes verdes* (cod in a green apple sauce). Exotic meats like kangaroo turn up on the menu too.

Can Conesa SNACKS €
(Map p828; 93 310 57 95; Carrer de la Llibreteria 1; rolls & toasted sandwiches €3-5; ❄Mon-Sat; MJaume I) This place has been doling out delicious *entrepans* (bread rolls with filling), frankfurters and toasted sandwiches here for more than 50 years – *barcelonins* swear by it and queue for them.

EL RAVAL

Bar Pinotxo TAPAS €€
(Map p828; Mercat de la Boqueria; meals €20; ❄6am-5pm Mon-Sat Sep-Jul; MLiceu) Of the half-dozen or so tapas bars and informal eateries within the market, this one near the Rambla entrance is about the most popular. Roll up to the bar and enjoy some people-watching as you munch on tapas assembled from the products on sale at the stalls around you.

Can Lluís CATALAN €€
(Map p828; 93 441 11 87; Carrer de la Cera 49; meals €30-35; ❄Mon-Sat Sep-Jul; MSant Antoni) Three generations have kept this spick-and-span old-time classic in business since 1929. Beneath the olive green beams in the back dining room you can see the spot where an anarchist's bomb went off in 1946, killing the then owner. Expect fresh fish and seafood.

Casa Leopoldo
CATALAN €€

(Map p828; ☎93 441 30 14; www.casaleopoldo.com; Carrer de Sant Rafael 24; meals €50; ☺lunch & dinner Tue-Sat, lunch Sun Sep-Jul; ☻) Several rambling dining areas with magnificent tiled walls and exposed timber-beam ceilings make this a fine option. The seafood menu is extensive and the local wine list strong. This is an old-town classic beloved of writers and artists down the decades.

LA RIBERA & WATERFRONT
La Barceloneta is the place to go for seafood; Passeig Joan de Borbó is lined with eateries but locals head for the back lanes.

TOP CHOICE Xiringuito d'Escribà
SEAFOOD

(off Map p824; ☎93 221 07 29; www.escriba.es; Ronda Litoral 42, Platja de Bogatell; meals €40-50; ☺lunch; Ⓜ Llacuna) The Barcelona pastry family serves up top-quality seafood at this popular waterfront eatery. This is one of the few places where one person can order from the selection of paella and *fideuá* (normally a minimum of two people).

Cal Pep
TAPAS €€

(Map p824; ☎93 310 79 61; www.calpep.com; Plaça de les Olles 8; meals €45-50; ☺lunch Tue-Sat, dinner Mon-Fri Sep-Jul; Ⓜ Barceloneta; ☻) It's getting a foot in the door here that's the problem. And if you want one of the five tables out the back, you'll need to call ahead. Most people are happy elbowing their way to the bar for some of the tastiest gourmet seafood tapas in town.

Les Cuines de Santa Caterina
INTERNATIONAL €€

(Map p828; ☎93 268 99 18; www.cuinessantacaterina.com; Mercat de Santa Caterina; meals €25-30; Ⓜ Jaume I; ☻☻) Peck at the sushi bar, tuck into classic rice dishes or go vegetarian in this busy market restaurant in the Mercat de Santa Caterina. A drawback is the speed with which they whisk barely finished plates away from you, but the range of dishes and bustling atmosphere are fun. It doesn't take reservations, so it's first come first served.

Suquet de l'Almirall
SEAFOOD €€

(Map p824; ☎93 221 62 33; Passeig de Joan de Borbó 65; meals €45-50; ☺lunch & dinner Tue-Sat, lunch Sun; Ⓜ Barceloneta, ☒17, 39, 57 or 64; ☻) A family business run by one of the acolytes of Ferran Adrià's El Bulli restaurant, the order of the day is top-class seafood. A good option is the pica pica marinera (a seafood mix; €38) or you could opt for the tasting menu (€44).

TOP CHOICE Tapaç 24
TAPAS €€

(Map p824; www.carlesabellan.com; Carrer de la Diputació 269; meals €30-35; ☺9am-midnight Mon-Sat; Ⓜ Passeig de Gràcia) Specials in this basement tapas temple include the *bikini* (toasted ham and cheese sandwich – here the ham is cured and the truffle makes all the difference!), a thick black *arròs negre de sípia* (squid ink black rice) and, for dessert, *xocolata amb pa, sal i oli* (delicious balls of chocolate in olive oil with a touch of salt and wafer).

Inopia
TAPAS €€

(Map p824; ☎93 424 52 31; www.barinopia.com; Carrer de Tamarit 104; meals €25-30; ☺dinner Tue-Sat, lunch Sat; Ⓜ Rocafort) Albert Adrià, brother of star chef Ferran, has his hands full with this constantly busy gourmet tapas temple. Select a *pintxo de cuixa de pollastre a l'ast* (chunk of rotisserie chicken thigh) or the lightly fried, tempura-style vegetables. Wash down with house red or Moritz beer.

Relais de Venise
MEAT €€

(Map p824; ☎93 467 21 62; Carrer de Pau Claris 142; meals €35; ☺Sep-Jul; Ⓜ Passeig de Gràcia; ☻) There's just one dish, a succulent beef entrecôte with a secret 'sauce Porte-Maillot' (named after the location of the original restaurant in Paris), chips and salad. It is served in slices and in two waves so that it doesn't go cold.

☷ Drinking

Barcelona abounds with day-time cafes, laid-back lounges and lively night-time bars. Closing time is generally 2am from Sunday to Thursday and 3am Friday and Saturday.

BARRI GÒTIC

TOP CHOICE Soul Club
MUSIC BAR

(Map p828; Carrer Nou de Sant Francesc 7; ☺10pm-2.30am Mon-Thu, to 3am Fri & Sat, 8pm-2.30am Sun; Ⓜ Drassanes) Each night the DJs change the musical theme, which ranges from deep funk to Latin grooves. The tiny front bar is for drinking and chatting (get in early for a stool or the sole lounge). Out back is where the dancing is done.

Marula Café
BAR

(Map p828; www.marulacafe.com; Carrer dels Escudellers 49; ☺11pm-5am Sun-Thu, to 5.30am Fri & Sat; Ⓜ Liceu) A fantastic new funk find in the heart of the Barri Gòtic, Marula will transport you to the 1970s and the best in black music, mostly funk and soul. James

Brown fans will think they've died and gone to heaven.

EL RAVAL

Boadas
COCKTAIL BAR

(Map p828; Carrer dels Tallers 1; ⊙noon-2am Mon-Thu, to 3am Fri & Sat; MCatalunya) Inside the unprepossessing entrance is one of the city's oldest cocktail bars (famed for its daiquiris). The bow-tied waiters have been serving up their poison since 1933; Joan Miró and Hemingway tippled here.

Casa Almirall
BAR

(Map p828; Carrer de Joaquín Costa 33; ⊙5.30pm-2.30am Sun-Thu, 7pm-3am Fri & Sat; MUniversitat) In business since the 1860s, this unchanged corner bar is dark and intriguing, with Modernista decor and a mixed clientele. There are some great original pieces in here, like the marble counter.

LA RIBERA

Gimlet
COCKTAIL BAR

(Map p824; Carrer del Rec 24; ⊙10pm-3am; MJaume l) White-jacketed bar staff with all the appropriate aplomb will whip you up a gimlet or any other classic cocktail (around €10) your heart desires. Barcelona cocktail guru Javier Muelas is behind this and several other cocktail bars around the city, so you can be sure of excellent drinks, some with a creative twist.

La Vinya del Senyor
WINE BAR

(Map p828; Plaça de Santa Maria del Mar 5; ⊙noon-1am Tue-Sun; MJaume l) The wine list is as long as *War and Peace*, and the terrace lies in the shadow of Santa Maria del Mar. You can crowd inside the tiny wine bar itself or take a bottle upstairs.

L'EIXAMPLE & GRÀCIA

Berlin
BAR

(Map p824; Carrer de Muntaner 240; ⊙10am-2am Mon-Wed, to 2.30am Thu, to 3am Fri & Sat; MDiagonal or Hospital Clínic) This elegant corner bar attracts waves of night animals starting up for a long night. In warmer weather you can sit outside on the footpath, or head downstairs into the basement if the bar's too crowded.

Dry Martini
COCKTAIL BAR

(Map p824; www.drymartinibcn.com; Carrer del Consell de Cent 247; ⊙5pm-3am; RFGC Provença) Well-dressed waiters serve up the best dry martini in town, or whatever else your heart desires, in this classic cocktail lounge. Sink into a leather lounge and nurse a huge G&T.

☆ Entertainment

To keep up with what's on, pick up a copy of the weekly listings magazine, *Guía del Ocio* (€1) from newsstands.

Nightclubs

Barcelona clubs are spread a little more thinly than bars across the city. They tend to open from around midnight until 6am. Entry can cost from nothing to €20 (one drink usually included).

TOP CHOICE Elephant
CLUB

(www.elephantbcn.com, in Spanish; Passeig dels Til.lers 1; Wed, Thu & Sun free, Fri & Sat €15; ⊙11.30pm-3am Wed, to 5am Thu-Sun; MPalau Reial; P) Getting in here is like being invited to some private Beverly Hills party. Models and wannabes mix freely, as do the drinks. A big tentlike dance space is the focus but mingle around the various garden bars too.

TOP CHOICE Terrrazza
CLUB

(Map p824; www.laterrrazza.com; Avinguda de Francesc Ferrer i Guàrdia; admission €10-20; ⊙midnight-5am Thu, to 6am Fri & Sat; MEspanya) One of the city's top summertime dance locations, Terrrazza attracts squadrons of the beautiful people, locals and foreigners alike, for a full-on night of music and cocktails partly under the stars inside the Poble Espanyol complex.

Moog
CLUB

(Map p828; www.masimas.com/moog; Carrer de l'Arc del Teatre 3; admission €10; ⊙midnight-5am; MDrassanes) This fun, minuscule club is a downtown hit. In the main downstairs dance area, DJs dish out house, techno and electro, while upstairs you can groove to indie and occasional classic pop.

Gay & Lesbian Venues

Barcelona's gay and lesbian scene is concentrated in the blocks around Carrers de Muntaner and Consell de Cent (dubbed Gayxample). Here you'll find ambience every night of the week in the bars, discos and drag clubs.

Party hard at classic gay discos such as **Arena Madre** (Map p824; www.arenadisco.com, in Spanish; Carrer de Balmes 32; MUniversitat) and **Metro** (Map p828; www.metrodiscobcn.com; Carrer de Sepúlveda 185; ⊙1am-5am Mon, midnight-5am Sun & Tue-Thu, midnight-6am Fri & Sat; MUniversitat).

Theatre

Most theatre in the city is in Catalan.

There are quite a few venues that stage vanguard drama and dance, including the

Teatre Nacional de Catalunya (Map p824; ☑93 306 57 00; www.tnc.cat; Plaça de les Arts 1; admission €12-32; ☺box office 3-7pm Wed-Fri, to 8.30pm Sat, to 5pm Sun & 1hr before show; Ⓜ Glòries or Monumental).

Live Music

 Harlem Jazz Club JAZZ
(Map p828; www.harlemjazzclub.es; Carrer de la Comtessa de Sobradiel 8; admission up to €10; ☺8pm-4am Tue-Thu & Sun, to 5am Fri & Sat; Ⓜ Drassanes) This narrow, smoky, old-town dive is one of the best spots in town for jazz. Every now and then it mixes it up with a little rock, Latin or blues. There are usually two sessions in an evening.

Sala Tarantos FLAMENCO
(Map p828; ☑93 319 17 89; www.masimas.net; Plaça Reial 17; admission from €7; ☺performances 8.30pm, 9.30pm & 10.30pm; Ⓜ Liceu) This basement locale is the stage for some of the best flamenco to pass through Barcelona.

Sport

FC Barcelona (Barça for aficionados) has one of the best stadiums in Europe – the 99,000-capacity **Camp Nou** (off Map p824; ☑902 189 900; Carrer d'Aristides Maillol; ☺box office 9am-1.30pm & 3.30-6pm Mon-Fri; Ⓜ Palau Reial or Collblanc) in the west of the city. Tickets for national-league games are available at the stadium, by phone or online. For the latter two options, nonmembers must book 15 days before the match.

Shopping

Most mainstream fashion stores are along a shopping 'axis' that runs from Plaça de Catalunya along Passeig de Gràcia, then left (west) along Avinguda Diagonal.

The El Born area in La Ribera is awash with tiny boutiques, especially those purveying young, fun fashion. There are plenty of shops scattered throughout the Barri Gòtic (stroll Carrer d'Avinyò and Carrer de Portaferrissa). For secondhand stuff, head for El Raval, especially Carrer de la Riera Baixa.

Joan Murrià FOOD & DRINK
(Map p824; www.murria.cat; Carrer de Roger de Llúria 85; Ⓜ Passeig de Gràcia) Ramon Casas designed the Modernista shop-front ads for this delicious delicatessen, where the shelves groan under the weight of speciality food from around Catalonia and beyond.

Els Encants Vells MARKET
('The Old Charms'; Map p824; www.encantsbcn.com, in Catalan; Plaça de les Glòries Catalanes;

7am-6pm Mon, Wed, Fri & Sat; Ⓜ Glòries) Bargain hunters love this free-for-all flea market.

Vinçon HOMEWARES
(Map p824; www.vincon.com; Passeig de Gràcia 96; ☺10am-8.30pm Mon-Sat; Ⓜ Diagonal) Vinçon has the slickest designs in furniture and household goods, local and imported. The building once belonged to the Modernista artist Ramon Casas.

Antonio Miró CLOTHING
(Map p824; www.antoniomiro.es, in Spanish; Carrer del Consell de Cent 349; ☺10am-8pm Mon-Sat; Ⓜ Passeig de Gràcia) Mr Miró is one of Barcelona's haute-couture kings. He concentrates on light, natural fibres to produce smart, unpretentious men's and women's fashion. High-end evening dresses and shimmering, smart suits lead the way.

Custo Barcelona CLOTHING
(Map p824; www.custo-barcelona.com; Plaça de les Olles 7; Ⓜ Jaume I) Custo bewitches people the world over with a youthful, psychedelic panoply of women's and men's fashion. It has several branches around town.

ⓘ Information

Dangers & Annoyances

Purse snatching and pickpocketing are major problems, especially around Plaça de Catalunya, La Rambla and Plaça Reial. See p902 for more information on general safety.

Emergency

Tourists who want to report thefts need to go to the Catalan police, known as the **Mossos d'Esquadra** (☑088; Carrer Nou de la Rambla 80), or the **Guàrdia Urbana** (Local Police; ☑092; La Rambla 43).

In an emergency, call ☑112.

Internet Access

Bornet (Carrer de Barra Ferro 3; per hr/10hr €2.80/20; ☺10am-11pm Mon-Fri, 2pm-11pm Sat & Sun & holidays; Ⓜ Jaume I) A cool little internet centre-cum-art gallery.

Medical Services

Call ☑010 to find the nearest late-opening duty pharmacy.

Farmàcia Clapés (La Rambla 98; Ⓜ Liceu)

Hospital Clínic i Provincial (☑93 227 54 00; Carrer de Villarroel 170; Ⓜ Hospital Clínic)

Money

Banks (with ATMs) and foreign-exchange offices abound in Barcelona. **Interchange** (Rambla dels Caputxins 74; ☺9am-11pm; Ⓜ Liceu) represents American Express.

SPAIN BARCELONA

Post
Main post office (Plaça d'Antoni López; ⊙8.30am-9.30pm Mon-Fri, to 2pm Sat; MJaume I)

Tourist Information
Oficina d'Informació de Turisme de Barcelona Main branch (www.barcelonaturisme.com; Plaça de Catalunya 17-S underground; ⊙9am-9pm); Aeroport del Prat (Terminals 1, 2B and 2A arrivals halls; ⊙9am-9pm); Estació Sants (⊙8am-8pm late Jun–late Sep, 8am-8pm Mon-Fri, 8am-2pm Sat, Sun & holidays Oct-May; MSants Estació); Town hall (Carrer de la Ciutat 2; ⊙9am-8pm Mon-Fri, 10am-8pm Sat, 10am-2pm Sun & holidays; MJaume I)

Regional tourist office (www.gencat.net/probert; Passeig de Gràcia 107; ⊙10am-7pm Mon-Sat, to 2.30pm Sun; MDiagonal)

ⓘ Getting There & Away
Air
Barcelona's airport, **El Prat de Llobregat** (☎902 404 704; www.aena.es), is 12km southwest of the city centre. Barcelona is a big international and domestic destination, with direct flights from North America as well as many European cities.

Boat
Regular passenger and vehicular ferries to/from the Balearic Islands, operated by **Acciona Trasmediterránea** (☎902 454 645; www.trasmediterranea.es), dock along both sides of the Moll de Barcelona wharf in Port Vell; see p905 for further information.

The Grimaldi group's **Grandi Navi Veloci** (☎in Italy 010 209 4591; www1.gnv.it; MDrassanes) runs high-speed, thrice-weekly luxury ferries between Barcelona and Genoa, while **Grimaldi Ferries** (☎902 531 333, in Italy 081 496444; www.grimaldi-lines.com) operates similar services to Civitavecchia (near Rome), Livorno (Tuscany) and Porto Torres (northwest Sardinia).

Bus
The main terminal for most domestic and international buses is the **Estació del Nord** (☎902 303 222; www.barcelonanord.com; Carrer d'Ali Bei 80; MArc de Triomf). ALSA goes to Madrid (€28.18, eight hours, up to 16 daily), Valencia (€25.34, 4½ hours to 6½ hours, up to 14 daily) and many other destinations.

Eurolines (www.eurolines.com) also offers international services from Estació del Nord and **Estació d'Autobusos de Sants** (Carrer de Viriat), which is next to Estació Sants Barcelona.

Car & Motorcycle
Autopistas (tollways) head out of Barcelona in most directions, including the C31/C32 to the southern Costa Brava; the C32 to Sitges; the C16 to Manresa (with a turn-off for Montserrat); and the AP7 north to Girona, Figueres and France, and south to Tarragona and Valencia (turn off along the AP2 for Lleida, Zaragoza and Madrid).

Train
Virtually all trains travelling to and from destinations within Spain stop at **Estació Sants** (MSants-Estació). High-speed trains to Madrid via Lleida and Zaragoza take as little as two hours and 40 minutes; prices vary wildly. Other trains run to Valencia (€38.50 to €43.10, three to 4½ hours, 15 daily) and Burgos (from €49, six to seven hours, four daily).

There are also international connections with French cities from the same station.

ⓘ Getting Around
To/From the Airport
The **A1 Aerobús** (☎93 415 60 20; one way €5) runs from Terminal 1 to Plaça de Catalunya from 6.05am to 1.05am, taking 30 to 40 minutes. A2 Aerobús does the same run from Terminal 2, from 6am to 12.30am. Buy tickets on the bus.

Renfe's R2 Nord train line runs between the airport and Passeig de Gràcia (via Estació Sants) in central Barcelona (about 35 minutes). Tickets cost €3, unless you have a T-10 multitrip public-transport ticket.

A taxi to/from the centre, about a half-hour ride depending on traffic, costs around €20 to €25.

Public Transport
Barcelona's metro system spreads its tentacles around the city in such a way that most places of interest are within a 10-minute walk of a station. Buses and suburban trains are needed only for a few destinations. A single metro, bus or suburban train ride costs €1.40, but a T-1 ticket, valid for 10 rides, costs €7.85.

Taxi
Barcelona's black-and-yellow taxis are plentiful and reasonably priced. The flag fall is €2. If you can't find a street taxi, call ☎93 303 30 33.

Monestir de Montserrat

The monks who built the Monestir de Montserrat (Monastery of the Serrated Mountain), 50km northwest of Barcelona, chose a spectacular spot. The Benedictine **monastery** (www.abadiamontserrat.net; ⊙9am-6pm) sits on the side of a 1236m-high mountain of weird, bulbous peaks. The monastery was founded in 1025 and pilgrims still come from all over Christendom to kiss the Black

Virgin (La Moreneta), the 12th-century wooden sculpture of the Virgin Mary.

The **Museu de Montserrat** (Plaça de Santa Maria; adult/student €6.50/5.50; ☉10am-6pm) has an excellent collection, ranging from an Egyptian mummy to art by El Greco, Monet, Degas and Picasso.

If you're around the basilica at the right time, you'll catch a brief performance by the **Montserrat Boys' Choir** (Escolania; www.escolania.net; admission free; ☉performances 1pm & 6.45pm Mon-Fri, 11am & 6.45pm Sun Sep-Jun).

You can explore the mountain above the monastery on a web of paths leading to some of the peaks and to 13 empty and rather dilapidated hermitages. Running every 20 minutes, the **Funicular de Sant Joan** (one way/return €4.50/7.20; ☉10am-5.40pm Apr-Oct, to 7pm mid-Jul–Aug, to 4.30pm Mar & Nov, 11am-4.30pm Dec, closed Jan-Feb) will carry you up the first 250m from the monastery.

ⓘ Getting There & Away

Montserrat is an easy day trip from Barcelona. The R5 line trains operated by FGC run from Plaça d'Espanya station in Barcelona to Monistrol de Montserrat up to 18 times daily starting at 5.16am. They connect with the rack-and-pinion train, or **cremallera** (www.cremallerademontserrat.com), which takes 17 minutes to make the upwards journey and costs €5.15/8.20 one way/return.

Girona

POP 92,200

A tight huddle of ancient arcaded houses, grand churches, climbing cobbled streets and medieval baths, all enclosed by defensive walls and a lazy river, constitute a powerful reason for visiting north Catalonia's largest city, Girona (Castilian: Gerona).

◉ Sights & Activities

Catedral
CHURCH

The billowing baroque facade of the cathedral stands at the head of a majestic flight of steps rising from Plaça de la Catedral. Repeatedly rebuilt and altered down the centuries, it has Europe's widest Gothic nave (23m). The cathedral's **museum** (www.catedraldegirona.org; adult/under 7yr €5/free, admission free Sun; ☉10am-8pm Apr-Oct, to 7pm Nov-Mar, 10am-2pm Sun & holidays), through the door marked 'Claustre Tresor', contains the masterly Romanesque *Tapís de la Creació* (Tapestry of the Creation) and a Mozarabic illuminated *Beatus* manuscript, dating from 975. The fee for the museum also admits you to the beautiful 12th-century Romanesque **cloister**.

TOP CHOICE **Passeig Arqueològic** GARDENS

Across the street from the Banys Àrabs, steps lead up into some heavenly gardens where town and plants merge into one organic masterpiece. The gardens follow the city walls up to the 18th-century Portal de Sant Cristòfol gate, from where you can walk back down to the cathedral.

The Call
HISTORIC DISTRICT

Until 1492 Girona was home to Catalonia's second-most important medieval Jewish community (after Barcelona), and its Jewish quarter, the Call, was centred on Carrer de la Força. For an idea of medieval Jewish life and culture, visit the **Museu d'Història dels Jueus de Girona** (Jewish History Museum, aka the Centre Bonastruc Ça Porta; Carrer de la Força 8; adult/child €2/free; ☉10am-8pm Mon-Sat Jun-Oct, 10am-6pm Mon-Sat Nov-May, 10am-3pm Sun & holidays).

⌖ Sleeping & Eating

TOP CHOICE **Hotel Llegendes de Girona**
HOTEL €€€

(☏972 22 09 05; www.llegendeshotel.com; Portal de la Barca 4; d €123; 'Fountain of Lovers' room

---

NO MORE BULLS?

On 28 July 2010 Catalonia became the first region in mainland Spain to ban bullfighting; the Canary Islands voted to make bullfighting illegal in 1991. The vote, which came as a result of a 180,000-strong petition, follows moves by 23 municipalities (including Barcelona) who have declared themselves to be antibullfighting cities in recent years. With Catalonia never the strongest bastion of bullfighting tradition and with Spain's major national political parties opposing Catalonia's ban, the chances of other Spanish regions following suit seem remote. However, other factors do pose a significant (albeit longer-term) threat to bullfighting. Recent surveys have found that around 50% of Spaniards oppose bullfighting, with the figures much higher among younger Spaniards. The recent global economic crisis has also taken its toll – there was a 50% drop in the number of bullfights in 2009, with many small towns forced to cancel their annual fiestas.

€288; P❂❄) This new hotel has so many hi-tech gadgets it's like sleeping in the Space Shuttle. The rooms are supremely comfort-able and the all-glass bathrooms with huge rain showers are minimalist. In each room is a little book detailing different tantric sex positions and in three of the rooms is an 'Eros' sofa...

Bed & Breakfast Bells Oficis   B&B €€

(☏972 22 81 70; www.bellsoficis.com; Carrer dels Germans Busquets 2; r incl breakfast €35-85; ❂❄) Up the wobbly winding staircase of an old building you'll discover six very desirable rooms. Some have unusual pebble art in the bathroom whilst others share bathrooms and some have views over the street.

Gro Hostel Girona   HOSTEL €

(☏972 31 20 45; www.equity-point.com; Plaça Cata-lunya 23; dm incl breakfast from €20, without bath-room from €18; ❂@❄) Part of a small chain of hostels (the others are in Barcelona and Ma-drid), it offers not just the cheapest night's kip in Girona but is also a great-value, colourful and friendly hostel in its own right.

TOP CHOICE Restaurant Txalaka   BASQUE €€

(☏972 22 59 75; Carrer Bonastruc de Porta 4; menú €33, mains €15-20, pintxos €2.50-4; ◷closed Sun) For sensational Basque cooking and *pintxos* (Basque tapas) washed down with txakoli (the fizzy, white wine from the Basque coast), poured from a great height the way it's supposed to be, don't miss this popular place on the edge of the new town.

L'Alqueria   RICE DISHES €€

(☏972 22 18 82; www.restaurantalqueria.com; Carrer Ginesta 8; mains €15-20; ◷lunch & dinner Wed-Sat, lunch Tue & Sun, closed Mon) This smart new restaurant serves the finest *arrós negre* (rice cooked in cuttlefish ink) and *arrós a la Catalan* in the city. It's wise to book ahead.

❶ Information

Tourist office (www.girona.cat; Jŏan Maragall 2; ◷8am-8pm Mon-Fri, 8am-2pm & 4-8pm Sat, 9am-2pm Sun)

❶ Getting There & Away

AIR **Girona-Costa Brava airport**, 11km south of the centre and just off the AP7 and A2, is Ryanair's Spanish hub.

TRAIN There are more than 20 trains per day to Figueres (€10.50 to €13.70, 30 to 40 minutes) and Barcelona (from €14.90, 1½ hours).

The Costa Brava

The Costa Brava (Rugged Coast) was Cata-lonia's first tourist centre, and after you visit its rocky coastline, romantic coves, tur-quoise waters and former fishing villages, you'll see why. Overdevelopment has ruined some stretches but much of the coast retains its spectacular beauty.

◉ Sights & Activities

The Costa Brava is all about picturesque inlets and coves – and there are many. Al-though buses run along much of the coast, the best way to uncover some of these gems is with your own wheels.

The first truly pretty stop on the Costa Brava when heading northeast from Barce-lona is **Tossa de Mar**, with its golden beach, ochre medieval village core and nearby coves. The coast road on to **Sant Feliu de Guíxols** is spectacular.

Further north are three gorgeous beach towns near Palafrugell: **Tamariu** (the small-

---

DALÍ'S CATALONIA

A short train ride north of Girona, Figueres is home to the zany **Teatre-Museu Dalí** (www.salvador-dali.org; Plaça de Gala i Salvador Dalí 5; adult/under 9yr €11/free; ◷9am-8pm Jul-Sep, 9.30am-6pm Mar-Jun & Oct, 10.30am-6pm Nov-Feb, closed Mon Oct-Jun), housed in a 19th-century theatre converted by Salvador Dalí (who was born here). 'Theatre-museum' is an apt label for this multidimensional trip through one of the most fertile (or disturbed) imaginations of the 20th century. It's full of surprises, tricks and illusions, and contains a substantial portion of Dalí's life's work.

Dalí fans will want to travel south to visit the equally kooky **Castell de Púbol** (☏972 48 86 55; www.salvador-dali.org; La Pera; adult/under 9yr €7/free; ◷10am-8pm, closed Jan–mid-Mar & Mon outside high season) at La Pera, 22km northwest of Palafrugell, and the **Casa Museu Dalí** (☏972 25 10 15; www.salvador-dali.org; Port Lligat; adult/child €10/free) at his summer getaway in Port Lligat (1.25km from Cadaqués), where entry is by advance reservation only.

est, least crowded and most exclusive), **Llafranc** (the biggest and busiest) and **Calella de Palafrugell**. There are further fine beaches and coves on the coast near Begur, a little further north.

North of the Costa Brava's main dive centre, **L'Estartit**, are the ruins of the Greek and Roman town of **Empúries** (www.mac.cat; adult/child €3/free; ⊙10am-8pm Jun-Sep, to 6pm Oct-May), 2km outside **L'Escala**.

Cadaqués, at the end of an agonising series of hairpin bends one hour from Figueres, is postcard perfect. Beaches are of the pebbly variety, so people spend a lot of time sitting at waterfront cafes or strolling. It's a pleasant 2km walk from central Cadaqués to Port Lligat, where you'll find Dalí's summer residence. Some 10km northeast of Cadaqués is **Cap de Creus**, an impressive cape that is Spain's easternmost point.

Of the many historic towns inland from the Costa Brava, the pretty walled town of **Pals**, 6km inland from Begur, and the nearby impeccably preserved medieval hamlet of **Peratallada** are the most charming.

🛏 Sleeping & Eating

TOSSA DE MAR

TOP **Hostal Cap d'Or**   HOTEL €€
CHOICE (☑972 34 00 81; www.hotelcapdor.com; Passeig de la Vila Vella 1; s/d incl breakfast €53/96; P❉❄) Rub up against the town's history in this spot right in front of the walls. Rooms are lovingly decorated in sea blues and whites, and the best look straight onto the beach.

Hotel Canaima   HOTEL €€
(☑972 34 09 95; www.hotelcanaima.com; Avendia de la Palma 24; s/d incl breakfast €37.50/75; ❉❄) Surrounded by super-sized package holiday hotels, this little family-run hotel offers something refreshingly different. Rooms are big and bright with little balconies and there's a laid-back cafe downstairs.

CADAQUÉS

TOP **Hostal Vehí**   BUDGET HOTEL €€
CHOICE (☑972 25 84 70; www.hostalvehi.com; Carrer de l'Església 5; s/d €77, without bathroom €30/55; ❉) Near the church in the heart of the old town, this simple but engaging *pensión* with clean as a whistle rooms tends to be booked up for July and August. Easily the cheapest deal in town, it's also about the best. In fact the only drawback we can come up with is that it's a pain to get to if you have a lot of luggage. Breakfast is €6 extra.

ℹ Information

There are tourist offices in **Palafrugell** (☑972 61 44 75; Carrer de les Voltes 6; ⊙10am-8pm Jul-Aug, shorter hours rest of year) and other towns on the coast and inland.

ℹ Getting There & Away

Sarfa (☑902 30 20 25; www.sarfa.com) runs buses from Barcelona, Girona and Figueres to most towns along the Costa Brava.

Tarragona

POP 134,160

Barcelona's senior in Roman times and a lesser medieval city, Tarragona is a provincial sort of place with some outstanding attractions: Catalonia's finest Roman ruins, a magnificent medieval cathedral in a pretty Old Town, and some decent beaches.

◎ Sights & Activities

Museu d'Història de Tarragona   ROMAN RUINS
(MHT; www.museutgn.com; adult/child per site €3/free, incl all MHT sites €10; ⊙9am-9pm Mon-Sat, to 3pm Sun Easter-Oct, shorter hours rest of year) To call the four sites that make up the Museu d'Història de Tarragona a museum is somewhat misleading as there are, in fact, four separate Roman sites (which since 2000 together have constituted a Unesco World Heritage site).

Start with the **Pretori i Circ Romans** (Plaça del Rei), which includes part of the vaults of the Roman circus, where chariot races were held. Near the beach is the crown jewel of Tarragona's Roman sites, the well-preserved **Amfiteatre Romà** (Plaça d'Arce Ochotorena), where gladiators battled each other, wild animals or Russell Crowe to the death. Southeast of Carrer de Lleida are remains of the **Fòrum Romà** (Carrer del Cardenal Cervantes), dominated by several imposing columns. The **Passeig Arqueològic** is a peaceful walk around part of the perimeter of the old town between two lines of city walls; the inner ones are mainly Roman.

Museu Nacional Arqueològic de Tarragona   MUSEUM
(www.mnat.es; Plaça del Rei 5; adult/child €2.40/free; ⊙10am-8pm Tue-Sat, 10am-2pm Sun & holidays Jun-Sep, shorter hours rest of year) This carefully presented museum gives further insight into Roman Tarraco. Exhibits include part of the Roman city walls, mosaics, frescos, sculpture and pottery.

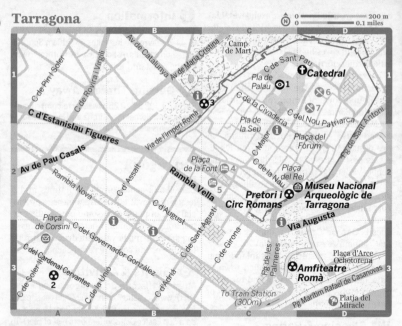

Catedral   CHURCH
(Pla de la Seu; adult/child €3.80/1.20; ⊙10am-7pm Mon-Sat, shorter hours Jul–mid-Oct) Sitting grandly at the top of the old town, Tarragona's cathedral demands a solid chunk of your time. Built between 1171 and 1331 on the site of a Roman temple, it combines Romanesque and Gothic features, as typified by the main facade on Pla de la Seu.

The entrance is by the cloister on the northwest flank of the building. The cloister and its perfectly presented gardens have Gothic vaulting and Romanesque carved capitals.

🛏 Sleeping & Eating

Look for tapas bars and inexpensive cafes on the Plaça de la Font. The Moll de Pescadors (Fishermen's Wharf) is the place to go for seafood restaurants.

Pensió Forum   PENSION €
(☑977 23 1718; Plaça de la Font 37; s/d €26/38) The small but oh so colourful rooms at this helpful pension perch above a restaurant and overlook the main square – views of which can be enjoyed from one of the rooms with a balcony.

Hotel Plaça de la Font   HOTEL €€
(☑977 24 61 34; www.hotelpdelafont.com; Plaça de la Font 26; s/d €55/70; ☀) Although a trifle cramped, the rooms here have a pleasing modern look, with soft colours, sturdy beds and, in the case of half of the rooms, little balconies overlooking the square.

Aq   MODERN CATALONIAN €€
(☑977 21 59 54; Carrer de les Coques 7; mains €15, menú del día from €18; ⊙Tue-Sat) A bubbly designer haunt with stark colour contrasts (black, lemon and cream linen), slick lines

and intriguing international plays on traditional cooking.

Quim Quima INTERNATIONAL €€
(📞977 25 21 21; Carrer de les Coques 1bis; meals €35, menú del día from €19.90; ⏰lunch Tue-Thu, lunch & dinner Fri & Sat) This renovated medieval mansion makes a marvellous setting for a meal. The playful menu is wide-ranging, including sausage-and-cheese crêpes and lasagne.

ℹ Information

Regional tourist office (Carrer de Fortuny 4; ⏰9am-2pm & 4-6.30pm Mon-Fri, 9am-2pm Sat)

Tourist office (www.tarragonaturisme.cat; Carrer Major 39; ⏰10am-8pm Mon-Sat, 10am-2pm Sun Jul-Oct, 10am-2pm & 4-7pm Mon-Sat)

ℹ Getting There & Away

BUS Bus services run to Barcelona, Valencia, Zaragoza, Madrid, Alicante, Pamplona, the main Andalucian cities, Andorra and the north coast. The bus station is around 1.5km northwest of the old town.

TRAIN At least 16 regional trains per day run to/from Barcelona's Passeig de Gràcia via Sants. The cheapest fares cost €13.80 to an average of €20 and the journey takes one to 1½ hours.

ARAGÓN, BASQUE COUNTRY & NAVARRA

This northeast area of Spain is brimming with fascinating destinations: the arid hills and proud history of Aragón; the lush coastline and gourmet delights of the Basque Country (País Vasco); and the wine country and famous festivals of Navarra.

Aragón

Zaragoza is the capital of the expansive Aragón region, though by no means is the city its only attraction. The national parks and pretty towns of the Pyrenees are well worth exploring too.

ZARAGOZA

POP 624,700 / ELEV 200M

Sitting on the banks of the mighty Ebro River, Zaragoza (a contraction of Caesaraugusta, the name the Romans gave to this city when they founded it in 14 BC) is a busy regional capital with a seemingly voracious appetite for eating out and late-night rev-

elry. The historic old centre, crowned by the majestic Basílica del Pilar, throws up echoes of its Roman and Muslim past. The Old Town is also home to El Tubo (The Tube), a maze of streets with countless tapas bars and cafes.

◉ Sights

FREE **Basílica de Nuestra Señora del Pilar** CHURCH
(Plaza del Pilar s/n; ⏰7am-8.30pm) Brace yourself for the saintly and the solemn in this great baroque cavern of Catholicism. It was here on 2 January 40 that Santiago (St James the Apostle) is believed to have seen the Virgin Mary descend atop a marble *pilar* (pillar). A chapel was built around the remaining pillar, followed by a series of ever-more-grandiose churches, culminating in the enormous basilica that you see today. Originally designed in 1681, it was greatly modified in the 18th century and the towers were not finished until the early 20th century. The exterior, with its splendid main dome lording over a flurry of 10 mini domes, each encased in chunky blue, green, yellow and white tiles, creates a kind of rugged Byzantine effect.

A **lift** (admission €2; ⏰10am-1.30pm & 4-6.30pm Tue-Sun) whisks you most of the way up the north tower (Torre Pilar) for fine views.

TOP CHOICE **Aljafería** PALACE
(Calle de los Diputados; adult/under 12yr €3/free, free Sun; ⏰10am-2pm Sat-Wed, 4.30-8pm Mon-Wed, Fri & Sat Jul & Aug, shorter hours rest of year) La Aljafería is Spain's finest Islamic-era edifice outside Andalucía. It's not in the league of Granada's Alhambra or Córdoba's Mezquita, but it's nonetheless a glorious monument. The Aljafería was built as a pleasure palace for Zaragoza's Islamic rulers, chiefly in the 11th century. After the city passed into Christian hands in 1118, Zaragoza's Christian rulers made alterations.

Inside the main gate, cross the rather dull introductory courtyard into a second, the **Patio de Santa Isabel**, once the central courtyard of the Islamic palace. Here you're confronted by the delicate interwoven arches typical of the geometric mastery of Islamic architecture.

La Seo CHURCH
(Catedral de San Salvador; Plaza de la Seo; admission €4; ⏰10am-6pm Tue-Fri, 10am-2pm & 3-6pm Sat, 10-11.30am & 2.30-6pm Sun Jun-Sep) La Seo may lack the fame of the Basílica de Nuestra Señora del Pilar, but its interior is easily

SPAIN ARAGÓN, BASQUE COUNTRY & NAVARRA

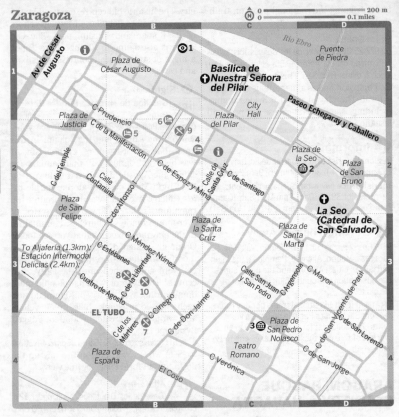

its architectural superior. Built between the 12th and 17th centuries, it displays a fabulous spread of architectural styles from Romanesque to baroque.

Museo del Foro de Caesaraugusta
MUSEUM

(Plaza de la Seo 2; admission €2.50; ☺9am-8.30pm Tue-Sat, 10am-2pm Sun Jun-Sep, shorter hours rest of year) The trapezoid building on Plaza de la Seo is the entrance to an excellent reconstruction of part of Roman Caesaraugusta's forum, now well below ground level.

Museo del Teatro de Caesaraugusta
ROMAN THEATRE, MUSEUM

(Calle de San Jorge 12; admission €3.50; ☺9am-8.30pm Tue-Sat, to 1.30pm Sun) Discovered during the excavation of a building site in 1972, the ruins of Zaragoza's Roman theatre are the focus of this interesting museum; the theatre once seated 6000 spectators.

🛏 Sleeping

TOP CHOICE **Hotel Las Torres** HOTEL €€
(Hotel Nastasi Basic ZGZ; ☎976 39 42 50; www.nastasibasiczgzhotel.com; Plaza del Pilar 11; s/d incl breakfast from €65/75; ❀🞀) This is easily Zaragoza's best place to stay. The rooms are designer cool with dazzling white furnishings and daring wallpaper. The bathroom have hydromassage showers, and the views of the square and basilica from the balconies in most rooms are simply stunning.

Hotel San Valero HOTEL €
(☎976 29 86 21; www.hotelsanvalero.com; Calle de la Manifestación 27; d €40-48; ❀🞀) It's difficult to believe the prices here. Centrally located, the rooms have a designer feel and while some could be larger, the value is unimpeachable. In short, it's a boutique hotel feel for *hostal* prices.

Zaragoza

⊙ Top Sights

⊙ Sights

🛏 Sleeping

✖ Eating

Sabinas APARTMENTS €€

(☎976 20 47 10; www.sabina.es; Calle de Alfonso I 43; d/apt from €58/68; P☀🌐) Apartments with a kitchen and sitting room styled with a contemporary look and a location a few steps off Plaza del Pilar make this a terrific option. The bathrooms are lovely and the price is extraordinarily good considering the location and size of the rooms. Standard doubles with a microwave are also available.

✗ Eating & Drinking

Zaragoza has some terrific tapas bars, with dozens of places on or close to Plaza de Santa Marta. Otherwise the narrow streets of El Tubo, north of Plaza de España, are tapas central.

Calle del Temple, southwest of Plaza del Pilar, is the spiritual home of Zaragoza's roaring nightlife. This is where the city's students head out to drink. There are more bars lined up along this street than anywhere else in Aragón.

TOP CHOICE **Casa Pascualillo** TAPAS €

(Calle de la Libertad 5; meals €15-25; ⊙lunch & dinner Tue-Sat, lunch Sun) The bar here groans under the weight of every tapa variety imaginable, with seafood and meat in abundance; the house speciality is El Pascualillo, a 'small' *bocadillo* (filled roll) of *jamón*, mushrooms and onion.

Taberna Doña Casta TAPAS €€

(Calle Estébanes 6; ⊙Tue-Sun) If you like your tapas without too many frills, this enduringly popular and informal *taberna* could become your culinary home in Zaragoza. The bottle of wine and six tapas for €23 is a terrific way to meet all your gastronomic needs at a reasonable price. The specialities are *croquetas* (croquettes) and egg-based dishes.

Casa Lac REGIONAL, TAPAS €€

(☎976 29 90 25; Calle de los Mártires 12; meals €30-35; ⊙Wed-Mon) The grand old lady of the Zaragoza dining scene, Casa Lac pays homage to the 19th century (it opened in 1825) with its seigniorial decor and impeccable service. The food revolves around Aragonese staples, although the lamb carpaccio with foie gras shows Casa Lac isn't averse to a little experimentation. Dine upstairs with the Who's Who of Zaragoza society, or downstairs in the more informal tapas bar.

El Rincón de Aragón REGIONAL €€

(☎976 20 11 63; Calle de Santiago 3-5; meals €20-35) There's no time for unnecessary elaborations here – the decor is basic and the food stripped down to its essence – but the eating is top-notch and ideal for finding out why people get excited about Aragonese cooking. One house speciality among many is the *ternasco asado con patatas a la pobre* (roasted suckling lamb ribs with 'poor man's potatoes').

ℹ Information

Municipal tourist office (www.zaragoza turismo.es; ⊙9am-9pm mid-Jun–mid-Oct, 10am-8pm mid-Oct–mid-Jun)

Oficina de Turismo de Aragón (www.turismo dearagon.com; Avenida de César Augusto 25; ⊙9am-2pm & 5-8pm Mon-Fri, from 10am Sat & Sun)

ℹ Getting There & Away

AIR Zaragoza-Sanjurjo airport (☎976 71 23 00) has domestic and international flights.

BUS Services from the bus station attached to the Estación Intermodal Delicias train station include Madrid (from €14.47, 3¾ hours) and Barcelona (€13.71, 3¾ hours).

TRAIN Zaragoza's **Estación Intermodal Delicias** (Calle Rioja 33) is connected by almost hourly high-speed AVE services to Madrid (€58.20, 1½ hours, 10 daily) and Barcelona (€63.70, from 1½ hours). There are also trains to Valencia (€28.60, 4½ hours, three daily) and Teruel (€15.90, 2¼ hours, four daily).

Around Aragón

In Aragón's south, little visited **Teruel** is home to some stunning Mudéjar architecture. Nearby, **Albarracín** is one of Spain's most beautiful villages.

In the north, the Pyrenees dominate and the **Parque Nacional de Ordesa y Monte Perdido** is excellent for hiking; the pretty village of **Torla** is the gateway. South of the hamlet of **La Besurta** is the great Maladeta massif, a superb challenge for experienced climbers. This forbidding line of icy peaks, with glaciers suspended from the higher crests, culminates in **Aneto** (3404m), the highest peak in the Pyrenees. There are plenty of hiking and climbing options for all levels in these mountain parks bordering France. Another enchanting base for exploration in the region is **Aínsa**, a hilltop village of stone houses.

In Aragón's northwest, **Sos del Rey Católico** is another gorgeous stone village draped along a ridge.

Basque Country

The Basques, whose language is believed to be among the world's oldest, claim two of Spain's most interesting cities – San Sebastián and Bilbao – as their own. Stately San Sebastián offers a slick seaside position and some of the best food Spain has to offer. The extraordinary Guggenheim Bilbao museum is that city's centrepiece.

SAN SEBASTIÁN
POP 183,300

Stylish San Sebastián (Donostia in Basque) has the air of an upscale resort, complete with an idyllic location on the shell-shaped Bahía de la Concha. The natural setting – crystalline waters, a flawless beach, green hills on all sides – is captivating. But this is one of Spain's true culinary capitals, with more Michelin stars per capita here than anywhere else on earth.

Sights & Activities

Beaches & Isla de Santa Clara   BEACHES

Fulfilling almost every idea of how a perfect city beach should be formed, **Playa de la Concha** and its westerly extension **Playa de Ondarreta** are easily among the best city beaches in Europe. The **Isla de Santa Clara**, about 700m from the beach, is accessible by boats that run every half-hour from June to September. Less popular, but just as showy, **Playa de Gros**, east of Río Urumea, is the city's main surf beach.

Museo Chillida Leku   MUSEUM, PARK

(www.museochillidaleku.com; adult/child €8.50/free; ⊙10.30am-8pm Mon-Sat, to 3pm Sun Jul & Aug, shorter hours rest of year) This open-air museum, south of San Sebastián, is the most engaging museum in rural Basque Country. Amid the beech, oak and magnolia trees, you'll find 40 sculptures of granite and iron created by the renowned Basque sculptor Eduardo Chillida. Many more of Chillida's works appear inside the renovated 16th-century farmhouse.

To get here, take the G2 bus (€1.35) for Hernani from Calle de Okendo in San Sebastián and get off at Zabalaga.

Aquarium   AQUARIUM

(www.aquariumss.com; Paseo del Muelle 34; adult/4-12yr €12/6; ⊙10am-8pm Mon-Fri, to 9pm Sat & Sun Apr-Jun & Sep, shorter hours rest of year) In the city's excellent aquarium you'll fear for your life as huge sharks bear down on you, and be tripped out by fancy fluoro jellyfish. The highlights of a visit are the cinema screen–sized deep ocean and coral reef exhibits, and the long tunnel, around which swim monsters of the deep.

Monte Igueldo   LOOKOUT

The views from the summit of Monte Igueldo, just west of town, will make you feel like a circling hawk staring over the vast panorama of the Bahía de la Concha and the surrounding coastline and mountains. The best way to get there is via the old-world **funicular railway** (return adult/under 7yr €2.60/1.90; ⊙10am-10pm mid-Jul & Aug, shorter hours rest of year).

Monte Urgull   CASTLE, MUSEUM

You can walk to the top of Monte Urgull, topped by low castle walls and a grand statue of Christ, by taking a path from Plaza de Zuloaga or from behind the aquarium. The views are breathtaking. The castle houses the well-presented **Mirando a San Sebastián** (admission free; ⊙11am-8pm May–mid-Sep, shorter hours rest of year), a small museum focusing on the city's history.

Sleeping

TOP CHOICE **Pensión Bellas Artes**

BOUTIQUE HOTEL €€

(☑943 47 49 05; www.pension-bellasartes.com; Calle de Urbieta 64; s/d from €75/95; ☞) To call this magnificent place a mere *pensión* is to do it something of a disservice. Its spacious rooms (some with glassed-in balconies) with exposed stone walls and excellent bathrooms should be the envy of many a more expensive hotel. It also has to be the friendliest hotel in town – the staff seem to genuinely love their job and city, and want to help you get the most out of your visit.

Pensión Aida   BOUTIQUE HOTEL €€
(☑943 32 78 00; www.pensionesconencanto.com; Calle de Iztueta 9; s/d €59/82, studio €145; ❉@☎) The owners of this excellent *pensión* read the rule book on what makes a good hotel and have complied exactly. The rooms are bright and bold, full of exposed stone, and everything smells fresh and clean. The communal area, stuffed with soft sofas and mountains of information, is a big plus.

Pensión Amaiur Ostatua   BOUTIQUE HOTEL €
(☑943 42 96 54; www.pensionamaiur.com; Calle de 31 de Agosto 44; s without bathroom €40-45, d without bathroom €50-65; @☎) Sprawling over three-floors of an old townhouse this excellent *pensión* continues to improve. The rooms, all of which share bathrooms, are fairly small but have had a great deal of thought put into them, and every room and every floor is different – maybe you'll get one with chintzy wallpaper or maybe you'll go for one with brazen primary colours.

Pensión Altair   PENSIÓN €€
(☑943 29 31 33; www.pension-altair.com; Calle Padre Larroca 3; s/d €60/84; ❉@☎) This brand-new *pensión* might well be the future of the San Sebastián accommodation scene. A beautifully restored townhouse with unusual arched windows that look like they've come from a church, and spacious minimalist rooms that are a world away from the fusty decor of the old town *pensión*s. Reception is closed between 1.30pm and 5pm.

✘ Eating

San Sebastián is paradise for food lovers. Considered the birthplace of *nueva cocina española* (Spanish nouvelle cuisine), this area is home to some of the country's top chefs. Yet not all the good food is pricey. Head to the Parte Vieja for San Sebastián's *pintxos,* Basque-style tapas.

Do what the locals do – crawls of the city centre's bars. *Pintxo* etiquette is simple. Ask for a plate and point out what *pintxos* (bar snacks – more like tasty mounds of food on little slices of baguette) you want. Keep the toothpicks and go back for as many as you'd like. Accompany with *txakoli,* a cloudy white wine poured like cider to create a little fizz. When you're ready to pay, hand over the plate with all the toothpicks and tell bar staff how many drinks you've had. It's an honour system that has stood the test of time. Expect to pay €2.50 to €3.50 for a *pintxo* and *txakoli.*

TOP CHOICE | La Cuchara de San Telmo   TAPAS €
(Calle de 31 de Agosto 28) This unfussy, hidden-away (and hard to find) bar offers miniature *nueva cocina vasca* (Basque nouvelle cuisine) from a supremely creative kitchen, where chefs Alex Montiel and Iñaki Gulin conjure up such delights as *carrílera de ternera al vino tinto* (calf cheeks in red wine), with meat so tender it starts to dissolve almost before it's past your lips.

TOP CHOICE | Arzak   BASQUE FINE DINING €€€
(☑943 27 84 65; www.arzak.info; Avenida Alcalde Jose Elosegui 273; meals around €150; ⊙closed last 2 weeks Jun & all Nov) With three shining Michelin stars, acclaimed chef Juan Mari Arzak takes some beating when it comes to *nueva cocina vasca* and his restaurant is, not surprisingly, considered one of the best places to eat in Spain. Arzak is now assisted by his daughter Elena and they never cease to innovate. Reservations, well in advance, are obligatory. The restaurant is about 1.5km east of San Sebastián.

Astelana   TAPAS €
(Calle de Iñigo 1) The *pintxos* draped across the counter in this bar, tucked into the corner of Plaza de la Constitución, stand out as some of the best in the city. Many of them are a fusion of Basque and Asian inspirations, but the best of all are perhaps the foie gras–based treats.

Restaurante Alberto   SEAFOOD €
(☑943 42 88 84; Calle de 31 de Agosto 19; menú €14; ⊙closed Tue) A charming old seafood restaurant with a fishmonger-style window display of the day's catch. It's small, dark and friendly, but much of the fish is sold by the kilo so bring a friend.

La Mejillonera   TAPAS €
(Calle del Puerto 15) If you thought mussels came only with garlic sauce, come here and discover mussels (from €3) by the thousand in all their glorious forms. Mussels not for you? Opt for the calamari and spicy *patatas bravas*. We promise you won't regret it.

❶ Information

Street signs are in Basque and Spanish.

Oficina de Turismo (☑943 48 11 66; www .sansebastianturismo.com; Alameda de Blvd 8;

San Sebastián

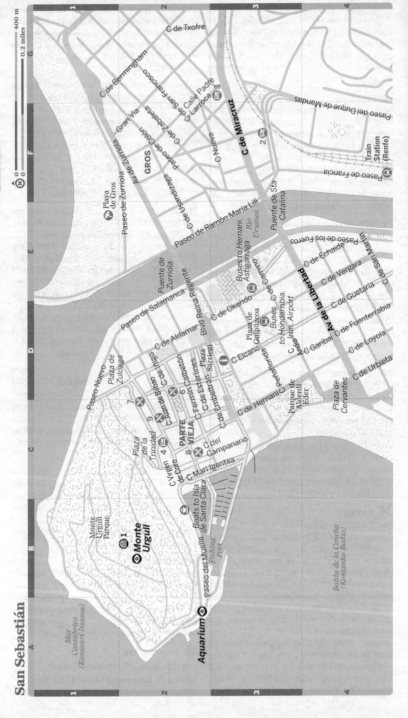

400 m
0.2 miles

Mar Cantábrico
(Kantauri Itsasoa)

C de Txofre

C de Bermingham

Gran Via

Calle Padre Larroca

C de San Francisco

C de Zabaleta

Paseo de Colón

GROS

C Nueva

C de Miracruz

Train Station (Renfe)

Paseo de Francia

Paseo del Duque de Mandas

AV de Zurriola

Playa de Gros

Paseo de Zurriola

C de Usandizaga

Paseo de Ramón María Lili

Río Urumea

Puente de Sta Catalina

Puente de Zurriola

Paseo de Salamanca

Paseo de los Fueros

Buses to Hernani, Astigarraga

C de Echaide

C de Okendo

C de Camino

Blvd Reina Regente

C de Vergara

AV de la Libertad

C de San Martin

Paseo Nuevo

Plaza de Zuloaga

C de Aldamar

Plaza de Guipúzcoa

Buses to Hondarribia, Irún, Airport

C de Guetaria

C de Elcano

C Peñaflorida

C Garibai

C de Fuenterrabia

Plaza de Bilbao

C Fermín Calbetón

C de Esterlines

Plaza Ekaitz-Sarriegi

C de Loyola

Plaza de la Trinidad

PARTE VIEJA

C de Embeltran

C del Campanario

C de Hernani

Parque de Alderdi Eder

Plaza de Cervantes

C de Urbieta

C Virgen de Coro

C Mari Igentea

Boats to Isla de Santa Clara

Plaza de Cervantes

Monte Urgull Parque

Monte Urgull

Paseo del Muelle

Fishing Port

Aquarium

Bahía de la Concha
(Kontxako Badia)

⊙9am-8pm Mon-Sat, 10am-7pm Sun Jun-Sep, 9am-1.30pm & 3.30-7pm Mon-Thu, 9.30am-7pm Fri & Sat, 10am-2pm Sun Oct-May)

❶ Getting There & Away

AIR The city's **airport** (☑902 40 47 04; www.aena.es) is 22km out of town, near Hondarribia. There are regular flights to Madrid and occasional charters to European cities.

BUS Daily bus services leave for Bilbao (€7.06 to €14, one hour), Bilbao Airport (€15.40, 1¼ hours), Biarritz (France; €8.50, 1¼ hours), Madrid (from €31.99, five hours) and Pamplona (€6.88, one hour).

TRAIN The main **Renfe train station** (Paseo de Francia) is just across Río Urumea. There are regular services to Madrid (from €52.60, five hours) and Barcelona (from €36.90, eight hours). There's only one direct train to Paris, but there are plenty more from the Spanish/French border town of Irun (or sometimes Hendaye) (€1.80, 25 minutes), which is also served by **Eusko Tren/Ferrocarril Vasco** (www.euskotren.es, in Spanish & Basque). Trains depart every half-hour from Amara train station, about 1km south of the city centre.

BILBAO

POP 354,200

The commercial hub of the Basque Country, Bilbao (Bilbo in Basque) is best known for the magnificent Guggenheim Museum. An architectural masterpiece by Frank Gehry, the museum was the catalyst of a turnaround that saw Bilbao transformed from an industrial port city into a vibrant cultural centre. After visiting this must-see temple to modern art, spend time exploring Bilbao's

SPAIN BASQUE COUNTRY

San Sebastián

◉ Top Sights

Casco Viejo (Old Quarter), a grid of elegant streets dotted with shops, cafes, *pintxos* bars and several small but worthy museums.

◎ Sights

TOP CHOICE Museo Guggenheim ART MUSEUM

(www.guggenheim-bilbao.es; Avenida Abandoibarra 2; adult/child €13/free; ⊙10am-8pm Jul & Aug, closed Mon Sep-Jun) Opened in September 1997, Bilbao's Museo Guggenheim lifted modern architecture and Bilbao into the 21st century – with sensation. Some might say, probably quite rightly, that structure overwhelms function here and that the Guggenheim is more famous for its architecture than its content. But Canadian architect Frank Gehry's inspired use of flowing canopies, cliffs, promontories, ship shapes, towers and flying fins is irresistible. The interior of the Guggenheim is purposefully vast. The cathedral-like atrium is more than 45m high. Light pours in through the glass cliffs. Permanent exhibits fill the ground floor and include such wonders as mazes of metal and phrases of light reaching for the skies.

For most people, though, it is the temporary exhibitions that are the main attraction (check the Guggenheim's website for a full program of upcoming exhibitions).

Museo de Bellas Artes ART MUSEUM

(Fine Arts Museum; www.museobilbao.com; Plaza del Museo 2; adult/child €6/free; admission free Wed; ⊙10am-8pm Tue-Sun) A mere five minutes from Museo Guggenheim is Bilbao's Museo de Bellas Artes. There are three main subcollections: Classical art, with works by Murillo, Zurbarán, El Greco, Goya and van Dyck; Contemporary art, featuring works by Gauguin, Francis Bacon and Anthony Caro; and Basque art, with the works of the great sculptors Jorge de Oteiza and Eduardo Chillida, and also strong paintings by the likes of Ignacio Zuloaga and Juan de Echevarria.

Casco Viejo OLD TOWN

The compact Casco Viejo, Bilbao's atmospheric old quarter, is full of charming streets, boisterous bars, and plenty of quirky and independent shops. At the heart of the Casco are Bilbao's original 'seven streets', Las Siete Calles, which date from the 1400s.

The 14th-century Gothic Catedral de Santiago (⊙10am-1pm & 4-7pm Tue-Sat, 10.30am-1.30pm Sun) has a splendid Renaissance portico and pretty little cloister. Further north, the 19th-century arcaded Plaza Nueva is a rewarding *pintxo* haunt.

Euskal Museoa (Museo Vasco) MUSEUM

(Museum of Basque Archaeology, Ethnography & History; www.euskal-museoa.org; Plaza Miguel Unamuno 4; adult/child €3/free, admission free Thu; ⊙11am-5pm Tue-Sat, to 2pm Sun) This is probably the most complete museum of Basque culture and history in all the Basque regions. The story kicks off back in the days of prehistory, and from this murky period the displays bound rapidly through to the modern age. The museum is housed in a fine old building, at whose centre is a peaceful cloister that was part of an original 17th-century Jesuit college.

🛏 Sleeping

The Bilbao tourism authority has a useful reservations department (☎902 877 298; www.bilbaoreservas.com) for accommodation.

TOP CHOICE Pensión Iturrienea Ostatua
BOUTIQUE HOTEL €€

(☎944 16 15 00; www.iturrieneaostatua.com; Calle de Santa María 14; d/tr €66/80; ☎) Easily the most eccentric hotel in Bilbao, it's part farmyard, part old-fashioned toyshop, and a work of art in its own right. Try to get a double room on the 1st floor (singles don't come with quite as many frills and ribbons); they are so full of character there'll be barely enough room for your own!

Hostal Begoña BOUTIQUE HOTEL €€

(☎944 23 01 34; www.hostalbegona.com; Calle de la Amistad 2; s/d from €54/63; @☎) The owners of this outstanding place don't need voguish labels for their very stylish and individual creation. Begoña speaks for itself with colourful rooms decorated with modern artworks, all with funky tiled bathrooms and wrought-iron beds. There's a car park nearby.

Gran Hotel Domine BOUTIQUE HOTEL €€€

(☎944 25 33 00; www.granhoteldominebilbao.com; Alameda Mazarredo 61; d from €140; P ✲ @ ☎) Designer chic all the way, from the Javier Mariscal main interiors to the Philippe Starck and Arne Jacobsen fittings – and that's just in the loos. This stellar showpiece of the Silken chain has views of the Guggenheim from some of its pricier rooms and from the roof terrace. Booking online beforehand can lead to big discounts.

✗ Eating

TOP CHOICE Rio-Oja BASQUE €

(☎944 15 08 71; Calle de Perro 4; mains €9-12) An institution that shouldn't be missed. It specialises in light Basque seafood and heavy inland fare, but to most foreigners the sheep brains and squid floating in pools of its own ink are the makings of a culinary adventure story they'll be recounting for years. Don't worry, though: it really does taste much better than it sounds.

TOP CHOICE Restaurante Guggenheim
BASQUE FINE DINING €€€
(☑944 23 93 33; www.restauranteguggenheim.com; bistro menu €20, restaurant menu €75, mains €30-35 ⊘closed Mon & Christmas period) El Goog's modernist, chic restaurant and cafe are under the direction of super chef Josean Martínez Alija. Needless to say, the *nueva cocina vasca* is breathtaking, and the ever-changing menu includes such mouth-waterers as Iberian pork meatballs with carrot juice and curry. Even the olives are vintage classics: all come from thousand-year-old olive trees! Reservations are essential in the evening, but at lunch it's a first-come, first-served basis from 1.30pm.

Café Iruña
BASQUE €
(cnr Calles de Colón de Larreátegui & Berástegui; menú del día €13.50) Moorish style and a century of gossip are the defining characteristics of this grand old dame. It's the perfect place to indulge in a bit of people-watching and while you're at it you might as well also indulge in a meal or, in the evening, some *pinchos morunos* (spicy kebabs with bread; €2.20).

❶ Information
Tourist office (www.bilbao.net/bilbaoturismo; Plaza del Ensanche 11; ⊘9am-2pm & 4-7.30pm Mon-Fri) Other branches at the Teatro Arriaga, Museo Guggenheim and airport.

❶ Getting There & Away
AIR Bilbao's airport (BIO), with domestic and a handful of international flights, is near Sondika, 12km northeast of the city. The airport bus Bizkaibus A3247 (€1.20, 30 minutes) runs to/from Termibus (bus station), where there is a tram stop and a metro station.

TRAIN Two Renfe trains runs daily to Madrid (from €48.60, six hours) and Barcelona (€62.30, six hours) from the Abando train station. Slow **FEVE** (www.feve.es) trains run from Concordia station next door, heading west into Cantabria and Asturias.

BUS Regular bus services operate to/from Madrid (€27.17, 4¾ hours), Barcelona (€41.90, seven hours), Pamplona (€13.40, two hours) and Santander (from €6.71, 1¼ hours).

Navarra

Navarra, historically and culturally linked to the Basque Country, is known for its fine wines and for the Sanfermines festival in Pamplona.

PAMPLONA
POP 195.800

Immortalised by Ernest Hemingway in *The Sun Also Rises,* the pre-Pyrenean city of Pamplona (Iruña in Basque) is home of the wild Sanfermines (aka Encierro or Running of the Bulls) festival, but is also an extremely walkable city that's managed to mix the charm of old plazas and buildings with modern shops and a lively nightlife.

◉ Sights

Cathedral
CHURCH
(Calle Dormitalería; guided tours adult/child €4.40/2.60; ⊘10am-7pm Mon-Fri, to 2pm Sat mid-Jul–mid-Sep, closed for lunch mid-Sep–mid-Jul) Pamplona's main cathedral stands on a rise just inside the city ramparts amid a dark thicket of narrow streets. It's a late-medieval Gothic gem spoiled only by its rather dull neoclassical facade, an 18th-century appendage. The real joys are the vast interior and the Gothic cloister, where there is marvellous delicacy in the stonework.

Ciudadela & Parks
PARK
(Avenida del Ejército) The walls and bulwarks of the grand fortified citadel, the star-shaped Ciudadela, lurk amid the verdant grass and trees in what is now a charming park, the portal to three more parks that unfold to the north and lend the city a beautiful green escape.

Museo Oteiza
MUSEUM
(www.museooteiza.org; Calle de la Cuesta 7; adult/student/child €4/2/free, all admission free Fri;

SURVIVING SANFERMINES

The Sanfermines festival is held from 6 to 14 July, when Pamplona is overrun with thrill-seekers, curious onlookers and, yes, bulls. The Encierro (Running of the Bulls) begins at 8am daily, when bulls are let loose from the Corralillos Santo Domingo. The 825m race lasts just three minutes, so don't be late. The safest place to watch the Encierro is on TV. If that's too tame for you, try to sweet-talk your way onto a balcony or book a room in a hotel with views.

SPAIN NAVARRA

⊙11am-7pm Tue-Sat, to 3pm Sun Jun-Sep) Around 9km northeast of Pamplona in the town of Alzuza, this impressive museum contains almost 3000 pieces by the renowned Navarran sculptor Jorge Oteiza. As well as his workshop, this beautifully designed gallery incorporates the artist's former home in a lovely rural setting. Three buses a day run to Alzuza from Pamplona's bus station.

🛏 Sleeping

Accommodation is hard to come by during Sanfermines – book months in advance. Prices below don't reflect the huge (up to fivefold) mark-up you'll find in mid-July.

TOP CHOICE | Palacio Guendulain

HISTORIC HOTEL €€€

(☎948 22 55 22; www.palacioguendulain.com; Calle Zapatería 53; d from €128; P❋📶) To call this stunning new hotel sumptuous is an understatement. Inside the converted former home of the Viceroy of New Granada, the rooms contain 'Princess and the Pea' soft beds, enormous showers and regal armchairs.

Hotel Puerta del Camino   BOUTIQUE HOTEL €€

(☎948 22 66 88; www.hotelpuertadelcamino.com; Calle dos de Mayo 4; s/d €70/82; P❋@) A very stylish new hotel inside a converted convent (clearly the nuns appreciated the finer things in life!) beside the northern gates to the old city. The functional rooms have clean, modern lines and it's positioned in one of the prettier, and quieter, parts of town.

Habitaciones Mendi   PENSION €

(☎948 22 52 97; Calle de las Navas de Tolosa 9; s/d €30/45) Full of the spirits of Pamplona past, this charming little guesthouse is a real find. Creaky, wobbly wooden staircases and equally creaky chintzy rooms make it just like being at your gran's, and the woman running it will cluck over you as if she were your gran.

✖ Eating & Drinking

Central streets such as Calle de San Nicolás and Calle de la Estafeta are lined with tapas bars, many of which morph into nightspots on weekends.

Baserri   BASQUE €

(Calle de San Nicolás 32; menú del día €14) This place has won enough pintxo awards that we could fill this entire book listing them. As you'd expect from such a certificate-studded bar, the pintxos are superb but sadly the full meals play something of a second fiddle in comparison.

Casa Otaño   BASQUE €

(☎948 22 50 95; Calle de San Nicolás 5; mains €15-18) A little pricier than many on this street but worth the extra. Its formal atmosphere is eased by the dazzling array of pink and red flowers spilling off the balcony. Great dishes range from the locally caught trout to heavenly duck dishes.

Mesón Pirineo   BASQUE €

(Calle de la Estafeta 41; mains €12-16) There's nothing fancy and modern about this place; it's just old Navarran style and superb *pintxos* all the way.

Café Iruña   HISTORIC CAFE

(Plaza del Castillo 44) Opened on the eve of Sanfermines in 1888, Café Iruña's dominant position, powerful sense of history and frilly belle époque decor make this by far the most famous and popular watering hole in the city.

ℹ Information

Tourist office (www.turismo.navarra.es; Calle de Esclava 1; ⊙9am-8pm Mon-Sat, to 2pm Sun)

ℹ Getting There & Away

AIR Pamplona's **airport** (☎948 16 87 00), about 7km south of the city, has regular flights to Madrid and Barcelona. Bus 21 (€1.10) travels between the city (from the bus station) and the airport.

BUS From the **main bus station** (Calle Conde Oliveto 8), buses leave for Bilbao (€13.40, two hours) and San Sebastián (€6.88, one hour).

TRAIN Pamplona's train station is linked to the city centre by bus 9 from Paseo de Sarasate every 15 minutes. Trains run to/from Madrid (€56, three hours, four daily) and San Sebastián (from €20.40, two hours, two daily).

CANTABRIA, ASTURIAS & GALICIA

With a landscape reminiscent of parts of the British Isles, 'Green Spain' offers great walks in national parks, seafood feasts in sophisticated towns and oodles of opportunities to plunge into the ice-cold waters of the Bay of Biscay.

Cantabria

Some 34km west of the regional capital, Santander, **Santillana del Mar** (www.santillana delmar.com) is a bijou medieval village and the obvious overnight base for visiting the nearby Cueva de Altamira.

The country's finest prehistoric art, in the Cueva de Altamira, 2km southwest of Santillana del Mar, is off-limits to all but the scientific community. Since 2001, however, the **Museo Altamira** (http://museodealtamira.mcu.es; adult/child, EU senior or student €3/free, Sun & from 2.30pm Sat free; ⌚9.30am-8pm Tue-Sat, to 3pm Sun & holidays) has allowed all comers to view the inspired, 14,500-year-old depictions of bison, horses and other beasts (or rather, their replicas) in this full-size, dazzling re-creation of the cave's most interesting chamber, the Sala de Polícromos (Polychrome Hall).

Buses run three to four times a day from Santander to Santilla del Mar.

Oviedo

POP 190,000

The elegant parks and modern shopping streets of Asturias' capital are agreeably offset by what remains of the *casco antiguo* (old town).

Just outside the city (within 3km) is a scattering of 9th-century, pre-Romanesque buildings, including the **Iglesia de San Julián de los Prados**, **Palacio de Santa María del Naranco** and the **Iglesia de San Miguel de Lillo**. Get information from the tourist offices in town.

⊙ Sights

FREE **Catedral de San Salvador** CHURCH
The mainly Gothic cathedral is home to the **Cámara Santa** (museum & cloister €3.50, free Thu afternoon); ⌚10am-1pm & 4-6pm Mon-Sat), a chapel built by Alfonso II to house holy relics. It contains some key symbols of medieval Spanish Christianity: Alfonso II presented the Cruz de los Ángeles (Cross of the Angels) to Oviedo in 808, and it's still the city's emblem; a century later, Alfonso III donated the Cruz de la Victoria (Cross of Victory), which in turn became the sign of Asturias.

Old Town HISTORIC AREA
The Old Town's nooks and crannies include **Plaza de la Constitución**, capped at one end by the Iglesia de San Isidoro and fronted by an eclectic collection of old shops, cafes and the 17th-century *ayuntamiento*. To the south, past the **Mercado El Fontán** food market, arcaded **Plaza Fontán** is equipped with a couple of *sidrerías* (cider houses). Other little squares include Plaza de Trascorrales, Plaza de Riego and Plaza del Paraguas.

WORTH A TRIP

PICOS DE EUROPA

These jagged mountains straddling Asturias, Cantabria and northeast Castilla y León amount to some of the finest walking country in Spain.

They comprise three limestone massifs (whose highest peak rises 2648m). The 647-sq-km **Parque Nacional de los Picos de Europa** (www.picosdeeuropa.com, in Spanish) covers all three massifs and is Spain's second-biggest national park.

There are numerous places to stay and eat all over the mountains. Getting here and around by bus can be slow going but the Picos are accessible from Santander and Oviedo (the latter is easier) by bus.

🛏 Sleeping & Eating

Oviedo's *sidrería* rules include getting good food at reasonable prices. Calle de la Gascona is a particularly happy hunting ground.

Hotel de la Reconquista HOTEL €€€
(☑985 24 11 00; www.hoteldelareconquista.com; Calle de Gil de Jaz 16; s/d from €131/157; ꟼ❄✳@🛜) The city's top lodgings, two blocks northwest of Campo de San Francisco, started life as an 18th-century hospice. Rooms come in different shapes and sizes, with timber furniture, floor-to-ceiling windows, and gentle ochre and white colour schemes.

Hotel Santa Cruz HOTEL €€
(☑985 22 37 11; www.santacruzoviedo.com; Calle de Marqués de Santa Cruz 6; s/d €50/65; ꟼ❄🛜) Only a couple of rooms overlook the lovely big green park across the street, and there's nothing inspired about the decor. But with well-sized, spotless rooms, friendly reception and a central location, this amounts to decent value.

TOP CHOICE **La Puerta Nueva** MEDITERRANEAN €€
(☑985 22 52 27; Calle de Leopoldo Alas 2; meals €40-60; ⌚lunch daily, dinner Thu-Sat; ❄) A gourmet experience, mixing northern with Mediterranean cooking in a homey, welcoming atmosphere. The best option is to tackle one of the tasting menus.

Tierra Astur SIDRERÍA €€
(☑985 20 25 02; Calle de la Gascona 1; meals €20-30) An especially atmospheric *sidrería*

restaurant, Tierra Astur is famed for its grilled meats and prize-winning cider. Folks queue for tables, or give up and settle for tapas at the bar. Platters of Asturian sausage, cheese or ham are a good starter option.

❶ Information

Oficina Municipal de Turismo (Plaza de la Constitución 4; ⏰9.30am-7.30pm)

Regional tourist office (www.infoasturias. com; Calle de Cimadevilla 4; ⏰10am-8pm Mon-Fri, to 7pm Sat & Sun, closed Sun mid-Sep–Jun)

❶ Getting There & Away

AIR The **Aeropuerto de Asturias** (☎902 404704) is at Santiago del Monte, 47km north-west of Oviedo and 40km west of Gijón. There are flights to European cities and around Spain. Buses run hourly to/from Oviedo's ALSA bus station (€6.35, 45 minutes).

BUS From the **ALSA bus station** (☎902 422242; Calle de Pepe Cosmen), 300m north-east of the train station, direct services head to Gijón (€2.15, 30 minutes) every 10 or 15 minutes. Other daily buses head to Asturian towns, Galicia, Cantabria and elsewhere.

TRAIN One **station** (Avenida de Santander) serves both train companies, Renfe and FEVE (for buses to Santander and Bilbao), the latter located on the upper level. **Renfe** (www.renfe .com) runs trains to León, Madrid and Barcelona at least once daily. For Gijón, Renfe *cercanías* (€2.75, 35 minutes) go once or twice an hour.

Santiago de Compostela

POP 79,000

The supposed burial place of St James (Santiago), Santiago de Compostela is a bewitching city. Christian pilgrims journeying along the Camino de Santiago often end up mute with wonder on entering its medieval centre. Fortunately, they usually regain their verbal capacities over a celebratory late-night foray into the city's lively bar scene.

◉ Sights

Catedral de Santiago de Compostela
CHURCH

(Praza do Obradoiro; www.catedraldesantiago.es; ⏰7am-9pm) The grand heart of Santiago, the cathedral soars above the city centre in a splendid jumble of moss-covered spires and statues. Though Galicia's grandest monument was built piecemeal through the centuries, its beauty is only enhanced by the mix of Romanesque, baroque and Gothic flourishes. What you see today is actually the fourth church to stand on this spot. The bulk of it was built between 1075 and 1211, in Romanesque style with a traditional Latin-cross layout and three naves.

The main entrance is via the lavish stair-case and facade on the Praza do Obradoiro, or through the south door on Praza de Praterías. The baroque Obradoiro facade was erected in the 18th century partly to protect the cathedral's original entrance, which is now just inside it – the artistically unparalleled **Pórtico de la Gloria** (Galician: Porta da Gloria), with its 200 Romanesque sculptures by Maestro Mateo.

Towards the far (west) end of the cathedral's main nave, to the right of the Churrigueresque **Altar Mayor** (Main Altar), a small staircase leads up above the altar to a 13th-century **statue of Santiago**, which the faithful queue up to embrace.

A special pilgrims' Mass is celebrated at noon daily. Other high-altar Masses take place at 10am, 6pm and (except Sunday) 7.30pm.

For an unforgettable bird's-eye view of the city, take the **cathedral rooftop tour** (☎981 55 29 85; www.santiagoturismo.com; per person €10; ⏰10am-2pm & 4-8pm).

Museo da Catedral MUSEUM

(Cathedral Museum; www.catedraldesantiago.es; Praza do Obradoiro; adult/student & pilgrim/child €5/3/free; ⏰10am-2pm & 4-8pm, closed Sun afternoon) The many-roomed Museo da Catedral, entered to the right of the Obradoiro facade, spreads over four floors and includes the cathedral's large 16th-century Gothic/plateresque cloister. You'll see Maestro Mateo's original stone choir (destroyed in 1603 but recently pieced back together), rooms of tapestries including a set from designs by Goya, the lavishly decorated 18th-century *sala capitular* (chapter house), and the richly decorated crypt beneath the Pórtico de la Gloria.

Around the Cathedral PLAZAS

The cathedral is surrounded by handsome plazas that invite you to wander through them. The grand **Praza do Obradoiro** (Workshop Plaza), to which most arriving Camino pilgrims instinctively find their way, earned its name from the stonemasons' workshops set up here while the cathedral was being built. At its northern end, the Renaissance **Hostal dos Reis Católicos** was built in the early 16th century. Today it shelters well-off travellers instead, as a luxurious *parador*. Along the western side of the square is the elegant 18th-century **Pazo de Raxoi**, now the city hall.

Around the corner, **Praza das Praterías** (Silversmiths' Square) is marked with the **Fuente de los Caballos** (1829) fountain, with the cathedral's south facade at the top of the steps. Curiously, the **Casa do Cabildo**, facing it on the lower side of the square, is no more than a 3m-deep facade, erected in 1758 to embellish the plaza.

FREE **Museo das Peregrinacións** MUSEUM (www.mdperegrinacions.com; Rúa de San Miguel 4; ⊙10am-8pm Tue-Fri, 10.30am-1.30pm & 5-8pm Sat, 10.30am-1.30pm Sun) This fine museum explores the pilgrim culture that has so shaped Santiago. Look out for the fascinating illuminated map showing pilgrimage destinations across the world.

Sleeping

Casa-Hotel As Artes HOTEL €€
(☎981 55 52 54; www.asartes.com; Travesía de Dos Puertas 2; r €102-130; ☎) On a quiet street close to the cathedral, As Artes' lovely stonewalled rooms exude a romantic rustic air. Breakfast (€10.80) is served in a homey dining room overlooking the street.

Parador Hostal dos Reis Católicos
HOTEL €€€
(☎981 58 22 00; www.parador.es; Praza do Obradoiro 1; r incl breakfast from €190; P🅿🛜) Opened in 1509 and rubbing shoulders with the cathedral, the palatial *parador* is Santiago's top hotel. Even if you don't book one of its regal rooms, stop in for tea at the elegant cafe.

Hotel Airas Nunes HOTEL €€
(☎981 56 93 50; www.pousadasdecompostela.com; Rúa do Vilar 17; d €97; 🅿@🛜) For laid-back elegance, this is a great choice, though it can be hard to get a room. The spiralling granite staircase leads to 10 appealing rooms with garnet-and-green colour schemes, buttery yellow walls, warm wooden furniture and wood-beam ceilings.

Meiga Backpackers HOSTEL €
(☎981 57 08 46; www.meiga-backpackers.es; Rúa dos Basquiños 67; dm incl breakfast €17-18; ☺@🛜) Clean, colourful, friendly and handily placed between the bus station and city centre, Meiga has spacious bunk dorms, a kitchen, a garden and no curfew. It's the only place you need consider if you're on the budget backpacking trail – unless you want a private room, in which case **Meiga Backpackers Pension** (☎981 59 64 01; www.meiga-backpackers.es; Rúa da

República del Salvador 32; d €36-42; ☺🛜), in the new town, could fit the bill nicely.

Eating

A Curtidoría GALICIAN €€
(☎981 55 43 42; Rúa da Conga 2-3; meals €25-50; ⊙closed Sun dinner; 🌱) Understatedly stylish and a favourite lunch spot with locals, A Curtidoría overlooks four streets from its two dining rooms and specialises in inventive but uncomplicated fish, meat and rice dishes like crab-stuffed peppers, grilled turbot with glazed vegies or entrecôte with wild mushroom sauce.

Mesón Ó 42 TAPAS €
(Rúa do Franco 42; raciones €5-18) With a solid list of favourite local *raciones* like *empanadas* (pies), shellfish, octopus and tortillas, as well as fish, meat and rice dishes, this popular place stands out from the crowd with its well-prepared food and good service.

Casa Rosalía TAPAS €
(Rúa do Franco 10; raciones €4-16) With a more contemporary style than other nearby bars, Rosalía draws crowds for tapas and *raciones* like scallop-and-monkfish brochette or Galician cheese salad. A selection of tempting snacks (€1.10 to €1.60) is ranged along the bar.

Drinking

If you're after tapas and wine, graze along Rúa do Franco and Rúa da Raíña. For people-watching, hit the cafes along Praza da Quintana and Rúa do Vilar. The liveliest area lies east of Praza da Quintana, especially along Rúa de San Paio de Antealtares, known as a hot spot for live music.

ℹ Information

City tourist office (www.santiagoturismo.com; Rúa do Vilar 63; ⊙9am-9pm)

Pilgrims' Reception Office (Oficina de Acogida de Peregrinos; ☎981 56 88 46; www.peregrinossantiago.es; Rúa do Vilar 1; ⊙9am-8pm)

Regional tourist office (www.turgalicia.es; Rúa do Vilar 30-32; ⊙10am-8pm Mon-Fri, 11am-2pm & 5-7pm Sat, 11am-2pm Sun)

ℹ Getting There & Around

AIR Flights from various Spanish and European destinations land at **Lavacolla airport** (☎981 54 75 00). Up to 36 Empresa Freire buses (€1.80) run daily between Lavacolla airport and Rúa do Doutor Teixeiro, in the new town southwest of Praza de Galicia.

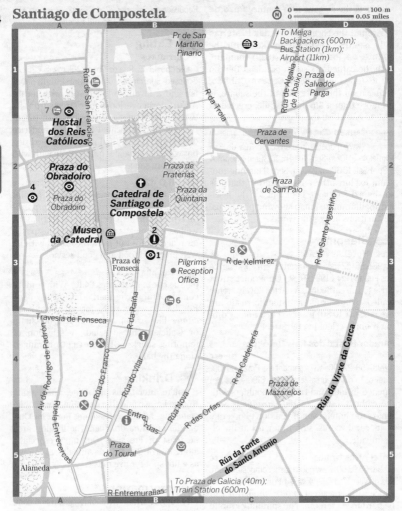

BUS The **bus station** (☎ 981 54 24 16; www.tussa.org, in Spanish; Praza de Camilo Díaz Baliño) is about a 20-minute walk northeast of the centre. Castromil-Monbus runs to destinations throughout Galicia. ALSA has services to Oviedo (€26 to €43, 4¾ to 5½ hours), San Sebastián (€58, 12½ to 13½ hours), León (€23 to €27, six hours) and Madrid (€42 to €60, eight to 9¾ hours). ALSA also has direct daily services to Porto (€29, three hours) and Lisbon (€50, seven to nine hours).

TRAIN From the **train station** (Avenida de Lugo), regional trains run up and down the coast, while a daytime Talgo and an overnight Trenhotel head to Madrid (€49.50, nine hours).

Around Galicia

Galicia's dramatic Atlantic coastline is one of Spain's best-kept secrets, with wild and precipitous cliffs and isolated fishing villages. The lively port city of **A Coruña** has a lovely city beach and fabulous seafood (a recurring Galician theme). It's also the gateway to the stirring landscapes of the **Costa da Morte** and **Rías Altas**; the latter's highlight among many is probably **Cabo Ortegal**. Inland Galicia is also worth exploring, especially the old town of **Lugo**, surrounded by what many consider to be the world's best preserved Roman walls.

Santiago de Compostela

VALENCIA & MURCIA

A warm climate, an abundance of seaside resorts, and interesting cities make this area of Spain a popular destination. The beaches of the Costa Blanca (White Coast) draw most of the visitors, but venture beyond the shore to get a real feel for the region.

Valencia

POP 814,200

Valencia, where paella first simmered over a wood fire, is a vibrant, friendly, slightly chaotic place. It has two outstanding fine-arts museums, an accessible old quarter, Europe's newest cultural and scientific complex, and one of Spain's most exciting nightlife scenes.

Head to the Barrio del Carmen, Valencia's oldest quarter, for quirky shops and the best nightlife. Other key areas are the nearby Plaza del Ayuntamiento, the Plaza de la Reina and the Plaza de la Virgen.

◉ Sights & Activities

TOP CHOICE **Ciudad de las Artes y las Ciencias**

SCIENCE CENTRE

(City of Arts & Sciences; ☑reservations 902 10 00 31; www.cac.es; combined ticket adult/child €31.50/24) The aesthetically stunning City of Arts & Sciences occupies a massive 350,000-sq-metre swath of the old Turia riverbed. It's mostly the work of stellar local architect, the world-renowned Santiago Calatrava. The complex includes the **Oceanogràfic** (adult/child €24/18; ☺10am-6pm), a stunning aquarium; **Hemisfèric** (adult/child €7.50/5.80), a planetarium and IMAX cinema; **Museo de las Ciencias Príncipe Felipe** (adult/child €7.50/6; ☺10am-7pm), an interactive science museum; and the extraordinary **Palau de les Arts Reina Sofía** (www.lesarts.com; Autovía a El Saler) concert hall. It's 3km southeast of the Plaza de la Virgen; take bus 35 from Plaza del Ayuntamiento or bus 95 from Torres de Serranos or Plaza de América.

Barrio del Carmen HISTORIC AREA

You'll see Valencia's best face by simply wandering around the Barrio del Carmen. Valencia's Romanesque-Gothic-baroque-Renaissance **catedral** (adult/child incl audioguide €4/2.70; ☺10am-5.30pm Mon-Sat, 2-5.30pm Sun) is a compendium of centuries of architectural history and home to the **Capilla del Santo Cáliz**, a chapel said to contain the Holy Grail (the chalice Christ supposedly used in the last supper). Climb the 207 stairs of the **Micalet bell tower** (Miguelete bell tower; adult/child €2/1; ☺10am-7pm) for sweeping city views.

Plaza del Mercado HISTORIC PLAZA

Over on Plaza del Mercado, two emblematic buildings, each a masterpiece of its era, face each other. Valencia's Modernista covered market, the **Mercado Central** (☺7.30am-2.30pm Mon-Sat) recently scrubbed and glowing as new, was constructed in 1928. With over 900 stalls, it's a swirl of smells, movement and colour. **La Lonja** (☺10am-2pm & 4.30-8.30pm Mon-Sat, 10am-3pm Sun) is a splendid late-15th-century building, a Unesco World Heritage site and was originally Valencia's silk and commodity exchange.

Instituto Valenciano de Arte Moderno (IVAM) CONTEMPORARY ART MUSEUM

(www.ivam.es; Calle de Guillem de Castro 118; adult/child €2/1; ☺10am-8pm Tue-Sun) IVAM (ee-bam) hosts excellent temporary exhibitions and houses an impressive permanent collection of 20th-century Spanish art.

FREE **Museo de Bellas Artes** FINE ARTS MUSEUM

(Calle San Pío V 9; ☺10am-8pm Tue-Sun) Bright and spacious, the Museo de Bellas Artes ranks among Spain's best. Highlights include the

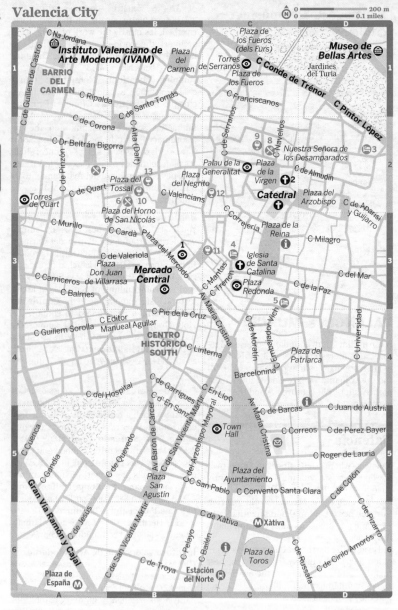

grandiose Roman *Mosaic of the Nine Muses*, a collection of magnificent late-medieval altarpieces and works by El Greco, Goya, Velázquez, Murillo, Ribalta and artists such as Sorolla and Pinazo of the Valencian Impressionist school.

Beaches

Playa de la Malvarrosa runs into **Playa de las Arenas**. Each is bordered by the **Paseo Marítimo** promenade and a string of restaurants. **Playa El Salér**, 10km south, is backed by shady pine woods. **Autocares**

SPAIN VALENCIA

Herca (☑96 349 12 50; www.autocaresherca.com, in Spanish) buses run between Valencia and Perelló hourly (half-hourly in summer), calling by El Salér village. The beaches lie east and southeast of the city centre.

🛏 Sleeping

TOP CHOICE **Ad Hoc** HOTEL €€
(☑96 391 91 40; www.adhochoteles.com; Calle Boix 4; s €65-101, d €76-125; ❄️📶) Friendly, welcoming Ad Hoc offers comfort and charm deep within the old quarter. The late-19th-century building has been restored to its former splendour with great sensitivity.

TOP CHOICE **Petit Palace Bristol** BOUTIQUE HOTEL €€
(☑96 394 51 00; www.hthoteles.com; Calle Abadía San Martín 3; r €60-130; ❄️@📶) Hip and minimalist, this lovely boutique hotel, a comprehensively made-over 19th-century mansion, retains the best of its past and does a particularly scrumptious buffet breakfast. Free bikes for guests.

Chill Art Jardín Botánico BOUTIQUE HOTEL €€
(☑96 315 40 12; www.hoteljardinbotanico.com; Calle Doctor Peset Cervera 6; s €94-133, d €94-149; ❄️📶) Welcoming and megacool, this intimate, 16-room hotel is furnished with great flair. Candles flicker in the lounge and each bedroom has original artwork. The Instituto Valenciano de Arte Moderno (IVAM) is nearby.

Hostal Antigua Morellana BUDGET HOTEL €
(☑96 391 57 73; www.hostalam.com; Calle En Bou 2; s €45-55, d €55-65; ❄️) The friendly, family-run 18-room Hostal Antigua Morellana is tucked away near the central market. Occupying a renovated 18th-century *posada* (where wealthier merchants could spend the night),

it has cosy, good-sized rooms, most with balconies.

Neptuno HOTEL €€€
(☑96 356 77 77; www.hotelneptunovalencia.com; Paseo de Neptuno 2; s €115-135, d €128-148; ❄️📶) Neptuno, ultramodern and ultracool, overlooks the beach and leisure port. It's ideal for mixing cultural tourism with a little beach frolicking.

✕ Eating

At weekends, locals in their hundreds head for Las Arenas, just north of the port, where a long line of restaurants overlooking the beach all serve up authentic paella in a three-course meal costing around €15.

TOP CHOICE **La Pepica** SEAFOOD €€
(☑96 371 03 66; Paseo Neptuno 6; meals around €25; ⊙lunch & dinner Mon-Sat, lunch Sun) More expensive than its competitors, La Pepica is renowned for its rice dishes and seafood. Here, Ernest Hemingway, among many other luminaries, once strutted. Between courses, browse through the photos and tributes that plaster the walls.

TOP CHOICE **Tridente** SPANISH FUSION €€€
(☑96 371 03 66; Paseo Neptuno; menú €45-65, mains €22-30; ⊙Tue-Sat & lunch Sun) Begin with an aperitif on the broad beachfront terrace, then move inside, where there's an ample à la carte selection but you won't find details of the day's *menús* in front of you – they're delivered orally by the maître d', who speaks good English. Dishes with their combinations of colours and blending of sweet and savoury are creative and delightfully presented, and portions are generous.

BURN BABY BURN

In mid-March, Valencia hosts one of Europe's wildest street parties: **Las Fallas de San José** (www.fallas.es, in Spanish). For one week (12 to 19 March), the city is engulfed by an anarchic swirl of fireworks, music, festive bonfires and all-night partying. On the final night, giant *ninots* (effigies), many of political and social personages, are torched in the main plaza.

If you're not in Valencia then, see the *ninots* saved from the flames by popular vote at the **Museo Fallero** (Plaza Monteolivete 4; adult/child €2/1; ⊙10am-2pm & 4.30-8pm Tue-Sat, 10am-3pm Sun).

Bar Pilar   TAPAS €
(C del Moro Zeit 13; ⊙noon-midnight) Cramped, earthy Bar Pilar is great for hearty tapas and *clóchinas,* small, juicy local mussels, available between May and August. For the rest of the year, *mejillones* are served, altogether fatter if less tasty. Ask for an *entero,* a platterful in a spicy broth that you scoop up with a spare shell.

Seu-Xerea   MEDITERRANEAN €€
(☑96 392 40 00; www.seuxerea.com; Calle Conde Almodóvar 4; menú €22-50, mains €16-19; ⊙lunch & dinner Mon-Fri, dinner Sat) This welcoming restaurant has a creative, regularly changing à la carte menu that features dishes both international and rooted in Spain. Wines are uniformly excellent.

L'Hamadríada   MEDITERRANEAN €€
(☑96 326 08 91; www.hamadriada.com, in Spanish; Plaza Vicente Iborra; lunch menú €13, menús €18-22, mains €12.50-16; ⊙lunch Sun-Tue, lunch & dinner Wed-Sat) Staff are well informed and attentive at the Wood Nymph, a local favourite. This slim white rectangle of a place does an innovative midday *menú,* perfectly simmered rice dishes, and grills where the meat, like the vegetables, is of prime quality.

🍷 Drinking

The Barrio del Carmen, the university area (around Avenidas de Aragón and Blasco Ibáñez), the area around the Mercado de Abastos and, in summer, the new port area and Malvarrosa are all jumping with bars and clubs.

TOP CHOICE **Sant Jaume**   CAFE BAR
(Plaza del Tossal) A converted pharmacy, its 1st floor is all quiet crannies and poky passageways

Café-Bar Negrito   CAFE BAR
(Plaza del Negrito) Recently redesigned, it traditionally attracts a more left-wing, intellectual clientele.

Café Lisboa   CAFE BAR
(Plaza del Doctor Collado 9) Another lively, student-oriented bar with a large, streetside terrace.

Café Infanta   CAFE BAR
(Plaza del Tossal) The interior is a clutter of cinema memorabilia while its external terrace is great for people-watching.

Café de las Horas   COCKTAIL BAR
(Calle Conde de Almodóvar 1) Offers a high baroque interior, tapestries, candelabras, music of all genres and a long list of exotic cocktails.

☆ Entertainment

Terraza Umbracle   LOUNGE, CLUB
(⊙midnight-6.30am Thu-Sat mid-May–mid-Oct) At the southern end of the Umbracle walkway within the City of Arts and Sciences, this is a cool, sophisticated spot to spend a hot summer night. Catch the evening breeze under the stars on the terrace, then drop below to **MYA**, a top-of-the-line club with an awesome sound system. Admission (€20 including first drink) covers both venues.

Dub Club   CLUB
(Calle Jesús 91; ⊙Thu-Sun) 'We play music not noise' is the slogan of this funky dive with its long, narrow bar giving onto a packed dance floor. And it indeed offers great music and great variety including live jazz jamming, reggae, dub, drum'n'bass, funk, breakbeat and more. It's around 1km southwest of the Plaza de la Virgen, just off Avenida Giorgeta.

Black Note   LIVE MUSIC
(Calle Polo y Peyrolón 15) Valencia city's most active jazz venue, Black Note has live music Monday to Thursday and good canned jazz, blues and soul on Friday and Saturday. Admission, including first drink, costs from €6 to €15 depending on who's grooving. It's 1.5km east of the Plaza de la Virgen, just off Avenida de Aragón.

ℹ Information

Regional tourist office (www.comunitatvalenciana.com; Calle Paz 48; ⊙9am-8pm Mon-Sat, 10am-2pm Sun)

Turismo Valencia (VLC) (www.turisvalencia.es; Plaza de la Reina 19; ⊙9am-7pm Mon-Sat, 10am-2pm Sun)

❶ Getting There & Away

AIR Valencia's **Aeropuerto de Manises** (📞96 159 85 00) is 10km west of the city centre. It's served by metro lines 3 and 5. Budget flights serve major European destinations.

BOAT Acciona Trasmediterránea (www .acciona-trasmediterranea.es) operates car and passenger ferries to Ibiza, Mallorca and Menorca; see p905.

BUS Valencia's **bus station** (📞96 346 62 66) is beside the riverbed on Avenida Menéndez Pidal. **Avanza** (www.avanzabus.com) operates hourly bus services to/from Madrid (€18 to €27, four hours). **ALSA** (www.alsa.es) has numerous buses to/from Barcelona (€26 to €30, 4½ hours) and Alicante (€21, 2½ hours), most passing by Benidorm (€14.50, 1¾ hours).

TRAIN From Valencia's Estación del Norte, major destinations include Alicante (€29, 1¾ hours, eight daily) and Barcelona (€39 to €43, three to 3½ hours, at least 12 daily). The AVE, the high-speed train, now links Madrid and Valencia, with up to 15 high-speed services daily and a journey time of around 1¾ hours.

❶ Getting Around

Metro line 5 connects the airport, city centre and port. The high-speed tram leaves from the FGV tram station, 500m north of the cathedral, at the Pont de Fusta. This is a pleasant way to get to the beach, the paella restaurants of Las Arenas and the port.

Alicante

POP 334,800

With its elegant, palm-lined boulevards, lively nightlife scene and easy-to-access beaches, Alicante (Alacant in Valenciano) is an all-in-one Spanish city. The city is at its most charming at night, when tapas bars and taverns in El Barrio (the Old Quarter) come alive.

◉ Sights & Activities

TOP CHOICE **Castillo de Santa Bárbara**   CASTLE
(☉10am-10pm) There are sweeping views over the city from this 16th-century castle, which will soon house the **Museo de la Ciudad de Alicante (MUSA)**, a new museum recounting the history of the city. A lift/elevator, reached by a footbridge opposite Playa del Postiguet, rises through the bowels of the mountain.

TOP CHOICE **Museo de Arte Contemporáneo de Alicante (MACA)**   ART MUSEUM
(Plaza Sta María 3; admission free; ☉10am-8pm Tue-Sat, to 2pm Sun) Closed for many years

while its premises, the splendid 17th-century Casa de la Asegurada, were renovated and enlarged, this splendid museum has an excellent collection of 20th-century Spanish art, including works by Dalí, Miró, Chillida, Sempere, Tàpies and Picasso.

Beaches   BEACHES
Immediately north of the port is the sandy beach of **Playa del Postiguet**. Easily reached by tram, **Playa de San Juan** is larger and usually less crowded.

🛏 Sleeping

TOP CHOICE **Hostal Les Monges Palace**
BUDGET HOTEL €
(📞96 521 50 46; www.lesmonges.net; Calle San Agustín 4; s €30-44, d €45-59; ✳@🤶) This agreeably quirky place is a treasure with its winding corridors, tiles, mosaics and antique furniture. Each room is individually decorated and reception couldn't be more welcoming. Look out for the small Dalí original beside the reception desk.

Guest House Antonio
BOUTIQUE BUDGET HOTEL €
(📞650 718353; www.guesthousealicante.com; Calle Segura 20; s €35-40, d €45-50; ✳🤶) A magnificent budget choice: eight large, tastefully decorated rooms, each with a safe, full-size fridge and free beverage-making facilities. The five apartments (€70 to €80), two with their own patio, have a mini-kitchen and washing machine, and are exceptional value.

🍴 Eating & Drinking

The old quarter around Catedral de San Nicolás is wall-to-wall bars. Down by the harbour, the Paseo del Puerto, tranquil by day, is a double-decker line of bars, cafes and night-time discos.

TOP CHOICE **Piripi**   VALENCIAN €€
(📞96 522 79 40; Avenida Oscar Esplá 30; mains €12-26) This highly regarded restaurant is strong on rice, seafood and fish, which arrives fresh and daily from the wholesale markets of Denia and Santa Pola. There's a huge variety of tapas and a *valenciano* speciality that changes daily. It's around 500m west of Plaza de Calvo Sotelo.

El Trellat   MODERN SPANISH €
(Calle de Capitán Segarra 19; lunch menú €10, dinner menús €10-25; ☉lunch Mon-Sat, dinner Fri & Sat) Beside the covered market, this small, friendly place has exceptionally creative, flexible *menús*: a serve-yourself first-course buffet, then an ample choice of inventive mains.

SPAIN VALENCIA & MURCIA

Alicante

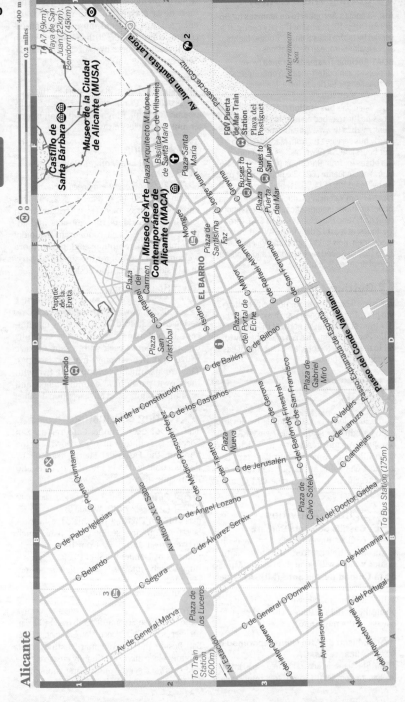

To A7 (9km);
Playa de San
Juan (22km):
Benidorm (45km)

Castillo de
Santa Bárbara

Museo de la Ciudad
de Alicante (MUSA)

Av Juan Bautista Lafora

Paseo de Gómiz

Mediterranean
Sea

Plaza Arquitecto M López

Basílica C de Villavieja
de Santa María

Plaza Santa
María

FGV Puerta
de Mar Train
Station

Playa del
Postiguet

Museo de Arte
Contemporáneo de
Alicante (MACA)

Monges

Plaza de
Santísima
Faz

Buses to
Airport

Buses to
San Juan

Plaza
Puerta
del Mar

EL BARRIO

Plaza
del Portal de
Elche

C de Bilbao

Plaza
del Rafael del
Carmen

C San Rafael de

Plaza
San
Cristóbal

S Isidro

C de Bailén

Mercado

Parque
de la
Ereta

Av de la Constitución

C de los Castaños

C de Gerona

C del Teatro

Plaza
Nueva

C de Médico Pascual Pérez

C de Jerusalén

C de Ángel Lozano

C de Álvarez Sereix

Av Alfonso X El Sabio

C de Pablo Iglesias

C Belando

C Segura

Plaza de
los Luceros

Av de General Marvá

C del Pintor Cabrera

C del Barón de Finestrat

C de San Francisco

Plaza de
Gabriel
Miró

C Valdés

C de Lanuza

Canalejas

Plaza de
Calvo Sotelo

Av del Doctor Gadea

Av del Estación

To Train
Station
(600m)

To Bus Station (175m)

C de General O'Donnell

Av Maisonnave

C de Alemania

C del Portugal

Paseo Esplanada de España

Paseo del Conde Vallellano

400 m

0.2 miles

Alicante

ⓘ Information

Municipal tourist office (www.alicanteturismo
.com) Branches at the bus station and train
station.

Regional tourist office (Rambla de Méndez
Núñez 23; ◷9am-8pm Mon-Sat, 10am-2pm
Sun)

ⓘ Getting There & Away

AIR Alicante's **El Altet airport**, gateway to the
Costa Blanca, is around 12km southwest of the
centre. It's served by budget airlines, charters
and scheduled flights from all over Europe.

BUS Destinations include Madrid (€27.50, 5¼
hours, at least 10 daily), Murcia (€5.50, one
hour, at least seven daily) and Valencia (€21, 2½
hours, 10 daily).

TRAIN Destinations from the main **Renfe
Estación de Madrid** (Avenida de Salamanca)
include Barcelona (€55, five hours, eight daily),
Madrid (€45, 3¾ hours, seven daily), Murcia
(€4.50, 1¼ hours, hourly) and Valencia (€29, 1¾
hours, eight daily).

TRAM (www.fgvalicante.com) Tram line 1 goes
to Benidorm (€4.40, one hour, every 30 minutes). Catch it from the Mercado stop beside
the covered market, changing at La Isleta or
Lucentum.

Costa Blanca

Clean white beaches, bright sunshine and
a rockin' nightlife have made the **Costa
Blanca** (www.costablanca.org) one of Europe's
favourite summer playgrounds. Many resorts are shamefully overbuilt, but it is still
possible to discover charming towns and

unspoilt coastline. Some of the best towns
to explore include **Benidorm**, a highrise
nightlife hot spot in summer (but filled to
the brim with pensioners the rest of the
year); **Altea**, whose church with its pretty
blue-tiled dome is its crowning glory; and
Calpe, known for the Gibraltar-like **Peñon
de Ifach** (332m). All are accessible by train
from Alicante.

Murcia

With its rural interior, small coastal resorts
and lively capital city, **Murcia** (www.murcia
turistica.es) is as authentically Spanish as it
gets. A conservative province, Murcia is
known for its fabulous local produce, rich
tapas and unusually warm coast.

MURCIA
POP 433,850

Murcia is a laid-back provincial capital
that comes alive during the weekend *paseo* (stroll). Bypassed by most tourists and
treated as a country cousin by too many
Spaniards, the city nevertheless merits a
visit. Head for the river, the cathedral and
the surrounding pedestrian streets.

◎ Sights & Activities

TOP CHOICE **Real Casino de Murcia**

HISTORIC BUILDING
(www.casinodemurcia.com; Calle Trapería 18; admission €5; ◷11.30am-9pm) Murcia's resplendent
casino first opened as a gentlemen's club in
1847. The building is a fabulous combination
of historical design and opulence, providing
an evocative glimpse of bygone aristocratic
grandeur.

FREE **Catedral de Santa María** CHURCH
(Plaza del Cardinal Belluga; ◷7am-1pm &
5-8pm) Murcia's cathedral was built in 1394
on the site of a mosque. The initial Gothic
architecture was given a playful baroque
facelift in 1748. The 15th-century **Capilla de
los Vélez** is a highlight; the chapel's flutes
and curls resemble piped icing.

⊨ Sleeping & Eating

TOP CHOICE **Hotel Casa Emilio** HOTEL €
(✆968 22 06 31; www.hotelcasaemilio.
com; Alameda de Colón 9; s/d €45/50; ℗❄⊛)
Across from the Floridablanca gardens, near
the river, this is an attractively designed and
well-maintained hotel with spacious, brightly lit rooms, large bathrooms and good firm
mattresses.

Arco de San Juan HISTORIC HOTEL €€
(☎968 21 04 55; www.arcosanjuan.com; Plaza de Ceballos 10; s/d €75/130; P❉☎) This four-star hotel in a former 18th-century palace hints at its palatial past with a massive 5m-high original door and some hefty repro columns. The rooms are classic and comfortable, with hardwood details and classy fabrics.

Figón de Alfaro TAPAS €
(Calle Alfaro 7; meals €12-15; ⊙lunch & dinner Mon-Sat, lunch Sun) Popular with all ages and budgets, Figón de Alfaro offers a chaotic bar area or a more sedate interconnecting dining room. Choose from full meals, a range of juicy *montaditos* (minirolls) or innovative one-offs such as *pastel de berejena con salsa de calabacín* (aubergine pie with a courgette sauce).

Los Zagales SPANISH €
(Calle Polo Medina 4; meals €10-15) Lying within confessional distance of the cathedral (since 1926), Los Zagales dishes up superb, inexpensive tapas, *raciones, platos combinados,* homemade desserts (and homemade chips). This is where the locals eat, so you may have to wait for a table. It's worth it.

Los Arroces del Romea RICE DISHES €€
(Plaza Romea; meals €20-25; ☎) Watch the speciality paella-style rice dishes being prepared in cartwheel-sized pans over the flames while you munch on circular *murciano* bread drizzled with olive oil.

ⓘ Information
Tourist office (www.murciaciudad.com; Plaza del Cardenal Belluga; ⊙10am-2pm & 5-9pm Mon-Sat, 10am-2pm Sun)

ⓘ Getting There & Away
AIR Murcia's San Javier airport is closer to Cartagena than Murcia city. There are numerous flights to/from the UK.
TRAIN Up to five trains travel daily to/from Madrid (€44.60, 4¼ hours).

BALEARIC ISLANDS

POP 1.07 MILLION
The Balearic Islands (Illes Balears in Catalan) adorn the glittering Mediterranean waters off Spain's eastern coastline. Beach tourism destinations *par excellence,* each of the four islands has a quite distinct identity and they have managed to retain much of their individual character and beauty. All boast beach-es second to none in the Med but each offers reasons for exploring inland too.

Check out websites like www.illesbalears. es, www.platgesdebalears.com and www.balearsculturaltour.com.

ⓘ Getting There & Away
Air
In summer, charter and regular flights converge on Palma de Mallorca and Ibiza from all over Europe. Major operators from the Spanish mainland include **Iberia** (www.iberia.es), **Air Europa** (www.aireuropa.com), **Spanair** (www.spanair .com), **Air Berlin** (www.airberlin.com) and **Vueling** (www.vueling.com).

Boat
Compare prices and look for deals at **Direct Ferries** (www.directferries.es). Ferries serving the Balearic Islands:

Acciona Trasmediterránea (☎902 454 645; www.trasmediterranea.es)
Baleària (☎902 160 180; www.balearia.com)
Cala Ratjada Tours (☎902 100 444; www .calaratjadatours.es, in Spanish)
Iscomar (☎902 119 128; www.iscomar.com)

The main ferry routes to the mainland:
Ibiza (Ibiza City) To/from Barcelona (Acciona Trasmediterránea, Baleària), Valencia (Acciona Trasmediterránea)
Ibiza (Sant Antoni) To/from Denia and Barcelona (Baleària), Valencia (Acciona Trasmediterránea, Baleària)
Mallorca (Palma de Mallorca) To/from Barcelona and Valencia (Acciona Trasmediterránea, Baleària), Denia (Baleària)
Menorca (Maó) To/from Barcelona and Valencia (Acciona Trasmediterránea, Baleària)

The main interisland ferry routes:
Ibiza (Ibiza City) To/from Palma de Mallorca (Acciona Trasmediterránea and Baleària)
Mallorca (Cala Ratjada) To/from Ciutadella (Cala Ratjada Tours)
Mallorca (Palma de Mallorca) To/from Ibiza City (Acciona Trasmediterránea and Baleària) and Maó (Acciona Trasmediterránea and Baleària)
Mallorca (Port d'Alcúdia) To/from Ciutadella (Iscomar)
Menorca (Ciutadella) To/from Cala Ratjada (Cala Ratjada Tours) and Port d'Alcúdia (Iscomar)
Menorca (Maó) To/from Palma de Mallorca (Acciona Trasmediterránea and Baleària)

Mallorca

The sunny, warm hues of the medieval heart of Palma de Mallorca (pop 401,300), the archipelago's capital, make a great introduction to the islands. The northwest coast, dominated by the Serra de Tramuntana mountain range, is a beautiful region of olive groves, pine forests and ochre villages, with a spectacularly rugged coastline. Most of Mallorca's best beaches are on the north and east coasts, and although many have been swallowed up by tourist developments, you can still find the occasional exception. There is also a scattering of fine beaches along the south coast.

🛈 Getting Around

BUS Most of the island is accessible by bus from Palma. All buses depart from or near the **bus station** (Carrer d'Eusebi Estada).

TRAIN Two train lines run from Plaça d'Espanya in Palma de Mallorca. The popular, old train runs to Sóller, a pretty ride. A standard train line runs inland to Inca (€1.80, 40 minutes, every half-hour), where the line splits with a branch to Sa Pobla (€2.40, one hour, hourly) and another to Manacor (€2.40, 1¼ hours, hourly).

PALMA DE MALLORCA
🎯 Sights & Activities

TOP CHOICE **Cathedral**   CHURCH
(La Seu; Carrer del Palau Reial 9; adult/child €4/3; ⊙10am-5.15pm Mon-Fri, 10am-2.15pm Sat) This awesome structure, completed in 1601, is predominantly Gothic, apart from the main facade (replaced after an earthquake in 1851) and parts of the interior. The cathedral's interior is stunning, with ranks of slender columns supporting the soaring ceiling and framing three levels of elaborate stained-glass windows. The front altar's centrepiece, a light, twisting wrought-iron sculpture suspended from the ceiling, is one of Gaudí's more eccentric creations. For once, Gaudí is upstaged by the island's top contemporary artist, Miquel Barceló, who reworked the **Capella del Santíssim i Sant Pere**, at the head of the south aisle, in a dream-fantasy, swirling ceramic rendition of the miracle of the loaves and fishes.

Palau de l'Almudaina   PALACE
(Carrer del Palau Reial s/n; adult/child €3.20/2.30, audioguide €2.50; ⊙10am-5.45pm Mon-Fri, 1.15pm Sat) Originally an Islamic fort, this mighty construction was converted into a residence for the Mallorcan monarchs at the end of the 13th century. It is still occasionally used for official functions when King Juan Carlos is in town. At other times, you can wander through a series of cavernous and austere stone-walled rooms, a chapel with a rare Romanesque entrance, and upstairs royal apartments adorned with Flemish tapestries and period furniture.

Es Baluard   ART MUSEUM
(Museu d'Art Modern i Contemporani; www.es baluard.org, in Spanish; Porta de Santa Catalina 10; adult/child €6/4.50, temporary exhibitions €4/3; ⊙10am-8pm Tue-Sun) This 21st-century concrete complex nests within Palma's grand Renaissance-era seaward fortifications. A playful game of light, surfaces and perspective, it makes the perfect framework for the works within.

Palau March   ART MUSEUM
(www.fundbmarch.es; Carrer de Palau Reial 18; adult/child €3.60/free; ⊙10am-6pm Mon-Fri, to 2pm Sat) This house, palatial by any definition, contains sculptures by 20th-century greats such as Henry Moore, Auguste Rodin, Barbara Hepworth and Eduardo Chillida which grace the outdoor terrace. Within is a set of Salvador Dalí prints.

FREE Museu d'Art Espanyol Contemporani   ART MUSEUM
(Museu Fundació Juan March; www.march.es/arte /palma; Carrer de Sant Miquel 11; ⊙10am-6.30pm Mon-Fri, 10.30am-2pm Sat) On permanent display within this 18th-century mansion are some 70 pieces that together constitute a veritable who's who of mostly 20th-century artists, including Picasso, Miró, Juan Gris (of cubism fame), Dalí and the sculptor Julio González.

🛏 Sleeping

TOP CHOICE **Hotel Santa Clara**   BOUTIQUE HOTEL €€€
(☎971 72 92 31; www.santaclarahotel .es; Carrer de Sant Alonso 16; s/d from €155/210; ❄@🖰) Boutique meets antique in this historic mansion, respectfully converted, where subdued greys, steely silvers and cream blend harmoniously with the warm stone walls, ample spaces and high ceilings of the original structure.

Hotel Born   HISTORIC HOTEL €€
(☎971 71 29 42; www.hotelborn.com; Carrer de Sant Jaume 3; s incl breakfast €52, d €76-97; ❄@🖰) A superb place in the heart of the city, this hotel is in an 18th-century palace. Rooms combine elegance and history with all mod cons. The best have an engaging view onto the palm-shaded patio.

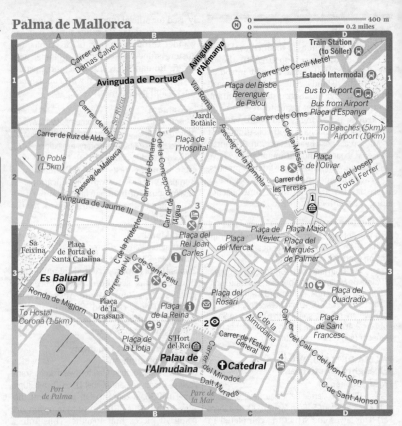

Hostal Corona

HOTEL €

(☎971 73 19 35; www.hostal-corona.com; Carrer de Josep Villalonga 22; s €30, d €45-60) With its palm trees and cornucopia of plants, the generous courtyard garden of this little hotel (the house was once a private villa) has a faraway feel. Rooms are simple, with timber furnishings and old tiled floors.

✗ Eating

TOP CHOICE Simply Fosh

INTERNATIONAL €€

(☎971 72 01 14; www.simplyfosh.com; Carrer de la Missió 7a; mains €14-26, dinner menús €52; ☺Mon-Sat) It's great gourmet cuisine at the restaurant of Michelin-starred British chef Marc Fosh. Quality is sustained right down to the cheese board, with its selection of the very best that Spain offers.

La Bodeguilla

SPANISH €€

(☎971 71 82 74; www.la-bodeguilla.com; Carrer de Sant Jaume 3; mains €17.50-19.50; ☺Mon-Sat) This gourmet restaurant does creative interpretations of dishes from across Spain (such as *cochinillo,* suckling pig, from Segovia, and *lechazo,* young lamb, baked Córdoba-style in rosemary).

Bon Lloc

VEGETARIAN €

(☎971 71 86 17; www.bonllocrestaurant.com, in Spanish; Carrer de Sant Feliu 7; menús €13.50; ☺lunch Mon-Sat; ☑) This 100% vegetarian place, where all produce is organic, is light, open and airy. There are no agonising decisions – just a satisfying, take-it-or-leave-it four-course menú. It's hugely popular so do ring to reserve.

13%

TAPAS €

(www.13porciento.com; Carrer Sant Feliu 13a; meals around €15; ☑) At the quieter end of the old town, this L-shaped barn of a place is both wine and tapas bar. Most items are organic and there's plenty of choice for vegetarians. Wines are displayed on racks and all can be purchased (both bar and takeaway prices are quoted so you know exactly the mark-up).

SPAIN MALLORCA

🍷 Drinking & Entertainment

The old quarter is the city's most vibrant nightlife zone. Particularly along the narrow streets between Plaça de la Reina and Plaça de la Drassana, you'll find an enormous selection of bars, pubs and bodegas. According to a much flouted law, bars should shut by 1am Sunday to Thursday (3am Friday and Saturday).

Vamos 365 (www.vamosmallorca365.com), a monthly freebie, has its finger on Palma's night-time pulse.

|TOP\ CHOICE| **Puro Beach** BAR

(www.purobeach.com; ⊙11am-2am Apr-Oct) This uber-laid-back, sunset chill lounge has a tapering outdoor promontory with an all-white bar that's perfect for sunset cocktails, DJ sessions and fusion food escapes. It is just a two-minute walk east of Cala Estancia (itself just east of Ca'n Pastilla). It's southeast of Palma de Mallorca along the coast.

Ca'n Joan de S'Aigo CAFE

(Carrer de Can Sanç 10; ⊙8am-9pm Wed-Mon) Dating from 1700, this is *the* place for a hot chocolate (€1.40) in what can only be described as an antique-filled milk bar. The house speciality is *quart,* a feather-soft sponge cake that children love with almond-flavoured ice cream.

Abaco BAR

(www.bar-abaco.com, in Spanish; Carrer de Sant Joan 1; ⊙from 9pm) Behind a set of ancient timber doors is the bar of your wildest dreams. Inside, a typical Mallorcan patio and candlelit courtyard are crammed with elaborate floral arrangements, cascading towers of fresh fruit and bizarre artworks.

❶ Information

Consell de Mallorca tourist office (☏971 71 22 16; www.infomallorca.net; Plaça de la Reina 2; ⊙8am-8pm Mon-Fri, 9am-2pm Sat)

Municipal tourist office (☏902 102365; ⊙9am-8pm Mon-Sat) Main office (Casal Solleric, Passeig d'es Born 27); branch office (train station)

AROUND MALLORCA

Mallorca's northwestern coast is a world away from the high-rise tourism on the other side of the island. Dominated by the Serra de Tramuntana, it's a beautiful region of olive groves, pine forests and small villages with shuttered stone buildings. There are a couple of highlights for drivers: the hair-raising road down to the small port of **Sa Calobra**, and the amazing trip along the peninsula leading to the island's northern tip, **Cap Formentor**.

Sóller is a good place to base yourself for hiking and the nearby village of **Fornalutx** is one of the prettiest on Mallorca.

From Sóller, it's a 10km walk to the beautiful hilltop village of **Deià** (www.deia.info), where Robert Graves, poet and author of *I Claudius,* lived for most of his life. From the village, you can scramble down to the small shingle beach of **Cala de Deià**. Boasting a fine monastery and pretty streets, **Valldemossa** (www.valldemossa.com) is further southwest down the coast.

Further east, **Pollença** and **Artà** are attractive inland towns. Nice beaches include those at **Cala Sant Vicenç**, **Cala Mondragó** and around **Cala Llombards**.

🛏 Sleeping & Eating

The **Consell de Mallorca tourist office** (☏971 71 22 16; www.infomallorca.net; Plaça de la Reina 2; ⊙8am-8pm Mon-Fri, 9am-2pm Sat) in Palma can supply information on rural and other types of accommodation around the island.

DEIÀ

Hostal Miramar
HOTEL €€

(📞971 63 90 84; www.pensionmiramar.com; Carrer de Ca'n Oliver; r incl breakfast €84, without bathroom €75; 🕙Mar–mid-Nov) Hidden within the lush vegetation above the main road and with views across to Deià's hillside church and sea beyond, this 19th-century stone house with gardens is a shady retreat with nine rooms.

El Barrigón de Xelini
TAPAS €

(Avinguda del Arxiduc Lluís Salvador 19; meals €20; 🕙Tue-Sun) You never quite know what to expect here, but tapas, more than 50 kinds drawn from all over Spain, are at the core. It has a penchant for mains of lamb too. On summer weekends, there's live jazz.

SÓLLER

The Sóller area has plenty of boutique hotels in historic buildings or country houses; many are listed on www.sollernet.com.

Hotel El Guía
HOTEL €€

(📞971 63 02 27; www.sollernet.com/elguia; Carrer del Castanyer 2; s/d €53/84) Right beside the train station and family run, this is a good place to meet fellow walkers. Its bright, simple rooms feature timber trims and modern bathrooms, and it runs a creditable restaurant.

Ca's Carreter
MALLORCAN €€

(📞971 63 51 33; Carrer del Cetre 9; menús €12, mains €16; 🕙lunch & dinner Tue-Sat, lunch Sun) Set in a leafy cart workshop (founded in 1914), this is a cool and welcoming spot for modest local cooking, with fresh fish and meat options.

EAST COAST

Hostal Playa Mondragó
BUDGET HOTEL €€

(📞971 65 77 52; www.playamondrago.com; Cala Mondragó; s/d incl breakfast €63/96; 🕙Easter-Oct; ❄️🌐🏊) Barely 50m back from one of the beaches, it's a tranquil option and the better rooms have balconies and fine sea views.

Ibiza

Ibiza (Eivissa in Catalan) is an island of extremes. Its formidable party reputation is completely justified, with some of the world's greatest clubs attracting hedonists from the world over. The interior and northeast of the island, however, are another world. Peaceful country drives, hilly green territory, a sprinkling of mostly laid-back beaches and coves, and some wonderful inland accommodation and eateries, are light years from the ecstasy-fuelled madness of the clubs that dominate the west.

ℹ️ Getting Around

AIR Ibiza's airport (Aeroport d'Eivissa), just 7km southwest of Ibiza City, receives direct flights from all over Europe.

BOAT Hourly ferries (one way/return €3.50/6) run to/from Playa d'en Bossa and Figueretes from May to October. Boats to Cala Llonga, Santa Eulària d'es Riu and Es Canar (all €13 return) run up to six times daily from May to mid-October.

BUS Buses to other parts of the island depart from the new bus station (nearing completion when we last visited) on Avenide de la Pau.

IBIZA CITY
🎯 Sights & Activities

Ibiza City's port area of Sa Penya is crammed with funky and trashy clothing boutiques and arty-crafty market stalls. From here, you can wander up into D'Alt Vila, the atmospheric old walled town.

Ramparts
HISTORIC AREA

A ramp leads from Plaça de Sa Font in Sa Penya up to the 1585 **Portal de ses Taules** gateway, the main entrance. The walls consist of seven artillery bastions joined by thick protective walls up to 22m in height. You can **walk** the entire perimeter of these impressive Renaissance-era walls, designed to withstand heavy artillery, and enjoy great views along the way.

Catedral
CHURCH

Ibiza's cathedral elegantly combines several styles: the original 14th-century structure is Catalan Gothic but the sacristy was added in 1592, and a major baroque renovation took place in the 18th century.

Centre d'Interpretació Madina Yasiba
MUSEUM

(Carrer Major 2; adult/child €2/1.50; 🕙10am-2pm & 6-8pm Tue-Sat, 10am-2pm Sun) A small display that replicates the medieval Muslim city of Madina Yasiba (Ibiza City), prior to the island's fall to Christian forces in 1235. Artefacts, audiovisuals and maps help transport us to those times.

🛏️ Sleeping

Many of Ibiza City's hotels and *hostales* are closed in the low season and heavily booked between April and October. Make sure you book ahead.

Hotel La Ventana
HISTORIC HOTEL €€€

(⌨971 30 35 37; www.laventanaibiza.com; Carrer de Sa Carossa 13; d from €165; ❋🛜) This charming 15th-century mansion is set on a little tree-shaded square in the old town. Some rooms come with stylish four-poster beds and mosquito nets. The rooftop terrace, trim gardens and restaurant are welcome extras.

Hostal La Marina
BUDGET HOTEL €€

(⌨971 31 01 72; www.hostal-lamarina.com; Carrer de Barcelona 7; r €68-125; ❋) Looking onto both the waterfront and bar-lined Carrer de Barcelona, this mid-19th-century building has all sorts of brightly coloured rooms. A handful of singles and some doubles look onto the street (with the predictable noise problem), with pricier doubles and attics with terraces and panoramic port and/or town views.

Casa de Huéspedes Navarro
BUDGET HOTEL €

(⌨971 31 07 71; Carrer de sa Creu 20; s/d without bathroom €28/55; ⊘May-Oct) Right in the thick of things, this simple option has eight rooms at the top of a long flight of stairs. The front rooms have harbour views, interior ones are quite dark (but cool in summer) and there's a sunny rooftop terrace. Bathrooms are shared but spotless.

✖ Eating

TOP CHOICE Comidas Bar San Juan
MEDITERRANEAN €

(Carrer de Guillem de Montgrí 8; meals €15-20; ⊘Mon-Sat) A family-run operation with two small dining rooms, this simple eatery offers outstanding value, with fish dishes for around €10 and many small mains for €6 or less. It doesn't take reservations so do arrive early.

Restaurant of Hotel Mirador de Dalt Vila
GOURMET €€

(⌨971 30 30 45; Plaça d'Espanya 4; menú €45, mains €26-30; ⊘Easter-Dec) At this intimate – do reserve – restaurant with its painted barrel ceiling and original canvases around the walls, you'll dine magnificently. Service is discreet yet friendly, dishes are creative, colourful and delightfully presented.

🍷 Drinking

Sa Penya is the nightlife centre. Dozens of bars keep the port area jumping. Alternatively, various bars at Platja d'en Bossa combine sounds, sand, sea and sangria.

Discobus (www.discobus.es; per person €3; ⊘midnight-6am Jun-Sep) runs around the major discos, bars and hotels in Ibiza City, Platja d'en Bossa, Sant Rafel, Es Canar, Santa Eulària and Sant Antoni.

Teatro Pereira
MUSIC BAR

(www.teatropereyra.com; Carrer del Comte de Rosselló 3; ⊘8am-4am) Away from the waterfront hubbub, this hugely atmospheric place, all stained wood and iron girders, was once the foyer of the long-abandoned 1893 theatre at its rear. Packed most nights with a more eclectic crowd than the standard preclubbing bunch, it offers nightly live music sessions. By day, it's a stylish place for a drink or snack.

Bora Bora Beach Club
BEACH BAR

(⊘noon-4am May-Sep) At Platja d'en Bossa, about 2km from the old town, this is *the* place – a long beachside bar where sun- and fun-worshippers work off hangovers and prepare new ones. Entry's free and the ambience is chilled, with low-key club sounds wafting over the sand.

❶ Information

Tourist office Main office (www.ibiza.travel; Passeig de Vara de Rei 1; ⊘9am-8pm Mon-Fri, to 7pm Sat); D'Alt Vila office (Carrer Major 2; ⊘9am-8pm Mon-Sat, to 3pm Sun)

AROUND IBIZA

Ibiza has numerous unspoiled and relatively undeveloped beaches. **Cala de Boix**, on the northeastern coast, is the only black-sand beach on the island, while further north are the lovely beaches of **S'Aigua Blanca**.

On the north coast near Portinatx, **Cala Xarraca** is in a picturesque, secluded bay, and near Port de Sant Miquel is the attractive **Cala Benirrás**.

In the southwest, **Cala d'Hort** has a spectacular setting overlooking two rugged rock islets, Es Verda and Es Verdranell.

The best thing about rowdy **Sant Antoni**, the island's second biggest town and north of Ibiza City, is heading to the small rock-and-sand strip on the north shore to join hundreds of others for sunset drinks at a string of chilled bars. The best known remains **Café del Mar** (www.cafedelmar.es; ⊘4pm-1am), our favourite, but it's further north along the pedestrian walkway.

Local **buses** (www.ibizabus.com) run to most destinations between May and October.

🛏 Sleeping & Eating

Check out rural accommodation at www.ibizaruralvillas.com and www.casasrurales ibiza.com (in Spanish). For more standard

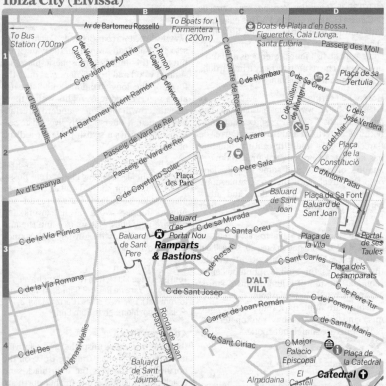

accommodation, start at www.ibizahotels guide.com.

TOP CHOICE **Hostal Cala Boix** BUDGET HOTEL €€
(☎971 33 52 24; www.hostalcalaboix.com; d incl breakfast €80; ☺May-Oct; ☀) Set uphill and back from the beach, this solitary place has big, cheap rooms and a hearty restaurant. On the beach you'll find a daytime bar in summer.

Hostal Es Alocs BUDGET HOTEL €
(☎971 33 50 79; www.hostalalocs.com; s/d €35/65; ☺May-Oct) Right on the beach at Platja Es Figueral. Rooms are simple, over a couple of floors. Downstairs it has a bar-restaurant with shady terrace.

Bar Anita BAR-RESTAURANT €
(mains €8-16) A timeless tavern opposite the village church in inland Sant Carles, this place offers anything from pizza to slabs of ~~~te con salsa de pimiento~~ (entrecôte ~~~er sauce; €15).

Menorca

Renowned for its pristine beaches and archaeological sites, tranquil Menorca was declared a Biosphere Reserve by Unesco in 1993. The capital, Maó, is known as Mahón in Castilian.

❶ Getting Around

TO/FROM THE AIRPORT Bus 10 (€1.60) runs between Menorca's airport, 7km southwest of Maó, and the city's bus station every half-hour. A taxi costs around €15.

BUS You can get to most destinations from Maó, but, with a few exceptions, services are infrequent and sluggish.

◉ Sights & Activities

Maó absorbs most of the tourist traffic. North of Maó, a drive across a lunar landscape leads to the lighthouse at **Cap de Favàritx**. South of the cape stretch some

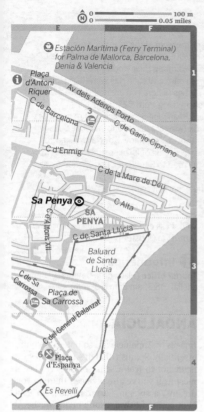

SPAIN MENORCA

🛏 Sleeping

Many accommodation options on the island are closed between November and April.

MAÓ

TOP CHOICE **Casa Alberti** HISTORIC HOTEL **€€**
(☑971 35 42 10; Carrer d'Isabel II 9; www
.casalberti.com; s/d incl breakfast from €80/100;
⊙Easter-Oct) Climb the central stairs with their striking wrought-iron banisters to your vast room with its white walls and whitest of white sheets. Each of the six bedrooms within this 18th-century mansion is furnished with traditional items, while bathrooms are designer-cool and contemporary.

CIUTADELLA

Hotel Gèminis HOTEL **€€**
(☑971 38 46 44; www.hotelgeminismenorca.com; Carrer de Josepa Rossinyol 4; s/d €65/96; ❈🅟🛜🖢) A friendly, stylish two-star place on a back-street, this graceful, three-storey, rose-and-white lodging offers comfortable if somewhat neutral rooms just a short walk away from the city centre.

Hostal-Residencia Oasis BUDGET HOTEL **€**
(☑971 38 21 97; Carrer de Sant Isidre 33; s/d €35/45) Run by a delightful elderly couple, this quiet place is close to the heart of the old quarter. Rooms, mostly with bathroom, are set beside a spacious garden courtyard. Their furnishings, though still trim, are from deep into the last century.

---

fine sandy bays and beaches, including **Cala Presili** and **Platja d'en Tortuga**, reachable on foot.

Ciutadella, with its smaller harbour and historic buildings, has a more distinctly Spanish feel to it and is the more attractive of the two. A narrow country road leads south of Ciutadella (follow the 'Platges' sign from the *ronda,* or ring road) and then forks twice to reach some of the island's loveliest beaches: (from west to east) **Arenal de Son Saura**, **Cala en Turqueta**, **Es Talaier**, **Cala Macarelleta** and **Cala Macarella**. As with most beaches, you'll need your own transport.

In the centre of the island, the 357m-high **Monte Toro** has great views; on a clear day you can see Mallorca.

On the northern coast, the picturesque town of **Fornells** is on a large bay popular with windsurfers.

CLUBBING IN IBIZA

In summer (late May to the end of September), the west of the island is a continuous party from sunset to sunrise and back again. In 2009 the International Dance Music Awards ranked two Ibiza clubs, Pacha and Space, among their worldwide top five.

The clubs operate nightly from around 1am to 6am and each has something different. Theme nights, fancy-dress parties and foam parties (where you are half-drowned in the stuff) are regular features. Admission can cost anything from €25 to €60.

The best include **Amnesia** (www.amnesia.es; ☺early Jun–Sep), located 4km north of Ibiza City on the road to Sant Rafel; **Es Paradis** (www.esparadis.com; Carrer de Salvador Espriu 2, Sant Antoni; ☺mid-May–Sep) in Sant Antoni de Portmany; **Pacha** (www.pacha.com; ☺nightly Jun-Sep, Fri & Sat Oct-May), on the north side of Ibiza port; **Privilege** (www.privilegeibiza.com), 5km north of Ibiza City on the road to Sant Rafel; and **Space** (www.space-ibiza.es; ☺Jun–mid-Oct).

A good website is **Ibiza Spotlight** (www.ibiza-spotlight.com).

✖ Eating & Drinking

The ports in both Maó and Ciutadella are lined with bars and restaurants.

MAÓ

El Varadero SPANISH €€
(☏971 35 20 74; Moll de Llevant 4; mains €11.50-17; ☺Easter-Nov) With such a splendid vista from the harbourside terrace, it must be tempting to simply sit on your laurels. But El Varadero doesn't. There's a range of tempting rice dishes and a short, select choice of fish and meat mains. If a full meal is too much, drop by for a tapa or two with a glass of wine and savour the view.

CIUTADELLA

[TOP CHOICE] **Cas Ferrer de Sa Font** MENORCAN €€
(☏971 48 07 84; www.casferrer.com; Carrer del Portal de Sa Font 16; meals €35; ☺Tue-Sun) Nowhere on the island will you find more authentic Menorcan cuisine based upon meats and vegetables from the owner's organic farm. Dine on the delightful interior patio of this charming 18th-century building or inside, below beams and soft curves, in what was once a blacksmith's forge.

Café des Museu COCKTAIL BAR
(Carreró d'es Palau 4; ☺10pm-3.30am) In the old town, this charming cocktail bar tucked away down a tight lane occasionally hosts live gigs – anything from acid jazz to bossanova.

FORNELLS

Es Port SEAFOOD €€
(☏971 37 64 03; Passeig Marítim 5; meals €30-35; ☺Sat-Thu Easter-Oct) Some fine fresh fish and seafood are done here. Of course, it does *caldereta de llagosta* (lobster stew; €64) as

well. Less expensive is the sizzling *paella de llomanto* (lobster paella; €35).

ℹ Information

Tourist office (Plaça de la Catedral 5, Ciutadella; ☺8.30am-3pm & 5-9pm)

ANDALUCÍA

Images of Andalucía are so potent, so quintessentially Spanish that it's sometimes difficult not to feel a sense of déjà vu. It's almost as if you've already been there in your dreams: a solemn Easter parade, an ebullient spring festival, exotic nights in the Alhambra. In the stark light of day the picture is no less compelling.

Seville

POP 703,000

A sexy, gutsy and gorgeous city, Seville is home to two of Spain's most colourful festivals, fascinating and distinctive *barrios* (neighbourhoods) and a local population that lives life to the fullest. A fiery place (as you'll soon see in its packed and noisy tapas bars), it is also hot climatewise – avoid July and August!

◉ Sights & Activities

Cathedral & Giralda CHURCH
(adult/concession/under 16yr €8/2/free; ☺11am-5.30pm Mon-Sat, 2.30-6.30pm Sun Sep-Jun, 9.30am-4.30pm Mon-Sat, 2.30-6.30pm Sun Jul & Aug) After Seville fell to the Christians in 1248, its main mosque was used as a church until 1401, when it was knocked down to make way for what would become one of

the world's largest cathedrals and an icon of Gothic architecture. The building wasn't completed until 1507. Over 90m high, the perfectly proportioned and exquisitely decorated **La Giralda** was the minaret of the mosque that stood on the site before the cathedral. The views from the summit are exceptional.

Inside, the **Capilla de San Antonio** contains Murillo's large 1666 canvas depicting the vision of St Anthony of Padua. Inside the southern door stands the elaborate **tomb of Christopher Columbus**, which Spain transferred here from Cuba in 1902. Towards the east end of the main nave is the **Capilla Mayor**, whose Gothic altarpiece is the jewel of the cathedral and reckoned to be the biggest altarpiece in the world with more than 1000 carved biblical figures. The **Sacristía de los Cálices** (Sacristy of the Chalices) contains Goya's 1817 painting of the Seville martyrs *Santas Justa y Rufina*. The room's centrepiece is the **Custodia de Juan de Arfe**, a huge 475kg silver monstrance made in the 1580s by Renaissance metalsmith Juan de Arfe. Displayed in a glass case are the city keys handed to the conquering Fernando III in 1248.

Alcázar CASTLE
(adult/child & concession €7.50/free; ⊙9.30am-7pm Apr-Sep, to 6pm Oct-Mar) Seville's Alcázar, a royal residence for many centuries, was founded in 913 as a Muslim fortress. The Alcázar has been expanded and rebuilt many times in its 11 centuries of existence. The Catholic Monarchs, Fernando and Isabel, set up court here in the 1480s as they prepared for the conquest of Granada. Later rulers created the Alcázar's lovely gardens. The Alcázar's highlights include exquisitely adorned patios and the showpiece **Palacio de Don Pedro**.

FREE **Archivo de Indias** MUSEUM
(Calle Santo Tomás, ⊙10am-4pm Mon-Sat, to 2pm Sun & holidays) On the western side of Plaza del Triunfo, the Archivo de Indias is the main archive on Spain's American empire, with 80 million pages of documents dating from 1492 through to the end of the empire in the 19th century: a most effective statement of Spain's power and influence during its Golden Age.

Barrio de Santa Cruz HISTORIC DISTRICT
Seville's medieval *judería*, east of the cathedral and Alcázar, is today a tangle of atmospheric, winding streets and lovely plant-decked plazas perfumed with orange blossom. Among its most characteristic plazas is **Plaza de Santa Cruz**, which gives the *barrio* its name. **Plaza de Doña Elvira** is another romantic perch, especially in the evening.

Museo del Baile Flamenco MUSEUM
(www.museoflamenco.com; Calle Manuel Rojas Marcos 3; adult/child €10/6; ⊙9.30am-7pm) The brainchild of Sevillana flamenco dancer Cristina Hoyos, Seville's newest museum is spread over three floors of an 18th-century palace, although at €10 a pop it's more than a little overpriced. Exhibits include sketches, paintings, photos of erstwhile (and contemporary) flamenco greats, plus a collection of dresses and shawls.

Parque de María Luisa & Plaza de España
PARK
(⊙8am-10pm) A large area south of the tobacco factory was transformed for Seville's 1929 international fair, the Exposición Iberoamericana, when architects adorned it with fantastical buildings, many of them harking back to Seville's past glory or imitating the native styles of Spain's former colonies. In its midst is the large Parque de María Luisa, a living expression of Seville's Moorish and Christian past.

✹ Festivals & Events

The first of Seville's two great festivals is **Semana Santa**, the week leading up to Easter Sunday. Throughout the week, thousands of members of religious brotherhoods parade in penitents' garb with tall, pointed *capirotes* (hoods) accompanying sacred images through the city, while huge crowds look on.

The **Feria de Abril**, a week in late April, is a welcome release after this solemnity: the festivities involve six days of music, dancing, horse riding and traditional dress, plus daily bullfights.

The city also stages Spain's largest flamenco festival, the month-long **Bienal de Flamenco**. It's held in September in even-numbered years.

WANT MORE?

For in-depth information, reviews and recommendations at your fingertips, head to the Apple App Store to purchase Lonely Planet's *Seville City Guide* iPhone app.

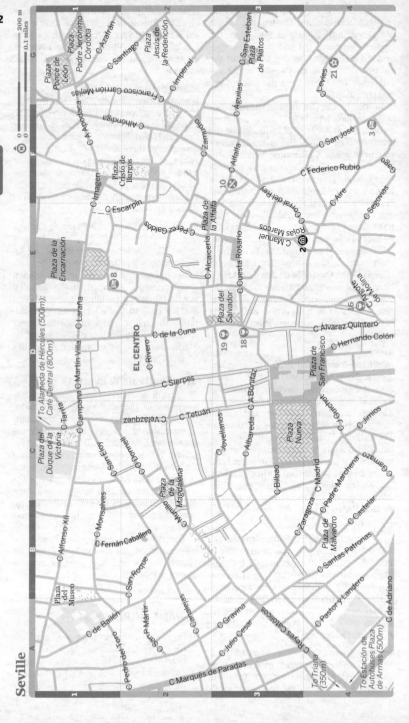

Seville

200 m
0.1 miles

G1 Plaza Ponce de León
Plaza Jerónimo Córdoba
C Azafrán
C Santiago
Plaza Jesús de la Redención
C Padre
C Apodaca
C Francisco Carrión Mejías
C Imperial

F C Alhóndiga
Plaza Cristo de Burgos
C Imagen
C Escarpín
C Zamudio
C Aguilas
C San Esteban
Plaza de Pilatos
C Alfalfa
C San José
C Federico Rubio
C Aire
C Segovias
Caso

E Plaza de la Encarnación
8
Laraña
C de la Cuna
Plaza de Perez Galdós
Plaza de la Alfalfa
C Alcaicería
C Cuesta Rosario
C Manuel Rojas Marcos
2
10
Corral del Rey
C Ábreu
C de Molina
C de Molina
6

D Plaza del Salvador
19 18
EL CENTRO
Rivero
C Martín Villa
C Álvarez Quintero
C Hernando Colón
Plaza de San Francisco

C Plaza del Duque de la Victoria
To Alameda de Hércules (500m);
Café Central (800m)
C Campana
C Tarifa
C Sierpes
C San Eloy
C O'Donnell
C Velázquez
C Tetuán
C Jovellanos
C Albareda
C A.Bonilla
Plaza Nueva
C Bilbao
C Zaragoza C Madrid
C Cuenca
C Jimios
C Gamazo

B Plaza del Museo
C Alfonso XII
C Monsalves
C Fernán Caballero
Plaza de la Magdalena
C Murillo
C San Roque
C Padre Marchena
Plaza de Malviedro
C Castelar
C Santas Patronas

A C de Bailén
C de Pedro del Toro
C San P. Mártir
C Canalejas
C Gravina
C Julio Cesar
C Reyes Católicos
C Marqués de Paradas
C Pastor y Landero
C de Adriano
To Triana (350m)
To Estación de Autobuses Plaza de Armas (500m)

21
3

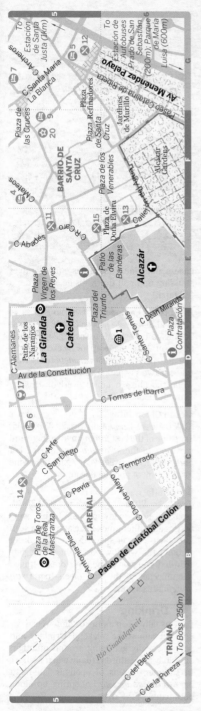

🛏 Sleeping

There's plenty of accommodation in the Barrio de Santa Cruz (close to the Alcázar), El Arenal and El Centro.

Prices over Semana Santa and the Feria de Abril can be up to double the high-season prices cited here. Accommodation is often full on weekends and is always booked solid during festivals, so book well ahead.

Hotel Amadeus   HOTEL €€
(☑954 50 14 43; www.hotelamadeussevilla.com; Calle Farnesio 6; s/d €85/95; P✳🤖) This musician family converted their 18th-century mansion into a stylish hotel with 14 elegant rooms of which Mozart would have been proud. A couple of the newer rooms have been soundproofed for piano or violin practice.

Las Casas de la Judería   HOTEL €€€
(☑954 41 51 50; www.casasypalacios.com; Callejón Dos Hermanas 7; s/d from €140/175; P✳🤖) At last a five-star that might actually be worth it. Countless patios and corridors link this veritable palace that was once 18 different houses situated on the cusp of the Santa Cruz quarter. The decor is exquisite, from the trickling fountains to the antique furniture and paintings.

Hotel Puerta de Sevilla   HOTEL €€
(☑954 98 72 70; www.hotelpuertadesevilla.com; Calle Puerta de la Carne 2; s/d from €66/86; P✳@🤖) A small shiny hotel in a great location, the Puerta de Sevilla has tin-glazed painted *azulejos* tiles, flower-pattern textiles and wrought-iron beds, all for one star. An extra bonus is the first-class but friendly service.

Pensión San Pancracio   PENSIÓN €
(☑954 41 31 04; Plaza de las Cruces 9; d €50, s/d without bathroom €25/35) An ideal budget option in Santa Cruz, this old rambling family house has plenty of different room options (all cheap) and a pleasant flower-bedecked patio/lobby. Friendliness makes up for the lack of luxury.

Hotel Simón   HOTEL €€
(☑954 22 66 60; www.hotelsimonsevilla.com; Calle García de Vinuesa 19; s €60-70, d €95-110; ✳) A typically grand 18th-century Sevillan house, with an ornate patio and spotless and comfortable rooms, this place gleams way above its two-star rating. Some of the rooms are embellished with rich *azulejos* tile-work.

Oasis Backpackers' Hostel   HOSTEL €
(☑954 29 37 77; www.oasissevilla.com; Plaza de la Encarnación 29; dm/d incl breakfast €15/50; ✳@🤖)

Seville's offbeat, buzzing backpacker central offers 24-hour free internet access. The new location is in Plaza Encarnación, a narrow street behind the Church of the Anunciación. Each dorm bed has a personal safe, and there is a small rooftop pool. There's no curfew. This is Spain!

Hotel Goya HOTEL €

(☎954 21 11 70 www.hotelgoyasevilla.com; Calle Mateos Gago 31; s/d €40/60; ❋@🛜) The gleaming Goya is more popular than ever. Book ahead.

✖ Eating

TOP CHOICE **Catalina** TAPAS €

(Paseo Catalina de Ribera 4; raciones €10) If your view of tapas is 'glorified bar snacks'; then your ideas could be blown out of the water here with a creative mix of just about every ingredient known to Iberian cooking. Start with the goat's cheese, aubergine and paprika special.

Bodega Santa Cruz TAPAS €

(Calle Mateos Gago; tapas €1.50-2) Forever crowded and with a mountain of paper on the floor, this place is usually standing room only with tapas and drinks enjoyed alfresco as you dodge the marching army of tourists squeezing through Santa Cruz's narrow streets.

Extraverde TAPAS €

(Plaza de Doña Elvira 8; tapas €2.50-4; ⊙10.30am-11.30pm) New on the scene, Extraverde is a unique bar/shop specialising in Andalucian products such as olive oil,

cheese and wine. You can taste free samples standing up or sit down inside and order a full tapa.

Restaurant La Cueva TRADITIONAL SPANISH €€

(☎954 21 31 43; Calle Rodrigo Caro 18 & Plaza de Doña Elvira 1; menú €16, mains €11-24) Slightly frosty service is made up for by excellent paella and a storming fish *zarzuela* (casserole; €30 for two people). The interior is roomy while the alfresco tables overlook dreamy Plaza de Doña Elvira.

Mesón Cinco Jotas TAPAS €

(Calle Castelar 1; tapas/media raciones €3.80/9.45) Try some of the best *jamón* in town here and move on to the *solomillo ibérico* (Iberian pork sirloin) in sweet Pedro Ximénez wine for the peak of porcine flavour.

Bar Alfalfa TAPAS €

(Cnr Calles Alfalfa & Candilejo; tapas €2-3) It's amazing how many people, hams, wine bottles and other knick-knacks you can stuff into such a small space. No matter; order through the window when the going gets crowded. You won't forget the tomato-tinged magnificence of the Italy-meets-Iberia *salmorejo* bruschetta.

🍷 Drinking

Bars usually open 6pm to 2am weekdays, 8pm till 3am at the weekend. Drinking and partying really get going around midnight on Friday and Saturday (daily when it's hot). In summer, dozens of open-air late-night bars *(terrazas de verano)* spring up along both banks of the river.

Plaza del Salvador is brimful of drinkers from mid-evening to 1am. Grab a drink from **La Antigua Bodeguita** or **La Sapotales** next door and sit on the steps of the Parroquia del Salvador.

Antigüedades
BAR

(Calle Argote de Molina 40) Blending mellow beats with offbeat decor, the tiled window seats with a view of the busy street are the best place to nurse your drink.

Casa Morales
BAR

(Garcia de Vinuesa 11) Founded in 1850, not much has changed in this defiantly old-world bar, with charming anachronisms wherever you look. Towering clay *tinajas* (wine storage jars) carry the chalked-up tapas choices of the day. Locals sweat it out on summer nights like true *sevillanos*.

Café Central
BAR

(Alameda de Hércules 64) One of the oldest and most popular along the street, Central has yellow bar lights, wooden flea-market chairs and a massive crowd that gathers at weekends.

☆ Entertainment

Seville is arguably Spain's flamenco capital and you're most likely to catch a spontaneous atmosphere (of unpredictable quality) in one of the bars staging regular nights of flamenco with no admission fee. *Soleares,* Flamenco's truest *cante jondo* (deep song), was first concocted in Triana; head here to find some of the more authentic clubs.

TOP CHOICE La Carbonería
FLAMENCO BAR

(Calle Levíes 18; admission free; ⊙8pm-4am) During the day there is no indication that this happening place is anything but a large garage. But come 8pm and this converted coal yard in the Barrio de Santa Cruz reveals two large bars, and nightly live flamenco (11pm and midnight) for no extra charge.

Casa de la Memoria de Al-Andalus
FLAMENCO SHOW

(☎954 56 06 70; Calle Ximénez de Enciso 28; tickets €15; ⊙9pm) This place in Santa Cruz is probably the most intimate and authentic nightly *tablao* (flamenco show), offering a wide variety of flamenco styles in a room of shifting shadows. Space is limited to 100, so reserve tickets in advance.

Casa Anselma
FLAMENCO BAR

(Pagés de Corro 49, Triana; ⊙midnight to late Mon-Sat) If you can squeeze in past the foreboding form of Anselma (a celebrated Triana flamenco dancer) at the door, you'll quickly realise that anything can happen in here. Casa Anslema (beware: there's no sign, just a doorway embellished with *azulejos* tiles) is the antithesis of a tourist flamenco *tablao,* with cheek-to-jowl crowds, thick cigarette smoke, zero amplification and spontaneous outbreaks of dexterous dancing. Pure magic.

❶ Information

Discover Sevilla (www.discoversevilla.com)

Explore Seville (www.exploreseville.com)

Regional tourist office Avenida de la Constitución (Avenida de la Constitución 21; ⊙9am-7pm Mon-Fri, 10am-2pm & 3-7pm Sat, 10am-2pm Sun, closed holidays); Estación de Santa Justa (⊙9am-8pm Mon-Fri, 10am-2pm Sat & Sun, closed holidays)

Seville Tourism (www.turismo.sevilla.org)

Turismo Sevilla (www.turismosevilla.org; Plaza del Triunfo 1; ⊙10.30am-7pm Mon-Fri)

❶ Getting There & Away

Air

A range of domestic and international flights land in Seville's **Aeropuerto San Pablo**, 7km from the city centre.

Bus

From the **Estación de Autobuses Prado de San Sebastián** (Plaza San Sebastián), there are 12 or more buses daily to/from Cádiz (€11.50, 1¾ hours), Córdoba (€10, two hours), Granada (€19, 3½ hours), Ronda (€11, 2½ hours, five or more daily) and Málaga (€15.75, 2¾ hours).

From the **Estación de Autobuses Plaza de Armas** (Avenida del Cristo de la Expiración), destinations include Madrid (€18.65, six hours, 14 daily), Mérida (€13, three hours, 12 daily), Cáceres (€15, four hours, six daily) and Portugal.

Train

The modern, efficient **Estación de Santa Justa** (Avenida Kansas City) is 1.5km northeast of the city centre. There's also a city-centre **Renfe ticket office** (Calle Zaragoza 29).

Twenty or more superfast AVE trains, reaching speeds of 280km/h, whiz daily to/from Madrid (€80.70, 2½ hours) and to Barcelona (€130, 6½ hours, one daily). Other services include Barcelona (€61 to €88, 10½ to 13 hours, three daily), Cádiz (€12.75, 1¾ hours, 13 daily), Córdoba (€16 to €32, 40 minutes to 1½ hours, 21 or more daily), Granada (€24, three hours, four daily), Málaga (€19.10 to €36.40, 2½ hours, five daily) and Mérida (€14, five hours, one daily).

ℹ Getting Around

Los Amarillos (www.losamarillos.es) runs buses between the airport and the Avenida del Cid near the San Sebastión bus station (€2.20 to €2.50, at 15 and 45 minutes past the hour). A taxi costs about €20.

Buses run by Seville's urban transport authority **Tussam** (www.tussam.es), C1, C2, C3 and C4, do useful circular routes linking the main transport terminals and the city centre.

Tussam's **Tranvia** (www.tussam.es, in Spanish), the city's sleek tram service, was launched in 2007. Individual rides cost €1.20, or you can buy a *Bono* (travel pass offering five rides for €5) from many newspaper stands and tobacconists.

SeVici (☎902 01 10 32; www.sevici.es; ☺7am-9pm) is a cycle-hire network comprising almost 200 fully automated pick-up/drop-off points dotted all over the city (clearly shown on a nifty folding pocket map). A one-week subscription costs €5. Your first 30 minutes cycling is free, the next hour costs €1, second and subsequent hours are €2 per hour.

Córdoba

POP 302,000

Córdoba was once one of the most enlightened Islamic cities on earth, and enough remains to place it in the contemporary top three Andalucian draws. The centrepiece is the gigantic and exquisitely rendered Mezquita. Surrounding it is an intricate web of winding streets, geranium-sprouting flower boxes and cool intimate patios that are at their most beguiling in late spring.

⊙ Sights & Activities

⌷ᴼᴾ Mezquita   CHURCH, MOSQUE
ᶜʜᴼᴵᶜᴱ (adult/child €8/4, free 8.30-10am Mon-Sat; ☺10am-7pm Mon-Sat Apr-Oct, 9-10.45am & 1.30-6.30pm Sun) Founded in 785, Córdoba's gigantic mosque is a wonderful architectural hybrid with delicate horseshoe arches making this unlike anywhere else in Spain. The main entrance is the **Puerta del Perdón**, a 14th-century Mudéjar gateway, with the

Córdoba

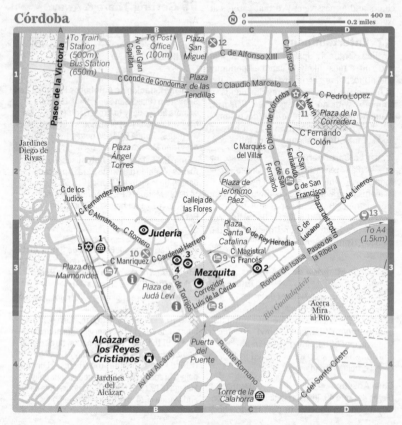

ticket office immediately inside. Also inside the gateway is the aptly named **Patio de los Naranjos** (Courtyard of the Orange Trees). Once inside, you can see straight ahead to the **mihrab**, the prayer niche in the mosque's *qibla* (the wall indicating the direction of Mecca) that was the focus of prayer. The first 12 transverse aisles inside the entrance, a forest of pillars and arches, comprise the original **8th-century mosque**.

Judería
HISTORIC DISTRICT

The medieval *judería,* extending northwest from the Mezquita almost to Avenida del Gran Capitán, is today a maze of narrow streets and whitewashed buildings with flowery window boxes. The beautiful little 14th-century **Sinagoga** (Calle de los Judíos 20; adult/EU citizen €0.30/free; ☺9.30am-2pm & 3.30-5.30pm Tue-Sat, 9.30am-1.30pm Sun & holidays) is one of only three surviving medieval synagogues in Spain and the only one in Andalucía.

In the heart of the *judería,* and once connected by an underground tunnel to the Sinagoga, is the 14th-century **Casa de Sefarad** (www.casadesefarad.es; admission €4; ☺10am-6pm Mon-Sat, 11am-2pm Sun) This small, beautiful museum is devoted to reviving interest in the Spanish Sephardic-Judaic tradition.

Alcázar de los Reyes Cristianos
CASTLE

(Castle of the Christian Monarchs; Campo Santo de Los Mártires s/n; adult/concession €4/2, free Fri; ☺10am-2pm & 5.30-7.30pm Tue-Sat, 9.30am-2.30pm Sun & holidays) Just southwest of the Mezquita, the Alcázar began as a palace and fort for Alfonso X in the 13th century. From 1490 to 1821 the Inquisition operated from here. Today its gardens are among the most beautiful in Andalucía.

Hammam Baños Árabes
BATHHOUSE

(☏957 48 47 46; www.hammamspain.com/cordoba; Calle del Corregidor Luis de la Cerda 51; bath/bath & massage €26/33; ☺2hr sessions 10am, noon, 2pm, 4pm, 6pm, 8pm & 10pm) Follow the lead of the medieval Cordobans and dip your toe in the beautifully renovated Arab baths, where you can enjoy an aromatherapy massage, with tea, hookah and Arabic sweets in the cafe later.

Medina Azahara
ISLAMIC RUINS

(Madinat al-Zahra; adult/EU citizen €1.50/free; ☺10am-6.30pm Tue-Sat, to 8.30pm May–mid-Sep, to 2pm Sun) Even in the cicada-shrill heat and stillness of a summer afternoon, the Medina Azahara whispers of the power and vision of its founder, Abd ar-Rahman III. The self-proclaimed caliph began the construction of a magnificent new capital 8km west of Córdoba around 936, and took up full residence around 945. Medina Azahara was a resounding declaration of his status, a magnificent trapping of power. It was destroyed in the 11th century and just 10% of the site has been excavated. A taxi costs €37 for the return trip, with one hour to view the site, or you can book a three-hour coach tour for €6.50 to €10 through many Córdoba hotels.

🛏 Sleeping

TOP CHOICE **Hotel Hacienda Posada de Vallina**
HOTEL €€

(☏957 49 87 50; ww.hhposadadevallinacordoba .com; Calle del Corregidor Luís de la Cerda 83; s/d €50/70; P❄@☎) In an enviable nook on

Córdoba

the quiet side of the Mezquita (the building actually predates it), this cleverly renovated hotel uses portraits and period furniture to enhance a plush and modern interior. The rooms make you feel comfortable but in-period (ie medieval Córdoba). Columbus allegedly once stayed here.

Hotel Amistad Córdoba   HOTEL €€€
(✆957 42 03 35; www.nh-hoteles.com; Plaza de Maimónides 3; s/d €125; ▣❄@☎) Occupying two 18th-century mansions with original Mudéjar patios, the Amistad is part of the modern NH chain with elegant rooms and all the requisite luxury hotel facilities including babysitting. Closed at the time of research, but renovations will have been completed by the time you read this.

Hostal La Fuente   HOTEL €
(✆957 48 78 27; www.hostallafuente.com; Calle San Fernando 51; s/d €35/50; ❄@☎) A journeyman hotel, though in Córdoba this means you get an airy patio, *azulejos* tiles, exposed brick and interesting architectural details. The rooms are clean and comfortable, and the staff quietly helpful.

Hotel Mezquita   HOTEL €€
(✆957 47 55 85; hotelmezquita.com; Plaza Santa Catalina 1; s/d €42/74; ❄) One of the best-value places in town, this hotel is right opposite the Mezquita itself. The 16th-century mansion has sparkling bathrooms and elegant rooms, some with views of the great mosque across the street.

✖ Eating & Drinking

Córdoba's liveliest bars are mostly scattered around the newer parts of town and come alive at about 11pm or midnight on weekends. Most bars in the medieval centre close around midnight.

TOP CHOICE Taberna San Miguel El Pisto   TAPAS €
(Plaza San Miguel 1; tapas €3, media raciones €5-10; ⊙closed Sun & Aug) Stand aside Seville. Fine wine, great atmosphere, professional old-school waiters, zero pretension and a clamorous yet handsome decor make El Pisto (the barrel) a Cordoban and Andalucian tapa classic. You can squeeze in at the bar or grab a jug of wine and grab a table out back.

Taberna Salinas   TAPAS €
(Calle Tundidores 3; tapas/raciones €2.50/8; ⊙closed Sun & Aug) Dating back to 1879, this large patio restaurant fills up fast. Try the delicious aubergines with honey or potatoes with garlic. The tavern side is quieter in the

early evening, and the friendly bar staff will fill your glass with local Montilla whenever you look thirsty.

Casa Pepe de la Judería   ANDALUCIAN €€€
(✆957 20 07 44; Calle Romero 1; tapas/media raciones €2.50-9.50, mains €11-18, menú €27) A great roof terrace with views of the Mezquita and a labyrinth of busy dining rooms. Down a complimentary glass of Montilla before launching into the house specials, including Cordoban oxtails or venison fillets.

Amapola   BAR
(Paseo de la Ribera 9; ⊙9am-3pm Mon-Fri, 5pm-4am Sat & Sun) This is where the young and beautiful lounge on green leather sofas consuming elaborate cocktails. DJs spin until the small hours.

Jazz Café   LIVE MUSIC
(Calle Espartería; ⊙8am-late) This fabulous, cavernous bar full of black-and-white jazz photos puts on regular free live jazz and jam sessions.It's also a good place for an early-morning hangover cure.

ℹ Information

Municipal tourist office (Plaza de Judá Levi; ⊙8.30am-2.30pm Mon-Fri)

Regional tourist office (Calle de Torrijos 10; ⊙9am-7.30pm Mon-Fri, 9.30am-3pm Sat, Sun & holidays)

ℹ Getting There & Away

BUS The **bus station** (Glorieta de las Tres Culturas) is 1km northwest of Plaza de las Tendillas. Destinations include Seville (€10.36, 1¾ hours, six daily), Granada (€12.52, 2½ hours, seven daily) and Málaga (€12.75, 2¾ hours, five daily).

TRAIN From Córdoba's **train station** (Avenida de América), destinations include Seville (€10.60 to €32.10, 40 to 90 minutes, 23 or more daily), Madrid (€52 to €66.30, 1¾ to 6¼ hours, 23 or more daily), Málaga (€21 to €39.60, one to 2½ hours, nine daily) and Barcelona (€59.40 to €133, 10½ hours, four daily).

Granada

POP 300,000 / ELEV 685M

Granada's eight centuries as a Muslim capital are symbolised in its keynote emblem, the remarkable Alhambra, one of the most graceful architectural achievements in the Muslim world. Islam was never completely expunged here, and today it seems more present than ever in the shops, restaurants, tearooms and mosque of a growing North African community in and around the maze of the Albayzín. The tapas bars fill to bursting with hungry and thirsty revellers, while flamenco dives resound to the heart-wrenching tones of the south.

⊙ Sights & Activities

TOP CHOICE **Alhambra** PALACE

(☎902 44 12 21; www.alhambra-tickets.es, www.servicaixa.com; adult/EU senior/EU student/under 8yr €12/9/9/free, Generalife only €6; ⊙8.30am-8pm 16 Mar-31 Oct, to 6pm 1 Nov-14 Mar) The mighty Alhambra is breathtaking. Much has been written about its fortress, palace, patios and gardens, but nothing can really prepare you for seeing the real thing.

The **Alcazaba**, the Alhambra's fortress, dates from the 11th to the 13th centuries. There are spectacular views from the tops of its towers. The **Palacio Nazaríes** (Nasrid Palace), built for Granada's Muslim rulers in their 13th- to 15th-century heyday, is the centrepiece of the Alhambra. The beauty of its patios and intricacy of its stuccoes and woodwork, epitomised by the **Patio de los Leones** (Patio of the Lions) and **Sala de las Dos Hermanas** (Hall of the Two Sisters), are stunning. The **Generalife** (Palace Gardens) is a great spot to relax and contemplate the complex from a little distance.

The Palacio Nazaríes is also open for **night visits** (⊙10pm-11.30pm Tue-Sat Mar-Oct, 8pm-9.30pm Fri & Sat Nov-Feb). Book for night visits the same way as for day visits.

Albayzín HISTORIC AREA

Exploring the narrow, hilly streets of the Albayzín, the old Moorish quarter across the river from the Alhambra, is the perfect complement to the Alhambra. The cobblestone streets are lined with gorgeous *cármenes* (large mansions with walled gardens, from the Arabic *karm* for garden). It survived as the Muslim quarter for several decades after the Christian conquest in 1492.

Head uphill to reach the **Mirador de San Nicolás** – a viewpoint with breathtaking vistas and a relaxed scene.

Capilla Real HISTORIC BUILDING

(www.capillareal.granada.com; Calle Oficios; admission €3.50; ⊙10.30am-1.30pm & 4-7.30pm Mon-Sat, 11am-1.30pm & 4-7pm Sun Apr-Oct) It's well worth exploring the streets and lanes surrounding Plaza Bib-Rambla, and visiting the chapel where Fernando and Isabel, the Christian monarchs who conquered Granada in 1492, are buried. The sacristy contains a small but impressive **museum** with royal memorabilia and lovely artworks, including Botticelli's *Prayer in the Garden of Olives*.

Next door to the chapel is Granada's **Catedral** (admission €3.50; ⊙10.45am-1.30pm & 4-8pm Mon-Sat, 4-8pm Sun), which dates from the early 16th century.

🛌 Sleeping

TOP CHOICE **Casa Morisca Hotel**

HISTORIC HOTEL €€€

(☎958 22 11 00; www.hotelcasamorisca.com; Cuesta de la Victoria 9; d interior/exterior €118/148; ❋@⊛) The Morisca could easily compete with the finest of Marrakech's *riads* with its 14 Alhambra-esque rooms occupying a gorgeous late-15th-century Albayzín mansion. Everything is arranged around an atmospheric patio with an ornamental pool and overlooking wooden galleries. The pinnacle: an exquisite Mirador suite, affording views of the great palace it-

ALHAMBRA TICKETS

Up to 6600 tickets to the Alhambra are available for each day. About one-third of these are sold at the ticket office on the day, but they sell out early and you need to start queuing by 7am to be reasonably sure of getting one. It's highly advisable to book in advance (you pay €1 extra per ticket). You can book up to a year ahead in two ways:

» **Alhambra Advance Booking** (☎national calls 902 88 80 01, international calls 0034 934 92 37 50; www.alhambra-tickets.es; ⊙8am-9pm)

» **Servicaixa** (www.servicaixa.com) Online booking in Spanish and English. You can also buy tickets in advance from Servicaixa cash machines (8am to 7pm March to October, 8am to 5pm November to February), but only in the Alhambra grounds

For internet or phone bookings you need a Visa card, MasterCard or Eurocard. You receive a reference number, which you must show, along with your passport, national identity card or credit card, at the Alhambra ticket office when you pick up the ticket on the day of your visit.

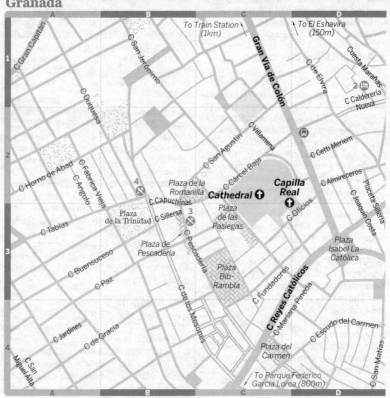

self. It's around 600m northeast of the Iglesia de Santa Ana, just off the Carrera del Darro.

Carmen de la Alcubilla HISTORIC HOTEL **€€€**
(☑958 21 55 51; www.alcubilladelcaracol.com; Aire Alta 12; s/d €100/120; 🕸@🛜) Tranquil Granadian beauty, this time perched on the Realejo hill in a restored Carmen (house with an internal garden) with a terraced garden overflowing with jasmine and lemon trees. The house is (almost refreshingly) light on antiques, but the views of the Sierra Nevada are stunning and the service flawless. It's on one of the southern slopes of the Alhambra, south of the Cuesta de Gomérez.

Parador de Granada HISTORIC HOTEL **€€€**
(☑958 22 14 40; www.parador.es; Calle Real de la Alhambra; r €315; P🕸@🛜) The most expensive *parador* in Spain can't be beaten for its location within the walls of the Alhambra and its historical connections (it was a former con-

vent). Live like a Nasrid king, for one night at least. Book ahead.

Hotel Casa del Capitel Nazarí HISTORIC HOTEL **€€**
(☑958 21 52 60; www.hotelcasacapitel.com; Cuesta Aceituneros 6; s/d €88/110; 🕸@🛜) More Albayzín magic in a 1503 Renaissance palace which is as much architectural history lesson as plush hotel. Rooms have Moroccan inflections and the courtyard hosts art exhibits.

Hostal Molinos HOTEL **€**
(☑958 22 73 67; www.hotelmolinos.es; Calle Molinos 12; s/d/tr €29/32/45; 🛜) Don't let the 'narrowest hotel in the world' moniker put you off (and yes, it actually is – and has a certificate from the *Guinness Book of Records* to prove it): there's plenty of breathing space in Molino's nine rooms and warm hospitality in its information-stacked lobby. Situated at the

TOP CHOICE **Restaurante Arrayanes** MOROCCAN €
(📞958 22 84 01; Cuesta Marañas 4; mains €8.50-19; ⊙from 8pm) The best Moroccan food in a city that is well known for its Moorish throwbacks? Recline on lavish patterned seating, try the rich fruity tagine casseroles and make your decision. No alcohol.

Parador de Granada INTERNATIONAL €€
(📞958 22 14 40; Calle Real de la Alhambra; mains €19-22; ⊙8am-11pm) Even a jaded, jilted, world-weary cynic would come over all romantic in this dreamy setting. The Spanish food has Moroccan and French influences, and it tastes all the better for being taken inside the Alhambra.

El Ají MODERN SPANISH €
(San Miguel Bajo 9; mains €12-20; 🍴) A cool, modern (tiny) interior, soft jazz, and a menu of nontraditional meat and vegetarian choices make Ají different in the way that only Granada can be. It's at the western end of the Albayzín, off Calle de Santa Isabel La Real.

Reca TAPAS €
(Plaza de la Trinidad; raciones €8; ⊙closed Tue) A tapas classic rightly famous for its *salmorejo* (thicker version of gazpacho) and its all-through-the-afternoon food service.

Oliver SEAFOOD €
(Calle Pescadería 12; mains €12-18; ⊙closed Sun) Sandwiched in between Plazas Bib-Rambla and Trinidad, this is a favourite lunchtime office-worker stop, revered for its fried fish.

☆ **Entertainment**

The excellent monthly *Guía de Granada* (€1), available from kiosks, lists entertainment venues and tapas bars.

foot of the Realejo, it makes an economical central option.

Oasis Backpackers' Hostel HOSTEL €
(📞958 21 58 48; www.oasisgranada.com; Placeta Correo Viejo 3; dm/d €18/40; ❄@🛜) Bohemian digs in a bohemian quarter, Oasis is seconds away from the bars on Calle de Elvira. There's free internet access, a rooftop terrace and personal safes. As backpacker's hostels go, it's a gem.

🍴 **Eating**

Granada is one of the last bastions of that fantastic practice of free tapas with every drink, and some have an international flavour. The labyrinthine Albayzín holds a wealth of eateries tucked away in the narrow streets. Calle Calderería Nueva is a fascinating muddle of *teterías* (tearooms) and Arabic-influenced takeaways.

Situated above and to the northwest of the city centre, and offering panoramic views over the Alhambra, the Sacromonte is Granada's centuries-old *gitano* (Roma) quarter. The Sacromonte caves harbour touristy flamenco haunts, which you can prebook through hotels and travel agencies; some offer free transport. Try the Friday or Saturday midnight shows at **Los Tarantos** (📞day 958 22 45 25, night 958 22 24 92; Camino del Sacromonte 9; admission €24) for a lively experience.

Peña de la Platería   FLAMENCO
(Placeta de Toqueros 7) Buried deep in the Albayzín warren, this is a genuine aficionados' club with a large outdoor patio. Dramatic 9.30pm performances take place on Thursday or Saturday in an adjacent room and cost €12.

El Eshavira   LIVE MUSIC
(Postigo de la Cuna 2; ⊙from 10pm) Duck down a spooky alley to this shadowy haunt of flamenco and jazz. It is jam-packed on Thursday and Sunday, the performance nights.

ℹ Information

Regional tourist office (www.turismodegra
nada.org; Plaza de Mariana Pineda 10; ⊙9am-8pm Mon-Fri, 10am-2pm & 4-7pm Sat, 10am-3pm Sun May-Sep)

Municipal tourist office (www.granadatur
.com; Calle Almona del Campillo, 2; ⊙9am-7pm Mon-Fri, to 6pm Sat, 10am-2pm Sun)

ℹ Getting There & Away

AIR Destinations from Granada's airport include Madrid, Barcelona, Milan and Bologna. **Autocares J González** (www.autocaresjose
gonzalez.com) runs buses between the airport and the city centre (€3, five daily) on Gran Vía de Colón.

BUS Granada's **bus station** (Carretera de Jaén) is 3km northwest of the city centre. **Alsina Graells** (📞902 42 22 42; www.alsa.
es) runs to Córdoba (€12.50, 2¾ hours direct, nine daily), Seville (€19.30, three hours direct, eight daily), Málaga (€9.75, 1½ hours direct, 16 daily) and Madrid (€16.30, five to six hours, 10 to 13 daily).

TRAIN The **train station** (Avenida de Andalucés) is 1.5km west of the centre. Trains run to/from Seville (€23.85, three hours, four daily), Almería (€15.90, 2¼ hours, four daily), Ronda (€13.50, three hours, three daily), Algeciras (€20.10, 4½ hours, three daily), Madrid (€66.80, four to five hours, one or two daily), Valencia (€50.60, 7½ to eight hours, one daily) and Barcelona (€62.10, 12 hours, one daily).

Costa de Almería

The coast east of Almería in eastern Andalucía is perhaps the last section of Spain's Mediterranean coast where you can have a beach to yourself. This is Spain's sunniest region – even in late March it can be warm enough to strip off and take in the rays.

⊙ Sights & Activities

Alcazaba   FORTRESS
(Calle Almanzor s/n; adult/EU citizen €1.50/free; ⊙9am-8.30pm Tue-Sun Apr-Oct, to 6.30pm Tue-Sun Nov-Mar) An enormous 10th-century Muslim fortress, the Alcazaba is the highlight of Almería City.

Cabo de Gata   BEACHES
The best thing about the region is the wonderful coastline and semidesert scenery of the **Cabo de Gata** promontory. All along the 50km coast from El Cabo de Gata village to Agua Amarga, some of the most beautiful and empty beaches on the Mediterranean alternate with precipitous cliffs and scattered villages. The main village is laid-back **San José**, with excellent beaches nearby, such as **Playa de los Genoveses** and **Playa de Mónsul**.

🛏 Sleeping & Eating

ALMERÍA CITY

Hotel Costasol   HOTEL €
TOP CHOICE
(📞950 23 40 11; www.hotelcostasol.com; Paseo de Almería 58; r €54; P❄@🗑) It's amazing what some red colour accents and a clean, simple but funky refurb can do. Factor in the sleek reception, enormous bathrooms, spacious communal areas and stylish basement restaurant, and you won't find a better hotel for this price in Andalucía.

Hotel Torreluz   HOTEL €€
(📞950 23 43 99; www.torreluz.com; Plaza de las Flores 2 & 3; s/d 2-star €39/64, 3-star €56/74; P❄🗑) Burnt-plum-coloured walls, comfortable beds and good prices make this one of Almería's best-value places to stay.

CABO DE GATA

Sanctuario San José   HOTEL €€
(📞902 87 73 88; www.elsantuariosanjose.es; Camino de Calahiguera 9, San José; s/d €64/79; P❄) This refurbished 28-room brilliant-white hotel offers minimal yet friendly design with attractive lounging and dining terraces. Its Anicette restaurant (mains €15 to €24) has a strong reputation locally.

Hostal Sol Bahía
HOTEL €€

(☎950 38 03 07; Avenida de San José, San José; d €40-70; ❄) The Sol Bahía and its sister establishment, Hostal Bahía Plaza across the street, are in the centre of San José and have functional, clean rooms in bright, modern buildings.

Restaurante Mediterraneo
SEAFOOD €€

(Puerto Deportivo de San José, San José; mains €10-22) Last stop in a run of similarly good seafood restaurants near the marina, this one has particularly friendly staff and a less frantic atmosphere than some of its neighbours.

ℹ Information

Regional tourist office (Parque de Nicolás Salmerón, Almería City; ◷9am-7pm Mon-Fri, 10am-2pm Sat & Sun)

ℹ Getting There & Away

AIR Almería **airport** (☎950 21 37 00), 10km east of the city centre, receives flights from several European countries, as well as Barcelona, Madrid and Melilla.

BOAT There are daily sailings to/from Melilla, Nador (Morocco) and Ghazaouet (Algeria). The tourist office has details.

BUS Destinations served from Almería's **bus station** (☎950 26 20 98) include Granada (€13.45, 2¼ hours, 10 daily), Málaga (€16, 3¼ hours, 10 daily), Murcia (€17.25, 2½ hours, 10 daily), Madrid (€25, seven hours, five daily) and Valencia (€35.65, 8½ hours, five daily).

TRAIN Daily trains run to Granada (€15.90, 2¼ hours), Seville (€38.15, 5½ hours) and Madrid (€44.10, 6¾ hours).

Málaga

POP 720,000

The exuberant port city of Málaga may be uncomfortably close to the overdeveloped Costa del Sol, but it's a wonderful amalgam of old Andalucian town and modern metropolis. The centre presents the visitor with narrow, old streets and wide, leafy boulevards, beautiful gardens and impressive monuments, fashionable shops and a burgeoning cultural life. The city's terrific bars and nightlife, the last word in Málaga *joie de vivre,* stay open very late.

◉ Sights & Activities

TOP CHOICE **Museo Picasso Málaga**
ART MUSEUM

(☎902 44 33 77; www.museopicassomalaga.org; Palacio de Buenavista, Calle San Agustín 8; permanent/temporary collection €6/4.50,

combined ticket €8, seniors & under-26 students half-price; ◷10am-8pm Tue-Thu & Sun, to 9pm Fri & Sat; ♿) The hottest attraction on Málaga's tourist scene is tucked away on a pedestrian street in what was medieval Málaga's *judería.* The Museo Picasso Málaga has 204 Picasso works and also stages high-quality temporary exhibitions on Picasso themes. The Picasso paintings, drawings, engravings, sculptures and ceramics on show (many never previously on public display) span almost every phase and influence of the artist's colourful career. Picasso was born in Málaga in 1881 but moved to northern Spain with his family when he was nine.

Casa Natal de Picasso (Plaza de la Merced 15; admission €1; ◷9.30am-8pm), Picasso's birthplace, is a centre for exhibitions and academic research on contemporary art, with a few compelling items of personal memorabilia and a well-stocked shop. Entrance is free with the Picasso museum combined ticket.

Cathedral
CHURCH

(www.3planalfa.es/catedralmalaga; Calle Molina Lario; admission €3.50; ◷10am-5.30pm Mon-Fri, to 5pm Fri, closed Sun & holidays) Preserved rather magnificently, like an unfinished Beethoven symphony, Málaga's cathedral was begun in the 16th century on the former site of the main mosque and never properly completed. Consequently the building exhibits a mishmash of architectural styles absorbed over two centuries of construction. The entrance is on Calle Císter.

Alcazaba
CASTLE

(Calle Alcazabilla; admission €2.10, incl Castillo de Gibralfaro €3.40; ◷9.30am-8pm Tue-Sun Apr-Oct) At the lower, western end of the Gibralfaro hill, the wheelchair-accessible Alcazaba was the palace-fortress of Málaga's Muslim governors, dating from 1057. The brick path winds uphill, interspersed with arches and stone walls, and is refreshingly cool in summer. Roman artefacts and fleeting views of the harbour and city enliven the walk, while honeysuckle, roses and jasmine perfume the air.

Castillo de Gibralfaro
CASTLE

(admission €2.10; ◷9am-9pm Apr-Sep, to 6pm Oct-Mar) Above the Alcazaba rises the older Castillo de Gibralfaro, built by Abd ar-Rahman I, the 8th-century Cordoban emir, and rebuilt in the 14th and 15th centuries. Nothing much remains of the castle's interior,

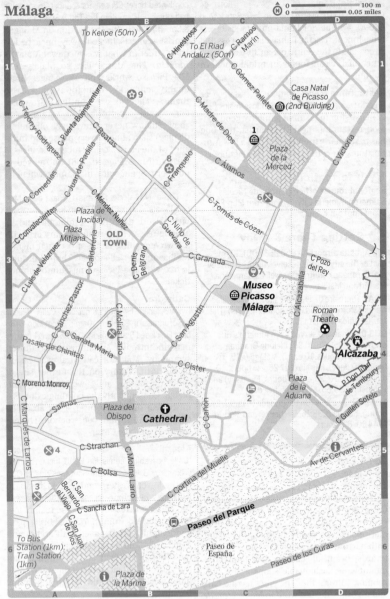

but the walkway around the ramparts affords exhilarating views and there's a tiny museum with a military focus.

Beaches BEACHES

Sandy city beaches stretch several kilometres in each direction from the port. **Playa de la Malagueta**, handy to the city centre, has some excellent bars and restaurants close by. **Playa de Pedregalejo** and **Playa del Palo**, about 4km east of the centre, are popular and reachable by bus 11 from Paseo del Parque.

Málaga

🛏 Sleeping

El Riad Andaluz   HOTEL €€
(✆952 21 36 40; www.elriadandaluz.com; Calle Hinestrosa 24; s/d €70/86; ❄@🖥) Colourful and exotic, this gorgeous restored monastery in the Centro Historico offers eight rooms with Moroccan decor set around an atmospheric patio, with tea and coffee on tap all day.

Parador Málaga Gibralfaro   HOTEL €€€
(✆952 22 19 02; www.parador.es; Castillo de Gibralfaro; r €160-171; P❄🖥≋) With an unbeatable location up on the pine-forested Gibralfaro hill, Málaga's modern but rustic *parador* provides spectacular views of city and harbour from its upper floors, excellent terrace restaurant and rooftop pool.

Hotel Sur   HOTEL €€
(✆952 22 48 03; www.hotel-sur.com; Calle Trinidad Grund 13; s/d/tr €52/76/100, s/d without bathroom €39/49; P❄🖥) A good location a goal kick away from the Plaza de la Marina adds kudos to the plain but pristine Hotel Sur's portfolio. More are added with friendly, polite staff and the availability of wi-fi in all of the rooms. It's around 250m southwest of Plaza de la Marina, off Alameda Principal.

Hotel Carlos V   HOTEL €
(✆952 21 51 20; www.hotel-carlosvmalaga.com; Calle Císter 10; s/d €36/59; P❄@) Close to the cathedral and Picasso Museum, the Carlos V is enduringly popular. Renovated in 2008,

bathrooms sparkle in their new uniform of cream-and-white tiles. Excellent standard for the price and helpful staff make this hotel a winner.

🍴 Eating

Most of the best eating places are sandwiched in the narrow streets between Calle Marqués de Larios and the cathedral.

La Rebaná   TAPAS €
(Calle Molina Lario 5; tapas €4.20-8.50, raciones €7-11.50) A great, noisy tapas bar near the Picasso Museum and the cathedral. Dark wood, tall windows and exposed brick walls create a modern, minimal but laid-back space. Try the foie gras with salted nougat for a unique tapa.

Gorki   TAPAS €€
(Calle Strachan 6; platos combinados €7.50-16) A popular upmarket tapas bar with pavement tables and a modern interior full of wine-barrel tables and stools. Creative tapas have a more *Sevillano* twist and the clientele is young and trendy.

Café Lepanto   CAFE, SNACKS €
(Calle Marqués de Larios 7) An old-world Italianate coffee/ice-cream bar that serves as Málaga's top *confitería,* Lepanto is insanely popular, probably because most of its sweets and pastries are highly addictive. Enjoy them in the art nouveau–embellished interior, served by athletic waiters in waistcoats.

Lechuga   TAPAS €
(Plaza de la Merced 1; tapas €2.50-3.50, raciones €8-10; 🖉) In this calm retreat, vegetables reign supreme and the chef does wonderful things with them, as with hummus, Indian-style *bhajis* and various inventive salads.

🍷 Drinking & Entertainment

On weekend nights, the web of narrow old streets north of Plaza de la Constitución comes alive. Look for bars around Plaza de la Merced, Plaza Mitjana and Plaza de Uncibay.

Málaga's substantial flamenco heritage has its nexus to the northwest of Plaza de la Merced. Venues here include **Kelipe** (✆692 82 98 85; www.kelipe.net; Calle Pena 11), a flamenco centre which puts on *muy puro* performances Thursday to Saturday at 9.30pm; entry of €15 includes one drink and tapa; reserve ahead. Intensive weekend courses in guitar and dance are also held. **Amargo** (Calle R Franquillo 3) offers Friday and Saturday night gigs, while **Vino Mio** (Calle Alamos) is a small restaurant with an international menu where musicians and dancers fill the wait for the food.

TOP CHOICE **Bodegas El Pimpi** BAR

(Calle Granada 62; ⊙11am-2am) A Málaga institution with a warren of charming rooms and mini patios, El Pimpi attracts a boisterous crowd of all nationalities and generations with its sweet wine and traditional music. Look out for the flamenco (last Monday of the month) and the signed photo of a young-looking Tony Blair.

ℹ️ Information

Municipal tourist office (www.malagaturismo.com, in Spanish) Plaza de la Marina (⊙9am-8pm Mar-Sep, to 6pm Oct-Feb); Casita del Jardinero (Avenida de Cervantes 1; ⊙9am-8pm Mar-Sep, to 6pm Oct-Feb)

Regional tourist office (Pasaje de Chinitas 4; www.andalucia.org; ⊙9am-7.30pm Mon-Fri, 10am-7pm Sat, 10am-2pm Sun)

ℹ️ Getting There & Away

AIR Málaga's busy **airport** (☎952 04 88 38), the main international gateway to Andalucía, receives flights by dozens of airlines from around Europe. The Aeropuerto train station on the Málaga–Fuengirola line is a five-minute walk from the airport. Trains run about every half-hour to Málaga-Renfe station (€2, 11 minutes) and Málaga-Centro station.

BUS Málaga's **bus station** (Paseo de los Tilos) is 1km southwest of the city centre. Frequent buses go to Seville (€16, 2½ hours), Granada (€9.75, 1½ to two hours), Córdoba (€12.50, 2½ hours) and Ronda (€9.50, 2½ hours).

TRAIN **Málaga-Renfe** (Explanada de la Estación), the main station, is around the corner from the bus station. The superfast AVE service runs to Madrid (€76.40 to €85, 2½ hours, six daily). Trains also go to Córdoba (€21 to €44, one hour, 10 daily), Seville (€19.10 to €36.40, 2½ hours, five daily) and Barcelona (€62.70 to €138, 13 or 6½ hours, two daily).

Ronda

POP 37,000 / ELEV 744M

Perched on an inland plateau riven by the 100m fissure of El Tajo gorge and surrounded by the beautiful Serranía de Ronda, Ronda is the most dramatically sited of Andalucía's *pueblos blancos* (white villages).

◎ Sights & Activities

The **Plaza de Toros** (built 1785), considered the national home of bullfighting, is a mecca for aficionados; inside is the small but fas-cinating **Museo Taurino** (Calle Virgen de la Paz; admission €6; ⊙10am-8pm Apr-Sep, to 6pm Oct-Mar).

The amazing 18th-century **Puente Nuevo** (New Bridge) is an incredible engineering feat crossing the gorge to the originally Muslim Old Town (La Ciudad). At the **Casa del Rey Moro** (House of the Moorish King; Calle Santo Domingo 17), a romantically crumbling 18th-century house, supposedly built over the remains of an Islamic palace, you can visit the cliff-top gardens and climb down La Mina, a Muslim-era stairway cut inside the rock, right to the bottom of the gorge.

Also well worth a visit are the beautiful 13th-century **Baños Arabes** (Arab Baths; Hoyo San Miguel; admission €3, free on Sun; ⊙10am-7pm Mon-Fri, to 3pm Sat & Sun). Nearby, the amusing **Museo del Bandolero** (Calle de Armiñán 65; admission €3; ⊙10.30am-8pm Apr-Sep, to 6pm Oct-Mar) is dedicated to the banditry for which central Andalucía was renowned in the 19th century.

🛏️ Sleeping & Eating

Hotel San Francisco HOTEL €

(☎952 87 32 99; www.hotelsanfranciscoronda.com; Calle María Cabrera 18; s/d incl breakfast €38/60; ❄️) This is the best budget option in Ronda, offering a warm welcome. It was recently refurbished and upgraded from *hostal* to hotel, with facilities to match including wheelchair access.

Hotel Alavera de los Baños HOTEL €€

(☎952 87 91 43; www.alaveradelosbanos.com; Hoyo San Miguel s/n; s/d incl breakfast €70/95; ❄️🏊) A magical hotel with style echoes of the Arab baths next door, this one-time tannery looks like it was decorated by a departing Moor, with a flower-filled patio and pool. The sultan-sized baths are carved from a type of stucco, and their pink tinge is due to natural pigments.

Parador de Ronda HOTEL €€€

(☎952 87 75 00; www.parador.es; Plaza de España s/n; r €160-171; P❄️@📶🏊) Acres of shining marble and deep-cushioned furniture give this modern *parador* a certain appeal. The terrace is a wonderful place to drink in views of the gorge with your coffee or wine, especially at night.

TOP CHOICE **Bodega San Francisco** TAPAS €

(Calle Ruedo Alameda; raciones €6-10) Taking price, food quality, ambience and local-to-tourist ratio into account, this is the best eating joint in town – hands down.

It's situated in the Barrio San Francisco just outside the old Carlos V gate and gets regular rave reviews from travellers who have sought it out.

ℹ Information

Municipal tourist office (www.turismoderonda.es; Paseo de Blas Infante; ☺10am-7.30pm Mon-Fri May-Sep, to 6pm Oct-Apr, 10.15am-2pm & 3.30-6.30pm Sat, Sun & holidays)

Regional tourist office (www.andalucia.org; Plaza de España 1; ☺9am-7.30pm Mon-Fri May-Sep, to 6pm Oct-Apr, 10am-2pm Sat)

ℹ Getting There & Away

BUS From the **bus station** (Plaza Concepción García Redondo 2), there are frequent services to/from Málaga (€9.20, two hours), Seville (€10.85, 2½ hours), Cádiz (€13.85, 2½ hours) and Málaga (€10.21, 1½ hours, at least three daily).

TRAIN From the **train station** (Avenida de Andalucía), trains run to/from Algeciras (€7.40 to €18.70, 1¾ hours, six daily), Granada (€13.50, 2½ hours, three daily), Córdoba (€31.50, 2½ hours, two daily) and Málaga (€9.75, two hours, one daily except Sunday).

Algeciras

POP 111,300

An unattractive industrial and fishing town between Tarifa and Gibraltar, Algeciras is the major port linking Spain with Morocco. Keep your wits about you, and ignore the legions of moneychangers, drug-pushers and ticket-hawkers who hang out here. The **tourist office** (Calle Juan de la Cierva s/n; ☺9am-7.30pm Mon-Fri, 9.30am-3pm Sat & Sun) is near the port.

ℹ Getting There & Away

BOAT **FRS** (☑956 68 18 30; www.frs.es) runs the fastest ferry services from Algeciras to Tangier (passenger/car/motorcycle €37/93/31, 70 minutes, eight daily).

BUS The bus station is on Calle San Bernardo. **Comes** (☑956 65 34 56) has buses for La Línea (for Gibraltar; €2, 30 minutes) every half-hour, Tarifa (€2, 30 minutes, 13 daily), Cádiz (€11, 2½ hours, 13 daily) and Seville (€17, 2½ hours, six daily).

TRAIN The **train station** (☑956 63 10 05) runs services to/from Madrid (€68.70, six or 11 hours, two daily) and Granada (€20.20, four hours, three daily).

Cádiz

POP 128,600

Cádiz, widely considered the oldest continuously inhabited settlement in Europe, is crammed onto the head of a promontory like an overcrowded ocean liner. Columbus sailed from here on his second and fourth voyages, and after his success in the Americas, the town grew into Spain's richest and most cosmopolitan city in the 18th century. The best time to visit is during the February *carnaval* (carnival), which rivals Rio in terms of outrageous exuberance.

◉ Sights & Activities

Catedral CHURCH
(Plaza de la Catedral; adult/student €5/3, free 7-8pm Tue-Fri, 11am-1pm Sun; ☺10am-6.30pm Mon-Sat, 1.30-6.30pm Sun) The yellow-domed 18th-century cathedral is the city's most striking landmark. From a separate entrance on Plaza de la Catedral, climb to the top of the **Torre de Poniente** (Western Tower; adult/child/senior €4/3/3; ☺10am-6pm, to 8pm mid-Jun–mid-Sep) for marvellous vistas.

You can also get your bearings by climbing up the baroque **Torre Tavira** (Calle Marqués del Real Tesoro 10; adult/student €4/3.30; ☺10am-6pm, to 8pm mid-Jun–mid-Sep), the highest of Cádiz' old watchtowers, which features sweeping views of the city.

Museo de Cádiz MUSEUM
(Plaza de Mina; adult/EU citizen €1.50/free; ☺2.30-8.30pm Tue, 9am-8.30pm Wed-Sat, 9.30am-2.30pm Sun) The Museo de Cádiz has a magnificent collection of archaeological remains, as well as an excellent fine-art collection.

For more history, the city's lively **central market** (Plaza de las Flores) is on the site of a former Phoenician temple.

Playa de la Victoria BEACH
The broad, sandy Playa de la Victoria, a lovely Atlantic beach, stretches about 4km along the peninsula from its beginning 1.5km beyond the Puertas de Tierra. Bus 1 'Plaza España–Cortadura' from Plaza de España will get you there.

🛏 Sleeping & Eating

TOP CHOICE **Hotel Argantonio** HOTEL €€
(☑956 21 16 40; www.hotelargantonio.com; Calle Argantonio 3; s/d incl breakfast €90/107; ❅@☎) A very attractive small new hotel in the old city with an appealing Mudéjar accent to its decor. Staff are welcoming, and

the rooms are comfortable with wi-fi access and flat-screen TVs.

Hospedería Las Cortes de Cádiz HOTEL €€€
(☎956 21 26 68; www.hotellascortes.com; Calle San Francisco 9; s/d incl breakfast €107/148; P❋@☎) This excellent hotel occupies a remodelled 1850s mansion. The 36 rooms, each themed around a figure, place or event associated with the Cortes de Cádiz, sport classical furnishings and modern comforts. The hotel also has a roof terrace, Jacuzzi and small gym.

Casa Caracol HOSTEL €
(☎956 26 11 66; www.caracolcasa.com; Calle Suárez de Salazar 4; dm/hammock incl breakfast €16/10; @☎) Casa Caracol is the only backpacker hostel in the old town. Friendly, as only Cádiz can be, it has bunk dorms for four and eight, a communal kitchen and a roof terrace with hammocks. Green initiatives include recycling, water efficiency and plans for solar panels.

Arrocería La Pepa RICE DISHES €€
(☎956 26 38 21; Paseo Maritimo 14; paella per person €12-17) To get a decent paella you have to leave the old town behind and head a few kilometres southeast along Playa de la Victoria – an appetite-rousing predinner walk or a quick ride on the number 1 bus. Either method is worth it. The fish in La Pepa's seafood paella tastes as if it's just jumped the 100 or so metres from the Atlantic onto your plate.

El Aljibe TAPAS €€
(www.pablogrosso.com; Calle Plocia 25; tapas €2-3.50, mains €10-15) Cadiz-native chef Pablo Grosso concocts delicious combinations of the traditional and the adventurous. Try the pheasant breast stuffed with dates and the *solomillo ibérico* (Iberian pork sirloin) with Emmental cheese, ham and piquant peppers. You can enjoy his creations as tapas in the stone-walled downstairs bar.

❶ Information

Municipal tourist office (Paseo de Canalejas s/n; ☉8.30am-6pm Mon-Fri, 9am-5pm Sat & Sun)

Regional tourist office (Avenida Ramón de Carranza s/n; ☉9am-7.30pm Mon-Fri, 10am-2pm Sat, Sun & holidays)

❶ Getting There & Away

BUS Destinations include Seville (€11, 1¾ hours, 10 daily), Tarifa (€8.46, two hours, five daily), Ronda (€13, three hours, two daily), Málaga (€20, four hours, six daily) and Granada (€28, five hours, four daily).

TRAIN From the **train station** (☎902 24 02 02) trains run daily to Seville (€12.75, two hours), three per day to Córdoba (€23.85 to €38.20, three hours) and two to Madrid (€70, five hours). High-speed AVE services to Madrid are slated for commencement by 2012.

Tarifa
POP 17,700

Windy, laid-back Tarifa is so close to Africa that you can almost hear the call to prayer issuing from Morocco's minarets. The town is a bohemian haven of cafes and crumbling Moorish ruins. There's also a lively windsurfing and kitesurfing scene.

Stretching west are the long, sandy (and largely deserted) beaches of the Costa de la Luz (Coast of Light), backed by cool pine forests and green hills.

◉ Sights

A wander round the old town's narrow streets, of mainly Islamic origin, is an appetiser for Morocco. The Mudéjar **Puerta de Jerez** was built after the Reconquista. Wind your way to the mainly 15th-century **Iglesia de San Mateo** (Calle Sancho IV El Bravo; ☉9am-1pm & 5.30-8.30pm). South of the church, the **Mirador El Estrecho**, atop part of the castle walls, has spectacular views across to Africa, only 14km away. The 10th-century **Castillo de Guzmán** (Calle Guzmán El Bueno; admission €2; ☉11am-4pm) is also worth a wander; tickets for the latter must be bought at the tourist office.

⚡ Activities

Beaches
On the isthmus leading out to Isla de las Palomas, tiny **Playa Chica** lives up to its name. Spectacular **Playa de los Lances** is a different matter stretching northwest for 10km to the huge sand dune at **Ensenada de Valdevaqueros**.

Kitesurfing & Windsurfing
Tarifa now has around 30 kitesurf and windsurf schools, many of them with offices or shops along Calle Batalla del Salado or on Calle Mar Adriático. Most rent equipment and run classes. Most of the action occurs along the coast between Tarifa and Punta Paloma, 11km northwest.

Horse Riding

Located on Playa de los Lances, **Aventura Ecuestre** (956 23 66 32; www.aventura ecuestre.com; Hotel Dos Mares, N340 Km79.5) and **Hurricane Hípica** (646 964279; Hurricane Hotel, N340 Km78) both rent well-kept horses with excellent guides. An hour's beach ride costs €30. Three- or four-hour inland rides cost €70.

Whale-watching

The Strait of Gibraltar is a top site for viewing whales and dolphins. Killer whales visit in July and August, huge sperm and fin whales lurk here from spring to autumn, and pilot whales and three types of dolphin stay all year. Several organisations in Tarifa run daily two- to 2½-hour boat trips to observe these marine mammals, and most offer a free second trip if you don't at least see dolphins. **Firmm** (956 62 70 08; www.firmm .org; Calle Pedro Cortés 4; Mar-Oct) is the best and uses every trip to record data.

🛏 Sleeping & Eating

TOP CHOICE **Posada La Sacristía** HISTORIC HOTEL €€
(956 68 17 59; www.lasacristia.net; Calle San Donato 8; r incl breakfast €115-135) Tarifa's most elegant accommodation is in a beautifully renovated 17th-century townhouse with both Moorish and Thai Buddhist influences. The 10 white rooms have some lovely details.

Hostal Africa HOTEL €
(956 68 02 20; Calle María Antonia Toledo 12; s/d €50/65, without bathroom €35/50; closed 24 Dec-31 Jan) The well-travelled owners of this revamped house know just what travellers need. Rooms are attractive and there's an expansive terrace with wonderful views. Short-term storage for boards, bicycles and baggage is available.

Arte Vida Hotel HOTEL €€€
(956 68 52 46; www.hotelartevidatarifa.com; N340 Km79.3; s/d incl breakfast €120/140; P) The stylish Arte Vida, just over 5km from the town centre, combines attractive, medium-sized rooms with an excellent restaurant that has stunning views. Its grassy garden opens right onto the beach.

Chilimoso ARABIC €
(Calle Peso 6; dishes €4-6;) This tiny place serves tasty vegan and vegetarian food with oriental leanings. Try the falafel with hummus, tzatziki and salad.

Mandrágora MOROCCAN, ARABIC €€
(956 68 12 91; Calle Independencia 3; Mains €12-18; from 8pm Mon-Sat) Follow the 'listed in Lonely Planet' sign to this intimate place with its Moroccan-Arabic-inspired menu. Try the fruity lamb tagine or monkfish in a wild mushroom sauce.

ℹ Information

Tourist office (www.aytotarifa.com, in Spanish; Paseo de la Alameda; 10am-2pm daily, 4-6pm Mon-Fri Oct-May, 6-8pm Mon-Fri Jun-Sep)

ℹ Getting There & Away

BUS Comes (956 68 40 38; Calle Batalla del Salado 13) runs daily buses to Cádiz (€8.45, 1¾ hours), Algeciras (€2, 30 minutes), La Línea de la Concepción (for Gibraltar; €3.83, 45 minutes), Seville (€17.05, three hours) and Málaga (€12.75, two hours).

BOAT FRS (956 68 18 30; www.frs.es; Estación Marítima) runs fast ferries between Tarifa and Tangier (passenger/car/motorcycle €37/93/31, 35 minutes, eight daily).

GIBRALTAR

POP 28,000

The British colony of Gibraltar is like 1960s Britain on a sunny day, with Bobbies, double-decker buses and fried-egg-and-chip-style eateries. In British hands since 1713, the island was the starting point for the Muslim conquest of Iberia a thousand years earlier. Spain has never fully accepted UK control of the island but, for the moment at least, talk of joint sovereignty seems to have gone cold. Inhabitants speak English and Spanish, and signs are in English.

◎ Sights & Activities

In town, the **Gibraltar Museum** (Bomb House Lane; adult/under 12yr £2/1; 10am-6pm Mon-Fri, to 2pm Sat), with its interesting historical collection and Muslim-era bathhouse, is worth a peek.

The large **Upper Rock Nature Reserve** (adult/child incl attractions £10/5, vehicle £2, pedestrian excl attractions £0.50; 9.30am-7.15pm, last entry 6.45pm), covering most of the upper rock, has spectacular views. The rock's most famous inhabitants are its colony of Barbary macaques, the only wild primates in Europe. Some of these hang around the **Apes' Den** near the middle cable-car station; others can often be seen at the top station or Great Siege Tunnels. Other attractions include **St**

Michael's Cave, a large natural grotto renowned for its stalagmites and stalactites, and the **Great Siege Tunnels**, a series of galleries hewn from the rock by the British during the Great Siege by the Spaniards (1779–83) to provide new gun emplacements.

Dolphin-watching is an option from April to September. Most boats go from Watergardens Quay or adjacent Marina Bay. The trips last about 1½ hours and cost around £20 per adult. Tourist offices have full details.

Sleeping & Eating

Compared with Spain, expect to pay through the nose for accommodation and food.

Bristol Hotel   HOTEL **€€**
(76800; www.bristolhotel.gi; 10 Cathedral Sq; s/d/tr £63/81/93;) Veterans of bucket-and-spade British seaside holidays can wax nostalgic at the stuck-in-the-'70s Bristol with its creaking floorboards, red patterned carpets and Hi-de-Hi reception staff. Arrivals from other climes will enjoy the attractive walled garden, small swimming pool and prime location just off the main street.

Cannon Hotel   HOTEL **€€**
(51711; www.cannonhotel.gi; 9 Cannon Lane; d incl breakfast £47, s/d without bathroom £26.50/38.50) This is a small, budget-priced hotel right in the main shopping area that recalls a kind of Britain of yesteryear with its flowery decor.

Clipper   BRITISH **€€**
(78B Irish Town; mains £3.50-9;) Full of that ubiquitous naval decor, the Clipper offers real pub grub, genuine atmosphere and Premier League football on big-screen TV. Picture a little piece of Portsmouth floated round the Bay of Biscay to keep the Brits happy. Full English breakfast is served from 9.30am to 11am.

House of Sacarello   INTERNATIONAL **€€**
(57 Irish Town; daily specials £7-11.50; 9am-7.30pm Mon-Fri, to 3pm Sat, closed Sun) A restaurant with many hats (and nooks) in a converted coffee warehouse that serves light lunches, pastas, salads, quiche and soup. Or you can linger over afternoon tea between 3pm and 7.30pm.

Information

Money
The currency is the Gibraltar pound. You can also use euros or pounds sterling.

Telephone
To dial Gibraltar from Spain, you precede the five-digit local number with the code 00350; from other countries, dial the international access code, then the Gibraltar country code (350) and local number. To phone Spain from Gibraltar, just dial the nine-digit Spanish number.

Tourist Information
Gibraltar Tourist Board (www.gibraltar.gov .uk; Duke of Kent House, Cathedral Sq; 9am-5.30pm Mon-Thu, to 5.15pm Fri)
Tourist office (Grand Casemates Sq; 9am-5.30pm Mon-Fri, 10am-3pm Sat, to 1pm Sun & holidays)

Visas
To enter Gibraltar, you need a passport or EU national identity card. EU, USA, Canadian, Australian, New Zealand and South African passport-holders are among those who do not need visas for Gibraltar.

Getting There & Away

AIR easyJet (www.easyjet.com) flies approximately 15 times weekly from London Gatwick, **British Airways** (www.ba.com) operate seven weekly flights from London Heathrow and **Monarch Airlines** (www.flymonarch.com) flies daily to/from London Luton and thrice weekly to/from Manchester.

BUS There are no regular buses to Gibraltar, but La Línea de la Concepción bus station is only a five-minute walk from the border.

CAR & MOTORCYCLE Snaking vehicle queues at the 24-hour border and congested traffic in Gibraltar often make it easier to park in La Línea and walk across the border. To take a car into Gibraltar (free) you need an insurance certificate, registration document, nationality plate and driving licence.

FERRY Transcoma (in Spain 902 10 41 01, in Gibraltar 200 61 720; www.transcomalines.com) operates ferries between Algeciras and Gibraltar (one way/return €8/14, five daily).

EXTREMADURA

A sparsely populated stretch of vast skies and open plains, Extremadura is far enough from most beaten tourist trails to give you a genuine sense of exploration.

Trujillo

POP 9800

With its medieval architecture, leafy courtyards, fruit gardens, churches and convents, Trujillo truly is one of the most captivating small towns in Spain. It can't be much bigger now than it was in 1529, when its most famous son, Francisco Pizarro, set off with his three brothers and a few buddies for an expedition that culminated in the bloody conquest of the Incan empire.

⦿ Sights

Plaza Mayor
SQUARE

A large equestrian **Pizarro statue** by American Charles Rumsey looks down over the spectacular Plaza Mayor. On the plaza's south side, carved images of Pizarro and his lover Inés Yupanqui (sister of the Inca emperor Atahualpa) decorate the corner of the 16th-century **Palacio de la Conquista**. Through a twisting alley above the Palacio de la Conquista is the **Palacio Juan Pizarro de Orellana** (admission free; ⊙10am-1pm & 4.30-6.30pm Mon-Sat, 10am-12.30pm Sun), converted from miniature fortress to Renaissance mansion by one of the Pizarro cousin conquistadors. Overlooking the Plaza Mayor from the northeast corner is the 16th-century **Iglesia de San Martín** (adult/under 12yr €1.40/free; ⊙10am-2pm & 4-7pm) with delicate Gothic ceiling tracing, stunning stained-glass windows and a grand organ (climb up to the choir loft for the best view).

Upper Town
HISTORIC AREA

The 900m of walls circling the upper town date from Muslim times and it was here that the newly settled noble families built their mansions and churches after the Reconquista.

The 13th-century **Iglesia de Santa María la Mayor** (adult/under 12yr €1.40/free; ⊙10am-2pm & 4-7pm) has a mainly Gothic nave and a Romanesque tower that you can ascend (all 106 steps) for fabulous views.

At the top of the hill, Trujillo's impressive **castle** (adult/under 12yr €1.40/free; ⊙10am-2pm & 4-7pm) has 10th-century Muslim origins (evident by the horseshoe-arch gateway just inside the main entrance) and was later strengthened by the Christians. Patrol the battlements for magnificent 360-degree sweeping views.

🛏 Sleeping & Eating

TOP CHOICE **Posada Dos Orillas** HISTORIC HOTEL €€
(⟋927 65 90 79; www.dosorillas.com; Calle de Cambrones 6; d €70-90 Sun-Thu, €80-107 Fri & Sat; ❀🕸) This tastefully renovated 16th-century mansion in the walled town once served as a silk-weaving centre. The rooms

replicate Spanish colonial taste; those in the older wing bear the names of the 'seven Trujillos' of Extremadura and the Americas. It has a pleasant courtyard restaurant.

El Mirador de las Monjas
HOTEL €€

(⟋927 65 92 23; www.elmiradordelasmonjas.com, in Spanish; Plaza de Santiago 2; s/d incl breakfast €50/60 Mon-Thu, €60/70 Fri-Sun; ❀) High in the old town, this contemporary six-room *hostería* has large, minimalist rooms with clean lines and stylish bathrooms.

TOP CHOICE Restaurante La Troya
TRADITIONAL SPANISH €

(Plaza Mayor 10; set menú €15) Mention Trujillo to anyone in Spain and chances are they'll have heard of La Troya – the restaurant is an *extremeño* institution. You will be directed to one of several dining areas and there be presented with plates of tortilla, chorizo, cheese and salad, followed by a three-course menu (with truly gargantuan portions), including wine and water.

Restaurante Pizarro
TRADITIONAL SPANISH €€

(Plaza Mayor 13; meals €30-40; ⊙Wed-Mon) Next door to La Troya, much quieter and with arguably better food (they've been winning gastronomic awards since 1985). The dining room is pleasantly unpretentious, while the menu includes dishes like chicken stuffed with truffles, and *frito de cordero* (lamb stew).

ℹ Information

Tourist office (www.trujillo.es, in Spanish; Plaza Mayor s/n; ⊙10am-2pm & 4-7pm Oct-May, 10am-2pm & 5-8pm Jun-Sep)

ℹ Getting There & Away

The **bus station** (⟋927 32 12 02; Avenida de Miajadas) is 500m south of Plaza Mayor. There are services to/from Madrid (€19.30 to €31.40, three to 4¼ hours, five daily), Cáceres (€4.20, 40 minutes, eight daily) and Mérida (€8.15, 1½ hours, three daily).

Cáceres

POP 89,100

Cáceres' *ciudad monumental* (old town), built in the 15th and 16th centuries, is perfectly preserved. The town's action centres on Plaza Mayor, at the foot of the Old Town, and busy Avenida de España, a short distance south.

⊙ Sights & Activities

Plaza de Santa María　　　　SQUARE

Enter the Old Town from Plaza Mayor through the 18th-century **Arco de la Estrella**, built with a wide span for the passage of carriages. The 15th-century Gothic cathedral, **Concatedral de Santa María** (Plaza de Santa María; admission €1; ⊙9.30am-2pm & 5.30-8.30pm Mon-Sat, 9.30-11.50am & 5.30-7.15pm Sun May-Sep), creates an impressive opening scene. Climb the **bell tower** (€1) for stunning views.

Also on the plaza are the **Palacio Episcopal** (Bishop's Palace), the **Palacio de Mayoralgo** and the **Palacio de Ovando**, all in 16th-century Renaissance style. Heading back through Arco de la Estrella, you can climb the 12th-century **Torre de Bujaco** (Plaza Mayor; adult/under 12yr €2/free; ⊙10am-2pm & 5.30-8.30pm Mon-Sat, 10am-2pm Sun Apr-Sep, 10am-2pm & 4.30-7.30pm Mon-Sat, 10am-2pm Sun Oct-Mar) for good stork's-eye views of the Plaza Mayor.

Plaza de San Mateo & Plaza de las Veletas　　　　SQUARE

From Plaza de San Jorge, Cuesta de la Compañía climbs to Plaza de San Mateo and the **Iglesia de San Mateo**, traditionally the church of the land-owning nobility and built on the site of the town's mosque.

Below the square is the excellent **Museo de Cáceres** (Plaza de las Veletas 1; adult/EU citizens €1.20/free; ⊙9am-2.30pm & 5-8.15pm Tue-Sat, 10.15am-2.30pm Sun) in a 16th-century mansion built over an evocative 12th-century *aljibe* (cistern), the only surviving element of Cáceres' Muslim castle. It has an impressive archaeological section and an excellent fine-arts display (open only in the mornings), with works by Picasso, Miró, Tapiès and other renowned Spanish painters and sculptors.

🛏 Sleeping & Eating

Hotel Casa Don Fernando

　　　　BOUTIQUE HOTEL €€

(☎927 21 42 79; www.casadonfernando.com; Plaza Mayor 30; d €60-140; ❋⃝) Arguably the classiest midrange choice in Cáceres, this boutique hotel sits on Plaza Mayor directly opposite the Arco de la Estrella. Spread over four floors, there are rooms on each floor with plaza views, and the designer rooms and bathrooms are tastefully chic. Parking is €9.

Hotel Iberia　　　　HOTEL €

(☎927 24 76 34; www.iberiahotel.com, in Spanish; Calle de los Pintores 2; s/d €46/60; ❋) Located in an 18th-century former palace just off Plaza Mayor, this friendly and family-run 36-room hotel has public areas that look like an old-world museum piece, decorated with antique furnishings. The rooms are more subdued with parquet floors, cream walls and pale-grey tiled bathrooms.

Mesón El Asador　　　TRADITIONAL SPANISH €€

(Calle de Moret 34; raciones €6-8, meals €20-30, set menus €15-26; ⊙closed Sun) Enter the dining room and you get the picture right away: one wall is covered with hung hams. It's often packed to the rafters with locals, not least because you won't taste better roast pork (or lamb) in town. Its bar also serves *bocadillos* and a wide range of *raciones*, while the *menú especial* (€26) is terrific value.

Restaurante Torre de Sande　　　FUSION €€

(☎927 21 11 47; www.torredesande.com, in Spanish; Calle Condes 3; meals €35-45; ⊙lunch & dinner Tue-Sat, lunch Sun) Dine in the pretty courtyard on dishes like *salmorejo de cerezas del jerte con queso de cabra* (cherry-based cold soup with goat's cheese) at this elegant gourmet restaurant. More modestly, stop for a drink and a tapa (€4) at the interconnecting Tapería.

ℹ Information

Junta de Extremadura tourist office (www .turismoextremadura.com; Plaza Mayor 3; ⊙8.30am-2.30pm & 4-6pm or 5-7pm Mon-Fri, 10am-2pm Sat & Sun)

Municipal tourist office (Calle de los Olmos 3; ⊙10am-2pm & 4.30-7.30pm or 5.30-8.30pm)

ℹ Getting There & Away

BUS The **bus station** (⊙927 23 25 50; Carretera de Sevilla) has services to Trujillo (€4.20, 40 minutes, eight daily) and Mérida (€5.35, 50 minutes, two to four daily).

TRAIN Up to five trains per day run to/from Madrid (€25.80 to €38.50, four hours), Plasencia (€5.55, 1½ hours) and Mérida (from €4.30, one hour).

Mérida

POP 74,900

Once the biggest city in Roman Spain, Mérida is home to more ruins of that age than anywhere else in the country and is a wonderful spot to spend a few archaeologically inclined days.

Sights

Roman Remains
RUINS

The **Teatro Romano** (Calle Alvarez S. de Buruaga; adult/under 12yr €8/free; ⏱9.30am-7.30pm Jun-Sep, 9.30am-1.45pm & 4-6.15pm Oct-May), built around 15 BC to seat 6000 spectators and set in lovely gardens, has a dramatic and well-preserved two-tier backdrop of Corinthian stone columns; the stage's facade (*scaenae frons*) was inaugurated in AD 105. The theatre hosts performances during the Festival del Teatro Clásico in summer. The adjoining **Anfiteatro**, opened in 8 BC for gladiatorial contests, had a capacity of 14,000.

Los Columbarios (Calle del Ensanche s/n; adult/under 12yr €4/free; ⏱9.30am-1.45pm & 5-7.15pm Jun-Sep, 9.30am-1.45pm & 4-6.15pm Oct-May) is a Roman funeral site. A footpath connects it with the **Casa del Mitreo** (Calle Oviedo s/n; adult/under 12yr €4/free; ⏱9.30am-1.45pm & 5-7.15pm Jun-Sep, 9.30am-1.45pm & 4-6.15pm Oct-May), a 2nd-century Roman house with several intricate mosaics and a well-preserved fresco.

Don't miss the extraordinarily powerful spectacle of the **Puente Romano** over the Río Guadiana, which at 792m in length with 60 granite arches is one of the longest bridges built by the Romans.

The **Templo de Diana** (Calle de Sagasta) stood in the municipal forum, where the city government was based. The restored **Pórtico del Foro**, the municipal forum's portico, is just along the road.

Museo Nacional de Arte Romano
MUSEUM

(museoarteromano.es; Calle de José Ramón Mélida; adult/child €3/free, EU seniors & students free; ⏱9.30am-3.30pm & 5.30-8.30pm Tue-Sun Jul-Sep, shorter hours rest of year) On no account miss this fabulous museum which has a superb collection of statues, mosaics, frescos, coins and other Roman artefacts. Designed by the architect Rafael Moneo, the soaring brick structure makes a remarkable home for the collection.

Alcazaba
FORTRESS

(Calle Graciano; adult/child €4/free; ⏱9.30am-1.45pm & 5-7.15pm Jun-Sep, 9.30am-1.45pm & 4-6.15pm Oct-May) This large Muslim fort was built in AD 835 on a site already occupied by the Romans and Visigoths. Down below, its *aljibe* (cistern) incorporates marble and stone slabs with Visigothic decoration that were recycled by the Muslims, while the ramparts look out over the Guadiana and

down into the Alcazaba's gardens. The 15th-century monastery in its northeast corner now serves as the Junta de Extremadura's presidential offices.

Sleeping & Eating

⭐ La Flor de al-Andalus
BUDGET HOTEL €

(☎924 31 33 56; www.laflordeal-andalus.es, in Spanish; Avenida de Extremadura 6; s/d €33/45; ✻🖥) If only all *hostales* were this good. Opened in May 2010 and describing itself as a 'boutique *hostal*', La Flor de al-Andalus has beautifully decorated rooms in Andalucían style, friendly service and a good location within walking distance of all the main sites. The buffet breakfast costs just €3.

⭐ Hotel Adealba
HOTEL €€

(☎924 38 83 08; www.hoteladealba.com; Calle Romero Leal 18; d incl breakfast from €96.30; ✿🖥✻) Opened in 2009, this stunning hotel occupies a 19th-century townhouse close to the Templo de Diana and does so with a classy, contemporary look. The designer rooms have strong, contrasting colours and there's a pillow menu to choose from. Parking is €12.

Tabula Calda
TRADITIONAL SPANISH €€

(www.tabulacalda.com; Calle Romero Leal 11; meals €20-25; ⏱lunch & dinner Mon-Sat, lunch Sun) This inviting space with tilework and abundant greenery serves up well-priced meals (including *menús* from €12 to €24.50) that cover most Spanish staples. The cooking effortlessly combines traditional home cooking, thoughtful presentation and subtle innovations.

Convivium
TAPAS, TRADITIONAL SPANISH €

(Calle de Sagasta 21; tortillinas €1, meals €15-20) Head straight for the pretty patio with tables set under a large lemon tree at this informal place where the speciality is *tortillinas* (mini omelettes with fillings including cod, salami, spinach, aubergines and prawns). The *tortillina*, gazpacho and drink for €2.50 has to be Mérida's best deal.

Information

Municipal tourist office (www.merida.es, in Spanish; Paseo de José Álvarez Sáenz de Buruaga s/n; ⏱9.30am-2pm & 5-7.30pm)

Getting There & Away

BUS From the **bus station** (☎924 37 14 04; Avenida de la Libertad), destinations include Seville (€13.10, 2½ hours, five daily), Cáceres (€5.35,

50 minutes, two to four daily), Trujillo (€8.15, 1¼ hours, three daily) and Madrid (€22.15 to €27, four to five hours, eight daily).

TRAIN Trains to Madrid (€31.80 to €36.30, 4½ to 6½ hours, five daily), Cáceres (from €4.30, one hour, six daily) and Seville (€14.10, four hours, one daily).

UNDERSTAND SPAIN

History

Ancient Civilisations

Spain's story is one of European history's grand epics, and it's a story that begins further back than most – the oldest pieces of human bone in Europe (dating back a mere 780,000 years) have been found in Spain, in the Sierra de Atapuerca near Burgos.

The point at which Spanish history really gets interesting, however, is when the great civilisations of the Ancient Mediterranean began to colonise what we now know as the Iberian Peninsula, from around 1000 BC. The sea-going Phoenicians founded a great seafaring empire which depended on the establishment of ports around the Mediterranean rim. One of these ports, Cádiz (p887), is widely believed to be Europe's oldest continuously inhabited settlement.

The Romans arrived in the 3rd century BC and while they took 200 years to subdue the peninsula, they would hold it for six centuries. Called Hispania, Roman Spain became an integral part of the Roman Empire, with its impact upon language, architecture and religion lasting to this day. Reminders of Roman times include Segovia's aqueduct (p811), the ancient theatres and other monuments of Mérida (p892) and Tarragona (p839), and the ruins of Zaragoza (p841).

Muslim Spain & the Reconquista

In 711 Muslim armies invaded the peninsula, most of which they would end up occupying. Muslim dominion would last almost 800 years in parts of Spain. In Islamic Spain (known as al-Andalus), arts and sciences prospered, new crops and agricultural techniques were introduced, and palaces, mosques, schools, public baths and gardens were built. The spirit of these times lives on most powerfully in Andalucía.

In 1085 Alfonso VI, king of Castile, took Toledo, the first definitive victory of the Reconquista (the struggle to wrestle Spain into Christian hands). By the mid-13th century, the Christians had taken most of the peninsula, except for the emirate of Granada.

The kingdoms of Castile and Aragón emerged as Christian Spain's two main powers, and in 1469 they were united by the marriage of Isabel, princess of Castile, and Fernando, heir to Aragón's throne. Known as the Catholic Monarchs, they laid the foundations for the Spanish Golden Age, but were also responsible for one of the darkest hours in Spain's history – the Spanish Inquisition, a witch-hunt to expel or execute Jews and other non-Christians. In 1492 the last Muslim ruler of Granada surrendered to them, marking the end of the Reconquista. In the same year, Jews were expelled from Spain, with Muslims sent into exile eight years later.

The Golden Age

In the same year that marked the end of the Reconquista, Christopher Columbus (Colón in Castilian) landed in the Bahamas and later Cuba. He never guessed he'd discovered new continents and changed the course of history. His voyages sparked a period of exploration and exploitation that was to yield Spain enormous wealth, while destroying the ancient American empires. Over the centuries that followed, Spain's growing confidence was reflected in an extravagant cultural outpouring, producing towering figures such as Velázquez and Cervantes. For three centuries, gold and silver from the New World were used to finance the rapid expansion of the Spanish empire but were not enough to prevent its slow decline. By the 18th century, the mighty Spanish empire was on its way out, the life sucked out of it by a series of unwise kings, a self-seeking noble class and ceaseless warfare.

Struggle for the Soul of Spain

By the early 19th century, Spain's royal court had descended into internecine squabbles over succession to the Spanish throne. The consequences for the rest of the country were profound.

In 1807–08 Napoleon's forces occupied a weakened Spain, and King Carlos IV abdicated without a fight. In his place Napoleon installed his own brother, Joseph Bonaparte. The Spaniards retaliated with a five-year war of independence (in which British forces under the Duke of Wellington played a key role). The French were expelled in 1813 after defeat at Vitoria. A Bourbon, Fernando VII, was restored to the Spanish throne – despite periods of interruption to their rule, the Bourbon royal family rule Spain to this day.

Independence may have been restored, but Spain spent much of the next century embroiled in wars at home and abroad. The Spanish-American War of 1898 marked the end of the Spanish empire. The USA crushed Spanish arms and took over its last overseas possessions – Cuba, Puerto Rico, Guam and the Philippines. Spain was in a dire state.

Franco's Spain

Begun in the 19th century, the battle between conservatives and liberals, and between monarchists and republicans came to a head in July 1936 when Nationalist plotters in the army rose against the Republican government, launching a civil war (1936–39) that would create bitter wounds that are still healing today. The Nationalists, led by General Francisco Franco (who stood at the head of an alliance of the army, Church and the Fascist-style Falange Party), received military support from Nazi Germany and Fascist Italy, while the elected Republican government received support from the Soviet Union and other foreign leftists.

The war ended in 1939, with Franco the victor. Some 350,000 Spaniards died in the war, most of them on the battlefield but many others in executions, prison camps or simply from disease and starvation. After the war, thousands of Republicans were executed, jailed or forced into exile, and Franco's 36-year dictatorship began with Spain isolated internationally and crippled by recession. It wasn't until the 1950s and '60s, when the rise in tourism and a treaty with the USA combined to provide much-needed funds, that the country began to recover, although Franco retained an iron grip over the country.

The New Spain

Franco died in 1975, having named Juan Carlos, the grandson of Alfonso XIII, as his successor. Despite Franco's careful grooming, King Juan Carlos opted for the creation of a constitutional monarchy and a democratic government. The first elections were held in 1977 and a new constitution was drafted in 1978. It was a dramatic shift and although deep schisms remain to this day, the country's democratic transition has been an extraordinary success.

Post-Franco Spain bore little resemblance to what went before and the country revelled in its new-found freedoms with all the zeal of an ex-convent schoolgirl. Seemingly everything – from political parties to drugs – was legalised and the 1980s, despite the spectre of killings by the Basque terrorist group ETA, was a period of great cultural innovation and Spain's reputation as Europe's party capital was born. Spain joined the European Community (EC) in 1986 and celebrated its return to the world stage in style in 1992, with Expo '92 in Seville and the Olympic Games in Barcelona.

At a political level, Spain was ruled from 1982 until 1996 by the Partido Socialista Obrero Español (Spanish Socialist Party; PSOE) of Felipe González. By 1996 the PSOE government stood accused of corruption and was swept from power by the centre-right Partido Popular (Popular Party; PP), led by José María Aznar. The PP went on to establish programs of economic decentralisation and liberalisation.

Spain Today

Long accustomed to terrorist attacks by ETA (which has killed more than 800 people in the past four decades), Spain was nonetheless shaken to its core by the largest-ever terrorist attack on Spanish soil (later claimed by al-Qaeda), in Madrid on 11 March 2004. In national elections held three days later, the PP lost the presidential election to the PSOE. Among his first actions as president, José Luís Rodríguez Zapatero withdrew Spanish troops from Iraq.

The Socialists embarked on something of a social revolution, legalising gay marriage, regularising the status of hundreds of thousands of illegal immigrants, removing the Church's role in religious education in schools, making abortions easier to obtain, and pushing through a law aimed at investigating the crimes and executions of the Franco years; the latter broke the 'pact of silence' that had prevailed throughout the transition to democracy in the late 1970s.

Zapatero also opened the way to increased devolution of powers to the regions but, again, not without controversy. The opposition PP took special exception to Catalonia's new Estatut (autonomy statutes). Indeed, the PP maintained a divisive campaign against the government until the 2008 elections, which Zapatero also won.

Within months of his re-election, years of economic boom came shuddering to an end amid the global financial crisis; unemployment jumped from around 7% in 2007 to above 20% in 2010. With the economy deep in recession, the Socialists' popularity plummeted. National elections are due in 2012.

Good news may be hard to come by, but the announcement of a ceasefire by a much-weakened ETA in September 2010 was welcomed by the government and opposition alike. Although ETA has returned to arms after similar ceasefires in the past, the move has nonetheless raised much-needed hopes that at least one source of conflict within Spanish society may soon come to an end.

People

Spain has a population of approximately 46 million, descended from all the many peoples who have settled here over the millennia, among them Iberians, Celts, Romans, Jews, Visigoths, Berbers, Arabs and 20th-century immigrants from across the globe. The biggest cities are Madrid (3.6 million), Barcelona (1.62 million), Valencia (814,200) and Seville (703,000). Each region proudly preserves its own unique culture, and some – Catalonia and the Basque Country in particular – display a fiercely independent spirit.

Religion

Only about 20% of Spaniards are regular churchgoers, but Catholicism is deeply ingrained in the culture and an estimated 94% of Spaniards identify themselves as Catholics. As the writer Unamuno said, 'Here in Spain we are all Catholics, even the atheists'.

However, many Spaniards have a deep-seated scepticism about the Church. During the civil war and the four decades of Franco's rule, the Catholic Church was, for the most part, a strong supporter of his policies and church-going was practically obligatory – those who shunned the Church were often treated as outcasts or targeted as delinquents by Franco's police. The Church retains a powerful public voice in national debates.

Spain's most significant (and growing) religious communities after the Catholics are Protestants and Muslims.

Arts

Literature

Miguel de Cervantes' novel *Don Quijote* is the masterpiece of the literary flowering of the 16th and 17th centuries, not to mention one of the world's great works of fiction.

The next high point of in the early 20th century grew out of the crisis of the Spanish-American War that spawned the intellectual Generation of '98. The towering figure was poet and playwright Federico García Lorca, who won international acclaim before he was murdered in the civil war for his Republican sympathies.

Popular contemporary authors include Arturo Pérez Reverte, whose *Capitán Alatriste* books are international best-sellers. Another writer with a broad following is Javier Marías. He has kept the country in thrall these past years with his 1500-page trilogy, *Tu Rostro Mañana* (Your Face Tomorrow).

Cinema

Modern Spanish cinema's best-known director is Pedro Almodóvar, whose humorous, cutting-edge films are often set amid the great explosion of drugs and creativity that occurred in Madrid in the 1980s. His *Todo Sobre Mi Madre* (All About My Mother; 1999) and *Habla Con Ella* (Talk to Her; 2002) are both Oscar winners, while *Volver* (2006) is his most acclaimed recent work.

Alejandro Amenábar, the young Chilean-born director of *Abre los Ojos* (Open Your Eyes; 1997), *The Others* (2001) and the Oscar-winning *Mar Adentro* (The Sea Inside; 2004), is Almodóvar's main competition for Spain's 'best director' title. That latter film's star, Javier Bardem, won the Oscar for Best Supporting Actor in the Coen brothers' disturbing *No Country for Old Men* in 2008.

Woody Allen set his *Vicky Cristina Barcelona* (2008), a light romantic comedy, largely in Barcelona; the Madrid-born actress Penélope Cruz won an Oscar for Best Supporting Actress for her role in the film.

Architecture

Spain resembles an open-air gallery that spans some of history's most important architectural styles.

The Muslims left behind some of the most splendid buildings in the Islamic world, particularly in Andalucía. Examples include Granada's Alhambra (p879), Córdoba's Mezquita (p876) and Seville's Alcázar (p871) – the latter is an example of Mudéjar architecture, the name given to Islamic artistry built in Christian-held territory. Outside of Andalucía, Zaragoza's Aljafería (p841) captures the same spirit, albeit on a smaller scale.

The first main Christian architectural movement was Romanesque, best seen in churches and monasteries across the north of the country. Later came the great Gothic cathedrals, such as those in Toledo (p818), Burgos (p817), León (p814), Ávila (p807), Salamanca (p808) and Seville (p870) of the 12th to 16th centuries. Spain then followed the usual path to baroque (17th and 18th centuries) and neoclassicism (19th century).

Around the turn of the 20th century, Catalonia produced its startling Modernista movement, so many of whose buildings adorn Barcelona's streets; Antoni Gaudí's La Sagrada Família (p832) is the most stunning example.

Of the daring contemporary structures appearing all over Spain, Valencia's Ciudad de las Artes y las Ciencias (p855) and Bilbao's Guggenheim (p848) are the most eye-catching.

Painting

Spain's painters rank among some of history's best-known European masters.

The giants of Spain's Golden Age (around 1550 to 1650) were Toledo-based El Greco (originally from Crete) and Diego Velázquez, considered Spain's best painter by greats including Picasso and Dalí. El Greco and Velázquez are well represented in Madrid's Museo del Prado (p785), as is the genius of the 18th and 19th centuries, Francisco Goya. Goya's versatility ranged from unflattering royal portraits and anguished war scenes to bullfight etchings and tapestry designs.

Catalonia was the powerhouse of early-20th-century Spanish art, claiming the hugely prolific Pablo Picasso (although born in Málaga, Andalucía), the colourful symbolist Joan Miró and surrealist Salvador Dalí. To get inside the latter's world, head for Figueres or the Castell de Púbol (for both, see the boxed text, p838). The two major museums dedicated to Picasso's work are the Museu Picasso (p834) in Barcelona and the Museo Picasso Málaga (p883), while his signature *Guernica* and other works are found in Madrid's Centro de Arte Reina Sofía (p790). The Reina Sofía also has works by Joan Miró, as does the Fundació Joan Miró (p827).

Important artists of the late 20th century include the Basque sculptor Eduardo Chillida; his Museo Chillida Leku (p844) is south of San Sebastián.

Flamenco

Most musical historians speculate that flamenco probably dates back to a fusion of songs brought to Spain by the *gitanos* (Roma people or gypsies) with music and verses from North Africa crossing into medieval Muslim Andalucía. Flamenco as we now know it first took recognisable form in the 18th and early 19th centuries among *gitanos* in western Andalucía. Suitably, for a place considered the cradle of the genre, the Seville–Jerez de la Frontera–Cádiz axis is still considered the flamenco heartland and it's here, purists believe, that you must go for the most authentic flamenco experience.

Environment

The Land

Spain is a geographically diverse country, with landscapes ranging from the near-deserts of Almería to the emerald green countryside of Asturias and deep coastal inlets of Galicia, from the rolling sunbaked plains of Castilla-La Mancha to the rugged Pyrenees. The country covers 84% of the Iberian Peninsula and spreads over 505,370 sq km, about 40% of which is high *meseta* (tableland).

FLAMENCO – THE ESSENTIAL ELEMENTS

A flamenco singer is known as a *cantaor* (male) or *cantaora* (female); a dancer is a *bailaor/a*. Most of the songs and dances are performed to a blood-rush of guitar from the *tocaor/a* (flamenco guitarist). Percussion is provided by tapping feet, clapping hands and sometimes castanets. Flamenco *coplas* (songs) come in many different types, from the anguished *soleá* or the intensely despairing *siguiriya* to the livelier *alegría* or the upbeat *bulería*. The first flamenco was *cante jondo* (deep song), an anguished instrument of expression for a group on the margins of society. *Jondura* (depth) is still the essence of pure flamenco.

The traditional flamenco costume – shawl, fan and long frilly *bata de cola* (tail gown) for women, flat Cordoban hats and tight black trousers for men – dates from Andalucian fashions in the late 19th century.

Wildlife

The brown bear, wolf, Iberian lynx (the world's most endangered cat species, although it's making a hesitant and much-assisted comeback) and wild boar all survive in Spain, although only the boar exists in abundance. Spain's high mountains harbour the chamois and Spanish ibex, and big birds of prey such as eagles, vultures and lammergeier. The marshy Ebro Delta and Guadalquivir estuary are important for waterbirds, among them the spectacular greater flamingo.

Environmental Issues

Spain faces some of the most pressing environmental issues of our time. Drought, massive overdevelopment of its coastlines, overexploitation of scarce water resources by tourism projects and intensive agriculture, and spiralling emissions of greenhouse gases are all major concerns. It's a slightly more nuanced picture than first appears – Spain is a leading player in the wind-power industry, it has locked away around 40,000 sq km of protected areas, including 14 national parks, and its system of public transport is outstanding – but the apparent absence of any meaningful political will to tackle these issues is storing up problems for future generations.

Food & Drink

Reset your stomach's clock in Spain unless you want to eat alone, with other tourists or, in some cases, not at all.

Most Spaniards start the day with a light *desayuno* (breakfast), perhaps coffee with a *tostada* (piece of toast) or *pastel/bollo* (pastry), although they might stop in a bar later for a mid-morning *bocadillo* (baguette). *La comida* (lunch) is usually the main meal of the day, eaten between about 2pm and 4pm. The *cena* (evening meal) is usually lighter and most locals won't sit down for it before 9pm. The further south you go, the later start times tend to be – anything from 10pm to midnight!

Staples & Specialities

The variety in Spanish cuisines is quite extraordinary, and each region has its own styles and specialities. One of the most characteristic dishes, from the Valencia region, is paella – rice, seafood, the odd vegetable and often chicken or meat, all sim-mered together and traditionally coloured yellow with saffron. *Jamón serrano* (cured ham) is a delicacy available in many different qualities.

Many would argue that tapas are Spain's greatest culinary gift to the world, not least because the possibilities are endless. Anything can be a tapa, from a handful of olives or a piece of *tortilla de patatas* (potato and onion omelette) to more elaborate and often intensely surprising combinations of tastes. For tapas, the cities of Andalucía are usually (but not always) bastions of tradition, while the undoubted king of tapas destinations is San Sebastián (p845), in Basque country, where they call tapas *'pintxos'*. It all comes together in Madrid (see the boxed text, p800).

 Drinks

Start the day with a strong coffee, either as a *cafe con leche* (half-coffee, half-milk), *cafe solo* (short black, espresso-like) or *cafe cortado* (short black with a little milk).

The most common way to order a *cerveza* (beer) is to ask for a *caña* (small draught beer). In Basque Country this is a *zurrito*. A larger beer (about 300mL) is often called a *tubo*. All these words apply to *cerveza de barril* (draught beer) – if you just ask for a *cerveza* you're likely to get bottled beer, which is a little more expensive.

Vino (wine) comes *blanco* (white), *tinto* (red) or *rosado* (rosé). Exciting wine regions include Penedès, Priorat, Ribera del Duero and La Rioja. There are also many regional specialities, such as *jerez* (sherry) in Jerez de la Frontera and *cava* (a sparkling wine) in Catalonia. Sangria, a sweet punch made of red wine, fruit and spirits, is a summer drink and especially popular with tourists. *Tinto de verano,* a kind of wine shandy, is a summer alternative.

Agua del grifo (tap water) is usually safe to drink.

Where to Eat & Drink

Bars and cafes are open all day (see p900 for detailed hours), serving coffees, pastries, *bocadillos* and usually tapas (which generally cost from €1.50 to €4). You can also order *raciones,* a large-sized serving of these snacks.

Spaniards like to eat out, and restaurants (which come in different styles and with different names such as *taberna, mesón, tasca* and *restaurante*) abound even in small towns. At lunchtime, most places

JAMÓN – A PRIMER

Unlike Italian prosciutto, Spanish *jamón* is a bold, deep red and well marbled with buttery fat. Like wines and olive oil, Spanish *jamón* is subject to a strict series of classifications. *Jamón serrano* refers to *jamón* made from white-coated pigs introduced to Spain in the 1950s. Once salted and semidried by the cold, dry winds of the Spanish sierra, most now go through a similar process of curing and drying in a climate-controlled shed for around a year. *Jamón serrano* accounts for approximately 90% of cured ham in Spain.

Jamón *ibérico* – more expensive and generally regarded as the elite of Spanish hams – comes from a black-coated pig indigenous to the Iberian Peninsula and a descendant of the wild boar. If the pig gains at least 50% of its body weight during the acorn-eating season, it can be classified as *jamón ibérico de bellota*, the most sought-after designation for *jamón*.

offer a *menú del día* – a fixed-price lunch menu and the traveller's best friend. For €8 to €12 you typically get three courses, bread and a drink. The *plato combinado* (combined plate) is a cousin of the *menú* and usually includes a meat dish with some vegetables.

After dinner, head for the bars where you can get coffee and tea. A *bar de copas* will sell beer and an endless array of *combinados* (drinks like vodka and orange or rum and Coke) and sometimes more sophisticated cocktails.

As of 1 January 2011, all bars and restaurants are smoke-free.

Vegetarians & Vegans

Vegetarians may have to be creative in Spain. You'll find dedicated vegetarian restaurants in larger cities and important student centres. Otherwise, most traditional restaurants will offer salads and egg tortillas, but little else for non-carnivores. Even salads may come laden with sausages or tuna. Pasta and pizza are readily available, as is seafood for those who eat it. Vegans will have an especially hard time away from the big cities (and not an easy time in them).

Directory A–Z

Accommodation

In this chapter, budget options include everything from dorm-style youth hostels to family-style *pensiones* and slightly better-heeled *hostales*. At the upper end of this category you'll find rooms with air-conditioning and private bathrooms. Midrange *hostales* and hotels are more comfortable and most offer standard hotel services. Business hotels, trendy boutique hotels and luxury hotels are usually in the top-end category.

Virtually all accommodation prices are subject to IVA *(impuesto sobre el valor añadido)*, the Spanish version of value-added tax, which is 7%. This may or may not be included in the quoted price. To check, ask: *Está incluido el IVA?* (Is IVA included?)

PRICE RANGES

Our reviews refer to double rooms with a private bathroom, except in hostels or where otherwise specified. Quoted rates are for **high season**, which is generally May to September (though this varies greatly from region to region).

€€€ more than €120 (more than €200 for Madrid/Barcelona)

€€ €60 to €120 (€70 to €200 for Madrid/Barcelona)

€ less than €60 (less than €70 for Madrid/Barcelona)

CAMPING

Spain has around 1000 officially graded *campings* (camping grounds) and they vary greatly in service, cleanliness and style. They're officially rated as first class (1ªC), second class (2ªC) or third class (3ªC). Camping grounds usually charge per person, per tent and per vehicle – typically €5 to €9 for each. Many camping grounds close from around October to Easter.

Useful websites:

Campings Online (www.campingsonline.com/espana) Booking service.

Campinguía (www.campinguia.com) Contains comments (mostly in Spanish) and links.

Guía Camping (www.guiacampingfecc.com) Online version of the annual *Guía Camping* (€13.60), which is available in bookshops around the country.

HOTELS, HOSTALES & PENSIONES

Most options fall into the categories of hotels (one to five stars, full amenities), *hostales* (high-end guesthouses with private bathroom; one to three stars) or *pensiones* (guesthouses, usually with shared bathroom; one to three stars).

Among the more tempting hotels for those with a little fiscal room to manoeuvre are the 90 or so **paradores** (☎in Spain 902 547 979; www.parador.es), a state-funded chain of hotels in often stunning locations, among them towering castles and former medieval convents. Boutique hotels are also all the rage.

YOUTH HOSTELS

Albergues juveniles (youth hostels) are cheap places to stay, especially for lone travellers. Expect to pay from €15 to €28 per night, depending on location, age and season. Spain's Hostelling International (HI) organisation, **Red Española de Albergues Juveniles** (REAJ; www.reaj.com), has around 250 youth hostels throughout Spain. Official hostels require HI membership (you can buy a membership card at virtually all hostels) and many have curfews.

🏃 Activities

HIKING

Spain is a hiker's paradise. You can read more about some of the best treks in the country in Lonely Planet's *Walking in Spain*. Useful for hiking, especially in the Pyrenees, are maps by Editorial Alpina. The series combines information booklets with detailed maps. Buy them at bookshops, sports shops and sometimes at petrol stations near hiking areas.

Throughout Spain, you'll find GR (*Grandes Recorridos,* or long distance) trails. These are indicated with red-and-white markers. The Camino de Santiago (St James' Way, with several branches) is perhaps Spain's best-known long-distance walk. In addition to this world-famous pilgrimage route across northern Spain, some of Spain's best hiking is in the Pyrenees, Picos de Europa and Andalucía.

SKIING

Skiing is cheaper but less varied than in much of the rest of Europe. The season runs from December to mid-April. The best resorts are in the Pyrenees, especially in northwest Catalonia and in Aragón. The Sierra Nevada in Andalucía offers the most southerly skiing in Western Europe.

SURFING, WINDSURFING & KITESURFING

The Basque Country has good surf spots, including San Sebastián, Zarautz and the legendary left at Mundaka. Tarifa (p888), with its long beaches and ceaseless wind, is generally considered to be the windsurfing capital of Europe. It's also a top spot for kitesurfing.

Business Hours

Reviews in this guidebook won't list business hours unless they differ from the following standards:

Banks 8.30am to 2pm Monday to Friday; some also open 4pm to 7pm Thursday and 9am and 1pm Saturday

Central post offices 8.30am to 9.30pm Monday to Friday, 8.30am to 2pm Saturday

Nightclubs midnight or 1am to 5am or 6am

Restaurants lunch 1pm to 4pm, dinner 8.30pm to midnight or later

Shops 10am to 2pm and 4.30pm to 7.30pm or 5pm to 8pm; big supermarkets and department stores generally open from 10am to 10pm Monday to Saturday

Embassies & Consulates

Australia (☎91 353 66 00; www.spain.embassy.gov.au; 24th fl, Paseo de la Castellana 259D, Madrid)

Canada (☎91 382 84 00; www.espana.gc.ca; Torre Espacio, Paseo de la Castellana 259D, Madrid)

Japan (☎91 590 76 00; www.es.emb-japan.go.jp; Calle de Serrano 109, Madrid)

New Zealand (☎91 523 02 26; www.nzembassy.com; Calle del Pinar 7, Madrid)

UK (☎91 714 63 00; http://ukinspain.fco.gov.uk; Torre Espacio, Paseo de la Castellana 259D, Madrid)

USA (☎91 587 22 00; http://madrid.usembassy.gov; Calle de Serrano 75, Madrid)

Food

Throughout this chapter, each place to eat is accompanied by one of the following symbols (the price relates to a three-course meal with house wine per person):

€€€ more than €50

€€ €20 to €50

€ less than €20

Gay & Lesbian Travellers

Homosexuality is legal in Spain. In 2005 the Socialist president, José Luis Rodríguez Zapatero, gave the country's conservative Catholic foundations a shake with the legalisation of same-sex marriages in Spain.

Lesbians and gay men generally keep a fairly low profile, but are quite open in the cities. Madrid (see the boxed text, p803), Barcelona (p834), Sitges, Torremolinos and Ibiza have particularly lively scenes.

Internet Access

Wi-fi is increasingly available at most hotels and in some cafes, restaurants and airports; generally (but not always) free.

Good cybercafes are increasingly hard to find; ask at the local tourist office. Prices per hour range from €1.50 to €3.

Language Courses

Among the more popular places to learn Spanish are Barcelona, Granada, Madrid, Salamanca and Seville.

The **Escuela Oficial de Idiomas** (EOI; www.eeooiinet.com, in Spanish) is a nationwide institution teaching Spanish and other local languages. On the website's opening page, hit 'Centros' under 'Comunidad' and then 'Centros en la Red' to get to a list of schools.

Legal Matters

Drugs Cannabis is legal but only for personal use and in very small quantities. Public consumption of any drug is illegal.

Legal driving age 18

Legal drinking age 18

Smoking Not permitted in any enclosed public space, including bars, restaurants and nightclubs.

Maps

If you're driving around Spain, consider investing in a road atlas with detailed road maps as well as maps of all the main towns and cities. Most travel shops stock them. Otherwise, some of the best maps for travellers are by Michelin, which produces the 1:1,000,000 *Spain Portugal* map and six 1:400,000 regional maps covering the whole country. Also good are the GeoCenter maps published by Germany's RV Verlag.

Money

ATMs Many credit and debit cards can be used for withdrawing money from *cajeros automáticos* (automatic teller machines) that display the relevant symbols such as Visa, MasterCard, Cirrus etc.

Cash Most banks will exchange major foreign currencies and offer the best rates. Ask about commissions and take your passport.

Credit & Debit Cards Can be used to pay for most purchases. You'll often be asked to show your passport or some other form of identification. The most widely accepted cards are Visa and MasterCard.

Moneychangers Exchange offices, indicated by the word *cambio* (exchange), offer longer opening hours than banks, but worse exchange rates and higher commissions.

Taxes & Refunds In Spain, value-added tax (VAT) is known as IVA (*ee*-ba; *impuesto sobre el valor añadido*). Visitors are entitled to a refund of the 16% IVA on purchases costing more than €90.16 from any shop if they are taking them out of the EU within three months.

Tipping Menu prices include a service charge. Most people leave some small change. Taxi drivers don't have to be tipped but a little rounding up won't go amiss.

Travellers Cheques Can be changed (for a commission) at most banks and exchange offices.

Post

The Spanish postal system, **Correos** (☎902 197 197; www.correos.es), is generally reliable, if a little slow at times. Ordinary mail to other Western European countries can take up to a week (although often as little as three days); to North America up to 10 days; and to Australia or New Zealand (NZ) between 10 days and three weeks.

Sellos (stamps) are sold at most *estancos* (tobacconists' shops with 'Tabacos' in yellow letters on a maroon background), as well as post offices.

A postcard or letter weighing up to 20g costs €1.07 from Spain to other European countries, and €1.38 to the rest of the world.

Public Holidays

The two main periods when Spaniards go on holida&y are Semana Santa (the week leading up to Easter Sunday) and July or August. At these times accommodation can be scarce and transport heavily booked.

There are at least 14 official holidays a year – some observed nationwide, some locally. National holidays:

Año Nuevo (New Year's Day) 1 January

Viernes Santo (Good Friday) March/April

Fiesta del Trabajo (Labour Day) 1 May

La Asunción (Feast of the Assumption) 15 August

Fiesta Nacional de España (National Day) 12 October

La Inmaculada Concepción (Feast of the Immaculate Conception) 8 December

Navidad (Christmas) 25 December

Regional governments set five holidays and local councils two more. Common dates:

Epifanía (Epiphany) or **Día de los Reyes Magos** (Three Kings' Day) 6 January

Día de San José (St Joseph's Day) 19 March

Jueves Santo (Good Thursday) March/April. Not observed in Catalonia and Valencia.

Corpus Christi June. The Thursday after the eighth Sunday after Easter Sunday.

Día de San Juan Bautista (Feast of St John the Baptist) 24 June

Día de Santiago Apóstol (Feast of St James the Apostle) 25 July

Día de Todos los Santos (All Saints Day) 1 November

Día de la Constitución (Constitution Day) 6 December

Safe Travel

Most visitors to Spain never feel remotely threatened, but a sufficient number have unpleasant experiences to warrant an alert. The main thing to be wary of is petty theft (which may of course not seem so petty if your passport, cash, travellers cheques, credit card and camera go missing). Stay alert and you can avoid most thievery techniques. Algeciras, Barcelona, Madrid and Seville are the worst offenders, as are popular beaches in summer (never leave belongings unattended). Common scams include the following:

» Kids crowding around you asking for directions or help.

» A person pointing out bird droppings on your shoulder (some substance their friend has sprinkled on you) – as they help clean it off they are probably emptying your pockets.

» The guys who tell you that you have a flat tyre. While your new friend and you check the tyre, his pal is emptying the car.

» The classic snatch-and-run. Never leave your purse, bag, wallet, mobile phone etc unattended or alone on a table.

» An old classic: the ladies offering flowers for good luck. We don't know how they do it, but your pockets always wind up empty.

Telephone

Blue public payphones are common and fairly easy to use. They accept coins, phonecards and, in some cases, credit cards. Phonecards come in €6 and €12 denominations and, like postage stamps, are sold at post offices and tobacconists.

International reverse-charge (collect) calls are simple to make: dial ☎900 99 followed by the appropriate code. For example: ☎900 99 00 61 for Australia, ☎900 99 00 44 for the UK, ☎900 99 00 11 (AT&T) for the USA etc.

To speak to an English-speaking Spanish international operator, dial ☎1008 (for calls within Europe) or ☎1005 (rest of the world).

MOBILE PHONES

All Spanish mobile phone companies (Telefónica's MoviStar, Orange and Vodafone) offer *prepagado* (prepaid) accounts for mobiles. The SIM card costs from €50, which includes some prepaid phone time.

Mobile phone numbers in Spain start with the number 6.

PHONE CODES

Telephone codes in Spain are an integral part of the phone number. All numbers are nine digits and you just dial that nine-digit number.

Numbers starting with 900 are national toll-free numbers, while those starting 901 to 905 come with varying costs; most can only be dialled from within Spain. In a similar category are numbers starting with 800, 803, 806 and 807.

Tourist Information

All cities and many smaller towns have an *oficina de turismo*. In the country's provincial capitals you'll sometimes find more than one tourist office – one specialising in information on the city alone, the other carrying mostly provincial or regional information. National and natural parks also often have visitor centres offering useful information.

Turespaña (www.spain.info) is the country's national tourism body.

Visas

Spain is one of 25 member countries of the Schengen Convention and Schengen visa rules apply.

Citizens or residents of EU & Schengen countries No visa required.

Citizens or residents of Australia, Canada, Israel, Japan, NZ and the USA No visa required for tourist visits of up to 90 days.

Other countries Check with a Spanish embassy or consulate.

To work or study in Spain A special visa may be required – contact a Spanish embassy or consulate before travel.

Work

Norwegian, Swiss, Icelandic and EU nationals may work in Spain without a visa. Everyone else is supposed to obtain a work permit (from a Spanish consulate in their country of residence) and, if they plan to stay more than 90 days, a residence visa. These procedures can be complex.

Teaching English is an obvious option; a TEFL (Teaching English as a Foreign Language) certificate will be a big help. Other possibilities include summer bar and restaurant work, as well as getting work on yachts in major ports.

Getting There & Away

Entering the Country

Immigration and customs checks usually involve a minimum of fuss, although there are exceptions. Your vehicle could be searched on arrival from Morocco; they're looking for controlled substances. Expect long delays at these borders, especially in summer.

The tiny principality of Andorra is not in the EU, so border controls (and rigorous customs checks for contraband) remain in place.

Air

Flights from all over Europe, including numerous budget airlines, serve main Spanish airports. All of Spain's airports share the user-friendly website and flight information telephone number of **Aena** (☏902 404 704; www.aena.es), the national airports authority. For more information on each airport on Aena's website, choose English and click on the drop-down menu of airports. Each airport's page has details on practical informa-

tion (such as parking and public transport) and a full list of (and links to) airlines using that airport.

Madrid's Aeropuerto de Barajas is Spain's busiest (and Europe's fourth-busiest) airport. Other major airports include Barcelona's Aeroport del Prat (BCN) and the airports of Palma de Mallorca (PMI), Málaga (AGP), Alicante (ALC), Girona (GRO), Valencia (VLC), Ibiza (IBZ), Seville (SVQ), Bilbao (BIO) and Zaragoza (ZAZ).

You'll find a list of major airlines operating throughout Europe on p1021.

Land

Spain shares land borders with France, Portugal and Andorra.

Apart from shorter cross-border services, **Eurolines** (www.eurolines.com) is the main operator of international bus services to Spain from most of Western Europe and Morocco.

In addition to the rail services connecting Spain with France and Portugal, there are direct trains between Zurich and Barcelona (via Bern, Geneva, Perpignan and Girona), and between Milan and Barcelona (via Turin, Perpignan and Girona). For these and other services, visit the website of **Renfe** (☏for international trips 902 24 34 02; www.renfe.com), the Spanish national railway company.

ANDORRA

Regular buses connect Andorra with Barcelona (including winter ski buses and direct services to the airport) and other destinations in Spain (including Madrid) and France.

FRANCE
Bus

Eurolines (www.eurolines.fr) heads to Spain from Paris and more than 20 other French cities and towns. It connects with Madrid (17¾ hours), Barcelona (14¾ hours) and many other destinations. There's at least one departure per day for main destinations.

Car & Motorcycle

The main road crossing into Spain from France is the highway that links up with Spain's AP7 tollway, which runs down to Barcelona and follows the Spanish coast south (with a branch, the AP2, going to Madrid via Zaragoza). A series of links cut across the Pyrenees from France and Andorra into Spain, as does a coastal route that runs from Biarritz in France into the Spanish Basque Country.

Train

The main rail lines into Spain cross the Franco–Spanish frontier along the Mediterranean coast and via the Basque Country. Another minor route runs inland across the Pyrenees from Latour-de-Carol to Barcelona.

In addition to the options listed below, TGV (high-speed) trains connect Paris Montparnasse with Irún, where you change to a normal train for the Basque Country and on towards Madrid. Up to three TGVs also put you on track to Barcelona (leaving from Paris Gare de Lyon), with a change at Montpellier or Narbonne.

There are plans for a high-speed rail link between Madrid and Paris by 2012. Major cross-border services in the meantime:

Paris Austerlitz to Madrid Chamartín (chair/sleeper class €166.50/194.20, 13½ hours, one daily) *Trenhotel Francisco de Goya* runs via Orléans, Blois, Poitiers, Vitoria, Burgos and Valladolid.

Paris Austerlitz to Barcelona Estacio de Franca (sleeper class €188, 12 hours, one daily) *Trenhotel Joan Miró* runs via Orléans, Limoges, Figueres and Girona.

Montpellier to Lorca (twice daily) Talgo service along the Mediterranean coast via Girona, Barcelona, Tarragona, Valencia, Alicante, Murcia and Cartagena.

PORTUGAL
Bus

Avanza (☑in Spain & Portugal 902 02 09 99; www.avanzabus.com) runs two daily buses between Lisbon and Madrid (€55.25, 7½ to nine hours, two daily).

Other bus services run north via Porto to Tui, Santiago de Compostela and A Coruña in Galicia. Local buses cross the border from towns such as Huelva in Andalucía, Badajoz in Extremadura and Ourense in Galicia.

Car & Motorcycle

The A5 freeway linking Madrid with Badajoz crosses the Portuguese frontier and continues on to Lisbon, and there are many other road connections up and down the length of the Hispano–Portuguese frontier.

Train

From Portugal, the main line runs from Lisbon across Extremadura to Madrid.

Lisbon–Madrid chair/sleeper class €58.60/83.20, 10½ hours, one daily

Lisbon–Irún chair/sleeper class €68.80/96.60, 14½ hours, one daily

Sea

Ferries run to mainland Spain regularly from the Canary Islands, Italy, North Africa (Algeria, Morocco and the Spanish enclaves of Ceuta and Melilla) and the UK. Most services are run by the Spanish national ferry company, **Acciona Trasmediterránea** (☑902 45 46 45; www.trasmediterranea.es). You can take vehicles on the following routes.

ALGERIA

Acciona Trasmediterránea runs the following services from late June to mid-September:

Almería–Ghazaouet eight hours, four weekly

Almería–Oran eight hours, two weekly

ITALY

Barcelona–Genoa 18 hours, three weekly

Barcelona–Civitavecchia (near Rome) 20½ hours, six to seven weekly

Barcelona–Livorno (Tuscany) 19½ hours, three weekly

Barcelona–Porto Torres (Sardinia) 12 hours, one daily

MOROCCO

In addition to the following services, there are also ferries to the Spanish enclaves of Melilla (from Almería and Málaga) and Ceuta (from Algeciras).

Tangier–Algeciras (70 minutes, up to eight daily) Buses from several Moroccan cities converge on Tangier to make the ferry crossing to Algeciras, and then fan out to the main Spanish centres.

Tangier–Barcelona 24 hours, weekly

Tangier–Tarifa 35 minutes, up to eight daily

Nador–Almería five to eight hours, up to three daily

For further information, head to shop.lonely planet.com to purchase a downloadable PDF of the Morocco chapter from Lonely Planet's *Mediterranean Europe* guide.

UK

From mid-March to mid-November, **Brittany Ferries** (☑0871 244 0744; www.brittany -ferries.co.uk) runs the following services:

Plymouth–Santander 24 to 35 hours, weekly

Portsmouth–Santander 24 to 35 hours, three weekly

Getting Around

Students and seniors are eligible for discounts of 30% to 50% on most types of transport within Spain.

Air

Domestic Spanish routes are operated by the following airlines:

Air Berlin (www.airberlin.com) German budget airline with flights from Madrid to Valencia, Palma de Mallorca, Seville, Jerez de la Frontera and Asturias.

Air Europa (www.aireuropa.com) Dozens of domestic Spanish routes.

easyJet (www.easyjet.com) To Ibiza from Madrid and Bilbao.

Iberia (www.iberia.es) Spain's national airline and its subsidiary, Iberia Regional-Air Nostrum, covering most of Spain.

Ryanair (www.ryanair.com) More than a dozen domestic Spanish routes.

Spanair (www.spanair.com) Numerous domestic Spanish services.

Vueling (www.vueling.com) Spanish low-cost company with loads of domestic flights within Spain.

Bicycle

Finding bikes to rent in Spain is a hit-and-miss affair, so it's best to bring your own. Getting hold of spare parts in case you need them, however, shouldn't be a problem.

All regional trains have space for carrying bikes, and they're also permitted on most *cercanías* (local area trains around big cities such as Madrid and Barcelona). On long-distance trains there are more restrictions. As a rule, you have to be travelling overnight in a sleeper or couchette to have the (dismantled) bike accepted as normal luggage.

Boat

Regular ferries connect the Spanish mainland with the Balearic Islands. For more details, see p905.

Bus

Spain's bus network is operated by countless independent companies, and reaches into the most remote towns and villages. Many towns and cities have one main station for arrivals and departures, which usually has an information desk. Tourist offices can also help with information on bus services.

Local services can get you nearly anywhere, but most buses connecting rural towns aren't geared to tourist needs. Frequent weekday services drop off to a trickle (or nothing) on Saturday and Sunday. It's not necessary, and often not possible, to make advance reservations for local bus journeys. It is, however, a good idea to turn up at least 30 minutes before the bus leaves to guarantee a seat.

Generally, bus fares are cheaper than on the faster, long-distance trains. For longer trips, you can and should buy your ticket in advance.

Among the hundreds of bus companies operating in Spain, the following have the largest networks:

ALSA (✆902 422 242; www.alsa.es)

Avanza (✆902 020 999; www.avanzabus.com)

Car & Motorcycle

Spain's roads vary enormously but are generally good. Fastest are the *autopistas;* on some, you have to pay hefty tolls. Minor routes can be slow going but are usually more scenic. Trying to find a parking spot in larger towns and cities can be a nightmare. *Grúas* (tow trucks) can and will tow your car. The cost of bailing out a car can be €200 or more.

Spanish cities do not have parking meters at every spot. Instead, if you park in a blue or green zone (frequently from 8am to 2pm or from 4pm to 8pm), you obtain a ticket from a street-side meter, which may be a block away. Display the ticket on the dashboard.

Petrol stations are easy to find along highways and *autopistas.*

AUTOMOBILE ASSOCIATIONS

The **Real Automóvil Club de España** (RACE; ✆902 404 545; www.race.es) is the national automobile club. They may well come to assist you in case of a breakdown, but in any event you should obtain an emergency telephone number for Spain from your own insurer.

DRIVING LICENCES

All EU member states' driving licences are recognised. Other foreign licences should be accompanied by an International Driving Permit. These are available from automobile clubs in your country and valid for 12 months.

HIRE

To rent a car in Spain you have to have a licence, be aged 21 or over and have a credit or debit card. Rates vary widely: the best deals tend to be in major tourist areas, including airports. Prices are especially competitive in the Balearic Islands. Expect a compact car to cost from €30 and up per day. See p1024 for information on major car-hire companies.

INSURANCE

Third-party motor insurance is a minimum requirement and it is compulsory to have an internationally recognised proof of insurance, which can be obtained from your insurer. Also ask your insurer for a European Accident Statement form, which can simplify matters in the event of an accident.

ROAD RULES

Blood-alcohol limit 0.05%.

Legal driving age for cars 18.

Legal driving age for motorcycles & scooters 16 (80cc and over) or 14 (50cc and under). A licence is required.

Motorcyclists Must use headlights at all times and wear a helmet if riding a bike of 125cc or more.

Side of the road Drive on the right.

Speed limits In built-up areas 50km/h (and in some cases, such as inner-city Barcelona, 30km/h), which increases to 100km/h on major roads and up to 120km/h on *autovías* and *autopistas* (toll-free and tolled dual-lane highways, respectively). Cars towing caravans are restricted to a maximum speed of 80km/h.

Train

Renfe (☏902 240 202; www.renfe.es) is the national railway company. Trains are mostly modern and comfortable, and late arrivals are the exception rather than the rule. The high-speed network is in constant expansion.

You can buy tickets and make reservations online, at stations, at travel agencies displaying the Renfe logo and in Renfe offices in many city centres.

Passes are valid for all long-distance Renfe trains; Inter-Rail users pay supplements on Talgo, InterCity and AVE trains. All passholders making reservations pay a small fee.

Among Spain's numerous types of trains:

Alaris, Altaria, Alvia, Arco and Avant Long-distance intermediate-speed services.

Cercanías For short hops and services to outlying suburbs and satellite towns in Madrid, Barcelona and 11 other cities.

Euromed Similar to the AVE trains, they connect Barcelona with Valencia and Alicante.

Regionales Trains operating within one region, usually stopping at all stations.

Talgo and Intercity Slower long-distance trains.

Tren de Alta Velocidad Española (AVE) High-speed trains that link Madrid with Barcelona, Burgos, Córdoba, Cuenca, Huesca, Lerida, Málaga, Seville, Valencia, Valladolid and Zaragoza. There is also a Barcelona–Seville service. In coming years Madrid–Cádiz and Madrid–Bilbao should come on line.

Trenhotel Overnight trains with sleeper berths.

CLASSES & COSTS

All long-distance trains have 2nd and 1st classes, known as *turista* and *preferente,* respectively. The latter is 20% to 40% more expensive.

Fares vary enormously depending on the service (faster trains cost considerably more) and, in the case of some high-speed services such as the AVE, on the time and day of travel. Tickets for AVE trains are by far the most expensive. A one-way trip in 2nd class from Madrid to Barcelona (on which route only AVE trains run) could cost as must as €115 (it works out slightly cheaper if you book online).

Children aged between four and 12 years are entitled to a 40% discount; those aged under four travel for free (except on high-speed trains, for which they pay the same as those aged four to 12). Buying a return ticket often gives you a 10% to 20% discount on the return trip. Students and people up to 25 years of age with a Euro<26 Card (Carnet Joven in Spain) are entitled to 20% to 25% off most ticket prices.

On overnight trips within Spain on *trenhoteles* it's worth paying extra for a *litera* (couchette; a sleeping berth in a six- or four-bed compartment) or, if available, single or double cabins in *preferente* or *gran clase* class. The cost depends on the class of accommodation, type of train and length of journey.

RESERVATIONS

Reservations are recommended for long-distance trips; you can make them in train stations, Renfe offices, travel agencies and online. A growing number of stations let you pick up prebooked tickets from machines scattered about the station concourse.

Turkey

Best Places to Stay

» Marmara Guesthouse (p920)
» Biber Evi (p932)
» Hotel Villa Mahal (p952)
» Tuvana Hotel (p957)
» Kelebek Hotel & Cave Pension (p970)

Best Places to Eat

» Cooking Alaturka (p921)
» Balıkçı (p933)
» Fish Market (p943)
» Ziggy's (p974)
» Kahvaltı Sokak (p979)

Why Go?

While many Turks see their country as European, Turkey packs in as many towering minarets and spice-trading bazaars as its Middle Eastern neighbours. This bridge between continents has absorbed Europe's modernism and sophistication, and Asia's culture and tradition. Travellers can enjoy historical hot spots, mountain outposts, expansive steppe and caravanserai-loads of the exotic, without forgoing comfy beds and buses.

Despite its reputation as a continental meeting point, Turkey can't be pigeonholed. Cappadocia, a dreamscape dotted with fairy chimneys, is unlike anywhere else on the planet. Likewise, spots like Mt Nemrut, littered with giant stone heads, and Olympos, where Lycian ruins peek from the undergrowth, are quintessentially Turkish mixtures of natural splendour and ancient remains.

The beaches and mountains offer enough activities to impress the fussiest Ottoman sultan. Worldy pleasures include the many historic hotels, meze to savour on panoramic terraces and, of course, Turkey's famous kebaps.

When to Go

Ankara

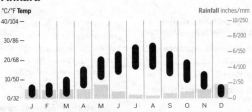

April–May Spring sunshine without summer crowds; tulips bloom in İstanbul.

September–October The crowds thin; autumn is perfect for walking and diving in the southwest.

December–January Ski, celebrate New Year and see Cappadocia in the snow.

Fast Facts

» **Area** 779,452 sq km

» **Capital** Ankara

» **Country code** ☎90

» **International access code** ☎00

» **Ambulance** ☎112
Fire ☎110 **Police** ☎155

Exchange rates

Australia	A$1	TL1.69
Canada	C$1	TL1.64
euro	€1	TL2.25
Japan	¥100	TL1.96
New Zealand	NZ$1	TL1.27
UK	UK£1	TL2.58
USA	US$1	TL1.60

Set Your Budget

» **Budget hotel room** Up to TL75

» **Two-course dinner** Midrange TL15 to TL20

» **Museum entrance** TL3 to TL15

» **Beer** TL5

» **City transport ticket** TL1 to TL

Resources

» www.cornucopia.net

» www.hurriyetdailynews.com

» www.todayszaman.com

Connections

İstanbul is well connected to Europe. Buses leave the otogar (bus station) for countries including Austria, Bulgaria, Germany, Greece, Macedonia, Romania and Slovenia, but trains and ferries are more romantic.

The most useful daily trains are the *Bosfor/Balkan Ekspresi* to Bucharest (Romania; with connections including Budapest, Hungary) via Dimitrovgrad (Bulgaria; with connections including Sofia, Bulgaria and Belgrade, Serbia); and the *Dostluk/Filia Express* to Thessaloniki (Greece; with connections to Athens). A suggested train route from London to İstanbul is the three-night journey via Paris, Munich, Budapest and Bucharest; see www.seat61.com/turkey for more information and other routes.

Ferries connect Turkey's Aegean and Mediterranean coasts with Greek islands, Northern Cyprus and Italy; İstanbul with Ukraine; and Trabzon on the Black Sea coast with Russia.

See p993 for more information.

ITINERARIES

One week

Devote two or three days to magical İstanbul, then head down the Aegean coast, via the Gallipoli battlefields, Ayvalık or Bergama (Pergamum), to marvel at the ruins of Ephesus.

Two weeks

From Ephesus, head inland to Pamukkale's shiny travertine formations, then return to the coast at laid-back Kaş and travel along the Mediterranean to Roman-Ottoman Antalya, checking out Olympos' tree houses en route. With more time or by skipping some of the above spots, work in a detour, on the way back to İstanbul, to Cappadocia's surreal valleys and fairy chimneys.

Essential Food & Drink

Far from the uninspiring kebaps and stuffed vine leaves you may have seen at home, Turkish food is a celebration of community and life in its home country. Kebaps are swooningly succulent, *yaprak dolması* (stuffed vine leaves) are filled with subtly spiced rice and cuisine is social, slow and seasonal. Food is taken very seriously indeed, with delicious results that vary between regions, meaning that travelling here will constantly surprise and seduce your taste buds.

Apart from *kebaps,* classic Turkish dishes and tipples include *köfte* (meatballs), meze, pide, *lahmacun* (Arabic pizza), *gözleme* (thin savoury crepes), *mantı* (Turkish ravioli), *börek* (filled pastries), baklava and *çay* (tea).

Rakı (a fiery, highly alcoholic aniseed drink) is best accompanied by meze, especially *beyaz peynir* (ewe- or goat's-milk cheese) and melon, and *balık* (fish).

For more on food and drink, see p985.

İSTANBUL

🎵0212 / POP 13 MILLION

Some ancient cities are the sum of their monuments. But others, such as İstanbul, factor a lot more into the equation. Here, you can visit Byzantine churches and Ottoman mosques in the morning, shop in chic boutiques during the afternoon and party at glamorous nightclubs through the night. In the space of a few minutes, you can hear the evocative strains of the call to prayer issuing from the Old City's minarets, the sonorous horn of a commuter ferry crossing between Europe and Asia, and the strident cries of a street hawker selling fresh seasonal produce. This marvellous metropolis is an exercise in sensory seduction like no other.

Ask locals to describe what they love about İstanbul and they'll shrug, give a small smile and say merely that there is no other place like it. Spend a few days here, and you'll know exactly what they mean.

In terms of orientation, the Bosphorus strait, between the Black Sea and the Sea of Marmara, divides Europe from Asia. On its western shore, European İstanbul is further divided by the Golden Horn (Haliç) into Old İstanbul in the southwest and Beyoğlu in the northeast.

Overlooked by the Galata Tower, the Galata Bridge (Galata Köprüsü) spans the Golden Horn between Eminönü, north of Sultanahmet in Old İstanbul, and Karaköy. Ferries depart from Eminönü and Karaköy for the Asian shore.

Beyoğlu, uphill from Karaköy, was once the 'new', or 'European', city. The Tünel funicular railway links Karaköy to the bottom of Beyoğlu's pedestrianised main street, İstiklal Caddesi. A tram climbs the İstiklal from there to Taksim Sq, the heart of 'modern' İstanbul and home to luxury hotels and airline offices.

History

Late in the 2nd century AD, the Roman Empire conquered the small city–state of Byzantium, which was renamed Constantinople in AD 330 after Emperor Constantine moved his capital there. The city walls kept out barbarians for centuries while the western part of the Roman Empire collapsed. When Constantinople fell for the first time in 1204, it was ransacked by the loot-hungry Europeans of the Fourth Crusade.

İstanbul only regained its former glory after 1453, when it was captured by Mehmet the Conqueror (Mehmet Fatih) and made capital of the Ottoman Empire. During the glittering reign of Süleyman the Magnificent (1520–66), the city was graced with many beautiful new buildings, and retained much of its charm even during the empire's long decline.

Occupied by Allied forces after WWI, the city came to be thought of as the decadent playpen of the sultans, notorious for its extravagant lifestyle, espionage and intrigue. As a result, when the Turkish Republic was proclaimed in 1923, Ankara became the new capital, in an attempt to wipe the slate clean. Nevertheless, İstanbul remains a commercial, cultural and financial centre, and is still Turkey's number-one city in all but name.

◉ Sights & Activities

OLD İSTANBUL

The Sultanahmet area is the centre of 'Old İstanbul', a Unesco-designated World Heritage site packed with so many wonderful sights you could spend several weeks here.

Blue Mosque   MOSQUE

(Sultan Ahmet Camii; Map p914; Hippodrome, Sultanahmet; ⊘closed during prayer times) Just southwest of the Aya Sofya, Sultan Ahmet I's mosque (built 1606 and 1616) is a voluptuous architectural feat, light and delicate compared with its squat neighbour. The graceful exterior is notable for its six slender minarets and cascade of domes and half domes; the interior is luminous blue, an effect created by stained-glass windows and tens of thousands of tiles.

İSTANBUL IN...

Two Days

On day one, visit the **Blue Mosque**, **Aya Sofya** and **Basilica Cistern** in the morning and the **Grand Bazaar** in the afternoon. Cross the Golden Horn from Sultanahmet for dinner in **Beyoğlu**.

Spend your second morning in **Topkapı Palace**, then board a private excursion boat for a **Bosphorus cruise**. Afterwards, walk up through Galata to **İstiklal Caddesi** to enjoy Beyoğlu's nightlife again.

BLACK SEA (KARADENİZ)

BULGARIA

Burgas

Kapıkule • Edirne • Kırklareli

Sinop

İnebolu

Cide

Amasra

Zonguldak

Safranbolu • Kastamonu

Karabük

Tosya • Osmancık

GREECE

İpsala • Tekirdağ • Çorlu • İstanbul

Kocaeli (İzmit)

Kurşunlu • Ilgaz

Keşan

The Bosphorus

Darıca

Adapazarı

Gerede

Çankırı • Çorum

Gelibolu

Yalova

Bolu

Sungurlu

Gallipoli Peninsula

Lapseki

Gemlik • İznik

Eskişehir

Ankara

Hattuş

Çanakkale • Bandırma

Bursa

Sakarya River

Gordion

Yozgat

Troy (Truva)

Uludağ (2543m)

Kırıkkale

Ayvacık

Edremit • Balıkesir

Kütahya

Polatlı

Kırşehir

Assos

Ayvalık

Lesvos

Bergama • Pergamum

Göreme

Chios • Yeni Foça • Aliağa

Manisa

Uşak

Afyon

Akşehir

Nevşehir • Ürg

Çeşme • İzmir • Sardis

Eğirdir Gölü

Mustafapaşa • Derinkuyu

Odemiş

Çivril

Aksaray

Cappadocia • Yahya

Selçuk

Aydın • Nazilli

Hierapolis/ Pamukkale

Isparta

Tuz Gölü (Salt Lake)

Niğde

Kuşadası • Priene • Ephesus

Beyşehir Gölü

Konya

Ereğli

Samos • Didyma • Milas • Yatağan

Afrodisias

Denizli

Burdur

Suğla Gölü

Ikaria

Güllük

Gökova (Akyaka) • Muğla

Çavdır

Perge • Aspendos

Karaman

Adan

Bodrum

Ortaca

Termessos

Akseki

Kırobası • Tarsus

Kos

Marmaris • Dalaman

Fethiye

Antalya • Side

Uzuncaburç

Mersin (İçel)

Ölüdeniz

Çıralı

Kemer

Alanya

Silifke • Kızkalesi

Patara Beach

Kaş • Olympos

Olukbaşı

Megiste • Kekova • Lycian Way

Finike

Anamurium

Anamur

Crete

Lefkoşa/ Lefkosia (Nicosia)

CYPRUS

MEDITERRANEAN SEA (AKDENİZ)

Turkey Highlights

1 Uncover **İstanbul** (p909), the glorious one-time Ottoman and Byzantine capital and one of the world's truly great cities.

2 Sleep in fairy chimneys and explore underground cities in jaw-droppingly bizarre and beautiful **Cappadocia** (p968).

3 Imagine the tourists streaming down the Curetes Way are wearing togas in **Ephesus** (p939), one of the greatest surviving Greco-Roman cities.

4 Hike through the Mediterranean countryside on a section of the 500km **Lycian Way** (p986).

5 Explore Turkey's exotic east at **Nemrut Dağı** (Mt Nemrut; p977), where decapitated stone heads litter a king's burial mound.

6 Cruise over a sunken Lycian city at **Kekova** (p957), one of many blue voyages offered at Aegean and Mediterranean harbours.

7 Wander the Roman-Ottoman old quarter of **Antalya** (p957), a stylish Mediterranean hub located on both the 'Turquoise Coast' and the 'Turkish Riviera'.

The Blue Mosque's *arasta* (row of shops near a mosque) to the southeast provides support for the mosque's upkeep and it's also a great for hassle-free shopping.

Great Palace Mosaic Museum   MUSEUM
(Map p914; ☎518 1205; Torun Sokak; admission TL8; ☺9am-6.30pm Tue-Sun Jun-Oct, to 4.30pm Nov-May) Behind the *arasta* is the entrance to this museum, which houses a spectacular stretch of mosaic Byzantine pavement featuring hunting scenes.

Topkapı Sarayı   PALACE
(Map p914; ☎512 0480; www.topkapisarayi.gov.tr/eng; Babıhümayun Caddesi; palace TL20, Harem TL15; ☺9am-6pm Wed-Mon, Harem closes 5pm) One of İstanbul's most iconic monuments, opulent Topkapı Palace features in more colourful stories than most of the world's royal residences put together. Mehmet the Conqueror started work on the palace shortly after the Conquest in 1453, and Ottoman sultans lived in this rarefied environment until the 19th century. It consists of four massive courtyards (the first was open to everyone and the third and fourth only to the royal family, VIPs and palace staff) and a series of imperial buildings. Make sure you visit the mind-blowing **harem**, the palace's most famous sight, and the **treasury**, which features an incredible collection of precious objects.

Grand Bazaar   BAZAAR
(Map p912; ☺8.30am-7.30pm Mon-Sat) Hone your haggling skills before dipping into Turkey's most mind-boggling *kapalı çarşı* (covered market). Just north of Divan Yolu, this labyrinthine medieval shopping mall consists of 2000-plus shops selling everything from *lokum* (Turkish delight) to *nazar boncuk* ('evil eye' beads and pendants), including carpets, silverware, jewellery, antiques and belly-dancing costumes. Starting from a small masonry *bedesten* (market enclosure) built during the time of Mehmet the Con-

İstanbul

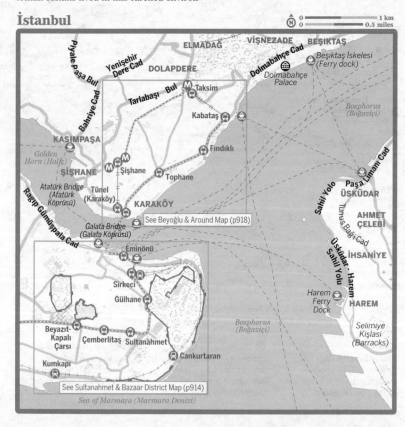

AYA SOFYA

No doubt you will gasp at the overblown splendour of the **Aya Sofya** (Map p914; ☑522 0989; Aya Sofya Meydanı; adult/child under 6 TL20/free, official guide (45min) TL30-50; ⊗9am-6pm Tue-Sun May-Oct, to 4pm Nov-Apr; upper gallery closes 15-30min earlier), also known as Sancta Sophia in Latin, Haghia Sofia in Greek and the Church of the Divine Wisdom in English, one of the world's most glorious buildings. Built as part of Emperor Justinian's effort to restore the greatness of the Roman Empire, it was completed in AD 537 and reigned as the grandest church in Christendom until the Conquest in 1453. The exterior does impress, but the interior, with its sublime domed ceiling soaring heavenward, is truly a knockout.

Supported by 40 decorated ribs, the dome was constructed of special hollow bricks made in Rhodes from a unique light, porous clay. These rest on huge pillars concealed in the interior walls, which creates an impression that the dome hovers unsupported.

queror, the bazaar has grown to cover a vast area. It's probably the most discombobulating and manic shopping precinct you could hope to experience. Sure, the touts are ubiquitous, but come in the right frame of mind and you'll realise it's part of the fun. With 16 *hans* (caravanserais) and 64 lanes, it's a great place to wander and get lost – which you will certainly do at least once.

Divan Yolu Caddesi
HISTORIC AREA

Walking or taking a tram westward to the Grand Bazaar from Sultanahmet, you'll pass various monuments, including a shady Ottoman cemetery with an attached tea garden, **Türk Ocağı Kültür ve Sanat Merkezi İktisadi İşletmesi Çay Bahçesi** (cnr Divan Yolu & Babıalı Caddesi). Also on the right, overlooking the tram stop of the same name, is the tall column known as **Çemberlitaş**, erected by the Emperor Constantine to celebrate the dedication of Constantinople as capital of the Roman Empire in 330.

Basilica Cistern
HISTORIC BUILDING

(Map p914; ☑522 1259; Yerebatan Caddesi 13; admission TL10; ⊗9am-7.30pm) Across the tram lines from Aya Sofya is the entrance to this majestic underground chamber, built by Justinian in AD 532 and visited by James Bond in *From Russia with Love*. The vast, atmospheric, column-filled cistern stored up to 80,000 cubic metres of water for the Great Palace and surrounding buildings. Its cavernous depths stay wonderfully cool in summer.

İstanbul Archaeology Museum
MUSEUM

(Map p914; ☑520 7740; Osman Hamdi Bey Yokuşu, Gülhane; admission TL10; ⊗9am-6pm Tue-Sun May-Sep, till 4pm Oct-Apr) Downhill from the Topkapı Palace, this superb museum complex is a must-see for anyone interested in the Middle East's ancient past. The Archaeology Museum houses an outstanding collection of classical statuary, including the magnificent sarcophagi from the Royal Necropolis at Side in Lebanon.

In a separate building, the **Museum of the Ancient Orient** houses Hittite and other pre-Islamic archaeological finds. Also in the complex is the **Tiled Kiosk** (1472), İstanbul's oldest non-religious Turkish building.

Hippodrome
PARK

(Atmeydanı; Map p914) In front of the Blue Mosque is the Hippodrome, where chariot races once took place. The centre of Byzantine life for 1200 years and Ottoman life for another four centuries, riots here led to the rewriting of the Ottoman constitution in 1909.

The following monuments' bases rest at the former ground level of the Hippodrome, some 2.5m below ground.

İstanbul's oldest monument, the pink granite **Obelisk of Theodosius** (Map p914) is an Egyptian temple column from Karnak. Emperor Theodosius had it brought here in 390 and placed on a ceremonial marble base.

To the south are the remains of a **spiral column** (Map p914) of intertwined snakes, originally erected at Delphi by the Greeks to celebrate their victory over the Persians.

The mysterious 4th-century **rough-stone obelisk** (Map p914) was once covered in bronze, subsequently stolen by the Crusaders.

Turkish & Islamic Arts Museum
MUSEUM

(Map p914; ☑518 1805; Atmeydanı 46; admission TL10; ⊗9am-4.30pm Tue-Sun) On the Hippodrome's western side, this museum is housed

Sultanahmet & Bazaar District

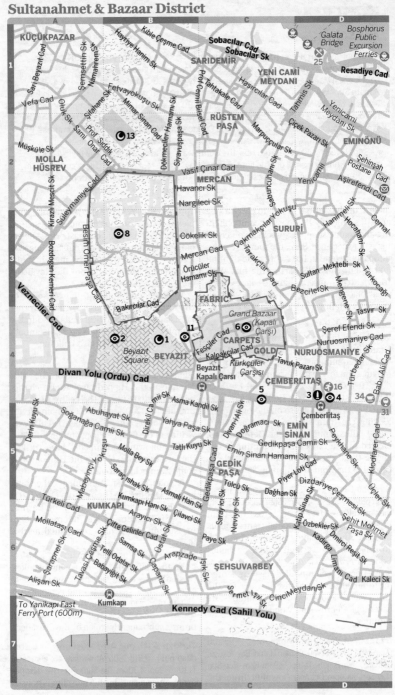

KÜÇÜKPAZAR

Kible Çeşme Cad

Sobacılar Cad
Sobacılar Sk

SARIDEMİR

Galata
Bridge

Bosphorus
Public
Excursion
Ferries

Resadiye Cad

YENİ CAMİ
MEYDANI

Şemsettin Sk
Sarı Beyazıt Cad
Namahrem Sk
Hayriye Hanım Sk

Hasırcılar Cad

Yenicami
Meydanı Sk

Vefa Cad

Fetvayokuşu Sk
Mimar Sinan Cad
Şifahane Cad
Prof. Siddik
Sami Onar Cad

Prof.Cemil Bilsel Cad

Tahtakale Cad

Marpuççular Sk

Çiçek Pazarı Sk

EMİNÖNÜ

Tahmis Sk

Sıyavuşpaşa Sk

Dökmeciler Hamamı Sk

RÜSTEM
PAŞA

Şehinşah
postane
Cad

Asırefendi Cad

Müşküle Sk

MOLLA
HÜSREV

Oluk Sk

13

Vasif Çınar Cad

MERCAN

Yenicamii

Kırazlı Mescit Sk

Süleymaniye Cad

Havancı Sk

Nargileci Sk

Çakmakçılar Yokuşu

Sabuncuhanı Sk

Hanımeli Sk
Hocahanı Sk
Türkocağı

Cemal

Bozdogan Kemeri Cad

Besim Ömer Paşa Cad

8

Çökelik Sk

Mercan Cad

SURURİ

Tarakçılar Cad

Sultan Mektebi Sk

Bezciler Sk

Mengene Sk

Tasvır Sk

Vezneciler Cad

Örücüler
Hamamı Sk

FABRIC

Grand Bazaar
(Kapalı
Çarşı)

Şeref Efendi Sk

Nuruosmaniye Cad

Bakırcılar Cad

11

6

CARPETS

NURUOSMANİYE

2

1

Beyazıt
Square

BEYAZIT

Fesçiler Cad

Kalpakçılar Cad

GOLD

Kürkçüler
Çarşısı

Tavuk Pazarı Sk

Türbedar Sk

Bab-ı Ali Cad

Divan Yolu (Ordu) Cad

Beyazıt-
Kapalı Çarşı

ÇEMBERLİTAŞ

16

3

4

34

31

Derin Kuyu Sk

Soğanağa Camii Sk

Abuhayat Sk

Dikeli Camii Sk

Asma Kandil Sk

5

Çemberlitaş

Divan-ı Ali Sk

Doğramacı Sk

EMİN
SİNAN

Peykhane Sk

Klodfarer Cad

Molla Bey Sk

Yahya Paşa Sk

Tatlı Kuyu Sk

Gedikpaşa Camii Sk

Emin Sinan Hamamı Sk

Üçler Sk

Saraç Ishak Sk

Mabeyinci Yokuşu Sk

Asmalı Han Sk

Gedikpaşa Cad

Tülcü Sk

GEDİK
PAŞA

Piyer Loti Cad

Dağhan Sk

Dizdariye Çeşmesi Sk

Katip Sinan Sk

Şehit Mehmet
Paşa Sk

Türkeli Cad

KUMKAPI

Kumkapı Hanı Sk

Arayıcı Sk

Çilavci Sk

Saray İçi Sk

Neviye Sk

Paye Sk

Özbekler Sk

Dmirci Reşit Sk

Mollataşı Cad

Çifte Gelinler Cad

Usta Sk

Kadirga
Limanı Cad

Kaleci Sk

Şarapnel Sk

Samsa Sk

Arapzade

Işık Sk

ŞEHSUVARBEY

Alişan Sk

Takvası Çeşme Sk

Telli Odalar Sk

Babayigit Sk

Caparız Sk

Cinci Meydanı Sk

Sermet Işık Sk

Kumkapı

Kennedy Cad (Sahil Yolu)

To Yanikapı Fast
Ferry Port (600m)

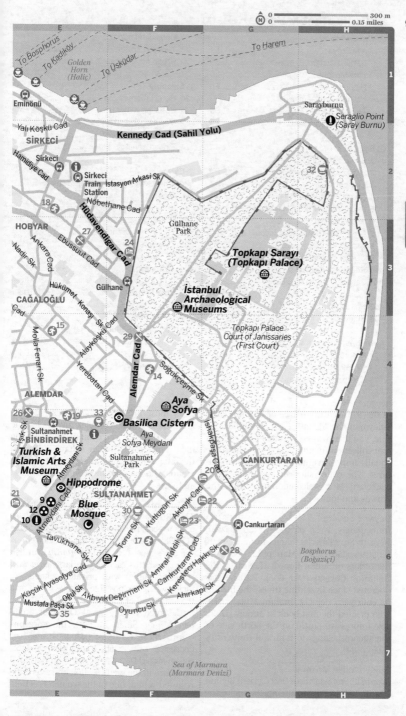

TURKEY

in the 16th-century palace of İbrahim Paşa, Süleyman the Magnificent's son-in-law. Inside, you'll be wowed by one of the world's best collections of antique carpets and some equally impressive manuscripts and miniatures. The coffee shop in the lovely green courtyard is a welcome refuge from the crowds and touts.

Beyazıt Square   HISTORIC AREA
Immediately west of the Grand Bazaar, Beyazıt Sq takes its name from **Beyazıt Mosque** (1501–1506; Map p912), built on the orders of Sultan Beyazıt II. Nearby, the **Sahaflar Çarşısı** (Old Book Bazaar) has operated since Byzantine times; the bust in its courtyard depicts İbrahim Müteferrika, who printed the first book in Turkey (1732). The impressive portal on the north side of the square belongs to **İstanbul University** (Map p914).

Süleymaniye Mosque   MOSQUE
(Map p912; Prof Sıddık Sami Onar Caddesi) Behind İstanbul University to the north, one of the city's most prominent landmarks and its grandest mosque complex overlooks the Golden Horn. It was commissioned by the most powerful Ottoman sultan, Süleyman the Magnificent, and designed by Mimar Sinan, who was the most famous imperial architect.

Hammams   HAMMAM
The 18th-century **Cağaloğlu Hamamı** (Map p914; Yerebatan Caddesi 34; bath, scrub & massage TL78-98; ⊙8am-10pm men, till 8pm women) is the city's most beautiful *hammam* (Turkish bath). Its baths each have a large *camekan* (reception area) with private, lockable cubicles where it's possible to have a nap or a tea at the end of your bath.

Designed by the great Ottoman architect Mimar Sinan in 1584, the gorgeous **Çemberlitaş Hamamı** (Map p914; Vezir Hanı Caddesi 8; bath, scrub & soap massage TL55; ⊙6am-midnight) has a splendid original *camekan* in the men's section and a recently restored/rebuilt one in the women's section.

Both *hammams* are pricey and touristy, but the surroundings are exquisite.

DOLMABAHÇE PALACE

Catch a tram across the Galata Bridge and along the Bosphorus shore to Kabataş, the last stop (also reachable from Taksim Sq on the funicular railway). Continuing northeast, you'll come to the grandiose **Dolmabahçe palace** (Map p912; ☎236 9000; Dolmabahçe Caddesi, Beşiktaş; adult/child TL20/1; ☺9am-4pm Tue-Wed & Fri-Sun summer, to 3pm winter), right on the waterfront. Built between 1843 and 1856, the palace housed some of the last Ottoman sultans and its neo-baroque and neoclassical flourishes reflect the decadence of the decaying empire. It was guaranteed a place in the Turkish history books when Atatürk died here on 10 November 1938 and all the palace clocks stopped.

Visitors are taken on a guided tour of two sections: the over-the-top **Selamlık** (ceremonial suites) and the slightly more restrained **Harem-Cariyeler** (harem and concubines' quarters). Afterwards, make sure you visit the **Crystal Palace**, with its fairy-tale-like conservatory featuring a crystal piano.

BEYOĞLU

Beyoğlu is the heart of modern İstanbul and *the* hot spot for galleries, cafes and boutiques, with hip new restaurants opening almost nightly, and more bars then a barhopper could hope to prop up in a lifetime. The neighbourhood is a showcase of cosmopolitan Turkey at its best – miss Beyoğlu and you haven't seen İstanbul.

İstiklal Caddesi
BOULEVARD

(Independence Ave; Map p918) Climbing from Tünel Sq to Taksim Sq, İstiklal Caddesi was known as the Grande Rue de Pera in the late 19th century, and now it carries the life of the modern city up and down its lively promenade. It's indisputably Turkey's most famous thoroughfare, and a stroll along its length is a must – or ride on the quaint antique tram that trundles up and down the pedestrianised boulevard.

About half-way along is the 19th-century school **Galatasaray Lycée** (Map p918), where students were taught in French as well as Turkish. Nearby, the **balık pazar** (fish market; Map p918) and, in the Cité de Pera building (1876), the **Çiçek Pasajı** (Flower Passage; Map p918) are must-sees. These days locals bypass the touts and the mediocre food at Çiçek Pasajı and make their way behind the passage to one of İstanbul's most colourful and popular eating and drinking precincts, **Nevizade Sokak**.

Galata Tower
LANDMARK

(Map p918, Galata Meydanı, Karaköy; admission TL10; ☺9am-8pm) Uphill from Karaköy, this cylindrical Beyoğlu landmark, originally constructed in 1348, was the highest point in the Genoese fortifications of Galata. It has survived several earthquakes, as well as the demolition of the rest of the Genoese walls in the mid-19th century. There are spectacular views from its vertiginous panoramic balcony, but the entry fee is a little inflated, so you may prefer the terrace of the Anemon Galata hotel opposite.

THE PLEASURES OF THE BATH

After a long day's sightseeing, few things could be better than relaxing in a *hammam*. The ritual is invariably the same. First, you'll be shown to a cubicle where you can undress, store your clothes and wrap the provided *peştamal* (cloth) around you. Then an attendant will lead you through to the hot room, where you can sit and simply sweat for a while.

It's cheapest to bring soap and a towel and wash yourself. The hot room will be ringed with individual basins that you fill from the taps above, before sluicing the water over yourself with a plastic scoop. But it's far more enjoyable to let an attendant do it for you, dousing you with warm water and scrubbing you with a coarse cloth mitten. You'll be lathered with a sudsy swab, rinsed off and shampooed.

When all this is complete, you'll likely be offered a massage, an experience worth having at least once during your trip.

Bath etiquette dictates that men should keep the *peştamal* on at all times.

Traditional *hammams* have separate sections for men and women or admit men and women at separate times. In tourist areas, many *hammams* are happy for foreign men and women to bathe together.

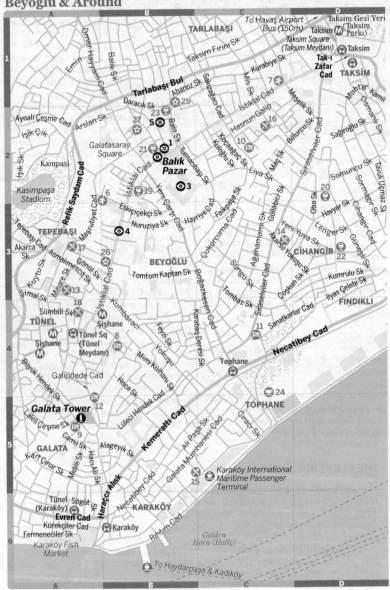

TURKEY İSTANBUL

BOSPHORUS

Don't leave İstanbul without exploring the Bosphorus on a cruise on one of the boats departing from Eminönü. **Private excursion boats** (TL10, 90 minutes) travel to Anadolu Hisarı and back, without stopping. İDO's **Bosphorus Public Excursion Ferry** (Map p914; www.ido.com.tr; Boğaz İskelesi; one way/return TL15/25; ⏰10.30am, plus noon & 1.30pm mid-Apr–Oct, 7.15pm Sat mid-Jun–early Aug) travels all the way to Anadolu Kavağı at the Black Sea (90 minutes one way), stopping en route on the European and Asian sides.

The shores are sprinkled with monuments and sights, including the Dolmabahçe Palace, the majestic Bosphorus Bridge, numerous mosques, lavish *yalıs* (waterfront wooden summer residences) and affluent suburbs on the hills above the strait.

PRINCES' ISLANDS (ADALAR)

With beaches, woodland, a couple of Greek monasteries, Victorian villas and transport by horse-drawn carriage or bicycle, this string of nine islands is İstanbul's favourite getaway. Unfortunately, day trippers have covered them with rubbish, but they make a convenient escape from the city's noise and hustle. In particular, the pier side of **Heybeliada** is pleasant, with seafront cafes and hilly streets of dilapidated *yalıs*. **Ferries** (TL3) leave from the Adalar İskelesi dock at Kabataş, opposite the tram stop. Try to go midweek to avoid the crowds.

🍴 Courses

Caferağa Medresesi   HANDICRAFTS
(Map p914; ☏ 528 0089; www.tkhv.org; Caferiye Sokak, Sultanahmet) The Turkish Cultural Services Foundation runs courses in techniques such as calligraphy, miniature painting, *ebru* (traditional Turkish marbling), binding and glass painting.

Cooking Alaturka   COOKING
(Map p914; ☏ 458 5919; www.cookingalaturka. com; Akbiyik Caddesi 72a, Sultanahmet; TL130 per person) İstanbul's first cooking school runs hands-on Turkish cooking classes, and the delicious results are enjoyed over lunch.

👉 Tours

İstanbul Walks   WALKING & CULTURAL TOURS
(Map p918; ☏ 292 2874; www.istanbulwalks.net; 5th fl, İstiklal Caddesi 53, Beyoğlu; walking tours adult/ child €20/free) This small cultural tourism specialist offers guided walking tours, including the excellent Grand Bazaar tour and 'Dining Out in a Turkish Way' evening (€60).

Urban Adventures   WALKING & CULTURAL TOURS
(Map p914; ☏ 512 7144; www.urbanadventures.com; 1st fl, Ticarethane Sokak 11, Sultanahmet; tours €25) Tours include a four-hour walk around Sultanahmet and the Bazaar District, and dinner with a local family in their home.

Istanbul Culinary Institute (Map p918; ☏ 251 2214; www.istanbulculinary.com; Meşrutiyet Caddesi 59, Tepebaşı) and **Turkish Flavours** (Map p914 ☏ 532 218 0653; www.turkishflavours. com; Apt 3, Vali Konağı Caddesi 14, Nişantaşı) offer foodie walking tours as well as cooking classes.

🛏 Sleeping

During low season (October to April, but not around Christmas or Easter) you should be able to negotiate discounts of at least 20%.

Before confirming bookings, ask if the hotel will give you a discount for cash payment (usually 5% or 10%) and whether there are discounts for extended stays. A pick-up from the airport is often included if you stay more than three nights. Book ahead from May to September.

SULTANAHMET & AROUND

The Sultanahmet area has the most budget and midrange options, as well as some more luxurious accommodation. Most have stunning views from their roof terraces, and are close to the Old City's sights.

TOP CHOICE Marmara Guesthouse　　PENSION €

(Map p914; ☎638 3638; www.marmaraguesthouse.com; Terbıyık Sokak 15, Cankurtaran; s/d from €35/45; ✴@) Charming manager Elif Aytekin and her family live on site and go out of their way to make guests feel welcome. Rooms have comfortable beds with feather doonas, double-glazed windows and safe boxes; some have sea views. There's a vine-covered terrace and a light-filled breakfast room. A gem.

Hotel Empress Zoe　　BOUTIQUE HOTEL €€

(Map p914; ☎518 2504; www.emzoe.com; Adliye Sokak 10, Cankurtaran; s/d/ste from €80/120/140; ✴) Named after the feisty Byzantine empress, this fabulous American-run place has individually and charmingly decorated

rooms, and a gorgeous flower-filled garden where breakfast is served. The rooftop lounge-terrace is a perfect spot for a sunset drink.

Hotel İbrahim Paşa　　BOUTIQUE HOTEL €€

(Map p914; ☎518 0394; www.ibrahimpasha.com; Terzihane Sokak 5, Binbirdirek; r €99-235; ✴@) Successfully combining Ottoman style with contemporary decor, this exemplary boutique hotel offers comfortable rooms, excellent service, gorgeous ground-floor common areas and a terrace bar with Blue Mosque views.

Osman Han Hotel　　HOTEL €

(Map p914; ☎458 7702; www.osmanhanhotel.com; Çetinkaya Sokak 1, Cankurtaran; s/d €45/75; ✴@) Apart from its low prices and lack of a bar, this pleasantly decorated seven-room hotel can almost claim boutique status. The ensuite rooms have minibar, tea and coffee facilities, satellite TV and rainfall showerheads. The pretty breakfast room and terrace have Sea of Marmara and Blue Mosque views.

Sirkeci Konak　　HOTEL €€€

(Map p914; ☎528 4344; Taya Hatun Sokak 5, Sirkeci; r €150-340; ✴@⊠) This terrific hotel overlooking Gülhane Parkı offers large, well-equipped rooms with tea and coffee facilities, satellite TV, quality toiletries and luxe linen. There's a basement wellness centre with pool, gym and *hammam* (a rarity on this side of town) plus complimentary walking tours, afternoon teas and Anatolian cooking lessons.

BEYOĞLU & AROUND

Stay here to avoid the Old City touts, and because buzzing, bohemian Beyoğlu has İstanbul's best wining, dining and shopping. Unfortunately the area doesn't have Sultanahmet's range and quality of accommodation – apart from an ever-increasing number of stylish apartment and suite hotels.

TOP CHOICE 5 Oda
BOUTIQUE HOTEL €€

(Map p918; ☎252 7501; www.5oda.com; Şahkulu Bostan Sokak 16, Tünel; s/d from €115/125; ✳@) 'Five Rooms' offers exactly that – in a seriously stylish suite hotel in fashionable Tünel. A great deal of thought has gone into the design: suites have an equipped kitchen, lounge with satellite TV, custom-designed furniture, large bed, black-out curtains and openable windows.

Witt İstanbul Hotel
BOUTIQUE HOTEL €€€

(Map p918; ☎293 1500; www.wittistanbul.com; Defterdar Yokuşu 26, Cihangir; ste €160-390; ✳@) Just uphill from the Tophane tram stop in trendy Cihangir, this stylish place has suites with fully equipped marble kitchenettes, seating areas with flat-screen satellite TVs, CD/DVD players, king-sized beds and huge bathrooms. Some look over to Sultanahmet, and there's a lobby bar and 24-hour reception.

Anemon Galata
HISTORIC HOTEL €€

(Map p918; ☎293 2343; www.anemonhotels.com; cnr Galata Meydanı & Büyükhendek Caddesi, Galata; s/d from €128/150; ✳@) Located on the attractive square surrounding the Galata Tower, this 19th-century wooden building has been rebuilt inside. The elegant, individually decorated rooms feature ornate painted ceilings, king-sized beds and antique-style desks. Large bathrooms have baths and marble basins, and the restaurant boasts one of İstanbul's best views. Request a room with a view.

İstanbul Apartments
APARTMENT €

(Map p918; ☎249 5065; www.istanbulapt.com; Tel Sokak 27, Taksim; d, tr & q €70-120; ✳@) On a quiet side street off İstiklal Caddesi, this well-run operation offers two- to six-person apartments. Each has a small lounge with equipped kitchenette, couch, dining table and satellite TV, plus one or two bedrooms

with comfortable beds and well-sized bathrooms. Antique rugs, objet d'art, paintings and textiles feature, along with a communal washing machine and dryer.

World House Hostel
HOSTEL €

(Map p918; ☎293 5520; www.worldhouseistanbul.com; Galipdede Caddesi 117, Tünel; dm €10-14, d €50;@) İstanbul is not endowed with many great hostels, but this place near the Galata Tower is small, friendly and calm. It's possible to grab a decent night's kip here even though it's close to Beyoğlu's nightlife. The four- to 14-bed dorms are clean and light and there's a cheerful ground-floor cafe.

✗ Eating

Teeming with affordable fast-food joints, cafes and restaurants, İstanbul is a food-lover's paradise. Unfortunately, Sultanahmet has the least impressive range of eating options, so we recommend crossing the Galata Bridge to join the locals.

İstanbul Eats (http://istanbuleats.com) is a good local foodie website.

SULTANAHMET & AROUND

The cheapest way to enjoy fresh fish from the waters around İstanbul is to buy a *balık ekmek* (fish kebap). On bobbing boats tied to the quay at the Eminönü end of the Galata Bridge (Map p914), cookers are loaded with fish fillets. Once cooked the fillets are crammed into quarter loafs of fresh bread and eaten on dry land. You can buy one for about TL4.

Avoid the rip-off eateries near the accommodation and bars on Akbıyık Caddesi.

TOP CHOICE Cooking Alaturka
ANATOLIAN €€

(Map p914; ☎458 5919; www.cookingalaturka.com; Akbıyık Caddesi 72a, Cankurtaran; set meal TL50; ☺lunch Mon-Sat, dinner Mon-Sat by reservation) This little haven in the midst of carpet-selling frenzy is run by a Dutch-born foodie who knows and loves Anatolian food. The set four-course menu changes daily according to the local markets and what produce is in season. Don't get it confused with Hotel Alaturka's touristy fish restaurant.

Ziya Şark Sofrası
ANATOLIAN €€

(Map p914; Alemdar Caddesi 28, Alemdar; kebaps TL13.50-23.50) On the busy road between Eminönü and Sultanahmet, the locals have discovered Ziya but tourists haven't. The food here is fresh and well cooked, the decor is cheerful and the service is friendly, albeit with an alcohol-free policy.

FREE THRILLS

İstanbul is such a richly cultural city that just wandering its streets and markets, marvelling at the mosques and smelling the kebaps, is a great way to a get a taste of the place. At these spots you can amble for free:

» İstiklal Caddesi (p917)
» Grand Bazaar (p912)
» Sahaflar Çarşısı (Old Book Bazaar; p916)
» Divan Yolu Caddesi (p913)
» Blue Mosque (p909)
» Hippodrome (p913)

Paşazade   ANATOLIAN €€
(Map p914; 513 3601; Cafariye Sokak; meze TL6-12, mains TL13-23) This *Osmanlı mutfağı* (Ottoman kitchen) serves well-priced Ottoman dishes in an attractive streetside restaurant and, with a view, on the rooftop terrace. The large portions are delicious, and service is attentive. Bravo.

Teras Restaurant   RESTAURANT €€€
(Map p914; 638 1370; Hotel Armada, Ahırkapı Sokak, Cankurtaran; mains TL24-37) This upmarket hotel restaurant's Turkish degustation menu (TL68) offers three courses of 'İstanbul cuisine', complemented by an excellent wine list. You can also order à la carte; the fish is particularly good. Book a terrace table with a Blue Mosque view.

Çiğdem Pastanesi   CAFE €
(Map p914; Divan Yolu Caddesi 62a) Serving locals since 1961, Çiğdem's *ay çöreği* (pastry with a walnut, sultana and spice filling) is the perfect accompaniment to a cappuccino; *su böreği* (white-cheese-and-parsley *börek*) goes well with tea or fresh juice.

BEYOĞLU & AROUND

Karaköy Lokantası   LOKANTA, MEYHANE €€
(Map p918; 292 4455; Kemankeş Caddesi 37, Karaköy; meals TL7-16; ⊗closed Sun) The tasty food is well priced and the service is friendly and efficient. It functions as a *lokanta* (eatery serving ready-made food) during the day, and at night morphs into a popular, slightly pricier *meyhane* (Turkish tavern).

Antiochia   ANATOLIAN €€
(Map p918; 292 1100; www.antiochiaconcept. com; Minare Sokak 21, Asmalımescit; mains TL12-19;

⊗closed Sun) This newcomer in fashionable Asmalımecit specialises in dishes from Antakya (Hatay). Sitting inside or in the quiet pedestrianised street, sample unusual and delicious kebaps, and salads dominated by wild thyme, pomegranate syrup, olives, walnuts, hot pepper and homemade yoghurt.

Mikla   MODERN TURKISH €€€
(Map p918; 293 5656; www.miklarestaurant. com; Marmara Pera Hotel, Meşrutiyet Caddesi 15, Tepebaşı; mains TL44-71; ⊗closed Sun) Local celebrity chef Mehmet Gürs is a master of perfectly executed Mediterranean cuisine. The Turkish accents he employs complete the experience, alongside the extraordinary views and luxe surrounds. In summer, request a table on the terrace.

Sofyalı 9   MEYHANE €€
(Map p918; 245 0362; Sofyalı Sokak 9, Tünel; mezes TL2.50-10; ⊗closed Sun) This welcoming little place on the city's most happening street serves up good *meyhane* food. Most guests stick to mezes; don't feel obliged to accept any that are placed on the table beforehand. Tables here are hot property on Friday and Saturday night.

Kahvedan   CAFE, BAR €€
(Map p918; Akarsu Caddesi 50, Cihangir; www. kahvedan.com; mains TL10-30; ⊗9am-2am;🛜) This expat haven serves dishes such as bacon and eggs, French toast, *mee goreng* and falafel wraps, with decent wine by the glass and good music. There's a happy hour every Tuesday (8pm to 11pm).

Medi Şark Sofrası   KEBAPCI €€
(Map p918; Küçük Parmak Kapı Sokak 46a; kebaps TL9-25) This excellent *kebapçı* off İstiklal Caddesi specialises in meat dishes from southeastern Turkey, served with house speciality *babam ekmek* (literally 'my father's bread'). Its renowned Adana and beyti kebaps are perfectly accompanied by *ayran* (yoghurt drink; alcohol is unavailable).

🍷 Drinking & Entertainment

For an overview of what's on, pick up *Time Out İstanbul* and visit **Biletix** (www.biletix.com), where you can buy tickets for most events using a credit card. To pick up or buy tickets, Biletix's city-wide outlets include **İstiklal Kitabevi** (Map p918; İstiklal Caddesi 55, Beyoğlu).

BEYOĞLU & AROUND
There's a thriving bar scene in Beyoğlu, which is almost permanently crowded with

locals who patronise the atmosphere-laden side-street bars and *meyhanes*. The most popular bar precincts are on or around Balo Sokak and Sofyalı Sokak, but there are also sleek bars on roof terraces on both sides of the İstiklal.

TOP CHOICE Tophane Nargileh NARGILEH CAFE
(Map p918; off Necatibey Caddesi, Tophane; ⊙24hr) Follow the enticing smell of apple tobacco to this atmospheric row of *nargileh* (water pipe) cafes opposite the Tophane tram stop. It's always packed with teetotallers, and is a fabulous place to come after a meal.

360 BAR, RESTAURANT
(Map p918; www.360istanbul.com; 8th fl, İstiklal Caddesi 311, Galatasaray) İstanbul's most famous bar. Shoot for one of the bar stools on the terrace: the view is truly extraordinary. It morphs into a club after midnight on Fridays and Saturdays.

Papillon BAR
(Map p918; 4th fl, Balo Sokak 31) A classic example of Beyoğlu's top-floor drinking dens, this laid-back hang-out is scattered with beanbags, pot plants, mirrorballs and psychedelic decor. The drinks are cheap, too. Head down Balo Sokak past the James Joyce Irish pub, and take the steps on the left just before the 'Balo' and 'Haydar Rock Bar' signs; it gets going after 10pm.

5 Kat BAR, RESTAURANT
(Map p918; www.5kat.com; 5th fl, Soğancı Sokak 7, Cihangir; ⊙10am-1.30am) With great views of the Bosphorus, this fifth-floor bar/restaurant in trendy Cihangir will suit those who can't stomach the style overload at 360 et al. In winter, drinks are served in the boudoir-style bar; in summer, action moves to the outdoor terrace.

Nightclubs

Araf CLUB
(Map p918; 5th fl, Balo Sokak 32) Popular among English teachers and Turkish-language students for the in-house gypsy band and cheap beer. There's no cover charge.

Ghetto CLUB
(Map p918; Kalyoncu Kulluk Caddesi 10) Behind Çiçek Pasajı, with bold postmodern decor and an interesting musical program featuring local and international acts.

SULTANAHMET
Sultanahmet isn't as happening as Beyoğlu, but it has a few watering holes, with backpacker offerings clustered on Akbıyık Caddesi. The area's alcohol-free, atmosphere-rich *çay bahçesi* (tea gardens) or *kahvehanes* (coffee houses) are great for relaxing and sampling that great Turkish institution, the *nargileh,* along with a *Türk kahvesi* (Turkish coffee) or *çay*.

Set Üstü Çay Bahçesi TEA GARDEN
(Map p914; Gülhane Parkı, Sultanahmet; ⊙10am-11pm) Particularly at weekends, follow the locals through Gülhane Parkı to this terraced tea garden, where you can enjoy *tost* (toasted sandwich) with spectacular water views. No *nargileh*.

Yeni Marmara NARGILEH CAFE
(Map p914; Çayıroğlu Sokak, Küçük Ayasofya; ⊙8am-midnight) With bags of character plus a terrace and wood stove, this cavernous teahouse is always packed with locals playing backgammon, sipping *çay* and puffing on *nargilehs*.

Cafe Meşale TEA GARDEN
(Map p914; Arasta Bazaar, Utangaç Sokak, Cankurtaran; ⊙24hr) In the sunken courtyard next to the Arasta Bazaar, generations of backpackers have joined *nargileh*-smoking locals on Meşale's stools. In summer there's live Turkish music between 8pm and 10pm nightly.

Sultan Pub PUB
(Map p914; Divan Yolu Caddesi 2; ⊙9.30pm-1am) Sultanahmet's English pub has been around for decades. The 30-to-40ish crowds sit at sun-drenched streetside tables and on the rooftop terrace. Nearby **Cosy Pub** (Divan Yolu Caddesi 66) is similar.

MEYHANES

A classic İstanbul night out involves carousing to live *fasıl*, a raucous local form of gypsy music, in Beyoğlu's *meyhanes*. A dizzying array of meze and fish dishes is on offer, washed down with *rakı*. On Friday and Saturday nights, *meyhane* precincts such as Nevizade and Sofyalı Sokaks literally heave with people and are enormously enjoyable places to be.

Good *meyhanes* include:

Cumhuriyet (Map p918; ☑293 1977; Sahne Sokak 4; set menu from TL55) In the Balık Pazar.

Demeti (Map p918; ☑244 0628; Şimşirci Sokak 6, Cihangir; set menu from TL55; ⊙closed Sun) Near Taksim Sq.

İstanbul is no more nor less safe than any large metropolis, but are there some dangers worth highlighting.

» Many İstanbullus drive like rally drivers, and there is no such thing as a generally acknowledged right of way for pedestrians, despite the little green man. As a pedestrian, give way to vehicles in all situations, even if you have to jump out of the way.

» Bag-snatching is a slight problem, especially on Galipdede Sokak in Tünel and İstiklal Caddesi's side streets.

» In Sultanahmet, if a shoe cleaner drops his brush, don't pick it up. He will insist on giving you a 'free' clean in return, before demanding an extortionate fee.

» Importantly, you should be aware of the long-standing nightlife scam targeting male visitors. Single men are approached in areas such as Sultanahmet and Taksim and lured to a bar by new 'friends'. The scammers may be accompanied by a fig leaf of a woman. When the bill arrives, the prices are astronomical and the proprietors can produce a menu showing the same prices. Drugging is also a risk, especially for lone men.

» The PKK (Kurdistan Workers Party) and other terrorist groups sporadically target İstanbul with bombings, normally aimed at affluent, touristy neighbourhoods. In October 2010, a Kurdish suicide bomber injured 32 people in Taksim Sq.

See also p1012.

ℹ Information

Emergency
Tourist police (527 4503; Yerebatan Caddesi 6, Sultanahmet)

Internet Access
Wi-fi is widespread, and hotels and hostels often offer a computer with internet access. There are internet cafes throughout İstanbul.

Medical Services
The following charge around TL180 for a standard consultation (credit card accepted).
American Hospital (Amerikan Hastanesi; 444 3777; Güzelbahçe Sokak 20, Nişantaşı)
German Hospital (Alman Hastanesi; 293 2150; Sıraselviler Caddesi 119, Taksim)

Money
Banks, ATMs and exchange offices are widespread, including next to Sultanahmet's Aya Sofya Meydanı and along İstiklal Caddesi in Beyoğlu. The exchange rates offered at the airport are usually as good as those offered in town.

Post
İstanbul's central post office is a few blocks southwest of Sirkeci train station. There are branch post, telephone and telegraph offices (PTTs) in the Grand Bazaar, in Beyoğlu near the Galata Bridge and off Taksim and Galatasaray Squares, and at both airports.

Telephone
İstanbul has two area codes: 0212 for the European side, 0216 for the Asian zone. All numbers here use the 0212 code unless otherwise indicated.

Tourist Information
Tourist offices are found in several locations.
Atatürk International Airport (International arrivals; ⊘24hr)
Sultanahmet (518 8754; ⊘8.30am-5pm) At the northeast end of the Hippodrome.

Travel Agencies
Both go to the Gallipoli Peninsula among other destinations.
Fez Travel (www.feztravel.com) Also operates the Fez Bus (see p994).
Trooper Tours (www.troopertours.com)

ℹ Getting There & Away

Air
Atatürk International Airport (465 5555; www.ataturkairport.com) Long-haul flights generally touch down here, 23km west of Sultanahmet.
Sabiha Gökçen International Airport (0216-585 5000; www.sgairport.com) Some 50km east of Sultanahmet, on the Asian side of the city, and popular with cut-price European carriers.

Boat
Yenikapı This is the main dock for (www.ido.com.tr) ferries across the Sea of Marmara to Yalova, Bursa and Bandırma (from where you can catch a train to İzmir or a bus to Çanakkale).

Bus

The aptly titled **Büyük İstanbul Otogarı** (Big İstanbul Bus Station; ☎658 0505; www.otoga ristanbul.com) is the city's main *otogar* (bus station) for intercity and international routes. Buses leave from here for virtually anywhere in Turkey and for international destinations including Austria, Bulgaria, Georgia, Germany, Greece, Iran, Macedonia, Romania and Slovenia.

It's in Esenler, about 10km northwest of Sultanahmet.

» Many bus companies offer a free *servis* (shuttle bus) to/from the *otogar*.

» The LRT (Light Rail Transport) service stops here between Atatürk International Airport and Aksaray, where you can pick up a tram to Beyoğlu via Sultanahmet.

» Bus 830/910 leaves for Taksim Sq/Eminönü (one hour) about every 20 minutes from 6am and 8.45pm.

» A taxi to Sultanahmet costs around TL25 (20 minutes); to Taksim Sq around TL30 (30 minutes).

Train

Trains from Edirne and Europe terminate at **Sirkeci train station** (Map p914; ☎520 6575), north of Sultanahmet on the Golden Horn near Eminönü. This will change with the Marmaray public transport project, aimed at relieving İstanbul's woeful traffic congestion, but this will not come about until late 2013 at the earliest.

Daily international **Turkish State Railways** (www.tcdd.gov.tr/tcdding/avrupa_ing.htm) services from Sirkeci:

Bosfor/Balkan Ekspresi Overnight to Bucharest (Romania), with connections including Budapest (Hungary). Change in Dimitrovgrad (Bulgaria) for Sofia (Bulgaria) and Belgrade (Serbia).

Dostluk/Filia Ekspresi Twice daily to Thessaloniki, Greece (first/second class from €26/39; 13 hours), with connections to Athens. Cancelled at the time of writing.

Trains from Anatolia and from countries to the east and south terminate at **Haydarpaşa train station** (☎0216-336 4470), on the Asian shore. From here, destinations include Adana, Ankara, Aleppo (Syria), Kars, Konya, Tatvan (Lake Van) and Tehran (Iran).

Ferries cross link Haydarpaşa with the European side and nearby Kadıköy. As part of Marmaray, services will eventually move to Söğütlüçeşme, near Üsküdar.

❶ Getting Around

Tickets on public transport in İstanbul generally cost TL1.75.

To/From the Airport

Airport Shuttle (www.istanbulairportshuttle. com; €10) Seven per day between the airports and Sultanahmet/Taksim. Book ahead and allow lots of time before your flight.

Havaş Airport Bus (☎444 0487; www.havas. com.tr; 40min) Half-hourly buses connect Cumhuriyet Caddesi near Taksim Sq with Atatürk (TL10, 40 minutes) and Sabıha Gökçen (TL13, one hour), leaving Atatürk from 4am until 1am and Sabıha Gökçen from 4am to midnight and thereafter when flights land.

LRT (Light Rail Transport; 50min to Sultanahmet, 85min to Taksim Sq) From Atatürk arrivals, follow the 'Rapid Transit' signs to the station and travel to Zeytinburnu, where you can connect with the tram to Sultanahmet and Beyoğlu.

Taxi From Atatürk/Sabıha Gökçen to the centre should cost around TL35/90, more if there's heavy traffic.

Boat

The most scenic and enjoyable way to cross İstanbul is by **İDO** (www.ido.com.tr) ferry. The main ferry docks are at the mouth of the Golden Horn (Eminönü, Sirkeci and Karaköy) and at Beşiktaş, a few kilometres northeast of the Galata Bridge, near Dolmabahçe Palace.

Bus

İstanbul's efficient bus system has major stations at Taksim Sq, Beşiktaş, Aksaray, Rüstempaşa-Eminönü, Kadıköy and Üsküdar. Most services run between 6.30am and 11.30pm. You must have a ticket before boarding; buy tickets from the white booths near major stops or, for a small mark-up, from some nearby shops (look for 'İETT *otobüs bileti satılır'* signs).

Funicular Railway

The one-stop Tünel funicular system climbs the hill from Karaköy to the bottom of İstiklal Caddesi (every 10 minutes from 7.30am to 9pm). A funicular railway also climbs from the Bosphorus shore at Kabataş (where it connects with the tram) to the metro station at Taksim Sq.

BUS ARRIVALS

If you're arriving from Anatolia, rather than travelling all the way to the Big İstanbul Bus Station, it's quicker to get out at the smaller **Harem Otogar** (☎0216-333 3763), north of Haydarpaşa train station on the Asian shore, and take the ferry to Sirkeci/ Eminönü.

LRT

A Light Rail Transport service connects Aksaray with the airport, stopping at 16 stations, including the *otogar*, along the way. It operates from 5.40am until 1.40am.

Taxi

İstanbul is full of yellow taxis, all of them with meters; do not let drivers insist on a fixed rate. From Sultanahmet to Taksim costs around TL12.

Tram

A *tramvay* (tramway) service runs from Zeytinburnu (where it connects with the airport LRT) to Kabataş (connecting with the funicular to Taksim Sq) via Sultanahmet, Eminönü and Karaköy (connecting with the funicular to Tünel). Trams run every five minutes or so from 6am to midnight.

A quaint antique tram rattles up and down İstiklal Caddesi in Beyoğlu, from the Tünel station to Taksim Sq via Galatasaray Lycée.

AROUND İSTANBUL

Since İstanbul is such a vast city, few places are within easy reach on a day trip. If you make an early start, however, it's just possible to see the sights of Edirne in Thrace (Trakya), the only bit of Turkey that is geographically within Europe. Ferries cross the Sea of Marmara to Bursa, although it's better to overnight there.

Edirne

☎ 0284 / POP 136,000

European Turkey's largest settlement outside İstanbul, Edirne is unwisely disregarded by all but a handful of travellers, who come to enjoy its stunning mosques. Edirne was the Ottoman capital before Constantinople (İstanbul), and many of its key buildings are in excellent shape. You can enjoy mosques as fine as almost any in İstanbul – without the crowds found by the Bosphorus. With Greece and Bulgaria a half-hour's drive away, Edirne is a bustling border town, its streets crowded with foreigners, locals and off-duty soldiers.

☉ Sights

Selimiye Camii   MOSQUE

Dominating Edirne's skyline is the Selimiye Mosque (1569–75), the finest work of the great Ottoman architect Mimar Sinan. Its lofty dome and four slender, 71m-high minarets create a dramatic perspective. There are two *madrasas* (Islamic schools) in the

complex, which have museums, including the **Selimiye Foundation Museum** (Selimiye Vakıf Müzesi; ☎212 1133; admission free; ⊙9am-5pm Tue-Sun), with displays covering the restoration of the mosque, metalwork, İznik tiles and seminary education.

Eski Cami   MOSQUE

Near Selimiye Camii in the centre of town, the Old Mosque (1403–14) has rows of arches and pillars supporting a series of small domes.

Üç Şerefeli Cami   MOSQUE

The Three-Balcony Mosque (1437–47), another example of architectural magnificence, has four strikingly different minarets. Its design is halfway between the Seljuk Turkish and truly Ottoman styles.

Beyazıt II complex   MOSQUE, MUSEUM

Featuring the excellent **Museum of Health** (Sağlık Müzesi; ☎224 0922; admission TL10; ⊙9am-5.30pm), this mosque complex (1484–88), built by the Ottoman architect Hayreddin, stands in splendid isolation by the Tunca River.

🛏 Sleeping & Eating

There's an assortment of eateries along Saraçlar and Maarif Caddesis. The riverside restaurants south of the centre are more atmospheric, but most open only in summer and are booked solid at weekends.

Selimiye Taşodalar   BOUTIQUE HOTEL €€

(☎212 3529; www.tasodalar.com.tr; Selimiye Arkası Hamam Sokak 3; s/d from €80/100; ❄@) Occupying a historic mansion, the 'Stone Rooms' are next to Selimiye Camii and a 14th-century *hammam*. A few pieces of kitsch decor jar with the Ottoman interiors, but antiques and cedar furniture abound.

OIL WRESTLING

One of the world's oldest and most bizarre sporting events takes place annually in late June/early July at Sarayiçi in northern Edirne. At the 650-year-old **Tarihi Kırkpınar Yağlı Güreş Festivali** (Historic Kırpınar Oil Wrestling Festival), muscular men, naked bar a pair of heavy leather shorts, coat themselves with olive oil and throw each other around. For more information, visit **Kırpınar Evi** (Kırpınar House; ☎212 8622; www.kirkpinar. com; ⊙10am-noon & 2-6pm) in Edirne or www.turkishwrestling.com.

Efe Hotel
BOUTIQUE HOTEL €€
(☎213 6166; www.efehotel.com; Maarif Caddesi 13; s/d TL85/125; ❀@) A stylish choice, filled with antiques, curios and artwork. Rooms are well equipped and the hotel features a bar-restaurant and pub.

Tuna Hotel
HOTEL €€
(☎214 3340; fax 214 3323; Maarif Caddesi 17; s/d TL60/85;❀) A dependable choice, from its comfortable rooms with small TV to the modest breakfast spread, served in a small courtyard by the back annexe.

❶ Getting There & Away
For the Bulgarian border crossing at Kapıkule, catch a *dolmuş* (minibus that follows a pre-scribed route; TL5, 25 minutes) from opposite the tourist office on Talat Paşa Caddesi. For the Greek border post at Pazarkule, catch a *dolmuş* (TL1, 20 minutes) from outside the tourist office on Maarif Caddesi.

Edirne's *otogar* is 9km southeast of the centre. There are regular buses to:

Çanakkale (TL30, four hours)

İstanbul (TL10, 2½ hours)

Bursa
☎0224 / POP 1.9 MILLION

Sprawling at the base of Uludağ, Bursa was the first capital of the Ottoman Empire. Today, İstanbul's favourite winter-sports weekend getaway mixes traditional Turkish flavour with modern vitality. Allow at least a day to take in the ancient mosques, tombs, *madrasas* and their enthralling designs. The thermal springs in the village-like sub-urb of Çekirge, 3km west of central Bursa, are the perfect salve after exploring the city or Uludağ's tree-clad slopes.

The city centre is along Atatürk Caddesi, between the Ulu Cami and, to the east, the main square, Cumhuriyet Alanı, commonly called Heykel.

⊙ Sights & Activities

Yeşil Cami
MOSQUE
About 1km east of Heykel is the supremely beautiful Green Mosque (1424) and its stun-ningly tiled **Yeşil Türbe** (Green Tomb; admis-sion free; ⊙8am-noon & 1-5pm).

Ulu Cami
MOSQUE
(Atatürk Caddesi) Right in the centre of the city, the 20-domed, Seljuk Grand Mosque (1396) is Bursa's most imposing mosque. Behind it, Bursa's sprawling **covered market** (*kapalı*

çarşı) is proudly local, especially if you find İstanbul's Grand Bazaar too touristy.

Bursa Citadel
CASTLE
Uphill and west of Ulu Cami, towards Çekirge, this oldest section of Bursa was once enclosed by stone ramparts and walls, parts of which survive. In a park are the **Tombs of Sultans Osman and Orhan**, founders of the Ottoman Empire. A kilo-metre beyond lies the delightful **Muradiye Complex**, with a 13th-century mosque and 12 decorated, 15th- and 16th-century tombs. With a shady park in front, it's a peaceful oasis in busy Bursa.

Uludağ
NATURE RESERVE
Whether it's winter or summer, it's worth taking a cable-car ride up the Great Moun-tain (2543m) to take advantage of the views and the cool, clear air of **Uludağ National Park**. As well as one of Turkey's most popular ski resorts (the season runs from December to early April), the park offers pine forests and the occasional snowy peak. Hiking to the summit of Uludağ takes three hours. To get to the **teleferik** (cable car; TL8 return) from Bursa, take a city bus from stop 1 or a *dolmuş* from behind the City Mu-seum (Kent Müzesi).

🛌 Sleeping
There are a few decent options in Bursa, mostly of the business hotel ilk. Consider Çekirge, which has tranquil hotels for some R&R. Prices here can be higher, but gener-ally include the use of the mineral baths. A *dolmuş* (in Bursa, these are cars as well as minibuses) to Çekirge from the terminal immediately south of Heykel costs TL1.50; a taxi is TL10.

TOP CHOICE Kitap Evi
BOUTIQUE HOTEL €€€
(Bookshop Hotel; ☎225 4160; www.kitapevi. com.tr; Kavaklı Mahallesi, Burç Üstü 21; s/d/ste €90/120/220; ❀@☎) Once a bookshop, this city-centre hotel has gorgeously appointed rooms, decorated with old-school panache and set in a refurbished Ottoman manse.

Safran Otel
PENSION €€
(☎224 7216; www.safranotel.com; Arka Sokak 4; s/d TL80/150; ❀☎) Near the Osman and Orhan tombs in a historic neighbourhood high above the city, this restored mansion is all golden tones trimmed with polished dark wood (although the Ottoman trappings don't quite extend to the rooms).

Kervansaray Termal   LUXURY HOTEL €€
(☎233 9300; www.kervansarayhotels.com; Çekirge; d from €87; ✱@✱) This sprawling pleasure-plex blends modern and Ottoman touches, and has a crumbling thermal *hammam*. For something stylish, upgrade from the past-their-prime standard rooms.

Otel Güneş   HOSTEL €
(☎222 1404; İnebey Caddesi 75; s/d TL28/48) One of Bursa's few options catering to penny pinchers, this lively joint in the heart of the city crams backpackers into a small space. Teeny rooms and shared toilets are the norm.

✖ Eating & Drinking

Make sure you spend an evening at one of the fish restaurants on Arap Şükrü (officially called Sakarya Caddesi), Bursa's most atmospheric eating precinct.

Kebapçı İskender   KEBAPÇI €€
(Ünlü Caddesi 7; İskender kebap TL18; ⊘lunch & dinner) A legend throughout Turkey, this dimly lit kebap shop opened its doors in 1867 serving Bursa's nationally famous meat platter, the *İskender kebap*. Choose between *bir porsyon* (one serving) and the belt-loosening *bir buçuk porsyon* (1½ portions). There are other branches around the city.

Cafe My Kitchen   INTERNATIONAL €€
(☎234 6200; www.cafemykitchen.com; Çekirge Caddesi 114; pizza TL11-18, mains TL17-24; ⊘lunch & dinner; 🛜) This snazzy restaurant serves international fare in a slick atmosphere. Lipstick-red awnings dangle above locals thumbing gossip mags and clinking drinks at the wine bar.

Kitap Evi   INTERNATIONAL €€€
(☎225 4160; www.kitapevi.com.tr; Kavaklı Mahallesi, Burç Üstü 21; mains TL15-30; ⊘breakfast, lunch & dinner; 🛜) The former bookshop's inner courtyard, with its high stone walls, trickling fountain and snaking olive grove, is an inspiring place indeed.

Gren   BAR, CAFE €
(☎223 6064; www.grencafe.com; Sakarya Caddesi 46) This 'photography cafe' is the closest Bursa gets to a hipster hang-out. With black-and-white snaps and antique cameras scattered about, it's great for relaxing after a meal along neighbouring Arap Şükrü.

Mahfel Mado   BAR, RESTAURANT €
(Namazgah Caddesi 2; mains TL5-10) Bursa's oldest cafe is set along a gorgeous ravine.

Snag a table amid chatty 20-somethings and shady trees, or grab your *dondurma* (ice cream) to go.

ℹ Information

There's a post office (with payphones) and ATMs on Atatürk Caddesi, and exchange offices in the covered market.

Tourist office (⊘9am-5pm Mon-Fri to 6pm Sat) Beneath Atatürk Caddesi, in the row of shops at the north entrance to Orhan Gazi Alt Geçidi. Expect a friendly welcome and fluctuating opening hours.

ℹ Getting There & Away

Bursa's *otogar* is 10km north of the centre; take bus 38 (TL2, 45 minutes) or a taxi (around TL25). Bus 96 goes to Çekirge.

FERRY The fastest route to **İstanbul** is the metro-bus combo to Maudanya, then an **İDO ferry** (www.ido.com.tr) across the Sea of Marmara to Kabataş or Yenikapı. Alternatively, take a bus to Yalova (TL9, 1¼ hours, half-hourly), then a ferry to Yenikapı. Catch a bus leaving Bursa's *otogar* at least 90 minutes before the scheduled boat departure. On both routes, to travel on a weekend or public holiday, purchase your ferry ticket in advance.

BUS *Karayolu ile* (by road) buses drag you around the Bay of İzmit (about TL20, four to five hours); *feribot ile* (by ferry) buses go to Topçular, east of Yalova, and then by ferry to Eskihisar near **İstanbul**, a quicker and more pleasant route.

THE AEGEAN COAST

Turkey's Aegean coast can convincingly claim more ancient ruins per square kilometre than any other region in the world. Since time immemorial, conquerors, traders and travellers have beaten a path to the mighty monuments, and few leave disappointed. Here you'll see the famous ruins of Troy, Ephesus and Pergamum (Bergama), and you can contemplate the devastation of war at the battlefield sites of Gallipoli.

Gallipoli (Gelibolu) Peninsula

☎0286

Antipodeans and many Brits won't need an introduction to Gallipoli; it is the backbone of the 'Anzac legend', in which an Allied campaign in 1915 to knock Turkey out of WWI and open a relief route to Russia turned into one of the war's greatest fiascos. Some 130,000 men died, a third from Allied forces and the rest Turkish.

Today the Gallipoli battlefields are peaceful places, covered in brush and pine forests. But the battles fought here nearly a century ago are still alive in many memories, both Turkish and foreign, especially Australians and New Zealanders, who view the peninsula as a place of pilgrimage. The Turkish officer responsible for the defence of Gallipoli was Mustafa Kemal (the future Atatürk); his victory is commemorated in Turkey on 18 March. On **Anzac Day** (25 April), a dawn service marks the anniversary of the Allied landings.

The easiest way to see the battlefields is with your own transport or an afternoon minibus tour from nearby Eceabat/Çanakkale (typically TL45/60) with **Crowded House Tours** (☏814 1565; www.crowdedhousegallipoli.com) or **TJs Tours** (☏814 3121; www.anzacgallipolitours.com). With a tour you get the benefit of a guide who can explain the battles as you go along.

Most people use Çanakkale or, on the Thracian (European) side of the strait, Eceabat as a base. Ferries link Çanakkale and Eceabat (see p929). From Eceabat, take a *dolmuş* (TL2.50) or taxi to the **Kabatepe Information Centre & Museum**, 750m from the bottom of the road up to the main battlefields.

Some travellers prefer to join an organised tour from İstanbul (p924).

Eceabat (Maydos)

☏0286 / POP 5500

Eceabat is a small, easy-going waterfront town with the best access to the main Gallipoli battlefields of any main centre.

Ferries dock by the main square, Cumhuriyet Meydanı, which has hotels, restaurants, ATMs, a post office, bus-company offices, *dolmuş* stands and taxi stands. Like most of the peninsula, Eceabat is swamped with students and tour groups at weekends from mid-March to mid-June and in late September.

⌁ Sleeping & Eating

TOP CHOICE **Hotel Crowded House** HOSTEL €
(☏814 1565; www.crowdedhousegallipoli.com; Hüseyin Avni Sokak 4; dm/s/d TL15/45/60; ❄@) Recommended by readers, this gem of a backpackers' has comfortable, spick-and-span rooms and dorms, plus a ground-floor

bar and mezzanine breakfast area. Best of all is the welcome and professional service.

Hotel Boss BUSINESS HOTEL €
(☏814 1464; www.heyboss.com; Cumhuriyet Meydanı 14; s/d TL40/70; ❄@) A cool, compact hotel with a black-and-white reception and some of Eceabat's best rooms. The helpful staff speak a little English.

TJs Hotel HOSTEL €
(☏814 3121; www.anzacgallipolitours.com; Cumhuriyet Meydanı; dm TL15; r per person TL25-50; ❄@) With rooms to suit every budget, from basic dorms to 'hotel' rooms with air-con and balcony, TJs' long corridors are rather institutional and the service can be shambolic, but the fifth-floor bar is fabulous.

TOP CHOICE **Liman Restaurant** SEAFOOD €€
(☏814 2755; İstiklal Caddesi 67; mains TL10) At the southern end of the main waterfront strip, Eceabat's best restaurant serves excellent meze and fish. The covered terrace is a delight in all weather.

❶ Getting There & Away

Çanakkale Hourly car ferries (from TL2, 25 minutes).

İstanbul Hourly buses (TL38, five hours).

Çanakkale

☏0286 / POP 86,600

The liveliest settlement on the Dardanelles, this sprawling harbour town would be worth a visit for its sights, nightlife and overall vibe even if it didn't lie opposite the Gallipoli Peninsula. Its sweeping waterfront promenade heaves during the summer months.

A good base for visiting Troy, Çanakkale has become a popular destination for week-ending Turks; during summer, try to visit midweek. The **tourist office** (☏217 1187; Cumhuriyet Meydanı; ⊗8.30am-5.30pm) is 150m from the ferry pier, and you can access the internet at **Araz Internet** (Fetvane Sokak 21; per hr TL1.50; ⊗9am-midnight).

◉ Sights

Military Museum PARK, MUSEUM
(Askeri Müze; ☏213 1730; Çimenlik Sokak; admission TL4; ⊗9am-5pm Tue, Wed & Fri-Sun; ℙ) An Ottoman castle and seafront building house this museum. It's situated in a park in the military zone at the southern end of the quay, among artefacts including a replica of the Nusrat minelayer.

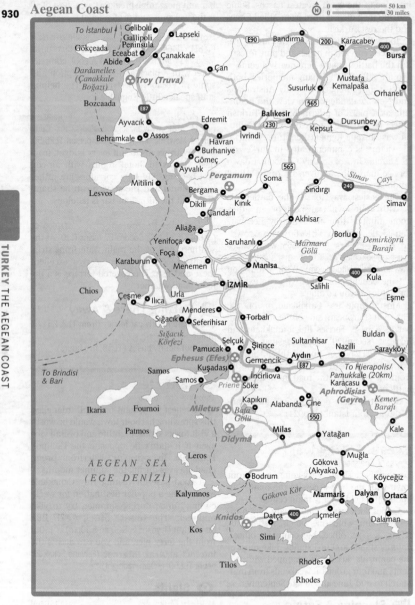

Archaeological Museum MUSEUM

(Arkeoloji Müzesi; ☎217 6565; 100 Yil Caddesi; admission TL5; ☉8am-5pm; P) Just over 1.5km south of the *otogar*, on the road to Troy, the Archaeological Museum holds artefacts from Troy and Assos.

🛏 Sleeping

Travellers should be aware that rooms in Çanakkale are expensive around Anzac Day, and they are also usually booked solid months before 25 April arrives.

TOP CHOICE **Hotel Kervansaray**   BOUTIQUE HOTEL €€

(📞217 8192; www.otelkervansaray.com; Fetvane Sokak 13; s/d/tr TL90/140/170; ❄@) This boutique caravanserai lays on Ottoman touches in keeping with the restored house (and sympathetic new annexe) it occupies. Rooms have a dash of character without being overdone.

Efes Hotel   PENSION €

(📞217 3256; www.efeshotelcanakkale.com; Fetvane Sokak 5; s/d TL40/50, breakfast TL5; ❄) Good for couples and lone women, the friendly Efes has a female touch, with cheerful rooms, small balconies and a fountain in the back garden.

Anzac Hotel   HOTEL €

(📞217 7777; www.anzachotel.com; Saat Kulesi Meydanı 8; s/d/tr €35/45/60; ❄@) The Kervansaray's three-star sister has an unbeatable position by the clock tower, a mezzanine cafe and Dardanelles views. Rooms have satellite TV, safe and minibar.

Hotel Akol   HOTEL €€€

(📞217 9456; www.hotelakol.com.tr; Kayserili Ahmet Paşa Caddesi; s/d/ste TL150/200/370; ❄❄) Near the Trojan Horse, this tower is easier on the eyes from the inside. Antique furniture dots the lobby, rooms are small but comfortable and there's a rooftop bar.

Yellow Rose Pension   HOSTEL €

(📞217 3343; www.yellowrose.4mg.com; Aslan Abla Sokak 5; dm/s/d/tr/q TL20/30/50/70/90; P@) This hostel on a quiet, central street has a lounge with monumental TV, and small rooms and dorms with effective garden-hose showers. The tiled floors and smell of disinfectant are rather spartan, but there's a kitchen.

🍴 Eating & Drinking

To eat on the hoof, browse the stalls along the waterfront, which offer corn on the cob, mussels and other simple items. Head to Fetvane and buzzing, pedestrianised Matbaa Sokaks for bars and soak-up-the-Efes eateries.

Anafartalar Kebap   KEBAPÇI €€

(📞214 9112; Kayserili Ahmet Paşa Caddesi 40; mains TL10; ⏱8am-11.30pm) Quieter and better value than the nearby waterfront fish restaurants, serving excellent pide and *İskender kebap*.

Café Notte   BAR, RESTAURANT €€

(📞214 9112; Kayserili Ahmet Paşa Caddesi 40; mains TL12; ⏱8am-11.30pm) In the trendier northern waterfront strip, this cool bar/bistro's cosmopolitan menu features fajitas, fish and chips, pizzas and cocktails.

Benzin   BAR, CAFE

(Eski Balıkhane Sokak 11; pizzas TL8-12.50;📶) This waterfront bar-cafe done out in 1960s decor is a relaxing spot for a drink and a bite, but gets crowded at weekends.

Time Out   LIVE MUSIC

(Kayserili Ahmet Paşa Caddesi) A rock club with pictures of Elvis et al, outside tables and a barman who plays sets.

❶ Getting There & Away

Bus

Ayvalık (TL25, 3½ hours, hourly)

Bandırma (TL20, 2½ hours, hourly)

İstanbul (TL35, six hours, frequent)

İzmir (TL35, 5½ hours, hourly)

Ferry

Eceabat See Eceabat, p929.

Troy (Truva)

📞0286

Of all the ancient centres in Turkey, the remains of the great city of Troy are in fact among the least impressive; you'll have to use your imagination. Still, for history buffs and fans of Homer's *Iliad*, it's an important site to tick off the list – and the wooden horse is fun.

Approaching the ruins of **Troy** (📞283 0536; per person TL15; ⏱8.30am-7pm May-15 Sep, to 5pm 16 Sep-end Apr) from the ticket booth, the first thing you see is a reconstruction of the Trojan Horse. The site is rather confusing for nonexpert eyes (guides are available), but the most conspicuous features include the **walls** from various periods; **megarons** (houses inhabited by the elite); the Roman **Odeon**, where concerts were held, and **sanctuaries** to ancient deities.

From Çanakkale, *dolmuşes* to Troy (TL4, 35 minutes, 9.30am to 4.30/7pm winter/summer) leave on the half-hour (less frequently at weekends) from a station at the northern end of the bridge over the Sarı River and arrive at the Troy ticket booth. Returning, *dolmuşes* leave on the hour (7am to 3pm/5pm winter/summer).

The travel agencies offering Gallipoli tours also offer morning trips to Troy (around TL60 per person).

Behramkale & Assos

☏0286

Behramkale, southwest of Ayvacık, is an old hilltop Greek village spread out around the ruins of the 6th-century BC Ionic **Temple of Athena** (admission TL5; ☺8am-7.30pm), which has spectacular views of Lesvos and the dazzling Aegean. Next to the temple ticket booth, the 14th-century **Hüdavendigar Camii** is a simple early Ottoman mosque.

Just before the entrance to the village, a road winds down the steep hill to Assos, the ideal place to unwind over a glass of *çay*. Overlooking the picture-perfect harbour, the old stone buildings have been transformed into hotels and fish restaurants.

The villages make a fine combination, but tourists pour in by the coachload at weekends and public holidays from the beginning of April to the end of August.

⨳ Sleeping

BEHRAMKALE

TOP CHOICE **Biber Evi**   BOUTIQUE HOTEL **€€€**
(☏721 7410; www.biberevi.com; s TL200-230, d TL240-270, mains TL30; ❋❄) This 150-year-old stone house has six rooms and a terrace with views of the temple and coast. The bar is stocked with single malts, and the breakfasts and dinners demonstrate care and creativity. Bookings need to be for a minimum of two nights.

Eris Pansiyon   PENSION **€€**
(☏721 7080; www.erispansiyon.com; s/d incl tea TL70/120) Set in a stone house with pretty gardens, the American-run Eris has three pleasant, peaceful rooms. Afternoon tea is served on a terrace with views over the hills.

Dolunay Pansiyon   PENSION **€€**
(☏721 7172; s/d TL50/100; ❋) On the village square, this homely affair has spotless, simple rooms, a pleasant courtyard and a pretty terrace with sea views.

ASSOS

In high season virtually all of the hotels here insist on *yarım pansiyon* (half-board).

Hotel Kervansaray   HOTEL **€€**
(☏721 7093; www.assoskervansaray.com; s/d with sea view TL120/140; ❋❄) A 19th-century acorn

store, the cavernous Kervansaray has smart rooms, outdoor and indoor pools, a sauna and jacuzzi.

Yıldız Saray Hotel   PENSION **€€**
(☏721 7025; www.yildizsaray-hotels.com; s/d/f TL80/120/200; ❋) Though some of its bedding looks rather '70s, the Star Palace's colourful carpets and walls hoist it above ordinary village pensions. Breakfast is served on a fantastic floating platform.

Dr No Antik Pansiyon   PENSION **€**
(☏721 7397; dr.noantikpansiyon@hotmail.com; s/d TL35/70; ❋) A Bond villain's hideaway it ain't, but this friendly budget option's rickety rooms are passable – if offensively green.

⨯ Eating

In contravention of the way these things usually work, the settlement at the bottom of the hill is actually the 'posh' part of town, where prices, if not standards, are higher. Be sure to check the cost of fish and bottles of wine before ordering. Mains typically cost less than TL10/over TL15 in Behramkale/Assos.

ⓘ Getting There & Away

Behramkale Regular buses run from Çanakkale to Ayvacık (TL10, 1½ hours), where you can pick up a *dolmuş* to Behramkale (TL3, 20 minutes). In low season, the *dolmuşes* run less frequently; a taxi from Ayvacık costs around TL25 to TL30.

Assos Some *dolmuşes* continue to Assos. In summer, there's a half-hourly shuttle service between the villages (TL1). In winter, *dolmuşes* occasionally link the two (TL7.50).

Ayvalık

☏0266 / POP 36,000

Back from the palm trees and fish restaurants on Ayvalık's waterfront, the tumbledown old Greek village provides a kind of outdoor museum. Horses and carts clatter down narrow streets, past headscarf-wearing women holding court outside picturesque shuttered houses.

Olive-oil production is the traditional business here, and the town is well known as a gateway to local islands and the Greek isle of Lesvos.

The tourist office is 1.5km southwest of the centre; between June and September, an information kiosk opens on the waterfront just south of the main square. Offshore is

Alibey Island (Alibey Adası; known locally as Cunda), which is lined with open-air fish restaurants and linked to the mainland by ferries (June to early September) and a causeway. Summer cruises (TL20 per person including lunch) include it in their day tours of the bay's islands, leaving Ayvalık around 11am and stopping here and there for sunbathing and swimming.

🛏 Sleeping & Eating

TOP CHOICE Annette's House　　PENSION €€
(📞312 5971; www.annetteshouse.com; Neşe Sokak 12; per person TL45, breakfast TL10; ⊛) On a quiet square (Thursdays excepted when it's the site of the village market), this oasis of calm and comfort, run by a personable retired teacher from Germany, combines white floors and colourful traditional decor.

Kelebek Pension　　PENSION €€
(📞312 3908; www.kelebek-pension.com; Mareşal Çakmak Caddesi 108; s/d/tr TL50/80/120; ✳) Winning praise from readers and with a good local reputation, the English- and German-speaking Kirayfamily's seven-room pension occupies a quaint, white-and-blue building with a terrace.

TOP CHOICE Balıkçı　　SEAFOOD €€
(📞312 9099; Balıkhane Sokak 7; mains TL17; ⊘dinner) This waterfront *balık* (fish) restaurant, run by a local association of fishermen and marine environmentalists, is the perfect place to grab a *rakı* (aniseed brandy) and understand the expression '*rakı, balık,* Ayvalık'.

Tarlakusu Gurmeko　　CAFE €€
(📞312 3312; Cumhuriyet Caddesi 53; ⊘8.30am-8.30pm; 🛈) Run by a clued-up İzmiri couple, this deli sells a range of teas and coffees, plus cookies, brownies, soup, salads, cheese plates and *börek*.

❶ Getting There & Away

Bus & Dolmuş
The *otogar* is 1.5km northeast of the centre.
Alibey Island *Dolmuş* taxis (white with red stripes) run from the south side of Ayvalık main square (TL2, 20 minutes).
Bergama (TL7, 1¾ hours, hourly) Bergama-bound buses pass through town, so you can jump on at the main square.
Çanakkale (TL13, 3¼ hours, five a day) Smaller companies may drop you on the main highway to hitch to Ayvalık centre.
İzmir (TL15, three hours, hourly)

Boat
Alibey Island (TL4; 15 minutes; every 15 minutes) From a quay behind the tourist kiosk just off Ayvalık main square.

Lesvos (one way/return €40/50, 1½ hours) Daily except Sunday between May and September, with three boats a week from October to May. Advance reservations are essential; contact **Jale Tour** (📞331 3170; www.jaletour. com; Gümrük Caddesi 24).

Bergama (Pergamum)

📞0232 / POP 58,200
As Selçuk is to Ephesus, so Bergama is to Pergamum: the workaday market town has become a major stop on the tourist trail because of its proximity to the remarkable ruins of Pergamum, site of ancient Rome's pre-eminent medical centre. During Pergamum's heyday (between Alexander the Great and the Roman domination of Asia Minor) it was one of the Middle East's richest and most powerful small kingdoms.

The elongated main street (İzmir/Cumhuriyet/Bankalar Caddesi) is where you'll find banks with ATMs and the PTT. Just north of the museum is a basic **tourist office** (📞631 2851; İzmir Caddesi; ⊘8.30am-noon & 1-5.30pm).

⊙ Sights

A new **cable car** (TL12 return) ascends to the Acropolis. A taxi from the centre to the Asclepion/Acropolis is TL7/15. A taxi tour, including waiting time at the Asclepion, Red Basilica and Acropolis, costs around TL50.

Asclepion　　RUINS
(Temple of Asclepios; admission/parking TL15/3; ⊘8.30am-5.30pm) About 3km uphill from the centre, the well-proportioned Asclepion was a famous medical centre, which came to the fore in the 2nd century. Treatments included mud baths, herbs and ointments, enemas, sunbathing and dream analysis.

Acropolis　　RUINS
(Akropol; admission TL20; ⊘8.30am-5.30pm) The ruins of the Acropolis, 5km from the ruined **Red Basilica** in the centre of Bergama, are equally striking. The hilltop setting is absolutely magical, and the well-preserved ruins are magnificent, especially the vertigo-inducing 10,000-seat **theatre** and the marble-columned **Temple of Trajan,** built during the reigns of Emperors Trajan and Hadrian and used to worship them as well as Zeus.

Archaeology Museum　　　MUSEUM
(Arkeoloji Müzesi; ☑631 2884; Cumhuriyet Caddesi; admission TL5; ☺8.30am-5.30pm Tue-Sun)
The excellent Archaeology Museum has a small but substantial collection of artefacts from the surrounding sites, including a collection of 4th-century BC statues from the Pergamum School.

🛌 Sleeping

TOP CHOICE Odyssey Guesthouse　　PENSION €
(☑631　3501;　www.odysseyguesthouse.com; Abacıhan Sokak 13; dm TL15, s/d from TL35/40, without bathroom from TL25/35, breakfast TL7) This 180-year-old house is full of crannies, corners and character, with a copy of Homer's *Odyssey* in every room. Up top is a terrace and a kitchenette for guest use.

Gobi Pension　　　PENSION €
(☑633 2518; www.gobipension.com; İzmir Caddesi 18; s/d TL40/65, s/d without bathroom TL25/45; @❄) On the main road behind a shady terrace draped in greenery, the family-run Gobi has bright, breezy rooms. It's well set up for travellers, with a kitchen and laundry service.

Hotel Anıl　　　HOTEL €€
(☑632 6352; www.anilhotelbergama.com; Hatuniye Caddesi 4; s/d/tr TL70/100/130; ❄) The central, pinkish Anıl has comfortable, well-equipped rooms, and winning Acropolis views from its third and fourth floors.

🍽 Eating

TOP CHOICE Kervan　　FAMILY RESTAURANT €€
(☑633 2632; İzmir Caddesi; mains TL12) Next to Gobi Pension, Kervan is popular for its large outdoor terrace and excellent food, including kebaps, pide, *çorba* (soup) and *künefe* (syrup-soaked dough and sweet cheese sprinkled with pistachio).

Köy Evi　　　LOKANTA €
(Village House; Galinos Caddesi 12; mantı TL5; ☺10am-7.30pm) At this cosy, family-run eatery, the home-cooked dishes typically include stuffed peppers, *mantı* and *patlıcan kebap* (meat grilled with aubergine).

ℹ Getting There & Away

Between 6am and 7pm, a free *servis* shuttles between Bergama's new *otogar*, 7km from the centre at the junction of the highway and the main road into town, and the central old *otogar*. A taxi costs about TL20.

Ayvalık (TL7.50, 1¼ hours, hourly)
İzmir (TL10, two hours, every 45 minutes)

İzmir

☎0232 / POP 2.7 MILLION

Though you will soon fall for Alsancak's student nightlife, shopping in the Kemeraltı Bazaar and catching ferries along the *kordon* (seafront), İzmir can take some getting used to. Certainly nowhere else in the region prepares you for the sheer size, sprawl and intensity of Turkey's third-largest city.

At the water's edge, İzmir's chronic traffic has been beaten back and the city really comes into its own. The wide, pleasant esplanade provides plenty of opportunities for eating, drinking and watching the sunset. With its Levantine and Jewish heritage, İzmir is a cosmopolitan, liberal place; spending a night or two here is one of the best things you can do in urban Turkey.

👁 Sights

Agora　　　RUINS
(Agora Caddesi; admission TL3; ☺8.30am-7pm, to 5.30pm Sat; P) Since most of old İzmir was destroyed after WWI by a Greek invasion and a fire, there's little to see here compared with other Turkish cities. It does, however, boast these sparse remains of an extensive 2nd-century Roman agora, just southeast of Kemeraltı Bazaar.

Kemeraltı Bazaar　　　BAZAAR
(☺8am-5pm) İzmir's modern bazaar largely sells unexotic goods, as well as a few more-intriguing items, like water pipes, beads and leather goods (a local speciality). It has plenty of atmosphere, with İzmiris crowding along its narrow, intertwining alleys. The restored caravanserai **Kızlarağası Han** (1744) has a cafe in the courtyard, where merchants once tethered their camels.

🛌 Sleeping

İzmir's waterfront is dominated by high-end business hotels, which fill up quickly during summer; inland are more budget and midrange options, particularly around the bazaar and Basmane train station. East of the station, 1368 Sokak is good for budget hotels.

MyHotel　　BOUTIQUE HOTEL €€€
(☑445　5241;　www.myhotel.com.tr;　Cumhuriyet Bulvarı 132; s/d €80/110; ❄@) The business-come-boutique MyHotel is super-stylish,

with glass floors, an ubercool lobby bar and minimalist rooms. It's near the waterfront but doesn't have sea views.

Konak Saray Hotel
BOUTIQUE HOTEL **€€**

(☑483 7755; www.konaksarayhotel.com; Anafartalar Caddesi 635; s/d TL60/90; ✳@) One of İzmir's best-value options, the Konak Saray occupies a restored Ottoman house. A hit with readers, its small, modern rooms have minibars, plasma-screen TVs and sound-proofing against bazaar noise. There's also a great top-floor restaurant.

Otel Antik Han
BOUTIQUE HOTEL **€€**

(☑489 2750; www.otelantikhan.com; Anafartalar Caddesi 600; s/d €45/65; @) This restored Ottoman building is one of İzmir's few historic hotels, with pleasant (if sometimes threadbare) rooms that have plasma-screen TVs and minibars. The tranquil courtyard is a retreat from the bustling bazaar outside.

Hotel Yaman
HOTEL **€€**

(☑421 1287; www.hotelyaman.com; 1440 Sokak 19; s/d €45/60; ✳) In an ideal location near Alsancak's cafes and bars, the no-frills Yaman is a good-value option for a short stay.

🍴 Eating & Drinking

For fresh fruit and veg, freshly baked bread and delicious savoury pastries, head for the canopied market just off Anafartalar Caddesi. *The* place to be seen on a romantic summer's evening is an outside table on the *kordon*, though you pay for the location. In Alsancak, you lose the sunset views but gain on atmosphere; head to the lanes linking Cumhuriyet Bulvarı and Kıbrıs Şehitleri Caddesi.

TOP CHOICE Sakız
MODERN TURKISH **€€**

(☑484 1103; Şehit Nevresbey Bulvarı 9a; mains TL12-22; ⊙12pm-2pm & 7.30pm-10pm Mon-Sat) With a wooden terrace, Sakız serves fresh meze, including *balık kokoreç* (fish intestines), and unusual mains. For lunch, choose between 35 vegetarian dishes (10 on Saturday).

Balık Pişiricisi
SEAFOOD **€**

(☑464 2705; Atatürk Caddesi 212; mains TL20; ⊙noon-10.30pm) The queues outside and galloping waiters reveal much about this fish restaurant. Simple and modern, its speciality is *dil şiş* (grilled sole).

Aksak Lounge
BAR

(1452 Sokak 10) In a typical İzmir mansion with high ceilings, balconies and a courtyard garden, Aksak attracts a cultured crowd to its Tuesday and Sunday jazz nights.

ℹ Information

Banks, ATMS, internet cafes and wi-fi networks are found throughout the centre.

Tourist office (☑483 5117; 1344 Sokak 2) Just off Atatürk Caddesi.

ℹ Getting There & Away

Air

There are many flights to İzmir's **Adnan Menderes Airport** (www.adnanmenderesairport.com) from European destinations. Turkish Airlines flies to/from İstanbul (both airports), Ankara and 11 other Turkish locations. Onur Air, Atlasjet, Pegasus Airlines, Sun Express and Izair also serve İzmir.

Bus

From the mammoth *otogar*, 6.5km northeast of the centre, frequent buses leave for nationwide destinations including:

Bergama (TL10, two hours)

Çeşme (TL12, 1¾ hours) Buses also leave from a local bus terminal in Üçkuyular, 6.5km southwest of Konak.

Kuşadası (TL15, 1¼ hours)

Selçuk (TL8, one hour)

Train

Most intercity services arrive at Basmane station, although Alsancak is being vamped up.

Ankara (TL27, 15 hours) Two a day in both directions; via Eskişehir (TL21, 11 hours).

Bandırma (TL17, six hours) Every afternoon in both directions. Apart from on Tuesday, morning trains coordinate with the ferry to/from İstanbul.

Manisa (TL3 to TL7.50, 1¾ hours) Six every day but Tuesday.

ℹ Getting Around

Main squares Konak Meydanı (Government House Sq) and Cumhuriyet Meydanı are on İzmir's two principal avenues: Atatürk Caddesi, known as *birinci* (first) *kordon*, which runs along the waterfront; and Cumhuriyet Bulvarı, the *ikinci* (second) *kordon*, which runs parallel a block inland.

Just inland from Konak Meydanı, Anafartalar Caddesi leads along the southern side of Kemeraltı Bazaar towards Basmane train station.

Shopping, restaurant and nightclub district Alsancak is north of Cumhuriyet Meydanı.

AIRPORT Havaş buses (TL10, 30 minutes) leave from Gaziosmanpaşa Bulvarı near the

Swissotel on the half hour; and from domestic arrivals 25 minutes after flights arrive.

BUS Intercity bus companies operate *servis* shuttles to/from the *otogar*. *Dolmuşes* run to the centre; to the *otogar*, take the metro to Bornova and catch bus 505.

FERRY (TL3) Roughly half-hourly services, with more at the beginning and end of the working day, link piers including Alsancak, Pasaport and Konak.

Çeşme Peninsula

☎0232

The Çeşme Peninsula is İzmir's summer playground, which means it fills with Turkish tourists over weekends and during school holidays. Çeşme itself is a family-orientated resort and transit point for the Greek island of Chios, 8km west. It's a pleasantly authentic port town with a dramatic Genoese fortress, although you may prefer to stay in boutique bolt-hole Alaçatı, with its old Greek stone houses and windsurfing beach.

Çeşme's **tourist office** (☎/fax 712 6653; İskele Meydanı 4; ☉8.30am-noon & 1-5.30pm Mon-Fri), ferry and bus ticket offices, banks with ATMs, restaurants and hotels are all within two blocks of the main square.

🛏 Sleeping

ÇEŞME

Barınak Pansiyon   PENSION **€**
(☎712 6670; 3052 Sokak 58; s/d TL30/50; 🗙) A good choice, next to Sahil Pansiyon, Barınak has spacious, spotless rooms with nice bathrooms and a little terrace.

Rıdvan Otel   HOTEL **€€**
(☎712 6336; www.ridvanotel.com; Cumhuriyet Meydanı 11; s/d TL60/100; 🗙) Rooms are slightly clinical, but their balconies overlook the sea or the castle and main square. Photos of old İzmir abound, and there's a ground-floor cafe with seating on the square.

ALAÇATI

Prices plummet out of season, although most hotels open only from mid-May to mid-October and for Christmas and New Year.

TOP CHOICE **Alaçatı Taş Otel**   BOUTIQUE HOTEL **€€€**
(☎716 7772; www.tasotel.com; Kemalpaşa Caddesi 132; s/d incl afternoon tea from €125/155; 🗙🗙) This former olive warehouse was the first of Alacatı's 100-plus boutique hotels. Rooms with elegant simplicity overlook a walled

garden and large swimming pool. Open year-round.

Değirmen Otel   BOUTIQUE HOTEL **€€€**
(☎716 6714; www.alacatidegirmen.com in Turkish; Değirmen Sokak 3; s/d TL100/180; 🗙) The Mill Hotel occupies four converted windmills on a hillock. Rustic in feel but beautifully decorated, the circular rooms are arranged around a first-floor pool and terrace restaurant.

Eating

ÇEŞME

On Çeşme waterfront are touristy restaurants specialising in seafood – and multilingual menus. For cheaper, more locally orientated places, head to İnkılap Caddesi.

Pasifik Otel Restaurant   SEAFOOD **€€**
(☎712 1767; Tekke Plajı Mevkii 16; mains TL10-15; ☉noon-midnight) This hotel restaurant, at the far northern end of the seafront, serves a great fish casserole at tables overlooking a small beach.

İmren Lokantası Restaurant   RESTAURANT **€€**
(☎712 7620; İnkılap Caddesi 6; mains TL15; ☉noon-9pm) Çeşme's first restaurant, opened in 1960, occupies a bamboo-roofed atrium with a fountain and plants. The traditional, high-quality Turkish dishes include stews.

No Problem Bar   EXPAT BAR
(☎712 9411; Çarşı Caddesi 14; ☉9am-midnight; 🛜) Decorated with British souvenir towels, No Problem offers tastes of Blighty such as a full English breakfast (TL10), pub quiz (8pm Monday) and a book exchange.

ALAÇATI

Restaurants here are mostly smart, gourmet affairs, with mains typically starting at around TL18. Many close for lunch, and open only at weekends (if at all) in low season. The cafes by the mosque serve cheaper fare.

ℹ Getting There & Around

Boat

Chios (one way/return €25/40, 1½ hours) Between mid-May and mid-September, **Ertürk** (☎712 6768; www.erturk.com.tr; Beyazıt Caddesi 6) sails once or twice daily; outside that period, twice a week.

Ancona (Italy; single from €215, 60 hours) Between May and September, **Marmara Lines** (☎712 2223; www.marmaralines.com; Turgut Özal Bulvarı 13D) sails on Thursdays, returning to Çeşme on Saturdays.

Bus

Buses from Çeşme *otogar* run every 15 minutes to İzmir *otogar* (TL12, 1¾ hours) and the smaller, western Üçkuyular terminal (TL10, 1½ hours). *Dolmuşes* link Çeşme and Alaçatı (TL3.50).

Selçuk

☎ 0232 / POP 27,300

The normal gateway to Ephesus, Selçuk is an atmospheric place with backlit minarets and soaring aqueduct ruins, as well as sights including one of the Seven Wonders of the Ancient World. The quiet town acts more as a weigh station for the throngs of passers-through than a vibrant tourist hub.

◉ Sights

FREE **Temple of Artemis** RUINS
(☺8am-5.30pm) In its day, this was the largest temple to Artemis, eclipsing even the Parthenon at Athens and becoming one of the Seven Wonders of the Ancient World. One enormous pillar remains on the peaceful site at the western end of Selçuk.

Ephesus Museum MUSEUM
(☎892 6010; Uğur Mumcu Sevgi Yolu Caddesi; admission TL5; ☺8.30am-6.30pm/4.30pm summer/winter) This excellent museum houses a striking collection of artefacts, including the effigy of Priapus, the Phallic God, which pops up in postcard racks throughout Turkey.

Basilica of St John HISTORIC BUILDING
(St Jean Caddesi; admission TL5; ☺8.30am-6.30pm summer, to 4.30pm winter) Emperor Justinian built this conspicuous 6th-century basilica, one of the superb monuments scattered around central Selçuk, on the site on Ayasuluk Hill where it was believed St John had been buried.

🛏 Sleeping

Competition between Selçuk's many pensions is intense, and the standard of service and value offered is higher than perhaps anywhere else in Turkey. Most cater to budget and midrange travellers.

Jimmy's Place HOTEL €€
(☎892 1982; www.jimmysplaceephesus.com; 1016 Sokak 19; d/ste from €30/70; ❄@☃) Near the bus station, Jimmy's Place is an inviting spot with five spacious floors of neatly renovated rooms. Staff are eager to please, offering a gut-busting breakfast and extras including a highly informative travel service.

Akay Hotel HOTEL €€
(☎892 3172; www.hotelakay.com; 1054 Sokak 7; s/d from €35/55; ❄@☃) Hand-cut stone foundations, white walls and inviting green doors wrap around friendly Akay's two wings of accommodation. A la carte dinners are served on the relaxing roof terrace.

Homeros Pension PENSION €
(☎892 3995; www.homerospension.com; 1048 Sokak 3; s/d/tr TL45/70/105; ❄@) On a quiet alley, Homeros' two houses are imprinted with the quirky character of the welcoming, kind-hearted owner. Traditional-style furniture mixes with hanging textiles and the roof terraces have good views.

WORTH A TRIP

PAMUKKALE

East of Selçuk, Pamukkale's gleaming white **travertines** (admission TL20; ☺daylight), calcite shelves with pools cascading down the plateau edge, are a World Heritage site. Next to this fragile wonder, you can tour the magnificent ruins of the Roman city of **Hierapolis**, an ancient spa resort with a theatre, colonnaded street, latrine building and necropolis.

You can bathe amid sunken columns at Hierapolis' **Antique Pool** (admission TL25; ☺9am-7pm) and visit the **Hierapolis Archaeology Museum** (admission TL3; ☺9am-12.30pm & 1.30-7pm Tue-Sun).

One of several budget pensions in the village, **Melrose Hotel** (☎272 2250; www.melroseresidence.com; Vali Vekfi Ertürk Caddesi 8; s/d TL50/60; ❄@☃) has cheery pastel rooms and hearty dinners on offer.

Buses connect local hub Denizli with Selçuk (TL18, three hours) and İzmir (TL20, four hours). Buses run between Denizli and Pamukkale every 15 minutes (TL2, 30 minutes). Touts taking commissions from hotels may try to get you to take a *dolmuş* from Denizli.

Selçuk

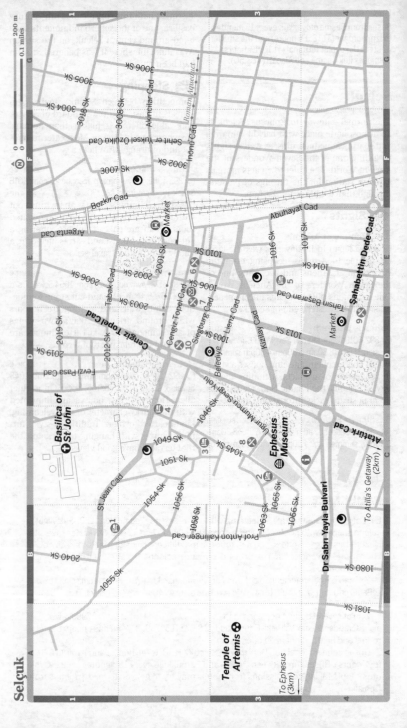

TURKEY THE AEGEAN COAST

200 m
0.1 miles

Basilica of St John

Temple of Artemis

Ephesus Museum

To Ephesus (3km)

To Atilla's Getaway (2km)

Roman Aqueduct

Atatürk Cad

Dr Sabri Yayla Bulvari

Şahabettin Dede Cad

Abuhayat Cad

Bozkir Cad

Argenta Cad

Cengiz Topel Cad

Uğur Mumcu Sevgi Yolu

Prof Anton Kallinger Cad

St Jean Cad

Fevzi Paşa Cad

Tabak Cad

Şehit er Yüksel Özülkü Cad

Akıncılar Cad

İnönü Cad

Tahsin Başaran Cad

Kızılay Cad

Lienz Cad

Siegburg Cad

3005 Sk
3006 Sk
3018 Sk
3004 Sk
3008 Sk
3007 Sk
3002 Sk
2001 Sk
2002 Sk
2003 Sk
2006 Sk
2012 Sk
2019 Sk
2019 Sk
2040 Sk
1055 Sk
1054 Sk
1056 Sk
1058 Sk
1049 Sk
1051 Sk
1045 Sk
1046 Sk
1063 Sk
1065 Sk
1066 Sk
1080 Sk
1081 Sk
1003 Sk
1006 Sk
1010 Sk
1013 Sk
1014 Sk
1016 Sk
1017 Sk

Market
Belediye
Market

Barım Pension PENSION €€
(☎892 6923; barim_pansiyon@hotmail.com; 1045 Sokak 34; s/d incl breakfast TL35/60; ❄@) Behind the unforgettable facade – a huge work of wire art replete with figurines and camels – this 140-year-old stone house is decorated with the metalworker-owners' art. Breakfasts are served in the adorable stone cloister amid dangling vines and potted shrubs.

Atilla's Getaway HOSTEL €
(☎892 3847; www.atillasgetaway.com; Acarlar Köyü; half-board dm/s/d TL35/40/45; ❄@☎) Selçuk's most unique accommodation, this chilled-out backpackers' 'resort' is 2.5km south of the centre, with a regular shuttle service.

Hotel Bella HOTEL €€
(☎892 3944; www.hotelbella.com; St Jean Caddesi 7; s/d from TL60/80; ❄@) The small rooms have clearly benefited from a designer's touch; Ottoman rugs and trinkets abound.

✖ Eating

Most pensions offer home-cooked dinners at reasonable prices. The fantastic Saturday **market**, behind the bus station, is a great place to stock up for a picnic.

Selçuk Köftecisi KÖFTECİ €
(Şahabettin Dede Caddesi; mains TL6-9) This family-run spot has been churning out bullet-sized meatballs since 1959. It's highly recommended despite being rather monopolised by tour groups.

Ejder Restaurant ANATOLIAN €€
(Cengiz Topel Caddesi 9/E; mains TL7-17) Run by a husband-and-wife team, this restaurant is popular for its delicious dishes (try the grilled chicken şiş or Anatolian meat platter) and setting under the arches of the Roman Aqueduct.

Sisçi Yaşar ın Yeri KÖFTECİ €
(Atatürk Caddesi; mains from TL6) With a small, shaded seating area around the back, this stall on the main road serves delicious köfte and kebaps.

Kebab House Mehmet & Alibaba KEBAPÇI €€
(1047 Sokak 4-A; mains TL5-16; ☎) This friendly joint dishes out Turkish treats like Adana kebap. Complimentary coffee and yoghurt sides are the norm.

Eski Ev ANATOLIAN €
(Old House Restaurant; 1005 Sokak 1/A; mains TL6-11) With tables in a little courtyard shaded by trees, this intimate place serves tasty Turkish dishes such as the house kebap, served sizzling on a platter.

❶ Information

Tourist office (www.selcuk.gov.tr; Agora Caddesi 35; ◷8am-noon & 1-5pm summer, Mon-Fri winter)

❶ Getting There & Away

Frequent *dolmuşes* run to Kuşa-dası (TL4, 30 minutes) and the beach at Pamucak (TL2.50, 10 minutes). Buses include:
İzmir (TL8, one hour, every 40 minutes in summer) If you ask in advance, you can usually be dropped at the junction of the road to Adnan Menderes Airport (a 2km walk or TL10 taxi).
Bodrum (TL25, 3¼ hours, two daily)

Ephesus (Efes)

Even if you're not an architecture buff, you can't help but be dazzled by the sheer beauty of the ruins of **Ephesus** (☎892 6010; admission/parking TL20/3; ◷8am-6.30pm May-Oct, 8am-4.30pm Nov-Apr), the best-preserved classical city in the eastern Mediterranean. Once the capital of the Roman province of Asia, with 250,000-plus inhabitants, today it's *the* place to get a feel for life in Greco-Roman times.

There's a couple of hours' worth of sights to explore, including the **Great Theatre**, reconstructed by the Romans between AD 41 and 117, and capable of holding 25,000

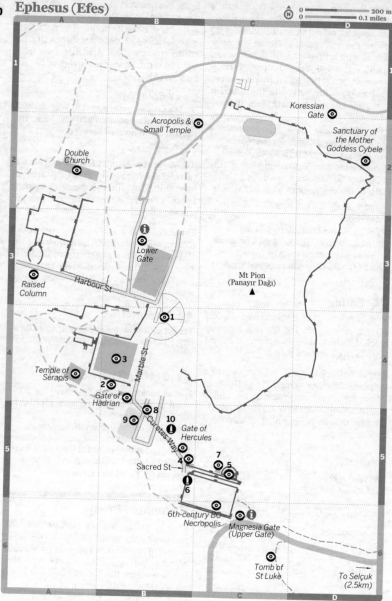

Map legend / labels:

- Koressian Gate
- Sanctuary of the Mother Goddess Cybele
- Acropolis & Small Temple
- Double Church
- Lower Gate
- Mt Pion (Panayır Dağı)
- Raised Column
- Harbour St
- Marble St
- 1
- Temple of Serapis
- 3
- 2
- Gate of Hadrian
- 8
- 9
- 10 Gate of Hercules
- Curetes Way
- 7
- 4
- 5
- Sacred St
- 6
- 6th-century BC Necropolis
- Magnesia Gate (Upper Gate)
- Tomb of St Luke
- To Selçuk (2.5km)

people; the 110-sq-m **Lower Agora**, a textile and food market; and the **Library of Celsus**, adorned with niches holding statues of the classical Virtues. Going up Ephesus' Champs Élysées, the **Curetes Way**, you can't miss the impressive Corinthian-style **Temple of Hadrian** on the left, its arches decorated with deities; the magnificent **Terraced Houses** (admission TL15), which are well worth the extra outlay; and the **Trajan Fountain**. At the top of the Curetes Way, the **Pollio Fountain** and **Memius Monument**

Ephesus (Efes)

◎ **Sights**

also hint at the lavish fountains that covered the ancient capital. Up the hill on the left are the very ruined remains of the **Prytaneum** (town hall) and the **Temple of Hestia Boulaea**, where vestal virgins tended to a perpetually burning flame. Beyond, the **Odeon**, a 5000-seat theatre with marble seats and carved ornamentation, was used for municipal meetings.

The mediocre audioguide is not recommended; nor are the 'guides' loitering at the entrances. Organise a guide in advance to bring the site to life. Bring your own snacks and water, as prices are high here. Heat and crowds can be problematic so come early or late and avoid weekends and public holidays.

Local law prohibits free lifts to Ephesus. A taxi from Selçuk costs about TL15. You may prefer to be dropped at the upper **Magnesia Gate** (the southern entrance or *güney kapısı*) so that you can walk back downhill (roughly 3km) through the ruins and out through the main **Lower Gate**.

We don't recommend walking from Selçuk: while the first 20 minutes are easy enough, the last part is an uphill climb along an unshaded stretch of highway. *Dolmuşes* frequently pass the Ephesus turn-off, a 20-minute walk from the Lower Gate.

Kuşadası

☏ 0256 / POP 54,660

The fourth busiest cruise port in the entire Mediterranean, Kuşadası has shed its fishing-village roots, offering a decent, if oft-crowded, beach, and some of the coast's headiest nightlife. Think Irish pubs, happy hours, sing-a-longs, tribute acts and swaying discos.

There's a PTT and several banks with ATMs on Barbaros Hayrettin Bulvarı, and a **tourist office** (İskele Meydanı, Liman Caddesi; ⊙8am-noon & 1-5pm Mon-Fri) near the wharf where the cruise ships dock, about 60m west of the caravanserai.

◎ Sights & Activities

Kuşadası is short on specific sights, although the minor **stone fortress** on an island connected to the mainland by a causeway makes a pleasant stroll. There's also **beaches** south of town, a tourist-orientated **bazaar**, Europe's largest water park, **Adaland** (☏618 1252; www.adaland.com; Çamlimanı Mevkii; adult/ child TL40/30; ⊙10am-6pm May-Oct), and PADI scuba-diving courses with **Aquaventure Diving Center** (☏612 7845; www.aquaventure. com.tr; Miracle Beach Club, Kadınlar Denizi).

Numerous operators offer trips to major attractions including Ephesus and Pamukkale (€45), and boat tours.

Priene, Miletus & Didyma   RUINS
(admission TL3; ⊙9am-7.30pm mid-May–mid-Sep, 9am-5.30pm mid-Sep–mid-May) Kuşadası makes a good base for visits to the superb ancient sites of Priene, Miletus and Didyma to the south. Perched high on the craggy slopes of Mt Mykale, Priene has a beautiful, windswept setting; Miletus boasts a spectacular theatre; and in Didyma is the stupendous Temple of Apollo. *Dolmuşes* do not run to Miletus; the easiest way to visit the sites is on a 'PMD' tour from Kuşadası (€50).

🛏 Sleeping

Kuşadası is brimming with accommodation: pensions and business hotels in the centre, and resorts on the bays extending north and south.

Hotel Ilayda   BUSINESS HOTEL €€
(☏614 3807; www.hotelilayda.com; Atatürk Bulvarı 46; s/d TL70/120, ❊@) A recent refurbishment has yielded hip results in the small rooms, and the good restaurant and record-low price tag make the central Ilayda unbeatable.

Atlantique Holiday Club   RESORT €
(☏633 1320; www.atlantiqueclub.com; Karaova Mevkii Sahil Setileri; full board per person from €35; ❊@☒) Seaside resort amenities (swimming pools, tennis courts and a private beach), a clean room with crisp white furnishings, and buffet meals are all included – at backpackers' prices. It's 7km south of the centre (take *dolmuş* No 6).

TURKEY KUŞADASI

Club Caravanserai HISTORIC HOTEL €€
(☎614 4115; www.kusadasihotelcaravanserail.
com; Atatürk Bulvarı 2; s/d/ste incl breakfast
€65/85/150; ✲) This grand 17th-century
caravanserai is a Kuşası landmark. Rooms
are appointed with authentic Ottoman dec-
orations, from handcrafted rugs to ornate
drapery.

✗ Eating & Drinking

The prime dining location is by the picturesque marina. Competition keeps bills
down, but ask in advance the price of seafood and wine.

For cheaper options, head inland. Kaleiçi,
the Old Town behind the post office, has
atmospheric dining rooms and cheap and
cheerful joints.

Barlar Sokak (Bar St) is chock-a-block
with Irish-theme pubs. Locals prefer Kaleiçi's bars and clubs in charming stone
houses and courtyards.

Bebop INTERNATIONAL €€
(☎618 0727; www.bebopjazzclub.com; mains from
TL9; ☺lunch & dinner) At the marina, you could
spend all day at the resort-like Bebop, with
its tantalising swimming pool and jazz beats
late in the evening.

Planet Yucca INTERNATIONAL €€
(☎612 0769; Sağlik Caddesi 56; mains TL12-26;
☺lunch & dinner) This 'Mexican-Chinese-
Turkish Restaurant' serves a veritable UN
of cuisine; stick with the Turkish dishes for
satisfying results. Free taxi pick-ups sweeten
the deal.

Köfteci Ali KÖFTECI €
(Arsanlar Caddesi 14; mains TL5; ☺9am-midnight
winter, summer 24hr) Situated near the entrance of Bar St, this simple street booth does
some terrific spicy wrapped pide kebaps.

❶ Getting There & Around

Boat

Samos All Kuşadası travel agents sell tickets
to the Greek island. Boats (one way/same-day
return €30/35) depart daily between April and
October.

Bus

Dolmuşes run up and down the coast road.
Heading out of Kuşadası, *dolmuşes* leave from
the central Adnan Menderes Bulvarı and the
otogar, out on the bypass road.

Bodrum In summer, three afternoon buses
(TL20, 2½ hours); in winter, take a *dolmuş* to
Söke (TL4).

Selçuk *Dolmuşes* (TL4, 30 minutes, every 15
minutes) via Pamucak and Ephesus.

Bodrum

☎0252 / POP 39,400

The beating heart of a holiday-happy peninsula, Bodrum is a famously posh paradise
where sun-kissed travellers dance the breezy
summer nights away. With laws restricting
the height of its buildings, the town has a
nice architectural uniformity; the idyllic
whitewashed houses with their bright-blue
trim call out to tourists' cameras. Even when
the clubs are bumpin' there's something
rather refined about the town.

◎ Sights & Activities

Day trips to big-ticket sights such as Ephesus and Pamukkale can be booked at travel
agencies and accommodation.

Castle of St Peter MUSEUM
(☎316 2516; www.bodrum-museum.com; admission TL10; ☺9am-noon & 1-5pm Tue-Sun) This
conspicuous castle is Bodrum's star attraction. Built in 1437 by the Knights Hospitaller,
it houses the **Museum of Underwater Archaeology**, arguably the most important
museum of its kind in the world; and other
attractions including, in the **Carian Princess Hall** (admission TL5; ☺10am-noon & 2-4pm
Tue-Sun), the possible remains of Queen Ada,
the last Carian queen.

Mausoleum of Halicarnassus RUINS
(Turgutreis Caddesi; admission TL8; ☺8.30am-
5.30pm Tue-Sun) Sadly there's little left of
the monumental tomb of the Carian leader
Mausolus, which was one of the Seven Wonders of the Ancient World.

Blue Cruises CRUISE
(Western Bay; around €12) Boats moored on
Neyzen Tevfik Caddesi run day trips to nearby spots including Karaada (Black Island),
where hot springs gush out of a cave and
swimmers rub the supposedly curative orange mud on their skin.

🛏 Sleeping

With an efficient shuttle system linking Bodrum to the rest of the peninsula, it's worth
checking out hotels on the other bays. The
town centre is dominated by cheap, usually
lacklustre pensions, with great inns and upmarket sleeps in the hills at the city's edge.
The closer you stay to the sea, the noisier it
is at night.

Su Otel
BOUTIQUE HOTEL €€

(☑316 6906; www.suhotel.net; Turgutreis Caddesi, 1201 Sokak; s/d/ste €55/90/125; ✳@☒) Follow the blue mosaic snake down the alley to find this cheery number with sun-filled bedrooms and radiant Aegean blooms on its blue trellises. Get cosy in the pillowed lounge amid trippy beats.

Mars Otel
PENSION €

(☑316 6559; www.marsotel.com; Turgutreis Caddesi, İmbat Çıkmazi 29; s/d €30/40; ✳@☒) The best budget option, located a five-minute walk from the sea, Mars is a mini-resort with a pool, lounge chairs, small bar and friendly staff. Free *otogar* and port transfers are offered.

Marmara Bodrum
LUXURY HOTEL €€€

(☑313 8130; www.themarmarahotels.com; Suluhasan Caddesi; r/ste incl breakfast from €180/600; ✳@☒) Easily the most upmarket option in town, the gorgeous Marmara Bodrum is perched high in the condo-clad bluffs. The sprawling hotel boasts elegant rooms and excellent amenities, such as the complimentary shuttle to a private beach.

Baç Pansiyon
PENSION €€

(☑316 1602; bacpansiyon@turk.net; Cumhuriyet Caddesi 16; r TL85-100; ✳) A gem amid the market maelstrom, Baç sits right along the water. Hallways are coated in dark marble and have great mood lighting; plasma TVs are an extra perk.

Kaya Pension
PENSION €€

(☑316 5745; www.kayapansiyon.com.tr; Cevat Şakir Caddesi, Eski Hükümet Sokak 14; r incl breakfast TL90; ✳@) Noticeably nicer than most of the other pensions in town (and slightly pricier), Kaya wins the adorable courtyard award, and its rooms are perfectly prim.

Otel Atrium
RESORT €€

(☑316 3926; www.atriumbodrum.com; Fabrika Sokak 21; s/d half-board from TL80/110; ✳@☒) For only a small step up from pension prices, Otel Atrium offers luscious gardens and an informal resort atmosphere, with a sociable pool area and friendly staff. It fills up quickly.

✗ Eating & Drinking

New restaurants emerge all the time, but most upmarket eats are found along the Western Bay; in the east you'll find filler food after a night at the adjacent bars and nightclubs.

Central Bodrum offers everything from pizza and sushi to local joints serving seasonal mezes and fresh-from-the-sea fish. Swing by the **fruit market** (Cevat Şakir Caddesi) during the day.

For drinking follow the normal rule of thumb: for cheap and cheerful head to the Eastern Bay; for expensive and classy, think Western Bay. Dr Alim Bey Caddesi and Cumhuriyet Caddesi function as Bodrum's waterfront 'Bar Street'.

TOP CHOICE Fish Market
SEAFOOD €€

(Cevat Şakir Caddesi; fish/meze TL20/from TL4; ⊙dinner Mon-Sat) This small network of back alleys overflows with tables and locals gorging on fish and *rakı*. Order drinks and mezes, then head to the fishmongers to select your catch (avoid the cheap farm fish), which the restaurant will cook for an extra TL4. Book in advance.

Orfoz
AEGEAN €€€

(☑316 4285; www.orfoz.com/bodrum.htm; Cumhuriyet Caddesi 177/B; mains from TL20; ⊙dinner) Across a backstreet from Halıkarnas, Orfoz is often lauded as Bodrum's best seafood restaurant. The homemade food is sensational, but served in small portions; with wine you're looking at about TL100 per person.

Döner Tepecik
FAST FOOD €

(Neyzen Tevfik Caddesi; döner TL4) Bodrum's best *döner* shop, this hole in the wall serves scrumptious snacks. Look for the striped white-and-blue awning directly across from the mosque and ask for your *döner* on homemade toasted bread.

La Pasión
SPANISH €€

(Restaurante Español; www.lapasion-bodrum.com; Atatürk Caddesi, Uslu Sokak 8; menu TL35; ⊙lunch & dinner) This inviting restaurant fills an old flower-strewn courtyard and a charming stone house. Bossa nova moves through air as Iberian-inspired platters are served.

Moonlight
BAR

(www.moonlightbodrum.com; Cumhuriyet Caddesi 60/B) Nurse your Efes right along the rolling tide at one of hectic Cumhuriyet Caddesi's more chilled out and atmospheric spots, down a side street opposite Körfez.

☆ Entertainment

Nightclubs such as kitschy **Halıkarnas** (www.halikarnas.com.tr; Cumhuriyet Caddesi 178; weekday/weekend TL35/40; ⊙10pm-5am summer) and the floating **Marine Club Catamaran**

Bodrum

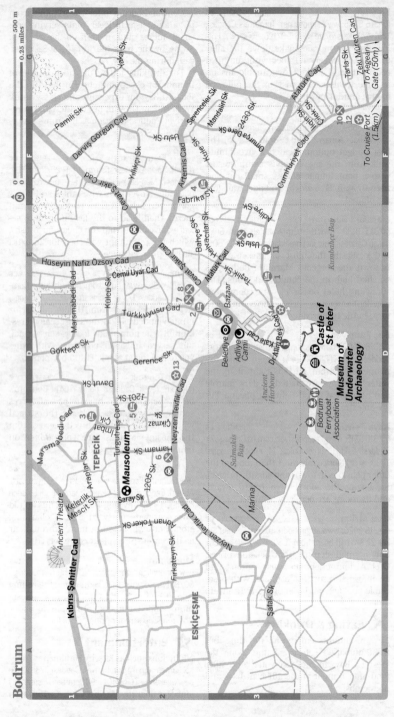

500 m
0.25 miles

Mausoleum

Castle of St Peter

Museum of Underwater Archaeology

Kumbahçe Bay

Salmakis Bay

Ancient Harbour

Marina

Bodrum Ferryboat Association

Ancient Theatre

TEPECİK

ESKİÇEŞME

Kıbrıs Şehitler Cad

Marsmabedi Cad

Arayapar Sk

Mescit Sk

Kelerlik

Saray Sk

1205 Sk

Hamam Sk

Adnan Toker Cad

Firkateyn Sk

Şafak Sk

Neyzen Tevfik Cad

Çıkmaz Sk

Turgutreis Cad

İmbat Çık

Davut Sk

1201 Sk

Göktepe Sk

Gerence Sk

Türkkuyusu Cad

Cemil Uyar Cad

Hüseyin Nafiz Özsoy Cad

Kulcu Sk

Marsmabedi Cad

Cevat Şakir Cad

Yıldırım Sk

Artemis Cad

Fabrika Sk

Bahçe Sk

Hevacılar Sk

Atatürk Cad

Taşlık Sk

Uslu Sk

Kadıye Sk

Cumhuriyet Cad

İğdır Sk

Çiçek Sk

Tarla Sk

Zeki Müren Cad

Atatürk Cad

Omurça Dere Sk

2490 Sk

Mandalın Sk

Sevenceler Sk

Krije Sk

Uslu Sk

Derviş Görgün Cad

Pamili Sk

Yaka Sk

Bazaar

Belediye

Adliye Camii

Dr Alim Bey Cad

Kale Cad

To Cruise Port (1.5km)

To Aegean Gate (50m)

Bodrum

◎ Top Sights

🛏 Sleeping

🍽 Eating

☕ Drinking

✦ Entertainment

(www.clubcatamaran.com; Dr Alimbey Caddesi; weekday/weekend TL35/40; ⊙10pm-4am mid-May–Sep) are famous party spots, but there are quieter clubs such as **Helva** (www.helvabodrum.com; Neyzen Tevfik Caddesi 54; ⊙2pm-3am), mostly aimed at Turkish trendsetters. As with eating and drinking, Eastern Bay venues are cheaper than the Western Bay.

❶ Information

Head to Cevat Şakir Caddesi for the PTT and ATMs.

Tourist office (Kale Meydanı; ⊙8am-6pm Mon-Fri, daily in summer) Beside the Castle of St Peter.

❶ Getting There & Away

Air

Airlines including Turkish Airlines and Atlasjet fly from İstanbul and elsewhere to Bodrum International Airport, which is 60km away and connected to Bodrum by Havaş shuttle bus (TL17).

Boat

For tickets and the latest times, contact the **Bodrum Ferryboat Association** (www.bodrum ferryboat.com; Kale Caddesi Cümrük Alanı 22).

Kos (one way or same-day return €28, one hour) Daily ferries to/from the Greek island.

Rhodes (Rhodos; one way or same-day return €60, 2¼ hours) From June to September there are two weekly hydrofoils to/from the Greek island.

Datça (single/return TL25/40, two hours) Daily ferries from mid-June to September; three weekly from April to mid-June and in October.

Bus

There are services to more or less anywhere you could wish to go.

İstanbul (TL60-81, 12 hours, 10 nightly)
Kuşadası (TL20, 2½ hours, four afternoon)
Marmaris (TL18, three hours, hourly)

THE MEDITERRANEAN COAST

The Western Mediterranean, known as the 'Turquoise Coast', is a region of endless azure sea lined with kilometres of sandy beaches and backed by mountains rising up to almost 3000m. It also has an embarrassment of ancient ruins strewn through the aromatic scrub and pine forests, and a sophisticated menu of sports and activities.

The Med's seamless mix of history and holiday inspires and excites. The most dramatic way to see this stretch of coastline is aboard a *gület* (traditional wooden yacht) or by walking sections of the 500km-long Lycian Way, high above the crystal waters known locally as the Akdeniz (White Sea).

The Eastern Mediterranean, meanwhile, has long lived in its more fashionable western neighbour's shadow. But the area facing Syria has Christian sites, Hittite settlements and Crusade castles between its timeless hillside villages, mountains and stunning coastline.

Marmaris

📞 0252 / POP 40,000

A popular resort town with a population that swells to more than 200,000 people during summer, in-your-face Marmaris is the closest thing Mediterranean Turkey has to Spain's Costa del Sol. Bar St offers unparalleled decadence and charter-boat touts will happily whisk you to Fethiye and beyond. Lord Nelson organised his fleet in the stunning natural harbour here before attacking the French at Abukir in 1798.

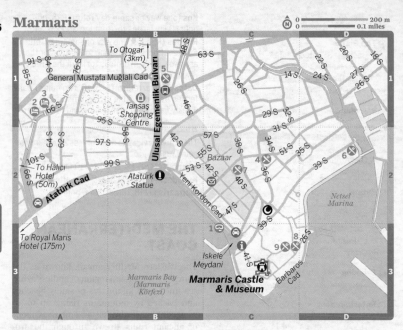

⊙ Sights & Activities

Castle   FORTRESS, MUSEUM
(admission TL3; ⊙8am-noon & 1-5pm Tue-Sun)
The small castle houses an archaeology museum and offers lovely views of Marmaris.

Datça and Bozburun Peninsulas   NATURE
Not far south, these deeply indented peninsulas, reached by *dolmuş* or boat, hide azure bays backed by pine-covered mountains and gorgeous fishing villages.

Boat Trips   CRUISE
Between May and October, numerous 'dolmuş boats' offer day tours of Marmaris Bay, its islands and beaches, usually for between TL25 and TL30 per person. Check where the excursion goes, which boat you'll be on and what's on the lunch menu.

To get off the beaten current, hiring a boat with a group will take you to quieter coves (around €300 for up to seven people). **Zeus Boat** (☑0532 247 4974; http://zeus-boat. netfirms.com) is reliable.

Overnight and two- and three-day excursions often go to Dalyan and Kaunos; longer, more serious charter trips go to Datça and Knidos or along the Bozburun Peninsula; and 'Blue Voyages' (p949) sail to Fethiye and beyond.

Marmaris

Diving   DIVING
Several centres along Yeni Kordon Caddesi offer scuba-diving excursions and courses (April to October). Also recommended:

Deep Blue Dive Center (☑0541 374 5881; www.sealung.com) Offers a three-day PADI open water course (€240) and day excursions (€29 including equipment, two dives and lunch).

🛏 Sleeping

Marmaris is geared towards all-in package tour groups, so good-value independent sleeping options are rare.

Royal Maris Hotel
HOTEL €€€
(☎412 8383; www.royalmarishotel.com; Atatürk Caddesi 34; s/d/tr TL110/170/200; P ✽ ❄ ⚴) A good-value choice, with two pools, a private beach, a *hammam* and fitness centre, a roof terrace and spacious balconies with stunning views.

Maltepe Pansiyon
PENSION €
(☎412 1629, 0532 346 4244; www.maltepepansiyon.com; 66 Sokak 9; s/d TL30/60; ✽ @) The shady garden is just one of the attractions of this long-time backpacker's favourite. Rooms are small but spotless, there's free use of the kitchen and a helpful manager.

Özcan Pansiyon
PENSION €
(☎412 7761; ozcanpansitonmarmaris@hotmail.com; 66 Sokak 17; s/d TL35/60; ✽) Resembling an old apartment block from the outside, this good-value pension has a pleasant garden terrace. Balconies and en suite bathrooms feature in some rooms.

Halıcı Hotel
HOTEL €€
(☎495 8201; www.halicihotel.com; Çam Sokak 1; s/d TL70/140; P ✽ @ ⚴) The enormous 'Carpet Seller Hotel's' bread and butter is package tours, so expect facilities from pools and bars to a tropical garden.

🍴 Eating & Drinking

Marmaris is a party town and hedonists should join the crowds at the aptly named **Bar St** (39 Sokak), where there are regular foam parties.

Ney
RESTAURANT €€
(☎412 0217; 26 Sokak 24; meze TL5-6, mains TL14-20) Tucked away up some steps from the marina is this tiny, delightful restaurant in a 250-year-old Greek house. The delicious home cooking includes *tavuklu mantı böreği* (Turkish ravioli with chicken).

Liman Restaurant
SEAFOOD €€
(☎412 6336; 40 Sokak 38; meze TL6-12, mains TL10-20; ⊙8am-1am) Something of an institution for its fish dishes, meze and *kavurma* (a kind of lamb stir fry), this lively restaurant is in the covered bazaar.

Panorama Restaurant & Bar
INTERNATIONAL €€
(☎413 4835; Hacı İmam Sokağı 40; mains TL10-15; ⊙9am-1am) Just off 26 Sokak, this favourite for a drink with a view also serves simple dishes, like pizza, pasta and omelettes, on its celebrated terrace overlooking the marina.

İdil Mantı Evi
LOCAL €€
(39 Sokak 140; meze TL5-6, mains TL8-20; ⊙4pm-5am) A great spot on Bar St for night nibbles.

Alin's Cafe and Restaurant
FAMILY RESTAURANT €€
(36 Sokak 23; mains TL5.90-14.90; ⊙8am-12.30am) This chain is full of Turkish families feasting on healthy grills, burgers and spuds.

Doyum
KEBAPÇI €€
(☎413 4977; Ulusal Egemenlik Bulvarı 14; mains TL4-12; ⊙24hr) A good place for early breakfasts and veggie dishes.

ℹ Information

Mavi Internet (☎413 4979; 26 Sokak 8; per hr TL2; ⊙9am-11pm) In the Old Town near Ney restaurant.

Tourist office (☎412 1035; İskele Meydanı 2; ⊙8am-noon & 1-5pm Mon-Fri, daily Jun–mid-Sep) Right below the castle; very unhelpful.

ℹ Getting There & Away

Air
The nearest airports are at Dalaman, reached on a shuttle bus, and Bodrum.

Boat
Rhodes (Greece; one way/same-day return from €43/45, 50 minutes) Catamarans sail twice daily from mid-April to October. The Sunday morning service runs sporadically in June and July. Buy tickets from Marmaris agencies at least one day in advance.

Bus
The *otogar* is 3km north of the centre, and there are ticket offices around the Tansaş Shopping Centre. Buses include:
Bodrum (TL18, 3¼ hours, at least every two hours)
Fethiye (TL16, three hours, half-hourly) via Ortaca (for Dalyan; TL10, 1½ hours)
İzmir (TL30, 4¼ hours, hourly)

Dalyan
☎0252 / POP 3000
Dalyan is a laid-back riverside community with a strong farming pedigree and a growing penchant for package tourism. It makes an excellent base for exploring the surrounding fertile waterways, in particular Lake Köyceğiz and the turtle-nesting grounds at İztuzu Beach.

In summer excursion boats go out to explore the river and the lake. You can save yourself a lot of money and hassle by taking a cruise or river *dolmuş* run by the **Dalyan Kooperatifi** (☎0541 505 0777), southwest of the main square. The cooperative's standard tour (about TL30 including lunch) takes in the **Sultaniye hot springs and mud baths** on the shores of Lake Köyceğiz, the ruined city of **Kaunos** (admission TL8; ⊘8.30am-5.30pm) and unspoilt **İztuzu Beach** on the Mediterranean coast.

🛏 Sleeping & Eating

The best accommodation is found along the main drag, Maraş Caddesi, and its continuation, Kaunos Sokak. Dalyan's restaurants vary greatly in quality, so be selective.

TOP **Happy Caretta** HOTEL €€
CHOICE
(☎284 2109; www.happycaretta.com; Kaunos Sokak 26; s/d TL100/150; ❄@) The magical garden has cypress trees, palms and caged songbirds, and the small, simple rooms are stylishly decorated with natural materials. There's also a lovely boat and leisure dock, night views of the illuminated King's Tombs, and superb home-cooked meals.

Kilim Hotel HOTEL €€
(☎284 2253; www.kilimhotel.com; Kaunos Sokak 11; s/d TL40/80; ❄☀) English owner Becky presides over this buzzing hotel filled with *kilims* (woven rugs) and art, with a somewhat rustic annexe near the river. There's a wheelchair ramp and daily yoga and aerobic workouts.

Dalyan Camping CAMPING GROUND €
(☎284 5316; Maraş Caddesi 144; per tent/caravan TL10/20, large/small bungalows per person TL20/25; ⊘Apr-Oct) This well-shaded, river-side site is centrally located opposite the tombs.

Kösk FAMILY RESTAURANT €€
(☎0537 352 4770; 84 2877; Maraş Caddesi; mains 10-14; ⊘8am-11pm) This little place is Dalyan's busiest eatery, thanks to its home-style meze and grills. Watch the evening parade from the forecourt.

ℹ Getting There & Away

From Cumhuriyet Meydanı near the mosque, minibuses go to Ortaca *otogar* (TL3, hourly/every 25 minutes in high/low season), for buses to locations including Dalaman (TL4, 15 minutes).
Dalaman airport A taxi costs TL75.

Fethiye

📞0252 / POP 74,000

In 1958 an earthquake levelled the harbour city of Fethiye, sparing only the ancient remains of Telmessos. Fifty years on, Fethiye is once again a prosperous and proud hub of the Western Mediterranean. Its natural harbour, tucked away in the southern reaches of a broad bay scattered with pretty islands, is perhaps the region's finest.

◉ Sights & Activities

Dolmuşes run southeast to the **Lycian ruins** dotting the countryside, including Pınara, Letoön and Xanthos.

Fethiye offers numerous water-based activities and tours, including the **12-Island Tour** (TL25 per person), the **Butterfly Valley tour** (TL25) via Ölüdeniz, and the **Dalyan tour** (TL45).

Telmessos RUINS
In central Fethiye, little remains of the city of Telmessos (400 BC) other than a **Roman theatre** and **Lycian sarcophagi**. The cliffs hold several rock-cut tombs, including the Ionic **Tomb of Amyntas** (admission TL8; ⊘8am-5pm). **Fethiye Museum** (505 Sokak; admission TL5; ⊘8.30am-5pm) has some small statues and votive stones from Telmessos and other Lycian sites.

Crusader Fortress FORTRESS
The ruined tower south of town belongs to this 15th-century fortress.

Lycian Way WALK
Fethiye is at the western end of this 500km walking trail (p986), which passes Ölüdeniz.

Kayaköy HISTORIC AREA
(admission TL8; ⊘8.30am-6pm) *Dolmuşes* run to this nearby open-air museum, an evocative Ottoman Greek 'ghost town' that was abandoned after the population exchange of 1923.

Saklıkent Gorge NATURE
Minibuses and tours (TL45) also run to this beautiful gorge, an 18km-long crack in the Akdağlar mountains too narrow, in places, for even sunlight to squeeze through.

Tlos RUINS
Saklıkent *dolmuşes* pass Güneşli – disembark for these **Lycian ruins** (admission TL8; ⊘8.30am-6pm).

Fethiye is the hub of Turkey's cruising scene, and the most popular route is the 'Blue Voyage' *(Mavi Yolculuk)* to Olympos: a four-day, three-night journey on a *gület* (traditional wooden sailing boat) that attracts young party animals. Boats usually call in at Ölüdeniz and Butterfly Valley and stop at Kaş, Kalkan and Kekova, with the final night at Gökkaya Bay opposite the eastern end of Kekova. A less common (but some say prettier) route is between Marmaris and Fethiye.

Depending on the season the price is €135 to €185 per person (food and water should be included). Make sure you shop around – there are many shoddy operators working the waters and wallets. Recommended operators include **Before Lunch Cruises** (☎0535-636 0076; www.beforelunch.com), **Ocean Turizm & Travel Agency** (☎612 4807; www.oceantravelagency.com) and **Olympos Yachting** (☎0242-892 1145; www.olymposyachting.com).

For more-ambitious trips you can charter the whole boat yourself, with or without crew, and set off wherever the fancy takes you. Fethiye and Marmaris are both good starting points.

🛏 Sleeping

Most accommodation is up the hill behind the marina in Karagözler or further west. Many pensions organise transport from the *otogar*.

TOP CHOICE **Yildirim Guest House**

HOSTEL, PENSION **€€**
(☎614 4627; www.yildirimguesthouse.com; Fevzi Çakmak Caddesi 37; dm/s/d/tr TL25/35/70/105; ❋@) Shipshape Yildirim includes four- to six-bed dorms and spotless rooms, some facing the harbour. Well-travelled host Omer offers excursions, laundry and dinner.

Ferah Pension

HOSTEL, PENSION **€**
(☎614 2816; www.ferahpension.com; Ortdu Caddesi 23; dm/s/d TL20/30/50; ❋@) 'Monica's place' has a leafy, glass-enclosed lobby terrace and little pool, with paintings and 'sexy dinners' by the owner. The sizeable, tidy rooms include two small dorms.

Villa Daffodil

PENSION **€€**
(☎614 9595; www.villadaffodil.com; Fevzi Çakmak Caddesi 139; s/d TL75/100; ❋) This large, Ottoman-styled, flowered-bedecked guest house is a rare survivor of the earthquake and development. Rooms are homely and have stylish furnishings; the best have balconies and sea views.

🍴 Eating & Drinking

Fethiye's enormous canalside Tuesday **market** takes place between Atatürk Caddesi and Pürşabey Caddesi next to the stadium.

Serious partygoers head to Hisarönü, an expat-choked suburb 12km to the southeast.

Fethiye's bars and nightclubs are mostly on Hamam Sokak in the Old Town, and along Dispanser Caddesi south of the Martyrs' Monument.

TOP CHOICE **Meğri Lokantasi**

LOKANTA **€€€**
(☎614 4047; www.megrirestaurant.com; Çarşı Caddesi 26; mains TL14-25; ◷8am-2am) Excellent at lunchtime, and with locals spilling onto the streets, the Meğri does hearty home-style cooking including *güveç* (casserole) at palatable prices.

Deniz Restaurant

SEAFOOD **€€**
(☎612 0212; Uğur Mumcu Parkı Yanı 10/1; mains TL12-25) Probably Fethiye's best seafood restaurant away from the market, the 'Sea' exhibits everything alive and swimming in tanks (the grouper is best). Meze such as *semizotu* (purslane) in yogurt and *ceviche* (fish preserved in lemon juice) are excellent.

Paşa Kebab

KEBAPÇI **€**
(☎614 9807; Çarşı Caddesi 42; meze, pide, kebaps & pizza TL4-13.50; ◷9am-1am) Considered locally to offer Fethiye's best kebabs, unpretentious Paşa has a well-priced menu with useful photos of dishes. Try the Paşa Special (TL12.50), a gigantic beef, tomato and cheese concoction.

Recep's Place

SEAFOOD **€€**
(☎614 8297; Hal ve Pazar Yeri 51; mains TL10-20; ◷10am-midnight) You can taste Fethiye's fabulous fish by purchasing your own (per kilo TL18 to TL25) from the fishmongers in the central covered market and getting it cooked at one of the restaurants opposite. Our favourite restaurant, Recep's, charges

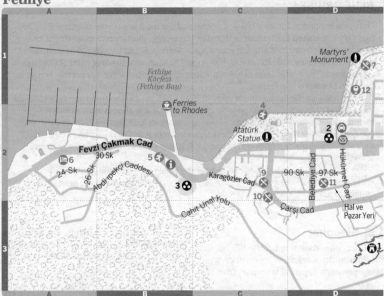

Fethiye Körfezi (Fethiye Bay)

TL5 for the service, with accompanying sauce, green salad, garlic bread, fruit and coffee.

Val's Cocktail Bar   BAR
(☎612 2363; Uğur Mumcu Parkı Yanı; ⊙9am-1am) Englishwoman Val's cute little bar stocks a mean selection of poison and strong coffee, as well as having a free lending library and a resident grey parrot.

ℹ Information

Millennium Internet Cafe (503 Sokak 2/A; per hr TL1.50; ⊙8am-midnight) Southeast of the Martyrs' Monument.

Tourist office (☎614 1527; İskele Meydanı; ⊙8am-noon & 1-5pm Mon-Fri) Helpful centre opposite the marina.

ℹ Getting There & Away

Boat

Rhodes (Greece; one way/same-day return €58/65, 1½ hours) Catamarans sail between mid-April and October.

Bus

Fethiye's *otogar* is 2.5km east of the centre.
Antalya (TL18, four hours) The inland *(yayla)* road is quicker than the coastal *(sahil)* route (TL25, 7½ hours, hourly in summer) via the following destinations.
Kalkan (TL10, 1½ hours)

Kaş (TL12, 2½ hours)
Olympos (TL22, five hours)

Dolmuş

From the stops near the mosque, minibuses run to local destinations including:
Ölüdeniz (TL4, 25 minutes)

Ölüdeniz

☎0252 / POP 2000

Ölüdeniz's many charms – a sheltered lagoon beside a lush national park, a long spit of sandy beach, and Baba Dağ (Mt Baba) casting its shadow across the sea – have been a curse as much as a blessing. Many people think package tourism has turned 'Dead Sea' into a Paradise Lost. But Ölüdeniz remains a good place to party before continuing to the less-frenetic Butterfly Valley.

The **lagoon** (admission TL4; ⊙8am-8pm) remains a lovely place to while away a few hours on the beach with mountains soaring above you. Ölüdeniz is also a hot spot for **paragliding** (and parasailing). Companies here offer tandem paragliding flights off Baba Dağ (1960m) for TL100 to TL160.

Day cruises (TL20) explore the coast, and shuttle boats head south to the beautiful **Butterfly Valley** (TL15 return). There are

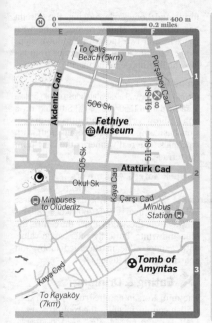

laid-back accommodation options in the valley and nearby Faralya and Kabak.

🛏 Sleeping & Eating

Ölüdeniz's camping grounds are almost like budget resorts, with comfortable and stylish bungalows.

TOP CHOICE Sugar Beach Club

CAMPING GROUND, RESORT €€
(☏617 0048; www.thesugarbeachclub.com; Ölüdeniz Caddesi 20; campsite/bungalow per person TL10/TL50-140; ❄@) The pick of the crop for backpackers, this ultra-chilled Turkish-Australian venture has a palm-shaded beach, lounging areas and a waterfront bar and restaurant. Canoes and pedalos can be hired, there's an on-site shop and barbecues are a regular occurrence. Non-guests can use the sun lounges, parasols and showers (TL5).

Oba Motel Restaurant FAMILY RESTAURANT €€
(☏617 0158; Mimar Sınan Caddesi; mains TL15-25; ☺8am-midnight) The leafy Oba Motel's log-cabin restaurant has a reputation for home-style food at reasonable prices, including six veggie dishes and homemade muesli with mountain yoghurt and local pine honey.

ⓘ Getting There & Away

Fethiye (TL4, 25 minutes) Frequent minibuses.

Patara

☏0242 / POP 950

With Turkey's longest uninterrupted beach, laid-back little Patara (Gelemiş) is the perfect spot to mix your ruin-rambling with some dedicated sand-shuffling. The extensive **ruins** (admission TL5; ☺9am-5pm) include a triple-arched triumphal gate and a necropolis containing Lycian tombs. All in all, the former hippy-trail stop offers a good combination of nature, culture and traditional village life.

🛏 Sleeping & Eating

Patara View Point Hotel HOTEL €€
(☏843 5184; www.pataraviewpoint.com; s/d TL60/90; ❄@☀) Uphill from the main road, this stylish hotel has killer views over the valley from its Ottoman-style cushioned terrace and rooms with balconies. There's also a daily tractor-shuttle to/from the beach.

Flower Pension PENSION €
(☏843 5164; www.pataraflowerpension.com; s/d/ apt from TL20/40/50; ❄@) On the road before the turn to the centre, the Flower

Pension has simple, airy rooms with balconies overlooking a garden. There's a free shuttle to the beach. Studios and apartments have kitchens.

Akay Pension PENSION €
(☏843 5055; www.pataraakaypension.com; s/d/t TL35/50/60; ✴@) Run by helpful Kazım and Ayşe, the Akay has well-maintained rooms with comfortable beds and balconies overlooking citrus groves. Ayşe's cooking is legendary and set meals are available from TL15.

Tlos Restaurant FAMILY RESTAURANT €€
(☏843 5135 meze €5, mains €12-20;⊙8am-midnight) The Tlos has an open kitchen and is shaded by a large plane tree. The *güveç* is recommended. It's BYO.

❶ Getting There & Away

Buses on the Fethiye–Kaş route drop you on the highway 4km from the village. From here hourly *dolmuşes* run to the village.

In season minibuses run from the beach through the village to:
Fethiye (TL10, 1½ hours)
Kalkan (TL5, 20 minutes)
Kaş (TL8, 45 minutes)

Kalkan
☏0242 / POP 3600

Kalkan is a stylish hillside harbour town overlooking a sparkling blue bay. It's as rightly famous for its restaurants as its small but pretty beach, and makes an upmarket alternative to neighbouring Kaş. Development continues on the hills, but the former Ottoman-Greek fishing village's charms are found in the compact Old Town.

🛌 Sleeping

TOP CHOICE Hotel Villa Mahal LUXURY HOTEL €€€
(☏844 3268; www.villamahal.com; d €180-290; ✴🛏) One of Turkey's most elegant and stylish hotels lies atop a cliff outside town. The individually designed, minimalist rooms have private terraces and breathtaking sea and sunset views. Steps lead to the sea and a bathing platform. There's a free water taxi into Kalkan.

Caretta Boutique Hotel HOTEL €€
(☏844 3435; www.carettaboutiquehotel.com; İskele Sokak 3; s/d from TL80/120; ✴@) A perennial favourite for its isolated swimming plat-

forms and home-style cooking, the Caretta has bright and sunny rooms, some with jacuzzis, and two tucked away down steps along the cliff. There's boat service from below the lighthouse in the marina.

White House Pension PENSION €€
(☏844 3738; www.kalkanwhitehouse.co.uk; 5 Nolu Sokak; s/d from TL50/100; ✴@) Situated on a quiet hilltop corner, this attentively run pension has compact, breezy rooms, four with balconies. The real winner is the view from the terrace.

Kelebek Hotel & Apartments HOTEL, APARTMENT €
(☏844 3770; www.butterflyholidays.co.uk; Mantese Mah 4; s/d/apt from TL30/50/60; ✴@🛏) Slightly away from the action above the centre, the blue-and-white 'Butterfly' offers good value, with a pool table in the tiled lobby and apartments with kitchens.

🍴 Eating & Drinking

The mini Korsan empire, run by a Turkish-British couple, includes the rooftop **Korsan Fish Terrace** (☏844 3076; www.korsankalkan. com; Atatürk Caddesi; mains TL25-32; ⊙10am-midnight), arguably Kalkan's finest seafood experience, with legendary homemade lemonade and live jazz on Tuesday night; **Korsan Meze** (☏844 3622; Yat Limanı; mains TL20-30; 🎵), serving modern Turkish and international cuisine opposite the beach; and **Korsan Kebap** (☏844 2116; Atatürk Caddesi; mains TL12-25; 🎵), with a harbourside terrace and upmarket kebaps and pide.

Maya FAMILY RESTAURANT €€€
(☏844 1145; Hasan Altan Caddesi; mains €19-26; ⊙7pm-midnight) Sevilay's homely eatery offers three different meze and four mains every day of the week. Shoot for a seat on the small roof terrace.

Öz Adana KEBAPÇI €€
(☏844 1140; Yalıboyu Mah; mains TL7-11) Just opposite the first roundabout and the turning to Kalamar, the 'Original Adana' serves Kalkan's best kebaps, pide and *lahmacun*.

Ali Baba MUTFAK €
(☏844 3627; Hasan Altan Caddesi; mains TL4-12.50; ⊙24hr/5am-midnight summer/winter) With generous opening hours and relatively low prices, everybody's favourite local cheapie does decent breakfasts and veggie dishes.

Moonlight Bar
BAR

(2844 3043; Süleyman Yılmaz Caddesi 17) Kalkan's oldest bar is still its most 'happening', though a good percentage of the people sitting outside and around the small dance floor are visitors.

ⓘ Getting There & Away

Minibuses go to:

Fethiye (TL10, 1½ hours)
Kaş (TL5, 35 minutes)
Patara (TL5, 25 minutes)

Kaş
☎0242 / POP 5930

A much more genuine destination than Kalkan, Kaş (literally 'cash') may not sport the finest beach culture in the region, but this yachties' haven has a wonderfully mellow atmosphere. The surrounding areas are ideal for day trips by sea or scooter, and a plethora of adventure sports are on offer, in particular some excellent wreck diving.

The **tourist office** (☎836 1238; ☺8amnoon & 1-5pm Mon-Fri) is on the main square; log on at **Computer World** (per hr TL2; ☺9am-11pm), opposite the PTT.

⊙ Sights & Activities

Apart from enjoying the small pebble beaches, you can walk west a few hundred metres to the well-preserved **Hellenistic theatre**. You also can walk to the **rock tombs** in the cliffs above town, left from the Lycian port of Antiphellos. It's well worth climbing the hilly street to the east of the main square to reach the **Lion Tomb**, a Lycian sarcophagus mounted on a high base. Overland excursions and *dolmuşes* go to Saklıkent Gorge.

Boat Trip
CRUISE

The most popular trip (TL50) is to Üçağız and Kekova, a three-hour bus-and-boat excursion that includes several interesting ruins as well as swimming stops. Other standard tours go to the Mavi Mağara (Blue Cave), Patara and Kalkan, or to Longos and several small nearby islands.

Bougainville Travel
WATER SPORTS

(☎836 3737; www.bougainville-turkey.com; İbrahim Selin Sokak 10) This long-established English-Turkish tour operator offers scuba-diving, paragliding, mountain biking, canyoning, sea-kayaking and canoeing. Kayaking over

the sunken ruins alongside Kekova Island is suitable for all fitness levels.

🛏 Sleeping

TOP CHOICE **Hideaway Hotel**
HOTEL €€

(☎836 1887; www.hotelhideaway.com; Amfitiyatro Sokak 7; s/d TL80/110; ❋@≋) The quiet, aptly named Hideaway is at the far end of town. Many of the comfortable rooms with a balcony face the sea, and there's a roof terrace overlooking the water and amphitheatre. Rooms have DVD players and honour-system bars. Cheap meals are available.

White House Pension
PENSION €€

(☎836 1513; www.orcholiday.com; Yeni Cami Caddesi 10; s/d TL65/100; ❋@) This stylish little gem in wood, wrought iron, marble and terracotta paint has attractive rooms – including an attic room with a lovely balcony – and a pretty terrace.

Gardenia Boutique Hotel
BOUTIQUE HOTEL €€€

(☎836 2368; www.gardeniahotel-kas.com; Hükümet Caddesi 41; r €80-110; ❋) This stylishly restrained hostelry is southeast of the centre, towards the beaches. Rooms have wicker, fringed lampshades and leather seating in reds and browns, and there's also a rooftop terrace.

Santosa Pansiyon
PENSION €

(☎836 1714; www.santosapension.com; Recep Bilgin Sokak 4; s/d TL45/70; ❋@) Clean, quiet and cheap, this backpacker hang-out has simple but attractively decorated rooms that are excellent value. The couple who run Santosa are cooks; try their barbecue or vegetarian set meals.

🍴 Eating

There are some excellent restaurants southeast of the main square, especially around Sandıkçı Sokak. A big outdoor Friday market takes place along the old road to Kalkan.

TOP CHOICE **İkbal**
MODERN TURKISH €€€

(☎836 3193; Sandıkçı Sokak 6; mains TL18-30; ☺9am-midnight) Kaş' best restaurant, run by a Turkish-German couple, serves excellent prepared fish dishes and slow-cooked leg of lamb. In addition to the small, well-chosen menu, there's a good selection of Turkish wines from Mediterranean vineyards.

Bi Lokma
MUTFAK €€

(☎836 3942; Hükümet Caddesi 2; mains TL9.50-20; ☺9am-midnight) 'Mama's Kitchen' has

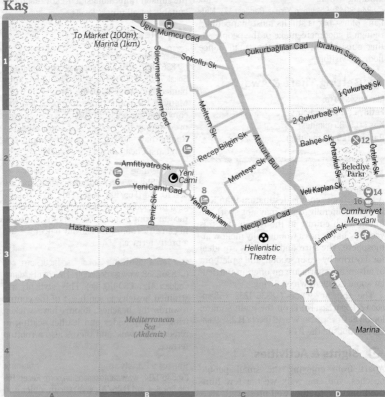

tables strewn around a terraced garden overlooking the harbour. The great traditional dishes include *mantı* and *börek*.

Cafe Mola CAFE €€
(☑836 1994; Emin Erdem Meydanı 3/B; dishes TL7-10; ☺9am-11pm) This convivial cafe with an espresso machine is great for Turkish breakfast, sandwiches, *mantı* and fresh lemonade.

Blue House MUTFAK €€
(☑836 1320; Sandıkçı Sokak 8; mains TL20-30) This blue-doored restaurant with a distinctive balcony has a great atmosphere and lovely views. The excellent meze are the main reason for coming. The ladies work from their home kitchen, which you pass through to reach the terrace.

Bahçe Restaurant LOCAL €€
(☑836 2370; Uzun Çarşı Sokak 31; mains TL14-30; ☺10am-midnight) Up behind the Lion Tomb, Bahçe has a pretty garden and serves excellent dishes at decent prices, including meze and fish in paper.

Drinking

There are a couple of buzzing bars in Kaş: not the kind of boisterous places you find elsewhere in southwest Turkey, but more civilised venues, heavy on atmosphere. Check out:

Hideaway Cafe & Bar (Cumhuriyet Caddesi 16/A) This enchanting cafe/garden is accessible from the street via a secret doorway opposite the Noel Baba Cafe.

Echo Cafe & Bar (Limanı Sokak) Sip fruit daiquiris with Kaş high society at this hip and stylish lounge. The airy upstairs sections hosts exhibitions and has nice little balconies overlooking the water.

Noel Baba Cafe (Cumhuriyet Meydanı 1) Occupying a shaded terrace on the main square with views of the harbour, this is a

favourite local meeting point – but it has become rather pricey in recent years.

Hi-Jazz Bar (Zümrüt Sokak 3) This mellow little bar has canned (and sometimes live) jazz. It's a very friendly and a cosy spot, but with no outside space it's not one for the height of summer.

❶ Getting There & Away

Boat
Meis (Kastellorizo) The **Meis Express** (☑836 1725; www.meisexpress.com; same-day return TL40; 20min) fast ferry sails daily throughout the year to the tiny Greek island. It's possible to spend the night there, or continue to Rhodes. Tickets can be bought from travel agencies or directly from Meis Express in the harbour.

Bus
İstanbul (TL65, 15 hours, daily)
Fethiye (TL12, 2½ hours, hourly in summer) Change here for Ankara and İzmir.

Dolmuş
There are regular *dolmuşes* to:
Antalya (TL16, 3½ hours)
Fethiye (TL12; 2½ hours)
Kalkan (TL5, 35 minutes)
Olympos (TL15, 2½ hours)
Patara (TL8, 45 minutes)

Olympos & Çirali
☑0242

Olympos has long had ethereal appeal to travellers. It was an important Lycian city in the 2nd century BC, when the Olympians devoutly worshipped Hephaestus (Vulcan), the god of fire. No doubt this veneration sprang from reverence for the mysterious Chimaera, an eternal flame that still burns in the ground nearby. Along with the other Lycian coastal cities, Olympos went into decline in the 1st century BC, before its fortunes twisted and turned through Roman rule, 3rd-century AD pirate attacks, and fortress building during the Middle Ages by the

Venetians and Genoese. By the 15th century the site had been abandoned.

Neighbouring Çıralı, over the mountain and the narrow Ulupınar Stream, is another gem of a place. While Olympos has a well-established party reputation (though it has gentrified considerably), Çıralı is a family-friendly place to experience the fine art of *keyif* (quiet relaxation).

◉ Sights & Activities

You can swim at the beach fronting the ruins of Olympos. Agencies and camps in Olympos offer activities including boat cruises, canyoning, jeep safaris, mountain biking, rock climbing, diving, sea kayaking and hiking.

Ruins of Olympos   RUINS

(admission TL3; ⊙9am-6pm) Set in a deep shaded valley running to the beach, these ruins appear undiscovered among the vines and flowered trees. Rambling along the trickling stream that runs through this rocky gorge is a treat.

Chimaera   NATURAL PHENOMENON

(admission TL3.50) This cluster of flames blaze from crevices on the rocky slopes of Mt Olympos, 7km from Olympos. Pensions and agencies offer lifts/tours (TL5/15).

🛏 Sleeping & Eating

OLYMPOS

Staying in an Olympos 'tree house' has long been the stuff of travel legend. The camps lining the valley have become overcrowded and institutionalised compared with their hippy-trail incarnations, and few huts are actually up in the trees. Still, they offer good value and an up-for-it party atmosphere in a lovely setting.

Unless specified otherwise, the prices listed here are for half-board per person. Bathrooms are generally shared, but some bungalows have private facilities and even air-conditioning. Not all tree houses have reliable locks, so store valuables at reception.

Be extra attentive to personal hygiene while staying here; every year some travellers get ill. Especially in summer, the huge influx of visitors can overwhelm the camps' capacity for proper waste disposal. Be vigilant about where and what you eat.

Şaban Tree Houses   CAMPING GROUND, PENSION €

(☑892 1265; www.sabanpansion.com; dm/tree house/en suite bungalow TL25/35/45; ❄@) In the

words of charming manager Meral, 'It's not a party place' and instead offers tranquillity, space and great home cooking. The hammocks in the shade of orange trees are perfect for snoozing.

Kadır's Yörük Top Treehouse

CAMPING GROUND, PENSION €

(☑892 1250; www.kadirstreehouses.com; dm/en suite bungalow from TL15/40; ❄@) The place that started it all looks like a Wild West boom town that just kept growing. The wooden bungalows, cabins and dorm rooms can accommodate 350, the Bull Bar is the valley's liveliest and there's an activities centre.

Bayrams   CAMPING GROUND, PENSION €

(☑892 1243; www.bayrams.com; dm/tree house/ bungalow from TL25/30/45; ❄@) Here guests relax on cushioned benches playing backgammon or reading in the garden or puff away on a *nargileh* at the bar. Come here if you want to socialise but not necessarily party.

Doğa Pansiyon   CAMPING GROUND, PENSION €

(☑892 1066; www.dogapansiyon.net; tree house/en suite bungalow from TL30/40) Smaller and more subdued than most camps, the new 'Nature' has well-built elevated huts with a lovely mountain backdrop.

Varuna   LOCAL €€

(☑892 1347; www.olymposvaruna.com; mains TL10-15; ⊙8am-midnight) Next to Bayrams, this popular restaurant serves dishes including pide, trout and *şiş kebaps* in an attractive open dining room.

ÇIRALI

Çıralı may initially look like two dirt roads lined with pensions, but it's a delightful beach community for nature lovers and post-backpackers. There are about 60 pensions here, some near the path up to the Chimaera and others close to the beach and the Olympos ruins.

Hotel Canada   HOTEL €€

(☑825 7233; www.canadahotel.net; d/4-person bungalow €55/80; ❄@≋) A beautiful hotel offering the quintessential Çıralı experience: warmth, friendliness and homemade honey. The garden is filled with hammocks, citrus trees and bungalows (ideal for families), and excellent set meals are available.

Arcadia Hotel   HOTEL €€€

(☑825 7340; www.arcadiaholiday.com; s/d from €70/90; ❄) With another five luxury bungalows at Arcadia 2 across the road, this verdant escape at the northern end of the beach is well laid out and managed. Its big circular restaurant with an open hearth serves quality food.

Sima Peace Pension   PENSION €
(📞825 7245; www.simapeace.com; s TL40-60, d 60-100; ❄@) For decades, this comfortable '60s throwback has been hiding in a pretty garden down from the beach. The upstairs rooms feel like they were lifted from an old village house, and Koko the parrot adds a troppo twist.

ℹ Getting There & Away

Buses and minibuses plying the Fethiye–Antalya road will halt at the stops near the Olympos and Çıralı junctions. From there, minibuses leave for both destinations (TL6). From October to April they wait until enough passengers arrive, which can sometimes take a while. Most of the accommodation listed above will pick you up from the highway if you ask in advance.

The most pleasant way to travel to Olympos from Fethiye is on a cruise (see the boxed text p949).

Antalya

📞0242 / POP 956,000

Once seen simply as the gateway to the 'Turkish Riviera', Antalya is generating a buzz among culture vultures. Situated on the Gulf of Antalya (Antalya Körfezi), the largest city on Turkey's Mediterranean coast is both stylishly modern and classically beautiful. It boasts the wonderfully preserved Roman-Ottoman quarter of Kaleiçi, a splendid Roman harbour, plus superb ruins in the surrounding Beydağları (Bey Mountains). The good-value boutique hotels are of an international standard, the museum is one of Turkey's finest, and there are excellent bars and clubs. The opera and ballet season at the Aspendos amphitheatre continues to draw attention.

◎ Sights & Activities

Antalya Museum   MUSEUM
(📞236 5688; Konyaaltı Caddesi 1; admission TL15; ⊙9am-5.30pm Tue-Sun) This comprehensive museum, about 2km west of the centre and accessible on the *tramvay* (tram), has a dozen large halls covering everything from the Stone and Bronze Ages to Byzantium. Highlights include finds from Lycian and Pamphylian cities, and the statues of Olympian gods, most found at Perge.

Around the harbour is the lovely historic district Kaleiçi (literally 'within the castle'). It's a charming area full of twisting alleys, huge stone walls, atmosphere-laden courtyards, souvenir shops and lavishly restored mansions. Cliffside vantage points, including Karaalioğlu Parkı, provide stunning views over the beautiful marina and soaring Beydağları. Kaleiçi is downhill from the main square at Kale Kapısı (Fortress Gate), with its old stone clock tower (*saat kalesi*).

Yivli Minare   LANDMARK
Antalya's symbol is this fluted 13th-century minaret, erected by the Seljuk sultan Aladdin Keykubad I. The complex's restored **Mevlevi tekke** (whirling dervish monastery) houses a gallery, and next door are two 14th-century **türbe** (tombs). The adjacent mosque is still in use.

Hadriyanüs Kapısı   LANDMARK
The monumental Hadrian's Gate was erected for the Roman emperor's visit to Antalya (130 BC).

Suna & İnan Kiraç Kaleiçi Museum   MUSEUM
(Kocatepe Sokak 25; admission TL3; ⊙9am-noon & 1-6pm Thu-Tue) The small but well-formed ethnography museum, housed in a restored mansion and Greek Orthodox church, has the usual Ottoman dioramas and a fine collection of Turkish ceramics.

Balık Pazarı Hamamı   HAMMAM
(Balık Pazarı Sokak; bath & scrub TL13; ⊙8am-11pm) The 700-year-old Fish Market Hammam is a great place to experience the joys of the traditional Turkish bath.

Kesik Minare   LANDMARK
The Truncated Minaret is a stump of a tower on the site of a ruined Roman temple.

Boat Trips   CRUISE
Excursion yachts tie up in the harbour, offering trips to the Gulf of Antalya islands and some beaches for a swim (TL20 to TL60).

🛏 Sleeping

The best place to stay is Kaleiçi, where signs point the way to some of Turkey's best guest houses.

TOP
CHOICE **Tuvana Hotel**   BOUTIQUE HOTEL €€€
(📞247 6015; www.tuvanahotel.com; Karanlık Sokak 18; r €140-300; ❄@⊛) Among the most beautiful and intimate hotels on the Turkish Mediterranean coast, this refined city hotel

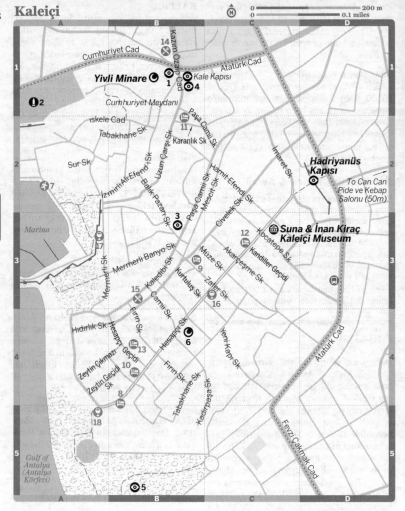

To Can Can
Pide ve Kebap
Salonu (50m)

occupies a discreet compound of six Ottoman houses. The plush rooms mix *kilims* with such mod-cons as DVD players.

White Garden Pansiyon PENSION €
(☎241 9115; www.whitegardenpansion.com; Hesapçı Geçidi 9; s/d TL35/45; ❈@☀) Metin's pension combines tidiness and class beyond its price level, with impeccable service. The building and courtyard have been charmingly restored.

Villa Perla PENSION €€
(☎248 9793; Hesapçı Sokak 26; s/d TL100/160; ❈☀) At this authentic Ottoman place hidden in a courtyard with pool and tortoises, the comfortable rooms are at the top of a staircase that starts with a 12th-century stone step. Wooden ceilings, four-poster beds and folk-painted cupboards feature.

Mediterra Art Hotel BOUTIQUE HOTEL €€
(☎244 8624; www.mediterraart.com; Zafer Sokak 5; s/d from €52/69; ❈@☀) This upmarket wood-and-stone masterpiece once housed a Greek tavern; 19th-century frescoes and graffiti adorn the restaurant wall. The small rooms are modestly luxurious, and ancient stone steps lead to an art gallery.

Kaleiçi

Sabah Pansiyon   PENSION €

(☎247 5345; www.sabahpansiyon.8m.com; Hesapçı Sokak 60; dm/s/d from TL20/30/40; ✳@) Long a budget stalwart, rooms here vary greatly so ask to see a couple. The shaded courtyard is perfect for meeting other travellers.

Hotel Blue Sea Garden   HOTEL €€

(☎248 8213; www.hotelblueseagarden.com; Hesapçı Sokak 65; s/d TL60/90; ✳@≋) The pool in the leafy courtyard is perfect for the heat of summer. Rooms are nothing special, with small bathrooms, but the elevated ones are more peaceful and the restaurant has a good reputation.

Eating

A nearly endless assortment of cafes and eateries is tucked in and around the harbour area. For cheap eating, cross Atatürk Caddesi to the commercial district.

Seraser   MEDITERRANEAN, MODERN TURKISH €€€

(www.seraserrestaurant.com; mains TL28-45) This restaurant at the Tuvana Hotel (see Sleeping) is arguably the city's best, offering international dishes with a Mediterranean slant in fine Ottoman surrounds. Try the grouper with rosemary and samphire or the quail with mustard honey glaze, and the Turkish coffee crème brûlée.

Parlak Restaurant   ANATOLIAN €€

(☎241 6553; www.parlakrestaurant.com; Zincirli Han, Kazım Özlap Caddesi 7; mains TL8-20) Opposite the jewellery bazaar and just off the pedestrian Kazım Özlap Caddesi, this sprawling open-air patio restaurant in an old caravanserai is famous locally for its slow-roasted chicken and meze.

Sim Restaurant   LOCAL €€

(☎248 0107; Kaledibi Sokak 7; mains TL12.50-20) Global graffiti gives a youthful pulse and eclectic antiques complement *köfte*, white-bean salads and glorious *çorba*. In fine weather, dine underneath the canopy in the narrow passageway, against Byzantine walls.

Can Can Pide ve Kebap Salonu   KEBAPÇI €

(☎243 2548; Arık Caddesi 4/A; pide TL3-4, dürüm TL5-6; ⊙9am-11pm Mon-Sat) Fantastically prepared *çorba*, pide and Adana *dürüm* (beef kebap rolled in pitta) at bargain prices; opposite the Plaza Cinema.

Drinking

Kaleiçi has a lot to offer after dark: buzzy beer gardens with million-dollar views, live music venues, as well as raunchy clubs and discotheques with outrageously expensive drinks and Russian prostitutes in full force.

It's worth seeking out the Kale Bar (Mermerli Sokak 2), attached to the CH Tükevi Hotel and commanding some of Antalya's best harbour and sea views; the lively bar/cafe Dem-Lik (Hesapçı Sokak 16), filled with students; and the clifftop Terrace Bar (Hıdırlık Sokak), where beer and coffee are accompanied by top-of-the-world views.

❶ Information

Owl Bookshop (Kocatepe Sokak 9; ⊙10am-7pm Mon-Sat) Secondhand bookshop stocked mostly with travellers' hand-me-downs.

Rıhtım Cafe (per hr TL1; ⊙9am-midnight) Internet access in a *nargileh* cafe north of Cumhuriyet Meydanı.

Tourist office (☎241 1747; Anafatlar Caddesi 31; ⊙8am-6pm Mon-Fri) Just north of the Seleker Shopping Centre and tram stop.

ⓘ Getting There & Away

Air

Antalya's airport is 10km east of the city centre on the Alanya highway.

İstanbul Turkish Airlines and budget Anadolu-Jet have a dozen daily flights year-round.

Ankara The same airlines have four daily flights year-round.

Bus

From the *otogar*, 4km north of the centre on the D650 highway to Burdur, regular buses head to:

Göreme/Ürgüp (TL40, nine hours)

Konya (TL25, five hours)

Side/Manavgat (TL15, 1½ hours)

From opposite the Sheraton Voyager Antalya Hotel, west of the centre:

Kaş (TI16, 3½ hours)

Olympos/Çıralı (TL13, 1½ hours)

Around Antalya

There are several magnificent Graeco-Roman ruins in the Mediterranean hinterland around Antalya. You can't help but be dazzled by the ruins of **Perge** (admission TL15; ⊙9am-5pm), one of the most important towns of ancient Pamphylia, located 17km east of Antalya and 2km north of Aksu. The site has a 12,000-seat stadium and a 14,000-seat theatre.

Another stunning place is **Aspendos** (admission TL15, parking TL5; ⊙9am-5.30pm), 47km east of Antalya. Here you'll see the world's best-preserved Roman theatre, dating from the 2nd century AD and still used for performances during the **Aspendos Opera & Ballet Festival** (www.aspendosfestival.gov.tr) every June.

The fierce Pisidians inhabited the ruined but still massive city of **Termessos** (admission TL10; ⊙8.30am-5pm) for centuries, and repelled Alexander the Great from this rugged mountain valley. The ruins, 34km northwest of Antalya, have a spectacular setting, but demand some vigorous walking and climbing.

The only drawback is that it's not convenient to get to these sights by public transport. The easiest way to see them is with your own transport or on a tour from Antalya. A tour to Perge and Aspendos should cost around TL90; an excursion/taxi tour to Termessos costs about TL60/90. There are plenty of agencies in Antalya hiring out cars.

The Roman ruins continue at **Köprülü Kanyon**, about 100km northeast of Antalya and deservedly popular for hiking and white-water rafting. Companies and pensions here offer rafting trips, including **Medraft** (⊉312 6296; www.medraft.com), which charges TL50 for a lesson, a four-hour trip and lunch.

The canyon is included in tours from Antalya (about TL90 per person) – your only option without your own wheels.

Side

⊉0242 / POP 20,100

To some, the once-docile fishing town of Side (pronounced *see*-day) is mass tourism at its worst: endless rows of souvenirs, sunbeds lined up along the beach, and '*Gute Deutsche küche*' (good German food) advertised everywhere.

But move a couple of streets over and you'll find a different side to Side. Entering the town though the monumental Vespasian Gate is like walking onto a film set; Roman and Hellenistic ruins mark out the road, and a rebuilt agora could just as easily contain togas as T-shirts. Adding to Side's appeal is the Temple of Athena, its resurrected columns marching towards the deep-blue sea.

⊙ Sights

Side's impressive structures include a 2nd-century AD **theatre** (admission TL10; ⊙9am-5.30pm) with 20,000 seats, one of the largest in the region; seaside **temples** to Apollo and Athena from the same era; and a 5th-century bathhouse, now **Side Museum** (admission TL10; ⊙9am-7.30pm Tue-Sun), with an excellent small collection of statues and sarcophagi. The town is also blessed with sandy **beaches**.

🛏 Sleeping & Eating

Some accommodation has parking; otherwise you have to use the car park just beyond the theatre (TL3/15 per hour/day).

TOP CHOICE **Beach House Hotel** HOTEL €€
(⊉753 1607; www.beachhouse-hotel.com; Barbaros Caddesi; s/d from TL35/75; [P][❄][@]) Once the celebrated Pamphylia Hotel, this personable Turkish-Australian operation has a prime seafront location and a steady flow of regulars. Most rooms face the sea; all have spacious balconies. The roof terrace has a jacuzzi and in the garden is a ruined Byzantine villa (as well as some rabbits).

Onur Pansiyon PENSION €
(⊉753 2328; www.onur-pansiyon.com; Karanfil Sokak 3; s/d TL35/60; [❄][@]) This excellent family-

owned pension has regulars year-round, drawn by the bright, cosy rooms and (in cooler months) cocktails by the fireplace.

Emir
FAMILY RESTAURANT €€

(✆753 2224; Menekşe Caddesi; mains TL16-22; ⊙9am-midnight) Almost leaning on the ruined Roman baths where Cleopatra is said to have dallied, the Emir's open kitchen produces excellent meze, grills and vegetarian dishes.

ℹ Getting There & Away

In summer, Side has daily buses to Ankara, İzmir and İstanbul. Otherwise, frequent minibuses connect Side with Manavgat *otogar*, 4km away, from where buses go to:

Antalya (TL8, 1½ hours)
Alanya (TL8, 1½ hours)
Konya (TL25, four hours)

Alanya
✆0242 / POP 86,800

Alanya has mushroomed from a sparsely populated highway town with a sandy beach to a densely populated tourist haven. Aside from a quick boat cruise or waterfront stroll, many visitors to Alanya shuffle between the airport shuttle and the hotel pool, venturing to the throbbing, laser-shooting nightclubs after dark. But Alanya has something special up its ancient sleeve. Looming high above the promontory south of the modern centre is an impressive fortress complex, with the remains of a Seljuk castle, some atmospheric ruins and active remnants of village life.

◉ Sights

Alanya Castle
FORTRESS

(admission TL10; ⊙9am-5pm) Alanya's crowning glory is the Seljuk fortress on the promontory, overlooking the city as well as the Pamphylian plain and the Cilician mountains.

Kızılkule
HISTORIC BUILDING

(admission TL3; ⊙9am-5pm) Seljuk Sultan Alaaddin Keykubad I, who also built the fortress, constructed the octagonal Red Tower down by the harbour in 1226.

🏃 Activities

Every day at around 10.30am **boats** (per person incl lunch TL30) leave from near Rıhtım Caddesi for a six-hour voyage around the

promontory, visiting several caves and Cleopatra's Beach.

Many local operators organise tours for landlubbers. A typical tour to sights including Aspendos and Side costs around TL65 per person, while a **4WD safari** in the Taurus Mountains costs about TL50.

🛏 Sleeping

Alanya has hundreds of hotels and pensions, almost all designed for groups and those in search of *apart oteller* (self-catering flats). The best alternatives are found along İskele Caddesi.

Kaptan Hotel
HOTEL €€

(✆513 4900; www.kaptanhotels.com; İskele Caddesi 70; s/d TL100/170; ❄☷) The four-star Kaptan has a large and somewhat slick lobby with a nautical theme and a pleasant bar. The clean and tidy rooms have all amenities; some have sea-facing balconies. The breakfast is excellent.

Seaport Hotel
BUSINESS HOTEL €€

(✆513 6487; www.hotelseaport.com; İskele Caddesi 82; s/d TL90/160; ❄) The last stop on the İskele hotel strip, just steps from the Red Tower, the Seaport offers efficient service and sea views from some rooms. Rooms are not huge but well appointed.

🍴 Eating & Drinking

The many hillside bar-cafes below the fortress offer stunning views and a welcome break from the party below.

TOP CHOICE İskele Sofrası
SEAFOOD €€

(✆0532 782 4647; Tophane Caddesi 2/B; mains TL18-30) For authentic Turkish seafood dining, eschew the harbour and head for this intimate place next to the Kaptan Hotel, serving six-dozen meze and fresh fish and shellfish. The terrace with harbour views is delightful.

Ottoman House
MODERN TURKISH €€

(✆511 1421; mains TL18-24) Alanya's most atmospheric eatery occupies a 100-year-old stone villa surrounded by lush gardens. The grilled fish dishes and traditional Ottoman *beğendili taş kebabı* (sauteed lamb served on aubergine puree) are testament to the kitchen's creativity. On Thursday and Sunday nights there's an all-you-can-eat fish barbecue; music is performed most summer evenings.

Köfte D Köfte KÖFTECI €€

(☎512 1270; Kale Yolu Caddesi; grills TL13-22; ☺8am-3am) At the bottom of the castle hill, this 'boutique' fast-food joint offers clean lines, attentive service and generous meat, rice and salad combinations. Try the omelettes.

Harem Cafe Bar LIVE MUSIC

(☎511 9225; www.haremcafebar.com; İskele Caddesi 46; ☺9am-3am) This Turkish music venue just up from the harbour fills with local lads and lasses sipping beers – more relaxed than anywhere down the hill. The music starts at 10pm.

ⓘ Information

Kısayol Internet Cafe (İskele Caddesi; per hr TL1.50; ☺9.30am-10pm)

Tourist office (☎513 1240; Damlataş Caddesi 1; ☺8am-5pm Mon-Fri) Opposite Alanya Museum, with a smaller branch (Damlataş Caddesi) between the *belediye* (town hall) and Kuyularönü Camii.

ⓘ Getting There & Away

Boat

Girne/Kyrenia (Northern Cyprus; one way/ return TL88/138) **Fergün Denizcilik** (☎511 5565; www.fergun.net; İskele Caddesi 84) runs ferries twice a week.

Bus

The *otogar* is on the coastal highway (Atatürk Caddesi), 3km west of the centre.

There are regular buses to:

Antalya (TL14, two hours)

Adana (TL35, 10 hours) Via Anamur.

Anamur

☎0324 / POP 35.900

Anamur has a pretty beach and waterfront at İskele, but the main reason to stop here is the ruined Byzantine city of **Anemurium** (admission TL3; ☺8am-5pm), 8.5km west of the town. A number of buildings are still identifiable and the occasional fragmented mosaic pokes through the topsoil. About 7km east of Anamur's main roundabout, **Mamure Castle** (admission TL3; ☺8am-5pm) is the biggest and best-preserved fortification on the Turkish Mediterranean coast. The 13th-century monolith retains all its original 39 towers.

Good sleeping options are **Hotel Ünlüselek** (☎814 1973; www.unluselekhotel.com; Fahri Görgülü Caddesi; s/d/tr from TL40/70/100; 🌣@) and **Hotel Luna Piena** (☎814 9045; www.hotellunapiena.com; Süleyman Bal Sokak; s/d from TL40/80; 🌣@).

Buses run to Alanya (TL20, three hours, Taşucu/Silifke (TL28, three hours) and Adana (TL30, six hours).

Kızkalesi

☎0324 / POP 1980

Wonderful 'Maiden's Castle', an inclusive and easygoing village with one of the region's loveliest sand beaches, is named after the astounding **Byzantine castle** (admission free) offshore, which looks from a distance as if it's suspended on top of the water. Unless you're up to swimming 300m, you'll need to take a boat (TL5) to get there. The ruins of **Korykos Castle** (admission TL3; ☺8am-5pm) are on the beach; the two were once linked by a causeway.

Yaka Hotel (☎523 2444; www.yakahotel.com. tr; s/d from TL50/60; 🌣@) is Kızkalesi's smartest and most welcoming hotel.

There are frequent buses from Kizkalesi to Silifke (TL3, 30 minutes).

From Taşucu, 11km southwest of Silifke, **Akgünler Denizcilik** (☎741 2303; www.akgunler.com.tr) *feribotlar* (car ferries; one way/ return from TL69/109; four to 10 hours; Sunday to Thursday) and faster *ekspresler* (hydrofoils; one way/return TL79/124; daily) depart for Girne (Kyrenia) in Northern Cyprus.

Adana

☎0322 / POP 1.52 MILLION

Turkey's fourth-largest city is a thoroughly modern affair, and its main use for travellers is as a transport hub. If you end up with some time to kill, a few mosques are worth a look, particularly the extravagant **Sabancı Merkez Cami**, built by the 20th-century tycoon Sakıp Sabancı; as are the ethnography and archaeology **museums**.

If you get stuck overnight, the riverfront boutique **Hotel Bosnalı** (☎359 8000; www.hotelbosnali.com; Seyhan Caddesi 29; s/d €75/85; 🌣) and budget **Otel Mercan** (☎351 2603; www.otelmercan.com; Küçüksaat Meydanı 5; s/d from TL25/40; 🌣) are dependable choices.

Şakirpaşa airport is 4km west of the centre; a taxi costs about TL15.

Trains run daily to İstanbul (TL40, 19 hours) via Konya (TL16, seven hours).

Adana's *otogar,* 2km beyond the airport, serves destinations throughout Turkey, including Antakya (TL18, 3½ hours), Konya (TL35, six hours), Ankara (TL35, seven hours) and İstanbul (TL50, 12 hours).

Antakya (Hatay)

📞 0326 / POP 212,700

Part of Syria until 1938, you might recognise Antakya from its biblical name, Antioch: the city vilified as the Roman Empire's most depraved outpost. Today's prosperous, modern city isn't that exciting, but Arab influences permeate local life, food and language, and the bazaars, back lanes and Orontes (Asi) River are well worth a wander.

The **tourist office** (📞216 6098; Muammer Ürgen Alanı; ⊙8am-noon & 1-5pm Mon-Fri) is on a roundabout at the end of Atatürk Caddesi, a 10-minute walk from the centre.

⊙ Sights

Archaeology Museum   MUSEUM
(Gündüz Caddesi 1; admission TL8; ⊙9am-noon & 12.30-4.30pm Tue-Sun) The museum contains one of the world's finest collections of Roman and Byzantine mosaics, many recovered almost intact from nearby Daphne (Harbiye) and Tarsus.

Church of St Peter   CHURCH
(admission TL8; ⊙9am-noon & 1-5pm) At this early Christian cave church, 2.5km northeast of town, Peter and Paul dropped by to do their bit in the war on debauchery.

🛌 Sleeping

Antik Beyazıt Hotel   BOUTIQUE HOTEL €€
(📞216 2900; www.antikbeyazitoteli.com; Hükümet Caddesi 4; s/d TL90/120; P❄) In a pretty French Levantine house, Antakya's first boutique hotel is looking frayed, though the antique furnishings and Oriental carpets still evoke an elegant past.

Mozaik Otel   HOTEL €€
(📞215 5020; www.mozaikotel.com; İstiklal Caddesi 18; s/d TL75/120) Rooms are decorated with folksy bedspreads and mosaic repros. The Mozaik is next to Hatay Sultan Sofrası restaurant – north of Ulus Alanı near the bazaar.

🍴 Eating

For restaurants head south of Ulus Alanı on Hürriyet Caddesi. Tea gardens are found in the park on the left bank of the Orontes, southwest of the museum.

Syrian influences permeate Antakya's cuisine. Handfuls of mint and wedges of lemon accompany many kebaps. Hummus is readily available and local specialities abound; including *künefe,* a cake of fine shredded wheat laid over a dollop of fresh, mild cheese, on a layer of sugar syrup, topped with chopped walnuts and baked. You can try it at several places near the Ulu Cami, including Kral Künefe.

Hatay Sultan Sofrası   LOCAL €€
(📞213 8759; İstiklal Caddesi 20/A; mains TL8-15; ⊙8am-midnight Mon-Sat) Antakya's premier spot for affordable local dishes. The articulate manager loves to guide diners through the menu.

ⓘ Getting There & Away

The new *otogar* is 7km northwest of the centre. Destinations include **Adana** (TL15, 3½ hours).

Syria

At the central old *otogar,* the **Jet Bus Company** (📞444 0277) has daily buses to:
Aleppo (TL10, three hours) 9am and noon.
Damascus (TL15, seven hours) Noon.

CENTRAL ANATOLIA

On central Turkey's hazy plains, the sense of history is so pervasive that the average kebap chef can remind you that the Romans preceded the Seljuks. This is, after all, the region where the whirling dervishes first swirled, Atatürk began his revolution, Alexander the Great cut the Gordion Knot and King Midas turned everything to gold. Julius Caesar came here to utter his famous line, *'Veni, vidi, vici'* ('I came, I saw, I conquered').

In Safranbolu and Amasya, drinking in the history involves sipping *çay* and gazing at the half-timbered Ottoman houses. While these are two of Turkey's most beautiful towns, offering Ottoman digs with cupboard bathrooms, other spots are so little visited that foreigners may find themselves entered as just *turist* (tourist) in hotel ledgers.

Ankara

📞 0312 / POP 4.5 MILLION

İstanbullus may quip that the best view in Ankara is the train home, but the Turkish capital has more substance than its reputation as a staid administrative centre

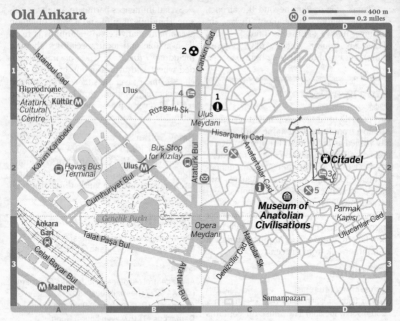

suggests. The capital established by Atatürk offers a mellower, more manageable vignette of urban Turkey than İstanbul, and claims two of the country's most important sights: the Anıt Kabir, Atatürk's hilltop mausoleum; and the Museum of Anatolian Civilisations, which will help you solve clues at sites left on the Anatolian plateau by Hittites, Phrygians and other ancient folk. Ankara can be a disjointed place, but two or three neighbourhoods have some charm:

the historic streets in the hilltop citadel; the chic Kavaklıdere district; and Kızılay, one of Turkey's hippest urban quarters.

◎ Sights

Museum of Anatolian Civilisations MUSEUM
(Map p964; ☎324 3160; Gözcü Sokak 2; admission TL15; ◎8.30am-5pm) Displaying artefacts cherry-picked from just about every significant archaeological site in Anatolia, all housed in a beautifully restored 15th-century *bedesten* (market vault), the museum is the perfect introduction to the complex weave of Turkey's chequered ancient past.

Citadel HISTORIC AREA
(Map p964) Just up the hill from the museum, it's also well worth exploring the side streets of the *hisar* (citadel), the most scenic part of Ankara. Inside, local people still live as if in a traditional Turkish village.

FREE Anıt Kabir MONUMENT
(◎9am-4pm) Pay your respects to the founder of modern Turkey and observe the Turks' enduring reverence for Atatürk at his monumental mausoleum, 2km west of Kızılay.

Roman Baths RUINS
(Map p964; admission TL3; ◎8.30am-12.30pm & 1.30-5.30pm) About 400m north of Ulus

Meydanı, these sprawling remains date back to the 3rd century. Southeast of the baths, you'll find more Roman ruins, including the **Column of Julian** (AD 363) in a square ringed by government buildings.

🛏 Sleeping

The Ulus area is undergoing a revamp, both inside and outside the citadel. If you want to go out for the evening, given that most of the restaurants and nightlife are in Kızılay and Kavaklıdere, and you will catch public transport and/or a taxi back to Ulus, upgrading to a room in Kızılay may cost the same overall. Good-value hotels abound in Kızılay; discounts are readily available.

TOP CHOICE Angora House Hotel   HISTORIC €€
(Map p964; ☑309 8380; Kalekapısı Sokak 16-18; s/d TL60/120; ☉Mar-Oct; @) Under new owners, this remains the pick of the Old Town and one of Ankara's most authentic accommodation options. The walled courtyard shields the tastefully decorated rooms from the citadel streets (apart from the noisy front room).

Ankara Regency Hotel   HOTEL €€
(Map p965; ☑419 4868; www.ankararegencyhotel.com; Selanik Caddesi 37; s/d TL80/120; ❄@) A winner in three key categories: pimping lobby, cheesy smiles on the staff and proximity to bars. The big rooms are cleverly laid out and blushed in 40-odd shades of tan, with floral patterns galore and flat-screen TVs.

Hotel Gold   HOTEL €€
(Map p965; ☑419 4868; www.ankaragoldhotel.com; Güfte Sokak 4; s/d/tr TL80/120/140; ❄@) The pillared entrance, rock-and-roll lobby and marbled lifts set the razzle-dazzle tone early, and it continues in the rooms with their candy-coloured bedspreads.

Hotel Oğultürk   HOTEL €
(Map p964; ☑309 2900; www.ogulturk.com; Rüzgarlı Eşdost Sokak 6; TL50/60/70; ❄) Just off Rüzgarlı Sokak, the Oğultürk is one of central Ulus' smarter options – on a par with many in Kızılay. It's professionally managed and good for lone women.

🍴 Eating & Drinking

Most Ulus options are cheap and basic. **Ulus Hali food market** sells provisions from oversized chilli peppers to jars of honey. In and around the citadel, inviting, atmospheric licensed restaurants occupy old wood-and-stone houses. Summer opening hours are around noon to midnight; live music adds atmosphere in the evening, although most reduce their hours in winter.

TOP CHOICE Le Man Kültür   INTERNATIONAL €
(Map p965; ☑310 8617; Konur Sokak 8a-b; mains TL6-11; ☉10am-11pm) Named (and decorated) in honour of a cult Turkish comic strip, this is the pre-party pick for a substantial feed. Drinks are reasonably priced and the speakers crank everything from indie-electo to Türk pop.

Kale Washington   INTERNATIONAL €€
(Map p964; ☑311 4344; Doyran Sokak 5-7; mains TL15-24) The Old Town's most elegant eatery, serving international and Turkish cuisine to visiting dignitaries. The views from the white table loths are most palatable.

Urfalı Kebap   KEBABS €
(Map p965; ☑418 9495; Karanfil Sokak 69; mains TL5-10) One of Ankara's best kebap restaurants.

Kızılay & Bakanlıklar

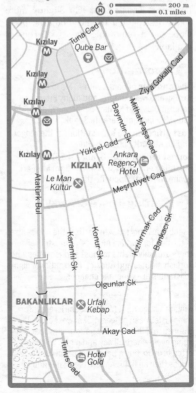

SAFRANBOLU & AMASYA

Safranbolu and Amasya, respectively 145km north and 270km northeast of Ankara, are slightly off the beaten Anatolian track, but beckon savvy travellers with their ethereal settings and historic atmosphere. Both retain many of their original Ottoman buildings.

Safranbolu is such an enchanting town that Unesco declared it a World Heritage site. It boasts a wonderful old Ottoman quarter bristling with 19th-century half-timbered houses; as part of the ongoing restoration, many have been turned into hotels or museums.

Blissfully located on riverbanks beneath cliffs carved with Pontic tombs, **Amasya** is one of Turkey's best-kept secrets, harbouring historic sites including a lofty citadel, Seljuk mosques and enough picturesque Ottoman piles to satisfy the fussiest sultan.

Both towns boast excellent accommodation, with a profusion of delightful pensions set in skilfully restored Ottoman mansions. In Safranbolu, travellers love **Bastoncu Pansiyon** (☑0370-712 3411; www.bastoncupension.com; Hıdırlık Yokuşu Sokak; dm/s/d/tr TL25/45/70/80; @). In Amasya, the new **Emin Efendi Konağı** (☑0358-212 6622; Ziyapaşa Bulvarı 2c; s/d/tr TL80/140; ❄@) has grand rooms.

There are buses from Ankara to Safranbolu (TL25, three hours) and Amasya (TL30, five hours), and from İstanbul.

Fast, friendly and seats 80-plus diners, from students to three-generation families.

Qube Bar　　　　　　　　　DESIGNER BAR
(Map p965; Bayındır Sokak 16b) Slightly more sophisticated than the neighbouring pubs, Qube has a removable glass roof. Food is available.

ℹ Information

There are lots of banks with ATMs in Ulus, Kızılay and Kavaklıdere, and many internet cafes in Ulus and Kızılay, particularly around Ulus Meydanı and Karanfıl Sokak.

Post offices In the train station, at the *otogar* and on Atatürk Bulvarı in Ulus.

Tourist office (☑310 8789/231 5572; Gazi Mustafa Kemal Bulvarı; ◷9am-5pm Mon-Fri, 10am-5pm Sat) Opposite the train station.

ℹ Getting There & Away

Air

Esenboğa airport, 33km north of the city centre, is the hub for Turkish Airlines' domestic network; there are daily flights to most Turkish cities with Turkish Airlines and Atlasjet. International flights to İstanbul are generally cheaper.

Bus

Ankara's huge AŞTİ (Ankara Şehirlerarası Terminali İşletmesi) *otogar*, 4.5km west of Kızılay, is the vehicular heart of the nation, with coaches going everywhere all day and night. You can often turn up, buy a ticket and be on your way in less than an hour. Ankara is a major hub for

buses throughout central Turkey. Buses to/from İstanbul (TL30, six hours).

Train

Train services between İstanbul and Ankara are the best in the country, and an even faster rail link is set to open imminently. Ankara Garı has a PTT, restaurant, snack shops, kiosks, ATMs, telephones and *emanet* (left-luggage room). Ankara services lines to many cities and towns, including İstanbul (seat/sleeper TL23/80, eight hours).

ℹ Getting Around

To/From the Airport

SHUTTLE BUS Havaş shuttle buses depart from Gate B at 19 May Stadium every half-hour between 4.30am and midnight daily (TL10, 45 minutes). They may leave sooner if they fill up, so be early. Havaş also links the airport and *otogar*.

TAXI Don't pay more than TL60.

Public Transport

BUS Buses marked 'Ulus' and 'Çankaya' run the length of Atatürk Bulvarı. Those marked 'Gar' go to the train station, those marked 'AŞTİ' to the *otogar*. You can buy tokens (TL3), valid for 45 minutes of multiple bus and subway journeys, from subway stations and major bus stops or anywhere displaying an EGO Bilet sign.

TAXI It costs about TL8 to cross the centre; charges rise at night.

UNDERGROUND TRAIN (one way TL1) The network has two lines: the Ankaray line running between AŞTİ *otogar* and Dikimevi via Kızılay, where it interconnects with the Metro line, which runs from Kızılay northwest via Sıhhiye and Ulus to Batıkent.

Konya

☎ 0332 / POP 762,000

Turkey's equivalent of the 'Bible Belt', conservative Konya treads a delicate path between its historical significance as the home town of the whirling dervish orders and a bastion of Seljuk culture on the one hand, and its modern importance as an economic boom town on the other. The city derives considerable charm from this juxtaposition of old and new, and boasts one of Turkey's finest and most characteristic sights, the Mevlâna Museum.

The centre stretches from Alaaddin Tepesi, the hill topped by the Seljuk Alaaddin Camii, along Mevlâna Caddesi to the Mevlâna Museum.

The two-week **Mevlâna Festival** culminates on 17 December, the anniversary of Mevlâna's 'wedding night' with Allah. **Semas** (dervish ceremonies) also take place at other times of year; contact the tourist office about both.

◉ Sights

Mevlâna Museum   HISTORIC BUILDING, MUSEUM
(admission TL2; ⊙9am-6.30pm Tue-Sun, 10am-6pm Mon) Join the pilgrims at this wonderful museum-come-shrine at the eastern end of Mevlâna Caddesi, where embroidered velvet shrouds cover the turban-topped tombs of eminent dervishes. The former lodge of the whirling dervishes, it is crowned by a brilliant turquoise-tiled dome – one of Turkey's most distinctive sights. Although it's virtually under siege from devout crowds, there's a palpable mystique here.

Museum of Wooden Artefacts & Stone Carving   MUSEUM
(☎351 3204; Adliye Bulvarı; admission TL3; ⊙9am-noon & 1.30-5.30pm) Housed in the 13th-century Seljuk İnce Minare Medresesi (Seminary of the Slender Minaret), the museum has an extraordinarily elaborate doorway, with bands of Arabic inscription.

FREE **Tombstone Museum**   MUSEUM
(☎353 4031; Sırçalı Caddesi; ⊙8.30am-5.30pm) One of several Seljuk buildings around Alaaddin Tepesi and in the narrow warren of streets to the south, the Sırçalı Medrese (Glass Seminary), named after its tiled exterior, houses this museum. The tombstones feature finely carved inscriptions.

🛏 Sleeping

TOP CHOICE **Ulusan Otel**   HOTEL €
(☎351 5004; Çarşı PTT Arkasi 4; s/d from TL40/70) Behind the post office is this brilliant little hotel with spotless rooms, graceful management and hearty breakfasts. The palatial shared bathrooms are immaculately kept.

Mevlâna Sema Otel   HOTEL €
(☎350 4623; www.semaotel.com; Mevlâna Caddesi 67; s/d/tr TL50/75/100; ❄) With a great position, some swanky decor and comfortable, beige rooms, the Mevlâna Sema has a lot going for it. Rooms at the rear are quieter.

Hotel Rumi   HOTEL €€
(☎353 1121; www.rumihotel.com; Durakfakih Sokak 5; s/d/tr/ste TL100/150/200/250; ❄@) Boasting a killer position near the Mevlâna Museum, the stylish Rumi's rooms have curvy chairs, slender lamps and mirrors. The breakfast room with Mevlâna views, the friendly staff and the *hammam* make this an oasis of calm.

Konya Deluxe Otel   HOTEL €€
(☎351 1546; Ayanbey Sokak 22; s/d/tr TL80/150; ❄) This new hotel down the road from the Rumi is clean and friendly with smallish rooms and spiffy bathrooms. A good option for solo travellers.

🍴 Eating & Drinking

Restaurants around the Mevlâna Museum and tourist office have great views, but their food is not recommended – with the exception of Gülbahçesi Konya Mutfağı. The fast-food restaurants on Adilye Bulvarı are lively places for a snack, but check the swift grub is thoroughly cooked.

Tea gardens dot the slopes of Alaaddin Tepesi.

Köşk Konya Mutfağı   TURKISH €
(☎352 8547; Mengüç Caddesi 66; mains TL8; ⊙11am-10pm) Southeast of the centre, this excellent traditional restaurant is run by the food writer Nevin Halıcı, who puts her personal twist on Turkish classics. The outside tables are situated next to vine-draped pillars and a fragrant rose garden.

Osmanlı Çarşısı   CAFE
(☎353 3257; İnce Minare Sokak) Looking like an apple-smoke-spewing pirate ship, this early-20th-century house near Alaaddin Tepesi has terraces and seats on the street, where students talk politics or just inhale a lungful.

ⓘ Information

You'll find numerous banks and internet cafes, including **Elma Net** (Çinili Sokak 14; per hr TL1; ⊙10am-11pm), around Alaaddin Tepesi.

Tourist office (☑353 4020; Mevlâna Caddesi 21; ⊙8.30am-5.30pm Mon-Sat) Gives out a city map and a leaflet covering the nearby Mevlâna Museum; can also organise guides.

ⓘ Getting There & Away

Air

There are three daily Turkish Airlines flights to/ from İstanbul. The airport is 13km northeast of the centre; TL40 by taxi.

Bus

From the *otogar*, 7km north of the centre and accessible by tram from Alaaddin Tepesi, regular buses serve all major destinations.

Ankara (TL20, four hours)
İstanbul (TL45, 11½ hours)
Kayseri (TL25, four hours)

Train

Three express trains link Konya with İstanbul via Afyon. A new direct, high-speed rail link between Konya and Ankara, scheduled to open in 2011, will trim the journey time from 10½ hours to 1¼ hours.

CAPPADOCIA (KAPADOKYA)

In extraordinary Cappadocia, Central Anatolia's mountain-fringed plains give way to a land of fairy chimneys and underground cities. The fairy chimneys – rock columns, pyramids, mushrooms and even a few shaped like camels – were formed, alongside the valleys of cascading white cliffs, when Erciyes Daği (Mt Erciyes) erupted.

The intervening millennia added to the remarkable Cappadocian canvas, with Byzantines carving out cave churches and subterranean complexes large enough to house thousands. You could spend days hiking through the canyons and admiring the rock-cut churches and their frescoes.

Between your lingering looks at the rocky remains of Cappadocia's unique history, it's worth checking out some further-flung sights including the seemingly lost valley of Ihlara and former Greek settlements such as Mustafapşa. Two hours' drive south of Göreme, Ala Dağlar National Park protects the rugged middle range of the Taurus Mountains. It's famous throughout the country for its extraordinary hiking routes, which make their way through craggy limestone ranges dotted with waterfalls.

When the day's done, spots such as Göreme and Ürgüp have some of Anatolia's best guest houses and restaurants. Whether it's a pension or a boutique hideaway with as few rooms as it has fairy chimneys, the accommodation allows guests to experience troglodyte living first hand.

☞ Tours

Most itineraries finish at a carpet shop, onyx factory or pottery workshop. It is interesting to see traditional Cappadocian craftsmen at work, but make it clear before the trip begins if you are not interested.

Most tour companies offer the following:

Full-day tours Often include one of the underground cities (which are best visited with a guide), a stretch of the Ihlara Valley and a caravanserai; some go to Soğanlı and Mustafapaşa.

Guided day-hikes Usually in the Rose, Sun, Red and/or Pigeon Valleys. Costs vary according to the destination, degree of difficulty and length, but should not exceed those of the full-day tours.

Ihlara Valley A full day, including a guided hike and lunch; most operators charge TL60 to TL70, but prices go up to TL90.

The following Göreme-based agencies offer good daily tours. There are also agencies in Avanos and Ürgüp; Nevşehir has a reputation for unscrupulous operators.

Yama Tours (☑271 2508; www.yamatours.com; Müze Caddesi 2) Also offers three-day trips to Nemrut Daği.

Middle Earth Travel (☑271 2559; www.middleearthtravel.com; Cevizler Sokak 20) The adventure-travel specialist offers climbing and treks from local, one-day expeditions to one-week missions.

Heritage Travel (☑271 2687; www.turkishheritagetravel.com; Yavuz Sokak 31) The knowledgeable Mustafa is highly recommended (TL60 for four people minimum and €100 for a private tour).

New Göreme Tours (☑271 2166; www.newgoreme.com; El Sanatlari Carsis 24) Fun and friendly private tours.

Nomad Travel (☑271 2767; www.nomadtravel.com.tr; Müze Caddesi 35) Offers an excellent Soğanlı tour.

ⓘ Getting There & Away

Air

There are two convenient airports. To travel between them and central Cappadocia, the easiest solution is to organise a transfer through your accommodation.

Kayseri airport Turkish Airlines and Onur Air fly to/from İstanbul daily; Sun Express flies to/from İzmir twice a week. Ürgüp agencies **Argeus Tours** (☑0384 341 4688; www.argeus.com.tr, www.cappadociaexclusive.com) and **Peerless Travel Services** (☑0384 341 6970; www.peerlessexcursions.com) respectively transfer Turkish Airlines passengers and those with Onur Air and Sun Express to/from Ürgüp (TL15), Göreme, Uçhisar, Avanos and Nevşehir (all TL20). You *must* pre-book, either through your accommodation or directly.

Nevşehir airport Turkish Airlines flies to/from İstanbul four times a week.

Bus

It's easy to get to Cappadocia by bus, although from İstanbul it will likely be an overnight journey. When you purchase your ticket, make sure it clearly states your final destination, as travellers have been deposited at Nevşehir *otogar* or even on the highway outside Avanos. The bus company should provide a free *servis* from Nevşehir to the surrounding villages. If you get stuck, phone your accommodation for a pick-up and do *not* book a tour in Nevşehir. A taxi to Göreme should cost around TL35.

Departing Cappadocia, Göreme and Ürgüp have *otogars* as well as Kayseri and Nevşehir. From Göreme buses go to:

Ankara (TL25, 4½ hours)
Antalya (TL35, nine hours)
İstanbul (TL40, 12 hours)
Konya (TL20, three hours)

ⓘ Getting Around

Travelling the quieter roads is a great way to cover the central sights and appreciate the landscape. Prices (in Göreme) for a day's rental:
Mountain bikes TL10 to TL15
Mopeds and scooters TL30 to TL45
Small Renault or Fiat car TL40 to TL100

Dolmuş

Belediye Bus Corp *dolmuşes* (about TL2) travel between Ürgüp and Avanos via Ortahisar, Göreme Open-Air Museum, Göreme village, Çavuşin and (on request) Paşabaği and Zelve. The services leave Ürgüp every two hours between 8am and 4pm (6pm in summer) and Avanos between 9am and 5pm (7pm in summer).

There's also an hourly *belediye* (municipal) bus from Avanos to Nevşehir (TL4) via Çavuşin (10 minutes), Göreme (15 minutes) and Uçhisar (30 minutes), leaving Avanos from 7am to 6pm.

Göreme

☑0384 / POP 6350

Göreme is the archetypal travellers' utopia: a beatific village where the surreal surroundings spread a fat smile on everyone's face. Beneath the honeycomb cliffs, the locals live in fairy chimneys – or increasingly, run hotels in them. The wavy white valleys in the distance, with their hiking trails, panoramic viewpoints and rock-cut churches, look like creamy tubs of soft-scoop ice cream. Rose Valley, meanwhile, lives up to its name; watching its pink rock slowly change colour at sunset is best accompanied by meze in one of the village's excellent eateries.

Tourism has inevitably changed this village, where you can start the day in a hot-air balloon before touring a valley of rock-cut Byzantine churches at Göreme Open-Air Museum. Nonetheless, you can still see rural life continuing in a place where, once upon a time, if a man couldn't lay claim to one of the rock-hewn pigeon houses, he would struggle to woo a wife.

All the services useful to travellers are in the centre, including the *otogar,* where there are four ATMs and a **tourist information booth** (☑271 2558; www.goreme.org); the **PTT** (off Bilal Eroğlu Caddesi), best for changing

---

DON'T MISS

GÖREME OPEN-AIR MUSEUM

Cappadocia's number one attraction and a World Heritage site, the **Göreme Open-Air Museum** (admission TL15; ⊙8am-5pm) has been a Christian pilgrimage destination for centuries. Byzantine frescoes can be seen in the rock-hewn monastic settlement where some 20 monks lived. The best-preserved churches are from the 10th to 13th centuries – notably the stunning 11th-century **Karanlık Kilise** (Dark Church). One of the most famous and fresco-filled churches, it's well worth the extra TL8 admission fee. Across the road from the main entrance, the **Tokalı Kilise** (Buckle Church), with an underground chapel and fabulous frescos, is included in the entrance fee.

money; and **Mor-tel Telekom** (Roma Kalesi Arkası; per hr TL2; ⏰9am-midnight), for internet and international calls.

👁 Sights & Activities

Valleys   HIKING

There are many hiking options around Göreme village. It's surrounded by a handful of gorgeous valleys that are easily explored on foot, allowing about one to three hours for each. The valleys are remote in places and it's easy to get lost in them, so walk with a companion if possible. Most pension owners will happily guide you on the trails for a small fee.

Horse Riding   HORSE RIDING

Cappadocia is excellent for horse riding, which allows you to access untrodden parts of the valleys. **Dalton Brothers** (📞0532-275 6869; 2hr TL50), run by the Göreme-born 'horse whisperer' Ekrem Ilhan and based behind the Anatolian Balloons office, uses sure-footed Anatolian horses from Erciyes Dağı (Mt Erciyes).

🛏 Sleeping

With about 100 hostels, pensions and hotels in Göreme, competition keeps prices low. If you're visiting between October and May, pack warm clothes as pension owners may delay putting the heating on, and ring ahead to check your choice is open.

TOP CHOICE Kelebek Hotel & Cave Pension
CAVE HOTEL €
(📞271 2531; www.kelebekhotel.com; Yavuz Sokak 31; fairy chimney s/d from €28/35; @🏊) Local guru Ali Yavuz leads a charming team at the village's original boutique hotel, which has seen a travel industry spring from beneath its stunning terrace. The pension proper spreads over two gorgeous stone houses with a fairy chimney protruding skyward, all skilfully restored and Anatolian-ised. Suites face a summer garden and private dining area where smitten guests recover from the luxurious *hammam*.

TOP CHOICE Koza Cave Hotel BOUTIQUE CAVE HOTEL €€
(📞271 2466; www.kozacavehotel.com; s/d from €70/90; @) After decades in Holland, owner Dervish has applied Dutch eco-sensibility to the beautiful new 'Cocoon'. Style and comfort aren't sacrificed in the pursuit of sustainable living: each stunning room is either handcrafted or uses recycled materials.

Köse Pension   HOSTEL €
(📞271 2294; www.kosepension.com; Ragıp Üner Caddesi; dm TL15, r TL25-90; 🏊🍴) This Scottish-Turkish family affair remains a travellers' favourite following a refurbishment in 2009. Spotless rooms suited to all budgets feature brilliant bathrooms, bright linens and comfortable beds. The TL15 three-course Turkish feast is great value and the pool and gardens are lovingly tended. A winner for families and independent folk alike.

Fairy Chimney Inn   CAVE HOUSE €
(📞271 2655; www.fairychimney.com; Güvercinlik Sokak 5-7; s/d/tr from €33/55/66; 🍴@) At the high point of Göreme, Dr Andus Emge and his lovely wife run this highbrow retreat, and offer academic asides to their wonderful hospitality. The tranquil gar-

---

ABOVE THE FAIRY CHIMNEYS

Cappadocia is one of the best places in the world to try hot-air ballooning, with favourable flight conditions and a wonderful network of valleys to explore. Flights take place at dawn, and balloons go up most days from the beginning of April to the end of November. The major drawback is that, with the activity's burgeoning popularity, as many as 70 balloons now fill the sky on typical mornings, and the numerous operators vary in expertise and safety standards. The following have good credentials:

Ez-Air Balloons (📞0384-341 7096; www.ezairballoons.com; Kavaklionu Mahallesi 8a, Ürgüp) Charges €160 for one hour minimum.

Butterfly Balloons (📞0384-271 3010; www.butterflyballoons.com; Uzundere Caddesi 29) Flights costs around €175 with this wing of Heritage Travel.

Kapadokya Balloons (📞0384-271 2442; www.kapadokyaballoons.com; Adnan Menderes Caddesi, Göreme) Flights cost from €175 (one hour).

Sultan Balloons (📞0384-353 5249; www.sultanballoons.com; Kaktus Sokak 21, Mustafapaşa Kasabası, Ürgüp) Charges €160 for one hour.

DR ANDUS EMGE: ANTHROPOLOGIST

Tell us what you do in Göreme.

I bought an old ramshackle cave dwelling, which functions as the base of the Cappadocia Academy and its Fairy Chimney guest house. I am involved in several pilot projects related to Cappadocia and continue my academic work on the region.

How can travellers get involved?

Travellers should take advantage of the region's unique characteristics by choosing traditional cave dwellings as accommodation and telling their hosts to serve local products to support a regional-sustainable agriculture.

What aspects of traditional cave life should we try to retain?

The local cave dwellings are not only good for storing, but also ideal for living. They are cool in summer and warm in winter. Instead of building new houses with AC, one could take advantage of that regional-typical characteristic.

What hopes do you have for Göreme?

I hope that subregional building characteristics don't get totally lost and the World Heritage site will present itself in a modern individual way, avoiding total Disneyfication of the tourism sector.

Describe your dream cave house.

After restoring an old cave house, I am now planning to realise a modern functional low-energy cave dwelling, combining aspects of current architectural design forms with the location-specific advantages.

den, where communal meals take place, has magnificent views; the simple furniture and traditional textiles have an understated Byzantine class.

Travellers' Cave Hotel   CAVE HOTEL €
(☎271 2780; www.travellerscave.com; Görçeli Sokak 7; s/d from €45/55; @) Friendly Bekir presides over this hideaway atop Aydınlı Hill, removed from the village hubbub. Rooms sprawl between, at, in, under and around stone staircases. The terrace is magnificent, the food reassuringly Turkish and the attentive staff arrange all sorts of tours. Bekir's cheaper pension on the other side of the village is also recommended.

Flintstones Cave   HOSTEL €
(☎271 2555; www.theflintstonescavehotel.com; dm TL20, s/d from TL20/40; @≋) Göreme's premium budget joint has outlived its party reputation. An expansion has created a spacious new wing with slick jacuzzi rooms, while dorms include a five-bedder with communal areas and private bathroom. The large pool is a sunbathing paradise with numerous reclining chairs. The huge bar comes with pool table and giant noticeboard, and the kitchen makes use of an organic vegie patch.

Cappadocia Cave Suites   CAVE HOTEL €€€
(☎271 2800; www.cappadociacavesuites.com; Ünlü Sokak 19; d/ste from TL210/340; @) A forerunner in luxury cave living, this open, inviting premises maintains its edge with uncomplicated service, a recommended restaurant, spacious, modern-meets-megalithic suite rooms and cool, converted stables. Avoid the double rooms if possible.

✕ Eating

There is a strip of eateries on the quiet side of the dry canal, away from the busy Bilal Eroğlu Caddesi.

TOP CHOICE Seten Restaurant   ANATOLIAN €€
(☎271 3025; www.setenrestaurant.com; Aydınlı Mah; mains TL15-25; ☉11am-11pm) This brand new project for the Kelebek crew is the centrepiece of a proposed cultural centre dedicated to preserving Göreme's historical flavour. Matching the glorious setting, the food is an education for newcomers to Anatolian cuisine and a treat for well-travelled tongues. Attentive service complements classic dishes and a dazzling array of mezes.

Orient Restaurant   TURKISH €€
(☎271 2346; Adnan Menderes Caddesi; mezes TL8, mains TL12-40, 4-course set menus TL20)

Couples nestle behind an extensive wine list at Göreme's most atmospheric restaurant. Juicy eye steaks, tender veal claypots and flavoursome pasta dishes head the impressive, meaty menu. The cold mezes are oily and the fish is dry, but the decent three-course set menu (TL20) is a safe bet is. Service is delightful.

Nazar Börek TURKISH €
(271 2441; Müze Caddesi; mains TL7) This expat and industry hang-out serves simple yet delicious meals, and the atmosphere is fun and friendly. Munch on fresh *gözleme* and *börek* such as *sosyete böreği* (stuffed spiral pastries served with yoghurt and tomato sauce) in the canal-side chill-out area.

Dibek ANATOLIAN €
(271 2209; Hakkı Paşa Meydanı 1; mains TL10-18; ⊙9am-11pm) An ancient agricultural theme pervades this family restaurant in a 475-year-old building, still churning out homemade wine. Diners sprawl on cushions in low-lit alcoves and feast on the signature dish, *testi* (pottery) kebap, with meat or mushrooms and vegetables cooked in a sealed terracotta pot, which is broken at the table. Book at least three hours ahead to try this.

Fırın Express TURKISH PIZZA €
(271 2266; Eski Belediye Yanı Sokak; mains TL8-13; ⊙11am-11pm) Göreme's best *lahmaçun* and *pide* are found in this local haunt, which also does *(paket)* takeaway. The cavernous wood oven fires up meat and vegetarian options and dishes doused with egg. Traditional stews are also available.

Local Restaurant TURKISH €
(271 2629; Müze Caddesi 38; mains TL11-20) The reliable Local stands on its own en route to Göreme Open-Air Museum, and is known for its meat dishes including stews, steaks, lamb shanks and *tavuklu mantarli krep* (chicken and mushroom pancake). The white tablecloths and stone-walled terrace are some consolation for the indifferent service.

Uçhisar

📞0384 / POP 6350

Between Göreme and Nevşehir is picturesque, laid-back yet stylish Uçhisar, built around a **rock castle** (admission TL3; ⊙8am-8.15pm) that offers panoramic views from its summit. The local 'kilometre zero' for Gallic gallivanters since Club Med revived the village's fortunes in the 1960s, Uçhisar is quieter than Göreme and worth considering as an alternative base.

There are some excellent places to stay, mostly with views of Pigeon Valley, Rose Valley and the rest of the rocky gang.

Hospitable to the last *nargileh,* the spacious **Kilim Pension** (📞219 2774; www.sisik.com; Tekelli Mahallesi; s/d/tr TL60/80/100) has hip, sparingly decorated rooms at the top of the village.

Underground passageways and secret doors add magic to **Kale Konak** (📞219 3133; www.kalekonak.com; Kale Sokak 9; r TL150; @), with a Roman arched terrace, marble *hammam* and luxurious brass beds in the shadow of Uçhisar castle.

The smallish rooms at the unassuming boutique hotel **Taka Ev** (📞532 740 4177; www.takaev.net; Kayabasi Sokak 43; s/d TL50/100; @) are brand new and spotless, with swanky bathrooms with powerful showers.

Zelve Valley

Three valleys of abandoned rock-cut churches and homes converge at the excellent **Zelve Open-Air Museum** (admission incl Paşabağı TL8, parking TL2; ⊙8am-5pm, last admission 4.15pm), off the road from Göreme to Avanos. Inhabited until 1952, its sinewy valley walls with rock antennae could have been made for poking around. In the same area, some of the finest fairy chimneys can be seen at **Paşabağı**, where you can climb inside one formation to a monk's quarters, decorated with Hellenic crosses; and **Devrent Valley**, also known as 'Imagination Valley' for its chimneys' anthropomorphic forms.

Avanos

📞0384 / POP 11,800

Avanos, 16km north of Nevşehir, is famous for pottery made with red clay from the Kızılırmak (Red River), which runs through its centre, and white clay from the mountains. Aside from the pottery-purchasing tour groups, the slow-paced provincial town is relatively devoid of foreign visitors, leaving you to ponder the Zelve sunset or your umpteenth riverside *çay*.

As well as the usual guided tours, **Kirkit Voyage** (📞511 3148; www.kirkit.com; Atatürk Caddesi 50) can arrange walking, cycling, canoeing, horse-riding and snowshoe trips.

Set in old stone houses around a lovingly restored courtyard, the long-running **Kirkit Pension** (☏511 3148; www.kirkit.com; Atatürk Caddesi; s/d/tr €30/40/55; @) is a low-key Cappadocian base with a recommended restaurant serving home-cooked meals. The smallish rooms are decorated with *kilims,* historical photographs of the region and Uzbek bedspreads.

Resident artist Hoja welcomes guests to the beautiful madness at **Sofa Hotel** (☏511 5186; www.sofa-hotel.com; Orta Mahallesi, Baklacı Sokak 13; s/d TL60/100), a collection of redesigned Ottoman houses. Staircases lead to bridges that wind through corridors and merge in terraced gardens with idiosyncrasies at every turn. Breakfast is a hit.

A basic but welcoming eatery on the main square, **Sanço-Panço Restaurant** (☏511 4184; Çarşi Sokak; mains TL6-7) is a great people-watching spot. Given Avanos' pottery trade, it's hardly surprising that the speciality is *güveç (*beef stew baked in a clay pot).

Near the bridge, the kebaps, pide and *künefe* are sensational at shiny, modern **Dayının Yeri** (☏511 6840; mains TL10).

Dine in a cave cellar, terrace, cave entrance or stone room at **Bizim Ev** (☏511 5525; Orta Mahallesi, Baklacı Sokak 1; mains TL11-15). Interesting selections include a clay pot of local trout and the surprisingly pleasant catfish skewers.

ℹ Information

The **tourist office** (☏511 4360; Atatürk Caddesi; ◷8.30am-5pm) is on the main street. To check your emails head to the **Hemi Internet Café** (Uğur Mumcu Caddesi; per hr TL1; ◷9am-midnight); there are banks with ATMs on and around the main square.

Ürgüp

☏0384 / POP 15,500

Eighty years after Ürgüp's Greek residents were evicted, international visitors are pained to leave their temporary boutique residences. Like your favourite Turkish aunt, Ürgüp is elegant without even trying. With a few fine restaurants, a fabulous *hammam,* an up-and-coming winery and valley views, the town is one of Turkey's hippest rural retreats, and the connoisseurs' base for exploring the heart of Cappadocia.

🛏 Sleeping

Most of the boutique hotels are on Esbelli Hill.

TOP CHOICE Esbelli Evi   BOUTIQUE HOTEL €€
(☏341 3395; www.esbelli.com; Esbelli Mahallesi Sokak 8; s/d/ste €90/120/200; ⊖❉@) Jazz in the bathroom, whiskey by the tub, secret tunnels to secret gardens lifted from photo shoots, privacy and company at alternate turns: Esbelli Evi is the crème de la crème of Cappadocian accommodation. Nine properties contain a highly cultured, yet unpretentious hotel. The detailed rooms feel like first-class holiday apartments for visiting dignitaries, and the breakfast spread is organic and delicious.

TOP CHOICE Serinn House   BOUTIQUE HOTEL €€
(☏341 6076; www.serinnhouse.com; Esbelli Mahallesi Sokak 36; d €100-140; @) This contemporary effort from jet-setter hostess Eren Serpen seamlessly merges Istanbul's European aesthetic with Turkish provincial life. The minimally furnished rooms feature tables too cool for coffee, the toiletries are top shelf, the restaurant ruled by a trained gourmet chef, and the achingly beautiful open courtyard elevates cave life to a new plane.

Hotel Elvan   BUDGET HOTEL €
(☏341 4191; www.hotelelvan.com; Barbaros Hayrettin Sokak 11; s/d/tr TL45/70/90; @) Ürgüp's best budget guest house is thankfully still a well-kept family secret. Rooms feature satellite TVs and minibars, and a congenial atmosphere runs through the shared lounges and leafy rooftop garden. Locals rate the small restaurant.

Hotel Kilim   HOTEL €€
(☏341 3131; www.hotelkilim.com; Dumlupinar Caddesi 50; s/d/tr from TL40/80/100; ❉@) Orderly, professional staff prepare bright rooms with private balconies and calming interiors, renovated in 2008. One of Ürgüp's better cheaper options, it's in the centre of town.

Yunak Evleri   LUXURY HOTEL €€
(☏341 6920; www.yunak.com; Yunak Mahallesi; d €100-115; ⊖@) Warranting its own postcode, Yunak is a labyrinth of good taste tumbling down the cliffside. Sections of the regal hotel date back to the 5th century. From the bronze desk lamps to the wireless entertainment systems and handcrafted wooden furniture, this is a hotel for connoisseurs of exceptional travel.

🍴 Eating & Drinking

The main square is the best place to grab an alcoholic or caffeinated beverage at an outside table and watch Cappadocia cruise by. *Pastanes* (patisseries) and cafes vie for attention with sweet eats and shiny window displays, overlooked by terrace restaurants. The pedestrian walkway running northeast from Ehlikeyf restaurant is full of cafes, bars and old men playing backgammon.

TOP CHOICE Ziggy's   MODERN TURKISH €€

(☑341 7107; Yunak Mahallesi, Teyfik Fikret Caddesi 24; mains TL15-18) Hosts Selim and Nuray, who sells her beautiful handmade jewellery downstairs, have created a winning menu, including Cappadocia's finest meze selection. The two-tiered terrace fills with humming tunes, strong cocktails and a hip clientele.

Han Çirağan Restaurant   TURKISH €€

(☑341 2566; Cumhuriyet Meydanı; mains TL14) This hugely improved restaurant has undergone a terrific renovation, with a cool bar added downstairs by new management. The terrace dining area is lovely (though lacks breeze) and the food is high quality; the lamb chops and trout are recommended.

Dimrit   TURKISH €€

(☑341 8585; Yunak Mahallesi, Teyfik Fikret Caddesi 40; mains TL10-21) One of Ürgüp's top choices for ambiance, Dimrit's long menu is not particularly illustrious for the price, but the divine presentation and hillside terrace more than compensate.

Ürgüp Pide Salonu   TURKISH PIZZA €

(☑341 8242; Terminal İçi, Onur İşhanı pide TL5-12) Beside the *otogar*, this Turkish pizza joint is one of the best in the region. It will deliver to your hotel free of charge.

Teras Cafe   TURKISH €

(☑341 2442; Cumhuriyet Meydanı 42; mains TL5-10; ☎) New owners and a renovation have improved this pleasant indoor/outdoor cafe, in a prime position at the foot of the hill. Outside are a big TV and comfy couches under giant, colourful umbrellas; inside and upstairs, the small restaurant dishes up dirt-cheap Turkish staples.

Mahzen Sarap Evi   WINE HOUSE

(☑341 6110; Istanbul Caddesi) This trendy number happily breaks the musty wine-house mould, with its sprightly female owner carrying coffee, booze and sandwiches to shared booths. After dark, Turkish indie and Kurdish electronica set the tone.

ℹ Information

Around Cumhuriyet Meydanı, the main square, you'll find banks with ATMs. There's internet access at **Teras Cafe** (per hr TL1) and the **tourist office** (☑341 4059; Kayseri Caddesi 37; ☺8am-5pm Mon-Fri) gives out a walking map and has a list of hotels.

Local travel agencies Argeus Tours and Peerless Travel Services (see p993) can arrange tours and transfers.

Mustafapaşa

☑0384 / POP 1600

Mustafapaşa is the sleeping beauty of Cappadocia – a peaceful village with pretty old stone-carved houses, some minor rock-cut churches and a handful of hotels. If you want to get away from it all, this is the place to base yourself. Until WWI it was called Sinasos and was a predominantly Ottoman-Greek settlement.

Perimasali Cave Hotel (☑353 5090; www.perimasalihotel.com; Davatlu Mahallesi, Sehit; s/d €60/120) is a dreamy renovation: an old Greek house on a quiet hill transformed into an opulent cave hideaway.

From the moment you enter the pretty vine-trellised courtyard, **Hotel Pacha** (☑353 5331; www.pachahotel.com; Sinasos Meydanı; s/d TL50/80) has old-fashioned, homestay-style appeal. The family-run pension offers a warm welcome and home cooking by the lady of the house, Demra.

Old **Greek House** (☑353 5306; www.oldgreekhouse.com; Şahin Caddesi; s/d from TL60/80; set menu TL20-30) is well known for its Ottoman-flavoured set menus, starring good versions of the usual suspects: *mantı, köfte,* lima beans, crispy salads and baklava. If the *Türk kahvesi* hasn't kicked in, the large bedrooms have polished floorboards and an antique feel.

Nine buses per day (three on Sundays) travel between Mustafapaşa and Ürgüp's Mustafapaşa *otogar* (TL1, 10 minutes), next to the main bus station.

Ihlara Valley

☑0382

A beautiful canyon full of greenery and rock-cut churches dating back to Byzantine times, Ihlara Valley (admission TL5; ☺8am-6.30pm) is an excellent, if popular, spot for a walk. Footpaths follow the course of the river, Melendiz Suyu, which flows for 13km between the narrow gorge at Ihlara village and the wide valley around **Selime Monastery** (⊙dawn-dusk).

The easiest way to see the valley is on a **day tour** (TL50 to TL60, see p968), which allows a few hours for a one-way walk through the stretch of the gorge with most churches. To get there by bus, you must change in Nevşehir and Aksaray, making it tricky to get there and back from Göreme and complete the walk in a day.

If you want to walk the whole valley – and it's definitely worth the effort – there are modest pensions at both ends: **Akar Pansion & Restaurant** (☑453 7018; www.ihlara-akarmotel.com; s/d/tr TL20/40/55; @) in Ihlara village and **Piri Pension** (☑454 5114; carpet_Mustafa@gmail.com; s/d TL20/40) in Selime. You can also break your journey with an overnight stay in Belisırma, which has three riverside camping grounds and **Vadi Pansiyon** (☑457 3067; d TL50). Note that all accommodation is closed out of season (December to March).

Ten *dolmuşes* a day travel down the valley from Aksaray, stopping in Selime, Belisırma and Ihlara village. In Belisırma, *dolmuşes* stop up on the plateau, and you have to hike a few hundred metres down into the valley.

To travel in the opposite direction, you have to catch a taxi. Between Ihlara village and Selime should cost about TL35; from Selime to Aksaray, about TL55.

Kayseri

☑0352 / POP 1.2 MILLION

Mixing Seljuk tombs, mosques and modern developments, Kayseri is both Turkey's most devoutly Islamic city after Konya and one of the economic powerhouses nicknamed the 'Anatolian tigers'. Colourful silk headscarfs are piled in the bazaar, one of the country's biggest, and businesses shut down at noon on Friday for prayer, but Kayseri's religious leanings are less prominent than its economic prowess. Its inhabitants are often less approachable than folk in Göreme et al, and this can be frustrating and jarring if you arrive fresh from the fairy chimneys. Nevertheless, if you are passing through this transport hub, it's worth taking a look at a Turkish boom town with a strong sense of its own history.

The citadel, just south of main square Cumhuriyet Meydanı, is the centre of the Old Town. The train station is 500m north, at the top of Atatürk Bulvarı.

◉ **Sights**

Citadel   FORTRESS
Now acting as an overflow valve for the nearby bazaar, the black, volcanic-stone *hisar* or *kale* was constructed in the early 13th century, during the Seljuk sultan Alaattin Keykubat's reign, then restored over the years (twice in the 15th century).

Kapalı Çarşı   MARKET
One of the largest built by the Ottomans, the vaulted bazaar remains the heart of the city and is well worth a wander.

Güpgüpoğlu Konağı   MUSEUM
(off Tennuri Sokak; admission TL3; ⊙8am-5pm Tue-Sun) Just southeast of the citadel is this wonderful 18th-century Ottoman stone mansion, which houses an interesting ethnographic museum.

Mahperi Hunat Hatun Complex
                                      HISTORIC BUILDING
(Seyyid Burhaneddin (Talas) Caddesi) Among Kayseri's distinctive features are important building complexes founded by Seljuk queens and princesses, including this austere-looking complex, east of the citadel. It comprises a *hammam* (still in use), mosque and *madrasa*.

Ulu Cami   MOSQUE
South the bazaar is Kayseri's Great Mosque (1205), a good example of early Seljuk style with one of Anatolia's first brick minarets.

Çifte Medrese   HISTORIC BUILDING
(Mimar Sinan Parkı) The Twin Seminaries, adjoining religious schools, date back to the 12th century.

Scattered about Kayseri are several conical **Seljuk tombs**.

🛏 **Sleeping**

Hotel Almer   HOTEL €€
(☑320 7970; www.almer.com.tr; Osman Kavuncu Caddesi 15; s/d/tr TL80/100/150; ❄@☎) Smoothly professional from the moment you reel through the revolving door, the Almer's relaxing reception has a backlit bar, little alcoves and a magazine rack. Rooms are quiet despite the busy road, and the restaurant (mains TL12, open 7pm to 11.30pm) is one of very few in Kayseri serving alcohol.

Hotel Çapari   HOTEL €€
(☑222 5278; www.hotelcapari.com; Gevher Nesibe Mahellesi Donanma Caddesi 12; s/d/tr/ste

TL60/90/110/120; ❄🛜) With thick red carpets and friendly staff, this three-star hotel on a quiet street off Atatürk Bulvarı is one of Kayseri's best deals. The well-equipped rooms have satellite TV and massive minibars.

Hotel Sur   HOTEL €

(☎222 4367; Talas Caddesi 12; s/d/tr TL40/60/75) Beyond the dark reception and institutional corridors, you'll find that the Sur's rooms are bright and comfortable. The withered international flags almost touch the ancient city walls.

Novotel   HOTEL €€

(☎207 3000; www.novotel.com; Kocasinan Bulvarı; s €120-135, d €140-155; ❄@) A good branch of the dependable international chain, featuring clean lines, bright colours and five-star service.

✖ Eating

The western end of Sivas Caddesi has a strip of fast-food joints that still seem to be pumping when everything else in town is quiet, including the fish-loving **İstanbul Balık Pazarı** (Sivas Caddesi; mains TL3).

Kayseri's best restaurants are **Tuana** (☎222 0565; 2nd fl, Sivas Caddesi; mains TL7), with views of the citadel and Erciyes Dağı and a roll call of classics such as kebaps and Kayseri *mantı*; and **Elmacıoğlu İskender et Lokantası** (☎222 6965; 1st & 2nd fl, Millet Caddesi 5; mains TL8-13), where *İskender* kebaps are the house speciality, available with *köfte* or in 'double' form. Other dishes include pide with local speciality *pastırma* (salted, sun-dried veal coated with *çemen*, a spicy concoction of garlic, red peppers, parsley and water).

ℹ Information

You'll find banks with ATMs and a helpful **tourist office** (☎222 3903; Cumhuriyet Meydanı; ⊘8am-5pm Mon-Fri) in the centre.

Soner Internet Café (Düvenönü Meydanı; per hr TL1.50; ⊘8am-midnight) West of the Old Town.

ℹ Getting There & Away

See also p993.

Bus

The *otogar* is about 3km northwest of the centre. On an important north–south and east–west crossroads, Kayseri has many services, including:

Göreme (TL10, 1½ hours)
Malatya (TL25, five hours)
Ürgüp (TL6, 1¼ hours)

Train

There are trains to Adana, Ankara, İstanbul, Kars, Kurtalan, Malatya, Tatvan and Iran, most of which are daily express services.

EASTERN TURKEY

Like a challenge? Eastern Turkey – vast, remote and culturally very Middle Eastern – is the toughest part of Turkey to travel in but definitely the most exotic, and certainly the least affected by mass tourism. Winter here can be bitterly cold and snowy.

Most of the region's key sights are found in mountainous southeastern Anatolia, near Turkey's borders with Syria, Iran and Iraq. Particularly near the latter country, a few places and roads are sometimes off-limits, but the southeast is mostly safe and accessible to independent travellers. What will linger longest in your memory is the incredibly warm-hearted welcome from the (predominantly Kurdish) locals.

SAFETY IN THE EAST

The conflict between the Turkish army and the PKK (Kurdistan Workers Party) separatist group has simmered down since the Kurdish rebellion during the 1980s and '90s. However, incidents do still occur, so it's worth checking your embassy's website for its current advice on southeastern Anatolia. After the PKK called off a 14-month ceasefire in 2010, fighting was focused on Hakkari and the border areas with Iraq, but activity also reached cities including Van and İstanbul.

Expect a significant military presence and keep your passport handy for army checkpoints. Road blocks can cause delays, but on the plus side, if there is any trouble, the military will not let you get anywhere near it.

Do your homework before you leave, keep your ear to the ground while travelling and monitor up-to-date information sources like Lonely Planet's Thorn Tree travel forum.

Mt Nemrut National Park

Nemrut Dağı Milli Parkı (admission TL6.50; ☉dawn-dusk) contains one of the country's most awe-inspiring sights. Two thousand years ago, right on top of **Nemrut Dağı** (Mt Nemrut; 2150m) and pretty much in the middle of nowhere, a meglomaniac Commagene king erected fabulous temples and a funerary mound. The fallen heads of the gigantic decorative statues of gods and kings, toppled by earthquakes, form one of the country's most enduring images.

There are a few possible bases for visiting Mt Nemrut. To the northwest is **Malatya**, where the **tourist office** (☎0422-323 2942; Atatürk Caddesi; ☉9am-5pm Mon-Fri) organises all-inclusive daily minibus tours (TL100, early May to late September/mid-October), with a night at the Güneş Hotel below the summit and visits to the heads at sunset and sunrise.

Alternatively, visit the mountain from the south via **Kahta**, where hotels and guest houses offer eight-hour sunrise and sunset trips, as well as the three-hour 'small tour'. This route is more scenic, but note that Kahta has a reputation for rip-offs so you need to be wary of what's on offer. Always check exactly what you will be seeing, and how long you'll be away. **Mehmet Akbaba** (☎0535-295 4445; akbabamehmet@hotmail.com) and **Nemrut Tours** (☎0416-725 6881; Hotel Nemrut, Mustafa Kemal Caddesi) offer informative English-speaking guides.

Tours (TL100 per person, minimum two people) from **Şanlıurfa** (Urfa), run by **Harran-Nemrut Tours** (☎0414-215 1575; www.aslankonukevi.com; Aslan Konak Evi, Demokrasi Caddesi 12), arrive at Nemrut around 10am. You're missing out on sunset or sunrise, but the upside is less people at the summit.

Some people take a two-day tour (about TL280) from Cappadocia, but it's a tedious drive. If you have enough time, it's better to opt for a three-day tour, which should also include a few stops, such as Harran and Şanlıurfa.

In the park, accommodation in **Karadut** offers return trips to the summit for TL50 to TL75 per vehicle.

🛏 Sleeping

MALATYA

Grand W Aksaç Hotel   HOTEL **€€**
(☎0422-324 6565; www.aksachotel.com, in Turkish; Saray Mahallesi, Ömer Efendi Sokak 19; s/d TL80/120; 🕸) This newly opened hotel supplements a quiet central location with spacious, shiny bathrooms and flash services including a *hammam*. Rooms feature flat-screen TVs, huge beds and there are also chocolate-covered apricots for sale – a winning combination if you've been travelling too quickly.

KAHTA

Hotel Kommagene & Camping
PENSION, CAMPING GROUND **€**
(☎0416-725 5385; www.nemruttours.info; Mustafa Kemal Caddesi 1; campsites per person TL8, caravans TL18, per person without/with bathroom TL18/25, breakfast TL7; 🕸) The most obvious choice for budget-minded travellers, less because of its inherent merits than its lack of competitors in this price bracket. Rooms are clean and secure, some with comfy new beds. Campers can pitch their tent on the parking lot, and the ablutions block is shipshape. Expect some insistent selling of tours including short and long Nemrut itineraries at some point. An all-inclusive deal incorporating one night's accommodation and a Nemrut trip is available.

KARADUT

Karadut Pension   PENSION, CAMPING GROUND **€**
(☎0416-737 2169, 0532-566 2857; www.karadut pansiyon.net; campsites/d per person TL5/25; 🕸@) This pension/hostel at the northern end of Karadut has neat, if compact, rooms, cleanish bathrooms and a shared kitchen. Meals are available and there's an alfresco terrace bar. The partially shaded rear camping plot has mountain views and a super-clean ablutions block. It's popular with overland tour groups, so book ahead.

Hotel Euphrat   HOTEL **€€**
(☎0416-737 2175; www.hoteleuphratnemrut.com, in Turkish; s/d half-board TL80/160; 🕸🕸) Popular with tour groups in peak season, recent renovations have made the low-rise Euphrat's rooms larger and more comfortable. The restaurant terrace and new pool have spectacular views and the food is good.

ŞANLIURFA

🔝 Aslan Konuk Evi   PENSION **€**
(☎0414-215 1575; www.aslankonukevi.com; Demokrasi Caddesi 12; s/d TL50/75, without bathroom per person TL25-30; 🕸@) Simple but spacious high-ceilinged rooms are arranged around a courtyard in a heritage Urfa building. Efficiently run by a local English teacher and guide, it's a good choice for female budget travellers, with free pick-ups from the *otogar*. Outside guests are welcome to dine in

the rooftop terrace restaurant, which serves excellent food (and cold beer!), but you need to book in the morning. The new private rooms are excellent value.

Hotel Arte   BOUTIQUE HOTEL **€€**
(☏314 7060; www.otel-arte.com Köprübaşı Caddesi; s/d TL60/100; ❄) Bringing style and sleekness to Urfa, the Arte's design-led interior has Barbie-esque plastic chairs in the lobby, laminated floors and contemporary furniture in the rooms – although a touch-up of paint here and there would be nice. The floor-to-ceiling windows afford superb views of the main drag.

ℹ Getting There & Away

Malatya, Kahta and Şanlıurfa are well connected, with regular buses to/from locations including Ankara, İstanbul and Kayseri.

Malatya and Şanlıurfa's airports both have daily Turkish Airlines flights to/from Ankara and İstanbul, and Onur Air also flies İstanbul-Malatya.

During the summer season, there are minibuses (TL10) around every two hours between Kahta and the Çeşme Pansion, about 6km from the summit, via Karadut. Pension owners can pick you up at Kahta's otogar (set the price beforehand).

Mardin

☏0482 / POP 55,000

Pretty-as-a-picture Mardin is an addictive, unmissable spot. With its minarets poking out of a labyrinth of brown lanes, its castle dominating the Old City, and the honey-coloured stone houses that cling to the hillside, Mardin emerges like a phoenix from the sun-roasted Mesopotamian plains. A mosaic of Kurdish, Yezidi, Christian and Syrian cultures, among others, it also has a fascinating cultural mix.

The city has started to become popular with Turkish travellers – get here before it becomes too touristy.

◎ Sights & Activities

Bazaar   MARKET
Strolling through the rambling bazaar, among charmingly decorated donkeys and saddle repairers, keep your eyes open for the secluded **Ulu Cami**, a 12th-century Iraqi Seljuk structure.

Mardin Museum   MUSEUM
(Cumhuriyet Caddesi; admission TL3; ◷8am-5pm Tue-Sun) A superbly restored late 19th-century mansion houses a collection including an Assyrian vase and Bronze Age finds.

Cumhuriyet Caddesi   ARCHITECTURE, HAMMAM
East of the museum, an ornately carved **house** with a three-arched facade is fabulous example of Mardin's domestic architecture. **Sultan İsa (Zinciriye) Medresesi** (1385) has an imposing recessed doorway, pretty courtyards and city views from the roof. Opposite the **post office**, housed in a 17th-century caravanserai, rises the elegant, slender minaret of the 14th-century **Şehidiye Camii**. It's superbly carved, with colonnades all around and three small bulbs superimposed at the summit. **Emir Hamamı** (treatments from T15; ◷men 6.30am-noon & 6.30-10pm, women noon-5.30pm) is one of Turkey's most atmospheric *hammams,* with history going back to Roman times and views of the plains from its terrace.

🛏 Sleeping & Eating

Mardin's popularity with Turkish tourists means that accommodation is expensive, and summer weekends are particularly busy. Rooms are often small and lacking natural light; ask the right questions when you're booking.

Antik Tatlıede Butik Hotel   BOUTIQUE HOTEL **€€**
(☏213 2720; www.tatlidede.com.tr, in Turkish; Medrese Mahalessi; s/d TL100/150; ❄) In a quiet location near the bazaar, this labyrinthine heritage mansion has rooms of varying sizes (mostly fairly spacious), filled with a rustic mix of old *kilims* and antique furniture. The expansive lobby flows to huge terraces with views across the plains.

TOP CHOICE Kamer Vakif   MUTFAK **€€**
(Cumhuriyet Caddesi; mains TL10-15) The Moon Foundation is a support organisation for women who are victims of domestic violence. In its terrific restaurant, one of eastern Turkey's best, different women cook on a rotating basis, dishing up authentic and tasty Kurdish bulgur wheat pilav and *köfte.*

ℹ Getting There & Away

AIR Any minibus to Kızıltepe can drop you at Mardin airport (TL2), 20km south of Mardin. Turkish Airlines has daily flights to/from İstanbul and Ankara.

DOLMUŞ There are frequent minibuses to Diyarbakır (TL8, 1¼ hours), Şanlıurfa (TL20, three hours), Nusaybin (for Syria; TL6, one hour) and Silopi (for Iraq; TL20, three hours).

Van

☎ 0432 / POP 391,000

Young couples walking hand in hand on the main drag, students flirting in the pastry shops, live bands knocking out Kurdish tunes in pubs, unscarved girls sampling ice cream and daring to make eye contact with foreigners: frontier towns never looked so liberal! Van is different in spirit from the rest of southeastern Anatolia – more urban, more casual – and boasts a brilliant location, near the eponymous lake.

◉ Sights

Castle
RUINS

(admission TL3; ☺9am-dusk) Try to visit Van's imposing castle at sunset for great views of the lake, it's situated about 3km west of the centre. On the southern side of the rock are the foundations of **Eski Van** (the old city).

Van Museum
MUSEUM

(Kişla Caddesi; admission TL3; ☺8am-noon & 1-5pm Tue-Sun) The small city museum has an outstanding collection of Urartian exhibits, with gold jewellery, bronze belts, helmets, horse armour and terracotta figures.

Akdamar Island
CHURCH

Van's 8th-century Armenian rulers took refuge on Akdamar Island in Van Gölü (Lake Van) when the Arab armies flooded through from the south. The carefully restored **Akdamar Kiliseli** (Church of the Holy Cross; admission TL3) is one of the wonders of Armenian architecture. The island, 3km out in the lake, is a day trip from Van by minibus and boat.

Hoşap Castle
FORTRESS

(admission TL3) A slightly longer day trip takes you southeast to the spectacular Hoşap Castle, a Kurdish fortification perched on a rocky outcrop. To get there, catch a Başkale- or Yüksekova-bound minibus on Cumhuriyet Caddesi (south of Büyük Asur Oteli) and get out at Hoşap (TL6). After seeing the castle, flag down a bus to Çavuştepe, where you can pick up a bus to Van. Frequent minibuses and buses ply the route.

🛏 Sleeping

Otel Bahar
HOTEL €

(☎215 5748, 0539 729 6838; Ordu Caddesi 20; s/d TL25/50) One of Van's best cheapies, the Bahar's simple rooms have clean bathrooms and compact balconies. When the nearby mosque wakes you, look down on the lanes with teashops and barbers. The friendly reception may be slightly offended when you forgo the OK breakfast for *kahvaltı* (see the boxed text, p979) just around the corner.

Büyük Asur Oteli
HOTEL €€

(☎216 8792; www.buyukasur.com; Cumhuriyet Caddesi, Turizm Sokak; s/d TL60/90; ✴) Even if you're on a tight budget, consider spending a little more to enjoy this reliable venture. The colourful rooms have fresh linen, TV and well-scrubbed bathrooms. The English-speaking staff can organise local tours, including Akdamar island and Hoşap Castle.

🍴 Eating & Drinking

Hotel Tamara
PUB €€

(Yüzbaşıoğlu Sokak; mains TL10-15; ☺5pm-late) A meal at **Tamara Ocakbaşı** is dizzying, especially for carnivores – each table has its own grill. High-quality meat and fish dishes feature prominently, but the meze menu is impressive. Also in the recommended business hotel, the **North Shield** pub is a slice of ersatz Tyneside, offering cold pints and a familiar English pub ambience.

Kebabistan
KEBAPÇI €€

(Sinemalar Sokak; mains TL6-10) Getting to this kebap eatery is as fun as its name: it's on a side street where men sit on low chairs, playing backgammon and drinking tea. The kitchen turns out expertly cooked kebaps (go for the *kuşbaşı*, with little morsels of beef) and, across the street, a second branch specialises in pide.

ℹ Information

Hotels, restaurants, ATMs, internet cafes, bus company offices, the PTT and the **tourist**

BREAKFAST OF CHAMPIONS

Van is famed for its tasty kahvaltı (breakfast), best tried on pedestrianised Eski Sümerbank Sokak, also called 'Kahvaltı Sokak' (Breakfast St). Here, a row of eateries offers complete Turkish breakfasts (around TL12 to TL15). Sample *otlu peynir* (cheese mixed with a tangy herb, Van's speciality), *beyaz peynir*, honey from the highlands, olives, *kaymak* (clotted cream), tomatoes, cucumbers, and *sucuklu yumurta* (omelette with sausage).

office (☎216 2530; Cumhuriyet Caddesi; ☉8.30am-noon & 1-5.30pm Mon-Fri) lie on and around Cumhuriyet Caddesi.

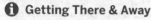

ℹ Getting There & Away

AIR The airport is 6km from the centre; a taxi there costs about TL20. There are daily flights to/from İstanbul and Ankara with Turkish Airlines and Pegasus Airlines.

BOAT A twice-daily ferry crosses Lake Van between Tatvan and Van (TL8, four hours), but there's no fixed schedule.

BUS Daily buses connect Van with Ankara (TL70, 22 hours), Malatya (TL50, 10 hours) and Şanlıurfa (TL40, nine hours).

TRAIN The twice-weekly *Vangölü Ekspresi* train from İstanbul and Ankara meets the ferry in Tatvan. The weekly *Trans Asya Ekspresi* connects İstanbul to Tehran (Iran) via Van; a train also runs to Tabriz (Iran) on Thursday.

UNDERSTAND TURKEY

History

The sheer weight and depth of history in Turkey is overwhelming. The Anatolian plateau features in various guises in both Homer's *Iliad* and the Bible; it has produced some of the world's longest-lasting empires, been instrumental in maintaining control in much of Europe and the Middle East for centuries, and still holds a strategic position at the meeting of two continents. Just look at the ruins littering the Aegean and Mediterranean coasts to glimpse the country's former glories.

By 7000 BC a Neolithic city, one of the oldest ever recorded, was established at Çatalhöyük, near Konya. The greatest of the early civilisations of Anatolia (Asian Turkey) was that of the Hittites, a force to be reckoned with from 2000 to 1200 BC, with their capital at Hattuşa, east of Ankara. Traces of their existence remain throughout central Turkey.

After the collapse of the Hittite empire, Anatolia splintered into several small states until the Graeco-Roman period, when parts of the country were reunited. Later, Christianity spread through Anatolia, carried by the apostle Paul, a native of Tarsus (near Adana).

Byzantine Empire & the Crusades

In AD 330, the Roman emperor Constantine founded a new imperial city at Byzantium (modern İstanbul). Renamed Constantinople, this strategic city became the capital of the Eastern Roman Empire and was the centre of the Byzantine Empire for 1000 years. During the European Dark Ages, the Byzantine Empire kept alive the flame of Western culture, despite threats from the empires of the East (Persians, Arabs and Turks) and West (the Christian powers of Europe).

The Byzantine Empire's decline came with the arrival of the Seljuk Turks and their defeat of the Byzantine forces in 1071. Seljuks overran most of Anatolia, and established a provincial capital at Konya, ruling domains that included today's Turkey, Iran and Iraq.

The Byzantines endeavoured to protect their capital and reclaim Anatolia, but, during the Fourth Crusade (1202–04), a combined Venetian and crusader force took and plundered Constantinople. They eventually regained the ravaged city in 1261.

Ottoman Empire

A Mongol invasion in the late 13th century ended Seljuk power, but new small Turkish states soon arose in western Anatolia. One, headed by Gazi Osman (1258–1326), grew into the Ottoman Empire. In 1453 Constantinople finally fell to the Ottoman sultan Mehmet II (the Conqueror), replacing Bursa as the capital of the dynasty.

A century later, under Süleyman the Magnificent, the Ottoman Empire reached its peak, spreading deep into Europe, Asia and North Africa. Ottoman success was based on military expansion; when their march westwards stalled at Vienna in 1683, the rot set in. By the 19th century, the great European powers had begun to covet the sultans' vast domains.

Nationalist ideas swept through Europe after the French Revolution. In 1829 the Greeks won their independence, followed by the Serbs, the Romanians and the Bulgarians. In the ensuing territorial scrambles, Italy took Tripolitania (now Libya) from Turkey, and in 1913 the Ottomans lost both Albania and Macedonia.

Having sided with the Axis powers in 1914, the Turks emerged from WWI stripped of their last non-Turkish provinces: Syria, Palestine, Mesopotamia (Iraq) and the Arabian peninsula. Most of Anatolia itself was to be parcelled out to the victorious Europeans, leaving the Turks with virtually nothing.

Mustafa Kemal Atatürk

At this low point (around 1920), Mustafa Kemal, the father of modern Turkey, took over. Atatürk, as he was later called, had made his name by repelling the Anzacs in their heroic but futile attempt to capture the strategic Dardanelles strait at Gallipoli during WWI.

Rallying the remnants of the Turkish army during the Turkish War of Independence that followed WWI, Kemal pushed the last of the Ottoman rulers aside and out-manoeuvred the Allied forces. The Turks finally won in 1922 by repelling the invading Greeks at Smyrna (present-day İzmir). In the ensuing population exchange, whole communities were uprooted as Greek-speaking people from Anatolia were shipped to Greece, while Muslim residents of Greece were transferred to Turkey. One result of this upheaval was the 'ghost villages' that were vacated but never reoccupied.

After the renegotiation of the WWI treaties, a new Turkish republic, reduced to Anatolia and part of Thrace, was born. Atatürk embarked on a rapid modernisation program, establishing a secular democracy, introducing the Latin script and European dress, and adopting equal rights for women (at least in theory). The capital was also moved from İstanbul to Ankara. Such sweeping changes did not come easily, and some of the disputes from that period have never been fully resolved.

Relations with Greece improved in the 1930s (the Greek president even nominated Atatürk for the Nobel Peace Prize), but soured again after WWII due to the conflict over Cyprus; particularly after the Greek-led anti-Makarios coup and the subsequent Turkish invasion in 1974.

Modern Turkey

After Atatürk's death on 10 November 1938, Turkey experienced three military coups and a lot of political turbulence; no fewer than 60 different governments have held office since independence. During the 1980s and '90s the country was wracked by the ongoing conflict with the PKK (Kurdistan Workers' Party), led by Abdullah Öcalan, who wanted the creation of a Kurdish state in southeastern Anatolia. The conflict led to an estimated 35,000 deaths and huge population shifts. In 1999 Öcalan was captured, but Kurdish discontent and terrorist activities continue.

In 2001 the Turkish economy collapsed in spectacular fashion. More than a million people lost their jobs, and the value of the Turkish lira slumped from TRL650,000 for US$1 to TRL1.6 million.

In 2002 the newly formed AKP (Islamic Justice and Development Party), a religious party dominated by one-time İstanbul mayor Recep Tayyip Erdoğan, won an unprecedented victory, becoming the first noncoalition government in 15 years and ousting 90% of the existing members of parliament. Only one other party won any seats at all.

With concerns over Erdoğan's controversial past (he was once jailed for inciting religious hatred, and was still banned from sitting in parliament at the time his party came to power), many people feared the AKP would bring hardline Islam to national politics. So far, the party has proved moderate, concentrating on stabilising the economy and strengthening the country's bid to join the EU. Although many Turks remain uneasy about the government's pro-Islamic leanings, the AKP is now serving its third term in office after winning the June 2011 elections.

Current Events

Terrorism and the increasing polarisation of the Eastern and Western worlds have reinforced Turkey's position as a United States ally and NATO member, and joining Europe remains a key priority for the country. The death penalty was abolished to meet EU criteria (incidentally reprieving PKK leader Öcalan) and the Kurdish minority has been granted greater rights and freedoms. Accession talks began in October 2005. The issue of Turkish-held North Cyprus, however, stands between Turkey and EU member states Greece and Cyprus, whose support Turkey will need in its bid.

Additionally, the negative press generated when Turkey's best-known author, Orhan Pamuk, was tried for 'insulting Turkishness' put the spotlight on the government's declared commitment to freedom of expression. With accession talks offering no guarantee of acceptance into the EU, it seems that Turkey may remain teetering on the edge of Europe for many years.

Following the AKP's re-election in mid-2007, the tussle between 'secularists' and 'Islamists' grew more heated. An unsuccessful legal case to close the AKP for 'nonsecular activities' brought tensions to boiling point. In mid-2008, police arrested scores of people associated with the ultranationalist Ergenekon movement, alleging they were planning a coup against the government, and a series of terrorist bombs exploded in İstanbul.

Relations have roller-coastered with Armenia, which has long pressured its western neighbour to acknowledge that Ottoman troops carried out genocide against Armenians in 1915. In 2008 president Abdullah Gul became the first Turkish leader to visit Armenia, but efforts to normalise the countries' relations faltered in 2010, and their border remains closed.

In 2009 the Turkish lira ditched the *yeni* (new) prefix introduced in 2005, signalling a stronger currency. The following year, Turkey saw the world's strongest economic growth after China.

International observers feared that Turkey was turning eastwards in 2010, as it voted against UN sanctions against Iran, instead brokering a nuclear fuel swap with its neighbour. Turkey also recalled its ambassador from Israel after Israeli troops stormed the Mavi Marmara, a Turkish vessel in a Gaza-bound aid flotilla, and killed nine activists. In September, Turks voted in favour of the AKP's proposed constitutional reform, which will lessen the military and judiciary's powers in what will hopefully be a move towards greater democracy. Critics, however, regard the reform as an attack on Turkey's bastions of Atatürk-inspired secularism.

People

Turkey's population (77.8 million) is predominantly made up of Turks, with a big Kurdish minority (about 15 million) and much smaller groups of Laz, Hemşin, Arabs, Jews, Greeks and Armenians. The Laz and Hemsin people are natives of the northeastern corner of Turkey on the Black Sea coast, while Arab influence is strongest in the Antakya (Hatay) area abutting Syria. Southeastern Turkey is pretty solidly Kurdish, although the problems of the last 30 years have led many to head west in search of a better life.

As a result of Atatürk's reforms, republican Turkey has largely adapted to a modern Westernised lifestyle, at least on the surface. In the big cities and coastal resorts, you will not feel much need to adapt to fit in. In smaller towns and villages, however, particularly in the east, you may find people warier and more conservative.

The gregarious, nationalistic Turks have an acute sense of pride and honour. They are fiercely proud of their history and heroes, especially Atatürk, whose portrait and statues are ubiquitous. The extended family still plays a key role and formality and politeness are important; if asked 'how is Turkey?', answer '*çok güzel*' (very beautiful).

Turkey is 99% Muslim, about 80% Sunni, with Shiites and Alevis mainly in the east. The religious practices of Sunnis and Alevis differ markedly, with the latter incorporating aspects of Anatolian folklore and less strict segregation of the sexes.

The country espouses a more relaxed version of Islam than many Middle Eastern nations. Many men drink alcohol (although almost no one touches pork) and many women uncover their heads.

The small Jewish community includes some 23,000 Jews in İstanbul. The Christian minority includes some 70,000 Armenians, also mostly in İstanbul, Greeks and ancient southeastern Anatolian communities, such as Chaldean Catholics and Aramaic-speaking adherents of the Syriac Orthodox Church.

Arts

As with everything else, Atatürk changed Turkey's cultural picture, encouraging painting, sculpture, Western music (he loved opera), dance and drama. Today's arts scene is a vibrant, if at times discordant, mix of the traditional, the innovative and the painfully modern.

Carpets

Turkey is famous for its beautiful carpets and *kilims* (woven rugs). It's thought that the Seljuk Turks introduced hand-woven carpet-making techniques to Anatolia in the 12th century. Traditionally, village women wove carpets for their family's use, or for their dowry; today, the dictates of the market rule, but carpets still incorporate traditional symbols and patterns. The Ministry of Culture has sponsored projects to revive aged weaving and dyeing methods in western Turkey; some shops stock these 'project carpets'.

Architecture

Turkey's architectural history encompasses everything from Hittite stonework and

Graeco-Roman temples to modern tower-blocks, but perhaps the most distinctively Turkish styles are Seljuk and Ottoman. The Seljuks left magnificent mosques, *madrasas* and *hans* (caravanserais), distinguished by their elaborate entrances. The Ottomans also built grand religious structures, and fine wood-and-stone houses in towns such as Safranbolu and Amasya (see the boxed text, p966).

Literature

The most famous Turkish novelists are Yaşar Kemal, nominated for the Nobel Prize for Literature on numerous occasions, and Orhan Pamuk, the Nobel Prize Laureate in 2006. Kemal's novels, which include *Memed, My Hawk, The Wind from the Plain* and *Salman the Solitary*, chronicle the desperate lives of villagers battling land-grabbing lords.

An inventive prose stylist, Pamuk's books include the Kars-set *Snow*, and the existential İstanbul whodunit *Black Book*, told through a series of newspaper columns. Other well-regarded contemporary writers include Elif Şafak *(The Flea Palace)*, Latife Tekin *(Dear Shameless Death)* and Buket Uzuner *(Long White Cloud, Gallipoli)*.

Cinema

Several Turkish directors have won world-wide recognition, most notably the late Yılmaz Güney, director of *Yol* (The Road) and *Duvar* (The Wall) and *Sürü*. Cannes favourite Nuri Bilge Ceylan probes the lives of village migrants in the big city in *Uzak* (Distant), and looks at male-female relationships in *İklimler* (Climates).

Ferzan Özpetek's *Hamam* addresses the hitherto hidden issue of homosexuality in Turkish society. Golden Bear-winning Fatih Akın ponders the Turkish experience in Germany in *Duvara Karsi* (Head On) and *Edge of Heaven*. Yılmaz Erdoğan's *Vizontele* is a black comedy about the first family to get a TV in a southeastern Anatolian town.

Music

The big pop stars include pretty-boy Tarkan, covered by Holly Valance, and chanteuse Sezen Aksu. Burhan Öçal is one of Turkey's

UNDERSTAND TURKEY ARTS

LOCAL KNOWLEDGE

CELAL COŞKUN: CARPET SELLER

Celal Coşkun learned to make carpets and *kilims* at his grandmother's knee in Malatya, before apprenticing as a carpet repairer in İstanbul and opening his shop in Fethiye, **Old Orient Carpet & Kilim Bazaar** (☑0532-510 6108; Karagözler Caddesi 5). We asked this veteran of the trade for his 10 top carpet tips.

» A carpet is for life; an investment that holds its value if treated properly.

» Know the basics: a carpet is wool or silk pile with single (Persian) or double (Turkish) knots; a *kilim* is a flat weave and is reversible; a *cicim* is a *kilim* with one side embroidered.

» Establish in advance your price range and what you want in terms of size, pattern and colour.

» Deal only with a seller who you feel you can trust, be it through reputation, recommendation or instinct.

» Counting knots is only important on silk-on-silk carpets, though a double-knotted wool carpet will wear better than a single-knotted one.

» Most reputable carpet shops can negotiate discounts of 5% to 10% depending on how you pay; anything higher than that and the price has been inflated.

» Carpets create a warm atmosphere, reduce echo and are more hygienic than fitted carpets; walking barefoot on a wool carpet reduces stress.

» To extend a carpet's length, remove your shoes when walking over it, and never beat it, as this breaks the knots and warp (vertical) and weft (horizontal) threads.

» If professional cleaning is too expensive and the traditional method (washing it with mild soap and water and drying it on wood blocks to allow air to circulate beneath) is too daunting, lay the carpet face (pattern) side down for a few minutes in fresh snow.

» Anything made by hand, including a carpet, can be repaired by hand.

finest percussionists; his seminal *New Dream* is a funky take on classical Turkish music.

With an Arabic spin, Arabesk is also popular. The genre's stars are Orhan Gencebay and the Kurdish former construction worker, İbrahim Tatlıses.

Two folk singers to listen out for are Kurdish chanteuses Aynur Doğan and the ululating Rojin.

For an excellent overview of Turkish music, watch Fatih Akın's documentary *Crossing the Bridge: the Sound of İstanbul,* which covers styles from rock and hip hop to *fasıl* (gypsy music), or listen to Baba Zulu's classic *Duble Oryantal.* Featuring *saz* (Turkish lute), electronic and pop, it's mixed by British dub master Mad Professor.

Sport

Turkish men are fanatical lovers of soccer, and will happily opine about English teams as well as domestic sides. Major teams include Bursaspor and the big İstanbul three, Galatasaray, Fenerbahçe and Beşiktaş.

The other main spectator sport is *yağlı güreş* (oil wrestling), where burly men in leather shorts grease themselves up with olive oil and grapple – most famously in Edirne (see p926).

Environment

The Land

The Dardanelles, the Sea of Marmara and the Bosphorus divide Turkey into Asian and European parts. Eastern Thrace (European Turkey) comprises only 3% of the country's 779,452-sq-km land area; the remaining 97% is Anatolia, a vast plateau rising eastward towards the Caucasus mountains. With more than 8300km of coastline, snow-capped mountains, rolling steppes, vast lakes and broad rivers, Turkey is geographically diverse. Turkey's 33 national parks include Uludağ National Park near Bursa, Cappadocia's Ala Dağlar National Park and Mt Nemrut National Park, northeast of Gaziantep.

Wildlife

Turkey's location at the junction between Asia and Europe and its varied geography has made it one of the most biodiverse temperate-zone countries, blessed with an exceptionally rich flora of more than 9000 species, 1200 of them endemic. In addition, some 400 bird species are found here, with about 250 of these passing through on migration from Africa to Europe.

In theory, you could see bears, deer, jackals, caracal, wild boars and wolves in Turkey, although you're unlikely to spot any wild animals unless you're hiking. Instead look out for Kangal dogs, originally bred to protect sheep from wolves and bears on mountain pastures. People wandering off the beaten track, especially in eastern Turkey, are often alarmed at the sight of these huge, yellow-coated, black-headed animals, especially as they often wear spiked collars to protect them against wolves.

Environmental Issues

Turkey's embryonic environmental movement is making slow progress; discarded litter and ugly concrete buildings (some half-finished) disfigure the west in particular.

Short of water and electricity, Turkey is one of the world's main builders of dams. The 22-dam Güneydoğu Anadolu Projesi (GAP) project is changing southeastern Anatolia's landscape as it generates hydroelectricity for industry. Parched valleys have become fish-filled lakes, causing an explosion of diseases such as malaria, and archaeological sites are disappearing under dam water. In 2008, plans to drown Hasankeyf saw the historic southeastern town named on the World Monuments Watch list. GAP has also generated problems with Syria and Iraq, the countries downriver.

Another major environmental challenge facing the country is the threat from maritime traffic along the Bosphorus. A noted *cause célèbre* is the loggerhead turtle *(caretta caretta),* whose beach nesting grounds such as İztuzu Beach at Dalyan, the Göksu Delta and Patara Beach have long been endangered by tourism and development. Various schemes are underway to protect these areas during the breeding season – look out for signs telling you when to avoid which stretches.

On the plus side, Turkey is slowly reclaiming its architectural heritage; Central Anatolia's Ottoman towns Safranbolu and Amasya are masterpieces of restoration. The country is doing well when it comes to beach cleanliness, with 300-plus beaches qualifying for Blue Flag status (which recognises success in areas such as water quality, environmental education and information, environmental management and safety); go to www.blueflag.org for the complete list.

İstanbul has a branch of Greenpeace Mediterranean (☏0212-292 7619; www. greenpeace.org/mediterranean).

Food & Drink

Afiyet olsun (good appetite)! Not without reason is Turkish food regarded as one of the world's greatest cuisines. Kebaps are, of course, the mainstay of restaurant meals; omnipresent *kebapçıs* (kebap restaurants) and *ocakbaşıs* (grill houses) sell a wide range of meat feasts. The ubiquitous *dürüm döner kebap* contains compressed meat (usually lamb) cooked on a revolving upright skewer over coals, then thinly sliced. When laid on pide bread, topped with tomato sauce and browned butter and with yoghurt on the side, *döner kebap* becomes *İskender kebap*. Equally ubiquitous are *şiş kebap* (roast skewered meat) and *köfte* (meatballs).

For a quick, cheap fill you could hardly do better than a Turkish pizza, a freshly cooked pide topped with cheese, egg or meat. Alternatively, *lahmacun* is a paper-thin Arabic pizza topped with chopped onion, lamb and tomato sauce. Other favourites are *gözleme* (thin savoury crepes) and *simit,* a small bread ring covered with sesame seeds. *Mantı* (Turkish ravioli) is perfect in winter but can be overly rich and heavy in hot weather.

Balık (fish) dishes, although excellent, are often expensive; always check the price before ordering.

For vegetarians, a meal made up of meze can be an excellent way to ensure a varied diet. Most restaurants will be able to rustle up at least *beyaz peynir* (ewe- or goat's-milk cheese), *sebze çorbası* (vegetable soup), *börek* (filled pastries – go for the white-cheese-and-parsley *su böreği*), *dolma* (stuffed vegetables), a *salata* (salad) such as the basic *çoban salatası* (shepherd's salad), *fasulye pilaki* (beans) and *patlıcan tava* (fried aubergine).

For dessert, try *fırın sütlaç* (rice pudding), *aşure* ('Noah's Ark' pudding), baklava (honey-soaked flaky pastry stuffed with walnuts or pistachios), *kadayıf* (dough soaked in syrup and topped with clotted cream) and *dondurma* (ice cream). The famously chewy *lokum* (Turkish delight) has been made here since the Ottoman sultans enjoyed it with their harems.

The national hot drink, *çay* (tea), is served in tiny tulip-shaped glasses with copious quantities of sugar. The wholly chemical *elma çay* (apple tea) is caffeine-free and only for tourists – locals wouldn't be seen dead drinking the stuff. If you're offered a tiny cup of traditional, industrial-strength Turkish *kahve* (coffee), you will be asked how sweet you like it: *çok şekerli* (very sweet), *orta şekerli* (middling), *az şekerli* (slightly sweet) or *sade* (not at all). Unfortunately, Nescafé is much more readily available than filter coffee or cappuccino. Don't miss the love-it-or-hate-it savoury dairy drink *ayran,* made by whipping up yoghurt with water and salt.

The Turks' meze accompaniment of choice is *rakı,* a fiery aniseed drink like the Greek *ouzo,* Arab *arak* or French *pastis.* Do as the Turks do and turn it milky white by adding water if you don't want to suffer ill effects. Turkish *şarap* (wine), both *kırmızı* (red) and *beyaz* (white), is improving in quality, particularly in Cappadocia and the Aegean island of Bozcaada. You can buy Tuborg or Efes Pilsen beers everywhere, although wine is less common and less Westernised towns may have only one licensed restaurant and/or liquor store.

SURVIVAL GUIDE

DIRECTORY A–Z
Accommodation

Hotels quote tariffs in Turkish lira or euros, sometimes both, so we've used the currency quoted by the business being reviewed.

In general, you will find more-Westernised spots such as İstanbul quote in euros, while less touristy locations use lira; most hotels happily accept either currency.

Virtually nowhere in Turkey is far from a mosque; light sleepers might want to bring earplugs for the early-morning call to prayer.

The rates quoted in this chapter are for high season (May to September) and include tax (KDV) and, unless otherwise mentioned, breakfast.

In tourist-dependent areas, such as the coast and Cappadocia, many accommodation options close from mid-October to late April. In those that remain open, rooms are discounted by about 20%, apart from during the Christmas period and major Islamic holidays.

PRICE RANGES

The prices ranges used in this chapter are based on the cost of a double room with en suite bathroom, and breakfast included:

€   Up to TL75

€€   TL75 to TL175

€€€   More than TL175

Prices in İstanbul are at the high ends of these brackets.

Listings are ordered by preference.

CAMPING

» Camping facilities are dotted about Turkey, mostly along the coasts and in Cappadocia and Mt Nemrut National Park.
» Pensions and hostels will often let you camp in their grounds and use their facilities for a small fee.

HOSTELS

» There are plenty of hostels with dormitories in popular destinations, where dorm beds usually cost about TL15 to TL20 per night.
» Turkey has no official hostel network, but there are Hostelling International members in İstanbul, Cappadocia and the Aegean and Western Mediterranean areas.

HOTELS

Budget In most cities and resort towns, good, inexpensive beds are readily available. The most difficult places to find good cheap rooms are İstanbul, Ankara, İzmir and package-holiday resort towns such as Alanya and Çeşme. The cheapest hotels, which charge around TL25 for a single, are mostly used by working-class Turkish men, and are not suitable for solo women.

RESIST THE TOUTS!

In small tourist towns such as Fethiye, Pamukkale and Selçuk, touts for pensions may approach you as you step from your bus, in the hope of extracting commission from a pension. Taxi drivers sometimes play this game, too. Avoid letting these faux friends make choices for you by deciding where you want to stay and sticking to your guns. Touts sometimes work for newly opened establishments offering cheap rates, but before viewing the pension in question, make it clear that you're only looking and are not obliged to stay.

Midrange One- and two-star hotels vary from TL70 to TL120 for a double room with shower. They are less oppressively masculine in atmosphere, even when the clientele is mainly male.

Top End Turkey offers top-notch boutique accommodation. Increasingly, old Ottoman mansions and other historic buildings are being refurbished, or completely rebuilt, as hotels equipped with all mod cons and bags of character. İstanbul and Cappadocia have some excellent boutique hotels, but almost every city boasts character-filled establishments.

PENSIONS

» Most tourist areas offer simple, family-run pensions where you can get a good, clean single or double for around TL40 or TL70.
» Pensions are often cosy and represent better value than hotels, distinguished from cheap hotels by extras such as a choice of simple meals, laundry service, international TV channels and staff who speak at least one foreign language.

TREE HOUSES

Olympos, on the Mediterranean coast, is famous for its 'tree houses', wooden shacks of minimal comfort in forested settings near the beach. Increasingly, these basic shelters are being converted into chalets with more comfort.

Activities

HIKING

Popular hiking destinations include Uludağ National Park near Bursa and southern Cappadocia's Ala Dağlar National Park. The spectacular valleys of central Cappadocia are excellent for day walks.

If you're a serious hiker, you could consider conquering Turkey's highest mountain, Mt Ararat (5137m), near Doğubayazıt, but you need a permit. Middle Earth Travel (p968) is a good contact.

Waymarked trails The *Sunday Times* chose the 500km Lycian Way, which runs around the coast and mountains of Lycia from Fethiye to Antalya, as one of the world's 10 best walks. The country's other waymarked path, the St Paul Trail (Perge to Lake Eğirdir), is a similar length. For more info on the trails, visit www.trekkinginturkey.com.

WATER & WIND SPORTS

All sorts of activities, including windsurfing, rafting and kayaking, are available on the Aegean and Mediterranean coasts. The best diving spots are Ayvalık, Kuşadası, Bodrum, Marmaris and Kaş. You can also try tandem paragliding in Ölüdeniz.

WINTER SPORTS

Most Turkish ski resorts are cheaper than their western European counterparts and offer good facilities, although they are much more basic than the better European resorts.

Palandöken, near Erzurum, has the best facilities, and pine-studded Sarıkamış, near Kars, has the most scenic runs. You can also ski on Uludağ, near Bursa, and Erciyes Dağı, above Kayseri.

RELAXING & REJUVENATING

Those of a lazier disposition may want to take a *gület* (p949) boat trip along the coast, stopping off to swim in bays along the way.

At the many *hammams* (p917), some in historic Seljuk or Ottoman buildings, you can get yourself scrubbed and massaged for a fraction of what it would cost in a Western spa.

Business Hours

In the areas covered by the following table, reviews in destination chapters only specify opening hours if they differ markedly from those listed here. Reviews of sights always list opening hours.

Most museums close on Monday and, from April to October, close 1½ to two hours later. The hours given here also experience seasonal variation; a bar is likely to open later in summer than in winter, and tourist offices in popular locations open longer hours and at weekends during summer.

The working day gets shortened during the holy month of Ramazan, which currently falls during summer. More Islamic cities such as Konya and Kayseri virtually shut down during noon prayers on Friday (the Muslim sabbath); apart from that, Friday is a normal working day.

Banks, post offices 8.30am-noon & 1.30-5pm Mon-Fri

Restaurants breakfast 8am-11am, lunch 12pm-4pm, dinner 6pm-10pm

Bars 4pm-late

Nightclubs & entertainment venues 9pm-late

Shops 9am-6pm Mon-Fri (longer in tourist areas and big cities – including weekend opening)

Children

Çocuklar (children) are the beloved centrepiece of family life and your children will be welcomed wherever they go.

However, Turkish safety consciousness rarely meets Western standards and children are not well catered for, although hotels and restaurants will often prepare special dishes for children.

Psychotic Turkish drivers and uneven surfaces can make using strollers, or just walking the streets with little ones, challenging. Other hazards include open power points and carelessly secured building sites.

Shops such as Migros supermarket sell baby food, although fresh milk is uncommon and formula is expensive.

Customs Regulations

IMPORT

Goods including the following can be imported duty-free:

» 200 cigarettes
» 50 cigars
» 200g of tobacco
» One 100cl or two 75cl bottles of wine or spirits

EXPORT

» It's illegal to export antiquities.
» Carpet shops should be able to provide a form certifying that your purchase is not antique.
» Ask for advice from vendors and keep receipts and paperwork.

Discount Cards

The following are available in Turkey but easier to get in your home country. They offer discounts on accommodation (typically 25%), eating, entertainment, shopping and transport.

International Student Identity Card (ISIC; www.isic.org)

International Youth Travel Card (IYTC; http://tinyurl.com/25tlbv7)

International Teacher Identity Card (ITIC; http://tinyurl.com/25tlbv7)

Embassies & Consulates

Foreign embassies are in Ankara but many countries also have consulates in İstanbul and elsewhere. In general they open from 8am or 9am to noon Monday to Friday, then after lunch until 5pm or 6pm. For more information, visit http://tinyurl.com/6ywt8a.

Australia Ankara (☎0312-459 9500; www.emb australia.org.tr; MNG Bldg, Uğur Mumcu Caddesi 88, Gaziosmanpaşa); İstanbul (☎0212-243 1333; Ritz Carlton Residences, Asker Ocağı Caddesi 15, Elmadağ)

Azerbaijan Ankara (☎0312-491 1681; www. mfa.gov.az/eng; Diplomatik Site, Baku Sokak 1, Oran); İstanbul (☎0212-325 8042; Sümbül Sokak 17, Levent 1)

Bulgaria Ankara (☎0312-467 2071; www. bulgaria.bg/en/; Atatürk Bulvarı 124, Kavaklıdere); İstanbul (☎0212-281 0115; www.bulgariancon-sulate-ist.org; Ahmet Adnan Saygun Caddesi 44, Ulus/Levent 2)

Canada Ankara (☎0312-409 2700; www. canadainternational.gc.ca; Cinnah Caddesi 58, Çankaya); İstanbul (☎0212-251 9838; 5th fl, İstiklal Caddesi 189, Beyoğlu)

France Ankara (☎0312-455 4545; www. ambafrance-tr.org; Paris Caddesi 70, Kavaklıdere); İstanbul (☎0212-334 8730; www.consulfrance -istanbul.org; İstiklal Caddesi 4, Taksim)

Georgia Ankara (☎0312-491 8030; www.turkey. mfa.gov.ge; Diplomatik Site, Kılıç Ali Sokak 12, Oran)

Germany Ankara (☎0312-455 5100; www. ankara.diplo.de; Atatürk Bulvarı 114, Kavaklıdere); İstanbul (☎0212-334 6100; İnönü Caddesi 16-18, Taksim)

Greece Ankara (☎0312-448 0647; www.mfa. gr; Zia Ur Rahman Caddesi 9-11, Gaziosmanpaşa); İstanbul (☎0212-393 8290; Akun Apt, İnönü Caddesi 39-8, Beyoğlu)

Iran Ankara (☎0312-468 2820; www.mfa.gov.ir; Tahran Caddesi 10, Kavaklıdere); İstanbul (☎0212-513 8230; Ankara Caddesi 1, Cağaloğlu)

Iraq Ankara (☎0312-468 7421; http://iraq missions.hostinguk.com; Turan Emeksiz Sokak 11, Gaziosmanpaşa); İstanbul (☎0212-299 0120; www.mofa.gov.iq; Köybaşı Caddesi 3, Yeniköy)

Ireland Ankara (☎0312-459 1000; www.embas syofireland.org.tr; MNG Bldg, Uğur Mumcu Caddesi 88, Gaziosmanpaşa); İstanbul (☎0212-482 1862; Ali Rıza Gürcan Caddesi 417)

Netherlands Ankara (☎0312-409 1800; http:// turkije.nlambassade.org; Hollanda Caddesi 5, Yıldız); İstanbul (☎0212-393 2121; http://istanbul. nlconsulate.org; İstiklal Caddesi 197, Beyoğlu)

New Zealand Ankara (☎0312-467 9054; www.nzembassy.com/turkey; İran Caddesi 13,

Kavaklıdere); İstanbul (☎0212-244 0272; İnönü Caddesi 48, Taksim)

Syria Ankara (☎0312-440 9657; Sedat Simavi Sokak 40, Çankaya); İstanbul (☎0212-232 6721; Ralli Apt 37, 3rd fl, Maçka Caddesi, Nişantaşı)

UK Ankara (☎0312-455 3344; http://ukinturkey. fco.gov.uk; Şehit Ersan Caddesi 46/A, Çankaya); İstanbul (☎0212-334 6400; Meşrutiyet Caddesi 34, Tepebaşı)

USA Ankara (☎0312-455 5555; http://turkey. usembassy.gov; Atatürk Bulvarı 110, Kavaklıdere); İstanbul (☎0212-335 9000; http://istanbul.uscon-sulate.gov; Kaplıcalar Mevkii 2, İstiniye)

Food

For more information on food and drink, see p985.

The prices ranges used in this book are based on the cost of a main course:

€   Up to TL9

€€   TL9 to TL17.50

€€€ More than TL17.50

Prices in İstanbul are at the high ends of these brackets.

Listings are ordered by preference.

Gay & Lesbian Travellers

Although not uncommon in a culture that traditionally separates men and women, overt homosexuality is not socially acceptable, except in a few small pockets in İstanbul, Ankara, Bodrum and some resorts. Some *hammams* are known to be gay meeting places.

Club Mancha (www.gayshareresorts.com) Resort in Bodrum for gay men.

Kaos GL (www.kaosgl.com) Ankara-based quarterly gay-and-lesbian magazine (in Turkish).

Lambda İstanbul (www.lambdaistanbul.org, in Turkish) LGBT support group.

Pride Travel Agency (www.turkey-gay-travel. com) Gay-friendly travel agent, with useful web links.

Health

In addition to the routine vaccinations that all travellers should have (see p1006), Typhoid and Hepatitis A and B are recommended for Turkey.

Rabies is endemic here, so if you will be travelling off the beaten track you might want to consider a vaccination.

Malaria is found in a few areas on the Syrian border.

Insurance

» A travel insurance policy covering theft, loss and medical expenses is a good idea.
» Some policies exclude 'dangerous activities', which can include scuba-diving, motorcycling and even hiking.
» Some policies may not cover you if you travel to regions of the country where your government warns against travel.
» If you decide to cancel your trip on the advice of an official warning against travel, your insurer may not cover you.

Internet Access

» Internet cafes are widespread.
» Fees are typically about TL2 per hour.
» Throughout the country, most accommodation options offer free wi-fi, as do many other businesses.
» We have used the internet icon (@) where the option provides a computer with internet access for guest use.
» In Eating and Drinking reviews, we have used the wi-fi icon (🛜) where the business has a network.

Language Courses

The most popular Turkish language courses are **Dilmer** (www.dilmer.com), near Taksim Sq in İstanbul, and the Ankara University-affiliated **Tömer** (www.tomer.com.tr), with branches throughout the country.

Legal Matters

» Technically, you should carry your passport at all times, but you may prefer to carry a photocopy.
» There are laws against treason, antiques smuggling and illegal drugs.

Maps

Maps are available at tourist offices and bookshops, such as the shops on and around İstiklal Caddesi in İstanbul; online, check Tulumba.com and Amazon.

Mep Medya's city, regional and touring maps are recommended.

Money

» Turkey's currency, the Türk Lirası (Turkish Lira; TL), replaced the Yeni Türk Lirası (New Turkish Lira; YTL) in January 2009.
» Lira come in notes of 5, 10, 20, 50 and 100, and 1 lira coins.
» One lira is worth 100 *kuruş*, which is available in 1, 5, 10, 25 and 50 coins.
» Watch out for people dumping their old-currency coins on you.
» Prices in this book are quoted in lira or €, depending on which currency is used by the business being reviewed.
» Lack of change is a constant problem; try to keep a supply of coins and small notes for minor payments.

ATMS

ATMs dispense Turkish lira, and occasionally euros and US dollars, to Visa, MasterCard, Cirrus and Maestro card holders. Machines are found in most towns.

It's possible to get around Turkey using only ATMs, if you draw out money in the towns to tide you through the villages, and keep some cash in reserve for the inevitable day when the ATM throws a wobbly.

Some banks levy high charges for the conversion and/or withdrawal, so check your bank's fees before you leave home.

CASH

» Euros and US dollars are the most readily accepted foreign currencies, and the easiest to change.
» Many exchange offices and banks will change other major currencies such as UK pounds and Japanese yen.
» Foreign currencies are accepted in shops, hotels and restaurants in many tourist areas.
» Taxi drivers accept foreign currencies for big journeys.

CREDIT CARDS

Visa and MasterCard are widely accepted by hotels, shops and restaurants, although often not by pensions and local restaurants outside main tourist areas.

You can also get cash advances on these cards.

American Express is more commonly accepted in top-end establishments.

Inform your credit card provider of your travel plans.

MONEYCHANGERS

» The Turkish lira is weak against Western currencies, and you will likely get a better exchange rate in Turkey than elsewhere.
» Exchange offices offer better rates than banks, and often don't charge commission. They offer the best rates in market areas. Offices are also found at some post offices, shops and hotels.

» Banks are more likely to change minor currencies, although often make heavy weather of it.

» Turkey has no black market.

TIPPING & BARGAINING

Turkey is fairly European in its approach to tipping and you won't be pestered with demands for baksheesh.

Round up metered taxi fares and leave waiters and masseurs around 10% to 15% of the bill. In more-expensive restaurants, check a *servis ücreti* (service charge) hasn't been automatically added to the bill.

Hotel prices are sometimes negotiable, and you should always bargain for souvenirs.

TRAVELLERS CHEQUES

Banks, shops and hotels usually see it as a burden to change travellers cheques, and will either try to persuade you to go elsewhere or charge you a premium. If you do have to change them, try one of the major banks.

Photography

» People in Turkey are generally receptive to having their photo taken, apart from when they are praying or performing other religious activities.

» As in most countries, do not take photos of military sites, airfields, police stations and so on.

Post

The Turkish postal service is known as the PTT. *Postanes* (post offices) are indicated by blue-on-yellow 'PTT' signs.

Postcards sent abroad cost TL0.80; letters cost from TL85.

If you are shipping something from Turkey, don't close your parcel before it has been inspected by a customs official.

Parcels sent by airmail to Europe cost around TL40 for the first kilo, then about TL4.50 per kilo (TL7.90 to the UK); to Australia/USA, TL42.90/29.10, then TL20.40/9.30.

Public Holidays

Public holidays in Turkey:

New Year's Day 1 January

National Sovereignty & Children's Day 23 April

Youth & Sports Day 19 May

Victory Day 30 August

Republic Day 28–29 October

Turkey also celebrates the main Islamic holidays, the most important of which are Şeker Bayramı (18–20 August 2012), which marks the end of the holy month of Ramazan; and about two months later, Kurban Bayramı (25–29 October 2012). Due to the fact that these holidays are celebrated according to the Muslim lunar calendar, they take place around 11 days earlier every year.

Safe Travel

Although Turkey is in no way a dangerous country to visit, it's always wise to be a little cautious, especially if you're travelling alone.

As a pedestrian, note that there is no such thing as a generally acknowledged right of way, despite the little green man. Give way to cars and trucks in all situations.

Drugging is a risk, especially for lone men, and most commonly in İstanbul. It may involve so-called friends, a bar, and perhaps a willowy temptress. Be a little cautious about who you befriend, especially when you're new to the country.

Receiving the hard sell from carpet salesmen in places such as İstanbul's Grand Bazaar can drive you to distraction. Remember you're under no obligation to look or buy.

There is often no such thing as a free kebap. 'Free' lifts and other suspiciously cheap services often lead to near-compulsory visits to carpet showrooms or hotel commission for touts.

Do not buy coins or other artefacts offered to you by touts at ancient sites such as Ephesus and Perge.

See the boxed text on p976 for advice on visiting Kurdish southeastern Anatolia. Sporadic bombings, linked to Kurdish separatist groups, target affluent areas frequented by tourists, including a double-bomb attack in İstanbul in 2008.

Nationalistic laws against insulting, defaming or making light of Atatürk, the Turkish flag and so on are taken seriously. Turks have been known to claim derogatory remarks were made in the heat of a quarrel, which is enough to get a foreigner carted off to jail.

Telephone

See p908 for important numbers.

Türk Telekom (www.telekom.gov.tr) has a monopoly on phone services, which are efficient if costly.

Payphones are found in many major public buildings and facilities, public squares and transport terminals.

International calls can be made from payphones, which require phonecards.

MOBILE PHONES

Turks just love *cep* (mobile) phones, and reception is generally excellent.

Mobile phone numbers start with a four-figure number beginning with ☑05.

If you set up a roaming facility with your home network, most mobiles can connect to Turkcell (the most comprehensive network), Vodafone and Avea.

To buy a Turkcell SIM card (TL25 to TL35), you need to show your passport and ensure the seller phones your details through to Turkcell.

If you use a Turkish SIM card in your home mobile, the network detects and bars foreign phones within a month. To avoid barring, register your phone by going to a certified mobile phone shop with your passport and filling out a short form declaring your phone in Turkey.

You can pick up a basic mobile phone for about TL50.

New Turkcell credit is readily available at shops displaying the company's blue-and-yellow logo, which can be found on every street corner.

PHONE CODES

» We have listed four-digit local area codes at the start of city and town sections. These should be followed by a seven-digit number.
» Numbers starting with 444 don't require area codes and, wherever you call from, are charged at the local rate.
» See also p908.

PHONECARDS

» Phonecards can be bought at telephone centres or, for a small mark-up, from some shops.
» The cheapest option for international calls is with phonecards such as IPC, available at post offices.
» If you're only going to make one quick call, it's easier to look for a booth with a sign saying '*kontörlü telefon*', where the cost of your call is metered.

Time

Standard Turkish time is two hours ahead of GMT/UTC – three during daylight saving (last Sunday in March until the last Sunday in October), when Turkish clocks go forward one hour.

Toilets

» Most hotels have sit-down toilets, but hole-in-the-ground models are common.
» Toilet paper is often unavailable, so keep some on you.
» In an emergency it's worth remembering that mosques have basic men and women's toilets.

Tourist Information

Local tourist offices, run by the **Ministry of Culture and Tourism** (www.goturkey.com), can rarely do more than hand out glossy brochures. There are exceptions, but tour operators, pension owners and so on are often better sources of information.

Travellers with Disabilities

Turkey is challenging for disabled (*engelli* or *özürlü*) travellers, and not just because of the scarce facilities. Obstacles lurk everywhere and crossing the road is tough even for the fully mobile, although Selçuk, Bodrum and Fethiye are relatively user-friendly.

Airlines and top hotels and resorts have some provision for wheelchair access, with discounts offered by Turkish Airlines.

Hotel Rolli (www.hotel-rolli.de) Specially designed for wheelchair users; in Anamur (p962).

Mephisto Voyage (www.mephistovoyage.com) Special tours of Cappadocia for mobility-impaired people, utilising the Joelette system.

Visas

Nationals of countries including Denmark, Finland, France, Germany, Israel, Italy, Japan, New Zealand, Sweden and Switzerland don't need a visa to visit Turkey for up to 90 days.

Nationals of countries including Australia, Austria, Belgium, Canada, Ireland, the Netherlands, Norway, Portugal, Spain, the UK and the USA need a visa, but it is just a sticker bought on arrival at the airport or border post.

The standard visa is valid for three months and, depending on your nationality, usually allows for multiple entries.

You must buy the visa before joining the queue for immigration.

The cost of the visa varies. At the time of writing, Australians and Americans paid US$20 (or €15), Canadians US$60 (or

€45) and British citizens UK£10 (or €15 or US$20).

You *must* pay in hard-currency cash. The customs officers expect to be paid in one of the above currencies, and don't give change.

Your passport must be valid for at least six months from the date you enter the country.

The bureaucracy and costs involved in applying for further visas mean that it's much easier to do a 'visa run', heading to a Greek island, perhaps, and returning on a fresh visa.

See the **Ministry of Foreign Affairs** (www.mfa.gov.tr) for the latest information.

Volunteering

Alternative Camp (www.alternativecamp.org) Runs camps for people with disabilities.

Gençlik Servisleri Merkezi (www.gsm-youth.org) Runs voluntary work camps.

Gençtur (www.genctur.com) A portal for volunteering schemes.

Ta Tu Ta (www.bugday.org/tatuta) Organises work and accommodation on organic farms.

Volunteer Abroad (www.volunteerabroad.com) Volunteering opportunities through international organisations.

Women Travellers

Turkish society is still basically sexually segregated, especially once you get away from the big cities and tourist resorts. Although younger Turks are questioning the old ways and women hold positions of authority (there's even been a female prime minister), foreign women can find themselves being harassed. It's mostly just catcalls and dubious remarks, but assaults do occasionally occur.

Travelling with companions usually improves matters, and it's worth remembering that Turkish women ignore men who speak to them in the street. Dressing appropriately will also reduce unwanted attention, and encourage most men to treat you with kindness and generosity.

Tailor your behaviour and your clothing to your surrounds. Look at what local women are wearing. On the streets of Beyoğlu (İstanbul) you'll see skimpy tops and tight jeans, but cleavage and short skirts without leggings are a no-no everywhere except nightclubs in İstanbul and heavily touristed destinations along the coast.

Bring a shawl to cover your head when visiting mosques.

On the street, you don't need to don a headscarf, but keeping your legs, upper arms and neckline covered is often a good idea, particularly in eastern Anatolia. Here, long sleeves and baggy long pants should attract the least attention, and you should keep your dealings with men formal and polite, not friendly.

Wearing a wedding ring and carrying a photo of your 'husband' and 'child' can help, as can wearing dark glasses to avoid eye contact.

Men and unrelated women are not supposed to sit together on long-distance buses, although the bus companies rarely enforce this in the case of foreigners. Lone women are often assigned seats at the front of the bus near the driver.

Restaurants and tea gardens that aim to attract women often set aside a family room or section. Look for the term *aile salonu* (family dining room), or just *aile*.

Stick to official campsites and camp where there are plenty of people around, especially out east. See p986 for more accommodation advice.

Work

Travellers sometimes work illegally for room and board in pensions, bars and other businesses in tourist areas. These jobs are generally badly paid and only last a few months maximum, but they are a fun way to stay in a place and get to know the locals.

Job hunters may have luck with:
» http://istanbul.craigslist.org
» www.sahibinden.com/en
» www.mymerhaba.com
» www.expatinturkey.com
» www.sublimeportal.com

NANNYING

One of the most lucrative nonspecialist jobs available to foreigners is nannying for the wealthy urban elite, with opportunities for English, French and German speakers.

You must be prepared for long hours and demanding employers.

Accommodation is normally included, but living with the family means you are always on call, and you may be based in the suburbs.

Anglo Nannies (www.anglonannies.com) The main agency.

TEACHING ENGLISH

There is lots of work available for qualified English teachers, although many employers are reluctant to deal with the bureaucratic headache of helping you get a work permit. You will have to be prepared to do 'visa runs' (see p991).

One of the best options is working for a university or a *dershane* (private school). This typically pays TL2000 to TL3500 per month, and also offers attractions such as accommodation (although it may be on or near the campus in the suburbs), a work permit and even flights. Jobs are mostly advertised in May and June, then run from September until the end of the academic year in June.

If you're looking for short-term opportunities or don't have any teaching qualifications, you could advertise yourself as a tutor on Craigslist and Sahibinden (TL35 to TL60 per hour) or try a language school (TL19 to TL35). Language schools are exploitative institutions untroubled by professional ethics; those with a particularly bad reputation are often 'blacklisted' on Craigslist.

Visit www.eslcafe.com and www.tefl.com.

Getting There & Away

Air

The cheapest fares for Turkey are usually to **İstanbul's Atatürk International Airport** (www.ataturkairport.com), 23km west of Sultanahmet, and **Sabiha Gökçen International Airport** (www.sgairport.com), 50km east of Sultanahmet on the Asian side of the city.

To reach other Turkish airports, you often have to transit in İstanbul.

Other international airports are at Ankara, Antalya, Bodrum, Dalaman and İzmir.

It's a good idea to book at least two months in advance if you plan to arrive between April and late August. If you plan to visit a resort, check with your local travel agents for flight and accommodation deals.

İstanbul is connected to most major European cities by Turkey's national carrier, **Turkish Airlines** (www.thy.com), its subsidiary **Sun Express** (www.sunexpress.com), its Turkish competitor **Pegasus Airlines** (www.flypgs.com) and European carriers including **easyJet** (www.easyjet.com).

See p994 for more Turkish airlines, many of which operate international flights.

In addition to Turkish Airlines, airlines linking Turkey with the following regions include:

Australasia Emirates Airlines, Malaysia Airlines, Singapore Airlines (or travel with a European airline via Europe)

Europe German charter airlines (try Condor, German Wings and Corendon Airlines), easyJet, Lufthansa, Pegasus Airlines, Sun Express

Middle East & Asia Armavia Airlines, Azerbaijan Airlines, Pegasus Airlines, Atlasjet, Emirates Airlines, Singapore Airlines

UK & Ireland Atlasjet, British Airways, charter flights (try www.justtheflight.co.uk and www.thomsonfly.com), easyJet, Pegasus Airlines

North America Air Canada, American Airlines, British Airways, Delta Airlines, KLM, Lufthansa (direct or via Europe)

Land

Turkey shares borders with Armenia (closed), Azerbaijan, Bulgaria, Georgia, Greece, Iran, Iraq and Syria. There are many routes into and out of the country.

BUS

Austria, Bulgaria, Germany, Greece, Macedonia and Romania have the most direct buses to İstanbul.

The Turkish companies **Varan Turizm** (www.varan.com.tr), **Metro Turizm** (www.metroturizm.com.tr) and **Öz Batu** (http://ozbatu turizm.com) operate on these routes.

If you're travelling from other European countries, you'll likely have to catch a connecting bus.

Sample one-way fares to/from İstanbul:

Berlin €140 (36 hours)

Sofia, Bulgaria TL50 (10 hours)

TRAIN

See p996 for information on the trains crossing the Greek and Bulgarian borders to/from İstanbul, and p908 for a suggested route between London and İstanbul.

Sea

Departure times change between seasons, with less ferries generally running in winter. For more information see the websites listed in the table or the relevant destinations.

Ferrylines (www.ferrylines.com) A good starting point for information.

Getting Around

Air

Turkey is well connected by air throughout the country, although many flights go via hubs İstanbul or Ankara. Internal flights are a good option in such a large country, and competition between the following Turkish airlines keeps tickets affordable.

Atlasjet (www.atlasjet.com) Limited network including Adana, Ankara, Antalya, Bodrum, Dalaman, İstanbul, İzmir, and Lefkoşa (North Nicosia), Northern Cyprus.

Anadolu Jet (www.anadolujet.com) Turkish Airlines subsidiary serving some 30 airports.

Onur Air (www.onurair.com.tr) Flies from İstanbul to Adana, Antalya, Bodrum, Dalaman, Diyarbakır, Erzurum, Gaziantep, İzmir, Malatya, Samsun and Trabzon.

Pegasus Airlines (www.pegasusairlines.com) Serves most of the locations mentioned in the above listings plus less-usual spots including Kayseri and Van.

Sun Express (www.sunexpress.com) Turkish Airlines subsidiary with an extensive network, particularly from Antalya, İstanbul and İzmir.

Turkish Airlines (www.thy.com) The main domestic network.

Bicycle

Riding a bike is a great way of exploring the countryside and archaeological sites, especially in touristy areas, where you can hire bikes from pensions and rental outfits. Road surfaces are generally acceptable, if a bit rough, though Turkey's notorious road-hog drivers are a hazard.

BACKPACKER BUS

An easy option, geared towards backpackers (don't expect to meet many Turks on it), is the **Fez Bus** (www.feztravel.com). The hop-on, hop-off bus service links the main resorts of the Aegean and the Mediterranean with İstanbul and Cappadocia.

Bus

The Turkish bus network is a pleasant surprise: coaches go just about everywhere, they're cheap and comfortable, smoking isn't permitted, drinks and snacks are often provided, and regular toilet stops are built into longer routes.

The premium companies have nationwide networks offering greater speed and comfort for slightly higher fares. They also have the best safety records. Departures on popular routes can be as frequent as every 15 minutes, with hourly services the norm from major cities. Fares vary according to distance and the popularity of the route; typically, from İstanbul to Çanakkale costs TL42, İstanbul to Ankara TL39 to TL49, and İstanbul to Göreme (Cappadocia) TL50 to TL60.

Although you can usually walk into an *otogar* (bus station) and buy a ticket for the next bus, it's wise to plan ahead for public holidays, at weekends and during the school holidays from mid-June to early September. You can reserve seats over the web with the better companies.

A town's *otogar* is often on the outskirts, but most bus companies provide free *servis* buses to/from the centre. Besides intercity buses, *otogars* often handle *dolmuşes* (see p996) to outlying districts or villages. Larger bus stations have an *emanetçi* (left luggage) room, which you can use for a nominal fee.

The best bus companies, with extensive route networks:

Kamil Koç (www.kamilkoc.com.tr, in Turkish) Good for western Turkey.

Metro Turizm (www.metroturizm.com.tr) Nationwide.

Ulusoy (www.ulusoy.com.tr) Nationwide.

Varan Turizm (www.varan.com.tr) Its 'bistro coach' between İstanbul and Ankara features a restaurant.

Car & Motorcycle

Public transport is a much easier and less stressful way of getting around the traffic-clogged cities. Turkey's main motoring organisation is the **Türkiye Turing ve Otomobil Kurumu** (Turkish Touring & Automobile Association; www.turing.org.tr).

BRINGING YOUR OWN VEHICLE

You can bring your vehicle into Turkey for six months without charge, but details of

ROUTE	FREQUENCY	DURATION	FARE (ONE WAY/RETURN)	COMPANY
Ayvalık–Lesvos, Greece	Mon-Sat May-Sep; 3 weekly Oct-May	1½hr	€40/50, car €60/70	Jale Tour (www.jale tour.com)
Alanya–Girne (Kyrenia), Northern Cyprus	2 weekly	3½hr	TL88/138	Fergün Denizcilik (www.fergun.net)
Bodrum–Kos, Greece	daily	1hr	€28/56	Bodrum Ferryboat Association (www. bodrumferryboat. com)
Bodrum–Rhodes, Greece	2 weekly Jun-Sep	2¼hr	€60/120	Bodrum Ferryboat Association (www. bodrumferryboat. com)
Çeşme–Chios, Greece	daily mid-May-mid-Sep; 2 weekly Sep-May	1½hr	€25/40, car €70/120	Ertürk (www.erturk. com.tr)
Çeşme–Ancona, Italy	weekly May-Sep	60hr	one way €215 to €505, car €260	Marmara Lines (www. marmaralines.com)
Datça–Rhodes	Sat May-Sep	45min	TL90/180	Knidos Yachting (www. knidosyachting.com)
Datça–Simi, Greece	hydrofoil Sat May-Sep, *gület* on demand	hydrofoil 15min, *gület* 70min	hydrofoil TLL60/120, *gület* one way TL120	Knidos Yachting (www. knidosyachting.com)
İstanbul–Sevastopol, Ukraine	weekly	32hr	return from €185	Sudostroyenie
Kaş–Meis (Kastellorizo), Greece	daily	20min	single or same-day return TL40	Meis Express (www. meisexpress.com)
Kuşadası–Samos, Greece	daily Apr-Oct	1¼hr	€30/50	Meander Travel (www. meandertravel.com)
Marmaris–Rhodes	2 daily Apr-Oct, twice weekly Nov-Mar	50min to 2hr	from €43/45, car from €95/120	Yeşil Marmaris Travel & Yachting (www. yesilmarmaris.com)
Taşucu–Girne (Kyrenia), Northern Cyprus	daily	2hr	TL79/124	Akgünler Denizcilik (www.akgunler.com.tr)
Trabzon–Sochi, Russia	weekly	12hr	one way €65	Apollonia II & Princess Victoria Lines
Turgutreis–Kalymnos, Greece	2 weekly	1¼hr	€43/86	Bodrum Ferryboat Association (www. bodrumferryboat. com)
Turgutreis–Kos, Greece	5 weekly	45min	€28/56	Bodrum Ferryboat Association (www. bodrumferryboat.com)

your car are stamped in your passport to ensure it leaves the country with you.

DRIVING LICENCES

An international driving permit (IDP) is not obligatory, but may be handy if your driving licence is from a country likely to seem obscure to a Turkish police officer.

FUEL & SPARE PARTS

Turkey has some of the world's most expensive fuel prices. Petrol and diesel both cost over TL3 per litre.

There are plenty of modern petrol stations in the west. In the east they are slightly less abundant and it's a good idea to have a full tank when you start out in the morning.

Yedek parçaları (spare parts) are readily available in the big cities and *sanayi bölgesi* (industrial zones) on the outskirts, especially for European models such as Renaults, Fiats and Mercedes-Benz. Repairs are usually quick and cheap.

CAR HIRE

Rental charges are similar to those in Continental Europe.

You normally need to be at least 21 years old, with a year's driving experience, to hire a car.

Most companies require a credit card.

The big international companies (including Avis, Budget, Europcar, Hertz, National and Sixt) are represented in the main cities, towns and airports. Particularly in eastern Anatolia, stick with these companies, as they have insurance and better emergency backup.

Economy Car Rentals (www.economycar rentals.com) Gets excellent rates with other companies, including Budget.

INSURANCE

You *must* have third-party insurance to drive in Turkey. If you don't have it, you can buy it at the border.

ROAD RULES & SAFETY

Turkey has one of the world's highest motor-vehicle accident rates.

Driving is hair-raising during the day because of fast, inappropriate driving and overladen trucks, and dangerous at night, when some drivers speed along with their headlights off.

Unless otherwise posted, maximum speed limits are 50km/h in towns, 90km/h on highways and 120km/h on an *otoyol* (motorway).

Drink-driving is a complete no-no.

Hitching

Although we don't recommend hitching *(otostop)*, short hitches are not uncommon in Turkey. If you need to get from the highway to an archaeological site, hitch a ride with whatever comes along, be it a tractor, lorry or private car.

Offer to pay something towards the petrol, although most drivers pick up foreign hitchers for their curiosity value.

Instead of sticking out your thumb for a lift you should face the traffic, hold your arm out towards the road, and wave it up and down as if bouncing a basketball.

Local Transport

Short-distance and local routes are usually served by medium-sized 'midibuses' or smaller *dolmuşes* (minibuses that follow prescribed routes), run by private operators.

A few cities, including Bursa and İzmir, have old-fashioned *taksi dolmuşes* (shared taxis).

Most towns have a municipal bus network; this may be supplemented by underground, tram, train and even ferry services in the largest cities.

Taxis are plentiful; they have meters – just make sure they're switched on.

Tours

Areas where an organised tour makes sense, particularly with limited time, include the Gallipoli, Troy and Cappadocia. There are unscrupulous operators, particularly in Sultanahmet, İstanbul, but also plenty of good outfits.

Train

Although most people still opt for buses as train journey times are notoriously long, the system is being overhauled and a few fast lines (such as İstanbul–Ankara) are in service.

A growing number of fans appreciate the no-rush travel experience of a train journey, such as the stunning scenery rolling by and immersion with fellow passengers.

The occasional unannounced hold-up and public toilets gone feral by the end of the long journey are all part of the adventure. If you're on a budget, an overnight train journey is a great way to save accommodation costs. The trick is not to attempt a trans-Turkey trip in one go, as the country is large and the trains slow.

Turkish State Railways (www.tcdd.gov.tr)

The Man in Seat Sixty-One (www.seat61.com/turkey2) Information and inspiration on Turkish train travel.

ROUTES

The train network covers the country fairly well, with the notable exception of the coastlines. The short stretch between İzmir and Selçuk is being upgraded. For the Aegean and Mediterranean coasts you can travel by train to either İzmir or Konya, and take the bus from there.

Useful routes include:
» İstanbul–Ankara
» İstanbul–İzmir (including ferry)
» İzmir–Ankara
» Konya–Ankara

Long-distance, overnight trips include:
» İstanbul-Adana, Kars, Konya and Tatvan (Lake Van)

Survival Guide

Directory A–Z

Accommodation

There's a vast choice of accommodation in Mediterranean Europe, ranging from world-famous five-star hotels to modest family rooms. The cheapest places to stay are camping grounds, followed by hostels and student dormitories. Guest houses, pensions and private rooms often offer good value, as do rooms in religious institutes. Self-catering flats and cottages are also worth considering for group stays, especially for longer sojourns. You can also bunk down in a B&B, stay on a farm or crash on a couch.

Unless otherwise stated, prices in this book are high-season rates for rooms with private bathrooms. All listings are ordered according to preference with the author's favourite place listed first.

Some general tips:

» High season rates apply at Easter, from June to August, and over Christmas and New Year. Prices are also high in April and May in many of the region's big cities. Conversely, many city hoteliers drop rates in August to lure punters away from the coast.

» Book ahead for peak holiday periods and year-round in big destinations such as Paris, Rome and Madrid – at least for the first night or two. Most places can be booked online, and many require credit card details in lieu of a deposit.

» It's often worth bargaining in the low season as, although they may not advertise the fact, many places reduce their rates.

» Many accommodation options on the coast close over winter, typically between November and March.

» Most airports and many large train stations have accommodation-booking desks, although they rarely cover budget hotels. Tourist offices can generally supply accommodation lists and some will even help you find a hotel. There's usually a small fee for this service, but if accommodation is tight it can save you hassle. Agencies offering private rooms are also worth considering.

» In some destinations locals wait at train stations or ferry terminals, touting rented rooms. Don't necessarily reject these out of hand, as in some places they're genuine offers. Before accepting though, make sure the accommodation isn't in a far-flung suburb or an outlying village that requires a difficult journey, and don't forget to confirm the price.

» It's always worth checking hotel websites for last-minute deals and discounts.

B&Bs

B&B accommodation is widely available across the region and usually provides excellent value. There's a huge selection of places, ranging from traditional B&B set-ups (private homes with a guest room or two) to smart boutique-style outfits offering quality accommodation at midrange and top-end prices. As a general rule, a B&B room will be cheaper than a hotel room of corresponding comfort.

Most B&Bs will give you a key, allowing you to come and go as you like, although some places might insist that you're back by a certain time. Most smarter B&Bs will have private bathrooms; in some you might have to share with other guests or the host family.

When booking, make sure you're happy with the location. City B&Bs are often not central, so check local transport connections; if it's in a remote rural spot, work out in advance how it fits in with your plans.

Contact tourist offices for lists of local B&Bs. Useful resources are:

International Bed and Breakfast Pages (www.ibbp.com)

Bed & Breakfast in Europe (www.bedandbreakfastineurope.com)

Europe and Relax (www.europeandrelax.com)

Camping

Camping is very popular in Mediterranean Europe, and there are thousands of campsites dotted around the region. These range from large, resort-style operations with swimming pools and supermarkets to more simple affairs in isolated countryside locations. National tourist offices and local camping organisations can provide lists.

If you're intent on camping around the region, consider the **Camping Card International** (CCI; www.campingcardinternational.com), an ID-style card that provides third-party insurance and entitles you to discounts of up to 25% at more than 1100 camping grounds across Europe. Note that in some cases discounts are not available if you pay by credit card. CCIs are issued by automobile associations, camping federations and, sometimes, on the spot at camping grounds.

Further considerations:

» At designated grounds, there are often charges per tent or site, per person and per vehicle.

» Many places have bungalows or cottages accommodating two to eight people.

» Free camping is often illegal without permission from the local authorities (the police or local council) or from the owner of the land. In some countries (eg France and Spain) it is illegal on all but private land, and in Greece, Croatia and Slovenia it's illegal altogether. This doesn't prevent hikers from occasionally pitching their tent for the night, and you'll usually get away with it if you have a small tent, stay only one or two nights, take the tent down during the day and don't light a campfire or leave rubbish. At worst, you'll be woken up by the police and asked to move on.

» Many campsites close over winter, typically between October and April.

» Carting your kit around with you is fine if you've got a car, but a real pain if you haven't.

» Most city camping grounds are some distance from the city centre, so the money you save on accommodation can quickly be eaten up in bus and train fares.

Couchsurfing & House Swapping

The cheapest way of staying in the region is sleeping on a local's couch – a practice known as couchsurfing. Through online agencies such as **Couch Surfing** (www.couchsurfing.org), **GlobalFreeloaders** (www.globalfreeloaders.com) or **Hospitality Club** (www.hospitalityclub.org), you can contact members across the world who'll let you sleep on their sofa or in their spare room for next to nothing.

Another cheap alternative is house swapping, whereby you sign up to an online agency such as **Home Exchange** (www.ihen.com) or **Global Home Exchange** (www.4homex.com) and arrange to swap houses with a fellow member for an agreed period of time.

Farm-stays

Farm-stays are an excellent way of escaping the crowds and experiencing the local countryside. They are particularly popular in Italy, where an *agriturismo* can be anything from a working farm to a luxurious rural resort in a converted castle. Italian tourist offices can provide lists for specific areas. Online information is available at **Agriturist** (www.agriturist.it).

Farm-stays are also popular in Slovenia – the **Slovenia Tourist Board** (www.slovenia.info) lists 260 tourist farms – and Portugal, where farmhouses and country homes are affiliated to the **Turihab** (www.turihab.pt) network.

In general:

» Room rates are usually much less than in hotels of comparable comfort.

» Many farm-stays offer activities such as horse riding, hiking and cycling, and serve delicious food.

» Country locations mean that most have plenty of space for kids to run around in, making them a good choice for families.

» You'll almost certainly need a car to get to them.

» Always book ahead, as in high season places fill quickly, while in low season many open only on request.

Guest Houses & Pensions

The distinction between a guest house and a hotel is fairly blurred. Most guest houses are simple family affairs offering basic rooms and shared bathrooms but more expensive guest houses can have rooms of hotel standard.

Pensions, which are widespread throughout the region, are basically small, modest hotels. In cities, they are often housed in converted flats that occupy one or two floors of a large apartment block. Rooms tend to be simple, often with just a basin and bidet.

Homestays & Private Rooms

Renting a room in a local home is generally a good, cheap option, especially for longer stays. It's not so good for solo travellers (most rooms are set up as doubles or triples) or for quick stopovers (many places levy hefty surcharges, typically 30% to 40%, for stays of under three or four days).

» Room quality and price vary considerably – some rooms come with private bathrooms, some have cooking facilities, some might even have both.

» When you book, make sure you check if the price is per room or per person, and whether or not breakfast is included. Also make sure you're happy with the location.

» You can book rooms either privately or through an agency (to whom you'll have to pay a fee). Once you've booked a room, it's always worth phoning ahead to say when you're arriving as, in many cases, the owners will pick you up at the station or port.

» Room rentals are particularly widespread in Albania, Bosnia & Hercegovina, Croatia, Greece and Montenegro.

Hostels

Hostels are widespread across the region and provide a cheap roof over your head. Hostels referred to as 'official' are affiliated with **Hostelling International** (HI; www.hihostels.com), while private hostels are just that and operate independently of HI.

Membership requirements To stay at an official hostel you'll need to be a HI member, although in practice you can usually stay by buying a 'welcome stamp' (generally about €3; buy six and you qualify for full HI membership) directly at the hostel. HI membership is available at affiliated hostels or through your national hostelling association – there's a full list on the HI website.

Beds & Facilities Alongside dorms of varying sizes – small ones typically for four or five people, larger ones for up to 12 people – many hostels offer hotel-standard private rooms with en suite bathrooms. Dorms may or may not be single sex. Typical facilities include a communal kitchen, a TV room, a laundry and internet access.

Rules Generally speaking, independent hostels are a lot less rule bound than HI hostels, some of which impose a maximum length of stay, a daytime lockout and a curfew. But with the rules come standards, and affiliated hostels have to comply with HI safety and cleanliness standards.

Age Limits These days few hostels impose age limits, although some may give priority to younger, student-age travellers in peak periods.

Meals Many hostels offer a complimentary breakfast and some serve an evening meal (about €10).

Reservations It's a good idea to book ahead whenever possible, especially in summer, when popular hostels are packed to the gills. The easiest way to book is online, either through individual hostel websites or the HI website. Many hostels also accept reservations over the phone or by fax (but during peak periods you will probably have to call to bag a bed). If you are heading on to another hostel, most places will book the next place for you for a small fee. Two useful websites that you can book through are **Hostelworld.com** (www.hostelworld.com) and **HostelPlanet.com** (www.hostelplanet.com).

Hotels

Hotels in the region range from dodgy fleapits with rooms to rent by the hour to some of the world's grandest five-star palaces.

Classification Each country operates its own hotel-classification system, so a three-star hotel in İstanbul might not correspond to a three-star hotel in Barcelona. Stars are awarded according to facilities only and give no indication of value, comfort, atmosphere or friendliness. As a rule, the hotels we recommend range from one to three stars.

Location Inexpensive hotels are often clustered around bus and train stations. These can be useful for late-night/early-morning

---

ALTERNATIVE ACCOMMODATION

In addition to typical accommodation in the region, there are various other options available.

Convents & Monasteries Particularly widespread in Italy, these are a good bet for cheap, modest lodging, often in historic buildings. You'll usually need your own transport to get to convents and monasteries in country locations outside of towns and cities. See p581.

Mountain Refuges A favourite with hikers, refuges offer high-altitude accommodation between July and September. Don't expect frills, but breakfast is generally included in the price and dinner is sometimes available. Bookings are usually required.

Pousadas These are former castles, monasteries or palaces providing simple accommodation in Portugal. See p738.

Tree Houses Olympos on Turkey's Mediterranean Coast is the place to go to stay in a tree house. Accommodation is pretty basic but the forest setting and nearby beaches are a major plus. See p987.

arrivals or departures, but are rarely the best options around. As a general rule, you'll do better looking elsewhere in town.

Rates Rates fluctuate enormously from high to low season, sometimes by up to 40 or 50%. Always make sure you know exactly what your room rate covers (eg air-con, breakfast, internet access). If breakfast is extra, bear in mind that you'll often be able to get a better, and cheaper, breakfast in a regular cafe.

Discounts Discounts are often available for groups or longer stays, particularly in the slower winter months. In slack periods, hoteliers may even be open to a little bargaining – it's worth trying. It's also worth checking hotel websites for last-minute deals and weekend discounts, as many business hotels (usually three stars and upwards) slash their rates by up to 40% on Friday and Saturday nights.

Reservations Well-known hotels in major destinations fill quickly in high season, so always book ahead. If you're not booking online, many hotels will insist on an email or faxed confirmation. Most will also require credit card details in place of a deposit. If you don't have a credit card you might be asked to send a money order to cover the first night's stay.

Payment To avoid embarrassing scenes at reception, always check that your hotel accepts credit cards. Most do, but it's dangerous to assume that a request for a credit card number with your booking means that the hotel accepts payment by plastic.

University Accommodation

Student accommodation is sometimes opened to travellers in the holidays and provides an alternative to sleeping in a hostel. Beds are available in single rooms but more commonly in doubles or triples. There might also be cooking facilities available. Enquire at the university, at student information services or at local tourist offices.

Activities

Beautiful beaches, tempting seas, mountains, lakes and rivers – Mediterranean Europe is a magnificent outdoor playground. Activities run the gamut, from gentle strolls to tough mountain hikes, and from windsurfing and scuba diving to mountain-biking, paragliding and white-water rafting.

For more specific details on the activities available in individual destinations see the relevant country chapter.

Cycling

» Cycling opportunities abound across the region – tourist offices can usually provide maps and local information.

» The best time for cycling is generally spring when the weather is sunny but not too hot and the countryside is at its most colourful. In summer, resorts in the Alps, Dolomites and Pyrenees offer excellent mountain biking.

» On a health note, never underestimate the effects of the heat. Always cover your head (helmets are mandatory in the region anyway) and make sure you drink plenty of fluids. Sunburn can be highly unpleasant and heatstroke very serious.

» See the relevant sections in the Transport chapter for information about transporting and hiring bikes.

Diving

The Med's warm waters with their abundant marine life, underwater caves and sunken shipwrecks are ideal for diving. Throughout the region there are hundreds of diving centres offering everything from beginners courses to trips exploring wrecks. Most dive schools hire out equipment.

Extreme Sports

» Hang-gliding, paragliding, caving, canyoning and hydrospeed (boogie boarding down a river) are among the adventure sports available across the region.

» Adventure sports are becoming increasingly popular in Slovenia and the Balkan countries with a growing number of ecotourism groups offering tailor-made activity packages.

» Climbing is also popular, particularly in the Alps, where the icy slopes attract mountaineers, rock climbers and ice climbers.

Hiking

» Keen hikers could spend a lifetime exploring Mediterranean Europe's many trails.

» As a rule spring and autumn are the best periods.

» Between June and September, the region's mountain chains offer stunning hiking with mountain refuges providing accommodation on many of the longer, high-altitude routes.

» While most high-level mountain paths are only open in the summer, there are possibilities for hiking in the winter snow.

» Contact tourist offices for information on routes and local guides.

Kayaking & Rafting

The region's lakes, rivers and reservoirs offer ample opportunities for sport for water lovers. In mountainous areas, kayaking and white-water rafting provide thrills (and possibly the odd spill).

Skiing & Snowboarding

» Winter sports are big business in southern Europe, and each year thousands take to the pistes to ski (downhill or cross-country), snowboard and snowshoe.

WINTER & SUMMER HOURS

Throughout this book we have quoted summer opening hours. In winter, hours are often reduced, typically with earlier evening closing times. In coastal areas, many seasonal businesses (hotels, souvenir shops, bars etc) close over winter, generally from November to March.

» For a ski holiday you'll need to budget for ski lifts, accommodation and the inevitable après-ski entertainment. You'll save a bit by bringing your own equipment, but often not enough to compensate for the hassle of lugging it around with you. As a general rule, cross-country skiing costs less than downhill.

» The ski season traditionally lasts from early December to late March, though at higher altitudes in the French and Italian Alps it may extend an extra month either way. Snow conditions vary greatly from one year to the next and from region to region, but January and February tend to be the best, busiest and most expensive months.

Surfing, Windsurfing & Kitesurfing

» Windsurfing is one of the most popular of the region's water sports. It's easy to rent sailboards in many tourist centres, and courses are usually available for beginners.

» Surfers can strut their stuff too, with excellent waves on the western seaboard off the coast of France, Spain and Portugal.

» Kitesurfing is also taking off in a big way and is readily available across the region.

Business Hours

Although there are no hard and fast rules respected by all the countries in this guide (or even by all the businesses in any one country), most Mediterranean countries do share some habits.

Banks Generally open early and either close for the day

at around 1.30pm or reopen for a brief two-hour window in the early afternoon, perhaps from 2.30pm to 4.30pm.

Museums Many are closed on Mondays.

Offices Usually operate from Monday to Friday and possibly Saturday morning; opening on Sunday is not unheard of, but it's not widespread.

Shops It's common, especially outside the main cities, for small shops to close for a long lunch. Typically a shop might open from 8am or 9am until 1.30pm, and then from about 4pm to 8pm. Larger department stores tend to stay open all day. See individual country directories for further information.

Children

Despite a dearth of child-friendly sights and activities, the Mediterranean is a great place to travel with children. Kids are universally adored, and are welcome just about everywhere.

» You should have no problems finding baby food, formulas or disposable nappies.

» Remember that shop opening hours might be different from those at home, so if you run out of nappies on Saturday afternoon you could be in for a messy weekend.

» Most car-rental firms have safety seats for hire at a nominal cost, but it's essential you book them in advance. The same goes for high chairs and cots – they're available in most restaurants

and hotels, but numbers will be limited.

» Don't overdo it on the beach – the Mediterranean sun is strong and sunburn is a risk, particularly in the first couple of days.

» For more information, see Lonely Planet's *Travel with Children,* or check out **TravelWithYourKids** (www.travelwithyourkids.com) or **Family Travel Network** (www.familytravelnetwork.com).

Customs Regulations

Travelling within the EU

Travelling from one EU country to another you're allowed to carry:

» 800 cigarettes

» 200 cigars or 1kg of loose tobacco

» 10L of spirits (anything more than 22% alcohol by volume)

» 20L of fortified wine or aperitif

» 90L of wine

Entering or Leaving the EU

You can carry the following duty-free:

» 200 cigarettes or 50 cigars or 250g of tobacco

» 1L of spirits (more than 22% alcohol) or 2L of fortified wine or aperitif

» 4L of still wine

» 16L of beer

» Goods, including perfume and electronic devices, up to a value of €430 for air and sea travellers, and €300 for land travellers

On leaving the EU, non-EU residents can reclaim value-added tax (VAT) on expensive purchases (see p1011).

Non-EU Countries

Non-EU countries each have their own regulations, although most forbid the exportation of antiquities and cultural treasures.

PRACTICALITIES

» The metric system is in use throughout Mediterranean Europe, so expect litres not gallons and kilometres rather than miles. In some countries, decimal points are represented by commas (eg 0,5) and to separate thousands a full point is used (eg 1.000.000 for one million).

» Smoking bans exist in all the countries listed in this book. The exact rules vary from place to place, so always check before lighting up.

» English-language newspapers and magazines are available in many of the region's big cities and popular resorts.

» Keep up to date with world news on BBC World Service, broadcast on shortwave radio or on local FM or AM frequencies, as well as via internet streaming.

» Satellite TV is common across the area and in many hotels you'll be able to pick up BBC World and CNN International.

» European DVDs are formatted to play on the PAL/Secam TV system rather than the NTSC system used in the US. They are also encoded with the regional code 2, so will only work on players set up for region 2 discs.

Discount Cards

Many major cities now offer cards that provide discounts on public transport and entry to selected sights. See individual city entries in the country chapters. Alternatively, **European Cities Marketing** (www.europeancitycards.com) sells cards for cities in Croatia, France, Italy, Portugal, Slovenia and Spain.

Senior Cards

» EU citizens over 65 are often entitled to free or discounted entry to museums and tourist attractions, provided proof of age can be shown. A passport or ID card is usually sufficient.

» There are a growing number of tour operators who specialise in senior travel and can provide information about special packages and discounts.

Student & Youth Cards

The **International Student Travel Confederation** (www.istc.org) issues three types of cards:

International Student Identity Card (ISIC) Available to full-time students and gappers who have a confirmed place at uni or college.

International Teacher Identity Card (ITIC) For teachers and professors.

International Youth Travel Card (IYTC) For non-students under 26.
All three offer worldwide discounts on transport, museum entry, youth hostels and even some restaurants, as well as access to a 24-hour emergency telephone help line.

The price varies from country to country but in the UK the cards cost UK£9, in Australia A$25 and in the USA US$22. See the ISTC website for details of worldwide issuing offices.

Other cards available are:

European Youth Card (www.euro26.org) Formerly known as the Euro<26 card, it is available to people aged under 30, and offers a wide selection of benefits and discounts. It costs €5–19 depending on the country of purchase.

International Student Exchange Card (www.isecards.com) Available to full-time students, teachers and under-26s, it costs US$25. Benefits include discounts, US medical insurance and a global phone card.
See p1001 for information on the Camping Card International.
Note also that membership of Hostelling International (p1002) also guarantees discounts and benefits.

1005

DIRECTORY A–Z DISCOUNT CARDS

Electricity

Voltages & Cycles

Most of Europe runs on 230V/50Hz AC (as opposed to, say, North America, where the electricity is 120V/60 Hz AC). Chargers for phones, iPods and laptops usually can handle any type of electricity. If in doubt, read the fine print.

Plugs & Sockets

Apart from Cyprus and Malta, which use UK-style plugs (three flat pins), the rest of Mediterranean Europe uses the 'europlug' (two round pins). If possible, purchase plug adaptors before travelling.

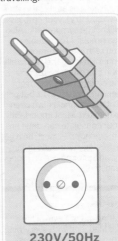

230V/50Hz

240v/50hz

Embassies & Consulates

As a traveller, it's important to realise what your embassy can and can't do for you. Remember, you're bound by the laws of the country you're in. If you end up in jail after committing a crime locally (even if such actions are legal in your own country), your embassy will not be sympathetic. Also remember if the trouble you're in is even remotely your own fault, they generally won't be much help. In genuine emergencies you might get some assistance, but only if other channels have been exhausted. Most importantly, your consulate can issue an emergency passport, help get a message to friends or family, and offer advice on money transfers.

Food

Eating out is a way of life on the Med, and with everything from Michelin-starred restaurants, beachside tavernas, designer bistros, cafes and bars, there's no shortage of

choices. If you're on a budget, look out for self-service canteens or roadside kiosks serving local snacks (think takeaway pizza in Italy or souvlaki in Greece) and shop at local markets.

Some region-wide food tips:

» Lunch remains the main meal of the day in most Mediterranean countries.

» Meals are eaten later in southern Europe than in more northerly climes – dinner is typically served from about 8pm.

» Children are usually welcome in all but the very smartest establishments. Kids menus are uncommon but you can often ask for half portions.

» Vegetarianism is not widespread in the region and vegetarians might have a hard time in Portugal and some of the eastern European countries.

» Eat better and save money by choosing seasonal dishes and local wines/beers/spirits.

See individual destination chapters for country-specific customs, habits and specialities.

Gay & Lesbian Travellers

Discretion is the key. Although homosexuality is acknowledged and in the large part tacitly accepted in Mediterranean Europe, attitudes remain conservative and overt displays of affection could elicit hostility, especially outside of main cities and in some eastern countries.

» Anti-discrimination legislation is in place everywhere except Morocco, where homosexuality is officially illegal, and Turkey.

» Same-sex relationships are recognised in Croatia, Slovenia, France, Spain and Portugal and same-sex marriages are legal in Spain and Portugal.

» Paris, Madrid, Barcelona, Lisbon and Athens all have thriving gay scenes and the Greek islands of Mykonos and Lesvos are popular gay beach destinations. Further information is listed in individual country directories. Useful resources are:

Damron (www.damron.com) Publishes various gay travel guides and apps.

Gay Journey (www.gay journey.com) Travel services (package deals, accommodation, insurance etc), gay-friendly listings and loads of links.

Spartacus International (www.spartacusworld.com) Produces the *Spartacus International Gay Guide* (€25.95, US$32.99, UK£19.99), a male-only directory of worldwide gay venues, as well as a guide to gay-friendly hotels and restaurants.

Health
Required Vaccinations

» No vaccinations are mandatory for any of the countries in this book.

» The World Health Organization (WHO) recommends that all travellers, regardless of their destination, should be covered for diphtheria, tetanus, measles, mumps, rubella and polio.

» Since most vaccines don't produce immunity until at least two weeks after they're given, visit a physician at least six weeks before departure.

Health Insurance

» With a **European Health Insurance Card** (www.ehic. org.uk), EU nationals are entitled to free or reduced cost public health care in EU countries. The card, available from health centres, UK post offices or through the website, does not cover private treatment or emergency repatriation.

» Non-EU citizens should find out if there is a reciprocal arrangement for free or reduced cost medical care between their country and the country visited. For example, Australian residents are entitled to subsidised medical treatment in Italy and Malta. US citizens should check whether their health insurance plan covers medical care abroad – many don't.

» As a rule, non-EU nationals are strongly advised to take out health insurance.

» If you do need health insurance, consider a policy that covers you for the worst possible scenario, such as an accident requiring an emergency flight home.

» Find out in advance if your insurance plan will make payments directly to providers, or will reimburse you later for overseas health expenditures. The former option is generally preferable, as it doesn't require you to be out of pocket in a foreign country.

Availability of Health Care

» Good health care is readily available throughout the region.

» For minor illnesses pharmacists can give valuable advice and sell over-the-counter medication. They can also advise when more specialised help is required and point you in the right direction.

» The standard of dental care is usually good; however, it is sensible to have a dental check-up before a long trip.

Common Problems
HEAT EXHAUSTION & HEATSTROKE

Heat exhaustion occurs when excessive fluid loss is combined with inadequate replacement of fluids and salt. Symptoms include headache, dizziness and tiredness. Dehydration is already happening by the time you feel thirsty – aim to drink sufficient water to produce pale, diluted urine. Replace lost fluids by drinking water and/or fruit juice, and cool the body with cold water and fans. Treat salt loss with salty fluids such as soup, or add a little more table salt to foods than usual.

Heatstroke is much more serious, resulting in irrational and hyperactive behaviour, and eventually loss of consciousness and death. Rapid cooling by spraying the body with water and fanning is ideal. Emergency fluid and electrolyte replacement by intravenous drip is recommended.

INSECT BITES & STINGS

Mosquitoes are found in most parts of Mediterranean Europe. They may not carry malaria, but they can cause irritation and infected bites. Use a DEET-based insect repellent.

Sandflies are found around Mediterranean beaches. They usually cause only a nasty, itchy bite, but can carry a rare skin disorder called cutaneous leishmaniasis.

TRAVELLER'S DIARRHOEA

If you develop diarrhoea, be sure to drink plenty of fluids, preferably an oral rehydration solution such as Dioralyte. You should seek medical attention if diarrhoea is bloody, persists for more than 72 hours, or is accompanied by a fever, shaking, chills or severe abdominal pain.

Insurance

Travel insurance to cover theft, loss and medical problems is highly recommended. It may also cover you for cancellation of and delays in your travel arrangements.

» There is a whole range of policies available so make sure you get one that's tailored to your needs – while one policy may be suitable if you're going skiing, if you're planning a beach holiday you'll need another – and always check the small print.

» Don't forget to keep all paperwork. If you have to claim for medical expenses you'll need all the relevant documentation. Similarly, to claim for a theft, you'll require a statement from the local police.

» Things to consider when choosing a policy:

* Are 'dangerous activities' (scuba diving, motorcycling and, for some policies, trekking) covered? Some policies might not cover you if you're riding a motorbike with a locally acquired motorcycle licence.

* Does the policy cover every country you're planning to visit? Some policies don't cover certain countries, such as Montenegro or BiH.

* Does it cover ambulance service or an emergency flight home?

TRAVEL HEALTH WEBSITES

Before travelling to the region, you can get up-to-date health advice from your government's website:

Australia (www.smartraveller.gov.au/tips/travelwell.html)
Canada (www.phac-aspc.gc.ca/tmp-pmv/index-eng.php)
New Zealand (www.safetravel.govt.nz/)
UK (www.fco.gov.uk/en/travel-and-living-abroad/staying-safe/health/)
USA (www.cdc.gov/travel/)
Another useful resource is www.mdtravelhealth.com, a US website with detailed destination advice.

CAN YOU DRINK THE TAP WATER?

Tap water is safe to drink in most of the countries listed in this book. However, in Albania, BiH, Montenegro, Turkey and Morocco, it's best to stick to bottled or purified water. Don't drink water from rivers or lakes, as it may contain bacteria or viruses that can cause diarrhoea or vomiting.

» The policies handled by STA Travel (www.statravel.com) and other student travel agencies are usually good value.

» Price comparison website Money Supermarket (www.moneysupermarket.com) compares 450 policies and comes up with the best for your needs. It also has a useful FAQ section and some good general information.

» Worldwide travel insurance is available at www.lonelyplanet.com/travel_services. You can buy, extend and claim online anytime – even if you're already on the road.

» For more information on health insurance see p1006; for car insurance refer to p1024.

Internet Access

» As wi-fi becomes increasingly common the number of internet cafes is decreasing, although you will still find them across the region. You might also be able to log on at department stores, post offices, libraries, tourist offices and universities. Costs range from about €1.50 to €5 per hour.

» Most hotels and hostels offer internet access of some sort – either a computer for communal use or wi-fi. Wi-fi is often free but some places might charge a small fee.

» Wi-fi is also increasingly available in public parks, at restaurants, and in railway stations and airports. To find regional hot spots, try **JiWire** (www.jiwire.com).

» If you're using your own kit, note that that you might need a power transformer (to convert from 110V to 220V if your computer isn't set up for dual voltage) and a plug adaptor.

» Throughout this book the internet icon (@) is used to denote accommodation with a computer for guest use, while the wi-fi icon (🛜) indicates the availability of wi-fi.

Language Courses

A language course is a great way of tapping into the local culture. Courses are available to foreigners at universities and in private language schools across the region.

France Details of language schools are available at www.diplomatie.gouv.fr and www.europa-pages.com/france.

Greece Try the **Athens Centre** (www.athenscentre.gr).

Italy The **Università per Stranieri** (www.unistrapg.it) in Perugia is a popular place to study, with hundreds of courses available to non-Italians.

Spain Look up schools on www.europa-pages.com/spain.

Information about courses is also available from the cultural institutes maintained by many European countries around the world, such as the Spanish **Istituto Cervantes** (www.cervantes.es, in Spanish). National tourist authorities, student-exchange organisations and student travel agencies should also be able to help. Ask about special holiday packages that include a course.

If you don't fancy a language course there are many other subjects to choose from – cooking, art, literature, architecture, drama, music, fashion and photography.

See the country chapters for specific details.

Legal Matters

Age of Consent Varies from country to country but ranges from 14 to 18. Travellers should note that they can be prosecuted under the law of their home country regarding the age of consent, even when abroad.

Drinking Minimum drinking ages vary from country to country, but are all between 16 and 18.

Driving The minimum driving age is 18 in most European countries, 17 in Turkey and 21 in Morocco. However, you probably won't be able to hire a car until you're 21. Drink driving laws apply and road checks are common in some areas. When driving make sure you have the correct documents at hand – see p1023 for further driving information.

Drugs Drugs are widespread and easy to come by. Legislation and local attitudes vary, but if you're caught with a small quantity of cannabis you might get away with a warning and/or a fine. Possession of hard drugs or quantities of cannabis deemed 'dealable' could lead to imprisonment. Note that prescription drugs that are legal in your home country might not be legal abroad – check before travelling.

Proof of Identity You are required by law to prove your identity if asked by police, so always carry your passport, or ID card if you're an EU citizen.

Theft If you have something stolen and you want to claim it on insurance, you must make a statement to the police, as insurance companies won't pay up without official proof of a crime.

Maps

» Proper road maps are essential if you're driving or cycling. Quality European map publishers include **Michelin** (www.viamichelin. com), **Freytag & Berndt** (www.freytagberndt.com) and **Kümmerly+Frey** (www. kuemmerly-frey.ch).

» As a rule, maps published by automobile associations (for example ACI in Italy or ELPA in Greece) are excellent, and are sometimes free if membership of your local association gives you reciprocal rights.

» Tourist offices are a good source of free, basic maps.

» Good maps are easy to find in bookshops throughout the region.

Money

Of the countries covered in this book, Cyprus (Republic), France, Greece, Italy, Malta, Montenegro, Portugal, Slovenia and Spain use the euro. The euro is also widely accepted in Albania, BiH, Croatia and North Cyprus.

There are seven euro notes (€5, €10, €20, €50, €100, €200 and €500) and eight euro coins (€1 and €2, then 1, 2, 5, 10, 20 and 50 cents); one euro is equivalent to 100 cents.

While travelling in the region, the best way to carry your money is to bring a mix of ATM cards, credit cards and cash, with travellers cheques as backup. Internet banking accounts are useful for tracking your spending – if you don't have one, set one up before you leave home.

ATMs

» Every country listed in this book has ATMs that allow you to withdraw cash.

TELL THE BANK

Before leaving home, always let your bank or credit card company know of your travel plans. If you don't, you risk having your card blocked, as banks often block cards as a security measure when they notice out-of-the-ordinary transactions.

They're widely available and easy to use (many have instructions in English). It's always prudent, though, to have a backup option in case something goes wrong with your card or you can't find a working ATM – in remote villages and islands they can be scarce.

» There are four types of card you can use in an ATM:

• **ATM Cards** Use to withdraw money from your home bank account. They can be used in ATMs linked to international networks such as Cirrus and Maestro.

• **Debit Cards** Like ATM cards but can also be used to make purchases over the counter.

• **Credit Cards** Can be used in ATMs displaying the appropriate logos.

• **Prepaid Travel Money Cards** Like credit cards, they can be used in ATMs displaying the appropriate logos.

» Note that you'll need a four-digit PIN (in numbers rather than letters) for most European ATMs. You might have difficulties if your card doesn't have a metallic chip – check with your bank.

» As a security measure, be wary of people who offer to help you use an ATM or, at ports or stations, people who claim that there are no ATMs at your destination.

» Note also that ATMs impose a limit on daily withdrawals, typically around €250.

Black Market

Black-market money exchange is relatively rare in Mediterranean Europe, although it's not totally absent. If you do encounter it, stay well clear. The rates rarely outweigh the risk of being caught, and by dealing with unofficial moneychangers you greatly increase your chances of being conned – many people offering illegal exchanges are professional thieves.

Cash

Nothing beats cash for convenience, or risk. If you lose it, it's gone forever and very few travel insurers will come to your rescue. Those that will insure you limit the amount to somewhere around US$300. As a general rule of thumb, carry no more than 10% to 15% of your total trip money in cash.

It's still a good idea, though, to bring some local currency in cash, if only to tide you over until you find an ATM.

Charges

When you withdraw money from an ATM, the amounts are converted and dispensed in local currency. However, you will be charged various fees. Typically, you'll be charged a transaction fee (usually around 3% with a minimum fee of €3 or more), as well as a 1% to 3% conversion charge. If you're using a credit card, you'll also be hit by interest on the cash withdrawn. Fees vary from company to company but the British firm Halifax charges no fees for cash withdrawals and foreign currency purchases and the US bank Capital One charges no fees for foreign currency transactions.

For more on card-related costs check out the British website **Money Supermarket** (www.moneysupermarket.com/travel-money).

Credit Cards

Credit cards are good for major purchases such as airline tickets or car hire, as well as for providing emergency cover. They also make life a lot easier if you need to book hotels while on the road – many places request a credit card number when you reserve a room.

They are widely accepted in most countries, although don't rely on them in small restaurants, shops or private accommodation in Albania, Croatia and Montenegro. As a general rule, Visa and MasterCard are more widely accepted in the region than American Express and Diners Club.

Other considerations:

» Some European countries now use a 'chip and PIN' system for credit and debit cards. If your card isn't enabled for this, as many US cards are not, or you don't know your card's PIN, you can often still sign a printed receipt in the usual way. However, you might find your card is refused in automatic payment machines at railway stations, petrol stations etc.

» Using your credit card in ATMs is costly. On every transaction there's a fee (which can reach US$10 with some credit-card issuers), as well as interest per withdrawal. Check the charges with your issuer before leaving home.

» Make sure you can always see your card when making transactions – it'll lessen the risk of fraud.

International Transfers

If you need money sent to you, international bank transfers are good for secure one-off movements of large amounts of money, but they might take three to five days and there will be a fee. Be sure to specify the name of the bank, plus the IBAN (International Bank Account Number) and the address of the branch where you'd like to pick up your money.

It's quicker and easier (although more expensive) to have money wired via **Western Union** (www.westernunion.com) or **MoneyGram** (www.moneygram.com).

A cheaper option is **Moneybookers** (www.moneybookers.com), a British money-transfer website that allows you to send and receive money via email.

Moneychangers

» US dollars, British pounds and the euro are the easiest currencies to exchange in Europe. You might have trouble exchanging Canadian, Australian and New Zealand dollars.

» Most airports, central train stations, big hotels and many border posts have exchange facilities. Post offices are another option, although while they'll always exchange cash, they might not change travellers cheques unless they're in the local currency.

» The best exchange rates are generally offered by banks. *Bureaux de changes* usually, but not always, offer worse rates or charge higher commissions. Hotels are almost always the worst places to change money.

Prepaid Travel Money Cards

As a backup to your debit or credit card, consider a prepaid travel money card, such as those offered by **Travelex** (www.cashpassport.com). Before you leave home, load the card with as much money as you want to spend and then use it to withdraw cash at ATMs – the money you withdraw comes off the card and not out of your account – or to make direct purchases. If necessary, you can then reload it via telephone or online. Note, however, that you'll still be stung by ATM and conversion fees, as well as reloading fees.

Tipping

There are no hard-and-fast rules about tipping.

» Many restaurants add service charges, making a tip discretionary. In such cases, it's common practice, and often expected of visitors, to round bills up. If the service was particularly good and you want to leave a tip, 5 to 10% is fine.

» There is usually no tipping when ordering at a bar.

» In some places, such as Croatia, tour guides expect to be tipped.

» See country chapters for further details.

Travellers Cheques

» Although outmoded by debit cards and ATMs, travellers cheques are safer than cash and are a

---

GET THE BILL IN LOCAL CURRENCY

Something to look out for when making payments with a credit card is what's known as 'dynamic currency conversion'. This is used when a vendor offers to convert your bill into your home currency rather than charging you in the local currency. The catch here is that the exchange rate used to convert your bill will usually be highly disadvantageous to you, and the vendor might well add his or her own commission fee. Always ask to be billed in the local currency.

TAX FREE SHOPPING

Tax free shopping is available across the region – look for signs in shop windows – and while it won't save you a fortune, it won't cost you anything extra.

Value added tax (VAT) is a sales tax imposed on most goods and services sold in Europe; it varies from country to country but is typically around 20%. In most countries, non-EU residents who spend more than a certain amount – ranging from €50 to €175 depending on the country – can claim VAT back on their purchases when they leave the EU. EU residents, however, are not entitled to a refund on goods bought in another EU country.

The procedure is straightforward. When you make your purchase ask the shop assistant for a tax-refund voucher (sometimes called a tax-free shopping cheque), which is filled in with the date of your purchase and its value. When you leave the EU, get this voucher stamped at customs – the customs agent might want to check the item so try to ensure you have it at hand – and take it to the nearest tax-refund counter. Here you can get an immediate refund, either in cash or onto your credit card. If there's no refund counter at the airport or you're travelling by sea or overland, you'll need to get the voucher stamped at the port or border crossing and mail it back for your refund.

useful emergency backup, especially as you can claim a refund if they're stolen. Keep a separate record of their numbers and all original purchase receipts.

» American Express, Visa and Travelex cheques are the most widely accepted, particularly in US dollars, British pounds or euros.

» It's becoming increasingly hard to find places to cash travellers cheques, especially outside of the main centres.

» When changing, ask about fees and commissions, as well as the exchange rate. There may be a service fee charged per cheque; a flat transaction fee; or a fee that's a percentage of the total amount.

Photography

As a rule, there are very few photographic restrictions in Mediterranean Europe. However:

» Photography is prohibited near military bases in Cyprus.

» Many museums, art galleries and churches ban (flash) photography.

» It's best to ask permission before photographing people, particularly in Morocco. Film is available everywhere in the region but most people now shoot digital. Things to bear in mind:

» Make sure you have at least 2GB of memory.

» If you run out of memory your best bet is to burn your photos onto a CD, which many photo stores will do for you.

» If you have a laptop, photo-enabled MP3 player, iPod or iPhone you can store photos on these.

» Remember that you might need a plug adaptor and transformer (to ensure the correct voltage) for your battery charger.

» For further tips, check out Lonely Planet's *Travel*

Post

» From major European centres, airmail typically takes about five days to North America and a week to Australasian destinations. It might be slower from countries such as Albania and BiH, which have three parallel postal services.

» Postage costs vary from country to country, as does post-office efficiency.

» Many central post offices offer poste restante services, which allow people to write to you care of the post office, but email has rendered this service largely obsolete. When collecting mail, you'll need your passport and you may have to pay a small fee. Post offices usually hold mail for about a month, but sometimes less.

» Courier services such as **DHL** (www.dhl.com) are best for essential deliveries.

Public Holidays

» Most holidays in the southern European countries are based on the Christian calendar.

» In the countries with a Muslim majority (Morocco and Turkey), the month-long holiday of Ramadan is celebrated, usually around September and October. Its exact timing depends on lunar events. See country directories for specific information.

» August is the peak holiday period for Mediterranean dwellers.

» The major school holidays run from July to September, and many businesses simply shut up shop for much of August. Schools also pause for breaks over Easter and Christmas.

» For details of the school calendar, check out the

Eurydice network (http://eacea.ec.europa.eu/education/eurydice), which lists holiday dates for many European countries.

Safe Travel

Travelling in Mediterranean Europe is pretty safe. Violent crime is rare and the region is relatively stable. However, travellers to Morocco should check on the latest security situation in North Africa and visitors to BiH should note the presence of unexploded landmines in certain areas of the country – see the country chapter for details. Petty crime is widespread in the region, however, so watch out for bag snatchers, pickpockets and scam artists. In cities, take note of any local crime hot spots (a particular neighbourhood, bus route, metro station etc) and areas to avoid after dark. As always, common sense and a little healthy scepticism are the best defence.

Scams

Mediterranean con artists are good at what they do and you should be on your guard against scams. Typical scenarios:

Bar scam Typically worked on solo male travellers. You're approached by a bloke who claims to be a lone out-of-towner like you but who's heard of a great bar. You go to the bar and enjoy a boozy evening with a crowd of new friends. At the end of the evening you're presented with an outrageous bill.

Druggings These are unlikely but do happen, especially on trains. A new 'friend' slips something into your drink or food and then fleeces you of your valuables as you sleep off the effects.

Flat-tyre ruse While driving you stop to help someone with a flat tyre (or someone stops to help you change your tyre, which they've just punctured). As you change the tyre, an accomplice takes valuables from the interior of your car.

Phoney cops These often appear as the end-play in cons involving money-changers or arguments about money. If approached by someone claiming to be a police officer, offer to go with them to the nearest police station.

Swapping banknotes You pay for a taxi fare or a train ticket with a €20 note. The taxi driver or ticket seller deftly palms the note and produces a €5 note, claiming that you paid with this. In your confusion you're not sure what you did and accept their word.

Touts and unofficial guides Be wary of people directing you to hotels or shops (they'll usually be collecting a commission) and people offering to show you around tourist sites (they'll demand hefty payment afterwards).

Theft

Theft is the biggest problem facing travellers in Mediterranean Europe. There's no need for paranoia but be aware that pickpockets and bag snatchers are out there.

» Don't store valuables in train-station lockers or at luggage-storage counters, and be careful if people offer to help you operate a locker.

» Be vigilant if someone offers to carry your luggage: they just might carry it away.

» Carry your own padlock for hostel lockers. Be careful even in hotels; don't leave any valuables lying around in your room.

» When going out, spread your valuables, cash and cards around your body or in different bags. A money belt with your essentials (passport, cash, credit cards, airline tickets) is usually a good idea. However, to avoid delving into it in public, carry a wallet with a day's cash.

» Don't flaunt watches, cameras and other expensive goods.

» Cameras and shoulder bags are an open invitation for snatch thieves, many of whom work from motorcycles or scooters. A small day pack is better, but watch your rear. Also be very careful at cafes and bars – always loop your bag's strap around your leg while seated.

» Pickpockets are particularly active in dense crowds, especially in busy train stations and on public transport. A common ploy is for one person to distract you while another whips through your pockets. Beware of gangs of dishevelled-looking kids waving newspapers and demanding attention. In the blink of an eye, a wallet or camera can go missing. Remember also that some of the best pickpockets are well dressed.

» Parked cars, especially those with foreign number plates or rental-agency stickers, are prime targets for

---

GOVERNMENT TRAVEL ADVICE

The following government websites offer travel advisories and information on current hot spots:

Australian Department of Foreign Affairs (www.smartraveller.gov.au)

British Foreign & Commonwealth Office (www.fco.gov.uk/en/travel-and-living-abroad)

Canadian Department of Foreign Affairs (http://dfait-maeci.gc.ca)

US State Department (http://travel.state.gov)

petty criminals. While driving through cities, beware of thieves at traffic lights; keep your doors locked and the windows rolled up.

» A favourite tactic of scooter snatchers is for a first rider to brush past your car, knocking the side mirror out of position; then, as you reach out to re-adjust the mirror, an accomplice on a second scooter will race past, snatching the watch off your wrist as he goes.

» In case of theft or loss, always report the incident to the police and ask for a statement. Without one, your travel insurance company won't pay up.

Telephone

» Direct international calls can be made from public payphones, which are widespread throughout the region, using prepaid phonecards. In some places you can also call from hotels, post offices, internet cafes (via Skype) and private call centres.

» Phoning from a post office or a public payphone is almost always cheaper than calling from a hotel. Private call centres often have good long-distance rates but always check before calling.

» To call abroad simply dial the international access code (IAC) of the country you're calling *from* (most commonly ⚀00), the country code (CC) of the country you're calling *to*, the local area code (usually, but not always dropping the leading zero if there is one) and then the number.

» To have someone else pay for your call, you can often dial directly to your home-country operator and make a reverse-charge (collect) call. Alternatively, you can use the Country Direct system (such as AT&T's USADirect), which lets you phone home by billing the long-distance carrier you use at home.

Home Direct numbers, which can often be dialled from public phones without even inserting a phonecard, vary from country to country.

Mobile Phones

» Most European mobile phones operate on the GSM 900/1800 system, which also covers Australia and New Zealand, but is not compatible with the North American GSM 1900 system. Some American GSM 1900/900 phones, however, do work in Europe, although high roaming charges make it an expensive option.

» If you have a GSM tri- or quad-band phone that you can unlock (check with your service provider), the easiest way of using it is to buy a prepaid SIM card in each country you visit.

» You can often buy European SIM cards in your home country but you'll generally pay less in Europe – see individual country chapters for price details.

» Note that most SIMs expire if not used within a certain time and that most country-specific SIMs can only be used in the country of origin.

» If you're using your smartphone (iPhone, Blackberry, Android etc) to access the internet and check your email note that high data-roaming fees quickly add up. A way around this is to turn off data roaming and use wi-fi to go online.

Phone Codes

Phone codes are listed in country chapters.

Toll-free numbers in Mediterranean Europe often have an ⚀0800 or ⚀800 prefix (also ⚀900 in Spain). You'll find toll-free emergency numbers listed in destination chapters.

Phonecards

» To call from a public payphone, you'll need a phonecard, available from post offices, telephone centres, news-stands and retail outlets.

» There's a wide range of local and international phonecards. Most international cards come with a toll-free number and a PIN code, which gives access to your prepaid credit. However, for local calls you're usually better off with a local phonecard.

» Cards sold at airports and train stations are rarely good value for money.

» Note that many cards have an expiry date.

» Both the International Student Identity Card (see p1005) and Hostelling International offer a range of phonecards and SIM cards – see www.isiconnect.ekit. com or www.hi.ekit.com for details.

» If you don't have a phonecard, you can often telephone from a booth inside a post office or telephone centre and settle your bill at the counter.

Time

Most of the countries covered in this book are on Central European Time (GMT/ UTC plus one hour) except

---

EMERGENCY NUMBERS

The EU-wide general emergency number is ⚀112. This can be dialled, toll-free, for emergencies in Cyprus, France, Greece, Italy, Malta, Portugal, Slovenia and Spain. In Turkey it is used for ambulances only. See the individual country directories for country-specific emergency numbers.

for Portugal, which runs on Western European Time (GMT/UTC); Morocco, which follows GMT/UTC, but does not observe daylight savings; and Cyprus, Greece and Turkey, which are on Eastern European Time (GMT/UTC plus two hours).

In most European countries, clocks are put forward one hour for daylight-saving time on the last Sunday in March and turned back again on the last Sunday in October. Thus, during daylight-saving time, Western European Time is GMT/UTC plus one hour, Central European Time GMT/UTC plus two hours and Eastern European Time GMT/UTC plus three hours.

Toilets

» Public toilets are pretty thin on the ground in much of the region. The best advice if you're caught short is to nip into a train station, fast-food outlet, bar or cafe and use their facilities.

» A small fee (typically €0.20 to €0.70) is often charged in public loos, so try to keep some small change handy.

» Most loos in the region are of the sit-down Western variety, but don't be surprised to find the occasional squat loo. And don't ever assume that public loos will have paper – they almost certainly won't.

Tourist Information

» Tourist information is widely available throughout the region. Most towns, big or small, have a tourist office of some description, which at the very least will be able to provide a rudimentary map and give information on accommodation. Some even provide a hotel-reservation service, which might or might not be free.

» In the absence of a tourist office, useful sources of information include travel agencies and hotel receptionists.

» Tourist-office staff will often speak some English in the main centres, but don't bank on it away from the tourist hot spots.

» For country-specific tourist information, see the country chapters.

Travellers With Disabilities

With the notable exception of Croatia, which has improved wheelchair access due to the large number of wounded war veterans, the region does not cater well to disabled travellers. Steep cobbled streets, ancient lifts and anarchic traffic all make life difficult for wheelchair-using visitors. Wheelchair access is often limited to the more expensive hotels and major airports; public transport is usually woefully ill-equipped; and tourist sites rarely cater well to those with disabilities.

However, it's not impossible to travel the region, even independently. If you're going it alone, pre-trip research and planning is essential:

☐ find out about facilities on public transport

☐ work out how to get to your hotel or hostel

☐ check if there are care agencies available and how much they cost

☐ give your wheelchair a thorough service before departing and prepare a basic tool kit, as punctures can be a problem

National support organisations can help. They often have libraries devoted to travel, and can put you in touch with travel agents who specialise in tours for the disabled. The following are also useful resources:

Flying with Disability (www.flying-with-disability.org) Comprehensive and easy-to-use site covering all aspects

of air travel – pre-trip planning, navigating the airport, boarding the flight, on the plane etc.

Global Access (www.globalaccessnews.com) A worldwide network for wheelchair users with a monthly e-zine and tons of reader-generated articles.

Lonely Planet (www.lonelyplanet.com) Check out the Travellers with Disabilities branch on the Thorn Tree travel forum.

Mobility International USA (www.miusa.org) Publishes guides and advises travellers with disabilities or mobility issues.

Society for Accessible Travel and Hospitality (www.sath.org) Has loads of useful information, including a need-to-know section and travel tips.

Visas

Citizens of the USA, Australia, New Zealand, Canada and the UK need only a valid passport to enter most of the countries in this guide for up to three months (90 days), provided they have some sort of onward or return ticket and/or 'sufficient means of support' (ie money).

France, Greece, Italy, Malta, Portugal, Slovenia and Spain have all signed the Schengen Agreement, which abolishes customs checks between signatory states. Cyprus has also signed the agreement, but has yet to implement the provisions.

For the purposes of visa requirements, the Schengen area should be considered a single unit, as all member states operate the same entry requirements. These include the following:

» Legal residents of one Schengen country do not need a visa for another Schengen country.

» Nationals of Australia, Canada, Israel, Japan, New Zealand and the USA do not need a visa for tourist or business visits of up to 90 days.

» The UK and Ireland are not part of the Schengen area but their citizens can stay indefinitely in other EU countries, and only need to fill in paperwork if they want to work long term or take up residency.

Of the non-Schengen countries in this book, only Turkey requires visas from Australian, Canadian, British and US nationals. They can be bought at any point of entry into the country. See p992 for details.

Apart from the Schengen visa, it's generally easier to get your visas as you go along, rather than arranging them all beforehand. Carry spare passport photos (you may need from one to four every time you apply for a visa).

Visa requirements change, and you should always check with the embassy of your destination country or a reputable travel agent before travelling.

For more information about work visas and permits see p1016.

Schengen Visa

If you do require a Schengen visa for a tourist visit, you'll need the category C short-stay visa. There are two versions of this:

» A single-entry visa which allows for an uninterrupted stay of up to 90 days within a six-month period (180 days).

» A multiple-entry visa which allows you to enter and leave the Schengen area as long as your combined stay in the area does not exceed 90 days in any 180-day period. In both cases, the clock starts ticking from the moment you enter the Schengen area. You cannot exit the Schengen area for a short period and start the clock on your return. Other rules:

» It's obligatory to apply for a Schengen visa in your country of residence at the embassy of your main destination country or, if you have no principal destination, of the first Schengen country you'll be entering.

» A visa issued by one Schengen country is generally valid for travel in other Schengen countries, but individual countries may impose restrictions on certain nationalities.

» You can only apply for two Schengen visas in any 12-month period.

» You cannot work in a Schengen country without a specific work permit.

» Always check which documents you'll need. You'll almost certainly require a passport valid for three months beyond the end of your proposed visit; a return air or train ticket; proof of a hotel reservation or similar accommodation arrangement; proof of your ability to support yourself financially; and medical insurance.

Volunteering

If you can afford it, a volunteer work placement is a great way to gain an insight into local culture. Typical volunteer jobs include working on conservation projects, participating in research programs, or helping out at animal-welfare centres. In some cases volunteers are paid a living allowance; sometimes they work for their keep; and sometimes volunteers are required to pay for the experience, typically from about US$300 per week.

Useful resources:

World Wide Opportunities on Organic Farms (WWOOF; www.wwoof.org) International organisation that puts volunteers in contact with organic farms across the world. In exchange for your labour, you'll receive free lodging and food.

The Big Trip Lonely Planet's *The Big Trip* provides advice and practical information on volunteering and working abroad.

Volunteer Abroad (www.volunteerabroad.com) A vast search engine listing volunteering opportunities across the world.

Women Travellers

It's sad to report, but machismo is alive and well in Mediterranean Europe, a region in which gender roles are still largely based on age-old social norms. But even if attitudes are not always very enlightened, a deep sense of hospitality runs through many Mediterranean societies, and travellers (of both sexes) are usually welcomed with warmth and genuine kindness. That said, women travellers continue to face more challenging situations than men do, most often in the form of unwanted harassment. Other things to bear in mind:

» Staring is much more overt in Mediterranean countries than in the more reticent northern parts of Europe, and although it is almost always harmless, it can become annoying.

» If you find yourself being pestered by local men and ignoring them isn't working, tell them you're waiting for your husband (marriage is highly respected in the area) and walk away. If they continue, call the police.

» Gropers, particularly on crowded public transport, can also be a problem. If you do feel someone start to touch you inappropriately, make a fuss – molesters are no more admired in Mediterranean Europe than they are anywhere else.

» In Muslim countries, where women's roles are clearly defined and unmarried men have little contact with women outside of their family unit, women travelling alone or with other women will attract attention. This is rarely dangerous, but you'll need to exercise common sense. Dress conservatively, avoid eye contact and, if possible, don't walk alone at night.

» Security for solo travellers is mainly a matter of common sense – watch your possessions, don't go wandering down dark alleys at night and be wary of overly friendly people you've just met. Good resources are:

Wanderlust & Lipstick (http://wanderlustandlipstick. com) Comprehensive site with loads of useful info. Also sells *The Essential Guide for Women Travelling Solo*, a good guide for nervous first-timers.

Journeywoman (www. journeywoman.com) An online women's travel magazine full of tips, anecdotes and recommendations.

Lonely Planet (www. lonelyplanet.com) Exchange thoughts and ideas on the Women Travellers branch of the Thorn Tree travel forum.

Women Travel Tips (www. womentraveltips101.com) US travel expert Marybeth Bond shares her experiences and provides plenty of on-the-road tips.

For further information, see the individual country directories.

Work

Finding work in Mediterranean Europe is not always easy. Unemployment in the region is high, and the ever growing immigrant population provides local employers with a ready pool of cheap labour, particularly for unskilled, seasonal agricultural work. However, it's not all gloom and doom, and with a bit of planning and determination you should be able to find something.

Permits

» EU citizens can work in any other EU country without a visa or specific permit. Paperwork, which can be complicated, only really becomes necessary for long-term employment or if you want to apply for residency.

» Non-EU nationals require work permits, which can be difficult to arrange, especially for temporary work. There are ways around this, though. If, for example, one of your parents or a grandparent was born in an EU country, you may have certain rights you never knew about. Get in touch with that country's embassy and ask about dual citizenship and work permits – if you go for citizenship, ask about any obligations, such as military service and residency. Be aware that your home country may not recognise dual citizenship.

Types of Work
SEASONAL WORK

Much of the temporary work offered in the region is seasonal – ski resorts provide winter opportunities, while beach bars, clubs, restaurants and hotels are a rich source of summer employment. Remember, though, that if you find a temporary job, the pay might be less than that offered to locals (little more than pocket money in some cases), although you might get board and lodging thrown in. Au pairing is a good way of ensuring accommodation for your stay.

TEACHING ENGLISH

Teaching English is a favourite option, although many schools now ask for a degree and a TEFL (Teaching English as a Foreign Language) certificate. There are no such requirements to give private lessons.

The British *Guardian* newspaper has a useful online TEFL section (www. guardian.co.uk/education/ tefl) and the *Times Educational Supplement* (www.tes. co.uk) has a comprehensive job database. Other useful sources of information:

TEFL International (www. teflinternational.org.uk)

British Council (www. teachingenglish.org.uk)

Berlitz (www.berlitz.com)

Inlingua (www.inlingua.com)

Wall Street Institute International (www.wall streetinstitute.com).

Resources

There are hundreds of guides dedicated to working abroad, but Susan Griffith's *Work Your Way Around the World* is usually considered the classic of the genre. Lonely Planet's *The Big Trip* also has information about work and volunteering across the world. Useful websites:

Gap Work (www.gapwork. com) Comprehensive website aimed at gappers. Has good advice, job searches and plenty of useful links.

Go Abroad (www.goabroad. com) Huge site with information on hundreds of jobs and volunteer opportunities.

Transitions Abroad (www. transitionsabroad.com) Publishes the comprehensive guide *Work Abroad: The Complete Guide to Finding a Job Overseas*.

Working Abroad (www. workingabroad.com) Has good job and volunteer information. For UK£29 you can get a personal report advising on the best jobs to suit your requirements and travel preferences.

The Big Guide to Living and Working Overseas (www.workingoverseas.com) The 1800-page *BIG Guide to Living and Working Overseas* provides advice for US and Canadian readers.

Transport

This chapter provides a general overview of transport in Mediterranean Europe. For more-detailed country-specific information, see the Getting There & Away and Getting Around sections in individual country chapters.

Unless otherwise specified, all telephone numbers are local and don't include international dialling codes.

GETTING THERE & AWAY

Getting to Mediterranean Europe is pretty easy. Most of the world's major airlines serve the region and there are plenty of budget airlines operating within Europe. Road and rail networks connect with countries in northern and eastern Europe, while ferries sail into the region from the UK and North Africa.

Flights, tours and rail tickets can be booked at www.lonelyplanet.com/bookings.

Entering the Region

There are no special entry requirements for EU citizens and nationals of Australia, Canada, New Zealand and the USA. For most places a valid passport is all you need for a stay of up to three months. Some nationalities, including South Africans, require visas for Schengen countries – see p1014 for further information.

Passport

Exact passport requirements vary from country to country, even within the EU, but as a rule non-EU nationals require a passport valid for three to six months after their period of stay. EU citizens travelling to Albania, Bosnia and Hercegovina, Greece, Morocco and Turkey, are also subject to minimum passport validity requirements. Check details on these government travel websites:

Australian Department of Foreign Affairs (www.smartraveller.gov.au)

British Foreign & Commonwealth Office (www.fco.gov.uk/en/travel-and-living-abroad)

Canadian Department of Foreign Affairs (http://dfait-maeci.gc.ca)

US State Department (http://travel.state.gov) Note that if travelling with a child, the child should either have their own passport (or ID card) or be registered on a parent's passport. As of June 2012, all children will be required to have their own passport.

Air

It's not difficult to find a flight to the Med. Most major airlines fly into the region, and there are currently 42 low-cost carriers operating between 360 European airports. In summer, charter flights add to the congestion.

Expect to pay high-season prices between June and September – the two months either side of this period are the shoulder seasons. Low season is November to March.

Many no-frills airlines use secondary provincial airports, see individual country chapters for details.

See p1021 for a list of the main budget airlines operating in Mediterranean Europe.

Tickets

Finding tickets to Mediterranean Europe isn't difficult, but to get the best deal you'll need to spend some time shopping around.

» Airline websites are an obvious starting point – they often list special online fares, and most European low-cost carriers operate solely on the web. There are also a whole host of travel websites which find the most competitive fares and enable you to book them. Lonely Planet has a flight search engine at www.lonelyplanet.com/bookings/flights.do.

» Note, that some low-cost airlines, most notably Ryanair, only accept bookings made on their own website.

» If you're planning a complex itinerary it's probably worth talking to a travel agent who can find you the best fares, advise on connections and sell travel insurance.

» Full-time students and people aged under 26

TICKET TIPS

For advice on booking tickets, check out **How to Buy Cheap Flights Online** (www.stanfords.co.uk/articles/how-to/how-to-buy-cheap-flights-online,264,AR.html), which has some excellent tips.

Other considerations to bear in mind:

» Buy early. If booking for high season (June to September) try to sort out your ticket by about March.

» Travelling mid-week generally costs less than at weekends.

» Flights to major hubs tend to be cheaper. If you're heading to eastern Europe consider taking a long-haul flight to a major western European airport and then picking up an onward budget flight.

» When working out the cost of your ticket, factor in all price extras, such as fuel surcharges, seat selection, luggage fees etc.

» Consider an open-jaw return when you fly into one city and exit from another. They are usually more expensive than simple returns but might save you in the long-run, particularly if travelling across the region. If, for example, you plan to fly into Rome and head across to Madrid, it might cost less to fly out of Madrid on an open-jaw ticket than to retrace your footsteps to Rome and fly out on a standard return ticket.

(under 30 in some countries) have access to discounted fares. You'll have to show a document proving your date of birth, such as a valid International Student Identity Card (ISIC) or an International Youth Travel Card (IYTC) when buying your ticket. See **International Student Travel Confederation** (www.istc.org) for more information.

» Almost all air tickets are now electronic tickets (e-tickets). In effect, these are just printouts of your booking details – the important thing is the e-ticket number.

Land

There are plenty of options for getting to Mediterranean Europe by car, bus or train. In most of the Western European countries, buses are generally cheaper than trains, which tend to be more comfortable and more frequent. However, in the Bal-

kan countries buses are the main form of long-distance travel, serving more destinations than the limited train networks.

Bicycle

Transporting your bike to the region poses no great problems.

» Different airlines have different rules – some insist that you pack your bike in a bike bag, others require you to remove the pedals and deflate the tyres, and some even sell specially designed bike boxes. Remember that the bike's weight will be included in your luggage allowance.

» Bikes can generally be carried on slower trains, subject to a small supplementary fee. On fast trains they might need to be sent as registered luggage and will probably end up on a different train from the one you take.

» In the UK, **European Bike Express** (☐ 014-3042 2111; www.bike-express.co.uk) is

a coach service on which cyclists can travel with their bikes. It runs in the summer from Stokesley in northeast England, to France and northern Spain, with pick-up and drop-off points en route. Standard return fares range from UK£227 to UK£247; singles cost UK£136. Members of the **Cyclists' Touring Club** (CTC; ☐ 0844 736 8450; www.ctc.org.uk; membership adult/senior/junior UK£37/23/12) qualify for a discount of UK£10 on return fares. The CTC can also offer advice and organise tours.

» If travelling from Britain to France by **Eurostar** (☐ in the UK 0870 518 6186, in France 08 92 35 35 39; www.eurostar.com) you can take a bike on as part of your luggage only if it's in a bike bag. Otherwise it must go as registered baggage, for which there's a UK£30 fee.

» **Eurotunnel** (☐ in the UK 0844 335 3535, in France 08 10 63 03 04; www.eurotunnel.com) runs two daily cycle services to the continent. These must be booked 24 hours in advance. The standard fares for cyclists are UK£16/32 for a single/return trip.

Border Crossings

Border crossings into the region are pretty stress-free.

» If entering France, Greece, Italy, Malta, Portugal, Slovenia or Spain from another Schengen country, there are officially no border controls. However, spot checks are not unusual, particularly on trains, and individual countries are within their rights to reinstate controls. As a precaution always have your passport or ID card ready to show when crossing a national border.

» Land crossings into the eastern Mediterranean countries are fairly straightforward, although delays are not uncommon between Albania and Greece, particularly in summer.

» Border crossings into Turkey often involve a one- to

three-hour delay. Passengers are usually required to get off the bus or train for checks of paperwork and baggage. Note that if you require a visa – see the Turkey chapter for details – you will need to buy it at the border crossing. Some crossings don't have ATMs or exchange facilities so ensure you have the money on hand.

» The Moroccan border with Algeria is closed.

For details of border crossings into individual countries, refer to country chapters. To check on visa requirements see p1014.

Bus

Bus links between Mediterranean Europe and the rest of Continental Europe are comprehensive.

Eurolines (www.eurolines. com) is a consortium of coach companies that operates across Europe and Morocco. You can book tickets through the website, which also has timetable information and details of ticket offices in each country.

At some border crossings you might be required to get off the bus to have your documents and bags checked.

Car & Motorcycle

Driving to the region from northern Europe is a definite possibility – the road network is good, border controls are simple and there are no special hazards. However, if you have to traverse the Alps, note that while the main mountain passes remain open year-round, some minor ones close over winter.

When driving make sure you have:

☐ a valid driving licence, and, if necessary, an International Driving Permit (IDP)

☐ vehicle registration documents

☐ insurance certificate

☐ passport or ID card

☐ any compulsory equipment (such as snow chains, a warning triangle etc)

For further details on road rules and legal driving requirements see Car and Motorcycle in the Getting Around section, p1023.

THE CHANNEL TUNNEL
To take your car through the Channel Tunnel, **Eurotunnel** (☑in the UK 0844 335 3535, in France 08 10 63 03 04; www. eurotunnel.com) operates between Folkestone and Calais. Trains run 24 hours, every day, with up to four departures an hour at peak times.

» To save money it makes sense to book in advance, although it is possible to drive into the terminal, buy a ticket and get on the next train.

» There are a dizzying array of tickets with fares starting at UK£44 one way for a car, including all passengers, unlimited luggage and taxes. Check the website for special promotions.

» Both terminals are directly linked to motorways (the M20 in the UK and the A16 in France) and both have petrol stations.

Train

The train is a viable option for getting to Mediterranean Europe, particularly if travelling from the UK.

The high-speed **Eurostar** (☑in the UK 0843 218 6186, in France 08 92 35 35 39; www. eurostar.com) passenger service runs from London to Paris, where you can pick up trains to destinations across Europe:

Routes Direct trains from London's St Pancras International Station, Ebbsfleet and Ashford in the UK to Paris' Gare du Nord station, Lille, Calais and Avignon. There are also services to Paris Disneyland, several Alpine ski resorts, and Brussels.

Journey Times Approximately one hour to Calais, 1½ hours to Lille, 2¼ hours to Paris, and 6¼ hours to Avignon.

Fares There are 10 ticket types (standard child/youth/senior, fully-/semi-/nonflexible etc), with a corresponding range of fares and restrictions. The cheapest are generally non-refundable returns with restrictions on departure times and length of stay. As a rough guide, fares to Paris start at UK£69. Always check the website for special deals.

Tickets Tickets are available direct from Eurostar, from travel agencies, at St Pancras, Ebbsfleet and Ashford, from other UK mainline stations, and from **Rail Europe** (☑in the UK 0844 848 4064; www.raileurope.co.uk), which also sells other European rail tickets.

You can also get trains to the region from Central and Eastern Asia. Allow at least eight days.

For more information, see country chapters.

Sea

The Mediterranean has an extensive ferry network. For timetables, routes, ports and prices, check out **aferry** (www.aferry.com).

EUROPEAN RAIL RESOURCES

German Deutsch Bahn (www.bahn.de) German Railway's excellent website with schedules for European trains.

The Man in Seat 61 (www.seat61.com) Encyclopedic site with information on how to get to Europe by train.

Thomas Cook European Timetable (www.european railtimetable.co.uk) Order timetables of train, bus and ferry services; updated monthly.

From North Africa

There are regular ferries from Morocco to Spain and France, and from Tunisia to Italy and France. Of Morocco's Mediterranean ports, the busiest is Tangier, from where ferries sail for the Spanish ports of Algeciras and Tarifa, and the French port of Sète. Ferries are often filled to capacity in summer, so book well in advance if you're taking a vehicle across.

Ferry companies operating to/from North Africa:

Acciona Trasmediterránea (✆in Spain 902 45 46 45; www.trasmediterranea. es) Tangier to Algeciras, Barcelona, Tarifa, Almería; Ceuta to Algeciras; Melilla to Almería and Málaga. There are also services from Ghazaouet and Oran (both Algeria) to Almería.

SNCM (✆in France 3260; www.sncm.fr) Services from Tunisia (Tunis) and Algeria (Algiers, Oran, Béjaia, Skikda and Annaba) to France (Marseille).

See country chapters for more information.

From the UK

There are several UK–France ferry routes:

» Dover–Calais (1¼ to 1½ hours)
» Newhaven–Dieppe (four hours),
» Poole–Cherbourg (4½ to 6½ hours)
» Portsmouth–Cherbourg (5½ hours)

See the Spain and France chapters for details.

Fares depend on the usual mix of factors – the time of day/year, the flexibility of the ticket and, if you're driving, the length of your vehicle. Vehicle tickets include the driver and often up to five passengers free. There are also plenty of reductions on off-peak crossings and advance-purchase tickets. On most routes there is generally little price advantage in buying a return ticket rather than two singles. To compare fares check out **Ferry Savers** (www.ferrysavers.com).

Rail pass-holders are entitled to discounts or free travel on some lines, and most ferry companies give discounts to drivers with disabilities.

Major ferry companies include:

Brittany Ferries (✆0871 244 0744; www.brittany-ferries. com) From Portsmouth to Caen, Cherbourg and St Malo (all France), Bilbao and Santander (Spain); from Poole to Cherbourg (France); and from Plymouth to Roscoff (France) and Santander (Spain).

Condor Ferries (✆0845 609 1024; www.condorferries. co.uk) From Portsmouth to Cherbourg (France); from Poole to St Malo (France); and from Weymouth to St Malo (France).

LD Lines (✆0844 576 8836; www.ldlines.co.uk) From Portsmouth to Le Havre (France)

Norfolk Line (✆0844 847 5042; www.norfolkline.com) From Dover to Dunkirk (France).

P&O Ferries (✆0871 664 5645; www.poferries. com) From Dover to Calais (France); and from Portsmouth to Bilbao (Spain).

SeaFrance (✆France 03 21 17 70 33; www.seafrance. net) From Dover to Calais (France).

Transmanche Ferries (✆0844 576 8836; www. transmancheferries.com) From Newhaven to Dieppe (France).

From the USA

Sailing the Atlantic is slow (typically between seven and 13 days) and not especially cheap. You can either sign up for an expensive passage on a cruise ship or hop on a freighter as a paying passenger. Freighters are cheaper, more frequent and offer more routes.

» Freighters usually carry up to 12 passengers (more than 12 would require a doctor to be on board), with passage typically costing between US$80 and US$140 per day.

» Vehicles can often be included for an additional fee.

» If you're not travelling with a car, you'll need to organise transport from the port to the centre of town – ask the port agent (who'll be on board when the vessel docks) to arrange a taxi for you.

» You'll need to be flexible as shipping schedules can change at very short notice due to weather conditions, delays in cargo loading, port congestion etc.

» Pills to prevent sea sickness are probably a good idea, as many cargo ships are not fitted with stabilisers.

» **Strand Travel** (✆in the UK 020-7802 2136; www. strandtravel.co.uk) is a good source of information, as is **A la Carte Freighter Travel** (www.freighter-travel.com).

GETTING AROUND

Getting around Mediterranean Europe poses no great difficulties. There's a comprehensive transport network, and relations between countries are generally good. Ensure that you have a valid passport and check any visa requirements before travelling – see p1014 and individual country directories.

Air

Flying around Mediterranean Europe is definitely an option. Alongside the main established carriers, there are currently 42 budget airlines operating out of 360 airports across Europe. You can usually pick up a reasonably priced flight, especially if you're prepared to fly very early in the morning or late at night.

Some considerations:

» Low-cost carriers rarely provide much in the way of comfort or service. Inflight food, checked-in baggage, airport check-in and priority boarding are all things you'll be charged extra for.

» When booking online, always ensure that you untick any add-on options you don't want. The default page settings of many airline websites have them automatically ticked.

» Check baggage weight allowances – they are often less than on the established airlines and they are enforced.

» Many budget carriers use provincial airports that might be some way from your destination city. For example, Ryanair's Venice flights actually land at Treviso, which is some 30km from the lagoon city. If you're arriving late at night, make sure you've checked transport options into town, otherwise you could end up forking out for an expensive taxi ride.
See p1017 for information on buying tickets, and destination chapters for country-specific information.

Airlines

Europe's no-frills carriers are the obvious first point of call when looking for bargain flights, but don't write off the bigger established airlines. If travelling with a lot of luggage at peak holiday periods, there's often very little difference between the price of a 'low-cost' ticket, complete with extra charges for checked-in luggage, online booking etc, and a ticket from an established airline.

Listed below are the main budget airlines operating in the region:

Air Berlin (AB; www.airberlin.com)

bmibaby (WW; www.bmibaby.com)

easyJet (U2; www.easyjet.com)

germanwings (4U; www.germanwings.com)

Jet2 (LS; www.jet2.com)

Ryanair (FR; www.ryanair.com)

Thomson Airways (BY; http://flights.thomson.co.uk)

TUIfly (X3; www.tuifly.com)

Vueling (VY; www.vueling.com)

Air Passes

If you're planning to do a lot of flying in the region and prefer to sort out your transport before you leave, check out the European air passes that many major airlines offer. They are generally only available to non-Europeans, who must purchase them in conjunction with a long-haul international return ticket. Typically, they involve the purchase of flight coupons (usually around US$60 to US$205 each) for travel between a number of European destinations.

The following are the main European passes:

EuropeByAir Pass (www.europebyair.com) Valid for one-way travel between 150 European cities, the non-refundable coupons cost US$99 to US$199 per flight. They are only available to non-Europeans, but are valid for 120 days and are very flexible – you can decide where and when to use them as you go along. Airport taxes are not included.

Oneworld Visit Europe Pass (www.oneworld.com) Available to non-Europeans who buy an intercontinental ticket with a Oneworld member airline. There's a minimum of two coupons (€55 to €240), although you must only confirm the first flight when you buy. Valid on routes between 160 cities in 45 countries.

SkyTeam Europe Pass (www.skyteam.com) Flight coupons (US$60 to US$205) are valid for flights in 44 countries. The pass is available with the purchase of an intercontinental flight with any of SkyTeam's 13 member carriers. Advance booking is only required for the first European flight.

Star Alliance European Air Pass (www.staralliance.com) Non-European residents who buy a round-trip international ticket with a Star Alliance operator can buy a minimum of three and a maximum of 10 coupons for one-way flights between 45 European countries. Coupons, the first of which you must reserve when you buy the pass, are valid for three months.

Bicycle

Although cycling is a popular sport in France, Spain and Italy, as a means of everyday transport it is not particularly common in Mediterranean Europe. Outside certain areas there are very few dedicated cycle lanes, and drivers tend to regard cyclists as an oddity. Poor road conditions, particularly in the Eastern European countries, and mountainous terrain provide further obstacles.

» There are no special road rules for cyclists, although it's advisable to carry a helmet, lights and a basic repair kit (containing spare brake and gear cables, spanners, Allen keys, spare spokes and some strong adhesive tape). Take a good lock and make sure you use it when you leave your bike unattended.

» Bike hire is available throughout the region – tourist offices can usually direct you to rental outlets. See the country chapters for details.

» There are plenty of shops selling new and secondhand bikes, although you'll need a specialist outlet for a touring bike. European prices are quite high; expect to pay from €100 for a new bike. For more information on cycling, see p1003, p1018 and individual country chapters.

Boat

The Mediterranean's modern ferry network is comprehensive, covering all corners of the region. There are routes between Morocco, Spain and France; between Italy, Spain, Greece, Croatia, Turkey and Malta; and between the hundreds of Mediterranean islands. See the relevant country chapters for further details. Popular routes get very busy in summer, so try to book ahead.

The following are the major Mediterranean companies and the main routes they serve:

Acciona Trasmediterránea (☑in Spain 902 45 46 45; www.trasmediterranea.es) Spanish company with services from Barcelona to Ibiza, Maó and Palma de Mallorca (all Spain), Civitavecchia and Livorno (both Italy); from Valencia to Palma de Mallorca, Maó and Ibiza (all Spain); and from Algeciras to Ceuta and Tangier (both Morocco).

Agoudimos (☑in Greece 210 414 1300, in Italy 0831 56 03 81; www.agoudimos-lines.com) Services from Bari (Italy) to Igoumenitsa, Patra and Corfu (all Greece); from Brindisi (Italy) to Igoumenitsa and Corfu (both Greece).

Corsica Ferries (☑in Italy 199 400 500; www.corsica-ferries.it) Services from Bastia (Corsica) to Toulon, Nice (both France), Savona and Livorno (both Italy); from Golfo Aranci (Sardinia) to Civitavecchia, Livorno and Piombino (all Italy).

Grandi Navi Veloci (☑in Italy 010 209 45 91; www.gnv.it) Services from Genoa (Italy) to Barcelona (Spain), Porto Torres and Olbia (both Sardinia), and Palermo (Sicily); and from Palermo and Livorno (both Italy) to Malta.

Grimaldi Lines (☑in Italy 081 464 444, in Spain 902 53 13 33; www.grimaldi-lines.com) Serv-ices from Barcelona (Spain) to Porto Torres (Sardinia), Civitavecchia and Livorno (both Italy); from Valencia (Spain) to Livorno (Italy) and Tangier (Morocco); from Civitavecchia (Italy) to Catania (Sicily) and Malta.

Endeavor Lines (☑in Italy 0831 52 76 67; www.endeavor-lines.com) Services from Brindisi (Italy) to Igoumenitsa, Patra, Corfu and Kefallonia (all Greece).

Jadrolinija (☑in Croatia 051-666 111; www.jadrolinija.hr) Services from Ancona (Italy) to Split (Croatia); from Bari (Italy) to Dubrovnik (Croatia).

Minoan Lines (☑in Italy 041 504 12 01, in Greece 210 426 000; www.minoan.gr) Ferries from Ancona (Italy) to Igoumenitsa and Patra (both Greece); from Venice (Italy) to Corfu, Igoumenitsa and Patra (all Greece).

SNAV (☑in Italy 081 428 55 55; www.snav.it) Italian company with services from Ancona to Split (Croatia) and from Pescara to Hvar Island and Split (both Croatia); from Naples to Palermo and the Aeolian Islands (all Sicily); from Civitavecchia to Olbia (Sardinia) and Palermo (Sicily).

Superfast Ferries (www.superfast.com) Services from Ancona (Italy) to Igoumenitsa and Patra (both Greece); from Bari (Italy) to Igoumenitsa, Patra and Corfu (all Greece).

Tirrenia (☑in Italy 892 123; www.tirrenia.it) Italian company with services from Genoa to Arbatax, Porto Torres and Olbia (all Sardinia); from Civitavecchia to Olbia, Arbatax and Cagliari (all Sardinia); from Naples to Palermo (Sicily) and Cagliari (Sardinia).

Bus

Travelling by bus is generally the cheapest way of getting around the region, although it's neither comfortable nor particularly quick. In some of the eastern countries, including BiH, Croatia and Montenegro, the rail networks are limited and buses tend to be quicker (and more expensive) than trains. Buses also cover more routes, especially away from the main coastal areas; in mountainous countries (eg Albania and Greece) they are sometimes the only option.

Eurolines (www.eurolines.com) is a network of 32 European coach operators serving 500 destinations throughout Europe and Morocco. Country contact details are as follows:

Bosnia & Hercegovina (☑033-464045)
Croatia (☑051-660 300)
France (☑08 92 89 90 91)
Italy (☑0861 199 19 00)
Morocco (☑022 43 82 82)
Spain (☑934 90 40 00)
Turkey (☑444 1888)

The Moroccan national bus line, **Compagnie des Transports Marocains** (CTM), operates buses from Spain, France and northern Italy to most large Moroccan towns.

London-based **Busabout** (www.busabout.com) runs bus tours around Europe, stopping off at major cities in Italy, France, Spain and other countries. Note, however, that you don't simply buy a ticket from A to B; rather, you pay for travel on a specified route, allowing you to hop off at any scheduled stop, then resume with a later bus. Busabout buses are often oversubscribed, so book each sector to avoid being stranded. Departures are every two days from May to October. See below for ticket information.

Individual country chapters have further information about long-distance buses.

Bus Passes

Bus passes make sense if you want to cover a lot of ground as cheaply as possible. However, they're not always as extensive or as flexible as rail passes, and to get your money's worth you will need to spend a lot of time crammed into a bus seat.

Eurolines Pass (www. eurolines-pass.com) Covers 43 European cities. Most of the trips must be international, although a few internal journeys are possible between major cities. There are two passes: one valid for 15 days (low/high season adult €205/345, under 26 €175/290) and one valid for 30 days (low/high season adult €310/455, under 26 €240/375).

Busabout (www.busabout. com) Has various ticket options: a pass for a single loop costs per adult/ student UK£322/310, two loops costs UK£552/532. A flexitrip pass allows you to choose where you want to go and buy tickets (flexistops) for those destinations. It's valid for the entire operating season (May to October) and costs per adult/student UK£280/271 for six flexistops. There are also a series of one-way route tickets, costing from UK£449/365 per adult/ student. Discounts are available for early booking. For more information on Busabout tours, see p1026.

Costs & Reservations

Booking a seat in advance is not usually obligatory, but if you already know when you want to travel it makes sense to do so. In summer it is always advisable to book if you want to travel popular routes.

As a rough guide, a one-way bus ticket from Paris to Rome costs about €90, and from Madrid to Lisbon approximately €40.

Car & Motorcycle

Travelling around the region by car or motorbike gives you increased flexibility and allows you to venture off the beaten path. On the downside you'll often have to deal with congestion, urban one-way systems, traffic-free zones and nonexistent city parking. In winter, ice and fog can prove hazardous, particularly in mountainous areas such as Albania and BiH, where roads are badly signposted and often in poor condition.

Mediterranean Europe is well suited to motorcycle touring, as it has an active motorcycling scene and plenty of panoramic roads. On ferries, motorcyclists can sometimes be squeezed in without a reservation, although booking ahead is advisable in peak travelling periods. Take note of local customs about parking on pavements.

Some useful motoring resources are:

AA (www.theaa.com) The British Automobile Association's site has a comprehensive travel section covering all aspects of driving in Europe.
British Motorcyclists Federation (www.bmf.co.uk) Click on the 'Touring' link for information on all aspects of European touring, including specialist tour operators, recommended maps and updated European fuel prices.
Idea Merge (www.ideamerge. com/motoeuropa) An extensive US guide to motoring in Europe, with information on renting, leasing and purchasing, and specific country-by-country details.
RAC (www.rac.co.uk/driving -abroad/) Has up-to-date country-by-country information, a route planner and a useful pre-trip checklist.

Bringing Your Own Vehicle

Bringing your own vehicle into the region is fairly straightforward if you're coming from elsewhere in mainland Europe. In addition to your vehicle registration document you'll need a valid driving licence and proof of third-party (liability) insurance.

Shipping a vehicle from the US or Canada is expensive and time-consuming. It will generally cost from US$3000 return for a car. For further information consult **Idea Merge** (www.idea merge.com/motoeuropa/).

Other considerations:
» Some countries require you to carry certain pieces of equipment. For example, you'll need a first-aid kit in Croatia, Greece and Slovenia; a warning triangle in Cyprus, Greece, Italy, Portugal and Slovenia; a fire extinguisher in Greece and Turkey; and a set of spare headlight bulbs in Croatia and Spain.
» Note that there's sometimes a maximum time limit (typically six or 12 months) you can keep your car in a foreign country.
» For more information contact the **RAC** (www.rac. co.uk) or **AA** (www.theaa.com) in the UK, or the **AAA** (www. aaa.com) in the USA.

Driving Licence

» A European Union driving licence is valid for driving throughout Europe.
» If you've got an old-style green UK licence or a licence issued by a non-EU country you'll need an International Driving Permit (IDP).
» To get an IDP, apply to your national automobile association – you'll need a passport photo and your home driving licence. They cost about US$15/UK£10 and are valid for 12 months. When driving in Europe, you should always carry your home licence with the IDP, as the IDP is not valid on its own.

Fuel & Spare Parts

» Fuel prices vary from country to country, but are almost always more expensive than in the US or Australia.
» Fuel is sold by the litre (one US gallon is 3.8 litres). It comes as either unleaded petrol or diesel. Diesel is cheaper than unleaded petrol.

» As a rough guide, reckon on anything from €1.23 in Spain to €1.57 in Greece for 1L of unleaded petrol; and from €1.09 in Spain to €1.36 in Italy for diesel. You can get updated fuel prices for many European countries at **AA Roadwatch** (www.aaroadwatch.ie/eupetrolprices).

» Prices tend to be higher at motorway service stations and lowest at supermarket petrol stations. You'll also save by filling up in the cheapest countries (for example, Spain rather than France).

» You should have no great problems getting spare parts if needed.

Hire

AGENCIES

Car-hire agencies are widespread across the region. **Avis** (www.avis.com), **Budget** (www.budget.com), **Europcar** (www.europcar.com) and **Hertz** (www.hertz.com) have offices throughout the Med, and there are any number of local firms.

Regulations vary but there's often a minimum hire age (typically 21 or 23) and sometimes a maximum age (usually about 65 or 70). The hire company might also insist that you've held your licence for at least a year. You'll almost certainly need a credit card.

Motorcycle and moped hire is common in Italy, Spain, Greece and the south of France. See the Getting Around section in individual country chapters for further details.

COSTS

The international agencies are generally more expensive, but guarantee reliable service and a good standard of vehicle. You'll also usually have the option of returning the car to a different outlet at the end of the rental period.

If you know in advance that you want a car, you'll get a better deal if you arrange it at home. Fly-drive packages and other programs are also worth considering.

A useful online resource is **TravelJungle** (www.traveljungle.co.uk), which finds the best rates available for your destination. Brokers, like those listed below, can also cut costs.

Autos Abroad (🖰in the UK 0844 826 6536; www.autosabroad.com)

Holiday Autos (🖰in Australia 1300 554 507, in the UK 0871 472 5229, in the USA 866 392 9288; www.holidayautos.com)

Kemwel Holiday Autos (🖰in the USA 877 820 0668; www.kemwel.com)

As an approximate guide, expect to pay from €25 (from €40 in some places) per day for a small car and from €210 per week. Also note there are very few automatic cars in Mediterranean Europe and that they cost a lot more to hire. Check individual chapters for country-specific prices.

LEASING

For longer stays, leasing can be cheaper. The **Renault Eurodrive** (www.renault-eurodrive.com) scheme provides new cars for non-EU residents for a period of between 17 and 170 days. Under this arrangement, a Renault Clio Campus for a month in France costs about US$1560, including comprehensive insurance and roadside assistance.

In the US, **Kemwel Holiday Autos** (www.kemwel.com) arranges similar deals.

Check out www.ideamerge.com for further information on leasing in Europe.

RENTAL AGREEMENTS

Always make sure that you understand what's included in your rental agreement (collision waiver, unlimited mileage etc). Most agreements provide basic insurance that you can supplement by purchasing additional coverage. This supplemental insurance is often expensive if bought directly from the hire agency. As an alternative, check if your home car insurance covers foreign hire or if your credit-card company offers insurance.

If you're going to be crossing national borders, make sure your insurance policy is valid from one country to the next.

RAIL-AND-DRIVE PASSES

You can combine train and car travel with a rail-and-drive pass. The **Eurail Select Drive Pass** (www.europeonrail.com) is a typical option, covering 1st class train travel and Avis or Hertz car hire. Available to US residents, it comes in various packages, allowing travel in three, four or five countries over a two-month period. Prices for a three-country deal start at US$744 for two adults.

Insurance

Insurance requirements for driving in Mediterranean Europe:

» You'll need third-party (liability) insurance – most UK motor insurance policies automatically provide this for EU countries.

» To drive in Albania, BiH, Morocco and Turkey you'll also need an International Insurance Certificate, commonly called a Green Card. This is a certificate attesting that your insurance policy meets the minimum legal requirements of the country you're visiting. When you get this, check with your insurance company that it covers all the countries you intend to visit, and if you're driving in Turkey, make sure that it covers the European and Asian parts of the country. Taking out a European motoring assistance policy to cover roadside assistance and emergency repair is a good idea. In the UK, both the **AA** (www.theaa.com) and the **RAC** (www.rac.co.uk/driving-abroad) offer such services. The price varies depending on the area you'll be travelling around, the age of your car and the number of passengers, but it's typically about UK£75 for two adults travelling for two weeks in a three-year-old car. Non-Europeans might find it cheaper to arrange international coverage with their national motoring organisation. Also ask about the services (eg free breakdown assistance) offered by European motoring organisations affiliated with your home motoring organisation.

In the event of an accident a useful document to have is a European Accident Statement form. Available from your insurance company, it allows each party at an accident to record identical information for insurance purposes.

Purchase

Buying a car in Mediterranean Europe is generally not worth the hassle. In EU countries you can only buy a car if you are a legal resident of the country or have a local tax registration number. For further information see www.ideamerge.com/motoeuropa/index.html.

Paperwork can be tricky wherever you buy, and many countries have compulsory roadworthy checks on older vehicles.

Road Conditions

Road conditions vary enormously across the region. At best, you'll find well-maintained four- or six-lane dual carriageways or motorways. At worst, you'll be driving on rough, badly signposted single-lane tracks. You'll encounter some pretty terrible roads in Albania and BiH, although conditions are improving all the time. Minor roads might also be less than smooth in Morocco, Malta and Greece.

Tolls are charged on motorways (*autoroutes, autostrade* etc) in many Mediterranean countries, including Croatia, France, Greece, Italy, Portugal, Slovenia, Spain and Turkey. You can generally pay by cash or credit card, and in some cases you can avoid the queues altogether by buying a prepaid card. See individual chapters for details.

Road Rules

Motoring organisations can supply members with country-by-country information on road rules. See www.ideamerge.com/motoeuropa/index.html for details on driving in Croatia, France, Greece, Italy, Portugal, Slovenia, Spain and Turkey. Some universal rules and considerations:

» Drive on the right, except in Malta and Cyprus.

» In European cars the steering wheel is on the left. If you're bringing over a UK or Irish right-hand-drive vehicle you should adjust its headlights (which are angled differently to those in Mediterranean Europe) to avoid blinding oncoming traffic at night.

» Some countries require you to have your headlights on even when driving during the day.

» Unless otherwise indicated, always give way to cars entering a junction from the left (except in Malta and Cyprus).

» Speed limits vary from country to country. You may be surprised at the apparent disregard for speed limits (and traffic regulations in general) in some places, but as a visitor it's always best to be cautious.

» Random police checks are common in some countries and many driving infringements are subject to on-the-spot fines. If you're clobbered with a fine, always ask for a receipt.

» Drink-driving laws are strict, with the blood-alcohol concentration (BAC) limit generally between 0.05% and 0.08%.

» It's obligatory to wear a helmet on two-wheel vehicles everywhere in Mediterranean Europe. It's also recommended that motorcyclists use their headlights during the day.

Hitching

Hitching is more common in northern Europe than in Mediterranean countries, and although it is possible, you'll need to be patient. It's never entirely safe, however, and we don't recommend it. If you do decide to go for it, there are a few simple steps you can take to minimise the risks:

» Travel in pairs – ideally with a man if you're a woman. A woman hitching on her own is taking a big risk.

» Let someone know where you're going and when you'll be on the road. If possible, carry a mobile phone.

» When a driver stops, ask where they're going before getting in. This gives you time to size up the driver and, if you don't like the look of them, to politely decline the ride.

» Don't let the driver put your backpack in the boot; if possible, keep it with you in the car.

Some further tips:

» Don't try to hitch from city centres – take public transport to suburban exit routes.

» Hitching is often illegal on motorways, so stand on the slip roads or approach drivers at petrol stations and truck stops.

» Look presentable and cheerful, and make a cardboard sign indicating the road you want to take or your destination. A sign will also mean you're less likely to use the wrong gesture – the thumbs-up sign, for example, means 'up yours' in Sardinia.

» Never hitch where traffic passes too quickly or where drivers can't stop without causing an obstruction. Drivers will want to check you out before stopping, so don't wear sunglasses.

» If your itinerary includes a ferry crossing, try to score a ride before the ferry rather than after, as vehicle tickets sometimes include all passengers free of charge.

» It is sometimes possible to arrange a lift in advance: scan student noticeboards in colleges, or contact car-sharing agencies such as **Allostop Provoya** (☑in France 01 53 20 42 42; www.allostop. net, in French) in Paris. Online resources are:

BUG (www.bugeurope.com) Has a page dedicated to hitching in Europe.

Digihitch (www.digihitch. com) A comprehensive site with hitchers' forums, links and country-specific information.

Local Transport

The region's local transport network is comprehensive and mostly pretty efficient. Services may be irregular in remote rural regions, but wait long enough and a bus will pass.

In many places you have to buy your ticket before you get on the bus/boat/train and then validate it once on board (if the driver hasn't already checked it). It's often tempting not to do this – many locals don't appear to – but if you're caught with an unvalidated ticket you risk a fine.

If you're going to use public transport frequently, check out the daily, weekly and monthly passes available.

Boat

In some parts of the region, jumping on a ferry is as common as taking a bus. In Venice, vaporetti (small passenger ferries) ply the city's canals, ferrying tourists and locals alike, while in İstanbul ferries are the cheapest way of getting around the city.

Bus

City buses usually require you to buy your ticket in advance from a kiosk or machine, and then validate it upon boarding. See the country chapters and individual city sections for more details on local bus routes.

Metro

All the region's major capitals (Athens, Paris, Madrid and Rome) have metro systems, as do several other large cities (Milan, Barcelona, İstanbul). While it can often be quicker to travel underground, it can get unpleasantly hot and crowded, especially in summer during rush hour.

Taxi

Taxis are generally metered and rates are uniformly high. There can also be additional charges depending on the pick-up location or time of day, or for luggage or extra passengers. As a rule, always insist on a metered fare rather than an agreed price. Set fares to airports are an exception to this general rule of thumb.

To catch a cab you'll usually have to phone for one or queue at a taxi rank, which are often found outside train stations and big hotels.

Tours

Tours exist for all ages, interests and budgets. Specialist operators offer everything you can imagine from tours of the region's gardens to island-hopping cruises, walking holidays and adventure-sports packages.

Established outfits include:

Austin-Lehman Adventures (☑in the USA 800 577 1540; www.austinlehman.com) A US tour operator specialising in adventure sports, walking and cycling holidays.

Has packages in Croatia, France, Greece, Italy and Slovenia.

Busabout (www.busabout. com) Best known for its European bus tours (see p1022), London-based Busabout also offers tours to Italy (from UK£179), Spain and Portugal (from UK£449), and the Balkans (from UK£519), as well as cruises in Greece (from UK£239) and Croatia (from UK£387).

Contiki (http://ie.contiki. com) Contiki runs a range of European tours for 18- to 35-year-olds, including city breaks, camping trips and island-hopping journeys. Also has its own resort on Mykonos.

Ramblers Holidays (☑in the UK 017-0733 1133; www. ramblersholidays.co.uk) A British-based outfit that offers hiking holidays, ski packages and much more.

Saga Holidays (www.saga. co.uk) Serving people aged over 50, Saga sells everything from travel insurance to bus tours, river cruises and special-interest holidays.

Top Deck (☑in the UK 020-8987 3300; www.topdeck travel.co.uk) This London-based outfit offers young travellers everything from Croatian coastal cruises to festival weekends and ski breaks.

Many national tourist offices organise trips ranging from one-hour city tours to excursions taking several days. While they often work out more expensive than a self-organised tour, they are sometimes worth it if you're pressed for time. A short city tour will give you a quick overview of the place and can be a good way to begin your visit.

Train

Trains are a popular way of getting around Mediterranean Europe. The region's rail network is comprehensive, and trains are comfortable, frequent and generally punctual. You'll have no trouble travelling between the region's main cities, although if you want to get off the beaten track, particularly in the eastern Balkan countries, you'll find the bus a better option. Other factors to bear in mind:

» The speed and cost of your journey depends on the type of train you take. Fast trains include the TGV in France, the Tren de Alta Velocidad Española (AVE) in Spain and the Eurostar Alta Velocità (ES AV) in Italy. Extra charges apply on fast trains, and it's often obligatory to make seat reservations. See individual country chapters for details.

» Most long-distance trains have a dining car or an attendant with a snack trolley. If possible, buy your food before travelling, as on-board prices tend to be high.

» You should be quite safe travelling on trains in Mediterranean Europe, but it pays to be security-conscious nonetheless. Keep an eye on your luggage at all times (especially when stopping at stations) and lock the compartment doors at night.

» Note that European trains sometimes split en route in order to service two destinations, so even if you're on the right train, make sure you're in the correct carriage.

To check train schedules in any European country get hold of the **Thomas Cook European Timetable** (www.europeanrailtimetable.co.uk), which lists train, bus and ferry times. Updated monthly, the timetable (UK£13.99) can be ordered online or bought from Thomas Cook outlets in the UK. Another useful publication is *European Planning & Rail Guide*, available to US residents from **Budget Europe Travel** (☑ in the USA 800 441 9413; www.budgeteuropetravel.com).

Other resources include **The Man in Seat 61** (www.seat61.com), an exhaustive website touching on every aspect of European rail travel, and **German Deutsch Bahn** (www.bahn.de), where you can get up-to-the-minute train times for services across Europe.

Classes

On most trains there are 1st- and 2nd-class carriages. As a rough guide, a 1st-class ticket generally costs about double the price of a 2nd-class ticket. In 1st-class carriages there are fewer seats and more luggage space. On overnight trains, your comfort depends less on which class you're travelling than on whether you've booked a regular seat, couchette or sleeper – see the Overnight Trains boxed text, p1027.

Costs

Rail travel throughout the region is generally pretty economical. How much you pay depends on the type of train you take (high-speed trains are more expensive), whether you travel 1st or 2nd class, the time of year (or even the time of day), and whether or not you have a seat, a couchette or a sleeper. As a rough guide, the following are approximate ticket prices for high-speed trains:

» Barcelona–Madrid, €115

» Paris–Marseille, €84
» Rome–Florence, €44
Discounts are often available online or if you book well in advance. Check country chapters for details.

Reservations

On many local services it's not possible to reserve a seat – just jump on and sit where you like. On faster, long-distance trains it's sometimes obligatory to make a reservation, although this will often be included in the ticket price. Regardless of whether it's necessary, it's a good idea to book on popular routes in peak periods. Most international trains require a seat reservation, and you'll also need to book sleeping accommodation on overnight trains. Bookings can be made for a small, nonrefundable fee (usually about €3) when you buy your ticket.

Supplements (applicable on some fast trains) and reservation costs are not covered by most rail passes.

Train Passes

There are a lot of rail passes for travel in the region but before you buy you should work out whether you really need one. Unless you're planning to cover a lot of ground in a short space of time, you'd probably do as well buying regular train tickets. Advance-purchase deals,

---

OVERNIGHT TRAINS

Overnight trains are often a good bet as they save you time and the price of a night's accommodation. They usually offer a choice of couchettes or sleepers.

» Couchettes are mixed sex, and are fitted with four or six bunks, for which pillows, sheets and blankets are supplied.

» Sleepers are for between one and four passengers, and are more expensive. They are generally single sex, come with towels and toiletries, and have a washbasin in the compartment.

On some routes, you can now get a private room with an en suite shower and toilet.

one-off promotions and special circular-route tickets are all available. Also, normal international tickets are valid for two months and allow you to stop as often as you like en route. However, rail passes do provide a degree of flexibility that many discount tickets do not.

When choosing a pass, consider how many countries you want to see, how flexible your travel dates are, if you want to travel 1st or 2nd class, and if you need a Eurail pass (for residents of non-European countries) or an InterRail pass (for European residents). Passes are available online or at travel agents. Prices vary, so it pays to shop around before committing yourself. Once you've purchased a pass, take care of it, as it cannot be replaced or refunded if it's lost or stolen.

Before travelling always check that the train you're taking doesn't require a supplement or seat reservation – these additional costs are not covered by most rail passes. Note also that passholders must always carry their passport for identification purposes.

Comprehensive information and online bookings are available at **Rail Europe** (www.raileurope.com) and **Rail Pass** (www.railpass.com).

PASSES FOR NON-EUROPEAN RESIDENTS

If you are resident in a non-European country you'll need a **Eurail** (www.eurail.com) pass. These are best bought before you leave home. You can buy them in Europe – provided you can prove you've been on the continent for less than six months – but sales outlets are limited and you'll pay up to 20% more than you would at home.

There are four types of passes (the Global Pass, Select Pass, Regional Pass and One Country Pass) and four fare types – adult (over

26), youth (12–25 years of age), family and saver. Prices quoted here are for the adult and youth versions; savers, available for two to five people travelling together, cost about 15% less than adult passes. With adult passes, children under four travel free, and kids aged between four and 11 travel for half price. Adult and saver passes provide 1st-class travel; the youth version is for 2nd class.

Eurail Global Pass

This provides unlimited rail travel in 22 countries – including Croatia, France, Greece, Italy, Portugal, Slovenia and Spain. It comes in two forms:

Continuous (15 days/3 months adult US$729/2025, youth US$475/1315) Provides travel each day for a period ranging from 15 days to three months.

Flexi (10/15 days adult US$865/1135, youth US$559/739) Opt for 10 or 15 non-consecutive travel days within a two-month period.

The pass is valid on some ferries between Italy and Greece. Before using the pass for the first time, you'll need to have it validated at a ticket counter (you'll need your passport to do this).

Eurail Select Pass

The **Select Pass** (4 countries 5/6/8/10 days adult US$515/565/659/749, youth US$335/365/429/489) allows travel between three, four or five bordering countries for five, six, eight or 10 days within a two-month period (the five-country pass also has a 15-day option). Countries covered include Croatia, France, Greece, Italy, Portugal, Montenegro, Slovenia and Spain.

Eurail Regional & One Country Passes

If you're going to stay in one country or plan on concentrating on a particular area it

makes sense to go for a One Country or Regional Pass, rather than the more expensive Global Passes.

Eurail has an extensive range of regional passes, including passes for Austria, Croatia and Slovenia; France and Italy; France and Spain; Greece and Italy; and Spain and Portugal. These provide for between four and 10 days unlimited travel within a two-month period. Prices vary, but as a rough guide:

Austria, Croatia & Slovenia (4/10 days adult US$269/509, youth US$195/369)

France & Spain (4/10 days adult US$379/645, youth US$245/419)

Greece & Italy (4/10 days adult US$359/579, youth US$235/379)

The One Country Pass is available for 17 countries, including Croatia, Greece, Italy, Portugal, Slovenia and Spain. The most popular pass, the **Italy Pass** (3/10 days adult US$209/385, youth US$169/315) covers between three and 10 days of travel within a two-month period.

Most of these passes can only be purchased prior to arrival in the country concerned.

PASSES FOR EUROPEAN RESIDENTS

European residents of at least six months' standing (passport identification is required) will need an **InterRail** (www.interrailnet.com) pass. There are two types of pass: the Global Pass and the One Country Pass.

Adult passes are available in 1st and 2nd class, while the youth (12–25 years of age) passes are for 2nd class only. With adult passes, children under four travel free, and kids aged between four and 11 travel for half price. Seniors (over 60) qualify for a 10% discount on the Global Pass.

InterRail Global Pass

The Global Pass is valid for travel in 30 countries, including BiH, Croatia, France, Greece, Italy, Montenegro, Portugal, Slovenia, Spain and Turkey. There are various options:

» Five days of travel within 10 days (adult/youth €169/259)

» 10 days of travel within 22 days (adult/youth €249/369)

» 15 days of travel (adult/youth €289/409)

» 22 days of travel (adult/youth €319/479)

» One month of travel (adult/youth €409/619) Before you start each trip, fill in the journey details on the provided form.

InterRail One Country Pass

There are InterRail One Country Passes for 27 European countries. These provide three, four, six or eight days travel within a one-month period. Among the most popular options are passes to Italy and Spain. The Greece Plus Pass also includes Superfast and Blue Star ferries to Italy.

Italy Pass (3/4/6/8 days adult €115/145/195/235, youth €75/95/125/155)

Spain Pass (3/4/6/8 days adult €269/299/389/459/, youth €119/139/169/199)

Greece Plus Pass (3/4/6/8 days adult €115/145/195/235, youth €75/95/125/155)

Language

This chapter offers basic vocabulary to help you get around Mediterranean Europe. If you read our coloured pronunciation guides as if they were English, you'll be understood. Note that the stressed syllables are indicated with italics.

Some of the phrases in this chapter have both polite and informal forms (indicated by the abbreviations 'pol' and 'inf' respectively). Use the polite form when addressing older people, officials or service staff. The abbreviations 'm' and 'f' indicate masculine and feminine gender respectively.

ALBANIAN

There are two main dialects of Albanian – Tosk (spoken in southern Albania, Greece, Italy and Turkey) and Gheg (spoken in northern Albania, Kosovo, Serbia, Montenegro and Macedonia). Tosk is the official language of Albania and is also used in this chapter.

Note that ew is pronounced as ee with rounded lips, uh as the 'a' in 'ago', dh as the 'th' in 'that', dz as the 'ds' in 'adds', and zh as the 's' in 'pleasure'. Also, ll and rr are pronounced stronger than when they are written as single letters.

Basics

Hello.	Tungjatjeta.	toon·dya·tye·ta
Goodbye.	Mirupafshim.	mee·roo·paf·sheem
Excuse me.	Më falni.	muh fal·nee
Sorry.	Më vjen keq.	muh vyen kech
Please.	Ju lutem.	yoo loo·tem
Thank you.	Faleminderit.	fa·le·meen·de·reet
Yes./No.	Po./Jo.	po/jo

WANT MORE?

For in-depth language information and handy phrases, check out Lonely Planet's *Mediterranean Europe Phrasebook*. You'll find it at **shop. lonelyplanet.com**, or you can buy Lonely Planet's iPhone phrasebooks at the Apple App Store.

Do you speak English?
A flisni anglisht?　　a flees·nee ang·leesht

I don't understand.
Unë nuk kuptoj.　　oo·nuh nook koop·toy

Accommodation

campsite	vend kampimi	vend kam·pee·mee
guesthouse	bujtinë	booy·tee·nuh
hotel	hotel	ho·tel

Do you have a singe/double room?
A keni një dhomë teke/dopjo?　　a ke·nee nyuh dho·muh te·ke dop·yo

How much is it per night/person?
Sa kushton për një natë/njeri?　　sa koosh·ton puhr nyuh na·tuh/nye·ree

Numbers – Albanian

1	një	nyuh
2	dy	dew
3	tre	tre
4	katër	ka·tuhr
5	pesë	pe·suh
6	gjashtë	dyash·tuh
7	shtatë	shta·tuh
8	tetë	te·tuh
9	nëntë	nuhn·tuh
10	dhjetë	dhye·tuh

Eating & Drinking

Is there a vegetarian restaurant near here?
A ka ndonjë restorant   a ka ndo·nyuh res·to·rant
vegjetarian   ve·dye·ta·ree·an
këtu afër?   kuh·too a·fuhr

I'd like the bill/menu, please.
Më sillni faturën/   muh seell·nee fa·too·ruhn
menunë, ju lutem.   me·noo·nuh yoo loo·tem

I'll have ...	*Dua ...*	doo·a ...
Cheers!	*Gëzuar!*	guh·zoo·ar

Emergencies

Help!
Ndihmë!   ndeeh·muh

Call a doctor/the police!
Thirrni doktorin/   theerr·nee dok·to·reen
policinë!   po·lee·tsee·nuh

I'm lost.
Kam humbur rrugën.   kam hoom·boor rroo·guhn

I'm ill.
Jam i/e sëmurë. (m/f)   yam ee/e suh·moo·ruh

Where are the toilets?
Ku janë banjat?   koo ya·nuh ba·nyat

Shopping & Services

I'm looking for ...
Po kërkoj për ...   po kuhr·koy puhr ...

How much is it?
Sa kushton?   sa koosh·ton

Transport & Directions

Where's the ...?
Ku është ...?   koo uhsh·tuh ...

What's the address?
Cila është adresa?   tsee·la uhsh·tuh a·dre·sa

a ... ticket	*Një biletë ...*	nyuh bee·le·tuh ...
one-way	*për vajtje*	puhr vai·tye
return	*kthimi*	kthee·mee

boat	*anija*	a·nee·ya
bus	*autobusi*	a·oo·to·boo·see
plane	*aeroplani*	a·e·ro·pla·nee
train	*treni*	tre·nee

CROATIAN

The national language of Croatia also has official status in Bosnia and Montenegro.

Note that r is a rolled sound, zh is pronounced as the 's' in 'pleasure', and the apostrophe (') indicates a slight y sound after a consonant.

Basics

Hello.	*Dobar dan.*	do·bar dan
Goodbye.	*Zbogom.*	zbo·gom
Excuse me.	*Oprostite.*	o·pro·sti·te
Sorry.	*Žao mi je.*	zha·o mi ye
Please.	*Molim.*	mo·lim
Thank you.	*Hvala.*	hva·la
Yes./No.	*Da./Ne.*	da/ne

Do you speak English?
Govorite/Govoriš li   go·vo·ri·te/go·vo·rish
engleski? (pol/inf)   li en·gle·ski

I don't understand.
Ja ne razumijem.   ya ne ra·zu·mi·yem

Accommodation

campsite	*kamp*	kamp
guesthouse	*privatni*	pri·vat·ni
	smještaj	smyesh·tai
hotel	*hotel*	ho·tel

Do you have a single/double room?
Imate li jednokrevetnu/   i·ma·te li yed·no· kre·vet·nu/
dvokrevetnu sobu?   dvo·kre·vet·nu so·bu

How much is it per night/person?
Koliko stoji po   ko·li·ko sto·yi po ...
noći/osobi?   no·chi/o·so·bi

Eating & Drinking

Do you have vegetarian food?
Da li imate   da li i·ma·te
vegetarijanski obrok?   ve·ge·ta·ri·yan·ski o·brok

I'd like the bill/menu, please.
Mogu li dobiti račun/   mo·gu li do·bi·ti ra·chun
jelovnik molim?   ye·lov·nik mo·lim

I'll have ...
Želim naručiti ...   zhe·lim na·ru·chi·ti ...

Cheers!
Živjeli!   zhi·vye·li

Emergencies

Help!
Upomoć!   u·po·moch

Call a doctor/the police!
Zovite liječnika/   zo·vi·te li·yech·ni·ka/
policiju.   po·li·tsi·yu

I'm lost.
Izgubio/Izgubila   iz·gu·bi·o/iz·gu·bi·la
sam se. (m/f)   sam se

I'm ill.
Ja sam bolestan/   ya sam bo·le·stan/
bolesna. (m/f)   bo·le·sna

Where are the toilets?
Gdje se nalaze zahodi   gdye se na·la·ze za·ho·di

Numbers – Croatian

1	jedan	ye·dan
2	dva	dva
3	tri	tri
4	četiri	che·ti·ri
5	pet	pet
6	šest	shest
7	sedam	se·dam
8	osam	o·sam
9	devet	de·vet
10	deset	de·set

Shopping & Services

I'm looking for ...
Tražim ... tra·zhim

How much is it?
Koliko stoji? ko·li·ko sto·yi

Transport & Directions

Where's the ...?
Gdje je ...? gdye ye ...

What's the address?
Koja je adresa? ko·ya ye a·dre·sa

One one-way/return ticket (to Sarajevo), please.
Jednu jednosmjernu/ yed·nu yed·no·smyer·nu/
povratnu kartu po·vrat·nu kar·tu
(do Sarajeva), molim. (do sa·ra·ye·va) mo·lim

boat	brod	brod
bus	autobus	a·u·to·bus
plane	avion	a·vi·on
train	vlak	vlak

FRENCH

French has official status in France, Belgium, Switzerland and Luxembourg.

French has nasal vowels (pronounced as if you're trying to force the sound through the nose), indicated in our pronunciation guides with o or u followed by an almost inaudible nasal consonant sound m, n or ng. Note also that air is pronounced as in 'fair', eu as the 'u' in 'nurse', ew as ee with rounded lips, r is a throaty sound, and zh is pronounced as the 's' in 'pleasure'.

Syllables in French words are, for the most part, equally stressed, but try adding a light stress on the final syllable of a word.

Basics

Hello.	Bonjour.	bon·zhoor
Goodbye.	Au revoir.	o·rer·vwa
Excuse me.	Excusez-moi.	ek·skew·zay·mwa
Sorry.	Pardon.	par·don

Please.	S'il vous plaît.	seel voo play
Thank you.	Merci.	mair·see
Yes./No.	Oui./Non.	wee/non

Do you speak English?
Parlez-vous anglais? par·lay·voo ong·glay

I don't understand.
Je ne comprends pas. zher ner kom·pron pa

Accommodation

campsite	camping	kom·peeng
guesthouse	pension	pon·syon
hotel	hôtel	o·tel

Do you have	Avez-vous	a·vey·voo
a ... room?	une chambre ...?	ewn shom·bre ...
single	à un lit	a un lee
double	avec un	a·vek ung
	grand lit	gron lee

How much is it per night/person?
Quel est le prix par kel ey le pree par
nuit/personne? nwee/pair·son

Eating & Drinking

Do you have vegetarian food?
Vous faites les repas voo fet ley re·pa
végétarien? vey·zhey·ta·ryun

I'd like the bill/menu, please.
Je voudrais l'addition/ zhe voo·drey la·dee·syon/
la carte s'il vous plaît. la kart seel voo pley

I'll have ...
Je prends ... zhe pron ...

Cheers!
Santé! son·tay

Emergencies

Help!
Au secours! o skoor

Call a doctor!
Appelez un médecin! a·play un mayd·sun

Call the police!
Appelez la police! a·play la po·lees

I'm lost.
Je suis perdu(e). (m/f) zhe swee·pair·dew

I'm ill.
Je suis malade. zher swee ma·lad

Where are the toilets?
Où sont les toilettes? oo son ley twa·let

Shopping & Services

I'd like to buy ...
Je voudrais acheter ... zher voo·dray ash·tay ...

How much is it?
C'est combien? say kom·byun

Numbers – French		
1	*un*	un
2	*deux*	der
3	*trois*	trwa
4	*quatre*	ka·trer
5	*cinq*	sungk
6	*six*	sees
7	*sept*	set
8	*huit*	weet
9	*neuf*	nerf
10	*dix*	dees

Transport & Directions

Where's ...?
Où est ...?   oo ay ...

What's the address?
Quelle est l'adresse?   kel ay la·dres

one-way ticket
billet simple   bee·yey sum·ple

return ticket
billet aller et retour   bee·yey a·ley ey re·toor

boat	*bateau*	ba·to
bus	*bus*	bews
plane	*avion*	a·vyon
train	*train*	trun

GREEK

Greek has official status in Greece and Cyprus.

Note that dh is pronounced as the 'th' in 'that', dz as the 'ds' in 'lads', and that gh and kh are both throaty sounds, similar to the 'ch' in the Scottish *loch*.

Basics

Hello.	Γεια σου.	yia su
Goodbye.	Αντίο.	a·di·o
Excuse me.	Με συγχωρείτε.	me sing·kho·ri·te
Sorry.	Συγνώμη.	si·ghno·mi
Please.	Παρακαλώ.	pa·ra·ka·lo
Thank you.	Ευχαριστώ.	ef·kha·ri·sto
Yes.	Ναι.	ne
No.	Οχι.	o·hi

Do you speak English?
Μιλάς Αγγλικά;   mi·las ang·gli·ka

I don't understand.
Δεν καταλαβαίνω.   dhen ka·ta·la·ve·no

Accommodation

campsite	χώρος για κάμπινγκ	kho·ros yia kam·ping
guesthouse	ξενώνας	kse·no·nas
hotel	ξενοδοχείο	kse·no·dho·hi·o

Do you have a single/double room?
Εχετε ένα μονό/   e·he·te e·na mo·no/
διπλό δωμάτιο;   dhi·plo dho·ma·ti·o

How much is it per night/person?
Πόσο είναι για κάθε   po·so i·ne yia ka·the
νύχτα/άτομο;   nikh·ta/a·to·mo

Eating & Drinking

Do you have vegetarian food?
Εχετε φαγητό για   e·he·te fa·yi·to yia
χορτοφάγους;   khor·to·fa·ghus

I'd like the bill/menu, please.
Θα ήθελα το μενού/   tha i·the·la to me·nu
λογαριασμό, παρακαλώ.   lo·gha·riaz·mo pa·ra·ka·lo

I'll have ... Θα πάρω ... tha pa·ro ...
Cheers! Εις υγείαν! is i·yi·an

Emergencies

Help!
Βοήθεια!   vo·i·thia

Call a doctor!
Κάλεσε ένα γιατρό!   ka·le·se e·na yia·tro

Call the police!
Κάλεσε την αστυνομία!   ka·le·se tin a·sti·no·mi·a

I'm ill.
Είμαι άρρωστος/   i·me a·ro·stos/
άρρωστη. (m/f)   a·ro·sti

Where are the toilets?
Που είναι η τουαλέτα;   pu i·ne i tu·a·le·ta

Shopping & Services

I'd like to buy ...
Θα ήθελα να αγοράσω ...   tha i·the·la na a·gho·ra·so ...

How much is it?
Πόσο κάνει;   po·so ka·ni

Transport & Directions

Where's ...?
Που είναι ...?   pu i·ne ...

What's the address?
Ποια είναι η διεύθυνση;   pia i·ne i dhi·ef·thin·si

a ... ticket	ενα εισιτίριο ...	e·na i·si·ti·ri·o ...
one-way	απλό	a·plo
return	με επιστροφή	me e·pi·stro·fi

Numbers – Greek

1	ένας	e·nas
2	δύο	dhi·o
3	τρεις	tris
4	τέσσερις	te·se·ris
5	πέντε	pe·de
6	έξι	ek·si
7	εφτά	ef·ta
8	οχτώ	okh·to
9	εννέα	e·ne·a
10	δέκα	dhe·ka

boat	πλοίο	pli·o
bus	λεωφορείο	le·o·fo·ri·o
plane	αεροπλάνο	a·e·ro·pla·no
train	τρένο	tre·no

ITALIAN

Italian is the official language in Italy and also has that status in Switzerland.

Italian vowel are generally shorter than those in English. Double consonants are pronounced more emphatically. Note that ow is pronounced as in 'how', dz as the 'ds' in 'lads', and r is a strong, rolled sound.

Basics

Hello.	Buongiorno.	bwon·jor·no
Goodbye.	Arrivederci.	a·ree·ve·der·chee
Excuse me.	Mi scusi. (pol)	mee skoo·zee
	Scusami. (inf)	skoo·za·mee
Sorry.	Mi dispiace.	mee dees·pya·che
Please.	Per favore.	per fa·vo·re
Thank you.	Grazie.	gra·tsye
Yes./No.	Sì./No.	see/no

Do you speak English?
Parla inglese?   par·la een·gle·ze

I don't understand.
Non capisco.   non ka·pee·sko

Accommodation

campsite	campeggio	kam·pe·jo
guesthouse	pensione	pen·syo·ne
hotel	albergo	al·ber·go

How much is it per night/person?
Quanto costa per   kwan·to kos·ta per
una notte/persona?   oo·na no·te/per·so·na

Do you have a single room?
Avete una   a·ve·te oo·na
camera singola?   ka·me·ra seen·go·la

Do you have a double room?
Avete una camera   a·ve·te oo·na ka·me·ra
doppia con letto   do·pya kon le·to
matrimoniale?   ma·tree·mo·nya·le

Eating & Drinking

Do you have vegetarian food?
Avete piatti   a·ve·te pya·tee
vegetariani?   ve·je·ta·rya·nee

I'd like the ..., please.
Vorrei il conto/ menù,   vo·ray eel kon·to/me·noo
per favore.   per fa·vo·re

I'll have ...	Prendo ...	pren·do ...
Cheers!	Salute!	sa·loo·te

Emergencies

Help!
Aiuto!   ai·yoo·to

Call a doctor!
Chiami un medico!   kya·mee oon me·dee·ko

Call the police!
Chiami la polizia!   kya·mee la po·lee·tsee·a

I'm lost.
Mi sono perso/a. (m/f)   mee so·no per·so/a

I'm ill.
Mi sento male.   mee sen·to ma·le

Where are the toilets?
Dove sono i gabinetti?   do·ve so·no ee ga·bee·ne·tee

Shopping & Services

I'm looking for ...
Sto cercando ...   sto cher·kan·do ...

How much is it?
Quant'è?   kwan·te

Transport & Directions

Where's ... ?
Dov'è ... ?   do·ve ...

What's the address?
Qual'è l'indirizzo?   kwa·le leen·dee·ree·tso

One ... ticket	Un biglietto ...	oon bee·lye·to...
one-way	di sola andata	dee so·la an·da·ta
return	di andata e ritorno	dee an·da·ta e ree·tor·no

Numbers – Italian

1	uno	oo·no
2	due	doo·e
3	tre	tre
4	quattro	kwa·tro
5	cinque	cheen·kwe
6	sei	say
7	sette	se·te
8	otto	o·to
9	nove	no·ve
10	dieci	dye·chee

boat	nave	na·ve
bus	autobus	ow·to·boos
plane	aereo	a·e·re·o
train	treno	tre·no

PORTUGUESE

Most vowel sounds in Portuguese have a nasal version (ie pronounced as if you're trying to force the sound through the nose), which is indicated in our pronunciation guides with ng after the vowel. Note also that oh is pronounced as the 'o' in 'note', ow as in 'how', rr is a throaty sound in Portuguese (similar to the French 'r'), and zh is pronounced as the 's' in 'pleasure'.

Basics

Hello.	Olá.	o·laa
Goodbye.	Adeus.	a·de·oosh
Excuse me.	Faz favor.	faash fa·vor
Sorry.	Desculpe.	desh·kool·pe
Please.	Por favor.	poor fa·vor
Thank you.	Obrigado. (m)	o·bree·gaa·doo
	Obrigada. (f)	o·bree·gaa·da
Yes./No.	Sim./Não.	seeng/nowng

Do you speak English?
Fala inglês?   faa·la eeng·glesh

I don't understand.
Não entendo.   nowng eng·teng·doo

Accommodation

campsite	parque de campismo	paar·ke de kang·peezh·moo
guesthouse	casa de hóspedes	kaa·za de osh·pe·desh
hotel	hotel	o·tel

Do you have a single/double room?
Tem um quarto de solteiro/casal?   teng oong kwaar·too de sol·tay·roo/ka·zaal

How much is it per night/person?
Quanto custa por noite/pessoa?   kwang·too koosh·ta poor noy·te/pe·so·a

Eating & Drinking

Do you have vegetarian food?
Tem comida vegetariana?   teng koo·mee·da ve·zhe·ta·ree·aa·na

I'll have ...	Eu queria ...	e·oo ke·ree·a ...
Cheers!	Saúde!	sa·oo·de

I'd like the ..., please.	Queria ..., por favor.	ke·ree·a ... poor fa·vor
bill	a conta	a kong·ta
menu	um menu	oong me·noo

Emergencies

Help!
Socorro!   soo·ko·rroo

Call a doctor!
Chame um médico!   shaa·me oong me·dee·koo

Call the police!
Chame a polícia!   shaa·me a poo·lee·sya

I'm ill.
Estou doente.   shtoh doo·eng·te

Where are the toilets?
Onde é a casa de banho?   ong·de e a kaa·za de ba·nyoo

Shopping & Services

I'd like to buy ...
Queria comprar ...   ke·ree·a kong·praar ...

How much is it?
Quanto custa?   kwang·too koosh·ta

Transport & Directions

Where's ...?
Onde é ...?   ong·de e ...

What's the address?
Qual é o endereço?   kwaal e oo eng·de·re·soo

one-way ticket
bilhete de ida   bee·lye·te de ee·da

return ticket
bilhete de ida e volta   bee·lye·te de ee·da ee vol·ta

boat	barco	baar·koo
bus	autocarro	ow·to·kaa·roo
plane	avião	a·vee·owng
train	comboio	kong·boy·oo

Numbers – Portuguese

1	um	oong
2	dois	doysh
3	três	tresh
4	quatro	kwaa·troo
5	cinco	seeng·koo
6	seis	saysh
7	sete	se·te
8	oito	oy·too
9	nove	no·ve
10	dez	desh

SLOVENE

We've used the symbols oh (as the 'o' in 'note') and ow (as in 'how') to help you pronounce vowels followed by the letters *l* and *v* in written Slovene – at the end of a syllable these combinations produce a sound similar to the 'w' in English.

Note also that uh is pronounced as the 'a' in 'ago', zh as the 's' in 'pleasure', r is rolled, and the apostrophe (') indicates a slight y sound.

Basics

Hello.	Zdravo.	zdra·vo
Goodbye.	Na svidenje.	na svee·den·ye
Excuse me.	Dovolite.	do·vo·lee·te
Sorry.	Oprostite.	op·ros·tee·te
Please.	Prosim.	pro·seem
Thank you.	Hvala.	hva·la
Yes./No.	Da./Ne.	da/ne

Do you speak English?
Ali govorite   a·lee go·vo·ree·te
angleško?   ang·lesh·ko

I don't understand.
Ne razumem.   ne ra·zoo·mem

Accommodation

campsite	kamp	kamp
guesthouse	gostišče	gos·teesh·che
hotel	hotel	ho·tel

Do you have a single/double room?
Ali imate   a·lee ee·ma·te
enoposteljno/   e·no·pos·tel'·no/
dvoposteljno sobo? dvo·pos·tel'·no so·bo

How much is it per night/person?
Koliko stane na   ko·lee·ko sta·ne na
noč/osebo?   noch/o·se·bo

Eating & Drinking

Do you have vegetarian food?
Ali imate   a·lee ee·ma·te
vegetarijansko   ve·ge·ta·ree·yan·sko
hrano?   hra·no

I'd like the bill/menu, please.
Želim račun/   zhe·leem ra·choon/
jedilni list, prosim. ye·deel·nee leest pro·seem

| I'll have ... | Jaz bom ... | yaz bom ... |
| Cheers! | Na zdravje! | na zdrav·ye |

Emergencies

Help!
Na pomoč!   na po·moch

Call a doctor/the police!
Pokličite zdravnika/ pok·lee·chee·te zdrav·nee·ka/
policijo!   po·lee·tsee·yo

I'm ill.
Bolan/Bolna sem. (m/f) bo·lan/boh·na sem

Where are the toilets?
Kje je stranišče?   kye ye stra·neesh·che

Shopping & Services

I'm looking for ...
Iščem ...   eesh·chem ...

How much is this?
Koliko stane?   ko·lee·ko sta·ne

Transport & Directions

Where's the ...?
Kje je ...?   kye ye ...

What's the address?
Na katerem naslovu je?   na ka·te·rem nas·lo·voo ye

one-way/return ticket
enosmerno/povratno   e·no·smer·no/pov·rat·no
vozovnico   o·zov·nee·tso

Numbers – Slovene

1	en	en
2	dva	dva
3	trije	tree·ye
4	štirje	shtee·rye
5	pet	pet
6	šest	shest
7	sedem	se·dem
8	osem	o·sem
9	devet	de·vet
10	deset	de·set

boat	ladja	ad·ya
bus	avtobus	av·to·boos
plane	letalo	le·ta·lo
train	vlak	vlak

SPANISH

Spanish vowels are generally pronounced short. Note that ow is pronounced as in 'how', kh as in the Scottish *loch* (a throaty sound), rr is rolled and stronger than in English, and v is a soft 'b' (pronounced between the English 'v' and 'b' sounds).

Basics

Hello.	Hola.	o·la
Goodbye.	Adiós.	a·dyos
Excuse me.	Perdón.	per·don
Sorry.	Lo siento.	lo see·en·to
Please.	Por favor.	por fa·vor
Thank you.	Gracias.	gra·thyas
Yes./No.	Sí./No.	see/no

Do you speak English?
¿Habla/Hablas   a·bla/a·blas
inglés? (pol/inf)   een·gles

I don't understand.
Yo no entiendo.   yo no en·tyen·do

Accommodation

campsite	terreno de cámping	te·re·no de kam·peeng
guesthouse	pensión	pen·syon
hotel	hotel	o·tel

Do you have a single/double room?
¿Tiene una habitación   tye·ne oo·na a·bee·ta·thyon
individual/doble?   een·dee·vee·dwal/do·ble

How much is it per night/person?
¿Cuánto cuesta por   kwan·to kwes·ta por
noche/persona?   no·che/persona

Eating & Drinking

Do you have vegetarian food?
¿Tienen comida   tye·nen ko·mee·da
vegetariana?   ve·khe·ta·rya·na

I'd like the ... please.	Quisiera ... por favor.	kee·sye·ra ... por fa·vor
bill	la cuenta	la kwen·ta
menu	el menú	el me·noo

| I'll have ... | Para mí ... | pa·ra mee ... |
| Cheers! | ¡Salud! | sa·loo |

Emergencies

Help!
¡Socorro!   so·ko·ro

Call a doctor!
¡Llame a un médico!   lya·me a oon me·dee·ko

Call the police!
¡Llame a la policía!   lya·me a la po·lee·thee·a

I'm ill.
Estoy enfermo/a. (m/f)   es·toy en·fer·mo/a

Where are the toilets?
¿Dónde están los   don·de es·tan los
servicios?   ser·vee·thyos

Shopping & Services

I'd like to buy ...
Quisiera comprar ...   kee·sye·ra kom·prar ...

How much is it?
¿Cuánto cuesta?   kwan·to kwes·ta

Transport & Directions

Where's ...?
¿Dónde está ...?   don·de es·ta ...

What's the address?
¿Cuál es la dirección?   kwal es la dee·rek·thyon

one-way ticket
billete sencillo   bee·lye·te sen·thee·lyo

return ticket
billete de   bee·lye·te de
ida y vuelta   ee·da ee vwel·ta

boat	barco	bar·ko
bus	autobús	ow·to·boos
plane	avión	a·vyon
train	tren	tren

Numbers – Spanish		
1	uno	oo·no
2	dos	dos
3	tres	tres
4	cuatro	kwa·tro
5	cinco	theen·ko
6	seis	seys
7	siete	sye·te
8	ocho	o·cho
9	nueve	nwe·ve
10	diez	dyeth

TURKISH

Turkish is the official language in Turkey and the northern part of Cyprus.

Double vowels are pronounced twice. Note that eu is pronounced as the 'u' in 'nurse', ew as 'ee' with rounded lips, uh as the 'a' in 'ago', zh as the 's' in 'pleasure', r is always rolled and v is a little softer than in English.

Basics

Hello.	Merhaba.	mer·ha·ba
Goodbye.	Hoşçakal. (by person leaving)	hosh·cha·kal
	Güle güle. (by person staying)	gew·le gew·le
Excuse me.	Bakar mısınız.	ba·kar muh·suh·nuhz
Sorry.	Özür dilerim.	eu·zewr dee·le·reem
Please.	Lütfen.	lewt·fen
Thank you.	Teşekkür ederim.	te·shek·kewr e·de·reem
Yes./No.	Evet./Hayır.	e·vet/ha·yuhr

Do you speak English?
İngilizce konuşuyor musunuz?
een·gee·leez·je ko·noo·shoo·yor moo·soo·nooz

I don't understand.
Anlamıyorum.
an·la·muh·yo·room

Accommodation

campsite	kamp yeri	kamp ye·ree
guesthouse	misafirhane	mee·sa·feer·ha·ne
hotel	otel	o·tel

Do you have a single/double room?
Tek/İki kişilik odanız var mı?
tek/ee·kee kee·shee·leek o·da·nuz var muh

How much is it per night/person?
Geceliği/Kişi başına ne kadar?
ge·je·lee·ee/kee·shee ba·shuh·na ne ka·dar

Eating & Drinking

Do you have vegetarian food?
Vejeteryan yiyecekleriniz var mı?
ve·zhe·ter·yan yee·ye·jek·le·ree·neez var muh

I'd like the bill/menu, please.
Hesabı/Menüyü istiyorum.
he·sa·buh/me·new·yew ees·tee·yo·room

I'll have ...	... alayım.	... a·la·yuhm
Cheers!	Şerefe!	she·re·fe

Emergencies

Help!
İmdat!
eem·dat

Call a doctor!
Doktor çağırın!
dok·tor cha·uh·ruhn

Call the police!
Polis çağırın!
po·lees cha·uh·ruhn

I'm lost.
Kayboldum.
kai·bol·doom

I'm ill.
Hastayım.
has·ta·yuhm

Where are the toilets?
Tuvaletler nerede?
too·va·let·ler ne·re·de

Shopping & Services

I'd like to buy ...
... almak istiyorum.
... al·mak ees·tee·yo·room

How much is it?
Ne kadar?
ne ka·dar

Transport & Directions

Where is ...?
... nerede?
... ne·re·de

What's the address?
Adresi nedir?
ad·re·see ne·deer

I'd like a ... ticket.	... bir bilet lütfen.	... beer bee·let lewt·fen
one-way	Gidiş	gee·deesh
return	Gidiş-dönüş	gee·deesh-deu·newsh
boat	vapur	va·poor
bus	otobüs	o·to·bews
plane	uçak	oo·chak
train	tren	tren

Numbers – Turkish		
1	bir	beer
2	iki	ee·kee
3	üç	ewch
4	dört	dert
5	beş	besh
6	altı	al·tuh
7	yedi	ye·dee
8	sekiz	se·keez
9	dokuz	do·kooz
10	on	on

behind the scenes

SEND US YOUR FEEDBACK

We love to hear from travellers – your comments keep us on our toes and help make our books better. Our well-travelled team reads every word on what you loved or loathed about this book. Although we cannot reply individually to postal submissions, we always guarantee that your feedback goes straight to the appropriate authors, in time for the next edition. Each person who sends us information is thanked in the next edition – and the most useful submissions are rewarded with a free book.

Visit **lonelyplanet.com/contact** to submit your updates and suggestions or to ask for help. Our award-winning website also features inspirational travel stories, news and discussions.

Note: We may edit, reproduce and incorporate your comments in Lonely Planet products such as guidebooks, websites and digital products, so let us know if you don't want your comments reproduced or your name acknowledged. For a copy of our privacy policy visit lonely planet.com/privacy.

OUR READERS

Many thanks to the travellers who used the last edition and wrote to us with helpful hints, useful advice and interesting anecdotes:

Yoram Adriaanse, Paul Beach, Bernhard, Nathan Billington, Geoff Block, Denis Bodnar, Ana Flavia Borges, Anette Jeroen Brugge-man, Munthe & Jan Bruusgaard, Colette Coumont, Blaž Cugmas, Abhishek Dubey, Albrecht Eisen, Bård Magnus Fauske, Lorraine Federico, Gaetan, Fiona Gall, Mantikas Georgios, Brian Gettings, Arnon Golan, Julian Gonzalez, Hamish Gray, Heiko Günther, Graham Hamilton, Mathilda Hermansson, Patrice Van Heyst, Florian Hinz, Lisa Johann, Russell Kim, Nancy Kinlock, Michelle Kirby, Ken Levine, Catherine Leung, Robert Lismanis, Christian Louis, Lorel Martin, Marvin, Marshall Mckinney, Ken Merk, Peter Moselund, Alan Nicholson, Mick Nishikawa, Kevin Paxter, Ivan Petryshyn, Shrikant Pusalkar, Helen Roach, Innes Rothel, Karlis Rozenkrons, Tim Schoof, John Soar, Reinier Spreen, Thomas Staempfli, Jason Stewart, Richard Stow, Julian Timm, David Torrance, Aileen Traves, Roald van Stijn, Gayna Vetter, Jennifer Vincent, Rachel Waldman, Lisa Warner, Jeffrey White, Aprilianto Wiria, Martins Zaprauskis

AUTHOR THANKS

Duncan Garwood

A big thank you to fellow authors James Bainbridge, Paul Clammer, Josephine Quintero and Neil Wilson for all their help and hard work, and to all the other Lonely Planet scribes who contributed to this big project. On the home front, I owe the usual vast debt of gratitude to Lidia and the boys, Ben and Nick. *Grazie di cuore.*

Alexis Averbuck

Once again, extensive, grateful thanks are due to Alexandra Stamopoulou for all of her insightful tips. Marijke Verstrepen and Margarita Kontzia provided helpful advice on festivals and hot happenings around the country. Dimitris Foussekis always shows me something new. And thank you Anthy and Costas for making Athens feel like home. Special thanks are also due to Craig McLachlan for seamlessly pulling our chapter together.

James Bainbridge

A hearty çok teşekkür to everyone who helped me in İstanbul and around Turkey: Selcuk Akgul, Yener and friends, Leyla Tabrizi, Funda Dagli, Pat, Ekrem and the Kelebek posse in Göreme, Ece in İzmir, Ziya, Bill and the gang in Eceabat, Melek Anne and Café

Pena in Edirne, Lütfi et al in Behramkale, Annette in Ayvalık, Mustafa in Bergama and Talat in Alaçatı. Thanks to Jen for teaching me backgammon, and to Leigh-Robin for coming on the adventure.

Paul Clammer

Shukran to all my Fassi 'family' – you know who you are. Thanks also to Jack, Ina and Youness in Figuig, and Cynthia Berning in Midelt.

Jayne D'Arcy

Thanks to fellow travellers Peter van der Brugghen and Marja Exterkate, familiar faces Mario Qytyku and Scott Logan, colleagues Carolyn Bain and Peter Dragičević and Lawrence and Mia Marzouk in Kosovo. Thanks to Tawan Sierek for the laughs during my third (!) visit to Butrint, to my dearest partner Sharik Billington for making sure young Miles was fed, watered and schooled until we were all together again, and to Miles. You guys rock.

Peter Dragičević

Thanks to Hayley Wright, Jack Delf and Amy Watson for helpful tips and contacts. Special thanks to Michael Woodhouse for finding Belgrade's campest accommodation and generally making the first week of research so enjoyable.

Mark Elliott

Many thanks to Snezhan in Trebinje, Vlaren at Tvrdoš Monastery, Semir in Blagaj, Nermen, Žika, Sanila and Narmina in Mostar, Branislav in Višegrad and so many more including the mysterious 'angel' who provided me with such insights to the Belašnica highland villages then disappeared without my ever knowing his name. As ever my greatest thanks go to my endlessly inspiring wife Dani Systermans and to my unbeatable parents who, three decades ago, had the crazy idea of driving me to Bosnia in the first place.

Steve Fallon

Thanks to Tatjana Radovič and Petra Stušek at the Ljubljana Tourist Board and Lucija Jager at the Slovenian Tourist Board. Slovenian Railways' Marino Fakin, Tone Plankar at the Ljubljana bus station and Tomaž Škofic of Adria Airways helped with transport and Dušan Brejc of the Wine Association of Slovenia with the right vintage(s). It was wonderful catching up with mates Domen Kalajžič of 3glav Adventures, Bled, and Aleš Hvala of Hotel Hvala, Kobarid. As always, my efforts here are dedicated to my partner, Michael Rothschild.

Anthony Ham

In eight years of living in Madrid, I have been welcomed and assisted by too many people to name and whose lives and stories have become a treasured part of the fabric of my own. It was my great fortune a week after arriving in Madrid to meet my wife and soulmate, Marina, who has made this city a true place of the heart. And to my daughters, Carlota and Valentina: truly you are Madrid's greatest gift of all.

Virginia Maxwell

Duncan Garwood and Ryan Ver Berkmoes gave me encouragement, expert advice and extended deadlines, for which I was extremely grateful. *Grazie mille!* Thanks also to my favourite travelling companion, Max Handsaker; to Peter for looking after the home front; and to Shelley, Roger, Moss, Dennis, Sophia, Theo, Freya, Filippo, Fabrizio and Elisabetta.

Craig McLachlan

A hearty thanks to all those who helped me out on the road, but most of all to my exceptionally beautiful wife Yuriko who let me know when I'd had enough Mythos each day! – and who also limited my daily intake of gyros pitta.

Anja Mutić

Hvala mama, for your home cooking and contagious laughter. *Gracias* to the Barcelona family. *Obrigada*, Hoji, for always being there. A huge *hvala* to my friends in Croatia who gave me endless contacts and recommendations. Lidija, you're always full of great ideas! Special thanks to Viviana Vukelić and her team at HTZ. A thank you also goes to Tom Masters for his flexibility. Finally, to the inspiring memory of my late father who travels with me still.

Josephine Quintero

Thanks to all the helpful folk in the various tourist offices, in particular Alexis Christodoulides from the CTO in Larnaka. Also thanks to Athina Papadoupoulou from the Nicosia Masterplan Office for her invaluable contribution. Thanks too, to coordinating author Duncan Garwood for his continued support.

Regis St Louis

Big thanks to maestro Ryan VB and *Portugal 8* co-authors Kate, Gregor and Adam, who proved a stellar team to work with. In Portugal, I'd like to thank João for deep insight into Lisboa, Paolo for the enlightening Castelo walk and the memorable meals, Bruno for the radical UMM experience, and the many locals who shared tips along the way. As always beijos to Cassandra and daughters Magdalena and Genevieve for their support.

Nicola Williams

Kudos to the exceptional commitment, creativity and cooperation of the *France 9* team of authors whose prose I cut and manicured to create the France chapter of this guide. *Un grand merci* to Parisians Laure Chouillou and Sophie Maisonnier; and at home bisous to Matthias and our three wonderfully travel-happy children, Niko (9), Mischa (6) and Kaya (10mths).

Neil Wilson

Thanks to the friendly and helpful tourist office staff in Malta and Gozo, and to all those people on the road who offered advice and recommendations.

ACKNOWLEDGMENTS

Climate map data adapted from Peel MC, Finlayson BL & McMahon TA (2007) 'Updated World Map of the Köppen-Geiger Climate Classification', *Hydrology and Earth System Sciences*, 11, 163344.

Cover photograph: Church with ocean in background. Fira, Santorini, Cyclades, Southern Aegean, Greece, Europe/Craig Pershouse/ Lonely Planet Images

Many of the images in this guide are available for licensing from Lonely Planet Images: www.lonelyplanetimages.com.

THIS BOOK

Many people have helped to create this 10th edition of Lonely Planet's *Mediterranean Europe* guidebook, which is part of Lonely Planet's Europe series. Other titles in this series include *Western Europe*, *Eastern Europe*, *Central Europe*, *Scandinavia* and *Europe on a Shoestring*. This guidebook was commissioned in Lonely Planet's London office, and produced by the following:

Commissioning Editors Joe Bindloss, Lucy Monie, Dora Whitaker

Coordinating Editor Sophie Splatt
Coordinating Cartographer Valentina Kremenchutskaya
Coordinating Layout Designer Carlos Solarte
Managing Editors Kirsten Rawlings, Tasmin Waby McNaughtan
Managing Cartographers Amanda Sierp, Dianne Duggan
Managing Layout Designer Chris Girdler

Assisting Editor Helen Yeates
Assisting Cartographers Katalin Dadi-Racz, Eve Kelly, Tom Webster
Cover Research Naomi Parker
Internal Image Research Aude Vauconsant
Language Content Branislava Vladisavljevic
Thanks to Justin Flynn, Lisa Knights, Ali Lemer, Annelies Mertens, Averil Robertson, John Taufa

index

INDEX C

how to use this book

These symbols will help you find the listings you want:

💿	Sights	🏳️	Tours	🍷	Drinking
🏊	Beaches	🎊	Festivals & Events	⭐	Entertainment
🏃	Activities	🛏️	Sleeping	🛍️	Shopping
🍴	Courses	✖️	Eating	ℹ️	Information/Transport

Look out for these icons:

 Our author's recommendation

FREE No payment required

🌱 A green or sustainable option

Our authors have nominated these places as demonstrating a strong commitment to sustainability – for example by supporting local communities and producers, operating in an environmentally friendly way, or supporting conservation projects.

These symbols give you the vital information for each listing:

🕿	Telephone Numbers	🛜	Wi-Fi Access	🚌	Bus
⌚	Opening Hours	🏊	Swimming Pool	⛴️	Ferry
Ⓟ	Parking	🥗	Vegetarian Selection	Ⓜ	Metro
⊖	Nonsmoking	📖	English-Language Menu	Ⓢ	Subway
❄️	Air-Conditioning	👪	Family-Friendly	⊖	London Tube
@	Internet Access	🐾	Pet-Friendly	🚋	Tram
				🚆	Train

Reviews are organised by author preference.

Map Legend

Sights
- 🏖️ Beach
- 🔴 Buddhist
- 🏯 Castle
- ✝️ Christian
- 🕉️ Hindu
- ☪️ Islamic
- ✡️ Jewish
- 🔵 Monument
- 🏛️ Museum/Gallery
- 🔴 Ruin
- 🍇 Winery/Vineyard
- 🦁 Zoo
- 🔵 Other Sight

Activities, Courses & Tours
- 🤿 Diving/Snorkelling
- 🛶 Canoeing/Kayaking
- ⛷️ Skiing
- 🏄 Surfing
- 🏊 Swimming/Pool
- 🚶 Walking
- 🏄 Windsurfing
- 🔵 Other Activity/Course/Tour

Sleeping
- 🛏️ Sleeping
- ⛺ Camping

Eating
- ✖️ Eating

Drinking
- 🍷 Drinking
- ☕ Cafe

Entertainment
- 🎭 Entertainment

Shopping
- 🛍️ Shopping

Information
- 📮 Post Office
- ℹ️ Tourist Information

Transport
- ✈️ Airport
- ⊗ Border Crossing
- 🚌 Bus
- ++🚠++ Cable Car/Funicular
- --⊛-- Cycling
- -⊙- Ferry
- Ⓜ Metro
- ==⊕== Monorail
- Ⓟ Parking
- Ⓢ S-Bahn
- 🚕 Taxi
- +🚉+ Train/Railway
- ==🚋== Tram
- ⊖ Tube Station
- ⓤ U-Bahn
- • Other Transport

Routes
- ▬ Tollway
- ▬ Freeway
- ▬ Primary
- ▬ Secondary
- ▬ Tertiary
- ▬ Lane
- ▬ Unsealed Road
- ▬ Plaza/Mall
- ⫶⫶⫶ Steps
- ⊐⊏ Tunnel
- ▬ Pedestrian Overpass
- ▬ Walking Tour
- ▬ Walking Tour Detour
- --- Path

Boundaries
- --- International
- ---- State/Province
- --- Disputed
- - - - Regional/Suburb
- ▬ Marine Park
- ▬ Cliff
- ▬ Wall

Population
- 🔴 Capital (National)
- ◉ Capital (State/Province)
- 🔴 City/Large Town
- 🔴 Town/Village

Geographic
- 🏠 Hut/Shelter
- 🔴 Lighthouse
- 🔵 Lookout
- ▲ Mountain/Volcano
- 🔵 Oasis
- 🔵 Park
-)(Pass
- 🔵 Picnic Area
- 🔵 Waterfall

Hydrography
- ⌒ River/Creek
- ⌒ Intermittent River
- ⌇ Swamp/Mangrove
- ⌒ Reef
- ⌒ Canal
- 🔵 Water
- 🔵 Dry/Salt/Intermittent Lake
- 🔵 Glacier

Areas
- ⬚ Beach/Desert
- +++ Cemetery (Christian)
- ××× Cemetery (Other)
- ⬚ Park/Forest
- ⬚ Sportsground
- ⬚ Sight (Building)
- ⬚ Top Sight (Building)

Anja Mutić

Croatia It's been more than 18 years since Anja left her native Croatia. The journey took her to several countries before she made New York City her base 11 years ago. But the roots are a'calling. She's been returning to Croatia frequently for work and play, intent on discovering a new place on every visit. On her last trip, she loved exploring Hvar's lavender-dotted interior. Anja blogs about her travels at www.everthenomad.com.

Read more about Anja at:
lonelyplanet.com/members/anjamutic

Josephine Quintero

Cyprus Josephine has visited Cyprus many times and finds the island fascinating; she also feels a real affinity with Cypriots from both sides of the Green Line. Highlights during this trip were visiting the incredible frescoed Byzantine churches in the Republic and a moonlit stroll around the north's Kyrenia harbour, a quintessential Mediterranean resort. Josephine also rediscovered the irresistible appeal of the traditional meze, washed down with local Cypriot wine from one of the growing number of wineries in the Troodos.

Read more about Josephine at:
lonelyplanet.com/members/josephinequintero

Regis St Louis

Portugal Regis' long-time admiration for wine, rugged coastlines and melancholic music made him easy prey for Portugal. He has travelled extensively across the country, most recently fêting Lisbon's favourite saint at the Festa de Santo Antonio, exploring gorgeous beaches in the Parque Natural da Arrábida and eating too many *pasteis de nata* (including six in one day—oops). Regis is the coordinating author of Lonely Planet *Portugal*, and his travel essays have appeared in newspapers, inflight magazines and online. He lives in Brooklyn, New York.

Read more about Regis at:
lonelyplanet.com/members/regisstlouis

Nicola Williams

France Nicola Williams has lived in France and written about it for more than a decade. From her hillside home on the southern shore of Lake Geneva, it's a quick flit to the Alps (call her a ski fiend...), Paris (... art buff), Provence (... food and wine lover). Paris this time meant stylish-apartment living in St-Germain des Prés with husband extraordinaire Matthias and three trilingual kids with ants in their pants. Nicola blogs at tripalong.wordpress.com and tweets at @Tripalong.

Read more about Nicola at:
lonelyplanet.com/members/nicolawilliams

Neil Wilson

Malta Researching this chapter provided Neil with the opportunity to enjoy Malta in perfect autumn weather, wandering the streets of Valletta and Vittoriosa, hiking the coast of Gozo, and tucking into fresh local food in places like Mahżen XII in Mdina. Neil is a full-time travel writer based in Edinburgh, Scotland, and has written more than 50 guidebooks, including Lonely Planet's *Malta & Gozo*.

Read more about Neil at:
lonelyplanet.com/members/neilwilson

Jayne D'Arcy

Albania Counting Albania's highlights every two years for the past six has led Jayne to the startling conclusion that Albania resembles a robust child's growth chart. Taking advantage of the growth are cyclists in remote corners, hikers turning the 'Accursed Mountains' into a 'must-hike' and backpacker hostels opening in the hottest spots. When she's not taking photos of vintage folding bikes in Albania, Jayne also writes about the southern hemisphere (*South East Asia on a Shoestring* and *Australia*) and rides her own vintage folding bike around Melbourne, Australia.

Peter Dragičević

Montenegro Among the two dozen or so Lonely Planet books that Peter's co-written are the first ever *Montenegro* country guide, *Western Balkans* and the two previous editions of this title. While it was family ties that first drew him to the Balkans, it's the history, natural beauty, convoluted politics, cheap *rakija* and intriguing people that keep bringing him back. This trip's highlight was a particularly dramatic trek through the clouds to the Njegoš monument on the top of Mt Lovćen.

Read more about Peter at:
lonelyplanet.com/members/peterdragicevich

Mark Elliott

Bosnia & Hercegovina British born travel-writer Mark Elliott was only 11 when his family dragged him to Sarajevo and stood him in the now defunct concrete footsteps of Gavrilo Princip. Fortunately no Austro-Hungarian emperors were passing at the time. He has since visited virtually every corner of BiH supping fine Hercegovinian wines, talking philosophy with Serb monks and Sufi mystics and drinking more Bosnian coffee than any healthy stomach should. When not writing he lives in Belgium with the lovely Danielle who he met while jamming blues harmonica in a Turkmenistan club.

Steve Fallon

Slovenia Steve has been travelling to Slovenia since the early 1990s, when almost everyone but the Slovenes had never heard of the place. Never mind, it was his own private Idaho for over a decade. Though *on še govori slovensko kot jamski človek* (he still speaks Slovene like a caveman), Steve considers part of his soul to be Slovenian and returns as often as he can for a glimpse of the Julian Alps in the sun, a dribble of *bučno olje* and a dose of the dual.

Read more about Steve at:
lonelyplanet.com/members/stevefallon

Anthony Ham

Spain In 2002, Anthony arrived in Madrid on a one-way ticket. He has called the city home ever since and now lives with his *madrileña* wife and two daughters overlooking their favourite plaza in the city. He has written more than fifty guidebooks for Lonely Planet, including *Spain* and *Madrid*. Researching this guide allowed him to rediscover his home city afresh (Malasaña is his new favourite *barrio*) and he particularly enjoyed losing himself in the villages of Aragón.

Read more about Anthony at:
lonelyplanet.com/members/anthony_ham

Virginia Maxwell

Italy Virginia has been travelling regularly in Italy for over 20 years, inspired by a love of Renaissance arts and architecture and an all-abiding passion for the country's food and wine. She is the coordinating author of Lonely Planet's *Tuscany & Umbria* book and has covered Rome, Lazio and Tuscany for the *Italy* guidebook.

Read more about Virginia at:
lonelyplanet.com/members/virginiamaxwell

Craig McLachlan

Greece Craig has researched the Greek Islands for four of the most recent Lonely Planet guidebooks to Europe. He is also a regular visitor to Greece as a tour leader, mainly guiding hiking groups in the mountains and gorges of Crete and around the Cyclades. A Kiwi, Craig spends the southern-hemisphere summer running an outdoor adventure company in Queenstown before heading north for the winter as a 'freelance anything'. He is also a karate instructor and Japanese interpreter. Check out www.craigmclachlan.com.

Read more about Craig at:
lonelyplanet.com/members/craigmclachlan

OUR STORY

A beat-up old car, a few dollars in the pocket and a sense of adventure. In 1972 that's all Tony and Maureen Wheeler needed for the trip of a lifetime – across Europe and Asia overland to Australia. It took several months, and at the end – broke but inspired – they sat at their kitchen table writing and stapling together their first travel guide, *Across Asia on the Cheap*. Within a week they'd sold 1500 copies. Lonely Planet was born.

Today, Lonely Planet has offices in Melbourne, London and Oakland, with more than 600 staff and writers. We share Tony's belief that 'a great guidebook should do three things: inform, educate and amuse'.

OUR WRITERS

Duncan Garwood

Coordinating author& Italy Ever since island-hopping around the Greek Islands as a student, Duncan has been fascinated by the Mediterranean and its wonderful mix of history, culture and endless sunshine. Many years later he can actually see the Med from the balcony of his hilltop apartment just outside Rome. Duncan moved to Italy in 1997 and after a few years teaching English – once, memorably, to Italy's Miss World candidate – took to the road as a Lonely Planet writer. He has since travelled extensively in Italy and contributed to a raft of titles as well as newspapers and magazines. This is the fifth edition of *Mediterranean Europe* he has worked on and with each one he discovers yet more reasons to love the region he now calls home.

Read more about Duncan at:
lonelyplanet.com/members/duncangarwood

Alexis Averbuck

Greece Alexis Averbuck lives in Hydra, Greece and makes any excuse she can to travel the isolated back roads of her adopted land. She is committed to dispelling the stereotype that Greece is simply a string of sandy beaches. A travel writer for two decades, Alexis has lived in Antarctica for a year, crossed the Pacific by sailboat and written books on her journeys through Asia and the Americas. She's also a painter – see her work at www.alexisaverbuck.com.

Read more about Alexis at:
lonelyplanet.com/members/alexisaverbuck

James Bainbridge

Turkey Coordinating two editions of Lonely Planet's *Turkey* took James from Aegean islands to the Anatolian plateau. He also spent most of 2010 living in İstanbul – trendy Cihangir to be exact – and learning to love suffixes on a Turkish course. Originally from England, he now lives in Cape Town (Turkey, give my South African girlfriend a visa next time!) and writes about Africa, the Middle East and Europe for worldwide publications. His other Lonely Planet credits include the previous edition of this guide and, most recently, coordinating *Morocco*.

Read more about James at:
lonelyplanet.com/members/james_bains

Paul Clammer

Morocco As a student, Paul had his first solo backpacking experience when he took a bus from his Cambridgeshire home all the way to Casablanca. After an interlude where he trained and worked as a molecular biologist, he returned to work as a tour guide, trekking in the Atlas and trying not to lose passengers in the Fez medina. The increasing number of budget airline routes from the UK to Morocco is one of his favourite recent travel innovations, allowing him to continue to hop over to Morocco on a regular basis.

Read more about Paul at:
lonelyplanet.com/members/paulclammer

OVER PAGE | MORE WRITERS

Published by Lonely Planet Publications Pty Ltd
ABN 36 005 607 983
10th edition – Oct 2011
ISBN 978 1 74179 677 3
© Lonely Planet 2011 Photographs © as indicated 2011
10 9 8 7 6 5 4 3 2 1
Printed in Singapore

MARS 2011